January 12–18, 2015
Mumbai, India



Association for Computing Machinery

*Advancing Computing as a Science & Profession*

POPL 2015

# POPL'15

Proceedings of the 42nd Annual ACM SIGPLAN-SIGACT Symposium on

## Principles of Programming Languages

*Sponsored by:*

*ACM SIGPLAN and ACM SIGACT*

*Supported by:*

*Microsoft Research, Flipkart.com, ACM India, Oracle Labs, IARCS, Facebook, Persistent, Samsung, Google, Jane Street, Tata Consultancy Services, IBM Research, TIFR, and Xerox*

Association for
Computing Machinery

*Advancing Computing as a Science & Profession*

**The Association for Computing Machinery**
**2 Penn Plaza, Suite 701**
**New York, New York 10121-0701**



**ISBN:** 978-1-4503-3300-9

Additional copies may be ordered prepaid from:

**ACM Order Department**
PO Box 30777
New York, NY 10087-0777, USA

Phone: 1-800-342-6626 (USA and Canada)
+1-212-626-0500 (Global)
Fax: +1-212-944-1318
E-mail: acmhelp@acm.org
Hours of Operation: 8:30 am – 4:30 pm ET

Printed in the USA

# Welcome to POPL 2015

It is our great pleasure to welcome you to the $42^{nd}$ *ACM Symposium on Principles of Programming Languages, POPL 2015,* held in Mumbai, India, at the beautiful Tata Institute for Fundamental Research. This year's program consists of 52 papers drawn from the 227 papers originally submitted at the July 2014 paper deadline. These papers cover a wide range of topics stretching from theoretical foundations concerning the lambda calculus, type theory and verification to applications in security, networking, and web programming. The program also features invited talks from Peter Buneman, Sumit Gulwani and Peter Lee.

While at POPL'15 in Mumbai, we encourage you to take part in the following co-located events:

- *ACM SIGPLAN Conference on Certified Programs and Proofs (CPP)*
- *International Workshop on Coq for Programming Languages (CoqPL)*
- *POPL Off the Beaten Track: New Frontiers for Programming Languages Research (OBT)*
- *ACM SIGPLAN Workshop on Partial Evaluation and Program Manipulation (PEPM)*
- *ACM SIGPLAN Programming Languages Mentoring Workshop (PLMW)*
- *International Conference on Verification, Model Checking and Abstract Interpretation (VMCAI)*
- *Programming Languages and Verification Technology for Networking (PLVNET)*
- *IMPECS-POPL Workshop on Emerging Research and Development Trends in Programming Languages (WEPL)*
- *Six tutorials.*

Putting *POPL'15* together was a team effort. The program committee for POPL consisted of 30 members, who reviewed an average of 21 papers each. We also used an external review committee of 66 members and 71 ad hoc, external reviewers. In addition, for the first time at POPL, we evaluated the artifacts that authors of accepted papers submitted. Arjun Guha and Jan Vitek led a team of 21 additional artifact reviewers in this process. They describe this new process in a note that follows this welcome. Last, many accepted papers were assigned "angels" from amongst the program committee members or other reviewers. Each angel agreed to help authors interpret their reviews, read a revised draft of their paper and provide additional feedback. All told, the reviewers for *POPL'15* put in an enormous effort and our community is better because of it. We cannot thank them enough.

We are also very thankful for work of the local organizers, lead by Paritosh Pandya, from TIFR, S. Akshay from IIT Bombay and Aditya Nori from Microsoft Research. Without their help, there would be no *POPL'15*. David Van Horn (Workshop Chair), Ross Tate (Treasurer), Ruzica Piskac and Viktor Vafeiadis (Publicity), and Matthew Parkinson (Student Activities) were also key to the vast organizational effort that makes a conference like *POPL'15* run smoothly. In addition, while organizing the conference, we called on the advice of the POPL steering committee and a number of other senior members of the community. We thank them all for their input.

Finally, we would like to thank our sponsors, ACM, ACM SIGPLAN and ACM SIGACT. We also had very generous corporate support from Microsoft Research, Flipkart.com, ACM India, Oracle Labs, IARCS, Facebook, Persistent, Samsung, Google, Jane Street, Tata Consultancy Services, IBM Research, TIFR and Xerox.

We hope that you find the *POPL'15* program thought-provoking and that the symposium provides you with a valuable opportunity to share ideas with other researchers from around the world.

**Sriram Rajamani**
*POPL'15 General Chair*
*Microsoft Research, India*

**David Walker**
*POPL'15 Program Chair*
*Princeton University, USA*

# Artifact Evaluation

It is our pleasure to report on the artifact evaluation process that we ran on the behalf of the Program Chair, David Walker. POPL'15 is the first in the long-running POPL conference series to have an Artifact Evaluation Committee (AEC).

Artifact evaluation is concerned with the byproducts of science. An "artifact" is something intended to support the scientific claims made in a paper. For instance, an artifact might be a program's source code, a data collection, a test suite, a proof, or a model. "Evaluation" is a best-effort attempt to reconcile a paper's artifacts with the claims made in the paper. A primary goal of the artifact evaluation process is to encourage authors to create artifacts that can be shared and used by others as bases for new activities. The process seeks other benefits as well. These include encouraging authors to be precise in their claims and publicly recognizing efforts toward making high-quality artifacts.

Three months before the POPL'15 paper submission deadline, the AEC chairs invited members of the POPL community to nominate PhD students and postdocs to serve on the AEC. The chairs selected **21** of these, based on their levels of experience and areas of expertise.

After the decisions for POPL'15 submissions were distributed, the authors of accepted papers were invited to submit artifacts for evaluation. (Thus, by design, the artifact evaluation process had no effect on which papers were chosen to appear at POPL.) Authors had one week, until October 6, to respond to the call for artifacts. The submission guidelines asked that each artifact be packaged so as to make evaluation as easy as possible. Typically, this involved the creation of a virtual machine image, but other means were also accepted. Each artifact was accompanied by the accepted version of its associated paper so that the AEC could evaluate each artifact against its paper's claims. A total of ***29*** artifacts were submitted for evaluation.

The AEC had almost three weeks, until October 26, to render judgments. The AEC expected artifacts to be "consistent with the paper; as complete as possible; documented well; and easy to reuse, facilitating further research." The AEC members bid on artifacts and the chairs selected two reviewers for each one. Artifact evaluation had two phases. During the first "installation phase", the committee simply tried to download, build, and launch the artifacts. The committee reported any errors that occurred in an initial review and authors had an opportunity to reply with solutions. During the second phase, the AEC tried to repeat some or all of the experiments described in the artifact's paper. AEC members were cognizant that it would be difficult to reproduce certain results, e.g., benchmarks that were run on high-performance machines. For four artifacts, the AEC purchased Amazon EC2 servers to recreate experimental conditions at a total cost of $310.10. Other artifacts ran successfully on the committee's personal computers. After all reviews were submitted, the AEC held an intense online discussion to decide, for each artifact, if it met, exceeded, or fell below the expectations set by its paper.

Of the ***29*** submitted artifacts, ***27*** were judged to meet or exceed expectations. The papers that describe these artifacts can be recognized by the AEC badge they bear (created by Matthias Hauswirth).

We thank the authors of the ***29*** submitted artifacts for their work in preparing and documenting their research output. We hope that they found the feedback from the AEC to be helpful. We also thank David Walker for his support, and the members of the AEC for their energy and enthusiasm.

**Arjun Guha**
*POPL'15 AEC Co-Chair*
*University of Massachusetts, Amherst, USA*

**Jan Vitek**
*POPL'15 AEC Co-Chair*
*Northeastern University, USA*

# Table of Contents

## Session 3A: Dynamic Verification

Session Chair: Jan Vitek *(Northeastern University)*



## Session 3B: Concurrency I

Session Chair: Ganesan Ramalingam *(Microsoft Research)*



## Session 4A: Compiler Correctness

Session Chair: Adam Chlipala *(Massachusetts Institute of Technology)*



## Session 4B: Types II

Session Chair: Deepak Garg *(Max Planck Institute for Software Systems)*



## Session 5A: Regular Languages and Automata

Session Chair: S Akshay *(IIT Bombay)*

## Session 5B: Programming Models I

Session Chair: Frank Pfenning *(Carnegie Mellon University)*



## Session 6A: Concurrency II

Session Chair: Nishant Sinha *(IBM Research India)*



## Session 6B: Semantics

Session Chair: Arjun Guha *(University of Massachusetts, Amherst)*



## Keynote Address II

Session Chair: David Walker *(Princeton University)*



## Keynote Address III

Session Chair: Paritosh Pandya *(Tata Institute for Fundamental Research)*



## Session 7A: Probabilistic Programs

Session Chair: Supratik Chakraborty *(IIT Bombay)*



## Session 7B: Programming Models II

Session Chair: Roberto Giacobazzi *(University of Verona)*

## Session 8A: Program Analysis II

Session Chair: Akash Lal *(Microsoft Research)*



## Session 8B: Verification

Session Chair: Sumit Gulwani *(Microsoft Research)*



## Session 9A: Concurrency III

Session Chair: Rupak Majumdar *(Max Planck Institute for Software Systems)*



## Session 9B: Synthesis

Session Chair: Swarat Chaudhuri *(Rice University)*

# POPL 2015: 42nd ACM SIGPLAN-SIGACT Symposium on Principles of Programming Languages

**General Chair:** Sriram Rajamani *(Microsoft Research, India)*

**Program Chair:** David Walker *(Princeton University, USA)*

**Local Arrangements Chair:** Paritosh Pandya *(Tata Institute of Fundamental Research, India)*

**Publicity Chairs:** Ruzica Piskac *(Yale University, USA)*
Viktor Vafeiadis *(MPI-SWS, Germany)*

**Workshop Chair:** David Van Horn *(University of Maryland, USA)*

**Treasurer:** Ross Tate *(Cornell University, USA)*

**Student Activities Chair:** Matthew Parkinson *(Microsoft Research, UK)*

**Artifact Evaluation Chairs:** Arjun Guha *(University of Massachusetts, Amherst, USA)*
Jan Vitek *(Northeastern University, USA)*

**Organizing Committee:** S Akshay *(IIT Bombay, India)*
Aditya Nori *(Microsoft Research, India)*

**Steering Committee:** Radhia Cousot *(École Normal Supérieure CNRS & Inria, France)*
Roberto Giacobazzi *(Universita di Verona, Italy)*
Jeremy Gibbons *(University of Oxford, UK)*
Graham Hutton *(University of Nottingham, UK)*
Suresh Jagannathan *(Purdue University, USA)*
Sriram Rajamani *(Microsoft Research, India)*
Peter Sewell *(University of Cambridge, UK)*
Jan Vitek *(Northeastern University, USA)*
Philip Wadler *(University of Edinburgh, UK)*
David Walker *(Princeton University, USA)*

**Program Committee:** Umut Acar *(Carnegie Mellon University, USA)*
Amal Ahmed *(Northeastern University, USA)*
Jade Alglave *(University College London, UK)*
Karthikeyan Bhargavan *(Inria, France)*
Rastislav Bodik *(University of California, Berkeley, USA)*
Giuseppe Castagna *(CNRS – Université Paris Diderot, France)*
Satish Chandra *(Samsung Electronics, USA)*
Swarat Chaudhuri *(Rice University, USA)*
Ravi Chugh *(University of California, San Diego, USA)*
Patrick Cousot *(CIMS, New York University, USA)*
Robby Findler *(Northwestern University, USA)*

**Program Committee (continued):**

Jeff Foster *(University of Maryland, USA)*
Cédric Fournet *(Microsoft Research, France)*
Deepak Garg *(MPI-SWS, Germany)*
Arjun Guha *(University of Massachusetts, Amherst, USA)*
Ralf Hinze *(University of Oxford, UK)*
Martin Hofmann *(Ludwig-Maximilians-Universitat, Germany)*
Joxan Jaffar *(National University of Singapore, Singapore)*
Patricia Johann *(Appalachian State University, USA)*
Naoki Kobayashi *(University of Tokyo, Japan)*
Gabriele Keller *(University of New South Wales and NICTA, Australia)*
Dan Licata *(Wesleyan University, USA)*
Mayur Naik *(Georgia Institute of Technology, USA)*
Madhusudan Parthasarathy *(University of Illinois at Urbana-Champaign, USA)*
David Pichardie *(ENS Rennes and IRISA, France)*
Brigitte Pientka *(McGill University, Canada)*
François Pottier *(Inria, France)*
Shaz Qadeer *(Microsoft Research, USA)*
Ganesan Ramalingam *(Microsoft Research, India)*
Greta Yorsh *(Queen Mary University of London, UK)*
Andreas Abel *(Gothenburg University, Sweden)*
Davide Ancona *(DIBRIS - Università di Genova, Italy)*
David Aspinall *(University of Edinburgh, UK)*
Michael Benedikt *(Oxford University, UK)*
Nick Benton *(Microsoft Research, UK)*
Josh Berdine *(Microsoft Research, UK)*
Emery Berger *(University of Massachusetts Amherst, USA)*
Lars Birkedal *(Aarhus University, Denmark)*
Supratik Chakraborty *(IIT Bombay, India)*
Bor-Yuh Evan Chang *(University of Colorado Boulder, UK)*
Arthur Charguéraud *(Inria, France)*
Avik Chaudhuri *(Facebook, USA)*
Wei-Ngan Chin *(National University of Singapore, Singapore)*
Stephen Chong *(Harvard University, USA)*
Michael Clarkson *(George Washington University, USA)*
Delphine Demange *(IRISA - University of Rennes 1, France)*
Alastair Donaldson *(Imperial College London, UK)*
Gabriel Dos Reis *(Microsoft, USA)*
Derek Dreyer *(Max Planck Institute for Software Systems, Germany)*
Michael Emmi *(IMDEA Software Institute, Spain)*
Xinyu Feng *(University of Science and Technology of China, China)*
Kathleen Fisher *(Tufts University, USA)*
Nate Foster *(Cornell University, USA)*
Pierre Genevès *(CNRS, France)*

**Extended Review Committee:**

**Artifact Evaluation Committee:** Andrew Cave *(McGill University, Canada)*
Chris Martens *(Carnegie Mellon University, USA)*
Christos Dimoulas *(Harvard University, USA)*
Cristian Gherghina *(Singapore U. of Technology and Design, Singapore)*
Duc-Hiep Chu *(National University of Singapore, Singapore)*
Emma F. Tosch *(University of Massachusetts Amherst, USA)*
Gregory Malecha *(Harvard University, USA)*
Heather Miller *(EPFL, Switzerland)*
Jean Yang *(MIT CSAIL, USA)*
Jed Liu *(Cornell University, USA)*
Joel Galenson *(University of California Berkeley, USA)*
John Wickerson *(Imperial College London, UK)*
Mahdi Eslamimehr *(SAP Labs, USA)*
Marc Brockschmidt *(Microsoft Research, UK)*
Nada Amin *(EPFL, Switzerland)*
Nathan Chong *(Imperial College London, UK)*
Neil Toronto *(University of Maryland, College Park, USA)*
Olle Fredriksson *(The University of Birmingham, UK)*
Vijayaraghavan Murali *(National University of Singapore, Singapore)*
Vincent Laporte *(Université Rennes, France)*
Yulei Sui *(UNSW, Australia)*

**Additional Reviewers:**

Aws Albarghouthi
Faouzi Atig
Greg Ballard
Gilles Barthe
Utpal Banerjee
Samik Basu
Lennart Beringer
Gianfranco Bilardi
Ahmed Bouajjani
Sebastian Burckhardt
Luís Caires
Pavol Cerny
Pierre-Évariste Dagand
David Doty
Doug Downey
Javier Esparza
Jerome Feret
Jonathan Fetter-Degges
Andrzej Filinski
Carsten Fuhs
Fabio Gadducci
Alexey Gotsman
Bjørn Grathwohl
Michael Greenberg
Matthew Hammer
Kevin Hammond
Danny Hendler
Ethan Jackson
Jinseong Jeon
Nick Johnson
Russ Joseph
Ali Sinan Koksal
Shriram Krishnamurthi
Viktor Kuncak
Akash Lal
Henry Lieberman
Ratul Mahajan
Anders Moller

**Additonal Reviewers (continued):**

Jacob Nelson
Phil Nguyen
ThanhVu Nguyen
Dejan Nickovic
Aditya Nori
Luca Padovani
Catuscia Palamidessi
Prakash Panangaden
Sanjay Rajopadhye
Ulrik Rasmussen
Julian Rathke
Brianna Ren
Martin Rinard
Atanas Rountev
Andrew Ruef
Gabriel Scherer
Sylvain Schmitz
Peter Selinger
Ilya Sergey
Zhong Shao
Filip Sieczkowski
Michael Spear
Charles Sutton
Neil Toronto
Tarmo Uustalu
Viktor Vafeiadis
David Van Horn
Jamie Vicary
Mingsheng Ying
Steve Zdancewic
Haoqi Zhang
Hai Zhou

# POPL 2015 Sponsors and Supporters

## Sponsors:

acm SIGPLAN

SIGACT

## Supporters:

Microsoft Research

flipkart.com

acm India

Oracle Labs

IARCS

facebook

PERSISTENT

SAMSUNG

Google

Jane Street

TATA
TATA CONSULTANCY SERVICES

IBM Research

tifr

xerox

# Automating Repetitive Tasks for the Masses

Sumit Gulwani
Microsoft Research
sumitg@microsoft.com

## Abstract

The programming languages (PL) research community has traditionally catered to the needs of professional programmers in the continuously evolving technical industry. However, there is a new opportunity that knocks our doors. The recent IT revolution has resulted in the masses having access to personal computing devices. More than 99% of these computer users are non-programmers and are today limited to being passive consumers of the software that is made available to them. Can we empower these users to more effectively leverage computers for their daily tasks? The formalisms, techniques, and tools developed in the PL and the formal methods research communities can play a pivotal role!

***Categories and Subject Descriptors*** D.1.2 [*Software*]: Programming Techniques—Automatic Programming; K.3.1 [*Computing Milieux*]: Computers and Education—Computer Uses in Education

***Keywords*** End-user Programming; Computer-aided Education; Programming by Examples; Programming by Natural Language; Program Synthesis; Domain-specific Languages; Search Algorithms

## What do masses struggle with?

There are several domains of repetitive tasks that large populations of people (with access to computational devices) struggle with in their daily lives. These can be identified via study of help forums [6], analyzing search engine query logs [9], conducting user studies, or partnering with domain experts. Following are two broad areas with great need to automate repetitive tasks.

### End-user Programming: Empowering IT workers

End users of computational devices, most of whom are non-programmers, often need to create small (and perhaps one-off) scripts to automate repetitive tasks. These users can easily specify their intent using examples and/or natural language. The opportunity here is to develop program synthesis techniques [3] that can translate the user's specification in the form of examples or natural language (which is often imprecise or ambiguous) into intended scripts. While program synthesis has been an old area of study, its application to end-user programming is very timely now, given the increased significance of this application, and the recent advances in computational power and algorithms to address the associated technical challenges.

***Programming by Examples (PBE)*** Several data manipulation tasks, including extraction [7], transformation [6] and formatting [10], are amenable to programming by examples. The IT revolution has resulted in digitization of massive amounts of data. Data is available in documents of various types, e.g., text/log files, spreadsheets, webpages, xml, pdf, and images. These documents offer great flexibility in storing and organizing hierarchical data by combining presentation/formatting with the underlying data model. However, this makes it hard to manipulate and reason about the underlying data. PBE has the potential to convert data wrangling into a delightful experience, thereby enabling users to discover new actionable insights about their data.

***Programming by Natural Language (PBNL)*** Natural language is a good fit for describing actions with side-effects as is the case in smartphone automation scripts [8]. Some data manipulation tasks such as filtering and summarization, are also best communicated using natural language [5].

### Computer-aided Education: Empowering teachers & students

Education has been one of the least technically impacted sectors. With recent disruption in the form of online educational platforms, blended classrooms, and one-tablet-per-child programs, technology stands to play a transformative role. For instance, technology can assist with repetitive tasks in Education like problem generation and feedback generation, for a variety of subjects including programming, algorithms, logic, mathematics, and language learning [4]. This can facilitate interactive and adaptive pedagogies in both standard and online classrooms.

***Problem generation*** Generating fresh problems that have specific solution characteristics (e.g., difficulty level, use of a certain set of concepts) is a tedious task for the teacher. Automating it can enable personalized workflows for students and also help prevent plagiarism (each student can be provided with a different problem with the same characteristics).

***Feedback generation*** This involves identifying whether the student's solution is incorrect and, if so, the nature of the error and potential fix. Automating it can save teachers time, and enable consistency in grading. It can also be used to provide immediate feedback to students thereby improving student learning.

## What role can PL technologies play?

***Domain-specific languages (DSL)*** The classic problem (in the PL community) of designing an appropriate domain-specific language is relevant to both End-user programming and Education domains. Several PBE and PBNL systems involve an underlying DSL that describes the space of programs to which the user's specification is mapped. Such a DSL is based on abstractions that can be


*POPL '15*, January 15–17, 2015, Mumbai, India.

ACM 978-1-4503-3300-9/15/01.
http://dx.doi.org/10.1145/2676726.2682621

used to *succinctly* describe the various tasks that the users hope to accomplish. On one hand, the DSL should be expressive enough to describe real-world tasks in the domain, while, on the other hand, it should be restricted enough to enable efficient synthesis. In case of problem generation, declarative DSLs allow for describing various kinds of (syntactic or solution-based) features associated with the problems that the teacher aims to generate.

***Symbolic reasoning and Search techniques*** Various symbolic reasoning and search techniques have been developed in the PL community as part of research on invariant generation and constraint solving. Such techniques can be brought to bear to deal with the challenging problem of searching for programs in a DSL that match the user's specification (in case of both PBE and PBNL). Such techniques can also be useful for generating models to queries expressed in declarative languages (in case of both End-user programming and Education domains).

***Test input generation techniques*** Automated test input generation is a well-studied topic in the PL community with great practical utility. Interestingly, these techniques can be useful in both End-user programming and Education domains. In End-user programming, they can drive an active learning user interface that prompts the user about behavior on *distinguishing* inputs that differentiate the multiple programs learned from the user's imprecise specification [3]. In Education, they can be used to generate counterexample based feedback for solutions to *conceptual* problems including constructions (of automata, grammars, programs) and proofs (in algebra, geometry). These techniques can also be used to generate practice problems for *procedural* content such as mathematical procedures taught in middle/high school (e.g., addition, long division, Gaussian elimination) and algorithmic procedures taught in undergraduate computer science, where students are expected to demonstrate their understanding of certain classic algorithms on specific inputs (e.g., breadth-first search, insertion sort, or regular expression to automaton conversion) [4]. For instance, the various concepts in teaching the addition procedure (such as adding single digits, adding numbers without carry, with a single carry, or with a double carry) correspond to specific sets of paths inside the loopy procedure for adding two numbers represented as arrays of digits—test input generation techniques can be used to generate inputs that traverse such a given set of paths.

## What are some future directions?

***Meta-frameworks*** Developing a robust end-to-end experience for a given domain often requires critical domain knowledge and non-trivial implementation effort. A key future direction is to develop general frameworks that can enable easy implementation of domain-specific technologies (for related domains in PBE, PBNL, problem generation, or feedback generation), say from a declarative specification of the domain knowledge. For instance, can we develop frameworks that allow construction of efficient synthesizers from a mere description of the underlying DSL, similar to how declarative parsing frameworks allow compiler writers to construct a parser from a mere description of the syntax of the underlying language. The SyGuS [1], Rosette [11], and FlashExtract [7] frameworks are great initial efforts in this direction.

***Data-driven research*** Leveraging large-scale field data to improve the robustness of systems is another key aspect. For instance, in case of Education domains, the student data can be leveraged to obtain different correct solutions to a problem (which in turn can be used to generate feedback [2]), or to discover effective learning pathways to guide problem selection. In case of End-user programming domains, the knowledge of common idiomatic computations (obtained from a large collection of programs constructed by end users) can be used to guide ranking of programs learned from user's imprecise or ambiguous specification.

***Multi-modality and Interactivity*** Another useful direction is to develop *multi-modal* systems that take as input various forms of specifications such as examples, logical specifications, natural language, and speech. An orthogonal challenge is to develop *interactive* systems that support debugging and allow the user to split the task into multiple steps in case of failure to completely automate the task. There is good inspiration to be drawn from work on interactive theorem proving and work that combines different modes of analysis such as static/deductive and dynamic/inductive.

## Acknowledgments

I thank Rishabh Singh and Ben Zorn for feedback on this article. I thank all my collaborators on projects in End-user programming and Education for believing in and driving the shared vision mentioned in this article.

## References

[1] R. Alur, R. Bodík, G. Juniwal, M. M. K. Martin, M. Raghothaman, S. A. Seshia, R. Singh, A. Solar-Lezama, E. Torlak, and A. Udupa. Syntax-guided synthesis. In *FMCAD*, 2013.

[2] E. Fast, C. Lee, A. Aiken, M. S. Bernstein, D. Koller, and E. Smith. Crowd-scale interactive formal reasoning and analytics. In *UIST*, 2013.

[3] S. Gulwani. Dimensions in program synthesis. In *PPDP*, 2010.

[4] S. Gulwani. Example-Based Learning in Computer-Aided STEM Education. *CACM*, 2014.

[5] S. Gulwani and M. Marron. NLyze: Interactive programming by natural language for spreadsheet data analysis and manipulation. In *SIGMOD*, 2014.

[6] S. Gulwani, W. Harris, and R. Singh. Spreadsheet data manipulation using examples. *CACM*, 2012.

[7] V. Le and S. Gulwani. FlashExtract: A framework for data extraction by examples. In *PLDI*, 2014.

[8] V. Le, S. Gulwani, and Z. Su. Smartsynth: Synthesizing smartphone automation scripts from natural language. In *MobiSys*, 2013.

[9] O. Polozov and S. Gulwani. LaSEWeb: Automating search strategies over semi-structured web data. In *KDD*, 2014.

[10] M. Raza, S. Gulwani, and N. Milic-Frayling. Programming by example using least general generalizations. In *AAAI*, 2014.

[11] E. Torlak and R. Bodík. A lightweight symbolic virtual machine for solver-aided host languages. In *PLDI*, 2014.

## Biography

Sumit Gulwani is a principal researcher at Microsoft Research, Redmond. He has expertise in formal methods and automated program analysis and synthesis techniques. His recent research interests lie in the cross-disciplinary areas of automating end-user programming (for systems like spreadsheets, smartphones, and robots), and building intelligent tutoring systems (for various subject domains including computer science, mathematics, and language learning). His programming-by-example work led to the Flash Fill feature in Microsoft Excel 2013 that is used by hundreds of millions of people. He was awarded the ACM SIGPLAN Robin Milner Young Researcher Award in 2014. He obtained his PhD in Computer Science from UC-Berkeley in 2005, and was awarded the ACM SIGPLAN Outstanding Doctoral Dissertation Award. He obtained his BTech in Computer Science and Engineering from IIT Kanpur in 2000, and was awarded the President's Gold Medal.

# Functors are Type Refinement Systems

Paul-André Melliès
CNRS, Université Paris Diderot
Sorbonne Paris Cité
mellies@pps.univ-paris-diderot.fr

Noam Zeilberger
MSR-Inria Joint Centre
noam.zeilberger@gmail.com

## Abstract

The standard reading of type theory through the lens of category theory is based on the idea of viewing a type system as a category of well-typed terms. We propose a basic revision of this reading: rather than interpreting type systems as categories, we describe them as *functors* from a category of typing derivations to a category of underlying terms. Then, turning this around, we explain how in fact *any* functor gives rise to a generalized type system, with an abstract notion of typing judgment, typing derivations and typing rules. This leads to a purely categorical reformulation of various natural classes of type systems as natural classes of functors.

The main purpose of this paper is to describe the general framework (which can also be seen as providing a categorical analysis of *refinement types*), and to present a few applications. As a larger case study, we revisit Reynolds' paper on "The Meaning of Types" (2000), showing how the paper's main results may be reconstructed along these lines.

***Categories and Subject Descriptors*** F.3.2 [*Semantics of Programming Languages*]

***Keywords*** type theory; category theory; refinement types

## 1. Introduction

One basic difficulty with type theory as a mathematical "theory" is that in practice, the word "type" actually covers two very different usages:

1. Sometimes, like the syntactician's *parts of speech*, types serve to define the basic grammar of well-formed expressions; in this usage, all expressions carry a type, and there is no need (or even sense) to consider the meaning of "untyped" expressions.
2. Other times, like the semanticist's *predicates*, types serve as a way of identifying subsets of expressions with certain desirable properties; in this usage, every expression carries an independent meaning, and typing judgments serve to assert some property of that meaning.


*POPL '15*, January 15–17, 2015, Mumbai, India.

ACM 978-1-4503-3300-9/15/01...$15.00.
http://dx.doi.org/10.1145/2676726.2676970

These two different uses of types are often associated respectively with Alonzo Church and Haskell Curry (hence "types à la Church" and "types à la Curry"), while John Reynolds referred to these as the *intrinsic* and the *extrinsic* views of typing in his book, *Theories of Programming Languages* [30].

Traditionally, readings of type theory through the lens of category theory have sided towards the intrinsic ("à la Church") view. This is natural given the analogy

$$\text{type system} \sim \text{category}$$

which observes for example that a well-typed term

$$x_1 : A_1, \ldots, x_n : A_n \vdash e : B$$

of the simply-typed lambda calculus may be interpreted as a morphism

$$A_1 \times \cdots \times A_n \xrightarrow{e} B$$

in a cartesian-closed category [17]. This favors the intrinsic interpretation, since any morphism of a category

$$A \xrightarrow{f} B$$

is intrinsically associated with a pair of types, namely, its domain $\mathrm{dom}(f) = A$ and codomain $\mathrm{cod}(f) = B$.

On the other hand, there are type-theoretic situations where such an interpretation is plainly problematic. For example, type systems including a notion of intersection or subtyping

$$\frac{\Gamma \vdash e : B \quad \Gamma \vdash e : C}{\Gamma \vdash e : B \cap C} \qquad \frac{\Gamma \vdash e : B \quad B \leq C}{\Gamma \vdash e : C}$$

involve making multiple judgments about the same expression, but in a category, it is not even *grammatical* to write the same morphism between a different pair of objects[1]

$$* \quad \begin{array}{l} A \xrightarrow{f} B \\ A \xrightarrow{f} C \end{array}$$

What Reynolds originally observed [29, 30] is that an intrinsic semantics for such a type system must really interpret *typing derivations* rather than terms. This leads to questions of *coherence* (i.e., whether two derivations of the same typing judgment have the same meaning), and in later work [31], Reynolds gave a particularly elegant proof of coherence, as a corollary to a pair of more general results (a logical relations theorem and a "bracketing" theorem) relating an intrinsic semantics of typing derivations to an *extrinsic* semantics defined directly on untyped terms.

[1] Here and below we adopt the linguist's practice of writing an asterisk to the left of an expression which is ungrammatical (with respect to some linguistic conventions made clear from context).

Conceptually, Reynolds' intrinsic semantics may be formulated as a functor

$$[\![-]\!]_D : \text{Derivations} \to \text{Meanings}$$

from a *category* of typing derivations to some semantic category of meanings, while his extrinsic semantics may be seen as a functor

$$[\![-]\!]_T : \text{Terms} \to \text{Meanings}$$

from a category of untyped terms to the same category of meanings. On the other hand, albeit somewhat hidden in Reynolds' original analysis, implicitly there is also a "forgetful" functor

$$\mathbf{U} : \text{Derivations} \to \text{Terms}$$

from typing derivations to terms, since every typing derivation is *about* some underlying term. The logical relations and bracketing theorems can then be phrased as describing relationships among these three functors.

Our starting point here will be the observation that this analysis may be turned around: in fact, *any* functor

$$\mathbf{U} : \mathcal{D} \to \mathcal{T}$$

may be alternatively viewed as a "type system" in a generalized sense, if we interpret the (arbitrary) category $\mathcal{D}$ as a category of typing derivations and the (arbitrary) category $\mathcal{T}$ as a category of terms. This will lead us to a purely categorical way of speaking about typing derivations and terms—but also conversely to a purely type-theoretic way of speaking about functors.

In some ways, this very abstract view goes back to ideas developed after Grothendieck, in particular by Jean Bénabou, who promoted the idea that any functor may be seen as a "generalized fibration" [2] (we will describe how Grothendieck fibrations themselves can be expressed quite naturally in type-theoretic terms, as type systems with "inverse image types"). Our approach is also closely related to—and partly inspired by—the concept of *refinement* in type theory, viewing $\mathbf{U}$ as the functor which forgets refinement information. In the paper, we will adopt some of the language typically used to speak about refinement type systems [27] in order to speak about general functors—in effect providing a simple and natural categorical semantics of refinement types.

## 2. Reading a functor as a refinement system

For completeness and in order to fix notations, we begin by recalling the formal definitions of *category* and *functor*.

**Definition 1.** A **category** consists of:

- A collection of *objects* $(A, B, \dots)$.
- A collection of *morphisms* $(f, g, \dots)$, together with operations dom and cod assigning to each morphism a unique source and target. We write $f : A \to B$ to indicate that $\text{dom}(f) = A$ and $\text{cod}(f) = B$.
- Composition and identity: for any pair of morphisms $f : A \to B$ and $g : B \to C$, a morphism $(f;g) : A \to C$, as well as for every object $A$, a morphism $\text{id}_A : A \to A$ (we often omit the subscript on id when it can be deduced from context).
- Such that associativity and unit laws hold:

$$(f;g);h = f;(g;h)$$
$$f;\text{id} = f = \text{id};f$$

**Definition 2.** Let $\mathcal{D}$ and $\mathcal{T}$ be categories. We say that $\mathbf{U}$ is a **functor** from $\mathcal{D}$ to $\mathcal{T}$ when it determines the following:

- for each object $S$ of $\mathcal{D}$, an object $\mathbf{U}(S)$ of $\mathcal{T}$, and
- for each morphism $\alpha : S \to T$ of $\mathcal{D}$, a morphism $\mathbf{U}(\alpha) : \mathbf{U}(S) \to \mathbf{U}(T)$ of $\mathcal{T}$,
- such that composition and identity are preserved:

$$\mathbf{U}(\alpha;\beta) = (\mathbf{U}(\alpha);\mathbf{U}(\beta))$$
$$\mathbf{U}(\text{id}_S) = \text{id}_{\mathbf{U}(S)}$$

■

Now, for the remainder of the section we will assume a fixed, arbitrary functor $\mathbf{U} : \mathcal{D} \to \mathcal{T}$, and consider various notions relative to $\mathbf{U}$.

**Definition 3.** We say that an object $S \in \mathcal{D}$ **refines** an object $A \in \mathcal{T}$ if $\mathbf{U}(S) = A$.

**Definition 4.** A **typing judgment** is a triple $(S, f, T)$ such that $S$ and $T$ refine the domain and codomain of $f$, respectively, i.e., such that $f : A \to B$, $\mathbf{U}(S) = A$ and $\mathbf{U}(T) = B$, for some arbitrary $A$ and $B$. In the special case where $f = \text{id}$ (implying that $\mathbf{U}(S) = \mathbf{U}(T)$), we also call this a **subtyping judgment**.

**Definition 5.** A **derivation** of a typing judgment $(S, f, T)$ is a morphism $\alpha : S \to T$ in $\mathcal{D}$ such that $\mathbf{U}(\alpha) = f$. ■

We emphasize again that these definitions are all parameterized by a fixed functor $\mathbf{U}$, and in some situations to be completely explicit we could speak of $\mathbf{U}$-refinement, $\mathbf{U}$-typing judgments, and so on. In fig. 1, we give a graphical illustration of the definitions relative to a few miniature examples.

Along with these definitions, we introduce some notation (also appearing in fig. 1) and conventions inspired from logic and proof theory:

1. We write $S \sqsubset A$ to indicate that $S$ refines $A$ (i.e., $\mathbf{U}(S) = A$). In general, we refer to objects of $\mathcal{T}$ as *types*, to objects of $\mathcal{D}$ as *refinement types*, and to morphisms of $\mathcal{T}$ as *terms*.
2. We write

$$S \underset{f}{\Longrightarrow} T$$

to indicate that $(S, f, T)$ is a typing judgment in the sense of Defn. 4 (i.e., $\mathbf{U}(S) = \text{dom}(f)$ and $\mathbf{U}(T) = \text{cod}(f)$), and

$$U \leq V$$

to indicate that $(U, \text{id}, V)$ is a subtyping judgment (i.e., $\mathbf{U}(U) = \mathbf{U}(V)$). Since subtyping is just a special case of typing, the two judgments

$$U \leq V \quad \text{and} \quad U \underset{\text{id}}{\Longrightarrow} V$$

have precisely the same meaning.
3. We write

$$S \overset{\alpha}{\underset{f}{\Longrightarrow}} T$$

to indicate that $\alpha$ is a derivation of the typing judgment $(S, f, T)$ in the sense of Defn. 5 (i.e., $\alpha : S \to T$ and $\mathbf{U}(\alpha) = f$). We also write

$$\vdash S \underset{f}{\Longrightarrow} T$$

to simply indicate that such a derivation *exists* (without naming it), or

$$\nvdash S \underset{f}{\Longrightarrow} T$$

to indicate the absence of such a derivation, in which case we say that the typing judgment is *valid* or *invalid*, respectively.

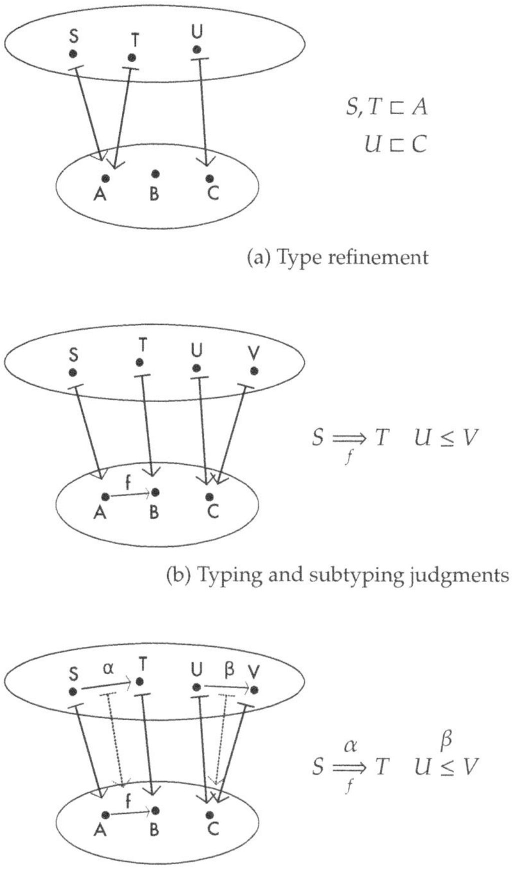


(a) Type refinement

(b) Typing and subtyping judgments

(c) Derivations of typing and subtyping judgments

Figure 1: An illustration of various type-theoretic concepts associated to a functor.

4. More generally, we say that a *typing rule*

$$\frac{S_1 \xRightarrow[f_1]{} T_1 \quad \dots \quad S_n \xRightarrow[f_n]{} T_n}{S \xRightarrow[f]{} T}$$

is valid if, given derivations of the premises, we can construct a derivation of the conclusion. We will sometimes give an explicit name to a typing rule (as a way of referring to the corresponding construction on derivations), by placing it to the right of the horizontal bar. For example, any derivation can be treated as a valid typing rule with no premises:

$$S \overset{\alpha}{\xRightarrow[f]{}} T \quad \Longleftrightarrow \quad \frac{}{S \xRightarrow[f]{} T}\,\alpha$$

**Proposition 6.** *The following typing rules are always valid:*

$$\frac{S \xRightarrow[f]{} T \quad T \xRightarrow[g]{} U}{S \xRightarrow[f;g]{} U}\,; \qquad \frac{}{S \xRightarrow[\mathrm{id}]{} S}\,\mathrm{id}$$

*Proof.* These are immediate consequences of the functoriality of $\mathbf{U}$. For example, suppose $\alpha$ is a derivation of $(S, f, T)$ and $\beta$ is a derivation of $(T, g, U)$. By definition, this means that $\alpha : S \to T$ and $\mathbf{U}(\alpha) = f$, and $\beta : T \to U$ and $\mathbf{U}(\beta) = g$. But then $(\alpha;\beta)$ is a derivation of $(S, (f;g), U)$, since $(\alpha;\beta) : S \to U$ and $\mathbf{U}(\alpha;\beta) = (\mathbf{U}(\alpha);\mathbf{U}(\beta)) = (f;g)$. □

**Proposition 7.** *Subtyping is reflexive and transitive, and admits rules of covariant and contravariant subsumption:*

$$\frac{}{S \le S} \qquad \frac{S \le T \quad T \le U}{S \le U} \qquad \frac{S \xRightarrow[f]{} T \quad T \le U}{S \xRightarrow[f]{} U} \qquad \frac{S \le T \quad T \xRightarrow[g]{} U}{S \xRightarrow[g]{} U}$$

*Proof.* Reflexivity of subtyping is by definition just another way of writing the id typing rule of Prop. 6, while transitivity and subsumption are all special cases of ";" with one or both of the terms (i.e., morphisms of $\mathcal{T}$) $f$ and $g$ set to the identity term id. □

As the proof of Prop. 7 illustrates, sometimes constructing a typing derivation involves reasoning about equality of terms (i.e., morphisms of $\mathcal{T}$). In general, we allow ourselves to work modulo this equality, but for clarity it is sometimes useful to make the move between equal terms explicit by indicating a *conversion step*:

$$\frac{S \xRightarrow[f]{} T}{S \xRightarrow[g]{} T}\,\sim$$

For example, the covariant subsumption rule of Prop. 7 can be more explicitly derived as follows:

$$\cfrac{\cfrac{S \xRightarrow[f]{} T \quad T \le U}{S \xRightarrow[f;\mathrm{id}]{} U}\,;}{S \xRightarrow[f]{} U}\,\sim$$

Finally, we should mention that the categorical axioms also imply various equations on typing derivations. For example, the associativity axioms imply that the derivation named by

$$\cfrac{\cfrac{S \overset{\alpha}{\xRightarrow[f]{}} T \quad T \overset{\beta}{\xRightarrow[g]{}} U}{S \xRightarrow[f;g]{} U}\,; \quad U \overset{\gamma}{\xRightarrow[h]{}} V}{S \xRightarrow[(f;g);h]{} V}\,;$$

is equal to the derivation named by

$$\cfrac{S \overset{\alpha}{\xRightarrow[f]{}} T \quad \cfrac{T \overset{\beta}{\xRightarrow[g]{}} U \quad U \overset{\gamma}{\xRightarrow[h]{}} V}{T \xRightarrow[g;h]{} V}\,;}{S \xRightarrow[f;(g;h)]{} V}\,;$$

while the unit laws imply that

$$\cfrac{\cfrac{S \overset{\alpha}{\xRightarrow[f]{}} T \quad T \overset{\beta}{\xRightarrow[g]{}} U}{S \xRightarrow[f;g]{} U}\,; \quad \cfrac{}{U \xRightarrow[\mathrm{id}]{} U}\,\mathrm{id}}{S \xRightarrow[(f;g);\mathrm{id}]{} U}\,; \quad = \quad \cfrac{S \overset{\alpha}{\xRightarrow[f]{}} T \quad T \overset{\beta}{\xRightarrow[g]{}} U}{S \xRightarrow[f;g]{} U}\,;$$

$$\cfrac{\cfrac{}{T \xRightarrow[\mathrm{id}]{} T}\,\mathrm{id} \quad \cfrac{T \overset{\beta}{\xRightarrow[g]{}} U \quad U \overset{\gamma}{\xRightarrow[h]{}} V}{T \xRightarrow[g;h]{} V}\,;}{T \xRightarrow[\mathrm{id};(g;h)]{} V}\,; \quad = \quad \cfrac{T \overset{\beta}{\xRightarrow[g]{}} U \quad U \overset{\gamma}{\xRightarrow[h]{}} V}{T \xRightarrow[g;h]{} V}\,;$$

These various simple observations motivate our adopting the following definition:

**Definition 8.** A **refinement system** is a functor $\mathbf{U} : \mathcal{D} \to \mathcal{T}$.

**Example 1.** To try to provide a bit of intuition for this way of reading functors, we will consider a simple and naive example, which is indeed perhaps the "folk model" of refinement types. For $\mathcal{T}$ we take the category **Set** of sets and functions, while for $\mathcal{D}$ we take the category **SubSet** of *subsets and image inclusions*. An object of **SubSet** is a pair $(A, S)$ of a set $A$ and a subset of that set $S \subseteq A$, while a morphism

$$(A, S) \to (B, T)$$

is a function between the underlying sets

$$f : A \to B$$

such that the image of the first subset is included in the second

$$\forall a.a \in S \Rightarrow f(a) \in T$$

As the functor $\mathbf{U}$ : **SubSet** $\to$ **Set** we take the first projection, sending a subset to its underlying set.

Putting aside formal questions of what exactly "sets" are (e.g., whether axiomatized by ZFC, etc.), by most interpretations, the category **Set** is already quite rich with types. For example we can probably suppose it contains types of natural numbers, integers, sequences of integers,

$$\mathbb{N}, \mathbb{Z}, \mathbb{Z}^{\mathbb{N}}$$

and many more besides. But if one could attribute a "philosophy" to type refinement, it is that rather than trying to say everything at once in the language of types, it is sometimes better to start from a rough statement, and then explore ways of making it more precise *while keeping the original statement*. So, for instance, we might consider the refinement types of *odd*, *even*, or *prime* natural numbers,[2]

$$odd \stackrel{\text{def}}{=} \{\, n \mid \exists k.n = 2k + 1 \,\} \sqsubset \mathbb{N}$$
$$even \stackrel{\text{def}}{=} \{\, n \mid \exists k.n = 2k \,\} \sqsubset \mathbb{N}$$
$$prime \stackrel{\text{def}}{=} \{\, n \mid n > 1 \wedge \forall k.(k > 1 \wedge k \mid n) \Rightarrow k = n \,\} \sqsubset \mathbb{N}$$

of *non-zero* or *non-negative* integers,

$$nonzero \stackrel{\text{def}}{=} \{\, x \mid x \neq 0 \,\} \sqsubset \mathbb{Z}$$
$$nonneg \stackrel{\text{def}}{=} \{\, x \mid x \geq 0 \,\} \sqsubset \mathbb{Z}$$

of *linear* or *bounded* sequences,

$$linear \stackrel{\text{def}}{=} \{\, f \mid \exists a, b \forall n.f(n) = a \cdot n + b \,\} \sqsubset \mathbb{Z}^{\mathbb{N}}$$
$$bounded \stackrel{\text{def}}{=} \{\, f \mid \exists x \forall n.f(n) \leq x \,\} \sqsubset \mathbb{Z}^{\mathbb{N}}$$

and so on. The point of the functor $\mathbf{U}$ : **SubSet** $\to$ **Set** is that these refinement types (in **SubSet**) will always be considered with respect to the original types (in **Set**) they refine.

For example, the question whether "every prime number is odd" may be sensibly posed as a subtyping problem,

$$prime \leq odd$$

whose answer happens to be negative (i.e., the judgment is invalid). On the other hand, the question of whether "every linear sequence is odd" is not really sensible without resort to some encoding, and the corresponding subtyping judgment

$$* \; linear \leq odd$$

is not well-formed, since the two sides refine different types. As another example, if we take

$$\lambda x.x^2 : \mathbb{Z} \to \mathbb{Z}$$

to be the squaring function on the integers, then the following three typing judgments are respectively valid, invalid, and ill-formed:

$$\vdash nonzero \underset{\lambda x.x^2}{\Longrightarrow} nonneg$$
$$\nvdash nonneg \underset{\lambda x.x^2}{\Longrightarrow} nonzero$$
$$* \; nonneg \underset{\lambda x.x^2}{\Longrightarrow} bounded$$

## 3. Monoidal and logical refinement systems

In the previous section, we described how an *arbitrary* functor gives rise to a "refinement system", in the sense of an abstract notion of typing judgment, typing rules, etc. Of course, if all we could say were restricted to such generalities, then we could not say very much. But we have several strategies for carving out richer *classes* of refinement systems $\mathbf{U} : \mathcal{D} \to \mathcal{T}$:

1. By asking for additional structure on $\mathcal{D}$ and $\mathcal{T}$, and that it is preserved by $\mathbf{U}$.
2. By asking for additional properties of $\mathbf{U}$ (like for instance that it is a fibration).
3. By considering specific (refinement) type signatures, under assumption of some existing structure and properties.

In this section we will pursue the first strategy (the others will be considered later on). We begin by recalling the standard definition of a *monoidal* category:

**Definition 9.** A **monoidal structure** on a category $\mathcal{D}$ consists of a functor (called the tensor product)

$$- \bullet - : \mathcal{D} \times \mathcal{D} \to \mathcal{D}$$

together with an object $I \in \mathcal{D}$, satisfying associativity and unity axioms up to natural isomorphism,

$$(A \bullet B) \bullet C \equiv A \bullet (B \bullet C) \qquad A \bullet I \equiv A \equiv I \bullet A$$

Moreover, these natural isomorphisms have to satisfy certain "coherence laws" which we omit here (see [21]). A **monoidal category** is a category equipped with a monoidal structure. ■

There are many examples of monoidal categories, and often the tensor product satisfies additional properties, such as being *symmetric* or *cartesian* [21]. However, here we just want to start from the most basic situation.

**Definition 10.** A **monoidal refinement system** is a functor $\mathbf{U} : \mathcal{D} \to \mathcal{T}$ between monoidal categories, preserving the monoidal structure in the strict sense that we have a pair of commutative squares:

$$\begin{array}{ccc} \mathcal{D} \times \mathcal{D} & \xrightarrow{\bullet_{\mathcal{D}}} & \mathcal{D} \\ {\scriptstyle \mathbf{U}\times\mathbf{U}} \downarrow & & \downarrow {\scriptstyle \mathbf{U}} \\ \mathcal{T} \times \mathcal{T} & \xrightarrow[\bullet_{\mathcal{T}}]{} & \mathcal{T} \end{array} \qquad \begin{array}{ccc} 1 & \xrightarrow{I_{\mathcal{D}}} & \mathcal{D} \\ \| & & \downarrow {\scriptstyle \mathbf{U}} \\ 1 & \xrightarrow[I_{\mathcal{T}}]{} & \mathcal{T} \end{array}$$

■

To read these conditions in type-theoretic language, we first allow ourselves to introduce another natural convention: we say that a *refinement rule*

$$\frac{S_1 \sqsubset A_1 \quad \dots \quad S_n \sqsubset A_n}{S \sqsubset A}$$

[2] Here we allow ourselves the slight abuse of writing $S \sqsubset A$, although strictly speaking the pair $(A, S)$ is the object of **SubSet**.

is valid if $\mathbf{U}(S_1) = A_1, \ldots, \mathbf{U}(S_n) = A_n$ implies that $\mathbf{U}(S) = A$. Then the commutative squares of defn. 10 translate straightforwardly to the following proposition (we omit subscripts on the monoidal operations, since they are always clear from context).

**Proposition 11.** *In any monoidal refinement system, the following refinement rules and typing rules are valid:*

$$\frac{S_1 \sqsubset A_1 \quad S_2 \sqsubset A_2}{S_1 \bullet S_2 \sqsubset A_1 \bullet A_2} \qquad \frac{}{I \sqsubset I} \qquad \frac{S_1 \underset{f_1}{\Longrightarrow} T_1 \quad S_2 \underset{f_2}{\Longrightarrow} T_2}{S_1 \bullet S_2 \underset{f_1 \bullet f_2}{\Longrightarrow} T_1 \bullet T_2}\bullet \qquad \frac{}{I \underset{I}{\Longrightarrow} I}\,I$$

Likewise, the axioms of monoidal categories translate to various equations on derivations constructed using the typing rules. We elide these here, and instead move on to considering what we call *logical* refinement systems. First we recall more standard material on category theory.

**Definition 12.** Let $A$ and $C$ be two objects of a monoidal category. A **left residual of** $C$ **by** $A$ is an object $B'$ equipped with a *left-evaluation map*

$$A \bullet B' \xrightarrow{\obslash} C$$

and a transformation $\lambda[-]$ from maps

$$A \bullet B \xrightarrow{f} C \tag{1}$$

(where $B$ is any object) to maps

$$B \xrightarrow{\lambda[f]} B' \tag{2}$$

called *left-currying*, such that for any $f : A \bullet B \to C$ and $g : B \to B'$ we have equations

$$((\mathrm{id} \bullet \lambda[f]); \obslash) = f \qquad g = \lambda[(\mathrm{id} \bullet g); \obslash]$$

These equations ensure that there is a one-to-one correspondence between maps of the form (1) and maps of the form (2). Similarly, for any two objects $B$ and $C$, a **right residual of** $C$ **by** $B$ is an object $A'$ equipped with a *right-evaluation map*

$$A' \bullet B \xrightarrow{\oslash} C$$

and a transformation $\rho[-]$ from maps

$$A \bullet B \xrightarrow{f} C$$

(where $A$ is any object) to maps

$$A \xrightarrow{\rho[f]} A'$$

called *right-currying*, such that for any $f : A \bullet B \to C$ and $g : A \to A'$ we have

$$((\rho[f] \bullet \mathrm{id}); \oslash) = f \qquad g = \rho[(g \bullet \mathrm{id}); \oslash]$$

**Proposition 13.** *Residuation is determined up to isomorphism, i.e., if $B$ and $B'$ are two left residuals of $C$ by $A$, then $B \cong B'$, and if $A$ and $A'$ are two right residuals of $C$ by $B$, then $A \cong A'$.*

Because of this proposition, we allow ourselves to speak of *the* left residual of $C$ by $A$ whenever it exists, writing $A \backslash C$ to denote it—and similarly $C \,/\, B$ for the right residual.

**Definition 14.** A **logical refinement system** is a monoidal refinement system $\mathbf{U} : \mathcal{D} \to \mathcal{T}$ which preserves left and right residuals. ■

It is worth mentioning that the definition of a logical refinement system in our sense does not require that *all* left and right residuals exist in $\mathcal{D}$ and $\mathcal{T}$ (i.e., that the categories are *closed*), but only that $\mathbf{U}$ *preserves* any which exist in $\mathcal{D}$.

$$\frac{S \sqsubset A \quad U \sqsubset C}{S \backslash U \sqsubset A \backslash C} \qquad \frac{}{S \bullet S \backslash U \underset{\obslash}{\Longrightarrow} U}\obslash \qquad \frac{S \bullet T \underset{f}{\Longrightarrow} U}{T \underset{\lambda[f]}{\Longrightarrow} S \backslash U}\lambda$$

$$\beta\quad \frac{\dfrac{\dfrac{}{S \underset{\mathrm{id}}{\Longrightarrow} S}\mathrm{id} \quad \dfrac{S \bullet T \underset{f}{\Longrightarrow} U}{T \underset{\lambda[f]}{\Longrightarrow} S \backslash U}\lambda}{S \bullet T \underset{\mathrm{id}\bullet\lambda[f]}{\Longrightarrow} S \bullet S \backslash U}\bullet \quad \dfrac{}{S \bullet S \backslash U \underset{\obslash}{\Longrightarrow} U}\obslash}{S \bullet T \underset{(\mathrm{id}\bullet\lambda[f]);\obslash}{\Longrightarrow} U}\,; \quad = \quad \overset{\beta}{S \bullet T \underset{f}{\Longrightarrow} U}$$

$$\overset{\eta}{T \underset{g}{\Longrightarrow} S \backslash U} \quad = \quad \frac{\dfrac{\dfrac{\dfrac{}{S \le S}\mathrm{id} \quad \overset{\eta}{T \underset{g}{\Longrightarrow} S \backslash U}}{S \bullet T \underset{\mathrm{id}\bullet g}{\Longrightarrow} S \bullet S \backslash U}\bullet \quad \dfrac{}{S \bullet S \backslash U \underset{\obslash}{\Longrightarrow} U}\obslash}{S \bullet T \underset{(\mathrm{id}\bullet g);\obslash}{\Longrightarrow} U}\,;}{T \underset{\lambda[(\mathrm{id}\bullet g);\obslash]}{\Longrightarrow} S \backslash U}\lambda$$

Figure 2: The defining rules of a logical refinement system (restricted to the rules involving left residuals).

In fig. 2, we illustrate how defn. 14 (limited to the part involving left residuals) may be equivalently formulated in the language of type theory, using the appropriate refinement rules, typing rules, and equations. These rules are actually quite standard in the literature on refinement types (see, for example, the system of "simple sorts" described by Pfenning [27, §6]), except for our use of the notation of the Lambek calculus [16] (justified by the fact that we are working in a general monoidal rather than a cartesian setting). Perhaps one rule from fig. 2 that bears emphasizing is the refinement rule:

$$\frac{S \sqsubset A \quad U \sqsubset C}{S \backslash U \sqsubset A \backslash C}$$

Under the conventions we have established, the rule simply restates the condition that the functor $\mathbf{U}$ preserves left residuals. In particular, the refinement rule should *not* be confused with the familiar rule of subtyping for function types, which mixes contravariance in the domain with covariance in the codomain:

**Proposition 15.** *The following subtyping rules are valid in any logical refinement system, if the corresponding residuals exist:*

$$\frac{S_2 \le S_1 \quad U_1 \le U_2}{S_1 \backslash U_1 \le S_2 \backslash U_2} \qquad \frac{U_1 \le U_2 \quad T_2 \le T_1}{U_1 \,/\, T_1 \le U_2 \,/\, T_2}$$

*Proof.* We can derive the rule for left residuals as follows (the case of right residuals is symmetric):

$$\frac{\dfrac{\dfrac{\dfrac{\dfrac{\dfrac{S_2 \le S_1 \quad \dfrac{}{S_1 \backslash U_1 \le S_1 \backslash U_1}\mathrm{id}}{S_2 \bullet S_1 \backslash U_1 \le S_1 \bullet S_1 \backslash U_1}\bullet \quad \dfrac{}{S_1 \bullet S_1 \backslash U_1 \underset{\obslash}{\Longrightarrow} U_1}\obslash}{S_2 \bullet S_1 \backslash U_1 \underset{\obslash}{\Longrightarrow} U_1}\,; \quad U_1 \le U_2}{S_2 \bullet S_1 \backslash U_1 \underset{\obslash}{\Longrightarrow} U_2}\,;}{S_1 \backslash U_1 \underset{\lambda[\obslash]}{\Longrightarrow} S_2 \backslash U_2}\lambda}{S_1 \backslash U_1 \le S_2 \backslash U_2}}{}\sim$$

□

**Example 2.** The refinement system **SubSet** → **Set** considered in Section 2 extends to a logical refinement system. The monoidal structure on **Set** is the usual cartesian structure,

$$A \bullet B \stackrel{\text{def}}{=} A \times B \qquad I \stackrel{\text{def}}{=} 1$$

which also lifts to a (cartesian) monoidal structure on **SubSet**:

$$(S \sqsubset A) \bullet (T \sqsubset B) \stackrel{\text{def}}{=} \{\, (a,b) \mid a \in S, b \in T \,\} \sqsubset A \times B$$
$$(I \sqsubset I) \stackrel{\text{def}}{=} \{\, * \,\} \sqsubset 1$$

Both categories are also closed, with left and right residuals both defined in terms of the function space (we describe only the underlying sets/subsets, not evaluation and currying):

$$A \setminus C \stackrel{\text{def}}{=} C^A \qquad C \,/\, B \stackrel{\text{def}}{=} C^B$$
$$(S \sqsubset A) \setminus (U \sqsubset C) \stackrel{\text{def}}{=} \{\, f \mid \forall a. a \in S \Rightarrow f(a) \in U \,\} \sqsubset C^A$$
$$(U \sqsubset C) \,/\, (T \sqsubset B) \stackrel{\text{def}}{=} \{\, f \mid \forall b. b \in T \Rightarrow f(b) \in U \,\} \sqsubset C^B$$

The forgetful functor **SubSet** → **Set** evidently sends products and residuals in **SubSet** to products and residuals in **Set**, and thus defines a logical refinement system.

As an example, writing $+ : \mathbb{N} \bullet \mathbb{N} \to \mathbb{N}$ for addition of natural numbers, we can state various easy arithmetic facts and non-facts as valid and invalid judgments:

$$\vdash odd \xRightarrow[\lambda[+]]{} odd \setminus even$$
$$\vdash odd \xRightarrow[\lambda[+]]{} even \setminus odd$$
$$\nvdash even \xRightarrow[\lambda[+]]{} prime \setminus odd$$

## 4. Reading Grothendieck in translation

In this section we will pursue the second strategy mentioned at the beginning of Section 3, and begin by recalling the definition of when a functor $\mathbf{U} : \mathcal{D} \to \mathcal{T}$ is a *fibration* à la Grothendieck [13].

**Definition 16.** A morphism $\alpha : T' \to T$ in $\mathcal{D}$ is said to be **cartesian** if for every object $S \in \mathcal{D}$ and every pair of morphisms $\beta : S \to T$ and $g : \mathbf{U}(S) \to \mathbf{U}(T')$ such that $\mathbf{U}(\beta) = g;\mathbf{U}(\alpha)$, there is a unique morphism $\beta' : S \to T'$ such that $\beta = \alpha;\beta'$ and $\mathbf{U}(\beta') = g$.

**Definition 17.** Let $f : A \to B$ be a morphism in $\mathcal{T}$, and $T$ be an object of $\mathcal{D}$ such that $\mathbf{U}(T) = B$. A morphism $\alpha$ in $\mathcal{D}$ is said to be a **cartesian lifting** of $f$ to $T$ if $\mathbf{U}(\alpha) = f$, $\mathrm{cod}(\alpha) = T$, and $\alpha$ is cartesian.

**Definition 18.** A functor $\mathbf{U} : \mathcal{D} \to \mathcal{T}$ is said to be a **fibration** if for every morphism $f : A \to B$ in $\mathcal{T}$ and object $T \in \mathcal{D}$ such that $\mathbf{U}(T) = B$, $f$ has a cartesian lifting to $T$.

The definition of fibration plays a fundamental role in category theory as well as in the semantics of dependent types, and we may thus wonder whether we can understand it from our point of view on refinement type systems. Again, we assume $\mathbf{U} : \mathcal{D} \to \mathcal{T}$ is fixed, with the notational and terminological conventions of Section 2 (we do not assume any other structure on $\mathcal{D}$ and $\mathcal{T}$).

**Definition 19.** Let $f : A \to B$ and $T \sqsubset B$. A **pullback** (or "inverse image") **of** $T$ **along** $f$ is a refinement type $T' \sqsubset A$ equipped with a pair of valid typing rules

$$\dfrac{}{T' \xRightarrow[f]{} T}\,L \qquad \dfrac{S \xRightarrow[g;f]{} T}{S \xRightarrow[g]{} T'}\,R$$

such that for all derivations

$$S \xRightarrow[g;f]{\beta} T \quad \text{and} \quad S \xRightarrow[g]{\eta} T'$$

we have a pair of equalities

$$\dfrac{\dfrac{S \xRightarrow[g;f]{\beta} T}{S \xRightarrow[g]{} T'}\,R \qquad \dfrac{}{T' \xRightarrow[f]{} T}\,L}{S \xRightarrow[g;f]{} T}\,; \quad = \quad S \xRightarrow[g;f]{\beta} T$$

and

$$S \xRightarrow[g]{\eta} T' \quad = \quad \dfrac{\dfrac{S \xRightarrow[g]{\eta} T' \qquad \dfrac{}{T' \xRightarrow[f]{} T}\,L}{S \xRightarrow[g;f]{} T}\,;}{S \xRightarrow[g]{} T'}\,R$$

■

Now, it is essentially immediate by unwinding the definitions that we have just redubbed Grothendieck to a type-theoretic soundtrack:

**Proposition 20.** *$\alpha : T' \to T$ is a cartesian lifting of $f$ to $T$ if and only if the triple $(T', L_\alpha, R_\alpha)$ is a pullback of $T$ along $f$, where $L_\alpha = \alpha$, and where $R_\alpha$ is defined using the universal property of $\alpha$.*

**Proposition 21.** *$\mathbf{U}$ is a fibration iff for every $f : A \to B$ and $T \sqsubset B$, there exists a pullback of $T$ along $f$.*

Somewhat remarkably, many standard facts about fibrations can be derived quite mechanically under this translation, reminiscent of proofs in the sequent calculus. We begin by showing in this proof-theoretic style that pullbacks are determined up to *vertical isomorphism*.

**Definition 22.** Let $S, T \sqsubset A$ be two refinements of a common type. We say that $S$ and $T$ are **vertically isomorphic** (written $S \equiv T$) when there exist a pair of subtyping derivations

$$\overset{\alpha}{S \leq T} \qquad \overset{\beta}{T \leq S}$$

which compose to the identity

$$\dfrac{\overset{\alpha}{S \leq T} \quad \overset{\beta}{T \leq S}}{S \leq S}\,; \; = \; \dfrac{}{S \leq S}\,\mathrm{id} \qquad \dfrac{\overset{\beta}{T \leq S} \quad \overset{\alpha}{S \leq T}}{T \leq T}\,; \; = \; \dfrac{}{T \leq T}\,\mathrm{id}$$

**Proposition 23.** *Any two pullbacks of $T$ along $f$ are vertically isomorphic.*

*Proof.* Let $T'$ and $T''$ both be pullbacks of $T$ along $f$, equipped with corresponding valid typing rules

$$\dfrac{}{T' \xRightarrow[f]{} T}\,LT' \qquad \dfrac{S \xRightarrow[g;f]{} T}{S \xRightarrow[g]{} T'}\,RT'$$

and

$$\dfrac{}{T'' \xRightarrow[f]{} T}\,LT'' \qquad \dfrac{S \xRightarrow[g;f]{} T}{S \xRightarrow[g]{} T''}\,RT''$$

Then we can build derivations of $T' \leq T''$ and $T'' \leq T'$ by

$$\dfrac{\dfrac{}{T' \xRightarrow[f]{} T}\,LT'}{T' \leq T''}\,RT'' \qquad \dfrac{\dfrac{}{T'' \xRightarrow[f]{} T}\,LT''}{T'' \leq T'}\,RT'$$

$$\frac{f : A \to B \quad T \sqsubset B}{f^* T \sqsubset A} \qquad \frac{}{f^* T \underset{f}{\Longrightarrow} T}\, Lf^* \qquad \frac{S \underset{g;f}{\Longrightarrow} T}{S \underset{g}{\Longrightarrow} f^* T}\, Rf^*$$

$$\dfrac{\dfrac{S \underset{g;f}{\overset{\beta}{\Longrightarrow}} T}{S \underset{g}{\Longrightarrow} f^* T}\, Rf^* \quad \dfrac{}{f^* T \underset{f}{\Longrightarrow} T}\, Lf^*}{S \underset{g;f}{\Longrightarrow} T}\, ; \;=\; S \underset{g;f}{\overset{\beta}{\Longrightarrow}} T \qquad S \underset{g}{\overset{\eta}{\Longrightarrow}} f^* T \;=\; \dfrac{\dfrac{S \underset{g}{\overset{\eta}{\Longrightarrow}} f^* T \quad \dfrac{}{f^* T \underset{f}{\Longrightarrow} T}\, Lf^*}{S \underset{g;f}{\Longrightarrow} T}\, ;}{S \underset{g}{\Longrightarrow} f^* T}\, Rf^*$$

Figure 3: The defining rules of pullback refinements.

$$\frac{S \sqsubset A \quad f : A \to B}{f\, S \sqsubset B} \qquad \frac{S \underset{f;g}{\Longrightarrow} T}{f\, S \underset{g}{\Longrightarrow} T}\, Lf \qquad \frac{}{S \underset{f}{\Longrightarrow} f\, S}\, Rf$$

$$\dfrac{\dfrac{}{S \underset{f}{\Longrightarrow} f\, S}\, Rf \quad \dfrac{S \underset{f;g}{\overset{\beta}{\Longrightarrow}} T}{f\, S \underset{g}{\Longrightarrow} T}\, Lf}{S \underset{f;g}{\Longrightarrow} T}\, ; \;=\; S \underset{f;g}{\overset{\beta}{\Longrightarrow}} T \qquad f\, S \underset{g}{\overset{\eta}{\Longrightarrow}} T \;=\; \dfrac{\dfrac{\dfrac{}{S \underset{f}{\Longrightarrow} f\, S}\, Rf \quad f\, S \underset{g}{\overset{\eta}{\Longrightarrow}} T}{S \underset{f;g}{\Longrightarrow} T}\, ;}{f\, S \underset{g}{\Longrightarrow} T}\, Lf$$

Figure 4: The defining rules of pushforward refinements.

and easily verify from the axioms that these two derivations compose to the identity. □

Because pullbacks are determined up to vertical isomorphism, we allow ourselves to speak of *the* pullback of $T$ along $f$ whenever one exists, writing $f^* T$ for the refinement type and $Lf^*$ and $Rf^*$ for the corresponding rules (see fig. 3).

We can now mechanically establish the following facts about pullbacks, which, in categorical jargon, go into showing that any fibration determines a pseudofunctor $\mathcal{T}^{\mathrm{op}} \to \mathbf{Cat}$:

**Proposition 24.** *Whenever the corresponding pullbacks exist:*

1. *the following subtyping rule is valid:*
$$\frac{T_1 \leq T_2}{f^* T_1 \leq f^* T_2}$$
2. *we have vertical isomorphisms*
$$(g; f)^* T \equiv g^* f^* T \qquad \mathrm{id}^* T \equiv T$$

*Proof.* 1.
$$\dfrac{\dfrac{\dfrac{\dfrac{}{f^* T_1 \underset{f}{\Longrightarrow} T_1}\, Lf^* \quad T_1 \leq T_2}{f^* T_1 \underset{f;\mathrm{id}}{\Longrightarrow} T_2}\, ;}{f^* T_1 \underset{\mathrm{id};f}{\Longrightarrow} T_2}\, \sim}{f^* T_1 \leq f^* T_2}\, Rf^*$$

2. For the left equation, we construct subtyping derivations in both directions by
$$\dfrac{\dfrac{\dfrac{}{(g;f)^* T \underset{g;f}{\Longrightarrow} T}\, L(g;f)^*}{(g;f)^* T \underset{g}{\Longrightarrow} f^* T}\, Rf^*}{(g;f)^* T \leq g^* f^* T}\, Rg^* \qquad \dfrac{\dfrac{\dfrac{}{g^* f^* T \underset{g}{\Longrightarrow} f^* T}\, Lg^* \quad \dfrac{}{f^* T \underset{f}{\Longrightarrow} T}\, Lf^*}{g^* f^* T \underset{g;f}{\Longrightarrow} T}\, ;}{g^* f^* T \leq (g;f)^* T}\, R(g;f)^*$$
and again by an easy calculation, we can show that these two derivations compose to the identity. The right equation $\mathrm{id}^* T \equiv T$ is essentially immediate (which also means that pullbacks along the identity always exist). □

Next, we give an analogous reconstruction of the dual concept of an *opfibration*.

**Definition 25.** Let $S \sqsubset A$ and $f : A \to B$. A **pushforward** (or "image") **of $S$ along $f$** is a refinement type $S' \sqsubset B$ equipped with a pair of valid typing rules
$$\frac{S \underset{f;g}{\Longrightarrow} T}{S' \underset{g}{\Longrightarrow} T}\, L \qquad \frac{}{S \underset{f}{\Longrightarrow} S'}\, R$$
such that for all derivations
$$S \underset{f;g}{\overset{\beta}{\Longrightarrow}} T \quad \text{and} \quad S' \underset{g}{\overset{\eta}{\Longrightarrow}} T$$
we have equalities
$$\dfrac{\dfrac{}{S \underset{f}{\Longrightarrow} S'}\, R \quad \dfrac{S \underset{f;g}{\overset{\beta}{\Longrightarrow}} T}{S' \underset{g}{\Longrightarrow} T}\, L}{S \underset{f;g}{\Longrightarrow} T}\, ; \quad = \quad S \underset{f;g}{\overset{\beta}{\Longrightarrow}} T$$
and
$$S' \underset{g}{\overset{\eta}{\Longrightarrow}} T \quad = \quad \dfrac{\dfrac{\dfrac{}{S \underset{f}{\Longrightarrow} S'}\, R \quad S' \underset{g}{\overset{\eta}{\Longrightarrow}} T}{S \underset{f;g}{\Longrightarrow} T}\, ;}{S' \underset{g}{\Longrightarrow} T}\, L$$

**Proposition 26.** **U** *is a Grothendieck opfibration iff for every $S \sqsubset A$ and $f : A \to B$, there exists a pushforward of $S$ along $f$.*

Since pushforwards are determined up to vertical isomorphism, we speak of *the* pushforward of $S$ along $f$, writing $f\, S$ for the refinement type and $Lf$ and $Rf$ for the corresponding rules (see fig. 4). Again, we can mechanically establish some basic facts about pushforwards (which go into showing that any opfibration determines a pseudofunctor $\mathcal{T} \to \mathbf{Cat}$):

**Proposition 27.** *Whenever the corresponding pushforwards exist:*

1. *the following subtyping rule is valid:*
$$\frac{S_1 \leq S_2}{f\, S_1 \leq f\, S_2}$$
2. *we have vertical isomorphisms*
$$(f; g)\, S \equiv g\, f\, S \qquad \mathrm{id}\, S \equiv S$$

**Proposition 28.** *Whenever the respective pushforwards and pullbacks exist, we have a three-way correspondence of interderivability,*
$$\vdash f\, S \leq T \quad \textit{iff} \quad \vdash S \underset{f}{\Longrightarrow} T \quad \textit{iff} \quad \vdash S \leq f^* T$$

**Example 3.** For the refinement system **SubSet** → **Set**, pushforward and pullback refinements may be constructed as suggested by the notation, via image and inverse image operations on subsets (along any function $f : A \to B$):
$$f\, S \overset{\mathrm{def}}{=} \{\, f(a) \mid a \in S \,\}$$
$$f^* T \overset{\mathrm{def}}{=} \{\, a \mid f(a) \in T \,\}$$

For example, the typing judgment

$$f^* T \underset{f}{\Longrightarrow} T$$

is obviously valid, reading as « $f$ maps anything in the inverse image of $T$ along $f$ to something in $T$ », while

$$S \underset{f}{\Longrightarrow} f\, S$$

reads as « $f$ maps anything in $S$ to something in the image of $S$ along $f$ ». Since these operations are defined for any $f : A \to B$, $S \sqsubset A$, and $T \sqsubset B$, the functor **SubSet** $\to$ **Set** is both a fibration and an opfibration, i.e., a *bifibration*.

**Example 4.** The general approach of Hoare logic [12] provides a natural class of examples of refinement systems, to a first approximation defined as follows (we will consider a more nuanced view in Section 5):

- Take $\mathcal{T}$ as a category with one object $W$ corresponding to the state space, and with morphisms $c : W \to W$ corresponding to program commands, identified with state transformers.
- Take $\mathcal{D}$ as a category whose objects are predicates $\phi$ over states, and whose morphisms $\phi \to \psi$ are pairs of a state transformer $c$ together with a verification that $c$ takes any state satisfying $\phi$ to a state satisfying $\psi$.
- Let $\mathbf{U} : \mathcal{D} \to \mathcal{T}$ be the evident forgetful functor, mapping every $\phi$ to $W$ and every verification about $c$ to $c$ itself.

Indeed, the induced notion of typing judgment for the functor $\mathbf{U} : \mathcal{D} \to \mathcal{T}$ corresponds exactly to the classical notion of Hoare triple $\{\phi\}c\{\psi\}$. One easily checks that the usual rules of sequential composition, pre-strengthening and post-weakening are valid by Propositions 6 and 7, and moreover that a pullback of $\psi$ along $c$ is precisely a *weakest precondition*, while a pushforward of $\phi$ along $c$ is a *strongest postcondition*:

$$wp(c, \psi) = c^* \psi$$
$$sp(c, \phi) = c\, \phi$$

On the other hand, it is not necessarily the case that $\mathcal{D} \to \mathcal{T}$ is a fibration and/or opfibration: whether weakest preconditions/strongest postconditions exist for *all* predicates and state transformers depends on the specifics of the class of predicates and the class of state transformers.

**Example 5.** The example of **SubSet** $\to$ **Set** can be generalized in terms of *enriched category theory* [15]. Let $(\mathcal{V}, \otimes_{\mathcal{V}}, I_{\mathcal{V}}, \multimap_{\mathcal{V}})$ be a symmetric monoidal closed category, let $\mathcal{V}$**Cat** be the (bi)category of $\mathcal{V}$-enriched categories, and let $\mathcal{V}$**Psh** the category of $\mathcal{V}$-presheaves, i.e., the category whose objects are $\mathcal{V}$-valued functors $S : A \to \mathcal{V}$ out of $\mathcal{V}$-enriched categories, and where a morphism from $S : A \to \mathcal{V}$ to $T : B \to \mathcal{V}$ is a pair of a ($\mathcal{V}$-)functor $f : A \to B$ together with a natural transformation $\alpha : S \Rightarrow (f; T)$. Then the refinement system given by the domain functor dom : $\mathcal{V}$**Psh** $\to$ $\mathcal{V}$**Cat** is a bifibration, with pullbacks simply defined by precomposition, and pushforwards computed as *coends*:

$$f^* T \stackrel{\text{def}}{=} a \mapsto T(fa)$$
$$f\, S \stackrel{\text{def}}{=} b \mapsto \int^a B(fa, b) \otimes_{\mathcal{V}} T(a)$$

Note that this is also an example of a logical refinement system—the (symmetric) closed monoidal structure on $\mathcal{V}$**Cat** is defined by constructing tensor product categories and functor categories

$$A \bullet B \stackrel{\text{def}}{=} A \otimes B \qquad A \setminus C \stackrel{\text{def}}{=} [A, C] \qquad C \,/\, B \stackrel{\text{def}}{=} [B, C]$$

while the tensor product of two presheaves is defined as their *external tensor product*,

$$S \bullet T : A \otimes B \to \mathcal{V}$$
$$S \bullet T \stackrel{\text{def}}{=} (a, b) \mapsto S(a) \otimes_{\mathcal{V}} T(b)$$

and the left and right residuals defined as *ends*:

$$S \setminus U : [A, C] \to \mathcal{V}$$
$$S \setminus U \stackrel{\text{def}}{=} f \mapsto \int_a S(a) \multimap_{\mathcal{V}} U(fa)$$
$$U \,/\, T : [B, C] \to \mathcal{V}$$
$$U \,/\, T \stackrel{\text{def}}{=} g \mapsto \int_b T(b) \multimap_{\mathcal{V}} U(gb)$$

**Example 6.** A trivial example of a bifibration is the unique functor $! : \mathcal{D} \to 1$ from any category $\mathcal{D}$ to the terminal category 1. Since there is only the identity arrow in 1, all pushforwards and pullbacks exist trivially. (If $\mathcal{D}$ is monoidal, this is also trivially a logical refinement system.) ■

## 5. Separation Logic and the Frame Rule

We have seen how a lot of general type theory can be reconstructed as a "theory of functors". In many ways, though, the really interesting phenomena arise by taking the various type constructors as building blocks, and using them to define specific *type signatures*. Effectively, this is a way of viewing refinement systems as a "logical framework", using them both to define theories and to construct models. In this section we will give some basic examples, describing how some aspects of Reynolds and O'Hearn's *separation logic* [32] can be usefully explained in terms of refinement systems.

Recall (Example 4) that Hoare logic may be considered as a refinement system where terms $c : W \to W \in \mathcal{T}$ are commands (state-transformers), refinements $\phi, \psi \sqsubset W$ are predicates over the state space, and where derivations

$$\phi \overset{\alpha}{\underset{c}{\Longrightarrow}} \psi$$

are proofs that the command $c$ will take any state satisfying $\phi$ to a state satisfying $\psi$. Although this description suggests that $\mathcal{T}$ is a one-object category, such a restriction is not really necessary, and it turns out to be useful to work more generally.

In particular, suppose we know that $\mathcal{T}$ is a monoidal category and that $W$ is a *monoid object* in $\mathcal{T}$, i.e., that it is equipped with operations

$$\circledast : W \bullet W \to W$$
$$e : 1 \to W$$

satisfying the monoid axioms. Then for any pair of refinements $\phi, \psi \sqsubset W$, we can define their *separating conjunction* $\phi * \psi \sqsubset W$ as a pushforward (along $\circledast$) of a tensor product:

$$\phi * \psi \stackrel{\text{def}}{=} \circledast\, (\phi \bullet \psi)$$

We similarly define the unit of the separating conjunction $emp \sqsubset W$ as a pushforward (along $e$) of the tensor unit:

$$emp \stackrel{\text{def}}{=} e\, I$$

Finally, for any $\phi, \tau \sqsubset W$ we define "magic wand" $\phi \mathrel{-\!\!*} \tau \sqsubset W$ as a pullback (along the currying of $\circledast$) of a residual:[3]

$$\phi \mathrel{-\!\!*} \tau \stackrel{\text{def}}{=} \lambda[\circledast]^* (\phi \setminus \tau)$$

[3] Incidentally, these kinds of definitions—where in order to define some logical structure of interest we rely on a similar structure in the

Now, interpreting this signature in the refinement system **SubSet** $\to$ **Set** (Examples 1 to 3) yields the basic set-theoretic semantics of the separation logic connectives:

$$\phi * \psi = \{ w_1 \circledast w_2 \mid w_1 \in \phi, w_2 \in \psi \}$$
$$emp = \{ e \}$$
$$\phi -\!\!* \tau = \{ w \mid \forall w'.\, w' \in \phi \Rightarrow w' \circledast w \in \tau \}$$

On the other hand, we can see that the abstract definition in terms of refinement systems is much more general. For example, interpreting the signature in $\mathcal{V}$**Psh** $\to$ $\mathcal{V}$**Cat** (Example 5) recovers the well-known *Day construction* for lifting a monoidal structure on a category to a closed monoidal structure on its category of presheaves. The next proposition describes the situation more abstractly.

**Proposition 29.** *Whenever the operations $\phi * -$ and $\phi -\!\!* -$ are defined (i.e., when the corresponding pushforwards, pullbacks, and residuals exist), they are functorial in the sense that subtyping rules*

$$\frac{\psi_1 \le \psi_2}{\phi * \psi_1 \le \phi * \psi_2} \qquad \frac{\tau_1 \le \tau_2}{\phi -\!\!* \tau_1 \le \phi -\!\!* \tau_2}$$

*are valid, and adjoint in the sense that the subtyping rule*

$$\frac{\phi * \psi \le \tau}{\psi \le \phi -\!\!* \tau}$$

*is both valid and invertible.*

This proposition is actually independent of whether $\circledast$ and $e$ satisfy the monoid axioms, and can even be adapted for a binary operation of arbitrary type $\circledast : A \bullet B \to C$.

The functoriality of $\phi * -$ expressed in Prop. 29 is a trivial instance of O'Hearn's *frame rule*, which can be expressed as follows for a general command $c$:

$$\frac{\psi_1 \underset{c}{\Longrightarrow} \psi_2}{\phi * \psi_1 \underset{c}{\Longrightarrow} \phi * \psi_2}\ \textit{frame}$$

There is no reason why the frame rule should be valid in an arbitrary refinement system, and it is impossible to derive it from the above axioms. On the other hand, in the presence of pullbacks or pushforwards, it is not difficult to see that the frame rule is equivalent to either one of two simple algebraic conditions on the command $c$:

$$\phi * c^* \psi \le c^* (\phi * \psi) \qquad c\,(\phi * \psi) \le \phi * c\,\psi$$

The correspondence between the frame rule and the left-hand side property was noticed already by O'Hearn and Yang [24]. Here, we would like to emphasize that the left-hand side property says that pullback along $c$, seen as an endofunctor

$$c^* : \mathcal{D}_W \to \mathcal{D}_W$$

on the fiber of $W$, is strong with respect to the action $\phi * -$ of the monoidal category $\mathcal{D}_W$ on itself. This correspondence connects the frame rule to the traditional description of locality as a monadic strength in the semantics of effects.

## 6. Reconstructing "The Meaning of Types"

As we mentioned in the introduction, John Reynolds wrote eloquently on the distinction between the "intrinsic" and "extrinsic" views of typing (as he did on many topics), and considered the relationship between these two views carefully in his paper on "The Meaning of Types" [31]. To conclude our paper, we want to revisit Reynolds' analysis, and describe how much of it may be expressed quite naturally in the language of refinement systems. The following Sections 6.1 to 6.5 track Sections 1–5 of [31].

### 6.1 Syntax and Typing Rules

*We define a category $\mathcal{T}$ and a functor $\mathbf{U} : \mathcal{D} \to \mathcal{T}$, representing the syntax and typing rules of a small language.*

The language Reynolds considers in the paper is a simple extension of the lambda calculus including primitive boolean and arithmetic operations, records, recursion, and subtyping. Since the language is meant to be illustrative rather than interesting of itself, we will further simplify here by getting rid of records, recursion, and a few of the primitive operations, in order to focus on the treatment of subtyping. We will also follow the LF approach [10] and use higher-order abstract syntax (rather than explicit identifiers) to describe binding operations, since this leads to an elegant analysis in terms of *cartesian* logical refinement systems.

**Definition 30.** A **cartesian logical refinement system** is a logical refinement system $\mathbf{U} : \mathcal{D} \to \mathcal{T}$ in which the monoidal structures on $\mathcal{D}$ and $\mathcal{T}$ are cartesian [21]. We write $X \times Y$ and $Y^X$ to denote cartesian products and exponentials.

The reason we must consider cartesian rather than arbitrary logical refinement systems is that in Reynolds' language variables can be used any number of times and in any order. Otherwise, though, whether one works with cartesian logical refinement systems or in the general monoidal setting, the structure of the analysis is essentially the same.

So, we begin by considering the category $\mathcal{T}$ of terms as a cartesian category freely generated from a single type $P$ of *phrases*, a pair of morphisms

$$lam : P^P \to P$$
$$app : P \to P^P$$

representing lambda and application, and morphisms

$$add, sub, lt : P \times P \to P$$
$$not : P \to P$$
$$zero, one, true, false : 1 \to P$$

representing the operations of addition, subtraction, comparison, negation, and the numerical and boolean constants.

We next define a functor $\mathbf{U} : \mathcal{D} \to \mathcal{T}$, as a cartesian logical refinement system freely generated from the following refinement rules

$$\frac{}{int \sqsubset P} \quad \frac{}{nat \sqsubset P} \quad \frac{}{bool \sqsubset P} \quad \frac{\theta_1 \sqsubset P \quad \theta_2 \sqsubset P}{fn[\theta_1, \theta_2] \sqsubset P}$$

the following subtyping rules

$$\frac{}{nat \le int}\ NI \quad \frac{}{nat \le bool}\ NB \quad \frac{\theta_1' \le \theta_1 \quad \theta_2 \le \theta_2'}{fn[\theta_1, \theta_2] \le fn[\theta_1', \theta_2']}\ Fn$$

a pair of typing rules for lambda and application

$$\frac{}{{\theta_2}^{\theta_1} \underset{lam}{\Longrightarrow} fn[\theta_1, \theta_2]}\ Lam \qquad \frac{}{fn[\theta_1, \theta_2] \underset{app}{\Longrightarrow} {\theta_2}^{\theta_1}}\ App$$

and a collection of typing rules for the primitive operations

$$\frac{}{nat \times nat \underset{add}{\Longrightarrow} nat}\ N+ \quad \frac{}{int \times int \underset{add}{\Longrightarrow} int}\ I+ \quad \frac{}{bool \times bool \underset{add}{\Longrightarrow} bool}\ B+$$

$$\frac{}{int \times int \underset{sub}{\Longrightarrow} int}\ I- \quad \frac{}{int \times int \underset{lt}{\Longrightarrow} bool}\ I< \quad \frac{}{bool \underset{not}{\Longrightarrow} bool}\ B\neg$$

logical framework—are a recurring pattern, and an example of the "microcosm principle" in the sense of Baez and Dolan. In Section 6.4 we will see this pattern again in the definition of the logical relation.

$$\frac{}{1 \underset{zero}{\Longrightarrow} nat}\,N0 \qquad \frac{}{1 \underset{one}{\Longrightarrow} nat}\,N1 \qquad \frac{}{1 \underset{true}{\Longrightarrow} bool}\,Bt \qquad \frac{}{1 \underset{false}{\Longrightarrow} bool}\,Bf$$

We emphasize that this signature should be read as specifying conditions on the category $\mathcal{D}$ and the functor $\mathbf{U}$. For example, the *NI* subtyping rule indicates that $\mathcal{D}$ contains a morphism $NI : nat \to int$ and that $\mathbf{U}$ maps $NI$ to $\mathrm{id}_P$, while the *App* rule says that $\mathcal{D}$ contains a morphism $App : fn[\theta_1, \theta_2] \to {\theta_2}^{\theta_1}$ (for every $\theta_1, \theta_2 \sqsubset P$) and that $\mathbf{U}$ maps *App* to *app*.

In the spirit of the LF approach (but now at the level of refinements, cf. [20, 26]), there is a lot that we *don't* have to mention in this signature. For example, we don't have to explicitly include Reynolds' subsumption rule, since it is valid in any refinement system (Prop. 7). On the other hand, observe that the *Fn* subtyping rule is *not* an instance of Prop. 15, since a priori we do not identify $fn[\theta_1, \theta_2]$ with the exponential object ${\theta_2}^{\theta_1}$ (the former refines $P$, the latter $P^P$).

**Example 7.** The function $dec = lam(\lambda[(\mathrm{id} \bullet one); sub])$ subtracting one from an integer may be typed by the following derivation (at the bottom we write $;Lam$ for the typing rule defined by post-composing with *Lam*):

$$\dfrac{\dfrac{\dfrac{\dfrac{}{int \underset{\mathrm{id}}{\Longrightarrow} int}\,\mathrm{id} \quad \dfrac{\dfrac{}{1 \underset{one}{\Longrightarrow} nat}\,N1 \quad \dfrac{}{nat \le int}\,NI}{1 \underset{one}{\Longrightarrow} int}\,;}{int \underset{\mathrm{id}\bullet one}{\Longrightarrow} int \times int}\,\bullet \qquad \dfrac{}{int \times int \underset{sub}{\Longrightarrow} int}\,I-}{int \underset{(\mathrm{id}\bullet one);sub}{\Longrightarrow} int}\,;}{1 \underset{\lambda[(\mathrm{id}\bullet one);sub]}{\Longrightarrow} int^{int}}\,\lambda}{1 \underset{dec}{\Longrightarrow} fn[int, int]}\,;Lam$$

**Example 8.** It is possible to have more than one typing derivation of the same typing judgment. For example, the typing judgment

$$nat \times nat \underset{add}{\Longrightarrow} bool$$

may be derived either as

$$\dfrac{\dfrac{}{nat \times nat \underset{add}{\Longrightarrow} nat}\,N{+} \qquad \dfrac{}{nat \le bool}\,NB}{nat \times nat \underset{add}{\Longrightarrow} bool}\,;$$

or as

$$\dfrac{\dfrac{\dfrac{}{nat \le bool}\,NB \quad \dfrac{}{nat \le bool}\,NB}{nat \times nat \le bool \times bool}\,\bullet \qquad \dfrac{}{bool \times bool \underset{add}{\Longrightarrow} bool}\,B{+}}{nat \times nat \underset{add}{\Longrightarrow} bool}\,;$$

### 6.2 An Intrinsic Semantics

*We define a cartesian closed functor* $[\![-]\!]_D : \mathcal{D} \to \mathbf{Dom}$ *from derivations to domains.*

In order to define the intrinsic semantics we assume domains $\mathbb{N}_\bot, \mathbb{Z}_\bot, \mathbb{B}_\bot$ of naturals, integers, and booleans, as well as operations

$$+_{\mathbb{N}} : \mathbb{N}_\bot \times \mathbb{N}_\bot \to \mathbb{N}_\bot \quad +_{\mathbb{Z}} : \mathbb{Z}_\bot \times \mathbb{Z}_\bot \to \mathbb{Z}_\bot \quad \vee_{\mathbb{B}} : \mathbb{B}_\bot \times \mathbb{B}_\bot \to \mathbb{B}_\bot$$
$$-_{\mathbb{Z}} : \mathbb{Z}_\bot \times \mathbb{Z}_\bot \to \mathbb{Z}_\bot \quad <_{\mathbb{Z}} : \mathbb{Z}_\bot \times \mathbb{Z}_\bot \to \mathbb{B}_\bot \quad \neg_{\mathbb{B}} : \mathbb{B}_\bot \to \mathbb{B}_\bot$$
$$0, 1 : 1 \to \mathbb{N}_\bot \quad tt, \mathit{ff} : 1 \to \mathbb{B}_\bot$$

standing for the *componentwise-strict* extensions of the evident operations on naturals, integers, and booleans. We also write $i : \mathbb{N}_\bot \to \mathbb{Z}_\bot$ for the evident inclusion, and $j : \mathbb{N}_\bot \to \mathbb{B}_\bot$ for the strict extension of the following map:

$$n \mapsto \begin{cases} tt & \text{if } n > 0 \\ \mathit{ff} & \text{if } n = 0 \end{cases}$$

Then we define the functor $[\![-]\!]_D : \mathcal{D} \to \mathbf{Dom}$ by:

$$[\![nat]\!] = \mathbb{N}_\bot \quad [\![int]\!] = \mathbb{Z}_\bot \quad [\![bool]\!] = \mathbb{B}_\bot \quad [\![fn[S,T]]\!] = [\![T]\!]^{[\![S]\!]}$$
$$[\![NI]\!] = i \quad [\![NB]\!] = j \quad [\![Fn[\alpha,\beta]]\!] = (f \mapsto [\![\alpha]\!]; f; [\![\beta]\!])$$
$$[\![Lam]\!] = \mathrm{id} \quad [\![App]\!] = \mathrm{id}$$
$$[\![N{+}]\!] = +_{\mathbb{N}} \quad [\![I{+}]\!] = +_{\mathbb{Z}} \quad [\![B{+}]\!] = \vee_{\mathbb{B}}$$
$$[\![I{-}]\!] = -_{\mathbb{Z}} \quad [\![I{<}]\!] = <_{\mathbb{Z}} \quad [\![B\neg]\!] = \neg_{\mathbb{B}}$$
$$[\![N0]\!] = 0 \quad [\![N1]\!] = 1 \quad [\![Bt]\!] = tt \quad [\![Bf]\!] = \mathit{ff}$$

Note that this data suffices for defining the cartesian closed functor $[\![-]\!]_D$, by the requirement that it preserves cartesian products and exponentials.

### 6.3 An Untyped Semantics

*We define a cartesian closed functor* $[\![-]\!]_T : \mathcal{T} \to \mathbf{Dom}$ *from terms to domains.*

In order to define the untyped semantics we assume a domain $U$ equipped with operations

$$\mathbb{Z}_\bot \underset{\Psi_p}{\overset{\Phi_p}{\rightleftarrows}} U \qquad U^U \underset{\Psi_f}{\overset{\Phi_f}{\rightleftarrows}} U$$

such that $\Phi_p; \Psi_p = \mathrm{id}$ and $\Phi_f; \Psi_f = \mathrm{id}$ (i.e., embedding-retraction pairs). We also suppose operations

$$tt_{\mathbb{Z}} : 1 \to \mathbb{Z}_\bot \quad <_{\mathbb{Z}} : \mathbb{Z}_\bot \times \mathbb{Z}_\bot \to \mathbb{Z}_\bot \quad \neg_{\mathbb{Z}} : \mathbb{Z}_\bot \to \mathbb{Z}_\bot$$

which must at minimum satisfy

$$\begin{aligned} tt_{\mathbb{Z}} &> 0 \\ (x <_{\mathbb{Z}} y) &> 0 && \text{when } x < y \\ (x <_{\mathbb{Z}} y) &= 0 && \text{when } x \ge y \\ (\neg_{\mathbb{Z}} x) &> 0 && \text{when } x = 0 \\ (\neg_{\mathbb{Z}} x) &= 0 && \text{when } x > 0 \end{aligned}$$

Then $[\![-]\!]_T$ is defined by:

$$[\![P]\!] = U \qquad [\![lam]\!] = \Phi_f \quad [\![app]\!] = \Psi_f$$
$$[\![add]\!] = (\Psi_p \bullet \Psi_p); +_{\mathbb{Z}}; \Phi_p \quad [\![sub]\!] = (\Psi_p \bullet \Psi_p); -_{\mathbb{Z}}; \Phi_p$$
$$[\![lt]\!] = (\Psi_p \bullet \Psi_p); <_{\mathbb{Z}}; \Phi_p \quad [\![not]\!] = (\Psi_p \bullet \Psi_p); \neg_{\mathbb{Z}}; \Phi_p$$
$$[\![zero]\!] = [\![false]\!] = 0; i; \Phi_p \quad [\![one]\!] = 1; i; \Phi_p \quad [\![true]\!] = tt_{\mathbb{Z}}; \Phi_p$$

As in Section 6.2, this data suffices for defining $[\![-]\!]_T$ as a cartesian closed functor.

### 6.4 Logical Relations

*We formalize Reynolds' logical relations theorem, connecting the intrinsic semantics to the untyped semantics.*

The logical relations theorem boils down to defining a cartesian closed functor $\rho : \mathcal{D} \to \mathbf{DRel}$ satisfying a pair of commuting squares:

$$\begin{array}{ccc} \mathcal{D} & \xrightarrow{\rho} & \mathbf{DRel} \\ \Vert & (0) & \downarrow{\scriptstyle \partial_0} \\ \mathcal{D} & \xrightarrow[{[\![-]\!]_D}]{} & \mathbf{Dom} \end{array} \qquad \begin{array}{ccc} \mathcal{D} & \xrightarrow{\rho} & \mathbf{DRel} \\ {\scriptstyle \mathrm{U}}\downarrow & (1) & \downarrow{\scriptstyle \partial_1} \\ \mathcal{T} & \xrightarrow[{[\![-]\!]_T}]{} & \mathbf{Dom} \end{array}$$

Here **DRel** is the category whose objects are chain-complete relations over domains (hence *domain-theoretic relations*) and whose morphisms are pairs of functions mapping related arguments to related results, while the $\partial_i$ are the evident projection functors. To define $\rho$, we take advantage of the fact that the pairing of the projection functors $(\partial_0, \partial_1) : \mathbf{DRel} \to$

**Dom** × **Dom** has the structure of a logical refinement system (with all pullbacks and some pushforwards)—so let us take a moment to describe this structure (cf. [14, Example 3(2)]).

A refinement $S \sqsubset (A, B)$ corresponds to a chain-complete relation $S \subseteq A \times B$ between domains, while a derivation of

$$S \underset{(f,g)}{\Longrightarrow} T$$

corresponds to a proof that

$$\forall a, b.\, a \sim_S b \Rightarrow f(a) \sim_T g(b)$$

Products, residuals, pullbacks and pushforwards are defined as follows on relations:

$$\begin{array}{rll} (a_1, a_2) \sim_{S \times T} (b_1, b_2) & \text{iff} & a_1 \sim_S b_1 \wedge a_2 \sim_T b_2 \\ f \sim_{T^S} g & \text{iff} & \forall a, b.\, a \sim_S b \Rightarrow f(a) \sim_T g(b) \\ a \sim_{(f,g)^* T} b & \text{iff} & f(a) \sim_T g(b) \\ c \sim_{(f,g) S} d & \text{iff} & \exists a, b.\, c = f(a) \wedge d = g(b) \wedge a \sim_S b \end{array}$$

Note that pushforward is a partial operation, because the relation $(f, g)\, S$ is not necessarily chain-complete. However, the pushforward along a pair of functions $(f, g)$ with flat codomains (or more generally, with codomains where every element is compact) is always defined.

Now, in order to satisfy the squares (0) and (1), the object part of the functor $\rho : \mathcal{D} \to$ **DRel** must assign to each $\theta \sqsubset P$ a relation $\rho[\theta] \sqsubset ([\![\theta]\!], U)$. Let $\Delta$ : **Dom** $\to$ **DRel** be the (cartesian closed) functor assigning the identity relation to any domain. We define $\rho[\theta]$ as follows (by induction on $\theta$):

$$\begin{array}{rl} \rho[int] & = (\mathrm{id}, \Psi_p)^*\, \Delta[\mathbb{Z}_\perp] \\ \rho[nat] & = (\mathrm{id}, \Psi_p)^*\, (\mathrm{id}, i)\, \Delta[\mathbb{N}_\perp] \\ \rho[bool] & = (\mathrm{id}, \Psi_p)^*\, (\mathrm{id}, i)\, (\mathrm{id}, j)^*\, \Delta[\mathbb{B}_\perp] \\ \rho[fn[\theta_1, \theta_2]] & = (\mathrm{id}, \Psi_f)^*\, \rho[\theta_2]^{\rho[\theta_2]} \end{array}$$

By unwinding the interpretation of the logical refinement system **DRel** $\to$ **Dom** × **Dom**, it is easy to check that these definitions agree with Reynolds' Definitions 4.1 and 4.2. For example, we have

$$\begin{array}{rll} b \sim_{\rho[bool]} p & \text{iff} & b \sim_{(\mathrm{id},i)\,(\mathrm{id},j)^*\,\Delta[\mathbb{B}]} \Psi_p(p) \\ & \text{iff} & \exists n. \Psi_p(p) = i(n) \wedge b \sim_{(\mathrm{id},j)^*\,\Delta[\mathbb{B}]} n \\ & \text{iff} & \exists n. \Psi_p(p) = i(n) \wedge b = j(n) \end{array}$$

We can now prove that $\rho$ extends to a functor and that the two squares (0) and (1) commute, which modulo our treatment of variables (using higher-order abstract syntax rather than explicit environments) is an exact transcription of Reynolds' Logical Relations Theorem (4.8).

**Theorem 31.** *If* $\theta_1 \overset{\alpha}{\underset{p}{\Longrightarrow}} \theta_2$ *then* $\vdash \rho[\theta_1] \underset{([\![\alpha]\!],[\![p]\!])}{\Longrightarrow} \rho[\theta_2]$.

*Proof.* By induction on $\alpha$. The content of the proof is basically identical with the proof in [31], but the trip through refinement systems gives the proof considerably more structure. We illustrate with a few cases:

- $\alpha = NI$:

$$\begin{array}{c} \hline \Delta[\mathbb{N}_\perp] \underset{(i,i)}{\Longrightarrow} \Delta[\mathbb{Z}_\perp] \quad \Delta[i] \\ \hline (\mathrm{id}, i)\, \Delta[\mathbb{N}_\perp] \underset{(i,\mathrm{id})}{\Longrightarrow} \Delta[\mathbb{Z}_\perp] \quad L(\mathrm{id}, i) \\ \hline (\mathrm{id}, \Psi_p)^*\, (\mathrm{id}, i)\, \Delta[\mathbb{N}_\perp] \underset{(i,\mathrm{id})}{\Longrightarrow} (\mathrm{id}, \Psi_p)^*\, \Delta[\mathbb{Z}_\perp] \quad (fun) \\ \hline\hline \rho[nat] \underset{([\![NI]\!],[\![\mathrm{id}]\!])}{\Longrightarrow} \rho[int] \end{array}$$

where we write a double line for expansion of definitions, (*fun*) for functoriality of pullbacks (Prop. 24), and $\Delta[i]$ for the application of the functor $\Delta$ to the map $i : \mathbb{N}_\perp \to \mathbb{Z}_\perp$.

- $\alpha = Lam$:

$$\begin{array}{c} \hline \rho[\theta_2]^{\rho[\theta_1]} \underset{(\mathrm{id},\mathrm{id})}{\Longrightarrow} \rho[\theta_2]^{\rho[\theta_1]} \quad \mathrm{id} \\ \hline \rho[\theta_2]^{\rho[\theta_1]} \underset{(\mathrm{id},(\Phi_f;\Psi_f))}{\Longrightarrow} \rho[\theta_2]^{\rho[\theta_1]} \quad \sim \\ \hline \rho[\theta_2]^{\rho[\theta_1]} \underset{(\mathrm{id},\Phi_f)}{\Longrightarrow} (\mathrm{id}, \Psi_f)^*\, \rho[\theta_2]^{\rho[\theta_1]} \quad R(\mathrm{id}, \Psi_f)^* \\ \hline\hline \rho[\theta_2{}^{\theta_1}] \underset{([\![Lam]\!],[\![lam]\!])}{\Longrightarrow} \rho[fn[\theta_1, \theta_2]] \end{array}$$

- $\alpha = N+$:

$$\begin{array}{c} \dfrac{}{\Delta[\mathbb{N}_\perp] \bullet \Delta[\mathbb{N}_\perp] \underset{(+_\mathbb{N},+_\mathbb{N})}{\Longrightarrow} \Delta[\mathbb{N}_\perp]}\,\Delta[+_\mathbb{N}] \quad \dfrac{}{\Delta[\mathbb{N}_\perp] \underset{(\mathrm{id},i)}{\Longrightarrow} (\mathrm{id}, i)\, \Delta[\mathbb{N}_\perp]}\,R(\mathrm{id}, i) \\ \hline \Delta[\mathbb{N}_\perp] \bullet \Delta[\mathbb{N}_\perp] \underset{(+_\mathbb{N},(+_\mathbb{N};i))}{\Longrightarrow} (\mathrm{id}, i)\, \Delta[\mathbb{N}_\perp] \quad ; \\ \hline \Delta[\mathbb{N}_\perp] \times \Delta[\mathbb{N}_\perp] \underset{(+_\mathbb{N},(i \bullet i;+_\mathbb{Z}))}{\Longrightarrow} (\mathrm{id}, i)\, \Delta[\mathbb{N}_\perp] \quad \sim \\ \hline \rho[nat] \times \rho[nat] \underset{(+_\mathbb{N},((\Psi_p \bullet \Psi_p);+_\mathbb{Z};\Phi_p))}{\Longrightarrow} \rho[nat] \quad (\dagger) \\ \hline\hline \rho[nat \times nat] \underset{([\![N+]\!],[\![add]\!])}{\Longrightarrow} \rho[nat] \end{array}$$

where at (†) we have elided several easy steps of reasoning, and at ~ we use the fact that $(+_\mathbb{N}; i) = (i \bullet i; +_\mathbb{Z})$.

□

### 6.5 Bracketing

*We formalize Reynolds' bracketing theorem, which combined with the logical relations theorem yields coherence.*

We begin by defining for each domain $[\![\theta]\!]$ in the image of the intrinsic semantics a pair of functions

$$[\![\theta]\!] \underset{\psi[\theta]}{\overset{\phi[\theta]}{\rightleftarrows}} U$$

which will turn out to be an embedding-retraction pair. The family is defined as follows (by induction on $\theta$):

$$\phi[int] = \Phi_p \quad \psi[int] = \Psi_p \quad \phi[nat] = i; \Phi_p \quad \psi[nat] = \Psi_p; i'$$

$$\phi[bool] = j'; i; \Phi_p \quad \psi[bool] = \Psi_p; i'; j$$

$$\phi[fn[\theta_1, \theta_2]] = \phi[\theta_2]^{\psi[\theta_1]}; \Phi_f \quad \psi[fn[\theta_1, \theta_2]] = \Psi_f; \psi[\theta_2]^{\phi[\theta_1]}$$

Here $g^f \overset{\mathrm{def}}{=} \lambda[f \bullet \mathrm{id}; \circledcirc; g]$, while $i' : \mathbb{Z}_\perp \to \mathbb{N}_\perp$ is the function sending non-negative integers to naturals and everything else to $\perp$, and $j' : \mathbb{B}_\perp \to \mathbb{N}_\perp$ is the strict extension of the function sending *tt* to 1 and *ff* to 0. Note that this family of pairs may be seen as a pair of transformations between functors

$$\phi : [\![-]\!]_D \Rightarrow (\mathbf{U}; [\![-]\!]_T) \qquad \psi : (\mathbf{U}; [\![-]\!]_T) \Rightarrow [\![-]\!]_D$$

albeit not a pair of *natural* transformations. Instead, $\phi$ and $\psi$ are related by Reynolds' *bracketing theorem*.

**Theorem 32** (Bracketing). *The two judgments*

$$\Delta[\![\theta]\!] \underset{(\mathrm{id},\phi_\theta)}{\Longrightarrow} \rho[\theta] \underset{(\mathrm{id},\psi_\theta)}{\Longrightarrow} \Delta[\![\theta]\!]$$

*are derivable for all* $\theta$.

*Proof.* By induction on $\theta$. Once again, the proof is highly structured, and we include it in full in Appendix A. □

Finally, by combining the bracketing theorem with the logical relations theorem, we can show that the intrinsic semantics is coherent, i.e., that any two derivations of the same judgment have the same interpretation (the following statements correspond to Reynolds' Theorem 5.7 and Corollary 5.8).

**Corollary 33** (Coherence). *We have:*

1. *If* $\theta_1 \overset{\alpha}{\underset{p}{\Longrightarrow}} \theta_2$ *then* $[\![\alpha]\!] = \phi_{\theta_1} ; [\![p]\!] ; \psi_{\theta_2}$.
2. *If* $\theta_1 \overset{\alpha_1}{\underset{p}{\Longrightarrow}} \theta_2$ *and* $\theta_1 \overset{\alpha_2}{\underset{p}{\Longrightarrow}} \theta_2$ *then* $[\![\alpha_1]\!] = [\![\alpha_2]\!]$.

## 7. Related work and conclusions

Refinement type systems are the higher-order version of Hoare logic, and as such, they are recognized today as a fundamental tool in program analysis and certification. An important contribution to this line of research has been the work by Frank Pfenning and his collaborators [9] who have developed along the years a comprehensive theory of refinement type systems, including a clean account of the relationship between extrinsic and intrinsic typing [27]. Here, by going back to Reynolds [31] we establish a very natural connection between refinement type systems and functorial semantics, based on the idea that every functor defines a refinement type system.

Functorial semantics is an old idea going back to Lawvere in algebra [18] and logic [19], and which plays a central role in the study of imperative languages since Reynolds and Oles [25, 28]. Functorial semantics has also played a defining role in the early development of separation logic [23] as well as in more recent extensions of the logic to higher-order imperative languages [3, 4]. One distinctive feature of the present work is to develop a formal language of typing judgments and derivations reflecting the basic reasoning principles of functorial semantics. This language has been designed in order to be amenable to mechanization and could eventually serve as an intermediate language in a proof assistant. We demonstrated the power of the language in Section 6, by recasting the sophisticated semantic arguments used by Reynolds [31] in a concise and highly structured way.

One of the original motivations for this language was to better understand effect type systems and their fibrational aspects, along the lines of [8, 14]. The idea of using product and implication-preserving fibrations in the study of logical predicates and logical relations may be traced back to Hermida [11], with later developments by Katsumata. Investigating effects and refinement type systems led us to replace fibrations by general functors, and in particular to appreciate the expressive power of closed functors. Together with the existence of *specific* pullbacks and pushforwards, one recovers many of the operations of dependent types but in a more flexible and general setting.

The principle of refining types while paying careful attention to the dual act of "forgetting" also appears in McBride's notion of *ornament* [22], which have been analyzed in fibrational terms [1, 6]. We would like to clarify the connection with our work in the future. Finally, the idea of using closed functors as a logical framework (capable of speaking about both "syntax" and "semantics" in a unified way) is very much in the spirit of de Groote's *abstract categorial grammars* [7], as well as Carette, Kiselyov and Shan's *tagless interpreters* [5].

## References


[1] Robert Atkey, Patricia Johann, and Neil Ghani. Refining Inductive Types. *LMCS*, 8:2, 2012.

[2] Jean Bénabou. Distributors at work. Notes from a course at TU Darmstadt in June 2000, taken by Thomas Streicher.

[3] Bodil Biering, Lars Birkedal, and Noah Torp-Smith. BI-Hyperdoctrines, Higher-order Separation Logic, and Abstraction. *ACM Trans. Program. Lang. Syst.*, 5:29, 2007.

[4] Lars Birkedal, Noah Torp-Smith, and Hongseok Yang. Semantics of Separation-Logic Typing and Higher-order Frame Rules for Algol-like languages. *LMCS*, 5:2, 2006.

[5] Jacques Carette, Oleg Kiselyov, and Chung-chieh Shan. Finally tagless, partially evaluated: Tagless staged interpreters for simpler typed languages. *JFP*, 5:19, 2009.

[6] Pierre-Evariste Dagand and Conor McBride. A Categorical Treatment of Ornaments. LICS 2013.

[7] Philippe de Groote. Towards Abstract Categorial Grammars. In *Assoc. for Computational Linguistics, 39th Annual Meeting*, 2001.

[8] Andrzej Filinski. Monads in Action. POPL 2010.

[9] Tim Freeman and Frank Pfenning. Refinement Types for ML. PLDI 1991.

[10] Robert Harper, Furio Honsell and Gordon Plotkin. A Framework For Defining Logics. *Journal of the ACM*, 40(1):143-184, 1993.

[11] Claudio Hermida. *Fibrations, Logical predicates and indeterminates*, PhD thesis, University of Edinburgh, November 1993.

[12] C.A.R. Hoare. An Axiomatic Basis for Computer Programming, *Communications of the ACM*, 12:10, 1969.

[13] Bart Jacobs. *Categorical Logic and Type Theory.* Studies in Logic and the Foundations of Mathematics 141. North Holland, 1999.

[14] Shin-ya Katsumata. Relating Computational Effects by ⊤⊤-Lifting. ICALP 2011.

[15] Max Kelly. *Basic concepts in enriched category theory*. CUP, 1982.

[16] Joachim Lambek. The mathematics of sentence structure. *American Mathematical Monthly*, 65:3, 1958.

[17] Joachim Lambek and Philip Scott. *Introduction to Higher-order Categorical Logic.* CUP, 1986.

[18] F. William Lawvere. *Functorial Semantics of Algebraic Theories*, PhD thesis, Columbia University, 1963.

[19] F. William Lawvere. Adjointness in Foundations, *Dialectica* 23, 1969, 281–296.

[20] William Lovas. *Refinement types for logical frameworks*, PhD thesis, Carnegie Mellon University, September 2010.

[21] Saunders Mac Lane. *Categories for the Working Mathematician.* Springer, 1971.

[22] Conor McBride. Ornamental Algebras, Algebraic Ornaments. *JFP* (to appear). 9/8/2010 version available on author's website.

[23] Peter W. O'Hearn and David J. Pym. The Logic of Bunched Implications. *BSL* 5:2, 1999.

[24] Peter W. O'Hearn and Hongseok Yang. A Semantic Basis for Local Reasoning. FOSSACS 2002.

[25] Frank J. Oles. *A Category-Theoretic Approach to the Semantics of Programming Languages*, PhD thesis, Syracuse University, 1982.

[26] Frank Pfenning. Refinement Types for Logical Frameworks. Workshop on Types for Proofs and Programs, May 1993.

[27] Frank Pfenning. Church and Curry: Combining Intrinsic and Extrinsic Typing. Studies in Logic 17, 2008, 303–338.

[28] John C. Reynolds. The Essence of Algol. *Algorithmic Languages*, 1981, 345–372.

[29] John C. Reynolds. The Coherence of Languages with Intersection Types, TACS 1991.

[30] John C. Reynolds. *Theories of Programming Languages.* CUP, 1998.

[31] John C. Reynolds. The Meaning of Types: from Intrinsic to Extrinsic Semantics. BRICS Report RS-00-32, Aarhus University, December 2000.

[32] John C. Reynolds. Separation logic: A Logic for Shared Mutable Data Structures. LICS 2002.

## A. Proof of the Bracketing Theorem

Recall that the bracketing theorem (Thm. 32) says that the pair of judgments

$$\Delta\llbracket\theta\rrbracket \underset{(\mathrm{id},\phi[\theta])}{\Longrightarrow} \rho[\theta] \underset{(\mathrm{id},\psi[\theta])}{\Longrightarrow} \Delta\llbracket\theta\rrbracket$$

are derivable in the logical refinement system **DRel** $\to$ **Dom** $\times$ **Dom**. We prove this by induction on $\theta$.

- (Case $\theta = fn[\theta_1, \theta_2]$).
  In one direction we build the following derivation:

$$\dfrac{\dfrac{\dfrac{\dfrac{\dfrac{\overset{i.h.}{\rho[\theta_1] \underset{(\mathrm{id},\psi[\theta_1])}{\Longrightarrow} \Delta\llbracket\theta_1\rrbracket} \quad \dfrac{}{\Delta\llbracket\theta_1\rrbracket \bullet \Delta\llbracket\theta_2\rrbracket^{\Delta\llbracket\theta_1\rrbracket} \underset{(\ogreaterthan,\ogreaterthan)}{\Longrightarrow} \Delta\llbracket\theta_2\rrbracket}\,\Delta[\ogreaterthan] \quad \overset{i.h.}{\Delta\llbracket\theta_2\rrbracket \underset{(\mathrm{id},\phi[\theta_2])}{\Longrightarrow} \rho[\theta_2]}}{\rho[\theta_1] \bullet \Delta\llbracket\theta_2\rrbracket^{\Delta\llbracket\theta_1\rrbracket} \underset{(\ogreaterthan,(\psi[\theta_1]\bullet\mathrm{id};\ogreaterthan;\phi[\theta_2]))}{\Longrightarrow} \rho[\theta_2]}\,(\dagger)}{\Delta\llbracket\theta_2\rrbracket^{\Delta\llbracket\theta_1\rrbracket} \underset{(\mathrm{id},\phi[\theta_2]^{\psi[\theta_1]})}{\Longrightarrow} \rho[\theta_2]^{\rho[\theta_1]}}\,\lambda}{\Delta\llbracket\theta_2\rrbracket^{\Delta\llbracket\theta_1\rrbracket} \underset{(\mathrm{id},(\phi[\theta_2]^{\psi[\theta_1]};\Phi_f;\Psi_f))}{\Longrightarrow} \rho[\theta_2]^{\rho[\theta_1]}}\,\sim}{\Delta\llbracket\theta_2\rrbracket^{\Delta\llbracket\theta_1\rrbracket} \underset{(\mathrm{id},(\phi[\theta_2]^{\psi[\theta_1]};\Phi_f))}{\Longrightarrow} (\mathrm{id},\Psi_f)^* \rho[\theta_2]^{\rho[\theta_1]}}\,R(\mathrm{id},\Psi_f)^*}{\Delta\llbracket fn[\theta_1,\theta_2]\rrbracket \underset{(\mathrm{id},\phi[fn[\theta_1,\theta_2]])}{\Longrightarrow} \rho[fn[\theta_1,\theta_2]]}$$

  where at (†) we apply composition twice (the order is irrelevant by associativity), after multiplying the leftmost premise by the identity on the right to bring it to the appropriate type.
  In the other direction we build the following derivation:

$$\dfrac{\dfrac{\dfrac{\dfrac{}{(\mathrm{id},\Psi_f)^* \rho[\theta_2]^{\rho[\theta_1]} \underset{(\mathrm{id},\Psi_f)}{\Longrightarrow} \rho[\theta_2]^{\rho[\theta_1]}}\,L(\mathrm{id},\Psi_f)^* \quad \dfrac{\overset{i.h.}{\Delta\llbracket\theta_1\rrbracket \underset{(\mathrm{id},\phi[\theta_1])}{\Longrightarrow} \rho[\theta_1]} \quad \overset{i.h.}{\rho[\theta_2] \underset{(\mathrm{id},\psi[\theta_2])}{\Longrightarrow} \Delta\llbracket\theta_1\rrbracket}}{\Delta\llbracket\theta_1\rrbracket \bullet \rho[\theta_2]^{\rho[\theta_1]} \underset{(\ogreaterthan,(\phi[\theta_1]\bullet\mathrm{id};\ogreaterthan;\psi[\theta_2]))}{\Longrightarrow} \Delta\llbracket\theta_2\rrbracket}\,L\backslash}{\Delta\llbracket\theta_1\rrbracket \bullet (\mathrm{id},\Psi_f)^* \rho[\theta_2]^{\rho[\theta_1]} \underset{(\ogreaterthan,(\phi[\theta_1]\bullet\Psi_f;\ogreaterthan;\psi[\theta_2]))}{\Longrightarrow} \Delta\llbracket\theta_2\rrbracket}\,(\dagger)}{(\mathrm{id},\Psi_f)^* \rho[\theta_2]^{\rho[\theta_1]} \underset{(\mathrm{id},(\Psi_f;\psi[\theta_2]^{\phi[\theta_1]}))}{\Longrightarrow} \Delta\llbracket\theta_2\rrbracket^{\Delta\llbracket\theta_1\rrbracket}}\,\lambda}{\rho[fn[\theta_1,\theta_2]] \underset{(\mathrm{id},\psi[fn[\theta_1,\theta_2]])}{\Longrightarrow} \Delta\llbracket fn[\theta_1,\theta_2]\rrbracket}$$

  where at (†) again we multiply the leftmost premise by the identity on the left before composing, and at $L\backslash$ we apply an instance of the following rule (which is valid in any logical refinement system):

$$\dfrac{S' \underset{v}{\Longrightarrow} S \quad U \underset{k}{\Longrightarrow} U'}{S' \bullet S \backslash U \underset{v\bullet\mathrm{id};\ogreaterthan;k}{\Longrightarrow} U'}\,L\backslash$$

- (Case $\theta = int$).

$$\dfrac{\dfrac{\dfrac{\dfrac{}{\Delta[\mathbb{Z}_\perp] \underset{(\mathrm{id},\mathrm{id})}{\Longrightarrow} \Delta[\mathbb{Z}_\perp]}\,\mathrm{id}}{\Delta[\mathbb{Z}_\perp] \underset{(\mathrm{id},(\Phi_p;\Psi_p))}{\Longrightarrow} \Delta[\mathbb{Z}_\perp]}\,\sim}{\Delta[\mathbb{Z}_\perp] \underset{(\mathrm{id},\Phi_p)}{\Longrightarrow} (\mathrm{id},\Psi_p)^* \Delta[\mathbb{Z}_\perp]}\,R(\mathrm{id},\Psi_p)^*}{\Delta\llbracket int\rrbracket \underset{(\mathrm{id},\phi[int])}{\Longrightarrow} \rho[int]} \qquad \dfrac{\dfrac{}{(\mathrm{id},\Psi_p)^* \Delta[\mathbb{Z}_\perp] \underset{(\mathrm{id},\Psi_p)}{\Longrightarrow} \Delta[\mathbb{Z}_\perp]}\,L(\mathrm{id},\Psi_p)^*}{\rho[int] \underset{(\mathrm{id},\psi[int])}{\Longrightarrow} \Delta\llbracket int\rrbracket}$$

- (Case $\theta = nat$).

$$\begin{array}{c}
\dfrac{\dfrac{\dfrac{}{\Delta[\mathbb{N}_\bot] \underset{(\mathrm{id},i)}{\Longrightarrow} (\mathrm{id},i)\,\Delta[\mathbb{N}_\bot]}\;R(\mathrm{id},i)}{\Delta[\mathbb{N}_\bot] \underset{(\mathrm{id},(i;\Phi_\mathrm{p};\Psi_\mathrm{p}))}{\Longrightarrow} (\mathrm{id},i)\,\Delta[\mathbb{N}_\bot]}\;\sim}{\Delta[\mathbb{N}_\bot] \underset{(\mathrm{id},(i;\Phi_\mathrm{p}))}{\Longrightarrow} (\mathrm{id},\Psi_\mathrm{p})^*\,(\mathrm{id},i)\,\Delta[\mathbb{N}_\bot]}\;R(\mathrm{id},\Psi_\mathrm{p})^* \\
\hline\hline
\Delta[\![nat]\!] \underset{(\mathrm{id},\phi[nat])}{\Longrightarrow} \rho[nat]
\end{array}
\qquad
\begin{array}{c}
\dfrac{\dfrac{\dfrac{\dfrac{}{\Delta[\mathbb{N}_\bot] \underset{(\mathrm{id},\mathrm{id})}{\Longrightarrow} \Delta[\mathbb{N}_\bot]}\;\mathrm{id}}{\Delta[\mathbb{N}_\bot] \underset{(\mathrm{id},(i;i'))}{\Longrightarrow} \Delta[\mathbb{N}_\bot]}\;\sim}{(\mathrm{id},i)\,\Delta[\mathbb{N}_\bot] \underset{(\mathrm{id},i')}{\Longrightarrow} \Delta[\mathbb{N}_\bot]}\;L(\mathrm{id},i)}{(\mathrm{id},\Psi_\mathrm{p})^*\,(\mathrm{id},i)\,\Delta[\mathbb{N}_\bot] \underset{(\mathrm{id},(\Psi_\mathrm{p};i'))}{\Longrightarrow} \Delta[\mathbb{N}_\bot]}\;L(\mathrm{id},\Psi_\mathrm{p})^*\,; \\
\hline\hline
\rho[nat] \underset{(\mathrm{id},\psi[nat])}{\Longrightarrow} \Delta[\![nat]\!]
\end{array}$$

- (Case $\theta = bool$).

$$\begin{array}{c}
\dfrac{\dfrac{\dfrac{\dfrac{\dfrac{\dfrac{}{\Delta[\mathbb{B}_\bot] \underset{(\mathrm{id},\mathrm{id})}{\Longrightarrow} \Delta[\mathbb{B}_\bot]}\;\mathrm{id}}{\Delta[\mathbb{B}_\bot] \underset{(\mathrm{id},(j';j))}{\Longrightarrow} \Delta[\mathbb{B}_\bot]}\;\sim}{\Delta[\mathbb{B}_\bot] \underset{(\mathrm{id},j')}{\Longrightarrow} (\mathrm{id},j)^*\,\Delta[\mathbb{B}_\bot]}\;R(\mathrm{id},j)^*}{\Delta[\mathbb{B}_\bot] \underset{(\mathrm{id},(j';i))}{\Longrightarrow} (\mathrm{id},i)\,(\mathrm{id},j)^*\,\Delta[\mathbb{B}_\bot]}\;;R(\mathrm{id},i)}{\Delta[\mathbb{B}_\bot] \underset{(\mathrm{id},(j';i;\Phi_\mathrm{p};\Psi_\mathrm{p}))}{\Longrightarrow} (\mathrm{id},i)\,(\mathrm{id},j)^*\,\Delta[\mathbb{B}_\bot]}\;\sim}{\Delta[\mathbb{B}_\bot] \underset{(\mathrm{id},(j';i;\Phi_\mathrm{p}))}{\Longrightarrow} (\mathrm{id},\Psi_\mathrm{p})^*\,(\mathrm{id},i)\,(\mathrm{id},j)^*\,\Delta[\mathbb{B}_\bot]}\;R(\mathrm{id},\Psi_\mathrm{p})^* \\
\hline\hline
\Delta[\![bool]\!] \underset{(\mathrm{id},\phi[bool])}{\Longrightarrow} \rho[bool]
\end{array}
\qquad
\begin{array}{c}
\dfrac{\dfrac{\dfrac{\dfrac{}{(\mathrm{id},j)^*\,\Delta[\mathbb{B}_\bot] \underset{(\mathrm{id},j)}{\Longrightarrow} \Delta[\mathbb{B}_\bot]}\;L(\mathrm{id},j)^*}{(\mathrm{id},j)^*\,\Delta[\mathbb{B}_\bot] \underset{(\mathrm{id},(i;i';j))}{\Longrightarrow} \Delta[\mathbb{B}_\bot]}\;\sim}{(\mathrm{id},i)\,(\mathrm{id},j)^*\,\Delta[\mathbb{B}_\bot] \underset{(\mathrm{id},(i';j))}{\Longrightarrow} \Delta[\mathbb{B}_\bot]}\;L(\mathrm{id},i)}{(\mathrm{id},\Psi_\mathrm{p})^*\,(\mathrm{id},i)\,(\mathrm{id},j)^*\,\Delta[\mathbb{B}_\bot] \underset{(\mathrm{id},(\Psi_\mathrm{p};i';j))}{\Longrightarrow} \Delta[\mathbb{B}_\bot]}\;L(\mathrm{id},\Psi_\mathrm{p})^*\,; \\
\hline\hline
\rho[bool] \underset{(\mathrm{id},\psi[bool])}{\Longrightarrow} \Delta[\![bool]\!]
\end{array}$$

# Integrating Dependent and Linear Types

Neelakantan R. Krishnaswami
University of Birmingham
<n.krishnaswami@cs.bham.ac.uk>

Pierre Pradic
ENS Lyon
<pierre.pradic@ens-lyon.fr>

Nick Benton
Microsoft Research
<nick@microsoft.com>

## Abstract

In this paper, we show how to integrate linear types with type dependency, by extending the linear/non-linear calculus of Benton to support type dependency.

Next, we give an application of this calculus by giving a proof-theoretic account of imperative programming, which requires extending the calculus with computationally irrelevant quantification, proof irrelevance, and a monad of computations. We show the soundness of our theory by giving a realizability model in the style of Nuprl, which permits us to validate not only the $\beta$-laws for each type, but also the $\eta$-laws.

These extensions permit us to decompose Hoare triples into a collection of simpler type-theoretic connectives, yielding a rich equational theory for dependently-typed higher-order imperative programs. Furthermore, both the type theory and its model are relatively simple, even when all of the extensions are considered.

***Keywords*** Linear types, dependent types, intersection types, proof irrelevance, separation logic, Hoare triples

## 1. Introduction

Two of the most influential research directions in language design are substructural logic and dependent type theory.

Substructural logics like linear logic [18] and separation logic [38] offer fine-grained control over the structural rules of logic (i.e., contraction and weakening), which means types control not only how a value of a given type is used, but also how often it is used. This permits giving a logical account of the notion of *resource*, and has been tremendously useful in giving modular and accurate specifications to stateful and imperative programs.

On the other hand, dependent type theory extends simple type theory by permitting terms to occur in types, permitting the expression of concepts like equality in types. This enables giving types which give a very fine-grained specification of the functional behaviour of their inhabitants.

We would like to fully integrate dependent and linear type theory. Linear type theory would permit us to extend the Curry-Howard correspondence to (for example) *imperative* programs, and type dependency permits giving very precise types to describe the precise functional behavior of those programs. The primary difficulty we face is precisely the interaction between type dependency and the structural rules. Since linear types ensure a variable occurs only once in a program, and dependent types permit variables to occur in both types and terms, how should we count occurrences of variables in types?

The key observation underpinning our approach is that *we do not have to answer this question!* We build on the work of Benton [7], which formulated models of intuitionistic linear logic in terms of a monoidal adjunction $F \dashv G$ between a monoidal closed category $\mathbb{L}$ and a cartesian closed category $\mathbb{C}$. The exponential $!A$ then decomposes as the composition of the $G(F(A))$. Syntactically, such a model then corresponds to a pair of lambda calculi, one intuitionistic, and one linear, which are related by a pair of modal operators $F$ and $G$.

In the linear/non-linear (LNL) calculus, we no longer have to view the intuitionistic function space $P \to Q$ through the lens of the Girard encoding $!P \multimap Q$. Instead, the intuitionistic arrow, $\to$, is a connective in its own right, independent of the linear function space, $\multimap$. Given such a separation, we can make the intuitionistic part of the language dependent, changing the type $X \to Y$ to the pi-type $\Pi x : X.\ Y$, without altering the linear function space $A \multimap B$. We then end up with a type theory in which linear types may depend on intuitionistic terms in quite sophisticated ways, but we never have to form a type dependent on an open linear term.

As an illustration, recall Girard's [19] classic motivating example of the resource reading of linear logic in which the proposition A represents spending a dollar, B represents obtaining a pack of Camels, and C obtaining a pack of Marlboro. The formula $A \multimap B\&C$ then expresses that one may spend a dollar and receive the option of a pack of Camels and of a pack of Marlboro, but only of these options may be exercised. In $\mathrm{LNL_D}$, from that assumption one can type, for example, a machine M that takes n dollars and produces its choice of something you can buy:

$$M : \Pi n : \mathbb{N}.\ \mathsf{tuple}\, n\, A \multimap \mathsf{F} m : \mathbb{N}, m' : \mathbb{N}, p : m + m' = n.\ \mathsf{tuple}\, m\, B \otimes \mathsf{tuple}\, m'\, C$$

where $\mathsf{tuple}\, n\, A$ is the (definable) n-fold linear tensor $A \otimes \cdots \otimes A$. The return type of the linear function space in the type of M is a linear dependent pair, which generalizes LNL's F modality for mapping intuitionistic values into linear ones. So M yields two integers $m$ and $m'$, a proof that their sum is $n$ and an $m$-tuple of Bs together with an $m'$-tuple of Cs.

***Contributions.*** In this paper, we make the following contributions:

- First, we describe a core type theory $\mathrm{LNL_D}$ that smoothly integrates both linearity and full type dependency, by ex-


*POPL '15*, January 15–17, 2015, Mumbai, India.

ACM 978-1-4503-3300-9/15/01...$15.00.
http://dx.doi.org/10.1145/2676726.2676969

$$\boxed{\Gamma\ \mathsf{ok}}$$

$$\frac{}{\cdot\ \mathsf{ok}} \qquad \frac{\Gamma\ \mathsf{ok} \qquad \Gamma \vdash X\ \mathsf{type}}{\Gamma, x : X\ \mathsf{ok}}$$

$$\boxed{\Gamma \vdash \Delta\ \mathsf{ok}}$$

$$\frac{}{\Gamma \vdash \cdot\ \mathsf{ok}} \qquad \frac{\Gamma \vdash \Delta\ \mathsf{ok} \qquad \Gamma \vdash A\ \mathsf{linear}}{\Gamma \vdash \Delta, a : A\ \mathsf{ok}}$$

$$\boxed{\Gamma \vdash X\ \mathsf{type}} \qquad \boxed{\Gamma \vdash A\ \mathsf{linear}}$$

$$\frac{\Gamma \vdash X : U_i}{\Gamma \vdash X\ \mathsf{type}} \qquad \frac{\Gamma \vdash A : L_i}{\Gamma \vdash A\ \mathsf{linear}}$$

$$\boxed{\Gamma \vdash X \equiv Y\ \mathsf{type}} \qquad \boxed{\Gamma \vdash A \equiv B\ \mathsf{linear}}$$

$$\frac{\Gamma \vdash X \equiv Y : U_i}{\Gamma \vdash X \equiv Y\ \mathsf{type}} \qquad \frac{\Gamma \vdash A \equiv B : L_i}{\Gamma \vdash A \equiv B\ \mathsf{linear}}$$

**Figure 1.** Structural judgements

tending the linear/non-linear calculus [7, 8]. Our type theory is an extensional type theory, which means that we consider the full βη-theory of the language, and furthermore, it also has a universe hierarchy, meaning that we support "full-spectrum" dependent types including large eliminations (i.e., computing types from terms).

Our approach to linear dependent type theory gives a simple proof-theoretic explanation of how the ad-hoc restrictions on the interaction of linearity in earlier approaches (such as Linear LF [10]) arise, by showing how they can be modelled in $\mathrm{LNL_D}$.

- Second, we show how to turn this calculus into a language for dependently-typed imperative programming (in the style of separation logic). The general idea is to combine linearity and type dependency to turn separation-logic style specifications into types, and to take imperative programs to be inhabitants of those types.

  Ensuring that programs have the appropriate operational behavior requires a number of extensions to the type system, including pointer types, implicit quantification (in the style of intersection and union types), and proof irrelevance for linear types.
- Once this is done, we not only have a very expressive type system for higher-order imperative programs, but we also can systematically give a natural equational theory for them via the βη-theory for each of the type constructors we use.
- Next, we give a realizability model in the style of Nuprl [20] to show the consistency of our calculus. Our model is very simple and easy to work with, but nevertheless simply and gracefully justifies the wide variety of the extensions we consider.
- Finally, we give a small implementation of our extended type theory, illustrating that it is possible to implement all of these constructions.

## 2. Core Dependent Linear Type Theory

In this section, we describe the core dependent linear/nonlinear calculus. The full grammar of terms and types is given later, in Figure 10, but here we present the calculus rule by rule.

$$\frac{}{\Gamma \vdash U_i : U_{i+1}} \qquad \frac{}{\Gamma \vdash L_i : U_{i+1}}$$

$$\frac{\Gamma \vdash X : U_i \qquad \Gamma, x : X \vdash Y : U_i}{\Gamma \vdash \Pi x : X.\ Y : U_i} \qquad \frac{\Gamma \vdash X : U_i \qquad \Gamma, x : X \vdash Y : U_i}{\Gamma \vdash \Sigma x : X.\ Y : U_i}$$

$$\frac{}{\Gamma \vdash 1 : U_i} \qquad \frac{\Gamma \vdash A : L_i}{\Gamma \vdash G\,A : U_i}$$

$$\frac{\Gamma \vdash X : U_i \qquad \Gamma \vdash e : X \qquad \Gamma \vdash e' : X}{\Gamma \vdash e =_X e' : U_i}$$

$$\frac{}{\Gamma \vdash I : L_i} \qquad \frac{\Gamma \vdash A : L_i \qquad \Gamma \vdash B : L_i}{\Gamma \vdash A \otimes B : L_i} \qquad \frac{\Gamma \vdash A : L_i \qquad \Gamma \vdash B : L_i}{\Gamma \vdash A \multimap B : L_i}$$

$$\frac{\Gamma \vdash X : U_i \qquad \Gamma, x : X \vdash A : L_i}{\Gamma \vdash \Pi x : X.\ A : L_i} \qquad \frac{\Gamma \vdash X : U_i \qquad \Gamma, x : X \vdash A : L_i}{\Gamma \vdash F x : X.\ A : L_i}$$

$$\frac{}{\Gamma \vdash \top : L_i} \qquad \frac{\Gamma \vdash A : L_i \qquad \Gamma \vdash B : L_i}{\Gamma \vdash A \,\&\, B : L_i}$$

**Figure 2.** Type Well-formedness

$$\frac{}{\Gamma, x : X, \Gamma' \vdash x : X} \qquad \frac{\Gamma \vdash e : Y \qquad \Gamma \vdash X \equiv Y\ \mathsf{type}}{\Gamma \vdash e : X} \qquad \frac{}{\Gamma \vdash () : 1}$$

$$\frac{\Gamma \vdash e : X \qquad \Gamma \vdash e' : [e/x]Y}{\Gamma \vdash (e, e') : \Sigma x : X.\ Y} \qquad \frac{\Gamma \vdash e : \Sigma x : X.\ Y}{\Gamma \vdash \pi_1\, e : X}$$

$$\frac{\Gamma \vdash e : \Sigma x : X.\ Y}{\Gamma \vdash \pi_2\, e : [\pi_1\, e/x]Y}$$

$$\frac{\Gamma \vdash \Pi x : X.\ Y\ \mathsf{type} \qquad \Gamma, x : X \vdash e : Y}{\Gamma \vdash \lambda x.\ e : \Pi x : X.\ Y}$$

$$\frac{\Gamma \vdash e : \Pi x : X.\ Y \qquad \Gamma \vdash e' : X}{\Gamma \vdash e\ e' : [e'/x]Y}$$

$$\frac{\Gamma \vdash e \equiv e' : X}{\Gamma \vdash \mathsf{refl} : e =_X e'} \qquad \frac{\Gamma; \cdot \vdash e : A}{\Gamma \vdash G\,e : G\,A}$$

**Figure 3.** Intuitionistic Typing

The basic structural judgements are given in Figure 1. The judgement $\Gamma$ ok is the judgement that a context $\Gamma$ of *intuitionistic hypotheses* is well-formed. As is standard, a well-formed context is either empty, or a context $\Gamma', x : X$ where $\Gamma'$ is well-formed and $X$ is an intuitionistic type well-formed in $\Gamma$. The judgement $\Gamma \vdash \Delta$ ok says that $\Delta$ is a well-formed *linear context*, whose linear types may depend (only) upon the intuitionistic variables in $\Gamma$. The judgements $\Gamma \vdash X$ type and $\Gamma \vdash A$ linear judge when a term is an intuitionistic or linear type, respectively. The equality judgements $\Gamma \vdash X \equiv Y$ type and $\Gamma \vdash A \equiv B$ linear determine whether two intuitionistic or linear types are definitionally equal, respectively.

Both $\Gamma \vdash X$ type and $\Gamma \vdash A$ linear work by immediately appealing to an ordinary typing judgement for an intuitionistic universe $U_i$ and a linear universe $L_i$. The type well-formedness rules are given in Figure 2, and the introduction and elimination rules are given in Figure 3, with the judgement $\Gamma \vdash e : X$.

Both linear and intuitionistic universes $L_i$ and $U_i$ are elements of the larger universe $U_{i+1}$. Note that $L_i$ is an element of $U_{i+1}$ — this is because a linear *type* is an intuitionistic *term*, since we do not wish to restrict how often type variables ranging over linear types can occur. (That is, we want polymorphic types like $\Pi\alpha : L_i.\ \alpha \multimap \alpha$ to be well-formed.)

$$\frac{}{\Gamma; a : A \vdash a : A} \qquad \frac{\Gamma;\Delta \vdash e : B \qquad \Gamma \vdash A \equiv B \ \text{linear}}{\Gamma;\Delta \vdash e : A}$$

$$\frac{}{\Gamma; \cdot \vdash () : \mathsf{I}} \qquad \frac{\Gamma;\Delta \vdash e : \mathsf{I} \qquad \Gamma;\Delta' \vdash e' : C}{\Gamma;\Delta,\Delta' \vdash \mathsf{let}\ () = e\ \mathsf{in}\ e' : C}$$

$$\frac{\Gamma;\Delta \vdash e : A \qquad \Gamma;\Delta' \vdash e' : B}{\Gamma;\Delta,\Delta' \vdash (e, e') : A \otimes B}$$

$$\frac{\Gamma;\Delta \vdash e : A \otimes B \qquad \Gamma;\Delta', a : A, b : B \vdash e' : C}{\Gamma;\Delta,\Delta' \vdash \mathsf{let}\ (a, b) = e\ \mathsf{in}\ e' : C}$$

$$\frac{\Gamma;\Delta, a : A \vdash e : B}{\Gamma;\Delta \vdash \lambda a.\, e : A \multimap B} \qquad \frac{\Gamma;\Delta \vdash e : A \multimap B \qquad \Gamma;\Delta' \vdash e' : A}{\Gamma;\Delta,\Delta' \vdash e\, e' : B}$$

$$\frac{\Gamma, x : X;\Delta \vdash e : A}{\Gamma;\Delta \vdash \hat{\lambda} x.\, e : \Pi x : X.\, A} \qquad \frac{\Gamma;\Delta \vdash e : \Pi x : X.\, A \qquad \Gamma \vdash e' : X}{\Gamma;\Delta \vdash e\, e' : [e'/x]A}$$

$$\frac{}{\Gamma;\Delta \vdash () : \top}$$

$$\frac{\Gamma;\Delta \vdash e_1 : A_1 \qquad \Gamma;\Delta \vdash e_2 : A_2}{\Gamma;\Delta \vdash (e_1, e_2) : A_1 \,\&\, A_2} \qquad \frac{\Gamma;\Delta \vdash e : A \,\&\, B}{\Gamma;\Delta \vdash \pi_1\, e : A}$$

$$\frac{\Gamma;\Delta \vdash e : A \,\&\, B}{\Gamma;\Delta \vdash \pi_2\, e : B}$$

$$\frac{\Gamma \vdash e : X \qquad \Gamma;\Delta \vdash t : [e/x]A}{\Gamma;\Delta \vdash \mathsf{F}\,(e, t) : \mathsf{F} x : X.\, A}$$

$$\frac{\Gamma;\Delta \vdash e : \mathsf{F} x : X.\, A \qquad \Gamma, x : X;\Delta', a : A \vdash e' : C}{\Gamma;\Delta,\Delta' \vdash \mathsf{let}\ \mathsf{F}\,(x, a) = e\ \mathsf{in}\ e' : C}$$

$$\frac{\Gamma \vdash e : \mathsf{G}\, A}{\Gamma; \cdot \vdash \mathsf{G}^{-1}\, e : A}$$

**Figure 4.** Linear Typing

$$\boxed{\Gamma \vdash e \equiv e' : X} \qquad \boxed{\Gamma;\Delta \vdash t \equiv t' : A}$$

$$\frac{\Gamma \vdash p : e =_X e'}{\Gamma \vdash e \equiv e' : X}$$

$$\frac{}{\Gamma \vdash (\lambda x.\, e)\, e' \equiv [e'/x]e : X} \qquad \frac{}{\Gamma \vdash e \equiv \lambda x.\, e\, x : \Pi x : X.\, Y}$$

$$\frac{}{\Gamma \vdash \pi_1\, (e, e') \equiv e : X} \qquad \frac{}{\Gamma \vdash \pi_2\, (e, e') \equiv e' : X}$$

$$\frac{}{\Gamma \vdash e \equiv (\pi_1\, e, \pi_2\, e) : \Sigma x : X.\, Y}$$

$$\frac{}{\Gamma \vdash e \equiv e' : 1}$$

$$\frac{}{\Gamma \vdash \mathsf{G}\,(\mathsf{G}^{-1}\, e) \equiv e : \mathsf{G}\, A}$$

$$\frac{}{\Gamma; \cdot \vdash \mathsf{G}^{-1}\,(\mathsf{G}\, t) \equiv t : A} \qquad \frac{}{\Gamma;\Delta \vdash (\lambda x.\, e)\, e' \equiv [e'/x]e : C}$$

$$\frac{}{\Gamma;\Delta \vdash e \equiv \lambda x.\, e\, x : A \multimap B}$$

$$\frac{}{\Gamma;\Delta \vdash (\hat{\lambda} x.\, e)\, e' \equiv [e'/x]e : C} \qquad \frac{}{\Gamma;\Delta \vdash e \equiv \hat{\lambda} x.\, e\, x : \Pi x : X.\, A}$$

$$\frac{}{\Gamma;\Delta \vdash e \equiv e' : \top}$$

$$\frac{}{\Gamma;\Delta \vdash \pi_1\, (e, e') \equiv e : A} \qquad \frac{}{\Gamma;\Delta \vdash \pi_1\, (e, e') \equiv e' : B}$$

$$\frac{}{\Gamma;\Delta \vdash e \equiv (\pi_1\, e, \pi_2\, e) : A \,\&\, B}$$

$$\frac{}{\Gamma;\Delta \vdash \mathsf{let}\ () = ()\ \mathsf{in}\ e \equiv e : C}$$

$$\frac{}{\Gamma;\Delta \vdash \mathsf{let}\ () = t\ \mathsf{in}\ [()/x]t' \equiv [t/x]t' : C}$$

$$\frac{}{\Gamma;\Delta \vdash \mathsf{let}\ (a, b) = (t_1, t_2)\ \mathsf{in}\ t' \equiv [t_1/a, t_2/b]t' : C}$$

$$\frac{}{\Gamma;\Delta \vdash \mathsf{let}\ (a, b) = t\ \mathsf{in}\ [(a, b)/x]t' \equiv [t/x]t' : C}$$

$$\frac{}{\Gamma;\Delta \vdash \mathsf{let}\ \mathsf{F}\,(x, a) = \mathsf{F}\,(e, t)\ \mathsf{in}\ t' \equiv [e/x, t/a]t' : C}$$

$$\frac{}{\Gamma;\Delta \vdash \mathsf{let}\ \mathsf{F}\,(x, a) = t\ \mathsf{in}\ [\mathsf{F}\,(x, a)/y]t' \equiv [t/y]t' : C}$$

**Figure 5.** $\beta\eta$-Equality

The intuitionistic types we consider are the dependent function space $\Pi x : X.\, Y$, with a lambda-abstraction and function application as its introduction and elimination rules; the dependent pair $\Sigma x : X.\, Y$, with pairing $(e, e')$ as its introduction, and the projective (or "strong") eliminations $\pi_1\, e$ and $\pi_2\, e$; the unit type 1; and the equality type $e =_X e'$. Equality is introduced with $\mathsf{refl}$, but has no explicit elimination form, since we are giving an extensional type theory with equality reflection. These rules are all standard for dependent type theory. Similarly, it is possible to add inductive types (such as natural numbers) to the calculus, including support for large eliminations, though we omit them from the rules in the paper for space reasons (rules and proofs are in the companion tech report).

The first place that linearity arises is with the the adjoint embedding of linear types into intuitionistic types $\mathsf{G}\, A$. Its (intuitionistic) introduction rule is $\mathsf{G}\, e$, which checks that $e$ has linear type $A$, in the empty linear context. (Intuitively, this reflects the fact that closed linear terms can be freely duplicated.) It is worth noting that our intuitionistic types are also essentially the same types as are found in the non-dependent LNL calculus, only we have changed $X \to Y$ to a pi-type, and $X \times Y$ to a sigma-type.

The typing judgement $\Gamma;\Delta \vdash e : A$ for linear terms says that $e$ has type $A$, assuming intuitionistic variables $\Gamma$ and linear variables $\Delta$. The well-formedness and typing rules for the MALL connectives $(\mathsf{I}, \otimes, \multimap, \&, \top)$ are all standard. The elimination form of the type $\mathsf{G}\, A$ is $\mathsf{G}^{-1}\, e$, which yields an $A$ in an empty linear context, which is the same as in Benton [7].

We depart from propositional LNL when we reach the dependent version of the other adjoint connective. Instead of a unary modal connective $\mathsf{F}(X)$, we introduce the *linear dependent pair type* $\mathsf{F} x : X.\, A[x]$. Its introduction form $\mathsf{F}\,(e, t)$ consists of a pair consisting of an intuitionistic term $e$ of type $X$, and a linear term $t$ of type $A[e]$ — observe the type of the linear term may depend on the intuitionistic first component. However, just as in the LNL calculus, this pair has a pattern matching eliminator $\mathsf{let}\ \mathsf{F}\,(x, a) = e\ \mathsf{in}\ e'$. Also, we add a dependent linear function space $\Pi x : X.\, A$, which is a function which takes an intuitionistic argument and returns a linear result (whose type may depend on the argument). We add this for essentially hygienic reasons — it gives us syntax for the equivalence $(\mathsf{F} x : X.\, A) \multimap C \simeq \Pi x : X.\, A \multimap C$.

The equality theory of our language is given in Figure 5. This gives the $\beta$ and $\eta$ rules for each of the connectives, including commuting conversions for all of the positive connectives (i.e., $\otimes$, $\mathsf{I}$ and $\mathsf{F}$). We also include the equality reflection rule of extensional type theory. For space reasons, we do not include any of the congruence rules, or the equivalence relation axioms (they are given in the technical report).

$$\frac{}{\Gamma \vdash \mathsf{Loc} : U_i} \qquad \frac{\Gamma \vdash e : \mathsf{Loc} \quad \Gamma \vdash X : U_i}{\Gamma \vdash e \mapsto X : L_i} \qquad \frac{\Gamma \vdash A : L_i}{\Gamma \vdash T(A) : L_i}$$

$$\frac{\Gamma \vdash A : L_i}{\Gamma \vdash [A] : L_i}$$

$$\frac{\Gamma \vdash X : U_i \quad \Gamma, x : X \vdash Y : U_i}{\Gamma \vdash \forall x : X.\, Y : U_i} \qquad \frac{\Gamma \vdash X : U_i \quad \Gamma, x : X \vdash Y : L_i}{\Gamma \vdash \forall x : X.\, Y : L_i}$$

$$\frac{\Gamma \vdash X : U_i \quad \Gamma, x : X \vdash Y : U_i}{\Gamma \vdash \exists x : X.\, Y : U_i} \qquad \frac{\Gamma \vdash X : U_i \quad \Gamma, x : X \vdash Y : L_i}{\Gamma \vdash \exists x : X.\, Y : L_i}$$

$$\frac{}{\Gamma \vdash T_I : U_i}$$

**Figure 6.** Well-formedness of extensions

$$\frac{\Gamma, x : X \vdash e : Y \quad x \notin FV(e)}{\Gamma \vdash e : \forall x : X.\, Y} \qquad \frac{\Gamma \vdash e : \forall x : X.\, Y \quad \Gamma \vdash e' : X}{\Gamma \vdash e : [e'/x]Y}$$

$$\frac{\Gamma, x : X, y : Y \vdash e : Z \quad x \notin FV(e)}{\Gamma, y : \exists x : X.\, Y \vdash e : Z}$$

$$\frac{\Gamma, x : X \vdash Y \text{ type} \quad \Gamma \vdash e' : X \quad \Gamma \vdash e : [e'/x]Y}{\Gamma \vdash e : \exists x : X.\, Y}$$

$$\frac{\Gamma, x : X; \Delta \vdash e : A \quad x \notin FV(e)}{\Gamma; \Delta \vdash e : \forall x : X.\, A}$$

$$\frac{\Gamma; \Delta \vdash e : \forall x : X.\, A \quad \Gamma \vdash e' : X}{\Gamma; \Delta \vdash e : [e'/x]A}$$

$$\frac{\Gamma, x : X; \Delta, a : A \vdash e : C \quad x \notin FV(e)}{\Gamma; \Delta, a : \exists x : X.\, A \vdash e : C}$$

$$\frac{\Gamma, x : X \vdash Y \text{ linear} \quad \Gamma \vdash e' : X \quad \Gamma; \Delta \vdash e : [e'/x]Y}{\Gamma; \Delta \vdash e : \exists x : X.\, Y}$$

$$\frac{\begin{array}{c}\Gamma, n : \mathbb{N} \vdash \Pi x : X[n].\, Y[n] \text{ type} \qquad \Gamma, f : \top_I, x : X(0) \vdash e : Y(0) \\ \Gamma, n : \mathbb{N}, f : \Pi x : X[n].\, Y[n], x : X[s(n)] \vdash e : Y[s(n)] \\ n \notin FV(\text{fix } f\ x = e)\end{array}}{\Gamma \vdash \text{fix } f\ x = e : \forall n : \mathbb{N}.\, \Pi x : X[n].\, Y[n]}$$

**Figure 7.** Intersection and Union Types

## 3. Internal Imperative Programming

There have been a number of very successful applications of dependent type theory to verify imperative programs using dependent types, such as XCAP, Bedrock and the Verified Software Toolchain [4, 11, 31]. These approaches all have the common feature that they are "external" methodologies for imperative programming. That is, within the metalogic of dependent type theory, an imperative language (such as C or assembly) and its semantics is defined, and a program logic for that language is specified and proved correct. So the type theory remains pure, and imperative programs are therefore objects of study rather than programs of the type theory.

We would like to investigate an internal, "proofs as programs", methodology for imperative programming, where we write functional programs which (a) have effects, but (b) nonetheless are inhabitants of the appropriate types.

***Pointers, Computations, and Proof Irrelevance*** In order to program with mutable state, we need types to describe both state and computation that manipulate it. To do this, we will follow the pattern of L3 [2], and introduce a type of *locations*, and a type of *reference capabilities*.

$$\frac{\Gamma \vdash e : \mathsf{Loc} \quad \Gamma; \Delta \vdash t : [e \mapsto X] \quad \Gamma, x : X; \Delta', a : [e \mapsto X] \vdash t' : C}{\Gamma; \Delta, \Delta' \vdash \text{let } (x, a) = \text{get}(e, t) \text{ in } t' : C}$$

$$\frac{\Gamma; \Delta \vdash e : A}{\Gamma; \Delta \vdash \text{val } e : T(A)} \qquad \frac{\Gamma; \Delta \vdash e : T(A) \quad \Gamma; \Delta', a : A \vdash e' : T(C)}{\Gamma; \Delta, \Delta' \vdash \text{let val } a = e \text{ in } e' : T(C)}$$

$$\frac{\Gamma \vdash e : X}{\Gamma; \cdot \vdash \text{new}_X\ e : T((Fx : \text{Loc}.\ [x \mapsto X]))}$$

$$\frac{\Gamma \vdash e : \mathsf{Loc} \quad \Gamma; \Delta \vdash t : [e \mapsto X]}{\Gamma; \Delta \vdash \text{free}(e, t) : T(I)}$$

$$\frac{\Gamma \vdash e : \mathsf{Loc} \quad \Gamma; \Delta \vdash t : [e \mapsto X] \quad \Gamma \vdash e' : Y}{\Gamma; \Delta \vdash e :=_t e' : T([e \mapsto Y])}$$

$$\frac{\Gamma; \Delta \vdash e \div A}{\Gamma; \Delta \vdash * : [A]} \qquad \frac{\Gamma; \Delta \vdash e : A}{\Gamma; \Delta \vdash e \div A}$$

$$\frac{\Gamma; \Delta \vdash e : [A] \quad \Gamma; \Delta', x : A \vdash e' \div C}{\Gamma; \Delta, \Delta' \vdash \text{let } [x] = e \text{ in } e' \div C}$$

$$\frac{\Gamma; \Delta \vdash e : [I] \quad \Gamma; \Delta' \vdash e' : C}{\Gamma; \Delta, \Delta' \vdash \text{let } [] = e \text{ in } e' : C}$$

$$\frac{\Gamma; \Delta \vdash e : [A \otimes B] \quad \Gamma; \Delta', a : [A], b : [B] \vdash e' : C}{\Gamma; \Delta, \Delta' \vdash \text{let } [a, b] = e \text{ in } e' : C}$$

**Figure 8.** Typing of Imperative Programs

$$\frac{\Gamma, x : X \vdash e \equiv e' : Y}{\Gamma \vdash e \equiv e' : \forall x : X.\, Y} \qquad \frac{\Gamma \vdash e \equiv e' : \forall x : X.\, Y \quad \Gamma \vdash t : X}{\Gamma \vdash e \equiv e' : [t/x]Y}$$

$$\frac{\Gamma \vdash e \equiv e' : [t/x]Y \quad \Gamma \vdash t : X}{\Gamma \vdash e \equiv e' : \exists x : X.\, Y}$$

$$\frac{\Gamma, x : X, y : Y \vdash e \equiv e' : Z \quad x \notin FV(e, e', Z)}{\Gamma, y : \exists x : X.\, Y \vdash e \equiv e' : Z}$$

$$\frac{}{\Gamma; \Delta \vdash \text{let val } x = \text{val } t \text{ in } t' \equiv [t/x]t' : T(C)}$$

$$\frac{}{\Gamma; \Delta \vdash \text{let val } x = t \text{ in val } x \equiv t : T(C)}$$

$$\frac{}{\Gamma; \Delta \vdash \begin{array}{c}\text{let val } y = (\text{let val } x = t_1 \text{ in } t_2) \text{ in } t_3 \\ \equiv \\ \text{let val } x = t_1 \text{ in let val } y = t_2 \text{ in } t_3\end{array} : T(C)}$$

$$\frac{}{\Gamma; \Delta \vdash e \equiv e' : [A]}$$

$$\frac{\Gamma, x : X; \Delta \vdash e \equiv e' : A}{\Gamma; \Delta \vdash e \equiv e' : \forall x : X.\, Y} \qquad \frac{\Gamma; \Delta \vdash e \equiv e' : \forall x : X.\, A \quad \Gamma \vdash t : X}{\Gamma; \Delta \vdash e \equiv e' : [t/x]A}$$

$$\frac{\Gamma; \Delta \vdash e \equiv e' : [t/x]A \quad \Gamma \vdash t : X}{\Gamma; \Delta \vdash e \equiv e' : \exists x : X.\, A}$$

$$\frac{\Gamma, x : X; \Delta, a : A \vdash e \equiv e' : C \quad x \notin FV(e, e', C)}{\Gamma \vdash \Delta, a : \exists x : X.\, A \equiv e : e'C}$$

$$\frac{}{\Gamma \vdash (\text{fix } f\ x = e)\ e' \equiv [(\text{fix } f\ x = e)/f, e'/x]e : Z}$$

**Figure 9.** Imperative Equality

The type Loc is an intuitionistic type of locations. This is a type of addresses, which may be freely duplicated and stored in data structures. Testing locations for equality is a pure computation, and for simplicity we do not consider address arithmetic. However, merely having a location is not sufficient to dereference it, since *a priori* we do not know if that location points to allocated memory.

The right to access a pointer is encoded in the capability type $e \mapsto X$. This says that the location $e$ holds a value of type $X$. This differs slightly from separation logic, whose points-to assertion $e \mapsto v$ says that $e$ points to the specific value $v$. However, since we have dependent types at our disposal, we can easily recover the separation logic assertion with the encoding $e \mapsto v \equiv e \mapsto (\Sigma x : X.\ x = v)$.

At this point, much of the descriptive power of separation logic is already available to us: as soon as we have locations and pointer capabilities, we can use the tensor product $P \otimes Q$ just like the separating conjunction $P * Q$.[1]

Next, we introduce a type $\mathsf{T}(A)$ of computations. That is, if $A$ is a linear type, then $\mathsf{T}(A)$ is a computation type which produces a result of type $A$. Note that $\mathsf{T}(A)$ is itself a linear type; intuitively, executing a computation modifies the current state so that it becomes a post-state of type $A$. The reason we treat computations monadically is because, naively, allocation and deallocation of memory violates linearity: for example, if we typed allocation as $\mathsf{F}x : \mathsf{Loc}.\ x \mapsto X$, the points-to assertion is "created from nothing". Since one of our design goals is precisely to keep the semantics (see section 4) as naive as possible, we introduce a linear computation type.

With the features we have introduced so far, a stateful computation $e$ might be given the type $\mathsf{G}(P \multimap \mathsf{T}(Q))$, representing a linearly-closed term which takes a pre-state of type $P$, and computes a result of type $Q$. While this is perfectly adequate from a props-as-types point of view, it is not quite right computationally.

In our approach, we encode reasoning about state using linear types, so that we can read the type $P' \multimap P$ as saying that the state $P'$ implies the state $P$. However, a proof $f$ of this entailment is a linear lambda term, and evaluating it *does computation*. So if we precompose the proof $f$ with the computation $e$, then we get a result which does different computation than $e$ did originally. This is quite different from the way that the rule of consequence works in Hoare logic.

To solve this problem, we introduce a form of linear proof irrelevance into our language. The type $[A]$ is a *squash type*, which erases all of the proof-relevant data about $A$ — we are left with only knowledge of its inhabitation. Our type system has a rule saying that $*$ is an inhabitant of $[A]$, if we can find evidence for it using the monadic judgement $\Gamma; \Delta \vdash e \div A$. This judgement lets us turn any derivation of $A$ as evidence of inhabitation, and lets us use evidence of proof-irrelevant inhabitation relevantly, as long as we stay in the irrelevance judgement. We also give a pair of rules to distribute proof-irrelevance through tensor products and units.[2]

[1] It is relatively easy to show that any formula in the logic of bunched implications [33] which does not interleave the ordinary implication $P \supset Q$ and the magic wand $P -\!\!* Q$ has a corresponding proof in linear logic, since interleaving the additive and multiplicative implications is the only way to create bunched contexts. However, the magic wand is rarely used in practice (though see [21]).

[2] Intuitionistically, the isomorphism $[A \times B] \simeq [A] \times [B]$ is derivable, but the proof relies on the fact that pairing has first and second projections. With the linear tensor product, this isomorphism has to be built into the syntax.

So we can type computations as $\mathsf{G}([P] \multimap \mathsf{T}(\mathsf{F}x : X.\ [Q]))$, representing computations that take (proof-irrelevant) pre-states $P$ to proof-irrelevant post-states, while returning values of type $X$.

We can now describe the typing rules for computations in Figure 8. Given a location and a proof-irrelevant capability to access it, we can now type a dereference operation. Dereferencing $\mathsf{let}\ (x, a) = \mathsf{get}(e, t)\ \mathsf{in}\ t'$ (in Figure 8) takes a location $e$ and a capability $t$, and then binds the contents to $x$, and the returned capability in the variable $a$, before evaluating the body $t'$.

The dereference operation is a pure linear term (i.e., has a non-monadic type), since it reads but does not modify the state. The other stateful operations are monadic. Allocation $\mathsf{new}_X\ e$ is a computation which returns a pair of location and an irrelevant capability to access that location. Deallocation $\mathsf{free}(e, e')$ takes a location and the capability to access it, and then deallocates the memory, returning a computation of unit type. Update $e :=_t e'$ takes a location and a capability to access it, and then updates the location, returning a new capability to access it. Since capabilities are linear, we are able to support *strong update* – assignment can change the type of a pointer. We also include standard monadic rules for returning pure values and sequencing computations.

As a simple example, consider the following term:

```
1  let val F (x, c₁) = new_ℕ 0 in
2  let val F (y, c₂) = new_bool false in
3  let (n, c₁') = get(x, c₁) in
4  let val c₂' = (y :=_c₂ n) in
5  val (F (x, c₁'), F (y, c₂'))
```

On the first two lines, this function allocates two pointers $x$ (pointing to 0) and $y$ (pointing to false), with access capabilities $c_1$ and $c_2$. On line 3, it dereferences $x$, binding the result to $n$. Furthermore, the linear capability $c_1$ is taken by the dereference operation, and returned (as the capability $c_1'$). On line 4, $y$ is updated to point to $n$, again taking in the capability $c_2$ and returning the capability $c_1$. This is a strong update, changing the type of $y$ so that it points to a natural number. Then, we return both pointers and their access capabilities on line 5, with an overall type of $\mathsf{T}((\mathsf{F}x : \mathsf{Loc}.\ [x \mapsto \mathbb{N}]) \otimes (\mathsf{F}y : \mathsf{Loc}.\ [y \mapsto \mathbb{N}]))$.

One point worth mentioning is that our computation monad is a *strong* monad, which is in some sense the essence of the frame rule of separation logic — the derivability of the map $(A \otimes \mathsf{T}(B)) \multimap \mathsf{T}((A \otimes B))$ means that a computation of $B$ that doesn't use the state $A$ can "fold it in" to produce a bigger computation of $A \otimes B$.

Another point worth mentioning is that our system only treats reading pointers as a pure linear action. Naively, one might expect writes could also be viewed as pure, since linearity ensures that there is at most one capability to modify a location. Unfortunately, this idea is incompatible with proof-irrelevance: squashing erases a term, and erasing terms which could modify the heap would be unsound.

***Intersection Types and Implicit Quantification*** At this point, we are close to being able to formulate specifications of imperative programs in an internal way. However, one still-missing feature of program logics is support of *logical variables*. These are variables which occur only in specifications, but which do not affect the evaluation of a program. Fortunately, these have also been studied extensively in lambda-calculus, albeit under a different name: *intersection types*.

We introduce the two type formers $\forall x : X.\ Y$ and $\exists x : X.\ Y$ (and their linear counterparts), corresponding to an $X$-indexed intersection and union, respectively. A term $e$ is an inhabitant of $\forall x : X.\ Y$ if it is an inhabitant of $Y$ for all $x$, and symmetrically, $e$ inhabits $\exists x : X.\ Y$ if there is some $v : X$ such that $e : [v/x]Y$. The precise rules are given in Figure 7 – the key constraint is that even though a new hypothesis becomes available in the context, it cannot occur in the term. This ensures that it cannot affect evaluation, even though it can appear in typing.

The classical intersection type $A \wedge B$ can be encoded using large elimination, as $\forall b : 2.\ \mathsf{if}(b, A, B)$, and the union type $A \vee B$ is $\exists b : 2.\ \mathsf{if}(b, A, B)$.

Now, we can introduce logical variables into our specifications (i.e., types) by simple quantification:

$$\forall x : X.\ \mathsf{G}\,([P] \multimap \mathsf{T}\,(\mathsf{F}y : Y.\ [Q]))$$

The variable $x$ can now range over both the pre- and the post-conditions without being able to affect the computation.

***Fixed Points*** Finally, we make use of intersection types to introduce a recursive function form $\mathsf{fix}\ f\ x = e$ (see Figure 7). This function is ascribed the type $\forall n : \mathbb{N}.\ \Pi x : X[n].\ Y[n]$, when (1) assuming $f$ has the type $\Pi x : X[n].\ Y[n]$ and $x$ has the type $X[\mathsf{s}(n)]$, then the body has the type $Y[\mathsf{s}(n)]$, and (2) we can show that the body has the type $Y[0]$ when the argument has type $X[0]$. (In the base case, we also assume that $f$ has a top type which cannot be used, to prevent recursive calls.)

This permits us to define recursive functions if we can supply a decreasing termination metric as a computationally-irrelevant argument. This is useful because the inductive eliminators require a proof-relevant argument, which we might not have!

### 3.1 Examples

With all of this machinery, we can now define a simple linked list predicate. For simplicity, we leave the data out, leaving only the link structure behind.

$$\begin{array}{lcl} \mathrm{LList} & : & \mathbb{N} \times \mathsf{Loc} \to \mathsf{L}_0 \\ \mathrm{LList}(0, l) & = & [l \mapsto \mathsf{inl}\,()] \\ \mathrm{LList}(n+1, l) & = & \mathsf{F}l' : \mathsf{Loc}.\ [l \mapsto \mathsf{inr}\,l'] \otimes \mathrm{LList}(n, l') \end{array}$$

This says that a list of length 0 is a pointer to a null value, and a list of length $n+1$ is a pointer to a list of length $n$. Note that this predicate is *proof-relevant*, in that a term of type $\mathrm{LList}(n, l)$ is a nested tuple including all the pointers in the linked list. As a result, we need to squash the predicate when giving specifications to programs. We will also make use of the fact that proof-relevant quantifiers inside of a squash can be turned into proof-irrelevant quantifiers outside of a squash: that is, the axiom $[\mathsf{F}x : X.\ A] \multimap \exists x : X.\ [A]$ is inhabited (by the term $\lambda x.\ *$). In particular, this lets us turn squashed coproducts into union types: $[A \oplus B] \multimap [A] \vee [B]$.

***List length*** As a first example, if we wanted to define a length function for linked lists, we would need to do it as:

```
len : ∀n : ℕ. Πl : Loc. G([LList(n, l)]
                    ⊸ (Fm : ℕ, pf : m = n. [LList(n, l)]))
len l = G(λc.
  let [c′] = ∗ in
  let [c₁, c₂] = c′ in
  let ((v, pf), c₁′) = get(l, c₁) in
  case(v,
    inl () → F (0, refl, ∗)
    inr l′ → let (F (m, pf, c″)) = G⁻¹ (len l′) ∗ in
             F (m + 1, refl, ∗)))
```

The type of this function says that if we are given a list of length $n$, then we can recursively traverse the linked list in order to get a computationally-relevant number equal to $n$. This turns out to be a very common pattern in specifications: we use computations to mediate between some logical fact about a piece of data (i.e., the index $n$) and computational data (in this case, the length $m$ of the list).

Obviously, this function cannot be defined with an eliminator on $n$, since the point is precisely to compute a relevant number equal to $n$, and the data we receive is merely a bare pointer, along with the right to traverse it.

Worth noting is that the squash type completely conceals almost all of the proof-related book-keeping related to manipulating the linked-list predicate LList. As a result, it is obvious what the computationally-relevant action is, though *why* things work can get quite tricky to figure out. In this case, on the first line, we making use of the fact that given a list $[\mathrm{LList}(n, l)]$ we can get out an element of the union type $\exists p : n = 0.\ [l \mapsto \mathsf{inl}\,() \otimes \mathsf{I}] \vee \exists k : \mathbb{N}, n = \mathsf{s}(k), l' : \mathsf{Loc}.\ [l \mapsto \mathsf{inr}\,l' \otimes \mathrm{LList}(k, l')]$. This is bound to $c'$, and then the body can be typechecked under both alternatives.

***List Append*** We can also write a type-theoretic version of in-place list append, one of the examples from the original paper on separation logic. First, let's write a rehead function, which changes the head pointer of a list:

```
rehead : ∀n : ℕ. Πl, l′ : Loc. G([l ↦ inl ()] ⊗ [LList(n, l′)]
                                  ⊸ T ([LList(n, l)]))
rehead l l′ = G(λc₁ c₂.
  let [c₂′, c₂″] = ∗ in
  let (v, c₂′) = get(l′, c₂′) in
  let val c₁ = (l :=_{c₁} v) in
  let val () = free (l′, c₂′) in
  val ∗)
```

This function simply assigns the contents the list to the first argument pointer, and then frees the head pointer of the second list. As usual, a small amount of bureaucracy is needed to split irrelevant arguments, but otherwise the code is very similar to what one might write in ML or Haskell.

```
append : ∀n, n′ : ℕ. Πl, l′ : Loc. G([[LList(n, l)] ⊗ [LList(n′, l′)]
                                     ⊸ T ([LList(n + n′, l)]))
append l l′ = G(λc₁ c₂.
  let [c₁′, c₁″] = ∗ in
  let (v, c₁′) = get(l, c₁′) in
  case(v,
    inl () → let val c = G⁻¹(rehead l l′) c₁′ c₂ in val ∗
    inr l″ → let val c = G⁻¹(append l″ l′) c₁″ c₂ in val ∗))
```

This walks to the end of a list, and then reheads the head of the second list to the tail of the first list. Then with some straightforward linearly-typed proof-programming, it's possible to show that this gives us a linked list of the appropriate shape (which is concealed in the val $*$ terms). The fact that we return only a squashed argument corresponds to the fact that this is an in-place algorithm, which modifies the state and returns only some linear knowledge about the new state.

***Data Abstraction*** Because we can quantify over types, our calculus also supports data abstraction, in the style of Nanevski et al. [29]. As an example, we can use our linked list to implement a stack as an abstract type. First, we define a function to grow a linked list by one element.

$$\mathsf{grow} : \Pi l : \mathsf{Loc}.\ \forall n : \mathbb{N}.\ \mathsf{G}(\mathrm{LList}(l, n) \multimap \mathsf{T}\,(\mathrm{LList}(l, n+1)))$$

$$\begin{array}{l} \mathsf{grow}\ l = \mathsf{G}(\lambda c. \\ \quad \mathsf{let}\ [c', c''] = * \ \mathsf{in} \\ \quad \mathsf{let}\ (v, c') = \mathsf{get}(l, c')\ \mathsf{in} \\ \quad \mathsf{case}(v, \\ \quad\ \ \mathsf{inl}\,() \to \mathsf{let\ val}\ (l_0, c_0) = \mathsf{new\ inl}\,()\ \mathsf{in} \\ \qquad\qquad\quad \mathsf{let\ val}\ c' = l :=_{c'} \mathsf{inr}\ l_0\ \mathsf{in} \\ \qquad\qquad\quad \mathsf{val}\, * \\ \quad\ \ \mathsf{inr}\ l'' \to \mathsf{let\ val}\ c = \mathsf{G}^{-1}(\mathsf{grow}\ l'')\ c''\ \mathsf{in\ val}\, *)) \end{array}$$

This iterates to the end of the list, and then adds one element to the tail, in order to preserve the identity of the list. Similarly, we can shrink a list by an element as well.

$$\begin{array}{l} \mathsf{shrink} : \Pi l : \mathsf{Loc}.\ \forall n : \mathbb{N}.\ \mathsf{G}(\mathsf{LList}(l, n+1) \multimap \mathsf{T}\,(\mathsf{LList}(l, n))) \\ \mathsf{shrink}\ l = \mathsf{G}(\lambda c. \\ \quad \mathsf{let}\ [c', c''] = * \ \mathsf{in} \\ \quad \mathsf{let}\ (l', c') = \mathsf{get}(l, c')\ \mathsf{in} \\ \quad \mathsf{let\ val}\ c' = l :=_{c'} \mathsf{inl}\,()\ \mathsf{in} \\ \quad \mathsf{G}^{-1}(\mathsf{rehead}\ l\ l')\ c'\ c'') \end{array}$$

This deletes an element of the list, using the rehead function to ensure that the head pointer remains unchanged.

Now, we can give a procedure to build a stack as an abstract type.

$$\begin{array}{l} \mathsf{make} : \mathsf{G}(\mathsf{T}(\mathsf{F}\ \mathsf{Stack} : \mathbb{N} \to \mathsf{L}_i, \\ \qquad\qquad\quad \mathsf{push} : \forall n : \mathbb{N}.\ \mathsf{G}\,\mathsf{Stack}\ n \multimap \mathsf{T}\,(\mathsf{Stack}(\mathsf{s}(n))), \\ \qquad\qquad\quad \mathsf{pop} : \forall n : \mathbb{N}.\ \mathsf{G}\,\mathsf{Stack}(\mathsf{s}(n)) \multimap \mathsf{T}\,(\mathsf{Stack}\ n). \\ \qquad\qquad\quad \mathsf{Stack}\ 0)) \\ \mathsf{make} = \mathsf{G}(\mathsf{T}(\mathsf{let\ val}\ \mathsf{F}\,(l, c) = \mathsf{new}\ 0\ \mathsf{in} \\ \qquad\qquad\quad \mathsf{val}\ \mathsf{F}\,(\lambda n.\ \mathsf{LList}(n, l), \mathsf{F}\,(\mathsf{grow}\ l, \mathsf{F}\,(\mathsf{shrink}\ l, c))))) \end{array}$$

This procedure allocates a new location initialized to 0, and then returns the grow and shrink operations at the types for push and pop. Importantly, the representation of the stack is completely hidden — there is no way to know a pointer represents the stack.

One particularly interesting feature of this specification is that the choice of representation invariant is *data-dependent*: our definition of the Stack predicate captures the actual location allocated as a free variable.

### 3.2 Equational Theory

So far, we have decomposed the Hoare triple $\{P\}x : X\{Q\}$ as the dependent linear type $\mathsf{G}\,([P] \multimap \mathsf{T}\,((\mathsf{F}x : X.\ [Q])))$. That is, we view elements of Hoare type as duplicable terms, which take a proof-irrelevant witness for the pre-state P, and then compute a result of type X, as well as a producing a proof-irrelevant witness for the post-state Q.

This is, admittedly, a zoo of connectives! However, such fine-grained decompositions have a number of benefits. Since each of the connectives we give has a very simple $\beta\eta$-theory, we can derive the equational theory for terms of Hoare type by joining up the $\beta\eta$-theory of its components.[3]

As a simple example, an immediate consequence of our decomposition is that all terms of type $\{0\}x : X\{Q\}$ (that is, the type of computations with a false precondition) are equal, simply via the eta-rule for functions and falsity.

Another consequence (which we rely upon in our examples) comes from our encoding of the points-to predicate of separation logic. Our basic pointer type $l \mapsto X$ says only that $l$ contains a value of type X. We encode the points-to of separation logic $l \mapsto v$ using the type $l \mapsto \Sigma x : X.\ x = v$. Then, the fact that the sigma-type is contractible (i.e., all its elements are equal) means that we know that any dereference of $l$ is equal to $(v, \mathsf{refl})$, without having to put explicit proofs into the terms (because of equality reflection).

In addition, moving things like preconditions out of the computation monad $\mathsf{T}(A)$ lets us give a very simple model for it, which means that we can easily show the soundness of equations such as eliminating duplicate gets

$$\Gamma; \Delta \vdash \begin{array}{c} \mathsf{let}\ (x, c) = \mathsf{get}(e, e')\ \mathsf{in}\ C[\mathsf{let}\ (x', c') = \mathsf{get}(e, c)\ \mathsf{in}\ e''] \\ \equiv \\ \mathsf{let}\ (x, c) = \mathsf{get}(e, e')\ \mathsf{in}\ C[[c/c', x/x']e''] \end{array} : A$$

and eliminating gets after sets:

$$\Gamma; \Delta \vdash \begin{array}{c} \mathsf{let\ val}\ c = e :=_{e''} e'\ \mathsf{in}\ C[\mathsf{let}\ (x', c') = \mathsf{get}(e, c)\ \mathsf{in}\ e'''] \\ \equiv \\ \mathsf{let\ val}\ c = e :=_{e''} e'\ \mathsf{in}\ C[[e'/x', c/c']e'''] \end{array} : \mathsf{T}(A)$$

### 3.3 Hoare Type Theory

Hoare type theory [28] gives an alternative internal approach to imperative programming, by *directly* embedding Hoare triples into type theory. The central idea is to use dependent types to specify imperative programs as elements of an indexed monad, where the index domain are formulas of separation logic. This approach has proven remarkably successful in verifying complex imperative programs (such as modern congruence closure algorithms [30]), but working out the equational theory of the Hoare type has proven to be an extremely challenging problem, to the point that Svendsen et al. [40] give a model without any equations.

To illustrate the connection more clearly, we note that each of the basic constants of Hoare type theory is definable in our calculus, with a type that is close to the image of the translation of its Hoare type. Below, we give allocation, dereference, assignment, and the rule of consequence to illustrate. (We leave out the terms, because they can be read off the types.) In each case, the Hoare type is on the top line, and the linear type is on the line below.

$$\begin{array}{ll} \mathsf{new}_1 : & \{\mathrm{emp}\}x : \mathsf{Loc}\{x \mapsto ()\} \\ & \mathsf{G}\,(\mathsf{T}\,((\mathsf{F}x : \mathsf{Loc}.\ [x \mapsto ()]))) \\ \mathsf{set} : & \Pi x : \mathsf{Loc}, v, v' : X.\ \{x \mapsto v\}1\{x \mapsto v'\} \\ & \forall v : X.\ \Pi x : \mathsf{Loc}, v' : X.\ \mathsf{G}\,([x \mapsto v] \multimap \mathsf{T}\,([x \mapsto v'])) \\ \mathsf{get} : & \Pi x : \mathsf{Loc}, v : X.\ \{x \mapsto v\}v' : X\{v' = v \wedge x \mapsto v\} \\ & \forall v : X.\ \Pi x : \mathsf{Loc}.\ \mathsf{G}\,([x \mapsto v] \multimap \mathsf{F}v' : X, \mathrm{pf} : v' = v.\ [x \mapsto v]) \\ \mathsf{con} : & \Pi P, P', Q, Q'.\ \begin{array}{l} (P \supset P') \to (Q' \supset Q) \to \\ \{P'\}x : X\{Q'\} \to \\ \{P\}x : X\{Q\} \end{array} \\ & \Pi P, P', Q, Q' : \mathsf{L}_i.\ \begin{array}{l} \mathsf{G}\,[P \multimap P'] \to \mathsf{G}\,[Q' \multimap Q] \to \\ \mathsf{G}\,([P'] \multimap \mathsf{F}x : X.\ [Q']) \to \\ \mathsf{G}\,([P] \multimap \mathsf{F}x : X.\ [Q]) \end{array} \end{array}$$

We can see that in some cases, the $\mathrm{LNL_D}$ typings have computational advantages. For example, for the set constant, we are able to use the implicit $\forall$ quantifier to make clear that while the pointer and the new value need to be passed as arguments, the old contents do not need to be passed in. This is not possible in HTT (due to the absence of intersections), and to work around this a two-state postcondition is used. As another example, the get constant doesn't have a monadic effect in $\mathrm{LNL_D}$.

[3] We say "the" equational theory because the $\beta\eta$-equality is canonical. However, there are many desirable equations (such as those arising from parametricity) which go far beyond it.

As a result, any (totally correct) program in Hoare type theory should in principle be translatable into $\text{LNL}_\text{D}$ (neglecting the much superior maturity and automation available for Hoare type theory).

***Caveat*** There is, however, a significant difference between $\text{LNL}_\text{D}$ and HTT: the latter supports general recursion, and deals with partial correctness. $\text{LNL}_\text{D}$ requires a termination metric on fixed point definitions and only deals with total correctness.

Most of the complexity in the model theory of HTT comes from its treatment of recursion, such as the need for $\top\top$-closure to ensure admissibility for fixed point induction. We have sidestepped these issues by focussing only on total correctness.

In fact, much of the subtlety in the design of $\text{LNL}_\text{D}$ lay in the effort needed to *rule out* general recursion — in languages with higher-order store, it is usually possible to write recursion operators by backpatching function pointers (aka "Landin's knot"), and so we had to carefully exploit linearity to prevent the typability of such examples. (This was originally observed by Ahmed et al. [2].) Another example is found in our fixed point operator, which defines recursive *functions* with an irrelevant termination metric. If we had given a general fixed point operator $\mathsf{fix}\ x.\ e$, even with an irrelevant termination metric, then looping computations would be definable. (This is connected to the ability of intersection types to detect evaluation order.)

As a result, to formally argue that our approach makes proving equations easier, we would need to give a version of our $T(-)$ monad which is partial, which would give a calculus corresponding more closely to HTT. We hope to investigate these questions more deeply in future work. As matters stand, all we can say is that our semantics is in many ways much less technically sophisticated than models such as the one of Petersen et al. [34], even though it permits us to prove a number of novel equations on programs.

## 4. Metatheory

We now establish the metatheory of our type system. Our approach integrates the ideas of Harper [20] and Ahmed et al. [2]. We begin by giving an untyped operational semantics for the language. In fact, we give three operational semantics: one for pure intuitionistic terms, one for pure linear terms, and one for monadic linear terms.

Next, we use this operational semantics to give a semantic realizability model, by defining the interpretation of each logical connective as a partial equivalence relation (PER). Because we have dependent types, we need to define the set of syntactic types mutually recursively with the interpretation of each type, in the style of an inductive-recursive definition. Furthermore, we have to interpret intuitionistic and linear terms differently: we use an ordinary PER on terms to interpret intuitionistic types, and a PER on machine configurations (terms plus store) to interpret linear types.

This gives a semantic interpretation of closed types. We extend this to an interpretation of contexts as sets of environments, and then prove the fundamental theorem of logical relations for our type system, which establishes the soundness and adequacy of our rules (including its equational theory).

### 4.1 Operational Semantics

The syntax for our language of untyped terms is given in Figure 10. For simplicity, all our types and terms live in the same syntactic category, regardless of whether they are intuitionistic and linear. The variable $v$ ranges over intuitionistic values, $u$ ranges over linear values, and $\sigma$ denotes heaps.

There are actually *three* operational semantics for our language. First, we have an evaluation relation $e \Downarrow v$ for intuitionistic terms, a a linear evaluation relation $\langle\sigma; e\rangle \Downarrow \langle\sigma'; u\rangle$ for linear terms, and a monadic evaluation relation $\langle\sigma; e\rangle \rightsquigarrow \langle\sigma'; \mathsf{val}\, u\rangle$ for evaluating monadic terms. Both the linear and monadic semantics are store-passing relations, because they are imperative computations which may depend upon the state of memory.

The intuitionistic evaluation relation $e \Downarrow v$ is a standard call-by-name big-step evaluation relation for the lambda calculus. We treat all types as values (and do not evaluate their subterms), and also include location values $l$ in the syntactic category of values. Though there are no typing rules for location values, they may arise during program evaluation when fresh memory cells are allocated.

The linear evaluation relation $\langle\sigma; e\rangle \Downarrow \langle\sigma'; u\rangle$ evaluates the machine configuration $\langle\sigma; e\rangle$ to $\langle\sigma'; u\rangle$. This is also a call-by-name big-step evaluator. However, there are many rules in this reduction relation, simply because we have many linear types in our language. The rules for functions (both linear $A \multimap B$ and dependent $\Pi x : X.\ A$) and pairs $A \,\&\, B$ follow the beta-rules of the equational theory, as expected. The let-style eliminators for $I$, $A \otimes B$ and $\mathsf{F}x : X.\ A$ are more verbose, but also line up with the beta-rules of the theory. The eliminator $\mathsf{G}^{-1}\, e$ evaluates $e$ to a term $\mathsf{G}\, t$, and then executes $t$, again following the beta-rule.

A nuisance in our rules is that we need operational rules for the let-style rules (i.e., $\mathsf{let}\ [a, b] = e\ \mathsf{in}\ e'$) distributing proof irrelevance through units and tensors. This has no computational content, since the argument $e$ is never evaluated, but nevertheless we must include evaluation rules for it.

Finally, we also have the dereference operation $\mathsf{let}\ (x, c') = \mathsf{get}(e, e')\ \mathsf{in}\ e''$. This rule evaluates $e$ to a location $l$, and $e'$ to an irrelevant value $*$. Then it looks up the value $v$ stored at $l$, and binds that to $x$, and binds $c'$ to the irrelevant value $*$ before evaluating the continuation $e''$.

One point worth making is that *none* of these rules affect the shape of the heap – we can dereference pointers in the pure linear fragment, but we cannot write or modify them. As a result, every linear reduction is really of the form $\langle\sigma; e\rangle \Downarrow \langle\sigma; u\rangle$. We could easily have have made this into a syntactic restriction, but having two configurations is slightly more convenient when giving the realizability semantics.

Finally, we have the monadic evaluation $\langle\sigma; e\rangle \rightsquigarrow \langle\sigma'; \mathsf{val}\, u\rangle$. The rule for let-binding $\mathsf{let}\ \mathsf{val}\, x = e\ \mathsf{in}\ e'$ is sequential composition: it evaluates the first argument to a monadic value, and then binds the result to $x$ before evaluating $e'$. The rule for $\mathsf{new}\, e$ evaluates its (intuitionistic) argument to a value $v$, and then allocates a fresh location $l$ to store it in, returning the location (and a dummy $*$ for the capability). The rule for assignments $e :=_{e''} e'$ evaluates $e$ to a location $l$, $e'$ to a value $v$, and $e''$ to a capability $*$. Then it modifies the heap so that $l$ points to $v$. Similarly, the rule for deallocation $\mathsf{free}\,(e, e')$ evaluates $e$ to $l$ and then deallocates the pointer. Note that all of these operations could get stuck, if the appropriate piece of heap did not exist — the soundness proof will establish that type-safe programs are indeed safe.

### 4.2 CPPOs and Fixed Points

Since types depend on terms in dependent type theory, we cannot define the grammar of types up front, before giving an interpretation their interpretations. Instead, what we need is morally an inductive-recursive definition. As a result, we

$$
\begin{array}{lcl}
e, t, X, A & ::= & \Pi x : X.\, Y \mid A \multimap B \mid \lambda x : C.\, e \mid e\ e' \mid \hat{\lambda} x.\, e \\
& \mid & 1 \mid I \mid () \mid \mathsf{let}\ () = e\ \mathsf{in}\ e' \\
& \mid & \Sigma x : X.\, Y \mid A \otimes B \mid (e, e') \\
& \mid & \pi_1\, e \mid \pi_2\, e \mid \mathsf{let}\ (x, y) = e\ \mathsf{in}\ e' \\
& \mid & \mathsf{G}\, e \mid \mathsf{G}^{-1}\, e \\
& \mid & \mathsf{F} x : X.\, A \mid \mathsf{F}\,(e, t) \mid \mathsf{let}\ \mathsf{F}\,(x, a) = t\ \mathsf{in}\ t' \\
& \mid & \top \mid A \,\&\, B \\
& \mid & \forall x : X.\, Y \mid \exists x : x.\, Y \\
& \mid & e =_X e' \mid \mathsf{refl} \\
& \mid & \mathbb{N} \mid 0 \mid \mathsf{s}(e) \mid \mathsf{iter}(e, 0 \to e_0, \mathsf{s}(x), y \to e_1) \\
& \mid & \mathsf{U}_i \mid \mathsf{L}_i \\
& \mid & x \mid \mathsf{fix}\ f\ x = e \\
& \mid & [A] \mid \mathsf{let}\ [x] = e\ \mathsf{in}\ e \mid * \\
& \mid & e \mapsto X \mid \mathsf{Loc} \mid \mathsf{new}_X\, e \mid \mathsf{free}\,(e, t) \mid l \\
& \mid & \mathsf{let}\ (x, a) = \mathsf{get}(e, e')\ \mathsf{in}\ e'' \mid e :=_{e''} e' \\
& \mid & \mathsf{T}\,(A) \mid \mathsf{val}\, e \mid \mathsf{let\ val}\ x = e\ \mathsf{in}\ e' \\
\\
v & ::= & \lambda x : A.\, e \mid () \mid (e, e) \mid \mathsf{refl} \mid \mathsf{G}\, e \mid l \mid * \mid 0 \mid \mathsf{s}(v) \\
& \mid & \Pi x : X.\, Y \mid A \multimap B \mid \top \mid A \,\&\, B \\
& \mid & 1 \mid I \mid \Sigma x : X.\, Y \mid A \otimes B \mid \mathsf{F} x : X.\, B \\
& \mid & e =_X e' \mid e \mapsto X \mid \mathsf{Loc} \mid \mathsf{U}_i \mid \mathsf{L}_i \\
\\
u & ::= & \lambda x.\, e \mid () \mid (e, e) \mid \mathsf{F}\,(e, e) \mid \hat{\lambda} x.\, e \mid (e, e') \\
& \mid & * \mid \mathsf{val}\, e \mid \mathsf{let\ val}\ x = e\ \mathsf{in}\ e \mid \mathsf{new}_X\, e \mid e :=_{e''} e' \\
\\
\sigma & ::= & \cdot \mid \sigma, l : v
\end{array}
$$

**Figure 10.** Terms $e, t, X, A$, values $v$, linear values $u$, stores $\sigma$

need to use a fixed theorem which is a little stronger than the standard Kleene or Knaster-Tarski fixed point theorems.

Recall that a *pointed partial order* is a triple $(X, \leqslant, \bot)$ such that $X$ is a set, $\leqslant$ is a partial order on $X$, and $\bot$ is the least element of $X$. A subset $D \subseteq X$ is a *directed set* when every pair of elements $x, y \in D$ has an upper bound in $D$ (i.e., there is a $z \in D$ such that $x \leqslant z$ and $y \leqslant z$). A pointed partial order is *complete* (i.e., forms a CPPO) when every directed set $D$ has a supremum $\bigsqcup D$ in $X$.

The following fixed point theorem[4] is in Harper [20], and is Theorem 8.22 in Davey and Priestley [13].

**Theorem 1.** *(Fixed Points on CPPOs) If $X$ is a CPPO, and $f : X \to X$ is a monotone function on $X$, then $f$ has a least fixed point.*

*Proof.* Construct the ordinal-indexed sequence $x_\alpha$, where:

$$
\begin{array}{lcl}
x_0 & = & \bot \\
x_{\beta+1} & = & f(x_\beta) \\
x_\lambda & = & \bigsqcup_{\beta < \lambda} x_\beta
\end{array}
$$

Because $f$ is monotone, we can show by transfinite induction that every initial segment is directed, which ensures the needed suprema exist and the sequence is well-defined.

Now, we know there must be a stage $\lambda$ such that $x_\lambda = x_{\lambda+1}$. If there were not, then we could construct a bijection between the ordinals and the strictly increasing chain of elements of the sequence $x$. However, the elements of the sequence $x$ are all drawn from $X$. Since $X$ is a set, it follows that the elements of $x$ must themselves form a set. Since the ordinals do not form a set (they are a proper class), this leads to a contradiction. Hence, $f$ must have a fixed point. □

### 4.3 Partial Equivalence Relations and Semantic Type Systems

We now need to define what our types are, and how to interpret them. Following the example of Nuprl, we will

$$\boxed{e \Downarrow v}$$

$$\frac{}{v \Downarrow v} \qquad \frac{e_1 \Downarrow \lambda x : A.\, e \qquad [e_2/x]e \Downarrow v}{e_1\ e_2 \Downarrow v}$$

$$\frac{e \Downarrow (e_1, e_2) \qquad e_1 \Downarrow v}{\pi_1\, e \Downarrow v} \qquad \frac{e \Downarrow (e_1, e_2) \qquad e_2 \Downarrow v}{\pi_2\, e \Downarrow v}$$

$$\frac{e \Downarrow v}{\mathsf{s}(e) \Downarrow \mathsf{s}(v)} \qquad \frac{e \Downarrow 0 \qquad e_0 \Downarrow v}{\mathsf{iter}(e, 0 \to e_0, \mathsf{s}(x), y \to e_1) \Downarrow v}$$

$$\frac{e \Downarrow \mathsf{s}(n) \qquad \mathsf{iter}(n, 0 \to e_0, \mathsf{s}(x), y \to e_1) \Downarrow v \qquad [n/x, v/y]e_1 \Downarrow v'}{\mathsf{iter}(e, 0 \to e_0, \mathsf{s}(x), y \to e_1) \Downarrow v'}$$

$$\frac{e \Downarrow \mathsf{fix}\ f\ x = e_0 \qquad [(\mathsf{fix}\ f\ x = e_0)/f, e'/x]e_0 \Downarrow v}{e\ e' \Downarrow v}$$

$$\boxed{\langle \sigma; e \rangle \Downarrow \langle \sigma'; u \rangle}$$

$$\frac{}{\langle \sigma; u \rangle \Downarrow \langle \sigma; u \rangle}$$

$$\frac{\langle \sigma; e_1 \rangle \Downarrow \langle \sigma'; \lambda x.\, e_1' \rangle \qquad \langle \sigma'; [e_2/x]e_1' \rangle \Downarrow \langle \sigma''; u'' \rangle}{\langle \sigma; e_1\ e_2 \rangle \Downarrow \langle \sigma''; u'' \rangle}$$

$$\frac{\langle \sigma; e_1 \rangle \Downarrow \langle \sigma'; \hat{\lambda} x.\, e \rangle \qquad \langle \sigma'; [e_2/x]e \rangle \Downarrow \langle \sigma''; u'' \rangle}{\langle \sigma; e_1\ e_2 \rangle \Downarrow \langle \sigma''; u'' \rangle}$$

$$\frac{\langle \sigma; e \rangle \Downarrow \langle \sigma'; (e_1, e_2) \rangle \qquad \langle \sigma'; e_1 \rangle \Downarrow \langle \sigma''; u'' \rangle}{\langle \sigma; \pi_1\, e \rangle \Downarrow \langle \sigma''; u'' \rangle}$$

$$\frac{\langle \sigma; e \rangle \Downarrow \langle \sigma'; (e_1, e_2) \rangle \qquad \langle \sigma'; e_2 \rangle \Downarrow \langle \sigma''; u'' \rangle}{\langle \sigma; \pi_2\, e \rangle \Downarrow \langle \sigma''; u'' \rangle}$$

$$\frac{\langle \sigma; e \rangle \Downarrow \langle \sigma'; () \rangle \qquad \langle \sigma'; e' \rangle \Downarrow \langle \sigma''; u \rangle}{\langle \sigma; \mathsf{let}\ () = e\ \mathsf{in}\ e' \rangle \Downarrow \langle \sigma''; u \rangle}$$

$$\frac{\langle \sigma; e \rangle \Downarrow \langle \sigma'; (e_1, e_2) \rangle \qquad \langle \sigma'; [e_1/a, e_2/b]e' \rangle \Downarrow \langle \sigma''; u \rangle}{\langle \sigma; \mathsf{let}\ (a, b) = e\ \mathsf{in}\ e' \rangle \Downarrow \langle \sigma''; u \rangle}$$

$$\frac{\langle \sigma; e \rangle \Downarrow \langle \sigma'; \mathsf{F}\,(e_1, e_2) \rangle \qquad \langle \sigma'; [e_1/x, e_2/a]e' \rangle \Downarrow \langle \sigma''; u \rangle}{\langle \sigma; \mathsf{let}\ \mathsf{F}\,(x, a) = e\ \mathsf{in}\ e' \rangle \Downarrow \langle \sigma''; u \rangle}$$

$$\frac{e \Downarrow \mathsf{G}\, e' \qquad \langle \sigma; e' \rangle \Downarrow \langle \sigma'; u \rangle}{\langle \sigma; \mathsf{G}^{-1}\, e \rangle \Downarrow \langle \sigma'; u \rangle} \qquad \frac{\langle \sigma; e \rangle \Downarrow \langle \sigma'; u' \rangle}{\langle \sigma; \mathsf{let}\ [] = e_0\ \mathsf{in}\ e \rangle \Downarrow \langle \sigma'; u' \rangle}$$

$$\frac{\langle \sigma; [*/a, */b]e \rangle \Downarrow \langle \sigma'; u' \rangle}{\langle \sigma; \mathsf{let}\ [a, b] = e_0\ \mathsf{in}\ e \rangle \Downarrow \langle \sigma'; u' \rangle}$$

$$\frac{e \Downarrow l \qquad \langle \sigma; e' \rangle \Downarrow \langle \sigma', l : v; * \rangle \qquad \langle \sigma', l : v; [v/x, */c]e'' \rangle \Downarrow \langle \sigma''; u \rangle}{\langle \sigma; \mathsf{let}\ (x, c) = \mathsf{get}(e, e')\ \mathsf{in}\ e'' \rangle \Downarrow \langle \sigma''; u \rangle}$$

$$\boxed{\langle \sigma; e \rangle \rightsquigarrow \langle \sigma'; \mathsf{val}\, v \rangle}$$

$$\frac{}{\langle \sigma; \mathsf{val}\, e \rangle \rightsquigarrow \langle \sigma; \mathsf{val}\, e \rangle}$$

$$\frac{\langle \sigma; e \rangle \Downarrow \langle \sigma'; u \rangle \qquad e \neq \mathsf{val}\, u_0 \qquad \langle \sigma; u \rangle \rightsquigarrow \langle \sigma''; \mathsf{val}\, u' \rangle}{\langle \sigma; e \rangle \rightsquigarrow \langle \sigma''; \mathsf{val}\, u' \rangle}$$

$$\frac{\langle \sigma; e \rangle \rightsquigarrow \langle \sigma_1; \mathsf{val}\, e_1 \rangle \qquad \langle \sigma_1; [e_1/x]e' \rangle \rightsquigarrow \langle \sigma'; \mathsf{val}\, v \rangle}{\langle \sigma; \mathsf{let\ val}\ x = e\ \mathsf{in}\ e' \rangle \rightsquigarrow \langle \sigma'; \mathsf{val}\, v \rangle}$$

$$\frac{e \Downarrow v \qquad l \not\in \mathrm{dom}(\sigma)}{\langle \sigma; \mathsf{new}_X\, e \rangle \rightsquigarrow \langle \sigma, l : v; \mathsf{val}\, \mathsf{F}\,(l, *) \rangle}$$

$$\frac{e \Downarrow l \qquad e' \Downarrow v \qquad \langle \sigma; e'' \rangle \Downarrow \langle \sigma', l : v'; * \rangle}{\langle \sigma, l : v'; e :=_{e''} e' \rangle \rightsquigarrow \langle \sigma', l : v; \mathsf{val}\, * \rangle}$$

$$\frac{e \Downarrow l \qquad \langle \sigma; t \rangle \Downarrow \langle \sigma', l : v; * \rangle}{\langle \sigma; \mathsf{free}\,(e, t) \rangle \rightsquigarrow \langle \sigma'; \mathsf{val}\, () \rangle}$$

**Figure 11.** Operational Semantics

[4] A constructive, albeit impredicative, proof of this theorem is possible: this is Pataraia's theorem [17].

interpret types as partial equivalence relations of terms, with the intuition that if $(e, e) \in X$, then $e$ is an element of the type X, and that if $(e, e') \in X$ then $e$ is equal to $e'$. Because of type dependency, we will then *simultaneously* define the PER of types, and an interpretation function sending each type to the PER it defines.

A *partial equivalence relation* (PER) is a symmetric, transitive relation on closed, terminating expressions. We further require that PERs be *closed under evaluation*. Given a PER R, we require that for all $e, e', v, v'$ such that $e \Downarrow v$ and $e' \Downarrow v'$, we have that $(e, e') \in R$ if and only if $(v, v') \in R$. Given a PER P, we write $P^*$ to close it up under evaluation. We extend this notation to functions, as well, so that given a function f into PERs, $f^*(x) = (f\ x)^*$. Finally, given a relation R, we write $R^\dagger$ to take its symmetric, transitive closure. We will use PERs to interpret intuitionistic types.

A *partial evaluation relation on configurations* (CPER) is a symmetric, transitive relation on terminating machine configurations $\langle \sigma; e \rangle$. We further require that they be *closed under linear evaluation*. Given a CPER M, we require that for all $\langle \sigma_1; e_1 \rangle$ such that $\langle \sigma_1; e_1 \rangle \Downarrow \langle \sigma_1'; u_1 \rangle$ and $\langle \sigma_2; e_2 \rangle$ such that $\langle \sigma_2; e_2 \rangle \Downarrow \langle \sigma_2'; u_2 \rangle$, we have $(\langle \sigma_1; e_1 \rangle, \langle \sigma_2; e_2 \rangle) \in M$ if and only if $(\langle \sigma_1'; u_1 \rangle, \langle \sigma_2'; u_2 \rangle) \in M$. We will use CPERs to interpret linear types, with the idea that the store components of each element of the PER corresponds to the resources owned by that term.

Note that since evaluation (both ordinary and linear) is deterministic, an evaluation-closed PER is determined by its sub-PER on values (or value configurations). As a result, we will often define PERs and functions on PERs by simply giving the relation for values.

A *semantic linear/non-linear type system* is a four-tuple $(I \in \text{PER}, L \in \text{PER}, \phi : |I| \to \text{PER}, \psi : |L| \to \text{CPER})$ such that $\phi$ respects I and $\psi$ respects L. We say that I are the *semantic intuitionistic types*, L are the *semantic linear types*, and $\phi$ and $\psi$ are *the type interpretation functions*.

The set of type systems forms a CPPO. The least element is the type system $(\emptyset, \emptyset, !_{\text{PER}}, !_{\text{CPER}})$ with an empty set of intuitionistic and linear types. The ordering $(I, L, \phi, \psi) \leqslant (I', L', \phi', \psi')$ is given by set inclusion on $I \subseteq I'$ and $L \subseteq L'$, when there is agreement between $\phi$ and $\phi'$ on the common part of their domains, and likewise for $\psi$ and $\psi'$ (which we write $\phi \sqsubseteq \phi'$ and $\psi \sqsubseteq \psi'$). Given a directed set, the join is given by taking unions pointwise (treating the functions $\phi$ and $\psi$ as graphs).

Next, our goal is to define a semantic type system to interpret our syntax. To do this, we will define a monotone type system operator $T_k$. Since type systems form a CPPO, we can define the semantic type system we use to interpret our syntax as the least fixed point of $T_k$.

First, we'll define some constructions on PERs in Figures 12 and 13. There is one construction for each of the type connectives in our language, explaining what each connective means "logical relations style" — though these constructions do not yet define a logical relation, since they are just constructions on PERs.

The intuitionistic constructions are given in Figure 12. The *Loc* relation relates each location to itself, and the unit relation $\hat{1}$ relates the unit value to itself. The identity relation $Id(a, b, E)$ is equal to $\{(\mathsf{refl}, \mathsf{refl})\}$ if a and b are in the relation E, and is empty otherwise. The $\Pi$ construction takes a PER E, and a function $\Phi$ from elements of E to PERs (which respects the relation E). From that data it returns the PER of function values $(f, f')$ which take E-related pairs $(a, a')$ to $(f\ a, f'\ a')$ in $E(a)$, with the $\Sigma(E, \Phi)$ construction working similarly for

$$
\begin{array}{lcl}
\mathit{Loc} & = & \{(l, l) \mid l \in \mathsf{Loc}\} \\
\hat{1} & = & \{((), ())\} \\
\mathit{Id}(a, b, E) & = & \{(\mathsf{refl}, \mathsf{refl}) \mid (a, b) \in E\} \\
\Pi(E, \Phi) & = & \{(v, v') \mid \forall (a, a') \in E.\ (v a, v' a') \in \Phi(a)\} \\
\Sigma(E, \Phi) & = & \{((a, b), (a', b')) \mid (a, a') \in E \wedge (b, b') \in \Phi(a)\} \\
G(C) & = & \{(\mathsf{G}\, e, \mathsf{G}\, e') \mid (\langle \cdot; e \rangle, \langle \cdot; e' \rangle) \in C\} \\
\hat{\forall}(E, \Phi) & = & \{(v, v') \mid \forall (e, e') \in E.\ (v, v') \in \Phi(e)\} \\
\hat{\exists}(E, \Phi) & = & \{(v, v') \mid \exists (e, e') \in E.\ (v, v') \in \Phi(e)\}^\dagger \\
\hat{\mathbb{N}} & = & \{(\mathsf{s}^k(0), \mathsf{s}^k(0)) \mid k \text{ is a natural number}\} \\
\hat{\top}_I & = & \{(v, v') \mid v \in \mathrm{Val} \wedge v' \in \mathrm{Val}\}
\end{array}
$$

**Figure 12.** Intuitionistic PER constructions

pairs. The intersection type $\hat{\forall}(E, \Phi)$ construction just takes the intersection over $\Phi(a)$ for all a in E, which is a PER since PERs are closed under intersection. The union type is a little more complicated; it takes the union of PERs, and then has to take the symmetric transitive closure because PERs are not closed under unions. The natural number relation $\hat{\mathbb{N}}$ relates numerals to themselves, and $\hat{\top}_I$ relates any two values.

The linear constructions are given in Figure 13. The $\hat{\top}$ relation relates two unit values under any stores at all, whereas the $\hat{1}$ relation relates two units only in the empty store. Similarly, the $A \mathbin{\hat{\&}} B$ relation relates two pairs, as long as the first components are related at A using all of the store, and the second components are related at B using all of the store. The tensor relation $C \mathbin{\hat{\otimes}} D$ relation, on the other hand, relates two pairs if their stores can divided into two disjoint parts, one relating the first components in the C relation, and the other relating the second components in the D relation. The semantic linear function space constructor $C \mathbin{\hat{\multimap}} D$ relates functions, such that if we have values in C with disjoint store, then the applications are related in D with the combined store (much like the "magic wand" of separation logic). The $F(E, \Psi)$ relation consists of pairs of stores and values $F(a, b)$ and $F(a', b')$, such that a and a' are intuitionistic terms related in E, and b and b' are related in $\Psi(a)$ using their whole stores. The $\Pi_L$ relation works similarly, except that it relates on dependent linear functions rather than pairs. The linear intersection and union type constructors work similarly to their intuitionistic counterparts.

The proof irrelevance relation $\mathit{Irr}(A)$ relates two squash tokens $*$ at some stores, if there are linear terms that could relate those stores at A. The pointer construction $\mathit{Ptr}(e, E)$ simply says that the heap consists of a single memory cell addressed by e, and whose contents are related at E. (Its only term is $*$, because we don't care about its value, as we use it solely to track capabilities.) The $\hat{T}(A)$ construction relates monadic computations, if each side reduces to a store/value configuration which is related by A. Furthermore, only "frame-respecting" computations can be related — if a computation works in a smaller store, it should also work in a larger store, without modifying that larger store.

We can now define an operator $T_k$ on type systems:

$$T_k(I, L, \phi, \psi) = (I'^*, L'^*, \phi'^*, \psi'^*)$$

where $I'$ and $L'$ are defined in Figure 14 and and where $\phi'$ and $\psi'$ are defined in Figure 15.

The definition of $I'$ and $L'$ includes each of the base types, and then for each of the higher-arity operations draws the argument types from I or L, so that (for example) $L'$ includes every $A \otimes B$ where A and B are in L. The definition of $\phi'$ and $\psi'$ is by analysis of the structure of the elements of $I'$ and $L'$, using the PER constructions we described earlier

$$
\begin{array}{lcl}
\hat{\top} & = & \{(\langle\sigma;()\rangle,\langle\sigma';()\rangle) \mid \sigma,\sigma' \in \mathrm{Store}\} \\
A \mathbin{\hat{\&}} B & = & \left\{ \begin{array}{l} (\langle\sigma;(a,b)\rangle, \\ \ \langle\sigma';(a',b')\rangle) \end{array} \middle| \begin{array}{l} (\langle\sigma;a\rangle,\langle\sigma';a'\rangle) \in A \wedge \\ (\langle\sigma;b\rangle,\langle\sigma';b'\rangle) \in B \end{array} \right\} \\
\hat{I} & = & \{(\langle\cdot;()\rangle,\langle\cdot;()\rangle)\} \\
(C \mathbin{\hat{\otimes}} D) & = & \left\{ \begin{array}{l} (\langle\sigma;(c,d)\rangle, \\ \ \langle\sigma';(c',d')\rangle) \end{array} \middle| \begin{array}{l} \exists\sigma_C,\sigma_D,\sigma_{C'},\sigma_{D'}. \\ \ \sigma = \sigma_C \cdot \sigma_D \wedge \\ \ \sigma' = \sigma'_C \cdot \sigma'_D \wedge \\ \ (\langle\sigma_C;c\rangle,\langle\sigma'_C;c'\rangle) \in C \wedge \\ \ (\langle\sigma_D;d\rangle,\langle\sigma'_D;d'\rangle) \in D \end{array} \right\} \\
(C \mathbin{\hat{\multimap}} D) & = & \left\{ \begin{array}{l} (\langle\sigma;u\rangle, \\ \ \langle\sigma';u'\rangle) \end{array} \middle| \begin{array}{l} \forall\sigma_0\#\sigma,\sigma'_0\#\sigma',c,c'. \\ \ \text{if } (\langle\sigma_0;c\rangle,\langle\sigma'_0;c'\rangle) \in C \\ \ \text{then} \begin{pmatrix} \langle\sigma\cdot\sigma_0;uc\rangle, \\ \langle\sigma'\cdot\sigma'_0;u'c'\rangle \end{pmatrix} \in D \end{array} \right\} \\
F(E,\Psi) & = & \left\{ \begin{array}{l} (\langle\sigma;F(a,b)\rangle, \\ \ \langle\sigma';F(a',b')\rangle) \end{array} \middle| \begin{array}{l} E(a,a') \wedge \\ (\langle\sigma;b\rangle,\langle\sigma';b'\rangle) \in \Psi(a) \end{array} \right\} \\
\Pi_L(E,\Psi) & = & \left\{ \begin{array}{l} (\langle\sigma;u\rangle, \\ \ \langle\sigma';u'\rangle) \end{array} \middle| \begin{array}{l} \forall(e,e') \in E. \\ \ (\langle\sigma;u\ e\rangle,\langle\sigma';u'\ e'\rangle) \in \Psi(e) \end{array} \right\} \\
\hat{\forall}_L(E,\Psi) & = & \left\{ \begin{array}{l} (\langle\sigma;u\rangle, \\ \ \langle\sigma';u'\rangle) \end{array} \middle| \begin{array}{l} \forall(e,e') \in E. \\ \ (\langle\sigma;u\rangle,\langle\sigma';u'\rangle) \in \Psi(e) \end{array} \right\} \\
\hat{\exists}_L(E,\Psi) & = & \left\{ \begin{array}{l} (\langle\sigma;u\rangle, \\ \ \langle\sigma';u'\rangle) \end{array} \middle| \begin{array}{l} \exists(e,e') \in E. \\ \ (\langle\sigma;u\rangle,\langle\sigma';u'\rangle) \in \Psi(e) \end{array} \right\}^{\dagger} \\
\hat{T}(A) & = & \left\{ \begin{array}{l} (\langle\sigma_1;e_1\rangle, \\ \ \langle\sigma_2;e_2\rangle) \end{array} \middle| \begin{array}{l} \forall\sigma_f\#\sigma_1,\sigma_g\#\sigma_2.\ \exists\sigma'_1,\sigma'_2,u_1,u_2. \\ \langle\sigma_1\cdot\sigma_f;e_1\rangle \rightsquigarrow \langle\sigma'_1\cdot\sigma_f;\mathsf{val}\,u_1\rangle \wedge \\ \langle\sigma_2\cdot\sigma_g;e_2\rangle \rightsquigarrow \langle\sigma'_2\cdot\sigma_g;\mathsf{val}\,u_2\rangle \wedge \\ (\langle\sigma'_1;u_1\rangle,\langle\sigma'_2;u_2\rangle) \in A \end{array} \right\} \\
\mathit{Ptr}(e,E) & = & \left\{ (\langle\sigma_1;*\rangle,\langle\sigma_2;*\rangle) \middle| \begin{array}{l} \sigma_1 = [l:v_1] \wedge \sigma_2 = [l:v_2] \wedge \\ (e,l) \in \mathit{Loc} \wedge (v_1,v_2) \in E \end{array} \right\} \\
\mathit{Irr}(A) & = & \{(\langle\sigma;*\rangle,\langle\sigma';*\rangle) \mid \exists a,a'.\ (\langle\sigma;a\rangle,\langle\sigma;a'\rangle) \in A\}
\end{array}
$$

**Figure 13.** Linear PER Constructions

to interpret each of the type constructors. Furthermore, in the definition of $\phi'$, when we write $\phi'(\mathsf{Loc})$, we actually mean any $\phi'(e)$ such that $I'(e, \mathsf{Loc})$. This is justified by the fact that evaluation is deterministic and relations are closed under evalution. (Similarly, we define $\psi'$ only on the values, extending it to all terms by determinacy and closure under evaluation.) Once we have this definition, we can then show that $T_k$ is a monotone type system operator.

**Lemma 1** ($T_k$ is monotone). *We have that* $T_k$ *is a monotone function on type systems.*

*Proof.* (Sketch) This lemma really makes two claims. First, that $T_k$ is indeed a function on semantic type systems (in particular, that $\phi'$ and $\psi'$ respect $I'$ and $L'$), and second, that it is monotone. Both of these follow from a case analysis on the shape of the possible elements of $I'$ and $L'$. See the technical report for details. □

Then, we can take the interpretation of the i-th universe $\mathcal{T}_i$ to be the least fixed point of $T_i$. Furthermore, we also have a cumulativity property:

**Lemma 2** (Universe Cumulativity). *If* $i \leqslant k$ *then* $\mathcal{T}_i \leqslant \mathcal{T}_k$.

We sometimes write $\mathcal{T}$ for the limit of the countable universe hierarchy, and write $U$, $L$, $\phi$, and $\psi$ for its components.

### 4.4 Semantic Environments

Our semantic type system $\mathcal{T}$ gives us an interpretation of closed types. Before we can prove the correctness of our typing rules, we have to extend our interpretation to open types and terms, and to do that, we have to give an interpretation of environments.

In Figure 16, we give the interpretation of contexts. The meaning of an intuitionistic context $[\![\Gamma]\!]$ is given as a set of binary substitutions $\gamma$. By binary substitution, we mean that for every $x \in \mathrm{dom}(\gamma)$, we have that $\gamma(x) = (e, e')$ for some

$$
\begin{array}{ll}
I' = & \{(\mathsf{Loc},\mathsf{Loc})\} \cup \\
& \{(\mathbb{N},\mathbb{N})\} \cup \\
& \{(\top_I,\top_I)\} \cup \\
& \{(e_1 =_X e_2, t_1 =_Y t_2) \mid I(X,Y) \wedge \Phi(X)(e_1,t_1) \wedge \Phi(X)(e_2,t_2)\} \cup \\
& \left\{ \begin{array}{l} (\Pi x:X.\ Y[x], \\ \ \Pi x:X'.\ Y'[x]) \end{array} \middle| \begin{array}{l} I(X,X') \wedge \\ \forall(v,v') \in \Phi(X).\ I(Y[v],Y'[v']) \end{array} \right\} \cup \\
& \left\{ \begin{array}{l} (\Sigma x:X.\ Y[x] \\ \ \Sigma x:X'.\ Y'[x]) \end{array} \middle| \begin{array}{l} I(X,X') \wedge \\ \forall(v,v') \in \Phi(X).\ I(Y[v],Y'[v']) \end{array} \right\} \cup \\
& \left\{ \begin{array}{l} (\forall x:X.\ Y[x] \\ \ \forall x:X'.\ Y'[x]) \end{array} \middle| \begin{array}{l} I(X,X') \wedge \\ \forall(v,v') \in \Phi(X).\ I(Y[v],Y'[v']) \end{array} \right\} \cup \\
& \left\{ \begin{array}{l} (\exists x:X.\ Y[x] \\ \ \exists x:X'.\ Y'[x]) \end{array} \middle| \begin{array}{l} I(X,X') \wedge \\ \forall(v,v') \in \Phi(X).\ I(Y[v],Y'[v']) \end{array} \right\} \cup \\
& \{(G\,A, G\,A') \mid L(A,A')\} \cup \\
& \{(U_i,U_i) \mid i < k\} \cup \\
& \{(L_i,L_i) \mid i < k\} \\
\\
L' = & \{(\mathsf{I},\mathsf{I})\} \cup \\
& \{(A \otimes B, A' \otimes B') \mid L(A,A') \wedge L(B,B')\} \cup \\
& \{(A \multimap B, A' \multimap B') \mid L(A,A') \wedge L(B,B')\} \cup \\
& \left\{ \begin{array}{l} (Fx:X.\ A[x], \\ \ Fx:X'.\ A'[x]) \end{array} \middle| \begin{array}{l} I(X,X') \wedge \\ \forall(v,v') \in \Phi(X).\ L(A[v],A'[v']) \end{array} \right\} \cup \\
& \left\{ \begin{array}{l} (\Pi x:X.\ A[x], \\ \ \Pi x:X'.\ A'[x]) \end{array} \middle| \begin{array}{l} I(X,X') \wedge \\ \forall(v,v') \in \Phi(X).\ L(A[v],A'[v']) \end{array} \right\} \cup \\
& \left\{ \begin{array}{l} (\forall x:X.\ A[x], \\ \ \forall x:X'.\ A'[x]) \end{array} \middle| \begin{array}{l} I(X,X') \wedge \\ \forall(v,v') \in \Phi(X).\ L(A[v],A'[v']) \end{array} \right\} \cup \\
& \left\{ \begin{array}{l} (\exists x:X.\ A[x], \\ \ \exists x:X'.\ A'[x]) \end{array} \middle| \begin{array}{l} I(X,X') \wedge \\ \forall(v,v') \in \Phi(X).\ L(A[v],A'[v']) \end{array} \right\} \cup \\
& \{(\top,\top)\} \cup \\
& \{(A \mathbin{\&} B, A' \mathbin{\&} B') \mid L(A,A') \wedge L(B,B')\} \cup \\
& \{(T(A),T(A')) \mid (A,A') \in L\} \cup \\
& \{(e \mapsto X, e' \mapsto X') \mid (e,e') \in \mathsf{Loc} \wedge (X,X') \in I\}
\end{array}
$$

**Figure 14.** Definition of type part of $T_k$

$$
\begin{array}{lcl}
\phi'(\mathsf{Loc}) & = & \mathit{Loc} \\
\phi'(\mathbb{N}) & = & \hat{\mathbb{N}} \\
\phi'(\top_I) & = & \hat{\top}_I \\
\phi'(e_1 =_X e_2) & = & \mathit{Id}(e_1,e_2,\phi(X)) \\
\phi'(\Pi x:X.\ Y[x]) & = & \Pi(\phi(X),\lambda v.\ \phi(Y[v])) \\
\phi'(\Sigma x:X.\ Y[x]) & = & \Sigma(\phi(X),\lambda v.\ \phi(Y[v])) \\
\phi'(\forall x:X.\ Y[x]) & = & \hat{\forall}(\phi(X),\lambda v.\ \phi(Y[v])) \\
\phi'(\exists x:X.\ Y[x]) & = & \hat{\exists}(\phi(X),\lambda v.\ \phi(Y[v])) \\
\phi'(G\,A) & = & G(\psi(A)) \\
\phi'(U_i) \text{ when } i < k & = & \mathsf{let}\ (\hat{U},\hat{L},\hat{\phi},\hat{\psi}) = \mathsf{fix}(T_i)\ \mathsf{in}\ \hat{U} \\
\phi'(L_i) \text{ when } i < k & = & \mathsf{let}\ (\hat{U},\hat{L},\hat{\phi},\hat{\psi}) = \mathsf{fix}(T_i)\ \mathsf{in}\ \hat{L} \\
\\
\psi'(\mathsf{I}) & = & \hat{I} \\
\psi'(A \otimes B) & = & \psi(A) \mathbin{\hat{\otimes}} \psi(B) \\
\psi'(\top) & = & \hat{\top} \\
\psi'(A \mathbin{\&} B) & = & \psi(A) \mathbin{\hat{\&}} \psi(B) \\
\psi'(A \multimap B) & = & \psi(A) \mathbin{\hat{\multimap}} \psi(B) \\
\psi'(Fx:X.\ A[x]) & = & F(\phi(X),\lambda v.\ \psi(A[v])) \\
\psi'(\Pi x:X.\ A[x]) & = & \Pi_L(\phi(X),\lambda v.\ \psi(A[v])) \\
\phi'(\forall x:X.\ A[x]) & = & \hat{\forall}_L(\phi(X),\lambda v.\ \psi(A[v])) \\
\phi'(\exists x:X.\ A[x]) & = & \hat{\exists}_L(\phi(X),\lambda v.\ \psi(A[v])) \\
\psi'(T(A)) & = & T(\psi(A)) \\
\psi'(e \mapsto X) & = & \mathit{Ptr}(e,\phi(X))
\end{array}
$$

**Figure 15.** Definition of $T_k$, interpretation part

$$
\begin{array}{lcl}
[\![\cdot]\!] & = & \{\langle\rangle\} \\
[\![\Gamma, x : X]\!] & = & \left\{ (\gamma, (e_1, e_2)/x) \;\middle|\; \begin{array}{l} \gamma \in [\![\Gamma]\!] \wedge \\ (\gamma_1(X), \gamma_2(X)) \in U \wedge \\ (e_1, e_2) \in \phi(\gamma_1(X)) \end{array} \right\}
\end{array}
$$

$$
\begin{array}{lcl}
[\![\cdot]\!] & = & \{(\langle\epsilon;\langle\rangle\rangle, \langle\epsilon;\langle\rangle\rangle)\} \\
[\![\Delta_1, \Delta_2]\!] & = & \left\{ \begin{array}{l} (\langle\sigma;\delta_1,\delta_2\rangle, \\ \langle\sigma';\delta_1',\delta_2'\rangle) \end{array} \;\middle|\; \begin{array}{l} \exists \sigma_1, \sigma_2, \sigma_1', \sigma_2'. \\ \sigma = \sigma_1 \cdot \sigma_2 \wedge \sigma' = \sigma_1' \cdot \sigma_2' \wedge \\ (\langle\sigma_1;\delta_1\rangle, \langle\sigma_1';\delta_1'\rangle) \in [\![\Delta_1]\!] \wedge \\ (\langle\sigma_2;\delta_2\rangle, \langle\sigma_2';\delta_2'\rangle) \in [\![\Delta_2]\!] \end{array} \right\} \\
[\![a : A]\!] & = & \left\{ (\langle\sigma;e/a\rangle, \langle\sigma';e'/a\rangle) \;\middle|\; \begin{array}{l} (A, A) \in L \wedge \\ (\langle\sigma;e\rangle, \langle\sigma;e'\rangle) \in \psi(A) \end{array} \right\}
\end{array}
$$

**Figure 16.** Interpretation of Environments

*pair* of terms. We write $\gamma_1$ for the ordinary unary substitution substituting the first projection of $\gamma$ for each variable in $\gamma$, and $\gamma_2$ for the ordinary substitution substituting the second projection. We write $\gamma(e)$ for the pair $(\gamma_1(e), \gamma_2(e))$.

The intepretation of the empty context is the empty substitution. The interpretation of $\Gamma, x : X$ is every substitution $(\gamma, (e, e')/x)$ where $\gamma \in [\![\Gamma]\!]$ and $\gamma_1(X)$ is a type in U, and $(e, e')$ are related by $\phi(\gamma_1(X))$.

The interpretation of linear contexts $\Delta$ is a little more complicated. Instead of a binary substitution, its elements consist of pairs of store/substitution pairs. Intuitively, a linear environment is a set of linear values for each linear variable, plus the store needed to interpret the value. So the interpretation of a single-variable context $a : A$ are all the pairs of configurations $(\langle\sigma; e/a\rangle, \langle\sigma'; e'/a\rangle)$, where $\langle\sigma; e\rangle$ and $\langle\sigma'; e'\rangle$ are related by $\psi(A)$ (and A is a linear type in L).

The interpretation of the empty linear context is similar to the interpretation for I; it relates two empty substitutions in empty heaps. Likewise, the interpretation of contexts $\Delta_1, \Delta_2$ is very similar to the interpretation of the tensor product. When we interpret a context $\Delta_1, \Delta_2$, we take it be a pair of $\langle\sigma; \delta_1, \delta_2\rangle$ and $\langle\sigma'; \delta_1', \delta_2'\rangle$, such that we can divide the stores so that $\sigma = \sigma_1 \cdot \sigma_2$ and $\sigma' = \sigma_1' \cdot \sigma_2'$, and $\langle\sigma_1; \delta_1\rangle$ is related to $\langle\sigma_1'; \delta_1'\rangle$ at $\Delta_1$, and likewise $\langle\sigma_2; \delta_2\rangle$ is related to $\langle\sigma_2'; \delta_2'\rangle$ at $\Delta_2$.

### 4.5 Fundamental Property

We can now state the fundamental lemma of logical relations:

**Theorem 2** (Fundamental Property).
*Suppose* $\Gamma$ ok *and* $\gamma \in [\![\Gamma]\!]$ *and* $\Gamma \vdash \Delta$ ok *and* $(\langle\sigma_1; \delta_2\rangle, \langle\sigma_1; \delta_2\rangle) \in [\![\gamma_1(\Delta)]\!]$. *Then we have that:*

1. *If* $\Gamma \vdash X$ type *then* $\gamma(X) \in U$.
2. *If* $\Gamma \vdash X \equiv Y$ type *then* $(\gamma_1(X), \gamma_2(Y)) \in U$.
3. *If* $\Gamma \vdash e : X$ *then* $\gamma(e) \in \phi(\gamma_1(X))$.
4. *If* $\Gamma \vdash e_1 \equiv e_2 : X$ *then* $(\gamma_1(e_1), \gamma_2(e_2)) \in \phi(\gamma_1(X))$.
5. *If* $\Gamma \vdash A$ linear *then* $\gamma(A) \in L$.
6. *If* $\Gamma \vdash A \equiv B$ linear *then* $(\gamma_1(A), \gamma_2(B)) \in L$.
7. *If* $\Gamma; \Delta \vdash e : A$ *then* $(\langle\sigma_1; \gamma_1(\delta_1(e))\rangle, \langle\sigma_2; \gamma_2(\delta_2(e))\rangle) \in \psi(\gamma_1(X))$.
8. *If* $\Gamma; \Delta \vdash e_1 \equiv e_2 : A$ *then* $(\langle\sigma_1; \gamma_1(\delta_1(e_1))\rangle, \langle\sigma_2; \gamma_2(\delta_2(e_2))\rangle) \in \psi(\gamma_1(X))$.
9. *If* $\Gamma; \Delta \vdash e \div A$ *then there are* t *and* t' *such that for each* $\gamma \in [\![\Gamma]\!]$ *and* $(\langle\sigma_1; \delta_1\rangle, \langle\sigma_2; \delta_2\rangle) \in [\![\gamma_1(\Delta)]\!]$, *we have* $(\langle\sigma_1; \delta_1(\gamma_1(t))\rangle, \langle\sigma_2; \delta_2(\gamma_2(t'))\rangle) \in \psi(\gamma_1(A))$.

*Proof.* The theorem follows by a massive mutual induction over all of the rules of all of the judgements in the system. The full proof is in the companion technical report.

Worth noting is that in many of the cases, we make the arbitrary choice to use the first projection of the substitution (i.e., $\gamma_1$ or $\delta_1$) rather than the second. Connosieurs of dependent types may worry that difficulties could be lurking in this choice. Happily, there are no problems, because we established that $\mathcal{T}$ is a semantic type system up front, and so we know that $\phi$ and $\psi$ respect I and U. □

Evaluation of all closed well-typed terms terminates. The fundamental property also implies consistency, since every well-typed term is in the logical relation and inconsistent types (like $0 = 1$) have empty relations. We also have adequacy — any two provably equal terms of natural number type will evaluate to the same numeral (and similarly for the linear type $Fn : \mathbb{N}.\ I$ and the monadic type $T((Fn : \mathbb{N}.\ I))$).

## 5. Implementation

We have written a small type checker for a version of our theory in Ocaml. We say "version of", because the type system we present in this paper is (extremely) undecidable, and so we have needed to make a number of modifications to the type theory to make it implementable. We emphasize that even though all of the modifications we made seem straightforward, we have done no proofs about the implementation: we still need to show that everything is consistent and conservative with respect to the extensional system.

***Equality Reflection*** Our implementation does not support equality reflection, or indeed most of the $\eta$ rules. Our system implements an untyped conversion relation, and opportunistically implements a few of the easier eta-rules (for example, $\lambda x.\ f\ x \equiv f$). So our implementation is really an intensional type theory, rather than an extensional one.

***Intersection and Union Types*** The formulation of intersections and unions in this paper is set up to optimize the simplicity of the side conditions — to check a term e against the type $\forall x : X.\ Y$, we just add $x : X$ to the context, and check that x does not occur free in e. However, eliminating an intersection type requires guessing the instantiation.

In our implementation, we have to write an explicit abstraction $\lambda x.\ e$ to introduce a universal quantifier $\forall x : X.\ Y$, and eliminating an intersection requires an explicit annotation, so that if $f : \forall x : X.\ Y$, and we want to instantiate it with $e : X$, then we need to write $f\ e : [e/x]Y$. Similarly, we give a syntax for implicit existentials $\exists x : X.\ Y$ where the introduction is an explicit pack $\mathsf{pack}(e, t)$, with $e : X$ and $t : [e/x]Y$, and the elimination is an unpack $\mathsf{let\ pack}(x, y) = e \mathsf{\ in\ } e'$.

However, we track which variables are computationally relevant or not: in both a forall-introduction $\lambda x.\ e$, and a exists-elimination $\mathsf{let\ pack}(x, y) = e \mathsf{\ in\ } e'$, the x is not computationally relevant, may only appear within type annotations, implicit applications and the first argument of packs. This restriction is in the style of the "resurrection operator" of Pfenning [35] (which was later extended to type dependency by Abel [1]). Our overall result also looks very much like ICC* [6], the variant of the implicit calculus of constructions [27] with decidable typechecking.

***Proof Irrelevance*** In this paper, we implement linear proof irrelevance with a "squashed" term $*$. To turn this into something we can typecheck, we note that the premise of the rule requires that we produce an irrelevant derivation $\Gamma; \Delta \vdash e \div A$. The rules of this judgement (see Figure 8) are actually a linear version of the monadic modality of Pfenning and Davies [36] (and in fact we borrow their notation). So, to turn this into something we can typecheck, all we have to do is to replace $*$ with a term $[e]$, where we can derive $\Gamma; \Delta \vdash e \div A$.

We should also extend definitional equality to equate all terms of type $[A]$, though we have not yet implemented this, as that requires a typed conversion relation.

***Evaluation*** Our preliminary experience is that equality is the most challenging issue for us. We had to postulate numerous equalities that are sound in our model, but not applied automatically, and this is quite noisy. For example, we needed to postulate function extensionality to make things work, since we formulate lists in terms of W-types [25], and they are not well-behaved intensionally. In addition, our by-hand derivations of uses $\mathsf{fix}\ f\ x = e$ often make use of equality reflection, but we have not yet found a completely satisfactory formulation of its typing rule that works well in an intensional setting. An easy fix is to add lists (and other inductive types) as a primitive to our system, and another possibility is to move to something like observational type theory [3].

## 6. Discussion and Related Work

We divide the discussion into several categories, even though many individual pieces of work straddle multiple categories.

***Dependent Types*** As an extensional type theory, our system is constructed in the Nuprl [12] tradition. Our metatheory was designed following the paper of Harper [20], and many of our logical connectives were inspired by work on Nuprl. For example, our treatment of intersection and union types is similar to the work of Kopylov [23] (as well as PER models of polymorphism such as the work of Bainbridge et al. [5]). Our treatment of proof irrelevance is also inspired by the "squash types" of Nogin [32], though because of the constraints of linearity we could not directly use his rules.

***Linearity*** Cervesato and Pfenning [10] proposed the *Linear Logical Framework*, a core type theory for integrating linearity and dependent types. This calculus consisted of the negative fragment of MALL ($\multimap$, $\&$, $\top$) together with a dependent function space $\Pi x : A.\ B$, with the restriction that in any application $f\ e$, the argument $e$ could contain no free linear variables. In our calculus, this type corresponds to $\Pi x : \mathsf{G}\,A.\ B$. This neatly explains why the argument of the application should not have any free linear variables; every LLF application $f\ e$ corresponds to an application $f\ (\mathsf{G}\ e)$ in our calculus!

Very recently, Vákár [42] has proposed an extension of Linear LF, in which he extends linear LF with an intuitionistic sigma-type $\Sigma x : \widehat{A}.\ B$, whose introduction form is a pair whose first component does not have any free linear variables. In our calculus, this can be encoded as $\mathsf{F}x : \mathsf{G}\,A.\ B$. This encoding yields a nice explanation of why the first component of the pair is intuitionistic, and also why the dependent pair has a let-style elimination rather than a projective eliminator. (He also extends the calculus with many other features such as equality types and universes, just as we have, but in both cases these extensions are straightforward and so there is nothing interesting to compare.) Instead of an operational semantics, he gives a categorical axiomatization, and in future work we will see if his semantics applies to our syntax.

***Polarization, Value Dependency and Proof Irrelevance*** Another extension of LLF is the *Concurrent Logical Framework* (or CLF) of Watkins et al. [43], which extends LLF with positive types (such as $A \oplus B$, $A \otimes B$, and the intuitionistic sigma types), as well as a *computational monad* $\{A\}$ to mediate between uses of positive and negative types. This seems to be an instance of *focalization*, in which a pair of adjoint modalities $\uparrow N$ and $\downarrow P$ are used to segregate positive and negative types, with the monadic type $\{A\}$ arising as the composite $\uparrow\downarrow P$.

The distinction between positive and negative corresponds to a value/computation distinction (c.f., [24, 44]). While the LNL calculus is also built on an adjunction, this adjunction reflects the linear/nonlinear distinction and not the value/computation distinction. As a result, our language is pure (validating the full $\beta\eta$ theory for all the connectives), and we can freely mix positive and negative types (e.g., $A \otimes B \multimap C$).

However, polarization remains interesting from both purely theoretical and more practical points of view. Spiwack [39] gives *dependent L*, a polarized, linear, dependent type theory from a purely proof-theoretic perspective. The key observation is that polarized calculi have a weaker notion of substitution (namely, variables stand for values, rather than arbitrary terms), and as a result, (a) dependent types may depend only on values (which forbids large eliminations), but (b) since contraction of closed values is "safe" (since no computations can occur in types), linear variables may be freely duplicated when they occur in types.

Similar ideas are also found in the $F^*$ language of Swamy et al. [41]. This is an extension of the $F^\#$ language with type dependency. Since $F^*$ is an imperative language in the ML tradition, for soundness dependency is restricted to value dependency, just as in dependent L. However, the treatment of dependency on linear variables is somewhat different — $F^*$ has a universe of proof-irrelevant (intuitionistic) types, and affine variables can appear freely in proof-irrelevant types.

***Imperative Programming with Capabilities*** In addition to languages exploring "full-spectrum" type dependency (including Hoare Type Theory, which we discuss in Section 3.3), there are also a number of languages which have looked at using linear types as a programming feature.

ATS with linear dataviews, by Zhu and Xi [45], is not a dependently-typed language, since it very strictly segregates its proof and programming language. However, it has an extremely extensive language of proofs, and this proof language includes linear types, which are used to control memory accesses in a fashion very similar to L3 or separation logic. Interestingly, the entire linear sublanguage is computationally irrelevant – linear proofs are proofs, and hence erased at runtime.

Similarly, the calculus of capabilities of Pottier [37] represents another approach towards integrating linear capabilities with a programming language. As with ATS, capabilities are linear and irrelevant, and this system also includes support for advanced features such as the anti-frame rule. (A simpler proof-irrelevant capability system can be found in the work of Militão et al. [26], who give a kernel linear capability calculus.)

At this point, it should be clear that the combination of proof irrelevance and linearity is something which has appeared frequently in the literature, in many different guises. Unfortunately, it has mostly been introduced on an ad-hoc basis, and is not something which has been studied in its own right. As a result, we cannot give a crisp comparison of our proof irrelevance modality with this other work, since the design space seems very complex.

***Other Work*** One piece of work we wish to draw attention to is the enriched effect calculus of Egger et al. [16]. This calculus is like the (non-dependent) LNL calculus, except that it restricts linear contexts to at most a single variable (so that they are stoups, in Girard's terminology). One striking coincidence is that EEC has a mixed pair $X\,!\!\otimes A$, which looks very much like our linear dependent pair $\mathsf{F}x : X.\ A$.

Another direction for future work is to enrich the heap model. Our model of imperative computations is a generalization of Ahmed et al. [2], which in turn builds a logical relation model on top of the basic heap model of separation logic [38]. However, over the past decade, this model of heaps has been vastly extended, both from a semantic perspective [9, 15], and from the angle of verification [14, 22].

## References


[1] A. Abel. Irrelevance in type theory with a heterogeneous equality judgement. In *Foundations of Software Science and Computational Structures*, pages 57–71. Springer, 2011.

[2] A. Ahmed, M. Fluet, and G. Morrisett. L3: A linear language with locations. *Fundamenta Informaticae*, 77(4):397–449, 2007.

[3] T. Altenkirch, C. McBride, and W. Swierstra. Observational equality, now! In *PLPV*, pages 57–68. ACM, 2007.

[4] A. Appel, R. Dockins, A. Hobor, L. Beringer, J. Dodds, G. Stewart, S. Blazy, and X. Leroy. *Program logics for certified compilers*. Cambridge University Press, 2014.

[5] E. S. Bainbridge, P. J. Freyd, A. Scedrov, and P. J. Scott. Functorial polymorphism. *Theoretical computer science*, 70(1):35–64, 1990.

[6] B. Barras and B. Bernardo. The implicit calculus of constructions as a programming language with dependent types. In *Foundations of Software Science and Computational Structures*, pages 365–379. Springer, 2008.

[7] N. Benton. A mixed linear and non-linear logic: Proofs, terms and models. In *Computer Science Logic (CSL)*, 1994.

[8] N. Benton and P. Wadler. Linear logic, monads and the lambda calculus. In *Logic in Computer Science (LICS)*, 1996.

[9] L. Birkedal, K. Støvring, and J. Thamsborg. A relational realizability model for higher-order stateful adts. *The Journal of Logic and Algebraic Programming*, 81(4):491–521, 2012.

[10] I. Cervesato and F. Pfenning. A linear logical framework. *Inf. Comput.*, 179(1):19–75, 2002.

[11] A. Chlipala. Mostly-automated verification of low-level programs in computational separation logic. *ACM SIGPLAN Notices*, 46(6):234–245, 2011.

[12] R. L. Constable. Constructive mathematics as a programming logic I: Some principles of theory. In *Annals of Mathematics*, volume 24, pages 21–37. Elsevier, 1985.

[13] B. A. Davey and H. A. Priestley. *Introduction to lattices and order*. Cambridge university press, 2002.

[14] T. Dinsdale-Young, L. Birkedal, P. Gardner, M. Parkinson, and H. Yang. Views: compositional reasoning for concurrent programs. *ACM SIGPLAN Notices*, 48(1):287–300, 2013.

[15] D. Dreyer, G. Neis, and L. Birkedal. The impact of higher-order state and control effects on local relational reasoning. *Journal of Functional Programming*, 22(4-5):477–528, 2012.

[16] J. Egger, R. E. Møgelberg, and A. Simpson. Enriching an effect calculus with linear types. In *Computer Science Logic*, pages 240–254. Springer, 2009.

[17] M. H. Escardó. Joins in the frame of nuclei. *Applied Categorical Structures*, 11(2):117–124, 2003.

[18] J.-Y. Girard. Linear logic. *Theoretical computer science*, 50(1):1–101, 1987.

[19] J.-Y. Girard. Linear logic: Its syntax and semantics. In *Advances in Linear Logic*, volume 222 of *London Mathematical Society Lecture Notes*. CUP, 1995.

[20] R. Harper. Constructing type systems over an operational semantics. *Journal of Symbolic Computation*, 14(1):71–84, 1992.

[21] A. Hobor and J. Villard. The ramifications of sharing in data structures. *ACM SIGPLAN Notices*, 48(1):523–536, 2013.

[22] J. B. Jensen and L. Birkedal. Fictional separation logic. In *Programming Languages and Systems*, pages 377–396. Springer, 2012.

[23] A. Kopylov. *Type Theoretical Foundations for Data Structures, Classes, and Objects*. PhD thesis, 2004.

[24] P. B. Levy. *Call-By-Push-Value: A Functional/Imperative Synthesis*, volume 2 of *Semantics Structures in Computation*. Springer, 2004.

[25] P. Martin-Lof and G. Sambin. *Intuitionistic type theory*. Bibliopolis Naples, 1984.

[26] F. Militão, J. Aldrich, and L. Caires. Substructural typestates. In *Proceedings of the ACM SIGPLAN 2014 workshop on Programming languages meets program verification*, pages 15–26. ACM, 2014.

[27] A. Miquel. The implicit calculus of constructions extending pure type systems with an intersection type binder and subtyping. In *TLCA*, pages 344–359. Springer, 2001.

[28] A. Nanevski, G. Morrisett, and L. Birkedal. Polymorphism and separation in hoare type theory. In J. H. Reppy and J. L. Lawall, editors, *ICFP*, pages 62–73. ACM, 2006.

[29] A. Nanevski, G. Morrisett, and L. Birkedal. Hoare type theory, polymorphism and separation. *Journal of Functional Programming*, 18(5-6):865–911, 2008.

[30] A. Nanevski, V. Vafeiadis, and J. Berdine. Structuring the verification of heap-manipulating programs. In M. V. Hermenegildo and J. Palsberg, editors, *POPL*, pages 261–274. ACM, 2010.

[31] Z. Ni, D. Yu, and Z. Shao. Using XCAP to certify realistic systems code: Machine context management. In *TPHOLs*, pages 189–206, 2007.

[32] A. Nogin. Quotient types: A modular approach. In *Theorem Proving in Higher Order Logics*, pages 263–280. Springer, 2002.

[33] P. W. O'Hearn and D. J. Pym. The logic of bunched implications. *Bulletin of Symbolic Logic*, 5(02):215–244, 1999.

[34] R. L. Petersen, L. Birkedal, A. Nanevski, and G. Morrisett. A realizability model for impredicative hoare type theory. In *Programming Languages and Systems*, pages 337–352. Springer, 2008.

[35] F. Pfenning. Intensionality, extensionality, and proof irrelevance in modal type theory. In *LICS 2001. Proceedings.*, pages 221–230. IEEE, 2001.

[36] F. Pfenning and R. Davies. A judgmental reconstruction of modal logic. *Mathematical structures in computer science*, 11(04): 511–540, 2001.

[37] F. Pottier. Syntactic soundness proof of a type-and-capability system with hidden state. *Journal of Functional Programming*, 23 (1):38–144, Jan. 2013.

[38] J. C. Reynolds. Separation logic: A logic for shared mutable data structures. In *Logic in Computer Science, 2002. Proceedings. 17th Annual IEEE Symposium on*, pages 55–74. IEEE, 2002.

[39] A. Spiwack. A dissection of L, 2014. URL `http://assert-false.net/arnaud/papers`.

[40] K. Svendsen, L. Birkedal, and A. Nanevski. Partiality, state and dependent types. In C.-H. L. Ong, editor, *TLCA*, volume 6690 of *Lecture Notes in Computer Science*, pages 198–212. Springer, 2011.

[41] N. Swamy, J. Chen, C. Fournet, P.-Y. Strub, K. Bhargavan, and J. Yang. Secure distributed programming with value-dependent types. In *ICFP*, pages 266–278, 2011.

[42] M. Vákár. Syntax and semantics of linear dependent types, 2014. URL `http://arxiv.org/abs/1405.0033`.

[43] K. Watkins, I. Cervesato, F. Pfenning, and D. Walker. A concurrent logical framework: The propositional fragment. In *TYPES*, pages 355–377, 2003.

[44] N. Zeilberger. On the unity of duality. *Ann. Pure Appl. Logic*, 153 (1-3):66–96, 2008.

[45] D. Zhu and H. Xi. Safe Programming with Pointers through Stateful Views. In *PADL*, pages 83–97, January 2005.

# Higher Inductive Types as Homotopy-Initial Algebras

Kristina Sojakova
Carnegie Mellon University
kristinas@cmu.edu

## Abstract

Homotopy Type Theory is a new field of mathematics based on the recently-discovered correspondence between Martin-Löf's constructive type theory and abstract homotopy theory. We have a powerful interplay between these disciplines - we can use geometric intuition to formulate new concepts in type theory and, conversely, use type-theoretic machinery to verify and often simplify existing mathematical proofs.

Higher inductive types form a crucial part of this new system since they allow us to represent mathematical objects, such as spheres, tori, pushouts, and quotients, in the type theory. We investigate a class of higher inductive types called W-suspensions which generalize Martin-Löf's well-founded trees. We show that a propositional variant of W-suspensions, whose computational behavior is determined up to a higher path, is characterized by the universal property of being a homotopy-initial algebra. As a corollary we get that W-suspensions in the strict form are homotopy-initial.

***Categories and Subject Descriptors*** F.4.1 [*Mathematical Logic and Formal Languages*]: Mathematical Logic

***Keywords*** homotopy-initial algebra; W-suspension; higher inductive type; homotopy type theory

## 1. Introduction

Homotopy Type Theory (HoTT) has recently generated significant interest among type theorists and mathematicians alike. It uncovers deep connections between Martin-Löf's dependent type theory ([17, 18]) and the fields of abstract homotopy theory, higher categories, and algebraic topology ([2, 6–9, 12, 14, 24–27]). Insights from homotopy theory are used to add new concepts to the type theory, such as the representation of various geometric objects as higher inductive types. Conversely, type theory is used to formalize and verify existing mathematical proofs using proof assistants such as Coq [5] and Agda [19]. Moreover, type-theoretic insights often help us discover novel proofs of known results which are simpler than their homotopy-theoretic versions: the calculation of $\pi_n(\mathbf{S}^n)$ ([11, 13]); the Freudenthal Suspension Theorem [23]; the Blakers-Massey Theorem [23], etc.

As a formal system, HoTT [23] is a generalization of intensional Martin-Löf Type Theory with two features motivated by abstract homotopy theory: Voevodsky's *univalence axiom* ([9, 26]) and *higher-inductive types* ([15, 20]). The slogan in HoTT is that *types are topological spaces, terms are points, and proofs of identity are paths between points.* The structure of an identity type in HoTT is thus far more complex than just consisting of reflexivity paths, despite the definition of $\mathsf{Id}_A(x, y)$ as an inductive type with a single constructor $\mathsf{refl}_A(x) : \mathsf{Id}_A(x, x)$. It is a beautiful, and perhaps surprising, fact that not only does this richer theory admit an interpretation into homotopy theory ([2], [9]) but that many fundamental concepts and results from mathematics arise naturally as constructions and theorems of HoTT.

For example, the unit circle $\mathbf{S}^1$ is defined as a higher inductive type with a point base and a loop loop based at base. It comes with a recursion principle which says that to construct a function $f : \mathbf{S}^1 \to X$, it suffices to supply a point $x : X$ and a loop based at $x$. The value $f(\mathsf{base})$ then computes to $x$. Such definitional computation rules are convenient to work with but also pose some conceptual difficulties. For instance, an alternative encoding of the circle as a higher inductive type $\mathbf{S}^1_a$ specifies two points south, north and two paths from north to south, called east and west. The recursion principle then says that in order to construct a function $f : \mathbf{S}^1_a \to X$, it suffices to supply two points $x, y : X$ and two paths between them. The values $f(\mathsf{north})$ and $f(\mathsf{south})$ then compute to $x$ and $y$ respectively.

We have a natural way of relating these two representations via an equivalence: in one direction, map base to north and loop to east; in the other direction, map both north and south to base and map east to loop and west to the identity path at base. Unfortunately, the types $\mathbf{S}^1$, $\mathbf{S}^1_a$ related this way, while equivalent, do *not* satisfy the same definitional laws, which poses a compatibility issue. Even more importantly, we do not have a way of *internalizing* these notions of a circle and working with them inside the type theory, since we can only talk about definitional equalities on the meta-level.

In this paper we thus study higher inductive types abstractly, as arbitrary types endowed with certain constructors and *propositional* computation behavior: in the case of $\mathbf{S}^1$, for example, we say that a type $C$ with constructors $b : C$ and $l : c = c$ satisfies the recursion principle for a circle if for any other type $X$, point $x : X$ and loop based at $x$, there exists a function $f : C \to X$ for which there is a *path between* $f(b)$ *and* $x$ (and which satisfies a higher coherence condition). We note that we require *no* change to the underlying type theory: the particular higher inductive type $\mathbf{S}^1$ just becomes a specific instance of the abstract definition of a circle, one whose computation rules happen to hold definitionally.

A major advantage of types with propositional computation rules is that we can internalize the definitions and reason about them within the type theory - and in particular, use proof assistants to verify the results. In this respect, our work is complementary to [16], which gives an external, category-theoretic semantics for a certain class of higher inductives. Another advantage of propositional computation behavior is portability: relaxing the computation laws satisfied by the types $\mathbf{S}^1$ and $\mathbf{S}^1_a$ to their propositional


*POPL '15*, January 15–17 2015, Mumbai, India.

http://dx.doi.org/10.1145/2676726.2676983

counterparts results in two notions of a circle that are equivalent. This in particular means that any type $C$ which is a circle in one sense is also a circle in the alternate sense. We can thus state and prove results about either of these specifications, knowing that the proofs carry over to any particular implementation - be it $\mathbf{S}^1$, $\mathbf{S}^1_a$, or a third one.

It further turns out that types with propositional rules tend to keep many of their desirable properties; for instance, it can be shown that the main result of [13], that the fundamental group of the circle is the group of integers, carries over to the case when *both* the circle and the integer types have propositional computational behavior. In addition, we can now show that higher inductive types are characterized by the universal property of being a *homotopy-initial algebra*. This notion was first introduced in [3], where an analogous result was established for the "ordinary" inductive type of well-founded trees (Martin-Löf's W-types). In the higher-dimensional setting, an *algebra* is a type $X$ together with a number of finitary operations $f, g, h \ldots$, which are allowed to act not only on $X$ but also on any higher identity type over $X$. An *algebra homomorphism* has to preserve all operations up to a higher homotopy. Finally, an algebra $\mathcal{X}$ is *homotopy-initial* if the type of homomorphisms from $\mathcal{X}$ to any other algebra $\mathcal{Y}$ is contractible.

Our main theorem is stated for a class of higher inductive types which we call W-suspensions; they generalize ordinary W-types as well as the higher inductive type $\mathbb{S}$ and others. We show that the induction principle for W-suspensions is equivalent (as a type) to homotopy-initiality. This extends the main result of [3] for "ordinary" inductive types to the important, and much more difficult, higher-dimensional case.

# 2. Basic Homotopy Type Theory

The core of HoTT is a dependent type theory with

- dependent pair types $\Sigma_{x:A}B(x)$ and dependent function types $\Pi_{x:A}B(x)$ (with the non-dependent versions $A \times B$ and $A \to B$). To stay consistent with the presentation in [23], we assume definitional $\eta$-conversion for functions but do not assume it for pairs.
- a cumulative hierarchy of universes $\mathcal{U}_0 : \mathcal{U}_1 : \mathcal{U}_2 : \ldots$ in the style of Russell.
- intensional identity types $\mathsf{Id}_A(x, y)$, also denoted $x =_A y$. We have the usual formation and introduction rules; the elimination and computation rules are recalled below:

$$\frac{E : \Pi_{x,y:A}\mathsf{Id}_A(x,y) \to \mathcal{U}_i \qquad d : \Pi_{x:A}E(x,x,\mathsf{refl}_A(x))}{\mathsf{J}(E,d) : \Pi_{x,y:A}\Pi_{p:\mathsf{Id}_A(x,y)}E(x,y,p)}$$

$$\frac{\begin{array}{c}E : \Pi_{x,y:A}\mathsf{Id}_A(x,y) \to \mathcal{U}_i \\ d : \Pi_{x:A}E(x,x,\mathsf{refl}_A(x)) \qquad a : A\end{array}}{\mathsf{J}(E,d)(a,a,\mathsf{refl}_A(a)) \equiv d(a) : E(a,a,\mathsf{refl}_A(a))}$$

These rules are, of course, applicable in any context $\Gamma$; we follow the standard convention of omitting it. If the type $\mathsf{Id}_A(x, y)$ is inhabited, we call $x$ and $y$ *equal*. If we do not care about the specific equality witness, we often simply say that $x =_A y$ or if the type $A$ is clear, $x = y$. A term $p : x =_A y$ will be often called a *path* and the process of applying the identity elimination rule will be referred to as *path induction*. Definitional equality between $x, y : A$ will be denoted as $x \equiv y : A$.

We emphasize that apart from the aforementioned identity rules, univalence, and higher inductive types there are no other rules governing the behavior of identity types - in particular, we assert neither any form of Streicher's K-rule [22] nor the identity reflection rule.

The rest of this section describes the univalence axiom and some key properties of identity types; higher inductive types are discussed in Section. 3. For a thorough exposition of homotopy type theory we refer the reader to [23].

## 2.1 Groupoid laws

Proofs of identity behave much like paths in topological spaces: they can be reversed, concatenated, mapped along functions, etc. Below we summarize a few of these properties:

- For any path $p : x =_A y$ there is a path $p^{-1} : y =_A x$, and we have $\mathsf{refl}_A(x)^{-1} \equiv \mathsf{refl}_A(x)$.
- For any paths $p : x =_A y$ and $q : y =_A z$ there is a path $p \cdot q : x =_A z$, and we have $\mathsf{refl}_A(x) \cdot \mathsf{refl}_A(x) \equiv \mathsf{refl}_A(x)$.
- Associativity of composition: for any paths $p : x =_A y$, $q : y =_A z$, and $r : z =_A u$ we have $(p \cdot q) \cdot r = p \cdot (q \cdot r)$.
- We have $\mathsf{refl}_A(x) \cdot p = p$ and $p \cdot \mathsf{refl}_A(y) = p$ for any $p : x =_A y$.
- For any $p : x =_A y$, $q : y =_A z$ we have $p \cdot p^{-1} = \mathsf{refl}_A(x)$, $p^{-1} \cdot p = \mathsf{refl}_A(y)$, and $(p^{-1})^{-1} = p$, $(p \cdot q)^{-1} = q^{-1} \cdot p^{-1}$.
- For any type family $P : A \to \mathcal{U}_i$ and path $p : x =_A y$ there are functions $p^P_* : P(x) \to P(y)$ and $p^*_P : P(y) \to P(x)$, called the *covariant transport* and *contravariant transport*, respectively. We furthermore have $\mathsf{refl}_A(x)^P_* \equiv \mathsf{refl}_A(x)^*_P \equiv \mathsf{id}_{P(x)}$.
- We have $(p^{-1})^P_* = p^*_P$, $(p^{-1})^*_P = p^P_*$ and $(p \cdot q)^P_* = q^P_* \circ p^P_*$, $(p \cdot q)^*_P = p^*_P \circ q^*_P$ for any family $P : A \to \mathcal{U}_i$ and paths $p : x =_A y$, $q : y =_A z$.
- For any function $f : A \to B$ and path $p : x =_A y$, there is a path $\mathsf{ap}_f(p) : f(x) =_B f(y)$ and we have $\mathsf{ap}_f(\mathsf{refl}_A(x)) \equiv \mathsf{refl}_B(f(x))$.
- We have $\mathsf{ap}_f(p^{-1}) = \mathsf{ap}_f(p)^{-1}$ and $\mathsf{ap}_f(p \cdot q) = \mathsf{ap}_f(p) \cdot \mathsf{ap}_f(q)$ for any $f : A \to B$ and $p : x =_A y$, $q : y =_A z$.
- We have $\mathsf{ap}_{g \circ f}(p) = \mathsf{ap}_g(\mathsf{ap}_f(p))$ for any $f : A \to B$, $g : B \to C$ and $p : x =_A y$.
- For a dependent function $f : \Pi_{x:A}B(x)$ and path $p : x =_A y$, there are paths $\mathsf{dap}_f(p) : p^B_*(f(x)) =_{B(y)} f(y)$ and $\mathsf{dap}^f(p) : p^*_B(f(y)) =_{B(x)} f(x)$. We also have $\mathsf{dap}_f(\mathsf{refl}_A(x)) \equiv \mathsf{dap}^f(\mathsf{refl}_A(x)) \equiv \mathsf{refl}_{B(x)}(f(x))$.
- All constructs respect propositional equality.

## 2.2 Homotopies between functions

A homotopy between two functions is in a sense a "natural transformation":

**Definition 1.** *For $f, g : \Pi_{x:A}B(x)$, we define the type*

$$f \sim g :\equiv \Pi_{a:A}(f(a) =_{B(a)} g(a))$$

*and call it the* type of homotopies *between $f$ and $g$.*

**Definition 2.** *For $f : A \to B$ and $g : A' \to B$, we define the type*

$$f \sim_{\mathcal{H}} g :\equiv \Pi_{a:A}\Pi_{a':A}(f(a) =_B g(a'))$$

*and call it the* type of heterogeneous homotopies *between $f$ and $g$.*

We now introduce some notation that will be needed later.

- For any $f, g : X \to Y$, $p : x =_X y$, $\alpha : f \sim g$, there is a path
$$\mathsf{nat}(\alpha, p) : \alpha(x) \cdot \mathsf{ap}_g(p) = \mathsf{ap}_f(p) \cdot \alpha(y)$$
- For any $f : X \to Z$, $g : Y \to Z$, $p : x_1 =_X x_2$, $q : y_1 =_Y y_2$, $\alpha : f \sim_{\mathcal{H}} g$, there is a path
$$\mathsf{nat}_{\mathcal{H}}(\alpha, p, q) : \alpha(x_1, y_1) \cdot \mathsf{ap}_g(q) = \mathsf{ap}_f(p) \cdot \alpha(x_2, y_2)$$

### 2.3 Truncation levels

In general, the structure of paths on a type $A$ can be highly nontrivial - we can have many distinct *0-cells* $x, y, \ldots : A$; there can be many distinct *1-cells* $p, q, \ldots : x =_A y$; there can be many distinct *2-cells* $\gamma, \delta, \ldots : p =_{x =_A y} q$; ad infinitum. The hierarchy of truncation levels describes those types which are, informally speaking, trivial beyond a certain dimension: a type $A$ of truncation level $n$ can be characterized by the property that all $m$-cells for $m > n$ with the same source and target are equal. From this intuitive description we can see that the hierarchy is cumulative.

It is customary to also speak of truncation levels $-2$ and $-1$, called *contractible types* and *mere propositions* respectively:

**Definition 3.** *A type $A : \mathcal{U}_i$ is called* contractible *if there exists a point $a : A$ such that any other point $x : A$ is equal to $a$:*

$$\mathsf{is\text{-}contr}(A) :\equiv \Sigma_{a:A}\Pi_{x:A}(a =_A x)$$

*A type $A : \mathcal{U}_i$ is called a* mere proposition *if all its inhabitants are equal:*

$$\mathsf{is\text{-}prop}(A) :\equiv \Pi_{x,y:A}(x =_A y)$$

Thus, a contractible type can be seen as having exactly one inhabitant, up to equality; a mere proposition can be seen as having at most one inhabitant, up to equality. Clearly:

**Lemma 4.** *If $A$ is contractible then $A$ is a mere proposition.*

The existence of a path between any two points implies more than just path-connectedness:

**Lemma 5.** *If $A$ is a mere proposition, then $x =_A y$ is contractible for any $x, y : A$.*

Thus, contractible types are in a sense the "nicest" possible: any two points are equal up to a *1-cell*, which itself is unique up to a *2-cell*, which itself is unique up to a *3-cell*, and so on. Mere propositions are the "nicest" ones after contractible spaces. We can now easily show:

**Corollary 6.** *For any $A$, $\mathsf{is\text{-}contr}(A)$ and $\mathsf{is\text{-}prop}(A)$ are mere propositions.*

### 2.4 Equivalences

A crucial concept in HoTT is that of an equivalence between types.

**Definition 7.** *A map $f : A \to B$ is called an* equivalence *if it has both a left and a right inverse:*

$$\mathsf{iseq}(f) :\equiv (\Sigma_{g:B\to A}(g \circ f \sim \mathsf{id}_A)) \times (\Sigma_{h:B\to A}(f \circ h \sim \mathsf{id}_B))$$

*We define*

$$(A \simeq B) :\equiv \Sigma_{f:A\to B}\mathsf{iseq}(f)$$

*and call $A$ and $B$* equivalent *if the above type is inhabited.*

Unsurprisingly, we can prove that $A$ and $B$ are equivalent by constructing functions going back and forth, which compose to identity on both sides[1]; this is also a necessary condition.

**Lemma 8.** *Two types $A$ and $B$ are equivalent if and only if there exist functions $f : A \to B$ and $g : B \to A$ such that $g \circ f \sim \mathsf{id}_A$ and $f \circ g \sim \mathsf{id}_B$.*

We will refer to such functions $f$ and $g$ as forming a *quasi-equivalence* and say that $f$ and $g$ are *quasi-inverses* of each other. From this we can easily show:

**Lemma 9.** *Equivalence of types is an equivalence relation.*

[1] Although the type of such functions itself is not equivalent to $A \simeq B$, see Chpt. 4 of [23].

We call $A$ and $B$ *logically equivalent* if there are exist functions $f : A \to B$, $g : B \to A$. It is immediate that if both types are mere propositions then logical equivalence implies $A \simeq B$. For example:

**Corollary 10.** *For any $A$, $\mathsf{is\text{-}contr}(A) \simeq (A \times \mathsf{is\text{-}prop}(A))$.*

Many "diagram-like" operations on paths turn out to be equivalences. For instance:

- For any $u : a =_X b$, $v : b =_X d$, $w : a =_X c$, $z : c =_X d$ there is a map
$$\mathbf{I}^1_\square : (u = w \cdot z \cdot v^{-1}) \to (u \cdot v = w \cdot z)$$
defined in the obvious way by induction on $v$ and $w$. This map is an equivalence.
- For any $u : a =_X b$, $v : b =_X d$, $w : a =_X c$, $z : c =_X d$ there is a map
$$\mathbf{I}^2_\square : (u = w \cdot z \cdot v^{-1}) \to (w^{-1} \cdot u = z \cdot v^{-1})$$
defined in the obvious way by induction on $v$ and $w$. This map is an equivalence.

### 2.5 Structure of path types

Let us first consider the product type $A \times B$. We would like for two pairs $c, d : A \times B$ to be equal precisely when their first and second projections are equal. By path induction we can easily construct a function

$${}^{=}\mathsf{E}^{\times}_{c,d} : (c = d) \to (\pi_1(c) = \pi_1(d)) \times (\pi_2(c) = \pi_2(d))$$

We can show:

**Lemma 11.** *The map ${}^{=}\mathsf{E}^{\times}_{c,d}$ is an equivalence for any $c, d : A \times B$.*

We will denote the quasi-inverse of ${}^{=}\mathsf{E}^{\times}_{c,d}$ by ${}^{\times}\mathsf{E}^{=}_{c,d}$. For brevity we will often omit the subscripts.

We have a similar correspondence for dependent pairs; however, the second projections of $c, d : \Sigma_{x:A}B(x)$ now lie in different fibers of $B$ and we employ (covariant) transport. By path induction we can define a map

$${}^{=}\mathsf{E}^{\Sigma}_{c,d} : (c = d) \to \Sigma_{(p:\pi_1(c)=\pi_1(d))}(p^B_*(\pi_2(c)) = \pi_2(d))$$

**Lemma 12.** *The map ${}^{=}\mathsf{E}^{\Sigma}_{c,d}$ is an equivalence for any $c, d : \Sigma_{x:A}B(x)$.*

We will denote the quasi-inverse of ${}^{=}\mathsf{E}^{\Sigma}_{c,d}$ by ${}^{\Sigma}\mathsf{E}^{=}_{c,d}$. We also have an analogous correspondence using a contravariant transport.

We would like for two types $A, B : \mathcal{U}_i$ to be equal precisely when they are equivalent. As before, we can easily obtain a function

$${}^{=}\mathsf{E}^{\simeq}_{A,B} : (A = B) \to (A \simeq B)$$

The univalence axiom now states that this map is an equivalence:

**Axiom 1** (Univalence)**.** *The map ${}^{=}\mathsf{E}^{\simeq}_{A,B}$ is an equivalence for any $A, B : \mathcal{U}_i$.*

We will denote the quasi-inverse of ${}^{=}\mathsf{E}^{\simeq}_{A,B}$ by ${}^{\simeq}\mathsf{E}^{=}_{A,B}$.

It follows from univalence that *equivalent types are equal* and hence they satisfy the same properties:

**Lemma 13.** *For any type family $P : \mathcal{U}_i \to \mathcal{U}_j$, and types $A, B : \mathcal{U}_i$ with $A \simeq B$, we have that $P(A) \simeq P(B)$. Thus in particular, $P(A)$ is inhabited precisely when $P(B)$ is.*

Finally, two functions $f, g : \Pi_{x:A}B(x)$ should be equal precisely when there exists a homotopy between them. Constructing a map

$${}^{=}\mathsf{E}^{\Pi}_{f,g} : (f = g) \to (f \sim g)$$

is easy. Showing that this map is an equivalence (or even constructing a map in the opposite direction) is much harder, and is in fact among the chief consequences of univalence:

**Lemma 14.** *The map* ${}^{=}\mathsf{E}^{\Pi}_{f,g}$ *is an equivalence for any* $f, g : \Pi_{x:A} B(x)$.

*Proof.* See Chpt. 4.9 of [23]. □

We will denote the quasi-inverse of ${}^{=}\mathsf{E}^{\Pi}_{f,g}$ by ${}^{\Pi}\mathsf{E}^{=}_{f,g}$.

## 3. Higher Inductive Types

In this section we describe some higher inductive types of interest and use these specific examples as an introduction to the terminology and methodology that will follow in Sect. 4.

An inductive type $X$ can be understood as being *freely generated* by a collection of constructors: in the familiar case of natural numbers, we have the two constructors for zero and successor. The property of being freely generated can be stated as an induction principle: in order to show that a property $P : \mathbb{N} \to \mathcal{U}_i$ holds for all $n : \mathbb{N}$, it suffices to show that it holds for zero and is preserved by the successor operation. As a special case, we get the recursion principle: in order to define a map $f : \mathbb{N} \to C$, is suffices to determine its value at zero and its behavior with respect to successor.

Higher inductive types generalize ordinary inductive types by allowing constructors involving *path spaces of* $X$ rather than just $X$ itself, as the next example shows.

### 3.1 The circle

The unit circle $\mathbf{S}^1$ is represented as an inductive type $\mathbb{S} : \mathcal{U}_0$ with two constructors [13]:

$$\mathsf{base} : \mathbb{S}$$
$$\mathsf{loop} : \mathsf{base} =_{\mathbb{S}} \mathsf{base}$$

pictured as

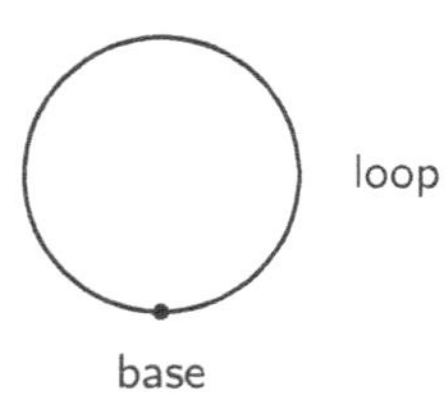


This in particular means that we have further paths, such as $\mathsf{loop}^{-1} \cdot \mathsf{loop} \cdot \mathsf{loop} \cdot \mathsf{refl}_{\mathbb{S}}(\mathsf{base})$ (which is equal to $\mathsf{loop}$).

We can reason about the circle using the principle of *circle recursion*, also called *simple elimination* for $\mathbb{S}$, which tells us that in order to construct a function out of $\mathbb{S}$ into a type $C$, it suffices to supply a point $c : C$ and a loop $s : c =_C c$.

$$\frac{C : \mathcal{U}_i \qquad c : C \qquad s : c =_C c}{\mathsf{rec}_{\mathbb{S}}(C, c, s) : \mathbb{S} \to C}$$

Furthermore, the recursor has the expected behavior on the 0-cell constructor $\mathsf{base}$ (we omit the premises):

$$\mathsf{rec}_{\mathbb{S}}(C, c, s)(\mathsf{base}) \equiv c : C$$

We also have a computation rule for the 1-cell constructor $\mathsf{loop}$:

$$\mathsf{ap}_{\mathsf{rec}_{\mathbb{S}}(C,c,s)}(\mathsf{loop}) =_{\mathsf{Id}_C(c,c)} s$$

This rule type-checks by virtue of the previous one. We note that in order to record the effect of the recursor on the path $\mathsf{loop}$, we use the "action-on-paths" construct $\mathsf{ap}$. Since this is a derived notion rather than a primitive one, we state the rule as a propositional rather than definitional equality.

We also have the more general principle of *circle induction*, also called *dependent elimination* for $\mathbb{S}$, which subsumes recursion. Instead of a type $C : \mathcal{U}_i$ we now have a type family $E : \mathbb{S} \to \mathcal{U}_i$. Where previously we required a point $c : C$, we now need a point $e : E(\mathsf{base})$. Finally, an obvious generalization of needing a loop $s : c =_C c$ would be to ask for a loop $d : e =_{E(\mathsf{base})} e$. However, this would be incorrect: once we have our desired inductor of type $\Pi_{x:\mathbb{S}} E(x)$, its effect on $\mathsf{loop}$ is not a loop at $e$ in the fiber $E(\mathsf{base})$ but a path from $\mathsf{loop}^E_*(e)$ to $e$ in $E(\mathsf{base})$ (or its contravariant version). The induction principle thus takes the following form:

$$\frac{E : \mathbb{S} \to \mathcal{U}_i \qquad e : E(\mathsf{base}) \qquad d : \mathsf{loop}^E_*(e) =_{E(\mathsf{base})} e}{\mathsf{ind}_{\mathbb{S}}(E, e, d) : \Pi_{x:\mathbb{S}} E(x)}$$

We have the associated computation rules:

$$\mathsf{ind}_{\mathbb{S}}(E, e, d)(\mathsf{base}) \equiv e : E(\mathsf{base})$$
$$\mathsf{dap}_{\mathsf{ind}_{\mathbb{S}}(E,e,d)}(\mathsf{loop}) =_{\mathsf{Id}_{E(\mathsf{base})}(\mathsf{loop}^E_*(e), e)} d$$

### 3.2 The circle, round two

We could have alternatively represented the circle as an inductive type $\mathbb{S}_a : \mathcal{U}_0$ with four constructors:

$$\mathsf{north} : \mathbb{S}_a$$
$$\mathsf{south} : \mathbb{S}_a$$
$$\mathsf{east} : \mathsf{north} =_{\mathbb{S}_a} \mathsf{south}$$
$$\mathsf{west} : \mathsf{north} =_{\mathbb{S}_a} \mathsf{south}$$

pictured as

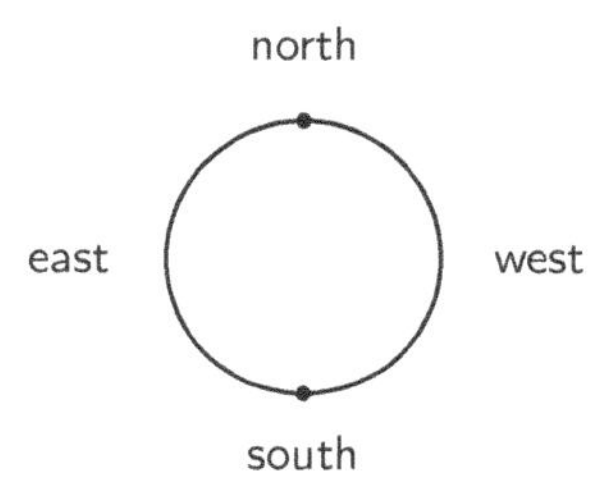


We now have the recursion principle

$$\frac{C : \mathcal{U}_i \qquad c : C \qquad d : C \qquad p : c =_C d \qquad q : c =_C d}{\mathsf{rec}_{\mathbb{S}_a}(C, c, d, p, q) : \mathbb{S}_a \to C}$$

with the computation rules

$$\mathsf{rec}_{\mathbb{S}_a}(C, c, d, p, q, \mathsf{north}) \equiv c : C$$
$$\mathsf{rec}_{\mathbb{S}_a}(C, c, d, p, q, \mathsf{south}) \equiv d : C$$

and

$$\mathsf{ap}_{\mathsf{rec}_{\mathbb{S}_a}(C,c,d,p,q)}(\mathsf{east}) = p$$
$$\mathsf{ap}_{\mathsf{rec}_{\mathbb{S}_a}(C,c,d,p,q)}(\mathsf{west}) = q$$

The corresponding induction principle is

$$\frac{\begin{array}{c} E : \mathbb{S}_a \to \mathcal{U}_i \qquad u : E(\mathsf{north}) \qquad v : E(\mathsf{south}) \\ \mu : \mathsf{east}^E_*(u) =_{E(\mathsf{south})} v \qquad \nu : \mathsf{west}^E_*(u) =_{E(\mathsf{south})} v \end{array}}{\mathsf{ind}_{\mathbb{S}_a}(E, u, v, \mu, \nu) : \Pi_{x:\mathbb{S}_a} E(x)}$$

with the associated computation rules

$$\mathsf{ind}_{\mathbb{S}_a}(E, u, v, \mu, \nu, \mathsf{north}) \equiv u : E(\mathsf{north})$$
$$\mathsf{ind}_{\mathbb{S}_a}(E, u, v, \mu, \nu, \mathsf{south}) \equiv v : E(\mathsf{south})$$

and

$$\mathsf{dap}_{\mathsf{ind}_{\mathbb{S}_a}(E,u,v,\mu,\nu)}(\mathsf{east}) = \mu$$
$$\mathsf{dap}_{\mathsf{ind}_{\mathbb{S}_a}(E,u,v,\mu,\nu)}(\mathsf{west}) = \nu$$

As expected, the two circle types are equivalent:

**Lemma 15.** *We have* $\mathbb{S} \simeq \mathbb{S}_a$.

*Proof sketch.* From left to right, map base to north and loop to east $\cdot$ west$^{-1}$. From right to left, map both north and south to base, east to loop, and west to $\mathsf{refl}_{\mathbb{S}}(\mathsf{base})$. Using the respective induction principles, show that these two mappings compose to identity on both sides and apply Lem. 8. □

### 3.3 Computation laws, revisited

By Lem. 15 the types $\mathbb{S}$ and $\mathbb{S}_a$ are equivalent and hence satisfy the same properties (see Lem. 13). We would thus expect the induction principle for $\mathbb{S}$ to carry over to $\mathbb{S}_a$, and vice versa. Indeed, with a little effort we can show the former:

**Lemma 16.** *The type* $\mathbb{S}_a$ *satisfies the induction and computation laws for* $\mathbb{S}$*, with* north *acting as the constructor* base *and* east $\cdot$ west$^{-1}$ *acting as the constructor* loop.

In the other direction, though, we hit a snag - the only obvious choice we have is to define both points north and south to be base, one of the paths west and east to be loop, and the other one the identity path at base. This, however, does not give us the desired induction principle: unless the two given points $u : E(\mathsf{base})$ and $v : E(\mathsf{base})$ happen to be definitionally equal, we will not be able to map base to both of them, as required by the computation rules.

This poses more than just a conceptual problem - in mathematics, we often have several possible definitions of a given notion, all of which are interchangeable from the point of view of a "user". Having two definitions of a circle which are not (known to be) interchangeable, however, can be problematic: any theorem we establish about or by appealing to $\mathbb{S}_a$ might no longer hold - or even type-check! - when using $\mathbb{S}$ instead. To see this, take the second computation law for $\mathbb{S}_a$, $\mathsf{dap}_{\mathsf{ind}_{\mathbb{S}_a}(E,u,v,\mu,\nu)}(\mathsf{west}) = \nu$. If we attempt to "implement" $\mathbb{S}_a$ using the circle $\mathbb{S}$ instead - by taking north, south := base, east := loop, west := $\mathsf{refl}_{\mathbb{S}}(\mathsf{base})$ as in the proof of Lem. 15 - the computation law is no longer well-typed since the left-hand side reduces to a reflexivity path whereas the right hand side is a path from $u$ to $v$.

This is one of the motivations for considering inductive types with *propositional* computation behavior: we now want to investigate types which "act like the circle" up to propositional equality. In the case of $\mathbb{S}$, such a type $C : \mathcal{U}_i$ should come with a point $b : C$ and loop $l : c =_C c$. In the case of $\mathbb{S}_a$, such a type should come with two points $n, s : C$ and two paths $e, w : n =_C s$. We can express this more concisely as follows:

**Definition 17.** *Define the type of* $\mathbb{S}$-algebras *on a universe* $\mathcal{U}_i$ *as*

$$\mathbb{S}\text{-}\mathsf{Alg}_{\mathcal{U}_i} := \Sigma_{C:\mathcal{U}_i} \Sigma_{b:C} (b = b)$$

**Definition 18.** *Define the type of* $\mathbb{S}_a$-algebras *on a universe* $\mathcal{U}_i$ *as*

$$\mathbb{S}_a\text{-}\mathsf{Alg}_{\mathcal{U}_i} := \Sigma_{C:\mathcal{U}_i} \Sigma_{n,s:C} (n = s) \times (n = s)$$

We are now interested in maps between algebras which in a suitable sense preserve the distinguished points and paths, i.e., *algebra homomorphisms.* A homomorphism between two $\mathbb{S}$-algebras $(C, c, p)$ and $(D, d, q)$ should be a function $f : C \to D$ for which we have a path $\beta : f(c) = d$. Furthermore, $f$ should also appropriately relate $p$ and $q$. To figure out what this means, we observe that if we map $p$ along $f$, we obtain a path $\mathsf{ap}_f(p) : f(c) = f(c)$. Each of the (identical) endpoints is equal to $d$, via the path $\beta$. Thus, we now have another path $\beta^{-1} \cdot \mathsf{ap}_f(p) \cdot \beta : d = d$. It is reasonable to require that this path be equal to $q$, i.e., that the following diagram commutes:

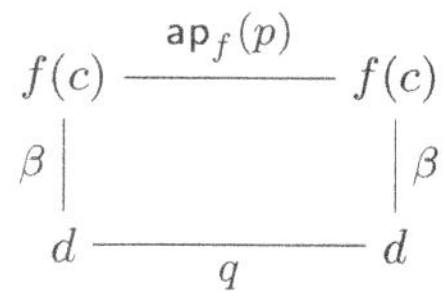


Likewise, a homomorphism between two $\mathbb{S}_a$-algebras $(C, a, b, p, q)$ and $(D, c, d, r, s)$ should be a function $f : C \to D$ for which we have paths $\beta : f(a) = c, \gamma : f(b) = d$ and for which the following diagrams commute:

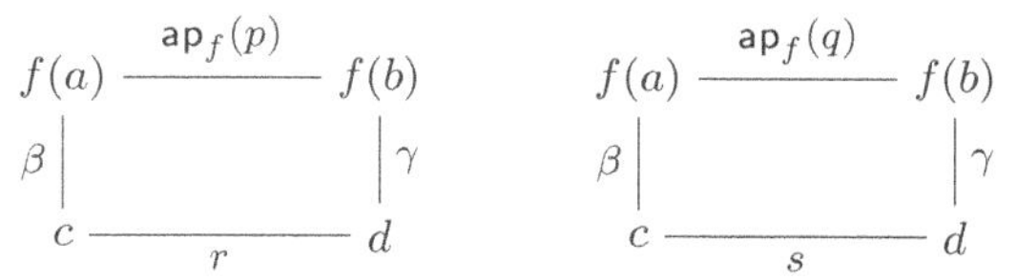


In other words, an $\mathbb{S}$- or $\mathbb{S}_a$-homomorphism behaves just like a function constructed by the appropriate circle recursion, albeit with propositional computation laws for points and paths. We can express this as follows:

**Definition 19.** *For algebras* $\mathcal{X} : \mathbb{S}\text{-}\mathsf{Alg}_{\mathcal{U}_i}$, $\mathcal{Y} : \mathbb{S}\text{-}\mathsf{Alg}_{\mathcal{U}_j}$*, define the type of* $\mathbb{S}$-homomorphisms *from* $\mathcal{X}$ *to* $\mathcal{Y}$ *by*

$$\mathbb{S}\text{-}\mathsf{Hom}\ (C, c, p)\ (D, d, q) := \Sigma_{f:C\to D} \Sigma_{\beta:f(c)=d} \big(\mathsf{ap}_f(p) \cdot \beta = \beta \cdot q\big)$$

**Definition 20.** *For algebras* $\mathcal{X} : \mathbb{S}_a\text{-}\mathsf{Alg}_{\mathcal{U}_i}$, $\mathcal{Y} : \mathbb{S}_a\text{-}\mathsf{Alg}_{\mathcal{U}_j}$*, define the type of* $\mathbb{S}_a$-homomorphisms *from* $\mathcal{X}$ *to* $\mathcal{Y}$ *by*

$$\mathbb{S}_a\text{-}\mathsf{Hom}\ (C, a, b, p, q)\ (D, c, d, r, s) := \Sigma_{f:C\to D} \Sigma_{\beta:f(a)=c} \Sigma_{\gamma:f(b)=d} \big(\mathsf{ap}_f(p) \cdot \gamma = \beta \cdot r\big) \times \big(\mathsf{ap}_f(q) \cdot \gamma = \beta \cdot s\big)$$

We note that to be able to form the type of homomorphisms as we just did, it is crucial to have the computation laws stated propositionally. The recursion principle now becomes a property internal to the type theory and can be expressed compactly as saying that there is a homomorphism into any other algebra $\mathcal{Y}$:

**Definition 21.** *An algebra* $\mathcal{X} : \mathbb{S}\text{-}\mathsf{Alg}_{\mathcal{U}_i}$ satisfies the $\mathbb{S}$-recursion principle *on a universe* $\mathcal{U}_j$ *if for any algebra* $\mathcal{Y} : \mathbb{S}\text{-}\mathsf{Alg}_{\mathcal{U}_j}$ *there exists a homomorphism from* $\mathcal{X}$ *to* $\mathcal{Y}$*:*

$$\mathsf{has}\text{-}\mathbb{S}\text{-}\mathsf{rec}_{\mathcal{U}_j}(\mathcal{X}) := \big(\Pi \mathcal{Y} : \mathbb{S}\text{-}\mathsf{Alg}_{\mathcal{U}_j}\big)\ \mathbb{S}\text{-}\mathsf{Hom}\ \mathcal{X}\ \mathcal{Y}$$

**Definition 22.** *An algebra* $\mathcal{X} : \mathbb{S}_a\text{-}\mathsf{Alg}_{\mathcal{U}_i}$ satisfies the $\mathbb{S}_a$-recursion principle *on a universe* $\mathcal{U}_j$ *if for any algebra* $\mathcal{Y} : \mathbb{S}_a\text{-}\mathsf{Alg}_{\mathcal{U}_j}$ *there exists a homomorphism from* $\mathcal{X}$ *to* $\mathcal{Y}$*:*

$$\mathsf{has}\text{-}\mathbb{S}_a\text{-}\mathsf{rec}_{\mathcal{U}_j}(\mathcal{X}) := \big(\Pi \mathcal{Y} : \mathbb{S}_a\text{-}\mathsf{Alg}_{\mathcal{U}_j}\big)\ \mathbb{S}_a\text{-}\mathsf{Hom}\ \mathcal{X}\ \mathcal{Y}$$

To express the induction principle in a similar fashion, we first need to introduce dependent or *fibered* versions of algebras and algebra homomorphisms:

**Definition 23.** *Define the type of* fibered $\mathbb{S}$-algebras *on a universe* $\mathcal{U}_j$ *over an algebra* $\mathcal{X} : \mathbb{S}\text{-}\mathsf{Alg}_{\mathcal{U}_i}$ *by*

$$\mathbb{S}\text{-}\mathsf{Fib}\text{-}\mathsf{Alg}_{\mathcal{U}_j}\ (C, c, p) := \Sigma_{E:C\to\mathcal{U}_j} \Sigma_{e:E(c)} \big(p^E_*(e) = e\big)$$

**Definition 24.** *Define the type of* fibered $\mathbb{S}_a$-algebras *on a universe* $\mathcal{U}_j$ *over an algebra* $\mathcal{X} : \mathbb{S}_a\text{-}\mathsf{Alg}_{\mathcal{U}_i}$ *by*

$$\mathbb{S}_a\text{-}\mathsf{Fib}\text{-}\mathsf{Alg}_{\mathcal{U}_j}\ (C, c, d, p, q) := \Sigma_{E:C\to\mathcal{U}_j} \Sigma_{u:E(c)} \Sigma_{v:E(d)} \big(p^E_*(u) = v\big) \times \big(q^E_*(u) = v\big)$$

**Definition 25.** *For algebras* $\mathcal{X} : \mathbb{S}\text{-}\mathsf{Alg}_{\mathcal{U}_i}$, $\mathcal{Y} : \mathbb{S}\text{-}\mathsf{Fib}\text{-}\mathsf{Alg}_{\mathcal{U}_j}\ \mathcal{X}$, *define the type of* fibered $\mathbb{S}$-homomorphisms *from* $\mathcal{X}$ *to* $\mathcal{Y}$ *by*

$$\mathbb{S}\text{-}\mathsf{Fib}\text{-}\mathsf{Hom}\ (C, c, p)\ (E, e, q) :=$$
$$\Sigma_{f:(\Pi x:C)E(x)} \Sigma_{\beta: f(c)=e} \big(\mathsf{dap}_f(p) \cdot \beta = \mathsf{ap}_{p^E_*}(\beta) \cdot q\big)$$

Pictorially, the last component witnesses the commuting diagram

$$\begin{array}{ccc} p^E_*(f(c)) & \overset{\mathsf{dap}_f(p)}{\text{———}} & f(c) \\ \mathsf{ap}_{p^E_*}(\beta) \Big| & & \Big| \beta \\ p^E_*(e) & \underset{q}{\text{———}} & e \end{array}$$

**Definition 26.** *For algebras* $\mathcal{X} : \mathbb{S}_a\text{-}\mathsf{Alg}_{\mathcal{U}_i}$, $\mathcal{Y} : \mathbb{S}_a\text{-}\mathsf{Fib}\text{-}\mathsf{Alg}_{\mathcal{U}_j}\ \mathcal{X}$, *define the type of* fibered $\mathbb{S}_a$-homomorphisms *from* $\mathcal{X}$ *to* $\mathcal{Y}$ *by*

$$\mathbb{S}_a\text{-}\mathsf{Fib}\text{-}\mathsf{Hom}\ (C, a, b, p, q)\ (D, c, d, r, s) := \Sigma_{f:(\Pi x:C)E(x)}$$
$$\Sigma_{\beta: f(a)=c} \Sigma_{\gamma: f(b)=d} \big(\mathsf{dap}_f(p) \cdot \gamma = \mathsf{ap}_{p^E_*}(\beta) \cdot r\big) \times$$
$$\big(\mathsf{dap}_f(q) \cdot \gamma = \mathsf{ap}_{q^E_*}(\beta) \cdot s\big)$$

Pictorially, the last two components witness the commuting diagrams

$$\begin{array}{ccc} p^E_*(f(a)) & \overset{\mathsf{dap}_f(p)}{\text{———}} & f(b) \\ \mathsf{ap}_{p^E_*}(\beta) \Big| & & \Big| \gamma \\ p^E_*(c) & \underset{r}{\text{———}} & d \end{array} \qquad \begin{array}{ccc} p^E_*(f(a)) & \overset{\mathsf{dap}_f(q)}{\text{———}} & f(b) \\ \mathsf{ap}_{p^E_*}(\beta) \Big| & & \Big| \gamma \\ p^E_*(c) & \underset{s}{\text{———}} & d \end{array}$$

The induction principle can now be expressed as saying that there is a fibered homomorphism into any fibered algebra $\mathcal{Y}$:

**Definition 27.** *An algebra* $\mathcal{X} : \mathbb{S}\text{-}\mathsf{Alg}_{\mathcal{U}_i}$ satisfies the $\mathbb{S}$-induction principle *on a universe* $\mathcal{U}_j$ *if for any fibered algebra* $\mathcal{Y} : \mathbb{S}\text{-}\mathsf{Alg}_{\mathcal{U}_j}\ \mathcal{X}$ *there exists a fibered homomorphism from* $\mathcal{X}$ *to* $\mathcal{Y}$:

$$\mathsf{has}\text{-}\mathbb{S}\text{-}\mathsf{ind}_{\mathcal{U}_j}(\mathcal{X}) := \big(\Pi \mathcal{Y} : \mathbb{S}\text{-}\mathsf{Fib}\text{-}\mathsf{Alg}_{\mathcal{U}_j}\big)\ \mathbb{S}\text{-}\mathsf{Fib}\text{-}\mathsf{Hom}\ \mathcal{X}\ \mathcal{Y}$$

**Definition 28.** *An algebra* $\mathcal{X} : \mathbb{S}_a\text{-}\mathsf{Alg}_{\mathcal{U}_i}$ satisfies the $\mathbb{S}_a$-induction principle *on universe* $\mathcal{U}_j$ *if for any fibered algebra* $\mathcal{Y} : \mathbb{S}_a\text{-}\mathsf{Alg}_{\mathcal{U}_j}\ \mathcal{X}$ *there exists a fibered homomorphism from* $\mathcal{X}$ *to* $\mathcal{Y}$:

$$\mathsf{has}\text{-}\mathbb{S}_a\text{-}\mathsf{ind}_{\mathcal{U}_j}(\mathcal{X}) := \big(\Pi \mathcal{Y} : \mathbb{S}_a\text{-}\mathsf{Fib}\text{-}\mathsf{Alg}_{\mathcal{U}_j}\big)\ \mathbb{S}_a\text{-}\mathsf{Fib}\text{-}\mathsf{Hom}\ \mathcal{X}\ \mathcal{Y}$$

### 3.4 Relating the two circles

We first note that the notions of $\mathbb{S}$-algebras and $\mathbb{S}_a$-algebras are in fact the same:

**Lemma 29.** *We have a function*

$$\mathbb{S}\text{-}\mathsf{to}\text{-}\mathbb{S}_a\text{-}\mathsf{Alg}_{\mathcal{U}_i} : \mathbb{S}\text{-}\mathsf{Alg}_{\mathcal{U}_i} \to \mathbb{S}_a\text{-}\mathsf{Alg}_{\mathcal{U}_i}$$

*which is an equivalence.*

*Proof.* Define the equivalence between $\mathbb{S}\text{-}\mathsf{Alg}_{\mathcal{U}_i}$ and $\mathbb{S}_a\text{-}\mathsf{Alg}_{\mathcal{U}_i}$ by the quasi-inverses

$$(C, c, p) \mapsto (C, c, c, p, \mathsf{refl}(c))$$
$$(C, a, b, p, q) \mapsto (C, a, p \cdot q^{-1})$$

□

Next, we note that the notions of fibered $\mathbb{S}$-algebras and fibered $\mathbb{S}_a$-algebras are the same, in the following sense:

**Lemma 30.** *For any algebra* $\mathcal{X} : \mathbb{S}\text{-}\mathsf{Alg}_{\mathcal{U}_i}$ *we have a function*

$$\mathbb{S}\text{-}\mathsf{to}\text{-}\mathbb{S}_a\text{-}\mathsf{Fib}\text{-}\mathsf{Alg}_{\mathcal{U}_i}(\mathcal{X}) :$$
$$\mathbb{S}\text{-}\mathsf{Fib}\text{-}\mathsf{Alg}_{\mathcal{U}_i}\ \mathcal{X} \to \mathbb{S}_a\text{-}\mathsf{Fib}\text{-}\mathsf{Alg}_{\mathcal{U}_i}\ \big(\mathbb{S}\text{-}\mathsf{to}\text{-}\mathbb{S}_a\text{-}\mathsf{Alg}_{\mathcal{U}_i}\ \mathcal{X}\big)$$

*which is an equivalence.*

*Proof.* Fix algebra $(C, c, p) : \mathbb{S}\text{-}\mathsf{Alg}_{\mathcal{U}_i}$. Define the equivalence between $\mathbb{S}\text{-}\mathsf{Fib}\text{-}\mathsf{Alg}_{\mathcal{U}_i}\ (C, c, p)$ and $\mathbb{S}_a\text{-}\mathsf{Fib}\text{-}\mathsf{Alg}_{\mathcal{U}_i}\ (C, c, c, p, \mathsf{refl}(c))$ by the quasi-inverses

$$(E, e, q) \mapsto (E, e, e, q, \mathsf{refl}(e))$$
$$(E, a, b, r, s) \mapsto (E, a, r \cdot s^{-1})$$

□

The notions of $\mathbb{S}$-homomorphisms and $\mathbb{S}_a$-homomorphisms also coincide:

**Lemma 31.** *For any algebras* $\mathcal{X} : \mathbb{S}\text{-}\mathsf{Alg}_{\mathcal{U}_i}$, $\mathcal{Y} : \mathbb{S}\text{-}\mathsf{Alg}_{\mathcal{U}_j}$ *we have*

$$\mathbb{S}\text{-}\mathsf{Hom}\ \mathcal{X}\ \mathcal{Y} \simeq \mathbb{S}_a\text{-}\mathsf{Hom}\ \big(\mathbb{S}\text{-}\mathsf{to}\text{-}\mathbb{S}_a\text{-}\mathsf{Alg}_{\mathcal{U}_i}\ \mathcal{X}\big)\ \big(\mathbb{S}\text{-}\mathsf{to}\text{-}\mathbb{S}_a\text{-}\mathsf{Alg}_{\mathcal{U}_i}\ \mathcal{Y}\big)$$

Finally, the respective fibered versions of $\mathbb{S}$-homomorphisms and $\mathbb{S}_a$-homomorphisms coincide:

**Lemma 32.** *For any algebras* $\mathcal{X} : \mathbb{S}\text{-}\mathsf{Alg}_{\mathcal{U}_i}$, $\mathcal{Y} : \mathbb{S}\text{-}\mathsf{Fib}\text{-}\mathsf{Alg}_{\mathcal{U}_j}\ \mathcal{X}$ *we have*

$$\mathbb{S}\text{-}\mathsf{Fib}\text{-}\mathsf{Hom}\ \mathcal{X}\ \mathcal{Y} \simeq$$
$$\mathbb{S}_a\text{-}\mathsf{Fib}\text{-}\mathsf{Hom}\ \big(\mathbb{S}\text{-}\mathsf{to}\text{-}\mathbb{S}_a\text{-}\mathsf{Alg}_{\mathcal{U}_i}\ \mathcal{X}\big)\ \big(\mathbb{S}\text{-}\mathsf{to}\text{-}\mathbb{S}_a\text{-}\mathsf{Fib}\text{-}\mathsf{Alg}_{\mathcal{U}_i}(\mathcal{X})\ \mathcal{Y}\big)$$

We can now show that $\mathbb{S}$-recursion is the same as $\mathbb{S}_a$-recursion, and likewise for induction:

**Lemma 33.** *For any* $\mathcal{X} : \mathbb{S}\text{-}\mathsf{Alg}_{\mathcal{U}_i}$ *we have*

$$\mathsf{has}\text{-}\mathbb{S}\text{-}\mathsf{rec}_{\mathcal{U}_j}(\mathcal{X}) \simeq \mathsf{has}\text{-}\mathbb{S}_a\text{-}\mathsf{rec}_{\mathcal{U}_j}(\mathbb{S}\text{-}\mathsf{to}\text{-}\mathbb{S}_a\text{-}\mathsf{Alg}_{\mathcal{U}_i}(\mathcal{X}))$$
$$\mathsf{has}\text{-}\mathbb{S}\text{-}\mathsf{ind}_{\mathcal{U}_j}(\mathcal{X}) \simeq \mathsf{has}\text{-}\mathbb{S}_a\text{-}\mathsf{ind}_{\mathcal{U}_j}(\mathbb{S}\text{-}\mathsf{to}\text{-}\mathbb{S}_a\text{-}\mathsf{Alg}_{\mathcal{U}_i}(\mathcal{X}))$$

**Corollary 34.** *The* $\mathbb{S}_a$*-algebra* $(\mathbb{S}, \mathsf{base}, \mathsf{base}, \mathsf{loop}, \mathsf{refl}_{\mathbb{S}}(\mathsf{base}))$ *satisfies the* $\mathbb{S}_a$*-induction principle on any universe* $\mathcal{U}_j$.

**Corollary 35.** *The* $\mathbb{S}$*-algebra* $(\mathbb{S}_a, \mathsf{north}, \mathsf{east} \cdot \mathsf{west}^{-1})$ *satisfies the* $\mathbb{S}$*-induction principle on any universe* $\mathcal{U}_j$.

### 3.5 Propositional truncation

Another example of a higher inductive type is the *propositional truncation* $||A|| : \mathcal{U}_i$ of a type $A : \mathcal{U}_i$, investigated in [1] in an extensional setting under the name *bracket types*. Intuitively, $||A||$ represents the "squashing" of $A$ which makes all the elements in $A$ equal. The need for such a type arises when we wish to hide information: having a term $a : A$ is very different from having a $b : ||A||$. In the latter case, we know that the *provable failure* of $A$ to be inhabited, that is, a term of type $A \to \mathbf{0}$, would lead to a contradiction. However, we do not have a generic way of constructing an inhabitant of $A$.

Formally, we define $||A||$ as the higher inductive type generated by a constructor $|\cdot|$, which projects a given element of $A$ down to $||A||$, and a truncation constructor, which states that $||A||$ is indeed a mere proposition[2]:

$$|\cdot| : A \to ||A||$$
$$\mathsf{sq} : \Pi_{x,y:||A||}(x =_{||A||} y)$$

As usual, the recursion principle states that given a structure of the same form, we have a function out of $||A||$ which preserves the constructors:

$$\frac{C : \mathcal{U}_j \qquad c : A \to C \qquad s : \Pi_{x,y:C}(x =_C y)}{\mathsf{rec}_{||A||}(C, c, s) : ||A|| \to C}$$

where for each $a : A$ we have

$$\mathsf{rec}_{||A||}(C, c, s, |a|) \equiv c(a) : C$$

[2] Hence the name *propositional* truncation; see Chpt. 6 of [23] for other kinds of truncation.

and for each $k, l : ||A||$ we have

$$\mathsf{ap}_{\mathsf{rec}_{||A||}(C,c,s)}(\mathsf{sq}(k,l)) = s\big(\mathsf{rec}_{||A||}(C,c,s,k), \mathsf{rec}_{||A||}(C,c,s,l)\big)$$

We note that we are only able to eliminate into types which are themselves mere propositions. This together with Lem. 5 implies that the second computation law always holds. We have included it nonetheless to illustrate the general pattern.

To state the induction principle, we need to suitably generalize the last hypothesis. As before, we note that once the desired map $f : \Pi_{x:||A||}E(x)$ is constructed, it will give us a path from $\mathsf{sq}(k,l)^E_*(f(k))$ to $f(l)$ in $E(l)$ for any $k, l : ||A||$. Hence, $E$ should already come equipped with such a family of paths - except, of course, we have no way of referring to $f(k)$ and $f(l)$ before $f$ is constructed. Thus, we simply require that such a path exists for *all* points $u : E(k)$ and $v : E(l)$:

$$\frac{E : ||A|| \to \mathcal{U}_j \qquad e : \Pi_{a:A}E(|a|) \qquad q : \Pi_{x,y:||A||}\Pi_{u:E(x)}\Pi_{v:E(y)}\big(\mathsf{sq}(x,y)^E_*(u) =_{E(y)} v\big)}{\mathsf{ind}_{||A||}(E,e,q) : \Pi_{x:||A||}E(x)}$$

where for each $a : A$ we have

$$\mathsf{ind}_{||A||}(E,e,q,|a|) \equiv e(a) : E(|a|)$$

and for each $k, l : ||A||$ we have

$$\mathsf{dap}_{\mathsf{ind}_{||A||}(E,e,q)}(\mathsf{sq}(k,l)) = q\big(k, l, \mathsf{ind}_{||A||}(E,e,q,k), \mathsf{ind}_{||A||}(E,e,q,l)\big)$$

The second rule again turns out to always hold, as we will see shortly.

### 3.6 Revisiting the truncation computation laws

We point out that the truncation $||A||$ as defined has its share of unexpected behavior. For instance, as the type $\mathbb{N}$ of natural numbers is inhabited, it follows that $||\mathbb{N}|| = \mathbf{1}$. It is not obvious, however, how to turn $\mathbf{1}$ itself into a truncation of $\mathbb{N}$, since the first computation law ought to hold *definitionally*. More surprising yet is the observation by N. Kraus in [10] that there exists a map $f$ such that $f \circ |\cdot| \equiv \mathsf{id}_{\mathbb{N}}$; this is another somewhat strange side effect of the definitional computation law for $|\cdot|$.

In light of these issues, we follow our methodology for circles and investigate types which "act like the type $||A||$" up to propositional equality. We have the following:

**Definition 36.** *Define the type of* $||A||$-algebras *on a universe* $\mathcal{U}_j$ *as*

$$||A||\text{-}\mathsf{Alg}_{\mathcal{U}_j} :\equiv \Sigma_{C:\mathcal{U}_j}(A \to C) \times \mathsf{is\text{-}prop}(C)$$

A natural definition of an algebra homomorphism between two $||A||$-algebras $(C, c, p)$ and $(D, d, q)$ is a map $f : C \to D$ together with path families

$$\beta : \Pi_{a:A}\big(f(c(a)) = d(a)\big)$$
$$\gamma : \Pi_{x,y:C}\big(\mathsf{ap}_f(p(x,y)) = q(f(x), f(y))\big)$$

However, the type $D$ is a mere proposition. Thus by Lem. 5 and the fact that a family of contractible types is itself contractible, it follows that both of the above types are equivalent to $\mathbf{1}$. Hence, we have the simple definition:

**Definition 37.** *For algebras* $\mathcal{X} : ||A||\text{-}\mathsf{Alg}_{\mathcal{U}_j}$, $\mathcal{Y} : ||A||\text{-}\mathsf{Alg}_{\mathcal{U}_k}$, *define the type of* $||A||$-homomorphisms *from* $\mathcal{X}$ *to* $\mathcal{Y}$ *by*

$$||A||\text{-}\mathsf{Hom}\ (C,c,p)\ (D,d,q) :\equiv C \to D$$

As before, the recursion principle states that there is a homomorphism to any other algebra $\mathcal{Y}$:

**Definition 38.** *An algebra* $\mathcal{X} : ||A||\text{-}\mathsf{Alg}_{\mathcal{U}_j}$ satisfies the recursion principle *on a universe* $\mathcal{U}_k$ *if for any algebra* $\mathcal{Y} : ||A||\text{-}\mathsf{Alg}_{\mathcal{U}_k}$ *there exists a* $||A||$*-homomorphism from* $\mathcal{X}$ *to* $\mathcal{Y}$*:*

$$\mathsf{has}\text{-}||A||\text{-}\mathsf{rec}_{\mathcal{U}_k}(\mathcal{X}) :\equiv \big(\Pi\mathcal{Y} : ||A||\text{-}\mathsf{Alg}_{\mathcal{U}_k}\big)\ ||A||\text{-}\mathsf{Hom}\ \mathcal{X}\ \mathcal{Y}$$

Based on the $||A||$-elimination rule, a natural definition of a fibered algebra over $(C, c, p)$ is a family of types $E : C \to \mathcal{U}_k$ endowed with a function $e : \Pi_{a:A}E(c(a))$ and path family

$$q : \Pi_{x,y:C}\Pi_{u:E(x)}\Pi_{v:E(y)}(p(x,y)^E_*(u) = v)$$

Using the fact that $C$ is a mere proposition, we can show, however, that the above type is equivalent to the condition that $E$ is a family of mere propositions, $\Pi_{x:C}\mathsf{is\text{-}prop}(E(x))$. We can thus define:

**Definition 39.** *Define the type of fibered* $||A||$*-algebras on a universe* $\mathcal{U}_k$ *over* $\mathcal{X} : ||A||\text{-}\mathsf{Alg}_{\mathcal{U}_j}$ *by*

$$||A||\text{-}\mathsf{Fib\text{-}Alg}_{\mathcal{U}_k}\ (C,c,p) :\equiv \Sigma_{E:C\to\mathcal{U}_k}\big(\Pi_{a:A}E(c(a))\big) \times \big(\Pi_{x:C}\mathsf{is\text{-}prop}(E(x))\big)$$

Analogously to the non-fibered case, a natural definition of a fibered $||A||$-homomorphism from $(C, c, p)$ to $(E, e, q)$ is a function $f : \Pi_{x:C}E(x)$ together with path families

$$\beta : \Pi_{a:A}\big(f(c(a)) = e(a)\big)$$
$$\gamma : \Pi_{x,y:C}\big(\mathsf{dap}_f(p(x,y)) = q(x, y, f(x), f(y))\big)$$

Since $E$ is a family of mere propositions, by exactly the same reasoning we get that both of the above types are equivalent to $\mathbf{1}$. Hence, we can define:

**Definition 40.** *For algebras* $\mathcal{X} : ||A||\text{-}\mathsf{Alg}_{\mathcal{U}_j}$, $\mathcal{Y} : ||A||\text{-}\mathsf{Alg}_{\mathcal{U}_k}\ \mathcal{X}$, *define the type of* fibered $||A||$-homomorphisms *from* $\mathcal{X}$ *to* $\mathcal{Y}$ *by*

$$||A||\text{-}\mathsf{Fib\text{-}Hom}\ (C,c,p)\ (E,e,q) :\equiv \Pi_{x:C}E(x)$$

As before, the induction principle states that there is a fibered homomorphism to any fibered algebra $\mathcal{Y}$:

**Definition 41.** *An algebra* $\mathcal{X} : ||A||\text{-}\mathsf{Alg}_{\mathcal{U}_j}$ satisfies the $||A||$-induction principle *on a universe* $\mathcal{U}_k$ *if for any fibered algebra* $\mathcal{Y} : ||A||\text{-}\mathsf{Alg}_{\mathcal{U}_k}\ \mathcal{X}$ *there exists a fibered homomorphism from* $\mathcal{X}$ *to* $\mathcal{Y}$*:*

$$\mathsf{has}\text{-}||A||\text{-}\mathsf{ind}_{\mathcal{U}_k}(\mathcal{X}) :\equiv \big(\Pi\mathcal{Y} : ||A||\text{-}\mathsf{Alg}_{\mathcal{U}_k}\ \mathcal{X}\big)\ ||A||\text{-}\mathsf{Fib\text{-}Hom}\ \mathcal{X}\ \mathcal{Y}$$

It is now easy to show that induction and recursion for $||A||$ are in fact equivalent. As we will see in the next section, this result is an analogue of our main theorem 53. The proof given below for truncations illustrates the basic idea behind the proof of Thm. 53.

We note that since universe levels are cumulative, the technical restriction that $k \geq j$ does not pose a problem.

**Lemma 42.** *For* $A : \mathcal{U}_i$*, the following conditions on an algebra* $\mathcal{X} : ||A||\text{-}\mathsf{Alg}_{\mathcal{U}_j}$ *are equivalent:*

- $\mathcal{X}$ *satisfies the induction principle on the universe* $\mathcal{U}_k$
- $\mathcal{X}$ *satisfies the recursion principle on the universe* $\mathcal{U}_k$

*for* $k \geq j$*. In other words, we have*

$$\mathsf{has}\text{-}||A||\text{-}\mathsf{ind}_{\mathcal{U}_k}(\mathcal{X}) \simeq \mathsf{has}\text{-}||A||\text{-}\mathsf{rec}_{\mathcal{U}_k}(\mathcal{X})$$

*provided* $k \geq j$*. Moreover, the two types above are mere propositions.*

*Proof.* The fact that the types are mere propositions is clear. The direction from right to left is obvious. For the other direction, fix algebras $(C, c, p) : ||A||\text{-}\mathsf{Alg}_{\mathcal{U}_j}$, $(E, e, q) : ||A||\text{-}\mathsf{Fib\text{-}Alg}_{\mathcal{U}_k}\ (C, c, p)$. The total space $\Sigma_{x:C}E(x) : \mathcal{U}_k$ is a mere proposition, we can thus apply recursion with the projection map $a \mapsto (c(a), e(a))$ to get a function $f : C \to \Sigma_{x:C} E(x)$. A homotopy $\alpha : \mathsf{fst} \circ f \sim \mathsf{id}_C$ exists as $C$ is a mere proposition. Applying second projection and transporting gives us a map $x \mapsto \alpha(x)_*^E(\pi_2(f(x)))$ and we are done. □

## 4. W-Suspensions as Homotopy-Initial Algebras

Here we consider a class of higher inductive types which we call W-*suspensions*; informally, they combine Martin-Löf's W-types [18], also known as well-founded trees, with (a generalized form of) suspensions ([23], Chpt. 6.5). Ordinary W-types allow proper induction on the level of points but have no higher-dimensional constructors. Suspensions, on the other hand, only provide vacuous induction on the point level, in the form of two nullary constructors; however, they allow us to specify an arbitrary number of path constructors between these two points. A suitable combination of these two classes of types keeps the phenomenons of induction and higher-dimensionality orthogonal, which gives us a well-behaved elimination principle.

### 4.1 W-suspensions

Formally, given types $A, C : \mathcal{U}_i$, a type family $B : A \to \mathcal{U}_i$, and functions $\mathtt{l}, \mathtt{r} : C \to A$, the W-suspension $\mathsf{W}(A, B, C, \mathtt{l}, \mathtt{r}) : \mathcal{U}_i$ is the higher inductive type generated by the constructors

$$\mathsf{sup} : \Pi_{a:A}\big(B(a) \to \mathsf{W}(A,B,C,\mathtt{l},\mathtt{r})\big) \to \mathsf{W}(A,B,C,\mathtt{l},\mathtt{r})$$
$$\mathsf{cell} : \Pi_{c:C}\Pi_{t:B(\mathtt{l}\ c)\to \mathsf{W}(A,B,C,\mathtt{l},\mathtt{r})}\Pi_{s:B(\mathtt{r}\ c)\to \mathsf{W}(A,B,C,\mathtt{l},\mathtt{r})} \; \mathsf{sup}(\mathtt{l}\ c, t) = \mathsf{sup}(\mathtt{r}\ c, s)$$

From now on we will write W instead of $\mathsf{W}(A, B, C, \mathtt{l}, \mathtt{r})$, unless indicated otherwise.

As in the case of ordinary W-types, the type $A$ can be thought of as the type of labels for points and for any $a : A$, the type $B(a)$ represents the arity of the label $a$, i.e., it is the index type for the arguments of $a$. Similarly, the type $C$ represents the type of labels for paths between points. For any $c : C$, the terms $\mathtt{l}(c)$ and $\mathtt{r}(c)$ determine the respective labels of the left and right endpoints of the paths labeled by $c$. As can be read off from the type of the constructor cell, each label $c : C$ determines a family of paths in W, one for each pair of terms $t : B(\mathtt{l}\ c) \to \mathsf{W}$ and $s : B(\mathtt{r}\ c) \to \mathsf{W}$.

An ordinary W-type $\mathsf{W}_{x:A}B(x)$ arises as a W-suspension in the obvious way by taking $A := A$, $B := B$, $C := \mathbf{0}$, and letting both $\mathtt{l}$ and $\mathtt{r}$ be the canonical function from $\mathbf{0}$ into $A$. We can encode the circle $\mathbb{S}$ by taking $A, C := \mathbf{1}$, $B(-) := \mathbf{0}$, $\mathtt{l}(-) := \star$, $\mathtt{r}(-) := \star$. The circle $\mathbb{S}_a$ arises when we take $A, C := \mathbf{2}$, $B(-) := \mathbf{0}$, $\mathtt{l}(-) := \top$, $\mathtt{r}(-) := \bot$. Other types which can be represented in this form include the interval type, suspensions - hence in particular all the higher spheres $\mathbf{S}^n$ - and of course all ordinary inductive types arising as W-types, e.g., natural numbers, lists, and so on.

As an additional example we consider positive integers modulo two. Let $\mathbf{4}$ be the inductive type with constructors $\mathsf{tt}, \mathsf{tf}, \mathsf{ft}, \mathsf{ff} : \mathbf{4}$. We put $A := \mathbf{4}$; $B(\mathsf{tt}) := \mathbf{0}$, $B(\mathsf{ff}) := \mathbf{0}$, $B(\mathsf{tf}) := \mathbf{1}$, $B(\mathsf{ft}) := \mathbf{1}$; $C := \mathbf{2}$; $\mathtt{l}(\top) := \mathsf{tt}$, $\mathtt{l}(\bot) := \mathsf{ff}$; $\mathtt{r}(\top) := \mathsf{tf}$, $\mathtt{r}(\bot) := \mathsf{ft}$. The nullary point labels tt and ff encode the positive integers one and two, respectively. The unary point label tf represents the function $n \mapsto 2n + 1$ and the unary point label ft represents the function $n \mapsto 2(n + 1)$. The path label $\top$ represents equations of the form $(\mathsf{tt}, -) = (\mathsf{tf}, -)$, to equate all odd positive integers. The path label $\bot$ represents equations of the form $(\mathsf{ff}, -) = (\mathsf{ft}, -)$, to equate all even positive integers.

W-suspensions come with the expected recursion principle: Given terms

- $E : \mathcal{U}_j$
- $e : \Pi_{a:A}(B(a) \to E) \to E$
- $q : \Pi_{c:C}\Pi_{u:B(\mathtt{l}\ c)\to E}\Pi_{v:B(\mathtt{r}\ c)\to E}\big(e(\mathtt{l}\ c, u) = e(\mathtt{r}\ c, v)\big)$

there is a recursor $\mathsf{rec}_\mathsf{W}(E, e, q) : \mathsf{W} \to E$. The recursor satisfies the computation laws

- $\mathsf{rec}_\mathsf{W}(E, e, q, \mathsf{sup}(a, t)) \equiv e\big(a, \mathsf{rec}_\mathsf{W}(E, e, q) \circ t\big)$

for any $a : A, t : B(a) \to \mathsf{W}$ and

- $\mathsf{ap}_{\mathsf{rec}_\mathsf{W}(E,e,q)}(\mathsf{cell}(c, t, s)) = q\Big(c, \mathsf{rec}_\mathsf{W}(E, e, q) \circ t, \mathsf{rec}_\mathsf{W}(E, e, q) \circ s\Big)$

for any $c : C, t : B(\mathtt{l}\ c) \to \mathsf{W}, s : B(\mathtt{r}\ c) \to \mathsf{W}$. Similarly, we have an induction principle: Given terms

- $E : \mathsf{W} \to \mathcal{U}_j$
- $e : \Pi_{a:A}\Pi_{t:B(a)\to\mathsf{W}}\big(\Pi_{b:B(a)}E(t\ b)\big) \to E(\mathsf{sup}(a, t))$
- $q : \Pi_{c:C}\Pi_{t:B(\mathtt{l}\ c)\to\mathsf{W}}\Pi_{u:(\Pi b:B(\mathtt{l}\ c))E(t\ b)}\Pi_{s:B(\mathtt{r}\ c)\to\mathsf{W}} \Pi_{v:(\Pi b:B(\mathtt{r}\ c))E(s\ b)}\big(\mathsf{cell}(c, t, s)_*^E\ e(\mathtt{l}\ c, t, u) = e(\mathtt{r}\ c, s, v)\big)$

there is an inductor $\mathsf{ind}_\mathsf{W}(E, e, q) : \Pi_{w:\mathsf{W}}E(w)$. The inductor satisfies the computation laws

- $\mathsf{ind}_\mathsf{W}(E, e, q, \mathsf{sup}(a, t)) \equiv e\big(a, t, \mathsf{ind}_\mathsf{W}(E, e, q) \circ t\big)$

for any $a : A, t : B(a) \to \mathsf{W}$ and

- $\mathsf{dap}_{\mathsf{ind}_\mathsf{W}(E,e,q)}(\mathsf{cell}(c, t, s)) = q\Big(c, t, \mathsf{ind}_\mathsf{W}(E, e, q) \circ t, s, \mathsf{ind}_\mathsf{W}(E, e, q) \circ s\Big)$

for any $c : C, t : B(\mathtt{l}\ c) \to \mathsf{W}, s : B(\mathtt{r}\ c) \to \mathsf{W}$.

Following the now-familiar pattern, we define W-suspension algebras and homomorphisms:

**Definition 43.** *Define the type of* W-algebras *on a universe* $\mathcal{U}_j$ *by*

$$\mathsf{W\text{-}Alg}_{\mathcal{U}_j}(A, B, C, \mathtt{l}, \mathtt{r}) := \textit{type of triples } (D, d, p)$$

*where*

- $D : \mathcal{U}_j$
- $d : \Pi_{a:A}(B(a) \to D) \to D$
- $p : \Pi_{c:C}\Pi_{u:B(\mathtt{l}\ c)\to D}\Pi_{v:B(\mathtt{r}\ c)\to D}\big(d(\mathtt{l}\ c, u) = d(\mathtt{r}\ c, v)\big)$

As before, we will keep the parameters $A, B, C, \mathtt{l}, \mathtt{r}$ implicit if no confusion arises in doing so.

**Definition 44.** *Define the type of* fibered W-algebras *on a universe* $\mathcal{U}_k$ *over* $\mathcal{X} : \mathsf{W\text{-}Alg}_{\mathcal{U}_j}$ *by*

$$\mathsf{W\text{-}Fib\text{-}Alg}_{\mathcal{U}_k}(D, d, p) := \textit{type of triples } (E, e, q)$$

*where*

- $E : D \to \mathcal{U}_k$
- $e : \Pi_{a:A}\Pi_{t:B(a)\to D}\big(\Pi_{b:B(a)}E(t\ b)\big) \to E(d(a, t))$
- $q : \Pi_{c:C}\Pi_{t:B(\mathtt{l}\ c)\to D}\Pi_{s:B(\mathtt{r}\ c)\to D}\Pi_{u:(\Pi b:B(\mathtt{l}\ c))E(t\ b)} \Pi_{v:(\Pi b:B(\mathtt{r}\ c))E(s\ b)}\Big(p(c, t, s)_*^E\ e(\mathtt{l}\ c, t, u) = e(\mathtt{r}\ c, s, v)\Big)$

In order to express the type of homomorphisms between two W-algebras, we again need to use propositional instead of definitional equality.

**Definition 45.** *For* $\mathcal{X} : \mathsf{W\text{-}Alg}_{\mathcal{U}_j}$ *and* $\mathcal{Y} : \mathsf{W\text{-}Alg}_{\mathcal{U}_k}$, *define the type of* W-homomorphisms *from* $\mathcal{X}$ *to* $\mathcal{Y}$ *by*

$$\mathsf{W\text{-}Hom}\ (D, d, p)\ (E, e, q) := \textit{type of triples } (f, \beta, \theta)$$

*where*

- $f : D \to E$
- $\beta : \Pi_{a:A}\Pi_{t:B(a)\to D}\big(f(d(a, t)) = e(a, f \circ t)\big)$

- $\theta : \Pi_{c:C}\Pi_{t:B(\mathtt{l}\ c)\to D}\Pi_{s:B(\mathtt{r}\ c)\to D}\Big(\mathsf{ap}_f(p(c,t,s)) = \beta(\mathtt{l}\ c,t) \cdot q(c, f\circ t, f\circ s) \cdot \beta(\mathtt{r}\ c,s)^{-1}\Big)$

Pictorially, $\theta(c,t,s)$ witnesses the commuting diagram:

$$\begin{array}{ccc} f(d(\mathtt{l}\ c,t)) & \xrightarrow{\quad \mathsf{ap}_f(p_{c,t,s}) \quad} & f(d(\mathtt{r}\ c,s)) \\ \Big\| \beta_{\mathtt{l}(c),t} & & \beta_{\mathtt{r}(c),s} \Big\| \\ e(\mathtt{l}\ c, f\circ t) & \xrightarrow[\quad q_{c,f\circ t,f\circ s} \quad]{} & e(\mathtt{r}\ c, f\circ s) \end{array}$$

**Definition 46.** *For $\mathcal{X}$ : $\mathsf{W\text{-}Alg}_{\mathcal{U}_j}$ and $\mathcal{Y}$ : $\mathsf{W\text{-}Fib\text{-}Alg}_{\mathcal{U}_k}$ $\mathcal{X}$, define the type of fibered* W-homomorphisms *from $\mathcal{X}$ to $\mathcal{Y}$ by*

$$\mathsf{W\text{-}Fib\text{-}Hom}\ (D,d,p)\ (E,e,q) :\equiv \textit{type of triples } (f,\beta,\theta)$$

*where*

- $f : \Pi_{x:D}E(x)$
- $\beta : \Pi_{a:A}\Pi_{t:B(a)\to D}\big(f(d(a,t)) = e(a,t,f\circ t)\big)$
- $\theta : \Pi_{c:C}\Pi_{t:B(\mathtt{l}\ c)\to D}\Pi_{s:B(\mathtt{r}\ c)\to D}\Big(\mathsf{dap}_f(p(c,t,s)) = \mathsf{ap}_{p(c,t,s)^E_*}(\beta(\mathtt{l}\ c,t)) \cdot q(c,t,s,f\circ t,f\circ s) \cdot \beta(\mathtt{r}\ c,s)^{-1}\Big)$

Pictorially, $\theta(c,t,s)$ witnesses the commuting diagram:

$$\begin{array}{ccc} (p_{c,t,s})^E_*(f(d(\mathtt{l}\ c,t))) & \xrightarrow{\quad \mathsf{dap}_f(p_{c,t,s}) \quad} & f(d(\mathtt{r}\ c,s)) \\ \Big\| \mathsf{ap}_{p(c,t,s)^E_*}(\beta_{\mathtt{l}(c),t}) & & \beta_{\mathtt{r}(c),s} \Big\| \\ (p_{c,t,s})^E_*(e(\mathtt{l}\ c,t,f\circ t)) & \xrightarrow[\quad q_{c,t,s,f\circ t,f\circ s} \quad]{} & e(\mathtt{r}\ c,s,f\circ s) \end{array}$$

The recursion and induction principles are defined as usual:

**Definition 47.** *An algebra $\mathcal{X}$ : $\mathsf{W\text{-}Alg}_{\mathcal{U}_j}$* satisfies the recursion principle *on a universe $\mathcal{U}_k$ if for any algebra $\mathcal{Y}$ : $\mathsf{W\text{-}Alg}_{\mathcal{U}_k}$ there exists a* W*-homomorphism from $\mathcal{X}$ to $\mathcal{Y}$:*

$$\mathsf{has\text{-}W\text{-}rec}_{\mathcal{U}_k}(\mathcal{X}) :\equiv \big(\Pi\mathcal{Y} : \mathsf{W\text{-}Alg}_{\mathcal{U}_k}\big)\ \mathsf{W\text{-}Hom}\ \mathcal{X}\ \mathcal{Y}$$

**Definition 48.** *An algebra $\mathcal{X}$ : $\mathsf{W\text{-}Alg}_{\mathcal{U}_j}$* satisfies the induction principle *on a universe $\mathcal{U}_k$ if for any fibered algebra $\mathcal{Y}$ : $\mathsf{W\text{-}Alg}_{\mathcal{U}_k}$ $\mathcal{X}$ there exists a fibered* W*-homomorphism from $\mathcal{X}$ to $\mathcal{Y}$:*

$$\mathsf{has\text{-}W\text{-}ind}_{\mathcal{U}_k}(\mathcal{X}) :\equiv \big(\Pi\mathcal{Y} : \mathsf{W\text{-}Fib\text{-}Alg}_{\mathcal{U}_k}\ \mathcal{X}\big)\ \mathsf{W\text{-}Fib\text{-}Hom}\ \mathcal{X}\ \mathcal{Y}$$

We will also need the following uniqueness properties which state that any two (fibered) homomorphisms into any (fibered) algebra $\mathcal{Y}$ are equal:

**Definition 49.** *An algebra $\mathcal{X}$ : $\mathsf{W\text{-}Alg}_{\mathcal{U}_j}$* satisfies the recursion uniqueness principle *on a universe $\mathcal{U}_k$ if for any other algebra $\mathcal{Y}$ : $\mathsf{W\text{-}Alg}_{\mathcal{U}_k}$ the type of* W*-homomorphisms from $\mathcal{X}$ to $\mathcal{Y}$ is a mere proposition:*

$$\mathsf{has\text{-}W\text{-}rec\text{-}uniq}_{\mathcal{U}_k}(\mathcal{X}) :\equiv \big(\Pi\mathcal{Y} : \mathsf{W\text{-}Alg}_{\mathcal{U}_k}\big)\ \mathsf{is\text{-}prop}(\mathsf{W\text{-}Hom}\ \mathcal{X}\ \mathcal{Y})$$

**Definition 50.** *An algebra $\mathcal{X}$ : $\mathsf{W\text{-}Alg}_{\mathcal{U}_j}$* satisfies the induction uniqueness principle *on a universe $\mathcal{U}_k$ if for any fibered algebra $\mathcal{Y}$ : $\mathsf{W\text{-}Alg}_{\mathcal{U}_k}$ $\mathcal{X}$ the type of* W*-homomorphisms from $\mathcal{X}$ to $\mathcal{Y}$ is a mere proposition:*

$$\mathsf{has\text{-}W\text{-}ind\text{-}uniq}_{\mathcal{U}_k}(\mathcal{X}) :\equiv \big(\Pi\mathcal{Y} : \mathsf{W\text{-}Fib\text{-}Alg}_{\mathcal{U}_k}\ \mathcal{X}\big)\ \mathsf{is\text{-}prop}(\mathsf{W\text{-}Fib\text{-}Hom}\ \mathcal{X}\ \mathcal{Y})$$

We now define the key concept of homotopy-initiality [3], which translates the notion of existence plus uniqueness into the homotopy type-theoretic setting as contractibility:

**Definition 51.** *An algebra $\mathcal{X}$ : $\mathsf{W\text{-}Alg}_{\mathcal{U}_j}$ is* homotopy-initial *on a universe $\mathcal{U}_k$ if for any other algebra $\mathcal{Y}$ : $\mathsf{W\text{-}Alg}_{\mathcal{U}_k}$ the type of* W*-homomorphisms from $\mathcal{X}$ to $\mathcal{Y}$ is contractible:*

$$\mathsf{is\text{-}W\text{-}hinit}_{\mathcal{U}_k}(\mathcal{X}) :\equiv \big(\Pi\mathcal{Y} : \mathsf{W\text{-}Alg}_{\mathcal{U}_k}\big)\ \mathsf{is\text{-}contr}(\mathsf{W\text{-}Hom}\ \mathcal{X}\ \mathcal{Y})$$

**Lemma 52.** *For any $\mathcal{X}$ : $\mathsf{W\text{-}Alg}_{\mathcal{U}_j}$ we have*

$$\mathsf{is\text{-}W\text{-}hinit}_{\mathcal{U}_k}(\mathcal{X}) \simeq \mathsf{has\text{-}W\text{-}rec}_{\mathcal{U}_k}(\mathcal{X}) \times \mathsf{has\text{-}W\text{-}rec\text{-}uniq}_{\mathcal{U}_k}(\mathcal{X})$$

### 4.2 Main result

Our main result establishes the equivalence between the universal property of being homotopy-initial and the satisfaction of the induction principle:

**Theorem 53.** *For $A, C : \mathcal{U}_i$, $B : A \to \mathcal{U}_i$, $\mathtt{l}, \mathtt{r} : C \to A$, the following conditions on an algebra $\mathcal{X}$ : $\mathsf{W\text{-}Alg}_{\mathcal{U}_j}(A,B,C,\mathtt{l},\mathtt{r})$ are equivalent:*

- *$\mathcal{X}$ satisfies the induction principle on the universe $\mathcal{U}_k$*
- *$\mathcal{X}$ is homotopy-initial on the universe $\mathcal{U}_k$*

*for $k \geq j$. In other words, we have*

$$\mathsf{has\text{-}W\text{-}ind}_{\mathcal{U}_k}(\mathcal{X}) \simeq \mathsf{is\text{-}W\text{-}hinit}_{\mathcal{U}_k}(\mathcal{X})$$

*provided $k \geq j$. Moreover, the two types above are mere propositions.*

By Lem. 52, homotopy-intiality is equivalent to the principles of recursion plus recursion uniqueness. The uniqueness condition is necessary since in general, the recursion principle does not fully determine an inductive type: the recursion principle for the circle, for example, is also satisfied by the disjoint union of *two* circles.

Before we proceed to the proof of the general case, we look at the analogue of the main theorem for propositional truncations. We can define homotopy-initial $||A||$-algebras as expected:

**Definition 54.** *An algebra $\mathcal{X}$ : $||A||\text{-}\mathsf{Alg}_{\mathcal{U}_j}$ is* homotopy-initial *on a universe $\mathcal{U}_k$ if for any other algebra $\mathcal{Y}$ : $||A||\text{-}\mathsf{Alg}_{\mathcal{U}_k}$ the type of $||A||$-homomorphisms from $\mathcal{X}$ to $\mathcal{Y}$ is contractible:*

$$\mathsf{is\text{-}}||A||\mathsf{\text{-}hinit}_{\mathcal{U}_k}(\mathcal{X}) :\equiv \big(\Pi\mathcal{Y} : ||A||\text{-}\mathsf{Alg}_{\mathcal{U}_k}\big)\ \mathsf{is\text{-}contr}(||A||\text{-}\mathsf{Hom}\ \mathcal{X}\ \mathcal{Y})$$

Since we operate in the setting of mere propositions, we do not have to formulate an analogous uniqueness condition, which is uniquely satisfied and hence redundant. Instead, we have:

**Lemma 55.** *For any $\mathcal{X}$ : $||A||\text{-}\mathsf{Alg}_{\mathcal{U}_j}$ we have*

$$\mathsf{is\text{-}}||A||\mathsf{\text{-}hinit}_{\mathcal{U}_k}(\mathcal{X}) \simeq \mathsf{has\text{-}}||A||\mathsf{\text{-}rec}_{\mathcal{U}_k}(\mathcal{X})$$

Thus, Lem. 42 is the analogue of our main result for truncations.

***Proof outline*** A crucial step of the proof is the characterization of the path space $\mu = \nu$ between two (fibered) W-homomorphisms $\mu, \nu : \mathcal{X} \to \mathcal{Y}$ in a more explicit form. For simplicity we only consider the non-fibered case here. We recall that a homomorphism between two algebras $(D,d,p)$, $(E,e,q)$ is a triple $(f,\beta,\theta)$, where $f : C \to D$ is a function between the carrier types, $\beta$ specifies the behavior of $f$ on the 0-cells, i.e., the value of $f(d(a,t))$, and $\theta$ specifies the behavior of $f$ on the 1-cells, i.e., the value of $\mathsf{ap}_f(p(c,t,s))$.

Using the characterization of paths between tuples together with function extensionality, the path space $(f,\beta,\theta) = (g,\gamma,\phi)$ between two homomorphisms should be equivalent to a type of triples $(\alpha,\eta,\psi)$, where $\alpha : f \sim g$ is a homotopy relating the two underlying mappings, and $\eta, \psi$ relate $\beta$ to $\gamma$ resp. $\theta$ to $\phi$ in an appropriate way. We will call such a triple $(\alpha, \eta, \psi)$ a W-*cell*. The recursion uniqueness condition on an algebra $\mathcal{X}$ can then be equivalently expressed as saying that for any algebra $\mathcal{Y}$ and homomorphisms $\mu, \nu$ from $\mathcal{X}$ to $\mathcal{Y}$, there exists a W-cell between $\mu$ and $\nu$.

We point out that this uniqueness condition can itself be understood as a certain form of induction, albeit a very specific one. The existence of a W-cell between any two homomorphisms $(f, \beta, \theta)$, $(g, \gamma, \phi)$ in particular guarantees the existence of a dependent function $\alpha : \Pi_{x:X}(f(x) = g(x))$ - the "inductor". The behavior of $\alpha$ on the 0-cells, i.e., the value of $\alpha(d(a, t))$, is specified by the term $\eta$, which thus serves as a witness for the first "computation rule". Finally, the behavior of $\alpha$ on the 1-cells, i.e., the value of $\mathsf{dap}_\alpha(p(c, t, s))$, is specified by the term $\psi$, which hence serves as a witness for the second "computation rule." We observe the same pattern in the case of propositional truncations: homomorphisms between $||A||$-algebras are just maps between the carrier types, hence there are no "computation rules" to speak of. A cell between $||A||$-homomorphisms $f$ and $g$ would just be a homotopy $\alpha : \Pi_{x:X}(f(x) = g(x))$ - the "inductor". The existence of such $\alpha$ is of course a moot point since we work with mere propositions.

We can thus see why the full induction principle for W-suspensions gives us homotopy-initiality: the latter essentially amounts to the recursion principle plus a specific form of induction, both of which are implied by the general induction principle. The hardest part of the proof is showing the converse, i.e., that the general induction principle can be recovered from homotopy-initiality.

We are now ready to give the formal definition of a W-cell. There is an analogous definition of a *fibered* W-*cell*, which uses the fibered versions of W-algebras and homomorphisms, and for which we refer the reader to [21].

**Definition 56.** *For algebras* $\mathcal{X}$ : $\mathsf{W\text{-}Alg}_{\mathcal{U}_j}$, $\mathcal{Y}$ : $\mathsf{W\text{-}Alg}_{\mathcal{U}_k}$ *and homomorphisms* $\mu, \nu$ : $\mathsf{W\text{-}Hom}\ \mathcal{X}\ \mathcal{Y}$*, we define the type of* W-cells *between* $\mu$ *and* $\nu$ *by*

$$\mathsf{W\text{-}Cell}\ (D, d, p)\ (E, e, q)\ (f, \beta, \theta)\ (g, \gamma, \phi) :=$$
$$\textit{type of triples}\ (\alpha, \eta, \psi)$$

*where*

- $\alpha : f \sim g$
- $\eta : \Pi_{a:A}\Pi_{t:B(a)\to D}\Big(\alpha(d(a,t)) = \beta(a,t) \cdot \mathsf{ap}_{e(a)}({}^{\Pi}\mathsf{E}^{=}(\alpha \circ t)) \cdot \gamma(a,t)^{-1}\Big)$
- $\psi$ *asserts the commutativity of the diagram in Fig. 1 for any* $c : C, t : B(\mathtt{l}\ c) \to D, s : B(\mathtt{r}\ c) \to D$.

Pictorially, $\eta(a, t)$ witnesses the commuting diagram:

$$\begin{array}{ccc} f(d(a,t)) & \xrightarrow{\ \alpha(d(a,t))\ } & g(d(a,t)) \\ \Big| \beta(a,t) & & \Big| \gamma(a,t) \\ e(a, f \circ t) & \xrightarrow[\ \mathsf{ap}_{e(a)}({}^{\Pi}\mathsf{E}^{=}(\alpha \circ t))\ ]{} & e(a, g \circ t) \end{array}$$

We will often leave the algebra arguments to a W-cell implicit.

*Remark:* Although the diagram in Fig. 1 does not explicitly mention the term $\mathsf{dap}_\alpha(p(c, t, s))$, it nevertheless specifies its value uniquely since this term is expressible using $\mathsf{nat}(\alpha, p(c, t, s))$.

**Lemma 57.** *For algebras* $\mathcal{X}$ : $\mathsf{W\text{-}Alg}_{\mathcal{U}_j}$, $\mathcal{Y}$ : $\mathsf{W\text{-}Alg}_{\mathcal{U}_k}$ *and homomorphisms* $\mu, \nu$ : $\mathsf{W\text{-}Hom}\ \mathcal{X}\ \mathcal{Y}$*, the path space* $\mu = \nu$ *is equivalent to the type of* W-cells *between* $\mu$ *and* $\nu$*:*

$$\mu = \nu \ \simeq\ \mathsf{W\text{-}Cell}\ \mu\ \nu$$

The proof of the main result now consists of the following steps:

1) *Show that the induction principle implies the recursion principle, that is for any* $\mathcal{X}$ : $\mathsf{W\text{-}Alg}_{\mathcal{U}_j}$ *we have*

$$\mathsf{has\text{-}W\text{-}ind}_{\mathcal{U}_k}(\mathcal{X}) \to \mathsf{has\text{-}W\text{-}rec}_{\mathcal{U}_k}(\mathcal{X})$$

2) *Show that the induction principle implies both uniqueness conditions, that is for any* $\mathcal{X}$ : $\mathsf{W\text{-}Alg}_{\mathcal{U}_j}$ *we have:*

$$\mathsf{has\text{-}W\text{-}ind}_{\mathcal{U}_k}(\mathcal{X}) \to \mathsf{has\text{-}W\text{-}ind\text{-}uniq}_{\mathcal{U}_k}(\mathcal{X})$$
$$\mathsf{has\text{-}W\text{-}ind}_{\mathcal{U}_k}(\mathcal{X}) \to \mathsf{has\text{-}W\text{-}rec\text{-}uniq}_{\mathcal{U}_k}(\mathcal{X})$$

3) *Show that the recursion plus recursion uniqueness principles imply the induction principle, that is for any* $\mathcal{X}$ : $\mathsf{W\text{-}Alg}_{\mathcal{U}_j}$ *we have:*

$$\mathsf{has\text{-}W\text{-}rec}_{\mathcal{U}_k}(\mathcal{X}) \times \mathsf{has\text{-}W\text{-}rec\text{-}uniq}_{\mathcal{U}_k}(\mathcal{X}) \to \mathsf{has\text{-}W\text{-}ind}_{\mathcal{U}_k}(\mathcal{X})$$

Using Lem. 52 we thus obtain a logical equivalence between $\mathsf{has\text{-}W\text{-}ind}_{\mathcal{U}_k}(\mathcal{X})$ and $\mathsf{is\text{-}W\text{-}hinit}_{\mathcal{U}_k}(\mathcal{X})$. It remains to show that both of these types are mere propositions. The latter is a mere proposition by Lem. 6. To show that $\mathsf{has\text{-}W\text{-}ind}_{\mathcal{U}_k}(\mathcal{X})$ is a mere proposition, it is sufficient to do so under the assumption that it is inhabited. Since $\mathcal{X}$ satisfies the induction principle, by the second step it satisfies the induction uniqueness principle. This means that for any fibered algebra $\mathcal{Y}$, the type $\mathsf{W\text{-}Fib\text{-}Hom}\ \mathcal{X}\ \mathcal{Y}$ is a mere proposition. Since a family of mere propositions is itself a mere proposition, this finishes the proof.

We now sketch the proof of the crucial part, step three. Fix an algebra $(D, d, p)$ : $\mathsf{W\text{-}Alg}_{\mathcal{U}_j}$ and assume that $\mathsf{has\text{-}W\text{-}rec}_{\mathcal{U}_k}(D, d, p)$ and $\mathsf{has\text{-}W\text{-}rec\text{-}uniq}_{\mathcal{U}_k}(D, d, p)$ hold. Fix any algebra $(E, e, q)$ fibered over $(D, d, p)$. In order to apply the recursion principle, we need to turn this into a non-fibered algebra $(E', e', q')$. The first component is easy: the only reasonable choice we have is to put $E' := \Sigma_{x:D}E(x)$; we note that since $D : \mathcal{U}_j$, $E : D \to \mathcal{U}_k$, and $j \leq k$, we indeed have $\Sigma_{x:D}E(x) : \mathcal{U}_k$ as needed. For the second component, we put $e'(a, u) := \big(d(a, \pi_1 \circ u), e(a, \pi_1 \circ u, \pi_2 \circ u)\big)$. The last component we omit for brevity. The recursion principle then gives us a homomorphism $(f, \beta, \theta)$, where in particular $f : D \to \Sigma_{x:D}E(x)$. We next show that the function $\pi_1 \circ f$ is in fact the identity on $D$ (up to a homotopy). We can do this by endowing both of the functions $\pi_1 \circ f$ and $\mathsf{id}_D$ with a homomorphism structure on the algebra $(D, d, p)$; by the recursion uniqueness principle it then follows that these homomorphisms are equal, and in particular they are equal as maps. Thus we have a homotopy $\alpha : \pi_1 \circ f \sim \mathsf{id}_D$ and the underlying map of our desired fibered homomorphism can be defined as $x \mapsto \alpha(x)_*^E(\pi_2(f(x)))$. Endowing this map with a homomorphism structure involves a significant amount of higher path manipulations.

To illustrate some of the issues that arise when dealing with higher paths, we show the proof of step one. Fix an algebra $(D, d, p)$ : $\mathsf{W\text{-}Alg}_{\mathcal{U}_j}$ and assume that $\mathsf{has\text{-}W\text{-}ind}_{\mathcal{U}_k}(D, d, p)$ holds. Fix any other algebra $(E, e, q)$. In order to apply the induction principle, we need to turn this into a fibered algebra $(E', e', q')$. The first two components are easy: put $E'(x) := E$ and $e'(a, t, u) := e(a, u)$. For the last component, we note that the transport between any two fibers of a constant type family is constant. We can thus define $q'(c, t, s, u, v)$ to be the path in Fig. 2 a). The induction principle then gives us a map $f : D \to E$, a path family $\beta : \Pi_{a:C}\Pi_{t:B(a)\to D}\big(f(d(a, t)) = e(a, f \circ t)\big)$, and for any $c : C$,

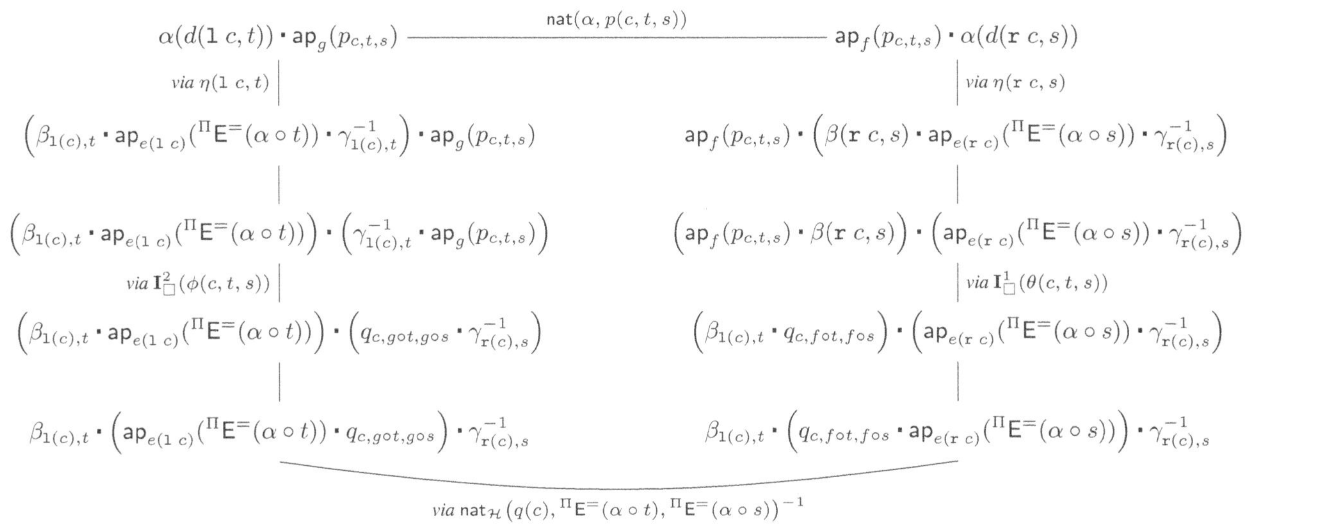


**Figure 1.** Diagram for the definition of a W-cell.

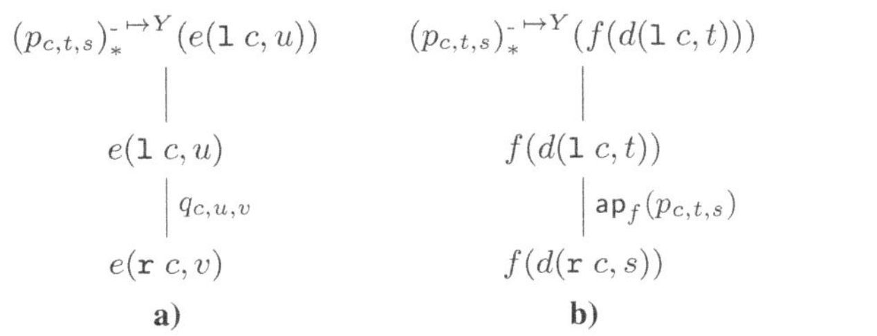


**Figure 2.**

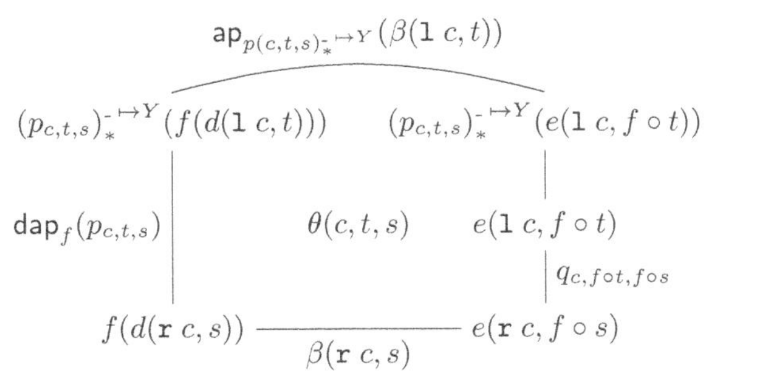


**Figure 3.**

$t : B(\mathtt{l}\ c) \to D$, $s : B(\mathtt{r}\ c) \to D$ a witness $\theta(c,t,s)$ for the commutativity of the diagram in Fig. 3. Using path induction we can express $\mathsf{dap}_f(p_{c,t,s})$ equivalently as the path in Fig. 2 b). Thus the outer rectangle in the diagram in Fig. 4 commutes. Suitable path induction shows that rectangle $A$ commutes; hence rectangle $B$ commutes too and we are done.

### 4.3 Definability

We now show how to derive the analogue of our main result for the circle $\mathbb{S}$; the cases of $\mathbb{S}_a$ and other inductive types presentable as W-suspensions follow the same methodology. In the rest of this section we work with a specific W-suspension $\mathsf{W}(A, B, C, \mathtt{l}, \mathtt{r}) : \mathcal{U}_0$ where $A, C :\equiv \mathbf{1}$, $B(-) :\equiv \mathbf{0}$, $\mathtt{l}(-) :\equiv \star$, $\mathtt{r}(-) :\equiv \star$.

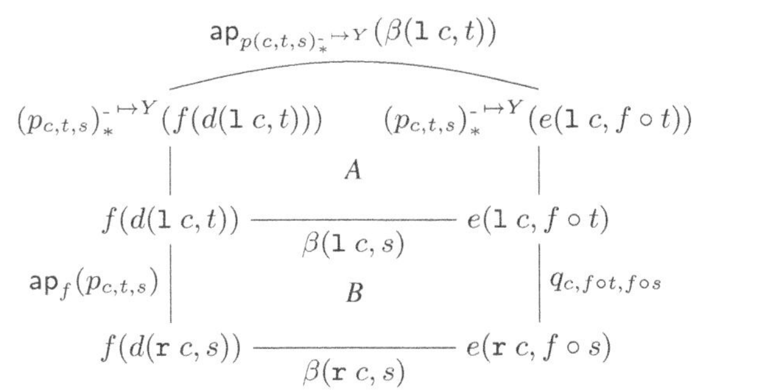


**Figure 4.**

**Definition 58.** *An algebra* $\mathcal{X} : \mathbb{S}\text{-}\mathsf{Alg}_{\mathcal{U}_j}$ *is* homotopy-initial *on a universe* $\mathcal{U}_k$ *if for any other algebra* $\mathcal{Y} : \mathbb{S}\text{-}\mathsf{Alg}_{\mathcal{U}_k}$ *the type of* $\mathbb{S}$-*homomorphisms from* $\mathcal{X}$ *to* $\mathcal{Y}$ *is contractible:*

$$\mathsf{is}\text{-}\mathbb{S}\text{-}\mathsf{hinit}_{\mathcal{U}_k}(\mathcal{X}) :\equiv \left(\Pi\mathcal{Y} : \mathbb{S}\text{-}\mathsf{Alg}_{\mathcal{U}_k}\right) \mathsf{is}\text{-}\mathsf{contr}(\mathbb{S}\text{-}\mathsf{Hom}\ \mathcal{X}\ \mathcal{Y})$$

**Lemma 59.** *We have a function*

$$\mathbb{S}\text{-}\mathsf{to}\text{-}\mathsf{W}\text{-}\mathsf{Alg}_{\mathcal{U}_i} : \mathbb{S}\text{-}\mathsf{Alg}_{\mathcal{U}_i} \to \mathsf{W}\text{-}\mathsf{Alg}_{\mathcal{U}_i}$$

*which is an equivalence.*

*Proof.* We define the function by the mapping

$$(D, d, p) \mapsto \left(D, \lambda_a\lambda_t d, \lambda_c\lambda_t\lambda_s p\right)$$

It is not hard to see that this is an equivalence. □

**Lemma 60.** *For any algebra* $\mathcal{X} : \mathbb{S}\text{-}\mathsf{Alg}_{\mathcal{U}_i}$ *we have a function*

$$\mathbb{S}\text{-}\mathsf{to}\text{-}\mathsf{W}\text{-}\mathsf{Fib}\text{-}\mathsf{Alg}_{\mathcal{U}_i}(\mathcal{X}) : \mathbb{S}\text{-}\mathsf{Fib}\text{-}\mathsf{Alg}_{\mathcal{U}_i}\ \mathcal{X} \to \mathsf{W}\text{-}\mathsf{Fib}\text{-}\mathsf{Alg}_{\mathcal{U}_i}\left(\mathbb{S}\text{-}\mathsf{to}\text{-}\mathsf{W}\text{-}\mathsf{Alg}_{\mathcal{U}_i}\ \mathcal{X}\right)$$

*which is an equivalence.*

*Proof.* Fix an algebra $(D, d, p) : \mathbb{S}\text{-}\mathsf{Alg}_{\mathcal{U}_i}$. We define the function by the mapping

$$(E, e, q) \mapsto \left(E, \lambda_a\lambda_t\lambda_u e, \lambda_c\lambda_t\lambda_u\lambda_s\lambda_v q\right)$$

It is not hard to see that this is an equivalence. □

**Lemma 61.** *For any algebras* $\mathcal{X} : \mathbb{S}\text{-Alg}_{\mathcal{U}_i}$, $\mathcal{Y} : \mathbb{S}\text{-Alg}_{\mathcal{U}_j}$ *we have*

$$\mathbb{S}\text{-Hom}\ \mathcal{X}\ \mathcal{Y} \simeq \text{W-Hom}\ (\mathbb{S}\text{-to-W-Alg}_{\mathcal{U}_i}\ \mathcal{X})\ (\mathbb{S}\text{-to-W-Alg}_{\mathcal{U}_i}\ \mathcal{Y})$$

**Lemma 62.** *For any algebras* $\mathcal{X} : \mathbb{S}\text{-Alg}_{\mathcal{U}_i}$, $\mathcal{Y} : \mathbb{S}\text{-Fib-Alg}_{\mathcal{U}_j}\ \mathcal{X}$ *we have*

$$\mathbb{S}\text{-Fib-Hom}\ \mathcal{X}\ \mathcal{Y} \simeq$$
$$\text{W-Fib-Hom}\ (\mathbb{S}\text{-to-W-Alg}_{\mathcal{U}_i}\ \mathcal{X})\ (\mathbb{S}\text{-to-W-Fib-Alg}_{\mathcal{U}_i}(\mathcal{X})\ \mathcal{Y})$$

**Lemma 63.** *For any* $\mathcal{X} : \mathbb{S}\text{-Alg}_{\mathcal{U}_i}$ *we have*

$$\text{has-}\mathbb{S}\text{-rec}_{\mathcal{U}_j}(\mathcal{X}) \simeq \text{has-W-rec}_{\mathcal{U}_j}(\mathbb{S}\text{-to-W-Alg}_{\mathcal{U}_i}(\mathcal{X}))$$
$$\text{has-}\mathbb{S}\text{-ind}_{\mathcal{U}_j}(\mathcal{X}) \simeq \text{has-W-ind}_{\mathcal{U}_j}(\mathbb{S}\text{-to-W-Alg}_{\mathcal{U}_i}(\mathcal{X}))$$
$$\text{is-}\mathbb{S}\text{-hinit}_{\mathcal{U}_j}(\mathcal{X}) \simeq \text{is-W-hinit}_{\mathcal{U}_j}(\mathbb{S}\text{-to-W-Alg}_{\mathcal{U}_i}(\mathcal{X}))$$

**Corollary 64.** *For an algebra* $\mathcal{X} : \mathbb{S}\text{-Alg}_{\mathcal{U}_i}$, *the following conditions are equivalent:*

- $\mathcal{X}$ *satisfies the induction principle on the universe* $\mathcal{U}_j$
- $\mathcal{X}$ *is homotopy-initial on the universe* $\mathcal{U}_j$

*In other words, we have*

$$\text{has-}\mathbb{S}\text{-ind}_{\mathcal{U}_j}(\mathcal{X}) \simeq \text{is-}\mathbb{S}\text{-hinit}_{\mathcal{U}_j}(\mathcal{X})$$

*Moreover, the two types above are mere propositions.*

*Proof.* We use Lem. 63 and 53. □

## 5. Conclusion

We have investigated higher inductive types with propositional computational behavior and shown that they can be equivalently characterized as homotopy-initial algebras. We have stated and proved this result for propositional truncations and for the so-called W-suspensions, which subsume a number of other interesting cases - ordinary W-types, the unit circle $\mathbf{S}^1$, the interval type $\mathbf{I}$, all suspensions, and thus all the higher spheres $\mathbf{S}^n$. The characterization of these individual types as homotopy-initial algebras can be easily obtained as a corollary to our main theorem. Furthermore, we can readily apply the method presented here to obtain an analogous result for set truncations and set quotients. We conjecture that similar results can be established for other higher inductive types - such as homotopy (co)limits, tori, group quotients, or real numbers - following the same methodology. We are planning to formalize the results presented here in the Coq proof assistant.

Finally, we remark that the entire field of Homotopy Type Theory is a subject of intense research and many questions pertaining to higher inductive types and univalence are yet to be satisfactorily answered. Two important open problems are finding a unifying schema for general higher inductive types (see [16] for progress towards this goal) and developing a computational interpretation of HoTT (partially answered by the cubical set model [4]).

## Acknowledgments

Thanks to Profs. Steve Awodey and Frank Pfenning. Support for this research was provided by the Fundação para a Ciência e a Tecnologia (Portuguese Foundation for Science and Technology) through the Carnegie Mellon Portugal Program, as well as by the National Science Foundation under award No. NSF-CCF-DMS 1351344. Any opinions, findings and conclusions or recommendations expressed in this material are those of the author and do not necessarily reflect the views of the National Science Foundation.

## References

[1] S. Awodey and A. Bauer. Propositions as [types]. *Journal of Logic and Computation*, 14(4):447–471, 2004.

[2] S. Awodey and M. Warren. Homotopy-theoretic models of identity types. *Mathematical Proceedings of the Cambridge Philosophical Society*, 146(1):45–55, 2009.

[3] S. Awodey, N. Gambino, and K. Sojakova. Inductive types in Homotopy Type Theory. In *Logic in Computer Science (LICS 2012)*, pages 95–104. IEEE Computer Society, 2012.

[4] M. Bezem, T. Coquand, and S. Huber. A model of type theory in cubical sets, 2014. Available at `http://www.cse.chalmers.se/~coquand/mod1.pdf`.

[5] Coq Development Team. *The Coq Proof Assistant Reference Manual, version 8.4pl3*. INRIA, 2012. Available at `coq.inria.fr`.

[6] N. Gambino and R. Garner. The identity type weak factorisation system. *Theoretical Computer Science*, 409(3):94–109, 2008.

[7] R. Garner. Two-dimensional models of type theory. *Mathematical Structures in Computer Science*, 19(4):687–736, 2009.

[8] M. Hofmann and T. Streicher. The groupoid interpretation of type theory. In *Twenty-five years of constructive type theory 1995*, volume 36 of *Oxford Logic Guides*, pages 83–111. Oxford Univ. Press, 1998.

[9] C. Kapulkin, P. Lumsdaine, and V. Voevodsky. The simplicial model of univalent foundations. Available as arXiv:1211.2851v1, 2012.

[10] N. Kraus. The truncation map $|\_| : \mathbb{N} \to ||\mathbb{N}||$ is nearly invertible, 2013. Post on the Homotopy Type Theory blog.

[11] D. Licata and G. Brunerie. $\pi_n(\mathbf{S}^n)$ in Homotopy Type Theory. In *Certified Programs and Proofs*, volume 8307 of *LNCS*, pages 1–16. Springer, 2013.

[12] D. Licata and R. Harper. Canonicity for 2-dimensional type theory. In *Principles of Programming Languages (POPL 2012)*, pages 337–348. ACM, 2012.

[13] D. Licata and M. Shulman. Calculating the fundamental group of the circle in Homotopy Type Theory. In *Logic in Computer Science (LICS 2013)*, pages 223–232. IEEE Computer Society, 2013.

[14] P. Lumsdaine. Weak $\omega$-categories from intensional type theory. *Logical Methods in Computer Science*, 6:1–19, 2010.

[15] P. Lumsdaine. Higher inductive types: a tour of the menagerie, 2011. Post on the Homotopy Type Theory blog.

[16] P. Lumsdaine and M. Shulman. Semantics of higher inductive types, 2012. Available at `http://uf-ias-2012.wikispaces.com/file/view/semantics.pdf`.

[17] P. Martin-Löf. An intuitionistic theory of types: Predicative part. In *Logic Colloquium 1973*, pages 73–118. North-Holland, 1975.

[18] P. Martin-Löf. Constructive mathematics and computer programming. In *Logic, Methodology, and Philosophy of Science*, pages 153–175. North-Holland, 1982.

[19] U. Norell. *Towards a practical programming language based on dependent type theory*. PhD thesis, Chalmers University of Technology, 2007.

[20] M. Shulman. Homotopy Type Theory, VI, 2011. Post on the n-category cafe blog.

[21] K. Sojakova. Higher inductive types as homotopy-initial algebras. Technical Report CMU-CS-14-101R, Carnegie Mellon University, 2014. Available at `http://reports-archive.adm.cs.cmu.edu/`.

[22] T. Streicher. Investigations into intensional type theory. Habilitation Thesis. Available from the authors web page, 1993.

[23] The Univalent Foundations Program, Institute for Advanced Study. *Homotopy Type Theory - Univalent Foundations of Mathematics*. Univalent Foundations Project, 2013.

[24] B. van den Berg and R. Garner. Types are weak $\omega$-groupoids. *London Mathematical Society*, 102(2):370–394, 2011.

[25] B. van den Berg and R. Garner. Topological and simplicial models of identity types. *ACM TOCL*, 13(1), 2012.

[26] V. Voevodsky. Univalent foundations of mathematics, 2011. Invited talk at the Workshop on Logic, Language, Information and Computation (WoLLIC 2011).

[27] M. Warren. *Homotopy-theoretic aspects of constructive type theory*. PhD thesis, Carnegie Mellon University, 2008.

# Runtime Enforcement of Security Policies on Black Box Reactive Programs

Minh Ngo Fabio Massacci
University of Trento, Italy
ngo@disi.unitn.it,Fabio.Massacci@unitn.it

Dimiter Milushev Frank Piessens
iMinds-DistriNet, KU Leuven, Belgium
{Dimiter.Milushev,Frank.Piessens}@cs.kuleuven.be

## Abstract

Security enforcement mechanisms like execution monitors are used to make sure that some untrusted program complies with a policy. Different enforcement mechanisms have different strengths and weaknesses and hence it is important to understand the qualities of various enforcement mechanisms.

This paper studies runtime enforcement mechanisms for reactive programs. We study the impact of two important constraints that many practical enforcement mechanisms satisfy: (1) the enforcement mechanism must handle each input/output event in finite time and on occurrence of the event (as opposed to for instance Ligatti's edit automata that have the power to buffer events for an arbitrary amount of time), and (2) the enforcement mechanism treats the untrusted program as a *black box*: it can monitor and/or edit the input/output events that the program exhibits on execution and it can explore alternative executions of the program by running additional copies of the program and providing these different inputs. It can *not* inspect the source or machine code of the untrusted program.

Such enforcement mechanisms are important in practice: they include for instance many execution monitors, virtual machine monitors, and secure multi-execution or shadow executions.

We establish upper and lower bounds for the class of policies that are enforceable by such black box mechanisms, and we propose a generic enforcement mechanism that works for a wide range of policies. We also show how our generic enforcement mechanism can be instantiated to enforce specific classes of policies, at the same time showing that many existing enforcement mechanisms are optimized instances of our construction.

***Categories and Subject Descriptors*** D.4.6 [*Operating Systems*]: Security and Protection

***General Terms*** Security

***Keywords*** Runtime Enforcement; Hypersafety Policy; Black Box Mechanism; Reactive Program


*POPL '15*, January 15–17, 2015, Mumbai, India.
Copyright © 2014 ACM 978-1-4503-3300-9/15/01...$15.00.
http://dx.doi.org/10.1145/2676726.2676978

## 1. Introduction

An *enforcement mechanism* is a mechanism to ensure that some untrusted program will comply with an independently specified security policy for that program. An interesting question that has received a considerable amount of attention over the past decade is: for what classes of policies do there exist *secure* and *precise* enforcement mechanisms? Roughly speaking, an enforcement mechanism is *secure* if it ensures that any program running under the enforcement mechanism complies with the policy. It is *precise* if it does not change the behavior of secure programs in any significant way, i.e. secure programs are not affected by the enforcement mechanism.

For purely static enforcement mechanisms (i.e. mechanisms that should accept or reject the program after some finite amount of analysis, possibly including verification of the code of the program, model checking of the program, or the execution of a finite number of test runs) it is known that they can enforce exactly the recursively decidable properties of programs (i.e. the class $\Pi_0$ of the arithmetic hierarchy) [15].

For dynamic (runtime) enforcement mechanisms, the picture is more complicated. At least in part this is the case because it is less clear what exactly runtime mechanisms are allowed to do. Can they only monitor the program and halt it on an observed policy violation? Or are they also allowed to change the program and/or its executions? And if so under what constraints? Obviously, the enforcement mechanism should not be allowed to make arbitrary changes if it is to be precise; it should preserve (in some sense) the behavior of secure programs.

For the important mechanism of *execution monitoring*, the mechanism can only observe executions of the program and terminate them (i.e. prevent any further actions) as soon as they are observed not to comply with the policy. The enforcement power of this mechanism was first studied by Schneider [25] and Schneider's results were later refined by Viswanathan et al. [28] and Hamlen et al. [15]. Roughly speaking, execution monitors can enforce the computable safety properties, but the details depend on the intervention power of the monitor (if there are certain events/actions that the monitor can not prevent from happening, such as the passing of time, this impacts the set of enforceable properties) [4, 15].

*Edit automata* are a generalization of execution monitors where the monitor can also suppress, insert or change actions that the program performs. They were shown to be strictly more powerful than execution monitors [19]. Edit automata can enforce the so-called *infinite renewal properties*, a class of properties that also includes some liveness properties. Yet, this is only possible at the expense of assuming that the monitor can buffer input/output events for an arbitrary amount of time. For reactive programs, it would be desirable if the enforcement mechanism handles each input/output event on occurrence of the event. Buffering an input/output event will often inhibit further progress of the reactive program: events happen in response to earlier events.

The main objective of this paper is to come to a better understanding of the enforcement power of dynamic enforcement mechanisms for deterministic reactive programs that satisfy two constraints that are important in practice. First, we require the enforcement mechanism to handle each input event in finite time and before processing the next input event (no buffering). Second, the enforcement mechanism does not analyze the code or runtime state of the program: it treats the program as a *black box*. The enforcement mechanism can intercept input/output events and possibly modify them. It can also run multiple copies of the program as in secure multi-execution [11] or shadow executions [7].

In summary, this paper makes the following contributions:

- we define the class of black box enforceable policies, a class of policies that is enforceable by only considering the I/O behaviour of a program (and hence *without* any analysis of the source or binary code of the program).
- we establish upper and lower bounds for this class.
- we develop a generic black box enforcement mechanism, and prove that it is secure and precise.
- we show how this generic enforcement mechanism can be instantiated to interesting policies.

The remainder of this paper is structured as follows: in Sections 2 and 3 we define reactive programs and security policies. In Section 4 we define and study the notion of black box enforceable policies, and construct a generic black box enforcement mechanism. In Section 5 we show specific useful and interesting instances of the generic construction, and we discuss some of the implications of our result in Section 6. Finally Sections 7 and 8 discuss related work and conclude.

# 2. A Model of Reactive Programs and Observations

We model reactive programs as states in a labeled transition system with a total computable deterministic transition relation. Programs are black boxes in the sense that the only observation one can do on a program is feeding it input and observing the corresponding output. This section formalizes these concepts.

## 2.1 Programs

Let $\mathbf{I}$ (resp. $\mathbf{O}$) be enumerable sets of input (resp. output) values. The metavariable $i$ (resp. $o$) ranges over $\mathbf{I}$ (resp $\mathbf{O}$).

A *stream of inputs* $I$ (resp. *stream of outputs* $O$) is defined coinductively from $[]$, the empty stream and the observation $i : I$ (resp. $o : O$) of a value $i$ and a tail stream $I$. The set of (finite and infinite) streams over $\mathbf{I}$ (resp. $\mathbf{O}$) is denoted $\mathbf{I}^\infty$ (resp. $\mathbf{O}^\infty$). The set of *finite* streams over $\mathbf{I}$ (resp. $\mathbf{O}$) is denoted $\mathbf{I}^\star$ (resp. $\mathbf{O}^\star$). We abuse notation and denote by $I : i$ the operation of appending value $i$ to the finite stream $I$. For simplicity we will abbreviate $[i_1 : [\ldots [i_n : []] \ldots]]$ as $[i_1 : \ldots : i_n]$ for $n \geq 1$.

**Definition 2.1.** *A* labelled transition system *(LTS) is a tuple* $\langle \mathbf{C}, \mathbf{I}, \mathbf{O}, \rightarrow \rangle$, *where* $\mathbf{C}$ *is the set of states and* $\rightarrow \subseteq \mathbf{C} \times (\mathbf{I} \times \mathbf{O}) \times \mathbf{C}$ *is a transition relation. We denote a transition as* $C \xrightarrow{i|o} C'$. *An LTS is* input-total *if for all* $C \in \mathbf{C}$, *and* $i \in \mathbf{I}$, *there exist* $C' \in \mathbf{C}$ *and* $o \in \mathbf{O}$ *such that* $C \xrightarrow{i|o} C'$. *An LTS is* deterministic *if for all* $C \in \mathbf{C}$ *and for all* $i \in \mathbf{I}$, *if* $C \xrightarrow{i|o} C'$ *and* $C \xrightarrow{i|o'} C''$ *then* $o = o'$ *and* $C' = C''$.

For this paper, program states $C$ are elements of the state set $\mathbf{C}$ of some input-total and deterministic LTS $\langle \mathbf{C}, \mathbf{I}, \mathbf{O}, \rightarrow \rangle$.

We assume throughout the paper that the function mapping any $(C, i)$ to $(o, C')$ such that $C \xrightarrow{i|o} C'$ holds is total and computable. The intuition is that if $C \xrightarrow{i|o} C'$ holds then program state $C$ will process input $i$, produce output $o$ in finite time, and transition to the new program state $C'$. We will often refer to states $C$ as programs, rather than program states.

Each program $C$ transduces an input stream $I$ into an output stream $O$. This process coinductively defines a relation $C \xrightarrow{I|O} C'$ by the rules specified below.

$$\text{NIL}\ \frac{}{C \xrightarrow{[]|[]} C} \qquad\qquad \text{CONS}\ \frac{C \xrightarrow{i|o} C'' \qquad C'' \xrightarrow{I|O} C'}{C \xrightarrow{i:I|o:O} C'}$$

This relation defines a function on finite input streams that maps any $(C, I)$ to some $(O, C')$. Since the function that processes an individual input is total and computable, also the function over streams is total and computable for finite input streams $I$. Therefore, we write $C(I) = O$ if there is some program $C'$ such that $C \xrightarrow{I|O} C'$ and say that program $C$, on input $I$, produces output $O$.

Programs run for ever in this model (every program state is ready to accept more inputs), but termination of a program can be modeled by producing a special $o_{end}$ output value ad infinitum for every input value.

Bohannon et al.'s model of reactive systems [6] allows divergence on a single input value. We impose the constraint that a program can not diverge on a single input value, because we want to impose that same constraint on enforcement mechanisms. The consequences of this choice are significant, and further discussed in Section 6.

Listing 1 shows an example program, specified as a function on an input value and on program state stored in a state variable.

**Listing 1.** A sum program

```
state var sum:Integer = 0
input(i:Integer) {
  sum := sum + i;
  output(sum)
}
```

This program maps for instance input stream $[1 : 2 : 3]$ on output stream $[1 : 3 : 6]$, and the infinite input stream $[1 : 1 : 1 : \ldots]$ on the infinite output stream $[1 : 2 : 3 : \ldots]$.

## 2.2 Finite observations on programs

A *primitive observation* is a pair $(I, O)$ where $I \in \mathbf{I}^*$ and $O \in \mathbf{O}^*$ are finite and of equal length. A program $C$ has the primitive observation $(I, O)$ iff $C(I) = O$.

An *observation* $M$ is a finite set of primitive observations, i.e. a partial mapping of finite input streams to finite output streams. A program $C$ has the observation $M$ (denoted by $M \subseteq C$) iff it has all the primitive observations in $M$.

The *prefix* of a primitive observation $(I : i, O : o)$ is $(I, O)$. An observation $M$ is *prefix-closed* if for each $(I : i, O : o) \in M$, it is also the case that $(I, O) \in M$. The *prefix closure* of $M$ (denoted as $\overline{M}$) is the smallest set that includes $M$ and is prefix-closed. It is straightforward to prove that if $M \subseteq C$, then $\overline{M} \subseteq C$.

We write inputs$(M)$ for the set $\{I \mid (I, O) \in M\}$. Given a finite set $Is$ of finite input streams, we define

$$\text{map}(C, Is) \quad = \quad \{(I, O) \mid I \in Is \wedge C(I) = O\}.$$

It is easy to see that $M \subseteq C$ iff map$(C, \text{inputs}(M)) = M$.

We say an observation $M$ is *possible* if there exists a program $C$ that has the observation $M$. For instance, $\{([1], [1]), ([1 : 2], [1 :$

$3])\}$ is possible because it is an observation on the sum program above, but the observation $\{([1],[1]),([1:2],[2:3])\}$ is not possible: any program that has primitive observation $([1:2],[2:3])$ must also have the primitive observation $([1],[2])$ and hence by determinism of programs it can not have observation $([1],[1])$.

**Proposition 2.1.** *An observation is possible if and only if its prefix-closure is deterministic i.e.* $(I,O) \in \overline{M}$ *and* $(I,O') \in \overline{M}$ *implies that* $O = O'$.

In the sequel, we only consider possible observations. We write **OBS** for the set of all possible observations, and use the metavariable $M \in \mathbf{OBS}$ to range over them.

**Definition 2.2.** *Two programs* $C$ *and* $C'$ *are* observationally equivalent *(denoted by* $C \sim C'$*) iff they have the same primitive observations.*

It follows that, if two programs $C$ and $C'$ are *not* observationally equivalent, there is some finite input $I$ such that $C(I) \neq C'(I)$.

## 3. Policies

A policy $\mathcal{P}$ can be defined very generally as the set of programs allowed by the policy. Membership of the policy is required to be compatible with observational equivalence: if $C \in \mathcal{P}$ then all programs observationally equivalent with $C$ must also be in $\mathcal{P}$. Hence, one can also think of a policy as a set of sets of primitive observations: a program satisfies the policy iff the set of primitive observations of the program is an element of the policy [10].

For black box dynamic enforcement mechanisms such as the ones in this paper, we are interested in the subset of policies for which violation of the policy can be detected by means of a finite observation, and for which the test of violation is decidable.

### 3.1 Hypersafety policies

The policies for which violation can be detected by a finite observation were formalized by Clarkson and Schneider [10] as the hypersafety policies: if $C$ is not in the policy then $C$ has a finite observation $M_{bad}$ that only programs disallowed by the policy have.

**Definition 3.1.** *A policy* $\mathcal{P}$ *is a* hypersafety policy *iff*

$$\forall C \notin \mathcal{P} \;\Rightarrow\; (\exists M_{bad} \in \mathbf{OBS}.\; M_{bad} \subseteq C \;\wedge\; (\forall C'.\; M_{bad} \subseteq C' \Rightarrow C' \notin \mathcal{P}))$$

If there is a bound $k$ on the cardinality of these bad observations, the policy is a $k$-safety policy.

**Definition 3.2.** *A policy* $\mathcal{P}$ *is a* $k$-safety policy *iff*

$$\forall C \notin \mathcal{P} \;\Rightarrow\; (\exists M_{bad} \in \mathbf{OBS}.\; M_{bad} \subseteq C \wedge |M_{bad}| \leq k \;\wedge\; (\forall C'.\; M_{bad} \subseteq C' \Rightarrow C' \notin \mathcal{P}))$$

Hypersafety policies can be specified by defining a set $\mathcal{M}$ of bad or disallowed observations. The corresponding policy $\mathcal{P}$ is then defined as: $C \notin \mathcal{P}$ if and only if $C$ has one of the specified bad observations $M_{bad} \in \mathcal{M}$. However, for a given hypersafety policy, $\mathcal{M}$ need not be unique. For example, one may choose $\mathcal{M}$ to be the set containing any one $M_{bad}$ for every $C \notin \mathcal{P}$.

**Example 1.** *Suppose there are two distinguished output values* $o_{send}$ *(the program is sending something over the network) and* $o_{read}$ *(the program initiates a read action on the file system). The 1-safety policy* no-send-after-read *(NSAR) can be specified by the following set of bad observations:*

$$\{\{(I,O)\} | sendAfterRead(O)\}$$

*where* $sendAfterRead(O)$ *is a boolean function defined as:*

$$\begin{aligned} sendAfterRead([]) &= false \\ sendAfterRead(o_{read}:O) &= occurs(o_{send},O) \\ sendAfterRead(\_:O) &= sendAfterRead(O) \end{aligned}$$

*where the boolean function* $occurs(o,O)$ *is true if the value* $o$ *occurs somewhere in finite stream* $O$.

*NSAR is 1-safety since every specified bad observation is a singleton containing 1 primitive observation.*

**Example 2.** *Noninterference (NI), the policy that low (L) outputs do not depend on high (H) inputs is a 2-safety policy, and can be specified by defining a set of disallowed observations as follows. Let* $lvl$ *be a function that assigns H or L to input and output values. Given a finite stream I, let* $I|_L$ *be the resulting stream after filtering out the input values* $i$ *with* $lvl(i) = H$ *(and similarly for* $O|_L$*).*

*Then a program* $C$ *is* noninterferent *(or* $C \in \mathcal{P}_{NI}$*) iff*

$$\forall I, I' \in \mathbf{I}^* : I|_L = I'|_L \implies O|_L = O'|_L,$$

*where* $C(I) = O$ *and* $C(I') = O'$.

*A set of bad observations that specifies* $\mathcal{P}_{NI}$ *is:*

$$\{\{(I,O),(I',O')\} \mid I|_L = I'|_L \wedge O|_L \neq O'|_L\}.$$

*A program* $C$ *that has an observation in this set is not NI. If* $C$ *does not have any such observation, then it is NI.*

*NI is a 2-safety hyperproperty since the bad observations in the set above all have cardinality 2.*

Here is an example of a $k$-safety policy for arbitrary $k$ [10].

**Example 3.** *Let* $o_i$ *be the act of outputting the* $i$*-th share of a secret (for* $0 < i \leq k$*). The policy that no observation on the program will ever reveal all* $k$ *shares can be specified by defining the following set of bad observations:*

$$\{\{(I_1,O_1),\ldots,(I_k,O_k)\} \mid occurs(o_1,O_1) \wedge \ldots \wedge occurs(o_k,O_k)\}$$

### 3.2 Testable hypersafety policies

To enforce a policy, it should be decidable whether an observation made on the program is allowed or not by the policy. For policies specified by a set of bad observations $\mathcal{M}$, this seems to imply we want membership of $\mathcal{M}$ to be decidable.

However, a hypersafety policy can be specified by different sets of bad observations, and membership can be decidable for some of these sets and not for others.

A canonical set of bad observations for a given policy is the *maximal* set.

**Definition 3.3.** *For a hypersafety policy* $\mathcal{P}$*, we define* $\mathcal{M}_{\mathcal{P}}$*, the* maximal *set of bad observations as:*

$$\mathcal{M}_{\mathcal{P}} = \{M_{bad} \mid \forall C : M_{bad} \subseteq C \implies C \notin \mathcal{P}\}$$

*An observation* $M$ *is* allowed *by a policy* $\mathcal{P}$ *iff* $M \notin \mathcal{M}_{\mathcal{P}}$.

It is *maximal* in the sense that any other set $\mathcal{M}$ that specifies the same policy $\mathcal{P}$ is a subset of $\mathcal{M}_{\mathcal{P}}$.

For any hypersafety policy $\mathcal{P}$, the maximal set $\mathcal{M}_{\mathcal{P}}$ always exists. *Yet*, it is possible that $\mathcal{P}$ can be specified by a computable set of disallowed observations, even if $\mathcal{M}_{\mathcal{P}}$ is not computable.

**Example 4.** *Let* $\mathbf{O}$ *be the set of closed terms* $t$ *of the untyped* $\lambda$*-calculus. Consider the policy that specifies that programs can only output valid reduction sequences (in some deterministic reduction relation): for any input, the next term on the output is a valid reduction of the previous term on the output stream. A program can therefore only emit a valid reduction of the term until it reaches normal form, and then no valid output is possible anymore. Recall from Section 2 that programs have to keep producing output (possibly stuttering on a specific output value to model termination).*

*Hence, the only programs satisfying the policy are the programs that output sequences starting with a λ-term whose reduction does not terminate, and ad infinitum output further reductions of this term.*

*We define two predicates* $isValidRS(O)$ *which holds iff* $O$ *is a* valid reduction sequence *and* $isValidNTRS(O)$ *which holds iff* $O$ *is a valid reduction sequence that ends in a term that is not normalizing (and hence can be further reduced indefinitely long).*

$$\begin{array}{rcl} isValidRS([]) & = & \textit{true} \\ isValidRS([t]) & = & \textit{true} \\ isValidRS(t_1 : t_2 : O) & = & t_1\ \lambda\text{-reduces to } t_2 \quad \wedge \\ & & isValidRS(t_2 : O) \\ isValidNTRS(O) & = & isValidRS(O) \wedge \\ & & last(O) \text{ not normalizing} \end{array}$$

*We can use the following set of bad observations:*

$$\{M \mid \exists (I,O) \in \overline{M}, \neg isValidRS(O)\}$$

*Membership in this set is computable and correctly captures the policy: any bad program will eventually have one of these bad observations. Yet, it is not maximal for the hypersafety policy it specifies: we can have observations (e.g. a program emitting a normalizing term), that are themselves not in the specified set of bad observations, but any program that has the observation is bound to eventually violate the policy. Once a program has output a normalizing term, it will eventually have to stop outputting valid reductions: it can reduce until it reaches normal form, but then the next element in the output cannot be obtained by a reduction of the former element, and the policy is violated.*

*The maximal set corresponding to this policy is:*

$$\{M \mid \exists (I,O) \in \overline{M}, \neg isValidNTRS(O)\}$$

*Any observation that is bound to eventually fail is in this set: as soon as a program outputs a term that will always terminate (i.e. is normalizing), the program is rejected. However, membership in this maximal set is not computable (as this would require deciding termination of λ-terms).*

**Definition 3.4.** *A hypersafety policy* $\mathcal{P}$ *is* testable *iff membership in* $\mathcal{M}_{\mathcal{P}}$ *is decidable.*

For the construction of enforcement mechanisms, we limit our attention to testable hypersafety policies. Such policies can be specified by giving a total computable boolean function reject($M$) that for an observation $M$ returns **true** iff $M \in \mathcal{M}_{\mathcal{P}}$.

It is non-trivial to check whether a set of bad observations specified by a reject function is actually maximal. For example, the set of bad observations that we specified in Example 2 for NI is *not* maximal. It does not contain observations that have violated the policy in the past but where things have "re-adjusted" as the execution progressed, as shown in the following example:

**Example 5.** *Suppose that* $\mathbf{I} = \mathbf{O} = \{0, 1\}$ *and that* $lvl(0) = L$ *whereas* $lvl(1) = H$. *Consider the following observation* $\{([0 : 1 : 0], [0 : 1 : 0]), ([1 : 0 : 0], [0 : 0 : 1])\}$. *This observation is possible and it satisfies the simple test presented in Example 2 because the outputs are equivalent* $[0 : 1 : 0]|_L = [0 : 0] = [1 : 0 : 0]|_L$. *However, no program that satisfies the NI policy can generate this observation because it will have to first generate the observation* $\{([0 : 1], [0 : 1]), ([1 : 0], [0 : 0])\}$ *which would violate the policy.*

Fortunately, the maximal set for NI is still decidable.

**Example 6** (NI, a testable 2-safety hyperproperty)**.** *For the NI policy discussed in Example 2, a reject predicate can be constructed as follows:*

$$reject(M) = \begin{cases} \textit{true} & \exists M_{bad} = \{(I,O),(I',O')\}, \\ & M_{bad} \subseteq \overline{M} \text{ s.t. } I|_L = I'|_L \text{ and } O|_L \neq O'|_L, \\ \textit{false} & \text{otherwise.} \end{cases}$$

*It is straightforward to check that this is a total computable function. We show that it specifies the maximal set of bad observations by contradiction.*

*Suppose that there is an observation* $M$ *such that* $reject(M) =$ ***false*** *and* $M \in \mathcal{M}_{\mathcal{P}}$. *By construction of the reject function we have that* $reject(\overline{M}) =$ ***false***. *Since* $\mathcal{M}_{\mathcal{P}}$ *is maximal,* $\overline{M} \in \mathcal{M}_{\mathcal{P}}$.

*By definition of* $\mathcal{M}_{\mathcal{P}}$, *all programs* $C$ *such that* $\overline{M} \subseteq C$ *must not belong to the policy. Consider now one of such programs* $C_{good}$ *such that for all* $(I,O) \in \overline{M}$, $C_{good}(I) = O$ *and otherwise it always outputs a value* $o$ *with* $lvl(o) = H$. *This program satisfies the policy. Contradiction.*

**Example 7.** *The policy in Example 4 is an example of a hypersafety policy that is not testable.*

### 3.3 Incrementally constructing observations allowed by a policy

An enforcement mechanism must not only decide whether or not an observation is rejected by the policy. It must also "correct" programs that turn out to have observations that are not allowed (for instance by terminating the program, or more generally by modifying the outputs of the program).

Given an observation $M$ of the untrusted program that is still allowed so far, when we find for the next input $i$ that the corresponding output will lead to a violation of the policy, we need to find another output that will *not* lead to a violation of the policy.

**Definition 3.5.** *Given a set of bad observations* $\mathcal{M}$ *that specifies a hypersafety policy, a function* $extend_{\mathcal{M}}(M, I, i)$ *is an* extension function *for* $\mathcal{M}$ *iff, for any observation* $M \notin \mathcal{M}$, *where* $(I,O) \in M$, *it returns an* $o \in \mathbf{O}$ *such that* $M \cup \{(I : i, O : o)\} \notin \mathcal{M}$.

Any extension function can be used for "correcting" outputs. Think of $I$ as the input processed so far, $i$ as the new input to be processed, and $M$ as the set of observations made on the program so far (possibly including primitive observations on alternative input streams). If the new output $o$ observed of the program makes $M \cup \{(I : i, O : o)\}$ a bad observation, then extend$_{\mathcal{M}}(M, I, i)$ can be used to replace this output.

One of the reasons why it is useful to work with the maximal set of bad observations to specify a policy is that for the maximal set, an extension function always exists.

**Proposition 3.1.** *For any hypersafety policy* $\mathcal{P}$, *there exists an extension function for the maximal set of bad observations* $\mathcal{M}_{\mathcal{P}}$.

*Proof.* If the policy $\mathcal{P}$ is empty then all observations are bad observations (in $\mathcal{M}_{\mathcal{P}}$) and therefore the precondition for the applicability of the extension function is false, and we are done.

If the policy is not empty, consider an observation $M$ that is allowed by $\mathcal{M}_{\mathcal{P}}$. By definition of maximal set of bad observations there must be a program $C_{good}$ such that $M \subseteq C_{good}$ and $C_{good} \in \mathcal{P}$ (if none existed $M$ would have been in $\mathcal{M}_{\mathcal{P}}$).

Let $I$ be an arbitrary input stream such that $(I,O) \in M$ and $i$ an arbitrary input value. By definition of observation on a program, it must be $C_{good}(I) = O$. Since programs are input total, $C_{good}(I : i)$ has the form $O : o$ for some $o \in \mathbf{O}$. Pick this $o$ as the return value for extend$_{\mathcal{M}_{\mathcal{P}}}(M, I, i)$.

Suppose now $M \cup \{(I : i, O : o)\} \in \mathcal{M}_{\mathcal{P}}$. Since $M \cup \{(I : i, O : o)\} \subseteq C_{good}$ by definition of maximal set of bad observation it should be $C_{good} \notin \mathcal{P}$. Contradiction. Therefore the set $M \cup \{(I : i, O : o)\}$ is also allowed by $\mathcal{M}_{\mathcal{P}}$. ∎

For a given hypersafety policy $\mathcal{P}$, we write extend$_{\mathcal{P}}(M, I, i)$ as an abbreviation for some function extend$_{\mathcal{M}_{\mathcal{P}}}(M, I, i)$ that is guaranteed to exist by the proposition above.

Interestingly, for testable hypersafety policies, there is always a *total computable* extension function.

**Proposition 3.2.** *Let $\mathcal{P}$ be a testable hypersafety policy, then there exists a total computable extension function for $\mathcal{M}_{\mathcal{P}}$.*

*Proof.* Let $M$ be an observation, $I$ be an arbitrary input stream in inputs$(M)$ and $i$ be an arbitrary input value. The total computable extension function is constructed as follows:

1. if the first argument $M$ already belongs to $\mathcal{M}_{\mathcal{P}}$ then the function returns an arbitrary output value; (in this case the precondition for the extension function is not satisfied, and we can return any value)
2. otherwise the function enumerates all output values $o$ and submits each observation $M \cup \{(I : i, O : o)\}$ to the total computable membership test for $\mathcal{M}_{\mathcal{P}}$ continuing until the reject function returns **false**.

Since (by Proposition 3.1) an $o_{good}$ exists such that $M \cup \{(I : i, O : o_{good})\}$ is not in $\mathcal{M}_{\mathcal{P}}$ this procedure terminates. ■

The function constructed in the proof of this proposition is not very efficient. Many policies admit much more efficient ways of extending allowed observations.

**Example 8.** *For the NSAR policy, extend$_{\mathcal{P}_{NSAR}}(M, I, i)$ can be defined to always return $o_{read}$: Appending $o_{read}$ to an allowed output stream is always allowed.*

**Example 9.** *For the NI policy, we can define extend$_{\mathcal{P}_{NI}}(M, I, i)$ as follows. Let $o_H$ be an arbitrary output value with $lvl(o_H) = H$.*

1. *if $(I : i, O : o)$ is in $\overline{M}$, then return $o$,*
2. *else if $lvl(i) = H$, then return $o_H$,*
3. *else if $lvl(i) = L$:*
   (a) *if there exists $(I' : i, O' : o')$ in $\overline{M}$ s.t. $I'|_L = I|_L$ then return $o'$*
   (b) *otherwise, return $o_H$.*

*We show that this is a correct extension function by contradiction.*

*Suppose there exists an input stream $I$, an input value $i$, and an output stream $O$ such that $(I, O) \in M$, reject$(M)$ = **false**, and reject$(M \cup \{(I : i, O : o)\})$ = **true**, where the reject predicate is specified as in Example 6 and $o$ = extend$_{\mathcal{P}_{NI}}(M, I, i)$ is the result of the above algorithm.*

*By construction of the reject function we also have reject$(\overline{M'})$ = reject$(M')$ for all $M'$. Let $M_1 = M \cup \{(I : i, O : o)\}$, then by hypothesis and the properties of the reject predicate we have that reject$(\overline{M_1})$ = **true**. Further, since $(I, O) \in M$ we have that $\overline{M_1} = \overline{M} \cup \{(I : i, O : o)\}$.*

- *If $(I : i, O : o)$ is in $\overline{M}$, then $\overline{M_1} = \overline{M}$. Thus, reject$(\overline{M})$ = **true**. Contradiction.*
- *If $lvl(i) = H$, then $o = o_H$, hence $lvl(o) = H$. Since reject$(M_1)$ = **true**, there exists $(I_b, O_b)$ in $\overline{M}$ s.t $I_b|_L = I : i|_L$ and $O_b|_L \neq O : o|_L$. Because $lvl(i) = lvl(o) = H$, it follows that $I : i|_L = I|_L$ and $O : o|_L = O|_L$. But then $I_b|_L = I|_L$ and $O_b|_L \neq O|_L$. Thus, reject$(\overline{M})$ = **true**. Contradiction.*
- *If $lvl(i) = L$ and there exists $(I' : i, O' : o')$ in $\overline{M}$ s.t. $I'|_L = I|_L$, then $o$ is $o'$. Since reject$(\overline{M_1})$ = **true**, there exists $(I_b, O_b)$ in $\overline{M}$ s.t $I_b|_L = I : i|_L$, and $O_b|_L \neq O : o|_L$. But $I' : i|_L = I : i|_L$ and $O' : o'|_L = O : o|_L$, and since both $(I_b, O_b)$ and $(I' : i, O' : o')$ are in $\overline{M}$ it follows that reject$(\overline{M})$ = **true**. Contradiction.*
- *If $lvl(i) = L$ and there is no $(I' : i, O' : o')$ in $\overline{M}$ s.t. $I'|_L = I|_L$, then $o = o_H$. Since reject$(\overline{M_1})$ = **true**, there must exist $I_b$ in inputs$(\overline{M})$ s.t $I_b|_L = I : i|_L$. Let $I'_b$ be the prefix of $I_b$ that removes all elements with level $H$ at the end of $I_b$. Then $I'_b$ is in inputs$(\overline{M})$, and it must have the form $I''_b : i$ and it must have $I''_b|_L = I_L$. Contradiction.*

# 4. Black Box Enforcement Mechanisms

## 4.1 Definition

We model enforcement mechanisms as total computable functions from programs to programs: they turn a program (that possibly does not satisfy the policy) into a program that definitely complies with the policy (the *security* property). Moreover, they do not have any observable impact on untrusted programs that *do* happen to satisfy the policy (the *precision* property). Finally, they should be *black box*, i.e. only depend on the externally observable behaviour of their input program.

**Definition 4.1.** *A* black box enforcement mechanism *for a policy $\mathcal{P}$ is a total computable function $\mathsf{E}_{\mathcal{P}}$ from programs to programs, which satisfies the following properties:*

- *Security: for all programs $C$, $\mathsf{E}_{\mathcal{P}}(C) \in \mathcal{P}$*
- *Precision: if $C \in \mathcal{P}$, then $C \sim \mathsf{E}_{\mathcal{P}}(C)$*
- *Black box: if $C_1 \sim C_2$, then $\mathsf{E}_{\mathcal{P}}(C_1) \sim \mathsf{E}_{\mathcal{P}}(C_2)$*

*A policy $\mathcal{P}$ is* black box enforceable *iff there exists a secure and precise black box enforcement mechanism for $\mathcal{P}$.*

Because enforcement mechanisms produce programs in our program model, they have to respond to any input event in finite time with an appropriate output event without buffering inputs or outputs.

In this section, we derive upper and lower bounds on the set of black box enforceable policies.

## 4.2 Upper bounds on black box enforceable policies

First, non-suprisingly, any policy that is black box enforceable is a hypersafety policy.

**Theorem 4.1.** *If an enforcement mechanism $\mathsf{E}_{\mathcal{P}}$ exists for a policy $\mathcal{P}$, then $\mathcal{P}$ is a hypersafety policy.*

*Proof.* Suppose $C \notin \mathcal{P}$. We have to construct an $M_{bad}$ such that (1) $M_{bad} \subseteq C$, and (2) $\forall C'.\ M_{bad} \subseteq C' \Rightarrow C' \notin \mathcal{P}$.

If $C \notin \mathcal{P}$, then, by security of the enforcement mechanism $\mathsf{E}_{\mathcal{P}}(C)$ is not observationally equivalent to $C$. Hence, there must be some finite input stream $I$ such that $C(I) \neq \mathsf{E}_{\mathcal{P}}(C)(I)$. Take as $M_{bad}$ the set of all primitive observations that $\mathsf{E}_{\mathcal{P}}$ has done on $C$ during the execution of $\mathsf{E}_{\mathcal{P}}(C)(I)$, and add the primitive observation $(I, C(I))$. This set is necessarily finite as $\mathsf{E}_{\mathcal{P}}(C)(I)$ must process the finite input $I$ in finite time.

It is clear that (1) holds, as $M_{bad}$ is constructed only using primitive observations on $C$.

In order to prove (2), suppose a program $C'$ has this same observation. Then $C'(I) = C(I)$, because $M_{bad}$ includes $(I, C(I))$. But also $\mathsf{E}_{\mathcal{P}}(C')(I) = \mathsf{E}_{\mathcal{P}}(C)(I)$, as $C'$ will respond exactly as $C$, to *all* the observations that $\mathsf{E}_{\mathcal{P}}$ does while processing the input stream $I$ and $\mathsf{E}_{\mathcal{P}}$ is a deterministic program. Hence $C'(I) \neq \mathsf{E}_{\mathcal{P}}(C')(I)$. By hypothesis the enforcement mechanism is precise and therefore $C' \notin \mathcal{P}$. ■

Obviously, the converse is not true: there are many hypersafety policies that are not enforceable. For instance, the non-testable policy in Example 4 is not enforceable: if the program outputs a first $\lambda$-term, the enforcement mechanism should output this term unmodified iff it is non-terminating. Obviously, it cannot decide this in finite time.

This upper bound can be substantially tightened. We say a hypersafety policy is *semi-testable* if membership in $\mathcal{M}_{\mathcal{P}}$ is co-recursively enumerable, i.e. we can enumerate all the observations that are allowed by the policy.

**Theorem 4.2.** *Let $\mathcal{P}$ be a hypersafety policy. If an enforcement mechanism $\mathsf{E}_{\mathcal{P}}$ exists for $\mathcal{P}$, then $\mathcal{P}$ is semi-testable.*

*Proof.* We have to provide an algorithm for the reject function that will return **false** for any observation $M$ that is not in $\mathcal{M}_{\mathcal{P}}$ and will return **true** or diverge for any observation $M$ that is in $\mathcal{M}_{\mathcal{P}}$.

Given an observation $M$, the algorithm enumerates all possible programs in some complete programming language for writing reactive programs. For each program, it applies the enforcement mechanism to inputs($M$) and then tries to observe $M$. It returns **false** if it can observe $M$ and otherwise continues with the next program.

If $M \in \mathcal{M}_{\mathcal{P}}$, then – by the security property of the enforcement mechanism – $M$ will never be observed, and the algorithm diverges.

If $M \notin \mathcal{M}_{\mathcal{P}}$, then – by the maximality of $\mathcal{M}_{\mathcal{P}}$ there exists some program $C_{good}$ that has $M$ and satisfies $\mathcal{P}$. By precision, the enforcement mechanism applied to $C_{good}$ will be observationally equivalent to $C_{good}$ and hence will have observation $M$. Hence, if $M \notin \mathcal{M}_{\mathcal{P}}$, we will eventually enumerate $C_{good}$, and the algorithm for the reject function will terminate with return value **false**. ∎

### 4.3 A lower bound on black box enforceable policies

For 1-safety policies it is obvious that testability (as defined in Definition 3.4) is a *sufficient* condition for enforceability. If membership of an observation in the maximal set of bad observations is decidable, then it is obviously possible to decide whether primitive observation $\{(I, O)\}$ is a bad observation. Therefore, one can simply use the reject function as a security automaton in the sense of Schneider [25]. At the point where the primitive observation corresponding to the current execution is about to violate the policy, one can use the extension function to correct the execution. Schneider considers only termination as a corrective measure (in the terminology of this paper, he assumes that outputting $o_{end}$ is never disallowed by any policy, and hence one can use the constant function on $o_{end}$ as an extension function). In cases where policies can talk about termination too [15], one can use another extension function. Only in the case where the policy is empty (and hence the maximal set of bad observations contains all observations), a testable 1-safety policy is not black box enforceable.

Surprisingly, testability is also a sufficient condition for black box enforceability for general hypersafety policies. We show that in this section by constructing a secure and precise enforcement mechanism for any testable hypersafety policy. We need to address two challenges: (1) testing a sufficient number of alternative executions, and (2) doing corrections in a consistent way.

#### 4.3.1 Generating sufficient test inputs

For $k$-safety policies with $k > 1$, it is not obvious that testability is a sufficient condition for enforceability. For such policies, the enforcement mechanism should not only look at the input/output streams $(I, O)$ of the current execution. For $k$-safety it should also make sure that other primitive observations that the policy defines to be incompatible with the current execution do not exist, and in general there will be infinitely many alternate input streams that can possibly lead to incompatible observations.

**Example 10.** *For the NI policy, for a given primitive observation $(I, O)$, the set of all other primitive observations that are incompatible with $(I, O)$ is:*

$$\{(I', O') \mid I|_L = I'|_L \wedge O'|_L \neq O|_L\}$$

*This set contains an infinite number of input streams $I'$, so the enforcement mechanism can not query the program $C$ with all of them in finite time.*

Fortunately, it is not necessary to check the behavior of the program on *all* input streams that might be potentially conflicting with the current input stream.

We introduce the notion of *test generator*, a function that computes a finite and sufficient set of alternative input streams to check.

**Definition 4.2.** *A* test generator *for a hypersafety policy $\mathcal{P}$ is a function $g : \mathbf{I}^\star \rightarrow$ finite $2^{\mathbf{I}^\star}$ s.t. for all $C \in \mathbf{C}$ and all $M_{bad} \in \mathcal{M}_{\mathcal{P}}$:*

$$(\forall I \in \mathit{inputs}(M_{bad}) : \mathit{map}(C, g(I) \cup \{I\}) \notin \mathcal{M}_{\mathcal{P}}) \Rightarrow M_{bad} \not\subseteq C$$

In other words, if a program $C$ has a bad observation $M_{bad}$, then there is at least one input stream $I \in \text{inputs}(M_{bad})$ for which $g(I)$ is a sufficiently large set of input streams such that testing the program $C$ on these input streams *in addition to* the actual input stream $I$ will detect a policy violation.

**Lemma 4.1.** *If, for every $I$, $\mathit{map}(C, g(I) \cup \{I\}) \notin \mathcal{M}_{\mathcal{P}}$, then $C \in \mathcal{P}$.*

*Proof.* Suppose $C \notin \mathcal{P}$. By definition, there is a bad observation $M_{bad} \in \mathcal{M}_{\mathcal{P}}$ such that $M_{bad} \subseteq C$.

From the property of generators in Definition 4.2, it follows that there exists an $I \in \text{inputs}(M_{bad})$ such that $\text{map}(C, g(I) \cup I) \in \mathcal{M}_{\mathcal{P}}$. But this contradicts the condition of the lemma. ∎

**Example 11.** *For 1-safety policies, $g(I) = \{\}$ is a test generator. Since a 1-safety policy defines a predicate on primitive observations, any $M_{bad}$ contains at least one $(I, O)$ that violates the predicate. Hence if $M_{bad} \subseteq C$, then at least one of the $\{(I, C(I))\}$ will be in $\mathcal{M}_{\mathcal{P}}$.*

**Example 12.** *For the NI policy from Example 2 (with reject specified in Example 6), $g(I) = \{I|_L\}$ is a test generator.*

*Let $M_{bad} \in \mathcal{M}_{\mathcal{P}_{NI}}$. This means there must exist $(I, O), (I', O') \in M_{bad}$ with $I|_L = I'|_L$ and $O|_L \neq O'|_L$.*

*Now, suppose $M_{bad} \subseteq C$, i.e. $C(I) = O$ and $C(I') = O'$. We show that $C$ has a bad observation either on inputs $I$ and $I|_L$, or on inputs $I'$ and $I'|_L$.*

*Consider the output $O''$ of $C$ on $I|_L = I'|_L$. Since $O|_L \neq O'|_L$, we must have either that $O'' \neq O|_L$ or $O'' \neq O'|_L$.*

- *If $O'' \neq O|_L$, then $C$ has a bad observation on inputs $I$ and $I|_L$.*
- *If $O'' \neq O'|_L$, then $C$ has a bad observation on inputs $I'$ and $I|_L$.*

*This implies that $g$ is a generator.*

*We can further reduce the size of the generator. Let us define $g'$ as follows:*

$$g'(I) = \text{if } I|_L = I \text{ then } \{\} \text{ else } \{I|_L\}$$

*Since for all $I$, $g(I) \cup I = g'(I) \cup I'$, it follows easily from Definition 4.2 that $g'$ is a generator if $g$ is a generator.*

#### 4.3.2 Consistently correcting executions

A second challenge that needs to be addressed is *how to correct executions*. While processing an input stream $I$, the enforcement mechanism will explore other input streams in order to check that there are no bad observations. So the output for input stream $I$ will be computed in different circumstances: while $\mathsf{E}_{\mathcal{P}}(C)$ is actually processing $I$, as well as while the mechanism's actual input is another stream $I'$ and the stream $I$ is only considered as a potential candidate jointly with $I'$ for membership in a bad set. The enforcement mechanism should compute the same output for $I$ in any of these circumstances.

**Example 13.** *Assume that* $\mathbf{I} = \mathbf{O} = \{0, 1\}$. $I \oplus I'$ *is defined for* $I$ *and* $I'$ *of equal length as a pair-wise xor of* $I$ *and* $I'$, *where* $(0 \oplus 1) = (1 \oplus 0) = 1$ *and* $(0 \oplus 0) = (1 \oplus 1) = 0$. *Similarly, we define* $O \oplus O'$. *Let* ***1*** *(resp.* ***0****) denote a stream consisting of only* 1 *values (resp.* 0 *values).*

*A program* $C$ *satisfies a policy* $\mathcal{P}_{xor}$ *iff*

$$\forall I, I' : I \oplus I' = \mathbf{1} \Rightarrow O \oplus O' = \mathbf{1}$$

*The reject function that decides* $\mathcal{M}_{\mathcal{P}_{xor}}$ *is as follows:*

$$reject(M) = \begin{cases} \textbf{\textit{true}} & \exists M_{bad} = \{(I, O), (I', O')\}, \\ & M_{bad} \subseteq \overline{M} \text{ s.t. } I \oplus I' = \mathbf{1} \text{ and } O \oplus O' \neq \mathbf{1}, \\ \textbf{\textit{false}} & \text{otherwise.} \end{cases}$$

*We define* $g(I) \triangleq \{I' \mid I \oplus I' = \mathbf{1}\}$. *Obviously, given an* $I$, *such* $I'$ *is unique. It is easy to show that it actually is a test generator.*

*Now consider a naive construction of an enforcement mechanism* $\mathsf{E}_{\mathcal{P}_{xor}}$ *that on execution of a program* $C$ *on input stream* $I$, *checks the behavior of* $C$ *also on* $g(I) = \{I'\}$. *If the enforcement mechanism finds that* $C(I) \oplus C(I') \neq \mathbf{1}$, *it corrects the output for* $C(I)$ *to make it compliant with the policy. For instance, let* $C$ *be the program that just outputs* 0 *for any input value (i.e.* $C(I) = \mathbf{0}$ *for any* $I$*). If* $\mathsf{E}_{\mathcal{P}_{xor}}(C)$ *is executed on* $[0]$, *the enforcement mechanism would see that* $C([0]) = [0]$ *and that* $C([1]) = [0]$, *and it would decide to correct the output for* $[0]$ *to* $[1]$. *It is easy to see that* $\mathsf{E}_{\mathcal{P}_{xor}}$ *is not a secure enforcement mechanism, because if* $\mathsf{E}_{\mathcal{P}_{xor}}(C)$ *is executed on* $[1]$, *it would see that* $C([1]) = [0]$ *and that* $C([0]) = [0]$, *and it would decide to correct the output for* $[1]$ *to* $[1]$. *Essentially* $\mathsf{E}_{\mathcal{P}_{xor}}(C)$ *will be a program that always outputs* 1 *on every input, and it violates the policy* $\mathcal{P}_{xor}$ *as badly as* $C$ *does.*

*This is an example of inconsistent corrections: on execution of* $\mathsf{E}_{\mathcal{P}_{xor}}(C)$ *on* $[0]$, *we are considering the alternate execution* $[1]$, *but we are not taking into account that the alternate execution might as well be corrected if it were ever executed.*

Guaranteeing consistency of corrections is challenging. One idea is to use recursive invocations of the enforcement mechanism while checking alternative inputs.

**Example 14.** *For the example above, if* $\mathsf{E}_{\mathcal{P}_{xor}}(C)$ *is executed on* $[0]$, *the enforcement mechanism would see that* $C([0]) = [0]$ *and then it should not check this against* $C([1])$, *but against* $\mathsf{E}_{\mathcal{P}_{xor}}(C)([1])$. *Unfortunately, for the given generator, this would lead to divergence, as* $\mathsf{E}_{\mathcal{P}_{xor}}(C)([1])$ *will again recursively call* $\mathsf{E}_{\mathcal{P}_{xor}}(C)([0])$.

We address the issue of divergence by means of the notion of well-founded test generator: a generator is *well-founded*, if there exists a well-founded partial order $\sqsubset$ on the set of finite input streams, such that:

- $I \sqsubset I : i$
- $\forall I' \in g(I), I' \sqsubset I$

Now, we can recursively call the enforcement mechanism on alternative input streams generated by the generator, and this will make sure that corrections are done consistently.

**Example 15.** *Consider again the* $\mathcal{P}_{xor}$ *policy. We now propose the following generator:* $g(I : 0) \triangleq \emptyset$ *and* $g(I : 1) \triangleq \{I' : 0 | I : 1 \oplus I' : 0 = \mathbf{1}\}$.

*This is a well-founded generator. The partial order* $\sqsubset$ *can be defined as (the transitive closure of)* $I \sqsubset I : i$ *and* $I : 0 \sqsubset I : 1$.

*Now consider again an enforcement mechanism* $\mathsf{E}_{\mathcal{P}_{xor}}$ *that on execution of an untrusted program* $C$ *on input stream* $I$, *checks the behaviour of* $\mathsf{E}_{\mathcal{P}_{xor}}(C)$ *also on* $g(I)$. *Now the enforcement mechanism will let any program* $C$ *do its original output on* 0*s and it will correct the output on* 1*s so that the policy is satisfied.*

*For instance, let* $C$ *again be the program that just outputs* 0 *for any input value. If* $\mathsf{E}_{\mathcal{P}_{xor}}(C)$ *is executed on* $[0]$, *the enforcement mechanism would output* $[0]$. *If* $\mathsf{E}_{\mathcal{P}_{xor}}(C)$ *is executed on* $[1]$, *our algorithm would see that* $C([1]) = [0]$ *and that* $\mathsf{E}_{\mathcal{P}_{xor}}(C)([0]) = [0]$, *and it would decide to correct the output for* $[1]$ *to* $[1]$. *Essentially* $\mathsf{E}_{\mathcal{P}_{xor}}(C)$ *will now be a program that echoes inputs on outputs, and hence it is a secure program. The recursive calls to* $\mathsf{E}_{\mathcal{P}_{xor}}(C)$ *always terminate thanks to the well-founded generator.*

**Lemma 4.2.** *Every non-empty testable hypersafety policy has a well-founded generator.*

*Proof.* Construct an enumeration of $\mathbf{I}^*$ (the set of finite streams of input values) that has the property that $I$ is enumerated before $I : i$ for all $i, I$. The constructed enumeration defines a total order on $\mathbf{I}^*$. Say $I \sqsubset I'$ if $I$ is enumerated before $I'$. Define the generator $g(I) = \{I' \mid I' \sqsubset I\}$. It is easy to check that this is a generator: for any $M_{bad}$, let $I$ be the maximal element in the set $inputs(M_{bad})$. Then $inputs(M_{bad}) \subseteq g(I) \cup \{I\}$. Since $C$ is deterministic and $inputs(M_{bad}) \subseteq g(I) \cup \{I\}$, if $M_{bad} \subseteq C$ then $M_{bad} \subseteq \text{map}(C, g(I) \cup \{I\})$, and hence $\text{map}(C, g(I) \cup \{I\}) \in \mathcal{M}_{\mathcal{P}}$ (from the property of maximal set of bad observations). ∎

### 4.3.3 A generic enforcement mechanism

We now have all the necessary ingredients to construct a secure and precise enforcement mechanism for any testable hypersafety policy. This construction will be useful in two ways. We will use it in Section 5 to construct enforcement mechanisms for interesting policies by constructing efficient well-founded generators for these policies. We will also use it to show a lower bound on enforceable policies (Theorem 4.6).

**Definition 4.3.** *Let* $\mathcal{P}$ *be a testable hypersafety policy (specified as a total computable* $reject(M)$ *predicate), with a total computable well-founded generator* $g(I)$ *and a total computable extension function* $extend_{\mathcal{P}}(M, I, i)$.

*We define a function* $\mathsf{E}_{\mathcal{P}}$ *from programs to programs as follows. A state of* $\mathsf{E}_{\mathcal{P}}(C)$ *is a tuple* $\langle I, C, C', O \rangle$, *where* $C$ *is the original program,* $C'$ *is the current state of the program after input* $I$, *and* $O$ *is a good output of the enforcement mechanism on* $I$ *(or* $\mathsf{E}_{\mathcal{P}}(C)(I) = O$*). The initial state of* $\mathsf{E}_{\mathcal{P}}(C)$ *is a tuple* $\langle [], C, C, [] \rangle$. *The transition relation of* $\mathsf{E}_{\mathcal{P}}(C)$ *is defined by the following rules:*

$$\text{OK}\ \frac{\begin{array}{c} M = map(\mathsf{E}_{\mathcal{P}}(C), g(I : i)) \\ C' \overset{i|o}{\to} C'' \quad reject(M \cup \{(I : i, O : o)\}) = \textbf{\textit{false}} \end{array}}{\langle I, C, C', O \rangle \overset{i|o}{\to} \langle I : i, C, C'', O : o \rangle}$$

$$\text{NOK}\ \frac{\begin{array}{c} M = map(\mathsf{E}_{\mathcal{P}}(C), g(I : i)) \\ reject(M \cup \{(I : i, O : o)\}) = \textbf{\textit{true}} \\ C' \overset{i|o}{\to} C'' \quad o' = extend_{\mathcal{P}}(M \cup \{(I, O)\}, I, i) \end{array}}{\langle I, C, C', O \rangle \overset{i|o'}{\to} \langle I : i, C, C''', O : o' \rangle}$$

The first rule says that, if the observation obtained by combining the recursive application of $\mathsf{E}_{\mathcal{P}}$ to $g(I : i)$ and the new observation that $C$ is producing are allowed by the policy, then we just release the output of $C$.

The second rule says that, if the obtained observation is not allowed, we will correct the execution. We correct it by selecting a new output using the consistent extension function $\text{extend}_{\mathcal{P}}$. The successor state for the monitored program can be an arbitrary program $C'''$: as the program being monitored is definitely not compliant with the policy, we do no longer have to care about precision. $C'''$ could for instance be a state that terminates (i.e. continuously emits the $o_{end}$ output). While $C'''$ can be chosen arbitrarily, the enforcement mechanism should choose it deterministically based only on its current state and input (in order to make $\mathsf{E}_{\mathcal{P}}(C)$ a deterministic program).

Notice that in the antecedent of our rules we do *not* check the output of the program $C$ on the additional inputs from the generator, but the output of $\mathsf{E}_{\mathcal{P}}(C)$. This avoids inconsistency of corrections as we had in Example 13.

We have to show that the rules OK and NOK are a proper definition for a program.

**Lemma 4.3.** *For every state $(I, C, C', O)$ of the enforcement mechanism, and for every input $i$, the transition relation is (1) total computable, and (2) deterministic.*

*Proof.* We show both properties by total induction on the well-founded order $\sqsubset$ on $\mathbf{I}^*$. So, suppose both properties (1) and (2) hold for all states $(I_0, C_0, C_0', O_0)$ and input $i_0$ with $I_0 : i_0 \sqsubset I : i$.

The transition from $(I, C, C', O)$ on input $i$ is total computable, because (a) the transition relation on $C$ is total computable, (b) the reject and extension functions are total computable, and (c) the computation of the map of $\mathsf{E}_{\mathcal{P}}(C)$ only needs a finite number of transitions on states $(I_0, C_0, C_0', O_0)$ and inputs $i_0$ such that $I_0 : i_0 \sqsubset I : i$ (this follows from the fact that $g$ is well-founded and hence all $I' \in g(I : i) \sqsubset I : i$). Hence by the induction hypothesis all these transitions are total computable.

The transition from $(I, C, C', O)$ on input $i$ is deterministic, because (a) the transition relation on $C$ is deterministic, (b) the computation of the map of $\mathsf{E}_{\mathcal{P}}(C)$ only needs transitions on states $(I_0, C_0, C_0', O_0)$ and inputs $i_0$ such that $I_0 : i_0 \sqsubset I : i$. Hence by the induction hypothesis all these transitions are deterministic. Now reject deterministically returns either true or false. For the false case, we are done. For the true case, since the extension function is indeed a function and its parameters are deterministically determined by the input state and input value, this function deterministically returns an $o'$. Finally, the state $C'''$ in the output state is chosen arbitrarily but deterministically based on current state and input value. ∎

Now that we have established that $\mathsf{E}_{\mathcal{P}}$ is a total computable function from programs to programs, we can prove its properties.

**Theorem 4.3** (Security). *Let $\mathcal{P}$ be a testable and non-empty hypersafety policy. Then $\mathsf{E}_{\mathcal{P}}(C) \in \mathcal{P}$ for any $C$.*

*Proof.* Let us say that a program $C$ is $I$-level secure if it does not have any bad observation $M_{bad}$ with for all $I' \in inputs(M_{bad})$, $I' \sqsubseteq I$.

We first show the following property: For all $I \in \mathbf{I}^*$, $\mathsf{E}_{\mathcal{P}}(C)$ is $I$-level secure. We prove this by complete induction on the well-founder order $\sqsubset$. So suppose the property holds for all inputs $I_1 \sqsubset I$. We prove it holds for $I$.

For the case where $I$ is empty: Since the empty list is a minimal element under the $\sqsubset$ relation, we just have to show that the primitive observation $([], [])$ is not in $\mathcal{M}_{\mathcal{P}}$. This follows from the fact that $\mathcal{P}$ is non-empty: there is a program $C \in \mathcal{P}$, and every $C$ has the observation $([], [])$.

For the case where $I$ has the form $I_1 : i$, we show that $\text{map}(\mathsf{E}_{\mathcal{P}}(C), g(I_1 : i) \cup \{I_1 : i\}) \notin \mathcal{M}_{\mathcal{P}}$.

- For the subcase where the last output on this input was derived by the OK rule, this follows from the fact that $\text{reject}(M \cup \{(I_1 : i, O : o)\}) = \textbf{false}$ for $M = \text{map}(\mathsf{E}_{\mathcal{P}}(C), g(I_1 : i))$.
- For the subcase where the last output on this input was derived by the NOK rule, we can use the induction hypothesis. All the input streams in $g(I_1 : i) \cup \{I_1\}$ are $\sqsubset I_1 : i$. Hence, the first argument to the extend function is an allowed observation.
  By the property of the extend function, we then also get for this subcase that $\text{map}(\mathsf{E}_{\mathcal{P}}(C), g(I_1 : i) \cup \{I_1 : i\}) \notin \mathcal{M}_{\mathcal{P}}$.

Now we can show that $\mathsf{E}_{\mathcal{P}}(C)$ is $I$-level secure. Suppose there is an $M_{bad}$ with all elements of $\text{inputs}(M_{bad}) \sqsubseteq I$. Then we can easily see that for all $I' \in inputs(M_{bad})$ it holds that $\text{map}(\mathsf{E}_{\mathcal{P}}(C), g(I) \cup \{I\}) \notin \mathcal{M}_{\mathcal{P}}$. (For $I' \sqsubset I$ this follows from the induction hypothesis and the fact that $g$ is well-founded, for $I' = I$ we have just shown it.) But then the definition of test generator tells us that $M_{bad} \notin \mathcal{M}_{\mathcal{P}}$.

Finally, using this fact that $\mathsf{E}_{\mathcal{P}}(C)$ is $I$-level secure for all $I$, we can apply Lemma 4.1 and we get that $\mathsf{E}_{\mathcal{P}}(C) \in \mathcal{P}$. ∎

**Theorem 4.4.** *$\mathsf{E}_{\mathcal{P}}(C)$ is precise.*

*Proof.* We have to show that $C$ and $\mathsf{E}_{\mathcal{P}}(C)$ have exactly the same primitive observations when $C \in \mathcal{P}$. We show this by complete induction on the well-founded partial order $\sqsubset$ on $\mathbf{I}^*$.

Assume that $C$ and $\mathsf{E}_{\mathcal{P}}(C)$ have the same primitive observations $(I', O')$ for all $I' \sqsubset I : i$. We have to show that $\mathsf{E}_{\mathcal{P}}(C)(I : i) = C(I : i)$.

From the induction hypothesis, it follows that the derivation of the last step of $\mathsf{E}_{\mathcal{P}}(C)$ processing input $I : i$ was done by the OK rule: $\mathsf{E}_{\mathcal{P}}(C)$ is applied only on $I' \sqsubset I : i$, hence the induction hypothesis applies, and $\mathsf{E}_{\mathcal{P}}(C)$ has the same outputs as $C$ on $g(I : i)$. Hence, $\text{map}(\mathsf{E}_{\mathcal{P}}(C), g(I : i) \cup \{(I : i, O : o)\})$ is actually an observation on $C$, and since $C \in \mathcal{P}$ it follows that $\text{map}(\mathsf{E}_{\mathcal{P}}(C), g(I : i)) \cup \{(I : i, O : o)\} \notin \mathcal{M}_{\mathcal{P}}$, and hence the call to reject must return false. As a consequence, the primitive observation of $\mathsf{E}_{\mathcal{P}}(C)$ on $I : i$ is the same as the primitive observation of $C$ on $I : i$. ∎

**Theorem 4.5.** *$\mathsf{E}_{\mathcal{P}}(C)$ is black box.*

*Proof.* By the same induction technique as in Lemma 4.3 one can show that $\text{map}(\mathsf{E}_{\mathcal{P}}(C_1), g(I : i))$ is equal to $\text{map}(\mathsf{E}_{\mathcal{P}}(C_2), g(I : i))$ if $C_1 \sim C_2$. ∎

### 4.3.4 A lower bound

Finally, we can establish an interesting lower bound for the set of black box enforceable policies.

**Theorem 4.6.** *Every non-empty testable hypersafety policy is black box enforceable.*

*Proof.* For any non-empty testable hypersafety policy:

- the reject predicate is total computable by definition of testable.
- Proposition 3.2 gives us a total computable extension function.
- Lemma 4.2 gives us a well-founded generator.

Hence, we can construct an enforcement mechanism as in Definition 4.3, and Theorems 4.3, 4.4 and 4.5 tell us that this enforcement mechanism is secure, precise and black box. ∎

Obviously, this construction is very inefficient, but from a theoretical point of view this lower bound on the class of black box enforceable policies is interesting. In the next section, we turn to constructing concrete enforcement mechanisms.

## 5. Instances

Given a hypersafety policy $\mathcal{P}$, the steps that need to be taken to enforce the policy using our generic enforcement mechanism are:

1. specify a total computable reject function that decides membership in $\mathcal{M}_{\mathcal{P}}$. Prove that the set of observations for which reject returns true is indeed maximal in the sense of definition 3.3.
2. specify a total computable test generator function, and prove it satisfies the property required of a test generator as stipulated in definition 4.2.
3. specify a total computable extension function, and prove that it has the property required of such a function as specified in definition 3.5. Since our enforcement mechanism only applies extend to observations $M$ with inputs($M$) of the form $g(I : i) \cup \{I\}$, it is sufficient to define extend for such input parameters.

In this section, we construct interesting instances and relate them to existing enforcement mechanisms. We also discuss some optimizations to improve the performance of the generic enforcement mechanism.

### 5.1 1-safety policies

The simplest instantiation of our mechanism is the case where $\mathcal{P}$ is a 1-safety policy.

1. The generator $g$ maps every $I$ on $\{\}$ (cfr Example 11).
2. The reject function can be simplified to just a boolean predicate on primitive observations. Maximality ensures that any primitive observation that is not rejected can be further extended in a way acceptable to the policy. Hence, reject is a *benevolent* detector in the sense of Hamlen et al. [15].
3. The extend function just takes a primitive observation $(I, O)$ and a new input $i$ and returns a valid output $o$.

Since $g$ always returns the empty set, no recursive calls of the enforcement mechanism are needed: processing an input/output event just requires one call to reject and one call to extend.

Even this simplest instantiation admits interesting examples.

**Example 16.** *For the NSAR policy, reject was specified in Example 1, the generator always returns the empty set, and an extend function was defined in Example 8.*

**Example 17.** *Consider the policy that forbids any primitive observation of length bigger than 5. (Also counting the $o_{end}$ output values) This policy is empty (no program complies), and hence not enforceable. The reject function for this policy is the constant function that returns true.*

*Suppose the policy requires termination after at most 5 steps. This policy is enforceable. The reject function is:*

$$reject((I, O)) \quad = \quad \exists o \neq o_{end} : occurs(o, (drop\ 5\ O))$$

*The extend function always returns the termination event.*

$$extend(I, O, i) = o_{end}$$

*If a program fails to terminate before its 5th step, the enforcement mechanism will force it to terminate. For instance the sum program from Listing 1 will process the input stream $[1 : 1 : 1 : \ldots]$ to the output stream $[1 : 2 : 3 : 4 : 5 : o_{end} : o_{end} : o_{end} : \ldots]$ when executed under this enforcement mechanism.*

### 5.2 Non-interference with two levels

Let $pr$ be a total idempotent function from finite input streams to finite input streams. That is, for all $I \in \mathbf{I}^\star$, $pr(I) = pr(pr(I))$. We think of $pr$ as a projection that removes confidential information from the input stream.

A program $C$ is *non-interferent w.r.t. pr* iff

$$\forall I, I' \in \mathbf{I}^\star : pr(I) = pr(I') \implies O|_L = O'|_L,$$

where $C(I) = O$ and $C(I') = O'$.

The projection $pr$ can be instantiated in many ways, and our enforcement mechanism can handle all these instantiations.

- $pr(I) = I|_{L,HD}$ where $I|_{L,HD}$ is the resulting stream after replacing the H input values in $I$ with default values: this is a variation of NI where *content* of input events is secret but the *occurrence* of the input event is not. With the optimizations in Section 5.4 our generic enforcement mechanism reduces to standard secure multi-execution [11, 22].
- $pr(I) = I|_L$: models standard NI as in Example 2. Our generic enforcement mechanism defines a reactive variant of secure multi-execution as in [5, 30].
- $pr$ can more generally project to values that depend on all previous values in the input stream. This can model for instance NI with stateful declassification policies [27]. Our generic enforcement mechanism even improves on the mechanism in [27], as it does not require declassify annotations for precision since in [27] a declassify operator is just a directive indicating that a particular value is computed by the release function.

Construction of the reject predicate and the test generator for this policy is similar to Example 6 and Example 12. For this more general case, the following definitions work:

$$\text{reject}(M) = \begin{cases} \textbf{true} & \exists M_{bad} = \{(I, O), (I', O')\}, \\ & M_{bad} \subseteq \overline{M} \text{ s.t. } pr(I) = pr(I') \\ & \quad \text{and } O|_L \neq O'|_L, \\ \textbf{false} & \text{otherwise.} \end{cases}$$

$$g(I) = \{pr(I)\} \setminus \{I\}$$

The well founded order for the generator is the smallest ordering such that for all $I$ and $i$, $I \sqsubset I : i$ and if $pr(I) \neq I$ then $pr(I) \sqsubset I$. A sufficient condition is that $pr$(I) has smaller or equal length as $I$, and this is satisfied in all instances for $pr$ mentioned above.

Since extend is only called for $M = \{(I, O), (I' : i', O' : o')\}$ where $pr(I : i) = I' : i'$, this function is as below where $o_H$ is an arbitrary value such that $lvl(o_H) = H$.

$$\text{extend}_{\mathcal{P}_{NI1}}(M, I, i) = \begin{cases} o_H & \text{if } lvl(i) = H \text{ where } lvl(o_H) = H \\ o' & \text{if } lvl(i) = L. \end{cases}$$

### 5.3 Non-interference for multiple levels

It is relatively straigtforward to extend all the variants of NI above to multiple confidentiality levels. We illustrate this for standard NI. Let $\langle \mathcal{L}, \leq \rangle$ be a complete lattice of security levels with a top level ($\top$) and a bottom level ($\bot$), and let $lvl$ be a function from $\mathbf{I} \cup \mathbf{O}$ to $\mathcal{L}$. A program $C$ is *non-interferent* with respect to $lvl$ iff $\forall I, I' \in \mathbf{I}^\star : I|_l = I'|_l \implies O|_l = O'|_l$, where $C(I) = O$ and $C(I') = O'$, and $I|_l$ filters out all $i$ with $lvl(i) \not\leq l$ (and similarly for $O|_l$).

$$\text{reject}(M) = \begin{cases} \textbf{true} & \exists M_{bad} = \{(I, O), (I', O')\}, \\ & M_{bad} \subseteq \overline{M} \text{ s.t. } I|_l = I'|_l \\ & \quad \text{and } O|_l \neq O'|_l, \text{ for some } l \\ \textbf{false} & \text{otherwise.} \end{cases}$$

$$g(I) = \{I|_l \quad | \quad l \in \mathcal{L}\} \setminus \{I\}$$

$$\text{extend}_{\mathcal{P}_{NI}}(M, I, i) = \begin{cases} o_\top & \text{if } lvl(i) \neq \bot \text{ where } lvl(o_\top) = \top, \\ o_\bot & \text{if } lvl(i) = \bot. \end{cases}$$

(taking into account that extend is only called for $M = \{(I, O)\} \cup \{(I' : i', O' : o') \mid I' : i' \in g(I : i)\}$ and $(I_\perp : i_\perp, O_\perp : o_\perp)$ is in $M$, where $I_\perp : i_\perp = (I : i)|_\perp$)

### 5.4 Optimizations and extensions.

The construction in Definition 4.3 is designed to minimize the state of the enforcement mechanism (thus making the security and precision proofs relatively simple). However, it is very suboptimal in terms of execution time. The recursive calls to the enforcement mechanism will often recompute observations on $\mathsf{E}_\mathcal{P}(C)$ over and over many times.

A standard optimization for such cases is *memoization*: cache the results of calls to $\mathsf{E}_\mathcal{P}(C)$ in some data structure and reuse them from the cache instead of recomputing them.

A data structure that is particularly well suited for optimization of our enforcement mechanism is an array of entries $\langle I_j, C_j, O_j \rangle$, where for each $j$, it holds that $\langle I_j, C, C_j, O_j \rangle$ is the state reached by the enforcement mechanism after processing input stream $I_j$. This data structure (1) caches all the output streams that $\mathsf{E}_\mathcal{P}(C)$ produces on any of the $I_j$ (or prefixes of $I_j$), and (2) it is efficient to update the data structure for growing $I_j$. Essentially, such a data structure maintains a set of alternative executions of $C$ (taking into account corrections to the execution where necessary), in a way that is very close to secure multi-execution [11]. Proving the correctness of this optimization for an arbitrary policy and relating it to secure multi-execution is an interesting avenue for future work.

Finally, our generic construction also constructs secure and precise enforcement mechanism for many other policies. However, it is not always obvious that efficient test generators exist. For example, the $k$-safety policy from Example 3 is enforceable, but we have not been able to come up with an efficient generator for this policy. Another interesting line of future work is to look for efficient generators for other hypersafety policies.

## 6. Discussion

Many enforcement mechanisms used in practice make no, or very limited use of analysis of the code of the programs they are monitoring. Operating system kernels, virtual machine monitors, and application firewalls treat the programs they are guarding as black boxes. Hence it is interesting to understand what exactly can be enforced under this black box constraint.

Figure 1 summarizes our results on upper and lower bounds for the class of black box enforceable policies. The shaded region corresponds to the class of policies that are black box enforceable as defined in Definition 4.1. First, in Theorem 4.1 we have shown that any policy that is black box enforceable must be hypersafety. More importantly, in Theorem 4.2 we have shown that such policies must be semi-testable hypersafety policies. Based on this theorem, the policy in Example 4 is not black box enforceable. Finally, in Theorem 4.6 we have shown that every non-empty testable hypersafety policy is black box enforceable. The empty policy is not enforceable since there is no program in this policy and the mechanism is just a program.

An interesting question is how tight the bounds we establish for black box enforceable policies are. There is a gap between the sufficient condition, i.e. that the policy is testable hypersafety, and the necessary condition, i.e. that the policy is semi-testable hypersafety. Clearly, the upper bound is not tight: an example 1-safety policy that is semi-testable but not enforceable is the policy that requires programs to only output terminating $\lambda$-terms. The complement of the maximal set of bad observations is recursively enumerable, hence the policy is semi-testable. However an enforcement mechanism would have to decide termination. The question now is whether the subset marked with ??? on Figure 1 is empty. For the

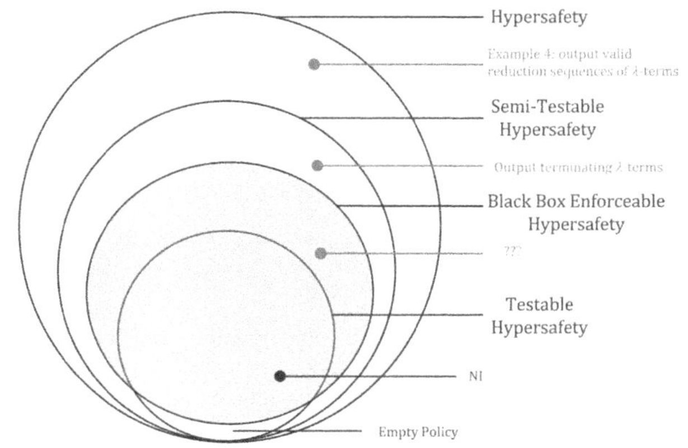


**Figure 1.** Lower and upper bounds of black box enforceable hypersafety policies.

lower bound, we believe it might actually be tight, but we have not been able to prove this yet.

One important aspect of our results is the fact that they hold for our specific model of reactive programs where programs can not diverge on a single input value. On the one hand, this is a positive aspect as many programs satisfy this constraint, and under this program model enforcement mechanisms can be guaranteed not to diverge while still being allowed to speculatively execute programs until the next observable output. Divergence of a program could perhaps be modeled by having the program react with a special output value $o_{busy}$ to any input value while diverging, but this *does* impact the policies that are enforceable, as output values such as $o_{busy}$ become observable, and hence policies have to take them into account. On the other hand, this constraint on programs makes enforcement easier, and some of our results will clearly not hold for programs that do diverge on some inputs. An important question for future work is to explore the impact of variations of the program model on our results.

Another interesting question to ask is: what is the relation between policies enforceable by program rewriting [15], and the black box enforceable policies (under our model of programs)? Clearly, the black box enforceable policies are also enforceable by rewriting. But rewriters seem to have additional power as they can inspect and transform the code of the program at will. However, we have not been able to find policies that are enforceable by rewriting but not black box enforceable. It seems that the power to edit input/output events and explore alternative runs is very close to the power to rewrite and inspect code – at least if one operates under the constraints that (1) the resulting enforcement mechanism must be secure and precise, and (2) programs must not diverge on single inputs.

Besides the bounds on enforceability, this article also introduces a general enforcement mechanism that can be used to build practical enforcement mechanisms. This was demonstrated in Section 5, where we have seen that several different flavors of enforcement mechanisms for NI are particular instances of our techniques with efficient test generators. We believe that the existence of efficient test generators is the key to practical enforceability. In fact, one can prove that the existence of an efficient enforcement mechanism implies the existence of an efficient test generator: one can take as $g(I)$ all the input streams $I'$ that the efficient enforcement mechanism feeds to the untrusted program while processing input $I$. It is not too hard to see that this defines a test generator. Hence, we believe one of the interesting conclusions of this work is that the key to developing a black box enforcement mechanism for a hypersafety policy is to come up with an efficient test generator.

# 7. Related Work

## 7.1 Enforcement power of enforcement mechanisms

Erlingsson and Schneider [12, 25] initiated the investigation of dynamic enforcement of security policies via execution monitoring (EM). Schneider [25] demonstrated that for a security policy to be enforceable by EM, the policy has to be a safety property on execution traces. He also introduced a class of monitors called *security automata* that can be used as recognizers for safety properties. Such an automaton is capable of observing system actions, recognizing violations and terminating the observed system (called the *target*) when it is about to perform a violation. A target system is allowed to perform a computation step if and only if the respective security automaton can transition to some next state by performing the same step. Our proposed mechanisms can be seen as a generalization of Schneider's enforceable security policies, as they can be instantiated on nonempty 1-safety policies.

Schneider's work was refined by Viswanathan [28] who showed that a property has to be decidable in order to be enforceable. Formally, Viswanathan argued that the class of dynamically enforceable policies with EM is actually equivalent to the class of co-recursively enumerable ($coRE$) properties, also known as the class $\Pi_1$ of the arithmetic hierarchy. However, it was later shown by Hamlen et al. [15] that $coRE$ is actually an upper bound on the class of EM enforceable properties. The reason is that some policies in $coRE$ are not enforceable because the monitor might not have enough power to intervene. For instance, it is impossible to enforce a policy that forbids all the interventions available to the EM.

Fong [14] analyzed the impact of memory-limitations on the enforcement mechanisms. He introduced *shallow history automata* which only store information about the occurrence of past events and *not* about their order. Despite this limitation, many interesting properties were shown to remain enforceable. Talhi et al. [26] extended Fong's work by introducing *bounded history automata*, combining features of security and edit automata and having bounded memory. In addition, they proposed an algorithm that decides whether there exists a bounded history automaton for a policy in a language from a subclass of the regular languages (called the locally testable languages [21]). Falcone et al. [13] investigated the properties that are recognizable by different automata models with a finite set of control states and enforcement operations in terms of the safety-progress hierarchy [9]. In addition, they presented a systematic technique to synthesize monitors from an automaton recognizing some safety, guarantee, obligation or response properties. Hamlen et al. [15] defined the class of security policies enforceable by program rewriting (RW) and called it $RW$-*enforceable*. However, they did not provide a precise characterization of this class and even argued that a characterization in complexity theoretic terms might not exist. Finally, Chabot et al. [8] explored the problem of policy enforcement w.r.t. a trace universe. They showed that a truncation enforcement mechanism is more powerful if it only considers the possible traces and not all traces in the trace universe. They also presented an algorithm that takes as an input a finite state automaton (i.e. the policy) and a finite state transition system (i.e. the target system) and checks if the policy is enforceable. Additionally, if the policy is found to be enforceable, the algorithm returns a secured version of the target system.

Ligatti et al. [18, 19] introduced edit automata, capable of enforcing a class of non-safety (including purely liveness) policies called *infinite renewal* properties. They argued that infinite renewal properties subsume the computable safety properties. Edit automata are a black box enforcement mechanism, capable of inserting and deleting system actions as well as terminating a target system in the case of a policy violation. The authors also showed how to construct an enforcement mechanism that provably enforces any "reasonable" infinite renewal property [18]. Edit automata are similar to our approach in that they offer a black box mechanism capable of monitoring and/or editing the input/output behavior of programs. However, to enforce infinite renewal properties, they have to buffer program actions – something that is undesirable for reactive programs. Also, edit automata are not capable of exploring alternative executions.

Unlike edit automata, mandatory-result automata [20] have an interface to interact with a target system: they get requests from the system and send outputs back to the system but do not enforce policies that are more expressive than those investigated by Basin et al. [4]. Basin and his coauthors revisited Schneider's work and proposed to distinguish between actions that are under the control of the enforcement mechanism and actions that are merely observable (for instance the passing of time), i.e. the mechanism cannot prevent their execution. For this refinement of the problem, the authors presented necessary and sufficient conditions to characterize when a policy is EM enforceable, based on their generalized notion of safety. In addition, they studied the problem of whether a policy is enforceable for several specification languages. They also showed how to synthesize an enforcement mechanism for a given enforceable policy and gave complexity results.

Clarkson and Schneider [10] were the first to propose *hyperproperties* (sets of trace properties) as a model for security policies. They generalized safety and liveness to hypersafety and hyperliveness, and proposed a static verification approach for verifying compliance with a hypersafety property. The fact that hypersafety aligns so well with black box enforceability is additional evidence that their classification of security policies as hypersafety or hyperliveness is a useful taxonomy of policies.

## 7.2 Existing black box enforcement mechanisms for non-interference

Besides the general purpose black box enforcement mechanisms (such as the different variants of execution monitors and edit automata) discussed above, a considerable amount of research has been done on dynamic enforcement of non-interference, some of it assuming only black box access to programs. Le Guernic's PhD thesis [17] presents an extensive survey of the state of the art in dynamic information flow control circa 2007. The major more recent results are presented next.

There have been several proposals for information flow runtime monitors. Sabelfeld et al. proposed such monitors for DOM-like structures [24], dynamic code evaluation [1] and timeouts [23]. Austin and Flanagen [2] presented alternative techniques that have the potential of being more permissive. All these monitors are useful and relatively efficient, however a common problem is that they are not precise, i.e. they over-approximate the problem and as a result sometimes block secure executions.

A secure and precise dynamic enforcement technique is secure multi-execution (SME), developed independently by several researchers [11, 16, 29]. Khatiwala et al. [16] proposed a technique called *Data Sandboxing*, which partitions the program into two programs at source-code level and then uses system call interposition to control the output channels. In a follow-up article, Capizzi et al. [29] abandoned source-code partitioning; instead, they proposed to run two processes for the public and secret levels respectively and as a result provide strong confidentiality guarantees. Devriese and Piessens [11] independently proposed the related technique that they called SME. The overall idea of SME is to keep a program secure by separating computations at different security levels. To that end, the original program is executed multiple times, once for each security level and giving inputs and outputs special treatment; this technique guarantees security and precision.

Austin and Flanagan [3] developed a more efficient implementation of SME based on multi-faceted evaluation. Rafnsson and Sabelfeld [22] upgraded the SME technique to distinguish between presence and content of secret messages on a channel, to perform declassification and to make SME precise for observers having access to more than one level. Zanarini et al. [30] proposed combining SME with execution monitoring. The idea is at each step to compare the current execution with what SME would produce in order to detect (and report) actions that offend the policy. Similarly to Rafnsson and Sabelfeld [22], they use a scheduling strategy that preserves the interleaving of events from different security levels, thus increasing the precision of SME. Vanhoef et al. [27] proposed an SME-based technique for enforcing information flow policies with support for stateful declassification for event-driven programs. They used a projection function to specify what information about an event can be declassified and a stateful release function to specify aggregate information about secret events seen so far that can be declassified. It is clear that the mechanisms presented in this work are a generalization and at the same time go beyond a number of flavors of SME, for instance the vanilla one with 2-levels, the one with n-levels [11], and with stateful declassification [27].

## 8. Conclusion

We have studied security policy enforcement mechanisms for deterministic reactive programs that respond to input events in finite time with an observable output event. Our enforcement mechanisms are *black box*: the enforcement mechanism only needs to be able to (1) intercept and edit the input/output events of the untrusted program, and (2) run multiple isolated copies of the untrusted program in order to test the behaviour of the program on alternative inputs. The enforcement mechanism can *not* do (or more positively: does not *need* to do) analysis on the source or machine code of the program.

We have given a constructive proof that under these assumptions any testable hypersafety policy is enforceable: if it is decidable whether an observation can not be produced by any program in the policy, then the policy is black box enforceable by a generic enforcement mechanism. The construction in the proof is inefficient, but one can construct more efficient enforcement mechanisms by providing a reject function, an efficient test generator and an extension function as inputs to the general construction.

We have also shown an upper bound on black box enforceable policies: any enforceable policy is a semi-testable hypersafety policy, i.e. the observations that are possible for *some* program in the policy are enumerable.

While these lower and upper bounds are of theoretical interest, we have also shown that our generic enforcement mechanism is of practical interest by instantiating it to concrete enforcement mechanisms for a number of relevant policies.

## Acknowledgments

The authors are grateful to Deepak Garg for proofreading this paper and suggesting numerous improvements. This research is partially funded by the Research Fund KU Leuven, by the Research Foundation - Flanders (FWO), by the Italian project TENACE PRIN (n. 20103P34XC), and by the project EU-IST-NOE-NESSOS.

## References

[1] A. Askarov and A. Sabelfeld. Tight enforcement of information-release policies for dynamic languages. In *CSF*, pages 43–59, 2009.

[2] T. H. Austin and C. Flanagan. Permissive dynamic information flow analysis. In *PLAS*, pages 3:1–3:12, 2010.

[3] T. H. Austin and C. Flanagan. Multiple facets for dynamic information flow. In *POPL*, pages 165–178, 2012.

[4] D. Basin, V. Jugé, F. Klaedtke, and E. Zălinescu. Enforceable security policies revisited. *TISSEC*, 16(1):3:1–3:26, June 2013.

[5] N. Bielova, D. Devriese, F. Massacci, and F. Piessens. Reactive non-interference for a browser model. In *5th International Conference on Network and System Security*, pages 97–104, 2011.

[6] A. Bohannon, B. C. Pierce, V. Sjöberg, S. Weirich, and S. Zdancewic. Reactive noninterference. In *CCS*, pages 79–90, 2009.

[7] R. Capizzi, A. Longo, V. N. Venkatakrishnan, and A. P. Sistla. Preventing information leaks through shadow executions. In *ACSAC*, pages 322–331, 2008.

[8] H. Chabot, R. Khoury, and N. Tawbi. Extending the enforcement power of truncation monitors using static analysis. *Computers & Security*, 30(4):194–207, June 2011.

[9] E. Y. Chang, Z. Manna, and A. Pnueli. Characterization of temporal property classes. In *ICALP*, pages 474–486, 1992.

[10] M. R. Clarkson and F. B. Schneider. Hyperproperties. *JCS*, 18:1157–1210, September 2010.

[11] D. Devriese and F. Piessens. Noninterference through secure multi-execution. In *IEEE S&P*, pages 109–124, 2010.

[12] U. Erlingsson and F. B. Schneider. Sasi enforcement of security policies: A retrospective. In *1999 Workshop on New Security Paradigms*, pages 87–95, 2000.

[13] Y. Falcone, L. Mounier, J.-C. Fernandez, and J.-L. Richier. Runtime enforcement monitors: composition, synthesis, and enforcement abilities. *Formal Methods in System Design*, 38(3):223–262, 2011.

[14] P. W. L. Fong. Access control by tracking shallow execution history. In *IEEE S&P*, pages 43–55, 2004.

[15] K. W. Hamlen, G. Morrisett, and F. B. Schneider. Computability classes for enforcement mechanisms. *TOPLAS*, 28(1):175–205, 2006.

[16] T. Khatiwala, R. Swaminathan, and V. N. Venkatakrishnan. Data sandboxing: A technique for enforcing confidentiality policies. In *ACSAC*, pages 223–234, 2006.

[17] G. Le Guernic. *Confidentiality Enforcement Using Dynamic Information Flow Analyses*. PhD thesis, Kansas State University, 2007.

[18] J. Ligatti, L. Bauer, and D. Walker. Edit automata: Enforcement mechanisms for run-time security policies. *Int. J. of Inf. Sec.*, 4(1–2):2–16, February 2005.

[19] J. Ligatti, L. Bauer, and D. Walker. Run-time enforcement of non-safety policies. *TISSEC*, 12(3):1–41, 2009.

[20] J. Ligatti and S. Reddy. A theory of runtime enforcement, with results. In *ESORICS*, pages 87–100, 2010.

[21] R. McNaughton and S. A. Papert. *Counter-Free Automata (M.I.T. Research Monograph No. 65)*. The MIT Press, 1971.

[22] W. Rafnsson and A. Sabelfeld. Secure multi-execution: fine-grained, declassification-aware, and transparent. In *CSF*, pages 33–48, 2013.

[23] A. Russo and A. Sabelfeld. Securing timeout instructions in web applications. In *CSF*, pages 92–106, 2009.

[24] A. Russo, A. Sabelfeld, and A. Chudnov. Tracking information flow in dynamic tree structures. In *ESORICS*, pages 86–103, 2009.

[25] F. Schneider. Enforceable security policies. *TISSEC*, 3(1):30–50, 2000.

[26] C. Talhi, N. Tawbi, and M. Debbabi. Execution monitoring enforcement under memory-limitation constraints. *Inf. Comput.*, 206(2-4):158–184, Feb. 2008.

[27] M. Vanhoef, W. De Groef, D. Devriese, F. Piessens, and T. Rezk. Stateful declassification policies for event-driven programs. In *CSF*, 2014.

[28] M. Viswanathan. *Foundations for the Run-time Analysis of Software Systems*. PhD thesis, University of Pennsylvania, 2000.

[29] A. R. Yumerefendi, B. Mickle, and L. P. Cox. Tightlip: Keeping applications from spilling the beans. In *4th USENIX Conference on Networked Systems Design & Implementation*, pages 12–12, 2007.

[30] D. Zanarini, M. Jaskelioff, and A. Russo. Precise enforcement of confidentiality for reactive systems. In *CSF*, pages 18–32, 2013.

# Higher-Order Approximate Relational Refinement Types for Mechanism Design and Differential Privacy

Gilles Barthe[⋆] Marco Gaboardi[‡] Emilio Jesús Gallego Arias[#]
Justin Hsu[#] Aaron Roth[#] Pierre-Yves Strub[⋆]

[⋆] IMDEA Software Institute [‡] University of Dundee, Scotland [#] University of Pennsylvania

## Abstract

*Mechanism design* is the study of algorithm design where the inputs to the algorithm are controlled by strategic agents, who must be *incentivized* to faithfully report them. Unlike typical programmatic properties, it is not sufficient for algorithms to merely satisfy the property—incentive properties are only useful if the strategic agents also *believe* this fact.

Verification is an attractive way to convince agents that the incentive properties actually hold, but mechanism design poses several unique challenges: interesting properties can be sophisticated *relational* properties of probabilistic computations involving expected values, and mechanisms may rely on other probabilistic properties, like *differential privacy*, to achieve their goals.

We introduce a relational refinement type system, called $\mathsf{HOARe}^2$, for verifying mechanism design and differential privacy. We show that $\mathsf{HOARe}^2$ is sound w.r.t. a denotational semantics, and correctly models $(\epsilon, \delta)$-differential privacy; moreover, we show that it subsumes *DFuzz*, an existing linear dependent type system for differential privacy. Finally, we develop an SMT-based implementation of $\mathsf{HOARe}^2$ and use it to verify challenging examples of mechanism design, including auctions and aggregative games, and new proposed examples from differential privacy.

***Categories and Subject Descriptors*** D.3.1 [*Programming Languages*]: Formal Definitions and Theory—Semantics; D.2.4 [*Software Engineering*]: Software/Program Verification.

***Keywords*** program logics; probabilistic programming

## 1. Introduction

When designing algorithms, we usually assume that the inputs are correctly reported. However, in the real world, inputs may be provided by people who may want to influence the outcome of the algorithm. *Mechanism design* is the field of algorithm design where the *inputs* to the algorithm (often called a *mechanism*) are controlled by *strategic agents* who may manipulate what their inputs. In this setting, it is not enough to design an algorithm which behaves correctly on correct input; the design of the mechanism must convince (*incentivize*) agents to provide their *correct* inputs to the algorithm.

The canonical application of mechanism design is auction design. In an auction, the algorithmic problem can be very simple: for instance, allocate some set of goods amongst a set of $n$ agents so as to maximize their sum value for the goods. The inputs to the algorithmic problem are simply the agents' values for the goods, but these are unknown to the algorithm designer. Instead, the mechanism must elicit bids. To incentivize agents to bid honestly, actions compute a price that each agent must pay. Auctions are generally designed so that the allocation and payment rules incentivize agents to bid their true value for the goods, *no matter what their opponents do*. An auction that satisfies this property is said to be *dominant strategy incentive compatible*, or simply *truthful*. This is among the most important *solution concepts*—predictions about behavior of strategic agents—in mechanism design.

Beyond auctions, mechanisms design can be used to handle more abstract games where agents have a variety of actions and a real-valued *utility function* based on the actions selected by all agents. In most settings, agents do not have any dominant strategies, and so we must be satisfied with weaker *solution concepts* like *Nash equilibria*. Informally, a set of actions, one for each player, forms a Nash equilibrium if no player can increase her utility unilaterally deviating to a different action *so long as no other player deviates*.[1] The hope is that strategic agents will collectively decide to play at an equilibrium: no single agent can gain by deviating.

However, Nash equilibria can be an unrealistic prediction of behavior. First of all, they are generally not unique: agents must somehow coordinate to play at a single equilibrium, but different agents might prefer different equilibrium outcomes. Second of all, in games with a large number of players, agents generally do not have complete knowledge about everyone's utility functions, and so may not even know what the Nash equilibria of the game are. To help players coordinate on an equilibrium, one approach is to design an equilibrium selection mechanism. Agents are asked to report their utility functions to some *mediator*, and the mediator suggests some action for them to play. Agents are strategic, so they are free to misreport their utility function, or disregard the mediator's suggestion. A well-designed mediator will incentivize agents to report truthfully and follow the recommendation.

A promising and recent tool for mediator design is *differential privacy* [18]. The original goal of differential privacy was to protect individuals privacy in data mining, by ensuring that answering the same query on two databases differing in a single person's data leads to results that are close in some sense. Seen another way, differential privacy limits any individual's *influence* on the result. This can be

[1] Contrast this with dominant strategies: in a truthful auction, no agent can gain by deviating *no matter what the other players play*.



*POPL '15*, January 15–17, 2015, Mumbai, India.

ACM 978-1-4503-3300-9/15/01... $15.00.
http://dx.doi.org/10.1145/10.1145/2676726.2677000

quite useful as a tool for mechanism design: If the mediator satisfies differential privacy, agents will have little incentive to deviate from truthful behavior since they can only change the selected equilibria to a small degree.

While this is a theoretically clean idea, there can be practical issues: currently proposed mechanisms are complex enough that agents may not be able to verify the promised incentive properties of the mediator. In general, if agents do not believe the incentive properties of a mechanism, then they may behave in unpredictable ways or decline to participate. Indeed, designers of an upcoming public radio spectrum auction have stressed "obviousness" as a key feature—the incentive features should be plainly apparent to any agent [39]. While this is a desirable goal for simple mechanisms, it is hard to achieve for complex mechanisms. For these cases, we propose an alternative approach: rather than simplify the mechanism, use formal verification to automatically check incentive properties.

However, mechanism design poses serious challenges for verification. First, both differential privacy and equilibria properties are *relational* properties of programs, which reason about more than one run of the same program; for instance, truthfulness states that the payoff of an agent in a run when she reports truthfully is at least its payoff in a run where she reports arbitrarily. Second, equilibria properties are significantly more involved than typical program verification properties. For randomized mechanisms, properties are stated in terms of *expected value* rather than more standard equivalences or relations between distributions. Finally, incentive properties of mediator mechanisms rest on non-trivial interactions between game-theoretic properties and differential privacy, so their formal verification must be conducted in a framework that is expressive enough to reason about differential privacy, game-theoretic properties, and interactions of the two.

***Contributions*** To handle these challenges, we present HOARe$^2$, a type-based framework for relational properties of higher-order probabilistic programs, like differential privacy, truthfulness, and approximate equilibrium. HOARe$^2$ is based on refinement types—an expressive type discipline that captures fine-grained properties of computations by enriching types with assertions [23]—and tightly integrates several features: relational refinements [4], refinements at higher types (where assertions constrain the behavior of functions), and a polymonadic representation of approximate refinements for probabilistic computations [3]. We demonstrate the theoretical and practical relevance of HOARe$^2$ through the following contributions:

- We demonstrate that HOARe$^2$ achieves desirable meta-theoretical properties, like soundness with respect to a denotational semantics (§ 3.3) and semantic subtyping. As a contribution of independent interest, we show that the logical interpretation of non-termination adopted by existing refinement type systems is inconsistent with semantic subtyping when refinements at higher order types are allowed.
- We define a type-preserving embedding of *DFuzz* [24]—a linear dependent type system for differential privacy—into HOARe$^2$, and recover soundness of *DFuzz* from soundness of HOARe$^2$ (§ 4). The embedding illustrates how semantic subtyping and refinements at higher types combine to internalize logical relations in HOARe$^2$.
- We implement a type-checker for HOARe$^2$ and verify examples drawn from differential privacy and mechanism design. For instance, we verify truthfulness properties of randomized auctions, and an equilibrium selection algorithm for aggregative games based on differential privacy. The implementation is fully automated, discharging assertions using SMT solvers.

We discuss related work in § 7, and conclude with possible future directions in § 8.

## 2. Relational refinements, informally

We will establish properties of programs by using refinement types, an expressive typing discipline introduced by Freeman and Pfenning [23]. As is typical in refinement type systems, we type expressions in two steps. First, we define a simply typed system in which the type of probabilistic computations are modeled using a probability monad $\mathfrak{M}[\cdot]$; for example, the expected value of a positive real-valued function w.r.t. a distribution is modeled by a function $\mathbf{E}$ of type: $\mathfrak{M}[T] \to (T \to \mathbb{R}^+) \to \overline{\mathbb{R}}^+$, where $\mathbb{R}^+$ denotes the type of positive reals and $\overline{\mathbb{R}}^+$ denotes $\mathbb{R}^+$ extended with $+\infty$.

Next, we define a relational refinement type system for simply typed expressions. Relational refinements [4] specify properties of *pairs* of values via types of the form $\{x :: T \mid \phi\}$, where $\phi$ is a *relational assertion*: a logical formula that can express facts involving the *left* instance $x_\triangleleft$ and the *right* instance $x_\triangleright$ of $x$. For instance, the type $\{x :: \mathbb{N} \mid |x_\triangleleft - x_\triangleright| \leqslant k\}$ models pairs of natural numbers which differ by at most $k$.

Both traditional and relational refinement type systems (e.g., [4]) often forbid refinements at higher types, like $\{x :: T \mid \phi\}$ where $T$ is a function type. However, such relational refinements are convenient to model properties of probabilistic operators. For instance, given a distribution $\mu :: \mathfrak{M}[T]$, the following types for $\mathbf{E}\,\mu$ capture monotonicity and linearity of expectation:

$$\{f :: T \to \mathbb{R}^+ \mid \forall z. f_\triangleleft z \leqslant f_\triangleright z\} \to \{r :: \overline{\mathbb{R}}^+ \mid r_\triangleleft \leqslant r_\triangleright\}$$
$$\{f :: T \to \mathbb{R}^+ \mid \forall z. f_\triangleleft z = k \cdot f_\triangleright z\} \to \{x :: \overline{\mathbb{R}}^+ \mid x_\triangleleft = k \cdot x_\triangleright\}$$

Relational refinements can also be used to model relations between pairs of distributions, like differential privacy. A probabilistic computation $F : T \to U$ is $(\epsilon, \delta)$-*differentially private* (w.r.t an adjacency relation $\Phi$) if for every $t_1, t_2 \in T$, and for every subset of outputs $E$,

$$t_1 \;\Phi\; t_2 \implies \Pr_{x \leftarrow F\,t_1}[x \in E] \leqslant \exp(\epsilon) \Pr_{x \leftarrow F\,t_2}[x \in E] + \delta.$$

The parameters $\epsilon$ and $\delta$ are non-negative real numbers controlling the strength of the privacy guarantee. Using relational refinement types, the type of $(\epsilon, \delta)$-differentially private computations from $T$ to $U$ is:

$$\{x :: T \mid x_\triangleleft \;\Phi\; x_\triangleright\} \to \{\mu :: \mathfrak{M}[U] \mid \Delta_\epsilon(\mu_\triangleleft, \mu_\triangleright) \leqslant \delta\},$$

where

$$\Delta_\epsilon(\mu_1, \mu_2) = \max_{E \subseteq U} \left( \Pr_{x \leftarrow \mu_1}[x \in E] - \exp(\epsilon) \Pr_{x \leftarrow \mu_2}[x \in E] \right)$$

is the $\epsilon$-*distance* [3] between two distributions $\mu_1$ and $\mu_2$ over $U$.

However, this modeling is not appropriate for practical program verification; indeed, the definition of $\epsilon$-distance uses probabilities and exponentials; it is possible to formalize basic properties for these concepts, but more advanced reasoning, which is required for some examples, is beyond the abilities of SMT solvers. Instead, we introduce a probabilistic polymonad [33], with a type constructor of the form $\mathfrak{M}_{\epsilon,\delta}[\cdot]$ and two operators unit and bind with respective types:

$$\begin{array}{lll} \mathsf{unit} & : & T \to \mathfrak{M}_{\epsilon,\delta}[T] \\ \mathsf{bind} & : & \mathfrak{M}_{\epsilon,\delta}[T] \to (T \to \mathfrak{M}_{\epsilon',\delta'}[U]) \to \mathfrak{M}_{\epsilon+\epsilon',\delta+\delta'}[U]. \end{array}$$

The main advantage of the polymonad versus the explicit formalization of $\epsilon$-distance is that all reasoning about probabilities is confined to the definition of valid judgment, and to the proof of soundness of the monadic rules. On the other hand, the refinement types $T$ and $U$ remain standard relational refinements, and do not need to refer to probabilities or exponentials.

The interpretation of $\mathfrak{M}_{\epsilon,\delta}[\cdot]$ is based on a lifting operator $\mathcal{L}_{\epsilon,\delta}(\cdot)$ that turns a relation $\Psi$ on $T_1 \times T_2$ into a relation $\mathcal{L}_{\epsilon,\delta}(\Psi)$ on $\mathfrak{M}[T_1] \times \mathfrak{M}[T_2]$; we will provide the formal definition in § 3.4.

A useful property of lifting [3] is that two distributions are related by $\mathcal{L}_{\epsilon,\delta}(=)$ iff their $\epsilon$-distance is upper bounded by $\delta$. In particular, $(\epsilon,\delta)$-differentially private computations can be modeled by the relational refinement:

$$\{x :: T \mid x_\triangleleft\ \Phi\ x_\triangleright\} \to \mathfrak{M}_{\epsilon,\delta}[\{y :: U \mid y_\triangleleft = y_\triangleright\}],$$

which leads to simpler verification conditions over individual outputs rather than sets of outputs.

Another advantage of this polymonadic approach is that the type of the bind operator captures the sequential composition theorem of differential privacy [18], and that it leads to an elegant type system in which quantitative reasoning related to differential privacy is confined to the rules of the polymonad. This is in contrast to some prior work where quantitative reasoning is pervasive in all rules of the system [3].

The last component of HOARe$^2$ is a monad $\mathfrak{C}[\cdot]$ to model diverging computations. While this is quite standard, this approach is key to reconcile semantic subtyping, and refinements at higher types. We elaborate on this point next.

### 2.1 An aside on non-termination and refinement types

Exploiting the power of refinement types requires the ability to draw useful inferences from assertions. These inferences are typically represented in typing derivations via a subtyping relation $\preceq$, and applied with a special typing rule, called *subsumption*, that changes the type of an expression to an arbitrary supertype. Ideally, the subtyping relation should be complete w.r.t. the denotational semantics of the type system—a property known as *semantic subtyping*. However, extending most existing refinement type systems with semantic subtyping can lead to an inconsistency, because semantic subtyping conflicts with typical logical treatments of non-termination.

Inconsistency can arise both in non-relational and relational settings; let us consider the non-relational case. Here, inconsistency manifests itself as an expression of type $\{x : \mathbb{N} \mid \bot\}$ in the empty context, with the expression reducing to a value. Existing refinement type systems such as F7, F$^\star$ and LIQUIDHASKELL assign the type $\{x : \mathbb{N} \mid x \neq 0\} \to \{y : \mathbb{N} \mid \bot\}$ to any recursive function $f$ that does not terminate on values $x \neq 0$, such as for instance $\texttt{letrec}\ g\ x = \texttt{case}\ x\ \texttt{with}\ [0 \Rightarrow 0 \mid s\ y \Rightarrow g\ x]$. On the other hand, semantic subtyping validates the equivalence FUN-SUB:

$$\{x : T \mid \phi\} \to \{y : U \mid \psi\} \simeq \{f : T \to U \mid \forall x : T. \phi \Longrightarrow \psi[f\ x/y]\}$$

where we write $T \simeq U$ iff $T \preceq U$ and $U \preceq T$. It follows that $f\ 0$ has the problematic type:

$$\dfrac{\dfrac{\dfrac{\dfrac{\vdash f : \{x : \mathbb{N} \mid x \neq 0\} \to \{y : \mathbb{N} \mid \bot\}}{\vdash f : \{g : \mathbb{N} \to \mathbb{N} \mid \forall x : \mathbb{N}. x \neq 0 \Longrightarrow \bot\}}}{\vdash f : \{g : \mathbb{N} \to \mathbb{N} \mid \forall x : \mathbb{N}. \bot\}}}{\vdash f : \mathbb{N} \to \{x : \mathbb{N} \mid \bot\}} \qquad \vdash 0 : \mathbb{N}}{\vdash f\ 0 : \{x : \mathbb{N} \mid \bot\},}$$

where the first three inferences are by subsumption (the first two by FUN-SUB, and the second by the standard rule of consequence—replacing an assertion by a logically weaker one).

This example shows that a naive combination of semantic subtyping with refinements at higher types is inconsistent with the use of $\bot$ to model diverging computation. We will follow a more semantically correct approach, by modeling non-termination as a (monadic) effect using a monad $\mathfrak{C}[\cdot]$ that distinguishes non-terminating and terminating computations. In this way, the inconsistency is avoided.

We conclude this discussion by noting that this counterexample is independent of the evaluation strategy. Accordingly, it complements the recent observation by Vazou et al. [52] that a logical interpretation of non-termination is unsound for call-by-name, even in languages without higher-order refinements. Vazou et al. [52] solve the issue by internalizing size types into refinement types to enforce termination.

## 3. The HOARe$^2$ System

### 3.1 Expressions

HOARe$^2$ is a relational type discipline for a $\lambda$-calculus with inductive types, unbounded recursion and monads for probabilities and partiality. For readability, we only present our calculus with some fixed inductive types.

Let $\mathcal{X} = \{x, y, \ldots\}$ be a countably infinite set of variables. The set $\mathbf{PCF}(\mathcal{X})$ of expressions with variables in $\mathcal{X}$ is defined as follows:

$$\begin{array}{rl} e ::= & x \mid n \in \mathbb{N} \mid \alpha \in \overline{\mathbb{R}}^+ \mid () \mid \epsilon \mid \cdot :: \cdot \mid \texttt{false} \mid \texttt{true} \\ \mid & e\ e \mid \lambda x.\, e \mid \texttt{let}\ x = e\ \texttt{in}\ e \mid \texttt{letrec}^{\mathfrak{m}}\ f\ x = e \\ \mid & \texttt{if}\ e\ \texttt{then}\ e\ \texttt{else}\ e \mid \texttt{case}\ e\ \texttt{with}\ [\epsilon \Rightarrow e \mid x :: x \Rightarrow e] \\ \mid & e_\uparrow \mid \texttt{let}_\uparrow\ x = e\ \texttt{in}\ e \mid \texttt{unit}_{\mathrm{M}}\ e \mid \texttt{bind}_{\mathrm{M}}\ x = e\ \texttt{in}\ e, \end{array}$$

where $\mathfrak{m} \in \{\downarrow, \cdot\}$ and $\overline{\mathbb{R}}^+$ stands for $\mathbb{R}^+$ augmented with the infinity $\infty$. We write $\mathbf{PCF}$ for $\mathbf{PCF}(\mathcal{X})$ when $\mathcal{X}$ is clear from the context.

Most of the syntax is standard. The expressions $\texttt{unit}_{\mathrm{M}}\ e$ and $\texttt{bind}_{\mathrm{M}}\ x = e\ \texttt{in}\ e$ corresponds to the unit and the multiplication of the *probabilistic monad*. Similarly, $e_\uparrow$ and $\texttt{let}_\uparrow\ x = e\ \texttt{in}\ e$ corresponds to the unit and the multiplication of the *partiality monad*. Finally, we have two expressions for building recursive definitions: one for terminating programs, the other for non terminating ones. We distinguish between them by means of the superscript $\mathfrak{m} \in \{\downarrow, \cdot\}$.

HOARe$^2$ distinguishes between *expressions* and *relational expressions*. The former are used in the subject of typing judgments, and correspond to the actual programs to which we can assign semantics. The latter are used in assertions.

**Definition 3.1** (Expressions and Relational Expressions)**.** Let $\mathcal{X}_\mathcal{R}$ and $\mathcal{X}_\mathcal{P}$ be two disjoint countably infinite sets of *relational* and *plain* variables. Associated with every relational variable $x \in \mathcal{X}_\mathcal{R}$, we have a left instance $x_\triangleleft$ and a right instance $x_\triangleright$. We write $\mathcal{X}_\mathcal{R}{}^{\bowtie}$ for $\bigcup_{x \in \mathcal{X}_\mathcal{R}} \{x_\triangleleft, x_\triangleright\}$ and $\mathcal{X}^{\bowtie}$ for $\mathcal{X}_\mathcal{R}{}^{\bowtie} \cup \mathcal{X}_\mathcal{P}$. The set of HOARe$^2$ *expressions* $\mathcal{E}$ is the set of expressions in $\mathbf{PCF}(\mathcal{X}_\mathcal{P})$. The set of HOARe$^2$ *relational expressions* $\mathcal{E}^{\bowtie}$ is the set of expressions in $\mathbf{PCF}(\mathcal{X}^{\bowtie})$, where only non-relational variables can be bound.

### 3.2 HOARe$^2$ Types

We introduce the types of HOARe$^2$ in two steps. First, we introduce simple types; for simplicity, we restrict instances of inductive types to base types. Then, we introduce relational refinement types, which express properties about two interpretations of an expression.

**Definition 3.2** (Types)**.** The sets $\mathbf{Ty}$ and $\mathbf{CoreTy}$ of (simple) types and core (simple) types are defined as follows:

$$\begin{array}{rcl} \tau, \sigma, \ldots \in \mathbf{Ty} & ::= & \tilde{\tau} \mid \mathfrak{M}[\tau] \mid \mathfrak{C}[\tau] \mid \tau \to \sigma \\ \tilde{\tau}, \tilde{\sigma}, \ldots \in \mathbf{CoreTy} & ::= & \bullet \mid \mathbb{B} \mid \mathbb{N} \mid \overline{\mathbb{R}} \mid \overline{\mathbb{R}}^+ \mid \tilde{\tau}\ \texttt{list}. \end{array}$$

The type $\mathfrak{M}[\tau]$ corresponds to the probability monad over the type $\tau$, while the type $\mathfrak{C}[\tau]$ corresponds to the partiality monad over the type $\tau$. Besides the standard function types $\tau \to \sigma$, the type language includes the unit type, booleans, integers, reals and lists.

Relational types extend the grammar of simple types with relational refinements, and use a dependent function type rather than standard function types.

**Definition 3.3.** The sets of *relational types* $\mathcal{T} = \{T, U, \ldots\}$ and *assertions* $\mathcal{A} = \{\phi, \psi, \ldots\}$ are defined as follows:

$$T, U \in \mathcal{T} ::= \tilde{\tau} \mid \mathfrak{M}_{\epsilon,\delta}[T] \mid \mathfrak{C}[T] \mid \Pi(x :: T).\, T \mid \{x :: T \mid \phi\}$$

$$\begin{aligned}\phi, \psi \in \mathcal{A} ::= {} & \mathcal{Q}\,(x : \tau).\, \phi \qquad (x \in \mathcal{X}_{\mathcal{P}}) \\ & \mathcal{Q}\,(x :: T).\, \phi \qquad (x \in \mathcal{X}_{\mathcal{R}}) \\ & \mathcal{C}(\phi_1, \ldots, \phi_n) \mid e^{\bowtie} = e^{\bowtie} \mid e^{\bowtie} \leqslant e^{\bowtie} \\ \mathcal{C} = {} & \{\top/0, \bot/0, \neg/1, \vee/2, \wedge/2, \Rightarrow/2\},\end{aligned}$$

where $\epsilon, \delta, e^{\bowtie} \in \mathcal{E}^{\bowtie}$, and $\mathcal{Q} \in \{\forall, \exists\}$.

The definitions of relational types and assertions are mutually recursive. For the latter, the constructors $\mathfrak{C}[.]$ and $\mathfrak{M}_{\epsilon,\delta}[.]$ capture the partiality monad and the probability polymonad for relational refinements. The type $\Pi(x :: T).\, U$ corresponds to the dependent type product of $T$ over $U$ indexed by $x$. As usual, we write $T \to U$ for $\Pi(x :: T).\, U$ when $x$ does not occur free in $U$. A type of the shape $\{x :: T \mid \phi\}$ *refines* the type $T$ using the assertion $\phi$. In both dependent and refinement types, we require the bound variable to be relational ($x \in \mathcal{X}_{\mathcal{R}}$).

Assertions are built from primitive assertions using the standard connectives and quantification; we allow quantification over both relational and plain variables. Primitive assertions are equalities and inequalities over relational expressions.

The notions of substitutions are defined largely as usual. Substitutions bind *pairs* of (non-relational) expressions to relational variables, and involve a special treatment of *refinement type constructors*, which must handle the relational expressions. For instance, for a substitution $\rho = \{y \mapsto (e_1, e_2)\}$, we define

$$\{x :: T \mid \phi\}\rho = \left\{ x :: T\rho \;\middle|\; \phi \begin{Bmatrix} y_{\lhd} \mapsto |e_1|_{\lhd} \\ y_{\rhd} \mapsto |e_2|_{\rhd} \end{Bmatrix} \right\},$$

where $|e|_{\lhd}$ (resp. $|e|_{\rhd}$) is obtained from $e$ by replacing all the free variables $x$ of $e$ by $x_{\lhd}$ (resp. $x_{\rhd}$).

### 3.3 Standard typing

We define the simply typed layer of HOARe$^2$, and prove its soundness w.r.t. a denotational semantics. Both the type system and the semantics are mostly standard.

***Static semantics*** The sole notable typing rules are for the two different `letrec` of our language:

$$\textsc{LetRec}\ \frac{\Gamma, f : \tau \to \mathfrak{C}[\sigma] \vdash \lambda x.\, e : \tau \to \mathfrak{C}[\sigma]}{\Gamma \vdash \mathtt{letrec}\ f\ x = e : \tau \to \mathfrak{C}[\sigma]}$$

$$\textsc{LetRecSN}\ \frac{\Gamma, f : \tau \to \sigma \vdash \lambda x.\, e : \tau \to \sigma \qquad \mathcal{SN}\text{-guard}}{\Gamma \vdash \mathtt{letrec}^{\downarrow}\ f\ x = e : \tau \to \sigma.}$$

The rule LetRec handles unrestricted recursion, and requires that the output type be in the partiality monad. On the contrary, the rule LetRecSN does not impose any restriction on the type, but the expression must pass a *termination guard*. We leave the termination guard unspecified; possible forms of enforcing the guard include sized types and syntactic criteria.

***Denotational semantics*** The denotational semantics is largely standard. Core types are interpreted in the standard way. The interpretation of types mixes a set-theoretical and cpo semantics in order to accommodate the partiality monad.

**Definition 3.4** (Interpretation of types)**.** The *interpretation* $[\![\tau]\!]$ of a type $\tau \in \mathbf{Ty}$ is inductively defined as follows:

$$[\![\mathfrak{M}[\tau]]\!] = \{\mu : [\![\tau]\!] \to \mathbb{R}^+ \mid \mathsf{dsupp}(\mu) \text{ discrete} \wedge \textstyle\sum_{x \in \tau} \mu\, x = 1\}$$

$$[\![\mathfrak{C}[\tau]]\!] = [\![\tau]\!]_{\bot} \qquad [\![\tau \to \sigma]\!] = [\![\tau]\!] \multimap [\![\sigma]\!],$$

where the *support* $\mathsf{dsupp}(\mu)$ of a distribution $\mu$ is the set of elements for which $\mu$ takes a non-zero value, and $\multimap$ represents a cpo-continuous function space when the codomain is equipped with a cpo structure, and the set-theoretical function space otherwise.

$$[\![\Gamma \vdash e_{\uparrow} : \mathfrak{C}[\tau]]\!]_\theta = [\![\Gamma \vdash e : \tau]\!]_\theta$$

$$[\![\Gamma \vdash \mathtt{let}_{\uparrow}\ x = e_1\ \mathtt{in}\ e_2 : \mathfrak{C}[\sigma]]\!]_\theta = \begin{cases} \bot & \text{if } d = \bot \\ [\![\Gamma \vdash e_2 : \mathfrak{C}[\sigma]]\!]_{\theta^d_x} & \text{otherwise} \end{cases}$$
$$\text{where } d = [\![\Gamma \vdash e_1 : \mathfrak{C}[\tau]]\!]_\theta$$

$$[\![\Gamma \vdash \mathtt{unit}_{\mathrm{M}}\ e : \mathfrak{M}[\tau]]\!]_\theta = x \mapsto \begin{cases} 1 & \text{if } x = [\![e]\!]_\theta \\ 0 & \text{otherwise} \end{cases}$$

$$[\![\Gamma \vdash \mathtt{bind}_{\mathrm{M}}\ x = e_1\ \mathtt{in}\ e_2 : \mathfrak{M}[\sigma]]\!]_\theta = d \mapsto \textstyle\sum_{g \in [\![\tau]\!]} ([\![e_1]\!]_\theta(g) \times [\![e_2]\!]_{\theta^g_x}(d))$$

$$[\![\Gamma \vdash \mathtt{letrec}^{\mathrm{m}}\ f\ x = e : \tau \to \sigma]\!]_\theta = \textstyle\bigcup_{n \in \mathbb{N}} F^n(\bot_{[\![\tau \to \sigma]\!]})$$
$$\text{where } F(d) = [\![\Gamma, f : \tau \to \sigma \vdash \lambda x.\, e : \tau \to \sigma]\!]_{\theta^d_f}$$

Figure 1: Interpretation of PCF Expressions

Types $\mathfrak{C}[\tau]$ and $\sigma \to \tau$ where $\tau$ is interpreted as a cpo are interpreted as cpos. However, types of the form $\mathfrak{M}[\tau]$ are not interpreted as cpos, because their interpretation is based on discrete distributions.[2]

We can now define the denotational interpretation of expressions.

**Definition 3.5.** A *valuation* $\theta$ is any finite map from $\mathcal{X}$ to $\bigcup_\tau [\![\tau]\!]$. A valuation $\theta$ *validates* an environment $\Gamma$, written $\theta \models \Gamma$, if $\forall x \in \mathrm{dom}(\Gamma)$, $x\theta \in [\![x\Gamma]\!]$. We denote by $[\![\Gamma \vdash e : \tau]\!]_\theta$ the interpretation of $\Gamma \vdash e : \tau$ with respect to $\theta \models \Gamma$.

The definition of the interpretation is mostly standard; Figure 1 gives the interpretation of the monadic constructions and of the two `letrec` operators. As expected, the static semantics is sound w.r.t the denotational one.

**Lemma 3.1.** *If* $\Gamma \vdash e : \tau$ *and* $\theta \models \Gamma$*, then* $[\![e]\!]_\theta \in [\![\tau]\!]$.

### 3.4 Refinement Typing

The key point of relational typing is its ability to relate a *pair* of expressions—which we call the *left* and *right* expressions—via relational assertions that appear as refinements in types. For instance, the type

$$\Pi(x :: \mathbb{N}).\, \{y :: \mathbb{N} \mid y_{\lhd} = x_{\lhd} + 1 \wedge y_{\rhd} = x_{\rhd}\}$$

represents a pair of integer to integer functions where the left function adds 1 to argument, and the right one returns its argument untouched.

In this section, we define the refinement type system of HOARe$^2$ in three steps. First, we give an interpretation for assertions and refinement types. Second, we define a subtyping relation that is complete w.r.t. this interpretation. Finally, we define the refinement type system, and prove its soundness w.r.t. a denotational semantics.

We start by defining relational contexts.

**Definition 3.6.** A *relational environment* $\mathcal{G}$ is any finite sequence of relational bindings $(x :: T)$ s.t. a variable is never bound twice and only variables of $\mathcal{X}_{\mathcal{R}}$ are bound. We use $\varnothing$ to denote the empty environment. A relational environment defines a finite mapping from

[2] It would have been possible to interpret them as sub-distributions and to define another `letrec` operator for probabilistic computations, at the cost of replacing $\delta + \delta'$ by $\exp(\epsilon')\ \delta + \exp(\epsilon)\ \delta'$ in the typing rule for bind. However, our examples do not require this additional generality.

$$
\begin{aligned}
\llbracket \mathcal{C}(\phi_1, \ldots, \phi_n) \rrbracket_\theta &= \overline{\mathcal{C}}(\llbracket \phi_1 \rrbracket_\theta, \ldots, \llbracket \phi_n \rrbracket_\theta) \\
\llbracket e_1^{\bowtie} = e_2^{\bowtie} \rrbracket_\theta &= \llbracket e_1^{\bowtie} \rrbracket_\theta = \llbracket e_2^{\bowtie} \rrbracket_\theta \\
\llbracket e_1^{\bowtie} \leqslant e_2^{\bowtie} \rrbracket_\theta &= \llbracket e_1^{\bowtie} \rrbracket_\theta \leqslant \llbracket e_2^{\bowtie} \rrbracket_\theta \\
\llbracket \forall\, (x : \tau).\, \phi \rrbracket_\theta &= \textstyle\bigwedge_{d \in \llbracket \tau \rrbracket} \llbracket \phi \rrbracket_{\theta_x^d} \\
\llbracket \forall\, (x :: T).\, \phi \rrbracket_\theta &= \textstyle\bigwedge_{(d_1, d_2) \in \llparenthesis T \rrparenthesis_\theta} \llbracket \phi \rrbracket_{\theta\left\{\substack{x_\lhd \mapsto d_1 \\ x_\rhd \mapsto d_2}\right\}} \\
\llbracket \exists\, (x : \tau).\, \phi \rrbracket_\theta &= \textstyle\bigvee_{d \in \llbracket \tau \rrbracket} \llbracket \phi \rrbracket_{\theta_x^d} \\
\llbracket \exists\, (x :: T).\, \phi \rrbracket_\theta &= \textstyle\bigvee_{(d_1, d_2) \in \llparenthesis T \rrparenthesis_\theta} \llbracket \phi \rrbracket_{\theta\left\{\substack{x_\lhd \mapsto d_1 \\ x_\rhd \mapsto d_2}\right\}}
\end{aligned}
$$

where $\overline{\mathcal{C}}$ stands for the $\mathcal{C}$-boolean operator.

Figure 2: Relational interpretation of assertions

$$
\frac{(d_1, d_2) \in \llbracket \widetilde{\tau} \rrbracket^2}{(d_1, d_2) \in \llparenthesis \widetilde{\tau} \rrparenthesis_\theta}
\qquad
\frac{(d_1, d_2) \in \llparenthesis T \rrparenthesis_\theta \qquad \llbracket \phi \rrbracket_{\theta\left\{\substack{x_\lhd \mapsto d_1 \\ x_\rhd \mapsto d_2}\right\}}}{(d_1, d_2) \in \llparenthesis \{x :: T \mid \phi\} \rrparenthesis_\theta}
$$

$$
\frac{\begin{array}{c}(f_1, f_2) \in \llbracket |T| \to |U| \rrbracket^2 \\ \forall (d_1, d_2) \in \llparenthesis T \rrparenthesis_\theta.\, (f_1(d_1), f_2(d_2)) \in \llparenthesis U \rrparenthesis_{\theta\left\{\substack{x_\lhd \mapsto d_1 \\ x_\rhd \mapsto d_2}\right\}}\end{array}}{(f_1, f_2) \in \llparenthesis \Pi(x :: T).\, U \rrparenthesis_\theta}
$$

$$
\frac{(d_1, d_2) \in \llparenthesis T \rrparenthesis_\theta \cup \{(\bot, \bot)\}}{(d_1, d_2) \in \llparenthesis \mathfrak{C}[T] \rrparenthesis_\theta}
\qquad
\frac{\begin{array}{c}\mu_1, \mu_2 \in \mathfrak{M}[|T|] \\ \mathcal{L}_{\epsilon,\delta}(\llparenthesis T \rrparenthesis_\theta)\ \mu_1\ \mu_2\end{array}}{(\mu_1, \mu_2) \in \llparenthesis \mathfrak{M}_{\epsilon,\delta}[T] \rrparenthesis_\theta}
$$

Figure 3: Relational interpretation of types

variables to relational types; we write $x\mathcal{G}$ for the application of the finite map $\mathcal{G}$ to $x$.

We define a *type erasure function* $|\cdot|$ from relational to simple types, which maps dependent products to function spaces, and erases refinements and the indexes of the probabilistic monad. The definition of $|\cdot|$ extends recursively to relational environments: $x|\mathcal{G}| = |x\mathcal{G}|$ for any $x \in \mathrm{dom}(\mathcal{G})$. We also define the *relational type erasure of* $\mathcal{G}$, written $\|\mathcal{G}\|$, by $x_\mathfrak{s}\|\mathcal{G}\| = x|\mathcal{G}|$ iff $x \in \mathrm{dom}(\mathcal{G})$, where $\mathfrak{s} \in \{\lhd, \rhd\}$. Note that given a relational binding $(x :: T)$, the relational type erasure $\|(x :: T)\|$ gives the environment $(x_\lhd : |T|, x_\rhd : |T|)$.

Next, we interpret assertions and refinement types.

**Definition 3.7** (Relational interpretation of refinement types). We say that a valuation $\theta$ *validates a relational environment* $\mathcal{G}$, written $\theta \Vdash \mathcal{G}$, if $\theta \models \|\mathcal{G}\|$ and $\forall x \in \mathrm{dom}(\mathcal{G}),\ (x_\lhd\theta, x_\rhd\theta) \in \llparenthesis x\mathcal{G} \rrparenthesis_\theta$. Figures 2 and 3 define the *relational interpretation* $\llbracket \phi \rrbracket_\theta \in \{\top, \bot\}$ (resp. $\llparenthesis T \rrparenthesis_\theta \in \llbracket |T| \rrbracket^2$) of an assertion $\phi$ (resp. of a relational type $T$) w.r.t a valuation $\theta \models \Gamma$ (resp. $\theta \models \|\mathcal{G}\|$).

Assertions are interpreted relationally in the expected way where some care is needed for quantifiers since the interpretation distinguishes between binders for relational and plain variables. Relational types are interpreted as sets of pairs of elements of the interpretation of the erased type. Formally, a pair $(d_1, d_2)$ is in the relational interpretation of a refinement $\{x :: T \mid \phi\}$ if the assertion $\phi$ holds in a relational context where $d_1$ and $d_2$ are assigned to $x_\lhd$ and $x_\rhd$, respectively.

The relational interpretation of the dependent product is defined in a *logical relation* style: it relates function elements $f_1, f_2$ that map related elements $d_1, d_2$ (in $\llparenthesis T \rrparenthesis_\theta$) to related elements (in $\llparenthesis U \rrparenthesis_{\theta\left\{\substack{x_\lhd \mapsto d_1 \\ x_\rhd \mapsto d_2}\right\}}$). A monadic type $\mathfrak{C}[T]$ is relationally interpreted as the set of pairs in the interpretation of $T$ plus the pair $(\bot, \bot)$. The polymonadic type $\mathfrak{M}_{\epsilon,\delta}[T]$ is interpreted using a lifting construction $\mathcal{L}_{\epsilon,\delta}(\cdot)$ that turns a relation $\Psi$ on $T_1 \times T_2$ into a relation $\mathcal{L}_{\epsilon,\delta}(\Psi)$ on $\mathfrak{M}[T_1] \times \mathfrak{M}[T_2]$.

**Definition 3.8** (Lifting of a relation). Given $\Psi \subseteq T_1 \times T_2$, we have $\mathcal{L}_{\epsilon,\delta}(\Psi)\ \mu_1\ \mu_2$ iff there is a distribution $\mu \in \mathfrak{M}[T_1 \times T_2]$ such that

1. $\mu\,(a, b) > 0$ implies $(a, b) \in \Psi$,
2. $\pi_1\,\mu \leqslant \mu_1 \wedge \pi_2\,\mu \leqslant \mu_2$, and
3. $\Delta_\epsilon(\mu_1, \pi_1\,\mu) \leqslant \delta, \wedge \Delta_\epsilon(\mu_2, \pi_2\,\mu) \leqslant \delta$ ,

where $\pi_1\,\mu = \lambda x.\, \sum_y \mu\,(x, y)$ and $\pi_2\,\mu = \lambda y.\, \sum_x \mu\,(x, y)$.

We next define subtyping between refinement types.

**Definition 3.9** (Subtyping). The *subtyping relation* $\mathcal{G} \vdash T \preceq U$ is defined by the rules of Figure 4.

$$
\textsc{Sub-Refl}\ \frac{\mathcal{G} \vdash T}{\mathcal{G} \vdash T \preceq T}
\qquad
\textsc{Sub-Trans}\ \frac{\begin{array}{c}\mathcal{G} \vdash T \preceq U \\ \mathcal{G} \vdash U \preceq V\end{array}}{\mathcal{G} \vdash T \preceq V}
$$

$$
\textsc{Sub-List}\ \frac{\mathcal{G} \vdash T \preceq U}{\mathcal{G} \vdash T\ \texttt{list} \preceq U\ \texttt{list}}
$$

$$
\textsc{Sub-C}\ \frac{\mathcal{G} \vdash T \preceq U}{\mathcal{G} \vdash \mathfrak{C}[T] \preceq \mathfrak{C}[U]}
\qquad
\textsc{Sub-Left}\ \frac{\mathcal{G} \vdash \{x :: T \mid \phi\}}{\mathcal{G} \vdash \{x :: T \mid \phi\} \preceq T}
$$

$$
\textsc{Sub-Right}\ \frac{\begin{array}{c}\mathcal{G} \vdash T \preceq U \qquad \|\mathcal{G}, x :: U\| \vdash \phi \\ \forall \theta.\, \theta \Vdash \mathcal{G}, x :: T \Rightarrow \llbracket \phi \rrbracket_\theta\end{array}}{\mathcal{G} \vdash T \preceq \{x :: U \mid \phi\}}
$$

$$
\textsc{Sub-M}\ \frac{\begin{array}{c}\mathcal{G} \vdash T \preceq U \qquad \|\mathcal{G}\| \vdash \epsilon_i : \overline{\mathbb{R}}^+ \qquad \|\mathcal{G}\| \vdash \delta_i : \overline{\mathbb{R}}^+ \\ \forall \theta.\, \theta \Vdash \mathcal{G}, x :: T \Rightarrow \llbracket \epsilon_1 \leqslant \epsilon_2 < \infty \wedge \delta_1 \leqslant \delta_2 < \infty \rrbracket_\theta\end{array}}{\mathcal{G} \vdash \mathfrak{M}_{\epsilon_1,\delta_1}[T] \preceq \mathfrak{M}_{\epsilon_2,\delta_2}[U]}
$$

$$
\textsc{Sub-Prod}\ \frac{\mathcal{G} \vdash T_2 \preceq T_1 \qquad \mathcal{G}, x :: T_2 \vdash U_1 \preceq U_2}{\mathcal{G} \vdash \Pi(x :: T_1).\, U_1 \preceq \Pi(x :: T_2).\, U_2}
$$

Figure 4: Relational Subtyping

A subtyping judgment $\mathcal{G} \vdash T \preceq U$ relates only relational types that erase to the same simple type, i.e. $|T| = |U|$. The rules SUB-LEFT and SUB-RIGHT allow erasing and reinforcing refinements. The rule SUB-M allows weakening the indices of the probabilistic polymonad, and the underlying refinements. Other rules are mostly standard. The definition of subtyping validates the relational counterpart of the equivalence FUN-SUB discussed in § 2. More generally, it is possible to define a normalization function that converts any refinement type $T$ into an equivalent type $\{x :: U \mid \phi\}$, where $U$ is a simple type, i.e. does not contain any refinement. The existence of the normalization function immediately entails semantic subtyping.

Finally, we present the HOARe$^2$ typing rules.

**Definition 3.10** (Relational Typing). The *refinement typing relation* $\mathcal{G} \vdash e_1 \sim e_2 :: T$ is defined in Figure 5. We use $\Gamma \vdash e :: T$ as a shorthand for $\Gamma \vdash e \sim e :: T$.

We briefly comment on some of the typing rules. As in relational Hoare logic [6], we distinguish between synchronous and asynchronous rules; the latter operate on both expressions of the

$$\textsc{Var}\ \frac{x \in \mathrm{dom}(\mathcal{G})}{\mathcal{G} \vdash x :: x\mathcal{G}} \qquad \textsc{Abs}\ \frac{\mathcal{G}, x :: T \vdash e :: U}{\mathcal{G} \vdash \lambda x.\, e :: \Pi(x :: T).\, U} \qquad \textsc{App}\ \frac{\mathcal{G} \vdash e_1 :: \Pi(x :: T).\, U \qquad \mathcal{G} \vdash e_2 :: T}{\mathcal{G} \vdash e_1\, e_2 :: U\{x \mapsto e_2\}}$$

$$\textsc{LetRecSN}\ \frac{\begin{array}{c}\mathcal{G}, f :: \Pi(x :: T).\, U \vdash \lambda x.\, e :: \Pi(x :: T).\, U \\ \mathcal{G} \vdash \Pi(x :: T).\, U \qquad \mathcal{SN}\text{-guard}\end{array}}{\mathcal{G} \vdash \mathtt{letrec}^{\downarrow}\ f\ x = e :: \Pi(x :: T).\, U} \qquad \textsc{LetRec}\ \frac{\begin{array}{c}\mathcal{G} \vdash \Pi(x :: T).\, \mathfrak{C}[U] \\ \mathcal{G}, f :: \Pi(x :: T).\, \mathfrak{C}[U] \vdash \lambda x.\, e :: \Pi(x :: T).\, \mathfrak{C}[U]\end{array}}{\mathcal{G} \vdash \mathtt{letrec}\ f\ x = e :: \Pi(x :: T).\, \mathfrak{C}[U]}$$

$$\textsc{Case}\ \frac{\begin{array}{c}\mathcal{G} \vdash T \qquad \mathcal{G} \vdash e :: \tilde{\tau}\ \mathtt{list} \qquad \forall \theta.\, \theta \models \mathcal{G} \Rightarrow [\![ (|e|_{\lhd} = \epsilon) \Leftrightarrow (|e|_{\rhd} = \epsilon) ]\!]_{\theta} \\ \mathcal{G} \vdash e_1 :: T \qquad \mathcal{G}, x :: \tilde{\tau}, y :: \tilde{\tau}\ \mathtt{list}, \{|e|_{\lhd} = x_{\lhd} :: y_{\lhd} \wedge |e|_{\rhd} = x_{\rhd} :: y_{\rhd}\} \vdash e_2 :: T\end{array}}{\mathcal{G} \vdash \mathtt{case}\ e\ \mathtt{with}\ [\epsilon \Rightarrow e_1 \mid x :: y \Rightarrow e_2] :: T} \qquad \textsc{UnitC}\ \frac{\mathcal{G} \vdash e :: T}{\mathcal{G} \vdash e_{\uparrow} :: \mathfrak{C}[T]}$$

$$\textsc{BindC}\ \frac{\begin{array}{c}\mathcal{G} \vdash e_1 :: \mathfrak{C}[T_1] \\ \mathcal{G} \vdash \mathfrak{C}[T_2] \qquad \mathcal{G}, x :: T_1 \vdash e_2 :: \mathfrak{C}[T_2]\end{array}}{\mathcal{G} \vdash \mathtt{let}_{\uparrow}\ x = e_1\ \mathtt{in}\ e_2 :: \mathfrak{C}[T_2]} \qquad \textsc{UnitM}\ \frac{\|\mathcal{G}\| \vdash \epsilon : \overline{\mathbb{R}}^{+} \qquad \|\mathcal{G}\| \vdash \delta : \overline{\mathbb{R}}^{+} \qquad \mathcal{G} \vdash e :: T}{\mathcal{G} \vdash \mathtt{unit}_{\mathrm{M}}\ e :: \mathfrak{M}_{\epsilon,\delta}[T]}$$

$$\textsc{BindM}\ \frac{\begin{array}{c}\mathcal{G} \vdash e_1 :: \mathfrak{M}_{\epsilon_1,\delta_1}[T_1] \\ \mathcal{G} \vdash \mathfrak{M}_{\epsilon_2,\delta_2}[T_2] \qquad \mathcal{G}, x :: T_1 \vdash e_2 :: \mathfrak{M}_{\epsilon_2,\delta_2}[T_2]\end{array}}{\mathcal{G} \vdash \mathtt{bind}_{\mathrm{M}}\ x = e_1\ \mathtt{in}\ e_2 :: \mathfrak{M}_{\epsilon_1+\epsilon_2,\delta_1+\delta_2}[T_2]} \qquad \textsc{Sub}\ \frac{\mathcal{G} \vdash e :: T \qquad \mathcal{G} \vdash T \preceq U}{\mathcal{G} \vdash e :: U}$$

$$\textsc{ARedLeft}\ \frac{e_1 \to e_1' \qquad \mathcal{G} \vdash e_1 \sim e_2 :: T}{\mathcal{G} \vdash e_1' \sim e_2 :: T}$$

$$\textsc{ACase}\ \frac{\begin{array}{c}\mathcal{G} \vdash T \qquad |\mathcal{G}| \vdash e : \tilde{\tau}\ \mathtt{list} \qquad |\mathcal{G}| \vdash e' : |T| \\ \mathcal{G}, \{|e|_{\lhd} = \epsilon\} \vdash e_1 \sim e' :: T \qquad \mathcal{G}, x :: \tilde{\tau}, y :: \tilde{\tau}\ \mathtt{list}, \{|e|_{\lhd} = x_{\lhd} :: y_{\lhd}\} \vdash e_2 \sim e' :: T\end{array}}{\mathcal{G} \vdash \mathtt{case}\ e\ \mathtt{with}\ [\epsilon \Rightarrow e_1 \mid x :: y \Rightarrow e_2] \sim e' :: T}$$

Figure 5: Relational Typing (Selected Rules)

judgments, whereas the former operate on a single expression and can relate expressions that have different shapes. Synchronous rules exist for the two monads, the two `letrec` and the dependent product. Note that the rule for application substitutes the argument of the application into the result type, and does not impose any value restriction.

The `case` construction is an example of a rule with both a synchronous and an asynchronous version. The synchronous rule requires a synchronicity condition: the same branch must be taken in the left and right expressions. For the case of lists, this is ensured by requiring that the matched lists are either both empty or both non-empty. In contrast, the asynchronous rule does not require this condition. The reduction rules close typing under reduction, and is useful to relate expressions that do not have the same shape.

Refinement typing is sound w.r.t. its denotational semantics.

**Theorem 3.1** (Soundness). *If $\mathcal{G} \vdash e_1 \sim e_2 :: T$, then for every valuation $\theta \models \mathcal{G}$ we have $([\![e_1]\!]_{\theta}, [\![e_2]\!]_{\theta}) \in (\!|T|\!)_{\theta}$.*

It follows that HOARe$^2$ accurately models differential privacy.

**Corollary 3.1** (Differential Privacy). *If $\vdash e :: \{x :: \sigma \mid \Phi\} \to \mathfrak{M}_{\epsilon,\delta}[\{y :: \tau \mid y_{\lhd} = y_{\rhd}\}]$ then $[\![e]\!]$ is $(\epsilon, \delta)$-differentially private w.r.t. adjacency relation $[\![\Phi]\!]$.*

We have completed a formalization of Theorem 3.1 in the Coq proof assistant, assuming an axiomatization of probabilities and lifting.

### 3.5 Type-checking

We have implemented a type-checker for HOARe$^2$. The type-checker generates proof obligations during type-checking; proof obligations are sent to SMT solvers via Why3. The type-checker uses a ML-like syntax and includes a few practical extensions like inductive datatypes, let expressions, as well as the ability to define logical predicates and core theories for the datatypes.

| Example | # Lines | Verif. time |
|---|---|---|
| `histogram` | 25 | 2.66 s. |
| `dummysum` | 31 | 11.95 s. |
| `noisysum` | 55 | 3.64 s. |
| `two-level-a` | 38 | 2.55 s. |
| `two-level-b` | 56 | 3.94 s. |
| `binary` | 95 | 18.56 s. |
| `idc` | 73 | 27.60 s. |
| `dualquery` | 128 | 27.71 s. |
| `competitive-b` | 81 | 2.80 s. |
| `competitive` | 75 | 4.19 s. |
| `fixedprice` | 10 | 0.90 s. |
| `summarization` | 471 | 238.42 s. |

Table 1: Benchmarks

All the programs presented in § 5 and § 6, as well as some additional examples from the DP literature (private histograms, sums, two level counters and IDC) were automatically type checked by the implementation, with the only help of top-level type annotations. See Table 1 for a summary.

Both the type-checker and the Coq formalization are available at `https://github.com/ejgallego/HOARe2/`.

## 4. Embedding *DFuzz*

*DFuzz* [24] is a linear dependently typed language that has been used to verify many examples of differential private algorithms. In this section, we define a type-preserving embedding from *DFuzz*

$$
\begin{array}{llll}
\kappa & ::= & \mathrm{r} \mid \mathrm{n} & \text{(kinds)} \\
S & ::= & i \mid 0 \mid S+1 & \text{(sizes)} \\
R & ::= & i \mid S \mid \mathbb{R}^{\geqslant 0} \mid \infty \mid R+R \mid R \cdot R & \text{(sensitivities)} \\
\sigma, \tau & ::= & \mathbb{R} \mid \mathbb{R}[R] \mid \sigma\ \mathtt{list}[S] \mid !_R\sigma \multimap \tau & \text{(types)} \\
 & \mid & \forall i : \kappa.\, \sigma \mid \mathfrak{M}[\mathbb{R}] & \\
e & ::= & x \mid \mathbb{N} \mid \mathbb{R}^{\geqslant 0} \mid \lambda x.\, e & \text{(expressions)} \\
 & \mid & \mathtt{letrec}\ f\ x = e \mid e_1\ e_2 \mid \Lambda i.\, e \mid e[R] & \\
 & \mid & \mathtt{case}\ e\ \mathtt{with}\ [\epsilon \Rightarrow e_1 \mid x :: xs_{[i]} \Rightarrow e_2] & \\
\Gamma, \Delta & ::= & \varnothing \mid \Gamma, x :!_R\sigma & \text{(environments)} \\
\phi, \psi & ::= & \varnothing \mid \phi, i : \kappa & \text{(sens. environments)} \\
\Phi, \Psi & ::= & \varnothing \mid S = 0 \mid S = i+1 \mid \Phi, \Phi & \text{(constraints)}
\end{array}
$$

Figure 6: *DFuzz* Types and Expressions

into $\mathsf{HOARe}^2$, and recover soundness of *DFuzz* from Theorem 3.1. The embedding is interesting for several reasons. First, it shows that $\mathsf{HOARe}^2$ is sufficiently expressive to capture all differentially private examples covered by *DFuzz*. Second, it relates two previously disconnected approaches for verifying differential privacy. Third, it shows how relational refinements can internalize logical relations.

For compactness, we only consider a terminating fragment of *DFuzz* with probabilities only over real numbers. Types and expressions are defined in Figure 6; both are parameterized by indexes, drawn from two distinct languages. The first one deals with *sensitivities* (interpreted as elements of $\overline{\mathbb{R}}^+$) and the second one deals with *sizes* (interpreted as natural numbers). Typing judgments are of the form $\phi; \Phi; \Gamma \vdash_D e : \sigma$, where $\phi$ is an environment that records the sensitivity and size variables, $\Phi$ is a set of constraints used in pattern matching, and $\Gamma$ is an environment containing assignments of the form $x :!_R\tau$. Figure 7 gives selected typing rules, where environments are combined by algebraic operations. The environment $R \cdot \Gamma$ is obtained by taking $x :!_{R \cdot R_i}\tau$ for every $x :!_{R_i}\tau \in \Gamma$, while environment addition is defined as:

$$
\begin{array}{ll}
(x :!_{R_1}\sigma, \Gamma) + (x :!_{R_2}\sigma, \Delta) = x :!_{R_1+R_2}\sigma, (\Gamma + \Delta) & \\
(x :!_R\sigma, \Gamma) + \Delta = x :!_R\sigma, (\Gamma + \Delta) & \text{if } x \notin \mathrm{dom}(\Delta) \\
\Gamma + (x :!_R\sigma, \Delta) = x :!_R\sigma, (\Gamma + \Delta) & \text{if } x \notin \mathrm{dom}(\Gamma).
\end{array}
$$

We refer to Gaboardi et al. [24] for definitions and further explanation of the typing rules.

In *DFuzz*, types $\sigma, \tau$ are interpreted as metric spaces, with associated metrics $d_\sigma, d_\tau$. Then, the *DFuzz* type system enforces metric preservation [24, 48]: if $e$ is well typed in context $\Gamma$, for arbitrary closing substitutions $\theta_1, \theta_2$ for $\Gamma$, the distance between the interpretations of $\theta_1(e)$ and $\theta_2(e)$ is upper bounded by the distance between $\theta_1$ and $\theta_2$. As a particular instance, *DFuzz* expressions of type $!_R\sigma \multimap \tau$ correspond to *R-sensitive* functions, i.e. functions $f$ such that for every pairs of inputs $v_1$ and $v_2$, $d_\tau(f\, v_1, f\, v_2) \leqslant R \cdot d_\sigma(v_1, v_2)$. We will present an embedding which captures metric preservation as a relational refinement type.

To this end, we first define the multiplication operation on sensitivities in more detail. We distinguish two sorts: sensitivities $\mathbb{R}_s = \mathbb{R}^{>0} \cup \{0_s, \infty\}$ and distances $\mathbb{R}_d = \mathbb{R}^{>0} \cup \{0_d, \perp\}$. We interpret sensitivities $R$ in *DFuzz* as sensitivities, while metrics (Figure 8) are interpreted as distances. We write $s$ and $d$ to range over the respective sorts. To interpret multiplication, we define a associative and commutative operator $\diamond$ that maps $\mathbb{R}_s \times \mathbb{R}_s \to \mathbb{R}_s$ and $\mathbb{R}_d \times \mathbb{R}_s \to \mathbb{R}_d$. The non-standard cases are those involving $0_s, 0_d$ and $\infty, \perp$:

$$
s \diamond \infty = \infty \qquad d \diamond \infty = \begin{cases} 0_d & \text{if } d = 0_d \\ \perp & \text{otherwise} \end{cases}
$$

$$
\perp \diamond s = \perp \qquad r \diamond r' = r \cdot r' \quad \text{if } r, r' \in \mathbb{R}^+.
$$

$$
\frac{}{\phi; \Phi; \Gamma, x :!_1\sigma \vdash_D x : \sigma} \qquad \frac{\phi; \Phi; \Gamma, x :!_R\sigma \vdash_D e : \tau}{\phi; \Phi; \Gamma \vdash_D \lambda x.\, e :!_R\sigma \multimap \tau}
$$

$$
\frac{\phi; \Phi; \Gamma \vdash_D e_1 :!_R\sigma \multimap \tau \qquad \phi; \Phi; \Gamma' \vdash_D e_2 : \sigma}{\phi; \Phi; \Gamma + R \cdot \Gamma' \vdash_D e_1\, e_2 : \tau}
$$

$$
\frac{\phi; \Phi; \Gamma \vdash_D e : \mathbb{R}}{\phi; \Phi; \infty \cdot \Gamma \vdash_D \mathbf{return}\, e : \mathfrak{M}[\mathbb{R}]}
$$

$$
\frac{\phi; \Phi; \Gamma, f :!_\infty(!_R\sigma \multimap \tau), x :!_R\sigma \vdash_D e_1 : \tau}{\phi; \Phi; \infty \cdot \Gamma \vdash_D \mathtt{letrec}\ f\ x = e :!_{R_2}\sigma \multimap \tau}
$$

$$
\frac{\phi, i : \kappa; \Phi; \Gamma, f :!_\infty(\forall i : \kappa.\, \sigma) \vdash_D e_1 : \sigma \qquad i \text{ fresh in } \Phi, \Gamma}{\phi; \Phi; \infty \cdot \Gamma \vdash_D \mathtt{letrec}\ f\ i = e : \forall i : \kappa.\, \sigma}
$$

$$
\frac{\phi; \Phi; \Gamma \vdash_D e_1 : \mathfrak{M}[\sigma] \qquad \phi; \Phi; \Gamma', x :!_\infty\sigma \vdash_D e_2 : \mathfrak{M}[\tau]}{\phi; \Phi; \Gamma + \Gamma' \vdash_D \mathtt{let}\ x = e_1\ \mathtt{in}\ e_2 : \mathfrak{M}[\tau]}
$$

$$
\frac{\phi, i : \kappa; \Phi; \Gamma \vdash_D e : \sigma \qquad i \text{ fresh in } \Phi, \Gamma}{\phi; \Phi; \Gamma \vdash_D \Lambda i : \kappa.\, e : \forall i : \kappa.\, \sigma} \qquad \frac{\phi; \Phi; \Gamma \vdash_D e : \forall i : \kappa.\, \sigma \qquad \phi \models S : \kappa}{\phi; \Phi; \Gamma \vdash_D e[S] : \sigma[S/i]}
$$

$$
\frac{\phi; \Phi; \Delta \vdash_D e : \sigma\ \mathtt{list}[S] \qquad \phi; \Phi, S = 0; \Gamma \vdash_D e_l : \sigma \qquad \phi, i : \mathrm{n}; \Phi, S = i+1; \Gamma, x :!_R\sigma, xs :!_R\sigma\ \mathtt{list}[i] \vdash_D e_r : \sigma}{\phi; \Phi; \Gamma + R \cdot \Delta \vdash_D \mathtt{case}\ e\ \mathtt{with}\ [\epsilon \Rightarrow e_l \mid x :: xs_{[i]} \Rightarrow e_r] : \sigma}
$$

Figure 7: *DFuzz* typing rules

$$
\begin{aligned}
\mathcal{D}_{\mathbb{R}}(d_1, d_2) &= |d_1 - d_2| \\
\mathcal{D}_{\sigma\ \mathtt{list}[S]}(d_1, d_2) &= \begin{cases} \sum_{i \leqslant n} \mathcal{D}_\sigma(d_1^i, d_2^i) & \text{if } \mathsf{sz}(d_1) = \mathsf{sz}(d_2) = S \\ \perp & \text{otherwise} \end{cases} \\
\mathcal{D}_{\mathbb{R}[R]}(d_1, d_2) &= \begin{cases} 0 & \text{if } d_1 = d_2 = R \\ \perp & \text{otherwise} \end{cases} \\
\mathcal{D}_{!_R\sigma \multimap \tau}(d_1, d_2) &= \max_{d_3, d_4 \in |\sigma|} \left( \begin{array}{c} \mathcal{D}_\tau d_1\, d_3, d_2\, d_4) \\ -R \diamond \mathcal{D}_\sigma(d_3, d_4) \end{array} \right) \\
\mathcal{D}_{\mathfrak{M}[\mathbb{R}]}(\mu_1, \mu_2) &= \max_{x \in \mathbb{R}} \left| \ln \left( \frac{\mu_1(x)}{\mu_2(x)} \right) \right| \\
\mathcal{D}_{\forall i : \kappa.\, \sigma}(d_1, d_2) &= \max_{d \in \kappa} \mathcal{D}_{\sigma[d/i]}(d_1\, d, d_2\, d)
\end{aligned}
$$

Figure 8: Metric induced by *DFuzz* types

Note that $\diamond$ with type $\mathbb{R}_d \times \mathbb{R}_d \to \mathbb{R}_d$ is never used.

Then, the expression $\mathcal{D}_\sigma : |\sigma| \times |\sigma| \to \mathbb{R}_d$ will capture the distance function for the *DFuzz* type $\sigma$ on our embedding, where $|\cdot|$ is the erasure function from *DFuzz* types to simple types. For the sake of readability, we define $\mathcal{D}_\sigma$ in usual mathematical style (see Figure 8), where $\mathsf{sz}$ denotes the length of a list.

The translation $\cdot^*$ is first defined on sensitivities and sizes, then on types and expressions, and finally on environments. Sensitivities and sizes are translated directly as expressions of type $\mathbb{R}_s$ and $\mathbb{N}$ respectively. More interestingly, the translation for types (given in Figure 9) uses refinements and dependent products to capture

$$
\begin{aligned}
(\mathbb{R}[R])^* &= \{x :: \mathbb{R} \mid x_\lhd = x_\rhd = R^*\} \\
(\sigma\ \mathtt{list}[S])^* &= \{x :: |\sigma|\ \mathtt{list} \mid \mathsf{sz}(x_\lhd) = \mathsf{sz}(x_\rhd) = S^*\} \\
(!_R\sigma \multimap \tau)^* &= \sigma^* \to \tau^* \\
(\forall i : \kappa.\ \sigma)^* &= \Pi(i :: \{x :: \kappa^* \mid x_\lhd = x_\rhd\}).\ \sigma^* \\
\mathfrak{M}[\mathbb{R}]^* &= \mathfrak{M}_{0,0}[\mathbb{R}]
\end{aligned}
$$

Figure 9: Translation of *DFuzz* types

size and sensitivity information. The translation of expressions is straightforward; the only interesting case are:

$$(e[S])^* = e^*\ S^* \qquad (\Lambda i.e)^* = \lambda i : \kappa.e^*$$

$$
\begin{aligned}
&(\mathtt{case}\ e\ \mathtt{with}\ [\epsilon \to e_1 \mid x :: xs_{[i]} \to e_2])^* \\
&\quad = \mathtt{case}\ e^*\ \mathtt{with}\ [\epsilon \to e_1^* \mid x :: xs \to e_2^*\{\mathsf{sz}(xs)/i\}].
\end{aligned}
$$

The translation of environments is defined inductively. We have $(\varnothing)^* = \varnothing$ for terms, index environments, and constraints. Moreover, we define:

$$
\begin{aligned}
(\Gamma, x :!_R\sigma)^* &= \Gamma^*, x :: \sigma^* \\
(\phi, i : \kappa)^* &= \phi^*, i :: \{x :: \kappa^* \mid x_\lhd = x_\rhd\} \\
(\Phi, S_1 = S_2) &= \Phi^*, \{\_ :: \mathbb{B} \mid S_1^* = S_2^*\}.
\end{aligned}
$$

Note that the translation of size and sensitivity environments requires the equivalence of the left and right instances of the relational variables. We can show soundness of the embedding.

**Theorem 4.1** (*DFuzz* Embedding). *If $\phi;\Phi;\Gamma \vdash_D e : \tau$ then*

$$\phi^*, \Phi^*, \Gamma^* \vdash e^* :: \{y :: \tau^* \mid \mathcal{D}_\tau(y_\lhd, y_\rhd) \leqslant \mathcal{D}_\Gamma(\Gamma^*_\lhd, \Gamma^*_\rhd)\},$$

*where $\mathcal{D}_\Gamma(\Gamma^*_\lhd, \Gamma^*_\rhd) = \sum_{x:!_R\sigma\in\Gamma} R \diamond \mathcal{D}_\sigma(x_\lhd, x_\rhd)$.*

*Proof.* By induction on the derivation of $\phi;\Phi;\Gamma \vdash_D e : \tau$. The cases for abstraction and application rely on the properties of semantics subtyping. In particular, using subtyping we can pass from

$$\Pi(x :: \sigma^*).\{y :: \tau^* \mid \mathcal{D}_\tau(y_\lhd, y_\rhd) \leqslant \mathcal{D}_{\Gamma,x:!_R\sigma}((\Gamma^*_\lhd, x_\lhd :: \sigma^*), (\Gamma^*_\rhd, x_\rhd :: \sigma^*))\}$$

to

$$\{f :: \Pi(x :: \sigma^*).\ \tau^* \mid \mathcal{D}_{!_R\sigma\multimap\tau}(f_\lhd, f_\rhd) \leqslant \mathcal{D}_\Gamma(\Gamma^*_\lhd, \Gamma^*_\rhd)\}$$

and vice versa. Higher order relational refinements are crucial here for internalizing the metric of *DFuzz* at the function type that is essentially a logical relation argument—this equivalence shows that *two functions are related if they map related inputs to related outputs*.

Similarly, for the probability distribution case, remembering that we consider only distributions over base types, we use subtyping to pass from

$$\mathfrak{M}_{0,0}[\{y :: \mathbb{R} \mid \mathfrak{D}_\mathbb{R}(y_1, y_2) \leqslant \mathcal{D}_\Gamma(\Gamma^*_\lhd, \Gamma^*_\rhd)\}]$$

to

$$\{z :: \mathfrak{M}[\mathbb{R}] \mid \mathcal{L}_{0,0}\Big(\mathfrak{D}_\mathbb{R}(y_1, y_2) \leqslant \mathcal{D}_\Gamma(\Gamma^*_\lhd, \Gamma^*_\rhd)\Big)\ z_\lhd\ z_\rhd\}$$

and vice versa.

The other cases are similar. Interestingly, the case of pattern matching does not require asynchronous reasoning. Indeed, the refinement type of the translation of the term under match ensures that the two runs will take the same branch. □

Hence typable *DFuzz* expressions are differentially private.

**Corollary 4.1.** *If $\varnothing;\varnothing;x :!_\epsilon\tau \vdash_D e : \mathfrak{M}[\mathbb{R}]$ then*

$$\{x :: \tau^* \mid \mathcal{D}(x_\lhd, x_\rhd) \leqslant 1\} \vdash e^* :: \mathfrak{M}_{\epsilon,0}[\{y :: \mathbb{R} \mid y_\lhd = y_\rhd\}].$$

*Proof.* By Theorem 4.1,

$$x :: \tau^* \vdash e^* :: \{y :: \mathfrak{M}_{0,0}[\mathbb{R}] \mid \mathcal{D}_{\mathfrak{M}[\mathbb{R}]}(y_\lhd, y_\rhd) \leqslant \mathcal{D}_\Gamma(x_\lhd, x_\rhd)\}$$

with $\Gamma \equiv x :!_\epsilon\tau$. Let $U = \{x :: \tau^* \mid \mathcal{D}_\tau(x_\lhd, x_\rhd) \leqslant 1\}$. By definition of $\mathcal{D}$ and elementary reasoning about probabilities,

$$x :: U \vdash e^* :: \{y :: \mathfrak{M}_{0,0}[\mathbb{R}] \mid \Delta_\epsilon(y_\lhd, y_\rhd) \leqslant 0\}.$$

Finally, by semantic subtyping:

$$x :: U \vdash e^* :: \mathfrak{M}_{\epsilon,0}[\{y :: \mathbb{R} \mid y_\lhd = y_\rhd\}].$$

□

Moreover, Theorem 4.1 and Theorem 3.1 give a direct proof of metric preservation for *DFuzz*.

**Theorem 4.2** (*DFuzz* Metric Preservation [24]). *If $\phi;\Phi;\Gamma \vdash_D e : \tau$ and $\theta \models \phi, \Phi$ and $\theta_1, \theta_2 \models [\![\Gamma]\!]_\theta$, then*

$$\mathfrak{D}_{[\![\tau]\!]_\theta}([\![e^*]\!]_{\theta_1,\theta}, [\![e^*]\!]_{\theta_2,\theta}) \leqslant \mathfrak{D}_{[\![\Gamma]\!]_\theta}(\theta_1, \theta_2).$$

Notice that the above theorem uses three valuations. The valuation $\theta$ is used for index variables which are equal in the two executions. The other two valuations $\theta_1, \theta_2$ are used to substitute related values in the two executions.

## 5. Differential Privacy

Theorem 4.1 establishes that every differentially private algorithm that can be modeled in *DFuzz* is also captured by HOARe$^2$. In addition, we present a few previously unverified algorithms demonstrating the features of our system.

In what follows, we will use some notational shorthands. We write **mlet/munit**, **clet/cunit** for the bind/return operations of the probabilistic and partiality monad. We write $\mathbb{R}^\geqslant$ for the type $\{x :: \mathbb{R} \mid x_\lhd \geqslant x_\rhd\}$. When a relational variable $x$ is assumed to be equal in both runs ($x_\lhd = x_\rhd$), we omit the projection and write $x$ for both $x_\lhd$ and $x_\rhd$.

### 5.1 Private Primitives

We review two differentially private mechanisms that are used in the next algorithms. The first mechanism is the *Laplace mechanism* [7], which releases a private version of a numeric value (which can differ in the two runs) by adding noise drawn from the Laplace distribution.

Formally, the $\epsilon$-private Laplace mechanism takes a real number $x$ as input and returns $x + \nu$, where $\nu$ is random noise drawn from the Laplace distribution, which has density function

$$F(\nu) = \frac{\epsilon}{2}\exp(-\epsilon|\nu|).$$

If $x$ can differ by at most $s$ in adjacent runs, then the Laplace mechanism is $(\epsilon s, 0)$ differentially private. We model this as an operator **lap** with the following type:

$$\Pi(x :: \mathbb{R}).\ \mathfrak{M}_{\epsilon\ |x_\lhd - x_\rhd|, 0}[\{u :: \mathbb{R} \mid u_\lhd = u_\rhd\}].$$

When the output range is non-numeric, a typical tool from differential privacy is the *Exponential mechanism* [38]. Let $B$ be the output range, and suppose there is a *quality score* $Q : B \to A \to \mathbb{R}$. On an input $a$, the exponential mechanism produces $b \in B$ approximately maximizing $Q\ b\ a$. If for every $b \in B$ and adjacent $a_1, a_2 \in A$ (wrt. an adjacency relation $\Phi$), the quality score $Q$ satisfies the condition

$$|Q\ b\ a_1 - Q\ b\ a_2| \leqslant s,$$

then the Exponential mechanism satisfies $(\epsilon s, 0)$-differential privacy. We model this as an operator `expmech` of type

$$\{a :: A \mid a_{\triangleleft} \Phi a_{\triangleright}\} \to \mathfrak{S} \to \mathfrak{M}_{\epsilon s,0}[\{b :: B \mid b_{\triangleleft} = b_{\triangleright}\}]$$

with the type $\mathfrak{S}$ of score functions defined as

$$\{b :: B \mid b_{\triangleleft} = b_{\triangleright}\} \to \{a :: A \mid a_{\triangleleft} \Phi a_{\triangleright}\} \to \{r :: \mathbb{R} \mid |r_{\triangleleft} - r_{\triangleright}| \leqslant s\} .$$

### 5.2 Dual Query Release

We first focus on the problem of privately answering a large set of queries. The Laplace mechanism is a simple solution, but it's known that this will add noise to each query proportional to $\sqrt{k}$ for $k$ queries under $(\epsilon, \delta)$-privacy. When $k$ is large, the large noise will make the released answers completely useless. Fortunately, there is a line of algorithms where noise is added in a carefully correlated manner, guaranteeing privacy while adding noise proportional only to $\log k$. We have verified the privacy of one such algorithm, called DualQuery [25]. The algorithm is parameterized by a natural number `s` and a set `qs` of queries to answer accurately. The input is the number of rounds `t` and database `db`, and the output is a private synthetic database that is accurate for the given queries. The code of the algorithm is given below:

```
let rec dualquery t db = match t with
  | 0        → munit []
  | 1 + t' →
    mlet curdb     = dualquery t' db           in
    let  quality   = build_quality t' curdb in
    mlet e         = expmech db quality        in
    mlet new_qry   = sampleN s e               in
    let  newrecord = opt new_qry               in
    munit (newrecord :: curdb)
```

We encode the database as a list of natural numbers; adjacent databases are lists of the same length whose distance w.r.t. $\mathcal{D}_{\mathbb{N}\ \mathtt{list}}$ is smaller than 1. Here we consider $\mathcal{D}_{\mathbb{N}\ \mathtt{list}}$ to be defined similarly to the distance $\mathcal{D}_{\sigma\ \mathtt{list}[n]}$ for list of size $n$ defined in Figure 8 but where the $n$ is provided implicitly by the length of the lists. We represent the output of the mechanism as a list of selected records, each encoded as a natural number.

The algorithm performs `t` steps, producing one record of the synthetic database in every round. For each round, we first build a *quality score* `quality`—a function from queries to real numbers—based on the previously produced records, using the auxiliary function `build_quality`. If we think of the current records as forming an approximate database, the quality score measures how poorly the approximation performs on each query. We then sample `s` queries using the exponential mechanism with this quality score; queries with higher error are more likely to be selected. These queries are fed into an optimization function `opt`, which chooses the next record to add to the approximate database.

The only private operation is the exponential mechanism. The quality score we generate at each round `i` has sensitivity `i`, and so a draw form the exponential mechanism is $\mathtt{i}\epsilon$-private. Since `i` is upper bounded by `t` and there are `s` samples per round, the privacy cost per round is bounded by $\mathtt{s} \cdot \mathtt{t} \cdot \epsilon$. With `t` rounds in total, the whole algorithm is $\mathtt{s} \cdot \mathtt{t}^2 \cdot \epsilon$-private. This guarantee is reflected in the type of `dualquery`:

$$\begin{aligned} &\{\mathtt{t} :: \mathbb{N} \mid \mathtt{t}_{\triangleleft} = \mathtt{t}_{\triangleright}\} \\ \to\ &\{\mathtt{db} :: \mathbb{N}\ \mathtt{list} \mid \mathcal{D}_{\mathbb{N}\ \mathtt{list}}(\mathtt{db}_{\triangleleft}, \mathtt{db}_{\triangleright}) \leqslant 1\} \\ \to\ &\mathfrak{M}_{\mathtt{s}\cdot\mathtt{t}^2\cdot\epsilon,0}[\{\mathtt{l} :: \mathbb{N}\ \mathtt{list} \mid \mathtt{l}_{\triangleleft} = \mathtt{l}_{\triangleright}\}]. \end{aligned}$$

The type states that for two runs with adjacent databases, `dualquery` will return synthetic databases that are $\mathtt{s} \cdot \mathtt{t}^2 \cdot \epsilon$ apart, where `t` is the number of iterations and `s` is the number of samples used.

### 5.3 Private Counters and the Partiality Monad

Our second example is a *private counter*. The program takes in a list of real numbers, and releases a list of running counts. This algorithm is also known as the *binary mechanism* due to Chan et al. [11] and has not been verified before; previous verification work focused on the *two-level* counter from the same paper.

Suppose the input stream has length $T = 2^n$. The binary mechanism will return a list of noisy sums, reusing noise to reduce the improve the accuracy of the sums. The algorithm proceeds via branching recursion. In the base case, we add Laplace noise to the single element of the input stream and return. In the recursive case, we split the input stream into a first and a second half and perform the recursive call on each half; we then return the noised sum of the whole stream together with the result of the recursive calls. Each output list contains the sums for one "level" of the tree; the first list contains a single sum of length $2^n$, the next contains the two sums of length $2^{n-1}$, and so on.

The algorithm terminates, but the simple guard condition implemented in our tool does not capture termination.[3] Hence its formalization is based on the partiality monad and its associated **cunit** and **clet** operations:

```
let rec binary n ls = match l with
  | []          → cunit (munit [])
  | x :: xs     → match xs with
    | []        → cunit (mlet sum = lap x in
                         munit ([sum] :: []))
    | y :: ys →
      let (left, right) = split l in
      clet cleftN       = binary (n - 1) left  in
      clet crightN      = binary (n - 1) right in
      cunit(mlet leftN  = cleftN               in
            mlet rightN = crightN              in
            mlet sum    = lap (sum l)          in
            munit ([sum] :: (leftN ++ rightN)))
```

The algorithm `binary` takes as input a natural number `n` and a list `ls` of reals with length $2^{\mathtt{n}}$ and returns a list of lists of reals. Formally, `binary` has type

$$\begin{aligned} &\{\mathtt{n} :: \mathbb{N} \mid \mathtt{n}_{\triangleleft} = \mathtt{n}_{\triangleright}\} \\ \to\ &\{\mathtt{l} :: \mathbb{R}\ \mathtt{list} \mid \mathtt{sz}(\mathtt{l}_{\triangleleft}) = \mathtt{sz}(\mathtt{l}_{\triangleright}) = 2^{\mathtt{n}} \wedge \mathcal{D}_{\mathbb{R}\ \mathtt{list}}(\mathtt{l}_{\triangleleft}, \mathtt{l}_{\triangleright}) \leqslant \mathtt{k}\} \\ \to\ &\mathfrak{C}[\mathfrak{M}_{\epsilon\cdot\mathtt{k}\cdot(\mathtt{n}+1),0}[\{\mathtt{l} :: (\mathbb{R}\ \mathtt{list})\ \mathtt{list} \mid \mathtt{l}_{\triangleleft} = \mathtt{l}_{\triangleright}\}]], \end{aligned}$$

where we write `n` for readability (since it is assumed equal in both runs) and where we use $\mathcal{D}_{\mathbb{R}\ \mathtt{list}}$ to the distance of lists at the type $\mathbb{R}$ `list` (defined analogously to $\mathcal{D}_{\mathbb{N}\ \mathtt{list}}$).

## 6. Auctions and Algorithmic Game Theory

We now study the verification of mechanisms with incentive properties. We start by describing the truthfulness property for deterministic mechanisms, then we proceed to the randomized case. The closing examples illustrates the problem of computing an approximate Nash equilibrium using differential privacy.

### 6.1 Truthful auctions

In the *digital goods* setting, there is an infinite supply of identical goods to be sold in auction. For instance, when selling music downloads, goods can be reproduced for free. We assume every agent (or *bidder*) $i$ has a secret value $v_i$, which is the price she values the item, and submits a single bid $b_i$ to the mechanism. Once all bids have been submitted, the mechanism selects a set of winning bidders and prices $p_i$ for each winner. Bidders aim to maximize their utility, which is 0 if they do not win and $v_i - p_i$ if they win and at price $p_i$.

[3] It is of course possible to prove termination using known techniques, but we want to demonstrate the partiality monad.

We want our mechanism to be *truthful*: given fixed bids of the other agents $b_{-i}$, the utility of agent $i$ is maximized when she bids her true valuation $b_i = v_i$. This feature makes bidding easy for bidders, and provides the algorithm designer with some assurance that she will see the correct inputs (the true values of the players). From a verification point of view, truthfulness is a *relational* property of programs: if the mechanism maps bids to outcomes and all but one of the bidders bids the same in both runs, then the remaining bidder should have higher utility when bidding truthfully than when bidding non-truthfully.

We start with the *fixed-price auction*, a very simple mechanism for this setting. First, we pick a price $p$ (the *reserve price*). Bidders then submit their bids, and we select all bidders who bid above $p$ to be winners. Each winning bidder is charged price $p$.

Informally, this process is truthful: a bidder's price does not depend on her own bid, so lowering her bid will never lower the price—it can only cause her to lose the item at a price that she would have wanted to pay. Similarly, increasing her bid above her value is never beneficial: If her truthful bid is winning, raising her bid does not change the outcome (she still wins, and pays the same price). If her truthful bid is losing, raising her bid can only cause her to win the item at a price that is higher than her value.

To model this with code, we will model a single bidder's utility when she deviates.[4] Note that each bidder is treated independently—her utility depends solely on her value, her bid, and the reserve price, and not on what any of the other bidders do. So, we can model this auction with the following function, which calculates a single bidder's utility:

```
let fixedprice b p = if b > p then v - p else 0
```

For clarity, we treat v as a parameter declared in context with refinement type $\{\mathsf{v} :: \mathbb{R} \mid \mathsf{v}_{\triangleleft} = \mathsf{v}_{\triangleright}\}$. Truthfulness of this auction follows from the type of fixedprice:

$$\{\mathsf{b} :: \mathbb{R} \mid \mathsf{b}_{\triangleleft} = \mathsf{v}\} \to \{\mathsf{p} :: \mathbb{R} \mid \mathsf{p}_{\triangleleft} = \mathsf{p}_{\triangleright}\} \to \{\mathsf{u} :: \mathbb{R} \mid \mathsf{u}_{\triangleleft} \geqslant \mathsf{u}_{\triangleright}\}.$$

The relational variable b is required to be equal to v in the first run, and arbitrary on the second run. Then, the final utility u cannot be higher on the second run, demonstrating truthfulness.

This example also demonstrates a boolean version of the asynchronous typing rule ACASE from Figure 5. Since the bid b is arbitrary in the second run, the two runs may take different branches. Indeed, these are the most interesting cases of the reasoning: If the same branch is taken in both runs, then the utility is the same in both runs (since the price is the same in both runs). When different branches are taken, we verify that truthfulness holds even when deviating from truthful bidding changes the outcome of the auction.

## 6.2 Universal Truthfulness and Randomized Mechanisms

While the fixed-price auction is very simple, it has poor revenue properties since the price is set independently of the bids. Setting it too high will lead to very few goods sold (and hence low revenue), and setting it too low may sell many goods, but at a price that is substantially less than bidders would have been willing to pay (again, low revenue). However, picking the price as a function of the bids can destroy the auction's truthfulness property. What to do?

It turns out that randomization is a useful way around this problem. In the random sampling auction due to Goldberg et al. [27], the bidders are randomly split into two groups $\mathsf{g}_1$ and $\mathsf{g}_2$. The fixed-price maximizing revenue is computed for each group, and then a fixed-price auction is run in each group—but using the price computed from the *other* group. Truthfulness holds since the price charged to any bidder remains independent of *her own* bid.

[4] While it is possible to code the full auction that calculates all the winners and charges all the prices, we verify the core guarantee of truthfulness, which deals with a *single* bidder's utility function.

Since the mechanism is randomized, we want to verify *truthfulness in expectation*: an individual's expected utility will never increase if she deviates from bidding her true value. In fact, the random sampling auction satisfies a stronger property, known as *universal truthfulness*: a bidder will never be able to gain by deviating from truthful bidding, even knowing the random coins of the mechanism.

To model the random sampling auction, we will treat as parameters the value $\mathsf{v} : \mathbb{R}$ of the single deviating bidder $*$ and the bids of the other bidders $\mathsf{bs} : \mathbb{R}\ \mathtt{list}$; these are again assumed to the same on both runs. We define a (deterministic) utility function that takes the bid (b) for the deviating bidder $*$, a coin (mygrp) indicating the group of $*$, and a list of coins (othergrp) indicating the groups of the other bidders. Then, utility for $*$ is computed using the fixed-price auction with reserve price from the bids in the other group; the optimal reserve price function is denoted by optfixed:

```
let utility b (mygrp, othergrp) =
  let (g1, g2) =
    split (mygrp :: othergrp) (b :: bs) in
  if mygroup
    then fixedprice b (optfixed g2)
    else fixedprice b (optfixed g1)
```

Universal truthfulness can be seen from the type of utility:

$$\{\mathsf{b} :: \mathbb{R} \mid \mathsf{b}_{\triangleleft} = \mathsf{v}_{\triangleleft}\} \to \{\mathsf{c} :: \mathbb{B} \times \mathbb{B}\ \mathtt{list} \mid \mathsf{c}_{\triangleleft} = \mathsf{c}_{\triangleright}\} \to \{\mathsf{u} :: \mathbb{R} \mid \mathsf{u}_{\triangleleft} \geqslant \mathsf{u}_{\triangleright}\}$$

The type shows that for any realization of the randomness, the utility is maximized by truthful reporting.

The main auction takes in the real-valued bid b of $*$, draws the booleans indicating the groups, and uses the expectation operation to compute the expected utility of $*$ on this distribution:

```
let auction b =
  mlet me     = flip            in
  mlet others = repeat N flip   in
  let  coins  = munit (me, others) in
  E coins (utility b)
```

Above, flip returns a uniformly random boolean, and has type

$$\mathfrak{M}_{0,0}[\{\mathsf{c} :: \mathbb{B} \mid \mathsf{c}_{\triangleleft} = \mathsf{c}_{\triangleright}\}].$$

The repeat function is used to generate a list of $N$ random booleans (where $N + 1$ is the total number of bidders) that are then used to split the other bidders into two groups.

Truthfulness for the random sampling auction is reflected by the type for auction, which computes the expected utility of $*$:

$$\{\mathsf{b} :: \mathbb{R} \mid \mathsf{b}_{\triangleleft} = \mathsf{v}_{\triangleleft}\} \to \{\mathsf{u} :: \mathbb{R} \mid \mathsf{u}_{\triangleleft} \geqslant \mathsf{u}_{\triangleright}\}.$$

To verify the truthfulness of this auction we rely on monotonicity of expectation, as captured by the refinement type from § 2.

## 6.3 Nash Equilibrium via Differential Privacy

In this section, we move beyond auctions and consider the more general setting of *games*. A game is played by a collection of $N$ agents indexed by $i$, each with a set of possible actions $A_i$ (the *action space*). Given a vector of actions (one for each player) $a = (a_1, \ldots, a_N)$, each agent receives a (possibly randomized) payoff $P_i(a_1, \ldots, a_N)$; agents seek to maximize their (expected) payoff. For an example, auctions can be considered as games where each agent's action space is the space of possible bids, and the payoff of each agent is their utility for the chosen outcome.

So far, we have considered mechanisms where one action (truthfully reporting) is a *dominant strategy*: a maximum payoff strategy no matter how the opponents play. In general games, like rock-paper scissors, dominant strategies usually do not exist. In this section, we consider a weaker solution concept: *approximate Nash equilibrium*.

```
let rec mkSums i br* br =
  mlet s  = lap (sign (br* i) (br i))    in
  match i with
    | 0      → munit [s]
    | i' + 1 →
      mlet ss = mkSums i' br* br         in
      munit (s :: ss)

let rec search i br* br sums =
  if |i - nth i sums| < T + 1/2
    then i
    else match i with
      | 0      → 0
      | i' + 1 → search i' br* br sums

let expay br* dev* br dev =
  E (mlet  sums = mkSums k br* br       in
      let  s•   = search k br* br sums in
      let  a*   = dev* (br* s•)         in
      let  a    = dev  (br  s•)         in
      let  p*   = pay* a* (sign a* a)  in
      munit p*) (λx. x)
```

Figure 10: Aggregative game mechanism

**Definition 6.1.** Let $\alpha \geqslant 0$. An assignment of agents to actions (a *strategy profile*) $(a_1, \ldots, a_N)$ is an *$\alpha$-approximate Nash equilibrium* if no single agent $i$ can gain more than $\alpha$ payoff from a unilateral deviation from $a_i$, assuming that all other players are playing according to $a$. That is, for all agents $i$ and actions $a'_i$,

$$\mathbf{E}[P_i(a_1, \ldots, a_i, \ldots a_N)] \geqslant \mathbf{E}[P_i(a_1, \ldots, a'_i, \ldots a_N)] - \alpha.$$

We consider an algorithm for computing an approximate Nash equilibrium when the payoffs are not publicly known. There are at least two difficulties: first, a general game may have several Nash equilibria; agents may prefer different equilibria among the many that exist. This may lead agents to misrepresent their payoff functions to influence which equilibrium is selected, something we want to prevent. Second, payoff functions may consist of sensitive information, and agents may be unwilling to reveal their payoffs to the mechanism if the output could disclose their private information.

Somewhat remarkably, using differential privacy to solve the second problem also solves the first: if we can compute a Nash equilibrium under differential privacy, then the profile of actions when agents truthfully report their payoff function is an approximate Nash equilibrium. A full discussion is beyond the scope of this paper; we present and verify the approximate Nash equilibrium property for a version of a mechanism due to Cummings et al. [13], which computes approximate Nash equilibrium of *aggregative games*.

In an aggregative game, payoffs are a function only of an agent's own action and a *signal*, a non-negative real number bounded by $k$ that depends on the aggregated actions of all players. That is, the payoff function for bidder $i$ is of the form $P_i(a_i, S(a_1, \ldots, a_N))$, where $S$ is a signal function of type $A_1 \times \cdots \times A_N \to [0, k]$. In code, we will write `sign` for the signal function and `k` for the bound; they are the same in both runs and we consider them implicit parameters.

The mechanism we have verified computes an equilibrium of an aggregative game, where the payoffs are reported by the agents. We want to show that reporting the true payoff *and* playing the action suggested by the mechanism is an approximate Nash equilibrium.

To keep the notation light, we think of all players as having the same action space, and we consider only two players with actions `a*` and `a`, respectively. We consider the player $*$ as the possibly deviating player, while the other agent is a meta-player, representing all of the other players in the aggregative game (who do not deviate).

The relevant code for the mechanism is in Figure 10. The function `expay` computes the expected pay-off for bidder $*$; it takes as inputs *best response functions* `br*` and `br` that map signals to an agent's highest payoff action (this is how agents report their payoff), and *deviation functions* `dev*` and `dev` that map recommended actions to actual actions. Agents also have a *true* payoff, `pay*` and `pay`, also considered as parameters since they are the same in both runs. The mechanism will not use these functions in the code; they are only referred to by the refinements.

The function `expay` performs the following steps:

1. Use `mkSums` to compute a noisy list `sums` of signals, using the Laplace mechanism;
2. compute a signal $s^\bullet$ such that if both agents choose their (self-reported) best action `br` $s^\bullet$ and `br*` $s^\bullet$ for signal $s^\bullet$, then the true signal based on strategy profiles `a` and `a*` (defined next) is close to $s^\bullet$;
3. apply the deviation functions `dev` and `dev*` to the recommended action `br` $s^\bullet$ and `br*` $s^\bullet$ of each player to produce the strategy profile `a` and `a*`;
4. calculate the true payoff `p*` for the deviating agent on the strategy profile;
5. compute the expectation of the payoff `p*` for the deviating agent.

Players have two opportunities to deviate: they could misreport their best response function, or they could choose a deviation function to play differently than their recommendation. We want to show that reporting the true best response function and following the recommendation (i.e., using the identity function for deviation) is an approximate Nash equilibrium. As before, we perform the verification by assigning `expay` a relational refinement type where $*$ behaves truthfully in the left execution, while in the right execution $*$ behaves arbitrarily. Assuming that $\mathsf{br*}_\triangleleft$ is the true best response function corresponding to `pay*`, and that $\mathsf{dev*}_\triangleleft$ is the identity function, and that `br` and `dev` coincide on both runs (we thus omit subscripts), we want to prove (according to Definition 6.1):

$$\mathsf{expay}\ \mathsf{br*}_\triangleleft\ \mathsf{dev}_\triangleleft\ \mathsf{br}\ \mathsf{dev} \quad \geqslant \quad \mathsf{expay}\ \mathsf{br*}_\triangleright\ \mathsf{dev*}_\triangleright\ \mathsf{br}\ \mathsf{dev} - \alpha$$

for some value $\alpha$. We do this by checking that `expay` has type:

$$\begin{array}{ll} & \{\mathsf{br*}\ :: \mathbb{R} \to A \mid \forall \mathsf{s}, \mathsf{a}.\ \mathsf{pay*}\ (\mathsf{br*}_\triangleleft\ \mathsf{s})\ \mathsf{s} \geqslant \mathsf{pay*}\ \mathsf{a}\ \mathsf{s}\} \\ \to & \{\mathsf{dev*} :: A \to A \mid \forall \mathsf{x}.\ \mathsf{dev*}_\triangleleft\ \mathsf{x} = \mathsf{x}\} \\ \to & \{\mathsf{br}\ :: \mathbb{R} \to A \mid \mathsf{br}_\triangleleft = \mathsf{br}_\triangleright\} \\ \to & \{\mathsf{dev}\ :: A \to A \mid \forall \mathsf{a}.\ \mathsf{dev}_\triangleleft\ \mathsf{a} = \mathsf{dev}_\triangleright\ \mathsf{a} = \mathsf{a}\} \\ \to & \{\mathsf{u}\ :: \overline{\mathbb{R}}^+ \mid \mathsf{u}_\triangleleft \geqslant \mathsf{u}_\triangleright - \alpha\}. \end{array}$$

We briefly comment on the two most interesting steps in the verification. First, when calculating $s^\bullet$, the algorithm computes `sums` by adding Laplace noise to each induced best response: we want to ensure that agents have a limited influence on the chosen signal (and hence have limited incentive to misreport their best response strategy). For the accuracy guarantee we need to show that this noise is not too large (which is the case if the signal and payoff functions satisfy certain low-sensitivity conditions captured with refinement types). This is modeled by assigning to the Laplace mechanism **`lap`** a refinement type capturing *accuracy*:

$$\Pi(\mathsf{x} :: \mathbb{R}).\ \mathfrak{M}_{\epsilon|\mathsf{x}_\triangleleft - \mathsf{x}_\triangleright|, \beta}[\{\mathsf{u} :: \mathbb{R} \mid \mathsf{u}_\triangleleft = \mathsf{u}_\triangleright \wedge |\mathsf{x}_\triangleleft - \mathsf{u}_\triangleleft| < T\}],$$

where $T$ is defined as $|\mathsf{x}_\triangleleft - \mathsf{x}_\triangleright| + \frac{1}{\epsilon}\log\frac{2}{\beta}$. Informally, this states that the added noise is less than $T$ with probability $1 - \beta$.

The second interesting point is taking the expected value. The expression payoff `p*` is randomized, and has type

$$\mathfrak{M}_{\epsilon', \delta'}[\{\mathsf{u} :: \mathbb{R}^+ \mid \mathsf{u}_\triangleleft \geqslant \mathsf{u}_\triangleright - \alpha'\}]$$

for some concrete values of $\epsilon', \delta'$ and $\alpha'$. The payoff above is a probability distribution on real numbers, related by the lifted inequality relation. We wish to take the expected value of these distributions, in order to relate the *expected* payoff on the two runs. However, a priori, it is not clear how the expected values of these distributions are related. Fortunately, the expected values are related in a rather simple way, as seen in the following refinement for $\mathbf{E}$:

$$\begin{array}{ll} & \mathfrak{M}_{\epsilon',\delta'}[\{x :: \mathbb{R}^+ \mid x_\triangleleft \geqslant x_\triangleright - \alpha'\}] \\ \to & \{\mathsf{f} :: \mathbb{R}^+ \to \mathbb{R}^+ \mid \mathsf{f}_\triangleleft = \mathsf{f}_\triangleright = \mathsf{id}\} \\ \to & \{\mathsf{u} :: \mathbb{R}^+ \mid \mathsf{u}_\triangleleft \geqslant \mathsf{u}_\triangleright - \alpha''\}, \end{array}$$

where $\alpha''$ is an expression computed from $\epsilon'$, $\delta'$, and $\alpha'$. That is, taking expectation of two distributions related by the *lifted* inequality relation yields two real numbers that are approximately related by the *unlifted*, standard inequality relation on real numbers. Though not obvious, the soundness of this refinement can be derived from the definition of expectation and lifting.

From this refinement on the expected payoff for $*$ computed by expay, we conclude that truthful reporting and following the recommended action is an approximate Nash equilibrium.

## 7. Related Work

Our work lies at the intersection of differential privacy, mechanism design, probabilistic programming languages, and verification. We briefly comment on the first three areas (which are too enormous to be covered here) and elaborate on the most relevant work in program verification.

***Differential privacy*** Differential privacy, first proposed by Blum et al. [7] and formally defined by Dwork et al. [20], has been an area of intensive research in the last decade. We have touched on a handful of private algorithms, including an algorithm for computing running sums [11] (part of a broader literature on streaming privacy), answering large classes of queries [25] (part of a broader literature on learning-theoretic approaches to data privacy). We refer readers interested in a more comprehensive treatment to the excellent surveys by Dwork [18, 19].

***Mechanism Design*** Mechanism design was introduced to the theoretical computer science community (with a new focus on efficient implementations) by the seminal work of Nisan and Ronen [41]; see Nisan et al. [42] for a textbook introduction. It is understood that truthfulness guarantees can be difficult to prove and verify, so there is a literature giving generic reductions from mechanism design to algorithm design in limited settings, but it is known that this is not possible in full generality [2, 12, 16, 32]. Differential privacy was first proposed as a tool in mechanism design by McSherry and Talwar [38], and has since found many applications; see Pai and Roth [44] for a survey of this area.

***Probabilistic programs*** There is a long line of work that develops models of probabilistic programs. The monadic representation of distributions originates from Giry [26] and was further developed in a programming language setting by later work [8, 34, 45, 47]. The connections with machine learning have recently triggered a surge of interest in probabilistic programming languages. We refer the reader to recent introductory articles [28, 29] for further information.

***Verification of higher-order programs*** The refinement type discipline was introduced by Freeman and Pfenning [23], and further developed by others [14, 17, 55]. Advances in SMT solvers have allowed practical systems that support refinement types through SMT back-ends, for instance F7 [5], F$^\star$ [51], and LIQUIDHASKELL [49]. Our work is mostly related to a recent variant of F$^\star$ called RF$^\star$ [4]. Like HOARe$^2$, RF$^\star$ supports relational reasoning of probabilistic computations. However, RF$^\star$ lacks support for approximate relational refinement types and higher-order refinements, which are both critical for verifying differential privacy and game-theoretic properties.

Dependent types is another expressive typing discipline that can be used to verify properties of functional programs—they also form the basis of proof assistants like Coq. Examples of dependently typed languages include Cayenne [1], Epigram [36], Idris [9] and Trellys [10]. Like our system, Trellys distinguishes between terminating and non-terminating expressions to ensure logical consistency.

Other prominent approaches for verifying functional programs include dynamic checking [22] (and its combination with static type-checking [30, 31, 54]), model-checking [43] and translating functional programs into logic [53].

***Verification of differential privacy and mechanism design*** There has been significant work on language-based techniques for verifying differentially privacy. Pierce [46] defines three categories: run-time enforcement (PINQ [37], AIRAVAT [50]), static enforcement (*Fuzz* [48], *DFuzz* [24]), and verification-based enforcement (CertiPriv [3]). Our work clearly falls into the last category. All these works are focused on privacy, rather than accuracy. See Barthe et al. [3], Pierce [46] for a more detailed account of related work.

There has been comparatively little work on language-based techniques for verifying mechanism design. Lapets et al. [35] give an interesting approach, by presenting a programming language for automatically verifying simple auction mechanisms. A key component of the language is a type analysis to determine if an algorithm is *monotone*; if bidders have a single real number as their value (*single-parameter domains*), then truthfulness is equivalent to a monotonicity property (e.g., see Mu'Alem and Nisan [40]). Their language can be extended by means of user-defined primitives that preserve monotonicity. The paper shows the use of the language for verifying two simple auction examples, but it is unclear how this approach scales to larger auctions.

Finally, Fang et al. [21] propose the use of program synthesis for verifying truthfulness of auctions. Their approach reduces the verification of auction to linear constraints that can be handled by an SMT solver. In this respect, their approach is similar in spirit to ours. However, the constraints they consider are linear and moreover their technique applies to imperative programs. The extension to higher order functions is not obvious.

## 8. Future Directions

HOARe$^2$ is an expressive system of relational refinement types that captures differential privacy, game-theoretic properties and other relational properties of probabilistic computations. An exciting direction for further work is to formally verify more complex mechanisms whose truthfulness guarantees are less standard. For example, it would be interesting to verify mechanisms that are merely *truthful in expectation*, for which universally truthful analogues do not exist (e.g., Dobzinski and Dughmi [15]). Such mechanisms use randomization in a crucial way for their incentive properties, and in addition to being interesting challenges for verification, are mechanism for which truthfulness is non-obvious. We also intend to develop a non-relational version of HOARe$^2$ for reasoning about the accuracy of probabilistic computations.

***Acknowledgements*** We thank Zhiwei Steven Wu for good discussions and in particular for suggesting the aggregative games example. We also thank the anonymous reviewers for their close reading and helpful comments. This research was supported by the European Community's Seventh Framework grant #272487, MINECO grant TIN2012-39391-C04-01 (StrongSoft), Madrid regional project S2009TIC-1465 (PROMETIDOS), and NSF grant CNS-1065060.

## References


[1] L. Augustsson. Cayenne – a language with dependent types. In *ACM SIGPLAN International Conference on Functional Programming (ICFP), Baltimore, Maryland*, pages 239–250, 1998. URL http://link.springer.com/chapter/10.1007%2F10704973_6.

[2] M.-F. Balcan, A. Blum, J. D. Hartline, and Y. Mansour. Reducing mechanism design to algorithm design via machine learning. *Journal of Computer and System Sciences*, 74(8):1245–1270, 2008. URL http://www.cs.cmu.edu/~ninamf/papers/ml_md_bbhm.pdf.

[3] G. Barthe, B. Köpf, F. Olmedo, and S. Zanella-Béguelin. Probabilistic relational reasoning for differential privacy. In *ACM SIGPLAN–SIGACT Symposium on Principles of Programming Languages (POPL), Philadelphia, Pennsylvania*, pages 97–110, 2012. URL http://certicrypt.gforge.inria.fr/2012.POPL.pdf.

[4] G. Barthe, C. Fournet, B. Grégoire, P.-Y. Strub, N. Swamy, and S. Zanella-Béguelin. Probabilistic relational verification for cryptographic implementations. In *ACM SIGPLAN–SIGACT Symposium on Principles of Programming Languages (POPL), San Diego, California*, pages 193–206, 2014. URL http://research.microsoft.com/en-us/um/people/nswamy/papers/rfstar.pdf.

[5] J. Bengtson, K. Bhargavan, C. Fournet, A. D. Gordon, and S. Maffeis. Refinement types for secure implementations. In *IEEE Computer Security Foundations Symposium, Pittsburgh, Pennsylvania*, 2008. URL http://dl.acm.org/citation.cfm?id=1890031.

[6] N. Benton. Simple relational correctness proofs for static analyses and program transformations. In *ACM SIGPLAN–SIGACT Symposium on Principles of Programming Languages (POPL), Venice, Italy*, pages 14–25, 2004. URL http://research.microsoft.com/en-us/um/people/nick/correctnessfull.pdf.

[7] A. Blum, C. Dwork, F. McSherry, and K. Nissim. Practical privacy: the SuLQ framework. In *ACM SIGACT–SIGMOD–SIGART Symposium on Principles of Database Systems (PODS), Baltimore, Maryland*, pages 128–138, 2005. URL http://research.microsoft.com/pubs/64351/bdmn.pdf.

[8] J. Bornholt, T. Mytkowicz, and K. S. McKlinley. Uncertain⟨t⟩: A first-order type for uncertain data. In *Asian Symposium on Programming Languages and Systems (APLAS), Salt Lake City, Utah*, 2014. URL http://research.microsoft.com/pubs/208236/asplos077-bornholtA.pdf.

[9] E. Brady. Idris, a general-purpose dependently typed programming language: Design and implementation. *Journal of Functional Programming*, 23(5):552–593, 2013. URL http://eb.host.cs.st-andrews.ac.uk/drafts/impldtp.pdf.

[10] C. Casinghino, V. Sjöberg, and S. Weirich. Combining proofs and programs in a dependently typed langauge. In *ACM SIGPLAN–SIGACT Symposium on Principles of Programming Languages (POPL), San Diego, California*, 2014. URL http://www.seas.upenn.edu/~ccasin/papers/combining-TR.pdf.

[11] T.-H. H. Chan, E. Shi, and D. Song. Private and continual release of statistics. *ACM Transactions on Information and System Security*, 14 (3):26, 2011. URL http://eprint.iacr.org/2010/076.pdf.

[12] S. Chawla, N. Immorlica, and B. Lucier. On the limits of black-box reductions in mechanism design. In *ACM SIGACT Symposium on Theory of Computing (STOC), New York, New York*, 2012. URL http://arxiv.org/abs/1109.2067.

[13] R. Cummings, M. Kearns, A. Roth, and Z. S. Wu. Privacy and truthful equilibrium selection for aggregative games. Technical report, 2014. URL http://arxiv.org/abs/1407.7740.

[14] R. Davies and F. Pfenning. Intersection types and computational effects. In *ACM SIGPLAN International Conference on Functional Programming (ICFP), Montréal, Québec*, pages 198–208, 2000. URL http://www.cs.cmu.edu/~fp/papers/icfp00.pdf.

[15] S. Dobzinski and S. Dughmi. On the power of randomization in algorithmic mechanism design. In *IEEE Symposium on Foundations of Computer Science (FOCS), Atlanta, Georgia*, pages 505–514. URL http://arxiv.org/abs/0904.4193.

[16] S. Dughmi and T. Roughgarden. Black-box randomized reductions in algorithmic mechanism design. *SIAM Journal on Computing*, 43 (1):312–336, 2014. URL http://theory.stanford.edu/~tim/papers/blackbox.pdf.

[17] J. Dunfield and F. Pfenning. Tridirectional typechecking. In *ACM SIGPLAN–SIGACT Symposium on Principles of Programming Languages (POPL), Venice, Italy*, pages 281–292. URL http://www.cs.cmu.edu/~joshuad/papers/tridirectional-typechecking/Dunfield04_tridirectional.pdf.

[18] C. Dwork. Differential privacy. In *International Colloquium on Automata, Languages and Programming (ICALP), Venice, Italy*, pages 1–12, 2006. URL http://citeseerx.ist.psu.edu/viewdoc/download?doi=10.1.1.83.7534&rep=rep1&type=pdf.

[19] C. Dwork. Differential privacy: A survey of results. In *Theory and Applications of Models of Computation (TAMC), Xi'an, China*, volume 4978 of *LNCS*, pages 1–19. Springer Berlin Heidelberg, 2008. URL http://research.microsoft.com/apps/pubs/default.aspx?id=74339.

[20] C. Dwork, F. McSherry, K. Nissim, and A. Smith. Calibrating noise to sensitivity in private data analysis. In *IACR Theory of Cryptography Conference (TCC), New York, New York*, pages 265–284, 2006. URL http://dx.doi.org/10.1007/11681878_14.

[21] Y. Fang, S. Chaudhuri, and M. Vardi. Computer-aided mechanism design, 2014. Poster at POPL'14.

[22] R. B. Findler and M. Felleisen. Contracts for higher-order functions. In *ACM SIGPLAN International Conference on Functional Programming (ICFP), Pittsburgh, Pennsylvania*, pages 48–59, 2002. URL http://www.eecs.northwestern.edu/~robby/pubs/papers/ho-contracts-techreport.pdf.

[23] T. Freeman and F. Pfenning. Refinement types for ML. In *ACM SIGPLAN Conference on Programming Language Design and Implementation (PLDI), Toronto, Ontario*, pages 268–277, 1991. URL https://www.cs.cmu.edu/~fp/papers/pldi91.pdf.

[24] M. Gaboardi, A. Haeberlen, J. Hsu, A. Narayan, and B. C. Pierce. Linear dependent types for differential privacy. In *ACM SIGPLAN–SIGACT Symposium on Principles of Programming Languages (POPL), Rome, Italy*, pages 357–370, 2013. URL http://dl.acm.org/citation.cfm?id=2429113.

[25] M. Gaboardi, E. J. Gallego Arias, J. Hsu, A. Roth, and Z. S. Wu. Dual query: Practical private query release for high dimensional data. In *International Conference on Machine Learning (ICML), Beijing, China*, 2014. URL http://arxiv.org/abs/1402.1526.

[26] M. Giry. A categorical approach to probability theory. *Categorical Aspects of Topology and Analysis*, pages 68–85, 1982.

[27] A. V. Goldberg, J. D. Hartline, A. R. Karlin, M. Saks, and A. Wright. Competitive auctions. *Games and Economic Behavior*, 55 (2), 2006. URL http://www.ime.usp.br/~yw/papers/games/goldberg2008-competitive-auctions.pdf.

[28] N. D. Goodman. The principles and practice of probabilistic programming. In *ACM SIGPLAN–SIGACT Symposium on Principles of Programming Languages (POPL), Rome, Italy*, pages 399–402, 2013. URL https://web.stanford.edu/~ngoodman/papers/POPL2013-abstract.pdf.

[29] A. D. Gordon, T. A. Henzinger, A. V. Nori, and S. K. Rajamani. Probabilistic programming. In *International Conference on Software Engineering (ICSE), Hyderabad, India*, pages 167–181, 2014. URL http://research.microsoft.com/pubs/208585/fose-icse2014.pdf.

[30] M. Greenberg, B. C. Pierce, and S. Weirich. Contracts made manifest. In *ACM SIGPLAN–SIGACT Symposium on Principles of Programming Languages (POPL), Madrid, Spain*, pages 353–364, 2010. URL http://www.cis.upenn.edu/~bcpierce/papers/contracts-popl.pdf.

[31] J. Gronski, K. Knowles, A. Tomb, S. N. Freund, and C. Flanagan. Sage: Hybrid checking for flexible specifications. In *Scheme and Functional Programming Workshop*, pages 93–104,

2006. URL http://galois.com/wp-content/uploads/2014/07/pub_AT_SAGEHybridChecking.pdf.

[32] J. D. Hartline and B. Lucier. Bayesian algorithmic mechanism design. In *ACM SIGACT Symposium on Theory of Computing (STOC), Cambridge, Massachusetts*, pages 301–310, 2010. URL http://arxiv.org/abs/0909.4756.

[33] M. Hicks, G. Bierman, N. Guts, D. Leijen, and N. Swamy. Polymonadic programming. In *Workshop on the Mathematical Foundations of Programming Semantics (MFPS), Ithaca, New York*, 2014. URL http://arxiv.org/abs/1406.2060.

[34] O. Kiselyov and Chung-Chieh Shan. Embedded probabilistic programming. In *DSL*, pages 360–384, 2009.

[35] A. Lapets, A. Levin, and D. Parkes. A Typed Truthful Language for One-dimensional Truthful Mechanism Design. Technical Report BUCS-TR-2008–026, 2008. URL http://cs-people.bu.edu/lapets/resource/typed-ec-mech.pdf.

[36] C. McBride. Epigram: Practical programming with dependent types. In *Advanced Functional Programming*, pages 130–170. Springer, 2005. URL http://cs.ru.nl/~freek/courses/tt-2010/tvftl/epigram-notes.pdf.

[37] F. McSherry. Privacy integrated queries. In *ACM SIGMOD International Conference on Management of Data (SIGMOD), Providence, Rhode Island*, 2009. URL http://research.microsoft.com/pubs/80218/sigmod115-mcsherry.pdf.

[38] F. McSherry and K. Talwar. Mechanism design via differential privacy. In *IEEE Symposium on Foundations of Computer Science (FOCS), Providence, Rhode Island*, pages 94–103, 2007. URL http://doi.ieeecomputersociety.org/10.1109/FOCS.2007.41.

[39] P. Milgrom and I. Segal. Deferred-acceptance auctions and radio spectrum reallocation. In *ACM SIGecom Conference on Economics and Computation (EC), Palo Alto, California*, pages 185–186, 2014. URL http://web.stanford.edu/~isegal/heuristic.pdf.

[40] A. Mu'Alem and N. Nisan. Truthful approximation mechanisms for restricted combinatorial auctions. *Games and Economic Behavior*, 64(2):612–631, 2008. URL http://authors.library.caltech.edu/13158/1/MUAgeb08preprint.pdf.

[41] N. Nisan and A. Ronen. Algorithmic mechanism design. In *ACM SIGACT Symposium on Theory of Computing (STOC), Atlanta, Georgia*, pages 129–140, 1999. URL http://www.cs.yale.edu/homes/jf/nisan-ronen.pdf.

[42] N. Nisan, T. Roughgarden, E. Tardos, and V. V. Vazirani. *Algorithmic game theory*. Cambridge University Press, 2007.

[43] C.-H. L. Ong and S. J. Ramsay. Verifying higher-order functional programs with pattern-matching algebraic data types. In *ACM SIGPLAN–SIGACT Symposium on Principles of Programming Languages (POPL), Austin, Texas*, volume 46, pages 587–598, 2011. URL https://www.cs.ox.ac.uk/files/3721/main.pdf.

[44] M. M. Pai and A. Roth. Privacy and mechanism design. *ACM SIGecom Exchanges*, 12(1):8–29, 2013. URL http://www.cis.upenn.edu/~aaroth/Papers/PrivacyMDSurvey.pdf.

[45] S. Park, F. Pfenning, and S. Thrun. A probabilistic language based upon sampling functions. In *ACM SIGPLAN–SIGACT Symposium on Principles of Programming Languages (POPL), Long Beach, California*, pages 171–182, 2005. URL https://www.cs.cmu.edu/~fp/papers/popl05.pdf.

[46] B. C. Pierce. Differential privacy in the programming languages community, 2012. Invited tutorial at DIMACS Workshop on Recent Work on Differential Privacy across Computer Science.

[47] N. Ramsey and A. Pfeffer. Stochastic lambda calculus and monads of probability distributions. In *ACM SIGPLAN–SIGACT Symposium on Principles of Programming Languages (POPL), Portland, Oregon*, pages 154–165, 2002. URL http://www.cs.tufts.edu/~nr/pubs/pmonad.pdf.

[48] J. Reed and B. C. Pierce. Distance makes the types grow stronger: A calculus for differential privacy. In *ACM SIGPLAN International Conference on Functional Programming (ICFP), Baltimore, Maryland*, 2010. URL http://dl.acm.org/citation.cfm?id=1863568.

[49] P. M. Rondon, M. Kawaguci, and R. Jhala. Liquid types. In *ACM SIGPLAN Conference on Programming Language Design and Implementation (PLDI), Tucson, Arizona*, pages 159–169, 2008. URL http://goto.ucsd.edu/~rjhala/papers/liquid_types.pdf.

[50] I. Roy, S. Setty, A. Kilzer, V. Shmatikov, and E. Witchel. Airavat: Security and privacy for MapReduce. In *USENIX Symposium on Networked Systems Design and Implementation (NDSI), San Jose, California*, 2010. URL http://dl.acm.org/citation.cfm?id=1855731.

[51] N. Swamy, J. Chen, C. Fournet, P.-Y. Strub, K. Bhargavan, and J. Yang. Secure distributed programming with value-dependent types. In *ACM SIGPLAN International Conference on Functional Programming (ICFP), Tokyo, Japan*, 2011. URL http://research.microsoft.com/pubs/150012/icfp-camera-ready.pdf.

[52] N. Vazou, E. L. Seidel, R. Jhala, D. Vytiniotis, and S. Peyton Jones. Refinement Types for Haskell. In *ACM SIGPLAN International Conference on Functional Programming (ICFP), Gothenburg, Sweden*, 2014. URL http://goto.ucsd.edu/~nvazou/refinement_types_for_haskell.pdf.

[53] D. Vytiniotis, S. Peyton Jones, K. Claessen, and D. Rosén. Halo: Haskell to logic through denotational semantics. In *ACM SIGPLAN–SIGACT Symposium on Principles of Programming Languages (POPL), Rome, Italy*, 2013. URL http://research.microsoft.com/en-us/people/dimitris/hcc-popl.pdf.

[54] P. Wadler and R. B. Findler. Well-typed programs can't be blamed. In *European Symposium on Programming (ESOP), York, England*, pages 1–16, 2009. URL http://homepages.inf.ed.ac.uk/wadler/papers/blame/blame.pdf.

[55] H. Xi and F. Pfenning. Dependent types in practical programming. In *ACM SIGPLAN–SIGACT Symposium on Principles of Programming Languages (POPL), San Antonio, Texas*, pages 214–227, 1999. URL http://www.cs.cmu.edu/~fp/papers/popl99.pdf.

# Differential Privacy: Now it's Getting Personal


Hamid Ebadi
Chalmers University of Technology
Göteborg, Sweden
hamid.ebadi@chalmers.se

David Sands
Chalmers University of Technology
Göteborg, Sweden
dave@chalmers.se

Gerardo Schneider
University of Gothenburg
Göteborg, Sweden
gerardo@cse.gu.se



## Abstract

Differential privacy provides a way to get useful information about sensitive data without revealing much about any one individual. It enjoys many nice compositionality properties not shared by other approaches to privacy, including, in particular, robustness against side-knowledge.

Designing differentially private mechanisms from scratch can be a challenging task. One way to make it easier to construct new differential private mechanisms is to design a system which allows more complex mechanisms (programs) to be built from differentially private building blocks in principled way, so that the resulting programs are guaranteed to be differentially private by construction.

This paper is about a new accounting principle for building differentially private programs. It is based on a simple generalisation of classic differential privacy which we call Personalised Differential Privacy (PDP). In PDP each individual has its own personal privacy level. We describe ProPer, a interactive system for implementing PDP which maintains a privacy budget for each individual. When a primitive query is made on data derived from individuals, the provenance of the involved records determines how the privacy budget of an individual is affected: the number of records derived from Alice determines the multiplier for the privacy decrease in Alice's budget. This offers some advantages over previous systems, in particular its fine-grained character allows better utilisation of the privacy budget than mechanisms based purely on the concept of global sensitivity, and it applies naturally to the case of a live database where new individuals are added over time.

We provide a formal model of the ProPer approach, prove that it provides personalised differential privacy, and describe a prototype implementation based on McSherry's PINQ system.



***Categories and Subject Descriptors*** D.3.2 [*Programming Languages*]: Language Classifications–Specialized application languages

***General Terms*** Design, Languages, Theory

***Keywords*** differential privacy, provenance





*POPL '15,* January 15 - 17 2015, Mumbai, India.
Copyright is held by the owner/author(s). Publication rights licensed to ACM.
ACM 978-1-4503-3300-9/15/01…$15.00.
http://dx.doi.org/10.1145/2676726.2677005


## 1. Introduction

Differential privacy is a relatively new notion of privacy [5–7]. The theory shows that by adding the right amount of noise to statistical queries, one can get useful results at the same time as providing a quantifiable notion of privacy. Its definition does not involve a syntactic condition on the data itself, but rather it is a condition formed by comparing the results of a query on any database with or without any one individual: a query $Q$ (a randomised function) is $\varepsilon$-differentially private if the difference in probability of any query outcome on a data-set only varies by a factor of $e^{\varepsilon}$ (approximately $1 + \varepsilon$ for small $\varepsilon$) whenever an individual is added or removed.

Research on differential privacy has developed a variety of query mechanisms that provide differential privacy for a useful range of statistical problems. A few works have focussed more on composition principles that allow new differential private mechanisms to design a system which allows more complex mechanisms (programs) to be built from differentially private building blocks in principled way, so that the resulting programs are guaranteed to be differentially private by construction [12, 17, 24]. PINQ [17] is the starting point for the present work.

***PINQ-style Global Privacy Budget*** PINQ is an implmentation of interactive differential privacy which ensures, at runtime, that queries adhere to a global privacy budget. Third-party client code freely decides how sensitive data sets should be processed and queried. The run-time system ensures that this does not break a specified privacy budget $\varepsilon$. PINQ builds on a collection of standard differentially private primitive queries, together with simple composition principles – mathematical properties enjoyed by the definition of differential privacy. One central principle is that multiple queries (e.g. with differential privacy $\varepsilon_1$ and $\varepsilon_2$ respectively) have an additive effect ($\varepsilon_1 + \varepsilon_2$) on the overall differential privacy. Another central idea is to track *sensitivity* of functions to measure how much a change in the input might affect the value of the data. Together, these components allow the system to track how much to deduct from the global privacy budget on each invocation of a primitive query.

***Limitations of the Global Privacy Budget*** In a batch system where all computations are described up-front as a monolithic program, a global budget is reasonable. In an interactive system, however, there are several limitations to this style of accounting. Imagine a scenario involving a large data set of individuals – a cross-set of the population – containing various information about health and lifestyle. Let us suppose, further, that we aim for $\varepsilon$-differential privacy for some specified value of $\varepsilon$. On Monday the analyst selects all the people from the database who have a particular blood type, $AB$-negative, and constructs an algorithm which extracts information about them as part of medical research. Since just 0.6% of the population have this blood type, the proportion of the database involved in this study is relatively small, but the database is known to be big enough for it to be meaningful. Let us suppose that the cost of this analysis, according to the system, is $\varepsilon_1$. Now on Tuesday the analyst gets a new task, to extract information about the lifestyle of smokers, towards an advertising campaign for nicotine gum. This is a significantly larger portion of the database, possibly overlapping Monday's research group. The analyst has $\varepsilon - \varepsilon_1$ left to spend. If $\varepsilon_1$ is large, the analyst has blown the budget by analysing the small group, even though that study did not touch the data of the larger part of the population. PINQ offers a way around this problem by adding nonstandard database primitives. Here we would partition the data into ($AB^-$, not $AB^-$) and perform the two studies in parallel, with cost being the maximum of the cost of the two studies.

This leads to a batch-style reasoning and an unnatural programming style. But it also has another limitation. What if the database is live – we obtain new data over time, or if data is continually being added? A global budget forces us to be unnecessarily pessimistic about new as-yet unexploited data.

***Personalised Differential Privacy*** This paper addresses these issues by offering a simple generalisation of differential privacy called *personalised differential privacy (PDP)* which permits each individual to have a personalised privacy budget. The definition supports generalised versions of the composition principles upon which systems like PINQ are based (§2), and moreover enjoys a number of properties which allow for less wasteful compositional principles (§3). For example, any query about the drinking habits of adults offers 0-differential privacy for Adrian, aged 13, as it does for any records of individuals which enter the database after the query has been made.

From these principles we design a system, in the style of PINQ, called ProPer (**Pro**venance for **Per**sonalised Differential Privacy- §4). The ProPer system maintains a personal budget for every record entering the system. Instead of using sensitivity, ProPer tracks the *provenance* of every record in the system, and uses the exact provenance to calculate how a query should affect the budgets of the individuals. Unlike PINQ, the system is described as an abstract formal model for which we prove personalised differential privacy. This is important because the correctness of ProPer is not obvious for two reasons. Firstly, the individual budgets become highly sensitive and how we handle them is novel. More specifically, if a query involves records that would break the budget of an individual they are silently dropped from the data set upon which the query is calculated. In the example above, Tuesday's analysis of smokers will automatically exclude data derived from any diseased individuals as soon as the cost of the queries exceeds their budgets. Secondly, it is necessary to restrict the domain of computations over data sets to a class which guarantees that the provenance of any derived record is *affine* (zero or one record), otherwise the number of records which might get excluded due to a small change in the input might be too big to give privacy guarantees.

The approach is suitable for integration with other systems, since we assume the existence of basic primitives providing classical differential privacy. We have implemented a prototype of the ProPer approach which extends the PINQ system (§6) with personalised budgets and the ability to input live data. We compare the performance of our provenance-based implementation with PINQ to show that the runtime overhead is not significant.

We conclude with a discussion of related work (§7), a summary of our contributions (§8), and the current limitations of the approach as well as directions for future work.

## 2. Differential Privacy

We begin by reviewing the classic definition of differential privacy, and its simple composition principles that allow the construction of new differentially-private algorithms from existing components. In this work the "data sets" will abstract representations of databases, modelled simply as multisets over some unspecified set of records. When we say that $A$ and $B$ differ on at most one record, also written $A \sim B$, we mean that they are either identical, or one can be obtained from the other by adding a single record.

**Definition 2.1.** *A randomised function $Q$ provides $\varepsilon$-differential privacy if for all data sets $A \sim B$, and any set of possible outputs $S \subseteq \mathsf{range}(Q)$, we have:*

$$Pr[Q(A) \in S] \leq Pr[Q(B) \in S] \times e^{\varepsilon}$$

Thus the likelihood of a given output to a query $Q$ only changes by a quantifiable amount with or without any individual. The smaller the $\varepsilon$ the better the privacy guarantee for the individual. The literature contains many examples of differentially private aggregate operations on data, achieving an appropriate balance between privacy and utility by the principled use of statistical noise. In this work we take the existence of such building blocks as given.

We will adopt the convention of writing $Q_\varepsilon$ to denote an $\varepsilon$-differentially private query. Queries will be algorithms rather than just abstract mathematical functions, so we assume that the range of $Q$ is finite and moreover the result of a query forms a discrete probabilistic distribution. Given this, we can simplify the conditions of the form $Q(A) \in S$ to $Q(A) = v$ for any value in the range of $Q$.

Definition 2.1 satisfies a number of useful properties that serve as building blocks for systems enforcing differential privacy [17], which we outline informally here.

***Query Composition*** If we apply two queries $Q_{\varepsilon_1}$ and then $Q_{\varepsilon_2}$ to a data set, then the combined result is $\varepsilon_1 + \varepsilon_2$ differentially private. This result holds even if $Q_{\varepsilon_2}$ is chosen in response to the result of $Q_{\varepsilon_1}$. Although useful, the sequential query composition principle can be very wasteful. If two queries are applied to disjoint sets of data then the privacy loss is the maximum of the privacy losses of the two queries. This observation prompted McSherry to include this as a nonstandard *parallel query* operation in PINQ.

***Pre-processing and Sensitivity*** What if we transform data before applying a query? A key compositionally concept is the *sensitivity* of a function [5] (it is also a key concept in the design of primitive differentially private operations [8], although that is not our focus here). Roughly speaking, a function $f$ has sensitivity $c$ (also known as *stability* $c$ [17]) if whenever the distance between two inputs is $n$, the distance between the results of applying $f$ is at most $c \times n$. For (multi-)sets, the distance between $A$ and $B$ is just the size of their symmetric difference. Not all functions have a bounded sensitivity. For example consider the cartesian product of two data sets: adding a record to one data set can add unboundedly many elements to the result – it depends on the size of the other argument.

We dub the following property the *sensitivity composition principle*:

> If data-set transformer $F$ has sensitivity $c$, then $Q_\varepsilon \circ F$ is $(\varepsilon \cdot c)$-differentially private.

The proof of this follows easily from the following scaling property of differential privacy: if data sets $A$ and $B$ differ by $k$ elements, then

$$Pr[Q(A) \in S] \leq Pr[Q(B) \in S] \times e^{(k \cdot \varepsilon)}.$$

***Post-processing*** A very simple – perhaps obvious – property is that a differentially private query is robust under post-processing:

> For any function $F$, $F \circ Q_\varepsilon$ is $\varepsilon$-differentially private.

This means that post-processing the result of a query cannot extract more private information than the query itself released. This is also the case when $F$ is chosen in response to other queries – or the result of other "side knowledge" about the data set.

## 3. Personalised Differential Privacy

Now we turn to the main concept introduced in this paper, *Personalised* or "big epsilon" differential privacy, and its analogous compositionality properties.

**Definition 3.1** (Personalised (Big Epsilon) Differential Privacy). *We say that data sets $A$ and $B$ differ on record $r$, written $A \stackrel{r}{\sim} B$, if $A$ can be obtained from $B$ by adding the record $r$, or vice-versa.*

*Let $\mathscr{E}$ be a function from records to non-negative real numbers. A randomized query $Q$ provides $\mathscr{E}$-*differential privacy *if for all records $r$, and all $A \stackrel{r}{\sim} B$, and any set of outputs $S \subseteq \mathsf{range}(Q)$, we have: $Pr[Q(A) \in S] \leq Pr[Q(B) \in S] \times e^{\mathscr{E}(r)}$*

Personalised differential privacy allows each individual (record) to have its own personal privacy level. This may turn out to be a useful concept in its own right, but its main purpose in this work is as a generalisation that permits a more fine-grained accounting in the construction of classical differentially private mechanisms, and one which plays well with dynamic databases. The following proposition summarises the relation to "small-epsilon" differential privacy:

**Proposition 3.2.**

*(i) If $Q$ is $\varepsilon$-differentially private, then $Q$ is $\lambda x.\varepsilon$-differentially private.*
*(ii) If $Q$ is $\mathscr{E}$-differentially private, and $\sup(\mathsf{range}(\mathscr{E})) = \varepsilon$ then $Q$ is $\varepsilon$-differentially private.*

Now we consider the composition principles analogous to those above. We keep the presentation informal since we will not apply these principles directly in our formal developments – rather they provide an intuition behind the approach. Most of the principles above generalise to personalised differential privacy.

***Query Composition*** In the sequential composition of queries, if $Q_1$ and $Q_2$ are $\mathscr{E}_1$ and $\mathscr{E}_2$-differentially private, respectively, then applied in sequence they yield a $\lambda x.\mathscr{E}_1(x) + \mathscr{E}_2(x)$-differentially private query. For parallel queries let us be a little more precise:

Let $\{R_i\}_{i \in I}$ be a partition of the set of all records, and $\{Q_i\}_{i \in I}$ be a set of queries. we define a parallel query $P(A) = \Pi_{i \in I} Q_i(A \cap R_i)$ where $\Pi$ is just the n-ary cartesian product of sets. Now we have the following natural generalisation of the parallel query principle:

> If $Q_i$ is $\mathscr{E}_i$-differentially private then $P$ is $\mathscr{E}$-differentially private, where $\mathscr{E}(r) = \mathscr{E}_i(r)$ if $r \in R_i$.

Now we introduce the first specialised principle which takes advantage of the fine-grained nature of personalised differential privacy, the *selection principle*:

> For set $A$, define $\mathsf{select}_A(x) = x \cap A$. If $Q$ is $\mathscr{E}$-differentially private, then $Q \circ \mathsf{select}_A$ is $\mathscr{E}[r \mapsto 0 \mid r \notin A]$-differentially private.

Here $\mathscr{E}[r \mapsto 0 \mid r \notin A]$ denotes the function which maps every element outside $A$ to 0, and behaves as $\mathscr{E}$ otherwise. In simple terms, a query which operates on $A$ is perfectly private for individuals outside of $A$. In contrast, the composition principle of $\varepsilon$-differential privacy has nothing helpful to say here: the sensitivity of the selection function is 1.

How does this help us? It can show how the sequential composition principle for $\mathscr{E}$-differential privacy gives greater accounting precision. Specifically, parallel composition is simply no longer necessary to give a reasonably accurate estimate of privacy cost. Suppose we compute $P(A)$ by sequentially computing $Q_i \circ \mathsf{select}_{R_i}$. Then the sequential composition principle calculates the cost of this iterated sequential composition as

$$\lambda x.\Sigma_{i \in I}(\text{if } x \in R_i \text{ then } \mathscr{E}_i(x) \text{ else } 0)$$

which is precisely the cost calculated for the parallel query.

***Sensitivity Composition*** The sensitivity composition principle also lifts into the world of personalised differential privacy:

> If data-set transformer $F$ has sensitivity $c$, and $Q$ is $\mathscr{E}$-differentially private, then $Q \circ F$ is $\lambda x.(\mathscr{E}(x) \times c)$-differentially private.

The proof analogously follows easily from the following scaling property: If data sets $A$ and $B$ differ on elements $C$, then

$$Pr[Q(A) \in S] \leq Pr[Q(B) \in S] \times \exp(\Sigma_{r \in C}\mathscr{E}(r)).$$

***The Personalised Sensitivity Principle*** A key feature of personalised differential privacy is that it supports a fine-grained composition property for a large and important class of functions, namely functions that are union preserving. A function $F$ from multisets to multisets is union preserving if $F(A \uplus B) = F(A) \uplus F(B)$, $A \uplus B$ denotes the additive union of multisets $A$ and $B$. In standard relational algebra, for example, all functions are union preserving in each of their arguments, with the exception of the (multi-)set difference operator which is not union preserving in its second argument. Complex union-preserving functions may be built from simple ones as they are closed under compositions. You will read more about supported compositions in section 4.3.

The characteristic property of union preserving functions is that their behaviour can be completely characterised by their behaviour on individual records. This gives us a completely precise way to compute the influence of a single record on the result of the function, since $F(A \uplus \{r\}) = F(A) \uplus F\{r\}$. This leads us to the following.

**Lemma 3.3.** *If $F$ is a union-preserving function and $Q$ is $\mathscr{E}$-differentially private, then $Q \circ F$ is $(\lambda x.\Sigma_{s \in F\{x\}}\mathscr{E}(s))$-differentially private.*

*Proof.* Follows easily from the scaling property. □

Taking $\mathscr{E} = \lambda r.\varepsilon$ yields the following useful corollary which is the core of our approach to combining existing differentially private mechanisms with our personalised approach:

**Corollary 3.4.** *If $F$ is a union-preserving function and $Q$ is $\varepsilon$-differentially private, then $Q \circ F$ is $(\lambda x.\mathsf{size}(F\{x\}) \times \varepsilon)$-differentially private.*

## 4. ProPer: Provenance for Personalised Privacy

In this section we provide an abstract model of the ProPer system. The ProPer system encapsulates sensitive databases and manages computations over them via an imperative API. It guarantees (as we shall prove) $\mathscr{E}$-differential privacy for the records which enter the system.

***Descriptive vs Prescriptive Systems*** The principles described in the previous section are a guide as to how we can build a system that allows non-expert analysts to compose new differentially private algorithms from differentially private components. In principle such systems can be of two kinds: *descriptive*, or *prescriptive*. In a descriptive system we can apply the principles to compute and *report* on the level of privacy achieved by a given run of a program. A prescriptive system, on the other hand, is given a goal – an amount of privacy that is to be achieved, and the system must use the principles and ensure that the privacy stays within the bound.[1] In a dy-

[1] In an approach based on static analysis, such as the type-system of Fuzz [12], one could say that these two approaches are unified.

namic system like PINQ, however, it is more natural to describe a prescriptive system – one which does not violate a preconceived level of privacy.

In a prescriptive system the desired amount of privacy can be thought of as a *budget*, and in the literature it is often referred to as such. For ProPer this is an amount of privacy per record as described by some function $\mathscr{E}$. But the principles described above know nothing of budgets – they are purely descriptive. It is therefore important to design a mechanism which is private even when the program fails to meet the intended goals. With personalised differential privacy this is a crucial question – because the budget itself is clearly a sensitive object. In a nutshell, the ProPer approach involves tracking the provenance of each record in any intermediate table (on which sensitive input record does it depend), and by silently dropping records from the arguments to statistical queries if the presence of those records would break the privacy budget of some individual. The provenance information is used to make that link.

We begin with an informal overview before describing the system in formal terms.

### 4.1 Overview of ProPer

The ProPer system is described in terms of two main components: the *protected system* which stores all sensitive data and its derivatives, and mediates all computation over that data, and *the client program* which queries the sensitive data, requests computations to be performed over the sensitive data, and drives the inclusion of new input records into the protected system. An illustration of the architecture is given in Figure 1.

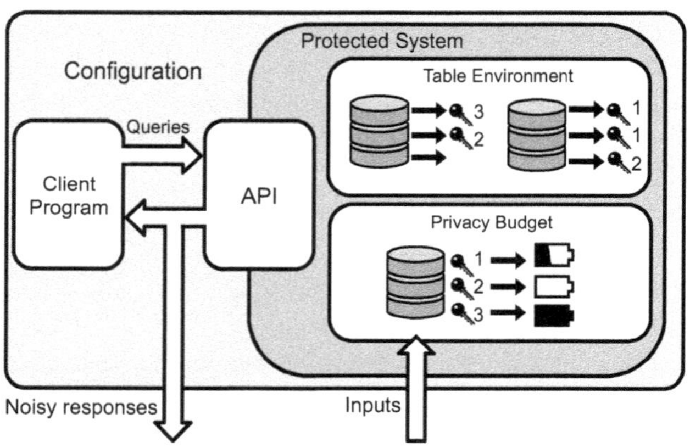


**Figure 1.** ProPer System Structure

From the viewpoint of a client program, the system just stores tables. Tables are referenced via *table variables*. A client program will issue a command to the protected system phrased in terms of table variables. These commands will represent *transformations* such as "Select all females from table A and assign the result to table B", or "Input some new records and assign them to table C", or *primitive differential-private queries* such as "Return the number of records in table C, with 0.5-differential privacy.".

The records that are input are the subject of our privacy concerns. We refer to those records as *individuals*. To provide $\mathscr{E}$-differential privacy for the individuals, the protected system needs to maintain more information than just the mapping between table variables and tables. For each individual $r$ that has been input to the system so far, a *privacy budget* for $r$ needs to be maintained. Initially the budget will be $\mathscr{E}(r)$. As queries are performed over time the budget for each individual may decrease.

There are two key issues that the system must address: (i) how much should the budget for each individual be decreased when a table is queried, and (ii) how do we prevent the budget from becoming negative (which would imply that we have violated privacy).

The solution to this is to track, together with each record, its *provenance*. The provenance of a given record is just the individual from which that record was derived (if any). Problem (i) is then solved by noting that the cost for individual $r$ is the privacy cost of the query multiplied by the number of elements in the table which have provenance $r$ (c.f. Corollary 3.4).

Before we can provide the formal definitions of the above sketch we need to define our basic domains and introduce some suitable notation.

### 4.2 Preliminary Definitions and Notation

Given sets $A$ and $B$, $A \rightharpoonup B$ denotes the set of partial functions between $A$ and $B$ with finite domain. If $f$ is (partial) function then $f[x \mapsto y]$ denotes the (partial) function which maps $x$ to $y$ and behaves as $f$ for all other arguments. We will also write partial functions (and updates) using a set-comprehension style notation, e.g. $[x \mapsto x+1 | x \in \{-1,0,1\}]$.

We assume an untyped set of records Rec, ranged over by $r$, $s$, etc. We will work extensively with multisets, in particular multisets of records. For a set $A$, we write $\mathsf{mset}(A)$ to denote the set of multisets over $A$ (isomorphic to functions $A \to \mathbb{N}$). More specifically, the set of tables $\mathrm{Table}$ is defined to be $\mathsf{mset}(\mathrm{Rec})$.

It will be convenient to introduce some notation for working with multisets. We use multiset brackets such as e.g. $A = \{\!\{5,5,6\}\!\}$, denoting a multiset $A$ containing two copies of 5 and one 6. We write multiset membership $a \overset{n}{\in} A$ to mean that there are exactly $n$ copies of $a$ in $A$, and $a \in A$ means $\exists n > 0.\, a \overset{n}{\in} A$. Analogous to set-comprehensions (set-builder notation) we will use multiset comprehensions, with the ability to express multiplicities. For example:

$$\{\!\{x^{[n]} \mid x \overset{n}{\in} \{\!\{5,5,-5\}\!\} \wedge x > 0\}\!\} = \{\!\{5,5\}\!\}.$$

But note that multiplicities may "sum up" as in this example:

$$\{\!\{0 \times x^{[n]} \mid x \overset{n}{\in} \{\!\{5,5,-5\}\!\}\}\!\} = \{\!\{0,0,0\}\!\}.$$

Given multisets $A$ and $B$, we write $A \uplus B$ to denote the additive union, which is the least multiset such that whenever $a \overset{n}{\in} A$ and $a \overset{m}{\in} B$ then $a \overset{m+n}{\in} (A \uplus B)$

***Multi-Relations*** Binary relations are to sets as multi-relations are to multisets. In other words a multi-relation is just a notation for a multiset of pairs [13].

We will use the concept of multi-relation extensively to model the records of a table together with their provenance. For example, a table containing just three copies of a record $r$, two of which where derived from individual Alice and one from individual Bob, will be modelled by a multi-relation $\{\!\{(r, \text{Alice}), (r, \text{Alice}), (r, \text{Bob})\}\!\}$.

Before we show how we use this in practice we need some notation to make reasoning with multi-relations more palatable.

Formally, given sets $A$ and $B$ we write $A \leftrightarrow B$ to denote $\mathsf{mset}(A \times B)$. If $R \in A \leftrightarrow B$ then we write $a \overset{n}{R}\, b$ to mean $a$ is related to $b$, $n$ times, i.e., $(a,b) \overset{n}{\in} R$.

**Definition 4.1** (Operations on Multi-relations). *Let $R$ and $S$ range over $X \leftrightarrow X$ for some $X$, let be $T$ is a subset of $X$, and $U \in \mathsf{mset}(X)$. We define the following operations involving multi-relations:*

| | |
|---|---|
| ***Domain of a Relation*** | $\mathsf{dom}(R) \stackrel{\text{def}}{=} \{\!\!\{ a^{[n]} \mid (a,b) \stackrel{n}{\in} R \}\!\!\}$ |
| ***Relation Composition*** | $R \,;\, S \stackrel{\text{def}}{=} \{\!\!\{ (a,c)^{[m \cdot n]} \mid a \stackrel{n}{R} b \wedge b \stackrel{m}{S} c \}\!\!\}$ |
| ***Application*** | $R \bullet U \stackrel{\text{def}}{=} \{\!\!\{ a^{[n \cdot m]} \mid a \stackrel{n}{R} b \wedge b \stackrel{m}{\in} U \}\!\!\}$ |
| ***Right Restriction*** | $R \rhd T \stackrel{\text{def}}{=} \{\!\!\{ (a,b)^{[n]} \mid a \stackrel{n}{R} b \wedge b \in T \}\!\!\}$ |

**Example 4.2.** *Given the following two multi-relations:*

$$R = \{\!\!\{ (x,y), (x,w), (x,w) \}\!\!\} \qquad S = \{\!\!\{ (y,z), (w,z), (w,v) \}\!\!\}$$

*then* $\mathsf{dom}(S) = \{\!\!\{ y, w, w \}\!\!\}$, $R \,;\, S = \{\!\!\{ (x,z)^{[3]}, (x,v)^{[2]} \}\!\!\}$, $R \rhd \{w\} = \{\!\!\{ (x,w)^{[2]} \}\!\!\}$, *and* $R \bullet \{\!\!\{ w^{[2]}, y \}\!\!\} = \{\!\!\{ x^{[5]} \}\!\!\}$.

The following properties are easily verified.

**Proposition 4.3.** *For all multi-relations $R$, $R'$, $S$, and $S'$, and set $T$,*

*(i) Composition is $\uplus$-preserving in both arguments:*

$$(R \uplus R') \,;\, S = (R \,;\, S) \uplus (R' \,;\, S)$$
$$R \,;\, (S \uplus S') = (R \,;\, S) \uplus (R \,;\, S'),$$

*(ii) restriction is $\uplus$-preserving in its first argument:*

$$(R \uplus S) \rhd T = (R \rhd T) \uplus (S \rhd T),$$

*(iii) restriction and composition associate as follows:*

$$(R \,;\, S) \rhd T = R \,;\, (S \rhd T),$$

*(iv) and finally:*

$$\mathsf{dom}(R \rhd T) = R \bullet T$$

Note that, as in (iv), we will freely use sets as if they were multisets without making the obvious injection operation explicit.

### 4.3 Provenance Tracing

As mentioned, we will track the provenance of each record derived. The key idea to achieve personalised differential privacy is that the provenance of a given record must be at most one record. We call this *affine* provenance.

***Supported operations*** As we explained, in this setting, records' provenance should be affine. This is achieved by simply requiring that all transformations are unary and $\uplus$-preserving i.e., transformations $F$ for which $F(A \uplus B) = F(A) \uplus F(B)$. This guarantees that provenance can be tracked by observing the action of $F$ on singletons, and (ii) provenance will always be a single element.

To give a simple syntactic characterisation of a class of unary $\uplus$-preserving functions, we can use a grammar of terms built from the standard operations of relational algebra, used here over multisets. The basic operators of relational algebra, transposed to multisets, are the set operations (multiset union $\uplus$, set difference $-$, cartesian product $\times$), together with record selection $\sigma_p$, which selects all elements satisfying property $p$, and projection $\pi_a$ which transforms each row by retaining only the columns given by schema $a$. We omit the details of the definitions and refer to [11] for definitions of multiset variants of these standard operations.

**Definition 4.4** (Affine Relational Terms). *Let $V$ range over sets of variables and $T$ over literal multisets. We define a family of variable-indexed relational algebra terms $A_V$ by the following grammar:*

$$A_V ::= x\ (\in V) \mid A_V \uplus A_V \mid A_V - A_{\{\}} \mid A_V \times A_{\{\}} \mid A_{\{\}} \times A_V$$
$$\mid \sigma_p(A_V) \mid \pi_a(A_V) \mid T$$

**Theorem 4.5.** *Any multiset transformation $F$ defined by $F(x) = A_{\{x\}}$ is $\uplus$-preserving.*

The proof follows by induction on the definition of $A_{\{x\}}$ using the union-preserving properties of the operators. The restrictions imposed by the grammar are due to the facts that all the operations preserve unions in each argument individually, except for the second argument of set difference, and that $\uplus$ preserves unions across its arguments simultaneously, whereas $\times$ does not (i.e. $(A \uplus A') \times (B \uplus B') \neq (A \times B) \uplus (A' \times B')$ ).

***Provenance Tables*** The fact that we will track affine provenance leads us to define a *provenance table* as a table in which the affine provenance of each element is recorded.

**Definition 4.6** (Provenance Table). *A provenance table is a multi relation of type* $\mathrm{ProvTable} \stackrel{\text{def}}{=} \mathrm{Rec} \leftrightarrow \mathrm{Rec}_\bot$, *where* $\mathrm{Rec}_\bot \stackrel{\text{def}}{=} \mathrm{Rec} \cup \{\bot\}$ *for some distinguished non-record* $\bot$.

The underlying table $T$ represented by a provenance table $D$ is obtained by simply taking the domain of $D$, i.e. $T = \mathsf{dom}(D)$. The provenance of each element $r$ of the table $T$ is given by the element to which they are related, viz, if $r D s$ then there is a copy of $r$ in $T$ that has provenance $s$. If some record $r$ is related to $\bot$ this signifies that $r$ is present in the table, but that it has no provenance (i.e. it was not derived from any individual).

In the remainder of this section we introduce the notation and techniques necessary to permit provenance to be traced across computation.

How do we build and maintain provenance tables? We need a way to create provenance tables from new tables, and we need a way to construct the provenance table of a table produced by a transformation applied to a (provenance) table.

When new records of individuals enter the system then their provenance table has a simple form: the provenance of each record is itself. When we create a new literal table (i.e. where the elements do not depend on individuals) then each record has provenance $\bot$. The following notation for these cases will be useful:

**Definition 4.7.** *For a set of records $R$, define the* identity provenance table

$$\mathsf{Id}_R \stackrel{\text{def}}{=} \{\!\!\{ (r,r) \mid r \in R \}\!\!\}.$$

*For a table $T$ define the* constant provenance table

$$\mathsf{Const}_T \stackrel{\text{def}}{=} \{\!\!\{ (r,\bot)^{[n]} \mid r \stackrel{n}{\in} T \}\!\!\}.$$

The final building block is to show how to lift a function $F$ which computes over tables to a function $\hat{F}$ which computes over provenance tables so that (in particular) the following diagram commutes:

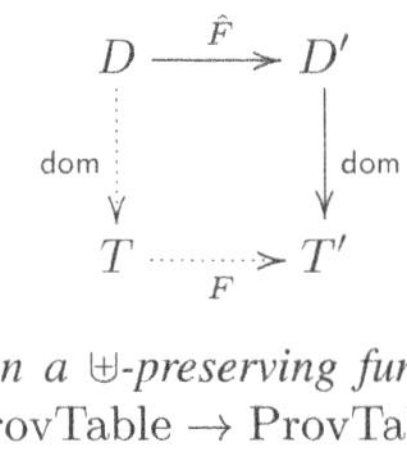


**Definition 4.8.** *Given a $\uplus$-preserving function* $F \in \mathrm{Table} \to \mathrm{Table}$, *define* $\hat{F} \in \mathrm{ProvTable} \to \mathrm{ProvTable}$ *by*

$$\hat{F}(D) \stackrel{\text{def}}{=} \widetilde{F} \,;\, D$$

*where* $\widetilde{F} \in \mathrm{Rec} \leftrightarrow \mathrm{Rec}$ *is defined by* $t \stackrel{n}{\widetilde{F}} s \Leftrightarrow t \stackrel{n}{\in} F(\{s\})$

The fact that the diagram above commutes is captured as follows:

**Lemma 4.9** (functional correctness). $\mathsf{dom}(\hat{F}(D)) = F(\mathsf{dom}(D))$

*Proof.* First we show that the relational representation of $F$ and the relational application operator behave as expected:

$$\widetilde{F} \bullet A = F(A) \tag{1}$$

$$\begin{aligned}
\widetilde{F} \bullet A &= \{\!|a^{[m \cdot n]} \mid a \overset{n}{\widetilde{F}} b, b \overset{m}{\in} A |\!\} \\
&= \{\!|a^{[m \cdot n]} \mid a \overset{n}{\in} F(\{b\}), b \overset{m}{\in} A |\!\} && \text{(Def. 4.8)} \\
&= \{\!|a^{[k]} \mid a \overset{k}{\in} F(A) |\!\} && (F \text{ preserves } \uplus) \\
&= F(A)
\end{aligned}$$

Now we show:

$$\mathsf{dom}(D \,;\, D') = D \bullet \mathsf{dom}(D') \tag{2}$$

$$\begin{aligned}
\mathsf{dom}(D \,;\, D') &= \mathsf{dom}(\{\!|(a,c)^{[m \cdot n]} \mid a \overset{m}{D} b, b \overset{n}{D'} c |\!\}) \\
&= \{\!|a^{[m \cdot n]} \mid a \overset{m}{D} b, b \overset{n}{D'} c |\!\} \\
&= \left\{\!\!\left| a^{[m \cdot k]} \;\middle|\; (a,b) \overset{m}{\in} D \wedge b \overset{k}{\in} \mathsf{dom}(D') \right|\!\!\right\} \\
&= D \bullet \mathsf{dom}(D')
\end{aligned}$$

Finally we calculate:

$$\begin{aligned}
\mathsf{dom}(\hat{F}(D)) &= \mathsf{dom}(\widetilde{F} \,;\, D) \\
&= \widetilde{F} \bullet \mathsf{dom}(D) && \text{(Eq. 2 )} \\
&= F(\mathsf{dom}(D)) && \text{(Eq. 1 )}
\end{aligned}$$

□

### 4.4 The System Model

The semantics of the overall system will be given by a probabilistic transition system described by combining the *client program* with the *protected system*.

***Protected System*** The protected system is a collection of states which encodes four pieces of information:

1. the set of individuals which have been input to the system so far,
2. a *privacy budget* (a positive real) for each of these individuals indicating how much of the personalised privacy remains,
3. a set of *table variables* TVar used to identify intermediate tables computed, and
4. a *table environment* which maps each *table variable* to the provenance table it represents.

The first two items are modelled by a partial function from individuals to budgets, and we assume that the set of table variables is fixed (and at least countable). This leads us to the formal definition of the states:

**Definition 4.10** (Protected System States)**.**

$$\text{States} \stackrel{\text{def}}{=} (\text{TVar} \to \text{ProvTable}) \times (\text{Rec} \rightharpoonup \mathbb{R}^+)$$

***Client Program Model*** We work with an abstract notion of a client program. A program is just a labelled transition system, subject to some restrictions, where the labels – the *actions* – represent the imperative API through which the program interacts with the protected system.

The program model, inspired by PINQ [17], is an imperative program that computes with tables by requesting that the commands $a \in \text{ProgAct}$ are performed. ProgAct is specified in figure 2.

Here we assume that $F$ ranges over an unspecified set denoting $\uplus$-preserving functions in Table $\to$ Table, and $Q_\varepsilon$ ranges over

$$\begin{aligned}
\text{ProgAct} ::=\; & \tau && \text{Silent step} \\
\mid\; & tv := \text{Expr} && \text{Assignment} \\
\mid\; & Q_\varepsilon(tv)?v && \text{Primitive Query returning } v \in \text{Val}
\end{aligned}$$

$$\begin{aligned}
\text{Expr} ::=\; & tv && \text{Table variable} \\
\mid\; & F(tv_1 \uplus \cdots \uplus tv_k) && \text{Transform} \\
\mid\; & T && \text{Table literal, } T \in \text{Table} \\
\mid\; & \mathsf{input} && \text{Reference to the input stream}
\end{aligned}$$

**Figure 2.** ProgAct: the labels of the transition system

an unspecified set of queries with the convention that $Q_\varepsilon$ denotes an $\varepsilon$-differentially private query. Note that we will not formally distinguish the name of a function (as used here to define the set of actions) from its denotation (as used in the specification of the semantics of the system below).

The idea is that programs have no direct access to tables, but make requests for the system to manipulate them on their behalf. This includes making a request for the system to collect new individuals via an `input` action (and place them in a table variable). The primitive query action is special. Firstly, it does not model a request, but rather a request and its result all in one. The reason for this is that it allows us to model value passing without needing to introduce any specific syntax for programs. Secondly, the value returned by the query is known to the program, and the program can act on it accordingly. From the perspective of the program and the protected system together, this value will be considered an observable output of the whole system. We also model internal actions of the program (and hence the passage of time) via the traditional silent action $\tau$. A program, then, is just a ProgAct-labelled transition system. However we impose some mild restrictions on the transition system which model the fact that (i) the query operation really is an input operation, so if the program issues a query, there must be a transition for that query with every possible value, and that (ii) the program is fully deterministic, so that at most one type of action is possible in any given state, and the action determines the next state.

**Definition 4.11** (Client Program)**.** *A client program (a program for short) is a labelled transition system $\langle \mathbb{P}, \to, P_0 \rangle$ where $\mathbb{P}$ is the set of program states with initial state $P_0$ and transition relation $\to \subseteq (\mathbb{P} \times \text{ProgAct} \times \mathbb{P})$, satisfying the following properties. Firstly it is deadlock free – a program can always make a transition, and secondly it satisfies the determinacy property:*

*For all states $P$, if $P \xrightarrow{a} P'$ and $P \xrightarrow{b} P''$ then*

1. *if $a = b$ then $P' = P''$,*
2. *if $a$ is not a query then $a = b$,*
3. *if $a = Q_\varepsilon(tv)?r$ then $b = Q_\varepsilon(tv)?r'$ for some $r'$, and for all $s$ there exists a $P_s$ such that $P \xrightarrow{Q_\varepsilon(tv)?s} P_s$.*

***Remark: Implicit parameters*** To avoid excessive parameterisation of definitions, in what follows we will fix some arbitrary client program $\langle \mathbb{P}, \to, P_0 \rangle$ and some arbitrary personal budget $\mathscr{E}$ and make definitions relative to these.

***Configuration Semantics*** Now we can provide the semantics of the combination of a program and the protected system – what we will call a *configuration*:

$$\mathbb{C} \in \text{Config} \stackrel{\text{def}}{=} \mathbb{P} \times (\text{TVar} \to \text{ProvTable}) \times (\text{Rec} \rightharpoonup \mathbb{R}^+)$$

We will write a configuration as a triple $\langle P, E, B\rangle$ where metavariable $E$ ranges over the table environment and $B$ ranges over the budget.

The behaviour of a configuration will be a form of probabilistic labelled transition system whose labels are the values of queries made by the program, the silent transition $\tau$, and the tables of unique individuals which are input by the environment.

**Definition 4.12** (Initial configuration). *The initial configuration is formed from the initial program state, the environment that maps every variable to the empty provenance table, and the empty budget table:*

$$\mathbb{C}_0 \stackrel{\text{def}}{=} \langle P_0, [tv \mapsto \{\!\!\}\ \mid tv \in \text{TVar}], []\rangle$$

**Definition 4.13** (Operational Semantics). *The operational semantics of configurations is given by a "probabilistic" labelled transition relation with transitions of the form $\mathbb{C} \xrightarrow{a}_p \mathbb{C}'$ where $a \in \text{Act} \stackrel{\text{def}}{=} \{\tau\} \cup \text{Val} \cup 2^{\text{Rec}}$, and (probability) $p \in [0,1]$. The definition is given by cases in Figure 3.*

We put "probability" in parentheses because the relation is not *a priori* probabilistic but something that must be proven; this is established in Lemma 4.16. First we provide some explanation of each nontrivial rule in turn.

***[Input]*** The program requests an input to be made and assigned to a table variable. The rule imposes a constraint on the records $T$ which are input: it must be a *set* of records, and this set must be disjoint from the records previously input (the domain of $B$). This reflects the idea that the input records are the subject of privacy and represent unique individuals. The transition of the configuration is labelled with $T$ to record that the environment chose to input $T$. The probability of the transition is 1, meaning that the choice of input is treated nondeterministically. The configuration is updated in two ways. Firstly, the table is converted to a provenance table by recording that the provenance of each record is itself. Secondly the budget for each new record is initialised from $\mathscr{E}$.

***[Assign]*** The program requests a transformation of existing data. Here we apply the mechanisms developed in Section 4.3 to lift the function (respectively, table) into the world of provenance tables.

***[Query]*** Here the program is requesting the value of a query $Q_\varepsilon(tv)$. To answer the query we must determine the *eligible* records, $L$, from the table $tv$, which can safely be involved in this query. To do this we first determine a *Cost map* $C$, which describes the privacy cost which would be inflicted upon individual $r$ by releasing the query $Q_\varepsilon(tv)$; the cost of an $\varepsilon$-differentially private query on $tv$ to an individual $r$ is $\varepsilon$ multiplied by the number of records in $tv$ which have provenance $r$. Given the cost map, we can determine $A$, the set of individuals for which this cost is *Acceptable* – i.e. those who have sufficient budget. Finally we can use $A$ to determine $L$: it is the sub-table of records which depend at most on records in $A$.

The probability of the transition is inherited from the probability that the query returns that particular value.

### 4.5 Trace semantics

The transition system on configuration $\mathbb{C} \xrightarrow{a}_p \mathbb{C}'$ is fully probabilistic in that $\mathbb{C}$ and the value of $a$ uniquely determine $p$ and, when $p > 0$, $\mathbb{C}'$. This makes it very straightforward to lift the single-step semantics to a probabilistic trace semantics.

In what follows let $\sigma$ range over *traces*, sequences of zero or more actions $\text{Act}^*$. The empty trace is denoted by $[]$ and $a\sigma$ denotes the trace starting with $a$ and continuing with $\sigma$.

**Definition 4.14** (Trace semantics). *Define the trace transition relation*

$$\Rightarrow\ \subseteq \text{Config} \times \text{Act}^* \times [0,1] \times \text{Config}$$

*inductively by the following rules:*

$$\mathbb{C} \stackrel{[]}{\Rightarrow}_1 \mathbb{C} \qquad \frac{\mathbb{C} \xrightarrow{a}_p \mathbb{C}' \quad \mathbb{C}' \stackrel{\sigma}{\Rightarrow}_q \mathbb{C}''}{\mathbb{C} \stackrel{a\sigma}{\Longrightarrow}_{p.q} \mathbb{C}''}$$

We write $\mathbb{C} \stackrel{\sigma}{\Rightarrow}_p$ to mean $\mathbb{C} \stackrel{\sigma}{\Rightarrow}_p \mathbb{C}'$ for some $\mathbb{C}'$.

Although we have a trace-labelled transition system involving numbers derived from probabilities, it remains to show in what sense we have specified a probabilistic system. We begin with a definition which describes when an input sequence is compatible with a given trace.

**Definition 4.15** (Input Compatibility). *An* input trace *$i$ is a sequence of mutually disjoint sets of records. We say that a trace $t$ is* compatible *with $i$, written $t \vdash i$ iff the subsequence of inputs in $t$ is a prefix of $i$.*

Now we can state the sense in which the transition system is probabilistic: it can be viewed as a probabilistic function of the input and the length of the trace observed:

**Lemma 4.16** (Traces are Probabilistic). *For all input traces $i$, and all $n \geq 0$,*

$$\Sigma\{\!\!\{p \mid \mathbb{C}_0 \stackrel{t}{\Rightarrow}_p\ \wedge t \vdash i \wedge \mathsf{size}(t) = n\}\!\!\} = 1$$

I.e. in response to a given input, the possible traces of a program of a given length form a probability distribution.

*Proof.* (sketch) A key here is the following determinacy property: whenever $\mathbb{C} \xrightarrow{a}_p \mathbb{C}'$ and $\mathbb{C} \xrightarrow{a}_q \mathbb{C}''$ for $p, q > 0$, then $\mathbb{C}' = \mathbb{C}''$ and $p = q$. This can be established by cases according to the transition, and depends crucially on the assumption that the program transitions are deterministic. From this it is straightforward to show that $\mathbb{C} \stackrel{t}{\Rightarrow}_p \mathbb{C}'$ and $\mathbb{C} \xrightarrow{t}_q \mathbb{C}''$ for $p, q > 0$, imply $p = q$ and $\mathbb{C}' = \mathbb{C}''$. The first clause($p = q$) is easily established by cases according to the rule inducing the transition, making use of determinism assumption about programs; the second clause ($\mathbb{C}' = \mathbb{C}''$) then follows easily from the first. Armed with these two properties, the proof follows by induction on $n$. □

So whenever $\mathbb{C} \stackrel{\sigma}{\Rightarrow}_p$, $p$ is the probability of observing $\sigma$ among traces of the same length and for which the input sequence is the same. We thus write $Pr(\mathbb{C} \stackrel{\sigma}{\Rightarrow}) = p$ to mean $\mathbb{C} \stackrel{\sigma}{\Rightarrow}_p$.

## 5. ProPer Provides $\mathscr{E}$-Differential Privacy

In this section we establish the main theorem for the system, which states that the trace semantics is an $\mathscr{E}$-differentially private function of its input. In order to state this in a convenient way we introduce some notation.

**Definition 5.1** ($r$-difference). *For any record $r$ and any tables $T$ and $T'$, we write $T \stackrel{r}{\sqsubset} T'$ to mean that $T \uplus \{\!\!\{r\}\!\!\} = T'$. We lift this relation to traces, writing $\sigma \stackrel{r}{\sqsubset} \sigma'$ to mean $\sigma = \sigma_1 T \sigma_2$ and $\sigma' = \sigma_1 T' \sigma_2$, for some $\sigma_1, \sigma_2, T, T'$ such that $T \stackrel{r}{\sqsubset} T'$.*

*We will further lift $T \stackrel{r}{\sqsubset} T'$ to various structures containing tables. In all cases we define the overloaded relation $\stackrel{r}{\sim}$ to be the symmetric closure of $\stackrel{r}{\sqsubset}$, so $T \stackrel{r}{\sim} T'$ iff either $T \stackrel{r}{\sqsubset} T'$ or $T' \stackrel{r}{\sqsubset} T$.*

So when $\sigma \stackrel{r}{\sim} \sigma'$ then $\sigma$ and $\sigma'$ differ in exactly one element, an input set, and and their difference is exactly the record $r$.

**Theorem 5.2** ($\mathscr{E}$-differential privacy for all traces). *If $\sigma \stackrel{r}{\sim} \sigma'$ and $\text{Pr}(\mathbb{C} \stackrel{\sigma}{\Rightarrow}) = p$ then $\text{Pr}(\mathbb{C} \stackrel{\sigma'}{\Rightarrow}) = q$ for some $q$ such that $p \leq q \cdot \exp(\mathscr{E}(r))$.*

$$\text{Input}\ \frac{P \xrightarrow{tv:=\mathsf{input}} P' \quad T \in 2^{\mathrm{Rec}} \quad T \cap \mathsf{dom}(B) = \emptyset}{\langle P, E, B\rangle \xrightarrow{T}_1 \langle P', E[tv \mapsto \mathsf{Id}(T)], B[r \mapsto \mathscr{E}(r) \mid r \in T]\rangle}$$

$$\text{Assign}\ \frac{P \xrightarrow{tv:=e} P'}{\langle P, E, B\rangle \xrightarrow{\tau}_1 \langle P', E[tv \mapsto D], B\rangle} \quad \text{where } D = \begin{cases} \hat{F}(E(tv_1) \uplus \cdots \uplus E(tv_n)) & \text{if } e = F(tv_1 \uplus \cdots \uplus tv_n) \\ \mathsf{Const}(T) & \text{if } e = T \\ E(tv') & \text{if } e = tv' \end{cases}$$

$$\text{Silent}\ \frac{P \xrightarrow{\tau} P'}{\langle P, E, B\rangle \xrightarrow{\tau}_1 \langle P', E, B\rangle}$$

$$\text{Query}\ \frac{P \xrightarrow{Q_\varepsilon(tv)?n} P'}{\langle P, E, B\rangle \xrightarrow{n}_p \langle P', E, B[r \mapsto B(r) - C(r) \mid r \in A]\rangle} \quad \text{where} \quad \begin{array}{rcl} C & = & [s \mapsto \varepsilon.\mathsf{size}(E(tv) \bullet \{s\}) \mid s \in \mathsf{dom}(B)] \\ A & = & \{r \mid B(r) \geq C(r)\} \\ L & = & E(tv) \bullet (A \cup \{\bot\}) \\ p & = & \Pr(Q_\varepsilon(L) = n) \end{array}$$

**Figure 3.** Operational Semantics

To prove the theorem (inevitably by an induction over the trace length) we must establish an invariant relation over configurations which generalises $T \overset{r}{\sqsubset} T'$. The most tricky and important of these is the relation between provenance tables.

**Definition 5.3.** $D \overset{r}{\sqsubset} D' \Leftrightarrow D \uplus (D' \rhd \{r\}) = D'$

This says that when $D \overset{r}{\sqsubset} D'$, the table represented by $D'$ has all the elements of $D$, with the same provenance, and that the elements of $D'$ which are not in $D$ all have provenance $r$.

This relation will be used to express a key invariant in the correctness proof, and can also be thought of (in the main proof) as establishing the correctness of the provenance information. Now we establish some basic properties of this relation on provenance tables.

**Proposition 5.4.** $D \overset{r}{\sqsubset} D' \Rightarrow \mathsf{dom}(D') = D' \bullet \{r\} \uplus \mathsf{dom}(D)$

*Proof.*

$$\begin{aligned} D \overset{r}{\sqsubset} D' &\Rightarrow (D' \rhd \{r\}) \uplus D = D' \\ &\Rightarrow \mathsf{dom}((D' \rhd \{r\}) \uplus D) = \mathsf{dom}(D') \\ &\Rightarrow \mathsf{dom}(D' \rhd \{r\}) \uplus \mathsf{dom}(D) = \mathsf{dom}(D') \\ &\Leftrightarrow D' \bullet \{r\} \uplus \mathsf{dom}(D) = \mathsf{dom}(D') && (4.3(iv))\ \square \end{aligned}$$

**Proposition 5.5.** $\forall i \in I.(D_i \overset{r}{\sqsubset} D'_i) \Rightarrow \biguplus_{i\in I} D_i \overset{r}{\sqsubset} \biguplus_{i\in I} D'_i$

*Proof.*

$$\begin{aligned} &\forall i \in I.(D'_i \rhd \{r\}) \uplus D_i = D'_i \\ &\Rightarrow \biguplus_i ((D'_i \rhd \{r\}) \uplus D_i) = \biguplus_i D'_i \\ &\Rightarrow \biguplus_i (D'_i \rhd \{r\}) \uplus (\biguplus_i D_i) = \biguplus_i D'_i \\ &\Leftrightarrow (\biguplus_i D'_i \rhd \{r\}) \uplus (\biguplus_i D_i) = \biguplus_i D'_i && (4.3(ii)) \\ &\Leftrightarrow \biguplus_{i\in I} D_i \overset{r}{\sqsubset} \biguplus_{i\in I} D'_i && (\text{def of } \overset{r}{\sqsubset})\quad \square \end{aligned}$$

The following establishes that computations over provenance tables preserves $\overset{r}{\sqsubset}$.

**Proposition 5.6.** $D \overset{r}{\sqsubset} D' \Rightarrow \hat{F}(D) \overset{r}{\sqsubset} \hat{F}(D')$

*Proof.* Assume premise.

$$\begin{aligned} \hat{F}(D') &= \widetilde{F} \,;\, D' && (\text{def.}) \\ &= \widetilde{F} \,;\, (D' \rhd \{r\} \uplus D) && (\text{premise}) \\ &= (\widetilde{F} \,;\, (D' \rhd \{r\})) \uplus (\widetilde{F} \,;\, D) && (4.3(i)) \\ &= ((\widetilde{F} \,;\, D') \rhd \{r\}) \uplus (\widetilde{F} \,;\, D) && (4.3(iii)) \\ &= ((\hat{F}(D')) \rhd \{r\}) \uplus \hat{F}(D) && (\hat{F}\text{ def.}) \end{aligned}$$

Hence $\Rightarrow \hat{F}(D) \overset{r}{\sqsubset} \hat{F}(D')$ as required. □

**Definition 5.7** (($r, \varepsilon$)-similarity for configurations)**.** *We define the following similarity relations for (the components of) configurations:*

- $E \overset{r}{\sqsubset} E' \iff \forall tv.\, E(tv) \overset{r}{\sqsubset} E'(tv) \vee E(tv) = E'(tv)$
- $B \overset{r,\varepsilon}{\sqsubset} B' \iff B[r \mapsto \varepsilon] = B' \wedge \varepsilon \in [0, \mathscr{E}(r)]$
- $\langle P, E, B\rangle \overset{r,\varepsilon}{\sqsubset} \langle P', E', B'\rangle \iff P = P' \wedge E \overset{r}{\sqsubset} E' \wedge B \overset{r,\varepsilon}{\sqsubset} B'$

*Finally, define* $\mathbb{C} \overset{r,\varepsilon}{\sim} \mathbb{C}'$ *iff* $\mathbb{C} \overset{r,\varepsilon}{\sqsubset} \mathbb{C}'$ *or* $\mathbb{C}' \overset{r,\varepsilon}{\sqsubset} \mathbb{C}$.

The generalised version of Theorem 5.2 establishes the invariant relation between configurations from which the Theorem is a straightforward corollary.

**Lemma 5.8.** *If* $\sigma \overset{r}{\sim} \sigma'$ *and* $\mathbb{C}_0 \overset{\sigma}{\Rightarrow}_p \mathbb{C}$*, then* $\mathbb{C}_0 \overset{\sigma'}{\Rightarrow}_q \mathbb{C}'$ *where* $\mathbb{C} \overset{r,\varepsilon}{\sim} \mathbb{C}'$ *for some* $\varepsilon$ *such that* $p \leq q.\exp(\mathscr{E}(r) - \varepsilon)$.

The proof is given in Appendix A.

## 6. Implementation and Experimental Results

In this section we start by briefly describing the implementation of ProPer. We continue with a small example to give a taste on how the tool is used, and finally we present some experimental results in terms of time and memory execution applied to a couple of benchmarks, comparing ProPer with PINQ.

### 6.1 Description of the Tool

We have implemented our PDP approach into the tool ProPer. The tool has been implemented in C#.

In order to interact with the tool, the user must be working on a programming environment (e.g., C#) and needs to create an instance of the ProPer class. After this, there are a number of constructs available thorough the ProPer API to initialise and manipulate data. ProPer is based on LINQ, and its interface has been designed having PINQ as inspiration so not surprisingly the way a user interacts with both tools is similar, modulo some syntactic differences.

Despite similarities there are important differences in the way PINQ and ProPer are implemented as explained below.

(i). When a new data set is given to ProPer, each record of the data set is assigned a unique key and an individual privacy budget. In PINQ records do not have a key and the privacy budget is global.

(ii). ProPer performs provenance tracking using the above mentioned record keys. One feature of this provenance tracking is that each record depends at most on one record from the input set.

(iii). Some transformations are implemented differently: In ProPer `Where` and `Select` are equipped with provenance tracking mechanisms, but this is not the case in PINQ.

(iv). Though the dynamic updating of databases (adding records) is possible in PINQ, the added records inherit the current global budget and thus they can be used as many times in queries as the old records. In ProPer, PDP guarantees that added records may participate in as many queries as their individual budget allows, not depending on others' record budget (or global budget).

In what follows we elaborate on how ProPer works. Let us assume the user has initialised a data set and wants to perform a number of transformations in order to make some queries. In order to do this, a ProPer object is first created, the data set is imported into ProPer, the transformations are applied to this object, and finally the user can then run arbitrary queries on that ProPer object. The above description is a simplification as ProPer only supports transformations where each resulting record depends on at most one record. If other transformations not respecting this constraint are neededthen a PINQ subroutine will be called, and treated like a primitive query.

In more detail, in ProPer, sensitive data is stored in a protected object with the generic type of `ProPer<T>` (in PINQ sensitive data is placed in a `PINQueryable<T>` object). When data is manipulated using $\uplus$-preserving transformations, provenance information is also transferred and attached to the resulting records. Two important supported transformations are `Where` and `Select` representing the *projection*($\pi$) and *selection*($\sigma$) primitive operators in relational algebra. When it comes to aggregation, records with sufficient privacy budget are selected and their privacy budget is reduced. Also when a transformation with unsupported type of provenance is issued, the data set may switch to classical differential privacy by calling `AsPINQ(double epsilon)`. This reduces the budget of each involved record by $\varepsilon$, and creates a protected object of type `PINQueryable<T>`. From this point the resulting `PINQueryable<T>` object can be used in other arbitrary transformations defined in classical differential privacy or contribute in other $\varepsilon$-differentially private aggregations.

### 6.2 Example

As mentioned previously, PINQ introduces a special parallel composition operation for applying queries to disjoint parts of a data set. We argued that personalised budgets implies that the analyst does not need to construct parallel queries (§3) – it is just as efficient to pose sequential queries. But in situations where there is no natural partition of data our approach is not only more convenient, but also gives strictly better results. Let us assume a data set on which we will perform three queries, each one with accuracy $\varepsilon$, and such that the pairwise intersection of the intended domains of these queries is nonempty but where we know that that the intersection of the 3 queries is empty (see Figure 4). In the universe where each person is allowed to have at most two roles, the queries

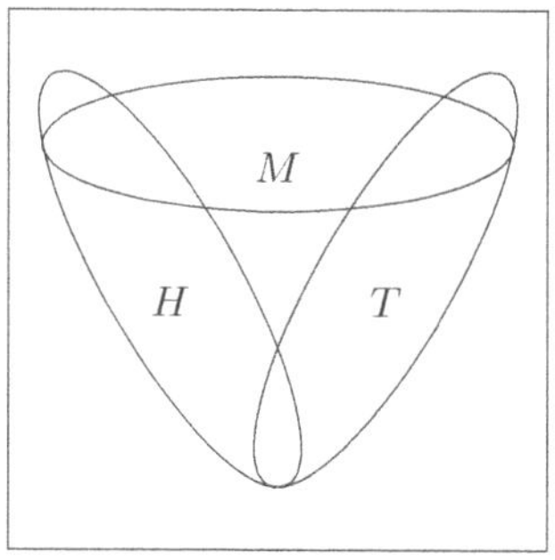


**Figure 4.** T=*Teachers*, M= *Managers* and H=*Headmasters*

*Teachers*, *Managers* and *Headmasters* are asking about individuals in different roles. In this case, we cannot use parallel composition (as in PINQ) since it would require that the queries are disjoint. If we run them sequentially it would consume $3\varepsilon$, whereas if we use PDP we will consume $2\varepsilon$. (Note, that in the case of 3 disjoint queries, the PDP approach would consume the same budget as in the parallel case ($\varepsilon$).) The above case may be generalised: Given $n$ queries such that each record is involved in at most $g$ queries, would give the following: parallel composition (*à la* PINQ) cannot be applied, PINQ sequential composition would consume $n \cdot \varepsilon$, while PDP would consume $g \cdot \varepsilon$.

As a simple example we demonstrate how this analysis can be implemented in ProPer. We use the structure described below to store an individual's information, where each individual has at most two different roles: role1 (e.g., Teacher), and role2 (e.g., Manager).

```
public struct Individual
{
    public string name;
    public string role1;
    public string role2;
}
```

To initialise and populate our database with sample data we can pass an array of type `Individual` as an argument to the constructor method:

```
Individual[] population = new Individual[]
{
    new Individual{ name = "Alice",
                    role1 = "Teacher" ,
                    role2 = "Headmaster"},
    new Individual{ name = "Bob",
                    role1 = "Manager" ,
                    role2 = "Teacher"},
    ...
}
var protectData = new ProPer<Individual>
     (population.AsQueryable(),budget);
```

To construct a ProPer protected object that only stores information about Teachers we can use the *selection* operation. Note that each record in the resulting ProPer has a dependency relation with exactly one record from the input data set:

```
var Admins = protectData.Where(person=>(
     person.role1.Equals("Teacher") ||
     person.role2.Equals("Teacher") ) );
```

Using the `Select` transformation we can modify an attribute's value or totally remove an attribute from a relation. For instance, as you can see in the following code, we transformed the table storing information about all Teachers into another table containing the length of their names:

```
var NameLengths = Admins.Select (person =>
     (person.name).Length );
```

Finally, to extract information from the above table we call the method **AsPINQ(epsilon)** which will reduce the budget of each individual record from the data set under consideration by $\varepsilon$, and will create a **PINQueryable** object with total budget $\varepsilon$.

Now it is possible to run a classical differential privacy query; the simplest one being to call an aggregation function with accuracy $\varepsilon$, as shown in the code below.

```
Console.WriteLine (NameLengths.NoisyAverage(epsilon,
    x =>x /20) * 20 );
```

Similarly, the ProPer object can be converted into a **PINQueryable** object as follows:

```
var pinqObj= NameLengths.AsPINQ(epsilon);
```

Note that **PINQueryable** objects can also be used in more complicated transformations like **Join** and **GroupBy**, available in PINQ.

As we have previously mentioned, another distinct feature of ProPer is its ability to deal with dynamic databases. For that, ProPer has the following available methods: **Update**, **Insert** and **Delete**. It is also possible for users to define their own methods to manipulate data if needed be. A function to refresh the contents of the database when it is called can be defined with the **SetRefresh()** method. The defined function is called by the client program each time **Refresh()** is called:

```
protectData.SetRefresh (obj=>(obj
    .Remove(predicate=>true))
    .Insert(newPopulation.AsQueryable() , epsilon)
    );
protectData.Refresh();
```

### 6.3 Experimental results

To have a space and execution time comparison we implemented the *k-means clustering* algorithm both in PINQ and ProPer. This algorithm only uses *projection* and *selection* primitives which makes it a perfect candidate for comparison. The k-means algorithm accepts four parameters: a list of records, the number of centres, the number of dimensions, and the number of iterations. For the purpose of this research we fixed three of the parameters (Number of dimensions = 4 , Number of centres = 4 , Number of iterations = 5), and modified the number of records to see its effect on execution time and memory usage.

The result of our experiments concerning time is shown in Figure 5, where it is possible to see the effect on execution time when varying the number of records. As it can be seen in the figure, adding provenance tracking (ProPer) has a negative effect on the execution time and slows down the system by around 15 percent. Concerning the memory usage, ProPer implementation of the k-means clustering algorithm uses twice as much memory as the PINQ implementation. This can be motivated by the fact that each record has the type **double**, and for each record a key with type **int** and a structure to keep track of privacy budget is needed. This high memory usage is justifiable since these extra structures (key and privacy budget) has almost the same size as the size of the record. More generally the overhead in memory will be the ratio of the size of the record with and without the provenance record key.

### 6.4 Limitations

The restriction of ProPer to unary union-preserving transformations means that in some cases we simply have to fall back to using PINQ routines. For example, in the network analysis example of McSherry and Mahajan [16] the first transformation of the dataset is to group network requests by IP address. If the number of possible IP addresses was small and statically known, then we could iterate over this list to select the elements corresponding to each IP. But since they are not, the list of groups clearly has multiple provenances and is thus not supported by our method. So in this example

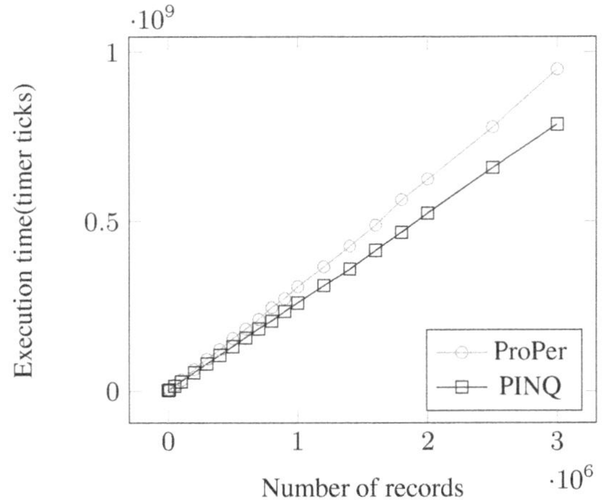


**Figure 5.** Comparing PINQ and ProPer wrt execution time

we immediately fall back to using a PINQ subprogram, and appear to get no benefit from personalised budgets. But potential benefits from personalised budgets are not far away. For example, if one decided to restrict analysis to a specific geolocation, then personalised budgets would ensure that we don't waste the budget of the rest of the world. Another example is if traffic data arrives continuously over time, in which case we would automatically filter the records which have an exhausted budget without requiring any visible bookkeeping at the level of the analyst code.

## 7. Related work

The literature on differential privacy, although only ten years old, is already vast. For an overview we refer to Dwork's surveys [6, 7]. We consider work related along four dimensions: general systems which provide mechanisms for constructing differentially private analyses, approaches to dealing with dynamic data, provenance and its connection to privacy, and approaches to improving the utilisation of privacy budget.

***Systems Enforcing Differential Privacy*** As mentioned earlier, the interactive style of our system is inspired by PINQ [17]. The implementation of PINQ has a number of side-channels as pointed out in [12]; these and other implementation weaknesses ([19]) are certainly present in our implementation and it has not been our goal to focus on those. Other systems of note include Airavat [24], which is a MapReduce-based framework for constructing differentially private programs. Untrusted client analysts construct mappers, and the system provides differentially private reducers. Note that mapping is restricted in Airavat (by modifying the JVM) to be a union-preserving operation ("only a single record is allowed to affect the key-value pairs output by the mapper"), so it would be interesting to explore personalised budgets in that setting since it could potentially improve the budget utilisation over time, and perhaps remove the need to statically decide and enforce the exact number of elements produced by the mapper. Another line of work developing the Fuzz and DFuzz prototypes [10, 12, 23] describes non-interactive differential privacy in which the whole computation over private data is described by a domain-specific functional program, and a sensitivity-based static type system determines statically whether the computation will be within budget. This approach would combine well with ours by using it as a (necessarily side-effect free) query sublanguage.

***Dynamic systems and data streams*** There are different senses in which a system might support dynamic data. In one sense the users are static, but their data arrive as a stream. One approach to privacy on streaming data is *Pan-privacy* [18], a stronger notion than differential privacy which ensures that the entire state of the system is private. Streaming PINQ is a version of PINQ that supports this kind of data [26]. GUPT introduces a novel concept of privacy which degrades over time. It seems that this is a feature that could be added to ProPer by periodic increase in the budgets of records.

Tschantz, Kaynar, and Datta [25] build a model and proof techniques for reasoning about interactive differential privacy with records that are input over time. They introduce a specific generalisation of differential privacy called differential noninterference. Their formal model of noninterference has similarities to ours, based on probabilistic transition systems. They develop bisimulation-like proof methods and similar ideas could be useful in our setting to refactor our main proof. In our setting the one system we reason about is parameterised over any program which uses the internal API. In the formal model of Tschantz *et al* the queries are supplied by the environment. Thus the model of the (malicious) analysis is the sequence of all possible queries (for all possible input sequences). A question mark over this model is that is does not capture the *strategy* of the user; for a probabilistic systems it is known from the noninterference literature that modelling the user using nondeterminism rather than a strategy can hide the presence of information leaks [20, 27]. One aspect of their model is not captured in our system, they model bounded memory. This causes an unexpected magnification in the privacy cost of computations, since addition of one record into an input stream will cause a full memory to change by two records (the record itself and the record that it displaces).

***Provenance and Lineage*** The notion of provenance that we use is more specifically called *what provenance* in the terminology of Cheney *et al* [2]. More specifically it is the *lineage* notion from Cui *et al* [3]. Union-preserving transformations are called *dispatchers* in that work.

Our main principle is the tracking of data from input to the point at which it is used in a query. Complementary to this, Birgisson, McSherry and Abadi [1] show how to improve privacy budgets by tracking from the result of a query to the final result of the (batch) program; if the query is not used to produce the final result then you don't need to count it's cost. In some sense this optimisation is already built into systems like Fuzz. Our model assumes that the results of intermediate queries are observed by the attacker, so using this principle would require us to refine our model, but it can be plugged straight into our implementation.

There are a number of other works which link the concepts of provenance and privacy, although these are mainly connected with answering queries about the provenance of data in a privacy preserving manner, e.g. [4].

***Improving the Budgeting Accuracy of Composition*** Many methods in differential privacy deal with improving the $\varepsilon$-bound that is attributed to a given class of computations. Some of these are related to the deficiency of the sequential query composition principle, and are typically much more specialised (and therefore more technically sophisticated) than the method of provenance tracing described here – see for example [14, 15, 28]. Palamidessi and Stronati [21] provide a compositional method for improving the sensitivity estimation for relational algebra terms. It would be interesting to investigate whether these ideas can be used alongside our personalised approach.

Proserpio, Goldberg and McSherry [22] introduced wPINQ, a framework for weighted datasets. In wPINQ, "problematic" records (those inducing extra noise to preserve privacy) are specially treated. The idea is that in order to better preserve privacy while not degrading the accuracy of the query result, the weight of those individual records in an aggregate query is scaled down, instead of scaling up the noise added to all records. Note that weights in wPINQ are associated with each and every record, whereas budgets in ProPer are associated just with individuals (the original inputs). By making weights part of every record, the privacy of the weights themselves will be protected by the requirements of the definition of differential privacy. Weights are used to track sensitivity at the level of each record level – similar to the fine-grained accounting achieved by tracking provenance. But the number of transformations that wPINQ supports is more than in PINQ. The price to pay is that every primitive query must be implemented to use the weights appropriately, and must be proven to be differentially private. In ProPer the correctness argument for the system itself has to be argued from first principles, but the method is able to reuse arbitrary differentially private queries as sub-programs without modification.

## 8. Conclusion

We have introduced a new concept of personalised differential privacy (PDP) that improves the bookkeeping regarding the cost of composed queries, and makes it easy to include dynamic expansion of the data base. We have realised this idea in the design of ProPer, a system which enforces PDP for all (deterministic) client programs that compute against a simple API. We have proved that the ProPer model provides personalised – and therefore also standard – differential privacy.

***On Limitations of Affine Provenance*** In our development of this work, the implementation preceded the theoretical development [9]. Our first implementation traced the provenance for a much more general class of (SQL) functions, i.e. we traced provenance across operations like join, which implies non affine provenance (the provenance of a record may be more than one input record). Through our formalisation we subsequently discovered that this in fact violates differential privacy. Used as a descriptive mechanism, where we record privacy debt rather than spend from a budget, this approach is still sound since it never needs to exclude any records from queries, but it is less clear how to deploy such a system. The restriction to unary union-preserving functions, on the other hand, limits the functionality of client programs, but seems no worse than Airavat's mapper restrictions. In section 4.3 you can see a list of relational algebra operations that guarantee to have records with affine provenance. In any case, when a subcomputation cannot be expressed via a union-preserving transformation we can still plug in any other black-box differential privacy mechanism. This was further discussed in Section 6.4.

***On Dynamic Data and Utility*** Perhaps the biggest advantage of PDP is that it smoothly supports dynamic databases in a PINQ style system – something that seems difficult to achieve in the presence of a single global budget. Our prototype implementation shows a 15% slowdown compared to PINQ, requiring just a constant space overhead per record.

Another potential advantage of PDP is precisely personalisation; each individual can set her own privacy budget. However we are cautious in our assessment of this as a feature in its own right rather than just a means to an end. What is missing in the theory of PDP is a proper treatment of utility. The personal budget determines how quickly a record will be "used up". This complicates the understanding of the utility of the information returned by queries. But even if we start out with every record being assigned the same budget, if the analyst has no prior on the data then it can be hard to say much about the utility of any given query.

One particular case where utility guarantees may be easy to give (without a prior) is the case when the rate at which new data enters the database is sufficiently high relative to the rate at which queries consume their budgets. Assume a stream of inputs with flow rate $f$, queue size $l$ and individual privacy budget of $b$. If we apply $\varepsilon$-differentially private queries at an execution rate below $\frac{b \times f}{l \times \varepsilon}$, then we can guarantee that ProPer can answer all queries without excessive noise caused by blocking too many old records from being used in queries. A more rigorous analysis of this idea is appropriate for future work.


### Acknowledgements

This research has been partially supported by a grant from the Swedish Foundation for Strategic Research (SSF). Many thanks to our colleagues in the ProSec and Formal Methods groups for many helpful discussions, and special thanks Raúl Pardo Jiménez for participation in the early stage of the research, and to Niklas Broberg for comments on an earlier draft. Thanks also to Cédric Fournet and the anonymous referees for helpful comments.


## References


[1] A. Birgisson, F. McSherry, and M. Abadi. Differential privacy with information flow control. In *Proceedings of the ACM SIGPLAN 6th Workshop on Programming Languages and Analysis for Security*, PLAS '11, pages 2:1–2:6. ACM, 2011.

[2] J. Cheney, L. Chiticariu, and W.-C. Tan. Provenance in databases: Why, how, and where. *Found. Trends databases*, 1(4):379–474, Apr. 2009. .

[3] Y. Cui and J. Widom. Lineage tracing for general data warehouse transformations. *The VLDB Journal The International Journal on Very Large Data Bases*, 12(1):41–58, 2003.

[4] S. B. Davidson, S. Khanna, S. Roy, J. Stoyanovich, V. Tannen, and Y. Chen. On provenance and privacy. In *Proceedings of the 14th International Conference on Database Theory*, pages 3–10. ACM, 2011.

[5] C. Dwork. Differential privacy. In *33rd International Colloquium on Automata, Languages and Programming, part II (ICALP 2006)*, volume 4052, pages 1–12. Springer Verlag, 2006.

[6] C. Dwork. Differential privacy: A survey of results. In *Theory and Applications of Models of Computation*, volume 4978 of *Lecture Notes in Computer Science*, pages 1–19. Springer Berlin Heidelberg, 2008.

[7] C. Dwork. A firm foundation for private data analysis. *Communications of the ACM*, 54(1):86–95, 2011.

[8] C. Dwork, F. McSherry, K. Nissim, and A. Smith. Calibrating noise to sensitivity in private data analysis. In *Theory of Cryptography*, pages 265–284. Springer, 2006.

[9] H. Ebadi. PINQuin, a framework for differentially private analysis. Master's thesis, Chalmers University of Technology, 2013.

[10] M. Gaboardi, A. Haeberlen, J. Hsu, A. Narayan, and B. C. Pierce. Linear dependent types for differential privacy. In *Proceedings of the 40th Annual ACM SIGPLAN-SIGACT Symposium on Principles of Programming Languages*, POPL '13, pages 357–370. ACM, 2013.

[11] P. W. Grefen and R. A. de By. A multi-set extended relational algebra: a formal approach to a practical issue. In *Data Engineering, 1994. Proceedings. 10th International Conference*, pages 80–88. IEEE, 1994.

[12] A. Haeberlen, B. C. Pierce, and A. Narayan. Differential privacy under fire. In *USENIX Security Symposium*, 2011.

[13] I. Hayes. Multi-relations in z. *Acta Informatica*, 29(1):33–62, 1992.

[14] G. Kellaris and S. Papadopoulos. Practical differential privacy via grouping and smoothing. In *Proceedings of the 39th international conference on Very Large Data Bases*, PVLDB'13, pages 301–312. VLDB Endowment, 2013.

[15] C. Li, M. Hay, V. Rastogi, G. Miklau, and A. McGregor. Optimizing linear counting queries under differential privacy. In *Proceedings of the Twenty-ninth ACM SIGMOD-SIGACT-SIGART Symposium on Principles of Database Systems*, PODS '10, pages 123–134. ACM, 2010.

[16] F. McSherry and R. Mahajan. Differentially-private network trace analysis. *SIGCOMM Comput. Commun. Rev.*, 40(4):123–134, 2010. ISSN 0146-4833.

[17] F. D. McSherry. Privacy integrated queries: an extensible platform for privacy-preserving data analysis. In *Proceedings of the 2009 ACM SIGMOD International Conference on Management of data*, pages 19–30. ACM, 2009.

[18] D. Mir, S. Muthukrishnan, A. Nikolov, and R. N. Wright. Pan-private algorithms via statistics on sketches. In *Proceedings of the Thirtieth ACM SIGMOD-SIGACT-SIGART Symposium on Principles of Database Systems*, PODS '11, pages 37–48. ACM, 2011.

[19] I. Mironov. On significance of the least significant bits for differential privacy. In *ACM Conference on Computer and Communications Security*. ACM, 2012.

[20] K. R. O'Neill, M. R. Clarkson, and S. Chong. Information-flow security for interactive programs. In *CSFW*, pages 190–201. IEEE Computer Society, 2006.

[21] C. Palamidessi and M. Stronati. Differential Privacy for relational algebra: improving the sensitivity bounds via constraint systems. In *QAPL - Tenth Workshop on Quantitative Aspects of Programming Languages*, volume 85 of *Electronic Proceedings in Theoretical Computer Science*, pages 92–105. Open Publishing Association, 2012.

[22] D. Proserpio, S. Goldberg, and F. McSherry. Calibrating data to sensitivity in private data analysis. *40th International Conference on Very Large Data Bases, VLDB'14*, 7(8):637–648, 2014.

[23] J. Reed and B. C. Pierce. Distance makes the types grow stronger: A calculus for differential privacy. In *Proceedings of the 15th ACM SIGPLAN International Conference on Functional Programming*, ICFP '10, pages 157–168. ACM, 2010.

[24] I. Roy, S. T. V. Setty, A. Kilzer, V. Shmatikov, and E. Witchel. Airavat: Security and privacy for mapreduce. In *NSDI*, pages 297–312. USENIX Association, 2010.

[25] M. C. Tschantz, D. Kaynar, and A. Datta. Formal verification of differential privacy for interactive systems (extended abstract). *Electron. Notes Theor. Comput. Sci.*, 276:61–79, Sept. 2011.

[26] L. Waye. Privacy integrated data stream queries. In *Proceedings of the 5th annual conference on Systems, programming, and applications: software for humanity*. ACM, 2014.

[27] J. T. Wittbold and D. M. Johnson. Information flow in nondeterministic systems. In *IEEE Symposium on Security and Privacy*, pages 144–161, 1990.

[28] Y. Xiao, L. Xiong, and C. Yuan. Differentially private data release through multidimensional partitioning. In *Proceedings of the 7th VLDB Conference on Secure Data Management*. Springer-Verlag, 2010.


## A. Proof of Main Lemma (5.8)

*Proof.* Assume that $\sigma \overset{r}{\sim} \sigma'$ and $\mathbb{C}_0 \overset{\sigma}{\Rightarrow}_p \mathbb{C}$. We proceed by induction on the length of the trace $\sigma$, and by cases according to the last step of the trace.

**Case 1:** $\sigma = []$. Vacuous since we cannot have $\sigma \overset{r}{\sim} \sigma'$ if there are no inputs.

**Case 2:** $\sigma = \sigma_1 a$. Suppose that $\mathbb{C}_0 \overset{\sigma_1}{\Rightarrow}_{p_1} \langle P_1, E_1, B_1 \rangle \overset{a}{\rightarrow}_{p_2} \langle P, E, B \rangle = \mathbb{C}$, and hence that $p = p_1 p_2$. We split this into two cases according to whether $r$ is input on the last step, or earlier in the trace:

**Case 2.1:** $\sigma' = \sigma_1 a'$ **and** $\{a, a'\} = \{T, T \cup \{r\}\}$. Suppose that $a = T$ (the other case is argued similarly). Then we must have $P_1 \xrightarrow{tv := \mathsf{input}} P$ for some $tv$, and hence:

$$\mathbb{C} = \langle P, E_1[tv \mapsto \mathsf{Id}(T)], B_1[s \mapsto \mathscr{E}(s) \mid s \in T] \rangle$$

$$\begin{aligned}\mathbb{C}' &= \langle P, E_1[tv \mapsto \mathsf{Id}(T \cup \{r\})], B_1[s \mapsto \mathscr{E}(s) \mid s \in (T \cup \{r\})] \rangle \\ &= \langle P, E_1[tv \mapsto \mathsf{Id}(T \cup \{r\})], B_1[s \mapsto \mathscr{E}(s) \mid s \in T][r \mapsto \mathscr{E}(r)] \rangle\end{aligned}$$

Hence $\mathbb{C} \overset{r,\mathscr{E}(r)}{\sim} \mathbb{C}'$. Since the probability of the input transition is 1 we have $p = q$ and hence $p \leq q.\exp(\mathscr{E}(r) - \mathscr{E}(r))$ as required.

**Case 2.2: $\sigma' = \sigma'_1 a$ and $\sigma_1 \overset{r}{\sim} \sigma'_1$.**

The induction hypothesis gives us $q_1$, $P_1$, $E'_1$, $B'_1$ and $\varepsilon_1$ such that

$$\mathbb{C}_0 \overset{\sigma'_1}{\Longrightarrow}_{q_1} \langle P_1, E'_1, B'_1 \rangle \tag{3}$$

$$E_1 \overset{r}{\sim} E'_1 \tag{4}$$

$$B_1 \overset{r,\varepsilon_1}{\sim} B'_1 \tag{5}$$

$$p_1 \leq q_1.\exp(\mathscr{E}(r) - \varepsilon_1) \tag{6}$$

From here we argue by cases according to the rule applied for the last transition $\langle P_1, E_1, B_1 \rangle \xrightarrow{a}_{p_2} \langle P, E, B \rangle$. In every case except for the query transition we will see that $p_2 = 1$, and that $\langle P_1, E_1, B_1 \rangle \xrightarrow{a}_1 \mathbb{C}'$ for some $\mathbb{C}'$. In those cases it follows that $p \leq q \cdot \exp(\mathscr{E}(r) - \varepsilon)$ by taking $\varepsilon = \varepsilon_1$ and using (6).

**Case 2.2.1: Input.** In this case $a = T$ and $P_1 \xrightarrow{\mathsf{input}} P$. Hence we have transitions

$$\langle P_1, E_1, B_1 \rangle \xrightarrow{T}_1 \mathbb{C}$$

$$\langle P_1, E'_1, B'_1 \rangle \xrightarrow{T}_1 \mathbb{C}'$$

where

$$\mathbb{C} = \langle P, E_1[tv \mapsto \mathsf{Id}(T)], B_1[s \mapsto \mathscr{E}(s) \mid s \in T] \rangle$$
$$\mathbb{C}' = \langle P, E'_1[tv \mapsto \mathsf{Id}(T)], B'_1[s \mapsto \mathscr{E}(s) \mid s \in T] \rangle$$

Since $r \notin T$, it follows easily from 4 and 5 that $\mathbb{C} \overset{r,\varepsilon_1}{\sim} \mathbb{C}'$.

**Case 2.2.2: Silent.** Similar (but simpler) argument to above – the only change in the configuration is the program component, so it follows directly from the IH.

**Case 2.2.3: Constant Transformation.** $P_1 \xrightarrow{tv:=T} P$ and hence $\langle P_1, E_1, B_1 \rangle \xrightarrow{\tau}_1 \mathbb{C}$ and $\langle P_1, E'_1, B'_1 \rangle \xrightarrow{\tau}_1 \mathbb{C}'$ where

$$\mathbb{C} = \langle P, E_1[tv \mapsto \mathsf{Const}(T)], B_1 \rangle$$
$$\mathbb{C}' = \langle P, E'_1[tv \mapsto \mathsf{Const}(T)], B'_1 \rangle$$

and we reason as for case 2.2.1.

**Case 2.2.4: Table variable.** Similar to the previous case, $P_1 \xrightarrow{tv:=tv'} P$ and hence $\langle P_1, E_1, B_1 \rangle \xrightarrow{\tau}_1 \mathbb{C}$ and $\langle P_1, E'_1, B'_1 \rangle \xrightarrow{\tau}_1 \mathbb{C}'$ where

$$\mathbb{C} = \langle P, E_1[tv \mapsto tv'], B_1 \rangle$$
$$\mathbb{C}' = \langle P, E'_1[tv \mapsto tv'], B'_1 \rangle$$

and we reason as for case 2.2.1.

**Case 2.2.5: $F$-Transformation.** Here $P_1 \xrightarrow{t:=F(t_1 \uplus \ldots \uplus t_n)} P$, and so we have

$$\mathbb{C} = \langle P, E_1[tv \mapsto \hat{F}(E_1(tv_1) \uplus \cdots \uplus E_1(tv_n))], B_1 \rangle$$
$$\mathbb{C}' = \langle P, E'_1[tv \mapsto \hat{F}(E'_1(tv_1) \uplus \cdots \uplus E'_1(tv_n))], B'_1 \rangle$$

Since, from 4 we have $E_1(tv_i) \overset{r}{\sim} E'_1(tv_i)$, $i \in \{1, \ldots, n\}$, and so from 5.6 and 5.5 it follows that $\hat{F}(E_1(tv_1) \uplus \cdots \uplus E_1(tv_n)) \overset{r}{\sim} \hat{F}(E'_1(tv_1) \uplus \cdots \uplus E'_1(tv_n))$ and hence we have that $\mathbb{C} \overset{r,\varepsilon_1}{\sim} \mathbb{C}'$.

**Case 2.2.6: Query.** Here we have a rule instance of the form

$$\text{Query}\,\frac{P_1 \xrightarrow{Q_\varepsilon(tv)?n} P}{\langle P_1, E_1, B_1 \rangle \xrightarrow{n}_{p_2} \mathbb{C}}$$

and thus there is an analogous transition

$$\langle P_1, E'_1, B'_1 \rangle \xrightarrow{n}_{q_2} \mathbb{C}'$$

where

$$\mathbb{C} = \langle P, E_1, B \rangle \qquad B = B_1[s \mapsto B_1(s) - C(s) \mid s \in A]$$
$$\mathbb{C}' = \langle P, E'_1, B' \rangle \qquad B' = B'_1[s \mapsto B'_1(s) - C'(s) \mid s \in A']$$

$$C = [s \mapsto \varepsilon \cdot \mathsf{size}(E_1(tv) \bullet \{s\}) \mid s \in \mathsf{dom}(B_1)]$$
$$C' = [s \mapsto \varepsilon \cdot \mathsf{size}(E'_1(tv) \bullet \{s\}) \mid s \in \mathsf{dom}(B'_1)]$$

$$A = \{s \mid B_1(s) \geq C(s)\} \qquad L = E_1(tv) \bullet A$$
$$A' = \{s \mid B'_1(s) \geq C'(s)\} \qquad L' = E'_1(tv) \bullet A'$$
$$p_2 = \Pr(Q_\varepsilon(L) = n) \qquad q_2 = \Pr(Q_\varepsilon(L') = n)$$

Since the environments are unchanged in this transition, $E_1 \overset{r}{\sim} E'_1$ follows immediately from the induction hypothesis. Suppose, without loss of generality, that $r$ is in $\mathbb{C}$. Then it remains to show that, for some $\varepsilon'$,

$$B \overset{r,\varepsilon'}{\sqsubset} B' \tag{7}$$

$$p_1 \cdot p_2 \leq q_1 \cdot q_2 \cdot \exp(\mathscr{E}(r) - \varepsilon') \tag{8}$$

Let us first compare the respective cost mappings $C$ and $C'$: $E_1 \overset{r}{\sqsubset} E'_1$ gives $\mathsf{size}(E_1(tv) \bullet \{tv\}) = \mathsf{size}(E'_1(tv) \bullet \{s\})$ whenever $s \neq r$. Hence the only difference between $C$ and $C'$ is a single mapping:

$$C = C'[r \mapsto \varepsilon \cdot \mathsf{size}(E_1(tv) \bullet \{r\})]. \tag{9}$$

Now consider $A$ and $A'$. Since $C$ and $C'$ only differ on $r$, then if $B_1(r) \geq C(r)$ then $A = A' \uplus \{r\}$. Otherwise $A = A'$. Consider these cases in turn:

**Case 2.2.6.1:** $A = A'$. and hence $L = L'$, and hence $p_2 = q_2$. By taking $\varepsilon'$ to be $\varepsilon_1$, requirement (8) follows from the induction hypothesis (6). Since the budget of $r$ is unchanged in either transition, then $B \overset{r,\varepsilon_1}{\sim} B'$ follows from the induction hypothesis (5).

**Case 2.2.6.2:** $A = A' \uplus \{r\}$.

$$\begin{aligned} L &= E_1(tv) \bullet (A' \uplus \{r\}) \\ &= E_1(tv) \bullet A' \uplus E_1(tv) \bullet \{r\} \\ L' &= E'_1(tv) \bullet A' \\ &= E_1(tv) \bullet A' \end{aligned}$$

where the last step follows since $r \notin A'$ and $E_1 \overset{r}{\sim} E'_1$. Hence $L = L' \uplus (E(tv) \bullet \{r\})$ – i.e. the difference in the size of the sets on which the respective queries are made is $\mathsf{size}(E(tv) \bullet \{r\})$. Since $Q_\varepsilon$ is $\varepsilon$-differentially private, it follows from the definition of vanilla differential privacy that

$$p_2 \leq q_2 \cdot \exp(\varepsilon \cdot \mathsf{size}(E(tv) \bullet \{r\})) \tag{10}$$

Combining this inequality with (6) we get

$$p_1 \cdot p_2 \leq q_1 \cdot q_2 \cdot \exp(\mathscr{E}(r) - \varepsilon_1) \cdot \exp(\varepsilon \cdot \mathsf{size}(E(tv) \bullet \{r\}))$$

Rearranging the exponents gives $p_1 \cdot p_2 \leq q_1 \cdot q_2 \cdot \exp(\mathscr{E}(r) - \varepsilon')$ when $\varepsilon' = \varepsilon_1 - \varepsilon \cdot \mathsf{size}(E(tv) \bullet \{r\})$. We complete the proof by showing that this value of $\varepsilon'$ gives $B \overset{r,\varepsilon'}{\sim} B'$. From the induction hypothesis (5) we have that $B_1$ and $B'_1$ agree on all values in their domains except $r$, and from (9) we have that the same holds for $C$ and $C'$. Thus $B$ and $B'$ only differ on $r$, for which

$$\begin{aligned} B(r) &= B_1(r) - C(r) \\ &= \varepsilon_1 - \varepsilon \cdot \mathsf{size}(E(tv) \bullet \{r\}) \end{aligned}$$

and hence $B \overset{r,\varepsilon'}{\sim} B'$ as required. □

# Summary-Based Context-Sensitive Data-Dependence Analysis in Presence of Callbacks

Hao Tang[1] Xiaoyin Wang[2] Lingming Zhang[3] Bing Xie[1] * Lu Zhang[1] Hong Mei[1]

[1]Key Laboratory of High Confidence Software Technologies, Ministry of Education, Peking University, Beijing, 100871, China
[2]Department of Computer Science, University of Texas at San Antonio, TX 78249, USA
[3]Department of Computer Science, University of Texas at Dallas, TX 75080, USA
{tanghao13, xiebing, zhanglu, meih}@sei.pku.edu.cn, xiaoyin.wang@utsa.edu, lingming.zhang@utdallas.edu

## Abstract

Building a summary for library code is a common approach to speeding up the analysis of client code. In presence of callbacks, some reachability relationships between library nodes cannot be obtained during library-code summarization. Thus, the library code may have to be analyzed again during the analysis of the client code with the library summary. In this paper, we propose to summarize library code with tree-adjoining-language (TAL) reachability. Compared with the summary built with context-free-language (CFL) reachability, the summary built with TAL reachability further contains *conditional reachability* relationships. The *conditional reachability* relationships can lead to much lighter analysis of the library code during the client code analysis with the TAL-reachability-based library summary. We also performed an experimental comparison of context-sensitive data-dependence analysis with the TAL-reachability-based library summary and context-sensitive data-dependence analysis with the CFL-reachability-based library summary using 15 benchmark subjects. Our experimental results demonstrate that the former has an 8X speed-up over the latter on average.

***Categories and Subject Descriptors*** F.3.2 [*Logics and Meanings of Programs*]: Semantics of Programming Languages - Program analysis; F.4.3 [*Mathematical Logic and Formal Languages*]: Formal Languages - Classes defined by grammars or automata

***General Terms*** Algorithms, Languages

***Keywords*** TAL reachability, CFL reachability, context-sensitive analysis, summary-based analysis, tree adjoining languages

## 1. Introduction

Leveraging libraries is ubiquitous in modern software development. The existence of various software libraries makes it possible for developers to reuse products of numerous previous software developers. As a result, a modern software application is typically composed of a large volume of library code and a small volume of client code. For example, *compress*, a typical Java based application from SPECjvm2008 benchmark suite [2], involves 17640 Control-Flow Graph nodes while 91.6% of them are from libraries. The huge size of used library code in an application becomes a burden for various program analysis tasks. One common approach to this problem is to build a summary for each used library. Based on the library summary, the analysis time of the client code becomes much shorter. The summary for the library can also be built once and reused many times for analyzing all its client applications.

Data-dependence analysis [15] aims to identify the def-use chains in a program, and has many applications, such as slicing [31] and impact analysis [3]. For context-sensitive data-dependence analysis, a typical way to build the summary of a library is to use context-free-language (CFL) reachability [29], where a CFL (typically the parenthesis-matching language) is used to filter out invalid paths in the dependence graph. However, the possible existence of callbacks[1] poses an obstacle for summarizing the library code with CFL reachability. When there are no callbacks, the analysis of a client application can be confined to the client code with only queries of the summary of the library code. That is to say, it suffices that we know all the reachability relationships between library nodes after summarizing the library code. In presence of callbacks, even with the library summary, the library code should still be analyzed as well as the client code, because callbacks may incur new reachability (i.e., dependence) between library nodes.

To further motivate our research, let us consider the following example for context-sensitive data-dependence analysis.

```
package library;
public abstract class AbstractClass {
      public final int method1(int x1) {
            int y1 = x1 + 1;
            int z1 = method2(y1) + 1;
            return z1;
      }
      private final int method2(int x2) {
            int y2 = x2 + 2;
            int z2 = method3(y2) + 2;
            return z2;
      }
      abstract public int method3(int x3);
}
```

* Corresponding author



*POPL'15* January 15-17 2015, Mumbai, India

http://dx.doi.org/10.1145/2676726.2676997

[1] Callbacks are invocations of the methods/functions in the client code from the library code. Due to the convenience of customizing/extending libraries, many major programming languages provide some mechanism (e.g., dynamic binding) to support callbacks.

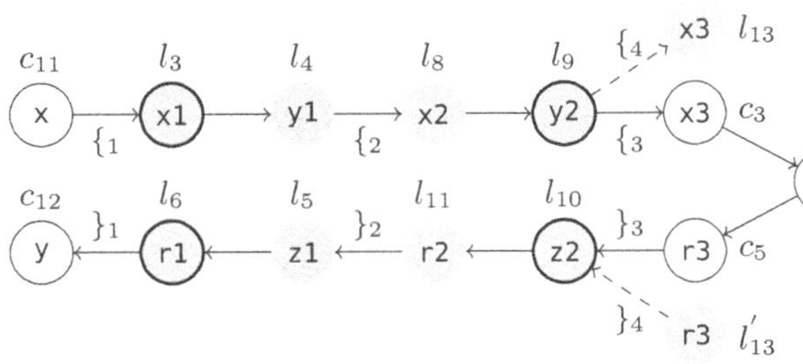


Figure 1: Data-Dependence Graph for the Example

As shown in the above code, there is an abstract class defined in the library. The abstract class provides a public method named `method1` for its clients, and requires its clients to implement a public method named `method3`, which may lead to a callback. The client code is listed below, where `ConcreteClass` extends the abstract class in the library with an implementation of `method3`, resulting in a callback.

```
1  package client;
2  class ConcreteClass extends library.AbstractClass {
3          public int method3(int x3) {
4                  int y3 = x3 * 3;
5                  return y3;
6          }
7  }
8  public class Main {
9          public static void main(String[] args) {
10                 ConcreteClass p = new ConcreteClass();
11                 int x = 4;
12                 int y = p.method1(x);
13                 System.out.println(y);
14         }
15 }
```

Supposing that it is required to determine whether the value of `y` in the `main` method after calling `method1` depends on the value of `x`. This problem can be turned into the problem of determining whether it is reachable from node $c_{11}$ to node $c_{12}$ in Figure 1, where the gray/white nodes are from the library/client code, and the $i$th line in client/library code is labeled as $c_i/l_i$. In this figure, the edges labeled with $\{_i/\}_i$ ($i \in [1,4]$) correspond to direct data dependence incurred by the four method invocations/returns[2]; and nodes $l_6$, $l_{11}$, and $c_5$ represent the result values immediately before the method returns (denoted as $r_1$, $r_2$, and $r_3$). Obviously, it is reachable from node $c_{11}$ to node $c_{12}$, if we use CFL reachability to analyze both the library code and the client code, i.e., the value of `y` depends on the value of `x`.

However, when summarizing only the library code with CFL reachability, as nodes $c_3$, $c_4$, and $c_5$ are not available yet, it is unknown whether it is reachable from node $l_3$ to node $l_6$. Only when the client code is available can it be determined that node $c_3$ is reachable to node $c_5$. Then the library graph should be analyzed again to determine that it is actually reachable from node $l_3$ to node $l_6$. With this information, node $c_{11}$ can be determined to be reachable to node $c_{12}$. Note that nodes $l_4$, $l_5$, $l_8$, and $l_{11}$ are essential here to determine this reachability relationship even if we already have the CFL-reachability-based summary of the library code. Without these four nodes, we cannot know that it is reachable from node $l_3$ to node $l_6$.

[2] Note that $\{_4/\}_4$ is marked as dashed line because it is the invocation/return to an abstract method.

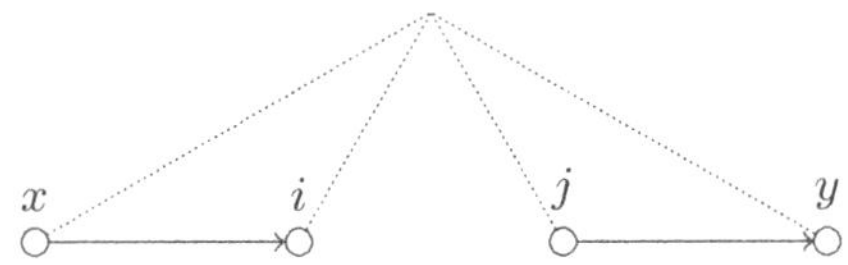


Figure 2: Graphical Representation of C-Reachable$_{i,j}(x,y)$

### 1.1 Our Solution

The basic idea of our approach is to further calculate *conditional reachability* relationships as well as unconditional reachability relationships[3] when summarizing the library code. Below, we define *conditional reachability* in Definition 1.1.

**DEFINITION** 1.1. ***(Conditional Reachability)*** *Let $G$ be a directed graph and $x$, $y$, $i$, and $j$ be four nodes in $G$. It is said that there is a conditional reachability relationship among $x$, $y$, $i$, and $j$ (denoted as C-Reachable$_{i,j}(x,y)$), if it is reachable from $x$ to $y$ when a new unconditional reachability relationship from $i$ to $j$ is added.*

For intuitiveness of presentation, if C-Reachable$_{i,j}(x, y)$, we also state that there is a *conditional reachability* relationship from $x$ to $y$ depending on the reachability from $i$ to $j$. Figure 2 depicts the graphical representation of C-Reachable$_{i,j}(x,y)$. Similar to the reachability relationships in CFL reachability, *conditional reachability* relationships can also be labeled with different symbols to distinguish *conditional reachability* relationships of different types.

For the motivating example, there is actually a *conditional reachability* relationship from node $l_3$ to node $l_6$ depending on the reachability from node $l_9$ to node $l_{10}$ (i.e., C-Reachable$_{l_9,l_{10}}(l_3,l_6)$). If we obtain this *conditional reachability* relationship when summarizing the library code, we can immediately determine that it is reachable from node $l_3$ to node $l_6$ after we analyze the client code to obtain the reachability from node $c_3$ to node $c_5$. That is, we turn the *conditional reachability* relationship into an unconditional one. In fact, calculating *conditional reachability* during library-code summarization has the following two benefits. First, we can save some computation when analyzing the client code, as such computation has already been performed when analyzing the library code. In our example, the computation for determining C-Reachable$_{l_9,l_{10}}(l_3,l_6)$ actually involves some computation for determining the reachability from node $l_3$ to node $l_6$ under CFL reachability. Second, since we have the *conditional reachability* relationship during library-code summarization, some nodes (i.e., nodes $l_4$, $l_5$, $l_8$, and $l_{11}$ in our example) in the library graph become unnecessary for analyzing client code. Thus, we can further avoid some unnecessary computation involving these nodes when analyzing the client code. Of course, calculating *conditional reachability* would incur extra computation during library-code summarization.

As a *conditional reachability* relationship involves four nodes in the graph, it is beyond the power of CFL reachability to calculate *conditional reachability*. Therefore, we turn the problem of summarizing *conditional reachability* relationships for the library code as a problem of calculating tree-adjoining-language (TAL) reachability. Tree-adjoining languages, each of which can be defined with a tree-adjoining grammar (TAG) [11], are a family of mildly context-sensitive languages that can represent much context sensitivity in natural languages[4]. As there are constructs (denoted as second-order non-terminals in this paper) in a TAG to represent two strings with some yet-unknown symbols between the two strings, such a construct can be used to represent

[3] To avoid ambiguity, we also refer to the reachability relationships calculated via CFL reachability as unconditional reachability relationships.

[4] Note that the meaning of *context sensitivity* in the formal language theory is completely different from that in program analysis.

*conditional reachability*, where the reachability between two library nodes depends on the reachability in client code.

Based on the definition of *conditional reachability*, we can summarize a library that contains at most one callback on any path. If multiple callbacks exist, our approach retains a small number of selected library nodes in the summary, and uses these nodes to chain multiple conditional reachability relationships. In such a case, the library is not fully-summarized because some analysis is still required on the selected library nodes during the client analysis phase. However, the client analysis phase can still be significantly accelerated (as validated in our evaluation) because only a small set of library nodes need to be analyzed.

To evaluate the performance enhancement that our approach achieves for analyzing client code, we empirically compared our approach with the approach that adopts CFL reachability to summarize the library code using 15 Java applications as subjects. Our evaluation results demonstrate that the analysis of client code using the TAL-reachability-based summary achieves an average 8X speed-up over the analysis using the CFL-reachability-based summary.

### 1.2 Contributions and Paper Organization

In summary, this paper makes the following main contributions:

- A concise formalism for defining tree-adjoining-language (TAL), serving as the Chomsky Normal Form for TAGs.
- The proposal of TAL reachability, and the first (polynomial) algorithm for calculating TAL reachability.
- A formalization of the problem of summarizing library code with callbacks for context-sensitive data-dependence analysis as a TAL-reachability problem.
- A sound technique for context-sensitive data-dependence analysis of client code based on the summary calculated with TAL reachability.
- An experimental evaluation of our approach on a number of benchmark subjects, comparing with the approach using CFL reachability to summarize the library code.

## 2. Tree-Adjoining Languages and Grammars

For natural language processing, researchers have investigated some formalisms to define mildly context-sensitive grammars to parse sentences in a natural language, which is typically a context-sensitive language. In particular, there are four intensively investigated formalisms for defining mildly context-sensitive grammars: tree-adjoining grammars [11], head grammars [23], linear indexed grammars [8], and combinatory categorial grammars [39]. According to [41], these four formalisms actually define the same family of languages, which are parsable in $O(n^6)$ time (where $n$ is the length of the sentence for parsing). Thus, in this paper, we refer to the language family described by all the four grammars as tree-adjoining languages (TALs). As all the four existing grammars are not suitable for defining TAL reachability in Section 3, we present a new and concise formalism that defines the same language family as TALs (proof given in the Appendix). Our formalism is actually the Chomsky Normal Form for TAGs, which is suitable for defining TAL reachability and analyzing its complexity.

We define our tree-adjoining grammars (TAGs) by extending the formalism for defining CFGs. A context-free grammar $G$ is typically defined as a four-tuple, denoted as $G{=}(N, T, P, S)$, where $N$ is a set of non-terminals, $T$ is a set of terminals, $P$ is a set of productions, and $S$ is a non-terminal in $N$. Each terminal in $T$ is a character and each non-terminal in $N$ represents a set of strings, each being the concatenation of some terminals.

In our formalism for TAGs, there is a new type of non-terminals, each of which represents a set of ordered pairs of strings. To distinguish the two types of non-terminals, we refer to non-terminals representing strings as first-order non-terminals and non-terminals representing ordered pairs of strings as second-order non-terminals in this paper. For the ease of presentation, we use upper-case letters (e.g., $A$) to denote first-order non-terminals, upper-case letters in the blackboard typeface (e.g., $\mathbb{A}$) to denote second-order non-terminals, and lower-case letters to denote terminals. Furthermore, for two strings (denoted as $\alpha$ and $\beta$), if the pair of $\alpha$ and $\beta$ is in the set of pairs of strings that $\mathbb{A}$ represents, we denote that $\mathbb{A}$ can represent $\alpha \circ \beta$. Note that, as each pair is ordered, $\alpha \circ \beta$ (indicating that $\alpha$ appears before $\beta$) and $\beta \circ \alpha$ (indicating that $\beta$ appears before $\alpha$) denote two different pairs. Similarly, if $\gamma$ is in the set of strings that $A$ represents, we denote that $A$ can represent $\gamma$.

In the formalism for defining CFGs, there is only one operator (i.e., the concatenation operator) to connect non-terminals (i.e., first-order non-terminals) and/or terminals. In the formalism of TAGs, there are a number of extra operators to connect second-order non-terminals and first-order non-terminals. Specifically, there is one operator to connect two second-order non-terminals, and the result is a set of pairs of strings. This operator is called the *adjoining operator*, whose semantics is defined in Definition 2.1.

**DEFINITION** 2.1. ***(Adjoining Operator)*** *Let $\mathbb{A}$ and $\mathbb{B}$ be two second-order non-terminals. The semantics of the adjoining operator is as follows:*

- $\Cap(\mathbb{A}, \mathbb{B}) \doteq \{\alpha\gamma \circ \delta\beta \mid \alpha \circ \beta \in \mathbb{A}, \gamma \circ \delta \in \mathbb{B}\}$.

In Definition 2.1 and throughout the rest of this paper, we adopt the convention in the formalism of CFGs to denote the concatenation operator. That is to say, when we put two symbols (each being a first-order non-terminal, a terminal, or a string) immediately side by side, we mean the concatenation between them. For example, we use $\alpha\beta$ to denote the concatenation of $\alpha$ and $\beta$.

The formalism of TAGs also includes four operators to connect a second-order non-terminal and a first-order non-terminal. The result of each such operator is also a set of pairs of strings. In fact, the four operators are extended from the concatenation operator between first-order non-terminals, and the differences lie in the position for concatenation. Thus, they are referred to as the extended concatenation operators. Definition 2.2 provides the semantics of the four operators.

**DEFINITION** 2.2. ***(Extended Concatenation Operators)*** *Let $\mathbb{A}$ be a second-order non-terminal and $B$ be a first-order non-terminal. The semantics of the four extended concatenation operators are as follows:*

- ${\triangleleft\!\cap}(\mathbb{A}, B) \doteq \{\gamma\alpha \circ \beta \mid \alpha \circ \beta \in \mathbb{A}, \gamma \in B\}$.
- ${\triangleright\!\cap}(\mathbb{A}, B) \doteq \{\alpha\gamma \circ \beta \mid \alpha \circ \beta \in \mathbb{A}, \gamma \in B\}$.
- ${\cap\!\triangleleft}(\mathbb{A}, B) \doteq \{\alpha \circ \gamma\beta \mid \alpha \circ \beta \in \mathbb{A}, \gamma \in B\}$.
- ${\cap\!\triangleright}(\mathbb{A}, B) \doteq \{\alpha \circ \beta\gamma \mid \alpha \circ \beta \in \mathbb{A}, \gamma \in B\}$.

These four extended concatenation operators can also be used for connecting a second-order non-terminal and a terminal. For example, ${\triangleleft\!\cap}(\mathbb{A}, a)$ represents all pairs of strings in the form of $a\alpha \circ \beta$.

The formalism of TAGs has an operator to construct a set of pairs of strings from two first-order non-terminals, referred to as the pairing operator, whose semantics is provided in Definition 2.3.

**DEFINITION** 2.3. ***(Pairing Operator)*** *Let $A$ and $B$ be two first-order non-terminals. The semantics of pairing operator is:*

- $\oplus(A, B) \doteq \{\alpha \circ \beta \mid \alpha \in A, \beta \in B\}$.

The pairing operator can also be used to the situation where either $A$ or $B$ is a terminal or $\epsilon$ (i.e., the empty string). For example, $\oplus(a, \epsilon)$ represents the pair $a \circ \epsilon$.

In contrast to the pairing operator, the formalism of TAGs has a de-pairing operator to obtain a set of strings from one second-order non-terminal. Definition 2.4 provides the semantics of the de-pairing operator.

**DEFINITION** 2.4. *(**De-Pairing Operator**) Let $\mathbb{A}$ be a second-order non-terminal. The semantics of de-pairing operator is:*

- $\ominus(\mathbb{A}) \doteq \{\alpha\beta \mid \alpha \circ \beta \in \mathbb{A}\}$.

Based on the preceding operators and the concatenation operator used for defining CFGs, the tree-adjoining grammars (TAGs) are defined in Definition 2.5.

**DEFINITION** 2.5. *(**Tree-Adjoining Grammar**) A tree-adjoining grammar $G$ is a five-tuple, denoted as $G = (N_1, N_2, T, P, S)$, where $N_1$ is a set of first-order non-terminals, $N_2$ is a set of second-order non-terminals, $T$ is a set of terminals, $P$ is a set of productions, and $S$ is a first-order non-terminal in $N_1$. Productions in $P$ conform to the following rules.*

- *The left-hand side of a production must be a first-order non-terminal or a second-order non-terminal.*
- *If the left-hand side of a production is a first-order non-terminal, the right-hand side of the production must be in one of the following forms: 1) the de-pairing operator on one second-order non-terminal, 2) the concatenation of two symbols (each of which is either a first-order non-terminal or a terminal), 3) one first-order non-terminal, 4) one terminal, or 5) $\epsilon$.*
- *If the left-hand side of a production is a second-order non-terminal, the right-hand side of the production must be in one of the following forms: 1) one adjoining operator on two second-order non-terminals, 2) one extended concatenation operator on one second-order non-terminal and one first-order non-terminal (or terminal), 3) the pairing operator on two symbols (each of which is a first-order non-terminal, a terminal, or $\epsilon$), or 4) one second-order non-terminal.*

**EXAMPLE** 2.1. *The following TAG defines $\{a^n b^n c^n d^n \mid n \geq 0\}$:*

$S \rightarrow \ominus(\mathbb{S}_0)$
$\mathbb{S}_0 \rightarrow \cap_{\triangleright}(\mathbb{S}_3, d) \mid \oplus(\epsilon, \epsilon)$
$\mathbb{S}_1 \rightarrow {}_{\triangleleft}\!\cap(\mathbb{S}_0, a)$
$\mathbb{S}_2 \rightarrow {}_{\triangleright}\!\cap(\mathbb{S}_1, b)$
$\mathbb{S}_3 \rightarrow \cap_{\triangleleft}(\mathbb{S}_2, c)$

**THEOREM** 2.1. *The language family defined by CFGs is a true subset of the language family defined by TAGs.*

**Proof**. The second rule in Definition 2.5 defines a normal form for each production whose left-hand side is a first-order non-terminal. Except for the de-pairing operator, this normal form is actually a variant of Chomsky Normal Form. Therefore, any CFG, when transformed to the normal form required by this rule, is actually a TAG with no second-order non-terminals. As we know that the language defined in Example 2.1 is not a CFL, the CFL family is a true subset of the TAL family. □

## 3. TAL Reachability

As demonstrated by Reps [30], the notion of CFL reachability can be generalized to $\mathcal{L}$-reachability, where $\mathcal{L}$ can be any family of languages. By confining $\mathcal{L}$ to the family of TALs, we have the problem of TAL reachability. In the following, we present, to our knowledge, the first algorithm for TAL reachability, which is actually a polynomial algorithm .

**ALGORITHM 1:** Calculate TAL Reachability

**Input**: Directed graph $G$ and productions of TAL language $L$.
**Output**: $TAL$-reachability relationships for $G$.
1 /***Initialize the work list***/
2 **for** *each edge* $e(i, j)$ *(labeled with* $a$ *and* $1 \leq i, j \leq n$*) in* $G$ **do**
3 | Add $(a, i, j)$ to $R_1$; Add $(a, i, j)$ to $W$;
4 **end**
5 **for** *each* $i$ $(1 \leq i \leq n)$ **do**
6 | Add $(\epsilon, i, i)$ to $R_1$; Add $(\epsilon, i, i)$ to $W$;
7 **end**
8 /***Add reachability for productions***/
9 **while** $W$ *is not empty* **do**
10 | Select and remove the first item (denoted as $\varpi$) from $W$;
11 | **if** $\varpi$ *is in the form of* $(X, i, j)$ **then**
12 | | Try $Z \rightarrow X$ for $(X, i, j)$
13 | | Try $Z \rightarrow XY$ for $(X, i, j)$
14 | | Try $Z \rightarrow YX$ for $(X, i, j)$
15 | | Try $\mathbb{Z} \rightarrow {}_{\triangleleft}\!\cap(\mathbb{Y}, X)$ for $(X, i, j)$
16 | | Try $\mathbb{Z} \rightarrow {}_{\triangleright}\!\cap(\mathbb{Y}, X)$ for $(X, i, j)$
17 | | Try $\mathbb{Z} \rightarrow \cap_{\triangleleft}(\mathbb{Y}, X)$ for $(X, i, j)$
18 | | Try $\mathbb{Z} \rightarrow \cap_{\triangleright}(\mathbb{Y}, X)$ for $(X, i, j)$
19 | | Try $\mathbb{Z} \rightarrow \oplus(X, Y)$ for $(X, i, j)$
20 | | Try $\mathbb{Z} \rightarrow \oplus(Y, X)$ for $(X, i, j)$
21 | **end**
22 | **else if** $\varpi$ *is in the form of* $(\mathbb{X}, i, j, k, l)$ **then**
23 | | Try $Z \rightarrow \ominus(\mathbb{X})$ for $(\mathbb{X}, i, j, k, l)$
24 | | Try $\mathbb{Z} \rightarrow \mathbb{X}$ for $(\mathbb{X}, i, j, k, l)$
25 | | Try $\mathbb{Z} \rightarrow {}_{\triangleleft}\!\cap(\mathbb{X}, Y)$ for $(\mathbb{X}, i, j, k, l)$
26 | | Try $\mathbb{Z} \rightarrow {}_{\triangleright}\!\cap(\mathbb{X}, Y)$ for $(\mathbb{X}, i, j, k, l)$
27 | | Try $\mathbb{Z} \rightarrow \cap_{\triangleleft}(\mathbb{X}, Y)$ for $(\mathbb{X}, i, j, k, l)$
28 | | Try $\mathbb{Z} \rightarrow \cap_{\triangleright}(\mathbb{X}, Y)$ for $(\mathbb{X}, i, j, k, l)$
29 | | Try $\mathbb{Z} \rightarrow \Cap(\mathbb{X}, \mathbb{Y})$ for $(\mathbb{X}, i, j, k, l)$
30 | | Try $\mathbb{Z} \rightarrow \Cap(\mathbb{Y}, \mathbb{X})$ for $(\mathbb{X}, i, j, k, l)$
31 | **end**
32 **end**

### 3.1 Algorithm

Our algorithm for TAL reachability (depicted in Algorithm 1) is a dynamic programming algorithm, which can be viewed as an extension of the work-list algorithm for CFL reachability proposed by Melski and Reps [20].

Our algorithm maintains a work list (i.e., $W$) containing two categories of items. Each item in the first category represents the adding of a terminal or a first-order non-terminal. Such an item is in the form of $(X, i, j)$, which represents the adding of $X$ between the $i$-th node and the $j$-th node in $G$. Each item in the second category represents the adding of a second-order non-terminal. Such an item is in the form of $(\mathbb{X}, i, j, k, l)$, which indicates the addition of a second-order non-terminal between $i, j, k$, and $l$. Furthermore, we use $R_1$ to store the calculated reachability information of terminals and first-order non-terminals, and $R_2$ to store the calculated reachability information of second-order non-terminals.

In Algorithm 1, the two initialization steps (Lines 2 to 7) add reachability information into $R_1$ and items into $W$ for 1) terminals labeled on edges of $G$, and 2) $\epsilon$ between a node and itself. The main body of the algorithm is a large loop (Lines 9 to 32), in which we iteratively deal with the items in $W$. We further divide each iteration of the loop into two parts. The first part (Lines 11 to 21) deals with items in the first category, and each line between Line 12 and Line 20 deals with one type of productions involving $X$ at the right-hand side. The second part (Lines 22 to 31) deals with items in the second category, and each line between Line 22 and Line 29 deals with one type of productions involving $\mathbb{X}$ at the right-hand side. Note that, Lines 12 to 14 deal with basic CFL productions, which has also been described in Melski and Reps's algorithm for CFL reachability [20].

**ALGORITHM 2:** Try $\mathbb{Z} \to \curvearrowleft\!\cap(\mathbb{Y}, X)$ for $(X, i, j)$

**for** *each production in the form of* $\mathbb{Z} \to \curvearrowleft\!\cap(\mathbb{Y}, X)$ **do**
  **for** *each* $(\mathbb{Y}, j, k, l, p)$ *in* $R_2$ $(1 \le k, l, p \le n)$ **do**
    **if** $(\mathbb{Z}, i, k, l, p) \notin R_2$ **then**
      Add $(\mathbb{Z}, i, k, l, p)$ to $R_2$;
      Add $(\mathbb{Z}, i, k, l, p)$ to $W$;
    **end**
  **end**
**end**

Algorithm 2 depicts the details of Line 15 in Algorithm 1. As the right-hand side of such a production indicates that $X$ appears immediately before the first string of $\mathbb{Y}$, Algorithm 2 looks for reachability information of $\mathbb{Y}$ in $R_2$ satisfying this requirement. If such information exists, we add reachability information of $\mathbb{Z}$ with the corresponding nodes. The algorithms for Lines 16, 17, and 18 are similar to Algorithm 2. The differences lie in the different ways that $X$ concatenates with $\mathbb{Y}$.

The details of Line 19 in Algorithm 1 are depicted in Algorithm 3. As such a production does not require $Y$ to be concatenated with $X$, Algorithm 3 looks for reachability information of $Y$ in $R_1$ with no further requirement. If such information exists, we add reachability information of $\mathbb{Z}$ with corresponding nodes. The details of Line 20 in Algorithm 1 are similar to Algorithm 3.

**ALGORITHM 3:** Try $\mathbb{Z} \to \oplus(X, Y)$ for $(X, i, j)$

**for** *each production in the form of* $\mathbb{Z} \to \oplus(X, Y)$ **do**
  **for** *each* $(Y, k, l)$ *in* $R_1$ $(1 \le k, l \le n)$ **do**
    **if** $(\mathbb{Z}, i, j, k, l) \notin R_2$ **then**
      Add $(\mathbb{Z}, i, j, k, l)$ to $R_2$;
      Add $(\mathbb{Z}, i, j, k, l)$ to $W$;
    **end**
  **end**
**end**

The details of Line 23 in Algorithm 1 are depicted in Algorithm 4. To concatenate the two strings represented by $\mathbb{X}$, we require that the first string should appear immediately before the second string. If this requirement is satisfied, we add reachability information of $Z$ between nodes $i$ and $l$.

Line 24 in Algorithm 1 is similar to Line 12 in Algorithm 1. The difference is that Line 24 deals with productions each having two second-order non-terminals, while Line 12 deals with productions each having two first-order non-terminals.

Line 25 to Line 28 in Algorithm 1 are similar to Line 15 to Line 18 in Algorithm 1. The difference is that, for Line 25 to Line 28, we look in $R_1$ for first-order non-terminal $Y$ that can concatenate with second-order non-terminal $\mathbb{X}$.

**ALGORITHM 4:** Try $Z \to \ominus(\mathbb{X})$ for $(\mathbb{X}, i, j, k, l)$

**for** *each production in the form of* $Z \to \ominus(\mathbb{X})$ **do**
  **if** $j{=}k \wedge (Z, i, l) \notin R_1$ **then**
    Add $(Z, i, l)$ to $R_1$;
    Add $(Z, i, l)$ to $W$;
  **end**
**end**

The details of Line 29 in Algorithm 1 are depicted in Algorithm 5. In particular, we look for reachability information of $\mathbb{Y}$ in $R_2$ such that the first string of $\mathbb{Y}$ appears immediately after the first string of $\mathbb{X}$ and the second string of $\mathbb{Y}$ appears immediately before the second string of $\mathbb{X}$. The details of Line 30 in Algorithm 1 are similar to Algorithm 5.

**ALGORITHM 5:** Try $\mathbb{Z} \to \Cap(\mathbb{X}, \mathbb{Y})$ for $(\mathbb{X}, i, j, k, l)$

**for** *each production in the form of* $\mathbb{Z} \to \Cap(\mathbb{X}, \mathbb{Y})$ **do**
  **for** *each* $(\mathbb{Y}, j, p, q, k)$ *in* $R_2$ $(1 \le p, q \le n)$ **do**
    **if** $(\mathbb{Z}, i, p, q, l) \notin R_2$ **then**
      Add $(\mathbb{Z}, i, p, q, l)$ to $R_2$;
      Add $(\mathbb{Z}, i, p, q, l)$ to $W$;
    **end**
  **end**
**end**

### 3.2 Time Cost

As our TAL-reachability algorithm does not allow one piece of reachability information to be added more than once, we have at most $O((|N_1|+|T|)*n^2)$ items in the form of $(X, i, j)$ and at most $O(|N_2|*n^4)$ items in the form of $(\mathbb{X}, i, j, k, l)$. Then, we focus on analyzing the asymptotic time cost of dealing with one item in the form of $(X, i, j)$ and one item in the form of $(\mathbb{X}, i, j, k, l)$, respectively. We summarize the result of our analysis as Theorem 3.1.

Lines 12 to 20 deal with each item in the form of $(X, i, j)$. Among them, Line 13 requires the same asymptotic time as Line 14; Line 15 requires the same asymptotic time as Line 16, 17, or 18; and Line 19 requires the same asymptotic time as Line 20. Executing Line 12 once requires $O(|N_1|)$ time asymptotically, because given $X$, there are at most $O(|N_1|)$ productions in the form of $Z \to X$. Given $X$, there are at most $O(|N_1|*(|N_1|+|T|))$ productions in the form of $Z \to XY$, and for each such production there are at most $O(n)$ distinct pieces of reachability information of $Y$ such that $X$ appears immediately before $Y$. Thus, executing Line 13 once requires $O(|N_1|*(|N_1|+|T|)*n)$ time asymptotically. Given $X$, there are at most $O(|N_2|^2)$ productions in the form of $\mathbb{Z} \to \curvearrowleft\!\cap(\mathbb{Y}, X)$, and for each such production there are at most $O(n^3)$ distinct pieces of reachability information of $\mathbb{Y}$ such that $X$ appears immediately before the first string of $\mathbb{Y}$. Thus, executing Line 15 once requires $O(|N_2|^2*n^3)$ time asymptotically. Given $X$, there are at most $O(|N_2|*(|N_1|+|T|))$ productions in the form of $\mathbb{Z} \to \oplus(X, Y)$, and for each such production there are at most $O(n^2)$ distinct pieces of reachability information of $Y$. Thus, executing Line 19 once requires $O(|N_2|*(|N_1|+|T|)*n^2)$ time asymptotically. In summary, Lines 12 to 20 deal with one item in the form of $(X, i, j)$ in $O((|N_1|+|N_2|+|T|)^2*n^3)$ time asymptotically.

Lines 23 to 30 deal with each item in the form of $(\mathbb{X}, i, j, k, l)$. Among them, Line 23 requires the same asymptotic time as Line 24; Line 25 requires the same asymptotic time as Line 26, 27, or 28; and Line 29 requires the same asymptotic time as Line 30. Executing Line 23 once requires $O(|N_2|)$ time asymptotically. Given $\mathbb{X}$, there are at most $O(|N_2|*(|N_1|+|T|))$ productions in the form of $\mathbb{Z} \to \curvearrowleft\!\cap(\mathbb{X}, Y)$, and for each such production there are at most $O(n)$ distinct pieces of reachability information of $Y$ such that $Y$ appears immediately before the first string of $\mathbb{X}$. Thus, executing Line 25 once requires $O(|N_2|*(|N_1|+|T|)*n)$ time asymptotically. Given $\mathbb{X}$, there are at most $O(|N_2|^2)$ productions in the form of $\mathbb{Z} \to \Cap(\mathbb{X}, \mathbb{Y})$, and for each such production there are at most $O(n^2)$ distinct pieces of reachability information of $\mathbb{Y}$ such that the first string of $\mathbb{Y}$ appears immediately after the first string of $\mathbb{X}$ and the second string of $\mathbb{Y}$ appears immediately before the second string of $\mathbb{X}$. Thus, executing Line 29 once requires $O(|N_2|^2*n^2)$ time asymptotically. In summary, Lines 22 to 30 deal with one item in the form of $(\mathbb{X}, i, j, k, l)$ in $O((|N_1|+|N_2|+|T|)^2*n^2)$ time asymptotically.

**THEOREM** 3.1. *The asymptotic time cost of our TAL-reachability algorithm is* $O(l^3*n^6)$, *where* $l$ *is* $|N_1|+|N_2|+|T|$ *and* $n$ *is the number of nodes in* $G$.

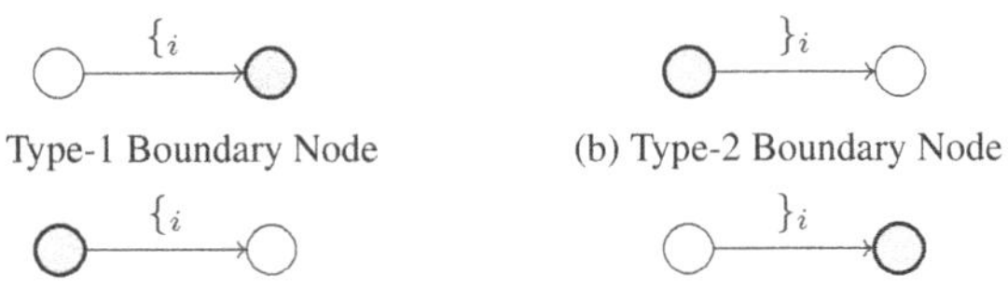


(a) Type-1 Boundary Node (b) Type-2 Boundary Node

(c) Type-3 Boundary Node (d) Type-4 Boundary Node

Figure 3: Four Types of Boundary Nodes in Summary

# 4. Context-Sensitive Data-Dependence Analysis with TAL Reachability

On top of TAL reachability, we propose a novel algorithm for context-sensitive data-dependence analysis to calculate the reachability relationships between each pair of client nodes. Our algorithm consists of three steps. First, we build a summary containing *conditional reachability* information via analyzing the library code (Section 4.1). Second, we further process the summary to make it suitable for the analysis of client code (Section 4.2). Third, we use CFL reachability to analyze the client code based on the post-processed summary (Section 4.3). In Section 4.4, we demonstrate the soundness of our algorithm.

## 4.1 Summarizing Library Code with TAL Reachability

Definition 4.1 defines the TAL that we use to summarize the library code. In this grammar, $S$ represents unconditional reachability with exactly matched parentheses, and $\mathbb{S}$ represents *conditional reachability* with exactly matched parentheses. Similarly, $S_1$ and $\mathbb{S}_1$ are for unconditional and conditional reachability with unmatched opening parentheses, and $S_2$ and $\mathbb{S}_2$ are for unconditional and conditional reachability with unmatched closing parentheses.

**DEFINITION** 4.1. ***(TAG for Library-Code Summarization)***

$S \rightarrow \ominus(\mathbb{S}) \mid SS \mid e$

$\mathbb{S} \rightarrow \Cap(\mathbb{S},\mathbb{S}) \mid \lhd\!\cap(\mathbb{S},S) \mid \rhd\!\cap(\mathbb{S},S) \mid \cap\!\lhd(\mathbb{S},S) \mid \cap\!\rhd(\mathbb{S},S) \mid \oplus(\{_i,\}_i)$

$S_1 \rightarrow \ominus(\mathbb{S}_1) \mid S_1S_1 \mid S_1S \mid SS_1 \mid \{_i$

$\mathbb{S}_1 \rightarrow \lhd\!\cap(\mathbb{S},S_1) \mid \cap\!\rhd(\mathbb{S},S_1) \mid \lhd\!\cap(\mathbb{S}_1,S_1) \mid \cap\!\rhd(\mathbb{S}_1,S_1)$

$S_2 \rightarrow \ominus(\mathbb{S}_2) \mid S_2S_2 \mid S_2S \mid SS_2 \mid \}_i$

$\mathbb{S}_2 \rightarrow \lhd\!\cap(\mathbb{S},S_2) \mid \cap\!\rhd(\mathbb{S},S_2) \mid \lhd\!\cap(\mathbb{S}_2,S_2) \mid \cap\!\rhd(\mathbb{S}_2,S_2)$

If we use the TAL defined in Definition 4.1 to calculate TAL reachability on a dependence graph $G$, we actually obtain exactly the same unconditional reachability relationships as we use the CFL[5] defined in Definition 4.2 to calculate CFL reachability on $G$. However, when calculating TAL reachability, we also obtain *conditional reachability* relationships as well as unconditional reachability relationships. In fact, our TAL-reachability algorithm always first determines a *conditional reachability* relationship, and if the *conditional reachability* relationship is in the form of C-Reachable$_{i,i}(x,\ y)$ for some $i$, our TAL-reachability algorithm (specifically Algorithm 4) then determines an unconditional reachability relationship from $x$ to $y$. Therefore, if we are summarizing a library, using the TAL in Definition 4.1 allows us to summarize more information than using the CFL in Definition 4.2.

**DEFINITION** 4.2. ***(CFG for Context-Sensitive Data-Dependence Analysis)***

$S \rightarrow SS \mid T_i\}_i \mid e$

$T_i \rightarrow \{_iS$

$S_1 \rightarrow S_1S_1 \mid S_1S \mid SS_1 \mid \{_i$

$S_2 \rightarrow S_2S_2 \mid S_2S \mid SS_2 \mid \}_i$

[5] If we use this CFL to analyze both the library code and the client code, we can calculate all the context-sensitive data-dependence relationships.

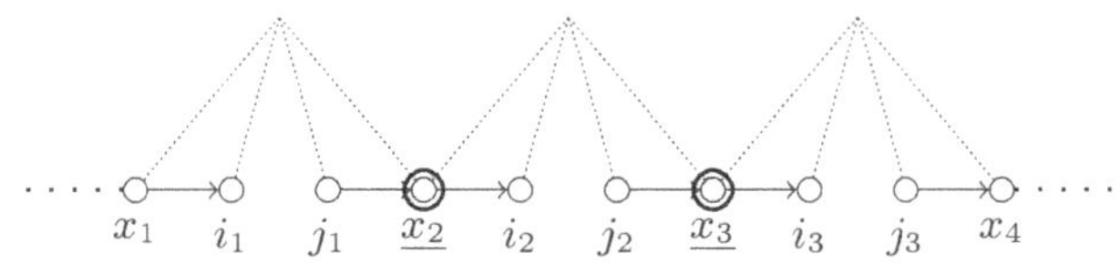


Figure 4: Chaining Nodes

## 4.2 Post-Processing

To make the summary obtained in Section 4.1 suitable for client-code analysis, we need to remove some unnecessary reachability relationships from the summary. Let us consider our example discussed in Section 1. Besides C-Reachable$_{l_9,l_{10}}(l_3,l_6)$, our TAL-reachability algorithm also calculates some other *conditional reachability* relationships using the TAL in Definition 4.1, e.g., C-Reachable$_{l_9,l_{10}}(l_4,l_5)$. In fact, C-Reachable$_{l_9,l_{10}}(l_4,l_5)$ does not provide further help for client-code analysis, but may incur unnecessary computation. To identify which information in the summary is unnecessary, we first identify in the summary a set of nodes such that only the reachability information among them is sufficient for client-code analysis. In this paper, we denoted these nodes as the *fundamental summary nodes*. It should be noted that, the post-processing is an important way to reduce the cost of client analysis when multiple callbacks exist. As the size of graph representing library summary shrinks, the graph will require much less unnecessary operations (adding non-terminals to edges) during client analysis.

### 4.2.1 Fundamental Summary Nodes

First, all the *boundary nodes* are *fundamental summary nodes*, since the reachability transfers between the summary and the client through them. Actually, there are four types of such *boundary nodes* in the summary. Figure 3, in which we use gray nodes to represent *boundary* nodes in the summary and white nodes to represent client nodes, depicts four boundary nodes each of a different type. The boundary node (referred to as the type-1 boundary node) in Figure 3(a) receives a value from the client via a call of a library method. The boundary node (referred to as the type-2 boundary node) in Figure 3(b) returns a value to the client via a method return. The boundary node (referred to as the type-3 boundary node) in Figure 3(c) passes a value to the client via a callback. The boundary node (referred to as the type-4 boundary node) in Figure 3(d) receives a value from the client via a return of a callback.

Second, it is still insufficient only keeping all the *boundary nodes*. Given one type-1 boundary node (denoted as $x$) and one type-2 boundary node (denoted as $y$) in the summary, there may be a chain of two or more *conditional reachability* relationships between them. If all the *conditional reachability* relationships in the chain are turned into unconditional, we have an unconditional reachability relationship between $x$ and $y$. Note that, as such a chain may depend on more than one unconditional reachability relationship provided by the client, it cannot be represented by just one *conditional reachability* relationship. Therefore, we need to keep all the nodes that may connect two or more *conditional reachability* relationships. We refer to these nodes as the *chaining nodes*. Figure 4 depicts a sub-chain. In this figure, both nodes $x_2$ and $x_3$ are *chaining nodes*.

Third, there are two ways for one *conditional reachability* relationship (denoted as C-Reachable$_{i,j}(x,y)$) to become unconditional. The first way is that the client provides an unconditional reachability relationship to make the *conditional reachability* relationship become unconditional. In such a case, $i$ must be a type-3 boundary node and $j$ a type-4 boundary node. The other way is that a chain of *conditional reachability* relationships eventually provides an unconditional reachability relationship to make the

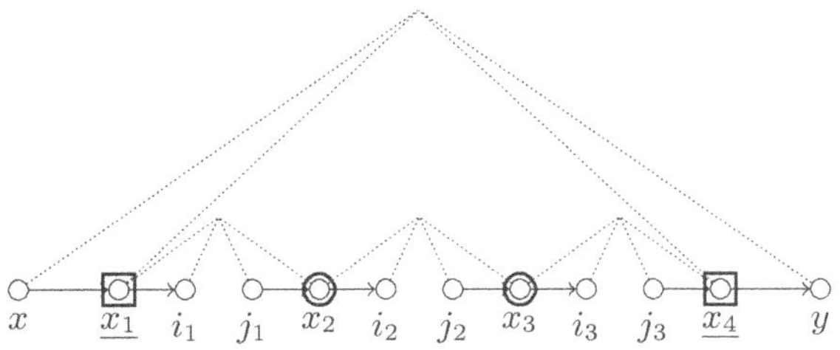


Figure 5: Hidden Chaining Nodes

*conditional reachability* relationship become unconditional. In such a case, either $i$ or $j$ may not be in the set of boundary nodes or the set of chaining nodes. We refer to such nodes as the *hidden chaining nodes*, which should also be kept in the summary. Figure 5, in which node $x_1$ and node $x_4$ are *hidden chaining nodes*, depicts such a situation. We further distinguish *hidden chaining nodes* into two types: type-1 and type-2. In Figure 5, $x_1$ is a type-1 and $x_4$ is a type-2 *hidden chaining node*.

Note that a *fundamental summary node* can be of multiple types, e.g., a type-3 *boundary node* may also be *chaining node*.

### 4.2.2 Identifying Fundamental Summary Nodes

*Chaining nodes* can be identified before calculating TAL reachability. The algorithm for identifying *chaining nodes* is depicted in Algorithm 6. Obviously, the asymptotical time cost of Algorithm 6 is $O(n+E)$, where $n$ is the number of nodes and $E$ is the number of edges. Essentially, a node with at least an incoming edge labeled with a closing parenthesis and at least an outgoing edge labeled with an opening parenthesis is a *chaining node*. However, due to the existence of edges labeled with $e$, we need to perform a propagation of edge labels (which is also based on a work-list algorithm) before checking the preceding condition. Algorithm 6 can ensure that, for any node (denoted as $x$) with at least an incoming edge labeled with a closing parenthesis and any node (denoted as $y$) with at least an outgoing edge labeled with an opening parenthesis, if there is a path from $x$ to $y$ with all edges labeled with $e$, there must be a *chaining node* along the path (including $x$ and $y$). Note that the change of edge labels in Algorithm 6 should be confined to the algorithm itself so as not to impact other parts of our analysis.

After identifying the *chaining nodes* and calculating TAL reachability, we identify *hidden chaining nodes* in the following way. Supposing there is a *conditional reachability* relationship among $x$, $y$, $i$, and $j$ (i.e., C-Reachable$_{i,j}(x,y)$) and the label is $\mathbb{S}$, if we know that $y$ is a *chaining node*, we mark $x$ as a type-1 *hidden chaining node*; and if we know that $x$ is a *chaining node*, we mark $y$ as a type-2 *hidden chaining node*.

It is straightforward to identify *boundary nodes*. The only issue for identifying *boundary nodes* is that we can only identify a set of potential boundary nodes when the client code is still unavailable. When the client code becomes available, we can refine the set to obtain real *boundary nodes*.

### 4.2.3 Discarding Unnecessary Reachability Information

As we keep only *fundamental nodes* in the summary, reachability information related to at least one node not being a *fundamental summary node* is naturally discarded. We further remove some reachability information as follows.

We keep all unconditional reachability relationships between two *fundamental summary nodes*. However, for a *conditional reachability* relationship in the form of C-Reachable$_{i,j}(x,y)$, we keep it in the summary only if both $x$ and $y$ are *fundamental summary nodes*; $i$ is a type-3 boundary node or a type-1 hidden chaining node; and $j$ is a type-4 boundary node or a type-2 hidden chaining node. All the other reachability information should be discarded.

**ALGORITHM 6:** Identify Chaining Nodes

**for** *each node $x$ with at least an incoming edge labeled with a closing parenthesis in $G$* **do**
  Add $x$ to $C$; Add $x$ to $W$;
**end**
**while** *$W$ is not empty* **do**
  Select and remove the first item (denoted as $\varpi$) from $W$;
  **for** *each outgoing edge (denoted as oe) labeled with e of $\varpi$* **do**
    Change the label of *oe* to an closing parenthesis;
    Suppose that *oe* connects $\varpi$ to $y$;
    **if** $y \notin C$ **then**
      Add $y$ to $C$; Add $y$ to $W$;
    **end**
  **end**
**end**
**for** *each node $x$ in $G$* **do**
  **if** *there is at least one incoming edge of $x$ labeled with a closing parenthesis and there is at least one outgoing edge of $x$ labeled with an opening parenthesis* **then**
    Mark $x$ as a *chaining node*
  **end**
**end**

Furthermore, if there is already an unconditional reachability relationship of a certain type (i.e., $S$, $S_1$, or $S_2$) between two nodes (denoted as $x$ and $y$), it is thus not useful to keep any *conditional reachability* relationships of the corresponding type (i.e., $\mathbb{S}$ for $S$, $\mathbb{S}_1$ for $S_1$, and $\mathbb{S}_2$ for $S_2$) in the form of C-Reachable$_{i,j}(x,y)$ for any $i$ and $j$. The reason is that the only aim to keep a *conditional reachability* relationship is that the *conditional reachability* relationship may become an unconditional one during client-code analysis. In fact, we use CFL reachability to calculate all the unconditional reachability relationships before calculating TAL reachability; and when there is already an unconditional reachability relationship from $x$ to $y$, we prevent our TAL-reachability algorithm from adding any *conditional reachability* relationship in the form of C-Reachable$_{i,j}(x,y)$ to $R_2$ in the first place.

### 4.3 Analyzing Client Code

With the post-processed summary, we use CFL reachability to analyze the client code. Specifically, we use the CFL defined in Definition 4.2 to analyze the graph composed of the client graph, the *fundamental summary nodes* with the reachability relationships among them, and edges each between a client node and a *boundary node* in the summary. Our CFL-reachability algorithm extends Melski and Reps's work-list algorithm [20] as follows.

First, for each unconditional reachability relationship in the summary, we put it into the work list during initialization, because it may trigger some productions in Definition 4.2 (e.g., $T_k \rightarrow \{_k S$, $S \rightarrow T_k\}_k$, and $S \rightarrow SS$).

Second, for each *conditional reachability* relationship in the summary, we do not put it into the work list, because we do not want to have new *conditional reachability* relationships. However, when we have a new unconditional reachability relationship between two summary nodes (denoted as $i$ and $j$), we check whether this unconditional reachability relationship can turn a *conditional reachability* relationship into unconditional. That is to say, we check whether there exist two summary nodes (denoted as $x$ and $y$) such that C-Reachable$_{i,j}(x, y)$.

### 4.4 Soundness

We demonstrate that our algorithm for context-sensitive data-dependency analysis using TAL-reachability-based summary is sound in Theorem 4.1.

**THEOREM 4.1.** ***(Soundness)*** *Our algorithm using TAL-reachability-based summary produces sound results for context-sensitive data-dependency analysis.*

In stead of directly proving Theorem 4.1, we prove that our algorithm produces exactly the same results as the CFL-reachability-based algorithm using the CFL defined in Definition 4.2 (i.e., Theorem 4.2). Since the CFL-reachability-based algorithm is sound, our algorithm is also sound.

**THEOREM 4.2.** ***(Equivalence)*** *Our algorithm using TAL-reachability-based summary produces exactly the same results for context-sensitive data-dependency analysis as the CFL-reachability-based algorithm using the CFL in Definition 4.2.*

**Proof**. To prove Theorem 4.2, we need to demonstrate that the following two properties hold for any two nodes (denoted as $x$ and $y$) in the client graph. First, if our algorithm determines a reachability relationship from $x$ to $y$, the CFL-reachability-based algorithm also determines such a reachability relationship. Second, if the CFL-reachability-based algorithm determines a reachability relationship from $x$ to $y$, our algorithm also determines such a reachability relationship. For conciseness, we consider only the reachability of exactly matched parentheses, as the proof for the other two types of reachability can be naturally extended from the current proof.

The first property obviously holds. In fact, when our algorithm determines a reachability from $x$ to $y$, our algorithm can ensure that there is at least a path from $x$ to $y$ labeled with exactly matched parentheses.

Let $G$ be the union of the client graph and the library graph, $N$ be the union of the set of client nodes and the set of $fundamental$ $summary\ nodes$, $x \in N$ and $y \in N$. We actually prove that if there is a parenthesis-matched path from $x$ to $y$ (denoted as $path_{x,y}$) in $G$, our algorithm determines a reachability relationship from $x$ to $y$. Note that this target property is stronger than the second property.

We prove the target property via mathematical induction on the basis of the number (denoted as $p$) of pairs of matched parentheses in $path_{x,y}$. When $p$=0, our target property obviously holds. Since there is no parenthesis in $path_{x,y}$, $path_{x,y}$ can be divided into a series of pieces, each of which is composed of nodes all in the library graph or nodes all in the client graph. As our algorithm keeps all the unconditional reachability between $boundary\ nodes$ in the library graph during library-code summarization and post-processing, our CFL-reachability algorithm for client-code analysis definitely determines $path_{x,y}$.

Let us assume that, for any $0 \leq r \leq q$, our target property holds when $p$=$r$. In the following, we prove that our target property holds when $p$=$q$+1. Let us denote the first opening parenthesis in $path_{x,y}$ as $OP$ and the closing parenthesis matched with $OP$ in $path_{x,y}$ as $CP$. There are four situations for $path_{x,y}$.

1. $OP$ does not connect two library nodes and $CP$ is not the last closing parenthesis in $path_{x,y}$.
2. $OP$ does not connect two library nodes and $CP$ is the last closing parenthesis in $path_{x,y}$.
3. $OP$ connects two library nodes and $CP$ is not the last closing parenthesis in $path_{x,y}$.
4. $OP$ connects two library nodes and $CP$ is the last closing parenthesis in $path_{x,y}$.

For Situation 1, let $CP$ connect node $i$ to node $j$. As $CP$ is not the last closing parenthesis, there is a parenthesis-matched sub-path from $x$ to $j$ in $path_{x,y}$, where the number of pairs of matched parentheses is at most $q$; and there is a parenthesis-matched sub-path from $j$ to $y$ in $path_{x,y}$, where the number of pairs of matched parentheses is at most $q$. Since $OP$ does not connect two library nodes, $CP$ must not connect two library nodes. Therefore, $j$ is a client node or a $boundary\ node$ in the library. According to the inductive assumption, our algorithm determines a reachability relationship from $x$ to $j$ and a reachability relationship from $j$ to $y$. As a result, our algorithm determines a reachability relationship from $x$ to $y$.

For Situation 2, let $OP$ connect node $i$ to node $j$ and $CP$ connect node $k$ to node $l$. Thus, there is a parenthesis-matched sub-path from $j$ to $k$ in $path_{x,y}$, where the number of pairs of matched parentheses is $q$. Since $OP$ does not connect two library nodes, $CP$ must not connect two library nodes. Therefore, $j$ is a client node or a $boundary\ node$ in the library, and so is $k$. According to the inductive assumption, our algorithm determines a reachability relationship from $j$ to $k$. As a result, our algorithm determines a reachability relationship from $x$ to $y$.

Situation 3 is similar to Situation 1. However, supposing that $CP$ connects node $i$ to node $j$, $j$ may not be a $fundamental$ $summary\ node$. Let us consider the first opening parenthesis (denoted as $OP'$) between $j$ and $y$ along $path_{x,y}$. Let $OP'$ connect node $k$ to node $l$. As $j$ is a library node and a library node can connect to a client node only through an edge labeled with a parenthesis, $k$ must be a library node and all the nodes between $j$ and $k$ along $path_{x,y}$ are library nodes. Thus, our Algorithm 6 can identify at least one $chaining\ node$ in the sub-path from $j$ to $k$. Note that, if $l$ is a client node, there must be another library node (denoted as $l'$) and an edge labeled with an opening parenthesis from $k$ to $l'$. Let node $u$ be such a chaining node. Our algorithm determines a reachability relationship from $x$ to $u$ and a reachability relationship from $u$ to $y$ based on the inductive assumption.

Situation 4 is similar to Situation 2 but more complicated. Supposing that $OP$ connects node $i$ to node $j$ and $CP$ connects node $k$ to node $l$, any of the four nodes may not be a $fundamental$ $summary\ node$. As there is no parenthesis between $x$ and $i$ along $path_{x,y}$, the entire sub-path from $x$ to $i$ is in the library graph. Similarly, the entire sub-path from $l$ to $y$ is in the library graph. Now, we consider all pairs of matched library parentheses nested with the pair of $OP$ and $CP$ along $path_{x,y}$. Let $OP'$ (connecting node $i'$ to node $j'$) and $CP'$ (connecting node $k'$ and node $l'$) denote the opening parenthesis and the closing parenthesis in the innermost pair. It can be proven that there exists a node (denoted as $u$) in the sub-path from $j'$ to $k'$ along $path_{x,y}$ such that $u$ is a type-3 boundary node or a type-1 hidden chaining node and there is no parenthesis between $j'$ and $u$ along $path_{x,y}$. Similarly, there exists a node (denoted as $v$) in the sub-path from $j'$ to $k'$ along $path_{x,y}$ such that $v$ is a type-4 boundary node or a type-2 hidden chaining node and there is no parenthesis between $v$ and $k'$ along $path_{x,y}$. According to the inductive assumption, our algorithm determines a reachability relationship from $u$ to $v$. Furthermore, our algorithm keeps a $conditional\ reachability$ relationship in the form of C-Reachable$_{u,v}(x,y)$.

To show the existence of $u$, let us consider the first opening parenthesis (denoted as $OP''$) in the sub-path from $j'$ to $k'$ along $path_{x,y}$. Supposing that $OP''$ connects node $i''$ to node $j''$ and the matched closing parenthesis of $OP''$ (denoted as $CP''$) connects node $k''$ to $l''$. If $j''$ is a client code, $i''$ is thus a type-3 boundary node and can serve as node $u$. Suppose that $j''$ is a library node. Then, $CP''$ must not be the last parenthesis in the sub-path from $j'$ to $k'$ along $path_{x,y}$; otherwise, the pair of $OP''$ and $CP''$ would nest inwardly with the pair of $OP'$ and $CP'$. Thus, we can find a $chaining\ node$ (denoted as $u'$) between $l''$ and $k'$ along $path_{x,y}$ such that there is no parenthesis between $l''$ and $u'$. Due to the existence of $u'$, $i''$ is thus a type-1 hidden chaining node and can serve as node $u$. □

## 5. Experimental Evaluations

In this section, we consider the cost our TAL-based approach in comparison with the CFL-based approach. As our main consideration is whether the TAL-reachability-based summary can boost client code analysis, our first experiment (**E1**) focuses on the cost comparison between our TAL-based approach and the CFL-based approach for analyzing *client code*. Furthermore, to understand how much more computation the calculation of TAL reachability would incur, our second experiment (**E2**) focuses on the cost comparison between our TAL-based approach and the CFL-based approach for summarizing *library code*. More details can be found in our project website at `http://www.utdallas.edu/~lxz144130/tal.html`.

### 5.1 Implementation

We implemented our TAL-Reachability algorithm in Java. More specifically, we use hash tables to store $R_1$ and $R_2$ in Algorithm 1 to 5 because reachability information in $R_1$ and $R_2$ is typically sparse. We use several indexing facilities to access reachability in $R_1$ and $R_2$ when trying different productions in Algorithm 1. For $R_1$, we use two hash tables to index all the reachability information in the form of $(X, i, j)$ by $<X, i>$ and $<X, j>$, respectively. For $R_2$, we use six hash tables to index $(\mathbb{X}, i, j, k, l)$ by $<\mathbb{X}, i>$, $<\mathbb{X}, j>$, $<\mathbb{X}, k>$, $<\mathbb{X}, l>$, $<\mathbb{X}, i, l>$ and $<\mathbb{X}, j, k>$, respectively. Here, we use HashSet and HashMap from the Java Standard Library to maintain the reachability information (i.e., $R_1$ and $R_2$) and the indexing information for $R_1$ and $R_2$, respectively.

Furthermore, we also implemented a TAL-based context-sensitive data-dependence analysis tool on top of Wala (version 1.3.5) [6] for Java applications. We used Wala to build the data dependence graph of the program. When building the data dependency graph, we do not directly perform alias analysis but retain all the information necessary for alias analysis (assignment information between object variables). Therefore, when TAL-reachability algorithm is applied, the alias information will be computed (in a flow-insensitive and field-insensitive but context-sensitive way) together with data dependence among various code elements. We chose to target Java applications, because Java is one of the most popular programming languages and callbacks are ubiquitous (even inevitable) in Java libraries due to the support of method overriding in Java. Our tool consists of (1) a summarization component that analyzes and generates TAL-based summaries for *library code*, and (2) an analysis component that performs context-sensitive data-dependence analysis for the *client code* using the generated summaries.

### 5.2 Experimental Setup

All our experiments were performed on a PC with 4-core 8-thread Intel Core i7-3770 CPU (3.4GHz) and 4 Gigabyte RAM running JVM 1.7.0-55 on Ubuntu Linux 13.10.

**Benchmarks.** We used 11 Java programs from SPECjvm2008 [2][7] as our benchmark. The SPECjvm benchmark suite has been widely used in the program analysis research [37, 38, 44, 45]. In addition, we also randomly selected 4 programs from GitHub [1] to evaluate our approach. The first 5 columns in Table 1 depict the statistics of the subjects used in our evaluation. Column 1 and 2 lists the subjects' name and size in lines of code; Columns 3 to 5 present the total number of nodes, the number of $fundamental\ summary\ nodes$, and the number of nodes in client code for each subject's data-dependence graph. Note that, each of our subjects contains a Java library and a client program that invokes the library in different ways. We analyze all the methods (in either client or library code) that are reachable from the main method of the client program, and we compute summaries for only the main Java library in the benchmark (while ignoring other invoked libraries such as java.lang). Our statistics are based on the part of client and library code that are involved in our analysis.

**Compared Techniques.** Since the summary information for library code is reusable, we may simply compare our approach in analyzing the client code with TAL-reachability-based summaries with the traditional CFL-based approach in analyzing the whole code base. However, that is not fair because the CFL-based approach can also pre-compute summary information for the part of library code that does not involve any callbacks. Note that, when using CFL reachability to summarize library code, if one node is labeled as not reachable to another node, the reachability is still possible during client-code analysis due to callbacks.

To enable a fair comparison between our TAL-based approach and the traditional CFL-based approach, we implemented a two-step CFL-based approach containing two components: (1) a summarization component that uses CFL reachability to pre-compute summary information for the *library code*, and (2) an analysis component that performs data-dependence analysis for the *client code* on the basis of the CFL-reachability-based library summaries. Similar to the implementation of our approach, we implemented the CFL-based approach using Melski and Reps's generic CFL-reachability algorithm [20]. Thus, we ensure that the CFL-based approach is the same with our approach except that it computes and uses CFL-reachability-based summaries instead of TAL-based summaries for library code.

To investigate the efficiency of our approach for analyzing client code (i.e., **E1**), we compared the second component of our approach with that of the CFL-based approach. Furthermore, to measure the overhead incurred by our TAL-based summary computation (i.e., **E2**), we compared our first component with that of the CFL-based approach.

**Measurements.** Similar to existing studies of CFL-reachability-based analysis [37, 44, 45], we measured both the time cost and the peak memory usage of our TAL-based analysis .

### 5.3 Results

The main experimental results are shown in Table 1. Columns 6 to 9 show the results for client code analysis (**E1**), and Columns 10 to 13 show the results for library summarization (**E2**).

**E1: Client-Code Analysis.** From Columns 6 to 9 of Table 1, we make the following observations. First, the time cost of our TAL-based approach is much lower than that of the CFL-based approach. For example, to analyze the client code for all the subjects, the CFL-based approach needs 7877 milliseconds, while our TAL-based approach needs only 956 milliseconds, indicating a speed-up of 8.24X. In an extreme case, our TAL-based approach achieves a speed-up of 25.83X for the $xml$ subject. In addition, our TAL-based approach outperforms the CFL-based approach for all the studied subjects in terms of time cost (with at least a speed-up of 2X). The reason is that, although our TAL-based approach leverages the same CFL-reachability algorithm when analyzing client code, it is able to utilize more intensive summaries for the library code, so that more parts of the library code need not to be analyzed again. Second, the peak memory consumption of the CFL-based approach is also larger than that of our TAL-based approach. This is also expected because our approach maintains reachability information between the $fundamental\ summary\ nodes$, whose number is much smaller than the number of all library nodes. As depicted in Table 1, in total, the number of $fundamental\ summary\ nodes$ is only 6.35% of the number of library nodes. Furthermore, for each subject, the number of $fundamental\ summary\ nodes$ is always less than 10% of the number of library nodes. In sum-

[6] http://wala.sourceforge.net

[7] Note that the $serial$ program is not included because our approach runs out of memory during library-code summarization.

| Subjects | Size (LOC) | #Nodes | | | Client-Code Analysis | | | | Library Summarization | | | |
|---|---|---|---|---|---|---|---|---|---|---|---|---|
| | | Total | Fund. | Client | CFL | | TAL | | CFL | | TAL | |
| | | | | | T(ms) | M(MB) | T(ms) | M(MB) | T(ms) | M(MB) | T(ms) | M(MB) |
| check | 10,672 | 19951 | 1539 | 3347 | 348 | 152 | 67 | 58 | 267 | 107 | 645 | 132 |
| compiler | 9,607 | 16726 | 1220 | 536 | 330 | 153 | 53 | 73 | 309 | 130 | 661 | 141 |
| compress | 10,058 | 17640 | 1309 | 1483 | 330 | 159 | 64 | 75 | 321 | 130 | 670 | 142 |
| crypto | 21,503 | 23310 | 1825 | 3216 | 459 | 174 | 73 | 66 | 339 | 126 | 773 | 207 |
| derby | 21,568 | 24513 | 1687 | 1106 | 684 | 250 | 78 | 93 | 435 | 194 | 998 | 610 |
| helloworld | 9,458 | 16299 | 1207 | 296 | 309 | 130 | 36 | 48 | 283 | 105 | 640 | 138 |
| mpegaudio | 40,246 | 56493 | 2175 | 27576 | 1047 | 378 | 215 | 196 | 575 | 239 | 4421 | 387 |
| scimark | 10,326 | 18297 | 1287 | 2027 | 331 | 161 | 67 | 78 | 322 | 131 | 665 | 149 |
| startup | 11,104 | 19933 | 1549 | 621 | 450 | 168 | 74 | 65 | 351 | 132 | 941 | 268 |
| sunflow | 9,102 | 15700 | 1121 | 85 | 290 | 123 | 33 | 44 | 293 | 100 | 663 | 127 |
| xml | 47,556 | 73786 | 4501 | 2312 | 2945 | 756 | 114 | 184 | 1433 | 587 | 5811 | 741 |
| btree | 5,168 | 7813 | 406 | 1103 | 105 | 80 | 48 | 56 | 179 | 68 | 264 | 155 |
| mushroom | 2,866 | 3865 | 272 | 7 | 80 | 64 | 8 | 48 | 169 | 76 | 183 | 93 |
| parser | 5,545 | 7968 | 385 | 112 | 108 | 86 | 13 | 53 | 199 | 74 | 269 | 158 |
| sample | 2,894 | 3969 | 247 | 28 | 61 | 64 | 13 | 48 | 162 | 73 | 184 | 99 |
| Total | 217,673 | 326263 | 20730 | 43855 | 7877 | | 956 | | 5637 | | 17788 | |

Table 1: Experimental results

mary, without sacrificing any precision, our approach is able to accelerate the context-sensitive data-dependence analysis on client code by almost a magnitude.

**E2: Library Summarization.** From Columns 10 to 13 of Table 1, we are able to make the following observations. First, the time cost of our approach is higher than that of the CFL-based approach when summarizing library code. Note that our TAL-based approach uses CFL reachability as a preprocessing step for summarizing the library code. To summarize the library code for all subjects, our TAL-based approach needs 17788 milliseconds, while the CFL-based approach needs only 5637 milliseconds, indicating an average slow-down of 3.16X. Second, the average peak memory consumption of our approach is 236.5MB, which is also higher than that of the CFL-based approach (i.e., 151.5MB). The reason for the slow-down and extra memory consumption is that our approach further computes the TAL-reachability information for library code as well as the CFL-reachability information. As this phase is typically performed much less frequently than the client-code analysis, the average slow-down of 3.16X can be affordable.

# 6. Discussion

## 6.1 Factors Affecting Client-Analysis Speed-up

Our experimental results in Section 5 demonstrate that the speed-up of our approach for client-code analysis varies much for different subjects (i.e., from 2X to 25X). Here, we further qualitatively investigate the factors that may affect the speed-up.

The first factor is the number of callbacks the client code provides. If the client does not provide any callbacks, our TAL-based summaries are essentially the same as the CFL-based summaries. Intuitively, the more callbacks the client provides, the more possibly our approach achieves a large speed-up. Also, since the impacts of different callbacks on the analysis are different, the overall impact does not depend only on the number of callbacks.

The second factor is the depth of nested method calls in the library code. Since our approach folds up nested method calls in library-code summarization, our client-code analysis can avoid analyzing those deeply nested method calls again. TAL reachability works best when some deeply nested method calls are callbacks.

The third factor is the number of long chains of *conditional reachability* relationships that are eventually turned into unconditional. Since our library-code summarization can speed up only the determination of each *conditional reachability* relationship to be unconditional in such a chain, the existence of many such long chains may affect our approach negatively.

## 6.2 Other Applications of TAL Reachability

Although we only investigate one application of TAL reachability, there may be many other applications in the following categories:

First, since many analyses can be modeled as CFL-reachability problems [3, 31, 40], TAL reachability should be useful for improving summary-based versions of these analyses. That is to say, we can use TAL reachability to calculate a more intensive summary of library code to boost client-code analysis.

Second, TAL reachability may provide further help for analyzing applications in which some code in the code base is not suitable for static analysis [43]. Two common cases are dynamically loaded code and dynamically generated code. Since dynamically loaded or generated code is typically impossible or very hard to analyze, to ensure the quality (e.g., reliability and security) of the whole program, dynamic analyzers and checkers are often enforced at run time. Similar to summarizing library code, it may be beneficial to acquire more intensive analysis results of the static code with TAL reachability so as to reduce the overhead of runtime enforcement.

Third, TAL reachability may be a useful tool for analyzing partial code. In other words, we can use TAL reachability to acquire useful properties of part of a code base regardless of the missing code (e.g., client code, dynamically loaded code, and dynamically generated code). For example, the *conditional reachability* information calculated by our algorithm can be easily extended to acquire the dependence between any two nodes in the library graph regardless of the client code: definite dependence, possible dependence, and impossible dependence. This dependence information can then be used for compiling and verifying the library.

Fourth, TAL reachability may also be useful for analyzing evolving software systems. Modern software systems usually undergo various revisions [5]. When the developers are changing some code files, they can run TAL-reachability-based analysis for the unchanged files (including libraries) meanwhile at the backend. Then, when the developers finish the revision, they can directly use the pre-computed information for unchanged files to speed-up program analysis for verifying the changed files.

## 6.3 Considering Field Sensitivity

In program analysis, field sensitivity is another important factor that impacts the precision of analysis [18, 37, 45]. Our approach performs flow-insensitive and field-insensitive data dependency analysis, and uses a simple heap abstraction that does not consider type structures. The rich heap abstractions that enable field-sensitivity can also be represented with CFL reachability. However, unfortunately, data-dependence analysis considering both kinds of sensitivity is undecidable [30]. One typical solution is to use a regular language to approximate one CFL and keep the other CFL intact. For example, we can regularize the CFL for field sensitivity (denoted as $RL_f$) and keep the CFL for context sensitivity (denoted as $CFL_c$) [12, 13]. Then, data-dependence analysis considering both kinds of sensitivity can be approximated as a CFL-reachability problem using $RL_f \cap CFL_c$. This paradigm can be extended to other constraints that can be represented as CFL reachability (e.g., synchronization sensitivity [26]). Of course, the generic algorithm by Melski and Reps [20] would typically not scale to large programs when using $RL_f \cap CFL_c$.

To extend our approach for field sensitivity, we can use a similar strategy: regularizing the CFL for field sensitivity to intersect it with our TAL in Definition 4.1 (denoted as $TAL_c$). Note that our TAL-reachability algorithm essentially provides a way to calculate the intersection of a regular language and a tree-adjoining language, as a regular language can be represented as paths in a graph. Similar to Melski and Reps's generic algorithm for CFL reachability, our generic algorithm for TAL reachability may also have scalability issues for large programs when using $RL_f \cap TAL_c$. One possible solution is to extend Kodumal and Aiken's regularly annotated set constraints [13] to TAL reachability.

## 7. Related Work

**CFL Reachability**. Based on the framework of CFL reachability proposed by Yannakakis [46], researchers used CFL reachability for various program-analysis problems, such as inter-procedural slicing [31], inter-procedural dataflow analysis [32], shape analysis [10, 28, 33], constant propagation [35] and pointer analysis [37, 45]. Researchers also investigated demand-driven algorithms for solving CFL-reachability problems [9, 38]. Reps [29] provided an early survey of program analysis based on CFL reachability. Rehof and Fähndrich [27] used CFL reachability to achieve an $O(n^3)$ algorithm for type-based flow analysis with polymorphic subtyping, which improves a previous $O(n^8)$ algorithm. Pratikakis et al. used CFL reachability for label-flow analysis [24] and race detection [25]. Zheng and Rugina [48] used CFL reachability for context-insensitive demand-driven alias analysis, which directly computes aliasing information without pre-computing points-to information. Chaudhuri [4] provided the first sub-cubic algorithm for CFL reachability. Some analyses require the consideration of satisfying multiple CFL reachability properties. However, it is undecidable considering two or more CFL reachability properties simultaneously [26, 30]. Therefore, it is needed to keep one CFL reachability property intact and approximate all the other CFL reachability properties as regular reachability properties [13, 37, 45]. In this paper, we propose TAL reachability via extending CFL reachability. TAL reachability allows us to calculate more intensive and compact summaries than CFL reachability for library code.

**Mildly Context-Sensitive Grammars**. As mentioned previously, researchers intensively investigated four formalisms for defining mildly context-sensitive grammars: tree-adjoining grammars [11], head grammars [23], linear indexed grammars [8], and combinatory categorial grammars [39]. According to [41], these four formalisms are actually four sets of different notations for defining the same family of mildly context-sensitive languages (i.e., the TAL family), which are parsable in $O(n^6)$ time (where $n$ is the length of the sentence for parsing) [36]. In this paper, we provide a concise formalism, which is the Chomsky Normal Form for defining the TAL family. Compared with the four existing formalisms, our formalism is more suitable for defining TAL reachability, which has not been investigated previously. There are also another two less intensively investigated formalisms (i.e., linear context-free rewriting systems [42] and minimalist grammars [17]) for defining a larger language family than the TAL family.

**Staged Program Analysis**. Summary-based analysis belongs to a wider notion of staged program analysis, where multiple passes of program analysis cooperate with each other to achieve the purpose.

We are aware of two research efforts on summary-based program analysis that try to build summaries for library code with callbacks. Specifically, Lattner et al. [16] leverages heap cloning to achieve context-sensitive stages analysis. However, their approach sacrifices context-sensitivity when recursion exists, while our approach achieves full context-sensitivity with recursions. Madhavan et al. [19] provide a general framework to deal with callbacks. Due to its generality, it identifies abstract domain parts affected by callbacks, and left these parts for analyses when client code is available, while our approach is able to generate partial summaries for these parts with conditional reachability, and the partial summaries are validated to be effective in our experiments. Our conditional reachability is relevant to conditional dependencies, which were defined and studied by Komondoor and Ramalingam [14] in another scenario. But the conditions in conditional dependencies refer to existing branch predicates, while the conditions in conditional reachability in our paper refer to the unknown client code.

Furthermore, CFL reachability [32] naturally provides a basis of summarizing library code. Dillig et al. [7] proposed a summary-based flow-sensitive analysis (for verifying program memory safety properties), in which strong updates are considered in summary building. However, their analysis does not consider callbacks. Researchers have also considered summarizing library code to speed up dataflow analysis [34]. However, their approach is based on the "functional approach" proposed by Sharir and Pnueli [22], and is not solvable in polynomial-time of the program size [32]. In addition, their approach simply folds intra-procedural nodes or invocation nodes which transitively invoke only library functions (no callbacks). Our TAL-based analysis can also be applied the folded graph produced by their approach to make data-flow analysis even faster, since our approach can reduce the analysis cost globally, e.g., our algorithm can also fold invocation nodes that can transitively invoke client code (dealing with callbacks).

For demand-driven interprocedural analysis, the main disadvantage of top-down approaches lies in repeated analysis and the main disadvantage of bottom-up approaches lies in analyzing information unnecessary for the demand [47]. Our approach is essentially a bottom-up approach. However, since we target analyzing reachability relationships between all pairs of nodes (not specific pairs of nodes), we do not need to avoid analysis unnecessary for any specific demand. Thus, it is natural to use bottom-up approach here.

Unlike summary-based program analysis, where library code is distinguished from client code, other staged analyses use different passes on the same code base. Naik and Aiken [21] proposed a two-stage analysis, where conditional must-not-aliasing information is calculated to ensure sound race detection. Xu et al. [45] proposed a two-stage points-to analysis, which uses conditional must-not-aliasing information to accelerate CFL-reachability calculation. Chugh et al. [6] proposed to use static information (i.e., residual policies) calculated in the first pass to reduce the runtime overhead for analyzing dynamically generated code in JavaScript.

## 8. Conclusion and Future Work

In this paper, we propose a novel framework for program analysis called TAL reachability. Based on this framework, we further propose a novel technique to summarize library code with callbacks for context-sensitive data-dependency analysis. Since our technique calculates *conditional reachability*, we have more intensive summary information without further approximation.

We further experimentally evaluated our approach on a set of Java benchmark programs, and our experimental results demonstrate that, compared with a similar CFL-based approach, our

TAL-based approach is able to achieve a speed-up of over 8X for client-code analysis on average. The largest speed-up even reaches over 25X. Our TAL-based approach naturally concedes some slow-down for library-code summarization; however our experimental results demonstrate that the slow-down is typically acceptable.

Since TAL reachability provides a new framework for static program analysis, we believe that there will be a lot of future work on top of TAL reachability. In the near future, we plan to investigate the following issues. First, although our current research focuses on data-dependence analysis, TAL reachability is applicable to various other program-analysis problems. We plan to investigate these problems (e.g., points-to analysis [37, 44, 45]) using TAL reachability. Second, our current algorithm for TAL reachability is a generic algorithm; it does not consider the special characteristics of the graph. We plan to investigate faster TAL-reachability algorithms, especially for specific program-analysis problems. Third, our current research considers only context sensitivity in our analysis. We plan to further consider field sensitivity in our analysis, where a major issue is to scale the field-sensitive, context-sensitive library-code summarization using TAL reachability. Fourth, when analyzing libraries, it is possible that library $l_1$ invokes another library $l_2$ whose summaries has been computed. We plan to handle this such cases by feeding the summaries of $l_2$ for TAL-reachability analysis of the client library $l_1$.

## Acknowledgment

The authors from Peking University are sponsored by the National 973 Program of China No. 2015CB352201, the National 863 Program of China No. 2013AA01A605, the Science Fund for Creative Research Groups of China No. 61121063, and the National Science Foundation of China No. 911118004, 61228203, and 61225007.

## References

[1] GitHub Home. `https://github.com/`.

[2] SPECjvm2008 Benchmark Suite. `http://www.spec.org/jvm2008/`.

[3] S. A. Bohner and R. S. Arnold. *Software Change Impact Analysis*. IEEE Computer Society Press, 1996.

[4] S. Chaudhuri. Subcubic algorithms for recursive state machines. In *Proc. POPL*, pages 159–169, 2008.

[5] L. Chen, J. Qian, Y. Zhou, P. Wang, and B. Xu. Identifying extract class refactoring opportunities for internetware. *Science China Information Sciences*, 57(7):1–18, 2014.

[6] R. Chugh, J. A. Meister, R. Jhala, and S. Lerner. Staged information flow for javascript. In *Proc. PLDI*, pages 50–62, 2009.

[7] I. Dillig, T. Dillig, A. Aiken, and M. Sagiv. Precise and compact modular procedure summaries for heap manipulating programs. In *Proc. PLDI*, pages 567–577, 2011.

[8] G. Gazdar. Applicability of indexed grammars to natural languages. In U. Reyle and C. Rohrer, editors, *Natural Language Parsing and Linguistic Theories*, pages 69–94, 1988.

[9] S. Horwitz, T. Reps, and M. Sagiv. Demand interprocedural dataflow analysis. In *Proc. FSE*, pages 104–115, 1995.

[10] S. Itzhaky, N. Bjørner, T. W. Reps, M. Sagiv, and A. V. Thakur. Property-directed shape analysis. In *Proc. CAV*, pages 35–51, 2014.

[11] A. K. Joshi, L. S. Levy, and M. Takahashi. Tree adjunct grammars. *Journal of Computer and System Sciences*, 10(1):136–163, 1975.

[12] J. Kodumal and A. Aiken. The set constraint/cfl reachability connection in practice. In *Proc. PLDI*, pages 207–218, 2004.

[13] J. Kodumal and A. Aiken. Regularly annotated set constraints. In *Proc. PLDI*, pages 331–341, 2007.

[14] R. Komondoor and G. Ramalingam. Recovering data models via guarded dependences. In *Proc. WCRE*, pages 110–119, 2007.

[15] D. J. Kuck, R. H. Kuhn, D. A. Padua, B. Leasure, and M. Wolfe. Dependence graphs and compiler optimizations. In *Proc. POPL*, pages 207–218, 1981.

[16] C. Lattner, A. Lenharth, and V. Adve. Making context-sensitive points-to analysis with heap cloning practical for the real world. In *Proc. PLDI*, pages 278–289, 2007.

[17] A. Lecomte and C. Retoré. Extending lambek grammars: a logical account of minimalist grammars. In *Proc. ACL*, pages 362–369, 2001.

[18] S. Litvak, N. Dor, R. Bodík, N. Rinetzky, and M. Sagiv. Field-sensitive program dependence analysis. In *Proc. FSE*, pages 287–296, 2010.

[19] R. Madhavan, G. Ramalingam, and K. Vaswani. Modular heap analysis for higher-order programs. In *Proc. SAS*, pages 370–387, 2012.

[20] D. Melski and T. Reps. Interconvertibility of a class of set constraints and context-free-language reachability. *TCS*, 248(1-2):29–98, 2000.

[21] M. Naik and A. Aiken. Conditional must not aliasing for static race detection. In *Proc. POPL*, pages 327–338, 2007.

[22] M. Pnueli. Two approaches to interprocedural data flow analysis. *Program flow analysis: Theory and applications*, pages 189–234, 1981.

[23] C. Pollard. *Gneralized Phrase Structure Grammars, Head Grammars and Natural Language*. PhD thesis, Stanford University, 1984.

[24] P. Pratikakis, J. S. Foster, and M. Hicks. Existential label flow inference via cfl reachability. In *Proc. SAS*, pages 88–106, 2006.

[25] P. Pratikakis, J. S. Foster, and M. W. Hicks. LOCKSMITH: Context-sensitive correlation analysis for race detection. In *Proc. PLDI*, pages 320–331, 2006.

[26] G. Ramalingam. Context-sensitive synchronization-sensitive analysis is undecidable. *TOPLAS*, 22(2):416–430, 2000.

[27] J. Rehof and M. Fähndrich. Type-based flow analysis: From polymorphic subtyping to CFL-reachability. In *Proc. POPL*, pages 54–66, 2001.

[28] T. Reps. Shape analysis as a generalized path problem. In *Proc. PEPM*, pages 1–11, 1995.

[29] T. Reps. Program analysis via graph reachability. *Information and Software Technology*, 40(11-12):701–726, 1998.

[30] T. Reps. Undecidability of context-sensitive data-dependence analysis. *TOPLAS*, 22(1):162–186, 2000.

[31] T. Reps, S. Horwitz, M. Sagiv, and G. Rosay. Speeding up slicing. In *Proc. FSE*, pages 11–20, 1994.

[32] T. Reps, S. Horwitz, and M. Sagiv. Precise interprocedural dataflow analysis via graph reachability. In *Proc. POPL*, pages 49–61, 1995.

[33] N. Rinetzky, A. Poetzsch-Heffter, G. Ramalingam, M. Sagiv, and E. Yahav. Modular shape analysis for dynamically encapsulated programs. In *Proc. ESOP*, pages 220–236, 2007.

[34] A. Rountev, S. Kagan, and T. Marlowe. Interprocedural dataflow analysis in the presence of large libraries. In *Proc. CC*, pages 2–16. Springer, 2006.

[35] M. Sagiv, T. Reps, and S. Horwitz. Precise interprocedural dataflow analysis with applications to constant propagation. *TCS*, 167(1-2): 131–170, 1996.

[36] Y. Schabes and K. Vijay-Shanker. Deterministic left to right parsing of tree adjoining languages. In *Proc. ACL*, pages 276–283, 1990.

[37] M. Sridharan and R. Bodík. Refinement-based context-sensitive points-to analysis for Java. In *Proc. PLDI*, pages 387–400, 2006.

[38] M. Sridharan, D. Gopan, L. Shan, and R. Bodík. Demand-driven points-to analysis for Java. In *Proc. OOPSLA*, pages 57–76, 2005.

[39] M. Steedman. Combinators and grammars. In R. Oehrle, E. Bach, and D. Wheeler, editors, *Categorial Grammars and Natural Language Structures*, pages 417–442, 1988.

[40] C. Sun, N. Xi, S. Gao, Z. Chen, and J. Ma. Automated enforcement for relaxed information release with reference points. *Science China Information Sciences*, 57(11):1–19, 2014.

[41] K. Vijay-Shanker and D. J. Weir. The equivalence of four extensions of context-free grammars. *Mathematical Systems Theory*, 27(6):511–546, 1994.

[42] D. Weir. *Characterizing mildly context-sensitive grammar formalisms*. PhD thesis, University of Pennsylvania, 1988.

[43] T. Xie, L. Zhang, X. Xiao, Y.-F. Xiong, and D. Hao. Cooperative software testing and analysis: Advances and challenges. *JCST*, 29(4): 713–723, 2014.

[44] G. Xu and A. Rountev. Merging equivalent contexts for scalable heap-cloning-based context-sensitive points-to analysis. In *Proc. ISSTA*, pages 225–235, 2008.

[45] G. Xu, A. Rountev, and M. Sridharan. Scaling CFL-reachability-based points-to analysis using context-sensitive must-not-alias analysis. In *Proc. ECOOP*, pages 98–122, 2009.

[46] M. Yannakakis. Graph-theoretic methods in database theory. In *Proc. PODS*, pages 230–242, 1990.

[47] X. Zhang, R. Mangal, M. Naik, and H. Yang. Hybrid top-down and bottom-up interprocedural analysis. In *Proc. PLDI*, pages 249–258, 2014.

[48] X. Zheng and R. Rugina. Demand-driven alias analysis for C. In *Proc. POPL*, pages 351–363, 2008.

## Appendix

**Theorem** 1. *Our formalism presented in Section 2 defines the same language family that TAGs define.*

In the following, we first present the formalism of Head Grammars [41], which is equivalent to the formalism of TAGs. Then, we prove that our formalism is equivalent to the formalism of Head Grammars, thus proving Theorem 1.

**Definition** 1. *(**Head Grammars** [41]) A head grammar $HG$ is a four tuple $G = (N, T, S, P)$, where $N$ is a finite set of non-terminals, $T$ is a finite set of terminals, $S \in N$ is the start symbol, and $P$ is a finite set of productions of the form $A \rightarrow f(\sigma_1, \sigma_2, ..., \sigma_n)$, where $A \in N, n \geq 1, f \in \{W, C_{1,n}, C_{2,n}, ..., C_{n,n}\}$, $\sigma_1, \sigma_2, ..., \sigma_n \in N \cup (T^* \times T^*)$, and $n = 2$ when $f = W$. $C_{i,n}$ and $W$ are defined as follows:*

- *$C_{i,n} : (T^* \times T^*)^n \rightarrow (T^* \times T^*)$ is a concatenation operation where $C_{i,n}(u_1 \uparrow v_1, ..., u_i \uparrow v_i, ..., u_n \uparrow v_n) = u_1 v_1 ... u_i \uparrow v_i ... u_n v_n$*
- *$W : (T^* \times T^*)^2 \rightarrow (T^* \times T^*)$ is the wrapping operation where $W(u_1 \uparrow v_1, u_2 \uparrow v_2) = u_1 u_2 \uparrow v_2 v_1$*

The language defined by $HG$ is $\{\mu\nu \in T^* | S \Rightarrow \mu \uparrow \nu\}$. Non-terminals in a Head Grammar are actually equivalent to second-order non-terminals in our formalism; and there is an implicit de-pairing operation on the start symbol to form a string in the language defined by the Head Grammar.

We transform Theorem 1 into the following two lemmas:

**Lemma** 1. *(**Backward Subsumption**) The language family defined by our formalism can be defined by the Head Grammars.*

**Lemma** 2. *(**Forward Subsumption**) The language family defined by the Head Grammars can be defined by our formalism.*

**Proof** (*Lemma 1*). We show that all the production rules in our formalism can be expressed by the rules in Head Grammars:

*Adjoining operator*. For any two string pairs $\mathbb{A}$ and $\mathbb{B}$ in the form $\alpha \circ \beta$ and $\gamma \circ \delta$, $\Cap(\mathbb{A}, \mathbb{B}) = \alpha\gamma \circ \delta\beta$. This can be exactly expressed by the $W$ operator in Head Grammars, since $W(\alpha \uparrow \beta, \gamma \uparrow \delta) = \alpha\gamma \uparrow \delta\beta$[8].

*Extended concatenation operators*. For a string pair in the form of $\alpha \circ \beta$ and a string in the form of $\gamma$, all the four extended concatenation operators can be expressed using the $W$ or $C_{i,n}$ operator in Head Grammars:

- ${\lhd}\!\cap(\alpha \circ \beta, \gamma) = \gamma\alpha \circ \beta$. This can be expressed by $C_{2,2}(\epsilon \uparrow \gamma, \alpha \uparrow \beta)$, which will produce $\epsilon\gamma\alpha \uparrow \beta$, and finally $\gamma\alpha \uparrow \beta$.
- ${\rhd}\!\cap(\alpha \circ \beta, \gamma) = \alpha\gamma \circ \beta$. This can be expressed by $W(\alpha \uparrow \beta, \gamma \uparrow \epsilon)$, which will produce $\alpha\gamma \uparrow \epsilon\beta$, and finally $\alpha\gamma \uparrow \beta$.
- $\cap\!{\lhd}(\alpha \circ \beta, \gamma) = \alpha \circ \gamma\beta$. This can be expressed by $W(\alpha \uparrow \beta, \epsilon \uparrow \gamma)$, which will produce $\alpha\epsilon \uparrow \gamma\beta$, and finally $\alpha \uparrow \gamma\beta$.
- $\cap\!{\rhd}(\alpha \circ \beta, \gamma) = \alpha \circ \beta\gamma$. This can be expressed by $C_{1,2}(\alpha \uparrow \beta, \epsilon \uparrow \gamma)$, which will produce $\alpha \uparrow \beta\epsilon\gamma$, and finally $\alpha \uparrow \beta\gamma$.

*Concatenation operator*. Although the formalism of Head Grammars contains only our second-order non-terminals, it can simulate the traditional concatenation operator as follows. We can use a non-terminal in Head Grammars representing $\alpha \uparrow \epsilon$ to simulate a non-terminal in CFGs (i.e., a first-order non-terminal in our formalism). Then the $W$ operator serves as the traditional concatenation operator for two such non-terminals.

*Pairing operator*. Let $A$ and $B$ be simulated by $\alpha \uparrow \epsilon$ and $\beta \uparrow \epsilon$, respectively. We can simulate $\oplus(A, B)$ as $C_{1,2}(\alpha \uparrow \epsilon, \beta \uparrow \epsilon)$.

*De-pairing operator*. In Head Grammars, there is actually an implicit de-pairing operator on the start symbol. Our formalism allows a first-order non-terminal de-paired from a second-order non-terminal to concatenate with other second-order non-terminals. The $C_{i,n}$ operator can simulate this situation. For example, de-pairing $\alpha \circ \beta$ can be expressed by $C_{2,2}(\alpha \uparrow \beta, \epsilon \uparrow \epsilon)$ since it will produce $\alpha\beta \uparrow \epsilon$. Note that we can use the $C_{i,n}$ operator together with $\epsilon{\uparrow}\epsilon$ and the $W$ operator to manipulate the concatenation position. For example, $W(\alpha{\uparrow}\beta, C_{2,2}(\gamma \uparrow \delta, \epsilon \uparrow \epsilon))$ results in $\alpha\gamma\delta \uparrow \beta$.

Therefore, all the production rules in our formalism can be expressed by the formalism of Head Grammars. □

**Proof** (*Lemma 2*). We further show that all the production rules in Head Grammars can be expressed by our formalism.

*$W$ operator*. As shown above, the $W$ operator in Head Grammars is equivalent to our adjoining operator $\Cap$, thus can be expressed by our formalism.

*$C_{i,n}$ operator*. We apply mathematical induction on $n$ ($n \geq 1$), and $i$ can be arbitrary integer within the range $[1, n]$.

- Case-1: $n = 1$, $i$ can only be 1:
  - $i = 1$: $C_{1,1}(u_1 \uparrow v_1) = u_1 \uparrow v_1$. This is the identity production rule and is trivially supported by our formalism.
- Case-2: $n = 2$, $i$ can be 1 or 2:
  - $i = 1$: $C_{1,2}(u_1 \uparrow v_1, u_2 \uparrow v_2) = u_1 \uparrow v_1 u_2 v_2$. This can be expressed by our formalism as: $\cap\!{\rhd}(u_1 \circ v_1, \ominus(u_2 \circ v_2))$.
  - $i = 2$: $C_{2,2}(u_1 \uparrow v_1, u_2 \uparrow v_2) = u_1 v_1 u_2 \uparrow v_2$. This can be expressed by our formalism as: ${\lhd}\!\cap(u_2 \circ v_2, \ominus(u_1 \circ v_1))$.
- Now we assume $C_{i,n}$ can be expressed by our formalism when $n = k$ ($k \geq 1$) for any $i \in [1, k]$, then for $n = k + 1$ and $i = i'$, $i' \in [1, k + 1]$:

$$\begin{aligned} & C_{i',k+1}(u_1 \uparrow v_1, ..., u_{i'} \uparrow v_{i'}, ..., u_{k+1} \uparrow v_{k+1}) \\ = \; & u_1 v_1 ... u_{i'} \uparrow v_{i'} ... u_{k+1} v_{k+1} \\ = \; & C_{2,2}(u_1 \uparrow v_1, C_{i'-1,k}(u_2 \uparrow v_2, ..., u_{i'} \uparrow v_{i'}, ..., u_{k+1} \\ & \uparrow v_{k+1})) \end{aligned}$$

According to Case-2, $C_{2,2}$ can be expressed by our formalism. In addition, $i' - 1$ is less than or equal to $k$. Then, according to our inductive assumption, $C_{i'-1,k}$ can also be expressed by our formalism. Thus, $C_{i,k+1}$ can be expressed by our formalism.

Based on mathematical induction, $C_{i,n}(n \geq 1, 1 \leq i \leq n)$ can be expressed by our formalism. □

[8] Note that the $\uparrow$ operator in Head Grammars is equivalent to our $\circ$ operator.

# Faster Algorithms for Algebraic Path Properties in Recursive State Machines with Constant Treewidth *

Krishnendu Chatterjee
Rasmus Ibsen-Jensen
Andreas Pavlogiannis
IST Austria (Institute of Science and Technology Austria) Klosterneuburg, Austria
{krish.chat, ribsen, pavlogiannis}@ist.ac.at

Prateesh Goyal
IIT Bombay (Indian Institute of Technology Bombay)
Mumbai, India
prateesh@iitb.ac.in

## Abstract

Interprocedural analysis is at the heart of numerous applications in programming languages, such as alias analysis, constant propagation, etc. Recursive state machines (RSMs) are standard models for interprocedural analysis. We consider a general framework with RSMs where the transitions are labeled from a semiring, and path properties are algebraic with semiring operations. RSMs with algebraic path properties can model interprocedural dataflow analysis problems, the shortest path problem, the most probable path problem, etc. The traditional algorithms for interprocedural analysis focus on path properties where the starting point is *fixed* as the entry point of a specific method. In this work, we consider possible multiple queries as required in many applications such as in alias analysis. The study of multiple queries allows us to bring in a very important algorithmic distinction between the resource usage of the *one-time* preprocessing vs for *each individual* query. The second aspect that we consider is that the control flow graphs for most programs have constant treewidth.

Our main contributions are simple and implementable algorithms that support multiple queries for algebraic path properties for RSMs that have constant treewidth. Our theoretical results show that our algorithms have small additional one-time preprocessing, but can answer subsequent queries significantly faster as compared to the current best-known solutions for several important problems, such as interprocedural reachability and shortest path. We provide a prototype implementation for interprocedural reachability and intraprocedural shortest path that gives a significant speed-up on several benchmarks.

***Categories and Subject Descriptors*** F.3.2 [*Logics and Meanings of Programs*]: Semantics of Programming Languages—Program Analysis

* This work has been supported by the Austrian Science Foundation (FWF) under the NFN RiSE (S11405), FWF Grant P23499-N23, ERC Start grant (279307: Graph Games), and Microsoft faculty fellows award.


*POPL '15*, January 15–17, 2015, Mumbai, India.

ACM 978-1-4503-3300-9/15/01... $15.00.
http://dx.doi.org/10.1145/2676726.2676979

***Keywords*** Interprocedural analysis, Constant treewidth graphs, Dataflow analysis, Reachability and shortest path.

## 1. Introduction

*Interprocedural analysis and RSMs.* Interprocedural analysis is one of the classic algorithmic problem in programming languages which is at the heart of numerous applications, ranging from alias analysis, to data dependencies (modification and reference side effect), to constant propagation, to live and use analysis [11, 14, 19, 22, 23, 29, 30, 32, 33, 36, 40, 45]. In seminal works [36, 40] it was shown that a large class of interprocedural dataflow analysis problems can be solved in polynomial time. A standard model for interprocedural analysis is *recursive state machines (RSMs)* [2] (aka *supergraph* in [36]). A RSM is a formal model for control flow graphs of programs with recursion. We consider RSMs that consist of component state machines (CSMs), one for each method that has a unique entry and unique exit, and each CSM contains boxes which are labeled as CSMs that allows calls to other methods.

*Algebraic path properties.* To specify properties of traces of a RSM we consider a very general framework, where edges of the RSM are labeled from a partially complete semiring (which subsumes bounded and finite distributive semirings), and we refer to the labels of the edges as weights. For a given path, the weight of the path is the semiring product of the weights on the edges of the path, and to choose among different paths we use the semiring plus operator. For example, (i) with Boolean semiring (with semiring product as AND, and semiring plus as OR) we can express the reachability property; (ii) with tropical semiring (with real-edge weights, semiring product as standard sum, and semiring plus as minimum) we can express the shortest path property; and (iii) with Viterbi semiring (with probability value on edges, semiring product as standard multiplication and semiring plus as maximum) we can express the most probable path property. The algebraic path properties expressed in our framework subsumes the IFDS/IDE frameworks [36, 40] which consider finite semirings and meet over all paths as the semiring plus operator. Since IFDS/IDE are subsumed in our framework, the large and important class of dataflow analysis problems that can be expressed in IFDS/IDE frameworks can also be expressed in our framework.

*Two important aspects.* In the traditional algorithms for interprocedural analysis, the starting point is typically *fixed* as the entry point of a specific method. In graph theoretic parlance, graph algorithms can consider two types of queries: (i) a *pair query* that given nodes $u$ and $v$ (called $(u, v)$-pair query) asks for the algebraic path property from $u$ to $v$; and (ii) a *single-source* query that given a node $u$ asks for the answer of $(u, v)$-pair queries for all nodes $v$. Thus the traditional algorithms for interprocedural analysis has focused on the answer for *one* single-source query. Moreover, the existing algorithms also consider that the input control flow graph is arbitrary, and do not exploit the fact that most control flow graphs satisfy several elegant structural properties. In this work, we consider two new aspects, namely, (i) *multiple* pair and single-source queries, and (ii) exploit the fact that typically the control flow graphs of programs satisfy an important structural property called the *constant treewidth property*. We describe in details the two aspects.

- *Multiple queries.* We first describe the relevance of pair and multiple pair queries, and then the significance of even multiple single-source queries. In alias analysis, the question is whether two pointers may point to the same object, which is by definition modeled as a question between a pair of nodes. Similarly, e.g., in constant propagation, given a function call, a relevant question is whether some variable remains constant within the entry and exit of the function (in general it can be between a pair of nodes of the program). This shows that the pair query problem, and the multiple pair queries are relevant in many applications. Finally, consider a run-time optimization scenario, where the goal is to decide whether a variable remains constant from *now on*, and this corresponds to a single-source query, where the starting point is the current execution point of the program. Thus multiple pair queries and multiple single-source queries are relevant for several important static analysis problems.
- *Constant treewidth.* A very well-known concept in graph theory is the notion of *treewidth* of a graph, which is a measure of how similar a graph is to a tree (a graph has treewidth 1 precisely if it is a tree) [39]. The treewidth of a graph is defined based on a *tree decomposition* of the graph [26], see Section 2 for a formal definition. Beyond the mathematical elegance of the treewidth property for graphs, there are many classes of graphs which arise in practice and have constant treewidth. The most important example is that the control flow graph for goto-free programs for many programming languages are of constant treewidth [42], and it was also shown in [24] that typically all Java programs have constant treewidth. An important property of constant-treewidth graphs is that the number of edges is at most a constant factor larger than the number of nodes. This has been considered in the comparison Tables 2 and 3.

*Our contributions.* In this work we consider RSMs where every CSM has constant treewidth, and the algorithmic question of answering multiple single-source and multiple pair queries, where each query is a *same-context* query (a same-context query starts and ends with an empty stack, see [16] for the significance of same-context queries). In the analysis of multiple queries, there is a very important algorithmic distinction between *one-time* preprocessing (denoted as the preprocessing time), and the work done for each individual query (denoted as the query time). There are two endpoints in the spectrum of tradeoff between the preprocessing and query resources that can be obtained by using the classical algorithms for one single-source query, namely, (i) the *complete preprocessing*, and (ii) the *no preprocessing*. In complete preprocessing, the single-source answer is precomputed with every node as the starting point (for example, in graph reachability this corresponds to computing the all-pairs reachability problem with the classical BFS/DFS algorithm [17], or with fast matrix multiplication [21]). In no preprocessing, there is no preprocessing done, and the algorithm for one single-source query is used on demand for each individual query. We consider various other possible tradeoffs in preprocessing vs query time. Our main contributions are as follows:

1. *(General result).* Since we consider arbitrary semirings (i.e., not restricted to finite semirings) we consider the stack height bounded problem, where the height of the stack is bounded by a parameter $h$. While in general for arbitrary semirings there does not exist a bound on the stack height, if the semiring contains subsets of a finite universe $D$, and the semiring plus operator is intersection or union, then solving the problem with sufficiently large bound on the stack height is equivalent to solving the problem without any restriction on stack height. Our main result is an algorithm where the one-time preprocessing phase requires $O(n \cdot \log n + h \cdot b \cdot \log n)$ semiring operations, and then each subsequent bounded stack height pair query can be answered in constant number of semiring operations, where $n$ is the number of nodes of the RSM and $b$ the number of boxes (see Table 1 and Theorem 3). If we specialize our result to the IFDS/IDE setting with finite semirings from a finite universe of distributive functions $2^D \to 2^D$, and meet over all paths as the semiring plus operator, then we obtain the results shown in Table 2 (Corollary 1). For example, our approach with a factor of $O(\log n)$ overhead for one-time preprocessing, as compared no preprocessing, can answer subsequent pair queries by a factor of $O(n \cdot |D|)$ faster. An important feature of our algorithms is that they are simple and implementable.
2. *(Reachability and shortest path).* We now discuss the significance of our result for the very important special cases of reachability and shortest path.
   - *(Reachability).* The result for reachability with full preprocessing, no preprocessing, and the various tradeoff that can be obtained by our approach is obtained from Table 2 by $|D| = 1$. For example for pair queries, full preprocessing requires quadratic time and space (for all-pairs reachability computation) and answers individual queries in constant time; no preprocessing requires linear time and space for individual queries; whereas with our approach (i) with almost-linear ($O(n \cdot \log n)$) preprocessing time and space we can answer individual queries in constant time, which is a significant (from quadratic to almost-linear) improvement over full preprocessing; or (ii) with linear space and almost-linear preprocessing time we can answer queries in logarithmic time, which is a huge (from linear to logarithmic) improvement over no preprocessing. For example, if we consider $O(n)$ pair queries, then both full preprocessing and no preprocessing in total require quadratic time, whereas our approach in total requires $O(n \cdot \log n + n \cdot \log n) = O(n \cdot \log n)$ time.
   - *(Shortest path).* We now consider the problem of shortest path, where the current best-known algorithm is for pushdown graphs [37, 38] and we are not aware of any better bounds for RSMs (that have unique entries and exits). The algorithm of [37] is a polynomial-time algorithm of degree four, and the full preprocessing requires $O(n^5)$ time and quadratic space, and can answer single-source (resp. pair) queries in linear (resp. constant time); whereas the no preprocessing requires $O(n^4)$ time and linear space for both single-source and pair queries. In contrast, we show that (i) with almost-quadratic ($O(n^2 \cdot \log n)$) preprocessing time and almost-linear space, we can answer single-source (resp. pair) queries in linear (resp. constant) time; or (i) with almost-quadratic preprocessing and linear space, we can answer single-source (resp. pair) queries in linear (resp. logarithmic) time. Thus our approach provides a significant theoretical improvement over the existing approaches.

   There are two facts that are responsible for our improvement, the first is that we consider that each CSM of the RSM has constant treewidth, and the second is the tradeoff of one-time preprocessing and individual queries. Also note that our results apply only to same-context queries.
3. *(Experimental results).* Besides the theoretical improvements, we demonstrate the effectiveness of our approach on several well-known benchmarks from programming languages. We use the tool for computing tree decompositions from [44], and all benchmarks of our experimental results have small treewidth. We have implemented our algorithms for reachabil-

| | Preprocessing time | Space | Single source query | Pair query | Reference |
|---|---|---|---|---|---|
| Our | $O(\log n \cdot (n + h \cdot b))$ | $O(n \cdot \log n)$ | $O(n)$ | $O(1)$ | Theorem 3 |
| Results | $O(\log n \cdot (n + h \cdot b))$ | $O(n)$ | $O(\log n)$ | $O(n)$ | Theorem 3 |

Table 1: Interprocedural same-context algebraic path problem on RSMs with $b$ boxes and constant treewidth, for stack height $h$.

| | Preprocessing time | Space | Single source query | Pair query | Reference |
|---|---|---|---|---|---|
| IDE/IFDS (complete preprocessing) | $O(n^2 \cdot \lvert D\rvert^3)$ | $O(n^2 \cdot \lvert D\rvert)$ | $O(\lvert D\rvert)$ | $O(n \cdot \lvert D\rvert)$ | [36, 40] |
| IDE/IFDS (no preprocessing) | - | $O(n \cdot \lvert D\rvert)$ | $O(n \cdot \lvert D\rvert^3)$ | $O(n \cdot \lvert D\rvert^3)$ | [36, 40] |
| Our | $O(\lvert D\rvert^2 \cdot \log n \cdot (n + b \cdot \lvert D\rvert))$ | $O(n \cdot \log n \cdot \lvert D\rvert^2)$ | $O(n \cdot \lvert D\rvert^2)$ | $O(\lvert D\rvert^2)$ | Corollary 1 |
| Results | $O(n \cdot \lvert D\rvert^2 + \log n \cdot (b \cdot \lvert D\rvert^3 + n))$ | $O(n \cdot \lvert D\rvert^2)$ | $O(n \cdot \lvert D\rvert^2)$ | $O(\log n \cdot \lvert D\rvert^2)$ | Corollary 1 |

Table 2: Interprocedural same-context algebraic path problem on RSMs with $b$ boxes and constant treewidth, where the semiring is over the subset of $|D|$ elements and the plus operator is the meet operator of the IFDS framework. The special case of reachability is obtained when $|D| = 1$.

| | Preprocessing time | Space | Single-source query | Pair query | Reference |
|---|---|---|---|---|---|
| GPR (complete preprocessing) | $O(n^5)$ | $O(n^2)$ | $O(n)$ | $O(1)$ | [37, 38] |
| GPR (no preprocessing) | - | $O(n)$ | $O(n^4)$ | $O(n^4)$ | [37, 38] |
| Our | $O(n^2 \cdot \log n)$ | $O(n \cdot \log n)$ | $O(n)$ | $O(1)$ | Corollary 2 |
| Results | $O(n^2 \cdot \log n)$ | $O(n)$ | $O(n)$ | $O(\log n)$ | Corollary 2 |

Table 3: Interprocedural same-context shortest path for RSMs with constant treewidth.

ity (both intraprocedural and interprocedural) and shortest paths (only intraprocedural), and compare their performance against complete and no preprocessing approaches for same-context queries. Our experimental results show that our approach obtains a significant improvement over the existing approaches (of complete and no preprocessing).

*Technical contribution.* Our main technical contribution is a dynamic algorithm (also referred to as incremental algorithm in graph algorithm literature) that given a graph with constant treewidth, after a preprocessing phase of $O(n \cdot \log n)$ semiring operations supports (1) changing the label of an edge with $O(\log n)$ semiring operations; and (2) answering pair queries with $O(\log n)$ semiring operations; and (3) answering single-source queries with $O(n)$ semiring operations. These results are presented in Theorem 2.

*Nice byproduct.* Several previous works such as [27] have stated the importance and asked for the development of data structures and analysis techniques to support dynamic updates. Though our main results are for the problem where the RSM is given and fixed, our main technical contribution is a dynamic algorithm that can also be used in other applications to support dynamic updates, and is thus also of independent interest.

### 1.1 Related Work

In this section we compare our work with several related work from interprocedural analysis as well as for constant treewidth property.

*Interprocedural analysis.* Interprocedural analysis is a classic algorithmic problem in static analysis and several diverse applications have been studied in the literature [11, 19, 22, 23, 29, 30, 32, 36, 40]. Our work is most closely related to the IFDS/IDE frameworks introduced in seminal works [36, 40]. In both IFDS/IDE framework the semiring is finite, and they study the algorithmic question of solving one single-source query. While in our framework the semiring is not necessarily finite, we consider the stack height bounded problem. We also consider the multiple pair and single-source, same-context queries, and the additional restriction that RSMs have constant treewidth. Our general result specialized to finite semirings (where the stack height bounded problem coincides with the general problem) improves the existing best known algorithms for the IFDS/IDE framework where the RSMs have constant treewidth. For example, the shortest path problem cannot be expressed in the IFDS/IDE framework [37], but can be expressed in the GPR framework [37, 38]. The GPR framework considers the more general problem of weighted pushdown graphs, whereas we show that with the restriction to constant treewidth RSMs the bounds for the best-known algorithm can be significantly improved. Finally, several works such as [27] ask for on-demand interprocedural analysis and algorithms to support dynamic updates, and our main technical contributions are algorithms to support dynamic updates in interprocedural analysis.

*Recursive state machines (RSMs).* Recursive state machines, which in general are equivalent to pushdown graphs, have been studied as a formal model for interprocedural analysis [2]. However, in comparison to pushdown graphs, RSMs are a more convenient formalism for interprocedural analysis. Games on recursive state machines with modular strategies have been considered in [3, 13], and subcubic algorithm for general RSMs with reachability has been shown in [15]. We focus on RSMs with unique entries and exits and with the restriction that the components have constant tree width. RSMs with unique entries and exits are less expressive than pushdown graphs, but remain a very natural model for efficient interprocedural analysis [36, 40].

*Treewidth of graphs.* The notion of treewidth for graphs as an elegant mathematical tool to analyze graphs was introduced in [39]. The significance of constant treewidth in graph theory is huge mainly because several problems on graphs become complexity-wise easier. Given a tree decomposition of a graph with low treewidth $t$, many NP-complete problems for arbitrary graphs can be solved in time polynomial in the size of the graph, but exponential in $t$ [4, 5, 8–10]. Even for problems that can be solved in polynomial time, faster algorithms can be obtained for low treewidth graphs, for example, for the distance problem [16]. The constant-treewidth property of graphs has also been used in the context of logic: Monadic Second Order (MSO) logic is a very expressive logic, and a celebrated result of [18] showed that for constant-treewidth graphs the decision questions for MSO can be solved in polynomial time; and the result of [20] shows that this can even be achieved in deterministic log-space. Dynamic algorithms for the special case of 2-treewidth graphs has been considered in [7] and extended to various tradeoffs by [25]; and [31] shows how to maintain the strongly connected component decomposition under edge deletions for constant treewidth graphs. However, none of these works consider RSMs or interprocedural analysis. Various other models (such as probabilistic models of Markov decision processes and games played on graphs for synthesis) with the constant-treewidth restriction have also been considered [12, 34]. The problem of computing a balanced tree decomposition for a constant treewidth graph was considered in [35], and we use this algorithm in our preprocessing phase. More importantly, in the context of programming languages, it was shown by [42] that the control flow graph for goto-free programs for many programming languages have constant treewidth. This theoretical result was subsequently followed up in several practical approaches, and it was shown in [24] that though in theory Java programs might not have constant treewidth, in practice Java programs do have constant treewidth. We also use the existing tree-decomposition tool developed by [44] in our experimental results.

## 2. Definitions

We will in this section give definitions related to semirings, graphs, and recursive state machines.

### 2.1 Semirings

**Definition 1** (Semirings). We consider partially complete *semirings* $(\Sigma, \oplus, \otimes, \overline{\mathbf{0}}, \overline{\mathbf{1}})$ where $\Sigma$ is a countable set, $\oplus$ and $\otimes$ are binary operators on $\Sigma$, and $\overline{\mathbf{0}}, \overline{\mathbf{1}} \in \Sigma$, and the following properties hold:

1. $\oplus$ is associative, commutative, and $\overline{\mathbf{0}}$ is the neutral element,
2. $\otimes$ is associative, and $\overline{\mathbf{1}}$ is the neutral element,
3. $\otimes$ distributes over $\oplus$,
4. $\oplus$ is infinitely associative,
5. $\otimes$ infinitely distributes over $\oplus$,
6. $\overline{\mathbf{0}}$ absorbs in multiplication, i.e., $\forall a \in \Sigma : a \otimes \overline{\mathbf{0}} = \overline{\mathbf{0}}$.

Additionally, we consider that semirings are equipped with a *closure* operator $^*$, such that $\forall s \in \Sigma : \ s^* = \overline{\mathbf{1}} \oplus (s \otimes s^*) = \overline{\mathbf{1}} \oplus (s^* \otimes s)$.

### 2.2 Graphs and tree decomposition

**Definition 2** (Graphs and weighted paths). Let $G = (V, E)$ be a finite directed graph where $V$ is a set of $n$ nodes and $E \subseteq V \times V$ is an edge relation of $m$ edges, along with a weight function $\mathsf{wt} : E \to \Sigma$ that assigns to each edge of $G$ an element from $\Sigma$. A path $P : u \rightsquigarrow v$ is a sequence of edges $(e_1, \ldots, e_k)$ and each $e_i = (x_i, y_i)$ is such that $x_1 = u$, $y_k = v$, and for all $1 \leq i \leq k-1$ we have $y_i = x_{i+1}$. The length of $P$ is $k - 1$. A path $P$ is *simple* if no node repeats in the path (i.e., it does not contain a cycle). A single node is by itself a 0-length path. Given a path $P = (e_1, \ldots, e_k)$, the weight of $P$ is $\otimes(P) = \bigotimes(\mathsf{wt}(e_1), \ldots, \mathsf{wt}(e_k))$ if $|P| \geq 1$ else $\otimes(P) = \overline{\mathbf{1}}$. Given nodes $u, v \in V$, the distance $d(u, v)$ is defined as $d(u,v) = \bigoplus_{P: u \rightsquigarrow v} \otimes(P)$, and $d(u, v) = \overline{\mathbf{0}}$ if no such $P$ exists.

**Definition 3** (Tree decomposition and treewidth [10, 39]). Given a graph $G = (V, E)$, a *tree-decomposition* $\mathrm{Tree}(G) = (V_T, E_T)$ is a tree such that the following conditions hold:

1. $V_T = \{B_0, \ldots, B_{n'-1} : \text{for all } 0 \leq i \leq n'-1, B_i \subseteq V\}$ and $\bigcup_{B_i \in V_T} B_i = V$.
2. For all $(u, v) \in E$ there exists $B_i \in V_T$ such that $u, v \in B_i$.
3. For all $i, j, k$ such that there exist paths $B_i \rightsquigarrow B_k$ and $B_k \rightsquigarrow B_j$ in $\mathrm{Tree}(G)$, we have $B_i \cap B_j \subseteq B_k$.

The sets $B_i$ which are nodes in $V_T$ are called bags. The *width* of a tree-decomposition $\mathrm{Tree}(G)$ is the size of the largest bag minus 1 and the *treewidth* of $G$ is the width of a minimum-width tree decomposition of $G$. It follows from the definition that if $G$ has constant treewidth, then $m = O(n)$.

**Example 1** (Graph and tree decomposition). The treewidth of a graph $G$ is an intuitive measure which represents the proximity of $G$ to a tree, though $G$ itself not a tree. The treewidth of $G$ is 1 precisely if $G$ is itself a tree [39]. Consider an example graph and its tree decomposition shown in Figure 1. It is straightforward to verify that all the three conditions of tree decomposition are met. Each node in the tree is a bag, and labeled by the set of nodes it contains. Since each bag contains at most three nodes, the tree decomposition by definition has treewidth 2.

*Intuitive meaning of tree decomposition.* In words, the tree-decomposition $\mathrm{Tree}(G)$ is a tree where every node (bag) is subset of nodes of $G$, such that: (1) every vertex in $G$ belongs to some bag; (2) every edge in $G$ also belongs to some bag; and (3) for every node $v$ of $G$, for every subpath in $\mathrm{Tree}(G)$, if $v$ appears in the endpoints of the path, then it must appear all along the path.

**Separator property.** Given a graph $G$ and its tree decomposition $\mathrm{Tree}(G)$, note that for each bag $B$ in $\mathrm{Tree}(G)$, if we remove the set of nodes in the bag, then the graph splits into possibly multiple components (i.e., each bag is a separator for the graph). In other words, every bag acts as a *separator* of the graph.

**Notations for tree decomposition.** Let $G$ be a graph, $T = \mathrm{Tree}(G)$, and $B_0$ be the root of $T$. Denote with $\mathsf{Lv}(B_i)$ the depth of $B_i$ in $T$, with $\mathsf{Lv}(B_0) = 0$. For $u \in V$, we say that a bag $B$ *introduces* $u$ if $B$ is the bag with the smallest level among all bags that contain $u$, i.e., $B_u = \arg\min_{B \in V_T:\, u \in B} \mathsf{Lv}(B)$. By definition, there is exactly one bag introducing each node $u$. We often write $B_u$ for the bag that introduces the node $u$, and denote with $\mathsf{Lv}(u) = \mathsf{Lv}(B_u)$. Finally, we denote with $B_{(u,v)}$ the bag of the highest level that introduces one of $u, v$. A tree-decomposition $\mathrm{Tree}(G)$ is *semi-nice* if $\mathrm{Tree}(G)$ is a binary tree, and every bag introduces at most one node.

**Example 2.** In the example of Figure 1, the bag $\{2, 8, 10\}$ is the root of $\mathrm{Tree}(G)$, the level of node 9 is $\mathsf{Lv}(9) = \mathsf{Lv}(\{8, 9, 10\}) = 1$, and the bag of the edge $(9, 1)$ is $B_{(9,1)} = \{1, 8, 9\}$.

**Theorem 1.** *(1) For every graph there exists a semi-nice tree decomposition that achieves the treewidth of G and uses $n' = O(n)$ bags [28]. (2) For constant treewidth graphs, a balanced tree decomposition can be obtained in $O(n \cdot \log n)$ time (i.e., every simple path $B_0 \rightsquigarrow B_i$ in $\mathrm{Tree}(G)$ has length $O(\log n)$) [35].*

**The algebraic path problem on graphs of constant treewidth.** Given $G = (V, E)$, a balanced, semi-nice tree-decomposition $\mathrm{Tree}(G)$ of $G$ with constant treewidth $t = O(1)$, a partially complete semiring $(\Sigma, \oplus, \otimes, \overline{\mathbf{0}}, \overline{\mathbf{1}})$, a weight function $\mathsf{wt} : E \to \Sigma$, the algebraic path problem on input $u, v \in V$, asks for the distance $d(u, v)$ from node $u$ to node $v$. In addition, we allow the weight function to change between successive queries. We measure the time complexity of our algorithms in number of operations, with each operation being either a basic machine operation, or an application of one of the operators of the semiring.

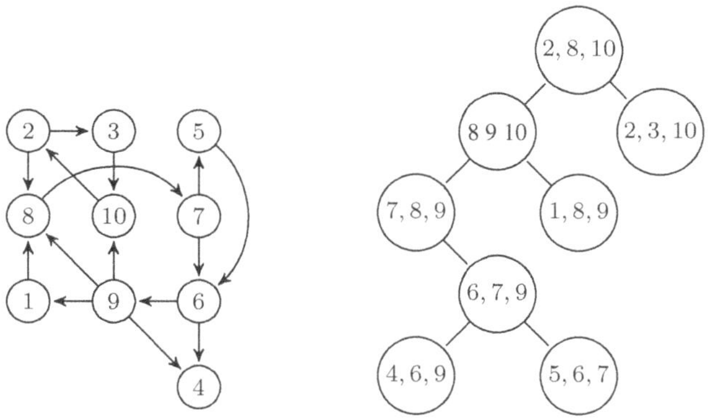


Figure 1: A graph $G$ with treewidth 2 (left) and a corresponding tree-decomposition $\text{Tree}(G)$ (right).

### 2.3 Recursive state machines

**Definition 4** (RSMs and CSMs). A *single-entry single-exit recursive state machine* (RSM from now on) over an alphabet $\Sigma$, as defined in [2], consists of a set $\{A_1, A_2, \ldots, A_k\}$, such that for each $1 \leq i \leq k$, the *component state machine* (CSM) $A_i = (B_i, Y_i, V_i, E_i, \mathsf{wt}_i)$, where $V_i = N_i \cup \{En_i\} \cup \{Ex_i\} \cup C_i \cup R_i$, consists of:

- A set $B_i$ of *boxes*.
- A map $Y_i$, mapping each box in $B_i$ to an index in $\{1, 2, \ldots, k\}$. We say that a box $b \in B_i$ *corresponds* to the CSM with index $Y_i(b)$.
- A set $V_i$ of *nodes*, consisting of the union of the sets $N_i$, $\{En_i\}$, $\{Ex_i\}$, $C_i$ and $R_i$. The number $n_i$ is the size of $V_i$. Each of these sets, besides $V_i$, are w.l.o.g. assumed to be pairwise disjoint.
  - The set $N_i$ is the set of *internal nodes*.
  - The node $En_i$ is the *entry node*.
  - The node $Ex_i$ is the *exit node*.
  - The set $C_i$ is the set of *call nodes*. Each call node is a pair $(x, b)$, where $b$ is a box in $B_i$ and $x$ is the entry node $En_{Y_i(b)}$ of the corresponding CSM with index $Y_i(b)$.
  - The set $R_i$ is the set of *return nodes*. Each return node is a pair $(y, b)$, where $b$ is a box in $B_i$ and $y$ is the exit node $Ex_{Y_i(b)}$ of the corresponding CSM with index $Y_i(b)$.
- A set $E_i$ of *internal edges*. Each edge is a pair in $(N_i \cup \{En_i\} \cup R_i) \times (N_i \cup \{Ex_i\} \cup C_i)$.
- A map $\mathsf{wt}_i$, mapping each edge in $E_i$ to a label in $\Sigma$.

**Definition 5** (Control flow graph of CSMs and treewidth of RSMs). Given a RSM $A = \{A_1, A_2, \ldots, A_k\}$, the *control flow graph* $G_i = (V_i, E'_i)$ for CSM $A_i$ consists of $V_i$ as the set of vertices and $E'_i$ as the set of edges, where $E'_i$ consists of the edges $E_i$ of $A_i$ and for each box $b$, each call node $(v, b)$ of that box (i.e. for $v = En_{Y_i(b)}$) has an edge to each return node $(v', b)$ of that box (i.e. for $v' = Ex_{Y_i(b)}$). We say that the RSM has *treewidth* $t$, if $t$ is the smallest integer such that for each index $1 \leq i \leq k$, the graph $G_i = (V_i, E'_i)$ has treewidth at most $t$. Programs are naturally represented as RSMs, where the control flow graph of each method of a program is represented as a CSM.

**Example 3** (RSM and tree decomposition). Figure 2 shows an example of a program for matrix multiplication consisting of two methods (one for vector multiplication invoked by the one for matrix multiplication). The corresponding control flow graphs, and their tree decompositions that achieve treewidth 2 are also shown in the figure.

**Box sequences.** For a sequence $L$ of boxes and a box $b$, we denote with $L \circ b$ the concatenation of $L$ and $b$. Also, $\emptyset$ is the empty sequence of boxes.

**Configurations and global edges.** A *configuration* of a RSM is a pair $(v, L)$, where $v$ is a node in $(N_i \cup \{En_i\} \cup R_i)$ and $L$ is a sequence of boxes. The *stack height* of a configuration $(v, L)$ is the number of boxes in the sequence $L$. The set of *global edges* $E$ are edges between configurations. The map $\mathsf{wt}$ maps each edge in $E$ to a label in $\Sigma$. We have that there is an edge between configuration $c_1 = (v_1, L_1)$, where $v_1 \in V_i$, and configuration $c_2 = (v_2, L_2)$ with label $\sigma = \mathsf{wt}(c_1, c_2)$ if and only if one of the following holds:

- **Internal edge:** We have that $v_2$ is an *internal* node in $N_i$ and each of the following (i) $L_1 = L_2$; and (ii) $(v_1, v_2) \in E_i$; and (iii) $\sigma = \mathsf{wt}_i((v_1, v_2))$.
- **Entry edge:** We have that $v_2$ is the *entry* node $En_{Y_i(b)}$, for some box $b$, and each of the following (i) $L_1 \circ b = L_2$; and (ii) $(v_1, (v_2, b)) \in E_i$; and (iii) $\sigma = \mathsf{wt}_i((v_1, (v_2, b)))$.
- **Return edge:** We have that $v_2 = (v, b)$ is a *return* node, for some exit node $v = Ex_i$ and some box $b$ and each of the following (i) $L_1 = L_2 \circ b$; and (ii) $(v_1, v) \in E_i$; and (iii) $\sigma = \mathsf{wt}_i((v_1, v))$.

Note that in a configuration $(v, L)$, the node $v$ cannot be $Ex_i$ or in $C_i$. In essence, the corresponding configuration is at the corresponding return node, instead of at the exit node, or corresponding entry node, instead of at the call node, respectively.

**Execution paths.** An *execution path* is a sequence of configurations and labels $P = \langle c_1, \sigma_1, c_2, \sigma_2 \ldots, \sigma_{\ell-1}, c_\ell \rangle$, such that for each integer $i$ where $1 \leq i \leq \ell - 1$, we have that $(c_i, c_{i+1}) \in E$ and $\sigma_i = \mathsf{wt}(c_i, c_{i+1})$. We call $\ell$ the *length* of $P$. Also, we say that the stack height of a execution path is the maximum stack height of a configuration in the execution path. For a pair of configurations $c, c'$, the set $c \rightsquigarrow c'$, is the set of execution paths $\langle c_1, \sigma_1, c_2, \sigma_2 \ldots, \sigma_{\ell-1}, c_\ell \rangle$, for any $\ell$, where $c = c_1$ and $c' = c_\ell$. For a set $S$ of execution paths, the set $B(S, h) \subseteq S$ is the subset of execution paths, with stack height at most $h$. Given a partially complete semiring $(\Sigma, \oplus, \otimes, \overline{\mathbf{0}}, \overline{\mathbf{1}})$, the *distance* of a execution path $P = \langle c_1, \sigma_1, c_2, \sigma_2 \ldots, \sigma_{\ell-1}, c_\ell \rangle$ is $\otimes(P) = \bigotimes(\sigma_1, \ldots, \sigma_{\ell-1})$ (the empty product is $\overline{\mathbf{1}}$). Given configurations $c, c'$, the *configuration distance* $d(c, c')$ is defined as $d(c, c') = \bigoplus_{P: c \rightsquigarrow c'} \otimes(P)$ (the empty sum is $\overline{\mathbf{0}}$). Also, given configurations $c, c'$ and a stack height $h$, where $c'$ is $h$-reachable from $c$, the *bounded height configuration distance* $d(c, c', h)$ is defined as $d(c, c', h) = \bigoplus_{P: B(c \rightsquigarrow c', h)} \otimes(P)$. Note that the above definition of execution paths only allows for so called *valid* paths [36, 40], i.e., paths that fully respect the calling contexts of an execution.

**The algebraic path problem on RSMs of constant tree-width.** Given (i) a RSM $A = \{A_1, A_2, \ldots, A_k\}$; and (ii) for each $1 \leq i \leq k$ a balanced, semi-nice tree-decomposition $\text{Tree}(A_i) := \text{Tree}((V_i, E'_i))$ with constant treewidth at most $t = O(1)$; and (iii) a partially complete semiring $(\Sigma, \oplus, \otimes, \overline{\mathbf{0}}, \overline{\mathbf{1}})$, the *algebraic path problem* on input nodes $u, v$, asks for the distance $d((u, \emptyset), (v, \emptyset))$, i.e. the distance between the configurations with the empty stack. Similarly, also given a height $h$, the *bounded height algebraic path problem* on input configurations $c, c'$, asks for the distance $d((u, \emptyset), (v, \emptyset), h)$. When it is clear from the context, we will write $d(u, v)$ to refer to the algebraic path problem of nodes $u$ and $v$ on RSMs.

*Remark* 1. Note that the empty stack restriction implies that $u$ and $v$ are nodes of the same CSM. However, the paths from $u$ to $v$ are, in general, interprocedural, and thus involve invocations and returns from other CSMs. This formulation has been used before in terms of *same-context* [15] and *same-level* [36] realizable paths and has several applications in program analysis, e.g. by capturing balanced parenthesis-like properties used in alias analysis [41].

### 2.4 Problems

We note that a wide range of interprocedural problems can be formulated as bounded height algebraic path problems.

1. *Reachability* i.e., given nodes $u$, $v$ in the same CSM, is there a path from $u$ to $v$? The problem can be formulated on the boolean semiring $(\{\mathsf{True}, \mathsf{False}\}, \vee, \wedge, \mathsf{False}, \mathsf{True})$.
2. *Shortest path* i.e., given a weight function $\mathsf{wt} : E \rightarrow \mathbb{R}_{\geq 0}$ and nodes $u$, $v$ in the same CSM, what is the weight of the minimum-weight path from $u$ to $v$? The problem can be formulated on the tropical semiring $(\mathbb{R}_{\geq 0} \cup \{\infty\}, \min, +, \infty, 0)$.
3. *Most probable path* i.e., given a probability function $P : E \rightarrow [0,1]$ and nodes $u$, $v$ in the same CSM, what is the probability of the highest-probable path from $u$ to $v$? The problem can be formulated on the Viterbi semiring $([0,1], \max, \cdot, 0, 1)$.
4. The class of *interprocedural, finite, distributive, subset (IFDS)* problems defined in [36]. Given a finite domain $D$, a universe of flow functions $F$ containing distributive functions $f : 2^D \rightarrow 2^D$, a weight function $\mathsf{wt} : E \rightarrow F$ associates each edge with a flow function. The weight of an interprocedural path is then defined as the composition $\circ$ of the flow functions along its edges, and the IFDS problem given nodes $u, v$ asks for the meet $\sqcap$ (union or intersection) of the weights of all $u \rightsquigarrow v$ paths. The problem can be formulated on the meet-composition semiring $(F, \sqcap, \circ, \emptyset, I)$, where $I$ is the identity function.
5. The class of *interprocedural distributive environment (IDE)* problems defined in [40]. This class of dataflow problems is an extension to IFDS, with the difference that the flow functions (called environment transformers) map elements from the finite domain $D$ to values in an infinite set (e.g., of the form $f : D \rightarrow \mathbb{N}$). An environment transformer is denoted as $f[d \rightarrow \ell]$, meaning that the element $d \in D$ is mapped to value $\ell$, while the mapping of all other elements remains unchanged. The problem can be formulated on the meet-environment-transformer semiring $(F, \sqcap, \circ, \emptyset, I)$, where $I$ is the identity environment transformer, leaving every map unchanged.

Note that if we assume that the set of weights of all interprocedural paths in the system is finite, then the size of this set bounds the stack height $h$. Additionally, several problems can be formulated as algebraic path problems in which bounding the stack height can be viewed as an approximation to them (e.g., shortest path with negative interprocedural cycles, or probability of reaching a node $v$ from a node $u$).

## 3. Dynamic Algorithms for Preprocess, Update and Query

In the current section we present algorithms that take as input a constant treewidth graph $G$ and a balanced, semi-nice tree-decomposition $\mathrm{Tree}(G)$ (recall Theorem 1), and achieve the following tasks:

1. Preprocessing the tree-decomposition $\mathrm{Tree}(G)$ of a graph $G$ to answer algebraic path queries fast.
2. Updating the preprocessed $\mathrm{Tree}(G)$ upon change of the weight $\mathsf{wt}(u,v)$ of an edge $(u,v)$.
3. Querying the preprocessed $\mathrm{Tree}(G)$ to retrieve the distance $d(u,v)$ of any pair of nodes $u, v$.

In the following section we use the results of this section in order to preprocess RSMs fast, with the purpose of answering interprocedural same-context algebraic path queries fast. Refer to Example 4 of Section 4 for an illustration on how these algorithms are executed on an RSM.

First we establish the following lemma which captures the main intuition behind tree decompositions, namely, that bags $B$ of the tree-decomposition $\mathrm{Tree}(G)$ are separators between nodes of $G$ that belong to disconnected components of $\mathrm{Tree}(G)$ once $B$ is removed.

**Lemma 1** (Separator property). *Consider a graph $G = (V,E)$ and a tree-decomposition* $\mathrm{Tree}(G)$. *Let $u, v \in V$, and $P' : B_1, B_2, \dots, B_j$ be the unique path in $T$ such that $u \in B_1$ and $v \in B_j$. For each $i \in \{1, \dots, j-1\}$ and for each path $P : u \rightsquigarrow v$, there exists a node $x_i \in (B_i \cap B_{i+1} \cap P)$.*

*Proof.* Fix a number $i \in \{1, \dots, j-1\}$. We argue that for each path $P : u \rightsquigarrow v$, there exists a node $x_i \in (B_i \cap B_{i+1} \cap P)$. We construct a tree $\mathrm{Tree}'(G)$, which is similar to $\mathrm{Tree}(G)$ except that instead of having an edge between bag $B_i$ and bag $B_{i+1}$, there is a new bag $B$, that contains the nodes in $B_i \cap B_{i+1}$, and there is an edge between $B_i$ and $B$ and one between $B$ and $B_{i+1}$. It is easy to see that $\mathrm{Tree}'(G)$ forms a tree decomposition of $G$. Let $\mathcal{C}_1$, $\mathcal{C}_2$ be the two components of $\mathrm{Tree}(G)$ separated be $B$, and w.l.o.g. $u \in \mathcal{C}_1$ and $v \in \mathcal{C}_2$. It follows by the definition of tree decomposition that $B$ is a separator of $\bigcup_{B' \in \mathcal{C}_1} B'$ and $\bigcup_{B' \in \mathcal{C}_2} B'$. Hence, each path $u \rightsquigarrow v$ must go through some node $x_i$ in $B$, and by construction $x_i \in B_i \cap B_{i+1}$. □

**Intuition and U-shaped paths.** A central concept in our algorithms is that of U-shaped paths. Given a bag $B$ and nodes $u, v \in B$ we say that a path $P : u \rightsquigarrow v$ is U-shaped in $B$, if one of the following conditions hold:

1. Either $|P| > 1$ and for all intermediate nodes $w \in P$, we have $\mathsf{Lv}(w) \geq \mathsf{Lv}(B)$,
2. or $|P| \leq 1$ and $B$ is $B_u$ or $B_v$.

Informally, given a bag $B$, a U-shaped path in $B$ is a path that traverses intermediate nodes that are introduced in $B$ and its descendants in $\mathrm{Tree}(G)$. In the following we present three algorithms for (i) preprocessing a tree decomposition, (ii) updating the data structures of the preprocessing upon a weight change $\mathsf{wt}(u,v)$ of an edge $(u,v)$, and (iii) querying for the distance $d(u,v)$ for any pair of nodes $u, v$. The intuition behind the overall approach is that for every path $P : u \rightsquigarrow v$ and $z = \mathsf{argmin}_{x \in P} \mathsf{Lv}(x)$, the path $P$ can be decomposed to paths $P_1 : u \rightsquigarrow z$ and $P_2 : z \rightsquigarrow v$. By Lemma 1, if we consider the path $P' : B_u \rightsquigarrow B_z$ and any bag $B_i \in P'$, we can find nodes $x, y \in B_i \cap P_1$ (not necessarily distinct). Then $P_1$ is decomposed to a sequence of U-shaped paths $P_1^i$, one for each such $B_i$, and the weight of $P_1$ can be written as the $\otimes$-product of the weights of $P_1^i$, i.e., $\otimes(P_1) = \bigotimes(\otimes(P_1^i))$. Similar observation holds for $P_2$. Hence, the task of preprocessing and updating is to summarize in each $B_i$ the weights of all such U-shaped paths between all pairs of nodes appearing in $B_i$. To answer the query, the algorithm traverses upwards the tree $\mathrm{Tree}(G)$ from $B_u$ and $B_v$, and combines the summarized paths to obtain the weights of all such paths $P_1$ and $P_2$, and eventually $P$, such that $\otimes(P) = d(u,v)$.

**Informal description of preprocessing.** Algorithm $\mathsf{Preprocess}$ associates with each bag $B$ a *local distance* map $\mathsf{LD}_B : B \times B \rightarrow \Sigma$. Upon a weight change, algorithm $\mathsf{Update}$ updates the local distance map of some bags. It will hold that after the preprocessing and each subsequent update, $\mathsf{LD}_B(u,v) = \bigoplus_{P:u \rightsquigarrow v}\{\otimes(P)\}$, where all $P$ are U-shaped paths in $B$. Given this guarantee, we later present an algorithm for answering $(u,v)$ queries with $d(u,v)$, the distance from $u$ to $v$. Algorithm $\mathsf{Preprocess}$ is a dynamic programming algorithm. It traverses $\mathrm{Tree}(G)$ bottom-up, and for a currently examined bag $B$ introducing a node $x$, it calls the method

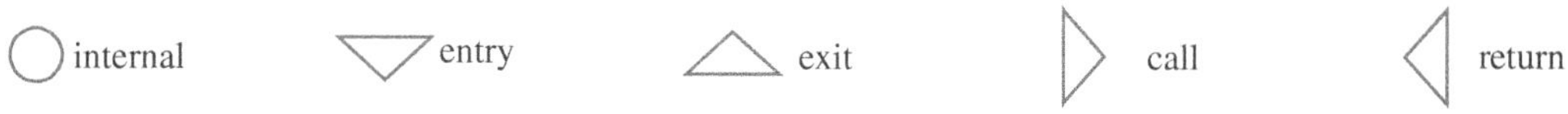


**Method:** dot_vector

**Input**: $x, y \in \mathbb{R}^n$
**Output**: The dot product $x^\top y$

```
1 result ← 0
2 for i ← 1 to n do
3     z ← x[i] · y[i]
4     result ← result + z
5 end
6 return result
```

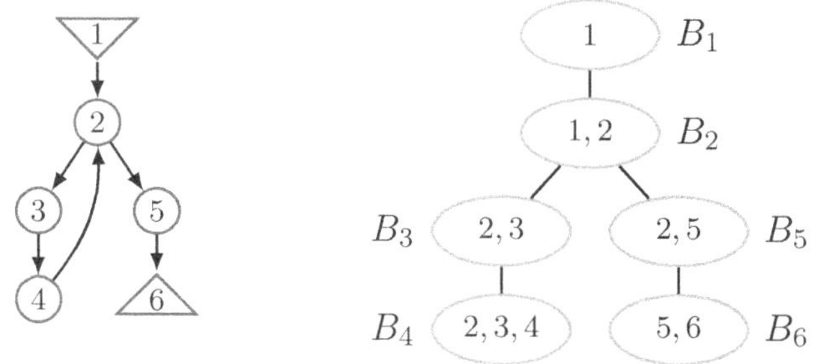


**Method:** dot_matrix

**Input**: $A \in \mathbb{R}^{n\times k}, B \in \mathbb{R}^{k\times m}$
**Output**: The dot product $A \times B$

```
1 C ← zero matrix of size n × m
2 for i ← 1 to n do
3     for j ← 1 to m do
4         Call dot_vector(A[i, :], B[:, j])
5         C[i, j] ← the value returned by the call of line 4
6     end
7 end
8 return C
```

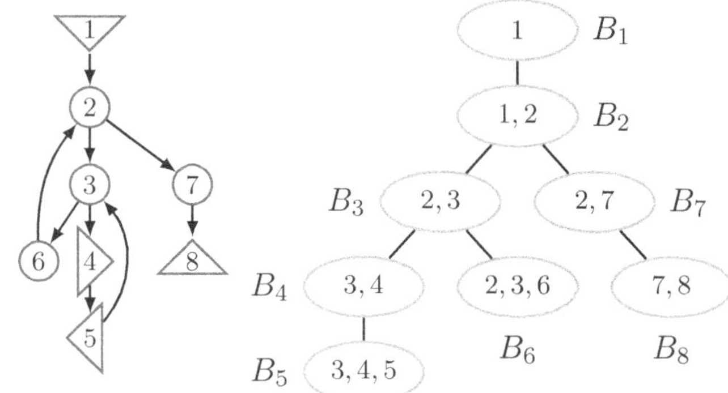


Figure 2: Example of a program consisting of two methods, their control flow graphs $G_i = (V_i, E_i')$ where nodes correspond to line numbers, and the corresponding tree decompositions, each one achieving treewidth 2.

Merge to compute the local distance map $\mathsf{LD}_B$. In turn, Merge computes $\mathsf{LD}_B$ depending only on the local distance maps $\mathsf{LD}_{B_i}$ of the children $\{B_i\}$ of $B$, and uses the closure operator $*$ to capture possibly unbdounded traversals of cycles whose smallest-level node is $x$. See Method 1 and Algorithm 2 for a formal description.

**Method 1:** Merge

**Input**: A bag $B_x$ with children $\{B_i\}$
**Output**: A local distance map $\mathsf{LD}_{B_x}$

1 Assign $\mathsf{wt}'(x,x) \leftarrow \left(\bigotimes\{\mathsf{LD}_{B_1}(x,x)^*, \dots, \mathsf{LD}_{B_j}(x,x)^*\}\right)^*$
2 **foreach** $u \in B_x$ *with* $u \neq x$ **do**
3     Assign $\mathsf{wt}'(x,u) \leftarrow \bigoplus\{\mathsf{wt}(x,u), \mathsf{LD}_{B_1}(x,u), \dots, \mathsf{LD}_{B_j}(x,u)\}$
4     Assign $\mathsf{wt}'(u,x) \leftarrow \bigoplus\{\mathsf{wt}(u,x), \mathsf{LD}_{B_1}(u,x), \dots, \mathsf{LD}_{B_j}(u,x)\}$
5 **end**
6 **foreach** $u, v \in B_x$ **do**
7     Assign $\delta \leftarrow \bigotimes(\mathsf{wt}'(u,x), \mathsf{wt}'(x,x), \mathsf{wt}'(x,v))$
8     Assign $\mathsf{LD}_{B_x}(u,v) \leftarrow \bigoplus\{\delta, \mathsf{LD}_{B_1}(u,v), \dots, \mathsf{LD}_{B_j}(u,v)\}$
9 **end**

**Lemma 2.** *At the end of* Preprocess, *for every bag $B$ and nodes $u, v \in B$, we have $\mathsf{LD}_B(u,v) = \bigoplus_{P:u\rightsquigarrow v}\{\otimes(P)\}$, where all $P$ are* U*-shaped paths in $B$.*

*Proof.* The proof is by induction on the parents. Initially, $B$ is a leaf introducing some node $x$, thus each such path $P$ can only go through $x$, and hence will be captured by Preprocess. Now assume that the algorithm examines a bag $B$, and by the induction hypothesis the statement is true for all $\{B_i\}$ children of $B_x$. The correctness follows easily if $B$ does not introduce any node, since every such $P$ is a U-shaped path in some child $B_i$ of $B$. Now consider that $B$ introduces some node $x$, and any U-shaped path $P' : u \rightsquigarrow v$ that additionally visits $x$, and decompose it to paths

**Algorithm 2:** Preprocess

**Input**: A tree-decomposition $\mathrm{Tree}(G) = (V_T, E_T)$
**Output**: A local distance map $\mathsf{LD}_B$ for each bag $B \in V_T$

1 Traverse $\mathrm{Tree}(G)$ bottom up and examine each bag $B$ with children $\{B_i\}$
2 **if** *$B$ introduces some node $x$* **then**
3     Assign $\mathsf{LD}_B \leftarrow$ Merge on $B$
4 **else**
5     **foreach** $u, v \in B$ **do**
6         Assign $\mathsf{LD}_B(u,v) \leftarrow \bigoplus\{\mathsf{LD}_{B_1}(u,v), \dots, \mathsf{LD}_{B_j}(u,v)\}$
7     **end**
8 **end**

$P_1 : u \rightsquigarrow x$, $P_2 : x \rightsquigarrow x$ and $P_3 : x \rightsquigarrow v$, such that $x$ is not an intermediate node in either $P_1$ or $P_3$, and we have by distributivity:

$$\bigoplus_{P'} \otimes(P') = \bigoplus_{P_1,P_2,P_3} \bigotimes(\otimes(P_1), \otimes(P_2), \otimes(P_3))$$

$$= \bigotimes\left(\bigoplus_{P_1}\otimes(P_1), \bigoplus_{P_2}\otimes(P_2), \bigoplus_{P_3}\otimes(P_3)\right)$$

Note that $P_1$ and $P_3$ are also U-shaped in one of the children bags $B_i$ of $B_x$, hence by the induction hypothesis in lines 3 and 2 of Merge we have $\mathsf{wt}'(u,x) = \bigoplus_{P_1}\otimes(P_1)$ and $\mathsf{wt}'(x,v) = \bigoplus_{P_3}\otimes(P_3)$. Also, by decomposing $P_2$ into a (possibly unbounded) sequence of paths $P_2^i : x \rightsquigarrow x$ such that $x$ is not intermediate node in any $P_2^i$, we get that each such $P_2^i$ is a U-shaped path in some child $B_{l_i}$ of $B$, and we have by distributivity and the induction hypothesis

$$\bigoplus_{P_2} \otimes(P_2) = \bigoplus_{P_2^1, P_2^2, \dots} \bigotimes \{\otimes(P_2^1), \otimes(P_2^2), \dots\}$$

$$= \bigoplus_{B_{l_1}, B_{l_2}, \dots} \bigotimes \left\{ \bigoplus_{P_2^1} \otimes(P_2^1), \bigoplus_{P_2^2} \otimes(P_2^2), \dots \right\}$$

$$= \bigoplus_{B_{l_1}, B_{l_2}, \dots} \bigotimes \left\{ \mathsf{LD}_{B_{l_1}}(x, x), \mathsf{LD}_{B_{l_2}}(x, x), \dots \right\}$$

and the last expression equals $\mathsf{wt}'(x, x)$ from line 1 of Merge. The above conclude that in line 6 of Merge we have $\delta = \bigoplus_{P'} \otimes(P')$.

Finally, each U-shaped path $P : u \rightsquigarrow v$ in $B$ either visits $x$, or is U-shaped in one of the children $B_i$. Hence after line 8 of Method Merge has run on $B$, for all $u, v \in B$ we have that $\mathsf{LD}_B(u, v) = \bigoplus_{P : u \rightsquigarrow v} \otimes(P)$ where all paths $P$ are U-shaped in $B$. The desired results follows. □

**Lemma 3.** Preprocess *requires* $O(n)$ *semiring operations.*

*Proof.* Merge requires $O(t^2) = O(1)$ operations, and Preprocess calls Merge at most once for each bag, hence requiring $O(n)$ operations. □

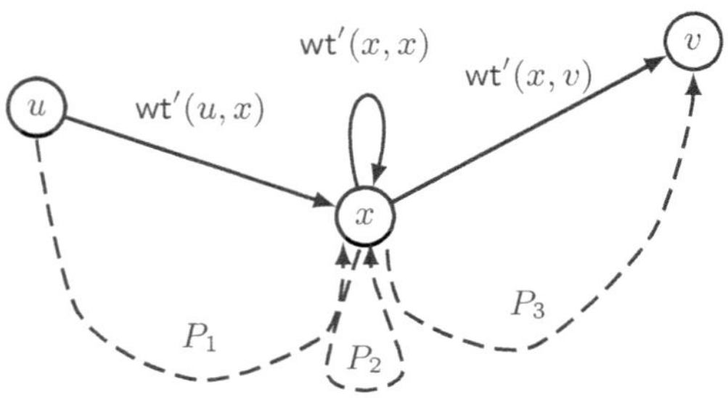


Figure 3: Illustration of the inductive argument of Preprocess.

**Informal description of updating.** Algorithm Update is called whenever the weight $\mathsf{wt}(x, y)$ of an edge of $G$ has changed. Given the guarantee of Lemma 2, after Update has run on an edge update $\mathsf{wt}(x, y)$, it restores the property that for each bag $B$ we have $\mathsf{LD}_B(u, v) = \bigoplus_{P : u \rightsquigarrow v} \{\otimes(P)\}$, where all $P$ are U-shaped paths in $B$. See Algorithm 3 for a formal description.

---

**Algorithm 3:** Update

---

**Input**: An edge $(x, y)$ with new weight $\mathsf{wt}(x, y)$
**Output**: A local distance map $\mathsf{LD}_B$ for each bag $B \in V_T$

Assign $B \leftarrow B_{(x,y)}$, the highest bag containing the edge $(x, y)$
**repeat**
    Call Merge on $B$
    Assign $B \leftarrow B'$ where $B'$ is the parent of $B$
**until** $\mathsf{Lv}(B) = 0$

---

**Lemma 4.** *At the end of each run of* Update, *for every bag* $B$ *and nodes* $u, v \in B$, *we have* $\mathsf{LD}_B(u, v) = \bigoplus_{P : u \rightsquigarrow v} \{\otimes(P)\}$, *where all* $P$ *are* U*-shaped paths in* $B$.

*Proof.* First, by the definition of a U-shaped path $P$ in $B$ it follows that the statement holds for all bags not processed by Update, since for any such bag $B$ and U-shaped path $P$ in $B$, the path $P$ cannot traverse $(u, v)$. For the remaining bags, the proof follows an induction on the parents updated by Update, similar to that of Lemma 2. □

**Lemma 5.** Update *requires* $O(\log n)$ *operations per update.*

*Proof.* Merge requires $O(t^2) = O(1)$ operations, and Update calls Merge once for each bag in the path from $B_{(u,v)}$ to the root. Recall that the height of Tree$(G)$ is $O(\log n)$ (Theorem 1), and the result follows. □

**Informal description of querying.** Algorithm Query answers a $(u, v)$ query with the distance $d(u, v)$ from $u$ to $v$. Because of Lemma 1, every path $P : u \rightsquigarrow v$ is guaranteed to go through the least common ancestor (LCA) $B_L$ of $B_u$ and $B_v$, and possibly some of the ancestors $B$ of $B_L$. Given this fact, algorithm Query uses the procedure Climb to climb up the tree from $B_u$ and $B_v$ until it reaches $B_L$ and then the root of Tree$(G)$. For each encountered bag $B$ along the way, it computes maps $\delta_u(w) = \bigoplus_{P_1} \{\otimes(P_1)\}$, and $\delta_v(w) = \bigoplus_{P_2} \{\otimes(P_2)\}$ where all $P_1 : u \rightsquigarrow w$ and $P_2 : w \rightsquigarrow v$ are such that each intermediate node $y$ in them has been introduced in $B$. This guarantees that for path $P$ such that $d(u, v) = \otimes(P)$, when Query examines the bag $B_z$ introducing $z = \mathsf{argmin}_{x \in P} \mathsf{Lv}(x)$, it will be $d(u, v) = \bigotimes(\delta_u(z), \delta_v(z))$. Hence, for Query it suffices to maintain a current best solution $\delta$, and update it with $\delta \leftarrow \bigoplus\{\delta, \bigotimes(\delta_u(x), \delta_v(x))\}$ every time it examines a bag $B$ introducing some node $x$. Figure 4 presents a pictorial illustration of Query and its correctness. Method 4 presents the Climb procedure which, given a current distance map of a node $\delta$, a current bag $B$ and a flag Up, updates $\delta$ with the distance to (if Up $=$ True), or from (if Up $=$ False) each node in $B$. See Method 4 and Algorithm 5 for a formal description.

---

**Method 4:** Climb

---

**Input**: A bag $B$, a map $\delta$, a flag Up
**Output**: A new map $\delta$

Remove from $\delta$ all $w \notin B$
Assign $\delta(w) \leftarrow \overline{0}$ for all $w \in B$ and not in $\delta$
**if** *B introduces node x* **then**
    **if** Up **then** /* Climbing up */
        Update $\delta$ with $\delta(w) \leftarrow \bigoplus\{\delta(w), \bigotimes(\delta(x), \mathsf{LD}_B(x, w))\}$
    **else** /* Climbing down */
        Update $\delta$ with $\delta(w) \leftarrow \bigoplus\{\delta(w), \bigotimes(\delta(x), \mathsf{LD}_B(w, x))\}$
    **end**
**return** $\delta$

---

**Lemma 6.** Query *returns* $\delta = d(u, v)$.

*Proof.* Let $P : u \rightsquigarrow v$ be any path from $u$ to $v$, and $z = \mathsf{argmin}_{x \in P} \mathsf{Lv}(x)$ the lowest level node in $P$. Decompose $P$ to $P_1 : u \rightsquigarrow z$, $P_2 : z \rightsquigarrow v$, and it follows that $\otimes(P) = \bigotimes(\otimes(P_1), \otimes(P_2))$. We argue that when Query examines $B_z$, it will be $\delta_u(z) = \bigoplus_{P_1} \otimes(P_1)$ and $\bigoplus_{P_2} \delta_v(z) = \otimes(P_2)$. We only focus on the $\delta_u(z)$ case here, as the $\delta_v(z)$ is similar. We argue inductively that when algorithm Query examines a bag $B_x$, for all $w \in B_x$ we have $\delta_u(w) = \bigoplus_{P'} \{\otimes(P')\}$, where all $P'$ are such that for each intermediate node $y$ we have $\mathsf{Lv}(y) \geq \mathsf{Lv}(x)$. Initially (line 1), it is $x = u$, $B_x = B_u$, and every such $P'$ is U-shaped in $B_u$, hence $\mathsf{LD}_{B_x}(x, w) = \bigoplus_{P'} \{\otimes(P')\}$ and $\delta_u(w) = \bigoplus_{P'} \{\otimes(P')\}$. Now consider that Query examines a bag $B_x$ (Lines 7 and 18) and the claim holds for $B_{x'}$ a descendant of $B_x$ previously examined by Query. If $x$ does not occur in $P'$, it is a consequence of Lemma 1 that $w \in B_{x'}$, hence by the induction hypothesis, $P'$ has been considered by Query. Otherwise, $x$ occurs in $P'$ and decompose $P'$ to $P'_1$, $P'_2$, such that $P'_1$ ends with the first occurrence of $x$ in $P'$, and it is $\otimes(P) = \bigotimes(\otimes(P'_1), \otimes(P'_2))$. Note that $P'_2$ is a U-shaped path in $B_x$, hence $\mathsf{LD}_{B_x}(x, w) = \bigoplus_{P'_2} \{\otimes(P'_2)\}$. Finally, as a consequence of Lemma 1, we have that $x \in B_{x'}$, and by the induction hypothesis, $\delta_u(x) = \bigoplus_{P'_1} \{\otimes(P'_1)\}$. It follows that af-

**Algorithm 5:** Query

**Input**: A pair $(u, v)$
**Output**: The distance $d(u, v)$ from $u$ to $v$

Initialize map $\delta_u$ with $\delta_u(w) \leftarrow \mathsf{LD}_{B_u}(u, w)$
Initialize map $\delta_v$ with $\delta_v(w) \leftarrow \mathsf{LD}_{B_v}(w, v)$
Assign $B_L \leftarrow$ the LCA of $B_u$, $B_v$ in Tree$(G)$
Assign $B \leftarrow B_u$
**repeat**
    Assign $B \leftarrow B'$ where $B'$ is the parent of $B$
    Call Climb on $B$ and $\delta_u$ with flag Up set to True
**until** $B = B_L$
Assign $B \leftarrow B_v$
**repeat**
    Assign $B \leftarrow B'$ where $B'$ is the parent of $B$
    Call Climb on $B$ and $\delta_v$ with flag Up set to False
**until** $B = B_L$
Assign $B \leftarrow B_L$
Assign $\delta \leftarrow \bigoplus_{x \in B_L} \otimes(\delta_u(x), \delta_v(x))$
**repeat**
    Assign $B \leftarrow B'$ where $B'$ is the parent of $B$
    Call Climb on $B$ and $\delta_u$ with flag Up set to True
    Call Climb on $B$ and $\delta_v$ with flag Up set to False
    **if** *$B$ introduces node $x$* **then**
        Assign $\delta \leftarrow \bigoplus\{\delta, \bigotimes(\delta_u(x), \delta_v(x))\}$
**until** $\mathsf{Lv}(B) = 0$
**return** $\delta$

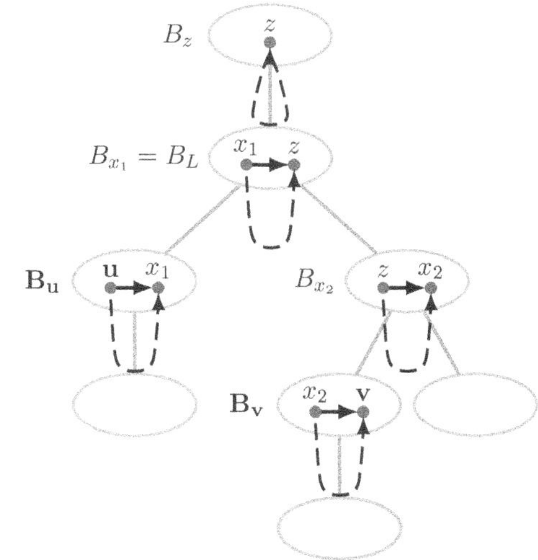


Figure 4: Illustration of Query in computing the distance $d(u, v) = \otimes(P)$ as a sequence of U-shaped paths, whose weight has been captured in the local distance map of each bag. When $B_z$ is examined, with $z = \mathsf{argmin}_{x \in P} \mathsf{Lv}(x)$, it will be $\delta_u(z) = d(u, z)$ and $\delta_v(z) = d(z, v)$, and hence by distributivity $d(u, v) = \bigotimes(\delta_u(z), \delta_v(z))$.

ter Query processes $B_x$, it will be $\delta_u(w) = \bigoplus_{P'}\{\otimes(P')\}$. By the choice of $z$, when Query examines the bag $B_z$, it will be $\delta_u(z) = \bigoplus_{P_1}\{\otimes(P_1)\}$. A similar argument shows that at that point it will also be $\delta_v(z) = \bigoplus_{P_2}\{\otimes(P_2)\}$, hence at that point $\delta = \bigotimes(\otimes(P_1), \otimes(P_2)) = d(u, v)$. □

**Lemma 7.** Query *requires $O(\log n)$ semiring operations.*

*Proof.* Climb requires $O(t^2) = O(1)$ operations and Query calls Climb once for every bag in the paths from $B_u$ and $B_v$ to the root. Recall that the height of Tree$(G)$ is $O(\log n)$ (Theorem 1), and the result follows. □

We conclude the results of this section with the following theorem.

**Theorem 2.** *Consider a graph $G = (V, E)$ and a balanced, semi-nice tree-decomposition* Tree$(G)$ *of constant treewidth. The following assertions hold:*

1. Preprocess *requires $O(n)$ semiring operations;*
2. Update *requires $O(\log n)$ semiring operations per edge weight update; and*
3. Query *correctly answers distance queries in $O(\log n)$ semiring operations.*

**Witness paths.** Our algorithms so far have only been concerned with returning the distance $d(u, v)$ of the pair query $u, v$. When the semiring lacks the closure operator (i.e., for all $s \in \Sigma$ it is $s^* = \overline{\mathbf{1}}$), as in most problems e.g., reachability and shortest paths with positive weights, the distance from every $u$ to $v$ is realized by an acyclic path. Then, it is straightforward to also obtain a witness path, i.e., a path $P : u \rightsquigarrow v$ such that $\otimes(P) = d(u, v)$, with some minor additional preprocessing. Here we outline how.

Whenever Merge updates the local distance $\mathsf{LD}_B(u, v)$ between two nodes in a bag $B$, it does so by considering the distances to and from an intermediate node $x$. It suffices to remember that intermediate node for every such local distance. Then, the witness path to a local distance in $B$ can be obtained straightforwardly by a top-down computation on Tree$(G)$ starting from $B$. Recall that in essence, Query answers a distance query $u, v$ by combining several local distances along the paths $B_u \rightsquigarrow B_z$ and $B_z \rightsquigarrow B_v$, where $z$ is the node with the minimum level in a path $P : u \rightsquigarrow v$ such that $\otimes(P) = d(u, v)$. Since from every such local distance a witness sub-path $P_i$ can be obtained, $P$ is reconstructed by juxtaposition of all such $P_i$. Finally, this process costs $O(|P|)$ time.

## 4. Algorithms for Constant Treewidth RSMs

In this section we consider the bounded height algebraic path problem on RSMs of constant treewidth. That is, we consider (i) an RSM $A = \{A_1, A_2, \dots, A_k\}$, where $A_i$ consists of $n_i$ nodes and $b_i$ boxes; (ii) a partially complete semiring $(\Sigma, \oplus, \otimes, \overline{\mathbf{0}}, \overline{\mathbf{1}})$; and (iii) a maximum stack height $h$. Our task is to create a datastructure that after some preprocessing can answer queries of the form: Given a pair $((u, \emptyset), (v, \emptyset))$ of configurations compute $d((u, \emptyset), (v, \emptyset), h)$ (also recall Remark 1). For this purpose, we present the algorithm RSMDistance, which performs such preprocessing using a datastructure $\mathcal{D}$ consisting of the algorithms Preprocess, Update and Query of Section 3. At the end of RSMDistance it will hold that algebraic path pair queries in a CSM $A_i$ can be answered in $O(\log n_i)$ semiring operations. We later present some additional preprocessing which suffers a factor of $O(\log n_i)$ in the preprocessing space, but reduces the pair query time to constant.

**Algorithm** RSMDistance**.** Our algorithm RSMDistance can be viewed as a Bellman-Ford computation on the call graph of the RSM (i.e., a graph where every node corresponds to a CSM, and an edge connects two CSMs if one appears as a box in the other). Informally, RSMDistance consists of the following steps.

1. First, it preprocesses the control flow graphs $G_i = (V_i, E_i')$ of the CSMs $A_i$ using Preprocess of Section 3, where the weight function $\mathsf{wt}_i$ for each $G_i$ is extended such that $\mathsf{wt}_i((en, b), (ex, b)) = \overline{\mathbf{0}}$ for all pairs of call and return nodes to the same box $b$. This allows the computation of $d(u, v, 0)$ for

all pairs of nodes $(u, v)$, since no call can be made while still having zero stack height.

2. Then, iteratively for each $\ell$, where $0 \leq \ell \leq h-1$, given that we have a dynamic datastructure $\mathcal{D}$ (concretely, an instance of the dynamic algorithms Update and Query from Section 3) for computing $d(u, v, \ell)$, the algorithm does as follows: First, for each $G_i$ whose entry to exit distance $d(En_i, Ex_i)$ has changed from the last iteration and for each $G_j$ that contains a box pointing to $G_i$, it updates the call to return distance of the corresponding nodes, using Query.
3. Then, it obtains the entry to exit distance $d(En_j, Ex_j)$ to see if it was modified, and continues with the next iteration of $\ell + 1$.

See Algorithm 6 for a formal description.

---

**Algorithm 6:** RSMDistance

---

**Input**: A set of control flow graphs $\mathcal{G} = \{G_i\}_{1 \leq i \leq k}$, stack height $h$

1 **foreach** $G_i \in \mathcal{G}$ **do**
2     Construct the tree-decomposition $\mathrm{Tree}(G_i)$
3     Call Preprocess on $\mathrm{Tree}(G_i)$
4 **end**
5 distances $\leftarrow$ [Call Query on $(En_i, Ex_i)$ of $G_i]_{1 \leq i \leq k}$
6 modified $\leftarrow \{1, \dots, k\}$
7 **for** $\ell \leftarrow 0$ **to** $h-1$ **do**
8     modified′ $\leftarrow \emptyset$
9     **foreach** $i \in$ modified **do**
10         **foreach** $G_j$ *that contains boxes* $b_{j_1}, \dots, b_{j_l}$ *s.t.* $Y_j(b_{j_x}) = i$ **do**
11             Call Update on $G_j$ for the weight change wt$((en, b_{j_l}), (ex, b_{j_x})) \leftarrow$ distances$[i]$
12             Call Query on $(En_j, Ex_j)$
13             **if** $d(En_j, Ex_j) \neq$ distances$[j]$ **then**
14                 modified′ $\leftarrow$ modified′ $\cup \{j\}$
15                 distances$[j] \leftarrow d(En_j, Ex_j)$
16             **end**
17         **end**
18     modified $\leftarrow$ modified′
19 **end**

---

**Correctness and logarithmic pair query time.** The algorithm RSMDistance is described so that a proof by induction is straightforward for correctness. Initially, running the algorithm Preprocess from Section 3 on each of the graphs $G_i$ allows queries for the distances $d(u, v, 0)$ for all pairs of nodes $(u, v)$, since no method call can be made. Also, the induction follows directly since for every CSM $A_i$, updating the distance from call nodes $(en, b)$ to the corresponding return nodes $(ex, b)$ of every box $b$ that corresponds to a CSM $A_j$ whose distance $d(En_j, Ex_j)$ was changed in the last iteration $\ell$, ensures that the distance $d(u, v, \ell+1)$ of every pair of nodes $u, v$ in $A_i$ is computed correctly. This is also true for the special pair of nodes $En_i$, $Ex_i$, which feeds the next iteration of RSMDistance. Finally, RSMDistance requires $O(\sum_{i=1}^{k}(n_i \cdot \log n_i))$ time to construct a balanced tree decomposition (Theorem 1), $O(n)$ time to preprocess all $G_i$ initially, and $O(\sum_{i=1}^{k}(b_i \cdot \log n_i))$ to update all $G_i$ for one iteration of the loop of Line 4 (from Theorem 2). Hence, RSMDistance uses $O(\sum_{i=1}^{k}(n_i \cdot \log n_i + h \cdot b_i \cdot \log n_i))$ preprocessing semiring operations. Finally, it is easy to verify that all preprocessing is done in $O(n)$ space.

After the last iteration of algorithm RSMDistance, we have a datastructure $\mathcal{D}$ that occupies $O(n)$ space and answers distance queries $d(u, v, h)$ in $O(\log n_i)$ time, with $u, v \in V_i$, by calling Query from Theorem 3 for the distance $d(u, v)$ in $G_i$.

**Example 4.** We now present a small example of how RSMDistance is executed on the RSM of Figure 2 for the case of reachability. In this case, for any pair of nodes $(u, v)$, we have $d(u, v) =$ True iff $u$ reaches $v$. Table 4(a) illustrates how the local distance maps $\mathsf{LD}_{B_x}$ look for each bag $B_x$ of each of the CSMs of the two methods dot_vector and dot_matrix. Each column represents the local distance map of the corresponding bag $B_x$, and an entry $(u, v)$ means that $\mathsf{LD}_{B_x}(u, v) =$ True (i.e., $u$ reaches $v$). For brevity, in the table we hide self loops (i.e., entries of the form $(u, u)$) although they are stored by the algorithms. Initially, the stack height $\ell = 0$, and Preprocess is called for each graph (line 3). The new reachability relations discovered by Merge are shown in bold. Note that at this point we have wt$(4, 5) =$ False in method dot_matrix, as we do not know whether the call to method dot_vector actually returns. Afterwards, Query is called to discover the distance $d(1, 6)$ in method dot_vector (line 5). Table 4(b) shows the sequence in which Query examines the bags of the tree decomposition, and the distances $\delta_1$, $\delta_6$ and $\delta$ it maintains. When $B_2$ is examined, $\delta =$ True and hence at the end Query returns $\delta =$ True. Finally, since Query returns $\delta =$ True, the weight wt$(4, 5)$ between the call-return pair of nodes $(4, 5)$ in method dot_matrix is set to True. An execution of Update (line 11) with this update on the corresponding tree decomposition (Table 4(a) for $\ell = 1$) updates the entries $(4, 5)$ and $(4, 3)$ in $\mathsf{LD}_{B_5}$ of method dot_matrix (shown in bold). From this point, any same-context distance query can be answered in logarithmic time in the size of its CSM by further calls to Query.

**Linear single-source query time.** In order to handle single-source queries, some additional preprocessing is required. The basic idea is to use RSMDistance to process the graphs $G_i$, and then use additional preprocessing on each $G_i$ by applying existing algorithms for graphs with constant treewidth. For graphs with constant treewidth, an extension of Lemma 7 from [16] allows us to precompute the distance $d(u, v)$ for every pair of nodes $u, v \in V_i$ that appear in the same bag of $\mathrm{Tree}(G_i)$. The computation required is similar to Preprocess, with the difference that this time $\mathrm{Tree}(G_i)$ is traversed top-down instead of bottom-up. Additionally, for each examined bag $B$, a Floyd-Warshall algorithm is run in the graph $G_i$ induced by $B$, and all pairs of distances are updated. It follows from Lemma 7 of [16] that for constant treewidth, this step requires $O(n_i)$ time and space.

After all distances $d(u, v)$ have been computed for each $B$, it is straightforward to answer single-source queries from some node $u$ in linear time. The algorithm simply maintains a map $A : V_i \to \Sigma$, and initially $A(v) = d(u, v)$ for all $v \in B_u$, and $A(v) = \overline{\mathbf{0}}$ otherwise. Then, it traverses $\mathrm{Tree}(G_i)$ in a BFS manner starting at $B_u$, and for every encountered bag $B$ and $v \in B$, if $A(v) = \overline{\mathbf{0}}$, it sets $A(v) = \bigoplus_{z \in B} \bigotimes(A(z), d(z, v))$. For constant treewidth, this results in a constant number of semiring operations per bag, and hence $O(n_i)$ time in total.

**Constant pair query time.** After RSMDistance has returned, it is possible to further preprocess the graphs $G_i$ to reduce the pair query time to constant, while increasing the space by a factor of $\log n_i$. For constant treewidth, this can be obtained by adapting Theorem 10 from [16] to our setting, which in turn is based on a rather complicated algorithmic technique of [1]. We present a more intuitive, simpler and implementable approach that has a dynamic programming nature. In Section 5 we present some experimental results obtained by this approach.

Recall that the extra preprocessing for answering single-source queries in linear time consists in computing $d(u, v)$ for every pair of nodes $u, v$ that appear in the same bag, at no overhead. To handle pair queries in constant time, we further traverse each $\mathrm{Tree}(G_i)$ one last time, bottom-up, and for each node $u$ we store maps $F_u, T_u : V_i^{B_u} \to \Sigma$, where $V_i^{B_u}$ is the subset of $V_i$ of nodes that appear in $B_u$ and its descendants in $\mathrm{Tree}(G_i)$. The maps are such that $F_u(v) = d(u, v)$ and $T_u = d(v, u)$. Hence, $F_u$ stores

| | dot_vector | | | | | | dot_matrix | | | | | | | |
|---|---|---|---|---|---|---|---|---|---|---|---|---|---|---|
| $\ell$/LD$_{B_x}$ | $B_1$ | $B_2$ | $B_3$ | $B_4$ | $B_5$ | $B_6$ | $B_1$ | $B_2$ | $B_3$ | $B_4$ | $B_5$ | $B_6$ | $B_7$ | $B_8$ |
| $\ell = 0$<br>(Preprocess) | – | $(1,2)$ | $(2,3)$ | $(2,3)$<br>$(3,4)$<br>$(4,2)$<br>$\mathbf{(2,4)}$ | $(2,5)$ | $(5,6)$ | – | $(1,2)$ | $(2,3)$ | $(3,4)$ | $(3,4)$<br>$(5,3)$ | $(2,6)$<br>$(3,6)$<br>$(6,2)$<br>$\mathbf{(3,2)}$ | $(2,7)$ | $(7,8)$ |
| $\ell = 1$<br>(Update) | – | $(1,2)$ | $(2,3)$ | $(2,3)$<br>$(3,4)$<br>$(4,2)$<br>$(2,4)$ | $(2,5)$ | $(5,6)$ | – | $(1,2)$ | $(2,3)$ | $(3,4)$ | $(3,4)$<br>$(5,3)$<br>$\mathbf{(4,5)}$<br>$\mathbf{(4,3)}$ | $(2,6)$<br>$(3,6)$<br>$(6,2)$<br>$(3,2)$ | $(2,7)$ | $(7,8)$ |

(a)

| | dot_vector | | | |
|---|---|---|---|---|
| | $B_6$ | $B_5$ | $B_2$ | $B_1$ |
| Query<br>$d(1,6)$ | $\delta_6 = \{5,6\}$<br>–<br>– | $\delta_6 = \{2,5\}$<br>–<br>– | $\delta_6 = \{1,2\}$<br>$\delta_1 = \{1,2\}$<br>$\delta =$ True | $\delta_6 = \{1\}$<br>$\delta_1 = \{1\}$<br>$\delta =$ True |

(b)

Table 4: Illustration of RSMDistance on the tree decompositions of methods dot_vector and dot_matrix from Figure 2. Table (a) shows the local distance maps for each bag and stack height $\ell = 0, 1$. Table (b) shows how the distance query $d(1,6)$ in method dot_vector is handled.

the distances from $u$ to nodes in $V_i^{B_u}$, and $T_u$ stores the distances from nodes in $V_i^{B_u}$ to $u$. The maps are computed in a dynamic programming fashion, as follows:

1. Initially, the maps $F_u$ and $T_u$ are constructed for all $u$ that appear in a bag $B$ which is a leaf of Tree$(G_i)$. The information required has already been computed as part of the preprocessing for answering single-source queries. Then, Tree$(G_i)$ is traversed up, level by level.
2. When examining a bag $B$ such that the computation has been performed for all its children, for every node $u \in B$ and $v \in V_i^B$, we set $F_u(v) = \bigoplus_{z \in B} \bigotimes\{d(u,z), F_z(v)\}$, and similarly for $T_u = \bigoplus_{z \in B} \bigotimes\{d(z,u), T_z(v)\}$.

An application of Lemma 1 inductively on the levels processed by the algorithm can be used to show that when a bag $B$ is processed, for every node $u \in B$ and $v \in V_i^B$, we have $T_u(v) = \bigoplus_{P: v \rightsquigarrow u} \otimes(P)$ and $F_u(v) = \bigoplus_{P: u \rightsquigarrow v} \otimes(P)$. Finally, there are $O(n_i)$ semiring operations done at each level of Tree$(G_i)$, and since there are $O(\log n_i)$ levels, $O(n_i \cdot \log n_i)$ operations are required in total. Hence, the space used is also $O(n_i \cdot \log n_i)$. We furthermore preprocess Tree$(G_i)$ in linear time and space to answer LCA queries in constant time (note that since Tree$(G_i)$ is balanced, this is standard). To answer a pair query $u, v$, it suffices to first obtain the LCA $B$ of $B_u$ and $B_v$, and it follows from Lemma 1 that $d(u,v) = \bigoplus_{z \in B} \bigotimes\{T_z(u), F_z(v)\}$, which requires a constant number of semiring operations.

We conclude the results of this section with the following theorem. Afterwards, we obtain the results for the special cases of the IFDS/IDE framework, reachability and shortest path.

**Theorem 3.** *Fix the following input: (i) a constant treewidth RSM $A = \{A_1, A_2, \dots, A_k\}$, where $A_i$ consists of $n_i$ nodes and $b_i$ boxes; (ii) a partially complete semiring $(\Sigma, \oplus, \otimes, \overline{\mathbf{0}}, \overline{\mathbf{1}})$; and (iii) a maximum stack height $h$.* RSMDistance *uses $O(\sum_{i=1}^k (n_i \cdot \log n_i + h \cdot b_i \cdot \log n_i))$ preprocessing semiring operations and*

1. *Using $O(n)$ space it correctly answers same-context algebraic pair queries in $O(\log n_i)$, and same-context algebraic single-source queries in $O(n_i)$ semiring operations.*
2. *Using $O(\sum_{i=1}^k (n_i \cdot \log n_i))$ space, it correctly answers same-context algebraic pair queries in $O(1)$ semiring operations.*

**IFDS/IDE framework.** In the special case where the algebraic path problem belongs to the IFDS/IDE framework, we have a meet-composition semiring $(F, \sqcap, \circ, \emptyset, I)$, where $F$ is a set of distributive flow functions $2^D \rightarrow 2^D$, $D$ is a set of data facts, $\sqcap$ is the meet operator (either union or intersection), $\circ$ is the flow function composition operator, and $I$ is the identity flow function. For a fair comparison, the $\circ$ semiring operation does not induce a unit time cost, but instead a cost of $O(|D|)$ per data fact (as functions are represented as bipartite graphs [36]). Because the set $D$ is finite, and the meet operator is either union or intersection, it follows that the image of every data fact will be updated at most $|D|$ times. Then, line 7 of RSMDistance needs to change so that instead of $h$ iterations, the body of the loop is carried up to a fixpoint. The amortized cost per $G_i$ is then $b_i \cdot \log n_i \cdot |D|^3$ (as there are $|D|$ data facts), and we have the following corollary (also see Table 2).

**Corollary 1** (IFDS/IDE). *Fix the following input a (i) constant treewidth RSM $A = \{A_1, A_2, \dots, A_k\}$, where $A_i$ consists of $n_i$ nodes and $b_i$ boxes; and (ii) a meet-composition semiring $(F, \sqcap, \circ, \emptyset, I)$ where $F$ is a set of distributive flow functions $D \rightarrow D$, $\circ$ is the flow function composition operator and $\sqcap$ is the meet operator.*

1. *Algorithm* RSMDistance *uses $O(\sum_{i=1}^k (n_i \cdot |D|^2 + b_i \cdot \log n_i \cdot |D|^3 + n_i \cdot \log n_i))$ preprocessing time, $O(n \cdot |D|^2)$ space, and correctly answers same-context algebraic pair queries in $O(\log n_i \cdot |D|^2)$ time, and same-context algebraic single-source queries in $O(n_i \cdot |D|^2)$ time.*
2. *Algorithm* RSMDistance *uses $O(\sum_{i=1}^k (n_i \cdot \log n_i \cdot |D|^2 + b_i \cdot \log n_i \cdot |D|^3))$ preprocessing time, $O(|D|^2 \cdot \sum_{i=1}^k (n_i \cdot \log n_i))$ space, and correctly answers same-context algebraic pair queries in $O(|D|^2)$ time, and same-context algebraic single-source queries in $O(n_i \cdot |D|^2)$ time.*

**Reachability**. The special case of reachability is obtained by setting $|D| = 1$ in Corollary 1.

**Shortest paths.** The shortest path problem can be formulated on the tropical semiring $(\mathbb{R}_{\geq 0} \cup \{\infty\}, \min, +, \infty, 0)$. We consider that both semiring operators cost unit time (i.e., the weights occurring in the computation fit in a constant number of machine words). Because we consider non-negative weights, it follows that the distance between any pair of nodes is realized by a path that traverses every entry node at most once. Hence, we set $h = k$ in Theorem 3, and obtain the following corollary for shortest paths (also see Table 3).

**Corollary 2** (Shortest paths). *Fix the following input a (i) constant treewidth RSM $A = \{A_1, A_2, \ldots, A_k\}$, where $A_i$ consists of $n_i$ nodes and $b_i$ boxes; (ii) a tropical semiring $(\mathbb{R}_{\geq 0} \cup \{\infty\}, \min, +, \infty, 0)$.* RSMDistance *uses $O(\sum_{i=1}^{k}(n_i \cdot \log n_i + k \cdot b_i \cdot \log n_i))$ preprocessing time and:*

1. *Using $O(n)$ space, it correctly answers same-context shortest path pair queries in $O(\log n_i)$, and same-context shortest path single-source queries in $O(n_i)$ time.*
2. *Using $O(\sum_{i=1}^{k}(n_i \cdot \log n_i))$ space, it correctly answers same-context shortest path pair queries in $O(1)$ time.*

**Interprocedural witness paths.** As in the case of simple graphs from Section 3, we can retrieve a witness path for any distance $d(u, v, h)$ that is realized by acyclic interprocedural paths $P : (u, \emptyset) \rightsquigarrow (v, \emptyset)$, without affecting the stated complexities. The process is straightforward. Let $A_i$ contain the pair of nodes $u, v$ on which the query is asked. Initially, we obtain the witness intraprocedural path $P' : u \rightsquigarrow v$, as described in Section 3. Then, we proceed recursively to obtain a witness path $P_j$ between the entry $En_j$ and exit $Ex_j$ nodes of every CSM $A_j$ such that $P'$ contains an edge between a call node $(en, b)$ and a return node $(ex, b)$ with $Y_i(B) = j$. That is, we reconstruct a witness path for every call to a CSM whose weight has been summarized locally in $A_i$. This process constructs an interprocedural witness path $P : u \rightsquigarrow v$ such that $\otimes(P) = d(u, v)$ in $O(|P|)$ time.

## 5. Experimental Results

**Set up.** We have implemented our algorithms for linear-time single-source and constant-time pair queries presented in Section 4 and have tested them on graphs obtained from the DaCapo benchmark suit [6] that contains several, real-world Java applications. Every benchmark is represented as a RSM that consists of several CSMs, and each CSM corresponds to the control flow graph of a method of the benchmark. We have used the Soot framework [43] for obtaining the control flow graphs, where every node of the graph corresponds to one Jimple statement of Soot, and the tool of [44] to obtain their tree decompositions. Our experiments were run on a standard desktop computer with a 3.4GHz CPU, on a single thread.

**Interprocedural reachability and intraprocedural shortest path.** In our experiments, we focus on the important special case of reachability and shortest path. We consider CSMs of moderate to large size (all CSMs with at least five hundred nodes), as for small CSMs the running times are negligible. The first step is to execute an interprocedural reachability algorithm from the program entry to discover all actual call to return edges $((en, b), (ex, b))$ of every CSM $A_i$ (i.e., all invocations that actually return), and then consider the control flow graphs $G_i$ independently.

- *(Reachability).* For every $G_i$, the complete preprocessing in the case of reachability is done by executing $n_i$ DFSs, one from each source node. The single-source query from $u$ is answered by executing one DFS from $u$, and the pair query $u, v$ is done similarly, but we stop as soon as $v$ is reached. We note that this methodology correctly answers interprocedural same-context reachability queries.
- *(Shortest path).* For shortest path we perform intraprocedural analysis on each $G_i$. We assign both positive and negative weights to each edge of $G_i$ uniformly at random from the range $[-10, 10]$. For general semiring path properties, the Bellman-Ford algorithm [17] is a very natural one, which in the case of shortest path can handle positive and negative weights, as long as there is no negative cycle. To have a meaningful comparison with Bellman-Ford (as a representative of a general semiring framework), we consider both positive and negative weights, but do not allow negative cycles. For complete preprocessing we run the classical Floyd-Warshall algorithm (which computes all-pairs shortest paths and is a generalization of Bellman-Ford). Under no preprocessing, for every single-source and pair query we run the Bellman-Ford algorithm.

**Results.** Our experimental results are shown in Table 5.

1. The average treewidth of control flow graphs is confirmed to be very small, and does not scale with the size of the graph. In fact, even the largest treewidth is four.
2. The preprocessing time of our algorithm is significantly less than the complete preprocessing, by factor of 1.5 to 4 times in case of reachability, and by orders of magnitude in case of shortest path.
3. In both reachability and shortest path, all queries are handled significantly faster after our preprocessing, than no preprocessing. We also note that for shortest path queries, Bellman-Ford answers single-source and pair queries in the same time, which is significantly slower than both our single-source and pair queries. Finally, we note that for single-source reachability queries, though we do not provide theoretical improvement over DFS (Table 2), the one-time preprocessing information allows for practical improvements.

Since our work focuses on same-context queries and the IFDS/IDE framework does not have this restriction, a direct comparison with the IFDS/IDE framework would be biased in our favor. In the experimental results for interprocedural reachability with same-context queries, we show that we are faster than even DFS (which is faster than IFDS/IDE).

**Description of Table 5.** In the table, the second (resp. third) column shows the average number of nodes (resp. treewidth) of CSMs of each benchmark. The running times of preprocessing are gathered by averaging over all CSMs in each benchmark. The running times of querying are gathered by averaging over all possible single-source and pair queries in each CSM, and then averaging over all CSMs in each benchmark.

## 6. Conclusions

In this work we considered constant treewidth RSMs since control flow graphs of most programs have constant treewidth. We presented algorithms to handle multiple same-context algebraic path queries, where the weights belong to a partially complete semiring. Our algorithms have small additional one-time preprocessing, but answer subsequent queries significantly faster than no preprocessing both in terms of theoretical bounds as well as in practice, even for basic problems such as reachability and shortest path. While in this work we focused on RSMs with unique entries and exits, an interesting theoretical question is to extend our results to RSMs with multiple entries and exists.

**Acknowledgements.** We thank anonymous reviewers for helpful comments to improve the presentation of the paper.

## References

[1] N. Alon and B. Schieber. Optimal preprocessing for answering on-line product queries. Technical report, Tel Aviv University, 1987.

[2] R. Alur, M. Benedikt, K. Etessami, P. Godefroid, T. W. Reps, and M. Yannakakis. Analysis of recursive state machines. *ACM Trans. Program. Lang. Syst.*, 2005.

[3] R. Alur, S. La Torre, and P. Madhusudan. Modular strategies for recursive game graphs. *Theor. Comput. Sci.*, 2006.

| Benchmarks | | | Interprocedural Reachability | | | | | | Intraprocedural Shortest path | | | | | |
|---|---|---|---|---|---|---|---|---|---|---|---|---|---|---|
| | | | Preprocessing | | Query | | | | Preprocessing | | Query | | | |
| | | | | | Single | | Pair | | | | Single | | Pair | |
| | $n$ | $t$ | Our | Complete | Our | No Prepr. | Our | No Prepr. | Our | Complete | Our | No Prepr. | Our | No Prepr. |
| antlr | 698 | 1.0 | 76316 | 136145 | 15.3 | 166.3 | 0.15 | 14.34 | 221578 | $1.13 \cdot 10^7$ | 251 | 24576 | 0.36 | 24576 |
| bloat | 696 | 2.3 | 27597 | 54335 | 3.9 | 72.5 | 0.10 | 14.34 | 87950 | $1.15 \cdot 10^7$ | 257 | 25239 | 0.37 | 25239 |
| chart | 1159 | 1.5 | 22191 | 90709 | 2.3 | 80.9 | 0.13 | 22.32 | 125468 | $1.24 \cdot 10^8$ | 398 | 88856 | 0.39 | 88856 |
| eclipse | 656 | 1.6 | 37010 | 138905 | 6.7 | 239.1 | 0.19 | 15.76 | 152293 | $1.07 \cdot 10^7$ | 533 | 23639 | 0.46 | 23639 |
| fop | 1209 | 1.7 | 30189 | 91795 | 2.9 | 60.6 | 0.12 | 43.0 | 153728 | $3.94 \cdot 10^8$ | 1926 | 113689 | 2.71 | 113689 |
| hsqldb | 698 | 1.0 | 55668 | 180333 | 13.0 | 219.0 | 0.14 | 13.89 | 215063 | $1.23 \cdot 10^7$ | 236 | 24322 | 0.36 | 24322 |
| jython | 748 | 1.5 | 43609 | 68687 | 7.2 | 85.7 | 0.11 | 12.84 | 159085 | $1.42 \cdot 10^7$ | 386 | 29958 | 0.32 | 29958 |
| luindex | 885 | 1.3 | 36015 | 142005 | 5.6 | 202.7 | 0.16 | 26.44 | 163108 | $2.97 \cdot 10^7$ | 258 | 51192 | 0.37 | 51192 |
| lusearch | 885 | 1.3 | 51375 | 189251 | 12.8 | 211.4 | 0.13 | 26.01 | 219015 | $2.90 \cdot 10^7$ | 254 | 50719 | 0.34 | 50719 |
| pmd | 644 | 1.4 | 31483 | 52527 | 2.5 | 83.9 | 0.13 | 12.5 | 140974 | $9.14 \cdot 10^6$ | 327 | 22572 | 0.37 | 22572 |
| xalan | 698 | 1.0 | 57734 | 138420 | 8.0 | 235.0 | 0.19 | 14.28 | 186695 | $1.10 \cdot 10^7$ | 380 | 24141 | 0.43 | 24141 |
| Jflex | 1091 | 1.6 | 51431 | 91742 | 3.1 | 50.8 | 0.11 | 20.46 | 154818 | $1.24 \cdot 10^8$ | 231 | 83093 | 0.36 | 83093 |
| muffin | 1022 | 1.7 | 29905 | 66708 | 2.6 | 52.7 | 0.10 | 18.57 | 125938 | $1.02 \cdot 10^8$ | 265 | 80878 | 0.38 | 80878 |
| javac | 711 | 1.8 | 32981 | 59793 | 4.8 | 75.2 | 0.11 | 11.86 | 117390 | $1.31 \cdot 10^7$ | 370 | 26180 | 0.34 | 26180 |
| polyglot | 698 | 1.0 | 68643 | 150799 | 12.2 | 184.5 | 0.14 | 14.14 | 228758 | $1.15 \cdot 10^7$ | 244 | 24400 | 0.35 | 24400 |

Table 5: Average statistics gathered from our experiments on the DaCapo benchmark suit. Times are in microseconds.


[4] S. Arnborg and A. Proskurowski. Linear time algorithms for NP-hard problems restricted to partial k-trees . *Discrete Appl Math*, 1989.

[5] M. Bern, E. Lawler, and A. Wong. Linear-time computation of optimal subgraphs of decomposable graphs. *J Algorithm*, 1987.

[6] S. M. e. a. Blackburn. The dacapo benchmarks: Java benchmarking development and analysis. In *OOPSLA*, 2006.

[7] H. Bodlaender. Dynamic algorithms for graphs with treewidth 2. In *Graph-Theoretic Concepts in Computer Science*, LNCS. Springer, 1994.

[8] H. Bodlaender. Discovering treewidth. In *SOFSEM 2005: Theory and Practice of Computer Science*, volume 3381 of *LNCS*. Springer, 2005.

[9] H. L. Bodlaender. Dynamic programming on graphs with bounded treewidth. In *ICALP*, LNCS. Springer, 1988.

[10] H. L. Bodlaender. A tourist guide through treewidth. *Acta Cybern.*, 1993.

[11] D. Callahan, K. D. Cooper, K. Kennedy, and L. Torczon. Interprocedural constant propagation. In *CC*. ACM, 1986.

[12] K. Chatterjee and J. Lacki. Faster algorithms for Markov decision processes with low treewidth. In *CAV*, 2013.

[13] K. Chatterjee and Y. Velner. Mean-payoff pushdown games. In *LICS*, 2012.

[14] K. Chatterjee, A. Pavlogiannis, and Y. Velner. Quantitative interprocedural analysis. In *POPL*, 2015.

[15] S. Chaudhuri. Subcubic algorithms for recursive state machines. In *POPL*, New York, NY, USA, 2008. ACM.

[16] S. Chaudhuri and C. D. Zaroliagis. Shortest Paths in Digraphs of Small Treewidth. Part I: Sequential Algorithms. *Algorithmica*, 1995.

[17] T. Cormen, C. Leiserson, R. Rivest, and C. Stein. *Introduction To Algorithms*. MIT Press, 2001.

[18] B. Courcelle. Graph rewriting: An algebraic and logic approach. In *Handbook of Theoretical Computer Science (Vol. B)*. MIT Press, Cambridge, MA, USA, 1990.

[19] P. Cousot and R. Cousot. Static determination of dynamic properties of recursive procedures. In E. Neuhold, editor, *IFIP Conf. on Formal Description of Programming Concepts*, 1977.

[20] M. Elberfeld, A. Jakoby, and T. Tantau. Logspace versions of the theorems of bodlaender and courcelle. In *FOCS*, 2010.

[21] M. J. Fischer and A. R. Meyer. Boolean Matrix Multiplication and Transitive Closure. In *SWAT (FOCS)*. IEEE Computer Society, 1971.

[22] R. Giegerich, U. Möncke, and R. Wilhelm. Invariance of approximate semantics with respect to program transformations. In *3rd Conference of the European Co-operation in Informatics (ECI)*, 1981.

[23] D. Grove and L. Torczon. Interprocedural constant propagation: A study of jump function implementation. In *PLDI*. ACM, 1993.

[24] J. Gustedt, O. Mæhle, and J. Telle. The treewidth of java programs. In *Algorithm Engineering and Experiments*, LNCS. Springer, 2002.

[25] T. Hagerup. Dynamic algorithms for graphs of bounded treewidth. *Algorithmica*, 2000.

[26] R. Halin. S-functions for graphs. *Journal of Geometry*, 1976.

[27] S. Horwitz, T. Reps, and M. Sagiv. Demand interprocedural dataflow analysis. *SIGSOFT Softw. Eng. Notes*, 1995.

[28] T. Kloks. *Treewidth, Computations and Approximations*. LNCS. Springer, 1994.

[29] J. Knoop and B. Steffen. The interprocedural coincidence theorem. In *CC*, 1992.

[30] J. Knoop, B. Steffen, and J. Vollmer. Parallelism for free: Efficient and optimal bitvector analyses for parallel programs. *ACM Trans. Program. Lang. Syst.*, 1996.

[31] J. Lacki. Improved deterministic algorithms for decremental reachability and strongly connected components. *ACM Transactions on Algorithms*, 2013.

[32] W. Landi and B. G. Ryder. Pointer-induced aliasing: A problem classification. In *POPL*. ACM, 1991.

[33] N. A. Naeem and O. Lhoták. Typestate-like analysis of multiple interacting objects. In *OOPSLA*, 2008.

[34] J. Obdrzálek. Fast mu-calculus model checking when tree-width is bounded. In *CAV*, 2003.

[35] B. A. Reed. Finding approximate separators and computing tree width quickly. In *STOC*, 1992.

[36] T. Reps, S. Horwitz, and M. Sagiv. Precise interprocedural dataflow analysis via graph reachability. In *POPL*, New York, NY, USA, 1995. ACM.

[37] T. Reps, S. Schwoon, S. Jha, and D. Melski. Weighted pushdown systems and their application to interprocedural dataflow analysis. *Sci. Comput. Program.*, 2005.

[38] T. Reps, A. Lal, and N. Kidd. Program analysis using weighted pushdown systems. In *FSTTCS 2007: Foundations of Software Technology and Theoretical Computer Science*, LNCS. 2007.

[39] N. Robertson and P. Seymour. Graph minors. iii. planar tree-width. *Journal of Combinatorial Theory, Series B*, 1984.

[40] M. Sagiv, T. Reps, and S. Horwitz. Precise interprocedural dataflow analysis with applications to constant propagation. *Theor. Comput. Sci.*, 1996.

[41] M. Sridharan, D. Gopan, L. Shan, and R. Bodík. Demand-driven points-to analysis for java. In *OOPSLA*, 2005.

[42] M. Thorup. All Structured Programs Have Small Tree Width and Good Register Allocation. *Information and Computation*, 1998.

[43] R. Vallée-Rai, P. Co, E. Gagnon, L. Hendren, P. Lam, and V. Sundaresan. Soot - a java bytecode optimization framework. In *CASCON '99*. IBM Press, 1999.

[44] T. van Dijk, J.-P. van den Heuvel, and W. Slob. Computing treewidth with libtw. Technical report, University of Utrecht, 2006.

[45] X. Zhang, R. Mangal, M. Naik, and H. Yang. Hybrid top-down and bottom-up interprocedural analysis. In *PLDI*, 2014.

# Predicting Program Properties from "Big Code"

Veselin Raychev
Department of Computer Science
ETH Zürich
veselin.raychev@inf.ethz.ch

Martin Vechev
Department of Computer Science
ETH Zürich
martin.vechev@inf.ethz.ch

Andreas Krause
Department of Computer Science
ETH Zürich
andreas.krause@inf.ethz.ch

## Abstract

We present a new approach for predicting program properties from massive codebases (aka "Big Code"). Our approach first learns a probabilistic model from existing data and then uses this model to predict properties of new, unseen programs.

The key idea of our work is to transform the input program into a representation which allows us to phrase the problem of inferring program properties as structured prediction in machine learning. This formulation enables us to leverage powerful probabilistic graphical models such as conditional random fields (CRFs) in order to perform *joint* prediction of program properties.

As an example of our approach, we built a scalable prediction engine called JSNICE[1] for solving two kinds of problems in the context of JavaScript: predicting (syntactic) names of identifiers and predicting (semantic) type annotations of variables. Experimentally, JSNICE predicts correct names for 63% of name identifiers and its type annotation predictions are correct in 81% of the cases. In the first week since its release, JSNICE was used by more than 30,000 developers and in only few months has become a popular tool in the JavaScript developer community.

By formulating the problem of inferring program properties as structured prediction and showing how to perform both learning and inference in this context, our work opens up new possibilities for attacking a wide range of difficult problems in the context of "Big Code" including invariant generation, de-compilation, synthesis and others.

## 1. Introduction

The increased amounts of freely available high quality programs in code repositories such as GitHub[2] (a situation termed "Big Code" [7] by a recent initiative) creates a unique opportunity for new kinds of programming tools based on statistical reasoning. These tools will extract useful information from existing codebases and will use that information to provide statistically likely solutions to problems that are difficult or impossible to solve with traditional rule based techniques.

[1] http://jsnice.org

[2] http://github.com


*POPL '15*, January 15–17, 2015, Mumbai, India.

http://dx.doi.org/10.1145/2676726.2677009

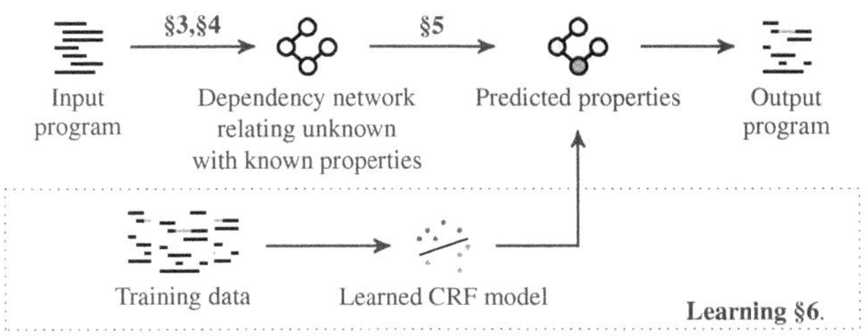


**Figure 1.** Statistical Prediction of Program Properties.

In this work we focus on the general problem of inferring program properties. We introduce a novel statistical approach which predicts properties of a given program by learning a probabilistic model from existing codebases already annotated with such properties. We use the term program property to encompass both: classic semantic properties of programs (*e.g.* type annotations) as well as syntactic program elements (*e.g.* identifiers or code). Our approach is fairly general and can serve as a basis for various kinds of statistical invariant predictions and statistical code synthesizers [24].

The core technical insight of our work is transforming the input program into a representation that enables us to formulate the problem of inferring program properties (be it semantic or syntactic) as structured prediction with conditional random fields (CRFs) [17], a powerful undirected graphical model successfully used in a wide variety of applications including computer vision, information retrieval, and natural language processing [4, 10, 17, 21, 22].

To our knowledge, this is the first work which shows how to leverage CRFs in the context of programs. By connecting programs to CRFs, our work also enables immediate reuse of state-of-the-art learning and inference algorithms [14] to the domain of programs.

Fig. 1 illustrates our two-phase structured prediction approach. In the prediction phase (shown on top), we are given an input program for which we are to infer properties of interest. In the next step, we convert the program into a representation which we call a dependency network. The essence of the dependency network is to capture relationships between program elements whose properties are to be predicted with elements whose properties are known. Once the network is obtained, we perform structured prediction and in particular, a query referred to as *Maximum a Posteriori (MAP)* inference [14]. This query makes a *joint* prediction for all elements together by optimizing a scoring function based on the learned CRF model. Making a joint prediction which takes into account structure and dependence is particularly important as properties of different elements are often related. A useful analogy is the ability to make joint predictions in image processing where the prediction of a pixel label is influenced by the predictions of neighboring pixels. To achieve good performance for the MAP inference, we developed a new algorithmic variant which targets the domain of programs (existing inference algorithms cannot efficiently deal with the combination of unrestricted network structure and massive number of possible predictions per element). Finally, we output a program where the newly predicted properties are incorporated. In the learning phase, we find a good scoring function by learning a CRF model from a large training set of programs. Here, because we deal with CRFs and MAP inference queries, we are able to leverage state-of-the-art max-margin CRF training methods [26].

**JSNICE : *name and type inference for JavaScript*** As an example of our approach, we built a system called JSNICE which addresses two important challenges in JavaScript: predicting (syntactic) identifier names and predicting (semantic) type annotations of variables. We focused on JavaScript for three reasons. First, in terms of type inference, recent years have seen extensions of JavaScript that add type annotations [6, 28]. However, these extensions rely on traditional type inference which does not scale to realistic programs that make use of dynamic evaluation and complex libraries (e.g. jQuery) [11]. Our work predicts likely type annotations for real world programs which can then be provided to the programmer or to a standard type checker. Second, much of JavaScript code found on the Web is obfuscated, making it difficult to understand what the code is doing. Our approach recovers likely identifier names thereby making the code readable again. Finally, JavaScript programs are readily available in source code repositories (e.g. GitHub) meaning that we can obtain a large set of high quality training programs.

***Main contributions*** The contributions of this paper are:

- A new approach for inferring likely program facts based on structured prediction with conditional random fields (CRFs).
- A new framework consisting of fast and approximate inference and learning algorithms tailored to structured prediction tasks in programs.
- A new system, JSNICE, which is an instance of our approach focusing on predicting names and type annotations of JavaScript programs. A week after its release[3], JSNICE was used by $> 30,000$ developers and has since become a popular tool in the JavaScript developer community.
- An evaluation on a range of real-world JavaScript programs. The experimental results indicate that JSNICE successfully predicts correct names for $63.4\%$ of program identifiers and $81.6\%$ of the guessed type annotations are correct.

***Paper structure*** The paper is organized as follows. Section 2 illustrates our approach on an example. Section 3 introduces the general prediction framework, while Section 4 describes JSNICE, an instantiation of that framework. Section 5 and Section 6 discuss our structured prediction and learning procedures. Section 7 presents a detailed experimental evaluation of JSNICE. In Section 8 we elaborate on our design choices and explain why and how we arrived at using structured prediction with CRFs. Finally, in Section 9 we discuss related work in detail and conclude in Section 10.

## 2. Overview

In this section we provide an informal description of our statistical inference approach on a running example. Consider the JavaScript program shown in Fig. 2(a). This is a program which has short, non-descriptive identifier names. Such names can be produced by both a novice inexperienced programmer or by an automated process known as minification (a form of obfuscation) which replaces identifier names with shorter names. In the case of client-side JavaScript, minification is a common process on the Web and is used to reduce the size of the code being transferred over the network and/or to prevent users from understanding what the program is actually doing. In addition to obscure names, variables in this program also lack annotated type information. The net effect is that it is difficult to understand what the program actually does, which is that it partitions an input string into chunks of given sizes and stores those chunks into consecutive entries of an array.

Given the program in Fig. 2(a), our system produced the program in Fig. 2(e). The output program has new identifier names and is annotated with predicted types for the parameters, the local variables and the return statement. Overall, it is easier to understand what that program does when compared to the input program. Next, we provide an overview of the prediction procedure. We focus on predicting names, but the process for predicting types is identical.

***Determine known and unknown properties*** Given the program in Fig. 2(a), we first determine the set of program elements for which we would like to infer properties. These are elements for which the properties to be inferred are currently *unknown*. For example, in the case of name inference, this set of elements includes the local variables of the input program: `e`, `t`, `n`, `r`, and `i`. We also determine the set of elements whose properties are *known*. One such element is the name of the field `length` in the input program or the names of the methods. Both kinds of elements are shown in Fig. 2(b). The goal of our prediction task is to predict the *unknown* properties based on: i) the obtained *known* properties, and ii) the relationship between various elements (discussed below).

***Build dependency network*** Next, we build a dependency network capturing various kinds of relationships between program elements. The dependency network is key to capturing structure when performing predictions and intuitively captures how properties which are to be predicted influence each other. For example, the link between known and unknown properties allows us to leverage the fact that many programs use common anchors (e.g. common API's such as JQuery) meaning that the unknown quantities we aim to predict are influenced by the way the known elements are used by the program. Further, the link between two unknown properties signifies that the prediction for the two properties is related in some way. Dependencies are triplets of the form ⟨`n`,`m`,`rel`⟩ where `n` and `m` are program elements and `rel` is the particular relationship between the two elements. In our work all dependencies are triplets, but in general, they can be extended to other more complex relationships.

In Fig. 2(c), we show three example dependencies between the program elements. For instance, the statement `i += t` generates a dependency ⟨`i`,`t`,**`L+=R`**⟩, because `i` and `t` are on the left and right side of a `+=` expression. Similarly, the statement **`var`** `r = e.length` generates several dependencies including ⟨`r`,`length`,**`L=_.R`**⟩ which designates that the left part of the relationship, denoted by **`L`**, appears before the de-reference of the right side denoted by **`R`** (we elaborate on the different types of relationships later in the paper). For clarity, in Fig. 2(c) we include only some of the relationships.

***MAP inference*** After obtaining the dependency network of a program, the next step is to infer the most likely values (according to a probabilistic model learned from data) for the nodes of the network, a query referred to as MAP inference [14]. As illustrated in Fig. 2(d), for the network of Fig. 2(c), our system infers the new names `step` and `len`. It also inferred that the previous name `i` was most likely.

Let us consider how we predicted the names `step` and `len`. Consider the network in Fig. 2(d). This is the same network as in Fig. 2(c) but with additional tables we elaborate on now (these tables are produced as an output of the learning phase). Each table is a function that scores the assignment of properties for the nodes connected by the corresponding edge. The function takes as input

[3] http://jsnice.org

```
function chunkData(e, t) {
  var n = [];
  var r = e.length;
  var i = 0;
  for (; i < r; i += t) {
    if (i + t < r) {
      n.push(e.substring(i, i + t));
    } else {
      n.push(e.substring(i, r));
    }
  }
  return n;
}
```

(a) JavaScript program with minified identifier names

```
/* str: string, step: number, return: Array */
function chunkData(str, step) {
  var colNames = []; /* colNames: Array */
  var len = str.length;
  var i = 0; /* i: number */
  for (; i < len; i += step) {
    if (i + step < len) {
      colNames.push(str.substring(i, i + step));
    } else {
      colNames.push(str.substring(i, len));
    }
  }
  return colNames;
}
```

(e) JavaScript program with new identifier names and types

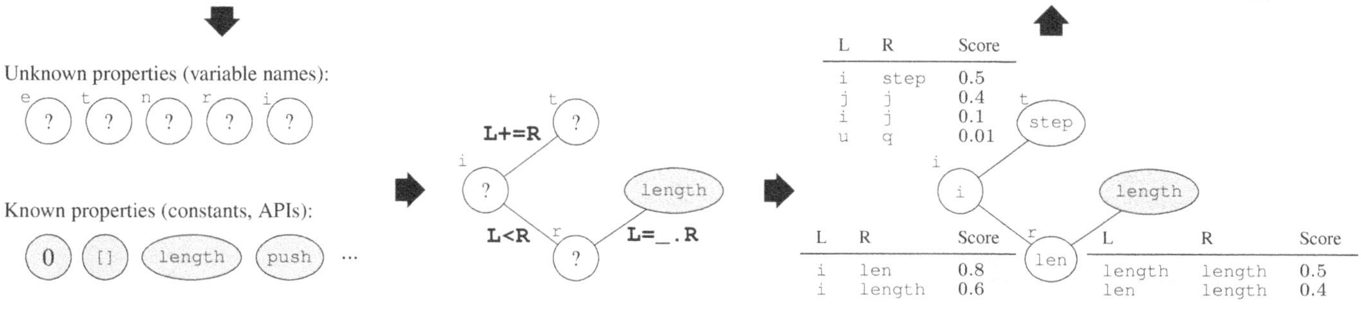


(b) Known and unknown name properties (c) Dependency network (d) Result of MAP inference

**Figure 2.** A JavaScript program with new names and type annotations, along with an overview of the name inference procedure.

two properties and returns the score for the pair (intuitively, how likely is the particular pair). In Fig. 2(d), each table shows possible functions for the three kinds of relationships we have.

Let us consider the topmost table. The first row says that the assignment of `i` and `step` is scored with 0.5. The MAP inference tries to find an assignment of properties to the nodes so that the assignment maximizes a particular scoring function. For the two nodes `i` and `t`, the inference ends up selecting the highest score from the table (i.e., the values `i` and `step`). Similarly for the nodes `i` and `r`. However, for nodes `r` and `length`, the inference *does not* select the topmost row but selects values from the second row. The reason is that if it had selected the topmost row, then the only viable choice (in order to match the value `length`) for the remaining relationship is the second row of that table (with value 0.6). However, the assignment 0.6 leads to a lower *combined* overall score. That is, the MAP inference must take into account the *structure* and dependencies between the nodes and cannot simply select the maximal score of each function and then stop.

***Output program*** Finally, after the new names are inferred, our system transforms the original program to use these names. The output of the entire inference process is captured in the program shown in Fig. 2(e). Notice how in this output program, the names tend to accurately capture what the program does.

***Predicting type annotations*** Even though we illustrated the inference process for variables names, the overall flow for predicting type annotations is identical. First, we define the program elements with unknown properties to infer type annotations for. Then, we define elements with known properties such as API names or variables with known types. Next, we build the dependency network (some of the relationships overlap with those for names) and finally we perform MAP inference and output a program annotated with the predicted type annotations. One can then run a standard type checker to check whether the predicted types are valid for that program. In our example program shown in Fig. 2(e), the predicted type annotations are indeed valid. In general, when automatically trying to predict semantic properties (such as types) where soundness is required, the approach presented here will have value as part of a guess-and-check loop.

***A note on name inference*** We note that our name inference process is independent of what the minified names are. In particular, the process will return the same names regardless of which minifier was used to obfuscate the original program (provided these minifiers always rename the *same set* of variables).

## 3. Structured Prediction for Programs

In this section we introduce our approach for predicting program properties. The key idea is to formulate the problem of inferring program properties as structured prediction with *conditional random fields* (CRFs). We first introduce CRFs, then show how the framing is done in a step-by-step manner, and finally discuss the specifics of inference and learning in the context of programs. The prediction framework presented in this section is fairly general and can potentially be instantiated to many different kinds of challenges (we instantiate it for two challenges in Section 4).

***Notation: programs, labels, predictions*** Let $x \in X$ be a program. As with standard program analysis, we will infer properties about program statements or expressions (referred to as program elements). For a program $x$, each element (e.g. a variable) is identified with an index (a natural number). We will usually need to separate the elements into two kinds: i) elements for which we are interested in inferring properties and ii) elements for which we already know their properties (e.g. these properties may have been obtained via standard program analysis or via manual annotation). We use two helper functions $n, m\colon X \to \mathbb{N}$ to return the appropriate number of program elements for a given program $x$: $n(x)$ returns the total number of elements of the first kind and $m(x)$ returns the total number of elements of the second kind. For convenience, we assume that elements of the first kind are indexed in the range $[1..n(x)]$ and elements of the second kind are indexed in the range

$[n(x)+1, n(x)+m(x)]$. To avoid clutter, when $x$ is clear from the context, we write $n$ instead of $n(x)$ and $m$ instead of $m(x)$.

We use the set $Labels_U$ to denote all possible values that a property can take. For instance, in type prediction, $Labels_U$ contains all possible types (e.g. number, string, etc). Then, for a program $x$, we use the notation $\mathbf{y} = (y_1, ..., y_{n(x)})$ to denote a vector of predicted program properties. Here, $\mathbf{y} \in Y$ where $Y = (Labels_U)^*$. That is, each entry $y_i$ in the vector $\mathbf{y}$ ranges over $Labels_U$ and denotes that program element $i$ has a property $y_i$.

***Problem definition*** Let $D = \{\langle x^{(j)}, \mathbf{y}^{(j)} \rangle\}_{j=1}^{t}$ denote the training data: a set of $t$ programs each with corresponding program properties. Our goal is to learn a model that captures the conditional probability $Pr(\mathbf{y} \mid x)$. Once the model is learned, we can predict properties of new programs by posing the following query (also known as MAP or Maximum a Posteriori query):

Given a **new** program $x$, find $\mathbf{y} = \text{argmax}_{\mathbf{y}' \in \Omega_x} Pr(\mathbf{y}' \mid x)$

That is, for a new program $x$, we aim to find the most likely assignment of program properties $\mathbf{y}$ according to the probabilistic distribution. Here, $\Omega_x \subseteq Y$ describes the set of possible assignments of properties $\mathbf{y}'$ for the program elements of $x$. The set $\Omega_x$ is important as it allows restricting the set of possible properties and is useful for encoding problem-specific constraints.

### 3.1 Conditional Random Fields (CRFs)

We now describe CRFs, a particular model for representing the conditional probability $Pr(\mathbf{y} \mid x)$. We consider the case where the factors are positive in which case, without loss of generality, any conditional probability of properties $\mathbf{y}$ given a program $x$ can be encoded as follows:

$$Pr(\mathbf{y} \mid x) = \frac{1}{Z(x)} \exp(score(\mathbf{y}, x))$$

where $score$ is a function that returns a real number indicating the score of an assignment of properties $\mathbf{y}$ for a program $x$. Assignments with higher score are more likely than assignments with lower score. $Z(x)$, called the partition function, ensures that the above expression does in fact encode a conditional distribution. It returns a real number depending only on the program $x$, such that the probabilities over all possible assignments $\mathbf{y}$ sum to 1, i.e.:

$$Z(x) = \sum_{\mathbf{y} \in \Omega_x} \exp(score(\mathbf{y}, x))$$

We consider $score$ functions that can be expressed as a composition of a sum of $k$ feature functions $f_i$ associated with weights $w_i$:

$$score(\mathbf{y}, x) = \sum_{i=1}^{k} w_i f_i(\mathbf{y}, x) = \mathbf{w}^T \mathbf{f}(\mathbf{y}, x)$$

Here, $\mathbf{f}$ is a vector of functions $f_i$ and $\mathbf{w}$ is a vector of weights $w_i$. The feature functions $f_i \colon Y \times X \to \mathbb{R}$ are used to score assignments of program properties. This representation of score functions is particularly suited for learning (as the weights $\mathbf{w}$ can be learned from data). Based on the definition above, we can now define a *conditional random field* [17].

**Definition 3.1** (Conditional Random Field (CRF)). *A model for the conditional probability of labels* $\mathbf{y}$ *given observations* $x$ *is called (log-linear) conditional random field, if it is represented as:*

$$Pr(\mathbf{y} \mid x) = \frac{1}{Z(x)} \exp(\mathbf{w}^T \mathbf{f}(\mathbf{y}, x))$$

***A note on feature functions*** Feature functions are key to controlling the likelihood of an assignment of properties $\mathbf{y}$ for a program $x$. For instance, a feature function can be defined in a way which prohibits or lowers the score of undesirable predictions: say if $f_i(\mathbf{y}^B, x) = -\infty$, the feature function $f_i$ (with weight $w_i > 0$) disables an assignment $\mathbf{y}^B$, thus resulting in $Pr(\mathbf{y}^B \mid x) = 0$.

We discuss how the feature functions are defined in the next subsection. Note that feature functions are defined *independently of the program* being queried, and are only based on the particular prediction problem we are interested in. For example, when we predict a program's types, we define one set of feature functions and when we predict identifier names, we define another set. Once defined, the feature functions are re-used for predicting the particular kind of property we are interested in for *any* input program.

### 3.2 Making Predictions for Programs

We next describe a step by step process for predicting program properties using CRFs where program elements are related with pairwise functions. We first show how to build a network between elements, then describe how to build the feature functions $f_i$ based on that network and finally illustrate how to score a prediction.

***Step 1: Build dependence network*** $G^x$ The first step in defining $f_i(\mathbf{y}, x)$ is to build what we refer to as a dependency network $G^x = \langle V^x, E^x \rangle$ from the input program $x$. This network captures dependencies between the predictions made for the program elements of interest. Here, $V^x = V_U^x \cup V_K^x$ denotes the set of program elements (e.g. variables) and consists of elements for which we would like to predict properties $V_U^x$ and elements whose properties we already know $V_K^x$. The set of edges $E^x \subseteq V^x \times V^x \times Rels$ denotes the fact that there is a relationship between two program elements and describes what that relationships is.

For a program $x$, we define the vector $\mathbf{z}^x = \{z_1^x, ..., z_m^x\}$ to capture the set of properties that are already known, that is, each element in $V_K^x$ is assigned a property from $\mathbf{z}^x$. Here, $z_i^x$ denotes the property of program element $n + i$. Each $z_i^x$ ranges over a set of properties $Labels_K$ which could potentially differ from the properties $Labels_U$ that we use for inference. For example, if the known properties are integer constants, $Labels_K$ will be all valid integers. To avoid clutter where $x$ is clear from the context, we use $\mathbf{z}$ instead of $\mathbf{z}^x$. We use $Labels = Labels_U \cup Labels_K$ to denote the set of all properties.

***Step 2: Define feature functions*** Once the network $G^x$ for a program $x$ is obtained, we use it to define the shape of the feature functions. We define the assignment vector $A = (\mathbf{y}, \mathbf{z})$ which is a concatenation of two assignments: the unknown properties $\mathbf{y}$ and the known properties $\mathbf{z}$. As usual, we access the property of the $j$'th element of the vector $A$ via $A_j$. We define a feature function $f_i$ as the sum of the applications of its corresponding pairwise feature function $\psi_i$ over the set of network edges obtained from step 1. That is, the formula below allows us to compute the value of a particular feature function for a given prediction $\mathbf{y}$:

$$f_i(\mathbf{y}, x) = \sum_{(a,b,rel) \in E^x} \psi_i((\mathbf{y}, \mathbf{z})_a, (\mathbf{y}, \mathbf{z})_b, rel)$$

Here, each $\psi_i \colon Labels \times Labels \times Rels \to \mathbb{R}$ is a pairwise feature function relating a *pair* of program properties as opposed to a larger number like $f_i$. Recall that each edge $(a, b, rel) \in E^x$ represents a pair of elements $a$ and $b$ and the kind of relationship $rel \in Rels$ between them. Then, every time we encounter an edge between two program elements, we apply the pairwise feature function passing in the appropriate relationship $rel$ as an argument. Conversely, if two program elements are unrelated there is no need to invoke the pairwise feature function for these two elements. Focusing on pairwise feature functions allows us to define $f_i$ directly on the network obtained from the program. Note again that pairwise feature functions $\psi_i$ are pre-defined once and for all *independently* of the program for which we are predicting properties. We will see particular instantiations of pairwise feature functions in later sections.

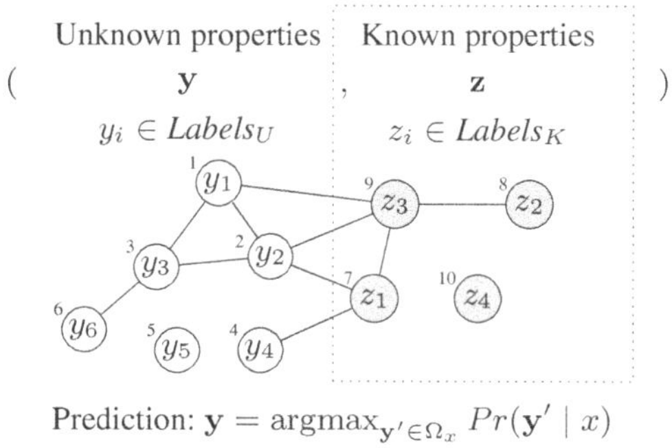


**Figure 3.** A general schema for building a network for a program $x$ and finding the best scoring assignment of program properties $\mathbf{y}$.

Although in this work we use pairwise feature functions, there is nothing specific in our approach which precludes us from using functions with higher arity.

***Step 3: Score a prediction*** $\mathbf{y}$ Based on the above definition of a feature function, we can now define how to obtain a total score for a prediction $\mathbf{y}$. By substitution, we obtain:

$$score(\mathbf{y}, x) = \sum_{(a,b,rel) \in E^x} \sum_{i=1}^{k} w_i \psi_i((\mathbf{y}, \mathbf{z})_a, (\mathbf{y}, \mathbf{z})_b, rel)$$

That is, for a program $x$ and its dependence network $G^x$, by using the pairwise functions $\psi_i$ and the learned weights $w_i$ associated with each $\psi_i$, we can obtain the score of a prediction $\mathbf{y}$.

***Example*** Let us illustrate the above steps as well as some key points on the simple example in Fig. 3. Here we have 6 program elements for which we would like to predict program properties. We also have 4 program elements whose properties we already know. Each program element is a node with an index shown outside the circles. The edges indicate relationships between the nodes and the labels inside the nodes are the predicted program properties or the already known properties. As explained earlier, the known properties $\mathbf{z}$ are fixed before the prediction process begins. In a structured prediction problem, the properties $y_1, \ldots, y_6$ of program elements $1 \ldots 6$ are predicted such that $Pr(\mathbf{y} \mid x)$ is maximal.

***Key Points*** Let us note three important points. First, predictions for a node (e.g. 5) disconnected from all other nodes in the network can be made independently of the predictions made for the other nodes. Second, nodes 2 and 4 are connected but only via nodes with known predictions. Therefore, the properties for nodes 2 and 4 can be assigned independently of one another. That is, the prediction $y_2$ of node 2 will not affect the prediction $y_4$ of node 4 with respect to the total score and vice versa. The reason why this is the case is due to a property in CRFs known as *conditional independence*. We say that the prediction for a pair of nodes $a$ and $b$ is conditionally independent given a set of nodes $C$ if the predictions for the nodes in $C$ are fixed and all paths between $a$ and $b$ go through a node in $C$. This is why the predictions for nodes 2 and 4 are conditionally independent of node 7. Conditional independence is an important property of CRFs and is leveraged by both the inference and the learning algorithms. We do not discuss conditional independence further but refer the reader to a standard reference [14]. Finally, a path between two nodes (not involving known nodes) means that the predictions for these two nodes may (and generally will) be dependent on one another. For example, nodes 2 and 6 are transitively connected (without going through known nodes) meaning that the prediction for node 2 can influence the prediction for node 6 and vice versa.

### 3.3 MAP inference

Recall that the key query we perform is MAP inference:

Given a program $x$, find $\mathbf{y} = \text{argmax}_{\mathbf{y}' \in \Omega_x} Pr(\mathbf{y}' \mid x)$

In a CRF, this amounts to the query:

$$\mathbf{y} = \underset{\mathbf{y}' \in \Omega_x}{\text{argmax}} \frac{1}{Z(x)} \exp(score(\mathbf{y}', x))$$

where:

$$Z(x) = \sum_{\mathbf{y}'' \in \Omega_x} \exp(score(\mathbf{y}'', x))$$

Note that $Z(x)$ does not depend on $\mathbf{y}'$ and as a result it does not affect the final choice for the prediction $\mathbf{y}$. This is an important observation, because computing $Z(x)$ is generally very expensive as it may need to sum over all possible assignments $\mathbf{y}''$. Therefore, we can exclude $Z(x)$ from the maximized formula. Next, we take into account the fact that exp is a monotonically increasing function enabling us to remove exp from the equation. This leads to an equivalent simplified query:

$$\mathbf{y} = \underset{\mathbf{y}' \in \Omega_x}{\text{argmax}}\, score(\mathbf{y}', x)$$

This means that an algorithm answering the MAP inference query must ultimately maximize the *score* function. For instance, for the example in Fig. 3, once we fix the labels $z_i$, we need to find labels $y_i$ such that *score* is maximized.

In principle, at this stage one can use any algorithm to answer the MAP inference query. For instance, a naïve but inefficient way to solve this query is by trying all possible outcomes $\mathbf{y}' \in \Omega_x$ and scoring each of them to select the highest scoring one. Other exact and inexact [14] inference algorithms exist if the network $G^x$ and the outcomes set $\Omega_x$ have certain restrictions (e.g. $G^x$ is a tree).

***Specifics of programs*** Unfortunately, the problem with existing inference algorithms is that they are too slow to be usable for our problem domain (i.e. programs). For example, in typical applications of CRFs [14], it is unusual to have more than a handful of possible assignments for an element (e.g. 10), while in our case there could potentially be thousands of possible assignments per element. Towards that, in Section 5 we present a fast and approximate MAP inference algorithm that is tailored to the specifics of dealing with programs: the shape of the feature functions, the unrestricted nature of $G^x$ and the massive set of possible assignments.

### 3.4 Learning

We briefly discuss how we learn the weights $\mathbf{w}$ that describe the scoring function *score*. To learn $\mathbf{w}$, we use an advanced learning technique that generalizes support vector machines. Given the training data $D = \{\langle x^{(j)}, \mathbf{y}^{(j)} \rangle\}_{j=1}^{t}$ of $t$ samples, our goal is to find $\mathbf{w}$ such that the given assignments $\mathbf{y}^{(j)}$ are the highest scoring assignments in as many training samples as possible subject to additional learning constraints. We discuss the learning procedure in detail in Section 6.

## 4. JSNICE: Predicting Names and Type Annotations for JavaScript

In this section we present an example of using our structured prediction approach presented in Section 3 for inferring two kinds of properties: (i) predicting names of local variables, and (ii) predicting type annotations of function arguments. We investigate the above challenges in the context of JavaScript, a popular language where addressing the above two questions is of significant importance. We do note however that much of the machinery discussed in this section applies almost as-is to other languages.

***Presentation Flow*** Recall that in Section 3, we defined a three-step process to obtaining a total score for a prediction, where the first step is to define the network $G^x = \langle V^x, E^x \rangle$ and the second step is to define the pairwise feature functions $\psi_i$. The combination of these two fully defines the feature functions $f_i$. In what follows, we first present the probabilistic name prediction and define $V^x$ for that problem. We then present the probabilistic type prediction and define $V^x$ in that context. Then, we define $E^x$: which program elements from $V^x$ are related as well as how they are related (that is, *Rels*). Some of these relationships are similar for both prediction problems and hence we discuss them in the same section. Finally, we discuss how to obtain the pairwise feature functions $\psi_i$.

### 4.1 Probabilistic Name Prediction

The goal of our name prediction task is to predict the (most likely) names of local variables in a given program $x$. The way we proceed to solve this problem in our framework is as follows. First, as outlined in Section 3, we identify the set of known program elements, referred to as $V_K^x$, as well as the set of unknown program elements for which we will be predicting new names, referred to as $V_U^x$.

For the name prediction problem, we take $V_K^x$ to be all constants, objects properties, methods and global variables of the program $x$. Each program element in $V_K^x$ can be assigned values from the set $Labels_K = JSConsts \cup JSNames$, where $JSNames$ is a set of all valid identifier names, and $JSConsts$ is a set of possible constants. We note that object property names and API names are modeled as constants, as the dot (`.`) operator takes an object on the left-hand size and a string constant on the right-hand size. We define the set $V_U^x$ to contain all local variables of a program $x$. Here, a variable name belonging to two different scopes leads to two program elements in $V_U^x$. Finally, $Labels_U$ ranges over $JSNames$.

To ensure the newly predicted names are semantic preserving, we ensure that the prediction satisfies the following constraints:

1. All references to a renamed local variable must be renamed to the same name.
2. The predicted identifier names must not be reserved keywords.
3. The prediction must not suggest the same name for two different variables in the same scope.

The first property is naturally enforced in the way we define $V_U^x$ where each element corresponds to a local variable as opposed to having a unique element for every variable occurrence in the program. The second property is enforced by making sure the set $Labels_U$ from which predicted names are drawn does not contain keywords. Finally, we enforce the third constraint by restricting $\Omega_x$ so that predictions with conflicting names are prohibited.

### 4.2 Probabilistic Type Annotation Prediction

Our second application involves probabilistic type annotation inference of function parameters. Focusing on function parameters is particularly important for JavaScript, a duck-typed language lacking type annotations. Without knowing the types of function parameters, a forward type inference analyzer will fail to derive precise and meaningful types (except the types of constants and those returned by common APIs such as DOM APIs). As a result, real-world programs using libraries cannot be analyzed precisely [11].

Instead, we propose to probabilistically predict the type annotations of function parameters. Here, our training data consists of a set of JavaScript programs that have already been annotated with types for function parameters. In JavaScript, these annotations are provided in a specially formatted comments known as JSDoc[4].

[4] https://developers.google.com/closure/compiler/docs/js-for-compiler

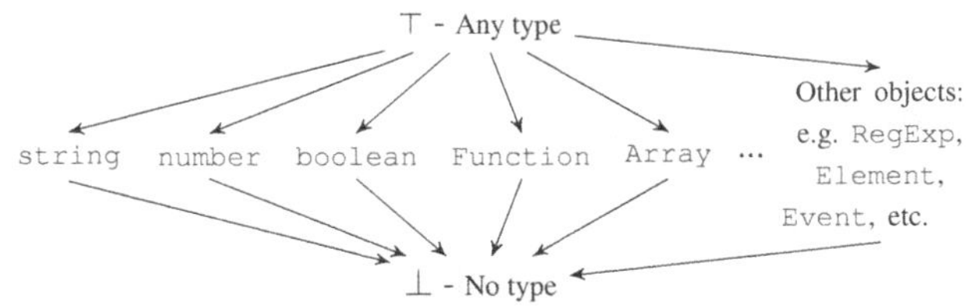


**Figure 4.** The lattice of types over which prediction occurs.

The simplified language over which we predict type annotations is defined as follows:

$$expr ::= val \mid var \mid expr_1(expr_2) \mid expr_1 \circledast expr_2 \qquad \textit{Expression}$$
$$val ::= \lambda var : \tau.expr \mid n \qquad \textit{Value}$$

Here, $n$ ranges over constants ($n \in JSConsts$), $var$ is a meta-variable ranging over the program variables, $\circledast$ ranges over the standard binary operators (`+`, `-`, `*`, `/`, `.`, `<`, `==`, `===`, etc.), and $\tau$ ranges over all possible variable types. That is, $\tau = \{?\} \cup L$ where $L$ is a set of types (we discuss how to instantiate $L$ below) and ? denotes the unknown type. To be explicit, we use the set $JSTypes$ where $JSTypes = \tau$. We use the function:

$$[]_x : expr \rightarrow JSTypes$$

to obtain the type of a given expression in a given program $x$. This map can be manually provided or built using program analysis. When the program $x$ is clear from the context we use $[e]$ as a shortcut for $[]_x(e)$.

***Defining known and unknown program elements*** As usual, our first step is to define the two sets of known and unknown elements. We define the set of unknown program elements as follows:

$$V_U^x = \{e \mid e \textbf{ is } var, [e] = ?\}$$
$$Labels_U = JSTypes$$

That is, $V_U^x$ contains variables whose type is unknown. We differentiate between the type $\top$ and the unknown type ? in order to allow for finer control over which types we would like to predict. For instance, a type may be $\top$ if a classic type inference algorithm fails to infer more precise types (usually, standard inference only discovers types of constants and values returned by common APIs, but fails to infer types of function parameters). A type may be denoted as unknown (i.e. ?) if the type inference did not even attempt to infer types for the particular expression (e.g. function parameters). Of course, in the above definition of $V_U^x$ we could also include $\top$ and use our approach to potentially refine the results of classic type inference.

Next, we define the set of known elements $V_K^x$. Note that $V_K^x$ can contain any expression, not just variables like $V_U^x$ above:

$$V_K^x = \{e \mid e \textbf{ is } expr, [e] \neq ?\} \cup \{n \mid n \textbf{ is } constant\}$$
$$Labels_K = JSTypes \cup JSConsts$$

That is, $V_K^x$ contains both, expressions whose types are known as well as constants. Currently, we do not apply any global restriction on the set of possible assignments $\Omega_x$, that is, $\Omega_x = (JSTypes)^n$ (recall that $n$ is a function which returns the number of elements whose property is to be predicted). This means that we rely entirely on the learning to discover the rules that will produce non-contradicting types. The only restriction (discussed below) that we apply is constraining $JSTypes$ when performing predictions.

***Defining*** $JSTypes$. So far, we have not discussed the exact contents of the set $JSTypes$ except to state that $JSTypes = \{?\} \cup L$ where $L$ is a set of types. The set $L$ can be instantiated

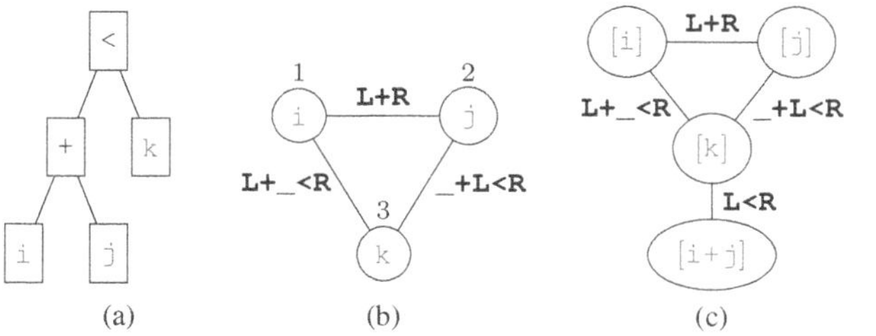


**Figure 5.** (a) the AST of expression `i+j<k`, and two dependency networks built from the AST relations: (b) for name predictions, and (c) for type predictions.

in various ways. In this work, we chose to define $L$ as $L = \mathcal{P}(T)$ where $\langle T, \sqsubseteq \rangle$ is a complete lattice of types with $T$ and $\sqsubseteq$ as defined in Fig. 4. In the figure we use "..." to denote a potentially infinite number of user-defined object types.

***Key points*** We note several important points here. First, the set $JSTypes$ is built during training from a finite set of possible types that are already manually provided or are inferred by the classic type inference. Therefore, for a given training data, $JSTypes$ is necessarily a finite set. Second, because $JSTypes$ may contain a subset of types $O \subseteq JSTypes$ specific to a particular program in the training data, it may be the case that when we are considering a new program whose types are to be predicted, the types found in $O$ are simply not relevant to that new program (for instance, the types in $O$ refer to names that do not appear in the new program). Therefore, when we perform prediction, we filter irrelevant types from the set $JSTypes$. This is the only restriction we consider when performing type predictions. Finally, because $L$ is defined as a powerset lattice, it encodes (in this case, a finite number of) disjunctions. That is, a variable whose type is to be predicted ranges over exponentially many subsets allowing many choices for the type. For example, a variable can have a type {`string`, `number`} which for convenience can also be written as `string` $\vee$ `number`.

### 4.3 Relating program elements

We next describe the relationships that we introduce between program elements. These relationships define how to build the set of edges $E^x$ of a program $x$. Since the program elements for both prediction tasks are similar (e.g. they both contain JavaScript constants, variables and expressions), we discuss the relationships we use for each task together. If a relationship is specific to a particular task, we explicitly state so when describing it.

#### 4.3.1 Relating Expressions

The first relationship we discuss is syntactic in nature: it relates two program elements based on the their syntactic relationship in the program's Abstract Syntax Tree (AST). Let us consider how we obtain the relationships for the expression `i+j<k`. First, we build the AST of the expression shown in Fig. 5 (a). Suppose we are interested in performing name prediction for variables `i`, `j` and `k` (denoted by program properties with indices 1, 2 and 3 respectively), that is, $V_U^x = \{1, 2, 3\}$. Then, we build the dependency network as shown in Fig. 5 (b) to indicate that the prediction for the three elements are dependent on one another (with the particular relationship shown over the edge). For example, the edge between `1` and `2` represents the relationships that these nodes participate in an expression **L+R** where **L** is a node for `1` and **R** is a node for `2`.

The relationships are defined using the following grammar:

$$rel_{ast} ::= rel_L(rel_R) \mid rel_L \circledast rel_R$$
$$rel_L ::= \mathbf{L} \mid rel_L(\_) \mid \_(rel_L) \mid rel_L \circledast \_ \mid \_ \circledast rel_L$$
$$rel_R ::= \mathbf{R} \mid rel_R(\_) \mid \_(rel_R) \mid rel_R \circledast \_ \mid \_ \circledast rel_R$$

All relationships $rel_{ast}$ are part of $Rels$, that is, $rel_{ast} \in Rels$. Here, as discussed earlier, $\circledast$ ranges over binary operators. All relationships derived using the above grammar have exactly one occurrence of **L** and **R**. For a relationship $r \in rel_{ast}$, let $r[x/\mathbf{L}, y/\mathbf{R}, e/\_]$ denote the expression where $x$ is substituted for **L**, $y$ is substituted for **R** and the expression $e$ is substituted for _. Then, given two program elements $a$ and $b$ and a relationship $r \in rel_{ast}$, a match is said to exist if $r[a/\mathbf{L}, b/\mathbf{R}, [expr]/\_] \cap Exp(x) \neq \emptyset$ (here, $[expr]$ denotes all possible expressions in the programming language and $Exp(x)$ is all expressions of program $x$). An edge $(a, b, r) \in E^x$ between two program elements $a$ and $b$ exists if there exists a match between $a$, $b$ and $r$.

Note that for a given pair of elements $a$ and $b$ there could be more than one relationship which matches, that is, both $r_1, r_2 \in rel_{ast}$ match where $r_1 \neq r_2$ (therefore, there could be multiple edges between $a$ and $b$ with different relationships).

The relationships described above are useful for both name and type inference. In the case of predicting names, the expressions being related are always variables, while for type annotations, the expressions need not be restricted to variables. For example, in Fig. 5(c) there is a relationship between the types of `k` and `i+j` via **L<R**. Note that our rules do not directly capture relationships between [`i`] and [`i+j`], but they are transitively dependent. Still, many useful and interesting direct relationships for type inference are present. For instance, in classic type inference, the relationship **L=R** implies a constraint rule [L] $\sqsupseteq$ [R] where $\sqsupseteq$ is the super-type relationship (indicated in Fig. 4). Interestingly, our inference model can learn such rules instead of providing them explicitly.

#### 4.3.2 Aliasing Relations

Another kind of (semantic) relationship we introduce is that of aliasing. Let $alias(e)$ denote the set of expressions that may alias with the expression $e$ (this information can be determined via standard alias analysis [25]).

***Argument-to-parameter*** We introduce the `ARG_TO_PM` relationship which relates arguments of a function invocation (the arguments can be arbitrary expressions) with parameters in the function declaration (variables whose names or types are to be inferred). Let $e_1(e_2)$ be an invocation of the function captured by the expression $e_1$. Then, for all possible declarations of $e_1$ (those are an over-approximation), we relate the argument of the call $e_2$ to the parameter in the declaration. That is, for any $v \in \{p \mid (\lambda p : \tau.e) \in alias(e_1)\}$, we add the edge $(e_2, v, \texttt{ARG\_TO\_PM})$ to $E^x$. In the case of predicting names $e_2$ is always a variable, while with predicting types $e_2$ is not restricted to variables.

***Transitive Aliasing*** Second, we introduce a transitive aliasing relationship referred to as $(r, \texttt{ALIAS})$ between variables which may alias. This is a relationship that we introduce only when predicting types. Let $a$ and $b$ be related via the relationship $r$ where $r$ ranges over the grammar defined earlier. Then, for all $c \in alias(b)$ where $c$ is a variable, we include the edge $(a, c, (r, \texttt{ALIAS}))$.

#### 4.3.3 Function name relationships

We also introduce two relationships referred to as `MAY_CALL` and `MAY_ACCESS`. These relationships are only used when predicting names and are particularly useful for predicting function names. The reason is that in JavaScript many of the local variables are function declarations. The `MAY_CALL` relationship relates a function name $f$ with names of other functions $g$ that $f$ may call (this semantic information can be obtained via program analysis). That is, if a function $f$ may call function $g$, we add the edge $(f, g, \texttt{MAY\_CALL})$ to the set of edges $E^x$. Similarly, if in a function $f$, there is an access to an object field named $fld$, we add the edge $(f, fld, \texttt{MAY\_ACCESS})$ to the set $E^x$. Naturally, $f$ and $g$ are allowed to only range over variables (as when predicting names the nodes represent variables and not arbitrary expressions), and the name of an object field $fld$ is a string constant.

### 4.4 Pairwise feature functions

Finally, we describe how to obtain and define the pairwise feature functions $\{\psi_i\}_{i=1}^{k}$. We obtain these functions as a pre-processing step before the *training phase* begins. Recall that our training set $D = \{\langle x^{(j)}, \mathbf{y}^{(j)}\rangle\}_{j=1}^{t}$ consists of $t$ programs where for each program $x$ we are given the corresponding properties $\mathbf{y}$. For each tuple $(x, \mathbf{y}) \in D$, we define the set of features as follows:

$$features(x, \mathbf{y}) = \{((\mathbf{y}, \mathbf{z})_a, (\mathbf{y}, \mathbf{z})_b, rel) \mid (a, b, rel) \in E^x\}$$

Then, for the entire training set we obtain all features as follows:

$$all\_features(D) = \bigcup_{j=1}^{t} features(x^{(j)}, \mathbf{y}^{(j)})$$

We then define the pairwise feature functions to be indicator functions of each feature triple $\langle l_i^1, l_i^2, rel_i\rangle \in all\_features(D)$:

$$\psi_i(l^1, l^2, rel) = \begin{cases} 1 & \textbf{if } l^1 = l_i^1 \textbf{ and } l^2 = l_i^2 \textbf{ and } rel = rel_i \\ 0 & \textbf{otherwise} \end{cases}$$

In addition to indicator functions, we have features for equality of program properties $\psi_{=}(l_1, l_2, rel)$ that return 1 if and only if the two related labels are equal. Our feature functions are fully inferred from the available training data and the network $G^x$ of each program $x$. After the feature functions are defined, in the training phase (discussed later), we learn their corresponding weights $\{w_i\}_{i=1}^{k}$ ($k$ is the number of pairwise functions). Note that the weights and the feature functions can vary depending on the training data $D$, but both are independent of the program for which we are trying to predict properties.

## 5. Prediction Algorithm

In this section we present our inference algorithm for making predictions (also referred to as MAP inference). Recall that predicting properties $\mathbf{y}$ of a program $x$ involves finding a $\mathbf{y}$ such that:

$$\mathbf{y} = \underset{\mathbf{y}' \in \Omega_x}{\operatorname{argmax}}\, Pr(\mathbf{y}' \mid x) = \underset{\mathbf{y}' \in \Omega_x}{\operatorname{argmax}}\, score(\mathbf{y}', x) = \underset{\mathbf{y}' \in \Omega_x}{\operatorname{argmax}}\, \mathbf{w}^T \mathbf{f}(\mathbf{y}', x)$$

When designing our inference algorithm, a key objective was optimizing the speed of prediction. There are two reasons why speed is critical. First, we expect prediction to be done interactively, as part of a program development environment or as a service (e.g., via a public web site such as JSNICE). This requirement renders any inference algorithm that takes more than a few seconds unacceptable. Second (as we will see later), the prediction algorithm is part of the inner-most loop of training, and hence its performance directly impacts an already costly and work-intensive training phase.

***Exact algorithms*** Exact inference in CRFs is generally NP-hard and computationally prohibitive in practice. This problem is well known and hard specifically for denser networks with no predefined shape like the ones we obtain from programs [14].

***Approximate algorithms*** Previous studies [8, 12] for MAP inference in networks of arbitrary shapes discuss loopy-belief propagation, greedy algorithms, combination approaches or graph-cut based algorithms. In their results, they show that advanced approximate algorithms may result in higher precision for the inference and the learning, however they also come at the cost of significantly more computation. Their experiments confirm that more advanced techniques such as belief propagation are consistently at least an order of magnitude slower than greedy algorithms.

As our focus is on performance, we proceeded with a greedy approach (also known as iterated conditional modes [4]). Our algorithm is tailored to the nature of our prediction task (especially when predicting names where we have a massive number of possible assignments for each element) in order to significantly improve the computational complexity over a naïve greedy approach. In particular, our algorithm leverages the shape of the feature functions discussed in Section 4.4. In essence, the approach works by selecting candidate assignments from a beam of $s$-best possible labels leading to significant gains in performance at the expense of slightly higher chance of obtaining non-optimal assignments.

**Algorithm 1:** Greedy Inference Algorithm

**Input**: network $G^x = \langle V^x, E^x\rangle$ of program $x$,
initial assignment of $n$ unknown properties $\mathbf{y}_0 \in \Omega_x$,
known properties $\mathbf{z}$
pairwise feature functions $\psi_i$ and their learned weights $w_i$
**Output**: $\mathbf{y} \approx \operatorname{argmax}_{\mathbf{y}' \in \Omega_x} (score(\mathbf{y}', x))$

1 **begin**
2   $\mathbf{y} \leftarrow \mathbf{y}_0$
3   **for** $pass \in [1..num\_passes]$ **do**
4     // for each node with unknown property in the graph $G^x$
5     **for** $v \in [1..n]$ **do**
6       $E_v \leftarrow \{(v, \_, \_) \in E^x\} \cup \{(\_, v, \_) \in E^x\}$
7       $score_v \leftarrow scoreEdges(E_v, (\mathbf{y}, \mathbf{z}))$
8       **for** $l' \in candidates(v, (\mathbf{y}, \mathbf{z}), E_v)$ **do**
9         $l \leftarrow y_v$   // get current label of $v$
10         $y_v \leftarrow l'$   // change label of $v$ in $\mathbf{y}$
11         $score'_v \leftarrow scoreEdges(E_v, (\mathbf{y}, \mathbf{z}))$
12         **if** $\mathbf{y} \in \Omega_x \wedge score'_v > score_v$ **then**
13           $score_v \leftarrow score'_v$
14         **else**
15           $y_v \leftarrow l$   // no score improvement: revert label.
16   return $\mathbf{y}$

### 5.1 Greedy inference algorithm

Algorithm 1 illustrates our greedy inference procedure. The inference algorithm has four inputs: i) a network $G^x$ obtained from a program $x$, ii) an initial assignment of properties for the unknown elements $\mathbf{y}_0$, iii) the obtained known properties $\mathbf{z}$, and iv) the pairwise feature functions and their weights. The way these inputs are obtained was already described earlier in Section 3. The output of the algorithm is an approximate prediction $\mathbf{y}$ which also conforms to the desired constraints $\Omega_x$. The algorithm also uses an auxiliary function called $scoreEdges$ defined as follows:

$$scoreEdges(E, A) = \sum_{(a,b,rel) \in E} \sum_{i=1}^{k} w_i \psi_i(A_a, A_b, rel)$$

The $scoreEdges(E, A)$ function is the same as $score$ defined earlier except that $scoreEdges$ works on a subset of the network edges $E \subseteq E^x$. Given a set of edges $E$ and an assignment of elements to properties $A$, $scoreEdges$ iterates over $E$, applies the appropriate feature function to each edge and sums up the results.

The basic idea of the algorithm is to start with an initial assignment $\mathbf{y}_0$ (Line 2) and to make a number of passes over all nodes in the network, attempting to improve the score of the current prediction $\mathbf{y}$. The algorithm works on a node by node basis: it selects a node $v \in [1..n]$ and then finds a label for that node which improves the score of the assignment. That is, once the node $v$ is selected, the algorithm first obtains the set of edges $E_v$ in which $v$ participates (shown on Line 6) and computes via $scoreEdges$ the contribution of the edges to the total score. Then, the inner loop starting at Line 8 tries new labels for the element $v$ from a set of candidate labels and accepts only labels that lead to a score improvement.

***Time Complexity*** The time complexity for one iteration of the prediction algorithm depends on the number of nodes, the number of adjacent edges for each node and the number of candidate labels. Since the total number of edges in the graph $|E^x|$ is a product of the number of nodes and the number of edges per node, then one iteration of the algorithm has $O(d|E^x|)$ time complexity, where $d$ is the total number of possible candidate assignment labels for a node (obtained on Line 8).

### 5.2 Obtaining Candidates

Our algorithm does not try all possible labels for a node. Instead, we define the function $candidates(v, A, E)$ which suggests candidate labels given a node $v$, assignment $A$, and a set of edges $E$. Recall that $all\_features(D)$ is a (large) set of triples $(l^1, l^2, r)$ obtained from the training data $D$ relating labels $l^1$ and $l^2$ via $r$. Further, our pairwise feature functions $\{\psi_i\}_{i=1}^k$ (where $k = |all\_features(D)|$) defined earlier are indicator functions meaning there is a one to one correspondence between a triple $(l^1, l^2, r)$ and a pairwise function. Recall that in the training phase (discussed later), we learn a weight $w_i$ associated with each function $\psi_i$ (and because of the one-to-one mapping, with each triple $(l^1, l^2, r)$). We use these weights in order to restrict the set of possible assignments we consider for a node $v$. Let $top_s$ be a function which given a set of features (triples) returns the top $s$ triples based on the respective weights. Let for convenience $F = all\_features(D)$. Then, we define the following auxiliary functions:

$$topL_s(lbl, rel) = top_s(\{t \mid t_l = lbl \wedge t_{rel} = rel \wedge t \in F\})$$
$$topR_s(lbl, rel) = top_s(\{t \mid t_r = lbl \wedge t_{rel} = rel \wedge t \in F\})$$

The above functions can be easily pre-computed for a fixed beam size $s$ and all triples in the training data $F$. Finally, we define:

$$candidates(v, A, E) =$$
$$= \bigcup_{\langle a,v,rel\rangle \in E} \{l^2 \mid \langle l^1, l^2, r\rangle \in topL_s(A_a, rel)\} \cup$$
$$\bigcup_{\langle v,b,rel\rangle \in E} \{l^1 \mid \langle l^1, l^2, r\rangle \in topR_s(A_b, rel)\}$$

The meaning of the above function is that for every edge adjacent to $v$, we consider at most $s$ of the highest scoring triples (according to the learned weights). This results in a set of possible assignments for $v$ used to drive the inference algorithm. The beam parameter $s$ controls a trade-off between precision and running time. Lower values of $s$ decrease the chance of predicting a good candidate label, while higher $s$ make the algorithm consider more labels and run longer. Our experiments show that good candidate labels can be obtained with fairly low values of $s$. Thanks to this observation, the prediction runs orders of magnitude faster than a naïve greedy algorithms that tries all possible labels.

***Monotonicity*** At each pass of our algorithm, we iterate over the nodes of $G^x$ and update the label of each node only if this leads to a score improvement (at Line 12). Since we always increase the score of the assignment $\mathbf{y}$, after a certain number of iterations, we reach a fixed point assignment $\mathbf{y}$ that can no longer be improved by the algorithm. The local optimum however, is not guaranteed to be a global optimum. Since we cannot give a complete optimality guarantee, to achieve further speed ups, we also cap the number of algorithm passes at a constant $num\_passes$.

***Additional Improvements*** To further decrease the computation time and possibly increase the precision of our algorithm, we made two improvements. First, if a node has more than a certain number of adjacent nodes, we decrease the size of the beam $s$. In our implementation we decrease the beam size by a factor of 16 if a node has more than 32 adjacent nodes. At almost no computation cost, we also perform optimizations on pairs of nodes in addition to individual nodes. In this case, for each edge in $G^x$, we use the $s$ best scoring features on the same type of edge in the training set and attempt to set the labels of the two elements connected by the edge to the values in each triple.

## 6. Learning

In this section we discuss the learning procedure we use for obtaining the weights $\mathbf{w}$ of the model $Pr(\mathbf{y} \mid x)$ from a data set. We assume that there is some underlying joint distribution $P(\mathbf{y}, x)$ from which the data set $D = \{\langle x^{(j)}, \mathbf{y}^{(j)}\rangle\}_{j=1}^t$ of $t$ programs is drawn independently and identically distributed. In addition to programs $x^{(j)}$, we assume a given assignment of labels $\mathbf{y}^{(j)}$ (names or type annotations in our case) is provided as well. We perform discriminative training (i.e., estimate $Pr(\mathbf{y} \mid x)$ directly) rather than generative training (i.e., estimate $Pr(\mathbf{y}, x)$, and deriving $Pr(\mathbf{y} \mid x)$ from this joint model), since latter requires estimating a distribution over programs $x$ – a challenging, and for our purposes unnecessary task.

The goal of learning is to then estimate the parameters $\mathbf{w}$ to achieve *generalization*: we wish that for a *new program* $x$ drawn from the same distribution $P$ – but generally *not* contained in the data set $D$ – its properties $\mathbf{y}$ are predicted accurately (using the prediction algorithm from Section 5). Several approaches to accomplish this task exist and can potentially be used.

One approach is to fit parameters in order to maximize the (conditional) likelihood of the data, that is, try to choose weights such that the estimated model $Pr(\mathbf{y} \mid x)$ accurately fits the true conditional distribution $P(\mathbf{y} \mid x)$ associated with the data-generating distribution $P$. Unfortunately, this task requires computation of the partition function $Z(x)$ which is a formidable task [14].

Instead, we perform what is known as *max-margin training*: we learn weights $\mathbf{w}$ such that the training data is classified correctly subject to additional constraints like margin and regularization. For this task, powerful learning algorithms are available [26, 27]. In particular, we use a variant of the *Structured Support Vector Machine (SSVM)*[5] [27] and we train it efficiently with the scalable subgradient descent algorithm proposed in [23].

***Structured Support Vector Machine*** The goal of SSVM learning is to find $\mathbf{w}$ such that for each training sample $\langle x^{(j)}, \mathbf{y}^{(j)}\rangle$ ($j \in [1, t]$), the assignment found by the classifier (i.e., maximizing the score) is equal to the given assignment $\mathbf{y}^{(j)}$, and there is a *margin* between the correct classification and any other classification:

$$\forall j, \forall \mathbf{y}' \in \Omega_{x^{(j)}}\ score(\mathbf{y}^{(j)}, x^{(j)}) \geq score(\mathbf{y}', x^{(j)}) + \Delta(\mathbf{y}^{(j)}, \mathbf{y}')$$

Here, $\Delta$: *Labels*$^*$ $\times$ *Labels*$^*$ $\rightarrow \mathbb{R}$ is a distance function (non-negative and satisfying triangle inequality). One can interpret $\Delta(\mathbf{y}^{(j)}, \mathbf{y}')$ as a (safety) margin between the given assignment $\mathbf{y}^{(j)}$ and any other assignment $\mathbf{y}'$, w.r.t. the score function. $\Delta$ is chosen such that slight mistakes (e.g., incorrect prediction of few properties) require less margin than major mistakes. For our appli-

[5] Structured Support Vector Machines generalize classical Support Vector Machines to predict many interdependent labels at once, as necessary when analyzing programs.

cations, we took $\Delta$ to return the number of different labels between the reference assignment $\mathbf{y}^{(j)}$ and any other assignment $\mathbf{y}'$.

Generally, it may not be possible to find weights achieving the above constraints. Hence, SSVMs attempt to find weights $\mathbf{w}$ that minimize the violation of the margin (i.e., maximize the goodness of fit to the data). At the same time, SSVMs control model complexity via *regularization*, penalizing the use of large weights. This is done to facilitate better generalization to unseen test programs.

### 6.1 Learning with stochastic gradient descent

Achieving the balance of data-fit and model complexity leads to a natural optimization problem:

$$\mathbf{w}^* = \underset{\mathbf{w}}{\text{argmin}} \sum_{j=1}^{t} \ell(\mathbf{w}; x^{(j)}, \mathbf{y}^{(j)}) \text{ s.t. } \mathbf{w} \in \mathcal{W}_\lambda \qquad (1)$$

where

$$\ell(\mathbf{w}; x^{(j)}, \mathbf{y}^{(j)}) = \max_{\mathbf{y}' \in \Omega_{x^{(j)}}} \mathbf{w}^T[\mathbf{f}(\mathbf{y}', x^{(j)}) - \mathbf{f}(\mathbf{y}^{(j)}, x^{(j)})] + \Delta(\mathbf{y}^{(j)}, \mathbf{y}')$$

is called the *structured hinge loss*. This nonnegative loss function measures the violation of the margin constraints caused for the $j$-th program, when using a particular set of weights $\mathbf{w}$. Thus, if the objective (1) reaches zero, all margin constraints are respected, i.e., accurate labels are returned for all training programs. Furthermore, the set $\mathcal{W}_\lambda$ encodes some constraints on the weights in order to control model complexity and avoid overfitting. In our work, we regularize by requiring all weights to be nonnegative and bounded by $1/\lambda$, hence we set

$$\mathcal{W}_\lambda = \{\mathbf{w} : w_i \in [0, 1/\lambda] \text{ for all } i\}.$$

The SSVM optimization problem (1) is *convex* (since the structured hinge loss is a pointwise maximum of linear functions, and $\mathcal{W}_\lambda$ is convex), suggesting the use of gradient descent optimization. In particular, we use a technique called *projected stochastic gradient descent*, which is known to converge to an optimal solution, while being extremely scalable for structured prediction problems [23].

The algorithm proceeds iteratively; in each iteration, it picks a random program with index $j \in [1..t]$ from $D$, computes the gradient (w.r.t. $\mathbf{w}$) of the loss function $\ell(\mathbf{w}; x^{(j)}, \mathbf{y}^{(j)})$ and takes a step in the negative gradient direction. If it ends up outside the feasible region $\mathcal{W}_\lambda$, it projects $\mathbf{w}$ to the closest feasible point.

In order to compute the gradient $\mathbf{g} = \nabla_{\mathbf{w}} \ell(\mathbf{w}; x^{(j)}, \mathbf{y}^{(j)})$ at $\mathbf{w}$ w.r.t. the $j$-th program, we must solve the problem

$$\mathbf{y}_{best} \leftarrow \underset{\mathbf{y}' \in \Omega_{x^{(j)}}}{\text{argmax}} \left( score(\mathbf{y}', x^{(j)}) + \Delta(\mathbf{y}^{(j)}, \mathbf{y}') \right), \qquad (2)$$

resulting in the gradient $\mathbf{g}$

$$\mathbf{g} \leftarrow \mathbf{f}(\mathbf{y}_{best}, x^{(j)}) - \mathbf{f}(\mathbf{y}^{(j)}, x^{(j)})$$

Hence, computing the gradient requires solving the *loss-augmented inference* problem (2). This problem can be (approximately) solved using the algorithm presented in Section 5.

After finishing the gradient computation, the weights $\mathbf{w}$ (used by $score$) are updated as follows:

$$\mathbf{w} \leftarrow \text{Proj}_{\mathcal{W}_\lambda}(\mathbf{w} - \alpha \mathbf{g})$$

where $\alpha$ is a learning rate constant and $\text{Proj}_{\mathcal{W}_\lambda}$ is a projection operation determined by the regularization described below.

### 6.2 Regularization

The function $\text{Proj}_{\mathcal{W}_\lambda} : \mathbb{R}^k \to \mathbb{R}^k$ projects its arguments to the point in $\mathcal{W}_\lambda$ that is closest in terms of Euclidean distance. This operation is used to place restrictions on the weights $\mathbf{w} \in \mathbb{R}^k$ such as non-negativity and boundedness. The goal of this procedure, known as *regularization*, is to avoid a problem known as *overfitting* – a case where $\mathbf{w}$ is good in predicting training data, but fails to generalize to unseen data. In our case, we perform $\ell^{\text{inf}}$ regularization, which can be efficiently done in closed form as follows:

$$\text{Proj}_{\mathcal{W}_\lambda}(\mathbf{w}) = \mathbf{w}' \quad \text{such that} \quad w'_i = \max(0, \min(1/\lambda, w_i))$$

This projection ensures that the learned weights are non-negative and never exceed a value $1/\lambda$, limiting the ability to learn too strong feature functions that may not generalize to unseen data. Our choice of $\ell^{\text{inf}}$ has the additional benefit that it operates on vector components independently. This allows for efficient implementation of the learning where we regularize only vector components that changed or components for which the gradient $\mathbf{g}$ is non-zero. This enables us to use a sparse representation of the vectors $\mathbf{g}$, avoiding iteration over all components of the vector $\mathbf{w}$ when projecting.

### 6.3 Complete training phase

In summary, our training procedure first iterates once over the training data and extracts features. We initialize each weight with $w_i = 1/(2\lambda)$. Then, we start with a learning rate of $\alpha = 0.1$ and iterate in multiple passes to learn their weights with stochastic gradient descent. In each pass, we compute gradients via inference, and apply regularization as described before. Additionally, we count the number of wrong labels in the pass and compare it to the number of wrong labels in the previous pass. If we do not observe improvement, we decrease the learning rate $\alpha$ by one half. In our implementation, we iterate over the data up to 24 times.

To speed up the training phase, we also parallelized the stochastic gradient descent on multiple threads as described in [29]. At each pass, we randomly split the data to threads where each thread $t_i$ updates its own version of the weights $\mathbf{w}^{t_i}$. At the end of each pass, the weights $\mathbf{w}^{t_i}$ are averaged to obtain the final weights $\mathbf{w}$.

## 7. Implementation and Evaluation

We implemented our approach in an end-to-end production quality interactive tool, called JSNICE, which targets name and type annotation prediction for JavaScript. JSNICE is integrated within the Google Closure Compiler [6], a tool which takes human-readable JavaScript with optional type annotations and typechecks it. It then returns an optimized, minified and human-unreadable JavaScript with stripped annotations.

To implement our system, we added a new mode to the compiler that aims to reverse its operation: given an optimized minified JavaScript code, JSNICE generates JavaScript code that is well annotated (with types) and as human-readable as possible (with useful identifier names). Our two applications for names and types were implemented as two models that can be run separately.

**JSNICE: *Impact on Developers*** A week after JSNICE was made publicly available, it was used by more than 30,000 developers, with the vast majority of feedback left in blogs and tweets being very positive (those can be found by a simple web search). We believe the combination of high speed and high precision achieved by the structured prediction approach were the main reasons for this positive reception.

***Experimental Evaluation*** We next present a detailed experimental evaluation of our statistical approach and demonstrate that the approach can be successfully applied to the two prediction tasks we described. Further, we evaluate how various knobs of our system affect the overall performance and precision of the predictions.

We collected two disjoint sets of JavaScript programs to form our training and evaluation data. For training, we downloaded 10,517 JavaScript projects from GitHub. For evaluation, we took the 50 JavaScript projects with the highest number of commits

| System | Names Accuracy | Types Precision | Types Recall |
|---|---|---|---|
| **all training data** | **63.4%** | **81.6%** | **66.9%** |
| 10% of training data | 54.5% | 81.4% | 64.8% |
| 1% of training data | 41.2% | 77.9% | 62.8% |
| all data, no structure | 54.1% | 84.0% | 56.0% |
| baseline - no predictions | 25.3% | 37.8% | 100% |

**Table 1.** Precision and recall for name and type reconstruction of minified JavaScript programs evaluated on our test set.

from BitBucket[6]. By taking projects from different repositories, we decrease the likelihood of overlap between training and evaluation data. We also searched in GitHub to check that the projects in the evaluation data are not included in the training data. Finally, we implemented a simple checker to detect and filter out minified and obfuscated files from the training and the evaluation data. After filtering minified files, we ended up with training data consisting of 324,501 files and evaluation data of 2,710 files. Next, we discuss how we trained and evaluated our system: first, we discuss parameter selection (Section 7.1), then precision (Section 7.2) and model sizes (Section 7.3), and finally the running times (Section 7.4).

### 7.1 Parameter selection

We used 10-fold cross-validation to select the best learning parameters of the system only based on the training data and not biased by any test set [20]. Cross-validation works by splitting the training data into 10 equal pieces called folds and evaluating the error rate on each fold by training a model on the data in the other 9 folds. Then, we trained and evaluated on a set of different training parameters and selected the parameters with the lowest error rate.

We tuned the values of two parameters that affect the learning: regularization constant $\lambda$, and presence of margin. Higher values of $\lambda$ mean that we regularize more, i.e. add more restrictions on the feature weights by limiting their maximal value to a lower value $1/\lambda$. The margin parameter determines if the margin function $\Delta$ (see Section 6) should return zero or the number of different labels between the two assignments. To reduce computation (since we must train and test a large number of parameters), we performed cross-validation on only 1% sample of the training data. The cross-validation procedure determined that the best value for $\lambda$ is 2.0 for names, 5.0 for types, and margin $\Delta$ should be applied to both tasks.

### 7.2 Precision

After choosing the parameters, we evaluated the precision of our system for predicting names and type annotations. Our experiments were performed by predicting the names and types in isolation on each of the 2,710 testing files. To evaluate precision, we first minified all 2,710 files with UglifyJS [7]. The process renames local variable identifiers to meaningless short names and removes whitespaces and type annotations. Each minified program is semantically equivalent (except when using `with` or `eval`) to the original program. Then, we used JSNICE to reconstruct name and type information. We compared the precision of the following configurations:

- The most powerful system works with all of the training data and performs structured prediction as described so far.
- Two systems using a fraction of the training data – one on 10% and one on 1% of the files.
- To evaluate the effect of structure when making predictions, we disabled relationships between unknown properties and performed predictions on that network (the learning phase still uses structure).
- A naïve baseline which does no prediction: it keeps names the same and sets all types to the most common type `string`.

#### 7.2.1 Name predictions

To evaluate the accuracy of name predictions, we took each of the minified programs and used the name inference in JSNICE to rename its local variables. Then, we compared the new names to the original names (before obfuscation) for each of the tested programs. The results for the name reconstruction are summarized in the second column of Table 1. Overall, our best system produces code with 63.4% of identifier names exactly equal to their original names. The systems trained on less data have significantly lower precision showing the importance of the amount of training data.

Not using structured prediction also drops the accuracy significantly and has about the same effect as an order of magnitude less data. Finally, not changing any identifier names produces accuracy of 25.3% – this is because minifying the code may not rename some variables (e.g. global variables) in order to guarantee semantic preserving transformations and occasionally one-letter local variable names stay the same (e.g. induction variable of a loop).

#### 7.2.2 Type annotation predictions

Out of the 2,710 test programs, 396 have type annotations for functions in a JSDoc. For these 396, we took the minified version with no type annotations and tried to rediscover all types in the function signatures. We first ran the closure compiler type inference, which produces no types for the function parameters. Then, we ran and evaluated JSNICE on inferring these function parameter types.

JSNICE does not always produce a type for each function parameter. For example, if a function has an empty body, or a parameter is not used, we often cannot relate the parameter to any known program properties and as a result, we make no prediction and return the unknown type (`?`). To take this effect into account, we present two metrics for types: recall and precision. Recall is the percentage of function parameters in the evaluation for which JSNICE made a prediction other than `?`. Precision refers to the percentage of cases – among the ones for which JSNICE made a prediction – where it was exactly equal to the manually provided JSDoc annotation of the test programs. We note that the manual annotations are not always correct, and as a result 100% precision is not necessarily a desired outcome.

We present our evaluation results for types in the last two columns of Table 1. Since we evaluate on production JavaScript applications that typically have short methods with complex relationships, the recall for predicting program types is only 66.9% for our best system. However, we note that none of the types we infer can be inferred by regular forward type analysis.

Since the total number of commonly used types is not as high as the number of names, the amount of training data has less impact on the system precision and recall. To increase the precision and recall of type prediction, adding more (semantic) relationships between program elements will be of higher importance than adding more training data. Dropping structure increases the precision of the predicted types slightly, but at the cost of a significantly reduced recall. The reason is that some types are related to known properties only transitively via other predicted types – relationships that non-structured approaches cannot capture. On the other end of the spectrum is a prediction system that suggests the most likely type

[6] http://bitbucket.org

[7] https://github.com/mishoo/UglifyJS

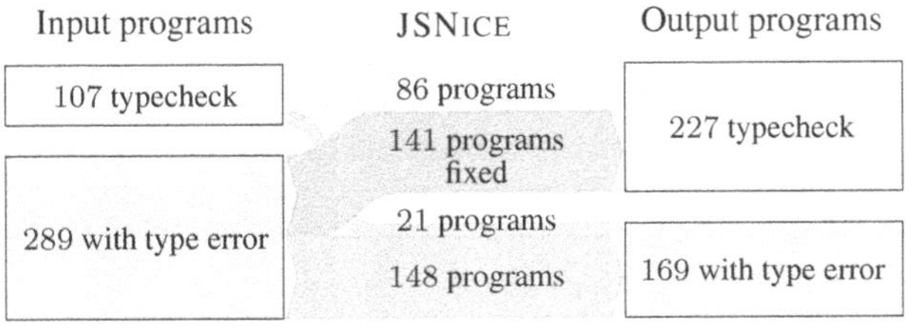


**Figure 6.** Evaluation results for the number of typechecking programs with manually provided types and with predicted types.

in JavaScript programs – `string`. Such a system produces a type for every variable (100% recall), but its precision is only 37.8%.

***Usefulness of type annotations*** To see if the predicted type annotations are useful, we compared them to the original types provided in the evaluated programs. First, we note that our evaluation data has 3, 505 type annotations for function parameters in 396 programs. After removing these annotations and reconstructing them with JSNICE, the number of annotations that are not ? increased to 4, 114 for the same programs. The reason JSNICE produces more types than originally present despite having only 66.3% recall is that not all functions in the original programs had manually provided type annotations.

Despite annotating more functions than in the original code, the output of JSNICE has fewer type errors. We summarize these findings in Fig. 6. For each of the 396 programs, we ran the typechecking pass of Google's Closure Compiler to discover type errors. Among others, this pass checks for incompatible types, calling into a non-function, conflicting and missing types, and non-existent properties on objects. For our evaluation, we kept all checks except the inexistent property check, which fails on almost all (even valid) programs, because it depends on annotating all properties of types – annotations that almost no program possesses.

When we ran typechecking on the input programs, we found the majority (289) to have typechecking errors. While surprising, this can be explained by the fact that JavaScript developers typically do not typecheck their annotations. Among others, we found the original code to have misspelled type names. Most typecheck errors occur due to missing or conflicting types. In a number of cases, the types provided were interesting for documentation, but were semantically wrong - e.g. a parameter is a `string` that denotes function *name*, but the manual annotation designates its type to be `Function`. In contrast, the types reconstructed by JSNICE make the majority (227) of the programs typecheck. In 141 of the programs that originally did not typecheck, JSNICE was able to infer correct types. On the other hand, JSNICE introduced type errors in 21 programs. We investigated some of these errors and found that not all of them were due to wrong types – in several cases the types were rejected due to imprecision of the type system.

### 7.3 Model sizes

Our models contain 7, 627, 484 features for names and 70, 052 features for types. Each feature is stored as a triple, along with its weight. As a result we need only 20 bytes per feature, resulting in a 145.5MB model for names and 1.3MB model for types. The dictionary which stores all names and types requires 16.8MB. As we do not data compress our model, the memory requirements for query processing are about as much as the model size.

### 7.4 Running times

We performed our performance evaluation on a 32-core machine with four 2.13GHz Xeon processors and running Ubuntu 12.04 with 64-Bit OpenJDK Java 1.7.0_51. The training phase for name

| Beam parameter | Name prediction | | Type prediction | |
|---|---|---|---|---|
| $b$ | Accuracy | Time | Precision | Time |
| 4 | 57.9% | 43ms | 80.6% | 36ms |
| 8 | 59.2% | 60ms | 80.9% | 39ms |
| 16 | 62.8% | 62ms | 81.6% | 33ms |
| 32 | 63.2% | 80ms | 81.3% | 37ms |
| 64 (**JSNICE**) | 63.4% | 114ms | 81.6% | 40ms |
| 128 | 63.5% | 175ms | 82.0% | 42ms |
| 256 | 63.5% | 275ms | 81.6% | 50ms |
| Naïve greedy, no beam | 62.8% | 115.2 s | 81.7% | 410ms |

**Table 2.** Trade-off between precision and runtime for the name and type predictions depending on beam search parameter $s$.

prediction took around 10 hours: 57 minutes to compile the input code and generate networks for the input programs and 23 minutes per SSVM (sub-) gradient descent optimization pass. Similarly for types, the compilation and network construction phase took 57 minutes and then we needed 2 minutes and 16 seconds per SSVM (sub-)gradient descent optimization pass. For all our training, we ran 24 gradient descent passes on the training data. All the training passes used 32 threads to utilize the cores of our machine.

***Running times of prediction*** We evaluated the effect of changing the beam size $s$ of our MAP inference algorithm (from Section 5), and the effect $s$ has on the prediction time. The average prediction times per program are summarized in Table 2. Each query is performed on a single core of our test machine. As expected, increasing $s$ improves prediction accuracy but requires more time. Removing the beam altogether and running naïve greedy iterated conditional modes [4] leads to running times of around two minutes per program for name prediction, unacceptable for an interactive tool such as JSNICE. Also, its precision trails some of the beam-based systems, because it does not perform optimization per pair of nodes, but only a node at a time. Due to the requirements for high performance, in our main evaluation and for our live server, we chose the value $s = 64$. This value provides a good balance between performance and precision suitable for our live system.

***Evaluation data metrics*** Our evaluation data consists of 381, 243 lines of JavaScript code with the largest file being 3, 055 lines. For each of the evaluated files, the constructed CRF for name prediction has on average 383.5 arcs and 29.2 random variables. For the type prediction evaluation tasks, each CRF has on average 109.5 arcs and 12.6 random variables.

## 8. Design Decisions

The problem of effectively learning from existing code and precisely answering interesting questions on new programs is non-trivial and requires careful interfacing between programs and sophisticated probabilistic models. As the overall machine can be fairly complex, here we state the important design choices that we made in order to arrive at the solution presented in the paper.

***From programs to random variables*** When predicting program properties, one needs to account for both, the program elements whose properties are to be predicted and the set of available properties from which we draw predictions. In JSNICE, the elements are local variables (for name prediction) and function parameters (for type prediction). In general however, one could instantiate our approach with any program element that ranges over program properties for which sufficient amount of training data is available.

We note that for our instantiation, JSNICE, a predicted program property always exists in the training data. In the case of names, large amounts of training data still allow us to predict meaningful and useful names. Because of the assumption that the property exists in the training data, we create one random variable per local variable of a program with the name to predict and the feature functions as described in Section 4.4. However, the framework from Section 3 can be instantiated (with different feature functions) to cases where a predicted variable name does not exist in the training data (e.g. is a concatenation of several existing words).

***The need for structure*** When predicting facts and properties of programs, it is important to observe that these properties are usually *dependent* on one another. This means that any predictions of these properties should be done *jointly* and not independently in isolation.

***Graphical models: Undirected over Directed*** A family of probabilistic models able to capture complex structural dependencies are graphical models such as Bayesian networks (directed models) and Markov networks (undirected models) [14]. In graphical models, nodes represent random variables and edges capture dependencies between these random variables. Therefore, graphical models are a natural fit for our problem domain where program elements are random variables and the edges capture a particular dependency between the properties to be inferred for these program elements. While we do need to capture dependence between two (or more) random variables, it is often not possible to decide a priori on the exact order (direction of the edges) of that dependence. In turn, this means that undirected models are a better match for our setting as they do not require specifying a direction of the dependence.

***Inference: MAP Inference over Marginals*** For a given program $x$ and a probabilistic model $P$, we are fundamentally interested in finding the most likely properties which should be assigned to program elements $V_U^x$ *given* the known, fixed values for the elements $V_K^x$. What is the right query for computing this most likely assignment? Should we try to find the value $v$ of each random variable $r_i \in V_U^x$ which maximizes its marginal probability $P(r_i = v)$ separately, or should we try to find the values $v_0, v_1, \ldots, v_n$ for *all* random variables $r_0, \ldots, r_n \in V_U^x$ *together* so that the joint probability is maximized, that is, $P(r_0 = v_0, r_1 = v_1, \ldots, r_n = v_n)$ (called MAP inference)?

We decided to use MAP inference over marginals for several reasons. First, we ultimately aim to find the best *joint* assignment and not make independent, potentially contradicting predictions. Second, it is easy to show that maximizing the marginal probability of each variable separately *does not* lead to the optimum assignment computed by MAP inference. Third, when computing marginals, it is difficult to enforce deterministic constraints such as $A \neq B$. It is often easier to incorporate such constraints with MAP inference. Finally, and as we discuss below, the decision to perform MAP inference over marginals enjoys a substantial benefit when it comes to training the corresponding probabilistic model.

An interesting point is that standard MAP inference algorithms are computationally expensive when the number of possible properties is large. Hence, we had to develop new algorithmic variants which can effectively deal with thousands of possible properties for a given random variable (e.g. many possible names).

***Training a Markov Network: Discriminative over Generative*** An important question when dealing with probabilistic models is deciding how the model should be trained. One approach is to train an undirected model in a generative way, thus obtaining a *joint* probability distribution over *both* $V_K^x$ and $V_U^x$ (this model is sometimes referred to as Markov Random Field). While possible in theory, this has a serious practical disadvantage: it requires placing prior probabilities on the known variables $V_K^x$. Providing such a prior distribution can however be very difficult in practice.

However, recall that our MAP inference query is in fact *conditional* on an existing assignment of the known elements $V_K^x$. This means that the underlying probabilistic model need only capture the *conditional* probability distribution of $V_U^x$ *given* $V_K^x$ and *not* the joint distribution. An undirected graphical model able to capture such conditional distributions is referred to as a Conditional Random Field (CRF) [17]. The CRF model admits *discriminative* training where priors on $V_K^x$ are no longer necessary, a key reason for why this model is so effective and popular in practice.

***Training a CRF: Max-Margin over Maximum Likelihood*** After deciding to use CRFs, we still need to find a scalable method for training and obtaining such CRF models from available data (e.g. "Big Code" in our setting). Training these models (say via maximum likelihood) is possible but can be computationally expensive (see Ch.20, [14]).

Recall that we are mainly interested in MAP inference queries where we do not need the exact probability value for the predicted assignment of $V_U^x$. Because of that, we are now able to leverage recent advances in scalable training methods for CRFs and in particular max-margin training [23, 26], a method geared towards answering MAP inference queries on the trained CRF model.

***Summary*** In summary, based on the above reasoning, we arrive at using MAP inference queries with Conditional Random Fields (CRFs), a probabilistic, undirected graphical model which we learn from the available data via an efficient max-margin training. We do note however that the translation of programs to networks and the feature functions we provide are directly reusable if one is interested in performing marginal queries and quantifying the uncertainty associated with the solutions.

### 8.1 Clustering vs. Probabilistic Models

It is instructive to understand that our approach is fundamentally *not* based on clustering. Given a program $x$, we do not try to find a similar (for some definition of similarity) program $s$ in the training corpus and then extract useful information from $s$ and integrate that information into $x$. Such an approach would be limiting as often there is not even a single program in the training corpus which contains all of the information we need to predict for program $x$. In contrast, with the approach presented here, it is possible to build a probabilistic model from multiple programs and then use that information to predict properties about a single program $x$.

## 9. Related Work

We next discuss some of the work most closely related to ours.

***Probabilistic models for code*** Recently, there has been interest in creating probabilistic models of programs based on large codebases [1, 19, 24]. In contrast to such *generative* models, in this work we model a conditional distribution over likely properties for any given program. Such *discriminative* approaches are often more scalable, in terms of their data requirements and computational efficiency [20], and enable us to capture complex relationships between program properties. While there are other probabilistic models [1, 2, 5, 13], they typically serve different purposes. CRFs, as we use here, are particularly well suited for making multiple, dependent predictions for complex, structured data like programs.

***Graphical models in programming*** Several works have used graphical models in the context of programs [3, 9, 15, 16, 18]. All of these works phrase the prediction problem as computing marginals. As we already discussed in Section 8, we find MAP inference to be the conceptually preferred problem formulation over marginals. Except for [15], none of these works *learn* the probabilistic models from data. If one is to pursue learning in their context, then this would essentially require new features which keep information common among programs (need some form of "anchors"). Further, because they frame the problem as computing marginal probabilities, these approaches do not allow for learning with loss functions, meaning that one has to model probabilities and compute the partition function at learning time. This would be prohibitively expensive for large datasets (such as ours) and does not allow for leveraging advanced methods for MAP inference based structured prediction (where one need not compute the partition function). Indeed, the learning method of [15] is extremely inefficient and suffers from the need to compute expectations w.r.t to the model which is generally very expensive and requires sampling, a procedure that is a lot less scalable than MAP inference.

In terms of particular applications, [16] aims to infer ownership values for pointers which range over a very small domain of 4 values: ro, co, and their negation. In contrast, we handle efficiently variables with thousands of possible assignments (for names) and even for types, the size of our domain is much greater. Further, their selection of feature functions make the inference process extremely slow. The reason is that one of the features (called the check factor, critical to the precision of their approach) requires running program analysis essentially on every iteration of the inference: this is devastating in an interactive setting (even with optimizations). Indeed, their follow-up work (section 3, [15]) mentions that the authors would like to find a better solution to this problem (unfortunately, pre-computing this feature is also practically infeasible due to the large numbers of possible combinations of values/variables). Similarly, [18] focuses on inferring likely tags for String methods (e.g. source, sink, regular, sanitizer), where values range over a small domain. The basic idea is to convert a graph extracted from a program (called the propagation graph) into a factor graph and to then perform marginal inference on that graph. This work does a little more than computing marginals: it selects the best marginals and conditions on them for re-computation of the rest, meaning that it can potentially encode constraints by conditioning on what is already computed. This approach is computationally very inefficient: it essentially requires running inference $N$ times for $N$ variables, instead of once. Further, the approach cannot compute optimal MAP inference. The paper [3] is similar to [18] in the sense that it infers permission annotations again ranging over a small set of values and both build factor graphs from programs. However, the inference algorithm in their paper just computes marginals directly and is simpler than the one in [18] (as it does not even iterate).

Overall, we believe that the problems these works address may benefit from considering MAP inference instead of computing marginals. Also, it seems that even with computing marginals, these works are not using state of the art inference methods (e.g. variational methods instead of the basic sum-product belief propagation which has no guarantees on convergence).

## 10. Conclusion

We presented a new statistical approach for predicting program properties by learning from massive codebases (aka "Big Code"). The core idea is to formulate the problem of property inference as structured prediction with conditional random fields (CRFs), enabling *joint* predictions of program properties. As an example of our approach, we built a system called JSNICE which is able to predict names and type annotations for JavaScript. JSNICE is practically effective: it was used by more than $30,000$ developers a week after its release and has now become a popular tool in the JavaScript developer community.

We believe the structured prediction approach presented in this work can serve as a basis for exploring approximate solutions to a variety of analysis and synthesis tasks in the context of "Big Code".

## References


[1] ALLAMANIS, M., AND SUTTON, C. Mining source code repositories at massive scale using language modeling. In *MSR* (2013).

[2] ANDRZEJEWSKI, D., MULHERN, A., LIBLIT, B., AND ZHU, X. Statistical debugging using latent topic models. In *ECML* (2007).

[3] BECKMAN, N. E., AND NORI, A. V. Probabilistic, modular and scalable inference of typestate specifications. PLDI '11, pp. 211–221.

[4] BESAG, J. On the Statistical Analysis of Dirty Pictures. *Journal of the Royal Statistical Society. Series B (Methodol.) 48*, 3 (1986), 259–302.

[5] BLEI, D., AND LAFFERTY, J. Topic models. In *Text Mining: Classification, Clustering, and Applications*. 2009.

[6] Closure compiler. https://developers.google.com/closure/compiler/.

[7] Mining big code to improve software reliability and construction. http://www.darpa.mil/NewsEvents/Releases/2014/03/06a.aspx.

[8] FINLEY, T., AND JOACHIMS, T. Training structural svms when exact inference is intractable. In *ICML* (2008), pp. 304–311.

[9] GULWANI, S., AND JOJIC, N. Program verification as probabilistic inference. POPL '07, ACM, pp. 277–289.

[10] HE, X., ZEMEL, R. S., AND CARREIRA-PERPIÑÁN, M. A. Multiscale conditional random fields for image labeling. CVPR '04.

[11] JENSEN, S. H., MØLLER, A., AND THIEMANN, P. Type analysis for javascript. In *SAS'09*.

[12] KAPPES, J. H., ET AL. A comparative study of modern inference techniques for discrete energy minimization problems. CVPR'13.

[13] KARAIVANOV, S., RAYCHEV, V., AND VECHEV, M. Phrase-based statistical translation of programming languages. Onward! '14.

[14] KOLLER, D., AND FRIEDMAN, N. *Probabilistic Graphical Models: Principles and Techniques*. MIT Press, 2009.

[15] KREMENEK, T., NG, A. Y., AND ENGLER, D. A factor graph model for software bug finding. IJCAI'07.

[16] KREMENEK, T., TWOHEY, P., BACK, G., NG, A., AND ENGLER, D. From uncertainty to belief: Inferring the specification within. OSDI '06, USENIX Association, pp. 161–176.

[17] LAFFERTY, J. D., MCCALLUM, A., AND PEREIRA, F. C. N. Conditional random fields: Probabilistic models for segmenting and labeling sequence data. ICML '01, pp. 282–289.

[18] LIVSHITS, B., NORI, A. V., RAJAMANI, S. K., AND BANERJEE, A. Merlin: Specification inference for explicit information flow problems. PLDI '09, ACM, pp. 75–86.

[19] MADDISON, C. J., AND TARLOW, D. Structured generative models of natural source code.

[20] MURPHY, K. P. *Machine learning: a probabilistic perspective*. Cambridge, MA, 2012.

[21] PINTO, D., MCCALLUM, A., WEI, X., AND CROFT, W. B. Table extraction using conditional random fields. SIGIR '03, pp. 235–242.

[22] QUATTONI, A., COLLINS, M., AND DARRELL, T. Conditional random fields for object recognition. In *NIPS* (2004), pp. 1097–1104.

[23] RATLIFF, N. D., BAGNELL, J. A., AND ZINKEVICH, M. (approximate) subgradient methods for structured prediction. In *AISTATS* (2007), pp. 380–387.

[24] RAYCHEV, V., VECHEV, M., AND YAHAV, E. Code completion with statistical language models. PLDI '14, ACM, pp. 419–428.

[25] STEENSGAARD, B. Points-to analysis in almost linear time. POPL '96, pp. 32–41.

[26] TASKAR, B., GUESTRIN, C., AND KOLLER, D. Max-margin markov networks. In *NIPS* (2003).

[27] TSOCHANTARIDIS, I., JOACHIMS, T., HOFMANN, T., AND ALTUN, Y. Large margin methods for structured and interdependent output variables. *Journal of Machine Learning Research 6, 2005*, 1453–1484.

[28] Typescript language. http://www.typescriptlang.org/.

[29] ZINKEVICH, M., WEIMER, M., LI, L., AND SMOLA, A. J. Parallelized stochastic gradient descent. In *NIPS* (2010), pp. 2595–2603.

# DReX: A Declarative Language for Efficiently Evaluating Regular String Transformations *

Rajeev Alur Loris D'Antoni Mukund Raghothaman
University of Pennsylvania
{alur, lorisdan, rmukund}@seas.upenn.edu

## Abstract

We present DReX, a declarative language that can express all regular string-to-string transformations, and can still be efficiently evaluated. The class of regular string transformations has a robust theoretical foundation including multiple characterizations, closure properties, and decidable analysis questions, and admits a number of string operations such as insertion, deletion, substring swap, and reversal. Recent research has led to a characterization of regular string transformations using a primitive set of function combinators analogous to the definition of regular languages using regular expressions. While these combinators form the basis for the language DReX proposed in this paper, our main technical focus is on the complexity of evaluating the output of a DReX program on a given input string. It turns out that the natural evaluation algorithm involves dynamic programming, leading to complexity that is cubic in the length of the input string. Our main contribution is identifying a consistency restriction on the use of combinators in DReX programs, and a single-pass evaluation algorithm for consistent programs with time complexity that is linear in the length of the input string and polynomial in the size of the program. We show that the consistency restriction does not limit the expressiveness, and whether a DReX program is consistent can be checked efficiently. We report on a prototype implementation, and evaluate it using a representative set of text processing tasks.

***Categories and Subject Descriptors*** D.3.2 [*Language Classifications*]: Specialized application languages; F.1.1 [*Theory of Computation*]: Models of Computation, Automata

***Keywords*** DReX, string transformations, declarative languages

## 1. Introduction

Programs that transform plain text are ubiquitous and used for many different tasks, from reformatting documents to translating data between different formats. String specific utilities such as sed, AWK, and Perl have been used to query and reformat text files for many years. Since these tools are Turing complete they can express very complex transformations, however this comes at the cost of not being amenable to algorithmic analysis. To address this issue, restricted languages have been proposed in the context of verification of string sanitizers [26] and string coders [13], and for the analysis and optimization of list-manipulating programs [15]. These languages build on variants of finite-state transducers, which are automata-based representations of programs mapping strings to strings, and each of these languages supports different algorithmic analyses that are enabled by the properties of the underlying transducer model. Due to the focus on analyzability, expressiveness is a limiting factor in all such languages and many programs, in particular those that reorder input chunks, cannot be represented. Moreover, these languages are not declarative and their semantics are tightly coupled to the transducer model, forcing the programmer to reason in terms of finite state machines and process the input left-to-right.

In the theory of string-to-string transformations the class of regular string transformations is a robust class that strikes a balance between decidability and expressiveness. In particular this class captures transformations that involve reordering of input chunks, it is closed under composition [9], it has decidable equivalence [21], and has several equivalent characterizations, such as one-way transducers with a finite set of write-only registers [1], two-way transducers [16] and monadic second-order definable graph transformations [10]. Recently Alur et al [3] proposed a set of combinators that captures the class of regular string transformations. In [3] the focus is on expressiveness and the paper does not provide an efficient procedure to evaluate programs written with these combinators. Efficient evaluation of such programs is the main focus of this paper.

Starting with the combinators presented in [3], we develop DReX, an expressive declarative language to describe string transformations. The base combinator of DReX, $\varphi \mapsto d$, maps any character $a$ that satisfies the predicate $\varphi$ to the string $d(a)$. This combinator symbolically extends the one proposed in [3] with predicates and can therefore succinctly model strings over large (and potentially infinite) alphabets, such as Unicode. The other combinators supported by DReX are: (*a*) `split`$(f, g)$ that unambiguously splits the input string into two parts and outputs the concatenation of the results obtained using $f$ on the first part and $g$ on the second part; (*b*) `iterate`$(f)$ that unambiguously splits the input string into multiple parts and outputs the concatenation of evaluating $f$ on each of such parts; (*c*) `combine`$(f, g)$ that applies both $f$ and $g$ to the input string and concatenates the obtained results; (*d*) the conditional $f$ `else` $g$ that first tries to apply $f$ to the input and if $f$ cannot be applied it applies $g$; (*e*) `chain`$(f, R)$ that unambiguously splits the string into multiple parts $\sigma = \sigma_1 \ldots \sigma_n$ each belonging to the language described by the regular expression $R$, applies $f$ to every two pair of adjacent chunks $\sigma_i \sigma_{i+1}$, and finally concatenates these results. In order to model operations such as reversing a string, the

---

* A prototype implementation of DReX may be downloaded from `http://www.cis.upenn.edu/~rmukund/drex/`. This research was partially supported by NSF Expeditions in Computing grant CCF 1138996.



*POPL '15*, January 15–17, 2015, Mumbai, India.
Copyright © 2015 ACM 978-1-4503-3300-9/15/01...$15.00.
http://dx.doi.org/10.1145/2676726.2676981

operators split, iteration and chained sum also have a *left-additive* version in which the outputs computed on each split of the string are concatenated in reverse order.

A straightforward algorithm to evaluate DReX programs involves "operationalizing" the semantics, i.e. use dynamic programming and evaluate each sub-program on each substring of the input. Unfortunately, this algorithm takes time cubic in the length of the input string, and does not scale to strings longer than approximately a thousand characters. Because of the analogy between DReX operators (split sum, conditionals, iteration, etc.) and regular expressions (concatenation, union, Kleene-*, etc.) one approach is to construct an automaton model for evaluating DReX programs similarly to the approach taken to evaluate regular expressions. This is not simple because of various reasons, such as: *(a)* the conditional operator, $f$ `else` $g$, applies the transformation $g$ to the input only if the input string is not accepted by $f$. To check whether a string is in the complement of the domain of $f$ one needs to determinize the domain automaton and this is an exponential time operation; and *(b)* the operator `combine`$(f, g)$ is only defined on the intersection of the domains of $f$ and $g$. Repeating automata intersections multiple times also causes an exponential blow-up.

The main technical challenge is to identify a fragment of DReX which does not sacrifice expressiveness, and still permits "fast" evaluation algorithms. We call this subset of DReX the *consistent* fragment. Intuitively, we require each operator to admit unambiguous parsing, and limit the operators' ability to express the complement and intersection of languages. For example, `split`$(f, g)$ is consistent iff the domains of $f$ and of $g$ are unambiguously concatenable, i.e. there is no string with multiple viable splits. In the case of a conditional $f$ `else` $g$, the domains of $f$ and $g$ are required to be disjoint, making the complementation of the domain of $f$ unnecessary. Similarly, for the operator `combine`$(f, g)$, we require the domains of $f$ and $g$ to be identical, so that the domain of the entire program is equal to the domain of its sub-expressions and no language intersection is required. For the `chain`$(f, R)$ operator to be consistent, the language $R^*$ is required to be unambiguous, and $f$ is required to be a `split` operator for which both the left and right hand sides are exactly defined on the language described by $R$. We show that consistency of a DReX program can be efficiently determined.

We present an algorithm that evaluates a consistent DReX program $f$ on an input string $\sigma$, in time polynomial in the size of $f$ and linear in the length of $\sigma$. Intuitively, we construct a machine for each sub-program which reads the input in a single left-to-right pass. Each machine keeps track of potential parse trees of $\sigma$ as multiple *threads*, and updates the threads on reading each input symbol. The goal of the algorithm is to have a number of threads that is linear in the size of the program but does not depend on the length of the input string. This bound is achieved using the consistency requirements to eagerly kill threads whenever they become inactive. For example, the machine for `split`$(f, g)$ outputs a result as soon as it discovers a single viable split of the input string $\sigma$, since the consistency rules guarantee the absence of any other split. If the program were not consistent the machine would need to delay the output causing the number of alive threads to depend on the length of the string. Similarly, the machine for $f$ `else` $g$ can output the results of $g$ whenever this is defined, because of the requirement that $f$ and $g$ have disjoint domains and cannot simultaneously emit results. We also present a dynamic programming algorithm that can handle all DReX programs, but is limited by its cubic time complexity in the length of the input string.

We implemented our evaluation and consistency-checking algorithms and evaluated them on several text transformations: deletion of comments from a program, insertion of quotes around words, tag extraction from XML documents, reversing dictionaries, and the reordering and aligning of misplaced fields in BibTeX files. The evaluation algorithm for consistent DReX scales to large inputs (less than for 8 seconds for $100,000$ characters), while the dynamic programming algorithm, due to the cubic complexity in the size of the input, does not scale in practice (more than 60 seconds for $5,000$ characters) and therefore has limited applicability. Finally, the consistency-checking algorithm is very fast in practice (less than $0.6$ seconds for programs of size $\approx 3,600$ subexpressions), and it is also very helpful in identifying sources of ambiguity in the implemented programs.

In summary we offer the following contributions.

1. DReX, a language for describing string transformations that extends the combinators proposed in [3] to model strings over arbitrary sorts, and consistent DReX, a fragment of DReX that admits efficient evaluation without sacrificing expressiveness (section 2);
2. an algorithm for evaluating consistent DReX programs in a single left-to-right pass that is linear in the size of the input string and polynomial in the size of the program (section 3);
3. a dynamic programming algorithm for evaluating unrestricted DReX programs that has cubic time complexity in the length of the input string (section 4);
4. a proof that adding a composition operator to DReX causes the evaluation problem to become PSPACE-complete, and the dynamic programming algorithm to run in time exponential in the size of the program (section 4); and
5. an implementation of DReX together with an evaluation of our algorithms on practical string transformations (section 5).

## 2. The Syntax and Semantics of DReX

### 2.1 Regular combinators for string transformations

Given a character $a \in \Sigma$, and an output string $d \in \Gamma^*$, the function $a \mapsto d : \Sigma^* \to \Gamma^*_\perp$ maps the single-character input string $\sigma = a$ to the output $d$, and is undefined for all other inputs:[1]

$$[\![a \mapsto d]\!](\sigma) = \begin{cases} d & \text{if } \sigma = a, \text{ and} \\ \perp & \text{otherwise.} \end{cases}$$

Another basic function is $\epsilon \mapsto d$ which maps the empty string $\epsilon$ to the output $d \in \Gamma^*$, and is undefined everywhere else. The final basic function `bottom` is undefined for all input strings.

The split sum operators are the counterparts of concatenation in regular expressions. Given an input string $\sigma$, if there exists a unique split $\sigma = \sigma_1\sigma_2$, such that both $[\![f_1]\!](\sigma_1)$ and $[\![f_2]\!](\sigma_2)$ are defined, then

$$[\![\texttt{split}(f_1, f_2)]\!](\sigma) = [\![f_1]\!](\sigma_1)[\![f_2]\!](\sigma_2), \text{ and}$$
$$[\![\texttt{left-split}(f_1, f_2)]\!](\sigma) = [\![f_2]\!](\sigma_2)[\![f_1]\!](\sigma_1).$$

For all other inputs (where there is either no split, or multiple viable splits), both functions are undefined. Note the insistence on a unique parse tree — this is so that programs define functions, rather than relations.

Given two DReX functions $f_1$ and $f_2$, the function $f_1$ `else` $f_2$ first tries to apply $f_1$, and if this fails, applies $f_2$:

$$[\![f_1 \texttt{ else } f_2]\!](\sigma) = \begin{cases} [\![f_1]\!](\sigma) & \text{if } [\![f_1]\!](\sigma) \neq \perp, \text{ and} \\ [\![f_2]\!](\sigma) & \text{otherwise.} \end{cases}$$

This is the unambiguous counterpart of the union operator of traditional regular expressions.

[1] We adopt the convention of saying $f(x) = \perp$ when $f$ is undefined for the input $x$, and write $A_\perp$ for $A \cup \{\perp\}$, when $\perp \notin A$.

Similarly, if both $[\![f_1]\!](\sigma)$ and $[\![f_2]\!](\sigma)$ are defined, then

$$[\![\texttt{combine}(f_1, f_2)]\!](\sigma) = [\![f_1]\!](\sigma)[\![f_2]\!](\sigma).$$

If either function is undefined for the input $\sigma$, $\texttt{combine}(f_1, f_2)$ is undefined as well. This combinator can be used to make multiple passes over the input string, and a typical example would be the function that copies the input string twice: $\sigma$ transformed into $\sigma\sigma$. In terms of the input domain, the operator `combine` is the counterpart of intersection in regular languages, and is necessary to achieve expressive parity with regular string transformations because of the non-commutativity of string concatenation.

If $f$ is a DReX program, and the input string $\sigma$ can be uniquely split into substrings $\sigma = \sigma_1\sigma_2 \dots \sigma_n$, with $n \geq 0$, and such that $[\![f]\!](\sigma_i) \neq \bot$, for each $i$, then

$$[\![\texttt{iterate}(f)]\!](\sigma) = [\![f]\!](\sigma_1)[\![f]\!](\sigma_2) \dots [\![f]\!](\sigma_n), \text{ and}$$
$$[\![\texttt{left-iterate}(f)]\!](\sigma) = [\![f]\!](\sigma_n)[\![f]\!](\sigma_{n-1}) \dots [\![f]\!](\sigma_1).$$

Otherwise (if the input $\sigma$ cannot be split, or if multiple viable splits exist), then both iterated sums are undefined. This is the counterpart of Kleene-* of regular expressions.

The chained sum operator allows us to "mix" outputs produced by different parts of the input string. This is a new operator, without a regular expression counterpart, and is necessary for expressive completeness. Let $R$ be a regular expression that defines the language $[\![R]\!] = L$, and $f$ be a DReX program. Given an input $\sigma$, if there is a unique split $\sigma = \sigma_1\sigma_2 \dots \sigma_n$, , such that $\sigma_i \in L$ for each $i$, then, if $n \geq 2$

$$\begin{aligned}[\![\texttt{chain}(f, R)]\!](\sigma) =& [\![f]\!](\sigma_1\sigma_2)[\![f]\!](\sigma_2\sigma_3) \dots \\ & [\![f]\!](\sigma_{n-1}\sigma_n), \text{ and} \\ [\![\texttt{left-chain}(f, R)]\!](\sigma) =& [\![f]\!](\sigma_{n-1}\sigma_n)[\![f]\!](\sigma_{n-2}\sigma_{n-1}) \dots \\ & [\![f]\!](\sigma_1\sigma_2).\end{aligned}$$

For notational convenience, we treat $\sigma\bot = \bot\sigma = \bot$, and so if $[\![f]\!](\sigma_i\sigma_{i+1})$ is undefined for any $i$, both functions are undefined. Furthermore, if a unique split of the input string $\sigma$ does not exist, both the chained and left-chained sums are undefined. Notice that the regular expression $R$ in $\texttt{chain}(f, R)$ defines the split of the input string, and $f$ is applied to each pair of adjacent splits.

The final operator is function composition. If $f_1$ and $f_2$ are DReX programs such that $[\![f_1]\!] : \Sigma^* \to \Gamma^*_\bot$, and $[\![f_2]\!] : \Gamma^* \to \Lambda^*_\bot$, are partial functions, $\texttt{compose}(f_1, f_2)$ is defined as

$$[\![\texttt{compose}(f_1, f_2)]\!](\sigma) = [\![f_2]\!]([\![f_1]\!](\sigma)),$$

with the notational convention that $[\![f_1]\!](\bot) = \bot$.

Recall that regular string transformations can be defined in multiple equivalent ways: as two-way finite state transducers, as one-way streaming string transducers, and as MSO-definable graph transformations. We summarize the main result of [3]:

**Theorem 1** (Expressive completeness). *For every finite input alphabet $\Sigma$, and output alphabet $\Gamma$, every regular string transformation $f : \Sigma^* \to \Gamma^*_\bot$ can be expressed by a DReX program.*

More precisely, when we include the chained sum, function composition is unnecessary for expressive completeness, while the chained sum can itself be expressed using function composition, and so if composition is included, the chained sum is unnecessary.

### 2.2 Character sorts and predicates

Consider the basic combinator $a \mapsto d$ we described in the previous subsection, which maps the input $\sigma = a$ to the output $d$. For large alphabets, such as the set of all Unicode characters, this approach of explicitly mentioning each character does not scale. Basic transformations in DReX may therefore also reference symbolic predicates and character functions, as we will now describe. This is inspired by the recent development of symbolic transducers [26], which has proved to be useful in several practical applications.

Let $\Sigma, \Gamma, \dots$ be a collection of character sorts. For each character sort $\Sigma$, we pick a (possibly infinite) collection of predicates $P_\Sigma$ such that *(a)* $P_\Sigma$ is closed under the standard boolean operations: for each $\varphi, \psi \in P_\Sigma$, $\neg\varphi, \varphi \wedge \psi, \varphi \vee \psi \in P_\Sigma$, and *(b)* the satisfiability of predicates is decidable: given $\varphi \in P_\Sigma$, whether there exists an $x \in \Sigma$ such that $\varphi(x)$ holds is decidable.

A simple example is the sort $\Sigma_2 = \{a, b\}$ together with the set of predicates $P_{\Sigma_2} = \{x = a, x = b, \texttt{true}, \texttt{false}\}$. Another example is the set of all integers $\mathbb{Z}$, and with $P_\mathbb{Z} = \{\texttt{odd}(x), \texttt{even}(x), \texttt{true}, \texttt{false}\}$. We will write $\mathbb{U}$ for the set of all Unicode characters, with the various character properties $P_\mathbb{U} = \{\texttt{uppercase}(x), \texttt{digit}(x), \dots\}$.

If $\varphi \in P_\Sigma$ and $d = [d_1, d_2, \dots, d_k]$ is a list of character transformations, i.e. $d_i : \Sigma \to \Gamma$, then $\varphi \mapsto d$ is a basic transformation which maps every single-character string $\sigma$ which satisfies $\varphi(\sigma)$ to the output string $d_1(\sigma)d_2(\sigma) \dots d_k(\sigma)$, and is undefined for all other strings.

For example, the function $\texttt{uppercase}(x) \mapsto \texttt{tolowercase}(x)$ transforms every upper-case Unicode character to lower-case, while the function $\texttt{uppercase}(x) \mapsto xx$ outputs two copies of an upper-case character. The function $x \geq 0 \mapsto x - 1$ transforms a non-negative integer by subtracting one from it. Given an input digit $x \in [2\text{-}9]$, the function $x \in [2\text{-}9] \mapsto x - 2$ subtracts 2 from it.

Note that the basic symbolic transformations can still only operate on individual characters in isolation, and cannot relate properties of adjacent characters. For example, we do not allow transformations such as $[x > 0, y > x] \mapsto x, y$, which outputs two consecutive symbols $x$ and $y$, if $x > 0$ and $y > x$. It is known that allowing such "multi-character predicates" makes several analysis questions undecidable [12].

### 2.3 Consistent DReX programs

We now define consistent DReX, a restricted class which still captures all regular string transformations but for which we can provide an efficient evaluation algorithm (section 3). Intuitively, we restrict each operator to only allow unambiguous parsing, and limit the operators' ability to express expensive automata operations such as intersection and complement. Since the purpose of the consistency rules is for the correctness of the evaluation algorithm, we defer their motivation to subsection 3.5.

#### 2.3.1 Consistent unambiguous regular expressions

The consistency rules we propose are based on the notion of consistent unambiguous regular expression (CURE). CUREs are similar to conventional regular expressions, but with the additional guarantee that all matched strings have unique parse trees. Unambiguous regular expressions have been studied in the literature [7, 8, 25] — we explicitly qualify them as consistent here to emphasize that there are no strings with multiple parse trees. They are defined inductively as follows:

1. $\bot$ and $\epsilon$ are CUREs. The language associated with $\bot$ is the empty set $[\![\bot]\!] = \emptyset$, and the language associated with $\epsilon$ is the singleton $[\![\epsilon]\!] = \{\epsilon\}$.
2. For each satisfiable predicate $\varphi \in P_\Sigma$, $\varphi$ is a CURE. The language $[\![\varphi]\!]$ associated with the CURE $\varphi$ is the set of all single-character strings $\{x \in \Sigma \mid \varphi(x) \text{ holds}\}$.
3. For each pair of non-empty CUREs $R_1$ and $R_2$, if the associated languages $L_1 = [\![R_1]\!]$ and $L_2 = [\![R_2]\!]$ are disjoint, then $R_1 \cup R_2$ is also a CURE, and $[\![R_1 \cup R_2]\!] = L_1 \cup L_2$.
4. Given a pair of non-empty CUREs $R_1$ and $R_2$, we say that they are *unambiguously concatenable*, if for each string $\sigma \in \Sigma^*$,

there is at most one split $\sigma = \sigma_1\sigma_2$ such that $\sigma_1 \in [\![R_1]\!]$ and $\sigma_2 \in [\![R_2]\!]$. If $R_1$ and $R_2$ are unambiguously concatenable, then $R_1 \cdot R_2$ is also a CURE, and $[\![R_1 \cdot R_2]\!] = [\![R_1]\!][\![R_2]\!]$.

5. A non-empty CURE $R$ is *unambiguously iterable* if for every string $\sigma$, there is at most one split $\sigma = \sigma_1\sigma_2 \dots \sigma_n$ into substrings such that $\sigma_i \in [\![R]\!]$ for each $i$. If $R$ is unambiguously iterable, then $R^*$ is also a CURE, and $[\![R^*]\!] = [\![R]\!]^*$.

For example, the regular expressions $\varphi$ and $(\neg\varphi)^*$ are unambiguously concatenable for every character predicate $\varphi$: every string $\sigma$ matching $\varphi \cdot (\neg\varphi)^*$ has to be split after the first character. On the other hand, $\Sigma^*$ is not unambiguously concatenable with itself: there are three ways to parse the string $aa$ in $\Sigma^* \cdot \Sigma^*$, because the left part of the concatenation can either match $\epsilon$, $a$, or $aa$. The regular expression $\Sigma^*$ is unambiguous — there is only one way to split each string $\sigma$ such that each substring is in $\Sigma$ — but $(\Sigma^*)^*$ is not unambiguous.[2]

We call two CUREs $R_1$ and $R_2$ *equivalent*, and write $R_1 \equiv R_2$, if $[\![R_1]\!] = [\![R_2]\!]$.

### 2.3.2 Consistency rules

A consistent DReX program is one that satisfies the rules defined in this section. One major effect of these rules is to guarantee that no string has multiple parse trees, so the word "unique" in the definitions of subsection 2.1 is unnecessary. The domain of a DReX program $f$ is the set containing every string $\sigma$ such that $[\![f]\!](\sigma)$ is defined. In the following rules, we assign each consistent DReX program a *domain type*, which is a representation of its domain as a CURE.

Most of the consistency rules are straight-forward, except for chained sum and `combine`. Recall from the definition of `chain` that for `chain`$(f, R)$ to be defined on a string $\sigma$, we must have a split $\sigma = \sigma_1\sigma_2 \dots \sigma_n$ with $n \geq 2$. Therefore the domain type of `chain`$(f, R)$ requires at least two matches of $R$: $R \cdot R \cdot R^*$. Next, we want expressions of the form `chain(combine(split(`$f_{11}, f_{12}$`), ... split(`$f_{k1}, f_{k2}$`)),` $R \cdot R$`)`, where $R$ is unambiguously concatenable with itself, and the domain type of each $f_{ij}$ is $R_{ij} \equiv R$, to be consistent. We therefore pay special attention to the rule for `combine`.

1. All basic functions `bottom`, $\epsilon \mapsto d$, and $\varphi \mapsto d$ (where $\varphi$ is satisfiable) are consistent. Their domain types are $\perp$, $\epsilon$ and $\varphi$ respectively.
2. If $f_1$ and $f_2$ are both consistent and have unambiguously concatenable domain types $R_1$ and $R_2$ respectively, then `split`$(f_1, f_2)$ and `left-split`$(f_1, f_2)$ are also both consistent and have the domain $R_1 \cdot R_2$.
3. If $f$ is consistent and has domain type $R$, and $R$ is unambiguously iterable, then `iterate`$(f)$ and `left-iterate`$(f)$ are both consistent, with domain $R^*$.
4. If $f_1$ and $f_2$ are consistent with disjoint domain types $R_1$ and $R_2$ respectively, then $f_1$ `else` $f_2$ is also consistent with the domain $R_1 \cup R_2$.
5. If $f$ is consistent, and has domain type $R_1 \cdot R_2$, such that $R_1 \equiv R_2 \equiv R$, where $R$ is an unambiguously iterable CURE, then `chain`$(f, R)$ and `left-chain`$(f, R)$ are both consistent, and have the domain $R \cdot R \cdot R^*$.
6. If $f_1$ and $f_2$ are consistent with domain types $R_1$ and $R_2$ respectively, and $R_1 \equiv R_2$, then `combine`$(f_1, f_2)$ is also consistent. Depending on the syntactic structure of the CUREs $R_1$ and $R_2$, the domain type of `combine`$(f_1, f_2)$ is defined as follows:
   (a) If $R_1 = R_{11} \cdot R_{12}$, and $R_2 = R_{21} \cdot R_{22}$, with $R_{11} \equiv R_{12} \equiv R_{21} \equiv R_{22}$, then the domain type of `combine`$(f_1, f_2)$ is $R_1$.
   (b) Otherwise, if $R_1$ is *not* of the form $R_{11} \cdot R_{12}$ with $R_{11} \equiv R_{12}$, then the domain type is $R_1$.
   (c) Otherwise, the domain type is $R_2$.

[2] To be consistent with the classic notation we write $\Sigma$ do denote the CURE that accepts all possible input characters, but formally in our definition the corresponding CURE is the predicate `true`.

We now strengthen the claim originally made in theorem 1. While consistency was not an explicit goal in the original proof of theorem 1, it is the case that every expression constructed was actually consistent, and we can therefore state:

**Theorem 2.** *For every finite input alphabet $\Sigma$, and output alphabet $\Gamma$, every regular function $f : \Sigma^* \to \Gamma^*_\perp$ can be expressed by a consistent DReX program.*

The consistency and domain computation rules are syntax-directed, and straightforward to implement directly. We need to be able to answer the following basic questions about unambiguous regular expressions:

1. "Given CUREs $R_1$ and $R_2$, are $R_1$ and $R_2$ unambiguously concatenable?", "Given a CURE $R$, is it unambiguously iterable?", "Given CUREs $R_1$ and $R_2$, are they disjoint, or equivalently, is $R_1 \cup R_2$ also a CURE?" Observe that the traditional algorithm [24] to convert regular expressions to NFAs converts unambiguous regular expressions to unambiguous NFAs, where each accepted string has exactly one accepting path. Whether a regular expression $R$ is unambiguous can therefore be checked in polynomial time [8]: take the product of the corresponding ($\epsilon$-transition free) NFA $A_R$ with itself, and check for the presence of a reachable state $(q, q')$, with $q \neq q'$, which can itself reach a pair of accepting states $(q_f, q'_f) \in F \times F$, where $F$ is the set of accepting states of $A_L$. Thus, if the input alphabet $\Sigma$ is finite, these questions can be answered in polynomial time. Otherwise, the same problems for symbolic automata (representing $R_1$, $R_2$, etc.) are also decidable in polynomial time assuming that we can check in polynomial time whether a predicate is satisfiable.
2. "Given CUREs $R_1$ and $R_2$, is $R_1 \equiv R_2$?" If $\Sigma$ is finite, then from [25], we have that this can be checked in time $\mathcal{O}(poly(|R_1|, |R_2|, |\Sigma|))$. Otherwise, if CUREs are expressed using the symbolic notation of section 2.2, they can be translated into symbolic automata, and the equivalence of symbolic automata is decidable in polynomial time in the size of $R_1$ and $R_2$ and exponential[3] in the number of predicates appearing in $R_1$ and $R_2$.

**Theorem 3.** *Given a DReX program $f$ over an input alphabet $\Sigma$, checking whether $f$ is consistent is decidable. Furthermore, if the input alphabet $\Sigma$ is finite, then the consistency of $f$ can be determined in time $\mathcal{O}(poly(|f|, |\Sigma|))$.*

Note specifically that programs involving function composition are not consistent. In the rest of this paper, to distinguish the class of consistent DReX programs from the bigger class of *all* DReX programs, we will qualify the latter as the unrestricted class.

[3] The algorithm proposed in [25] can check in polynomial time whether two unambiguous NFAs are equivalent. The algorithm requires the alphabet to be finite, and using the Minterm generation technique proposed in [14] one can make a symbolic alphabet finite by constructing the Boolean combinations of the predicates in the automaton. This operation however can cause an exponential blow-up.

### 2.4 Examples of consistent DReX programs

The simplest non-trivial DReX program is the identity function $id = \texttt{iterate}(\texttt{true} \mapsto x)$. Several variations of this program are also useful: $\texttt{iterate}(\texttt{lowercase}(x) \mapsto \texttt{touppercase}(x))$ maps strings of lower-case characters to upper-case, and $id_{\neg\texttt{space}} = \texttt{iterate}(\neg\,\texttt{space}(x) \mapsto x)$ is the identity function restricted to strings not containing a space.

More interesting functions can be constructed using the conditional operator: the function $\textit{sw-case} = \texttt{uppercase}(x) \mapsto \texttt{tolowercase}(x)\ \texttt{else}\ \texttt{lowercase}(x) \mapsto \texttt{touppercase}(x)$ flips the case of a single input character, and so $\texttt{iterate}(\textit{sw-case})$ switches the case of each character in the input string.

Given a string of the form "*First-name Last-name*", the function $\textit{echo-first} = \texttt{split}(id_{\neg\texttt{space}}, \texttt{space}(x) \mapsto \epsilon, \texttt{iterate}(\texttt{true} \mapsto \epsilon))$ outputs "*First-name*". Similarly, the function *echo-last* which outputs the last name could be written, and the two can be combined into $\texttt{combine}(\textit{echo-last}, \textit{echo-first})$, which outputs "*Last-name First-name*". Note that the space in between is omitted — the expression $\texttt{combine}(\texttt{split}(\textit{echo-last}, \epsilon \mapsto \texttt{" "}), \textit{echo-first})$ preserves this space. An example of the use of the left-additive operators is in string reversal: the function $\texttt{left-iterate}(\texttt{true} \mapsto x)$ reverses the input string.

Finally, to present an example of the chained sum combinator, we consider the situation of misaligned titles in BibTeX files. Assume that, by mistake, the title of the first entry appears in the second entry, the title of the second entry appears in the third entry, and so on. Let $R_{bib}$ be the unambiguous regular expression matching a BibTeX entry. Let $f_{bib}$ be the DReX program which examines pairs of adjacent BibTeX entries and outputs the title of the second entry and all other fields from the first entry. Then $\texttt{chain}(f_{bib}, R_{bib})$ corrects the misaligned text in the input file. We now outline the construction of $f_{bib}$. Let *echo-header* be the function which maps each BibTeX entry to its header (such as "@book{"), and *echo-title* be the function which maps each BibTeX entry to its title. Then $\textit{make-title} = \texttt{split}(\textit{echo-header}, \textit{echo-title})$ copies the header from the first BibTeX entry and the title from the second. Similarly, if *copy-body* echoes all the fields of a BibTeX entry except the title, and *delete-entry* maps an entire BibTeX entry to the empty string $\epsilon$, then $\textit{make-body} = \texttt{split}(\textit{copy-body}, \textit{delete-entry})$ completes the body of the output using the fields of the first BibTeX entry. We can then write $f_{bib} = \texttt{combine}(\textit{make-title}, \textit{make-body})$.

The reader is referred to appendix A for a description of the consistent DReX programs used in our evaluation.

## 3. A Single-Pass Algorithm for Consistent DReX

In this section, we present the main technical contribution of this paper: a single-pass linear time algorithm to evaluate consistent DReX programs. We describe the intuition and present the idea of *function evaluators* in subsection 3.1, and then construct the evaluators for each DReX combinator. We conclude with subsection 3.5, a brief discussion of why this algorithm does not work with unrestricted DReX programs. Full proofs, and the omitted case of the chained sum will be included in the full version of this paper.

### 3.1 Intuition and the idea of function evaluators

Given a consistent DReX program $f$, we construct an evaluator $T$ which computes the associated function $[\![f]\!]$. The evaluator $T$ processes the input string from left-to-right, one character at a time. After reading each character, it outputs the value of $f$ on the string read so far, if it is defined.

To understand the input / output specifications of $T$, we consider the example program $\texttt{split}(f, g)$. In this case, $T$ is given the sequence of input signals $(\textit{Start}, 0), (\sigma_1, 1), (\sigma_2, 2), \ldots, (\sigma_n, n)$. The first signal $(\textit{Start}, 0)$ indicates the beginning of the string, and

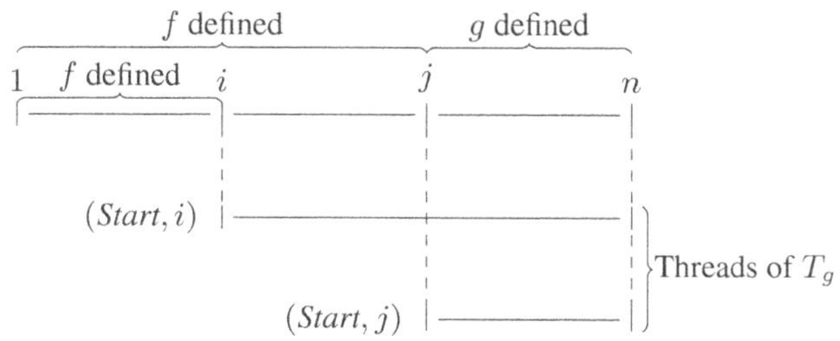


Figure 3.1: Example run of the evaluator $T$ for $\texttt{split}(f, g)$ over a string $\sigma$. The evaluator $T_f$ emits a result at indices $i$ and $j$ of the input string. The evaluator $T_g$ for $g$ may simultaneously be processing multiple threads, corresponding to different potential parse trees of the input string $\sigma$. From the consistency rules, we know that at most one thread may return a result at each index, and so $T$ can safely emit a result in response to getting a result from $T_g$.

each character $\sigma_i$ is annotated with its index $i$ in the input string. After reading $(\sigma_i, i)$, $T$ responds with the value of $\texttt{split}(f, g)$ on $\sigma_1\sigma_2\ldots\sigma_i$, if it is defined.

Assume that $f$ and $g$ are consistent, and have unambiguously concatenable domain types $R_f$ and $R_g$ respectively. The evaluator $T$ maintains two sub-evaluators $T_f$ and $T_g$ for the functions $f$ and $g$ respectively. Each time $T$ receives the input $(a, i)$, it forwards this signal to both $T_f$ and $T_g$. Whenever $T_f$ reports a result, i.e. that $f$ is defined on the input string read so far, $T$ sends the signal *Start* to $T_g$ to start processing the suffix. Consider the situation in figure 3.1, where $f$ is defined for the prefixes $\sigma_1\sigma_2\ldots\sigma_i$ and $\sigma_1\sigma_2\ldots\sigma_j$. The input to the sub-evaluator $T_g$ is then the sequence $(\sigma_1, 1)$, $(\sigma_2, 2), \ldots, (\sigma_i, i), (\textit{Start}, i), (\sigma_{i+1}, i+1), \ldots, (\sigma_j, j), (\textit{Start}, j), \ldots, (\sigma_n, n)$.

For each signal $(\textit{Start}, i)$ occurring in the input string, we call the subsequent sequence of characters $\sigma_{i+1}\sigma_{i+2}\ldots$ the *thread* beginning at index $i$. Note that each thread corresponds to a potential parse tree of $\sigma$, and that $T_g$ may be processing multiple such threads simultaneously. The main challenge is to ensure that the number of active threads in $T_g$ is bound by $\mathcal{O}(|g|)$, and is independent of the length of the input string. After reading $\sigma_n$, $T_g$ reports a result to $T$, the evaluator for the $\texttt{split}(f, g)$. To uniquely identify the thread $j$ reporting the result, the result signal $(\textit{Result}, j, \gamma_g)$ is annotated with the index $j$ at which the corresponding *Start* was received.

Note that the consistency rules guarantee that, after reading each input symbol, $T_g$ emits at most one result, for otherwise the prefix of the input string read so far would have multiple parse trees.

When $T$ receives this result signal from $T_g$, it combines it with the response $(\textit{Result}, 0, \gamma_f)$ initially obtained from $f$ at position $j$, and itself emits the result $(\textit{Result}, 0, \gamma_f\gamma_g)$. To do this, it maintains a set $th_g$ (for threads) of triples $(i_{0f}, i_{0g}, \gamma_f)$, where $i_{0f}$ is the index along the input string at which $T_f$ was started, $i_{0g}$ was the index at which $T_f$ reported a result and $T_g$ was started, and $\gamma_f$ was the result reported by $T_f$. In order to prevent this set $th_g$ from becoming too large, $T_g$ emits *kill signals*. Say that, at index $k$, $T_g$ discovers that for every possible suffix $\tau \in \Sigma^*$, $g$ will be undefined for the string $\sigma_{i+1}\sigma_{i+2}\ldots\sigma_k\tau$, and so the thread $(\textit{Start}, i)$ of $T_g$ initiated at the input index $i$ can never return a result. It then emits $(\textit{Kill}, i)$ to signal to $T$ that the relevant entries in the set $th_g$ can be deleted.

***Formal specification of the evaluator.*** The input alphabet to each evaluator is therefore $\textit{In} = (\Sigma \cup \{\textit{Start}\}) \times \mathbb{N}$ and the output alphabet is $\textit{Out} = (\{\textit{Result}\} \times \mathbb{N} \times \Gamma^*) \cup (\{\textit{Kill}\} \times \mathbb{N})$, where $\Sigma$ is the input and $\Gamma$ is the output alphabet of the DReX program.

While constructing the evaluator $T$ for a DReX program $f$, we assume the following condition of *input validity*: for each prefix of the input stream *in*, there is at most one thread for which $f$ is defined. Thus, for example, $T$ can never see two consecutive $(\textit{Start}, i)$ signals for the same $i$. In return, we make the following guarantees:

**Correctness of results.** After reading each input signal $(\sigma_j, j)$ in *in*, we report the result $(\textit{Result}, i, \gamma)$ exactly for that thread $(\textit{Start}, i)$ such that $[\![f]\!](\sigma_{i+1}\sigma_{i+2}\ldots\sigma_j) = \gamma$, if it exists.

**Eagerness of kills.** Every thread $\sigma$ beginning at $(\textit{Start}, i)$ of *in*, such that there is no suffix $\tau$ for which $f(\sigma\tau)$ is defined, is killed exactly once while reading *in*. Furthermore, there are always at most $\mathcal{O}(|f|)$ active threads, where $|f|$ is the size of $f$.

If an evaluator $T$ satisfies these requirements for $f$, then we say that the evaluator *computes* $f$. On the input $(\textit{Start}, 0), (\sigma_1, 1), (\sigma_2, 2), \ldots, (\sigma_n, n)$, the evaluator outputs a result $\gamma$ in exactly those cases when $f$ is defined, and in that case, $[\![f]\!](\sigma) = \gamma$. We will ensure that the evaluator $T$ processes each input signal in time $\mathcal{O}(poly(|f|))$.[4]

### 3.2 Basic evaluators

The simplest case is when $f = \texttt{bottom}$. The evaluator $T_\perp$ is defined by the following rules:

1. On input $(\textit{Start}, i)$, respond with $(\textit{Kill}, i)$.
2. On input $(a, i)$, for $a \in \Sigma$, do nothing.

Next, we consider the evaluator $T_{\epsilon \mapsto d}$, for the case when $f = \epsilon \mapsto d$, for some $d \in \Gamma^*$. Intuitively, this evaluator returns a result immediately on receiving a start signal, but can only kill the thread after reading the next symbol. It therefore maintains a set $th \subseteq \mathbb{N}$ of currently active threads, which are to be killed on reading the next input symbol. The set $th$ is initialized to $\emptyset$.

1. On input $(\textit{Start}, i)$, respond with $(\textit{Result}, i, d)$. Update $th := th \cup \{i\}$.
2. On input $(a, i)$, for $a \in \Sigma$, respond with $(\textit{Kill}, j)$, for each thread start index $j \in th$. Update $th := \emptyset$.

Observe that by the condition of input validity, we can never observe two consecutive start signals in the input stream. Therefore, $|th| \leq 1$, and the response time of $T_{\epsilon \mapsto d}$ to each input signal is bounded by a constant.

The final basic function is $f = \varphi \mapsto d$ for some character predicate $\varphi$ and $d : (\Sigma \to \Gamma)^*$. The evaluator $T_{\varphi \mapsto d}$ maintains two sets $th, th' \subseteq \mathbb{N}$ of thread start indices, initialized to $th = th' = \emptyset$. $th$ is the set of threads for which no symbol has yet been seen, while $th'$ is the set of threads for which one input symbol has been seen, and that input symbol satisfied the predicate $\varphi$.

1. On input $(\textit{Start}, i)$, update $th := th \cup \{i\}$.
2. On input $(a, i)$, for $a \in \Sigma$:
   (a) Emit $(\textit{Kill}, j)$, for each thread $j \in th'$.
   (b) If $a$ satisfies the predicate $\varphi$, for each thread $j \in th$, emit $(\textit{Result}, j, d(a))$. Update $th' := th$, and $th := \emptyset$.
   (c) If $a$ does not satisfy the predicate $\varphi$, then for each thread $j \in th$, emit $(\textit{Kill}, j)$. Update $th := \emptyset$, and $th' := \emptyset$.

Just as in the case of $\epsilon \mapsto d$, we have $|th|, |th'| \leq 1$, and so $T_{\varphi \mapsto d}$ responds to each input signal in time bounded by some constant.

[4] We assume a representation for strings with concatenation requiring only constant time. Specifically, strings are only concatenated symbolically using a pointer representation. Such "lazily" represented strings can be converted into the traditional sequence-of-characters representation in time linear in the string length.

### 3.3 State-free evaluators: combination and conditionals

The simplest non-trivial evaluator is for $\texttt{combine}(f, g)$. Recall that, by the consistency requirements, we have $R_f \equiv R_g$ for the domain types $R_f$ and $R_g$ of the sub-expressions. Thus, all state can be maintained by the sub-evaluators $T_f$ and $T_g$ and $T_{\texttt{combine}(f,g)}$ can be entirely state-free. It has the following behavior:

1. On input $(\textit{Start}, i)$, send the signal $(\textit{Start}, i)$ to both sub-evaluators $T_f$ and $T_g$.
2. On input $(a, i)$, send the signal $(a, i)$ to both $T_f$ and $T_g$.
3. On receiving the result $(\textit{Result}, i, \gamma_f)$ from $T_f$ and the result $(\textit{Result}, i, \gamma_g)$ from $T_g$ (which, according to the consistency requirements for $\texttt{combine}(f, g)$, have to occur simultaneously), respond with $(\textit{Result}, i, \gamma_f\gamma_g)$.
4. On receiving the kill signals $(\textit{Kill}, i)$ from $T_f$ and $T_g$ (by the consistency rules, necessarily simultaneously), emit the kill signal $(\textit{Kill}, i)$.

The evaluator $T_{f\ \texttt{else}\ g}$ maintains two sub-evaluators $T_f$ and $T_g$. In addition, it maintains two sets $th_f, th_g \subseteq \mathbb{N}$ of threads currently active in $T_f$ and $T_g$ respectively. Both sets are initialized to $\emptyset$. The behavior of $T_{f\ \texttt{else}\ g}$ is defined as follows:

1. On receiving the input $(\textit{Start}, i)$, update $th_f := th_f \cup \{i\}$, and $th_g := th_g \cup \{i\}$. Send the start signal $(\textit{Start}, i)$ to both $T_f$ and $T_g$.
2. On receiving the input $(a, i)$ for some $a \in \Sigma$, send the input $(a, i)$ to both $T_f$ and $T_g$.
3. When either $T_f$ or $T_g$ respond with the result $(\textit{Result}, i, \gamma)$ (by the consistency rules, we know that the other sub-evaluator is not responding with a result), emit the result $(\textit{Result}, i, \gamma)$.
4. If a kill signal $(\textit{Kill}, i)$ is received from $T_f$ (resp. $T_g$), update $th_f := th_f \setminus \{i\}$ (resp. $th_g := th_g \setminus \{i\}$). If $i \notin th_f$ and $i \notin th_g$, then kill the thread by emitting $(\textit{Kill}, i)$.

The sizes of $th_f$ and $th_g$ are bounded by the number of active threads of $T_f$ and $T_g$ respectively, and hence it follows that $T_{f\ \texttt{else}\ g}$ responds to each input signal in time $\mathcal{O}(|f| + |g|) + t_f + t_g$, where $t_f$ and $t_g$ are the response times of $T_f$ and $T_g$ respectively.

### 3.4 Stateful evaluators: iteration and split sum

We now construct evaluators for $\texttt{iterate}(f)$ and $\texttt{split}(f, g)$. The evaluators for $\texttt{left-iterate}(f)$ and $\texttt{left-split}(f, g)$ are symmetric with respect to concatenation and can be constructed similarly.

First, we build the evaluator $T_{\texttt{iterate}(f)}$, where $f$ is consistent and has the unambiguously iterable domain type $R_f$. Whenever $T_{\texttt{iterate}(f)}$ receives a start signal $(\textit{Start}, i)$, or an input signal $(a, i)$, this is passed to $T_f$. Consider a sequence of input signals $\sigma$, as shown in figure 3.2. After reading each input symbol, say $(\sigma_n, n)$, $T_f$ may report that $f$ is defined for a suffix of the input stream $(\textit{Start}, k), (\sigma_{k+1}, k+1), \ldots, (\sigma_n, n)$ seen so far. The evaluator $T_{\texttt{iterate}(f)}$ responds by initiating a new thread of $T_f$ by sending it the start signal $(\textit{Start}, n)$. Furthermore, it has to record the result $(\textit{Result}, k, \gamma_3)$ just reported by $T_f$. It does this by adding the entry $(i, n, \gamma_1\gamma_2\gamma_3)$ to the set $th$. Each entry $(i_0, j_0, \gamma) \in th$ refers to an active thread $j_0$ of $T_f$, the index of the signal $(\textit{Start}, i_0)$ received by $T_{\texttt{iterate}(f)}$, and the cumulative result $\gamma$ obtained so far.

Formally, the set $th \subseteq \mathbb{N} \times \mathbb{N} \times \Gamma^*$ is initialized to $\emptyset$. The evaluator $T_{\texttt{iterate}(f)}$ does the following:

1. On input $(\textit{Start}, i)$:
   (a) Update $th := th \cup \{(i, i, \epsilon)\}$.

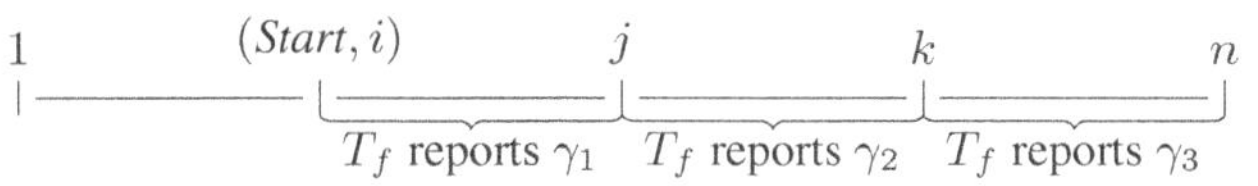


Figure 3.2: For each thread $(\mathit{Start}, i_0)$ of the evaluator $T_{\texttt{iterate}(f)}$, there may be multiple potential parse trees. The evaluator $T_{\texttt{iterate}(f)}$ maps individual threads $(\mathit{Start}, i)$ of $T_f$ to the corresponding start signal $(\mathit{Start}, i_0)$ in $T_{\texttt{iterate}(f)}$ through the entry $(i_0, i, \gamma)$ in the set *th*. Thus, after obtaining the response from $T_f$ at index $n$, $T_{\texttt{iterate}(f)}$ updates $\mathit{th} := \mathit{th} \cup \{(i, n, \gamma_1\gamma_2\gamma_3)\}$.

  (b) Send $(\mathit{Start}, i)$ to $T_f$. Assert that $T_f$ does not respond with a result $(\mathit{Result}, i, \gamma)$, because by the consistency rules, $f(\epsilon)$ is undefined for $R_f$ to be unambiguously iterable.

  (c) Respond with the result $(\mathit{Result}, i, \epsilon)$.

2. On input $(a, i)$, send the signal $(a, i)$ to $T_f$. For each response of $T_f$, do the following:

  (a) If the response is a result, $(\mathit{Result}, j, \gamma_f)$, then, find the corresponding entry $(j_0, j, \gamma) \in \mathit{th}$, for some values of $j_0$ and $\gamma$. Assert (by the invariant that *th* records the active threads of $T_f$) that this entry exists, and is unique.

    i. Update $\mathit{th} := \mathit{th} \cup \{(j_0, i, \gamma\gamma_f)\}$.

    ii. Send the signal $(\mathit{Start}, i)$ to $T_f$. Confirm that $T_f$ does not respond with a result $(\mathit{Result}, i, 0, \gamma'_f)$, for that would violate the consistency requirements.

    iii. Respond with the result $(\mathit{Result}, j_0, \gamma\gamma_f)$.

  (b) If the response is a kill signal, $(\mathit{Kill}, j)$:

    i. Let *kill-ring* be the set of all tuples $(j_0, j, \gamma) \in \mathit{th}$, for some values of $j_0$ and $\gamma$. By the consistency requirements, *kill-ring* is asserted to be a singleton set.

    ii. Update $\mathit{th} := \mathit{th} \setminus \mathit{kill\text{-}ring}$.

    iii. For every entry $(j_0, j, \gamma) \in \mathit{kill\text{-}ring}$ if there is no entry of the form $(j_0, j', \gamma') \in \mathit{th}$, then emit the kill signal $(\mathit{Kill}, j_0)$.

Observe that an element is added to *th* exactly when it is sent a start signal, and an entry is deleted exactly when $T_{\texttt{iterate}(f)}$ receives a kill signal. Thus, the entries of *th* correspond to the active threads of $T_f$, and its size is bounded by $\mathcal{O}(|f|)$. The response time of $T_{\texttt{iterate}(f)}$ to each input signal is therefore $\mathcal{O}(|f|) + t_f$, where $t_f$ is the response time of $T_f$.

The evaluator $T_{\texttt{split}(f,g)}$ for $\texttt{split}(f, g)$ is similar, except that it maintains two sets: the first set $\mathit{th}_f \subseteq \mathbb{N}$ is the set of thread start indices which are still active in $T_f$, and the second set $\mathit{th}_g \subseteq \mathbb{N} \times \mathbb{N} \times \Gamma^*$ is the set of triples $(i_0, i, \gamma_f)$ which indicates, for each active thread in $T_g$, the index $i$ at which $T_g$ was signaled to start, the index $i_0$ of the original start received by $T_{\texttt{split}(f,g)}$, when $T_f$ was started, and the value $\gamma_f$ returned by $T_f$ on the prefix. Both sets are initialized to $\emptyset$, and $T_{\texttt{split}(f,g)}$ follows the following rules:

1. On input $(\mathit{Start}, i)$:

  (a) Update $\mathit{th}_f := \mathit{th}_f \cup \{i\}$.

  (b) Send $(\mathit{Start}, i)$ to $T_f$. Let $\mathit{Rsp}_f$ be the responses from $T_f$. Let $\mathit{Rsp}_g = \emptyset$.

2. On input $(a, i)$:

  (a) Send $(a, i)$ to $T_f$. Let $\mathit{Rsp}_f$ be the set of responses from $T_f$.

  (b) Send $(a, i)$ to $T_g$. Let $\mathit{Rsp}_g$ be the set of responses from $T_g$.

3. For each response $r \in \mathit{Rsp}_f \cup \mathit{Rsp}_g$, do the following:

  (a) If $r$ is a result $(\mathit{Result}, j_0, \gamma_f)$ from $T_f$,

    i. Update $\mathit{th}_g := \mathit{th}_g \cup \{(j_0, i, \gamma_f)\}$.

    ii. Send the signal $(\mathit{Start}, i)$ to $T_g$. Update $\mathit{Rsp}_g := \mathit{Rsp}_g \cup \mathit{Rsp}'_g$, where $\mathit{Rsp}'_g$ is the set of responses from $T_g$.

  (b) If $r$ is a result $(\mathit{Result}, j, \gamma_g)$ from $T_g$, let $(j_0, j, \gamma_f)$ be the (by the consistency rules, necessarily unique) corresponding record in $\mathit{th}_g$. Respond with $(\mathit{Result}, j_0, \gamma_f\gamma_g)$.

  (c) If $r$ is a kill signal $(\mathit{Kill}, j_0)$ from $T_f$,

    i. Update $\mathit{th}_f := \mathit{th}_f \setminus \{j_0\}$.

    ii. If there is no element of the form $(j_0, j, \gamma_f) \in \mathit{th}_g$, for some values of $j$, $\gamma_f$, kill the thread: $(\mathit{Kill}, j_0)$.

  (d) Finally, if $r$ is a kill signal $(\mathit{Kill}, j)$ from $T_g$,

    i. Let *kill-ring* be the set of tuples $(j_0, j, \gamma_f) \in \mathit{th}_g$ for some values of $j_0$, $\gamma_f$.

    ii. Update $\mathit{th}_g := \mathit{th}_g \setminus \mathit{kill\text{-}ring}$.

    iii. For every record $(j_0, j, \gamma_f) \in \mathit{kill\text{-}ring}$, if there is no longer a record of the form $(j_0, j', \gamma'_f) \in \mathit{th}_g$, and $j_0 \notin \mathit{th}_f$, kill the thread beginning at $j_0$: $(\mathit{Kill}, j_0)$.

Observe that $|\mathit{th}_f|$ is bound by the number of active threads of $T_f$ and $|\mathit{th}_g|$ is bound by the number of active threads of $T_g$. Thus, $T_{\texttt{split}(f,g)}$ responds to each input signal in time $\mathcal{O}(|f| + |g|) + t_f + t_g$, where $t_f$ and $t_g$ are the response times of $T_f$ and $T_g$ respectively.

### 3.5 What breaks with unrestricted DReX programs?

First, notice that the function composition operator is un-amenable to the evaluator model we just described. We wish to process each character in bounded time, regardless of the length of the input string. Consider the case of $\texttt{compose}(f, g)$: when the evaluator $T_f$ returns a result $(\mathit{Result}, i, \gamma)$, we have to pass the *entire* intermediate result string $\gamma$ to $T_g$, and this is possibly as long as the input seen so far. Notice that this limitation should be unsurprising, because nested function compositions — such as the transformation $\sigma \mapsto \sigma\sigma$ composed with itself $k$ times — can cause an exponential blowup in the length of the output string.

Next, consider a potential evaluator $T$ for $\texttt{split}(f, g)$, in the absence of any consistency requirement. Thus, there might exist strings $\sigma = \sigma_1\sigma_2 \ldots \sigma_n$ which admit two splits $\sigma = \tau_1\tau_2 = \tau'_1\tau'_2$, such that all of $[\![f]\!](\tau_1)$, $[\![f]\!](\tau'_1)$, $[\![g]\!](\tau_2)$, and $[\![g]\!](\tau'_2)$ are defined. In this case, $\texttt{split}(f, g)$ is undefined for the entire string $\sigma$. We have to drop the requirement of input validity, because the nested evaluator $T_g$ emits *two Result* signals after reading $\sigma_n$. We could conceivably modify $T$ to emit an output signal when exactly one thread of $T_g$ returns a result. Unfortunately, it turns out that this modification is insufficient, as the induction hypothesis now breaks — the evaluator $T$ has to perform additional book-keeping to report results correctly. The consistency rules provide an easy way to avoid this non-trivial book-keeping.

Finally, note that unrestricted use of the chained sum operator does not satisfy the output bound $|[\![f]\!](\sigma)| = \mathcal{O}(\mathit{poly}(|f|)\,|\sigma|)$, while every consistent DReX program obeys $|[\![f]\!](\sigma)| \leq |f|\,|\sigma|$.

## 4. The Complexity of Unrestricted DReX

In this section we first describe the dynamic programming algorithm to evaluate DReX programs. We show that it has time complexity cubic in the size of the input string, and when function composition is allowed, requires time exponential in the size of the program. We then show that the evaluation problem for DReX programs with composition is PSPACE-complete, and is thus computationally hard. Finally, we argue that for unrestricted DReX programs, even when disallowing composition, there is no evaluation algorithm for which the complexity is linear in the length of the input string and polynomial in the size of the program.

### 4.1 Evaluation by dynamic programming

We now describe the dynamic programming algorithm to evaluate unrestricted DReX programs. This algorithm also works on programs containing the function composition operator. The algorithm mimics the semantics of DReX by computing the following functions (represented as lookup tables). Given a program $f$, and a string $\sigma$, for any two numbers $i$ and $j$ the algorithm computes the function $\text{OUT}(f, \sigma, i, j)$ representing the output of $f$ on the substring[5] $\sigma[i, j]$, $[\![f]\!](\sigma[i, j])$. To evaluate the operator $\texttt{iterate}(f)$ we also need to compute the function $\text{COUNT}(\texttt{iterate}(f), \sigma, i, j)$ that counts the number of possible ways to split $\sigma[i, j]$ so that each split is accepted by $f$, and to evaluate the operator $\texttt{chain}(f, R)$ we compute the function $\text{BEL}(R, \sigma, i, j)$ which checks whether a substring $\sigma[i, j]$ belongs to the language $[\![R]\!]$. Every function OUT, COUNT, and BEL is represented by a table and for each string $\sigma$, and each sub-program $g$ of $f$, each table will have $\mathcal{O}(|\sigma|^2)$ entries, corresponding to the substrings of $\sigma$. The final output of the algorithm is $\text{OUT}(f, \sigma, 1, |\sigma| + 1)$.

We explain the intuition of the algorithm by showing how the entries are computed for the iteration and composition operators. The value $\text{OUT}(\texttt{iterate}(f), \sigma, i, j)$ corresponding to the output of $\texttt{iterate}(f)$ on the string $\sigma' = \sigma[i, j]$ is defined iff there is a unique way to split the string $\sigma'$ into multiple chunks so that $f$ is defined on each chunk, i.e. iff $\text{COUNT}(\texttt{iterate}(f), \sigma, i, j) = 1$. If this is the case, then we know that there is a unique value $k$, such that $i \leq k < j$, for which both $\gamma_{pre} = \text{OUT}(\texttt{iterate}(f), \sigma, i, k)$ and $\gamma_{post} = \text{OUT}(f, \sigma, k, j)$ are defined, and $\gamma_{pre}\gamma_{post}$ is the output of $\texttt{iterate}(f)$ on $\sigma[i, j]$. Looking for this witness $k$ takes at most $|\sigma|$ steps if all the required table entries have already been computed. Similarly, the entry $\text{COUNT}(\texttt{iterate}(f), \sigma, i, j)$ can be computed in at most $|\sigma|$ steps by counting for how many values of $l$ the function $\text{COUNT}(\texttt{iterate}(f), \sigma, i, l)$ is greater than 0 and the functions $\text{OUT}(f, \sigma, l, j)$ is defined.

The rule for computing $\text{OUT}(\texttt{compose}(f_1, f_2), \sigma, i, j)$ is what causes an exponential blow-up in the evaluation time. To compute the output of $\texttt{compose}(f_1, f_2)$ on $\sigma[i, j]$, we first need to compute the output $\tau = \text{OUT}(f_1, \sigma, i, j)$ of the program $f_1$ on the string $\sigma[i, j]$ and then the output $\text{OUT}(f_2, \tau, 1, |\tau| + 1)$ of the program $f_2$ on the string $\tau$. As we will show, when using the composition operator the size of the output $\tau$ may grow exponentially, and since computing each entry of the table $\text{OUT}(f_2, \tau, \cdot, \cdot)$ requires $\mathcal{O}(\tau)$ steps, the resulting complexity is also exponential.

We now bound the output length of programs containing the composition operator.

**Lemma 4** (Output size). *Given a program $f$ and an input string $\sigma \in \Sigma^*$ such that $\tau = [\![f]\!](\sigma)$ is defined, we have $|\tau| \leq |f|^{d+1} |\sigma|$. Here $d$ is the number of composition operators appearing in $f$.*

We now state the complexity of the dynamic programming routine to evaluate DReX programs.

**Theorem 5** (Complexity of dynamic programming). *Given a program $f$, and an input string $\sigma \in \Sigma^*$, the output $[\![f]\!]$ can be computed in time $\mathcal{O}(|f|^{2d^2+5d+4} |\sigma|^{2d+3})$ where $d$ is the number of composition operators in $f$. If $d = 0$ we can show that the algorithm has complexity $\mathcal{O}(|f| |\sigma|^3)$.*

*Proof sketch.* For a particular string $\sigma$ and if the program $f$ that does not contain any composition operators ($d = 0$), computing each entry of the tables OUT, COUNT, and BEL takes time $\mathcal{O}(|\sigma|)$ and since there are $|f| |\sigma|^2$ entries the algorithm has complexity $\mathcal{O}(|f| |\sigma|^3)$. In the presence of composition operators which can produce intermediate results, for each intermediate string $\tau$, a new table of size $|\tau|^2$ must be created. By lemma 4 we know that an intermediate result has size at most $\mathcal{O}(|f|^{d+1} |\sigma|)$, hence the complexity is exponential in $d$. □

### 4.2 DReX evaluation with composition is PSPACE-complete

While the main appeal of the algorithm in subsection 4.1 is ease of implementation, it can use exponential space. It turns out that, even in the presence of composition, DReX programs can be evaluated in PSPACE. First observe that, since the output computed by a program has at most exponentially many characters (lemma 4), the index of each character in the output is only polynomially many bits long. We therefore adopt an implicit representation of strings with the following operations (in contrast with the traditional explicit list-of-characters representation of strings): (*a*) check whether $\sigma$ is defined; (*b*) compute the length of $\sigma$; and (*c*) given an index $i$, compute the $i$-th character of $\sigma$. Finally, by structural induction on the DReX program $f$, and given an implicit representation of the input string $\sigma$, we build an implicit representation of $[\![f]\!](\sigma)$ using only polynomial space. For example, the implicit representation of $[\![f \texttt{ else } g]\!](\sigma)$ would function as follows: (*a*) to check whether the output is defined, simply determine whether either $[\![f]\!](\sigma)$ or $[\![g]\!](\sigma)$ is defined; (*b*) to compute the length of the output, if $[\![f]\!](\sigma)$ is defined, return the length of $[\![f]\!](\sigma)$, and otherwise, return the length of $[\![g]\!](\sigma)$; and (*c*) to compute the $i$-th character of $[\![f \texttt{ else } g]\!](\sigma)$, if $\tau_1 = [\![f]\!](\sigma)$ is defined, then return the $i$-th character of $\tau_1$, and otherwise, return the $i$-th character of $\tau_2 = [\![g]\!](\tau)$. Observe that since both nested implicit representations $[\![f]\!](\sigma)$ and $[\![g]\!](\sigma)$ consume only polynomial space, $[\![f \texttt{ else } g]\!](\sigma)$ is itself evaluated in polynomial space. The most interesting case is $\texttt{compose}(f, g)$ where we simply connect the implicit representation of the output of $[\![f]\!](\sigma)$ to the input of the function $g$. The only non-trivial case is when $f = \texttt{iterate}(g)$. To check whether $f$ is defined on the input $\sigma$, we need to determine whether there is exactly one way to split $\sigma$ such that $g$ is defined on each split. Consider each position in the string $\sigma$ as a vertex in a graph, with an edge between two vertices iff $g$ is defined on the substring between them. Then each path from the initial to the final node of this graph corresponds to a viable split of $\sigma$, and thus $f$ is defined on $\sigma$ iff there is a unique path from the initial node to the final node in this implicitly represented graph of potentially exponential size. This problem can be solved in PSPACE.

**Theorem 6.** *Given a DReX program $f$, and strings $\sigma \in \Sigma^*$ and $\tau \in \Gamma^*$, the problem of determining whether $[\![f]\!](\sigma) = \tau$ is in* PSPACE.

Finally, we show that when we allow the use of composition operators polynomial space is required, and the problem of evaluating a DReX program is PSPACE-complete.

**Theorem 7.** *The following problems are* PSPACE*-complete:*

1. *given a program $f$ in DReX check whether $[\![f]\!](\epsilon)$ is defined;*
2. *given a program $f$ in DReX and a string $\sigma \in \Sigma^*$ check whether $[\![f]\!](\sigma)$ is defined;*
3. *given a program $f$ in DReX, a string $\sigma \in \Sigma^*$, and a string $\tau \in \Gamma^*$, check whether $[\![f]\!](\sigma) = \tau$;*

*Proof sketch of* PSPACE*-hardness.* To show that the first problem is PSPACE-hard we reduce from the validity problem for quantified Boolean formulas (QBF). Intuitively given a QBF $\Phi = \forall x_1 \exists x_2 \ldots \exists x_n \varphi(x_1, \ldots, x_n)$ we construct a DReX program $f_\Phi$ such that $[\![f_\Phi]\!](\epsilon)$ is defined iff $\Phi$ is valid. The program $f_\Phi$ is the composition of three programs $f_{01}$, $f_{3\text{CNF}}$ and $f_Q$ where:

[5] We define the substring $\sigma[i, j]$ of $\sigma$ as $\sigma_i \sigma_{i+1} \ldots \sigma_{j-1}$, so that $\sigma[i, i] = \epsilon$, for each $i$, and $\sigma[1, |\sigma| + 1]$ is the entire string $\sigma$.

1. $f_{01}$ takes as input $\epsilon$ and outputs all the strings in $\{0,1\}^n$ in lexicographic order and separated by a #; this program generates all the possible assignments of the boolean variables.
2. $f_{3CNF}$ takes as input the string of all the assignments produced by $f_{01}$ and replaces each assignment in $a \in \{0,1\}^n$ with $T$ if the assignment $a$ satisfies the 3SAT formula $\varphi$ and $F$ otherwise.
3. $f_Q$ takes as input the string over $(\{T,F\}\#)^*$ and checks whether such a sequence of satisfying assignments is valid for the quantified formula $\Phi$. If it is valid it outputs $\epsilon$ and otherwise it is undefined.

The other problems can be reduced to the first problem using the composition operator. □

### 4.3 Single-pass algorithms for unrestricted DReX

In the proof of theorem 5 we showed that in the absence of the function composition combinator the dynamic programming algorithm has complexity $\mathcal{O}(f|\sigma|^3)$ where $\sigma$ is the input string and $f$ the program. In this section we argue that, if one wants to obtain an algorithm that is linear in the size of the input, it is necessary to pay at least an exponential complexity in the size of the program.

DReX operators are similar to those offered by regular expressions (iteration, split, etc. are the broad analogues of Kleene-*, concatenation, etc.). Since one can evaluate regular expressions efficiently by transforming them into nondeterministic finite automata one can try to construct an automaton model corresponding to DReX programs. Unfortunately as we discussed in section 2, DReX combinators can also express language intersection and other complex operations. In the presence of such operations, directly constructing an automaton model from the program seems hard (see [23], where the author summarizes the state-of-the-art on matching regular expressions extended with an intersection operator). The following is currently the best claim we can make about evaluating unrestricted DReX programs with a single linear time pass over the input string:

**Theorem 8.** *Given a DReX program $f$ and an input string $\sigma \in \Sigma^*$, we can compute the output $[\![f]\!](\sigma)$ in time linear in the length of the input string $\sigma$, and a tower of exponentials with height $\mathcal{O}(|f|)$.*

The algorithm compiles $f$ into an equivalent streaming string transducer (SST) [1] using the procedure described in [3]. An SST is a finite state machine that reads the input in a left-to-right fashion and stores intermediate results inside variables. The final output is a combination of such variables. An SST $A$ can be evaluated on an input string $\sigma$ in one pass in time $\mathcal{O}(|A|\,|\sigma|)$. Since SSTs are deterministic, operations such as concatenation and iteration (even in the absence of function composition) cause an exponential blow-up, making the overall complexity non-elementary.

## 5. Evaluation

We implemented the algorithms described in this paper, and evaluated their performance on a representative set of text and BibTeX file transformations. We show that

1. the evaluation algorithm for consistent DReX scales to inputs with more than 100,000 characters (subsection 5.2.1), and
2. the dynamic programming algorithm presented in section 4.1 *does not* scale for inputs with more than 3,000 characters (subsection 5.2.2).

Finally, we remark on the subjective experience of expressing string transformations using DReX (subsection 5.3).

### 5.1 Implementation details

The prototype implementation of DReX was written in Java and uses the recently released Java SE 8. We used the symbolic automata library SVPAlib [11] to implement the symbolic operations required by the consistency-checking algorithm (theorem 3). The set of characters were all 16-bit UTF-16 code units, and the predicates were unions of character intervals (such as `[a-z, A-Z, 0-9]`).

The experiments were run on regular contemporary hardware: Windows 7 running on a 64-bit quad-core Intel Core i7-2600 CPU, at 3.40 GHz with 8 GB of RAM. Each experiment was run 10 times and the results reported are the mean of the obtained running times.

The dynamic programming (DP) algorithm for the extended version of DReX (theorem 5) is implemented lazily. Each entry $\text{OUT}(f,\sigma,i,j)$ is only computed and allocated when its value is required by another entry. Without this technique the algorithm runs out of memory for inputs of length smaller than 1,000. We also optimize the DP algorithm to take advantage of the consistency-checking; for consistent programs the algorithm does not need to check whether there is more than one way to match a string.

| Program name | Size | CC (ms) |
|---|---|---|
| *delete_comm* | 28 | 12 |
| *insert_quotes* | 28 | 6 |
| *get_tags* | 31 | 6 |
| *reverse* | 5 | 1 |
| *swap_bibtex* | 1663 | 262 |
| *align_bibtex* | 3652 | 537 |

Table 1: Evaluated programs with sizes and time to check consistency.

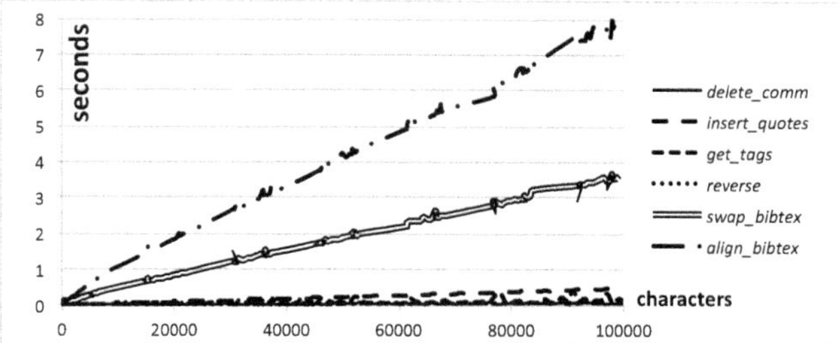


Figure 5.1: Evaluation time for the single-pass algorithm.

### 5.2 Benchmark programs

Table 1 shows the programs we considered in our evaluation together with their sizes and the running time of the consistency-checking algorithm. These programs are described in appendix A. Observe that for every program the consistency-checking algorithm terminates in less than 600 ms.

We evaluated the first four programs on randomly generated text files of size varying between 1 and 100,000 characters, and evaluated the more complex functions *swap_bibtex* and *align_bibtex* on actual BibTeX files of size also varying between 1 and 100,000 characters. We set a timeout of 60 seconds for each operation.

#### 5.2.1 Single-pass algorithm for consistent DReX

Figure 5.1 shows how the running time for the algorithm presented in section 3 depends linearly on the size of the input. For inputs up to 100,000 characters each program takes less than 8 seconds to compute the output. Also observe that the evaluation algorithm can successfully handle reasonably large programs such as *align_bibtex* which has an AST with 3652 nodes.

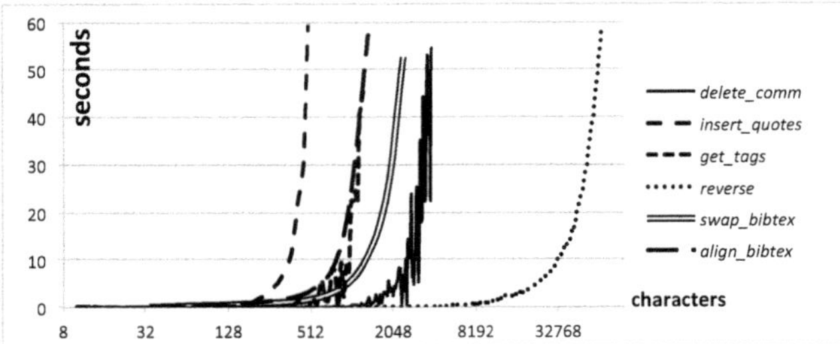


Figure 5.2: Evaluation time for dynamic programming algorithm. Note that the $x$-axis in log-scale.

### 5.2.2 Dynamic programming for unrestricted DReX

Figure 5.2 shows the running time for the dynamic programming algorithm presented in section 4.1. The $x$-axis is shown in log scale to better appreciate the difference between the different programs. From the figure we can see that the running time depends polynomially on the length of the input and, as a consequence, all the considered programs time out for inputs with more than 70,000 characters. In some cases large programs such as *swap_bibtex* execute faster than smaller programs such as *get_tags*. This is due to the fact that our implementation uses some optimizations that may depend on the shape of the program: for example in the case of programs that are only defined on strings of a fixed length $k$, the algorithm is evaluated only for those $i$ and $j$ such that $j - i = k$. In conclusion, although all DReX programs can be evaluated using the dynamic programming algorithm presented in section 4.1, the procedure does not scale to large inputs.

### 5.3 User experience and comparison to existing tools

We were able to easily program several non-trivial string-to-string transformations without having to worry about efficiency. The main restrictions of the streaming evaluation algorithm are that programs cannot use compositions and have to be consistent. In our case study we did not find instances where composition was required and all the natural implementations of our programs were consistent. Moreover, in many cases the consistency algorithm helped us in identifying sources of ambiguity that caused our program to be incorrect. As an anecdotal account, we had mistakenly concatenated the sub-program *copy_spaces* $= \texttt{iterate}(\texttt{space}(x) \mapsto x)$, which copies all whitespace characters (including tabs and newlines), with itself. In this case, the type-checker warned us that this concatenation was ambiguous on the input string "`\n`". This was clearly a bug in our script, and would have led to unexpected behavior even if we had used the dynamic programming evaluation algorithm.

We also programmed the benchmark transformations in sed, AWK, and Perl. Regular-expression based substitution, as present in all of these tools, is very efficient and usable to substitute or delete substrings based on patterns. This includes the benchmark programs *delete_comm* and *insert_quotes*, for which the sed implementations were $\approx$ 6 times faster than the DReX ones. On the other hand, *reverse*, *swap_bibtex* and *align_bibtex* were hard to express in line-based tools such as sed and AWK. The Perl implementations of these functions were $\approx 2$ times faster than ours.

## 6. Related Work

***Regular string transformations.*** This class of string-to-string transformations is robust and has many equivalent characterizations, including deterministic two-way string transducers [16, 18], streaming string transducers [1], transducers with origin information [6], and MSO-definable string transformations [10]. Regular string transformations are also closed under composition [9], and enjoy decidable equivalence [21]. Alur et al proposed a set of combinators that captures the set of regular string-to-string transformations [3] and this paper builds on it. The results in [3] only focus on expressiveness and do not try to answer questions about complexity. In particular the transformation to streaming string transducers proposed in [3] has non-elementary complexity in the size of the program. In this paper, however, we are primarily driven by issues related to the complexity of evaluation.

***DSLs for string transformations.*** DSLs for string transformations mainly fall into two classes: string specific utilities such as sed, AWK, and Perl, and transducer-based languages [13, 15, 26].

Utilities such as sed, AWK, and Perl provide the programmer with powerful programming constructs to manipulate strings. These languages are Turing-complete and in general cannot be efficiently compiled into fast executable code and are not amenable to algorithmic analysis. We also argued in section 5.3 that some of the programs that can be naturally expressed in DReX are actually hard to define using these tools.

All the existing transducer-based languages simply act as frontends to an underlying transducer model that they use to reason about the implemented programs. BEK uses symbolic finite transducers [26] and it has been used to analyze string sanitization functions. BEX is a frontend for extended symbolic finite transducers [12, 13] and it has been used to prove the correctness of string encoders and decoders such as Base64. FAST is based on symbolic tree transducers with regular look-ahead [15] and it is used to reason about programs that manipulate strings and trees over arbitrary domains. While these languages enable powerful analysis and verification techniques, (*a*) their semantics are tightly coupled to the transducer model, forcing the programmer to think in terms of a finite state machine, and a left-to-right reading of the input string, and (*b*) they only capture a strict subset of the class of regular string transformations; none of these models can reverse a string.

Another language based on automata is Boomerang, a bidirectional programming language for string editing [5]. Bidirectional programs contain combinators for extracting a view from a concrete input and then reconstructing an updated input from the updated view. Boomerang also supports extractions where each record is associated with a "key". Although Boomerang has a similar type-system to that of DReX (it forces unambiguous operations), we are not aware of a complexity analysis for the problem of evaluating a Boomerang program. The goals of Boomerang and DReX are orthogonal: the former focuses on bidirectional transformations, while the latter focuses on efficiently evaluating all regular string transformations. Despite this difference we believe that Boomerang could benefit from the evaluation techniques proposed in this paper.

***Efficient string manipulation.*** Little effort has been devoted to design languages and algorithms to efficiently evaluate string transformations in linear time. The general approach has been to identify an automaton model that processes the string in a single left-to-right pass and can express interesting programs. However, all existing tools that use this approach [13, 15, 26] take advantage of composition or combination operators that make the compilation to transducers exponential in the size of the program. Streaming string transducers (SST) [1] capture all programs that can be written in DReX and can be executed in a single left-to-right pass over the input. However, transforming DReX programs into SSTs also causes an super-exponential blow-up in the size of the input program.

In the context of XML processing numerous languages or fragments have been proposed for efficiently querying (XPath, XQuery), stream processing (STX [4]), and manipulating (XSLT) XML trees. Some of these languages particularly focus on efficiently processing the input in a linear time left-to-right pass. Although in the case of XML documents with bounded depth some XML transformations can be described in DReX, the main goal of DReX remains that of providing a well-defined fragment (regular) of *string* (and not tree) transformations that can be efficiently executed.

***Future Directions.*** A major motivation for choosing the class of regular string transformations was the decidability of analysis questions. In particular, consider regular type-checking: given a program $f$ and two regular languages $I$ and $O$, is it the case that for every input $\sigma \in I$, $[\![p]\!](\sigma) \in O$? Such a tool would be helpful to audit string sanitizers against specific kinds of attacks. Implementing these procedures is an open research direction.

In FlashFill [20] simple string transformations can be synthesized from examples. The expressiveness of the combinators used in FlashFill has not been characterized. Can DReX programs be efficiently learnt or synthesized from input-output examples?

Recently Mytkowicz et al. [22] proposed new techniques for evaluating finite automata in a data-parallel fashion. Can these techniques be used to parallelize the evaluation algorithm proposed in this paper?

Extending our techniques to tree transformations is another open problem. Streaming tree transducers (STTs) [2] are to regular tree transformations (or equivalently macro tree transducers [19], and MSO-definable tree transformations [17]) as SSTs are related to regular string transformations. Can we design a similar declarative language to express regular tree transformations?

Finally, certain operations such as counting the number of substring matches, sorting the elements of a dictionary, or deleting duplicate entries in a list are *not* regular string transformations. Extending DReX with non-regular primitives but which can still be efficiently evaluated is an interesting direction of future work.

## 7. Conclusion

We presented DReX, a declarative language for describing regular string transformations. The basic transformers are symbolic, so DReX can succinctly express transformations even over large alphabets such as Unicode. We demonstrated that the evaluation problem for unrestricted DReX is PSPACE-complete, and so we considered a restricted fragment, *consistent* DReX which permits a fast single-pass evaluation algorithm, and still retains expressive completeness. In experiments over representative string transformations such as BibTeX file manipulations the evaluation algorithm for consistent DReX scaled to process thousands of characters per second.

## References


[1] R. Alur and P. Černý. Streaming transducers for algorithmic verification of single-pass list-processing programs. In *Proceedings of the 38th Annual ACM SIGPLAN-SIGACT Symposium on Principles of Programming Languages*, pages 599–610. ACM, 2011.

[2] R. Alur and L. D'Antoni. Streaming tree transducers. In A. Czumaj, K. Mehlhorn, A. Pitts, and R. Wattenhofer, editors, *Automata, Languages, and Programming*, volume 7392 of *Lecture Notes in Computer Science*, pages 42–53. Springer, 2012.

[3] R. Alur, A. Freilich, and M. Raghothaman. Regular combinators for string transformations. In *Proceedings of the Joint Meeting of the 23rd EACSL Annual Conference on Computer Science Logic (CSL) and the 29th Annual ACM/IEEE Symposium on Logic in Computer Science (LICS)*, CSL-LICS '14, pages 9:1–9:10. ACM, 2014.

[4] O. Becker. Streaming transformations for xml-stx. In *XMIDX*, volume 24 of *LNI*, pages 83–88. GI, 2003.

[5] A. Bohannon, N. Foster, B. Pierce, A. Pilkiewicz, and A. Schmitt. Boomerang: Resourceful lenses for string data. In *Proceedings of the 35th Annual ACM SIGPLAN-SIGACT Symposium on Principles of Programming Languages*, pages 407–419. ACM, 2008.

[6] M. Bojańczyk. Transducers with origin information. In *Automata, Languages, and Programming*, volume 8573 of *Lecture Notes in Computer Science*, pages 26–37. Springer, 2014.

[7] R. Book, S. Even, S. Greibach, and G. Ott. Ambiguity in graphs and expressions. *IEEE Transactions on Computers*, 20(2):149–153, February 1971.

[8] A. Brüggemann-Klein. Regular expressions into finite automata. In *LATIN '92*, volume 583 of *Lecture Notes in Computer Science*, pages 87–98. Springer, 1992.

[9] M. Chytil and V. Jákl. Serial composition of 2-way finite-state transducers and simple programs on strings. In *Automata, Languages, and Programming*, volume 52 of *Lecture Notes in Computer Science*, pages 135–147. Springer, 1977.

[10] B. Courcelle. Monadic second-order definable graph transductions: a survey. *Theoretical Computer Science*, 126(1):53 – 75, 1994.

[11] L. D'Antoni and R. Alur. Symbolic visibly pushdown automata. In *Computer Aided Verification*, volume 8559 of *Lecture Notes in Computer Science*, pages 209–225. Springer, 2014.

[12] L. D'Antoni and M. Veanes. Equivalence of extended symbolic finite transducers. In *Computer Aided Verification*, volume 8044 of *Lecture Notes in Computer Science*, pages 624–639. Springer, 2013.

[13] L. D'Antoni and M. Veanes. Static analysis of string encoders and decoders. In *Verification, Model Checking, and Abstract Interpretation*, volume 7737 of *Lecture Notes in Computer Science*, pages 209–228. Springer, 2013.

[14] L. D'Antoni and M. Veanes. Minimization of symbolic automata. In *Proceedings of the 41st ACM SIGPLAN-SIGACT Symposium on Principles of Programming Languages*, pages 541–553, New York, NY, USA, 2014. ACM.

[15] L. D'Antoni, M. Veanes, B. Livshits, and D. Molnar. Fast: A transducer-based language for tree manipulation. In *Proceedings of the 35th ACM SIGPLAN Conference on Programming Language Design and Implementation*, pages 384–394. ACM, 2014.

[16] J. Engelfriet and H. J. Hoogeboom. MSO definable string transductions and two-way finite-state transducers. *ACM Transactions on Computational Logic*, 2(2):216–254, April 2001.

[17] J. Engelfriet and S. Maneth. Macro tree transducers, attribute grammars, and MSO definable tree translations. *Information and Computation*, 154(1):34–91, 1999.

[18] J. Engelfriet, G. Rozenberg, and G. Slutzki. Tree transducers, L systems, and two-way machines. *Journal of Computer and System Sciences*, 20(2):150 – 202, 1980.

[19] J. Engelfriet and H. Vogler. Macro tree transducers. *Journal of Computer and System Sciences*, 31(1):71–146, 1985.

[20] S. Gulwani. Automating string processing in spreadsheets using input-output examples. In *Proceedings of the 38th Annual ACM SIGPLAN-SIGACT Symposium on Principles of Programming Languages*, pages 317–330. ACM, 2011.

[21] E. Gurari. The equivalence problem for deterministic two-way sequential transducers is decidable. In *21st Annual Symposium on Foundations of Computer Science*, pages 83–85, 1980.

[22] T. Mytkowicz, M. Musuvathi, and W. Schulte. Data-parallel finite-state machines. In *Proceedings of the 19th International Conference on Architectural Support for Programming Languages and Operating Systems*, pages 529–542. ACM, 2014.

[23] G. Rosu. An effective algorithm for the membership problem for extended regular expressions. In *Foundations of Software Science and Computational Structures*, volume 4423 of *Lecture Notes in Computer Science*, pages 332–345. Springer, 2007.

[24] M. Sipser. *Introduction to the Theory of Computation*. Cengage Learning, 3rd edition, 2012.

[25] R. Stearns and H. Hunt. On the equivalence and containment problems for unambiguous regular expressions, grammars, and automata. In *Proceedings of the 22nd Annual Symposium on Foundations of Computer Science*, pages 74–81. IEEE Computer Society, 1981.

[26] M. Veanes, P. Hooimeijer, B. Livshits, D. Molnar, and N. Bjorner. Symbolic finite state transducers: Algorithms and applications. In *Proceedings of the 39th Annual ACM SIGPLAN-SIGACT Symposium on Principles of Programming Languages*, pages 137–150. ACM, 2012.

## A. Examples of Consistent DReX Programs

This appendix contains simplified descriptions of the consistent DReX programs that we used in our experiments in section 5. We will use the following macros in our definitions.

$$\begin{aligned}
\texttt{copy}(\varphi) &= \varphi(x) \mapsto [x]\\
\texttt{del}(\varphi) &= \varphi(x) \mapsto [\,]\\
\texttt{iterate-plus}(f) &= \texttt{split}(\texttt{iterate}(f), f)\\
\texttt{split}(f_1,\ldots,f_n) &= \texttt{split}(f_1, \texttt{split}(\ldots,f_n))
\end{aligned}$$

$\texttt{copy}(\varphi)$ and $\texttt{del}(\varphi)$ respectively copy or delete a character matching $\varphi$. When the predicate is of the form $x = c$ we simply write $c$. $\texttt{iterate-plus}(f)$ repeats the function $f$ one or more times. The last macro simply repeats the split sum operator on all the arguments.

### A.1 Delete one-line comments from a program

This program deletes all one-line comments from a file (i.e. the lines starting with `//`). We define each component of the program separately. The program *del_comm_line* deletes strings of the form "$//\sigma\backslash\texttt{n}$", where $\sigma$ does not contain any occurrence of the new line character "`\n`".

$$\begin{aligned}
\textit{del_slashes} &= \texttt{split}(\texttt{del}(\texttt{'/'}), \texttt{del}(\texttt{'/'})),\\
\textit{del_non_nl} &= \texttt{iterate}(\texttt{del}(x \neq \texttt{'\textbackslash n'})),\\
\textit{del_comm} &= \texttt{split}(\textit{del_slashes}, \textit{del_non_nl}),\\
\textit{del_comm_line} &= \texttt{split}(\textit{del_comm}, \texttt{del}(\texttt{'\textbackslash n'})).
\end{aligned}$$

The program *copy_line* copies strings of the form "$\sigma\backslash\texttt{n}$", where the string $\sigma$ is either the empty string, or it does not start with the character `'/'`.

$$\begin{aligned}
\textit{copy_non_nl} &= \texttt{iterate}(\texttt{copy}(x \neq \texttt{'\textbackslash n'})),\\
\textit{copy_txt} &= \texttt{split}(\texttt{copy}(x \neq \texttt{'/'}), \textit{copy_non_nl}),\\
\textit{copy_line} &= \texttt{copy}(\texttt{'\textbackslash n'})\,\texttt{else}\,\texttt{split}(\textit{copy_txt}, \texttt{copy}(\texttt{'\textbackslash n'})).
\end{aligned}$$

The program *process_line* reads a line and deletes it if it is a comment line and copies it otherwise. The last line might not end with a '`\n`' and the program *process_last_line* deals with this exception. Finally the program *delete_comm* repeats *process_line* and at the end processes the last line, therefore deleting all the one-line comments in the input.

$$\begin{aligned}
\textit{process_line} &= \textit{del_comm_line}\,\texttt{else}\,\textit{copy_line},\\
\textit{last_line} &= \textit{del_comm}\,\texttt{else}\,\textit{copy_txt},\\
\textit{process_last_line} &= \textit{process_line}\,\texttt{else}\,\textit{last_line},\\
\textit{process_lines} &= \texttt{iterate}(\textit{process_line}),\\
\textit{delete_comm} &= \texttt{split}(\textit{process_lines}, \textit{process_last_line}).
\end{aligned}$$

### A.2 Insert quotes around words

This program inserts quotes (`'"'`) around every alphabetic substring appearing in the input. The program *add_qts_skip*, given a string $\sigma_1\sigma_2$ where $\sigma_1$ is alphabetic and $\sigma_2$ does not contain any letter, outputs the string "$"\sigma_1"\sigma_2$".

$$\begin{aligned}
\textit{copy_astr} &= \texttt{iterate-plus}(\texttt{copy}([\texttt{a-zA-Z}])),\\
\textit{copy_nastr} &= \texttt{iterate-plus}(\texttt{copy}(x \notin [\texttt{a-zA-Z}])),\\
\textit{add_qt} &= \epsilon \mapsto [\texttt{'"'}],\\
\textit{add_qts} &= \texttt{split}(\textit{add_qt}, \textit{copy_astr}, \textit{add_qt}),\\
\textit{add_qts_skip} &= \texttt{split}(\textit{add_qts}, \textit{copy_nastr}).
\end{aligned}$$

The program *insert_quotes* repeats the *add_qts* function. Since the string might start with a symbol that is not alphabetic the program *start* deals with this case. Similarly the program *ending* checks whether the string does not end with an alphabetic sequence. Finally, the program *insert_quotes* inserts quotes around every alphabetic substring in the input.

$$\begin{aligned}
\textit{start} &= \texttt{iterate}(\texttt{copy}(x \notin [\texttt{a-zA-Z}])),\\
\textit{ending} &= \textit{add_qts}\,\texttt{else}\,\epsilon \mapsto [],\\
\textit{repeat_add} &= \texttt{iterate}(\textit{add_qts_skip}),\\
\textit{insert_quotes} &= \texttt{split}(\textit{start}, \textit{repeat_add}, \textit{ending}).
\end{aligned}$$

### A.3 Extracting tags from a malformed XML file

This program extracts and concatenates all the substrings of the form $<\sigma>$ where $\sigma$ does not contain any character $<$ or $>$ (this is a generalization of a program shown in [26]). For simplicity we assume that the string does not contain occurrences of the substring "$<>$". The program *copy_match* copies any string of the form $<\sigma>$ where $\sigma$ does not contain any character $<$ or $>$.

$$\begin{aligned}
\textit{copy_ntag} &= \texttt{iterate-plus}(\texttt{copy}(x \notin [\texttt{<>}])),\\
\textit{copy_match} &= \texttt{split}(\texttt{copy}(\texttt{'<'}), \textit{copy_ntag}, \texttt{copy}(\texttt{'>'})).
\end{aligned}$$

The program *del_not_match* deletes any string that does not contain a substring of the form $<s>$ where $s$ does not contain any character $<$ or $>$. The program *del_not_match* looks for the following pattern: $s = \sigma_1\texttt{>}\cdots\texttt{>}\sigma_i\texttt{<}\cdots\texttt{<}\sigma_n$ (with $i \geq 1$). Its sub-program *del_close_op* deletes all the string of the described form containing at least one open character (`'<'`).

$$\begin{aligned}
\textit{del_not_opn} &= \texttt{iterate}(\texttt{del}(x \neq \texttt{'<'})),\\
\textit{del_not_cls} &= \texttt{iterate}(\texttt{del}(x \neq \texttt{'>'})),\\
\textit{del_opn_not_cls} &= \texttt{split}(\texttt{del}(\texttt{'<'}), \texttt{iterate}(\texttt{del}(x \neq \texttt{'>'}))),\\
\textit{del_close_op} &= \texttt{split}(\textit{del_not_opn}, \textit{del_opn_not_cls}),\\
\textit{del_not_match} &= \textit{del_not_opn}\,\texttt{else}\,\textit{del_close_op}.
\end{aligned}$$

The program *find_match* keeps looking for tags and removes eventual non-matches at the end of the string. Finally, *get_tags* repeats *find_match*, and therefore outputs all the substrings of the form $<\sigma>$.

$$\begin{aligned}
\textit{find_match} &= \texttt{split}(\textit{del_not_match}, \textit{copy_match}),\\
\textit{repeat_get_tags} &= \texttt{iterate}(\textit{find_match}),\\
\textit{get_tags} &= \texttt{split}(\textit{repeat_get_tags}, \textit{del_not_match}).
\end{aligned}$$

### A.4 Reversing a dictionary

Given a dictionary of the form $\sigma_1\texttt{;}\sigma_2\texttt{;}\cdots\texttt{;}\sigma_n\texttt{;}$ we want to output the reverse $\sigma_n\texttt{;}\sigma_{n-1}\texttt{;}\cdots\texttt{;}\sigma_1\texttt{;}$. The program *copy_stretch* copies a string of the form $\sigma\texttt{;}$ such that $\sigma$ does not contain a '`;`'. The program *reverse* implements the final transformation by left iterating *copy_stretch*.

$$\begin{aligned}
\textit{copy_stretch} &= \texttt{split}(\texttt{iterate}(\texttt{copy}(x \neq \texttt{';'})), \texttt{copy}(\texttt{';'})),\\
\textit{reverse} &= \texttt{left-iterate}(\textit{copy_stretch}).
\end{aligned}$$

### A.5 Reformatting BibTeX files

In this section we define two functions that operate over BibTeX files. The first function, *swap_bibtex*, reorders attributes within each BibTeX entry by moving the title to the top. The second function, *align_bibtex*, rearranges a *misaligned* file by moving the title of each entry inside the previous entry.

To do so we first define a few auxiliary functions that are used for copying and deleting alphabetic strings, spaces, and delimiters.

$$\begin{aligned}
\textit{copy_astr} &= \texttt{iterate-plus}(\texttt{copy}([\texttt{a-zA-Z}])),\\
\textit{copy_anum} &= \texttt{iterate-plus}(\texttt{copy}([\texttt{a-zA-Z0-9}])),\\
\textit{copy_spaces} &= \texttt{iterate}(\texttt{copy}([\texttt{\textbackslash n \textbackslash r \textbackslash b \textbackslash t}])),\\
\textit{del_astr} &= \texttt{iterate-plus}(\texttt{del}([\texttt{a-zA-Z}])).
\end{aligned}$$

```
@book{Gal1638 ,
    publisher = {Elzevir},
    place = {Leiden},
    year = {1638},
    title = {Two New Sciences},
    author = {Galileo},
}
```

```
@book{Gal1638 ,
    title = {Two New Sciences},
    publisher = {Elzevir},
    place = {Leiden},
    year = {1638},
    author = {Galileo},
}
```

Figure A.1: Example application of the transformation *swap_bibtex* from the entry on the left to the entry on the right.

It is easy to see how given a DReX program that copies a pattern, one can easily define a DReX program that deletes the same pattern. To simplify the presentation in the following we assume that for every program of the form *copy_something* there is an analogous program *del_something* that is defined on the same input as *copy_something* but always outputs the empty string.

The program *copy_header* copies the header of an entry. In the example of figure A.1, it copies the string "`@book{Gal1638`" along with the following spaces.

$$\mathit{copy\_header} = \texttt{split}(\texttt{copy}(\texttt{'@'}), \mathit{copy\_astr}, \texttt{copy}(\texttt{'\{'}), \\ \mathit{copy\_anum}, \texttt{copy}(\texttt{','}), \mathit{copy\_spaces}).$$

We now define macros for copying and deleting a particular string $s$ or a set of strings.

$$\texttt{copy}(s) = \texttt{split}(\texttt{copy}(s[1]), \ldots, \texttt{copy}(s[|s|])), \\ \texttt{copy}(\{\sigma_1, \ldots, \sigma_n\}) = \texttt{copy}(\sigma_1)\,\texttt{else}\ldots\texttt{else}\,\texttt{copy}(\sigma_n).$$

The program *copy_title* copies the string "`title`", and the program *copy_non_title* copies every attribute name different from "`title`". We omit the full list of attributes for readability.

$$\mathit{copy\_title} = \texttt{copy}(\texttt{'title'}), \\ \mathit{copy\_non\_title} = \texttt{copy}(\{\texttt{'author'}, \texttt{'year'}, \texttt{'place'}, \ldots\}).$$

The program *copy_att_value* copies the value of an attribute along with the surrounding parentheses (i.e. "` = { Elzevir},`").

$$\mathit{copy\_non\_par} = \texttt{iterate}(\texttt{copy}(x \notin [\}\{])), \\ \mathit{copy\_att\_value} = \texttt{split}(\mathit{copy\_spaces}, \texttt{copy}(\texttt{'='}), \\ \mathit{copy\_spaces}, \texttt{copy}(\texttt{'\{'}), \mathit{copy\_non\_par}, \\ \texttt{copy}(\texttt{'\}'}), \texttt{copy}(\texttt{','}), \mathit{copy\_spaces}).$$

The program *copy_title_att* copies a complete title attribute (i.e. "`title = {Two New Sciences},`"), while *copy_non_title_att* copies a complete non-title attribute.

$$\mathit{copy\_title\_att} = \texttt{split}(\mathit{copy\_title}, \mathit{copy\_att\_value}), \\ \mathit{copy\_non\_title\_att} = \texttt{split}(\mathit{copy\_non\_title}, \mathit{copy\_att\_value}).$$

Given a list of attributes, the program *title_only* copies the title and deletes all the non-title attributes, the program *all_but_title* deletes the title and copies all the other attributes, and the program *copy_attrs* copies the entire list.

$$\mathit{title\_only} = \texttt{iterate}(\mathit{copy\_title}\,\texttt{else}\,\mathit{del\_non\_title}), \\ \mathit{all\_but\_title} = \texttt{iterate}(\mathit{del\_title}\,\texttt{else}\,\mathit{copy\_non\_title}), \\ \mathit{all\_but\_title} = \texttt{iterate}(\mathit{copy\_title}\,\texttt{else}\,\mathit{copy\_non\_title}).$$

### A.5.1 Polishing a BibTeX file

The following function defines a typical transformation a paper author may perform on BibTeX files. The program *swap_bibtex* moves the title attribute to the top of each entry of an input BibTeX file. Figure A.1 shows the result of applying *swap_bibtex* to a particular BibTeX entry. In this presentation we assume that every attribute is followed by a comma.[6] The program *title_first* copies the title first and then all the other attributes, therefore obtaining the desired attribute reordering.

$$\mathit{title\_first} = \texttt{combine}(\mathit{title\_only}, \mathit{all\_but\_title}).$$

The program *swap_entry* performs the operation of figure A.1 for a single BibTeX entry.

$$\mathit{swap\_entry} = \texttt{split}(\mathit{copy\_header}, \mathit{title\_first}, \\ \texttt{copy}(\texttt{'\}'}), \mathit{copy\_spaces}).$$

Finally, the program *swap_bibtex* applies the transformation to all the entries in the file.

$$\mathit{swap\_bibtex} = \texttt{iterate}(\mathit{swap\_entry}).$$

### A.5.2 Aligning titles in a misaligned BibTeX file

Assume that by mistake the titles of a BibTeX file have been misaligned: the title of the first entry now appears in the second one, the second title appears in the third entry and so on. The function *align_bibtex*, given such a misaligned file, moves the title of each entry $i+1$ to the correct entry $i$, and since the last entry would now not have a title, it gets deleted. This program requires the use of the chained sum operator in order to process two BibTeX entries at a time (first and second, second and third, and so on). The program *header_only_entry*, given a single BibTeX entry, copies only the header and deletes the rest of the entry.

$$\mathit{header\_only\_entry} = \texttt{split}(\mathit{copy\_header}, \mathit{del\_attrs}, \\ \texttt{del}(\texttt{'\}'}), \mathit{del\_spaces}).$$

The program *title_only_entry*, given a single BibTeX entry, copies only the title and deletes the rest of the entry, while the program *all_but_title_entry*, deletes the header, the title, and copies the rest of the entry.

$$\mathit{title\_only\_entry} = \texttt{split}(\mathit{del\_header}, \mathit{title\_only}, \\ \texttt{del}(\texttt{'\}'}), \mathit{del\_spaces}), \\ \mathit{all\_but\_title\_entry} = \texttt{split}(\mathit{del\_header}, \mathit{all\_but\_title}, \\ \texttt{copy}(\texttt{'\}'}), \mathit{copy\_spaces}).$$

The program *delete_entry* deletes a single BibTeX entry.

$$\mathit{delete\_entry} = \texttt{split}(\mathit{del\_header}, \mathit{del\_attrs}, \\ \texttt{del}(\texttt{'\}'}), \mathit{del\_spaces}).$$

The program *move_title*, given two BibTeX entries outputs the first entry where the title has been replaced with the title of the second entry: it first copies the header of the first entry, then the title of the second entry, and then the remaining attributes of the first entry.

$$\mathit{move\_title} = \texttt{combine}( \\ \texttt{split}(\mathit{header\_only\_entry}, \mathit{title\_only\_entry}), \\ \texttt{split}(\mathit{all\_but\_title\_entry}, \mathit{delete\_entry})).$$

Finally, the program *align_bibtex* applies the transformation to all the entries in the file. We omit the regular expression describing the format of an entry in the chain operator since DReX can infer it automatically.

$$\mathit{align\_bibtex} = \texttt{chain}(\mathit{move\_title}).$$

[6] The actual program used for the experiments is able to deal with missing commas.

# Data-Parallel String-Manipulating Programs

Margus Veanes    Todd Mytkowicz    David Molnar    Benjamin Livshits
Microsoft Research
{margus,toddm,dmolnar,livshits}@microsoft.com

## Abstract

String-manipulating programs are an important class of programs with applications in malware detection, graphics, input sanitization for Web security, and large-scale HTML processing. This paper extends prior work on BEK, an expressive domain-specific language for writing string-manipulating programs, with algorithmic insights that make BEK both *analyzable* and *data-parallel*. By analyzable we mean that unlike most general purpose programming languages, many algebraic properties of a BEK program are decidable (i.e., one can check whether two programs commute or compute the inverse of a program). By data-parallel we mean that a BEK program can compute on arbitrary *subsections* of its input in parallel, thus exploiting parallel hardware. This latter requirement is particularly important for programs which operate on large data: without data parallelism, a programmer cannot hide the latency of reading data from various storage media (i.e., reading a terabyte of data from a modern hard drive takes about 3 hours). With a data-parallel approach, the system can split data across multiple disks and thus hide the latency of reading the data.

A BEK program is expressive: a programmer can use conditionals, switch statements, and registers—or local variables—in order to implement common string-manipulating programs. Unfortunately, this expressivity induces data dependencies, which are an obstacle to parallelism. The key contribution of this paper is an algorithm which automatically removes these data dependencies by mapping a BEK program into a intermediate format consisting of symbolic transducers, which extend classical transducers with symbolic predicates and symbolic assignments. We present a novel algorithm that we call *exploration* which performs *symbolic loop unrolling* of these transducers to obtain simplified versions of the original program. We show how these simplified versions can then be lifted to a *stateless* form, and from there compiled to data-parallel hardware.

To evaluate the efficacy of our approach, we demonstrate up to $8x$ speedups for a number of real-world, BEK programs, (e.g., HTML encoder and decoder) on data-parallel hardware. To the best of our knowledge, these are the first data parallel implementation of these programs. To validate that our approach is correct, we use an automatic testing technique to compare our generated code to the original implementations and find no semantic deviations.


*POPL '15*, January 15–17, 2015, Mumbai, India.

http://dx.doi.org/10.1145/2676726.2677014

***Categories and Subject Descriptors*** D.3.1 [*Formal Definitions and Theory*]: Semantics; D.3.2 [*Language Classifications*]: Specialized application languages; F.1.1 [*Models of Computation*]: Automata; F.4.3 [*Formal Languages*]: Decision problems

***Keywords*** Symbolic Automaton; Symbolic Trandsducer; Satisfiability Modulo Theories; Data-Parallel; State Space Exploration

## 1. Introduction

BEK is a popular DSL for string-manipulating programs [15]. Because of its expressiveness and popularity, we have chosen to use it for our experiments. While much of our results can be applied broadly to symbolic finite-state transducers, our focus is on providing correct and performant implementations of symbolic finite-state transducers; BEK gives us a platform for doing so. The reader can browse some BEK programs online at http://rise4fun.com/Bek or read the BEK tutorial [23] to build his or her intuition. Typical BEK programs are string encoders and decoders, security sanitizers, etc.

**Why BEK:** The advantage of a domain-specific language is that, unlike most general-purpose languages, many algebraic properties are *decidable* for basic BEK (BEK programs that do not use registers). In particular, one can check whether such BEK programs commute or are idempotent; one can compute the inverse of a BEK program, and given an output, compute all inputs that lead to it.

While previous work has focused on algorithms for reasoning about basic BEK programs [15, 32], they did not provide a clear strategy for either *running* BEK on a variety of platforms, thus hindering its adoption, or providing algorithms that first transform BEK programs to their basic analyzable form. These are important problems as BEK programs are useful tools that developers use to secure both client-side web browsers and Internet scale web services. The goal of this paper is to demonstrate how to compile a BEK program to their basic form. Then, as a concrete application we show how to compile BEK programs into scalable data-parallel code.

Previous work has shown that special state variables, called *registers* in BEK, are often needed to express common functionality (Section 3). Unfortunately registers introduce data dependencies that are obstacles to parallelism and also make many forms of BEK analysis undecidable. Manually removing registers requires developers to reason about complex state, which is error-prone and time-consuming.

**Exploration:** A key contribution of this work is a novel *exploration* algorithm that is a form of loop unrolling combined with symbolic function composition. Loops are unrolled symbolically while data dependencies exist between consecutive iterations. Such unrolling is achieved by introducing new states for finite projections of registers. In this process, several characters may be grouped together into tokens by folding some part of a register symbolically into labels, while another part is folded into concrete states. Intuitively, grouping changes the granularity of what is to be considered as a single input element. For example, if we take a program such as a UTF8 decoder, then grouping would create tokens that correspond to subsequences between 1 and 4 bytes,[1] while for a Base64 decoder it would create subsequences of fixed length 4.

While the algorithm is not guaranteed to work in all cases because it is undecidable, e.g. it is easy to encode reachability of two counter machines which is undecidable [16], when it does work, it produces a transducer that is behaviorally equivalent to the original up to grouping of the input sequence, but *without* register variables. We have not found any typical BEK programs, such as sanitizers, encoders or decoders, for which the technique would fail to terminate. A case when it does not work is a loop that for example counts the number of elements in the input or, in general, has arbitrarily long dependencies between input elements.

**Data parallelism:** There are two key benefits to a BEK program after exploration. First, registers induce data dependencies which limit parallelism and thus exploration is a necessary first step in exploiting parallelism. Second, after exploration, by construction, a BEK program has little intermediate state (e.g., complexity of a program is pushed to the edges rather than encoded as states). The overhead of our data parallel implementation of a BEK program is linearly related to the size of the BEK program's intermediate state and thus exploration enables the automatic transformation from an expressive BEK program, with registers, into a data parallel one. This ultimately relieves the programmer from the burden of explicitly describing parallelism in a BEK program, an error-prone and difficult task.

### 1.1 Contributions

This paper makes the following contributions.

- Previous work on BEK introduced an extension to symbolic transducers with *registers* [32]. Use of registers is essential for modeling real sanitizers but makes their analysis difficult. In this paper, we present a novel *exploration* algorithm that is a form of symblic loop unrolling that works modulo *arbitrary decidable* background theories. The algorithm terminates for a class of transduces that only need a bounded lookahead and the algorithm outputs a new transducer that is equivalent to the input transducer but does not need registers.
- We integrated the exploration algorithm into a BEK to symbolic finite transducer (SFT) compiler. It has several interesting features. First, it uses an SMT solver as an oracle during the exploration algorithm, both for satisfiability checking and for model (witness) generation. Second, it combines exploration with *grouping*. Third, it uses the simplification mechanism present in modern SMT solvers for code generation of conditions and update functions.
- We demonstrate how exploration enables data parallelism. In particular, we show how to encode a BEK program, with infinite alphabets and registers, into one with a finite set of equivalence classes and no registers. Further, we demonstrate a data parallel implementation of this registerless intermediate form based on recent work in parallel finite state machines[25]. To the best of our knowledge, this is the first fully-automatic parallelization of string-manipulating code that combines advanced automata theory with state-of-the-art SMT technology to produce a parallel implementation.
- We have experimented with a number of BEK programs. We frequently observed exponential reductions in the number of states due to the application of our exploration algorithm. To validate the correctness of our translation, we used random testing of thousands of strings, observing no semantic differences when compared to independent C# serial implementations. For the range of hardware configurations we have experimented with, we observe a near-linear speedups as significant as $8x$.

[1] Assuming standard Unicode text processing where code points are limited to $\texttt{10FFFF}_{16}$, in which case 4 bytes are enough, otherwise longer encodings up to 6 bytes are possible.

```
private static string EncodeHtml(string t) {
  if (t == null) { return null; }
  if (t.Length == 0) { return string.Empty; }
  StringBuilder builder =
    new StringBuilder("", t.Length*2);
  foreach (char c in t) {
    if ((((c>'`')&&(c<'{')) ||
        ((c>'@')&&(c<'[')) || (c==' ') ||
        ((c>'/')&&(c<':')) || (c=='.') ||
        (c==',') || (c=='-') || (c=='_')) {
        builder.Append(c);
      } else {
        builder.Append("&#" +
          ((int)c).ToString() + ";");
      }
    }
    return builder.ToString();
}
```

**Figure 1.** Code for `AntiXSS.EncodeHtml` version 2.0.

The background theories that were relevant for us during this work, were theories over linear arithmetic, bit-vectors, tuples, and lists. These theories were used to represent characters, tokens and strings. However, there were no dependencies on these particular theories. For example, one could also consider reals, rationals and arrays. Pragmatically speaking, any theory, or combination of theories, that is supported by an SMT solver works.

## 2. Background and Motivation

**String-manipulating programs:** Much of the practical motivation for analyzing string-manipulating routines comes from the need to analyze *security sanitizers* [15], such as the one shown in Figure 1. These are key in protecting against cross site scripting ("XSS") attacks, which plague today's web applications. These attacks happen because the applications take data from untrusted users, and then echo this data to other users of the application. Because web pages mix markup and JavaScript, this data may be interpreted as code by a browser, leading to arbitrary code execution with the privileges of the victim.

The first line of defense against XSS is the practice of *sanitization*, where untrusted data is passed through a *sanitizer*, a function that escapes or removes potentially dangerous strings. Multiple widely used Web frameworks offer sanitizer functions in libraries, and developers often add additional custom sanitizers due to performance or functionality constraints.

Sanitizers are typically a small amount of code, perhaps tens of lines. Furthermore, application developers know when they are writing a new, custom sanitizer or set of sanitizers. Experience has shown that if developers are willing to spend a little more time on sanitizers, they can obtain fast and precise analyses of sanitizer behavior, along with actual sanitizer code ready to be integrated into both server- and client-side applications. Our approach here is BEK, a language for modeling string transformations. The language is designed to be (a) sufficiently expressive to model real-world code, and (b) sufficiently restricted to allow fast, precise analysis, without needing to approximate the behavior of the code.

Unfortunately, implementing sanitizers *correctly* is surprisingly difficult. Anecdotally, in dozens of code reviews performed across various industries, just about any custom-written sanitizer was flawed with respect to security. SANER, for example, shows flaws in custom-written sanitizers used by ten web applications [2]. Incorrect sanitization may be worse than no sanitization by *enabling* rather than *disabling* JavaScript execution [4, 21].

The problem becomes even more complicated when considering that a web application may *compose* multiple sanitizers in the course of creating a web page. In a recent empirical analysis, it has been found that a large web application often applied the same sanitizers twice, despite these sanitizers not being idempotent [29]. This analysis also found that the order of applying different sanitizers could vary, leading to questions about whether composition of sanitizers is commutative.

BEK has been previously used to perform security-specific analyses of sanitizers. For example, one can use BEK to determine whether there exists an input to a sanitizer that yields any member of a publicly available database of strings [27] (XSS Cheat Sheet) known to result in cross site scripting attacks. Our analysis is fast in practice; for example, we take two seconds to check the commutativity of the entire set of Internet Explorer 8 XSS filters, and less than 39 seconds to check an implementation of the `HTMLEncode` sanitization function against target strings from the XSS Cheat Sheet [15].

**Beyond strings:** BEK has been demonstrated as being useful for applications beyond security sanitization. Other uses have been proposed, as diverse as image blurring and geo-location privacy, which fall outside the scope of this paper. The interested reader can see [32] for more details.

**Performance:** To realize why performance is a concern in this context, consider large-scale distributed data processing in the cloud. Encoding is paramount in Web applications, especially with large volumes of data. Google Docs or Office Web Apps, for example, store multi-megabyte files from *millions* of users. XSS caused by insufficient data sanitization has been discovered in these large-scale cloud apps before. [2] To avoid XSS, these services must encode all user files before displaying them on the web.

```
function E(x)=
  ite(x<=25,x+65,
    ite(x<=51,x+71,
      ite(x<=61,x-4,ite(x==62,'+','/'))));

program b64e(input){
  return iter(x in input)[s:=0;r:=0;]{
    case(x>0xFF): raise ERROR;
    case(s==2): yield(E((r|(x>>6))), E(x&0x3F));
      s:=0; r:=0;
    case(true): yield(E(ite(s==0,x>>2,r|(x>>4))));
      r:=ite(s==0,(x&3)<<4,(x&0xF)<<2); s:=s+1;
    end case(s==1): yield (E(r),'=','=');
    end case(s==2): yield (E(r),'=');
    end case(true): yield (); //may be omitted
  };
}
```

**Figure 2.** BEK program for Base64 encoding.

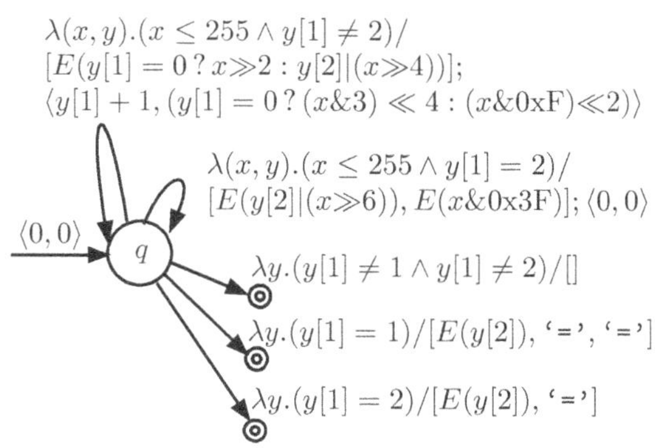


**Figure 3.** ST of the program `b64e` in Figure 2.

## 3. Symbolic Transducers

The semantics of BEK programs are given by symbolic transducers. The goal of this section is to recap the BEK language in Section 3.1. In Section 3.2, we develop a formal treatment required to precisely express these semantics. Pragmatically-inclined readers may wish to save Section 3.2 for later reading.

### 3.1 Intuition

We briefly describe the BEK domain-specific language for writing string transformations such as shown in Figure 1. An example BEK program is in Figure 2. As introduced in [15], the core construct in BEK is iteration over each character in an input string. Programs can then have case statements that describe different behavior for different input characters. Typically the program will perform some local computation, then *yield*, or output, a new character. A new string is built up based on the characters of the input string.

**Registers:** Programs can also have *register variables* that keep state during the iteration. Figure 2 shows a sample BEK program that checks each character and then updates a register variable $r$. Depending on input character, the program may then output the contents of the register, or it may simply pass through the character unchanged. An `end case` statement takes care of any remaining final output suffix after the end of the input has been reached For more details on BEK we refer to previous work or to the online BEK evaluator [23]. While the language is limited, it still is expressive enough to capture a wide range of string-manipulating functions, including many of the functions commonly used in Web sanitization and functions used in graphics processing [15, 32].

**ST representation:** The semantics of the program in Figure 2 is captured by a *symbolic transducer* in Figure 3. Symbolic transducers are a generalization of classic finite transducers, which allow arbitrary underlying label theories [32].

**Exploration and Data-Parallelism:** The register variables in BEK are important for making it easy to translate string-manipulating functions written in C# or other languages to BEK, because existing functions typically keep state through an iteration. These variables are also convenient for writing functions in BEK directly. Unfortunately, these register variables are enemies of data-parallelism, because they introduce control flow that depends on the registers and not on the individual character.

### 3.2 Formalism

We now formally define symbolic transducers or STs and give examples of how STs capture behavior of programs. We assume a *background structure* that has an effectively enumerable *background universe* $\boldsymbol{U}$, and is equipped with a language of function and relation symbols with fixed interpretations. Definitions below are given with $\boldsymbol{U}$ as an implicit parameter. We assume closure under Boolean operations and equality. Operations that are specific to $\boldsymbol{U}$ do not affect the results. We use $\lambda$-expressions for dealing with

[2] The reader may consult these links for examples:
https://www.cogmotive.com/blog/office-365-tips/vulnerability-in-office-365-allows-unauthorised-administrator-access,
http://xs-sniper.com/blog/2008/04/14/google-xss/,
http://ha.ckers.org/blog/20070617/another-google-xss-in-google-documents/.

anonymous functions that we call $\lambda$-*terms*. In general, we use standard first-order logic and follow the notational conventions that are consistent with [32]. The universe is multi-typed with $\boldsymbol{\tau}$ denoting the subuniverse of elements of type $\tau$. We make use of the *empty tuple type* $\mathtt{T0}$ such that $\mathbf{T0} = \{\langle\rangle\}$. We use a variant of the definition of STs where the control state component of STs is explicit. We write $\Psi(\sigma)$ for the set of $\sigma$-predicates. We write $\Lambda(\sigma \to \gamma)$ for $\lambda$-terms $f$ that denote functions $\boldsymbol{f} : \boldsymbol{\sigma} \to \boldsymbol{\gamma}$. We write $\Lambda(\sigma \to \gamma)^*$ for $\bigcup_{k \geq 0} \Lambda(\sigma \to \gamma^k)$. In other words, for any $\lambda$-term $f \in \Lambda(\sigma \to \gamma)^*$ the length of the output sequence may not depend of the input, but must be fixed.

**Definition 1:** A *Symbolic Transducer* or *ST* with input type $\sigma$ output type $\gamma$ and register type $\tau$ is a tuple $A = (Q, q^0, r^0, R)$, where $Q$ is a finite set of *states*; $q^0 \in Q$ is the *initial state*; $r^0 \in \boldsymbol{\tau}$ is the *initial register value*; $R$ is a finite set of *rules* $R = \Delta \cup F$ where $\Delta \subseteq (Q \times \Psi(\sigma \times \tau) \times \Lambda(\sigma \times \tau \to \gamma)^* \times \Lambda(\sigma \times \tau \to \tau)$ is a set of *transitions* and $F \subseteq (Q \times \Psi(\tau) \times \Lambda(\tau \to \gamma))$ is a set of *finalizers*. ⊠

A transition $(q, \varphi, o, u, p)$ is also written $q \xrightarrow{\varphi/o;u} p$ where $q$ is the *start* state, $\varphi$ the *guard*, $o$ the *output*, $u$ the *update*, and $p$ the *end* state. A finalizer $(q, \varphi, o)$ is also written $q \xrightarrow{\varphi/o} \circledcirc$ with $q$ as the state, $\varphi$ as the guard, $o$ as the output. Finalizers generalize final states.

**Example 1** Let $\sigma = \gamma$ be unsigned bitvectors (or natural numbers) N and let $\tau$ be the type N × N. The operation '$\ll$' is shift-left, '$\gg$' is shift-right, '&' is bit-wise-AND, '|' is bit-wise-OR. The ST in Figure 3 has the above types and is the direct mapping of the BEK program in Figure 2 where $s = y[1]$ and $r = y[2]$. $Q = \{q\}$, $r^0 = \langle 0, 0\rangle$, and the ST has two transitions and three finalizers. It computes Base64 encoding of byte sequences. Base64 is a standard encoding that is used to transfer binary data over textual media. ■

The semantics of $A$ is given by the following concrete transition relation. Let $q, p \in Q$, $r \in \boldsymbol{\tau}$, $a \in \boldsymbol{\sigma}$. Then $(q, r) \xrightarrow{[a]/\boldsymbol{o}(a,r)}_A (p, \boldsymbol{u}(a, r))$ denotes that there exists a transition $q \xrightarrow{\varphi/o;u} p$ such that $\varphi(a, r)$ holds. Similarly, $(q, r) \xrightarrow{\epsilon/\boldsymbol{o}(r)}_A \circledcirc$ denotes that there exists a finalizer $q \xrightarrow{\varphi/o} \circledcirc$ such that $\varphi(r)$ holds.

Now, the *reachability relation* $p \overset{\bar{a}/\bar{b}}{\twoheadrightarrow}_A p'$ for $\bar{a} \in \boldsymbol{\sigma}^*$, $\bar{b} \in \boldsymbol{\gamma}^*$, and $p, p' \in (Q \times \boldsymbol{\tau}) \cup \{\circledcirc\}$ is defined through the closure under the following conditions, where '$\cdot$' is concatenation of sequences, note that $\epsilon \cdot \bar{x} = \bar{x} \cdot \epsilon = \bar{x}$:

- If $p \xrightarrow{\bar{a}/\bar{b}}_A p'$ then $p \overset{\bar{a}/\bar{b}}{\twoheadrightarrow}_A p'$.
- If $p \overset{\bar{a}/\bar{b}}{\twoheadrightarrow}_A p_1 \overset{\bar{a}'/\bar{b}'}{\twoheadrightarrow}_A p_2$ then $p \overset{\bar{a}\cdot\bar{a}'/\bar{b}\cdot\bar{b}'}{\twoheadrightarrow}_A p_2$.

**Definition 2:** The *transduction* of $A$, denoted $\mathscr{T}_A$, is the following function from $\boldsymbol{\sigma}^*$ to $2^{(\boldsymbol{\gamma}^*)}$:

$$\mathscr{T}_A(\bar{a}) \stackrel{\text{def}}{=} \{\bar{b} \mid (q_A^0, r_A^0) \overset{\bar{a}/\bar{b}}{\twoheadrightarrow}_A \circledcirc\}$$

$A$ is *single-valued* when $|\mathscr{T}_A(\bar{a})| \leq 1$ for all $\bar{a} \in (\boldsymbol{\sigma})^*$ and $A$ is *deterministic* when, for all $\bar{a}, \bar{b}_1, \bar{b}_2, p, p_1, p_2$, if $p \xrightarrow{\bar{a}/\bar{b}_1}_A p_1$ and $p \xrightarrow{\bar{a}/\bar{b}_2}_A p_2$ then $\bar{b}_1 = \bar{b}_2$ and $p_1 = p_2$. We write $\mathscr{T}_A(\bar{a}, \bar{b})$ for $\bar{b} \in \mathscr{T}_A(\bar{a})$. ⊠

Finalizers can be omitted at the expense of allowing nondeterminism. However, nondeterminism is undesired because determinization of STs is in general not possible and analysis of (or even code generation from) nondeterministic STs is very difficult.

It is easy to show that determinism implies single-valuedness. Deterministic STs form a practically important subclass of STs and in the examples and case studies we only consider deterministic STs. For the data-parallel translation explained in Section 5 the STs are required to be deterministic, that is naturally the case for the kinds of string transformations we have in mind with this approach.

**Example 2** Let $A$ be the ST in Figure 3. Let $y = \langle 0, 0\rangle$ and $x =$ `'A'` $= 1000001_2$. So $x \leq 255$ and $y[1] \neq 2$. We have $E(x \gg 2) = E(10000_2) = E(16) = 16 + 65 =$ `'Q'` and $((x \& 3) \ll 4) = (1 \ll 4) = 10000_2 = 16$, so there is a concrete transition

$$(q, \langle 0, 0\rangle) \xrightarrow{[\text{'A'}]/[\text{'Q'}]} (q, \langle 1, 16\rangle)$$

If we do one more step from configuration $(q, \langle 1, 16\rangle)$ with input `'B'` we get the concrete transition

$$(q, \langle 1, 16\rangle) \xrightarrow{[\text{'B'}]/[\text{'U'}]} (q, \langle 2, 8\rangle)$$

Suppose that the input sequence ends here. Then we use the last finalizer that gives us the concrete transition:

$$(q, \langle 2, 8\rangle) \xrightarrow{\epsilon/[\text{'I'},\text{'='}]} \circledcirc$$

By using the derived reachability relation we have

$$(q, \langle 0, 0\rangle) \overset{[\text{'A'},\text{'B'}]/[\text{'Q'},\text{'U'},\text{'I'},\text{'='}]}{\twoheadrightarrow} \circledcirc$$

Thus, $\mathscr{T}_A($`"AB"`$) = \{$`"QUI="`$\}$. ■

## 4. Compilation of STs to SFTs

We assume that an ST is given. The ST may for example be the result of a translation from a BEK program. Sample BEK program and corresponding ST are illustrated in Figure 2 and Figure 3. Our goal is to compile the ST into an SFT (if possible), where an SFT is an ST *without* registers, or formally, whose register type $\tau$ is $\mathtt{T0}$. In the SFT we may group some characters into *combined characters* or *tokens* so that, if the input type of the ST is $\sigma$ then the input type of the SFT is $\sigma^{\leq k}$ for some $k \geq 1$ (sequences over $\sigma$ of length $l$, $1 \leq l \leq k$). In our compilation we maintain the following equivalence between the given *ST* and the resulting *SFT*. We use *flatten*$([u_i]_{i=1}^n)$, where $u_i$ has type $\sigma^{\leq k}$, to denote the sequence $u_1 \cdot u_2 \cdots u_n$ in $\boldsymbol{\sigma}^+$.

**Definition 3:** *ST* and *SFT* are *equivalent modulo grouping* if $\forall \bar{a}, \bar{b}$, $\mathscr{T}_{ST}(\bar{a}, \bar{b}) \Leftrightarrow \exists \bar{u} : \bar{a} = \mathit{flatten}(\bar{u}), \mathscr{T}_{SFT}(\bar{u}, \bar{b})$. ⊠

In other words, the outputs of *ST* and *SFT* must be equal for some grouping of the input characters in *SFT*. The compiler uses two phases, *grouping* and *exploration*. The phases are interleaved into a single algorithm, but intuitively, they serve two distinct purposes:

**Grouping:** The idea is as follows. Two consecutive transitions $p \xrightarrow{\varphi/o;u} q' \xrightarrow{\varphi'/o';u'} q$ can be lifted into a single transition that reads more inputs in one atomic step

$$p \xrightarrow{\substack{\lambda(x,y).\varphi_1(x[1],y) \wedge \varphi'(x[2],u(x[1],y))/ \\ \lambda(x,y).o(x[1],y)\cdot o'(x[2],u(x[1],y)); \\ \lambda(x,y).u'(x[2],u(x[1],y))}} q$$

where $x[i]$ reads the $i$'th element from $x$ (suppose first element has index 1). Thereby, the state $q'$ becomes eliminated (if this is the only occurrence of $q'$). The lifted transition may also become *unsatisfiable*, in which case it is eliminated. The input character of the new transition is a pair of the original characters.

**Exploration:** Exploration starts from the initial configuration $(q^0, r^0)$ where $q^0$ is the initial state and $r^0$ is the initial register value of the ST. If an update to a register is a fixed value $r$ that is *independent* of the input values in a given target state $q$ of the ST, then the configuration $(q, r)$ is treated as a state

```python
1  #algo.py
2  from z3 import *
3  Z = Solver()
4
5  class ST: #encapsulates a symbolic transducer
6    def __init__(self, q0, r0, T, F, x, y, ax):
7      self.q0 = q0           #initial state
8      self.r0 = r0           #initial register
9      self.T = T             #transitions
10     self.F = F             #finalizers
11     self.x = x             #label variable
12     self.y = y             #register variable
13     self.ax = ax           #background axioms
14
15   def Delta(self,q):       #transitions from q
16     for t in self.T:
17       if t[0] == q: yield t
18
19   def Fin(self,q):         #finalizers from q
20     for f in self.F:
21       if f[0] == q: yield f
22
23 def IsSat(f):
24   Z.push();Z.add(f);res=Z.check();Z.pop();
25   return res != unsat
26
27 def Choose(f, t):
28   Z.push();Z.add(f);Z.check();
29   v = Z.model().evaluate(t, True);
30   Z.pop(); return v
31
32 def GetUniqueValue(st, phi, t, k):
33   x_ = lambda i:Const('x%d'%(i+1),st.x.sort())
34   z_ = lambda i:Const('z%d'%(i+1),st.x.sort())
35   theta = [(x_(i),z_(i)) for i in range(k)]
36   t1 = substitute(t, *theta)
37   phi1 = substitute(phi, *theta)
38   if IsSat(And(phi,phi1,t!=t1)): return None
39   else: return Choose(phi, t)
40
41 def Group(st, q, r, k, phi, out):
42   for (qS, G, O, U, qE) in st.Delta(q):
43     xk = Const('x%d'%k, st.x.sort())
44     theta = [(st.x, xk),(st.y, r)]
45     c1 = And(phi, substitute(G, *theta))
46     if IsSat(c1):
47       o1 = [substitute(o, *theta) for o in O]
48       r1 = substitute(U, *theta)
49       v1 = GetUniqueValue(st, c1, r1, k)
50       if v1 != None:
51         yield (c1, out+o1, k, qE, v1)
52       else:
53         for tr in Group(st,qE,r1,k+1,c1,out+o1):
54           yield tr
55   for (qF, G, O) in st.Fin(q):
56     cF = And(phi, substitute(G,(st.y, r)))
57     if IsSat(cF):
58       oF = [substitute(o,(st.y,r)) for o in O]
59       yield (cF, out+oF, k-1, None, None)
60
61 def Explore(st): #Exploration algorithm
62   Z.add(st.ax)  #add the axioms to the solver
63   W, sft = {0},[]
64   nextStateId = 1
65   stateMap = {0 : (st.q0, st.r0)}
66   stateIdMap = {(st.q0, str(st.r0)) : 0}
67   while len(W) > 0:
68     qS = W.pop()
69     (q, r) = stateMap[qS]; tt = BoolVal(True)
70     for (g,o,k,q1,r1) in Group(st,q,r,1,tt,[]):
71       qE = None
72       if q1 != None:
73         if (q1,str(r1)) in stateIdMap:
74           qE = stateIdMap[(q1, str(r1))]
75         else:
76           qE = nextStateId; nextStateId += 1
77           stateMap[qE] = (q1,r1)
78           stateIdMap[(q1, str(r1))] = qE
79           W.add(qE)
80       sft.append((qS, g, o, k, qE))
81   return sft
```

**Figure 4.** ST exploration algorithm in Z3 Python.

of the explored SFT and the configuration (if new) is pushed to the search stack for continued exploration. If an update does not have a fixed value then grouping is invoked in an attempt to localize the use of the register update.

The overall effect is that registers which are used to encode local dependencies between consecutive characters are redundant and thus can be eliminated. We refer to the full algorithm also as *exploration* when it is clear from the context that the combined algorithm is meant. The complete self-contained algorithm is given by the (executable) Python script in Figure 4. Although the algorithm is given in a concrete executable form in Python (using the Z3 module) it is virtually identical to an abstract mathematical formulation and we have therefore decided to present only the concrete version, although it requires a bit of extra effort to get used to the notational differences compared to the formalism above. We illustrate the exploration algorithm in Example 3, where, for explanatory purposes, grouping and exploration are presented as two separate phases. The function `GetUniqueValue`, called on line 49, shows how Z3 is used to decide if the register is going to have a concrete value, i.e., if the term $r_1$ representing the value is constant with respect to the constraint $c_1$. If not then grouping is invoked recursively.

**Example 3** Take the ST in Figure 3. Project $\tau$ into $\tau_1 = \mathrm{N}$ as the first element $y[1]$ of $y$ and $\tau_2 = \mathrm{N}$ as the second element $y[2]$ of $y$. This projection happens automatically in the combined exploration algorithm. Exploration will now partially evaluate all the rules, by using depth first search, and integrate $y[1]$ into the states $q_{y[1]}$ in

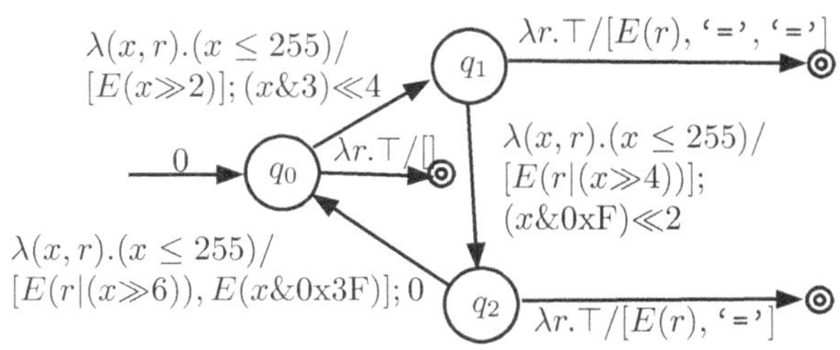


**Figure 5.** ST after exploration of ST in Figure 3.

such a way that a rule $q \xrightarrow{\lambda(x,y).\ell(x,y)} q$ is replaced by one or more rules of the form $q_a \xrightarrow{\lambda(x,z).\ell_{ab}(x,z)} q_b$ where $a, b \in \tau_1$ and the register $z$ has type $\tau_2$. The main technical insight is that it is possible to compute such $b$ and $\ell_{ab}$ for the given $a$ through *finite* case analysis over $x$ even though $\sigma$, $\gamma$ and $\tau_2$ may be infinite.

If we apply exploration to the ST in Figure 3 we get the equivalent ST in Figure 5. We can now apply grouping to this ST. To illustrate grouping, consider the path $q_0 \xrightarrow{f} q_1 \xrightarrow{g} q_2 \xrightarrow{h} q_0$ of transitions. First apply grouping to $q_0 \xrightarrow{f} q_1 \xrightarrow{g} q_2$ to obtain $q_0 \xrightarrow{f\circ g} q_2$ and then we apply grouping to $q_0 \xrightarrow{f\circ g} q_2 \xrightarrow{h} q_0$ to obtain $p_0 \xrightarrow{f\circ g\circ h} p_0$. At this point the composed label $f \circ g \circ h$ be-

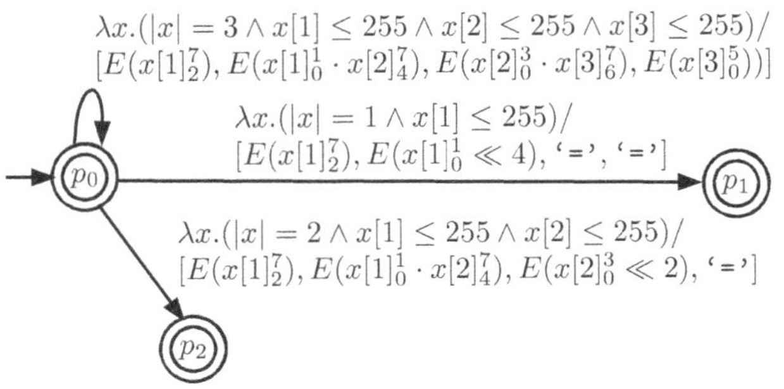


**Figure 6.** SFT after grouping of ST in Figure 5; $y_n^m$ denotes extraction of bits from $m$ to $n$ from $y$; $y \cdot z$ denotes bit-append.

comes independent of the register $r$ because $r$ is only used to glue $f$ with $g$ and $g$ with $h$.

A similar step is applied to transitions followed by finalizers to get composed transitions that lead from $p_0$ to *sink* states $p_1$ and $p_2$ (states without outgoing transitions and with trivial finalizers that yield empty outputs). Finally, all resulting rules are independent of the register and so the register can be eliminated and we have constructed an SFT illustrated in Figure 6. An important point is that the construction of the SFT would not be possible by only using grouping or only using naive exploration. The new combined exploration algorithm is needed. ■

The first point we address next is: *The reason we are interested in SFTs.* The second point is: *When does the exploration algorithm terminate?* The third point is: *Does the algorithm meet our needs for parallelization?* As it turns out, the third question needs more work – because, except for some special cases when the lookahead is fixed, the assumption that the input is tokenized up front is not fully realistic in a parallel setting because then there is no way to calculate where the next token starts without having processed the previous tokens.

### 4.1 Succinctness

Figure 7 compares the sizes of the state machines needed to achieve the different encoding and decoding tasks.

| | Size | | |
|---|---|---|---|
| **Encoder** | **SFT** | **SFT$^+$** | **$k$-SFT** |
| `UTF8encode` | 16 | 6 | 9 |
| `UTF8decode` | 6371 | 10 | 27 |
| `BASE64encode` | 105 | 6 | 14 |
| `BASE64decode` | 1161 | 6 | 23 |
| `HTMLencode` | 3 | 3 | 7 |
| `HTMLdecode` | 113 | 10 | 31 |

**Figure 7.** Exploration sizes in total nr of transitions. SFT is naive exploration. SFT$^+$ is grouped exploration. $k$-SFT is creation of $k$-SFT after SFT$^+$.

The table indicates the advantages of using the exploration algorithm. Without this dramatic reduction in the size of the SFT, we would not be able to compile the SFT to exploit data parallel finite state machines presented below, where the approach requires that the number of states in the transducer is *small*, which our compilation scheme provides, while the label theory may potentially allow infinite character domains. In particular, it is shown in [32, Figure 8(a)], that in HTML decoding, the number of states in the SFT grows exponentially in the length of $k$ for supporting decoding of patterns $\&\#[0-9]\{k\}$; that makes naive exploration to SFTs impractical in this case. This exponential blowup is avoided with the new exploration algorithm. The final column in the table shows the size of the $k$-SFT obtained after the final phase of the algorithm discussed below.

**Definition 4:** A *$k$-SFT* has a finite state space $Q$ and has transitions $p \xrightarrow{\varphi/f} q$ where $p, q \in Q$, $\varphi$ is a $\sigma$-predicate, and $f \in \Lambda(\sigma^m \to \gamma^n)$ is a $\lambda$-term for some fixed $m \geq 0$ and $n \geq 0$. We assume that the $k$-SFT is *deterministic* meaning that if there are two transitions $p \xrightarrow{\varphi_1/f_1} q_1$ and $p \xrightarrow{\varphi_2/f_2} q_2$ such that $\varphi_1 \wedge \varphi_2$ is satisfiable, then $f_1 = f_2$ and $q_1 = q_2$. A $k$-SFT has also finalizers of the form $q \xrightarrow{f} \circledcirc$ with $f$ as above and where (to maintain determinism) there is at most one finalizer for each state $q$. The case $m = 0$ means that there is no input dependence, so $f$ is a fixed output sequence. ⊠

The semantics of a transition $p \xrightarrow{\varphi/f} q$ is that $\varphi$ is applied in state $p$ to the current character in the input sequence $\bar{c}$, say $c_i$. There is an implicit well-definedness criterion that, if the state is $p$ and $\varphi(c_i)$ is true then $i \geq m$, where $m$ is the arity of $f$. If $\varphi(c_i)$ holds then $f$ is applied to $(c_{i-m+1}, c_{i-m+2}, \ldots, c_{i-1}, c_i)$ to produce the next subsequence of the output. For finalizers the semantics is that $f$ is applied to $(c_{l-m+1}, c_{l-m+2}, \ldots, c_{l-1}, c_l)$ to produce the suffix of the output, where $c_l$ is the last character.

### 4.2 Termination and Limitations

The exploration algorithm does not terminate if there are unbounded dependencies between successive characters in the input. In other words, if the register is needed to remember some input element for arbitrarily many following input elements. For example, if the register is used to sum all "digits" seen in the input, then the exploration algorithm does not terminate.

An *$m$-grouping* of a nonempty sequence $\bar{a}$ over $\boldsymbol{\sigma}$ is a sequence $\bar{u}$ over $\boldsymbol{\sigma}^{\leq m}$ whose flattened form equals $\bar{a}$. For example, the sequence $[[1,2],[3,4,5],[6]]$ is a 3-grouping of the sequence $[1,2,3,4,5,6]$.

**Definition 5:** ST $A$ has the *bounded lookahead property* if there is a finite subset $P \subseteq Q \times \boldsymbol{\tau}$, $p_0 = (q^0, r^0) \in P$, and there exists $m > 0$ such that for all input sequences $\bar{a}$ over $\boldsymbol{\sigma}$ accepted by $A$ there exists an $m$-grouping $[u_i]_{i=1}^n$ of $\bar{a}$ such that $p_{i-1} \xrightarrow{u_i/} p_i$ for some $p_i \in P$ for $i < n$ and $p_n = \circledcirc$. ⊠

**Theorem 1:** *Exploration algorithm terminates iff the ST has the bounded lookahead property. The output SFT is equivalent modulo grouping to the input ST.*

We write *SFT$^+$* for the intermediate result that the exploration algorithm produces. Namely, SFT$^+$ stands for the SFT whose input characters have been grouped, i.e., whose character type is $\sigma^{\leq m}$, for some $m > 0$, where $\sigma$ is the character type of the input SFT.

There is a class of STs for which the exploration algorithm does not terminate although an equivalent $k$-SFT exists. Roughly speaking, this situation arises when *bounded lookback* cannot be turned into *bounded lookahead*. Thus, even if the ST could, in principle, be compiled into an equivalent $k$-SFT, there exists no intermediate SFT$^+$ over grouped characters.

The following example illustrates such a case.

**Example 4** Consider standard `HtmlEncode` over full Unicode. An input to the encoder is a UTF-16 encoded string. An input is *malformed* if it contains a *bad surrogate* $b$:

- $b$ is a high surrogate (in range $\psi_H \stackrel{\text{def}}{=} \lambda x.55296 \leq x \leq 56319$) that is not immediately followed by a low surrogate (in range $\psi_L \stackrel{\text{def}}{=} \lambda x.56320 \leq x \leq 57343$), or
- $b$ is a low surrogate that is not immediately preceded by a high surrogate.

Some encoders use the following *correcting rule* as a robustness feature rather than rejecting malformed strings (e.g., `HtmlEncode` in `System.Net.WebUtility` in .NET Framework 4.5). The Unicode replacement character � (`\uFFFD`) is used to replace bad surrogates so that the string is not malformed. Such a correcting phase can be described by the ST in Figure 8(a), say `Rep`. For efficiency,

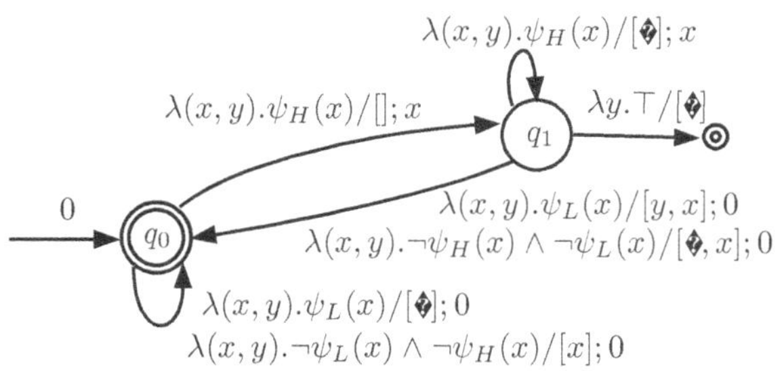


(a) Using an ST

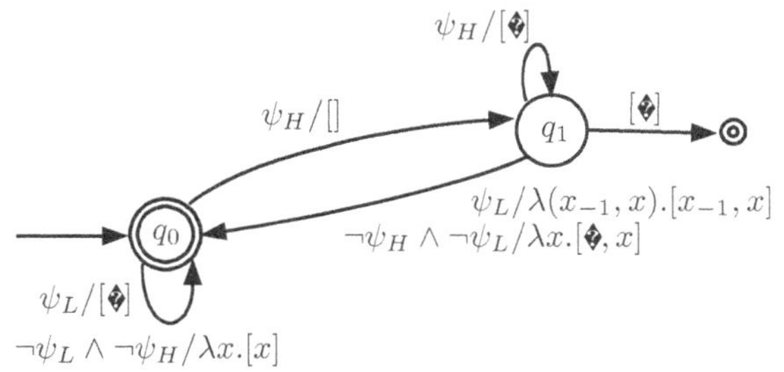


(b) Using a 2-SFT

**Figure 8.** Replacing bad surrogates with �.

existing hand-optimized encoders integrate `Rep` into the logic for the encoder, but here we think of it as a separate preprocessing step over the input. In some versions of `HtmlEncode` the replacement character � itself is also encoded, in others it is not.

The difficulty with `Rep` is that there is no fixed length lookahead window to decide, if the last character in the window is the last consequtive high surrogate. However, the 2-SFT in Figure8(b) is equivalent to `Rep` and is parallelizable with the approach described below. The variable $x_{-1}$ refers to the previous character in the input while $x$ refers to the current character, so the lookback window size for determining the output is 2. ■

To be completely accurate, the exploration algorithm *does* terminate for the `Rep` ST in Figure 8(a) because there are a finite number of high surrogates (1024). But this is not the point. The point is that the exploration creates a state space that is unreasonably large. Moreover, if $\psi_H(x)$ and $\psi_L(x)$ were defined as ($x \bmod 2 = 0$) and ($x \bmod 2 = 1$) then the algorithm would not terminate because `Rep` would not have the bounded lookahead property: suppose there exists $m$ and $P$ as in Definition 5 and consider the input $[c]_{i=1}^{m}$ for some $c$ such that $\psi_H(c)$ holds. Then $(q_1, c) \in P$, but there are infinitely many such $c$, contradicting that $P$ is finite.

It is an open problem how to decide such cases. The particular case of `Rep` in Figure 8(a) seems easy to detect, but consider the small variant of `Rep` where the $q_1$-loop is replaced by $q_1 \xrightarrow{\psi_H(x)/[]} q_1$, i.e., the intermediate high surrogates are ignored. Then there exists no fixed lookback $k+1$ for the symbol $x_{-k}$ in the corresponding transition from $q_1$ to $q_0$ in the $(k+1)$-SFT in Figure 8(b).

The way we deal with this problem is by using composition. The encoder STs we consider, are defined under the assumption that the input string is valid, i.e., it has no bad surrogates. The exploration algorithm is used to produce a SFT$^+$ that is then transformed into an equivalent $k$-SFT, say $M$. Finally, $M$ is *composed* with `Rep` (the 2-SFT in Figure 8(b)) to produce $M' = \lambda x.M(\texttt{Rep}(x))$. Although $k$-SFTs are, in general, not closed under compositon, in this particular case they are. So the actual input to parallelization is $M'$. Not only is this easier to program, but it is also less error prone because the corner cases of what to do with bad surrogates are completely avoided. Moreover, there is no loss in efficiency because the two transformations are automatically composed into one, essentially eliminating the intermediate corrected string, as a form of deforestation [34].

Example 4 illustrates a case when it is not possible to construct *SFT*$^+$ from *ST* because there is no grouping bound, although an equivalent *k-SFT* exists. Another difficulty is that it is not always possible to turn an *SFT*$^+$ into a *k-SFT* (that is required for parallelization unless all groups have a fixed length). As discussed below, such a transformation requires *monadic decomposition* of predicates [33] in order to decompose $n$-ary relations used as guards in the *SFT*$^+$ into Boolean combinations of monadic relations that will guard the transitions in the *k-SFT*. In general this is not possible, e.g., if the predicate is $x = y$. Moreover, the problem of deciding if such a decomposition exists is, in general, undecidable even when assuming (as we do) that the theory over labels is decidable. The latter undecidability follows from a result in [20, Proposition 2.b].

### 4.3 Parallelizability

The exploration algorithm presented above transforms an ST into an SFT at the expense of grouping several input characters into one token. Thus, formally the input language of the SFT is a nested sequence where the inner sequences or character groups are tokens. If all tokens have the same length $k$, as in Base64 decoding where $k = 4$, then it is possible to process the original input in parallel by reading the input tokens from offsets $km$ for $m > 0$. In general, as for example with HTML encoding or UTF8 encoding, the tokens have variable length and this simple solution does not work. Also, storing inputs in registers breaks parallelizability and takes us back to square one.

Instead, we transform the SFT$^+$ into a $k$-SFT with *lookback* building on the idea of $k$-SLTs introduced in [7]. The algorithm that we use does not introduce registers and maintains the property that transition guards only reference the current character, but output functions may refer back to $k$ prior input characters. The resulting $k$-SFT is a special kind of a $k$-SLT. The main benefit is that the transition graph of the domain of a $k$-SFT is an SFA over the original characters. This enables the parallelization approach presented in Section 5 and the output computation still works because the lookback is bounded and can be applied in parallel.

We illustrate the algorithm below using an example. The input to the algorithm is an SFT over tokens or subsequences of characters. This SFT is first decomposed so that all transitions are split into predicates over singleton characters. To achieve this, the algorithm uses *monadic decomposition* of predicates from [33]. Then the split transitions are merged back together into a deterministic $k$-SFT. Finally, the $k$-SFT is compiled into C# code that is used by the subsequent parallelization step.

**Example 5** We consider here a cut down version of a UTF8 decoder to illustrate $k$-SFT construction. Suppose that the SFT$^+$ produced by exploration has a single state $q_0$ and three transitions: $q_0 \xrightarrow{\psi/\lambda x.[x]} q_0$, $q_0 \xrightarrow{\varphi/f} q_0$, and $q_0 \xrightarrow{\gamma/g} q_0$, where

- $\psi$ reads *one* byte and checks that it is in the ASCII range and the character is output as is,
- $\varphi$ reads *two* bytes and checks that they form a valid 2-byte encoding, $f$ computes the code point from the two bytes,

- $\gamma$ reads *three* bytes and checks that they form a valid 3-byte encoding, $g$ computes the code point from the three bytes.

The first transition is kept as is. The second and the third transitions are split into transitions that read one character at a time and the output calculation is delayed to the last transition. In order to do so, the predicates are first decomposed by using monadic decomposition. The decomposed forms of the predicates are as follows (using hexadecimal notation for numbers and interval notations)

$$
\begin{aligned}
dec(\varphi(\bar{x})) &= x_1 \in \texttt{C2-DF} \wedge x_2 \in \texttt{80-BF} \\
dec(\gamma(\bar{x})) &= (x_1 = \texttt{E0} \wedge x_2 \in \texttt{A0-BF} \wedge x_3 \in \texttt{80-BF}) \vee \\
&\quad (x_1 = \texttt{ED} \wedge x_2 \in \texttt{80-9F} \wedge x_3 \in \texttt{80-BF}) \vee \\
&\quad (x_1 \in \texttt{EE|EF|E1-EC} \wedge x_2 \in \texttt{80-BF} \wedge x_3 \in \texttt{80-BF})
\end{aligned}
$$

The $k$-SFT construction algorithm introduces intermediate states for each transition after reading each symbol, considering one disjunct at a time in the DNF. It then merges the transitions into a single deterministic $k$-SFT. In this case the result is a 3-SFT shown in Figure 9. There would be additional states for the case of 4 byte encodings resulting in a 4-SFT, and more states and larger lookback if even longer encodings (up to 6 bytes) were allowed. ■

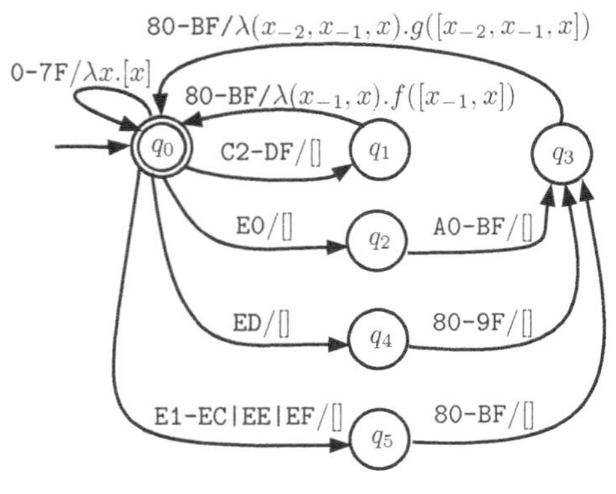


**Figure 9.** 3-SFT constructed from a UFT8 decoder that decodes up to three byte encodings.

## 5. Data-Parallel Translation

In the prior sections we demonstrated how to remove registers from ST and turn them into $k$-SFTs. In this section we describe how to run $k$-SFTs on data-parallel hardware. In particular, we demonstrate an end to end compilation of $k$-SFTs to a data parallel version capable of exploiting multiple cores via threads.

Here we frame the evaluation of finite state transducers as associative operations over vectors and matrices. Because these operations are associative, they can take advantage of data-parallel hardware. The number of states in the SFT must be small for efficiency. Our key insight that allows us to combine STs with the data-parallel approach is that we first transform the ST into a $k$-SFT, using the pipeline of algorithms discussed above. In effect, ST to $k$-SFT compilation pushes the complexity of the ST into the edges, which in turn allows us to efficiently target data-parallel hardware.

In the sections that follow, we demonstrate an automatic approach that compiles a BEK program into a SFT and then down into the data parallel formulation that runs on multicore hardware.

### 5.1 Data-Parallel Operators

To aid our discussion, we introduce two higher-order data-parallel primitives. First, `zip` takes a binary function and maps that function over two sequences of equal sized length. For example, to pairwise add the numbers in two sequences we could use

$$\texttt{zip}(+, [0,1,2], [3,4,5]) = [3,5,7]$$

Second, `scan` applies a binary *associative* function, $\oplus$, over every prefix of a sequence, i.e., given a sequence $[x_1, x_2, \ldots, x_n, x_{n+1}]$, and an identity element $\imath$ such that $\imath \oplus x = x$, `scan` produces

$$[\imath, x_1, (x_1 \oplus x_2), (x_1 \oplus x_2 \oplus x_3), \ldots, (x_1 \oplus \cdots \oplus x_n)]$$

For explanatory purposes we use a related function `scanf` that takes a function $\oplus : Q \times \boldsymbol{\sigma} \to Q$, a value $q \in Q$, a sequence $[s_1, \ldots, s_n, s_{n+1}] \in \boldsymbol{\sigma}^*$ and produces the sequence

$$[q, q \oplus s_1, ((q \oplus s_1) \oplus s_2), \ldots, (((q \oplus s_1) \oplus s_2) \cdots \oplus s_n)]$$

in $Q^*$ of length $n+1$. Finally, we use the function `split` to split a given sequence $\boldsymbol{s}$ according to a sequence $\boldsymbol{m}$ of lookback offsets as follows into a sequence of tuples (or subsequences):

$$\texttt{split}([s_i]_{i=1}^n, [m_i]_{i=1}^n) = [(s_{i+1-m_i}, s_{i+2-m_i}, \ldots, s_i)]_{i=1}^n$$

We next show how to define SFTs in terms of these primitives.

### 5.2 Describing SFTs With Higher-Order Functions

Recall that a $k$-SFT $M$ is a tuple $(Q, q^0, R)$ where $q^0$ is the initial state, and $R = \Delta \cup F$ is a finite set of rules, consisting of *transitions* $\Delta$ and *finalizers* $F$. Here we require $M$ to be deterministic. Moreover, for ease of presentation and without loss of generality, we assume that all finalizers of $M$ are trivial in the sense that they produce the empty output and are thus treated as final states in the classical sense. For example the 2-SFT in Figure 8(b) is deterministic. We assume that we work with an extended alphabet where there is an end-of-input (`EOI`) symbol and all valid input sequences end with `EOI`, so that finalizers are not needed. For each transition $p \xrightarrow{\varphi/f} q$ we refer to the arity of $f$ as the *lookback* of the transition, that is denoted by $\ell(p,a)$ where $a \in [\![\varphi]\!]$. We represent normal characters by their code points as (non-negative) integers. `EOI` has code $-1$. We refer to $f$ by $\phi(p,a)$, i.e., $\phi(p,a)$ takes $\ell(p,a)$ arguments.

Thus, the rules define a transition *function* from a given input and state to an output and a new state. Let $\delta(q,a)$ be the *state function*, implicitly defined by the rule set $R$, which takes as arguments a state $q$ and an input $a$ and produces a new state.

To transduce an input sequence $s$, $M$ starts in state $q_1 = q^0$ and sequentially reads the symbols of $s$. When $M$ reads the $i$'th symbol $s_i$ from $s$ in state $q_i$ (first symbol being $s_1$), it enters state $q_{i+1} = \delta(q_i, s_i)$ and calls the *output function* $\phi(q_i, u)$, where $u = [s_{i+1-\ell(q_i,s_i)}, s_{i+2-\ell(q_i,s_i)}, \ldots, s_i]$, which maps to a finite (possibly empty) sequence of symbols in the output alphabet. We call the algorithm to transduce a string by $M$, `Transduce`, it takes as input $M$ and a sequence $s$ and produces the output sequence.

$$
\begin{aligned}
&\texttt{Transduce}(M, s) = \\
&\quad \textit{let } \boldsymbol{q} = \texttt{scanf}(\delta, q^0, s) \textit{ in} \\
&\quad \textit{let } \boldsymbol{m} = \texttt{zip}(\ell, \boldsymbol{q}, s) \textit{ in} \\
&\quad \texttt{flatten}(\texttt{zip}(\phi, \boldsymbol{q}, \texttt{split}(s, \boldsymbol{m})))
\end{aligned}
$$

where `flatten` is defined in Section 4.

**Example 6** Consider the 2-SFT `Rep` in Figure 8(b). We first extend `Rep` so that it has the final state $q_2$ and we assume that all valid inputs end with `EOI`. We write $h$ for $\psi_H$. We write $\$$ for $\lambda x.(x = \texttt{EOI})$ and we write $\hbar$ for $\lambda x.\neg\$(x) \wedge \neg h(x)$. We also add a fourth state $q_3$ that corresponds to an *error state* (in practice this state may often be omitted, but we include it here for clarity). Let $? \stackrel{\text{def}}{=} [\blacklozenge]$, $f \stackrel{\text{def}}{=} \lambda x.[\textit{if } \psi_L(x) \textit{ then } \blacklozenge \textit{ else } x]$ and let $g \stackrel{\text{def}}{=} \lambda(x_{-1}, x).[(\textit{if } \psi_L(x) \textit{ then } x_{-1} \textit{ else } \blacklozenge), x]$. The extended 2-SFT is depicted in Figure 10. Let $a = \texttt{D83D}_{16}$ and $b = \texttt{DE0A}_{16}$. So $h(a)$ holds and $\psi_L(b)$ (thus also $\hbar(b)$) holds. Take the input

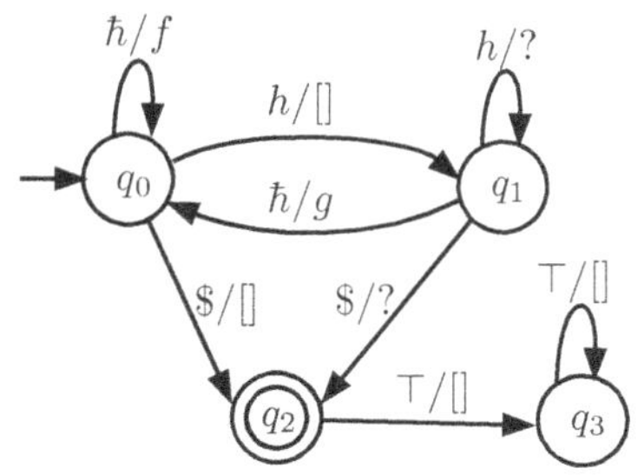


**Figure 10.** 2-SFT Rep extended with EOI. The state $q_2$ is the final state, meaning that it has the trivial finalizer $q_2 \xrightarrow{[]} \circledcirc$.

sequence $s = [b, a, a, b, a, \mathtt{EOI}]$. We get that

$$\begin{array}{rl} s = & [b\ , a\ , a\ , b\ , a\ , \mathtt{EOI}] \\ \mathtt{scanf}(\delta, q_0, s) = \ \boldsymbol{q} = & [q_0\ , q_0\ , q_1\ , q_1\ , q_0\ , q_1\ ] \\ \mathtt{zip}(\ell, \boldsymbol{q}, s) = \boldsymbol{m} = & [1\ , 0\ , 0\ , 2\ , 0\ , 0\ ] \\ \mathtt{split}(s, \boldsymbol{m}) = \ \boldsymbol{u} = & [(b)\ , ()\ , ()\ , (a, b)\ , ()\ , ()\ ] \\ \mathtt{zip}(\phi, \boldsymbol{q}, \boldsymbol{u}) = \ \boldsymbol{v} = & [[\text{�}]\ , []\ , [\text{�}]\ , [a, b]\ , []\ , [\text{�}]\ ] \end{array}$$

and so $\mathtt{flatten}(\boldsymbol{v})$ is the valid Unicode string $[\text{�}, \text{�}, a, b, \text{�}]$ that would be displayed similar to "��☺�" where $(a, b)$ is the surrogate pair UTF16 encoding of the code point $\mathtt{1F60A}_{16}$ that is a smiley in the emoticon alphabet.[3] ∎

### 5.3 Data-Parallel $k$-SFT

The prior section formalized $k$-SFT in terms of higher-order data parallel primitives. If the function on which these primitives operate are not *associative*, they must execute sequentially. If the BEK code contains registers, then in general it is not possible to directly write the resulting $k$-SFT with associative generalization of $\delta$. Fortunately, as we saw in the previous section, our compilation algorithm can remove registers in many cases.

We compile $\delta$ into an associative operation on matrices. Because matrix multiplication is an associative operation that encodes graph traversals, this representation is amenable to data parallelism. The main idea is to lift `scanf` above to its associative counterpart `scan` by representing both states and symbols as matrices (so that we can talk about associativity to begin with). We build on known techniques from [14, 19, 25].

**Graph Traversals with Matrix Multiplication:** A convenient way to view $k$-SFT is as a graph where nodes in the graph are states and there exists an edge from state $i$ to state $j$ on symbol $s$ if $\delta(i, s) = j$. A graph is simple to represent as an adjacency matrix: the set of allowed transitions for each symbol $s$ in our input alphabet can be described by $M_s$, a $n \times n$ adjacency matrix, where $n$ is the number of states, such that $(M_s)_{ij} = 1$ if state $i$ transitions to state $j$ on symbol $s$, and $(M_s)_{ij} = 0$, otherwise. In other words, an adjacency matrix is a symbolic representation of how a symbol from the input alphabet transitions *every* state in a $k$-SFT.

In order to deal with a potentially infinite alphabet $\boldsymbol{\sigma}$, we first divide the input alphabet $\boldsymbol{\sigma}$ into a finite set of equivalence classes $\boldsymbol{\sigma}_\sim$ such that the state transitions are invariant under $\sim$. Thus, we end up with one matrix $M_C$ per equivalence class $C \in \boldsymbol{\sigma}_\sim$. We write $\widetilde{a}$ for the equivalence class containing the symbol $a$. But how do we actually compute the equivalence relation $\sim$? Let all the guards of the $k$-SFT be $\Psi = \{\varphi_1, \ldots, \varphi_m\}$. The equivalence relation $\sim$ can be effectively obtained by constructing all the *satisfiable* Boolean combinations over $\Psi$, for this we use the *minterm* algorithm from [9].

[3] See http://unicode.org/charts/PDF/U1F600.pdf.

**Example 7** Consider the 2-SFT Rep in Figure 10. Rep uses four guards. The minterms are $\{h, \hbar, \$\}$ because they are all pairwise disjoint and their union equals $\top$. The SFA corresponding to Rep looks exactly the same as Rep but with output functions omitted. Since there are three equivalence classes, say $A = [\![h]\!]$, $B = [\![\hbar]\!]$, and $C = [\![\$]\!]$, we have three adjacency matrices ($M_A$, $M_B$ and $M_C$) that describe how every state in the SFA transitions when reading symbols $a \in A$, $b \in B$ and $c \in C$, respectively.

$$M_A = \begin{pmatrix} 0 & 1 & 0 & 0 \\ 0 & 1 & 0 & 0 \\ 0 & 0 & 0 & 1 \\ 0 & 0 & 0 & 1 \end{pmatrix} \quad M_B = \begin{pmatrix} 1 & 0 & 0 & 0 \\ 1 & 0 & 0 & 0 \\ 0 & 0 & 0 & 1 \\ 0 & 0 & 0 & 1 \end{pmatrix} \quad M_C = \begin{pmatrix} 0 & 0 & 1 & 0 \\ 0 & 0 & 1 & 0 \\ 0 & 0 & 0 & 1 \\ 0 & 0 & 0 & 1 \end{pmatrix}$$

Given $a$ and $b$ as in Example 6, we have $a \in A$ and $b \in B$. ∎

Given this formulation, we use matrix multiplication '$\cdot$' as a mechanism for graph traversal. Assume the identity matrix I encodes the initial state of the SFA. Then adjacency matrix that encodes the state of the SFA after reading the first symbol $a$ in an input sequence $s$ is $I \cdot M_{\widetilde{a}}$. Further, the adjacency matrix that encodes the state of the SFA after reading the second symbol, $b$ of $s$ is $I \cdot M_{\widetilde{a}} \cdot M_{\widetilde{b}}$, etc.

**From $k$-SFTs to matrices:** To transform a $k$-SFT to operations on vectors and matrices, we define the following two functions, `inflate` and `project`; `inflate` generates the matrix $M_{\widetilde{a}}$ for each symbol $a \in \boldsymbol{\sigma}$; `project` extracts from matrix $M_w$ the state of the (underlying) SFA, where $M_w$ is obtained after reading the input sequence $w$, starting from state $q^0 = 0$:

$$\mathtt{project}(M_w) = V_0 \cdot M_w \cdot V_F$$

where $V_0$ is an $n$-component *row* vector

$$V_0 = (1, 0, \ldots, 0)$$

and $V_F$ is an $n$-component *column* vector

$$V_F^T = (0, 1, \ldots, n-1).$$

So $V_0 \cdot M_w$ extracts the first row, say $X$, of $M_w$, where $X$ has exactly one element $j$ that is 1 while all the other elements are 0 because the SFA is deterministic, where $j$ is the state reached from $q^0$ after reading $w$. Thus $X \cdot V_F$ equals that state $j$.

Given this formulation, we implement an associative version $\hat{\delta}$ of the transition function $\delta$ that uses "inflated" symbols instead of actual symbols. Thus, instead of using the actual alphabet, the transduction uses the inflated alphabet $\{M_{\widetilde{a}} \mid a \in \boldsymbol{\sigma}\}$ and the input sequence is mapped to the inflated alphabet through the *initial inflation* of the input sequence $\mathtt{map}(\mathtt{inflate}, s)$:

$$\hat{\delta}(M, M_{\widetilde{a}}) \stackrel{\text{def}}{=} M \cdot M_{\widetilde{a}}$$

where $M$ is a matrix that encodes the state of the SFA, and $M_{\widetilde{a}}$ is the inflated symbol $a$. Thus, the function $\hat{\delta}$ is associative by associativity of matrix multiplication and enables us to implement a data parallel version of Transduce as:

$$\begin{array}{l} \mathtt{Transduce}(k\text{-SFT}, s) \stackrel{\text{def}}{=} \\ \quad \textit{let } S = \mathtt{map}(\mathtt{inflate}, s) \textit{ in} \\ \quad \textit{let } \boldsymbol{q} = \mathtt{map}(\mathtt{project}, \mathtt{scan}(\hat{\delta}, S)) \textit{ in} \\ \quad \textit{let } \boldsymbol{m} = \mathtt{zip}(\ell, \boldsymbol{q}, S) \textit{ in} \\ \quad \mathtt{flatten}(\mathtt{zip}(\phi, \boldsymbol{q}, \mathtt{split}(s, \boldsymbol{m}))) \end{array}$$

An important point to note is that $\phi$ must be applied to the *original* (non-inflated) sequence $s$ because the output functions of the rules of the SFT depend on the actual input, while both $\ell$ and $\delta$ are lifted to work directly on the equivalence classes.

### 5.4 An Efficient Matrix Representation

While matrix multiplication is associative, it unfortunately has a high overhead. Even an optimized implementation requires a significant amount of computation and memory—matrix multiplication runs in $O(m^3)$ where $m$ is the number of states in a finite state automaton and requires $m^2$ memory.

To reduce this overhead such that it is linear in the number of states (both time and space), we exploit the fact that all of our adjacency matrices are square binary matrices with exactly one 1 in each row (and zeros elsewhere). We follow recent work and succinctly represent this type of adjacency matrix as an array where the value of the array at index $i$ (staring from 0) is equal to the index of the column that contains a 1 for row $i$ [25]. This is possible because each row contains *exactly* one 1.

In other words, the matrix is encoded as a one-dimensional array indexed by states. For example, the matrices $M_A$ and $M_B$ from the prior section, represented as arrays are $[1, 1, 3, 3]$ and $[0, 0, 3, 3]$, respectively. With this flattened representation, matrix multiplication of $M_A$ with $M_B$ reorders (with replacement) the elements of $M_B$ according to $M_A$: $M_A \cdot M_B = [0, 0, 3, 3]$

To implement this efficient form of matrix multiplication is simple; we re-order the elements of one array by the elements of another:

```
void Multiply(char Ma[K], char Mb[K], char Mab[K]) {
  for(int i = 0; i < K; i++) Mab[i] = Mb[Ma[i]]; }
```

Because multiplying two matrices of this form produces another matrix of this form, we always represent matrices as linear arrays indexed by state which requires only $m$ memory locations and a running time of $O(m)$.

### 5.5 Translating $k$-SFT to $\delta$, $\ell$ and $\phi$

To summarize, we produce the following pipeline. First, a programmer writes string manipulating functions in BEK. Next, we compile from BEK into an ST and then compile the ST into a $k$-SFT. Finally, we compile from the $k$-SFT to C# functions which encode $\phi$, $\delta$ and $\ell$.

These functions can then be applied as part of our data-parallel computation. As an integrated part of the pipeline, we also need a constraint solver, e.g., an SMT solver [3, 11], to construct the finite equivalence relation $\sim$ and to construct a classifier that decides membership of actual inputs in the $\sim$-equivalence classes.

**Example 8** Consider again the 2-SFT in Figure 10. Recall the matrices $M_A$, $M_B$ and $M_C$ from Example 7. Let $s$ be as in Example 6. So $S = \texttt{map(inflate}, s) = [M_B, M_A, M_A, M_B, M_A, M_C]$ and

$$\begin{aligned}&\texttt{map(project}, \texttt{scan}(\hat{\delta}, S))\\ &\quad = \texttt{map(project}, [I, M_B, M_B \cdot M_A, M_B \cdot M_A \cdot M_A, \ldots])\\ &\quad = [q_0, q_0, q_1, q_1, q_0, q_1]\end{aligned}$$

The rest of the output computation is the same as illustrated in Example 6. ■

The actual code generation to C# is discussed below. The code template for the generated C# is shown in Figure 13. The field `delta` corresponds to $\hat{\delta}$, the field `lookback` corresponds to $\ell$ (lifted to symbols), and the field `output` corresponds to $\phi$. The semantics of `Transduce` is the implementation of `Encoder.Apply`. The implementation of `GetSymbol` uses predicates that have been generated by Z3 and then mapped to C# expressions to decide which symbol a concrete character maps to. The symbols are unique identifiers for the equivalence classes of $\sim$ as discussed above.

## 6. Evaluation

This section demonstrates the efficacy of our algorithms by investigating their correctness and performance. Section 6.1 explains the setup of the evaluation experiment. Section 6.2 empirically demonstrates that our generated programs produce consistent outputs compared to those available in existing system libraries. Section 6.3 provides a baseline performance comparison of our generated programs with existing library functions in the sequential case, demonstrating that our generated programs are comparable in performance. Finally, Section 6.4 demonstrates multi-factor speedups on a variety of real-world string transformation programs.

We use three encoder and decoder pairs in the following experiments, `HtmlEncode` and `HtmlDecode`, `Utf8Encode` and `Utf8Decode`, and finally, `Base64Encode` and `Base64Decode`. Each pair performs the logical inverse of the other (i.e., the output of an encoder is the input to the corresponding decoder). We also use sanitizers from the `AntiXss` library [22] in our sequential baseline comparison. All system encoders that we use are listed in Figure 11. There are several variations of some of them and they differ behaviorally. For example `HtmlEncode` in `AntiXss` is different than both the one in `HttpUtility` and the one in `WebUtility`. In particular, the latter two do not encode control characters or the replacement character � while the former does. However, the latter two encode all non-ASCII characters such as ä while the former does not encode all of them. In total, the latter two encode 101 characters out of all of the 256 extended ASCII characters, while the former encodes only 72. Since we have no bias in selecting one before the other, we compare against all of them in our experiments.

| Routine | Library |
|---|---|
| HtmlEncode | AntiXss.AntiXssEncoder |
| HtmlDecode | AntiXss.AntiXssEncoder |
| CssEncode | AntiXss.AntiXssEncoder |
| JavaScriptStringEncode | AntiXss.AntiXssEncoder |
| HtmlEncode | System.Net.WebUtility |
| HtmlDecode | System.Net.WebUtility |
| HtmlEncode | System.Web.HttpUtility |
| HtmlDecode | System.Web.HttpUtility |
| JavaScriptStringEncode | System.Web.HttpUtility |
| ToBase64String | System.Convert |
| FromBase64String | System.Convert |
| UTF8.GetBytes (encoder) | System.Text.Encoding |
| UTF8.GetString (decoder) | System.Text.Encoding |

**Figure 11.** Pre-existing encoders used for comparison. All encoders are from .NET Framework 4.5.

### 6.1 Setup

The concrete input to each individual experiment is the intermediate representation of the BEK program under consideration. It is an ST, as an instance of the `ST` python class in Figure 4. For example, the BEK intermediate representation of `Base64Encode` is shown in Figure 12. It corresponds to the ST shown in Figure 3. It has a single state $q = 0$, a register that is a pair of numbers, two transitions $\{r_1, r_2\}$ and three finalizers $\{f_1, f_2, f_3\}$. The initial register value is the pair $(0, 0)$. Notice that the function $E$ is defined as a Z3 axiom. Such axioms are either inlined or used to define corresponding methods during code generation.

The python function `st2cs` in Figure 12 is the entry point that generates the final C# code. First, it invokes `Explore` (as defined in Figure 4) to construct the equivalent (modulo grouping) SFT$^+$. It then decomposes the transitions of the SFT$^+$ by introducing lookback and constructs a deterministic $k$-SFT. In the case of encoders whose input is assumed to be a valid UTF16 string, the resulting $k$-SFT is composed with the 2-SFT `Rep`, as shown in Figure 8(b), to lift the input strings to arbitrary sequences of characters (as opposed to valid UTF16 strings only, recall the discussion at the end

```
#genBase64Encode.py
from st2cs import *

def Base64Encode():
  bvs =  BitVecSort(16); q = 0
  C = lambda c:BitVecVal(ord(c),bvs)
  Register = Datatype('Register')
  Register.declare('Pair',('Fst',bvs),('Snd',bvs))
  Register = Register.create()
  P=Register.Pair; F=Register.Fst; S=Register.Snd
  Edef = lambda x: If(x <= 25, x + 65,
           If(x <= 51, x + 71,
             If(x <= 61, x - 4,
               If(x == 62, C('+'), C('/')))))
  E = Function('Encode',bvs,bvs)
  v = Const('v',bvs)
  axiom = ForAll(v,(E(v)==Edef(v)),patterns=[E(v)])
  x = Var(1,bvs) #input character variable
  y = Var(0,Register) #register variable
  #transitions
  r1 = (q, And(x <= 255,F(y)!=2),
      [If(F(y)==0,E(x >> 2),E(S(y)|(x>>4)))],
      P(F(y)+1,If(F(y)==0,(x&3)<<4,(x&0xF)<<2)),q)
  r2 = (q, And(x <= 255,F(y)==2),
      [E(S(y)|(x>>6)),E(x&0x3F)],P(0,0),q)
  #finalizers
  f1 = (q, And(F(y) != 1, F(y) != 2), [])
  f2 = (q, F(y)==1,[E(S(y)),C('='),C('=')])
  f3 = (q, F(y)==2,[E(S(y)),C('=')])
  st = ST(q,P(0,0),[r1,r2],[f1,f2,f3],x,y,[axiom])
  return st

st2cs("Base64Encode",Base64Encode())
```

**Figure 12.** `Base64Encode` intermediate representation.

of Section 4.2). The generated C# is taylored for the subsequent parallelization step.

### 6.2 Consistency

To demonstrate that our synthesized encoders are correct, we checked the consistency of the BEK-generated output against independent implementations with the same functionality. We generate a set of 100 1-MB strings and evaluate both the independent output and the BEK generated code on each input.

The strings are chosen randomly. We used independently-produced implementations listed in Figure 11 for comparison. In each case we implemented a corresponding equivalent BEK program and automatically generated the code as explained above. For each individual input we compared that the output of the BEK generated program is equal to the output returned by the corresponding system encoder. We found no discrepancies. The system encoders, listed in Figure 11, came from .NET 4.5 core libraries and the `AntiXss` encoder library.

### 6.3 Sequential BEK

The generic code template for the generated sequential C# code for a given BEK encoder is shown in Figure 13. It exercises the same interface of the $k$-SFT that is used by the parallel implementation. The method `Encoder.Apply` implements the sequential routine. Concrete characters $x$ are mapped to a finite set of symbols through `GetSymbol`. Each symbol identifies the equivalence class in which the input behaves similarly (recall the discussion from Section 5.3). The maximal lookback is $k$. The initial state is 0. Given a state $q$ and a symbol $s$, $\texttt{delta}[q][s]$ is the next state. Output is computed from a given state $q$ and symbol $s$ by invoking $\texttt{output}[q][s](x_1,\ldots,x_m)$ where $(x_1,\ldots,x_m)$ is the subsequence of $m$ previous characters, $m = \texttt{lookback}[q][s]$, note that $m \leq k$. We have not optimized for the case when the input grouping size

```
namespace Experiments
{
 public static class Encoder
 {
  public const int finalSymbol = ...;
  public const int finalState = ...;
  public const int k = ...;
  public static int[][] delta = ...;
  public static int[][] lookback = ...;
  public static Func<int[],int>[][][] output = ...;
  public static int GetSymbol(int x) {...};

  public static string Apply(string s)
  {
   int L = s.Length;
   StringBuilder sb = new StringBuilder();
   var xs = new int[k];
   int state = 0;
   for (int i = 0; i < L; i++)
   {
    var x = s[i];
    var symbol = GetSymbol(x);
    int n = output[state][symbol].Length;
    if (n > 0)
    {
     var m = lookback[state][symbol];
     for (int j = 0; j < m; j++)
      xs[j] = s[i - m + 1 + j];
     for (int j = 0; j < n; j++)
      sb.Append((char)output[state][symbol][j](xs));
    }
    state = delta[state][symbol];
   }
   var m_end = lookback[state][finalSymbol];
   for (int j = 0; j < m_end - 1; j++)
    xs[j] = s[L - m_end + 1 + j];
   var n_end = output[state][finalSymbol].Length;
   for (int j = 0; j < n_end; j++)
    sb.Append((char)output[state][finalSymbol][j](xs));
   return sb.ToString();
  }
 }
}
```

**Figure 13.** Code template for generated C#.

is fixed (as with `Base64Decode`) but iterate one character at a time over the input.

For each of the *string to string* encoders in Figure 11 (the top 9 rows) we compared the running time with the corresponding BEK generated encoder `Encoder.Apply` over 100 randomly generated 1-megabyte strings (over extended ASCII). To get statistically significant results, we ran each experiment 10 times and report the mean $m$ and the standard error $e$ of the running time as $m(\pm e)$. For `HtmlEncode` we use a different version of BEK encoder in the case of `AntiXss` to match the semantics, while we use another BEK encoder for the other two libraries. For `HtmlDecode` we used the same BEK encoder in all three instances. As input to the decoder we used the output from the corresponding encoder, i.e., from the random inputs we generate inputs to the decoders using the corresponding encoders: inputs for `HtmlDecode` in `AntiXss` are generated with `HtmlEncode` in `AntiXss`, inputs for `HtmlDecode` in `WebUtility` are generated with `HtmlEncode` in `WebUtility`, etc. The Html decoder in BEK supports up to 3 digit decimal encodings, which is why we restricted this experiment to extended ASCII. We see no reason why supporting longer encodings would affect the sequential running time in any significant manner. The experiments were carried out on a Lenovo X1 Carbon laptop with Intel i7 2GHz processor having 8GB of RAM and running 64-bit Windows 8.1.

The results are shown in Figure 14. The sequential performance of our generated encoders are on par with existing hand-optimized codes. Our code is sometimes faster and sometimes slower than

| Routine | Library | $t$(sec) | $t_{Bek}$(sec) | $t_{Bek}/t$ |
|---|---|---|---|---|
| `HtmlEncode` | `AntiXss` | $2.7(\pm.02)$ | $4.6(\pm.1)$ | 1.7 |
| `HtmlDecode` | `AntiXss` | $8.0(\pm.1)$ | $3.5(\pm.03)$ | 0.4 |
| `CssEncode` | `AntiXss` | $3.4(\pm.03)$ | $9.5(\pm.05)$ | 2.8 |
| `JSSEncode` | `AntiXss` | $3.6(\pm.1)$ | $3.7(\pm.03)$ | 1.0 |
| `HtmlEncode` | `WebUtility` | $6.9(\pm.1)$ | $4.6(\pm.07)$ | 0.7 |
| `HtmlDecode` | `WebUtility` | $11(\pm.2)$ | $4.4(\pm.06)$ | 0.4 |
| `HtmlEncode` | `HttpUtility` | $6.8(\pm.07)$ | $4.5(\pm.04)$ | 0.7 |
| `HtmlDecode` | `HttpUtility` | $11(\pm.1)$ | $4.4(\pm.04)$ | 0.4 |
| `JSSEncode` | `HttpUtility` | $3.6(\pm.07)$ | $3.8(\pm.05)$ | 1.0 |
| `Geomean :` | | | | 0.92 |

**Figure 14.** Sequential comparison over 100x1MB strings.

these standard libraries. Consider `HtmlDecode`: BEK is significantly faster than the `AntiXss` baseline as this decoder has many corner cases which makes it difficult to hand-optimize (and thus points to the benefits of an automated compiler). However, consider `CssEncode` where BEK is almost 3x slower `AntiXss`. This is because all encodings have the form \0000$XY$ and use the loop over function calls in `output` in Figure 13 to append '\' and four '0's to `sb`, one at a time. We could amortize this huge overhead through simple optimizations (i.e., inlining function calls instead of indirectly calling them through a table), however, because this paper is about extracting data parallelism from BEK codes with registers, we left this simple optimization for future work.

The encoder producing inputs for `HtmlDecode` in the `AntiXss` experiment encodes less data than in the other two `HtmlDecode` experiments, as was explained above, which explains the BEK time difference of almost 1 second in those experiments.

To summarize, the geometric mean of all speedup experiments is 0.92 and at the 95% confidence interval, ranges from 0.57 to 1.46. So our approach is neither statistically faster nor slower than these hand-optimized baselines.

### 6.4 Data Parallel BEK

In this section we demonstrate multi-factor performance improvements over sequential baselines by utilizing multiple threads on multi-core hardware. It is worth noting our approach is not limited to multiple cores as it is data parallel and thus it can target many forms of data parallel hardware (e.g., GPUs or Hadoop clusters).

**Platform:** We conducted all experiments on an unloaded Intel 2 GHz (E5-2650) workstation with 64 GB of RAM and 32 logical processors (2 sockets with 16 physical cores).

**Inputs:** For both the `HTML` and `Utf8` encoder/decoder pair, we encode (and then decode) a 1GB subset of Wikipedia's HTML while for the `Base64` encoder/decoder pair, we encode (and then decode) a 100 MB SQL server executable. We measured the time it takes to execute a BEK program *after* reading the input from disk. Many of our performance numbers are faster than a commodity disk and thus we did not want our experiments to be IO bound. To compute throughput numbers, we measure both bytes read *and* bytes written as both numbers are required to understand a BEK program's performance. To get statistically significant results, we ran each experiment 10 times and reported the mean and 95% confidence interval of the mean.

**Throughput:** Our data-parallel BEK programs exploit parallel hardware and are fast. As shown in Figure 15, with 32 logical threads, our encoders and decoders are able to process data at speeds of anywhere from 250 to 600 MB/sec. In contrast, the serial baselines are anywhere from 30 to 100 MB/sec. Secondly, even with small input data (i.e., `Base64` encoder only encodes 100 MB) we still see significant throughput. This implies that the cost to

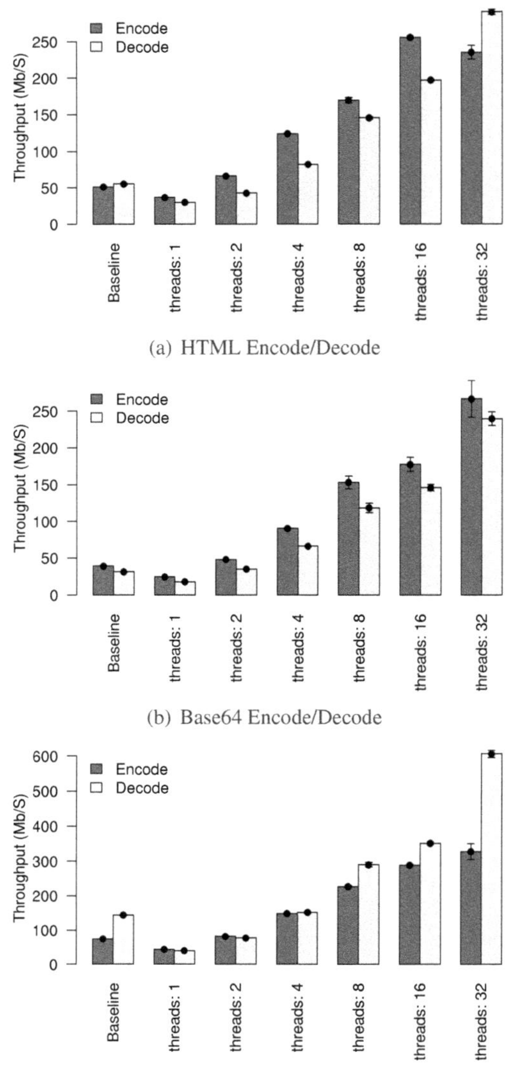

(a) HTML Encode/Decode

(b) Base64 Encode/Decode

(c) UTF8 Encode/Decode

**Figure 15.** Throughput of various BEK encoders shown in MB/sec on the $y$ axis, as function of threads.

create and manage threads does not dominate the computation. Lastly, our single-threaded implementation is *slower* than the baseline. This result is pedagogical: our implementation requires each thread do two passes over the input and with a single-thread our implementation does twice as much work as the sequential baseline. A real user of our system would never run with a single thread.

**Speedup:** Our data-parallel BEK programs provide nearly linear speedups for up to 8 physical cores and moderate speedups after that, up through 16 cores. Figure 16 details the speedup of $x$ processors over a single processor. With 16 threads, our implementation is just shy of $8x$ speedup across the various encoders and decoders. Our approach saturates at 16 physical threads because the latency of reading data from shared caches and RAM becomes a bottleneck. Because our approach is data parallel, we could amortize this latency by using more physical machines such that each machine more effectively utilizes both caches and RAM. To summarize, these order-of-magnitude throughput improvements and speedups across a wide range of BEK programs are significant and enable data parallel processing of large amounts of data.

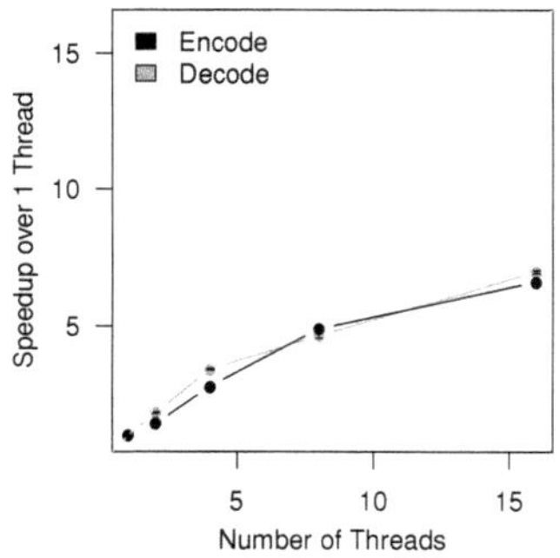


(a) HTML Encode/Decode

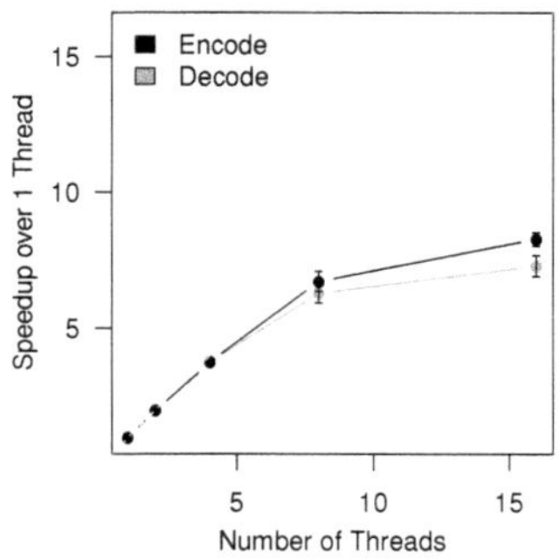


(b) Base64 Encode/Decode

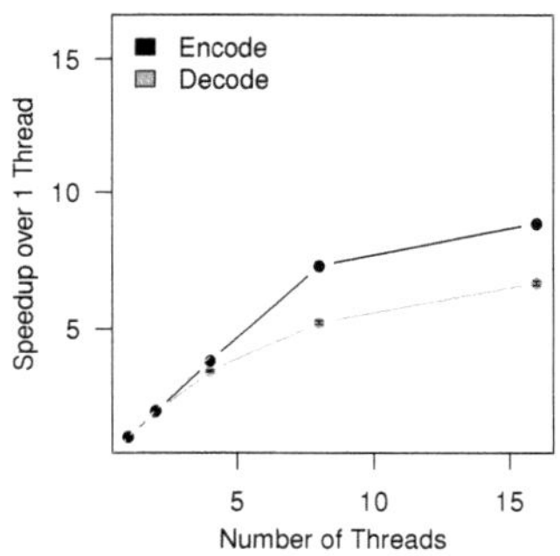


(c) UTF8 Encode/Decode

**Figure 16.** Speedup of various BEK encoders, relative to a sequential baseline, as a function of threads.

## 7. Related Work

Symbolic finite transducers (SFTs) and BEK were originally introduced in [15] with a focus on security analysis of sanitizers. The formal foundations and the theoretical analysis of the underlying SFT algorithms, in particular, an algorithm for deciding equivalence of single-valued SFTs, modulo a decidable background theory is studied in [32], where Symbolic Transducers (STs) are also introduced as an extension of SFTs with registers, but exploration of STs and code generation are not studied in [15, 32]. In contrast, the focus of this paper and its motivation is efficient transformation from STs to SFTs and $k$-SFTs with the particular application of *code generation* that supports efficient parallel execution. Another recent extension of SFTs, *extended* SFTs [8], is SFTs with *lookahead* where the primary motivation is to allow lookahead without introducing registers; unlike SFTs, ESFTs are not closed under composition. The grouping idea was originally exploited in [8] where it is used as a heuristic for lifting ESFTs to SFTs, but it is not integrated with exploration. A model similar to $k$-SFTs is $k$-SLTs, $k$-SLTs are introduced in [7], and use lookback instead of lookahead and, unlike ESFTs, step one symbol at a time. Our model of $k$-SFTs can be seen as a special class of parallelizable $k$-SLTs. A key property that we use here is monadicity of the predicates [33], which is needed for a $k$-SLTs to be translatable into a $k$-SFTs. The general case of deciding if a predicate is monadic is undecidable, which follows from [20, Proposition 2.b].

In recent years there has been considerable interest in automata over infinite languages [17, 30]. Finite words over an infinite alphabet are often called *data words* in the literature. Other related automata models are *pebble automata* [26] and *data automata* [6]. Several characterizations of logics with respect to different models of data word automata are studied in [5]. This line of work focuses on fundamental questions about definability, decidability, complexity, and expressiveness on classes of automata on one hand and fragments of logic on the other hand. A different line of work on automata with infinite alphabets introduces *lattice automata* [12] that are finite state automata whose transitions are labeled by elements of an atomic lattice with motivation coming from verification of symbolic communicating machines. *Streaming transducers* [1] is another recent symbolic extension of finite transducers. We do not know of prior work that has investigated the use of symbolic extensions of transducers for code generation.

In our implementation we use the off-the-shelf SMT solver Z3 [10] for incrementally solving label constraints that arise during the exploration algorithm. Similar applications of SMT techniques have been introduced in the context of symbolic execution of programs by using path conditions to represent under and over approximations of reachable states [13]. The distinguishing feature of our exploration algorithm is that it computes a transformation that is behaviorally *equivalent* to the original ST with respect to the transduction semantics, which is important for correct code generation.

Finite state transducers have been used for dynamic and static analysis to validate sanitization functions in web applications in [2]. Other types of security analyses use string analysis [24, 35]. Yu et.al. show how multiple automata can be composed to model looping code [36]. Our work is complementary to previous efforts in using SMT solvers to solve problems related to list transformations. HAMPI [18] and Kaluza [28] extend the STP solver to handle equations over strings and equations with multiple variables. We are not aware of previous work investigating the use of finite state transducers for efficient code generation. One explanation for this is that classical finite state transducers are not directly suited for this purpose because SFTs can be exponentially more succinct with respect to the alphabet size.

Parallel algorithms for finite state machines, akin to the one presented in this work, have been known for a long time [14, 19]. Like this paper, Ladner and Fischer build a parallel implementation by phrasing finite state machine computation as matrix multiplication. Their approach targets applications with small finite state machines and thus they ignore the resulting cubic (in the number of states) overhead [19]. Hillis and Steele describe an improved algorithm based on parallel prefix sum which reduces this overhead to linear in the number of states [14]. To the best of our knowledge, none of these approaches allow infinite alphabets, neither were implemented on real hardware nor are they used with a larger framework for transducing. This paper builds on these theoretical insights, fits into a larger compilation framework which lets programmers use an expressive language to write encoders and decoders, and then evaluates those programs on large scale, parallel machines.

Finally, stream processing is a programming model which organizes programs by independent filters that communicate over data channels. Programmers need not think about parallelism as it is implicit in the programming model; a streaming program is the successive composition of independent filters and the runtime maps these independent computations to hardware parallelism [31, 37].

Unlike the programming model in this paper, streaming based programming models are not analyzable nor do they *break* data dependencies to expose data parallelism like we do in this work. In particular, streaming languages can only run as fast as hardware can expose a stream. Thus, it is not clear how they can hide I/O from reading large files from multiple disks.

## 8. Conclusions

This paper demonstrates how to compile an expressive domain-specific language, BEK to produce consistent and fast encoders and sanitizers. We use symbolic transducers as an intermediate formalism, and then introduce a novel algorithm which performs a symbolic partial exploration of these transducers to obtain simplified, stateless versions of the original BEK program.

We then show how to compile the resulting stateless transducers to data-parallel hardware. Our compilation results indicate significant runtime improvements: our data-parallel compilation speedups are up to $8x$ faster compared to a sequential implementation, when run on a 16-node commodity desktop.

## References


[1] R. Alur and P. Cerný. Streaming transducers for algorithmic verification of single-pass list-processing programs. In *Proceedings of the 38th Annual ACM SIGPLAN-SIGACT Symposium on Principles of Programming Languages*, POPL '11. ACM, 2011.

[2] D. Balzarotti, M. Cova, V. Felmetsger, N. Jovanovic, E. Kirda, C. Kruegel, and G. Vigna. Saner: Composing static and dynamic analysis to validate sanitization in web applications. In *IEEE Oakland Security and Privacy*, 2008.

[3] C. Barrett and C. Tinelli. Satisfiability modulo theories. In E. Clarke, T. Henzinger, and H. Veith, editors, *Handbook of Model Checking*. Springer, 2014. (to appear).

[4] D. Bates, A. Barth, and C. Jackson. Regular expressions considered harmful in client-side xss filters. In *Proceedings of the 19th international conference on World wide web*, WWW '10. ACM, 2010.

[5] M. Benedikt, C. Ley, and G. Puppis. Automata vs. logics on data words. In *Proceedings of the 24th international conference/19th annual conference on Computer Science Logic (CSL'10/EACSL'10)*, volume 6247 of *LNCS*, pages 110–124. Springer, 2010.

[6] M. Bojańczyk, A. Muscholl, T. Schwentick, L. Segoufin, and C. David. Two-variable logic on words with data. In *Proceedings of the 21st Annual IEEE Symposium on Logic in Computer Science (LICS'06)*, pages 7–16. IEEE, 2006.

[7] M. Botinčan and D. Babić. Sigma*: symbolic learning of input-output specifications. In *Proceedings of the 40th annual ACM SIGPLAN-SIGACT symposium on Principles of programming languages*, POPL'13, pages 443–456. ACM, 2013.

[8] L. D'Antoni and M. Veanes. Static analysis of string encoders and decoders. In *14th International Conference on Verification, Model Checking, and Abstract Interpretation, VMCAI 2013*, volume 7737 of *LNCS*, pages 209–228. Springer, 2013.

[9] L. D'Antoni and M. Veanes. Minimization of symbolic automata. In *Proceedings of the 41st ACM SIGPLAN-SIGACT Symposium on Principles of Programming Languages*, POPL'14, pages 541–553. ACM, 2014.

[10] L. de Moura and N. Bjørner. Z3: An efficient SMT solver. In C. Ramakrishnan and J. Rehof, editors, *Tools and Algorithms for the Construction and Analysis of Systems*, volume 4963 of *LNCS*. Springer, 2008.

[11] L. De Moura and N. Bjørner. Satisfiability modulo theories: Introduction and applications. *Commun. ACM*, 54(9):69–77, 2011.

[12] T. L. Gall and B. Jeannet. Lattice automata: A representation for languages on infinite alphabets, and some applications to verification. In *SAS 2007*, volume 4634 of *LNCS*, pages 52–68, 2007.

[13] P. Godefroid. Compositional dynamic test generation. In *Proceedings of the 34th annual ACM SIGPLAN-SIGACT symposium on Principles of programming languages*, POPL'13, pages 47–54, 2007.

[14] W. D. Hillis and G. L. Steele. Data parallel algorithms. In *Commun. ACM*, volume 29, pages 1170–1183, Dec 1986.

[15] P. Hooimeijer, B. Livshits, D. Molnar, P. Saxena, and M. Veanes. Fast and precise sanitizer analysis with Bek. In *USENIX Security*, August 2011.

[16] J. E. Hopcroft and J. D. Ullman. *Introduction to Automata Theory, Languages, and Computation*. Addison Wesley, 1979.

[17] M. Kaminski and N. Francez. Finite-memory automata. In *31st Annual IEEE Symposium on Foundations of Computer Science*, volume 2 of *FOCS'90*, pages 683–688. IEEE, 1990.

[18] A. Kiezun, V. Ganesh, P. J. Guo, P. Hooimeijer, and M. D. Ernst. HAMPI: a solver for string constraints. In *International Symposium on Software Testing and Analysis*, 2009.

[19] R. E. Ladner and M. J. Fischer. Parallel prefix computation. *Journal of the ACM*, 27(4):831–838, 1980.

[20] L. Libkin. Variable independence for first-order definable constraints. *ACM Transactions on Computational Logic*, 4(4):431–451, 2003.

[21] D. Lindsay and E. V. Nava. Universal XSS via IE8's XSS filters. In *Black Hat Europe*, 2010.

[22] *Anti-Cross Site Scripting Library*. Microsoft Corporation, . http://msdn.microsoft.com/en-us/security/aa973814.aspx.

[23] *Bek guide*. Microsoft Research, . http://rise4fun.com/bek/tutorial.

[24] Y. Minamide. Static approximation of dynamically generated web pages. In *WWW '05*, pages 432–441, 2005.

[25] T. Mytkowicz, M. Musuvathi, and W. Schulte. Data-parallel finite-state machines. In *Proceedings of the 19th International Conference on Architectural Support for Programming Languages and Operating Systems*, ASPLOS '14, pages 529–542, New York, 2014. ACM.

[26] F. Neven, T. Schwentick, and V. Vianu. Finite state machines for strings over infinite alphabets. *ACM Trans. CL*, 5:403–435, 2004.

[27] *XSS Filter Evasion Cheat Sheet*. OWASP. http://ha.ckers.org/xss.html.

[28] P. Saxena, D. Akhawe, S. Hanna, S. McCamant, F. Mao, and D. Song. A symbolic execution framework for JavaScript. In *IEEE Security and Privacy*, 2010.

[29] P. Saxena, D. Molnar, and B. Livshits. Scriptgard: Preventing script injection attacks in legacy web applications with automatic sanitization. Technical Report MSR-TR-2010-128, Microsoft Research, August 2010.

[30] L. Segoufin. Automata and logics for words and trees over an infinite alphabet. In Z. Ésik, editor, *EACSL Annual Conference on Logic in Computer Science, CSL*, volume 4207 of *LNCS*, pages 41–57, 2006.

[31] W. Thies, M. Karczmarek, and S. P. Amarasinghe. Streamit: A language for streaming applications. In *Proceedings of the 11th International Conference on Compiler Construction*, volume 2304 of *LNCS*, pages 179–196. Springer, 2002.

[32] M. Veanes, P. Hooimeijer, B. Livshits, D. Molnar, and N. Bjorner. Symbolic finite state transducers: Algorithms and applications. In *Proceedings of the 39th Annual ACM SIGPLAN-SIGACT Symposium on Principles of Programming Languages*, POPL '12. ACM, 2012.

[33] M. Veanes, N. Bjørner, L. Nachmanson, and S. Bereg. Monadic decomposition. In *International Conference on Computer Aided Verification*, volume 8559 of *LNCS*, pages 628–645. Springer, 2014.

[34] P. Wadler. Deforestation: transforming programs to eliminate trees. In *Proceedings of the Second European Symposium on Programming*, pages 231–248, 1988.

[35] G. Wassermann, D. Yu, A. Chander, D. Dhurjati, H. Inamura, and Z. Su. Dynamic test input generation for web applications. In *International Symposium on Software Testing and Analysis*, 2008.

[36] F. Yu, T. Bultan, and O. H. Ibarra. Relational string verification using multi-track automata. In *Conference on Implementation and Application of Automata*, CIAA'10, pages 290–299, 2011.

[37] D. Zhang, Q. J. Li, R. Rabbah, and S. Amarasinghe. A lightweight streaming layer for multicore execution. *SIGARCH Comput. Archit. News*, 36(2):18–27, May 2008.

# Ur/Web: A Simple Model for Programming the Web

Adam Chlipala
MIT CSAIL
adamc@csail.mit.edu

## Abstract

The World Wide Web has evolved gradually from a document delivery platform to an architecture for distributed programming. This largely unplanned evolution is apparent in the set of interconnected languages and protocols that any Web application must manage. This paper presents Ur/Web, a domain-specific, statically typed functional programming language with a much simpler model for programming modern Web applications. Ur/Web's model is **unified**, where programs in a single programming language are compiled to other "Web standards" languages as needed; supports novel kinds of **encapsulation** of Web-specific state; and exposes **simple concurrency**, where programmers can reason about distributed, multithreaded applications via a mix of transactions and cooperative preemption. We give a tutorial introduction to the main features of Ur/Web and discuss the language implementation and the production Web applications that use it.

***Categories and Subject Descriptors*** D.2.2 [*Software Engineering*]: Design Tools and Techniques - Modules and interfaces; D.3.2 [*Programming Languages*]: Language Classifications - Concurrent, distributed, and parallel languages; Applicative (functional) languages

***Keywords*** Web programming languages; encapsulation; transactions; remote procedure calls; message passing; relational databases; functional-reactive programming

## 1. Introduction

The World Wide Web is a very popular platform today for programming certain kinds of distributed applications with graphical user interfaces (GUIs). Today's complex ecosystem of "Web standards" was not planned monolithically. Rather, it evolved gradually, from the starting point of the Web as a delivery system for static documents. The result is not surprising: there are many pain points in implementing rich functionality on top of the particular languages that browsers and servers speak. At a minimum, today's rich applications must generate HTML, for document structure; CSS, for document formatting; JavaScript, a scripting language for client-side interactivity; and HTTP, a protocol for sending all of the above and more, to and from browsers. Most recent, popular applications also rely on a language like JSON for serializing complex datatypes for network communication, and on a language or API like SQL for storing persistent, structured data on servers. Code fragments in these different languages are often embedded within each other in complex ways, and the popular Web development tools provide little help in catching inconsistencies.

These complaints are not new, nor are language-based solutions. The Links project [7, 11] pioneered the "tierless programming" approach, combining all the pieces of dynamic Web applications within one statically typed functional language. More recent designs in the mainstream reap some similar benefits, as in Google's Web Toolkit[1] and Closure[2] systems, for adding compilation on top of Web-standard languages; and Microsoft's LINQ [27], for type-safe querying (to SQL databases and more) within general-purpose languages.

Such established systems provide substantial benefits to Web programmers, but there is more we could ask for. This paper focuses on a language design that advances the state of the art by addressing two key desiderata. First, we bring **encapsulation** to rich Web applications, supporting program modules that treat key pieces of Web applications as private state. Second, we expose a **simple concurrency** model to programmers, while supporting the kinds of nontrivial communication between clients and servers that today's applications take advantage of. Most Web programmers seem unaware of either property as something that might be worth asking for, so part of our mission in this paper is to evangelize for them.

We present the **Ur/Web** programming language, an extension of the Ur language [8], a statically typed functional language inspired by dependent type theory. A prior paper described Ur and its type system, but did not discuss the Web-specific extensions. Open-source implementations of Ur/Web have been available since 2006, and several production Web applications use the language, including at least one profitable commercial site.

Ur/Web reduces the nest of Web standards to a simple programming model, coming close to retaining just the essence of the Web as an application platform, from the standpoints of security and performance.

- An application is a program in one language (Ur/Web) that runs on one **server** and many **clients**, with automatic compilation of parts of programs into the languages appropriate to the different nodes (e.g., JavaScript). The server is completely under the programmer's control, while clients may deviate arbitrarily from code we provide to them to run. For reasons of performance scaling or reliability, we may use multiple physical machines to implement server functionality, but it is sound for the programmer to imagine all server code running in a single isolated machine.
- All objects passed between parts of the application are **strongly typed**. Applications may be written with no explicit marshaling


*POPL '15*, January 15–17, 2015, Mumbai, India.

ACM 978-1-4503-3300-9/15/01... $15.00.
http://dx.doi.org/10.1145/2676726.2677004

[1] `http://www.gwtproject.org/`

[2] `https://developers.google.com/closure/`

or other conversion of data between formats. Where snippets of code appear as first-class values, they are presented as abstract syntax trees, ruling out flaws like *code injection vulnerabilities* that rely on surprising consequences of concatenating code-as-strings.

- The only persistent state in the server sits in an SQL database, accessed through a strongly typed SQL interface.
- The server exposes a set of typed functions that are callable remotely. A client begins interacting with the application in a new browser tab by **making a remote procedure call to one of these functions, with arbitrary correctly typed arguments**. The server runs the associated function **atomically**, with no opportunity to observe interference by any other concurrent operations, generating an HTML page that the client displays.
- The HTML page in a client may contain traditional *links* to other pages, which are represented as **suspended calls to other remotely callable functions**, to be forced when a link is followed, to generate the new HTML page to display.
- Any HTML page may also contain **embedded Ur/Web code** that runs in the client. Such code may spawn as many client-side threads as is convenient, and the threads obey a **cooperative multithreading** semantics, where one thread runs at a time, and we only switch threads during well-defined blocking operations. Threads may modify the GUI shown to the user, via a **functional-reactive programming** system that mixes dataflow programming with imperative callbacks.
- Client-side thread code may also make blocking **remote procedure calls** treated similarly to those for regular links. Such a call may return a value of any function-free type, not just HTML pages; and the thread receiving the function result may compute with it to change the visible GUI programmatically, rather than by loading a completely new page. As before, every remote procedure call appears to execute **atomically** on the server.
- Server code may allocate **typed message-passing channels**, which may be both stored in the database and returned to clients via remote function calls. The server may send values to a channel, and a client that has been passed the channel may receive those values asynchronously. Channel sends are included in the guarantee of atomicity for remote calls on the server; all sends within a single call execution appear to transfer their messages to the associated channels atomically.

The next section expands on these points with a tutorial introduction to Ur/Web. We highlight the impact on the language design of our goals to support **encapsulation** and **simple concurrency**. Next, we describe key implementation techniques in the Ur/Web compiler and runtime system, and we evaluate the effectiveness of the language, partly through surveying deployed applications that use it.

The open-source implementation of Ur/Web is available at:

`http://www.impredicative.com/ur/`

## 2. A Tutorial Introduction to Ur/Web

We will introduce the key features of Ur/Web through a series of refinements of one example, a multiuser chat application. Visitors to the site choose from a selection of chat rooms, each of which maintains a log of messages. Any visitor to a chat room may append any line of text to the log, and there should be some way for other users to stay up-to-date on log additions. We start with a simple implementation, in the style of 20th-century Web applications, before it became common to do significant client-side scripting. We evolve toward a version with instant updating upon all message additions, where a chat room runs within a single HTML page updated incrementally by client-side code. Along the way, we highlight our running themes of **encapsulation** and **simple concurrency**.

```
table room : { Id : int, Title : string }
table message : { Room : int, When : time,
                  Text : string }

fun chat id =
 let
  fun say r =
   dml (INSERT INTO message (Room, When, Text)
     VALUES ({[id]}, CURRENT_TIMESTAMP, {[r.Text]}));
   chat id
 in
  title <- oneRowE1 (SELECT (room.Title) FROM room
                     WHERE room.Id = {[id]});
  log <- queryX1 (SELECT message.Text FROM message
                  WHERE message.Room = {[id]}
                  ORDER BY message.When)
                 (fn r => <xml>{[r.Text]}<br/></xml>);
  return <xml><body>
   <h1>Chat Room: {[title]}</h1>

   <form>
    Add message: <textbox{#Text}/>
    <submit value="Add" action={say}/>
   </form>

   <hr/>

   {log}
  </body></xml>
 end

fun main () =
 rooms <- queryX1 (SELECT * FROM room
                   ORDER BY room.Title)
          (fn r => <xml><li><a link={chat r.Id}>
                   {[r.Title]}</a></li></xml>);
 return <xml><body>
  <h1>List of Rooms</h1>

  {rooms}
 </body></xml>
```

**Figure 1.** A simple chat-room application

### 2.1 HTML and SQL

Mainstream modern Web applications manipulate code in many different languages and protocols. Ur/Web hides most of them within a unified programming model, but we decided to expose two languages explicitly: **HTML**, for describing the structure of Web pages as trees, and **SQL**, for accessing a persistent relational database on the server. In contrast to mainstream practice, Ur/Web represents code fragments in these languages as first-class, strongly typed values. We use the type system of Ur [8] to define rich syntax tree types, where the generic type system is sufficient to enforce the typing rules of the embedded languages, HTML and SQL. Going into the details of type encoding would take us off-track in this paper, so the reader may pretend that Ur/Web includes special built-in support for type-checking HTML and SQL.

Figure 1 gives our first chat-room implementation, relying on embedding of HTML and SQL code. While in general Ur/Web programs contain code that runs on both server and clients, all code from this figure runs on the server, where we are able to enforce that it is run exactly as written in the source code.

The first two lines show declarations of SQL tables, which can be thought of as mutable global variables of type "multiset of records." Table `room`'s records contain integer IDs and string titles, while table `message`'s records contain integer room IDs, timestamps, and string messages. The former table represents the set of available chat rooms, while the latter represents the set of all (timestamped) messages sent to all rooms.

It is unusual for a programming language to treat SQL tables as declared within the language. The more common view is that the SQL database exists as a resource "out there somewhere," and the programming language merely connects to it. Our strange choice has important consequences for encapsulation, which we will get to shortly.

We direct the reader's attention now to the declaration of function `main`, near the end of Figure 1. Here we see Ur/Web's syntax extensions for embedded SQL and HTML code. Such notation is desugared into calls to constructors of abstract syntax tree types, at which point the normal Ur type-checker may validate the type-correctness of embedded fragments. The `main` definition demonstrates two notations for "antiquoting," or inserting Ur code within a quoted code fragment. The notation `{e}` asks to evaluate expression `e` to produce a subfragment to be inserted at that point, and notation `{[e]}` adds a further stage of formatting `e` as a literal of the embedded language (using type classes [37] as in Haskell's `show`). Note that we are *not* exposing syntax trees to the programmer as strings, so neither antiquoting form presents any danger of *code injection attacks*, where we accidentally interpret user input as code.

What exactly does the `main` definition do? First, we run an SQL query to list all chat rooms. In our tutorial examples, we will call a variety of functions from Ur/Web's standard library, especially various higher-order functions for using SQL query results. We adopt a typographic convention for documenting each library function briefly, starting with `queryX1`, used in `main`:

`queryX1` Run an SQL query that returns columns from a single table (leading to the `1` in the identifier), calling an argument function on every result row. Since just a single table is involved, the input to the argument function can be a record with one field per column returned by the query. The argument function should return XML fragments (leading to the `X` in the identifier), and all such fragments are concatenated together, in order, to form the result of `queryX1`.

Note that a remotely callable function like `main` lives in a distinguished monad for input-output [29] as in Haskell, since Ur is purely functional. Thus, we use the `<-` notation to run an effectful computation and bind its result to a variable, and we call the `return` function to lift pure values into trivial computations.

The remaining interesting aspect of `main` is in its use of an HTML `<a>` tag to generate a hyperlink. Instead of denoting a link via a URL as in standard HTML, we use a `link` attribute that accepts a *suspended Ur/Web remote function call*. In this case, we call `chat`, which is defined earlier. The Ur/Web implementation handles proper marshaling of arguments in suspended calls.

Now let us examine the implementation of function `chat`, providing a page for viewing the current message log of a chat room. First, there is a nested definition of a function `say`, which will be called to append a message to the log.

`dml` Run a piece of SQL code for its side effect of mutating the database. The function name refers to SQL's **d**ata **m**anipulation **l**anguage.

This particular invocation of `dml` inserts a new row into the `message` table with the current timestamp, after which we display the same page as `chat` itself would generate. Note that `say`, like all remotely callable functions, appears to execute **atomically**, so the programmer need not worry about interleavings between concurrent operations by different clients. To tune performance, programmers might want to indicate the boundaries of atomic execution units explicitly, but we have found that it works well to make the atomic units be precisely the remote calls, which saves programmers from needing to write any explicit code to begin or end transactions.

The main body of `chat` runs appropriate queries to retrieve the room name and the full, sorted message log.

`oneRowE1` Run an SQL query that should return just one result row containing just a single column (justifying the `1`) that is computed using an arbitrary SQL **e**xpression (justifying the `E`). That one result value becomes the result of the `oneRowE1` call.

We antiquote the query results into the returned page in an unsurprising way. The only new feature involves HTML forms. In general, we tag each input widget with a *record field name*, and then the submit button of the form includes, in its `action` attribute, an Ur/Web function that should be called upon submission, on *a record built by combining the values of all the input widgets*. We will not say any more about HTML forms, which to some extent represent a legacy aspect of HTML that has been superseded by client-side scripting. Forms are a non-Turing-complete language for input solicitation, and these days it is more common to use a Turing-complete language (JavaScript) for the same task.

Note that this first example already displays a small bit of encapsulation: the local function `say` may only be referenced within the declaration of `chat`. Clients may ignore the intended order of link-following and visit `say` directly, but we at least know our application itself will not accidentally generate links to `say` outside the intended scope.

Compiling an application to run on the real Web platform requires exposes remotely callable functions (like `main`, `chat`, and `say`) via URLs. Ur/Web automatically generates pleasing URL schemes by *serializing the function-call expressions* that appear in places like `link` attributes. For instance, the link to `chat` in the declaration of `main` is compiled to a URL `/chat/NN`, where `NN` is a textual representation of the room ID. The link to `say` within the `submit` button above is compiled like `/say/NN`, including the value of a local variable `id` implicitly captured in the function.

The Ur/Web compiler handles generation of URL schemes in such a way that it is guaranteed that no two functions will wind up with conflicting schemes. This approach contrasts sharply with the manual URL routing found in most mainstream frameworks. There are serious costs to modularity when composing two libraries requires understanding their URL schemes.

Some other systems, like the PLT Scheme Web Server [20] and Links [11], avoid the problem by generating non-human-readable URLs, standing for continuation references. We prefer to keep URLs readable, since they serve as a common interface with the broader Internet world. However, Links pioneered many of the other design elements on display in Figure 1, including type-safe combination of HTML and database code within a single language. One further key difference is that Ur/Web works with direct embedding of SQL code, whereas Links compiles to SQL from a subset of itself, presented as a monadic query language [7].

The key distinguishing elements of Ur/Web's design, in comparison to past languages, become clearer when we turn to taking better advantage of encapsulation. Before doing so, we pause to discuss some relative strengths and weaknesses of the HTML and SQL encodings in Ur/Web.

Ur/Web effectively encodes XML with algebraic datatypes, which are not expressive enough to capture all of the constraints associated with XML schemas. *Regular expression types* [19] are an established approach to enforcing the rules of XML more literally, and they have been integrated with ML-style languages in the OCamlDuce project [16]. Programmers may benefit from that style of more precise type-checking. On the other hand, more complex static checking of XML may be more difficult for programmers

```
structure Room : sig
 type id
 val rooms : transaction (list {Id : id,
                                Title : string})
 val chat : id -> transaction page
end = struct
 (* ...copies of old definitions of room, message,
      and chat... *)

 val rooms = queryL1 (SELECT * FROM room
                      ORDER BY room.Title)
end

fun main () =
 rooms <- Room.rooms;
 return <xml><body>
  <h1>List of Rooms</h1>

  {List.mapX (fn r =>
    <xml><li><a link={Room.chat r.Id}>
      {[r.Title]}</a></li></xml>) rooms}
 </body></xml>
```

**Figure 2.** A modular factorization of the first application

to understand. An additional benefit of Ur/Web's approach is that XML checking need not be built into the language (as it is in, e.g., OCamlDuce) but is instead encoded as a library using Ur's rich but general-purpose type system [8]. We use row types to encode context constraints on XML elements, so that the generic Ur type-inference engine may do the rest of the work.

A similar comparison may be drawn with other approaches to encoding relational database queries. The *language-integrated query* approach represents queries within a restricted subset of the host programming language, rather than working with explicit embedded syntax of a language like SQL. Microsoft's LINQ [27] is the well-known example that gives the approach its name, but the contemporaneous Links language [7, 11] uses static type checking and term rewriting to provide more principled guarantees about which expressions will compile to SQL successfully. Ur/Web encodes SQL as a library, with no special type-inference support required in the compiler, and the programmer benefits from the explicit control over exactly which code will be passed to the database system. Performance fine-tuning may be most effective with this sort of direct approach. On the other hand, explicit manipulation of query syntax can be more tedious than writing query code directly in the host language, relying on compilation to the language of a database system; and the use of multiple languages encourages some amount of duplicate definition of library functions. Overall, on this comparison point the author is agnostic and could imagine a successor to Ur/Web being developed with language-integrated query.

### 2.1.1 Adding More Encapsulation

The application in Figure 1 is rather monolithic. The database state is exposed without restrictions to all parts of the application. We would not tolerate such a lack of encapsulation in a large traditional application. Chunks of functionality should be modularized, e.g. into classes implementing data structures. The database tables here are effectively data structures, so why not try to encapsulate them as well?

The answer is that, as far as we are aware, no prior language designs allow it! As we wrote above, the general model is that the SQL database is a preexisting resource, and any part of the application may create an interface to any part of the database. We analogize such a scheme to an object-oriented language where all class fields are public; it forecloses on some very useful styles of modular reasoning. It is important that modules be able to *create their own private database tables*, without requiring any changes to other source code, application configuration files, etc., for the same reason that we do not want client code of a dictionary class to change, when the dictionary switches to being implemented with hash tables instead of search trees.

Figure 2 shows a refactoring of our application code, to present the chat-room table as a mutable abstract data type. We use Ur/Web's module system, which is in the ML tradition [23]. We have *modules* that implement *signatures*, which may impose information hiding by not exposing some members or by making some types *abstract*. Figure 2 defines a module `Room` encapsulating all database access.

The signature of `Room` appears bracketed between keywords `sig` and `end`. We expose an abstract type `id` of chat-room identifiers. Ur/Web code in other program modules will not be able to take advantage of the fact that `id` is really `int`, and thus cannot fabricate new IDs out of thin air. The signature exposes two methods: `rooms`, to list the IDs and titles of all chat rooms; and `chat`, exactly the remotely callable function we wrote before, but typed in terms of the abstract type `id`. Each method's type uses the `transaction` monad, which is like Haskell's IO monad, but with support for executing all side effects **atomically** in a remote call.

The implementation of `Room` is mostly just a copying-and-pasting of the bulk of the code from Figure 1. We only need to add a simple implementation of the `rooms` method.

`queryL1` Return as a list (justifying the `L`) the results of a query that only returns columns of one table (justifying the `1`).

`List.mapX` Apply an XML-producing function to each element of a list, then concatenate together the resulting XML fragments to compute the result of `mapX`.

The code for `main` changes to call methods of `Room`, instead of inlining database access.

This sort of separation of a data model is often implemented as part of the "model-view-controller" pattern. To our knowledge, that pattern had not previously been combined with guaranteed encapsulation of the associated database tables. It also seems to be novel to apply ML-style type abstraction to database results, as in our use of an `id` type here. We hope this example has helped convey one basic take-away message: giving first-class status to key pieces of Web applications makes it easy to apply standard language-based encapsulation mechanisms.

Strong encapsulation is not automatic when using conventional database engines. The database server will generally be configured to allow ad-hoc querying by humans and other applications, where the data abstraction in a particular Ur/Web application need not be respected. We imagine a future version of Ur/Web with tighter data storage integration, where by default only an application itself may access particular tables. For now, though, data abstraction for SQL tables remains useful as a way to reason about Ur/Web programs, and it is possible to associate each application with a new database user whose authentication credentials are only given to the application daemon. The Ur/Web compiler will automatically initialize the schema of a database, and each application checks on start-up that the schema matches what is present in its source code.

## 2.2 Client-Side GUI Scripting

We will develop two more variations of the chat-room application. Our modifications will be confined to the implementation of the `Room` module. Its signature is already sufficient to enable our experiments, and we will keep the same `main` function code for the rest of the tutorial.

Our first extension takes advantage of *client-side scripting* to make applications more responsive, without the need to load a completely fresh page after every user action. Mainstream Web applications are scripted with JavaScript, but, as in Links and similar

```
structure Log : sig
  type t
  val create : transaction t
  val append : t -> string -> transaction {}
  val render : t -> xbody
end = struct
  datatype log =
      Nil
    | Cons of string * source log

  type t = {Head : source log,
            Tail : source (source log)}

  val create =
    s <- source Nil;
    s' <- source s;
    return {Head = s, Tail = s'}

  fun append t text =
    s <- source Nil;
    oldTail <- get t.Tail;
    set oldTail (Cons (text, s));
    set t.Tail s;

    log <- get t.Head;
    case log of
      Nil => set t.Head (Cons (text, s))
    | _ => return ()

  fun render' log =
    case log of
      Nil => <xml/>
    | Cons (text, rest) => <xml>
        {[text]}<br/>
        <dyn signal={log <- signal rest;
                     return (render' log)}/>
      </xml>

  fun render t = <xml>
    <dyn signal={log <- signal t.Head;
                 return (render' log)}/>
  </xml>
end
```

**Figure 3.** A module implementing a GUI for an append-only log

languages, Ur/Web scripting is done in the language itself, which is compiled to JavaScript as needed.

### 2.2.1 Reactive GUIs

Ur/Web GUI programming follows the **functional-reactive** style. That is, to a large extent, the visible page is described via *dataflow*, as a pure function over some primitive streams of values. As the primitive streams evolve, the language runtime system automatically rerenders just those parts of the page that are affected. Languages like Flapjax [28] and Elm [14] adopt the stream metaphor literally, where the primitive streams represent, e.g., mouse clicks made by the user. Ur/Web adopts a less pure style, where we retain the *event callbacks* of imperative programming. These callbacks modify *data sources*, which are a special kind of mutable reference cells. The only primitive streams are effectively *the sequences of values that data sources take on*, where new entries are pushed into the streams mostly via imperative code in callbacks.

As a basic orientation to these concepts in Ur/Web, here is their type signature. We write :: to ascribe a *kind* to a type-level identifier, where, for instance, Type → Type indicates a *type family* parameterized over one type argument. We write : to ascribe a type to a value-level identifier. As types and values occupy different namespaces, we often reuse an identifier (e.g., source) to stand for both a type and the run-time operation for allocating one of its instances.

$$
\begin{array}{rcl}
\mathsf{source} & :: & \mathsf{Type} \to \mathsf{Type} \\
\mathsf{source} & : & \forall \alpha.\ \mathsf{transaction}\ (\mathsf{source}\ \alpha) \\
\mathsf{get} & : & \forall \alpha.\ \mathsf{source}\ \alpha \to \mathsf{transaction}\ \alpha \\
\mathsf{set} & : & \forall \alpha.\ \mathsf{source}\ \alpha \to \alpha \to \mathsf{transaction}\ \{\}
\end{array}
$$

$$
\begin{array}{rcl}
\mathsf{signal} & :: & \mathsf{Type} \to \mathsf{Type} \\
\mathsf{s\_m} & : & \mathsf{monad\ signal} \\
\mathsf{signal} & : & \forall \alpha.\ \mathsf{source}\ \alpha \to \mathsf{signal}\ \alpha
\end{array}
$$

That is, data sources are a polymorphic type family, with operations for allocating them and reading or writing their values. All such operations live inside the `transaction` monad, which contains imperative side effects in the manner of Haskell's IO monad [29]. *Signals*, or time-varying values, are another polymorphic type family, which happens to form a monad with appropriate operations, as indicated by the presence of a first-class dictionary s_m witnessing their monadhood. One more key operation with signals is producing them from sources, via the value-level signal function, which turns a source into a stream that documents changes to the source's contents.

Figure 3 demonstrates these constructs in use, in a module implementing a GUI widget for append-only logs. The module signature declares an abstract type `t` of logs. We have methods `create`, to allocate a new log; `append`, to add a new string to the end of a log; and `render`, to produce the HTML representing a log. The type of `render` may be deceiving in its simplicity; Ur/Web HTML values (as in the `xbody` type of HTML that fits in a document body) actually are all implicitly parameterized in the dataflow style, and they are equipped to rerender themselves after changes to the data sources they depend on.

The workhorse data structure of logs is an algebraic datatype `log`, which looks almost like a standard definition of lists of strings. The difference is that the tail of a nonempty `log` has type `source log`, rather than just `log`. We effectively have a type of lists that supports imperative replacement of list tails, but not replacement of heads.

The type `t` of logs is a record of two fields. Field `Head` is a modifiable reference to the current log state, and `Tail` is a "pointer to a pointer," telling us which source cell we should overwrite next to append to the list. Methods `create` and `append` involve a bit of intricacy to update these fields properly, but we will not dwell on the details. We only mention that the point of this complexity is to avoid rerendering the whole log each time an entry is appended; instead, only a constant amount of work is done per append, to modify the document tree at the end of the log. That sort of pattern is difficult to implement with pure functional-reactive programming.

The most interesting method definition is for `render`. Our prior examples only showed building HTML fragments that are vacuously dataflow-parameterized. We create dependencies via an HTML pseudotag called `<dyn>`. The `signal` attribute of this tag accepts a signal, a time-varying value telling us what content should be displayed at this point on the page at different times. Crucially, the `signal` monad rules out imperative side effects, instead capturing pure dataflow programming. Since it is a monad, we have access to the usual monad operations `<-` and `return`, in addition to the `signal` function for lifting sources into signals.

Let us first examine the definition of `render'`, a recursive helper function for `render`. The type of `render'` is `log -> xbody`, displaying a log as HTML. Empty logs are displayed as empty HTML fragments, and nonempty logs are rendered with their textual heads followed by recursive renderings of their tails. However, the recursive call to `render'` is not direct. Instead it appears inside a `<dyn>` pseudotag. We indicate that this subpage depends on the current value of the tail (a data source), giving the computation to translate from the tail's value to HTML. Now it is easy to define `render`, mostly just duplicating the last part of `render'`.

An important property of this module definition is that a `render`ed log automatically updates in the browser after every call to `append`, even though we have not coded any explicit coupling between these methods. The Ur/Web runtime system takes care of the details, once we express GUIs via parameterized dataflow.

*Client code may use logs without knowing implementation details.* The standard Web model involves imperative mutation of the document tree, which is treated as a public global variable. Mistakes in one code module may wreck subtrees that other modules believe they control. For instance, subtrees are often looked up by string ID, creating the possibility for two different libraries to choose the same ID unwittingly for different subtrees. With the Ur/Web model, the author of module Log may think of it as *owning* particular subtrees of the HTML document as private state. Standard module encapsulation protects the underlying data sources from direct modification by other modules, and rendered logs only have dataflow dependencies on the values of those sources.

Classic pure functional-reactive frameworks provide similar advantages, but it can be challenging to fit a full application into the model of pure stream transformers. In our experience, many programmers find the callback style easier to wrap their heads around. Consider the example of the Log module. We *could* express the log creation or rendering method as a function over a stream of requests to append entries. However, building these streams in practice may be nontrivial, forcing explicit demultiplexing of the variety of user actions and network responses that may produce log entries. (We see an example of multiple log-entry sources in the next subsection.) The usual modularity advantages of mutable state fit well in this GUI domain, and they are compatible with maintaining the dataflow part of functional-reactivity. Flapjax [28] supports the imperative model, via a method for pushing events into *any* stream (even those that we might wish client code saw as read-only), but this method is suggested for use only in interfacing with legacy, callback-based code.

### 2.2.2 Remote Procedure Calls

The GUI widget for displaying the chat log is only one half of the story, if we are to write an application that runs within a single page. We also need a way for this application to contact the server, to trigger state modifications and receive updated information. Ur/Web's first solution to that problem is *remote procedure calls (RPCs)*, allowing client code to run particular function calls as if they were executing on the server, with access to shared database state. Client code only needs to wrap such calls to remotely callable functions within the `rpc` keyword, and the Ur/Web implementation takes care of all network communication and marshaling. Every RPC appears to execute **atomically**, just as for other kinds of remote calls.

Figure 4 reimplements the `Room` module to take advantage of RPCs and the `Log` widget.

`List.foldl` As in ML, step through a list, applying a function $f$ to each element, so that, given an initial accumulator $a$ and a list $[x_1, \ldots, x_n]$, the result is $f(x_n, \ldots f(x_1, a) \ldots)$.

`List.app` Apply an effectful function to every element of a list, in order.

The code actually contains few new complexities. Our basic strategy is for each client to maintain the timestamp of the *most recent* chat message it has received. The textbox for user input is associated with a freshly allocated `source string`, via the `<ctextbox>` pseudotag ("c" is for "client-side scripting"). Whenever the user

```
structure Room : sig
 type id
 val rooms : transaction (list {Id : id,
                                Title : string})
 val chat : id -> transaction page
end = struct
 table room : { Id : int, Title : string }
 table message : { Room : int, When : time,
                   Text : string }
 val rooms = queryL1 (SELECT * FROM room
                      ORDER BY room.Title)

 (* New code w.r.t. Figure 2 starts here. *)

 fun chat id =
  let
   fun say text lastSeen =
    dml (INSERT INTO message (Room, When, Text)
         VALUES ({[id]}, CURRENT_TIMESTAMP, {[text]}));
    queryL1 (SELECT message.Text, message.When
             FROM message
             WHERE message.Room = {[id]}
               AND message.When > {[lastSeen]}
             ORDER BY message.When DESC)

   val maxTimestamp =
    List.foldl (fn r acc => max r.When acc) minTime
  in
   title <- oneRowE1 (SELECT (room.Title) FROM room
                      WHERE room.Id = {[id]});
   initial <- queryL1 (SELECT message.Text,
                        message.When
                       FROM message
                       WHERE message.Room = {[id]}
                       ORDER BY message.When DESC);
   text <- source "";
   log <- Log.create;
   lastSeen <- source (maxTimestamp initial);

   return <xml><body onload={
     List.app (fn r => Log.append log r.Text) initial}>
    <h1>Chat Room: {[title]}</h1>

    Add message: <ctextbox source={text}/>
    <button value="Add" onclick={fn _ =>
     txt <- get text;
     set text "";
     lastSn <- get lastSeen;
     newMsgs <- rpc (say txt lastSn);
     set lastSeen (maxTimestamp newMsgs);
     List.app (fn r => Log.append log r.Text)
      newMsgs}/>
    <hr/>
    {Log.render log}
   </body></xml>
  end
end
```

**Figure 4.** A client-code-heavy chat-room application

modifies the text shown in this box, the associated source is automatically mutated to contain the latest text. When the user clicks a button to send a message, we run the callback code in the button's `onclick` attribute, *on the client*, whereas the code for this example outside of `on*` attributes runs on the server. This code makes an RPC, telling the server both the new message text and the last timestamp that the client knows about. The server sends back a list of all chat messages newer than that timestamp, and client code iterates over that list, adding each message to the log; and then updates the last-seen timestamp accordingly, taking advantage of the fact that the RPC result list will never be empty, as it always contains at least the message that this client just sent. An `onload` event handler in the `body` tag initialized the log in the first place, appending each entry returned by an initial database query.

Note how seamless is the use of the `Log` module. We allocate a new log, drop its rendering into the right part of the page, and peri-

```
fun main () =
 tag <- source "";
 image <- source <xml/>;

 return <xml><body>
  Tag: <ctextbox source={tag}
   onchange={tag <- get tag;
    found <- rpc (tagExists tag);
    if found then
     set image <xml>
      <img src={url (serveImage tag)}/></xml>
    else return ()}/><br/>
  <dyn signal={signal image}/>
```

Figure 5. Partial Ur/Web code for image-lookup example

odically append to it. Pure functional-reactive programming would require some acrobatics to interleave the event streams generated as input to the log system, from the two syntactically distinct calls to `Log.append`. Another challenge is fitting effectful RPCs into a pure functional-reactive framework. Elm [14] supports injection of RPCs in pure stream-transformation code, with a novel mechanism to allow local computation to continue while waiting for RPC responses. It is not clear how to extend such a technique for impure RPCs, which are useful for precisely the kind of call we use in Figure 4, to modify a shared database. For pure RPCs, we can realize similar semantics to Elm's merely by spawning RPCs in their own threads, which write to sources after RPCs complete.

For instance, consider the third example from a paper about Elm [14], where users type text into a textbox, and an image on the same page updates according to the result of an image-search query to a remote server, using the latest text. Here is an excerpt of the Elm code.

```
(inputField, tags) = Input.text "Enter a tag"

getImage tags =
  lift (fittedImage 300 200)
       (syncGet (lift requestTag tags))

... async (getImage tags) ...
```

Built-in function `syncGet` makes an HTTP request, and built-in function `async` causes evaluation to run in a separate thread. The essential dataflow action in this example is from `tags`, a stream recording successive contents of a freshly created textbox, into the details of the HTTP request to be made via `syncGet`.

We can actually duplicate the same functionality in Ur/Web, in an equally pure way, by taking advantage of the fact that the HTML `<img>` tag already has built into it the idea of contacting a remote server to retrieve an image by URL. A dynamically varying piece of HTML may simply contain different `<img>` tags at different times, and the browser handles retrieving images as usual. However, for a fairer comparison, we should consider an interaction that does require some custom logic. Figure 5 shows Ur/Web code for a variant approach, where, whenever the contents of the tag textbox change, we first ask the server by RPC if any image exists matching that tag. If none exists, we make no changes to which image is displayed. If a match is found, we change to the new image, using the built-in function `url`, which coerces a remote function call into an abstract type of URLs. In this case, the URL is for a server-side function that computes an image based on input text. All of the reactive computation happens inside an `onchange` handler for the textbox, called whenever the text changes.

The code in Figure 5 blocks the whole client-side application while an RPC runs, but that problem is easily solved by putting the whole `onchange` attribute code snippet into a new thread, with the `spawn` keyword that we say more about in the next subsection. Overall, the Ur/Web version of this functionality is moderately more complicated than the Elm version, but all of the imperative side effects can be encapsulated within a module in the style of Log from Figure 3, creating an observationally pure image-search widget. Some functionality, like that of the `Log` module itself, is inherently easier to orchestrate modularly with mutable state, allowing widely separated parts of a program, with their own private state, to create data flows into a shared component, with no explicit fan-in merging their different streams.

```
structure Room : sig
 type id
 val rooms : transaction (list {Id : id,
                                Title : string})
 val chat : id -> transaction page
end = struct
 table room : { Id : int, Title : string }
 table message : { Room : int, When : time,
                   Text : string }
 val rooms = queryL1 (SELECT * FROM room
                      ORDER BY room.Title)

 (* New code w.r.t. Figure 2 starts here. *)

 table subscriber : { Room : int,
                      Chan : channel string }

 fun chat id =
  let
   fun say text =
    dml (INSERT INTO message (Room, When, Text)
         VALUES ({[id]}, CURRENT_TIMESTAMP, {[text]}));
    queryI1 (SELECT subscriber.Chan FROM subscriber
             WHERE subscriber.Room = {[id]})
            (fn r => send r.Chan text)
  in
   chan <- channel;
   dml (INSERT INTO subscriber (Room, Chan)
        VALUES ({[id]}, {[chan]}));

   title <- oneRowE1 (SELECT (room.Title) FROM room
                      WHERE room.Id = {[id]});
   initial <- queryL1 (SELECT message.Text,
                         message.When
                       FROM message
                       WHERE message.Room = {[id]}
                       ORDER BY message.When DESC);

   text <- source "";
   log <- Log.create;

   return <xml><body onload={
    let
     fun listener () =
      text <- recv chan;
      Log.append log text;
      listener ()
    in
     spawn (listener ());
     List.app (fn r => Log.append log r.Text) initial
    end}>
    <h1>Chat Room: {[title]}</h1>

    Add message: <ctextbox source={text}/>
    <button value="Add" onclick={fn _ =>
     txt <- get text;
     set text "";
     rpc (say txt)}/>

    <hr/>

    {Log.render log}
   </body></xml>
  end
end
```

Figure 6. Final chat-room application

### 2.3 Message-Passing from Server to Client

Web browsers make it natural for clients to contact servers via HTTP requests, but the other communication direction may also be useful. One example is our chat application, where only the server knows when a client has posted a new message, and we would like the server to notify all other clients in the same chat room. Clients can *poll* the server with periodic HTTP requests, guaranteeing that the lag to learn of a new message will not exceed the polling period. Real-world applications often use a technique called *long polling*, where a client opens a connection and is willing to wait an arbitrary period of time for the server's response. The server can hold all of these long-poll connections open until there is a new event to distribute. The mechanics are standardized in recent browsers with the WebSockets protocol, providing an abstraction of bidirectional streams between clients and servers. Ur/Web presents an alternative abstraction (implemented with long polling) where servers are able to send typed *messages* directly to clients.

The messaging abstraction is influenced by concurrent programming languages like Erlang [1] and Concurrent ML [31]. Communication happens over unidirectional *channels*. Every channel has an associated client and a type. The server may *send* any value of that type to the channel, which conceptually adds the message to a queue on the client. Clients asynchronously *receive* messages from channels for which they have handles, conceptually dequeuing from local queues, blocking when queues are empty. Any remote call may trigger any number of sends to any number of channels. All sends in a single remote call appear to take place **atomically**. Atomicity will be important in our chat-room example, to preserve a consistent global view of message order, when many simultaneous RPCs may be notifying the same set of clients with different messages.

The API for channels is straightforward:

$$\begin{array}{rcl} \mathsf{channel} & :: & \mathsf{Type} \to \mathsf{Type} \\ \mathsf{channel} & : & \forall\alpha.\ \mathsf{transaction}\ (\mathsf{channel}\ \alpha) \\ \mathsf{recv} & : & \forall\alpha.\ \mathsf{channel}\ \alpha \to \mathsf{transaction}\ \alpha \\ \mathsf{send} & : & \forall\alpha.\ \mathsf{channel}\ \alpha \to \alpha \to \mathsf{transaction}\ \{\} \end{array}$$

One wrinkle is that channel and send may only be called in server-side code, while recv may only be called in client-side code. A compiler analysis makes sure that functions are not called in the wrong places, and we have considered changing the types of the basic operations in a future Ur/Web version, so that standard type inference verifies sidedness properties.

Figure 6 gives another reimplementation of `Room`, this time using channels to keep clients synchronized at all times, modulo small amounts of lag. We retain the same `room` and `message` tables as before, but we also add a new table `subscriber`, tracking which clients are listening for notifications about which rooms. (Thanks to Ur/Web's approach to encapsulation of database tables, we need not change any other source or configuration files just because we add a new private table.) Every row of `subscriber` has a room ID `Room` and a channel `Chan` that is able to receive strings.

Now the `chat` method begins by allocating a fresh channel with the `channel` operation, which we immediately insert into `subscriber`. Compared to Figure 4, we drop the client-side timestamp tracking. Instead, the server will use channels to notify all clients in a room, each time a new message is posted there. In particular, see the tweaked definition of `say`.

`queryI1` Run an SQL query returning columns from just a single table (justifying the `1`), applying a function to each result in order, solely for its **i**mperative side effects (justifying the `I`).

We loop over all channels associated with the current room, sending the new message to each one.

There is one last change from Figure 4. The `onload` attribute of our `<body>` tag still contains code to run immediately after the page is loaded. This time, before we initialize the `Log` structure, we also create a new thread with the `spawn` primitive. That thread loops forever, blocking to receive messages from the freshly created channel and add them to the log.

Threads follow a simple *cooperative* semantics, where the programming model says that, at any moment in time, at most one thread is running *across all clients of the application*. Execution only switches to another thread when the current one terminates or executes a blocking operation, among which we have RPCs and channel `recv`. Of course, the Ur/Web implementation will run many threads at once, with an arbitrary number on the server and one JavaScript thread per client, but the implementation ensures that no behaviors occur that could not also be simulated with the simpler one-thread-at-a-time model.

This simple approach has pleasant consequences for program modularity. The example of Figure 6 only shows a single program module taking advantage of channels. It is possible for channels to be used freely throughout a program, and the Ur/Web implementation takes care of routing messages to clients, while maintaining the simple thread semantics. For instance, the `Log` module could use channels privately, without disrupting the use of channels in `Room`. Manual long-polling approaches require explicit dispatching logic, to the different parts of an application waiting for server notifications, because in practice a client can only afford to have one long-polling connection active at once.

Figure 6 contains no explicit deallocation of clients that have stopped participating. The Ur/Web implementation detects client departure using a heartbeating mechanism. When a client departs, the runtime system *atomically deletes from the database all references to that client's channels*. In this respect, channels in the database act like weak pointers. A database row with a field typed like `channel T` will be deleted outright when the owning client departs. When a row contains a field of type `option (channel T)`, which may hold either a channel or a null value, references to dead channels are merely nulled out. All clean-up operations described in the last two sentences commute with each other, so there is no need to specify the order in which different channel references for a single departed client are dealt with. Automatic deletion of channel references provides a kind of modularity similar to what garbage collection provides for heap-allocated objects.

Before wrapping up the tutorial part of the paper, we want to emphasize how this sequence of examples has demonstrated key Ur/Web design principles. Early in the sequence, we settled on one interface for the `Room` module. As we progressed through fancier implementations, no changes were required to the `main` function or any global application configuration file. Strong **encapsulation** of module state guarantees that code outside the module cannot distinguish between alternatives. Throughout all versions of the application, we also maintained the **simple concurrency** abstraction of one thread running at a time, with context switches only at well-defined points.

## 3. Implementation

The Ur/Web compiler is implemented in Standard ML, in about 55,000 lines of code. It compiles Ur/Web source files to run on the server, as native POSIX Threads binaries via C; and on the client, as JavaScript. Compiled applications are linked with a runtime system, with both a server part, in about 5,000 lines of C; and a client part, in about 1,500 lines of JavaScript.

We summarize here some of the less obvious aspects of the implementation.

### 3.1 Atomic Execution of Database Operations

The focus on atomic execution in Ur/Web is inspired by the database community's decades of experience with *transactions* [17], an idea that originated in that world. Many production-quality database servers support various flavors of atomicity. Since version 9.1, PostgreSQL has supported truly atomic (serializable) transactions [30]. In other words, it looks to arbitrary database clients as if their sequences of SQL operations execute without interference by other threads. We recommend using Ur/Web with PostgreSQL, but it is also possible to use other backends that do not quite provide serializable transactions, at the cost of weakening Ur/Web's operational semantics.

We have been surprised at the near absence of programming frameworks that take advantage of serializable or almost-serializable database transactions. Typically, database engines implement these abstractions with combinations of locking and optimistic concurrency. In either case, it is possible for operations to encounter serialization failures (with locking because of deadlock, and with optimistic concurrency because a conflict is detected). Popular SQL client libraries indicate serialization failure as just another error code returnable by any operation. Applications must check for this code after every operation, being prepared to do something sensible when it appears.

In contrast, Ur/Web hides serialization failures completely. Any serialization failure in an Ur/Web transaction execution *undoes and restarts the transaction*. The `transaction` monad is carefully designed so that all side effects may be undone as necessary. The Ur/Web runtime system uses C's `setjmp/longjmp` to allow reverting to the start of a transaction, from arbitrary code running within it. Since server threads share state only through the database, it is easy to run each remote call with a fresh private heap, so that undoing heap effects is a constant-time operation.

By hiding serialization failures automatically, Ur/Web is able to present to programmers the clean transactional abstraction sketched in the last section.

### 3.2 Message Routing with Channels

It would violate the transactional abstraction to send messages to clients immediately during `send` operations. Instead, `send`s are appended to a thread-local log. At a transaction's *commit* point, where all operations have completed without serialization failures, we atomically execute all message sends.

The server may not connect directly to clients to hand off messages. Instead, clients periodically open long-polling connections to the server. If a client is connected at the point where the server wants to hand off a message, the message is written directly to the client, and the connection is closed. Otherwise, messages for clients are appended to server-side buffers maintained per client. If a client connects again when its buffer is nonempty, all queued messages are sent immediately as the HTTP response, and the connection is closed.

The last (implicit) ingredient of message routing is garbage-collecting dead channels. A heartbeat mechanism detects dead clients. For each application, the compiler generates a C function parameterized on a client ID, to remove all database references to that client. Whenever a client departs, that C function is run inside a transaction of its own. Since client data structures may be reused across departures, this use of database transactions interacts critically with transactions for normal remote calls, to ensure that messages are not accidentally sent to new clients who have taken over the data structures of intended recipients who have already departed. From the perspective of an atomic remote call, any client is either fully present or fully absent, for the whole transaction.

### 3.3 Implementing Functional-Reactive GUIs

In earlier sections, we discussed how Ur/Web HTML fragments are implicitly instrumented for incremental recomputation via the `signal` monad. Each fragment is conceptually a function over the current values of all data sources, and the runtime system should understand well enough *which* sources matter for each fragment, to avoid wasteful recomputation of fragments that do not depend on a set of source changes. Implementing this semantics requires using custom data structures that are periodically transformed and installed into browsers' normal data structures for dynamic HTML trees, called the Document Object Model (DOM).

One key data structure appears in the JavaScript parts of the runtime system. Rather than representing HTML fragments as strings, we instead use what is morally an algebraic datatype with 3 constructors. The simplest constructor injects literal HTML strings. A two-argument constructor concatenates two values. Finally, one constructor injects a JavaScript function (compiled from Ur/Web code) that will be used as an event handler or signal, e.g. in an `onclick` or `<dyn> signal` attribute. This datatype is easily forced into normal HTML code, but the explicit closures within it force the JavaScript garbage collector to keep alive any objects that the handlers depend on.

A crucial piece of logic appears in the implementation of the `<dyn>` pseudotag, which injects signals into HTML fragments. The runtime system begins by evaluating the signal with the current data source values, producing a value in the datatype from the prior paragraph. That value is then forced into a normal HTML string, replacing all closure references with reads from positions of a global array where we have stashed the closures. In the new DOM tree node created from this code, we also record which slots in that closure array we have used. Additionally, the signal evaluation process saved the set of sources that were read. We only need to rerun the signal if any of these sources change. This set of sources is also saved in the new DOM node.

Data sources are represented as records containing data values and *sets of DOM nodes that are listening for changes*. Whenever a source changes, all listening nodes must be recomputed. Recomputation needs to deallocate the old HTML contents of a node, including freeing its global closures and removing it and its subtrees from the listener sets of sources. It is precisely to enable this cleanup that we save sets of closure slots and sources in each DOM node. Recomputation must also update these sets appropriately.

## 4. Evaluation

In this section, we evaluate the effectiveness of the Ur/Web implementation as a practical programming tool, considering both performance and programmer productivity. We start with a discussion of some microbenchmarks and then turn to a summary of deployed Ur/Web applications.

### 4.1 Microbenchmarks

Readers might worry that Ur/Web's higher abstraction level vs. mainstream frameworks may bring an unacceptable performance cost. We briefly consider performance via microbenchmarks, where in important cases we find exactly the opposite comparison to less abstract frameworks.

An Ur/Web solution was entered into the TechEmpower Web Framework Benchmarks[3], a third-party comparison initiative run independently of the author of this paper, using contributed benchmark solutions from different communities, including an Ur/Web solution written in part by the author. Evaluation centers on *throughput* of Web applications, or how many concurrent requests

[3] `http://www.techempower.com/benchmarks/`

their server-side pieces can handle per second. *Latency* (time to service a single request) is also measured, but not highlighted as much on the results pages.

Ur/Web does particularly poorly on a test with many database writes. Most frameworks in the competition do not enforce transactional semantics as Ur/Web does, and on every remote call we pay a performance cost for runtime analysis of transactional operations, paying the even higher cost of transaction restart when there is much contention. We hope to convince the benchmark coordinators to add a version of this test where implementations are required to use transactions.

However, on more realistic workloads, Ur/Web does very well. Exactly one test (`fortunes`) involves actual generation of HTML pages, based on results of database queries. On the benchmark's highest-capacity server, with 40 hardware threads all running Ur/Web server threads, Ur/Web achieves the best latency (2.1 ms) and the 4th-best throughput (about 110,000 requests per second) among all frameworks. This test (in Round 9 of the benchmarks) involved about 70 different configurations of about 60 different frameworks, including almost all of the most popular frameworks for real-world applications. We think these results are particularly encouraging given that our competitors are mostly not running within SQL transactions (i.e., they provide weaker semantics that make programming more challenging).

### 4.2 Deployed Applications

The Ur/Web implementation has been available as open source for long enough to develop a modest community of users. Beside the author of this paper, 12 users have contributed patches. Several serious Ur/Web applications have also been deployed on the Web. In this subsection, we summarize the ones we are aware of. Each is written by programmers outside the core Ur/Web development team, and there are no duplicate authors among the applications we survey, with one exception as noted below. Table 1 lists the applications and their URLs and authors. Nearly all of these applications also use Ur/Web's *foreign function interface (FFI)*, for interfacing with C and JavaScript libraries.

We especially want to highlight the first entry in the table, a profitable business based on an Ur/Web application. **BazQux Reader** is a Web-based reader for feeds of syndicated content, via formats like RSS and Atom. It provides similar functionality to the late Google Reader, but with many extras, like reading comments on feeds in the same interface. BazQux mostly uses Ur/Web's reactive GUI features and RPCs, interfacing via our FFI to a Riak[4] database that is kept up-to-date by a separate Haskell feed fetcher. As of this writing, there are about 2500 active BazQux users with paid subscriptions. Average load on the application is about 10 requests/second, with busy-period peaks above 150 requests/second. The Ur/Web source code of BazQux Reader is available publicly on GitHub[5].

The next two applications were developed by a single author. Both relate to the cryptographic currency bitcoin. The **Bitparking Namecoin Exchange** previously allowed visitors to trade bitcoins to do the equivalent of registering Internet domain names, within an alternative decentralized protocol for name mapping. It was decommissioned recently after 2 years of operation. The developer notes that most similar services were plagued by generic Web security problems (e.g., cross-site request forgery) in that period, but the Ur/Web-based exchange maintained a spotless record. The **Bitcoin Merge Mining Pool** has been running since 2011, managing a confederation of bitcoin miners. At its peak in 2013, about 10% of global progress in bitcoin mining worked through this application. It serves about 400 requests per second on average. This family of applications has mostly stressed Ur/Web's SQL interface, RPC system, and foreign-function interface (to connect to implementations of nontrivial cryptographic protocols).

The **Big Map of Latin America** is an animated presentation of that region's history. The user moves a slider widget to step through time, which places various icons around a colorful map, indicating events in categories like economics and the environment. Clicking on an icon opens an overlay with an illustrated article going into more detail. There is also a less-polished administrative interface for editing the history database with conventional HTML forms.

**Ecosrv** serves firmware upgrades for CGNAT network hardware devices, which connect to the Ur/Web application via an HTTP-based API. A more traditional GUI also displays statistics on recent activity. Ur/Web source code is available on GitHub[6].

**Logitext** is a graphical interface to sequent-calculus proofs, intended for use in teaching logic to undergraduates. Proof problems appear embedded within tutorial documents. Each solution is a tree of deduction steps, where the user adds a new step by clicking on the right subformula. The trees appear rendered in classic inference-rule notation. The backend for executing proof steps is the Coq proof assistant, invoked via RPCs and the FFI with some Haskell code involved.

Most of these applications' developers have no special connection to the Ur/Web development team, so their decisions to adopt Ur/Web provide some validation of the language design. We asked developers what they saw as the biggest positive and negative points of Ur/Web. There was a clear consensus that the biggest plus was the simple model for coding client-side GUIs that interact easily with server-side code. The most mentioned pain point was the way that the Ur/Web compiler checks that server-side code does not call functions that only make sense in the client, or vice versa. In designing the language, we were worried that it would be too complex to extend the type system to track such constraints, tagging monadic computation types with sidedness information. However, the approach we adopted instead, with ad-hoc static analysis on whole programs at compile time, leads to error messages that confuse even experienced Ur/Web programmers. In general, improvements to error messages and performance of the compiler (which does specialized whole-program optimization) are high on our list of future priorities.

One of the main motivations for designing the Ur language [8] was supporting complex metaprogramming, with detailed compile-time checking of metaprograms inspired by dependent type theory. As far as we know, the production Ur/Web applications are currently making only modest use of metaprogramming, e.g. for small convenience operations related to polymorphic record and variant types. The HTML and SQL encodings make extensive use of type-system features that go beyond those of ML and Haskell, but there has not yet been much direct adoption of such features outside the Ur/Web standard library.

## 5. Related Work

MAWL [2] was an early domain-specific language for safe programming of form-based Web applications. The MAWL compiler did static verification of HTML validity and of compatibility between forms and handlers. MAWL included no features for building libraries of abstractions, as it tied together forms and handlers via fixed sets of template files.

Continuation-based Web application systems make a different set of trade-offs than Ur/Web does in supporting abstraction. The PLT Scheme Web Server [20] provides completely first-class sup-

[4] `http://basho.com/riak/`

[5] `http://github.com/bazqux/bazqux-urweb`

[6] `http://github.com/grwlf/urweb-econat-srv`

| Application | URL | Author |
|---:|---|---|
| BazQux Reader | `http://www.bazqux.com/` | Vladimir Shabanov |
| Big Map of Latin America | `http://map.historyisaweapon.com/` | Daniel Patterson |
| Bitcoin Merge Mining Pool | `http://mmpool.org/` | Chris Double |
| Bitparking Namecoin Exchange [now defunct] | `http://exchange.bitparking.com/` | Chris Double |
| Ecosrv | `http://ecosrv.hit.msk.ru/` | Sergey Mironov |
| Logitext | `http://logitext.mit.edu/` | Edward Z. Yang |

**Table 1.** Deployed Ur/Web applications

port for continuations-as-URLs, making it very easy to construct many useful abstractions. This platform works without a static type system, fitting the preferences of many programmers today. As a consequence, however, many kinds of strong encapsulation are impossible; for instance, the ability of programs to generate arbitrary HTML and JavaScript as strings means that any client-side component discipline can be subverted. Seaside [15] provides strong encapsulation guarantees at the expense of not exposing continuations as first-class URLs. Seaside's component system also only runs server-side; client-side code uses the normal JavaScript model, with the document exposed as a mutable global variable, with subtrees assigned names from a global namespace.

As far as we are aware, no continuation-based systems give persistent resources like database tables first-class status, which prevents encapsulation of these resources. That design decision makes it easier to build on top of existing programming languages and provide simpler libraries. We expect that different developers will prefer different positions in this design space. We hope that many fans of strong encapsulation in object-oriented and functional languages will prefer the style advocated in this paper. We have not found any previous recommendations of that style, so part of our mission in this paper is to add such a recommendation to the larger debate.

Mutable state enables new modularity disciplines. Web cells [26] are a variant of mutable references (implemented in the PLT Web Server) that provide the abstraction of each Web page having its own copy of the heap, while admitting efficient implementation. Initial Web cells implementations only worked with server-side storage of all continuations, which imposes significant storage requirements. More recent work [25] has shown how to represent Web-cell-using continuations compactly enough that these continuations may be serialized in full within URLs. Ur/Web's more static approach makes it possible for an algorithm to find all possible entry points to an application, enabling rigorous verification and testing as in some past work doing static analysis on Ur/Web code for security [9], while the PLT approach is more lightweight and easier for mainstream programmers to learn.

The Links [11] language pioneered strong static checking of multiple-tier Web applications, where the code for all tiers is collected in a single language. Where Ur/Web includes explicit markers (e.g., `rpc`) of control transfer between client and server, Links follows a more implicit approach [13], where different first-class functions are tagged as belonging to different sides and are automatically run on those sides when called. Links also includes a novel means of abstraction for HTML forms based on idioms [12]. Still, much of Ur/Web is inspired closely by Links and can be thought of as layering modularity features upon that foundation. Links does not include a module system or other vehicle for type abstraction, and any piece of Links code may access any database table or DOM subtree by referring to its textual name. Some other similar systems have been presented, including JWIG [10], which is a Java extension based around new types and program analysis.

Hop [33] is another unified Web programming language, this time dynamically typed and based on Scheme. Many elements are quite similar to the patterns demonstrated in our Ur/Web examples, including a simple RPC syntax (to server endpoints called *services*) and a quotation and antiquotation convention for easy mixing of server- and client-side code. GUI interaction follows the usual browser model, where a page is a mutable tree that can be walked arbitrarily by any client-side code. Hop is based on no distinguished database integration, instead supporting access to a variety of database systems via libraries. Hop servers support a novel means of configurable concurrency for pipeline execution [32], but we do not believe that any transaction-based model has been implemented, and it does not seem obvious how to implement such a configuration without more fundamental language support. The HipHop extension [5] uses synchronous reactive programming to support a different declarative style of organizing interactions between stages of processes that span clients and servers.

Ocsigen [3, 4] is an OCaml-based platform for building dynamic Web sites in a unified language, with static typing that rules out many potential programming mistakes. The concurrency model [36] is cooperative multithreading, on both client and server. The Ocsigen ecosystem includes libraries for both statically typed SQL database access and server-to-client message passing, the latter via a mechanism called *buses*. There is no support for grouping the two sorts of actions into transactions; rather, the semantics is the usual interleaving one, with cooperative context-switch points. The SQL library also allows arbitrary access to any table from any module that knows its string name, even allowing different modules to declare different versions of a table with different, incompatible types. There is optional library support for a functional-reactive GUI programming style.

The Opa language[7] is another statically typed unified language for database-backed Web applications. Its database integration is with the nonrelational system MongoDB[8], which does not support transactions, so Opa inherits a semantics that exposes interleaving of concurrent requests. Opa supports a precursor to the sort of database table encapsulation that we have described, where modules may declare private components of the database state. However, the Opa mechanism forces programmers to assign components names in a global namespace. The compiler will prevent duplicate use of a name, which thwarts threats against encapsulation, but which also forces authors of different modules to coordinate on a naming scheme. Similar issues arise in Opa's use of a mostly standard model of client-side GUIs, where elements are assigned textual names in a global namespace, and where the visible page is changed by mutating elements directly.

Strong encapsulation has been supported through capability systems [22], including the Capsules system [21] for isolating Web servlets. Capsules is built on top of Java, so, compared to Ur/Web, it provides an easier migration path for mainstream programmers. However, Capsules does not support database access, and, among cookies and other persistent values that are supported, true encapsulation is not possible. The reason is that a Capsules application must

[7] `http://opalang.org/`

[8] `http://www.mongodb.org/`

contain trusted code to delegate persistent resources to components, which implies that a component must know which resources its subcomponents use. In Ur/Web, components use special declarations like `table` to, in effect, seed their initial capability sets in a static and modular way.

Some ostensibly capability-safe subsets of JavaScript have been proposed, including Caja[9]. Formal analysis using operational semantics [24] has uncovered holes in some of these languages and suggested practical formal conditions that guarantee absence of holes. That line of work is complementary to our approach from this paper, as it provides a simple foundation without suggesting which abstractions should be built on it. With Ur/Web's current implementation, we depend on the fact that all modules are compiled from type-checked Ur/Web source. Instead, we could target some common safe JavaScript subset, ensuring safe interoperation with components built directly in JavaScript or with other compilers.

Several other languages and frameworks support functional-reactive programming for client-side Web GUIs, including Flapjax [28], which is available in one flavor as a JavaScript library; and Elm [14], a new programming language. These libraries implement the original, "pure" version of functional-reactive programming, where key parts of programs are written as pure functions that transform input streams into streams of visible GUI content. Such a style is elegant in many cases, but it does not seem compatible with the modularity patterns we demonstrated in Section 2.2.1, where it is natural to spread input sources to a single stream across different parts of a program. Ur/Web supports that kind of modularity by adopting a hybrid model, with imperative event callbacks that trigger recomputation of pure code.

As far as we are aware, Ur/Web was the first Web programming tool to support impure functional-reactive programming, but the idea of reactive GUI programming in JavaScript is now mainstream, and too many frameworks exist to detail here.

One popular JavaScript framework is Meteor[10], distinguished by its support for a particular reactive programming style. It integrates well with mainstream Web development tools and libraries, which is a nontrivial advantage for most programmers. Its standard database support is for MongoDB, with no transactional abstraction or other way of taming simultaneous complex state updates. Like Opa, Meteor allows modules to encapsulate named database elements, but an exception is thrown if two modules have chosen the same string name for their elements; module authors must coordinate on how to divide a global namespace. Meteor supports automatic publishing of server-side database changes into client-side caches, and then from those caches into rendered pages. In addition to automatic updating of pages based on state changes, a standard DOM-based API for walking document structure and making changes imperatively is provided, though it is not very idiomatic. Meteor's machinery for reactive page updating involves a more complex API than in Ur/Web. Its central concept is of *imperative* functions that need to be rerun when any of their dependencies change, where Ur/Web describes reactive computations in terms of *pure* code within the signal monad, such that it is easy to rerun only *part* of a computation, when not all of its dependencies have changed. Forcing purity on these computations helps avoid the confusing consequences of genuine side effects being repeated on each change to dependencies. The 7 lines of code near the start of Section 2.2.1, together with the `<dyn>` pseudotag, give the complete interface for reactive programming in Ur/Web, in contrast with tens of pages of documentation (of dynamically typed functions) for Meteor.

[9] `http://code.google.com/p/google-caja/`

[10] `http://www.meteor.com/`

Other popular JavaScript frameworks include Angular.js[11], Backbone[12], Ractive[13], and React[14]. A commonality among these libraries seems to be heavyweight approaches to the basic structure of reactive GUIs, with built-in mandatory concepts of models, views, controllers, templates, components, etc. In contrast, Ur/Web has its 7-line API of sources and signals. These mainstream JavaScript frameworks tend to force elements of reactive state to be enumerated explicitly as fields of some distinguished object, instead of allowing data sources to be allocated dynamically throughout the modules of a program and kept as private state of those modules.

Microsoft's TouchDevelop [6, 35] is another recent Web language design, intended to appeal to novices. TouchDevelop allows client code to manipulate distributed data structures directly, applying distributed-systems techniques automatically to enforce eventual consistency. Consequences of such changes flow automatically into affected parts of documents, in a partly functional-reactive style. Allowing direct manipulation of data structures by clients raises security concerns, which Ur/Web avoids by funneling all such manipulations through RPCs from client to server, running code in a trusted environment where appropriate checks may be applied, with the chance to use message-passing channels to notify clients of updates in a globally consistent order. In general, the TouchDevelop model seems superior for newcomers to Web programming, while Ur/Web offers better robustness in a few senses.

The transactional abstraction has also been exposed in high-level programming languages via the software transactional memory model [34], for instance in GHC Haskell [18]. Such systems provide a transactional interface over the classic model of mutable, linked objects in a garbage-collected heap. Ur/Web's `transaction` monad is actually much closer to the original idea of transactions from databases. The only mutable server-side state in an Ur/Web application is in the SQL database (where columns have only primitive types) and in message queues of channels, so there is no need to do, e.g., conflict analysis on traces of accesses to pointer-based data structures.

## 6. Conclusion

We have presented the design of Ur/Web, a programming language for Web applications, focusing on a few language-design ideas that apply broadly to a class of distributed applications. Our main mission is to promote two desiderata that programmers should be asking for in their Web frameworks, but which seem almost absent from mainstream discussion. First, while mainstream practice is drifting further away from the conceptual simplicity of transactions and atomic execution of units of concurrent work, we suggest holding on to simple concurrency models, unless forced away from them by performance concerns. Second, while language-enforced encapsulation is widely praised for conventional data structures, we suggest that it ought to be generalized to key pieces of Web applications, like database tables and HTML subtrees, importing familiar software-engineering benefits with new twists. Ur/Web is already being used in serious production applications, and we hope languages adopting our principles can continue to help programmers realize nontrivial functionality with less effort and more confidence in correctness.

[11] `https://angularjs.org/`

[12] `http://backbonejs.org/`

[13] `http://www.ractivejs.org/`

[14] `http://facebook.github.io/react/`

## Acknowledgments

For their bug reports, feature requests, patches, and enthusiasm, we thank the early adopters of Ur/Web, including the application authors acknowledged earlier but also many others. We also thank Gergely Buday, Jason Gross, Arjun Guha, Barbara Liskov, Clément Pit–Claudel, and the anonymous referees for their helpful feedback on drafts of this paper. This work has been supported in part by National Science Foundation grant CCF-1217501.

## References

[1] J. Armstrong. Erlang – a survey of the language and its industrial applications. In *Proc. INAP*, pages 16–18, 1996.

[2] D. Atkins, T. Ball, M. Benedikt, G. Bruns, K. Cox, P. Mataga, and K. Rehor. Experience with a domain specific language for form-based services. In *Proc. DSL*, 1997.

[3] V. Balat. Ocsigen: typing Web interaction with Objective Caml. In *Proc. ML Workshop*, 2006.

[4] V. Balat, J. Vouillon, and B. Yakobowski. Experience report: Ocsigen, a Web programming framework. In *Proc. ICFP*, pages 311–316. ACM, 2009.

[5] G. Berry and M. Serrano. Hop and HipHop: Multitier web orchestration. In *Proc. ICDCIT*, pages 1–13, 2014.

[6] S. Burckhardt, M. Fahndrich, P. de Halleux, S. McDirmid, M. Moskal, N. Tillmann, and J. Kato. It's alive! Continuous feedback in UI programming. In *Proc. PLDI*, pages 95–104. ACM, 2013.

[7] J. Cheney, S. Lindley, and P. Wadler. A practical theory of language-integrated query. In *Proc. ICFP*, pages 403–416. ACM, 2013.

[8] A. Chlipala. Ur: Statically-typed metaprogramming with type-level record computation. In *Proc. PLDI*, pages 122–133. ACM, 2010.

[9] A. Chlipala. Static checking of dynamically-varying security policies in database-backed applications. In *Proc. OSDI*, pages 105–118, 2010.

[10] A. S. Christensen, A. Møller, and M. I. Schwartzbach. Extending Java for high-level Web service construction. *TOPLAS*, 25(6):814–875, November 2003.

[11] E. Cooper, S. Lindley, P. Wadler, and J. Yallop. Links: Web programming without tiers. In *Proc. FMCO*, pages 266–296, 2006.

[12] E. Cooper, S. Lindley, P. Wadler, and J. Yallop. The essence of form abstraction. In *Proc. APLAS*, pages 205–220. Springer-Verlag, 2008.

[13] E. E. Cooper and P. Wadler. The RPC Calculus. In *Proc. PPDP*, pages 231–242. ACM, 2009.

[14] E. Czaplicki and S. Chong. Asynchronous functional reactive programming for GUIs. In *Proc. PLDI*, pages 411–422. ACM, 2013.

[15] S. Ducasse, A. Lienhard, and L. Renggli. Seaside – a multiple control flow Web application framework. In *European Smalltalk User Group – Research Track*, 2004.

[16] A. Frisch. OCaml + XDuce. In *Proc. ICFP*, pages 192–200. ACM, 2006.

[17] J. Gray. The transaction concept: Virtues and limitations (invited paper). In *Proc. VLDB*, pages 144–154, 1981.

[18] T. Harris, S. Marlow, S. Peyton-Jones, and M. Herlihy. Composable memory transactions. In *Proc. PPoPP*, pages 48–60. ACM, 2005.

[19] H. Hosoya, J. Vouillon, and B. C. Pierce. Regular expression types for XML. In *Proc. ICFP*, pages 11–22. ACM, 2000.

[20] S. Krishnamurthi, P. W. Hopkins, J. McCarthy, P. T. Graunke, G. Pettyjohn, and M. Felleisen. Implementation and use of the PLT Scheme Web Server. *Higher Order Symbol. Comput.*, 20(4):431–460, 2007.

[21] A. Krishnamurthy, A. Mettler, and D. Wagner. Fine-grained privilege separation for Web applications. In *Proc. WWW*, 2010.

[22] H. M. Levy. *Capability-Based Computer Systems*. Butterworth-Heinemann, Newton, MA, USA, 1984. ISBN 0932376223.

[23] D. MacQueen. Modules for Standard ML. In *Proc. LFP*, pages 198–207. ACM, 1984.

[24] S. Maffeis, J. Mitchell, and A. Taly. Object capabilities and isolation of untrusted Web applications. In *Proc. IEEE S&P*, pages 125–140, 2010.

[25] J. McCarthy. Automatically RESTful Web applications or, marking modular serializable continuations. In *Proc. ICFP*. ACM, 2009.

[26] J. McCarthy and S. Krishnamurthi. Interaction-safe state for the Web. In *Proc. Scheme and Functional Programming*, 2006.

[27] E. Meijer, B. Beckman, and G. Bierman. LINQ: Reconciling objects, relations and XML in the .NET framework. In *Proc. SIGMOD*, pages 706–706. ACM, 2006.

[28] L. A. Meyerovich, A. Guha, J. Baskin, G. H. Cooper, M. Greenberg, A. Bromfield, and S. Krishnamurthi. Flapjax: A programming language for Ajax applications. In *Proc. OOPSLA*, pages 1–20. ACM, 2009.

[29] S. L. Peyton Jones and P. Wadler. Imperative functional programming. In *Proc. POPL*, pages 71–84. ACM, 1993.

[30] D. R. K. Ports and K. Grittner. Serializable Snapshot Isolation in PostgreSQL. *Proc. VLDB Endow.*, 5(12):1850–1861, Aug. 2012.

[31] J. H. Reppy. *Concurrent Programming in ML*. Cambridge University Press, 1999. ISBN 0-521-48089-2.

[32] M. Serrano. Hop, a fast server for the diffuse web. In *Proc. COORDINATION*, pages 1–26. Springer-Verlag, 2009.

[33] M. Serrano, E. Gallesio, and F. Loitsch. Hop, a language for programming the Web 2.0. In *Proc. DLS*, 2006.

[34] N. Shavit and D. Touitou. Software transactional memory. In *Proc. PODC*, pages 204–213. ACM, 1995.

[35] N. Tillmann, M. Moskal, J. de Halleux, and M. Fahndrich. TouchDevelop: Programming cloud-connected mobile devices via touchscreen. In *Proc. ONWARD*, pages 49–60. ACM, 2011.

[36] J. Vouillon. Lwt: A cooperative thread library. In *Proc. ML Workshop*, pages 3–12. ACM, 2008.

[37] P. Wadler and S. Blott. How to make ad-hoc polymorphism less ad hoc. In *Proc. POPL*, pages 60–76. ACM, 1989.

# Safe & Efficient Gradual Typing for TypeScript

Aseem Rastogi *
University of Maryland
College Park
aseem@cs.umd.edu

Nikhil Swamy    Cédric Fournet
Microsoft Research
{nswamy, fournet}@microsoft.com

Gavin Bierman *
Oracle Labs
Gavin.Bierman@oracle.com

Panagiotis Vekris *
University of California
San Diego
pvekris@cs.ucsd.edu

## Abstract

Current proposals for adding gradual typing to JavaScript, such as Closure, TypeScript and Dart, forgo soundness to deal with issues of scale, code reuse, and popular programming patterns.

We show how to address these issues in practice while retaining soundness. We design and implement a new gradual type system, prototyped for expediency as a 'Safe' compilation mode for TypeScript. Our compiler achieves soundness by enforcing stricter static checks and embedding residual runtime checks in compiled code. It emits plain JavaScript that runs on stock virtual machines. Our main theorem is a simulation that ensures that the checks introduced by Safe TypeScript (1) catch any dynamic type error, and (2) do not alter the semantics of type-safe TypeScript code.

Safe TypeScript is carefully designed to minimize the performance overhead of runtime checks. At its core, we rely on two new ideas: *differential subtyping*, a new form of coercive subtyping that computes the minimum amount of runtime type information that must be added to each object; and an *erasure modality*, which we use to safely and selectively erase type information. This allows us to scale our design to full-fledged TypeScript, including arrays, maps, classes, inheritance, overloading, and generic types.

We validate the usability and performance of Safe TypeScript empirically by type-checking and compiling around 120,000 lines of existing TypeScript source code. Although runtime checks can be expensive, the end-to-end overhead is small for code bases that already have type annotations. For instance, we bootstrap the Safe TypeScript compiler (90,000 lines including the base TypeScript compiler): we measure a 15% runtime overhead for type safety, and also uncover programming errors as type safety violations. We conclude that, at least during development and testing, subjecting JavaScript/TypeScript programs to safe gradual typing adds significant value to source type annotations at a modest cost.

## 1. Introduction

Originally intended for casual scripting, JavaScript is now widely used to develop large applications. Using JavaScript in complex codebases is, however, not without difficulties: the lack of robust language abstractions such as static types, classes, and interfaces can hamper programmer productivity and undermine tool support. Unfortunately, retrofitting abstraction into JavaScript is difficult, as one must support awkward language features and programming patterns in existing code and third-party libraries, without either rejecting most programs or requiring extensive annotations (perhaps using a PhD-level type system).

Gradual type systems set out to fix this problem in a principled manner, and have led to popular proposals for JavaScript, notably Closure, TypeScript and Dart (although the latter is strictly speaking not JavaScript but a variant with some features of JavaScript removed). These proposals bring substantial benefits to the working programmer, usually taken for granted in typed languages, such as a convenient notation for documenting code; API exploration; code completion; refactoring; and diagnostics of basic type errors. Interestingly, to be usable at scale, all these proposals are *intentionally unsound*: typeful programs may be easier to write and maintain, but their type annotations do not prevent runtime type errors.

Instead of giving up on soundness at the outset, we contend that a sound gradual type system for JavaScript is practically feasible. There are, undoubtedly, some significant challenges to overcome. For starters, the language includes inherently type-unsafe features such as eval and stack walks, some of JavaScript's infamous "bad parts". However, recent work is encouraging: Swamy et al. (2014) proposed TS$^\star$ a sound type system for JavaScript to tame untyped adversarial code, isolating it from a gradually typed core language. Although the typed fragment of TS$^\star$ is too limited for large-scale JavaScript developments, its recipe of coping with the bad parts using type-based memory isolation is promising.

In this work, we tackle the problem of developing a sound, yet practical, gradual type system for a large fragment of JavaScript, confining its most awkward features to untrusted code by relying implicitly on memory isolation. Concretely, we take TypeScript as our starting point. In brief, TypeScript is JavaScript with optional type annotations: every valid JavaScript program is a valid TypeScript program. TypeScript adds an object-oriented gradual type system, while its compiler erases all traces of types and emits JavaScript that can run on stock virtual machines. The emitted code is syntactically close to the source (except for type erasure), hence TypeScript and JavaScript interoperate with the same performance.

TypeScript's type system is intentionally unsound; Bierman et al. (2014) catalog some of its unsound features, including bivariant subtyping for functions and arrays, as well as in class and interface extension. The lack of soundness limits the benefits of writing type annotations in TypeScript, making abstractions hard to enforce and leading to unconventional programming patterns, even for programmers who steer clear of the bad parts. Consider for instance the following snippet from TouchDevelop (Tillmann et al. 2012), a mobile programming platform written in TypeScript:

```
private parseColorCode (c:string) {
  if (typeof c !== "string") return −1; . . . }
```

* This work was done at Microsoft Research.


*POPL '15*, January 15–17, 2015, Mumbai, India.

ACM 978-1-4503-3300-9/15/01...$15.00.
http://dx.doi.org/10.1145/2676726.2676971

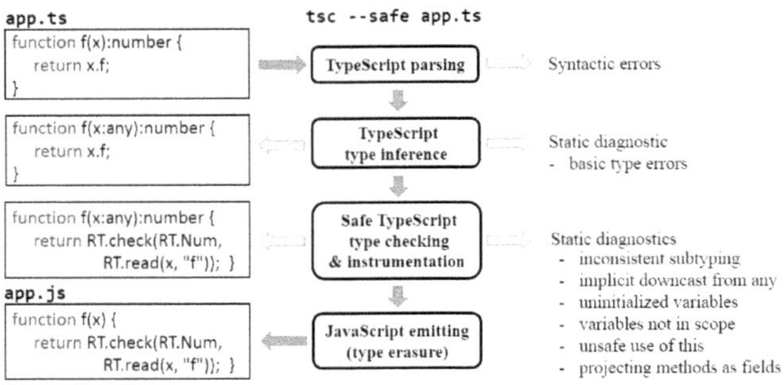


Figure 1: Architecture of Safe TypeScript

Despite annotating the formal parameter c as a string, the prudent TypeScript programmer must still check that the argument received is indeed a string using JavaScript reflection, and deal with errors.

## 1.1 Safe TypeScript

We present a new type-checker and code generator for a subset of TypeScript that guarantees type safety through a combination of static and dynamic checks. Its implementation is fully integrated as a branch of the TypeScript-0.9.5 compiler. Programmers can opt in to Safe TypeScript simply by providing a flag to the compiler (similar in spirit to JavaScript's strict mode, which lets the programmer abjure some unsafe features). As with TypeScript, the code generated by Safe TypeScript is standard JavaScript and runs on stock virtual machines.

Figure 1 illustrates Safe TypeScript at work. A programmer authors a TypeScript program, `app.ts`, and feeds it to the TypeScript compiler, `tsc`, setting the `--safe` flag to enable our system. The compiler initially processes `app.ts` using standard TypeScript passes: the file is parsed and a type inference algorithm computes (potentially unsound) types for all subterms. For the top-level function f in the figure, TypeScript infers the type (x:any)⇒number, using by default the dynamic type any for its formal parameter. (It may infer more precise types in other cases.) The sub-term x.f is inferred to have type any as well. In TypeScript, any-typed values can be passed to a context expecting a more precise type, so TypeScript silently accepts that x.f be returned at type number. Since TypeScript erases all types, x.f need not be a number at runtime, which may cause callers of f to fail later, despite f's annotation.

In contrast, when using Safe TypeScript, a second phase of type-checking is applied to the program, to confirm (soundly) the types inferred by earlier phases. This second phase may produce various static errors and warnings. Once all static errors have been fixed, Safe TypeScript rewrites the program to instrument objects with runtime type information (RTTI) and insert runtime checks based on this RTTI. In the example, the rewriting involves instrumenting x.f as RT.readField(x, `"f"`), a call into a runtime library RT used by all Safe TypeScript programs. Although the static type of x is any, the RTTI introduced by our compiler allows the runtime library to determine whether it is safe to project x.f, and further (using RT.check) to ensure that its content is indeed a number. Finally, the dynamically type-safe JavaScript code is emitted by a code generator that strips out type annotations and desugars constructs like classes, but otherwise leaves the program unchanged.

Underlying Safe TypeScript are two novel technical ideas:

***(1) Partial erasure.*** Many prior gradual type systems require that a single dynamic type (variously called dynamic, dyn, $*$, any, $\top$, etc.) be a universal super-type and, further, that any be related to all other types by subtyping and coercion. We relax this requirement: in Safe TypeScript, any characterizes only those values that are tagged with RTTI. Separately, we have a modality for *erased types*, whose values need not be tagged with RTTI. Erased types are not subtypes of any, nor can they be coerced to it, yielding four important capabilities. First, *information hiding*: we show how to use erased types to encode private fields in an object and prove a confidentiality theorem (Theorem 2). Second, *user-controlled performance*: through careful erasure, the user can minimize the overhead of RTTI operations. Third, *modularity*: erased-types allow us to ensure that objects owned by external modules do not have RTTI. And, fourth, *long-term evolution*, allowing us to scale Safe TypeScript up to a language with a wide range of typing features.

***(2) Differential subtyping.*** In addition, we rely on a form of coercive subtyping (Luo 1999) that allows us to attach *partial* RTTI on any-typed objects, and is vital for good runtime performance.

## 1.2 Main contributions

We present the first sound gradual type system with a formal treatment of objects with mutable fields and immutable methods, addition and deletion of computed properties from objects, nominal class-based object types, interfaces, structural object types with width-subtyping, and partial type erasure.

***Formal core** (§3).* We develop SafeTS: a core calculus for Safe TypeScript. Our formalization includes the type system, compiler and runtime for a subset of Safe TypeScript, and also provides a dynamic semantics suitable for a core of both TypeScript and Safe TypeScript. Its metatheory establishes that well-typed SafeTS programs (with embedded runtime checks) simulate programs running under TypeScript's semantics (without runtime checks), except for the possibility of a failed runtime check that stops execution early (Theorem 1). Pragmatically, this enables programmers to switch between 'safe' and 'unsafe' mode while testing and debugging.

***Full-fledged implementation for TypeScript** (§4).* Relying on differential subtyping and erasure, we extend SafeTS to the full Safe TypeScript language, adding support for several forms of inheritance for classes and interfaces; structural interfaces with recursion; support for JavaScript's primitive objects; auto-boxing; generic classes, interfaces and functions; arrays and dictionaries with mutability controls; enumerated types; objects with optional fields; variadic functions; and a simple module system. In all cases, we make use of a combination of static checks and RTTI-based runtime checks to ensure dynamic type safety.

***Usability and Performance Evaluation** (§5).* We report on our experience using Safe TypeScript to type-check and safely compile about 120,000 lines of source code, including bootstrapping the Safe TypeScript compiler itself. In doing so, we found and corrected several errors that were manifested as type safety violations in the compiler and in a widely used benchmark. Quantitatively, we evaluate Safe TypeScript's tagging strategy against two alternatives, and find that differential subtyping (and, of course, erasure) offers significant performance benefits.

We conclude that large TypeScript projects can easily be ported to Safe TypeScript, thereby increasing the benefits of existing type annotations; that Safe TypeScript can reveal programming bugs both statically and dynamically; that statically typed code incurs negligible overhead; and that selective RTTI can ensure type safety with modest overhead.

We provide the full formal development and proofs of SafeTS, and more experimental details, in an accompanying technical report (Rastogi et al. 2014). Source code of our compiler and all our benchmarks are available at `https://github.com/nikswamy/SafeTypeScript`. We also provide an in-browser demo of Safe TypeScript in action at `http://research.microsoft.com/en-us/um/people/nswamy/Playground/TSSafe/`.

## 2. An overview of Safe TypeScript

Being sound, Safe TypeScript endows types with many of the properties that Java or C# programmers might expect but not find in TypeScript. On the other hand, Safe TypeScript is also intended to be compatible with JavaScript programming. As a language user, understanding what type safety means is critical. As a language designer, striking the right balance is tricky. We first summarize some important consequences of type safety in Safe TypeScript.

***An object implements the methods in its type.*** Objects in JavaScript are used in two complementary styles. First, as mutable dictionaries, they use field-names to represent keys. Second, in a more object-oriented style, they expose methods to operate on their state. Safe TypeScript supports both styles. In less structured code, dictionary-like objects may be used: the type system ensures that fields have the expected type *when defined*. In more structured code, objects may expose their functionality using methods: the type system guarantees that an object always implement calls to the methods declared in its type, i.e., methods are *always defined* and *immutable*. The two styles can be freely mixed, i.e., a dictionary may have both methods and fields with functional types.

***Values can be undefined.*** Whereas languages like C# and Java have one null-value included in all reference types, JavaScript has two: null and undefined. Safe TypeScript rationalizes this aspect of JavaScript's design, in effect removing null from well-typed programs while retaining only undefined. (Retaining only null is possible too, but less idiomatic.) For existing programs that may use null, our implementation provides an option to permit null to also be a member of every reference type. Note that undefined is also included in all native types, such as boolean and number. This supports, e.g., the pervasive use in JavaScript of undefined for false.

***Type safety as a foundation for security.*** JavaScript provides a native notion of dynamic type safety. Although relatively weak, it is the basis of many dynamic security enforcement techniques. For instance, the inability to forge object references is the basis of capability-based security techniques (Miller et al. 2007). By compiling to JavaScript, Safe TypeScript (like TypeScript itself) still enjoys these properties. Moreover, Safe TypeScript provides higher level abstractions for encapsulation enforced with a combination of static and dynamic checks. For example, TypeScript provides syntax for classes with access qualifiers to mark certain fields as private, but does not enforce them, even in well-typed code. In §2.4, we show how encapsulations like private fields can be easily built (and relied upon!) in Safe TypeScript. Looking forward, Safe TypeScript's type safety should provide a useful basis for more advanced security-oriented program analyses.

***Static safety and canonical forms.*** For well-typed program fragments that do not make use of the any type, Safe TypeScript ensures that no runtime checks are inserted in the code (although some RTTI may still be added). For code that uses only erased types, neither checks nor RTTI are added, ensuring that code runs at full speed. When adding RTTI, we are careful not to break JavaScript's underlying semantics, e.g., we preserve object identity. Additionally, programmers can rely on a canonical-form property. For example, if a value $v$ is defined and has static type {ref:number}, then the programmer can conclude that $v$.ref contains a number (if defined) and that $v$.ref can be safely updated with a number. In contrast, approaches to gradual typing based on higher-order casts do not have this property. For example, in the system of Herman et al. (2010), a value $r$ with static type ref number may in fact be another value wrapped with a runtime check—attempting to update $r$ with a number may cause a dynamic type error.

In the remainder of this section, we illustrate the main features of Safe TypeScript using several small examples.

### 2.1 Nominal classes and structural interfaces

JavaScript widely relies on encodings of class-based object-oriented idioms into prototype-based objects. To this end, TypeScript provides syntactic support for declaring classes with single inheritance and multiple interfaces (resembling constructs in Java or C#) and its code generator desugars class declarations to prototypes using well-known techniques. Safe TypeScript retains TypeScript's classes and interfaces, with a few important differences illustrated on the code below:

```
interface Point { x:number; y:number }
class MovablePoint implements Point {
  constructor(public x:number, public y:number) {}
  public move(dx:number, dy:number) { this.x += dx; this.y += dy; }
}
function mustBeTrue(x:MovablePoint) {
  return !x || x instanceof MovablePoint;
}
```

The code defines a Point to be a pair of numbers representing its coordinates and a class MovablePoint with two public fields x and y (initialized to the arguments of the constructor) and a public move method. In TypeScript, all types are interpreted structurally: Point and MovablePoint are aliases for $t_p$ ={x:number; y:number} and $t_o$ ={x:number; y:number; move(dx:number, dy:number): void}, respectively. This structural treatment is pleasingly uniform, but it has some drawbacks. First, a purely structural view of class-based object types is incompatible with JavaScript's semantics. One might expect that every well-typed function call mustBeTrue(v) returns true. However, in TypeScript, this need not be the case. Structurally, taking v to be the object literal {x:0, y:0, move(dx:number, dy:number){}}, mustBeTrue(v) is well-typed, but v is not an instance of MovablePoint (which is decided by inspecting v's prototype) and the function returns false.

To fix this discrepancy, Safe TypeScript treats class-types nominally, but let them be viewed structurally. That is, MovablePoint is a subtype of both $t_p$ and $t_o$, but neither $t_p$ nor $t_o$ are subtypes of MovablePoint. Interfaces in Safe TypeScript remain, by default, structural, i.e., Point is equivalent to $t_p$. In §4, we show how the programmer can override this default. Through the careful use of nominal types, both with classes and interfaces, programmers can build robust abstractions and, as we will see in later sections, minimize the overhead of RTTI and runtime checks.

### 2.2 A new style of efficient, RTTI-based gradual typing

Following TypeScript, Safe TypeScript includes a dynamic type any, which is a supertype of every non-erased type $t$. When a value of type $t$ is passed to a context expecting an any (or vice versa), Safe TypeScript injects runtime checks on RTTI to ensure that all the $t$-invariants are enforced. The particular style of RTTI-based gradual typing developed for Safe TypeScript is reminiscent of prior proposals by Swamy et al. (2014) and Siek and Vitousek (2013), but makes important improvements over both. Whereas prior approaches require all heap-allocated values to be instrumented with RTTI (leading to a significant performance overhead, as discussed in §5), in Safe TypeScript RTTI is added to objects only as needed. Next, we illustrate the way this works in a few common cases.

The source program shown to the left of Figure 2 defines two types: Point and Circle, and three functions: copy, f and g. The function g passes its Circle-typed argument to f at the type any.

Clearly there is a latent type error in this code: in line 10, the function is expected to return a number, but circ.center is no longer a Point (since the assignment at line 7 mutates the circle and changes its type). Safe TypeScript cannot detect this error statically: the formal parameter q has type any and any property access on any-typed objects is permissible. However, Safe TypeScript does detect this error at runtime; the result of compilation is the instrumented code shown to the right of Figure 2.

```
1  interface Point { x:number; y:number }
2  interface Circle { center:Point; radius:number }
3  function copy(p:Point, q:Point) { q.x=p.x; q.y=p.y; }
4  function f(q:any) {
5      var c = q.center;
6      copy(c, {x:0, y:0});
7      q.center = {x:"bad"}; }
8  function g(circ:Circle) : number {
9      f(circ);
10     return circ.center.x; }
```

```
1  RT.reg("Point",{"x":RT.num,"y":RT.num});
2  RT.reg("Circle",{"center":RT.mkRTTI("Point"), "radius":RT.num});
3  function copy(p, q) { q.x=p.x; q.y=p.y; }
4  function f(q) {
5      var c = RT.readField(q,"center");
6      copy(RT.checkAndTag(c, RT.mkRTTI("Point")),{x:0,y:0});
7      RT.writeField(q, "center", {x:"bad"}); }
8  function g(circ) {
9      f(RT.shallowTag(circ, RT.mkRTTI("Circle")));
10     return circ.center.x; }
```

Figure 2: Sample source TypeScript program (left) and JavaScript emitted by the Safe TypeScript compiler (right)

As we aim for statically typed code to suffer no performance penalty, it must remain uninstrumented. As such, the copy function and the statically typed field accesses circ.center.x are compiled unchanged. The freshly allocated object literal {x:0,y:0} is inferred to have type Point and is also unchanged (in contrast to Swamy et al. (2014) and Siek and Vitousek (2013), who instrument *all* objects with RTTI). We insert checks only at the boundaries between static and dynamically typed code and within dynamically typed code, as detailed in the 4 steps below.

***(1) Registering user-defined types with the runtime.*** The interface definitions in the source program (lines 1–2) are translated to calls to RT, the Safe TypeScript runtime library linked with every compiled program. Each call to RT.reg registers the runtime representation of a user-defined type.

***(2) Tagging objects with RTTI to lock invariants.*** Safe TypeScript uses RTTI to express invariants that must be enforced at runtime. In our example, g passes circ:Circle to f, which uses it at an imprecise type (any); to express that circ must be treated as a Circle, even in dynamically typed code, before calling f in the generated code (line 9), circ is instrumented using the function RT.shallowTag whose implementation is shown (partially) below.

```
function shallowTag(c, t) {
  if (c!==undefined) { c.rtti = combine(c.rtti, t); }
  return c; }
```

The RTTI of an object is maintained in an additional field (here called rtti) of that object. An object's RTTI may evolve at runtime—Safe TypeScript guarantees that the RTTI decreases with respect to the subtyping relation, never becoming less precise as the program executes. At each call to shallowTag(c,t), Safe TypeScript ensures that c has type t, while after the call (if c is defined) the old RTTI of c is updated (using the function combine) to also recall that c has type t (Circle, in our example). Importantly for performance, shallowTag does not descend into the structure of c tagging objects recursively—a single tag at the outermost object suffices; nested objects need not be tagged with RTTI (a vital difference from prior work).

***(3) Propagating invariants in dynamically typed code.*** Going back to our source program (line 5), the dynamically typed read q.center is rewritten to RT.readField(q,"center"), whose definition is shown (partially) below.

```
function readField(o,f) {
  if (f==="rtti") die("reserved name");
  return shallowTag(o[f], fieldType(o.rtti, f)); }
```

Reading a field f out of an object requires tagging the value stored in o.f with the invariants expected of that field by the enclosing object. In our example, we tag the object stored in q.center with RTTI indicating that it must remain a Point. The benefit we gain by not descending into the structure of an object in shallowTag is offset, in part, by the cost of propagating RTTI as the components of an object are accessed in dynamically typed code—empirically, we find that it is a good tradeoff (see §2.3 and §5).

***(4) Establishing invariants by inspecting and updating RTTI.*** When passing c to copy (line 6), we need to check that c is a Point, as expected by copy. We do this by calling another runtime function RT.checkAndTag that (unlike shallowTag) descends into the structure of c, checks that c is structurally a Point and, if it succeeds, tags c with RTTI recording that it is a Point. We outline below the (partial) implementation of RT.checkAndTag with a simplified signature. In our example, where f is called only from g, the check succeeds.

```
function checkAndTag(v, t) {
  if (v === undefined) return v;
  if (isPrimitive(t)) {
    if (t === typeof v) return v;
    else die("Expected a " + t);
  } else if (isObject(t)) {
    for (var f in fields(t)) {
      checkAndTag(v[f.name], f.type);
    }; return shallowTag(v, t);
  } . . . }
```

Finally, we come to the type-altering assignment to q.center: it is instrumented using the RT.writeField function (at line 7 in the generated code), whose partial definition is shown below.

```
function writeField(o, f, v) {
  if (f==="rtti") die("reserved name");
  return (o[f]=checkAndTag(v,fieldType(o.rtti,f))); }
```

The call writeField(o, f, v) ensures that the value v being written into the f field of object o is consistent with the typing invariants expected of that field—these invariants are recorded in o's RTTI, specifically in fieldType(o.rtti, f). In our example, this call fails since {x:"bad"} cannot be typed as a Point.

## 2.3 Differential subtyping

Tagging objects can be costly, especially with no native support from JavaScript virtual machines. Prior work on RTTI-based gradual typing suggests tagging every object, as soon as it is allocated (cf. Siek and Vitousek 2013 and Swamy et al. 2014). Following their approach, our initial implementation of Safe TypeScript ensured that every object carries a tag. We defer a detailed quantitative comparison until §5.1 but, in summary, this variant can be 3 times slower than the technique we describe below.

Underlying our efficient tagging scheme is a new form of coercive subtyping, called differential subtyping. The main intuitions are as follows: (1) tagging is unnecessary for an object as long as it is used in compliance with the static type discipline; and (2) even if an object is used dynamically, its RTTI need not record a full description of the object's typing invariants: only those parts used outside of the static type discipline require tagging.

Armed with these intuitions, consider the program in Figure 3, which illustrates width subtyping. The triple of numbers p in toOrigin3d (a 3dPoint) is a subtype of the pair (a Point) expected by toOrigin, so the program is accepted and compiled to the code at the right of the figure. The only instrumentation occurs at the use of subtyping on the argument to toOrigin: using shallowTag, we tag p with RTTI that records just the z:number field—the RTTI need

```
function toOrigin(q:{x:number;y:number}) { q.x=0;q.y=0; }
function toOrigin3d(p:{x:number;y:number;z:number}) {
    toOrigin(p); p.z=0; }
toOrigin3d({x:17, y:0, z:42});
```

```
function toOrigin(q) { q.x=0; q.y=0; }
function toOrigin3d(p) {
    toOrigin(RT.shallowTag(p, {"z":RT.num})); p.z=0; }
toOrigin3d({x:17, y:0, z:42});
```

Figure 3: Width-subtyping in a source TypeScript program (left) and after compilation to JavaScript (right)

not mention x or y, since the static type of toOrigin's parameter guarantees that it will respect the type invariants of those fields. Of course, neglecting to tag the object with z:number would open the door to dynamic type safety violations, as in the previous section.

***Differential width-subtyping.*** To decide what needs to be tagged on each use of subtyping, we define a three-place subtyping relation $t_1 <: t_2 \rightsquigarrow \delta$, which states that the type $t_1$ is more precise than $t_2$, and that $\delta$ is (to a first approximation) the difference in precision between $t_1$ and $t_2$. We let $\delta$ range over types, or $\emptyset$ when there is no loss in precision. We speak of $t_1$ as a $\delta$-subtype of $t_2$. For width-subtyping on records, the relation includes the 'splitting' rule $\{\overline{x:t}; \overline{y:t'}\} <: \{\overline{x:t}\} \rightsquigarrow \{\overline{y:t'}\}$, since the loss between the two record types is precisely the omitted fields $\overline{y:t'}$. On the other hand, for a record type $t$, we have $t <: \mathsf{any} \rightsquigarrow t$, since in this case the loss is total. At each use of subtyping, the Safe TypeScript compiler computes $\delta$, and tags objects with RTTI that record just $\delta$, rather than the full type $t_1$.

***Taking advantage of primitive RTTI.*** Our definition of differential subtyping is tailored specifically to the RTTI available in Safe TypeScript and, more generally, in JavaScript—on other platforms, the relation would likely be different. For primitive types such as numbers, for instance, the JavaScript runtime already provides primitive RTTI (typeof n evaluates to "number" for any number n) so there is no need for additional tagging. Thus, although number is more precise than any, we let $\mathsf{number} <: \mathsf{any} \rightsquigarrow \emptyset$.

Similarly, for prototype-based objects, JavaScript provides an instanceof operator to test whether an object is an instance of a class (cf. §2.1); also a form of primitive RTTI. Hence, for a class-based object type $C$, we have $C <: \mathsf{any} \rightsquigarrow \emptyset$, meaning that Safe TypeScript does not tag when subtyping is used on a class-based object type. As such, our subtyping relation computes the loss between two types that may not already be captured by RTTI, hence subtyping is non-coercive on types with primitive RTTI.

***Controlling differences to preserve object identity.*** Besides performance, differential subtyping helps us ensure that our instrumentation does not alter the semantics of TypeScript. Consider subtyping for function types. One might expect a value f:(x:Point)⇒3dPoint to be usable at type (x:3dPoint)⇒Point via a standard lifting of the width-subtyping relation to function types. Given that differential subtyping is coercive (tags must be added), the only way to lift the tagging coercions to functions is by inserting a wrapper. For example, we might coerce f to the function g below, which tags the z field of the argument and then tags that field again on the result.

```
function g(y) {
  var t = {"z":RT.Num};
  return shallowTag(f(shallowTag(y, t)),t); }
```

Unfortunately, for a language like TypeScript in which object identity is observable (functions are a special case of objects), coercive wrappers like the one above are inadmissible—the function g is not identical to f, the function it wraps. Our solution is to require that higher order subtyping only use *$\emptyset$-subtypes* for relating function arguments, i.e., only non-coercive subtyping is fully structural. Thus, we exclude (x:Point)⇒3dPoint $<:$ (x:3dPoint)⇒Point from the subtyping relation. Conversely, given $t = (x{:}t_1) \Rightarrow t_2$ and $t' = (x{:}t_1') \Rightarrow t_2'$, we have $t <: t' \rightsquigarrow t$, when $t_1' <: t_1 \rightsquigarrow \emptyset$ and $t_2 <: t_2' \rightsquigarrow \emptyset$, since the $\emptyset$-difference ensures that no identity-breaking wrappers need to be inserted. Subtyping on functions is still coercive, however. In the relation above, notice that the difference is computed to be $t$, the type of the left-hand side. Thus, we coerce f : $t$ to $t'$ using shallowTag(f,$t$), which sets $t$ in the rtti field of the function object f, thereby capturing the precise type of f in its RTTI.

### 2.4 A modality for type erasure

Selective tagging and differential subtyping enable objects with partial RTTI. Going further, it is useful to ensure that some objects *never* carry RTTI, both for performance and for modularity. To this end, Safe TypeScript introduces a new modality on types to account for RTTI-free objects.

***User-controlled erasure.*** Consider a program that calls toOrigin3d on a large array of 3dPoints: the use of width-subtyping in the body of toOrigin3d causes every object in the array to get tagged with RTTI recording a z number field. This is wasteful, inasmuch as the usage of each 3dPoint is type-safe without any instrumentation. To avoid unnecessary tagging, the programmer may write instead:

```
function toOrigin(q:•Point) { q.x=0;q.y=0; }
```

The type •Point is the type of *erased* Points, i.e., objects that have number-typed fields x and y, but potentially no RTTI.[1] Subtyping towards erased types is non-coercive; i.e., 3dPoint<:•Point⇝ $\emptyset$. So, along one dimension, erased types provide greater flexibility, since they enable more subtyping at higher-order. However, without RTTI, the runtime system cannot enforce the typing invariants of $\bullet t$ values; so, along another dimension, erased types are more restrictive, since they exclude dynamic programming idioms (like field extension, reflection, or deletion) on values with erased types. In particular, $\bullet t$ is not a subtype of any. Balancing these tradeoffs requires some careful thinking from the programmer, but it can boost performance and does not compromise safety.

***Information hiding with erased types.*** Since values of erased types respect a static type discipline, programmers can use erasure to enforce deeper invariants through information hiding. JavaScript provides just a single mechanism for information hiding: closures. Through the use of erased types, Safe TypeScript provides another, more idiomatic, form of hiding, illustrated below. Consider a monotonic counter object with a private v field hidden from its clients, and a public inc method for incrementing the counter.

```
var ctr: •{inc():number} = {v:0, inc(){ return ++this.v;} };
```

By introducing the newly allocated object ctr at an erased type, its client code is checked (statically and dynamically) to ensure conformance with its published API: only inc is accessible, not v. Without the erasure modality, clients could mutate the v field using statements like ctr["v"] = −17. We show an encoding of abstract types using erased types in §3.4 (Theorem 2).

***Erasure, modularity, and trust.*** TypeScript programs rarely run in isolation; their environment includes APIs provided by primitive JavaScript arrays and strings, the web browser's document object model (DOM), JQuery, the file system for server-side JavaScript, etc. The default library used for typing TypeScript programs includes about 14,000 lines of specifications providing types to these

[1] §4 discusses how we fit erased types into TypeScript without any modifications to its concrete syntax; until then, we use the • to mark erased types.

external libraries, and even more comprehensive TypeScript library specifications are available online.[2] Recompiling all these libraries with Safe TypeScript is not feasible; besides, sometimes these libraries are not even authored in JavaScript. Nevertheless, being able to use these libraries according to their trusted specifications from within Safe TypeScript is crucial in practice.

The erasure modality can help: we mark such external libraries as providing objects with erased type, for two purposes: (1) since these external objects carry no RTTI, this ensures that their use within Safe TypeScript is statically checked for compliance with their specification; (2) the erased types ensure that their objects are never tagged—adding new fields to objects owned by external libraries is liable to cause those libraries to break.

As such, the type safety for typical Safe TypeScript programs is guaranteed only modulo the compliance of external libraries to their specifications. In scenarios where trust in external code poses an unacceptable risk, or when parts of the program need to carefully utilize features of JavaScript like eval that are outside our type-safe language, one might instead resort to the type-based isolation mechanism of TS$^\star$ (Swamy et al. 2014). Specifically, TS$^\star$ proposes the use of an abstract type Un to encapsulate untyped adversarial code and a family of type-directed coercions to safely manipulate Un-values. This mechanism is complementary to what Safe TypeScript offers. In fact, as discussed in §3.4, Safe TypeScript's erased types generalize their Un type. In particular, from Theorem 2, we have that the type $\bullet\{\}$ is the Safe TypeScript analog of Un.

***Gradually evolving Safe TypeScript using erased types.*** Over the course of last year, as we were developing Safe TypeScript, TypeScript added several advanced features to its type system, notably generic types. Keeping pace with TypeScript is a challenge made easier through the use of erased types. Recall that values of erased types must be programmed with statically, since erased types are invisible to the runtime system. Adding TypeScript's generic class types to Safe TypeScript requires significant changes to the interplay between the Safe TypeScript compiler and its runtime. One way to minimize this upheaval is to add generic types to Safe TypeScript in two steps, first to the static type system only, where generics are well understood, and only thereafter to the runtime system, if needed. §4 explains how we completed the first step by treating all generic types as erased. This allows Safe TypeScript programmers to use generic types statically, promoting code reuse and reducing the need for (potentially expensive) subtyping. By restricting the interaction between generic types and any, the system remains simple and sound. So far, preventing the use of polymorphic values in dynamically typed code has not been a significant limitation.

## 3. SafeTS: the formal core of Safe TypeScript

SafeTS models a sizeable fragment of Safe TypeScript including erased types, primitive types, structural objects, and nominal classes and interfaces. In this section we define the SafeTS syntax, type system, and dynamic semantics. We model compilation as a translation from SafeTS to itself that inserts dynamic type checks. Due to space constraints, we cover only the subset of SafeTS without classes and interfaces; full details can be found in the technical report (Rastogi et al. 2014). The following section (§4) outlines the parts of SafeTS omitted here, and informally explains how our implementation extends SafeTS to all of Safe TypeScript.

Our main results are expressed as a weak forward-simulation (meaning that runtime checks do not alter the behavior of well-typed programs, except when a dynamic type safety violation is detected) and an information-hiding theorem (letting programmers build robust abstractions despite JavaScript's dynamic features).

[2] https://github.com/borisyankov/DefinitelyTyped

$$
\begin{array}{rlcl}
\text{Type} & \tau & ::= & t \mid \bullet\, t \\
\text{Dynamic type} & t & ::= & c \mid \mathsf{any} \mid \{M;F\} \mid \ldots \\
\text{Primitive} & c & ::= & \mathsf{void} \mid \mathsf{number} \mid \mathsf{string} \mid \mathsf{boolean} \\
\text{Method types} & M & ::= & \cdot \mid m(\overline{\tau_i}) : \tau \mid M_1; M_2 \\
\text{Field types} & F & ::= & \cdot \mid f{:}\tau \mid F_1; F_2 \\
\text{Expression} & e & ::= & v \mid \{\tilde{M}, \tilde{F}\} \mid e.f \mid e[e'] \\
 & & \mid & e.m(\overline{e_i}) \mid e[e'](\overline{e_i}) \mid \langle t\rangle e \mid \mathit{RT}(\overline{e \mid \tau}) \\
\text{Value} & v & ::= & \ell \mid x \mid \mathsf{c}_t \\
\text{Method defns.} & \tilde{M} & ::= & \cdot \mid m(\overline{x_i{:}\tau_i}) : \tau\ \{s; \mathsf{return}\ e\} \mid \tilde{M}_1, \tilde{M}_2 \\
\text{Field defns.} & \tilde{F} & ::= & \cdot \mid f :_\tau e \mid \tilde{F}_1, \tilde{F}_2 \\
\text{Statement} & s & ::= & e \mid \mathsf{skip} \mid s_1; s_2 \mid \mathsf{var}\ x{:}\tau = e \\
 & & \mid & x = e \mid e.f = e' \mid e[e'] = e''
\end{array}
$$

### 3.1 Syntax

The syntax for SafeTS is given above. We stratify types into those that may be used dynamically and those that may be erased. Dynamic types $t$ include primitive types $c$, any, and structural object types $\{M;F\}$ where $F$ is a sequence of field names $f$ and their types $\tau$ and $M$ is a sequence of method names $m$ and their method types[3] written $(\overline{\tau_i}) : \tau$. As expected in TypeScript, methods also take an implicit this argument with the type of the enclosing object.

Like JavaScript, SafeTS separates expressions from statements. Expressions include values $v$, literals, static and dynamic field projections, static and dynamic method calls, and type casts. The form $\mathit{RT}(\overline{e \mid \tau})$ranges over the runtime functions (with several expression or type arguments) used to instrument compiled programs, modeled as primitives in SafeTS. As such, the *RT* form is excluded from source programs.

Values include memory locations $\ell$, variables $x$ (including the distinguished variable this), and literals, ranged over by the metavariable $\mathsf{c}_t$. To reflect their primitive RTTI provided by JavaScript (and returned by typeof), we may subscript literals with their type, writing, e.g., $\mathsf{undefined}_{\mathsf{void}}$. Object literals are sequences of explicitly typed method and field definitions. (In our implementation, those types are first inferred by the TypeScript compiler, as shown in Figure 1.) Method definitions are written $m(\overline{x_i{:}\tau_i}) : \tau\ \{s; \mathsf{return}\ e\}$. For simplicity, method bodies consist of a statement $s$ and a return expression $e$; void-returning methods return undefined. Field definitions are written $f :_\tau e$ where $\tau$ is the type inferred by TypeScript and is not concrete syntax.

Statements include expressions, skip, sequences, typed variable definitions, variable assignments, and static & dynamic field assignments. Conditional statements and loops are trivial, so we relegate them to the full technical report.

Like TypeScript, SafeTS models functions as objects with a single method named call. Thus, functions in concrete syntax function $(\overline{x_i : t_i}){:}t\ \{s;\ \mathsf{return}\ e\}$ become $\{\mathsf{call}(\overline{x_i : t_i}){:}t\ \{s;\ \mathsf{return}\ e\}\}$ and function calls $e(\overline{e_i})$ become $e.\mathsf{call}(\overline{e_i})$.

### 3.2 Static semantics

Figure 4 presents a core of the static semantics of SafeTS. The main judgments involve the typing and compilation for expressions $\Gamma \vdash e : \tau \hookrightarrow e'$ and for statements $\Gamma \vdash s \hookrightarrow s'$ where the source and target terms are both included in SafeTS. (The embedding of compiled SafeTS to a formal semantics of JavaScript is beyond the scope of this work.)

The type system of SafeTS has two fragments: a fairly standard static type discipline that applies to most terms, and a more permissive discipline that applies to the more dynamic terms, such as dynamic field projection. Figure 4 gives the most interesting rules

[3] Although TypeScript provides different notation for methods and fields, it makes no semantic distinction between the two. In concrete syntax, the formal parameters in a method type must be named, although arguments are still resolved by position.

$$\boxed{\tau <: \tau' \rightsquigarrow \delta, \qquad \Gamma \vdash e : \tau \hookrightarrow e', \qquad \Gamma \vdash \tilde{M} \hookrightarrow \tilde{M}', \qquad \Gamma \vdash \tilde{F} \hookrightarrow \tilde{F}', \qquad \Gamma \vdash s \hookrightarrow s'}$$

$$\textsc{S-Refl}\ \frac{}{\tau <: \tau} \qquad \textsc{S-Void}\ \frac{}{\mathsf{void} <: \tau} \qquad \textsc{S-PAny}\ \frac{}{c <: \mathsf{any}} \qquad \textsc{S-RAny}\ \frac{}{\{M;F\} <: \mathsf{any} \rightsquigarrow \{M;F\}}$$

$$\textsc{S-Rec}\ \frac{\{M;F\} \neq \{M';F'\} \qquad F' \subseteq F \qquad \forall m(\overline{\tau_i'}) : \tau' \in M'.\exists m(\overline{\tau_i}) : \tau \in M.\tau <: \tau' \wedge \forall i.\tau_i' <: \tau_i}{\{M;F\} <: \{M';F'\} \rightsquigarrow \{M \setminus M'; F \setminus F'\}} \qquad \textsc{S-Erased}\ \frac{t <: t' \rightsquigarrow \delta}{[\bullet]t <: \bullet t'}$$

$$\frac{x : \tau \in \Gamma}{\Gamma \vdash x : \tau \hookrightarrow x}\ \textsc{T-Env} \qquad \frac{\tau = sig(\{\tilde{M},\tilde{F}\}) \qquad \Gamma, \mathsf{this}{:}\tau \vdash \tilde{M} \hookrightarrow \tilde{M}' \qquad \Gamma \vdash \tilde{F} \hookrightarrow \tilde{F}'}{\Gamma \vdash \{\tilde{M},\tilde{F}\} : \tau \hookrightarrow \{\tilde{M}',\tilde{F}'\}}\ \textsc{T-Rec} \qquad \frac{\Gamma \vdash e : \tau' \hookrightarrow e' \qquad \tau' <: \tau \rightsquigarrow \delta}{\Gamma \vdash f :_\tau e \hookrightarrow f :_\tau \mathsf{shallowTag}(e', \delta)}\ \textsc{T-Fd}$$

$$\frac{\Gamma' = \Gamma, \overline{x_i{:}\tau_i}, \mathsf{locals}(s) \qquad \Gamma' \vdash s \hookrightarrow s' \qquad \Gamma' \vdash e : \tau' \hookrightarrow e' \qquad \tau' <: \tau \rightsquigarrow \delta}{\Gamma \vdash m(\overline{x_i{:}\tau_i}) : \tau\ \{s; \mathsf{return}\ e\} \hookrightarrow m(\overline{x_i{:}\tau_i}) : \tau\ \{s'; \mathsf{return\ shallowTag}(e', \delta)\}}\ \textsc{T-Md} \qquad \frac{\Gamma \vdash e : \tau' \hookrightarrow e' \qquad f{:}\tau \in \mathsf{fields}(\tau')}{\Gamma \vdash e.f : \tau \hookrightarrow e'.f}\ \textsc{T-Rd}$$

$$\textsc{T-Call}\ \frac{\Gamma \vdash e : \tau \hookrightarrow e' \qquad m(\overline{\tau_i}) : \tau_r \in \mathsf{methods}(\tau) \qquad \forall i.\Gamma \vdash e_i : \tau_i' \hookrightarrow e_i' \qquad \forall i.\tau_i' <: \tau_i \rightsquigarrow \delta_i}{\Gamma \vdash e.m(\overline{e_i}) : \tau_r \hookrightarrow e'.m(\mathsf{shallowTag}(\overline{e_i'}, \overline{\delta_i}))} \qquad \textsc{T-Wrx}\ \frac{\Gamma \vdash e : \tau' \hookrightarrow e' \qquad \tau' <: \Gamma(x) \rightsquigarrow \delta}{\Gamma \vdash x = e \hookrightarrow x = \mathsf{shallowTag}(e', \delta)}$$

$$\frac{\Gamma \vdash e_1 : \tau_1 \hookrightarrow e_1' \qquad f{:}\tau \in \mathsf{fields}(\tau_1) \qquad \Gamma \vdash e_2 : \tau_2 \hookrightarrow e_2' \qquad \tau_2 <: \tau \rightsquigarrow \delta}{\Gamma \vdash e_1.f = e_2 \hookrightarrow e_1'.f = \mathsf{shallowTag}(e_2', \delta)}\ \textsc{T-Wr} \qquad \frac{\forall j \in \{1,2,3\}.\Gamma \vdash e_j : t_j \hookrightarrow e_j'}{\Gamma \vdash e_1[e_2] = e_3 \hookrightarrow \mathsf{write}(e_1', t_1, e_2', e_3', t_3)}\ \textsc{T-DWr}$$

$$\textsc{T-DRd}\ \frac{\forall j \in \{1,2\}.\Gamma \vdash e_j : t_j \hookrightarrow e_j'}{\Gamma \vdash e_1[e_2] : \mathsf{any} \hookrightarrow \mathsf{read}(e_1', t_1, e_2')} \qquad \textsc{T-DCall}\ \frac{\forall j \in \{1,2,i\}.\Gamma \vdash e_j : t_j \hookrightarrow e_j'}{\Gamma \vdash e_1[e_2](\overline{e_i}) : \mathsf{any} \hookrightarrow \mathsf{invoke}(e_1', t_1, e_2', \overline{e_i'}, \overline{t_i})} \qquad \frac{\Gamma \vdash e : t' \hookrightarrow e'}{\Gamma \vdash \langle t \rangle e : t \hookrightarrow \mathsf{checkAndTag}(e', t', t)}\ \textsc{T-C}$$

Figure 4: Typing and compiling a core of SafeTS, where $\delta ::= t \mid \emptyset$ and $\Gamma ::= \cdot \mid x{:}\tau \mid \Gamma, \Gamma'$ and $\tau <: \tau' \triangleq \tau <: \tau' \rightsquigarrow \emptyset$

from both fragments; we discuss them in turn. (Due to space constraints, we omit routine rules, such as those for typing literals.)

***Differential subtyping*** is a ternary relation $\tau_1 <: \tau_2 \rightsquigarrow \delta$. As a shorthand, we write $\tau_1 <: \tau_2$ when $\delta = \emptyset$. Subtyping is reflexive (S-REFL) and is provably transitive. Via S-VOID, the undefined value inhabits all types—in a stricter setting, one may choose to omit this rule. The rules S-PANY, S-RANY and S-REC enforce any as a supertype for all primitive and object types, as well as subtyping on object types, as discussed in §2.3. Rule S-ERASED stands for two rules: both $t$ and $\bullet t$ are subtypes of $\bullet t'$, so long as $t$ is a subtype of $t'$. Although there is a loss of precision ($\delta$) when using this rule, uses of $\bullet t'$-terms have to be typed statically, so there is no need to add RTTI—hence the $\emptyset$-difference in the conclusion.

As we will see shortly, the use of subtyping when typing expressions and statements is carefully controlled—each use of subtyping may introduce a loss in precision which gets reflected into the RTTI of the compiled term by shallowTag(e, $\delta$). Although not shown in the rules, when $\delta = \emptyset$ the call to shallowTag is optimized away.

***Variables*** are typed and compiled to themselves using T-ENV.

***Objects*** are typed using T-REC, by typing their method and field definitions in turn. The auxiliary function $sig(\{\tilde{M},\tilde{F}\})$ computes the type of the object itself for the this reference (discussed further in the next paragraph). Fields are typed using T-FD: the initializer must be a subtype of the field type. The loss in precision $\delta$ due to the use of subtyping is reflected into the RTTI of $e'$ using shallowTag. Methods are typed using T-MD. In the first premise, we extend $\Gamma$ to contain not only the parameter bindings, but also bindings for local variables of the method body, denoted by locals($s$). This models JavaScript's hoisting of local variables in method bodies. The rule then types $s$ and the return expression $e$. The use of subtyping for the result is manifested in the compiled code by a call to shallowTag.

***Restricting the use of* this:** Foreshadowing the dynamic semantics, in a normal method call $v.m()$, the body of m executes with the implicit parameter this bound to $v$. For a function call $g()$, however, JavaScript's semantics for resolving the this-parameter is much more subtle—broadly speaking, the body of $g$ executes with this bound to a global object. As such, relying on any properties of this in $g$ is unsafe. We preclude the use of this in a non-method function $g = \mathsf{call}(\overline{x_i{:}\tau_i}){:}\tau\ \{\ s;\mathsf{return}\ e\ \}$ by typing it using this : $\bullet\{\}$, the type of an abstract reference to an object (see Theorem 2). Specifically, we define $sig(g) = \bullet\{\}$, whereas for all other objects $sig(\{\tilde{M},\tilde{F}\}) = \{M;F\}$, the point-wise erasure of method- and field-definitions to their types.

***Field projections, method calls, local variable assignments, and field assignments*** are statically typed by T-RD, T-CALL, T-WRX, and T-WR, respectively. These rules are routine apart from their use of shallowTag at each use of subtyping.

***The dynamic fragment*** of SafeTS includes the rules T-DWR, T-DRD, T-DCALL and T-C. In each case, we restrict the types of each sub-term involved to dynamic types $t$—erased types $\bullet t$ must respect the static discipline. When compiling the term, we generate a runtime check that mediates the dynamic operation in question, passing to the check the sub-terms and (some of) their static types as RTTI. In the next subsection, we discuss how each check makes use of RTTI to ensure dynamic type safety.

### 3.3 Dynamic semantics

Figure 5 presents selected rules from our small-step operational semantics, of the form $\mathbb{C} \longrightarrow \mathbb{C}'$ where each runtime configuration $\mathbb{C}$ is a pair of a state $\mathcal{C}$ and a program statement $s$. Our semantics models the execution of SafeTS programs both before and after compilation—the former is intended as a model of the dynamic semantics of a core of TypeScript, while the latter is a model of Safe TypeScript.

A state $\mathcal{C}$ is a quadruple $H; T; X; L$ consisting of a heap $H$ mapping locations $\ell$ to mutable objects $O$ and values $v$; a tag heap $T$ mapping *some* of these locations to RTTI $t$ (when executing source programs, the tag heap is always empty); a call stack $X$

where each element consists of a local store $L$ and an evaluation context $E$; and a local store $L$ mapping variables $x$ to locations $\ell$ for the current statement. We use the notation $\mathcal{C}.H$ for the heap component of $\mathcal{C}$, $\mathcal{C} \triangleleft H$ for $\mathcal{C}$ with updated heap $H$, and use similar notations for the other components and also for $\mathbb{C}$.

Our runtime representation of objects includes a prototype field, a sequence of method definitions sharing a captured closure environment $L$, and a sequence of field definitions. For simplicity, we treat return e as a statement, although it can only occur at the end of a method body. Finally, we define evaluation contexts, $E$, as follows for both statements and expressions, embodying a strict left-to-right evaluation order.

$$\begin{array}{lcl} E & ::= & \langle\rangle \mid E.f \mid E[e] \mid v[E] \mid RT(\overline{v|t}, E, \overline{e|t}) \mid \ldots \\ & \mid & E; s \mid \mathsf{var}\ x : t = E \mid \mathsf{return}\ E \mid \ldots \end{array}$$

***Context rules.*** Figure 5 begins with E-DIE, where die is a distinguished literal that arises only from the failure of a runtime check; the failure bubbles up and terminates the execution. We omit the other, standard rules for evaluation contexts.

***Field projection and update.*** Static field projection $\ell.f$ (E-RD) involves a prototype traversal using the *lookup* function, whose definition we omit. Dynamic field reads split into two cases; we show only the former: when an object reference $\ell'$ is used as a key into the fields of $\ell$ (E-DRD), as in JavaScript, $\ell'$ is coerced to a string by calling toString; when the key is a literal and $H$ maps $\ell$ to an object, we return either its corresponding field, if any, or undefined. Dynamic field writes also have two cases; we show only the latter (E-DWR): we expect $\mathcal{C}.H(\ell)$ to contain an object, and we update its field $f_c$ with $v$. (We write $f_c$ for JavaScript's primitive coercion of a literal c to a field name.)

***The calling convention and closures.*** E-DCALL shows a dynamic call of the method c in object $\ell$. In the first premise, we use the auxiliary function *lookup_m_this* to traverse the prototype chain to find the method $m$ and to implement JavaScript's semantics for resolving the implicit this argument to $\ell'$. Usually $\ell = \ell'$, except when $m$ = call (i.e., a bare function call), when $\ell'$ defaults to a global object—this is safe since the type system ensures that functions do not use this in their bodies. Next, we gather all the local variables $\overline{y_j}$ from the method body s, and allocate slots for them and the function parameters in the heap. Locals and parameters are mutable (as shown in the next rule, E-WRX) and are shared across all closures that capture them, so we use one indirection and promote their contents to the heap. In the conclusion of E-DCALL, we push one stack frame, set the current local store to the captured closure environment (extended with the locals and parameters) and proceed to the method body. Dually, E-RET pops the stack and returns the value $v$ to the suspended caller's context. Rule E-OBJ allocates objects: a fresh location in the heap is initialized with an object O whose prototype is set to a distinguished location $\hat{\ell}$, representing, concretely, Object.prototype in JavaScript. Initializing the methods involves capturing the current local store $\mathcal{C}.L$ as a closure environment. Initializing the fields is straightforward.

***Two sources of RTTI for enforcing dynamic type safety.*** The main novelty of our dynamic semantics is in the remaining six rules, which enforce SafeTS's notion of dynamic type safety using RTTI. RTTI in SafeTS comes in two forms—there is *persistent* RTTI, associated with objects in the tag heap or available primitively on literals; and *instantaneous* RTTI, provided by the compiler among the arguments to the *RT* functions. The most precise view of an object's invariants available to a runtime check is obtained by combining both forms of RTTI, using the auxiliary partial function *combine* (Figure 6). An invariant of our system ensures that it is always possible to combine the persistent and instantaneous RTTI consistently, e.g., it is impossible for the tag heap to claim that an object has a field $f$ : number while the instantaneous RTTI claims $f$ : any. Additionally, our invariants ensure that the method types in the persistent RTTI are never less precise than the instantaneous method types—recall that any loss in precision due to subtyping on methods is recorded in the RTTI using shallowTag.

***Reads and writes.*** E-READ mediates reading $f_c$ from an object reference $\ell{:}t$; similarly, E-WRITE mediates writing $v{:}t'$ to $f_c$ of $\ell{:}t$. In both cases, we combine any persistent RTTI stored at $T[\ell]$ (defined as $T(\ell)$ when $\ell \in dom(T)$ and $\{\cdot;\cdot\}$ otherwise) with $t$, the instantaneous RTTI of $\ell$ provided by the compiler, and then use the partial function *fieldType* to compute the type of $f_c$. If the field is present in the RTTI, we simply use its type $t_f$; unless the field name clashes with a known method name, the field type defaults to any; otherwise, *fieldType* is not defined, and both E-READ and E-WRITE are stuck—in this case, the configuration steps to die; we omit these routine rules. Given $t_f$, in E-READ, we project the field and then propagate $t_f$ into the persistent RTTI of the value that is read before returning it. In E-WRITE, before updating $f_c$, we check that $v{:}t'$ is compatible with the expected type $t_f$.

***Method and function invocations.*** E-INVM and E-INVF mediate these invocations. In E-INVM, the goal is to safely invoke method $f_c$ on $\ell{:}t$ with parameters $\overline{v_i{:}t_i}$. If we find the method in $\ell$'s combined RTTI, we invoke it after checking that the parameters have the expected types, and then propagate the result type into the RTTI of the result. In E-INVF, the goal is to call a function-typed field of $\ell{:}t$. The handling is similar, except that instead of looking up a method, we traverse the prototype chain, project the field, and inspect that field's RTTI for a call signature. If we find the signature, we call the function just as in E-INVM. In both rules, if the method or function is not found, the configuration steps to die.

***Propagating and checking tags.*** Finally we have two workhorses for the semantics: shallowTag (E-ST) and checkAndTag (E-CT). The semantics of the former is given by $[\![\mathsf{shallowTag}(v,\delta)]\!]_T$, an interpretation function on tag heaps. When $\delta = \emptyset$ or $v$ = c, there is no tag propagation and the function is the identity. On structural types, we use the *combine* function to update the tag heap—an invariant ensures that persistent RTTI evolves monotonically, i.e., it never gets less precise. Whereas shallowTag never fails, the interpretation $[\![\mathsf{checkAndTag}(v,t,t')]\!]_{T,H}$ is a partial function that either evaluates to a new tag heap or returns $\bot$. The interpretation is given by the function *ctaux*. The most interesting case involves checking whether $\ell$ can be given the type $\{M;F\}$. To do this, we consult $\{M';F'\}$, the combined view of $\ell$'s RTTI, and if $\{M';F'\} <: \{M;Fc\} \rightsquigarrow \delta$ where $Fc$ are the fields shared between $F$ and $F'$, we tag $\ell$ with the loss in precision (if any); we then recursively checkAndTag $\ell$'s fields for each of the fields in $F'$ not in $F$ ($F_{new}$); and, if that succeeds, we finally propagate $F_{new}$ to $\ell$'s RTTI. We prove that *ctaux* always terminates, even in the presence of cycles in the object graph.

### 3.4 Metatheory

Our main result is that compilation is a weak forward-simulation, which also implies subject reduction for well-typed programs. Our second theorem is an abstraction property for values of erased types, rewarding careful programmers with robust encapsulation. Our results apply to full SafeTS, including classes and nominal interfaces. In full SafeTS, runtime states $\mathcal{C}$ are *five*-tuples $S;H;T;X;L$ where the additional $S$ is a signature that contains all class and interface declarations. The runtime functions like checkAndTag are parameterized by $S$ as well, and use it to implement dynamic type safety for these constructs. Pragmatically, some runtime checks on classes can be more efficient, since they can be implemented primitively (e.g., using instanceof).

$$\text{E-DIE}\ \frac{\mathcal{C}; s \longrightarrow \mathcal{C}'; \mathsf{die}}{\mathcal{C}; E\langle s\rangle \longrightarrow \mathcal{C}'; \mathsf{die}} \qquad \frac{lookup_{\mathcal{C}.H}(\ell, f) = v}{\mathcal{C}; \ell.f \longrightarrow \mathcal{C}; v}\ \text{E-RD} \qquad \frac{}{\mathcal{C}; \ell[\ell'] \longrightarrow \mathcal{C}; \ell[\ell'.\mathsf{toString}()]}\ \text{E-DRD} \qquad \frac{H' = \mathcal{C}.H[\ell \mapsto \mathcal{C}.H(\ell)[f_{\mathsf{c}} \mapsto v]]}{\mathcal{C}; \ell[\mathsf{c}] = v \longrightarrow \mathcal{C} \triangleleft H'; v}\ \text{E-DWR}$$

$$\frac{lookup\_m\_this_H(\ell, f_c) = L'.m(\overline{x_i : \tau_i}) : \tau\{s\}, \ell' \quad \mathsf{locals}(s) = \overline{y_j} \quad \overline{\ell_j}, \overline{\ell_i}\ \text{fresh} \quad H' = H[\overline{\ell_i \mapsto v_i}, \overline{\ell_j \mapsto \mathsf{undefined}}]}{H; T; X; L; E\langle \ell[\mathsf{c}](\overline{v_i})\rangle \longrightarrow H'; T; (X; L.E); (L', \mathsf{this} \mapsto \ell', \overline{x_i \mapsto \ell_i}, \overline{y_j \mapsto \ell_j}); s}\ \text{E-DCALL}$$

$$\text{E-WRX}\ \frac{H' = \mathcal{C}.H[\mathcal{C}.L(x) \mapsto v]}{\mathcal{C}; x = v \longrightarrow \mathcal{C} \triangleleft H'; \mathsf{skip}} \qquad \text{E-RET}\ \frac{\mathcal{C}.X = X'; L.E}{\mathcal{C}; \mathsf{return}\ v \longrightarrow \mathcal{C} \triangleleft X'; L; E\langle v\rangle} \qquad \frac{\ell\ \text{fresh} \quad H' = \mathcal{C}.H[\ell \mapsto \{\mathtt{proto}{:}\hat{\ell},\ \mathtt{m}{:}\mathcal{C}.L.\tilde{M},\ \mathtt{f}{:}\overline{f_i = v_i}\}]}{\mathcal{C}; \{\tilde{M}; \overline{f_i = v_i}\} \longrightarrow \mathcal{C} \triangleleft H'; \ell}\ \text{E-OBJ}$$

$$\text{E-READ}\ \frac{t_f = fieldType(f_{\mathsf{c}}, combine(\mathcal{C}.T[\ell], t)) \quad t_f <: \mathsf{any} \rightsquigarrow \delta}{\mathcal{C}; \mathsf{read}(\ell, t, \mathsf{c}) \longrightarrow \mathcal{C}; \mathsf{shallowTag}(\ell[\mathsf{c}], \delta)} \qquad \frac{t_f = fieldType(f_{\mathsf{c}}, combine(\mathcal{C}.T[\ell], t))}{\mathcal{C}; \mathsf{write}(\ell, t, \mathsf{c}, v, t') \longrightarrow \mathcal{C}; \ell[\mathsf{c}] = \mathsf{checkAndTag}(v, t', t_f)}\ \text{E-WRITE}$$

$$\frac{f_{\mathsf{c}}(\overline{t_i'}) : t' \in \mathsf{methods}(combine(\mathcal{C}.T[\ell], t)) \quad t' <: \mathsf{any} \rightsquigarrow \delta}{\mathcal{C}; \mathsf{invoke}(\ell, t, \mathsf{c}, \overline{v_i}, \overline{t_i}) \longrightarrow \mathcal{C}; \mathsf{shallowTag}(\ell[\mathsf{c}](\overline{\mathsf{checkAndTag}(v_i, t_i, t_i')}), \delta)}\ \text{E-INVM} \qquad \frac{T' = [\![\mathsf{shallowTag}(v, \delta)]\!]_{\mathcal{C}.T}}{\mathcal{C}; \mathsf{shallowTag}(v, \delta) \longrightarrow \mathcal{C} \triangleleft T'; v}\ \text{E-ST}$$

$$\frac{lookup_{\mathcal{C}.H}(\ell, f_{\mathsf{c}}) = \ell' \quad \mathsf{call}(\overline{t_i'}) : t' \in \mathsf{methods}(\mathcal{C}.T[\ell']) \quad t' <: \mathsf{any} \rightsquigarrow \delta}{\mathcal{C}; \mathsf{invoke}(\ell, t, \mathsf{c}, \overline{v_i}, \overline{t_i}) \longrightarrow \mathcal{C}; \mathsf{shallowTag}(\ell[\mathsf{c}](\overline{\mathsf{checkAndTag}(v_i, t_i, t_i')}), \delta)}\ \text{E-INVF} \qquad \frac{T' = [\![\mathsf{checkAndTag}(v, t, t')]\!]_{\mathcal{C}.T, \mathcal{C}.H}}{\mathcal{C}; \mathsf{checkAndTag}(v, t, t') \longrightarrow \mathcal{C} \triangleleft T'; v}\ \text{E-CT}$$

Figure 5: Selected rules from SafeTS's dynamic semantics: $\mathcal{C}; s \longrightarrow \mathcal{C}'; s$

$$\begin{array}{lcl}
fieldType(f, t) & = & \text{if } f{:}t' \in \mathsf{fields}(t) \text{ then } t' \\
 & & \text{else if } f \notin \mathsf{methods}(t) \text{ then } \mathsf{any} \\
 & & \text{else } \bot \\
combine(t, t') & = & t \ \text{ if } t' = c \text{ or } t' = \mathsf{any} \\
combine(\{M; F\}, \{M'; F'\}) & = & \{M \cup \{m{:}\tau \in M' \mid m{:}_ \notin M\}; \\
 & & F \uplus F'\} \\
[\![\mathsf{shallowTag}(v, \emptyset)]\!]_T & = & T \\
[\![\mathsf{shallowTag}(\mathsf{c}, \delta)]\!]_T & = & T \\
[\![\mathsf{shallowTag}(\ell, \{M; F\})]\!]_T & = & T[\ell \mapsto combine(T[\ell], \{M; F\})] \\
[\![\mathsf{checkAndTag}(v, t, t')]\!]_{T,H} & = & ctaux(v, t, t', T, H)
\end{array}$$

$$\begin{array}{lcl}
ctaux(\mathsf{undefined}, t, t', T, H) & = & T \\
ctaux(\mathsf{c}_c, t, c, T, H) & = & T \\
ctaux(v, t, \mathsf{any}, T, H) & = & T \\
ctaux(v, t, \bullet t', T, H) & = & ctaux(v, t, t', T, H) \\
ctaux(\ell, t, \{M; F\}, T, H) & = & \\
\multicolumn{3}{l}{\quad \text{let } \{M'; F'\} = combine(T[l], t)} \\
\multicolumn{3}{l}{\quad \text{let } F_C = \{f{:}t \in F \mid f \in dom(F')\}, F_{new} = F \setminus F_C} \\
\multicolumn{3}{l}{\quad \text{check } (\{M'; F'\} <: \{M; F_C\} \rightsquigarrow \delta)} \\
\multicolumn{3}{l}{\quad \text{let } T_0 = [\![\mathsf{shallowTag}(\ell, \delta)]\!]_T \text{ and}} \\
\multicolumn{3}{l}{\quad \forall f_i{:}t_i \in F_{new}.T_i = ctaux(H[\ell][f_i], \mathsf{any}, t_i, T_{i-1}, H)} \\
\multicolumn{3}{l}{\quad [\![\mathsf{shallowTag}(\ell, \{\cdot; F_{new}\})]\!]_{T_n}} \\
ctaux(v, t, t', T, H) & = & \bot \text{ if none of the above}
\end{array}$$

Figure 6: Auxiliary functions used in dynamic semantics

***Compiling configurations.*** We extend the typing and compiling relation of Figure 4 to runtime configurations, writing $\mathbb{C} : \tau \hookrightarrow_\Sigma \mathbb{C}'$ where $\Sigma$ is a heap-typing and $\tau$ is the type of the result of the stack of evaluation contexts. The main technicality is in the compilation of statements that include free heap-locations. In particular, when compiling $\mathcal{C}; s$ to $\mathcal{C}'; s'$, we relate the statements using a generalization of statement typing of the form $S; \Sigma; \mathcal{C}'.T; \Gamma \vdash s \hookrightarrow s'$, where $\Gamma$ is derived from $\mathcal{C}.L$ and $\Sigma$. Intuitively, the heap typing $\Sigma$ records the static type of a location at the instant it was allocated, while $\mathcal{C}'.T$ records the dynamic RTTI of a location, which evolves according to Definition 1 below.

To translate heap locations, we introduce the following rule:

$$\frac{combine_S(T[\ell], \Sigma(\ell)) = combine_S(T[\ell], t)}{S; \Sigma; T; \Gamma \vdash \ell : t \hookrightarrow \ell}\ \text{T-LOC}$$

This rule captures the essence of differential subtyping. In traditional systems with subtyping, we would type a location $\ell$ using any super-type of $\Sigma(\ell)$. With differential subtyping, however, any loss in precision due to subtyping must be reflected in the RTTI of $\ell$, i.e., in $T[\ell]$. In T-LOC, we are trying to relate a source configuration $\mathcal{C}; \ell$ to a given target configuration $\mathcal{C}'; \ell$ (where $T = \mathcal{C}'.T$). So, we must pick a type $t$, such that the loss in precision in $t$ relative to $\Sigma(\ell)$ is already captured in the persistent RTTI at $T[\ell]$. In fact, $t$ may be more precise or even unrelated to $\Sigma(\ell)$, so long as, taken together with $T[\ell]$, there is no loss (or gain) in precision—the premise of T-LOC makes this intuition precise. Since *combine* is a partial function, the rule is applicable only when the persistent RTTI of $\ell$ is consistent with its static type.

The following relation constrains how tag heaps evolve. In particular, the information about a location $\ell$ never grows less precise. The auxiliary relation $\Sigma \sim T$ (in the full paper) states that $\Sigma(\ell)$ is consistent with $T(\ell)$ for each location $\ell$ in the domain of $T$, i.e., its static and dynamic types are never in contradiction.

**Definition 1 (Tag heap evolution).** *$\Sigma_1; T_1$ evolves to $\Sigma_2; T_2$, written $\Sigma_1; T_1 \triangleright \Sigma_2; T_2$, when $\Sigma_2 \supseteq \Sigma_1$; $\Sigma_1 \sim T_1$; $\Sigma_2 \sim T_2$; and, for all $\ell \in \mathsf{dom}(T_2)$, we have either (1) $\ell \notin \mathsf{dom}(T_1)$, or (2) $T_1(\ell) = T_2(\ell)$, or (3) $T_1(\ell) = \{M_1; F_1\}$ and $T_2(\ell) = \{M_2; F_2\}$ with $M_1 \subseteq M_2$ and $F_1 \subseteq F_2$.*

Intuitively, our main theorem states that, if a source configuration $\mathbb{C}$ is typed at $\tau$ and compiled to $\mathbb{C}_1$, then every step taken by $\mathbb{C}$ is matched by one or more steps by $\mathbb{C}_1$, unless $\mathbb{C}_1$ detects a violation of dynamic type safety.

**Theorem 1 (Forward Simulation).** *If we have* $\mathbb{C} : \tau \hookrightarrow_{\Sigma_1} \mathbb{C}_1$ *then either both* $\mathbb{C}$ *and* $\mathbb{C}_1$ *are terminal; or, for some* $\mathbb{C}'$ *and* $\mathbb{C}'_1$*, we have* $\mathbb{C} \longrightarrow \mathbb{C}'$, $\mathbb{C}_1 \longrightarrow^+ \mathbb{C}'_1$*, and either* $\mathbb{C}'_1.s = \mathsf{die}$ *or for some* $\Sigma'_1 \supseteq \Sigma_1$ *we have* $\mathbb{C}' : \tau \hookrightarrow_{\Sigma'_1} \mathbb{C}'_1$ *and* $\Sigma_1; \mathbb{C}_1.T \rhd \Sigma'_1; \mathbb{C}'_1.T$.

An immediate corollary of the theorem is the canonical forms property mentioned in §2. We can also read off the theorem a type safety property for target configurations, stated below, where $\Sigma \vdash \mathbb{C} : \tau$ abbreviates $\exists \mathbb{C}_0.\mathbb{C}_0 : \tau \hookrightarrow_\Sigma \mathbb{C}$.

**Corollary 1 (Type Safety).** *If* $\Sigma \vdash \mathbb{C} : \tau$ *then either* $\mathbb{C}$ *is terminal or for some* $\Sigma' \supseteq \Sigma$ *we have* $\mathbb{C} \longrightarrow^+ \mathbb{C}'$ *and* $\Sigma' \vdash \mathbb{C}' : \tau$.

***Information hiding.*** Our second theorem states that values with type $\bullet\{\}$ are immutable and perfectly secret in well-typed contexts. The theorem considers two well-typed configurations $\mathbb{C}_1$ and $\mathbb{C}_2$ that differ only in the contents of location $\ell{:}\bullet\{\}$ and shows that their reductions proceed in lock-step. It provides a baseline property on which to build more sophisticated, program-specific partial abstractions. For example, the monotonic counter from §2.4 chooses to allow the context to mutate it in a controlled manner and to reveal the result.

**Theorem 2 (Abstraction of $\bullet\{\}$).** *If* $\Sigma(l) = \bullet\{\}$ *and for* $i \in \{1,2\}$ *we have* $\Sigma \vdash \mathbb{C} \lhd H[\ell \mapsto O_i] : \tau$ *; then, for* $n \geq 0$,

$$\begin{array}{ll} \mathbb{C} \lhd H[\ell \mapsto O_1] \longrightarrow^n \mathbb{C}' \lhd H'[\ell \mapsto O_1] & \textit{if and only if} \\ \mathbb{C} \lhd H[\ell \mapsto O_2] \longrightarrow^n \mathbb{C}' \lhd H'[\ell \mapsto O_2]. & \end{array}$$

Theorem 2 also clarifies the similarity between type $\bullet\{\}$ and type Un from TS* (Swamy et al. 2014): both types are abstract to the context. However, erased types are more general. Type •f:number contains more information (it has a field f with type number), whereas Un is an abstract type with no more information.

# 4. Scaling to Safe TypeScript

TypeScript has a multitude of features for practical programming and we adapt them all soundly for use in Safe TypeScript. Of particular interest are the many forms of polymorphism: inheritance for classes and interfaces, ad hoc subtyping with recursive interfaces, prototype-based JavaScript primitive objects, implicit conversions, ad hoc overloading, and even parametric polymorphism. Space constraints prevent a detailed treatment of all these features: we select a few representatives and sketch how SafeTS can be extended gracefully to handle them.

By restricting more advanced typing features (e.g., parametric polymorphism) to erased types, we improve the expressiveness of the static fragment of the language, while ensuring that these features do not complicate the (delicate) runtime invariants of Safe TypeScript and its interface with the type-checker.

## 4.1 Encoding type qualifiers

Since TypeScript does not syntactically support type qualifiers, we used a simple (though limited) encoding for the erasure modality. For instance, we give below the concrete syntax for the function toOrigin with erased types presented in §2.4.

```
module STS { interface Erased {} . . . } //Safe TypeScript library
// client code
interface ErasedPoint extends Point, STS.Erased {}
function toOrigin(q:ErasedPoint) { q.x=0;q.y=0; }
function toOrigin3d(p:3dPoint) { toOrigin(p); p.z = 0; }
```

To mark a type $t$ as erased, we define a new interface $I$ that extends both $t$ and STS.Erased, a distinguished empty interface defined in the standard library. (We discuss inheritance of classes and interfaces in more detail, shortly.) In TypeScript, the type $I$ has all the fields of t, and no others, so $I$ is convertible to $t$. In Safe TypeScript, however, we interpret $I$ (and, transitively, any type that extends STS.Erased) as an erased type. We use similar encodings to mark types as being immutable or nominal. While these encodings fit smoothly within TypeScript, they have obvious limitations, e.g., only named types can be qualified.

## 4.2 Inheritance

***Class and interface extension.*** SafeTS provides a simple model of classes and interfaces—in particular, it has no support for inheritance. Adding inheritance is straightforward. As one would expect, since fields are mutable, classes and interfaces are not permitted to override inherited field types. Method overrides are permissible, as long as they respect the subtyping relation.[4] Specifically, when class $C_1$ extends $C_0$, we require that every overriding method $m$ in $C_1$ be a subtype of the method that it overrides in $C_0$ (which in-turn enforces method arguments and return types to be related by $\emptyset$-subtyping). We refer to this as the *override-check*; it is analogous to rule S-REC in §3.

***Implements clauses.*** Class inheritance in TypeScript is desugared directly to prototype-based inheritance in JavaScript. As an object may have only one prototype, multiple inheritance for classes is excluded. As in languages like Java or C#, a substitute for multiple inheritance is ad hoc subtyping, using classes that implement multiple interfaces. Unlike Java or C#, however, an instance of a class $C$ can implicitly be viewed as an instance of a structurally-compatible interface $I$, even when $C$ does not declare that it implements $I$. Nevertheless, in TypeScript, class declarations may be augmented with implements clauses mentioning one or more interfaces. For each such declaration, Safe TypeScript checks that the class provides every field and method declared in these interfaces, using the override-check above.

***Extending $\emptyset$-subtyping with nominal interfaces.*** $\emptyset$-subtyping on the arguments and results of methods in the override-check can sometimes be too restrictive. As explained in §2.4, using erased types may help: their subtyping is non-coercive, since they need not carry RTTI. Dually, subtyping towards class- or primitive-types is also non-coercive, since their values always carry RTTI. Safe TypeScript makes use of implements-clauses to also provide non-coercive subtyping towards certain interfaces. By default, interface types are structural, but some of them can be qualified as *nominal*. Nominal interfaces are inhabited only by instances of classes specifically declared to implement those interfaces (as would be expected in Java or C#). More importantly, nominal interfaces are inhabited only by class instances with primitive RTTI, thereby enabling non-coercive subtyping and making S-REC and the overrides-check more permissive.

***JavaScript's primitive object hierarchy.*** Aside from inheritance via classes and interfaces, we also capture the inheritance provided natively in JavaScript. Every object type (a subtype of $\{\}$) extends the nominal interface Object, the base of the JavaScript prototype chain that provides various methods (toString, hasOwnProperty, ...). Likewise, every function (an object with a call method in Safe TypeScript) extends the nominal interface Function. For instance, our subtyping relation includes $t <: \bullet\{\mathsf{toString}() : \mathsf{string}\} \rightsquigarrow \emptyset$.

***Arbitrary prototype chains.*** Finally, we discuss a feature excluded from Safe TypeScript: programmers cannot build arbitrary prototype chains using JavaScript's __proto__ property, or using arbitrary functions as object constructors. The former (forbidden in the JavaScript standard, but implemented by several VMs) is prevented by treating __proto__ as a reserved property and forbidding its access both statically (where detectable) and at runtime. The latter is pre-

[4] TypeScript, more liberally, permits inheritance that overrides both fields and methods using an unsound *assignability* relation (Bierman et al. 2014).

vented by requiring that new be called only on objects with a constructor signature, only present on class types.

### 4.3 Generic interfaces, functions, and classes

The code below illustrates several valid uses of generic types in Safe TypeScript.

```
1  interface Pair⟨A,B⟩ { fst: A; snd: B }
2  function pair⟨A,B⟩(a:A,b:B): Pair⟨A,B⟩ {return { fst: a, snd: b }; }
3  declare var Array:{ new⟨A⟩(len:number):Array⟨A⟩; . . . }
4  interface Array⟨T⟩ {
5    push(...items:T []) : number; . . .
6    [key:number] : T }
7  class Map⟨A,B⟩ {
8    private map: Array⟨Pair⟨A, B⟩⟩;
9    constructor() { this.map = new Array(10); }
10   public insert(k:A,v:B) { this.map.push(pair(k,v)); } }
```

We have a declaration of a generic interface for pairs (line 1) and a generic function for constructing pairs (line 2), showing how types can be abstracted. Line 3 declares an external symbol Array (provided by the JavaScript runtime) at an implicitly erased type that includes a generic constructor—types can be abstracted at method signatures too. The constructor in Array builds a value of type Array⟨A⟩, an interface (partially defined at lines 4–6) that provides a push function, which receives a variable number of T-typed arguments, adds them all to the end of the array, and returns the new length of the array. The type Array⟨T⟩ also contains an *index signature* (line 6), which states that each Array⟨T⟩ is a map from number-typed keys to T-typed values, indicating that an array as:Array⟨T⟩ can be subscripted using a[i], for i:number. Finally, line 7 defines a generic class Map⟨A,B⟩.

***Typing generics.*** Except for erasure (explained next), our static treatment of generic types is fairly straightforward: we extend the context with type variables, and allow type abstraction at interfaces, classes, and method/function boundaries. To enable instantiations of type variables at arbitrary types, including erased types, their subtyping only includes reflexivity (since erased types may not even be subtypes of any). We also support bounded quantification to extend subtyping for type variables. Type instantiations are inferred by TypeScript's inference algorithm, e.g., at line 9, TypeScript infers Pair⟨A,B⟩ for the arguments of new Array and, at line 10, Pair ⟨A,B⟩ and A, B for the arguments of push and pair, respectively.

***Erasing generic types.*** To keep the interface between our compiler and runtime system simple, we erase all generic types, and we forbid subtyping from generic types to any. Take the pair function or the Array value, for example. Were we to allow it to be used at type any, several tricky issues arise. For instance, how to compute type instantiations when these values are used at type any? Conversely, should any be coercible to the type of pair? Ahmed et al. (2011) propose a solution based on dynamic seals, but it is not suitable here since dynamic seals would break object identity. Erasing generics types and forbidding their use in dynamically typed contexts sidesteps these issues. On the other hand, instances of generic interfaces need not always be erased. For example, Pair⟨number, string⟩ is a subtype of {fst:number; snd:string}, and vice versa. The latter type can be viewed structurally, and safely handled at type any, with the difference computed as usual. Thus, the erasure modality safely allows us to extend SafeTS with generics.

### 4.4 Arrays

TypeScript types arrays using the generic Array⟨T⟩ interface outlined in §4.3. Given their pervasive use, Safe TypeScript extends SafeTS with array types, written t[]. Arrays in JavaScript are instances of a primitive object called Array. However, all instances of arrays, regardless of their generic instantiation, share the same prototype Array.prototype. Thus, in contrast with Object and Function, we do not treat Array as a nominal interface type. Instead, we have $t[] <: \mathsf{any} \rightsquigarrow t[]$, meaning that array instances are tagged with RTTI as required by subtyping.

Further complications arise from subtyping. In TypeScript, array subtyping is both covariant (as in Java and C#) and contravariant, allowing for instance $\mathsf{number}[] <: \mathsf{any}[] <: \mathsf{string}[]$. More conservatively, Safe TypeScript supports sound covariant subtyping for immutable arrays, based on a type CheckedArray in the standard library and a type qualifier for tracking immutability. Specifically, we have $t[] <: \mathsf{CheckedArray}\langle s\rangle \rightsquigarrow t[]$ as long as $t <: s \rightsquigarrow \emptyset$. The type CheckedArray includes only a subset of the methods of Array, for instance keeping map but excluding push. Additionally, the compiler inserts checks to prevent assignments on instances of CheckedArray. Finally, the runtime provides a function mutateArray ⟨S,T⟩(a:CheckedArray⟨S⟩): T[], which allows an immutable array a to be coerced back to an array with a different element type, after checking the RTTI of a for safety.

## 5. Experimental evaluation

We summarize below the experiments we conducted to measure the performance implications of our design choices, and to gain insight into how Safe TypeScript fares when used in practice.

*1.* We compared differential subtyping to a variant of Safe TypeScript that tags objects with RTTI as they are created. We find that RTTI-on-creation incurs a slow down by a factor of 1.4–3x.

*2.* We compared two implementation strategies for the tag heap: one using JavaScript's weak maps to maintain a global RTTI table "off to the side"; the other uses an additional field in tagged objects. We find the latter to be faster by a factor of 2.

*3.* To gain experience migrating from JavaScript, we ported six benchmarks from the Octane suite (`http://octane-benchmark.googlecode.com/`) to Safe TypeScript. We observe that, at least for these examples, migration is straightforward by initially typing the whole program using any. Even so, Safe TypeScript's variable scoping rules statically discovered a semantic bug in one of the benchmarks (navier-stokes), which has subsequently been fixed independently. For more static checking, we gradually added types to the ported benchmarks, and doing so also restored performance of the Safe TypeScript version to parity with the original JavaScript.

*4.* Finally, we gained significant experience with moving a large TypeScript codebase to Safe TypeScript. In particular, we migrated the 90KLOC Safe TypeScript compiler (including about 80KLOC from TypeScript-0.9.5) originally written in TypeScript. While doing so, Safe TypeScript reported 478 static type errors and 26 dynamic type errors. Once fixed, we were able to safely bootstrap Safe TypeScript—the cost of dynamic type safety is a performance slowdown of 15%.

### 5.1 Exploring the design space of tagging

***Differential subtyping vs. RTTI-on-creation.*** Prior proposals for RTTI-based gradual typing suggest tagging every object (e.g. Swamy et al. 2014). We adapted this strategy to Safe TypeScript and implemented a version of the compiler, called STS*, that tags every object, array and function that has a *non-erased* type with RTTI upon creation. Thus STS* also benefits from the use of erased types, one of the main innovations of Safe TypeScript. In code that makes heavy use of class-based objects, Safe TypeScript and STS* have essentially the same characteristics—in both strategies, all class-based objects have RTTI (via their prototype chain) as soon as they are allocated. Finally, STS* has a few limitations, particularly when used with generic interfaces. Consider the function pair from §4.3. In Safe TypeScript, the function call pair(0,1) (correctly) allocates a pair $v$ with no tags. Later, if we were to use subtyping and view $v$ at type any, Safe TypeScript (again, correctly) tags $v$ with the type {fst:number; snd:number}. In contrast, STS* fails to allocate the correct RTTI for v, since doing so would require passing explicit type parameters to pair so as to tag it with the correct type at the allocation site. Thus, STS* is not suitable for deployment, but it provides a conservative basis against which to measure the performance benefit of differential subtyping.

***Object instrumentation vs. weak maps.*** Our default implementation strategy is to add a field to every object that carries RTTI. This strategy has some advantages as well as some drawbacks. On the plus side, accessing RTTI is fast since it is co-located with the object. However, we must ensure that well-typed code never accesses this additional field. To this end, we use a hard-to-guess, reserved field name, and we instrument the read, write, and invoke functions, as well as property enumerations, to exclude this reserved name. However, this strategy is brittle when objects with RTTI are passed to external, untrusted code. An alternative strategy to sidestep these problems makes use of WeakMap, a new primitive in the forthcoming ES6 standard for JavaScript already available in some (experimental) JavaScript environments: WeakMap provides a mapping from objects to values in which the keys are weakly held (i.e., they do not impede garbage collection). This allows us to associate RTTI with an object in state that is private to the Safe TypeScript runtime library. For class instances, we retain a field in the object's prototype. We refer to our implementation that use WeakMap as STS$^{\dagger}$.

The performance evaluation in the remainder of this section compares Safe TypeScript with its variants, STS* and STS$^{\dagger}$, on Node.js-0.10.17, Windows 8.1, and an HP z-820 workstation.

### 5.2 Octane benchmarks

Octane is an open JavaScript benchmark suite. It contains 14 JavaScript programs, ranging from simple data structures and algorithms (like splay trees and ray-tracers) implemented in a few hundred lines, to large pieces of JavaScript code automatically generated by compilers, and even compilers implemented in JavaScript for compiling other languages to JavaScript.

The table alongside lists 6 programs we picked from the Octane benchmark, each a human-authored program a few hundred lines long which we could port to TypeScript with reasonable effort. All these programs use a JavaScript encoding of classes using prototypes. In porting them to Safe TypeScript, we reverted these encodings and used classes instead (since direct manipulation of prototype chains cannot be proven type-safe in Safe TypeScript); the 'classes' column indicates the number of classes we reverted; the number in parentheses indicates the number of abstract classes added while typechecking the program. We then added type annotations, primarily to establish type safety and recover good performance; the 'types' column indicates their number.

| Name | LOC | classes | types |
|---|---|---|---|
| splay | 394 | 2 | 15 |
| navier-stokes | 409 | 1(1) | 41 |
| richards | 539 | 7(1) | 30 |
| deltablue | 883 | 12 | 61 |
| raytrace | 904 | 14(1) | 48 |
| crypto | 1531 | 8(1) | 142 |

Without any type annotations, we pay a high cost for enforcing dynamic type safety. For the six unannotated Octane benchmarks, the slowdown spans a broad range from a factor of 2.4x (splay) to 72x (crypto), with an average of 22x. However, with the addition of types, we recover the lost performance—the slowdown for the typed versions is, on average only 6.5%. On benchmarks that make almost exclusive use of classes (e.g., raytrace and crypto) the performance of Safe TypeScript and STS* is, as expected, the same.

In untyped code, the cost of additional tagging in STS* is dwarfed by the large overhead of checks. However, in typed code, STS* incurs an average slowdown of 66%, and sometimes as much as 3.6x. Finally, in dynamically typed code (involving many RTTI operations), STS$^{\dagger}$ is significantly slower than Safe TypeScript: 2x on average, parity in the best case, and 3.2x in the worst case. We have spent some effort on simple optimizations, mainly inlining runtime checks: this had a measurable impact on dynamically typed code, improving performance by 16% on average. However, there is still substantial room for applying many optimizations targeted towards detecting and erasing redundant checks.

We draw a few conclusions from our performance evaluation. First, differential subtyping is clearly preferable to RTTI-on-creation when trying to ensure good performance for statically typed code. Second, better type inference would significantly improve the experience of migrating from JavaScript to Safe TypeScript. Currently, we rely solely on TypeScript's support for local type inference within method bodies. Most of the annotations we added manually were for top-level functions and for uninitialized variables (where TypeScript defaults to inferring any). Inferring better types for these based on usage sites is left as future work. Whilst weak maps are an attractive implementation choice in principle, their performance overhead in STS$^{\dagger}$ is still too substantial for practical use, although as ES6 is more widely implemented, this option may become viable.

### 5.3 Bootstrapping Safe TypeScript

Our most substantial experience with Safe TypeScript to date has been with the Safe TypeScript compiler itself, which contains about 80 KLOC of code authored by the developers of TypeScript, and about 10 KLOC written by us. TypeScript supports an option (`--noImplicitAny`) that causes the compiler to report a warning if the type of any variable was inferred to be any without an explicit user annotation, and their compiler was developed with this option enabled. Thus, much of the code is carefully annotated with types.

***Static error detection*** Bootstrapping the Safe TypeScript code base resulted in 478 static type errors. It took one author about 8 hours to diagnose and fix all these static errors, summarized below.

We detected 98 uses of bivariant subtyping of arrays: we fixed the covariant cases through the use of the immutable CheckedArray type (§4.4), and the contravariant cases by local code rewriting. Covariant subtyping of method arguments was observed 130 times, mostly in a single file that implemented a visitor pattern over an AST and due to binary methods in class inheritance. We fixed them all through the use of a runtime check. Variable scoping issues came up 128 times, which we fixed by manually hoisting variable declarations, and in 3 cases uncovering almost certain bugs on hard-to-reach code paths. Programmers confused methods and functions 52 times, e.g., projecting a method when passing a parameter to a higher-order function; which we fixed by local code rewriting. We lack the space to discuss the long tail of remaining error classes.

***Dynamic type safety violations*** were detected 26 times, each a failed checkAndTag operation while running the compiler test suite. Five of these were due to attempted dynamic uses of covariant subtyping of mutable fields, primarily in code that was written by us—even when experts write code with type safety in mind, it is easy to make mistakes! Many failed downcasts (erased by TypeScript) were found in the existing code of TypeScript-0.9.5, which we fixed by rewriting the code slightly. Interestingly, two classes of dynamic type errors we discovered were in the new code we added. In order to implement Safe TypeScript, we had to reverse engineer some of the invariants of the TypeScript compiler. In some cases, we got this slightly wrong, expecting some values to be instances of a particular class, when they were not—the failed checks pointed directly to our mistakes. Another class of errors was related to a bug in the subtyping hierarchy we introduced while evolving the system with generic types, and which had not manifested itself earlier because of the lack of checked casts.

***The performance overhead of safely bootstrapping*** the compiler (relative to bootstrapping the same code base with all runtime checks disabled) was a slowdown of only 15%. The added cost of runtime checks was easily paid for by the dozens of bugs found in heavily tested production code. We also bootstrapped the compiler using $STS^{\dagger}$ and $STS^{\star}$, observing a further slowdown of 14% and 40%, respectively—the compiler makes heavy use of classes, for which we do not use weak maps or RTTI-on-creation, so the difference is noticeable, but not enormous.

We conclude that, at least during development and testing, opting in to Safe TypeScript's sound gradual type system can significantly improve code quality. For a code base that is already annotated with types (as most TypeScript developments are), the cost of migrating even a large codebase to Safe TypeScript can be reasonable: a day or two's worth of static error diagnosis followed by dynamic error detection with only slightly slower runtimes. On the other hand, to be fair, understanding the root cause of errors requires some familiarity with our type system, i.e., a developer interested in using Safe TypeScript effectively would probably have to understand (at least the informal parts of) this paper.

***Experience with the TypeScript v1.1 compiler*** While we were working on Safe TypeScript, the TypeScript team released a new version, TypeScript-1.1, of the compiler. TypeScript-1.1 is comparatively much smaller (18K LOC) and faster (4x) (Turner 2014). It is a complete rewrite of the old compiler, including a design shift from being class-based to structural record- and interface-based. We have type-checked TypeScript-1.1 using Safe TypeScript, in the process providing inputs to the TypeScript team about the type errors found by Safe TypeScript. In preliminary experiments of using the instrumented version of TypeScript-1.1, we found that the overhead of the dynamic checks is much higher as compared to Safe TypeScript, which is based on TypeScript-0.9.5. The reason is that runtime checks are more expensive for structural types than for nominal class types. We are currently in the process of porting our type checker to TypeScript-1.1.

## 6. Related work

There has been considerable work on combining static and dynamic type-checking in a variety of language, too much to provide a comprehensive survey here—we discuss a few highlights.

***Classic work on mixing static and dynamic types.*** Abadi et al. (1989) were among the first to study the semantics of a (simply) typed calculus with the explicit addition of a dynamic type. Around the same time, Fagan (1990) and Cartwright and Fagan (1991) considered adding static checks to a dynamically typed language. Their soft typing approach involved using a static type system to detect suspicious fragments of an unannotated program at compile time and guard them with runtime checks for dynamic type safety. Wright and Cartwright (1997) developed an implementation of soft typing for Scheme. Also related is the work of Henglein and Rehof (1995), who develop a system to translate a subset of Scheme to ML, while also handling polymorphism.

***Static type systems for JavaScript.*** Given its ever-growing popularity over the last two decades, the earlier focus on LISP and Scheme has grown to include JavaScript. Early proposals for the addition of types to JavaScript were made by Thiemann (2005) who used singleton types and first-class record labels, and Anderson et al. (2005) who focused on type inference.

Guha et al. (2011) proposed a flow-sensitive static type system that refines types based on the control flow (typeof checks, comparison with undefined, etc.). The most recent incarnation of this line of work is TeJaS (Lerner et al. 2013), an extensible framework for exploring a range of static type systems for JavaScript. TeJaS features a sophisticated base type system (including bounded quantification, intersection and union types, mutable references, type-level functions, recursive types, object types, and a kind system). Despite this sophistication, or perhaps because of it, the base type system and its user-defined extensions come without a soundness argument.

Chugh et al. (2012) used both refinement and heap types to statically check some highly dynamic programming idioms of JavaScript: however, again, no soundness argument is given. Swamy et al. (2013) used an encoding of JavaScript (following a translation semantics by Guha et al. 2010) into a general-purpose, sound system of monadic refinement types to verify JavaScript safety.

***Gradual typing.*** Siek and Taha (2006) popularized the term "gradual typing" for classifying systems that mix static and dynamic idioms while allowing the programmer to control their interaction using a language of type annotations and runtime checks. Tobin-Hochstadt and Felleisen (2006) introduced similar ideas almost simultaneously. The addition of runtime checks can cause hard-to-diagnose failures, particularly with higher-order types. To address this problem, Wadler and Findler (2009) present a notion of *blame* for gradual type systems, which allows failed runtime checks to identify the module in a program responsible for the failure. Blame may be less important in Safe TypeScript, inasmuch as it does not involve (identity-breaking) higher order wrappers, an important source of difficulty for error diagnosis.

Typed Scheme (Tobin-Hochstadt and Felleisen 2008) departs from the no-annotations, no-rejected-programs philosophy of Soft Scheme; it allows programmers to decorate their code with optional types and provides a control-flow sensitive type system to enforce them using a combination of static and dynamic checks. Takikawa et al. (2012) describe and formalize Typed Racket, the latest version of Typed Scheme. Their type system is similar in scope to Safe TypeScript in that it deals with methods, mutable fields, and structural subtyping. It also supports mixins and their subtle interaction with inheritance. It tracks flows of information between the typed and untyped spaces, relying on row polymorphism and (identity-breaking) sealed contracts to deal with mixins. It offers blame tracking should errors occur. Mixins in Typed Racket are reminiscent of dynamic field extension in Safe TypeScript; they may be coded in our system using a mixture of static types, runtime checks, and reflection.

Swamy et al. (2014) propose a gradual type system called $TS^{\star}$ for JavaScript and utilize RTTI as a mechanism for ensuring type safety. As discussed in §1 and §2.4, the two systems are somewhat complementary. Safe TypeScript focuses on scale and flexibility; it incorporates new typing mechanisms leading to a more permissive type systems with lower runtime overhead. $TS^{\star}$ focuses on isolation of untrusted code, and safe interoperability with code outside the fragment covered by Safe TypeScript. As an alternative to isolation, or in concert, one may also reduce trust in external code by resorting to the techniques of Feldthaus and Møller (2014), who develop tools to specifically check the correctness of a large TypeScript type definition repository.

Vitousek et al. (2014) present Reticulated Python, a framework for experimenting with gradual type systems in Python. They consider three cast semantics: (a) the well-known wrapper semantics, which breaks object identity; (b) a *transient semantics* that involves inserting runtime checks at call sites, function definitions, etc.; and (c) a *monotonic semantics* that locks objects with evolving field types. The transient semantics is not formalized and its soundness is unclear. The monotonic semantics is reminiscent of Swamy et al. (2014) and Safe TypeScript, except that types evolve with respect to an (intentionally) naïve subtyping hierarchy.

Allende et al. (2013) study three cast insertion strategies (placing casts at the call-site, the callee or a mix of the two) for Gradualtalk, a gradually-typed Smalltalk, and observe fluctuating performance when interacting with variously typed libraries. To mitigate this unexpected behavior, they recently present Confined Gradual Typing (Allende et al. 2014), an extension of a gradual typing with type qualifiers to track values between typed and untyped spaces. One of these qualifiers is similar to the erasure modality of Safe TypeScript, in that both exclude subtyping to any. However, their use of higher-order casts does not preserve object identity.

Wrigstad et al. (2010) advocate *like-types*, another mechanism for mixing static and dynamically typed code. They extend Thorn by allowing every (nominal) class type $C$ to be qualified as Like$C$. Functions taking Like $C$ parameters are statically checked against $C$'s interface, whereas their callers are unconstrained. Hence, type safety involves dynamic checks on like-typed expressions. Richards et al. (2014) recently proposed like-types for JavaScript, building on TypeScript. Their model does not cover higher-order fields, method arguments, and references (their objects are purely functional). Our type system is more expressive, and our semantics more faithful to TypeScript. On the other hand, they use type information as a source of optimizations in the VM, an interesting aspect complementary to our work.

As discussed in §1, gradual type systems are starting to see industrial adoption. Microsoft's TypeScript has a gradual type system similar to the system of Siek and Taha (2007), but adds a number of unsound typing rules to support particular programming patterns, and erases all types during compilation, thereby excluding dynamic checks (Bierman et al. 2014). Google's Dart similarly relaxes soundness, and also normally compiles to JavaScript by erasing all types, but it has a checked mode that embeds ad-hoc runtime checks for early detection of some common errors. Facebook has released Hack, a gradual type system for PHP. Again, types are erased, and there is no soundness guarantee in the presence of any types.

## 7. Conclusions

Safe TypeScript is the first, large-scale, sound gradual type system for JavaScript. We have already argued for the benefits it provides to application developers, at a modest performance penalty. We also expect our work to be useful for researchers developing JavaScript program analyses, who may consider using Safe TypeScript as a baseline on which to build more sophisticated analyses. A large community effort continues to be expended on designing and implementing static analyses for JavaScript, and each must wrestle with the inherent dynamism of the language. Starting from Safe TypeScript may render static analysis problems more tractable, delegating to our compiler the task of reining JavaScript's dynamism and allowing the tool developer to focus on higher level properties.

Some challenges remain. Notably, JavaScript and TypeScript are moving targets: both languages evolve continuously, with the new standard of JavaScript (ES6) due in a few months and newer versions of TypeScript also expected. Whether or not the goodness of a sound type system will be embraced by the growing JavaScript and TypeScript community of developers, and evolve along with those languages, remains to be seen.

***Acknowledgments*** Our thanks to Martín Abadi, Mads Torgersen and the TypeScript team for several useful discussions; to the anonymous reviewers of the paper and artifact for their valuable feedback; and to Matthias Felleisen, Shriram Krishnamurthi, and Sam Tobin-Hochstadt for suggesting improvements to our discussion of related work.

## References

M. Abadi, L. Cardelli, B. Pierce, and G. Plotkin. Dynamic typing in a statically-typed language. In *Proceedings of POPL*, 1989.

A. Ahmed, R. B. Findler, J. G. Siek, and P. Wadler. Blame for all. In *Proceedings of POPL*, 2011.

E. Allende, J. Fabry, and É. Tanter. Cast insertion strategies for gradually-typed objects. In *Proceedings of DLS*, 2013.

E. Allende, J. Fabry, R. Garcia, and É. Tanter. Confined gradual typing. In *Proceedings of OOPSLA*, 2014.

C. Anderson, P. Giannini, and S. Drossopoulou. Towards type inference for JavaScript. In *Proceedings of ECOOP*, 2005.

G. Bierman, M. Abadi, and M. Torgersen. Understanding TypeScript. In *Proceedings of ECOOP*, 2014.

R. Cartwright and M. Fagan. Soft typing. In *Proceedings of PLDI*, 1991.

R. Chugh, D. Herman, and R. Jhala. Dependent types for JavaScript. In *Proceedings of OOSLA*, 2012.

M. Fagan. *Soft Typing: An Approach to Type Checking for Dynamically Typed Languages*. PhD thesis, 1990.

A. Feldthaus and A. Møller. Checking correctness of TypeScript interfaces for JavaScript libraries. In *Proceedings of OOPSLA*, 2014.

A. Guha, C. Saftoiu, and S. Krishnamurthi. The essence of JavaScript. In *Proceedings of ECOOP*, 2010.

A. Guha, C. Saftoiu, and S. Krisnamurthi. Typing local control and state using flow analysis. In *Proceedings of ESOP*, 2011.

F. Henglein and J. Rehof. Safe polymorphic type inference for Scheme: Translating Scheme to ML. In *Proceedings of FPCA*, 1995.

D. Herman, A. Tomb, and C. Flanagan. Space-efficient gradual typing. *Higher Order Symbol. Comput.*, 2010.

B. S. Lerner, J. G. Politz, A. Guha, and S. Krishnamurthi. TeJaS: Retrofitting type systems for JavaScript. In *Proceedings of DLS*, 2013.

Z. Luo. Coercive subtyping. *J. Log. Comput.*, 9(1):105–130, 1999.

M. S. Miller, M. Samuel, B. Laurie, I. Awad, and M. Stay. Caja: Safe active content in sanitized JavaScript. Unpublished paper, 2007.

A. Rastogi, N. Swamy, C. Fournet, G. Bierman, and P. Vekris. Safe & efficient gradual typing for TypeScript, MSR-TR-2014-99, 2014.

G. Richards, F. Z. Nardelli, C. Rouleau, and J. Vitek. Types you can count on. Unpublished paper, 2014.

J. G. Siek and W. Taha. Gradual typing for functional languages. In *Proceedings of Scheme and functional programming workshop*, 2006.

J. G. Siek and W. Taha. Gradual typing for objects. In *Proceedings of ECOOP*, 2007.

J. G. Siek and M. M. Vitousek. Monotonic references for gradual typing. Unpublished paper, 2013.

N. Swamy, J. Weinberger, C. Schlesinger, J. Chen, and B. Livshits. Verifying higher-order programs with the Dijkstra monad. In *Proceedings of PLDI*, 2013.

N. Swamy, C. Fournet, A. Rastogi, K. Bhargavan, J. Chen, P.-Y. Strub, and G. Bierman. Gradual typing embedded securely in JavaScript. In *Proceedings of POPL*, 2014.

A. Takikawa, T. S. Stickland, C. Dimoulas, S. Tobin-Hochstadt, and M. Felleisen. Gradual typing for first-class classes. In *Proceedings of OOPSLA*, 2012.

P. Thiemann. Towards a type systems for analyzing JavaScript programs. In *Proceedings of ESOP*, 2005.

N. Tillmann, M. Moskal, J. de Halleux, M. Fähndrich, and S. Burckhardt. Touchdevelop: app development on mobile devices. In *Proceedings of FSE*, 2012.

S. Tobin-Hochstadt and M. Felleisen. Interlanguage migration: from scripts to programs. In *Proceedings of DLS*, 2006.

S. Tobin-Hochstadt and M. Felleisen. The design and implementation of Typed Scheme. In *Proceedings of POPL*, 2008.

J. Turner. Announcing TypeScript 1.1 CTP, 2014. http://blogs.msdn.com/b/typescript/archive/2014/10/06/announcing-typescript-1-1-ctp.aspx.

M. M. Vitousek, A. M. Kent, J. G. Siek, and J. Baker. Design and evaluation of gradual typing for Python. In *Proceedings of DLS*, 2014.

P. Wadler and R. B. Findler. Well-typed programs can't be blamed. In *Proceedings of ESOP*, 2009.

A. K. Wright and R. Cartwright. A practical soft type system for scheme. *ACM Trans. Program. Lang. Syst.*, 19(1):87–152, Jan. 1997. .

T. Wrigstad, F. Z. Nardelli, S. Lebresne, J. Östlund, and J. Vitek. Integrating typed and untyped code in a scripting language. In *Proceedings of POPL*, 2010.

# Space-Efficient Manifest Contracts

Michael Greenberg
Princeton University
mg19@cs.princeton.edu

## Abstract

The standard algorithm for higher-order contract checking can lead to unbounded space consumption and can destroy tail recursion, altering a program's asymptotic space complexity. While space efficiency for gradual types—contracts mediating untyped and typed code—is well studied, sound space efficiency for manifest contracts—contracts that check stronger properties than simple types, e.g., "is a natural" instead of "is an integer"—remains an open problem.

We show how to achieve sound space efficiency for manifest contracts with strong predicate contracts. The essential trick is breaking the contract checking down into *coercions*: structured, blame-annotated lists of checks. By carefully preventing duplicate coercions from appearing, we can restore space efficiency while keeping the same observable behavior.

***Categories and Subject Descriptors*** D.3.3 [*Software*]: PROGRAMMING LANGUAGES—Language Constructs and Features

***Keywords*** contracts; pre- and post-conditions; function proxy; coercions; space efficiency

## 1. Introduction

Types are an extremely successful form of lightweight specification: programmers can state their intent—e.g., plus is a function that takes two numbers and returns another number—and then type checkers can ensure that a program conforms to the programmer's intent. Types can only go so far though: division is, like addition, a function that takes two numbers and returns another number... so long as the second number isn't zero. Conventional type systems do a good job of stopping many kinds of errors, but most type systems cannot protect partial operations like division and array indexing. Advanced techniques—singleton and dependent types, for example—can cover many of these cases, allowing programmers to use types like "non-zero number" or "index within bounds" to specify the domains on which partial operations are safe. Such techniques are demanding: they can be difficult to understand, they force certain programming idioms, and they place heavy constraints on the programming language, requiring purity or even strong normalization.


*POPL '15*, January 15–17, 2015, Mumbai, India.

ACM 978-1-4503-3300-9/15/01...$15.00.
http://dx.doi.org/10.1145/2676726.2676967

*Contracts* are a popular compromise: programmers write type-like contracts of the form $\mathsf{Int} \rightarrow \{x{:}\mathsf{Int} \mid x \neq 0\} \rightarrow \mathsf{Int}$, where the predicates $x \neq 0$ are written in code. These type-like specifications can then be checked at runtime [5]. Models of contract calculi have taken two forms: latent and manifest [12]. We take the manifest approach here, which means checking contracts with *casts*, written $\langle T_1 \Rightarrow T_2\rangle^l\ e$. Checking a *predicate contract* (also called a *refinement type*, though that term is overloaded) like $\{x{:}\mathsf{Int} \mid x \neq 0\}$ on a number $n$ involves running the predicate $x \neq 0$ with $n$ for $x$. Casts from one predicate contract to another, $\langle\{x{:}B \mid e_1\} \Rightarrow \{x{:}B \mid e_2\}\rangle^l$, take a constant $k$ and check to see that $e_2[k/x] \longrightarrow^* \mathsf{true}$. It's hard to know what to do with function casts at runtime: in $\langle T_{11} \rightarrow T_{12} \Rightarrow T_{21} \rightarrow T_{22}\rangle^l\ e$, we know that $e$ is a $T_{11} \rightarrow T_{12}$, but what does that tell us about treating $e$ as a $T_{21} \rightarrow T_{22}$? Findler and Felleisen's insight is that we must defer checking, waiting until the cast value $e$ gets an argument [5]. These deferred checks are recorded on the value by means of a *function proxy*, i.e., $\langle T_{11} \rightarrow T_{12} \Rightarrow T_{21} \rightarrow T_{22}\rangle^l\ e$ is a value when $e$ is a value; applying a function proxy unwraps it contravariantly. We check the domain contract $T_1$ on $e$, run the original function $f$ on the result, and then check that result against the codomain contract $T_2$:

$$(\langle T_{11} \rightarrow T_{12} \Rightarrow T_{21} \rightarrow T_{22}\rangle^l\ e_1)\ e_2 \longrightarrow$$
$$\langle T_{12} \Rightarrow T_{22}\rangle^l\ (e_1\ (\langle T_{21} \Rightarrow T_{11}\rangle^l\ e_2))$$

Findler and Felleisen neatly designed a system for contract checking in a higher-order world, but there is a problem: contract checking is space inefficient [15].

Contract checking's space inefficiency can be summed up as follows: **function proxies break tail calls**. Calls to an unproxied function from a tail position can be optimized to not allocate stack frames. Proxied functions, however, will unwrap to have codomain contracts—breaking tail calls. We discuss other sources of space inefficiency below, but breaking tail calls is the most severe. Consider factorial written in accumulator passing style. The developer may believe that the following can be compiled to use tail calls:

$$\begin{array}{l}\mathsf{fact} : \{x{:}\mathsf{Int} \mid x \geq 0\} \rightarrow \{x{:}\mathsf{Int} \mid x \geq 0\} \rightarrow \{x{:}\mathsf{Int} \mid x \geq 0\}\\ \quad = \lambda x{:}\{x{:}\mathsf{Int} \mid \mathsf{true}\}.\ \lambda y{:}\{y{:}\mathsf{Int} \mid \mathsf{true}\}.\\ \qquad \mathsf{if}\ x = 0\ \mathsf{then}\ y\ \mathsf{else\ fact}\ (x - 1)\ (x * y)\end{array}$$

A cast insertion algorithm [29] might produce the following non-tail recursive function:

$$\begin{array}{l}\mathsf{fact} =\\ \quad \langle\{x{:}\mathsf{Int} \mid \mathsf{true}\} \rightarrow \{y{:}\mathsf{Int} \mid \mathsf{true}\} \rightarrow \{z{:}\mathsf{Int} \mid \mathsf{true}\} \Rightarrow\\ \quad \{x{:}\mathsf{Int} \mid x \geq 0\} \rightarrow \{y{:}\mathsf{Int} \mid y \geq 0\} \rightarrow \{z{:}\mathsf{Int} \mid x \geq 0\}\rangle^{l_{\mathsf{fact}}}\\ \quad \lambda x{:}\{x{:}\mathsf{Int} \mid \mathsf{true}\}.\ \lambda y{:}\{y{:}\mathsf{Int} \mid \mathsf{true}\}.\\ \qquad \mathsf{if}\ x = 0\ \mathsf{then}\ y\ \mathsf{else}\\ \qquad\quad (\langle\{x{:}\mathsf{Int} \mid x \geq 0\} \Rightarrow \{x{:}\mathsf{Int} \mid \mathsf{true}\}\rangle^{l_{\mathsf{fact}}}\ (\mathsf{fact}\ \ldots))\end{array}$$

Tail-call optimization is essential for usable functional languages. Space inefficiency has been one of two significant obstacles for pervasive use of higher-order contract checking. (The other is state, which we do not treat here.)

In this work, we show how to achieve semantics-preserving space efficiency for non-dependent contract checking. Our approach is inspired by work on *gradual typing* [27], a form of (manifest) contracts designed to mediate dynamic and simple typing—that is, gradual typing (a) allows the dynamic type, and (b) restricts the predicates in contracts to checks on type tags. Herman et al. [15] developed the first space-efficient gradually typed system, using Henglein's coercions [14]; Siek and Wadler [28] devised a related system supporting blame. The essence of the solution is to allow casts to merge: given two adjacent casts $\langle T_2 \Rightarrow T_3\rangle^{l_2}$ $(\langle T_1 \Rightarrow T_2\rangle^{l_1}\ e)$, we must somehow combine them into a single cast. Siek and Wadler annotate their casts with an intermediate type representing the greatest lower bound of the types encountered. Such a trick doesn't work in our more general setting: simple types plus dynamic form a straightforward lattice using type precision as the ordering, but it's less clear what to do when we have arbitrary predicate contracts.

We define two modes of a single calculus, $\lambda_H$. The <u>c</u>*lassic* mode is just the conventional, inefficient semantics; the <u>e</u>*idetic* mode annotates casts with *refinement lists* and *function coercions*—a new form of coercion inspired by Greenberg [9]. The coercions keep track of checking so well that the type indices and blame labels on casts are unnecessary:

$$\langle T_2 \overset{c_2}{\Rightarrow} T_3\rangle^\bullet\ (\langle T_1 \overset{c_1}{\Rightarrow} T_2\rangle^\bullet\ e) \longrightarrow_{\mathsf{E}} \langle T_1 \overset{\mathsf{join}(c_1,c_2)}{\Rightarrow} T_3\rangle^\bullet\ e$$

These coercions form a skew lattice: refinement lists have ordering constraints that break commutativity. Eidetic $\lambda_H$ is space efficient and observationally equivalent to the classic mode.

Eidetic $\lambda_H$ is the first manifest contract calculus that is both *sound* and *space efficient* with respect to the classic semantics—a result contrary to Greenberg [9], who conjectured that such a result is impossible. We believe that space efficiency is a critical step towards the implementation of practical languages with manifest contracts.

We do not prove a blame theorem [30], since we lack the clear separation of dynamic and static typing found in gradual typing. We conjecture that such a theorem could be proved. Our model has two limits worth mentioning: we do not handle dependency, a common and powerful feature in manifest systems; and, our bounds for space efficiency are *galactic*—they establish that contracts consume constant space, but do nothing to reduce that constant [20]. Our contribution is showing that sound space efficiency is *possible* where it was believed to be impossible [9]; we leave evidence that it is *practicable* for future work.

Our proofs are available in the extended version [10], Appendices A–C.

Readers who are very familiar with this topic can read Figures 1, 2, and 3 and then skip directly to Section 4. Readers who understand the space inefficiency of contracts but aren't particularly familiar with manifest contracts can skip Section 2 and proceed to Section 3.

## 2. Function proxies

Space inefficient contract checking breaks tail recursion—a show-stopping problem for realistic implementations of pervasive contract use. Racket's contract system [22], the most widely used higher-order contract system, takes a "macro" approach to contracts: contracts typically appear only on module interfaces, and aren't checked within a module. Their approach comes partly out of a philosophy of breaking invariants inside modules but not out of them, but also partly out of a need to retain tail recursion within modules. Space inefficiency has shaped the way their contract system has developed. They do not use our "micro" approach, wherein annotations and casts permeate the code.

Tail recursion aside, there is another important source of space inefficiency: the unbounded number of function proxies. Hierarchies of libraries are a typical example: consider a list library and a set library built using increasingly sorted lists. We might have:

$$\begin{array}{rcll}
\mathsf{null} & : & \alpha\ \mathsf{List}{\rightarrow}\{x{:}\mathsf{Bool} \mid \mathsf{true}\} & = \ldots \\
\mathsf{head} & : & \{x{:}\alpha\ \mathsf{List} \mid \mathsf{not}\ (\mathsf{null}\ x)\}{\rightarrow}\alpha & = \ldots \\
\\
\mathsf{empty} & : & \alpha\ \mathsf{Set}{\rightarrow}\{x{:}\mathsf{Bool} \mid \mathsf{true}\} & = \mathsf{null} \\
\mathsf{min} & : & \{x{:}\alpha\ \mathsf{Set} \mid \mathsf{not}\ (\mathsf{empty}\ x)\}{\rightarrow}\alpha & = \mathsf{head}
\end{array}$$

Our code reuse comes with a price: even though the precondition on min is effectively the same as that on head, we must have two function proxies, and the non-emptiness of the list representing the set is checked twice: first by checking empty, and again by checking null (which is the same function). Blame systems like those in Racket encourage modules to declare contracts to avoid being blamed, which can result in redundant checking like the above when libraries requirements imply sub-libraries' requirements.

Or consider a library of drawing primitives based around painters, functions of type Canvas→Canvas. An underlying graphics library offers basic functions for manipulating canvases and functions over canvases, e.g., primFlipH is a painter transformer—of type (Canvas→Canvas)→(Canvas→Canvas)—that flips the generated images horizontally. A wrapper library may add derived functions while re-exporting the underlying functions with refinement types specifying a canvas's square dimensions, where $\mathsf{SquareCanvas} = \{x{:}\mathsf{Canvas} \mid \mathsf{width}(x) = \mathsf{height}(x)\}$:

$$\begin{array}{l}
\mathsf{flipH}\ p = \langle \mathsf{Canvas}{\rightarrow}\mathsf{Canvas}{\Rightarrow} \\
\qquad\qquad \mathsf{SquareCanvas}{\rightarrow}\mathsf{SquareCanvas}\rangle^l \\
\qquad\qquad (\mathsf{primFlipH} \\
\qquad\qquad\quad (\langle \mathsf{SquareCanvas}{\rightarrow}\mathsf{SquareCanvas}{\Rightarrow} \\
\qquad\qquad\qquad \mathsf{Canvas}{\rightarrow}\mathsf{Canvas}\rangle^l\ p))
\end{array}$$

The wrapper library only accepts painters with appropriately refined types, but must strip away these refinements before calling the underlying implementation—which demands Canvas→Canvas painters. The wrapper library then has to cast these modified functions *back* to the refined types. Calling flipH (flipH $p$) yields:

$$\begin{array}{l}
\langle \mathsf{Canvas}{\rightarrow}\mathsf{Canvas}{\Rightarrow}\mathsf{SquareCanvas}{\rightarrow}\mathsf{SquareCanvas}\rangle^l \\
\quad (\mathsf{primFlipH} \\
\quad\quad (\langle \mathsf{SquareCanvas}{\rightarrow}\mathsf{SquareCanvas}{\Rightarrow}\mathsf{Canvas}{\rightarrow}\mathsf{Canvas}\rangle^l \\
\quad\quad\quad (\langle \mathsf{Canvas}{\rightarrow}\mathsf{Canvas}{\Rightarrow}\mathsf{SquareCanvas}{\rightarrow}\mathsf{SquareCanvas}\rangle^l \\
\quad\quad\quad\quad (\mathsf{primFlipH} \\
\quad\quad\quad\quad\quad (\langle \mathsf{SquareCanvas}{\rightarrow}\mathsf{SquareCanvas}{\Rightarrow} \\
\quad\quad\quad\quad\quad\quad \mathsf{Canvas}{\rightarrow}\mathsf{Canvas}\rangle^l\ p)))))
\end{array}$$

That is, we first cast $p$ to a plain painter and return a new painter $p'$. We then cast $p'$ into and then immediately out of the refined type, before continuing on to flip $p'$. All the while, we are accumulating many function proxies beyond the wrapping done by the underlying implementation of primFlipH. Redundant wrapping can become quite extreme, especially for continuation-passing programs. Function proxies are the essential problem: nothing bounds their accumulation. Unfolding unboundedly many function proxies creates stacks of unboundedly many checks—which breaks tail calls. A space-efficient scheme for manifest contracts bounds the number of function proxies that can accumulate.

## 3. Classic manifest contracts

The standard manifest contract calculus, $\lambda_H$, is originally due to Flanagan [7]. We give the syntax for the non-dependent fragment in Figure 1. We have highlighted in yellow the four syntactic forms relevant to contract checking. This paper paper discusses two modes of $\lambda_H$: classic $\lambda_H$, mode C,and eidetic $\lambda_H$, mode E. Each of these languages uses the syntax of Figure 1, while the typing rules

**Modes**
$m ::= \mathsf{C}$ classic $\lambda_H$; Section 3
$\mid \mathsf{E}$ eidetic $\lambda_H$; Section 4

**Types**
$B ::= \mathsf{Bool} \mid \ldots$
$T ::= \{x{:}B \mid e\} \mid T_1 \rightarrow T_2$
**Terms**
$e ::= x \mid k \mid \lambda x{:}T.\ e \mid e_1\ e_2 \mid op(e_1, \ldots, e_n) \mid \langle T_1 \overset{a}{\Rightarrow} T_2 \rangle^l\ e \mid \langle \{x{:}B \mid e_1\}, e_2, k\rangle^l \mid \Uparrow l \mid \langle \{x{:}B \mid e_1\}, s, r, k, e\rangle^\bullet$
**Annotations: type set, coercions, and refinement lists**
$a ::= \bullet \mid c$
$c ::= r \mid c_1 \mapsto c_2$
$r ::= \mathsf{nil} \mid \{x{:}B \mid e\}^l, r$
**Statuses**
$s ::= \checkmark \mid ?$
**Locations**
$l ::= \bullet \mid l_1 \mid \ldots$

**Figure 1.** Syntax of $\lambda_H$

and operational semantics are indexed by the mode $m$. The proofs and metatheory are also mode-indexed. In an extended version of this work, we develop two additional modes with slightly different properties from eidetic $\lambda_H$, filling out a "framework" for space-efficient manifest contracts [10]. We omit the other two modes here to save space for eidetic $\lambda_H$, which is the only mode that is sound with respect to classic $\lambda_H$.

The metavariable $B$ is used for base types, of which at least Bool must be present. There are two kinds of types. First, *predicate contracts* $\{x{:}B \mid e\}$, also called *refinements of base types* or just *refinement types*, denotes constants $k$ of base type $B$ such that $e[k/x]$ holds—that is, such that $e[k/x] \longrightarrow^*_m \mathsf{true}$ for any mode $m$. Function types $T_1 \rightarrow T_2$ are standard.

The terms of $\lambda_H$ are largely those of the simply-typed lambda calculus: variables, constants $k$, abstractions, applications, and operations should all be familiar. The first distinguishing feature of $\lambda_H$'s terms is the *cast*, written $\langle T_1 \overset{a}{\Rightarrow} T_2 \rangle^l\ e$. Here $e$ is a term of type $T_1$; the cast checks whether $e$ can be treated as a $T_2$—if $e$ doesn't cut it, the cast will use its label $l$ to raise the uncatchable exception $\Uparrow l$, read "blame $l$". Our casts also have annotations $a$. Classic doesn't need annotations—we write $\bullet$ and say "none". Eidetic $\lambda_H$ uses coercions $c$, based on coercions in Henglein [14]. We explain coercions in greater detail in Section 4, but they amount to lists of blame-annotated refinement types $r$ and function coercions.

The three remaining forms—active checks, blame, and coercion stacks—only occur as the program evaluates. Casts between refinement types are checked by *active checks* $\langle \{x{:}B \mid e_1\}, e_2, k\rangle^l$. The first term is the type being checked—necessary for the typing rule. The second term is the current status of the check; it is an invariant that $e_1[k/x] \longrightarrow^*_m e_2$. The final term is the constant being checked, which is returned wholesale if the check succeeds. When checks fail, the program raises *blame*, an uncatchable exception written $\Uparrow l$. A *coercion stack* $\langle \{x{:}B \mid e_1\}, s, r, k, e\rangle^\bullet$ represents the state of checking a coercion; we only use it in eidetic $\lambda_H$, so we postpone discussing it until Section 4.

### 3.1 Core operational semantics

Our mode-indexed operational semantics for our manifest calculi comprise three relations: $\mathsf{val}_m\ e$ identifies terms that are values in mode $m$ (or $m$-values), $\mathsf{result}_m\ e$ identifies $m$-results, and $e_1 \longrightarrow_m e_2$ is the small-step reduction relation for mode $m$. Figure 2 defines the core rules. The rules for classic $\lambda_H$ ($m = \mathsf{C}$) are in salmon; the shared space-efficient rules are in periwinkle. To save space, we pass over standard rules.

The mode-agnostic value rules are straightforward: constants are always values (V_CONST), as are lambdas (V_ABS). Each mode defines its own value rule for function proxies, V_PROXY$m$. The classic rule, V_PROXYC, says that a function proxy

$$\langle T_{11} \rightarrow T_{12} \overset{\bullet}{\Rightarrow} T_{21} \rightarrow T_{22} \rangle^l\ e$$

is a C-value when $e$ is a C-value. That is, function proxies can wrap lambda abstractions and other function proxies alike. Eidetic $\lambda_H$ only allows lambda abstractions to be proxied. All of the space-efficient calculi in the literature take our approach, where a function cast applied to a value *is* a value; some space inefficient ones do, too [5, 12, 13]. In other formulations of $\lambda_H$ in the literature, function proxies are implemented by introducing a new lambda as a wrapper à la Findler and Felleisen's $\overline{wrap}$ operator [1, 5, 7, 27]. Such an $\eta$-expansion semantics is convenient, since then applications only ever reduce by $\beta$-reduction. But it wouldn't suit our purposes at all: space efficiency demands that we combine function proxies. We can also imagine a third, ungainly semantics that looks into closures rather than having explicit function proxies. Results don't depend on the mode: $m$-values are always $m$-results (R_VAL); blame is always a result, too (R_BLAME).

E_BETA applies lambda abstractions via substitution, using a call-by-value rule. Note that $\beta$ reduction in mode $m$ requires that the argument is an $m$-value. The reduction rule for operations (E_OP) defers to operations' denotations, $[\![op]\!]$; since these may be partial (e.g., division), we assign types to operations that guarantee totality (see Section 3.2). That is, partial operations are a potential source of stuckness, and the types assigned to operations must guarantee the absence of stuckness. Robin Milner famously stated that "well typed expressions don't go wrong" [21]; his programs could go wrong by (a) applying a boolean like a function or (b) conditioning on a function like a boolean. Systems with more base types can go wrong in more ways, some of which are hard to capture in standard type systems. Contracts allow us to bridge that gap. Letting operations get stuck is a philosophical stance—contracts expand the notion of "wrong".

E_UNWRAP applies function proxies to values, contravariantly in the domain and covariantly in the codomain. We also split up each cast's annotation, using $\mathsf{dom}(a)$ and $\mathsf{cod}(a)$—each mode is discussed in its respective section. E_CHECKNONEC turns a cast between refinement types into an active check with the same blame label. We discard the source type—we already know that $k$ is a $\{x{:}B \mid e_1\}$—and substitute the scrutinee into the target type, $e_2[k/x]$, as the current state of checking. We must also hold onto the scrutinee, in case the check succeeds. We are careful to not apply this rule in eidietc $\lambda_H$, which must generate annotations before running checks. Active checks evaluate by the congruence rule E_CHECKINNER until one of three results adheres: the predicate returns $\mathsf{true}$, so the whole active check returns the scrutinee (E_CHECKOK); the predicate returns $\mathsf{false}$, so the whole active check raises blame using the label on the chceck (E_CHECKFAIL); or blame was raised during checking, and we propagate it via E_CHECKRAISE. Checks in eidetic $\lambda_H$ use slightly different forms, described in Section 4.

The core semantics includes several other congruence rules: E_APPL, E_APPR, and E_OPINNER. Since space bounds rely not only on limiting the number of function proxies but also on accumulation of casts on the stack, the core semantics doesn't include a cast congruence rule. The congruence rule for casts in classic $\lambda_H$, E_CASTINNERC, allows for free use of congruence. In the space-efficient calculus, the use of congruence is instead limited by the rules E_CASTINNERE and E_CASTMERGEE. Cast arguments only take congruent steps when they aren't casts themselves. A cast ap-

**Values and results** $\boxed{\mathsf{val}_m\ e}$ $\boxed{\mathsf{result}_m\ e}$

$$\frac{}{\mathsf{val}_m\ k}\ \textsc{V\_Const} \qquad \frac{}{\mathsf{val}_m\ \lambda x{:}T.\ e}\ \textsc{V\_Abs} \qquad \frac{\mathsf{val}_{\mathsf{C}}\ e}{\mathsf{val}_{\mathsf{C}}\ \langle T_{11}\to T_{12} \overset{\bullet}{\Rightarrow} T_{21}\to T_{22}\rangle^l\ e}\ \textsc{V\_ProxyC} \qquad \frac{\mathsf{val}_m\ e}{\mathsf{result}_m\ e}\ \textsc{R\_Val} \qquad \frac{}{\mathsf{result}_m\ \Uparrow l}\ \textsc{R\_Blame}$$

**Shared operational semantics** $\boxed{e_1 \longrightarrow_m e_2}$

$$\frac{\mathsf{val}_m\ e_2}{(\lambda x{:}T.\ e_{12})\ e_2 \longrightarrow_m e_{12}[e_2/x]}\ \textsc{E\_Beta} \qquad \frac{\mathsf{val}_m\ e_1\ \dots\ \mathsf{val}_m\ e_n}{op(e_1,\ \dots,\ e_n) \longrightarrow_m [\![op]\!]\,(e_1,\ \dots,\ e_n)}\ \textsc{E\_Op}$$

$$\frac{\mathsf{val}_m\ \langle T_{11}\to T_{12} \overset{a}{\Rightarrow} T_{21}\to T_{22}\rangle^l\ e_1 \quad \mathsf{val}_m\ e_2}{(\langle T_{11}\to T_{12} \overset{a}{\Rightarrow} T_{21}\to T_{22}\rangle^l\ e_1)\ e_2 \longrightarrow_m \langle T_{12} \overset{\mathsf{cod}(a)}{\Rightarrow} T_{22}\rangle^l\ (e_1\ (\langle T_{21} \overset{\mathsf{dom}(a)}{\Rightarrow} T_{11}\rangle^l\ e_2))}\ \textsc{E\_Unwrap}$$

$$\begin{aligned} \mathsf{dom}(\bullet) &= \bullet \\ \mathsf{dom}(c_1 \mapsto c_2) &= c_1 \end{aligned} \qquad \begin{aligned} \mathsf{cod}(\bullet) &= \bullet \\ \mathsf{cod}(c_1 \mapsto c_2) &= c_2 \end{aligned}$$

$$\frac{}{\langle \{x{:}B \mid e_1\} \overset{\bullet}{\Rightarrow} \{x{:}B \mid e_2\}\rangle^l\ k \longrightarrow_{\mathsf{C}} \langle \{x{:}B \mid e_2\}, e_2[k/x], k\rangle^l}\ \textsc{E\_CheckNoneC}$$

$$\frac{}{\langle \{x{:}B \mid e\}, \mathsf{true}, k\rangle^l \longrightarrow_m k}\ \textsc{E\_CheckOK} \qquad \frac{}{\langle \{x{:}B \mid e\}, \mathsf{false}, k\rangle^l \longrightarrow_m \Uparrow l}\ \textsc{E\_CheckFail}$$

$$\frac{e_1 \longrightarrow_m e_1'}{e_1\ e_2 \longrightarrow_m e_1'\ e_2}\ \textsc{E\_AppL} \qquad \frac{\mathsf{val}_m\ e_1 \quad e_2 \longrightarrow_m e_2'}{e_1\ e_2 \longrightarrow_m e_1\ e_2'}\ \textsc{E\_AppR}$$

$$\frac{\mathsf{val}_m\ e_1\ \dots\ \mathsf{val}_m\ e_{i-1} \quad e_i \longrightarrow_m e_i'}{op(e_1, \dots, e_{i-1}, e_i, \dots, e_n) \longrightarrow_m op(e_1, \dots, e_{i-1}, e_i', \dots, e_n)}\ \textsc{E\_OpInner}$$

$$\frac{e \longrightarrow_{\mathsf{C}} e'}{\langle T_1 \overset{\bullet}{\Rightarrow} T_2\rangle^l\ e \longrightarrow_{\mathsf{C}} \langle T_1 \overset{\bullet}{\Rightarrow} T_2\rangle^l\ e'}\ \textsc{E\_CastInnerC} \qquad \frac{e_2 \longrightarrow_m e_2'}{\langle \{x{:}B \mid e_1\}, e_2, k\rangle^l \longrightarrow_m \langle \{x{:}B \mid e_1\}, e_2', k\rangle^l}\ \textsc{E\_CheckInner}$$

$$\frac{e_2 \longrightarrow_{\mathsf{E}} e_2' \quad e_2 \neq \langle T_1 \overset{a'}{\Rightarrow} T_2\rangle^{l'}\ e_2''}{\langle T_2 \overset{a}{\Rightarrow} T_3\rangle^l\ e_2 \longrightarrow_{\mathsf{E}} \langle T_2 \overset{a}{\Rightarrow} T_3\rangle^l\ e_2'}\ \textsc{E\_CastInnerE} \qquad \frac{c_3 = \mathsf{join}(c_1, c_2)}{\langle T_2 \overset{c_2}{\Rightarrow} T_3\rangle^l\ (\langle T_1 \overset{c_1}{\Rightarrow} T_2\rangle^{l'}\ e_2) \longrightarrow_{\mathsf{E}} \langle T_1 \overset{c_3}{\Rightarrow} T_3\rangle^l\ e_2}\ \textsc{E\_CastMergeE}$$

$$\frac{}{\Uparrow l\ e_2 \longrightarrow_m \Uparrow l}\ \textsc{E\_AppRaiseL} \qquad \frac{\mathsf{val}_m\ e_1}{e_1 \Uparrow l \longrightarrow_m \Uparrow l}\ \textsc{E\_AppRaiseR} \qquad \frac{}{\langle T_1 \overset{\mathcal{S}}{\Rightarrow} T_2\rangle^l \Uparrow l' \longrightarrow_m \Uparrow l'}\ \textsc{E\_CastRaise}$$

$$\frac{\mathsf{val}_m\ e_1\ \dots\ \mathsf{val}_m\ e_{i-1}}{op(e_1, \dots, e_{i-1}, \Uparrow l, \dots, e_n) \longrightarrow_m \Uparrow l}\ \textsc{E\_OpRaise} \qquad \frac{}{\langle \{x{:}B \mid e\}, \Uparrow l, k\rangle^{l'} \longrightarrow_m \Uparrow l}\ \textsc{E\_CheckRaise}$$

**Figure 2.** Core operational semantics of $\lambda_{\mathrm{H}}$; classic $\lambda_{\mathrm{H}}$ rules are salmon; space-efficient rules are periwinkle

plied to another cast *merges*, using the join function. Each space-efficient calculus uses a different annotation scheme, so each one has a different merge function. We are careful to define join only over coercions, so E_CASTMERGEE won't apply on the empty annotation, • (read "none"). We have E_CASTMERGEE arbitrarily retain the label of the outer cast. This choice is ultimately irrelevant, since eidetic $\lambda_{\mathrm{H}}$ won't need to keep track of blame labels on casts themselves (Section 4). In addition to congruence rules, there are blame propagation rules, which are universal: E_APPRAISEL, E_APPRAISER, E_CASTRAISE, E_OPRAISE. These rules propagate the uncatchable exception $\Uparrow l$ while obeying call-by-value rules.

### 3.2 Type system

All modes share a type system, given in Figure 3. All judgments are universal and simply thread the mode through—except for annotation well formedness $\vdash_m a \parallel T_1 \Rightarrow T_2$, which is mode specific, and a single eidetic-specific rule given in Figure 4. The type system comprises several relations: context well formedness $\vdash_m \Gamma$ and type well formedness $\vdash_m T$; type compatibility $\vdash T_1 \parallel T_2$, a mode-less comparison of the *skeleton* of two types; annotation well formedness $\vdash_m a \parallel T_1 \Rightarrow T_2$; and term typing $\Gamma \vdash_m e : T$.

Context well formedness is entirely straightforward; type well formedness requires some care to get base types off the ground. We establish as an axiom that the *raw* type $\{x{:}B \mid \mathsf{true}\}$ is well formed for every base type $B$ (WF_BASE); we then use raw types to check that refinements are well formed: $\{x{:}B \mid e\}$ is well formed in mode $m$ if $e$ is well typed as a boolean in mode $m$ when $x$ is a value of type $B$ (WF_REFINE). Without WF_BASE, WF_REFINE wouldn't have a well formed context. Function types are well formed in mode $m$ when their domains and codomains are well formed in mode $m$. (Unlike many recent formulations, our functions are not dependent—we leave dependency as future work.) Type compatibility $\vdash T_1 \parallel T_2$ identifies types which can be cast to each other: the types must have the same "skeleton". It is reasonable to try to cast a non-zero integer $\{x{:}\mathsf{Int} \mid x \neq 0\}$ to a positive integer $\{x{:}\mathsf{Int} \mid x > 0\}$, but it is senseless to cast it to a boolean $\{x{:}\mathsf{Bool} \mid \mathsf{true}\}$ or to a function type $T_1 \to T_2$. Every cast must be between compatible types; at their core, $\lambda_{\mathrm{H}}$ programs are simply typed lambda calculus programs. Type compatibility

**Context and type well formedness** $\boxed{\vdash_m \Gamma}$ $\boxed{\vdash_m T}$

$$\frac{}{\vdash_m \emptyset}\ \text{WF\_EMPTY} \qquad \frac{\vdash_m \Gamma \quad \vdash_m T}{\vdash_m \Gamma, x{:}T}\ \text{WF\_EXTEND}$$

$$\frac{}{\vdash_m \{x{:}B \mid \mathsf{true}\}}\ \text{WF\_BASE} \qquad \frac{x{:}\{x{:}B \mid \mathsf{true}\} \vdash_m e : \{x{:}\mathsf{Bool} \mid \mathsf{true}\}}{\vdash_m \{x{:}B \mid e\}}\ \text{WF\_REFINE} \qquad \frac{\vdash_m T_1 \quad \vdash_m T_2}{\vdash_m T_1 \to T_2}\ \text{WF\_FUN}$$

**Type compatibility and annotation well formedness** $\boxed{\vdash T_1 \parallel T_2}$ $\boxed{\vdash_m a \parallel T_1 \Rightarrow T_2}$

$$\frac{}{\vdash \{x{:}B \mid e_1\} \parallel \{x{:}B \mid e_2\}}\ \text{S\_REFINE} \qquad \frac{\vdash T_{11} \parallel T_{21} \quad \vdash T_{12} \parallel T_{22}}{\vdash T_{11} \to T_{12} \parallel T_{21} \to T_{22}}\ \text{S\_FUN} \qquad \frac{\vdash T_1 \parallel T_2 \quad \vdash_m T_1 \quad \vdash_m T_2}{\vdash_m \bullet \parallel T_1 \Rightarrow T_2}\ \text{A\_NONE}$$

**Expression typing** $\boxed{\Gamma \vdash_m e : T}$

$$\frac{\vdash_m \Gamma \quad x{:}T \in \Gamma}{\Gamma \vdash_m x : T}\ \text{T\_VAR} \qquad \frac{\vdash_m T_1 \quad \Gamma, x{:}T_1 \vdash_m e_{12} : T_2}{\Gamma \vdash_m \lambda x{:}T_1.\ e_{12} : T_1 \to T_2}\ \text{T\_ABS} \qquad \frac{\vdash_m \Gamma \quad \vdash_m T}{\Gamma \vdash_m \Uparrow l : T}\ \text{T\_BLAME}$$

$$\frac{\vdash_m \Gamma \quad \vdash_m \{x{:}B \mid e\} \quad \mathsf{ty}(k) = B \quad e[k/x] \longrightarrow_m^* \mathsf{true}}{\Gamma \vdash_m k : \{x{:}B \mid e\}}\ \text{T\_CONST} \qquad \frac{\mathsf{ty}(op) = T_1 \to \ldots \to T_n \to T \quad \Gamma \vdash_m e_i : T_i}{\Gamma \vdash_m op(e_1, \ldots, e_n) : T}\ \text{T\_OP}$$

$$\frac{\Gamma \vdash_m e_1 : (T_1 \to T_2) \quad \Gamma \vdash_m e_2 : T_1}{\Gamma \vdash_m e_1\ e_2 : T_2}\ \text{T\_APP} \qquad \frac{\vdash_m a \parallel T_1 \Rightarrow T_2 \quad \Gamma \vdash_m e : T_1}{\Gamma \vdash_m \langle T_1 \overset{a}{\Rightarrow} T_2 \rangle^l\ e : T_2}\ \text{T\_CAST}$$

$$\frac{\vdash_m \Gamma \quad \vdash_m \{x{:}B \mid e_1\} \quad \mathsf{ty}(k) = B \quad \emptyset \vdash_m e_2 : \{x{:}\mathsf{Bool} \mid \mathsf{true}\} \quad e_1[k/x] \longrightarrow_m^* e_2}{\Gamma \vdash_m \langle \{x{:}B \mid e_1\}, e_2, k\rangle^l : \{x{:}B \mid e_1\}}\ \text{T\_CHECK}$$

**Figure 3.** Universal typing rules of $\lambda_H$

is reflexive, symmetric, and transitive; i.e., it is an equivalence relation.

Our family of calculi use different annotations. All source programs (defined below) begin without annotations—we write the empty annotation $\bullet$, read "none". The universal annotation well formedness rule just defers to type compatibility (A_NONE); it is an invariant that $\vdash_m a \parallel T_1 \Rightarrow T_2$ implies $\vdash T_1 \parallel T_2$.

As for term typing, the T_VAR, T_ABS, T_OP, and T_APP rules are entirely conventional. T_BLAME types blame at any (well formed) type. A constant $k$ can be typed by T_CONST at any type $\{x{:}B \mid e\}$ in mode $m$ if: (a) $k$ is a $B$, i.e., $\mathsf{ty}(k) = B$; (b) the type in question is well formed in $m$; and (c), if $e[k/x] \longrightarrow_m^* \mathsf{true}$. As an immediate consequence, we can derive the following rule typing constants at their raw type, since $\mathsf{true} \longrightarrow_m^* \mathsf{true}$ in all modes and raw types are well formed in all modes (WF_BASE):

$$\frac{\vdash_m \Gamma \qquad \mathsf{ty}(k) = B}{\Gamma \vdash_m k : \{x{:}B \mid \mathsf{true}\}}$$

This approach to typing constants in a manifest calculus is novel: it offers a great deal of latitude with typing, while avoiding the subtyping of some formulations [7, 12, 17, 18] and the extra rule of others [1]. We assume that $\mathsf{ty}(k) = \mathsf{Bool}$ iff $k \in \{\mathsf{true}, \mathsf{false}\}$.

We require in T_OP that $\mathsf{ty}(op)$ only produces well formed first-order types, i.e., types of the form $\vdash_m \{x{:}B_1 \mid e_1\} \to \ldots \to \{x{:}B_n \mid e_n\}$. We require that the type is consistent with the operation's denotation: $[\![op]\!]\,(k_1, \ldots, k_n)$ is defined iff $e_i[k_i/x] \longrightarrow_m^* \mathsf{true}$ for all $m$. For this evaluation to hold for every system we consider, the types assigned to operations can't involve casts that both (a) stack and (b) can fail. We believe this is not so stringent a requirement: the types for operations ought to be simple, e.g. $\mathsf{ty}(\mathsf{div}) = \{x{:}\mathsf{Real} \mid \mathsf{true}\} \to \{y{:}\mathsf{Real} \mid y \neq 0\} \to \{z{:}\mathsf{Real} \mid \mathsf{true}\}$, and stacked casts only arise in stack-free terms due to function proxies. In general, it is interesting to ask what refinement types to assign to constants, as careless assignments can lead to circular checking (e.g., if division has a codomain cast checking its work with multiplication and vice versa).

The typing rule for casts, T_CAST, relies on the annotation well formedness rule: $\langle T_1 \overset{a}{\Rightarrow} T_2 \rangle^l\ e$ is well formed in mode $m$ when $\vdash_m a \parallel T_1 \Rightarrow T_2$ and $e$ is a $T_1$. Allowing any cast between compatible base types is conservative: a cast from $\{x{:}\mathsf{Int} \mid x > 0\}$ to $\{x{:}\mathsf{Int} \mid x \leq 0\}$ always fails. Earlier work has used SMT solvers to try to statically reject certain casts and eliminate those that are guaranteed to succeed [2, 7, 18]; we omit these checks, as we view them as secondary—a static analysis offering bug-finding and optimization, and not the essence of the system.

The final rule, T_CHECK, is used for checking active checks, which should only occur at runtime. In fact, they should only ever be applied to closed terms; the rule allows for any well formed context as a technical device for weakening.

Active checks $\langle \{x{:}B \mid e_1\}, e_2, k\rangle^l$ arise as the result of casts between refined base types, as in the following classic $\lambda_H$ evaluation of a successful cast:

$$\begin{aligned} \langle \{x{:}B \mid e\} \overset{\bullet}{\Rightarrow} \{x{:}B \mid e'\} \rangle^l\ k &\longrightarrow_C \langle \{x{:}B \mid e'\}, e'[k/x], k\rangle^l \\ &\longrightarrow_C^* \langle \{x{:}B \mid e'\}, \mathsf{true}, k\rangle^l \\ &\longrightarrow_C k \end{aligned}$$

If we are going to prove type soundness via syntactic methods [32], we must have enough information to type $k$ at $\{x{:}B \mid e'\}$. For this reason, T_CHECK requires that $e_1[k/x] \longrightarrow_m^* e_2$; this way, we know that $e'[k/x] \longrightarrow_m^* \mathsf{true}$ at the end of the previous derivation, which is enough to apply T_CONST. The other premises of T_CHECK ensure that the types all match up: that the target refinement type is well formed; that $k$ has the base type in question; and that $e_2$, the current state of the active check, is also well formed.

To truly say that our languages share a syntax and a type system, we highlight a subset of type derivations as *source program* type derivations. We show that source programs well typed in one mode are well typed in the all modes [10].

**3.1 Definition [Source program]:** A source program type derivation obeys the following rules:

– T_CONST only ever assigns the type $\{x{:}\mathsf{ty}(k) \mid \mathsf{true}\}$. Variations in each mode's evaluation aren't reflected in the (source program) type system. (We could soundly relax this requirement to allow $\{x{:}\mathsf{ty}(k) \mid e\}$ such that $e[k/x] \longrightarrow_m^* \mathsf{true}$ for any mode $m$.)

– Casts have empty annotations $a = \bullet$. Casts also have blame labels, and not empty blame (also written $\bullet$).

– T_CHECK, T_STACK (Section 4), and T_BLAME are not used—these are for runtime only.

Note that source programs don't use any of the typing rules that defer to the evaluation relation (T_CHECK and T_STACK), so we can maintain a clear phase distinction between type checking programs and running them.

### 3.3 Metatheory

One distinct advantage of having a single syntax with parameterized semantics is that some of the metatheory can be done once for all modes. Each mode proves its own canonical forms lemma—since each mode has a unique notion of value—and its own progress and preservation lemmas for syntactic type soundness [32]. But other standard metatheoretical machinery—weakening, substitution, and regularity—can be proved for all modes at once (see Section A.1). To wit, we prove syntactic type soundness in Appendix A.2 for classic $\lambda_H$ in just three mode-specific lemmas: canonical forms, progress, and preservation. In every theorem statement, we include a reference to the lemma number where it is proved in the appendix. In PDF versions, this reference is hyperlinked.

**Lemma [Classic canonical forms (A.11)]:** If $\emptyset \vdash_C e : T$ and $\mathsf{val}_C\ e$ then:

– If $T = \{x{:}B \mid e'\}$, then $e = k$ and $\mathsf{ty}(k) = B$ and $e'[e/x] \longrightarrow_C^* \mathsf{true}$.

– If $T = T_1 \rightarrow T_2$, then either $e = \lambda x{:}T.\ e'$ or $e = \langle T_{11} \rightarrow T_{12} \overset{\bullet}{\Rightarrow} T_{21} \rightarrow T_{22} \rangle^l\ e'$.

**Lemma [Classic progress (A.12)]:** If $\emptyset \vdash_C e : T$, then either:

1. $\mathsf{result}_C\ e$, i.e., $e = \Uparrow l$ or $\mathsf{val}_C\ e$; or
2. there exists an $e'$ such that $e \longrightarrow_C e'$.

**Lemma [Classic preservation (A.13)]:** If $\emptyset \vdash_C e : T$ and $e \longrightarrow_C e'$, then $\emptyset \vdash_C e' : T$.

## 4. Eidetic space efficiency

Eidetic $\lambda_H$ uses *coercions*. Coercions do two critical things: they retain check order, and they track blame. Our coercions are ultimately inspired by those of Henglein [14]; we discuss the relationship between our coercions and his in related work (Section 7). Recall the syntax of coercions from Figure 1:

$$c ::= r \mid c_1 \mapsto c_2$$
$$r ::= \mathsf{nil} \mid \{x{:}B \mid e\}^l, r$$

Coercions come in two flavors: blame-annotated refinement lists $r$—zero or more refinement types, each annotated with a blame label—and function coercions $c_1 \mapsto c_2$. We write them as comma separated lists, omitting the empty refinement list nil when the refinement list is non-empty. We define the coercion well formedness rules, an additional typing rule, and reduction rules for eidetic $\lambda_H$ in Figure 4. To ease the exposition, our explanation doesn't mirror the rule groupings in the figure.

As a general intuition, coercions are plans for checking: they contain precisely those types to be checked. Refinement lists are well formed for casts between $\{x{:}B \mid e_1\}$ and $\{x{:}B \mid e_2\}$ when: (a) every type in the list is a blame-annotated, well formed refinement of $B$, i.e., all the types are of the form $\{x{:}B \mid e\}^l$ and are therefore similar to the indices; (b) there are no duplicated types in the list; and (c) the target type $\{x{:}B \mid e_2\}$ is implied by some other type in the list. Note that the input type for all refinement lists can be any well formed refinement—this corresponds to the intuition that base types have no negative parts, i.e., casts between refinements ignore the type on the left. Finally, we simply write "no duplicates in $r$"—it is an invariant during the evaluation of source programs. Function coercions, on the other hand, have a straightforward (contravariant) well formedness rule.

The E_COERCE rule translates source-program casts to coercions: $\mathsf{coerce}(T_1, T_2, l)$ is a coercion representing exactly the checking done by the cast $\langle T_1 \overset{\bullet}{\Rightarrow} T_2 \rangle^l$. All of the refinement types in $\mathsf{coerce}(T_1, T_2, l)$ are annotated with the blame label $l$, since that's the label that would be blamed if the cast failed at that type. Since a coercion is a complete plan for checking, a coercion annotation obviates the need for type indices and blame labels. To this end, E_COERCE drops the blame label from the cast, replacing it with an empty label. We keep the type indices so that we can reuse E_CASTMERGEE from the universal semantics, and also as a technical device in the preservation proof.

The actual checking of coercions rests on the treatment of refinement lists: function coercions are expanded as functions are applied by E_UNWRAP, so they don't need much special treatment beyond a definition for dom and cod. Eidetic $\lambda_H$ uses *coercion stacks* $\langle \{x{:}B \mid e_1\}, s, r, k, e_2 \rangle^\bullet$ to evaluate refinement lists. Coercion stacks are type checked by T_STACK (in Figure 4). We explain the operational semantics before explaining the typing rule. Coercion stacks are runtime-only entities comprising five parts: a target type, a status, a pending refinement list, a constant scrutinee, and a checking term. We keep the target type of the coercion for preservation's sake. The status bit $s$ is either ✓ or ?: when the status is ✓, we are currently checking or have already checked the target type $\{x{:}B \mid e_1\}$; when it is ?, we haven't. The pending refinement list $r$ holds those checks not yet done. When $s = ?$, the target type is still in $r$. The scrutinee $k$ is the constant we're checking; the checking term $e$ is *either* the scrutinee $k$ itself, or it is an active check on $k$.

The evaluation of a coercion stack proceeds as follows. First, E_COERCESTACK starts a coercion stack when a cast between refinements meets a constant, recording the target type, setting the status to ?, and setting the checking term to $k$. Then E_STACKPOP starts an active check on the first type in the refinement list, using its blame label on the active check—possibly updating the status if the type being popped from the list is the target type. The active check runs by the congruence rule E_STACKINNER, eventually returning $k$ itself or blame. In the latter case, E_STACKRAISE propagates the blame. If not, then the scrutinee is $k$ once more and E_STACKPOP can fire again. Eventually, the refinement list is exhausted, and E_STACKDONE returns $k$.

Now we can explain T_STACK's many jobs. It must recapitulate A_REFINE, but not exactly—since eventually the target type will be checked and no longer appear in $r$. The status $s$ differentiates what our requirement is: when $s = ?$, the target type is in $r$. When $s = $ ✓, we either know that $k$ inhabits the target type or that we are currently checking the target type (i.e., an active check of the target type at some blame label reduces to our current checking term).

Finally, we need to define how to merge casts. We use the join operator, which is very nearly concatenation on refinement lists and a contravariant homomorphism on function coercions. It's not

**Coercion implication predicate: axioms** $\boxed{\{x{:}B \mid e_1\} \supset \{x{:}B \mid e_2\}}$

**(Reflexivity)** If $\vdash_{\mathsf{E}} \{x{:}B \mid e\}$ then $\{x{:}B \mid e\} \supset \{x{:}B \mid e\}$.
**(Transitivity)** If $\{x{:}B \mid e_1\} \supset \{x{:}B \mid e_2\}$ and $\{x{:}B \mid e_2\} \supset \{x{:}B \mid e_3\}$ then $\{x{:}B \mid e_1\} \supset \{x{:}B \mid e_3\}$.
**(Adequacy)** If $\{x{:}B \mid e_1\} \supset \{x{:}B \mid e_2\}$ then $\forall k \in \mathcal{K}_B.\ e_1[k/x] \longrightarrow^*_{\mathsf{E}} \mathsf{true}$ implies $e_2[k/x] \longrightarrow^*_{\mathsf{E}} \mathsf{true}$.
**(Decidability)** For all $\vdash_{\mathsf{E}} \{x{:}B \mid e_1\}$ and $\vdash_{\mathsf{E}} \{x{:}B \mid e_2\}$, it is decidable whether $\{x{:}B \mid e_1\} \supset \{x{:}B \mid e_2\}$.

**Coercion well formedness and term typing** $\boxed{\vdash_m c \parallel T_1 \Rightarrow T_2}$ $\boxed{\Gamma \vdash_m e : T}$

$$\frac{\begin{array}{l}\vdash_{\mathsf{E}} \{x{:}B \mid e_1\} \quad \vdash_{\mathsf{E}} \{x{:}B \mid e_2\} \\ \forall \{x{:}B \mid e\} \in r.\ \vdash_{\mathsf{E}} \{x{:}B \mid e\} \quad \text{no duplicates in } r \\ \exists \{x{:}B \mid e\} \in r.\ \{x{:}B \mid e\} \supset \{x{:}B \mid e_2\}\end{array}}{\vdash_{\mathsf{E}} r \parallel \{x{:}B \mid e_1\} \Rightarrow \{x{:}B \mid e_2\}}\ \text{A\_REFINE}$$

$$\frac{\vdash_{\mathsf{E}} c_1 \parallel T_{21} \Rightarrow T_{11} \quad \vdash_{\mathsf{E}} c_2 \parallel T_{12} \Rightarrow T_{22}}{\vdash_{\mathsf{E}} c_1 \mapsto c_2 \parallel (T_{11} \to T_{12}) \Rightarrow (T_{21} \to T_{22})}\ \text{A\_FUN}$$

$$\frac{\begin{array}{l}\vdash_{\mathsf{E}} \Gamma \quad \vdash_{\mathsf{E}} \{x{:}B \mid e_1\} \quad \mathsf{ty}(k) = B \quad \emptyset \vdash_{\mathsf{E}} e_2 : \{x{:}B \mid e_3\} \quad \forall \{x{:}B \mid e\} \in r.\ \vdash_{\mathsf{E}} \{x{:}B \mid e\} \\ s = \checkmark \text{ implies } e_1[k/x] \longrightarrow^*_{\mathsf{E}} \mathsf{true} \vee (\exists \{x{:}B \mid e\}.\ \exists l.\ \{x{:}B \mid e\} \supset \{x{:}B \mid e_1\} \wedge \langle \{x{:}B \mid e\}, e[k/x], k\rangle^l \longrightarrow^*_{\mathsf{E}} e_2) \\ s = {?} \text{ implies } (\exists \{x{:}B \mid e\} \in r.\ \{x{:}B \mid e\} \supset \{x{:}B \mid e_1\})\end{array}}{\Gamma \vdash_{\mathsf{E}} \langle \{x{:}B \mid e_1\}, s, r, k, e_2\rangle^\bullet : \{x{:}B \mid e_2\}}\ \text{T\_STACK}$$

**Values and operational semantics** $\boxed{\mathsf{val}_{\mathsf{E}}\ e}$ $\boxed{e_1 \longrightarrow_{\mathsf{E}} e_2}$

$$\frac{}{\mathsf{val}_{\mathsf{E}}\ \langle T_{11} \to T_{12} \overset{c_1 \mapsto c_2}{\Rightarrow} T_{21} \to T_{22}\rangle^\bullet\ \lambda x{:}T.\ e}\ \text{V\_PROXYE}$$

$$\frac{}{\langle T_1 \overset{\bullet}{\Rightarrow} T_2\rangle^l\ e \longrightarrow_{\mathsf{E}} \langle T_1 \overset{\mathsf{coerce}(T_1, T_2, l)}{\Rightarrow} T_2\rangle^\bullet\ e}\ \text{E\_COERCE}$$

$$\frac{}{\langle \{x{:}B \mid e_1\} \overset{r}{\Rightarrow} \{x{:}B \mid e_2\}\rangle^\bullet\ k \longrightarrow_{\mathsf{E}} \langle \{x{:}B \mid e_2\}, ?, r, k, k\rangle^\bullet}\ \text{E\_COERCESTACK}$$

$$\frac{}{\langle \{x{:}B \mid e\}, s, (\{x{:}B \mid e'\}^l, r), k, k\rangle^\bullet \longrightarrow_{\mathsf{E}} \langle \{x{:}B \mid e\}, s \vee (e = e'), r, k, \langle \{x{:}B \mid e'\}, e'[k/x], k\rangle^l\rangle^\bullet}\ \text{E\_STACKPOP}$$

$$\frac{e' \longrightarrow_{\mathsf{E}} e''}{\langle \{x{:}B \mid e\}, s, r, k, e'\rangle^\bullet \longrightarrow_{\mathsf{E}} \langle \{x{:}B \mid e\}, s, r, k, e''\rangle^\bullet}\ \text{E\_STACKINNER}$$

$$\frac{}{\langle \{x{:}B \mid e\}, s, r, k, \Uparrow l'\rangle^\bullet \longrightarrow_{\mathsf{E}} \Uparrow l'}\ \text{E\_STACKRAISE}$$

$$\frac{}{\langle \{x{:}B \mid e\}, \checkmark, \mathsf{nil}, k, k\rangle^\bullet \longrightarrow_{\mathsf{E}} k}\ \text{E\_STACKDONE}$$

**Cast translation and coercion operations**

$$\begin{array}{rcl}\mathsf{dom}(c_1 \mapsto c_2) &=& c_1 \\ \mathsf{cod}(c_1 \mapsto c_2) &=& c_2\end{array}$$

$$\begin{array}{rcl}\mathsf{coerce}(\{x{:}B \mid e_1\}, \{x{:}B \mid e_2\}, l) &=& \{x{:}B \mid e_2\}^l \\ \mathsf{coerce}(T_{11} \to T_{12}, T_{21} \to T_{22}, l) &=& \mathsf{coerce}(T_{21}, T_{11}, l) \mapsto \mathsf{coerce}(T_{12}, T_{22}, l)\end{array}$$

$$\begin{array}{rcl}\mathsf{join}(\{x{:}B \mid e\}^l, \mathsf{nil}) &=& \{x{:}B \mid e\}^l \\ \mathsf{join}(\{x{:}B \mid e\}^l, r) &=& \{x{:}B \mid e\}^l, \mathsf{drop}(r, \{x{:}B \mid e\})\end{array}$$

$$\begin{array}{rcl}\mathsf{join}(\mathsf{nil}, r_2) &=& r_2 \\ \mathsf{join}(\{x{:}B \mid e\}^l, r_1, r_2) &=& \mathsf{join}(\{x{:}B \mid e\}^l, \mathsf{join}(r_1, r_2)) \\ \mathsf{join}(c_{11} \mapsto c_{12}, c_{21} \mapsto c_{22}) &=& \mathsf{join}(c_{21}, c_{11}) \mapsto \mathsf{join}(c_{12}, c_{22})\end{array}$$

$$\begin{array}{rcl}\mathsf{drop}(\mathsf{nil}, \{x{:}B \mid e\}) &=& \mathsf{nil} \\ \mathsf{drop}((\{x{:}B \mid e_1\}^l, r), \{x{:}B \mid e\}) &=& \begin{cases}\mathsf{drop}(r, \{x{:}B \mid e\}) & \{x{:}B \mid e\} \supset \{x{:}B \mid e_1\} \\ \{x{:}B \mid e_1\}^l, \mathsf{drop}(r, \{x{:}B \mid e\}) & \{x{:}B \mid e\} \not\supset \{x{:}B \mid e_1\}\end{cases}\end{array}$$

$$\begin{array}{rcl}\checkmark \vee (e_1 = e_2) &=& \checkmark \\ ? \vee (e_1 = e_2) &=& \begin{cases}\checkmark & e_1 = e_2 \\ ? & \text{otherwise}\end{cases}\end{array}$$

**Figure 4.** Typing rules and operational semantics for eidetic $\lambda_{\mathrm{H}}$

concatenation because it uses an implication predicate, the pre-order $\supset$, to eliminate duplicates (because $\supset$ is reflexive) and hide subsumed types (because $\supset$ is adequate). We read $\{x{:}B \mid e_1\} \supset \{x{:}B \mid e_2\}$ as "$\{x{:}B \mid e_1\}$ implies $\{x{:}B \mid e_2\}$". When eliminating types, join always chooses the leftmost blame label. Contravariance means that $\mathsf{join}(c_1, c_2)$ takes leftmost labels in positive positions and rightmost labels in negative ones. The coerce metafunction and join operator work together to make sure that the refinement lists are correctly ordered. As we show below, 'correctly ordered' means the positive parts take older labels and negative parts take newer ones. E_CASTMERGEE is slightly subtle—we never merge casts with $\bullet$ as an annotation because such merges aren't defined.

In Figure 4, we only give the axioms for $\supset$: it must be an adequate, decidable pre-order. Syntactic type equality is the simplest implementation of the $\supset$ predicate, but the reflexive transitive closure of any adequate decidable relation would work.

By way of example, consider a cast from $T_1 = \{x{:}\mathsf{Int} \mid x \geq 0\} \to \{x{:}\mathsf{Int} \mid x \geq 0\}$ to $T_2 = \{x{:}\mathsf{Int} \mid \mathsf{true}\} \to \{x{:}\mathsf{Int} \mid x > 0\}$. For brevity, we refer to the domains as $T_{i\,1}$ and the codomains as $T_{i\,2}$. We find that $(\langle T_1 \overset{\bullet}{\Rightarrow} T_2\rangle^l\ v_1)\ v_2$ steps in classic $\lambda_{\mathrm{H}}$ to:

$$\begin{array}{l}\langle \{x{:}\mathsf{Int} \mid x \geq 0\} \overset{\bullet}{\Rightarrow} \{x{:}\mathsf{Int} \mid x > 0\}\rangle^l \\ \quad (v_1\ (\langle \{x{:}\mathsf{Int} \mid \mathsf{true}\} \overset{\bullet}{\Rightarrow} \{x{:}\mathsf{Int} \mid x \geq 0\}\rangle^l\ v_2))\end{array}$$

$$
\begin{aligned}
e = {} & \langle \{x{:}\mathsf{Int} \mid x \bmod 2 = 0\} \overset{\bullet}{\Rightarrow} \{x{:}\mathsf{Int} \mid x \neq 0\} \rangle^{l_3} \\
& \quad (\langle \{x{:}\mathsf{Int} \mid x \geq 0\} \overset{\bullet}{\Rightarrow} \{x{:}\mathsf{Int} \mid x \bmod 2 = 0\} \rangle^{l_2} \\
& \quad\quad (\langle \{x{:}\mathsf{Int} \mid \mathsf{true}\} \overset{\bullet}{\Rightarrow} \{x{:}\mathsf{Int} \mid x \geq 0\} \rangle^{l_1} \ {-1})) \\
& \hfill (\text{E\_COERCE}) \\
\longrightarrow_{\mathsf{E}} {} & \langle \{x{:}\mathsf{Int} \mid x \bmod 2 = 0\} \overset{\{x:\mathsf{Int} \mid x \neq 0\}^{l_3}}{\Rightarrow} \{x{:}\mathsf{Int} \mid x \neq 0\} \rangle^{l_3} \\
& \quad (\langle \{x{:}\mathsf{Int} \mid x \geq 0\} \overset{\bullet}{\Rightarrow} \{x{:}\mathsf{Int} \mid x \bmod 2 = 0\} \rangle^{l_2} \\
& \quad\quad (\langle \{x{:}\mathsf{Int} \mid \mathsf{true}\} \overset{\bullet}{\Rightarrow} \{x{:}\mathsf{Int} \mid x \geq 0\} \rangle^{l_1} \ {-1})) \\
& \hfill (\text{E\_CASTINNER/E\_COERCE}) \\
\longrightarrow_{\mathsf{E}} {} & \langle \{x{:}\mathsf{Int} \mid x \bmod 2 = 0\} \overset{\{x:\mathsf{Int} \mid x \neq 0\}^{l_3}}{\Rightarrow} \{x{:}\mathsf{Int} \mid x \neq 0\} \rangle^{l_3} \\
& \quad (\langle \{x{:}\mathsf{Int} \mid x \geq 0\} \overset{\{x:\mathsf{Int} \mid x \bmod 2 = 0\}^{l_2}}{\Rightarrow} \{x{:}\mathsf{Int} \mid x \bmod 2 = 0\} \rangle^{l_2} \\
& \quad\quad (\langle \{x{:}\mathsf{Int} \mid \mathsf{true}\} \overset{\bullet}{\Rightarrow} \{x{:}\mathsf{Int} \mid x \geq 0\} \rangle^{l_1} \ {-1})) \\
& \hfill (\text{E\_CASTMERGEE}) \\
\longrightarrow_{\mathsf{E}} {} & \langle \{x{:}\mathsf{Int} \mid x \geq 0\} \overset{r'}{\Rightarrow} \{x{:}\mathsf{Int} \mid x \neq 0\} \rangle^{l_3} \\
& \quad (\langle \{x{:}\mathsf{Int} \mid \mathsf{true}\} \overset{\bullet}{\Rightarrow} \{x{:}\mathsf{Int} \mid x \geq 0\} \rangle^{l_1} \ {-1}) \\
& \text{where } r' = \{x{:}\mathsf{Int} \mid x \bmod 2 = 0\}^{l_2}, \{x{:}\mathsf{Int} \mid x \neq 0\}^{l_3} \\
& \hfill (\text{E\_CASTINNER/E\_COERCE}) \\
\longrightarrow_{\mathsf{E}} {} & \langle \{x{:}\mathsf{Int} \mid x \geq 0\} \overset{r'}{\Rightarrow} \{x{:}\mathsf{Int} \mid x \neq 0\} \rangle^{l_3} \\
& \quad (\langle \{x{:}\mathsf{Int} \mid \mathsf{true}\} \overset{\{x:\mathsf{Int} \mid x \geq 0\}^{l_1}}{\Rightarrow} \{x{:}\mathsf{Int} \mid x \geq 0\} \rangle^{l_1} \ {-1}) \\
& \hfill (\text{E\_CASTMERGEE}) \\
\longrightarrow_{\mathsf{E}} {} & \langle \{x{:}\mathsf{Int} \mid \mathsf{true}\} \overset{r}{\Rightarrow} \{x{:}\mathsf{Int} \mid x \neq 0\} \rangle^{l_3} \ {-1} \\
& \text{where } r = \{x{:}\mathsf{Int} \mid x \geq 0\}^{l_1}, r' \\
& \hfill (\text{E\_COERCESTACK}) \\
\longrightarrow_{\mathsf{E}} {} & \langle \{x{:}\mathsf{Int} \mid x \neq 0\}, ?, r, -1, -1 \rangle^{\bullet} \\
& \hfill (\text{E\_STACKPOP}) \\
\longrightarrow_{\mathsf{E}} {} & \langle \{x{:}\mathsf{Int} \mid x \neq 0\}, ?, r', -1, \\
& \quad \langle \{x{:}\mathsf{Int} \mid x \geq 0\}, -1 \geq 0, -1 \rangle^{l_1} \rangle^{\bullet} \\
\longrightarrow_{\mathsf{E}}^{*} {} & \Uparrow l_1
\end{aligned}
$$

**Figure 5.** Example of eidetic $\lambda_H$

Note that $T_1$'s domain is checked but its codomain isn't; the reverse is true for $T_2$. When looking at a cast, we can read off which refinements are checked by looking at the positive parts of the target type and the negative parts of the source type. The relationship between casts and polarity is not a new one [4, 9, 13, 15, 31]. Unlike casts, coercions directly express the sequence of checks to be performed. Consider the coercion generated from the cast above, recalling that $T_{i\,1}$ and $T_{i\,2}$ are the domains and codomains of $T_1$ and $T_2$:

$$
\begin{aligned}
& ((\langle T_1 \overset{\bullet}{\Rightarrow} T_2 \rangle^{l} \ v_1) \ v_2 \\
\longrightarrow_{\mathsf{E}} \ & ((\langle T_1 \overset{c}{\Rightarrow} T_2 \rangle^{\bullet} \ v_1) \ v_2 \\
& \quad \text{where } c = \{x{:}\mathsf{Int} \mid x \geq 0\}^{l} \mapsto \{x{:}\mathsf{Int} \mid x > 0\}^{l} \\
\longrightarrow_{\mathsf{E}} \ & ((\langle T_{11} \rightarrow T_{12} \overset{c}{\Rightarrow} T_{21} \rightarrow T_{22} \rangle^{\bullet} \ v_1) \ v_2 \\
\longrightarrow_{\mathsf{E}} \ & \langle T_{12} \overset{\{x:\mathsf{Int} \mid x > 0\}^{l}}{\Rightarrow} T_{22} \rangle^{\bullet} \ (v_1 \ (\langle T_{21} \overset{\{x:\mathsf{Int} \mid x \geq 0\}^{l}}{\Rightarrow} T_{11} \rangle^{\bullet} \ v_2))
\end{aligned}
$$

In this example, there is only a single blame label, $l$. Tracking blame labels is critical for exactly matching classic $\lambda_H$'s behavior. The examples rely on $\supset$ being reflexive. First, we return to our example from before in Figure 5. Throughout the merging, each refinement type retains its own original blame label, allowing eidetic $\lambda_H$ to behave just like classic $\lambda_H$.

We offer a final pair of examples, showing how coercions with redundant types are merged. The intuition here is that positive positions are checked covariantly—oldest (innermost) cast first—while negative positions are checked contravariantly—newest (outermost) cast first. Consider the classic $\lambda_H$ term:

$$
\begin{aligned}
T_1 &= \{x{:}\mathsf{Int} \mid e_{11}\} \rightarrow \{x{:}\mathsf{Int} \mid e_{21}\} \\
T_2 &= \{x{:}\mathsf{Int} \mid e_{12}\} \rightarrow \{x{:}\mathsf{Int} \mid e_{22}\} \\
T_3 &= \{x{:}\mathsf{Int} \mid e_{13}\} \rightarrow \{x{:}\mathsf{Int} \mid e_{22}\} \\
e &= \langle T_2 \overset{\bullet}{\Rightarrow} T_3 \rangle^{l_2} \ (\langle T_1 \overset{\bullet}{\Rightarrow} T_2 \rangle^{l_1} \ v)
\end{aligned}
$$

Note that the casts run inside-out, from old to new in the positive position, but they run from the outside-in, new to old, in the negative position.

$$
\begin{aligned}
e \ v' \longrightarrow_{\mathsf{C}} \ & \langle \{x{:}\mathsf{Int} \mid e_{22}\} \overset{\bullet}{\Rightarrow} \{x{:}\mathsf{Int} \mid e_{22}\} \rangle^{l_2} \\
& \quad (\langle \{x{:}\mathsf{Int} \mid e_{21}\} \overset{\bullet}{\Rightarrow} \{x{:}\mathsf{Int} \mid e_{22}\} \rangle^{l_1} \\
& \quad\quad (v \ (\langle \{x{:}\mathsf{Int} \mid e_{12}\} \overset{\bullet}{\Rightarrow} \{x{:}\mathsf{Int} \mid e_{12}\} \rangle^{l_1} \\
& \quad\quad\quad (\langle \{x{:}\mathsf{Int} \mid e_{13}\} \overset{\bullet}{\Rightarrow} \{x{:}\mathsf{Int} \mid e_{12}\} \rangle^{l_2} \ v'))))
\end{aligned}
$$

The key observation for eliminating redundant checks is that only the check run first can fail—there's no point in checking a predicate contract twice on the same value. So eidetic $\lambda_H$ merges like so:

$$
\begin{aligned}
e \ \longrightarrow_{\mathsf{E}}^{*} \ & \langle T_2 \overset{\{x:\mathsf{Int} \mid e_{12}\}^{l_2} \mapsto \{x:\mathsf{Int} \mid e_{22}\}^{l_2}}{\Rightarrow} T_3 \rangle^{\bullet} \\
& \quad (\langle T_1 \overset{\{x:\mathsf{Int} \mid e_{11}\}^{l_1} \mapsto \{x:\mathsf{Int} \mid e_{22}\}^{l_1}}{\Rightarrow} T_2 \rangle^{\bullet} \ v) \\
\longrightarrow_{\mathsf{E}} \ & \langle T_1 \overset{c}{\Rightarrow} T_3 \rangle^{\bullet} \ v
\end{aligned}
$$

where

$$
\begin{aligned}
c = {} & \mathsf{join}(\{x{:}\mathsf{Int} \mid e_{12}\}^{l_2}, \{x{:}\mathsf{Int} \mid e_{11}\}^{l_1}) \mapsto \\
& \mathsf{join}(\{x{:}\mathsf{Int} \mid e_{22}\}^{l_1}, \{x{:}\mathsf{Int} \mid e_{22}\}^{l_2}) \\
= {} & \{x{:}\mathsf{Int} \mid e_{12}\}^{l_2}, \{x{:}\mathsf{Int} \mid e_{11}\}^{l_1} \mapsto \{x{:}\mathsf{Int} \mid e_{22}\}^{l_1}
\end{aligned}
$$

The coercion merge operator eliminates the redundant codomain check, choosing to keep the one with blame label $l_1$. Choosing $l_1$ makes sense here because the codomain is a positive position and $l_1$ is the older, innermost cast. We construct a similar example for merges in negative positions.

$$
\begin{aligned}
T_1 &= \{x{:}\mathsf{Int} \mid e_{11}\} \rightarrow \{x{:}\mathsf{Int} \mid e_{21}\} \\
T_2' &= \{x{:}\mathsf{Int} \mid e_{11}\} \rightarrow \{x{:}\mathsf{Int} \mid e_{22}\} \\
T_3' &= \{x{:}\mathsf{Int} \mid e_{13}\} \rightarrow \{x{:}\mathsf{Int} \mid e_{23}\} \\
e' &= \langle T_2' \overset{\bullet}{\Rightarrow} T_3' \rangle^{l_2} \ (\langle T_1 \overset{\bullet}{\Rightarrow} T_2' \rangle^{l_1} \ v)
\end{aligned}
$$

Again, the unfolding runs the positive parts inside-out and the negative parts outside-in when applied to a value $v'$:

$$
\begin{aligned}
& \langle \{x{:}\mathsf{Int} \mid e_{22}\} \overset{\bullet}{\Rightarrow} \{x{:}\mathsf{Int} \mid e_{23}\} \rangle^{l_2} \\
& \quad (\langle \{x{:}\mathsf{Int} \mid e_{21}\} \overset{\bullet}{\Rightarrow} \{x{:}\mathsf{Int} \mid e_{22}\} \rangle^{l_1} \\
& \quad\quad (v \ (\langle \{x{:}\mathsf{Int} \mid e_{11}\} \overset{\bullet}{\Rightarrow} \{x{:}\mathsf{Int} \mid e_{11}\} \rangle^{l_1} \\
& \quad\quad\quad (\langle \{x{:}\mathsf{Int} \mid e_{13}\} \overset{\bullet}{\Rightarrow} \{x{:}\mathsf{Int} \mid e_{11}\} \rangle^{l_2} \ v'))))
\end{aligned}
$$

Running the example in eidetic $\lambda_H$, we reduce the redundant checks in the domain:

$$
\begin{aligned}
e' \ \longrightarrow_{\mathsf{E}}^{*} \ & \langle T_2' \overset{\{x:\mathsf{Int} \mid e_{11}\}^{l_2} \mapsto \{x:\mathsf{Int} \mid e_{23}\}^{l_2}}{\Rightarrow} T_3' \rangle^{\bullet} \\
& \quad (\langle T_1 \overset{\{x:\mathsf{Int} \mid e_{11}\}^{l_1} \mapsto \{x:\mathsf{Int} \mid e_{22}\}^{l_1}}{\Rightarrow} T_2' \rangle^{\bullet} \ v) \\
\longrightarrow_{\mathsf{E}} \ & \langle T_1 \overset{c}{\Rightarrow} T_3' \rangle^{\bullet} \ v
\end{aligned}
$$

where

$$
\begin{aligned}
c = {} & \mathsf{join}(\{x{:}\mathsf{Int} \mid e_{11}\}^{l_2}, \{x{:}\mathsf{Int} \mid e_{11}\}^{l_1}) \mapsto \\
& \mathsf{join}(\{x{:}\mathsf{Int} \mid e_{22}\}^{l_1}, \{x{:}\mathsf{Int} \mid e_{23}\}^{l_2}) \\
= {} & \{x{:}\mathsf{Int} \mid e_{12}\}^{l_2} \mapsto \{x{:}\mathsf{Int} \mid e_{22}\}^{l_1}, \{x{:}\mathsf{Int} \mid e_{23}\}^{l_2}
\end{aligned}
$$

Following the outside-in rule for negative positions, we keep the blame label $l_2$ from the newer, outermost cast.

### 4.1 Metatheory

The proof of type soundness is a standard syntactic proof, relying on a few small lemmas concerning refinement list well formedness and the generic metatheory described in Section 3.3. The full proofs are in Appendix A.3.

**Lemma [Eidetic canonical forms (A.15)]:** If $\emptyset \vdash_{\mathsf{E}} e : T$ and $\mathsf{val}_{\mathsf{E}}\ e$ then:

- If $T = \{x{:}B \mid e'\}$, then $e = k$ and $\mathsf{ty}(k) = B$ and $e'[e/x] \longrightarrow^*_{\mathsf{E}} \mathsf{true}$.
- If $T = T_{21} \to T_{22}$, then either $e = \lambda x{:}T.\ e'$ or $e = \langle T_{11} \to T_{12} \overset{c_1 \mapsto c_2}{\Rightarrow} T_{21} \to T_{22}\rangle^{\bullet}\ \lambda x{:}T_{11}.\ e'$.

**Lemma [Eidetic progress (A.16)]:** If $\emptyset \vdash_{\mathsf{E}} e : T$, then either:

1. $\mathsf{result}_{\mathsf{E}}\ e$, i.e., $e = \Uparrow l$ or $\mathsf{val}_{\mathsf{E}}\ e$; or
2. there exists an $e'$ such that $e \longrightarrow_{\mathsf{E}} e'$.

**Lemma [Eidetic preservation (A.20)]:** If $\emptyset \vdash_{\mathsf{E}} e : T$ and $e \longrightarrow_{\mathsf{E}} e'$ then $\emptyset \vdash_{\mathsf{E}} e' : T$.

Eidetic $\lambda_{\mathrm{H}}$ shares source programs (Definition 3.1) with classic $\lambda_{\mathrm{H}}$. We can therefore say that classic and eidetic $\lambda_{\mathrm{H}}$ are really just *modes* of a single language.

**Lemma [Source program typing for eidetic $\lambda_{\mathrm{H}}$ (A.21)]:** Source programs are well typed in $\mathsf{C}$ iff they are well typed in $\mathsf{E}$, i.e.:

- $\Gamma \vdash_{\mathsf{C}} e : T$ as a source program iff $\Gamma \vdash_{\mathsf{E}} e : T$ as a source program.
- $\vdash_{\mathsf{C}} T$ as a source program iff $\vdash_{\mathsf{E}} T$ as a source program.
- $\vdash_{\mathsf{C}} \Gamma$ as a source program iff $\vdash_{\mathsf{E}} \Gamma$ as a source program.

## 5. Soundness for space efficiency

We want space efficiency to be *sound*: it would be space efficient to never check anything. Classic $\lambda_{\mathrm{H}}$ is normative: the more a mode behaves like classic $\lambda_{\mathrm{H}}$, the "sounder" it is.

A single property summarizes how a space-efficient calculus behaves with respect to classic $\lambda_{\mathrm{H}}$: cast congruence. In classic $\lambda_{\mathrm{H}}$, if $e_1 \longrightarrow_{\mathsf{C}} e_2$ then $\langle T_1 \overset{\bullet}{\Rightarrow} T_2\rangle^l\ e_1$ and $\langle T_1 \overset{\bullet}{\Rightarrow} T_2\rangle^l\ e_2$ behave identically. This cast congruence principle is easy to see, because E_CASTINNERC applies freely. In eidetic $\lambda_{\mathrm{H}}$, however, E_CASTINNER can only apply when E_CASTMERGEE doesn't. Merged casts may not behave the same as running the two casts separately. Eidetic $\lambda_{\mathrm{H}}$ recovers a complete cast congruence, just like classic $\lambda_{\mathrm{H}}$ has. Diagrammatically:

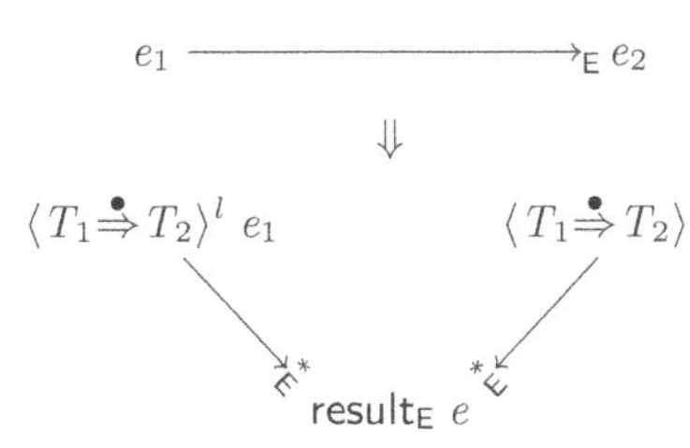

The proof is in Appendix B, but it is worth observing here that eidetic $\lambda_{\mathrm{H}}$ needs a proof of idempotency to justify the way it uses reflexivity to eliminate redundant coercions: checking a property once is as good as checking it twice. Naturally, this property only holds without state.

Our proofs relating classic $\lambda_{\mathrm{H}}$ and eidetic $\lambda_{\mathrm{H}}$ are by logical relations, found in Figure 6. In the extended version, the soundness proofs for all three different space-efficient modes use a single mode-indexed logical relation. Here we give its restriction to eidetic $\lambda_{\mathrm{H}}$. As far as alternative techniques go, an induction over evaluation derivations wouldn't give us enough information about evaluations that return lambda abstractions. Other contextual equivalence techniques (e.g., bisimulation) would probably work, too.

**Value rules** $\boxed{e_1 \sim_{\mathsf{E}} e_2 : T}$

$$\begin{array}{rcl} k \sim_{\mathsf{E}} k : \{x{:}B \mid e\} & \iff & \mathsf{ty}(k) = B \wedge e[k/x] \longrightarrow^*_{\mathsf{E}} \mathsf{true} \\ e_{11} \sim_{\mathsf{E}} e_{21} : T_1 \to T_2 & \iff & \mathsf{val}_{\mathsf{C}}\ e_1 \wedge \mathsf{val}_{\mathsf{E}}\ e_2 \wedge \\ & & \forall e_{12} \sim_{\mathsf{E}} e_{22} : T_1.\ e_{11}\ e_{12} \simeq_{\mathsf{E}} e_{21}\ e_{22} : T_2 \end{array}$$

**Term rules** $\boxed{e_1 \simeq_{\mathsf{E}} e_2 : T}$

$$e_1 \simeq_{\mathsf{E}} e_2 : T \iff \begin{pmatrix} e_1 \longrightarrow^*_{\mathsf{C}} \Uparrow l \wedge \\ e_2 \longrightarrow^*_{\mathsf{E}} \Uparrow l \end{pmatrix} \vee \begin{pmatrix} e_1 \longrightarrow^*_{\mathsf{C}} e_1' \wedge \mathsf{val}_{\mathsf{C}}\ e_1' \wedge \\ e_2 \longrightarrow^*_{\mathsf{E}} e_2' \wedge \mathsf{val}_{\mathsf{E}}\ e_2' \wedge \\ e_1' \sim_{\mathsf{E}} e_2' : T \end{pmatrix}$$

**Type rules** $\boxed{T_1 \sim_{\mathsf{E}} T_2}$

$$\begin{array}{l} \{x{:}B \mid e_1\} \sim_{\mathsf{E}} \{x{:}B \mid e_2\} \iff \\ \forall e_1' \sim_{\mathsf{E}} e_2' : \{x{:}B \mid \mathsf{true}\}.\ e_1[e_1'/x] \simeq_{\mathsf{E}} e_2[e_2'/x] : \{x{:}\mathsf{Bool} \mid \mathsf{true}\} \\ T_{11} \to T_{12} \sim_{\mathsf{E}} T_{21} \to T_{22} \iff T_{11} \sim_{\mathsf{E}} T_{21} \wedge T_{12} \sim_{\mathsf{E}} T_{22} \end{array}$$

**Closing substitutions and open terms** $\boxed{\Gamma \models_{\mathsf{E}} \delta}$ $\boxed{\Gamma \vdash e_1 \simeq_{\mathsf{E}} e_2 : T}$

$$\begin{array}{rcl} \Gamma \models_{\mathsf{E}} \delta & \iff & \forall x \in \mathsf{dom}(\Gamma).\ \delta_1(x) \sim_{\mathsf{E}} \delta_2(x) : \Gamma(x) \\ \Gamma \vdash e_1 \simeq_{\mathsf{E}} e_2 : T & \iff & \forall \Gamma \models_{\mathsf{E}} \delta.\ \delta_1(e_1) \simeq_{\mathsf{E}} \delta_2(e_2) : T \end{array}$$

**Figure 6.** Blame-exact, symmetric logical relation between classic $\lambda_{\mathrm{H}}$ and eidetic $\lambda_{\mathrm{H}}$

| Mode | Cast size | Pending casts |
|---|---|---|
| Classic ($m = \mathsf{C}$) | $2W_h + L$ | $\infty$ |
| Eidetic ($m = \mathsf{E}$) | $s2^{L+W_B}$ | $\|e\|$ |

**Table 1.** Space efficiency of $\lambda_{\mathrm{H}}$

**Lemma [Similar casts are logically related (B.3)]:** If $T_1 \sim_{\mathsf{E}} T_1'$ and $T_2 \sim_{\mathsf{E}} T_2'$ and $e_1 \sim_{\mathsf{E}} e_2 : T_1$, then $\langle T_1 \overset{\bullet}{\Rightarrow} T_2\rangle^l\ e_1 \simeq_{\mathsf{E}} \langle T_1' \overset{\bullet}{\Rightarrow} T_2'\rangle^l\ e_2 : T_2$.

**Lemma [Relating classic and eidetic source programs (B.4)]:**

1. If $\Gamma \vdash_{\mathsf{C}} e : T$ as a source program then $\Gamma \vdash e \simeq_{\mathsf{E}} e : T$.
2. If $\vdash_{\mathsf{C}} T$ as a source program then $T \sim_{\mathsf{E}} T$.

## 6. Bounds for space efficiency

We have claimed that eidetic $\lambda_{\mathrm{H}}$ is space efficient: what do we mean? What sort of space efficiency have we achieved? We summarize the results in Table 1; proofs are in Appendix C. From a high level, there are only a finite number of types that appear in our programs, and this set of types can only reduce as the program runs. We can effectively code each type in the program as an integer, allowing us to efficiently run the $\supset$ predicate.

Suppose that a type of height $h$ can be represented in $W_h$ bits and a label in $L$ bits. (Type heights are defined in Figure 7 in Appendix C.) Casts in classic $\lambda_{\mathrm{H}}$ each take up $2W_h + L$ bits: two types and a blame label. Coercions in eidetic $\lambda_{\mathrm{H}}$ have a different form: the only types recorded are those of height 1, i.e., refinements of base types. Pessimistically, each of these may appear at every position in a function coercion $c_1 \mapsto c_2$. We use $s$ to indicate the "size" of a function type, i.e., the number of positions it has. As a first pass, a set of refinements and blame labels take up $2^{L+W_1}$ space. But in fact these coercions must all be between refinements *of the same base type*, leading to $2^{L+W_B}$ space per coercion, where $W_B$ is the highest number of refinements of any single base type. We now have our worst-case space complexity: $s2^{L+W_B}$. A more precise bound might track which refinements appear in which parts of a function type, but in the worst case—each refinement appears in every position—it degenerates to the bound we give here. Classic $\lambda_H$ can have an infinite number of "pending casts"—casts and function proxies—in a program. Eidetic $\lambda_H$ can have no more than one pending cast per term node. Abstractions are limited to a single function proxy, and E_CASTMERGEE merges adjacent pending casts.

The text of a program $e$ is finite, so the set of types appearing in the program, $\mathsf{types}(e)$, is also finite. Since reduction doesn't introduce types, we can bound the number of types in a program (and therefore the size of casts). We can therefore fix a numerical coding for types at runtime, where we can encode a type in $W = \log_2(|\mathsf{types}(e)|)$ bits. In a given cast, $W$ over-approximates how many types can appear: the source, target, and annotation must all be compatible, which means they must also be of the same height. We can therefore represent the types in casts with fewer bits: $W_h = \log_2(|\{T \mid T \in \mathsf{types}(e) \wedge \mathsf{height}(T) = h\}|)$. In the worst case, we revert to the original bound: all types in the program are of height 1. Even so, there are never casts between different base types $B$ and $B'$, so $W_B = \max_B \log_2(|\{\{x{:}B \mid e\} \in \mathsf{types}(e)\}|)$. Eidetic $\lambda_H$'s coercions never hold types greater than height 1. The types on its casts are erasable once the coercions are generated, because coercions drive the checking.

### 6.1 Representation choices

The bounds we find here are *galactic*. Having established that contracts are theoretically space efficient, making an implementation practically space efficient is a different endeavor, involving careful choices of representations and calling conventions.

Eidetic $\lambda_H$'s space bounds rely only on the reflexivity of the $\supset$ predicate, since we leave it abstract. We have identified one situation where the relation allows us to find better space bounds: mutual implication.

If $\{x{:}B \mid e_1\} \supset \{x{:}B \mid e_2\}$ and $\{x{:}B \mid e_2\} \supset \{x{:}B \mid e_1\}$, then these two types are equivalent, and only one ever need be checked. Which to check could be determined by a compiler with a suitably clever cost model. Note that our proofs don't entirely justify this optimization. By default, our join operator will take whichever of $\{x{:}B \mid e_1\}$ and $\{x{:}B \mid e_2\}$ was meant to be checked first. Adapting join to always choose one based on some preference relation would not be particularly hard, and we believe the proofs adapt easily.

Other analyses of the relation seem promising at first, but in fact do not allow more compact representations. Suppose we have a program where $\{x{:}B \mid e_1\} \supset \{x{:}B \mid e_2\}$ but not vice versa, and that $B$ is our worst case type. That is, $W_B = 2$, because there are 2 different refinements of $B$ and fewer refinements of other base types. The worst-case representation for a refinement list is 2 bits, with bit $b_i$ indicating whether $e_i$ is present in the list. Can we do any better than 2 bits, since $e_1$ can stand in for $e_2$? Could we represent the two types as just 1 bit? We cannot when (a) there are constants that pass one type but not the other and (b) when refinement lists are in the reverse order of implication. Suppose there is some $k$ such that $e_2[k/x] \longrightarrow^*_{\mathsf{E}}$ true and $e_1[k/x] \longrightarrow^*_{\mathsf{E}}$ false. Now we consider a concatenation of refinement lists in the reverse ordering: $\mathsf{join}(\{x{:}B \mid e_2\}^l, \{x{:}B \mid e_1\}^{l'})$. We must retain both checks, since different failures lead to different blame. The $k$ that passes $e_2$ but not $e_1$ should raise $\Uparrow l'$, but other $k'$ that fail for both types should raise $\Uparrow l$. One bit isn't enough to capture the situation of having the coercion $\{x{:}B \mid e_2\}^l, \{x{:}B \mid e_1\}^{l'}$.

Finally, what is the right representation for a function? When calling a function, do we need to run coercions or not? Jeremy Siek suggested a "smart closure" which holds the logic for branching inside its own code; this may support better branch prediction than an indirect jump or branching at call sites.

## 7. Related work

Some earlier work uses first-class casts, whereas our casts are always applied to a term [1, 17]. It is of course possible to $\eta$-expand a cast with an abstraction, so no expressiveness is lost. Leaving casts fully applied saves us from the puzzling rules managing how casts work on other casts in space-efficient semantics, like: $\langle T_{11} \to T_{12} \overset{\bullet}{\Rightarrow} T_{21} \to T_{22} \rangle^l \; \langle T_{11} \overset{\bullet}{\Rightarrow} T_{12} \rangle^{l'} \longrightarrow_{\mathsf{F}} \langle T_{21} \overset{\bullet}{\Rightarrow} T_{22} \rangle^l$.

Previous approaches to space-efficiency have focused on gradual typing [27]. This work uses coercions [14], casts, casts annotated with intermediate types a/k/a *threesomes*, or some combination of all three [8, 16, 24, 26, 28]. Recent work relates all three frameworks, making particular use of coercions [25]. Our type structure differs from that of gradual types, so our space bounds come in a somewhat novel form. Gradual types, without the more complicated checking that comes with predicate contracts, allow for simpler designs. Siek and Wadler [28] can define a simple recursive operator on labeled types with a strong relationship to subtyping, the fundamental property of casts. We haven't been able to discover a connection in our setting. Instead, we ignore the type structure of functions and focus our attention on managing labels in lists of first-order predicate contracts. In the gradual world, only Rastogi et al. [23] take a similar approach, "recursively deconstruct[ing] higher-order types down to their first-order parts" when they compute the closure of flows into and out of type variables. Gradual types occasionally have simpler proofs, too, e.g., by induction on evaluation [24]; even when strong reasoning principles are needed, the presence of dynamic types leads them to use bisimulation [8, 25, 28]. We use logical relations because $\lambda_H$'s type structure is readily available, and because they allow us to easily reason about how checks evaluate.

Our coercions are inspired by Henglein's coercions for modeling injection to and projection from the dynamic type [14]. Henglein's primitive coercions tag and untag values, while ours represent checks to be performed on base types; both our formulation and Henglein's use structural function coercions.

Greenberg [9], the most closely related work, offers a coercion language combining the dynamic types of Henglein's original work with predicate contracts; his EFFICIENT language does not quite achieve "sound" space efficeincy. Rather, it is forgetful, occasionally dropping casts. He omits blame, though he conjectures that blame for coercions reads left to right (as it does in Siek and Garcia [26]); our eidetic $\lambda_H$ verifies this conjecture. While Greenberg's languages offer dynamic, simple, and refined types, our types here are entirely refined. His coercions use Henglein's ! and ? syntax for injection and projection, while our coercions lack such a distinction. In our refinement lists, each coercion simultaneously projects from one refinement type and injects into another (possibly producing blame). We reduce notation by omitting the interrobang '‽'.

Dimoulas et al. [3] introduce *option contracts*, which offer a programmatic way of turning off contract checking, as well as a controlled way to "pass the buck", handing off contracts from component to component. Option contracts address time efficiency, not space efficiency. Findler et al. [6] studied space and time efficiency for datatype contracts, as did Koukoutos and Kuncak [19].

Racket contracts have a mild form of space efficiency: the `tail-marks-match?` predicate[1] checks for exact duplicate contracts and blame at tail positions. The redundancy it detects seems

[1] From `racket/collects/racket/contract/private/arrow.rkt`.

to rely on pointer equality. Since Racket contracts are (a) module-oriented "macro" contracts and (b) first class, this optimization is somewhat unpredictable—and limited compared with our eidetic calculus, which can handle differing contracts and blame labels.

## 8. Conclusion and future work

Semantics-preserving space efficiency for manifest contracts is possible—leaving the admissibility of state as the final barrier to practical utility. We established that eidetic $\lambda_H$ behaves exactly like its classic counterpart without compromising space usage.

We believe it would be easy to design a latent version of eidetic $\lambda_H$, following the translations in Greenberg et al. [11].

In our simple (i.e., not dependent) case, our refinement types close over a single variable of base type. Space efficiency for a dependent calculus remains open. The first step towards dependent types would be extending $\supset$ with a context (and a source of closing substitutions, a serious issue [1]). In a dependent setting the definition of what it means to compare closures isn't at all clear. Closures' environments may contain functions, and closures over extensionally equivalent functions may not be intensionally equal. A more nominal approach to contract comparison may resolve some of the issues here. Comparisons might be more straightforward when contracts are explicitly declared and referenced by name. Similarly, a dependent $\supset$ predicate might be more easily defined over some explicit structured family of types, like a lattice. Findler et al. [6] has made some progress in this direction.

Finally, a host of practical issues remain. Beyond representation choices, having expensive checks makes it important to predict *when* checks happen. The $\supset$ predicate compares closures and will surely have delicate interactions with optimizations.

## Acknowledgments

Comments from Rajeev Alur, Ron Garcia, Fritz Henglein, Greg Morrisett, Stephanie Weirich, Phil Wadler, and Steve Zdancewic improved a previous version of this work done at the University of Pennsylvania. Some comments from Benjamin Pierce led me to realize that a cast formulation was straightforward. Discussions with Atsushi Igarashi, Robby Findler, and Sam Tobin-Hochstadt greatly improved the quality of the exposition. Phil Wadler encouraged me to return to coercions to understand the eidetic formulation. The POPL reviewers had many excellent suggestions, and Robby Findler helped once more with angelic guidance. Hannah de Keijzer proofread the paper.

This work was supported in part by the NSF under grants TC 0915671 and SHF 1016937 and by the DARPA CRASH program through the United States Air Force Research Laboratory (AFRL) under Contract No. FA8650-10-C-7090. The views expressed are the author's and do not reflect the official policy or position of the Department of Defense or the U.S. Government.

## References

[1] J. F. Belo, M. Greenberg, A. Igarashi, and B. C. Pierce. Polymorphic contracts. In *European Symposium on Programming (ESOP)*, 2011.

[2] G. M. Bierman, A. D. Gordon, C. Hriţcu, and D. Langworthy. Semantic subtyping with an SMT solver. In *International Conference on Functional Programming (ICFP)*, 2010.

[3] C. Dimoulas, R. Findler, and M. Felleisen. Option contracts. In *OOPSLA*, pages 475 – 494, 2013.

[4] R. B. Findler. Contracts as pairs of projections. In *Symposium on Logic Programming*, 2006.

[5] R. B. Findler and M. Felleisen. Contracts for higher-order functions. In *International Conference on Functional Programming (ICFP)*, 2002.

[6] R. B. Findler, S.-Y. Guo, and A. Rogers. Lazy contract checking for immutable data structures. In *Implementation and Application of Functional Languages*, pages 111–128. 2008. .

[7] C. Flanagan. Hybrid type checking. In *Principles of Programming Languages (POPL)*, 2006.

[8] R. Garcia. Calculating threesomes, with blame. In *International Conference on Functional Programming (ICFP)*, 2013.

[9] M. Greenberg. *Manifest Contracts*. PhD thesis, University of Pennsylvania, November 2013.

[10] M. Greenberg. Space-efficient manifest contracts, 2014. URL `http://arxiv.org/abs/1410.2813`. Technical report.

[11] M. Greenberg, B. C. Pierce, and S. Weirich. Contracts made manifest. In *Principles of Programming Languages (POPL)*, 2010.

[12] M. Greenberg, B. C. Pierce, and S. Weirich. Contracts made manifest. *Journal of Functional Programming (JFP)*, 22(3):225–274, May 2012.

[13] J. Gronski and C. Flanagan. Unifying hybrid types and contracts. In *Trends in Functional Programming (TFP)*, 2007.

[14] F. Henglein. Dynamic typing: Syntax and proof theory. *Sci. Comput. Program.*, 22(3):197–230, 1994.

[15] D. Herman, A. Tomb, and C. Flanagan. Space-efficient gradual typing. In *Trends in Functional Programming (TFP)*, pages 404–419, 2007.

[16] D. Herman, A. Tomb, and C. Flanagan. Space-efficient gradual typing. *Higher Order Symbol. Comput.*, 23(2):167–189, June 2010.

[17] K. Knowles and C. Flanagan. Hybrid type checking. *ACM Trans. Prog. Lang. Syst.*, 32:6:1–6:34, 2010.

[18] K. Knowles, A. Tomb, J. Gronski, S. N. Freund, and C. Flanagan. Sage: Hybrid checking for flexible specifications. In *Scheme and Functional Programming Workshop*, 2006.

[19] E. Koukoutos and V. Kuncak. Checking data structure properties orders of magnitude faster. In *Runtime Verification*, pages 263–268. 2014. .

[20] R. Lipton, October 2010. URL `http://goo.gl/6GrgtO`.

[21] R. Milner. A theory of type polymorphism in programming. *Journal of Computer and System Sciences*, 17:348–375, Aug. 1978.

[22] PLT. Racket contract system, 2013. URL `http://pre.plt-scheme.org/docs/html/guide/contracts.html`.

[23] A. Rastogi, A. Chaudhuri, and B. Hosmer. The ins and outs of gradual type inference. In *Principles of Programming Languages (POPL)*, 2012. .

[24] J. Siek, R. Garcia, and W. Taha. Exploring the design space of higher-order casts. In *Programming Languages and Systems*, volume 5502 of *LNCS*, pages 17–31. 2009.

[25] J. Siek, P. Thiemann, and P. Wadler. Blame, coercion, and threesomes: Together again for the first time. Draft., 2014. URL `http://homepages.inf.ed.ac.uk/wadler/topics/blame.html#coercions`.

[26] J. G. Siek and R. Garcia. Interpretations of the gradually-typed lambda calculus. In *Scheme and Functional Programming (SFP)*, 2012.

[27] J. G. Siek and W. Taha. Gradual typing for functional languages. In *Scheme and Functional Programming Workshop*, September 2006.

[28] J. G. Siek and P. Wadler. Threesomes, with and without blame. In *Principles of Programming Languages (POPL)*, pages 365–376, 2010.

[29] N. Swamy, M. Hicks, and G. M. Bierman. A theory of typed coercions and its applications. In *International Conference on Functional Programming (ICFP)*, pages 329–340, 2009. ISBN 978-1-60558-332-7.

[30] S. Tobin-Hochstadt and M. Felleisen. Interlanguage migration: From scripts to programs. In *OOPSLA*, 2006. .

[31] P. Wadler and R. B. Findler. Well-typed programs can't be blamed. In *European Symposium on Programming (ESOP)*, 2009.

[32] A. K. Wright and M. Felleisen. A syntactic approach to type soundness. *Information and Computation*, 115:38–94, 1994.

## A. Proofs of type soundness

This appendix includes the proofs of type soundness for all four modes of $\lambda_H$; we first prove some universally applicable metatheoretical properties.

### A.1 Generic metatheory

**A.1 Lemma [Weakening]:** If $\Gamma_1, \Gamma_2 \vdash_m e : T$ and $\vdash_m T'$ and $x$ is fresh, then $\vdash_m \Gamma_1, x{:}T', \Gamma_2$ and $\Gamma_1, x{:}T', \Gamma_2 \vdash_m e : T$.

**A.2 Lemma [Substitution]:** If $\Gamma_1, x{:}T', \Gamma_2 \vdash_m e : T$ and $\emptyset \vdash_m e' : T'$, then $\Gamma_1, \Gamma_2 \vdash_m e[e'/x] : T$ and $\vdash_m \Gamma_1, \Gamma_2$.

**A.3 Lemma [Regularity]:** If $\Gamma \vdash_m e : T$, then $\vdash_m \Gamma$ and $\vdash_m T$.

**A.4 Lemma [Similarity is reflexive]:** If $\vdash T \parallel T$.

**Proof:** By induction on $T$.

($T = \{x{:}B \mid e\}$) By S_REFINE.
($T = T_1 \to T_2$) By S_FUN and the IHs.

□

**A.5 Lemma [Similarity is symmetric]:** If $\vdash T_1 \parallel T_2$, then $\vdash T_2 \parallel T_1$.

**Proof:** By induction on the similarity derivation.

(S_REFINE) By S_REFINE.
(S_FUN) By S_FUN and the IHs.

□

**A.6 Lemma [Similarity is transitive]:** If $\vdash T_1 \parallel T_2$ and $\vdash T_2 \parallel T_3$, then $\vdash T_1 \parallel T_3$.

**Proof:** By induction on the derivation of $\vdash T_1 \parallel T_2$.

(S_REFINE) The other derivation must also be by S_REFINE; by S_REFINE.
(S_FUN) The other derivation must also be by S_FUN; by S_FUN and the IHs.

□

**A.7 Lemma [Well formed type sets have similar indices]:** If $\vdash_m \mathcal{S} \parallel T_1 \Rightarrow T_2$ then $\vdash T_1 \parallel T_2$.

**Proof:** Immediate, by inversion. □

**A.8 Lemma [Type set well formedness is symmetric]:** $\vdash_m a \parallel T_1 \Rightarrow T_2$ iff $\vdash_m a \parallel T_2 \Rightarrow T_1$ for all $m \neq \mathsf{E}$.

**Proof:** We immediately have $\vdash_m T_1$ and $\vdash_m T_2$, and $\vdash T_1 \parallel T_2$ iff $\vdash T_2 \parallel T_1$ by Lemma A.5.

If $m = \mathsf{C}$ or $m = \mathsf{F}$, then by A_NONE and symmetry of similarity (Lemma A.5.

If $m = \mathsf{H}$, then let $T \in \mathcal{S}$ be given. The $\vdash_{\mathsf{H}} T$ premises hold immediately; we are then done by transitivity (Lemma A.6) and symmetry (Lemma A.5) of similarity ($\vdash T \parallel T_1$ iff $\vdash T \parallel T_2$ when $\vdash T_1 \parallel T_2$). □

**A.9 Lemma [Type set well formedness is transitive]:** If $\vdash T_1 \parallel T_2$ and $\vdash_m a \parallel T_2 \Rightarrow T_3$ and $\vdash_m T_1$ and $m \neq \mathsf{E}$ then $\vdash_m a \parallel T_1 \Rightarrow T_3$.

**Proof:** We immediately have $\vdash_m T_1$ and $\vdash_m T_3$; we have $\vdash T_1 \parallel T_3$ by transitivity of similarity (Lemma A.6).

If $m = \mathsf{C}$ or $m = \mathsf{F}$, we are done immediately by A_NONE.

If, on the other hand, $m = \mathsf{H}$, let $T \in \mathcal{S}$ be given. We know that $\vdash_{\mathsf{H}} T$ and $\vdash T \parallel T_2$; by symmetry (Lemma A.5) and transitivity (Lemma A.6) of similarity, we are done by A_TYPESET. □

### A.2 Classic type soundness

**A.10 Lemma [Classic determinism]:** If $e \longrightarrow_{\mathsf{C}} e_1$ and $e \longrightarrow_{\mathsf{C}} e_2$ then $e_1 = e_2$.

**Proof:** By induction on the first evaluation derivation. □

**A.11 Lemma [Classic canonical forms]:** If $\emptyset \vdash_{\mathsf{C}} e : T$ and $\mathsf{val}_{\mathsf{C}}\ e$ then:

– If $T = \{x{:}B \mid e'\}$, then $e = k$ and $\mathsf{ty}(k) = B$ and $e'[e/x] \longrightarrow^*_{\mathsf{C}} \mathsf{true}$.
– If $T = T_1 \to T_2$, then either $e = \lambda x{:}T.\ e'$ or $e = \langle T_{11} \to T_{12} \overset{\bullet}{\Rightarrow} T_{21} \to T_{22} \rangle^l\ e'$.

**A.12 Lemma [Classic progress]:** If $\emptyset \vdash_{\mathsf{C}} e : T$, then either:

1. $\mathsf{result}_{\mathsf{C}}\ e$, i.e., $e = \Uparrow l$ or $\mathsf{val}_{\mathsf{C}}\ e$; or
2. there exists an $e'$ such that $e \longrightarrow_{\mathsf{C}} e'$.

**Proof:** By induction on the typing derivation. □

**A.13 Lemma [Classic preservation]:** If $\emptyset \vdash_{\mathsf{C}} e : T$ and $e \longrightarrow_{\mathsf{C}} e'$, then $\emptyset \vdash_{\mathsf{C}} e' : T$.

**Proof:** By induction on the typing derivation. □

### A.3 Eidetic type soundness

**A.14 Lemma [Determinism of eidetic $\lambda_H$ ]:** If $e \longrightarrow_{\mathsf{E}} e_1$ and $e \longrightarrow_{\mathsf{E}} e_2$ then $e_1 = e_2$.

**Proof:** By induction on the first evaluation derivation. In every case, only a single step can be taken. □

**A.15 Lemma [Eidetic canonical forms]:** If $\emptyset \vdash_{\mathsf{E}} e : T$ and $\mathsf{val}_{\mathsf{E}}\ e$ then:

– If $T = \{x{:}B \mid e'\}$, then $e = k$ and $\mathsf{ty}(k) = B$ and $e'[e/x] \longrightarrow^*_{\mathsf{E}} \mathsf{true}$.
– If $T = T_{21} \to T_{22}$, then either $e = \lambda x{:}T.\ e'$ or $e = \langle T_{11} \to T_{12} \overset{c_1 \mapsto c_2}{\Rightarrow} T_{21} \to T_{22} \rangle^\bullet\ \lambda x{:}T_{11}.\ e'$.

**A.16 Lemma [Eidetic progress]:** If $\emptyset \vdash_{\mathsf{E}} e : T$, then either:

1. $\mathsf{result}_{\mathsf{E}}\ e$, i.e., $e = \Uparrow l$ or $\mathsf{val}_{\mathsf{E}}\ e$; or
2. there exists an $e'$ such that $e \longrightarrow_{\mathsf{E}} e'$.

**Proof:** By induction on the typing derivation. □

**A.17 Lemma [Extended refinement lists are well formed]:** If $\vdash_{\mathsf{E}} \{x{:}B \mid e\}$ and $\vdash_{\mathsf{E}} r \parallel \{x{:}B \mid e_1\} \Rightarrow \{x{:}B \mid e_2\}$ then $\vdash_{\mathsf{E}} \mathsf{join}(\{x{:}B \mid e\}^l, r) \parallel \{x{:}B \mid e_1\} \Rightarrow \{x{:}B \mid e_2\}$.

**Proof:** By cases on the rule used.

(A_REFINE) All of the premises are immediately restored except in one tricky case. When $\{x{:}B \mid e\} \supset \{x{:}B \mid e'\}$ where $\{x{:}B \mid e'\} \in r$ is the only type implying $\{x{:}B \mid e_2\}$. Then $\mathsf{drop}(r, \{x{:}B \mid e\})$ isn't well formed on its own, but adding $\{x{:}B \mid e\}^l$ makes it so by transitivity. If not, then we know that $\mathsf{drop}(r, \{x{:}B \mid e\})$ is well formed, and so is its extensions by assumption.

We know that there are no duplicates by reflexivity of $\supset$.
(A_FUN) Contradictory.

□

**A.18 Lemma [Merged coercions are well formed]:** If $\vdash_{\mathsf{E}} c_1 \parallel T_1 \Rightarrow T_2$ and $\vdash_{\mathsf{E}} c_2 \parallel T_2 \Rightarrow T_3$ then $\vdash_{\mathsf{E}} \mathsf{join}(c_1, c_2) \parallel T_1 \Rightarrow T_3$.

**Proof:** By induction on $c_1$'s typing derivation.

(A_REFINE) By the IH, Lemma A.17, and A_REFINE.
(A_FUN) By the IHs and A_FUN.

□

**A.19 Lemma [$\mathsf{coerce}$ generates well formed coercions]:** If $\vdash T_1 \parallel T_2$ then $\vdash_{\mathsf{E}} \mathsf{coerce}(T_1, T_2, l) \parallel T_1 \Rightarrow T_2$.

**Proof:** By induction on the similarity derivation.

(S_REFINE) By A_REFINE, with $\mathsf{coerce}(\{x{:}B \mid e_1\}, \{x{:}B \mid e_2\}, l) = \{x{:}B \mid e_2\}^l$.
(S_FUN) By A_FUN and the IHs.

□

**A.20 Lemma [Eidetic preservation]:** If $\emptyset \vdash_{\mathsf{E}} e : T$ and $e \longrightarrow_{\mathsf{E}} e'$ then $\emptyset \vdash_{\mathsf{E}} e' : T$.

**Proof:** By induction on the typing derivation. □

**A.21 Lemma [Source program typing for eidetic $\lambda_{\mathsf{H}}$ ]:** Source programs are well typed in C iff they are well typed in E, i.e.:

- $\Gamma \vdash_{\mathsf{C}} e : T$ as a source program iff $\Gamma \vdash_{\mathsf{E}} e : T$ as a source program.
- $\vdash_{\mathsf{C}} T$ as a source program iff $\vdash_{\mathsf{E}} T$ as a source program.
- $\vdash_{\mathsf{C}} \Gamma$ as a source program iff $\vdash_{\mathsf{E}} \Gamma$ as a source program.

**Proof:** By mutual induction on $e$, $T$, and $\Gamma$. □

# B. Proofs of space-efficiency soundness

**B.1 Lemma [Idempotence of coercions]:** If $\emptyset \vdash_{\mathsf{E}} k : \{x{:}B \mid e_1\}$ and $\vdash_{\mathsf{E}} \mathsf{join}(r_1, r_2) \parallel \{x{:}B \mid e_1\} \Rightarrow \{x{:}B \mid e_2\}$, then for all $\mathsf{result}_{\mathsf{E}}\ e$, we have $\langle \{x{:}B \mid e_1\} \overset{\mathsf{join}(r_1, \mathsf{drop}(r_2, \{x:B \mid e_1\}))}{\Rightarrow} \{x{:}B \mid e_2\}\rangle^\bullet\ k \longrightarrow^*_{\mathsf{E}} e$ iff $\langle \{x{:}B \mid e_1\} \overset{\mathsf{join}(r_1, r_2)}{\Rightarrow} \{x{:}B \mid e_2\}\rangle^\bullet\ k \longrightarrow^*_{\mathsf{E}} e$.

**Proof:** By induction on their evaluation derivations: the only difference is that the latter derivation performs some extra checks that are implied by $e_1[k/x] \longrightarrow^*_{\mathsf{E}}$ true—which we already know to hold. □

As before, cast congruence is the key lemma in our proof—in this case, the strongest property we have: reduction to identical results.

**B.2 Lemma [Cast congruence (single step)]:** If

- $\emptyset \vdash_{\mathsf{E}} e_1 : T_1$ and $\vdash_{\mathsf{E}} c \parallel T_1 \Rightarrow T_2$ (and so $\emptyset \vdash_{\mathsf{E}} \langle T_1 \overset{c}{\Rightarrow} T_2\rangle^\bullet\ e_1 : T_2$),
- $e_1 \longrightarrow_{\mathsf{E}} e_2$ (and so $\emptyset \vdash_{\mathsf{E}} e_2 : T_1$),

then for all $\mathsf{result}_{\mathsf{E}}\ e$, we have $\langle T_1 \overset{c}{\Rightarrow} T_2\rangle^\bullet\ e_1 \longrightarrow^*_{\mathsf{E}} e$ iff $\langle T_1 \overset{c}{\Rightarrow} T_2\rangle^\bullet\ e_2 \longrightarrow^*_{\mathsf{E}} e$.

**Proof:** By cases on the step taken to find $e_1 \longrightarrow_{\mathsf{E}} e_2$. □

Our proof strategy is as follows: we show that the casts between related types are applicative, and then we show that well typed source programs in classic $\lambda_{\mathsf{H}}$ are logically related to their translation. Our definitions are in Figure 6. Our logical relation is *blame-exact*. Like our proofs relating forgetful and heedful $\lambda_{\mathsf{H}}$ to classic $\lambda_{\mathsf{H}}$, we use the space-efficient semantics in the refinement case and use space-efficient type indices.

**B.3 Lemma [Similar casts are logically related]:** If $T_1 \sim_{\mathsf{E}} T_1'$ and $T_2 \sim_{\mathsf{E}} T_2'$ and $e_1 \sim_{\mathsf{E}} e_2 : T_1$, then $\langle T_1 \overset{\bullet}{\Rightarrow} T_2\rangle^l\ e_1 \simeq_{\mathsf{E}} \langle T_1' \overset{\bullet}{\Rightarrow} T_2'\rangle^l\ e_2 : T_2$.

**Proof:** By induction on the invariant relation, using coercion congruence in the function case when $e_2$ is a function proxy. □

**B.4 Lemma [Relating classic and eidetic source programs]:**

1. If $\Gamma \vdash_{\mathsf{C}} e : T$ as a source program then $\Gamma \vdash e \simeq_{\mathsf{E}} e : T$.
2. If $\vdash_{\mathsf{C}} T$ as a source program then $T \sim_{\mathsf{E}} T$.

**Proof:** By mutual induction on the typing derivations. □

**Term type extraction** $\boxed{\mathsf{types}(e) : \mathcal{P}(T)}$

$$\begin{aligned}
\mathsf{types}(x) &= \emptyset \\
\mathsf{types}(k) &= \emptyset \\
\mathsf{types}(\lambda x{:}T.\ e) &= \mathsf{types}(T) \cup \mathsf{types}(e) \\
\mathsf{types}(\langle T_1 \overset{a}{\Rightarrow} T_2\rangle^l\ e) &= \mathsf{types}(T_1) \cup \mathsf{types}(T_2) \cup \\
&\quad\ \mathsf{types}(a) \cup \mathsf{types}(e) \\
\mathsf{types}(e_1\ e_2) &= \mathsf{types}(e_1) \cup \mathsf{types}(e_2) \\
\mathsf{types}(op(e_1, \ldots, e_n)) &= \textstyle\bigcup_{1 \le i \le n} \mathsf{types}(e_i) \\
\mathsf{types}(\langle \{x{:}B \mid e_1\}, e_2, k\rangle^l) &= \mathsf{types}(\{x{:}B \mid e_1\}) \cup \mathsf{types}(e_2) \\
\mathsf{types}(\langle \{x{:}B \mid e_1\}, s, r, k, e\rangle^\bullet) &= \\
&\quad\ \mathsf{types}(\{x{:}B \mid e_1\}) \cup \mathsf{types}(r) \cup \mathsf{types}(e) \\
\mathsf{types}(\Uparrow l) &= \emptyset
\end{aligned}$$

**Type, type set, and coercion type extraction**

$\boxed{\mathsf{types}(T) : \mathcal{P}(T)}$

$$\begin{aligned}
\mathsf{types}(\{x{:}B \mid e\}) &= \{\{x{:}B \mid e\}\} \cup \mathsf{types}(e) \\
\mathsf{types}(T_1 \to T_2) &= \{T_1 \to T_2\} \cup \\
&\quad\ \mathsf{types}(T_1) \cup \mathsf{types}(T_2)
\end{aligned}$$

$\boxed{\mathsf{types}(a) : \mathcal{P}(T)}$

$$\begin{aligned}
\mathsf{types}(\bullet) &= \emptyset \\
\mathsf{types}(\mathsf{nil}) &= \emptyset \\
\mathsf{types}(\{x{:}B \mid e\}^l, r) &= \{\{x{:}B \mid e\}\} \cup \mathsf{types}(r) \\
\mathsf{types}(c_1 \mapsto c_2) &= \mathsf{types}(c_1) \cup \mathsf{types}(c_2)
\end{aligned}$$

**Type height** $\boxed{\mathsf{height}(T)}$

$$\begin{aligned}
\mathsf{height}(\{x{:}B \mid e\}) &= 1 \\
\mathsf{height}(T_1 \to T_2) &= 1 + \max_{i \in \{1,2\}} \mathsf{height}(T_i)
\end{aligned}$$

**Figure 7.** Type extraction and type height

# C. Proofs of bounds for space-efficiency

This section contains our definitions for collecting types in a program and the corresponding proof of bounded space consumption (for all modes at once).

We define a function collecting all of the distinct types that appear in a program in Figure 7. If the type $T = \{x{:}\mathsf{Int} \mid x \ge 0\} \to \{y{:}\mathsf{Int} \mid y \ne 0\}$ appears in the program $e$, then $\mathsf{types}(e)$ includes the type $T$ itself along with its subparts $\{x{:}\mathsf{Int} \mid x \ge 0\}$ and $\{y{:}\mathsf{Int} \mid y \ne 0\}$.

**C.1 Lemma:** $\mathsf{types}(e[e'/x]) \subseteq \mathsf{types}(e) \cup \mathsf{types}(e')$

**Proof:** By induction on $e$. □

**C.2 Lemma:** $\mathsf{types}(\mathsf{dom}(a)) \subseteq \mathsf{types}(a)$

**Proof:** This property is trivial when $a = \bullet$.
Immediate when $a = c_1 \mapsto c_2$. □

**C.3 Lemma:** $\mathsf{types}(\mathsf{cod}(a)) \subseteq \mathsf{types}(a)$

**Proof:** Similar to Lemma C.2. □

**C.4 Lemma [Coercing types doesn't introduce types]:** $\mathsf{types}(\mathsf{coerce}(T_1, T_2, l)) \subseteq \mathsf{types}(T_1) \cup \mathsf{types}(T_2)$

**Proof:** By induction on $T_1$ and $T_2$. When they are refinements, we have the coercion just being $\{x{:}B \mid e_2\}^l$. When they are functions, by the IH. □

**C.5 Lemma [Dropping types doesn't introduce types]:** $\mathsf{types}(\mathsf{drop}\,(r, \{x{:}B \mid e\})) \subseteq \mathsf{types}(r)$

**Proof:** By induction on $r$.

($r = \mathsf{nil}$) The two sides are immediately equal.

($r = \{x{:}B \mid e'\}^l, r'$) If $\{x{:}B \mid e'\} \not\supset \{x{:}B \mid e\}$, then the two are identical. If not, then we have $\mathsf{types}(r') \subseteq \mathsf{types}(r)$ by the IH.

□

**C.6 Lemma [Coercion merges don't introduce types]:** $\mathsf{types}(\mathsf{join}(r_1, r_2)) \subseteq \mathsf{types}(r_1) \cup \mathsf{types}(r_2)$

**Proof:** By induction on $r_1$.

($r_1 = \mathsf{nil}$) The two sides are immediately equal.

($r_1 = \{x{:}B \mid e\}^l, r_1'$) Using Lemma C.5, we find:

$$\begin{aligned}
\mathsf{types}(\mathsf{join}(r_1, r_2)) &= \{\{x{:}B \mid e\}\} \cup \\
&\quad \mathsf{types}(\mathsf{join}(r_1', \mathsf{drop}\,(r_2, \{x{:}B \mid e\}))) \\
&\subseteq \{\{x{:}B \mid e\}\} \cup \mathsf{types}(r_1') \cup \\
&\quad \mathsf{types}(\mathsf{drop}\,(r_2, \{x{:}B \mid e\})) \\
&\subseteq \{\{x{:}B \mid e\}\} \cup \mathsf{types}(r_1') \cup \mathsf{types}(r_2) \\
&= \mathsf{types}(r_1) \cup \mathsf{types}(r_2)
\end{aligned}$$

□

**C.7 Lemma [Reduction doesn't introduce types]:** If $e \longrightarrow_m e'$ then $\mathsf{types}(e') \subseteq \mathsf{types}(e)$.

**Proof:** By induction on the step taken. □

# Manifest Contracts for Datatypes


Taro Sekiyama
Graduate School of Informatics
Kyoto University
t-sekiym@kuis.kyoto-u.ac.jp

Yuki Nishida
Graduate School of Informatics
Kyoto University
nishida@fos.kuis.kyoto-u.ac.jp

Atsushi Igarashi
Graduate School of Informatics
Kyoto University
igarashi@kuis.kyoto-u.ac.jp



## Abstract

We study algebraic datatypes in a manifest contract system, a software contract system where contract information occurs as refinement types. We first compare two simple approaches: refinements on type constructors and refinements on data constructors. For example, lists of positive integers can be described by $\{l{:}\mathsf{int\ list} \mid \mathsf{for\_all}\,(\lambda y.y > 0)\,l\}$ in the former, whereas by a user-defined datatype $\mathsf{pos\_list}$ with cons of type $\{x{:}\mathsf{int} \mid x > 0\} \times \mathsf{pos\_list} \rightarrow \mathsf{pos\_list}$ in the latter. The two approaches are complementary: the former makes it easier for a programmer to write types and the latter enables more efficient contract checking. To take the best of both worlds, we propose (1) a syntactic translation from refinements on type constructors to equivalent refinements on data constructors and (2) dynamically checked casts between different but compatible datatypes such as $\mathsf{int\ list}$ and $\mathsf{pos\_list}$. We define a manifest contract calculus $\lambda^H_{\mathtt{dt}}$ to formalize the semantics of the casts and prove that the translation is correct.



***Categories and Subject Descriptors*** D.3.1 [*Programming Languages*]: Formal Definitions and Theory; D.3.3 [*Programming Languages*]: Language Constructs and Features—Data types and structures; D.2.4 [*Software Engineering*]: Software/Program Verification—Programming by contracts

***General Terms*** Languages, Design, Theory

***Keywords*** algebraic datatypes, datatype translation, contract checking, refinement types


## 1. Introduction

### 1.1 Background: Software Contracts

*Software contracts* are a prominent tool to develop robust software. Contracts allow programmers to write specifications in the same programming language as that used to write programs, making it possible to check such specifications at run time. They are provided as libraries or primitive constructs in various practical programming languages. For example, the C language provides the assert macro to check at run time that a given Boolean expression evaluates to true and the Eiffel language [21] provides a dedicated construct to specify and check pre- and postconditions of methods and class invariants. Racket is a representative functional language with higher-order contracts, based on the seminal work by Findler and Felleisen [9].

Although contracts were originally conceived as a mechanism to check software properties dynamically, it was also clear that contract checking could cause significant overhead for various reasons and that it would be desirable to find contract violations earlier than run time. A lot of research has been conducted to address these problems. For example, Herman, Tomb, and Flanagan [16] and Siek and Wadler [25] address the space-efficiency problem that inserting contract checking can degrade tail calls into non-tail calls; Findler, Guo, and Rogers [10] introduce lazy contract checking to address the problem that naive contract checking for datatypes can make asymptotic time complexity worse; and there is a lot of work on static analysis/verification of contracts [11, 15, 18, 22, 32, 33] to find out statically which contract checking always succeeds in order to eliminate such successful contract checking for optimization. The last line of work is also closely related to static refinement checking [17, 24, 27, 31].

In this paper, we revisit the problem of contract checking on datatypes, especially in the context of *manifest contracts* [4, 11, 13, 14, 18].

### 1.2 Manifest Contracts and Two Approaches to Datatypes

In a manifest contract system, unlike more traditional (dubbed *latent* by Greenberg, Pierce, and Weirich [14]) contract systems, contract information occurs as *refinement types* of the form $\{x{:}T \mid e\}$. This form of type denotes the subset of values $v$ of type $T$ satisfying the Boolean expression $e$, namely, $e\,\{v/x\}$ reduces to $\mathsf{true}$. For example, $\{x{:}\mathsf{int} \mid x > 0\}$ denotes positive integers. Refinement types can be introduced by using *casts*, which involve run-time checking. A cast $\langle T \Leftarrow S\rangle^{\ell}$ means that, when applied to a value of the source type $S$, it is checked that the value can behave as a value of the target type $T$. For example, the cast application $\langle\{x{:}\mathsf{int} \mid x > 0\} \Leftarrow \mathsf{int}\rangle^{\ell}\,5$ succeeds, after confirming $5 > 0$ returns true, and returns $5$. If a cast fails, an uncatchable exception will be raised with the label $\ell$ to identify which cast has failed. Computational calculi of manifest contracts have been studied as theoretical frameworks for hybrid contract checking [11, 18], in which contract checking is performed both statically and dynamically. The idea behind hybrid contract checking is to check, for each cast $\langle T \Leftarrow S\rangle^{\ell}$, whether it is an upcast, or equivalently, $S$ is a subtype of $T$. Upcasts are proved to be contextually equivalent to the identity functions and so safe to be eliminated. The other casts are still subject to run-time check.

There are two approaches to specifying contracts for data structures. One is to put refinements on the type constructor for a plain data structure and the other is to put refinements on (types for) data constructors. For example, a type $\mathsf{slist}$ for sorted integer lists can be written $\{x{:}\mathsf{int\ list} \mid \mathsf{sorted}\ x\}$ in which $\mathsf{sorted}$ is a familiar Boolean function that returns whether the argument list is sorted



*POPL '15*, January 15–17, 2015, Mumbai, India.



ACM 978-1-4503-3300-9/15/01... $15.00.
http://dx.doi.org/10.1145/2676726.2676996

in the former, or defined as another datatype with refined cons of type $x{:}\mathsf{int} \times \{xs{:}\mathsf{slist} \mid \mathsf{nil}\ xs\ \mathsf{or}\ x \leq \mathsf{head}\ xs\} \rightarrow \mathsf{slist}$ in the latter. Here, the argument type is a dependent product type, expressing the relationship between the two components in the pair. However, as pointed out by Findler, Guo, and Rogers [10], neither approach by itself is very satisfactory.

On the one hand, the former approach, which is arguably easier for ordinary programmers, may cause significant overhead in contract checking to make asymptotic time complexity worse. To see how it happens, let us consider function **insert_sort** for insertion sort. The sorting function and its auxiliary function insert can be defined in the ML-like syntax as follows.

```
type slist1 = {x:int list | sorted x}

let rec insert (x:int) (l:slist1) : slist1 =
  match l with
  | []     -> ⟨slist1 ⇐ int list⟩^ℓ1 [x]
  | y::ys ->
    if x <= y then ⟨slist1 ⇐ int list⟩^ℓ2 (x::l)
    else ⟨slist1 ⇐ int list⟩^ℓ3
      (y::(insert x (⟨slist1 ⇐ int list⟩^ℓ4 ys)))

let rec insert_sort (l:int list) : slist1 =
  match l with
  | []     -> []
  | x::xs -> insert x (insert_sort xs)
```

Without gray-colored casts, **insert_sort** would be an ordinary insertion-sort function. However, in **insert**, the four subexpressions `[x]`, `x::l`, `y::(insert x ys)` and `ys`, which are given type `int list`, are actually expected to have type **slist1** by the context. To fill the gap[1], we have to check whether these subexpressions satisfy the contract **sorted**. Notice that these casts cannot be eliminated by simple subtype checking because `int list` is obviously not a subtype of **slist1**. As far as we understand, existing technologies cannot verify these casts will be successful, at least, without giving hints to the verifier. Unfortunately, leaving these casts (especially ones with $\ell_2, \ell_3$, and $\ell_4$) has an unpleasant effect: They traverse the entire lists to check sortedness, even though the lists have already been sorted, making the asymptotic time complexity of **insert** from $O(m)$ to $O(m^2)$, where $m$ stands for the length of the input.

On the other hand, the latter approach, which exploits refinement in argument types of data constructors, does not have this efficiency problem (if not always). For example, we can define sorted lists as a datatype with refined constructors:

```
type slist2 =
  SNil
| SCons of
    x:int × {xs:slist2 | nil xs or x <= head xs}
```

Here, **nil** and **head** are functions[2] that return whether a given list is empty and the first element of a given list, respectively, and a type of the form $x{:}T_1 \times T_2$ is a dependent product type, which denotes pairs $(v_1, v_2)$ of values such that $v_1$ and $v_2$ are of types $T_1$ and $T_2\,\{v_1/x\}$, respectively. So, **SCons** takes an integer **x** and a (sorted) list whose head (if any) is equal to or greater than **x**. Using **slist2**, we can modify the functions **insert** and **insert_sort** to perform less dynamic checking.

```
let rec insert' (x:int) (l:slist2) : slist2 =
  match l with
  | SNil -> SCons (x,⟨slist_x ⇐ slist2⟩^ℓ SNil)
  | SCons (y, ys) ->
    if x <= y then SCons (x,⟨slist_x ⇐ slist2⟩^ℓ l)
    else SCons
           (y,⟨slist_y ⇐ slist2⟩^ℓ (insert' x ys))

let rec insert_sort' (l:int list) : slist2 =
  match l with
  | []    -> SNil
  | x::xs -> insert' x (insert_sort' xs)
```

Here, $\texttt{slist}_e$ stands for `{xs:slist2 | nil xs or e <= head xs}`. Since the contract in the cast $\langle \texttt{slist}_\texttt{x} \Leftarrow \texttt{slist2}\rangle^\ell$ does not traverse **xs**, it is more efficient than the first definition; in fact, the time complexity of **insert'** remains to be $O(m)$. Moreover, it would be possible to eliminate the cast on **l** by collecting conditions (**l** is equal to `SCons(y, ys)` and `x <= y`) guarding this branch [24]. (It is more difficult to eliminate the other cast because the verifier would have to know that the head of the list returned by the recursive call to **insert'** is greater than **y**.)

However, this approach has complementary problems. First, we have to maintain the predicate function **sorted** and the corresponding type definition **slist2** separately. Second, it may not be a trivial task to write down the specification as data constructor refinement. For example, consider the type of lists whose elements contain a given integer $n$. A refinement type of such lists can be written `{l:int list | member n l}` using the familiar **member** function. One possible datatype definition corresponding to the refinement type above would be given by using an auxiliary datatype, parameterized over an integer **n** and a Boolean flag **p** to represent whether **n** has to appear in a list.

```
type incl_aux⟨p:bool, n:int⟩ =
  LNil  of {unit | not p}
| LCons of x:int × incl_aux⟨not (x=n) and p, n⟩

type list_including⟨n:int⟩ = incl_aux⟨true,n⟩
```

(Notice that `incl_aux⟨false,n⟩` is essentially `int list` and, if a list without $n$ is given type $\texttt{incl\_aux}\langle p,n\rangle$, then $p$ must be **false**.) We do not think it is as easy to come up with a datatype definition like this as the refinement type above.

Another issue is interoperability between a plain type and its refined versions: Just as casts between **slist1** and `int list` are allowed, we would hope that the language supports casts between **slist2** and `int list`, even when they have different sets of data constructors. Such interoperability is crucial for code reuse [10]—without it, we must reimplement many list-processing functions, such as **sort**, **member**, **map**, etc., every time a refined datatype is given. As pointed out in Vazou, Rondon, and Jhala [27], one can give one generic datatype definition, which is parameterized over predicates on components of the datatype, and instantiate it to obtain plain and sorted list types but, as we will show later, refined datatype definitions may naturally come with more data constructors than the plain one, in which case parameterization would not work (the number of constructors is the same for every instantiation).

In short, the two approaches are complementary.

### 1.3 Our Contributions

Our work aims at taking the best of both worlds. First, we give a provably correct syntactic translation from refinements on type constructors, such as the Boolean function **sorted**, to equivalent type definitions where data constructors are refined, namely, **slist2**. This translation is closely related to the work by Atkey, Johann, and Ghani [3] and McBride [20], also concerned about

---

[1] Actually, there are subexpressions whose expected types are `int list` but actual types are `slist1`. We assume that `slist1` can be converted to `int list` for free.

[2] Precisely speaking, these functions have to be defined together with `slist2` but we omit them for brevity.

systematic generation of a new datatype; see Section 5 for comparison. Second, we extend casts so that casts between similar but different datatypes (what we call compatible types, which are declared explicitly in datatype definitions) are possible. For example, $\langle$`slist2` $\Leftarrow$ `int list`$\rangle^\ell$`(1 :: 2 :: [])` yields `SCons(1, SCons(2, SNil))`, whereas $\langle$`slist2` $\Leftarrow$ `int list`$\rangle^\ell$ `(1 :: 0 :: [])` raises blame $\ell$. Thanks to the two ideas, a programmer can automatically derive a datatype definition from a familiar Boolean function, exploit the resulting datatype for less dynamic checking as we saw in the example of insertion sort, and also use it, when necessary, as if it were a refinement type using the Boolean function.

We formalize these ideas as a manifest contract calculus $\lambda^H_{\mathtt{dt}}$ and prove basic properties such as subject reduction and progress. We follow the existing approach, advocated by Belo et al. [4], to defining a manifest calculus without subtyping but improve it by modifying the semantics of casts slightly and simplifying the type equivalence relation. These changes play a crucial role in proving subject reduction and other semantic properties such as parametricity. We also give a first *syntactic* proof of the property that "if a program is given a refinement type $\{x{:}T \mid e\}$ and it results in a value $v$, then $v$ satisfies the predicate $e$" in the context of manifest calculi. This property was proved by using semantic methods in the literature [14, 18]. A syntactic proof would have been possible for a polymorphic manifest calculus $F_H$ [4] but the metatheory of $F_H$ depends on a few conjectures, which unfortunately turned out to be false recently (personal communication).

Our contributions are summarized as follows:

- We propose casts between compatible datatypes to enhance interoperability among a plain datatype and its refined versions.
- We define a manifest contract calculus $\lambda^H_{\mathtt{dt}}$ to formalize the semantics of the casts.
- We formally define a translation from refinements on type constructors to type definitions where data constructors are refined and prove the translation is correct.

We also have a toy implementation of $\lambda^H_{\mathtt{dt}}$ on top of OCaml and Camlp4 and it is available at `http://www.fos.kuis.kyoto-u.ac.jp/~t-sekiym/papers/rech/`. A full version with proofs is also found there.

We note that this work gives type translation but does *not* give translation from a program with refinement types to one with refined datatypes, so if a programmer has a program with, for example, `slist1`, then he has to rewrite it to one with a datatype like `slist2` by hand. Automatic program transformation is left as future work.

The rest of the paper is organized as follows. Section 2 gives an overview of our datatype mechanism and Section 3 formalizes $\lambda^H_{\mathtt{dt}}$ and shows its type soundness. Then, Section 4 gives a translation from refinement types to datatypes and proves its correctness. We discuss related work in Section 5 and conclude in Section 6.

## 2. Overview

In this section, we informally describe our proposals of datatype definitions, casts between compatible datatypes, and translation, mainly by means of examples.

As we have seen already in the example of sorted lists, our datatype definition allows the argument types of data constructors to be refined using the set comprehension notation $\{x{:}T \mid e\}$ and dependent product types $x{:}T_1 \times T_2$. We also allow parameterization over terms as in `incl_aux` in the previous section.

### 2.1 Casts for Datatypes

As we have discussed in the introduction, in order to enhance interoperability between refined datatypes, we allow casts between two different datatypes if they are "compatible"; in other words, compatibility is used to disallow casts between unrelated types (for example, the integer type and a function type). Compatibility for types other than datatypes means that two types are the same by ignoring refinements; compatibility for datatypes means that there is a correspondence between the sets of the data constructors from two datatypes and the argument types of the corresponding constructors are also compatible. In our proposal, a correspondence between constructors has to be explicitly declared. So, the type `slist2` in the previous section is actually written as follows:

```
type slist2 =
  SNil  || []
| SCons || (::) of
    x:int × {xs:slist2 | nil xs or x <= head xs}
```

The symbol `||` followed by a data constructor from an existing datatype declares how constructors correspond. The types `int list` and `slist2` are compatible because both `SNil` and `[]` take no arguments and the argument type `x:int × {xs:slist2 | nil xs or x <= head xs}` of `SCons` is compatible with `int × int list` of `(::)`. (Precisely speaking, compatibility is defined coinductively.) Readers may think that explicit declaration of a correspondence of data constructors seems cumbersome. However, we could replace these declarations by a compatibility declaration for type names as `slist2 || int list` and let the system infer the correspondence between data constructors. Such inference is easy for many cases, where the argument types of data constructors are of different shapes, as in this example.

A cast for datatypes converts data constructors to the corresponding ones and puts a new cast on components. For example, $\langle \mathsf{slist} \Leftarrow \mathsf{int\ list}\rangle^\ell\,(1 :: 2 :: 3 :: [\,])$ reduces to $\mathsf{SCons}\,(1, \mathsf{SCons}\,(2, \mathsf{SCons}\,(3, \mathsf{SNil})))$ as follows:

$$\begin{array}{l}
\langle \mathsf{slist} \Leftarrow \mathsf{int\ list}\rangle^\ell\,(1 :: 2 :: 3 :: [\,])\\
\rightarrow \mathsf{SCons}(\langle x{:}\mathsf{int} \times \{xs{:}\mathsf{slist} \mid \mathsf{nil}\ xs\ \mathsf{or}\ x \leq \mathsf{head}\ xs\} \Leftarrow \mathsf{int} \times \mathsf{int\ list}\rangle^\ell\\
\qquad\qquad (1, 2 :: 3 :: [\,]))\\
\rightarrow \mathsf{SCons}(1, \langle \{xs{:}\mathsf{slist} \mid \mathsf{nil}\ xs\ \mathsf{or}\ 1 \leq \mathsf{head}\ xs\} \Leftarrow \mathsf{int\ list}\rangle^\ell\,(2 :: 3 :: [\,]))\\
\rightarrow \ldots\\
\rightarrow \mathsf{SCons}\,(1, \mathsf{SCons}\,(2, \mathsf{SCons}\,(3, \mathsf{SNil})))
\end{array}$$

In the example above, the correspondence between data constructors is bijective but we actually allow nonbijective correspondence, too. This means that a new datatype can have two or more (or even no) data constructors corresponding to a single data constructor from an existing type. For example, an alternative definition of `list_including` is as follows:

```
type list_including⟨n:int⟩ =
  LConsEq  || (::) of {x:int|x=n} × int list
| LConsNEq || (::) of
                  {x:int|x<>n} × list_including⟨n⟩
```

This version of `list_including` has no constructors compatible to `Nil` because the empty list does not include `n`. By contrast, there are two constructors, `LConsEq` and `LConsNEq`, both compatible to `(::)`. The constructor `LConsEq` is used to construct lists where the head is equal to $n$, and `LConsNEq` to construct lists where the head is not equal to $n$ but the tail list includes $n$. A cast to the new version of `list_including` works by choosing either `LConsEq` or `LConsNEq`, depending on the head of the input list:

$$\begin{array}{ll}
\langle \mathsf{list_including}\langle 0\rangle \Leftarrow \mathsf{int\ list}\rangle^\ell\,[\,] & \longrightarrow^* \quad \Uparrow\ell\\
\langle \mathsf{list_including}\langle 0\rangle \Leftarrow \mathsf{int\ list}\rangle^\ell\,(2 :: 0 :: 1 :: [\,]) & \longrightarrow^*\\
\qquad\qquad \mathsf{LConsNEq}\,(2, (\mathsf{LConsEq}\,(0, 1 :: [\,])))
\end{array}$$

This cast does not have to traverse a given list when it succeeds (notice int list in the argument type of LConsEq and $1 :: []$ in the second example above).

Although it is fairly clear how to choose an appropriate constructor in the example above, it may not be as easy in general. In the formal semantics we give in this paper, we model these choices as oracles. In practice, a constructor choice function is specified along with a datatype definition either manually or often automatically—in fact, we will show that a constructor choice function can be systematically derived when a new datatype is generated from our translation. More interestingly, the asymptotic time complexity of the cast from a plain list to the generated datatype is no worse than the cast to the original refinement type. In this sense, the translation preserves efficiency of casts. This efficiency preservation lets us conjecture that, when a programmer rewrites a program with the refinement type to one with the generated datatype, the asymptotic time complexity of the latter program becomes no worse than the former. We discuss efficiency preservation in detail in Section 4.3.

Allowing nonbijective correspondence between constructors simplifies our translation and makes dynamic contract checking more efficient as in the example above.

### 2.2 Ideas for Translation

We informally describe the ideas behind our translation through the example of list_including above. We start with the refinement type $\{x{:}\mathsf{int\ list} \mid \mathsf{member}\ n\ x\}$, where `member n x` is a usual function, which returns whether `n` appears in list `x`:

```
let rec member (n:int) (l:int list) =
  match l with
  | []      -> false
  | x::xs ->
     if x = n then true
              else member n xs
```

Through this paper, we always suppose that some logical operations such as `&&` and `||` are desugared to simplify our formalization, and so here we write `if x = n then true else member n xs` instead of `x = n || member n xs`. We examine how list_including corresponds to `member`. For reference, the definition of list_including is shown below again:

```
type list_including⟨n:int⟩ =
| LConsEq  || (::) of {x:int|x=n} × int list
| LConsNEq || (::) of
              {x:int|x<>n} × list_including⟨n⟩
```

We expect that a value of list_including$\langle n\rangle$ returns true when it is passed to `member n` (modulo constructor names).

It is not difficult to observe two things. First, each constructor and its argument type represent when the predicate returns true. In this example, there are two reasons that `member n x` returns true: either (1) `n` is equal to the first element of `x` or (2) `n` is not equal to the first element of `x` but `member n` is true for the tail of `x`. The constructors LConsEq and LConsNEq and their argument types represent these conditions. Since `member n x` never returns true when `x` is the empty list, there is no constructor in list_including. Second, a recursive call on a substructure corresponds to type-level recursion: `member n xs` in the `else`-branch in `member` is represented by list_including$\langle n\rangle$ in the argument type of LConsNEq.

So, the basic idea of our translation scheme is to analyze the body of a given predicate function and collect guarding conditions on branches reaching `true`. As mentioned above, recursive calls on the tail become type-level recursion. This correspondence between execution paths and data constructors is also useful to derive a constructor choice function for a cast. For example, a cast to list_including$\langle n\rangle$ will choose LConsEq when (the list being checked is not empty and) the head is equal to $n$, just because LConsEq corresponds to the path guarded by `x=n` in the definition of `member`.

**Types**

$T \quad ::= \quad \mathsf{Bool} \mid x{:}T_1 \to T_2 \mid x{:}T_1 \times T_2 \mid \{x{:}T \mid e\} \mid \tau\langle e\rangle$

**Constants, Values, Terms**

$c \quad ::= \quad \mathsf{true} \mid \mathsf{false}$

$v \quad ::= \quad c \mid \mathtt{fix}\, f(x{:}T_1){:}T_2 = e \mid \langle T_1 \Leftarrow T_2\rangle^\ell \mid (v_1, v_2) \mid C\langle e\rangle v$

$e \quad ::= \quad c \mid x \mid \mathtt{fix}\, f(x{:}T_1){:}T_2 = e \mid e_1\, e_2 \mid (e_1, e_2) \mid e.1 \mid e.2 \mid C\langle e_1\rangle e_2 \mid \mathsf{match}\ e\ \mathsf{with}\ \overline{C_i\, x_i \to e_i}^{\,i} \mid \mathsf{if}\ e_1\ \mathsf{then}\ e_2\ \mathsf{else}\ e_3 \mid \langle T_1 \Leftarrow T_2\rangle^\ell$

**Datatype definitions**

$\varsigma \quad ::= \quad \tau\langle x{:}T\rangle = \overline{C_i : T_i}^{\,i} \mid \tau\langle x{:}T\rangle = \overline{C_i \parallel D_i : T_i}^{\,i}$

$\Sigma \quad ::= \quad \varnothing \mid \Sigma, \varsigma$

**Figure 1.** Program syntax.

| | |
|---|---|
| $\mathit{TypDefOf}_\Sigma(\tau)$ | The definition of $\tau$. |
| $\mathit{ArgTypeOf}_\Sigma(\tau)$ | The parameter name and its type of $\tau$. |
| $\mathit{CtrsOf}_\Sigma(\tau)$ | The set of constructors that belong to $\tau$. |
| $\mathit{TypSpecOf}_\Sigma(C)$ | The type specification of $C$. |
| $\mathit{TypNameOf}_\Sigma(C)$ | The data type that $C$ belongs to. |
| $\mathit{CtrArgOf}_\Sigma(C)$ | The argument type of $C$. |

**Table 1.** Lookup functions.

## 3. A Manifest Contract Calculus $\lambda^H_{\mathsf{dt}}$

We formalize a manifest contract calculus $\lambda^H_{\mathsf{dt}}$ of datatypes with its syntax, type system, and operational semantics, and prove its type soundness. Following Belo et al. [4], we drop subtyping and subsumption from the core of the calculus. to simplify the definition and metatheory.

In the following, we write a sequence with an overline: for example, $\overline{C_i}^{\,i\in\{1,\dots,n\}}$ means a sequence $C_1, \dots, C_n$ of data constructors. We often omit the index set $\{1, \dots, n\}$ when it is clear from the context or not important. Given a binary relation $R$, the relation $R^*$ denotes the reflexive transitive closure of $R$.

### 3.1 Syntax

We present the program syntax of $\lambda^H_{\mathsf{dt}}$ in Figure 1, where there are various metavariables: $T$ ranges over types, $\tau$ names of datatypes, $C$ and $D$ constructors, $c$ constants, $x$, $y$, $z$, $f$, etc. variables, $v$ values, $e$ terms, $\ell$ blame labels, $\Gamma$ typing contexts, $\varsigma$ datatype definitions, $\Sigma$ type definition environments.

Types consist of base types (we have only Boolean here but addition of other base types causes no problems), dependent function types, dependent product types, refinement types, and datatypes. In a dependent function type $x{:}T_1 \to T_2$ and a dependent product type $x{:}T_1 \times T_2$, variable $x$ is bound in $T_2$. A refinement type $\{x{:}T \mid e\}$, in which $x$ is bound in $e$, denotes the subset of type $T$ whose value $v$ satisfies the Boolean contract $e$, that is, $e\,\{v/x\}$ evaluates to true. Finally, a datatype $\tau\langle e\rangle$ takes the form of an application of $\tau$ to a term $e$.

Note that, unlike some refinement type systems [17, 24, 27, 28, 30, 31], which aim at decidable static verification, the predicate $e$ is allowed to be an arbitrary Boolean expression, which may diverge or raise blame. As we will see soon, however, no computation is involved with typing rules for source programs and it is easy to show decidability of typing for source programs. In fact, two types with different predicates such as $\{x{:}\mathsf{int} \mid x > 2\}$ and $\{x{:}\mathsf{int} \mid x > 1 + 1\}$ are always distinguished and a cast is required to convert from one type to the other. Static verification amounts to checking a given cast is in fact an upcast, where the source type is a subtype of the target, and subtyping is not, in general, decidable but the language is not equipped with subsumption.

Terms are basically those from the $\lambda$-calculus with Booleans, recursive functions, products, datatypes, and casts. A term $\mathtt{fix}\, f(x{:}T_1){:}T_2 = e$ represents a recursive function in which variables $x$ and $f$ denote an argument and the function itself, respectively, and are bound in $e$. We often omit type annotations. A data constructor application $C\langle e_1 \rangle e_2$ takes two arguments: $e_1$ represents one for the type definition and $e_2$ for data constructors, respectively. A match expression $\mathsf{match}\, e\, \mathsf{with}\, \overline{C_i\, x_i \rightarrow e_i}^{\,i}$ is as usual and binds each variable $x_i$ in $e_i$.

The last form is a cast $\langle T_1 \Leftarrow T_2 \rangle^{\ell}$, consisting of a target type $T_1$, a source type $T_2$ and a label $\ell$, and, when applied to a value $v$ of type $T_2$, checks that the value $v$ can behave as $T_1$. The label $\ell$ is used to identify the cast when it is blamed.

A datatype definition $\varsigma$ can take two forms. The form $\tau\,\langle x{:}T \rangle = \overline{C_i : T_i}^{\,i}$, where $x$ is bound in $\overline{T_i}^{\,i}$, declares a datatype $\tau$, parameterized over $x$ of type $T$, with data constructors $C_i$ whose argument types are $T_i$. The other form $\tau\,\langle x{:}T \rangle = \overline{C_i \parallel D_i : T_i}^{\,i}$ is the same except that it declares that $C_i$ is compatible with $D_i$ from another datatype.

A type definition environment $\Sigma$ is a sequence of datatype definitions. We assume that datatype and constructor names declared in a type definition environment are distinct. Table 1 shows metafunctions to look up information on datatype definitions. Their definitions are omitted since they are straightforward. A type specification, returned by *TypSpecOf* and written $x{:}T_1 \rightarrowtail T_2 \rightarrowtail \tau\langle x \rangle$, of a constructor $C$ consists of the datatype $\tau$ that $C$ belongs to, the parameter $x$ of $\tau$ and the type $T_1$ of $x$, and the argument type $T_2$ of $C$. In other words, $\tau = \mathit{TypNameOf}_{\Sigma}(C)$, $x{:}T_1 = \mathit{ArgTypeOf}_{\Sigma}(\tau)$ and $T_2 = \mathit{CtrArgOf}_{\Sigma}(C)$. We omit the subscript $\Sigma$ from these metafunctions for brevity if it is clear from the context.

We use the following familiar notations. We write $\mathsf{FV}(e)$ to denote the set of free variables in a term $e$, and $e\,\{e'/x\}$ capture avoiding substitution of $e'$ for $x$ in $e$. We apply similar notations to values and types. We say that a term/value/type is closed if it has no free variables, and identify $\alpha$-equivalent ones. In addition, we introduce several shorthands. A function type $T_1 \rightarrow T_2$ means $x{:}T_1 \rightarrow T_2$ where the variable $x$ does not occur free in $T_2$. We write $\lambda\, x{:}T_1.e$ to denote $\mathtt{fix}\, f(x{:}T_1){:}T_2 = e$ if $f$ does not occur in the term $e$. A let-expression $\mathsf{let}\, x = e_1\, \mathsf{in}\, e_2$ denotes $(\lambda\, x{:}T.e_2)\; e_1$ where $T$ is an appropriate type. Finally, a datatype $\tau$ is said to be *monomorphic* if the definition of $\tau$ does not refer to a type argument variable, and then we abbreviate $\tau\langle e \rangle$ to $\tau$.

### 3.2 Type System

This section introduces a type system for source programs in $\lambda^{H}_{\mathtt{dt}}$; later we extend the syntax to include run-time terms to define operational semantics and give additional typing rules for those terms. The type system consists of three judgments: context well-formedness $\Sigma \vdash \Gamma$, type well-formedness $\Sigma; \Gamma \vdash T$, and typing $\Sigma; \Gamma \vdash e : T$. Here, a typing context $\Gamma$ is a sequence of variable declarations:

$$\Gamma ::= \varnothing \mid \Gamma, x{:}T$$

where declared variables are pairwise distinct. We show inference rules in Figure 2, where a type definition environment $\Sigma$ in judgments are omitted for simplification. Typing rules for atomic terms, such as Booleans, variables, etc. demand that types of a typing context of a judgment be well-formed; in other rules, well-formedness of a typing context and a type of a term is shown as a derived property.

Inference rules for context and type well-formedness judgments are standard except for WT_DATATYPE, which requires an argument to a datatype $\tau$ to be typed at the declared argument type.

Most of typing rules are also standard or similar to the previous work [4]. The rule T_CAST means that the source and target types in a cast have to be compatible. Intuitively, two types are compatible when a cast from one type to the other may succeed. More formally, type compatibility, written $T_1 \parallel T_2$, is the least congruence satisfying rules in the bottom of Figure 2: the rule C_REFINEL allows casts from and to refinement types; and the rule C_DATATYPE says that if datatypes are declared to be compatible in the type definition, then they are compatible. The typing rule T_CTR demands that arguments $e_2$ and $e_1$ respect the argument types of $C$ and the datatype that $C$ belongs to, respectively. The rule T_MATCH for match expressions demands the matched term $e_0$ to be typed at a datatype $\tau\langle e \rangle$. Using the metafunction *CtrsOf*, the rule demands that the patterns $\overline{C_i\, x_i}^{\,i}$ be exhaustive. Moreover, each branch $e_i$ has to be given the same type $T$, which cannot contain pattern variables $x_i$ (and so is well formed under $\Gamma$).

### 3.3 Semantics

The semantics of $\lambda^{H}_{\mathtt{dt}}$ is given in the small-step style by using two relations over closed terms: the reduction relation ($\rightsquigarrow$), which represents basic computation such as $\beta$-reduction, and the evaluation relation ($\longrightarrow$), in which a subexpression is reduced.

The semantics is parameterized by a type definition environment and a *constructor choice function* $\delta$, which is a partial function that maps a term of the form $\langle \tau_1\langle e_1 \rangle \Leftarrow \tau_2\langle e_2 \rangle \rangle^{\ell}\, C_2\langle e \rangle v$ to a constructor $C_1$. We introduce this function as an oracle to decide which constructor a given constructor is converted to by a cast between datatypes, as discussed in Section 2. The constructor $C_1$ has to not only belong to $\tau_1$ but also be compatible with $C_2$. We will give a more precise condition on $\delta$ later.

Precisely speaking, the two relations are parameterized by $\Sigma$ and $\delta$ but we fix certain $\Sigma$ and $\delta$ in what follows and usually omit them from relations and judgments.

Before reduction and evaluation rules, we introduce several run-time terms to express dynamic contract checking in the semantics. These run-time terms are assumed not to appear in a source program (or datatype definitions). The syntax is extended as below:

$$e \;::=\; \ldots \mid {\Uparrow}\ell \mid \langle \{x{:}T \mid e_1\}, e_2, v \rangle^{\ell} \mid \langle\!\langle \{x{:}T \mid e_1\}, e_2 \rangle\!\rangle^{\ell}$$

The term ${\Uparrow}\ell$ denotes a cast failure blaming $\ell$, which identifies which cast failed. An active check $\langle \{x{:}T \mid e_1\}, e_2, v \rangle^{\ell}$ verifies that the value $v$ of type $T$ satisfies the contract $e_1$. The term $e_2$ represents an intermediate state of a check, which starts by reducing $e_1\,\{v/x\}$. If the check succeeds, namely $e_2$ reduces to $\mathsf{true}$, then the active check evaluates to $v$; otherwise, if $e_2$ reduces to $\mathsf{false}$, then it is blamed with $\ell$. A waiting check $\langle\!\langle \{x{:}T \mid e_1\}, e_2 \rangle\!\rangle^{\ell}$, which appears when an application of a cast to a refinement type is reduced, checks that the value of $e_2$ satisfies $e_1$. Waiting checks are introduced to avoid a technical problem recently found in Belo et al. [4]. We will discuss it in more detail at the end of this section.

Figure 3 shows reduction and evaluation rules. Reduction rules are standard except for those about casts and active/waiting checks. There are six reduction rules for casts. The rule R_BASE means that a cast between the same base type simply behaves like an identity function. The rule R_FUN, which shows that casts between function types behave like function contracts [6, 14], produces a lambda abstraction which wraps the value $v$ with the contravariant cast $\langle T_{21} \Leftarrow T_{11} \rangle^{\ell}$ between the argument types and the covariant cast $\langle T_{12} \Leftarrow T_{22} \rangle^{\ell}$ between the return types. To avoid capture of the bound variable of $T_{12}$, we take a fresh variable $y$ and rename

$\boxed{\vdash \Gamma}$ **Typing Context Well-Formedness Rules**

$$\frac{}{\vdash \varnothing}\ \text{WC\_EMPTY} \qquad \frac{\vdash \Gamma \quad \Gamma \vdash T}{\vdash \Gamma, x{:}T}\ \text{WC\_EXTENDVAR}$$

$\boxed{\Gamma \vdash T}$ **Type Well-Formedness Rules**

$$\frac{\vdash \Gamma}{\Gamma \vdash \mathsf{Bool}}\ \text{WT\_BASE} \qquad \frac{\Gamma \vdash T_1 \quad \Gamma, x{:}T_1 \vdash T_2}{\Gamma \vdash x : T_1 \to T_2}\ \text{WT\_FUN} \qquad \frac{\Gamma \vdash T_1 \quad \Gamma, x{:}T_1 \vdash T_2}{\Gamma \vdash x{:}T_1 \times T_2}\ \text{WT\_PROD}$$

$$\frac{\Gamma \vdash T \quad \Gamma, x{:}T \vdash e : \mathsf{Bool}}{\Gamma \vdash \{x{:}T \mid e\}}\ \text{WT\_REFINE} \qquad \frac{\mathit{ArgTypeOf}(\tau) = x{:}T \quad \Gamma \vdash e : T}{\Gamma \vdash \tau\langle e\rangle}\ \text{WT\_DATATYPE}$$

$\boxed{\Gamma \vdash e : T}$ **Typing Rules**

$$\frac{\vdash \Gamma \quad c \in \{\mathsf{true}, \mathsf{false}\}}{\Gamma \vdash c : \mathsf{Bool}}\ \text{T\_CONST} \qquad \frac{\vdash \Gamma \quad x{:}T \in \Gamma}{\Gamma \vdash x : T}\ \text{T\_VAR} \qquad \frac{\Gamma, f{:}(x{:}T_1 \to T_2), x{:}T_1 \vdash e : T_2 \quad f \notin \mathsf{FV}(T_2)}{\Gamma \vdash \mathtt{fix}\, f(x{:}T_1){:}T_2 = e : x{:}T_1 \to T_2}\ \text{T\_ABS}$$

$$\frac{\Gamma \vdash T_1 \quad \Gamma \vdash T_2 \quad T_1 \parallel T_2}{\Gamma \vdash \langle T_1 \Leftarrow T_2\rangle^{\ell} : T_2 \to T_1}\ \text{T\_CAST} \qquad \frac{\Gamma \vdash e_1 : x{:}T_1 \to T_2 \quad \Gamma \vdash e_2 : T_1}{\Gamma \vdash e_1\, e_2 : T_2\{e_2/x\}}\ \text{T\_APP}$$

$$\frac{\Gamma, x{:}T_1 \vdash T_2 \quad \Gamma \vdash e_1 : T_1 \quad \Gamma \vdash e_2 : T_2\{e_1/x\}}{\Gamma \vdash (e_1, e_2) : x{:}T_1 \times T_2}\ \text{T\_PAIR} \qquad \frac{\Gamma \vdash e : x{:}T_1 \times T_2}{\Gamma \vdash e.1 : T_1}\ \text{T\_PROJ1} \qquad \frac{\Gamma \vdash e : x{:}T_1 \times T_2}{\Gamma \vdash e.2 : T_2\{e.1/x\}}\ \text{T\_PROJ2}$$

$$\frac{\Gamma \vdash e_1 : \mathsf{Bool} \quad \Gamma \vdash e_2 : T \quad \Gamma \vdash e_3 : T}{\Gamma \vdash \mathsf{if}\ e_1\ \mathsf{then}\ e_2\ \mathsf{else}\ e_3 : T}\ \text{T\_IF} \qquad \frac{\begin{array}{c}\mathit{TypSpecOf}(C) = x{:}T_1 \rightarrowtail T_2 \rightarrowtail \tau\langle x\rangle \\ \Gamma \vdash e_1 : T_1 \quad \Gamma \vdash e_2 : T_2\{e_1/x\} \quad \Gamma \vdash \tau\langle e_1\rangle\end{array}}{\Gamma \vdash C\langle e_1\rangle e_2 : \tau\langle e_1\rangle}\ \text{T\_CTR}$$

$$\frac{\begin{array}{c}\Gamma \vdash e_0 : \tau\langle e\rangle \quad \Gamma \vdash T \quad \mathit{CtrsOf}(\tau) = \overline{C_i}^{\,i \in \{1,\dots,n\}} \quad \mathit{ArgTypeOf}(\tau) = y{:}T' \\ \text{for all } i,\ \mathit{CtrArgOf}(C_i) = T_i \quad \text{for all } i,\ \Gamma, x_i{:}T_i\{e/y\} \vdash e_i : T\end{array}}{\Gamma \vdash \mathsf{match}\ e_0\ \mathsf{with}\ \overline{C_i\, x_i \to e_i}^{\,i \in \{1,\dots,n\}} : T}\ \text{T\_MATCH}$$

$\boxed{T_1 \parallel T_2}$ **Type Compatibility**

$$\frac{T_1 \parallel T_2}{\{x{:}T_1 \mid e_1\} \parallel T_2}\ \text{C\_REFINEL} \qquad \frac{\mathit{TypDefOf}(\tau_1) = (\mathsf{type}\ \tau_1\ \langle x{:}T\rangle = \overline{C_i \parallel D_i : T_i}^{\,i}) \quad \text{for all } i,\ \mathit{TypNameOf}(D_i) = \tau_2}{\tau_1\langle e_1\rangle \parallel \tau_2\langle e_2\rangle}\ \text{C\_DATATYPE}$$

**Figure 2.** Type system.

variable $x$ in $T_{22}$ to it. Similar renaming is performed in R_PROD. The rule R_PROD means that elements $v_1$ and $v_2$ are checked by covariant casts obtained by decomposing the source and target types. The rules R_FORGET and R_PRECHECK are applied when source and target types of a cast are refinement types, respectively: the rule R_FORGET peels the outermost refinement of the source type; and the rule R_PRECHECK means that inner refinements in the target type are first checked and then the outermost one is. The side condition in R_PRECHECK are needed to make the semantics deterministic. For example, the term $\langle\{x{:}\mathsf{int} \mid 0 < x + 1\} \Leftarrow \{x{:}\mathsf{int} \mid 0 < x\}\rangle^{\ell}\, v$ reduces to $\langle\!\langle\{x{:}\mathsf{int} \mid 0 < x + 1\}, \langle\mathsf{int} \Leftarrow \mathsf{int}\rangle^{\ell}\, v\rangle\!\rangle^{\ell}$ by applying first R_FORGET and then R_PRECHECK. A waiting check turns into an active check when its second argument becomes a value (R_CHECK).

There are three rules R_DATATYPE, R_DATATYPEMONO and R_DATATYPEFAIL, for datatype casts. The rule R_DATATYPE is applied when the choice function $\delta$ gives the constructor $C_1$; then the original constructor argument $v$ is passed to a cast between the argument types of $C_2$ and $C_1$. Here, note that $e_1$ and $e_2$ are substituted for variables $x_1$ and $x_2$ in the argument types of $C_1$ and $C_2$, respectively, because these types depend on these variables. The rule R_DATATYPEMONO is similar to R_BASE. The rule R_DATATYPEFAIL says that, if the choice function $\delta$ is undefined for the cast, the cast application is blamed with $\ell$.

The last three rules R_CHECK, R_OK and R_FAIL follow the intuitive meaning of active checks explained above.

Evaluation rules are also shown in Figure 3. Here, evaluation contexts [8], ranged over by $E$, are defined as usual:

$$\begin{array}{l} E ::= [\,] \mid E\, e_2 \mid v_1\, E \mid (E, e_2) \mid (v_1, E) \mid E.1 \mid E.2 \mid C\langle e_1\rangle E \mid \\ \quad \mathsf{match}\ E\ \mathsf{with}\ \overline{C_i\, x_i \to e_i}^{\,i} \mid \mathsf{if}\ E\ \mathsf{then}\ e_2\ \mathsf{else}\ e_3 \mid \\ \quad \langle\{x{:}T \mid e\}, E, v\rangle^{\ell} \mid \langle\!\langle\{x{:}T \mid e\}, E\rangle\!\rangle^{\ell} \end{array}$$

The rule E_RED means that evaluation proceeds by reducing the redex indicated by an evaluation context; the rule E_BLAME means that a raised blame will abort program execution.

### 3.4 Type Soundness

We show type soundness of $\lambda^{H}_{\mathtt{dt}}$. As usual, type soundness means that a well-typed term does not go wrong and is proved via subject reduction and progress [23, 29]. Moreover, we will show that, if a term is given a refinement type, its value (if it exists) satisfies the contract. This last property, which was proved by using semantic methods [4, 18], is proved purely syntactically for the first time.

Before stating the type soundness theorem, we start with extending the type system to run-time terms, and define well-formedness of type definition environments and constructor choice functions.

#### 3.4.1 Typing for Run-time Terms

Typing rules for run-time terms are shown in Figure 4. The rule T_BLAME means that a blame $\Uparrow\ell$ can have any type because it is an exception. In the rule T_ACHECK for an active check $\langle\{x{:}T \mid e_1\}, e_2, v\rangle^{\ell}$, the last premise $e_1\{v/x\} \longrightarrow^{*} e_2$ means that $e_2$ is an intermediate state of checking, which started from

$\boxed{e_1 \rightsquigarrow e_2}$ **Reduction Rules**

$$(\mathtt{fix}\, f(x{:}T_1){:}T_2 = e)\, v \;\rightsquigarrow\; e\,\{v/x, \mathtt{fix}\, f(x{:}T_1){:}T_2 = e/f\} \qquad \text{R\_BETA}$$

$$(v_1, v_2).1 \rightsquigarrow v_1 \qquad \text{R\_PROJ1} \qquad\qquad \mathsf{if\ true\ then}\ e_1\ \mathsf{else}\ e_2 \rightsquigarrow e_1 \qquad \text{R\_IFTRUE}$$

$$(v_1, v_2).2 \rightsquigarrow v_2 \qquad \text{R\_PROJ2} \qquad\qquad \mathsf{if\ false\ then}\ e_1\ \mathsf{else}\ e_2 \rightsquigarrow e_2 \qquad \text{R\_IFFALSE}$$

$$\mathsf{match}\ C_j\langle e\rangle v\ \mathsf{with}\ \overline{C_i\, x_i \to e_i}^{\,i} \;\rightsquigarrow\; e_j\,\{v/x_j\} \qquad (\text{where } C_j \in \overline{C_i}^{\,i}) \qquad \text{R\_MATCH}$$

$$\langle \mathsf{Bool} \Leftarrow \mathsf{Bool}\rangle^{\ell}\, v \;\rightsquigarrow\; v \qquad \text{R\_BASE}$$

$$\langle x{:}T_{11} \to T_{12} \Leftarrow x{:}T_{21} \to T_{22}\rangle^{\ell}\, v \;\rightsquigarrow\; (\lambda x{:}T_{11}.\mathsf{let}\ y = \langle T_{21} \Leftarrow T_{11}\rangle^{\ell}\, x\ \mathsf{in}\ \langle T_{12} \Leftarrow (T_{22}\,\{y/x\})\rangle^{\ell}\,(v\, y))$$
$$(\text{where } y \text{ is fresh}) \qquad \text{R\_FUN}$$

$$\langle x{:}T_{11} \times T_{12} \Leftarrow x{:}T_{21} \times T_{22}\rangle^{\ell}\,(v_1, v_2) \;\rightsquigarrow\; \mathsf{let}\ x = \langle T_{11} \Leftarrow T_{21}\rangle^{\ell}\, v_1\ \mathsf{in}\ (x, \langle T_{12} \Leftarrow (T_{22}\,\{v_1/x\})\rangle^{\ell}\, v_2) \qquad \text{R\_PROD}$$

$$\langle T_1 \Leftarrow \{x{:}T_2 \mid e\}\rangle^{\ell}\, v \;\rightsquigarrow\; \langle T_1 \Leftarrow T_2\rangle^{\ell}\, v \qquad \text{R\_FORGET}$$

$$\langle \{x{:}T_1 \mid e\} \Leftarrow T_2\rangle^{\ell}\, v \;\rightsquigarrow\; \langle\!\langle \{x{:}T_1 \mid e\}, \langle T_1 \Leftarrow T_2\rangle^{\ell}\, v\rangle\!\rangle^{\ell} \qquad \text{R\_PRECHECK}$$
$$(\text{where } T_2 \text{ is not a refinement type})$$

$$\langle \tau_1\langle e_1\rangle \Leftarrow \tau_2\langle e_2\rangle\rangle^{\ell}\, C_2\langle e\rangle v \;\rightsquigarrow\; C_1\langle e_1\rangle(\langle T_1'\,\{e_1/x_1\} \Leftarrow T_2'\,\{e_2/x_2\}\rangle^{\ell}\, v) \qquad \text{R\_DATATYPE}$$
$$(\text{where } \tau_1 \neq \tau_2 \text{ or } \tau_1 \text{ is not monomorphic, and } \delta(\langle \tau_1\langle e_1\rangle \Leftarrow \tau_2\langle e_2\rangle\rangle^{\ell}\, C_2\langle e\rangle v) = C_1 \text{ and}$$
$$\mathit{ArgTypeOf}(\tau_i) = x_i{:}T_i \text{ and } \mathit{CtrArgOf}(C_i) = T_i' \text{ for } i \in \{1,2\}\,)$$

$$\langle \tau \Leftarrow \tau\rangle^{\ell}\, v \;\rightsquigarrow\; v \qquad \text{R\_DATATYPEMONO}$$

$$\langle \tau_1\langle e_1\rangle \Leftarrow \tau_2\langle e_2\rangle\rangle^{\ell}\, v \;\rightsquigarrow\; \Uparrow\ell \qquad \text{R\_DATATYPEFAIL}$$
$$(\text{where } \tau_1 \neq \tau_2 \text{ or } \tau_1 \text{ is not monomorphic, and } \delta(\langle \tau_1\langle e_1\rangle \Leftarrow \tau_2\langle e_2\rangle\rangle^{\ell}\, v) \text{ is undefined}\,)$$

$$\langle\!\langle \{x{:}T \mid e\}, v\rangle\!\rangle^{\ell} \;\rightsquigarrow\; \langle \{x{:}T \mid e\}, e\,\{v/x\}, v\rangle^{\ell} \qquad \text{R\_CHECK}$$

$$\langle \{x{:}T \mid e\}, \mathsf{true}, v\rangle^{\ell} \rightsquigarrow v \qquad \text{R\_OK} \qquad\qquad \langle \{x{:}T \mid e\}, \mathsf{false}, v\rangle^{\ell} \rightsquigarrow \Uparrow\ell \qquad \text{R\_FAIL}$$

$\boxed{e_1 \longrightarrow e_2}$ **Evaluation Rules**

$$\frac{e_1 \rightsquigarrow e_2}{E[e_1] \longrightarrow E[e_2]}\ \text{E\_RED} \qquad\qquad \frac{E \neq [\,]}{E[\Uparrow\ell] \longrightarrow \Uparrow\ell}\ \text{E\_BLAME}$$

**Figure 3.** Semantics.

$\boxed{\Gamma \vdash e : T}$

$$\frac{\vdash \Gamma \quad \varnothing \vdash T}{\Gamma \vdash \Uparrow\ell : T}\ \text{T\_BLAME} \qquad \frac{\begin{array}{c}\vdash \Gamma \quad \varnothing \vdash \{x{:}T \mid e_1\} \quad \varnothing \vdash v : T \\ \varnothing \vdash e_2 : \mathsf{Bool} \quad e_1\,\{v/x\} \longrightarrow^{*} e_2\end{array}}{\Gamma \vdash \langle \{x{:}T \mid e_1\}, e_2, v\rangle^{\ell} : \{x{:}T \mid e_1\}}\ \text{T\_ACHECK} \qquad \frac{\vdash \Gamma \quad \varnothing \vdash \{x{:}T \mid e_1\} \quad \varnothing \vdash e_2 : T}{\Gamma \vdash \langle\!\langle \{x{:}T \mid e_1\}, e_2\rangle\!\rangle^{\ell} : \{x{:}T \mid e_1\}}\ \text{T\_WCHECK}$$

$$\frac{\vdash \Gamma \quad \varnothing \vdash e : T_1 \quad T_1 \equiv T_2 \quad \varnothing \vdash T_2}{\Gamma \vdash e : T_2}\ \text{T\_CONV} \qquad \frac{\vdash \Gamma \quad \varnothing \vdash v : \{x{:}T \mid e\}}{\Gamma \vdash v : T}\ \text{T\_FORGET} \qquad \frac{\begin{array}{c}\vdash \Gamma \quad \varnothing \vdash \{x{:}T \mid e\} \quad \varnothing \vdash v : T \\ e\,\{v/x\} \longrightarrow^{*} \mathsf{true}\end{array}}{\Gamma \vdash v : \{x{:}T \mid e\}}\ \text{T\_EXACT}$$

**Figure 4.** Typing rules for run-time terms.

$e_1\,\{v_1/x\}$. This reference to the semantics in the typing rule is unusual but is important in Belo et al.'s syntactic approach. The rule T_WCHECK for a waiting check is easy to understand. The rule T_FORGET is needed because R_FORGET peels off the refinements in the source type of a cast. The rule T_EXACT allows a value which succeeds in dynamic checking to be typed at a refinement type.

Finally, T_CONV—the heart of the approach by Belo et al.—is introduced as a technical device to prove subject reduction. To see why this rule is required, let us consider an application term $v_1\, e_2$. From T_APP, the type of $v_1\, e_2$ is $T_2\,\{e_2/x\}$ for some $T_2$ and $x$. If $e_2$ reduces to $e_2'$, then the type of the application term changes to $T_2\,\{e_2'/x\}$. Since $T_2\,\{e_2/x\} \neq T_2\,\{e_2'/x\}$ in general, subject reduction would not hold. The rule T_CONV bridges the gap by allowing a term to be typed at another, but "equivalent" type. The type equivalence (denoted by $\equiv$) is given as follows.

**Definition 1** (Type Equivalence).

1. *The* common subexpression reduction relation $\Rrightarrow$ *over types is defined as follows:* $T_1 \Rrightarrow T_2$ *iff there exist some* $T$, $x$, $e_1$ *and* $e_2$ *such that* $T_1 = T\,\{e_1/x\}$ *and* $T_2 = T\,\{e_2/x\}$ *and* $e_1 \longrightarrow e_2$.
2. *The* type equivalence $\equiv$ *is the symmetric transitive closure of* $\Rrightarrow$.

The type equivalence given here relates fewer terms than that by Belo et al., but is sufficient to prove subject reduction.

The fact that typing contexts in premises are empty reflects that run-time terms are closed; however, they can appear under binders as part of types (notice term substitution in the typing rules) and so weakening is needed.

### 3.4.2 Well-formed Type Definition Environments

Intuitively, a type definition environment is well formed when the parameter type is well formed, constructor argument types are well formed, and the argument types of compatible constructors are compatible.

**Definition 2** (Well-Formed Type Definition Environments).

1. *Let* $\varsigma = \tau\langle x{:}T\rangle = \overline{C_i : T_i}^{i\in\{1,\dots,n\}}$. *A type definition* $\varsigma$ *is* well formed under a type definition environment $\Sigma$ *if it satisfies the followings: (a)* $0 < n$. *(b)* $\Sigma;\varnothing \vdash T$ *holds. (c) For any* $i \in \{1,\dots,n\}$, $\Sigma,\varsigma;x{:}T \vdash T_i$ *holds.*
2. *Let* $\varsigma = \tau\langle x{:}T\rangle = \overline{C_i \parallel D_i : T_i}^{i\in\{1,\dots,n\}}$. *A type definition* $\varsigma$ *is* well formed under a type definition environment $\Sigma$ *if it satisfies the followings: (a)* $0 < n$. *(b)* $\Sigma;\varnothing \vdash T$ *holds. (c) For any* $i \in \{1,\dots,n\}$, $\Sigma,\varsigma;x{:}T \vdash T_i$ *holds. (d) There exists some datatype* $\tau'$ *in* $\Sigma$ *such that constructors* $\overline{D_i}^{i\in\{1,\dots,n\}}$ *belong to it. (e) For any* $i \in \{1,\dots,n\}$, $T_i$ *is compatible with the argument type of* $D_i$ *under* $\Sigma,\varsigma$, *that is,* $\Sigma,\varsigma \vdash T_i \parallel \mathit{CtrArgOf}_\Sigma(D_i)$ *holds.*
3. *A type definition environment* $\Sigma$ *is* well formed *if for any* $\Sigma_1$, $\varsigma$ *and* $\Sigma_2$, $\Sigma = \Sigma_1,\varsigma,\Sigma_2$ *implies that* $\varsigma$ *is well formed under* $\Sigma_1$. *We write* $\vdash \Sigma$ *to denote that* $\Sigma$ *is well formed.*

Intuitively, a constructor choice function is well formed when it returns a constructor related by $\parallel$ in type definitions and respects term equivalence, which is defined similarly to type equivalence.

**Definition 3** (Compatible Constructors). *The compatibility relation* $\parallel$ *over constructors is the least equivalence relation satisfying the following rule.*

$$\frac{\mathit{TypNameOf}(C_i) = \tau \qquad \mathit{TypDefOf}(\tau) = \mathsf{type}\,\tau\langle y{:}T\rangle = \overline{C_j \parallel D_j : T_j}^{j}}{C_i \parallel D_i}$$

*The function CompatCtrsOf, which maps a datatype* $\tau$ *and a constructor* $C$ *to the set of compatible constructors of* $\tau$, *is defined as follows:*

$$\mathit{CompatCtrsOf}(\tau, C) = \{D \mid C \parallel D \text{ and } \mathit{TypNameOf}(D) = \tau\}.$$

**Definition 4** (Term Equivalence).

1. *The* common subexpression reduction relation $\Rrightarrow$ *over terms is defined as follows:* $e_1 \Rrightarrow e_2$ *iff there exist some* $e$, $x$, $e_1'$ *and* $e_2'$ *such that* $e_1 = e\{e_1'/x\}$ *and* $e_2 = e\{e_2'/x\}$ *and* $\langle\Sigma,\delta\rangle \vdash e_1' \longrightarrow e_2'$.
2. *The* term equivalence $\equiv$ *is the symmetric transitive closure of* $\Rrightarrow$.

**Definition 5** (Well-Formed Constructor Choice Functions). *A constructor choice function* $\delta$ *is* well formed *iff*

1. *if* $C_1 = \delta(\langle\tau_1\langle e_1\rangle \Leftarrow \tau_2\langle e_2\rangle\rangle^\ell\, C_2\langle e\rangle v)$, *then* $C_1 \in \mathit{CompatCtrsOf}(\tau_1, C_2)$; *and*
2. *for any* $e_1$, $e_2$ *and* $C$, *if* $e_1 \equiv e_2$ *and* $\delta(e_1) = C$, *then* $\delta(e_2) = C$.

We suppose that the type definition environment and the choice function are well formed in what follows.

**Lemma 1** (Subject Reduction). *If* $\varnothing \vdash e : T$ *and* $e \longrightarrow e'$, *then* $\varnothing \vdash e' : T$.

**Lemma 2** (Progress). *If* $\varnothing \vdash e : T$, *then one of the followings holds: (1)* $e \longrightarrow e'$ *for some* $e'$; *(2) e is a value; or (3)* $e = \Uparrow\ell$ *for some* $\ell$.

To show the additional property mentioned above about refinement types, we need to show that the term equivalence respects the semantics in the following sense.

**Lemma 3** (Cotermination). *Suppose* $e_1 \Rrightarrow^* e_2$.

1. *If* $e_1 \longrightarrow^* v_1$, *then there exist some* $v_2$ *such that* $e_2 \longrightarrow^* v_2$ *and* $v_1 \Rrightarrow^* v_2$.
2. *If* $e_2 \longrightarrow^* v_2$, *then there exist some* $v_1$ *such that* $e_1 \longrightarrow^* v_1$ *and* $v_1 \Rrightarrow^* v_2$.

**Theorem 1** (Type Soundness). *If* $\varnothing \vdash e : T$, *then one of the followings holds: (1) there exists* $v$ *such that* $e \longrightarrow^* v$ *and* $\varnothing \vdash v : T$; *(2)* $e \longrightarrow^* \Uparrow\ell$ *for some* $\ell$; *or (3) there is an infinite sequence of evaluation* $e \longrightarrow e_1 \longrightarrow \cdots$. *Moreover, if* $T$ *is a refinement type* $\{x{:}T_0 \mid e_0\}$ *and (1) holds, then* $e_0\{v/x\} \longrightarrow^*$ $\mathsf{true}$.

*Proof.* (1)–(3) follow from subject reduction and progress. For the additional property, it suffices to show that if $\varnothing \vdash v : T$, then $v$ satisfies all contracts of type $T$. We proceed by induction on the derivation of $\varnothing \vdash v : T$. In the case of T_CONV, we use Lemma 3 and the fact that for any $v'$, if $v' \Rrightarrow^* \mathsf{true}$ or $\mathsf{true} \Rrightarrow^* v'$, then $v' = \mathsf{true}$. □

#### 3.4.3 Remark on Semantics of Casts

As we have mentioned, our semantics of casts for nested refinement types is slightly different from the one for $F_H$ [4] in the following respects. First, they had a rule to remove reflexive casts

$$\langle T \Leftarrow T\rangle^\ell\, v \longrightarrow v$$

(for *any* type, including function and refinement types) and a rule to start an active check:

$$\langle\{x{:}T \mid e\} \Leftarrow T\rangle^\ell\, v \longrightarrow \langle\{x{:}T \mid e\}, e\{v/x\}, v\rangle^\ell$$

Second, they define type equivalence $\equiv$ based on parallel reduction. They also left the cotermination property as a conjecture. However, with these rules, cotermination does not quite hold. Consider $e = \langle\{x{:}\mathsf{Bool} \mid y\} \Leftarrow \{x{:}\mathsf{Bool} \mid \mathsf{false}\}\rangle^\ell\, v$. Then,

$$e\{\mathsf{false}/y\} \equiv e\{1 = 0/y\} \text{ and}$$
$$e\{\mathsf{false}/y\} \longrightarrow v \text{ (by removing the reflexive cast), but}$$
$$e\{1 = 0/y\} \longrightarrow^* \langle\{x{:}\mathsf{Bool} \mid 1 = 0\}, 1 = 0, v\rangle^\ell \longrightarrow^* \Uparrow\ell,$$

which is a counterexample to cotermination.[3] It is easy to construct a similar counterexample using the second rule above. This is quite bad because the cotermination property is quite important to show semantic properties such as (3) of Theorem 1 or parametricity for $F_H$.

The problem seems to stem from the fact that reduction of a subterm (in this case $1 = 0$) can change the cast rule to be applied. Our calculus $\lambda^H_{\mathsf{dt}}$ is carefully designed to avoid this problem by restricting reflexive casts (R_BASE and R_DATATYPEMONO) and introducing waiting checks. The price we pay is that we have to *prove* that reflexive casts can be eliminated.

## 4. Translation from Refinement Types to Datatypes

We give a translation from refinement types to datatypes and prove that the datatype obtained by the translation has the same meaning as the refinement type in the sense that a cast from the refinement type to the datatype always succeeds, and vice versa. We formalize our translation and prove its correctness using integer lists for simplicity and conciseness but our translation scheme can be generalized to other datatypes. We will informally discuss a more general case of binary trees later.

In this section, we assume that we have $\mathsf{unit}$ and $\mathsf{int}$ as base types and $\mathsf{int\ list}$ with [] and infix cons $x :: y$ as constructors. For

[3] Note that replacing $\equiv$ based on parallel reduction with one based on common subexpression reduction would not help. We should also note that subject reduction and progress of $F_H$ still hold because they do not depend on cotermination.

$$
\begin{array}{lcl}
\mathit{GenContracts}(\mathsf{true}) = \{(\mathit{None}, \mathsf{true})\} & & \mathit{GenContracts}(\mathsf{false}) = \varnothing \\
\mathit{GenContracts}(\mathsf{if}\ f\ e_1\ z_2\ \mathsf{then}\ e_2\ \mathsf{else}\ e_3) & = & \{(\mathit{Some}\ e_1, e_2)\} \cup \\
& & \{(e_{\mathbf{opt}}, \mathsf{if}\ f\ e_1\ z_2\ \mathsf{then\ false\ else}\ e_3') \mid (e_{\mathbf{opt}}, e_3') \in \mathit{GenContracts}(e_3)\} \\
& & \hfill (\text{if } \mathsf{FV}(e_1) \subseteq \{y, z_1\}) \\
\mathit{GenContracts}(\mathsf{if}\ e_1\ \mathsf{then}\ e_2\ \mathsf{else}\ e_3) & = & \{(e_{\mathbf{opt}}, \mathsf{if}\ e_1\ \mathsf{then}\ e_2'\ \mathsf{else\ false}) \mid (e_{\mathbf{opt}}, e_2') \in \mathit{GenContracts}(e_2)\} \cup \\
& & \{(e_{\mathbf{opt}}, \mathsf{if}\ e_1\ \mathsf{then\ false\ else}\ e_3') \mid (e_{\mathbf{opt}}, e_3') \in \mathit{GenContracts}(e_3)\} \\
& & \hfill (\text{if a term of the form } f\ e\ z_2 \text{ occurs in } e_2 \text{ or } e_3) \\
\mathit{GenContracts}(\mathsf{match}\ e_0\ \mathsf{with}\ \overline{C_i\ x_i \to e_i}^{i \in \{1,\ldots,n\}}) & = & \bigcup_{j \in \{1,\ldots,n\}} \{(e_{\mathbf{opt}}, \mathsf{match}\ e_0\ \mathsf{with}\ \overline{C_i\ x_i \to e_i'}^{i \in \{1,\ldots,n\}}) \mid \\
& & \quad (e_{\mathbf{opt}}, e_j') \in \mathit{GenContracts}(e_j) \land \forall i \neq j.\ e_i' = \mathsf{false}\} \\
& & \hfill (\text{if a term of the form } f\ e\ z_2 \text{ occurs in some } e_i) \\
\mathit{GenContracts}(e) & = & \{(\mathit{None}, e)\} \hfill (\text{otherwise})
\end{array}
$$

**Figure 6.** Generation of base contracts and arguments to recursive calls.

*Trans*
**input:**
$\mathtt{fix}\, f(y{:}T, x{:}\mathsf{int\ list}) = \mathsf{match}\ x\ \mathsf{with}\ [\,] \to e_1 \mid z_1 :: z_2 \to e_2$
**returns:**

1 **let** $\tau$ be a fresh type name **in**

2 **let** $\{T_i\}_i =$

$$\left\{ z_1{:}\mathsf{int} \times \{z_2{:}T_0 \mid e_0\} \;\middle|\; \begin{array}{l} (e_{\mathbf{opt}}, e) \in \mathit{GenContracts}(e_2), \\ (T_0, e_0) = \mathit{Aux}(\tau, e_{\mathbf{opt}}, e) \end{array} \right\} \ \mathbf{in}$$

3 **let** $D$ and $\overline{D_i}^{i}$ be fresh constructor names, and $z$ be a fresh variable **in**

4 $\mathsf{type}\ \tau\,\langle y{:}T\rangle = D \parallel [\,] : \{z{:}\mathsf{unit} \mid e_1\} \mid \overline{D_i \parallel (::) : T_i}^{i}$

where
$\mathit{Aux}(\tau, e_{\mathbf{opt}}, e) =$
**let** $e' = e\,\{\mathtt{fix}\, f(y{:}T, x{:}\mathsf{int\ list}) = \ldots / f\}$ **in**
**match** $e_{\mathbf{opt}}$ **with**
$\mid \mathit{Some}\ e'' \to (\tau\langle e''\rangle, \mathsf{let}\ z_2 = \langle \mathsf{int\ list} \Leftarrow \tau\langle e''\rangle\rangle^{\ell}\ z_2\ \mathsf{in}\ e')$
$\mid \mathit{None} \to (\mathsf{int\ list}, e')$

**Figure 5.** Translation.

simplicity, we also assume that the input predicate function is well typed and of the following form:

$$\mathtt{fix}\, f(y{:}T, x{:}\mathsf{int\ list}) = \mathsf{match}\ x\ \mathsf{with}\ [\,] \to e_1 \mid z_1 :: z_2 \to e_2$$

where $x \notin \mathsf{FV}(e_1) \cup \mathsf{FV}(e_2)$. We will use `sorted` as a running example. For expository reasons, the definition is slightly verbose; the nested `if` expression at the end is essentially `z1 <= y && sorted () z2`.

```
let rec sorted (y:unit, x:int list) =
  match x with
  | []      -> true
  | z1::z2 -> e2
```

where
$e_2^{\mathtt{sorted}} =$

```
match z2 with
| []      -> true
| y::ys -> if z1 <= y then
             if sorted () z2 then true
                else false
           else false
```

## 4.1 Translation, Formally

We show the translation function *Trans* in Figure 5 and the auxiliary function *GenContracts* in Figure 6. The main function *Trans* takes a recursive function as an input and returns a corresponding datatype definition (on line 4).

On line 2, information on how $e_2$, which is the contract for ::, can evaluate to true is gathered by the auxiliary function *GenContracts*. In the definition, variables $f$, $y$, $z_1$, and $z_2$ come from the input function and are fixed names. This function takes an expression as an input and returns a set of pairs $(e_{\mathbf{opt}}, e_2')$, each of which expresses one execution path that returns true in $e_2$. $e_2'$ is derived from $e_2$ by substituting false for all but one path and $e_{\mathbf{opt}}$ is the first argument to a recursive call (if any) on this path. Intuitively, conjunction of $e_2'$ and $f\ e_{\mathbf{opt}}\ z_2$ gives one sufficient condition for $e_2$ to be true and disjunction of the pairs in the returned set is logically equivalent to $e_2$. For example, $\mathit{GenContracts}(e_2^{\mathtt{sorted}})$ returns a set consisting of $(\mathit{None}, e_{21})$ where $e_{21}$ is

```
match z2 with [] -> true | y::ys -> false
```

and $(\mathit{Some}\,(), e_{22})$ where $e_{22}$ is

```
match z2 with
  []      -> false
| y::ys -> if z1 <= y then true else false .
```

(Gray bits show differences from $e_2^{\mathtt{sorted}}$.) The first expression means that a (non-empty) list `x` is sorted when the tail is empty; and the second means that `x` is sorted when the head `z1` is equal to or smaller than the second element `y` and the recursive call `sorted () z2` returns true. *GenContracts* performs a kind of disjunctive normal form translation and each disjunct will correspond to a data constructor in the generated datatype.

Now let us take a look at the definition of *GenContracts*. The first two clauses are trivial: if the expression is true, then it returns the trivial contract and if it is false, then this branch should not be taken and hence the empty sequence is returned. The third clause deals with a conditional on a recursive call $f\ e_1\ z_2$ on the tail. In this case, it returns $\mathit{Some}\ e_1$, to signal there is a designated recursive call in this branch, with the additional condition $e_2$ and also the condition when the recursive call returns false but $e_3$ is true. The following two clauses are for the other cases where the input expression is case analysis. In this case, from each branch, *GenContracts* recursively collects execution paths and reconstruct conditional expressions by replacing other branches with false. The side conditions on these clauses mean that we can stop DNF translation if there is no recursive calls on the tail and simply return the given contract as it is, by calling for the last clause, which deals with other forms of expressions.

The collected execution path information is further transformed into dependent product types with the help of another auxiliary function *Aux*. This function takes a pair $(e_{\mathbf{opt}}, e)$ (obtained by *GenContracts*) together with the new datatype name $\tau$ as an input and returns the base type and its refinement for the tail part. If there was no recursive call on the tail in a given execution path (namely, $e_{\mathbf{opt}} = None$), then the base type is int list and the refinement is $e'$, obtained from $e$ by replacing other recursive occurrences of $f$ with the function itself. Otherwise, the base type is the new datatype applied t the first argument $e''$ to the recursive call; the refinement is essentially $e'$ (except a cast back to int list). For example, for `sorted`, we obtain

$$T_1 = z_1\text{:int} \times \{z_2\text{:int list} \mid e_{21}\}$$

from $(None, e_{21})$ and

$$T_2 = z_1\text{:int} \times \{z_2\text{:}\tau \mid \text{let } z_2 = \langle \text{int list} \Leftarrow \tau \rangle^{\ell}\ z_2 \text{ in } e_{22}\}$$

from $(Some\,(), e_{22})$. $T_1$ is a type for singleton lists, which are trivially sorted and $T_2$ is a type for a list where the head is equal to or less than the second element and the tail is of type $\tau$, which is supposed to represent sorted lists.

Finally, we combine $T_i$ to make a complete datatype definition. The translation of `sorted` will be:

```
type sorted_t =
  SNil   || []   of {z:unit|true}
| SCons1 || (::) of z1:int × {z2:int list|e21}
| SCons2 || (::) of
    z1:int ×
    {z2:sorted_t|
     let z2 = ⟨int list ⇐ sorted_t⟩^ℓ z2 in e22}
```

Although the datatype `sorted_t` certainly represents sorted lists, its type definition is different from `slist2` given in Section 1. The difference comes from the fact that the case for (::) has a case analysis, one of whose branch has a recursive call. While it is possible to "merge" the argument types for `SCons1` and `SCons2` to make a two-constructor datatype, it is difficult in general. It is interesting future work, however, to investigate how to generate type definitions closer to programmers' expectation.

### 4.2 Correctness

We prove that the translation is correct in the sense that the cast from a refinement type to the datatype obtained by the translation always succeeds and vice versa. We use a metavariable $F$ to denote the recursive function used to define the refinement type in the typing judgment and the evaluation relation. We write $\langle \Sigma, \delta \rangle; \Gamma \vdash e : T$ and $\langle \Sigma, \delta \rangle \vdash e_1 \longrightarrow e_2$ to make a type definition environment $\Sigma$ and a constructor choice function $\delta$ explicit in the typing judgment and the evaluation relation.

First of all, the translation *Trans* always generates a well-formed datatype definition:

**Lemma 4** (Translation Generates Well-formed Datatype). *Let $\Sigma$ be a well-formed type definition environment, $\Sigma; \varnothing \vdash F : T \rightarrow$ int list $\rightarrow$ Bool. Then, the type definition $gen(Fvar)$ is well formed under $\Sigma$.*

The next theorem states that a cast from a refinement type to the generated datatype always succeeds.

**Theorem 2** (From Refinement Types to Datatypes). *Let $\Sigma$ be a well-formed type definition environment, $\Sigma; \varnothing \vdash F : T \rightarrow$ int list $\rightarrow$ Bool, $\tau$ be the name of the datatype $Trans\,(F)$. Then, there exists some computable well-formed choice function $\delta$ such that, for any $e = \langle \tau \langle e_0 \rangle \Leftarrow \{x\text{:int list} \mid F\ e_0\ x\} \rangle^{\ell}\ v$, if $(\Sigma, Trans\,(F)); \varnothing \vdash e : \tau\langle e_0 \rangle$, then $\langle (\Sigma, Trans\,(F)), \delta \rangle \vdash e \longrightarrow^{*} v'$ for some $v'$.*

It is a bit trickier to prove the converse because the first argument to a predicate function is always evaluated whereas a parameter to a datatype is not. So, the converse holds under the following termination condition on a datatype.

**Definition 6** (Termination). *Let $\Sigma$ be a type definition environment and $\delta$ be a constructor choice function. A closed term $e$* terminates at a value under $\Sigma$ and $\delta$, *written as $\langle \Sigma, \delta \rangle \vdash e\downarrow$, if $\langle \Sigma, \delta \rangle \vdash e \longrightarrow^{*} v$ for some $v$. We say that* argument terms to datatype $\tau$ in $v$ terminate at values under $\Sigma$ and $\delta$, *written as $v\downarrow_{\tau}$, if, for any $E$, $C \in CtrsOf(\tau)$, $e_1$ and $v_2$, $v = E[C\langle e_1 \rangle v_2]$ implies $\langle \Sigma, \delta \rangle \vdash e_1\downarrow$.*

**Theorem 3** (From Datatypes to Refinement Types). *Let $\Sigma$ be a well-formed type definition environment, $\Sigma; \varnothing \vdash F : T \rightarrow$ int list $\rightarrow$ Bool, $\tau$ be the name of the datatype $Trans\,(F)$. Then, there exists some computable well-formed choice function $\delta$ such that, for any $e = \langle \{x\text{:int list} \mid F\ e_0\ x\} \Leftarrow \tau\langle e_0 \rangle \rangle^{\ell}\ v$, if $\langle (\Sigma, Trans\,(F)), \delta \rangle; \varnothing \vdash e : \{x\text{:int list} \mid F\ e\ x\}$ and $v\downarrow_{\tau}$, then $e$ terminates at a value under $\langle (\Sigma, Trans\,(F)), \delta \rangle$ and $\delta$.*

We expect that the termination condition would not be needed if we change the semantics to evaluate argument terms to datatypes.

### 4.3 Efficiency Preservation

In addition to correctness of the translation, we are also concerned with the following question "When I rewrite my program so that it uses the generated datatype, is it as efficient as the original one?" To answer this question positively, we consider the asymptotic time complexity of a cast *for successful inputs* (which we simply call the complexity of a cast), and show that the complexity of a cast from int list to its refinement is the same as that of a cast from int list to the datatype obtained from its refinement. Here, we consider only successful inputs because we are mainly interested in programs (or program runs) that do not raise blame, where checks caused by casts are successful.[4]

This efficiency preservation is obtained from Theorem 2 and the following observation. As stated in Theorem 2, we can construct a *computable* choice function. In fact, the algorithm of the choice function can be read off from the proof of Theorem 2: it returns constructors of the generated datatype from the execution trace of the refinement checking. Moreover, the orders of both the execution time of the algorithm and the size of output constructors from the algorithm are linear in the size of the input execution trace, which is proportional to the execution time of the refinement checking. Thus, the asymptotic time complexities of computation of the constructors and constructor replacement are no worse than that of the refinement checking.

From this observation, we can implement the cast from int list to the generated datatype by (1) checking the refinement (given to the translation) and (2) the constructor generation and replacement described above. Since the complexity of the second step is the same as that of the refinement checking, the complexities of the cast from int list to a refinement type and the generated datatype are the same.

### 4.4 Extension: Binary Trees

We informally describe how to extend the translation algorithm for lists to trees, a kind of data structure with a data constructor which has more than one recursive part. Here, we take binary trees as an example and show how to obtain a datatype for binary search trees from a predicate function. Although this section deals with only binary trees, this extension can be adapted for other data structures.

A datatype for binary trees and a recursive predicate function which returns whether an argument binary tree is a binary search tree or not are defined as follows:

```
type bt = L | N of int * t * t
```

[4] We conjecture that, for inputs that lead to blame, the time complexity is also preserved by the translation but a proof is left for future work.

```
let rec bst (min,max:int*int) (t:bt) =
 match t with
 | L            -> true
 | N (x,l,r) -> min<=x and x<=max and
                    bst (min,x) l and bst (x,max) r
```

Let $\tau$ be a name for the new datatype.

The translation algorithm first calls *GenContracts* with the second branch of `bst`. Observing the predicate function `bst`, we find that the body calls `bst` itself recursively for different recursive parts (`l` and `r`) with different auxiliary arguments (`(min,x)` and `(x,max)`). Thus, *GenContracts* for binary trees looks for the first argument to each recursive call, unlike *GenContracts* for lists, which stops searching for a recursive call after finding one recursive call. For our running example, taking the branch for constructor `N`, *GenContracts* for binary trees returns the singleton set $\{(\mathit{Some}\,(min, x), \mathit{Some}\,(x, max), min \le x\,\mathsf{and}\,x \le max)\}$ (where we use the operator and instead of if expression for brevity), of which the first two optional terms denote arguments for left and right subtrees, respectively.

Next, for each element in the output from *GenContracts*, a dependent product type will be built. In this case, we obtain $T = x{:}\mathsf{int} \times l{:}\tau\langle(min, x)\rangle \times \{r{:}\tau\langle(x, max)\rangle \mid min \le x\,\mathsf{and}\,x \le max\}$. As we have seen for lists, casts from $\tau\langle e\rangle$ back to bt may have to be inserted.

Finally, the translation makes a datatype definition by using these type arguments and the contract. For `bst`, the corresponding datatype is given as follows:

```
type t ⟨min:int,max:int⟩ =
 | SL
 | SN of x:int × l:t⟨min,x⟩ ×
            {r:t⟨x,max⟩|min<=x and x<=max}
```

### 4.5 Discussion

The translation algorithm works "well" for list-processing functions, in the sense that there is no reference to the input predicate function in the generated datatype, if their definitions meet the two requirements: (1) recursive calls are given the tail part of the input list and occur linearly for each execution path; and (2) free variables in arguments to recursive calls are only the argument variable $y$ and the head variable $z_1$. Specifically, translation works as we expect if given functions are written in the `fold_left` form, or more generally, in the primitive recursion form where the result of a recursive call is used at most once for each execution path. In contrast, there can remain recursive calls to an input predicate function in the generated datatype when the predicate function does not meet these requirements. This happens when there is a recursive call on lists other than the tail of the input or, as in the following (admittedly quite artificial) example, when recursive calls which return true occur twice or more in one execution path:

```
let rec f () (l:int list) =
  match x with
  | []     -> true
  | x::xs -> f () xs and f () xs
```

or when $e_2$ includes non-branching constructs as in

```
let rec f (y:int) (x:int list) =
  match x with
  | []       -> true
  | z1::z2 -> let z = 5 + y in f z z2
```

In these cases, generation of a datatype itself succeeds but the obtained datatype is probably not what we expect because `f` is not eliminated.

Although our translation works well for many predicates, there is a lot of room to improve. First, the current translation algorithm could generate a datatype with too many constructors even if some of them can be "merged". For example, we demonstrated that the translation generated a datatype with three constructors from predicate function `sorted`, but we can give a datatype with only two constructors for it as shown in Section 2.1. Second, our translation algorithm works only for a single recursive Boolean function and so we cannot obtain a datatype from other forms of refinements, for example, conjunction of two predicate function calls. This also means that the translation cannot deal with a predicate function that returns additional information by using, say, an option type.

Our translation assumes an input refinement to be of a certain form. We think, however, that it is not so restrictive, because we can transform refinements before applying our method. For example, a predicate function of the form

$$\mathsf{if}\ e_1\ \mathsf{then}\ (\mathsf{match}\ x\ \mathsf{with}\ [\,] \to e_{11} \mid z_1 :: z_2 \to e_{12})\ \mathsf{else}\ e_2$$

can be transformed to

$$\begin{array}{l} \mathsf{match}\ x\ \mathsf{with}\ [\,] \quad \to \mathsf{if}\ e_1\ \mathsf{then}\ e_{11}\ \mathsf{else}\ e_2 \mid \\ \qquad\qquad z_1 :: z_2 \to \mathsf{if}\ e_1\ \mathsf{then}\ e_{12}\ \mathsf{else}\ e_2. \end{array}$$

Even if such transformation cannot be applied, we can always insert pattern matching on the input list in the beginning of a predicate refinement. (It may be the case, though, that we do not obtain an expected type definition.)

## 5. Related Work

***Contracts for datatypes.*** There has been much work about lambda calculi with higher-order contracts since the seminal work by Findler and Felleisen [9], but little of them considers algebraic datatypes in detail and compare the two approaches to datatypes with contracts. In particular, as far as we know there is no work on conversion between compatible datatypes. One notable exception is Findler et al. [10], who compare the two approaches to datatypes and introduce lazy contract checking in an eager language. Lazy contract checking delays contract checking for arguments to data constructor until they are used. As they already point out, one drawback of lazy contract checking is that it is not suitable for checking, where relationship between elements in a data structure is important. For example, if we take the head of an arbitrary list, which is subject to sortedness checking, it simply returns its head discarding the tail without verifying the tail is sorted. Chitil [7] also made a similar observation in the work on lazy contracts in a lazy language.

Knowles et al. [19] developed Sage, a programming language based on a manifest contract calculus with first-class types and dynamic type. Sage can deal with datatypes with refined constructors by Church-encoding, but does not formalize them in its core calculus. In particular, Knowles et al. did not clarify how casts between datatypes work. Dminor [5], proposed by Bierman et al., is a first-order functional programming language with refinement types, type-test and semantic subtyping. The combination of these features is as powerful as various types such as algebraic datatypes, intersection types, and union types can be encoded. Unlike our calculus, Dminor does not deal with higher-order functions and dynamic checking with type conversion.

Xu [32] developed a hybrid contract checker for OCaml. In the static checking phase, the checker performs symbolic simplification of program components wrapped by contracts, with the help of context information, to remove blames. If a blame remains in the simplified programs, the compiler reports errors, or it issues warnings and leaves contract checking to run time. Although the checker supports variant types (i.e., datatypes where constructors have no refinements), it does not take care of relationship between elements in data structures nicely. For example, it seems that it cannot prove statically that the tail of a sorted list is also sorted unless programmers give axioms about sorted lists.

In a different line of work, Miranda [26], a statically typed functional programming language, provides datatypes with laws, which are rules to reconstruct data structures according to certain specifications. For example, we suppose that a datatype integer has three constructors Zero, Succ integer and Pred integer, and then a law converts Succ (Pred $x$) to $x$. More interestingly, Miranda can control application of laws by giving them conditional expressions. Using laws with conditionals, we can define lists which are sorted automatically. Both Miranda and our calculus provide a mechanism to convert data structures, but the purposes are different: in our work, type conversion is used only to check contracts, and so does not change "structures".

***Systematic derivation of datatype definitions.*** As mentioned in Section 1, there is closely related work, in which systematic derivation of (indexed) datatype definitions is studied.

McBride [20] propose the notion of *ornaments*, which provide a mechanism to extend and to refine datatypes in a dependently-typed programming language. For example, the definition of lists can be derived from that of natural numbers by adding an element type; and the definition of lists indexed by their lengths can be derived. As far as we understand, he does not consider deriving new type definitions by changing the number of data constructors, as is the case for our work. Also, it is not clear whether partial refinements (the case where an index cannot be assigned to some values of the original datatype) can be dealt with in this framework. Partial refinements are important in our setting because our refinement types are for excluding some values in the underlying types.

Atkey et al. [3] developed derivation of inductive types from refinement types from a category-theoretic point of view. Moreover, it can deal with partial refinements. Our translation seems to be a concrete, syntactic instance of this framework. However, being abstract, their technique is not concerned about concrete representations of datatypes, which are significant when efficiency of casts is taken into account.

A similar idea is found in Kawaguchi et al. [17], who develop a refinement type system for static verification of programs dealing with datatypes. They allow programmers to write special terminating functions called measures, which will be used as hints to the verifier by indexing a datatype with the measure information.

***Dependent and/or refinement type systems.*** The term "refinement types" seems to have many related but subtly different meanings in the literature. We use this term for types to denote subsets in some way or another. Refinement types are intensively studied in the context of static program verification.

In Freeman and Pfenning [12], datatypes can be refined by giving data constructors appropriate types. For example, one may give [] a special type null and cons a special type int $\rightarrow$ null $\rightarrow$ singleton_list, which means that, if cons takes an element and the empty list, then it yields a singleton list. Here, null and singleton_list are atomic type names. They did not allow refinement types to take arbitrary contracts to make type checking and type inference decidable. On the other hand, they combined refinement types with intersection types to express overloaded functionality of a single constructor.

Xi and Pfenning [30, 31] have designed and developed practical programming languages which support a restricted form of dependent types. Kawaguchi et al. [17] and Vazou et al. [27] have devised type inference algorithms for statically typed lambda calculi with refinement types and recursive refinements, which provides recursive types with refinements, and have implemented it for OCaml and Haskell, respectively. The refinements used there are derived from decidable languages such as (extensions of) Presburger arithmetic because their main focus is static verification. Our type system allows arbitrary Boolean predicates.

Our datatypes resemble *inductive datatypes* found in interactive proof assistants such as Coq [2] or Agda [1]. Aside from compatibility relation and casts, our syntax treats a formal argument $\langle x \rangle$ to a datatype to be parametric (notice that only argument types of data constructors have to be given). However, since $x$ can appear in a refinement, conditions on the value of $x$ can be enforced and so we do not lose much expressiveness.

## 6. Conclusion

We have proposed datatypes for manifest contracts with the mechanism of casts between different but compatible datatypes, and prove type soundness of a manifest contract calculus $\lambda_{\mathtt{dt}}^{H}$ with datatypes. In particular, the property that the value of a term of a refinement type satisfies the contract in the refinement type is proved for the first time in a purely syntactic manner. We have also given a formal translation from a refinement on lists to a datatype definition with refined constructors and proved the translation is correct. Moreover, the translation preserves the efficiency of casts.

As a proof of concept, we have implemented our casts using Camlp4. Our implementation does not support derivation of datatypes yet and a constructor choice function works by trial and error with backtracking but we are planning to extend the implementation with derivation of datatypes and an accompanying constructor choice function.

There are many directions of future work. First, we would like to investigate static contract checking using datatypes. A key theoretical property is upcast elimination: a property that removing upcasts—casts from a type to its supertype—does not change the behavior of a program in a certain sense, similarly to previous work [4, 18]. We expect refining constructor argument types is useful also for static checking [17]. Second, a proof that a generalized version of the translation given in Section 4 is correct remains as future work (although we do have translation). Third, it is worth investigating intersection types (or even Boolean operations) in this setting so that properties on data structures can be easily combined.

## Acknowledgments

We thank Kohei Suenaga for valuable comments on an earlier draft. We are grateful to the anonymous reviewers for their fruitful comments and to Robby Findler for being our angel. Michael Greenberg encouraged us during the visit to our laboratory. This work was supported in part by Grant-in-Aid for Scientific Research (B) No. 25280024 from MEXT of Japan.

## References

[1] The Agda 2 homepage. `http://wiki.portal.chalmers.se/agda/pmwiki.php`.

[2] The Coq proof assistant. `http://coq.inria.fr/`.

[3] R. Atkey, P. Johann, and N. Ghani. Refining inductive types. *Logical Methods in Computer Science*, 8(2:9):1–30, 2012.

[4] J. F. Belo, M. Greenberg, A. Igarashi, and B. C. Pierce. Polymorphic contracts. In *Proc. of ESOP*, volume 6602 of *LNCS*, pages 18–37, 2011.

[5] G. M. Bierman, A. D. Gordon, C. Hriţcu, and D. Langworthy. Semantic subtyping with an SMT solver. In *Proc. of ACM ICFP*, pages 105–116, 2010.

[6] M. Blume and D. A. McAllester. Sound and complete models of contracts. *J. Funct. Program.*, 16(4–5):375–414, July 2006.

[7] O. Chitil. A semantics for lazy assertions. In *Proc. of ACM PEPM*, pages 141–150, 2011.

[8] M. Felleisen and R. Hieb. The revised report on the syntactic theories of sequential control and state. *Theor. Comput. Sci.*, 103(2):235–271, Sept. 1992.

[9] R. B. Findler and M. Felleisen. Contracts for higher-order functions. In *Proc. of ACM ICFP*, pages 48–59, 2002.

[10] R. B. Findler, S. Guo, and A. Rogers. Lazy contract checking for immutable data structures. In *Proc. of IFL*, volume 5083 of *LNCS*, pages 111–128, 2008.

[11] C. Flanagan. Hybrid type checking. In *Proc. of ACM POPL*, pages 245–256, 2006.

[12] T. Freeman and F. Pfenning. Refinement types for ML. In *Proc. of ACM PLDI*, pages 268–277, 1991.

[13] M. Greenberg. *Manifest Contracts*. PhD thesis, University of Pennsylvania, 2013.

[14] M. Greenberg, B. C. Pierce, and S. Weirich. Contracts made manifest. In *Proc. of ACM POPL*, pages 353–364, 2010.

[15] J. Gronski, K. Knowles, A. Tomb, S. N. Freund, and C. Flanagan. Sage: Hybrid checking for flexible specifications. In *Scheme and Functional Programming Workshop*, pages 93–104, 2006.

[16] D. Herman, A. Tomb, and C. Flanagan. Space-efficient gradual typing. In *Trends in Functional Prog. (TFP)*, 2007.

[17] M. Kawaguchi, P. M. Rondon, and R. Jhala. Type-based data structure verification. In *Proc. of ACM PLDI*, pages 304–315, 2009.

[18] K. Knowles and C. Flanagan. Hybrid type checking. *ACM TOPLAS*, 32(2:6):1–34, Feb. 2010.

[19] K. Knowles, A. Tomb, J. Gronski, S. N. Freund, and C. Flanagan. Sage: Unified hybrid checking for first-class types, general refinement types, and dynamic (extended report). Technical report, UCSC, 2007.

[20] C. McBride. Ornamental algebras, algebraic ornaments. *J. Funct. Program.*, 2014. To appear.

[21] B. Meyer. *Object-Oriented Software Construction, 1st Edition*. Prentice-Hall, 1988. ISBN 0-13-629031-0.

[22] P. C. Nguyen, S. Tobin-Hochstadt, and D. Van Horn. Soft contract verification. In *ACM ICFP*, 2014.

[23] B. C. Pierce. *Types and Programming Languages*. The MIT Press, Cambridge, MA, USA, 2002. ISBN 0-262-16209-1.

[24] P. M. Rondon, M. Kawaguchi, , and R. Jhala. Liquid types. In *ACM PLDI*, 2008.

[25] J. G. Siek and P. Wadler. Threesomes, with and without blame. In *Proc. of ACM POPL*, pages 365–376, 2010.

[26] D. A. Turner. Miranda: A non-strict functional language with polymorphic types. In *Proc. of ACM FPCA*, volume 201 of *LNCS*, pages 1–16, 1985.

[27] N. Vazou, P. M. Rondon, and R. Jhala. Abstract refinement types. In *Proc. of ESOP*, volume 7792 of *LNCS*, pages 209–228, 2013.

[28] N. Vazou, E. L. Seidel, R. Jhala, D. Vytiniotis, and S. Peyton Jones. Refinement types for Haskell. In *ACM ICFP*, 2014.

[29] A. K. Wright and M. Felleisen. A syntactic approach to type soundness. *Information and Computation*, 115(1):38–94, 1994.

[30] H. Xi. Dependent ML: An approach to practical programming with dependent types. *J. Funct. Program.*, 17(2):215–286, Mar. 2007.

[31] H. Xi and F. Pfenning. Dependent types in practical programming. In *Proc. of ACM POPL*, pages 214–227, 1999.

[32] D. N. Xu. Hybrid contract checking via symbolic simplification. In *Proc. of ACM PEPM*, pages 107–116, 2012.

[33] D. N. Xu, S. L. Peyton Jones, and K. Claessen. Static contract checking for Haskell. In *Proc. of ACM POPL*, pages 41–52, 2009.

# Common Compiler Optimisations are Invalid in the C11 Memory Model and what we can do about it


Viktor Vafeiadis
MPI-SWS

Thibaut Balabonski
INRIA

Soham Chakraborty
MPI-SWS

Robin Morisset
INRIA

Francesco Zappa Nardelli
INRIA



## Abstract

We show that the weak memory model introduced by the 2011 C and C++ standards does not permit many common source-to-source program transformations (such as expression linearisation and "roach motel" reorderings) that modern compilers perform and that are deemed to be correct. As such it cannot be used to define the semantics of intermediate languages of compilers, as, for instance, LLVM aimed to. We consider a number of possible local fixes, some strengthening and some weakening the model. We evaluate the proposed fixes by determining which program transformations are valid with respect to each of the patched models. We provide formal Coq proofs of their correctness or counterexamples as appropriate.



***Categories and Subject Descriptors*** D.3.1 [*Programming Languages*]: Formal Definitions and Theory; D.3.3 [*Programming Languages*]: Language Constructs and Features

***Keywords*** Concurrency; Weak memory models; C/C++; Compilers; Program transformations


## 1. Introduction

Programmers want to understand the code they write, compilers (and hardware) try hard to optimise it. Alas, in concurrent systems even simple compiler optimisations like constant propagation can introduce unexpected behaviours! The *memory models* of programming languages are designed to resolve this tension, by governing which values can be returned when the system reads from shared memory. However, designing memory models is hard: it requires finding a compromise between providing an understandable and portable execution model for concurrent programs to programmers, while allowing common compiler optimisations.

It is well-known that only racy programs (that is, programs in which two threads can access the same resource concurrently in conflicting ways) can observe normal compiler and hardware optimisations. A common approach for a programming language is thus to require that race-free code must exhibit only sequentially-consistent (that is, interleaving) behaviours, while racy code is undefined and has no semantics. This approach, usually referred to as *DRF (data race freedom)*, is appealing to the programmer because under the hypothesis that the shared state is properly protected by locks he has to reason only about interleaving of memory accesses. It is also appealing to the compiler because it can optimise code freely provided that it respects synchronisations. A study byŠ evčík [18] shows that it is indeed the case that in an idealised DRF model common compiler optimisations are correct. These include elimination and reorderings of non-synchronising memory accesses, and the so-called *"roach motel" reorderings* [10]: moving a memory access after a lock or before an unlock instruction. Intuitively, the latter amounts to enlarging a critical section, which should be obviously correct.

Although the idealised DRF design is appealing, integrating it into a complete language design is not straightforward because additional complexity has to be taken into account. For instance, Java relies on unforgeability of pointers to enforce its security model, and the Java memory model (JSR-133) [10] must impose additional restrictions to ensure that all programs (including racy programs) enjoy some basic memory safety guarantees. The resulting model is intricate, and fails to allow some optimisations implemented in the HotSpot reference compiler [17]. Despite ongoing efforts, no satisfactory fix to JSR-133 has been proposed yet.

The recent memory model for the C and C++ languages [8, 7], from now on referred to as C11, is also based on the DRF model. Since these languages are not type safe, the Java restrictions are unnecessary and both languages simply state that racy programs have undefined behaviour. However, requiring all programs to be well-synchronised via a locking mechanism is unacceptable when it comes to writing low-level high-performance code, for which C and C++ are often the languages of choice. An escape mechanism called *low-level atomics* was built into the model. The idea is to not consider conflicting atomic accesses as races, and to specify their semantics by attributes annotated on each memory access. These range from *sequentially consistent* (SC), which imposes a total ordering semantics, to weaker ones as *release* (REL) and *acquire* (ACQ), which can be used to efficiently implement message passing, and *relaxed* (RLX), whose purpose is to allow performing single hardware loads and stores without the overhead of memory barrier instructions. As a result, RLX accesses do not synchronise with one another and provide extremely weak ordering guarantees.

A common belief is that the C11 memory model enables all common compiler optimisations, and indeed Morisset et al. [11] proved thatŠ evčík's correctness theorem for eliminations and reorderings of non-atomic accesses holds in the C11 memory model.




*POPL'15,* January 15–17, 2015, Mumbai, India.



ACM 978-1-4503-3300-9/15/01... $15.00.
http://dx.doi.org/10.1145/2676726.2676995

The authors however did not consider transformations involving low-level atomic memory accesses.

Nowadays mainstream compilers are becoming aggressive in performing optimisations that involve atomic accesses; for instance in gcc 4.10, reorderings of SC atomic loads with non-atomic loads can be observed as a side effect of partial-redundancy elimination, while clang 3.5 routinely reorders non-atomic and RLX accesses. A complete understanding of the validity of compiler optimisations in the C11 memory model is now a necessity to guide not only the future standard evolution but also current compiler development.

In this paper we set out to perform an in-depth study of optimisations in the C11 memory model. In particular we build on, and extend, the results of [11] by considering optimisations that involve atomic accesses. Unexpected surprises lurked behind the corner.

***Standard Source-to-Source Transformations are Invalid in C11.*** Surprisingly, and contradicting the common belief, we discovered that the C11 model, as defined in the C/C++ standards and formalised by Batty et al. [4], does not validate a number of source-to-source transformations that are routinely performed by compilers and are intended to be correct. As an appetiser, in what follows we show that *sequentialisation*, a simple transformation that adds synchronisation by sequentialising two concurrent accesses:

$$C_1 \| C_2 \rightsquigarrow C_1 ; C_2$$

is unsound even when $C_1$ consists of a single non-atomic variable access. Most of our counterexamples exploit the counterintuitive *causality cycles* allowed by the C11 semantics. To understand these, first consider the following code:

$$\begin{array}{l||l} r_1 = x.\mathsf{load}(\mathrm{RLX}); & r_2 = y.\mathsf{load}(\mathrm{RLX}); \\ y.\mathsf{store}(1, \mathrm{RLX}); & x.\mathsf{store}(1, \mathrm{RLX}); \end{array} \qquad (\mathsf{LB})$$

(in all our examples all variables are initialised to 0 before the parallel composition, unless specified otherwise). Since relaxed atomic accesses by design do not race and do not synchronise, it is perfectly reasonable to get $r_1 = r_2 = 1$ at the end of some execution: the memory accesses in each thread are independent and the compiler or the hardware might have reordered them.

The C11 standard keeps track of relative ordering between the memory accesses performed during program execution via the *happens-before* relation (shortened hb), defined as the transitive closure of the program order and of the synchronisations between actions of different threads.[1] Non-atomic loads must return the last write in the hb relation: this is unique in race-free programs and guarantees a sequentially consistent semantics for race-free programs with only non-atomic accesses. For relaxed atomic accesses the intentions of the standard are more liberal and basically state that a relaxed load can see any other write which does not happen after it (according to hb), and which is not shadowed by another write, effectively allowing the outcome $r_1 = r_2 = 1$ above.

Unfortunately, the definition above enables some controversial behaviours. For instance, the program below can terminate with $x = y = 1$ as well:

$$\begin{array}{l||l} \mathsf{if}\ (x.\mathsf{load}(\mathrm{RLX})) & \mathsf{if}\ (y.\mathsf{load}(\mathrm{RLX})) \\ \quad y.\mathsf{store}(1, \mathrm{RLX}); & \quad x.\mathsf{store}(1, \mathrm{RLX}); \end{array} \qquad (\mathsf{CYC})$$

Again there are no synchronisations, and relaxed loads can see arbitrary stores. However, justifying this in terms of compiler or hardware optimisations is harder: the first thread might speculate that $x$ has value 1 tentatively executing the store to $y$, while the second thread speculates that the value of $y$ is 1 tentatively executing the store to $x$. The two threads then check if the speculation was correct, seeing each other's tentative stores that justify the speculation.

[1] For simplicity, we assume there are no consume atomic accesses.

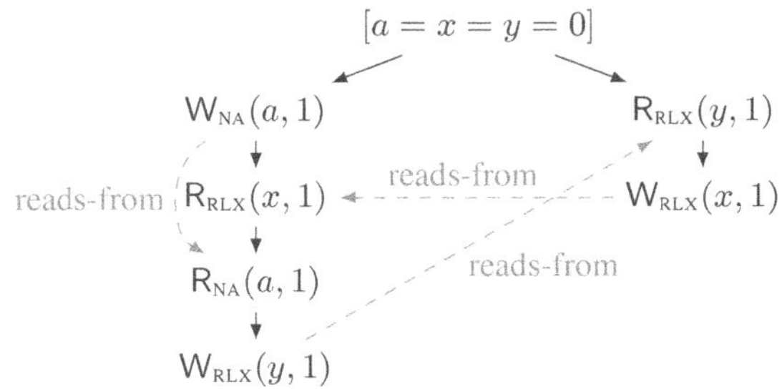


**Figure 1.** Execution resulting in $a = x = y = 1$.

Several authors have observed that causality cycles make code verification infeasible [2, 12, 16]. We show that the situation is even worse than that, because we can exploit them to show that standard program transformations are unsound. Consider:

$$a = 1; \;\Bigg\|\; \begin{array}{l} \mathsf{if}\ (x.\mathsf{load}(\mathrm{RLX})) \\ \quad \mathsf{if}\ (a) \\ \quad\quad y.\mathsf{store}(1, \mathrm{RLX}); \end{array} \;\Bigg\|\; \begin{array}{l} \mathsf{if}\ (y.\mathsf{load}(\mathrm{RLX})) \\ \quad x.\mathsf{store}(1, \mathrm{RLX}); \end{array} \qquad (\mathsf{SEQ})$$

First, notice that there is no execution (*consistent execution* in the terminology of Section 2) in which the load of $a$ occurs. We show this by contradiction. Suppose that there is an execution in which a load of $a$ occurs. In such an execution the load of $a$ can only return 0 (the initial value of $a$) because the store $a = 1$ does not happen before it (because it is in a different thread that has not been synchronised with) and non-atomic loads must return the latest write that happens before them. Therefore, in this execution the store to $y$ does not happen, which in turn means that the load of $y$ cannot return 1 and the store to $x$ also does not happen. Then, $x$ cannot read 1, and thus the load of $a$ does not occur. As a consequence this program is *not racy*: since the load of $a$ does not occur in any execution, there are no executions with conflicting accesses on the same non-atomic variable. We conclude that the only possible final state is $a = 1 \wedge x = y = 0$.

Now, imagine we apply sequentialisation, collapsing the first two threads and moving the assignment to the start:

$$\begin{array}{l||l} a = 1; & \\ \mathsf{if}\ (x.\mathsf{load}(\mathrm{RLX})) & \mathsf{if}\ (y.\mathsf{load}(\mathrm{RLX})) \\ \quad \mathsf{if}\ (a) & \quad x.\mathsf{store}(1, \mathrm{RLX}); \\ \quad\quad y.\mathsf{store}(1, \mathrm{RLX}); & \end{array}$$

Running the resulting code can lead to an execution, formally depicted in Figure 1, in which the load of $a$ actually returns the value 1 since the store to $a$ now happens before (via program-order) the load. This results in the final state $a = x = y = 1$, which is not possible for the initial program.

***Consequences.*** The example above is an instance of *source-to-source* program transformation: the semantics of both the source and target code are defined by the C11 memory model. It might be argued that the main purpose of compiler is not to perform a source-to-source translation but rather compile C11 programs to x86/ARM/Power assembler (to cite three widespread architectures), and a correctness statement for a compiler should relate the C11 semantics of the source program to the x86/ARM/Power semantics of the generated assembler. Indeed if we compile the transformed code above using the standard mapping for low-level atomics for x86 [4] or ARM/Power [13], then the problematic new behaviour does not arise in practice. To the best of our knowledge no modern relaxed architecture allows the causality cycle (or the other idiosyncrasies of the C11 model we exploit) built by the program labelled by (CYC) to terminate with $x = y = 1$. This implies that our counterexamples do not break C11-to-assembly compiler correctness statements, in contrast to what happens in Java [17].

However compilers rarely compile C code into assembly code in just one pass. Our counterexamples imply that the C11 memory model cannot be used to give semantics to the intermediate languages used internally by a compiler, as for instance the Clang/LLVM compiler aimed to. They also imply that reasoning about the correctness of program transformations cannot be done at the C11 level but must take into account the actual mapping of atomic accesses to a particular architecture, forbidding architecture independent reasoning and preventing compositional reasoning about compiler passes.

The design of a memory model that forbids causality cycles while enabling common compiler optimisation is currently a Holy Grail quest. Our counterexamples exploit a precise form of causality cycles (involving control dependencies) and not the most general form [6]; unfortunately it turns out that there is no simple local fix to the C11 model that makes all these transformations valid.

***Contributions and Outline.***

- We show that several source-to-source transformations intended to be correct, can introduce new behaviours in the C11 memory model. The transformations we consider include sequentialisation, strengthening, and roach motel reorderings; we present them and demonstrate that C11 forbids them in Section 3.
- We explore a number of possible local fixes to the C11 model, some strengthening and some weakening the model. These involve replacing one C11 consistency axiom by another; we formalise them in Section 4 and study their basic metatheory in Section 5. These include the acyclicity condition advocated by Boehm and Demsky [6] as well as weaker conditions.

  For each patched model, in Sections 6 and 7, we conduct an in-depth study of the soundness of a wide class of program transformations, involving reordering and eliminations of both non-atomic and atomic variables. For each we either provide a proof of its correctness formalised in the Coq proof assistant (with one exception), or a counterexample. For the condition in [6], under an additional condition on sequentially consistent accesses, all the intended transformations are valid. The weaker conditions either disallow some transformations or do not satisfy the DRF theorem. Additionally we show that the side conditions on the memory attributes of the operations involved in each sound optimisation are locally maximal, in that we have counterexamples for any weakening of them.
- We show that "Write-after-Read" elimination of atomic accesses is unsound in the C11 memory model, both in the current formulation and in the patched models (Section 7.1).
- Our investigation also highlighted some corner cases of the C11 model which break important metatheory properties. We discuss them, together with possible fixes, in Sections 4.3 and 5.4.

To make the paper self-contained we recall the presentation of the C11 memory model and the setup to reason about program transformations in Section 2. We finally discuss related work in Section 8. The Coq proof scripts and our appendix with the counterexamples are available at the following URL:

`http://plv.mpi-sws.org/c11comp/`

## 2. Abstract Optimisations in C11

In this paper, we are not looking at the actual algorithms used to implement compiler optimisations. Rather, we are concerned by the *effects* of compiler optimisations on *program executions*. We thus build on the representation of *abstract optimisations* introduced by Ševčík [18] and adapted to the C11 memory model in Morisset et al. [11], which we recall below. The subsection headings refer to the relevant files in our Coq development.

### 2.1 Representation of Programs [`actions.v`, `opsemsets.v`]

To abstract from the syntax complexity of the C language, we identify a source program with a set of descriptions of what *actions* it can perform when executed in an arbitrary context.

More precisely, in a source program each thread consists of a sequence of *instructions*. We assume that, for each thread, a thread-local semantics associates to each *instruction instance* zero, one, or more shared memory accesses, which we call *actions*. The actions we consider, ranged over by $act$, are of the form:

$$\begin{aligned}\Phi ::= &\ \mathsf{skip} \mid \mathsf{W}_{(\text{SC}|\text{REL}|\text{RLX}|\text{NA})}(\ell, v) \mid \mathsf{R}_{(\text{SC}|\text{ACQ}|\text{RLX}|\text{NA})}(\ell, v) \\ &\mid \mathsf{C}_{(\text{SC}|\text{REL-ACQ}|\text{ACQ}|\text{REL}|\text{RLX})}(\ell, v, v') \mid \mathsf{F}_{(\text{ACQ}|\text{REL})} \mid \mathsf{A}(\ell) \\ act ::= &\ tid : \Phi\end{aligned}$$

where $\ell$ ranges over memory locations, $v$ over values and $tid \in \{1..n\}$ over thread identifiers. We consider atomic and non-atomic loads from (denoted R) and stores to (W) memory, fences (F), read-modify-writes (C), and allocations (A) of memory locations. To simplify the statement of some theorems, we also include a no-op (skip) action. Each action specifies its thread identifier $tid$, the location $\ell$ it affects, the value read or written $v$ (when applicable), and the memory-order (written as a subscript, when applicable).[2] We assume a labelling function, $lab$, that associates action identifiers (ranged over by $a, b, r, w, \ldots$) to actions. In the drawings we usually omit thread and action identifiers.

We introduce some terminology regarding actions. A *read action* is a load or a read-modify-write (RMW); a *write* is a load or an RMW; a *memory access* is a load, store or RMW. Where applicable, we write $\mathsf{mode}(a)$ for the memory order of an action, $\mathsf{tid}(a)$ for its thread identifier, and $\mathsf{loc}(a)$ for the location accessed. We say an action is *non-atomic* iff its memory-order is NA, and *SC-atomic* iff it is SC. An *acquire* action has memory-order ACQ or stronger, while a *release* has REL or stronger. The *is stronger* relation, written $\sqsupseteq : \mathcal{P}(MO \times MO)$, is defined to be the least reflexive and transitive relation containing SC $\sqsupseteq$ REL-ACQ $\sqsupseteq$ REL $\sqsupseteq$ RLX, and REL-ACQ $\sqsupseteq$ ACQ $\sqsupseteq$ RLX.

The thread local semantics captures control flow dependencies via the *sequenced-before* ($sb$) relation, which relates action identifiers of the same thread that follow one another in control flow. We have $sb(a, b)$ if $a$ and $b$ belong to the same thread and $a$ precedes $b$ in the thread's control flow. Even among actions of the same thread, the sequenced-before relation is not necessarily total because the order of evaluation of the arguments of functions, or of the operands of most operators, is underspecified in C and C++. The thread local semantics also captures thread creation via the *additional-synchronised-with* ($asw$) relation, that orders all the action identifiers of a thread after the corresponding thread fork (which can be represented by a skip action).

Summarising, the thread local semantics identifies each program execution a triple $O = (lab, sb, asw)$, called an *opsem*. As an example, Figure 4 depicts one opsem for the program on the left and one for the program on the right. Both opsems correspond to the executions obtained from an initial state where $y$ holds 3, and

[2] We omit *consume* atomics and sequentially consistent fences. The semantics of the former is intricate and at the time of writing no major compiler profits from their weaker semantics, treating consume as acquire; the semantics of the latter is unclear. Despite their name, SC fences do not guarantee sequential consistency even when placed between every two instructions. This is because while they rule out the relaxed behaviour of the SB (store buffering) example, they permit those of the IRIW (independent reads of independent writes) example.

$$\mathsf{isread}_{\ell,v}(a) \stackrel{\mathsf{def}}{=} \exists X, v'.\ lab(a) \in \{\mathsf{R}_X(\ell,v), \mathsf{C}_X(\ell,v,v')\}$$
$$\mathsf{iswrite}_{\ell,v}(a) \stackrel{\mathsf{def}}{=} \exists X, v'.\ lab(a) \in \{\mathsf{W}_X(\ell,v), \mathsf{C}_X(\ell,v',v)\}$$
$$\mathsf{isfence}(a) \stackrel{\mathsf{def}}{=} lab(a) \in \{\mathsf{F}_{\mathsf{ACQ}}, \mathsf{F}_{\mathsf{REL}}\}$$
$$\mathsf{sameThread}(a,b) \stackrel{\mathsf{def}}{=} \mathsf{tid}(a) = \mathsf{tid}(b)$$
$$\mathsf{rsElem}(a,b) \stackrel{\mathsf{def}}{=} \mathsf{sameThread}(a,b) \vee \mathsf{isrmw}(b)$$

$$\mathsf{isread}_{\ell}(a) \stackrel{\mathsf{def}}{=} \exists v.\ \mathsf{isread}_{\ell,v}(a)$$
$$\mathsf{iswrite}_{\ell}(a) \stackrel{\mathsf{def}}{=} \exists v.\ \mathsf{iswrite}_{\ell,v}(a)$$
$$\mathsf{isaccess}(a) \stackrel{\mathsf{def}}{=} \mathsf{isread}(a) \vee \mathsf{iswrite}(a)$$
$$\mathsf{isrmw}(a) \stackrel{\mathsf{def}}{=} \mathsf{isread}(a) \wedge \mathsf{iswrite}(a)$$
$$\mathsf{isAcq}(a) \stackrel{\mathsf{def}}{=} \mathsf{mode}(a) \sqsupseteq \mathrm{ACQ}$$

$$\mathsf{isread}(a) \stackrel{\mathsf{def}}{=} \exists \ell.\ \mathsf{isread}_{\ell}(a)$$
$$\mathsf{iswrite}(a) \stackrel{\mathsf{def}}{=} \exists \ell.\ \mathsf{iswrite}_{\ell}(a)$$
$$\mathsf{isNA}(a) \stackrel{\mathsf{def}}{=} \mathsf{mode}(a) = \mathrm{NA}$$
$$\mathsf{isSC}(a) \stackrel{\mathsf{def}}{=} \mathsf{mode}(a) = \mathrm{SC}$$
$$\mathsf{isRel}(a) \stackrel{\mathsf{def}}{=} \mathsf{mode}(a) \sqsupseteq \mathrm{REL}$$

$$\mathsf{rseq}(a,b) \stackrel{\mathsf{def}}{=} a = b \vee \mathsf{rsElem}(a,b) \wedge mo(a,b) \wedge (\forall c.\ mo(a,c) \wedge mo(c,b) \Rightarrow \mathsf{rsElem}(a,c))$$
$$\mathsf{sw}(a,b) \stackrel{\mathsf{def}}{=} \exists c, d.\ \begin{array}{l}\neg\mathsf{sameThread}(a,b) \wedge \mathsf{isRel}(a) \wedge \mathsf{isAcq}(b) \wedge \mathsf{rseq}(c, rf(d)) \\ \wedge\, (a = c \vee \mathsf{isfence}(a) \wedge sb^+(a,c)) \wedge (d = b \vee \mathsf{isfence}(d) \wedge sb^+(d,b))\end{array}$$
$$\mathsf{hb} \stackrel{\mathsf{def}}{=} (sb \cup \mathsf{sw} \cup asw)^+$$
$$\mathsf{Racy} \stackrel{\mathsf{def}}{=} \exists a, b.\ \begin{array}{l}\mathsf{isaccess}(a) \wedge \mathsf{isaccess}(b) \wedge \mathsf{loc}(a) = \mathsf{loc}(b) \wedge a \neq b \\ \wedge(\mathsf{iswrite}(a) \vee \mathsf{iswrite}(b)) \wedge (\mathsf{isNA}(a) \vee \mathsf{isNA}(b)) \wedge \neg(\mathsf{hb}(a,b) \vee \mathsf{hb}(b,a))\end{array}$$
$$\mathsf{Observation} \stackrel{\mathsf{def}}{=} \{(a,b) \mid mo(a,b) \wedge \mathsf{loc}(a) = \mathsf{loc}(b) = \mathtt{world}\}$$

**Figure 2.** Auxiliary definitions for a C11 execution $(lab, sb, asw, rf, mo, sc)$.

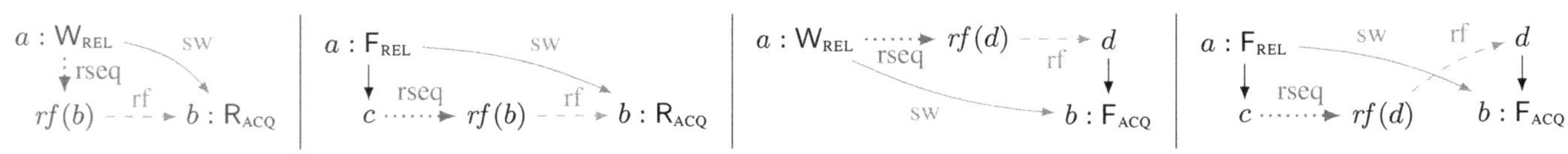

**Figure 3.** Illustration of the "synchronizes-with" definition: the four cases inducing an sw edge.

the environment does not perform any write to the shared variables (each read returns the last value written).

The set of all the opsems of a program is an *opsemset*, denoted by $S$. We require opsemsets to be *receptive*: $S$ is receptive if, for every opsem $O$, for every read action $r$ in the opsem $O$, for all values $v'$ there is an opsem $O'$ in $S$ which only differs from $O$ because the read $r$ returns $v'$ rather than $v$, and for the actions that occur after $r$ in $sb \cup asw$. Intuitively an opsemset is receptive if it defines a behaviour for each possible value returned by each read.

We additionally require opsemsets to be prefix-closed, assuming that a program can halt at any time. Formally, we say that an opsem $O'$ is a prefix of an opsem $O$ if there is an injection of the actions of $O'$ into the actions of $O$ that behaves as the identity on actions, preserves $sb$ and $asw$, and, for each action $x \in O'$, whenever $x \in O$ and $(sb \cup asw)(y, x)$, it holds that $y \in O'$.

***Program Transformations.*** Opsemsets abstract the syntax of programs by identifying each program with the set of actions it can perform in an arbitrary environment. We can then characterise the effect of an arbitrary source code transformation directly on opsemsets. On a given opsem, the effect of any transformation of the source code is to *eliminate*, *reorder*, or *introduce* actions and modifying the $sb$ and $asw$ relations accordingly.

In the example in Figure 4, taken from Morisset et al. [11], the loop on the left is optimised into the code on the right by loop invariant code motion. As we said, the figure shows opsems for the initial state $z = 0$, $y = 3$ assuming that the code is not run in parallel with an interfering context. Observe that the effect of the optimisation on the first opsem is to eliminate the shaded actions, and to reorder the stores to x, thus mapping the opsem of the unoptimised code into an opsem of the optimised code.

An opsem captures a possible execution of the program, so by applying a transformation to an opsem we are actually optimising one particular execution. Lifting pointwise this definition of *semantic transformations* to opsemsets enables optimising all the execution paths of a program, one at a time, thus abstracting from actual source program transformation.

Soundness of program transformations can then be formalised by identifying the set of conditions under which eliminating, reordering or introducing actions in the opsems of an opsemset does

```
for (i=0; i<2; i++) {          t = y; x = t;
  z = z + y + i;          ⇝    for (i=0; i<2; i++) {
  x = y;                         z = z + t + i;
}                              }
```

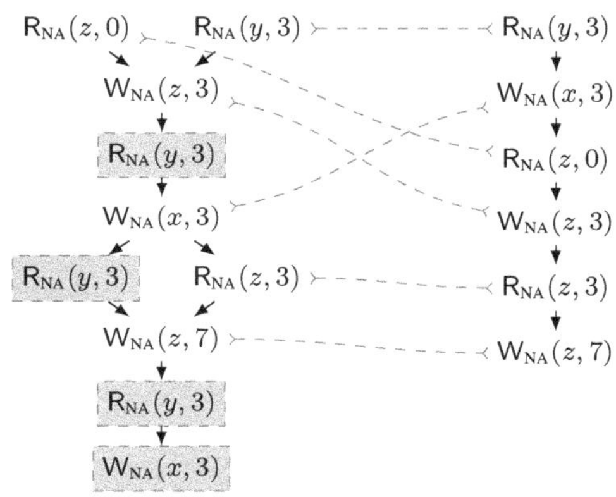

**Figure 4.** Effect of loop invariant code motion on an opsem.

not introduce new observable behaviours. We must thus define what it means to *execute* an opsemset.

### 2.2 Executing Programs [c11.v, lang.v]

The mapping of programs to opsemsets only takes into account the structure of each thread's statements, not the semantics of memory operations. In particular, the values of reads are chosen arbitrarily, without regard for writes that have taken place. (In our Coq development, we present such a mapping from programs to opsemsets for a concurrent WHILE language.)

The C11 memory model then filters inconsistent opsems by constructing additional relations and checking the resulting candidate executions against the axioms of the model. For the subset of C11 we consider, a witness $W$ for an opsem $O$ contains the following additional relations:[3]

[3] The full model includes two additional relations, dd (data dependency) and dob (dependency ordered before), used to define hb for consume reads.

$$\forall a, b.\ sb(a,b) \implies \mathsf{tid}(a) = \mathsf{tid}(b) \qquad \text{(ConsSB)}$$

$$\mathsf{order}(\mathsf{iswrite}, mo) \land \forall \ell.\ \mathsf{total}(\mathsf{iswrite}_\ell, mo) \qquad \text{(ConsMO)}$$

$$\mathsf{order}(\mathsf{isSC}, sc) \land \mathsf{total}(\mathsf{isSC}, sc) \land (\mathsf{hb} \cup mo) \cap (\mathsf{isSC} \times \mathsf{isSC}) \subseteq sc \qquad \text{(ConsSC)}$$

$$\forall b.\ (\exists c.\ rf(b) = c) \iff \exists \ell, a.\ \mathsf{iswrite}_\ell(a) \land \mathsf{isread}_\ell(b) \land \mathsf{hb}(a,b) \qquad \text{(ConsRFdom)}$$

$$\forall a, b.\ rf(b) = a \implies \exists \ell, v.\ \mathsf{iswrite}_{\ell,v}(a) \land \mathsf{isread}_{\ell,v}(b) \qquad \text{(ConsRF)}$$

$$\forall a, b.\ rf(b) = a \land (\mathsf{isNA}(a) \lor \mathsf{isNA}(b)) \implies \mathsf{hb}(a,b) \qquad \text{(ConsRFna)}$$

$$\forall a, b.\ rf(b) = a \land \mathsf{isSC}(b) \implies \mathsf{imm}(\mathsf{scr}, a, b) \lor \neg\mathsf{isSC}(a) \land \nexists x.\ \mathsf{hb}(a,x) \land \mathsf{imm}(\mathsf{scr}, x, b) \qquad \text{(SCReads)}$$

$$\nexists a.\ \mathsf{hb}(a,a) \qquad \text{(IrrHB)}$$

$$\nexists a, b.\ rf(b) = a \land \mathsf{hb}(b,a) \qquad \text{(ConsRFhb)}$$

$$\nexists a, b.\ \mathsf{hb}(a,b) \land mo(b,a) \qquad \text{(CohWW)}$$

$$\nexists a, b.\ \mathsf{hb}(a,b) \land mo(rf(b), rf(a)) \qquad \text{(CohRR)}$$

$$\nexists a, b.\ \mathsf{hb}(a,b) \land mo(rf(b), a) \qquad \text{(CohWR)}$$

$$\nexists a, b.\ \mathsf{hb}(a,b) \land mo(b, rf(a)) \qquad \text{(CohRW)}$$

$$\forall a, b.\ \mathsf{isrmw}(a) \land rf(a) = b \implies \mathsf{imm}(mo, b, a) \qquad \text{(AtRMW)}$$

$$\forall a, b, \ell.\ lab(a) = lab(b) = \mathsf{A}(\ell) \implies a = b \qquad \text{(ConsAlloc)}$$

where $\mathsf{order}(P, R) \stackrel{\text{def}}{=} (\nexists a.\ R(a,a)) \land (R^+ \subseteq R) \land (R \subseteq P \times P)$

$\mathsf{total}(P, R) \stackrel{\text{def}}{=} (\forall a, b.\ P(a) \land P(b) \implies a = b \lor R(a,b) \lor R(b,a))$

$\mathsf{imm}(R, a, b) \stackrel{\text{def}}{=} R(a,b) \land \nexists c.\ R(a,c) \land R(c,b)$

$\mathsf{scr}(a, b) \stackrel{\text{def}}{=} sc(a,b) \land \mathsf{iswrite}_{\mathsf{loc}(b)}(a)$

**Figure 5.** Axioms satisfied by consistent C11 executions, $\mathsf{Consistent}(lab, sb, asw, rf, mo, sc)$.

- The *reads-from* map ($rf$) maps every read action $r$ to the write action $w$ that wrote the value read by $r$.
- The *modification-order* ($mo$) relates writes to the same location; for every location, it is a total order among the writes to that location.
- The *sequential-consistency* order ($sc$) is a total order over all SC-atomic actions. (The standard calls this relation $S$.)

From these relations, C11 defines a number of derived relations (written in sans-serif font), the most important of which are: the *synchronizes-with* relation and the *happens-before* order.

- *Synchronizes-with* (sw) relates each release write with the acquire reads that read from some write in its release sequence (rseq). This sequence includes the release write and certain subsequent writes in modification order that belong to the same thread or are RMW operations. The sw relation also relates fences under similar conditions. Roughly speaking, a release fence turns succeeding writes in $sb$ into releases and an acquire fence turns preceding reads into acquires. (For details, see the definition in Figure 2 and the illustration in Figure 3.)
- *Happens-before* (hb) is a partial order on actions formalising the intuition that one action was completed before the other. In the C11 subset we consider, $\mathsf{hb} = (sb \cup \mathsf{sw} \cup asw)^+$.

We refer to a pair of an opsem and a witness $(O, W)$ as a *candidate execution*. A candidate execution is said to be *consistent* if it satisfies the axioms of the memory model, which will be presented shortly. The model finally checks if none of the consistent executions contains an *undefined behaviour*, arising from a *race* (two conflicting accesses not related by hb)[4] or a *memory error* (accessing an unallocated location), where two accesses are conflicting if they are to the same address, at least one is a write, and at least one is non-atomic. Programs that exhibit an undefined behaviour in one of their consistent executions are undefined; programs that do not exhibit any undefined behaviour are called *well-defined*, and their semantics is given by the set of their consistent executions.

***Consistent Executions.*** According to the C11 model, a candidate execution $(lab, sb, asw, rf, mo, sc)$ is consistent if all of the properties shown in Figure 5 hold.

(ConsSB) Sequenced-before relates only same-thread actions.

(ConsMO) Writes on the same location are totally ordered by $mo$.

(ConsSC) The $sc$ relation must be a total order over SC actions and include both hb and $mo$ restricted to SC actions. This in effect means that SC actions are globally synchronised.

(ConsRFdom) The reads-from map, $rf$, is defined for those read actions for which the execution contains an earlier write to the same location.

(ConsRF) Each entry in the reads-from map, $rf$, should map a read to a write to the same location and with the same value.

(ConsRFna) If a read reads from a write and either the read or the write are non-atomic, then the write must have happened before the read. Batty et al. [4] additionally require the write to be *visible*: i.e. not to have been overwritten by another write that happened before the read. This extra condition is unnecessary, as it follows from (CohWR).

(SCReads) SC reads are restricted to read only from the immediately preceding SC write to the same location in $sc$ order or from a non-SC write that has not happened before that immediately preceding SC write.

(IrrHB) The happens-before order, hb, must be irreflexive: an action cannot happen before itself.

(ConsRFhb) A read cannot read from a future write.

(CohWW, CohRR, CohWR, CohRW) Next, we have four coherence properties relating $mo$, hb, and $rf$ on accesses to the same location. These properties require that $mo$ never contradicts hb or the observed read order, and that $rf$ never reads values that have been overwritten by more recent actions that happened before the read.

(AtRMW) Read-modify-write accesses execute atomically: they read from the immediately preceding write in $mo$.

(ConsAlloc) The same location cannot be allocated twice by different allocation actions. (This axiom is sound because for simplicity we do not model deallocation. The C11 model by Batty et al. [4, 3] does not even model allocation.)

***Observable Behaviour.*** The *observable behaviour* of a candidate execution is the restriction of the $mo$ relation to the distinguished `world` location. If none of the candidate executions of a program exhibit an undefined behaviour, then its observable behaviour is the set of all observable behaviours of its candidate executions. In our counterexamples, we often distinguish executions based on the final values of memory—this is valid because there could be a context program reading those values and writing them to `world`.

[4] The standard distinguishes between races arising from accesses of different threads, which it calls *data races*, and from those of the same thread, which it calls *unsequenced races*. The standard says unsequenced races can occur even between atomic accesses.

| | | | |
|---|---|---|---|
| $x$.store(1, RLX);<br>$x$.store(2, SC);<br>$y$.store(1, SC); | $x$.store(3, RLX);<br>$y$.store(2, SC); | $y$.store(3, SC);<br>$r = x$.load(SC); | $s_1 = x$.load(RLX);<br>$s_2 = x$.load(RLX);<br>$s_3 = x$.load(RLX);<br>$t_1 = y$.load(RLX);<br>$t_2 = y$.load(RLX);<br>$t_3 = y$.load(RLX); |

**Behaviour in question:** $r = s_1 = t_1 = 1 \wedge s_2 = t_2 = 2 \wedge s_3 = t_3 = 3$

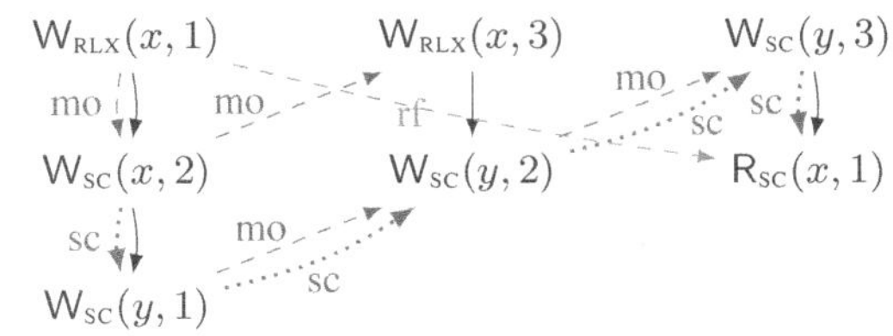


**Figure 6.** A weird consequence of the SCReads axiom: strengthening the $x$.store(3, RLX) into $x$.store(3, SC) introduces new behaviour.

## 3. Invalid Source-to-Source Transformations

In the introduction we discussed how *sequentialisation*, a simple transformation rewriting $C_1 \| C_2 \rightsquigarrow C_1; C_2$ can introduce new behaviours in C11 programs. Here we present other surprising problems that arise from innocent-looking program transformations.

***Strengthening is Unsound.*** A desirable property of a memory model is that adding synchronisation to a program introduces no new behaviour (other than deadlock). The following example shows however that replacing a relaxed atomic store with a release atomic store is unsound in C11. Consider:

| | | |
|---|---|---|
| $a = 1$;<br>$z$.store(1, RLX); | if ($x$.load(RLX))<br>  if ($z$.load(ACQ))<br>    if ($a$)<br>      $y$.store(1, RLX); | if ($y$.load(RLX))<br>  $x$.store(1, RLX); |

As in the SEQ program from Section 1, the load of $a$ cannot return 1 because the store to $a$ does not happen before it (and this time we can name the axiom responsible for this: ConsRFna). Therefore, the only final state is $a = z = 1 \wedge x = y = 0$. If, however, we make the store of $z$ a release store, then it synchronises with the acquire load, and it is easy to build a consistent execution with final state $a = z = x = y = 1$. A symmetric counterexample can be constructed for strengthening a relaxed load to an acquire load.

What is more interesting is that *even in the absence of causality cycles*, strengthening an atomic access into a sequentially consistent one is unsound in general. Consider, for example, the program in Figure 6, where coherence of the relaxed loads in the final thread forces the *mo*-orderings to be as shown in the execution on the right of the figure. Now, the question is whether the SC-load can read from the first store to $x$ and return $r = 1$. In the program as shown, it cannot, because that store happens before the $x$.store(2, SC) store, which is the immediate *sc*-preceding store to $x$ before the load. If, however, we also make the $x$.store(3, RLX) be sequentially consistent, then it becomes the immediately *sc*-preceding store to $x$, and hence reading $r = 1$ is no longer blocked.

***Roach Motel Reorderings are Unsound.*** Roach motel reorderings are a class of optimisations that let compilers move accesses to memory into synchronised blocks, but not move them out: the intuition is that it is always safe to move more computations (including memory accesses) inside critical sections. In the context of C11, roach motel reorderings would allow moving non-atomic accesses after an acquire read (which behaves as a lock operation) or before a release write (which behaves as an unlock operation).

However the following example program shows that in C11 it is unsound to move a non-atomic store before a release store.

| | | |
|---|---|---|
| $z$.store(1, REL);<br>$a = 1$; | if ($x$.load(RLX))<br>  if ($z$.load(ACQ))<br>    if ($a$)<br>      $y$.store(1, RLX); | if ($y$.load(RLX))<br>  $x$.store(1, RLX); |

As before, the only possible final state of this program is $a = z = 1$ and $x = y = 0$. If, however, we reorder the two stores in the first thread, we get a consistent execution leading to the final state

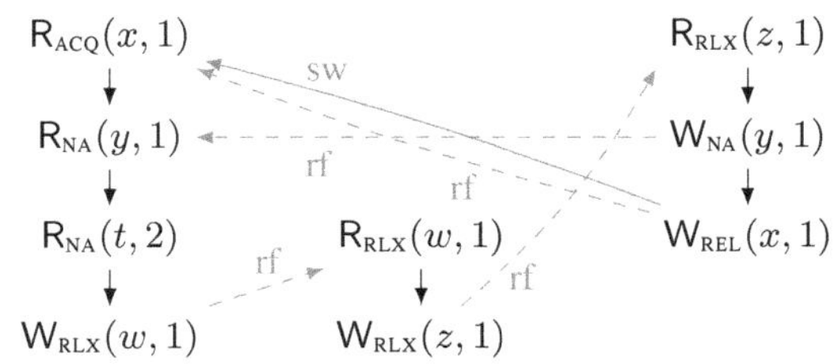


**Figure 7.** Execution generating new behaviour if the expression evaluation order is linearised.

$a = z = x = y = 1$. Again, we can construct a similar example showing that reordering over an acquire load is also not allowed by C11.

***Expression Linearisation is Unsound.*** A simple variation of sequentialisation is expression evaluation order *linearisation*, a transformation that adds an *sb* arrow between two actions of the same thread and that every compiler is bound to perform. This transformation is unsound as demonstrated below:

| | | |
|---|---|---|
| $t = x$.load(ACQ)$+y$;<br>if ($t == 2$)<br>  $w$.store(1, RLX); | if ($w$.load(RLX))<br>  $z$.store(1, RLX); | if ($z$.load(RLX))<br>  $y = 1$;<br>  $x$.store(1, REL); |

The only possible final state for this program has all variables, including $t$, set to zero. Indeed, the store $y = 1$; does not happen before the load of $y$, which can then return only 0. However, if the $t = x$.load(ACQ) $+ y$; is linearised into $t = x$.load(ACQ); $t = t + y$;, then a synchronisation on $x$ induces an order on the accesses to $y$, and the execution shown in Figure 7 is allowed.

## 4. Further C11 Weaknesses and Proposed Fixes

In this section, we consider possible solutions to the problems identified in the previous section, as well as to two other weaknesses with the C11 model, which however do not manifest themselves as invalid program transformations. (All of the models in this section as well as the relationships among them are formalised in `c11.v`.)

### 4.1 Resolving Causality Cycles and the ConsRFna Axiom

We first discuss possible solutions for the most important problem with C11, namely the interaction between causality cycles and the ConsRFna axiom.

***Naive Fix.*** A first, rather naive solution is to permit causality cycles, but drop the offending ConsRFna axiom. As we will show in Sections 6 and 7, this solution allows all the optimisations that were intended to be sound on C11. It is, however, of dubious usefulness as it gives extremely weak guarantees to programmers.

The DRF theorem—stating that programs whose sequential consistent executions have no data races, have no additional relaxed behaviours besides the SC ones—does not hold. As a counterexample, take the CYC program from the introduction, replacing the relaxed accesses by non-atomic ones.

***Arf: Forbidding* ($\mathsf{hb} \cup rf$) *Cycles.*** A second, much more reasonable solution is to try to rule out causality cycles. Ruling out causality cycles, while allowing non-causal loops in $\mathsf{hb} \cup rf$ is, however, difficult and cannot be done by stating additional axioms over single executions. This is essentially because the offending execution of the CYC program from the introduction is also an execution of the LB program, also from the introduction.

As an approximation, we can rule out all ($\mathsf{hb} \cup rf$) cycles, by stating the following axiom:

$$\mathsf{acyclic}(\mathsf{hb} \cup \{(a, b) \mid rf(b) = a\}) \qquad (\mathsf{Arf})$$

This solution has been proposed before by Boehm and Demsky [6] and also by Vafeiadis and Narayan [16]. Here, however, we take a subtly different approach from the aforementioned proposals in that besides adding the Arf axiom, we also drop the problematic ConsRFna axiom.

In Sections 6 and 7 we show that this model allows the same optimisations as the naive one (i.e., all the intended ones), except the reordering of atomic reads over atomic writes.

It is however known to make relaxed accesses more costly on ARM/Power, as there must be either a bogus branch or a lightweight fence between every shared load and shared store [6].

***Arfna: Forbidding Only Non-Atomic Cycles.*** Another approach is to instead make more behaviours consistent, so that the non-atomic accesses in the SEQ example from the introduction can actually occur and race. The simplest way to do this is to replace ConsRFna by

$$\mathsf{acyclic}(\mathsf{hb} \cup \{(rf(b), b) \mid \mathsf{isNA}(b) \vee \mathsf{isNA}(rf(b))\}) \qquad (\mathsf{Arfna})$$

A non-atomic load can read from a concurrent write, as long as it does not cause a causality cycle.

This new model has several nice properties. First, it is weaker than C11 in that it allows all behaviours permitted by C11. This entails that any compilation strategy proved correct from C11 to hardware memory models, such as to x86-TSO and Power, remains correct in the modified model (contrary to the previous fix).

**Theorem 1.** *If* $\mathsf{Consistent}_{\mathsf{C11}}(X)$, *then* $\mathsf{Consistent}_{\mathsf{Arfna}}(X)$.

*Proof.* Straightforward, since by the ConsRFna condition,

$$\{(rf(b), b) \mid \mathsf{isNA}(b) \vee \mathsf{isNA}(rf(b))\} \subseteq \mathsf{hb}$$

and hence Arfna follows from IrrHB. □

Second, this model is not much weaker than C11. More precisely, it only allows more racy behaviours.

**Theorem 2.** *If* $\mathsf{Consistent}_{\mathsf{Arfna}}(X)$ *and not* $\mathsf{Racy}(X)$, *then* $\mathsf{Consistent}_{\mathsf{C11}}(X)$.

Note that the definition of racy executions, $\mathsf{Racy}(X)$, does not depend on the axioms of the model, and is thus the same for all memory models considered here.

Finally, it is possible to reason about this model as most reasoning techniques on C11 remain true. In particular, in the absence of relaxed accesses, this model is equivalent to the Arf model. We are thus able to use the program logics that have been developed for C11 (namely, RSL [16] and GPS [15]) to also reason about programs in the Arfna model.

However, we found that reordering non-atomic loads past non-atomic stores is forbidden in this model, as shown by the following example:

| | |
|---|---|
| if ($x$.load(RLX)) {<br>  $t = a$;<br>  $b = 1$;<br>  if ($t$) $y$.store(1, RLX);<br>} | if ($y$.load(RLX))<br>  if ($b$) {<br>    $a = 1$;<br>    $x$.store(1, RLX);<br>  } |

In this program, the causality cycle does not occur, because for it to happen, an ($\mathsf{hb} \cup rf$)-cycle must also occur between the $a$ and $b$ accesses (and that is ruled out by our axiom). However, if we swap the non-atomic load of $a$ and store of $b$ in the first thread, then the causality cycle becomes possible, and the program is racy. Introducing a race is clearly unsound, so compilers are not allowed to do such reorderings (note that these accesses are non-atomic and adjacent). It is not clear whether such a constraint would be acceptable in C/C++ compilers.

### 4.2 Correcting the SCReads Axiom

As we have seen in the counterexample of Figure 6, the SCReads axiom places an odd restriction on where a sequentially consistent read can read from. The problem arises from the case where the source of the read is a non-SC write. In this case, the axiom forbids that write to happen before the immediately $sc$-preceding write to the same location. It may, however, happen before an earlier write in the $sc$ order.

We propose to strengthen the SCReads axiom by requiring there not to be a happens before edge between $rf(b)$ and any same-location write $sc$-prior to the read, as follows:

$$\begin{array}{l}\forall a, b.\ rf(b) = a \wedge \mathsf{isSC}(b) \implies \\ \mathsf{imm}(\mathsf{scr}, a, b) \vee \neg\mathsf{isSC}(a) \wedge \nexists x.\ \mathsf{hb}(a, x) \wedge \mathsf{scr}(x, b)\end{array} \qquad (\mathsf{SCread}')$$

Going back to the program in Figure 6, this stronger axiom rules out reading $r = 1$, a guarantee that is provided by the suggested compilations of C11 atomic accesses to x86/Power/ARM.

We also considered an even stronger version where instead of hb, the axiom mentions $mo$, as in the coherence axioms, but this axiom is unsound for the suggested compilation of C11 atomic accesses to the Power and ARM architectures.

### 4.3 Strengthening the Release Sequence Definition

The definition of release sequences in the C11 model is too weak, as shown be the following example.

| | | |
|---|---|---|
| $x$.store(2, RLX); | $y = 1$;<br>$x$.store(1, REL);<br>$x$.store(3, RLX); | if ($x$.load(ACQ) == 3)<br>  print($y$); |

In this program, assuming the test condition holds, the acquire load of $x$ need not synchronise with the release store even though it reads from a store that is sequenced after the release, and hence the program is racy. The reason is that the seemingly irrelevant store of $x$.store(2, RLX) can interrupt the release sequence as shown in the following execution snippet.

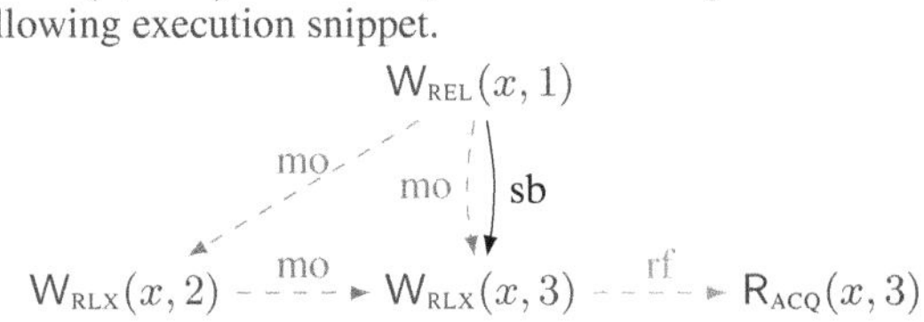


In the absence, however, of the first thread, the acquire and the release do synchronise and the program is well-defined.

As a fix for the release sequences definition, we propose to replace the definition of release sequences by the least fixed point of the following recursive definition (with respect to $\subseteq$) :

$$\begin{array}{rl}\mathsf{rseq}_{\mathsf{RSnew}}(a, b) \stackrel{\text{def}}{=} & a = b \vee \mathsf{sameThread}(a, b) \wedge mo(a, b) \\ & \vee\ \mathsf{isrmw}(b) \wedge \mathsf{rseq}_{\mathsf{RSnew}}(a, rf(b))\end{array}$$

Our release sequences are not defined in terms of $mo$ sequences, but rather in terms of $rf$ sequences. Either $b$ should belong to the same thread as $a$, or there should be a chain of RMW actions reading from one another connecting $b$ to a write in the same thread as $a$.

In the absence of uninitialised RMW accesses, this change strengthens the semantics. Every consistent execution in the revised model is also consistent in the original model. Despite being a strengthening, it does not affect the compilation results to x86, Power, and ARM. The reason is that release sequences do not play any role on x86, while on Power and ARM the compilation of release writes and fences issues a memory barrier that affects all later writes of the same thread, not just an uninterrupted $mo$-sequence of such writes.

### 4.4 Allowing Intra-Thread Synchronisation

A final change is to remove the slightly odd restriction that actions from the same thread cannot synchronise.[5] This change allows us to give meaning to more programs. In the original model, the following program has undefined behaviour:

$$\#\mathsf{define}\ f(x,y)\ (x.\mathsf{CAS}(1,0,\textsc{acq})?(y{+}{+}, x.\mathsf{store}(1,\textsc{rel})) : 0)$$
$$f(x,y) + f(x,y)$$

That is, although $f$ uses $x$ as a lock to protect the increments of $y$, and therefore the $y$ accesses could never be adjacent in an interleaving semantics, the model does not treat the $x$-accesses as synchronising because they belong to the same thread. Thus, the two increments of $y$ are deemed to race with one another.

As we believe that this behaviour is highly suspicious, we have also considered an adaptation of the C11 model, where we set

$$\mathsf{sameThread}_{\mathsf{STnew}}(a,b) \stackrel{\text{def}}{=} sb^{+}(a,b)$$

rather than $\mathsf{tid}(a) = \mathsf{tid}(b)$. We have proved that with the new definition, we can drop the $\neg\mathsf{sameThread}(a,b)$ conjunct from the sw definition without affecting hb.

Since, by the ConsSB axiom, every $sb$ edge has the same thread identifiers, the change also strengthens the model by assigning defined behaviour to more programs.

### 4.5 Summary of the Models to be Considered

As the four problems are independent and we have proposed fixes to each problem, we consider the product of the fixes:

$$\begin{pmatrix}\mathsf{ConsRFna}\\ \mathsf{Naive}\\ \mathsf{Arfna}\\ \mathsf{Arf}\end{pmatrix} \times \overbrace{\begin{pmatrix}\mathsf{SCorig}\\ \mathsf{SCnew}\end{pmatrix}}^{\S4.2} \times \overbrace{\begin{pmatrix}\mathsf{RSorig}\\ \mathsf{RSnew}\end{pmatrix}}^{\S4.3} \times \overbrace{\begin{pmatrix}\mathsf{STorig}\\ \mathsf{STnew}\end{pmatrix}}^{\S4.4}$$

We use tuple notation to refer to the individual models. For example, we write (ConsRFna, SCorig, RSorig, STorig) for the model corresponding to the 2011 C and C++ standards.

In Sections 5, 6 and 7, we show that the RSnew and STnew components, despite further constraining the set of consistent executions, permit all the transformations allowed by the RSorig and STorig components respectively.

## 5. Basic Metatheory of the Corrected C11 Models

In this section, we develop basic metatheory of the various corrections to the C11 model, which will assist us in verifying the program transformations in the next sections. The subsection headings mention the Coq source file containing the corresponding proofs.

### 5.1 Semiconsistent Executions [cmon.v]

We observe that in the monotone models (see Definition 3) the happens-before relation appears negatively in all axioms except for the $\Longleftarrow$ direction of the ConsRFdom axiom. It turns out, however, that this apparent lack of monotonicity with respect to happens-before does not cause problems as it can be circumvented by the following lemma.

[5] This restriction breaks monotonicity in the presence of consume reads.

**Definition 1** (Semiconsistent Executions). *An execution is* semiconsistent *with respect to a model $M$ iff it satisfies all the axioms of the model except for the $\Longleftarrow$ direction of the* ConsRFdom *axiom.*

**Lemma 1** (Semiconsistency). *Given a semiconsistent execution $(O, rf, mo, sc)$ with respect to $M$ for $M \neq (\mathsf{ConsRFna}, \_, \_, \_)$, there exists $rf' \subseteq rf$ such that $(O, rf', mo, sc)$ is consistent with respect to $M$.*

*Proof.* We pick $rf'$ as the greatest fixed point of the functional:

$$F(rf)(x) := \begin{cases} rf(x) & \text{if } \exists y.\ \mathsf{hb}(y,x) \wedge \mathsf{iswrite}_{\mathsf{loc}(x)}(y) \\ \text{undefined} & \text{otherwise}\end{cases}$$

that is smaller than $rf$ (with respect to $\subseteq$). Such a fixed point exists by Tarski's theorem as the function is monotone. By construction, it satisfies the ConsRFdom axiom, while all the other axioms follow easily because they are antimonotone in $rf$. □

### 5.2 Monotonicity [cmon.v]

We move on to proving the most fundamental property of the corrected models: *monotonicity*, saying that if we weaken the access modes of some of the actions of a consistent execution and/or remove some $sb$ edges, the execution remains consistent.

**Definition 2** (Access type ordering). *Let $\sqsubseteq : \mathcal{P}(MO \times MO)$ be the least reflexive and transitive relation containing* RLX $\sqsubseteq$ REL $\sqsubseteq$ REL-ACQ $\sqsubseteq$ SC, *and* RLX $\sqsubseteq$ ACQ $\sqsubseteq$ REL-ACQ.

*We lift the access order to memory actions, $\sqsubseteq : \mathcal{P}(EV \times EV)$, by letting $act \sqsubseteq act$, $\mathsf{R}_X(\ell,v) \sqsubseteq \mathsf{R}_{X'}(\ell,v)$, $\mathsf{W}_X(\ell,v) \sqsubseteq \mathsf{W}_{X'}(\ell,v)$, $\mathsf{C}_X(\ell,v,v') \sqsubseteq \mathsf{C}_{X'}(\ell,v,v')$, $\mathsf{F}_X \sqsubseteq \mathsf{F}_{X'}$, and $\mathsf{skip} \sqsubseteq \mathsf{F}_{X'}$, whenever $X \sqsubseteq X'$. We also lift this order to functions pointwise: $lab \sqsubseteq lab'$ iff $\forall a.\ lab(a) \sqsubseteq lab'(a)$.*

Monotonicity does not hold for all the models we consider, but only after some necessary fixes have been applied. We call those corrected models monotone.

**Definition 3.** *We call a memory model, $M$,* monotone, *iff $M \neq (\mathsf{ConsRFna}, \_, \_, \_)$ and $M \neq (\_, \mathsf{SCorig}, \_, \_)$.*

**Theorem 3** (Monotonicity). *For a monotone memory model $M$, if $\mathsf{Consistent}_M(lab, sb, asw, rf, mo, sc)$ and $lab' \sqsubseteq lab$ and $sb' \subseteq sb$, then there exist $rf' \subseteq rf$ and $sc' \subseteq sc$ such that $\mathsf{Consistent}_M(lab', sb', asw, rf', mo, sc')$.*

*Proof sketch.* From Lemma 1, it suffices to prove that the execution $(lab', sb', asw, rf, mo, sc')$ is semiconsistent. We can show this by picking:

$$sc'(x,y) \stackrel{\text{def}}{=} sc(x,y) \wedge \mathsf{isSC}(lab'(x)) \wedge \mathsf{isSC}(lab'(y))$$

We can show that $\mathsf{hb}' \subseteq \mathsf{hb}$, and then all the axioms of the model follow straightforwardly. □

From Theorem 3, we can immediately show the soundness of three simple kinds of program transformations:

- *Expression evaluation order linearisation* and *sequentialisation*, because in effect they just add $sb$ edges to the program;
- *Strengthening of the memory access orders*, such as replacing a relaxed load by an acquire load; and
- *Fence insertion*, because this can be seen as replacing a skip node (an empty fence) by a stronger fence.

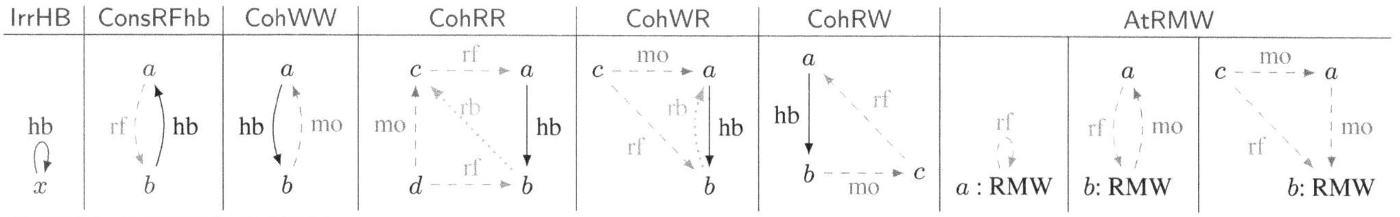


**Figure 8.** Executions violating the coherence axioms: all contain a cycle in $\{(a, b) \in \mathsf{hb} \mid \mathsf{loc}(a) = \mathsf{loc}(b)\} \cup \mathsf{com}$.

### 5.3 Alternative Presentation of the Coherence Axioms [coherence.v]

Next, we consider equivalent alternative presentations of the coherence axioms, which can be used to gain better understanding of the models and to simplify some proofs about them.

Since $mo$ is a total order on writes to the same location, and hb is irreflexive, the CohWW axiom is actually equivalent to the following one:

$$\forall a, b, \ell.\ \mathsf{hb}(a, b) \wedge \mathsf{iswrite}_\ell(a) \wedge \mathsf{iswrite}_\ell(b) \implies mo(a, b) \qquad (\mathsf{ConsMOhb})$$

The equivalence can be derived by a case analysis on how $mo$ orders $a$ and $b$. (For what it is worth, the C/C++ standards as well as the formal model of Batty et al. [4] include both axioms even though, as we show, one of them is redundant.)

Next, we show that the coherence axioms can be restated in terms of a single acyclicity axiom. To state this axiom, we need some auxiliary definitions. We say that a read, $a$, *reads before*[6] a different write, $b$, denoted $\mathsf{rb}(a, b)$, if and only if $a \neq b$ and $mo(rf(a), b)$. (Note that we need the $a \neq b$ condition because RMW actions are simultaneously both reads and writes.) We define the communication order, com, as the union of the modification order, the reads-from map, and the reads-before relation.

$$\mathsf{rb}(a, b) \stackrel{\mathsf{def}}{=} mo(rf(a), b) \wedge a \neq b$$
$$\mathsf{com}(a, b) \stackrel{\mathsf{def}}{=} mo(a, b) \vee rf(b) = a \vee \mathsf{rb}(a, b)$$

In essence, for every location $\ell$, $\mathsf{com}^+$ relates the writes to and initialised reads from that location, $\ell$. Except for uninitialised reads and loads reading from the same write, $\mathsf{com}^+$ is a total order on all accesses of a given location, $\ell$.

We observe that all the violations of the coherence axioms are cyclic in $\{(a, b) \in \mathsf{hb} \mid \mathsf{loc}(a) = \mathsf{loc}(b)\} \cup \mathsf{com}$ (see Figure 8). This is not accidental: from Shasha and Snir [14] we know that any execution acyclic in $\mathsf{hb} \cup \mathsf{com}$ is sequentially consistent, and coherence essentially guarantees sequential consistency on a per-location basis.

Based on this observation, we consider the following axiom stating that the union of hb restricted to relate same-location actions and com is acyclic.

$$\mathsf{acyclic}(\{(a, b) \in \mathsf{hb} \mid \mathsf{loc}(a) = \mathsf{loc}(b)\} \cup \mathsf{com}) \qquad (\mathsf{Coh})$$

This axiom is equivalent to the conjunction of seven C11 axioms as shown in the following theorem:

**Theorem 4.** *Assuming* ConsMO *and* ConsRF *hold, then*

$$\mathsf{Coh} \iff \begin{pmatrix} \mathsf{IrrHB} \wedge \mathsf{ConsRFhb} \wedge \mathsf{CohWW} \wedge \\ \mathsf{CohRR} \wedge \mathsf{CohWR} \wedge \mathsf{CohRW} \wedge \mathsf{AtRMW} \end{pmatrix}.$$

*Proof (sketch).* In the ($\Rightarrow$) direction, it is easy to see that all the coherence axiom violations exhibit cycles (see Fig. 8). In the other direction, careful analysis reveals that these are the only possible cycles—any larger ones can be shortened as $mo$ is a total order. □

[6] Alglave et al. [1] call this relation "from-read."

Although the alternative presentation of the coherence axioms developed here is much more concise than the original one, it is of limited use in verifying the program transformations, because we need to reason about yet another transitive closure (besides hb).

### 5.4 Prefixes of Consistent Executions [prefixes.v]

Another basic property we would like to hold for a memory model is for any prefix of a consistent execution to also form a consistent execution. Such a property would allow, for instance, to execute programs in a stepwise operational fashion generating the set of consistent executions along the way. It is also very useful in proving the DRF theorem and the validity of certain optimisations by demonstrating an alternative execution prefix of the program that contradicts the assumptions of the statement to be proved (e.g., by containing a race).

One question remains: Under which relation should we be considering execution prefixes? To make the result most widely applicable, we want to make the relation as small as possible, but at the very least we must include (the dependent part of) the program order, $sb$ and $asw$, in order to preserve the program semantics, as well as the reads from relation, $rf$, in order to preserve the memory semantics. Moreover, in the case of RSorig models, as shown in the example from Section 4.3, we must also include $mo$-prefixes.

**Definition 4** (Prefix closure). *We say that a relation, $R$, is* prefix closed *on a set, $S$, iff $\forall a, b.\ R(a, b) \wedge b \in S \implies a \in S$.*

**Definition 5** (Prefix opsem). *An opsem $(lab', sb', asw')$ is a* prefix *of another opsem $(lab, sb, asw)$ iff $lab' \subseteq lab$, $sb' = sb \cap (\mathsf{dom}(lab') \times \mathsf{dom}(lab'))$, $asw' = asw \cap (\mathsf{dom}(lab') \times \mathsf{dom}(lab'))$, and $sb$ and $asw$ are prefix closed on $\mathsf{dom}(lab')$.*

**Theorem 5.** *Given a model $M$, opsems $O$ and $O' = (lab', \_, \_)$ and a witness $W = (rf, mo, sc)$, if $\mathsf{Consistent}_M(O, W)$ and $O'$ is a prefix of $O$ and $\{(a, b) \mid rf(b) = a\}$ is prefix-closed on $\mathsf{dom}(lab')$ and either $M = (\_, \_, \mathsf{RSnew}, \_)$ or $mo$ is prefix-closed on $\mathsf{dom}(lab')$, then there exists $W'$ such that $\mathsf{Consistent}_M(O', W')$.*

*Proof (sketch).* We pick $W'$ to be $W$ restricted to the actions in $\mathsf{dom}(lab')$. Then, we show $\mathsf{hb}' = \mathsf{hb} \cap (\mathsf{dom}(lab') \times \mathsf{dom}(lab'))$ and that each consistency axiom is preserved. □

To be able to use such a theorem in proofs, the relation defining prefixes should be acyclic. This is because we would like there to exist a maximal element in the relation, which we can remove from the execution and have the resulting execution remain consistent. This means that, for example, in the Arf model, we may want to choose $\mathsf{hb} \cup rf$ as our relation. Unfortunately, however, this does not quite work in the RSorig model and requires switching to the RSnew model.

## 6. Verifying Instruction Reorderings

We proceed to the main technical results of the paper, namely the proofs of validity for the various program transformations. Having already discussed the simple monotonicity-based ones, we now

| $\downarrow a \setminus b \rightarrow$ | $\mathsf{R}_{\mathrm{NA}\mid\mathrm{RLX}\mid\mathrm{ACQ}}(\ell')$ | $\mathsf{R}_{\mathrm{SC}}(\ell')$ | $\mathsf{W}_{\mathrm{NA}}(\ell')$ | $\mathsf{W}_{\mathrm{RLX}}(\ell')$ | $\mathsf{W}_{\mathrm{REL}\mid\mathrm{SC}}(\ell')$ | $\mathsf{C}_{\mathrm{RLX}\mid\mathrm{ACQ}}(\ell')$ | $\mathsf{C}_{\sqsupseteq\mathrm{REL}}(\ell')$ | $\mathsf{F}_{\mathrm{ACQ}}$ | $\mathsf{F}_{\mathrm{REL}}$ |
|---|---|---|---|---|---|---|---|---|---|
| $\mathsf{R}_{\mathrm{NA}}(\ell)$ | ✓Thm.6 | ✓Thm.6 | ✓Thm.6/?/✗C | ✓Thm.6/?/✗C | ✗A.1 | ✓Thm.6/?/✗C | ✗A.2 | ✓Thm.6 | ✗A.7 |
| $\mathsf{R}_{\mathrm{RLX}}(\ell)$ | ✓Thm.6 | ✓Thm.6 | ✓Thm.6/?/✗C | ✓Thm.6/✗B/✗C | ✗A.1 | ✓Thm.6/✗B/✗C | ✗A.2 | ✗A.6 | ✗A.7 |
| $\mathsf{R}_{\mathrm{ACQ}\mid\mathrm{SC}}(\ell)$ | ✗A.3 | ✗A.3 | ✗A.3 | ✗A.3 | ✗A.1 | ✗A.3 | ✗A.3 | ✓Thm.7 | ✗A.7 |
| $\mathsf{W}_{\mathrm{NA}\mid\mathrm{RLX}\mid\mathrm{REL}}(\ell)$ | ✓Thm.6 | ✓Thm.6 | ✓Thm.6 | ✓Thm.6 | ✗A.1 | ✓Thm.6 | ✗A.2 | ✓Thm.6 | ✗A.7 |
| $\mathsf{W}_{\mathrm{SC}}(\ell)$ | ✓Thm.6 | ✗A.4 | ✓Thm.6 | ✓Thm.6 | ✗A.1 | ✓Thm.6 | ✗A.2 | ✓Thm.6 | ✗A.7 |
| $\mathsf{C}_{\mathrm{RLX}\mid\mathrm{REL}}(\ell)$ | ✓Thm.6 | ✓Thm.6 | ✓Thm.6/?/✗C | ✓Thm.6/✗B/✗C | ✗A.1 | ✓Thm.6/✗B/✗C | ✗A.2 | ✗A.6 | ✗A.7 |
| $\mathsf{C}_{\sqsupseteq\mathrm{ACQ}}(\ell)$ | ✗A.3 | ✗A.3 | ✗A.3 | ✗A.3 | ✗A.1 | ✗A.3 | ✗A.2 | ✓Thm.7 | ✗A.7 |
| $\mathsf{F}_{\mathrm{ACQ}}$ | ✗A.5 | ✗A.5 | ✗A.5 | ✗A.5 | ✗A.5 | ✗A.5 | ✗A.5 | = | ✗A.9 |
| $\mathsf{F}_{\mathrm{REL}}$ | ✓Thm.6 | ✓Thm.6 | ✓Thm.6 | ✗A.8 | ✓Thm.8 | ✗A.8 | ✓Thm.8 | ✓Thm.6 | = |

**Table 1.** Allowed parallelisations $a\,;b \rightsquigarrow a \parallel b$ in monotone models, and therefore reorderings $a\,;b \rightsquigarrow b\,;a$. We assume $\ell \neq \ell'$. Where multiple entries are given, these correspond to Naive/Arfna/Arf. Ticks cite the appropriate theorem, crosses the counterexample. Question marks correspond to unknown cases. (We conjecture these are valid, but need a more elaborate definition of opsem prefixes to prove.)

focus on transformations that reorder adjacent instructions that do not access the same location.

We observe that for monotone models, a reordering can be decomposed into a parallelisation followed by a linearisation:

$$a\,;b \xrightarrow{\text{under some conditions}} a \parallel b \xrightarrow{\text{By Theorem 3}} b\,;a$$

We summarise the allowed reorderings/parallelisations in Table 1. There are two types of allowed updates:

**(§6.1)** "Roach motel" instruction reorderings, and

**(§6.2)** Fence reorderings against the roach motel semantics.

For the negative cases, we provide counterexamples in the appendix.

### 6.1 Roach Motel Instruction Reorderings [reorder.v]

The "roach motel" reorderings are the majority among those in Table 1 and are annotated by '✓Thm.6.' This category contains all reorderable pairs of actions, $a$ and $b$, that are adjacent according to $sb$ and $asw$. We say that two actions $a$ and $b$ are *adjacent* according to a relation $R$ if (1) every action directly reachable from $b$ is directly reachable from $a$; (2) every action directly reachable from $a$, except for $b$, is also directly reachable by $b$; (3) every action that reaches $a$ directly can also reach $b$ directly; and (4) every action that reaches $b$ directly, except for $a$, can also reach $a$ directly. Note that adjacent actions are not necessarily related by $R$.

**Definition 6** (Adjacent actions). *Two actions $a$ and $b$ are* adjacent *in a relation $R$, written* $\mathsf{Adj}(R, a, b)$*, if for all $c$, we have:*
*(1) $R(b,c) \Rightarrow R(a,c)$, and (2) $R(a,c) \wedge c \neq b \Rightarrow R(b,c)$, and (3) $R(c,a) \Rightarrow R(c,b)$, and (4) $R(c,b) \wedge c \neq a \Rightarrow R(c,a)$.*

Two actions $a$ and $b$ are *reorderable* if (1) they belong to the same thread; (2) they do not access the same location, (3) $a$ is not an acquire access or fence, (4) $b$ is not a release access or fence, (5) if the model is based on Arfna or Arf and $a$ is a read, then $b$ is not a write, (6) if $a$ is a release fence, then $b$ is not an atomic write, (7) if $b$ is an acquire fence, then $a$ is not an atomic read, and (8) $a$ and $b$ are not both SC actions.

**Definition 7** (Reorderable pair). *Two distinct actions $a$ and $b$ are* reorderable *in a memory model $M$, written* $\mathsf{Reord}_M(a, b)$*, if*
*(1)* $\mathsf{tid}(a) = \mathsf{tid}(b)$
*and (2)* $\mathsf{loc}(a) \neq \mathsf{loc}(b)$
*and (3)* $\neg\mathsf{isAcq}(a)$
*and (4)* $\neg\mathsf{isRel}(b)$
*and (5i)* $\neg(M = (\mathsf{Arfna}, \_, \_, \_) \wedge \mathsf{isread}(a) \wedge \mathsf{iswrite}(b))$
*and (5ii)* $\neg(M = (\mathsf{Arf}, \_, \_, \_) \wedge \mathsf{isread}(a) \wedge \mathsf{iswrite}(b))$
*and (6)* $\neg(\mathsf{isFenceRel}(a) \wedge \mathsf{isAtomicWrite}(b))$
*and (7)* $\neg(\mathsf{isAtomicRead}(a) \wedge \mathsf{isFenceAcq}(b))$
*and (8)* $\neg(\mathsf{isSC}(a) \wedge \mathsf{isSC}(b))$

**Theorem 6.** *For a monotone $M$, if* $\mathsf{Consistent}_M(lab, sb, asw, W)$, $\mathsf{Adj}(sb, a, b)$, $\mathsf{Adj}(asw, a, b)$, *and* $\mathsf{Reord}_M(a, b)$, *there exists $W'$,*
*(i)* $\mathsf{Consistent}_M(lab, sb \cup \{(a,b)\}, asw, W')$,
*(ii)* $\mathsf{Observation}(lab', W') = \mathsf{Observation}(lab, W)$*, and*
*(iii)* $\mathsf{Racy}_M(lab, sb, W) \Rightarrow \mathsf{Racy}_M(lab, sb \cup \{(a,b)\}, W')$.

*Proof (sketch).* By Lemma 1, it suffices to show semiconsistency. The main part is then proving that $\mathsf{hb} = \mathsf{hb}' \cup \{(a,b)\}$, where $\mathsf{hb}$ (resp. $\mathsf{hb}'$) denotes the happens-before relation in $(lab, sb \cup \{(a,b)\}, asw, W)$ (resp. $(lab, sb, asw, W)$). Hence these transformations do not really affect the behaviour of the program, and the preservation of each axiom is a simple corollary. □

The proof of Theorem 6 (and similarly those of Theorems 7 and 8 in Section 6.2), require only conditions (1) and (3) from the definition of adjacent actions; Conditions (2) and (4) are, however, important for the theorems of Section 7.1, and so, for simplicity, we presented a single definition of when two actions are adjacent.

### 6.2 Non-RM Reorderings with Fences [fenceopt.v]

The second class is comprised of a few valid reorderings between a fence and a memory access of the same or stronger type. In contrast to the previous set of transformations, these new ones remove some synchronisation edges but only to fence instructions. As fences do not access any data, there are no axioms constraining these incoming and outgoing synchronisation edges to and from fences, and hence they can be safely removed.

**Theorem 7.** *For a monotone $M$, if* $\mathsf{Consistent}_M(lab, sb, asw, W)$, $\mathsf{Adj}(sb, a, b)$, $\mathsf{Adj}(asw, a, b)$, $\mathsf{isAcq}(a)$, *and* $lab(b) = \mathsf{F}_{\mathrm{ACQ}}$, *then*
*(i)* $\mathsf{Consistent}_M(lab, sb \cup \{(a,b)\}, asw, W)$ *and*
*(ii)* $\mathsf{Racy}_M(lab, sb, W) \Rightarrow \mathsf{Racy}_M(lab, sb \cup \{(a,b)\}, W)$.

**Theorem 8.** *For a monotone $M$, if* $\mathsf{Consistent}_M(lab, sb, asw, W)$, $\mathsf{Adj}(sb, a, b)$, $\mathsf{Adj}(asw, a, b)$, $lab(a) = \mathsf{F}_{\mathrm{REL}}$ *and* $\mathsf{isRel}(b)$, *then*
*(i)* $\mathsf{Consistent}_M(lab, sb \cup \{(a,b)\}, asw, W)$ *and*
*(ii)* $\mathsf{Racy}_M(lab, sb, W) \Rightarrow \mathsf{Racy}_M(lab, sb \cup \{(a,b)\}, W)$.

That is, we can reorder an acquire command over an acquire fence, and a release fence over a release command.

$$\mathsf{acq}\,;\mathsf{F}_{\mathrm{ACQ}} \xrightarrow{\text{Thm. 7 \& 3}} \mathsf{F}_{\mathrm{ACQ}}\,;\mathsf{acq} \qquad \mathsf{F}_{\mathrm{REL}}\,;\mathsf{rel} \xrightarrow{\text{Thm. 8 \& 3}} \mathsf{rel}\,;\mathsf{F}_{\mathrm{REL}}$$

## 7. Verifying Instruction Eliminations

Next, we consider eliminating redundant memory accesses, as would be performed by standard optimisations such as common subexpression elimination or constant propagation. To simplify the presentation (and the proofs), in §7.1, we first focus on the cases where eliminating an instruction is justified by an adjacent instruction (e.g., a repeated read, or an immediately overwritten write). In §7.2, we will then tackle the general case.

Consider the following program:

$$x = y = 0;$$

$y$.store(1, RLX); ∥ $t_2 = x$.CAS(0, 1, ACQ);
fence(REL); ∥ $t_3 = y$.load(RLX);
$t_1 = x$.load(RLX);
$x$.store($t_1$, RLX);

$$t_4 = x\text{.load(RLX)};$$

The outcome

$$t_1 = 0,\ t_2 = 0,\ t_3 = 0,\ t_4 = 1$$

is not possible. If, however, we remove the $x$.store(...) then this outcome becomes possible.

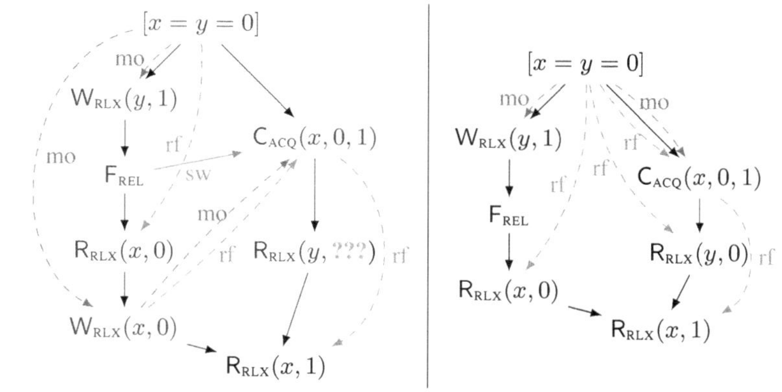


**Figure 9.** Counterexample for the 'write after read' elimination optimisation.

### 7.1 Elimination of Redundant Adjacent Accesses `[celim.v]`

***Repeated Read.*** The first transformation we consider is eliminating the second of two identical adjacent loads from the same location. Informally, if two loads from the same location are adjacent in program order, it is possible that both loads return the value written by the same store. Therefore, if the loads also have the same access type, the additional load will not introduce any new synchronisation, and hence we can always remove one of them, say the second.

$$\mathsf{R}_X(\ell, v)\,;\mathsf{R}_X(\ell, v) \rightsquigarrow \mathsf{R}_X(\ell, v)\,;\mathsf{skip} \qquad \text{(RAR-adj)}$$

Formally, we say that $a$ and $b$ are adjacent if $a$ sequenced before $b$ and they adjacent according to $sb$ and $asw$. That is:

$$\mathsf{Adj}(a, b) \stackrel{\text{def}}{=} sb(a, b) \wedge \mathsf{Adj}(sb, a, b) \wedge \mathsf{Adj}(asw, a, b)$$

We can prove the following theorem:

**Theorem 9** (RaR-Adjacent). *For a monotone memory model $M$, if* $\mathsf{Consistent}_M(lab, sb, asw, W)$, $\mathsf{Adj}(a, b)$, $lab(a) = \mathsf{R}_X(\ell, v)$, $lab(b) = \mathsf{skip}$, *and* $lab' = lab[b := \mathsf{R}_X(\ell, v)]$, *then there exists $W'$ such that*
*(i)* $\mathsf{Consistent}_M(lab', sb, asw, W')$,
*(ii)* $\mathsf{Observation}(lab', W') = \mathsf{Observation}(lab, W)$, *and*
*(iii)* $\mathsf{Racy}_M(lab, sb, asw, W) \Rightarrow \mathsf{Racy}_M(lab', sb, asw, W')$.

This says that any consistent execution of the target of the transformation can be mapped to one of the program prior to the transformation. To prove this theorem, we pick $rf' := rf[b \mapsto rf(a)]$ and extend the $sc$ order to include the $(a, b)$ edge in case $X = \textsc{sc}$.

***Read after Write.*** Similarly, if a load immediately follows a store to the same location, then it is always possible for the load to get the value from that store. Therefore, it is always possible to remove the load.

$$\mathsf{W}_X(\ell, v)\,;\mathsf{R}_Y(\ell, v) \rightsquigarrow \mathsf{W}_X(\ell, v)\,;\mathsf{skip} \qquad \text{(RAW-adj)}$$

Formally, we prove the following theorem:

**Theorem 10** (RaW-Adjacent). *For a monotone memory model $M$, if* $\mathsf{Consistent}_M(lab, sb, asw, W)$, $\mathsf{Adj}(a, b)$, $lab(a) = \mathsf{W}_X(\ell, v)$, $lab(b) = \mathsf{skip}$, $lab' = lab[b := \mathsf{R}_Y(\ell, v)]$ *and either* $Y \neq \textsc{sc}$ *or* $M \neq (\_, \_, \mathsf{STorig}, \_)$, *then there exists $W'$ such that*
*(i)* $\mathsf{Consistent}_M(lab', sb, asw, W')$,
*(ii)* $\mathsf{Observation}(lab', W') = \mathsf{Observation}(lab, W)$, *and*
*(iii)* $\mathsf{Racy}_M(lab, sb, asw, W) \Rightarrow \mathsf{Racy}_M(lab', sb, asw, W')$.

***Overwritten Write.*** If two stores to the same location are adjacent in program order, it is possible that the first store is never read by any thread. So, if the stores have the same access type we can always remove the first one. That is, we can do the transformation:

$$\mathsf{W}_X(\ell, v')\,;\mathsf{W}_X(\ell, v) \rightsquigarrow \mathsf{skip}\,;\mathsf{W}_X(\ell, v) \qquad \text{(OW-adj)}$$

To prove the correctness of the transformation, we prove the following theorem saying that any consistent execution of the target program corresponds to a consistent execution of the source program.

**Theorem 11** (OW-Adjacent). *For a monotone memory model $M$, if* $\mathsf{Consistent}_M(lab, sb, asw, W)$ *and* $\mathsf{Adj}(a, b)$ *and* $lab(a) = \mathsf{skip}$ *and* $lab(b) = \mathsf{W}_X(\ell, v)$ *and* $lab' = lab[a := \mathsf{W}_X(\ell, v')]$ *and* $\ell \neq \texttt{world}$, *then there exists $W'$ such that*
*(i)* $\mathsf{Consistent}_M(lab', sb, asw, W')$,
*(ii)* $\mathsf{Observation}(lab', W') = \mathsf{Observation}(lab, W)$, *and*
*(iii)* $\mathsf{Racy}_M(lab, sb, asw, W) \Rightarrow \mathsf{Racy}_M(lab', sb, asw, W')$.

Note that as a special case of this transformation, if the two stores are identical, we can alternatively remove the second one:

$$\mathsf{W}_X(\ell,v)\,;\mathsf{W}_X(\ell,v) \overset{\text{(OW-adj)}}{\rightsquigarrow} \mathsf{skip}\,;\mathsf{W}_X(\ell,v) \overset{\text{reorder}}{\rightsquigarrow} \mathsf{W}_X(\ell,v)\,;\mathsf{skip}$$

***Write after Read.*** The next case to consider is what happens when a store immediately follows a load to the same location, and writes the same value as observed by the load.

$$\mathsf{R}_X(\ell, v)\,;\mathsf{W}_{\text{RLX}}(\ell, v) \rightsquigarrow \mathsf{R}_X(\ell, v)\,;\mathsf{skip}$$

In this case, can we eliminate the redundant store?

Well, actually, no, we cannot. Figure 9 shows a program demonstrating that the transformation is unsound. The program uses an atomic read-modify-write instruction, CAS, to update $x$, in parallel to the thread that reads $x$ to be 0 and then writes back 0 to $x$.

Consider an execution in which the load of $x$ reads 0 (enforced by $t_1 = 0$), the CAS succeeds (enforced by $t_2 = 0$) and is in modification order after the store to $x$ (enforced by $t_4 = 1$ and the CohWR axiom). Then, because of the atomicity of CAS (axiom AtRMW), the CAS must read from the first thread's store to $x$, inducing a synchronisation edge between the two threads. As a result, by the CohWR axiom, the load of $y$ cannot read the initial value (i.e., necessarily $t_3 \neq 0$).

If, however, we remove the store to $x$ from the left thread, the outcome in question becomes possible as indicated by the second execution shown in Figure 9.

In essence, this transformation is unsound because we can force a operation to be ordered between the load and the store (according to the communication order). In the aforementioned counterexample, we achieved this by the atomicity of RMW instructions.

We can also construct a similar counterexample without RMW operations, by exploiting SC fences, a more advanced feature of C11, which for simplicity we do not model in this paper.

### 7.2 Elimination of Redundant Non-Adjacent Operations

We proceed to the general case, where the removed redundant operation is in the same thread as the operation justifying its removal, but not necessarily adjacent to it.

In the appendix, we have proved three theorems generalising the theorems of Section 7.1. The general set up is that we consider two actions $a$ and $b$ in program order (i.e., $sb(a, b)$), accessing the same location $\ell$ (i.e., $\mathsf{loc}(a) = \mathsf{loc}(b) = \ell$), without any intermediate actions accessing the same location (i.e., $\nexists c.\ sb(a,c) \wedge sb(c,b) \wedge \mathsf{loc}(c) = \ell$). In addition, for the generalisations of Theorems 9 and 10 (respectively, of Lemma 11), we also require there to be no acquire (respectively, release) operation in between.

Under these conditions, we can reorder the action to be eliminated (using Theorem 6) past the intermediate actions to become adjacent to the justifying action, so that we can apply the adjacent elimination theorem. Then we can reorder the resulting "skip" node back to the place the eliminated operation was initially.

## 8. Related Work

The C11 model was introduced by the 2011 revisions of the C and C++ standards [8, 7]. A rigorous mathematical formalisation of the C11 memory model was given by Batty et al. [4] and was later extended to cover read-modify-write and fence instructions [13].

Sample compilation schemes for atomic accesses have been proved correct both for the x86-TSO architecture [4] and for the Power/ARM architecture [3, 13]. The aim here was to study how expensive it is to enforce the intended C11 semantics on widespread architectures: the idealised compiler considered naively applies a one-to-one mapping from C memory accesses to machine memory accesses, attempting no optimisations at all.

Out-of-thin-air behaviours are being recognised as the most troublesome corner of the design of modern language memory models. The Java memory model [10] tried to effectively prohibit out-of-thin-air results in its specification. Complicated causality rules were introduced for this purpose, which turned out to forbid some program transformations that the reference HotSpot compiler actually performs [19]. The work ofŠ evčík is closely bound to the specificities of the Java memory model, and his counterexamples cannot be translated to C. The existence of causality cycles is vaguely acknowledged in the C and C++ language standards, and is stated clearly in [4, Sec. 4]. Since then, independent lines of research, including program logics [2, 16] and model checkers [12] bumped into issues related to causality cycles; it is today acknowledged that code verification is infeasible in their presence.

It turns out that it is very difficult to define a language memory model that both allows programmers to take full advantage of weakly-ordered memory accesses but still correctly disallows out-of-thin-air results. The quest for an updated model for Java is still open; it is the objective of the OpenJDK JEP 188 but no concrete design has yet been proposed. Surprisingly, the simpler requirements of the C language did not lead to a quick fix. A brute-force solution preventing relaxed loads from being reordered with subsequent relaxed stores has been proposed by Boehm [5, 6] and by Vafeiadis and Narayan [16], which we also studied in this paper. This condition imposes a non-negligible cost on some architectures (ARM, GPUs) and its adoption in the standard is unclear.

As already mentioned, the study of correctness of compiler optimisations in an idealised DRF model was done byŠ evčík [18] and later adapted to C11 for some optimisations by Morisset et al. [11]. This paper uses the same setup but explores in a far greater depth the interaction between optimisations and low-level atomic accesses, with the surprising results presented.

The certified compilers CompCert [9] and CompCertTSO [20] (the latter extending an earlier version of the former to concurrent shared memory programming with a TSO-based memory semantics) share the same memory model for all the intermediate languages. A hypothetical CompCertC11 compiler could not use the C11 memory model for this purpose: expression linearisation is performed in the first pass of CompCert and, as we have shown, it cannot be proved correct in the C11 model. Unless the C11 model is fixed along the lines we discussed, the hypothetical CompCertC11 would have to expand the compilation of atomic accesses immediately after parsing, and then reason in terms of the target architecture memory model. This is not an option for an efficiently implementable, general purpose, programming language: hardware memory models are not DRF models and prevent most optimisations on memory accesses.

## Acknowledgements

This work is supported by the EC FP7 FET project ADVENT and the ANR grant WMC (ANR-11-JS02-011). We would like to thank Brian Demsky, Jean-Jacques Lévy, Peter Sewell and the anonymous reviewers for their helpful feedback.

## References

[1] J. Alglave, L. Maranget, and M. Tautschnig. Herding cats: modelling, simulation, testing, and data-mining for weak memory. *TOPLAS*, 36(2):7:1–7:74, 2014.

[2] M. Batty, M. Dodds, and A. Gotsman. Library abstraction for C/C++ concurrency. In *POPL*, 2013.

[3] M. Batty, K. Memarian, S. Owens, S. Sarkar, and P. Sewell. Clarifying and compiling C/C++ concurrency: From C++11 to POWER. In *POPL*, 2012.

[4] M. Batty, S. Owens, S. Sarkar, P. Sewell, and T. Weber. Mathematizing C++ concurrency. In *POPL*, 2011.

[5] H.-J. Boehm. N3710: Specifying the absence of "out of thin air" results, 2013. Available at `http://www.open-std.org/jtc1/sc22/wg21/docs/papers/2013/n3710.html`.

[6] H.-J. Boehm and B. Demsky. Outlawing ghosts: avoiding out-of-thin-air results. In *MSPC*, 2014.

[7] ISO/IEC 14882:2011. Programming language C++, 2011.

[8] ISO/IEC 9899:2011. Programming language C, 2011.

[9] X. Leroy. Formal verification of a realistic compiler. *CACM*, 52(7):107–115, 2009.

[10] J. Manson, W. Pugh, and S. V. Adve. The Java memory model. In *POPL*, 2005.

[11] R. Morisset, P. Pawan, and F. Zappa Nardelli. Compiler testing via a theory of sound optimisations in the C11/C++11 memory model. In *PLDI*, 2013.

[12] B. Norris and B. Demsky. CDSChecker: Checking concurrent data structures written with C/C++ atomics. In *OOPSLA*, 2013.

[13] S. Sarkar, K. Memarian, S. Owens, M. Batty, P. Sewell, L. Maranget, J. Alglave, and D. Williams. Synchronising C/C++ and POWER. In *PLDI 2012*, pages 311–322. ACM, 2012.

[14] D. Shasha and M. Snir. Efficient and correct execution of parallel programs that share memory. *TOPLAS*, 10(2):282–312, 1988.

[15] A. Turon, V. Vafeiadis, and D. Dreyer. GPS: Navigating weak-memory with ghosts, protocols, and separation. In *OOPSLA*, 2014.

[16] V. Vafeiadis and C. Narayan. Relaxed separation logic: A program logic for C11 concurrency. In *OOPSLA*, 2013.

[17] J.Š evčík. The Sun Hotspot JVM does not conform with the Java memory model. Technical Report EDI-INF-RR-1252, School of Informatics, University of Edinburgh, 2008.

[18] J.Š evčík. Safe optimisations for shared-memory concurrent programs. In *PLDI*, 2011.

[19] J.Š evčík and D. Aspinall. On validity of program transformations in the Java memory model. In *ECOOP*, 2008.

[20] J.Š evčík, V. Vafeiadis, F. Zappa Nardelli, S. Jagannathan, and P. Sewell. CompCertTSO: A verified compiler for relaxed-memory concurrency. *J. ACM*, 60(3):22:1–22:50, June 2013.

# From Communicating Machines to Graphical Choreographies

Julien Lange
Imperial College London, UK
j.lange@imperial.ac.uk

Emilio Tuosto
University of Leicester, UK
emilio@le.ac.uk

Nobuko Yoshida
Imperial College London, UK
n.yoshida@imperial.ac.uk

## Abstract

Graphical choreographies, or global graphs, are general multiparty session specifications featuring expressive constructs such as forking, merging, and joining for representing application-level protocols. Global graphs can be directly translated into modelling notations such as BPMN and UML. This paper presents an algorithm whereby a global graph can be constructed from asynchronous interactions represented by communicating finite-state machines (CFSMs). Our results include: a sound and complete characterisation of a subset of safe CFSMs from which global graphs can be constructed; an algorithm to translate CFSMs to global graphs; a time complexity analysis; and an implementation of our theory, as well as an experimental evaluation.

***Categories and Subject Descriptors*** D.3.1 [*Programming Languages*]: Formal Definitions and Theory; F.3.2 [*Semantics of Programming Languages*]: Process Models

***Keywords*** multiparty session types, choreography, communicating finite-state machines, global graphs, theory of regions

## 1. Introduction

***Context*** Choreographies, models of interactions among software components from a global point of view, have been advocated as a conceptual and practical tool to tackle the complexity of designing, analysing, and implementing modern applications (see e.g., [3, 12, 18, 27]). As noted in [18], besides yielding a global perspective of the coordination of applications supporting the development and verification of single components, a global specification can also be projected so to obtain the local behaviour of components. The software engineering methodology associated with choreographies is usually a uni-directional (top-down) approach to software development life cycle (SDLC). Such a methodology appeals to industry [3, 4, 18] since it allows developers to check components against the corresponding projections of the choreography. However, choreography-based approaches do not fully support SDLC. For example, the 'conform direction' of *testable architectures* [3] lacks algorithms to obtain global models when modifying local projections.


*POPL '15*, January 15–17, 2015, Mumbai, India.

http://dx.doi.org/10.1145/2676726.2676964

To address this limitation we propose an algorithm to construct choreographies from a set of behavioural specifications of components interacting through asynchronous message passing. We consider the following two scenarios to motivate the practical applicability of our algorithm.

- Distributed service architectures envisage software as a provision made available (through a public interface that hides implementation details) to be dynamically searched by and composed. The choreography of such systems cannot therefore be designed in advance and has to be established and checked at binding-time to attain automatic composition.
- A frequent problem practitioners have to face is the integration of newly developed software with legacy code. Typically, the latter often do not come with a global specification and changes with time. Therefore, it is difficult to assess how modifications to newly developed components fit within the system.

Relying on a modelling notations used in industry, our algorithm enables a bi-directional (top-down and bottom-up) choreography-driven SDLC: a developer can visualise a global viewpoint; thus, when an unexpected choreography emerges, either existing components or the global specification may be refined. Modified choreographies can be projected again so to be compared with the original projections.

***Our approach*** We adopt *communicating finite-state machines* (CFSMs) as suitable behavioural specifications of distributed components from which a choreography can be built. CFSMs are a conceptually simple model, based on asynchronous FIFO message-passing communication, and are well-established for analysing properties of distributed systems. They are also widely used in industry tools and can be seen as end-point specifications.

We define an algorithm that, given a set of CFSMs, yields a choreography expressed as a *global graph* [20], a graphical model closely related to BPMN 2.0 Choreography, advocated as a suitable notation for services [1]. The system $S_{re}$ in Figure 1 will be the running example to illustrate our approach; $S_{re}$ consists of four CFSMs, each having *three* buffers to communicate with the other participants, that realise a protocol of a fictive game where:

1. `Alice` (`A`) sends either *bwin* to `Bob` (`B`) or *cwin* to `Carol` (`C`) to decide who wins the game. In the former case, `A` fires the transition `AB`!*bwin* whereby the message *bwin* is put in the FIFO buffer `AB` from `A` to `B`, and likewise in the latter case.
2. If `B` wins (that is the message *bwin* is on top of the queue `AB` and `B` consumes it by taking the transition `AB`?*bwin*), then he sends a notification (*close*) to `C` to notify her that she has lost. Symmetrically, `C` notifies `B` of her victory (*blose*).
3. During the game, `C` notifies `Dave` (`D`) that she is *busy*.
4. After `B` and `C` have been notified of the outcome of the game, `B` sends a signal (*sig*) to `A`, while `C` sends a message (*msg*) to `A`.

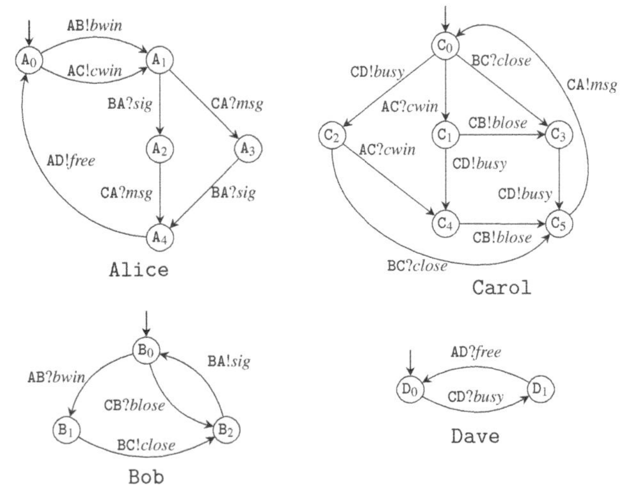


**Figure 1.** Communicating System $S_{re}$

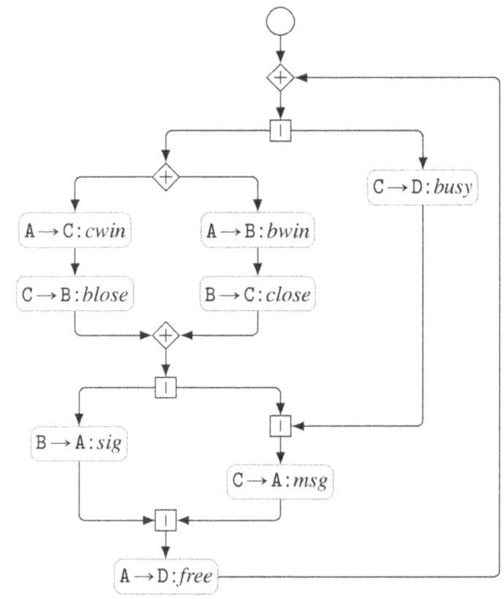


**Figure 2.** Global Graph $G_{re}$

5. Once the result is sent, A notifies D that C is now *free* and a new round starts.

The underlying protocol of $S_{re}$ shows that CFSMs capture many coordination constructs: in 1, A (non-deterministically) chooses the winner; in 2, B has a sequential behaviour; in 3, the parallel behaviour of C is rendered with the interleaving of transition CD!*busy*; in 4 and 5, threads join and finally the protocol loops.

Understanding the global model of $S_{re}$ is not easy. A much clearer specification is given by the global graph $G_{re}$ (constructed by our algorithm) in Figure 2. There, the choreography of the four components is explicit and it is possible to identify sequentially ordered, independent, or exclusive interactions. For instance, from $G_{re}$, it is evident that interaction A→B:*bwin* must precede B→C:*close*, while interaction C→D:*busy* is independent of the former two. On the other hand, A→B:*bwin* and A→C:*cwin* are exclusive, i.e., only one of them may be executed in each round of the game.

Establishing properties of CFSMs such as

> *Is $S_{re}$ deadlock-free? will any sent message be eventually consumed? will each participant eventually receive any message s/he is waiting for?*

is generally undecidable [14] or computationally hard, and not immediate even for the simple scenario in Figure 1. We give a decidable condition, called *generalised multiparty compatibility* (GMC) that characterises a set of systems for which the questions above can be decided. Our algorithm can produce a global graph from any set of generalised multiparty compatible CFSMs. The global graph is constructed through a transformation of the CFSMs into a safe Petri net, using the algorithm in [19]. The transformation preserves the original CFSMs, which can be recovered by projecting the global graph. Noteworthy, most of the systems we found in the literature enjoy GMC and very few of them do not (cf. § 5).

***Contributions*** To the best of our knowledge, this is the first work to build graphical choreographies from CFSMs and to characterise the set of CFSMs from which such choreographies can be built. Our theory is supported by a tool (which we evaluated against protocols from the literature).

Recently the construction of syntactic (non-graphical) multiparty session types [24] from local specifications has been studied in [21, 25] for a less general framework with no support for *local concurrency*; for instance in Figure 1, C can send message *busy* while concurrently receiving either *cwin* or *close* (similarly A can execute input actions CA?*msg* and BA?*sig* in parallel). We argue that catering for a general form of local concurrency (which is in fact supported by threads in many programming languages) is crucial for modelling real-world systems.

In [11, 12] conditions for communicating systems to be safe are given; however, they do not address the problem of constructing choreographies and consider a form of local concurrency more restrictive than ours due to a *single* receiving buffer per participant. We use two uni-directional queues for each couple of participants so that a component can concurrently communicate with many other components accessing different FIFO queues (as, e.g., supported in the TCP protocol suite).

***Synopsis*** § 2 reviews CFSMs. § 3 defines generalised multiparty compatibility, analyses its complexity (Proposition 3.1 and Proposition 3.2), and its soundness (Theorem 3.1). § 3.3 discusses how our condition can be used to suggest amendments to fix non-GMC systems. The construction algorithm, its complexity (Proposition 4.1), and its completeness (Theorem 4.1) are in § 4. The tool and experimental evaluation are in § 5. We conclude and discuss future work in § 7, after discussing more related work in § 6. The full version of this paper [5] include full proofs of our results and benchmark protocols; our tool is available online [6].

## 2. Communicating Finite-State Machines

This section reviews definitions and properties of CFSMs. Throughout the paper we use the following sets and notations. Fix a finite set $\mathcal{P}$ of *participants* (ranged over by p, q, r, s, etc.) and a finite alphabet $\mathbb{A}$. The set of *channels* is $C \stackrel{\text{def}}{=} \{\mathtt{pq} \mid \mathtt{p},\mathtt{q} \in \mathcal{P} \text{ and } \mathtt{p} \neq \mathtt{q}\}$ while $Act \stackrel{\text{def}}{=} C \times \{!,?\} \times \mathbb{A}$ is the set of *actions* (ranged over by $\ell$), $\mathbb{A}^*$ (resp. $Act^*$, ranged over by $\varphi$) is the set of finite words on $\mathbb{A}$ (resp. $Act$). Also, $\varepsilon$ ($\notin \mathbb{A} \cup Act$) is the empty word, $|\varphi|$ denotes the length of $\varphi$, and $\varphi\varphi'$ is the concatenation of $\varphi$ and $\varphi'$ (we overload these notations for words over $\mathbb{A}$).

**Definition 2.1** (CFSM)**.** A *communicating finite-state machine* is a finite transition system given by a 4-tuple $M = (Q, q_0, \mathbb{A}, \delta)$ where $Q$ is a finite set of *states*, $q_0 \in Q$ is the initial state, and $\delta \subseteq Q \times Act \times Q$ is a set of *transitions*. $\diamond$

The transitions of a CFSM are labelled by actions; label $\mathtt{sr}!a$ represents the *sending* of message $a$ from machine $\mathtt{s}$ to $\mathtt{r}$ and, dually, $\mathtt{sr}?a$ represents the *reception* of $a$ by $\mathtt{r}$. We write $\mathcal{L}(M) \subseteq Act^*$ for the language on $Act$ accepted by the automaton corresponding to machine $M$ where each state of $M$ is an accepting state. A state $q \in Q$ with no outgoing transition is *final*; $q$ is a *sending* (resp. *receiving*) state if all its outgoing transitions are labelled with sending (resp. receiving) actions, and $q$ is a *mixed* state otherwise.

A CFSM $M = (Q, q_0, \mathbb{A}, \delta)$ is *deterministic* if for all states $q \in Q$ and all actions $\ell \in Act$, if $(q, \ell, q'), (q, \ell, q'') \in \delta$ then $q' = q''$.[1] A CFSM $M$ is *minimal* if there is no machine $M'$ with fewer states and transitions than $M$ such that $\mathcal{L}(M) = \mathcal{L}(M')$. Hereafter, we only consider deterministic and minimal CFSMs.

**Definition 2.2** (Communicating systems). Given a CFSM $M_\mathtt{p} = (Q_\mathtt{p}, q_{0\mathtt{p}}, \mathbb{A}, \delta_\mathtt{p})$ for each $\mathtt{p} \in \mathcal{P}$, the tuple $S = (M_\mathtt{p})_{\mathtt{p}\in\mathcal{P}}$ is a *communicating system (CS)*. A *configuration* of $S$ is a pair $s = (\vec{q}; \vec{w})$ where $\vec{q} = (q_\mathtt{p})_{\mathtt{p}\in\mathcal{P}}$ with $q_\mathtt{p} \in Q_\mathtt{p}$ and where $\vec{w} = (w_{\mathtt{pq}})_{\mathtt{pq}\in C}$ with $w_{\mathtt{pq}} \in \mathbb{A}^*$; component $\vec{q}$ is the *control state* and $q_\mathtt{p} \in Q_\mathtt{p}$ is the *local state* of machine $M_\mathtt{p}$. The *initial configuration* of $S$ is $s_0 = (\vec{q_0}; \vec{\varepsilon})$ with $\vec{q_0} = (q_{0\mathtt{p}})_{\mathtt{p}\in\mathcal{P}}$. $\diamond$

Hereafter, we fix a machine $M_\mathtt{p} = (Q_\mathtt{p}, q_{0\mathtt{p}}, \mathbb{A}, \delta_\mathtt{p})$ for each participant $\mathtt{p} \in \mathcal{P}$ and let $S = (M_\mathtt{p})_{\mathtt{p}\in\mathcal{P}}$ be the corresponding system.

**Definition 2.3** (Reachable states and configurations). A configuration $s' = (\vec{q}'; \vec{w}')$ is *reachable* from another configuration $s = (\vec{q}; \vec{w})$ by *firing transition* $\ell$, written $s \xrightarrow{\ell} s'$ (or $s \rightarrow s'$ if the label is immaterial), if there is $a \in \mathbb{A}$ such that either:

1. $\ell = \mathtt{sr}!a$ and $(q_\mathtt{s}, \ell, q'_\mathtt{s}) \in \delta_\mathtt{s}$ and
   (a) $q'_\mathtt{p} = q_\mathtt{p}$ for all $\mathtt{p} \neq \mathtt{s}$, and
   (b) $w'_{\mathtt{sr}} = w_{\mathtt{sr}}.a$ and $w'_{\mathtt{pq}} = w_{\mathtt{pq}}$ for all $\mathtt{pq} \neq \mathtt{sr}$; or
2. $\ell = \mathtt{sr}?a$ and $(q_\mathtt{r}, \ell, q'_\mathtt{r}) \in \delta_\mathtt{r}$ and
   (a) $q'_\mathtt{p} = q_\mathtt{p}$ for all $\mathtt{p} \neq \mathtt{r}$, and
   (b) $w_{\mathtt{sr}} = a.w'_{\mathtt{sr}}$ and $w'_{\mathtt{pq}} = w_{\mathtt{pq}}$ for all $\mathtt{pq} \neq \mathtt{sr}$.

The reflexive and transitive closure of $\rightarrow$ is $\rightarrow^*$. We write $s_1 \xrightarrow{\ell_1\cdots\ell_m} s_{m+1}$ when, for some $s_2, \ldots, s_m$, $s_1 \xrightarrow{\ell_1} s_2 \cdots s_m \xrightarrow{\ell_m} s_{m+1}$. A sequence of transitions is *k-bounded* if no channel of any intermediate configuration on the sequence contains more than $k$ messages. The set of *reachable configurations of* $S$ is $RS(S) = \{s \mid s_0 \rightarrow^* s\}$. The *k-reachability set of* $S$ is the largest subset $RS_k(S)$ of $RS(S)$ within which each configuration $s$ can be reached by a $k$-bounded execution from $s_0$. $\diamond$

Condition (1b) in Definition 2.3 puts $a$ on channel $\mathtt{sr}$, while (2b) gets $a$ from channel $\mathtt{sr}$. Note that, for every integer $k$, the set $RS_k(S)$ is finite and computable.

We now recall several definitions about communicating systems $S$ and their configurations $s = (\vec{q}; \vec{w})$. We say that $s$ is a *deadlock configuration* [17, Def. 12] if $\vec{w} = \vec{\varepsilon}$, there is $\mathtt{r} \in \mathcal{P}$ such that $(q_\mathtt{r}, \mathtt{sr}?a, q'_\mathtt{r}) \in \delta_\mathtt{r}$, and for every $\mathtt{p} \in \mathcal{P}$, $q_\mathtt{p}$ is a receiving or final state, i.e., all the buffers are empty, there is at least one machine waiting for a message, and all the other machines are either in a final or receiving state. Configuration $s$ is an *orphan message configuration* if all $q_\mathtt{p} \in \vec{q}$ are final but $\vec{w} \neq \vec{\varepsilon}$, i.e., there is at least a non-empty buffer and each machine is in a final state. Finally, $s$ is an *unspecified reception configuration* [17, Def. 12] if there exists $\mathtt{r} \in \mathcal{P}$ such that $q_\mathtt{r}$ is a receiving state, and $(q_\mathtt{r}, \mathtt{sr}?a, q'_\mathtt{r}) \in \delta_\mathtt{r}$ implies that $|w_{\mathtt{sr}}| > 0$ and $w_{\mathtt{sr}} \notin a\mathbb{A}^*$, i.e., $q_\mathtt{r}$ is prevented from receiving any message from any of its buffers.

[1] Sometimes, a CFSM is considered deterministic when $(q, \mathtt{sr}!a, q') \in \delta$ and $(q, \mathtt{sr}!a', q'') \in \delta$ then $a = a'$ and $q' = q''$. Here, we follow a different definition [17] in order to represent branching type constructs.

**Definition 2.4** (Safe CS). System $S$ is *safe* if for each $s \in RS(S)$, $s$ is not a deadlock, an orphan message, nor an unspecified reception configuration. $\diamond$

The following definitions are new and instrumental for § 3 where we characterise a subset of safe CS from which a global graph can be constructed. A key point to give our condition for a CS to be safe is to identify sets of concurrent actions. Below, we define an equivalence relation on transitions of a CFSM. Given $q, q' \in Q$, let $act(q, q') \stackrel{\text{def}}{=} \{\ell \mid (q, \ell, q') \in \delta\}$ and define $\diamond, \blacklozenge \subseteq \delta \times \delta$ as the smallest equivalence relations that respectively contain the relations $\underline{\diamond}$ and $\underline{\blacklozenge}$ where

- $(q_1, \ell, q_2) \underline{\diamond} (q'_1, \ell, q'_2)$ iff $\ell \notin act(q_1, q'_1) = act(q_2, q'_2) \neq \varnothing$
- $(q_1, \ell, q_2) \underline{\blacklozenge} (q'_1, \ell, q'_2)$ iff $(q_1, \ell, q_2) \underline{\diamond} (q'_1, \ell, q'_2)$ and for all $(q, \ell, q') \in [(q_1, \ell, q_2)]^\diamond$, $act(q_1, q) = act(q_2, q') \wedge act(q'_1, q) = act(q'_2, q')$

where $[(q, \ell, q')]^\diamond$ denotes the equivalence class of $(q, \ell, q')$ wrt $\diamond$.

Intuitively, two transitions are $\blacklozenge$-related if they refer to the same action up-to interleaving.

**Example 2.1.** Consider the CFSM below.

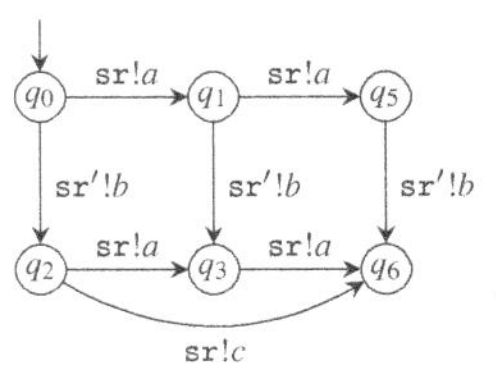


$$(q_0, \mathtt{sr}!a, q_1) \underline{\diamond} (q_2, \mathtt{sr}!a, q_3) \quad (1)$$
$$(q_0, \mathtt{sr}!a, q_1) \blacklozenge (q_2, \mathtt{sr}!a, q_3) \quad (2)$$
$$\neg((q_0, \mathtt{sr}!a, q_1) \underline{\diamond} (q_1, \mathtt{sr}!a, q_5)) \quad (3)$$
$$(q_0, \mathtt{sr}'!b, q_2) \underline{\diamond} (q_1, \mathtt{sr}'!b, q_3) \quad (4)$$
$$\neg((q_0, \mathtt{sr}'!b, q_2) \blacklozenge (q_1, \mathtt{sr}'!b, q_3)) \quad (5)$$

The relations in (1-2) hold since both transitions are interleaved with $\mathtt{sr}'!b$. The relation in (3) does not hold since the transition between the source of one ($q_0$) and the source of the other ($q_1$) passes through $\mathtt{sr}!a$ itself. The two transitions in (3) are *sequential* rather than concurrent. The relation in (4) holds, but the relation in (5) does not because there is $(q_5, \mathtt{sr}'!b, q_6)$ in the $\diamond$-equivalence classes of $(q_0, \mathtt{sr}'!b, q_2)$ for which the condition does not hold (due to the transition with label $\mathtt{sr}!c$).

In Figure 1, $(\mathtt{C}_0, \mathtt{AC}?cwin, \mathtt{C}_1) \blacklozenge (\mathtt{C}_2, \mathtt{AC}?cwin, \mathtt{C}_4)$ since both transitions represent the same action interleaved with $\mathtt{CD}!busy$. In each machine in Figure 1, a set of transitions $(q, \ell, q')$ with the same label $\ell$ forms a $\blacklozenge$-equivalence class, e.g., in $\mathtt{Alice}$, $\{(\mathtt{A}_1, \mathtt{CA}?msg, \mathtt{A}_3), (\mathtt{A}_2, \mathtt{CA}?msg, \mathtt{A}_4)\}$ is a $\blacklozenge$-equivalence class labelled by $\mathtt{CA}?msg$.

## 3. CFSMs Characterisation of Global Graphs

### 3.1 Synchronous transition system

Systems amenable to be transformed into global graphs are identified through *their synchronous transition system* (cf. Definition 3.2) where nodes consist of a vector of local states and transitions are labelled by elements in the set of *events* $\mathcal{E} \stackrel{\text{def}}{=} \bigcup_{\mathtt{s},\mathtt{r}\in\mathcal{P}} Q_\mathtt{s} \times Q_\mathtt{r} \times \{(\mathtt{s}, \mathtt{r})\} \times \mathbb{A}\}$. Intuitively, an event $(q_\mathtt{s}, q_\mathtt{r}, \mathtt{s}, \mathtt{r}, a) \in \mathcal{E}$, written $(q_\mathtt{s}, q_\mathtt{r}, \mathtt{s} \rightarrow \mathtt{r} : a)$ for short, indicates that machines $\mathtt{s}$ and $\mathtt{r}$ can exchange message $a$ when they are respectively in state $q_\mathtt{s}$ and $q_\mathtt{r}$. Indexing events with the local states of the machines permits to distinguish two occurrences of the same communication at two different points in a global graph. To single out parallelism at the machine level, we introduce an equivalence relation over events that identifies events whose underlying local transitions are $\blacklozenge$-equivalent.

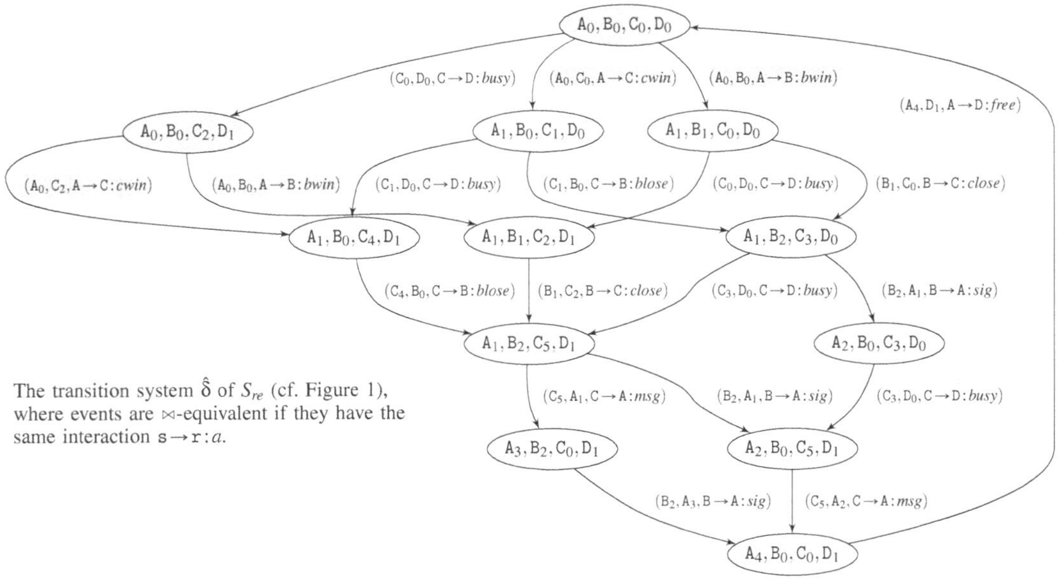


**Figure 3.** Transition graph of $\hat{\delta}$ and $TS(S_{re})$

**Definition 3.1** ($\mathcal{E}$-equivalence)**.** The *event equivalence* is the relation $\bowtie \stackrel{\text{def}}{=} \bowtie_{\mathtt{s}} \cap \bowtie_{\mathtt{r}} \subseteq \mathcal{E} \times \mathcal{E}$ where

$$(q_1,q_2,\mathtt{s}\to\mathtt{r}:a) \bowtie_{\mathtt{s}} (q_1',q_2',\mathtt{s}\to\mathtt{r}:a) \iff \forall (q_1,\mathtt{sr}!a,q_3),(q_1',\mathtt{sr}!a,q_3') \in \delta_{\mathtt{s}} : (q_1,\mathtt{sr}!a,q_3) \blacklozenge (q_1',\mathtt{sr}!a,q_3')$$

$$(q_1,q_2,\mathtt{s}\to\mathtt{r}:a) \bowtie_{\mathtt{r}} (q_1',q_2',\mathtt{s}\to\mathtt{r}:a) \iff \forall (q_2,\mathtt{sr}?a,q_4),(q_2',\mathtt{sr}?a,q_4') \in \delta_{\mathtt{r}} : (q_2,\mathtt{sr}?a,q_4) \blacklozenge (q_2',\mathtt{sr}?a,q_4')$$

We let $[e]$ denote the $\bowtie$-equivalence class of event $e$. ◇

**Example 3.1.** Consider the communicating system below:

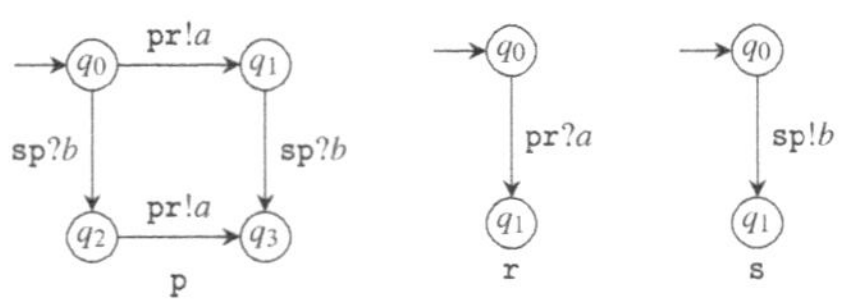


Its synchronous transition system (cf. Definition 3.2 below) is the labelled transition system:

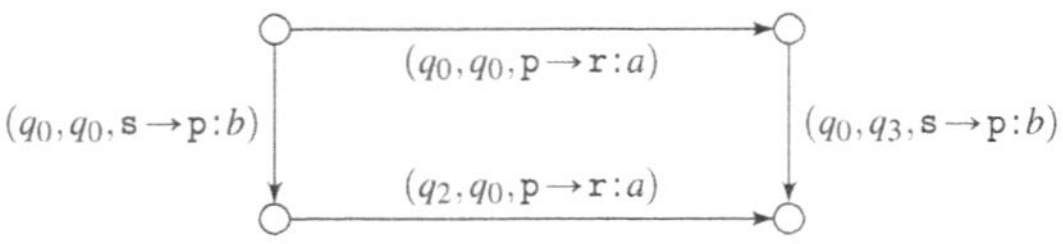


We have $(q_0,q_0,\mathtt{p}\to\mathtt{r}:a) \bowtie (q_2,q_0,\mathtt{p}\to\mathtt{r}:a)$ and $(q_0,q_0,\mathtt{s}\to\mathtt{p}:b) \bowtie (q_0,q_3,\mathtt{s}\to\mathtt{p}:b)$. Considering equivalent the events on the "vertical" transitions and those on the "horizontal" ones equivalent allows us to identify a pair of concurrent interactions; while still differentiating them from other occurences of communications $\mathtt{p}\to\mathtt{r}:a$ and $\mathtt{s}\to\mathtt{p}:b$.

In our running example (cf. Figure 1), we have $(\mathtt{C}_5,\mathtt{A}_2,\mathtt{C}\to\mathtt{A}:msg) \bowtie (\mathtt{C}_5,\mathtt{A}_1,\mathtt{C}\to\mathtt{A}:msg)$ since the underlying transitions of A are $\blacklozenge$-equivalent, i.e., $(\mathtt{A}_1,\mathtt{CA}?msg,\mathtt{A}_3) \blacklozenge (\mathtt{A}_2,\mathtt{CA}?msg,\mathtt{A}_4)$, and the underlying transition of C is the same for both events, i.e., $(\mathtt{C}_5,\mathtt{CA}!msg,\mathtt{C}_0)$.

Hereafter, we let $n,n',\ldots$ denote vectors of local states and $n[\mathtt{p}]$ denote the state of $\mathtt{p}\in\mathcal{P}$ in $n$.

**Definition 3.2** (Synchronous transition system)**.** Given a system $S=(M_{\mathtt{p}})_{\mathtt{p}\in\mathcal{P}}$, let $N \stackrel{\text{def}}{=} \{\vec{q} \mid (\vec{q};\vec{\varepsilon}) \in RS_1(S)\}$,

$$\hat{\delta} \stackrel{\text{def}}{=} \left\{(n,e,n') \mid (n;\vec{\varepsilon}) \xrightarrow{\mathtt{sr}!a} \xrightarrow{\mathtt{sr}?a} (n';\vec{\varepsilon}) \wedge e = (n[\mathtt{s}],n[\mathtt{r}],\mathtt{s}\to\mathtt{r}:a)\right\}$$

and $E \stackrel{\text{def}}{=} \{e \mid \exists n,n' \in N : (n,e,n') \in \hat{\delta}\} \subseteq \mathcal{E}$.
The *synchronous transition system of* $S$ is $TS(S) = (N, n_0, E/\bowtie, \Rightarrow)$ where $n_0 = \vec{q}_0$ is the initial state, and $n \stackrel{[e]}{\Longrightarrow} n' \iff (n,e,n') \in \hat{\delta}$. We fix a set $\hat{E}$ of representative elements of each $\bowtie$-equivalence class (i.e., $\hat{E} \subseteq E$ and $\forall e \in E\ \exists! e' \in \hat{E} : e' \in [e]$) and write $n \stackrel{e'}{\Longrightarrow} n'$ for $n \stackrel{[e]}{\Longrightarrow} n'$ when $e' \in [e] \cap \hat{E}$. Sequences of events are ranged over by $\pi$ and we extend the notation on $\to$ in Definition 2.3 to $\Rightarrow$ (e.g., if $\pi = e_1 \cdots e_k$, $n_1 \stackrel{\pi}{\Longrightarrow} n_{k+1}$ iff $n_1 \stackrel{e_1}{\Longrightarrow} n_2 \stackrel{e_2}{\Longrightarrow} \cdots \stackrel{e_k}{\Longrightarrow} n_{k+1}$). ◇

$TS(S)$ represents all the possible synchronous executions of system $S$; and each transition is labelled by an event $e$, taken up-to $\blacklozenge$-equivalence so to distinguish different occurrences of a same communication, while preserving the parallelism of local machines. The synchronous transition system for our running example is given in Figure 3.

**Definition 3.3** (Projections)**.** The projection of an event $e$ onto participant p, denoted by $e\downharpoonright_{\mathtt{p}}$, is defined as follows:

$$(q_{\mathtt{s}}, q_{\mathtt{r}}, \mathtt{s}\to\mathtt{r}:a)\downharpoonright_{\mathtt{p}} \stackrel{\text{def}}{=} \begin{cases} \mathtt{pr}!a & \text{if } \mathtt{s}=\mathtt{p} \\ \mathtt{sp}?a & \text{if } \mathtt{r}=\mathtt{p} \\ \varepsilon & \text{otherwise} \end{cases}$$

Projection is defined on sequences of events in the obvious way. The projection of $TS(S) = (N, n_0, \hat{E}, \Rightarrow)$ on participant p, written $TS(S)\downharpoonright_{\mathtt{p}}$, is the automaton $(Q, q_0, \mathbb{A}, \delta)$ where $Q = N$, $q_0 = n_0$, and $\delta \subseteq Q \times Act \cup \{\varepsilon\} \times Q$ is s.t. $(n_1, e\downharpoonright_{\mathtt{p}}, n_2) \in \delta \iff n_1 \stackrel{e}{\Longrightarrow} n_2$. ◇

### 3.2 Generalised multiparty compatibility

We introduce *generalised multiparty compatibility* (GMC) as a sound and complete condition for constructing global graphs. Hereafter, we fix a system $S = (M_{\mathtt{p}})_{\mathtt{p}\in\mathcal{P}}$ with $TS(S) = (N, n_0, \hat{E}, \Rightarrow)$. Essentially, GMC relies on two conditions, (1) *representability* (cf.

Definition 3.4): for each machine, each trace and each choice are represented in $TS(S)$; and (2) *branching property* (Definition 3.5): whenever there is a choice in $TS(S)$, a unique machine takes the decision and each of the other participants is either made aware of which branch was chosen or not involved in the choice. Representability guarantees that $TS(S)$ contains enough information to decide safety properties of any (asynchronous) execution of $S$; and the branching property ensures that, if a branching in $TS(S)$ represents a choice, then this choice is "well-formed".

For a language $\mathcal{L}$, $hd(\mathcal{L})$ returns the first actions of $\mathcal{L}$ (if any).

$$hd(\mathcal{L}) \stackrel{\text{def}}{=} \{\ell \mid \exists \varphi \in Act^* : \ell \cdot \varphi \in \mathcal{L}\} \qquad hd(\{\varepsilon\}) \stackrel{\text{def}}{=} \{\varepsilon\}$$

Given $n \in N$, let $TS(S)\langle n \rangle$ be the transition system $TS(S)$ where the initial state $n_0$ is replaced by $n$. We write $LT(S,n,\mathtt{p})$ for $\mathcal{L}(TS(S)\langle n \rangle \downarrow_{\mathtt{p}})$; that is $LT(S,n,\mathtt{p})$ is the language obtained by setting the initial node of $TS(S)$ to $n$ and then projecting this new transition system onto $\mathtt{p}$.

**Definition 3.4** (Representability)**.** System $S$ is *representable* if

1. $\mathcal{L}(M_{\mathtt{p}}) = LT(S,n_0,\mathtt{p})$ and
2. $\forall q \in Q_{\mathtt{p}}\ \exists n \in N : n[\mathtt{p}] = q \wedge \bigcup_{(q,\ell,q') \in \delta_{\mathtt{p}}} \{\ell\} \subseteq hd(LT(S,n,\mathtt{p}))$.

for all $\mathtt{p} \in \mathcal{P}$. ◇

Condition (1) in Definition 3.4 is needed to ensure that each trace of each machine is represented in $TS(S)$; while condition (2) is necessary to ensure that every choice in each machine is represented in $TS(S)$.

**Proposition 3.1.** *Given a system $S = (M_{\mathtt{p}})_{\mathtt{p} \in \mathcal{P}}$, checking whether $S$ satisfies the representability condition is computable in*

$$O(\sum_{\mathtt{p} \in \mathcal{P}} 2^{|N|+|Q_{\mathtt{p}}|}) \text{ time, with } |N| = \prod_{\mathtt{p} \in \mathcal{P}} |Q_{\mathtt{p}}|$$

In the worst case, the time complexity of checking the representability of $S$ is exponential. This is solely due to the language equivalence check (condition (1) in Definition 3.4) between each machine and its projection from $TS(S)$. However, as observed in [13], in practice algorithms for language equivalence behave very efficiently. In addition, we can remove some states from the projection of $TS(S)$, e.g., those that are on chains of $\varepsilon$-transitions only, while preserving its language, thus reducing the exponent $|N|$.

We give a few auxiliary definitions before formalising the branching property. For $n \neq n' \in N$, we define $n \prec n'$ iff $n \Rightarrow^* n'$ and for all paths $n_0 \Rightarrow n_1 \Rightarrow \ldots \Rightarrow n_{k-1} \Rightarrow n_k = n$ in $TS(S)$ such that $n_0, \ldots, n_k$ are pairwise distinct, $n' \neq n_h$ for all $0 \leqslant h \leqslant k$. Intuitively, $n \prec n'$ holds if $n'$ is reachable from $n$ and no simple path from $n_0$ to $n$ goes through $n'$; note that $\prec$ is not a preorder in general. The *last nodes* reachable from $n \in N$ with $e_1 \neq e_2 \in \hat{E}$ are

$$ln(n,e_1,e_2) \stackrel{\text{def}}{=} \left\{ (n_1,n_2) \;\middle|\; \begin{array}{l} \exists n' \in N : \forall i \in \{1,2\} : n \Rightarrow^* n' \stackrel{e_i}{\Rightarrow} n_i \\ \quad \wedge\ \forall n'' \in N : n' \Rightarrow n'' \\ \qquad \Longrightarrow \forall j \in \{1,2\} : \neg(n' \prec n'' \stackrel{e_j}{\Rightarrow}) \end{array} \right\}$$

If $(n_1,n_2) \in ln(n,e_1,e_2)$, then $n_i$ is a $\stackrel{e_i}{\Rightarrow}$-successor ($i = 1,2$) of a node $n'$ on a path from $n$ whose successors are either not able to fire both $e_1$ and $e_2$ or not $\prec$-related to $n'$.

**Example 3.2.** Consider the synchronous transition system below.

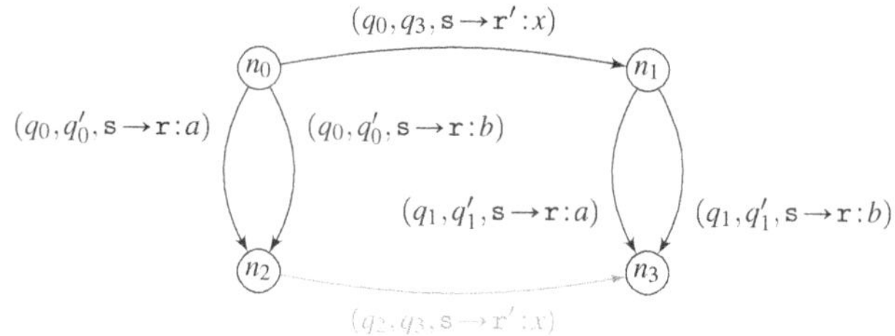


If $q_0 = q_1$ and $q'_0 = q'_1$, we have $ln(n_0,(q_0,q'_0,\mathtt{s}\to\mathtt{r}:a),(q_0,q'_0,\mathtt{s}\to\mathtt{r}:b)) = \{(n_3,n_3)\}$. In this case, both branches on $a$ and $b$ from nodes $n_0$ and $n_1$ are considered equivalent (they are only interleaved with the exchange of message $x$). However, if the edge from $n_2$ to $n_3$ is removed and $q_0 \neq q_1$ and $q'_0 \neq q'_1$, then $ln(n_0,(q_0,q'_0,\mathtt{s}\to\mathtt{r}:a),(q_0,q'_0,\mathtt{s}\to\mathtt{r}:b)) = \{(n_2,n_2)\}$. In this case the two branches are not equivalent since one of them prevents $x$ to be ever exchanged.

In our running example (cf. Figure 3), we have:

$$\begin{array}{l} ln((\mathtt{A}_0,\mathtt{B}_0,\mathtt{C}_0,\mathtt{D}_0),(\mathtt{A}_0,\mathtt{B}_0,\mathtt{A}\to\mathtt{B}:bwin),(\mathtt{A}_0,\mathtt{C}_0,\mathtt{A}\to\mathtt{C}:cwin)) \\ \qquad = \{((\mathtt{A}_1,\mathtt{B}_1,\mathtt{C}_2,\mathtt{D}_1),(\mathtt{A}_1,\mathtt{B}_0,\mathtt{C}_4,\mathtt{D}_1))\} \end{array}$$

Recall that $(\mathtt{A}_0,\mathtt{C}_2,\mathtt{A}\to\mathtt{C}:cwin) \bowtie (\mathtt{A}_0,\mathtt{C}_0,\mathtt{A}\to\mathtt{C}:cwin)$; i.e., the pair of events can be fired from both $(\mathtt{A}_0,\mathtt{B}_0,\mathtt{C}_0,\mathtt{D}_0)$ and $(\mathtt{A}_0,\mathtt{B}_0,\mathtt{C}_2,\mathtt{D}_1)$.

For an event $e = (q_{\mathtt{s}},q_{\mathtt{r}},\mathtt{s}\to\mathtt{r}:a) \in \mathcal{E}$, let $\iota(e) = \mathtt{s}\to\mathtt{r}:a$ and define a dependency relation $\lhd \subseteq \mathcal{E} \times \mathcal{E}$ on events:

$$e \lhd e' \iff \iota(e) = \mathtt{s}\to\mathtt{r}:a \wedge (\iota(e') = \mathtt{s}\to\mathtt{r}:a' \vee \iota(e') = \mathtt{r}\to\mathtt{r}':a')$$

Intuitively, $e$ and $e'$ are $\lhd$-related if there exists a dependency relation between the two interactions, from the point of view of the receiver. We define a relation $e \blacktriangleleft e'$ in $\pi$ if there is a $\lhd$-relation between $e$ and $e'$ in $\pi$, i.e.,

$$e \blacktriangleleft e' \text{ in } \pi \iff \begin{cases} (e \lhd e'' \wedge e'' \blacktriangleleft e' \text{ in } \pi') \vee e \blacktriangleleft e' \text{ in } \pi' & \text{if } \pi = e'' \cdot \pi' \\ e \lhd e' & \text{otherwise} \end{cases}$$

also, $dep(\iota(e),\pi,\iota(e'))$ iff

$$\begin{array}{c} (\pi = \pi_1 \cdot e \cdot \pi_2 \cdot e' \cdot \pi' \wedge (\_,\_,\iota(e)) \notin \pi_1 \wedge (\_,\_,\iota(e')) \notin \pi_2) \\ \Longrightarrow e \blacktriangleleft e' \text{ in } \pi_2 \end{array}$$

which checks whether there is a dependency between two interactions on a path $\pi$ (if these interactions do appear in $\pi$). Below we give the second condition for GMC, which ensures that each "global choice" is made by exactly one participant and that all the other participants are either made aware of the choice or not involved in/affected by the choice.

**Definition 3.5** (Branching property)**.** System $S$ has the *branching property* if for all $n \in N$ and for all $e_1 \neq e_2 \in \hat{E}$ such that $n \stackrel{e_1}{\Rightarrow} n_1$ and $n \stackrel{e_2}{\Rightarrow} n_2$, then we have that

1. either there is $n' \in N$ such that $n_1 \stackrel{e_2}{\Rightarrow} n'$ and $n_2 \stackrel{e_1}{\Rightarrow} n'$, or
2. for each $(n'_1,n'_2) \in ln(n,e_1,e_2)$, letting

   $L^i_{\mathtt{p}} \stackrel{\text{def}}{=} hd(\{e_i \downarrow_{\mathtt{p}} \cdot \varphi \mid \varphi \in LT(S,n'_i,\mathtt{p})\})$ with $i \in \{1,2\}$ and $\mathtt{p} \in \mathcal{P}$,

   conditions (2a), (2b), and (2c) below hold.

   (a) *choice-awareness*: $\forall \mathtt{p} \in \mathcal{P}$: either

      i. $L^1_{\mathtt{p}} \cap L^2_{\mathtt{p}} \subseteq \{\varepsilon\}$ and $\varepsilon \in L^1_{\mathtt{p}} \iff \varepsilon \in L^2_{\mathtt{p}}$, or

      ii. $\exists n' \in N, \pi_1, \pi_2$ :
      $n'_1 \stackrel{\pi_1}{\Rightarrow} n' \wedge n'_2 \stackrel{\pi_2}{\Rightarrow} n' \wedge (e_1 \cdot \pi_1) \downarrow_{\mathtt{p}} = (e_2 \cdot \pi_2) \downarrow_{\mathtt{p}} = \varepsilon$

   (b) *unique selector*: $\exists! \mathtt{s} \in \mathcal{P} : L^1_{\mathtt{s}} \cap L^2_{\mathtt{s}} = \varnothing \wedge \exists \mathtt{sr}!a \in L^1_{\mathtt{s}} \cup L^2_{\mathtt{s}}$

   (c) *no race*: $\forall \mathtt{r} \in \mathcal{P} : L^1_{\mathtt{r}} \cap L^2_{\mathtt{r}} = \varnothing$

$$\Longrightarrow \forall \mathtt{s_1 r}?a_1 \in L^1_{\mathtt{r}}, \forall \mathtt{s_2 r}?a_2 \in L^2_{\mathtt{r}} : \forall i \neq j \in \{1,2\} : n'_i \xrightarrow{\pi_i}$$
$$\Longrightarrow dep(\mathtt{s}_i \to \mathtt{r} : a_i,\ e_i \cdot \pi_i,\ \mathtt{s}_j \to \mathtt{r} : a_j) \quad \diamond$$

Definition 3.5 ensures that every branching either is (1) the concurrent execution of two events; or, for each participant p, (2(a)i) if p does not terminates before $n$, then the first actions of p in two different branches are disjoint; or (2(a)ii) p is not involved in the choice, i.e., the branches merge before p does any action; (2b) there is a unique participant s making the decision; and (2c) for each participant r involved in the choice, there cannot be a race condition between the messages that r can receive. The *no race* condition notably ensures that in any (asynchronous) execution of $S$, if a machine has more than one non-empty buffers, then it can read from them in any order (interleaving is possible). Note that if a machine r receives all its messages from a same sender, then there is a $\lhd$-relation between all its actions.

In system $S_{re}$, case (1) of Definition 3.5 applies to all branching nodes except $n_0 = (\mathtt{A}_0, \mathtt{B}_0, \mathtt{C}_0, \mathtt{D}_0)$ and $n = (\mathtt{A}_0, \mathtt{B}_0, \mathtt{C}_2, \mathtt{D}_1)$, highlighted in Figure 3, for which case (2) applies. For $e_1 = (\mathtt{A}_0, \mathtt{B}_0, \mathtt{A} \to \mathtt{B} : bwin)$ and $e_2 = (\mathtt{A}_0, \mathtt{C}_0, \mathtt{A} \to \mathtt{C} : cwin)$, we have $ln(n_0, e_1, e_2) = ln(n, e_1, e_2) = \{((\mathtt{A}_1, \mathtt{B}_1, \mathtt{C}_2, \mathtt{D}_1), (\mathtt{A}_1, \mathtt{B}_0, \mathtt{C}_4, \mathtt{D}_1))\}$. Hence, case (2a) holds for $n_0$ iff it holds for $n$. Following (2a), we check that every participant satisfies either (2(a)i) or (2(a)ii):

- A executes different (sending) actions in both branches (AB!*bwin* and AC!*cwin*),
- B executes different (receiving) actions (AB?*bwin* and CB?*blose*),
- C executes different (receiving) actions (AC?*cwin* and BC?*close*),

hence case (2(a)i) applies to A, B, and C. While case (2(a)ii) applies to D since there is a node $n' = (\mathtt{A}_1, \mathtt{B}_2, \mathtt{C}_5, \mathtt{D}_1)$ such that D does not execute any action on either path from $n$ to $n'$ (through nodes $(\mathtt{A}_1, \mathtt{B}_1, \mathtt{C}_2, \mathtt{D}_1)$ and $(\mathtt{A}_1, \mathtt{B}_0, \mathtt{C}_4, \mathtt{D}_1)$, respectively). Also, condition (2b) is satisfied since A is the unique sender that executes different actions in both branches $e_1$ and $e_2$.

Condition (2c) is satisfied for B and C due to the existence of dependency chains from AB?*bwin* to CB?*blose* (and vice versa) and from AC?*cwin* to BC?*close* (and vice versa). For instance, the dependency chain $\mathtt{B} \to \mathtt{C} : close \lhd \mathtt{C} \to \mathtt{A} : msg \lhd \mathtt{A} \to \mathtt{C} : cwin$ prevents C to delay the reception of *close* (sent by B) until she can receive message *cwin* (sent by A); C must send a message *msg* (to A) before she can receive the outcome of a new round of the game.

Finally, note that $ln(n_0, e_1, e_2)$ ensures that checking the branching between $e_1$ and $e_2$ at node $n_0$ is delayed until the interaction $\mathtt{C} \to \mathtt{D} : busy$ does not interfere with the choice. Hence, the behaviours of C and D are checked only once they have exchanged the *busy* message.

**Proposition 3.2.** *Given a system $S = (M_{\mathtt{p}})_{\mathtt{p} \in \mathcal{P}}$, checking whether $S$ satisfies the branching property is computable in*

$$O\left( |\Rightarrow|^2 \times |\Rightarrow|! \times \sum_{\mathtt{r} \in \mathcal{P}} \left( |\delta_{\mathtt{r}}|^2 \right) \right) \text{ time.}$$

Checking the branching property is factorial in the size of $TS(S)$ because it requires the enumeration of paths of $TS(S)$ (cf. (2c) of Definition 3.5). We remark that the above is a rather coarse approximation obtained under worst case assumptions oblivious of the typical structure of $TS(S)$; our experiments show good performances (cf. § 5). Finally, we observe that $TS(S)$ is generally much smaller than, e.g., the one-bounded transition system of $S$ (where each queue may contain at most one message).

**Definition 3.6** (Generalised multiparty compatibility). A system $S$ is *generalised multiparty compatible* (*GMC*) if it is representable and has the branching property. $\diamond$

**Example 3.3.** We show the interplay between the representability and branching conditions by exhibiting unsafe systems satisfying only one of the properties. Consider the following machines:

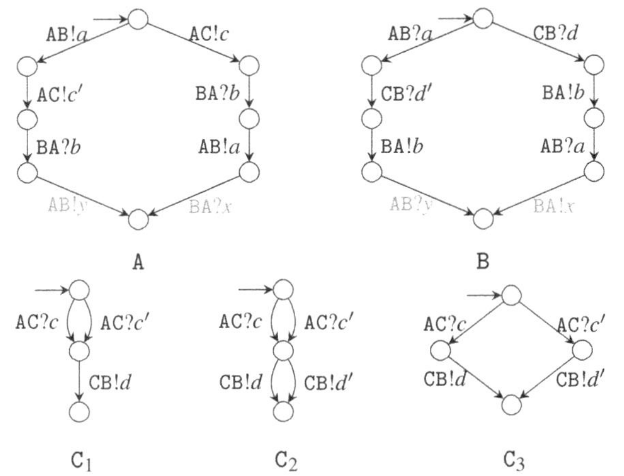


**(1)** System $S_1 = (\mathtt{A}, \mathtt{B}, \mathtt{C}_1)$ with $d = d'$ is not safe: whenever the left-hand side branch of A and the right-hand side branch of B are taken in a same execution, $S_1$ will reach an orphan message configuration where messages $x$ and $y$ are never consumed. In fact, $S_1$ is not GMC because there is a branching node from which B can execute, as first actions, either AB?$a$ or CB?$d$, and there is no dependency between the reception of $a$ and that of $d'$ (with $d = d'$) in the left-hand side branch, i.e., $\neg(\mathtt{A} \to \mathtt{B} : a \lhd \mathtt{A} \to \mathtt{C} : c' \lhd \mathtt{C} \to \mathtt{B} : d')$. Thus the branching property does not hold.

**(2)** System $S_2 = (\mathtt{A}, \mathtt{B}, \mathtt{C}_2)$ with $d \neq d'$ is not safe: as before, whenever the left-hand side branch of A and the right-hand side branch of B are taken in a same execution this system reaches an orphan message configuration. These two branches are not mutually exclusive since $\mathtt{C}_2$ can receive $c'$ then send $d$. This system is not GMC since there is no node in $TS(S_2)$ such that actions CB!$d$ and CB!$d'$ are the first actions executed by C. Hence the representability condition does not hold.

**(3)** System $S_3 = (\mathtt{A}, \mathtt{B}, \mathtt{C}_3)$ with $d \neq d'$ is safe and is GMC. In $S_3$, the left-hand side branch of A and the right-hand side branch of B are always mutually exclusive, while in $S_1$ and $S_2$ they are only mutually exclusive in synchronous executions.

We remark that systems $S_1$ and $S_2$ may be easily changed so that they are "safe" in any $k$-bounded execution but not safe in a $k+1$-bounded execution. This may be done by making A and B exchange $k+1$ messages consecutively, e.g., by replacing every AB!$a$ (resp. AB?$a$) transitions in A (resp. B) by a sequence of $k+1$ transitions AB!$a_i$ (resp. AB?$a_i$), for $1 \leqslant i \leqslant k+1$.

**Theorem 3.1** (Soundness). *If $S$ is GMC, then it is* safe *(no orphan message, deadlock, and unspecified reception configurations).*

Theorem 3.1 says that no (asynchronous) execution of $S$ will result in an orphan message, deadlock or unspecified reception configurations. Relying on representability (every transition and branching in each machine is represented in $TS(S)$), the proof shows that, for each branching node $n$, the function $ln(n, e_1, e_2)$ allows enough branches to be verified against the branching property. Then, it shows that any sent message is eventually received and that a machine in a receiving state eventually receives a message it expected, by Definition 3.5.

**Example 3.4.** The *unsafe* system below has the branching property and validates condition (1) of Definition 3.4, but *not* condition (2). This system can reach an orphan message configuration, where messages $x$ and $y$ are never received.

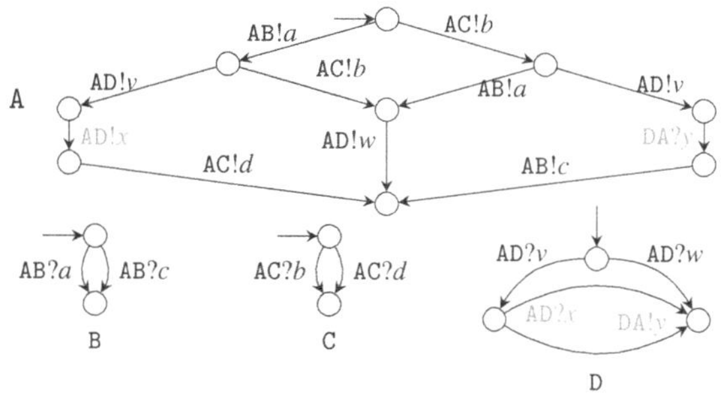


This example illustrates the importance of condition (2) of Definition 3.4 to ensure safety. In the *TS* of this system (isomorphic to machine A), the branches corresponding to DA!$y$ and AD?$x$ of machine D are not checked against each other for the branching property.

### 3.3 Amending communicating systems

When a system is not GMC, our algorithm can be used to suggest different ways of transforming it, so to validate the condition. By Definition 3.6, we first note:

**Proposition 3.3.** *If S satisfies all but* (1) *in Definition 3.4, then the system consisting of the (minimised) projections of TS(S) is GMC.*

This means that, in such a case, a new *safe* system may be automatically obtained from the projections of *TS*. For instance, system $S_2$ in Example 3.3 is not GMC because (1) in Definition 3.4 does not hold. However, the system corresponding to the projections of $TS(S_2)$ is exactly system $S_3$, which is GMC.

In case the projections of $TS(S)$ do not provide a viable alternative, then the language equivalence check allows to highlight which transitions (or paths) of each machine are not represented in $TS(S)$. Similarly, local states and transitions violating it can be singled out, according to condition (2) in Definition 3.4. For instance, in Example 3.4, we can highlight all transitions over $x$ and $y$, as well as the states where they are enabled.

When the branching property (Definition 3.5) is violated, then our analysis permits to give precise information on where the problem occurs. First, we can give the vector of local states and the two branching events for which the problem occurs as well as a witnessing execution that leads to the offending configuration.

- If the choice-awareness condition (2a) is violated, then we can list the machines for which the condition is not satisfied. If a machine has a first same receiving action in both branches, then it may be corrected by simply renaming some messages. These renamings can be automatically suggested while checking for the branching property. If the condition fails because a machine terminates in one branch but not in the other, then we can suggest to add a new label and a transition to the final state in the terminated branch; as well as a dual transition in a sending machine.
- If condition (2b) is violated, we can highlight the set of machines sending messages at this branching node. A solution may be found by identifying the genuine selecting machine and add communications from this machine to the others.
- If condition (2c) is violated, then we can highlight, for each machine violating the condition, on which messages a race condition may occur; and suggest to add an acknowledgement message between the two corresponding actions.

Note that since CFSMs are specification or abstraction of programs, it is generally not desirable to automatically repair non-GMC systems. Indeed, some corrections may not be reflected easily in the program or might have side effects in the corresponding implementation, analogously to concurrent programming where automatic corrections are not generally appealing, even if some deadlocks may be detected automatically (at run or compile time).

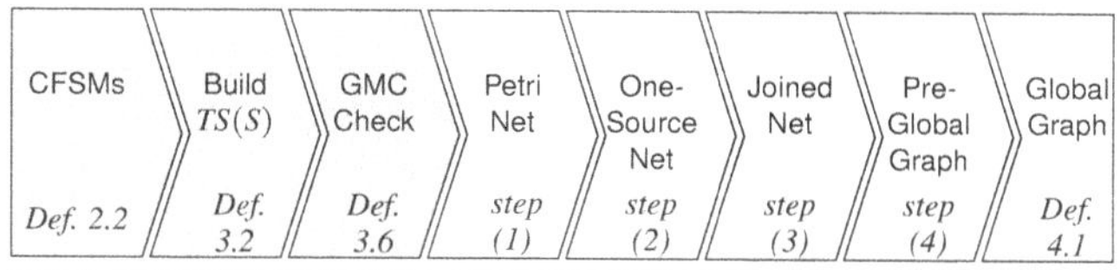


**Figure 4.** Work-flow of the construction

## 4. Building Global Graphs

In § 3, we construct the synchronous transition system $TS(S)$ of a communicating system $S$, and check whether it is GMC. We now describe the construction algorithm and its properties; Figure 4 summarises the work-flow of the transformations.

The algorithm to construct a global graph $G$ from a synchronous transition system $TS(S)$ consists of the following steps:

**(1)** we apply the algorithm of Cortadella et al. [19] to *derive* a Petri net $\mathbb{N}$ from $TS(S)$;

**(2)** we transform $\mathbb{N}$ so that its initial marking consists of exactly one place;

**(3)** we join transitions whenever possible, so to make explicit join and fork points of the work-flow;

**(4)** we transform the net of (3) into a pre-global graph; finally, we "clean-up" the pre-global graph of unnecessary vertexes so to obtain a global graph.

For the sake of the presentation and because the transformations are rather mechanical, we explain them through our running example. The formal definitions of the transformations and additional results are given in Appendix B.

For (1), it is enough for the reader to know that the algorithm in Cortadella et al. [19] is based on the theory of regions [8] and transforms a transition system into a safe and extended free-choice *labelled* Petri net, whose reachability graph is bisimilar to the original transition system. Basically, this algorithm transforms events of $TS(S)$ into transitions of $\mathbb{N}$ while the places are built out of *regions*, i.e., sets of states having a uniform behaviour wrt events. We assume in this section that each $TS(S)$ is *self-loop free*[2], i.e., $\forall n, n' \in N : n \Rightarrow n' \implies n \neq n'$. The algorithm of [19] is applicable on a self-loop free $TS(S)$, since every event $e \in \hat{E}$ has an occurrence in $TS(S)$ by construction and every state $n$ is reachable from $n_0$, as stated in Lemma 4.1 below. The Petri net obtained from $TS(S_{re})$ in Figure 3 is given in Figure 5 (left).

**Lemma 4.1.** *If $S$ is GMC and $TS(S) = (N, n_0, \hat{E}, \Rightarrow)$, then $\forall n \in N : n_0 \Rightarrow^* n$.*

In step (2), we transform a Petri net obtained from Cortadella's algorithm into a Petri net whose initial marking consists of exactly one place. This allows us to construct a global graph that has a unique starting point. In our running example, the Petri net on the left of Figure 5 is transformed by adding a fresh place ($p_0$), initially

[2] In $TS(S)$, if an event $e$ self-loops, then any transition labelled by $e$ is a self-loop. Hence, we can easily lift the self-loop free assumption by decomposing each self-loop into two (pointed) transitions in $TS(S)$ and recompose them once the global graph is constructed.

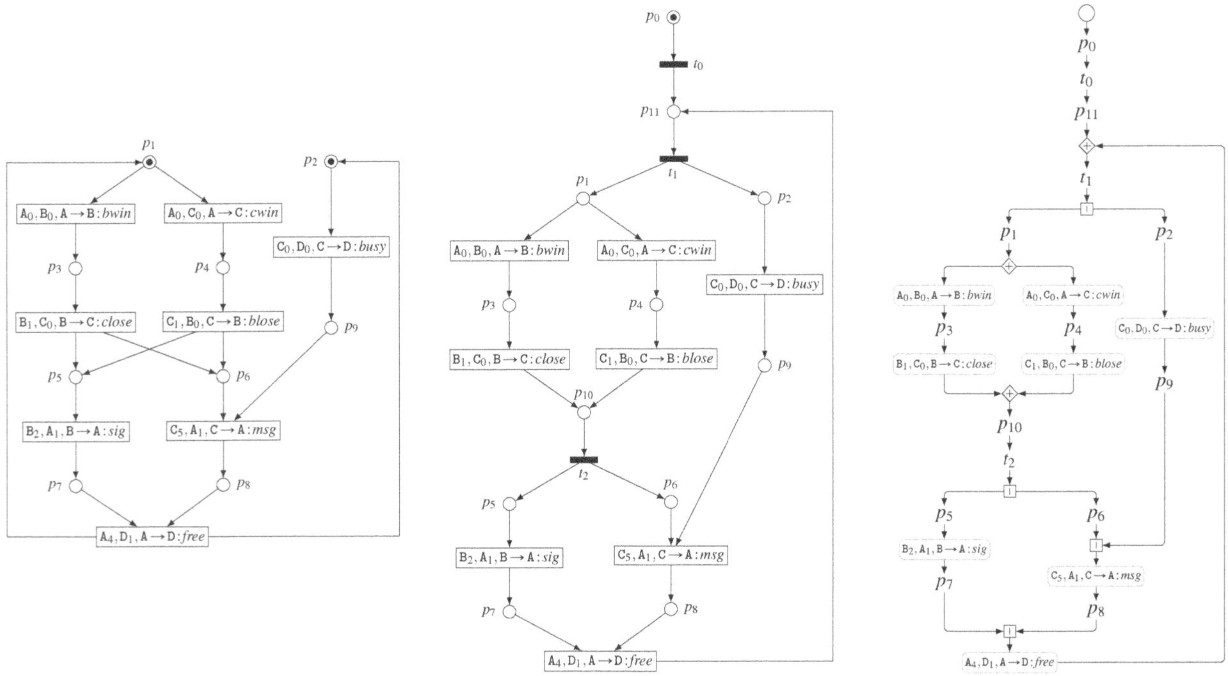


**Figure 5.** Derived net (left), net after transformations (middle), and pre-global graph (right)

marked, and a fresh (silent) transition ($t_0$) connected to places $p_1$ and $p_2$ (this simple transformation is not illustrated in Figure 5).

In step (3), a transformation ensures that parallel gates are used "as much as possible" in the graph (instead of mixing choice and parallel gates). In fact, the transformation joins sets of places that have the same preset or postset to minimise the number of choice gates. The Petri net in the middle of Figure 5 is the net obtained from the left-hand side net after applying step (2) and (3). In the second transformation, we add *(i)* $t_1$ and $p_{11}$ so to join $p_1$ and $p_2$ which have the same preset, i.e., $t_0$ and the transition with label $(\mathtt{A}_4, \mathtt{D}_1, \mathtt{A} \to \mathtt{D}: \mathit{free})$; and *(ii)* we add $t_2$ and $p_{10}$ so to join $p_5$ and $p_6$ which have the same preset, i.e., the transitions with labels $(\mathtt{C}_1, \mathtt{B}_0, \mathtt{C} \to \mathtt{B}: \mathit{blose})$ and $(\mathtt{B}_1, \mathtt{C}_0, \mathtt{B} \to \mathtt{C}: \mathit{close})$. Both $t_1$ and $t_2$ are silent transitions.

Let $\approx$ be the weak bisimilarity relation on reachability graphs (i.e., $\approx$ is the bisimilarity up-to silent transitions, cf. Appendix A).

**Lemma 4.2.** *Let $\mathbb{N}_1$ be the Petri net obtained after step (1), let $\mathbb{N}_2$ (resp. $\mathbb{N}_3$) be obtained by applying step (2) (resp. (3)) to $\mathbb{N}_1$ (resp. $\mathbb{N}_2$). If $T_i$ is the reachability graph of $\mathbb{N}_i$ (for $i = 1,2,3$) then $T_1 \approx T_2 \approx T_3$.*

We now define global graphs (a superclass of the generalised global types of [20] that allows each gate to be connected to more than two predecessors or successors).

**Definition 4.1** (Global graph). A *global graph* (over $\mathcal{P}$ and $\mathbb{A}$) is a labelled graph $\langle V, A, \Lambda \rangle$ with set of vertexes $V$, set of edges $A \subseteq V \times V$, and labelling function $\Lambda$ from $V$ to $\{\bigcirc, \circledcirc, \diamondplus, \boxbar\} \cup \{\mathtt{s} \to \mathtt{r}{:}a \mid \mathtt{s}, \mathtt{r} \in \mathcal{P} \wedge a \in \mathbb{A}\}$ such that, $\Lambda^{-1}(\bigcirc)$ is a singleton, and for each $v \in V$, if $\Lambda(v)$ is of the form $\mathtt{s} \to \mathtt{r}: a$ then $v$ has unique incoming and unique outgoing edges, and if $\Lambda(v) \in \{\diamondplus, \boxbar\}$, $v$ has at least one incoming and one outgoing edge while $v$ has no outgoing edges if $\Lambda(v) = \circledcirc$. $\diamond$

Label $\mathtt{s} \to \mathtt{r}: a$ represents an interaction where $\mathtt{s}$ sends a message $a$ to $\mathtt{r}$. A vertex with label $\bigcirc$ represents the source of the global graph, $\circledcirc$ represents the termination of a branch or of a thread, $\boxbar$ indicates forking or joining threads, and $\diamondplus$ marks vertexes corresponding to branch or merge points, or to entry points of loops.

In step (4), a *pre-global graph* is obtained from the Petri net obtained after step (3) via a transformation which consists in, firstly, creating a vertex in the global graph for each place, transition, and element of the flow relation. Then these vertexes are connected via gates: a source vertex is connected to a vertex without predecessor, a sink vertex is connected to any vertex without successors, while transitions (resp. places) are connected to a $\boxbar$-gate (resp. $\diamondplus$-gate) if they have more than one predecessors or successors. Finally, each component of the graph is connected by merging "ports" corresponding to elements of the flow relation. The pre-global graph for $S_{re}$ (Figure 1) is given in Figure 5 (right).

A global graph is obtained from a pre-global graph by removing all unnecessary nodes (i.e., former places and transitions such as $p_0$ and $t_0$ in Figure 5) and relabelling events into interactions ($e$ is replaced by $\iota(e)$); e.g., the pre-global graph in Figure 5 becomes the global graph in Figure 2.

**Proposition 4.1.** *Steps (2) to (4) are computable in polynomial time in the size of $\mathbb{N}$.*

We give the main result regarding the construction of a global graph from CFSMs. In Theorem 4.1 below, we formalise the relationship between the machines from which a global graph is constructed and its projections. Projecting a global graph $G$ can be done in two ways: *(i)* $G$ can be transformed into a Petri net whose reachability graph may be projected, similarly to the projection of $TS(S)$ (cf. Definition 3.3); or *(ii)* $G$ can be transformed into an automaton whose states are the nodes of $G$ and each transition is labelled by $(\mathtt{s} \to \mathtt{r}{:}a) \downharpoonright_{\mathtt{p}}$ if the source state corresponds to a vertex with label $\mathtt{s} \to \mathtt{r}: a$, and by $\varepsilon$ otherwise. In order to recover local concurrency, we take the parallel composition of the automata resulting of the projection of each successor of a $\boxbar$-gate. Finally, the resulting automaton is minimised wrt. language equivalence.

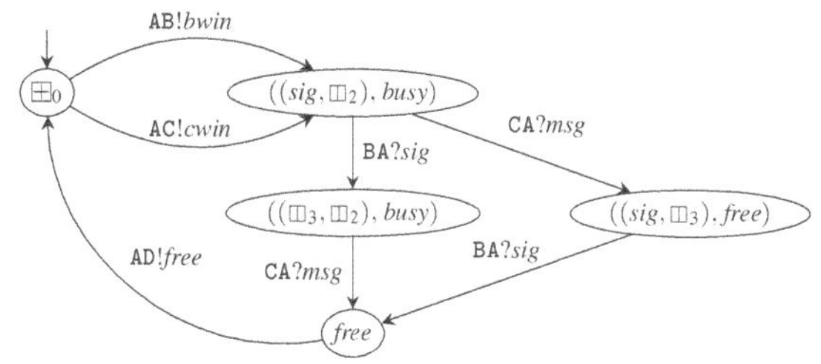


**Figure 6.** Projection of $G_{re}$ onto A

We write $G\downarrow_{\mathtt{p}}$ for the projection of $G$ onto p, and give the formal definition in [5]. As an example, Figure 6 shows the minimised projection of $G_{re}$ (cf. Figure 2) onto A.

**Theorem 4.1** (Completeness). *Given a GMC system $S = (M_{\mathtt{p}})_{\mathtt{p}\in\mathcal{P}}$, let $G$ be the global graph built from $S$ and let $TS(S) = (N, n_0, \hat{E}, \Rightarrow)$. If $TS(S)$ is self-loop free (i.e. $\forall n, n' \in N : n \Rightarrow n' \implies n \neq n'$), then $S$ is isomorphic to $(G\downarrow_{\mathtt{p}})_{\mathtt{p}\in\mathcal{P}}$, the system made of the projection of $G$.*

The proof of Theorem 4.1 (cf. [5]) relies on the fact that each machine is preserved during the construction, i.e., (1) the projection of $TS(S)$ onto each p is language equivalent with $M_{\mathtt{p}}$, (2) the net obtained from $TS(S)$ via the algorithm in [19] is bisimilar to $TS(S)$, (3) each transformation preserves (weak) bisimilarity with the derived net, cf. Lemma 4.2, and (4) the transformation to a global graph is sound since the net is extended free choice.

## 5. Implementation and Experimental Evaluation

In order to assess the applicability of our work and to estimate the effectiveness of checking for the GMC condition as well as constructing a global graph, we have developed a prototype tool supporting our theory [6]. The tool (implemented in Haskell) takes as input a textual representation of a communicating system $S$, then builds $TS(S)$ on which the representability condition and branching property are concurrently checked for (using HKC [13] to check for language equivalence). Then the tool constructs a global graph from $TS(S)$ relying on Petrify [2] (to derive a Petri net from $TS(S)$), and Graphviz (to render global graphs).

Table 1 summarises the results of experiments conducted on a few real-world protocols mainly taken from the literature. For each protocol, the table reports the number of machines, the number of nodes and transitions in $TS(S)$, whether it validates the GMC condition, the size of the constructed global graph, and the time it takes to check the condition *and* render its global graph (executions were on a 3.40GHz Intel i7 CPU with 16GB of RAM).

On most of the protocols the execution takes only a few seconds. To generate larger interesting examples, we tested systems consisting of the parallel composition of two protocols, e.g., *Running Example* ×2 is the parallel composition of two instances of the running example. Graphical representations of these protocols are in [5]. Observe that in general the size of the constructed global graph (i.e., the number of vertices) is significantly smaller than the size of $TS(S)$, see *Running Example* ×2 for instance. We note that it is slightly more expensive to check the *Running Example* and the *Logistic* protocols. This is due to the fact that each of these protocols features at least one participant for which checking condition (2c) of Definition 3.5 is not trivial, because they receive information about a choice from different participants, e.g., Carol in $S_{re}$. On the other hand, checking the *Alternating 3-bit* protocol is more time consuming due to larger ◆-equivalence classes.

| $S$ | $\lvert\mathcal{P}\rvert$ | $\lvert N\rvert$ | $\lvert\Rightarrow\rvert$ | GMC | $\lvert G\rvert$ | Time (s) |
|---|---|---|---|---|---|---|
| Running Example | 4 | 12 | 19 | ✓ | 16 | 0.184 |
| Running Example × 2 | 8 | 144 | 456 | ✓ | 32 | 22.307 |
| Bargain | 3 | 4 | 4 | ✓ | 8 | 0.103 |
| Bargain × 2 | 6 | 16 | 32 | ✓ | 16 | 0.161 |
| Alternating 2-bit [20] | 2 | 8 | 12 | ✓ | 13 | 0.161 |
| Alternating 2-bit × 2 | 4 | 64 | 192 | ✓ | 24 | 0.355 |
| Alternating 3-bit [20] | 2 | 24 | 48 | ✓ | 18 | 3.164 |
| Alternating 3-bit × 2 | 4 | 576 | 2304 | ✓ | 34 | 12.069 |
| TPMContract v2 [23] | 2 | 5 | 8 | ✓ | 15 | 0.142 |
| TPMContract v2 × 2 | 4 | 25 | 80 | ✓ | 30 | 0.362 |
| Sanitary Agency [31] | 4 | 17 | 21 | ✓ | 22 | 0.241 |
| Sanitary Agency × 2 | 8 | 196 | 476 | ✓ | 44 | 3.165 |
| Health System [15] | 6 | 10 | 11 | ✓ | 14 | 0.17 |
| Health System × 2 | 12 | 100 | 220 | ✓ | 28 | 1.702 |
| Filter Collaboration [33] | 2 | 3 | 5 | ✓ | 10 | 0.118 |
| Filter Collaboration × 2 | 4 | 9 | 30 | ✓ | 20 | 0.178 |
| Logistic [1] | 4 | 13 | 17 | ✓ | 27 | 0.276 |
| Logistic × 2 | 8 | 169 | 442 | ✓ | 54 | 2.155 |
| Cloud System v4 [22] | 4 | 7 | 8 | ✓ | 12 | 0.14 |
| Cloud System v4 × 2 | 8 | 49 | 112 | ✓ | 24 | 0.432 |

**Table 1.** Experiment results; $\lvert\mathcal{P}\rvert$ is the number of machines, $\lvert N\rvert$ (resp. $\lvert\Rightarrow\rvert$) is the number of nodes (resp. transitions) in $TS(S)$, and $\lvert G\rvert$ is the number of *vertices* in $G$.

## 6. Related Work

***Session Types*** In the context of multiparty session types, [28] first suggested a construction of a global protocol from a set of local session types, up to asynchronous sub-typing. A typing system which infers a global type [24] from a set of session types is given in [25]. Recursive constructions are restricted in this work, due to an inherently syntax-driven typing system, and multi-threaded participants are not supported (i.e., in terms of CFSMs, this means that mixed states are *not* allowed).

**Example 6.1.** Consider the GMC system of three machines below. Machine s chooses to either continue interacting with machine r (sending *cont*), or notify r that it wants to terminate (sending *end*), before collecting some information from machine p (*collect*).

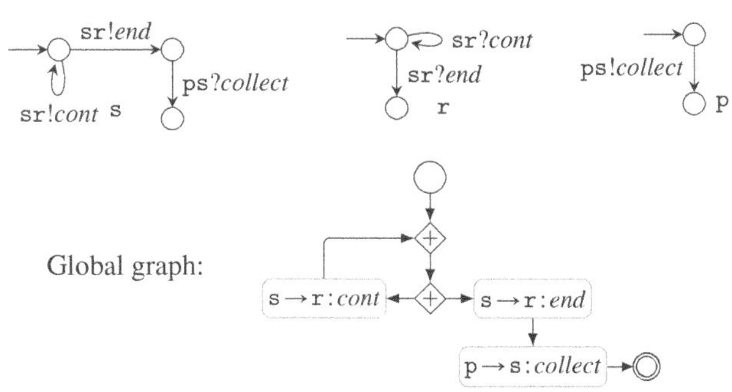


This system is not accepted by the typing system in [25] because machine p is not involved in the recursion (cf. rules [$\mu$] and [**x**] in [25]).

In [21], the authors study the *synthesis* of global types from *basic* CFSMs, that is deterministic, non-mixed (each state is either sending or receiving), and directed (for each state, its outgoing transitions are all labelled by an action sending to, or receiving from, the same participant). Basic CFSMs do not allow to model general concurrency at the local level, since a machine cannot have mixed states. Note that machines A, B, and C in Figure 1 are not directed. The present work covers a much larger set of global protocols than [21, 25, 28]: we support mixed and non-directed states (hence, multi-threaded participants are allowed), recursive protocols are no longer restricted by a syntax oriented formalism, and explicit fork/join control points may be constructed.

The first translation from generalised global types into CFSMs was given in [20], where only sound properties were presented. The generalised global types of [20] are strictly included in GMC systems (Definition 3.6). The complete characterisation of global graphs and a construction algorithm were left as open problems. This paper solves these problems.

***Choreographies*** Other recent works [10–12, 16, 23] study the relationship between global and local specifications, but *do not* consider the problem of building global specifications from local ones. Namely, in [11], *synchronisable* systems are shown to preserve some reachability properties regardless the communication being asynchronous or synchronous. Essentially, systems are synchronisable if their synchronous behaviour is equivalent to their one-bounded asynchronous behaviour (considering send actions only). In [12], the authors tackle the problem of determining whether a choreography is realisable. Essentially, a choreography is realisable if "it is possible to build a distributed system that communicates exactly as the choreography specifies". Choreographies in their work take the form of *conversation protocols*, that are finite state machines specifying the allowable sequence of interactions. A conversation protocol is akin to a global graph but without explicit construct for concurrent interactions, i.e., concurrent interactions must be specified by interleaving them.

We observe that both synchronisability and realisability conditions require strong properties on message ordering. In comparison, the GMC condition requires (*i*) the existence of a synchronous execution that encompasses all paths in each machine, and (*ii*) that each machine is either made aware every time a choice occurs or is not involved in the choice. In addition, a subtle difference between our machines and the machines in [11, 12] is that each of the latter machines has a unique buffer from which it can receive messages. Namely, their model is not suitable to reason about a CS as the interleaving of several multiparty sessions (where each participant has different receiving buffers in each session). In particular, their model cannot be used to represent programs which communicate via point-to-point communications, such as TCP connections between pairs of participants. We discuss a few examples that illustrate the main differences between the two communication models.

**Example 6.2.** Consider the GMC system below.

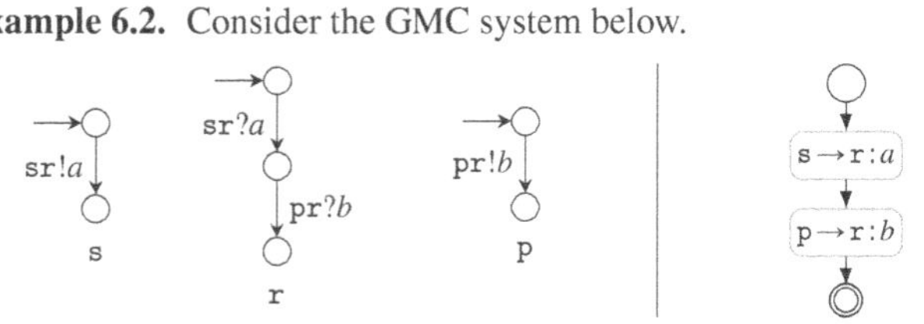


In our model, machine `r` receives messages from `s` and `p` from two different buffers; therefore, this system is safe (since machine `r` is always able to read message *a* and then consume *b* regardless of the order in which the messages from `s` and `p` arrive). In a model where machine `r` has only one FIFO buffer to receive both messages from `s` and `p`, machine `r` will end up in an unspecified reception configuration if message *b* reaches the queue before *a*. The system above is *not synchronisable*, since its synchronous execution differs from its one-bounded asynchronous execution (considering send actions only). Symmetrically, its choreography is *not realisable*.

Observe that the system $(\mathtt{A},\mathtt{B},\mathtt{C}_1)$, from Example 3.3, is unsafe in our communication model, but safe in theirs (where it is *synchronisable*). In that model, safety follows from the fact that machine `B` would have only one buffer. Hence, if `A` chooses the left-hand side branch, message *a* will be in `B`'s queue before, thus `B` must execute its left-hand side branch; while if `A` chooses the right-hand side branch, *d* will appear on `B`'s queue first and the latter will then execute its right-hand side branch. Finally, note that the GMC system (resp. choreography) in Example 6.1 is not synchronisable (resp. realisable) either due to the "race" between the send actions from machines `s` and `p`.

***Automata & MSC*** The term *synthesis* of CFSMs has been used to describe the reduction of CS to a more manageable (and decidable) model, e.g., with partial order approaches (see [30] for a summary of recent results). The acceptation of the term *synthesis* in this context is to identify a system of CFSMs that realises a protocol described by an incomplete specification (such as in [9, 29]). These approaches do not yield a global specification as instead achieved by our algorithm. In addition, our approach enables the verification of trace-based properties surveyed in [30]. For instance, the closed synthesis of CFSMs can be reduced to the construction from a regular language $L$ of a machine satisfying certain conditions related to buffer boundedness, deadlock-freedom, and words swapping.

In [27] a tool chain is given to synthesise an orchestrator (i.e., a message forwarder) from a set of finite-state machines communicating synchronously. This is transformed into a BPMN diagram via a Petri net transformation based on [19]. The work [32] gives an algorithm to compose several services. Each service is presented as an automaton and a set of automata are composed by a parallel product. The composite automaton is then transformed into a Petri net, using [19]. In both works, no result regarding safety or preservation of the behaviour of the original machines is given.

The work [7] studies whether Message Sequence Charts (MSC) imply unspecified scenarios (where MSCs are implemented by concurrent automata, but do not necessarily feature order-preserving communications). It gives conditions on MSCs for their implementation to be deadlock-free and realisable. MSCs are realisable if no other MSC may be inferable from them. It does not attempt to give an exhaustive global view of a distributed system, but focuses on identifying its possible misbehaviours.

## 7. Conclusions & Future Work

We have given a complete algorithm whereby one can build a global graph (choreography) from any *generalised multiparty compatible* (GMC) system. GMC systems form a new class of communicating systems, and we have proved that any system in this class is safe and there exist efficient algorithms to check GMC. Our work effectively uses the theory of regions [19], bridging a gap between a set of distributed uncontrolled behaviours (represented by CFSMs) and well-structured graphical session types, while offering a scalable implementation for our framework.

Since the original machines can be recovered by projecting the constructed global graph (by Theorem 4.1), we can use our framework to develop a software development life cycle based on choreographies: a specification written as a choreography is projected onto a set of local models which will then be refined against their implementations. Such an approach can also be used to reverse-engineer existing distributed systems. We are currently collaborating with the Zero Deviation Lifecyle project [4] which proposes a platform to attain "near-zero defect leakage across the various phases of the software development lifecycle". Updating global scenarios against local models plays an important role in different stages of software life cycle in this architecture. Our framework applies naturally to this platform, which notably uses BPMN 2.0 Choreography [1] specifications and tools.

We also plan to investigate a relaxed version of the GMC condition which would allow to build global graphs whose projections are equivalent to the original system, up-to asynchronous order-preserving communication [28].

## Acknowledgments

We thank Pierre-Malo Deniélou for initial discussions on this work and the ZDLC team at Cognizant for their stimulating conversations. This work is partially supported by UK EPSRC projects EP/K034413/1, EP/K011715/1, and EP/L00058X/1; and by EU 7FP projects under grant agreements 295261 (MEALS) and 612985 (UPSCALE) and COST Action IC1201: Behavioural Types for Reliable Large-Scale Software Systems (BETTY).

## References

[1] Business Process Model and Notation. http://www.bpmn.org.

[2] Petrify. http://www.lsi.upc.edu/~jordicf/petrify/.

[3] SAVARA Testable Architecture. http://www.jboss.org/savara.

[4] Zero Deviation Lifecycle. http://www.zdlc.co.

[5] Full version of this paper. http://www.doc.ic.ac.uk/~jlange/papers/lty15.pdf, 2014.

[6] GMC-Synthesis. https://bitbucket.org/julien-lange/gmc-synthesis, 2014.

[7] R. Alur, K. Etessami, and M. Yannakakis. Inference of Message Sequence Charts. *IEEE Trans. Software Eng.*, 29(7):623–633, 2003.

[8] E. Badouel and P. Darondeau. Theory of regions. In *Petri Nets*, volume 1491 of *LNCS*, pages 529–586. Springer, 1996.

[9] C. Baier, J. Klein, and S. Klüppelholz. Synthesis of reo connectors for strategies and controllers. *Fundam. Inform.*, 130(1):1–20, 2014.

[10] S. Basu and T. Bultan. Choreography conformance via synchronizability. In *WWW*, pages 795–804. ACM, 2011.

[11] S. Basu, T. Bultan, and M. Ouederni. Synchronizability for verification of asynchronously communicating systems. In *VMCAI*, volume 7148 of *LNCS*. Springer, 2012.

[12] S. Basu, T. Bultan, and M. Ouederni. Deciding choreography realizability. In *POPL*, pages 191–202. ACM, 2012.

[13] F. Bonchi and D. Pous. Checking nfa equivalence with bisimulations up to congruence. In *POPL*, pages 457–468. ACM, 2013.

[14] D. Brand and P. Zafiropulo. On communicating finite-state machines. *JACM*, 30(2):323–342, 1983.

[15] A. Bucchiarone, H. Melgratti, and F. Severoni. Testing service composition. In *Proceedings of the 8th Argentine Symposium on Software Engineering (ASSE07)*, 2007.

[16] G. Castagna, M. Dezani-Ciancaglini, and L. Padovani. On global types and multi-party session. *LMCS*, 8(1), 2012.

[17] G. Cécé and A. Finkel. Verification of programs with half-duplex communication. *I&C*, 202(2):166–190, 2005.

[18] W. W. W. Consortium. Web services choreography description language version 1.0. http://www.w3.org/TR/ws-cdl-10/, 2005.

[19] J. Cortadella, M. Kishinevsky, L. Lavagno, and A. Yakovlev. Deriving Petri Nets for Finite Transition Systems. *IEEE Trans. Computers*, 47 (8):859–882, 1998.

[20] P. Deniélou and N. Yoshida. Multiparty session types meet communicating automata. In *ESOP*, volume 7211 of *LNCS*, pages 194–213. Springer, 2012.

[21] P.-M. Deniélou and N. Yoshida. Multiparty compatibility in communicating automata: Characterisation and synthesis of global session types. In *ICALP*, volume 7966 of *LNCS*, pages 174–186, 2013.

[22] M. Güdemann, G. Salaün, and M. Ouederni. Counterexample guided synthesis of monitors for realizability enforcement. In *ATVA*, volume 7561 of *LNCS*, pages 238–253, 2012.

[23] S. Hallé and T. Bultan. Realizability analysis for message-based interactions using shared-state projections. In *SIGSOFT FSE*, pages 27–36. ACM, 2010.

[24] K. Honda, N. Yoshida, and M. Carbone. Multiparty asynchronous session types. In *POPL*, pages 273–284. ACM, 2008.

[25] J. Lange and E. Tuosto. Synthesising Choreographies from Local Session Types. In *CONCUR*, volume 7454 of *LNCS*, pages 225–239. Springer, 2012.

[26] R. Lanotte, A. Maggiolo-Schettini, and A. Troina. Weak bisimulation for probabilistic timed automata. *Theor. Comput. Sci.*, 411(50):4291–4322, 2010.

[27] S. McIlvenna, M. Dumas, and M. T. Wynn. Synthesis of orchestrators from service choreographies. In *APCCM*, volume 96 of *CRPIT*, pages 129–138. ACS, 2009.

[28] D. Mostrous, N. Yoshida, and K. Honda. Global principal typing in partially commutative asynchronous sessions. In *ESOP*, volume 5502 of *LNCS*, pages 316–332. Springer, 2009.

[29] M. Mukund, K. N. Kumar, and M. A. Sohoni. Synthesizing distributed finite-state systems from MSCs. In *CONCUR*, volume 1877 of *LNCS*, pages 521–535. Springer, 2000.

[30] A. Muscholl. Analysis of communicating automata. In *LATA*, volume 6031 of *LNCS*, pages 50–57. Springer, 2010.

[31] G. Salaün, L. Bordeaux, and M. Schaerf. Describing and reasoning on web services using process algebra. In *ICWS*, pages 43–. IEEE Computer Society, 2004.

[32] Y. Wang, A. Nazeem, and R. Swaminathan. On the optimal Petri net representation for service composition. In *ICWS*, pages 235–242. IEEE Computer Society, 2011.

[33] D. M. Yellin and R. E. Strom. Protocol specifications and component adaptors. *ACM Trans. Program. Lang. Syst.*, 19(2):292–333, 1997.

## A. Equivalences between Petri Nets

We give the formal definitions of the reachability graph of a Petri net and weak-bisimulation, which are used in Section 4.

**Definition A.1** (Reachability graph [19]). Given $\mathbb{N} = (P, T, F, m_0)$, we say that a transition $t \in T$ is enabled at marking $m_1$ if all its input places are marked. An enabled transition $t$ may fire, producing a new marking $m_2$ with one less token in each input place and one more token in each output place. We write $m_1 \xrightarrow{t} m_2$, if $m_2$ is reachable from $m_1$ by firing $t$, and write $\rightarrow^*$ for the reflexive transitive closure of $\rightarrow$.

The *reachability graph* of $\mathbb{N}$ is the transition system $RG(\mathbb{N}) = (M, m_0, \hat{E}, \rightarrow)$ such that $M = \{m \mid m_0 \rightarrow^* m\}$;

- $\rightarrow = \{(m_1, lab(t), m_2) \mid m_1, m_2 \in M \wedge m_1 \xrightarrow{t} m_2\}$ (where $lab(t) = \varepsilon$ if the label of $t$ is $\varepsilon$, and return the label $e$ of $t$ otherwise); and
- $\hat{E} = \{e \mid \exists (m_1, e, m_2) \in \rightarrow \wedge e \neq \varepsilon\}$;

Let $m \xrightarrow{e} m'$ iff $(m, e, m') \in \rightarrow$ and $m \overset{e}{\Rightarrow} m'$ iff $m (\xrightarrow{\varepsilon})^* \xrightarrow{e} (\xrightarrow{\varepsilon})^* m'$, with $e \neq \varepsilon$. ◇

The notion of weak bisimulation between two transition systems is given in Definition A.2 (adapted from [26])

**Definition A.2** (Weak bisimulation). Let $T = (M, m_0, \hat{E}, \rightarrow)$ be a transition system. A weak bisimulation on $T$ is an equivalence relation $\mathcal{B} \subseteq M \times M$ s.t. for all $(m_1, m_2) \in \mathcal{B}$, the following holds

- $m_1 \xrightarrow{e} m_1'$ implies that there is $m_2'$ such that $m_2 \overset{e}{\Rightarrow} m_2'$ and $(m_1', m_2') \in \mathcal{B}$; and
- $m_2 \xrightarrow{e} m_2'$ implies that there is $m_1'$ such that $m_1 \overset{e}{\Rightarrow} m_1'$ and $(m_1', m_2') \in \mathcal{B}$.

Two states $m_1$ and $m_2$ are called *weakly bisimilar* on $T$, written $m_1 \approx_T m_2$, iff $(m_1, m_2) \in \mathcal{B}$ for some weak bisimulation $\mathcal{B}$.

Two transition systems $T_i = (M_i, m_0^i, \hat{E}_i, \rightarrow_i)$, $i \in \{1, 2\}$, such that $M_1 \cap M_2 = \emptyset$, are weakly bisimilar, written $T_1 \approx T_2$, if given

- $M' = M_1 \cup M_2 \cup \{m_0\}$ and $\hat{E}' = \hat{E}_1 \cup \hat{E}_2$,
- $T' = (M', m_0, \hat{E}', \rightarrow_1 \cup \rightarrow_2 \cup \{(m_0, \varepsilon, m_0^1), (m_0, \varepsilon, m_0^2)\})$

$m_0^1 \approx_{T'} m_0^2$ holds. ◇

## B. From Petri Nets to Global Graphs

In this section we give the detailed transformations omitted in Section 4. The algorithm to construct a global graph $G$ from a synchronous transition system $TS(S)$ consists of the following steps: (1) using the algorithm of Cortadella et al. [19], we derive a Petri net $\mathbb{N}$ from $TS(S)$; (2) we transform $\mathbb{N}$ so that its initial marking consists of exactly one place (Transformation B.1 below); (3) we join transitions whenever possible, so to make joins and forks explicit (Transformation B.2 below); (4) we transform the net of (3) into a pre-global graph (Transformation B.3 below); finally, we "clean-up" the pre-global graph of any unnecessary vertexes so to obtain a global graph (Transformation B.4 below).

**Definition B.1** (Labelled net). A *labelled Petri net*, or net, $\mathbb{N}$ is a quadruple $(P,T,F,m_0)$ with $P$ a set of places (ranged over by $p$), $T$ a set of transitions (ranged over by $t$), $F \subseteq (P \times T) \cup (T \times P)$ the flow relation, and $m_0$ the initial marking. Each transition $t \in T$ is labelled with an event $e \in \hat{E}$, or marker $\varepsilon$ (the latter representing a silent transition). We let $x$ range over elements of $P \cup T$. As usual, ${}^\bullet x$ (resp. $x^\bullet$) is the preset (resp. postset) of $x$. A net is called *safe* if, for all reachable markings, no more than one token can appear in each place; in which case the reachable markings (including $m_0$) are sets of places. A net is *extended free-choice* if $\forall p \in P, \forall t \in T : (p,t) \in F \implies ({}^\bullet t \times p^\bullet) \subseteq F$. ◇

In the second step (2), we transform a Petri net obtained from Cortadella's algorithm into a Petri net whose initial marking consists of exactly one place. This allows us to construct a global graph that has a unique starting point (source).

**Transformation B.1** (One-source net). Given a labelled Petri net $\mathbb{N} = (P,T,F,m_0)$, the *one-source net* of $\mathbb{N}$ is $\mathbb{N}' = (P \cup \{p_0\}, T \cup \{t'\}, F', \{p_0\})$ such that $p_0 \notin P$, $t' \notin T$ is labelled by $\varepsilon$, and $F' = F \cup \{(p_0,t')\} \cup \bigcup_{p \in m_0} \{(t',p)\}$.

**Proposition B.1.** *Transformation B.1 is computable in linear time in the size of $m_0$.*

We can now state the following result, formalising the soundness of Transformation B.1.

**Lemma B.1.** *If $T$ is the reachability graph of the Petri net $\mathbb{N}$ obtained from $TS(S)$ via the algorithm in [19], and $T'$ is the reachability graph of the Petri net obtained after applying Transformation B.1, then $T \approx T'$.*

Next, Transformation B.2 ensures that parallel gates are used "as much as possible" in the graph (instead of mixing choice and parallel gates). In fact, Transformation B.2 joins sets of places having the same preset or postset to decrease the number of choice gates.

**Transformation B.2** (Joined net). The *joined net* of $\mathbb{N} = (P,T,F,m_0)$ is a net $\mathbb{N}' = (P',T',F',m_0)$ such that the following transformations are applied repeatedly:

1. for all maximal $X \subseteq P$ s.t. $|X| > 1$ and $\forall p_1, p_2 \in X : {}^\bullet p_1 = {}^\bullet p_2 \wedge |{}^\bullet p_1| > 1$, $P' = P \cup \{p'\}$ and $T' = T \cup \{t'\}$ with $p' \notin P$ and $t' \notin T$ and labelled by $\varepsilon$; also, chosen $p \in X$, $F' = \{(p',t')\} \cup ({}^\bullet p \times \{p'\}) \cup (\{t'\} \times X) \cup F \setminus \bigcup_{x \in X} {}^\bullet x \times \{x\}$
2. for all maximal $X \subseteq P$ s.t. $|X| > 1$ and $\forall p_1, p_2 \in X : p_1{}^\bullet = p_2{}^\bullet \wedge |p_1{}^\bullet| > 1$, $P' = P \cup \{p'\}$ and $T' = T \cup \{t'\}$ with $p' \notin P$ and $t' \notin T$ and labelled by $\varepsilon$; also, chosen $p \in X$, $F' = \{(t',p')\} \cup (\{p'\} \times p^\bullet) \cup (X \times \{t'\}) \cup F \setminus \bigcup_{x \in X} \{x\} \times x^\bullet$.

Note that the definition of $F'$ does not depend on the choice of $p$.

**Proposition B.2.** *Transformation B.2 is computable in polynomial time in the size of $\mathbb{N}$.*

Since we are working with *safe* nets, we have the result below.

**Lemma B.2.** *If $T$ (resp. $T'$) is the reachability graph of the Petri net $\mathbb{N}$ obtained after Transformation B.1 (resp. Transformation B.2), then $T \approx T'$.*

**Definition B.2** (Graph composition). Let $\mathbb{N}_i = (P_i, T_i, F_i, m_{0_i})$ with $i \in \{1,2\}$ be two nets and $G_i = \langle V_i, A_i, \Lambda_i \rangle$ two graphs such that $V_i = P_i \cup T_i \cup F_i$, $i \in \{1,2\}$, the *composition of $G_1$ and $G_2$*, denoted by $G_1 \uplus G_2$ is a graph $\langle V, A, \Lambda \rangle$ defined as:

- $V = \{v \in V_1 \mid v \in F_1 \implies v \notin V_2\} \cup \{v \in V_2 \mid v \in F_2 \implies v \notin V_1\}$
- $A = ((A_1 \cup A_2) \cap V \times V) \cup \{(v,v') \mid \exists v'' \in F_i : (v,v'') \in A_i, (v'',v') \in A_j \wedge i \neq j \in \{1,2\}\}$ ◇

Intuitively, the composition of the graphs consists of (1) the union of the two sets of vertexes, except flow elements $(p,t)$ and $(t,p)$ if they appear in both $V_1$ and $V_2$; and (2) the union of the two sets of arcs between vertexes in $V$, and each pair of arcs of the form $(v,(x,x'))$ or $((x,x'),v')$ is replaced by a single arc $(v,v')$.

**Transformation B.3** (Pre-global graph). The *pre-global graph* of $\mathbb{N} = (P,T,F,\{p_0\})$ is a tuple $\langle V,A,\Lambda \rangle$ such that $V = P \cup T \cup F$, $\Lambda$ is a labelling function such that $\Lambda(v) = v$ if $v \in P \cup F$ or $v \in T$ labelled by $\varepsilon$, and $\Lambda(v) \in \hat{E} \cup \{◎, ○, \oplus, ⊡\}$ otherwise; and $A$ is given by:

$$T_g(\mathbb{N}) = \biguplus_{x \in P \cup T} T_i(x) \uplus T_o(x) \qquad \text{where, given } x \in P \cup T:$$

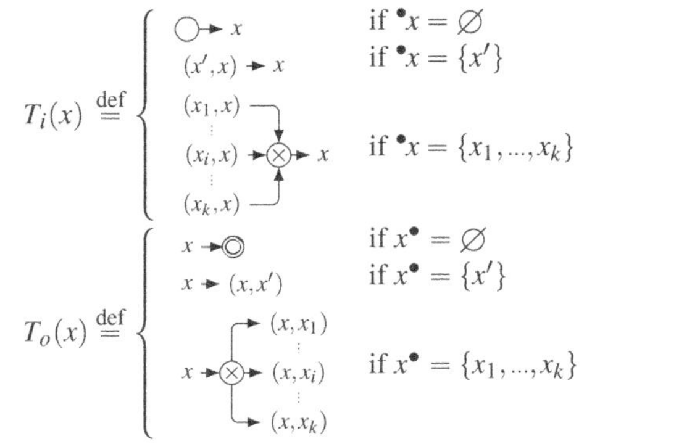


with $k > 1$, $\otimes = \oplus$ if $x \in P$, and $\otimes = ⊡$ if $x \in T$.

The pre-global graph of $S_{re}$ (Figure 1) is given in Figure 5 (right). Observe that all the vertexes of the form $(x,x')$, corresponding to an element of the flow relation, are removed as part of the graph composition (Definition B.2).

**Proposition B.3.** *Transformation B.3 is computable in polynomial time in the size of $\mathbb{N}$.*

We define the final transformation which cleans up a pre-global graph by removing unnecessary vertexes and arcs.

**Transformation B.4.** A global graph $G = \langle V,A,\Lambda \rangle$ is obtained from a pre-global graph $\langle P \cup T \cup F, A', \Lambda' \rangle$ by applying the following transformation: (1) replace each pair of transition $(x,p),(p,x') \in A'$ by $(x,x') \in A$; (2) replace each pair of transition $(x,t),(t,x') \in A'$, with $t$ labelled by $\varepsilon$, by $(x,x') \in A$; and (3) label each $t$ which is labelled by $(q_{\mathtt{s}}, q_{\mathtt{r}}, \mathtt{s} \to \mathtt{r} : a)$ in $\mathbb{N}$, by $\mathtt{s} \to \mathtt{r} : a$.

**Proposition B.4.** *Transformation B.4 is computable in polynomial time in the size of $\mathbb{N}$.*

# A Scalable, Correct Time-Stamped Stack

Mike Dodds
University of York
mike.dodds@york.ac.uk

Andreas Haas
University of Salzburg
ahaas@cs.uni-salzburg.at

Christoph M. Kirsch
University of Salzburg
ck@cs.uni-salzburg.at

## Abstract

Concurrent data-structures, such as stacks, queues, and deques, often implicitly enforce a total order over elements in their underlying memory layout. However, much of this order is unnecessary: linearizability only requires that elements are ordered if the insert methods ran in sequence. We propose a new approach which uses timestamping to avoid unnecessary ordering. Pairs of elements can be left unordered if their associated insert operations ran concurrently, and order imposed as necessary at the eventual removal.

We realise our approach in a new non-blocking data-structure, the TS (timestamped) stack. Using the same approach, we can define corresponding queue and deque data-structures. In experiments on x86, the TS stack outperforms and outscales all its competitors – for example, it outperforms the elimination-backoff stack by factor of two. In our approach, more concurrency translates into less ordering, giving less-contended removal and thus higher performance and scalability. Despite this, the TS stack is linearizable with respect to stack semantics.

The weak internal ordering in the TS stack presents a challenge when establishing linearizability: standard techniques such as linearization points work well when there exists a total internal order. We present a new stack theorem, mechanised in Isabelle, which characterises the orderings sufficient to establish stack semantics. By applying our stack theorem, we show that the TS stack is indeed linearizable. Our theorem constitutes a new, generic proof technique for concurrent stacks, and it paves the way for future weakly ordered data-structure designs.

***Categories and Subject Descriptors*** D.1.3 [*Programming languages*]: Programming techniques – concurrent programing; E.1 [*Data Structures*]: Lists, stacks, and queues; F.3.1 [*Logics and Meanings of Programs*]: Specifying and Verifying and Reasoning about Programs

***Keywords*** concurrent stack; linearizability; timestamps; verification


*POPL '15*, January 15–17, 2015, Mumbai, India.

http://dx.doi.org/10.1145/2676726.2676963

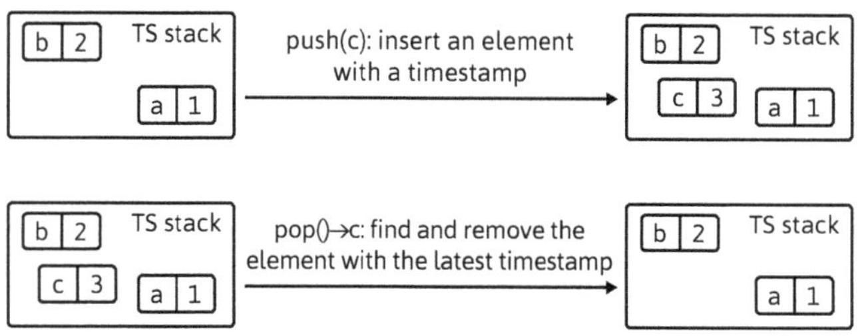


Figure 1: TS stack push and pop operations.

## 1. Introduction

This paper presents a new approach to building ordered concurrent data-structures, a realisation of this approach in a high-performance stack, and a new proof technique required to show that this algorithm is linearizable with respect to sequential stack semantics.

Our general approach is aimed at pool-like data-structures, e.g. stacks, queues and deques. The key idea is for insertion to attach timestamps to elements, and for these timestamps to determine the order in which elements should be removed. This idea can be instantiated as a stack by removing the element with the youngest timestamp, or as a queue by removing the element with the oldest timestamp. Both kinds of operation can be combined to give a deque. For most of this paper we will focus on the TS (timestamped) stack variant (the TS queue / deque variants are discussed briefly in §7). The TS stack push and pop are illustrated in Figure 1.

One might assume that generating a timestamp and adding an element to the data-structure has to be done together, atomically. This intuition is wrong: linearizability allows concurrent operations to take effect in any order within method boundaries – only sequential operations have to keep their order [14]. Therefore we need only order inserted elements if the methods inserting them execute sequentially. We exploit this fact by splitting timestamp generation from element insertion, and by allowing unordered timestamps. Two elements may be timestamped in a different order than they were inserted, or they may be unordered, but *only* when the surrounding methods overlap, meaning the elements could legitimately be removed in either order. The only constraint is that elements of sequentially executed insert operations receive ordered timestamps.

By separating timestamp creation from adding the element to the data-structure, our insert method can avoids two expensive synchronisation patterns – atomic-write-after-read (AWAR) and read-after-write (RAW). We take these patterns from [2], and refer to them collectively as *strong synchronisation*. Timestamping can be done by a stuttering counter or a hardware instruction like the x86 `RDTSCP` instruction, neither of which require strong synchronization. Timestamped elements can be stored in per-thread single-producer multiple-consumer pools. Such pools also do not require strong synchronization in the insert operation. Thus stack insertion avoids strong synchronization, radically reducing its cost.

The lack of synchronization in the insert operation comes at the cost of contention in the remove operation. Indeed, [2] proves that stacks, queues, and deques cannot be implemented without some strong synchronisation. Perhaps surprisingly, this problem can be mitigated by reducing the ordering between timestamps: intuitively, less ordering results in more opportunities for parallel removal, and thus less contention. To weaken the element order, we associate elements with *intervals* represented by pairs of timestamps. Interval timestamps allow our TS stack to achieve performance and scalability better than state-of-the-art concurrent stacks. For example, we believe the elimination-backoff stack is the current world leader; in our experiments on x86, the TS stack outperforms it by a factor of two.

Establishing correctness for the TS stack presents a challenge for existing proof methods. The standard approach would be to locate *linearization points*, syntactic points in the code which fix the order that methods take effect. This simply does not work for timestamped structures, because the order of overlapping push operations is fixed by the order of future pop operations. In the absence of pop operations, elements can remain entirely unordered. We solve this with a new theorem, mechanised in the Isabelle proof assistant, which builds on Henzinger et al.'s aspect-oriented technique [12]. Rather than a total order, we need only generate an order from push to pop operations, and vice versa, which avoids certain violations. This order *can* be generated from syntactic points in the TS stack code, allowing us to show that it is correct. Our stack theorem is generic, not tied to the TS stack. By generalising away from linearization points, it paves the way for future concurrent data-structures which weaken internal ordering.

***Contribution.*** To summarise, our contributions are:

- A new class of data-structure based on timestamping, realised as a stack, queue, and deque.
- A new optimisation strategy, interval timestamping, which exploits the weak ordering permitted by timestamped data-structures.
- A new proof technique for establishing the linearizability of concurrent stacks, and a mechanisation of the core theorem in Isabelle.
- A detailed application of this proof technique to show that the TS stack is linearizable with respect to its sequential specification.
- An experimental evaluation showing our TS stack outperforms the best existing concurrent stacks.

***Artifacts.*** We have produced two research artifacts:

- The TS stack itself, implemented in C, along with queue and deque variants, and benchmark code used to test it.
- The Isabelle mechanisation of our stack theorem.

Both artifacts are included with the supplementary material on the ACM digital library, and are also available from the TS stack webpage:

`http://scal.cs.uni-salzburg.at/tsstack/`

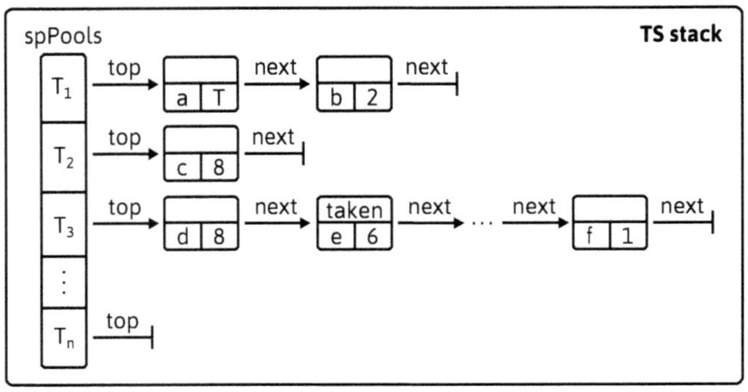


Figure 2: The TS stack data-structure.

***Paper structure.*** §2 describes the key ideas behind the TS stack, then in §3 we describe the algorithm in detail. In §4 we describe our proof technique, while in §5 we use it to establish that the TS stack is linearizable. In §6 we discuss our experiments. §7 discusses TS queue and deque variants. §8 surveys the related work. §9 concludes.

Longer proofs and other auxiliary material are included in supplementary appendices, available on the ACM digital library. Appendix A discusses the Isabelle proof of our core stack theorem. Appendix B gives further details about our TS stack linearizability proof. Appendix C gives a proof of correctness for our intermediate TS buffer data-structure.

## 2. Key Ideas

***Algorithm structure.*** The TS stack marks elements with timestamps recording the order they were pushed. Elements are popped according to this timestamp order. Figure 2 shows the stack's internal structure. Each thread $T_1$–$T_n$ which is accessing the stack has an associated single-producer multi-consumer pool, implemented as a linked list (we call these *SP pools*). These are linked from a common array `spPools`. Every element on the stack is stored in the SP pool of the thread that pushed it.

Pushing to the TS stack involves (1) adding a node to the head of the thread's SP pool, (2) generating a new timestamp, and (3) attaching the timestamp to the node. Thus un-timestamped nodes are visible to other threads – we write these in Figure 2 as the maximal value, $\top$. As nodes are only added by one thread to each SP pool, elements in a single pool are totally ordered by timestamp, and no synchronisation is needed when pushing.

Popping from the TS stack involves (1) searching all the SP pools for an element with a maximal timestamp, and (2) attempting to remove it. This process repeats until an element is removed successfully. As each SP pool is ordered, searching only requires reading the head of each pool in turn. Timestamps in different pools may be mutually unordered – for example when two timestamps are equal. Thus more than one element may be maximal, and in this case, either can be chosen. To remove a node, the thread writes to a flag in the node marking it as taken. Multiple threads may try to remove the same node, so an atomic compare-and-swap (CAS) instruction ensures at most one thread succeeds.

Accessing the heads of multiple per-thread pools imposes a cost through cache contention. However, our experiments show that this can be less expensive than contention on a single location with an opportunistic compare-and-swap approach. In our experiments, we mitigate contention and thereby improve performance by introducing a small `NOP` delay to the pop search loop. However, even without this optimisation, the TS stack outperforms the EB stack by a factor of two.

We have experimented with various implementations for timestamping itself. Most straightforwardly, we can use a strongly-synchronised fetch-and-increment counter. We can avoid unnecessary increments by using a compare-and-swap to detect when the counter has already been incremented. We can avoid strong synchronisation entirely by using a vector of thread-local counters, meaning the counter may stutter (many elements get the same timestamp). We can also use a hardware timestamping operation – for example the `RDTSCP` instruction which is available on all modern x86 hardware. Our benchmarks show that hardware timestamping provides the best push performance. However, the picture is more complicated in the presence of optimisation. See §6 for our experiments.

***Optimisations.*** Timestamping enables several optimisations of the TS stack, most importantly elimination (a standard strategy in the literature), and interval timestamping (a contribution of this paper).

In a stack, a concurrent push and pop can always soundly eliminate each other, irrespective of the state of the stack [9]. Therefore a thread can remove any concurrently inserted element, not just the stack top. Unlike [9], our mechanism for detecting elimination exploits the existence of timestamps. We read the current time at the start of a pop; any element with a later timestamp has been pushed during the current pop, and can be eliminated.

Surprisingly, it is not optimal to insert elements as quickly as possible. The reason is that removal is quicker when there are many unordered maximal elements, reducing contention and avoiding failed CASes. To exploit this, we define timestamps as *intervals*, represented by a pair of start and end times. Overlapping interval timestamps are considered unordered, and thus there can be *many* top elements in the stack. To implement this, the algorithm includes a delay for a predetermined interval after generating a start timestamp, then generates an end timestamp.

Pausing allows us to trade off the performance of push and pop: an increasing delay in insertion can reduce the number of retries in pop (for evidence see §6.2). Though pausing may appear as an unnecessary overhead to a push, our experiments show that optimal delay times (4 µs - 8 µs) are actually shorter than e.g. an atomic fetch-and-inc on a contended memory location. By weakening the order of stored elements, interval timestamping can substantially increase overall throughput and decrease the latency of pops.

Similarly, although interval timestamping increases the non-determinism of removal (i.e. the variance in the order in which pushed elements are popped), this need not translate into greater overall non-determinism compared to other high-performance stacks. A major source of non-determinism in existing concurrent data-structures is in fact contention [7]. While interval timestamping increases the potential for non-determinism in one respect, it decreases it in another.

***Performance vs. Elimination-Backoff stack.*** To the best of our knowledge the Elimination-Backoff (EB) stack [9] is the fastest stack previously proposed. In our experiments (§6.1) the TS stack configured with elimination and interval timestamping outperforms the EB stack by a factor of two. Several design decisions contribute to this success. The lack of insert-contention and mitigation of contention in the remove makes our stack fast even without elimination. Also, timestamping allows us to integrate elimination into normal stack code, rather than in separate back-off code.

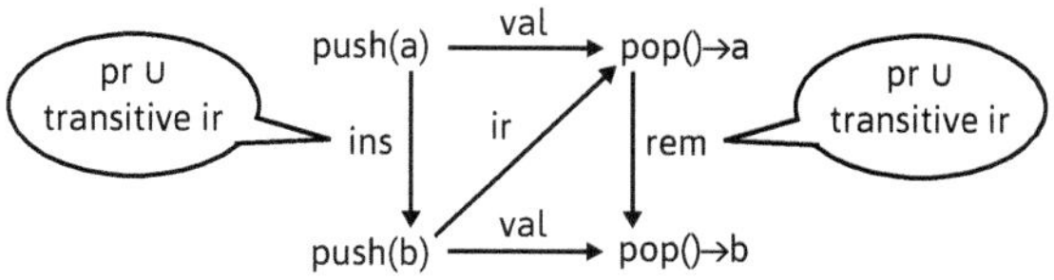


Figure 3: Non-LIFO behaviour forbidden by stack theorem.

***Algorithm correctness.*** Intuitively, the TS stack is correct because any two push operations that run sequentially receive ordered timestamps, and are therefore removed in LIFO order. Elements arising from concurrent push operations may recieve unordered timestamps, and may be removed in either order, but this does not affect correctness.

To formally prove that a stack is correct, i.e. linearizable with respect to stack semantics, we need to show that for any execution there exists a total linearization order. However, proving this directly is challenging, because the order between parallel push operations can be fixed by the order on later pop operations, while the order between parallel pop operations can likewise be fixed by earlier pushes.

Instead, we use a new *stack theorem* which removes the need to find a total linearization order. Intuitively, our theorem requires that if two elements are on the stack, then the younger element is popped first (i.e. LIFO ordering).

It is important that all operations take a consistent view on which elements are on the stack. To express this, our stack theorem require a relation which states whether a push takes logical effect before or after a pop. We call this ir, for 'insert-remove'. The ir relation is the crux of the linearization order: surprisingly, our theorem shows that it is the only part that matters. Thus, the stack theorem relieves us of the need to resolve problematic ordering between parallel push or parallel pop operations.

The stack theorem also uses two other relations: *precedence*, pr, which relates methods that run in sequence; and *value*, val, which relates a push to the pop removing the associated value. Loosely, the theorem has the following form:

> *If for every execution there exist* ir, pr, val *relations that are order-correct, then the algorithm is linearizable with respect to sequential stack semantics.*[1]

Order-correctness rules out non-LIFO behaviour. Intuitively, the situation shown in Figure 3 is forbidden: if push($a$) and push($b$) are ordered, and push($b$) is related to pop()$\to a$ in ir, then the two pops cannot also be ordered pop()$\to a$ before pop()$\to b$ – this would violate LIFO ordering.

As pr and val can easily be extracted from an execution, establishing linearizability amounts to showing the existence of a consistent ir. This is analogous to finding the linearization order, but ir can be constructed much more easily for the TS stack. We use a modified version of the linearization point method, but rather than a single order, we identify two and combine them to build ir.

- vis (for 'visibility'). A push($a$) and pop are ordered by vis if the value $a$ inserted by push was in a SP pool when the pop started, and so could have been visible to it.

[1] Additionally, the full theorem requires the algorithm is linearizable with respect to sequential set semantics. This guarantees non-LIFO properties such as absence of duplication.

- rr (for 'remove-remove'). Two operations pop()→$a$ and pop()→$b$ are ordered in rr if elements $a$ and $b$ are removed in order from the underlying SP pools.

Building ir is more than just merging these two relations because they may contradict one another. Instead, ir is built by taking vis as a core, and using rr to correct cases that contradict LIFO order. Our proof of correctness (§5) shows that this is always possible, which establishes that the TS stack is linearizable.

## 3. The TS Stack in Detail

We now present our TS stack algorithm in detail. Listing 1 shows the TS stack code. This code manages the collection of thread-specific SP pools linked from the array **spPools**. We factor the SP pool out as a separate data-structure supporting the following operations:

- **insert** – insert an element without attaching a timestamp, and return a reference to the new node.
- **getYoungest** – return a reference to the node in the pool with the youngest timestamp, together with the **top** pointer of the pool.
- **remove** – tries to remove the given node from the pool. Return **true** and the element of the node or **false** and **NULL** depending whether it succeeds.

We describe our implementation of the SP pool in §3.1. Listing 1 also assumes the timestamping function **newTimestamp** – various implementations are discussed in §3.2.

We can now describe Listing 1. To push an element, the TS stack inserts an un-timestamped element into the current thread's pool (line 13), generates a fresh timestamp (line 14), and sets the new element's timestamp (line 15).

A pop iteratively scans over all SP pools (line 35-54) and searches for the node with the youngest timestamp in all SP pools (line 48-53). The binary operator $<_{TS}$ is timestamp comparison. This is just integer comparison for non-interval timestamps – see §3.2. If removing the identified node succeeds (line 63) then its element is returned (line 26). Otherwise the iteration restarts.

For simplicity, in Listing 1 threads are associated statically with slots in the array **spPools**. To support a dynamic number of threads, this array can be replaced by a linked list for iteration in pop, and by a hashtable or thread-local storage for fast access in push.

***Elimination and emptiness checking.*** Code in gray in Listing 1 handles elimination and emptiness checking.

Elimination [9] is an essential optimisation in making our stack efficient. It is permitted whenever a push and pop execute concurrently. To detect opportunities for elimination, a pop reads the current time when it starts (line 20). When searching through the SP pools, any element with a later timestamp must have been pushed during the current pop, and can be eliminated immediately (lines 46-47).

To check whether the stack is empty, we reuse an approach from [8]. When scanning the SP pools, if a pool indicates that it is empty, then its **top** pointer is recorded (lines 40-43). If no candidate for removal is found then the SP pools are scanned again to check whether their **top** pointers have changed (lines 56-60). If not, the pools must have been empty between the first and second scan. The linearizability of this emptiness check has been proved in [8].

Listing 1: TS stack algorithm. The SP pool is defined in Listing 2 and described in §3.1, timestamps are discussed in §3.2. The gray highlighted code deals with the emptiness check and elimination.

```
1  TSStack{
2   Node{
3     Element element,
4     Timestamp timestamp,
5     Node next,
6     Bool taken
7   };
8
9   SPPool[maxThreads] spPools;
10
11  void push(Element element){
12    SPPool pool=spPools[threadID];
13    Node node=pool.insert(element);
14    Timestamp timestamp=newTimestamp();
15    node.timestamp=timestamp;
16  }
17
18  Element pop(){
19    // Elimination
20    Timestamp startTime=newTimestamp();
21    Bool success;
22    Element element;
23    do{
24      <success,element>=tryRem(startTime);
25    } while (!success);
26    return element;
27  }
28
29  <Bool,Element> tryRem(Timestamp startTime){
30    Node youngest=NULL;
31    Timestamp timestamp=-1;
32    SPPool pool;
33    Node top;
34    Node[maxThreads] empty;
35    for each(SPPool current in spPools){
36      Node node;
37      Node poolTop;
38      <node,poolTop>=current.getYoungest();
39      // Emptiness check
40      if(node==NULL){
41        empty[current.ID]=poolTop;
42        continue;
43      }
44      Timestamp nodeTimestamp=node.timestamp;
45      // Elimination
46      if(startTime <TS nodeTimestamp)
47        return current.remove(poolTop,node);
48      if(timestamp <TS nodeTimestamp){
49        youngest=node;
50        timestamp=nodeTimestamp;
51        pool=current;
52        top=poolTop;
53      }
54    }
55    // Emptiness check
56    if(youngest==NULL){
57      for each(SPPool current in spPools){
58        if(current.top!=empty[current.ID])
59          return <false,NULL>;
60      }
61      return <true,EMPTY>;
62    }
63    return pool.remove(top,youngest);
64  }
65 }
```

Listing 2: SP pool algorithm. The gray highlighted code deals with the unlinking of taken nodes.

```
66 SPPool{
67  Node top;
68  Int ID; // The ID of the owner thread.
69
70  init(){
71    Node sentinel=
72      createNode(element=NULL,taken=true);
73    sentinel.next=sentinel;
74    top=sentinel;
75  }
76
77  Node insert(Element element){
78    Node newNode=
79      createNode(element=element,taken=false);
80    newNode.next=top;
81    top=newNode;
82    Node next=newNode.next; // Unlinking
83    while(next->next!=next && next.taken)
84      next=next->next;
85    newNode.next=next;
86    return newNode;
87  }
88
89  <Node,Node> getYoungest(){
90    Node oldTop=top;
91    Node result=oldTop;
92    while(true){
93      if(!result.taken)
94        return <result,oldTop>;
95      else if (result.next==result)
96        return <NULL,oldTop>;
97      result=result.next;
98    }
99  }
100
101 <Bool,Element> remove(Node oldTop, Node node){
102   if(CAS(node.taken,false,true)){
103     CAS(top,oldTop,node); // Unlinking
104     // Unlink nodes before node in the list.
105     if(oldTop!=node)
106       oldTop.next=node;
107     // Unlink nodes after node in the list.
108     Node next=node.next;
109     while(next->next!=next && next.taken)
110       next=next->next;
111     node.next=next;
112     return <true,node.element>;
113   }
114   return <false,NULL>;
115 }
116 }
```

### 3.1 SP Pool

The SP pool (Listing 2) is a singly linked list of nodes accessed by a **top** pointer. A node consists of a **next** pointer for the linked list, the **element** it stores, the **timestamp** assigned to the element, and a **taken** flag. The singly linked list is closed at its end by a sentinel node pointing to itself (line 73). Initially the list contains only the sentinel node. The **taken** flag of the sentinel is set to **true** indicating that the sentinel does not contain an element. The **top** pointer is annotated with an ABA-counter to avoid the ABA-problem [13].

Elements are inserted into the SP pool by adding a new node (line 78) at the head of the linked list (line 80-81). To remove an element the **taken** flag of its node is set atomically with a **CAS** instruction (line 102). **getYoungest** iterates over the list (line 90-98) and returns the first node which is not marked as taken (line 94). If no such node is found, **getYoungest** returns **<NULL,oldTop>** (line 96).

***Unlinking taken nodes.*** Nodes marked as **taken** are considered removed from the SP pool and are therefore ignored by **getYoungest** and **remove**. However, to reclaim memory and to reduce the overhead of iterating over **taken** nodes, nodes marked as **taken** are eventually unlinked either in **insert** (line 82-85) or in **remove** (line 103-111).

To unlink we redirect the **next** pointer from a node $a$ to a node $b$ previously connected by a sequence of **taken** nodes (line 85, line 106, and line 111). In **insert** the nodes between the new node and the next un-**taken** node are unlinked, and in **remove** the nodes between the old top node and the removed node, and between the removed node and the next un-**taken** node are unlinked. Additionally **remove** tries to unlink all nodes between **top** and the removed node (line 103). By using **CAS**, we guarantee that no new node has been inserted between the **top** and the removed node.

### 3.2 Timestamping Algorithms

***TS-atomic:*** This algorithm takes a timestamp from a global counter using an atomic fetch-and-increment instruction. Such instructions are available on most modern processors – for example the **LOCK XADD** instruction on x86.

***TS-hardware:*** This algorithm uses the x86 **RDTSCP** instruction [16] to read the current value of the TSC register. The TSC register counts the number of processor cycles since the last reset.

TSC was not originally intended for timestamping, so an obvious concern is that it might not be synchronised across cores. In this case, relaxed-memory effects could lead to stack-order violations. We believe this is not a problem for modern CPUs. Ruan et al. [20] have tested **RDTSCP** on various x86 systems as part of their transactional memory system. Our understanding of [20] and the Intel x86 architecture guide [16] is that **RDTSCP** should provide sufficient synchronisation on recent multi-core and multi-socket machines. We have also observed no violations of stack semantics in our experiments across different machines. Aside from **RDTSCP**, we use C11 sequentially consistent atomics throughout, forbidding all other relaxed behaviours.

However, we have anecdotal reports that **RDTSCP** is not synchronised on older x86 systems. Furthermore, memory order guarantees offered by multi-processors are often underspecified and inaccurately documented – see e.g. Sewell et. al.'s work on a formalized x86 model [21] (which does not cover **RDTSCP**). Implementors should test **RDTSCP** thoroughly before using it to generate timestamps on substantially different hardware. We hope the TS stack will motivate further research into TSC, **RDTSCP**, and hardware timestamp generation more generally.

***TS-stutter:*** This algorithm uses thread-local counters which are synchronized by Lamport's algorithm [17]. To generate a new timestamp a thread first reads the values of all thread-local counters. It then takes the maximum value, increments it by one, stores it in its thread-local counter, and returns the stored value as the new timestamp. Note that the TS-stutter algorithm does not require strong synchronization. TS-stutter timestamping may return the same timestamp multiple times, but only if these timestamps were generated concurrently.

Listing 3: TS-CAS algorithm. The gray highlighted code is an optimisation to avoid unnecessary **CAS**.

```
117 TS_cas{
118  int counter=1;
119
120  Timestamp newTimestamp(){
121    int timestamp=counter;
122    pause(); // delay optimisation.
123    int timestamp2=counter;
124    if(timestamp != timestamp2)
125      return [timestamp,timestamp2-1];
126    if(CAS(counter,timestamp,timestamp+1))
127      return [timestamp,timestamp];
128    return [timestamp,counter-1];
129  }
130 }
```

***TS-interval:*** This algorithm does not return one timestamp value, but rather an interval consisting of a pair of timestamps generated by one of the algorithms above. Let $[a, b]$ and $[c, d]$ be two such interval timestamps. They are ordered $[a, b] <_{\mathsf{TS}} [c, d]$ if and only if $b < c$. That is, if the two intervals overlap, the timestamps are unordered. The TS-interval algorithm is correct because for any two interval timestamps $[a, b]$ and $[c, d]$, if these intervals are generated sequentially, then $b$ is generated before $c$ and therefore $b < c$, as discussed above.

In our experiments we use the TS-hardware algorithm (i.e. the x86 **RDTSCP** instruction) to generate the start and end of the interval, because it is faster than TS-atomic and TS-stutter. Adding a delay between the generation of the two timestamps increases the size of the interval, allowing more timestamps to overlap and thereby reducing contention during element removal. The effect of adding a delay on overall performance is analyzed in Section 6.2.

***TS-CAS:*** This algorithm is an optimisation of TS-atomic combined with interval timestamps. It exploits the insight that the shared counter needs only be incremented by *some* thread, not necessarily the current thread. In a highly concurrent situation, many threads using TS-atomic will increment the counter unnecessarily. The TS-CAS algorithm instead uses CAS failure to detect when the counter has been incremented. CAS failure without retrying is comparatively inexpensive, so this scheme is fast despite using strong synchronisation.

Source-code for TS-CAS is given in Listing 3. The algorithm begins by reading the counter value (line 121). If the CAS in line 126 succeeds, then the timestamp takes the counter's original value as its start and end (line 127). If the CAS fails, then another concurrent call must have incremented the counter, and TS-CAS does not have to. Instead it returns an interval starting at the original counter value and ending at the new value minus one (line 128). This interval will overlap with concurrent calls to **newTimestamp**, but will not overlap with any intervals created later.

Similar to TS-interval, adding a small delay between reading the counter value and attempting the CAS can improve performance. Here this not only increases the number of overlapping intervals, but also reduces contention on the global counter. Contention is reduced further by line 123-125, a standard CAS optimisation. If the value of **counter** changed during the delay, then the CAS in line 126 is guaranteed to fail. Instead of executing the CAS we can immediately return an interval timestamp. Our experiments show that in high-contention scenarios the performance of TS-CAS with a delay is up to 3x faster than without a delay.

## 4. Correctness Theorem for Stacks

Linearizability [14] is the *de facto* standard correctness condition for concurrent algorithms.[2] It ensures that every behaviour observed by an algorithm's calling context could also have been produced by a sequential (i.e. atomic) version of the same algorithm. We call the ideal sequential version of the algorithm the *specification*, e.g. below we define a sequential stack specification.

Interactions between the algorithm and calling context in a given execution are expressed as a *history*. Note that our formulation is specialised to pool-like data-structures, because the val relation embeds the connection between an operation which inserts a value, and the operation that receives it (e.g. a push and corresponding pop).

**Definition 1.** *A* history $\mathcal{H}$ *is a tuple* $\langle \mathcal{A}, \mathsf{pr}, \mathsf{val} \rangle$ *where* $\mathcal{A}$ *is a finite set of operations (for example, push(5)), and* $\mathsf{pr}, \mathsf{val} \subseteq \mathcal{A} \times \mathcal{A}$ *are the* precedence *and* value *relations, respectively. A history is* sequential *if* $\mathsf{pr}$ *is a total order.*

A history is extracted from a *trace*, $\mathcal{T}$, the interleaved sequence of events that took place during an execution of the algorithm. To extract the history, we first generate the set $\mathcal{A}$ of executed operations in the trace (as is standard in linearizability, assume that all calls have corresponding returns). A pair $(x, y)$ is in $\mathsf{pr}$ if the return event of operation $x$ is ordered before the call event of $y$ in $\mathcal{T}$. A pair $(x, y)$ is in $\mathsf{val}$ if $x$ is an insert, $y$ a remove, and the value inserted by $x$ was removed by $y$. Note that we assume that values are unique.

Linearizability requires that algorithms only interact with their calling context through call and return events. Therefore, a history captures all interactions between algorithm and context. We thus define a data-structure specification as just a set of histories (e.g. STACK is the set of histories produced by an ideal sequential stack). Linearizability is defined by relating implementation and specification histories.

**Definition 2.** *A history* $\langle \mathcal{A}, \mathsf{pr}, \mathsf{val} \rangle$ *is* linearizable *with respect to some specification* $\mathcal{S}$ *if there exists a* linearization order $\mathsf{pr}^T$ *such that* $\mathsf{pr} \subseteq \mathsf{pr}^T$, *and* $\langle \mathcal{A}, \mathsf{pr}^T, \mathsf{val} \rangle \in \mathcal{S}$.

*An implementation $C$ is linearizable with respect to $\mathcal{S}$ if any history $\mathcal{H}$ arising from the algorithm is linearizable with respect to $\mathcal{S}$.*

***The problem with linearization points.*** Proving that a concurrent algorithm is linearizable with respect to a sequential specification amounts to showing that, for every possible execution, there exists a total linearization order. The standard strategy is a simulation-style proof where the implementation and specification histories are constructed in lock-step. The points where the specification 'takes effect' are known as *linearization points* – to simplify the proof,

[2] Our formulation of linearizability differs from the classic one [14]. Rather than have a history record the total order on calls and returns, we convert this information into a strict partial order $\mathsf{pr}$. Likewise, linearizability between histories is defined by inclusion on orders, rather than by reordering call and return events. This approach, taken from [4], is convenient for us because our stack theorem is defined by constraints on orders. However, the two formulations are equivalent.

these are often associated with points in the implementation's syntax. Conceptually, when a linearization point is reached, the method is appended to the linearization order.

It has long been understood that linearization points are a limited approach. Simulation arguments work poorly for many non-blocking algorithms because the specification history is not precisely determined by the implementation. Algorithms may have linearization points dictated by complex interactions between methods, or by non-deterministic future behaviour. The TS stack is a particularly acute example of this problem. Two push methods that run concurrently may insert elements with unordered timestamps, giving no information to choose a linearization order. However, if the elements are later popped sequentially, an order is imposed on the earlier pushes. Worse, ordering two pushes can implicitly order other methods, leading to a cascade of linearizations back in time.

Consider the following history. Horizontal lines represent execution time, ↓ represents calls, and ↑ returns.

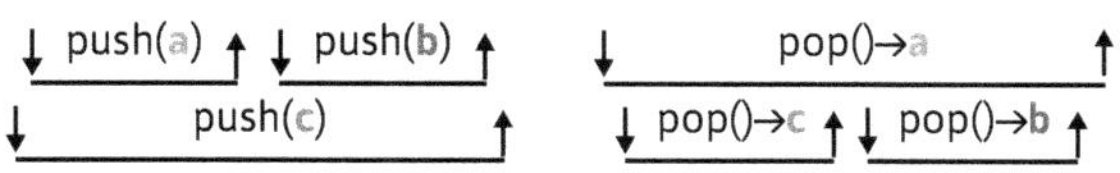


This history induces the precedence order pr represented by solid lines in the following graph.

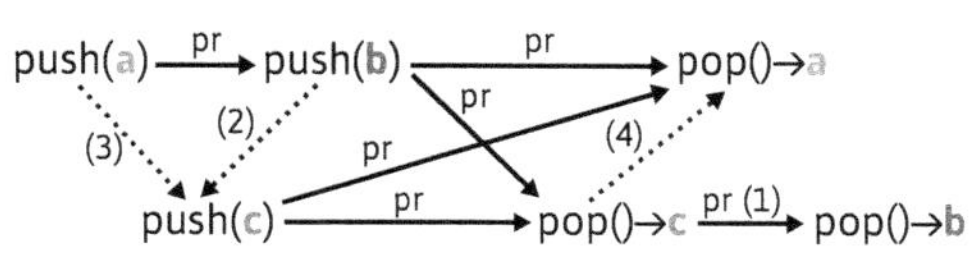


First consider the history immediately before the return of pop()→$c$ (i.e. without order (1) in the graph). As push($b$) and push($c$) run concurrently, elements $b$ and $c$ may have unordered timestamps. At this point, there are several consistent ways that the history might linearize, even given access to the TS stack's internal state.

Now consider the history after pop()→$b$. Dotted edges represent linearization orders forced by this operation. As $c$ is popped before $b$, LIFO order requires that push($b$) has to be linearized before push($c$) – order (2). Transitivity then implies that push($a$) has to be ordered before push($c$) – order (3). Furthermore, ordering push($a$) before push($c$) requires that pop()→$c$ is ordered before pop()→$a$ – order (4). Thus a method's linearization order may be fixed long after it returns, frustrating any attempt to identify linearization points.

***Specification-specific conditions (AKA aspects).*** For a given sequential specification, it may not be necessary to find the entire linearization order to show that an algorithm is linearizable. A degenerate example is the specification which contains all possible sequential histories; in this case, we need not find a linearization order, because any order consistent with pr will do. One alternative to linearization points is thus to invent special-purpose conditions for particular sequential specifications.

Henzinger et al. [12] have just such a set of conditions for queues. They call this approach *aspect-oriented.* One attractive property of their approach is that their queue conditions are mostly expressed using precedence order, pr. In other words, most features of queue behaviour can be checked without locating linearization points at all. (The exception is emptiness checking, which also requires special treatment in our approach – see below.)

***Stack and set specifications.*** Our theorem makes use of two sequential specifications: STACK, and a weaker specification SET that does not respect LIFO order. We define the set of permitted histories by defining updates over abstract states. Assume a set of values Val. Abstract states are finite sequences in $\mathsf{Val}^*$. Let $\sigma \in \mathsf{Val}^*$ be an arbitrary state. In STACK, push and pop have the following sequential behaviour ('$\cdot$' means sequence concatenation):

- push(v) – Update the abstract state to $\sigma \cdot [\mathrm{v}]$.
- pop() – If $\sigma = []$, return EMPTY. Otherwise, $\sigma$ must be of the form $\sigma' \cdot [v']$. Update the state to $\sigma'$, return $v'$.

In SET, push is the same, but pop behaves as follows:

- pop() – If $\sigma = []$, return EMPTY. Otherwise, $\sigma$ must be of the form $\sigma' \cdot [v'] \cdot \sigma''$. Update the state to $\sigma' \cdot \sigma''$, return $v'$.

### 4.1 The Stack Theorem

We have developed stack conditions sufficient to ensure linearizability with respect to STACK. Unlike [12], our conditions are not expressed using only pr (indeed, we believe this would be impossible – see §4.2). Rather we require an auxiliary insert-remove relation ir which relates pushes to pops and vice versa, but that does not relate pairs of pushes or pairs of pops. In other words, our theorem shows that for stacks it is sufficient to identify just *part* of the linearization order.

We begin by defining the helper orders ins and rem over push operations and pop operations, respectively. Informally, ins and rem are fragments of the linearization order that are imposed by the combination of ir and the precedence order pr. In all the definitions in this section, assume that $\mathcal{H} = \langle \mathcal{A}, \mathsf{pr}, \mathsf{val} \rangle$ is a history. Below we write $+a, +b, +c$ etc. for push operations, and $-a, -b, -c$ etc. for pop operations.

**Definition 3** (derived orders ins and rem)**.** *Assume an insert-remove relation* ir*.*

- *For all* $+a, +b \in \mathcal{A}$, $+a \xrightarrow{\mathsf{ins}} +b$ *if either* $+a \xrightarrow{\mathsf{pr}} +b$ *or there exists an operation* $-c \in \mathcal{A}$ *with* $+a \xrightarrow{\mathsf{pr}} -c \xrightarrow{\mathsf{ir}} +b$.
- *For all* $-a, -b \in \mathcal{A}$, $-a \xrightarrow{\mathsf{rem}} -b$ *if either* $-a \xrightarrow{\mathsf{pr}} -b$ *or there exists an operation* $+c \in \mathcal{A}$ *with* $-a \xrightarrow{\mathsf{ir}} +c \xrightarrow{\mathsf{ir}} -b$.

The order ins expresses ordering between pushes imposed either by precedence, or transitively by insert-remove. Likewise rem expresses ordering between pops. Using ins and rem, we can define order-correctness, which expresses the conditions necessary to achieve LIFO ordering in a stack.

In our formulation ins is weaker than rem – note the pr rather than ir in the final clause. However, our stack theorem also holds if the definitions are inverted, with rem weaker than ins. The version above is more convenient in verifying the TS stack.

**Definition 4** (alternating)**.** *We call a relation $r$ on $\mathcal{A}$* alternating *if every pair $+a, -b \in \mathcal{A}$ consisting of one push and one non-empty pop is ordered, and no other pairs are ordered.*

**Definition 5** (order-correct)**.** *We call $\mathcal{H}$* order-correct *if there exists an alternating relation* ir *on $\mathcal{A}$, and derived orders* ins *and* rem*, such that:*

1. $\mathsf{ir} \cup \mathsf{pr}$ *is cycle-free; and*
2. *Let* $+a, -a, +b \in \mathcal{A}$ *with* $+a \xrightarrow{\mathsf{val}} -a$ *and* $+a \xrightarrow{\mathsf{pr}} -a$. *If* $+a \xrightarrow{\mathsf{ins}} +b \xrightarrow{\mathsf{ir}} -a$, *then there exists* $-b \in \mathcal{A}$ *with* $+b \xrightarrow{\mathsf{val}} -b$ *and* $-a \not\xrightarrow{\mathsf{rem}} -b$;

Condition (2) is at the heart of our proof approach. It forbids the non-LIFO behaviour illustrated in Figure 3.

Order-correctness *only* imposes LIFO ordering; it does not guarantee non-LIFO correctness properties. For a stack these are (1) elements should not be lost; (2) elements should not be duplicated; (3) popped elements should come from a corresponding push; and (4) pop should report EMPTY correctly. The last is subtle, as it is a global rather than pairwise property: pop should return EMPTY only at a point in the linearization order where the abstract stack is empty.

Fortunately, these properties are also orthogonal to LIFO ordering: we just require that the algorithm is linearizable with respect to SET (simple to prove for the TS stack). For properties (1)-(3) it is trivial why this is sufficient. For emptiness checking, any history satisfying SET can be split into sub-histories free of pop-empty. As a pop-empty can only occur when no elements are in the data-structure, any such partitioning is also valid in STACK. Thus, the correctness of emptiness checking can be established separately from LIFO ordering.

**Theorem 1** (stack correctness). *Let C be a concurrent algorithm. If every history arising from C is order-correct, and C is linearizable with respect to* SET, *then C is linearizable with respect to* STACK.

*Proof.* Here we only sketch five stages of the proof. For full details see supplementary Appendix A. (1) Order all pop operations which do not return empty and which are ordered with their matching push operation in the precedence order. (2) Adjust the ir relation to deal with the definition of ins discussed above. Again we ignore all push-pop pairs with overlapping execution times. (3) Order all push operations which remain unordered after the first two stages and show that the resulting order is within STACK. (4) Show that push-pop pairs with overlapping execution times can always be added to a correct linearization order without violating STACK. (5) Show that also pop operations which return EMPTY can always be added to a correct linearization order as long as they are correct with respect to SET. □

For the TS stack, the advantage of Theorem 1 is that problematic orderings need not be resolved. In the example discussed above, push(a) and push(c) can be left unordered in ir, removing the need to decide their eventual linearization order; likewise pop()→$a$ and pop()→$c$. As we show in the next section, the ir relation *can* be extracted from the TS stack using an adapted version of the linearization point method.

Our stack theorem is generic, not tied to the TS stack. It characterises the internal ordering sufficient for an algorithm to achieve stack semantics. As well as sound, it is complete – for any linearizable stack, ir can be trivially projected from the linearization order. For CAS-based stacks such as Treiber's famous non-blocking stack [22] it is simple to see intuitively why the theorem applies. If two pushes are ordered, then their CASes are ordered. As a result their elements will be ordered in the stack representation and removed in order.

Intuitively, our theorem seems close to the lower bound for stack ordering. The next section (§4.2) provides evidence for this by ruling out the class of weaker formulations without ir. Intuitively, we would expect any concurrent stack to enforce orders as strong as the ones in our theorem. Thus, Theorem 1 points towards fundamental constraints on the structure of concurrent stacks.

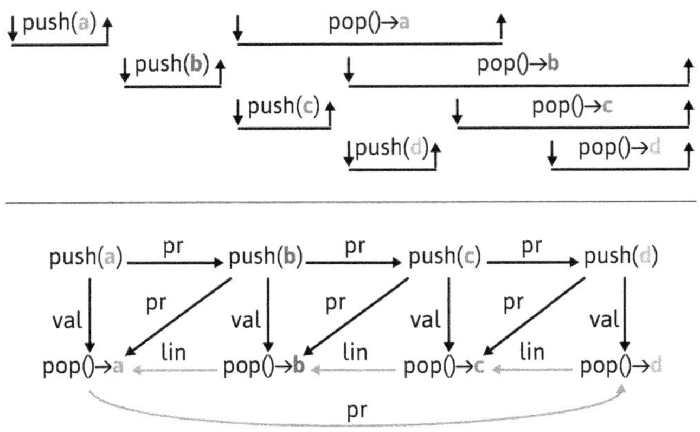


Figure 4: Top: example non-linearizable execution exhibiting non-local behaviour. Bottom: corresponding graph projecting out pr, val, and lin relations.

***Mechanisation.*** We have mechanised Theorem 1 in the Isabelle theorem prover. The source files for this proof are provided in supplementary file `stackthm.tgz`. Supplementary Appendix A discusses the structure of our mechanisation alongside with an informal proof of the theorem.

### 4.2 Why the Insert-Remove Relation is Necessary

Theorem 1 builds on a similar theorem for queues proved by Henzinger et al. [12]. As in our definition of order-correctness (Definition 5), their theorem forbids certain bad orderings between operations. However, their conditions are defined purely in terms of precedence, pr, and value, val – they do not require the auxiliary insert-remove relation ir.

We believe that any stack theorem similar in structure to ours must require some additional information like ir (and as a corollary, that checking linearizability for stacks is fundamentally harder than for queues). By 'similar', we mean a local theorem defined by forbidding a finite number of finite-size bad orderings. It is this locality that makes our theorem and Henzinger's so appealing. It reduces data-structure correctness from global ordering to ruling out a number of specific bad cases.

Our key evidence that the insert-remove relation is needed is the execution shown in Figure 4 (top). This execution as a whole is not linearizable – this can be seen more clearly in corresponding graph in Figure 4 (bottom), which projects out the pr and val relations. Here lin is the linearization order forced by LIFO ordering. The pr ∪ lin edges form a cycle, contradicting the requirement that linearization order is acyclic and includes pr.

However, if for any $i \in \{a, b, c, d\}$ the corresponding push($i$)–pop($i$) pair is deleted, the execution becomes linearizable. Intuitively, doing this breaks the cycle in lin ∪ pr that appears above. Thus, any condition based on precedence that is smaller than this whole execution cannot forbid it – otherwise it would forbid legitimate executions. Worse, we can make arbitrarily large bad executions of this form. Thus no theorem based on finite-size condition can define linearizability for stacks. Our insert-remove relation introduces just enough extra structure to let us define a local stack theorem.

This kind of execution is not a problem for queues because ordering an insert-remove pair cannot constrain the insert-insert or remove-remove order of any other pair.

## 5. Proving the TS Stack Correct

We now prove the TS Stack correct. We use a two-level argument to separate concerns in the proof. By verifying a lower-level structure first, we hide the complexities of the data-structure from the higher-level proof.

1. Prove the linearizability of an intermediate structure called the *TS buffer*. This shows that the SP pools combine to form a single consistent pool, but does not enforce LIFO ordering.
2. Use our stack theorem (Theorem 1) to prove the TS stack is linearizable with respect to LIFO stack semantics. Linearizability lets us use the lower-level TS buffer in terms of its sequential specification.

### 5.1 TS Buffer Linearizability

The TS buffer is a 'virtual' intermediate data-structure, i.e. a proof convenience that does not exist in the algorithm syntax. (It would be easy to add, but would make our code more complex). The TS buffer methods are the lines in push and pop which modify the `spPools` array and thread-specific pools. Proving the TS buffer linearizable means these lines can be treated as atomic. We name the TS buffer operations as follows – line numbers refer to Listing 1. Note that where possible these names coincide with names in Listing 1.

- `ins` – inserts an element into an SP pool (line 13).
- `newTimestamp` – generates a new timestamp (line 14).
- `setTimestamp` – assign a timestamp to a SP pool element (line 15).
- `getStart` – record the current time at the beginning of a pop (line 20).
- `tryRem` – search through the SP pools and try to remove the element with the youngest timestamp (line 24).

Note that `newTimestamp` and `getStart` have the same underlying implementation, but different abstract specifications. This is because they play different roles in the TS stack: respectively, generating timestamps for elements, and controlling elmination.

The abstract state of the TS buffer hides individual SP pools by merging all the elements into a single pool. As elements may be eliminated depending on when the method started, the abstract state also records snapshots representing particular points in the buffer's history.

As with STACK and SET, we define the sequential specification TSBUF by tracking updates to abstract states. Formally, we assume a set of *buffer identifiers*, ID, representing individual buffer elements; and a set of *timestamps*, TS, with strict partial order $<_{\mathsf{TS}}$ and top element $\top$. A TSBUF abstract state is a tuple $(B, S)$. $B \in \mathsf{Buf}$ is a partial map from identifiers to value-timestamp tuples, representing the current values stored in the buffer. $S \in \mathsf{Snapshots}$ is a partial map from timestamps to Buf, representing snapshots of the buffer at particular timestamps.

$$\mathsf{Buf}: \mathsf{ID} \rightharpoonup (\mathsf{Val} \times \mathsf{TS}) \qquad \mathsf{Snapshots}: \mathsf{TS} \rightharpoonup \mathsf{Buf}$$

We implicitly assume that all timestamps in the buffer were previously generated by `newTimestamp`.

Snapshots are used to support globally consistent removal. To remove from the buffer, pop first calls `getStart` to generate a timestamp `t` – abstractly, $[\mathtt{t} \mapsto B]$ is added to the library of snapshots. When pop calls `tryRem(t)`, elements that were present when `t` was generated may be removed normally, while elements added or timestamped more recently than `t` may be eliminated out of order. The stored snapshot $S(\mathtt{t})$ determines which element should be removed or eliminated.

The TS buffer functions have the following specifications, assuming $(B, S)$ is the abstract state before the operation:

- `newTimestamp()` – pick a timestamp $t \neq \top$ such that for all $t' \neq \top$ already in $B$, $t' <_{\mathsf{TS}} t$. Return $t$.

  Note that this means many elements can be issued the same timestamp if the thread is preempted before writing it into the buffer.
- `ins(v)` – Pick an ID $i \notin \mathrm{dom}(B)$. Update the state to $(B[i \mapsto (v, \top)], S)$ and return $i$.
- `setTimestamp(i,t)` – assume that `t` was generated by `newTimestamp()`. If $B(\mathtt{i}) = (v, \top)$, then update the abstract state to $(B[\mathtt{i} \mapsto (v, \mathtt{t})], S)$. If $B(\mathtt{i}) = \bot$, do nothing.
- `getStart()` – pick a timestamp $\mathtt{t} \neq \top$ such that $\mathtt{t} \notin \mathrm{dom}(S)$ or $\mathtt{t} \in \mathrm{dom}(S)$ and $S(\mathtt{t}) = B$. If $\mathtt{t} \notin \mathrm{dom}(S)$, update the state to $(B, S[\mathtt{t} \mapsto B])$. Return `t`.
- `tryRem(t)` – Assume $\mathtt{t} \in \mathrm{dom}(S)$. There are four possible behaviours:
  1. *failure.* Non-deterministically fail and return $\langle \mathsf{false}, \mathsf{null} \rangle$. This corresponds to a failed SP pool `remove` preempted by another thread.
  2. *emptiness check.* If the map is empty (i.e. $\mathrm{dom}(B) = \emptyset$) then return $\langle \mathsf{true}, \mathsf{EMPTY} \rangle$.
  3. *normal removal.* Pick an ID $i$ with $i \in \mathrm{dom}(S(\mathtt{t})) \cap \mathrm{dom}(B)$ and $B(i) \mapsto (v_i, t_i)$ such that $t_i$ is maximal with respect to other unremoved elements from the snapshot, i.e.

     $$\nexists i', t'.\, i' \in (\mathrm{dom}(S(\mathtt{t})) \cap \mathrm{dom}(B)) \wedge B(i') = (\_, t') \wedge t_i <_{\mathsf{TS}} t'$$

     Update the abstract state to $(B[i \mapsto \bot], S)$ and return $\langle \mathsf{true}, v_i \rangle$. Note that there may be many maximal elements that could be returned.
  4. *elimination.* Pick an ID $i$ such that $i \in \mathrm{dom}(B)$, and either $i \notin \mathrm{dom}(S(\mathtt{t}))$ and $B(i) \mapsto (v, \_)$; or $S(\mathtt{t})(i) \mapsto (v, \top)$. Update the abstract state to $(B[i \mapsto \bot], S)$ and return $\langle \mathsf{true}, v \rangle$.

     This corresponds to the case where $v$ was inserted or timestamped after pop called `getStart`, and $v$ can therefore be removed using elimination.

**Theorem 2.** *TS buffer operations are linearizable with respect to the specification* TSBUF.

*Proof.* The concrete state of the TS buffer consists of the array `spPools`, where each slot points to a SP pool, i.e. a linked list of nodes. For the abstract state, the mapping Buf is easily built by erasing taken nodes. We build Snapshots by examining the preceding trace. Snapshots are generated from the state of the buffer at any point `getStart` is called.

`ins` and `setTimestamp` are SP pool operations which take effect atomically because they build on atomic operations, i.e. the assignment to `top` in line 81, and to `timestamp` in line 15, respectively.

`newTimestamp` and `getStart` both build on the same timestamping operation. Only concurrent timestamp requests can generate overlapping timestamps. As timestamps have to be generated and then added to the buffer separately, at the call of `newTimestamp` and `getStart` an overlapping timestamp cannot be in the buffer. For `getStart`, the snapshot is correctly constructed automatically as a consequence of the mapping from concrete to abstract state.

The most complex proof is for `tryRem`, where the linearization point is in the call to `remove`. `tryRem` always removes a valid element because any element in the snapshot is guaranteed to be contained in one of the SP pools before `tryRem` starts its search for the youngest element. Any removed element not in the snapshot must have been added since the start of the search, and thus satisfies the elimination case of the specification. Further details are given in supplementary Appendix C. □

### 5.2 TS Stack Linearizability

We now prove that the TS stack is correct. We first define two orders vis and rr on push and pop operations. These orders are extracted from executions using a method analogous to linearization points, except that we generate two, possibly conflicting orders. The points chosen correspond to TS buffer operations. In §5.1 we proved that the TS buffer is linearizable, so we can treat these points as atomic.

- vis ('visibility' – the element inserted by a push was visible to a pop). A push and non-empty pop are ordered in vis if SP pool insertion in the push (line 13) is ordered before recording the current time in the pop (line 20).
- rr ('remove-remove' – two pops removed elements in order). Two non-empty pop operations are ordered in rr if their final successful `tryRem` operations (line 24) are similarly ordered in the execution.

As with ins / rem in the stack theorem, it is useful to define a helper order ts ('timestamp') on push operations. This order is imposed by precedence and vis transitivity. Informally, if two push operations are ordered in ts their elements are ordered in $<_{\mathsf{TS}}$.

**Definition 6** (derived order ts). *Assume a history* $\mathcal{H} = \langle \mathcal{A}, \mathsf{pr}, \mathsf{val} \rangle$ *and order* vis *on* $\mathcal{A}$. *Two operations* $+a, +b \in \mathcal{A}$ *are related* $+a \xrightarrow{\mathsf{ts}} +b$ *if:* $+a \xrightarrow{\mathsf{pr}} +b$*; or* $+a \xrightarrow{\mathsf{pr}} -c \xrightarrow{\mathsf{vis}} +b$ *for some* $-c \in \mathcal{A}$*; or* $+a \xrightarrow{\mathsf{pr}} +d \xrightarrow{\mathsf{vis}} -c \xrightarrow{\mathsf{vis}} -b$ *for some* $-c, +d \in \mathcal{A}$.

To apply Theorem 1 and to show that the TS stack is correct we need to show that any history arising from the TS stack is *order-correct* (Definition 5). The following lemma connects vis, rr and ts to this notion of order-correctness.

**Lemma 3.** *Let* $\mathcal{H} = \langle \mathcal{A}, \mathsf{pr}, \mathsf{val} \rangle$ *be a history. Assume* vis, *an alternating order on* $\mathcal{A}$, *and* rr, *a total order on non-empty pop operations in* $\mathcal{A}$. *Assume the derived order* ts. *If:*

1. $\mathsf{pr} \cup \mathsf{vis}$ *and* $\mathsf{pr} \cup \mathsf{rr}$ *are cycle-free; and*
2. *for all* $+a, -a, +b \in \mathcal{A}$ *such that* $+a \xrightarrow{\mathsf{val}} -a$, $+a \xrightarrow{\mathsf{pr}} -a$, *and* $+a \xrightarrow{\mathsf{ts}} +b \xrightarrow{\mathsf{vis}} -a$, *there exists* $-b \in \mathcal{A}$ *such that* $+b \xrightarrow{\mathsf{val}} -b$ *and* $-b \xrightarrow{\mathsf{rr}} -a$*;*

*then* $\mathcal{H}$ *is order-correct according to Definition 5.*

*Proof.* The proof works by using vis, rr and ts to construct a relation ir witnessing that $\mathcal{H}$ is order-correct. Either vis is such a witness, or vis can be adjusted locally such that it becomes a witness. Adjustment works iteratively by identifying triples of operations which violate order-correctness, then pushing one of the operations earlier or later in the relation to remove the violation. The detail of the proof consists of a case analysis showing that for any execution, such adjustments are always possible and eventually terminate. Further details are given in supplementary Appendix B. □

**Lemma 4.** *TS stack is linearizable with respect to* SET.

*Proof.* Straightforward from the fact that the TS buffer is linearizable with respect to TSBUF. We take the linearization point for push as the call to `ins` and the linearization point for pop as the call to `tryRem`. Correctness follows from the specification of TSBUF. □

**Theorem 5.** *TS stack is linearizable with respect to* STACK.

*Proof.* Follows by applying our stack theorem. Lemma 4 deals with the first clause of Theorem 1. The other clause requires the existence of an ir relation that satisfies order-correctness. It suffices to show that vis, rr, and ts satisfy the preconditions of Lemma 3. The first requirement that $\mathsf{pr} \cup \mathsf{vis}$ and $\mathsf{pr} \cup \mathsf{rr}$ are cycle-free, follows from the fact that the instructions used to define vis and rr are linearization points of the TS buffer. The second requirement for the lemma follows from the fact that ordering in ts implies ordering in $<_{\mathsf{TS}}$, and the fact that the TS stack removes elements in an order that respects $<_{\mathsf{TS}}$. Further details are given in supplementary Appendix B. □

**Theorem 6.** *The TS stack is lock-free.*

*Proof.* Straightforward from the structure of `tryRem`: removal can only fail when another thread succeeds. □

## 6. Performance Analysis

Our experiments compare the performance and scalability of the TS stack with two high-performance concurrent stacks: the Treiber stack [22] because it is the de-facto standard lock-free stack implementation; and the elimination-backoff (EB) stack [9] because it is the fastest concurrent stack we are aware of.[3] We configured the Treiber and EB stacks to perform as well as possible on our test machines: see below for the parameters used.

We ran our experiments on two x86 machines:

- an Intel-based server with four 10-core 2GHz Intel Xeon processors (40 cores, 2 hyperthreads per core), 24MB shared L3-cache, and 128GB of UMA memory running Linux 3.8.0-36; and
- an AMD-based server with four 16-core 2.3GHz AMD Opteron processors (64 cores), 16MB shared L3-cache, and 512GB of cc-NUMA memory running Linux 3.5.0-49.

Measurements were done in the Scal Benchmarking Framework [5]. To avoid measurement artifacts the framework uses a custom memory allocator which performs cyclic allocation [19] in preallocated thread-local buffers for objects smaller than 4096 bytes. Larger objects are allocated with the standard allocator of glibc. All memory is allocated cache-aligned when it is beneficial to avoid cache artifacts.

[3] Of course, other high-performance stacks exist. We decided against benchmarking the DECS stack [3] because (1) no implementation is available for our platform and (2) according to their experiments, in peak performance it is no better than a Flat Combining stack. We decided against benchmarking the Flat Combining stack because the EB stack outperforms it when configured to access the backoff array before the stack itself.

| | 40-core machine | 64-core machine |
|---|---|---|
| *high-contention:* | | |
| TS-interval stack | 7 µs | 6 µs |
| TS-CAS stack | 6 µs | 10.5 µs |
| *low-contention:* | | |
| TS-interval stack | 4.5 µs | 4.5 µs |
| TS-CAS stack | 3 µs | 9 µs |

Table 1: Benchmark delay times for TS-interval / TS-CAS.

The framework is written in C/C++ and compiled with gcc 4.8.1 and -O3 optimizations.

Scal provides implementations of the Treiber stack and of the EB stack. Unlike the description of the EB stack in [9] we access the elimination array *before* the stack – this improves scalability in our experiments. We configured the EB stack such that the performance is optimal in our benchmarks when exercised with 80 threads on the 40-core machine, or with 64 threads on the 64-core machine. These configurations may be suboptimal for lower numbers of threads. Similarly, the TS stack configurations we discuss later are selected to be optimal for 80 and 64 threads on the 40-core and 64-core machine, respectively. On the 40-core machine the elimination array is of size 16 with a delay of 18 µs in the high-contention benchmark, and of size 12 with a delay of 18 µs in the low contention benchmark. On the 64-core machine the elimination array is of size 32 with a delay of 21 µs in the high-contention benchmark, and of size 16 with a delay of 18 µs in the low contention benchmark.

On the 64-core machine the Treiber stack benefits from a backoff strategy which delays the retry of a failed `CAS`. On this machine, we configured the Treiber stack with a constant delay of 300 µs in the high-contention experiments and a constant delay of 200 µs in the low-contention experiments, which is optimal for the benchmark when exercised with 64 threads. On the 40-core machine performance decreases when a backoff delay is added, so we disable it.

We compare the data-structures in producer-consumer microbenchmarks where threads are split between dedicated producers which insert 1,000,000 elements into the data-structure, and dedicated consumers which remove 1,000,000 elements from the data-structure. We measure performance as total execution time of the benchmark. Figures show the total execution time in successful operations per millisecond to make scalability more visible. All numbers are averaged over 5 executions. To avoid measuring empty removal, operations that do not return an element are not counted.

The contention on the data-structure is controlled by a computational load which is calculated between two operations of a thread. In the high-contention scenario the computational load is a $\pi$-calculation in 250 iterations, in the low-contention scenario $\pi$ is calculated in 2000 iterations. On average a computational load of 1000 iterations corresponds to a delay of 2.3 µs on the 40-core machine.

### 6.1 Performance and Scalability Results

Figures 5a and 5b show performance and scalability in a producer-consumer benchmark where half of the threads are producers and half of the threads are consumers. These figures show results for the high-contention scenario. Results for the low-contention scenario are similar, but less pronounced – see Figure 7 in the supplementary material.

For TS-interval timestamping and TS-CAS timestamping we use the optimal delay when exercised with 80 threads on the 40-core machine, and with 64 threads on the 64-core machine, derived from the experiments in Section 6.2. The delay thus depends on the machine and benchmark. The delay times we use in the benchmarks are listed in Table 1. The impact of different delay times on performance is discussed in Section 6.2.

***Comparison between implementations.*** TS-interval is faster than the other timestamping algorithms in the producer-consumer benchmarks with an increasing number of threads. Interestingly the TS-atomic stack is faster than the TS-hardware stack in the high-contention producer-consumer benchmark. The reason is that since the push operations of the TS-hardware stack are so much faster than the push operations of the TS-atomic stack, elimination is possible for more pop operations of the TS-atomic stack (e.g. 41% more elimination on the 64-core machine, see Table 2 in the supplementary appendix), which results in a factor of 3 less retries of `tryRem` operations than in the TS-hardware stack. On the 40-core machine the TS-stutter stack is significantly slower than the TS-atomic stack, while on the 64-core machine the TS-stutter stack is faster. The reason is that on the 40-core machine TS-stutter timestamping is significantly slower than TS-atomic timestamping (see Figure 5c). On the 40-core machine the TS-CAS stack is much faster than the TS-hardware stack, TS-atomic stack, and TS-stutter stack, on the 64-core machine it is slightly faster. The reason is that on the 64-core machine a `CAS` is slower in comparison to other instructions than on the 40-core machine.

***Comparison with other data-structures.*** With more than 16 threads all TS stacks are faster than the Treiber stack. On both machines the TS-interval stack and the TS-CAS stack outperform the EB stack in the high-contention producer-consumer benchmark with a maximum number of threads, on the 64-core machine also the TS-stutter stack and the TS-atomic stack are sightly faster than the EB stack.

We believe TS-interval's and TS-CAS's performance increase with respect to the EB stack comes from three sources: (a) more elimination; (b) faster elimination; (c) higher performance without elimination. As shown in producer-only and consumer-only experiments, the lack of push-contention and mitigation of contention in pop makes our stack fast even without elimination. Additional experiments show that for example the TS-interval stack eliminates 7% and 23% more elements than the EB stack in high-contention scenarios on the 40-core and on the 64-core machine, respectively. Thus we improve on EB in both (a) and (c). (b) is difficult to measure, but we suspect integrating elimination into the normal code path introduces less overhead than an elimination array, and is thus faster.

***Push performance.*** We measure the performance of push operations of all data-structures in a producer-only benchmark where each thread pushes 1,000,000 element into the stack. The TS-interval stack and the TS-CAS stack use the same delay as in the high-contention producer-consumer benchmark, see Table 1:

Figure 5c and Figure 5d show the performance and scalability of the data-structures in the high-contention producer-only benchmark. The push performance of the TS-hardware stack is significantly better than the push of the other stack implementations. With an increasing number of threads the push operation of the TS-interval stack is faster than the

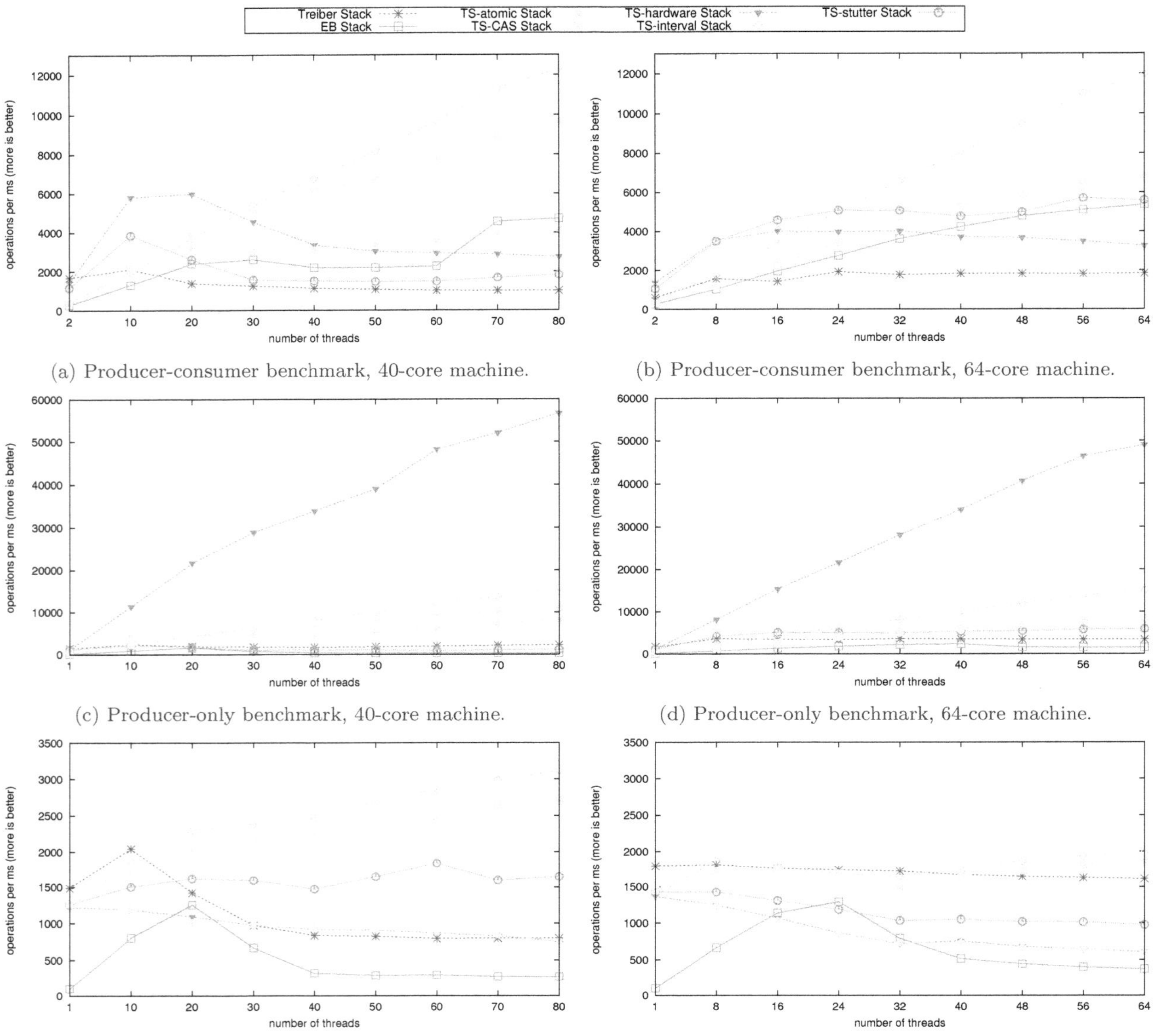


(a) Producer-consumer benchmark, 40-core machine.

(b) Producer-consumer benchmark, 64-core machine.

(c) Producer-only benchmark, 40-core machine.

(d) Producer-only benchmark, 64-core machine.

(e) Consumer-only benchmark, 40-core machine.

(f) Consumer-only benchmark, 64-core machine.

Figure 5: TS stack performance in the high-contention scenario on 40-core machine (left) and 64-core machine (right).

push operations of the TS-atomic stack and the TS-stutter stack, which means that the delay in the TS-interval timestamping is actually shorter than the execution time of the TS-atomic timestamping and the TS-stutter timestamping. Perhaps surprisingly, TS-stutter, which does not require strong synchronisation, is slower than TS-atomic, which is based on an atomic fetch-and-increment instruction.

***Pop performance.*** We measure the performance of pop operations of all data-structures in a consumer-only benchmark where each thread pops 1,000,000 from a pre-filled stack. Note that no elimination is possible in this benchmark. The stack is pre-filled concurrently, which means in case of the TS-interval stack and TS-stutter stack that some elements may have unordered timestamps. Again the TS-interval stack uses the same delay as in the high-contention producer-consumer benchmark.

Figure 5e and Figure 5f show the performance and scalability of the data-structures in the high-contention consumer-only benchmark. The performance of the TS-interval stack is significantly higher than the performance of the other stack implementations, except for low numbers of threads. The performance of TS-CAS is close to the performance of TS-interval. The TS-stutter stack is faster than the TS-atomic and TS-hardware stack due to the fact that some elements share timestamps and therefore can be removed in parallel. The TS-atomic stack and TS-hardware stack show the same performance because all elements have unique timestamps and therefore have to be removed sequentially. Also in the Treiber stack and the EB stack elements have to be removed sequentially. Depending on the machine, removing elements sequentially from a single list (Treiber stack) is sometimes less and sometimes as expensive as removing elements sequentially from multiple lists (TS stack).

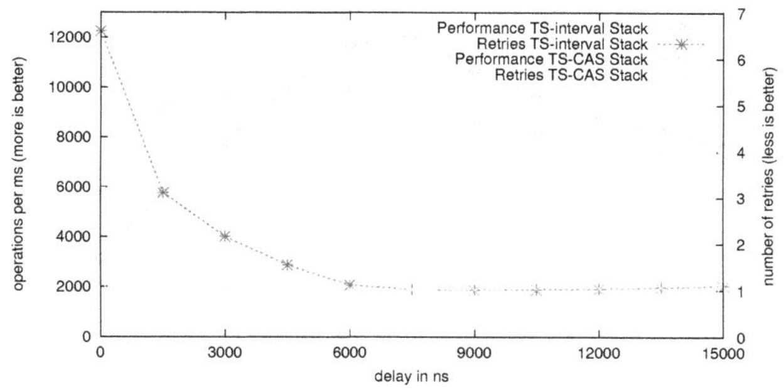


Figure 6: High-contention producer-consumer benchmark using TS-interval and TS-CAS timestamping with increasing delay on the 40-core machine, exercising 40 producers and 40 consumers.

### 6.2 Analysis of Interval Timestamping

Figure 6 shows the performance of the TS-interval stack and the TS-CAS stack along with the average number of `tryRem` calls needed in each pop (one call is optimal, but contention may cause retries). These figures were collected with an increasing interval length in the high contention producer-consumer benchmark on the 40-core machine. We used these results to determine the delays for the benchmarks in Section 6.1.

Initially the performance of the TS-interval stack increases with an increasing delay time, but beyond 7.5 µs the performance decreases again. After that point an average push operation is slower than an average pop operation and the number of pop operations which return `EMPTY` increases.

For the TS-interval stack the high performance correlates strongly with a drop in `tryRem` retries. We conclude from this that the impressive performance we achieve with interval timestamping arises from reduced contention in `tryRem`. For the optimal delay time we have 1.009 calls to `tryRem` per pop, i.e. less than 1% of pop calls need to scan the SP pools array more than once. In contrast, without a delay the average number of retries per pop call is more than 6.

The performance of the TS-CAS stack increases initially with an increasing delay time. However this does not decrease the number of `tryRem` retries significantly. The reason is that without a delay there is more contention on the global counter. Therefore the performance of TS-CAS with a delay is actually better than the performance without a delay. However, similar to TS-interval timestamping, with a delay time beyond 6 µs the performance decreases again. This is the point where an average push operation becomes slower than an average pop operations.

## 7. TS Queue and TS Deque Variants

In this paper, we have focussed on the stack variant of our algorithm. However, stored timestamps can be removed in any order, meaning it is simple to change our TS stack into a queue / deque. Doing this requires three main changes:

1. Change the timestamp comparison operator in `tryRem`.
2. Change the SP pool such that `getYoungest` returns the oldest / right-most / left-most element.
3. For the TS queue, remove elimination in `tryRem`. For the TS deque, enable it only for stack-like removal.

The TS queue is the second fastest queue we know of. In our experiments the TS-interval queue outperforms the Michael-Scott queue [18] and the flat-combining queue [10] but the lack of elimination means it is not as fast as the LCRQ [1].

The TS-interval deque is the fastest deque we know of, although it is slower than the corresponding stack / queue. However, it still outperforms the Michael-Scott and flat-combining queues, and the Treiber and EB stacks.

## 8. Related Work

***Timestamping.*** Our approach was initially inspired by Attiya et al.'s Laws of Order paper [2], which proves that any linearizable stack, queue, or deque necessarily uses the RAW or AWAR patterns in its remove operation. While attempting to extend this result to insert operations, we were surprised to discover a counter-example: the TS stack. We believe the Basket Queue [15] was the first algorithm to exploit the fact that enqueues need not take effect in order of their atomic operations, although unlike the TS stack it does not avoid strong synchronisation when inserting.

Gorelik and Hendler use timestamping in their AFC queue [6]. As in our stack, enqueued elements are timestamped and stored in single-producer buffers. Aside from the obvious difference in kind, our TS stack differs in several respects. The AFC dequeue uses flat-combining-style consolidation – that is, a combiner thread merges timestamps into a total order. As a result, the AFC queue is blocking. The TS stack avoids enforcing an internal total order, and instead allows non-blocking parallel removal. Removal in the AFC queue depends on the expensive consolidation process, and as a result their producer-consumer benchmark shows remove performance significantly worse than other flat-combining queues. Interval timestamping lets the TS stack trade insertion and removal cost, avoiding this problem. Timestamps in the AFC queue are Lamport clocks [17], not hardware-generated intervals. (We also experiment with Lamport clocks – see TS-stutter in §3.2). Finally, AFC queue elements are timestamped *before* being inserted – in the TS stack, this is reversed. This seemingly trivial difference enables timestamp-based elimination, which is important to the TS stack's performance.

The LCRQ queue [1] and the SP queue [11] both index elements using an atomic counter. However, dequeue operations do not look for *one of* the youngest elements as in our TS stack, but rather for the element with the enqueue index that matches the dequeue index *exactly*. Both approaches fall back to a slow path when the dequeue counter becomes higher than the enqueue counter. In contrast to indices, timestamps in the TS stack need not be unique or even ordered, and the performance of the TS stack does not depend on a fast path and a slow path, but only on the number of elements which share the same timestamp.

Our use of the x86 `RDTSCP` instruction to generate hardware timestamps is inspired by work on testing FIFO queues [7]. There the `RDTSC` instruction is used to determine the order of operation calls. (Note the distinction between the synchronised `RDTSCP` and unsynchronised `RDTSC`). `RDTSCP` has since been used in the design of an STM by Ruan et al. [20], who investigate the instruction's multi-processor synchronisation behaviour.

***Correctness.*** Our stack theorem lets us prove that the TS stack is linearizable with respect to sequential stack semantics. This theorem builds on Henzinger et al. who have a similar theorem for queues [12]. Their theorem is defined (almost) entirely in terms of the sequential order on methods – what we call precedence, pr. That is, they need not generate a linearization order. In contrast, our stack theorem requires a relation between inserts and removes. We suspect it is impossible to define such a theorem for stacks without an auxiliary insert-remove relation (see §4.2).

A stack must respect several non-LIFO correctness properties: elements should not be lost or duplicated, and pop should correctly report when the stack is empty. Henzinger et al. build these properties into their theorem, making it more complex and arguably harder to use. Furthermore, each `dequeue` that returns EMPTY requires a partition 'before' and 'after' the operation, effectively reintroducing a partial linearization order. However, these correctness properties are orthogonal to LIFO ordering, and so we simply require that the algorithm also respects set semantics.

***Implementation features.*** Our TS stack implementation reuses concepts from several previous data-structures.

Storing elements in multiple partial data-structures is used in the distributed queue [8], where insert and remove operations are distributed between partial queues using a load balancer. One can view the SP pools as partial queues and the TS stack itself as the load balancer. The TS stack emptiness check also originates from the distributed queues. However, the TS stack leverages the performance of distributed queues while preserving sequential stack semantics.

Elimination originates in the elimination-backoff stack [9]. However, in the TS stack, elimination works by comparing timestamps rather than by accessing a collision array. As a result, in the TS stack a pop which eliminates a concurrent push is faster than a normal uncontended pop. In the elimination-backoff stack such an eliminating pop is slower, as synchronization on the collision array requires at least three successful `CAS` operations instead of just one.

## 9. Conclusions and Future Work

We present a novel approach to implementing ordered concurrent data-structures like queues, stacks, and deques; a high-performance concurrent algorithm, the TS stack; and a new proof technique required to show the TS stack is correct. The broad messages that we draw from our work are:

- In concurrent data-structures, total ordering on internal data imposes a performance cost and is unnecessary for linearizability.
- However, weakened internal ordering makes establishing correctness more challenging. Specification-specific theorems such as our stack theorem can solve this problem.

Our work represents an initial step in designing and verifying timestamped data-structures. In future work, we plan to experiment with relaxing other internal ordering constraints; with dynamically adjusting the level of order in response to contention; with correctness conditions weaker than linearizability; and with relaxing the underlying memory model.

## Acknowledgments

We thank Ana Sokolova for feedback, Frank Zeyda for help with the Isabelle formalization, and Michael Lippautz for help with Scal. We also thank the POPL referees for their thoughtful comments. This work has been supported by the National Research Network RiSE on Rigorous Systems Engineering (Austrian Science Fund (FWF): S11404-N23).

## References

[1] Y. Afek and A. Morrison. Fast concurrent queues for x86 processors. In *PPoPP*. ACM, 2013.

[2] H. Attiya, R. Guerraoui, D. Hendler, P. Kuznetsov, M. Michael, and M. Vechev. Laws of order: expensive synchronization in concurrent algorithms cannot be eliminated. In *POPL*, 2011.

[3] G. Bar-Nissan, D. Hendler, and A. Suissa. A dynamic elimination-combining stack algorithm. In *OPODIS*, 2011.

[4] M. Batty, M. Dodds, and A. Gotsman. Library abstraction for C/C++ concurrency. In *POPL*, 2013.

[5] Computational Systems Group, University of Salzburg. Scal framework. URL `http://scal.cs.uni-salzburg.at`.

[6] M. Gorelik and D. Hendler. Brief announcement: an asymmetric flat-combining based queue algorithm. In *PODC*, 2013.

[7] A. Haas, C. Kirsch, M. Lippautz, and H. Payer. How FIFO is your concurrent FIFO queue? In *RACES*. ACM, 2012.

[8] A. Haas, T. Henzinger, C. Kirsch, M. Lippautz, H. Payer, A. Sezgin, and A. Sokolova. Distributed queues in shared memory—multicore performance and scalability through quantitative relaxation. In *CF*. ACM, 2013.

[9] D. Hendler, N. Shavit, and L. Yerushalmi. A scalable lock-free stack algorithm. In *SPAA*. ACM, 2004.

[10] D. Hendler, I. Incze, N. Shavit, and M. Tzafrir. Flat combining and the synchronization-parallelism tradeoff. In *SPAA*, 2010.

[11] T. Henzinger, H. Payer, and A. Sezgin. Replacing competition with cooperation to achieve scalable lock-free FIFO queues. Technical Report IST-2013-124-v1+1, IST Austria, 2013.

[12] T. A. Henzinger, A. Sezgin, and V. Vafeiadis. Aspect-oriented linearizability proofs. In *CONCUR*, 2013.

[13] M. Herlihy and N. Shavit. *The Art of Multiprocessor Programming*. Morgan Kaufmann Publishers Inc., 2008.

[14] M. Herlihy and J. Wing. Linearizability: a correctness condition for concurrent objects. *TOPLAS*, 12(3), 1990.

[15] M. Hoffman, O. Shalev, and N. Shavit. The baskets queue. In *OPODIS*. Springer, 2007.

[16] Intel. Intel 64 and ia-32 architectures software developer's manual, volume 3b: System programming guide, part 2, 2013. URL `http://download.intel.com/products/processor/manual/253669.pdf`.

[17] L. Lamport. Time, clocks, and the ordering of events in a distributed system. *Communications ACM*, 21, July 1978.

[18] M. Michael and M. Scott. Simple, fast, and practical non-blocking and blocking concurrent queue algorithms. In *PODC*. ACM, 1996.

[19] H. H. Nguyen and M. Rinard. Detecting and eliminating memory leaks using cyclic memory allocation. In *ISMM*. ACM, 2007.

[20] W. Ruan, Y. Liu, and M. Spear. Boosting timestamp-based transactional memory by exploiting hardware cycle counters. In *TRANSACT*, 2013.

[21] P. Sewell, S. Sarkar, S. Owens, F. Z. Nardelli, and M. O. Myreen. x86-TSO: a rigorous and usable programmer's model for x86 multiprocessors. *Commun. ACM*, 53(7), 2010.

[22] R. Treiber. Systems programming: Coping with parallelism. Technical Report RJ5118, IBM Almaden Research Center, April 1986.

# A Formally-Verified C Static Analyzer

Jacques-Henri Jourdan
Inria Paris-Rocquencourt
jacques-henri.jourdan@inria.fr

Vincent Laporte
IRISA and U. Rennes 1
vincent.laporte@irisa.fr

Sandrine Blazy
IRISA and U. Rennes 1
sandrine.blazy@irisa.fr

Xavier Leroy
Inria Paris-Rocquencourt
xavier.leroy@inria.fr

David Pichardie
IRISA and ENS Rennes
david.pichardie@irisa.fr

## Abstract

This paper reports on the design and soundness proof, using the Coq proof assistant, of Verasco, a static analyzer based on abstract interpretation for most of the ISO C 1999 language (excluding recursion and dynamic allocation). Verasco establishes the absence of run-time errors in the analyzed programs. It enjoys a modular architecture that supports the extensible combination of multiple abstract domains, both relational and non-relational. Verasco integrates with the CompCert formally-verified C compiler so that not only the soundness of the analysis results is guaranteed with mathematical certitude, but also the fact that these guarantees carry over to the compiled code.

***Categories and Subject Descriptors*** D.2.4 [*Software Engineering*]: Software/Program Verification—*Assertion checkers, Correctness proofs*; F.3.1 [*Logics and meanings of programs*]: Specifying and Verifying and Reasoning about Programs—*Mechanical verification*

***Keywords*** static analysis; abstract interpretation; soundness proofs; proof assistants

## 1. Introduction

Verification tools are increasingly used during the development and validation of critical software. These tools provide guarantees that are always independent from those obtained by more conventional means such as testing and code review; often stronger; and sometimes cheaper to obtain (rigorous testing can be very expensive). Verification tools are based on a variety of techniques such as static analysis, model checking, deductive program proof, and combinations thereof. The guarantees they provide range from basic memory safety to full functional correctness. In this paper, we focus on static analyzers for low-level, C-like languages that establish the absence of run-time errors such as out-of-bound array accesses, null pointer dereference, and arithmetic exceptions. These basic properties are essential both for safety and security. Among the various verification techniques, static analysis is perhaps the one that scales best to large existing code bases, with minimal intervention from the programmer.

Static analyzers can be used in two different ways: as sophisticated bug finders, discovering potential programming errors that are hard to find by testing; or as specialized program verifiers, establishing that a given safety or security property holds with high confidence. For bug-finding, the analysis must be precise (too many false alarms render the tool unusable for this purpose), but no guarantee is offered nor expected that all bugs of a certain class will be found. For program verification, in contrast, *soundness* of the analysis is paramount: if the analyzer reports no alarms, it must be the case that the program is free of the class of run-time errors tracked by the analyzer; in particular, all possible execution paths through the program must be accounted for.

To use a static analyzer as a verification tool, and obtain certification credit in regulations such as DO-178C (avionics) or Common Criteria (security), evidence of soundness of the analyzer must therefore be provided. Owing to the complexity of static analyzers and of their input data (programs written in "big" programming languages), rigorous testing of a static analyzer is very difficult. Even if the analyzer is built on mathematically-rigorous grounds such as abstract interpretation [14], the possibility of an implementation bug remains. The alternative we investigate in this paper is *deductive formal verification of a static analyzer*: we apply program proof, mechanized with the Coq proof assistant, to the implementation of a static analyzer in order to prove its soundness with respect to the dynamic semantics of the analyzed language.

Our analyzer, called Verasco, is based on abstract interpretation; handles most of the ISO C 1999 language, with the exception of recursion and dynamic memory allocation; combines several abstract domains, both non-relational (integer intervals and congruences, floating-point intervals, points-to sets) and relational (convex polyhedra, symbolic equalities); and is entirely proved to be sound using the Coq proof assistant. Moreover, Verasco is connected to the CompCert C formally-verified compiler [26], ensuring that the safety guarantees established by Verasco carry over to the compiled code.

Mechanizing soundness proofs of verification tools is not a new idea. It has been applied at large scale to Java type-checking and bytecode verification [25], proof-carrying code infrastructures [1, 12], and verification condition generators for C-like languages [20, 23], among other projects. The formal verification of static analyzers based on dataflow analysis or abstract interpretation is less developed. As detailed in section 10, earlier work in this area either


*POPL '15*, January 15–17, 2015, Mumbai, India.

ACM 978-1-4503-3300-9/15/01... $15.00.
http://dx.doi.org/10.1145/2676726.2676966

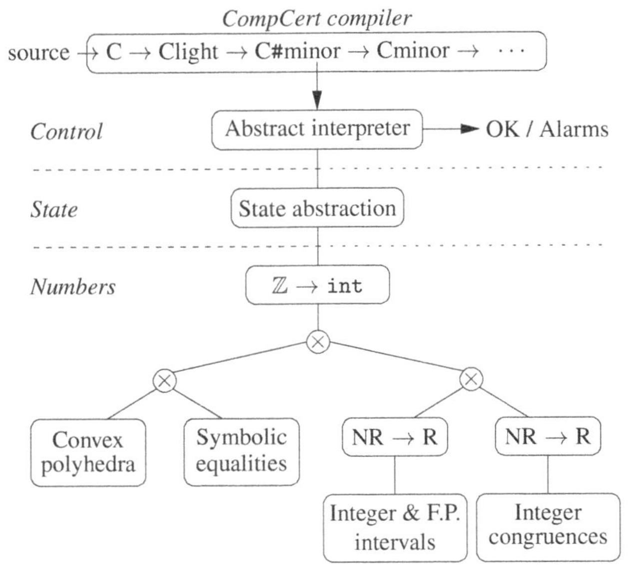


**Figure 1.** Modular architecture of the Verasco static analyzer

focuses on simple static analyses (dataflow analyses, no widening, non-relational domains only) or on mini-languages such as IMP. Compared with this earlier work on verified static analyzers, Verasco is a quantitative jump: the source language analyzed (most of C) is much more complex, and the static analysis technique used (combination of several abstract domains, including relational domains) is much more sophisticated.

This paper reports on the design and Coq verification of the Verasco static analyzer. In addition to the the quantitative jump mentioned above, we emphasize as a contribution the modular architecture of the analyzer and its verification, including fully-specified interfaces for the various components that makes it easy to connect new abstract domains to Verasco, as well as to reuse Verasco's domains in other projects. The full Coq development is available at `http://compcert.inria.fr/verasco/`.

The paper is organized as follows. Section 2 presents the general architecture of the analyzer. The next five sections give more details on the source language (§3), the abstract interpreter (§4), the state and memory abstraction (§5), the numerical abstract domains (§6) and how multiple domains communicate (§7). We finish by some notes on the Coq development (§8), preliminary experimental results (§9), discussion of related work (§10), and conclusions and perspectives (§11).

## 2. Architecture of the analyzer

The general architecture of the Verasco analyzer is depicted in figure 1. It is inspired by that of ASTRÉE [6] and is structured in three layers. At the top sits the abstract interpreter that infers abstract states at every program point and checks for potential run-time errors, raising alarms along the way. The abstract interpreter operates over the C#minor intermediate language described in section 3. This language is the second intermediate language in the CompCert compilation pipeline. The Verasco analyzer reuses the CompCert front-end to produce C#minor from the source C code. The semantics preservation theorem of CompCert guarantees that any safety property established on the C#minor intermediate language carries over to the assembly code generated by CompCert. Combining this theorem with the soundness theorem for Verasco, we obtain that any C#minor program that passes analysis without raising an alarm compiles to assembly code that is free of run-time errors. The Verasco abstract interpreter proceeds by fixpoint iteration that follows the structure of the C#minor program. Section 4 gives more details on this abstract interpreter and its soundness proof.

The middle layer of Verasco is an abstract domain for execution states, tracking the values of program variables, the contents of memory locations, and the chain of function calls. This state abstract domain is described in section 5. It is a parameter of the abstract interpreter, and has a well-defined interface (in terms of abstract operations provided and their specifications) outlined below. This parameterization makes it possible to experiment with several state domains of various precision, even though we currently have only one implementation of the state domain. Concerning values that arise during program execution, the domain tracks pointer values itself via points-to analysis, but delegates the tracking of numerical values to a numerical domain (bottom layer).

At the bottom layer of Verasco, the numerical abstract domain is itself an extensible combination of several domains. Some are non-relational, such as intervals and congruences, and track properties of the (integer or floating-point) value of a single program variable or memory cell. Others are relational, such as convex polyhedra and symbolic equalities, and track relations between the values of several variables or cells. Two domain transformers perform adaptation over domains: the "NR → R" transformer gives a relational interface to a non-relational domain, and the "$\mathbb{Z} \to$ `int`" transformer handles the overflow and wrap-around behaviors that occur when mathematical integers (type $\mathbb{Z}$) and their arithmetic operations are replaced by machine integers ($n$-bit vectors) and their modulo-$2^n$ arithmetic. Section 6 describes these abstract domains and their verification; section 7 explains how they are combined and how they can exchange information during analysis.

Supporting such a modular composition of formally-verified abstract domains requires that they adhere to well-defined *interfaces*. Figure 2 shows one of the three major interfaces used in Verasco (slightly simplified), the one for "machine" relational domains that acts as gateway between the numerical domains and the state domain. All Verasco interfaces are presented as Coq's type classes. A machine relational domain consists of a type `t` equipped with a semi-lattice structure: a decidable ordering `leb`, a `top` element, a `join` operation that returns an upper bound of its arguments (but not necessarily the least upper bound), and a `widen` operation used to accelerate the convergence of fixpoint iteration with widening. There is no bottom element in Verasco's domains: instead, when we need to represent unreachability, we use the type `t+`$\bot$ that adds a generic `Bot` element to the domain `t`.

The three most important operations are `forget`, `assign` and `assume`. The `forget` $x$ $A$ operation removes all information associated with the variable $x$ in state $A$, simulating a nondeterministic assignment to $x$. The type `var` of variables is another parameter of the class: it can be instantiated by program variables or, as the state abstract domain does, by abstract memory cells.

The `assign` $x$ $e$ $A$ operation updates $A$ to reflect the assignment of expression $e$ to variable $x$. Numerical expressions $e$ are built upon variables and constants using the arithmetic, logical and comparison operators of C#minor. (They are similar to C#minor expressions except that they do not feature memory loads and that intervals can occur instead of numerical constants, capturing some amount of nondeterminism.) When analyzing source-level assignments, it is crucial that the numerical domains receive a numerical expression as close as possible to the right-hand side of the source-level assignment, typically the same expression modulo the replacement of memory loads by variables representing the memory cells accessed; then, each domain can treat it to the best of its abilities. For example, on treating `x = y + z`, an interval domain will simply set `x` to the sum of the intervals associated with `y`

```
Class ab_machine_env (t var: Type): Type :=
  { leb: t → t → bool
  ; top: t
  ; join: t → t → t
  ; widen: t → t → t
  ; forget: var → t → t+⊥
  ; assign: var → nexpr var → t → t+⊥
  ; assume: nexpr var → bool → t → t+⊥
  ; nonblock: nexpr var → t → bool
  ; concretize_int: nexpr var → t → int_set+⊤+⊥

  ; γ : t → ℘ (var→num_val)
  ; gamma_monotone: forall x y,
    leb x y = true → γ x ⊆ γ y;
  ; gamma_top: forall x, x ∈ γ top;
  ; join_sound: forall x y,
    γ x ∪ γ y ⊆ γ (join x y)
  ; forget_correct: forall x ρ n ab,
    ρ ∈ γ ab →
    (upd ρ x n) ∈ γ (forget x ab)
  ; assign_correct: forall x e ρ n ab,
    ρ ∈ γ ab →
    n ∈ eval_nexpr ρ e →
    (upd ρ x n) ∈ γ (assign x e ab)
  ; assume_correct: forall e ρ ab b,
    ρ ∈ γ ab →
    of_bool b ∈ eval_nexpr ρ e →
    ρ ∈ γ (assume e b ab)
  ; nonblock_correct: forall e ρ ab,
    ρ ∈ γ ab →
    nonblock e ab = true →
    block_nexpr ρ e →
    False
  ; concretize_int_correct: ∀ e ρ ab i,
    ρ ∈ γ ab →
    NVint i ∈ eval_nexpr ρ e →
    i ∈ γ (concretize_int e ab)
}.
```

**Figure 2.** The interface for machine relational domains (slightly simplified).

and z, while a polyhedral domain will record the two inequalities $\mathtt{x} \leq \mathtt{y}+\mathtt{z} \wedge \mathtt{x} \geq \mathtt{y}+\mathtt{z}$.

Finally, `assume` $e\ b\ A$ refines the abstract state $A$ to reflect the fact that expression $e$ evaluates to the truth value $b$ (either `true` or `false`). It is used when analyzing conditional statements (`if`, `switch`) to keep track of the value of the discriminating expression.

Two query operations are provided to help the abstract interpreter detect potential run-time errors and raise alarms appropriately: `nonblock` $e\ A$ returns `true` if $e$ is guaranteed to evaluate safely and `false` if it can cause a run-time error (such as a division by zero) when evaluated in a concrete state matching $A$; and `concretize_int` $e\ A$ returns the set of possible integer values for the expression $e$ that can be deduced from the information in abstract state $A$.

The interface in figure 2 also specifies the soundness conditions for the abstract operations above. The specification uses a *concretization function* $\gamma$ that maps abstract states $A$ to sets of concrete environments `var` → `num_val` mapping variables to values. Here, values are the tagged union of 32-bit integers, 64-bit integers, and double-precision floating-point numbers (IEEE754 `binary64` format), that is, the numerical types offered by C#minor. As customary in Coq, the type $\wp(\mathtt{t})$ of sets of `t`'s is encoded as `t` → `Prop`, so that $\gamma$ is really a two-place predicate relating abstract states and concrete environments. The specification does not use a full Galois connection $A \underset{\gamma}{\overset{\alpha}{\leftrightarrows}} \wp(C)$ because the abstraction function $\alpha$ is problematic in a constructive logic such as Coq's: first, it is not a computable function as soon as the type $C$ of concrete "things" is infinite; second, for some domains, $\alpha$ is not well defined.[1]

The lack of an abstraction function $\alpha$ changes the style of specification of abstract operators, focusing the specification on soundness conditions and freeing us from the obligation to prove relative optimality. For example, the specification of `forget` in Galois-connection style would be

$$\mathtt{forget}\ x\ A = \alpha\{\rho[x \leftarrow v] \mid \rho \in \gamma(A), v \in \mathit{Values}\}$$

Instead, in $\gamma$-only style we state soundness as

$$\forall \rho, v,\ \rho \in \gamma(A) \Rightarrow \rho[x \leftarrow v] \in \gamma(\mathtt{forget}\ x\ A)$$

(condition `forget_correct` in figure 2). We could also state relative optimality using $\gamma$ only:

$$\forall A',\ (\forall \rho, v,\ \rho \in \gamma(A) \Rightarrow \rho[x \leftarrow v] \in \gamma(A')) \Rightarrow \mathtt{forget}\ x\ A \sqsubseteq A'$$

However, we elected to mechanize proofs of soundness only, leaving relative optimality optional.

The other two major interfaces of Verasco are similar in spirit to what is described above, with the following differences. The interface for "ideal" numerical relational domains concretizes not to machine numbers, but to the sum of mathematical integers (type $\mathbb{Z}$) and FP numbers. It also supports communication channels between domains, as described in section 7. The interface for abstract execution states that mediates between the abstract interpreter and the state domain uses full C#minor expressions, including memory loads; adds abstract operations to handle memory stores and to push and pop function calls in a call context; and concretizes to C#minor memory states and local variable environments (section 5).

## 3. The C#minor language

C#minor is the second intermediate language in the CompCert compilation pipeline, immediately preceding Cminor, the entry language of the CompCert back-end described in [27]. Classically, C#minor is structured in functions, statements, and expressions.

Expressions:

| | |
|---|---|
| $e ::= t$ | reading a temporary variable |
| $\mid \&x$ | address of a variable |
| $\mid cst$ | constants |
| $\mid op_1(e) \mid op_2(e, e')$ | arithmetic operations |
| $\mid \mathtt{load}(\tau, e)$ | memory load with size $\tau$ |

Statements:

| | |
|---|---|
| $s ::= \mathtt{skip}$ | |
| $\mid t := e$ | assignment |
| $\mid \mathtt{store}(\tau, e_1, e_2)$ | memory store with size $\tau$ |
| $\mid t := e(e_1, \ldots, e_n)$ | function call |
| $\mid (s_1; s_2)$ | sequence |
| $\mid \mathtt{if}\ e\ s_1\ \mathtt{else}\ s_2$ | conditional |
| $\mid \mathtt{loop}\ s$ | infinite loop |
| $\mid \mathtt{block}\ s$ | |
| $\mid \mathtt{exit}\ n$ | terminate $n+1$ enclosing `block`s |
| $\mid L : s$ | define label $L$ |
| $\mid \mathtt{goto}\ L$ | jump to label $L$ |
| $\mid \mathtt{return} \mid \mathtt{return}\ e$ | function return |

[1] For example, in the domain of linear rational inequalities, the set of pairs $\{(x, y) \mid x^2 + y^2 \leq 1\}$ has no best approximation as a polyhedron [28].

Functions:

$f ::= name\ (\ldots p_i \ldots)\ \{$
  `vars` $\ldots x_i[size_i] \ldots$ local variables
  `temps` $\ldots t_i \ldots$ temporary variables
  $s$ function body
$\}$

A program is composed of function definitions and global variable declarations. Variables are of two kinds: addressable (their address can be taken with the `&` operator) and temporary (not resident in memory). Expressions have no side effects: assignments, memory stores and function calls are statements. The arithmetic, logical, comparison, and conversion operators are roughly those of C, but without overloading: for example, distinct operators are provided for integer multiplication and FP division. Likewise, there are no implicit casts: all conversions between numerical types are explicit.

Statements offer both structured control and `goto` with labels. C loops as well as `break` and `continue` statements are encoded as infinite loops with a multi-level `exit` $n$ that jumps to the end of the $(n+1)$-th enclosing `block`.

The first passes of CompCert perform the following transformations to produce C#minor from C sources. First, side effects are pulled outside of expressions, and temporaries are introduced to hold their values. For example, `z = f(x) + 2 * g(y)` becomes

```
t1 = f(x);  t2 = g(y);  z = t1 + 2 * t2;
```

This transformation effectively picks one evaluation order among the several orders allowed in C. Second, local variables of scalar types whose addresses are never taken are "pulled out of memory" and turned into temporaries. Third, all type-dependent behaviors are made explicit: operator overloading is resolved, implicit conversions are materialized, and array and `struct` accesses become `load` and `store` operations with explicit address computations. Fourth and last, C loops are encoded using `block` and `exit`, as outlined in [7].

The dynamic semantics of C#minor is given in small-step style as a transition relation $C \xrightarrow{\nu} C'$ between configurations $C$. The optional $\nu$ label is an observable event possibly produced by the transition, such as accessing a `volatile` variable. A typical configuration $C$ comprises a statement $s$ under consideration, a continuation $k$ that describes what to do when $s$ terminates (e.g., "move to the right part of a sequence", "iterate a loop once more", or "return from current function"), and a dynamic state $\rho$ mapping temporaries to their values, local and global variables to their addresses, and memory cells to their contents. The continuation $k$ encodes both a context (where does $s$ occur in the currently-executing function) and a call stack (the chain of pending function calls). Some transition rules actually perform computations (e.g., an assignment); others are refocusing rules that change $s$ and $k$ to focus on the next computation.

The transition rules for C#minor are omitted from this paper, but resemble those for Cminor given in [27, section 4]. The semitone difference between Cminor and C#minor is that every Cminor function has exactly one addressable variable called the stack data block, while a C#minor function has zero, one or several variables bound to logically separated memory blocks.

## 4. The abstract interpreter

Exploring all execution paths of a program during static analysis can be achieved in two ways: the control flow graph (CFG) approach and the structural approach. In the CFG approach, a control flow graph is built with program points as nodes, and edges carrying elementary commands (assignments, tests, ...). The transfer function $T$ for the analysis is defined for elementary commands. The analyzer, then, sets up a system of inequations

$$A_{p'} \sqsupseteq T\ c\ A_p \quad \text{where } p \xrightarrow{c} p' \text{ is a CFG edge}$$

with unknowns $A_p$, the abstract states associated to every program point $p$. This system is then solved by global fixpoint iteration over the whole CFG.

In contrast, the structural approach applies to languages with structured control and compound statements such as `if` and loops. There, the transfer function $T$ is defined over basic as well as compound statements: given the abstract state $A$ "before" the execution of statement $s$, it returns $T\ s\ A$, the abstract state "after" the execution of $s$. For sequences, we have $T\ (s_1; s_2)\ A = T\ s_2\ (T\ s_1\ A)$. For loops, $T$ takes a local fixpoint of the transfer function for the loop body.

Since C#minor is a mostly structured language (only `goto` statements are unstructured), the abstract interpreter for C#minor follows the structural approach. This obviates the need to define program points for C#minor (a nontrivial task). Moreover, structural abstract interpreters use less memory than CFG-based ones, maintaining only a few different abstract states at any time, instead of one per program point. However, the transfer function for our abstract interpreter is more involved than usual, because control can enter and leave a C#minor statement in several ways. The statement $s$ can be entered normally at the beginning, or via a `goto` that branches to one of the labels defined in $s$. Likewise, $s$ can terminate either normally by running to the end, or prematurely by executing a `return`, `exit`, or `goto` statement. Consequently, the transfer function is of the form

$$T\ s\ (A_i, A_l) = (A_o, A_r, A_e, A_g)$$

where $A_i$ (input) is the abstract state at the beginning of $s$, $A_o$ (output) is the abstract state after $s$ terminates normally, $A_r$ (return) is the state if it returns, and $A_e$ (exits) maps exit numbers to the corresponding abstract states. The `goto` statements are handled by two maps from labels to abstract states: $A_l$ (labels) and $A_g$ (gotos), the first representing the states that can flow to a label defined in $s$, the second representing the states at `goto` statements executed by $s$. Figure 3 excerpts from the definition of $T$ and shows all these components in action.

The `loop` case computes a post-fixpoint with widening and narrowing, starting at $\bot$ and iterating at most $N_{\text{widen}}$ times. The `pfp` iterator is, classically, defined as

$$\texttt{pfp}\ F\ A\ N = \begin{cases} \top & \text{if } N = 0 \\ \texttt{narrow}\ F\ A\ N_{\text{narrow}} & \text{if } A \sqsupseteq F\ A \\ \texttt{pfp}\ F\ (A\ \nabla\ F\ A)\ (N-1) & \text{otherwise} \end{cases}$$

$$\texttt{narrow}\ F\ A\ N = \begin{cases} A & \text{if } N = 0 \\ \texttt{narrow}\ F\ (F\ A)\ (N-1) & \text{if } A \sqsupseteq F\ A \\ A & \text{otherwise} \end{cases}$$

Each iteration of `pfp` uses the widening operator $\nabla$ provided by the abstract domain to speed up convergence. Once a post-fixpoint is found, $F$ is iterated up to $N_{\text{narrow}}$ times in the hope of finding a smaller post-fixpoint.

In both widening and narrowing iterations, we use "fuel" $N$ to convince Coq that the recursions above are terminating, and to limit analysis time. We did not attempt to prove termination of iteration with widening: it would require difficult proofs over the widening operators of all our abstract domains [35], for no gain in soundness. Alternatively, we could delegate the computation of a candidate post-fixpoint $A$ to an untrusted iterator written in Caml, then check $A \sqsupseteq F\ A$ in a verified Coq function. This would cost one more invocation of the $F$ function, and it is unclear how the Caml implementation could be made more efficient than the `pfp` function above, written and verified in Coq.

$$T\ (x := e)\ (A_i, A_l) = (\texttt{assign}\ x\ e\ A_i, \bot, \bot, \bot)$$

$$T\ (s; s')\ (A_i, A_l) = (A'_o, A_r \sqcup A'_r, A_e \sqcup A_e, A_g \sqcup A'_g) \text{ where } \begin{cases} (A_o, A_r, A_e, A_g) = T\ s\ (A_i, A_l) \\ (A'_o, A'_r, A'_e, A'_g) = T\ s'\ (A_o, A_l) \end{cases}$$

$$T\ (\texttt{if}(e)\ s\ \texttt{else}\ s')\ (A_i, A_l) = T\ s\ (\texttt{assume}\ e\ \texttt{true}\ A_i, A_l) \sqcup T\ s'\ (\texttt{assume}\ e\ \texttt{false}\ A_i, A_l)$$

$$T\ (\texttt{loop}\ s)\ (A_i, A_l) = (\bot, A_r, A_e, A_g) \text{ where } (A_o, A_r, A_e, A_g) = \texttt{pfp}\ (\lambda(X_o, X_r, X_e, X_g).\ T\ s\ (A_i \sqcup X_o, A_l))\ \bot\ N_{\text{widen}}$$

$$T\ (\texttt{exit}\ n)\ (A_i, A_l) = (\bot, \bot, (\lambda n'.\ \texttt{if}\ n' = n\ \texttt{then}\ A_i\ \texttt{else}\ \bot), \bot)$$

$$T\ (\texttt{block}\ s)\ (A_i, A_l) = (A_o \sqcup A_e(0), A_r, (\lambda n.\ A_e(n+1)), A_g) \text{ where } (A_o, A_r, A_e, A_g) = T\ s\ (A_i, A_l)$$

$$T\ (\texttt{goto}\ L)\ (A_i, A_l) = (\bot, \bot, \bot, (\lambda L'.\ \texttt{if}\ L' = L\ \texttt{then}\ A_i\ \texttt{else}\ \bot))$$

$$T\ (L : s)\ (A_i, A_l) = T\ s\ (A_i \sqcup A_l(L), A_l)$$

**Figure 3.** Representative cases of the C#minor abstract interpreter

Optionally, the abstract interpreter can unroll loops on the fly: the $N$ first iterations of the loop are analyzed independently in sequence; the remaining iterations are analyzed with a `pfp` fixpoint. This delays widening and gains precision. The unrolling factor $N$ is currently given by an annotation in the source code.

In addition to the analysis of `loop` statements, a post-fixpoint is computed for every C#minor function to analyze `goto` statements. This function-global iteration ensures that the abstract states at `goto` statements are consistent with those assumed at the corresponding labeled statements. In other words, if $s$ is the body of a function and $T\ s\ (A_i, A_l) = (A_o, A_r, A_e, A_g)$ is its analysis, the analysis iterates until $A_g(L) \sqsubseteq A_l(L)$ for every label $L$. When this condition holds, the abstraction of the function maps entry state $A_i$ to exit state $A_o \sqcup A_r$ corresponding to the two ways a C#minor function can return (explicitly or by reaching the end of the function body).

Concerning functions, the abstract interpreter reanalyzes the body of a function at every call site, effectively unrolling the function definition on demand. We use fuel again to limit the depth of function unrolling. Moreover, since the state abstract domain does not handle recursion, it raises an alarm if a recursive call can occur.

The abstract interpreter is written in monadic style so that alarms can be reported during analysis. We use a logging monad: when an alarm is raised, it is collected in the log, but analysis continues. This is better than stopping at the first alarm like an error monad would do: often, widening reaches a state that causes an alarm, but the subsequent narrowing steps cause this alarm to go away.

The soundness proof for the abstract interpreter is massive, owing to the complexity of the C#minor language. To keep the proof manageable, we break it in two parts: 1- the definition and soundness proof of a suitable Hoare logic for C#minor, and 2- a proof that the abstract interpreter infers Hoare "triples" that are valid in this logic.

We first explain the approach in a simplified case, that of the IMP-like subset of C#minor, without `goto`, `exit` and `return`. In this subset, statements can only be entered at the beginning and exited at the end, and the transfer function is of the form $T\ s\ A = A'$. Intuitively, we expect this transfer function to be sound if, for any statement $s$ and initial abstract state $A$ such that the analysis $T\ s\ A$ raises no alarm, the execution of $s$ started in any concrete state $\rho \in \gamma(A)$ does not go wrong, and if it terminates in state $\rho'$, then $\rho' \in \gamma(T\ s\ A)$. The way we prove this property is first to show that if the analysis $T\ s\ A$ raises no alarms, then the weak Hoare triple $\{\gamma(A)\}\ s\ \{\gamma(T\ s\ A)\}$ can be derived in an appropriate program logic [5]. Then, we show that this program logic is sound with respect to the operational semantics of the language: if $\{P\}\ s\ \{Q\}$ can be derived in the logic, then the execution of $s$, started in a state satisfying $P$, does not go wrong, and if it terminates, it does so on a state satisfying $Q$.

The approach outlined above extends to the whole C#minor language, but not without elbow grease. C#minor statements can terminate in multiple ways: normally, or prematurely on an `exit`, `return` or `goto` statement. They can also be entered in two ways: at the beginning of the statement, or via a `goto` to a label defined within. Consequently, our program logic for C#minor manipulates Hoare "heptuples" of the form

$$\{P,\ P_l\}\ s\ \{Q,\ Q_r,\ Q_e,\ Q_g\}$$

where $P$ is the precondition if $s$ is entered normally, $P_l(L)$ the precondition if $s$ is entered by a `goto` $L$, $Q$ the postcondition if $s$ terminates normally, $Q_r(v)$ the postcondition if $s$ terminates by a `return` of value $v$, $Q_e(i)$ the postcondition if $s$ terminates by `exit`$(i)$, and $Q_g(L)$ the postcondition if $s$ terminates by `goto` $L$. We omit the rules of this program logic from this paper, as they are similar to those of the program logics for Cminor and Clight by Appel and Blazy [2, 3] (without the separation logic aspects).

THEOREM 1 (Soundness of the abstract interpreter). *Assume that the analysis $T\ s\ (A_i, A_l)$ returns $(A_o, A_r, A_e, A_g)$ without raising an alarm. Then, the heptuple*

$$\{\gamma(A_i), \gamma(A_l)\}\ s\ \{\gamma(A_o), \gamma(A_r), \gamma(A_e), \gamma(A_g)\}$$

*is derivable in the C#minor program logic.*

It remains to show the soundness of the program logic with respect to the continuation-based small-step semantics of C#minor. Taking inspiration from the work of Appel *et al.* on step-indexed semantics [3, 4], we say that a configuration $(s, k, \rho)$ is safe for $n$ steps if no sequence of at most $n$ transitions starting from $(s, k, \rho)$ triggers a run-time error: it either performs $n$ transitions or reaches a final configuration after $n' < n$ transitions. We say that a continuation $k$ is safe for $n$ steps with respect to the postconditions $(Q,\ Q_r,\ Q_e,\ Q_g)$ if:

$$Q\ \rho \Rightarrow (\texttt{skip}, k, \rho) \text{ safe for } n \text{ steps}$$
$$Q_r\ v\ \rho \Rightarrow (\texttt{return}(v), k, \rho) \text{ safe for } n \text{ steps}$$
$$Q_e\ i\ \rho \Rightarrow (\texttt{exit}(i), k, \rho) \text{ safe for } n \text{ steps}$$
$$Q_g\ L\ \rho \Rightarrow (\texttt{goto}\ L, k, \rho) \text{ safe for } n \text{ steps}$$

We can then state and prove soundness of the C#minor program logic as follows.

THEOREM 2 (Soundness of the program logic). *Assume that the heptuple* $\{P,\ P_l\}\ s\ \{Q,\ Q_r,\ Q_e,\ Q_g\}$ *is derivable in the program logic. Further assume that* $k$ *is safe for* $n$ *steps with respect to* $(Q,\ Q_r,\ Q_e,\ Q_g)$*. If* $\rho$ *satisfies* $P$*, then* $(s, k, \rho)$ *is safe for* $n$ *steps. Moreover, if* $\rho$ *satisfies* $P_l\ L$ *and* $L$ *is the label of sub-statement* $s'$ *of* $s$*, in continuation* $k'$ *extending* $k$*, then* $(s', k', \rho)$ *is safe for* $n$ *steps.*

## 5. The state abstract domain

The state abstraction in Verasco tracks values contained both in memory and in temporary variables. Each value is attached to an abstract memory cell, or "cell" for short, representing one unit of storage: either a temporary variable or a scalar part of a local or global variable. A scalar part is either the whole variable if it is of scalar type, or an element of scalar type in this variable (*e.g.*, a field in a structure, an element in an array). Therefore, a cell is given by the kind and the name of the variable it belongs to, the name of the function in which this variable is declared (unless it is global), and an offset and a value size (unless it is a temporary variable).

| | | |
|---|---|---|
| Cells: | $c ::=$ `temp`$(f, t)$ | the temporary $t$ in function $f$ |
| | \| `local`$(f, x, \delta, \tau)$ | slice of size $\tau$ at offset $\delta$ in the local variable $x$ of function $f$ |
| | \| `global`$(x, \delta, \tau)$ | slice of size $\tau$ at offset $\delta$ in the global variable $x$ |

The state abstract domain interacts with three specific abstract domains: an abstract value $(\mathtt{tp}, \mathtt{pt}, \mathtt{nm})$ is a triple in `types` $\times$ `points-to` $\times$ `num`. First, type information is tracked for every memory cell in order to disambiguate, when possible, the behavior of C#minor operators. For example addition of integer or pointer values has various behaviors depending on the actual types of its arguments: adding two integers yields an integer; adding an integer to a pointer yields a pointer in the same block; and adding two pointers is undefined (therefore raises an alarm). In addition this type information is used to prove that values are not undefined, for instance when loaded from the memory.

Then, a points-to graph associates to each memory cell a set of memory blocks the cell may point to. A cell whose content is not a pointer may be associated with any set.

Finally, we track properties of the numbers contained in cells. The abstract state domain is parameterized by a relational numerical abstract domain following the interface from figure 2. Cells act as variables for this numerical domain, which therefore abstracts environments $\rho$ mapping cells to numbers. The number associated with a cell is its content if it is of numerical type, or, if it contains a pointer, the byte offset part of this pointer. Driving a relational numerical abstract domain requires special care because we must feed it with rich numerical commands, as we now illustrate. Consider the following C#minor assignment occurring in a function `f`.

```
s := s + load(int32, &T + 8×i + 4)
```

Here, `s` and `i` are temporary variables (*i.e.*, the memory cell related to `s` is `temp(f,s)`) and `T` is a global variable of array type.

Type analysis computes that `&T` is a pointer whereas `s` and `i` are integers. Points-to analysis infers that `s` and `i` do not point to any block, but `&T` definitely points to the block of `T`. In order to feed the relational numerical domain with the assignment, we must transform the `load(int32, &T + 8×i + 4)` expression into its corresponding cells. We query the points-to domain to determine which memory blocks may be accessed during this load, yielding the block of `T`. We also query the numerical domain to obtain the possible values of `8×temp(f,i) + 4`, that is, the byte offsets that may be accessed during the load. Assume this query returns the set $\{4, 12\}$. We then approximate the load expression by the two cells `global(T,4,int32)` and `global(T,12,int32)`, send the numerical domain the two assignments

```
temp(f,s) := temp(f,s) + global(T,4,int32)
temp(f,s) := temp(f,s) + global(T,12,int32)
```

and finally take the join of the two new numerical abstract states thus obtained.

For a memory store $\mathtt{store}(\tau, e_l, e_r)$, we perform a similar technique and generate a set $\{c_l^1, \ldots, c_l^p\}$ of $p$ cells that may be modified during this store, and a set $\{e_r^1, \ldots, r_r^q\}$ of numerical expressions that capture the concrete value computed by expression $e_r$. When $p = 1$, we can perform a strong update that overwrites the previous value of the cell $c_l^1$. Otherwise, we must perform a weak (conservative) update and assume that any cell in $\{c_l^1, \ldots, c_l^p\}$ may still hold its old value after the update.

***Concretization*** The types and points-to domains concretize to functions from cells to values whereas the numerical domain concretizes to purely numerical values. To combine them into one concretization, the last one is lifted using an agreement relation $\sim_{\mathtt{tp}}$ (parameterized by the types information) ensuring that types and numerical values agree and that values bound by $\rho$ match the numerical values bound by $\rho'$. In particular, if the value $\rho(c)$ is a pointer, the number $\rho'(c)$ is the byte offset part of this pointer.

More precisely, a function $\rho$ from cells to values is in the concretization of an abstract value $(\mathtt{tp}, \mathtt{pt}, \mathtt{nm})$ iff 1) it is in the concretization $\gamma(\mathtt{tp})$ of the types domain $\mathtt{tp}$, 2) it is in the concretization $\gamma(\mathtt{pt})$ of the points-to domain (which means that for every cell $c$ that contains a pointer value with a block pointer $b$, then $b \in \mathtt{pt}(c)$) and 3) in the concretization $\gamma(\mathtt{nm})$ of the numerical domain, there exists a concrete mapping $\rho'$ from cells to numerical values that agrees with $\rho$:

$$\rho \in \gamma(\mathtt{tp}, \mathtt{pt}, \mathtt{nm}) \Leftrightarrow \rho \in \gamma(\mathtt{tp}) \cap \gamma(\mathtt{pt}) \wedge \exists \rho' \in \gamma(\mathtt{nm}),\ \rho \sim_{\mathtt{tp}} \rho'$$

Finally, a function $\rho$ from cells to values can be related to a C#minor execution state (call stack and memory state): the call stack determines a mapping from `temp` cells to values and from `local` and `global` cells to memory locations, and the memory state gives values to these locations.

***Inter-procedural analysis*** To analyze a function call such as `x:=f(args)`, where `f` is an expression, the function is first resolved, then the abstract state at function entry is prepared, and finally the function body is (recursively) analyzed from this state. There, the analysis of `return` statements will compute the abstract state after the call and assignment to `x`.

Function resolution uses points-to information to compute a set of functions that expression `f` may point to.

The `push_frame` operation of the state abstract domain performs the assignments corresponding to argument passing: arguments are evaluated in the context of the caller and then assigned to local variables of the callee.

Since local variables are identified by their names and the functions they belong to, the call chain is remembered as an abstract stack. In addition, to be able to distinguish local from global variables in expressions, the set of variables local to each function is remembered in this abstract stack.

Symmetrically, the `pop_frame` operation is used when analyzing `return` $e$ statements. The expression $e$ is analyzed in the callee context and assigned to a temporary in the caller context. Then, `pop_frame` simulates the freeing of local variables on function exit: this consists in invalidating the information associated to them, as well as invalidating pointers that may point to them.

As an illustration, consider the following program.

```
int f(int *p) { return *p; }
int main(void) {
```

```
  int x = 1;
  int t = f(&x); return t; }
```

When analyzing the call to the function `f`, the argument expression is processed and the local variable `p` of `f` is assigned in the three abstract domains. In particular, `p` is assigned to the constant zero (the value of its offset) in the numerical domain and to the block `local(main,x)` in the points-to domain. Therefore, the return expression of `f` is known to access exactly one cell, about which information can be queried in the various domains. This information is then assigned back to the temporary `t` of `main`.

***Progress verification*** At the same time we transform abstract states, we perform verifications to prove that every C#minor expression evaluates safely (without blocking) in its evaluation context. In particular, we check that every load and store is performed within bounds and with the correct alignment. We also check that every deallocation of local variables at function returns is performed on valid pointers, as well as various other side conditions (*e.g.* function pointers must have a null offset).

# 6. The numerical abstract domains

## 6.1 Intervals and congruences

The first numerical domains verified in Verasco are non-relational domains of intervals ($x \in [a, b]$) and congruences ($x \bmod n = p$). They abstract numbers consisting of the union of mathematical integers (type $\mathbb{Z}$) and double-precision floating-point (FP) numbers (IEEE754's `binary64` format). Treating both kinds of numbers at once facilitates the analysis of conversions between integers and FP numbers. Analyzing mathematical, exact integers instead of machine integers greatly simplifies the implementation and proof of abstract integer operations. In contrast, there is no benefit in analyzing FP numbers using a more mathematical type such as rationals: FP operations (with rounding) behave well with respect to FP ordering, and abstract operations that use rationals are costly.

***Integer intervals*** Integer intervals are either $[a, b]$ with $a, b \in \mathbb{Z}$ or $\top$, standing for $(-\infty, \infty)$. We do not represent the semi-open intervals $[a, \infty)$ nor $(-\infty, b]$. The implementation of arithmetic and comparison operators over integer intervals is standard, with comparisons returning sub-intervals of $[0, 1]$. We go to great lengths, however, to derive tight intervals for bit-wise logical operations ("and", "or", "not", ...). The widening operator does not jump immediately to $(-\infty, \infty)$ but first tries to replace the upper bound by the next higher number in a list of well-chosen thresholds (zero and some powers of 2), and likewise replacing the lower bound by the next lower threshold [16]. The implementation and soundness proof build on Coq's `ZArith` library, which defines $\mathbb{Z}$ from first principles, essentially as lists of bits; no untrusted big integer library is involved.

***Floating-point intervals*** Likewise, FP intervals are either $[a, b]$ where $a$ and $b$ are non-NaN but possibly infinite FP numbers, or $\top$. Not-a-Number (NaN) belongs in $\top$ but not in $[a, b]$. Interval analysis for FP arithmetic is complicated by the various special FP numbers (NaN, infinities, signed zeroes), but remains surprisingly close to reasoning over real numbers. IEEE754 specifies FP arithmetic operations as "compute the exact result as a real, then round it to a representable FP number". For example, addition of two finite FP numbers $x, y$ is defined as $x \oplus y = \circ(x + y)$, where $\circ$ is one of the rounding modes defined in IEEE754. Crucially, all these rounding modes are *monotonic* functions. Therefore, if $x \in [a, b]$ and $y \in [c, d]$,

$$x \oplus y = \circ(x + y) \in [\circ(a + c), \circ(b + d)] = [a \oplus c, b \oplus d]$$

This property provides tight bounds for $\oplus$ and other FP operations, provided the rounding mode is known statically. This is the case for C#minor, which specifies round to nearest, ties to even, and gives no way for the program to dynamically change the rounding mode. Likewise, and unlike ISO C, C#minor specifies exactly the precision used by FP operations and the places where conversions between precisions occur. Therefore, the FP interval domain does not need to account for excess precision and possible double rounding.

The implementation and proof of the FP interval domain build on the Flocq library, which provides first-principles specifications and implementations of FP arithmetic in terms of mathematical integers and reals [9].

***Integer congruences*** The congruence domain abstracts integers as pairs $(n, m)$ of a modulus $m$ and a constant $n$, representing all integers equal to $n$ modulo $m$:

$$\gamma(n, m) = \{x \in \mathbb{Z} \mid \exists k, x = n + km\}$$

The case $m = 1$ corresponds to $\top$. The case $m = 0$ is meaningful and corresponds to constant propagation: $\gamma(n, 0) = \{n\}$. Tracking constants this way enables more precise analysis of multiplications and divisions. This domain of congruences is crucial to analyze the safety of memory accesses, guaranteeing that they are properly aligned.

## 6.2 From non-relational to relational domains

The non-relational domains of intervals and congruences share a common interface, specifying a type `t` of abstract values; a concretization $\gamma$ to the union of $\mathbb{Z}$ integers and double-precision floats; functions to abstract constants; and functions to perform "forward" and "backward" analysis of C#minor operators. The following excerpt from the interface gives the flavor of the "forward" and "backward" functions.

```
forward_unop: i_unary_operation → t+⊤ → t+⊤+⊥;
backward_unop:
  i_unary_operation → t+⊤ → t+⊤ → t+⊤+⊥;
forward_unop_sound: ∀ op x x_ab, x ∈ γ x_ab →
  eval_iunop op x ⊆ γ (forward_unop op x_ab);
backward_unop_sound: ∀ op x x_ab, x ∈ γ x_ab →
  ∀ res res_ab, res ∈ γ res_ab →
  eval_iunop op x res →
  x ∈ γ (backward_unop op res_ab x_ab);
```

The "forward" functions compute an abstraction of the result given abstractions for the arguments of the operator. The "backward" functions take abstractions for the result and the arguments, and produce possibly better approximations for the arguments. For example, the backward analysis of $[0, 1] + [1, 2]$ with result $[0, 1]$ produces $[0, 0]$ for the first argument and $[1, 1]$ for the second one.

A generic domain transformer turns any non-relational domain satisfying this interface into a relational domain. Abstract environments are implemented as sparse finite maps from variables to non-$\top$ abstract values. Mappings from a variable to $\top$ are left implicit to make abstract environments smaller. The `assign` $x$ $e$ $A$ operation of the relational domain first computes an abstract value $a$ for expression $e$, looking up abstract values $A(y)$ for variables $y$ occurring in $e$ and using the forward operators provided by the non-relational domain. The result is the updated abstract environment $A[x \leftarrow a]$.

The `assume` $e$ $b$ $A$ operation of the relational domain abstractly evaluates $e$ "in reverse", starting with an expected abstract result that is the constant 1 if $b$ is true and the constant 0 otherwise. The expected abstract result $a_{res}$ is propagated to the leaves of $e$ using the backward operators of the non-relational domain. When encountering a variable $y$ in $e$, the abstract value of $y$ is refined, giving $A' = A[y \leftarrow A(y) \sqcap a_{res}]$.

This simple construction makes it easy to add other non-relational domains and combine them with relational domains.

### 6.3 Convex polyhedra

To exercise the interface for relational numerical domains, Verasco includes a relational domain of convex polyhedra. It builds on the VPL library of Fouilhé *et al.* [18], which implements all required operations over convex polyhedra represented as conjunctions of linear inequalities with rational coefficients. VPL is implemented in Caml using GMP rational arithmetic, and therefore cannot be trusted. However, every operation produces a Farkas certificate that can easily be checked by a validator written and proved sound in Coq [19]. For example, the `join` operation, applied to polyhedras $P_1, P_2$, returns not only a polyhedron $P$ but also Farkas certificates proving that the system of inequations $(P_1 \vee P_2) \wedge \neg P$ is unsatisfiable. Therefore, any concrete state $\rho \in \gamma(P_1) \cup \gamma(P_2)$ is also in $\gamma(P)$, establishing the soundness of `join`.

This is, currently, the only instance of verified validation a posteriori in Verasco. While simpler abstract domains can be verified directly with reasonable proof effort, verified validation is a perfect match for this domain, avoiding proofs of difficult algorithms and enabling efficient implementations of costly polyhedral computations.

### 6.4 Symbolic equalities

The relational domain of symbolic equalities records equalities $x = e_c$ between a variable $x$ and a conditional expression $e_c$, as well as facts $e_c = \texttt{true}$ or $e_c = \texttt{false}$ about the Boolean value of an expression. Conditional expressions $e_c$ extend numerical expressions $e$ with zero, one or several if-then-else selectors in prenex position:

$$e_c ::= e \mid e_c \mathrel{?} e_c : e_c$$

On its own, this domain provides no numerical information that can be used to prove absence of run-time errors. Combined with other numerical domains via the communication mechanism of section 7, symbolic equalities enable these other domains to analyze `assume` operations more precisely. A typical example comes from the way CompCert compiles C's short-circuit Boolean operators `&&` and `||`. The pass that pulls side effects outside of expressions transforms these operators into assignments to temporary Boolean variables. For example, "`if (f(x) > 0 && y < z) { s; }`" becomes, in C#minor,

```
t1 = f(x);
if (t1 > 0) { t2 = y < z; } else { t2 = 0; }
if (t2) { s; }
```

The symbolic equality domain infers $\texttt{t}_2 = \texttt{t}_1 > 0 \mathrel{?} \texttt{y} < \texttt{z} : 0$ at the second `if`. Assuming $\texttt{t}_2 = \texttt{true}$ in `s` adds no information in the interval and polyhedra domains. Noticing this fact, these domains can query the domain of equalities, obtain the symbolic equality over $\texttt{t}_2$ above, and learn that $\texttt{y} < \texttt{z}$ and $\texttt{t}_1 > 0$.

A set of equalities $x = e_c$ and facts $e_c = b$ concretizes to all concrete environments that validate these equations:

$$\gamma(\mathit{Eqs}, \mathit{Facts}) = \left\{ \rho \,\middle|\, \begin{array}{l} (x = e_c) \in \mathit{Eqs} \;\Rightarrow \rho(x) \in \texttt{eval}\ \rho\ e_c \\ (e_c = b) \in \mathit{Facts} \Rightarrow b \in \texttt{eval}\ \rho\ e_c \end{array} \right\}$$

A new equation is added by `assign`, and a new fact is added by `assume`. All equations and facts involving variable $x$ are removed when doing `assign` or `forget` over $x$. We do not track previous values of assigned variables the way value numbering analyses do. Likewise, we do not treat equalities between variables $x = y$ specially.

The clever operation in this domain is the join between two abstract states: this is where conditional expressions are inferred. Computing (optimal) least upper bounds between sets of symbolic equalities is known to be difficult [21], so we settle for an over-approximation. Equations and facts that occur in both abstract states (using syntactic equality for comparison) are kept. If one state contains an equality $x = e'_c$ and a fact $e_c = \texttt{true}$, and the other state contains $x = e''_c$ and $e_c = \texttt{false}$, the equality $x = e_c \mathrel{?} e'_c : e''_c$ is added to the joined state. All other equalities and facts are discarded. Widening is similar to join, except that new conditional expressions are not inferred.

### 6.5 Handling machine integers

Numerical domains such as intervals and polyhedra are well understood as abstractions of unbounded mathematical integers. However, most integer types in programming languages are bounded, with arithmetic overflows treated either as run-time errors or by "wrapping around" and taking the result modulo the range of the type. In C#minor, integer arithmetic is defined modulo $2^N$ with $N = 32$ or $N = 64$ depending on the operation. Moreover, C#minor does not distinguish between signed and unsigned integer types: both are just $N$-bit vectors. Some integer operations such as division or comparisons come in two flavors, one that interprets its arguments as unsigned integers and the other as signed integers; but other integer operations such as addition and multiplication are presented as a single operator that handles signed and unsigned arguments identically.

All these subtleties of machine-level integer arithmetic complicate static analysis. For specific abstract domains such as intervals and congruences, ad hoc approaches are known, such as strided intervals [36], wrapped intervals [31], or reduced product of two intervals of $\mathbb{Z}$, tracking signed and unsigned interpretations respectively [8]. These approaches are difficult to extend to other domains, especially relational domains. In Verasco, we use a more generic construction that transforms any relational domain over mathematical integers $\mathbb{Z}$ into a relational domain over $N$-bits machine integers with modulo-$2^N$ arithmetic.

We first outline the construction on a simple, non-relational example. Consider the familiar domain of intervals over $\mathbb{Z}$, with concretization $\gamma([l, h]) = \{x : \mathbb{Z} \mid l \le x \le h\}$. To adapt this domain to the analysis of 4-bit machine integers (type `int4`), we keep the same abstract values $[l, h]$ with $l, h \in \mathbb{Z}$, but concretize them to machine integers as follows:

$$\gamma_m([l, h]) = \{b : \texttt{int4} \mid \exists n : \mathbb{Z},\ n \in \gamma([l, h]) \wedge b = n \bmod 2^4\}$$

In other words, the mathematical integers in $\gamma([l, h])$, that is, $l, l+1, \ldots, h-1, h$, are projected modulo 16 into bit vectors.

All arithmetic operations that are compatible with equality modulo $2^4$ can be analyzed using the standard abstract operations over $\mathbb{Z}$-intervals. For example, 4-bit addition `add` is such that $\texttt{add}\ b_1\ b_2 = (b_1 + b_2) \bmod 2^4$. If it is know that $x \in [0, 2]$, we analyze $\texttt{add}\ x\ 15$ like we would analyze $x + 15$ (addition in $\mathbb{Z}$), obtaining $[0, 2] + [15, 15] = [15, 17]$. This interval $[15, 17]$ concretizes to three 4-bit vectors, $\{15, 0, 1\}$ with unsigned interpretation and $\{-1, 0, 1\}$ with signed interpretation. An overflow occurred in the unsigned view, but the $\mathbb{Z}$-interval arithmetic tracks it correctly. The same technique of analyzing machine operations as if they were exact works for addition, subtraction, and bitwise operations (and, or, not), without loss of precision, and also for multiplication and left shift, possibly with loss of precision.

Other arithmetic operations such as division, right shifts, and comparisons are not compatible with equality modulo $2^4$. (These are exactly the operations that must come in two flavors, unsigned and signed, at the machine level.) For example, $-1 \le 0$ but $15 \not\le 0$, even though $-1 = 15 \pmod{2^4}$. To analyze these operations, we first try to reduce the intervals for their arguments to the interval $[L, H)$ expected by the operation: $[0, 15]$ for an unsigned operation and $[-8, 7]$ for a signed operation. To this end, we just add an appropriate multiple of 16 to the original interval; this operation does not change its $\gamma_m$ concretization. Continuing the example above, $\mathtt{add}\ x\ 15 \in [15, 17]$, viewed as a signed integer, can be reduced to the interval $\mathtt{add}\ x\ 15 \in [-1, 1]$ by subtracting 16. Therefore, the signed comparison $\mathtt{le\_s}\ (\mathtt{add}\ x\ 15)\ 4$ can be analyzed as

$$\mathtt{le\_s}\ (\mathtt{add}\ x\ 15)\ 4 \in ([-1, 1] \leq [4, 4]) = \mathtt{true}$$

If we need to view $\mathtt{add}\ x\ 15 \in [15, 17]$ as an unsigned 4-bit integer, the best contiguous interval we can give is $[0, 15]$. Therefore, the unsigned comparison $\mathtt{le\_u}\ (\mathtt{add}\ x\ 15)\ 4$ is analyzed as

$$\mathtt{le\_u}\ (\mathtt{add}\ x\ 15)\ 4 \in ([0, 15] \leq [4, 4]) = \top$$

In the signed comparison case, the unsigned overflow during the computation of $\mathtt{add}\ x\ 15$ is benign and does not harm the precision of the analysis. In the unsigned comparison case, the overflow is serious and makes the result of the comparison unpredictable.

On the example of intervals above, our construction is very close to wrapped intervals [31]. However, our construction generalizes to any relational domain that satisfies the Verasco interface for "ideal" numerical domains. Such domains abstract ideal environments $\rho : \mathtt{var} \to \mathbb{Z} + \mathtt{float64}$ where integer-valued variables range over mathematical integers, not machine integers. Consider such a domain, with abstract states $A$ and concretization function $\gamma$. We now build a domain that abstracts machine environments $\rho_m : \mathtt{var} \to \mathtt{int32} + \mathtt{int64} + \mathtt{float64}$ where integer-valued variables are 32- or 64-bit machine integers with wrap-around arithmetic. We keep the same type $A$ of abstract states, but interpret them as sets of machine environments via

$$\gamma_m(A) = \{\rho_m \mid \exists \rho \in \gamma(A),\ \forall v,\ \rho_m(v) \cong \rho(v)\}$$

The agreement relation $\cong$ between a machine number and an ideal number is defined as

$$\begin{array}{rcll} b \in \mathtt{int32} & \cong & n \in \mathbb{Z} & \text{iff } b = n \bmod 2^{32} \\ b \in \mathtt{int64} & \cong & n \in \mathbb{Z} & \text{iff } b = n \bmod 2^{64} \\ f \in \mathtt{float64} & \cong & f' \in \mathtt{float64} & \text{iff } f = f' \end{array}$$

The abstract operations $\mathtt{assign}_m$, $\mathtt{assume}_m$ and $\mathtt{forget}_m$ over the machine domain are defined in terms of those of the underlying ideal domain after translation of the numerical expressions involved:

$$\begin{aligned} \mathtt{assign}_m\ x\ e\ A &= \mathtt{assign}\ x\ [\![e]\!]_A\ A \\ \mathtt{assume}_m\ e\ b\ A &= \mathtt{assume}\ [\![e]\!]_A\ b\ A \\ \mathtt{forget}_m\ x\ A &= \mathtt{forget}\ x\ A \end{aligned}$$

The translation of expressions inserts just enough normalizations so that the ideal transformed expression $[\![e]\!]_A$ evaluates to an ideal number that matches (up to the $\cong$ relation) the value of $e$ as a machine number. Variables and constants translate to themselves. Arithmetic operators that are compatible with the $\cong$ relation, such as integer addition and subtraction, and all FP operations, translate isomorphically. Other arithmetic operators have their arguments reduced in range, as explained below.

$$\begin{aligned} &[\![x]\!]_A = x \\ &[\![\mathtt{add}\ e_1\ e_2]\!]_A = [\![e_1]\!]_A + [\![e_2]\!]_A \\ &[\![\mathtt{le\_u}\ e_1\ e_2]\!]_A = \\ &\quad \mathtt{reduce}_A [\![e_1]\!]_A\ [0, 2^{32}) \leq \mathtt{reduce}_A\ [\![e_2]\!]_A\ [0, 2^{32}) \\ &[\![\mathtt{le\_s}\ e_1\ e_2]\!]_A = \\ &\quad \mathtt{reduce}_A\ [\![e_1]\!]_A\ [-2^{31}, 2^{31}) \leq \mathtt{reduce}_A\ [\![e_2]\!]_A\ [-2^{31}, 2^{31}) \end{aligned}$$

The purpose of $\mathtt{reduce}_A\ e\ [L, H)$, where $[L, H)$ is an interval of width $2^N$, is to reduce the values of $e$ modulo $2^N$ so that they fit the interval $[L, H)$. To this end, it uses a $\mathtt{get\_itv}\ e\ A$ operation of the ideal numerical domain that returns a variation interval of $e$. From this interval, it determines the number $q$ of multiples of $2^N$ that must be subtracted from $e$ to bring it back to the interval $[L, H)$. This is not always possible, in which cases $[L, H)$ is returned as the reduced expression. (Remember that numerical expressions in Verasco are nondeterministic and use intervals as constants.)

$$\begin{aligned} &\mathtt{reduce}_A\ e\ [L, H) = \\ &\quad \mathtt{let}\ [l, h) = \mathtt{get\_itv}\ e\ A\ \mathtt{in} \\ &\quad \mathtt{if}\ h - l \geq 2^N\ \mathtt{then}\ [L, H)\ \mathtt{else} \\ &\quad\quad \mathtt{let}\ q = \lfloor (l - L)/2^N \rfloor\ \mathtt{in} \\ &\quad\quad \mathtt{if}\ h + q.2^N \leq H\ \mathtt{then}\ e - q.2^N\ \mathtt{else}\ [L, H) \end{aligned}$$

The translation of expressions is sound in the following sense.

LEMMA 3. *Assume $\rho_m \in \gamma_m(A)$, $\rho \in \gamma(A)$ and $\rho_m(x) \cong \rho(x)$ for all variables $x$. Then, for all machine expressions $e$,*

$$v_m \in \mathtt{eval}_m\ \rho_m\ e \Rightarrow \exists v,\ v \in \mathtt{eval}\ \rho\ [\![e]\!]_A\ \wedge v_m \cong v$$

It follows that the $\mathtt{assign}_m$ and $\mathtt{assume}_m$ operations of the transformed domain are sound.

## 7. Communication between domains

Several abstract domains are used in order to keep track of different kinds of properties. For example, we need interval information to check that array accesses are within bounds. We use a congruence domain to check alignment of memory accesses. A domain of symbolic equalities helps us dealing with boolean expressions.

All those domains need to communicate. For example, only the interval domain is able to infer numerical information for all operators, including bitwise operators, division and FP operations; however, all other domains may need to use this information. Another example is the symbolic equalities domain: if the condition of a test is just a variable, another domain can substitute the variable with a boolean expression provided by this symbolic domain in order to refine their abstract states.

The classic approach to combining two abstract domains and make them exchange information is the *reduced product* [15]. Implementations of reduced products tend to be specific to the two domains being combined, and are difficult to scale to the combination of $n > 2$ domains. Reduced products are, therefore, not a good match for the modular architecture of Verasco. Instead, we use a system of inter-domain communications based on channels, inspired by that of ASTRÉE [17]. We define an input channel as follows:

```
Record in_chan : Type :=
  { get_itv: iexpr var → IdealIntervals.abs+⊥;
    get_eq_expr: var → option (mux_iexpr var) }.
```

An input channel is a record of functions. Each function corresponds to a specific kind of query: `get_itv` returns an interval of variation for an expression, while `get_eq_expr` returns an expression that evaluates to the same value as the variable it is called on. This type of channels is meant to be extended when needed. For example, one could add a query for a linear approximation of an expression, which could be answered by a dedicated domain and used by linear relational domains.

Like abstract states, channels have a concretization function. Intuitively, an environment $\rho : \mathtt{var} \to \mathbb{Z} + \mathtt{float64}$ is in the concretization of a channel if all answers to queries are valid in $\rho$:

```
Record in_chan_gamma chan ρ : Prop :=
  { get_itv_correct:
      ∀ e, eval_iexpr ρ e ⊆ γ (chan.(get_itv) e);
    get_eq_expr_correct:
      ∀ x e, chan.(get_eq_expr) x = Some e →
             eval_mux_iexpr ρ e (ρ x) }.
```

Channels are used by domains when they need information from another domain. When an operation of a domain receives as argument an abstract value, it also receives a channel corresponding to

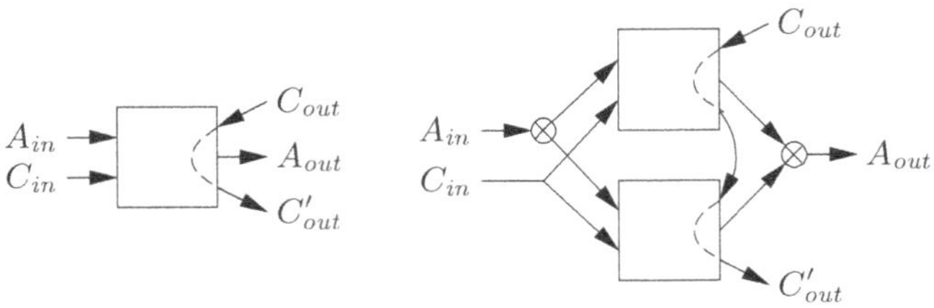


**Figure 4.** Communication channels between abstract operators. Left: single operator. Right: composition of two operators from different domains.

the same concrete environments. (Channel $C_{in}$ in figure 4.) Symmetrically, each transfer function that returns a new abstract value also returns a channel $C'_{out}$ that other domains can query to obtain information on the state after the execution of the transfer function. Finally, yet another channel $C_{out}$ is provided as extra argument to each transfer function. Querying this channel will provide information on the state after the execution of transfer functions from other domains. Only abstract domains having already computed these function can answer these queries. In other words, the domain operation produces $C'_{out}$ by enriching information already present in $C_{out}$ with information of its own. For example, the `assign` transfer function, which corresponds, in the concrete, to an assignment of an expression to a variable, has the following type:

```
assign: var → iexpr var → t * in_chan →
        in_chan → (t * in_chan)+⊥;
```

The first and second arguments are the assigned variable and expression. The third argument is a pair representing the initial states: an abstract value and the channel $C_{in}$. The fourth argument is the channel $C_{out}$ representing the current information about the final state after the assignment. If no contradiction is found, `assign` returns the final abstract state and the enriched channel $C'_{out}$. The specification of `assign` is as follows:

```
assign_correct: ∀ x e ab chan ρ n,
    n ∈ eval_iexpr ρ e →
    ρ ∈ γ ab →
    (upd ρ x n) ∈ γ chan →
    (upd ρ x n) ∈ γ (assign x e ab chan);
```

Here, we extend $\gamma$ to pairs of abstract values and channels, taking `γ (x, y) = γ x ∩ γ y` and using Coq type classes. This specification of `assign` is analogous to the one in figure 2. The difference is that we add an hypothesis stating that the two channels given as parameters are correct with respect to initial and final states respectively. Moreover, we demand that the returned channel be correct with respect to the final state.

An implementation of such a specification has to create a channel. For each query, the implementation can choose to forward it to the channel received as its fourth parameter, effectively forwarding it to another domain, or to answer it using its own information, or to do both and combine the information. For example, an interval domain will answer `get_itv` queries but not `get_eq_expr` queries, forwarding the latter to other domains.

This interface for channel-aware transfer functions such as `assign` makes it easy to combine two domains and have them communicate. Verasco provides a generic combinator (pictured as ⊗ in figure 1) that takes two abstract domains over ideal numerical environments and returns a product domain where information coming from both domains is stored, and where the two domains can communicate via channels. The definition of `assign` for the product is the following:

```
assign v e (ab:(A*B)*in_chan) chan :=
  let '((a, b), abchan) := ab in
  (* Computation on the first component *)
  do_bot retachan <- assign v e (a, abchan) chan;
  let '(reta, chan) := retachan in
  (* Computation on the second component,
     using the new input channel *)
  do_bot retbchan <- assign v e (b, abchan) chan;
  let '(retb, chan) := retbchan in
  NotBot ((reta, retb), chan)
```

The "plumbing" implemented here is depicted in figure 4, right part. As shown there, the $C_{out}$ channel passed to the second abstract domain is the $C'_{out}$ channel generated by the first abstract domain. This enables the second abstract domain to query the first one.

Using this product construction, we can build trees (nested products) of cooperating domains. As depicted in figure 1, the input to the "$\mathbb{Z} \to$ `int`" domain transformer described in section 6.5 is such a combination of numerical domains. Abstract states of this combination are pairs of, on the one hand, nested pairs of abstract states from the individual numerical domains, and, on the other hand, a channel. The channel is not only used when calling abstract transfer functions, but also directly in order to get numerical information such as variation intervals. When the "$\mathbb{Z} \to$ `int`" domain transformer calls a transfer function, it simply passes as initial $C_{out}$ channel a "top" channel whose concretization contains all concrete environments: `assign x e v in_chan_top`.

One final technical difficulty is comparison between abstract states, such as the subsumption test $\sqsubseteq$ used during post-fixpoint computation. In the upper layers, abstract states comprise (nested pairs of) abstract values plus a channel. Therefore, it seems necessary to compare two channels, or at least one channel and one abstract state. However, channels being records of functions, comparison is not decidable. Our solution is to maintain the invariant that *channels never contain more information than what is contained in the abstract values they are paired with.* That is, at the top of the combination of domains, when we manipulate a pair `(ab, chan)` of an abstract value and a channel, we will make sure that `γ(ab) ⊆ γ(chan)` holds. In order to check whether one such pair `(ab1, chan1)` is smaller than another `(ab2, chan2)`, we only need to check that `γ(ab1, chan1) ⊆ γ(ab2)`, which is easily decidable. Thus, the type of the comparison function for abstract values is:

```
leb: t * in_chan → t → bool
```

Note that it is useful to provide `leb` with a channel for its first argument: an abstract domain can, then, query other domains in order to compare abstract values.

However, the constraint `γ(ab) ⊆ γ(chan)` is too strong for real abstract domains: it makes it impossible for a domain to forward a query to another domain. Instead, we use a weaker constraint for every transfer function. In the case of `assign`, we prove:

```
∀ x e in chan0 ab chan,
  assign x e in chan0 = NotBot (ab, chan) →
  γ chan0 ∩ γ ab ⊆ γ(chan)
```

That is, the returned channel contains no more information than what is contained in the returned abstract value and the given channel. When `chan0` is `in_chan_top`, it follows that `γ(ab) ⊆ γ(chan)`, ensuring the soundness of the `leb` comparison function.

The property that limits the amount of information contained in channels is useful beyond the proof of soundness for comparisons: it is also a sanity check, ensuring that the returned channel only depends on the abstract value and on the channel given as the last argument, but not for instance on channels or abstract values

| | Specs | Proofs | Overall |
|---|---|---|---|
| Interfaces | 1081 | 139 | 3% |
| Abstract interpreter | 2335 | 2204 | 13% |
| State abstraction | 2473 | 3563 | 17% |
| Numerical domains | 7805 | 8563 | 48% |
| Domain combinators | 1305 | 1826 | 9% |
| Intervals | 1489 | 2224 | 10% |
| Congruences | 403 | 288 | 2% |
| Polyhedra (validator) | 4038 | 3598 | 22% (from [19]) |
| Symbolic equalities | 570 | 627 | 3% |
| Miscellaneous libraries | 3153 | 3329 | 19% |
| **Total** | 16847 | 17040 | 33887 lines |

**Table 1.** Size of the Coq development

previously computed. This is important for efficiency, because if the closures contained in the channel made references to previous channels or abstract values, this would make the analyzer keep old abstract values in memory, leading to bad memory behavior.

## 8. Implementation and mechanization

The Coq development for Verasco is about 34 000 lines, excluding blanks and comments. An additional 6 000 lines of Caml implement the operations over poyhedra that are validated a posteriori. The Coq sources split equally between proof scripts, on the one hand, and algorithms, specifications and statements of theorems on the other. Table 1 shows the relative sizes of the various components of Verasco. The parts reused from CompCert (e.g., syntax and semantics of C#minor) are not counted.

The interfaces that provide the backbone of Verasco are pleasantly lean. The bulk of the development is the abstract domains for states and (especially) for numbers, which involve large case analyses and difficult proofs over integer and F.P. arithmetic.

The Coq proofs are essentially constructive. The axiom of excluded middle and the axiom of functional extensionality are used in a few places, for convenience rather than by necessity. However, floating-point arithmetic is specified using Coq's theory of real numbers, which relies on classical logic axioms.

Except for the operations over polyhedra, the algorithms used by Verasco are implemented directly in Coq's specification language as function definitions in purely functional style. An executable analyzer is obtained by automatic extraction of Caml code from these function definitions and those of CompCert.

## 9. Experimental results

We conducted preliminary experiments with the executable C#minor static analyzer obtained as described in section 8. We ran the analyzer on a number of small test C programs (up to a few hundred lines). The purpose was to verify the absence of run-time errors in these programs. To exercise further the analyzer, we added support for a built-in function `verasco_assert(e)` to explicitly ask the analyzer to prove invariants that are expressible as C expressions `e`.

To model inputs, we added support for two other built-in functions: `any_int64` and `any_double`, which nondeterministically return a value of the requested type. They are often coupled to the built-in function `verasco_assume(b)`[2] to further constrain their results. These functions are also used to model library functions, whose code is not available or trusted.

[2] We only consider program executions where the boolean expression `b` is true when `verasco_assume(b)` is reached.

The following describes representative programs that we analyzed. The other examples have similar characteristics and lead to comparable observations.

***Function integration*** The example `integr.c` is a small program adapted from a CompCert benchmark. Most of its code is given below.

```
typedef double (*fun)(double);
fun functions[N] = { id, square, fabs, sqrt };

double
integr(fun f, double low, double high, int n) {
    double h, x, s; int i;
    h = (high - low) / n; s = 0;
    for (i = n, x = low; i > 0; i--, x += h)
        s += f(x);
    return s * h;
}

int main(void) {
    for (int i = 0; i < any_int(); ++i) {
        double m = any_double();
        verasco_assume( 1. <= m );
        int n = any_int();
        verasco_assume (0 < n);
        integr(functions[i % N], 0., m, n);
  }
  return 0;
}
```

This program repeatedly computes an approximation of the integral of a function between zero and some number greater than one. The function in question is picked from a constant array. It stresses various aspects of the analyzer such as function pointers, arrays, floating point and machine arithmetic.

***Numerical simulations*** Two programs of a few hundred lines taken from the CompCert benchmark, `nbody.c` and `almabench.c`, feature heavy numerical (floating point) computations and array manipulation.

***Cryptographic routines*** The `smult.c` example performs scalar multiplication. It is taken from the cryptography library NaCl. Scalars and group elements are stored in arrays of bytes or unsigned integers. Many of these arrays are initialized within a loop. Understanding that such an array is indeed properly initialized at the end of the loop would require a dedicated analysis beyond the scope of this paper [22]. Instead, we annotated the program to request full unrolling of these loops during analysis, thus preventing fixpoint computations.

***Preliminary results*** On the examples described above, Verasco was able to prove the absence of run-time errors. This is encouraging, since these examples exercise many delicate aspects of the C language: arrays, pointer arithmetic, function pointers, and floating-point arithmetic. As summarized in the table below, analysis times are high. Section 11 discusses possible directions to speed up the analyzer.

| Program | Size | Time[3] |
|---|---|---|
| `integr.c` | 42 lines | 0.1s |
| `smult.c` | 330 lines | 86.0s |
| `nbody.c` | 179 lines | 30.8s |
| `almabench.c` | 352 lines | 328.6s |

[3] Xeon E3-1240 processor, 3.4GHz, 8Mo cache, 16Go RAM.

## 10. Related work

Early work on the mechanized verification of static analyses was conducted in the framework of dataflow analyses. This includes Klein and Nipkow's verified Java bytecode verifier [25], Cachera *et al.*'s Coq formalization of dataflow analysis [11], and the verified dataflow analyses that support optimizations in CompCert [27]. Only non-relational abstract domains are considered, and there is no widening to accelerate the convergence of fixpoint iterations. Hofmann *et al.* verify a generic fixpoint solver usable in this context [24].

The first attempt to mechanize abstract interpretation in its full generality is Monniaux's master's thesis [30]. Using the Coq proof assistant and following the orthodox approach based on Galois connections, he runs into difficulties with $\alpha$ abstraction functions being nonconstructive, and with the calculation of abstract operators being poorly supported by Coq. Later, Pichardie's Ph.D. thesis [34, 35] mechanizes the $\gamma$-only presentation of abstract interpretation that we use in Verasco. Widening in fixpoint iterations as well as relational domains are supported, but the applications to Java static analysis presented in [34] use only non-relational domains. Blazy *et al.* use Pichardie's approach to verify an interval analysis for the RTL intermediate language of CompCert [8]. Bertot [5] and Nipkow [33] give alternate presentations of this approach, respectively in Coq and in Isabelle/HOL, resulting in pedagogical abstract interpreters for the IMP mini-language.

Many of the formalizations mentioned above run into serious complications to prove the termination of widened fixpoint iteration, using either integer measures [33] or well-founded orderings [11, 35]. The proof obligations related to termination account for much of the difficulty of constructing modular hierarchies of abstract domains. In Verasco, we forego termination proofs and elect to verify partial correctness only.

The ongoing project closest to Verasco in terms of ambitions is SparrowBerry by Cho *et al.* [13]. Rather than proving the soundness of a static analyzer, they follow a proof-carrying code approach: the existing, untrusted SparseSparrow C static analyzer is instrumented to produce analysis certificates, which are checked for correctness by a validator proved correct in Coq. Validation *a posteriori* reduces the overall proof effort to some extent. Indeed, we use it locally in Verasco to implement the polyhedral domain. However, we were reluctant to validate the analysis of a whole program by fear that the resulting certificates would be very large and take too long to check. (One of the claimed reasons why Astrée scales [16] is that it keeps few abstract states in memory at any given time.) This fear may be unfounded in light of the very good checking times reported for SparrowBerry [13]. We note, however, that SparrowBerry implements only one, non-relational domain (integer intervals), and that it does not handle a number of C features that Verasco handles (floating-point arithmetic, unions, wrap-around in unsigned integer arithmetic, pointer comparisons, and function pointers).

## 11. Conclusions and perspectives

Here is the final theorem in the Coq verification:

```
Theorem vanalysis_correct :
 forall prog res tr,
 vanalysis prog = (res, nil) →
 program_behaves (semantics prog) (Goes_wrong tr) →
 False.
```

Paraphrasing: if the whole-program analyzer `vanalysis` returns an empty list of alarms as its second result, the execution of the program cannot get stuck on a run-time error, regardless of the trace of inputs `tr` given to the program.

Verasco is an ongoing experiment, but at this stage of the project it already demonstrates the feasibility of formally verifying a realistic static analyzer based on abstract interpretation. Having to write Coq specifications and proofs did not preclude Verasco from handling a large source language (the subset of C typically used in critical embedded systems) nor from supporting multiple, nontrivial numerical abstract domains. Rather, this requirement that everything is specified and proved sound steered us towards a highly modular architecture, with well-specified interfaces and generic combinators to mix and adapt abstract domains. Most of these domains and domain combinators can be reused in other tool verification projects; some of them also act as reference implementations for advanced techniques for which no implementation was publically available before, such as the channel-based combination of abstractions.

The current Verasco analyzer can be extended in many directions. First, the algorithmic efficiency of the analyzer needs improvement. Currently, Verasco can take several minutes to analyze a few hundred lines of C. There are numerous sources of inefficiencies, which we are currently analyzing. One is Coq's integer and FP arithmetic, built from first principles (lists of bits). It should be possible to parameterize Verasco over arithmetic libraries such that more efficient big integer libraries and processor-native FP numbers can be used as an alternative. Another potential source of inefficiency is the purely functional data structures (AVL trees, radix-2 trees) used for maps and sets. ASTRÉE scales well despite using similar, purely functional data structures, but only because their implementations take advantage from *physical sharing* within and between tree data structures [16]. In Verasco, we already obtained good speedups by preserving preexisting sharing between the arguments of join operations. Going further, we could re-share a posteriori using general hash-consing [10].

Extending Verasco on the source language side, dynamic memory allocation could probably be handled by extending the memory abstraction so that one abstract memory cell can stand for several concrete memory locations, such as all the blocks created by a `malloc` inside a loop. Recursion raises bigger challenges: both the memory abstraction and the abstract interpreter would require heavy modifications so that they can merge the abstract states from multiple, simultaneously-active invocations of a recursive function, perhaps using call strings in the style of $k$-CFA [32].

Concerning the C#minor abstract interpreter, precision of the analysis would be improved by smarter unverified heuristics for loop unrolling, not relying on programmer-inserted annotations. The more elegant and powerful method would certainly be provided by a general trace partitioning mechanism [37]. Also, the nested fixpoint iterations arising out of the analysis of nested loops can be costly. It should be possible to accelerate convergence by starting the inner iterations not at $\perp$ but at the post-fixpoint found at the previous outer iteration. The starting points could be provided by an external, untrusted oracle written in imperative Caml.

The hierarchy of numerical abstractions is set up to accommodate new abstract domains easily. High on our wish list is a domain of *octagons*: linear inequalities of the form $\pm x \pm y \leq c$ [28]. Octagons are algorithmically more efficient than convex polyhedra. Moreover, using floating-point numbers for the coefficients of their difference bound matrices, octagons can infer inequalities involving floating-point program variables and not just integer variables. Such a use of FP arithmetic in a static analyzer is fraught with danger of numerical inaccuracy and deserves a formal proof of soundness. Just like convex polyhedra, octagons also need expression linearization heuristics [29] to extract more information out of nonlinear expressions.

## Acknowledgments

This work is supported by Agence Nationale de la Recherche, grant ANR-11-INSE-003. A. Fouilhé, S. Boulmé, D. Monniaux and M. Périn developed the VPL library and the verified validator mentioned in section 6.3. J. Feret and A. Miné provided advice based on their experience with Astrée.

## References


[1] A. Ahmed, A. W. Appel, C. D. Richards, K. N. Swadi, G. Tan, and D. C. Wang. Semantic foundations for typed assembly languages. *ACM Trans. Program. Lang. Syst.*, 32(3), 2010.

[2] A. W. Appel. *Program Logics for Certified Compilers*. Cambridge University Press, 2014.

[3] A. W. Appel and S. Blazy. Separation logic for small-step Cminor. In *TPHOLs*, volume 4732 of *LNCS*, pages 5–21. Springer, 2007.

[4] A. W. Appel and D. A. McAllester. An indexed model of recursive types for foundational proof-carrying code. *ACM Trans. Program. Lang. Syst.*, 23(5):657–683, 2001.

[5] Y. Bertot. Structural abstract interpretation: A formal study using Coq. In *Language Engineering and Rigorous Software Development, LerNet Summer School*, pages 153–194. Springer, 2008.

[6] B. Blanchet, P. Cousot, R. Cousot, J. Feret, L. Mauborgne, A. Miné, D. Monniaux, and X. Rival. A static analyzer for large safety-critical software. In *PLDI*, pages 196–207. ACM, 2003.

[7] S. Blazy, Z. Dargaye, and X. Leroy. Formal verification of a C compiler front-end. In *Formal Methods*, volume 4085 of *LNCS*, pages 460–475. Springer, 2006.

[8] S. Blazy, V. Laporte, A. Maroneze, and D. Pichardie. Formal verification of a C value analysis based on abstract interpretation. In *SAS*, volume 7935 of *LNCS*, pages 324–344. Springer, 2013.

[9] S. Boldo and G. Melquiond. Flocq: A unified library for proving floating-point algorithms in Coq. In *ARITH*, pages 243–252. IEEE, 2011.

[10] T. Braibant, J.-H. Jourdan, and D. Monniaux. Implementing and reasoning about hash-consed data structures in Coq. *J. Autom. Reasoning*, 53(3):271–304, 2014.

[11] D. Cachera, T. P. Jensen, D. Pichardie, and V. Rusu. Extracting a data flow analyser in constructive logic. *Theor. Comput. Sci.*, 342(1):56–78, 2005.

[12] A. Chlipala. Modular development of certified program verifiers with a proof assistant,. *J. Funct. Program.*, 18(5-6):599–647, 2008.

[13] S. Cho, J. Kang, J. Choi, C.-K. Hur, and K. Yi. SparrowBerry: A verified validator for an industrial-strength static analyzer. `http://ropas.snu.ac.kr/sparrowberry/`, 2013.

[14] P. Cousot and R. Cousot. Abstract interpretation: A unified lattice model for static analysis of programs by construction or approximation of fixpoints. In *POPL*, pages 238–252. ACM, 1977.

[15] P. Cousot and R. Cousot. Systematic design of program analysis frameworks. In *POPL*, page 269–282. ACM, 1979.

[16] P. Cousot, R. Cousot, J. Feret, L. Mauborgne, A. Miné, and X. Rival. Why does Astrée scale up? *Formal Methods in System Design*, 35(3):229–264, 2009.

[17] P. Cousot, R. Cousot, J. Feret, L. Mauborgne, A. Miné, D. Monniaux, and X. Rival. Combination of abstractions in the Astrée static analyzer. In *ASIAN*, volume 4435 of *LNCS*, pages 272–300. Springer, 2006.

[18] A. Fouilhé, D. Monniaux, and M. Périn. Efficient generation of correctness certificates for the abstract domain of polyhedra. In *SAS*, volume 7935 of *LNCS*, pages 345–365. Springer, 2013.

[19] A. Fouilhé and S. Boulmé. A certifying frontend for (sub)polyhedral abstract domains. In *VSTTE*, volume 8471 of *LNCS*, pages 200–215. Springer, 2014.

[20] D. Greenaway, J. Andronick, and G. Klein. Bridging the gap: Automatic verified abstraction of C. In *ITP*, volume 7406 of *LNCS*, pages 99–115. Springer, 2012.

[21] S. Gulwani, A. Tiwari, and G. C. Necula. Join algorithms for the theory of uninterpreted functions. In *FSTTCS*, volume 3328 of *LNCS*, pages 311–323. Springer, 2004.

[22] N. Halbwachs and M. Péron. Discovering properties about arrays in simple programs. In *PLDI*, pages 339–348. ACM, 2008.

[23] P. Herms, C. Marché, and B. Monate. A certified multi-prover verification condition generator. In *VSTTE*, volume 7152 of *LNCS*, pages 2–17. Springer, 2012.

[24] M. Hofmann, A. Karbyshev, and H. Seidl. Verifying a local generic solver in Coq. In *SAS*, volume 6337 of *LNCS*, pages 340–355, 2010.

[25] G. Klein and T. Nipkow. A machine-checked model for a Java-like language, virtual machine, and compiler. *ACM Trans. Program. Lang. Syst.*, 28(4):619–695, 2006.

[26] X. Leroy. Formal verification of a realistic compiler. *Comm. ACM*, 52(7):107–115, 2009.

[27] X. Leroy. A formally verified compiler back-end. *J. Automated Reasoning*, 43(4):363–446, 2009.

[28] A. Miné. The octagon abstract domain. *Higher-Order and Symbolic Computation*, 19(1):31–100, 2006.

[29] A. Miné. Symbolic methods to enhance the precision of numerical abstract domains. In *VMCAI*, volume 3855 of *LNCS*, pages 348–363. Springer, 2006.

[30] D. Monniaux. Réalisation mécanisée d'interpréteurs abstraits. Master's thesis, U. Paris 7, 1998.

[31] J. A. Navas, P. Schachte, H. Søndergaard, and P. J. Stuckey. Signedness-agnostic program analysis: Precise integer bounds for low-level code. In *APLAS*, volume 7705 of *LNCS*, pages 115–130. Springer, 2012.

[32] F. Nielson, H. Nielson, and C. Hankin. *Principles of Program Analysis*. Springer, 2005.

[33] T. Nipkow. Abstract interpretation of annotated commands. In *ITP*, volume 7406 of *LNCS*, pages 116–132. Springer, 2012.

[34] D. Pichardie. *Interprétation abstraite en logique intuitionniste: extraction d'analyseurs Java certifiés*. PhD thesis, U. Rennes 1, 2005.

[35] D. Pichardie. Building certified static analysers by modular construction of well-founded lattices. *Electr. Notes Theor. Comput. Sci.*, 212:225–239, 2008.

[36] T. W. Reps, G. Balakrishnan, and J. Lim. Intermediate-representation recovery from low-level code. In *PEPM*, pages 100–111. ACM, 2006.

[37] X. Rival and L. Mauborgne. The trace partitioning abstract domain. *ACM Trans. Program. Lang. Syst.*, 29(5), 2007.

# Analyzing Program Analyses

Roberto Giacobazzi
Dipartimento di Informatica
University of Verona, Italy
& Irdeto Canada

Francesco Logozzo
Microsoft Research
Redmond, WA, USA

Francesco Ranzato
Dipartimento di Matematica
University of Padova, Italy

*Dedicated to Radhia Cousot*

## Abstract

We want to prove that a static analysis of a given program is complete, namely, no imprecision arises when asking some query on the program behavior in the concrete (*i.e.*, for its concrete semantics) or in the abstract (*i.e.*, for its abstract interpretation). Completeness proofs are therefore useful to assign confidence to alarms raised by static analyses. We introduce the completeness class of an abstraction as the set of all programs for which the abstraction is complete. Our first result shows that for any nontrivial abstraction, its completeness class is not recursively enumerable. We then introduce a stratified deductive system $\vdash_A$ to prove the completeness of program analyses over an abstract domain $A$. We prove the soundness of the deductive system. We observe that the only sources of incompleteness are assignments and Boolean tests — unlikely a common belief in static analysis, joins do not induce incompleteness. The first layer of this proof system is generic, abstraction-agnostic, and it deals with the standard constructs for program composition, that is, sequential composition, branching and guarded iteration. The second layer is instead abstraction-specific: the designer of an abstract domain $A$ provides conditions for completeness in $A$ of assignments and Boolean tests which have to be checked by a suitable static analysis or assumed in the completeness proof as hypotheses. We instantiate the second layer of this proof system first with a generic nonrelational abstraction in order to provide a sound rule for the completeness of assignments. Orthogonally, we instantiate it to the numerical abstract domains of Intervals and Octagons, providing necessary and sufficient conditions for the completeness of their Boolean tests and of assignments for Octagons.

***Categories and Subject Descriptors*** D.2.4 [*Software Engineering*]: Software/Program Verification—correctness proofs, formal methods; D.3.1 [*Programming Languages*]: Formal Definitions and Theory—semantics; F.3.2 [*Logics and Meanings of Programs*]: Semantics of Programming Languages—program analysis;

***General Terms*** Languages.

***Keywords*** Abstract interpretation; abstract domain.



*POPL '15*, January 15–17, 2015, Mumbai, India.
Copyright © 2015 ACM 978-1-4503-3300-9/15/01...$15.00.
http://dx.doi.org/10.1145/2676726.2676987

## 1. Introduction

Consider the typical creative process faced by Alice, the designer of a new static analysis $\mathcal{A}$. Alice starts with a set of "representative" programs and properties to be checked, *e.g.*, the absence of certain runtime errors or of infinite computations. She designs the static analysis—equivalently the abstract domain—that best fits her initial dataset. Next, she will try the analysis $\mathcal{A}$ on a new set of programs, validate the results, and carefully refine the abstract domain or improve the efficiency as needed. When $\mathcal{A}$ becomes precise and fast enough it is shipped to external users.

A major part of the design of $\mathcal{A}$ is the tuning of the cost/precision trade-off—the analysis should deliver the expected answer on a set $\mathbb{T}$ of test programs without asking too many computational (time, space) resources. To achieve it, Alice gives up some of the precision, *i.e.*, she consciously introduces incompleteness into $\mathcal{A}$. The rationale for this design choice is that $\mathbb{T}$ represents real-world programs and as such she needs $\mathcal{A}$ to be complete for them. We denote this set of programs with $\mathbb{C}(A)$, where $A$ is the abstraction, or a set of abstractions, employed by the static analysis $\mathcal{A}$. On the other hand, the incompleteness of the analysis will only manifest in less common or pathological programs.

Ideally, given a program $P$, Alice wants to know whether $P$ is in $\mathbb{C}(A)$ or not. In fact, if $P \in \mathbb{C}(A)$ then the analysis will be precise and it will answer exactly to any query $q$ on the behaviour of $P$ which is expressible in the language of $A$. As a consequence, any alarm raised by the static analysis $\mathcal{A}$ on $P$ will be a true alarm, and $\mathcal{A}$ can then be used as an effective program verifier for $P$.

***The Problem.*** We are interested in proving that $P \in \mathbb{C}(A)$. For instance, let us consider the basic abstract domain $\mathsf{Null} = \{\bot, \mathit{Null}, \mathit{NotNull}, \top\}$ for nullness analysis of variables [1]. The non-null analysis will infer that, for the (intentionally very simple) program $\mathit{NN}$ in Figure 1, $x$ is not null after the conditional—if the true branch is taken, $x$ is null but it is assigned a freshly allocated memory location; otherwise $x$ maintains its non-null value. Intuitively, $\mathit{NN} \in \mathbb{C}(\mathsf{Null})$: both the Boolean guard $x = \mathit{null}$ and its negation $x \neq \mathit{null}$ are exactly representable in $\mathsf{Null}$; **new** is complete w.r.t. nullness: we do not know what happens to the heap (abstraction), but we know for sure it returns a non-null value (complete abstraction); **skip** does not affect the current state; and, eventually, the join does not introduce imprecision.

Next, let us consider the program *Dec* in Figure 2. Let us assume to analyze it using the abstract domain of intervals, $\mathsf{Int}$ [3], *without* loop unrolling and widening—in this case, the number of abstract iterations is finite. The analysis will report that $x \in [0, 0]$ at the loop exit, which is the most precise answer. Why is this the case? At first, one may argue that since the inferred invariant is a singleton it is necessarily the most precise one. However, this way of reasoning is incorrect in general. For instance, a program point may be unreachable, so that the concrete set of states at that point is

```
if(x = null)
    x := new object();
else skip;
// query: x ≠ null?
```

**Figure 1.** The program *NN*: an example where the nullness abstraction is complete.

```
x := 9;
while(x > 0)
    x := x − 1;
// query: x = 0?
```

**Figure 2.** The program *Dec*: an example where intervals are complete, but the proof is not trivial.

```
x := 9;
while(x > 0)
    x := x − 2;
// query: x = −1?
```

**Figure 3.** The program *Dec*$_2$: an example where intervals are incomplete, and a naif proof system may deduce the opposite.

$\varnothing$, and for any abstraction $A$ every abstract value different from the bottom value $\bot_A$ will be correct yet incomplete. Also, one could reason as follows: the assignment $x := 9$ with a constant is precise with intervals; both Boolean guards $x > 0$ and $x \leq 0$ can be exactly represented with intervals, resp. by $[1, +\infty)$ and $(-\infty, 0]$; the decrement operation $x := x - 1$ on intervals is precise, *e.g.*, $[3, 9] - [1, 1] = [2, 8]$. Therefore, one may conclude that this is why the analysis of *Dec* with intervals is complete. However, this way of reasoning is wrong. Consider the program *Dec*$_2$ in Figure 3. In its concrete semantics, at the loop exit point we have that $x \in [-1, -1]$, whereas in its analysis with $\mathsf{Int}$, the *most precise* invariant we can obtain, *even without widenings*, is $x \in [-1, 0]$. Therefore, *Dec*$_2 \notin \mathbb{C}(\mathsf{Int})$. By contrast, here, the same (intuitive) argument as for the *Dec* program still holds: assignment $x := 9$ is precise with $\mathsf{Int}$; both $x > 0$ and $x \leq 0$ can be exactly represented with $\mathsf{Int}$; the decrement $x := x - 2$ on intervals is precise, *e.g.*, $[3, 9] - [2, 2] = [1, 7]$.

Where is the problem with the above reasoning? It turns out that, even if the guard $x \leq 0$ can be exactly represented with intervals, its transfer function $[\![x \leq 0]\!] : \wp(\mathbb{Z}) \rightarrow \wp(\mathbb{Z})$ is not complete with respect to $\mathsf{Int}$. To give an example, let us consider the set of concrete values $S = \{-1, 1, 3, 5, 7, 9\}$, which is the set of values of $x$ computed by the while-loop of *Dec*$_2$. Hence, if the input to $[\![x \leq 0]\!]$ is $S$ then we obtain in $\mathsf{Int}$:

$$\begin{aligned}\mathsf{Int}([\![x \leq 0]\!]S) &= \mathsf{Int}(\{x \mid x \leq 0\} \cap S)\\ &= \mathsf{Int}(\{-1\}) = [-1, -1].\end{aligned}$$

On the other hand, if the input to $[\![x \leq 0]\!]$ is instead the abstraction $\mathsf{Int}(S)$ then we have:

$$\begin{aligned}\mathsf{Int}([\![x \leq 0]\!]\mathsf{Int}(S)) &= \mathsf{Int}([\![x \leq 0]\!][-1, 9])\\ &= \mathsf{Int}([-1, 0]) = [-1, 0],\end{aligned}$$

that is, the transfer function $[\![x \leq 0]\!]$ is not complete on $\mathsf{Int}$. Therefore, we cannot use mere syntactic arguments to prove whether $P \in \mathbb{C}(A)$ because they may lead to wrong conclusions.

***Our Solution.*** As a first step, one may think to design a deductive system for proving that a program $P$ is complete for an abstraction $A$ which requires that all the assignments and Boolean guards of $P$ are complete for $A$. Such a deductive system will be sound, but definitely too strong. For instance, we cannot use it to prove that the analysis of very simple programs as *Dec* in Figure 2 is complete—this deductive system can deduce completeness of *NN* in Figure 1, though.

Instead, we propose a layered proof system for completeness. Roughly, the layered proof system pushes the completeness proof of the analysis from the program statements up to the assignments and Boolean guards, and then it may use a further analysis to prove their completeness. For instance, in the example of Figure 2, the analysis of the program *Dec* is complete if both the initialization and the while loop are complete. The analysis of the initialization $x := 9$ is trivially complete for intervals. The analysis of the while loop is complete if the analysis of the Boolean guard, of its negation, and of the body are. With a little bit of effort, we can prove that the analysis of the body $x := x - 1$ is complete for intervals. The problem comes with the Boolean guards $x > 0$ and $x \leq 0$. We observed before that, in general, intervals are not complete for those guards. We will show that incompleteness happens when there is a "hole" in the concrete set of values *and* the Boolean guard discerns among those: in fact, in our counterexample above, $S$ has a hole between $-1$ and $1$ and the guard mentions 0. In the program *Dec*, there is no such a hole, because the variable $x$ assumes, in the concrete, all the values between 0 and 9. Thus, the analysis of the Boolean tests of *Dec* with intervals is complete. We can use a static analysis to prove this, and to conclude that the interval analysis of *Dec* is complete.

We should be careful in defining what "holes" are. Consider the program *DecInc* in Figure 4. Here, both $x$ and $y$ uniformly assume all the values between 0 and 9 and at the end of the loop we have that $x = 0$ and $y = 9$. However, the analysis of *DecInc* with intervals will determine at best that $y \in [0, +\infty)$. Once again, the source of incompleteness is the Boolean guard. In fact, the transfer function of $x \leq 0$, which is the negation of the guard $x > 0$, is not complete for intervals with the set of input pairs $(x, y)$ of concrete values $S = \{(9, 0), (8, 1), \ldots, (1, 8), (0, 9)\}$. It is worth remarking that this incompleteness does not originate from a perceived imprecision in the abstract join of intervals: in fact, the abstract lub $\sqcup_A$ of any abstraction $A$ is *always* complete, meaning that $\alpha(X \cup Y) = \alpha(X) \sqcup_A \alpha(Y)$ always holds—since abstraction functions in Galois connections always preserve joins [3]. On the other hand, using the abstract domain of Octagons [20], the guard $x > 0$ and its negation $x \leq 0$ are instead complete for the input set $S$.

A further issue arises with assignments. For relational abstractions as Octagons, it turns out that assignments like $z := x + y$ and $x := 2 * y$ are incomplete even if $x + y$ and $2 * y$ are complete considered as numerical expressions. Indeed, we will show that the only assignments which are complete for Octagons have the following shape: $x := a * y + k$ and $x := a * x + k$ for $a \in \{-1, 0, 1\}$ and $k \in \mathbb{Z}$.

Given an abstraction, it is therefore natural to ask: (i) which conditions on assignments/Boolean expressions and their input concrete states ensure completeness of the analysis; and (ii) how to

```
x := 9; y := 0;
while(x > 0)
  {x := x − 1; y := y + 1}
// query: y = 9?
```

**Figure 4.** The program *DecInc*: an example where Intervals are incomplete whereas Octagons are complete.

statically check these conditions so that the we can prove that the analysis is complete. We will address these issues in the article.

***Vision.*** This work originates from our experience in building real world-static analyses. We want to be able to prove that the static analysis on a given abstraction in some cases will infer an invariant which is complete, and therefore use this information for alarm ranking: alarms originating from analyses that cannot be proved complete should be ranked lower. Therefore, we advocate a new methodology for designing static analyses. In addition to the "main" static analysis for property checking, Alice also provides one or more completeness conditions, to be used to validate the completeness of the analysis for a given program. Our goal is ambitious because, as we will see in the paper, a proof of completeness relies upon the determination of the best correct approximation for all the statements occurring in the program. While this requirement can be bypassed for the fundamental constructs for program composition—that is, sequential composition, branching and guarded iteration, for the latter two by requiring completeness of their Boolean guards—for generic assignments this is still an open problem, as there exist (relational) abstract domains where the best correct approximation of the assignment for certain expressions is not known yet.

***Results.*** Firstly, we recall the necessary basic notions of abstract interpretation and completeness of abstract domains (Section 2), and we define the syntax, concrete semantics and abstract semantics for a basic imperative language (Section 3). We introduce the notion of completeness class for an abstraction $A$ as the set of programs for which the analysis over $A$ is complete; we show that for all nontrivial abstractions the corresponding completeness class is infinite, nontrivial, nonextensional, and in particular it is a productive set, namely it shares the same structure of the enumerations of true sentences in first order arithmetics, therefore inheriting Gödel's incompleteness (Section 4). We provide the core proof system for completeness; we prove that it is sound for all nonrelational abstract domains and argue that completeness of Boolean guards can be regarded as the hardest part in these completeness proofs (Section 5). We then analyze the soundness of the proof system for relational abstractions, in particular for the case of Octagons. We introduce a further layer in the proof system to prove completeness of assignments and Boolean guards; we instantiate it with the Interval and Octagon abstractions; we characterize the assignments which are complete for Octagons; we provide necessary and sufficient conditions for the completeness of Intervals and Octagons when handling Boolean guards (Section 6). We conclude by comparing our work to previous one (Section 7) and by discussing other possible applications of completeness proofs (Section 8).

## 2. Background

***Orders.*** Given a function $f : X \to Y$ and a subset $S \subseteq X$ then $f(S) \triangleq \{f(s) \in Y \mid s \in S\}$ denotes the image of $f$ on $S$. A complete lattice $C$ w.r.t. an ordering relation $\leq$ is denoted by $\langle C, \leq\rangle$. The pointwise ordering relation $\sqsubseteq$ between two functions $f, g : X \to C$ whose co-domain is a complete lattice $C$, is defined by $f \sqsubseteq g$ if for any $x \in X$, $f(x) \leq_C g(x)$. A function $f : C \to D$ between complete lattices is additive (co-additive) when $f$ preserves arbitrary lub's (glb's), while it is continuous when $f$ preserves lub's of chains. Given a function $f : C \to C$ on a complete lattice $C$, $\mathsf{lfp}(f)$ and $\mathsf{gfp}(f)$ denote, respectively, the least and greatest fixpoints of $f$, when they exist. Recall that least and greatest fixpoints always exist for monotone functions.

***Abstract Domains.*** In standard abstract interpretation [3, 4], abstract domains, also called abstractions, are specified by Galois connections/insertions (GCs/GIs for short). Concrete and abstract domains, $\langle C, \leq_C\rangle$ and $\langle A, \leq_A\rangle$, are assumed to be complete lattices which are related by abstraction and concretization maps $\alpha : C \to A$ and $\gamma : A \to C$ that give rise to a GC $(\alpha, C, A, \gamma)$, that is, for all $a \in A$ and $c \in C$, $\alpha(c) \leq_A a \Leftrightarrow c \leq_C \gamma(a)$. A GC is a GI when $\alpha \circ \gamma = \lambda x.x$. We use $\mathrm{Abs}(C)$ to denote all the possible abstractions of $C$: $A \in \mathrm{Abs}(C)$ means that $A$ is an abstract domain of $C$ specified by some GC/GI, while the notations $A_\alpha \in \mathrm{Abs}(C)$ and $A_{\alpha,\gamma} \in \mathrm{Abs}(C)$ are used to emphasize the underlying abstraction and concretization functions $\alpha$ and $\gamma$.

If $\alpha : C \to A$ is additive then we obtain a GC $(\alpha, C, A, \alpha^+)$ by considering its right-adjoint $\alpha^+ \triangleq \lambda a. \vee_C \{c \in C \mid \alpha(c) \leq_A a\}$. Dually, if $\gamma : C \to A$ is co-additive then $(\gamma^-, C, A, \gamma)$ is a GC where $\gamma^- \triangleq \lambda c. \wedge_A \{a \in A \mid c \leq_C \gamma(a)\}$ is the left-adjoint of $\gamma$. We recall well known properties of a GC $(\alpha, C, A, \gamma)$: (1) $\alpha$ is additive; (2) $\gamma$ is co-additive; (3) $\gamma \circ \alpha : C \to C$ is a closure operator, *i.e.*, it is monotone, idempotent, and increasing (*i.e.*, $x \leq \gamma(\alpha(x))$); (4) if $\mu : C \to C$ is a closure operator then $(\mu, C, \mu(C), id)$ is a GI.

If $A_1, A_2 \in \mathrm{Abs}(C)$ then $A_1$ is equivalent to $A_2$, denoted $A_1 \cong A_2$, when $\gamma_{A_1}(A_1) = \gamma_{A_2}(A_2)$. The quotient $\mathrm{Abs}(C)_{/\cong}$ is called the lattice of abstractions [4] because it turns out to be a complete lattice w.r.t. the relative precision ordering $\sqsubseteq$: $A_1 \sqsubseteq A_2$ iff for any $c \in C$, $\gamma_{A_1}(\alpha_{A_1}(c)) \leq_C \gamma_{A_2}(\alpha_{A_2}(c))$. $A_1 \sqsubseteq A_2$ means that $A_1$ is a more precise abstraction of the concrete domain $C$ than $A_2$, or, equivalently, that $A_2$ abstracts $A_1$. A lub $\sqcup_i A_i$ in the lattice of abstractions is therefore the most precise domain in $\mathrm{Abs}(C)_{/\cong}$ which abstracts all $A_i$'s. The glb $\sqcap_i A_i$ is the most abstract (*i.e.*, less precise) domain in $\mathrm{Abs}(C)_{/\cong}$ which is more precise than all $A_i$'s, and is also called reduced product of the $A_i$'s.

***Intervals.*** The interval abstraction was introduced by Cousot and Cousot [2] and it is still a widely used nonrelational abstraction since it is efficient and yet able to give useful information to prove, *e.g.*, the absence of arithmetic overflows or out-of-bounds array accesses. Let $\mathbb{Z}^\star \triangleq \mathbb{Z} \cup \{-\infty, +\infty\}$ and assume that the standard ordering $\leq$ on $\mathbb{Z}$ is extended to $\mathbb{Z}^\star$ in the usual way. Hence:

$$\mathsf{Int} \triangleq \{[a, b] \mid a, b \in \mathbb{Z}^\star,\ a \leq b\} \cup \{\bot\}$$

endowed with the standard ordering $\leq_{\mathsf{Int}}$ induced by interval containement gives rise to a complete lattice, where $\bot$ is the bottom element and $[-\infty, +\infty]$ is the top element. Then, consider the function $min : \wp(\mathbb{Z}) \to \mathbb{Z}^\star$ defined as follows:

$$min(X) \triangleq \begin{cases} x & \text{if } \exists x \in X. \forall y \in X. x \leq y \\ -\infty & \text{otherwise} \end{cases}$$

while $max : \wp(\mathbb{Z}) \to \mathbb{Z}^\star$ is dually defined. The abstraction map $\alpha : \wp(\mathbb{Z}) \to \mathsf{Int}$ defined by:

$$\alpha(X) \triangleq \begin{cases} \bot & \text{if } X = \varnothing \\ [min(X), max(X)] & \text{if } X \neq \varnothing \end{cases}$$

preserves arbitrary unions in $\wp(\mathbb{Z})$ and therefore gives rise to a GI, *i.e.*, $\mathsf{Int}_\alpha \in \mathrm{Abs}(\langle \wp(\mathbb{Z}), \subseteq\rangle)$.

It is straightforward to define the nonrelational lift of intervals to $n$-dimensions, with $n > 1$. If $\vec{x} \in \mathbb{Z}^n$ is a $n$-dimensional vector of integers and $i \in [1, n]$ then $\vec{x}_i \in \mathbb{Z}$ denotes the $i$-th component of $\vec{x}$. In turn, if $X \in \wp(\mathbb{Z}^n)$ is a set of vectors then $X_i \triangleq \{\vec{x}_i \in \mathbb{Z} \mid \vec{x} \in \mathbb{Z}\}$ denotes the $i$-th projection of $X$. Then, the $n$-dimensional interval abstraction is $\mathsf{Int}^n \triangleq \mathsf{X}_1^n \mathsf{Int}$, endowed with the component-wise ordering of $\mathsf{Int}$. The following component-wise abstraction map $\alpha : \wp(\mathbb{Z}^n) \to \mathsf{Int}^n$ defined as $\alpha(X) \triangleq \langle \alpha_{\mathsf{Int}}(X_1), \ldots, \alpha_{\mathsf{Int}}(X_1)\rangle$ yields an abstract domain $\mathsf{Int}_\alpha^n \in \mathrm{Abs}(\langle \wp(\mathbb{Z}^n), \subseteq\rangle)$.

***Octagons.*** The octagon abstract domain [19, 20] is a relational refinement of the interval abstraction which is able to represent variable relations of the form $\pm x \pm y \leq k$ while keeping an acceptable efficiency by exploiting a representation based on a modification of so-called difference bound matrices. The terminology "octagon" comes from the fact that in two dimensions an abstract element is a polyhedron with at most eight sides. Given $n \geq 1$, a difference bound matrix (DBM) $\boldsymbol{m} \in \text{DBM}_n$ is a $n \times n$ square matrix having entries $\boldsymbol{m}_{i,j} \in \mathbb{Z} \cup \{+\infty\}$. Then, any $\boldsymbol{m} \in \text{DBM}_{2n}$ induces, according to the canonical representation described in [20], a $n$-dimensional octagon $\mathsf{oct}_{\boldsymbol{m}} \in \wp(\mathbb{Z}^n)$ defined as follows:

$$\mathsf{oct}_{\boldsymbol{m}} \triangleq \big\{\langle x_1, \ldots, x_n\rangle \in \mathbb{Z}^n \mid \forall i, j \in [1, n]. \\ x_i - x_j \leq \boldsymbol{m}_{2i-1,2j-1},\ x_i + x_j \leq \boldsymbol{m}_{2i-1,2j}, \\ -x_i + x_j \leq \boldsymbol{m}_{2i,2j-1},\ -x_i - x_j \leq \boldsymbol{m}_{2i,2j}\big\}.$$

Observe that interval bounds like $x_i \geq a$ and $x_i \leq b$ can be encoded, respectively, by $-x_i - x_i \leq -2a$ and $x_i + x_i \leq 2b$, so that a $n$-dimensional interval is a particular octagon. Let us also recall that DBM representations are not unique, so that it can happen that for different DBMs $\boldsymbol{m} \neq \boldsymbol{m}'$, we have that $\mathsf{oct}_{\boldsymbol{m}} = \mathsf{oct}_{\boldsymbol{m}'}$. The $n$-dimensional octagon abstract domain is defined to be:

$$\mathsf{Oct}^n \triangleq \{\mathsf{oct}_{\boldsymbol{m}} \in \wp(\mathbb{Z}^n) \mid \boldsymbol{m} \in \text{DBM}_{2n}\}$$

and turns out to be a complete lattice wr.t. the subset relation. Observe that octagons are closed under arbitrary set intersections but not under set unions, so that $\langle \mathsf{Oct}^n, \subseteq\rangle$ is a complete lattice which is not a join sublattice of $\wp(\mathbb{Z}^n)$. $\alpha : \wp(\mathbb{Z}^n) \to \mathsf{Oct}^n$ is the abstraction given by $\alpha(X) \triangleq \bigcap\{O \in \mathsf{Oct}^n \mid X \subseteq O\}$. It is well defined and, being a closure operator, it is additive, so that it yields a GI, namely, we have that $\mathsf{Oct}^n_\alpha \in \text{Abs}(\langle\wp(\mathbb{Z}^n), \subseteq\rangle)$. Clearly, octagons are a refinement of intervals, *i.e.*, $\mathsf{Oct}^n \sqsubseteq \mathsf{Int}^n$.

***Correctness.*** Let $f : C \to C$ be some concrete monotone function—to keep notation simple, we consider 1-ary functions—and let $f^\sharp : A \to A$ be a corresponding monotone abstract function defined on some abstraction $A_{\alpha,\gamma} \in \text{Abs}(C)$. Then, $f^\sharp$ is a correct (or sound) abstract interpretation of $f$ on $A$ when $\alpha \circ f \sqsubseteq f^\sharp \circ \alpha$ holds. If $f^\sharp$ is correct for $f$ then we also have fixpoint correctness, that is, $\alpha(\mathsf{lfp}(f)) \leq_A \mathsf{lfp}(f^\sharp)$. The abstract function

$$f^\alpha \triangleq \alpha \circ f \circ \gamma : A \to A$$

is called the best correct approximation of $f$ on $A$, because any abstract function $f^\sharp$ is correct iff $f^\alpha \sqsubseteq f^\sharp$. Hence, $f^\alpha$ plays the role of the best possible approximation of $f$ on the abstraction $A$.

***Completeness.*** An abstract function $f^\sharp$ is a complete abstract interpretation of $f$ on $A$ when $\alpha \circ f = f^\sharp \circ \alpha$ holds [4]. When $f^\sharp$ is an abstract transfer function on the abstraction $A$ used by a static analysis, completeness intuitively encodes the greatest precision for $f^\sharp$, meaning that the abstract behaviour of $f^\sharp$ on $A$ exactly matches the abstraction in $A$ of the concrete behaviour of $f$. If $f^\sharp$ is complete for $f$ then we have fixpoint completeness (also called fixpoint transfer): $\alpha(\mathsf{lfp}(f)) = \mathsf{lfp}(f^\sharp)$. It turns out that completeness $\alpha \circ f = f^\sharp \circ \alpha$ holds iff

$$\alpha \circ f = \alpha \circ f \circ \gamma \circ \alpha.$$

Thus, the possibility of defining a complete approximation $f^\sharp$ of $f$ on some $A \in \text{Abs}(C)$ only depends on the concrete function $f$ and on the abstraction $A$ [13]. We will use both $A$ is complete for $f$ and $f$ is complete on $A$ to refer to the completeness equation $\alpha \circ f = \alpha \circ f \circ \gamma \circ \alpha$.

The problem of making abstract domains complete has been addressed in [13]. A constructive characterization of the most abstract refinement, called complete shell, and of the most concrete simplification, called complete core, of any abstract domain $A \in \text{Abs}(C)$, making it complete for a given continuous function $f : C \to C$, is given as a fixpoint solution of an abstract domain equation derived from $f$ and $A$. Let us recall this definition for the case of the complete shell refinement. This is the abstract domain refinement $\mathsf{Shell}_f : \text{Abs}(C) \to \text{Abs}(C)$ defined as:

$$\mathsf{Shell}_f(A) \triangleq \mathsf{gfp}(\lambda X.\, A \sqcap R_f(X))$$

where, for any domain $X_{\alpha,\gamma} \in \text{Abs}(C)$, $R_f(X)$ is the most abstract domain which contains the maximal inverse image of $f$ on $X$, namely, $R_f(X) \supseteq \bigcup_{y \in X} \max(\{c \in C \mid f(c) \leq \gamma(y)\})$. As a consequence, the following characterization of complete abstract domains holds: the abstraction $A$ is complete for $f$ iff for any $y \in A$, $\alpha(\max(\{c \in C \mid f(c) \leq \gamma(y)\})) \in A$.

## 3. Language and Abstract Semantics

***Syntax.*** We consider a basic deterministic while-language $\mathsf{Imp}$ with arithmetic and Boolean expressions, as defined, e.g., in [25], whose syntax is as follows:

$$\text{AExp} \ni a ::= v \in \mathbb{Z} \mid x \in \mathit{Var} \mid a + a \mid a - a \mid a * a$$
$$\text{BExp} \ni b ::= \mathbf{t} \mid \mathbf{f} \mid a = a \mid a > a \mid b \wedge b \mid \neg b$$
$$\mathsf{Imp} \ni C ::= \mathbf{skip} \mid x := a \mid C; C \mid \mathbf{if}\ b\ \mathbf{then}\ C \mid \mathbf{while}\ b\ \mathbf{do}\ C$$

Programs are commands in $\mathsf{Imp}$. The set of variables occurring in some syntactic object is $\mathit{svars}(s) \subseteq \mathit{Var}$.

***Concrete Semantics.*** We let $\mathbb{S} \triangleq \mathit{Var} \to \mathbb{Z}$ denote the set of program stores. We will often represent a store $\rho \in \mathbb{S}$ as a tuple $\langle x_1/v_{x_1}, \ldots, x_n/v_{x_n}\rangle$.

The semantics of arithmetic expressions is the function $(\!|a|\!) : \mathbb{S} \to \mathbb{Z}$ defined as usual. Similarly, the semantics of Boolean predicates is the function $(\!|b|\!) : \mathbb{S} \to \{\mathbf{t}, \mathbf{f}\}$.

The collecting semantics of an arithmetic expression $a$ is the function $[\![a]\!] : \wp(\mathbb{S}) \to \wp(\mathbb{Z})$ defined as $[\![a]\!]S \triangleq \{(\!|a|\!)\rho \mid \rho \in S\}$. Similarly, the collecting semantics of a predicate $b$ is the function $[\![b]\!] : \wp(\mathbb{S}) \to \wp(\mathbb{S})$ defined as $[\![b]\!]S \triangleq \{\rho \in S \mid (\!|b|\!)\rho = \mathbf{t}\}$. Intuitively, $[\![b]\!]S$ filters the concrete states of $S$ which make $b$ true.

The collecting denotational semantics of a command $C$ is the function $[\![C]\!] : \wp(\mathbb{S}) \to \wp(\mathbb{S})$ defined as

$$[\![\mathbf{skip}]\!]S \triangleq S$$
$$[\![x := a]\!]S \triangleq \{\rho[x \mapsto (\!|a|\!)\rho] \mid \rho \in S\}$$
$$[\![C_1; C_2]\!]S \triangleq [\![C_2]\!]([\![C_1]\!]S)$$
$$[\![\mathbf{if}\ b\ \mathbf{then}\ C]\!]S \triangleq [\![C]\!][\![b]\!]S \cup [\![\neg b]\!]S$$
$$[\![\mathbf{while}\ b\ \mathbf{do}\ C]\!]S \triangleq [\![\neg b]\!]\big(\mathsf{lfp}(\lambda T.\, S \cup [\![C]\!][\![b]\!]T)\big).$$

Please observe that nontermination is encoded by the empty set: A program $C \in \mathsf{Imp}$ does not terminate on an input $S \in \wp(\mathbb{S})$ when $[\![C]\!]S = \varnothing$. In the following, we make the hypothesis that the inputs to semantic functions, *i.e.*, the sets of stores in $\wp(\mathbb{S})$ are recursively enumerable sets.

***Store Abstractions.*** A store abstraction is specified by a GC $A_{\alpha,\gamma} \in \text{Abs}(\langle\wp(\mathbb{S}), \subseteq\rangle)$ on sets of stores. Variable projection (a.k.a. existential abstraction) of a set of stores on a set of variables $V \subseteq \mathit{Var}$ is defined by the following mapping $\exists_V : \wp(\mathbb{S}) \to \wp(\mathbb{S})$:

$$\exists_V(S) \triangleq \{\rho \in \mathbb{S} \mid \exists \eta \in S. \forall y \notin V.\, \rho(y) = \eta(y)\}.$$

Variable projection on a single variable $x \in \mathit{Var}$ is denoted by $\exists_x$. We will consider store abstractions with a complete variable projection, namely, an abstract domain $A \in \text{Abs}(\wp(\mathbb{S}))$ such that for any $V \subseteq \mathit{Var}$, $\alpha \circ \exists_V = \alpha \circ \exists_V \circ \gamma \circ \alpha$. Completeness of variable projection is satisfied by virtually any store abstraction used in practice, *e.g.*, this property holds for all known nonrelational and relational numerical store abstractions like $\mathsf{Sign}$, $\mathsf{Int}$, $\mathsf{Oct}$, congruences [14], Karr's domain of linear equalities [16], etc. Any store abstraction $A$ (which is complete for variable renaming—the easy formalization of variable renaming is omitted here) can be also viewed as an abstraction of sets of integer values in $\langle\wp(\mathbb{Z}), \subseteq\rangle$ by considering stores that "focus" on a single variable (call it $y$): this is determined by the abstraction map $\alpha^{\mathbb{Z}} : \wp(\mathbb{Z}) \to A$ defined as $\alpha^{\mathbb{Z}}(Z) \triangleq \alpha(\{\rho \in \mathbb{S} \mid \rho(y) \in Z\})$. Hence, in the following, the store abstraction $A$ is also viewed and used as an abstraction of sets of integers.

***Abstract Semantics.*** We define the best correct abstract semantics for a generic store abstraction $A_{\alpha,\gamma} \in \mathrm{Abs}(\langle\wp(\mathbb{S}), \subseteq\rangle)$. We assume that $\sqcup$ is the join in $A$.

The best correct abstract semantics $[\![a]\!]^{\alpha} : A \to A$ for an arithmetic expression $a \in \mathrm{AExp}$ is $[\![a]\!]^{\alpha} S^{\sharp} \triangleq \alpha([\![a]\!]\gamma(S^{\sharp}))$. It is worth noting that, in general, the best correct abstract semantics is not the standard compositional definition $[\![\cdot]\!]^{\alpha_c}$ of the abstract semantics of expressions. For instance, the compositional definition of a binary integer operation $op$ is:

$$[\![a_1\, op\, a_2]\!]^{\alpha_c} S^{\sharp} \triangleq [\![a_1]\!]^{\alpha_c} S^{\sharp}\ op^{\alpha}\ [\![a_2]\!]^{\alpha_c} S^{\sharp}.$$

When instantiating such a definition for the intervals Int, it turns out that:

$$\begin{aligned}
[\![x + x * (-1)]\!]^{\mathsf{Int}} \langle x/[1,2]\rangle &= [0,0] \sqsubset \\
[\![x + x * (-1)]\!]^{\mathsf{Int}_c} \langle x/[1,2]\rangle &= [1,2] + ([1,2] * [-1,-1]) \\
&= [-1,1]
\end{aligned}$$

The best correct abstract semantics for a predicate $b \in \mathrm{BExp}$ on $A$ is the abstract function $[\![b]\!]^{\alpha} : A \to A$ defined as

$$[\![b]\!]^{\alpha} S^{\sharp} \triangleq \alpha([\![b]\!]\gamma(S^{\sharp})).$$

We derive the best correct abstract semantics $[\![C]\!]^{\alpha} : A \to A$ of a program $C \in \mathsf{Imp}$ as the best correct approximation of its concrete semantics. We exploit two well-known facts: (i) the composition of two complete functions is complete; and, (ii) in a GC, the abstract join is always the best correct approximation of the concrete join. Let $S^{\sharp} \in A$ be an abstract store:

$$\begin{aligned}
[\![\mathbf{skip}]\!]^{\alpha} S^{\sharp} &\triangleq S^{\sharp} \\
[\![x := a]\!]^{\alpha} S^{\sharp} &\triangleq \alpha(\{\rho[x \mapsto (\!| a |\!)\rho] \mid \rho \in \gamma(S^{\sharp})\}) \\
[\![C_1; C_2]\!]^{\alpha} S^{\sharp} &\triangleq [\![C_2]\!]^{\alpha}([\![C_1]\!]^{\alpha} S^{\sharp}) \\
[\![\mathbf{if}\ b\ \mathbf{then}\ C]\!]^{\alpha} S^{\sharp} &\triangleq [\![\neg b]\!]^{\alpha} S^{\sharp} \sqcup [\![C]\!]^{\alpha}([\![b]\!]^{\alpha} S^{\sharp}) \\
[\![\mathbf{while}\ b\ \mathbf{do}\ C]\!]^{\alpha} S^{\sharp} &\triangleq [\![\neg b]\!]^{\alpha}(\mathsf{lfp}(\lambda X^{\sharp}.\, S^{\sharp} \sqcup [\![C]\!]^{\alpha}[\![b]\!]^{\alpha} X^{\sharp}))
\end{aligned}$$

Let us comment on the definition: (i) The best correct approximation of an assignment $[\![x := a]\!]^{\alpha}$ does not rely on the best correct abstract semantics $[\![a]\!]^{\alpha}$ of the arithmetic expression $a$; (ii) In the least fixpoint definition for $[\![\mathbf{while}\ b\ \mathbf{do}\ C]\!]^{\alpha}$, the abstract function $\lambda X^{\sharp}.\, S^{\sharp} \sqcup [\![C]\!]^{\alpha}[\![b]\!]^{\alpha} X^{\sharp}$ turns out to be the best correct approximation on $A$ of the concrete function $\lambda T.\, S \cup [\![C]\!][\![b]\!]T$; (iii) In the abstract function $\lambda X^{\sharp}.\, S^{\sharp} \sqcup [\![C]\!]^{\alpha}[\![b]\!]^{\alpha} X^{\sharp}$, practical static analyzers replace the abstract lub $\sqcup$ with a widening operator $\nabla$ to accelerate or force the convergence of the iterations in the abstract domain $A$ [3], thus losing the property of having the best correct abstract semantics of programs.

***Complete Abstractions.*** A store abstraction $A_{\alpha} \in \mathrm{Abs}(\wp(\mathbb{S}))$ is complete for an arithmetic expression $a \in \mathrm{AExp}$, a Boolean test $b \in \mathrm{BExp}$ and a program $C \in \mathsf{Imp}$, when for any set of stores $S \in \wp(\mathbb{S})$:

$$\begin{aligned}
\alpha([\![a]\!]S) &= [\![a]\!]^{\alpha}\alpha(S), \\
\alpha([\![b]\!]S) &= [\![b]\!]^{\alpha}\alpha(S), \\
\alpha([\![C]\!]S) &= [\![C]\!]^{\alpha}\alpha(S).
\end{aligned}$$

## 4. The Class of Complete Abstractions

***Completeness, Queries and Alarms.*** The goal of a static analysis/verification tool is to soundly answer some questions on the dynamic (concrete) execution of programs. For instance, common queries to static analysis tools are: "*Is this variable not-null?*", "*Is this variable non-negative?*", "*Does this loop ever terminate?*". The first two are examples of safety properties, the third of a liveness property. Here, we focus on safety properties. Given a program $P$, a set of input stores $I \subseteq \mathbb{S}$ and a store query (*i.e.*, a store predicate) $q$, we are interested to know whether the final states of $P$ satisfy the query $q$, *i.e.*, whether the following formula holds:

$$\forall \rho \in \mathbb{S}.\, \rho \in [\![P]\!]I \Rightarrow q(\rho) = \mathbf{true},$$

or, equivalently, by denoting with $[\![q]\!] \subseteq \mathbb{S}$ the stores satisfying $q$, whether $[\![P]\!]I \subseteq [\![q]\!]$. Obviously, we cannot decide this for each possible query. Therefore, static analyses over-approximate the collecting semantics $[\![P]\!]$ and under-approximate the query $[\![q]\!]$. In general, the abstractions used for these two approximations may be different—for instance, this happens when a numerical abstract domain (like intervals or octagons) is used to infer variable bounds and a SMT solver is used to check the absence of buffer overruns. We are interested in the case where there is no under-approximation of the query, that is, we require: (i) the two abstract domains to coincide; and (ii) the query $q$ to be exactly represented in this abstract domain, namely, $\gamma(\alpha([\![q]\!])) = [\![q]\!]$. For instance, a query like $x \geq y \wedge y \geq 0$ is exactly represented with octagons but not with intervals—the best approximation with intervals being $x \geq 0 \wedge y \geq 0$.

The key observation is that if a program query $q$ is exactly representable in a store abstraction $A \in \mathrm{Abs}(\wp(\mathbb{S}))$ and the abstract semantics on $A$ for a program $P$ is complete, then answering the query $q$ in the abstract is the same as answering $q$ in the concrete, *i.e.*, no imprecision in answering $q$ for $P$ is introduced by the abstraction $A$. Thus, completeness of a static analysis of $P$ implies that no false alarm can arise for queries which are representable in $A$. This is summarized by the following lemma, which comes straight from the definitions. If $[\![q]\!]^{\alpha} \triangleq \alpha([\![q]\!]) \in A$ is the abstraction of $[\![q]\!]$, $q$ is *representable in* $A$ when $[\![q]\!] = \gamma([\![q]\!]^{\alpha})$.

**Lemma 4.1.** *If $A_{\alpha} \in \mathrm{Abs}(\wp(\mathbb{S}))$ is complete for $P$ and $q$ is representable in $A$ then, for any $I \in \wp(\mathbb{S})$*

$$[\![P]\!]I \subseteq [\![q]\!] \Leftrightarrow [\![P]\!]^{\alpha}\alpha(I) \leq_A [\![q]\!]^{\alpha}.$$

*Proof.* Let $A_{\alpha,\gamma} \in \mathrm{Abs}(\wp(\mathbb{S}))$ be complete for $P$ and $q$ be representable in $A$.
($\Rightarrow$) By monotonicity of $\alpha$, from $[\![P]\!]I \subseteq [\![q]\!]$ we obtain, by using the completeness and representability hypotheses, $\alpha([\![P]\!]I) = [\![P]\!]^{\alpha}\alpha(I) \leq_A \alpha([\![q]\!]) = \alpha(\gamma([\![q]\!]^{\alpha})) \leq [\![q]\!]^{\alpha}$.
($\Leftarrow$) Since $[\![P]\!]^{\alpha}$ is always correct we have that $[\![P]\!]^{\alpha}\alpha(I) \leq_A [\![q]\!]^{\alpha} \Rightarrow \alpha([\![P]\!]I) \leq_A \alpha([\![q]\!])$. Thus, by applying $\gamma$ to both sides of the inequality, we obtain $[\![P]\!]I \subseteq \gamma(\alpha([\![P]\!]I)) \subseteq \gamma(\alpha([\![q]\!])) = [\![q]\!]$. □

Note that the proof of $[\![P]\!]^{\alpha}\alpha(I) \leq_A [\![q]\!]^{\alpha} \Rightarrow [\![P]\!]I \subseteq [\![q]\!]$ does not make use of the completeness hypothesis, since this implication is a straight consequence of the soundness of the best correct approximation $[\![P]\!]^{\alpha}$. On the other hand, completeness is crucial for proving the reverse implication. Completeness can be therefore read as follows: if a complete static analysis of $P$ raises an alarm in answering a representable query $q$ then this alarm is surely real:

$$[\![P]\!]^{\alpha}\alpha(I) \not\leq_A [\![q]\!]^{\alpha} \Rightarrow [\![P]\!]I \not\subseteq [\![q]\!].$$

**Example 4.2.** Consider the program *DecInc* in Figure 4 and the final query $q \equiv y < 9$, which is representable by the intervals $\langle x \in (-\infty, +\infty), y \in (-\infty, 8]\rangle$, and therefore by an octagon as well.

The static analysis of *DecInc* on Int raises an alarm for $q$, meaning that $[\![DecInc]\!]^{\mathsf{Int}}\top_{\mathsf{Int}} = \langle x \in [0,0], y \in [0,+\infty)\rangle \not\leq_{\mathsf{Int}} [\![y < 9]\!]$. However, since Int is not complete for *DecInc*, Lemma 4.1 does not allow us to conclude that this is a false alarm. On the other hand, the static analysis on Oct also raises an alarm for $q$, because $[\![DecInc]\!]^{\mathsf{Oct}}\top_{\mathsf{Oct}} = \langle x \in [0,0], y \in [9,9]\rangle \not\leq_{\mathsf{Oct}} [\![y < 9]\!]$, and in this case Lemma 4.1 tells us that this is a real alarm. □

***Classes of Completeness.*** From Lemma 4.1 it is therefore natural to reason on the precision of an abstraction $A$ in terms of the set of programs that are complete for the program properties represented by $A$. This is the class of programs which represents at best (and uniquely) the potential of an abstract domain in answering questions on their behavior. We therefore introduce the notion of completeness class as a mapping from abstract domains to sets of programs: those for which the abstraction is complete. An analogous completeness class is defined for arithmetic expressions and Boolean predicates.

**Definition 4.3** (Completeness Class). Given $A_\alpha \in \mathrm{Abs}(\wp(\mathbb{S}))$, its *completeness class* $\mathbb{C}(A)$ (for commands) is defined as:

$$\mathbb{C}(A) \triangleq \{P \in \mathsf{Imp} \mid \alpha([\![P]\!]) = [\![P]\!]^\alpha\}.$$

Similarly, the completeness classes of $A$ for arithmetic, Boolean, and generic expressions are:

$$\mathbb{A}(A) \triangleq \{a \in \mathrm{AExp} \mid \alpha([\![a]\!]) = [\![a]\!]^\alpha\}$$
$$\mathbb{B}(A) \triangleq \{b \in \mathrm{BExp} \mid \alpha([\![b]\!]) = [\![b]\!]^\alpha\}.$$ □

Roughly, the completeness class $\mathbb{C}(A)$ is defined to be the set of all programs whose static analysis on a given abstraction $A$ will never produce false alarms for queries representable in $A$. This is therefore a property of programs with respect to a fixed abstraction. It is worth noting that this property is infinite and non-extensional (cf. [23]). It is infinite because for any abstract domain $A$ whose abstraction function is computable we have that $|\mathbb{C}(A)| = \omega$. This is shown by a straightforward padding argument by observing that **skip** $\in \mathbb{C}(A)$ for any $A$ and because sequential composition of complete commands is still complete. It is also non-extensional, *i.e.*, it is not an index set for partial recursive functions, because there always exist programs $P$ and $Q$ such that: $P$ is complete for $A$, $[\![P]\!] = [\![Q]\!]$, and $Q$ is not complete for $A$. This phenomenon is known in static analysis where semantics preserving program transformations may lose precision of analyses (e.g., see [12, 17]).

**Example 4.4.** Consider the abstract domain for sign analysis of integer variables $\mathsf{Sign} = \{\mathbb{Z}, -, 0, +, \varnothing\}$, which is a straightforward abstraction of $\langle\wp(\mathbb{Z}), \subseteq\rangle$. We consider the standard nonrelational lifting of Sign to a store abstraction in $\mathrm{Abs}(\langle\wp(\mathbb{S}), \subseteq\rangle)$. Consider the following two programs:

$$P \equiv y := 2; z := 3; x := y * z$$
$$Q \equiv y := 2; z := 3; x := y * (z-1) + y$$

Obviously, we have that $[\![P]\!] = [\![Q]\!]$. However, since Sign is complete for multiplication and incomplete for addition, it turns out that

$$[\![x := y * z]\!]^{\mathsf{Sign}}\langle x/\mathbb{Z},\ y/+, z/+\rangle = \langle x/+, y/+, z/+\rangle$$
$$[\![x := y * (z-1) + y]\!]^{\mathsf{Sign}}\langle x/\mathbb{Z},\ y/+, z/+\rangle = \langle x/\mathbb{Z}, y/+, z/+\rangle$$

so that

$$[\![P]\!]^{\mathsf{Sign}}\varnothing = \langle x/+, y/+, z/+\rangle, \quad [\![Q]\!]^{\mathsf{Sign}}\varnothing = \langle x/\mathbb{Z}, y/+, z/+\rangle.$$

Thus, $P \in \mathbb{C}(\mathsf{Sign})$ while $Q \notin \mathbb{C}(\mathsf{Sign})$. □

It turns out that the relative precision of abstract domains—encoded by the ordering $\sqsubseteq$ on the lattice of abstractions—and the corresponding classes of completeness are not related. In particular, it may well happen that for an abstraction $A$ which is complete for a given $P$, a generic refinement $A^{\mathrm{ref}}$ of $A$, *i.e.*, $A^{\mathrm{ref}} \sqsubseteq A$, turns out to be instead incomplete for the same program $P$. This phenomenon is well known in static program analysis and it corresponds to the fact that coarse abstractions may induce a complete static analysis for some program where more precise ones instead fail for that same program. In the following, we assume that the set $\mathbb{S}$ of all stores is infinite. If we consider a *trivial store abstraction*, *i.e.*, there is no abstraction at all or any set of stores is abstracted into a single (top) value corresponding to the "don't know" answer, then the corresponding completeness class turns out to be the whole set of programs Imp. Let $id \in \mathrm{Abs}(\wp(\mathbb{S}))$ denote the trivial identical store abstraction (*i.e.*, for any $S$, $id(S) = S$) and $\top_{\mathbb{S}} \in \mathrm{Abs}(\wp(\mathbb{S}))$ denote the trivial "don't know" store abstraction (*i.e.*, for any $S$, $\top_{\mathbb{S}}(S) = \mathbb{S}$). Also, let $\wp^{\mathrm{re}}(\mathbb{S})$ denote the set of all recursively enumerable subsets of $\mathbb{S}$. Let us point out that any static program analysis always relies on recursive, namely decidable, abstractions $A_\alpha \in \mathrm{Abs}(\wp(\mathbb{S}))$, meaning that: (i) for any store $\rho \in \mathbb{S}$, $\alpha(\{\rho\})$ is computable; and (ii) for any $S \in \wp^{\mathrm{re}}(\mathbb{S})$ and $\rho \in \mathbb{S}$, $\rho \in^? \alpha(S)$ is decidable.

**Theorem 4.5.** *If* $A \in \mathrm{Abs}(\wp(\mathbb{S}))$ *is recursive then* $\mathbb{C}(A) = \mathsf{Imp}$ *iff* $A \in \{id, \top_{\mathbb{S}}\}$.

*Proof.* The trivial abstractions $id$ and $\top_{\mathbb{S}}$ are complete for any program, so that if $A = id$ or $A = \top_{\mathbb{S}}$ then $\mathbb{C}(A) = \mathsf{Imp}$. Assume now that $\mathbb{C}(A) = \mathsf{Imp}$ and $A \neq id$ and $A \neq \top_{\mathbb{S}}$. Hence, there exists some $S \in \wp^{\mathrm{re}}(\mathbb{S})$ such that $S \subsetneq \gamma(\alpha(S)) \subsetneq \mathbb{S}$. Since $A$ is a decidable abstraction, we have that $S$ and $\gamma(\alpha(S))$ are recursively enumerable. Hence, there exist programs $P_S$ and $P_{\alpha(S)}$ on a single integer variable $x$ such that $[\![P_S]\!]\,\mathbb{S} = S$ and $[\![P_{\alpha(S)}]\!]\,\mathbb{S} = \gamma(\alpha(S))$. We pick some $b \in \mathbb{S} \smallsetminus \gamma(\alpha(S))$ and some $c \in \gamma(\alpha(S)) \smallsetminus S$. Then, let us consider the program $Q_{bc}$ associated with the following partial recursive function $\psi_{bc} : \mathbb{S} \to \mathbb{S}$:

$$\psi_{bc}(x) \triangleq \begin{cases} x & \text{if } x \in S \\ b & \text{if } x = c \\ \text{undefined} & \text{otherwise} \end{cases}$$

Observe that if $x \notin S$ then $[\![Q_{bc}]\!]\{x\} \neq \{x\}$, since $c \neq b$. Then, it turns out that $\alpha([\![Q_{bc}]\!]S) = \alpha(S)$ and $\alpha([\![Q_{bc}]\!]\gamma(\alpha(S))) = \alpha(S \cup \{b\})$. Moreover, since $S \subsetneq \gamma(\alpha(S)) \subseteq \gamma(\alpha(S \cup \{b\}))$, by GC, we obtain that $\alpha(S) \lneq \alpha(S \cup \{b\})$. Thus, we have shown that there exists a set of stores $S \in \wp^{\mathrm{re}}(\mathbb{S})$ such that:

$$\alpha([\![Q_{bc}]\!]S) \lneq \alpha([\![Q_{bc}]\!]\gamma(\alpha(S))) \leq [\![Q_{bc}]\!]^\alpha \alpha(S).$$

This means[1] that $Q_{bc} \notin \mathbb{C}(A)$ which contradicts the hypothesis that $\mathbb{C}(A) = \mathsf{Imp}$. □

Informally, the result above states that for all nontrivial abstractions there exists a program for which the abstraction is incomplete. Moreover, by a straightforward padding argument, any of these programs (e.g., $Q_{bc}$ in the proof of Theorem 4.5) can be extended to an infinite set of programs for which the abstraction is incomplete. This means that any nontrivial abstraction has an infinite set of programs for which it is incomplete. We show that $\mathbb{C}(A)$ and its complement $\overline{\mathbb{C}(A)}$, for any nontrivial abstraction $A$, are *productive* sets. Recall that a set $S$ is productive if there exists a general effective method (*i.e.*, a total recursive function) which enables us to find, for any recursively enumerable subset $Y \subseteq X$, an element

[1] Note that, for generic recursively enumerable sets $S$ and $\gamma(\alpha(S))$ such that $S \subsetneq \gamma(\alpha(S))$, the set $\gamma(\alpha(S)) \smallsetminus S$ may not be recursively enumerable. This means that (due to the $c \in \gamma(\alpha(S)) \smallsetminus S$) the program $Q_{bc}$ exists but we may not have a constructive computable way for building it. The mere existence of $Q_{bc}$ as a mathematical object is enough for the purpose of this proof.

$x \in X \smallsetminus Y$ (see [10, 23]). It follows that no productive set can be recursively enumerable. This proves that, for a nontrivial abstraction $A$, both $\mathbb{C}(A)$ and its complement $\overline{\mathbb{C}(A)}$ are intrinsically nonrecursively enumerable sets having a structure which is similar to the set of Gödel numbers of true sentences in first-order arithmetics.

**Theorem 4.6.** *If $A \in \mathrm{Abs}(\wp(\mathbb{S}))$ is nontrivial and recursive then $\mathbb{C}(A)$ and $\overline{\mathbb{C}(A)}$ are productive sets.*

*Proof.* In the following, without loss of generality, we assume that programs in $\mathsf{Imp}$ have a single variable ranging over $\mathbb{N}$, so that $\mathbb{S} = \mathbb{N}$. If $P$ is a program and $S \in \wp(\mathbb{S})$, we denote by $[\![P]\!](S)^{\downarrow \leq n}$ the fact that $P$ terminates with any input in $S$ in less than $n$ steps. Let $\mathfrak{g} : \mathsf{Imp} \to \mathbb{N}$ be an enumeration of programs. This induces a corresponding enumeration $\mathfrak{g} : \wp^{\mathrm{re}}(\mathbb{S}) \to \mathbb{N}$ of recursively enumerable sets. Consider the representation in $\mathsf{Imp}$ of the halting problem of Turing machines (cf. [23]):

$$K \triangleq \{P \in \mathsf{Imp} \mid \exists n \in \mathbb{N}.\, [\![P]\!](\{\mathfrak{g}(P)\})^{\downarrow \leq n}\}.$$

We first prove that $\mathbb{C}(A)$ is productive. The proof relies on a many-to-one reduction of $\overline{K}$ to $\mathbb{C}(A)$, denoted by $\overline{K} \preceq_m \mathbb{C}(A)$, and means that there exists a total recursive function $f : \mathsf{Imp} \to \mathsf{Imp}$ such that $x \in \overline{K}$ iff $f(x) \in \mathbb{C}(A)$.

Let $A_{\alpha,\gamma} \in \mathrm{Abs}(\wp(\mathbb{S}))$ be recursive and nontrivial. As in Theorem 4.5, there exists $S \in \wp^{\mathrm{re}}(\mathbb{S})$ such that $S \subsetneq \gamma(\alpha(S)) \subsetneq \mathbb{S}$. Let $b \in \mathbb{S} \smallsetminus \gamma(\alpha(S))$, $c \in \gamma(\alpha(S)) \smallsetminus S$, and consider the program $Q_{bc}$ as in the proof of Theorem 4.5, where we proved that $Q_{bc} \notin \mathbb{C}(A)$. Since $\alpha$ is recursive, there exists $P^\top \in \mathsf{Imp}$ such that $\alpha([\![P^\top]\!]\varnothing) = \mathbb{S}$. By monotonicity of $\alpha$, for any $X \in \wp(\mathbb{S})$ we have that $\alpha([\![P^\top]\!]X) = \mathbb{S}$. Clearly, $P^\top \in \mathbb{C}(A)$ holds. Consider the partial recursive function $\psi : \mathsf{Imp} \times \wp^{\mathrm{re}}(\mathbb{S}) \to \wp^{\mathrm{re}}(\mathbb{S})$:

$$\psi(P, X) \triangleq \begin{cases} [\![Q_{bc}]\!](X) & \text{if } [\![P]\!](\{\mathfrak{g}(P)\})^{\downarrow \leq \mathfrak{g}(X)} \\ [\![P^\top]\!](X) & \text{otherwise} \end{cases}$$

Since $\psi$ is partial recursive, there exists a program $R \in \mathsf{Imp}$ such that $[\![R]\!](P, X) = \psi(P, X)$. By the s-m-n Theorem, there exists a total recursive function $f : \mathsf{Imp} \times \mathsf{Imp} \to \mathsf{Imp}$ such that for any $P \in \mathsf{Imp}$ and $X \in \wp^{\mathrm{re}}(\mathbb{S})$ we have that $[\![f(R, P)]\!](X) = [\![R]\!](P, X) = \psi(P, X)$. Consider a generic program $P \in \mathsf{Imp}$. If $P \in K$ then there exists $n \in \mathbb{N}$ such that $[\![P]\!](\{\mathfrak{g}(P)\})^{\downarrow \leq n}$. Let $\mathcal{I}^{\alpha}_{Q_{bc}}$ denote the set of all sets of stores for which $A_\alpha$ is not complete for $Q_{bc}$:

$$\mathcal{I}^{\alpha}_{Q_{bc}} \triangleq \{X \in \wp^{\mathrm{re}}(\mathbb{S}) \mid \alpha([\![Q_{bc}]\!]X) \neq [\![Q_{bc}]\!]^{\alpha}\alpha(X)\}.$$

It is easy to see that $\mathcal{I}^{\alpha}_{Q_{bc}}$ is infinite. In particular, as shown in the proof of Theorem 4.5, $S \in \mathcal{I}^{\alpha}_{Q_{bc}}$. It is also easy to derive that for any $x \in \mathbb{S}$ such that $x \neq c$ we have that $S \cup \{x\} \in \mathcal{I}^{\alpha}_{Q_{bc}}$. Therefore, since $|\,\mathbb{S}\,| = \omega$, we also have that $|\mathcal{I}^{\alpha}_{Q_{bc}}| = \omega$. This implies that there exists $X \in \mathcal{I}^{\alpha}_{Q_{bc}}$ such that $n \leq \mathfrak{g}(X)$ and therefore $[\![P]\!](\{\mathfrak{g}(P)\})^{\downarrow \leq \mathfrak{g}(X)}$. Hence, $[\![f(R, P)]\!](Y) = [\![Q_{bc}]\!](Y)$ for some $Y \in \mathcal{I}^{\alpha}_{Q_{bc}} \subset \wp(\mathbb{S})$. Therefore, $f(R, P) \notin \mathbb{C}(A)$. If $P \notin K$ then, for any $n \in \mathbb{N}$, we have that $[\![P]\!](\{\mathfrak{g}(P)\})$ does not converge in less than $n$ steps. Therefore, for any $X \in \wp^{\mathrm{re}}(\mathbb{S})$ we have that $\psi(P, X) = [\![P^\top]\!]X$ and therefore $[\![f(R, P)]\!] = [\![P^\top]\!]$, which implies that $f(R, P) \in \mathbb{C}(A)$.

Because $\lambda P \in \mathsf{Imp}.\, f(R, P)$ above is total recursive, we have that $K \preceq_m \overline{\mathbb{C}(A)}$, which is equivalent to $\overline{K} \preceq_m \mathbb{C}(A)$. This proves that $\mathbb{C}(A)$ is productive (see Theorem VII §7.5 in [23] and Theorem 4.5 in [24]). The proof that also $\overline{\mathbb{C}(A)}$ is productive is analogous and it is based on a many-to-one reduction $K \preceq_m \mathbb{C}(A)$ which exploits the partial recursive function:

$$\psi'(P, X) \triangleq \begin{cases} [\![P^\top]\!](X) & \text{if } [\![P]\!](\{\mathfrak{g}(P)\})^{\downarrow \leq \mathfrak{g}(X)} \\ [\![Q_{bc}]\!](X) & \text{otherwise} \end{cases}$$

□

As a consequence, neither $\mathbb{C}(A)$ nor its complement $\overline{\mathbb{C}(A)}$ turn out to be recursively enumerable sets. Let us notice that the proof of the previous theorem provides a further insight into the structure of $\mathbb{C}(A)$. Given a nontrivial and recursive abstraction $A \in \mathrm{Abs}(\wp(\mathbb{S}))$, it is always possible to systematically and effectively transform any algorithmic procedure attempting to enumerate $\mathbb{C}(A)$ into a program $P$ such that $P \notin \mathbb{C}(A)$. The same holds for $\overline{\mathbb{C}(A)}$. This can be read as follows: automating the proof that an abstraction is complete or incomplete for a given program—*i.e.*, a static program analysis can produce or cannot produce false alarms—is impossible. The completeness class of an abstraction is therefore a nontrivial property of programs for which no recursively enumerable procedure may exist which is able to enumerate all of its elements. In the following, we provide recursively enumerable under-approximations of $\mathbb{C}(A)$, namely systematic, and possibly automatic, proof systems such that if the proof succeeds for some program $P$ and nontrivial abstraction $A$, then $P \in \mathbb{C}(A)$.

## 5. Proving Completeness of Programs

Given a store abstraction $A \in \mathrm{Abs}(\wp(\mathbb{S}))$, our goal is to prove whether $P \in \mathbb{C}(A)$. To this aim, we design a layered proof system parametric on the abstraction $A$. The first layer is a compositional proof system $\vdash_A$ for a generic abstraction $A$. It deals with the fundamental constructs for program composition: sequential composition, branching, and guarded iteration. The second layer is instead domain-specific. It deals with the completeness of the assignments and of the Boolean guards — The handling of the assignments depends on whether the store abstraction is relational or not.

Let us remark that the abstract domain $A$ here is fixed. An approach based on complete shell refinements (or complete core simplifications) of the abstraction $A$, as recalled in Section 2, would therefore be orthogonal. A complete refinement of $A$ for all the assignments and Boolean guards (and their negations) occurring in $P$ would generate an abstract domain which is complete for all the programs that can be constructed by combining through sequential compositions, conditionals and loops, and for all the possible sets of input stores—in most practical cases, the abstraction $A$ would likely be refined to the concrete domain.

### 5.1 The Core Proof System

We report in Figure 5 the core proof system $\vdash_A$ for proving the completeness w.r.t. a generic store abstraction $A_{\alpha,\gamma} \in \mathrm{Abs}(\wp(\mathbb{S}))$. This deductive system is fully compositional on the program's syntax. A no-op command is trivially complete for all abstractions ([**skip**]). The rule [**seq**] states that the sequential composition of two complete commands is complete, too. It is worth remarking that the composition of the best correct approximations of two functions $f$ and $g$, in general, is not the best correct approximation of their composition $f \circ g$, while this indeed holds when these best correct approximations of $f$ and $g$ are indeed complete. The rule [**if**] asserts that a conditional statement is complete when its body, its Boolean guard *together with* its negation are complete. Loop statements are handled by the rule [**while**]: Iteration is complete if its body is complete as well as the loop guard and its negation. It is worth remarking that the rules for branching and loop commands imply that the abstract join operation *never* injects incompleteness in the analysis, unlike a common belief in static program analysis. Let us show that these rules are sound for proving completeness in $A$.

**Theorem 5.1.** *For any $A \in \mathrm{Abs}(\wp(\mathbb{S}))$ the rules in $\vdash_A$ are sound.*

*Proof.* [**skip**]: **skip** $\in \mathbb{C}(A)$ always holds.

$$\frac{}{\vdash_A \textbf{skip}}\,[\textbf{skip}] \qquad \frac{\vdash_A P \quad \vdash_A Q}{\vdash_A P;Q}\,[\textbf{seq}] \qquad \frac{\vdash_A C \quad b \in \mathbb{B}(A) \quad \neg b \in \mathbb{B}(A)}{\vdash_A \textbf{if } b \textbf{ then } C}\,[\textbf{if}] \qquad \frac{\vdash_A C \quad b \in \mathbb{B}(A) \quad \neg b \in \mathbb{B}(A)}{\vdash_A \textbf{while } b \textbf{ do } C}\,[\textbf{while}]$$

**Figure 5.** The core proof system $\vdash_A$.

[**seq**]: If $A$ is complete for $C_1$ and $C_2$ then $A$ is complete for $C_1; C_2$:

$$\begin{aligned}\alpha(\llbracket C_1; C_2\rrbracket S) &= \alpha(\llbracket C_2\rrbracket(\llbracket C_1\rrbracket S))\\ &= \llbracket C_2\rrbracket^\alpha \alpha(\llbracket C_1\rrbracket S))\\ &= \llbracket C_2\rrbracket^\alpha \llbracket C_1\rrbracket^\alpha \alpha(S)\\ &= \llbracket C_1; C_2\rrbracket^\alpha \alpha(S).\end{aligned}$$

[**if**]: If $A$ is complete for $b$, $\neg b$ and $C$ then $A$ is complete for **if** $b$ **then** $C$:

$$\begin{aligned}\alpha(\llbracket \textbf{if } b \textbf{ then } C\rrbracket S) &= \alpha(\llbracket C\rrbracket \llbracket b\rrbracket S \cup \llbracket\neg b\rrbracket S)\\ &= \alpha(\llbracket C\rrbracket \llbracket b\rrbracket S) \sqcup \alpha(\llbracket\neg b\rrbracket S)\\ &= \llbracket C\rrbracket^\alpha \alpha(\llbracket b\rrbracket S) \sqcup \llbracket\neg b\rrbracket^\alpha \alpha(S)\\ &= \llbracket C\rrbracket^\alpha \llbracket b\rrbracket^\alpha \alpha(S) \sqcup \llbracket\neg b\rrbracket^\alpha \alpha(S)\\ &= \llbracket \textbf{if } b \textbf{ then } C\rrbracket^\alpha \alpha(S).\end{aligned}$$

[**while**]: If $A$ is complete for $b$, $\neg b$ and $C$ then $A$ is complete for **while** $b$ **do** $C$. We first show that

$$\alpha \circ (\lambda T. S \cup \llbracket C\rrbracket\llbracket b\rrbracket T) = (\lambda X^\sharp.\alpha(S) \sqcup \llbracket C\rrbracket^\alpha \llbracket b\rrbracket^\alpha X^\sharp) \circ \alpha$$

For any $T \in \wp(\mathbb{S})$, we have that:

$$\begin{aligned}\alpha(S \cup \llbracket C\rrbracket\llbracket b\rrbracket T) &= \alpha(S) \sqcup \alpha(\llbracket C\rrbracket\llbracket b\rrbracket T)\\ &= \alpha(S) \sqcup \llbracket C\rrbracket^\alpha \alpha(\llbracket b\rrbracket T)\\ &= \alpha(S) \sqcup \llbracket C\rrbracket^\alpha \llbracket b\rrbracket^\alpha \alpha(T),\end{aligned}$$

so that

$$\alpha \circ (\lambda T. S \cup \llbracket C\rrbracket\llbracket b\rrbracket) = (\lambda X^\sharp.\alpha(S) \sqcup \llbracket C\rrbracket^\alpha \llbracket b\rrbracket^\alpha X^\sharp) \circ \alpha.$$

Hence, by fixpoint transfer (cf. Section 2):

$$\alpha(\mathsf{lfp}(\lambda T. S \cup \llbracket C\rrbracket\llbracket b\rrbracket T)) = \mathsf{lfp}(\lambda X^\sharp.\alpha(S) \sqcup \llbracket C\rrbracket^\alpha \llbracket b\rrbracket^\alpha X^\sharp).$$

We therefore obtain:

$$\begin{aligned}\alpha(\llbracket \textbf{while } b \textbf{ do } C\rrbracket S) &= \alpha(\llbracket\neg b\rrbracket(\mathsf{lfp}(\lambda T. S \cup \llbracket C\rrbracket\llbracket b\rrbracket T)))\\ &= \llbracket\neg b\rrbracket^\alpha \alpha(\mathsf{lfp}(\lambda T. S \cup \llbracket C\rrbracket\llbracket b\rrbracket T))\\ &= \llbracket\neg b\rrbracket^\alpha \mathsf{lfp}(\lambda X^\sharp.\alpha(S) \sqcup \llbracket C\rrbracket^\alpha \llbracket b\rrbracket^\alpha X^\sharp)\\ &= \llbracket \textbf{while } b \textbf{ do } C\rrbracket^\alpha \alpha(S).\end{aligned}$$ □

Let us point out that for a Boolean guard $b$ occuring in a program $P$, the rules of $\vdash_A$ require both $b$ and $\neg b$ to be complete on $A$ for any possible set of input stores. It is therefore important to remark that Boolean guards are a major source of incompleteness, even in seemingly innocuous cases, as shown by the following example:

**Example 5.2.** Let us consider the loop guard in the program *Dec* in Figure 2. Assume that the body of the while loop $x := x - 1$ is complete for the interval abstraction Int—this will be formally proved later on. The proof of completeness for *Dec* in $\vdash_{\mathsf{Int}}$ would need the hypotheses $x > 0 \in^? \mathbb{B}(\mathsf{Int})$ and $x \leq 0 \in^? \mathbb{B}(\mathsf{Int})$ stating the completeness of the guards of *Dec*. However, is is not true, in general, that intervals are complete for a guard like $x > 0$, even if $x > 0$ is exactly representable in Int. In fact, we have that:

$$\begin{aligned}\alpha_{\mathsf{Int}}(\llbracket x > 0\rrbracket\{0,2,3\}) &= \alpha_{\mathsf{Int}}(\{2,3\}) = [2,3]\\ &\sqsubset \llbracket x > 0\rrbracket^{\alpha_{\mathsf{Int}}} \alpha_{\mathsf{Int}}(\{0,2,3\})\\ &= \llbracket x > 0\rrbracket^{\alpha_{\mathsf{Int}}}[0,3] = [1,3].\end{aligned}$$

Therefore, $x > 0 \notin \mathbb{B}(\mathsf{Int})$. A similar counterexample may show that $x \leq 0 \notin \mathbb{B}(\mathsf{Int})$.
Let us also observe that even a simple equality test $\llbracket x = y\rrbracket$ between different variables cannot be complete in a relational abstraction such as octagons Oct which is able to represent precisely a variable relation like $x = y$. It is enough to note that:

$$\begin{aligned}\alpha_{\mathsf{Oct}}(\llbracket x = y\rrbracket\{(x/0, y/2), (x/2, y/0)\}) &= \alpha_{\mathsf{Oct}}(\varnothing) = \bot_{\mathsf{Oct}}\\ &\sqsubset \llbracket x = y\rrbracket^{\alpha_{\mathsf{Oct}}} \alpha_{\mathsf{Oct}}(\{(x/0, y/2), (x/2, y/0)\})\\ &= \llbracket x = y\rrbracket^{\alpha_{\mathsf{Oct}}} \langle 0 \leq x \leq 2,\ 0 \leq y \leq 2, x + y = 2\rangle\\ &= \langle x = 1, y = 1\rangle.\end{aligned}$$

A similar example may show that the test $\llbracket x = y\rrbracket$ is not complete for intervals as well, although this could be somewhat expected since intervals are not relational. □

### 5.2 Proving Completeness of Assignments

Assignment commands are not handled by the core proof system $\vdash_A$. The deductive system $\vdash_A$ is compositional on program's syntax and the problem for assignments stems from the fact a compositional rule for deriving the completeness of $x := a$ from the completeness of the expression $a$ (and/or $x - a$) cannot be sound for a generic abstract domain $A$. This is shown by the following example dealing with the relational octagon abstraction.

**Example 5.3.** Let $Var = \{x, y, z\}$ and let us represent a generic store $(x/v_x, y/v_y, z/v_z)$ simply by $(v_x, v_y, v_z) \in \mathbb{Z}^3$. We consider the arithmetic expression $x + y \in$ AExp and the abstraction Oct. It turns out that $x + y \in \mathbb{A}(\mathsf{Oct})$. In fact, for any nonempty set of stores $S \in \wp(\mathbb{S})$, consider the constraint $m \leq x + y \leq n$ which is expressed by $\mathsf{Oct}(S)$: this means that there exist $\rho_1, \rho_2 \in S$ such that $m = \rho_1(x) + \rho_1(y)$, $n = \rho_2(x) + \rho_2(y)$, and for any $\rho \in S$, $m \leq \rho(x) + \rho(y) \leq n$. Thus, $\mathsf{Oct}(\llbracket x + y\rrbracket S) = [m, n]$. On the other hand, since, for any $\rho \in \mathsf{Oct}(S)$, $m \leq \rho(x) + \rho(y) \leq n$, we also have that $\mathsf{Oct}(\llbracket x + y\rrbracket \mathsf{Oct}(S)) = [m, n]$.

Let us consider now $S = \{(2, 1, 0), (1, 4, 2)\} \in \wp(\mathbb{S})$ and the assignment $z := x + y \in$ Imp, whose concrete semantics on $S$ gives $\llbracket z := x + y\rrbracket S = \{(2, 1, 3), (1, 4, 5)\}$. The abstraction of $\llbracket z := x + y\rrbracket S$ in Oct is therefore as follows:

$$\begin{aligned}\mathsf{Oct}(\llbracket z := x + y\rrbracket S) = \langle &1 \leq x \leq 2, 1 \leq y \leq 4, 3 \leq z \leq 5,\\ &3 \leq x + y \leq 5, -3 \leq x - y \leq 1, 5 \leq x + z \leq 6,\\ &-4 \leq x - z \leq -1, 4 \leq y + z \leq 9, -2 \leq y - z \leq -1\rangle.\end{aligned}$$

On the abstract side, the abstraction of $S$ in Oct is as follows:

$$\begin{aligned}\mathsf{Oct}(S) = \langle &1 \leq x \leq 2, 1 \leq y \leq 4, 0 \leq z \leq 2,\\ &3 \leq x + y \leq 5, -3 \leq x - y \leq 1, 2 \leq x + z \leq 3,\\ &-1 \leq x - z \leq 2, 1 \leq y + z \leq 6, 1 \leq y - z \leq 2\rangle.\end{aligned}$$

Here $(2, 3, 1) \in \mathsf{Oct}(S)$ and $(2, 3, 5) \in \llbracket z := x + y\rrbracket \mathsf{Oct}(S) \subseteq \mathsf{Oct}(\llbracket z := x + y\rrbracket \mathsf{Oct}(S))$. But $(2, 3, 5) \notin \mathsf{Oct}(\llbracket z := x + y\rrbracket S)$ because the relation $5 \leq x + z \leq 6$ is not satisfied. Hence, $\mathsf{Oct}(\llbracket z := x + y\rrbracket S) \subsetneq \mathsf{Oct}(\llbracket z := x + y\rrbracket \mathsf{Oct}(S))$, namely $z := x + y \notin \mathbb{C}(\mathsf{Oct})$. □

***Nonrelational Abstractions.*** An abstraction $A_\alpha \in \mathrm{Abs}(\wp(\mathbb{S}))$ is nonrelational when it does not take into account any relationship between different variables. Let us formalize this notion. For any

$x \in Var$, let $\bar{x} \triangleq Var \setminus \{x\}$ and let $\alpha^x : \wp(\mathbb{S}) \to A$ be defined as $\alpha^x(S) \triangleq \alpha(\exists_{\bar{x}}(S))$. Then, $A$ is defined to be nonrelational when:

$$\forall S \in \wp(\mathbb{S}).\, \alpha(S) = \bigwedge_{x \in Var} \alpha^x(S).$$

Null, Sign and Int are examples of nonrelational abstractions, while Oct is not nonrelational. For a nonrelational abstraction $A$, we introduce the following compositional rule for assignments:

$$\frac{a \in \mathbb{A}(A)}{\vdash_A x := a}\ [\textbf{assignNR}]$$

We denote by $\vdash_A^{\mathbf{NR}}$ the core proof system $\vdash_A$ enhanced with the rule [**assignNR**] and we show its soundness for deriving completeness.

**Theorem 5.4.** *For any nonrelational abstraction $A \in \mathrm{Abs}(\wp(\mathbb{S}))$, $\vdash_A^{NR}$ is sound,* i.e., *if $\vdash_A P$ then $P \in \mathbb{C}(A)$.*

*Proof.* The soundness of the rules in $\vdash_A$ follows by Theorem 5.1. The soundness of [**assignNR**] follows from these equalities:

$$\begin{aligned}
&\alpha([\![x := a]\!]S) = \\
&= \alpha^x([\![x := a]\!]S) \wedge \bigwedge_{y \neq x} \alpha^y([\![x := a]\!]S) \\
&= \alpha(\exists_{\bar{x}}([\![x := a]\!]S)) \wedge \bigwedge_{y \neq x} \alpha(\exists_{\bar{y}}([\![x := a]\!]S)) \\
&\qquad [\text{by def. of variable projection and } \alpha^{\mathbb{Z}}] \\
&= \alpha^{\mathbb{Z}}([\![a]\!]S) \wedge \bigwedge_{y \neq x} \alpha(\exists_{\bar{y}}(S)) \\
&\qquad [\text{by } a \in \mathbb{A}(A) \text{ and completeness of } \exists_{\bar{y}}] \\
&= \alpha^{\mathbb{Z}}([\![a]\!]\gamma(\alpha(S))) \wedge \bigwedge_{y \neq x} \alpha(\exists_{\bar{y}}(\gamma(\alpha(S)))) \\
&\qquad [\text{by def. of variable projection and } \alpha^{\mathbb{Z}}] \\
&= \alpha(\exists_{\bar{x}}([\![x := a]\!]\gamma(\alpha(S)))) \wedge \bigwedge_{y \neq x} \alpha(\exists_{\bar{y}}([\![x := a]\!]\gamma(\alpha(S)))) \\
&= \alpha^x([\![x := a]\!]\gamma(\alpha(S))) \wedge \bigwedge_{y \neq x} \alpha^y([\![x := a]\!]\gamma(\alpha(S))) \\
&= \alpha([\![x := a]\!]\gamma(\alpha(S))).
\end{aligned}$$

□

Thus, for nonrelational abstract domains $A$, $\vdash_A^{\mathbf{NR}}$ is a fully compositional proof system for checking completeness of programs. Let us give a simple example of derivation in $\vdash_A^{\mathbf{NR}}$.

**Example 5.5.** Let us consider the nonrelational abstract domain Null for nullness analysis described in Section 1 and the simple program

$$P \equiv x := 0; \textbf{if } (x = 0) \textbf{ then } x := 1$$

where, with a slight abuse of notation, we assume that 0 stands for a null reference while 1 for a non-null reference. The proof tree in Figure 6 can be derived in $\vdash_{\mathsf{Null}}^{\mathbf{NR}}$, and this entails that the abstract semantics of $P$ on the abstraction Null is complete. Let us stress that the key point in proving the completeness of $P$ is that the abstraction Null is complete for the Boolean guard $x = 0$ *and* its negation $\neg(x = 0)$. □

Nevertheless, for the program *Dec* in Figure 2, we are still not able to derive that $\vdash_{\mathsf{Int}}$ *Dec*: the rule [**assignNR**] allows us to derive that the assignment $x := x - 1$ is complete for Int, but this is not enough since the Boolean guard $x > 0$ is not complete (cf. Example 5.2). The fact that $\mathbb{C}(A)$ is a productive set even for (nontrivial) nonrelational abstractions implies that an effective complete proof system for deriving completeness of programs cannot be defined. The proof system $\vdash_A^{\mathbf{NR}}$ is indeed sound but not complete, and the program *Dec* shows this incompleteness.

***Relational Abstractions.*** As shown in Example 5.3, the completeness of an expression $a$ does not imply that an assignment $x := a$ is complete for a relational abstract domain. It can be shown that more restrictive hypotheses such as the assumption that $x \notin vars(a)$ and the completeness of the Boolean expression $x = a$ on $A$, would imply that $x := a$ is complete on $A$ (the proof is omitted). However, this would yield a sound but far too restrictive derivation rule. Indeed, although the syntactic condition $x \notin vars(a)$ can always be met for any program $P$ simply by replacing an assignment $x := a$ where $x \in vars(a)$ with the composition $x' := a; x := x'$, where $x'$ is a fresh variable, this rule would require the hypothesis $(x = y) \in \mathbb{B}(A)$, and we observed in Example 5.2 that the equality test is not complete even for most known abstract domains.

Thus, for the generic case of a nonrelational abstraction $A$, it can be argued that a reasonable rule for deriving the completeness of assignments $x := a$ from the completeness of some other arithmetic expression and/or Boolean guard and/or command induced by $x := a$ simply cannot be found. Hence, a nonrelational abstraction therefore needs a specific analysis of the completeness of its assignments. We present a significant sample of this analysis for the case of the octagon abstraction.

***Octagon Abstraction.*** In Example 5.3 we have shown that the assignment $z := x + y$ is not complete for Oct. A similar example can be found for $x := x + y$. These observations show that any generic linear assignment $x := a_1 * x_1 + \ldots + a_n * x_n$ is not complete for Oct when $n \geq 2$. The intuitive reason is that for a relation $a \leq x + y \leq b$, the substitution of $x$ with $a_1 * x_1 + \ldots + a_n * x_n$ provides a relation for more than two variables which cannot be represented by Oct. A fortiori, this is also true for nonlinear assignments like $x := y * y$.

Thus, we are left to scrutinize linear assignments of the following shape: $x := a * y + k$ and $x := a * x + k$. If $a \notin \{-1, 0, 1\}$, *e.g.*, $x := 2 * y$, the following example shows that, as expected, we do not have completeness.

**Example 5.6.** We follow the notation of Example 5.3 where $Var = \{x, y, z\}$. Let us consider the assignment $x := 2 * y \in \mathsf{Imp}$ and the set of input stores $S = \{(0, 2, 0), (3, 0, 4)\} \in \wp(\mathbb{S})$. On the concrete side, we have that $[\![x := 2 * y]\!]S = \{(4, 2, 0), (0, 0, 4)\}$. The abstraction of $[\![x := 2 * y]\!]S$ in Oct is therefore as follows:

$$\begin{aligned}
&\mathsf{Oct}([\![x := 2 * y]\!]S) = \\
&\qquad \langle 0 \leq x \leq 4, 0 \leq y \leq 2, 0 \leq z \leq 4, \\
&\qquad 0 \leq x + y \leq 6, 0 \leq x - y \leq 2, x + z = 4, \\
&\qquad -4 \leq x - z \leq 4, 2 \leq y + z \leq 4, -4 \leq y - z \leq 2\rangle.
\end{aligned}$$

On the abstract side, the abstraction of $S$ in Oct is as follows:

$$\begin{aligned}
&\mathsf{Oct}(S) = \langle 0 \leq x \leq 3, 0 \leq y \leq 2, 0 \leq z \leq 4, \\
&\qquad 2 \leq x + y \leq 3, -2 \leq x - y \leq 3, 0 \leq x + z \leq 7, \\
&\qquad -1 \leq x - z \leq 0, 2 \leq y + z \leq 4, -4 \leq y - z \leq 2\rangle.
\end{aligned}$$

We consider the store $(1, 2, 2) \in \mathsf{Oct}(S)$ so that $(4, 2, 2) \in [\![x := 2 * y]\!]\mathsf{Oct}(S) \subseteq \mathsf{Oct}([\![x := 2 * y]\!]\mathsf{Oct}(S))$. However, we have that $(4, 2, 2) \notin \mathsf{Oct}([\![x := 2 * y]\!]S)$ because the relation $x + z = 4$ is not satisfied. This shows that $\mathsf{Oct}([\![x := 2 * y]\!]S) \subsetneq \mathsf{Oct}([\![x := 2 * y]\!]\mathsf{Oct}(S))$, *i.e.*, $x := 2 * y \notin \mathbb{C}(\mathsf{Oct})$. □

It turns out that the remaining assignments are the only which are complete for octagons.

**Lemma 5.7.** *The only complete assignments for* Oct *are: $x := a * y + k$ and $x := a * x + k$, where $a \in \{-1, 0, 1\}$ and $k \in \mathbb{Z}$.*

$$\dfrac{\dfrac{0 \in \mathbb{A}(\mathsf{Null})}{\vdash^{\mathbf{NR}}_{\mathsf{Null}} x := 0} \qquad \dfrac{(x = 0) \in \mathbb{B}(\mathsf{Null}) \quad \neg(x = 0) \in \mathbb{B}(\mathsf{Null}) \quad \dfrac{1 \in \mathbb{A}(\mathsf{Null})}{\vdash^{\mathbf{NR}}_{\mathsf{Null}} x := 1}}{\vdash^{\mathbf{NR}}_{\mathsf{Null}} \mathbf{if}\ (x = 0)\ \mathbf{then}\ x := 1}}{\vdash^{\mathbf{NR}}_{\mathsf{Null}} P \equiv x := 0;\ \mathbf{if}(x = 0)\ \mathbf{then}\ x := 1}$$

**Figure 6.** The derivation tree proving the completeness of the program $P$ on the abstraction $\mathsf{Null}$.

*Proof.* Consider $x := a * y + k$ with $a \in \{-1, 0, 1\}$. By the characterization of completeness given in [13] and recalled in Section 2, we have that $[\![x := a * y + k]\!] \in \mathbb{C}(\mathsf{Oct})$ iff for any octagon $\mathsf{oct} \in \mathsf{Oct}$:

$$\max(\{T \in \wp(\mathbb{S}) \mid [\![x := a * y + k]\!]T \subseteq \mathsf{oct}\}) \in \mathsf{Oct}.$$

We observe that this maximal set of store can be obtained from $\mathsf{oct}$ by replacing in any relation involving the variable $x$ the expression $ay + k$. If $a = 0$ then it is clear that this replacement still provides relations of the shape $\pm x \pm y \leq k$. It turns out that this also happens for $a \in \{-1, 1\}$. Let us consider the case $a = 1$, namely $x := y + k$. The following cases are possible. The replacement for $a \leq x \leq b$ provides the relation $a - k \leq y \leq b - k$; for $a \leq x - y \leq b$ the relation $a \leq k \leq b$, which can be true or false (and in this case we obtain the empty octagon); for $a \leq x + y \leq b$ the relation $a - k \leq 2y \leq b - k$, which is equivalent (integer variables) to $\lceil (a - k)/2 \rceil \leq y \leq \lfloor (b - k)/2 \rfloor$; for $a \leq x \pm z \leq b$, where $z \neq y$, we obtain $a - k \leq y \pm z \leq b - k$. Thus, in each case we obtain a variable relation of the shape $\pm x \pm y \leq k$, *i.e.*, $\max(\{T \in \wp(\mathbb{S}) \mid [\![x := y + k]\!]T \subseteq \mathsf{oct}\})$ is an octagon. A similar analysis applies to the remaining cases $x := -y + k$ and $x := \pm x + k$. $\square$

Lemma 5.7 therefore provides an exhaustive (static) analysis of the completeness of assignments for the octagon abstraction. It is worthwhile to observe that [20, Figure 15] describes algorithms that compute the best correct approximations (called exact approximations in [20]) on octagons for precisely the set of complete assignments characterized by Lemma 5.7. This may suggest an interesting relationship between the property of being complete for an assignment and that of admitting a computable best correct approximation.

## 6. Proving Completeness of Guards

We argued that the main problem in proving $\vdash_A P$ lies in the fact that in general it is hard to prove that $b \in \mathbb{B}(A)$ and $\neg b \in \mathbb{B}(A)$ for an arbitrary store abstraction $A$. Actually, most of the times, only trivial guards—true, false, nondeterministic choices and, e.g., $x = \mathit{Null}$ in the nullness domain—turn out to be complete. For instance, one may expect that a Boolean condition which is exactly representable in some abstraction, as $x > 0$ in $\mathsf{Int}$, turns out to be complete. However, in general, this is not the case, as shown by Example 5.2. Our goal is to take into account explicitly the Boolean guards of programs by adding suitable assumptions to completeness proofs in $\vdash_A$. Thus, we derive a conditional proof of completeness in $A$ for a program $P$, whose assumptions on the completeness of the Boolean guards of $P$ then need to be validated in a further distinct step.

Let us consider a store abstraction $A_{\alpha,\gamma} \in \mathrm{Abs}(\wp(\mathbb{S}))$ and a Boolean predicate $b \in \mathrm{BExp}$. We use the following notation: $[\![b]\!]^{\mathbf{t}} \triangleq \{\rho \in \mathbb{S} \mid (\!|b|\!)\rho = \mathbf{t}\}$. If $\alpha([\![b]\!]S) = [\![b]\!]^{\alpha}\alpha(S)$ holds for a given $S \in \wp(\mathbb{S})$ then $b$ is called complete for $A$ in $S$. Since this condition is equivalent to $\alpha([\![b]\!]S) = \alpha([\![b]\!]\gamma(\alpha(S)))$ and $[\![b]\!]S = [\![b]\!]^{\mathbf{t}} \cap S$, we have that $b$ is complete for $A$ in $S$ when $\alpha([\![b]\!]^{\mathbf{t}} \cap S) = \alpha([\![b]\!]^{\mathbf{t}} \cap \gamma(\alpha(S)))$.

Now, let us consider some $b \in \mathrm{BExp}$ which is representable in the abstract domain $A$, that is, $[\![b]\!]^{\mathbf{t}} = \gamma(\alpha([\![b]\!]^{\mathbf{t}}))$ holds — we call them $A$-Boolean expressions. For example, $x \leq k_1 \wedge y > k_2$ is a $\mathsf{Int}$- and $\mathsf{Oct}$-Boolean expression, while $k \leq x \wedge x \leq y$ is a $\mathsf{Oct}$-Boolean expression but not a $\mathsf{Int}$-Boolean expression. In this case, it turns out that

$$\begin{aligned}\alpha([\![b]\!]^{\mathbf{t}} \cap \gamma(\alpha(S))) &= \alpha(\gamma(\alpha([\![b]\!]^{\mathbf{t}})) \cap \gamma(\alpha(S)))\\ &= \alpha(\gamma(\alpha([\![b]\!]^{\mathbf{t}}) \wedge_A \alpha(S))) = \alpha([\![b]\!]^{\mathbf{t}}) \wedge_A \alpha(S)\end{aligned}$$

so that completeness of $b$ for $A$ in $S$ corresponds to require:

$$\alpha([\![b]\!]^{\mathbf{t}} \cap S) = \alpha([\![b]\!]^{\mathbf{t}}) \wedge_A \alpha(S).$$

We instrument our proof system $\vdash_A$ with suitable assumptions that guarantee that the sets of possible input states for a Boolean guard make it complete. This allows us to derive a conditional proof of completeness for a program $P$ under these assumptions on the completeness of the Boolean guards of $P$. These proof assumptions can then be proved in a later step, *e.g.* by a static analysis focused on Boolean guards. Let $\mathrm{BExp}(P)$ denote the set of Boolean guards occurring in some program point of $P$ and assume that the set $\Gamma_P$ of Boolean guards of $P$ which are not complete on $A$, *i.e.*, $\Gamma_P \triangleq \{b \in \mathrm{BExp}(P) \mid b \notin \mathbb{B}(A)\}$, consists of $A$-Boolean expressions only. If $\nvdash_A P$ then the completeness proof for $P$ may fail along some guard $b \in \Gamma_P$. If we are able to guarantee that this guard $b$ is complete for any set $S$ of possible input stores at the program point where the guard $b$ occurs in $P$ then we can safely conclude that $b$ is complete on $A$ for the purpose of proving that $P$ is complete on $A$. We therefore add the following conditional meta-rule **[gc]** for the completeness of guards $b \in \Gamma_P$:

$$\frac{\mathit{assume}[S : \alpha([\![b]\!]^{\mathbf{t}} \cap S) = \alpha([\![b]\!]^{\mathbf{t}}) \wedge_A \alpha(S)]}{b \in \mathbb{B}(A)}\ \textbf{[gc]}$$

Hence, a conditional completeness proof of $P$ in $\vdash_A \cup \{\textbf{[gc]}\}$ depends on the collection $\mathcal{G}_P$ of all the assumptions made for the guards $b \in \Gamma_P$. The next step consists in designing some domain-specific—possibly statically checkable—conditions that allow to validate all the assumptions in $\mathcal{G}_P$ made in a conditional proof of $P$, so as to establish an unconditional proof for $P$ on $A$.

### 6.1 Completeness of Int- and Oct-Boolean Guards

Given a set of store, we want to provide a characterization of the completeness of Boolean expressions which are representable as intervals or octagons. Namely, we characterize the sets of stores $S$ that make a $\mathsf{Int}$- and $\mathsf{Oct}$-Boolean expression complete, hence providing specific conditions for the assumptions of the conditional rule **[gc]** for $\mathsf{Int}$ and $\mathsf{Oct}$.

In order to keep the notation as simple as possible, in what follows we consider the abstractions $\mathsf{Int}$ and $\mathsf{Oct}$ on stores over two variables $(x, y)$, *i.e.*, $\mathbb{S} = \mathbb{Z}^2$ and $\mathsf{Int}, \mathsf{Oct} \in \mathrm{Abs}(\langle \wp(\mathbb{Z}^2), \subseteq \rangle)$. Moreover, for any set of concrete points $S \in \wp(\mathbb{Z}^2)$, we use $\mathsf{Int}(S), \mathsf{Oct}(S) \in \wp(\mathbb{Z}^2)$ to denote the corresponding interval and octagon abstractions. The generalization to $N > 2$ variables is conceptually simple but notationally tedious. In two variables, a (possibly infinite) interval is a (possibly infinite) rectangle $R$ in the

$(x, y)$ plane. A rectangle $R$ can be represented by its set of edges, denoted by edges$(R)$, which are at most four (this is the case of finite rectangles). Similarly, an octagon $O$ in two variables can be represented by its edges in edges$(O)$, which are at most eight. Any $E \in$ edges$(R)$ determines a line in the $(x, y)$ integer plane which is denoted by $l_E$. If $l$ is a line in the $(x, y)$ integer plane and $S \in \wp(\mathbb{Z}^2)$ is any set of points then $\pi^l(S)$ denotes the orthogonal projection of $S$ onto $l$. Completeness of Int-Boolean guards is then geometrically characterized as follows.

**Theorem 6.1.** *Let $R$ be a* Int*-Boolean expression. Then, $R$ is complete for* Int *in a set of stores $S \in \wp(\mathbb{Z}^2)$ if and only if the following condition holds:*

$$\forall E \in \text{edges}(R).\ \pi^{l_E}(\mathsf{Int}(S) \cap R) \subseteq \mathsf{Int}(\pi^{l_E}(S \cap R)). \quad (*)$$

*Proof.* Since $\mathsf{Int}(S \cap R) \subseteq \mathsf{Int}(\mathsf{Int}(S) \cap R) = \mathsf{Int}(S) \cap R$ always holds, let us first observe that $R$ is not complete for Int in $S$ when

$$\mathsf{Int}(S \cap R) \neq \mathsf{Int}(\mathsf{Int}(S) \cap R) \Leftrightarrow$$
$$\mathsf{Int}(S \cap R) \neq \mathsf{Int}(S) \cap R \Leftrightarrow$$
$$\mathsf{Int}(S \cap R) \subsetneq \mathsf{Int}(S) \cap R.$$

Moreover, it turns out that the rectangle $\mathsf{Int}(S \cap R)$ is strictly contained into the rectangle $\mathsf{Int}(S) \cap R$ iff there exists an edge $E' \in$ edges$(\mathsf{Int}(S) \cap R)$ such that $\pi^{l_{E'}}(\mathsf{Int}(S \cap R)) \subsetneq E' = \pi^{l_{E'}}(\mathsf{Int}(S) \cap R)$. The following figure helps in explaining this, where $S$ is given by the set of bullets, $\mathsf{Int}(S \cap R)$ is the (red) dashed inner rectangle, and $\mathsf{Int}(S) \cap R$ is the (blue) dotted rectangle.

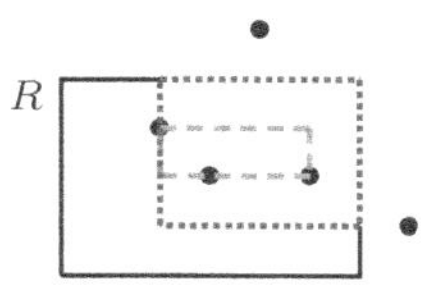


Since the rectangle $\mathsf{Int}(S) \cap R$ is contained in $R$, the last condition $\mathsf{Int}(S \cap R) \subsetneq \mathsf{Int}(S) \cap R$ holds iff there exists an edge $E \in$ edges$(R)$ such that $\pi^{l_E}(\mathsf{Int}(S \cap R)) \subsetneq \pi^{l_E}(\mathsf{Int}(S) \cap R)$. Also, the orthogonal projection $\pi^{l_E}$ onto the line $l_E$ satisfies the following property: $\pi^{l_E}(\mathsf{Int}(S \cap R)) = \mathsf{Int}(\pi^{l_E}(S \cap R))$, so that $\mathsf{Int}(S \cap R) \subsetneq \mathsf{Int}(S) \cap R$ holds iff $\mathsf{Int}(\pi^{l_E}(S \cap R)) \subsetneq \pi^{l_E}(\mathsf{Int}(S) \cap R)$. It is now easy to check that this latter condition holds iff the negation of $(*)$ holds. □

Observe that in the condition $(*)$ we have that $\pi^{l_E}(\mathsf{Int}(S) \cap R)$ is always an interval because $\mathsf{Int}(S) \cap R$ is always a rectangle. Furthermore, if $S$ is already a rectangle, namely $\mathsf{Int}(S) = S$, then condition $(*)$ holds so that we have completeness. Let us also observe that $(*)$ is trivially satisfied when one of the following conditions hold: $\mathsf{Int}(S) \cap R = \varnothing$ or $S \subseteq R$ or $R \subseteq S$. Finally, if $S \cap R = \varnothing$ but $\mathsf{Int}(S) \cap R \neq \varnothing$, then $(*)$ boils down to $\forall E \in$ edges$(R).\ \pi^{l_E}(\mathsf{Int}(S) \cap R) = \varnothing$, which is always false, so that completeness does not hold.

**Example 6.2.** In the following pictures, the set of points $S$ in the $(x, y)$ plane is given by the set of bullets. Let us first consider the following example.

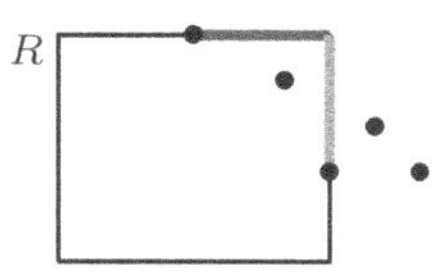


In this case, the rectangle $R$ turns out to be complete for Int in $S$. In fact, for any edge $E \in$ edges$(R)$, the two projections $\pi^{l_E}(\mathsf{Int}(S) \cap R)$ and $\pi^{l_E}(S \cap R)$ give the same intervals, which are depicted with (blue and red) thick lines. Let us now consider the following modified picture, where the rightmost point of $S$ is moved one step down.

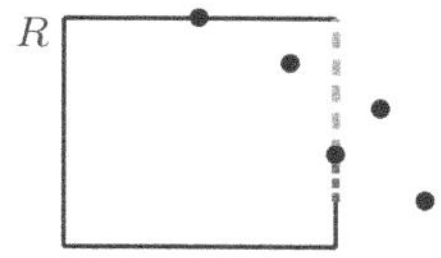


Here, completeness of $R$ for Int in $S$ is lost. In fact, for the rightmost vertical edge $E \in$ edges$(R)$, $\mathsf{Int}(\pi^{l_E}(S \cap R))$ is the (red) dashed interval which is strictly contained in the interval $\pi^{l_E}(\mathsf{Int}(S) \cap R)$ obtained by projecting $S$ onto $E$: the gap between these two intervals is depicted by the (blue) dotted segment. □

Of course, Theorem 6.1 can be stated in general for a $N$-dimensional space, with $N \geq 1$: in the general geometric formulation, $R$ is a $N$-dimensional hyperrectangle (also called orthotope), $S \in \wp(\mathbb{Z}^N)$ is any set of points in the $N$-dimensional space, edges of $R$ are replaced by the $2N$ facets of the hyperrectangle $R$ and lines determined by edges are the $(N-1)$-dimensional hyperplanes determined by facets.

Furthermore, Theorem 6.1 also holds for octagons with the same statement where the abstraction Oct replaces Int. Here, in the 2-dimensional case, the edges of an octagon are at most eight while the abstraction in Oct of a projection onto a line boils down to an interval abstraction. Thus, if $O$ is a Oct-Boolean guard then $O$ is complete for Oct in $S$ iff the following condition holds:

$$\forall E \in \text{edges}(O).\ \pi^{l_E}(\mathsf{Oct}(S) \cap O) \subseteq \mathsf{Int}(\pi^{l_E}(S \cap O)). \quad (*)$$

**Example 6.3.** In the following picture, the octagon $O$ is complete for Oct in the set $S$ of points depicted as bullets. In the picture, $\mathsf{Oct}(S)$ is depicted with (blue) dotted edges, while $\mathsf{Oct}(S \cap O)$ is depicted with (red) dashed edges. Condition $(*)$ holds: for example, for the edge $E \in$ edges$(O)$ in the picture $\pi^{l_E}(\mathsf{Oct}(S) \cap O) = \mathsf{Int}(\pi^{l_E}(S \cap O))$ is the (red) dashed interval.

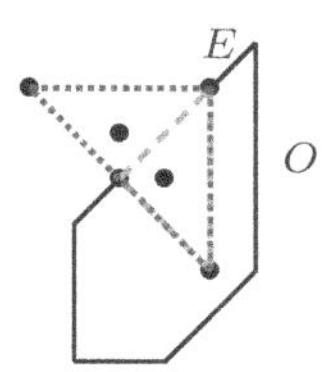


On the other hand, let us consider the following modified picture, where the leftmost point of $S$ is moved two steps down.

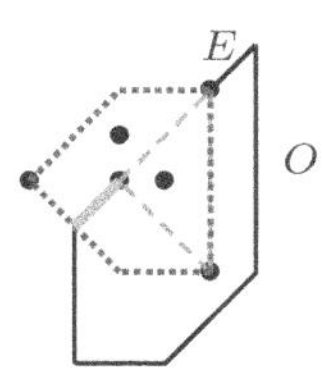


Here, completeness of $O$ for Oct in $S$ is lost: the gap between the two orthogonal projections on the edge $E \in$ edges$(O)$ is depicted with a (gray) thick segment, *i.e.*, condition $(*)$ does not hold. □

Theorem 6.1 explains precisely why the Int/Oct-Boolean expression $R \equiv x \leq 0$, which is the negation of the loop guard of the program *DecInc* in Figure 4 discussed in Section 1, is not complete for Int in the set of input stores $S = \{(9,0), (8,1), \ldots, (0,9)\}$. Here, $\mathsf{Int}(S) \cap R = \langle x = 0,\ 0 \leq x \leq 9\rangle$ and $S \cap R = \{(0,9)\}$, and for the edge $E \equiv \langle x = 0\rangle \in$ edges$(R)$, we have that $\pi^{l_E}(\mathsf{Int}(S) \cap R) = \langle x = 0,\ 0 \leq y \leq 9\rangle$ is not contained in $\mathsf{Int}(\pi^{l_E}(S \cap R)) = \{(0,9)\}$. Instead, this incompleteness does not arise with Oct because $\pi^{l_E}(\mathsf{Oct}(S) \cap R) = \{(0,9)\} = \mathsf{Int}(\pi^{l_E}(S \cap R))$.

***Validating Assumptions on Guards.*** Consider the following program template

$$P \triangleq x := k_1; y := k_2; \textbf{while } (x, y \in R) \textbf{ do } \{x := a_1; y := a_2\}$$

which subsumes the examples of Figures 2, 3 and 4. We assume that: (i) $k_i \in \mathbb{Z}$ are constant values; (ii) $R$ is any (finite or infinite) 2-dimensional rectangle in $\mathsf{Int}$ such that its complement $\neg R$ is a rectangle as well; (iii) the arithmetic expressions $a_i \in \mathrm{AExp}$ are complete for $\mathsf{Int}$, *i.e.*, $a_i \in \mathbb{A}(\mathsf{Int})$. By assumption (i):

$$\dfrac{\dfrac{k_1 \in \mathbb{A}(\mathsf{Int})}{\vdash^{\mathbf{NR}}_{\mathsf{Int}} x := k_1} \quad \dfrac{k_2 \in \mathbb{A}(\mathsf{Int})}{\vdash^{\mathbf{NR}}_{\mathsf{Int}} y := k_2}}{\vdash^{\mathbf{NR}}_{\mathsf{Int}} x := k_1; y := k_2}$$

Also, by assumption (iii), the body of the while-loop can be proved complete for $\mathsf{Int}$:

$$\dfrac{\dfrac{a_1 \in \mathbb{A}(\mathsf{Int})}{\vdash^{\mathbf{NR}}_{\mathsf{Int}} x := a_1} \quad \dfrac{a_2 \in \mathbb{A}(\mathsf{Int})}{\vdash^{\mathbf{NR}}_{\mathsf{Int}} y := a_2}}{\vdash^{\mathbf{NR}}_{\mathsf{Int}} x := a_1; y := a_2}$$

Let us then consider the set $S$ of stores, *i.e.*, concrete $(x, y)$-points, computed by the body of the while-loop of $P$, *i.e.*, if $I = \{(k_1, k_2)\} \in \wp(\mathbb{Z}^2)$ is the set of input stores for the while-loop then $S$ is given by

$$S = \mathsf{lfp}(\lambda X. I \cup [\![x := a_1; y := a_2]\!][\![R]\!]X).$$

We thus have a conditional proof $\vdash^{\mathbf{NR}}_{\mathsf{Int}} P$ which depends on the assumptions on the Boolean guard $R$ and its negation $\neg R$:

$$\textit{assume}[S : \mathsf{Int}(R \cap S) = R \cap \mathsf{Int}(S)],$$
$$\textit{assume}[S : \mathsf{Int}(\neg R \cap S) = \neg R \cap \mathsf{Int}(S)].$$

We apply Theorem 6.1 to derive the validity of these assumptions. Let us consider the following cases.

(A) If $[\![R]\!]I \neq I$, *i.e.* $[\![R]\!]I = \varnothing$, then the while-loop is not entered, so that $S = I$, and $R \cap S = \varnothing$ and $\neg R \cap S = S$. For example, this happens with:

$$x := 2; y := 4; \textbf{while } (x < 0) \textbf{ do } \{x := x + 1; y := y + 1\}$$

In this case, completeness of $R$ and $\neg R$ for $S$ is a trivial case of condition $(*)$ in Theorem 6.1.

(B) If $[\![R]\!]I = I$ then the while-loop is entered. If $S$ is an infinite set then we have nontermination. This means that $S \subseteq R$ and $\neg R \cap S = \varnothing$. This happens, for example, with the program:

$$x := 2; y := 4; \textbf{while } (x > 0) \textbf{ do } \{x := x + 1; y := y + 1\}$$

Here, condition $(*)$ for $R$ and $\neg R$ follows trivially because we have that, respectively, $S \subseteq R$ and $\neg R \cap S = \varnothing$.

(C) If $[\![R]\!]I = I$ and $S$ is finite then the while-loop is entered and we have termination. This means that $R \cap S \neq \varnothing$ and $\neg R \cap S \neq \varnothing$. This is the case of the following two programs:

$$P_1 \triangleq x := 2; y := 4; \textbf{while } (x > 0) \textbf{ do} \{x := x - 1; y := y - 1\}$$
$$P_2 \triangleq x := 2; y := 4; \textbf{while } (x > 0) \textbf{ do } \{x := x - 1; y := y\}$$

Here, we have that:

$$S_{P_1} = \{(2,4), (1,3), (0,2)\}; \quad S_{P_2} = \{(2,4), (1,4), (0,4)\}.$$

By condition $(*)$, we obtain that $R$ is not complete for $S_{P_1}$ while both $R$ and $\neg R$ are complete for $S_{P_2}$. While for $P_1$ the assumptions of its conditional proof cannot be validated, the assumptions for $P_2$ are validated by Theorem 6.1, hence we have $\vdash^{\mathbf{NR}}_{\mathsf{Int}} P_2$.

(D) Finally, let us consider the analyses of the programs $P_1$ and $P_2$ of point (C) for the abstraction Oct. In this case, by Lemma 5.7, we have that all the assignments in $P_1$ and $P_2$ are complete for Oct. Moreover, while $\vdash_{\mathsf{Oct}} P_2$ can obviously be inferred as in point (C), here we are also able to infer that $\vdash_{\mathsf{Oct}} P_1$. In fact, since the set $S_{P_1}$ is an octagon, *i.e.*, $\mathsf{Oct}(S_{P_1}) = S_{P_1}$, the condition $(*)$ is trivially satisfied both for $R$ and $\neg R$, so that the assumptions for $R$ and $\neg R$ of the conditional proof of $P_1$ can be validated.

## 7. Related Work

To the best of our knowledge, this is the first attempt to systematically extract a property concerning the precision of a static program analysis through a proof system. The subject of our analysis is a given abstract interpretation of a program, while the property to analyze is the completeness of this abstract interpretation. Completeness for an abstract interpretation is particularly important because it formalizes the absence of false alarms, and therefore it is deeply related with the quality of the program analysis. The most related approach is in [13], where the authors define a constructive optimal abstraction refinement for deriving the most abstract complete domain which refines a given (incomplete) abstraction for a generic program statement. Our method follows an orthogonal pattern. We are not interested in refining an abstract domain for obtaining completeness with respect to a given class of programs, but rather in studying the class of programs for which a given abstraction is complete. This different starting point leads us to design a deductive system for deriving a completeness proof for programs on a given abstraction. This new perspective allows us to decompose the problem of attaining a complete abstraction for a given program, which becomes modular and inductive on the program's syntax. The ubiquity of completeness properties in static analysis is also studied in [22], where it is argued how completeness can play a beneficial role for designing static analyses by reasoning on the completeness properties of their underlying abstract domains.

Provably precise static analyses usually make some assumption on the syntactic form of the analyzed program. For instance the precise interprocedural analysis of [21] computes, for each program point, all the affine relations among program variables. What the authors call "precision" is effectively our notion of completeness. They achieve precision by focusing on a particular class of programs, namely affine programs. Affine programs are such that: (i) all guards are non-deterministic; and (ii) the right-hand side of assignments are either affine expressions or unknown values. Similarly, in type systems, it is customary to ignore the guards in order to prove the completeness of the type inference algorithm, *e.g.*, in [9]. We argued in this article that the main problem for proving completeness is the handling of assignments and of Boolean guards.

Our research follows the lines of a recent approach by Cousot and Cousot [5] who put forward a type system for typing the structure of an abstract interpretation. A type represents inductively the way an abstraction has been built by composing simpler abstractions through systematic domain operations like reduced product. It could be interesting to investigate the possibility of combining our proof system with a structural type system for abstract interpretations as in [5], with the aim of providing along a derivation in $\vdash_A$ some additional information about the used sub-domains and their composition through domain operations.

## 8. Conclusion

Static analysis is, by design, incomplete. Nevertheless, experience has shown that it can be made precise enough to be used for verification [6, 11]. We envision static analyses which in addition to the inferred invariants also provide completeness certificates. The completeness certificate is used to provide confidence to the analysis of alarms. As a foundational step towards this goal, we introduced a theoretical framework to prove the completeness of a static analysis. We have shown that the source of incompleteness lies in the handling of Boolean guards and, for relational abstractions, in assignments. For nonrelational abstractions we introduced an abstraction-independent core proof system which pushes the completeness of the analysis to the numerical expressions and the Boolean guards of conditionals and loops. For relational abstractions, instead, the structure of complete assignments has to be derived in advance in order to obtain a sound proof system. We argued that the designer of a static analyzer should also provide completeness conditions for the Boolean guards and that these conditions could be automatically checked by further, yet less sophisticated, static analyses—we leave the design of such automated analyses for future work. We studied the completeness of Boolean guards in widely used numerical abstractions such as Intervals and Octagons. Most known abstract domains have been indeed designed to precisely capture properties of some given programs. This is justified by the fact that the class of completeness $\mathbb{C}(A)$ of any abstraction $A$ is always an infinite set. Therefore, deriving an abstract domain which is complete for a specific program $P$ provides at the same time a domain which is complete for an infinite class of programs.

As future work, we think that proving completeness of static analyses could be also beneficial to: (i) automatically apply abstract code repairs [18]—if the analysis of the original and the repaired programs can both be proven complete, then the repair is very likely to have fixed a concrete bug; (ii) validate refactorings [8]—among different program refactorings one may only keep the one(s) for which she can prove it preserves the completeness of the analysis; (iii) provide a better understanding of why over-approximating analyses of arrays [7] works well in practice even without performing under-approximations, argued as necessary in [15].

## Acknowledgments

Roberto Giacobazzi and Francesco Ranzato have been partially supported by the Microsoft Research Software Engineering Innovation Foundation 2013 Award (SEIF 2013).

## References

[1] COUSOT, P., AND COUSOT, R. Static verification of dynamic type properties of variables. Research Report no. 25, Laboratoire IMAG, University of Grenoble, France, 1975.

[2] COUSOT, P., AND COUSOT, R. Static determination of dynamic properties of programs. In *Proceedings of the 2nd International Symposium on Programming* (1976), Dunod, Paris, pp. 106–130.

[3] COUSOT, P., AND COUSOT, R. Abstract interpretation: A unified lattice model for static analysis of programs by construction or approximation of fixpoints. In *Conference Record of the 4th ACM Symposium on Principles of Programming Languages (POPL '77)* (1977), ACM Press, pp. 238–252.

[4] COUSOT, P., AND COUSOT, R. Systematic design of program analysis frameworks. In *Conference Record of the 6th ACM Symposium on Principles of Programming Languages (POPL '79)* (1979), ACM Press, pp. 269–282.

[5] COUSOT, P., AND COUSOT, R. A Galois connection calculus for abstract interpretation. In *Conference Record of the 41st ACM Symposium on Principles of Programming Languages (POPL '14)* (2014), S. Jagannathan and P. Sewell, Eds., ACM Press, pp. 3–4.

[6] COUSOT, P., COUSOT, R., FERET, J., MAUBORGNE, L., MINÉ, A., MONNIAUX, D., AND RIVAL, X. The ASTRÉE analyzer. In *Proceedings of the European Symposium on Programming (ESOP '05)* (2005), vol. 3444 of *Lecture Notes in Computer Science*, Springer, pp. 21–30.

[7] COUSOT, P., COUSOT, R., AND LOGOZZO, F. A parametric segmentation functor for fully automatic and scalable array content analysis. In *Conference Record of the 38th ACM Symposium on Principles of Programming Languages (POPL '11)* (2011), ACM Press, pp. 105–118.

[8] COUSOT, P., COUSOT, R., LOGOZZO, F., AND BARNETT, M. An abstract interpretation framework for refactoring with application to extract methods with contracts. In *Proceedings of the 27th ACM Inter. Conference on Object Oriented Programming Systems Languages and Applications (OOPSLA '12)* (2012), ACM Press, pp. 213–232.

[9] DAMAS, L., AND MILNER, R. Principal type-schemes for functional programs. In *Conference Record of the 9th ACM Symposium on Principles of Programming Languages (POPL '82)* (1982), ACM Press, pp. 207–212.

[10] DEKKER, J. C. E. Productive sets. *Trans. of the American Mathematical Society 78* (1955), 129–149.

[11] FAHNDRICH, M., AND LOGOZZO, F. Static contract checking with abstract interpretation. In *Proceedings of the Internat. Conf. on Formal Verification of Object-oriented Software (FoVeOOS 10)* (2010), Springer.

[12] GIACOBAZZI, R. Hiding information in completeness holes – New perspectives in code obfuscation and watermarking. In *Proc. of the 6th IEEE International Conferences on Software Engineering and Formal Methods (SEFM '08)* (2008), IEEE Press, pp. 7–20.

[13] GIACOBAZZI, R., RANZATO, F., AND SCOZZARI, F. Making abstract interpretation complete. *Journal of the ACM 47*, 2 (2000), 361–416.

[14] GRANGER, P. Static analysis of arithmetical congruences. *Intern. J. Computer Math. 30* (1989), 165–190.

[15] GULWANI, S., MCCLOSKEY, B., AND TIWARI, A. Lifting abstract interpreters to quantified logical domains. In *Conference Record of the 35th ACM Symposium on Principles of Programming Languages (POPL '08)* (2008), ACM Press, pp. 35–46.

[16] KARR, M. Affine relationships among variables of a program. *Acta Informatica 6* (1976), 133–151.

[17] LAVIRON, V., AND LOGOZZO, F. Refining abstract interpretation-based static analyses with hints. In *Proc. of the 2009 Asian Symp. on Programming Languages and Systems (APLAS '09)* (2009), vol. 5904 of *Lecture Notes in Computer Science*, Springer, pp. 343–358.

[18] LOGOZZO, F., AND BALL, T. Modular and verified automatic program repair. In *Proceedings of the 27th ACM Internat. Conference on Object Oriented Programming Systems Languages and Applications (OOPSLA '12)* (2012), ACM Press, pp. 133–146.

[19] MINÉ, A. A new numerical abstract domain based on difference-bound matrices. In *Proc. of the 2nd Symp. on Programs as Data Objects (PADO '01)* (2001), vol. 2053 of *Lecture Notes in Computer Science*, Springer, pp. 155–172.

[20] MINÉ, A. The octagon abstract domain. *Higher Order and Symbolic Computation 19*, 1 (2006), 31–100.

[21] MÜLLER-OLM, M., AND SEIDL, H. Precise interprocedural analysis through linear algebra. In *Conference Record of the 31st ACM Symposium on Principles of Programming Languages (POPL '04)* (2004), ACM Press, pp. 330–341.

[22] RANZATO, F. Complete abstractions everywhere. In *Proc. of the 14th International Conference on Verification, Model Checking and Abstract Interpretation (VMCAI'13)* (2013), vol. 7737 of *Lecture Notes in Computer Science*, Springer, pp. 15–26.

[23] ROGERS, H. *Theory of Recursive Functions and Effective Computability.* The MIT press, 1992.

[24] SOARE, R. I. *Recursively Enumerable Sets and Degrees.* Springer-Verlag, 1980.

[25] WINSKEL, G. *The Formal Semantics of Programming Languages: an Introduction.* MIT press, 1993.

# Compositional CompCert

Gordon Stewart Lennart Beringer Santiago Cuellar Andrew W. Appel
Princeton University
{jsseven,eberinge,scuellar,appel}@princeton.edu

## Abstract

This paper reports on the development of Compositional CompCert, the first verified separate compiler for C.

Specifying and proving separate compilation for C is made challenging by the coincidence of: compiler optimizations, such as register spilling, that introduce compiler-managed (private) memory regions into function stack frames, and C's stack-allocated addressable local variables, which may *leak* portions of stack frames to other modules when their addresses are passed as arguments to external function calls. The CompCert compiler, as built/proved by Leroy *et al.* 2006–2014, has proofs of correctness for whole programs, but its simulation relations are too weak to specify or prove separately compiled modules.

Our technical contributions that make Compositional CompCert possible include: language-independent linking, a new operational model of multilanguage linking that supports strong semantic contextual equivalences; and structured simulations, a refinement of Beringer *et al.*'s logical simulation relations that enables expressive module-local invariants on the state communicated between compilation units at runtime. All the results in the paper have been formalized in Coq and are available for download together with the Compositional CompCert compiler.

***Categories and Subject Descriptors*** F.3.1 [*Specifying and Verifying and Reasoning about Programs*]: Mechanical verification

***General Terms*** Verification

***Keywords*** CompCert, Compiler Correctness

## 1. Introduction

Verified separate compilation is the process of independently translating a program's components in a way that preserves correctness of the program as a whole. In the most general case, a verified separate compiler supports heterogeneous source programs, in which some modules are written in a high-level source language like C while others are written in a lower-level language such as assembly. A verified separate compiler in this context is one that preserves the behavior of the entire source program, comprising the C and assembly-language modules, when the C code is compiled.

Separate compilation has numerous practical benefits. It speeds up development cycles by enabling recompilation of just those

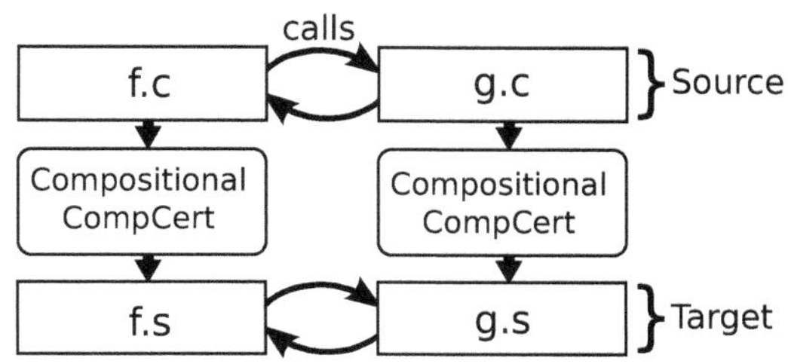


**Figure 1.** Compositional CompCert

source modules that have been edited by the programmer. It enables shared libraries—separately compiled modules mapped at runtime into the virtual address spaces of multiple processes. It promotes modularity in the large, by enabling programmers to write applications containing logically distinct translation units, each composed at a different level of abstraction or even in a different programming language altogether.

But perhaps equally important are applications of verified separate compilers to *modular verification*: proving a whole program correct by specifying and verifying its modules independently (with respect to the specifications of the other modules). Compiling verified modules with a semantics-preserving separate compiler results in correctness not only of each compiled module, but also of the target whole program linked and running on the machine.

In this paper, we present *Compositional CompCert*, a fully verified separate compiler from CompCert's (Leroy 2009) Clight language to x86 assembly. Each phase uses the *exact same* compilation function as CompCert 2.1, but a significantly strengthened specification that supports verified separate compilation of multimodule programs. In contrast, original CompCert's specification is limited to whole programs and fails to account for general shared-memory interaction. That is, CompCert is not certified for calls to other modules, especially if two modules might access the same memory locations. We certify the correctness of such calls.

Compositional CompCert builds on work of (Beringer et al. 2014), which showed how to adapt CompCert to support shared-memory interaction between a single compilation unit and its environment, under the restriction that the environment was not itself compiled. The technical innovations that enabled the adaptation to shared memory were twofold: First, a novel flavor of operational semantics, called *interaction semantics* ("core semantics" in (Beringer et al. 2014)), for modeling a module's interactions with its environments; and second, a new proof method, called *logical simulation relations (LSRs)*, for proving correctness of compiler phases with respect to the interaction semantics interface. LSRs supported *interlanguage* reasoning between the source, intermediate, and target languages of an optimizing compiler by modeling all languages uniformly, as interaction semantics. LSRs also composed *vertically*, or transitively, which made it possible to break down the correctness proof of a multiphase compiler into


*POPL '15*, January 15 - 17 2015, Mumbai, India.

ACM 978-1-4503-3300-9/15/01... $15.00.
http://dx.doi.org/10.1145/2676726.2676985

proofs of the individual compiler phases. (Leroy's original CompCert was also vertically compositional, but only because stack-allocated memory was not observable.)

The main deficiency of LSRs was that they did not compose *horizontally*: It was not possible, in general, to infer correct compilation of a whole program from the correct compilation of its modules. The reason was that LSRs, like CompCert's original simulation relations, imposed assumptions (relies) on the evolution of memory over external function calls, such as "spilled local variables are unmodified," but did not show that compiled code preserved the corresponding guarantees. This asymmetry between relies and guarantees made LSRs inapplicable whenever a module and its environment were both compiled—a situation that occurs not only when libraries are compiled, but also whenever there is a cyclic dependency between the modules of a program.

***Contributions.*** In Compositional CompCert we overcome these difficulties, and achieve horizontal compositionality, with the following innovations over previous work:

1. **Language-Independent Linking** is an extension of interaction semantics that gives the operational interpretation of horizontal composition. By abstracting from the details of how modules are implemented (or even in which language they are implemented), language-independent linking models the interactions of modules in different languages, even those with different calling conventions.
2. **Structured Simulations** refine LSRs to support the rely-guarantee relationship necessary for horizontal composition, while maintaining vertical compositionality. The key ingredients of structured simulations are: fine-grained *subjective invariants* on the state communicated between modules at runtime, and a *leakage* protocol that ensures that structured simulation proofs respect the reachability relation induced by C pointers.

Compositional CompCert's top-level correctness theorem is a variant of contextual equivalence between source and compiled multi-module programs in which contexts are specified *semantically*, as (nearly) arbitrary observations on the memory state at external call points. Contexts are not limited to programs in C or x86 but include mathematical relations expressed in Gallina.

In addition to sketching formal results that relate linking semantics, structured simulations, and contextual equvalence, we outline the instantiation of interaction semantics to the source and target languages of our compiler, Clight and x86, and present an overview of the adaptation of the relevant proofs of the CompCert phases.

All results in this paper have been proved formally in Coq, and are available, along with the Compositional CompCert compiler itself, on GitHub.[1] Before proceeding with the technical details, we briefly discuss some key aspects of the above innovations.

## 1.1 Key Ideas

*Language-independent linking* provides a generic operator $\mathcal{L}$ for composing interaction semantics, independent of the language level of individual modules. Our statements of separate compilation and contextual equivalence (Sections 3 and 6) are *cross-language* in the sense that they apply even to the situation in which a multilanguage source program is compiled to a multilanguage target program.

Informally, imagine a source program $P_S$ consisting of source modules $S_1, \cdots, S_n$, each in a different language. Then if target modules $P_T = T_1 \cdots T_n$ are shown related to $S_1 \cdots S_n$ (*e.g.*, by $n$ different structured simulations), the results of Sections 3 and 6 give us that the target "linked" program $P_T$ is contextually equivalent to the source "linked" program $P_S$ (under certain restrictions on the $S_i$ and $T_i$, explained in Section 3), for a strong semantic notion of program context. Of course, it's not clear *a priori* what it means to link multilanguage programs, at least not in any operational sense; answering this question is the subject of the first part of Section 3. In principle, these results mean that the target modules $T_1 \cdots T_n$ need not be generated by any particular compiler—our contextual equivalence results depend only on the existence of the simulations. In practice in Compositional CompCert, the $S_i$ are programs in Clight or hand-written assembly while the $T_i$ are x86 assembly programs.

*Structured simulations* evolve from LSRs by lifting the restriction to fixed environments, in two steps: First, we impose a rely-guarantee discipline (inspired in part by the rely-guarantee simulations used by Liang *et al.* (Liang et al. 2012) to prove contextual refinement of concurrent programs) on the interactions of program modules. The rely-guarantee discipline ensures that module compilation preserves the same properties that modules themselves assume about the behavior of external functions (those defined in other modules). This, in turn, makes it possible to implement external functions or libraries with code that is itself compiled, as in Figure 1. Second, we enrich the simulation relations with additional "ownership" data, which makes it possible to distinguish memory regions that are reorganized during compilation of distinct translation units. For example, the portion of the stack frame reserved for spilling during compilation of a function $A.f$ can be distinguished from the spill region reserved for a second function $B.g$, defined in a distinct translation unit $B$.

A key insight here is that the invariants that apply to distinct regions of memory—such as the regions reserved by the compiler for $A.f$'s and $B.g$'s spilled locals—are *subjective*: function $A.f$ can write to its own spilled locals but not to $B.g$'s, and vice versa for $B.g$ with respect to $A.f$'s spills. Structured simulations deal with this subjectivity by imposing an "us vs. them" discipline on compiler correctness invariants: Each structured simulation distinguishes the parts of the state that it controls (the "us") from the parts of the state controlled by the environment (the "them"). This discipline is reminiscent in some ways of Ley-Wild and Nanevski's subjective concurrent separation logic (SCSL) (Ley-Wild and Nanevski 2013), though here we apply a rely-guarantee discipline to the *two-program* invariants used to prove compiler correctness rather than to the verification of concurrent programs. To ensure that structured simulations validate contextual equivalences, and thus are reusable in many different program contexts, we make them parametric in nearly all state updates that can occur to the "them" portion of the state at external call points.

Another ingredient is a "leakage" protocol, which ensures that the views of the memory state imposed by the compiler invariants for different modules remain consistent. For example, when $A.f$ calls $B.g$ with arguments $\vec{v}$, we require that $A.f$'s compilation invariant "give up exclusive control" of all the memory regions reachable from $\vec{v}$ (*i.e.*, following pointer chains rooted in $\vec{v}$). This condition represents the guarantee that, while later compilation stages of $A.f$ can still reorganize parts of the state reachable from $\vec{v}$ (*e.g.*, by changing the order in which memory regions are allocated), they cannot remove these memory regions entirely (*e.g.*, by dead code/memory analysis): the existence of the memory regions in question has been leaked irrevocably to the environment. Similarly, at external function return points, memory regions reachable from the return value are "leaked in" to the caller's compilation invariant—representing the rely that these regions will never later be removed by compilation of the environment. Our language-independent linking semantics and contextual equivalence proof ensure that these conditions are in rely-guarantee relation.

[1] https://github.com/PrincetonUniversity/compcomp.

Interestingly, this leakage protocol bears much in common with the *system-level semantics* of Ghica and Tzevelekos (Ghica and Tzevelekos 2012). There, Ghica and Tzevelekos define a game semantics for a C-like language that avoids imposing so-called combinatorial (*i.e.*, syntactic) restrictions on the moves of the environment, by applying what they call "epistemic" restrictions instead. These epistemic conditions, which parallel our leakage conditions, allow the environment to update the state in nearly any way as long as the updates are to memory regions leaked to the environment during previous interactions with the client program. This leads to a strong *semantic* notion of program context similar to the one we develop in Section 3. While Ghica and Tzevelekos were interested in modeling open C-like programs and their environments, not compiler correctness in this setting, we view the coincidence of our leakage conditions with their system-level semantics as evidence of the naturalness of our leakage protocol (Section 4).

***Overview.*** We begin by reviewing *interaction semantics*, an operational model of shared-memory module and thread interaction. Section 3 employs interaction semantics to define the operational semantics of multilanguage linked programs, and semantic contextual equivalence. Then, we introduce structured simulations in Section 4. Section 5 presents the main theoretical results: vertical and horizontal compositionality, and contextual equivalence for CompCert. Section 6 describes the Compositional CompCert compiler itself, with a discussion of the effort required to port CompCert's existing languages and proofs to structured simulations.

## 2. Interaction Semantics

*Interaction semantics* (called *core semantics* in (Beringer et al. 2014)) are a protocol-oriented operational semantics of thread interaction, for modeling both multithread concurrent and multimodule programs. Interaction semantics grew from the insight that interaction, between well-synchronized concurrent threads or between modules, can be viewed as occuring exclusively at external function call points, that is, via calls to functions declared in one module but defined in another. This gives a compiler or weakly consistent memory model the freedom to optimize between interaction points.[2]

Here we give a brief overview of interaction semantics, which we build on in later sections to model language-independent linking. First, we describe the interaction semantics protocol. Then, we give representative encodings of interaction semantics, in this case, of CompCert's Clight and x86 assembly languages. In Compositional CompCert, all language semantics are encoded in this way, as interaction semantics.

### 2.1 Protocol

In a multithread concurrent program, threads are spawned, take normal (*i.e.*, unobservable) steps, yield at synchronization points (*e.g.*, call to `unlock`), and eventually halt or (silently) diverge. The same protocol applies to module interactions: a C program is initialized by spawning a new "thread" with a function pointer to `main`. This sequential thread (which we sometimes call a *core*) takes normal, unobservable steps by evaluating `main` or by calling other internal functions defined in the same translation unit, "yields" to the environment by calling external functions defined in other modules, "blocks" until the external function returns, and halts or nonterminates just as a concurrent thread does. At external-call interaction points, nearly anything can happen: For example, the (shared) memory state might be updated arbitrarily by an external function.

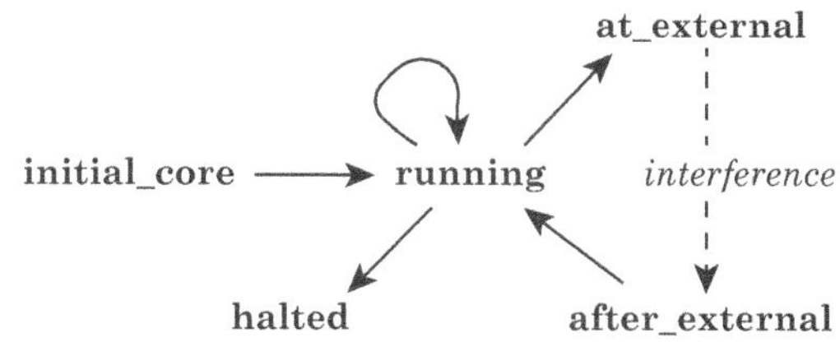


$$\mathsf{Semantics}\,(G\ C\ M : \mathsf{Type}) : \mathsf{Type} \triangleq \left\{\begin{array}{lcl} \mathsf{initial\_core} & : & G \to \mathcal{V} \to \mathsf{list}\ \mathcal{V} \to \mathsf{option}\ C \\ \mathsf{at\_external} & : & C \to \mathsf{option}\ (\mathcal{F} \times \mathsf{list}\ \mathcal{V}) \\ \mathsf{after\_external} & : & \mathsf{option}\ \mathcal{V} \to C \to \mathsf{option}\ C \\ \mathsf{halted} & : & C \to \mathsf{option}\ \mathcal{V} \\ \mathsf{corestep} & : & G \to C \to M \to C \to M \to \mathsf{Prop} \end{array}\right.$$

**Figure 2.** Interaction semantics interface. The types $G$ (global environment), $C$ (core state), and $M$ (memory) are parameters to the interface. $\mathcal{F}$ is the type of external function identifiers. $\mathcal{V}$ is the type of CompCert values.

Figure 2 summarizes the protocol. Each interaction semantics is parameterized by five types: $G$ is the type of global environments. $C$ is the type of internal, or "core" states. Core states can be instantiated to, *e.g.*, the register file, instruction stream, and processor flags for a language like x86, or to local variable environment and control continuation for a higher-level language like C. $M$ is the type of memories. In the models of the CompCert languages that we employ in Compositional CompCert, $M$ is instantiated to mem, the type of CompCert memories. (In semantic models of program logics such as the Verified Software Toolchain's *Verifiable C* (Appel et al. 2014), $M$ is instantiated to a step-indexed model of state used to model function pointer specifications and other higher-order features.) $\mathcal{F}$ is the type of external function identifiers. $\mathcal{V}$ is the type of values. $\mathcal{V}$ is usually just CompCert's value type.

The five functions at the bottom of Figure 2, together with a few governing axioms (not shown), encode the interaction protocol described above. New cores are initialized with initial_core $ge\ v\ \overrightarrow{v}$. The $v$ is a value, typically a function pointer, while $\overrightarrow{v}$ are the initial arguments to $v$. initial_core may fail with None when, *e.g.*, the function spawned is not defined in the global environment $ge$. at_external interrogates core state $c$ to determine whether $c$ is "blocked" at an external function call interaction point. When at_external succeeds, it does so with the name of the external function being called (of type $\mathcal{F}$) and the arguments (of type list $\mathcal{V}$). The after_external function is used to inject the return value of an external call into the calling at_external core state, producing a new core state as result. halted $c$ returns Some $v$ with return value $v$ if $c$ is halted, otherwise None. corestep gives the small-step internal transition relation of the interaction semantics. We use the syntax $ge \vdash c, m \longmapsto c', m'$ to denote this relation.

### 2.2 Examples: Clight & x86 Assembly

Figures 3 and 4 give the syntax of Clight and CompCert x86 assembly, the source and target language of Compositional CompCert, respectively. Both languages are adapted from CompCert's original Clight and x86 and have straightforward operational semantics, which we do not present here (but see the code that accompanies this paper for the complete definitions). Here we focus on the adaptations required to turn these two languages into interaction semantics: First, we give the core, or internal, states for each language; then, we provide an overview of the definitions of the interface functions, *e.g.*, at_external and after_external.

[2] Our model is designed to support shared-memory concurrency, although this paper does not yet do concurrency. Well-synchronized (Dijkstra-Hoare) programs can be proved in Concurrent Separation Logic, and from such proofs we can derive (virtual) permission changes at interaction points (Appel et al. 2014, Ch. 44). Racy programs can be accommodated as long as racy loads/stores can be modelled via permission changes (future work).

*Statements*

| | | | |
|---|---|---|---|
| $s$ | ::= | Sskip | no-op |
| | \| | Sassign $a_1$ $a_2$ | lval ← rval |
| | \| | Sset $id$ $a$ | temp ← rval |
| | \| | Scall $optid$ $a$ $\overrightarrow{a}$ | function call |
| | \| | Sbuiltin $optid$ $f$ $\overrightarrow{\tau}$ $\overrightarrow{a}$ | intrinsic |
| | \| | Ssequence $s_1$ $s_2$ | sequence |
| | \| | Sifthenelse $a$ $s_1$ $s_2$ | conditional |
| | \| | Sloop $s_1$ $s_2$ | infinite loop |
| | \| | Sbreak \| Sreturn $a_{opt}$ | break/return |
| | \| | Scontinue $s$ | continue statement |
| | \| | Switch $s$ \| Slabel $l$ $s$ \| Sgoto $l$ | |

*Internal & External Functions*

| | | | |
|---|---|---|---|
| $\tau$ | ::= | int \| long \| ptr $\tau$ \| $\cdots$ | C types |
| $\gamma$ | ::= | $\cdot$ \| $(id, \tau), \gamma$ | typing environments |
| $f_i$ | ::= | $\tau$ | function return type |
| | | $\gamma$ | function parameter typing |
| | | $\gamma_v$ | local variable typing |
| | | $\gamma_t$ | temporary variable typing |
| | | $s$ | function body |
| $f$ | ::= | Internal $f_i$ \| External $id_f$ $\overrightarrow{\tau}$ $\tau$ | |

*Continuations*

| | | | |
|---|---|---|---|
| $\kappa$ | ::= | Kstop | safe termination |
| | \| | Kseq $s$ $\kappa$ | sequential composition |
| | \| | Kloop $s_1$ $s_2$ $\kappa$ | loop continuation |
| | \| | Kswitch $\kappa$ | catch switch break |
| | \| | Kcall $optid$ $f_i$ $\rho_v$ $\rho_t$ $\kappa$ | catch function return |

*Core States*

| | | | |
|---|---|---|---|
| $\rho_v$ | ::= | $\cdot$ \| $(id, (loc \times \tau)), \rho_v$ | addressed var. environment |
| $\rho_t$ | ::= | $\cdot$ \| $(id, v), \rho_t$ | temporaries environment |
| $c$ | ::= | State$_{\mathsf{CL}}$ $f_i$ $s$ $\kappa$ $\rho_v$ $\rho_t$ | |
| | \| | CallState $f$ $\overrightarrow{v}$ $\kappa$ \| ReturnState $v$ $\kappa$ | |

**Figure 3.** Syntax and semantics of Clight (excerpts). Continuations and core states appear only in the operational semantics.

*Registers*

| | | | |
|---|---|---|---|
| $r_i$ | ::= | EAX \| EBX \| ECX \| EDX | integer registers |
| | \| | ESI \| EDI \| EBP \| ESP | |
| $r_f$ | ::= | XMM0 \| $\cdots$ \| XMM7 | floating-point registers |
| $cr_{state}$ | ::= | ZF \| CF \| PF \| SF \| OF | control register state |
| $r$ | ::= | PC \| IR $r_i$ \| FR $r_f$ \| ST0 \| CR $cr_{state}$ \| RA | |
| $rs$ | ::= | $\cdot$ \| $(r, v), rs$ | register environments |

*Instructions*

| | | | |
|---|---|---|---|
| $p$ | ::= | MOV$_{\mathsf{RR}}$ $r_i$ $r_i$ \| MOV$_{\mathsf{RI}}$ $r_i$ $i$ \| $\cdots$ | moves |
| | \| | JMP$_{\mathsf{L}}$ $l$ \| JMP$_{\mathsf{S}}$ $id$ \| JMP$_{\mathsf{c}}$ $cond$ $l$ \| $\cdots$ | jumps |
| | \| | CALL$_{\mathsf{S}}$ $id$ \| CALL$_{\mathsf{R}}$ $r_i$ \| RET \| $\cdots$ | calls/return |
| | \| | $\cdots$ moves with conversion, integer arithmetic, *etc.* | |

*Core States*

| | | | |
|---|---|---|---|
| $d$ | ::= | State$_{\mathsf{ASM}}$ $\tau_0$ $rs$ | normal states |
| | \| | MarshallState$_{\mathsf{In}}$ $id_f$ $\overrightarrow{v}$ | marshall args. in |
| | \| | MarshallState$_{\mathsf{Out}}$ $(id_f, \overrightarrow{\tau_0}, \tau_0)$ $\overrightarrow{v}$ $rs$ | marshall args. out |

**Figure 4.** Syntax and semantics of CompCert x86 assembly (excerpts). Core states appear only in the operational semantics. Intfloatness types $\tau_0$ (used for value decoding) are int, float, long, or single.

Clight's language of expressions, statements, internal function definitions, and external function declarations is given in the top half of Figure 3. Statements $s$ are as in CompCert, and rely on a language of expressions $a$ that includes the usual binary and unary operators. C control-flow constructs like while loops are derived forms (not shown). The semantics of Clight depends on continuations $\kappa$, described in the figure, and core states $c$, which come in three varieties: Normal states State$_{\mathsf{CL}}$ $f_i$ $s$ $k$ $\rho_v$ $\rho_t$ model the "running" states of a Clight program, during evaluation of anything but function calls, and consist of the name of the current function being executed $f_i$, the function body $s$, the control continuation $\kappa$, and two environments, $\rho_v$ for mapping address-taken stack variables to their locations in memory, and $\rho_t$ for mapping temporary variables to their values. CallState $f$ $\overrightarrow{v}$ $\kappa$ models Clight programs that are about to call function $f$ (either internal or external) with arguments $\overrightarrow{v}$ and continuation $\kappa$. ReturnState $v$ $\kappa$ gives the state that results after returning from function calls (either internal or external). $v$ is the value returned by the callee; $\kappa$ is the continuation to be executed after the call returns.

Adapting Clight to the interaction-semantics interface is straightforward. For example, here is the definition of Clight after_external:

```
cl_after_external v_opt c ≜
    case c of CallState f v⃗ κ →
        case f of Internal _ → None
            | External id_f τ⃗ τ →
              case v_opt of
                 | None → Some (ReturnState v_undef κ)
                 | Some v → Some (ReturnState v κ)
    | _ → None
```

First, we check whether $c$ is a CallState, with continuation $\kappa$. If it is, and the function that was being called was external, then we produce a ReturnState with return value $v_{undef}$ (whenever $v_{opt}$ was None) and $v$ (whenever $v_{opt}$ was Some $v$). In all other cases, we just return None.

The definition of initial_core $ge$ $v$ $\overrightarrow{v}$ is simple, since function arguments are passed not on the stack but abstractly, without reference to memory: we check that $v$ is a valid pointer to a defined function $f_i$, check that the arguments $\overrightarrow{v}$ are defined and match $f_i$'s type signature, then introduce state CallState (Internal $f_i$) $\overrightarrow{v}$ Kstop, which immediately steps to the body of function $f_i$ with the initial local variable environment $\rho_v$ that maps the function's formal parameters to its arguments $\overrightarrow{v}$. The definitions of initial_core in the languages below Clight follow a similar regime—all the way down to CompCert's Linear language, which uses an environment of abstract *locations* such as incoming parameter stack slots to represent the state of the stack and registers.

Adapting x86 assembly (Figure 4) is a bit trickier, since arguments must be passed concretely, on the stack. (The same applies to CompCert's Mach language.) As we will see in Section 3, we use the initial_core function of the interaction semantics interface to model both program initialization (*i.e.*, by the loader) and the function calls that occur at cross-module function invocations. If we knew that all modules in our program were written in x86 assembly and used, *e.g.*, the standard `cdecl` calling convention, then modeling cross-module invocations would be less of an issue: The shared calling convention would mean that arguments to one function (say, $B.g$) would be placed by a caller $A.f$ on the stack or in registers exactly as expected by $B.g$.

But the restriction to a shared calling convention/ABI is rather limiting. We want to be able to model, at least abstractly, the interactions of modules in a variety of languages, at both higher and lower levels of abstraction. To accomplish this, we apply a "marshalling" transformation to the x86 language: To initialize a new x86 core calling function $id_f$ with arguments $\overrightarrow{v}$, we produce

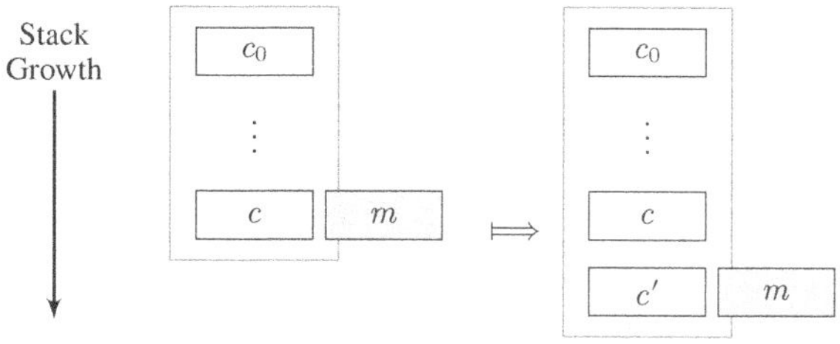


**Figure 5.** CALL case of the linking corestep relation. The outer boxes are "stacks-of-cores." Core state $c$ is at_external calling function $id_f$. Assuming $l$.plt $id_f$ = Some $idx$ and $ge\ id_f$ = Some $b_f$, initializing module $idx$ with function pointer Vptr $b_f$ results in initial core $c'$ being pushed onto the stack.

state MarshallState$_{\text{In}}$ $id_f\ \overrightarrow{v}$, which immediately steps to a running State. As a side effect of this step, however, we allocate a "dummy" stack frame in memory in which we store the incoming arguments $\overrightarrow{v}$, in right-to-left `cdecl` order as expected by CompCert and `gcc`. (MarshallState$_{\text{Out}}$ performs the symmetric step of marshalling arguments out of memory.)

Concretely, for x86 modules all sharing the same calling convention, this modeling step does not occur on a real machine (nor does the compiler output any "marshalling" code). But by sticking to the abstract "calling convention" imposed by initial_core, in which values are passed abstractly instead of in memory and registers according to a particular calling convention, we gain flexibility to model the interactions of modules in a wide variety of languages, not only Clight and x86 but also x86 modules following different calling conventions, such as, *e.g.*, `cdecl` and Microsoft `fastcall`.

## 3. Linking and Contextual Equivalence

In the previous section, we introduced *interaction semantics* as a means of interpreting the behavior of isolated modules. In this section, we define an abstract operator $\mathcal{L}([\![S_0]\!], [\![S_1]\!], \ldots, [\![S_{N-1}]\!])$ over interaction semantics that defines the linked behavior of a *set* of interacting modules, as given by a multimodule program $P = S_0, S_1, \cdots, S_{N-1}$.

As input, $\mathcal{L}$ takes $N$ interaction semantics, each with (perhaps) a different global environment and core state type (*i.e.*, modules programmed in perhaps different languages). The output of $\mathcal{L}$ is a new interaction semantics $[\![P]\!] = \mathcal{L}([\![S_0]\!], [\![S_1]\!], \ldots, [\![S_{N-1}]\!])$ that models the execution of the linked program by maintaining as its own core state a (heterogeneous) stack of the modules' core states. Each "frame" on the stack corresponds to a runtime invocation of one of the modules in the program. Cross-module function calls result in new cores being pushed onto the stack (initialized via initial_core); returning from such a function pops the top core from the stack and injects the return value into the state of the caller, using after_external.

The modules $S_i$ are written in different languages, whose states may have different (Coq) types. In order to treat these modules uniformly in $\mathcal{L}$, we wrap their interaction semantics by *existentially* quantifying over the core state types of each module, an operation we encapsulate in the type Modsem.

$$\mathsf{Modsem} \triangleq \left\{ \begin{array}{lcl} \mathsf{F,V,C} & : & \mathsf{Type} \\ \mathsf{ge} & : & \mathsf{Genv\ F\ V} \\ \mathsf{sem} & : & \mathsf{Semantics\ (Genv\ F\ V)\ C\ mem} \end{array} \right.$$

In this dependently typed record, the types of ge and sem depend on F, V, and C. This module is written in programming language F (*e.g.*, Clight or x86), whose global variables have type-specification language V (*e.g.*, Clight types or unit); and whose core states have type C (*e.g.*, Clight nonaddressable locals and control stack, or x86 register bank). We also existentially bind the global environment ge that was statically initialized for this module. It maps addresses to global variables and function-bodies.[3]

The final component is sem, an interaction semantics. It defines the interface functions initial_core, at_external, *etc.*, as well as a step relation ge $\vdash c, m \longmapsto c', m'$. Modules in the same language will typically have identical $\cdot \vdash \cdot \longmapsto \cdot$ relations, specialized by different ge components that map disjoint sets of addresses to internal function bodies (as opposed to external function declarations). In what follows, we use $[\![\cdot]\!]$ to refer interchangeably to the interaction semantics of modules and their Modsem wrappers.

The output of $\mathcal{L}$ is an interaction semantics in the LinkedState "language." LinkedState is parameterized by *modules*, a map from module indices in the range $[0, N)$ to module semantics, where $N$ is the (nonzero) number of translation units in the program.

$$\mathsf{Core}\ (N : \mathsf{pos})\ (modules : I_N \to \mathsf{Modsem}) \triangleq \left\{ \begin{array}{lcl} \mathsf{idx} & : & I_N \\ \mathsf{core} & : & \mathsf{C}\ (modules\ \mathsf{idx}) \end{array} \right.$$

Core models the runtime state of a sequential execution thread. $I_N$ is the (dependent) type of integers in range $[0, N)$. The idx of a Core is the index of the module from which the core was initialized.

The runtime state of a linked program is then:

$$\mathsf{LinkedState}\ (N : \mathsf{pos})\ (modules : I_N \to \mathsf{Modsem}) \triangleq \left\{ \begin{array}{lcl} \mathsf{plt} & : & \mathsf{ident} \to \mathsf{option}\ I_N \\ \mathsf{stack} & : & \mathsf{Stack}\ (\mathsf{Core}\ N\ modules) \end{array} \right.$$

The two fields of LinkedState are: the procedure linkage table plt—mapping function names (type ident) to the indices of the modules in which the functions are defined, if any (option $I_N$)—and a stack of cores. We model the plt as a field in the LinkedState record, as opposed to deriving it from $N$ and *modules*, to retain flexibility to do dynamic linking in the future. The stack is always nonempty; all cores except the topmost one are at_external ($\forall c \in$ (pop stack). at_external $c$ = Some $-$).

Figure 6 gives the step relation. There are three rules. The STEP rule deals with the case in which the topmost core on the call stack ($c$ = peek $l$.stack) takes a normal internal step ($ge_c \vDash c, m \longmapsto c', m'$). $ge_c$ is the global environment associated with the module from which $c$ was initialized. In this case, we just propagate the new core state $c'$ and memory $m'$ to the result state of the overall linking judgment. The notation $l$ **with** {stack := push $c'$ (pop $l$.stack)} updates the topmost core state on the stack. For readability, we elide the operations required to propagate the idx field of Core records.

The second rule, CALL, handles the case in which the topmost core on the stack is at_external (at_external $c$ = Some ($id_f, \overrightarrow{v}$)) making a cross-module function call. In this case, we use the initial_core function of the module semantics that defines function $id_f$ ($l$.plt $id_f$ = Some $idx$) to initialize a new core state to handle the function call (initial_core ($modules\ idx$) (Vptr $b_f$) $\overrightarrow{v}$ = Some $c'$). The core $c'$ is then pushed onto the stack ($l$ **with** {stack := push $c'$ $l$.stack}) to become the new running core.

The RETURN rule models external function returns. Here, the core state $c$ is halted with return value $v$ ($l$ **with** {stack := push $c'$ $l$.stack}). To resume execution, we use the after_external function exposed by the caller's semantics $c'$ = peek (pop $l$.stack) to inject the return value $v$ (after_external (Some $v$) $c'$ =

[3] All the inputs to $\mathcal{L}$ must have ge functions that map exactly the same global addresses (modules that fail to declare some unused external global variables or functions can always be made to do so, by safety monotonicity).

$$\boxed{ge \models c, m \Longmapsto c', m'}$$

$$\frac{c = \mathsf{peek}\ l.\mathsf{stack} \qquad ge_c \models c, m \longmapsto c', m'}{ge \models l, m \Longmapsto l\ \textbf{with}\ \{\mathsf{stack} := \mathsf{push}\ c'\ (\mathsf{pop}\ l.\mathsf{stack})\}, m'}\ (\text{STEP})$$

$$\frac{\begin{array}{c} c = \mathsf{peek}\ l.\mathsf{stack} \qquad \mathsf{at\_external}\ c = \mathsf{Some}\ (id_f, \overrightarrow{v}) \\ l.\mathsf{plt}\ id_f = \mathsf{Some}\ idx \qquad ge\ id_f = \mathsf{Some}\ b_f \\ \mathsf{initial\_core}\ (modules\ idx)\ (\mathsf{Vptr}\ b_f)\ \overrightarrow{v} = \mathsf{Some}\ c' \end{array}}{ge \models l, m \Longmapsto l\ \textbf{with}\ \{\mathsf{stack} := \mathsf{push}\ c'\ l.\mathsf{stack}\}, m}\ (\text{CALL})$$

$$\frac{\begin{array}{c} \mathsf{size}\ l.\mathsf{stack} > 1 \qquad c = \mathsf{peek}\ l.\mathsf{stack} \\ \mathsf{halted}\ c = \mathsf{Some}\ v \qquad c' = \mathsf{peek}\ (\mathsf{pop}\ l.\mathsf{stack}) \\ \mathsf{after\_external}\ (\mathsf{Some}\ v)\ c' = \mathsf{Some}\ c'' \end{array}}{ge \models l, m \Longmapsto l\ \textbf{with}\ \{\mathsf{stack} := \mathsf{push}\ c''\ (\mathsf{pop}\ (\mathsf{pop}\ l.\mathsf{stack}))\}, m}\ (\text{RETURN})$$

**Figure 6.** Corestep relation of program linking semantics $\mathcal{L}$.

$\mathsf{Some}\ c''$). State $c$ is then popped from the stack, and state $c'$ is updated to $c''$ ($l$ **with** $\{\mathsf{stack} := \mathsf{push}\ c''\ (\mathsf{pop}\ (\mathsf{pop}\ l.\mathsf{stack}))\}$).

The stack is an abstraction of the activation-record stack of a C or assembly program. Internal calls (within one module) do not push on our stack; they transition from one core (and memory) to another core (and memory) within the same top stack element. But of course this core/memory may be the abstraction/implementation of pushing and popping (module-local) activation records. Different modules may or may not share a "real" activation-record stack.

The final piece of linking semantics is the definition of the interface functions: initial_core, at_external, after_external, and halted. We do not have space to give the full definitions here (they are in the Coq code); instead, we briefly describe them.

A linking semantics is initialized (initial_core) by spawning a new core to handle the entry point function that was called. The linking semantics is at_external when the topmost core on the stack is at_external calling a function defined by none of the modules (otherwise, we would have initialized and pushed a new core to handle the function). To inject a return value into linker states (after_external), we inject the value into the topmost core state on the stack ($\mathsf{after\_external}\ v_{opt}\ c = \mathsf{Some}\ c'$). Finally, a linking semantics is halted when the stack contains a singleton halted core state ($\mathsf{halted}\ c$ and $\mathsf{size}\ l.\mathsf{stack} = 1$), *i.e.*, the topmost core is halted but has no return context.

***Contextual Equivalence.*** Linking semantics leads to a natural notion of semantic context: Take program contexts $C$ to be arbitrary module semantics Modsem. Then the application of a program context to an (open) multimodule program $P$ is just the semantics that results from linking the program with that context: $\mathcal{L}(C, [\![P]\!])$!

This notion of context-as-interaction-semantics is quite general: it supports the definition of program contexts in arbitrary languages, *e.g.*, Clight and x86 but also Coq's Gallina. (It is straightforward to define an interaction semantics whose step relation is an arbitrary Coq relation; the code that accompanies this paper includes one such example.)

Eliding some details related to global environments and memories, contextual equivalence of two open multimodule programs $P_S$ and $P_T$ may be defined as equitermination (halted in interaction semantics)—when initialized at matching entry points—in all contexts:

**Definition 1** (Contextual Equivalence).

$$P_S \sim P_T \triangleq \forall C.\ \mathcal{L}(C, [\![P_S]\!]) \Downarrow \iff \mathcal{L}(C, [\![P_T]\!]) \Downarrow$$

The context $C$ observes the state of memory (and the arguments to external calls) when the program interacts with the environment. To distinguish $P_S$ and $P_T$, $C$ can, *e.g.*, get stuck (as opposed to safely terminating) at one of these interaction points if the memory state and arguments fail to satisfy a specified predicate.

## 4. Structured Simulations

Section 3 showed how to define the semantics of open multimodule programs, and what contextual equivalence meant in that setting. Now we show how to *prove* contextual equivalences for CompCert. We briefly review logical simulation relations (Beringer et al. 2014), and then show our new enhancement, *structured simulations*.

LSRs established compiler correctness by showing that compilation preserved the protocol structure of interaction semantics, using CompCert's original match relations $\sim_f$ with memory injections $f$ to relate source and target states. For internal execution steps, they followed CompCert's forward simulation proofs. For external calls, they asserted that the two modules call the same function with related arguments, and that the simulation relation is reestablished at return points whenever the environment provides related return values, subject to a few constraints on how memory could evolve over the external calls.

The two most crucial of these constraints were that (1) in the source execution, external calls did not modify any memory region the compiler wished to remove;[4] and that (2) in the target execution, external calls did not modify locations that were unreachable from the source memory (an "unreachable" target location is one that does not correspond to a readable location in the source memory). Condition (2), in particular, enabled the proof of compiler phases such as spilling, which introduces new unreachable spill locations into a target program's stack frames. A deficiency of CompCert's simulation proofs and of LSRs was that they assumed conditions (1) and (2) at external calls, but did not prove that these properties were preserved by compilation.

Directly imposing constraints (1) and (2) onto the simulation clauses for internal steps does not work, however. A compiled function should be allowed to write to its *own* spill locations—just not to those of its caller.

To capture the difference in perspective between caller and callee, we make three adjustments to the LSR framework. First, to index the match relation $\sim$, we use *structured injections* $\mu$ instead of CompCert's original injections $f$. The additional structure in $\mu$ maintains the block-level ownership information necessary to tell a callee's (or other environmental) blocks apart from caller blocks. Second, we decorate the internal step relation of interaction semantics with *modification effects* $E$ such that locations not contained in $E$ are guaranteed not to be modified (*i.e.* written to, or freed) by the step in question. Third, we impose a *restriction* axiom onto $\sim$ that ensures compilation invariants depend only on memory regions either allocated by the module being compiled, or leaked to it via pointers returned from external calls. The details are as follows.

***Structured Injections.*** In CompCert, memory is allocated in regions, or *blocks*. Within each block, memory bytes are addressed using integer offsets (pointer arithmetic is allowed only within blocks). CompCert's memory injections $f$ : $\mathsf{block} \rightarrow$

[4] For example, if a source-language variable is represented in memory on the stack, and in the translation to intermediate language the compiler chooses to use a register (unaddressable local variable) instead, then we say this memory region is removed by the compiler.

$$
\begin{array}{l}
\mathsf{Ownership} \triangleq \mathsf{Priv} \mid \mathsf{Pub} \mid \mathsf{Frgn} \mid \mathsf{Invis} \mid \mathsf{None} \\
\mu \in \mathsf{StructuredInjection} : \mathsf{Type} \triangleq \\
\quad \left\{ \begin{array}{l}
\mathsf{own}_S : \mathsf{block} \rightarrow \mathsf{Ownership} \\
\mathsf{own}_T : \mathsf{block} \rightarrow \mathsf{Ownership} \\
\mathsf{f_{us}} : \mathsf{block} \rightarrow \mathsf{option}\ (\mathsf{block} \times \mathcal{Z}) \\
\mathsf{f_{them}} : \mathsf{block} \rightarrow \mathsf{option}\ (\mathsf{block} \times \mathcal{Z})
\end{array} \right.
\end{array}
$$

$$
\begin{array}{rcl}
\mathsf{owned}_i & \triangleq & \{b \mid \mathsf{own}_i(b) \in \{\mathsf{Priv}, \mathsf{Pub}\}\}, i \in \{S, T\} \\
\mathsf{shared}_i & \triangleq & \{b \mid \mathsf{own}_i(b) \in \{\mathsf{Pub}, \mathsf{Frgn}\}\}, i \in \{S, T\} \\
\mathsf{vis}_i & \triangleq & \mathsf{owned}_i \cup \mathsf{shared}_i, i \in \{S, T\} \\
f \lfloor_X & \triangleq & \lambda b.\ \textbf{if}\ b \in X\ \textbf{then}\ f\ b\ \textbf{else None} \\
\mu \lfloor_X & \triangleq & \mu\ \textbf{with}\ \{\mathsf{f_{us}} := \mathsf{f_{us}} \lfloor_X\}\{\mathsf{f_{them}} := \mathsf{f_{them}} \lfloor_X\}
\end{array}
$$

**Figure 7.** Structured injections.

option (block $\times\ \mathcal{Z}$) relate source and target memories. For example, the memory injection that maps $b$ to Some $(b', \delta)$ associates source address $(b, 8)$ with target address $(b', 8 + \delta)$.

Structured injections $\mu$ (Figure 7) strengthen CompCert's memory injection relations with additional ownership structure. They have four components: Two *ownership* functions $\mathsf{own}_S, \mathsf{own}_T$ : block $\rightarrow$ Ownership, which map blocks (in the source and target memories, respectively, of a related pair of program states) to values of an inductive Ownership type; and two CompCert-style memory injections: $\mathsf{f_{us}}$ and $\mathsf{f_{them}}$. $\mathsf{f_{us}}$ records the source–target mapping of blocks that were allocated by the current module; $\mathsf{f_{them}}$ maps external blocks (those allocated by other modules).

The Ownership modes are: Priv, for memory regions (blocks) allocated by the module being compiled but which haven't been leaked to the environment; Pub, for allocated blocks that *have* been leaked at a previous interaction point; Frgn, for foreign blocks leaked into $\mu$ at external calls; Invis, for blocks that have been allocated (by another module) but not leaked in; and None for blocks that may not yet have been allocated. A block is (locally) owned by $\mu$ in the source or target memory when $\mathsf{own}_S(b)$ (resp. $\mathsf{own}_T(b)$) is either Pub or Priv. *External* blocks in source and target are those mapped by $\mathsf{own}_{\{S,T\}}$ to Frgn or Invis. Likewise, a block is shared if its ownership is either Pub or Frgn. The *visible* source blocks of $\mu$ are those in the set $\mathsf{vis}_S \triangleq \mathsf{owned}_S \cup \mathsf{shared}_S$ (and likewise for $\mathsf{vis}_T$). We use notation $\mathsf{foreign}_{\{S,T\}}$ and $\mathsf{public}_{\{S,T\}}$ to denote the blocks with foreign and public ownership, respectively.

We track ownership of *blocks*, rather than ownership byte-by-byte, because the CompCert languages and memory model permit pointer arithmetic within blocks. Once a location within a block has been made public, the whole block is made public as well.

Complementing the data in Figure 7 are axioms that ensure proper interaction of ownership, leakage, and compilation. These axioms (not shown) enforce that $\mathsf{f_{us}}$ and $\mathsf{f_{them}}$ (1) operate exclusively on blocks of appropriate ownership (*i.e.* $\mathsf{f_{us}}$ only maps owned blocks, to owned blocks, and similarly for $\mathsf{f_{them}}$ and external blocks); and (2) are total on their portion of shared blocks: $\mathsf{f_{us}}$ must map all $\mathsf{Pub}_S$ blocks, and must map them to $\mathsf{Pub}_T$ blocks, and similarly for $\mathsf{f_{them}}$ and Frgn. The result is that blocks which have been leaked to/from the environment in one compilation stage cannot be removed by later stages.

At interaction points between a module and its environment, we adjust the structured injections so that (at these points) the shared regions are closed under pointer arithmetic and dereferencing (there are no pointers from the shared to the nonshared region). We maintain as an additional invariant that the source visible set $\mathsf{vis}_S$ is always closed under pointer dereferencing and pointer arithmetic.

***Simulation Structures.*** Figure 8 presents the two core clauses of structured simulations $\preceq$, those for internal (*i.e.* unobservable) steps (*Internal Steps*) and for external interactions with the environment (*External Steps*) (the clauses for initial_core, at_external, and halted are not shown). In the Figure, $\sim_\mu$ is existentially quantified. There is no single definition of $\sim_\mu$, but instead, one per compilation phase—Figure 8 defines the laws that each such $\sim_\mu$ relation must satisfy.[5]

*Internal Steps*

$$
\begin{array}{l}
\langle c, m \rangle \sim_\mu \langle d, tm \rangle \wedge ge_S \vdash c, m \xrightarrow{E_S} c', m' \rightarrow \\
\exists d'\ tm'\ \mu'. \\
\quad (1)\ \mu \sqsubseteq_{\mathsf{us}} \mu' \wedge \\
\quad (2)\ \mathsf{separated}\ \mu\ \mu'\ m\ tm \wedge \\
\quad (3)\ \mathsf{locally\_allocated}\ \mu\ \mu'\ m\ tm\ m'\ tm' \wedge \\
\quad (4)\ \langle c', m' \rangle \sim_{\mu'} \langle d', tm' \rangle \wedge \\
\quad (5)\ \exists E_T.\ ge_T \vdash d, tm \xrightarrow{E_T}{}^{+} d', tm' \wedge \\
\quad (6)\ E_S \subseteq \mathsf{vis}_S\ \mu \rightarrow \\
\qquad (6a)\ E_T \subseteq \mathsf{vis}_T\ \mu \wedge \\
\qquad (6b)\ \forall b_t\ z_t.\ (b_t, z_t) \in E_T \wedge b_t \notin \mathsf{owned}_T\ \mu \rightarrow \\
\qquad\qquad \exists b_s\ \delta.\ \mathsf{f_{them}}(b_s) = \mathsf{Some}\ (b_t, \delta) \wedge (b_s, z_t - \delta) \in E_S
\end{array}
$$

*External Steps*

*(at-external)*

$$
\left( \begin{array}{l}
\langle c, m \rangle \sim_\mu \langle d, tm \rangle \wedge \\
\mathsf{inject}\ \mu\ \overrightarrow{v_s}\ \overrightarrow{v_t} \wedge \mathsf{inject}\ \mu\ m\ tm \wedge \\
\mathsf{at\_external}\ c = \mathsf{Some}\ (id_f, \overrightarrow{v_s}) \wedge \\
\mathsf{at\_external}\ d = \mathsf{Some}\ (id_f, \overrightarrow{v_t}) \wedge \\
\nu \triangleq \textbf{leak\_out}\ \mu\ \overrightarrow{v_s}\ \overrightarrow{v_t}\ m\ tm
\end{array} \right) \rightarrow
$$

*(environment)*

$$
\forall \nu'\ v_s\ v_t\ m'\ tm'. \\
\left( \begin{array}{l}
\nu \sqsubseteq_{\mathsf{them}} \nu' \wedge \\
\mathsf{separated}\ \nu\ \nu'\ m\ tm \wedge \mathsf{valid}\ \nu'\ m'\ tm' \wedge \\
\mathsf{inject}\ \nu'\ v_s\ v_t \wedge \mathsf{inject}\ \nu'\ m'\ tm' \wedge \\
\mathsf{forward}\ m\ m' \wedge \mathsf{forward}\ tm\ tm' \wedge \\
\textbf{unchanged\_on}\ \{(b, z) \mid \mathsf{own}_S\ \nu\ b = \mathsf{Priv}\}\ m\ m' \wedge \\
\textbf{unchanged\_on}\ (\textbf{local\_out\_of\_reach}\ \nu\ m)\ tm\ tm' \wedge \\
\mu' \triangleq \textbf{leak\_in}\ \nu'\ v_s\ v_t\ m'\ tm'
\end{array} \right) \rightarrow
$$

*(after-external)*

$$
\begin{array}{l}
\exists c'\ d'.\ \mathsf{after\_external}\ v_s\ c = \mathsf{Some}\ c' \\
\quad \wedge\ \mathsf{after\_external}\ v_t\ d = \mathsf{Some}\ d' \\
\quad \wedge\ \langle c', m' \rangle \sim_{\mu'} \langle d', tm' \rangle
\end{array}
$$

**Figure 8.** Structured simulations, internal and external step cases.

The structure of the internal diagram (which is simplified in the figure to elide stuttering source steps) is familiar from traditional forward simulation proofs: Assume we are in matching initial states $\langle c, m \rangle \sim_\mu \langle d, tm \rangle$ and we take a source step $ge_S \vdash c, m \xrightarrow{E_S} c', m'$ with effect $E_S$. Then there exists a matching $d'$, $tm'$, and Kripke-extended structured injection $\mu'$ such that $ge_T \vdash d, tm \xrightarrow{E_T}{}^{+} d', tm'$ and $\langle c', m' \rangle \sim_{\mu'} \langle d', tm' \rangle$.Clause (1) (Kripke extension, $\mu \sqsubseteq_{\mathsf{us}} \mu'$) says that $\mu'$ may map more owned blocks than $\mu$ (in order to deal with allocations) but otherwise is equal to $\mu$. Clauses (2) and (3) are side conditions that are not important for understanding the key ideas.

Clause (6) is the **guarantee condition**. Clause (6a) asserts that the target effects $E_T$ are contained in $\mathsf{vis}_T\ \mu$, assuming that $E_S \subseteq$

[5] In most Compositional CompCert phases, the $\preceq_\mu$ relation is equality up to the injection of memory regions, the addition, removal, and merging of certain memory regions, and invariants on private memory regions. As in original CompCert, we say that nonpointer values such as integers are related only if they are actually equal.

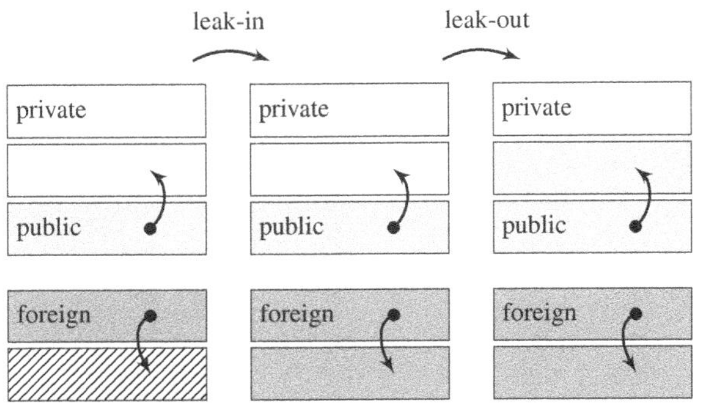


**Figure 9.** Graphical representation of the structured injection leakage operations. The thick black arrows are pointers in memory. The white private and light gray public boxes are owned ("us") blocks. The dark gray boxes are foreign ("them") blocks. The striped box is an Invis memory region that was allocated by another module but not yet leaked in. The leak-in operation marks the reachable invisible region as foreign. The leak-out operation marks as public a private region reachable from a public pointer.

$\mathsf{vis}_S\ \mu$. In other words, the compiler preserves the property of "writing to, and freeing, only visible locations."

Clause (6b) guarantees that writes to (and frees of) memory locations in the target that are not owned by $\mu$ ($b_t \notin \mathsf{owned}_T\ \mu$) can be "tracked back" to corresponding writes and frees in the source ($\exists b_s\ \delta.\ \mathsf{f}_{\mathsf{them}}(b_s) = \mathsf{Some}\ (b_t, \delta)$ and $(b_s, z_t - \delta) \in E_S$). Writes/frees of locations in blocks *owned* by the module being compiled are always permitted, which enables the compiler to introduce reloading code (for spilled variables) or to add function prologue/epilogue code that saves/restores callee-save registers.

The $E_S$ and $E_T$ that appear in clause (5) and in step judgments are *effect annotations*. For example, $ge_S \vdash c, m \xrightarrow{E_S} c', m'$ means: configuration $c, m$ steps to $c', m'$, writing to or freeing exactly the locations $E_S$. Locations not contained in this set are guaranteed not to be modified.

We state these "does not modify" guarantees intensionally in this way, as effect annotations, in order to prove vertical composition. The problem with a more extensional interpretation of effects (*e.g.*, as input–output "unchanged on" conditions) is that effects no longer "decompose": If a program takes two steps, from $m$ to $m''$ with effect set $E_1$ and from $m''$ to $m'$ with effect set $E_2$, with overall extensional effect $E$, it may be the case that $E_1 \cup E_2 \nsubseteq E$ if, for example, the second step restored a value that was overwritten by the first step. Decomposition is used in the internal step case of the proof that structured simulations compose vertically.

We track only write and free effects, and not read effects, because compiler correctness invariants do not, in general, depend on which locations another module merely reads. Proving more general program refinements (*e.g.*, between multiple implementations of an ADT), or that the compiler does not introduce additional memory reads—a property useful in security contexts—would most likely require a generalization to read effects.

The external step diagram occupies the bottom half of Figure 8. It relates an $\mathsf{at\_external}$ source–target configuration pair $\langle c, m\rangle \sim_\mu \langle d, tm\rangle$ with the $\mathsf{after\_external}$ configuration pair $\langle c', m'\rangle \sim_{\mu'} \langle d', tm'\rangle$ that results from making an external call. The basic premise is: For any source–target return values $v_s$, $v_t$, return memories $m'$ and $tm'$, and structured injection $\nu'$ satisfying the listed conditions, it's possible to inject $v_s$ and $v_t$ into states $c$ and $d$, resulting in the new states $c'$ and $d'$ which match in $\mu'$, $m'$, and $tm'$ ($\langle c', m'\rangle \sim_{\mu'} \langle d', tm'\rangle$). The $\nu \sqsubseteq_{\mathsf{them}} \nu'$ is dual to the $\sqsubseteq_{\mathsf{us}}$ condition used in the internal step diagram. It says that $\nu'$ may

*Reachability*

$$
\begin{array}{l}
\mathsf{reach}\ :\ \mathsf{mem} \to \mathsf{set\ block} \to \mathsf{list\ block} \to \mathsf{set\ block}\\
\mathsf{reach}\ m\ R\ \mathsf{nil} \triangleq R\\
\mathsf{reach}\ m\ R\ ((b', z') :: L) \triangleq\\
\quad \{b \mid b' \in \mathsf{reach}\ m\ R\ L \wedge \mathsf{perm}\ m\ b'\ z' = \mathsf{Readable}\\
\qquad \wedge\ \exists z.\ m(b', z') = \mathsf{Vptr}\ (b, z)\ \}\\
\mathsf{REACH}\ m\ R \triangleq \{b \mid \exists L.\ b \in \mathsf{reach}\ m\ R\ L\}
\end{array}
$$

*Export/Import*

$$
\begin{array}{l}
\mathsf{export}_i\ \mu\ B\ :\ \mathsf{StructuredInjection} \triangleq \mu\ \textbf{with}\ \{\mathsf{own}_i :=\\
\quad \lambda b.\ \textbf{if}\ b \in B\ \textbf{then}\ \mathsf{Pub}\ \textbf{else}\ \mathsf{own}_i\ \mu\ b\}, i \in \{S, T\}\\
\mathsf{import}_i\ \mu\ B\ :\ \mathsf{StructuredInjection} \triangleq \mu\ \textbf{with}\ \{\mathsf{own}_i :=\\
\quad \lambda b.\ \textbf{if}\ b \in B\ \textbf{then}\ \mathsf{Frgn}\ \textbf{else}\ \mathsf{own}_i\ \mu\ b\}, i \in \{S, T\}
\end{array}
$$

*Leakage*

$$
\begin{array}{l}
\mathsf{leak\_out}\ \mu\ \vec{v_s}\ \vec{v_t}\ m\ tm\ :\ \mathsf{StructuredInjection} \triangleq\\
\quad \textbf{let}\ L_S \triangleq \mathsf{REACH}\ m\ (\mathsf{blocksOf}\ \vec{v_S} \cup \mathsf{shared}_S\ \mu)\\
\qquad\qquad\qquad \cap\ \mathsf{owned}_S\ \mu\\
\qquad\quad L_T \triangleq \mathsf{REACH}\ tm\ (\mathsf{blocksOf}\ \vec{v_T} \cup \mathsf{shared}_T\ \mu)\\
\qquad\qquad\qquad \cap\ \mathsf{owned}_T\ \mu\\
\quad \textbf{in}\ \mathsf{export}_T\ (\mathsf{export}_S\ \mu\ L_S)\ L_T\\
\mathsf{leak\_in}\ \mu\ v_s\ v_t\ m\ tm\ :\ \mathsf{StructuredInjection} \triangleq\\
\quad \textbf{let}\ L_S \triangleq \mathsf{REACH}\ m\ (\mathsf{blocksOf}\ [v_s] \cup \mathsf{shared}_S\ \mu)\\
\qquad\qquad\qquad \cap\ \mathsf{owned}_S\ \mu\\
\qquad\quad L_T \triangleq \mathsf{REACH}\ tm\ (\mathsf{blocksOf}\ [v_T] \cup \mathsf{shared}_T\ \mu)\\
\qquad\qquad\qquad \cap\ \mathsf{owned}_T\ \mu\\
\quad \textbf{in}\ \mathsf{import}_T\ (\mathsf{import}_S\ \mu\ L_S)\ L_T
\end{array}
$$

**Figure 10.** Reachability and leakage.

map more external blocks than $\nu$—in order to deal with allocations performed by the environment—but otherwise is equal to $\nu$. The other nonbolded conditions are adapted from CompCert, and follow in our Coq proofs directly from symmetric conditions on the match-state relation and the internal step diagram.

The conditions listed in bold together compose the **structured simulation rely**. The predicate $\mathsf{unchanged\_on}\ U\ m\ m'$ specifies that memories $m$ and $m'$ are equal (same contents and permissions) at the locations in set $U$. In the source execution, we use $\mathsf{unchanged\_on}\ \{(b, z) \mid \mathsf{own}_S\ \nu\ b = \mathsf{Priv}\}\ m\ m'$ to ensure that $m$ and $m'$ are equal at locations in the private blocks of the injection $\nu$, which is built from $\mu$ by updating leakage information as described below. The target-execution condition $\mathsf{unchanged\_on}\ (\mathsf{local\_out\_of\_reach}\ \nu\ m)\ tm\ tm'$ says that $tm$ and $tm'$ are equal at owned target locations that either (1) do not correspond to readable source locations, or (2) are mapped from private source locations. By using $\mathsf{unchanged\_on}$ here, we stipulate the nonmodification conditions of the rely extensionally.

The structured injection $\nu$ is built from $\mu$—the injection that originally related $\mathsf{at\_external}$ states $\langle c, m\rangle \sim_\mu \langle d, tm\rangle$—using the $\mathsf{leak\_out}$ function depicted graphically in Figure 9 and defined in Figure 10. The idea is: $\mathsf{leak\_out}$ "leaks" to the public (other modules) blocks that are reachable by following pointer paths either from the arguments $\vec{v_i}$ to the external call ($\mathsf{blocksOf}\ \vec{v_i}$) or from blocks that were previously shared ($\mathsf{shared}_i\ \mu$). This is a consistency condition: It says that structured simulations may not assume anything about the contents of leaked blocks (the $\mathsf{unchanged\_on}$ conditions that form the rely satisfied by the environment apply only to private blocks). The functions $\mathsf{reach}$ and $\mathsf{REACH}$ defined at the top of Figure 10 calculate the transitive closure of the points-to relation on CompCert memories. In the definition of $\mathsf{leak\_out}$, we use the auxiliary function $\mathsf{export}$ to update the ownership functions of an injection $\mu$ to map blocks in the reachable set to $\mathsf{Pub}$.

The leak_in function used to define $\mu'$ at the end of the external step diagram plays a role analogous to that of leak_out, except that here, we are leaking into $\mu'$ new *foreign* blocks reachable from the return value $v_i$ of the external call. Likewise, the import function is almost equivalent to export, except that it updates the ownership functions of a structured injection to map the block set $B$ to Frgn as opposed to Pub.

***Restriction.*** The final consistency condition is: the simulation relation $\sim_\mu$ is independent of the Invis (and None) blocks. This condition is used, *e.g.*, in the proof of vertical composition (transitivity, Theorem 1). Technically, we enforce Invis-independence by requiring that $\sim_\mu$ be closed under restrictions to reach-closed supersets of the visible blocks, an operation defined in Figure 7 as $\mu\lfloor_X$ (with $X$ a block set). $\mu\lfloor_X$ denotes the structured injection obtained by restricting the maps $\mathsf{f_{us}}$ and $\mathsf{f_{them}}$ to the domain $X$. The closure condition says that if $\langle c, m\rangle \sim_\mu \langle d, tm\rangle$, then $\langle c, m\rangle \sim_{\mu\lfloor_X} \langle d, tm\rangle$ for any block set $X$ that contains at least $\mathsf{vis}_\mu$ and is closed under pointer dereferencing and arithmetic in $m$.

## 5. Main Results: Compositionality and Contextual Equivalence

***Vertical Composition (Transitivity).*** One can compose compiler phases (Figure 13). The proof that structured simulations compose vertically follows the same outline as that of LSRs (Beringer et al. 2014). As discussed in Section 4, the proof of transitivity of the internal-step diagram is tightly dependent on our treatment of effect annotations. Proving transitivity of the external-call clause (lower half of Figure 8) requires the construction of an interpolating after_external memory $m_2'$ in the intermediate execution between source and target.

**Theorem 1** (Transitivity). *Let $L_1$, $L_2$, and $L_3$ be effect-annotated interaction semantics. If $L_1 \preceq L_2$ is a structured simulation from $L_1$ to $L_2$ and $L_2 \preceq L_3$ a structured simulation from $L_2$ to $L_3$, then there exists a structured simulation $L_1 \preceq L_3$ from $L_1$ to $L_3$.*

***Horizontal Composition (Linking).*** The second kind of compositionality is *horizontal*: We would like to know that composing the simulation relations established by independently compiling the modules in a program results in an overall simulation between the (linked) multimodule source and target programs. We give the theorem statement first, then explain some of the subtleties, in particular, the restriction to *reach-closed* source semantics, which enforces the single-program conditions corresponding to the structured simulation guarantees of Section 4, and to *valid* target semantics (a technical property related to the CompCert memory model, explained below).

**Theorem 2** (Linking).

- *If $P_S = S_0, S_1, \cdots, S_{N-1}$ is a multimodule program with $N$ translation units, each of which is* ***reach-closed****, and*
- *$P_S$ is compiled to $P_T = T_0, T_1, \cdots, T_{N-1}$ (possibly by $N$ different compilation functions) such that $[\![S_i]\!] \preceq [\![T_i]\!]$ for each source–target pair, and each of the $T_i$ is* ***valid****, then*
- *there is a simulation relation $\mathcal{L}([\![P_S]\!]) \leq \mathcal{L}([\![P_T]\!])$ between the source and target programs that result from linking the $S_i$ and independently linking the $T_i$.*

The $\leq$ in the theorem denotes forward simulation on whole programs. Whole program simulations are as in Figure 8, but without clauses (1-3) in the internal step diagram, without clauses for at_external and after_external, and without effects. As Corollary 1 will show, establishing $\leq$ is sufficient for proving contextual equivalence of open multimodule programs. A *valid* semantics is one that never stores *invalid* pointers into memory. Invalid pointers, in CompCert parlance, are those that refer to memory regions that have not yet been allocated (freed pointers are never invalid). All CompCert x86 programs are valid in this way. Validity is required, in the proof of Theorem 2, to maintain the invariant that the set of valid target blocks is reach-closed.

***Reach-Closed Semantics.*** The restriction to reach-closed semantics (Figure 11) is best motivated with an example. Consider the program:

```
//Module A                    //Module B
void g(void);                   .globl _g
void h(int* x) {};            _g:
void f(void) {                  pushl %ebp
  int a=0;                      movl  %esp, %ebp
  if (a) {h(&a);}               movl  42,(0x28ac1c)
  g();}                         popl  %ebp
void main(void){f();}           ret
```

in which `A.f` calls (assembly function) `B.g`, passing no arguments. The strange bit is `B.g`: All it does is write the value `42` into memory at address `0x28ac1c`, which just happens to be the address at which local variable `a` is allocated on the stack in Windows.

Now imagine we compile module `A` through a compiler phase like dead code elimination, which results in `a` (which was previously addressed in dead code `if (a){h(&a);}` and therefore stack-allocated) being removed from memory. Since `0x28ac1c` is `a`'s address before dead code elimination, the unoptimized program above does not get stuck (the write succeeds, to location `&a`, without significant effect). After optimization, the program will fail, probably because the write to `&a` now overwrites the return address stored in `g`'s stack frame. (Incidentally, this program succeeds when compiled with `gcc -O0` but seg-faults under `gcc -O1`. This is not a bug in `gcc`; instead, it is evidence that the `gcc` developers agree with us that `Module B` is an ill-formed program context.)

One might object that `if (a){h(&a);}` is actually *not* dead code, because it results in `a` being stack-allocated, which in turn results in the safe execution of the (admittedly contrived) overall program. But *that way madness lies*. The point of a compositional compiler is to enable local modular compilation, which should depend only on translation-unit-local analyses. Correctness of optimizations like dead code elimination should be independent of the larger program context in which a module is executed.

The challenge, then, is coming up with a characterization of the source modules $S_0, S_1, \cdots, S_{N-1}$ that *does* admit linking as in Theorem 2. We do this in general, for arbitrary interaction semantics, by observing that the write to `0x28ac1c` is ill-formed not because it goes wrong (though it *will* lead to going wrong in most program contexts) but because it's a write to a location that the assembly program shouldn't have known about in the first place. Put another way, address `0x28ac1c` was not reachable via pointer arithmetic either from `g`'s initial arguments, from global variables, or from the return values of external calls `g` may have made previously.[6] This condition—no writes or frees to locations that are not "visible"—is the analogue of the $E_S \subseteq \mathsf{vis}_S\ \mu$ in clause (6) of Figure 8, but stated as a single-program property, independent of any particular structured injection $\mu$. We formalize the notion of a semantics that respects this characterization of visible locations as an extension of interaction semantics called *reach-closed semantics*, defined by the existence of an invariant $\mathcal{R}$ satisfying the laws in Figure 11. From the perspective of compiler correctness proofs, the

[6] It might seem strange to say "not reachable via pointer arithmetic" in the context of an assembly program, since in most assembly models the entire address space is "reachable". Here we mean "not reachable" in the instrumented semantics of x86 assembly used by CompCert, in which memory is allocated in blocks, as in CompCert's Clight, and interblock pointer arithmetic is disallowed.

*Reach-Closed Invariant*

$$\mathcal{R} : C \rightarrow \mathsf{mem} \rightarrow \mathsf{set\ block} \rightarrow \mathsf{Prop}$$

*Reach-Closed Initial Core*

$$\mathsf{initial\_core}\ ge\ v\ \vec{v} = \mathsf{Some}\ c \rightarrow \forall m.\ \mathcal{R}\ c\ m\ (\mathsf{blocksOf}\ \vec{v})$$

*Reach-Closed Step*

$$\mathsf{roots}\,(ge : G)\ (B : \mathsf{set\ block}) \triangleq \mathsf{globalBlocks}\, ge \cup B$$

$$\begin{array}{l}\mathcal{R}\ c\ m\ B\ \wedge\ ge \vdash c, m \overset{E}{\longmapsto} c', m' \rightarrow \\ (1)\ E \subseteq \mathsf{REACH}\ m\ (\mathsf{roots}\, ge\ B) \wedge \\ (2)\ \mathcal{R}\ c'\ m'\ (\mathsf{REACH}\ m'\ (\mathsf{freshblks}\ m\ m' \\ \qquad\qquad \cup\ \mathsf{REACH}\ m\ (\mathsf{roots}\ ge\ B)))\end{array}$$

*Reach-Closed After External*

$$\begin{array}{l}\mathcal{R}\ c\ m\ B \wedge \\ \mathsf{at\_external}\ c = \mathsf{Some}\ (id_f, \vec{v}) \wedge \\ \mathsf{after\_external}\ v_{opt}\, c = \mathsf{Some}\ c' \rightarrow \\ \textbf{let}\ B' \triangleq \textbf{case}\ v_{opt}\ \textbf{of} \\ \qquad \mid \mathsf{None} \rightarrow B \\ \qquad \mid \mathsf{Some}\ v \rightarrow \mathsf{blocksOf}\ (v :: \mathsf{nil}) \cup B \\ \textbf{in}\ \mathcal{R}\ c'\ m'\ B'\end{array}$$

**Figure 11.** Reach-closed semantics maintain an additional internal invariant $\mathcal{R}$ on states $c$, memories $m$, and block sets $B$ that satisfies the laws above. The definitions are parameterized by types $G$ and $C$, by a global environment $ge : G$, and by an interaction semantics of type Semantics $G$ $C$ mem that defines step relation $\longmapsto$ and functions after_external and initial_core (at_external and halted are elided).

restriction to reach-closed contexts is what *enables* program transformations: It would be unsound, for example, to remove a dead memory allocation if the larger program context depended on it, as in the example program above.

The $\mathcal{R}$ invariant of reach-closed semantics quantifies over: Core states of the argument semantics $c : C$, the memory $m$ : mem, and a set $B$ that records the blocks exposed to the semantics at interaction points (via pointers in the initial argument list, in the return values of external function calls, and by local allocation). We use the notation $sem_{rc}$, for *reach-closed semantics*, to denote a semantics $sem$ that exhibits such an $\mathcal{R}$.

The roots of a block set $B$ and global environment $ge$ are the union of $B$ and the global blocks of $ge$. The operative conditions of reach-closed semantics are those that characterize the reach-closed step relation (clauses 1 and 2). In particular, clause (1), which ensures that reach-closed semantics satisfy the structured simulation guarantees of Section 4, instruments the step relation of the underlying semantics with the additional condition that the effects $E$ produced by the step above clause (1) are a subset of the locations reachable in $m$ from the current roots.

Clause (2) asserts that the invariant can be reestablished after the step for: the blocks reachable (in $m'$) from newly allocated blocks (freshblks $m$ $m'$), if any, as well as from the blocks that were originally reachable in $m$ (REACH $m$ (roots $ge$ $c$)). This last condition ensures that the reachable set grows monotonically at each step, by not "forgetting" locations that were previously reachable.

The other interface laws modify $B$ as specified above. For example, the clause for after_external asserts that $\mathcal{R}$ can be reestablished for $B'$ equal to $B$ union the blocks exposed by the return values of external calls (blocksOf ($v$ :: nil)). initial_core asserts that the invariant can be established initially, with $B$ equal to the blocks exposed in the initial arguments. at_external and halted (not shown) assert that the arguments to external calls and return values, respectively, are not undefined.

As a corollary of Theorem 2, we get the following contextual equivalence result when the source modules are reach-closed, stated in terms of a variation of Definition 1 in which contexts satisfy a few additional properties.

**Definition 2** (Reach-Closed Contextual Equivalence).

$$\begin{array}{l}P_S \sim_{\mathsf{rc}} P_T \triangleq \\ \quad \forall C_{\mathsf{rc}}.\ C \preceq C \wedge \mathsf{det}\ C \wedge \mathsf{valid}\ C \wedge \mathsf{safe}\ \mathcal{L}(C, [\![P_S]\!]) \rightarrow \\ \qquad \mathcal{L}(C, [\![P_S]\!]) \Downarrow \iff \mathcal{L}(C, [\![P_T]\!]) \Downarrow\end{array}$$

**Corollary 1** (Simulation Implies Contextual Equivalence). *Let*

- $P_S = S_0, S_1, \cdots, S_{N-1}$*; and*
- $P_T = T_0, T_1, \cdots, T_{N-1}$

*for reach-closed source modules* $S_0, S_1, \cdots, S_{N-1}$ *and valid deterministic target modules* $T_0, T_1, \cdots, T_{N-1}$*. If for each i,* $[\![S_i]\!] \preceq [\![T_i]\!]$*, then* $P_S \sim_{\mathsf{rc}} P_T$*.*

In the above, we assume *closing contexts* $C$ (those that do not themselves call external functions not defined by any of the modules; callbacks into $P_S$ and $P_T$ are permitted). $C$ must also be valid. Safety of the source linked program and determinism of the target modules are required to prove the backward direction of the equivalence (the forward direction holds without these assumptions). The $C \preceq C$ condition says that $C$ commutes with memory injections: If $C$ is initialized twice with injected arguments, both executions either go wrong, nonterminate, or equiterminate with injected results. Although this condition follows directly from the form of Theorem 2, it is strongly motivated: We *should not* allow contexts to distinguish source and target programs based solely on bijective renamings of memory blocks exposed to the context (pointer arithmetic is not allowed *between* blocks, only within blocks). The consistency conditions on structured injections and simulations that we described in Section 4 mean that in the proof of $C \preceq C$, the context may assume that all public blocks leaked by the program are mapped from source to target (they are never removed during compilation of the program).

Nor is the reach closure condition imposed above an unrealistic proof obligation. One can show, for example, that all Clight programs satisfy the restrictions imposed in Figure 11.

**Theorem 3** (Safe Clight Programs are Reach-Closed). *There exists an* $\mathcal{R}$*, specialized to Clight states* $c$ *and the Clight step relation, that satisfies the laws given in Figure 11.*

The proof of this (perhaps counterintuitive) theorem relies on the fact that Clight programs never fabricate nonnull pointers, *e.g.*, by casting an integer to a pointer and then dereferencing it. (Even in standard C, casting an integer to a pointer, or vice versa, is only implementation defined, except when the pointer is `null`. See, *e.g.*, the C11 standard (C11 2011, 6.3.2.3).) □

The main difficulty in proving Theorem 2 (and Corollary 1) is in devising a simulation invariant to relate the stacks-of-cores runtime states of the linked programs $P_S$ and $P_T$. The situation is presented schematically in Figure 12. In the source linked program, we have a stack of core states, growing downwards, with $c$ in callee position with respect to a (direct or indirect) caller core $c_0$, which may be implemented in a different language. We must relate this stack of cores to the corresponding stack in the target linked program. We use $\mu$ to denote the structured simulation that relates the callees $c$ and $d$, and $\nu$ to denote the injection that relates callers $c_0$ and $d_0$. For simplicity, we elide the memories (for callers, the memory at the call point is existentially quantified). A caller core may be a callee with respect to another caller higher on the callstack.

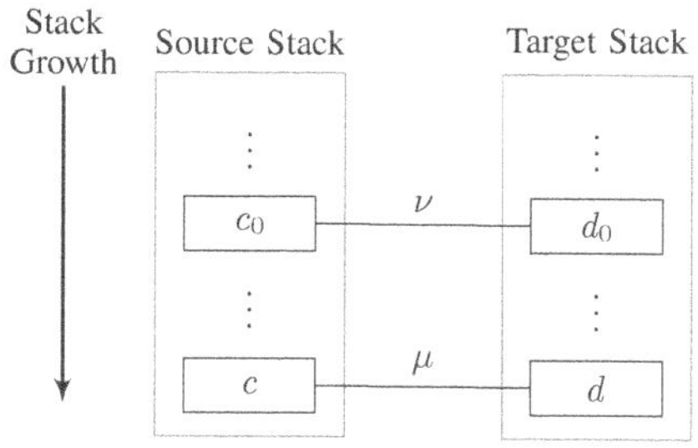


**Figure 12.** Schematic representation of the stacks-of-cores linking invariant. The inner white boxes are core states. Source core $c$ and target core $d$ are callees at the bottom of the LinkedState callstack, related by structured injection $\mu$ (memory is elided). Cores $c_0$ and $d_0$ are caller cores related by $\nu$.

The key rely–guarantee condition is to ensure that blocks labeled as foreign, or leaked-in, by callee injections $\mu$ are always labeled as public by caller injections $\nu$:

$$\mathsf{foreign}_S\ \mu \cap \mathsf{owned}_S\ \nu \subseteq \mathsf{public}_S\ \nu \tag{1}$$

From the fact that source modules are reach-closed

$$E_S \subseteq \mathsf{REACH}\ m\ (\mathsf{roots}\ ge\ B) \tag{2}$$

we then can show that the memory effects of the running callee core at the top of the callstack are confined to callee-allocated (owned) and foreign blocks. This implies that private caller memory regions in $\nu$, which are disjoint from the blocks marked as public by $\nu$, remain unmodified.

A difficulty here is how to relate the root sets of source modules to the visible sets $\mathsf{vis}_S$ used in the simulation relations. We do this by maintaining the following two invariants:

$$\mathsf{roots}\ ge\ B \subseteq \mathsf{vis}_S\ \mu \tag{3}$$

$$\mathsf{REACH}\ m\ (\mathsf{vis}_S\ \mu) \subseteq \mathsf{vis}_S\ \mu \tag{4}$$

Invariant (3) says that the root set of the source semantics is a subset of the visible source blocks in $\mu$. This invariant holds initially, for incoming block set $\mathsf{REACH}\ m\ (\mathsf{roots}\ ge\ (\mathsf{blocksOf}\ \overrightarrow{v}))$, and is maintained at external function calls and returns. Condition (4), which we maintain as an invariant of all structured simulations, says that the visible set is closed under reachability. These two conditions, plus (2) and monotonicity of the REACH relation, imply that $E_S$ is a subset of $\mathsf{vis}_S\ \mu$. This fact, together with condition (1) above, is sufficient to prove the unchanged_on relies of Figure 8 at the point at which the running core returns to its calling context.

## 6. Compositional CompCert

The proved-correct phases of the Compositional CompCert compiler are shown in Figure 13, with optimization phases in gray. The main differences with standard CompCert are: (1) We compile Clight to x86 assembly, whereas standard CompCert compiles a slightly higher-level language (CompCert C) to multiple assembly targets (x86, PowerPC, and ARM); and (2) standard CompCert includes three additional RTL-level optimizations (common subexpression elimination, constant propagation, and function inlining);[7] the adaptation of their proofs is ongoing work. The toplevel theorems we prove are the following.

**Theorem 4** (Compiler Correctness). *Let* CompCert *denote the compilation function that composes the phases in Figure 13 in order. If* $\mathsf{CompCert}(S) = \mathsf{Some}\ T$, *for Clight module $S$ and x86 module $T$, then* $[\![S]\!] \preceq [\![T]\!]$.

*Proof.* By transitive composition of the simulation proofs for the individual phases in Figure 13 using Theorem 1. □

**Corollary 2** (Compositional Compiler Correctness). *Let* $S_0$, $S_1$, $\ldots$, $S_{N-1}$ *be a set of Clight modules such that* $\mathsf{CompCert}(S_i) = \mathsf{Some}\ T_i$ *for each* $i$. *Then* $S_0, S_1, \ldots, S_{N-1} \sim_{\mathsf{rc}} T_0, T_1, \ldots, T_{N-1}$.

*Proof.* By Corollary 1, Theorem 3, Theorem 4, and determinism and validity of CompCert x86 assembly. □

The process of making the proof of a transformation phase compositional typically proceeded as follows: We refined CompCert's internal match-state notion $\sim_f$ (and the auxiliary relations for activation records, frame stacks, *etc.*) to relations $\sim_\mu$ indexed by structured injections. In particular, because external function call interactions may introduce memory regions related by memory injections in Compositional CompCert, the simulation relations of passes that were previously proved as memory equality or memory extension phases had to be reformulated as injection phases. Particular care was needed to assign correct ownership and visibility information to compiler-introduced memory blocks.

In addition, we had to add to each $\sim_\mu$ relation the clauses: $\mathsf{vis}_\mu$ is closed under reachability, and the relation $\sim_\mu$ is closed under restriction to the visible set ($\mu\ \downharpoonleft_{\mathsf{vis}_\mu}$). To ensure that global blocks were always mapped by each compiler phase, we treated them as Frgn to all modules. While the addition of these extra invariants proceeded in a mostly uniform manner across all phases, the refinement of $\sim_f$ to $\sim_\mu$ was phase-by-phase, due to the considerable internal differences between the various CompCert passes.

An issue that required special attention was the treatment of compiler builtins. Here we had to sharpen the distinction between, on the one hand, processor-specific 64-bit helpers and `memcpy`—these functions are typically inlined, and should never yield at_external despite being axiomatized as external calls by mainline CompCert—and true external functions, which are never inlineable, on the other. To sharpen this distinction, we modified the definition of the CminorSel language to ensure that the compiler-introduced calls to 64-bit helpers were unobservable.

All in all, porting the CompCert phases in Figure 13 to structured simulations took approximately 10 person-months. Much of this time was spent at the "boundaries" of the proof, updating the interfaces that connected our linking semantics and proofs to structured simulations. In general, the porting time decreased as as the project went on. Adapting the first few phases of the compiler took a few weeks to a month per phase, whereas the later phases went much more quickly (a day or two per phase). This was due in part to greater familiarity with CompCert, but also to the accumulation of a library of general-purpose lemmas that will remain useful as we continue to adapt the last few optimization passes.

As another measure of effort, we give lines-of-code for representative files in the development (Figure 14). Proofs of individual phases ("new") were on the order of 5klocs. By contrast, CompCert 2.1's ("old") proofs are about 2× smaller. The increase in proof lines is due mostly to the additional invariants we prove. However, we have not yet applied much proof automation at all, so we believe there is room for improvement. The increase in specification size is due to the use of duplicate language definitions: In order to add effects to the CompCert languages we duplicate the step relation of each semantics (once with, and once without, effects), then prove that the two semantics coincide. This results in specification counts that are larger than necessary.

[7] Inlining, which merges function stack frames, requires a slightly more general simulation relation than that of Figure 8 (without separated). We have done this generalization in a way that supports inlining and all previously proved phases but have not yet completed this proof in Coq.

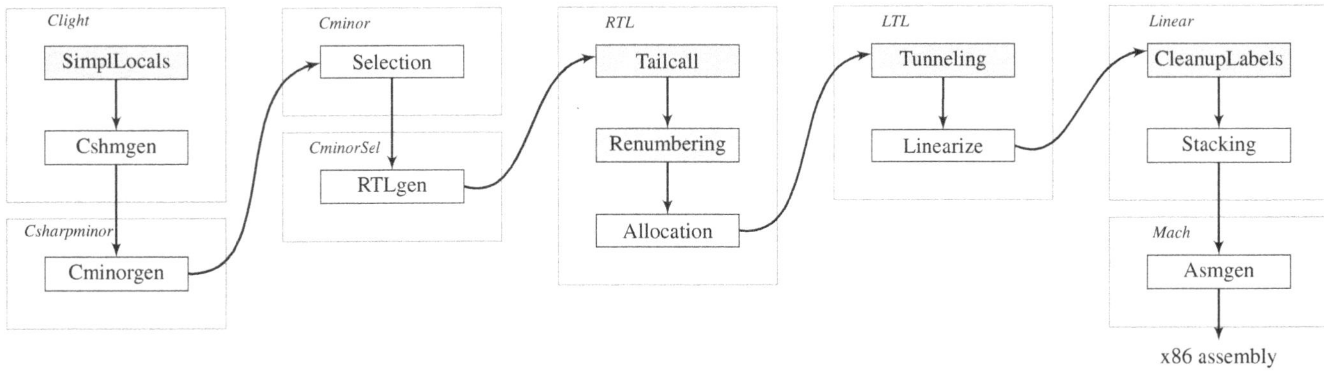


**Figure 13.** The phases of Compositional CompCert. Boxes in gray are optimization passes. Outer boxes indicate source languages.

| | Specs. | | Proofs | |
|---|---|---|---|---|
| *Compiler Phases:* | old | new | old | new |
| SimplLocals | 725 | 1004 | 2168 | 4572 |
| Cminorgen | 1619 | 1695 | 2796 | 5018 |
| RTLgen | 961 | 1355 | 1475 | 4883 |
| Tailcall | 441 | 637 | 628 | 1769 |
| Stacking | 712 | 1679 | 2906 | 6657 |
| *Theories:* | | | | |
| Structured Injs. (§4) | | 55 | | 2051 |
| Structured Sims. (§4) | | 763 | | 7967 |
| Transitivity (§5) | | 105 | | 5274 |
| Linking (§3, §5) | | 1651 | | 8459 |

**Figure 14.** Lines of code for selected parts of the development.

## 7. Related Work

Compiler verification is one of the "big problems" of computer science, as evidenced by the large body of research it has spawned in the 45 years or so since McCarthy and Painter (McCarthy and Painter 1967). We cannot hope to give a complete survey here (see (Dave 2003)). Instead, we focus on the most closely related work.

***Verified Whole-Program Compilers.*** Moore (Moore 1989) was one of the first to mechanically verify a programming language implementation (a compiler for a language called Piton). The most well-known work in this vein since Moore is Leroy's CompCert C compiler in Coq (Leroy 2009), upon which Compositional CompCert is based. Chlipala has also built verified compilers in Coq—first, from lambda calculus to idealized assembly language (Chlipala 2007), and then, later, for an impure functional language (Chlipala 2010). But both Chlipala and Leroy's compilers were limited to whole programs—they did not provide correctness guarantees, as we do in this work, about the behavior of separately compiled multimodule programs.

***Compositional Compilation.*** Benton and Hur were two of the first to explicitly do compositional specification of compilers and low-level code fragments, first for a compiler from a simply typed function language to a variant of Landin's SECD machine (Benton and Hur 2009), then for a functional language with polymorphism (Benton and Hur 2010). Benton and Hur's work was followed by a string of papers—by Dreyer, Hur, and collaborators—that resulted in refinements of the basic techniques (step-indexed logical relations and biorthogonality). The refinements included extensions to step-indexed *Kripke* logical relations, for dealing with state in the context of more realistic ML-like languages (Hur and Dreyer 2011), and more recently, to relation transition systems (RTSs) (Hur et al. 2012) and the related parametric bisimulations (Hur et al. 2013). RTSs demonstrated that it was possible to do bisimulation-style reasoning in the possible-worlds style of Kripke logical relations and state transition systems; parametric bisimulations refined RTSs by removing some technical restrictions. Both parametric bisimulations and RTSs compose transitively, like our structured simulations but unlike Kripke logical relations.

Although the context of their work is different, some of the techniques used by Benton, Dreyer, Hur, and their collaborators draw interesting parallels in our own work. Our "us vs. them" protocol is at least superficially similar to the "local vs. global knowledge" distinction that's made in RTSs. One difference is, we distinguish between local and external invariants on the *state* shared by modules, whereas in RTSs the local vs. global distinction is really about different notions of term equivalence. Also, our "them" invariants—which encapsulate one structured simulation's view of the memory regions allocated by external funcions—are not quite "global" in the same sense as Hur *et al.*'s global knowledge. Perhaps more fruitfully, one can view interaction semantics—and the structured simulations that are "indexed to" interaction semantics—as an analogue of the type structure used to index standard logical relations, but here applied to imperative languages with impoverished type systems: C, x86, and the other languages of CompCert. As in Kripke logical relations, structured simulations use Kripke-style possible worlds to model, *e.g.*, memory allocation.

An alternative to language-independent interaction semantics is *multi-language semantics* (Ahmed and Blume 2011), which combines several languages of a compiler into a single host language via syntactic boundary casts in the syle of Matthews and Findler (Matthews and Findler 2007). This makes it possible to state the correctness of a separate compiler as contextual equivalence in the combined language, as Perconti and Ahmed have recently done for a two-phase compiler from System F with existential and recursive types (Perconti and Ahmed 2014). But where Perconti and Ahmed define contexts syntactically, as one-hole terms in the combined language, we define contexts semantically, as interaction semantics. McKay's variation of Perconti and Ahmed's approach replaces explicit boundary conversion with programmatic conversion expressed as terms of the combined language, but considers only a single transformation, closure conversion (McKay 2014). Recently, Wang *et al.* (Wang et al. 2014) built a compositional compiler from a restricted C-like language, Cito, to Bedrock. In contrast to our work, compiler correctness in (Wang et al. 2014) is tied to the specifics of the Cito program logic.

***Concurrency.*** Liang *et al.*'s work (Liang et al. 2012) on verifying concurrent program transformations inspired our use of a rely-guarantee discipline, but the complexity of stack frame management, spilling, and block coalescing in CompCert made it difficult to apply their ideas directly in our setting. Ley-Wild and Nanevski's SCSL (Ley-Wild and Nanevski 2013), which we mentioned in the introduction, used subjective rely-guarantee invariants on auxiliary state to verify coarse-grained concurrent programs, such as parallel increment. Later work by Nanevski *et al.* extended the techniques to support verification of fine-grained concurrent programs (Nanevski et al. 2014). These subjective invariants made their proofs robust to the thread structure of the environment. Our "us vs. them" invariants serve a similar purpose—to prevent module-local structured simulations from being sensitive to the exact composition of their environment (other modules).

Lochbihler verified a whole-program compiler for multithreaded Java (Lochbihler 2012). Sevcík *et al.* built CompCertTSO (Sevcík et al. 2013), which adapted CompCert's correctness proofs to x86-TSO in order to reason about compilation of racy C code. Mansky's PTRANS framework (Mansky 2014) models optimizations as rewrite operations on parallel control flow graphs, specified using temporal logic formulae. While all three of these projects are whole-program, there are some similarities with our work. For example, both CompCertTSO and PTRANS lift program refinements from individual threads to whole programs, as we do for interacting modules, under certain noninterference conditions on shared state. A difference from our work is that PTRANS and CompCertTSO state the noninterference conditions as whole-system invariants. Our horizontal composition results instead rely only on a module-local characterization of noninterference, in the form of reach-closed semantics. That said, it would be interesting to investigate whether the compositional compilation approach we advocate could be applied to compilation with weak memory models.

## 8. Conclusion

CompCert is one of the great successes of formal methods for software verification. But as the authors of CompCert put it: "[CompCert's]... formal guarantees of semantic preservation apply only to whole programs that have been compiled as a whole by [the] CompCert C [compiler]." (Leroy 2014) We overcome this restriction.

## Acknowledgments

We thank the POPL anonymous reviewers, the members of the Princeton and Yale PL groups, Amal Ahmed, Robert Dockins, Dan Ghica, Robbert Krebbers, Xavier Leroy, and David Pichardie for valuable feedback. We especially thank Tahina Ramananandro for numerous insightful conversations. This material is based on research sponsored by DARPA under agreement number FA8750-12-2-0293. The U.S. Government is authorized to reproduce and distribute reprints for Governmental purposes notwithstanding any copyright notation thereon. The views and conclusions contained herein are those of the authors and should not be interpreted as necessarily representing the official policies or endorsements, either expressed or implied, of DARPA or the U.S. Government.

## References

A. Ahmed and M. Blume. An equivalence-preserving CPS translation via multi-language semantics. In *ICFP'11: The 16th ACM SIGPLAN International Conference on Functional Programming*, 2011.

A. W. Appel, R. Dockins, A. Hobor, L. Beringer, J. Dodds, G. Stewart, S. Blazy, and X. Leroy. *Program Logics for Certified Compilers*. Cambridge, 2014.

N. Benton and C.-K. Hur. Biorthogonality, step-indexing and compiler correctness. In *ICFP'09: The 14th ACM SIGPLAN International Conference on Functional Programming*, 2009.

N. Benton and C.-K. Hur. Realizability and compositional compiler correctness for a polymorphic language. Technical Report MSR-TR-2010-62, Microsoft Research, 2010.

L. Beringer, G. Stewart, R. Dockins, and A. W. Appel. Verified compilation for shared-memory C. In *ESOP'14: The 23rd European Symposium on Programming*, 2014.

C11. C11 draft standard. `http://www.open-std.org/jtc1/sc22/wg14/www/docs/n1570.pdf`, April 2011.

A. Chlipala. A certified type-preserving compiler from lambda calculus to assembly language. In *PLDI 2007: Programming Language Design and Implementation*, 2007.

A. Chlipala. A verified compiler for an impure functional language. In *POPL'10: The 37th ACM SIGACT-SIGPLAN Symposium on Principles of Programming Languages*, 2010.

M. A. Dave. Compiler verification: A bibliography. *SIGSOFT Software Engineeering Notes*, 28(6), 2003.

D. Ghica and N. Tzevelekos. A system-level game semantics. In *MFPS'12: The 28th Conference on the Mathematical Foundations of Programming Semantics*, 2012.

C. Hur, D. Dreyer, G. Neis, and V. Vafeiadis. The marriage of bisimulations and Kripke logical relations. In *POPL'12: The 39th ACM SIGACT-SIGPLAN Symposium on Principles of Programming Languages*, 2012.

C. Hur, G. Neis, D. Dreyer, and V. Vafeiadis. Parametric bisimulations: A logical step forward. In *POPL'13: The 40th ACM SIGACT-SIGPLAN Symposium on Principles of Programming Languages*, 2013.

C.-K. Hur and D. Dreyer. A Kripke logical relation between ML and assembly. In *POPL'11: The 38th ACM SIGACT-SIGPLAN Symposium on Principles of Programming Languages*, 2011.

X. Leroy. Formal verification of a realistic compiler. *Communications of the ACM*, 52(7):107–115, 2009.

X. Leroy. The CompCert C compiler website. `http://compcert.inria.fr/compcert-C.html`, 2014.

R. Ley-Wild and A. Nanevski. Subjective auxiliary state for coarse-grained concurrency. In *POPL'13: The 40th ACM SIGACT-SIGPLAN Symposium on Principles of Programming Languages*, 2013.

H. Liang, X. Feng, and M. Fu. A rely-guarantee-based simulation for verifying concurrent program transformations. In *POPL'12: The 39th ACM SIGACT-SIGPLAN Symposium on Principles of Programming Languages*, 2012.

A. Lochbihler. *A Machine-Checked, Type-Safe Model of Java Concurrency: Language, Virtual Machine, Memory Model, and Verified Compiler*. PhD thesis, Karlsruher Institut für Technologie, July 2012.

W. E. Mansky. *Specifying and Verifying Program Transformations with PTRANS*. PhD thesis, University of Illinois, 2014.

J. Matthews and R. B. Findler. Operational semantics for multi-language programs. In *POPL'07: The 34th ACM SIGACT-SIGPLAN Symposium on Principles of Programming Languages*, 2007.

J. McCarthy and J. Painter. Correctness of a compiler for arithmetic expressions. *Mathematical Aspects of Computer Science*, 1, 1967.

M. McKay. Compiler correctness via contextual equivalence. Undergraduate thesis, Carnegie Mellon University, May 2014.

J. S. Moore. A mechanically verified language implementation. *Journal of Automated Reasoning*, 5(4):461–492, 1989.

A. Nanevski, R. Ley-Wild, I. Sergey, and G. A. Delbianco. Communicating state transition systems for fine-grained concurrent resources. In *ESOP'14: The 23rd European Symposium on Programming*, 2014.

J. T. Perconti and A. Ahmed. Verifying an open compiler using multi-language semantics. In *ESOP'14: The 23rd European Symposium on Programming*, 2014.

J. Sevcík, V. Vafeiadis, F. Z. Nardelli, S. Jagannathan, and P. Sewell. CompCertTSO: A verified compiler for relaxed-memory concurrency. *J. ACM*, 60(3):22, 2013.

P. Wang, S. Cuellar, and A. Chlipala. Compiler verification meets cross-language linking via data abstraction. In *OOPSLA'14: Proceedings of the 2014 ACM International Conference on Object Oriented Programming Systems Languages and Applications*, 2014.

# Polymorphic Functions with Set-Theoretic Types

## Part 2: Local Type Inference and Type Reconstruction

Giuseppe Castagna[1] Kim Nguyễn[2] Zhiwu Xu[1,3] Pietro Abate[1]

[1]CNRS, PPS, Univ Paris Diderot, Sorbonne Paris Cité, Paris, France
[2]LRI, Université Paris-Sud, Orsay, France [3]TEC, Guangdong Power Grid Co., Guangzhou, China

**Abstract.** This article is the second part of a two articles series about the definition of higher-order polymorphic functions in a type system with recursive types and set-theoretic type connectives (unions, intersections, and negations).

In the first part, presented in a companion paper, we defined and studied the syntax, semantics, and evaluation of the explicitly-typed version of a calculus, in which type instantiation is driven by explicit instantiation annotations. In this second part we present a local type inference system that allows the programmer to omit explicit instantiation annotations for function applications, and a type reconstruction system that allows the programmer to omit explicit type annotations for function definitions.

***Categories and Subject Descriptors*** D.3.3 [*Programming Languages*]: Language Constructs and Features—Polymorphism

***Keywords*** Types, XML, intersection types, type constraints.

## 1. Introduction

Many XML processing languages, such as XDuce, ℂDuce, XQuery, OcamlDuce, XHaskell, XAct, are statically-typed functional languages. However, none of them provides full-fledged parametric polymorphism even though this feature has been repeatedly requested in different standardization groups. A major stumbling block to such an extension —*ie*, the definition of a subtyping relation for regular tree types with type variables— was lifted by Castagna and Xu [4]. In Part 1 of this work, presented in the previous edition of POPL [3], we described how to take full advantage of Castagna and Xu's system by defining a calculus with higher-order polymorphic functions and recursive types with union, intersection, and negation connectives. The approach is general and goes well beyond the sole application to XML processing languages. As a matter of fact, the motivating example we gave in Part 1 [3] does not involve XML, but looks like a rather classic display of functional programming specimens:

```
map :: (α -> β) -> [α] -> [β]
map f l = case l of
          | [] -> []
          | (x : xs) -> (f x : map f xs)

even :: (Int->Bool) ∧ ((α\Int) -> (α\Int))
even x = case x of
          | Int -> (x ‘mod‘ 2) == 0
          |   _ -> x
```

The first function is the classic map function defined in Haskell (we use Greek letters to denote type variables). The second would be an Haskell function were it not for two oddities: its type declaration contains type connectives (type intersection "∧" and type difference "\"); and the pattern in the `case` expression is a type, meaning that it matches all values returned by the matched expression that have that type. So what does the `even` function do? It checks whether its argument is an integer; if it is so it returns whether the integer is even or not, otherwise it returns its argument as it received it. Although the definition of `even` may seem weird, it follows a very common pattern used to manipulate functional data-structures. Two examples are Okasaki's functional implementation of red-black trees (for which our system provides a far better typing) and the transformation of XML documents whose elements are modified or left unchanged according to their tag/type (see actual code in Section 3.3 later on and in Appendix A included in the electronic appendix available on-line). Furthermore it is a perfect minimal example to illustrate all the aspects of our system.

In Part 1 [3] we showed that the system presented there is expressive enough to define the two functions above and to verify that they have the types declared in their signatures. That `map` has the declared type will come as no surprise (in practice, we actually want the system to infer this type even in the absence of a signature given by the programmer: see Section 7). That `even` was given an intersection type means that it must have all the types that form the intersection. So it must be a function that when applied to an integer it returns a Boolean and that when applied to an argument of a type that does not contain any integer, it returns a result of the same type. In other terms, `even` is a polymorphic (dynamically bounded) overloaded function. However, the system in Part 1 [3] is not able to *infer* (without the help of the programmer) the type of the partial application of `map` to `even`, which must be equivalent to

```
map even :: ([Int] -> [Bool]) ∧
            ([γ\Int] -> [γ\Int]) ∧                     (1)
            ([γ∨Int] -> [(γ\Int)∨Bool])
```

since `map even` returns a function that when applied to a list of integers it returns a list of Booleans; when applied to a list that does not contain any integer, then it returns a list of the same type (actually, the same list); and when it is applied to a list that may contain some integers (*eg*, a list of reals), then it returns a list of the same type, without the integers but with some Booleans instead (in the case of reals, a list with Booleans and reals that are not integers).

Typing `map even` is difficult because it demands to infer several different instantiations[1] of the type of `map` and then take their intersection. This is why the calculus in [3] includes explicit type substitutions: the programmer must explicitly provide the type-substitutions used to instantiate the types of the terms that form an application, a requirement that makes the system of [3] not usable in practice, yet. In this paper we remove this limitation by defining a sound and complete inference system that deduces the type-substitutions that a programmer should insert in a program

[1] For `map even` we need to infer just two instantiations, namely, $\{{}^{(\gamma\backslash\mathtt{Int})}/_{\alpha}, {}^{(\gamma\backslash\mathtt{Int})}/_{\beta}\}$ and $\{{}^{(\gamma\vee\mathtt{Int})}/_{\alpha}, {}^{(\gamma\backslash\mathtt{Int})\vee\mathtt{Bool}}/_{\beta}\}$. The type in (1) is redundant since the first type of the intersection is an instance (*eg*, for $\gamma$=`Int`) of the third. We included it just for the sake of the presentation.



*POPL '15*, January 15–17 2015, Mumbai, India.
Copyright is held by the owner/author(s). Publication rights licensed to ACM.
ACM 978-1-4503-3300-9/15/01...$15.00.
http://dx.doi.org/10.1145/2676726.2676991

of [3] to make it well typed. In other words, we define "local type inference"[2] for [3], namely, we solve the problem of checking whether there exist some type-substitutions that make the types of a function and of its arguments compatible and, if so, of inferring the type of the application as we did for (1). In particular, we show that local type inference for [3] reduces to the problem of finding two *sets* of type substitutions $\{\sigma_i \mid i{\in}I\}$ and $\{\sigma'_j \mid j{\in}J\}$ such that for two given types $s$ and $t$ the relation $\bigwedge_{i\in I} s\sigma_i \leq \bigwedge_{j\in J} t\sigma'_j$ holds, and we give a sound and complete algorithm for this problem. We also show how the same algorithm can be used to perform type reconstruction and infer types more precise than those inferred by the type systems of the ML family. The paper is accompanied by an electronic appendix available at http://dl.acm.org which contains all detailed proofs and complete definitions. The system is fully implemented and, at the moment of writing, in alpha-test. It will be distributed in the next public release of the ℂDuce language [2]. In the meanwhile, the current version can be tested by compiling the master branch of the ℂDuce git repository: `git clone` https://git.cduce.org/cduce (we recommend to check the bugtracker for current issues).

Next section outlines the various problems to be faced in this research and succinctly describes the system of [3]. The reader acquainted with the work in [3] can skip directly to Section 2.1.

## 2. Overview

The aim of this research is the definition an XML processing functional language with high-order polymorphic functions, that is, in the specific, a polymorphic version of the language ℂDuce [2]. ℂDuce is a strongly-typed programming language that eases the manipulation of data in XML format. Issued from academic research it is used in production, available on different platforms, and included in all major Linux distributions. The essence of ℂDuce is a $\lambda$-calculus with pairs, explicitly-typed recursive functions, and a type-case expression. Its types can be recursively defined and include basic, arrow, and product type *constructors* and the intersection, union, and negation type *connectives*. In this work we omit for brevity recursive functions and product types constructors and expressions (our results can be easily extended to them as sketched in Section 5 and detailed in the appendixes) and add type variables. So in the rest of this work we study a calculus whose types and expressions are described by the next two following definitions.

**Definition 2.1** (Types). *Types are the regular trees coinductively generated by the following productions:*

$$t ::= b \mid t \to t \mid t \wedge t \mid t \vee t \mid \neg t \mid \mathbb{0} \mid \mathbb{1} \mid \alpha \qquad (2)$$

*and such that every infinite branch contains infinitely many occurrences of "$\rightarrow$" constructor. We use $\mathscr{T}$ to denote the set of all types.*

In the definition, $b$ ranges over basic types (*eg*, `Int`, `Bool`), $\alpha$ ranges over type variables, and $\mathbb{0}$ and $\mathbb{1}$ respectively denote the empty (that types no value) and top (that types all values) types. Coinduction accounts for recursive types and the condition on infinite branches bars out ill-formed types such as $t = t \vee t$ (which does not carry any information about the set denoted by the type) or $t = \neg t$ (which cannot represent any set). It also ensures that the binary relation $\rhd \subseteq \mathscr{T}^2$ defined by $t_1 \vee t_2 \rhd t_i$, $t_1 \wedge t_2 \rhd t_i$, $\neg t \rhd t$ is Noetherian. This gives an induction principle on $\mathscr{T}$ that we will use without any further explicit reference to the relation. We use $\mathsf{var}(t)$ to denote the *set of type variables* occurring in a type $t$. A type $t$ is said to be *ground* or *closed* if and only if $\mathsf{var}(t)$ is empty. The subtyping relation for these types is the one defined by Castagna and Xu [4]. For this work it suffices to consider that ground types are interpreted as sets of *values* (*ie*, either constants or $\lambda$-abstractions) that have that type, and that subtyping is set containment (a ground type $s$ is a subtype of a ground type $t$ if and only if $t$ contains all the values of type $s$). In particular, $s{\to}t$ contains all $\lambda$-abstractions that when applied to a value of type $s$, if the computation terminates, then they return a result of type $t$ (*eg*, $\mathbb{0}{\to}\mathbb{1}$ is the set of all functions[3] and $\mathbb{1}{\to}\mathbb{0}$ is the set of functions that diverge on every argument). Type connectives (*ie*, union, intersection, negation) are interpreted as the corresponding set-theoretic operators (*eg*, $s \vee t$ is the union of the values of the two types). For what concerns non-ground types (*ie*, types with variables occurring in them) all the reader needs to know for this work is that the subtyping relation of Castagna and Xu is preserved by substitution of the type variables. Namely, if $s \leq t$, then $s\sigma \leq t\sigma$ for every type-substitution $\sigma$ (the converse does not hold in general, while it holds for *semantic* type-substitutions in convex models: see [4]). Two types are equivalent if they are subtype one of each other (type equivalence is denoted by $\simeq$). Finally, notice that in this system $s \leq t$ if and only if $s{\wedge}\neg t \leq \mathbb{0}$.

**Definition 2.2** (Expressions). *Expressions are the terms inductively generated by the following grammar*

$$e ::= c \mid x \mid ee \mid \lambda^{\wedge_{i\in I} s_i \to t_i} x.e \mid e{\in}t\,?\,e : e \qquad (3)$$

*and such that in every expression $e{\in}t\,?\,e_1 : e_2$ the type $t$ is closed.*

In the definition, $c$ ranges over constants (*eg*, `true`, `false`, `1`, `2`, ...) which are values of basic types (we use $b_c$ to denote the basic type of the constant $c$); $x$ ranges over expression variables; $e{\in}t\,?\,e_1 : e_2$ denotes the type-case expression that evaluates either $e_1$ or $e_2$ according to whether the value returned by $e$ (if any) is of type $t$ or not; $\lambda^{\wedge_{i\in I} s_i \to t_i} x.e$ is a value of type $\wedge_{i\in I} s_i \to t_i$ and denotes the function of parameter $x$ and body $e$. An expression has an intersection type if and only if it has all the types that compose the intersection. Therefore, intuitively, $\lambda^{\wedge_{i\in I} s_i \to t_i} x.e$ is a well-typed value if for all $i{\in}I$ the hypothesis that $x$ is of type $s_i$ implies that the body $e$ has type $t_i$, that is to say, it is well typed if $\lambda^{\wedge_{i\in I} s_i \to t_i} x.e$ has type $s_i \to t_i$ for all $i \in I$.

As we said at the beginning of the section, the functional core of ℂDuce [2] has exactly the same types and expressions as the above except for two single differences: ($i$) its types do not contain type variables and ($ii$) it includes product types and recursive functions, which we omitted here for brevity. The reasons why in ℂDuce (and in its polymorphic extension we study here) there is a type-case expressions and why $\lambda$-expressions are explicitly annotated by their intersection types are explained in details in the companion paper that presents the first part of this work [3] and to which the reader can refer. The novelty of this research with respect to ℂDuce, thus, is to allow type variables to occur in the types that annotate $\lambda$-abstractions. It becomes thus possible to define the polymorphic identity function as $\lambda^{\alpha\to\alpha}x.x$, while the classic "auto-application" term is written as $\lambda^{((\alpha\to\beta)\wedge\alpha)\to\beta}x.xx$. The intended meaning of using a type variable, such as $\alpha$, is that a (well-typed) $\lambda$-abstraction not only has the type specified in its label (and by subsumption all its super-types) but also all types obtained by instantiating the type variables occurring in its label. So $\lambda^{\alpha\to\alpha}x.x$ has not only type $\alpha \to \alpha$ but by subsumption also, for instance, the types $\mathbb{0}{\to}\mathbb{1}$ (the type of all functions, which is a super-type of $\alpha{\to}\alpha$) and $\neg$`Int` (the type of all non integer values), and by instantiation the

[2] There are different definitions for *local type inference*. Here we use it with the meaning of finding the type of an expression in which not all type annotations are specified. This is the acceptation used in Scala where, like in C# and Java, type parameters for polymorphic/generic method calls can be omitted. In our specific problem, we will omit —and, thus, infer— the annotations that specify how the types of a function and of its argument can be made compatible. As explained in Section 6 it is more general than Pierce and Turner's local type inference for arguments types [14].

[3] Actually, for every type $t$, all types of the form $\mathbb{0}{\to}t$ are equivalent and each of them denotes the set of all functions.

types $\texttt{Int}\to\texttt{Int}$, $\texttt{Bool}\to\texttt{Bool}$, etc. The addition of type variables and instantiation makes the calculus a full-fledged intersection type system (see Section 3.5 in [3]): for instance, by combining intersections, instantiation, and subtyping, it is possible to deduce that $\lambda^{\alpha\to\alpha}x.x$ has type $(\texttt{Int}\to\texttt{Int}) \wedge (\texttt{Bool}\to\texttt{Bool}) \wedge \neg\texttt{Int}$.

The key problem to be solved, then, is to define an *explicitly-typed* $\lambda$-calculus with intersection types and a type-case expression. This is technically quite challenging because of three main reasons: $(i)$ type instantiation must be explicit, $(ii)$ it may require the use of *sets* of type-substitutions, and $(iii)$ it cannot always be immediately propagated to the body of a function. A detailed description of these reasons can be found in [3] but, in a nutshell:

$(i)$ instantiation must be explicit because of the presence of a type-case: we check the type of a function by checking its type annotation, thus any type-substitution of variables of an annotation must be explicitly propagated. That is, to apply $\lambda^{\alpha\to\alpha}x.x$ to $42$ we must first apply the type-substitution $\{\texttt{Int}/\alpha\}$ to it, yielding $\lambda^{\texttt{Int}\to\texttt{Int}}x.x$, and only then we can apply the function to $42$.

$(ii)$ sets of type-substitutions are needed because of intersection types. A function that expects arguments of type $(\texttt{Int}\to\texttt{Int}) \wedge (\texttt{Bool}\to\texttt{Bool})$ can be safely applied to $\lambda^{\alpha\to\alpha}x.x$, but the latter must be previously instantiated by a *set* of two type-substitutions $[\{\texttt{Int}/\alpha\}, \{\texttt{Bool}/\alpha\}]$, yielding $\lambda^{(\texttt{Int}\to\texttt{Int})\wedge(\texttt{Bool}\to\texttt{Bool})}x.x$ (the application of a set of substitution to a type $t$ returns the intersection of all types obtained by applying each substitutions in the set to $t$).

$(iii)$ type-substitutions cannot be immediately applied to the body of a function since this may yield ill-typed terms. For instance, consider the following "daffy" definition of the identity function

$$(\lambda^{\alpha\to\alpha}x.(\lambda^{\alpha\to\alpha}y.x)x) \tag{4}$$

and apply it to the same set of substitutions as before, namely, $[\{\texttt{Int}/\alpha\}, \{\texttt{Bool}/\alpha\}]$. This yields the following term

$$(\lambda^{(\texttt{Int}\to\texttt{Int})\wedge(\texttt{Bool}\to\texttt{Bool})}x.(\lambda^{(\texttt{Int}\to\texttt{Int})\wedge(\texttt{Bool}\to\texttt{Bool})}y.x)x) \tag{5}$$

which is not well typed: to type it one should prove that under the hypothesis $x:\texttt{Int}$ the term $(\lambda^{(\texttt{Int}\to\texttt{Int})\wedge(\texttt{Bool}\to\texttt{Bool})}y.x)x$ has type $\texttt{Int}$, and that under the hypothesis $x:\texttt{Bool}$ this same term has type $\texttt{Bool}$, but both checks fail because, in both cases, $\lambda^{(\texttt{Int}\to\texttt{Int})\wedge(\texttt{Bool}\to\texttt{Bool})}y.x$ is ill-typed (it neither has type $\texttt{Int}\to\texttt{Int}$ when $x:\texttt{Bool}$, nor has it type $\texttt{Bool}\to\texttt{Bool}$ when $x:\texttt{Int}$).

To cope with these three problems we proposed in Part 1 [3] that the instantiation of the body of a function changes according to the type of the argument of the function. For instance, when we apply the daffy identity function to an integer we must instantiate its body by the type-substitution $\{\texttt{Int}/\alpha\}$, while the type-substitution $\{\texttt{Bool}/\alpha\}$ must be used when the function argument is a Boolean value. To obtain this behavior, in Part 1 [3] we introduced and studied a "lazy" instantiation of function bodies, which delays the propagation of a set of substitutions to the function body until the precise type of the function argument is known. This is obtained by decorating $\lambda$-abstractions by (sets of) type-substitutions. For example, in order to pass our daffy identity function (4) to a function that expects arguments of type $(\texttt{Int}\to\texttt{Int}) \wedge (\texttt{Bool}\to\texttt{Bool})$ we first "lazily" instantiate it as follows:

$$(\lambda^{\alpha\to\alpha}_{[\{\texttt{Int}/\alpha\},\{\texttt{Bool}/\alpha\}]}x.(\lambda^{\alpha\to\alpha}y.x)x). \tag{6}$$

The annotation that subscripts the outer "$\lambda$" indicates that the function must be relabeled and, therefore, that we are using the particular instance whose type is the one in the "interface" (*ie*, $\alpha\to\alpha$) to which we apply the set of type-substitutions in the annotation. The relabeling will be actually propagated to the body of the function at the moment of the reduction, only if and when the function is applied (relabeling is thus lazy). However, the new annotation is statically used by the type system to check type soundness.

Formally, this is obtained in Part 1 [3] by adding explicit sets of type-substitutions (ranged over by $[\sigma_j]_{j\in J}$) to the grammar (3) of Definition 2.2. Sets of type-substitutions can be applied directly to expressions (to produce a particular expansion/instantiation of the type variables occurring in them) or, as in (6), they can be used to annotate $\lambda$'s (to implement the lazy relabeling of the function body). This yields a calculus whose syntax is

$$e ::= c \mid x \mid ee \mid \lambda^{\wedge_{i\in I}s_i\to t_i}_{[\sigma_j]_{j\in J}}x.e \mid e{\in}t\,?\,e : e \mid e[\sigma_j]_{j\in J} \tag{7}$$

where types are those in Definition 2.1 and with the restriction that the type tested in type-case expressions is closed. We call this calculus and its expressions the *explicitly-typed* calculus and expressions, respectively, in order to differentiate it from the one of Definition 2.2 which does not have explicit type-substitutions and, therefore, is called the *implicitly-typed* calculus.

Henceforth, given a $\lambda$-abstraction $\lambda^{\wedge_{i\in I}s_i\to t_i}_{[\sigma_j]_{j\in J}}x.e$ we call the type $\bigwedge_{i\in I} s_i\to t_i$ the *interface* of the function and the set of type-substitutions $[\sigma_j]_{j\in J}$ the *decoration* of the function. We write $\lambda^{\wedge_{i\in I}t_i\to s_i}x.e$ for short when the decoration is a singleton containing just the empty substitution. We use $v$ to range over *values*, that is, either constants or $\lambda$-abstractions. Let $e$ be an expression: we use $\mathsf{fv}(e)$ and $\mathsf{bv}(e)$ respectively to denote the sets of *free expression variables* and *bound expression variables* of the expression $e$; we use $\mathsf{tv}(e)$ to denote the set of *type variables* occurring in $e$.

As customary, we assume bound expression variables to be pairwise distinct and distinct from any free expression variable occurring in the expressions under consideration. Polymorphic variables can be bound by interfaces, but also by decorations: for example, in $\lambda^{\beta\to\beta}_{[\{\alpha/\beta\}]}x.(\lambda^{\alpha\to\alpha}y.y)x$, the $\alpha$ occurring in the interface of the inner abstraction is "bound" by the decoration $[\{\alpha/\beta\}]$, and the whole expression is $\alpha$-equivalent to $(\lambda^{\beta\to\beta}_{[\{\gamma/\beta\}]}x.(\lambda^{\gamma\to\gamma}y.y)x)$. If a type variable is bound by an outer abstraction, it cannot be instantiated; such a type variable is called *monomorphic*. We assume that polymorphic type variables are pairwise distinct and distinct from any monomorphic type variable in the expressions under consideration. In particular, when substituting a value $v$ for a variable $x$ in an expression $e$, we suppose the polymorphic type variables of $e$ to be distinct from the monomorphic and polymorphic type variables of $v$ thus avoiding unwanted capture.

Both static and dynamic semantics for the explicitly-typed expressions in (7) are defined in [3] in terms of a *relabeling* operation "@" which takes an expression $e$ and a set of type-substitutions $[\sigma_j]_{j\in J}$ and pushes $[\sigma_j]_{j\in J}$ down to all outermost $\lambda$-abstractions occurring in $e$ (and collects and composes with the sets of type-substitutions it meets). Precisely, $e@[\sigma_j]_{j\in J}$ is defined for $\lambda$-abstractions and applications of type-substitutions as

$$\begin{aligned}(\lambda^{\wedge_{i\in I}t_i\to s_i}_{[\sigma_k]_{k\in K}}x.e)@[\sigma_j]_{j\in J} &\stackrel{\text{def}}{=} \lambda^{\wedge_{i\in I}t_i\to s_i}_{[\sigma_j]_{j\in J}\circ[\sigma_k]_{k\in K}}x.e\\ (e[\sigma_i]_{i\in I})@[\sigma_j]_{j\in J} &\stackrel{\text{def}}{=} e@([\sigma_j]_{j\in J}\circ[\sigma_i]_{i\in I})\end{aligned}$$

(where $\circ$ denotes the pairwise composition of all substitutions of the two sets). It erases the set of type-substitutions when $e$ is either a variable or a constant, and it is homomorphically applied on the remaining expressions (see [3] for comprehensive definitions). The dynamic semantics is given by the following notions of reduction (where $v$ denotes a *value*), applied by a leftmost-outermost strategy:

$$e[\sigma_j]_{j\in J} \rightsquigarrow e@[\sigma_j]_{j\in J} \tag{8}$$

$$(\lambda^{\wedge_{i\in I}t_i\to s_i}_{[\sigma_j]_{j\in J}}x.e)v \rightsquigarrow (e@[\sigma_j]_{j\in P})\{v/x\} \tag{9}$$

$$v{\in}t\,?\,e_1 : e_2 \rightsquigarrow \begin{cases} e_1 & \text{if } \vdash v : t\\ e_2 & \text{otherwise}\end{cases} \tag{10}$$

where in (9) we have $P \stackrel{\text{def}}{=} \{j{\in}J \mid \exists i{\in}I, \vdash v : t_i\sigma_j\}$.

The first rule (8) performs relabeling, that is, it propagates the sets of type-substitutions down into the decorations of the outermost $\lambda$-abstractions. The second rule (9) states the semantics of applications: this is standard call-by-value $\beta$-reduction, with the dif-

(ALG-CONST)
$$\frac{}{\Delta\,⨾\,\Gamma \vdash_{\mathscr{A}} c : b_c}$$

(ALG-VAR)
$$\frac{}{\Delta\,⨾\,\Gamma \vdash_{\mathscr{A}} x : \Gamma(x)}$$

(ALG-INST)
$$\frac{\Delta\,⨾\,\Gamma \vdash_{\mathscr{A}} e : t}{\Delta\,⨾\,\Gamma \vdash_{\mathscr{A}} e[\sigma_j]_{j\in J} : \bigwedge_{j\in J} t\sigma_j}\ \sigma_j \sharp \Delta$$

(ALG-APPL)
$$\frac{\Delta\,⨾\,\Gamma \vdash_{\mathscr{A}} e_1 : t \qquad \Delta\,⨾\,\Gamma \vdash_{\mathscr{A}} e_2 : s}{\Delta\,⨾\,\Gamma \vdash_{\mathscr{A}} e_1 e_2 : t \cdot s}\ \begin{array}{l} t \leq \mathbb{0} \to \mathbb{1} \\ s \leq \mathsf{dom}(t)\end{array}$$

(ALG-ABSTR)
$$\frac{\Delta \cup \Delta'\,⨾\,\Gamma, (x : t_i\sigma_j) \vdash_{\mathscr{A}} e@[\sigma_j] : s'_{ij}}{\Delta\,⨾\,\Gamma \vdash_{\mathscr{A}} \lambda^{\wedge_{i\in I} t_i \to s_i}_{[\sigma_j]_{j\in J}} x.e : \bigwedge_{i\in I, j\in J} (t_i\sigma_j \to s_i\sigma_j)}\ \begin{array}{l} \Delta' = \mathsf{var}(\wedge_{i\in I, j\in J} t_i\sigma_j \to s_i\sigma_j) \\ s'_{ij} \leq s_i\sigma_j, \quad i\in I, \quad j\in J\end{array}$$

(ALG-CASE-FST)
$$\frac{\Delta\,⨾\,\Gamma \vdash_{\mathscr{A}} e : t' \qquad \Delta\,⨾\,\Gamma \vdash_{\mathscr{A}} e_1 : s_1}{\Delta\,⨾\,\Gamma \vdash_{\mathscr{A}} (e\in t\,?\,e_1 : e_2) : s_1}\ t' \leq t$$

(ALG-CASE-SND)
$$\frac{\Delta\,⨾\,\Gamma \vdash_{\mathscr{A}} e : t' \qquad \Delta\,⨾\,\Gamma \vdash_{\mathscr{A}} e_2 : s_2}{\Delta\,⨾\,\Gamma \vdash_{\mathscr{A}} (e\in t\,?\,e_1 : e_2) : s_2}\ t' \leq \neg t$$

(ALG-CASE-BOTH)
$$\frac{\Delta\,⨾\,\Gamma \vdash_{\mathscr{A}} e : t' \qquad \Delta\,⨾\,\Gamma \vdash_{\mathscr{A}} e_1 : s_1 \qquad \Delta\,⨾\,\Gamma \vdash_{\mathscr{A}} e_2 : s_2}{\Delta\,⨾\,\Gamma \vdash_{\mathscr{A}} (e\in t\,?\,e_1 : e_2) : s_1 \vee s_2}\ \begin{array}{l} t' \not\leq \neg t \\ t' \not\leq t\end{array}$$

**Figure 1.** Typing algorithm

ference that the substitution of the argument for the parameter is performed on the *relabeled* body of the function. Notice that relabeling depends on the type of the argument and keeps only those type-substitutions that make the type of the argument $v$ match (at least one of) the input types defined in the interface of the function (*ie*, the set $P$ which contains all substitutions $\sigma_j$ such that the argument $v$ has type $t_i\sigma_j$ for some $i$ in $I$: the type system statically ensures that $P$ will never be empty). For instance, take the daffy identity function (4), instantiate it as in (6) by both Int and Bool, and apply it to 42 —*ie*, $(\lambda^{\alpha\to\alpha}_{[\{\mathtt{Int}/_{\alpha}\},\{\mathtt{Bool}/_{\alpha}\}]} x.(\lambda^{\alpha\to\alpha} y.x)x)\mathtt{42}$—, then it reduces to $(\lambda^{\alpha\to\alpha}_{[\{\mathtt{Int}/_{\alpha}\}]} y.\mathtt{42})\mathtt{42}$, (which is observationally equivalent to $(\lambda^{\mathtt{Int}\to\mathtt{Int}} y.\mathtt{42})\mathtt{42}$) since the reduction discards the $\{\mathtt{Bool}/_{\alpha}\}$ substitution. Finally, the third rule (10) checks whether the value returned by the expression in the type-case matches the specified type and selects the branch accordingly.

The static semantics is given by the rules in Figure 1 which form an algorithmic system (as stressed by the $\mathscr{A}$ subscript in $\vdash_{\mathscr{A}}$ and by the names of the rules): in every case at most one rule applies, either because of the syntax of the term or because of mutually exclusive side conditions. We invite the reader to consult [3] for more details (there the reader will also find a non-algorithmic —and far more readable— system defined in terms of subsumption). Here we just comment the rules interesting for this second part, that is, (ALG-ABSTR), (ALG-INST), and (ALG-APP). First of all notice the presence of $\Delta$ in judgments. This is the set of *monomorphic type variables*, that is, the variables that occur in the type of some outer $\lambda$-abstraction and, as such, cannot be instantiated; this set must contain all the type variables occurring in $\Gamma$. Rule (ALG-ABSTR) checks that $\lambda^{\wedge_{i\in I} t_i\to s_i}_{[\sigma_j]_{j\in J}} x.e$ has the type declared by (the combination of) its interface and its decoration, that is, $\wedge_{i\in I, j\in J} t_i\sigma_j \to s_i\sigma_j$. To do that it first adds all the variables occurring in this type to the set $\Delta$, (in the function body these variables are monomorphic). Then, it checks that for every possible input type —*ie*, for every possible combination of $t_i$ and $\sigma_j$— the function body $e$ relabeled with the single type-substitution $\sigma_j$ under consideration (*ie*, $e@[\sigma_j]$), has (a subtype of) the corresponding output type.

Rule (ALG-INST) infers for $e[\sigma_j]_{j\in J}$ the type obtained by applying the set of type-substitutions to the type of $e$, provided that the type-substitutions do not instantiate monomorphic variables (*ie*, for all $j\in J$, $\mathsf{dom}(\sigma_j) \cap \Delta = \varnothing$, noted as $\sigma_j \sharp \Delta$).

Rule (ALG-APPL) for applications checks that the type $t$ of the function is a functional type (*ie*, $t \leq \mathbb{0}\to\mathbb{1}$). Then it checks that the type of the argument is a subtype of the domain of $t$ (denoted by $\mathsf{dom}(t)$). Finally, it infers for the application the type $t \cdot s \stackrel{\text{def}}{=} \min\{u \mid t \leq s \to u\}$, that is, the smallest result type that can be obtained by subsuming $t$ to an arrow type with domain $s$.[4] Even if $t \leq \mathbb{0}\to\mathbb{1}$, in general, $t$ does not have the form of an arrow type (it could also be a union or an intersection or a negation of types) and the definition of $\mathsf{dom}(t)$ is not immediate. Formally, if $t \leq \mathbb{0}\to\mathbb{1}$, then $t \simeq \bigvee_{i\in I}(\bigwedge_{p\in P_i}(s_p \to t_p) \wedge \bigwedge_{n\in N_i} \neg(s_n \to t_n) \wedge \bigwedge_{q\in Q_i} \alpha_q \wedge \bigwedge_{r\in R_i} \neg\beta_r)$ where all $P_i$'s are not empty (see Castagna and Xu [4]), and, for such a type $t$, the domain is defined as $\mathsf{dom}(t) \stackrel{\text{def}}{=} \bigwedge_{i\in I} \bigvee_{p\in P_i} s_p$ (see Part 1 [3]).

The type system is sound (it satisfies both subject reduction and progress), it subsumes existing intersection type systems, and type inference is decidable. Furthermore the calculus can be compiled into an intermediate language which executes relabeling only by need and, thus, can be efficiently evaluated (again, see Part 1 [3]).

Before proceeding we stress again that in this calculus type-substitutions and, thus, instantiation are *explicit*: $(\lambda^{\alpha\to\alpha} x.x)[\{\mathtt{Int}/_{\alpha}\}]$ has type $\mathtt{Int}\to\mathtt{Int}$, but $(\lambda^{\alpha\to\alpha} x.x)$ does not (contrary to ML, the semantic subtyping relation $\leq$ does not account for instantiation).

### 2.1 Overview and contributions of this article (Part 2)

Recall that we want the programmer to use the implicitly-typed expressions of grammar (3), and not those of grammar (7) which would require the programmer to write explicit type-substitutions. Therefore in Section 3 we define a local type inference system that, given an implicitly-typed expression produced by the grammar (3), checks whether and where some sets of type-substitutions can be inserted in this expression so as to make it a well-typed explicitly-typed expression of grammar (7). Thus, our local type inference consists of a type-substitution reconstruction system, insofar as it has to reconstruct the sets of type-substitutions that make an expression of grammar (3) a well-typed expression of grammar (7). In order to avoid ambiguity we reserve the word "reconstruction" for the problem of reconstructing *type* annotations (in particular, function interfaces) and speak of *inference of type-substitutions* for the problem of local type inference. In particular, we show that this problem can be reduced to the problem of deciding whether for two types $s$ and $t$ there exist two sets of type-substitutions $[\sigma_i]_{i\in I}$ and $[\sigma'_j]_{j\in J}$ such that $s[\sigma_i]_{i\in I} \leq t[\sigma'_j]_{j\in J}$. We prove that when the cardinalities of $I$ and $J$ are given, the problem above is decidable and reduces to the problem of finding all substitutions $\sigma$ such that $s'\sigma \leq t'\sigma$ for two given types $s'$ and $t'$ (we dub this latter problem the *tallying problem*). We show how to produce a sound and complete set of solutions for the latter problem. This is done by generating *sets* of constraint-sets that are then *normalized*, *merged*, and *solved*. The solution of the tallying problem immediately yields a semi-decision procedure (that tries all the cardinalities for $I$, $J$) for the local type inference system. Henceforth, to enhance readability, we will systematically use the metavariable "$a$" to denote expressions of the implicitly-typed calculus (*ie*, those of grammar (3)) and reserve the metavariable "$e$" for expressions of the explicitly-typed calculus (*ie*, those of grammar (7)). Finally, in Section 4 we show that the theory and algorithms developed in Section 3 can be reused to do ML-like type reconstruction, that is, to infer the interface of unannotated $\lambda$-expressions in a pure $\lambda$-calculus with type-case.

In summary, the results of this paper make it possible to program in the implicitly-typed calculus (3), by compiling it into well-typed explicitly-typed expressions (7) defined in [3]. Let us show

[4] For every type $t$ such that $t \leq \mathbb{0}\to\mathbb{1}$ and type $s$ such that $s \leq \mathsf{dom}(t)$, the type $t \cdot s$ exists and can be effectively computed.

the details on the motivating example of the introduction. First, note that in the implicitly-typed calculus (3) `even` can be defined as

$$\lambda^{(\texttt{Int}\to\texttt{Bool})\wedge(\alpha\backslash\texttt{Int}\to\alpha\backslash\texttt{Int})}x\,.\,x{\in}\texttt{Int}\,?\,(x \bmod 2) = 0 : x \tag{11}$$

(where $s\backslash t$ is syntactic sugar for $s\wedge\neg t$) while —with the products and recursive function definitions given in the appendix— `map` is

$$\begin{array}{l}\mu m^{(\alpha\to\beta)\to[\alpha]\to[\beta]}\ f = \\ \qquad \lambda^{[\alpha]\to[\beta]}\ell\,.\,\ell{\in}\texttt{nil}\,?\,\texttt{nil} : (f(\pi_1\ell),mf(\pi_2\ell))\end{array} \tag{12}$$

where the type `nil` tested in the type case denotes the singleton type that contains just the constant `nil`, and $[\alpha]$ denotes the regular type that is the least solution of $X = (\alpha, X) \vee \texttt{nil}$.

If we feed these two expressions to the type-checker (the rules in Figure 1 suffice since no local type inference is needed to type these two functions) it confirms that both are well typed and have the types declared in their interfaces. To apply (the expression (12) defining) `map` to (the expression (11) defining) `even` we need to instantiate `map`, that is, to perform local type inference. The inference system of Section 3 infers the following set of type-substitutions $[\{(\gamma\backslash\texttt{Int})/_\alpha, (\gamma\backslash\texttt{Int})/_\beta\}, \{\gamma\vee\texttt{Int}/_\alpha, (\gamma\backslash\texttt{Int})\vee\texttt{Bool}/_\beta\}]$ and textually inserts it between the two terms (so that the type-substitutions apply to the type variables of `map`) yielding a typing equivalent to the one in (1). The expression with the inserted set of type-substitutions is compiled into the intermediate language defined in Section 5 of Part 1 [3] and executed as efficiently as if it were a monomorphic expression. Finally, in Section 4 we show that we could allow the programmer to omit the type declaration for `map` —*ie*, `map :: (`$\alpha$` -> `$\beta$`) -> [`$\alpha$`] -> [`$\beta$`]`—, since it is possible to reuse the algorithms developed in Section 3 to reconstruct for `map` a type slightly more precise than the one above.

***Contributions:*** The overall contribution of this work (Parts 1 and 2) is the definition of a statically-typed calculus with polymorphic higher-order functions in a type system with recursive types and union, intersection, and negation type connectives, and local type inference. The technical contributions of this Part 2 are:

- the definition of an algorithm that for any pair of polymorphic regular tree types $t_1$ and $t_2$ produces a sound and complete set of solutions to the problem of deciding whether there exists a type-substitution $\sigma$ such that $t_1\sigma \leq t_2\sigma$. This is obtained by using the set-theoretic interpretation of types to reduce the problem to a unification problem on regular tree types.
- the definition of a type-substitution inference system sound and complete w.r.t. the system of the explicitly-typed calculus of [3].
- the definition of a sound and complete algorithm for local type inference for the calculus. The algorithm yields a semi-decision procedure for the typeability of a $\lambda$-calculus with intersection and recursive types and with explicitly-typed $\lambda$-abstractions.
- the definition of a type reconstruction algorithm that uses the machinery developed for local type inference and improves reconstruction defined for ML languages.

We also provide two different implementations: a prototype implementation of the calculus presented here and the polymorphic extension of the compiler of ℂDuce, a production-grade language.

## 3. Inference of type-substitutions

Since we want the programmer to program in the implicitly-typed calculus (3), then it is the task of the type-substitution inference system to check whether it is possible to insert some type-substitutions in appropriate places of the expression written by the programmer so that the resulting expression is a well-typed explicitly-typed expression of the grammar in (7). To define the type-substitution inference system we proceed in two steps. First, we define a syntax-directed deduction system for the implicitly-typed calculus by modifying the one in Figure 1: whenever the old system checks a subtyping relation, the new system tries to guess some explicit type-substitutions to insert in that position. Second, we show how to compute the operations used by the deduction system defined in the first step. Each of these steps is developed in one of the following subsections.

### 3.1 Type substitution assignment

In this section we define an inference system for the implicitly-typed calculus of Definition 2.2. The system will be sound and complete with respect to explicitly-typed one modulo a single exception: we will not try to insert type-substitutions in decorations, that is, we will consider only expressions in the explicitly-typed calculus in which all decorations are absent (*ie*, they are a singleton set that contains only the empty type-substitution). There is no technical problem to infer also type-substitutions in decorations. Not doing so is just a design choice suggested by common sense so as to match the programmer's intuition: if we write an expression such as $\lambda^{\alpha\to\alpha}x.3$ we want to infer that it is ill-typed (as, say, Haskell does); but if we allowed to infer decorations, then the expression could be typed by inserting a decoration as in $\lambda^{\alpha\to\alpha}_{[\{\texttt{Int}/_\alpha\}]}x.3$. Likewise, if the programmer specified the signature `map::(`$\alpha$`->`$\beta$`)->`$\gamma$, we expect the system to answer that the definition of `map` does not conform this signature, rather than it conforms the signature by substituting `[`$\alpha$`]->[`$\beta$`]` for $\gamma$ (alternatively, we must omit the signature altogether and let the system infer it: see Section 4 on reconstruction).

We have to define a system that guesses where sets of type-substitutions must be inserted so that an implicitly-typed expression is transformed into an explicitly-typed expression that is well typed in the system of Figure 1. The general role of type-substitutions is to make the type of some expression satisfy some subtyping constraints. Examples of this are the type of the body of a function which must match the result type declared in the interface, or the type of the argument of a function which must be a subtype of the domain of the function. Actually *all* the cases in which subtyping constraints must be satisfied are enumerated in Figure 1: they coincide with the subtyping relation checks that occur in the rules. Figure 1 is our Ariadne's thread through the definition of the type-substitution inference system: the rule (ALG-INST) must be removed and wherever the typing algorithm in Figure 1 checks whether for some types $s$ and $t$ the relation $s \leq t$ holds, then the type-substitution inference system must check whether there exists a set of type-substitutions $[\sigma_i]_{i\in I}$ for the polymorphic variables (*ie*, those not in $\Delta$) that makes $s[\sigma_i]_{i\in I} \leq t$ hold. The reader may wonder why we apply the type-substitution only on the smaller type and not on both types. The reason can be understood by looking at the rules in Figure 1 and seeing that whenever a subtyping relation is specified, the right-hand side type cannot be instantiated: either because it is a ground type (rules (ALG-CASE-*)) or because it is a type in an interface and inferring a type-substitution for it would correspond to inferring a type-substitution in a decoration (rule (ALG-ABSTR)). The only exception to this is the rule (ALG-APPL) for application, but for it we will introduce a specific operator later in this section.

In order to ease the presentation it is handy to introduce a family of preorders $\sqsubseteq_\Delta$ that combine subtyping and instantiation:

**Definition 3.1.** *Let $s$ and $t$ be two types, $\Delta$ a set of type variables, and $[\sigma_i]_{i\in I}$ a set of type-substitutions. We define:*

$$\begin{array}{rcl}[\sigma_i]_{i\in I} \Vdash s \sqsubseteq_\Delta t & \stackrel{\text{def}}{\iff} & \bigwedge_{i\in I} s\sigma_i \leq t \textit{ and } \forall i{\in}I.\,\sigma_i \sharp \Delta \\ s \sqsubseteq_\Delta t & \stackrel{\text{def}}{\iff} & \exists[\sigma_i]_{i\in I} \textit{ such that } [\sigma_i]_{i\in I} \Vdash s \sqsubseteq_\Delta t\end{array}$$

Intuitively, it suffices to replace $\leq$ by $\sqsubseteq_\Delta$ and $\not\leq$ by $\not\sqsubseteq_\Delta$ in the algorithmic rules of Figure 1 (where $\Delta$ is the set of monomorphic variables used in the premises) to obtain the corresponding rules of type-substitution inference. This yields the system formed by the rules in Figure 2 (we subscripted the turnstile symbol by $\mathscr{I}$

$$\text{(INF-ABSTR)}\quad \frac{\Delta \cup \Delta' \,;\, \Gamma, x : t_i \vdash_{\mathscr{I}} a : s_i'}{\Delta \,;\, \Gamma \vdash_{\mathscr{I}} \lambda^{\wedge_{i\in I} t_i \to s_i} x.a : \bigwedge_{i\in I}(t_i \to s_i)} \quad \begin{array}{l}\Delta' = \mathsf{var}(\wedge_{i\in I} t_i \to s_i) \\ s_i' \sqsubseteq_{\Delta\cup\Delta'} s_i, \quad i\in I\end{array}$$

$$\text{(INF-CASE-BOTH)}\quad \frac{\Delta \,;\, \Gamma \vdash_{\mathscr{I}} a : t' \qquad \Delta \,;\, \Gamma \vdash_{\mathscr{I}} a_1 : s_1 \qquad \Delta \,;\, \Gamma \vdash_{\mathscr{I}} a_2 : s_2}{\Delta \,;\, \Gamma \vdash_{\mathscr{I}} (a{\in}t\,?\,a_1 : a_2) : s_1 \vee s_2} \quad \begin{array}{l} t' \not\sqsubseteq_\Delta \neg t \\ t' \not\sqsubseteq_\Delta t \end{array}$$

$$\text{(INF-CASE-FST)}\quad \frac{\Delta \,;\, \Gamma \vdash_{\mathscr{I}} a : t' \quad \Delta \,;\, \Gamma \vdash_{\mathscr{I}} a_1 : s_1}{\Delta \,;\, \Gamma \vdash_{\mathscr{I}} (a{\in}t\,?\,a_1 : a_2) : s_1}\, t' \sqsubseteq_\Delta t$$

$$\text{(INF-CASE-SND)}\quad \frac{\Delta \,;\, \Gamma \vdash_{\mathscr{I}} a : t' \quad \Delta \,;\, \Gamma \vdash_{\mathscr{I}} a_2 : s_2}{\Delta \,;\, \Gamma \vdash_{\mathscr{I}} (a{\in}t\,?\,a_1 : a_2) : s_2}\, t' \sqsubseteq_\Delta \neg t$$

$$\text{(INF-APPL)}\quad \frac{\Delta \,;\, \Gamma \vdash_{\mathscr{I}} a_1 : t \quad \Delta \,;\, \Gamma \vdash_{\mathscr{I}} a_2 : s}{\Delta \,;\, \Gamma \vdash_{\mathscr{I}} a_1 a_2 : u}\, u {\in} (t \bullet_\Delta s)$$

**Figure 2.** Inference system for type-substitutions

to stress that it is the $\mathscr{I}$nference system for type-substitutions) plus the rules for constants and variables (omitted: they are the same as in Figure 1). Of particular interest is the rule (INF-ABSTR) which has become simpler than in Figure 1 since it works under the hypothesis that $\lambda$-abstractions have empty decorations, and which uses the $\Delta{\cup}\Delta'$ set to compare the types of the body with the result types specified in the interface ($s_i' \sqsubseteq_{\Delta\cup\Delta'} s_i$). Notice that we do not require the sets of type-substitutions that make $s_i' \sqsubseteq_{\Delta\cup\Delta'} s_i$ satisfied to be the same for all $i{\in}I$: this is not a problem since the case of different sets of type-substitutions corresponds to using their union as sets of type-substitutions (*ie*, to intersecting them point-wise: see Definition B.9 and Corollary B.12 —henceforth, references starting with letters refer to appendixes).

It still remains the most delicate rule, (INF-APPL), the one for application. It is difficult because not only it must find two distinct sets of type-substitutions (one for the function type the other for the argument type) but also because the set of type-substitutions for the function type must enforce two distinct constraints: the type resulting from applying the set of type-susbstitutions to the type of the function must be a subtype of $\mathbb{0}{\to}\mathbb{1}$, and its domain must be compatible with (*ie*, a supertype of) the type inferred for the argument. In order to solve all these constraints we collapse them into a single definition which is the algorithmic counterpart of the set of types used in Section 2 to define the operation $t \cdot s$ occurring in the rule (ALG-APPL). Precisely, we define $t{\bullet_\Delta}s$ as the set of types for which there exist two sets of type-substitutions (for variables not in $\Delta$) that make $s$ compatible with the domain of $t$:

$$t \bullet_\Delta s \stackrel{\text{def}}{=} \left\{ u \;\middle|\; \begin{array}{l} [\sigma_j]_{j\in J} \Vdash t \sqsubseteq_\Delta \mathbb{0}{\to}\mathbb{1} \\ [\sigma_i]_{i\in I} \Vdash s \sqsubseteq_\Delta \mathsf{dom}(t[\sigma_j]_{j\in J}) \\ u = t[\sigma_j]_{j\in J} \cdot s[\sigma_i]_{i\in I} \end{array} \right\}$$

In practice, this set takes all the pairs of sets of type-substitutions that make $t$ a function type, and $s$ an argument type compatible with $t$ and collects all the possible result types. This set is closed by intersection (see Lemma B.8) which is an important property since it ensures that if we find two distinct solutions to type an application, then we can also use their intersection. Unfortunately, this property is not enough to ensure that this set has a minimum type (for that we also need to prove that the intersection of all the types in the set can be expressed as a *finite* intersection) which would imply the existence of a principal type (which is still an open problem). For the application of a function of type $t$ to an argument of type $s$, the inference system deduces every type in $t \bullet_\Delta s$. This yields the inference rule (INF-APPL) of Figure 2.

These type-substitution inference rules are sound and complete with respect to the typing algorithm, modulo the restriction that all the decorations in the $\lambda$-abstractions are empty. Both of these properties are stated in terms of the *erase*(.) function that maps expressions of the explicitly-typed calculus into expressions of the implicitly-typed one by erasing in the former all occurrences of sets of type-substitutions.

**Theorem 3.2** (Soundness of inference). *Let $a$ be an implicitly-typed expression. If $\Delta \,;\, \Gamma \vdash_{\mathscr{I}} a : t$, then there exists an explicitly-typed expression $e$ such that $erase(e) = a$ and $\Delta \,;\, \Gamma \vdash_{\mathscr{A}} e : t$.*

The proof of the soundness property is constructive: it builds along the derivation for the implicitly-typed expressions $a$ an explicitly-typed expression $e$ that satisfies the statement of the theorem; this expression is the one that is then compiled in the intermediate language we defined in Part 1 [3] and evaluated. Notice that $\sqsubseteq_\Delta$ gauges the generality of the solutions found by the inference system: the smaller the type found, the more general the solution is. As a matter of fact, adding to the system in Figure 2 a subsumption rule that uses the relation $\sqsubseteq_\Delta$ that is:

$$\text{(SUBSUMPTION)}\quad \frac{\Delta \,;\, \Gamma \vdash_{\mathscr{I}} a : t_1 \quad t_1 \sqsubseteq_\Delta t_2}{\Delta \,;\, \Gamma \vdash_{\mathscr{I}} a : t_2}$$

is sound. This means that the set of solutions is upward closed with respect to $\sqsubseteq_\Delta$ and that from smaller solutions it is possible (by such a subsumption rule) to deduce the larger ones. In that respect, the completeness theorem that follows states that the inference system can always deduce for the erasure of an expression a solution that is at least as good as the one deduced for that expression by the type system for the explicitly-typed calculus.

**Theorem 3.3** (Completeness of inference). *Let $e$ be an (explicitly-typed) expression in which all decorations are empty. If $\Delta \,;\, \Gamma \vdash_{\mathscr{A}} e : t$, then there exists a type $t'$ such that $\Delta \,;\, \Gamma \vdash_{\mathscr{I}} erase(e) : t'$ and $t' \sqsubseteq_\Delta t$.*

The inference system is syntax directed and describes an algorithm that is parametric in the decision procedures for $\sqsubseteq_\Delta$ and $\bullet_\Delta$. The problem of deciding these two relations is tackled next.

### 3.2 Type tallying

We define the tallying problem as follows

**Definition 3.4** (Tallying problem). *Let $C$ be a* constraint-set, *that is, a finite set of pairs of types (these pairs are called* constraints*), and $\Delta$ a finite set of type variables. A type-substitution $\sigma$ is a solution for the* tallying problem of $C$ and $\Delta$ *(noted $\sigma \Vdash_\Delta C$) if $\sigma \sharp \Delta$ and for all $(s,t) \in C$, $s\sigma \leq t\sigma$ holds.*

Thus a *constraint-set* corresponds to the *logical conjunction* of the constraints that compose it, and the tallying problem searches for a type-substitution that satisfies this conjunction. The definition of the tallying problem is the cornerstone of our type-substitution inference system, since every problem we have to solve to "implement" the rules of Figure 2 is reduced to different instances of this problem.

With the exception of (INF-APPL), it is not difficult to show that the "implementation" of the rules of the type-substitution inference system $\vdash_{\mathscr{I}}$ corresponds to finding and solving a particular tallying problem. First, notice that for the remaining rules the problem we have to solve is to prove (or disprove) the relation $s \sqsubseteq_\Delta t$ for given $s$ and $t$. By definition this corresponds to finding a set of $n$ type-substitutions $[\sigma_i]_{i\leq n}$ such that $\bigwedge_{i\leq n} s\sigma_i \leq t$. We can split each type-substitution $\sigma_i$ in two: a *renaming type-substitution* $\rho_i$ that maps each variable of $s$ not in $\Delta$ into a *fresh* type variable, and a type substitution $\sigma_i'$ such that $\sigma_i = \sigma_i' \circ \rho_i$. Thus the inequation becomes $\bigwedge_{i\leq n}(s\rho_i)\sigma_i' \leq t$. The domains of $\sigma_i'$ are

0. $\mathsf{norm}(t, M) =$
1. if $t \in M$ then return $\{\varnothing\}$ else
2. if $t = \bigwedge_{p\in P} t_p \wedge \bigwedge_{n\in N} \neg t_n \wedge \bigwedge_{q\in P'} \alpha_q \wedge \bigwedge_{r\in N'} \neg\alpha_r$ and $\alpha_k$ is the smallest variable (wrt $\preccurlyeq$) for $k$ in $P' \cup N'$ then return $\{\mathsf{single}(\alpha_k, t)\}$ else
3. if $t = \bigwedge_{p\in P} b_p \wedge \bigwedge_{n\in N} \neg b_n$ then ( if $\bigwedge_{p\in P} b_p \leq \bigvee_{n\in N} b_n$ then return $\{\varnothing\}$ else return $\varnothing$) else
4. if $t = \bigwedge_{p\in P}(s_p \to t_p) \wedge \bigwedge_{n\in N} \neg(s_n \to t_n)$ then return
5. $\displaystyle\bigsqcup_{n\in N}\Big(\mathsf{norm}(s_n \wedge \bigwedge_{p\in P} \neg s_p, M\cup\{t\}) \sqcap \Big(\bigsqcap_{P'\subset P} (\mathsf{norm}(s_n \wedge \bigwedge_{p\in P'} \neg s_p, M\cup\{t\}) \sqcup \mathsf{norm}(\bigwedge_{p\in P\setminus P'} t_p \wedge \neg t_n, M\cup\{t\}))\Big)\Big)$ else
6. if $t = \bigvee_{i\in I} t_i$ then return $\bigsqcap_{i\in I} \mathsf{norm}(t_i, M)$ else let $t'$ be the disjunctive normal form of $t$ in return $\mathsf{norm}(t', M)$

**Figure 3.** Constraint normalization

by construction pairwise disjoint (they are formed of distinct fresh variables) and disjoint from the variables in $t$; thus we can merge them into a single substitution $\sigma = \bigcup_{i\leq n} \sigma_i'$ and apply it to $t$ with no effect, yielding the inequation $(\bigwedge_{i\leq n} s\rho_i)\sigma \leq t\sigma$. Let $u_n = \bigwedge_{i\leq n} s\rho_i$, we have just transformed the problem of proving the relation $s \sqsubseteq_\Delta t$ into the problem of finding an $n$ for which there exists a solution to the tallying problem for $\{u_n \leq t\}$ and $\Delta$. The way to proceed to find $n$ is explained in Section 3.2.3.

The (INF-APPL) rule deserves a special treatment since it needs to solve a more difficult problem. A "solution" for the (INF-APPL) rule problem is *a pair* of sets of type-substitutions $[\sigma_i]_{i\in I}$, $[\sigma_j]_{j\in J}$ for variables not in $\Delta$ such that both $\bigwedge_{i\in I} t\sigma_i \leq \mathbb{0}\to\mathbb{1}$ and $\bigwedge_{j\in J} s\sigma_j \leq \mathsf{dom}(\bigwedge_{i\in I} t\sigma_i)$ hold. In this section we give an algorithm that produces a set of solutions for the (INF-APPL) rule problem that is sound (it finds only correct solutions) and complete (any other solution can be derived from those returned by the algorithm). To this end we proceed in three steps: $(i)$ given a tallying problem, we show how to effectively produce a finite set of solutions that is sound (it contains only correct solutions) and complete (every other solution of the problem is less general—in the usual sense of unification, *ie*, it is larger wrt $\sqsubseteq$— than some solution in the set); $(ii)$ we show that if we fix the cardinalities of $I$ and $J$, then it is possible to reduce the (INF-APPL) rule problem to a tallying problem; $(iii)$ from this we deduce a sound and complete algorithm to semi-decide the general (INF-APPL) rule problem and thus the whole inference system.

We solve each problem in one of the next subsections, but before we recall an important property of semantic subtyping systems [4, 10] which states that every type is equivalent to (and can be effectively transformed into) a type in *disjunctive normal form*, that is, a union of *uniform* intersections of *literals*. A literal is either an arrow, or a basic type, or a type variable, or a negation thereof. An intersection is uniform if it is composed of literals with the same constructor, that is, either it is an intersection of arrows, type variables, and their negations or it is an intersection of basic types, type variables, and their negations. In summary, a disjunctive normal form is a union of summands whose form is either

$$\bigwedge_{p\in P} b_p \wedge \bigwedge_{n\in N} \neg b_n \wedge \bigwedge_{q\in P'} \alpha_q \wedge \bigwedge_{r\in N'} \neg\alpha_r \qquad (13)$$

or

$$\bigwedge_{p\in P} (s_p \to t_p) \wedge \bigwedge_{n\in N} \neg(s_n \to t_n) \wedge \bigwedge_{q\in P'} \alpha_q \wedge \bigwedge_{r\in N'} \neg\alpha_r \qquad (14)$$

When either $P'$ or $N'$ is non empty, we call the variables $\alpha_q$'s and $\alpha_r$'s the *top-level variables* of the normal form.

### 3.2.1 Solution of the tallying problem.

In order to solve the tallying problem for given $\Delta$ and $C$, we first fix some total order $\preccurlyeq$ —any will do— on the type variables occurring in $C$ and not in $\Delta$ (from now on, when speaking of type variables we will mean type variables not in $\Delta$), order that will be used to ensure that all inferred types satisfy the contractivity condition of Definition 2.1. Next, we produce *sets of* constraint-sets (as a single constraint-set corresponds to logical conjunction, so a set of constraint-sets corresponds to disjunction of the corresponding conjunctions) in a particular form by proceeding in four steps: first, we **normalize** the constraint-sets (so that at least one of the two types of every constraint is a type variable); second, we **merge** constraints that are on the same variables; third, we **solve** all these constraint-sets by producing solvable sets of equations equivalent to the original problem and then solving these equations; fourth, we combine these three steps into an **algorithm** that produces a sound and complete set of solutions of the tallying problem. To this end we define two operations on sets of constraint-sets:

**Definition 3.5.** *Let* $\mathscr{S}_1, \mathscr{S}_2 \subseteq \mathscr{P}(\mathscr{T} \times \mathscr{T})$ *be two sets of constraint-sets. We define*

$$\mathscr{S}_1 \sqcap \mathscr{S}_2 \stackrel{\text{def}}{=} \{C_1 \cup C_2 \mid C_1 \in \mathscr{S}_1, C_2 \in \mathscr{S}_2\}$$
$$\mathscr{S}_1 \sqcup \mathscr{S}_2 \stackrel{\text{def}}{=} \mathscr{S}_1 \cup \mathscr{S}_2$$

By convention the empty set of constraint-sets is unsolvable (it denotes failure in finding a solution), while the set containing the empty set is always satisfied.

We also define an auxiliary function $\mathsf{single}$ that singles out a given top-level variable of a normal form. More precisely, given a type $t$ which is a summand of a normal form, that is, $t = \bigwedge_{p\in P} t_p \wedge \bigwedge_{n\in N} \neg t_n \wedge \bigwedge_{q\in P'} \alpha_q \wedge \bigwedge_{r\in N'} \neg\alpha_r$ and $k \in P' \cup N'$, we define $\mathsf{single}(\alpha_k, t)$ as the constraint equivalent to $t \leq \mathbb{0}$ in which $\alpha_k$ is "singled-out", that is,[5]

$\bigwedge_{p\in P} t_p \wedge \bigwedge_{n\in N} \neg t_n \wedge \bigwedge_{q\in P'} \alpha_q \wedge \bigwedge_{r\in (N'\setminus\{k\})} \neg\alpha_r \leq \alpha_k$
when $k \in N'$ and
$\alpha_k \leq \bigvee_{p\in P} \neg t_p \vee \bigvee_{n\in N} t_n \vee \bigvee_{q\in (P'\setminus\{k\})} \neg\alpha_q \wedge \bigvee_{r\in N'} \alpha_r$
when $k \in P'$. Henceforth, to enhance readability we will often write $s \leq t$ for the constraint $(s, t)$, as we did above.

EXAMPLE. *We will show the various phases of the process by solving the tallying problem for the following constraint-set:*
$C = \{(\alpha \to \mathtt{Bool}, \beta \to \beta)\ ,\ (\mathtt{Int}\vee\mathtt{Bool} \to \mathtt{Int}, \alpha \to \beta)\}$
*and assume that* $\alpha \preccurlyeq \beta$.

***1. Constraint normalization.*** We define a function $\mathsf{norm}$ that takes a type $t$ and generates a set of *normalized* constraint-sets —*ie*, constraint-sets formed by constraints whose form is either $\alpha \leq s$ or $s \leq \alpha$— whose set of solutions is sound and complete w.r.t. the constraint $t \leq \mathbb{0}$. This function is parametric in a set $M$ of visited types (needed to handle coinduction) and the algorithm to compute it is given in Figure 3. If the input type $t$ is not in normal form, then the algorithm is applied to the disjunctive normal form $t'$ of $t$ (end of line 6). Since a union is empty if and only if every summand that composes it is empty, then the algorithm generates a new constraint-set for the problem that equates all the summands of a normal form to $\mathbb{0}$ (beginning of line 6). If a summand contains a top-level variable, then the smallest (wrt $\preccurlyeq$) top-level variable is singled out (line 2). If there is no top-level variable and there are only basic types, then the algorithm checks

[5] Equivalence of $t \leq \mathbb{0}$ and the two following constraints is easily derived from the De Morgan's laws and the property $t_1 \leq t_2 \iff t_1 \wedge \neg t_2 \leq \mathbb{0}$.

the constraint by calling the subtyping algorithm and, accordingly, it returns either the unsatisfiable set of constraint-sets ($\varnothing$) or the one that is always satisfied ($\{\varnothing\}$) (line 3). Finally, if there are only intersections of arrows and their negations, then the problem is decomposed into a set of subproblems by using the decomposition rule of the subtyping algorithm for semantic subtyping (see [10] for details), after having added $t$ to the set $M$ of visited types. The regularity of types ensures that the algorithm always terminates (see Lemma C.14). Notice that, in line 2 the algorithm always singles out the smallest variable. Therefore, by construction, if norm generates a constraint $(\alpha, t)$ or $(t, \alpha)$, then every variable smaller than or equal to $\alpha$ may occur in $t$ only under an arrow (equivalently, every top-level variable of $t$ is strictly larger than $\alpha$).

REMARK 3.1. *There is the special case of $(\alpha, t)$ or $(t, \alpha)$ in which $t$ is itself a variable. In that case we give priority to the smallest variable and consider the larger variable be a bound for the lower one but not vice-versa. This point will be important for* merge.

A constraint-set in which all constraints satisfy this property is said to be *well ordered* (*cf.* Definition C.16).

EXAMPLE (Cont'd). *The function* norm *works on single constraints (actually, on a type $t$ representing the constraint $t \leq \mathbb{0}$), so let us apply it on the first constraint of the example. We want to normalize the constraint $\alpha{\to}\texttt{Bool} \leq \beta{\to}\beta$, and thus we apply* norm *to the type $(\alpha{\to}\texttt{Bool}) \wedge \neg(\beta{\to}\beta)$. Now, this constraint has two distinct solutions: either $(i)$ $\beta$ is the empty set, in which case the larger type becomes $\mathbb{0}{\to}\mathbb{0}$ that is the type of all functions (see Footnote 3) which contains every arrow type, in particular $\alpha{\to}\texttt{Bool}$, or $(ii)$ the types satisfy the usual covariant-contravariant rule for arrows, that is, $\beta \leq \alpha$ and $\texttt{Bool} \leq \beta$. Since there are* two *distinct solutions, then* norm *generates a set of* two *constraint-sets. Precisely* norm$((\alpha{\to}\texttt{Bool}) \wedge \neg(\beta{\to}\beta), \varnothing)$ *returns* $\{\ \{\ (\beta, \mathbb{0})\ \}\ ,\ \{\ (\beta, \alpha)\ ,\ (\texttt{Bool}, \beta)\ \}\ \}$. *Both constraint-sets are normalized and are computed by Line 5 in Figure 3: the first constraint-set is computed by the rightmost recursive call of* norm *(notice that $P'{=}\varnothing$ —since it ranges over the* strict *subsets of $P$ which, in this case, is a singleton—so it requires $s_n$,* ie *$\beta$, to be empty), while the second constraint-set is obtained by the union of the first two recursive calls (which require $s_n \leq s_p$ and $t_p \leq t_n$).*

**2. *Constraint merging.*** Take a normalized constraint-set. Each constraint of this set isolates one particular variable. However, the same variable can be isolated by several distinct constraints in the set. We next want to transform this constraint-set into an equivalent one (*ie*, a constraint-set with exactly the same set of solutions) in which every variable is isolated in at most two constraints, one where the variable is on the left-hand side and the other where it is on the right-hand side. In other words, we want to obtain a normalized constraint-set in which each variable has at most one upper bound and at most one lower bound. In practice, this set represents a set of constraints of the form $\{\, s_i{\leq}\alpha_i{\leq}t_i \mid i \in I\,\}$ where the $\alpha_i$'s are pairwise distinct. This is done by the function merge$(C, M)$ where $C$ is a normalized constraint-set and $M$ a set containing the types already visited by the function.

merge$(C, M)$ =

1. Rewrite $C$ by applying as long as possible the following rules according to the order $\preccurlyeq$ on the variables (smallest first) :
   - if $(\alpha, t_1)$ and $(\alpha, t_2)$ are in $C$, then replace them by $(\alpha, t_1 \wedge t_2)$;
   - if $(s_1, \alpha)$ and $(s_2, \alpha)$ are in $C$, then replace them by $(s_1{\vee}s_2, \alpha)$;
2. if there exist two constraints $(s, \alpha)$ and $(\alpha, t)$ in $C$ s.t. $s{\wedge}\neg t \notin M$,
   then let $\mathscr{S} = \{C\} \sqcap$ norm$(s{\wedge}\neg t, \varnothing)$
   in return $\bigsqcup_{C' \in \mathscr{S}}$ merge$(C', M{\cup}\{s{\wedge}\neg t\})$
   else return $\{C\}$

The function merge performs two steps. In the first step it scans (using $\preccurlyeq$ so as to give priority to smaller variables, *cf.* Remark 3.1) the variables isolated by the normalized constraint-set $C$ and for each such variable it merges all the constraints by taking the union of all its lower bounds and the intersection of all its upper bounds. For instance, if $C$ contains the following five constraints for $\alpha$: $(s_1, \alpha)$, $(s_2, \alpha)$, $(\alpha, t_1)$, $(\alpha, t_2)$, $(\alpha, t_3)$, then the first step replaces them by $(s_1{\vee}s_2, \alpha)$ and $(\alpha, t_1{\wedge}t_2{\wedge}t_3)$, which corresponds to having the constraint $s_1{\vee}s_2 \leq \alpha \leq t_1{\wedge}t_2{\wedge}t_3$. Such a constraint is satisfiable only if the constraint that the lower bound of $\alpha$ is smaller than its upper bound is satisfiable. This is checked in the second step, which looks for pairs of constraints of the form $(s, \alpha)$ and $(\alpha, t)$ (thanks to the first step we know that for each variable there is at most one such pair) and then adds the constraint $(s, t)$ to $C$. This constraint is equivalent to $(s{\wedge}\neg t, \mathbb{0})$ but neither it or $(s, t)$ is normalized. Thus before adding it to $C$ we normalize it by calling norm$(s{\wedge}\neg t, \varnothing)$. Recall that norm returns a *set* of constraint-sets, each constraint-set corresponding to a distinct solution. So we add the constraints that are in $C$ to all the constraint-sets that are the result of norm$(s{\wedge}\neg t, \varnothing)$ via the $\sqcap$ operator (this is why merge returns a set of constraint-sets rather than a single one). The constraint-sets so obtained are normalized but they may be not merged, yet. So we recursively apply merge to all of them (via the operator $\bigsqcup$) and we record $s{\wedge}\neg t$ in $M$. Of course, this step 2 is done only if the constraint $(s, t)$ was not already embedded in $C$ before, that is, only if $s{\wedge}\neg t$ is not already in $M$. Note that merge preserves the property that in every constraint $(\alpha, t)$ or $(t, \alpha)$, every variable smaller than or equal to $\alpha$ may occur in $t$ only under an arrow.

EXAMPLE (Cont'd). *If we apply* norm *also to the second constraint of our example we obtain a second set of constraint-sets:* $\{\ \{\ (\alpha, \mathbb{0})\ \}\ ,\ \{\ (\alpha, \texttt{Int}{\vee}\texttt{Bool})\ ,\ (\texttt{Int}, \beta)\ \}\ \}$. *To obtain a sound and complete set of solutions for our initial $C$ we have to consider all the possible combinations (see* Step 1 *of the constraint solving algorithm later on) of the two sets obtained by normalizing $C$, that is, a set of* four *constraint-sets:*

$$\begin{array}{ll}\{ & \{\ (\alpha, \mathbb{0}), (\beta, \mathbb{0})\ \}\ ,\\ & \{\ (\alpha, \texttt{Int}{\vee}\texttt{Bool})\ ,\ (\texttt{Int}, \beta)\ ,\ (\beta, \mathbb{0})\ \}\ ,\\ & \{\ (\texttt{Bool}, \beta)\ ,\ (\beta, \alpha)\ ,\ (\alpha, \mathbb{0})\ \}\ ,\\ & \{\ (\texttt{Bool}, \beta)\ ,\ (\texttt{Int}, \beta)\ ,\ (\beta, \alpha)\ ,\ (\alpha, \texttt{Int}{\vee}\texttt{Bool})\ \}\ \ \}\end{array}$$

*The application of* merge *to the first set leaves it unchanged. Merge on the second one returns an empty set of constraint-sets since at the second step it tries to solve $\texttt{Int} \leq \mathbb{0}$. The same happens for the third since it first adds $\beta \leq \mathbb{0}$ and at the recursive call tries to solve $\texttt{Bool} \leq \mathbb{0}$. The fourth one is more interesting: in step 1 it replaces $(\texttt{Bool}, \beta)$ and $(\texttt{Int}, \beta)$ by $(\texttt{Int}{\vee}\texttt{Bool}, \beta)$ and at the second step adds $(\beta, \texttt{Int}{\vee}\texttt{Bool})$ obtained from $(\beta, \alpha)$ and $(\alpha, \texttt{Int}{\vee}\texttt{Bool})$ (it also checks $(\texttt{Int}{\vee}\texttt{Bool}, \texttt{Int}{\vee}\texttt{Bool})$ which is always satisfied). So after* merge *we have* $\{\ \{(\alpha,\mathbb{0})\ ,(\beta,\mathbb{0})\}\ ,\ \{(\beta, \alpha)\ ,(\alpha, \texttt{Int}{\vee}\texttt{Bool})\ ,\ (\texttt{Int}{\vee}\texttt{Bool}, \beta)\ ,(\beta, \texttt{Int}{\vee}\texttt{Bool})\ \}\ \}$. *Notice that* we did not *merge $(\beta, \alpha)$ and $(\beta, \texttt{Int}{\vee}\texttt{Bool})$ into $(\beta, \alpha{\wedge}(\texttt{Int}{\vee}\texttt{Bool}))$: since $\alpha \preccurlyeq \beta$, then $\alpha$ is not considered an upper bound of $\beta$ (see Remark 3.1) and thanks to that the resulting constraint-set is well ordered.*

**3. *Constraint solving.*** norm and merge yield a set in which every constraint-set is of the form $C = \{s_i{\leq}\alpha_i{\leq}t_i \mid i \in I\}$ where $\alpha_i$ are pairwise distinct variables and $s_i$ and $t_i$ are respectively $\mathbb{0}$ or $\mathbb{1}$ whenever the corresponding constraint is absent. If there is a constraint on two variables, then again priority is given to the smaller variable. For instance, if $\alpha \preccurlyeq \beta$, then $\{(\alpha, \beta)\}$ will be considered to represent $\{(\mathbb{0}{\leq}\alpha{\leq}\beta), (\mathbb{0}{\leq}\beta{\leq}\mathbb{1})\}$. Thanks to this assumption the system so obtained is well ordered, that is, for every constraint $s{\leq}\alpha{\leq}t$ in it, the top-level variables of $s$ and $t$ are strictly larger than $\alpha$. Notice that in doing that we do not lose any information: the bounds for larger variables are still recorded in those of smaller ones and any bound for larger variables obtained by transitivity on the smaller variables is already in the system by step 2 of merge.

The last step is to *solve* this constraint-set, that is, to transform it into a solvable set of equations that then we solve by a Unify algorithm that exploits the particular form of the equations obtained from a well-ordered constraint-set. Let $C$ be a well-ordered constraint-set of the above form; we define $\mathsf{solve}(C)$ as follows:

$$\mathsf{solve}(C) = \{\alpha = (s \vee \beta) \wedge t \mid (s \leq \alpha \leq t) \in C, \beta \text{ fresh}\}$$

The function $\mathsf{solve}(C)$ takes every constraint $s \leq \alpha \leq t$ in $C$ and replaces it by $\alpha = (s \vee \beta) \wedge t$ (with $\beta$ fresh). It is clear that the constraint-set $C$ has a solution for every possible assignment of $\alpha$ included between $s$ and $t$ if and only if the new constraint-set has a solution for every possible (unconstrained) assignment of $\beta$. At the end, the constraint-set $\{s_i{\leq}\alpha_i{\leq}t_i \mid i \in I\}$ has become a set of equations of the form $\{\alpha_i = u_i \mid i \in I\}$ where the $\alpha_i$'s are pairwise distinct. By construction, this set of equations has the property that every variable that is smaller than or equal to (wrt $\preccurlyeq$) $\alpha_i$ may occur in $u_i$ only under an arrow (as for constraint-sets we say that the set of equations is *well ordered*). This last property ensures the contractivity of the equation defining the smallest type variable. By Courcelle [5] (and Lemma C.44) there exists a solution of this set, namely, a substitution from the type variables $\alpha_1, ..., \alpha_n$ into (possibly recursive regular) types $t_1, ..., t_n$ whose variables are contained in the fresh $\beta_i$'s variables introduced by $\mathsf{solve}$ (all universally quantified, *ie*, no upper or lower bound) and the type variables in $\Delta$. This solution is given by the following Unify procedure in which we use $\mu$-notation to denote regular types and where $E$ is a well-ordered set of equations.

Unify($E$)=
if $E = \varnothing$ then return $\{\}$ else
- select in $E$ the equation $\alpha = t_\alpha$ for the smallest $\alpha$ (wrt $\preccurlyeq$)
- let $E'$ be the set of equations obtained by replacing in $E \backslash \{\alpha = t_\alpha\}$ every occurrence of $\alpha$ by $\mu X.(t_\alpha\{^X/_\alpha\})$ ($X$ fresh)
- let $\sigma = \mathsf{Unify}(E')$ in return $\{\alpha = (\mu X.t_\alpha\{^X/_\alpha\})\sigma\} \cup \sigma$

Thanks to the well-ordering of $E$, Unify generates a set of solutions in which all types satisfy the contractivity condition on infinite branches of Definition 2.1. It solves the (contractive) recursive equation of the smallest variable $\alpha$ defined by $E$ (if $\alpha$ does not occur in $t_\alpha$, then the $\mu$-abstraction can be omitted), replaces this solution in the remaining equations, solves this set of equations, and applies the solution so found to the solution of $\alpha$ so as to solve the other variables occurring in its definition.

***4. The complete algorithm.*** The algorithm to solve the tallying problem for $C$ and variables not in $\Delta$, then, proceeds in three steps:

Step 1. Let $\mathscr{N} = \bigsqcap_{(s,t)\in C} \mathsf{norm}(s{\wedge}\neg t, \varnothing)$. If $\mathscr{N} = \varnothing$ then **fail** else proceed to the next step.

Step 2. Let $\mathscr{M} = \bigsqcup_{C\in\mathscr{N}} \mathsf{merge}(C, \varnothing)$. If $\mathscr{M} = \varnothing$ then **fail** else proceed to the next step.

Step 3. Let $\mathscr{S} = \bigsqcup_{C\in\mathscr{M}} \mathsf{solve}(C)$. Return $\{\mathsf{Unify}(E) \mid E{\in}\mathscr{S}\}$.

Let $\mathsf{Sol}_\Delta(C)$ denote the set of all substitutions obtained by the previous algorithm. They form a sound and complete set of solutions for the tallying problem:

**Theorem 3.6** (Soundness and completeness).

$$\sigma \in \mathsf{Sol}_\Delta(C) \quad\Rightarrow\quad \sigma \Vdash_\Delta C$$
$$\sigma \Vdash_\Delta C \quad\Rightarrow\quad \exists\sigma' \in \mathsf{Sol}_\Delta(C), \sigma'', \textit{ s.t. } \sigma \approx \sigma'' \circ \sigma'$$

where $\approx$ means that the two substitutions map the same variable into equivalent types. Regularity of types ensures the termination of the algorithm and, hence, the decidability of the tallying problem (the proof of these properties combines proofs of soundness, completeness, and termination of each step: see Appendix C).

EXAMPLE (End). *After Step 1 and 2 our initial tallying problem* $\{(\alpha{\to}\mathtt{Bool}, \beta{\to}\beta)\ ,\ (\mathtt{Int}{\vee}\mathtt{Bool} \to \mathtt{Int}, \alpha{\to}\beta)\}$ *has become* $\{\ \{(\alpha,\mathbb{0}), (\beta,\mathbb{0})\}\ ,\ \{(\beta,\alpha), (\alpha, \mathtt{Int}{\vee}\mathtt{Bool}), (\mathtt{Int}{\vee}\mathtt{Bool}, \beta), (\beta, \mathtt{Int}{\vee}\mathtt{Bool})\}\ \}$. *Let us apply Step 3. The first constraint-set is trivial and it is easy to see that it yields the solution* $\{^{\mathbb{0}}/_\alpha, ^{\mathbb{0}}/_\beta\}$. *The second constraint-set is* $\{\ (\beta{\leq}\alpha{\leq}\mathtt{Int}{\vee}\mathtt{Bool})\ ,\ (\mathtt{Int}{\vee}\mathtt{Bool}{\leq}\beta \leq \mathtt{Int}{\vee}\mathtt{Bool})\ \}$. *We apply* solve *to the constraints for* $\alpha$ *obtaining* $\{\alpha = (\gamma{\vee}\beta){\wedge}(\mathtt{Int}{\vee}\mathtt{Bool})\}$. *We find the solution for* $\beta$ *(no need to substitute* $\alpha$ *since it does not occur in the constraints for* $\beta$*) which is* $\{\beta = \mathtt{Int}{\vee}\mathtt{Bool}\}$. *We replace* $\beta$ *in the solution of* $\alpha$ *obtaining* $\{\alpha = (\gamma{\vee}\mathtt{Int}{\vee}\mathtt{Bool}){\wedge}(\mathtt{Int}{\vee}\mathtt{Bool})\}$. *The solution for this second constraint-set is then* $\{^{\mathtt{Int}\vee\mathtt{Bool}}/_\alpha, ^{\mathtt{Int}\vee\mathtt{Bool}}/_\beta\}$, *which with* $\{^{\mathbb{0}}/_\alpha, ^{\mathbb{0}}/_\beta\}$ *forms a sound and complete set of solutions for our initial tallying problem.*

Finally, $\mathsf{solve}$ introduces several fresh polymorphic variables which can be cleaned up after that the substitutions have been applied to obtain the types deduced by inference system: all variables that occur only in covariant (resp. contravariant) position in a type, can be replaced by $\mathbb{0}$ (resp. $\mathbb{1}$). This is what we implicitly did in our example to solve $\beta$ and eliminate $\gamma$ from the constraint of $\alpha$.

### *3.2.2 Solution for application with fixed cardinalities*

It remains to solve the problem for the (INF-APPL) rule. We recall that given two types $s$ and $t$, a solution for this problem is *a pair* of sets of type-substitutions $[\sigma_i]_{i\in I}$, $[\sigma_j]_{j\in J}$ for variables not in $\Delta$ that make both of these two inequations

$$\bigwedge_{i\in I} t\sigma_i \leq \mathbb{0}{\to}\mathbb{1} \qquad\qquad \bigwedge_{j\in J} s\sigma_j \leq \mathsf{dom}(\bigwedge_{i\in I} t\sigma_i) \qquad (15)$$

hold. Two complications are to be dealt with: $(i)$ we must find *sets* of type substitutions, rather than a single substitution as in the tallying problem and $(ii)$ we have to get rid of the $\mathsf{dom}()$ function. If $I$ and $J$ have fixed cardinalities, then both difficulties can be easily surmounted and the whole problem be reduced to a tallying problem. To see how, consider the two inequations in (15). Since the two sets of substitutions are independent, then without loss of generality we can split each substitution $\sigma_k$ (for $k{\in}I{\cup}J$) in two substitutions: a renaming substitution $\rho_k$ that maps each variable in the domain of $\sigma_k$ into a different fresh variable, and a second substitution $\sigma'_k$ defined such that $\sigma_k = \sigma'_k \circ \rho_k$. The two inequations thus become $\bigwedge_{i\in I}(t\rho_i)\sigma'_i \leq \mathbb{0}{\to}\mathbb{1}$ and $\bigwedge_{j\in J}(s\rho_j)\sigma'_j \leq \mathsf{dom}(\bigwedge_{i\in I}(t\rho_i)\sigma'_i)$. Since the various $\sigma'_k$ (for $k \in I{\cup}J$) have disjoint domains, then we can take their union to get a single substitution $\sigma = \bigcup_{k\in I\cup J} \sigma'_k$, and the two inequations respectively become $(\bigwedge_{i\in I} t\rho_i)\sigma \leq \mathbb{0}{\to}\mathbb{1}$ and $(\bigwedge_{j\in J} s\rho_j)\sigma \leq \mathsf{dom}((\bigwedge_{i\in I} t\rho_i)\sigma)$. Now if we fix the cardinalities of $I$ and $J$ since the $\rho_k$ are generic renamings, we have just transformed the problem in (15) into the problem of finding for two given types $t_1$ and $t_2$ all substitutions $\sigma$ such that[6]

$$t_1\sigma \leq \mathbb{0}{\to}\mathbb{1} \qquad \text{and} \qquad t_2\sigma \leq \mathsf{dom}(t_1\sigma) \qquad (16)$$

hold. Finally, we can prove (see Lemmas C.49 and C.50) that a type-substitution $\sigma$ solves (16) if and only if it solves

$$t_1\sigma \leq \mathbb{0}{\to}\mathbb{1} \qquad \text{and} \qquad t_1\sigma \leq (t_2{\to}\gamma)\sigma \qquad (17)$$

with $\gamma$ fresh. We transformed the application problem (with fixed cardinalities) into the tallying problem for $\{(t_1, \mathbb{0}{\to}\mathbb{1}), (t_1, t_2{\to}\gamma)\}$, whose set of solutions is a sound and complete set of solutions for the (INF-APPL) rule problem when $I$ and $J$ have fixed cardinalities.

### *3.2.3 Solution of the application problem*

The algorithm to solve the general problem for the (INF-APPL) rule explores all the possible combinations of the cardinalities of $I$

[6] Precisely, we have $t_1 = \bigwedge_{i=1..|I|} t_i^1$ and $t_2 = \bigwedge_{i=1..|J|} t_i^2$ where for $h = 1, 2$ each $t_i^h$ is obtained from $t_h$ by renaming the variables not in $\Delta$ into fresh variables.

and $J$ by, say, a dove-tail order. More precisely, we start with both $I$ and $J$ at cardinality 1 and:

*Step A*: Generate the constraint-set $\{(t_1, t_2 \to \gamma)\}$ as explained in Subsection 3.2.2 (the constraint $t_1 \leq \mathbb{0} \to \mathbb{1}$ is implied by this one since $\mathbb{0} \to \mathbb{1}$ contains every arrow type) and apply the tallying algorithm described in Subsection 3.2.1, yielding either a solution (a substitution for variables not in $\Delta$) or a failure.

*Step B*: If all the constraint-sets failed at Step 1 of the algorithm of Subsection 3.2.1, then fail (the expression is not typeable). If they all failed but at least one did not fail in *Step 1*, then increase the cardinalities of $I$ and $J$ to their successor in the dove-tail order and start from *Step A* again. Otherwise all substitutions found by the algorithm are solutions of the application problem.

Notice that the algorithm returns a failure only if all the constraint-sets fail at Step 1 of the algorithm for the tallying problem. The reason is that up to Step 1 all the constraints at issue are on distinct occurrences of type variables: if they fail, there is no possible expansion that can make the constraint-set satisfiable. In Step 2, instead, constraints of different occurrences of some variable are merged. Thus even if the constraints fail, it may be the case that they will be satisfied by expanding different occurrences of some variable into different variables. Therefore an expansion is tried. Solving the problem for $s \sqsubseteq_\Delta t$ is similar (there is just one set whose cardinality has to be increased at each step instead of two).

This constitutes a sound and complete semi-decision procedure for the application problem and, thus, for the type-substitution inference system (Theorem C.54). We defined some heuristics (omitted for space reasons: see Section C.2.3) to stop the algorithm when a solution seems unlikely. Whether these (or some coarser) halting conditions preserve completeness, that is, whether type-substitutions inference is decidable, is an open problem. We believe the system to be decidable. However, we fail to prove it when the type of the argument of an application is a union: its expansion distributes the union over the intersections thus generating new combinations of types. It comes as no surprise that the definitions of our heuristics are based on the cardinalities and depths of the unions occurring in the argument type.

Let us apply the algorithm to `map even`. We start with the constraint set $\{(\alpha_1 \to \beta_1) \to [\alpha_1] \to [\beta_1] \leq t \to \gamma\}$ where $t = (\texttt{Int} \to \texttt{Bool}) \wedge (\alpha \backslash \texttt{Int} \to \alpha \backslash \texttt{Int})$ is the type of `even` (we just renamed the variables of the type of `map`). After *Step A* the algorithm generates a set of nine constraint-sets (see Section 10.2.2 of [18] for more details on this example): one is unsatisfiable since it contains the constraint $t \leq \mathbb{0}$ (an intersection of arrows is never empty since it always contains $\mathbb{1} \to \mathbb{0}$ the type of the diverging functions); four of these are less general than some other (their solutions are included in the solutions of the other) and the remaining four are obtained by adding the constraint $\gamma \geq [\alpha_1] \to [\beta_1]$ respectively to $\{\alpha_1 \leq \mathbb{0}\}$, $\{\alpha_1 \leq \texttt{Int}, \texttt{Bool} \leq \beta_1\}$, $\{\alpha_1 \leq \alpha \backslash \texttt{Int}, \alpha \backslash \texttt{Int} \leq \beta_1\}$, $\{\alpha_1 \leq \alpha \vee \texttt{Int}, (\alpha \backslash \texttt{Int}) \vee \texttt{Bool} \leq \beta_1\}$, yielding the following four solutions for $\gamma$: $\{\gamma = [\,] \to [\,]\}$, or $\{\gamma = [\texttt{Int}] \to [\texttt{Bool}]\}$, or $\{\gamma = [\alpha \backslash \texttt{Int}] \to [\alpha \backslash \texttt{Int}]\}$, or $\{\gamma = [\alpha \vee \texttt{Int}] \to [(\alpha \backslash \texttt{Int}) \vee \texttt{Bool}]\}$. Of these solutions only the last two are minimal. Since both are valid we could stop here and take their intersection, yielding the type expected in the introduction. If instead we strictly follow the algorithm, then we have to perform a further iteration, expand the type of the function, yielding $\{((\alpha_1 \to \beta_1) \to [\alpha_1] \to [\beta_1]) \wedge ((\alpha_2 \to \beta_2) \to [\alpha_2] \to [\beta_2]) \leq t \to \gamma\}$ for which the minimal solution is, as expected:
$\{\gamma = ([\alpha \backslash \texttt{Int}] \to [\alpha \backslash \texttt{Int}]) \wedge ([\alpha \vee \texttt{Int}] \to [(\alpha \backslash \texttt{Int}) \vee \texttt{Bool}])\}$

A final remark on completeness. The theorem states that for every solution of the inference problem, our algorithm finds a solution that is more general. However this solution is not necessary the first one found by the algorithm: even if we find a solution, continuing with a further expansion may yield a more general solution. We have just seen that in the case of `map even` the good solution is the second one, although this solution could already have been deduced by intersecting the first minimal solutions we found. A simple example that shows that carrying on after a first solution may yield a better solution is the application of a function of type $(\alpha \times \beta) \to (\beta \times \alpha)$ to an argument of type $(\texttt{Int} \times \texttt{Bool}) \vee (\texttt{Bool} \times \texttt{Int})$. For this applications our algorithm (extended with product types) returns after one iteration the type $(\texttt{Int} \vee \texttt{Bool}) \times (\texttt{Int} \vee \texttt{Bool})$ (since it unifies $\alpha$ with $\beta$) while one further iteration would deduce the more precise type $(\texttt{Int} \times \texttt{Bool}) \vee (\texttt{Bool} \times \texttt{Int})$. Of course this raises the problem of the existence of principal types (notice that the type $t'$ in the statement of Theorem 3.3 is not unique): may an infinite sequence of increasingly general solutions exist? This is a problem we did not tackle in this work, but if the answer to the previous question were negative, then it would be easy to prove the existence of a principal type: since at each iteration there are only finitely many solutions, then the principal type would be the intersection of the minimal solutions of the last iteration.

Finally, notice that we did not give any reduction semantics for the implicitly-typed calculus. The reason is that its semantics is defined in terms of the semantics of the explicitly-typed calculus: the relabeling at run-time is an essential feature —independently from the fact that we started from an explicitly-typed expression or not— and we cannot avoid it. If we denote by $\mathit{erase}^{-1}(a)$ the set of expressions $e$ that satisfy the statement of Theorem 3.2, then the (big-step) semantics for an implicitly-typed expression $a$ is given in terms of $\mathit{erase}^{-1}(a)$: if an expression in $\mathit{erase}^{-1}(a)$ reduces to $v$, so does $a$. As we see the result of computing an implicitly-typed expression is a value of the explicitly-typed calculus (so $\lambda$-abstractions may contain non-empty decorations) and this is unavoidable since it may be the result of a partial application (this can be made transparent for the programmer by returning just the type and the "value" `<fun>` as in OCaml's toplevel). Also notice that the semantics is not univocally determined since different expressions in $\mathit{erase}^{-1}(a)$ may yield different results. However this may happen only in one particular case, namely, when an occurrence of a polymorphic function flows into a type-case and its type is tested. For instance the application $(\lambda^{(\texttt{Int} \to \texttt{Int}) \to \texttt{Bool}} f. f \in \texttt{Bool} \to \texttt{Bool} \,?\, \texttt{true} : \texttt{false})(\lambda^{\alpha \to \alpha} x.x)$ results into `true` or `false` according to whether the polymorphic identity at the argument is instantiated by $[\{^{\texttt{Int}}/_{\alpha}\}]$ or by $[\{^{\texttt{Int}}/_{\alpha}\}, \{^{\texttt{Bool}}/_{\alpha}\}]$. Once more this is unavoidable in a calculus that can dynamically test the types of polymorphic functions that admit several sound instantiations. This does not happen in practice since the inference algorithm always choose one particular instantiation (the existence of principal types would make this choice canonical and remove any residual latitude). So in practice the semantics is deterministic but implementation dependent.

In summary, programming in the implicitly-typed calculus corresponds to programming in the explicitly-typed one with the difference that we delegate to the system the task to write type-substitutions for us and with the caveat that by doing that we make the dynamic test of the type of a polymorphic function to be implementation dependent. Of course, forbidding the dynamic test of the type of polymorphic functions (or of functions *tout court*) make this problem disappear (and yields much a simpler implementation).

### 3.3 Examples and experiments

We developed two implementations (see the last page of the appendix for download instructions), a complete but non-optimized prototype with products and arrow type constructors, and an extension of the full $\mathbb{C}$Duce language which is highly optimized (types are stored in hash-consed binary decision trees to avoid the cost of normalization, pattern-matching has optimal implementation, static analyses are used to minimize the impact of polymorphism and so on). In this section we show examples of the latter, that is of ℂDuce syntax extended with type variables.[7] In this extension `map` has type $(\alpha \to \beta) \to$ `[`$\alpha$`*]` $\to$ `[`$\beta$`*]` since in ℂDuce sequence types are denoted by brackets whose content is described by a regular expression on types. Functions are explicitly typed and thus must specify both their input and output types

```
let pretty (x: Int): String = string_of x
```

or the whole interface when they are typed by an intersection type:

```
let even (Int->Bool ; (α\Int)->(α\Int))
  | x & Int -> (x mod 2) = 0
  | x -> x
```

The type returned for the partial application `map even` is then

`([(α\Int)*]`→`[(α\Int)*])&([(α|Int)*]`→`[(α\Int|Bool)*])`

(unions and intersections are denoted by `|` and `&`, respectively) while the one for `map pretty` is `([]`→`[])&([Int*]->[String*])`. While the right-hand side arrow of this intersection is the type an ML programmer would expect, our inference algorithm also deduces the special case `[]`→`[]`, stating that the function maps the empty list into itself. Interestingly, the solver does not need to know the *body* of `map` to deduce it; this is because ℂDuce encodes lists by recursive union types (`[`$\alpha$`*]` stands for $\mu X.$`nil`$\vee(\alpha, X)$ where `nil` denotes the empty list) and our system tries to infer a result for every type in the union. Instantiation works as expected as the following snippet of ℂDuce interactive toplevel shows ("`#`" is the prompt of the toplevel while its output is displayed in italics):

```
# let g ((Int -> Int) -> Int -> Int ;
        (Bool -> Bool) -> Bool -> Bool) x -> x;;
val g : (Bool -> Bool) -> Bool -> Bool
      & (Int -> Int) -> Int -> Int = <fun>

# let id ('a -> 'a) x -> x;;
val id : 'a -> 'a = <fun>

# g id;;
- : (Bool -> Bool) & (Int -> Int) = <fun>

# id (id g) ;;
- : (Bool -> Bool) -> Bool -> Bool
  & (Int -> Int) -> Int -> Int = <fun>
```

Our system includes singleton types (types that contain a single value) and thus the type returned, for instance, for

```
let churchtrue (x: α)(y: β): α = x in churchtrue 42;;
```

is $\beta \to 42$ (*ie*, the type of functions that accept any argument and return 42) and, likewise, `id 42` has type 42. More surprising may be the case for a function such as `max` (whose definition uses the ℂDuce's polymorphic comparison operator `>>` "greater than"):

```
# let max (x: α)(y: α): α = if (x >> y) then x else y;;
val max : α -> α -> α = <fun>
```

An ML programmer would probably expect the partial application `max 42` to be typed as `42`→`42` or `Int`→`Int` (at least, *we* were naively expecting that). Instead, for this application the system returns the type `(`$\beta$`|42)`→`(`$\beta$`|42)`, and rightly so. The point is that our system includes union types and, therefore, an application such as `max 42 "3"` is well typed: it suffices to instantiate the variable $\alpha$ in the type of `max` by the union type `Int|String`. To give the final instantiation for $\alpha$ the type system must know the type of *both* arguments of `max`, therefore in the case of the partial application, it instantiates $\alpha$ with $\beta$`|42` stating that it knows that $\alpha$ contains *at least* the value 42 and waits for the second argument to instantiate the missing part, represented by $\beta$; and the type returned for `max 42 "3"` is `42|"3"`. In this example we specified the type $\alpha$`->`$\alpha$`->`$\alpha$ for `max`, since this is what an ML programmer would have written. However, in a system with polymorphic union types a more meaningful type for `max` is $\alpha$`->`$\beta$`->`$\alpha$`|`$\beta$: if we specify such a type for `max`, then the type deduced for the partial application `max 42` is, more intuitively, $\beta$`->(`$\beta$`|42)`. The fact that $\alpha$`->`$\beta$`->`$\alpha$`|`$\beta$ and $\alpha$`->`$\alpha$`->`$\alpha$ cannot, from any practical point of view, be distinguished seems a nice feature of our system. Nevertheless notice that the same type deduction as for `max` would have happened if in the definition of `churchtrue` we had used $\alpha$ instead of $\beta$; in that case `churchtrue 42 "3"` would have been typed by the (less precise) union type `42|"3"`, too. Thus, in order to achieve precise typing, it is important to use distinct type variables for distinct parameters.

Finally, we said in the introduction that the typing of `even` follows a pattern that is common in programming functional data structures. This can be seen by examining Okasaki's implementation of red-black trees [13]. These are balanced binary search trees whose nodes are colored either in black or in red and such that every red node has two (possibly empty) black children; a red node with a red child is a "wrong" tree. Insertions must keep the tree balanced and the key definition is a function `balance` which transforms every "unbalanced" tree —*ie*, a black-rooted tree with a "wrong" child— into a red-rooted tree, and leaves all other trees unchanged. Okasaki gives a very compact and elegant definition of `balance` consisting of a pattern matching with two cases (for a union and for a capture variable), but current type systems are not expressive enough to verify that his code, without any modification, satisfies color invariants. Our types, instead, can do it as follows:

```
type RBtree = Btree | Rtree
type Btree  = <blk elem=α>[ RBtree RBtree ] | []
type Rtree  = <red elem=α>[ Btree  Btree ]
type Unbal  = <blk elem=α>( [ Wrong RBtree ]
                          | [ RBtree Wrong ])
type Wrong  = <red elem=α>( [ Rtree Btree ]
                          | [ Btree Rtree ])

let balance ( Unbal->Rtree ; (β\Unbal)->(β\Unbal) )
  | <blk (z)>[ <red (y)>[ <red (x)>[ a b ] c ] d ]
  | <blk (z)>[ <red (x)>[ a <red (y)>[ b c ] ] d ]
  | <blk (x)>[ a <red (z)>[ <red (y)>[ b c ] d ] ]
  | <blk (x)>[ a <red (y)>[ b <red (z)>[ c d ] ] ]
      -> <red (y)>[  <blk (x)>[ a b ]  <blk (z)>[ c d ] ]
  | x -> x
```

The only (irrelevant) difference of this definition with Okasaki's definition of `balance` is that we used ℂDuce's syntax for trees, that is, XML elements tagged by their color, with an attribute `elem` for their content, and that delimit sequences of two sub-trees. The type of `balance` (which has the same form as the type of `even`) precisely describes the behavior of the function and this type information is enough to prove that the insertion function has type $\alpha$→`Btree`→`Btree`, that is, that when it inserts an $\alpha$-element into a well-formed black-rooted red-black it returns another well-formed black-rooted red-black tree (see Appendix A for the complete code and how to run it on the development version of ℂDuce).

Transposing the results and algorithms of this paper, to full-fledged ℂDuce was not easy. Adapting the internal representation of types and its algorithms is challenging (to give an idea of such a challenge, consider that a simple type variable is internally represented as a hash-consed union of 7 binary decision diagrams each intersecting the top type of a type constructor) and so are type pretty printing and error message generation. For what is specific to this work, the main challenge is not only to extend the typing rules of Figure 2 to missing data structures and expressions (XML trees, general pattern matching, products, ...) but, above all, to modify the rules so that they return expressions decorated with sets of explicit types substitutions. Also the various internal languages used by the compiler must be modified (the ℂDuce compiler performs several passes that translate each intermediate language into a lower level one) and each transformation phase must be enriched with specific static analyses to optimize the evaluation of polymorphic expres-

[7] Following the OCaml convention, in the concrete syntax type variables start by a quote. To enhance readability here we pretty print them by Greek letters and so write $\alpha \to \beta$ rather than `'a -> 'b`.

sions. Finally, the propagation of type substitutions must be lazily implemented for all constructed values (*ie*, pairs and XML documents). The main modifications are summarized in Appendix E.

For what concerns performances, the results of some preliminary experiments are reported in Appendix F. In summary, we generated a test suite of 1 859 applications of higher-order polymorphic functions by taking all the 43 functions exported by the List module of OCaml, and cross applying one to each other. Whenever a given function can be applied (*ie*, the application type-checks in OCaml) to two other functions, then we applied it to their intersection and their union; whenever two functions can be applied to the same function then we applied their union and their intersection to it; and so on so forth up to a maximum of 15 top-level connectives. We also tested all applications resulting ill-typed in OCaml, so as to check cases in which local type-inference may fail. The results are significant and encouraging. The test suite was defined to maximize the possible exponential blow up (which is essentially due to the presence of arrows and intersections that may trigger multiple expansions). The combinations of the functions of the List module cover a wide range of use cases and involve recursive types (specifically, polymorphic lists), and the limit of 15 connectives on arrows more than doubles what we ever met in practice. To type check the 1 859 applications on an average laptop took 27 secs with an average time for application of 14ms and 2.1ms of median time. This means that apart from few pathological cases (which took a couple of seconds) our implementation performs local type inference within acceptable delays. We also verified that our implementation smoothly handles the application of curried functions to 20 arguments (*cf.*, OCaml standard library whose functions have at most 5 arguments). Furthermore, the room for improvement is still important. Our implementation uses the highly-optimized data-structures of ℂDuce types and aggressive memoization, however normalization and constraint generation are implemented as described in this paper. In particular, as in Line 5 in Figure 3, normalization performs a full expansion. By modifying the algorithms so that, like in the subtyping algorithm, normalization and constraint generation are performed lazily, we hope to improve performance by an order of magnitude.

## 4. Type reconstruction

The theory of type tallying we developed in Section 3 can be reused to perform type reconstruction, that is, to assign a type to functions whose interface is not specified. The idea is to type the body of a function under the hypothesis that the function has the generic type $\alpha \to \beta$ and deduce the corresponding constraints. Formally, we consider expressions produced by the following grammar:

$$m ::= c \mid x \mid mm \mid \lambda x.m \mid m{\in}t\,?\,m : m$$

together with the judgment $\Gamma \vdash_{\mathscr{R}} m : t \rightsquigarrow \mathscr{S}$ that states that under the typing environment $\Gamma$, $m$ has type $t$ under the constraints in $\mathscr{S}$, provided that $\mathscr{S}$ is satisfiable (the turnstile subscript $\mathscr{R}$ indicates that this is a type $\mathscr{R}$econstruction system). These judgments are derived by the rules in Figure 4. These are quite standard apart from the fact that they derive multiple constraint-sets, rather than just one. This is due to the type reconstruction rule for type-cases, which explores four possible alternatives ($m_0$ diverges, it can match only the first, the second, or both cases). In this system the type of a well-typed expression is a type and a set of type-substitutions (*ie*, the set of all substitutions that are solutions of the satisfiable constraint-sets in $\mathscr{S}$) and thus it is an intersection type obtained by applying this set of type-substitutions to the type.

The soundness of this system is a consequence of the results on the type-substitution inference of the previous sections. As a matter of facts, this system is precisely the same system as the one in the previous sections with the only difference that all interfaces are of the form $\alpha \to \beta$ and, to compensate that, we infer type-substitutions

$$\frac{}{\Gamma \vdash_{\mathscr{R}} c : b_c \rightsquigarrow \{\varnothing\}}\text{(R-CONST)} \qquad \frac{}{\Gamma \vdash_{\mathscr{R}} x : \Gamma(x) \rightsquigarrow \{\varnothing\}}\text{(R-VAR)}$$

$$\frac{\Gamma \vdash_{\mathscr{R}} m_1 : t_1 \rightsquigarrow \mathscr{S}_1 \qquad \Gamma \vdash_{\mathscr{R}} m_2 : t_2 \rightsquigarrow \mathscr{S}_2}{\Gamma \vdash_{\mathscr{R}} m_1 m_2 : \alpha \rightsquigarrow \mathscr{S}_1 \sqcap \mathscr{S}_2 \sqcap \{\{(t_1 \leq t_2 \to \alpha)\}\}}\text{(R-APPL)}$$

$$\frac{\Gamma, x : \alpha \vdash_{\mathscr{R}} m : t \rightsquigarrow \mathscr{S}}{\Gamma \vdash_{\mathscr{R}} \lambda x.m : \alpha \to \beta \rightsquigarrow \mathscr{S} \sqcap \{\{(t \leq \beta)\}\}}\text{(R-ABSTR)}$$

(R-CASE)
$$\begin{array}{rl} \mathscr{S} = & (\mathscr{S}_0 \sqcap \{\{(t_0 \leq \mathbb{0})\}\}) \\ \sqcup & (\mathscr{S}_0 \sqcap \mathscr{S}_1 \sqcap \{\{(t_0 \leq t), (t_1 \leq \alpha)\}\}) \\ \sqcup & (\mathscr{S}_0 \sqcap \mathscr{S}_2 \sqcap \{\{(t_0 \leq \neg t), (t_2 \leq \alpha)\}\}) \\ \sqcup & (\mathscr{S}_0 \sqcap \mathscr{S}_1 \sqcap \mathscr{S}_2 \sqcap \{\{(t_1 \vee t_2 \leq \alpha)\}\}) \end{array}$$
$$\frac{\Gamma \vdash_{\mathscr{R}} m_0 : t_0 \rightsquigarrow \mathscr{S}_0 \qquad \Gamma \vdash_{\mathscr{R}} m_1 : t_1 \rightsquigarrow \mathscr{S}_1 \qquad \Gamma \vdash_{\mathscr{R}} m_2 : t_2 \rightsquigarrow \mathscr{S}_2}{\Gamma \vdash_{\mathscr{R}} (m_0{\in}t\,?\,m_1 : m_2) : \alpha \rightsquigarrow \mathscr{S}}$$

where $\alpha$, $\alpha_i$ and $\beta$ in each rule are fresh type variables.

**Figure 4.** Type reconstruction rules

in decorations (we also used a different and more standard presentation to stress constraint generation). Of course, completeness does not hold: far from that. For instance, it is impossible, in general, to deduce for a function without type annotations the type $\mathbb{1} \to \mathbb{0}$ — the type of all diverging functions— since this would correspond to decide the halting problem (though our algorithm returns for $\mu f\, x{=}f(x)$ the same type as in ML, that is, $\alpha \to \beta$). Likewise, completeness would imply decidability of reconstruction and thus imply decidability for intersection type systems, which are undecidable. Similarly, our reconstruction system cannot type the paradoxical functions we pointed out in the first part of this work (see Section 2 in [3]). However, if a function can be typed in ML-like type systems, then our type reconstruction rules can deduce a type at least as good as the ML one. Indeed, if we restrict our attention to the first four rules, the system produces a singleton set of constraints that is the same as in ML system (*cf.* [15]) and when constraint-sets are not circular (*ie*, their solution does not require recursive types), then our constraint solving algorithm coincides with unification (all fresh variables introduced by solve are simplified as we described at the end of Section 3.2.1 and solve directly produces a set of equations that are, in Martelli and Montanari's terminology [11], in *solved form*). Furthermore, since the types considered here are much richer than in ML (since they include unions, intersections, and negations), then our reconstruction may infer slightly better types. Type connectives alone bring, in particular, two advantages for type reconstruction: $(i)$ the system deduces *sets* of type-substitutions (and thus deduces intersection types) and $(ii)$ pattern matching (which can be seen as a type-case with singleton types) is typed more precisely (thanks in particular to intersections and negations). For instance, and contrary to ML, our type reconstruction can type auto-application $\lambda x.xx$ for which it returns the recursive type $t = \mu X.(\alpha \wedge (X \to \beta)) \to \beta$. This type is a subtype of —thus, it is more precise than— the classic (non-recursive) typing of auto-application in intersection type systems $t \leq (\alpha \wedge (\alpha \to \beta)) \to \beta$ (though it is not as precise as its subtype $\mu X.(\alpha \vee (X \to \beta)) \to \beta$ which can also type auto-application). As a final example, if we apply our type reconstruction algorithm (extended with products and recursive functions) to the type erasure of the map function defined in equation (12), then we obtain the type (in CDuce's syntax) $((\alpha \to \beta) \to$ `[α*]`$\to$`[β*]`$) \wedge ((\mathbb{0} \to \mathbb{1}) \to$ `[]`$\to$`[]`$)$ (see the complete unfolding of the algorithm in Appendix D). Thanks to the precise typing of the type-case, our type is slightly more accurate than the ML type, since it states that the application of `map` to any function and the empty list returns the empty list.

Finally, the "type" returned by the type reconstruction algorithm is not always very readable and often needs to be simplified. For instance, the type we showed for `map` was obtained after applying some simplifications —one of which was done by hand—, and defining an algorithm that does the right simplifications is not obvious (*eg*, how to detect that the type $(\alpha\wedge(\alpha\rightarrow\beta))\rightarrow\beta$ is much more readable than the type $\mu X.(\alpha\wedge(X\rightarrow\beta))\rightarrow\beta$ reconstructed for auto-application by our algorithm?). The simplification of types (or of type constraints) is a stand alone research topic that deserves further investigation. Nevertheless our reconstruction algorithm can already be used as is, to make type declaration of local functions optional. Indeed for local functions the system is not required to return a "readable" type to the programmer, but just to check whether there exists a typing for local functions that is compatible with their usage; and, for that, our system is enough, even though we will probably have to couple it with bidirectional typing techniques [7] to provide informative error messages when the check fails.

## 5. Extensions

In this presentation we omitted two key features: pairs and recursive functions. Recursive functions do not pose any particular problem in the inference of type-substitutions and are dealt with in a standard way, while pairs are more challenging. The rule for pairs in inference system $\vdash_{\mathscr{I}}$ is the same as in the explicitly-typed calculus (this corresponds to disregarding sets of type-substitutions applied inside a pair, as they can equivalently be inferred outside the pair: $t_i \not\simeq \mathbb{0}$ and $(t_1{\times}t_2) \sqsubseteq_\Delta (s_1{\times}s_2) \Leftrightarrow t_i \sqsubseteq_\Delta s_i$). Instead, as expected, the rule for projection $\pi_i e$ needs some special care since if the type inferred for $e$ is, say, $t$, then we need to find a set of substitutions $[\sigma_i]_{i\in I}$ such that $\bigwedge_{i\in I} t\sigma_i \leq \mathbb{1}\times\mathbb{1}$. This problem can be solved by using the very same technique we introduced for $\bullet_\Delta$, namely by solving a sequence of tallying problems generated by increasing at each step the cardinality of $I$ (see the appendix).

In the first part of this work [3] we studied the extension of the explicitly-typed calculus with `let`-polymorphism, in particular, its typing and efficient execution (see Section 5.4 of [3]). There we distinguished `let`-bound variables by underlining them. Reconstruction is mostly useful when combined with `let`-polymorphism. To extend our reconstruction to `let` we use a separate type environment $\Phi$ for these variables (while we reserve $\Gamma$ for $\lambda$-abstracted variables). As in Damas-Milner $\mathscr{W}$ algorithm [6] we need to define $\overline{\Gamma}(t)$, the generalization (*closure* in [6]) of a type $t$ wrt the type environment $\Gamma$, that is, $\overline{\Gamma}(t) \stackrel{\text{def}}{=} t[\{\gamma_i/_{\alpha_i} \mid \alpha_i \in \mathsf{var}(t)\backslash\mathsf{var}(\Gamma)\}]$ where $\gamma_i$ are fresh. Then the rules for type reconstruction are

$$\textit{(let-var)}\ \frac{}{\Phi\,;\Gamma \vdash_{\mathscr{R}} \underline{x} : \overline{\Gamma}(\Phi(\underline{x})) \rightsquigarrow \{\varnothing\}}$$

$$\textit{(let)}\ \frac{\Phi\,;\Gamma \vdash_{\mathscr{R}} e_1 : t_1 \rightsquigarrow \mathscr{S} \qquad \Phi, (\underline{x} : t_1)\,;\Gamma \vdash_{\mathscr{R}} e_2 : t_2 \rightsquigarrow \mathscr{S}'}{\Phi\,;\Gamma \vdash_{\mathscr{R}} \texttt{let}\ \underline{x} = e_1\ \texttt{in}\ e_2 : t_2 \rightsquigarrow \mathscr{S} \sqcap \mathscr{S}'}$$

## 6. Related work

This section discusses related work on constraint-based type inference and inference for intersection/union type systems. Discussion about work on explicitly-typed intersection type systems and on XML processing languages can be found in Part 1 of this work [3].

Type inference in ML has essentially been considered as a constraint solving problem [12, 15]. We use a similar approach to solve the problem of type unification: finding a proper substitution that makes the type of the domain of a function compatible with (*ie*, a supertype of) the type of the argument it is applied to. Our type unification problem is essentially a specific set constraint problem [1]. This is applied in a much more complex setting with a complete set of type connectives and a rich set-theoretic subtyping relation. In particular, because of the presence of intersection types, solving the problem of application demands to find *sets* of substitutions rather than just one substitution. This is reflected by the definition of our $\sqsubseteq$ relation which is much more thorough than the corresponding relation used in ML inference insofar as it encompasses instantiation, expansion, and subtyping. The important novelty of our work comes from the use of set-theoretic connectives, which allows us to turn sets of constraints of the form $s{\leq}\alpha{\leq}t$ into sets of equations of the form $\alpha = (\beta \vee s) \wedge t$, a technique that, in our ken, is original to our work. This set of equations is then solved using Courcelle's work on infinite trees [5]. The use of type connectives also implies that we solve multiple sets of constraints, which account for different alternatives. Finally, it is worth noticing that [12, 15] use a richer language of constraints that includes binding. This allows separating constraint generation and constraint solving without compromising efficiency. Therefore an interesting direction of future research is either to re-frame our work into a richer language of constraints or to extend the work in [12, 15] to encompass our richer setting. This could be a first step towards the study of efficient constraint solving algorithms for our system.

Feature-wise the programming language closest to our language —*ie*, polymorphic ℂDuce— is Typed Racket [16, 17] since it has recursive types, union types, top and singleton types, subtyping, dynamic type-cases (called *occurrence typing* in [16, 17]), and explicitly-typed polymorphic functions. The goal of Typed Racket is to type an existing untyped programming language and it is superior to our system in that it allows the combination of both typed and untyped code in a single program. For what concerns typed features, however, Typed Racket is just a small fragment of our system: type-cases can only test basic types and tests for just *some* constructed types can be encoded by using Boolean connectives; there are no intersection types (thus, no overloaded functions); there are no negation or difference types; union types and their subtyping are quite naive (*eg*, a type is a subtype of a union of types only if it is a subtype of some type of the union, distribution laws over type constructors are absent, etc.). The typing of Typed Racket is internally defined in terms of propositional logic where atoms are the elements of a type environment (*eg*, $x : \tau$). The use of logical formulas coincides in ℂDuce to computing the types of capture variable of patterns (*cf.* the operator $t /\!\!/ p$ in Appendix E or in [9]): the use of propositional logic corresponds to the use of Boolean connectives in ℂDuce's patterns and unsatisfiability of a formula to type emptiness. This is why all the examples in the "Challenges" section of [17] can be easily defined and precisely typed in our system (straightforwardly with the syntactic sugar defined in the Appendix E of Part 1 [3]). Actually, these examples can already be defined and typed in monomorphic ℂDuce [2] since it already captures all the features characteristics of Typed Racket (recursive and union types, subtyping, occurrence typing, etc.) with the sole exception of polymorphism, a gap filled by this work. Typed Racket uses a limited form of local type inference: the application of a function to a polymorphic argument requires the application of an explicit type substitution to the argument. We do not have this limitation thanks to our tallying procedure that computes instantiations (type substitutitions) both for the function and for its argument. It is not clear whether using generic SMT solvers for typing (as suggested by [17]) also in ℂDuce case (where subtyping is checked by type emptiness) would yield a better (sub)typing algorithm.

Local type inference was first formalized, as far as we know, by Pierce and Turner [14]. They consider $(i)$ a type system with type variables, arrow, top, and bottom types, $(ii)$ an *internal language* with explicitly typed polymorphic functions that, to be applied, must be explicitly instantiated, and $(iii)$ an *external language* in which some or all such instantiations can be omitted. Then they show how to infer type instantiations for programs of the external language in order to obtain, when possible, well-typed programs of the internal language. Our work shares much of the philosophy and goals of Pierce and Turner [14]: expressions of grammar (3) form our external language, those of grammar (7) the internal one, and our sets of type-substitutions generalize Pierce and Turner's instantiations. Our work extends and generalizes Pierce and Turner's one in several ways. First, in an application we infer instantiation/type-substitutions both for the function *and* for the argument, while [14] does just the former (Typed Racket does the same). As a consequence while the application of the polymorphic identity $\lambda^{\alpha\to\alpha}x.x$ to a function $f$ of type (Int→Int)→Int can be typed in their systems (by inferring the instantiation $\{^{(\mathtt{Int}\to\mathtt{Int})\to\mathtt{Int}}/_{\alpha}\}$) the application of the same $f$ to the polymorphic identity cannot be typed (while our system types it by instantiating *the argument* by the substitution $\{^{\mathtt{Int}}/_{\alpha}\}$). Second, our system accounts for more expressive types, expressions, and subtyping relations. For instance, [14] essentially solves the tallying problem for simple constraint-sets whose form is the same as those obtained after applying our merge; instead we manipulate sets of constraint-sets (to account for alternatives generated to check either the typing of type-cases or the subtyping relation) and iterate the tallying problem with different cardinalities because of the presence of intersection types. Third, [14] synthesizes an instantiation for a type variable only if its occurrences are either all positive or all negative and fails otherwise, while our system, thanks to the use of type connectives and recursive types, always generates a set of solvable equations.

Finally, we want to stress as a caveat that works on type reconstruction for intersection type systems are weakly related to our study. The reason is that the core of our technique consists in solving type (in-)equations by *recursive types*. With recursive types pure intersection type systems *are trivially decidable* since all terms can be typed by the type $\mu X.X\to X$. The problem we tackle here, thus, is fundamentally different, namely, we check whether it is safe to apply to each other, expressions of two *explicitly given* (and possibly recursive) types in which some *basic types* may occur. There are however a few similarities with some techniques developed for pure intersection type systems that are thoroughly discussed in the extended version of this paper available on line.

## 7. Conclusion

The work presented here, together with the one in [3], provides the theoretical bases and all the algorithmic tools needed to design and implement polymorphic languages for semi-structured data and, more generally, generic functional languages with recursive types and set-theoretic unions, intersections, and negations. In particular, our results made the polymorphic extension of ℂDuce [2] possible and pave the way to the definition of a *real* type system for XQuery 3.0 [8] (not the current one in which all higher-order functions have type "function()"). Thanks to type reconstruction, these languages can have a syntax and semantics close to those of OCaml or Haskell, but also include primitives (in particular, complex patterns) that exploit the great expressive power of full-fledged set-theoretic types. Symmetrically, as the red-black trees and max examples in Section 3.3 demonstrates, OCaml and Haskell would certainly benefit from the addition of set-theoretic type connectives: we plan to study such an extension in the near future.

Some problems are still open, notably the decidability of type-substitution inference, but these are of theoretical nature and, as our experiments hitherto confirm, should not have any impact in practice. The only problem open in this second part of the work, that is the non determinism of the implicitly typed calculus, should have a negligible practical impact, insofar as it is theoretical (in practice, the semantics is deterministic but implementation dependent) and it concerns only the case when the type of (an instance of) a polymorphic function is tested at run-time: in our programming experience with ℂDuce we never met a single typecase for a function type. Nevertheless, it may be interesting to study how to remove such a latitude either by defining a canonical choice for the instances deduced by the inference system (a problem related to the existence of principal types), or by imposing reasonable restrictions, or by checking the flow of polymorphic functions by a static analysis.

On the practical side, by implementing the polymorphic extension of ℂDuce and applying it we realized that it would be useful to allow monomorphic type variables to occur in patterns (see Appendix A for examples) which in this work this would correspond to have a type case on types that may contain monomorphic type variables. How to do it is not straightforward and looks as a promising research direction. Other interesting practically-oriented directions of research are the study of heuristics to simplify types generated from constraints, so as to make type reconstruction for top-level functions human friendly; the generation of meaningful type error messages; the study of efficient implementation of constraint-solving; the extension of the bridge between OCaml and ℂDuce to include polymorphic types and, later on, the inclusion of GADTs.

***Acknowledgments.*** We want to thank the reviewers of POPL who gave detailed suggestions to improve our presentation. This work was partially supported by the ANR TYPEX project n. ANR-11-BS02-007. Zhiwu Xu was also partially supported by an Eiffel scholarship of French Ministry of Foreign Affairs and by the grant n. 61070038 of the National Natural Science Foundation of China.

## References

[1] A. Aiken and E. L. Wimmers. Type inclusion constraints and type inference. In *FPCA '93*, pages 31–41, 1993.

[2] V. Benzaken, G. Castagna, and A. Frisch. CDuce: an XML-friendly general purpose language. In *ICFP '03*. ACM Press, 2003.

[3] G. Castagna, K. Nguyễn, Z. Xu, H. Im, S. Lenglet, and L. Padovani. Polymorphic functions with set-theoretic types. Part 1: Syntax, semantics, and evaluation. In *POPL '14*, January 2014.

[4] G. Castagna and Z. Xu. Set-theoretic Foundation of Parametric Polymorphism and Subtyping. In *ICFP '11*, 2011.

[5] B. Courcelle. Fundamental properties of infinite trees. *Theoretical Computer Science*, 25:95–169, 1983.

[6] L. Damas and R. Milner. Principal type-schemes for functional programs. In *POPL '82*, pages 207–212, 1982.

[7] R. Davies. *Practical Refiniment-Type Checking*. PhD thesis, Carnegie Mellon University, 2005.

[8] J. Robie et al. XQuery 3.0: An XML query language (working draft 2010/12/14), 2010. http://www.w3.org/TR/xquery-30/.

[9] A. Frisch. *Théorie, conception et réalisation d'un langage de programmation fonctionnel adapté à XML*. PhD thesis, U. Paris 7, 2004.

[10] A. Frisch, G. Castagna, and V. Benzaken. Semantic subtyping: dealing set-theoretically with function, union, intersection, and negation types. *The Journal of ACM*, 55(4):1–64, 2008.

[11] A. Martelli and U. Montanari. An efficient unification algorithm. *ACM TOPLAS*, 4(2):258–282, 1982.

[12] M. Odersky, M. Sulzmann, and M. Wehr. Type inference with constrained types. *TAPOS*, 5(1):35–55, 1999.

[13] C. Okasaki. *Purely Functional Data Structures*. CUP, 1998.

[14] B.C. Pierce and D.N. Turner. Local type inference. *ACM Trans. Program. Lang. Syst.*, 22(1):1–44, 2000.

[15] F. Pottier and D. Rémy. The essence of ML type inference. In B.C. Pierce, editor, *Advanced Topics in Types and Programming Languages*, chapter 10, pages 389–489. MIT Press, 2005.

[16] S. Tobin-Hochstadt and M. Felleisen. The design and implementation of typed scheme. In *POPL '08*, 2008.

[17] S. Tobin-Hochstadt and M. Felleisen. Logical types for untyped languages. In *ICFP '10*, 2010.

[18] Z. Xu. *Parametric Polymorphism for XML Processing Languages*. PhD thesis, Université Paris Diderot, 2013. Available at http://tel.archives-ouvertes.fr/tel-00858744.

# Principal Type Schemes for Gradual Programs

Ronald Garcia *
Software Practices Lab
Department of Computer Science
University of British Columbia
rxg@cs.ubc.ca

Matteo Cimini †
Indiana University
mcimini@indiana.edu

## Abstract

Gradual typing is a discipline for integrating dynamic checking into a static type system. Since its introduction in functional languages, it has been adapted to a variety of type systems, including object-oriented, security, and substructural. This work studies its application to implicitly typed languages based on type inference. Siek and Vachharajani designed a gradual type inference system and algorithm that infers gradual types but still rejects ill-typed static programs. However, the type system requires local reasoning about type substitutions, an imperative inference algorithm, and a subtle correctness statement.

This paper introduces a new approach to gradual type inference, driven by the principle that gradual inference should only produce static types. We present a static implicitly typed language, its gradual counterpart, and a type inference procedure. The gradual system types the same programs as Siek and Vachharajani, but has a modular structure amenable to extension. The language admits let-polymorphism, and its dynamics are defined by translation to the Polymorphic Blame Calculus (Ahmed et al. 2009, 2011).

The principal types produced by our initial type system mask the distinction between static parametric polymorphism and polymorphism that can be attributed to gradual typing. To expose this difference, we distinguish static type parameters from gradual type parameters and reinterpret gradual type consistency accordingly. The resulting extension enables programs to be interpreted using either the polymorphic or monomorphic Blame Calculi.

## 1. Introduction

Interest in integrating static and dynamic checking is increasing among language researchers and industrial language designers. (e.g. (Bierman et al. 2010; Gronski et al. 2006; Swamy et al. 2014; Tobin-Hochstadt and Felleisen 2008; Wrigstad et al. 2010)) Among the proposed foundations for such languages, *gradual typing*, due to Siek and Taha (2006) has been used to integrate dynamic checks into a variety of type structures, including object-oriented (Siek and Taha 2007), substructural (Wolff et al. 2011), and ownership types (Sergey and Clarke 2012). The key technical pillars of gradual typing are the unknown type, ?, the *consistency* relation among gradual types, and support for the entire spectrum between purely dynamic and purely static checking. A gradual type checker rejects type inconsistencies in programs, accepts statically safe code, and instruments code that could plausibly be safe with runtime checks.

This paper applies the gradual typing approach to implicitly typed languages, like Standard ML, OCaml, and Haskell, where a type inference (a.k.a. type reconstruction) procedure is integral to type checking. This problem was investigated first by Siek and Vachharajani (2008), defining $\lambda^{?\alpha}_{\rightarrow}$, a gradual type inference system and algorithm that infers gradual types, but rejects ill-typed static programs.[1] This groundbreaking paper outlines principles that a gradual implicitly typed language should satisfy, demonstrates how several plausible approaches fail, and ultimately produces a compelling type system and type inference algorithm. Though the results satisfy the criteria for gradual typing, the type system requires special care in its handling of type variables, subtle statements and proofs of correctness, and a special-purpose imperative inference algorithm. These complexities make it unclear how to adopt, adapt, and extend this approach with modern features of implicitly typed languages, like let-polymorphism, row-polymorphism, and first-class polymorphism. Furthermore, extending an existing implicitly typed language implementation with support for gradual typing would require a rewrite or substantial overhaul of the type inferencer.

To support the extension of implicitly typed languages with support for gradual typing, this paper introduces a new foundation for gradual implicit typing. In particular, we make the following contributions:

1. We introduce a specification of static implicit typing that emphasizes the input-output modes of the type system. In particular the types of subterms are viewed as opaque, and we rely on partial functions to structure the system. This structure leads to a natural conception of gradual implicit typing that is easy to reason about and extend. The key insight underlying the design is to only allow fully static types to be implicit: gradual types, in our approach, must originate in the program text.
2. Siek and Vachharajani's type system is based explicitly on inferring gradual types and emphasizing type precision, a substantially different conceptual foundation. Nonetheless, we prove that the two foundations coincide: both type systems accept exactly the same programs.

* Partially funded by an NSERC discovery grant.
† Partially funded by NSF grant 1360694.


*POPL '15*, January 15–17, 2015, Mumbai, India.
Copyright is held by the owner/author(s). Publication rights licensed to ACM.
ACM 978-1-4503-3300-9/15/01... $15.00.
http://dx.doi.org/10.1145/2676726.2676992

[1] Rastogi et al. (2012) also combine gradual typing and type inference, but focus on improving performance rather than detecting inconsistencies (Sec. 13).

3. We define a corresponding constraint typing judgment and constraint solver. Central to its design is that we choose to limit the type inference problem to deducing only static types. In addition to the standard equality constraints between static types, we require consistency constraints between gradual types; our solver naturally extends unification to support them.
4. To confirm the extensibility of the type system, we extend it with support for let-polymorphism, using the standard approach off the shelf. We give the language dynamics by translating it to the Polymorphic Blame Calculus (Ahmed et al. 2009, 2011). The translation mirrors the analogous translation of Hindley/Milner typing to System F, suggesting that recent approaches to first-class polymorphism may also apply.
5. We observe that the principal types of the initial system mask the distinction between static parametric polymorphism and polymorphism due to gradual typing. To expose this difference, we distinguish static type parameters from gradual type parameters and reinterpret gradual type consistency accordingly. The resulting language can be interpreted using either a monomorphic or polymorphic intermediate language.

## 2. Implicit Typing and Type Inference

This section briefly introduces the Implicitly Typed Static Language (ITSL). Its main purpose is to introduce the core type system that we extend with gradual typing, as well as to briefly review the principles of implicit typing. We highlight some particular details of our presentation that are important to the overall approach.

$$A \in \text{TPARAM}, \quad T \in \text{TYPE}, \quad x \in \text{VAR}, \quad b \in \text{BOOL}, \quad n \in \mathbb{Z}, \quad t \in \text{TERM}, \quad v \in \text{VALUE} \quad \Gamma \in \text{VAR} \rightharpoonup \text{TYPE}$$

$$\begin{array}{rcll} T & ::= & A \mid \mathsf{Int} \mid \mathsf{Bool} \mid T \to T & \text{(types)} \\ t & ::= & n \mid t + t \mid b \mid \mathsf{if}\ t\ \mathsf{then}\ t\ \mathsf{else}\ t & \text{(terms)} \\ & \mid & x \mid \lambda x.t \mid \lambda x : T.t \mid t\ t \mid t :: T & \\ v & ::= & n \mid b \mid x \mid \lambda x.t \mid \lambda x : T.t & \text{(syntactic values)} \end{array}$$

**Figure 1.** Static Language (ITSL): Syntax

Fig. 1 presents the syntax for ITSL. By *implicit typing* we mean that the language is statically typed, but programmers may omit type annotations. In particular, this language provides function expressions $\lambda x.t$ that require no type annotation on their parameter, in contrast to the annotated form $\lambda x : T.t$, which it also supports. As a convenience, the language also provides type ascriptions $t :: T$, which could already be simulated as $((\lambda x : T.x)\ t)$.

The implications of these language features become clearer in the type system specification, presented in Fig. 2. The (T$\lambda$:) rule uses the type annotation on a function parameter to type its body. The (T$\lambda$) rule, on the other hand, types a function's body with any parameter type that works. The broader impact of this is that a function like $\lambda x : \mathsf{Int}.x$ has only one legal type, $\mathsf{Int} \to \mathsf{Int}$, but a function like $\lambda x.x$ can be given many types, specifically any type of the form $T \to T$. This flexibility reduces the annotation overhead for programmers while retaining static safety, and increases the expressiveness of the language if a polymorphic let construct is added (see Sec. 10).

***Presentation Style*** There are some notable differences between the presentation in Fig. 2 and the typical textbook presentation (c.f. (Pierce 2002)). They do not affect the meaning of this type system definition, but they play an important structuring role that we exploit when we extend it to support gradual typing.

The type system definition pays particular attention to the *mode* of the typing judgment, in the sense of logic programming (Debray and Warren 1988). In particular, the type context and term are interpreted as *inputs* to the typing judgment, while the term's type is

$$\text{(Tx)}\frac{x : T \in \Gamma}{\Gamma \vdash x : T} \qquad \text{(Tn)}\frac{}{\Gamma \vdash n : \mathsf{Int}} \qquad \text{(Tb)}\frac{}{\Gamma \vdash b : \mathsf{Bool}}$$

$$\text{(Tapp)}\frac{\Gamma \vdash t_1 : T_1 \quad \Gamma \vdash t_2 : T_2 \quad dom(T_1) = T_2}{\Gamma \vdash t_1\ t_2 : cod(T_1)}$$

$$\text{(Tif)}\frac{\Gamma \vdash t_1 : T_1 \quad \Gamma \vdash t_2 : T_2 \quad \Gamma \vdash t_3 : T_3 \quad T_1 = \mathsf{Bool}}{\Gamma \vdash \mathsf{if}\ t_1\ \mathsf{then}\ t_2\ \mathsf{else}\ t_3 : cmb(T_2, T_3)}$$

$$\text{(T+)}\frac{\Gamma \vdash t_1 : T_1 \quad \Gamma \vdash t_2 : T_2 \quad T_1 = \mathsf{Int} \quad T_2 = \mathsf{Int}}{\Gamma \vdash t_1 + t_2 : \mathsf{Int}}$$

$$\text{(T}\lambda\text{)}\frac{\Gamma, x : T_1 \vdash t : T_2}{\Gamma \vdash (\lambda x.t) : T_1 \to T_2}$$

$$\text{(T}\lambda\text{:)}\frac{\Gamma, x : T_1 \vdash t : T_2}{\Gamma \vdash (\lambda x : T_1.t) : T_1 \to T_2} \qquad \text{(T::)}\frac{\Gamma \vdash t : T \quad T = T_1}{\Gamma \vdash (t :: T_1) : T_1}$$

$$\begin{array}{ll} dom : \text{TYPE} \rightharpoonup \text{TYPE} & cod : \text{TYPE} \rightharpoonup \text{TYPE} \\ dom(T_1 \to T_2) = T_1 & cod(T_1 \to T_2) = T_2 \\ dom(T) \text{ undefined otherwise} & cod(T) \text{ undefined otherwise} \end{array}$$

$$\begin{array}{l} cmb : \text{TYPE} \times \text{TYPE} \rightharpoonup \text{TYPE} \\ cmb(T, T) = T \\ cmb(T_1, T_2) \text{ undefined otherwise} \end{array}$$

**Figure 2.** Static Language (ITSL): Type System

viewed as an *output*. The impact of this interpretation on the structure of the definition is as follows, and can be seen in the (Tapp) rule. Though the structure of the terms $t$ in the conclusions of rules are analyzed using pattern-matching-style syntax, the type position of each typing judgment in the premise is stated abstractly as *some* type $T$. For instance, the type rule for application usually has a premise $\Gamma \vdash t_1 : T_{11} \to T_{12}$, but in contrast the (Tapp) rule only assumes that the result is a type $T_1$. In lieu of pattern matching on a function type, the rules appeal to *partial* functions that are defined only for types with the proper shape. These partial functions name the result type of a term (e.g., $cod(T_1)$) and assert properties that must hold between interacting types (e.g., $dom(T_1) = T_2$).[2]

Our partial functions are partly responsible for imposing requirements on types. For instance, reference to $dom(T_1)$ in a rule implies that $T_1 = T_{11} \to T_{12}$ for some $T_{11}, T_{12}$, so this requirement does not need to be explicitly stated in the rule. If $dom(T_1)$ is undefined, then the (Tapp) rule does not apply. Using partial functions to abstract away type requirements is critical to our subsequent development of gradual typing.

A particularly interesting example of this phenomenon arises in the (Tif) rule. The requirement that $T_1$ must be $\mathsf{Bool}$ is standard, but the result type of the term is a partial function $cmb(T_2, T_3)$, that is defined only when the two types are equal, in which case it is the type itself. Typically, this rule is expressed by using pattern matching on the results of typing $t_2$ and $t_3$ to force them into the same type, and then providing that type as the final result. Instead, we keep the result types abstract and appeal to a partial function to "combine" them.

In summary, we use predicates only to express relationships between types that do not imply some result type. For all cases where we need to determine a type in terms of subterm types, we defer to a partial function.

[2] In propositions that refer to partial functions, we interpret = as Kleene equality: both sides of the equation must either be defined and equal, or undefined.

### 2.1 Type Polymorphism

As we mentioned earlier, a function like $\lambda x.x$ can be given the types $\mathsf{Int} \to \mathsf{Int}$, $\mathsf{Bool} \to \mathsf{Bool}$, and any other type of the form $T \to T$. We would like to express this polymorphism somehow, but our language does not support first-class polymorphism: each type is concrete. For this purpose we endow the language with a set of *type parameters* $A$, which are uninterpreted types in the sense that the type system gives them no special treatment. As a consequence any situation where a type parameter $A$ is used, any other particular type could appear. Let us formalize this observation.

**Definition 1.** *Let* $S^A \in \text{ASUBST} = \text{TPARAM} \to \text{TYPE}$ *denote type parameter substitutions, or* $A$-substitutions.

**Notation.** *If* $S$ *is some sort of substitution function, then we use* $\widehat{S}(T)$, $\widehat{S}(\Gamma)$, *and* $\widehat{S}(t)$ *to denote the compatible closure of substitution over types, type contexts, and terms, respectively.*

The $A$-substitutions give meaning to type parameters. With this we can treat them as representatives for type polymorphism.

**Proposition 1.** *If* $\Gamma \vdash t : T$ *then* $\widehat{S^A}(\Gamma) \vdash \widehat{S^A}(t) : \widehat{S^A}(T)$ *for any* $S^A \in \text{ASUBST}$.

*Proof.* Straightforward induction on derivations of $\Gamma \vdash t : T$. □

Prop. 1 shows us that a type with parameters can be made more specific arbitrarily. Regarding the dual consideration, we can ask about the presence of a *most general* type for a program.

**Definition 2** (Principal Type). *If* $\Gamma \vdash t : T$, *then we say that* $T$ *is a* principal type *of* $\Gamma$ *and* $t$ *if whenever* $\Gamma \vdash t : T_0$ *holds, then* $T_0 = \widehat{S^A}(T)$ *for some* $A$*-substitution* $S^A$.

Principal types succinctly summarize all possible types of a program. This particular language has principal types for every typeable program. We establish this once and for all in the gradually typed setting.

### 2.2 Type Inference

While this type system specification has great appeal, the question arises as to whether it can be effectively type checked. Indeed it can, and a broad array of literature has discussed approaches to doing so. We desire even more flexibility than the language provides as-is. To do so, we generalize the problem beyond purely elided type annotations.

To check implicit types, we must deduce types that are not present in the program text. To represent this problem in a broader context, we introduce notions of *type variables* and *type expressions*:

$$X \in \text{TVAR}, \quad T^{\mathsf{X}} \in \text{TYPEEXP}$$
$$T^{\mathsf{X}} ::= X \mid A \mid \mathsf{Int} \mid \mathsf{Bool} \mid T^{\mathsf{X}} \to T^{\mathsf{X}}$$

A type variable is a placeholder for one or more possible types, directly analogous to variables in secondary school algebra. Then a type expression $T^{\mathsf{X}}$ is just a type where some of its substructure has been filled with type variables. This idea extends to term expressions $t^{\mathsf{X}} \in \text{TERMEXP}$ and *type expression contexts* $\Gamma^{\mathsf{X}} \in \text{VAR} \rightharpoonup \text{TYPEEXP}$. We write $\text{Vars}(T^{\mathsf{X}})$ for the set of type variables in $T^{\mathsf{X}}$. The function Vars extends to terms and type contexts in the expected way, and in the remainder of the paper we simply write $\text{Vars}(o_1, o_2, \dots, o_n)$ for $\text{Vars}(o_1) \cup \text{Vars}(o_2) \dots \cup \text{Vars}(o_n)$, for some $n \geq 0$ and where $o_i$ can be a type, a term or a type context, for $0 \leq i \leq n$.

Note that type variables and type parameters are distinct concepts. Type parameters actually *are* types, while type variables are merely placeholders, just as variables in algebra are not numbers. However, all types count as type expressions too (i.e. $\text{TYPE} \subset \text{TYPEEXP}$); the analogous status also holds for term expressions

$$(\text{Var})\frac{x : U \in \Gamma}{\Gamma \vdash x : U} \qquad (\text{Abs})\frac{\Gamma, x : U_1 \vdash t : U_2}{\Gamma \vdash (\lambda x : U_1 . t) : U_1 \to U_2}$$

$$(\text{AppU})\frac{\Gamma \vdash t_1 : U_{11} \to U_{12} \qquad \Gamma \vdash t_2 : U_1 \qquad U_{11} \sim U_1}{\Gamma \vdash t_1\ t_2 : U_{12}}$$

$$(\text{App?})\frac{\Gamma \vdash t_1 : ? \qquad \Gamma \vdash t_2 : U_2}{\Gamma \vdash t_1\ t_2 : ?}$$

**Figure 3.** $\lambda^{?}_{\to}$: Simply Typed Gradual Calculus

and type expression contexts.[3] We give all of these expression forms meaning by substituting types for type variables.

**Definition 3.** *Let* $S^{\mathsf{X}} \in \text{XSUBST} = \text{TVAR} \to \text{TYPE}$ *type variable substitutions, or* $X$*-substitutions.*

Observe that these substitutions produce real types, terms, and type contexts in accordance with the source language.

**Definition 4.** *Let* $S_1^{\mathsf{X}}$ *and* $S_2^{\mathsf{X}}$ *be two type variable substitutions and let* $\mathcal{X} \subseteq \text{TVAR}$. *We say that* $S_2^{\mathsf{X}}$ agrees with $S_1^{\mathsf{X}}$ over $\mathcal{X}$ *whenever for all variables* $X \in \mathcal{X}$, *it holds that* $S_1^{\mathsf{X}}(X) = S_2^{\mathsf{X}}(X)$.

In algebra, we use variables to write down equation expressions, which are problems that may have solutions. By analogy, we use our expressions to formalize the *type inference problem* and to characterize its solutions.

**Definition 5** (Type Inference Problem). *Given a type expression context* $\Gamma^{\mathsf{X}}$ *and a term expression* $t^{\mathsf{X}}$, *the* type inference problem *for ITSL asks if* $\widehat{S^{\mathsf{X}}}(\Gamma^{\mathsf{X}}) \vdash \widehat{S^{\mathsf{X}}}(t^{\mathsf{X}}) : T$ *for some* $X$*-substitution* $S^{\mathsf{X}}$ *and type* $T$.

Only the context and term are expressions here.

A type inferencer, then, is a decision procedure for the type inference problem. We do not present a type inference algorithm for this static language. However, such an algorithm can be extracted directly from the gradual type inferencer we present below.

## 3. Introduction to Gradual Typing

Gradual typing is a type discipline, introduced by Siek and Taha, to extend an existing type system with seamless support for static and dynamic checks. Such a language supports both extremes of checking, fully static and fully dynamic, as well as any point in between. The gradual type system uses available type information to detect inconsistencies between types. Typing conditions that cannot be determined statically are checked at runtime using casts.

To achieve these goals, gradual typing extends an existing type system with an *unknown type* ?. For example, the corresponding gradual types for the language from the last section are as follows:

$$U \in \text{GTYPE}$$
$$U ::= ? \mid A \mid \mathsf{Int} \mid \mathsf{Bool} \mid U \to U \quad \text{(gradual types)}$$

Based on this definition, every static type is also a gradual type.

Fig. 3 presents the type system for $\lambda^{?}_{\to}$, the simply typed gradual calculus (Siek and Taha 2006). The rules for variables and functions are standard, but the rules for function application are not. The (App?) rule applies when the operator has the unknown type. Since the result could plausibly be a function, the program type checks, and the result type of the application is unknown in turn.

The (AppU) rule applies when the operator has some function type. Unlike static typing, the rule does not require that the operand have the same type as the domain of the operator, but simply that two types be *consistent*, written $U \sim U$. We define consistency as

[3] Some presentations of type inference use a single entity for both concepts. We distinguish them for clarity and to support our development in Sec. 12.

follows.

$$\frac{}{\mathsf{Int} \sim \mathsf{Int}} \qquad \frac{}{\mathsf{Bool} \sim \mathsf{Bool}} \qquad \frac{}{A \sim A} \qquad \frac{}{? \sim U}$$

$$\frac{}{U \sim ?} \qquad \frac{U_{11} \sim U_{21} \quad U_{12} \sim U_{22}}{U_{11} \to U_{12} \sim U_{21} \to U_{22}}$$

The intuition behind this definition is that two consistent gradual types need only agree on their statically known parts. Consistency is one of the key innovations of the gradual typing approach.

The type system must be a conservative extension of the underlying type system. This means that programs without any dynamism must type according to the underlying static type system. Since consistency reduces to equality in the absence of ?, it follows that the type system conservatively extends its pre-existing simply typed counterpart. A programmer, development environment, or syntactically-sugared source language then introduces dynamism by ascribing ? to program subterms (see Sec. 6).

In addition to consistency, gradual types impose a notion of *type precision* as a partial order $\sqsubseteq$, which indicates that one type is less unknown than another.

$$\frac{}{U \sqsubseteq ?} \qquad \frac{}{U \sqsubseteq U} \qquad \frac{U_{11} \sqsubseteq U_{21} \quad U_{12} \sqsubseteq U_{22}}{U_{11} \to U_{12} \sqsubseteq U_{21} \to U_{22}}$$

This relation coincides with the "naïve subtyping" relation of (Wadler and Findler 2009).[4]

To support gradual typing, programs are instrumented with type-directed runtime checks that ensure that consistency checks that cannot be fully resolved at type-checking time are dynamically verified.

In short, a gradual type system takes an optimistic approach to checking that two types are compatible, only statically rejecting combinations that exhibit inconsistencies, and dynamically verifying any remaining checks.

## 4. A Gradual Implicitly Typed Language

This section presents our conception of gradual typing for an implicitly typed language. The ideas from the last two sections combine to yield a design that differs from $\lambda^{?\alpha}_{\to}$ in its foundations, but is ultimately equivalent.

Fig. 4 presents the syntax of the Implicitly Typed Gradual Language (ITGL). As with standard practice, the singular difference is lifting of static types $T$ to gradual types $U$. Every static type annotation can now be replaced with a gradual type annotation.

$$A \in \textsc{TParam}, \quad T \in \textsc{Type}, \quad U \in \textsc{GType}, \quad x \in \textsc{Var},$$
$$b \in \textsc{Bool}, \quad n \in \mathbb{Z}, \quad t \in \textsc{Term}, \quad v \in \textsc{Value}$$

$$\begin{array}{rcll} T & ::= & A \mid \mathsf{Int} \mid \mathsf{Bool} \mid T \to T & \text{(static types)} \\ U & ::= & ? \mid A \mid \mathsf{Int} \mid \mathsf{Bool} \mid U \to U & \text{(gradual types)} \\ t & ::= & n \mid t + t \mid b \mid \mathsf{if}\ t\ \mathsf{then}\ t\ \mathsf{else}\ t & \text{(terms)} \\ & \mid & x \mid \lambda x.t \mid \lambda x : U.t \mid t\ t \mid t :: U & \\ v & ::= & n \mid b \mid x \mid \lambda x.t \mid \lambda x : U.t & \text{(syntactic values)} \end{array}$$

**Figure 4.** Gradual Language (ITGL): Syntax

$$(\text{Ux})\frac{x : U \in \Gamma}{\Gamma \vdash x : U} \qquad (\text{Un})\frac{}{\Gamma \vdash n : \mathsf{Int}} \qquad (\text{Ub})\frac{}{\Gamma \vdash b : \mathsf{Bool}}$$

$$(\text{Uapp})\frac{\Gamma \vdash t_1 : U_1 \quad \Gamma \vdash t_2 : U_2 \quad \widetilde{dom}(U_1) \sim U_2}{\Gamma \vdash t_1\ t_2 : \widetilde{cod}(U_1)}$$

$$(\text{Uif})\frac{\Gamma \vdash t_1 : U_1 \quad \Gamma \vdash t_2 : U_2 \quad \Gamma \vdash t_3 : U_3 \quad U_1 \sim \mathsf{Bool}}{\Gamma \vdash \mathsf{if}\ t_1\ \mathsf{then}\ t_2\ \mathsf{else}\ t_3 : U_2 \sqcap U_3}$$

$$(\text{U+})\frac{\Gamma \vdash t_1 : U_1 \quad \Gamma \vdash t_2 : U_2 \quad U_1 \sim \mathsf{Int} \quad U_2 \sim \mathsf{Int}}{\Gamma \vdash t_1 + t_2 : \mathsf{Int}}$$

$$(\text{U}\lambda)\frac{\Gamma, x : T_1 \vdash t : U_2}{\Gamma \vdash (\lambda x.t) : T_1 \to U_2}$$

$$(\text{U}\lambda:)\frac{\Gamma, x : U_1 \vdash t : U_2}{\Gamma \vdash (\lambda x : U_1.t) : U_1 \to U_2} \qquad (\text{U::})\frac{\Gamma \vdash t : U \quad U \sim U_1}{\Gamma \vdash (t :: U_1) : U_1}$$

$$\begin{array}{ll} \widetilde{dom} : \textsc{GType} \rightharpoonup \textsc{GType} & \widetilde{cod} : \textsc{GType} \rightharpoonup \textsc{GType} \\ \widetilde{dom}(U_1 \to U_2) = U_1 & \widetilde{cod}(U_1 \to U_2) = U_2 \\ \widetilde{dom}(?) = ? & \widetilde{cod}(?) = ? \\ \widetilde{dom}(U) \text{ undefined otherwise} & \widetilde{cod}(U) \text{ undefined otherwise} \end{array}$$

$$\begin{array}{l} \sqcap : \textsc{GType} \times \textsc{GType} \rightharpoonup \textsc{GType} \\ T \sqcap T = T \\ ? \sqcap U = U \sqcap ? = U \\ (U_{11} \to U_{12}) \sqcap (U_{21} \to U_{22}) = (U_{11} \sqcap U_{21}) \to (U_{12} \sqcap U_{22}) \\ U_1 \sqcap U_2 \text{ undefined} \quad \text{otherwise} \end{array}$$

**Figure 5.** Gradual Language (ITGL): Type System

The type system, presented in Fig. 5 builds on the ITSL type system from Sec. 2. Most of the rules have the same structure, except their static types have been lifted to gradual types, and the predicates and partial functions on static types have been lifted to consistent predicates and partial functions on gradual types. A straightforward example of this is the (U+) rule, which replaces type equality with type consistency, and static types with gradual types.

If we compare this type system to $\lambda^{?}_{\to}$, we notice that the former has one rule for function application, (Uapp), while the latter has two, (AppU) and (App?). In this case, the $\widetilde{dom}$ partial function provides the necessary abstraction to combine the two rules into one. The $\widetilde{dom}$ function is defined with two cases: folding them into the (Uapp) rule, along with $\widetilde{cod}$ would recover the two rules of $\lambda^{?}_{\to}$.

Consider the (Uif) rule. Most of the structure is as expected, but its result type is $U_2 \sqcap U_3$, the greatest lower bound (or *meet*) of $U_2$ and $U_3$ according to the precision relation. In fact, the meet is the gradual partial function that corresponds to *cmb*. To see how, consider the two gradual types $? \to \mathsf{Int}$ and $\mathsf{Bool} \to ?$. The only hope for some $U$ to be a well-defined result of combining them is for $U$ to be $\mathsf{Bool} \to \mathsf{Int}$. Naturally, one can always coerce two inconsistent branches to type-check using type ascriptions.

***Implicit types must be static types*** The (U$\lambda$) rule embodies implicit typing in ITGL. The corresponding ITSL rule types the body of the function using some arbitrary type, and the gradual type system does the same. To understand why the arbitrary type is static rather than gradual, consider the program $\lambda x.x\ x$. This program has no unknown type annotations, so it is in the language of the ITSL type system, which cannot type it. As such, the gradual type system must reject it as well. If the gradual type system could arbitrarily type $x$ as ?, however, then this function would type check, even though the programmer introduced no ? annotations. The key insight is that dynamicity is introduced only via program annotations. The type system itself must never introduce ? of its own accord. As we see next, this insight has broader implications.

### 4.1 Gradual Inference of Static Types

As with ITSL, we generalize type inference, taking into account the insight that our type system need only infer static types. To state the gradual type inference problem, we introduce corresponding type expressions, term expressions, and type context expressions. For

[4] We avoid calling it "subtyping" because it does not characterize substitutability.

brevity, we present only the gradual type expressions.

$$U^{\mathsf{X}} \in \text{GTYPEEXP}$$
$$U^{\mathsf{X}} ::= ? \mid X \mid A \mid \mathsf{Int} \mid \mathsf{Bool} \mid U^{\mathsf{X}} \to U^{\mathsf{X}}$$

Gradual type expressions $U^{\mathsf{X}}$ now include ?, since we are in a gradually-typed language. However, we do not update the definition of $X$-substitutions: type variables map to static types. This property generalizes the reasoning underlying the (U$\lambda$) rule: we only allow gradual types to be explicitly introduced in a program as a means to ensure that the type system cannot introduce dynamism without prompt and thereby compromise inconsistency checking.

**Definition 6** (Gradual Type Inference Problem). *Given a gradual type expression context* $\Gamma^{X}$ *and a term expression* $t^{X}$, *the* gradual type inference problem *asks if there is an* $X$*-substitution* $S^{X}$ *and gradual type* $U$ *such that* $\widehat{S^{x}}(\Gamma^{X}) \vdash \widehat{S^{x}}(t^{X}) : U$.

In contrast, $\lambda^{?\alpha}_{\to}$ (Siek and Vachharajani 2008) infers gradual types, albeit with restrictions. In the next section, we reconcile this difference.

## 5. $\lambda^{?\alpha}_{\to}$ types the same programs

Siek and Vachharajani (2008) analyze the concept of gradual type inference and design a language $\lambda^{?\alpha}_{\to}$ that formalizes and substantiates their approach. The $\lambda^{?\alpha}_{\to}$ language and types correspond to our gradual type expressions, but the type theoretic foundations differ substantially. In particular, $\lambda^{?\alpha}_{\to}$ is based on inferring *gradual* types, not just static types, but in a controlled manner. To formalize this, we introduce a new notion of substitutions.

$$S^{G} \in \text{GSUBST} = \text{TVAR} \to \text{GTYPE}$$
$$\mathcal{X} \in \mathcal{P}(\text{TVAR})$$

The $\lambda^{?\alpha}_{\to}$ type system is presented in Fig. 6.[5] It is based on the judgment $S^{G}; \Gamma^{\mathsf{X}} \vdash t^{\mathsf{X}} : U^{\mathsf{X}} \mid \mathcal{X}$, which intuitively means that $S^{G}$ and $\widehat{S^{G}}(U^{\mathsf{X}})$ solve a constrained variant of the type inference problem $\Gamma^{\mathsf{X}}$ and $t^{\mathsf{X}}$ for $\lambda^{?}_{\to}$ (Sec. 3), where extra variables $\mathcal{X}$ and their mappings are involved in the typing process. More precisely it means that in $\lambda^{?}_{\to}$, $\widehat{S^{G}}(\Gamma^{\mathsf{X}}) \vdash \widehat{S^{G}}(t^{\mathsf{X}}) : \widehat{S^{G}}(U^{\mathsf{X}})$ *and moreover* every type variable $X$ used to type $t^{\mathsf{X}}$ (i.e. present in $t^{\mathsf{X}}$ or $\mathcal{X}$) must map to some $S^{G}(X)$ such that $S^{G}(X) \sqsubseteq U$ for every gradual type $U$ that it is consistent with according to the typing derivation. The first criteria is essentially the standard type inference problem, but with gradual types in the substitution; the second criteria is their approach to preventing the type system from introducing unplanned dynamism. Every type variable's mapping is constrained by the static types it interacts with, but types that originate in the program text are unconstrained.

**Notation.** *We write* $\perp\left(\prod_{i<n} \mathcal{X}_i\right)$ *to mean that the given variable sets are mutually disjoint, i.e.,* $\forall i < n. \forall j < n. i \neq j \Rightarrow \mathcal{X}_i \cap \mathcal{X}_j = \emptyset$.

Most of the typing rules are standard in structure. The (Gapp) rule for function application is the most interesting. Where $\lambda^{?}_{\to}$ imposes a consistency relation between the type of the operand and the operator, this type system appeals to a judgment $S^{G} \models U^{\mathsf{X}}_1 \simeq U^{\mathsf{X}}_2$, which means that $\widehat{S^{G}}(U^{\mathsf{X}}_1) \sim \widehat{S^{G}}(U^{\mathsf{X}}_2)$ and moreover that $S^{G}$ respects the aforementioned lower-bound criteria for all variables in $U^{\mathsf{X}}_1$ and $U^{\mathsf{X}}_2$. The judgment decomposes type expressions to check for consistency. Upon reaching a type variable, it appeals to the judgment $S^{G} \models U \sqsubseteq U^{\mathsf{X}}_2$, which means that $U \sqsubseteq \widehat{S^{G}}(U^{\mathsf{X}}_2)$. The key rule of this judgment is the variable case. If $U \sqsubseteq S^{G}(X)$, then the converse—which is our global criterion—holds only if the two types are equal.

[5] The presentation has been adjusted to match this paper.

$$\boxed{S^{G}; \Gamma^{\mathsf{X}} \vdash t^{\mathsf{X}} : U^{\mathsf{X}} \mid \mathcal{X}} \quad \perp(\mathcal{X}, \text{Vars}(t^{\mathsf{X}}))$$

$$(\text{Gx})\frac{x : U^{\mathsf{X}} \in \Gamma^{\mathsf{X}}}{S^{G}; \Gamma^{\mathsf{X}} \vdash x : U^{\mathsf{X}} \mid \emptyset} \qquad (\text{Gn})\frac{}{S^{G}; \Gamma^{\mathsf{X}} \vdash n : \mathsf{Int} \mid \emptyset}$$

$$(\text{Gb})\frac{}{S^{G}; \Gamma^{\mathsf{X}} \vdash b : \mathsf{Bool} \mid \emptyset}$$

$$(\text{Gapp})\frac{\begin{array}{cc} S^{G}; \Gamma^{\mathsf{X}} \vdash t_1 : U^{\mathsf{X}}_1 \mid \mathcal{X}_1 & S^{G}; \Gamma^{\mathsf{X}} \vdash t_2 : U^{\mathsf{X}}_2 \mid \mathcal{X}_2 \\ S^{G} \models U^{\mathsf{X}}_1 \simeq U^{\mathsf{X}}_2 \to X & \perp(\{X\}, \mathcal{X}_1, \mathcal{X}_2) \end{array}}{S^{G}; \Gamma^{\mathsf{X}} \vdash t_1\ t_2 : X \mid \{X\} \cup \mathcal{X}_1 \cup \mathcal{X}_2}$$

$$(\text{G}\lambda{:})\frac{S^{G}; \Gamma^{\mathsf{X}}, x : U^{\mathsf{X}}_1 \vdash t : U^{\mathsf{X}}_2 \mid \mathcal{X}}{S^{G}; \Gamma^{\mathsf{X}} \vdash (\lambda x : U^{\mathsf{X}}_1 . t) : U^{\mathsf{X}}_1 \to U^{\mathsf{X}}_2 \mid \mathcal{X}}$$

$$\boxed{S^{G} \models U^{\mathsf{X}} \simeq U^{\mathsf{X}}}$$

$$\frac{}{S^{G} \models \mathsf{Bool} \simeq \mathsf{Bool}} \qquad \frac{}{S^{G} \models \mathsf{Int} \simeq \mathsf{Int}}$$

$$\frac{}{S^{G} \models A \simeq A} \qquad \frac{}{S^{G} \models U^{\mathsf{X}} \simeq ?} \qquad \frac{}{S^{G} \models ? \simeq U^{\mathsf{X}}}$$

$$\frac{S^{G} \models U^{\mathsf{X}}_{11} \simeq U^{\mathsf{X}}_{21} \qquad S^{G} \models U^{\mathsf{X}}_{12} \simeq U^{\mathsf{X}}_{22}}{S^{G} \models U^{\mathsf{X}}_{11} \to U^{\mathsf{X}}_{12} \simeq U^{\mathsf{X}}_{21} \to U^{\mathsf{X}}_{22}}$$

$$\frac{S^{G} \models \widehat{S^{G}}(X) \sqsubseteq U^{\mathsf{X}}_2}{S^{G} \models X \simeq U^{\mathsf{X}}_2} \qquad \frac{S^{G} \models \widehat{S^{G}}(X) \sqsubseteq U^{\mathsf{X}}_1}{S^{G} \models U^{\mathsf{X}}_1 \simeq X}$$

$$\boxed{S^{G} \models U \sqsubseteq U^{\mathsf{X}}}$$

$$\frac{\widehat{S^{G}}(X) = U}{S^{G} \models U \sqsubseteq X} \qquad \frac{}{S^{G} \models \mathsf{Bool} \sqsubseteq \mathsf{Bool}} \qquad \frac{}{S^{G} \models \mathsf{Int} \sqsubseteq \mathsf{Int}}$$

$$\frac{}{S^{G} \models A \sqsubseteq A} \qquad \frac{}{S^{G} \models U \sqsubseteq ?}$$

$$\frac{S^{G} \models U^{\mathsf{X}}_{11} \sqsubseteq U^{\mathsf{X}}_{21} \qquad S^{G} \models U^{\mathsf{X}}_{12} \sqsubseteq U^{\mathsf{X}}_{22}}{S^{G} \models U^{\mathsf{X}}_{11} \to U^{\mathsf{X}}_{12} \sqsubseteq U^{\mathsf{X}}_{21} \to U^{\mathsf{X}}_{22}}$$

**Figure 6.** $\lambda^{?\alpha}_{\to}$: Type System

This type system satisfies the goals of gradual type inference, but its structure is unorthodox. A substitution is incorporated explicitly into the judgment, instead of simply appearing in the statement of the type inference problem. This non-modular structure leaks into the corresponding constraint typing relation and constraint-solver. The result is a type inference procedure that differs significantly from a common type inferencer: existing type inference systems and procedures would be hard to extend with this approach.

Fortunately, and surprisingly, the type inference problems for $\lambda^{?\alpha}_{\to}$ and ITGL coincide, even though $\lambda^{?\alpha}_{\to}$ is allowed to infer gradual types. The key to understanding this is that the $\lambda^{?\alpha}_{\to}$ type system must reject any program that has a static inconsistency even after taking its type annotations into account. The type system cannot infer a ? that resolves such a conflict. As such, any ? that appears in an inferred type must be superfluous and replaceable with a static type. The propositions below formalize this insight.[6]

**Definition 7.** *We use the name* unknown substitution *to refer to those* $A$*-substitutions* $S^{?}$ : TPARAM $\to$ GTYPE *such that either* $S^{?}(A) = A$ *or* $S^{?}(A) = ?$.

[6] These theorems consider only the corresponding subset of ITGL.

We use unknown substitutions to show that ? is never needed in practice. The property we exploit is that all substitutions $S^G$ can be factored into some $X$-substitution composed with some unknown substitution $S^G = \widehat{S^?} \circ S^X$, and any such factoring will do.

**Proposition 2.**

1. *Suppose* $S^G = \widehat{S^?} \circ S^X$. *Then* $S^G \models \widehat{S^G}(U_1^X) \sqsubseteq U_2^X$ *implies* $S^X \models \widehat{S^X}(U_1^X) \sqsubseteq U_2^X$.
2. *Suppose* $S^G = \widehat{S^?} \circ S^X$. *Then* $S^G \models U_1^X \simeq U_2^X$ *implies* $S^X \models U_1^X \simeq U_2^X$.
3. *Suppose* $S^G = \widehat{S^?} \circ S^X$. *Then* $S^G; \Gamma^X \vdash t^X : U^X$ *implies* $S^X; \Gamma^X \vdash t^X : U^X$.

*Proof.* By induction on derivations. □

Prop. 2 tells us that with regards to solving the type inference problem for $\lambda^{?\alpha}_{\rightarrow}$, we need only look to $X$-substitutions $S^X$, just as for ITGL. Thus, we restrict consideration to $X$-substitutions for the $\lambda^{?\alpha}_{\rightarrow}$ type system, which allows us to connect the two type systems more directly.

**Proposition 3** (Completeness). *If* $S^X; \Gamma^X \vdash t^X : U^X \mid \mathcal{X}$ *then* $\widehat{S^X}(\Gamma^X) \vdash \widehat{S^X}(t^X) : U$ *for some* $U$ *such that* $\widehat{S^X}(U^X) \sqsubseteq U$.

*Proof.* By induction on $S^X; \Gamma^X \vdash t^X : U^X \mid \mathcal{X}$. □

The intuition behind this proposition is that since $\lambda^{?\alpha}_{\rightarrow}$ imposes only a consistency on the type of (Gapp), the result type can be an arbitrary static type if the codomain of the operator is ?; in contrast, ITGL propagates the gradual domain of the operator verbatim.

**Proposition 4** (Soundness). *If* $\widehat{S^X}(\Gamma^X) \vdash \widehat{S^X}(t^X) : U$ *then given any finite* $\mathcal{X}_0$ *that contains* $\mathrm{Vars}(t^X, \Gamma^X)$, $S_0^X; \Gamma^X \vdash t^X : U^X \mid \mathcal{X}$ *where* $\bot(\mathcal{X}_0, \mathcal{X})$ *for some* $S_0^X$ *that agrees with* $S^X$ *except at* $\mathcal{X}$, *and* $\widehat{S_0^X}(U^X) = U$.

*Proof.* By induction on $\widehat{S^X}(\Gamma^X) \vdash \widehat{S^X}(t^X) : U$. □

We have designed an interesting gradual type system with support for implicit typing, and have established that it types the same programs as $\lambda^{?\alpha}_{\rightarrow}$. In Section 7 we deduce a type inference process that corresponds naturally to our type system and conservatively extends the corresponding static procedure.

## 6. Application: Interlanguage Migration

Now that we have seen the syntax and static semantics of ITGL, the question remains: what can we do with it? We have already seen that ITGL conservatively extends ITSL, accepting and rejecting programs in the ITSL syntax exactly as that type system does. Furthermore, the last section demonstrates that ITGL subsumes $\lambda^{?\alpha}_{\rightarrow}$, and Siek and Vachharajani (2008) demonstrate how statically-inclined programmers can leverage the flexibility of gradual typing to write programs that would not be accepted by a purely static type system. As such, ITGL shares $\lambda^{?\alpha}_{\rightarrow}$'s example programs, and we defer to that paper for static-leaning applications.

In this section, we consider the converse question: how does ITGL serve the dynamically-inclined programmer? Gradual typing's goal is to serve both communities, filling the space between static and dynamic while subsuming both. We demonstrate how ITGL addresses the dynamic side of this goal. We present a dynamic counterpart to ITSL and demonstrate by a result of Siek and Taha (2006), that it amounts to a syntactic discipline over ITGL. We then present a hybrid surface language that is suitable for migration between dynamic and static programs. These language designs are straightforward embeddings into ITGL.

### 6.1 A Dynamic Language

If we reconsider the ITSL static language, the syntax of its natural dynamic counterpart, which we call DL, simply amounts to eliding type information:

$$\begin{array}{lcll} e \in \textsc{Dynamic} & & & \\ e & ::= & n \mid e + e \mid b \mid \mathsf{if}\ e\ \mathsf{then}\ e\ \mathsf{else}\ e & \text{(terms)} \\ & \mid & x \mid \lambda x.e \mid e\ e & \end{array}$$

It's immediately clear that $\textsc{Dynamic} \subset \textsc{Term}$: every DL program looks exactly like an ITSL program, but looks can be deceiving. In particular, one consistent property of dynamic languages is that any program in the syntax of the language has semantics. In contrast, ITSL only gives meaning to programs that are well-typed. For instance, $(\lambda x.x\ x)$ is a fine DL program, but it is not a legal ITSL program because it is not well-typed. The field of linguistics has a term for this: two similar-looking expressions, sometimes in different languages, that might be mistaken for having the same meaning, but do not, are called *false friends* (Crystal 2008). In natural languages they lead to misunderstandings between native speakers of different languages: in programming languages, the phenomenon recurs.

How do we reconcile these syntactic similarities but semantic differences between ITSL and DL? The key lies in ITGL: we define both languages by translation to ITGL. The translation for ITSL is trivial because it embeds immediately. The translation for DL (Siek and Taha 2006), on the other hand, has substance:

$$\begin{array}{l} \mathcal{G}[\![\cdot]\!] : \textsc{Dynamic} \rightarrow \textsc{Term} \\ \mathcal{G}[\![n]\!] = n :: ? \qquad \mathcal{G}[\![b]\!] = b :: ? \qquad \mathcal{G}[\![x]\!] = x :: ? \\ \mathcal{G}[\![e_1 + e_2]\!] = (\mathcal{G}[\![e_1]\!] + \mathcal{G}[\![e_2]\!]) :: ? \\ \mathcal{G}[\![\mathsf{if}\ e_1\ \mathsf{then}\ e_2\ \mathsf{else}\ e_3]\!] = (\mathsf{if}\ \mathcal{G}[\![e_1]\!]\ \mathsf{then}\ \mathcal{G}[\![e_2]\!]\ \mathsf{else}\ \mathcal{G}[\![e_3]\!]) :: ? \\ \mathcal{G}[\![\lambda x.e]\!] = (\lambda x :: ?.\mathcal{G}[\![e]\!]) :: ? \\ \mathcal{G}[\![e_1\ e_2]\!] = (\mathcal{G}[\![e_1]\!]\ \mathcal{G}[\![e_2]\!]) :: ? \end{array}$$

Under this translation, $\mathcal{G}[\![\lambda x.x\ x]\!] = (\lambda x : ?.(x :: ?)\ (x :: ?)) :: ?$, which is a well-typed ITGL program, as are all embeddings of DL programs.

**Proposition 5** (Siek and Taha (2006)). *Let* X *be the free variables of* $e$ *and* $\Gamma = \{ x : ? \mid x \in X \}$. *Then* $\Gamma \vdash \mathcal{G}[\![e]\!] : ?$.

As we desire, all terms in $\textsc{Dynamic}$ are well-defined DL programs.

### 6.2 A Hybrid Language for Interlanguage Migration

Armed with a translational semantics for DL and a (trivial) translational semantics for ITSL, we can now combine them. The result is a hybrid multi-language semantics, which we call HL, that seamlessly supports migration between the DL and ITSL languages (Matthews and Findler 2009; Tobin-Hochstadt and Felleisen 2006; Wadler and Findler 2009):

$$\begin{array}{lcll} e^d \in \textsc{Dynamic} & e^s \in \textsc{Static} & & \\ e^s & ::= & n \mid e^s + e^s \mid b \mid \mathsf{if}\ e^s\ \mathsf{then}\ e^s\ \mathsf{else}\ e^s & \text{(static)} \\ & \mid & x \mid \lambda x.e^s \mid \lambda x : T.e^s \mid e^s\ e^s \mid e^s :: T & \\ & \mid & \llcorner e^d \lrcorner & \\ e^d & ::= & n \mid e^d + e^d \mid b \mid \mathsf{if}\ e^d\ \mathsf{then}\ e^d\ \mathsf{else}\ e^d & \text{(dynamic)} \\ & \mid & x \mid \lambda x.e^d \mid e^d\ e^d \mid \ulcorner e^s \urcorner & \end{array}$$

The HL syntax combines ITSL and DL, allowing each to include the other. Its semantics is defined by combining the two translations to ITGL, yielding a coarse-grained gradual language where each type is either precisely static or completely unknown.

Taking the dynamic language as primary, HL clearly differentiates between the dynamic program $(\lambda x.x\ x)$, the hybrid program $\ulcorner \lambda x.\llcorner x\ x \lrcorner \urcorner$ and the static *non*-program $\ulcorner \lambda x.x\ x \urcorner$.

DL and HL have close ties to research on using types to improve the performance of dynamic languages (Cartwright and Fagan 1991; Rastogi et al. 2012; Swamy et al. 2014). By analogy, the goal in that approach is to transform a DL program into a corresponding HL program by automatically inserting transitions to the static language for as much code as possible while retaining well-typing and behaviour. This problem has been approached using type-based analyses that do infer unknown types.

# 7. Constraints and Constraint Generation

We have specified an implicit type system, demonstrated its expressiveness, and formalized the type inference problem for it: now we must solve the problem. To do so, we follow the approach of (Wand 1987a): generate constraints for typeability and solve them. Guided by the definition of the ITGL type system and properties of our gradual partial functions and predicates, we define a *constraint typing judgment*, which indicates what constraints must hold for a particular type expression-and-context pair to be typeable.

## 7.1 Constraint Typing Judgments

We first introduce a set of constraints $C$ that need to be solved during type inference (Fig. 7). There are two kinds of constraints: the standard equality constraints on static types, and new *consistency constraints* on gradual types. Ultimately we want to determine whether a set of constraints can be instantiated affirmatively using some substitution.

**Definition 8** (Constraint Satisfaction).

1. $S^X \models U_1^X \mathrel{\dot\sim} U_2^X$ *if and only if* $\widehat{S^X}(U_1^X) \sim \widehat{S^X}(U_1^X)$;
2. $S^X \models T_1^X \doteq T_2^X$ *if and only if* $\widehat{S^X}(T_1^X) = \widehat{S^X}(T_2^X)$;
3. $S^X \models C^\star$ *if and only if* $S^X \models C$ *for each* $C \in C^\star$.

***Constraint Typing*** Fig. 7 presents the constraint typing judgment $\Gamma^X \vdash t^X : U^X \mid C^\star \mid \mathcal{X}$. It means that the type expression context $\Gamma^X$ and term expression $t^X$, can be given type expression $U^X$ so long as the constraints $C^\star$ can be satisfied, where $\mathcal{X}$ are any extra variables needed to express the constraints. Since it involves type variables, the constraint typing judgment denotes a problem.

**Definition 9** (Constraint Typing Problem). *Given a gradual type expression context* $\Gamma^X$ *and a term expression* $t^X$, *the* constraint typing problem *asks if there is a* $S^X$ *such that* $\Gamma^X \vdash t^X : U^X \mid C^\star \mid \mathcal{X}$ *and* $S^X \models C^\star$.

***Auxiliary Constraint Typing*** Constraint typing appeals to three auxiliary constraint judgments, which reduce complex conditions to consistency constraints on gradual types and equality constraints on static types. They are presented in Figs. 8,9, and 10.

The $\widetilde{cod}(U_1^X) \doteq U_2^X \mid C^\star \mid \mathcal{X}$ judgment means that the codomain of gradual type expression $U_1^X$ is $U_2^X$ so long as the constraints $C^\star$ can be satisfied. The $\widetilde{dom}(U_1^X) \mathrel{\dot\sim} U_2^X \mid C^\star \mid \mathcal{X}$ judgment means that the domain of gradual type expression $U_1^X$ is consistent with $U_2^X$ so long as the constraints $C^\star$ can be satisfied. Finally the $U_1^X \sqcap U_2^X \doteq U_3^X \mid C^\star \mid \mathcal{X}$ judgment means that the meet of gradual type expressions $U_1^X$ and $U_2^X$ is $U_3^X$ so long as the constraints $C^\star$ can be satisfied. In each case, $\mathcal{X}$ names any extra type variables needed to express the constraints. The rules for these judgments are based on the properties of the corresponding gradual operations.

These constraint judgments are not defined for all inputs. For instance, the constraint meet judgment is not defined for Int and Bool. Any result would be contrived, so rather than relating these type

$$\boxed{\Gamma^X \vdash t^X : U^X \mid C^\star \mid \mathcal{X}} \quad \bot(\mathcal{X}, \mathrm{Vars}(t^X, \Gamma^X))$$

$$(\mathrm{Cx})\frac{x : U^X \in \Gamma^X}{\Gamma^X \vdash x : U^X \mid \emptyset \mid \emptyset} \qquad (\mathrm{Cn})\frac{}{\Gamma^X \vdash n : \mathsf{Int} \mid \emptyset \mid \emptyset}$$

$$(\mathrm{Cb})\frac{}{\Gamma^X \vdash b : \mathsf{Bool} \mid \emptyset \mid \emptyset}$$

$$(\mathrm{C+})\frac{\begin{array}{c}\Gamma^X \vdash t_1^X : U_1^X \mid C_1^\star \mid \mathcal{X}_1 \qquad \Gamma^X \vdash t_2^X : U_2^X \mid C_2^\star \mid \mathcal{X}_2 \\ \bot(\mathcal{X}_1, \mathcal{X}_2) \qquad C^\star = C_1^\star \cup C_2^\star \qquad \mathcal{X} = \mathcal{X}_1 \cup \mathcal{X}_2\end{array}}{\Gamma^X \vdash t_1^X + t_2^X : \mathsf{Int} \mid C^\star \cup \{\, U_1^X \mathrel{\dot\sim} \mathsf{Int}, U_2^X \mathrel{\dot\sim} \mathsf{Int} \,\} \mid \mathcal{X}}$$

$$(\mathrm{Cif})\frac{\begin{array}{c}\Gamma^X \vdash t_1^X : U_1^X \mid C_1^\star \mid \mathcal{X}_1 \qquad \Gamma^X \vdash t_2^X : U_2^X \mid C_2^\star \mid \mathcal{X}_2 \\ \Gamma^X \vdash t_3^X : U_3^X \mid C_3^\star \mid \mathcal{X}_3 \qquad U_2^X \sqcap U_3^X \doteq U_4^X \mid C_4^\star \mid \mathcal{X}_4 \\ \bot(\mathcal{X}_1, \mathcal{X}_2, \mathcal{X}_3, \mathcal{X}_4) \qquad \mathcal{X} = \mathcal{X}_1 \cup \mathcal{X}_2 \cup \mathcal{X}_3 \cup \mathcal{X}_4 \\ C^\star = C_1^\star \cup C_2^\star \cup C_3^\star \cup C_4^\star\end{array}}{\Gamma^X \vdash \mathsf{if}\ t_1^X\ \mathsf{then}\ t_2^X\ \mathsf{else}\ t_3^X : U_4^X \mid C^\star \cup \{\, U_1^X \mathrel{\dot\sim} \mathsf{Bool} \,\} \mid \mathcal{X}}$$

$$(\mathrm{Capp})\frac{\begin{array}{c}\Gamma^X \vdash t_1^X : U_1^X \mid C_1^\star \mid \mathcal{X}_1 \qquad \Gamma^X \vdash t_2^X : U_2^X \mid C_2^\star \mid \mathcal{X}_2 \\ \widetilde{cod}(U_1^X) \doteq U_3^X \mid C_3^\star \mid \mathcal{X}_3 \qquad \widetilde{dom}(U_1^X) \mathrel{\dot\sim} U_2^X \mid C_4^\star \mid \mathcal{X}_4 \\ \bot(\mathcal{X}_1, \mathcal{X}_2, \mathcal{X}_3, \mathcal{X}_4) \qquad \mathcal{X} = \mathcal{X}_1 \cup \mathcal{X}_2 \cup \mathcal{X}_3 \cup \mathcal{X}_4 \\ C^\star = C_1^\star \cup C_2^\star \cup C_3^\star \cup C_4^\star\end{array}}{\Gamma^X \vdash t_1^X\ t_2^X : U_3^X \mid C^\star \mid \mathcal{X}}$$

$$(\mathrm{C}\lambda)\frac{\Gamma^X, x : X \vdash t^X : U^X \mid C^\star \mid \mathcal{X} \qquad \bot(\mathcal{X}, \{\, X \,\})}{\Gamma^X \vdash (\lambda x.t^X) : X \to U^X \mid C^\star \mid \mathcal{X} \cup \{\, X \,\}}$$

$$(\mathrm{C}\lambda{:})\frac{\Gamma^X, x : U_1^X \vdash t^X : U_2^X \mid C^\star \mid \mathcal{X}}{\Gamma^X \vdash (\lambda x : U_1^X.t^X) : U_1^X \to U_2^X \mid C^\star \mid \mathcal{X}}$$

$$(\mathrm{C}{::})\frac{\Gamma^X \vdash t^X : U^X \mid C^\star \mid \mathcal{X}}{\Gamma^X \vdash (t^X :: U_1^X) : U_1^X \mid C^\star \cup \{\, U^X \mathrel{\dot\sim} U_1^X \,\} \mid \mathcal{X}}$$

$$C \in \textsc{Constraint}$$
$$C^\star \in \mathcal{P}(\textsc{Constraint})$$
$$C ::= U^X \mathrel{\dot\sim} U^X \mid T^X \doteq T^X$$

**Figure 7.** Constraint Typing Judgment

$$\boxed{\widetilde{cod}(U_1^X) \doteq U_2^X \mid C^\star \mid \mathcal{X}} \quad \bot(\mathcal{X}, \mathrm{Vars}(U_1^X))$$

$$\frac{}{\widetilde{cod}(X) \doteq X_2 \mid \{\, X \doteq X_1 \to X_2 \,\} \mid \{\, X_1, X_2 \,\}}$$

$$\frac{}{\widetilde{cod}(U_1^X \to U_2^X) \doteq U_2^X \mid \emptyset \mid \emptyset} \qquad \frac{}{\widetilde{cod}(?) \doteq\ ? \mid \emptyset \mid \emptyset}$$

**Figure 8.** Constraint Codomain Judgment

$$\boxed{\widetilde{dom}(U_1^X) \mathrel{\dot\sim} U_2^X \mid C^\star \mid \mathcal{X}} \quad \bot(\mathcal{X}, \mathrm{Vars}(U_1^X, U_2^X))$$

$$\frac{}{\widetilde{dom}(X) \mathrel{\dot\sim} U_2^X \mid \{\, X \doteq X_1 \to X_2, X_1 \mathrel{\dot\sim} U_2^X \,\} \mid \{\, X_1, X_2 \,\}}$$

$$\frac{}{\widetilde{dom}(U_{11}^X \to U_{12}^X) \mathrel{\dot\sim} U_2^X \mid \{\, U_{11}^X \mathrel{\dot\sim} U_2^X \,\} \mid \emptyset}$$

$$\frac{}{\widetilde{dom}(?) \mathrel{\dot\sim} U_2^X \mid \{\, ? \mathrel{\dot\sim} U_2^X \,\} \mid \emptyset}$$

**Figure 9.** Constraint Domain Consistency Judgment

$$\boxed{U_1^{\mathtt{X}} \sqcap U_2^{\mathtt{X}} \doteq U_3^{\mathtt{X}} \mid C^\star \mid \mathcal{X}} \quad \bot(\mathcal{X}, \mathrm{Vars}(U_1^{\mathtt{X}}, U_2^{\mathtt{X}}))$$

$$\frac{}{\mathsf{Int} \sqcap \mathsf{Int} \doteq \mathsf{Int} \mid \emptyset \mid \emptyset} \qquad \frac{}{\mathsf{Bool} \sqcap \mathsf{Bool} \doteq \mathsf{Bool} \mid \emptyset \mid \emptyset}$$

$$\frac{}{A \sqcap A \doteq A \mid \emptyset \mid \emptyset} \qquad \frac{}{U_1^{\mathtt{X}} \sqcap ? \doteq U_1^{\mathtt{X}} \mid \{ U_1^{\mathtt{X}} \mathrel{\dot\sim} ? \} \mid \emptyset}$$

$$\frac{}{? \sqcap U_2^{\mathtt{X}} \doteq U_2^{\mathtt{X}} \mid \{ ? \mathrel{\dot\sim} U_2^{\mathtt{X}} \} \mid \emptyset}$$

$$\frac{}{X_1 \sqcap U_2^{\mathtt{X}} \doteq X_1 \mid \{ X_1 \mathrel{\dot\sim} U_2^{\mathtt{X}} \} \mid \emptyset}$$

$$\frac{U_1^{\mathtt{X}} \notin \mathrm{TVAR}}{U_1^{\mathtt{X}} \sqcap X_2 \doteq X_2 \mid \{ U_1^{\mathtt{X}} \mathrel{\dot\sim} X_2 \} \mid \emptyset}$$

$$\frac{\begin{array}{ccc} U_{11}^{\mathtt{X}} \sqcap U_{21}^{\mathtt{X}} \doteq U_1^{\mathtt{X}} \mid C_1^\star \mid \mathcal{X}_1 & & U_{12}^{\mathtt{X}} \sqcap U_{22}^{\mathtt{X}} \doteq U_2^{\mathtt{X}} \mid C_2^\star \mid \mathcal{X}_2 \\ C^\star = C_1^\star \cup C_2^\star & \bot(\mathcal{X}_1, \mathcal{X}_2) & \mathcal{X} = \mathcal{X}_1 \cup \mathcal{X}_2 \end{array}}{(U_{11}^{\mathtt{X}} \to U_{12}^{\mathtt{X}}) \sqcap (U_{21}^{\mathtt{X}} \to U_{22}^{\mathtt{X}}) \doteq U_1^{\mathtt{X}} \to U_2^{\mathtt{X}} \mid C^\star \mid \mathcal{X}}$$

**Figure 10.** Constraint Meet Judgment

expressions to an arbitrary variable and unsatisfiable constraint, the judgment simply fails to hold.

### 7.2 Correctness and Decidability of Constraint Typing

We must prove for each constraint judgment that if a substitution can satisfy the given constraints, then that substitution, and the program type that it produces, solves the type inference problem.

**Proposition 6** (Constraint Soundness).
*If* $\Gamma^{\mathtt{X}} \vdash t : U^{\mathtt{X}} \mid C^\star \mid \mathcal{X}$ *and* $S^{\mathtt{X}} \models C^\star$ *then* $\widehat{S^{\mathtt{X}}}(\Gamma^{\mathtt{X}}) \vdash \widehat{S^{\mathtt{X}}}(t) : \widehat{S^{\mathtt{X}}}(U^{\mathtt{X}})$.

*Proof.* By induction on $\Gamma^{\mathtt{X}} \vdash t : U^{\mathtt{X}} \mid C^\star \mid \mathcal{X}$ with lemmas to address auxiliary constraint judgments. □

**Proposition 7** (Constraint Completeness).
*If* $\widehat{S^{\mathtt{X}}}(\Gamma^{\mathtt{X}}) \vdash \widehat{S^{\mathtt{X}}}(t^{\mathtt{X}}) : U$ *then for finite* $\mathcal{X}_0$ *s.t.* $\mathrm{Vars}(\Gamma^{\mathtt{X}}, t^{\mathtt{X}}) \subseteq \mathcal{X}_0$, $\Gamma^{\mathtt{X}} \vdash t^{\mathtt{X}} : U^{\mathtt{X}} \mid C^\star \mid \mathcal{X}$ *where* $\bot(\mathcal{X}_0, \mathcal{X})$, *and furthermore there is an* $S_0^{\mathtt{X}}$ *that agrees with* $S^{\mathtt{X}}$ *except at* $\mathcal{X}$, *where* $S_0^{\mathtt{X}} \models C^\star$ *and* $\widehat{S_0^{\mathtt{X}}}(U^{\mathtt{X}}) = U$.

*Proof.* By induction on $\widehat{S^{\mathtt{X}}}(\Gamma^{\mathtt{X}}) \vdash \widehat{S^{\mathtt{X}}}(t^{\mathtt{X}}) : U$. with lemmas to address auxiliary constraint judgments. □

The constraint completeness proposition must account for the extra variables $\mathcal{X}$ used by constraint typing, which do not necessarily hold for an arbitrary substitution that solves the type inference problem. The key is that given an arbitrary substitution $S^{\mathtt{X}}$ that solves the type inference problem, it's always possible to massage it into a slightly different $S_0^{\mathtt{X}}$ that produces the same solution but also satisfies the constraints.

## 8. Gradual Unification

In this section we present a procedure that generalizes unification (Robinson 1965) to account for consistency constraints and relates constraints to solutions, where possible. Since each rule of the judgment is invertible and simplifies the constraints, together they induce a straightforward decision procedure (bottom-up proof search) for gradual constraints.

**Proposition 8** (Consistency Inversion).

1. *If* $U_1 \sim U_2$ *then* $U_2 \sim U_1$*;*
2. *If* $T_1 \sim T_2$ *then* $T_1 = T_2$*;*
3. *if* $U_{11} \to U_{12} \sim U_{11} \to U_{12}$*; then* $U_{11} \sim U_{21}$ *and* $U_{12} \sim U_{21}$*;*

*Proof.* Straightforward. □

$$\mathcal{U} \in \mathcal{P}(\textsc{Constraint}) \times \textsc{XSubst}$$

$$\frac{}{\emptyset \,\mathcal{U}\, S_{\mathcal{A}}} \qquad \frac{C^\star \,\mathcal{U}\, S^{\mathtt{X}}}{C^\star \cup \{ X \mathrel{\dot\sim} X \} \,\mathcal{U}\, S^{\mathtt{X}}}$$

$$\frac{C^\star \,\mathcal{U}\, S^{\mathtt{X}}}{C^\star \cup \{ ? \mathrel{\dot\sim} U^{\mathtt{X}} \} \,\mathcal{U}\, S^{\mathtt{X}}} \qquad \frac{C^\star \,\mathcal{U}\, S^{\mathtt{X}}}{C^\star \cup \{ U^{\mathtt{X}} \mathrel{\dot\sim} ? \} \,\mathcal{U}\, S^{\mathtt{X}}}$$

$$\frac{C^\star \,\mathcal{U}\, S^{\mathtt{X}}}{C^\star \cup \{ \mathsf{Int} \mathrel{\dot\sim} \mathsf{Int} \} \,\mathcal{U}\, S^{\mathtt{X}}} \qquad \frac{C^\star \,\mathcal{U}\, S^{\mathtt{X}}}{C^\star \cup \{ \mathsf{Bool} \mathrel{\dot\sim} \mathsf{Bool} \} \,\mathcal{U}\, S^{\mathtt{X}}}$$

$$\frac{C^\star \cup \{ U_{11}^{\mathtt{X}} \mathrel{\dot\sim} U_{21}^{\mathtt{X}}, U_{12}^{\mathtt{X}} \mathrel{\dot\sim} U_{22}^{\mathtt{X}} \} \,\mathcal{U}\, S^{\mathtt{X}}}{C^\star \cup \{ U_{11}^{\mathtt{X}} \to U_{12}^{\mathtt{X}} \mathrel{\dot\sim} U_{21}^{\mathtt{X}} \to U_{22}^{\mathtt{X}} \} \,\mathcal{U}\, S^{\mathtt{X}}}$$

$$\frac{\begin{array}{c} C^\star \cup \{ X \mathrel{\dot\sim} U^{\mathtt{X}} \} \,\mathcal{U}\, S^{\mathtt{X}} \\ U^{\mathtt{X}} \notin \mathrm{TVAR} \end{array}}{C^\star \cup \{ U^{\mathtt{X}} \mathrel{\dot\sim} X \} \,\mathcal{U}\, S^{\mathtt{X}}} \qquad \frac{\begin{array}{c} C^\star \cup \{ X \doteq U^{\mathtt{X}} \} \,\mathcal{U}\, S^{\mathtt{X}} \\ U^{\mathtt{X}} \in \{ \mathsf{Int}, \mathsf{Bool} \} \end{array}}{C^\star \cup \{ X \mathrel{\dot\sim} U^{\mathtt{X}} \} \,\mathcal{U}\, S^{\mathtt{X}}}$$

$$\frac{\begin{array}{c} \{ X_1, X_2 \}\ \mathbf{fresh} \qquad X \notin \mathrm{Vars}(U_1^{\mathtt{X}} \to U_2^{\mathtt{X}}) \\ C^\star \cup \{ X \doteq X_1 \to X_2, X_1 \mathrel{\dot\sim} U_1^{\mathtt{X}}, X_2 \mathrel{\dot\sim} U_2^{\mathtt{X}} \} \,\mathcal{U}\, S^{\mathtt{X}} \end{array}}{C^\star \cup \{ X \mathrel{\dot\sim} U_1^{\mathtt{X}} \to U_2^{\mathtt{X}} \} \,\mathcal{U}\, S^{\mathtt{X}}}$$

$$\frac{C^\star \,\mathcal{U}\, S^{\mathtt{X}}}{C^\star \cup \{ \mathsf{Int} \doteq \mathsf{Int} \} \,\mathcal{U}\, S^{\mathtt{X}}} \qquad \frac{C^\star \,\mathcal{U}\, S^{\mathtt{X}}}{C^\star \cup \{ \mathsf{Bool} \doteq \mathsf{Bool} \} \,\mathcal{U}\, S^{\mathtt{X}}}$$

$$\frac{C^\star \cup \{ T_{11} \doteq T_{21}, T_{12} \doteq T_{22} \} \,\mathcal{U}\, S^{\mathtt{X}}}{C^\star \cup \{ T_{11} \to T_{12} \doteq T_{21} \to T_{22} \} \,\mathcal{U}\, S^{\mathtt{X}}}$$

$$\frac{\begin{array}{c} C^\star \cup \{ X \doteq T \} \,\mathcal{U}\, S^{\mathtt{X}} \\ X \notin \mathrm{Vars}(T) \end{array}}{C^\star \cup \{ T \doteq X \} \,\mathcal{U}\, S^{\mathtt{X}}} \qquad \frac{C^\star \,\mathcal{U}\, S^{\mathtt{X}}}{C^\star \cup \{ X \doteq X \} \,\mathcal{U}\, S^{\mathtt{X}}}$$

$$\frac{\widehat{[X \mapsto T]}(C^\star) \,\mathcal{U}\, S^{\mathtt{X}} \qquad X \notin \mathrm{Vars}(T)}{C^\star \cup \{ X \doteq T \} \,\mathcal{U}\, \widehat{S^{\mathtt{X}}} \circ [X \mapsto T]}$$

**Figure 11.** Unification

Fig. 11 presents the gradual unification judgment $C^\star \,\mathcal{U}\, S^{\mathtt{X}}$, which means that the $X$-substitution $S^{\mathtt{X}}$ satisfies the constraints in $C^\star$. Recall that satisfaction was defined in Sec. 7.1. Throughout, we assume that $C^\star \cup \{ C \}$ implies $C \notin C^\star$.

Most of the cases are straightforward. The most interesting case is for $X \mathrel{\dot\sim} U_1^{\mathtt{X}} \to U_2^{\mathtt{X}}$. Since $X$ represents a static type, we expand it to $X_1 \to X_2$ and make each component consistent to its corresponding gradual type. Equality would not work in general since the type on the right hand side is gradual. Furthermore, the added consistency checks ensure that any ?s contained within the underlying types are ignored.

We let $S_{\mathcal{A}} : \mathrm{TVAR} \to \mathrm{TPARAM}$ denote a bijective map from type variables to type parameters. This function is responsible for transforming any unconstrained type variables into type parameters.

**Notation.**

1. *The notation* $\mathcal{X}$ **fresh** *means that if the consequent of the rule is* $C^\star \,\mathcal{U}\, S$*, then* $\mathcal{X} \notin \mathrm{Vars}(C^\star)$.
2. *The notation* $[X \mapsto T]$ *stands for* $S_{id}[X \mapsto T]$*, the type substitution that is identity everywhere except for* $X$*, which it maps to* $T$.

**Proposition 9** (Unification Soundness). *If* $C^\star \,\mathcal{U}\, S$ *then* $S \models C^\star$.

*Proof.* By induction on the structure of $C^\star \boldsymbol{\mathcal{U}}\, S$. □

**Proposition 10** (Unification Completeness). *If $S_1^X \models C^\star$ then $C^\star \boldsymbol{\mathcal{U}}\, S_2^X$ for some $S_2^X$ and furthermore $S_1^X = \widehat{S^A} \circ S_2^X$ for some $S^A$.*

*Proof.* By induction on the breakdown of constraint sets $C^\star$ by the unification rules. This is dependent on that decomposition structure being well-ordered. □

**Proposition 11** (Unification is Decidable). *Backward proof search on $C^\star \boldsymbol{\mathcal{U}}\, S^X$ driven by $C^\star$ is decidable.*

*Proof.* Consider the relation on constraint sets determined by how each rule (read bottom-up) transforms them. Given soundness and completeness, it suffices to prove that this relation is a well-order.

Unlike other unification relations, the search structure cannot be lexicographically ordered on the number of type variables. Instead, we can represent the set of constraints as a directed graph of constraint *paths* and show that a metric on the graph decreases at every step. □

## 9. Principal Types

We establish our notion of principal types using the standard notion, adapted to account for the separation between type variables and type parameters.

**Definition 10** (Substitution Pre-order). *Let $S_1^X$ and $S_2^X$ be $X$-substitutions. Then $S_1^X \leq S_2^X$ if and only if $S_2^X = \widehat{S^A} \circ S_1^X$ for some $A$-substitution $S^A$.*

**Definition 11** (Principal Solution/Type). *$(S^X, U)$ is a* principal solution *for a gradual type inference problem if $S^X$ is least among the substitutions of all other solutions to the problem. In that case, $U$ is a* principal type *for the problem.*

**Proposition 12** (Principal Types). *Suppose $\Gamma^X \vdash t^X : U^X \mid C^\star \mid \mathcal{X}$. Then $S_1^X \models C^\star$ for some $S_1^X$, implies that $C^\star \boldsymbol{\mathcal{U}}\, S_2^X$, and $(S_2^X, \widehat{S_2^X}(U^X))$ is a principal solution for $\Gamma^X$ and $t^X$.*

*Proof.* Follows from Prop. 10. □

This proposition establishes that our type inference procedure produces the best type possible, which implies that the type system indeed has a well-defined notion of "best" types.

## 10. Let Polymorphism

Implicitly typed functional programming languages usually support let-polymorphism, introduced by Milner (1978). Siek and Vachharajani (2008) left this as an open problem for gradual type inference. Here we demonstrate that supporting let polymorphism follows the same approach as for a static implicitly typed language (Ohori 1989; Wright 1995; Wright and Felleisen 1994).

To extend ITGL with let-polymorphism, we introduce two new rules:

$$(\text{Uletp})\ \frac{\Gamma \vdash v : U_1 \qquad \Gamma \vdash [v/x]t : U_2}{\Gamma \vdash \mathsf{let}\ x = v\ \mathsf{in}\ t : U_2}$$

$$(\text{Ulet})\ \frac{t_1 \notin \textsc{Value} \qquad \Gamma \vdash (\lambda x.t_2)\ t_1 : U}{\Gamma \vdash \mathsf{let}\ x = t_1\ \mathsf{in}\ t_2 : U}$$

If the bound expression is a syntactic value, then it is treated polymorphically; otherwise, the value is given a monomorphic type according to the standard let translation.[7] These typing rules yield the corresponding constraint generation rules.

$$(\text{Cletp})\ \frac{\Gamma^{\mathsf{X}} \vdash v^{\mathsf{X}} : U_1^{\mathsf{X}} \mid C_1^\star \mid \mathcal{X}_1 \qquad \Gamma^{\mathsf{X}} \vdash [v^{\mathsf{X}}/x]t^{\mathsf{X}} : U_2^{\mathsf{X}} \mid C_2^\star \mid \mathcal{X}_2 \qquad \bot(\mathcal{X}_1, \mathcal{X}_2)}{\Gamma^{\mathsf{X}} \vdash \mathsf{let}\ x = v^{\mathsf{X}}\ \mathsf{in}\ t^{\mathsf{X}} : U_2^{\mathsf{X}} \mid C_1^\star \cup C_2^\star \mid \mathcal{X}_1 \cup \mathcal{X}_2}$$

$$(\text{Clet})\ \frac{t_1^{\mathsf{X}} \notin \textsc{Value} \qquad \Gamma^{\mathsf{X}} \vdash (\lambda x.t_2^{\mathsf{X}})\ t_1^{\mathsf{X}} : U \mid C^\star \mid \mathcal{X}}{\Gamma^{\mathsf{X}} \vdash \mathsf{let}\ x = t_1^{\mathsf{X}}\ \mathsf{in}\ t_2^{\mathsf{X}} : U \mid C^\star \mid \mathcal{X}}$$

The substitution-based presentation of let polymorphism is simple and clear, but impractical for implementations, so we also present an equivalent presentation based on *type schemes*, representatives of type polymorphism in the language. In the next section, we use this type system to endow ITGL with dynamic semantics.

The Schematic ITGL type system is modeled after (Milner 1978). It has the same terms and types as the original, but the typing judgment changes. The key difference is that the type context now maps variables to type schemes $\forall \overline{X}.U^{\mathsf{X}}$ instead of types.

$$\sigma \in \textsc{TypeScheme}$$
$$\Gamma^\forall \in \textsc{Var} \rightarrow \textsc{TypeScheme}$$
$$\sigma ::= \forall \overline{X}.U^{\mathsf{X}}$$

This allows us to type polymorphic let expressions, without resorting to substitution, by introducing polymorphic assumptions. We can represent a type $U$ as a vacuous type scheme $\forall \emptyset.U$. By convention, all type schemes must be closed. The type system then requires a few changes (Fig. 12).

$$(\sigma\lambda{:})\ \frac{\Gamma^\forall, x : \forall\emptyset.U_1 \vdash^\forall t : U_2}{\Gamma^\forall \vdash^\forall \lambda x : U_1.t : U_1 \rightarrow U_2}$$

$$(\sigma\lambda)\ \frac{\Gamma^\forall, x : \forall\emptyset.T_1 \vdash^\forall t : U_2}{\Gamma^\forall \vdash^\forall \lambda x.t : T_1 \rightarrow U_2} \qquad (\sigma\text{x})\ \frac{x : \forall\overline{X_i}.U^{\mathsf{X}} \in \Gamma^\forall}{\Gamma^\forall \vdash^\forall x : [\overline{T_i}/\overline{X_i}]U^{\mathsf{X}}}$$

$$(\sigma\text{let})\ \frac{\Gamma^\forall \vdash^\forall (\lambda x.t_2)\ t_1 : U \qquad t_1 \notin \textsc{Value}}{\Gamma^\forall \vdash^\forall \mathsf{let}\ x = t_1\ \mathsf{in}\ t_2 : U}$$

$$(\sigma\text{letp})\ \frac{\Gamma^\forall \vdash^\forall v_1 : U_1 \qquad \Gamma^\forall, x : \sigma \vdash^\forall t_2 : U_2 \qquad \sigma = \forall\overline{X_i}.[\overline{X_i}/\overline{A_i}]U_1 \qquad \overline{A_i} \notin \Gamma^\forall}{\Gamma^\forall \vdash^\forall \mathsf{let}\ x = v_1\ \mathsf{in}\ t_2 : U_2}$$

**Figure 12.** Schematic Typing: Key Rules

The $(\sigma\lambda{:})$ and $(\sigma\lambda)$ rules now introduce type schemes into the context when typing function bodies. The $(\sigma\text{x})$ rule magically instantiates a variable's corresponding type scheme to some gradual type. In the substitution-based system, this variable would have been replaced with a full syntactic value, which conveys its polymorphism implicitly. As we'll see, this corresponds directly to the translation from let-polymorphism to parametric polymorphism. Type schemes with no type variables naturally instantiate to their underlying type. The $(\sigma\text{letp})$ rule exploits the polymorphism of type parameters, abstracting some that are unconstrained (i.e. do not appear in the type context) to form the type scheme that is used to type the body. This formulation corresponds directly to the substitution-based specification.

**Definition 12.** *Let $\forall : \textsc{GType} \rightarrow \textsc{TypeScheme}$ be $\forall(U) = \forall\emptyset.U$; For notational convenience, we write $\forall(\Gamma) \equiv \forall \circ \Gamma$.*

[7] Here we assume a call-by-value semantics, but in general that is not necessary.

$$A \in \textsc{TParam}, \quad U \in \textsc{GType}, \quad X \in \textsc{TVar}, \quad x \in \textsc{Var},$$
$$b \in \textsc{Bool}, \quad n \in \mathbb{Z}, \quad t \in \textsc{Term}, \quad v \in \textsc{Value}$$

$$\begin{array}{lcll}
U & ::= & ? \mid X \mid A \mid \mathsf{Int} \mid \mathsf{Bool} \mid U \to U \mid \forall X.U & \text{Types} \\
t & ::= & n \mid t + t \mid b \mid \mathsf{if}\ t\ \mathsf{then}\ t\ \mathsf{else}\ t & \text{(terms)} \\
 & \mid & x \mid \lambda x : U.t \mid t\ t \mid \Lambda X.t \mid t[U] & \\
 & \mid & \mathsf{let}\ x : U = t\ \mathsf{in}\ t \mid \langle U \Leftarrow U \rangle\, t & \\
v & ::= & n \mid b \mid x \mid \lambda x : U.t \mid \Lambda X.v & \text{(syntactic values)}
\end{array}$$

**Figure 13.** Polymorphic Blame Calculus (PBC): Syntax

**Proposition 13** (Schematic Substitution).
*If* $\Gamma \vdash v : [\overline{A_i}/\overline{X_i}]U^X$ *for* $\overline{A_i} \notin \Gamma$ *and* $\forall(\Gamma), x : \forall\overline{X_i}.U^X \vdash^{\forall} t : U$ *then* $\Gamma \vdash [v/x]t : U$

*Proof.* By induction on the structure of $t$. □

**Proposition 14** (Schematic Abstraction). *If* $\forall(\Gamma) \vdash^{\forall} [v/x]t : U_1$ *and* $\forall(\Gamma) \vdash^{\forall} v : U_2$ *for some* $U_2$ *then* $\forall(\Gamma) \vdash^{\forall} v : [\overline{A_i}/\overline{X_i}]U^X$ *and* $\forall(\Gamma), x : \forall\overline{X_i}.U^X \vdash^{\forall} t : U_1$ *for some* $U^X$, $\overline{A_i} \notin \forall(\Gamma)$, *and* $\overline{X_i}$.

*Proof.* By induction on the structure of $t$. □

**Proposition 15.** $\Gamma \vdash t : U$ *if and only if* $\forall(\Gamma) \vdash^{\forall} t : U$.

*Proof.* Both directions are by induction on the structure of the corresponding typing judgment. □

## 11. Dynamic Semantics

Gradually typed languages are defined by type-directed translation to an intermediate language with runtime casts. We do not need to develop a new intermediate cast calculus for ITGL: we can translate it to the Polymorphic Blame Calculus (PBC) (Ahmed et al. 2009, 2011)

Fig. 13 presents the syntax of PBC, adapted to our notation. The language extends the polymorphic lambda calculus (Girard 1972; Reynolds 1974) with support for runtime casts. At runtime, the calculus also uses runtime sealing to encapsulate polymorphically typed values in an effort to enforce representation-independence, even in the face of casts (Matthews and Ahmed 2008). The language supports first-class polymorphism using type-abstracted terms $\Lambda X.t$ and types, $\forall X.U^X$, which resemble type schemes, but only abstract a single type variable, and can be open.

Fig. 14 presents the type system of the polymorphic blame calculus. For the most part the type system is standard, but it also supports casts $\langle U_2 \Leftarrow U_1 \rangle\, t$. To type casted terms, the polymorphic blame calculus presents a more complex consistency relation, but in the absence of first-class polymorphism, it reduces to $\sim$.

Fig. 15 presents a type-directed translation from the Schematic typing judgment for ITGL to PBC. In practice, the type derivation is produced by type inference. Most of the rules are straightforward compositional translations. Type abstractions and applications are introduced where necessary. Several of the rules insert casts, as needed, in positions where consistency is needed. The $\langle\langle U \Leftarrow U \rangle\rangle t$ function inserts a cast when the type translation is nontrivial.

**Definition 13** (Context Translation).

$$\begin{array}{rcl}
[\![\epsilon]\!]^X & ::= & \epsilon \\
[\![x : \forall\overline{X}.U^X, \Gamma^{\forall}]\!]^X & ::= & [\![\Gamma^{\forall}]\!]^X \\
[\![X, \Gamma^{\forall}]\!]^X & ::= & X, [\![\Gamma^{\forall}]\!]^X \\
[\![\epsilon]\!]^x & ::= & \epsilon \\
[\![x : \forall\overline{X}.U^X, \Gamma^{\forall}]\!]^x & ::= & x : \overline{\forall X}.U^X, [\![\Gamma^{\forall}]\!]^x \\
[\![X, \Gamma^{\forall}]\!]^x & ::= & [\![\Gamma^{\forall}]\!]^x
\end{array}$$

$$(\forall x)\frac{x : U \in \Gamma}{\Omega \mid \Gamma \vdash x : U} \qquad (\forall n)\frac{}{\Omega \mid \Gamma \vdash n : \mathsf{Int}}$$

$$(\forall b)\frac{}{\Omega \mid \Gamma \vdash b : \mathsf{Bool}}$$

$$(\forall app)\frac{\Omega \mid \Gamma \vdash t_1 : U_1 \to U_2 \quad \Omega \mid \Gamma \vdash t_2 : U_1}{\Omega \mid \Gamma \vdash t_1\ t_2 : U_2}$$

$$(\forall if)\frac{\Omega \mid \Gamma \vdash t_1 : \mathsf{Bool} \quad \Omega \mid \Gamma \vdash t_2 : U \quad \Omega \mid \Gamma \vdash t_3 : U}{\Omega \mid \Gamma \vdash \mathsf{if}\ t_1\ \mathsf{then}\ t_2\ \mathsf{else}\ t_3 : U}$$

$$(\forall +)\frac{\Omega \mid \Gamma \vdash t_1 : \mathsf{Int} \quad \Omega \mid \Gamma \vdash t_2 : \mathsf{Int}}{\Omega \mid \Gamma \vdash t_1 + t_2 : \mathsf{Int}}$$

$$(\forall\lambda{:})\frac{\Omega \mid \Gamma, x : U_1 \vdash t : U_2}{\Omega \mid \Gamma \vdash (\lambda x : U_1.t) : U_1 \to U_2}$$

$$(\forall\Lambda)\frac{\Omega, X \mid \Gamma \vdash t : U}{\Omega \mid \Gamma \vdash \Lambda X.t : \forall X.U} \qquad (\forall[])\frac{\Omega \mid \Gamma \vdash t : \forall X.U}{\Omega \mid \Gamma \vdash t[U_0] : [U_0/X]U}$$

$$(\forall\Leftarrow)\frac{\Omega \mid \Gamma \vdash t : U_1 \quad U_1 \sim U_2}{\Omega \mid \Gamma \vdash \langle U_2 \Leftarrow U_1 \rangle\, t : U_2}$$

**Figure 14.** Polymorphic Blame Calculus (PBC): Type System

**Proposition 16** (Well-typed Translation). *If* $\Gamma^{\forall} \vdash^{\forall} t \rightsquigarrow t' : U$ *then* $[\![\Gamma^{\forall}]\!]^X \mid [\![\Gamma^{\forall}]\!]^x \vdash t' : U$.

*Proof.* By induction on the derivation of $\Gamma^{\forall} \vdash^{\forall} t \rightsquigarrow t' : U$ □

In principle ITGL's semantics can also be defined using the substitutive approach, which essentially monomorphises programs at the expense of code explosion. Taking this approach, the image of the translation is the Blame Calculus (Siek et al. 2009; Wadler and Findler 2009), which is the monomorphic fragment of the PBC.

## 12. Static and Gradual Polymorphism

This section revisits Siek and Vachharajani's analysis of gradual type inference. Their intuitions about parametric polymorphism led them to design an inference algorithm that does not always yield principal types. Our analysis of that variance uncovers a distinction among type parameters. We extend our type system and inference procedure to expose this distinction, and thereby give firmer foundation to this idea.

To motivate their design, Siek and Vachharajani consider how best to answer the following type inference problem:

$$\lambda x : ?.(\lambda y : X.y)\ x$$

Clearly this program is typeable, but what type should $X$ get? Our type inferencer makes it a type parameter, producing the type $? \to A$, but Siek and Vachharajani's type inference algorithm produces $? \to ?$. Their reasoning is that the type $? \to A$ implies parametric polymorphism, and with it the idea that the type can be changed arbitrarily without affecting the program's behavior. However, this simple program gets the value of $y$ from a value of type ?, which, assuming a naïve casting model, could trigger a cast error depending on which type is assigned to $X$.[8] In their view, type signatures with type parameters should indicate static parametric polymorphism, and this type does not.

This observation suggests a distinction that we currently suppress. Sometimes type parameters indicate parametric polymorphic in the traditional sense: irrelevant to program execution. Other

[8] Their system precedes PBC and its dynamics had no runtime sealing.

$$(\sigma\mathrm{x})\ \frac{x : \forall\overline{X_i}.U^{\mathtt{x}} \in \Gamma^{\forall}}{\Gamma^{\forall} \vdash^{\forall} x \leadsto x[\overline{T_i}] : [\overline{T_i}/\overline{X_i}]U^{\mathtt{x}}}$$

$$(\sigma\mathrm{n})\ \frac{}{\Gamma^{\forall} \vdash^{\forall} n \leadsto n : \mathsf{Int}} \qquad (\sigma\mathrm{b})\ \frac{}{\Gamma^{\forall} \vdash^{\forall} b \leadsto b : \mathsf{Bool}}$$

$$(\sigma\mathrm{app})\ \frac{\begin{array}{c}\Gamma^{\forall} \vdash^{\forall} t_1 \leadsto t_1' : U_1 \quad \Gamma^{\forall} \vdash^{\forall} t_2 \leadsto t_2' : U_2 \\ \widetilde{dom}(U_1) \sim U_2\end{array}}{\begin{array}{l}\Gamma^{\forall} \vdash^{\forall} t_1\ t_2 \leadsto \qquad\qquad\qquad : \widetilde{cod}(U_1) \\ \quad (\langle\!\langle \widetilde{dom}(U_1) \to \widetilde{cod}(U_1) \Leftarrow U_1 \rangle\!\rangle t_1') \\ \quad (\langle\!\langle \widetilde{dom}(U_1) \Leftarrow U_2 \rangle\!\rangle t_2')\end{array}}$$

$$(\sigma\mathrm{if})\ \frac{\begin{array}{c}\Gamma^{\forall} \vdash^{\forall} t_1 \leadsto t_1' : U_1 \qquad \Gamma^{\forall} \vdash^{\forall} t_1 \leadsto t_2' : U_2 \\ \Gamma^{\forall} \vdash^{\forall} t_1 \leadsto t_3' : U_3 \quad U_1 \sim \mathsf{Bool} \quad U = U_2 \sqcap U_3\end{array}}{\begin{array}{l}\Gamma^{\forall} \vdash^{\forall} \mathsf{if}\ t_1\ \mathsf{then}\ t_2\ \mathsf{else}\ t_3 \leadsto \\ \quad \mathsf{if}\ \langle\!\langle \mathsf{Bool} \Leftarrow U_1 \rangle\!\rangle t_1 \\ \quad \mathsf{then}\ \langle\!\langle U \Leftarrow U_2 \rangle\!\rangle t_2\ \mathsf{else}\ \langle\!\langle U \Leftarrow U_3 \rangle\!\rangle t_3 : U\end{array}}$$

$$(\sigma+)\ \frac{\begin{array}{cc}\Gamma^{\forall} \vdash^{\forall} t_1 \leadsto t_1' : U_1 & \Gamma^{\forall} \vdash^{\forall} t_1 \leadsto t_2' : U_2 \\ U_1 \sim \mathsf{Int} & U_2 \sim \mathsf{Int}\end{array}}{\Gamma^{\forall} \vdash^{\forall} t_1 + t_2 \leadsto (\langle\!\langle \mathsf{Int} \Leftarrow U_1 \rangle\!\rangle t_1) + (\langle\!\langle \mathsf{Int} \Leftarrow U_2 \rangle\!\rangle t_2) : \mathsf{Int}}$$

$$(\sigma\lambda:)\ \frac{\Gamma^{\forall}, x : \forall\emptyset.U_1 \vdash^{\forall} t \leadsto t' : U_2}{\Gamma^{\forall} \vdash^{\forall} \lambda x : U_1.t \leadsto \lambda x : U_1.t' : U_1 \to U_2}$$

$$(\sigma\lambda)\ \frac{\Gamma^{\forall}, x : \forall\emptyset.T_1 \vdash^{\forall} t \leadsto t' : U_2}{\Gamma^{\forall} \vdash^{\forall} \lambda x.t \leadsto \lambda x : T_1.t' : T_1 \to U_2}$$

$$(\sigma\mathrm{let})\ \frac{\Gamma^{\forall} \vdash^{\forall} (\lambda x.t_2)\ t_1 \leadsto t' : U \qquad t_1 \notin \textsc{Value}}{\Gamma^{\forall} \vdash^{\forall} \mathsf{let}\ x = t_1\ \mathsf{in}\ t_2 \leadsto t' : U}$$

$$(\sigma\mathrm{letp})\ \frac{\begin{array}{ll}\Gamma^{\forall} \vdash^{\forall} v_1 \leadsto v_1' : U_1 & \Gamma^{\forall}, x : \sigma \vdash^{\forall} t_2 \leadsto t_2' : U_2 \\ \sigma = \forall\overline{X_i}.[\overline{X_i}/\overline{A_i}]U_1 & \overline{A_i} \notin \Gamma^{\forall}\end{array}}{\begin{array}{l}\Gamma^{\forall} \vdash^{\forall} \mathsf{let}\ x = v_1\ \mathsf{in}\ t_2 \leadsto \\ \quad (\lambda x : \sigma.t_2')\ (\overline{\Lambda X_i}.[\overline{X_i}/\overline{A_i}]v_1') : U_2\end{array}}$$

$$(\sigma::)\ \frac{\Gamma^{\forall} \vdash^{\forall} t : U \leadsto t' : U \qquad U \sim U_1}{\Gamma^{\forall} \vdash^{\forall} (t :: U_1) \leadsto \langle\!\langle U_1 \Leftarrow U \rangle\!\rangle t : U_1}$$

$$\langle\!\langle U \Leftarrow U \rangle\!\rangle t = t$$

$$\langle\!\langle U_2 \Leftarrow U_1 \rangle\!\rangle t = \langle U_2 \Leftarrow U_1 \rangle\, t \text{ if } U_1 \neq U_2$$

**Figure 15.** Gradual Language: Schematic Translation

times, type parameters indicate that a value's only constraint is that it may be cast to and from ?, which may introduce casts. We distinguish this latter circumstance as an instance of *gradual polymorphism*, the exact circumstance that the Polymorphic Blame Calculus was designed to address.

To clearly delineate this type-level distinction, we extend our languages with another class of type parameters: in addition to the *gradual type parameters* $A$, we introduce *static type parameters* $B$ (Fig. 16).

In ITSL, these type parameters would all be equivalent. However, when we transition to gradual typing, these types are distinguished from their forebears.

The gradual types extend the static types as usual, thereby creating the universe of types for this language. The type distinction, however, leads to several families of static and gradual types. Castable types $W$ are those static types that can be passed to the dynamic world. Their two salient properties are the absence of the unknown type ? and the static type parameter $B$, which may not pass to the dynamic world. Indeed there is a gradual counterpart $Y$.

$$\begin{array}{l}B \in \textsc{STParam}, \quad T \in \textsc{Type}, \quad U \in \textsc{GType}, \\ W \in \textsc{Castable}, \quad Y \in \textsc{GCastable} \\ V \in \textsc{StaticType} = \textsc{Type} \setminus \textsc{Castable} \\ Z \in \textsc{GStaticType} = \textsc{GType} \setminus \textsc{GCastable} \\ T ::= A \mid B \mid \mathsf{Int} \mid \mathsf{Bool} \mid T \to T \\ U ::= ? \mid A \mid B \mid \mathsf{Int} \mid \mathsf{Bool} \mid T \to T \\ W ::= A \mid \mathsf{Int} \mid \mathsf{Bool} \mid T \to T \\ Y ::= ? \mid A \mid \mathsf{Int} \mid \mathsf{Bool} \mid T \to T\end{array}$$

**Figure 16.** Gradual and Static Type Parameters: Syntax

The static and gradual types that do not appear in these sets make up the *static types* $V$ and *gradual static types* $Z$. These latter two refer to those types that represent pure parametric polymorphism.

In this new model, the unknown type ? no longer represents all possible static types, but only the types in GCASTABLE. In particular, they do not include the *static types*: any type that contains a static type parameter.

The most immediate change that results from this interpretation is that not all types are consistent with ?. In particular, $Z \not\sim\ ?$ for any $Z \in \textsc{GStaticType}$. In fact, it hereditarily follows that any type containing a static type parameter $B$ is not consistent with ?. The relevant changes to consistency are as follows.

$$\frac{}{B \sim B} \qquad \frac{}{? \sim Y} \qquad \frac{}{Y \sim ?}$$

Static type parameters are consistent to themselves, as is standard, but now ? is consistent to only the *castable* gradual types $Y$, not all gradual types $U$.

In ITSL, the consequence is that the language has more type variables, which to date has not been a problem in practice. For instance, the program $\lambda x.x$ may be given type $A \to A$, using the gradual type parameters, but our earlier program can at best be given the type $B \to B$ using static type parameters.

Furthermore, this extension changes the nature of our type polymorphism theorem:

**Definition 14.**

1. *Let* $S^A \in \textsc{ASubst} = \textsc{TParam} \to \textsc{Castable}$ *denote the gradual type parameter substitutions, or* $A$*-substitutions.*
2. *Let* $S^B \in \textsc{BSubst} = \textsc{STParam} \to \textsc{Type}$ *denote the static type parameter substitutions, or* $B$*-substitutions.*
3. *Let* $S^P \in \textsc{PSubst} =$ $\{ S^A \cup S^B \mid S^A \in \textsc{ASubst}, S^B \in \textsc{BSubst} \}$ *denote the type parameter substitutions, or* $P$*-substitutions.*

These two substitutions distill the semantics of polymorphism. Gradual type parameters $A$ represent castable types $W$; conversely, static type parameters $B$ represent all static types, including the gradual type parameters $A$. In practice, we are interested in substitutions $S^P = S^A \cup S^B$ which simultaneously map gradual and static type parameters to castable types and static types, respectively. These $P$-substitutions capture our new notion of type polymorphism.

**Proposition 17.**

1. *If* $\Gamma \vdash t : U$ *then* $\widehat{S^P}(\Gamma) \vdash \widehat{S^P}(t) : \widehat{S^P}(U)$ *for any* $S^P \in \textsc{PSubst}$.

*Proof.* Straightforward induction on derivations $\Gamma \vdash t : U$. □

### 12.1 Type Inference for Pure Parametric Polymorphism

Now that we have described an implicitly typed language with two tiers of parametric polymorphism, how do we infer these two types? Conveniently, doing so requires only a small extension to our type inference approach. Our type inferencer up to now has simply discarded constraints that require a type to be consistent with ?, since this was true of every type. Now we must consider them, because they make the difference between a static parametric type and a gradual one.

To account for the type distinction, we extend the unification relation to be a ternary relation

$$\mathcal{U} \in \mathcal{P}(\text{GTypeExp}) \times \mathcal{P}(\text{Constraint}) \times \text{TSubst},$$

where $\mathcal{T} \mid C^\star \; \mathcal{U} \; S$ means that the constraints $C^\star$ plus $(U^\mathtt{X} \sim ?)$ for each $U^\mathtt{X} \in \mathcal{T}$ are unified by $S$. We modify the previous unification relation as follows:

$$\frac{}{\mathcal{T} \mid \emptyset \; \mathcal{U} \; \widehat{S_\mathcal{B}} \circ [\overline{\text{Vars}(\mathcal{T}) \mapsto A_i}]} \qquad \frac{\mathcal{T} \cup \{U^\mathtt{X}\} \mid C^\star \; \mathcal{U} \; S}{\mathcal{T} \mid C^\star \cup \{? \stackrel{.}{\sim} U^\mathtt{X}\} \; \mathcal{U} \; S}$$

$$\frac{\mathcal{T} \cup \{U^\mathtt{X}\} \mid C^\star \; \mathcal{U} \; S}{\mathcal{T} \mid C^\star \cup \{U^\mathtt{X} \stackrel{.}{\sim} ?\} \; \mathcal{U} \; S}$$

First, we no longer discard constraints that $U^\mathtt{X} \sim ?$ because we must now ensure that $\widehat{S}(U^\mathtt{X}) \in \text{GCastable}$ to secure the type distinction. Second, to satisfy an empty constraint set, the corresponding substitution $S$ must map all type variables in $\mathcal{T}$ to gradual type parameters $A_i$. The remaining type variables have no constraints, so they can safely be mapped to static type parameters $B_i$.

With these few extensions, the corresponding notions of soundness and completeness of unification, as well as principal types, hold.

**Proposition 18** (Principal Types). *Suppose* $\Gamma^\mathtt{X} \vdash t^\mathtt{X} : U^\mathtt{X} \mid C^\star \mid \mathcal{X}$. *Then if* $S_1^\mathtt{X} \models C^\star$ *for some* $S_1^\mathtt{X}$, *it follows that* $\emptyset \mid C^\star \; \mathcal{U} \; S_2^\mathtt{X}$, *and* $(S_2^\mathtt{X}, \widehat{S_2^\mathtt{X}}(U^\mathtt{X}))$ *is a principal solution for* $\Gamma^\mathtt{X}$ *and* $t^\mathtt{X}$.

*Proof.* Follows from Completeness of Unification. □

This proposition establishes that our type inference procedure produces the best type possible, and along the way proves that the type system has a well-defined notion of "best" types.

### 12.2 Dynamic Semantics

This new type distinction suggests two more interpretations of ITGL. These interpretations differ with respect to whether or not they enforce representation-independence at runtime, and conversely with respect to the complexity of the necessary runtime support.

Our language from Sec. 11 corresponds to interpreting both static and gradual type parameters using runtime sealing. A more refined language could use static parametric polymorphism for static type parameters and reserve runtime sealing only for gradual type parameters.

Viewed from this perspective, Siek and Vachharajani interpret all gradual type parameters as ?, leaving only the static type parameters. This language model can be translated to the (monomorphic) Blame Calculus, erasing static type parameters in the standard way. Note, however, that this translation of $B$s to ?s implies a syntactic reinterpretation of our programs. In particular, since our type system does not infer gradual types, this reinterpretation corresponds to a refinement process on programs that introduces new type annotations to a program that change some parameters to gradual types. The $\lambda^{?\alpha}_{\rightarrow}$ language interprets these types without incident since gradual types were always inferrable, but at the cost of a complex type system and inferencer.

## 13. Discussion

Construction of the type system and inference was systematic and driven by underlying principles of the static type system. The structure of ITSL sheds light on the structure of the Simply Typed Gradual Calculus' type system, in particular the origin of the two typing rules for function application.

The constraint typing judgment does not hold for every context–term pair. This property falls out of our decision to reduce all gradual predicates and functions to consistency constraints on gradual types and equality constraints on static types. Alternatively, we could have produced constraints that directly correspond to those operators. Doing so would force us to also support gradual type variables, at least to account for the meet operator when typing if expressions. This design simplifies the constraint typing judgment, at the expense of the unification judgment, which would have to process more constraints, and be mindful of the order in which they are processed. Reducing constraints up-front imposes fewer extensions on the corresponding static unification judgment.

The ITGL type system can be easily shown to conservatively extend the ITSL type system. In particular, the gradual operators all reduce to their static counterparts when applied to static types. In contrast, Siek and Vachharajani (2008) requires explicit reasoning to establish this property.

Distinguishing type parameters from type variables was central to understanding the distinction between static polymorphism and gradual polymorphism, both of which are orthogonal to the type inference problem. This distinction explains Siek and Vachharajani's observation about assigning the unknown type. Such types are not principal according to their type system, but they arise naturally from interpreting gradual type parameters in our system as ?.

The ease with which ITGL extends with let-polymorphism suggests that the language may be amenable to other common features of Hindley-Milner type systems, like row polymorphism (Wand 1987b) and restricted first-class polymorphism (Peyton Jones et al. 2007). We intend to explore some of these more advanced features in the future. Furthermore, we believe that the connection between this system and its underlying static language suggests that it may be reasonable to extend an existing language implementation to support gradual type inference.

Although ITGL can be safely translated to either the Blame Calculus (BC) or the Polymorphic Blame Calculus (PBC), we do not yet understand all the tradeoffs involved. The BC imposes less runtime overhead since it does not require runtime sealing, but the PBC enforces representation-independence. Extending the language with first-class polymorphism, and implementing gradual type inference in a real language, may provide further insight.

***Related Work*** Aside from (Siek and Vachharajani 2008), the most closely related work to ours is Rastogi et al. (2012). It presents an approach to flow-based type inference for a variant of the ActionScript language that combines static and dynamic checking. Although both works involve graduality and inference, the two have essential differences that make them complementary.

First, the two approaches start with different kinds of languages. We begin with an implicitly typed functional language, for which types are typically inferred using unification. Rastogi et al. start from a subtyping-based object-oriented language, for which unification is insufficient to infer types.

Second, the two approaches start from different conceptual foundations. Rastogi et al. begin with a gradually typed language in the style of (Siek and Taha 2006), where missing type annotations are syntactic sugar for ? annotations, and extend it with support for type inference. To do so, they reinterpret missing type annotations as type variables and solve for gradual types using a flow-directed algorithm. We begin with an implicitly typed language and extend it with gradual typing. In doing so, we infer the same static types as the underlying language. It is interesting to observe, however, that Siek and Vachharajani (2008) start from similar foundations to Rastogi et al., but arrive at a type system like ours.

Third, the two approaches have distinct goals. Rastogi et al. are interested in reducing the performance overhead of gradual typing by removing dynamic checks where possible without changing the runtime error behaviour of programs. We are interested in consistency-based reasoning about programs in terms of the underlying pre-existing type system.

Ultimately, the two approaches are complementary. In particular, we believe that techniques similar to Rastogi et al. could be applied to ITGL to reduce runtime overhead. One open problem in this direction is the interaction between flow-based inference and runtime sealing.

## 14. Conclusion

Dynamic checking is often characterized as the practice of checking at runtime those expressions that lack type annotations. Static checking, on the other hand, is associated with introducing type annotations to achieve more safety. This paper investigates the combination of dynamic and static checking, and finds that the tables reverse in the foundations of gradual type inference: there can be no dynamism without annotation.

## 15. Acknowledgments

The authors would like to thank Suzanna Crage, Jeremy Siek, Éric Tanter, Sam Tobin-Hochstadt, Amal Ahmed, Bob Harper, and the anonymous reviewers for comments and suggestions about this work.

## References

A. Ahmed, R. B. Findler, J. Matthews, and P. Wadler. Blame for all. In *Proc. 1st Workshop on Script to Program Evolution*, STOP '09, pages 1–13, New York, NY, USA, 2009. ACM. .

A. Ahmed, R. B. Findler, J. G. Siek, and P. Wadler. Blame for all. In *Proc. Symposium on Principles of Programming Languages*, POPL '11, pages 201–214, New York, NY, USA, 2011. ACM. .

G. Bierman, E. Meijer, and M. Torgersen. Adding dynamic types to C#. In T. D'Hondt, editor, *Proc. 24th European Conference on Object-oriented Programming (ECOOP 2010)*, number 6183 in Lecture Notes in Computer Science, pages 76–100, Maribor, Slovenia, June 2010. Springer-Verlag.

R. Cartwright and M. Fagan. Soft typing. In *Proc. Conference on Programming Language Design and Implementation*, PLDI '91, pages 278–292, New York, NY, USA, 1991. ACM.

D. Crystal. *A dictionary of linguistics and phonetics*. Blackwell, 2008.

S. K. Debray and D. S. Warren. Automatic mode inference for logic programs. *Journal of Logic Programming*, 5(3):207–229, Sept. 1988.

J.-Y. Girard. *Interprtation fonctionelle et limination des coupures de l'arithmtique d'ordre suprieur.* PhD thesis, Universit Paris VII, 1972.

J. Gronski, K. Knowles, A. Tomb, S. N. Freund, and C. Flanagan. Sage: Hybrid checking for flexible specifications. In *Proc. Scheme and Functional Programming Workshop*, pages 93–104, 2006.

J. Matthews and A. Ahmed. Parametric polymorphism through run-time sealing or, theorems for low, low prices! In *Proc. European Conference on Programming Languages and Systems*, ESOP'08/ETAPS'08, pages 16–31, Berlin, Heidelberg, 2008. Springer-Verlag.

J. Matthews and R. B. Findler. Operational semantics for multi-language programs. *ACM Transactions on Programming Languages and Systems*, 31(3):12:1–12:44, Apr. 2009.

R. Milner. A theory of type polymorphism in programming. *Journal of Computer and System Sciences*, 17:348–375, Aug. 1978.

A. Ohori. A simple semantics for ml polymorphism. In *Proc. International Conference on Functional Programming Languages and Computer Architecture*, FPCA '89, pages 281–292, New York, NY, USA, 1989. ACM. .

S. Peyton Jones, D. Vytiniotis, S. Weirich, and M. Shields. Practical type inference for arbitrary-rank types. *Journal of Functional Programming*, 17(1):1–82, Jan. 2007. .

B. C. Pierce. *Types and programming languages*. MIT Press, Cambridge, MA, USA, 2002.

A. Rastogi, A. Chaudhuri, and B. Hosmer. The ins and outs of gradual type inference. In *Proc. Symposium on Principles of Programming Languages*, pages 481–494, New York, NY, USA, 2012. ACM. .

J. C. Reynolds. Towards a theory of type structure. In *Programming Symposium, Proceedings Colloque Sur La Programmation*, pages 408–423, London, UK, UK, 1974. Springer-Verlag.

J. A. Robinson. A machine-oriented logic based on the resolution principle. *J. ACM*, 12(1):23–41, Jan. 1965. ISSN 0004-5411. .

I. Sergey and D. Clarke. Gradual ownership types. In H. Seidl, editor, *Proc. European Symposium on Programming Languages and Systems*, volume 7211 of *ESOP '12*, pages 579–599, Tallinn, Estonia, 2012. Springer-Verlag.

J. Siek and W. Taha. Gradual typing for objects. In E. Ernst, editor, *Proc. European Conference on Object-oriented Programming*, number 4609 in ECOOP '07, pages 2–27, Berlin, Germany, July 2007. Springer-Verlag.

J. Siek, R. Garcia, and W. Taha. Exploring the design space of higher-order casts. In *Proc. European Symposium on Programming Languages*, ESOP '09, pages 17–31, Berlin, 2009. Springer-Verlag.

J. G. Siek and W. Taha. Gradual typing for functional languages. In *Proc. Scheme and Functional Programming Workshop*, pages 81–92, Sept. 2006.

J. G. Siek and M. Vachharajani. Gradual typing with unification-based inference. In *Proc. 2008 Symposium on Dynamic Languages*, DLS '08, pages 7:1–7:12, New York, NY, USA, 2008. ACM. .

N. Swamy, C. Fournet, A. Rastogi, K. Bhargavan, J. Chen, P.-Y. Strub, and G. Bierman. Gradual typing embedded securely in JavaScript. In *Proc. 41st ACM SIGPLAN-SIGACT symposium on Principles of programming languages (POPL 2014)*, pages 425–437, San Diego, CA, USA, Jan. 2014. ACM Press.

S. Tobin-Hochstadt and M. Felleisen. Interlanguage migration: From scripts to programs. In *Companion to the 21st ACM SIGPLAN Symposium on Object-oriented Programming Systems, Languages, and Applications*, OOPSLA '06, pages 964–974, New York, NY, USA, 2006. ACM. ISBN 1-59593-491-X.

S. Tobin-Hochstadt and M. Felleisen. The design and implementation of Typed Scheme. In *Proc. 35th ACM SIGPLAN-SIGACT Symposium on Principles of Programming Languages (POPL 2008)*, pages 395–406, San Francisco, CA, USA, Jan. 2008. ACM Press.

P. Wadler and R. B. Findler. Well-typed programs can't be blamed. In *Proc. European Symposium on Programming Languages*, ESOP '09, pages 1–16, Berlin, 2009. Springer-Verlag.

M. Wand. A simple algorithm and proof for type inference. *Fundamenta Infomaticae*, 10:115–122, 1987a.

M. Wand. Complete type inference for simple objects. In *Proc. 2nd IEEE Symposium on Logic in Computer Science*, pages 37–44, 1987b.

R. Wolff, R. Garcia, É. Tanter, and J. Aldrich. Gradual typestate. In M. Mezini, editor, *Proc. European Conference on Object-oriented Programming*, volume 6813 of *Lecture Notes in Computer Science*, pages 459–483, Lancaster, UK, July 2011. Springer-Verlag.

A. K. Wright. Simple imperative polymorphism. *Lisp Symb. Comput.*, 8(4): 343–355, Dec. 1995. ISSN 0892-4635. .

A. K. Wright and M. Felleisen. A syntactic approach to type soundness. *Journal of Information and Computation*, 115(1):38–94, Nov. 1994.

T. Wrigstad, F. Zappa Nardelli, S. Lebresne, J. Östlund, and J. Vitek. Integrating typed and untyped code in a scripting language. In *Proc. 37th annual ACM SIGPLAN-SIGACT symposium on Principles of programming languages (POPL 2010)*, pages 377–388, Madrid, Spain, Jan. 2010. ACM Press.

# Dependent Information Flow Types

Luísa Lourenço Luís Caires
CITI and NOVA Laboratory for Computer Science and Informatics
Faculdade de Ciências e Tecnologia
Universidade Nova de Lisboa

## Abstract

In this paper, we develop a novel notion of dependent information flow types. Dependent information flow types fit within the standard framework of dependent type theory, but, unlike usual dependent types, crucially allow the security level of a type, rather than just the structural data type itself, to depend on runtime values.

Our dependent function and dependent sum information flow types provide a direct, natural and elegant way to express and enforce fine grained security policies on programs, including programs that manipulate structured data types in which the security level of a structure field may depend on values dynamically stored in other fields, still considered a challenge to security enforcement in software systems such as data-centric web-based applications.

We base our development on the very general setting of a minimal $\lambda$-calculus with references and collections. We illustrate its expressiveness, showing how secure operations on relevant scenarios can be modelled and analysed using our dependent information flow type system, which is also shown to be amenable to algorithmic type checking. Our main results include type-safety and non-interference theorems ensuring that well-typed programs do not violate prescribed security policies.

***Categories and Subject Descriptors*** D.3.3 [*Programming Languages*]: Language Constructs and Features; D.4.6 [*Operating Systems*]: Security and Protection – Information Flow Controls; F.3.3 [*Logics and Meanings of Programs*]: Type Structure

***Keywords*** Information Flow; Dependent Type Systems

## 1. Introduction

Among the main challenges currently posed to software development one inevitably finds security enforcement, particularly relevant for the construction of data-centric applications to be made available on the web, or on mobile computing environments. Many reported security leaks in globally used information systems, including email management or social network systems, turn out in many cases to result from programming errors introducing insecure information flows in complex and heterogeneous software layers. A relevant research issue consists on finding improved techniques to ensure trustworthy confidentiality in the presence of multi-tenancy and container sharing, as e.g., when logically different security compartments are not statically mapped to different physical or data structure compartments, but are instead dynamic and dependent on runtime data, including on configuration parameters.

In this paper, we develop the notion of *dependent information flow types*. Dependent information flow types provide a direct, natural and elegant way to express and statically enforce fine grained security policies on programs, including programs that manipulate structured data types in which the security level of a structure field may depend on values dynamically stored in other fields, still considered a challenge to security enforcement in software systems such as data-centric web-based applications. In standard information flow type systems [1, 8, 10, 12, 28], a type has the form $\tau^{\mathtt{s}}$, where the structural type $\tau$ is tagged with a security label $\mathtt{s}$, an element of a security lattice modelling an hierarchy of security compartments or levels. For example, one defines $(\mathtt{int}^{\top} \rightarrow \mathtt{int}^{\top})^{\perp}$ as the type of a low security ($\perp$) function that maps a high security ($\top$) integer to a high security integer. However, as already suggested, it is often the case that the security level of data values depends on the manipulated data itself; such dependencies are obviously not expressible by such basic security labelling approaches.

The key idea behind dependent information flow types is fairly simple. We propose to extend dependent types in such a way that not only the (structural) type assigned to a computation may depend on values but also its security level, expressed by associating to a data type a value dependent security label [17], instead of a plain security label, as described above. To achieve this goal, we present in this paper a novel theory of dependent information flow types within the framework of dependent type theory, including sum and function dependent types, aiming to capture the general essence of value dependent security classification. A simple example of a dependent (function) information flow type is

$$\Pi x{:}\mathtt{string}^{\perp}.\mathtt{string}^{\mathtt{usr}(x)}$$

One could assign such a type to the function `get_passwd` that given a user name (a string) returns its password (a string). Although the security level of user "pat" is public ($\perp$), pat's password itself belongs to the security level usr("pat"), where $\mathtt{usr}(x)$ is a value dependent security label. For another simple example, consider the following dependent (labeled product) information flow type:

$$\Sigma[\mathtt{uid} : \mathtt{string}^{\perp} \times \mathtt{passwd} : \mathtt{string}^{\mathtt{usr(uid)}}]$$

This would type records in which the security level of `passwd` field depends on the actual value assigned to the `uid` field. Value dependent security labels, such as $\mathtt{usr}(x)$, denote concrete security levels in the given security lattice, along standard lines, but allow security levels to be indexed by program values, useful to express security constraints to depend on dynamically determined data values. In such a setting, we would expect the security levels usr("joe") and usr("pat") to be incomparable, thus avoiding insecure infor-


*POPL '15*, January 15–17, 2015, Mumbai, India.
Copyright © 2015 ACM 978-1-4503-3300-9/15/01...$15.00.
http://dx.doi.org/10.1145/2676726.2676994

mation flows between the associated security compartments, representing the private knowledge of users joe and pat respectively. In particular the security level of the password returned by the call **get_passwd**("joe") is **usr**("joe") rather than, say, just **usr**, which in our setting could be denoted by the label $\mathtt{usr}(\top)$, representing the security level of the information available from any user. Thus dependent types together with value indexed security labels allows secure computations to be expressed with extra precision.

Other key feature of our type system is the way it allows us to capture general data-dependent security constraints within data structures containing elements classified at different security levels, as necessary to represent, e.g., realistic rich security policies on structured documents or databases. Typically, it is required to flexibly inspect, select, and compose such structure elements during computations, while enforcing all the intended information flow policies. For example, consider a (global) password file **users** modelled by a collection (e.g. a list) of records of dependent type. The type assigned to such a collection would be:

$$\mathtt{users} : \Sigma[\mathtt{uid} : \mathtt{string}^{\perp} \times \mathtt{passwd} : \mathtt{string}^{\mathtt{usr(uid)}}]^{*\perp}$$

(notice that $s^*$ is the type of collections (lists) of values of type $s$). Then, consider the following function

```
let getPasswords = λ(u).
   foreach (x in users) with acum = {} do
     if x.uid = u then x.pwd :: acum else acum
```

The function getPasswords extracts from the global data structure **users** the collection of passwords associated to a user id (the **foreach** iterator is a familiar functional collection fold combinator [3]; x is the current item/cursor and acum denotes the value accumulated from previous iteration, with initial value $\{\}$). Notice that although the collection **users** contains passwords classified in different security levels, the security level of the collection returned by the function is always $\mathtt{usr}(u)$, with $u$ the user id string passed as argument. Then, the following typing holds:

$$\mathtt{getPasswords} : \Pi u{:}\mathtt{string}^{\perp}.\mathtt{string}^{*\mathtt{usr}(u)}$$

We base our development on a minimal $\lambda$-calculus with records, (general) imperative references, and collections. Although extremely parsimonious, we show that our programming language and its dependent information flow type system is already quite expressive, allowing practically relevant scenarios to be modelled and analysed against natural value dependent information flow policies.

Although approaching a substantial level of simplicity, our type system tackles relevant technical challenges, necessary to handle heterogeneously classified data structures and security level dependency. As in classical approaches (e.g., [1, 12]), both a type $\tau$ and a security label $\mathsf{s}$ are assigned to expressions by our typing judgment $\Delta \vdash^{\mathsf{r}}_{S} e : \tau^{\mathsf{s}}$, reflecting the fact that the value of $e$ does not depend on data classified with security levels above $\mathsf{s}$ or incomparable with $\mathsf{s}$, where $\mathsf{s}$ is in general a value dependent label. The analysis of implicit flows is also particularly interesting in our setting, even if we adopt standard techniques to track the computational context security level $\mathsf{r}$ (the "program counter"). The additional component $S$ represents a set of the equational constraints, used to refine label indices, and establish type equality.

We summarise the contributions of this paper. First, we motivate, introduce, and develop a type-based information flow analysis for a $\lambda$-calculus with references and collections. We build on a new notion of dependent information flow types, developed along the lines of a standard dependent type theory but where the security level (not just the structure) of data types may depend on values (Section 2). Second, we illustrate the expressiveness of our language and analysis using several examples (Section 3). Third, we present our main technical results: type safety (preservation and progress) (Theorems 5.4 and 5.5) and a non-interference (Theorem 5.11), which together imply that well-typed programs do not break data confidentiality according to the security policies prescribed by dependent information flow types (Section 5). After discussing algorithmic type checking (Section 6), we overview key related work (Section 7), and offer some concluding remarks (Section 8).

## 2. Dependent Information Flow Types

In this section, we motivate dependent (function and sum) information flow types by means of several examples, providing an informal overview of the approach developed in the paper.

As in any information flow analysis, we are concerned about insecure flows that might arise during the execution of a program but not with how data is accessed (which concerns access control). Our analysis associates security levels $\mathsf{s}$ to types $\tau$ to classify expressions $e$, so typing an expression at security level $\mathsf{s}$, denoted $\Delta \vdash e : \tau^{\mathsf{s}}$, means that data used or computed by expression $e$ will only be affected by data classified at security levels up to $\mathsf{s}$. We proceed by illustrating our programming language, a simple $\lambda$-calculus with references, using as toy example, a typical data centric web application: a conference manager.

In this scenario, a user of the system can be either a registered user, an author user, or a programme committee (PC) member user. The system stores data concerning its users' information, their submissions, and the reviews of submissions in "database tables" which we will represent in our core programming language as lists of (references to) records (e.g., mutable lists), as shown in Figure 1d for the types declared in Figure 1a: Users stores information for each registered user; Submissions keeps track of each submission in the system by storing its id, the author's id, and the contents of the submission; and Reviews stores information regarding the evaluation of each submission namely: the id of the PC member reviewing the submission, the id of the submission, the comments for the other PC members, and the comments and grade to be delivered to the author. The system offers operations to add new data as well as some listing operations. We exemplify some of them.

---

**Example 2.1** Operation assignReviewer assigns a PC member to review a given submission, initialising the remaining fields.

```
let assignReviewer = λ (u, s).
   let new_rec = ref_δa
     [uid=u, sid=s, PC_only= "", review="", grade=""]
   in Reviews := new_rec :: !Reviews
```

**Example 2.2** Operation viewAuthorPapers iterates the Submissions collection to build a list of all records with a given author id

```
let viewAuthorPapers = λ (uid_a).
  foreach(x in !Submissions) with y = {} do
    let tuple = !x in
      if tuple.uid = uid_a then tuple::y else y
```

**Example 2.3** Operation viewAssignedPapers simulates a join operation between collections Reviews and Submissions to obtain the list of submissions assigned to the PC member with the given id.

```
let viewAssignedPapers = λ (uid_r).
   foreach (x in !Reviews) with res_x = {} do
     let tuple_rev = !x in
       if tuple_rev.uid = uid_r then
         (foreach(y in !Submissions) with res_y = {} do
            let tuple_sub = !y in
              if tuple_sub.sid = tuple_rev.sid then
                 tuple_sub::res_y else res_y )::res_x
     else res_x
```

---

$$\tau_a \stackrel{\text{def}}{=} [\texttt{uid} : \texttt{int} \times \texttt{name} : \texttt{str} \times \texttt{univ} : \texttt{str} \times \texttt{email} : \texttt{str}]$$

$$\sigma_a \stackrel{\text{def}}{=} [\texttt{uid} : \texttt{int} \times \texttt{sid} : \texttt{int} \times \texttt{title} : \texttt{str} \times \texttt{abs} : \texttt{str}^* \times \texttt{paper} : \texttt{int}^*]$$

$$\delta_a \stackrel{\text{def}}{=} [\texttt{uid} : \texttt{int} \times \texttt{sid} : \texttt{int} \times \texttt{PC\_only} : \texttt{str}^* \times \texttt{review} : \texttt{str}^* \times \texttt{grade} : \texttt{int}]$$

(a) Purely structural types (not expressing security levels)

$$\tau_b \stackrel{\text{def}}{=} [\texttt{uid} : \bot \times \texttt{name} : \texttt{U} \times \texttt{univ} : \texttt{U} \times \texttt{email} : \texttt{U}]$$

$$\sigma_b \stackrel{\text{def}}{=} [\texttt{uid} : \bot \times \texttt{sid} : \bot \times \texttt{title} : \texttt{A} \times \texttt{abs} : \texttt{A} \times \texttt{paper} : \texttt{A}]$$

$$\delta_b \stackrel{\text{def}}{=} [\texttt{uid} : \bot \times \texttt{sid} : \bot \times \texttt{PC\_only} : \texttt{PC} \times \texttt{review} : \texttt{A} \times \texttt{grade} : \texttt{A}]$$

(b) Standard security types for information flow (e.g., [1, 12]) - we omit base types

$$\tau_c \stackrel{\text{def}}{=} \Sigma[\texttt{uid} : \bot \times \texttt{name} : \texttt{U(uid)} \times \texttt{univ} : \texttt{U(uid)} \times \texttt{email} : \texttt{U(uid)}]$$

$$\sigma_c \stackrel{\text{def}}{=} \Sigma[\texttt{uid} : \bot \times \texttt{sid} : \bot \times \texttt{title} : \texttt{A(uid,sid)} \times \texttt{abs} : \texttt{A(uid,sid)} \times \texttt{paper} : \texttt{A(uid,sid)}]$$

$$\delta_c \stackrel{\text{def}}{=} \Sigma[\texttt{uid} : \bot \times \texttt{sid} : \bot \times \texttt{PC\_only} : \texttt{PC(uid,sid)} \times \texttt{review} : \texttt{A}(\top,\texttt{sid}) \times \texttt{grade} : \texttt{A}(\top,\texttt{sid})]$$

(c) Dependent information flow types

```
let Users = ref_{ref(τ(·))*⊥} (ref_{τ(·)} [] )::{} in
let Submissions=ref_{ref(σ(·))*⊥} (ref_{σ(·)} [] )::{} in
let Reviews = ref_{ref(δ(·))*⊥} (ref_{δ(·)} [] )::{}
```

(d) Declaration of (mutable) collections of mutable records (replace (·) with a, b or c for according type)

Figure 1: Expressing security policies

The **foreach** primitive computes the accumulated value of a list's elements. For instance, `foreach(x in viewAuthorPapers(03))with count = 0 do count + 1`, returns the number of submissions of author with id `03`.

Our goal is to statically ensure by typing the confidentiality of the data stored in the conference manager system. As in classical approaches (e.g., [1, 12]), both a type $\tau$ and a security label s are assigned to expressions by our typing judgment $\Delta \vdash e{:}\tau^{\mathsf{s}}$, expressing the fact that the value of $e$ will only be affected by computations interfering at security levels $\leq$ s. As is usual in information flow analysis, a partial order (the so-called security lattice) relating security levels is defined, and information is only allowed to flow upwards (in the order). For the purpose of static code analysis, the given security lattice could be declared as a preamble to the code to be checked. To specify security policies for our system, we thus classify the data manipulated by our conference manager with security levels from a suitable security lattice (omitting data types when not necessary, for simplicity). We assume security lattices are bounded by a top, $\top$, and bottom, $\bot$ element denoting the most restrictive (no one can observe) and most permissive (public data, anyone can observe) security levels, respectively. For the conference manager we can then specify, say, that information is classified in three additional security levels: `U` for the data that can be disclosed to any registered user; `A` for data observable to authors; and `PC` for data that only programme committee members can see. In such simple case, we may let $\bot$<`U`<`A`<`PC`<$\top$ and specify the according security policy for each conference manager entity as shown in Figure 1d for the types declared in Figure 1b. Such policy states that a registered user's information is observable from security level `U`, meaning any registered user (including authors and PC members) can see it; that the content of a paper can be seen by authors; and, finally, regarding a submission's review we have that comments to the PC are observable only to its members and reviews and grade of the submission can be seen by authors.

This policy, however, is not precise enough to protect the confidentiality of the data. An author, who has at least the security level `A`, is able to execute the operation `viewAuthorPapers` (Example 2.2) using a different id than his own, which clearly violates confidentiality. Thus, the security policy that we need is the following: a registered user's information is *only* observable *by himself*; the content of a paper can be seen by *its author as well as its reviewers*; and regarding a submission's review, we have that comments to the PC can *only* be observable to the other members that are *also reviewers of the submission*, and that comments and grade of the submission can be seen by *its author only*. To express these kind of data-dependent policies and make sure that operations that depend on them are secure according to the given policies (such as the operation illustrated above), we introduce a general notion of dependent information flow type, which builds on the notion of *indexed* security label [17]. Using indexed security labels we may partition security levels by indexing labels $\ell$ with values $v$, so that each partition $\ell(v)$ classify data at a specific level, depending on the value $v$. For example, we can partition the security level `U` into $n$ security compartments, each representing a single registered user of the system, so security level `U(01)` represents the security compartment of the registered user with id `01`. Of course, one may also consider indexed labels of arbitrary arity, for instance for security level `A` (author) we can index with both the author's id and submission's id so `A(42,70)` would stand for the security compartment of data relating to author (with id `42`) and his submission (with id `70`).

Going back to our example, we assume the following defined security levels: `U(uid)`, for registered users with id `uid`; `A(uid,sid)`, for author of submission with id `sid` and whose user id is `uid`; and `PC(uid,sid)`, for PC members assigned to review submission with id `sid` and whose user id is `uid`. In general, the security lattice is required to enforce $\ell(\overline{v}, u, \overline{w}) \leq \ell(\overline{v}, \top, \overline{w})$ and $\ell(\overline{v}, \bot, \overline{w}) \leq \ell(\overline{v}, u, \overline{w})$, for all $u$, $\overline{v}$ and $\overline{w}$. So, e.g, for all `uid` we have `U(`$\bot$`)` $\leq$ `U(uid)` $\leq$ `U(`$\top$`)`; we can see `U(`$\top$`)` as the approximation (from above) of any `U(uid)`, e.g, standing for the standard label `U` (Figure 1b). Levels `A(`$\bot$`,`$\bot$`)`, and `PC(`$\bot$`,`$\bot$`)` stand for the security compartment accessible to any author and any PC member, respectively; but `A(`$\top$`,`$\top$`)`, and `PC(`$\top$`,`$\top$`)` respectively represent the compartments containing the information of all authors and all PC members; level `A(uid,`$\top$`)` stands for registered users with id `uid` that are authors; `A(`$\top$`,sid)` represents the security compartment of authors of submission with id `sid`; `A(uid,`$\bot$`)` means a registered author with no authority over submitted papers; and so on. We define the declarations in Figure 1d for the types declared in Figure 1c, and the partial order defining the sample security lattice by the following axioms (quantifiers ranging over natural numbers):

```
∀uid,sid. U(uid)≤ A(uid,sid)
∀uid1,uid2,sid. A(uid1,sid)≤ PC(uid2,sid)
```

We proceed our motivation of dependent information flow types with a series of code snippets relevant for our conference manager scenario.

Consider then the following code

**Example 2.4**

```
let t = first((foreach(x in !Submissions) with y={} do
       let t_sub = !x in
        if t_sub.uid = 42 and t_sub.sid = 70 then
          t_sub.title::y else y ))
in (foreach(x in !Submissions) with y = {} do
     let t_sub = !x in
       if t_sub.sid = 70 and t_sub.uid = 42 then
        let new_rec = [uid=t_sub.uid, title=t+"!", ...]
        in x:= new_rec )
```

In this example Submissions is a (mutable) collection of references of type $\sigma_c$ (Figure 1c). The type $\sigma_c$ is a dependent sum type where the security level of some fields depends on the actual values bound to other fields (as already explained in the Introduction). For example, notice that the security level of the title field is declared as A(uid,sid) where uid and sid are other fields of the (thus dependent) record type. Also, t gets security level A(42,70) since we are retrieving a record with uid value 42 and sid value 70. To type the record initialising the reference new_rec, we need to obtain type [uid:$\bot\times$sid:$\bot\times$title:A(uid,sid)$\times$...], which in turn needs to check the type of expression t+"!" for field title. But since we know t has security level A(42,70) and that t_sub.sid=70 and t_sub.uid=42 (so fields uid and sid have value 42 and 70, respectively, in new_rec), we can deem secure the assignment x:=new_rec.

On the other hand, if we change the last conditional to be **if** t_sub.sid = 24, then we would be attempting to associate data of security level A(42,70), value t, within the security compartment A(24,$\top$) for author with uid 24. So, in other words, data from author 42's submission is being associated to submissions of author 24, inducing an illegal flow of information.

For brevity, as in the example above, when writing new record values based on existing ones, we just mention the fields being assigned a new value, and a sample field indicating the record value from which the other values are to be copied. For example, in [uid=t_sub.uid, title=t + "!",...] we mean that fields sid, abs, and paper are just copied from t_sub as uid=t_sub.uid, e.g, sid=t_sub.sid, etc. Consider now the following code fragment

```
foreach (x in !Submissions) with y = {} do
  let t_sub = !x in
    if (t_sub.uid = 42) then
      [uid = t_sub.uid, sid = t_sub.sid,
                     title = t_sub.title]::y else y
```

The result of evaluating this program is a collection of records of sum type (resulting from projecting part of submission records of type $\sigma_c$). The expected type, given the definition of $\sigma_c$, is [uid:$\bot$ $\times$ sid:$\bot$ $\times$ title: A(uid, sid) ]. However, our type system can track value dependencies and constraints imposed by programs, so a more precise type is assigned in this case, namely $\Sigma$[uid:$\bot$ $\times$ sid:$\bot$ $\times$ title: A(42,sid)]. Such ability to track dependencies is crucial to rigorously analyse fine grained security policies. For instance, in order to check if PC member with id 10 could observe the result of the above operation, we need to establish that A(42,sid)$\leq$ PC(10,sid), which would not be possible had we approximated the field sid with $\top$.

Let us consider the following code for a function viewUserProfile

```
let viewUserProfile = λ (uid_a).
  foreach(x in !Users) with y = {} do
    let usr = !x in
      if usr.uid = uid_a then usr::y else y
```

Function viewUserProfile returns a collection of records of dependent sum type whose security labels on fields title, abs, and paper depend on the value of the parameter uid_a. A precise typing for viewUserProfile is $\Pi$(uid_a:$\bot$).
$\Sigma$[uid:$\bot\times$name:U(uid_a)$\times$univ:U(uid_a)$\times$email:U(uid_a)]*. Notice that the return type depends on the value of the function argument, so the type of viewUserProfile is a functional dependent type. Then the expression **first**(viewUserProfile(42)).email has type U(42).

**Example 2.5** The addCommentSubmission operation is used by the PC members to add comments to submissions. The types ensure that only PC members assigned to the particular paper will see such comments.

```
let addCommentSubmission = λ(uid_r: ⊥, sid_r: ⊥).
 foreach (p in viewAssignedPapers(uid_r)) with _ do
  if p.sid = sid_r then
   foreach(y in !Reviews) with _ do
    let t_rev = !y in
     if t_rev.sid = p.sid then
      let up_rec =
       [uid=t_rev.uid,PC_only=comment(p.uid,p.sid,p),...]
      in y := up_rec
```

Function viewAssignedPapers has type ($\Pi$(uid_r:$\bot$).C, where type C is $\Sigma$[uid:$\bot\times$sid:$\bot\times$title:A(uid,sid)$\times$abs:A(uid,sid) $\times$ paper:A(uid,sid)]* (Example 2.3). Since there is no dependency (uid_r not free in C), we may abbreviate the functional type by $\texttt{Int}^{\bot}\rightarrow$ C, thus identifier p has type C. Function *comment* returns a given paper's PC comments, and has type $\Pi$ u:$\bot$.$\Pi$s:$\bot$.$\Pi$r:C.A(u,s). Notice that its return type in the call *comment*(p.uid,p.sid,p) has security label A(p.uid,p.sid).

Additionally, we know t_rev has the type of the collection's references (type $\delta_c$ of Figure 1c). So, in order to type check the assignment expression, y := up_rec, we need to check that up_rec has the same type as the prescribed type for the collection's elements, type $\delta_c$. Namely, we have to check if *comment*(p.uid, p.sid,p) has type PC(t_rev.uid,p.sid).

As we said, the type for *comment*(p.uid, p.sid,p) has security label A(p.uid, p.sid) but since it has field dependencies, we need to infer values for them. In this case, we cannot infer a value for field uid so we approximate to $\top$ obtaining A($\top$,p.sid). However, because we know by the conditional that t_rev.sid = p.sid, we can index the security level by field sid instead, which allows us to type the assignment operation since field sid is bounded by the dependent sum type of the record being used for the assignment.

Then we can type *comment*(p.uid, p.sid,p) with type A($\top$,p.sid) and thus, due to A($\top$,p.sid) $\leq$ PC($\bot$, p.sid), we can up-classify *comment*(p.uid, p.sid,p) with PC(t_rev.uid, p.sid). Notice that this up-classification is only possible to PC members assigned to the paper whose sid is p.sid, so only those PC members will be able to see the added comment. So we can, finally, type the record up_rec with the dependent sum type $\Sigma$ [uid:$\bot$ $\times$sid:$\bot$ $\times$PC_only:PC(uid,sid) $\times$review:A($\top$,sid) $\times$grade:A($\top$,sid)]. We refer back to this example in Example 4.3, where we detail the relevant steps taken by the system to typecheck the program. Without dependent types, we would lose precision in the typing of *comment*(p.uid, p.sid,p) (obtaining A($\top$,$\top$) instead) and not be able to raise the security level to the required level, thus addCommentSubmission would not type check despite being secure.

After introducing our core language and dependent information flow types, we now formally introduce its syntax and semantics.

| | | |
|---|---|---|
| $e ::=$ | | *(expression)* |
| | $\mid e.m$ | (field access) |
| | $\mid$ **let** $x = e_1$ **in** $e_2$ | (let) |
| | $\mid e_1(e_2)$ | (application) |
| | $\mid$ **if** $c$ **then** $e_1$ **else** $e_2$ | (conditional) |
| | $\mid [\overline{m = e}]$ | (record) |
| | $\mid \overline{e}$ | (collection) |
| | $\mid e_1{::}e_2$ | (cons) |
| | $\mid$ **foreach**$(e_1, e_2, x.y.e_3)$ | (iteration) |
| | $\mid$ **ref**$_{\tau^s}$ $e$ | (reference) |
| | $\mid e_1 := e_2$ | (assign) |
| | $\mid !e$ | (deref) |
| | $\mid x$ | (identifier) |
| | $\mid v$ | (value) |

| | | |
|---|---|---|
| $v ::=$ | | *(values)* |
| | $\overline{v}$ | (collection) |
| | $\mid [\overline{m = v}]$ | (record) |
| | $\mid \lambda(x{:}\tau^s).e$ | (abstraction) |
| | $\mid$ **true** | (true) |
| | $\mid$ **false** | (false) |
| | $\mid ()$ | (unit) |
| | $\mid l$ | (locations) |

| | | |
|---|---|---|
| $c ::=$ | | *(conditions)* |
| | $\mid \neg c$ | (negation) |
| | $\mid c_1 \vee c_2$ | (disjunction) |
| | $\mid V = V$ | (equality) |
| | $\mid V$ | (term) |
| $V ::=$ | | *(terms)* |
| | $\overline{V}$ | (collection) |
| | $\mid [\overline{m = V}]$ | (record) |
| | $\mid \lambda(x{:}\tau^s).e$ | (abstraction) |
| | $\mid$ **true** | (true) |
| | $\mid$ **false** | (false) |
| | $\mid x$ | (identifier) |
| | $\mid ()$ | (unit) |
| | $\mid V.m$ | (field access) |

Figure 2: Syntax: expressions, values, conditions, terms

## 3. Core Language

Our core language (Figure 2) is a higher-order functional language with references and primitive collections. Primitive values ($v$) include abstractions, booleans, records, collections (lists of values, also present in languages such as DMinor [3]), and locations. We consider two values $v, u$ equal, $v = u$, when they are the same up to reordering of record labels, and assume intensional equality on lambda abstractions. Expressions ($e$) include let-expression, conditional, application, field access, cons operator to add an element to a collection, collection iterator, values, variables, locations, references, dereference and assignment. These primitives are to be understood as usual, namely the collection iterator `foreach` computes the accumulated value of a list's elements, as showed in the examples of Section 2. For readability purposes, we sometimes use the more natural concrete syntax adopted in the previous section. We assume other basic data types (integers, strings) and associated operations, such as `first(-)` and `rest(-)` for collections (but omit standard details). To illustrate primitive types, we will usually include just booleans in our formal presentation. As for abbreviations, we use an overbar to represented indexed sets of syntactic elements. Concretely, $[\overline{m = e}]$ stands for $[m_1{=}e_1, \ldots, m_n{=}e_n]$, and $\overline{e}$ stands for $\{e_1, \ldots, e_n\}$. Logical conditions $c$ are used in conditionals, which we require to be pure (side-effect free). We also consider terms $V$, used in conditions, e.g., terms are values that may be checked for equality. Pure expressions are those side-effect free, in concrete, all expressions except assignment, reference expressions and deference.

Programs in our language are closed expressions. The operational semantics is defined using a reduction relation, defined by the rules in Figure 3, which basically extend the standard ones for a call-by-value $\lambda$-calculus. Reduction is defined between configurations of the form $(S; e)$, where $S$ is a store, and $e$ is an expression. A reduction step of the form $(S; e) \longrightarrow (S'; e')$ states that expression $e$ under state $S$ evolves in one computational step to expression $e'$ under state $S'$. A store $S$ is a mapping from *locations* to values. Reduction rules follow predictable lines, we briefly comment on the less standard ones. Rules (*foreach-left*) and (*foreach-right*) reduce the first and second expressions of the list iterator operator, respectively. These rules, together with rule (*foreach*), imply an evaluation order from left to right. Evaluation of (store independent) logical conditions is given by the map $\mathcal{C} : c \rightarrow \{\textbf{true}, \textbf{false}\}$, using an auxiliary evaluation map for closed terms $\mathcal{T} : V \rightarrow v$, defined as expected (see [34] for more details).

## 4. Type System

As already discussed above, our type system for information flow builds on fairly traditional concepts from information flow type systems [1, 12], but crucially explores a notion of type dependency on security labels, in a way that cleanly fits within a standard framework of dependent type theory with canonical dependent functional and sum types. We assume a multilevel security approach that classifies information into security compartments, according to some given security lattice, and mediates users access to data according to the security clearance they possess. As in typical type-based information flow analyses, types are annotated with a security label. In our system, we consider value dependent security labels $\ell(\overline{\mathsf{v}})$, so our types take the form $\tau^{\mathsf{s}}$ where $\tau$ is a data type and $\mathsf{s}$ is a (indexed) security label $\ell(\overline{\mathsf{v}})$ - non-indexed labels may be represented by $\ell(\top)$.

If an expression $e$ is assigned type $\tau^{\mathsf{s}}$ then the system must ensure that only users with enough permissions to read information at security level $\mathsf{s}$ have access to the value computed by $e$. Otherwise, the result of $e$ is assumed to be opaque and thus cannot be observed by such an user. As for the attacker model, we assume an attacker can observe information, including stored data, that has security level $\bot$ (public), and may be a user of the system. So interaction with the system is possible using the core language we show here. This view is extended to any given security level, so that attackers with access to data classified at security level $\mathsf{s}$ can only observe information classified up to $\mathsf{s}$.

***Security Labels and Security Lattice.*** Security labels, which we consider in general to be value dependent, have the form $\ell(\overline{\mathsf{v}})$, where $\overline{\mathsf{v}}$ is a list of security label indexes. Label indexes are given by:

| | | | | |
|---|---|---|---|---|
| $\mathsf{v} ::=$ | | (label indexes) | | |
| | $\mid \top$ | (top) | $\mid \bot$ | (bot) |
| | $\mid$ **true** | (true) | $\mid$ **false** | (false) |
| | $\mid \overline{v}$ | (collection) | $\mid [\overline{m : v}]$ | (record) |
| | $\mid x.m$ | (field selection) | $\mid x$ | (variable) |
| | $\mid m$ | (field identifier) | | |

We call *concrete* a security label if all of its indexes is $\bot, \top$, or a value $v$, not a (record) field identifier $m$ or a variable $x$. As made clear below, labels indexed by a simple field identifier, e.g., $\ell(m)$, only make sense in the scope of a field $m$ in a dependent sum type.

We consider a general notion of security lattice. We require the lattice $\mathcal{L}$ elements to be concrete security labels, with $\top$ the top element (the most restrictive security level), and $\bot$ the bottom element (the most permissive security level), and $\sqcup, \sqcap$, denote the join and meet operations respectively. The lattice partial order is noted $\leq$ and $<$ its strict part; we write $\mathsf{s}\#\mathsf{s}'$ to assert that neither $\mathsf{s} \leq \mathsf{s}'$ nor $\mathsf{s}' \leq \mathsf{s}$. As suggested above, dependent security labels $\ell(\overline{\bot})$ and $\ell(\overline{\top})$ are interpreted as approximations to the "standard" non-value dependent label $\ell$. We thus require that for any values $v_1, \ldots, v_n$ that make the label $\ell(v_1, \ldots, v_n)$ concrete, $\ell(\overline{\bot}) \leq \ell(v_1, \ldots, v_n) \leq \ell(\overline{\top})$ holds in the given security lattice *(app-left)* $$\frac{(S;e_1) \longrightarrow (S';e'_1)}{(S;e_1(e_2)) \longrightarrow (S';e'_1(e_2))}$$

*(app-right)* $$\frac{(S;e_2) \longrightarrow (S';e'_2)}{(S;(\lambda(x:\tau_1^{\mathsf{s}_1}).e)(e_2)) \longrightarrow (S',(\lambda(x:\tau_1^{\mathsf{s}_1}).e)(e'_2))}$$

*(app)* $$(S;(\lambda(x:\tau_1^{\mathsf{s}_1}).e)(v)) \longrightarrow (S;e\{v/x\})$$

*(if-true)* $$\frac{\mathcal{C}[\![c]\!]}{(S;\textbf{if } c \textbf{ then } e_1 \textbf{ else } e_2) \longrightarrow (S;e_1)}$$

*(if-false)* $$\frac{\neg\mathcal{C}[\![c]\!]}{(S;\textbf{if } c \textbf{ then } e_1 \textbf{ else } e_2) \longrightarrow (S;e_2)}$$

*(ref-left)* $$\frac{(S;e) \longrightarrow (S';e')}{(S;\textbf{ref}_{\tau^s}\, e) \longrightarrow (S';\textbf{ref}_{\tau^s}\, e')}$$

*(ref-right)* $$\frac{l \notin dom(S)}{\begin{array}{c}(S;\textbf{ref}_{\tau^s}\, v) \longrightarrow \\ (S \cup \{l \mapsto v\};\ l)\end{array}}$$

*(assign-left)* $$\frac{(S;e_1) \longrightarrow (S';e'_1)}{(S;e_1 := e_2) \longrightarrow (S';e'_1 := e_2)}$$

*(assign-right)* $$\frac{(S;e_2) \longrightarrow (S';e'_2)}{(S;l := e_2) \longrightarrow (S';l := e'_2)}$$

*(assign)* $$\frac{l \in dom(S)}{(S;l := v) \longrightarrow (S[l \mapsto v];())}$$

*(deref-left)* $$\frac{(S;e) \longrightarrow (S';e')}{(S;!e) \longrightarrow (S';!e')}$$

*(deref)* $$\frac{S(l) = v}{(S;!l) \longrightarrow (S;v)}$$

*(foreach-left)* $$\frac{(S;e_1) \longrightarrow (S';e'_1)}{\begin{array}{l}(S;\textbf{foreach}(e_1,\ e_2,\ x.y.e_3) \longrightarrow \\ (S';\textbf{foreach}(e'_1,\ e_2,\ x.y.e_3))\end{array}}$$

*(foreach-right)* $$\frac{(S;e_2) \longrightarrow (S';e'_2)}{\begin{array}{l}(S;\textbf{foreach}(v,\ e_2,\ x.y.e_3) \longrightarrow \\ (S';\textbf{foreach}(v,\ e'_2,\ x.y.e_3))\end{array}}$$

*(foreach)* $$\frac{v_l = h{::}hs}{\begin{array}{l}(S;\textbf{foreach}(v_l,\ v,\ x.y.e_3) \longrightarrow \\ (S;\textbf{foreach}(hs,\ e_3\{h/x\}\{v/y\},\ x.y.e_3))\end{array}}$$

*(foreach-base)* $$(S;\textbf{foreach}(\{\},\ v,\ x.y.e_3) \longrightarrow (S;v)$$

*(let-left)* $$\frac{(S;e_1) \longrightarrow (S';e'_1)}{(S;\textbf{let } x = e_1 \textbf{ in } e_2) \longrightarrow (S';\textbf{let } x = e'_1 \textbf{ in } e_2)}$$

*(let-right)* $$(S;\textbf{let } x = v \textbf{ in } e_2) \longrightarrow (S;e_2\{v/x\})$$

*(field-right)* $$(S[\ldots m{:}v \ldots].m) \longrightarrow (S;v)$$

*(record)* $$\frac{(S;e) \longrightarrow (S';e')}{(S;[\ldots m{:}e \ldots]) \longrightarrow (S';[\ldots m{:}e' \ldots])}$$

*(list)* $$\frac{(S;e) \longrightarrow (S';e')}{(S;\{\ldots e \ldots\}) \longrightarrow (S';\{\ldots e' \ldots\})}$$

*(field-left)* $$\frac{(S;e) \longrightarrow (S';e')}{(S;e.m) \longrightarrow (S';e'.m)}$$

*(cons-left)* $$\frac{(S;e_1) \longrightarrow (S';e'_1)}{(S;e_1{::}e_2) \longrightarrow (S';e'_1{::}e_2)}$$

*(cons-right)* $$\frac{(S;e_2) \longrightarrow (S';e'_2)}{(S;v{::}e_2) \longrightarrow (S';v{::}e'_2)}$$

*(cons)* $$(S;v{::}\{v_1,\ldots,v_n\}) \longrightarrow (S;\{v,v_1,\ldots,v_n\})$$

Figure 3: Reduction

$$\begin{array}{rlr}
\mathsf{s},\mathsf{r},\mathsf{t},\mathsf{q} ::= & \ell(\overline{\mathsf{v}}) & \text{security label} \\
\tau^{\mathsf{s}},\sigma^{\mathsf{s}} ::= & \mid \mathtt{Bool}^{\mathsf{s}} & \text{bool type} \\
& \mid (\Pi x{:}\tau^{\mathsf{s}}.\mathsf{r};\sigma^{\mathsf{q}})^{\mathsf{t}} & \text{dependent function type} \\
& \mid \Sigma[\overline{m:\tau^{\mathsf{s}}}]^{\mathsf{r}} & \text{dependent sum type} \\
& \mid \tau^{*\mathsf{s}} & \text{collection type} \\
& \mid \mathtt{ref}(\tau^{\mathsf{s}})^{\mathsf{t}} & \text{reference type} \\
& \mid \mathtt{cmd}^{\mathsf{s}} & \text{command type}
\end{array}$$

Figure 4: Types

$\mathcal{L}$, and that the ordering between labels is well defined and satisfies the lattice property (i.e., well defined meets and joins, etc). We assume that the intended lattice (required for each particular security analysis) is specified by a list of schematic assertions of the form $\forall\overline{x}.\ell_1(\overline{u}) \leq \ell_2(\overline{v})$, where the (optional) $\overline{x}$ may occur in $\overline{u},\overline{v}$. We already gave examples of lattice assertions in Section 2.

***Types.*** The type structure (Figure 4) includes boolean, unit (or command), reference, dependent sum, dependent function, and collection types. In collection type $\tau^{*\mathsf{s}}$ each collection element has type $\tau^{\mathsf{s}}$. We assume other basic types, such as integers and strings with their associated operations, not formalised for the sake of simplicity, but used in examples. Dependent sum types and dependent functional types assume a key role in our type system as they allows us to express (runtime) value dependency on security labels, as already highlighted. A dependent sum type has the form

$$\Sigma[m_1{:}\tau_1^{\mathsf{s}_1} \times \ldots \times m_n{:}\tau_n^{\mathsf{s}_n}]^{\mathsf{t}}$$

where any of the security labels $\mathsf{s}_i$ with $i > 1$ may be dependent on previous fields (via the field identifier). For instance, the type

$$\Sigma[\mathtt{uid}{:}\bot \times \mathtt{name}{:}\mathtt{user}(\mathtt{uid})]^{\bot}$$

is a dependent sum type where field `name` has the value dependent security level, `user(uid)`, which is indexed by the (runtime) value in field `uid`. A dependent functional type has the general form

$$(\Pi x{:}\tau^{\mathsf{s}}.\mathsf{r};\sigma^{\mathsf{q}})^{\mathsf{t}}$$

where the (security level of) the codomain type $\sigma^{\mathsf{q}}$ may depend on the value of the argument (denoted by the bound variable $x$). Level $\mathsf{r}$ specifies a lower bound on the security level of the function effects (writes), if omitted it is assumed to be $\bot$. When $x$ does not occur free in $\sigma^{\mathsf{q}}$ we write $(\tau^{\mathsf{s}} \xrightarrow{\mathsf{r}} \sigma^{\mathsf{q}})^{\mathsf{t}}$ for the type above, or simply $(\tau^{\mathsf{s}} \to \sigma^{\mathsf{q}})^{\mathsf{t}}$ if $\mathsf{r}$ is $\bot$. Notice that in source types and programs non-concrete security labels may only occur in the context of dependent sum types and dependent functional types. Also, even if types for collections are homogeneous, due to the presence of dependent sum types, the system accommodates collections of elements containing data in different, possibly incomparable, security compartments.

***Dependencies in Security Labels.*** As stated earlier, and for natural reasons, the security lattice only relates concrete labels. As such, at some points, our type system is required to approximate runtime values to eliminate dependencies occurring in security labels. For example, should we project field `name` of a record typed with $\Sigma[\mathtt{uid}:\bot \times \mathtt{name}:\mathtt{user}(\mathtt{uid})]^{\bot}$, then we would need to eliminate the field dependency in the resulting type's security label, `user(uid)`, into either `user(s)` if the actual name `s` can be deduced from the computational context as is often the case, or, at least, by `user(`$\top$`)`. Dually, it may also be necessary to capture value dependencies in security labels, e.g., if we declare a reference of type $\Sigma[\mathtt{uid}:\bot \times \mathtt{name}:\mathtt{user}(\mathtt{uid})]^{\bot}$ and then initialise with a record with type $\Sigma[\mathtt{uid}:\bot \times \mathtt{name}:\mathtt{user}(0)]^{\bot}$, then we would need to introduce the field dependency in `user(0)`. We achieve such introduction and elimination of dependencies in security labels by: (1) tracking knowledge regarding dependencies in a constraint set $\mathcal{S}$ carried along in typing judgements; (2) using a equational theory to entail runtime values or dependencies, depending whether we are eliminating or capturing dependencies in security labels.

A constraint set $\mathcal{S}$ is a finite set of equational constraints of the form $e \doteq e'$ where $e, e'$ are pure (without side-effects) expressions. We assume a decidable sound equational theory, talking about basic data such as booleans, integers, records, etc, and write $\mathcal{S} \models e \doteq e'$

$$\frac{\ell(\top) \leq \mathsf{s}}{\tau^{\ell(\mathsf{v})} <: \tau^{\mathsf{s}}}\ (\textit{s-indexLeft}) \qquad \frac{\mathsf{s} \leq \ell(\bot)}{\tau^{\mathsf{s}} <: \tau^{\ell(\mathsf{v})}}\ (\textit{s-indexRight}) \qquad \frac{\forall_i\ \tau_i^{\mathsf{s}_i} <: \tau_i^{\mathsf{s}_i'} \quad \mathsf{t}' \leq \mathsf{t}}{\Sigma[\overline{m : \tau^{\mathsf{s}}}]^{\mathsf{t}} <: \Sigma[\overline{m : \tau^{\mathsf{s}'}}]^{\mathsf{t}'}}\ (\textit{s-record})$$

$$\frac{\mathsf{s} \leq \mathsf{s}'}{\tau^{\mathsf{s}} <: \tau^{\mathsf{s}'}}\ (\textit{s-expr}) \qquad \frac{\tau^{\mathsf{s}'} <: \tau^{\mathsf{s}} \quad \sigma^{\mathsf{q}} <: \sigma^{\mathsf{q}'} \quad \mathsf{r}' \leq \mathsf{r}}{(\Pi x{:}\tau^{\mathsf{s}}.\mathsf{r}; \sigma^{\mathsf{q}})^{\mathsf{t}} <: (\Pi x{:}\tau^{\mathsf{s}'}.\mathsf{r}'; \sigma^{\mathsf{q}'})^{\mathsf{t}}}\ (\textit{s-arrow})$$

Figure 5: (Key) Subtyping rules

for the entailment of $e \doteq e'$ given the constraints in $\mathcal{S}$. We also naturally require $\doteq$ to be compatible with reduction in the sense that for any $e, e'$ pure if $(S; e) \longrightarrow (S; e')$ then $\models e \doteq e'$. As for any equational theory, we assume that $S \models E$ and $\mathcal{S} \cup \{E\} \models E'$ implies $S \models E'$ (deduction closure). We denote by $\mathcal{S}\{x \doteq e\}$ the set $\mathcal{S} \cup \{x \doteq e\}$ if $e$ is a pure expression, and $\mathcal{S}$ otherwise. For instance, $\{x.\texttt{uid}{\doteq}\texttt{uid\_r}, \texttt{uid\_r}{\doteq}42\}{\models}x.\texttt{uid} \doteq 42$. For the purpose of this work we consider constraint solving issues inside a black-box, subject to the mentioned general requirements. We do not specify any particular equational theory since its precise formulation is orthogonal to our analysis, as long as it is decidable and sound (the more complete the theory the better).

***Typing Judgements and Rules.*** A typing judgment has the form

$$\Delta \vdash^{\mathsf{r}}_{\mathcal{S}} e : \tau^{\mathsf{s}}$$

It asserts that expression $e$ has type $\tau^{\mathsf{s}}$ under typing environment $\Delta$, given constraints $\mathcal{S}$. The label $\mathsf{s}$ states that the value of expression $e$ does not depend on data classified with security levels above $\mathsf{s}$ or incomparable with $\mathsf{s}$. As expected from type-based approaches to information flow analysis, our type system ensures that information only flows upwards the security lattice, e.g., only from a level $\mathsf{l}$ to a level $\mathsf{h}$ such that $\mathsf{l} \leq \mathsf{h}$. Label $\mathsf{r}$ is concrete and expresses the security level of the computational context (cf. the "program counter" [18, 22]), a familiar technique to prevent implicit flows. Typing declarations assign types to identifiers $x{:}\tau^{\mathsf{s}}$, and types to locations, $l{:}\tau^{\mathsf{s}}$. A typing environment $\Delta$ is a list of typing declarations. In Figure 6 we show the typing rules. The system also relies on a simple subtyping relation, denoted $<:$, which allows up-classification of security labels, defined in Figure 5. Rules *s-indexLeft/Right/expr* rely on the lattice order, where we consider $\mathsf{s} \leq \mathsf{s}'$ to be an instance of a lattice assertion, in rule *s-expr* we assume $\tau$ not to be dependent type. We also define well-formed types and well-formedness definition of typing contexts, denoted as as $\Delta \vdash \diamond$. Well-formed types are denoted by judgment $\Delta \vdash^{\mathcal{N}} \tau^{\mathsf{s}}$, stating that type $\tau^{\mathsf{s}}$ is well-formed under typing context $\Delta$, given names set $\mathcal{N}$. The full set of rules defining well-formed types can be found in [34].

We avoid commenting on typing rules standard for any typed $\lambda$-calculus and focus on key typing rules specific to our system. For simplicity and w.l.o.g we consider in our presentation that security labels are indexed by a single label index, assuming the obvious extension of type rules to deal with labels with multiple indexes, when necessary, e.g, in examples. In rule (*t-record*) we require the security label of record values to be, at most, the greatest lower bound of all the security labels occurring in their fields, otherwise implicit flows could occur on assignments of record values. Since a field's security label $\mathsf{s}$ may have dependencies, we approximate the values they denote with $\bot$, via $|\mathsf{s}|^{\downarrow}$. Notice that this allows (but does not force) records storing both private and public data to be classified as public. Such a scenario is in fact, secure, as will only leak, at most, information that a record is present, but not the field contents (except those classified as public). We will get back to this discussion below. Rule (*t-app*) is the expected rule for any value dependent function application where free occurrences of $x$ in the result type are replaced with a value $\mathsf{v}$. In our system we approximate the argument value $\mathsf{v}$ of $e_2$ via constraint entailment given the additional knowledge $x \doteq e_2$, otherwise we set $\mathsf{v} = \top$. In rule (*t-foreach*), we require the security level of all sub expressions to be the same. This is required to disallow insecure programs such as, e.g., in which one could count the elements of a collection classified with a high security level, and assign the result to a low level.

---

**Example 4.1** Suppose we have collection `top_secrets` with elements classified at security level $\top$ and consider the code snippet.

```
foreach (x in top_secrets) with count = 0 do count+1
```

This code can only be typed as $\texttt{int}^{\top}$. If we allowed the body of the foreach loop to be typed at a level lower that $\top$, we could type the result of the above program at security level $\bot$ since the computation only involves values at that level. That, however, would represent an implicit flow since one could then observe some information about collection `top_secrets` at level $\bot$, namely its number of elements, breaking noninterference. On the other hand, assume `boxed` to be a collection of records typed as $\texttt{boxed} : (\Sigma[\texttt{secret} : \texttt{string}^{\top}])^{*\bot}$. All fields contents of the collection's records are classified as high ($\top$), but the records themselves and the collection itself is classified as low ($\bot$). In this case, it is possible to type

```
foreach (x in boxed) with count = 0 do count+1
```

with type $\texttt{int}^{\bot}$. This means that the collection and its records (borders) are visible entities at level $\bot$, while the actual record field contents are concealed from the same level. With this spec, it would be allowed to a low observer to observe the collection size, but not the contents of the `secret` fields, preserving non-interference.

---

Rule (*t-if*) is as expected: to prevent implicit flows from occurring, we raise the security level of the computational context to the least upper bound of its current level with the logical condition's security level. Moreover, we enforce the security level of both branches and the logical condition to be the same, and track knowledge to the constraint set $\mathcal{S}$ about the condition's value in each branch. Rules (*t-refineRecord*) and (*t-unrefineRecord*), adequate to our dependent labeled sum types, correspond to introduction and elimination rule for (value-dependent) existential types. Rule (*t-refineRecord*) potentially introduces a dependent sum type by indexing a label with field $m_j$, given that a concrete witness value $\mathsf{v}$ can be identified from $m_j$ via constraint entailment. The converse is achieved with rule (*t-unrefineRecord*), that is, one may eliminate a field dependency (and potentially a dependent sum type) by replacing such a field with a concrete value witness, derivable as discussed for the (*t-refineRecord*) rule. We illustrate with some examples.

---

**Example 4.2** Recall the `viewAuthorPapers` from Example 2.2,

```
let viewAuthorPapers = λ (uid_a).
  foreach(x in !Submissions) with y = {} do
    let tuple = !x in
      if tuple.uid = uid_a then tuple::y else y
```

While typing expression `tuple::y`, while typing the **then** branch, we obtain type $\Sigma$`[uid:`$\bot$ $\times$ `sid:`$\bot$ $\times$ `title:A(uid,sid)` $\times$ `abs:A(uid,sid)` $\times$ `paper:A(uid,sid)]`$^{*\bot}$. However, at this point, we know that `tuple.uid = uid_a`, which was added to the constraint set $\mathcal{S}$ according to rule (*t-if*). So, to type `tuple`, we can apply rule (*t-unrefineRecord*), adding a new constraint $\{x \doteq \text{tuple}\}$ for a fresh identifier $x$, and entail
$\mathcal{S} \cup \{\texttt{tuple.uid=uid\_a} \doteq \texttt{true},\ x \doteq \texttt{tuple}\} \models x.\texttt{uid}{\doteq}\texttt{uid\_a}$
to eliminate the field dependency `uid` in the security label, obtaining the type $\Sigma$`[uid:`$\bot$ $\times$ `sid:`$\bot$ $\times$ `title:A(uid_a,sid)` $\times$ `abs:A(uid_a,sid)` $\times$ `paper:A(uid_a,sid)]`$^{\bot}$.

$$\textit{(t-field)}\quad \frac{\Delta \vdash^{\mathsf{r}}_{\mathcal{S}} e : \Sigma[\ldots \times m_i{:}\tau_i^{\mathsf{s}_i} \times \ldots]^{\mathsf{s}'}}{\Delta \vdash^{\mathsf{r}}_{\mathcal{S}} e.m_i : \tau_i^{\mathsf{s}_i}} \qquad \textit{(t-record)}\quad \frac{\forall_i\ \Delta \vdash^{\mathsf{r}}_{\mathcal{S}} e_i : \tau_i^{\mathsf{s}_i}}{\Delta \vdash^{\mathsf{r}}_{\mathcal{S}} [\ldots, m_i{=}e_i, \ldots] : \Sigma[\ldots \times m_i{:}\tau_i^{\mathsf{s}_i} \times \ldots]^{\sqcap|\mathsf{s}_i|^{\downarrow}}}$$

$$\textit{(t-refineRecord)}\quad \frac{\Delta \vdash^{\mathsf{r}}_{\mathcal{S}} e : \Sigma[\ldots \times m_j{:}\tau_j^{\mathsf{s}_j} \times \ldots \times m_i{:}\tau_i^{\ell_i(\mathsf{v})} \times \ldots]^{\mathsf{s}} \quad \mathcal{S}\{x \doteq e\} \models x.m_j \doteq \mathsf{v}}{\Delta \vdash^{\mathsf{r}}_{\mathcal{S}} e : \Sigma[\ldots \times m_j : \tau_j^{\mathsf{s}_j} \times \ldots \times m_i : \tau_i^{\ell_i(m_j)} \times \ldots]^{\mathsf{s}}}$$

$$\textit{(t-unrefineRecord)}\quad \frac{\Delta \vdash^{\mathsf{r}}_{\mathcal{S}} e : \Sigma[\ldots \times m_j{:}\tau_j^{\mathsf{s}_j} \times \ldots \times m_i{:}\tau_i^{\ell_i(m_j)} \times \ldots]^{\mathsf{s}} \quad \mathcal{S}\{x \doteq e\} \models x.m_j \doteq \mathsf{v}}{\Delta \vdash^{\mathsf{r}}_{\mathcal{S}} e : \Sigma[\ldots \times m_j : \tau_j^{\mathsf{s}_j} \times \ldots \times m_i : \tau_i^{\ell_i(\mathsf{v})} \times \ldots]^{\mathsf{s}}}$$

$$\textit{(t-sub)}\quad \frac{\Delta \vdash^{\mathsf{r}}_{\mathcal{S}} e : \tau^{\mathsf{s}} \quad \tau^{\mathsf{s}} <: \tau^{\mathsf{s}'} \quad \mathsf{r}' \leq \mathsf{r}}{\Delta \vdash^{\mathsf{r}'}_{\mathcal{S}} e : \tau^{\mathsf{s}'}} \qquad \textit{(t-let)}\quad \frac{\Delta \vdash^{\mathsf{r}}_{\mathcal{S}} e_1 : \tau^{\mathsf{s}} \quad \Delta, x : \tau^{\mathsf{s}} \vdash^{\mathsf{r}}_{\mathcal{S}\{x \doteq e_1\}} e_2 : \tau'^{\mathsf{s}'}}{\Delta \vdash^{\mathsf{r}}_{\mathcal{S}} \textbf{let } x = e_1 \textbf{ in } e_2 : \tau'^{\mathsf{s}'}}$$

$$\textit{(t-app)}\quad \frac{\Delta \vdash^{\mathsf{r}}_{\mathcal{S}} e_1 : (\Pi x{:}\tau^{\mathsf{s}}.\mathsf{r}'\sigma^{\mathsf{q}})^{\mathsf{t}} \quad \Delta \vdash^{\mathsf{r}}_{\mathcal{S}} e_2 : \tau^{\mathsf{s}} \quad (\mathsf{v} = \top) \vee (\mathcal{S}\{x \doteq e_2\} \models x \doteq \mathsf{v}) \quad \mathsf{r} \leq \mathsf{r}'}{\Delta \vdash^{\mathsf{r}}_{\mathcal{S}} e_1(e_2) : \sigma\{\mathsf{v}/x\}^{\mathsf{q}\{\mathsf{v}/x\} \sqcup \mathsf{t}}}$$

$$\textit{(t-lambda)}\quad \frac{\Delta, x : \tau^{\mathsf{s}} \vdash^{\mathsf{r}}_{\mathcal{S}} e : \sigma^{\mathsf{q}}}{\Delta \vdash^{\mathsf{r}}_{\mathcal{S}} \lambda(x : \tau^{\mathsf{s}}).e : (\Pi x{:}\tau^{\mathsf{s}}.\mathsf{r}; \sigma^{\mathsf{q}})^{\perp}} \qquad \textit{(t-collection)}\quad \frac{\forall_i \quad \Delta \vdash^{\mathsf{r}}_{\mathcal{S}} e_i : \tau^{\mathsf{s}}}{\Delta \vdash^{\mathsf{r}}_{\mathcal{S}} \{e_1, \ldots, e_n\} : \tau^{*\mathsf{s}}} \qquad \textit{(t-cons)}\quad \frac{\Delta \vdash^{\mathsf{r}}_{\mathcal{S}} e_1 : \tau^{\mathsf{s}} \quad \Delta \vdash^{\mathsf{r}}_{\mathcal{S}} e_2 : \tau^{*\mathsf{s}}}{\Delta \vdash^{\mathsf{r}}_{\mathcal{S}} e_1{::}e_2 : \tau^{*\mathsf{s}}}$$

$$\textit{(t-foreach)}\quad \frac{\Delta \vdash^{\mathsf{r}}_{\mathcal{S}} e_1 : \tau^{*\mathsf{s}} \quad \Delta \vdash^{\mathsf{r}}_{\mathcal{S}} e_2 : \tau'^{\mathsf{s}} \quad \Delta, x : \tau^{\mathsf{s}}, y : \tau'^{\mathsf{s}} \vdash^{\mathsf{r}}_{\mathcal{S}} e_3 : \tau'^{\mathsf{s}}}{\Delta \vdash^{\mathsf{r}}_{\mathcal{S}} \textbf{foreach } (e_1,\ e_2,\ x.y.e_3) : \tau'^{\mathsf{s}}}$$

$$\textit{(t-if)}\quad \frac{\Delta \vdash^{\mathsf{r}}_{\mathcal{S}} c : \mathtt{Bool}^{\mathsf{s}} \quad \Delta \vdash^{\mathsf{r}\sqcup\mathsf{s}}_{\mathcal{S}\cup\{c \doteq \mathtt{true}\}} e_1 : \tau^{\mathsf{s}} \quad \Delta \vdash^{\mathsf{r}\sqcup\mathsf{s}}_{\mathcal{S}\cup\{c \doteq \mathtt{false}\}} e_2 : \tau^{\mathsf{s}}}{\Delta \vdash^{\mathsf{r}}_{\mathcal{S}} \textbf{if } c \textbf{ then } e_1 \textbf{ else } e_2 : \tau^{\mathsf{s}}} \qquad \textit{(t-or)}\quad \frac{\Delta \vdash^{\mathsf{r}}_{\mathcal{S}} c_1 : \mathtt{Bool}^{\mathsf{s}} \quad \Delta \vdash^{\mathsf{r}}_{\mathcal{S}} c_2 : \mathtt{Bool}^{\mathsf{s}}}{\Delta \vdash^{\mathsf{r}}_{\mathcal{S}} c_1 \vee c_2 : \mathtt{Bool}^{\mathsf{s}}} \qquad \textit{(t-not)}\quad \frac{\Delta \vdash^{\mathsf{r}}_{\mathcal{S}} c : \mathtt{Bool}^{\mathsf{s}}}{\Delta \vdash^{\mathsf{r}}_{\mathcal{S}} \neg c : \mathtt{Bool}^{\mathsf{s}}}$$

$$\textit{(t-equal)}\quad \frac{\Delta \vdash^{\mathsf{r}}_{\mathcal{S}} V_1 : \tau^{\mathsf{s}} \quad \Delta \vdash^{\mathsf{r}}_{\mathcal{S}} V_2 : \tau^{\mathsf{s}}}{\Delta \vdash^{\mathsf{r}}_{\mathcal{S}} V_1 = V_2 : \mathtt{Bool}^{\mathsf{s}}} \qquad \textit{(t-true)}\quad \frac{}{\Delta \vdash^{\mathsf{r}}_{\mathcal{S}} \textbf{true} : \mathtt{Bool}^{\perp}} \qquad \textit{(t-false)}\quad \frac{}{\Delta \vdash^{\mathsf{r}}_{\mathcal{S}} \textbf{false} : \mathtt{Bool}^{\perp}} \qquad \textit{(t-unit)}\quad \frac{}{\Delta \vdash^{\mathsf{r}}_{\mathcal{S}} () : \mathtt{cmd}^{\perp}}$$

$$\textit{(t-ref)}\quad \frac{\Delta \vdash^{\mathsf{r}}_{\mathcal{S}} e : \tau^{\mathsf{s}} \quad \mathsf{r} \leq \mathsf{s}}{\Delta \vdash^{\mathsf{r}}_{\mathcal{S}} \textbf{ref}_{\tau^{\mathsf{s}}}\ e : \mathtt{ref}(\tau^{\mathsf{s}})^{\perp}} \qquad \textit{(t-deref)}\quad \frac{\Delta \vdash^{\mathsf{r}}_{\mathcal{S}} e : \mathtt{ref}(\tau^{\mathsf{s}})^{\mathsf{s}'} \quad \mathsf{s}' \leq \mathsf{s}}{\Delta \vdash^{\mathsf{r}}_{\mathcal{S}} !e : \tau^{\mathsf{s}}}$$

$$\textit{(t-assign)}\quad \frac{\Delta \vdash^{\mathsf{r}}_{\mathcal{S}} e_1 : \mathtt{ref}(\tau^{\mathsf{s}})^{\mathsf{s}'} \quad \Delta \vdash^{\mathsf{r}}_{\mathcal{S}} e_2 : \tau^{\mathsf{s}} \quad \mathsf{r} \sqcup \mathsf{s}' \leq \mathsf{s}}{\Delta \vdash^{\mathsf{r}}_{\mathcal{S}} e_1 := e_2 : \mathtt{cmd}^{\perp}} \qquad \textit{(t-loc)}\quad \frac{}{\Delta, l : \tau^{\mathsf{s}} \vdash^{\mathsf{r}}_{\mathcal{S}} l : \mathtt{ref}(\tau^{\mathsf{s}})^{\perp}}$$

Figure 6: Typing Rules

Finally, in both branches, `y` is typed as the collection type with element type the dependent sum type above (since we are adding `tuple` to `y` and the conditional branches must have the same type). So function `viewAuthorPapers` is assigned type Π `(uid_a:⊥).Σ[uid:⊥× sid:⊥× title:A(uid_a,sid)× ...]*⊥`.

---

**Example 4.3** We now refer back to Example 2.5. For clarity, we abbreviate dependent sum types and mention only the record fields relevant for the discussion.

```
let addCommentSubmission = λ(uid_r: ⊥, sid_r: ⊥).
 foreach (p in viewAssignedPapers(uid_r)) with _ do
  if p.sid = sid_r then
   foreach(y in !Reviews) with _ do
    let t_rev = !y in
     if t_rev.sid = p.sid then
      let up_rec =
       [uid=t_rev.uid,PC_only=comment(p.uid,p.sid,p),...]
      in y := up_rec
```

To typecheck `y:= up_rec` we need to type `up_rec` with the declared type for the elements of collection `Reviews`, which is type $\delta_c$ in Figure 1c. As shown in Example 2.5, identifier `p` has type

`Σ[uid:⊥ × sid:⊥ × ... × title:A(uid,sid)]`

The type for *comment*`(p.uid,p.sid,p)` has level `A(p.uid,p.sid)`. By the lattice order `A(p.uid,p.sid)≤ PC(⊥,p.sid)` and by (*t-indexRight*) we get `PC(⊥,p.sid) ≤ PC(t_rev.uid,p.sid)`, hence `A(p.uid,p.sid)≤ PC(t_rev.uid,p.sid))`. We may then type the `PC_only` record field with `PC(t_rev.uid,p.sid)`. At this point, we tracked the following knowledge (via conditionals and let-expressions) into the following constraint set:

```
{ p.sid ≐ sid_r, t_rev.sid ≐ p.sid,
  up_rec ≐ [uid = t_rev.uid, sid = t_rev.sid,
            PC_only = comment(p.uid,p.sid,p), ...] }
```

Let us typecheck `up_rec` in the context of the assignment `y:= up_rec`. After typing the record value, we eliminate field dependencies, adding to $\mathcal{S}$ the constraint $\{x \doteq$ `up_rec`$\}$, for a fresh $x$. Then, we can derive the entailments

$\mathcal{S}, x \doteq$ `up_rec` $\models x.$`sid` $\doteq$ `p.sid`

$\mathcal{S}, x \doteq$ `up_rec` $\models x.$`uid` $\doteq$ `t_rev.uid`.

So we refine the type of the `PC_only` field to `PC(uid,sid)` by (*t-refineRecord*) and type the record bound to `up_rec` with the dependent type `Σ[uid:⊥,sid:⊥, PC_only:PC(uid,sid), ...]`, thus matching the expected type of reference `y`.

---

By allowing the (*t-refineRecord*) and (*t-unrefineRecord*) rules to approximate the security label to a field identifier of another record, as we just did in Example 4.3, we retrieve essential precision in our analysis, required to obtain the correct typing for `PC_only`, `PC(uid,sid)`, and to typecheck function `addCommentSubmission`.

We briefly overview the remaining typing rules. Rule (*t-ref*) imposes a lower bound on the security level of the expression initializing the reference allocation to the computational context security level. Otherwise, illegal implicit flows could occur. For instance, in **let** `x = (`**if** `high` **then** **ref**$_{\tau^\perp}$ `low)` **in** `!x`, we would be able to observe that a new reference was allocated. Rule (*t-deref*) sets the reference's security level as the lower bound for the deference's security level, to prevent implicit flows since references are typed initially at security level ⊥ but may raise to a different security level, given the computational context. For instance, **let** `x =` **ref**$_{\tau^\perp}$ `low` **in** `(`**let** `y = (`**if** `high` **then** `x` **else** **ref**$_{\tau}^{\top}$ `0)` **in** `!y)`, would leak the value of `high` at low level, but does not typecheck . In (*t-assign*), we require that the least upper bound of the computational context security label and the reference's security level to be the lower bound of the content's security level. This way one can safely type basic values and commands at the $\bot$ level, even at higher computational contexts.

## 5. Type Preservation and Non-Interference

In this section we present our main technical results: Theorem 5.4 (Type Preservation) - types are preserved by the reduction relation; Theorem 5.5 (Progress) - well-typed expressions are either a value or have a reduction step; and Theorem 5.11 (Non-interference) - well-typed expressions preserve non-interference. Our results establish that our system ensures that well-typed programs do not leak confidential information under the security policy prescribed by the assumed security lattice. In other words, data does not flow from a security compartment to another if they are unrelated or if it is a down-flow in the security lattice. For detailed proofs see [34].

***Type Safety.*** We start by introducing some preliminary definitions.

**Definition 5.1 (Store Consistency)** Let $\Delta$ be a typing environment and $S$ a store, we say store $S$ is consistent with respect to typing environment $\Delta$, denoted as $\Delta \vdash S$, if $dom(S) \subseteq dom(\Delta)$ and $\forall l \in dom(S)$ then $\Delta \vdash^{\mathsf{r}}_{\mathcal{S}} S(l) : \Delta(l)$.

**Definition 5.2 (Well-typed Configuration)** A configuration $(S; e)$ is well-typed in typing environment $\Delta$ if $\Delta \vdash S$ and $\Delta \vdash^{\mathsf{r}}_{\mathcal{S}} e{:}\tau^{\mathsf{s}}$.

Theorem 5.4 says that well-typed configurations remain well-typed after a reduction step, and possibly the final configuration is extended with new locations in the state.

**Lemma 5.3 (Substitution Lemma)**
If $\Delta, x{:}\tau'^{\mathsf{s}'} \vdash^{\mathsf{r}}_{\mathcal{S}} e{:}\tau^{\mathsf{s}}$ and $\Delta \vdash^{\mathsf{r}'}_{\mathcal{S}} v{:}\tau'^{\mathsf{s}'}$ then $\Delta \vdash^{\mathsf{r}}_{\mathcal{S}} e\{v/x\}{:}(\tau^{\mathsf{s}})\{v/x\}$.

**Theorem 5.4 (Type Preservation)**
*Let $fv(e) \cup fv(\tau^{\mathsf{s}}) = \emptyset$, $vars(\Delta) = \emptyset$, $\Delta \vdash S$ and $\Delta \vdash^{\mathsf{r}}_{\mathcal{S}} e{:}\tau^{\mathsf{s}}$. If $(S; e) \longrightarrow (S'; e')$ then there is $\Delta'$ such that $\Delta' \vdash^{\mathsf{r}}_{\mathcal{S}} e' : \tau^{\mathsf{s}}$, $\Delta' \vdash S'$ and $\Delta \subseteq \Delta'$.*

Theorem 5.5, states that well-typed programs never get stuck.

**Theorem 5.5 (Progress)**
*Let $\Delta \vdash^{\mathsf{r}}_{\mathcal{S}} e{:}\tau^{\mathsf{s}}$ and $\Delta \vdash S$. If $e$ is not a value then $(S; e) \longrightarrow (S'; e')$.*

***Noninterference Theorem.*** To develop our main noninterference result, we now introduce some relevant concepts. The first is the relation of store equivalence up to a security level $\mathsf{s}$. Auxiliary function $redact(\Delta, S, \mathsf{s})$ returns the store obtained by "redacting" (replacing with a dummy value $\star$) all stored values in $S$ with security level higher than $\mathsf{s}$, or incomparable with $\mathsf{s}$ (detailed definitions in [34]). Two well-typed stores $S_1, S_2$ are said to be equivalent up to level $\mathsf{s}$, written $S_1 =_{\mathsf{s}} S_2$, if $redact(\Delta, S_1, \mathsf{s}) = redact(\Delta, S_2, \mathsf{s})$.

**Definition 5.6 (Store Equivalence)** Let $\Delta \vdash S_1$ and $\Delta \vdash S_2$. Then $S_1$ is equivalent to $S_2$ up to level $\mathsf{s}$ (written $S_1 =_{\mathsf{s}} S_2$) if and only if $redact(\Delta, S_1, \mathsf{s}) = redact(\Delta, S_2, \mathsf{s})$.

**Example 5.7** Assume `user(42)`$\#$`user(666)`, and let $S_1$ and $S_2$ be stores containing location `private_file`. Also, let `private_file` have type `Σ[uid:`$\bot$ $\times$ `content:user(uid)]` under typing environment $\Delta$, which also types both stores.
Then if $S_1$`(private_file) = {(42, "xpto"), (666, "fire")}`, and $S_2$`(private_file) = {(42, "puppies"), (666, "fire")}`.
We have $S_1 =_{\texttt{user(666)}} S_2$ since the values `"xpto"` and `"puppies"`, classified as `user(42)`, are not visible at level `user(666)`, because $redact$`(`$\Delta$`,`$S_1$`,user(666)) = {(42,`$\star$`),(666,"fire")} =` $redact$`(`$\Delta$`,`$S_2$`,user(666))`.
However, $S_1$ and $S_2$ are not equivalent at security level `user(42)`, $S_1 \neq_{\texttt{user(42)}} S_2$, since the values `"xpto"` and `"puppies"` are visible at level `user(42)`.
In fact, $redact$`(`$\Delta$`,`$S_1$`,user(42)) = {(42,"xpto"), (666,`$\star$`)}` $\neq$ `{(42,"puppies"),(666,`$\star$`) }=`$redact$`(`$\Delta$`,`$S_2$`,user(42))`.

(e-val)

$$\frac{\Delta \vdash^{\mathsf{r}}_{\mathcal{S}_1} v : \tau^{\mathsf{s}'} \quad \Delta \vdash^{\mathsf{r}}_{\mathcal{S}_2} v : \tau^{\mathsf{s}'}}{\Delta \vdash^{\mathsf{r}}_{\mathcal{S}_1,\mathcal{S}_2} v \cong_{\mathsf{s}} v : \tau^{\mathsf{s}'}}$$

(e-exprOpaque)

$$\frac{\Delta \vdash^{\mathsf{r}}_{\mathcal{S}_1} e_1 : \tau^{\mathsf{s}'} \quad \Delta \vdash^{\mathsf{r}}_{\mathcal{S}_2} e_2 : \tau^{\mathsf{s}'} \quad \mathsf{s} < \mathsf{s}' \sqcap \mathsf{r}}{\Delta \vdash^{\mathsf{r}}_{\mathcal{S}_1,\mathcal{S}_2} e_1 \cong_{\mathsf{s}} e_2 : \tau^{\mathsf{s}'}}$$

(e-refineRecord)

$$\frac{\Delta \vdash^{\mathsf{r}}_{\mathcal{S}_1,\mathcal{S}_2} e \cong_{\mathsf{s}} e' : \Sigma[\ldots \times m_j : \tau_j^{\mathsf{s}_j} \times \ldots \times m_i : \tau_i^{\ell_i(\mathsf{v})}, \ldots]^{\mathsf{s}'} \quad \mathcal{S}_1\{x \doteq e\} \models x.m_j \doteq \mathsf{v} \quad \mathcal{S}_2\{x \doteq e'\} \models x.m_j \doteq \mathsf{v}}{\Delta \vdash^{\mathsf{r}}_{\mathcal{S}_1,\mathcal{S}_2} e \cong_{\mathsf{s}} e' : \Sigma[\ldots \times m_j : \tau_j^{\mathsf{s}_j} \times \ldots \times m_i : \tau_i^{\ell_i(m_j)}, \ldots]^{\mathsf{s}'}}$$

(e-sub)

$$\frac{\Delta \vdash^{\mathsf{r}'}_{\mathcal{S}_1,\mathcal{S}_2} e \cong_{\mathsf{s}} e' : \tau^{\mathsf{s}''} \quad \tau^{\mathsf{s}''} <: \tau^{\mathsf{s}'} \quad \mathsf{r} \leq \mathsf{r}'}{\Delta \vdash^{\mathsf{r}}_{\mathcal{S}_1,\mathcal{S}_2} e \cong_{\mathsf{s}} e' : \tau^{\mathsf{s}'}}$$

Figure 7: Equivalence of expressions up to level $\mathsf{s}$ (sample rules)

Useful to formulations of non-interference results is the introduction of a relation of expression equivalence, relating expressions at the same type and security level. Technically, program expressions $e_1$ and $e_2$ are equivalent up to level $\mathsf{s}$ if they only differ in subexpressions classified at higher (or incomparable) security levels (being indistinguishable to attackers constrained to see only up to level $\mathsf{s}$). We say two expressions, $e_1, e_2$, are equivalent up to a security level $\mathsf{s}$, asserted by $\Delta \vdash^{\mathsf{r}}_{\mathcal{S}_1,\mathcal{S}_2} e_1 \cong_{\mathsf{s}} e_2{:}\tau^{\mathsf{s}'}$, if they compute the same result under all stores equivalent up to $\mathsf{s}$.

**Definition 5.8 (Expression Equivalence)** Expression equivalence of $e_1$ and $e_2$ up to $\mathsf{s}$ is asserted by $\Delta \vdash^{\mathsf{r}}_{\mathcal{S}_1,\mathcal{S}_2} e_1 \cong_{\mathsf{s}} e_2{:}\tau^{\mathsf{s}'}$.

Notice that two expressions may be equivalent up to level $\mathsf{s}$ even if they are typed at a different level $\mathsf{s}'$. We show key rules for expression equivalence in Figure 7 (see [34] for the complete definition). We may now present our non-interference theorems.

**Lemma 5.9 (Non-interference Step)** Let $vars(\Delta) = \emptyset$, $\Delta \vdash S_1$, $\Delta \vdash S_2$, $S_1 =_{\mathsf{s}} S_2$, $\Delta \vdash^{\mathsf{r}}_{\mathcal{S}_1,\mathcal{S}_2} e_1 \cong_{\mathsf{s}} e_2{:}\tau^{\mathsf{s}'}$. If $(S_1, e_1) \rightarrow (S_1', e_1')$ and $(S_2, e_2) \rightarrow (S_2', e_2')$, then exists $\Delta'$ such that $\Delta \subseteq \Delta'$, $\Delta' \vdash S_1'$, $\Delta' \vdash S_2'$, $S_1' =_{\mathsf{s}} S_2'$, $\Delta' \vdash^{\mathsf{r}}_{\mathcal{S}_1,\mathcal{S}_2} e_1' \cong_{\mathsf{s}} e_2'{:}\tau^{\mathsf{s}'}$.

**Proof**: By induction on the derivation of $\Delta \vdash^{\mathsf{r}}_{\mathcal{S}_1,\mathcal{S}_2} e_1 \cong_{\mathsf{s}} e_2{:}\tau^{\mathsf{s}'}$.

Lemma 5.9 states that if two equivalent programs can both perform a step under stores that differ only on information with higher (or incomparable) security level than $\mathsf{s}$, then the resulting stores remain indistinguishable up to security level $\mathsf{s}$, and the resulting program residuals remain equivalent at the same level.

**Lemma 5.10 (Value-Step-Equivalence)** Let $\Delta \vdash^{\mathsf{r}}_{\mathcal{S}_1,\mathcal{S}_2} v \cong_{\mathsf{s}} e{:}\tau^{\mathsf{s}'}$, $vars(\Delta) = \emptyset$, $\Delta \vdash S_1$, $\Delta \vdash S_2$ and $S_1 =_{\mathsf{s}} S_2$. If $(S_2, e) \longrightarrow (S_2', e')$ then there is $\Delta'$ such that $\Delta \subseteq \Delta'$, $\Delta' \vdash S_1$, $\Delta' \vdash S_2'$, $S_1 =_{\mathsf{s}} S_2'$ and $\Delta' \vdash^{\mathsf{r}}_{\mathcal{S}_1,\mathcal{S}_2} v \cong_{\mathsf{s}} e'{:}\tau^{\mathsf{s}'}$ (and symmetrically).

We can then prove our non-interference theorem:

**Theorem 5.11 (Non-interference)** *Let $\Delta \vdash^{\mathsf{r}}_{\mathcal{S}_1,\mathcal{S}_2} e_1 \cong_{\mathsf{s}} e_2{:}\tau^{\mathsf{s}'}$, with $vars(\Delta) = \emptyset$, $\Delta \vdash S_1$, $\Delta \vdash S_2$ and $S_1 =_{\mathsf{s}} S_2$. If $(S_1, e_1) \xrightarrow{m} (S_1', v_1)$, and $(S_2, e_2) \xrightarrow{n} (S_2', v_2)$ then there is $\Delta'$ such that $\Delta \subseteq \Delta'$, $\Delta' \vdash S_1'$, $\Delta' \vdash S_2'$, $S_1' =_{\mathsf{s}} S_2'$ and $\Delta' \vdash^{\mathsf{r}}_{\mathcal{S}_1,\mathcal{S}_2} v_1 \cong_{\mathsf{s}} v_2{:}\tau^{\mathsf{s}'}$.*

**Proof**: By induction on $m + n$, using Lemma 5.9 in the case $m > 0$ and $n > 0$. For $m = 0$ and $n > 0$ we rely on Lemma 5.10.

Suppose we apply theorem Theorem 5.11 to a program $e = e_1 = e_2$ (so $\Delta \vdash^{\mathsf{r}}_{\mathcal{S}_1,\mathcal{S}_2} e \cong_{\mathsf{s}} e{:}\tau^{\mathsf{s}'}$ holds by reflexivity). Then, if $\mathsf{s} \not< \mathsf{s}'$, we must have $v_1 = v_2$ (since *e-exprOpaque* is not applicable to derive $\Delta' \vdash^{r}_{\mathcal{S}_1,\mathcal{S}_2} v_1 \cong_{s} v_2{:}\tau^{s'}$). One can thus conclude that an attacker "located" at security level s never distinguishes the result of a program executed under stores that only differ in data that should be considered confidential for level s (data classified at any level l such that $l \not\leq s$.) We now illustrate our noninterference results.

---

**Example 5.12** Recall our conference manager from Section 2, and consider the following program that retrieves the profile of author with `uid 42` and then inserts a new profile in collection `Users` using some of the information previously retrieved.

$\tau_c \stackrel{\text{def}}{=} \Sigma[\texttt{uid} : \bot \times \texttt{name} : \texttt{U(uid)} \times \texttt{univ} : \texttt{U(uid)} \times \texttt{email} : \texttt{U(uid)}]$

```
let Users = ref_{ref(τc)*⊥} (ref_{τc} [] )::{} in
let p = first(viewUserProfile(42)) in
Users := [uid = 42, sid = p.sid, name = p.name,
          unit = p.univ, email = p.email] :: !Users
```

Since the new record value is associating information of security level `U(42)` (value `p`) with user id `42`, this program should be deemed secure and the noninterference property checked.

We apply the theorem to check. The evaluation of the assignment operation is the relevant part of this program since the program does not compute a value but changes the state at location `Users`. Thus, to illustrate the compliance of the noninterference theorem, we will just analyse this part of the program's evaluation, referring back to the assignment operation as expression $e$.
Assume `U(42)`#`U(666)`, and let $S_1$ and $S_2$ be stores such that
$S_1(\texttt{Users}) = \{(\texttt{42,70},A_1,A_2,A_3),(\texttt{666,9},B_1,\ B_2,B_3)\}$ and
$S_2(\texttt{Users}) = \{(\texttt{42,70},C_1,C_2,C_3),(\texttt{666,9},B_1,B_2,B_3)\}$.
We have $S_1 =_{\texttt{U(666)}} S_2$ since the values $A_i$ and $C_i$, classified as `U(42)`, are not visible at level `U(666)`, by definition of store equivalence and `U(42)`#`U(666)`. Also, we have $\Delta \vdash^{r}_{\mathcal{S}_1,\mathcal{S}_2} e \cong_{\texttt{U(666)}} e{:}\texttt{cmd}^{\bot}$.
Let us, then, consider the reductions $(S_1; e) \longrightarrow (S_1'; ())$ and $(S_2; e) \longrightarrow (S_2'; ())$. Then the resulting stores are the following

$S_1'(\texttt{Users}) = \{(\texttt{42,70},A_1,A_2,A_3),\ (\texttt{666,9},B_1,B_2,B_3),\ (\texttt{42,70},A_1,A_2,A_3)\}$ and
$S_2'(\texttt{Users}) = \{(\texttt{42,70},C_1,C_2,C_3),\ (\texttt{666,9},\ B_1,B_2,B_3),\ (\texttt{42,70},C_1,C_2,C_3)\}$

which means noninterference is satisfied, because we have
$\mathit{redact}(\Delta,S_1',\texttt{U(666)}) = \{(\texttt{42,70},\star,\star,\star),(\texttt{666,9},B_1,B_2,B_3),(\texttt{42,70},\star,\star,\star)\} = \mathit{redact}(\Delta,S_2',\texttt{U(666)})$.
That is, $S_1' =_{\texttt{U(666)}} S_2'$. So, the effects of expression $e$ are not visible at security level `U(666)`, as expected.

Now consider a slight modification to the presented code, where we replace expression e with another assignment operation (which we shall refer as $e'$):

```
Users := [uid = 666, sid = p.sid, name = p.name,
          unit = p.univ, email = p.email] :: !Users
```

Using subexpression $e'$ instead of $e$ in the main program will now associate the contents of the profile of author with id `42` to a profile of author with id `666`. This clearly violates confidentiality, among other things, and is disallowed by the security lattice since `U(42)`#`U(666)`, so the program using this subexpression should be considered insecure. Let us look this in detail.
Again, we have $\Delta \vdash^{r}_{\mathcal{S}_1,\mathcal{S}_2} e' \cong_{\texttt{U(666)}} e'{:}\texttt{cmd}^{\bot}$. After the reduction steps $(S_1; e') \longrightarrow (S_1'; ())$ and $(S_2; e') \longrightarrow (S_2'; ())$, we have

$S_1'(\texttt{Users}) = \{(\texttt{42,70},A_1,A_2,A_3),\ (\texttt{666,9},B_1,B_2,B_3),\ (\texttt{666,70},A_1,A_2,A_3)\}$ and
$S_2'(\texttt{Users}) = \{(\texttt{42,70},C_1,C_2,C_3),\ (\texttt{666,9},\ B_1,B_2,B_3),\ (\texttt{666,70},C_1,C_2,C_3)\}$

But now, $S_1' \neq_{\texttt{U(666)}} S_2'$ since after executing $e'$ the values $A_i$ and $C_i$ of the new record are observable at level `U(666)`. This is captured by the notion of store equivalence because now we have

$\mathit{redact}(\Delta,S_1',\texttt{U(666)}) = \{(\texttt{42,70},\star,\star,\star),\ (\texttt{666,9},B_1,B_2,B_3),\ (\texttt{666,70},A_1,A_2,A_3)\}$
and
$\mathit{redact}(\Delta,S_2',\texttt{U(666)}) = \{(\texttt{42,70},\star,\star,\star),\ (\texttt{666,9},B_1,B_2,B_3),\ (\texttt{666,70},C_1,C_2,C_3)\}$

As expected, the thesis of non-interference theorem is not satisfied.

---

Of course, insecure programs like Example 5.12 are rejected by our type system. In this particular case, it would not be possible to give the perhaps expected dependent type $\tau_c$, to record `[uid = 666, sid= p.sid, name = p.name, univ = p.univ, email = p.email]` using rule *(t-refineRecord)* because the security level of `p.name`, `p.univ`, and `p.email` is `U(42)` but field `uid` has value `666`.

# 6. Algorithmic Typechecking

We briefly discuss a type-checking algorithm for a suitable annotated version of our core language (Figure 8, remaining cases in [34]). The algorithm already allows us to verify many interesting examples, including those in paper, and support a prototype implementation [35]. For pragmatic reasons, we require type annotations on reference creation, record fields, and bound variables, leaving for future work possible inference. We introduce type cast constructs, of the forms $\lceil\tau^{s}\rceil e$ and $\rceil s\lceil e$, useful to manually up-classify primitive values and raise the level of the computational context, respectively.

The algorithm depends on subsidiary procedures to check subtyping, which we represent by the $\sigma <: \tau$ tests, and on a constraint solving procedure, which we represent by $\mathcal{S} \models V \doteq U$ tests. The auxiliary procedure $\mathit{unref}(\mathcal{S}, [\ldots, m_i{:}\tau_i^{s_i} = e_i, \ldots])$ eliminates field dependencies on the given (possibly dependent) record type, and returns an unrefined record type by attempting the most precise possible approximations to the field values $\mathsf{v}_i$ given by each expression $e_i$, using $\mathcal{S}\{x \doteq e_i\} \models x \doteq \mathsf{v}_i$.

The subtyping test essentially implements the subtyping rules, given a suitable security lattice. In our prototype implementation the security lattice can be user-defined, in a preamble to the code to be type checked. As far as constraint solving is concerned, our current prototype relies on an encoding of the required entailment checks on queries for the Z3 SMT solver [7]. The completeness of the algorithm is relative to the completeness of the required constraint solving problem.

# 7. Related Work

Language-based information flow analysis has attracted substantial research effort for a long time (see e.g., [22]). In early works the focus was on imperative languages [23, 28], $\lambda$-calculus [1, 12, 21], object-oriented languages [18], and concurrent languages [13, 30]. More recently, there has been a growing interest in studying secure information flows in the context of data-centric applications, namely in web scripting languages like Javascript (JS) as well as more general-purpose data manipulation languages (DML). While the work in this paper is not focused on reasoning about information flow analysis for data-centric applications, our core language can easily encode common DML high-level operation and thus our analysis is general enough to ensure noninterference on such applications involving expressive security policies, depending on runtime values as often required in realistic applications.

Static approaches have also been employed for secure information flows in data-centric applications, to cite a few of the relevant work: [3–5, 15], these works do not provide any kind of value-dependent information flow analysis, as we do here.

$$tc(\Delta, \mathcal{S}, \mathsf{r}, \mathbf{true}) \stackrel{\text{def}}{=} \mathtt{Bool}^{\perp}$$

$$tc(\Delta, \mathcal{S}, \mathsf{r}, 1) \stackrel{\text{def}}{=} \mathtt{Int}^{\perp}$$

$$tc(\Delta, \mathcal{S}, \mathsf{r}, x) \stackrel{\text{def}}{=} \Delta(x)$$

$$\begin{array}{l} tc(\Delta, \mathcal{S}, \mathsf{r}, [\tau^{\mathsf{s}}]e) \stackrel{\text{def}}{=} \mathbf{if}\ tc(\Delta, \mathcal{S}, \mathsf{r}, e) <: \tau^{\mathsf{s}} \\ \qquad\qquad\qquad\qquad \mathbf{then}\ \tau^{\mathsf{s}}\ \mathbf{else}\ \mathtt{typerror} \end{array}$$

$$tc(\Delta, \mathcal{S}, \mathsf{r}, ]\mathsf{s}[e) \stackrel{\text{def}}{=} \mathbf{if}\ \mathsf{r} \leq \mathsf{s}\ \mathbf{then}\ tc(\Delta, \mathcal{S}, \mathsf{s}, e)\ \mathbf{else}\ \mathtt{typerror}$$

$$\begin{array}{l} tc(\Delta, \mathcal{S}, \mathsf{r}, \lambda(x{:}\tau^{\mathsf{s}}).e) \stackrel{\text{def}}{=} \\ \quad \mathbf{let}\ \sigma^{\mathsf{t}} = tc(\Delta \cup \{x{:}\tau^{\mathsf{s}}\}, \mathcal{S}, \mathsf{r}, e)\ \mathbf{in}\ (\Pi x{:}\tau^{\mathsf{s}}.\mathsf{r}; \sigma^{\mathsf{t}})^{\perp} \end{array}$$

$$\begin{array}{l} tc(\Delta, \mathcal{S}, \mathsf{r}, e_1(e_2)) \stackrel{\text{def}}{=} \\ \quad \mathbf{if}\ tc(\Delta, \mathcal{S}, \mathsf{r}, e_1) = (\Pi x{:}\tau^{\mathsf{s}}.\mathsf{r}'; \sigma^{\mathsf{t}})^{\mathsf{q}}\ \mathbf{and} \\ \qquad tc(\Delta, \mathcal{S}, \mathsf{r}, e_2) <: \tau^{\mathsf{s}}\ \mathbf{and}\ \mathsf{r} \leq \mathsf{r}'\ \mathbf{then} \\ \qquad\quad \mathbf{if}\ \mathcal{S} \models e_2 \doteq \mathsf{v}\ \mathbf{then}\ \sigma^{\mathsf{t}}\{\mathsf{v}/x\}\ \mathbf{else}\ \sigma^{\mathsf{t}}\{\top/x\} \\ \quad \mathbf{else}\ \mathtt{typerror} \end{array}$$

$$\begin{array}{l} tc(\Delta, \mathcal{S}, \mathsf{r}, [\ldots, m_i{:}\tau_i^{\mathsf{s}_i} = e_i, \ldots]) \stackrel{\text{def}}{=} \\ \quad \mathbf{let}\ \Sigma[\ldots \times m_i{:}\tau_i'^{\mathsf{s}_i'} \times \ldots]^{\mathsf{s}} = \mathit{unref}(\mathcal{S}, [\ldots, m_i{:}\tau_i^{\mathsf{s}_i} = e_i, \ldots]) \\ \quad \mathbf{in}\ \mathbf{if}\ (\mathtt{forall}\ e_i.\ \sigma_i^{\mathsf{t}} = tc(\Delta, \mathcal{S}, \mathsf{r}, e_i)\ \mathbf{and}\ \sigma_i^{\mathsf{t}} <: \tau_i'^{\mathsf{s}_i'}) \\ \qquad \mathbf{then}\ \Sigma[\ldots \times m_i{:}\tau_i^{\mathsf{s}_i} \times \ldots]^{\mathsf{s}}\ \mathbf{else}\ \mathtt{typerror} \end{array}$$

$$\begin{array}{l} tc(\Delta, \mathcal{S}, \mathsf{r}, e.m) \stackrel{\text{def}}{=} \mathbf{let}\ \tau^{\mathsf{s}} = tc(\Delta, \mathcal{S}, \mathsf{r}, e)\ \mathbf{in} \\ \quad \mathbf{if}\ \tau = \Sigma[\ldots \times m{:}\sigma^{\ell(n)} \times \ldots]\ \mathbf{then} \\ \quad\ (\ \mathbf{if}\ \mathcal{S}\{f \doteq e\} \models f.n \doteq \mathsf{v}\ \mathbf{then}\ \sigma^{\ell(\mathsf{v})}\ \mathbf{else}\ \sigma^{\ell(\top)}\ ) \\ \quad \mathbf{else}\ \mathtt{typerror} \end{array}$$

$$\begin{array}{l} tc(\Delta, \mathcal{S}, \mathsf{r}, \mathbf{if}\ e_1\ \mathbf{then}\ e_2\ \mathbf{else}\ e_3) \stackrel{\text{def}}{=} \\ \quad \mathbf{let}\ \tau^{\mathsf{s}} = tc(\Delta, \mathcal{S}, \mathsf{r}, e_1)\ \mathbf{in} \\ \quad \mathbf{if}\ \tau = \mathtt{Bool}\ \mathbf{then} \\ \quad\ (\ \mathbf{let}\ {\tau_2}^{\mathsf{s}_2} = tc(\Delta, \mathcal{S} \cup \{e_1 \doteq \mathtt{true}\}, \mathsf{r} \sqcup \mathsf{s}, e_2)\ \mathbf{in} \\ \qquad \mathbf{let}\ {\tau_3}^{\mathsf{s}_3} = tc(\Delta, \mathcal{S} \cup \{e_1 \doteq \mathtt{false}\}, \mathsf{r} \sqcup \mathsf{s}, e_3)\ \mathbf{in} \\ \qquad \mathbf{if}\ \tau_2 = \tau_3\ \mathbf{then}\ \tau_2^{\mathsf{s} \sqcup \mathsf{s}_2 \sqcup \mathsf{s}_3}\ \mathbf{else}\ \mathtt{typerror} \\ \quad\ )\ \mathbf{else}\ \mathtt{typerror} \end{array}$$

$$\begin{array}{l} tc(\Delta, \mathcal{S}, \mathsf{r}, \mathbf{ref}_{\tau^{\mathsf{s}}}\ e) \stackrel{\text{def}}{=} \mathbf{let}\ \sigma^{\mathsf{t}} = tc(\Delta, \mathcal{S}, \mathsf{r}, e)\ \mathbf{in} \\ \quad \mathbf{if}\ \sigma^{\mathsf{t}} <: \tau^{\mathsf{s}}\ \mathbf{and}\ \mathsf{r} \leq \mathsf{s}\ \mathbf{then}\ (\mathtt{ref}_{\tau^{\mathsf{s}}})^{\perp}\ \mathbf{else}\ \mathtt{typerror} \end{array}$$

$$\begin{array}{l} tc(\Delta, \mathcal{S}, \mathsf{r}, !e) \stackrel{\text{def}}{=} \mathbf{let}\ \sigma^{\mathsf{t}} = tc(\Delta, \mathcal{S}, \mathsf{r}, e)\ \mathbf{in} \\ \quad \mathbf{if}\ \sigma^{\mathsf{t}} <: (\mathtt{ref}_{\tau^{\mathsf{s}}})^{\mathsf{t}}\ \mathbf{and}\ \mathsf{t} \leq \mathsf{s}\ \mathbf{then}\ \tau^{\mathsf{s}}\ \mathbf{else}\ \mathtt{typerror} \end{array}$$

$$\begin{array}{l} tc(\Delta, \mathcal{S}, \mathsf{r}, e_1 := e_2) \stackrel{\text{def}}{=} \mathbf{let}\ \sigma^{\mathsf{t}} = tc(\Delta, \mathcal{S}, \mathsf{r}, e_1)\ \mathbf{in} \\ \ \ \mathbf{let}\ \tau^{\mathsf{s}} = tc(\Delta, \mathcal{S}, \mathsf{r}, e_2)\ \mathbf{in} \\ \quad \mathbf{if}\ \sigma^{\mathsf{t}} <: (\mathtt{ref}_{\tau^{\mathsf{s}}})^{\mathsf{t}}\ \mathbf{and}\ \mathsf{r} \sqcup \mathsf{t} \leq \mathsf{s}\ \mathbf{then}\ \mathtt{Cmd}^{\perp}\ \mathbf{else}\ \mathtt{typerror} \end{array}$$

Figure 8: Typechecking algorithm

Two interesting ideas put forward recently are the specification of security policies that rely on runtime first-class representations of principals, by Tse and Zdancewic [27], and security labels that can dynamically change, by Zheng and Myers in [32]. The former is based on the (seminal) decentralised label model (DLM) introduced by Myers and Liskov in [19], and presents a typed $\lambda$-calculus where principals are values and thus can be used during program execution, for e.g. for conditional testing, increasing the expressiveness of the security policy model. The authors also prove a noninterference result for an information flow type system using this notion of runtime principals. Although it is conceivable that some dynamically enforced form of value dependent security label could be encoded in some version of the DLM (e.g., using label passing [2]) in this work we deliberately focus on a direct and lightweight static approach.

The second work, introduces a static type-based information flow analysis where security labels can change during execution time and are case-analysed via a label-test primitive. This construction is used to add label constraints that are statically checked by the type checker. In our work we do not consider runtime principals nor dynamically changing labels but, instead, use runtime values to index security labels to ensure data dependent security policies. With our label model, we are able to specify security labels that depend on the actual program's (stored) data.

To the best of our knowledge, dependent information flow types in the sense introduced here, leading to a general non-interference theorem, are novel; we have no perspective on how to conveniently and precisely express valued dependent security classification in existing dependent type systems.

Several recent works explore applications of dependent types [20, 25, 26] to language-based security in the context of stateful static information flow. In [25] Swamy *et. al.* present FINE, a general-purpose and very expressive dependently typed language based on Fable [24], and suggest several encodings in the language of high-level security concerns such as information flow and access control policies. To express an information flow analysis in such setting, the programmer is required to hardcode the security labels as well as the lattice and all its operations/axioms (meet, join, partial order relation, etc) into inductive types and logic formulae within a module that internalizes the intended information flow policy inside the framework. In [25] a value abstraction result is presented, stating that code within a module does not interfere with another module's protected code, which is different from the (standard) notion of noninterference used in our work, and does not primitively and explicitly address the fundamental notion of value dependent classification through dependent typing, which is the core contribution of our work (which, in addition, covers a language with general imperative features). Moreover, the use of dependent types to express security properties in such line of work relies on refinement types and relative logical encodings of meta properties, which is very different from what we do here, that does not involve refinement types, and adopts a simple and primitive notion of value dependent classification directly at the level of the type structure, leading to an absolute non-interference theorem.

In [20], Nanevski *et. al.*, use a very expressive relational Hoare type theory (RHTT) to reason about access control and information flow in stateful programs. Besides standard dependent types, this work introduces a special dependent type, `STsec`, to specify security policies via pre and post-conditions, using higher-order logic formulae capable of expressing heap union disjointness. The `STsec` type is used to type potentially side-effectful operations, but the relevant part *w.r.t.* to information flow analysis is the post-condition that specifies the behaviour of two different runs of the program, relating the outputs, input heaps and output heaps of any two terminating executions of the program. Another interesting work, based on [26] and [20], is RF* [33], where the authors introduce the notion of relational refinement types. The key idea of relational refinement types consists in extending classic refinement types to relational formulae, which in turn enables to relate the left and right value of every program variable in scope through projections L and R. With this setting, the author's type system is able to relate expressions at a relational refined type that can describe the results of both expressions. A distinguishing feature of these latter approaches is that data is not classified with security labels (as expected from traditional information flow analyses). Instead, and similarly to the approach of [25], the noninterference property is expressed directly in the post-condition via detailed assertions that relate the initial heap with the final heap as well as the output values for any two runs of the program. While it might be conceivable, in principle, to express value-dependent information flow policies in such a framework, and in fact, in any sufficiently expressive logical framework for imperative programs supporting general functional properties, the goal of our work follows a much lightweight and tractable type-based approach, and aims to single out and address in a direct and explicit way the core notion of value dependent information classification.

A concept of indexed security label was introduced in [17], as an useful yet isolated feature to express security policies in a domain specific language with high-level monolithic data manipulation operations, much less general and expressive than what we achieve here. The developments in this paper put forward, in a principled way and for the first time, the notion of data/state dependent information flow in terms of a fairly canonical dependent type theory with first-order sum and arrow types, defined by a set of simple type rules, and for a parsimonious $\lambda$-calculus with references and collections.

Several proposals for dynamic information flow analysis on web languages have been put forward such as [6, 9, 11, 14, 16, 31]. In this work we focus on static certification techniques, developing the new notion of dependent information flow types. In future work it would be interesting to study combinations of static and dynamic typing in the context of our dependent type system.

## 8. Concluding Remarks

In this paper, we have motivated, introduced and studied a novel theory of dependent information flow types, which provide a direct, natural and elegant way to express and statically enforce fine grained security policies on programs. In our framework, the security level of data types, rather than just the data types themselves, may depend on runtime values, unlike in traditional dependent type systems. We have illustrated, including by means of many examples, how the proposed approach provides a general, expressive and fine grained way to formulate realistic, yet challenging, security policies. Our development is carried out on top of a minimalistic $\lambda$-calculus with general references and collections, thus adding generality and application scope to the approach. Our main technical results are expressed by type safety and non-interference theorems, which ensure the soundness of our value dependent information flow analysis: well-typed programs do not disclose information in ways violating the prescribed security polices.

Reasoning about the identity of dependent security labels, e.g, necessary to eliminate dependent sum type field dependencies or approximate dependent function argument values, requires runtime values to be approximated by a given constraint system. It may also be the case that the elimination of a dependent sum type results in replacing field dependencies with another dependent sum type's field identifier (e.g., an assignment operation in a conditional's then branch whose logical condition relates the field dependency with another record field, instead of a value), as long the final type remains well-formed. The constraint system used to deduce approximations of runtime values can only contain pure expressions thus disallowing constraints containing dereferences, however, this is a natural restriction that in our experience does not seem to limit much the expressiveness of the approach, but that deserves further study. We have also briefly discussed some algorithmic aspects of our approach, that has led to a prototype implementation [35], which can already be used to check examples, including those in this paper.

Adding variant types to our language is a trivial exercise, and would be important also for practical reasons. It would be interesting to investigate formulations of our type system integrating notions of type refinement (e.g, [29]), and type inference. As another follow up topic, as information flow analysis per se is not enough to ensure full data security guarantees, we would like to investigate the combination of our dependent information flow types with an adequate form of role-based access control.

*Acknowledgments.* We thank the anonymous reviewers for their insightful comments and suggestions. We also thank Jorge A. Perez and João C. Seco for related discussions. This work is supported by CITI PEst-OE/EEI/UI0527/2014, FCT/MEC grant SFRH/BD/68801/2010, and FLEX-Agile grant by OutSystems SA.

## References

[1] M. Abadi, A. Banerjee, N. Heintze, and J. G. Riecke:. A Core Calculus of Dependency. In *POPL* 1999.

[2] O. Arden, M. D. George, J. Liu, K. Vikram, A. Askarov, and A. C. Myers. Sharing mobile code securely with information flow control. In *IEEE SSP 2012*.

[3] G. M. Bierman, A. D. Gordon, C. Hritcu, and D. E. Langworthy. Semantic Subtyping with an SMT Solver. *J. Funct. Program.*, 2012.

[4] A. Chlipala. Static Checking of Dynamically-Varying Security Policies in Database-Backed Applications. In *USENIX OSDI* 2010.

[5] B. J. Corcoran, N. Swamy, and M. W. Hicks. Cross-tier, Label-based Security Enforcement for Web Applications. In *ACM SIGMOD Int. Conf. on Management of Data*, 2009.

[6] B. Davis and H. Chen. DBTaint: Cross-Application Information Flow Tracking via Databases. In *USENIX WebApps* 2010.

[7] L. M. de Moura and N. Bjørner. Z3: An efficient smt solver. In *TACAS 2008*.

[8] D. E. Denning and P. J. Denning. Certification of Programs for Secure Information Flow. *Comm. of the ACM*, 1977.

[9] W. Enck, P. Gilbert, B. Chun, L. P. Cox, J. Jung, P. M., and A. Sheth. TaintDroid: An Information-Flow Tracking System for Realtime Privacy Monitoring on Smartphones. In *USENIX OSDI* 2010.

[10] J. A. Goguen and J. Meseguer. Security Policies and Security Models. In *IEEE SSP* 1982.

[11] D. Hedin and A. Sabelfeld. Information-Flow Security for a Core of JavaScript. In *IEEE CSF 2012*.

[12] N. Heintze and J. G. Riecke. The SLam Calculus: Programming with Secrecy and Integrity. In *POPL* 1998.

[13] K. Honda, V. T. Vasconcelos, and N. Yoshida. Secure information flow as typed process behaviour. In *ESOP 2000*, LNCS.

[14] C. Hritcu, M. Greenberg, B. Karel, B. C. Pierce, and G. Morrisett. All your ifcexception are belong to us. In *IEEE SSP 2013*.

[15] P. Li and S. Zdancewic. Practical information-flow control in web-based information systems. In *IEEE CSFW 2005*.

[16] J. Liu, M. D. George, K. Vikram, X. Qi, L. Waye, and A. C. Myers. Fabric: a platform for secure distributed computation and storage. In *ACM SOSP 2009*.

[17] L. Lourenço and L. Caires. Information Flow Analysis for Valued-Indexed Data Security Compartments. In *TGC 2013*.

[18] A. C. Myers. JFlow: Practical Mostly-Static Information Flow Control. In *POPL* 1999.

[19] A. C. Myers and B. Liskov. A Decentralized Model for Information Flow Control. In *ACM SOSP* 1997.

[20] A. Nanevski, A. Banerjee, and D. Garg. Verification of Information Flow and Access Control Policies with Dependent Types. In *IEEE SSP* 2011.

[21] F. Pottier and V. Simonet. Information flow inference for ML. In *POPL 2002*.

[22] A. Sabelfeld and A. C. Myers. Language-Based Information-Flow Security. *IEEE JSAC*, 21(1):5-19, Jan. 2003.

[23] A. Sabelfeld and D. Sands. A Per Model of Secure Information Flow in Sequential Programs. *Higher-Order and Symbolic Computation*, 2001.

[24] N. Swamy, B. J. Corcoran, and M. Hicks. Fable: A language for enforcing user-defined security policies. In *IEEE SSP 2008*.

[25] N. Swamy, J. Chen, and R. Chugh. Enforcing Stateful Authorization and Information Flow Policies in Fine. In *ESOP 2010*.

[26] N. Swamy, J. Chen, C. Fournet, P. Strub, K. Bhargavan, and J. Yang. Secure Distributed Programming with Value-dependent Types. In *ICFP 2011*.

[27] S. Tse and S. Zdancewic. Run-time Principals in Information-flow Type Systems. *ACM Trans. Program. Lang. Syst.*, 2007.

[28] D. M. Volpano, C. E. Irvine, and G. Smith. A Sound Type System for Secure Flow Analysis. *Journal of Computer Security*, 1996.

[29] H. Xi and F. Pfenning. Dependent Types in Practical Programming. In *POPL* 1999.

[30] S. Zdancewic and A. C. Myers. Observational determinism for concurrent program security. In *IEEE CSFW 2003*.

[31] N. Zeldovich, S. Boyd-Wickizer, and D. Mazières. Securing Distributed Systems with Information Flow Control. In *USENIX NSDI 2008*.

[32] L. Zheng and A. C. Myers. Dynamic Security Labels and Static Information Flow Control. *Int. J. Inf. Sec.*, 2007.

[33] G. Barthe, C. Fournet, B. Grégoire, P. Strub, N. Swamy and S. Z. Béguelin. Probabilistic relational verification for cryptographic implementations. In *POPL 2014*.

[34] L. Lourenço and L. Caires. Dependent Information Flow Types. Technical report, UNL, 2014.

[35] DIFT Prototype. `http://ctp.di.fct.unl.pt/DIFTprototype`.

# Abstract Symbolic Automata

## Mixed syntactic/semantic similarity analysis of executables

Mila Dalla Preda[1] Roberto Giacobazzi[1,3] Arun Lakhotia[2] Isabella Mastroeni[1]

[1]University of Verona [2]University of Louisiana [3] Irdeto Canada

mila.dallapreda@univr.it, roberto.giacobazzi@univr.it, arun@louisiana.edu, isabella.mastroeni@univr.it

## Abstract

We introduce a model for mixed syntactic/semantic approximation of programs based on symbolic finite automata (SFA). The edges of SFA are labeled by predicates whose semantics specifies the denotations that are allowed by the edge. We introduce the notion of abstract symbolic finite automaton (ASFA) where approximation is made by abstract interpretation of symbolic finite automata, acting both at syntactic (predicate) and semantic (denotation) level. We investigate in the details how the syntactic and semantic abstractions of SFA relate to each other and contribute to the determination of the recognized language. Then we introduce a family of transformations for simplifying ASFA. We apply this model to prove properties of commonly used tools for similarity analysis of binary executables. Following the structure of their control flow graphs, disassembled binary executables are represented as (concrete) SFA, where states are program points and predicates represent the (possibly infinite) I/O semantics of each basic block in a constraint form. Known tools for binary code analysis are viewed as specific choices of symbolic and semantic abstractions in our framework, making symbolic finite automata and their abstract interpretations a unifying model for comparing and reasoning about soundness and completeness of analyses of low-level code.

***Categories and Subject Descriptors*** D.3.1 [*Programming Languages*]: Formal Definitions and Theory; F.3.2 [*Logics and Meanings of Programs*]: Semantics of Programming Languages—program analysis

***General Terms*** Languages.

***Keywords*** Symbolic automata, abstract interpretation.

## 1. Introduction

**The problem.** Similarity analysis is a key component in mining and understanding huge software enclaves, including code, e,g., coming from malware repositories, specifications, analyses and other heterogeneous meta-data. This is particularly relevant when dealing with binary executables, which, besides representing a large portion of existing malware, also represent a highly malleable often hard to analyze carrier. This is due to its unstructured nature, allowing self-modification, overlapping instructions, and untyped computations where data and code coexist without any predefined (static) boundary.

In order to mine both semantic meanings and syntactic patterns from programs, existing tools for similarity analysis of binary executables always employ mixed syntactic/symbolic and semantic representations of programs. At syntactic level properties concerning the control flow graph, such as in *BinHunt* [15] and *BinDiff* [12, 25], or feature vectors concerning sequences of instructions, are used together with graph-isomorphism, sequence comparison algorithms, and hash functions for extracting structural similarities in code. At semantic level, more advanced semantic properties such as those extracted from symbolic executions, dynamic analysis and emulation, such as those used in *BinJuice* [18] and *BinHunt* [15], are employed for bypassing semantic preserving code transformations for code obfuscation, e.g., for similarity analysis in malware detection. The use of mixed syntactic/semantic representation of code in similarity analysis is becoming a good practice because pure semantic similarity is too complex and often undecidable while pure syntactic similarities is too imprecise and prone to false negatives due to code obfuscation techniques. This is precisely what happens in most known tools and methods for dissecting and comparing programs in order to extract semantic similarities from syntactically different code. However, none of these tools have a formal semantic model in which relative precision and soundness can be formally proved. This paper is intended to fill this gap.

**Our contribution.** We attack this problem by observing that most known methods employed in similarity analysis of disassembled binaries can be seen as peculiar abstract interpretations of *symbolic finite state automata* (SFA). Symbolic finite automata, introduced in [23] and further developed in [8, 9], provide the ideal formal setting in order to treat within the same model the abstraction of both the syntactic structure of programs and their intended semantics.

SFA have been introduced as an extension of traditional finite state automata for modeling languages with a potential infinite alphabet. Transitions in SFA are therefore modeled as constraints interpreted in a given Boolean algebra, providing the semantic interpretation of constraints, and therefore the (potentially infinite) structural components of the language recognized (see [9, 23]).

Our main contribution is the introduction of the notion of *abstract symbolic finite automaton*, where approximation is made by abstract interpretation of standard SFA. Abstract interpretation here acts both at syntactic (predicate), topological (graph), and semantic (denotation) level. We investigate in details how the syntactic, topological, and semantic abstractions of SFA relate to each other and interfere when automata, at different levels of abstractions, are compared with respect to their recognized language.

The abstraction respectively on syntactic predicates and semantic structures corresponds precisely to the abstract interpretation of the underlying Boolean algebra of a concrete SFA $M$, resulting in a



*POPL '15*, January 15–17, 2015, Mumbai, India.

http://dx.doi.org/10.1145/2676726.2676986

different SFA $A$ whose language recognized is an over approximation of the language of $M$. The key aspect here is to maintain a relative compatibility between syntactic abstractions on predicates and constraint formulae and the abstractions of their semantics. This intuitively means that the approximate predicates and their interpretation provide, one over the others, coherent partitions of objects (respectively interpretations and predicates).

Topological abstraction means instead changing the graph structure of SFA, yet keeping correctness, namely providing an over approximation of the recognized language of $M$. This is achieved by generalizing a minimization algorithm proposed in [9] with respect to a family of equivalence relations on SFA states. The result is a simplification of $M$ which is still correct in the sense of abstract interpretation with respect to $M$.

Abstract SFA provide a general enough model for representing syntactic and semantic properties of arbitrary programming languages. We apply our model in the attempt to formalize and prove properties of two commonly used tools for similarity analysis of binary executables, notably *BinJuice* [18] and *BinDiff.* Following the structure of their control flow graphs, disassembled binary executables are represented as (concrete) SFA, where states are program points between basic blocks and predicates represent the (possibly infinite) I/O semantics of each basic block in a constraint form. Tools for binary-level similarity analysis are then formalized as abstract interpretations of these concrete SFA. By studying the properties of the corresponding abstractions we can provide a first unifying model for formally proving properties for these tools. Moreover, our model suggests potential refinements of similarity analyses for disassembled binaries such as the possibility of extracting minimal SFA from binaries as canonical signatures for code fragments.

## 2. Preliminaries

***Mathematical Notation.*** Given two sets $S$ and $T$, we denote with $\wp(S)$ the powerset of $S$, $\wp^{\mathtt{re}}(S)$ the set of recursive enumerable (r.e.) subsets of $S$, with $S \smallsetminus T$ the set-difference between $S$ and $T$, with $S \subset T$ strict inclusion and with $S \subseteq T$ inclusion. $S^*$ denotes the set of all finite sequences of elements in $S$. A set $L$ with ordering relation $\leq$ is a poset and it is denoted as $\langle L, \leq\rangle$. A poset $\langle L, \leq\rangle$ is a lattice if $\forall x.y \in L$ we have that $x \vee y$ and $x \wedge y$ belong to $L$. A lattice $\langle L, \leq\rangle$ is complete when for every $X \subseteq L$ we have that $\bigvee X, \bigwedge X \in L$. As usual a complete lattice $L$, with ordering $\leq$, least upper bound (lub) $\vee$, greatest lower bound (glb) $\wedge$, greatest element (top) $\top$, and least element (bottom) $\bot$ is denoted by $\langle L, \leq, \vee, \wedge, \top, \bot\rangle$. Given $f : S \longrightarrow T$ and $g : T \longrightarrow Q$ we denote with $g \circ f : S \longrightarrow Q$ their composition, i.e., $g \circ f = \lambda x.g(f(x))$. $f : L \longrightarrow D$ on complete lattices is *additive (co-additive)* if for any $Y \subseteq L, f(\vee_L Y) = \vee_D f(Y)$ $(f(\wedge_L Y) = \wedge_D f(Y))$. Continuity holds when $f$ preserves *lubs*'s of chains. Co-continuity is dually defined. For a continuous function $f$: $lfp(f) = \bigwedge\{\, x \mid x = f(x) \,\} = \bigvee_{n\in\mathbb{N}} f^n(\bot)$ where $f^0(\bot) = \bot$ and $f^{n+1}(\bot) = f(f^n(\bot))$.

***Abstract Interpretation.*** Abstract domains can be equivalently formalized either as Galois connections or closure operators on a given concrete domain which is a complete lattice $C$ (cf. [4]). Let $C$ and $A$ be complete lattices, a pair of monotone functions $\alpha : C \longrightarrow A$ and $\gamma : A \longrightarrow C$ forms a *Galois connection (GC)* between $C$ and $A$ if for every $x \in C$ and $y \in A$ we have $\alpha(x) \leq_A y \Leftrightarrow x \leq_C \gamma(y)$. $\alpha$ (resp. $\gamma$) is the *left-adjoint* (resp. *right-adjoint*) to $\gamma$ (resp. $\alpha$) and it is additive (resp. co-additive). If $\langle\alpha, \gamma\rangle$ is a GC between $C$ and $A$ then $\gamma \circ \alpha \in uco(C)$. If $\rho \in uco(C)$ then $\langle\rho, \mathtt{id}\rangle$ is a CG between $C$ and $\rho(C)$. Given an additive (resp. co-additive) function $\alpha$ (resp. $\gamma$) we have a GC $\langle\alpha, \alpha^+\rangle$ (resp. $\langle\gamma^-, \gamma\rangle$) by considering its right (resp. left) adjoint $\alpha^+ = \lambda x. \bigvee\{y \mid \alpha(y) \leq x\}$ (resp. $\gamma^- = \lambda x. \bigwedge\{y \mid x \leq \gamma(y)\}$). An *upper closure operator* (or simply a *closure*) on a poset $\langle L, \leq\rangle$ is an operator $\rho : L \longrightarrow L$ which is monotone, idempotent, and extensive (i.e., $x \leq \rho(x)$). We denote with $uco(L)$ the set of all closure operators on the poset $L$. If $C$ is a complete lattice, then $\langle uco(C), \sqsubseteq, \sqcup, \sqcap, \lambda x.\, C, \mathtt{id}\rangle$ forms a complete lattice [24], which is the set of all possible abstractions of $C$, where the bottom is $\mathtt{id} = \lambda x.x$ and for every $\rho, \eta \in uco(C)$, $\rho$ is *more concrete than* $\eta$ iff $\rho \sqsubseteq \eta$ iff $\forall y \in C.\ \rho(y) \leq \eta(y)$ iff $\eta(C) \subseteq \rho(C)$, $(\sqcap_{i\in I}\rho_i)(x) = \wedge_{i\in I}\rho_i(x)$; $(\sqcup_{i\in I}\rho_i)(x) = x$ iff $\forall i \in I.\ \rho_i(x) = x$. $\rho \in uco(C)$ is disjunctive when $\rho(C)$ is a join-sublattice of $C$ which holds iff $\rho$ is additive (cf. [4]). $\rho \in uco(\wp(C))$ is *partitioning* (or induces a partition) if it is additive and $\{\rho(\{c\})\}_{c\in C}$ is a partition of $C$ [17]. If $\rho \in uco(\wp(C))$ then the most abstract partitioning closure containing $\rho$:

$$\Pi(\rho) \stackrel{\text{def}}{=} \bigsqcup\{\, \beta \in uco(\wp(C)) \mid \beta \sqsubseteq \rho \wedge \beta \text{ is partitioning } \,\}.$$

The key aspect of partitioning closures is that they preserve the structure of Boolean algebras.
If $f : C \longrightarrow C$ is a continuous function and $\rho \in uco(C)$ is an abstraction, then $f$ always has a *best correct approximation* in $\rho(C)$ which is $f^\rho \stackrel{\text{def}}{=} \rho \circ f \circ \rho$. Any approximation $f^\sharp : \rho(C) \longrightarrow \rho(C)$ of $f$ in $\rho(C)$ is *sound* if $f^\rho \sqsubseteq f^\sharp$. In this case we have the fixpoint soundness $\rho(lfp f) \leq lfp(f^\rho) \leq lfp(f^\sharp)$(cf. [3]). $f^\sharp$ is *complete* when $\rho \circ f = f^\sharp \circ \rho$ which holds iff $\rho \circ f = \rho \circ f \circ \rho$ (cf. [16]). Therefore the possibility of defining a complete approximation $f^\sharp$ of $f$ on some abstract domain $\rho$ only depends on $f$ and $\rho$. In this case we have: $\rho(lfp f) = lfp(f^\rho) = lfp(f^\sharp)$. In the following, for any semantics $[\![\cdot]\!] : \mathcal{S} \longrightarrow \mathcal{D}$ mapping syntactic objects in $\mathcal{S}$ into denotations in $\mathcal{D}$ such that $[\![\cdot]\!]$ is an element in the set of fixpoint semantics $\mathfrak{S} \subseteq \mathcal{S} \longrightarrow \mathcal{D}$ inductively defined as follows

$$\mathfrak{S} \quad ::= \quad f : \mathcal{S} \longrightarrow \mathcal{D} \mid lfp(\mathfrak{S}) \mid \mathfrak{S} \circ \mathfrak{S}$$

and if $\rho \in uco(\mathcal{D})$, we denote by $[\![\cdot]\!]^\rho \in \mathfrak{S}^\rho \subseteq \mathcal{S} \longrightarrow \rho(\mathcal{D})$ the corresponding best correct approximation which is defined inductively on the structure of $\mathfrak{S}$ as follows:

$$\mathfrak{S}^\rho \quad ::= \quad \rho \circ f \circ \rho \mid lfp(\mathfrak{S}^\rho) \mid \mathfrak{S}^\rho \circ \mathfrak{S}^\rho$$

It is known that $[\![\cdot]\!]^\rho$ is sound and, whenever $\rho$ is complete for the basic semantic operators $f$ defining $[\![\cdot]\!] \in \mathfrak{S}$, then $[\![\cdot]\!]^\rho$ is complete, i.e. for any $s \in \mathcal{S}$: $\rho([\![s]\!]) = [\![s]\!]^\rho$ (cf. [4, 16]).

***Symbolic Finite Automata.*** Symbolic automata and finite state transducers have been introduced to deal with specifications involving a potentially infinite alphabet of symbols [8, 9, 23]. We follow [9] in specifying symbolic automata in terms of effective Boolean algebra. Consider an effective Boolean algebra $\mathcal{A} = \langle\mathfrak{D}_\mathcal{A}, \Psi_\mathcal{A}, [\![\cdot]\!], \bot, \top, \wedge, \vee, \neg\rangle$, with domain elements in a r.e. set $\mathfrak{D}_\mathcal{A}$, a r.e. set of predicates $\Psi_\mathcal{A}$ closed under boolean connectives $\wedge$, $\vee$ and $\neg$. The semantic function $[\![\cdot]\!] : \Psi_\mathcal{A} \longrightarrow \wp(\mathfrak{D}_\mathcal{A})$ is a partial recursive function such that $[\![\bot]\!] = \varnothing$, $[\![\top]\!] = \mathfrak{D}_\mathcal{A}$, and $\forall\varphi, \phi \in \Psi_\mathcal{A}$ we have that $[\![\varphi \vee \phi]\!] = [\![\varphi]\!] \cup [\![\phi]\!]$, $[\![\varphi \wedge \phi]\!] = [\![\varphi]\!] \cap [\![\phi]\!]$, and $[\![\neg\varphi]\!] = \mathfrak{D}_\mathcal{A} \smallsetminus [\![\varphi]\!]$. In the following we abuse notation by denoting with $[\![\cdot]\!]$ also its additive lift to $\wp(\Psi_\mathcal{A})$, i.e., for any $\Phi \in \wp(\Psi_\mathcal{A})$: $[\![\Phi]\!] = \{\, [\![\varphi]\!] \mid \varphi \in \Phi \,\}$. For $\varphi \in \Psi_\mathcal{A}$ we write $IsSat(\varphi)$ when $[\![\varphi]\!] \neq \varnothing$ and say that $\varphi$ is *satisfiable*. $\mathcal{A}$ is decidable if $IsSat$ is decidable.

DEFINITION 2.1. *A symbolic automaton (SFA) is $\langle\mathcal{A}, Q, q_0, F, \Delta\rangle$ where $\mathcal{A}$ is an effective Boolean algebra, $Q$ is a finite set of states, $q_0 \in Q$ is the initial state, $F \subseteq Q$ is the set of final states and $\Delta \subseteq Q \times \Psi_\mathcal{A} \times Q$ is a finite set of transitions.*

A transition in $M = \langle\mathcal{A}, Q, q_0, F, \Delta\rangle$ labeled $\varphi$ from state $p$ to state $q$, $(p, \varphi, q) \in \Delta$ is often denoted $p \xrightarrow{\varphi} q$. $\varphi$ is called the *guard* of the transition. An $a$-move of a SFA $M$ is a transition $p \xrightarrow{\varphi} q$ such that $a \in [\![\varphi]\!]$, also denoted $p \xrightarrow{a} q$. The language recognized by a state $q \in Q$ in $M$ is defined as:

$$\mathscr{L}_q(M) = \left\{ a_1, \ldots, a_n \in \mathfrak{D}_{\mathcal{A}} \;\middle|\; \begin{array}{l} \forall 1 \leq i \leq n.\, p_{i-1} \xrightarrow{a_i} p_i \\ p_0 = q,\, p_n \in F \end{array} \right\}$$

in this case, $\mathscr{L}(M) = \mathscr{L}_{q_0}(M)$. We assume *complete SFA*, namely where all states hold an out-going $a$-move, for any character $a \in \mathfrak{D}$. This can be simply achieved by adding a shaft-state $q_\perp \in Q$ such that $q_\perp \xrightarrow{\top} q_\perp \in \Delta$ and for all states $q$ lacking an out-going $a$-move, for $a \in \mathfrak{D}$, then $q \xrightarrow{\neg\beta} q_\perp \in \Delta$ with $\beta = \bigvee \{ \varphi \mid q \xrightarrow{\varphi} p \wedge p \in Q \}$.

The following terminology holds for SFA: $M$ is *deterministic* whenever $p \xrightarrow{\varphi} q, p \xrightarrow{\beta} q' \in \Delta$: if $IsSat(\varphi \wedge \beta)$ then $q = q'$. $M$ is *clean* if for all $p \xrightarrow{\varphi} q \in \Delta$: $p$ is reachable from $q_0$ and $IsSat(\varphi)$. $M$ is *normalized* if for all $p, q \in Q$: there is at most one move from $p$ to $q$. $M$ is *minimal* if $M$ is deterministic, clean, normalized and for all $p, q \in Q$:

$$p = q \Leftrightarrow \mathscr{L}_q(M) = \mathscr{L}_p(M)$$

Given a SFA $M = \langle \mathcal{A}, Q, q_0, F, \Delta \rangle$ and $\equiv \subseteq Q \times Q$, we define the *quotient SFA* $M_{/\equiv} \stackrel{\text{def}}{=} \langle \mathcal{A}, Q', q_0', F', \Delta' \rangle$ as follows: $Q' = \{ [q]_\equiv \mid q \in Q \}$, $\Delta' \subseteq Q' \times \Psi_{\mathcal{A}} \times Q'$ is such that $\Delta' = \{ ([q]_\equiv, \Phi, [q']_\equiv) \mid (p, \Phi, q') \in \Delta, p \in [q]_\equiv \}$, $q_0' = [q_0]_\equiv$, and $F' = \{ [q]_\equiv \mid q \in F \}$.

## 3. Abstracting Symbolic Automata

Approximating symbolic automata means building different automata recognizing an upper approximation of the original recognized language. This can be achieved by abstract interpretation of the underlying effective Boolean algebra $\mathcal{A}$ and by approximating the automaton's structure. When acting on the Boolean algebra we may either approximate the domain of denotations $\mathfrak{D}_{\mathcal{A}}$ where formulae and predicates are interpreted, or approximate the predicates in $\Psi_{\mathcal{A}}$ where formulae are built. In both cases we need to obtain as result an abstract effective Boolean algebra.

### 3.1 Abstract effective Boolean algebras

The duality of syntax and semantics is perfectly encoded in SFA by the underlying algebraic structure of effective Boolean algebras. They represent the universe of predicates and formulae (later called *syntax*) as well as the domain for their interpretation and semantics, providing the structure for expressing the language recognized by the given SFA. The abstraction of syntactic and semantic structures applies on sets of predicates and semantic structures representing, as usual in abstract interpretation, properties respectively of predicates and semantics. In the following $\mathcal{A} = \langle \mathfrak{D}_{\mathcal{A}}, \Psi_{\mathcal{A}}, [\![\cdot]\!], \perp, \top, \wedge, \vee, \neg \rangle$ is an effective Boolean Algebra.

DEFINITION 3.1 (Semantic abstraction). *Let $\mathcal{A}$ be an effective Boolean Algebra and $\rho \in uco(\wp(\mathfrak{D}_{\mathcal{A}}))$ be a partitioning abstraction of its domain of denotations. The semantic abstraction of $\mathcal{A}$ w.r.t. $\rho$, denoted $(\!|\rho|\!)$-abstraction, is the effective Boolean algebra*

$$\mathcal{A}^\rho = \langle \mathfrak{D}^\rho_{\mathcal{A}}, \Psi_{\mathcal{A}}, [\![\cdot]\!]^\rho, \rho(\perp), \top, \wedge, \vee^\rho, \neg^\rho \rangle$$

*where:*

$\mathfrak{D}^\rho_{\mathcal{A}} = \bigcup \{ \rho(d) \mid d \in \mathfrak{D}_{\mathcal{A}} \}$

$[\![\cdot]\!]^\rho : \Psi_{\mathcal{A}} \longrightarrow \wp(\mathfrak{D}^\rho_{\mathcal{A}})$ *such that*

$$[\![\varphi]\!]^\rho = \rho([\![\varphi]\!]) = \bigcup \{ \rho(d) \mid d \in [\![\varphi]\!] \}$$

$\varphi_1, \varphi_2 \in \Psi_{\mathcal{A}} : [\![\varphi_1 \vee^\rho \varphi_2]\!]^\rho = [\![\varphi_1]\!]^\rho \cup [\![\varphi_2]\!]^\rho$

$\varphi \in \Psi_{\mathcal{A}} : [\![\neg^\rho \varphi]\!]^\rho = \mathfrak{D}^\rho_{\mathcal{A}} \setminus [\![\varphi]\!]^\rho$

Before abstracting predicates, i.e., syntax, we have to guarantee the effectiveness of symbolic computation in the SFA. Next lemma proves that if $S$ is a set, whenever $\eta \in uco(\wp(S))$ is additive $\eta$ maps any r.e. subset $X$ of $S$ into a r.e. (abstract) subset $\eta(X)$ of $S$.

LEMMA 3.2. *If $X \subseteq S$ is r.e. and $\eta \in uco(\wp(S))$ is additive, then $\eta(X)$ is r.e., namely $\eta \in uco(\wp^{\mathtt{re}}(S))$.*

By Lemma 3.2, because $\eta$ is a recursive function, and by Kleene's characterization of recursive enumerable sets, the range of $\eta$ over r.e. sets is itself r.e. (see [21]).

THEOREM 3.3. *If $S$ is a set and $\eta \in uco(\wp^{\mathtt{re}}(S))$ is additive then $\{ \eta(X) \mid X \subseteq S \wedge X \text{ is r.e.} \}$ is r.e.*

DEFINITION 3.4 (Syntactic abstraction). *Let $\mathcal{A}$ be an effective Boolean Algebra and let $\eta \in uco(\wp^{\mathtt{re}}(\Psi_{\mathcal{A}}))$ be an additive abstraction of predicates. The syntactic abstraction of $\mathcal{A}$ w.r.t. $\eta$, denoted $\langle\eta\rangle$-abstraction, is the effective Boolean algebra*

$$\mathcal{A}_\eta = \langle \mathfrak{D}_{\mathcal{A}}, \eta(\wp^{\mathtt{re}}(\Psi_{\mathcal{A}})), [\![\cdot]\!], \perp, \top, \wedge, \vee, \neg \rangle$$

*where $[\![\cdot]\!] : \eta(\wp^{\mathtt{re}}(\Psi_{\mathcal{A}})) \longrightarrow \wp(\mathfrak{D}_{\mathcal{A}})$ is defined as in SFA.*

If we have both a $(\!|\rho|\!)$-abstraction and a $\langle\eta\rangle$-abstraction of an effective Boolean algebra $\mathcal{A}$, then we define the combined abstraction $(\!|\rho|\!)\langle\eta\rangle$-abstraction of $\mathcal{A}$ by combining them as follows. Let $\rho \in uco(\wp(\mathfrak{D}_{\mathcal{A}}))$ and $\eta \in uco(\wp^{\mathtt{re}}(\Psi_{\mathcal{A}}))$. The abstraction of $\mathcal{A}$ w.r.t. $\rho$ and $\eta$ is the effective Boolean algebra

$$\mathcal{A}^\rho_\eta = \langle \mathfrak{D}^\rho_{\mathcal{A}}, \eta(\wp^{\mathtt{re}}(\Psi_{\mathcal{A}})), [\![\cdot]\!]^\rho, \rho(\perp), \top, \wedge, \vee^\rho, \neg^\rho \rangle$$

It is clear that $\mathcal{A}_\eta = \mathcal{A}^{\mathtt{id}}_\eta$ and $\mathcal{A}^\rho = \mathcal{A}^\rho_{\mathtt{id}}$. In the following of the paper we assume that $(\!|\rho|\!)$- and $\langle\eta\rangle$-abstractions satisfy the hypothesis in Definition 3.1 and 3.4 respectively.

THEOREM 3.5. *If $\mathcal{A}$ is decidable then for any $\rho \in uco(\wp(\mathfrak{D}_{\mathcal{A}}))$ and $\eta \in uco(\wp^{\mathtt{re}}(\Psi_{\mathcal{A}}))$, $\mathcal{A}^\rho_\eta$ is decidable.*

Note that, in the definition of symbolic automata there is a strong relation in the underlying effective Boolean algebra $\mathcal{A}$ between the domain of denotations $\mathfrak{D}_{\mathcal{A}}$ and the set of predicates $\Psi_{\mathcal{A}}$ used to symbolically represent them. This means that, if we abstract the domain of denotations by considering $\rho \in uco(\wp(\mathfrak{D}_{\mathcal{A}}))$, leaving unchanged $\Psi_{\mathcal{A}}$ we are implicitly changing the interpretation of predicates in $\mathfrak{D}_{\mathcal{A}}$. On the other hand, if we abstract the predicates by considering $\eta \in uco(\wp^{\mathtt{re}}(\Psi_{\mathcal{A}}))$ we explicitly describe how symbols are abstracted and the semantics is simply the collection of all the semantics denoting the same abstracted predicate. This leads to the following notion of *compatible abstractions*.

### 3.2 Compatible syntactic and semantic abstractions

Let us consider a $(\!|\rho|\!)$-abstraction of $\mathcal{A}$, we aim at characterizing the syntactic abstractions that produce abstract predicates which may have semantics in $\mathfrak{D}^\rho_{\mathcal{A}}$. This is captured by the notion of $(\!|\rho|\!)$-compatibility of a syntactic abstraction. Any semantic $(\!|\rho|\!)$-abstraction naturally induces a corresponding syntactic $\langle\Omega(\rho)\rangle$-abstraction with $\Omega(\rho) \in uco(\wp(\Psi_{\mathcal{A}}))$ defined as follows:

$$\Omega(\rho) \stackrel{\text{def}}{=} \lambda\Phi.\, \bigcup \{ \Phi' \mid [\![\Phi']\!] \subseteq [\![\Phi]\!]^\rho \}$$

Analogously, any syntactic $\langle\eta\rangle$-abstraction naturally induces a corresponding semantic $(\!|\mho(\eta)|\!)$-abstraction with $\mho(\eta) \in uco(\wp(\mathfrak{D}^\rho_{\mathcal{A}}))$. In order to characterize when and how a syntactic abstraction induces a semantic abstraction, we need to characterize the syntactic abstraction that precisely corresponds to the semantics $[\![\cdot]\!]$, namely the abstraction collecting all the predicates having the same semantics $[\![\cdot]\!]$. This is precisely $\Omega(\mathtt{id})$, which can be rewritten as $\lambda\Phi.\, [\![[\![\Phi]\!]]\!]^+$. Here $[\![\cdot]\!]^+$ is the *adjoint semantic function* defined as follows:

$$[\![\cdot]\!]^+ \stackrel{\text{def}}{=} \lambda X \in \wp(\mathfrak{D}_{\mathcal{A}}).\, \bigcup \{ \Phi \mid [\![\Phi]\!] \subseteq X \}$$

Then we can define the induced $\langle\!|\mho(\eta)|\!\rangle$-abstraction:

$$\mho(\eta) \stackrel{\text{def}}{=} \lambda X. \bigcup \{ \, Y \mid \llbracket Y \rrbracket^{+} \subseteq \eta(\llbracket X \rrbracket^{+}) \, \}$$

Observe that, when $\llbracket\cdot\rrbracket : \Psi_{\mathcal{A}} \rightarrow \wp(\mathfrak{D}_{\mathcal{A}})$ is surjective, namely when there exists at least one predicate for each possible semantics in $\wp(\mathfrak{D}_{\mathcal{A}})$ we have that $\mho(\texttt{id}) = \texttt{id}$. Indeed, $\texttt{id} \in uco(\wp^{\texttt{re}}(\Psi_{\mathcal{A}}))$ considers every single predicate and we have a predicate for each semantic object so in this case we have no effects on the semantics and $\mho(\texttt{id})$ return precisely the identity on the semantics.

Compatibility of a $\langle\eta\rangle$-abstraction w.r.t. $\langle\!|\rho|\!\rangle$-abstraction can therefore be defined in terms of relative abstraction of $\eta$ and $\Omega(\rho)$, or analogously, in terms of relative abstraction of $\rho$ and $\mho(\eta)$.

DEFINITION 3.6 (Semantic compatibility). *Given a $\langle\!|\rho|\!\rangle$-abstracted effective Boolean algebra $\mathcal{A}^{\rho}$ and a syntactic abstraction $\eta \in uco(\wp^{\texttt{re}}(\Psi_{\mathcal{A}}))$, $\eta$ is $\langle\!|\rho|\!\rangle$-compatible if:*

$$\eta \sqsubseteq \Omega(\rho) \tag{1}$$

Intuitively we have semantic compatibility when the syntactic abstraction is more concrete than the semantic abstraction, when they are compared on the domain of abstractions of predicates. Indeed, semantic compatibility means that the way a syntactic abstraction $\eta$ partitions the set of predicates of $\mathcal{A}$ is a refinement of the partition induced by the syntactic abstraction $\Omega(\rho)$ that corresponds to the semantic abstraction $\rho$. We can say that when we have semantic compatibility the abstraction of the syntax distinguishes programs with the same abstract semantics, namely the abstract program provides an under-approximation of the abstract program behavior.

THEOREM 3.7. *Let $\rho \in uco(\wp(\mathfrak{D}_{\mathcal{A}}))$, then $\Omega(\rho)$ is the most abstract syntactic abstraction $\langle\!|\rho|\!\rangle$-compatible.*

Note that $\mathcal{A}^{\Omega(\rho)}$ may not be an effective Boolean algebra because $\Omega(\rho)(\wp^{\texttt{re}}(\Psi_{\mathcal{A}}))$ may not be a r.e. set.

EXAMPLE 3.8. *Consider the domains depicted in Fig. 1 (the missing point labels are the set union of smaller elements). The first three domains on the left represent possible syntactic abstractions of $\wp(\Psi_{\mathcal{A}})$, where*

$$\Psi_{\mathcal{A}} \stackrel{\text{def}}{=} \{x+y>3, x\geq 3, y\geq 0, x+y>3 \wedge x\geq 3 \wedge y \geq 0\}.$$

*The last domain on the right represents possible semantic abstractions of $\wp(\mathfrak{D}_{\mathcal{A}})$, where*

$$\mathfrak{D}_{\mathcal{A}} \stackrel{\text{def}}{=} \{\llbracket x+y>3\rrbracket, \llbracket x\geq 3\rrbracket, \llbracket y\geq 0\rrbracket\}.$$

*Consider for instance the semantic abstraction $\rho$ of $\wp(\mathfrak{D}_{\mathcal{A}})$, depicted with circles on the last domain on the right. The corresponding syntactic abstraction $\Omega(\rho)$ is depicted on the three syntactic domain on the left. Considering the closures depicted on the first domain on the left we observe that the closure $\eta_1 \in \wp(\Psi_{\mathcal{A}})$ is $\langle\!|\rho|\!\rangle$-compatible being more concrete that $\Omega(\rho)$. This means that the syntactic abstraction can distinguish predicates with the same abstract semantics. In particular, while $\rho(\llbracket x+y>3\rrbracket) = \rho(\llbracket x\geq 3\rrbracket)$ we have that $\eta_1(x+y>3) = \{x+y>3, x\geq 3\}$ while $\eta_1(x\geq 3) = \{x \geq 3\}$.*

Now consider a $\langle\eta\rangle$-compatible abstraction of $\mathcal{A}$. We introduce the notion of $\langle\eta\rangle$-compatibility of a semantic abstraction.

DEFINITION 3.9 (Syntactic compatibility). *A semantic abstraction $\rho \in uco(\wp(\mathfrak{D}_{\mathcal{A}}))$ is $\langle\eta\rangle$-compatible for a syntactic $\langle\eta\rangle$-abstraction $\mathcal{A}_{\eta}$ if:*

$$\eta \sqsupseteq \Omega(\rho) \tag{2}$$

Intuitively we have syntactic compatibility when the syntactic abstraction is more abstract than the semantic abstraction when they are compared on the domain of abstractions of predicates.

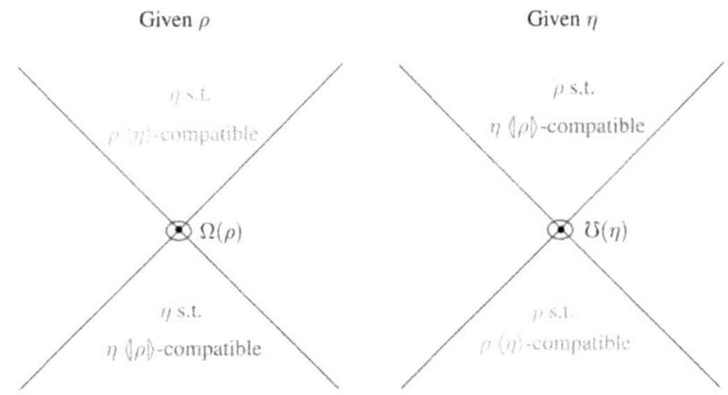


**Figure 2.** Relation between compatibilities.

Indeed, syntactic compatibility means that the semantic abstraction $\rho$ corresponds to a syntactic abstraction $\Omega(\rho)$ and that the partition on the set of predicates of $\mathcal{A}$ induced by $\Omega(\rho)$ is a refinement of the partition induced by $\eta$. In other words, when we have syntactic compatibility the abstraction $\eta$ of the syntax collapses programs with different abstract semantics $\rho$, hence capturing behaviors that, according to $\rho$, are not related with the program to analyze, yet providing an over-approximation of the abstract program behavior.

THEOREM 3.10. *Let $\eta \in uco(\wp^{\texttt{re}}(\Psi_{\mathcal{A}}))$, then $\mho(\eta)$ is the most concrete semantic abstraction $\langle\eta\rangle$-compatible.*

EXAMPLE 3.11. *Consider again the example in Fig. 1 introduced in Example 3.8. Consider in this case the syntactic abstraction $\eta_3$ depicted on the third domain . We observe that $\rho$ is $\langle\eta_3\rangle$-compatible since $\eta_3$ is more abstract than $\Omega(\rho)$. This means that $\eta_3$ induces a further semantic abstraction collapsing elements with different $\rho$ abstract semantics. In particular, $\rho(\llbracket x+y>3 \wedge x\geq 3 \wedge x \geq 3\rrbracket) \neq \rho(\llbracket x\geq 3\rrbracket)$ while $\eta_3(x+y>3 \wedge x\geq 3 \wedge y\geq 0) = \eta_3(x\geq 3) = \top$. In this example we can also observe a syntactic abstraction $\eta_2$ (depicted on the second domain) which fails both the compatibilities since it not comparable with $\Omega(\rho)$.*

Finally, we show when a syntactic abstraction does induce an abstraction of the semantic denotations and vice versa.

LEMMA 3.12. *Let $\eta \in uco(\wp^{\texttt{re}}(\Psi_{\mathcal{A}}))$:*

1. $\eta \sqsupseteq \Omega(\texttt{id})$ *iff* $\forall \Phi \in \wp^{\texttt{re}}(\Psi_{\mathcal{A}}).\ \llbracket\llbracket\eta(\Phi)\rrbracket\rrbracket^{+} = \eta(\Phi)$
2. $\eta \sqsubseteq \Omega(\texttt{id})$ *iff* $\forall \Phi \in \wp^{\texttt{re}}(\Psi_{\mathcal{A}}).\ \eta(\llbracket\llbracket\Phi\rrbracket\rrbracket^{+}) = \llbracket\llbracket\Phi\rrbracket\rrbracket^{+}$

THEOREM 3.13. *Let $\eta \in uco(\wp^{\texttt{re}}(\Psi_{\mathcal{A}}))$, then*

$$\eta \sqsubseteq \Omega(\texttt{id}) \Rightarrow \mho(\eta) = \texttt{id}$$

This result tells us that when we have a syntactic abstraction distinguishing predicates with the same semantics, then we cannot abstract the semantics.

We prove that we can characterize compatibilities both in the domain of semantic abstractions and in the domain of syntactic abstractions.

THEOREM 3.14. *Let $\eta \in uco(\wp^{\texttt{re}}(\Psi_{\mathcal{A}}))$ be such that $\eta \sqsupseteq \Omega(\texttt{id})$, and $\rho \in uco(\wp(\mathfrak{D}_{\mathcal{A}}))$:*

$$\Omega(\rho) \sqsubseteq \eta \quad \textit{iff} \quad \rho \sqsubseteq \mho(\eta)$$

In Fig. 2 we can see the relation between the two compatibilities. In particular we observe that the two transformers, form syntax to semantics and viceversa, show a relation similar to an adjunction, as observed in the following result.

PROPOSITION 3.15. *Let $\eta \in uco(\wp^{\texttt{re}}(\Psi_{\mathcal{A}}))$ and $\rho \in uco(\wp(\mathfrak{D}_{\mathcal{A}}))$ the following conditions holds:*

$$(1)\ \mho(\Omega(\rho)) \sqsupseteq \rho \qquad\qquad (2)\ \Omega(\mho(\eta)) \sqsubseteq \eta.$$

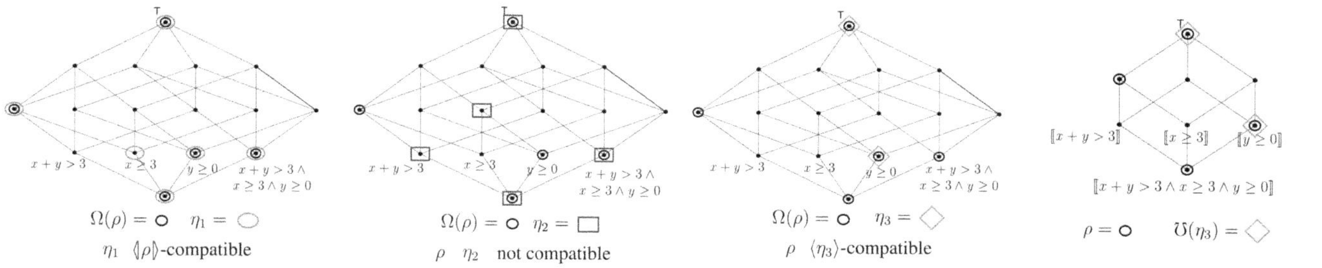


**Figure 1.** Compatible abstractions.

EXAMPLE 3.16. *Consider again the example in Fig. 1. For $\eta_3$ which satisfies the hypotheses of Th. 3.14, we have a corresponding semantic abstraction $\mho(\eta_3)$ (depicted on the right) which is indeed more abstract than $\rho$.*

As a corollary of the previous results we show when a $\llparenthesis\rho\rrparenthesis\langle\eta\rangle$-abstraction of $\mathcal{A}$ satisfies both the compatibilities. The computational cost of making analyses compatible is still to be explored.

PROPOSITION 3.17. *Let $\eta \in uco(\wp^{\mathtt{re}}(\Psi_{\mathcal{A}}))$ and $\rho \in uco(\wp(\mathfrak{D}_{\mathcal{A}}))$ such that $\Omega(\rho) \in uco(\wp^{\mathtt{re}}(\Psi_{\mathcal{A}}))$, the following facts are equivalent:*

1. *$\eta$ is $\llparenthesis\rho\rrparenthesis$-compatible and $\rho$ is $\langle\eta\rangle$-compatible;*
2. *$\eta = \Omega(\rho)$;*
3. *$\rho = \mho(\eta)$.*

### 3.3 Abstracting symbolic automata

Consider a SFA $M = \langle \mathcal{A}, Q, q_0, F, \Delta \rangle$ and the $\llparenthesis\rho\rrparenthesis\langle\eta\rangle$-abstraction of the effective Boolean algebra $\mathcal{A}$, denoted as $\mathcal{A}^{\rho}_{\eta}$. We define the symbolic finite automaton corresponding to $M$ on the abstract effective Boolean algebra $\mathcal{A}^{\rho}_{\eta}$ as $M^{\rho}_{\eta} \stackrel{\text{def}}{=} \langle \mathcal{A}^{\rho}_{\eta}, Q, q_0, F, \Delta_{\eta} \rangle$ where:

$$\Delta_{\eta} \stackrel{\text{def}}{=} \{ (q, \eta(\varphi), q') \mid (q, \varphi, q') \in \Delta \}$$

Note that $M_{\eta} = M^{\mathtt{id}}_{\eta}$ and $M^{\rho} = M^{\rho}_{\mathtt{id}}$. In the following we prove that when abstracting the underling effective Boolean algebra of an SFA we over-approximate the recognized language, providing a sound approximation in the sense of abstract interpretation.

THEOREM 3.18. *Given a SFA $M = \langle \mathcal{A}, Q, q_0, F, \Delta \rangle$, two closures $\eta \in uco(\wp^{\mathtt{re}}(\Psi_{\mathcal{A}}))$ and $\rho \in uco(\wp(\mathfrak{D}_{\mathcal{A}}))$, the abstract effective Boolean algebra $\mathcal{A}^{\rho}_{\eta}$ and the corresponding SFA $M^{\rho}_{\eta} = \langle \mathcal{A}^{\rho}_{\eta}, Q, q_0, F, \Delta_{\eta} \rangle$. Then: $\mathscr{L}(M) \subseteq \mathscr{L}(M^{\rho}_{\eta})$.*

For this reason is the following we abuse terminology and refer to the SFA whose underlying Boolean algebra is an $\llparenthesis\rho\rrparenthesis\langle\eta\rangle$-abstraction of a Boolean algebra $\mathcal{A}$ as an $\llparenthesis\rho\rrparenthesis\langle\eta\rangle$-abstract SFA. Moreover, we can observe that given two abstract Boolean algebra $\mathcal{A}^{\rho_1}_{\eta_1}$ and $\mathcal{A}^{\rho_2}_{\eta_2}$ and an SFA $M$ on $\mathcal{A}$, then the relation between the languages recognized respectively by $M^{\rho_1}_{\eta_1}$ and by $M^{\rho_2}_{\eta_2}$ corresponds to the relation existing between the best correct approximation of the semantics $[\![\cdot]\!]$ with respect to the pair of abstractions $\rho_1, \eta_1$ and $\rho_2, \eta_2$. This is formally stated in the following Proposition.

PROPOSITION 3.19. *Consider a SFA $M = \langle \mathcal{A}, Q, q_0, F, \Delta \rangle$, the closures $\eta_1, \eta_2 \in uco(\wp^{\mathtt{re}}(\Psi_{\mathcal{A}}))$ and $\rho_1, \rho_2 \in uco(\wp(\mathfrak{D}_{\mathcal{A}}))$, then:*

$$\begin{aligned} \mathscr{L}(M^{\rho_1}_{\eta_1}) \subseteq \mathscr{L}(M^{\rho_2}_{\eta_2}) \quad &\Leftrightarrow \quad \rho_1 \circ [\![\cdot]\!] \circ \eta_1 \sqsubseteq \rho_2 \circ [\![\cdot]\!] \circ \eta_2 \\ &\Leftarrow \quad \rho_1 \sqsubseteq \rho_2 \wedge \eta_1 \sqsubseteq \eta_2 \end{aligned}$$

## 4. Minterms

A notion which plays a central role in our transformations of SFA is the notion of *minterm*. This notion has been introduced in [9] for providing a minimal and univocal representation of the predicates in a given set of predicates, e.g., the guards of a given program. In this context we observe some peculiar properties of minterms which make them powerful tools for reasoning on semantics in a syntactic way. A minterm is a minimal satisfiable boolean combination of all predicates occurring in a given SFA. Minterms can be generated from a set of predicates by the algorithm proposed in [9] and reported in Fig. 3. As observed in [9] the set of minterms of an SFA may be expensive to compute, indeed in the worst case the complexity of the algorithm that computes the minterms is exponential in the number of guards of the SFA.

```
MINTERMS_A(Φ) ≝
    tree := new Tree(⊤_A, null, null);
    foreach φ in Φ tree.Refine(φ);
        return Leaves(tree);
    //The minterms are the leaf predicates
class Tree
    Predicate ψ; Tree left; Tree right;
    Refine(φ) ≝
    if (IsSat_A(ψ ∧ φ) and IsSat_A(ψ ∧ ¬φ))
        if (left = null)      // If the tree is a leaf then split ψ
            left := new Tree(ψ ∧ φ, null, null);
            right := new Tree(ψ ∧ ¬φ, null, null);
        else left.Refine(φ); right.Refine(φ);
```

**Figure 3.** Minterm generation algorithm.

### 4.1 Basic properties of Minterms

The minterm generation for a formula $\varphi$ produces a tree $T_{\varphi}$ that satisfies the following basic properties.

PROPOSITION 4.1. *Let* tree *be the tree built during the minterm generation, starting from a set $\Phi \in \wp^{\mathtt{re}}(\Psi_{\mathcal{A}})$ of predicates. Given $\varphi \in \Psi_{\mathcal{A}}$, let us denote by $T_{\varphi}$ the subtree of* tree *having $\varphi$ as root. Then the following properties hold:*

1. *Let $Leaves(T_{\varphi}) = \{\varphi_1, \ldots, \varphi_k\}$, then $\varphi \Leftrightarrow \bigvee_{i \in \{1..k\}} \varphi_i$;*
2. *Any $\varphi \in$ MINTERMS$(\Phi)$ $\varphi$ satisfiable implies that for all $\varphi' \in$ MINTERMS$(\Phi) \smallsetminus \{\varphi\}$ is not satisfiable.*
3. *For all $\varphi_1, \varphi_2 \in \Phi$ we have that $\varphi_1 \wedge \varphi_2$ is satisfiable iff $Leaves(T_{\varphi_1}) \cap Leaves(T_{\varphi_2}) \neq \varnothing$;*
4. *For any $\varphi_1, \varphi_2 \in \Phi$ we have that $\varphi_1 \Rightarrow \varphi_2$ is satisfiable with $\varphi_1$ satisfiable iff $Leaves(T_{\varphi_1})_{\mathrm{SAT}} \subseteq Leaves(T_{\varphi_2})$[1];*

The following proposition shows that the semantics of minterms is a partition of the domain $\mathfrak{D}_{\mathcal{A}}$ of denotations.

[1] where $\mathrm{Leaves}(T_{\varphi_1})_{\mathrm{SAT}} \stackrel{\text{def}}{=} \{ \varphi \in \mathrm{Leaves}(T_{\varphi_1}) \mid \varphi \text{ is satisfiable } \}$.

PROPOSITION 4.2. *Let $\mathcal{A} = \langle \mathfrak{D}_\mathcal{A}, \Psi_\mathcal{A}, [\![\cdot]\!], \bot, \top, \wedge, \vee, \neg \rangle$ be an effective Boolean algebra, then $\{ [\![\varphi]\!] \mid \varphi \in \text{MINTERMS}(\Psi_\mathcal{A}) \}$ is a partition of $\mathfrak{D}_\mathcal{A}$.*

### 4.2 Approximated Minterms

Minterms change their structure when the underlying Boolean algebra is approximated by abstract interpretation. We consider an effective Boolean algebra $\mathcal{A} = \langle \mathfrak{D}_\mathcal{A}, \Psi_\mathcal{A}, [\![\cdot]\!], \bot, \top, \wedge, \vee, \neg \rangle$, where the semantic function $[\![\cdot]\!] : \Psi_\mathcal{A} \to \wp(\mathfrak{D}_\mathcal{A})$ is surjective. Consider a subset $\Psi \subseteq \Psi_\mathcal{A}$ of such predicates, for example the set of predicates that label a given SFA. We define the syntactic abstraction $\eta_\Psi \in uco(\wp^{\mathtt{re}}(\Psi_\mathcal{A}))$ as that abstraction of predicates that observes precisely only the predicates in $\Psi$ and abstract in $\top$ any other predicate. Let $\varphi \in \Psi_\mathcal{A}$, then $\eta_\Psi$ is formally defined as additive lift of:

$$\eta_\Psi(\{\varphi\}) \stackrel{\text{def}}{=} \begin{cases} \{\varphi\} & \text{if } \varphi \in \Psi \\ \top & \text{otherwise} \end{cases}$$

Note that the fixpoints of $\eta_\Psi$ is $\eta_\Psi(\wp^{\mathtt{re}}(\Psi_\mathcal{A})) = \wp(\Psi) \cup \{\top\}$. Of course $\eta_\Psi$ corresponds to an abstraction $\mho(\eta_\Psi)$ on the semantics that precisely observes only the semantics of the predicates in $\Psi$, as stated by the following result.

LEMMA 4.3. *Let $\mathcal{A} = \langle \mathfrak{D}_\mathcal{A}, \Psi_\mathcal{A}, [\![\cdot]\!], \bot, \top, \wedge, \vee, \neg \rangle$ be an effective Boolean algebra and consider $\eta_\Psi \in uco(\wp^{\mathtt{re}}(\Psi_\mathcal{A}))$ which is $(\!|\mathtt{id}|\!)$-compatible, then:*

$$\mho(\eta_\Psi)(\wp(\mathfrak{D}_\mathcal{A})) = \{ [\![\Phi]\!] \mid \Phi \in \wp^{\mathtt{re}}(\Psi_\mathcal{A}) \}$$

Observe that $\eta_\Psi$ is $(\!|\mathtt{id}|\!)$-compatible if whenever there is a predicate in $\Psi$ then $\Psi$ contains also all the predicates with the same semantics. The closure $\mho(\eta_\Psi) \in uco(\wp(\mathfrak{D}_\mathcal{A}))$ may not be partitioning in general, so we consider $\Pi(\mho(\eta_\Psi))$ and we observe that the equivalence classes of the partition induced by $\Pi(\mho(\eta_\Psi))$ on $\mathfrak{D}_\mathcal{A}$ are precisely the semantics of the minterms of $\Psi$.

PROPOSITION 4.4. *Let $\mathcal{A} = \langle \mathfrak{D}_\mathcal{A}, \Psi_\mathcal{A}, [\![\cdot]\!], \bot, \top, \wedge, \vee, \neg \rangle$ be an effective Boolean algebra, and consider $\Psi \subseteq \Psi_\mathcal{A}$ such that the abstraction $\eta_\Psi \in uco(\wp^{\mathtt{re}}(\Psi_\mathcal{A}))$ is $(\!|\mathtt{id}|\!)$-compatible, then:*

$$\{ [\![\varphi]\!] \mid \varphi \in \text{MINTERMS}(\Psi) \} = \{ \Pi(\mho(\eta_\Psi))(d) \mid d \in \mathfrak{D}_\mathcal{A} \}$$

It is now interesting to observe what happens when we consider a generic syntactic abstraction $\eta \in uco(\wp^{\mathtt{re}}(\Psi_\mathcal{A}))$ such that $\eta_\Psi \sqsubseteq \eta$, namely that further abstracts the set of predicates $\Psi$ that we are considering. In this case, the semantics of the minterms of the approximated predicates $\eta(\Psi)$ are precisely given by the abstraction $\Pi(\mho(\eta))$ of the semantics of the minterms of $\Psi$.

THEOREM 4.5. *Let $\mathcal{A} = \langle \mathfrak{D}_\mathcal{A}, \Psi_\mathcal{A}, [\![\cdot]\!], \bot, \top, \wedge, \vee, \neg \rangle$ be an effective Boolean algebra, and consider $\Psi \subseteq \Psi_\mathcal{A}$ such that the abstraction $\eta_\Psi \in uco(\wp^{\mathtt{re}}(\Psi_\mathcal{A}))$ is $(\!|\mathtt{id}|\!)$-compatible, and an abstraction $\eta \in uco(\wp^{\mathtt{re}}(\Psi_\mathcal{A}))$ such that $\eta_\Psi \sqsubseteq \eta$. Then:*

$$\{ [\![\varphi]\!] \mid \varphi \in \text{MINTERMS}(\eta(\Psi)) \} = \{ \Pi(\mho(\eta))([\![\varphi]\!]) \mid \varphi \in \text{MINTERMS}(\Psi) \}$$

This means that the semantics of the minterms of a set of abstract predicates is precisely the abstraction of the semantics of the original predicates.

EXAMPLE 4.6. *Let $\mathcal{A} = \langle \mathfrak{D}_\mathcal{A}, \Psi_\mathcal{A}, [\![\cdot]\!], \bot, \top, \wedge, \vee, \neg \rangle$ be an effective Boolean algebra where $\Psi_\mathcal{A} = \{ x \in N \mid N \subseteq \mathbb{Z} \}$, and the semantic function $[\![\cdot]\!] : \Psi_\mathcal{A} \to \wp(\mathbb{Z})$ is naturally defined as $[\![x \in N]\!] = N$.*
*Let us consider the following subset of $\Psi_\mathcal{A}$:*

$$\Psi = \{ x \in \{4,6\}, x \in \{5,6\}, x \in \{-5\}, x \in \{-8\} \}$$

*the corresponding set of minterms is* MINTERMS($\Psi$)*:*

$$\begin{aligned} \{ & (x \in \{4,6\} \wedge x \in \{5,6\}), \\ & (x \in \{4,6\} \wedge \neg x \in \{5,6\}), \\ & (\neg x \in \{4,6\} \wedge x \in \{5,6\}), \\ & (\neg x \in \{4,6\} \wedge \neg x \in \{5,6\} \wedge x \in \{-5\}), \\ & (\neg x \in \{4,6\} \wedge \neg x \in \{5,6\} \wedge \neg x \in \{-5\} \wedge x \in \{-8\}), \\ & (\neg x \in \{4,6\} \wedge \neg x \in \{5,6\} \wedge \neg x \in \{-5\} \wedge \neg x \in \{-8\})\} \end{aligned}$$

*observe that:*

$$\{ [\![\varphi]\!] \mid \varphi \in \text{MINTERMS}(\Psi) \} = \{ \{4\}, \{6\}, \{5\}, \{-5\}, \{-8\}, \mathbb{Z} \setminus \{4,6,5,-5,-8\} \}$$

*the closure $\eta_\Psi \in uco(\wp^{\mathtt{re}}(\Psi_\mathcal{A}))$ is defined as the additive lift of:*

$$\eta_\Psi(\{x \in N\}) \stackrel{\text{def}}{=} \begin{cases} \{x \in N\} & \text{if } \{x \in N\} \in \Psi \\ \top & \text{otherwise} \end{cases}$$

*and, as states in Proposition 4.4 we have that:*

$$\{ \Pi(\mho(\eta_\Psi))(d) \mid d \in \mathbb{Z} \} = \{ \{4\}, \{6\}, \{5\}, \{-5\}, \{-8\}, \mathbb{Z} \setminus \{4,6,5,-5,-8\} \}$$

*Let $\mathbb{Z}^+ \stackrel{\text{def}}{=} \{ v \mid v \geq 0 \}$ and $\mathbb{Z}^- \stackrel{\text{def}}{=} \{ v \mid v < 0 \}$ and let the closure $\eta_{Sign} \in uco(\wp^{\mathtt{re}}(\Psi_\mathcal{A}))$ defined as the additive lift of:*

$$\eta_{Sign}(\{x \in N\}) \stackrel{\text{def}}{=} \begin{cases} \{x \in \mathbb{Z}^+\} & \text{if } N \subseteq \mathbb{Z}^+ \\ \{x \in \mathbb{Z}^-\} & \text{if } N \subseteq \mathbb{Z}^- \\ \top & \text{otherwise} \end{cases}$$

*Observe that the* MINTERMS($\eta_{Sign}(\Psi)$) *is the set*

$$\{ \{x \in \mathbb{Z}^+\}, \{x \in \mathbb{Z}^-\} \}$$

*and the semantics of the minterms of $\eta_{Sign}(\Psi)$ is:*

$$\{ [\![\varphi]\!] \mid \varphi \in \text{MINTERMS}(\eta_{Sign}(\Psi)) \} = \{\mathbb{Z}^+, \mathbb{Z}^-\}$$

*Moreover, as shown in Theorem 4.5:*

$$\{ \Pi(\mho(\eta_{Sign}))([\![\varphi]\!]) \mid \varphi \in \text{MINTERMS}(\Psi) \} = \{\mathbb{Z}^+, \mathbb{Z}^-\}$$

## 5. Topological SFA abstraction

In Section 3 we have seen how an SFA can be abstracted by abstracting its underlying Boolean algebra. This abstraction does not influence directly the topological structure of SFA. When dealing with automata, the natural way of thinking about automata simplification (or abstraction) is the merge of states. In general, we can define a simplification operation on automata that collapses states wrt a given equivalence relation over states. Namely, the equivalence relation establish the criteria that the simplification uses for merging states.

DEFINITION 5.1. *Consider a SFA $M = \langle \mathcal{A}, Q, q_0, F, \Delta \rangle$ and an equivalence relation $R \subseteq Q \times Q$ over its states. We denote with $Sim_R(M)$ the SFA obtained by simplifying $M$ wrt $R$, namely the SFA computed as the quotient of $M$ wrt $R$, i.e., $Sim_R(M) = M_{/R}$.*

Thus, SFA simplification is the operation of quotient made parametric on the equivalence relation used to merge states. It is easy to observe that for every equivalence relation $R$, the SFA $Sim_R(M)$ resulting from SFA simplification recognizes at least the language recognized by $M$. Indeed when we merge states we keep all the transitions of the original SFA and we may add some new *spurious* ones.

PROPOSITION 5.2. *Consider a SFA $M = \langle \mathcal{A}, Q, q_0, F, \Delta \rangle$. For any equivalence relation $R \subseteq Q \times Q$ we have that $\mathscr{L}(M) \subseteq \mathscr{L}(Sim_R(M))$.*

Given two equivalence relations $R$ and $R'$, we write $R \preceq R'$ when $R$ is a refinement of $R'$. Of course the coarser is the equivalence relation the wider is the language recognized by the corresponding simplified SFA.

PROPOSITION 5.3. *Consider a SFA $M = \langle \mathcal{A}, Q, q_0, F, \Delta \rangle$ and two equivalence relations $R, R' \subseteq Q \times Q$ such that $R \preceq R'$. Then $\mathscr{L}(Sim_R(M)) \subseteq \mathscr{L}(Sim_{R'}(M))$.*

Another important property of topological abstractions is that they do not change the set of minterms, since they do not change the predicates. In the following we report a simplification algorithm where the predicates of the SFA to simplify are first rewritten as disjunction of minterms (line 3-7). Thus, whenever the equivalence relation $R$ deals with properties of the languages of strings that reaches or starts from a state, it may be easier to check these properties on minterms instead of checking them on the language of denotations. (Examples will be provided in the following).

**Simplify**$(M, R)$

1. Input: $M = \langle \mathcal{A}, Q, q_0, F, \Delta \rangle$, $R \subseteq Q \times Q$,
2. $\quad \mathcal{A} = \langle \mathfrak{D}_{\mathcal{A}}, \Psi_{\mathcal{A}}, [\![\cdot]\!], \bot, \top, \wedge, \vee, \neg \rangle$
3. $\mathcal{M}t(M) \stackrel{\text{def}}{=} \text{MINTERMS}\left(\left\{ \psi \;\middle|\; \begin{array}{l} \exists p, q \in Q. \\ p \stackrel{\psi}{\longrightarrow} q \in \Delta \end{array} \right\}\right)$
4. $M' = \langle \mathcal{A}', Q, q_0, F, \Delta' \rangle$:
5. $\quad \mathcal{A}' \stackrel{\text{def}}{=} \langle \mathfrak{D}_{\mathcal{A}}, \mathcal{M}t(M), [\![\cdot]\!], \bot, \top, \wedge, \vee, \neg \rangle$
6. $\quad \mu(\psi) \stackrel{\text{def}}{=} \bigvee \{ \varphi \in \mathcal{M}t(M) \mid \varphi \in \text{Leaves}(T_\psi) \}$
7. $\quad \Delta' \stackrel{\text{def}}{=} \left\{ p \stackrel{\mu(\psi)}{\longrightarrow} q \;\middle|\; \exists \psi .\, p \stackrel{\psi}{\longrightarrow} q \right\}$
8. Output: $M'' = M'_{/R}$

## 5.1 Examples of SFA Simplifications

***Minimization.*** D'Antoni and Veanes in [9] have extended the standard algorithm of Hopcroft for finite state automata minimization to SFA. This operation is based on the idea of refining an initial partition by checking all the possible moves depending on the considered alphabet symbol. In FSA this is feasible because they have a finite alphabet. In SFA the alphabet is r.e., hence in general infinite. For this reason the algorithm proposed iterates this check on predicates/symbols in a way that makes the number of possible iteration finite: instead of checking transitions for each alphabet symbol, the check is made for each minterm (see [9] for details).

Observe that this SFA minimization algorithm can be seen as a simplification wrt. the equivalence relation that relates all and only the states that are reached exactly by the same language of minterms. Consider a SFA $M = \langle \mathcal{A}, Q, q_0, F, \Delta \rangle$, and for every $q \stackrel{\psi}{\longrightarrow} p \in \Delta$ let $\mu(\psi)$ be the predicate $\psi$ written as a disjunction of minterms (namely as the disjunction of the leaves of the subtree $T_\psi$ with root $\psi$ of the tree generated during the construction of the minterms of the considered SFA). We define the language of strings of minterms that reaches a state $q$ as:

$$\dot{\mathscr{L}}(q) \stackrel{\text{def}}{=} \left\{ \mu(\psi_1) \dots \mu(\psi_{n-1}) \;\middle|\; \begin{array}{l} \exists n \in \mathbb{N} : \exists q_1 \dots q_n \in Q : \\ \forall i \in [1, n[. q_i \stackrel{\mu(\psi_i)}{\longrightarrow} q_{i+1} \in \Delta \\ q_n = q \end{array} \right\}$$

Let $\doteq \subseteq Q \times Q$ be such that $q \doteq p$ iff $\dot{\mathscr{L}}(q) = \dot{\mathscr{L}}(p)$. Observe that for the properties of minterms proved in the previous section, we have that checking the language of minterms or checking the language of denotations is equivalent, since minterms provide a minimal and unequivocal representation of predicates. Let $Min(M)$ denote the minimization of $M$.

PROPOSITION 5.4. $Min(M) = Sim_{\doteq}(M)$.

***k-Minimization.*** According to the above formalization of SFA minimization, we can weaken minimization by defining a relation over states that observes the language of stings of minterms of a fixed length $k$ that reaches a given state. To this end, given an SFA $M = \langle \mathcal{A}, Q, q_0, F, \Delta \rangle$, and for every $q \stackrel{\psi}{\longrightarrow} p \in \Delta$ let $\mu(\psi)$ be the predicate $\psi$ written as a disjuction of minterms, we define the language $\dot{\mathscr{L}}_k(q)$, which is the language of strings of length $k$ that can reach the state $q$:

$$\dot{\mathscr{L}}_k(q) \stackrel{\text{def}}{=} \left\{ \mu(\psi_1) \dots \mu(\psi_{k-1}) \;\middle|\; \begin{array}{l} \exists q_1 \dots q_k \in Q : \\ \forall i \in [1, .k[. q_i \stackrel{\mu(\psi_i)}{\longrightarrow} q_{i+1} \in \Delta \\ q_k = q \end{array} \right\}$$

Let $\doteq_k \subseteq Q \times Q$ be such that $q \doteq_k p$ iff $\dot{\mathscr{L}}_k(q) = \dot{\mathscr{L}}_k(p)$. Let $Min_k(M)$ denote the simplification of $M$ wrt $\doteq_k$. The following examples illustrate the difference between minimization and $k$-minimization.

EXAMPLE 5.5. *Consider the SFA $M$ in Fig. 4 on the left. It is clear that the predicates* $x$ odd *and* $(x+1)$ even *are equivalent, as well as predicates* $y$ even *and* $(y+1)$ odd. *This is captured by the minimization algorithm of D'Antoni and Veanes that correctly collapses state $q_4$ with $q_5$ and $q_7$ with $q_8$. The minimized algorithm $Min(M)$ is shown in Fig. 4 at the top on the right. Observe that the edge between $q_2$ and $\{q_4, q_5\}$, as well as the edge between $\{q_7, q_8\}$ and $q_9$, is labeled by one of the two equivalent predicates. Of course, the SFA $M$ and $Min(M)$ recognize the same language. In order to clarify the difference between minimization and $k$-minimization at the bottom right of Fig. 4 we report the result obtained by applying the simplification algorithm wrt $\doteq_k$ where $k = 1$ at the SFA $M$. Observe that the simplification algorithm with $k = 1$ merges the state $q_6$ with the states $q_7$ and $q_8$, as shown in the resulting SFA $Min_1(M)$. Indeed, the states $q_6$, $q_7$ and $q_8$ are reached by the same language of strings of length 1 (in this simple case all the denotations with $y$ positive). The edge between $\{q_6, q_7, q_8\}$ and $q_9$ is labeled by* true *since it corresponds to* $y$ odd $\vee$ $y$ even. *We can observe that the language recognized by $Min_1(M)$ is greater than the one recognized by $M$. Let us consider the pairs $(n_1, n_2)$ with $n_1, n_2 \in \mathbb{Z}$ where the first number denotes the values of $x$ and the second the values of $y$. For example we have that the string of pairs $(1,2)(2,4)(4,8)(8,16) \in \mathscr{L}(Min_1(M))$ while it does not belong to $\mathscr{L}(M) = \mathscr{L}(Min(M))$.*

Of course when the value of $k$ increases it increases also the precision of the simplification wrt $\doteq_k$ by collapsing states that are equivalent, namely at the limit with $k$ increasing the $k$-minimization becomes minimization.

THEOREM 5.6. *Given two states $p$ and $q$ we have that $p \doteq q$ iff $\forall k \in \mathbb{N}.\, p \doteq_k q$.*

EXAMPLE 5.7. *Observe that if we compute the simplification of the SFA $M$ in the example in Fig. 4 wrt $\doteq_k$ and $k = 2$ we obtain the minimized SFA, namely $Min(M) = Min_2(M)$. Indeed, if we consider the language of words of length 2 that reach a given state we can no longer merge $q_6$ with $q_7$ and $q_8$.*

***k-Invariant.*** Minterms provide a systematic simplification of SFA based on the extraction of invariant properties that hold for the language of strings that reach (or start) from a given state. Consider an SFA $M = \langle \mathcal{A}, Q, q_0, F, \Delta \rangle$, and for every $q \stackrel{\psi}{\longrightarrow} p \in \Delta$ let $\mu(\psi)$ be the predicate $\psi$ written as a disjunction of minterms. Consider a state $q \in Q$. For every string $\mu(\psi_1) \dots \mu(\psi_k) \in \dot{\mathscr{L}}_k(q)$ of length $k$ that reaches the state $q$ we have that $IsSat(\bigwedge_{i \in [1,k]} \mu(\psi_i))$ is true iff all the disjunctions $\mu(\psi_i)$ of minterms share at least one minterm. This because, thanks to the properties of minterms, only

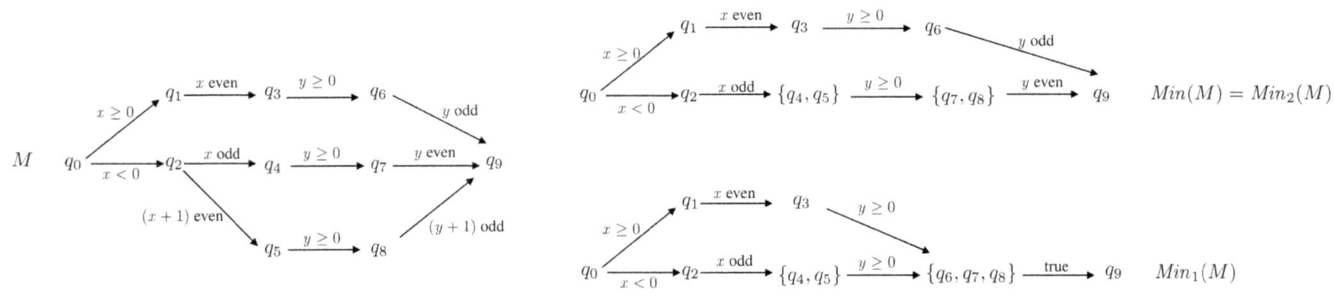


**Figure 4.** Minimization and $k$-Minimization

one minterm at the time can be true. Let

$$Inv\{\mu(\psi_i)\}_{i\in[1,k]} \stackrel{\text{def}}{=} \{\ \varphi \in \text{MINTERMS} \mid \forall i \in [1,k].\ \mathit{IsSat}(\varphi \wedge \mu(\psi_i))\ \}$$

It is the set of *all* the minterms shared by *all* the $\mu(\psi_i)$, which provides the invariant property of the corresponding string. Indeed, thanks to minterms this satisfiability can be checked syntactically. We can therefore define the following equivalence relation $\stackrel{\text{inv}}{\equiv}_k \subseteq Q \times Q$ such that $q \stackrel{\text{inv}}{\equiv}_k p$ iff $\Im_k(q) = \Im_k(p)$ where

$$\Im_k(q) = \{\ Inv\{\mu(\psi_i)\}_{i\in[1,k]} \mid \mu(\psi_1)\ldots\mu(\psi_k) \in \dot{\mathscr{L}}_k(q)\ \}$$

Thus, $\stackrel{\text{inv}}{\equiv}_k$ collapses states reached by paths that have the same $k$-invariant property. We can observe that, if two states share the same $k$-language then they surely share the same $k$-invariant, while the opposite may not be true since the language fixes an order in the constraints that the commutativity of the conjunction relaxes.

THEOREM 5.8. *Given two states $p$ and $q$, and $k \in \mathbb{N}$, we have that $p \dot{\equiv}_k q$ implies $\forall k' \leq k.\ p \stackrel{\text{inv}}{\equiv}_{k'} q$.*

EXAMPLE 5.9. *Consider again the automaton $M$ in Fig. 4. The minterms generated by its predicates are given in the table in Fig. 5: each $i$ denotes the minterm $M_i$ obtained as the conjunction between the constraint on $x$ and on $y$, for instance 3 stays for the minterm $M_3 = (x \text{ even } \wedge x \geq 0 \wedge y \text{ even } \wedge y < 0)$. In Fig. 5 we rewrite $M$ where on each edge the predicates are denoted as the set of the minterms specifying it. For instance $x \geq 0 \equiv \bigvee_{i\in[1,8]} M_i$. Note that on this automaton the $k$-invariant generates the same transformation as the $k$-minimization as showed in Fig. 4. Consider instead the automaton $M_1$ on the right. In this case, the languages recognized by $q_7$ and $q_8$ are different, for instance the trace $(-1,3)(3,-4)(3,5) \in \dot{\mathscr{L}}_3(q_7)$ is not in $\dot{\mathscr{L}}_3(q_8)$ since $(3,-4)$ does not satisfy the predicate between $q_2$ and $q_5$ in $M_1$, i.e., $y \geq 0$. If we consider 3-invariant then we observe that the invariant on the path $q_0q_2q_4q_7$ is $M_{13} \wedge M_{14}$ and the same is for the path $q_0q_2q_5q_8$, hence we can collapse the states $q_7$ and $q_8$.*

## 5.2 Topological abstraction of abstract SFA

It is worth noting that abstraction in SFA may influence the automata simplification. In this section we prove that the efficacy of simplification, and in particular of minimization and $k$-minimization, in SFA is strictly related with the degree of abstraction of their semantics or syntax.

EXAMPLE 5.10. *Consider the SFA $M$ in Fig. 4 and assume that we want to abstract from the parity of $y$. Hence we define abstraction $\eta_1$ on the predicates of $M$ as $\eta_1(y\,\text{odd}) = \eta_1(y\,\text{even}) = \eta_1((y+1)\,\text{odd}) = \text{true}$ and as the identity on the other predicates. In this example we do not abstract the semantics and we consider $\rho = \texttt{id}$. Let $M_{\eta_1}$ be the SFA wrt the considered abstraction (where the predicates of $M$ are substituted with their abstraction according to $\eta_1$). By applying minimization to this SFA we obtain the SFA $Min(M_{\eta_1})$ depicted at the top left of Fig. 6. We can observe that, due to the predicate abstraction $\eta_1$, the minimization of $M_{\eta_1}$ collapses more states than the minimization of $M$ and therefore: $\mathscr{L}(Min(M)) \subseteq \mathscr{L}(Min(M_{\eta_1}))$. For example the string of pairs $(1,2)(2,4)(4,8)(8,16) \in \mathscr{L}(Min(M_{\eta_1}))$ while it does not belong to $\mathscr{L}(Min(M))$.*

*We have an analogous situation in the case of $k$-minimization. Consider the predicate abstraction $\eta_2$ such that $\eta_1(x\,\text{odd}) = \eta_1(x\,\text{even}) = \eta_1((x+1)\,\text{even}) = \text{true}$ and as the identity on the other predicates, and let $\rho = \texttt{id}$. By applying the simplification algorithm wrt. $\dot{\equiv}_k$ with $k = 1$ to the SFA $M_{\eta_2}$ we obtain the SFA at the top right of Fig. 6. Also in this case, due to the abstraction $\eta_2$ the simplification algorithm collapses more states and therefore: $\mathscr{L}(Min_1(M)) \subseteq \mathscr{L}(Min_1(M_{\eta_2}))$. For example the string of pairs $(1,2)(3,6)(5,10)(7,14) \in \mathscr{L}(Min_1(M_{\eta_2}))$ while it does not belong to $\mathscr{L}(Min_1(M))$.*

Let $\mathbb{S}$ denote the set of SFA and let us define the following ordering relation $\dot{\leq}$ on $\mathbb{S}$ modeling precisely the relative precision of SFA with respect to language containment and size of the automaton, where given $M_1 = \langle \mathcal{A}, Q_1, q_0^1, F_1, \Delta_1\rangle$ and $M_2 = \langle \mathcal{A}, Q_2, q_0^2, F_2, \Delta_2\rangle \in \mathbb{S}$ we have that:

$$M_1 \dot{\leq} M_2 \Leftrightarrow \mathscr{L}(M_1) \subseteq \mathscr{L}(M_2) \vee \mathscr{L}(M_1) = \mathscr{L}(M_2) \wedge |Q_2| \leq |Q_1|$$

It is immediate to observe that $\langle \mathbb{S}, \dot{\leq}\rangle$ is a possibly non-complete lattice. Given the SFA simplification $Sim_R : \mathbb{S} \to \mathbb{S}$, a SFA $M = \langle \mathcal{A}, Q, q_0, F, \Delta\rangle$ and a $\langle\!|\rho|\!\rangle\langle\eta\rangle$-abstraction of the effective Boolean algebra $\mathcal{A}$ we wonder when the diagram in Fig. 7 commutes. In general we have that when we simplify the SFA after the abstraction of the underlying algebra we obtain an SFA that is more abstract than the one obtained by applying simplification before the abstraction. The intuition beyond this is that the abstraction of the underlying Boolean algebra could make equivalent edges of the original SFA that are not equivalent and this may cause the merge of states that would not be merged when simplifying original SFA.

PROPOSITION 5.11. *Given $M = \langle \mathcal{A}, Q, q_0, F, \Delta\rangle \in \mathbb{S}$, the closures $\eta \in uco(\wp(\Psi_{\mathcal{A}}))$ and $\rho \in uco(\wp(\mathfrak{D}_{\mathcal{A}}))$ and a relation $R$, we have that: $Sim_R(M)^{\rho}_{\eta} \dot{\leq} Sim_R(M^{\rho}_{\eta})$.*

EXAMPLE 5.12. *At the bottom left of Fig. 6 we show the result of abstracting the Boolean algebra after the SFA minimization. We observe that even if $Min(M_{\eta_1})$ and $Min(M)_{\eta_1}$ recognize the same language the automata obtained by minimizing after the abstraction of the underlying Boolean algebra has less states than the one computed by abstracting the Boolean algebra after the minimization. We have a similar result for $k$-minimization as we*

| y \ x | even + | odd + | even - | odd - |
|---|---|---|---|---|
| even + | 1 | 5 | 9 | 13 |
| odd + | 2 | 6 | 10 | 14 |
| even - | 3 | 7 | 11 | 15 |
| odd - | 4 | 8 | 12 | 16 |

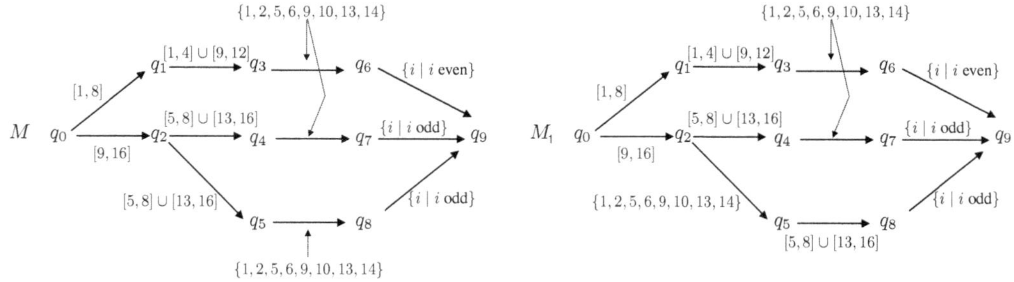


**Figure 5.** $k$-Invariant transformation

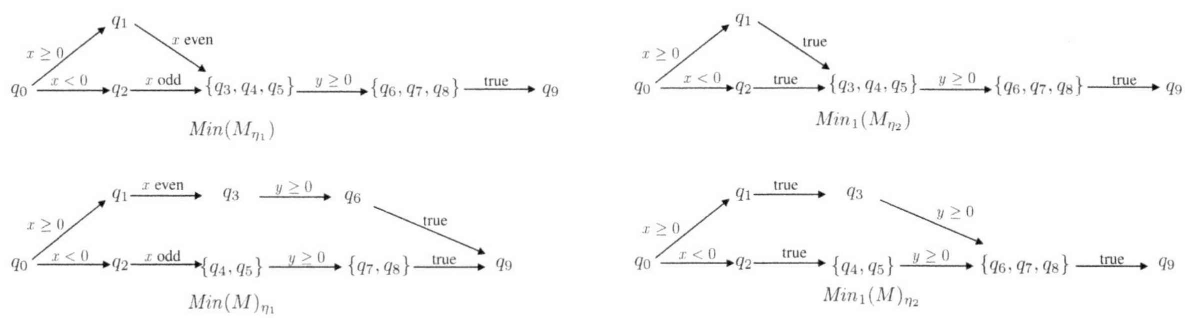


$\eta_1(y\,\texttt{even}) = \eta_1(y, \texttt{odd}) = \eta_1((y+1)\,\texttt{odd}) = \texttt{true}$

$\eta_2(x\,\texttt{even}) = \eta_2(x\,\texttt{odd}) = \eta_2((x+1)\,\texttt{even}) = \texttt{true}$

**Figure 6.** Minimization and $k$-Minimization in presence of Abstraction

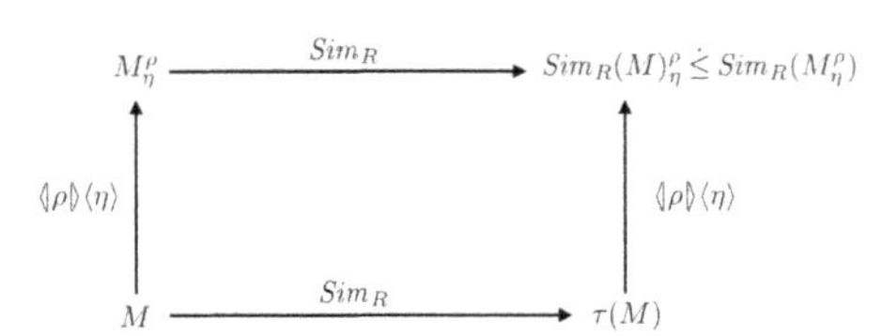


**Figure 7.** Completeness of SFA simplification

*can see by comparing the SFA at the bottom right and top right of Fig. 6.*

## 6. Programs as SFA

In this section we specify the approximate semantics of a program as the language recognized by a SFA. We consider programs in imperative computational model and assume to have access their correct control flow graph (CFG). The CFG of a program is a graph where nodes are given by sequences of non branching instructions. More formally, let $\mathbf{I}$ be the instruction set containing both branching and non-branching instructions. We denote with $\mathbb{I} \subseteq \mathbf{I}$ the set of non-branching instructions and with $\mathbb{C}$ the set of boolean expressions over program states that are guards of the branching instructions. Let $\texttt{c}$ range over $\mathbb{C}$ and $\texttt{b}$ range over $\mathbb{I}^*$. The CFG of a program $P \in \mathbf{I}^*$ is a graph $G_P = (N_P, E_P)$ where the set $N_P \subseteq \mathbb{I}^*$ of nodes specifies the basic blocks of $P$, namely the maximal sequences of sequential instructions of $P$, while the set of edges $E_P \subseteq N_P \times \mathbb{C} \times N_P$ denotes the guarded transitions of $P$. In particular, a labeled edge $(\texttt{b}, \texttt{c}, \texttt{b}') \in E_P$ means that the execution of $P$ flows from $\texttt{b}$ to $\texttt{b}'$ when the execution of $\texttt{b}$ leads to a program state that satisfies condition $\texttt{c}$. When a basic block $\texttt{b}$ has no outgoing edges in $E_P$ we say that it is final, denoted $\texttt{b} \in Final[G_P]$. We denote with $in[\texttt{b}]$ and $out[\texttt{b}]$ respectively the entry and exit point of the basic block $\texttt{b}$, and with $\mathbb{PP}[G_P]$ the block delimiters of $G_P$, namely the set of all the entry and exit points of the basic blocks of $G_P$, namely:

$$\mathbb{PP}[G_P] \stackrel{\text{def}}{=} \{\, in[\texttt{b}] \mid \texttt{b} \in N_P \,\} \cup \{\, out[\texttt{b}] \mid \texttt{b} \in N_P \,\}$$

Let $\Sigma$, ranged over by $s$, be the set of possible program states. Let $\texttt{exec} : \mathbb{I}^* \longrightarrow \wp^{\texttt{re}}(\Sigma \times \Sigma)$ be the function that defines the semantics of basic blocks, namely the pairs of input/output states that model the execution of sequences of instructions. When $(s, s') \in \texttt{exec}(\texttt{b})$ it means that the execution of the sequence of instructions $\texttt{b}$ transforms state $s$ into state $s'$. Let us denote with $s \models \texttt{c}$ the fact that the boolean condition $\texttt{c}$ is satisfied by state $s \in \Sigma$.

We define the set of executions of the CFG of a program $P$ the sequences of basic blocks and guards that can be encountered along a path of $G_P = (N_P, E_P)$. Formally:

$$Exe[G_P] \stackrel{\text{def}}{=} \left\{ \texttt{b}_0\texttt{c}_1\texttt{b}_1\texttt{c}_2 \ldots \texttt{c}_k\texttt{b}_k \;\middle|\; \begin{array}{l} \forall 0 \leq i < k : \\ (\texttt{b}_i, \texttt{c}_{i+1}, \texttt{b}_{i+1}) \in E_P \end{array} \right\} \quad (3)$$

We consider a safety semantics, namely the semantics of all prefixes of execution traces of a given program $P$ [19]. The execution trace semantics of a program $P$, denoted $[\![P]\!]$, is therefore the set of all finite executions starting from the entry point of the starting basic block $\texttt{b}_0$ in the CFG $G_P$ of $P$. Let $Init_P \subseteq \Sigma$ be the set of possible initial states of program $P$. Formally, for each $s_0 \in Init_P$:

$$\begin{aligned} [\![P]\!](s_0) \stackrel{\text{def}}{=} \{ & (s_0, s_1)(s_1, s_1)(s_1, s_2) \ldots (s_k, s_k)(s_k, s_{k+1}) \mid \\ & \texttt{b}_0\texttt{c}_1\texttt{b}_1 \ldots \texttt{c}_k\texttt{b}_k \in Exe[G_P], \\ & \forall 0 < i \leq k : s_i \models \texttt{c}_i, (s_{i-1}, s_i) \in \texttt{exec}(\texttt{b}_{i-1}) \} \end{aligned}$$

$$[\![P]\!] \stackrel{\text{def}}{=} \bigcup \{\, [\![P]\!](s_0) \mid s_0 \in Init_P \,\}$$

In order to define the SFA that corresponds to the CFG semantics of a given program we need to define an effective Boolean algebra that it is suitable for the representation of program execution. For this reason we define the following effective Boolean algebra where predicates are either basic blocks of instructions or guards of branching instructions, representing the syntactic structure of the program, and the denotations are pairs of input/output states:

$$\mathfrak{P} \stackrel{\text{def}}{=} \langle \Sigma \times \Sigma, \mathbb{I}^* \cup \mathbb{C}, \{\!|\cdot|\!\}, \bot, \top, \wedge, \vee, \neg \rangle$$

where the semantic function $\{\!|\cdot|\!\} : \mathbb{I}^* \cup \mathbb{C} \longrightarrow \wp^{\text{re}}(\Sigma \times \Sigma)$ is defined as follows for $\varphi \in \mathbb{I}^* \cup \mathbb{C}$:

$$\{\!|\varphi|\!\} \stackrel{\text{def}}{=} \begin{cases} \{ (s, s') \mid (s, s') \in \texttt{exec(b)} \} & \text{if } \varphi = \texttt{b} \in \mathbb{I}^* \\ \{ (s, s) \mid s \models \texttt{c} \} & \text{if } \varphi = \texttt{c} \in \mathbb{C} \end{cases}$$

we denote with $\{\!|\cdot|\!\}$ also its point-wise extension to $\wp^{\text{re}}(\mathbb{I}^* \cup \mathbb{C})$.

DEFINITION 6.1. *Let $P$ be a program with CFG $G_P$. The SFA associated with $P$ is*

$$M(P) \stackrel{\text{def}}{=} \langle \mathfrak{P}, \mathbb{PP}[G_P], in[\mathfrak{b}_0], \{out[\mathfrak{b}] \mid \mathfrak{b} \in Final[G_P]\}, \Delta_P \rangle$$

*where $\mathfrak{b}_0$ is the starting basic block of $G_P$ and $\Delta_P$ is defined as:*

$$\Delta_P \stackrel{\text{def}}{=} \{ (in[\mathfrak{b}], \mathfrak{b}, out[\mathfrak{b}]) \mid \mathfrak{b} \in N_P \} \cup \{ (out[\mathfrak{b}], \mathtt{c}, in[\mathfrak{b}']) \mid (\mathfrak{b}, \mathtt{c}, \mathfrak{b}') \in E_P \}$$

PROPOSITION 6.2. *If $P$ is a program then $M(P)$ is a deterministic SFA. $M(P)$ is clean if no dead-block is included in $G_P$.*

The language $\mathscr{L}(M(P)) \in \wp^{\text{re}}((\Sigma \times \Sigma)^*)$ recognized by the SFA $M(P)$ approximates the concrete program semantics $[\![P]\!]$ in a language of sequences of infinitely many possible input/output relations associated with each basic block. This is formally stated by the following theorem.

THEOREM 6.3. *If $P$ is a program then for any $s_0 \in Init_P$: $[\![P]\!](s_0) \in \mathscr{L}(M(P))$.*

Given the SFA $M(P)$ that represents the CFG of a program $P$ then it is possible to approximate the semantics of $P$ by abstracting either the predicates, namely the syntax, or the semantics of the effective Boolean algebra underlying $M(P)$.

Let us consider the minimization simplifications. Given compatible abstractions $\rho \in uco(\wp(\Sigma \times \Sigma))$ and $\eta \in uco(\wp^{\text{re}}(\mathbb{I}^* \cup \mathbb{C}))$ and $k \in \mathbb{N}$ we have that

$$M(P) \dot{\leq} Min(M_\eta^\rho(P)) \dot{\leq} Min_k(M_\eta^\rho(P))$$

This provides a reduction of the original SFA, and therefore CFG, providing at the same time a unique approximate representation of the abstract semantics of $P$. This is possible thanks to the combined syntactic and semantic approximation, acting both on the code and on its interpretation. Two programs $P$ and $Q$ can then be considered *similar* if they have the same reduced abstract SFA up to $k \in \mathbb{N}$:

$$P \approxeq_k Q \text{ iff } k = \max \{ n \mid Min_n(M_\eta^\rho(P)) = Min_n(M_\eta^\rho(Q)) \}$$

This weaker notion of similarity can be improved by considering minimal SFA as canonical representation of the approximate syntax and semantics of programs:

$$P \approxeq Q \text{ iff } Min(M_\eta^\rho(P)) = Min(M_\eta^\rho(Q))$$

The following theorem is therefore immediate by construction.

THEOREM 6.4. *Let $P$ and $Q$ be programs, then $P \approxeq Q$ iff $\forall k \in \mathbb{N} : P \approxeq_k Q$.*

It is clear that, for decidable $\langle\!|\rho|\!\rangle\!\langle\eta\rangle$-abstractions, there exists $k \in \mathbb{N}$ such that $P \approxeq_k Q \implies P \approxeq Q$.

## 7. Formal similarity analysis of executables

The idea of *BinJuice* [18] is that the *juice* of a binary forms a template that is expected to be identical regardless of code variations due to register renaming, memory address allocation, and constant replacement. Similar ideas have been employed in *BinDiff* [12] where executables are treated as graphs of graphs: a control flow graph where each block is itself represented as a graph, which is the sequence of its instructions. While the subset of *BinDiff* considered here is sound and semantic compatible, it is computationally expensive. For large size executables, this problem has been tackled in *BinJuice* which adds a further level of abstraction to make the resulting abstract SFA more compact. In contrast to other similar tools for similarity analysis such as *DarunGrim2*, *Rdiff*, *Patchdiff*, and *Radar2*, all designed to find differences in variants of the same program for the purpose of creating patches, *BinJuice* and *BinDiff* are motivated by a different problem: Find similar code in binaries that are not known to be related. This necessitates more advanced abstractions acting on both code and semantics, therefore better showing the potential of abstract SFA.

### 7.1 *BinJuice*

*BinJuice* performs symbolic transformations on the source disassembled binary in order to transform each basic block of assembly code into a corresponding symbolic representation. The idea of symbolic execution is that the operations encoded by the assembly instructions are immediately performed when the arguments are integers, in a sort of partial evaluation local to each basic block, otherwise the same operation keeps its symbolic structure. Consider for example the following fragment of binary code and the result of its disassembly:

| Binary | Assembly |
|---|---|
| `401290: b8 05 00 00 00` | `mov eax,0x5` |
| `401295: c3 04 00 00 00` | `add ebx,0x4` |
| `40129b: 6b c3` | |

*BinJuice* performs algebraic manipulation of instructions in order to reach a canonical form. Thus, the result of symbolic execution with algebraic simplification of the previous example is:

| Normalized State Updates | Constraints |
|---|---|
| `eax=5` | |
| `ebx=def(ebx)`×`5 + 20` | `20 = 4` × `5` |

where `def(ebx)` denotes the value of `ebx` before the execution of the basic block, namely at the entry of the basic block. The syntactic information lost during symbolic execution is actually added back by the constraints on numerical values. In other words, the symbolic execution of basic blocks augmented with numerical constraints is actually an isomorphism. The key abstraction in *BinJuice* is generalization, whose idea is to use typed logical variables in order to be independent from register names. The generalization is performed by consistently replacing register names with logical variables. The replacement is consistent in that two occurrences of the same register name are always replaced by the same variable. Observe that this replacement is a purely syntactic operation. In addition to abstracting the registers used, also constants are abstracted. *BinJuice* associates a type with each logical variable to keep track of type of the original register. In the example considered before the generalization phase of *BinJuice* produces the following juice:

| Juice |
|---|
| $A = V_1$ |
| $B = \texttt{def}(B) \times N_1 + N_2$ |
| constraints: $N_2 = N_1 \times N_3$ |
| types: $\texttt{type}(A) = \texttt{type}(B) = \texttt{reg32}$ |

Let us consider the function $\mathcal{G}$ that generalizes a single basic block.

$$\mathcal{G} : \mathbb{I}^* \longrightarrow \wp^{\mathtt{re}}(\mathit{SUpd}) \times \wp^{\mathtt{re}}(\widehat{\mathbb{C}}) \times \wp^{\mathtt{re}}(\mathcal{T})$$

where $\wp^{\mathtt{re}}(\mathit{SUpd})$ is the domain of normalized symbolic updates while $\wp^{\mathtt{re}}(\widehat{\mathbb{C}})$ is the set of constraints where register names and numerical values have been replaces by symbolic variables, and $\wp^{\mathtt{re}}(\mathcal{T})$ denotes the domain of type declarations.

We say that $\mathcal{G}(\mathtt{b})$ is the *juice* of the basic block $\mathtt{b}$. Observe that $\mathcal{G}$ acts as an abstraction since there may be more than one basic block sharing the same juice. In particular, $\mathcal{G}$ can be associated with an upper closure $\mathscr{G} \in uco(\wp^{\mathtt{re}}(\mathbb{I}^*))$ as follows:

$$\mathscr{G}(B) \stackrel{\text{def}}{=} \{\ \mathtt{b}' \mid \exists \mathtt{b} \in B.\, \mathcal{G}(\mathtt{b}) = \mathcal{G}(\mathtt{b}')\ \}$$

approximating in one single symbolic representation all basic blocks that have the same juice. We can therefore model the generalization process that *BinJuice* operates on the CFG of the disassembled binaries as an $\langle \mathscr{G} \rangle$-abstraction of the predicates of the effective Boolean algebra $\mathfrak{P}$ introduced in Section 6 for representing the CFG of programs as SFA. Here, we consider the extension of $\mathscr{G}$ to branching conditions on which it behaves like identity, $\mathscr{G} \in uco(\wp^{\mathtt{re}}(\mathbb{I}^* \cup \mathbb{C}))$. The resulting *BinJuice* symbolic automaton on the Boolean algebra $\mathfrak{P}_{\mathscr{G}}$ associated with a disassembled program $P$ is:

$$M_{\mathscr{G}}(P) = \langle \mathfrak{P}_{\mathscr{G}}, \mathbb{PP}[G_P], in[b_0], \{out[b] \mid b \in Final[G_P]\}, \Delta_{\mathscr{G}} \rangle$$

where $\mathfrak{P}_{\mathscr{G}} = \langle \Sigma \times \Sigma, \mathscr{G}(\wp^{\mathtt{re}}(\mathbb{I}^* \cup \mathbb{C})), \{\!|\cdot|\!\}, \bot, \top, \wedge, \vee, \neg \rangle$,

$$\begin{aligned}\Delta_{\mathscr{G}} = &\{\ (in[\mathtt{b}], \mathscr{G}(\mathtt{b}), out[\mathtt{b}]) \mid (in[\mathtt{b}], \mathtt{b}, out[\mathtt{b}]) \in \Delta_P\ \}\\ &\cup \{\ (out[\mathtt{b}], \mathtt{c}, in[\mathtt{b}']) \mid (out[\mathtt{b}], \mathtt{c}, in[\mathtt{b}']) \in \Delta_P\ \}\end{aligned}$$

and the semantic function $\{\!|\cdot|\!\}$ is the same as defined in Section 6 but now with a reduced abstracted domain:

$$\{\!|\cdot|\!\} : \mathscr{G}(\wp^{\mathtt{re}}(\mathbb{I}^* \cup \mathbb{C})) \longrightarrow \wp^{\mathtt{re}}(\Sigma \times \Sigma)$$

We observe that, $\mathscr{G}$ is neither syntactic nor semantic compatible (Def. 3.6, Def. 3.9) since:

(1) it collapses simplified updates with different semantics by abstracting values and variables, for example $\mathscr{G}(eax = 5) = \mathscr{G}(eax = 7) = (X = N)$;

(2) it still distinguishes between different simplified updates sharing the same semantics, as for example $\mathscr{G}(eax = ebx * 2) \neq \mathscr{G}(eax = ebx + ebx)$. But also

$$\begin{aligned}\mathscr{G}(eax = 2 * ebx + 10, &\text{constraint: } 10 = 5 * 2) =\\ X = N_1 * Y + N_2, &\text{constraint: } N_2 = N_3 * N_4\end{aligned}$$

and

$$\begin{aligned}\mathscr{G}(eax = 2 * ebx + 10, &\text{constraint: } 10 = 5 + 5) =\\ X = N_1 * Y + N_2, &\text{constraint: } N_2 = N_3 + N_4\end{aligned}$$

Indeed, $\mathscr{G}$ is not comparable with $\Omega(\mathtt{id})$.

PROPOSITION 7.1. *$\mathscr{G}$ is is neither syntactic nor semantic compatible.*

This observation is also related to the incorrectness of *BinJuice* in detecting similar basic blocks indeed *BinJuice* can lead to both false positives (blocks miss-classified as equivalent) and false negatives (blocks that are erroneously classified as different).

As observed before there are two causes of semantic incompatibility: (1) merging updates with different semantics and (2) distinguishing updates with the same semantics. We are interested in over-approximating $\Omega(\mathtt{id})$, namely obtaining a closure $\eta$ such that $\Omega(\mathtt{id}) \sqsubseteq \eta$, therefore avoiding (2) yet keeping (1).

A possible way for making $\mathscr{G}$ semantic compatible is to erase from the domain $\wp^{\mathtt{re}}(\mathbb{I}^* \cup \mathbb{C})$ all the elements that have the same generalized symbolic updates but different constraints. Namely by erasing all syntactic constraints. In the example above, it means for instance to restrict to the blocks that have generalized update $X = N_1 * Y + N_2$ while abstracting from the constraints on $N_2$. It is possible to prove that *BinJuice* is semantic compatible when considering this restricted domain of blocks. This highlights the fact that *BinJuice* is sensible to the structure of the constraints. Indeed, the constraints keep track of how the numerical values present in the update have been computed and is therefore tight to the particular way in which the basic block has computed them. This means that *BinJuice* can be foiled by an attacker that changes the structure of the constraints.

Define $\pi_1 : \wp^{\mathtt{re}}(\mathit{SUpd}) \times \wp^{\mathtt{re}}(\widehat{\mathbb{C}}) \times \wp^{\mathtt{re}}(\mathcal{T}) \to \wp^{\mathtt{re}}(\mathit{SUpd})$ as the projection on the first element of the tuple of the juice. Based on this, given $\mathtt{b} \in \mathbb{I}^*$ we define the predicate abstraction $\mathcal{U}[b] \in uco(\wp(\mathbb{I}^*))$ that keeps only the blocks that have the same generalized update of $\mathtt{b}$ and abstract in $\top$ every other block:

$$\mathcal{U}[\mathtt{b}](\mathtt{b}') \begin{cases} \mathtt{b}' & \text{if } \pi_1(\mathscr{G}(\mathtt{b})) = \pi_1(\mathscr{G}(\mathtt{b}')) \\ \top & \text{otherwise} \end{cases}$$

As expected, for every basic block $\mathtt{b}$ we have that the predicate abstraction $\mathscr{G} \circ \mathcal{U}[\mathtt{b}]$, that extracts the juice of blocks that have the same generalized updates of $\mathtt{b}$, is such that $\mho(\mathcal{U}[\mathtt{b}])$ is syntactic $\langle \mathscr{G} \circ \mathcal{U}[\mathtt{b}] \rangle$-compatible, as stated by the following result.

THEOREM 7.2. *$\forall b \in \mathbb{I}^*$ we have that $\Omega(\mho(\mathcal{U}[\mathtt{b}])) \sqsubseteq \mathscr{G} \circ \mathcal{U}[\mathtt{b}]$*

This result is a direct consequence of the definitions of $\mathcal{U}[\mathtt{b}]$ and of $\mathscr{G}$, and by Prop. 3.15-(2). Once again, this formally proves that *BinJuice* over-approximates the set of blocks with the same semantics when we restrict to blocks that have the same symbolic update.

### 7.2 *BinDiff*

We consider a subset of *BinDiff*, employing *instruction permutation* and *same string reference* (i.e., instructions and nodes can be matched by common string references, e.g., indicating functions that all contain code referring to the same string). All these equivalences correspond straightforwardly to abstractions of the SFA acting at syntactic and topological level. Consider the SFA $M(P)$ and the following abstractions:

**Permutation.** Let $\tau : \mathbb{I} \longrightarrow \mathcal{T}$ be a function associating the mnemonic op-code in $\mathcal{T}$ at each instruction in $\mathbb{I}$. Consider the lift of $\tau$ to multi-sets. Define an equivalence relation on basic blocks, viz., predicates in $M(P)$, such that for any $\mathtt{b}, \mathtt{b}' \in \mathbb{I}^* \cup \mathbb{C}$: $\mathtt{b} \equiv \mathtt{b}'$ if $\tau(\mathtt{b}) = \tau(\mathtt{b}')$. This clearly induces a partition which is a (partitioning) closure operator, denoted $\eta_\tau$ on predicates in $\mathbb{I}^* \cup \mathbb{C}$. In other words, $\tau$ forgets the order and the arguments of instructions. It is therefore clear that $\eta_\tau(\mathtt{b}) = \eta_\tau(\mathtt{b}') \not\Rightarrow \{\!|\mathtt{b}|\!\} = \{\!|\mathtt{b}'|\!\}$, namely $\eta_\tau$ may collapse blocks with different semantics meaning that it is not semantic compatible, i.e., $\eta_\tau \not\sqsubseteq \Omega(\mathtt{id})$. On the other hand, since $\eta_\tau$ observes precisely the multi-set of instructions, we could have blocks with the same semantics but written with different sets of instructions, i.e., $\{\!|\mathtt{b}|\!\} = \{\!|\mathtt{b}'|\!\} \not\Rightarrow \eta_\tau(\mathtt{b}) = \eta_\tau(\mathtt{b}')$ meaning that $\eta_\tau$ fails also the syntactic compatibility.

**Same reference.** Let $\mathcal{N}$ be a set of strings and $\xi : \mathbf{I} \longrightarrow \wp(\mathcal{N})$ the function associating with each basic block $\mathtt{b}$ the set of strings of $\mathcal{N}$ appearing in $\mathtt{b}$. This is clearly the left-adjoint of a GC, therefore inducing a closure $\eta_\xi$ on predicates which is also a partition. This abstraction forgets any instruction considering only a set of string manipulated in the block. Again, it is quite straightforward to observe that this abstraction can both collapse blocks with different semantics and distinguish blocks with the same semantics, for instance a string may be computed without writing it explicitly. Hence also $\eta_\xi$ fails both the compatibilities.

In order to make *permutations* syntactic compatible, we can indeed restrict the domain of the permutation abstraction similarly to what we have done on *BinJuice* and forcing syntactic compatibility. Let $\mathit{Instr}(B) \stackrel{\text{def}}{=} \{\, \mathtt{b}' \mid \exists \mathtt{b} \in B.\, \eta_\mathcal{T}(\mathtt{b}') = \eta_\mathcal{T}(\mathtt{b}) \,\}$ and

$$\mathcal{S}[\mathtt{b}](\mathtt{b}') = \begin{cases} \mathtt{b}' & \text{if } \mathit{Instr}(\mathtt{b}) = \mathit{Instr}(\mathtt{b}') \\ \top & \text{otherwise} \end{cases}$$

As expected, for every basic block $\mathtt{b}$ we have that the predicate abstraction $\mathit{Instr} \circ \mathcal{S}[\mathtt{b}]$, that collects blocks that have the same set of instructions of $\mathtt{b}$, is such that $\mho(\mathcal{S}[\mathtt{b}])$ is syntactic $\langle \mathit{Instr} \circ \mathcal{S}[\mathtt{b}] \rangle$-compatible, as stated by the following result which is a consequence of the definitions of $\mathcal{S}[\mathtt{b}]$ and of *Instr*, and by Prop. 3.15-(2).

THEOREM 7.3. $\forall \mathtt{b} \in \mathbb{I}^*$ *we have that* $\Omega(\mho(\mathcal{S}[\mathtt{b}])) \sqsubseteq \mathrm{Instr} \circ \mathcal{S}[\mathtt{b}]$.

## 8. Related Works

To the best of our knowledge, this is the first application of abstract interpretation to symbolic finite automata and of abstract symbolic automata to similarity analysis of binary executables. The most related work is [14], where the authors introduced the notion of *lattice automata*. Lattice automata, like SFA, allow languages over an infinite alphabet. In contrast to abstract SFA, lattice automata do not distinguish between symbolic/syntactic abstractions and semantic ones. Indeed transitions in lattice automata are constrained by elements in an atomic lattice $L$, which provide precisely the allowed alphabet-set along that transition. SFA are in this context strictly more general as they separate the symbolic constraints and their semantics, allowing in principle separate approximations for them.

The idea of approximating the program's data in a so called *predicate abstraction* is nowadays common practice in static program analysis. The roots of this idea are in automatic software verification (see [1, 13]). Observe that, given a program $P$, predicate abstraction abstracts the semantics (states) of $P$ into a set of predicates $E$ and then it derives an abstract program $P$-bool that models how the execution of $P$ affects $E$. Thus, predicate abstraction corresponds to a semantic abstraction $\rho$ that groups states w.r.t. to $E$, and $P$-bool is a possible way of representing the syntactic compatible abstraction $\Omega(\rho)$ of $P$. As observed in [2] predicate abstraction considers only finite abstractions, while the semantic abstraction of denotations in abstract SFA can be an infinite domain. Moreover, predicate abstraction does not allow to change the CFG of the program.

The relation between the approximation of symbolic/syntactic structures and their semantics is well known in the literature (see [6] and [11] for a recent account). In particular in [22] the authors study this relation for the systematic synthesis of optimal symbolic predicate transformers, as introduced in [20]. None of these consider the case of abstract interpretation of SFA. In [7] the authors model disassembled binaries as finite state automata (FSA). A widening of FSA is introduced for extracting syntactic code invariants in self-modifying metamorphic programs. This construction lacks of abstractions concerning the semantics of sequences of instructions.

## 9. Conclusion

We have studied how to weaken symbolic finite automata by abstract interpretation. The results is a general theory of approximated SFA which is parametric on the chosen abstraction. The purpose is to provide a compact and effective representation of code approximations acting both at syntactic and semantic level. Interestingly, for a Turing complete programming language, there is no syntactic abstraction which induces a compatible semantic abstraction. This follows from a simple padding argument, and it is indeed a common underlying problem in most known methods for program similarity analysis, such as *BinDiff* and *BinJuice*. Observe that the existing tools either abstract the syntax independently from the semantics, like in *BinDiff*, or represent into the syntax the abstraction of the semantics, like in predicate abstraction. In the first case we risk to fall far away form the meaning of the program to analyze, in the second case the analysis may be too much bound to the semantics without having the possibility of exploiting better syntax properties necessary in similarity analysis (e.g. in *BinDiff* and *BinJuice*). Compatibility bridges these two aspects. By semantic compatibility the abstraction of the syntax distinguishes programs with the same abstract semantics, namely the abstract program provides an under-approximation of the program behavior. By syntactic compatibility the abstraction of the syntax collapses programs with different semantics, hence capturing behaviors that are not related with the program to analyze, therefore providing an over-approximation of the program behavior. Interestingly, in our model we can restrict the form of predicates in order to have compatibility. This is what we proved in *BinJuice* and *BinDiff*, thus showing the limits of existing tools for code similarity and the possibility of systematically deriving conditions for making them syntactic compatible.

Another direction of future research is in the use of topological abstractions of SFA for extracting signatures of self-modifying code as recently studied in [7]. This requires the extension of widening operations, such as those introduced in [5, 10, 14], to abstract SFA. In this case approximate SFA provide advanced signatures in metamorphic malware analysis, incorporating both properties of way code changes during program execution (the invariant of the metamorphic engine) and additional semantic information, such as the values passed in system-calls. This may reduce the false positives occurring in [7] in signature-based detection of metamorphic malware.


## Acknowledgments

This work has been conceived when Mila, Roberto, and Isabella were visiting Arun at the University of Louisiana at Lafayette USA. They thank the Center for Advanced Computer Studies for the kind hospitality. This work is partly supported by the Air Force Research Laboratory and DARPA project: AFRL FA8750-10-C-0171 and by the MIUR FIRB project FACE (Formal Avenue for Chasing malwarE) RBFR13AJFT.


## References


[1] T. Ball, R. Majumdar, T. D. Millstein, and S. K. Rajamani. Automatic predicate abstraction of C programs. In M. Burke and M. L. Soffa, editors, *PLDI*, pages 203–213. ACM, 2001. ISBN 1-58113-414-2.

[2] P. Cousot. Verification by abstract interpretation. In *Verification: Theory and Practice, Essays Dedicated to Zohar Manna on the Occasion of His 64th Birthday*, volume 2772, pages 243–268. Springer, 2003.

[3] P. Cousot and R. Cousot. Abstract interpretation: A unified lattice model for static analysis of programs by construction or approximation of fixpoints. In *Conference Record of the 4th ACM Symposium on Principles of Programming Languages (POPL '77)*, pages 238–252. ACM Press, 1977.

[4] P. Cousot and R. Cousot. Systematic design of program analysis frameworks. In *Conference Record of the 6th ACM Symposium on Principles of Programming Languages (POPL '79)*, pages 269–282. ACM Press, 1979.

[5] P. Cousot and R. Cousot. Formal language, grammar and set-constraint-based program analysis by abstract interpretation. In *Proceedings of the Seventh ACM Conference on Functional Programming Languages and Computer Architecture*, pages 170–181. ACM Press, New York, NY, 25–28 June 1995.

[6] P. Cousot, R. Cousot, and L. Mauborgne. Theories, solvers and static analysis by abstract interpretation. *J. ACM*, 59(6):31, 2012.

[7] M. Dalla Preda, R. Giacobazzi, S. K. Debray, K. Coogan, and G. M. Townsend. Modelling metamorphism by abstract interpretation. In *Proc. of the 19th Int. Static Analysis Symp.* (*SAS '10*), volume 6337 of *Lecture Notes in Computer Science*, pages 218–235. Springer-Verlag, Berlin, 2010.

[8] L. D'Antoni and M. Veanes. Equivalence of extended symbolic finite transducers. In N. Sharygina and H. Veith, editors, *CAV*, volume 8044 of *Lecture Notes in Computer Science*, pages 624–639. Springer, 2013. ISBN 978-3-642-39798-1.

[9] L. D'Antoni and M. Veanes. Minimization of symbolic automata. In S. Jagannathan and P. Sewell, editors, *POPL*, pages 541–554. ACM, 2014. ISBN 978-1-4503-2544-8.

[10] V. D'Silva. Widening for automata. Diploma Thesis, Institut Fur Informatick, Universitat Zurich, 2006.

[11] V. D'Silva, L. Haller, and D. Kroening. Abstract satisfaction. In S. Jagannathan and P. Sewell, editors, *POPL*, pages 139–150. ACM, 2014. ISBN 978-1-4503-2544-8.

[12] H. Flake. Structural comparison of executable objects. In U. Flegel and M. Meier, editors, *DIMVA*, volume 46 of *LNI*, pages 161–173. GI, 2004. ISBN 3-88579-375-X.

[13] C. Flanagan and S. Qadeer. Predicate abstraction for software verification. In *Proc. of Conf. Record of the 29th ACM Symp. on Principles of Programming Languages* (*POPL '02*), pages 191–202. ACM Press, 2002.

[14] T. L. Gall and B. Jeannet. Lattice automata: A representation for languages on infinite alphabets, and some applications to verification. In H. R. Nielson and G. Filé, editors, *SAS*, volume 4634 of *Lecture Notes in Computer Science*, pages 52–68. Springer, 2007. ISBN 978-3-540-74060-5.

[15] D. Gao, M. Reiter, and D. Song. BinHunt: Automatically finding semantic differences in binary programs. In *Proceedings of the 10th International Conference on Information and Communications Security*, ICICS '08, pages 238–255. Springer-Verlag, 2008.

[16] R. Giacobazzi, F. Ranzato, and F. Scozzari. Making abstract interpretation complete. *Journal of the ACM*, 47(2):361–416, March 2000.

[17] S. Hunt and I. Mastroeni. The PER model of abstract non-interference. In C. Hankin and I. Siveroni, editors, *Proc. of The 12th Internat. Static Analysis Symp. (SAS '05)*, volume 3672 of *Lecture Notes in Computer Science*, pages 171–185. Springer-Verlag, 2005.

[18] A. Lakhotia, M. Dalla Preda, and R. Giacobazzi. Fast location of similar code fragments using semantic 'juice'. In *2nd Workshop on Program Protection and Reverse Engineering PPREW 2013*. ACM, 2013.

[19] I. Mastroeni and R. Giacobazzi. An abstract interpretation-based model for safety semantics. *Int. J. Comput. Math.*, 88(4):665–694, 2011.

[20] T. W. Reps, S. Sagiv, and G. Yorsh. Symbolic implementation of the best transformer. In B. Steffen and G. Levi, editors, *VMCAI*, volume 2937 of *Lecture Notes in Computer Science*, pages 252–266. Springer, 2004. ISBN 3-540-20803-8.

[21] H. Rogers. *Theory of recursive functions and effective computability*. The MIT press, 1992.

[22] A. V. Thakur, M. Elder, and T. W. Reps. Bilateral algorithms for symbolic abstraction. In A. Miné and D. Schmidt, editors, *SAS*, volume 7460 of *Lecture Notes in Computer Science*, pages 111–128. Springer, 2012. ISBN 978-3-642-33124-4.

[23] M. Veanes, P. Hooimeijer, B. Livshits, D. Molnar, and N. Bjørner. Symbolic finite state transducers: algorithms and applications. In J. Field and M. Hicks, editors, *POPL*, pages 137–150. ACM, 2012. ISBN 978-1-4503-1083-3.

[24] M. Ward. The Closure Operators of a Lattice. *Annals of Mathematics*, 43(2):191–196, 1942.

[25] Zynamics. BinDiff3.2manual., 2004. URL `http://www.zynamics.com/bindiff/manual/`.

# A Coalgebraic Decision Procedure for NetKAT

Nate Foster
Cornell University

Dexter Kozen
Cornell University

Matthew Milano
Cornell University

Alexandra Silva
Radboud University Nijmegen

Laure Thompson
Cornell University

## Abstract

NetKAT is a domain-specific language and logic for specifying and verifying network packet-processing functions. It consists of Kleene algebra with tests (KAT) augmented with primitives for testing and modifying packet headers and encoding network topologies. Previous work developed the design of the language and its standard semantics, proved the soundness and completeness of the logic, defined a PSPACE algorithm for deciding equivalence, and presented several practical applications.

This paper develops the coalgebraic theory of NetKAT, including a specialized version of the Brzozowski derivative, and presents a new efficient algorithm for deciding the equational theory using bisimulation. The coalgebraic structure admits an efficient sparse representation that results in a significant reduction in the size of the state space. We discuss the details of our implementation and optimizations that exploit NetKAT's equational axioms and coalgebraic structure to yield significantly improved performance. We present results from experiments demonstrating that our tool is competitive with state-of-the-art tools on several benchmarks including all-pairs connectivity, loop-freedom, and translation validation.

***Categories and Subject Descriptors*** F.4.3 [*Formal Languages*]: Classes defined by grammars or automata

***Keywords*** Coalgebra; Kleene algebra with tests; Brzozowski derivatives; automata; network verification; NetKAT.

## 1. Introduction

Networks have received widespread attention in recent years as a target for domain-specific language design. The emergence of *software-defined networking* (SDN) as a popular paradigm for network programming has led to the appearance of a number of SDN programming languages including Frenetic, Nettle, NetCore, Pyretic, Maple, and PANE, among others [10–12, 26, 27, 39, 40]. The details of these languages differ, but each seeks to provide high-level abstractions to simplify the task of specifying the packet-processing behavior of a network. In addition to SDN languages, a number of verification tools including HSA, VeriFlow, FlowLog, and VeriCon are also being actively developed [2, 16, 17, 28]. As SDN is being deployed in production enterprise, data center, and wide-area networks [14, 19, 20], it is becoming clear that SDN is the next major step in the evolution of network technology and is destined to have a significant impact.

Previous work by Anderson et al. [1] introduced NetKAT, a language and logic for specifying and verifying the packet-processing behavior of networks. NetKAT provides general-purpose programming constructs such as parallel and sequential composition, conditional tests, and iteration, as well as special-purpose primitives for querying and modifying packet headers and encoding network topologies. The language allows the desired behavior of a network to be specified equationally. In contrast to competing approaches, NetKAT has a formal mathematical semantics and an equational deductive system that is sound and complete over that semantics, as well as a PSPACE decision procedure. It is based on Kleene algebra with tests (KAT), an algebraic system for propositional program verification that has been extensively studied for nearly two decades [22]. Several practical applications of NetKAT have been developed, including algorithms for testing reachability and non-interference and a syntactic correctness proof for a compiler that translates programs to hardware instructions for SDN switches.

This paper develops the coalgebraic theory of NetKAT, defines a new algorithm for deciding equivalence based on this technology, and presents a full implementation in OCaml. The new algorithm is significantly more efficient than the previous naive algorithm [1], which was PSPACE in the best case and the worst case, as it was based on the determinization of a nondeterministic algorithm.

The contributions of this paper are both theoretical and practical. On the theoretical side, we introduce a new coalgebraic model of NetKAT, including a specialized version of the Brzozowski derivative in both semantic and syntactic forms. We prove a version of Kleene's theorem for NetKAT that shows that the coalgebraic model is equivalent to the standard packet-processing and language models introduced previously [1]. A highlight of our theoretical development is a representation theorem showing that the Brzozowski derivative can be concisely encoded in matrix form. On the practical side, we develop a new coalgebraic decision procedure for term equivalence based on our theoretical results, along with a full implementation in OCaml. The algorithm constructs a bisimulation between coalgebras built from NetKAT expressions via the Brzozowski derivative. The matrix representation enables us to exploit sparseness to obtain a significant reduction in the size of the state space. The implementation is very efficient in practice—it can verify reachability in a real-world campus network in less than a


*POPL '15*, January 15–17, 2015, Mumbai, India.

http://dx.doi.org/10.1145/10.1145/2676726.2677011

second on a laptop. We demonstrate the real-world applicability of our tool by using it to decide common network verification questions such as all-pairs connectivity, loop-freedom, and translation validation—all pressing questions in modern networks. The results of experiments on these benchmarks demonstrates that our implementation compares favorably with the state of the art.

The rest of this paper is organized as follows. In §2 we briefly review the syntax and semantics of NetKAT [1]. In §3 we introduce NetKAT coalgebras along with a variant of the Brzozowski derivative. In §4 we prove our main theoretical result on which the correctness of our equivalence algorithm is based: a generalization of Kleene's theorem relating NetKAT expressions and NetKAT coalgebras. In §5 we discuss a streamlined representation of NetKAT coalgebras using matrices, which is needed for our implementation. In §6 we present the details of our implementation, focusing on how we exploit the NetKAT axioms and coalgebraic structure to achieve significant performance improvements over the naive algorithm defined previously [1]. In §7 we describe three applications developed from our coalgebraic theory, which are used in the evaluation of our implementation. In §8 we report on the results of experiments. In §9 we discuss related work, and in §10 we present conclusions and identify directions for future research.

## 2. Overview

In this section we briefly review the syntax and semantics of NetKAT, along with other results that are needed to understand our coalgebraic algorithm described in the following sections [1].

NetKAT is based on Kleene algebra with tests (KAT) [22], a generic equational system for reasoning about partial correctness of programs. KAT is Kleene algebra (KA), the algebra of regular expressions, augmented with Boolean tests. Formally, a KAT is a two-sorted structure $(K, B, +, \cdot, ^*, ^-, 0, 1)$, where $B \subseteq K$ and

- $(K, +, \cdot, ^*, 0, 1)$ is a Kleene algebra
- $(B, +, \cdot, ^-, 0, 1)$ is a Boolean algebra
- $(B, +, \cdot, 0, 1)$ is a subalgebra of $(K, +, \cdot, 0, 1)$.

The Kleene algebra operators are choice $(+)$; sequential composition $(\cdot)$, which is often elided in expressions; iteration $(^*)$; fail (0), and skip (1). Elements of $B$ are called *tests*. On tests, choice, sequential composition behave as Boolean disjunction and conjunction, respectively, and 0 and 1 stand for falsity and truth, respectively. The operator $^-$ is the Boolean negation operator, sometimes written as $\neg$. The axioms of Kleene algebra are as follows:

$$\begin{array}{ll} p + (q + r) = (p + q) + r & p(qr) = (pq)r \\ p + q = q + p & 1 \cdot p = p \cdot 1 = p \\ p + 0 = p + p = p & p \cdot 0 = 0 \cdot p = 0 \\ p(q + r) = pq + pr & (p + q)r = pr + qr \\ 1 + pp^* \leq p^* & q + px \leq x \Rightarrow p^*q \leq x \\ 1 + p^*p \leq p^* & q + xp \leq x \Rightarrow qp^* \leq x \end{array}$$

where $p \leq q \Leftrightarrow p + q = q$. The axioms of Boolean algebra are

$$\begin{array}{ll} a + (bc) = (a + b)(a + c) & ab = ba \\ a + 1 = 1 & a + \bar{a} = 1 \\ a \cdot \bar{a} = 0 & aa = a \end{array}$$

in addition to the axioms of Kleene algebra above. KAT can model standard imperative programming constructs,

$$\begin{aligned} p\,; q &= pq \\ \textsf{if } b \textsf{ then } p \textsf{ else } q &= bp + \bar{b}q \\ \textsf{while } b \textsf{ do } p &= (bp)^*\bar{b} \end{aligned}$$

as well as Hoare partial correctness assertions

$$\{b\}\, p\, \{c\} \;\Leftrightarrow\; bp \leq pc \;\Leftrightarrow\; bp = bpc \;\Leftrightarrow\; bp\bar{c} = 0.$$

Hoare-style rules become universal Horn sentences in KAT. For example, the Hoare while-rule

$$\frac{\{bc\}\, p\, \{c\}}{\{c\} \textsf{ while } b \textsf{ do } p\, \{\bar{b}c\}}$$

becomes the universal Horn sentence

$$bcp \leq pc \;\Rightarrow\; c(bp)^*\bar{b} \leq (bp)^*\bar{b}\bar{b}c.$$

KA and KAT have standard language models consisting of, respectively, the regular sets of finite-length strings over a finite alphabet and the regular sets of *guarded strings* over disjoint finite alphabets of test and action symbols. These language models play an important role in that they are the free models on their generators, which means that they exactly characterize the equational theory. There are other useful models, including binary relation and trace models used in programming language semantics. KAT is complete for the equational theory of binary relation models. The equational theories of KA and KAT are both PSPACE complete.

NetKAT extends KAT with network-specific primitives for filtering, modifying, and forwarding packets, along with additional axioms for reasoning about programs built using those primitives. More formally, NetKAT is KAT with primitive actions and tests

- $x \leftarrow n$ (assignment)
- dup (duplication)
- $x = n$ (test)

We also use id and drop for 1 and 0, respectively. Intuitively, the assignment $x \leftarrow n$ assigns the value $n$ to the field $x$ in the current packet. The test $x = n$ tests whether field $x$ of the current packet contains the value $n$. The action dup duplicates the packet in the packet history, which keeps track of the path the packet takes through the network. As an example, the expression

$$switch = 6\,; port = 8\,; ipDst \leftarrow 10.0.1.5\,; port \leftarrow 5$$

encodes the command: "For all packets located at port 8 of switch 6, set the destination IP address to 10.0.1.5 and forward the packet out on port 5."

The NetKAT axioms consist of the KAT axioms as well as the following axioms, which govern the behavior of tests, assignments, duplication, and the interactions between them:

$$\begin{array}{rcll} x \leftarrow n\,; y \leftarrow m &=& y \leftarrow m\,; x \leftarrow n & (\text{if } x \neq y) \\ x \leftarrow n\,; y = m &=& y = m\,; x \leftarrow n & (\text{if } x \neq y) \\ x = n\,; \textsf{dup} &=& \textsf{dup}\,; x = n & \\ x \leftarrow n\,; x = n &=& x \leftarrow n & \\ x = n\,; x \leftarrow n &=& x = n & \\ x \leftarrow n\,; x \leftarrow m &=& x \leftarrow m & \\ x = n\,; x = m &=& 0 \quad (\text{if } n \neq m) & \\ \left(\sum_n x = n\right) &=& 1 & \end{array}$$

Intuitively, the first axiom states that assignments to distinct fields may be done in either order. The third axiom says that when a packet is duplicated, the values of the fields in the head packet are preserved in the history. The other axioms have similar intuitive interpretations.

There are many models that satisfy the NetKAT axioms, but the standard model of NetKAT is formulated in terms of packet-processing functions. A *packet* $\pi$ is a record whose fields assign constant values $n$ to fields $f$. A *packet history* is a nonempty sequence of packets

$$\pi_1 :: \pi_2 :: \cdots :: \pi_k,$$

in which the *head packet* is $\pi_1$. Operationally, only the head packet exists in the network, but in the logic we keep track of the packet's history to enable precise specification of forwarding behavior involving specific paths through the network. Every NetKAT expression $e$ denotes a function:

$$[\![e]\!] : H \to 2^H$$

where $H$ is the set of all packet histories. Intuitively, the expression $e$ takes an input packet history $\sigma$ and produces a set of output packet histories $[\![e]\!](\sigma)$.

The semantics of the primitive actions and tests are as follows. For a packet history $\pi :: \sigma$ with head packet $\pi$,

$$\begin{aligned}
[\![x \leftarrow n]\!](\pi :: \sigma) &= \{\pi[n/x] :: \sigma\} \\
[\![x = n]\!](\pi :: \sigma) &= \begin{cases} \{\pi :: \sigma\} & \text{if } \pi(x) = n \\ \varnothing & \text{if } \pi(x) \neq n \end{cases} \\
[\![\mathsf{dup}]\!](\pi :: \sigma) &= \{\pi :: \pi :: \sigma\}
\end{aligned}$$

where $\pi[n/x]$ denotes packet $\pi$ with the field $x$ rebound to the value $n$. Note that a test $x = n$ drops the packet if the test is not satisfied and passes it through unaltered if it is satisfied—i.e., tests behave as filters on packets. The dup construct duplicates the head packet $\pi$, yielding a fresh copy that can be modified by other constructs. Hence, in this standard model, the dup construct can be used to encode paths through the network, with each occurrence of dup marking an intermediate hop.

The KAT operations are interpreted as follows:

$$\begin{aligned}
[\![p + q]\!](\sigma) &= [\![p]\!](\sigma) \cup [\![q]\!](\sigma) \\
[\![p \cdot q]\!](\sigma) &= \bigcup_{\tau \in [\![p]\!](\sigma)} [\![q]\!](\tau) \\
[\![p^*]\!](\sigma) &= \bigcup_n [\![p^n]\!](\sigma) \\
[\![1]\!](\sigma) &= \{\sigma\} \\
[\![0]\!](\sigma) &= \varnothing \\
[\![\neg b]\!](\sigma) &= \begin{cases} \{\sigma\} & \text{if } [\![b]\!](\sigma) = \varnothing \\ \varnothing & \text{if } [\![b]\!](\sigma) = \{\sigma\} \end{cases}
\end{aligned}$$

The interpretation of sequential composition is often called *Kleisli composition*, as it is composition in the Kleisli category of the powerset monad. The $+$ operator accumulates actions. Thus the expression $(port \leftarrow 8) + (port \leftarrow 9)$ describes the behavior of a switch that outputs a copy of the packet on ports 8 and 9. Note that this is a departure from the usual Kleene algebra interpretation of $+$ as nondeterministic choice—NetKAT treats it as conjuctive rather than disjunctive. Nevertheless, it is not difficult to show that the axioms of KAT and NetKAT are sound over this interpretation.

The proof of completeness is more difficult, and uses a language model that plays a similar role as the regular sets of strings do for KA and the regular sets of guarded strings do for KAT [1]. The language model for NetKAT consists of the regular sets of *reduced strings* of the form

$$\alpha p_0 \,\mathsf{dup}\, p_1 \,\mathsf{dup}\, p_2 \cdots p_{n-1} \,\mathsf{dup}\, p_n, \quad n \geq 0,$$

where $\alpha$ is a *complete test* $x_1 = n_1 ; \cdots ; x_k = n_k$, the $p_i$ are *complete assignments* $x_1 \leftarrow n_1 ; \cdots ; x_k \leftarrow n_k$, and $x_1, \ldots, x_k$ are all of the fields in some arbitrary but fixed order.[1] Every NetKAT expression can be rewritten to an equivalent *reduced expression* in which every test is a complete test and every assignment is a complete assignment. Likewise, every string of primitive actions and tests is equivalent to a reduced string modulo the NetKAT axioms. The set of reduced strings is described by the expression $\mathsf{At} \cdot P \cdot (\mathsf{dup} \cdot P)^*$, where At is the set of complete tests and $P$ the set of complete assignments. The complete tests are the atoms (minimal nonzero elements) of the Boolean algebra generated by the primitive tests. Complete tests and complete assignments are in one-to-one correspondence determined by the sequence of values $n_1, \ldots, n_k$.

It is straightforward to show that every NetKAT expression $e$ can be interpreted as a regular set of reduced strings $G(e)$. The NetKAT axioms can be expressed in a simpler form for reduced strings. Let $\alpha_p$ be the complete test corresponding to the complete assignment $p$. Likewise, let $p_\beta$ be the complete assignment corresponding to the complete test $\beta$. The NetKAT axioms for reduced strings are as follows:

$$\alpha \,\mathsf{dup} = \mathsf{dup}\, \alpha \qquad p\alpha_p = p \qquad \alpha p_\alpha = \alpha$$

$$\alpha\alpha = \alpha \qquad \alpha\beta = 0,\ \alpha \neq \beta \qquad qp = p \qquad \textstyle\sum_{\alpha \in \mathsf{At}} \alpha = 1.$$

See the previous paper on NetKAT [1] for a comprehensive treatment of the language model, including proofs of the claims above.

## 3. NetKAT Coalgebra

Coalgebra is a general framework for modeling and reasoning about state-based systems [4, 5, 30, 33, 36]. A central aspect of coalgebra is the characterization of equivalence in terms of *bisimulation*. Our work is motivated by recent experiences with bisimulation-based decision procedures for KA and KAT [4, 5, 30]. However, to apply these techniques to NetKAT, we must first develop its coalgebraic theory. This will provide a combinatorial view of NetKAT similar to classical automata theory for KA and automata on guarded strings for KAT. This section develops this theory, which provides the necessary structure for our bisimulation-based decision procedure.

For background on the general theory of coalgebra in modeling state-based systems, see the survey article by Rutten [34]. The only general knowledge needed from this domain is the following:

1. Coalgebras are usually defined in terms of a set of *states* along with *observation* and *continuation* maps. The observation map gives information about each state while the continuation map specifies transition(s) from one state to the next states(s). The nature of these maps varies depending on the type of the system being modeled.
2. Two states are considered *bisimilar* if the observation maps yield identical information for both states and the continuation map leads again to bisimilar states.
3. A *homomorphism* is a map between coalgebras that preserves the structure of observations and continuations.
4. There is often a *final coalgebra* into which there is a unique homomorphism from any other coalgebra of the same type. Two states are bisimilar if and only if this homomorphism maps them to the same state in the final coalgebra.

As an example, a deterministic automaton over a finite alphabet $\Sigma$ is a coalgebra with an observation map $S \to 2$ that indicates whether a state is an accepting state and a continuation map $S \times \Sigma \to S$ that specifies the transitions of the automaton. The final coalgebra is $2^{\Sigma^*}$, the powerset of the set of all strings over $\Sigma$, with observation and continuation maps given by the (semantic) Brzozowski derivative $\varepsilon : 2^{\Sigma^*} \to 2$ such that $\varepsilon(L) = 1$ if and only if $L$ contains the null string and $\delta(L, a) = \{w \mid aw \in L\}$ for $a \in \Sigma$ and $w \in \Sigma^*$. The unique homomorphism from an

[1] Note that we will use metavariables $p$ to range over NetKAT expressions as well as complete tests. The intended meaning will be clear from context.

automaton to the final coalgebra takes a state $s$ to the set of strings that would be accepted by the automaton if $s$ were the start state.

There is also a *syntactic* Brzozowski derivative defined inductively on regular expressions Exp over $\Sigma$:

$$D_a(e_1{+}e_2) = D_a(e_1) + D_a(e_2)$$
$$D_a(e_1e_2) = D_a(e_1)\cdot e_2 + E(e_1)\cdot D_a(e_2)$$
$$D_a(e^*) = D_a(e)\cdot e^*$$
$$D_a(1) = D_a(0) = 0 \qquad D_a(b) = [b = a]$$

$$E(e_1{+}e_2) = E(e_1) + E(e_2)$$
$$E(e_1e_2) = E(e_1)\cdot E(e_2)$$
$$E(e^*) = 1$$
$$E(1) = 1 \qquad E(0) = E(a) = 0,\ a \in \Sigma,$$

where $[\varphi] = 1$ or 0 according as $\varphi$ is true or false, respectively. The map taking a regular expression $e$ to the set of strings it represents is the unique homomorphism to the final coalgebra.

### 3.1 Definitions

A NetKAT coalgebra consists of a set of states $S$ along with *continuation* and *observation maps*

$$\delta_{\alpha\beta} : S \to S \qquad\qquad \varepsilon_{\alpha\beta} : S \to 2$$

for $\alpha, \beta \in \mathsf{At}$. A deterministic NetKAT automaton is simply a finite-state NetKAT coalgebra with a distinguished start state $s \in S$. (There are also corresponding notions of nondeterministic automaton and a determinization procedure, but we will not need these for our formal development in this paper.) The inputs to the automaton are reduced strings belonging to the set $U = \mathsf{At}\cdot P\cdot(\mathsf{dup}\cdot P)^*$. That is, $U$ contains strings of the form

$$\alpha p_0\ \mathsf{dup}\ p_1\ \mathsf{dup}\cdots\mathsf{dup}\ p_n$$

for some $n \geq 0$. Intuitively, $\delta_{\alpha\beta}$ attempts to consume $\alpha p_\beta$ dup from the front of the input string and move to a new state with a residual input string. This succeeds if and only if the reduced string is of the form $\alpha p_\beta\ \mathsf{dup}\ x$ for some $x \in (P\cdot\mathsf{dup})^*\cdot P$, in which case the automaton moves to a new state as determined by $\delta_{\alpha\beta}$ with residual input string $\beta x$. The observation map $\varepsilon_{\alpha\beta}$ determines whether the string $\alpha p_\beta$ should be accepted in the current state.

Formally, acceptance is determined by a coinductively defined predicate $\mathsf{Accept} : S \times U \to 2$:

$$\mathsf{Accept}(t, \alpha p_\beta\ \mathsf{dup}\ x) = \mathsf{Accept}(\delta_{\alpha\beta}(t), \beta x)$$
$$\mathsf{Accept}(t, \alpha p_\beta) = \varepsilon_{\alpha\beta}(t).$$

A reduced string $x \in U$ is *accepted* by the automaton if $\mathsf{Accept}(s, x)$, where $s$ is the start state. A NetKAT coalgebra is a coalgebra for the set endofunctor

$$FX = X^{\mathsf{At}\times\mathsf{At}} \times 2^{\mathsf{At}\times\mathsf{At}} \tag{3.1}$$

The continuation and observation maps comprise the structure map of the coalgebra:

$$(\delta, \varepsilon) : X \to FX.$$

One can see immediately from equation (3.1) that $X^{\mathsf{At}\times\mathsf{At}}$ and $2^{\mathsf{At}\times\mathsf{At}}$ are isomorphic to the families of square matrices over $X$ and 2, respectively, with rows and columns indexed by At. Indeed, in §5, we will exploit the one-to-one correspondence between $P$ and At to express $\delta$ and $\varepsilon$ in matrix form.

The reader familiar with coalgebra might notice that the final coalgebra of the above functor is not exactly reduced NetKAT strings. However, the semantics of a NetKAT automaton as acceptor of reduced NetKAT strings can be recovered coalgebraically by doing a generalized powerset construction [38] in which one of the atoms in the argument of $\delta$ is hidden in the state. This is analogous to the situation for nondeterministic finite automata: these are (compact) acceptors of languages which need to be made deterministic in order to recover language semantics as the canonical equivalence. For space reasons and to keep the presentation simple, we will not explain the generalized powerset construction involved in recovering the language semantics categorically, but rather give the concrete definitions of the semantic map and syntactic structure on expressions.

### 3.2 The Brzozowski Derivative

This section develops a variant of the Brzozowski derivative for NetKAT. The derivative comes in two versions: semantic and syntactic. The semantic version is defined on subsets of $U$ and gives rise to a NetKAT coalgebra $(2^U, \delta, \varepsilon)$. The syntactic version is defined on expressions and also gives rise to a coalgebra $(\mathsf{Exp}, D, E)$. There is a unique language interpretation $G : \mathsf{Exp} \to 2^U$.

***Language Semantics.*** The language semantics for NetKAT is given by the semantic derivative:

$$\delta_{\alpha\beta} : 2^U \to 2^U \qquad\qquad \varepsilon_{\alpha\beta} : 2^U \to 2$$
$$\delta_{\alpha\beta}(A) = \{\beta x \mid \alpha p_\beta\ \mathsf{dup}\ x \in A\} \quad \varepsilon_{\alpha\beta}(A) = [\alpha p_\beta \in A].$$

***Syntactic Coalgebra.*** There is also a syntactic derivative:

$$D_{\alpha\beta} : \mathsf{Exp} \to \mathsf{Exp} \qquad\qquad E_{\alpha\beta} : \mathsf{Exp} \to 2,$$

where Exp is the set of reduced NetKAT expressions.[2] It is defined inductively as follows:

$$D_{\alpha\beta}(p) = 0 \qquad D_{\alpha\beta}(b) = 0 \qquad D_{\alpha\beta}(\mathsf{dup}) = \alpha\cdot[\alpha = \beta]$$
$$D_{\alpha\beta}(e_1 + e_2) = D_{\alpha\beta}(e_1) + D_{\alpha\beta}(e_2)$$
$$D_{\alpha\beta}(e_1e_2) = D_{\alpha\beta}(e_1)\cdot e_2 + \sum_\gamma E_{\alpha\gamma}(e_1)\cdot D_{\gamma\beta}(e_2)$$
$$D_{\alpha\beta}(e^*) = D_{\alpha\beta}(e)\cdot e^* + \sum_\gamma E_{\alpha\gamma}(e)\cdot D_{\gamma\beta}(e^*)$$

$$E_{\alpha\beta}(p) = [p = p_\beta] \qquad E_{\alpha\beta}(b) = [\alpha = \beta \leq b]$$
$$E_{\alpha\beta}(\mathsf{dup}) = 0 \qquad E_{\alpha\beta}(e_1 + e_2) = E_{\alpha\beta}(e_1) + E_{\alpha\beta}(e_2)$$
$$E_{\alpha\beta}(e_1e_2) = \sum_\gamma E_{\alpha\gamma}(e_1)\cdot E_{\gamma\beta}(e_2)$$
$$E_{\alpha\beta}(e^*) = [\alpha = \beta] + \sum_\gamma E_{\alpha\gamma}(e)\cdot E_{\gamma\beta}(e^*).$$

Note that the definitions for * are circular, but both are well-defined if we take the least fixpoint of the system of equations.

## 4. Kleene's Theorem for NetKAT

In this section we prove that a subset of $U$ is $G(e)$ for some NetKAT expression $e$ if and only if it is the set of strings accepted by some finite NetKAT automaton. This result is the generalization of Kleene's theorem, which relates regular expressions and automata, to NetKAT.

[2] Readers familiar with previous work on NetKAT [1] may notice that the syntactic derivative is actually defined on a superset of reduced NetKAT expressions that includes arbitrary tests $b$. The definition given here illustrates the connection to previous work on derivatives in the context of KAT [23] and remains correct when restricted to complete tests.

### 4.1 From Automata to Expressions

Let $M = (S, \delta, \varepsilon, s)$ be a finite NetKAT automaton. Consider a graph $H$ with nodes $(S \times \mathsf{At}) \cup \{\mathsf{halt}\}$ and labeled edges

$$(u, \alpha) \xrightarrow{p_\beta \mathsf{dup}} (v, \beta), \qquad \text{if } \delta_{\alpha\beta}(u) = v$$
$$(u, \alpha) \xrightarrow{p_\beta} \mathsf{halt}, \qquad \text{if } \varepsilon_{\alpha\beta}(u) = 1.$$

We claim that for $x \in (P \cdot \mathsf{dup})^* \cdot P$,

$$(t, \alpha) \xrightarrow{x} \mathsf{halt} \Leftrightarrow \mathsf{Accept}(t, \alpha x). \tag{4.1}$$

This can be proved by induction on the length of $x$. For the basis,

$$(t, \alpha) \xrightarrow{p_\beta} \mathsf{halt} \Leftrightarrow \varepsilon_{\alpha\beta}(t) = 1 \Leftrightarrow \mathsf{Accept}(t, \alpha p_\beta).$$

For the induction step,

$$\begin{aligned}(t, \alpha) \xrightarrow{p_\beta \mathsf{dup} x} \mathsf{halt} &\Leftrightarrow \exists u\, (t, \alpha) \xrightarrow{p_\beta \mathsf{dup}} (u, \beta) \xrightarrow{x} \mathsf{halt} \\ &\Leftrightarrow \exists u\, \delta_{\alpha\beta}(t) = u \wedge \mathsf{Accept}(u, \beta x) \\ &\Leftrightarrow \mathsf{Accept}(\delta_{\alpha\beta}(t), \beta x) \\ &\Leftrightarrow \mathsf{Accept}(t, \alpha p_\beta\ \mathsf{dup}\ x).\end{aligned}$$

The set of labels of paths in $H$ from $(t, \alpha)$ to $\mathsf{halt}$ is a regular subset of $(P \cdot \mathsf{dup})^* \cdot P$ and is described by a regular expression $e(t, \alpha)$. These expressions can be computed by taking the star of $H$ considered as a square matrix. By (4.1), the set of strings accepted by $M$ is the regular subset of $U$ described by $e = \sum_\alpha \alpha \cdot e(s, \alpha)$.

As shown previously [1], if $R(e) \subseteq U$, where $R$ is the canonical interpretation of regular expressions as regular sets of strings, then $R(e) = G(e)$. Hence, we have the following theorem.

**Theorem 1.** *Let $M$ be a finite NetKAT automaton. There exists a NetKAT expression $e$ such that the set of reduced strings accepted by $M$ is $G(e)$.*

### 4.2 From Expressions to Automata

For the other direction, we show how to construct a finite NetKAT automaton $M_e$ from an expression $e$. The states of the automaton are NetKAT expressions modulo associativity, commutativity, and idempotence (ACI), with $e$ as the start state. The continuation and observation maps are the syntactic derivative introduced in §3.2.

**Lemma 1.** *The set accepted by $M_e$ is $G(e)$.*

*Proof.* By Lemma 4, $G$ is a coalgebra homomorphism from the syntactic coalagebra $(\mathsf{Exp}, D, E)$ to the set-theoretic coalgebra $(2^U, \delta, \varepsilon)$. Proceeding by induction on the length of the string, we have the following:

$$\begin{aligned}\mathsf{Accept}(e, \alpha p_\beta) &\Leftrightarrow E_{\alpha\beta}(e) = 1 \\ &\Leftrightarrow G(E_{\alpha\beta}(e)) = 1 \\ &\Leftrightarrow \varepsilon_{\alpha\beta}(G(e)) = 1 \\ &\Leftrightarrow \alpha p_\beta \in G(e), \\ \mathsf{Accept}(e, \alpha p_\beta\ \mathsf{dup}\ x) &\Leftrightarrow \mathsf{Accept}(D_{\alpha\beta}(e), \beta x) \\ &\Leftrightarrow \beta x \in G(D_{\alpha\beta}(e)) \\ &\Leftrightarrow \beta x \in \delta_{\alpha\beta}(G(e)) \\ &\Leftrightarrow \alpha p_\beta\ \mathsf{dup}\ x \in G(e).\end{aligned}$$ □

It remains to show that $M_e$ is finite. This follows from the fact that $e$ has finitely many derivatives up to ACI. We defer the proof of this fact to Lemma 6 in the next section, as it depends on some details of our data representation.

**Theorem 2.** *For every NetKAT expression $e$, there is a deterministic NetKAT automaton $M_e$ with at most $|\mathsf{At}| \cdot 2^\ell$ states accepting the set $G(e)$, where $\ell$ is the number of occurrences of* dup *in $e$.*

## 5. Term and Automata Representations

In this section, we develop a collection of concrete structures that are useful for representing NetKAT automata and will lead to a practical implementation. They also provide further theoretical insights into the structure of the NetKAT language.

### 5.1 Matrices

The reader has probably noticed that many of the operations used to define the syntactic derivative $D_{\alpha\beta}$ and $E_{\alpha\beta}$ closely resemble matrix operations. Indeed, if we regard the types of the coalgebra operations as having the following types:

$$\delta : X \to X^{\mathsf{At} \times \mathsf{At}} \qquad \varepsilon : X \to 2^{\mathsf{At} \times \mathsf{At}},$$

then we can view $\delta(t)$ as an $\mathsf{At} \times \mathsf{At}$ matrix over $X$ and $\varepsilon(t)$ as an $\mathsf{At} \times \mathsf{At}$ matrix over 2. Moreover, if $X$ is a KAT, then the family of $\mathsf{At} \times \mathsf{At}$ matrices over $X$ again forms a KAT, denoted $\mathsf{Mat}(\mathsf{At}, X)$, under the standard matrix operations [9]. Thus we have

$$\delta : X \to \mathsf{Mat}(\mathsf{At}, X) \qquad \varepsilon : X \to \mathsf{Mat}(\mathsf{At}, 2).$$

So the syntactic coalgebra defined in §3.2 takes the following form:

$$\begin{gathered}D(p) = 0 \qquad D(b) = 0 \qquad D(\mathsf{dup}) = J \\ D(e_1 + e_2) = D(e_1) + D(e_2) \\ D(e_1 e_2) = D(e_1) \cdot I(e_2) + E(e_1) \cdot D(e_2) \\ D(e^*) = E(e^*) \cdot D(e) \cdot I(e^*),\end{gathered}$$

where $I(e)$ is the diagonal matrix with $e$ on the main diagonal and 0 elsewhere and $J$ is the matrix with $\alpha$ on the main diagonal in position $\alpha\alpha$ and 0 elsewhere. Similarly, we have:[3]

$$\begin{gathered}E(\mathsf{dup}) = 0 \qquad E(e_1 + e_2) = E(e_1) + E(e_2) \\ E(e_1 e_2) = E(e_1) \cdot E(e_2) \qquad E(e^*) = E(e)^*.\end{gathered}$$

Note that in this form $E$ becomes a KAT homomorphism from $\mathsf{Exp}$ to $\mathsf{Mat}(\mathsf{At}, 2)$.

Likewise, we can regard the set-theoretic coalgebra presented in §3.2 as having type:

$$\delta : 2^U \to \mathsf{Mat}(\mathsf{At}, 2^U) \qquad \varepsilon : 2^U \to \mathsf{Mat}(\mathsf{At}, 2).$$

Again, in this form, $\varepsilon$ becomes a KAT homomorphism:

**Lemma 2.**

(i) $\varepsilon(1) = I$
(ii) $\varepsilon(A \cup B) = \varepsilon(A) + \varepsilon(B)$
(iii) $\varepsilon(A \cdot B) = \varepsilon(A) \cdot \varepsilon(B)$
(iv) $\varepsilon(A^*) = \varepsilon(A)^*$

*Proof.* These properties follow straightforwardly from the definitions in §3.2. For example, for (iii) and (iv), we have

$$\begin{aligned}\varepsilon(AB)_{\alpha\beta} &= [\alpha p_\beta \in AB] \\ &= [\exists \gamma\ \alpha p_\gamma \in A \wedge \gamma p_\beta \in B] \\ &= \sum_\gamma [\alpha p_\gamma \in A] \cdot [\gamma p_\beta \in B] \\ &= \sum_\gamma \varepsilon(A)_{\alpha\gamma} \cdot \varepsilon(B)_{\gamma\beta} \\ &= (\varepsilon(A) \cdot \varepsilon(B))_{\alpha\beta}\end{aligned}$$

$$\varepsilon(A^*) = \varepsilon(\textstyle\bigcup_n A^n) = \sum_n \varepsilon(A)^n = \varepsilon(A)^*.$$ □

[3] Here, we elide the cases for tests $b$ and complete assignments $p$.

The next lemma characterizes $\delta$ on the regular operators.

**Lemma 3.**

(i) $\delta(\bigcup_n A_n) = \sum_n \delta(A_n)$
(ii) $\delta(AB) = \delta(A) \cdot I(B) + \varepsilon(A) \cdot \delta(B)$
(iii) $\delta(A^*) = \varepsilon(A^*) \cdot \delta(A) \cdot I(A^*)$

*where $I(A)$ is the matrix with the set $A$ on the main diagonal and $\varnothing$ elsewhere, and the matrix sum in (i) is componentwise union.*

*Proof.* We argue (ii) and (iii) explicitly; (i) follows from linearity.

(ii) By definition, $\delta_{\alpha\beta}(AB) = \{\beta x \mid \alpha p_\beta \text{ dup } x \in AB\}$. To show that $\alpha p_\beta$ dup $x \in AB$, the string must be the product of two reduced strings, one from $A$ and one from $B$. Depending on which of these strings contains the first occurrence of dup, one of the following must occur: (1) there exists $\gamma$ such that $\alpha p_\beta \text{ dup } x = \alpha p_\gamma \cdot \gamma p_\beta \text{ dup } x$ with $\alpha p_\gamma \in A$ and $\gamma p_\beta \text{ dup } x \in B$; or (2) there exist $\gamma$, $y$, and $z$ such that $\alpha p_\beta \text{ dup } x = \alpha p_\beta \text{ dup } y p_\gamma \cdot \gamma z$ with $\alpha p_\beta \text{ dup } y p_\gamma \in A$, $\gamma z \in B$, and $x = y p_\gamma \gamma z$.

In the first case, we have $\varepsilon_{\alpha\gamma}(A) = 1$ and $\beta x \in \delta_{\gamma\beta}(B)$, hence $\beta x \in \varepsilon_{\alpha\gamma}(A) \cdot \delta_{\gamma\beta}(B)$. In the second case, we have $\beta y p_\gamma \in \delta_{\alpha\beta}(A)$ and $\gamma z \in B$, hence $\beta x = \beta y_\gamma \gamma z \in \delta_{\alpha\beta}(A) \cdot B$. Thus

$$\delta_{\alpha\beta}(AB) = \delta_{\alpha\beta}(A) \cdot B \cup \textstyle\bigcup_\gamma \varepsilon_{\alpha\gamma}(A) \cdot \delta_{\gamma\beta}(B).$$

Abstracting over indices, we obtain the matrix equation (ii).

(iii) From (i) and (ii):

$$\begin{aligned}\delta(A^*) &= \delta(1 + AA^*) = 0 + \delta(AA^*)\\ &= \delta(A) \cdot I(A^*) + \varepsilon(A) \cdot \delta(A^*).\end{aligned}$$

The derivative is the least fixpoint of this equation, which by an axiom of KAT is the right-hand side of (iii). □

The following lemma says that $G$ is a coalgebra morphism from the syntactic coalgebra $(\mathsf{Exp}, D, E)$ to $(2^U, \delta, \varepsilon)$.

**Lemma 4.**

(i) $G(D(e)) = \delta(G(e))$
(ii) $E(e) = \varepsilon(G(e))$

*where $G$ is extended componentwise to matrices.*

*Proof.* By induction on $e$.

(i) For primitive terms $p$, $b$ and dup,

$$\begin{aligned}G(D_{\alpha\beta}(p)) &= G(0) = \varnothing\\ &= \{\beta x \mid \alpha p_\beta \text{ dup } x \in \{\gamma p \mid \gamma \in \mathsf{At}\}\}\\ &= \delta_{\alpha\beta}(\{\gamma p \mid \gamma \in \mathsf{At}\}) = \delta_{\alpha\beta}(G(p))\\ G(D_{\alpha\beta}(b)) &= G(0) = \varnothing\\ &= \{\beta x \mid \alpha p_\beta \text{ dup } x \in \{\beta p_\beta \mid \beta \le b\}\}\\ &= \delta_{\alpha\beta}(\{\beta p_\beta \mid \beta \le b\}) = \delta_{\alpha\beta}(G(b)).\\ G(D_{\alpha\beta}(\mathsf{dup})) &= G(\alpha \cdot [\alpha = \beta])\\ &= \{\beta p_\beta \mid \alpha = \beta\}\\ &= \{\beta x \mid \alpha p_\beta \text{ dup } x \in \{\gamma p_\gamma \text{ dup } p_\gamma \mid \gamma \in \mathsf{At}\}\}\\ &= \delta_{\alpha\beta}(\{\gamma p_\gamma \text{ dup } p_\gamma \mid \gamma \in \mathsf{At}\})\\ &= \delta_{\alpha\beta}(G(\mathsf{dup}))\end{aligned}$$

The case $e_1 + e_2$ is straightforward, since $G$, $\delta$, and $D$ are linear. For products, using Lemma 3 (ii),

$$\begin{aligned}G(D(e_1e_2)) &= G(D(e_1) \cdot I(e_2)) + G(E(e_1) \cdot D(e_2))\\ &= G(D(e_1)) \cdot G(I(e_2)) + G(E(e_1)) \cdot G(D(e_2))\\ &= \delta(G(e_1)) \cdot I(G(e_2)) + \varepsilon(G(e_1)) \cdot \delta(G(e_2))\\ &= \delta(G(e_1) \cdot G(e_2))\\ &= \delta(G(e_1e_2))\end{aligned}$$

$$\begin{aligned}lrsp(e_1 + e_2) &= lrsp(e_1) \cup lrsp(e_2)\\ lrsp(e_1e_2) &= \{(\ell, re_2) \mid (\ell, r) \in lrsp(e_1)\} \cup\\ &\quad\ \{(e_1\ell, r) \mid (\ell, r) \in lrsp(e_2)\}\\ lrsp(e^*) &= \{(e^*\ell, re^*) \mid (\ell, r) \in lrsp(e)\}\\ lrsp(\mathsf{dup}) &= \{(1, 1)\}\\ lrsp(b) &= lrsp(p) = \varnothing.\end{aligned}$$

**Figure 1.** NetKAT left-right spines.

For star, the system defining $D(e^*)$ is

$$D(e^*) = D(e) \cdot I(e^*) + E(e) \cdot D(e^*)$$

whose least solution is

$$D(e^*) = E(e^*) \cdot D(e) \cdot I(e^*).$$

Using Lemma 3 (iii),

$$\begin{aligned}G(D(e^*)) &= G(E(e^*) \cdot D(e) \cdot I(e^*))\\ &= G(E(e^*)) \cdot G(D(e)) \cdot G(I(e^*))\\ &= \varepsilon(G(e)^*) \cdot \delta(G(e)) \cdot I(G(e)^*)\\ &= \delta(G(e^*)).\end{aligned}$$

(ii) For $p$, $b$ and dup,

$$\begin{aligned}E_{\alpha\beta}(p) &= [p = p_\beta]\\ &= \varepsilon_{\alpha\beta}(\{\gamma p \mid \gamma \in \mathsf{At}\}) = \varepsilon(G(p)).\\ E_{\alpha\beta}(b) &= [\alpha = \beta \le b]\\ &= \varepsilon_{\alpha\beta}(\{\alpha p_\alpha \mid \alpha \le b\})\\ &= \varepsilon_{\alpha\beta}(G(b)).\\ E_{\alpha\beta}(\mathsf{dup}) &= 0\\ &= \varepsilon_{\alpha\beta}(\{\gamma p_\gamma \text{ dup } p_\gamma \mid \gamma \in \mathsf{At}\})\\ &= E_{\alpha\beta}(G(\mathsf{dup}))\end{aligned}$$

The case $e_1 + e_2$ is straightforward, since $G$, $\varepsilon$, and $E$ are linear. For products, using Lemma 2 (iii),

$$\begin{aligned}E_{\alpha\beta}(e_1e_2) &= \sum_\gamma E_{\alpha\gamma}(e_1) \cdot E_{\gamma\beta}(e_2)\\ &= (E(e_1) \cdot E(e_2))_{\alpha\beta}\\ &= (\varepsilon(G(e_1)) \cdot \varepsilon(G(e_2)))_{\alpha\beta}\\ &= (\varepsilon(G(e_1) \cdot G(e_2)))_{\alpha\beta}\\ &= \varepsilon_{\alpha\beta}(G(e_1e_2))\end{aligned}$$

For star, using Lemma 2 (iv),

$$E(e^*) = E(e)^* = \varepsilon(G(e))^* = \varepsilon(G(e^*)). \quad \square$$

### 5.2 Spines

As was just shown, matrices provide an elegant and compact way to express and encode NetKAT derivatives. It turns out that the set of derivatives of an expression is finite and can be bounded as a function of the size of the expression itself. To prove this, we develop the notion of the *spines* of a term $e$ and show that derivatives can always be represented as sums of spines. In our implementation, both of these representations are put to work: we encode the Brzozowski derivative using matrices whose elements are sets of spines.

Intuitively, the spines of an expression can be obtained by locating the occurrences of dup and forming a pair of expressions built from the expressions appearing to the left and right of the dup. The left component of the pair is called the *left spine* and the right component is called the *right spine*. The spines are related to the derivative in the following way: the left spine represents the expression that must be consumed before the occurrence of dup can be consumed itself, and the right spine indicates the expression that remains after doing so. For example, the set of spines of the expression $a \cdot \mathsf{dup} \cdot b$ is just $\{(a, b)\}$, and indeed, $a$ is the expression that must be consumed before the dup and $b$ is the expression that remains after it is consumed.

The inductive definition of the left-right spines of $e$, denoted $lrsp(e)$, is given in Figure 1. In many situations, just the right spines are useful. They can be defined more simply as follows (to lighten the notation, we write $A \cdot e$ for $\{de \mid d \in A\}$ and $e \cdot A$ for $\{ed \mid d \in A\}$ where $A \subseteq \mathsf{Exp}$ and $e \in \mathsf{Exp}$):

$$\begin{aligned} rsp(e_1 + e_2) &= rsp(e_1) \cup rsp(e_2) \\ rsp(e_1 e_2) &= rsp(e_1) \cdot e_2 \cup rsp(e_2) \\ rsp(e^*) &= rsp(e) \cdot e^* \\ rsp(\mathsf{dup}) &= \{1\} \\ rsp(b) &= rsp(p) = \varnothing. \end{aligned}$$

It is easy to show that every right spine in $rsp(e)$ has the form $1 \cdot e_1 \cdot e_2 \cdots e_n$, where the $e_i$ are subexpressions of $e$, and that there is one spine of $e$ for every occurrence of dup in $e$.

The next lemma relates the derivative of $e$ and its right spines:

**Lemma 5.** *For any $\alpha, \beta$,*

$$D_{\alpha\beta}(e) = \{\beta r \mid (\ell, r) \in lrsp(e),\ E_{\alpha\beta}(\ell) = 1\}.$$

*Thus the derivative $D_{\alpha\beta}(e)$ is a sum of terms of the form $\beta r$, where $r \in rsp(e)$.*

*Proof.* The proof is by induction on the structure of $e$. Abusing notation slightly by representing sums of terms as sets,[4] we argue the cases for products and star explicitly.

For products, we have the following equalities:

$$\begin{aligned} & D_{\alpha\beta}(e_1 e_2) \\ &= D_{\alpha\beta}(e_1) \cdot e_2 \cup \textstyle\bigcup_{E_{\alpha\gamma}(e_1)=1} D_{\gamma\beta}(e_2) \\ &= \{\beta r \mid (\ell, r) \in lrsp(e_1),\ E_{\alpha\beta}(\ell) = 1\} \cdot e_2 \\ &\qquad \cup \textstyle\bigcup_{E_{\alpha\gamma}(e_1)=1} \{\beta r \mid (\ell, r) \in lrsp(e_2),\ E_{\gamma\beta}(\ell) = 1\} \\ &= \{\beta r e_2 \mid (\ell, r) \in lrsp(e_1),\ E_{\alpha\beta}(\ell) = 1\} \\ &\qquad \cup \{\beta r \mid (\ell, r) \in lrsp(e_2),\ E_{\alpha\beta}(e_1 \ell) = 1\} \\ &= \{\beta r \mid (\ell, r) \in lrsp(e_1 e_2),\ E_{\alpha\beta}(\ell) = 1\}, \end{aligned}$$

where we use the induction hypothesis in the second step.

For star, we have the following equalities:

$$\begin{aligned} & D_{\alpha\beta}(e^*) \\ &= \textstyle\bigcup_{E_{\alpha\gamma}(e^*)=1} D_{\gamma\beta}(e) \cdot e^* \\ &= \textstyle\bigcup_{E_{\alpha\gamma}(e^*)=1} \{\beta r \mid (\ell, r) \in lrsp(e),\ E_{\gamma\beta}(\ell) = 1\} \cdot e^* \\ &= \{\beta r e^* \mid (\ell, r) \in lrsp(e),\ E_{\alpha\beta}(e^* \ell) = 1\} \\ &= \{\beta r \mid (\ell, r) \in lrsp(e^*),\ E_{\alpha\beta}(\ell) = 1\}. \end{aligned}$$ □

The final lemma presented in this section shows that the spines of spines of $e$ are themselves spines of $e$. Hence, taking repeated derivatives does not introduce new terms.

**Lemma 6.** *If $d \in rsp(e)$, then $rsp(\beta d) \subseteq rsp(e)$.*

[4] This is a convenient abuse which we take with impunity as we are working modulo ACI. The representation of the Brzozowski derivative in this form is often called the *Antimirov derivative*.

*Proof.* The argument for sums is straightforward. For products,

$$\begin{aligned} & d \in rsp(e_1 e_2) = rsp(e_1) \cdot e_2 \cup rsp(e_2) \\ &\Rightarrow d \in rsp(e_1) \cdot e_2 \text{ or } d \in rsp(e_2) \\ &\Rightarrow (d = c e_2 \text{ and } c \in rsp(e_1)) \text{ or } d \in rsp(e_2) \\ &\Rightarrow (d = c e_2 \text{ and } rsp(\beta c) \subseteq rsp(e_1)) \\ &\qquad \text{or } rsp(\beta d) \subseteq rsp(e_2) \\ &\Rightarrow rsp(\beta d) = rsp(\beta c e_2) = rsp(\beta c) \cdot e_2 \cup rsp(e_2) \\ &\qquad \subseteq rsp(e_1) \cdot e_2 \cup rsp(e_2) = rsp(e_1 e_2) \\ &\qquad \text{or } rsp(\beta d) \subseteq rsp(e_2) \subseteq rsp(e_1 e_2) \\ &\Rightarrow rsp(\beta d) \subseteq rsp(e_1 e_2). \end{aligned}$$

For star,

$$\begin{aligned} & d \in rsp(e^*) = rsp(e) \cdot e^* \\ &\Rightarrow d = c e^* \text{ and } c \in rsp(e) \\ &\Rightarrow rsp(\beta d) = rsp(\beta c e^*) = rsp(\beta c) e^* \cup rsp(e^*) \\ &\qquad \subseteq rsp(e) \cdot e^* \cup rsp(e^*) = rsp(e^*). \end{aligned}$$

For dup,

$$\begin{aligned} & d \in rsp(\mathsf{dup}) = \{1\} \\ &\Rightarrow d = 1 \\ &\Rightarrow rsp(\beta d) = rsp(\beta) = \varnothing \subseteq rsp(\mathsf{dup}). \end{aligned}$$

Note that we cannot have $d \in rsp(b)$ or $d \in rsp(p)$, since these sets are empty. □

Taken together, these lemmas show that repeated derivatives of $e$ can all be represented as sums of terms of the form $\beta d$, where $d \in rsp(e)$. Thus the number of derivatives of $e$ is at most $|\mathsf{At}| \cdot 2^\ell$, where $\ell$ is the number of occurrences of dup in $e$. Moreover, these terms can be represented compactly as a pair of an atom and a subset of $rsp(e)$. Using these representations to build NetKAT automata provides a solid foundation for building an efficient implementation, as is described in the next section.

## 6. Implementation

We have built a system that decides NetKAT equivalence. Given two NetKAT terms, it first converts these terms into automata using Brzozowski derivatives, and then tests whether the automata are bisimilar. Our implementation consists of 4500 lines of OCaml code and includes a parser, pretty printer, and a simple visualizer. We have also integrated our decision procedure into the Frenetic SDN controller platform. This integration enables automated verification of important properties for real-world network topologies and configurations.

Our implementation incorporates a number of important enhancements and optimizations that avoid potential sources of combinatorial blowup. In particular, the derivative and matrix-based algorithms described in the preceding sections are formulated in terms of the NetKAT language model consisting of sets of reduced strings of complete tests and assignments. Building a direct implementation of these algorithms would require constructing square matrices indexed by the universe of possible complete tests and assignments, which is exponential in the number of constants in the terms. Following such a strategy would be impractical, even for small terms. Instead, our implementation uses a symbolic representation that exploits symmetry and sparseness and incorporates optimizations to aggressively prune away values that do not contribute to the final outcome. Although the algorithm is still exponential in the worst case—which is unavoidable, as the problem is PSPACE-complete—the constrained nature of real-world networks allows our tool to perform well in many common cases.

### 6.1 Data Structures

The foundation of our implementation is based on a collection of data structures that provide symbolic representations for building and analyzing NetKAT automata.

***Bases.*** Bases represent sets of pairs of complete tests and assignments symbolically, typically avoiding having to enumerate every possible packet value. Let $e$ be a NetKAT term and let $x_1, \ldots, x_n$ be the collection of fields appearing in it. Likewise, let $U_i$ be the universe of all values associated with $x_i$ either by a test $x_i = n$ or an assignment $x_i \leftarrow n$. A *base* is a pair of sequences $X_1, \ldots, X_m; o_1, \ldots, o_m$, where the $X_i \subseteq U_i$ are sets of values and the $o_i \in U_i$ are optional values. The set represented by a base contains all tests where the value of the test for field $x_i$ is drawn from $X_i$ and the value for the assignment to $x_i$ is either $n_i$ if $o_i$ is defined and equal to $n_i$, or the same value as the test otherwise.

***Matrices.*** Using bases, it is straightforward to build a sparse matrix representation in which the rows and columns are indexed by complete tests and assignments. To encode a 0-1 matrix, we simply use a set of bases. To encode a matrix over a set, we use finite maps from bases to elements of the set. For example, when constructing the $E$ matrix for a term $e$, tests $x_i = m_i$ are represented by

$$U_1, \ldots, U_{i-1}, \{m_i\}, U_{i+1}, \ldots, U_n; ?, \ldots, ?,$$

where ? denotes a missing optional value. Similarly, assignments $x_i \leftarrow m_i$ are represented by

$$U_1, \ldots, U_n; ?, \ldots, ?, m_i, ?, \ldots, ?.$$

Sums and products can be obtained using matrix addition and multiplication as implemented using base sets. The product of bases $(X_1, \ldots, X_n; o_1, \ldots, o_n)$ and $(Y_1, \ldots, Y_n; q_1, \ldots, q_n)$ is nonzero if there exists a complete assignment in the left base that matches a complete test in the right for each field. If $o_i = ?$, then the intersection of $X_i$ and $Y_i$ must be nonempty, otherwise the tests corresponding to the $i$th field will drop all packets produced by the left base. On the other hand, if $o_i \neq ?$, then its value must belong to $Y_i$. If these conditions hold, the resulting product $Z_1, \ldots, Z_n; w_1, \ldots, w_n$ is defined as follows:

$$Z_i = \begin{cases} X_i & \text{if } o_i \neq ? \\ X_i \cap Y_i & \text{if } o_i = ? \end{cases} \qquad w_i = \begin{cases} o_i & \text{if } o_i \neq ? \text{ and } q_i = ? \\ q_i & \text{if } q_i \neq ? \\ ? & \text{if } o_i = q_i = ? \end{cases}$$

Using the product operation on bases, it is easy to build other matrix operations. For example, multiplication can be implemented by folding over the base sets, and fixpoints can be computed using an iterative loop that multiplies at each step or by repeated squaring.

### 6.2 Algorithms

The two core pieces of our implementation are (i) an algorithm that computes automata using Brzozowski derivatives, and (ii) another that checks bisimilarity of automata.

***Brzozowski derivative.*** Our implementation of Brzozowski derivatives uses the *spines* introduced in §5.2. Recall that there is one spine for every occurrence of dup in $e$. If $\sigma$ denotes an occurrence of dup, let $\ell_\sigma$ and $r_\sigma$ denote the left spine and right spine, respectively, of that occurrence. It is straightforward to show that

$$D_{\alpha\beta}(e) = \bigcup\{\beta r_\sigma \mid \sigma \text{ an occurrence of dup}, \ E_{\alpha\beta}(\ell_\sigma) = 1\}$$

or more succinctly,

$$D(e) = \sum_\sigma E(\ell_\sigma) \cdot J \cdot I(r_\sigma). \qquad (6.1)$$

To further streamline the computation of $D(e)$, we can avoid adding the $\beta r_\sigma$ term to $D_{\alpha\beta}(e)$ when $\beta r_\sigma$ is zero, or equivalently when there exists no element of $G(r_\sigma)$ of the form $\beta x$. Let $\Phi$ be a function that replaces all occurrences of dup with 1 as follows:

$$\Phi(p) = p \qquad \Phi(b) = b \qquad \Phi(\mathsf{dup}) = 1$$

$$\Phi(e_1 + e_2) = \Phi(e_1) + \Phi(e_2)$$

$$\Phi(e_1 e_2) = \Phi(e_1) \cdot \Phi(e_2) \qquad \Phi(e^*) = \Phi(e)^*.$$

It is easy to show that for any $\alpha$, the set $\{\alpha \mid \alpha x \in G(e)\}$ is equal to $\{\alpha \mid \alpha x \in G(\Phi(e))\}$. Hence, $\beta x \notin G(r_\sigma)$ is equivalent to $\beta x \notin G(\Phi(r_\sigma))$. Moreover, because $\Phi(r_\sigma)$ does not contain dup, the set $\{\alpha \mid \alpha x \in G(e)\}$ is described by the left-hand sequences $(A_1, \ldots, A_n)$ in the base set representation of $E(\Phi(r_\sigma))$. Hence the derivative can be described as:

$$D(e) = \sum_\sigma E(\ell_\sigma) \cdot E'(\Phi(r_\sigma)) \cdot J \cdot I(r_\sigma),$$

where $E'(\Phi(r_\sigma))$ is obtained from $E(\Phi(r_\sigma))$ by replacing each base $(A_1, \ldots, A_n; k_1, \ldots, k_n)$ with $(A_1, \ldots, A_n; ?, \ldots, ?)$.

This formulation, which is used in our implementation, has a number of advantages. First, it is expressed entirely in terms of simple matrix operations involving the $E$, $I$, and $J$ matrices. Second, it aggressively filters away intermediate terms that do not contribute to the overall result. In particular, if the $\alpha\beta$ entry of $E(\ell_\sigma)$ is 0, then the occurrence of dup indicated by $\sigma$ does not contribute to the first dup in any reduced string denoted by $e$, so the derivative is also 0. Third, since the spines of spines of $e$ are spines of $e$, we can calculate the left-right spines once and for all when we construct the term, and subsequent derivatives are guaranteed to have the form of (6.1).

***Bisimulation.*** The other step in our NetKAT decision procedure tests the bisimilarity of the automata constructed using Brzozowski derivatives. Once we have the coalgebraic structure, this algorithm is fairly standard. Given two NetKAT terms $e_1$ and $e_2$, we first compare the matrices $E(e_1)$ and $E(e_2)$ and check whether they are identical, returning false immediately if they are not. Otherwise, we calculate all derivatives of $e_1$ and $e_2$ and recursively check each of the resulting pairs. The algorithm halts when we have tested every possible derivative reachable transitively from the initial terms. The bounds derived in §5.2 guarantee that the algorithm terminates. This coinductive algorithm can be implemented in almost linear time in the combined size of the automata using the union-find data structure [13].

### 6.3 Optimizations

To further improve performance, our implementation incorporates a number of optimizations designed to reduce the overhead of representing and computing with terms, bases, sparse matrices, etc.

***Hash consing and memoization.*** Encoding real-world network topologies and configurations as NetKAT terms often leads to many repetitions. Our implementation exploits this insight by using aggressive normalization and hash consing so that (many) semantically equivalent terms are represented by the same syntactic term. For instance, we represent products as lists, which gives multiplicative associativity for free, and we represent sums as sets, which gives additive associativity, commutativity, and idempotence for free. We also use smart constructors that recognize identities involving 0 and 1 (along with several others) to further optimize the representations of terms. We calculate term metadata such as left-right spines and the $E$ matrix lazily and store the results alongside the term itself.

***Sparse multiplication.*** The straightforward way to represent matrix multiplication in terms of base sets would be to use nested folds over the sets—the product of two base sets is simply their point-wise cross-product. Sadly, this naive algorithm gives poor performance, and much of the effort is wasted multiplying bases whose product is always 0. We instead implement an algorithm which, rather than iterating over all pairs of bases, instead proactively filters the sets, only retaining elements which could produce a nonzero result. This is done as follows. (i) We first build an association from assignments to their originating bases from the left matrix. (ii) For each base in the right matrix, we intersect all test value sets in this base with the set of all assignments in the left matrix (per field). We will call the result of this operation the set of potential matches. (iii) We multiply each base in the right matrix with the bases corresponding to its potential matches to produce the overall product. These operations allow us to associate each base in the right operand with a small set of left operand bases, significantly limiting the number of pairs we multiply.

***Base compaction.*** There can be many representations of a set of complete tests and assignments, and as base sets are multiplied, those representations tend to grow. Hence, another key optimization for making matrix multiplication (and many other operations) fast is to compact the base sets whenever possible. Two bases can be merged when (i) one is a subset of the other or (ii) they are adjacent, in the following senses. The base $b_1 = X_1, \ldots, X_n; o_1, \ldots, o_n$ is a *subset* of base $b_2 = Y_1, \ldots, Y_n; q_1, \ldots, q_n$ when for all fields $i$, we have $X_i \subseteq Y_i$ and $o_i = q_i$. In this case, $b_1$ and $b_2$ can be replaced with just $b_2$. The base $b_1$ is *adjacent* to $b_2$ if there exists a field $i$ such that $o_i = q_i$ and for all other fields $j$ both $X_j = Y_j$ and $o_j = q_j$. The result of merging these two bases is $Y_1, \ldots, X_i \cup Y_i, \ldots, Y_n; q_1, \ldots, q_n$. Although both of these merging optimizations require bases with identical assignments, we can efficiently reduce the number of bases we attempt to merge by sorting base sets by their assignments. This yields a fast optimization that dramatically compacts the base sets that must be maintained in our implementation.

***Fast fixpoints.*** The algorithm for calculating the $E$ matrix presented in §5.1 uses a fixpoint, which is a potentially expensive operation. Our implementation incorporates several optimizations that greatly increase the efficiency of calculating this fixpoint by exploiting the structure of terms encoding networks. Generally speaking, network terms are of the form $in \cdot (p \cdot t)^* \cdot p \cdot out$, where $in$ and $out$ are edge policies that describe the packets entering and leaving the network, $p$ is a policy the describes the behavior of the switches, and $t$ encodes the topology. The edge policies are typically very small compared to $p$ or $t$. Hence, we can use the edge policies to cut down the size of the $(p \cdot t)^*$ term as we take its fixpoint. We first unfold $in \cdot (p \cdot t)^* \cdot p \cdot out$ to $in \cdot out + in \cdot (p \cdot t)^* \cdot out$ and then find the $in \cdot (p \cdot t)^*$ fixpoint by calculating $in \cdot p \cdot t + in \cdot p \cdot t \cdot p \cdot t + \cdots + in \cdot (p \cdot t)^i$, stopping when we have reached a fixpoint. We have determined empirically that when $in$ and $out$ are relatively small this process converges much faster than other techniques for computing fixpoints, such as repeatedly squaring the $(p \cdot t)$ term.

## 7. Additional Applications

The utility of NetKAT's coalgebraic theory is not limited to checking equivalence via bisimulation. The $E$ and $D$ matrices are also useful for solving many other practical verification problems directly. This section discusses several such applications: all-pairs connectivity, loop freedom, and translation validation.

***Connectivity.*** Reachability—whether host $A$ can communicate with host $B$—is a fundamental property of a network. Indeed, there are now many automated tools that can check reachability properties involving individual locations; see §9 for a survey. Connectivity is a slightly stronger property that asks whether *every* host in a network can communicate with every other host. In other words, connectivity tests whether a network provides the functionality of one "big switch" that forwards traffic between all of its ports.

As connectivity cares only about the end-to-end properties of a network, it is agnostic to paths. Hence, it can be modeled in NetKAT by simply setting all occurrences of dup to 1 using $\Phi$ from §6 and checking the following:

$$\Phi(in \cdot (p \cdot t)^* \cdot p \cdot out) = \sum_{(sw, sw', pt, pt')} \begin{pmatrix} switch = sw \cdot port = pt \cdot \\ switch \leftarrow sw' \cdot port \leftarrow pt' \end{pmatrix}$$

where $p$ encodes the switch policy, $t$ encodes the topology, and in the summation, $(sw, pt)$ and $(sw', pt')$ range over all outward-facing switch-port pairs, that is, those adjacent to a host. Intuitively, the left-hand side of the equation encodes the end-to-end forwarding behavior of the network—forwarding that starts from a state matching $in$ and traverses the switch policy and topology any number of times and eventually reaches a state matching $out$—while the right-hand side represents a specification of a network that forwards directly between every outward-facing switch-port pair. Because connectivity does not involve keeping track of paths, it can be verified simply by checking equality of $E$ matrices.

***Forwarding loops.*** A network has a *forwarding loop* if some packets traverse a cycle repeatedly. Forwarding loops are a frequent source of error in networks and have been identified as the cause of outages both in local-area networks, where loops are often produced by protocols for computing broadcast spanning trees, and on the broader Internet, where inter-domain protocols such as BGP can easily produce loops during periods of reconvergence [15]. Making matters worse, forwarding loops are often masked by features such as TTL (time-to-live) fields, a run-time mechanism that enforces an upper bound on the length of any loop by decrementing a counter at each hop and dropping the packet when the counter reaches 0.

To check whether a packet has a loop, we need to determine if there exists a packet that can reach the same location with the same value twice. One possible way to express this is with the equation $in \cdot (p \cdot t)^{2^n} = 0$, where $p$ is the switch policy, $t$ is the topology, and $n$ is the number of complete tests which occur in the program. The intuition behind this equation is that there are only $2^n$ distinct packet values, so any packet that traverses the network more than $2^n$ times must have been in some state at least twice, and thus will loop forever. However, while this equation is correct, checking it directly is inefficient, as exponentiation is an expensive operation.

To make the problem more tractable, we can recast it into an equivalent formulation using a quantifier:

$$\forall \alpha.\ prefix(in \cdot (p \cdot t)^*) \cdot \alpha \cdot p \cdot t \cdot (p \cdot t)^* \cdot \alpha = 0,$$

where *prefix* is the prefix closure operation. This equation directly encodes a packet that visits the same state twice, allowing us to avoid an expensive exponentiation operation. Moreover, it is not hard to show that the inner term is already prefix-closed, as it ends with a star. So we can reformulate our test to:

$$\forall \alpha.\ in \cdot (p \cdot t)^* \cdot \alpha \cdot p \cdot t \cdot (p \cdot t)^* \cdot \alpha = 0.$$

After converting to matrices, we obtain:

$$\forall (\alpha, \beta) \in E(\Phi(in \cdot (p \cdot t)^*)).\ \beta \cdot (p \cdot t) \cdot (p \cdot t)^* \cdot \beta = 0.$$

We then observe that for any complete test $\beta$ and term $x$, we have $\beta \cdot x \cdot \beta = 0$ if and only if $E_{\beta\beta}(\Phi(x)) = 0$. This yields a fast algorithm for determining loop freedom. We iterate through the sets of possible $\alpha$ and $\beta$ with nonzero entries in $E(\Phi(in \cdot (p \cdot t)^*))$ and check the entry in $E(\Phi(p \cdot t \cdot (p \cdot t)^*))$. If it is also nonzero, then the network has a loop. We have used this algorithm to check for loops

| Topology | Term Size | # Switches | Largest Policy | Parse Time | Loop Freedom | Connectivity | Translation |
|---|---|---|---|---|---|---|---|
| Airtel | 2412 | 15 | 112 | 0.102 | 3.386 | 1.755 | 10.424 |
| Uran | 5000 | 23 | 264 | 0.327 | 5.905 | 5.757 | 71.18 |
| GtsSlovakia | 10388 | 34 | 385 | 0.99 | 25.361 | 25.166 | 258.83 |
| Uunet | 20350 | 48 | 539 | 6.684 | 138.147 | 143.387 | 2007.68 |
| Telcove | 41474 | 72 | 781 | 32.826 | 280.413 | 300.265 | 6959.08 |
| Oteglobe | 56844 | 92 | 838 | 93.045 | 944.955 | 944.555 | 26292.8 |
| Pern | 131092 | 126 | 4757 | 311.644 | 2140.63 | 2478.24 | 83245.7 |

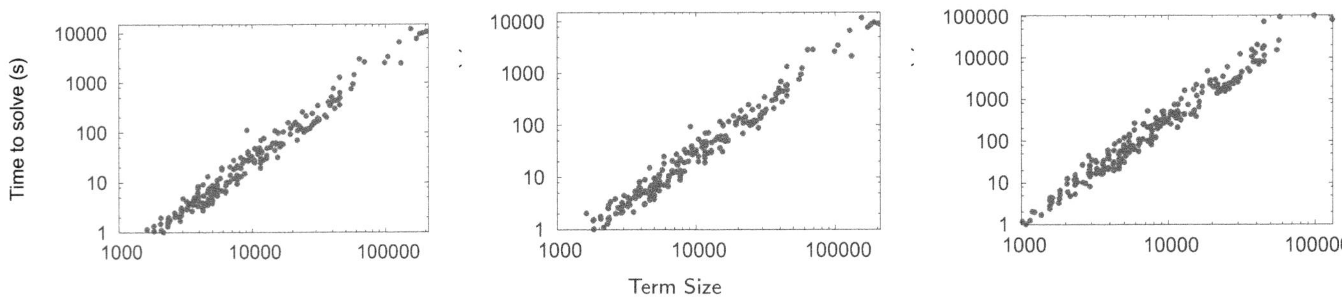


(a) connectivity (b) loop freedom (c) translation validation

**Figure 2.** Topology Zoo experimental results.

in networks with topologies containing thousands of switches and configurations with thousands of forwarding rules on each switch.

***Translation validation.*** One technique for checking the correctness of a compiler, often called *translation validation*, is to test whether the instructions it emits have same semantics as the programs provided as input [29]. We can use translation validation to check the NetKAT compiler itself, which is used by the Frenetic controller [11]. Unlike the applications just discussed, which only depend on analyzing $E$ matrices and do not require bisimulation, translation validation uses the full NetKAT decision procedure. This is due to the fact that it must check the equivalence of the paths generated by the compiler rather than just checking end-to-end forwarding.

We have developed a simple application that uses bisimulation to validate the output of the Frenetic compiler. It takes an input policy $p$ and invokes the NetKAT compiler to convert it to a sequence of OpenFlow forwarding rules, one for each switch. As was shown in the original NetKAT paper [1], the language is expressive enough to encode these rules, so we can reflect them back into NetKAT terms as nested cascades of conditionals,

$$c \;=\; \text{if } pat_1 \text{ then } acts_1 \text{ else} \\ \ldots \\ \text{if } pat_k \text{ then } acts_k \text{ else } 0$$

where each $pat_i$ is a positive conjunction of tests and each $act_i$ is a sequence of modifications. To verify equivalence, we simply check whether $p = (c \cdot t)^* \cdot c$, where $t$ is the topology. If this succeeds, we know that the forwarding rules emitted by the compiler encode the same paths as those specified in the program.

## 8. Evaluation

To evaluate the performance of our implementation, we conducted experiments on a variety of benchmarks. These experiments were designed to answer the following questions: Can our coalgebraic decision procedure effectively answer practical questions about real-world network topologies and configurations? How does its performance scale as the inputs grow in size? How does its performance compare to other network verification tools?

***Benchmarks.*** We ran experiments on the following benchmarks:

- *Topology Zoo* [18]: This public dataset contains a collection of 261 actual network topologies from around the world, mostly for regional ISPs and carrier networks. The topologies range in size from 5 nodes (ARPANET) to over 196 nodes (Cogentco).[5] We generated forwarding policies by placing hosts into the topology at random and computing paths that forward between all pairs of hosts. This benchmark provides the ability to experiment with a wide variety of topologies, ranging from trees, to stars, to meshes, and even seemingly random structures.
- *FatTrees*: These topologies, which are commonly used in data center networks, consist of a tree-structured hierarchy in which the switches at each level have multiple redundant connections to switches at the next higher level. We wrote a Python script to generate FatTrees for a given pair of depth and fanout parameters as well as a NetKAT policy that provides connectivity between hosts. This benchmark provides the ability to experiment with the scalability of our tool on a commonly used topology at varying sizes.
- *Stanford Backbone* [16]: This includes the 16-node topology of the Stanford campus backbone network as well as the actual configurations of each router. This benchmark provides an example of a complete real-world network and provides a means to compare performance directly against other verification tools, such as Header Space Analysis (HSA) [16].

***Properties.*** Our experiments focused on checking the following properties and used the applications described in §7:

- *Connectivity*: Does the network establish connectivity between all pairs of hosts?
- *Loop-Freedom*: Does the network have forwarding loops?
- *Translation Validation*: Does the NetKAT compiler translate high-level policies into equivalent OpenFlow forwarding rules?

For the Stanford benchmark, to facilitate a head-to-head comparison with HSA, we also performed a reachability query from a source to single destination.

[5] We omitted one outlier topology, Kdl, which is the largest topology and significantly larger than the next-largest topology in the Zoo.

| Fanout | Depth | Term Size | # of Switches | Largest Policy | Parse Time | Connectivity | Translation | Loop Freedom |
|---|---|---|---|---|---|---|---|---|
| 4 | 2 | 311 | 6 | 16 | 0.004000 | 0.031 | 0.042 | 0.054 |
| 10 | 2 | 2807 | 15 | 590 | 0.052003 | 0.699997 | 1.511 | 2.742 |
| 20 | 2 | 17207 | 30 | 3880 | 0.636040 | 38.246 | 74.17 | 165.548 |
| 30 | 2 | 52207 | 45 | 8670 | 6.256391 | 435.082 | 832.18 | 1891.75 |
| 46 | 2 | 173519 | 69 | 21781 | 126.051878 | 5858.85 | 11338.7 | 25179.1 |

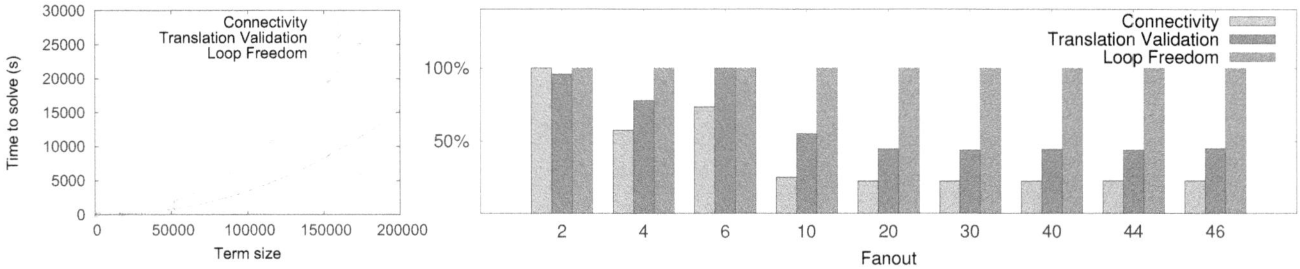


(a) scalability (b) relative performance

**Figure 3.** FatTree experimental results.

***Methodology.*** We ran our experiments on a small cluster of Dell r720 servers with four eight-core 2.70GHz Intel Xeon CPU E5-2680 processors and 64GB of RAM running Ubuntu 12.04.4 LTS. We restricted each experiment to run on a single core. We collected running times using the Unix `time` command for total process times and the OCaml function `Sys.time()` for sub-process times. In each experiment, we exclude the time required to parse inputs and generate policies and only report the amount of time used for the actual verification task.

***Results and Analysis.*** The results of our experiments on the Topology Zoo and FatTree benchmarks are depicted in Figures 2 and 3. We plot the running times of the benchmarks on inputs of varying size and also provide a sampling of data points in a table. All times are reported in seconds.

For the Topology Zoo benchmark, we see that our implementation is able to check small topologies with dozens of switches and policies with hundreds of rules on each switch in tens of seconds, and it scales to topologies with hundreds of switches and policies with thousands of rules without difficulty. The graphs in Figure 2 plot the running time of all three applications against the size of the NetKAT input term. Note that the plots use a semi-logarithmic scale to show the overall trend. The performance of loop detection is similar to connectivity. The performance of translation validation is slower, taking about an order of magnitude longer on large inputs, taking tens of hours for topologies with thousands of switches. This is expected, as translation validation involves invoking the full bisimulation algorithm, a step not required to perform most practical verification tasks. However, our tool is still able to complete and produce the correct result.

For the FatTree benchmark, we measured the scalability of our tool as the size of the network increases from a small number of nodes to several hundred nodes. The graph on the left of Figure 3 plots the performance of all three applications against the size of the NetKAT input term. We observe similar scaling as for the Topology Zoo benchmarks: small networks complete in seconds, while larger networks can take up to several hours. The graph on the right of Figure 3 compares the performance of our three applications, giving the relative running time compared to the slowest application—loop freedom—on FatTrees of increasing size. On small inputs, all three applications take roughly the same amount of time, whereas on larger inputs, connectivity is fastest, loop detection is about half as fast, and translation validation is again half as fast.

For our final benchmark, we compared the running time of our tool against the HSA network property-checking tool [16]. HSA works by doing a symbolic ternary simulation of the space of possible packet values through the policy. It incorporates numerous optimizations to prune the space and keep the representation compact. HSA is able to answer simple queries like reachability and loop detection involving a single host or port, but it does not check full equivalence, unless one performs iterated reachability queries over the entire state space. Nevertheless, for many properties of interest, HSA is able to produce an answer in a few seconds.

To facilitate a comparison with HSA, we made several further improvements to our tool. First, we wrote a front end to parse router configurations for the Stanford backbone. Second, we wrote a tool to convert configurations based on IP prefix matching into policies that only test concrete IP values. This tool works by computing a partitioning of the space of all possible IP addresses that respects the constants mentioned in the program and then replacing each IP prefix with the union of representatives of the equivalence classes it includes. Third, we developed an optimization that statically analyzes NetKAT policies and determines which fields are static, using the NetKAT axioms and partial evaluation to considerably reduce the size of the search space. For example, if a policy matches on IP destination addresses and never modifies those addresses, then for any particular address we can partially evaluate the policy to obtain a smaller policy that is specialized to that host. This analysis and optimization is integrated into our algorithm for constructing NetKAT automata and applied automatically during the computation of fixpoints for Kleene star.

With these enhancements, our tool is able to answer a reachability query involving a single source host in 0.67 seconds. Note that this query is evaluated on the production Stanford backbone network with 16 routers and thousands of forwarding rules. In the original HSA paper, the authors report 13 seconds for a single reachability query. We were able to replicate this number on our own testbed. Since publishing their original paper, the authors have built a hand-optimized version of HSA in C that can answer the same query in 0.5 seconds, but we were not able to replicate this figure at the time of the writing of this paper.

***Discussion.*** Overall, our experiments demonstrate that our tool for deciding NetKAT equivalence is able to scale to real-world network topologies and configurations and provides good performance on many common properties. Although the general problem of NetKAT equivalence is PSPACE complete, our implementation is still fast enough to be used for offline verification of production networks and can answer simpler questions such as point-to-point reachability in well under a second, making it also suitable for more dynamic situations.

## 9. Related Work

NetKAT [1] is the latest in a series of domain-specific languages for SDN programming developed as a part of the Frenetic project [11, 12, 26, 27]. NetKAT largely inherits its syntax, semantics, and application methodology from these earlier efforts but adds a complete deductive system and PSPACE decision procedure [1]. These new results in NetKAT build on the strong connection to earlier algebraic work in KA and KAT [21, 22, 24]. The present paper extends work on NetKAT further, developing the coalgebraic theory of the language and engineering an implementation of these ideas in an OCaml prototype. The overall result is the first practical implementation for deciding NetKAT equivalence.

The coalgebraic theories of KA and KAT and related systems have been studied extensively in recent years [8, 23, 33, 36], uncovering strong relationships between the algebraic/logical view of systems and the combinatorial/automata-theoretic view. We have exploited these ideas heavily in the development of NetKAT coalgebra and NetKAT automata. Finally, in our implementation, we have borrowed many ideas and optimizations from the coalgebraic implementations of KA and KAT and other related systems [4, 5, 30] to provide enhanced performance, making automated decision feasible even in the face of PSPACE completeness. Recent work by Pous developed symbolic techniques for constructing KAT automata and deciding equivalence using binary-decision diagrams (BDDs) [31]. It would be interesting to investigate extending these techniques to NetKAT in the future.

A large number of languages for SDN programming have been proposed in recent years. Nettle [39] applies ideas from functional reactive programming to SDN programming, and focuses on making it easy to express dynamic programs using time-varying signals rather than event loops and callbacks as in most other systems. PANE [10] exposes an interface that allows individual hosts in a network to request explicit functionality such as increased bandwidth for a large bulk transfer or bounded latency for a phone call. Internally PANE uses hierarchical tables to represent and manage the set of requests and a compiler inspired by NetCore [26]. Maple [40] provides a high-level programming interface that enables programmers to express network programs directly in Java, using a special library to match and modify packet headers. Under the hood, the Maple compiler builds up representations of network traffic flows using a tree structure and then compiles these to hardware-level forwarding rules. Several different network programming languages based on logic programming have been proposed including NDLog [25] and FlowLog [28]. The key difference between all of these languages and the system presented in this paper is that NetKAT has a formal mathematical semantics along with a sound and complete deductive apparatus that supports automated reasoning about program equivalence.

Lastly, there is a growing body of work focused on applications of formal methods ranging from lightweight testing to full-blown verification to SDN. The NICE tool [7] uses a model checker and symbolic execution to find bugs in network programs written in Python. Automatic Test Packet Generation [42] constructs a set of packets that provide coverage for a given network-wide configuration. The SDN Troubleshooting System [35] uses techniques inspired by delta debugging to reduce bugs to minimal causal sequences. The VeriCon [2] system uses first-order logic and a notion of admissible topologies to automatically check network-wide properties. It uses the Z3 SMT solver as a back-end decision procedure. Several different systems have proposed techniques for checking network reachability properties including seminal work by Xie et al. [41], Header Space Analysis [16], and VeriFlow[17]. These tools either translate reachability problems into problem instances for other tools, or they use custom decision procedures that extend basic satisfiability checking or ternary simulation with domain-specific optimizations to obtain improved performance. Compared to these tools, NetKAT is unique in its focus on algebraic and coalgebraic structure of network programs. Moreover, as shown in the original NetKAT paper, many properties including reachability can be reduced to equivalence.

## 10. Conclusion

This paper develops the coalgebraic theory of NetKAT and a new decision procedure based on bisimulation. The coalgebraic theory includes a definition of NetKAT automata, a variant of the Brzozowski derivative, and a version of Kleene's theorem relating terms and automata. A novel aspect of the theory is the concise representation of the Brzozowski derivative in terms of matrices and spines. Our implementation improves on a previous naive algorithm [1] and initial experimental results are promising. In the future, we intend to continue to make further enhancements and perform extensive testing on additional practical examples [1]. A straightforward extension is to incorporate well-studied algorithmic enhancements to the bisimulation construction such as up-to techniques [4, 32]. We also plan to explore extending alternative algorithms for deciding equivalence of KAT expressions [6, 37]. Another possible direction is to study nondeterministic NetKAT automata, which could provide more compact representations, or algorithms for deciding equivalence [3, 4]. We also intend to deploy our tool in the Frenetic SDN controller [11].

***Acknowledgments.*** The authors wish to thank our angel, Ralf Hinze, as well as Nikolaj Bjørner, Rebecca Coombes, Arjun Guha, Andrew Myers, Mark Reitblatt, Ross Tate, Konstantinos Mamouras, Dimitrios Vytiniotis, and the Cornell PLDG for many insightful discussions and helpful comments. Our work is supported by the National Security Agency; the National Science Foundation under grants CNS-1111698, CNS-1413972, DGE-1144153, and SHF-1422046; the Office of Naval Research under grant N00014-12-1-0757; the Dutch Research Foundation (NWO) under project numbers 639.021.334 and 612.001.113; a Sloan Research Fellowship; and a gift from Fujitsu Labs.

## References

[1] Carolyn Jane Anderson, Nate Foster, Arjun Guha, Jean-Baptiste Jeannin, Dexter Kozen, Cole Schlesinger, and David Walker. NetKAT: Semantic foundations for networks. In *POPL*, pages 113–126, January 2014.

[2] Thomas Ball, Nikolaj Bjorner, Aaron Gember, Shachar Itzhaky, Aleksandr Karbyshev, Mooly Sagiv, Michael Schapira, and Asaf Valadarsky. Vericon: Towards verifying controller programs in software-defined networks. In *PLDI*, pages 282–293, June 2014.

[3] Filippo Bonchi, Marcello M. Bonsangue, Jan J. M. M. Rutten, and Alexandra Silva. Brzozowski's algorithm (co)algebraically. In *Logic and Program Semantics–Essays Dedicated to Dexter Kozen on the Occasion of His 60th Birthday*, pages 12–23, April 2012.

[4] Filippo Bonchi and Damien Pous. Checking NFA equivalence with bisimulations up to congruence. In *POPL*, pages 457–468, January 2013.

[5] Thomas Braibant and Damien Pous. Deciding Kleene algebras in Coq. *Logical Methods in Computer Science*, 8(1:16):1–42, 2012.

[6] Sabine Broda, António Machiavelo, Nelma Moreira, and Rogério Reis. On the average size of Glushkov and equation automata for KAT expressions. In *FCT*, pages 72–83, August 2013.

[7] Marco Canini, Daniele Venzano, Peter Perešíni, Dejan Kostić, and Jennifer Rexford. A NICE way to test OpenFlow applications. In *NSDI*, April 2012.

[8] Hubie Chen and Riccardo Pucella. A coalgebraic approach to Kleene algebra with tests. In *CMCS*, pages 94–109, July 2003.

[9] Ernie Cohen, Dexter Kozen, and Frederick Smith. The complexity of Kleene algebra with tests. Technical Report TR96-1598, Computer Science Department, Cornell University, July 1996.

[10] Andrew D. Ferguson, Arjun Guha, Chen Liang, Rodrigo Fonseca, and Shriram Krishnamurthi. Participatory networking: An API for application control of SDNs. In *SIGCOMM*, pages 327–338, August 2013.

[11] Nate Foster, Rob Harrison, Michael J. Freedman, Christopher Monsanto, Jennifer Rexford, Alec Story, and David Walker. Frenetic: A network programming language. In *ICFP*, pages 279–291, September 2011.

[12] Arjun Guha, Mark Reitblatt, and Nate Foster. Machine-verified network controllers. In *PLDI*, pages 483–494, June 2013.

[13] John E. Hopcroft and Richard M. Karp. A linear algorithm for testing equivalence of finite automata. Technical Report 71-114, University of California, 1971.

[14] Sushant Jain, Alok Kumar, Subhasree Mandal, Joon Ong, Leon Poutievski, Arjun Singh, Subbaiah Venkata, Jim Wanderer, Junlan Zhou, Min Zhu, Jonathan Zolla, Urs Hölzle, Stephen Stuart, and Amin Vahdat. B4: Experience with a globally-deployed software defined WAN. In *SIGCOMM*, pages 3–14, August 2013.

[15] Ethan Katz-Bassett, Colin Scott, David R. Choffnes, Ítalo Cunha, Vytautas Valancius, Nick Feamster, Harsha V. Madhyastha, Thomas Anderson, and Arvind Krishnamurthy. LIFEGUARD: Practical repair of persistent route failures. In *SIGCOMM*, pages 395–406, August 2012.

[16] Peyman Kazemian, George Varghese, and Nick McKeown. Header space analysis: Static checking for networks. In *NSDI*, April 2012.

[17] Ahmed Khurshid, Xuan Zou, Wenxuan Zhou, Matthew Caesar, and P. Brighten Godfrey. VeriFlow: Verifying network-wide invariants in real time. In *NSDI*, April 2013.

[18] S. Knight, H.X. Nguyen, N. Falkner, R. Bowden, and M. Roughan. The internet topology zoo. *IEEE Selected Areas in Communications*, 29(9):1765–1775, October 2011.

[19] Teemu Koponen, Keith Amidon, Peter Balland, Martín Casado, Anupam Chanda, Bryan Fulton, Igor Ganichev, Jesse Gross, Natasha Gude, Paul Ingram, Ethan Jackson, Andrew Lambeth, Romain Lenglet, Shih-Hao Li, Amar Padmanabhan, Justin Pettit, Ben Pfaff, Rajiv Ramanathan, Scott Shenker, Alan Shieh, Jeremy Stribling, Pankaj Thakkar, Dan Wendlandt, Alexander Yip, and Ronghua Zhang. Network virtualization in multi-tenant datacenters. In *NSDI*, April 2014.

[20] Teemu Koponen, Martin Casado, Natasha Gude, Jeremy Stribling, Leon Poutievski, Min Zhu, Rajiv Ramanathan, Yuichiro Iwata, Hiroaki Inoue, Takayuki Hama, and Scott Shenker. Onix: A distributed control platform for large-scale production networks. In *OSDI*, pages 351–364, October 2010.

[21] Dexter Kozen. A completeness theorem for Kleene algebras and the algebra of regular events. *Information and Computation*, 110(2):366–390, May 1994.

[22] Dexter Kozen. Kleene algebra with tests. *Transactions on Programming Languages and Systems*, 19(3):427–443, May 1997.

[23] Dexter Kozen. On the coalgebraic theory of Kleene algebra with tests. Technical Report `http://hdl.handle.net/1813/10173`, Computing and Information Science, Cornell University, March 2008.

[24] Dexter Kozen and Frederick Smith. Kleene algebra with tests: Completeness and decidability. In *CSL*, pages 244–259, September 1996.

[25] Boon Thau Loo, Joseph M. Hellerstein, Ion Stoica, and Raghu Ramakrishnan. Declarative routing: Extensible routing with declarative queries. In *SIGCOMM*, pages 289–300, August 2005.

[26] Christopher Monsanto, Nate Foster, Rob Harrison, and David Walker. A compiler and run-time system for network programming languages. In *POPL*, pages 217–230, January 2012.

[27] Christopher Monsanto, Joshua Reich, Nate Foster, Jennifer Rexford, and David Walker. Composing software-defined networks. In *NSDI*, April 2013.

[28] Tim Nelson, Andrew D. Ferguson, Michael J. G. Scheer, and Shriram Krishnamurthi. Tierless programming and reasoning for software-defined networks. In *NSDI*, April 2014.

[29] Amir Pnueli, Michael Siegel, and Eli Singerman. Translation validation. In *TACAS*, pages 151–166, March 1998.

[30] Damien Pous. Relational algebra and KAT in Coq, February 2013. Available at `http://perso.ens-lyon.fr/damien.pous/ra`.

[31] Damien Pous. Symbolic algorithms for language equivalence and Kleene algebra with tests. In *POPL*, January 2015. To appear.

[32] Jurriaan Rot, Marcello M. Bonsangue, and Jan J. M. M. Rutten. Coalgebraic bisimulation-up-to. In *SOFSEM*, pages 369–381, January 2013.

[33] Jan J. M. M. Rutten. Automata and coinduction (an exercise in coalgebra). In *CONCUR*, pages 194–218, September 1998.

[34] Jan J. M. M. Rutten. Universal coalgebra: a theory of systems. *Theoretical Computer Science*, 249:3–80, 2000.

[35] Colin Scott, Andreas Wundsam, Barath Raghavan, Aurojit Panda, Andrew Or, Jefferson Lai, Eugene Huang, Zhi Liu, Ahmed El-Hassany, Sam Whitlock, H.B. Acharya, Kyriakos Zarifis, and Scott Shenker. Troubleshooting blackbox SDN control software with minimal causal sequences. In *SIGCOMM*, pages 395–406, August 2014.

[36] Alexandra Silva. *Kleene Coalgebra*. PhD thesis, University of Nijmegen, 2010.

[37] Alexandra Silva. Position automata for Kleene algebra with tests. *Scientific Annals of Computer Science*, 22(2):367–394, 2012.

[38] Alexandra Silva, Filippo Bonchi, Marcello M. Bonsangue, and Jan J. M. M. Rutten. *Logical Methods in Computer Science*, 9(1):9, 2013.

[39] Andreas Voellmy and Paul Hudak. Nettle: Functional reactive programming of OpenFlow networks. In *PADL*, pages 235–249, January 2011.

[40] Andreas Voellmy, Junchang Wang, Y. Richard Yang, Bryan Ford, and Paul Hudak. Maple: Simplifying SDN programming using algorithmic policies. In *SIGCOMM*, pages 87–98, August 2013.

[41] Geoffrey G. Xie, Jibin Zhan, David A. Maltz, Hui Zhang, Albert G. Greenberg, Gísli Hjálmtýsson, and Jennifer Rexford. On static reachability analysis of IP networks. In *INFOCOM*, March 2005.

[42] Hongyi Zeng, Peyman Kazemian, George Varghese, and Nick McKeown. Automatic test packet generation. In *CoNEXT*, pages 241–252, December 2012.

# Symbolic Algorithms for Language Equivalence and Kleene Algebra with Tests

Damien Pous *

Plume team – CNRS, ENS de Lyon, Université de Lyon, INRIA, UMR 5668, France

Damien.Pous@ens-lyon.fr

## Abstract

We propose algorithms for checking language equivalence of finite automata over a large alphabet. We use symbolic automata, where the transition function is compactly represented using (multi-terminal) binary decision diagrams (BDD). The key idea consists in computing a bisimulation by exploring reachable pairs symbolically, so as to avoid redundancies. This idea can be combined with already existing optimisations, and we show in particular a nice integration with the disjoint sets forest data-structure from Hopcroft and Karp's standard algorithm.

Then we consider Kleene algebra with tests (KAT), an algebraic theory that can be used for verification in various domains ranging from compiler optimisation to network programming analysis. This theory is decidable by reduction to language equivalence of automata on guarded strings, a particular kind of automata that have exponentially large alphabets. We propose several methods allowing to construct symbolic automata out of KAT expressions, based either on Brzozowski's derivatives or on standard automata constructions.

All in all, this results in efficient algorithms for deciding equivalence of KAT expressions.

***Categories and Subject Descriptors*** F.4.3 [*Mathematical Logic*]: Decision Problems; F.1.1 [*Models of computation*]: Automata; D.2.4 [*Program Verification*]: Model Checking

***Keywords*** Binary decision diagrams (BDD), symbolic automata, Disjoint set forests, union-find, language equivalence, Kleene algebra with tests (KAT), guarded string automata, Brzozowski's derivatives, Antimirov' partial derivatives.

* We acknowledge support from the following ANR projects: 2010-BLAN-0305 PiCoq and 12IS02001 PACE.



*POPL '15*, January 15–17 2015, Mumbai, India.

Copyright © 2015 ACM 978-1-4503-3300-9/15/01... $15.00.

http://dx.doi.org/10.1145/2676726.2677007

## 1. Introduction

A wide range of algorithms in computer science build on the ability to check language equivalence or inclusion of finite automata. In model-checking for instance, one can build an automaton for a formula and an automaton for a model, and then check that the latter is included in the former. More advanced constructions need to build a sequence of automata by applying a transducer, and to stop whenever two subsequent automata recognise the same language [7]. Another field of application is that of various extensions of Kleene algebra, whose equational theories are reducible to language equivalence of various kinds of automata: regular expressions and finite automata for plain Kleene algebra [26], "closed" automata for Kleene algebra with converse [5, 15], or guarded string automata for Kleene algebra with tests (KAT) [28].

The theory of KAT has been developed by Kozen et al. [12, 27, 28], it has received much attention for its applications in various verification tasks ranging from compiler optimisation [29] to program schematology [3], and very recently for network programming analysis [2, 17]. Like for Kleene algebra, the equational theory of KAT is PSPACE-complete, making it a challenging task to provide algorithms that are computationally practical on as many inputs as possible.

A difficulty with KAT is that the underlying automata work on an input alphabet which is exponentially large in the number of variables of the starting expressions. As such, it renders standard algorithms for language equivalence intractable, even for reasonably small inputs. This difficulty is shared with other fields where various people proposed to work with *symbolic automata* to cope with large, potentially infinite, alphabets [10, 41]. By symbolic automata, we mean finite automata whose transition function is represented using a compact data-structure, typically binary decision diagrams (BDDs) [9, 10], allowing one to explore the automata in a symbolic way.

D'Antoni and Veanes recently proposed a minimisation algorithm for symbolic automata [13], which is much more efficient than the adaptations of the traditional algorithms [22, 31, 32]. However, to our knowledge, the simpler problem of language equivalence for symbolic automata has not been covered yet. We say 'simpler' because language equivalence can be reduced trivially to minimisation—it suffices to minimise the disjoint union of the automata and to check whether the corresponding initial states are equated—but minimisation has complexity $n \ln n$ while Hopcroft and Karp's algorithm for language equivalence [23] is almost linear [40]. (This latter algorithm for checking language equivalence of finite automata can be seen as an instance of Huet's first-order unification algorithm without occur-check [24, Section 5.8]: one tries to unify the two automata recursively, keeping track of the generated equivalence classes of states using an efficient union-find data-structure.)

Our main contributions are the following:

- We propose a simple coinductive algorithm for checking language equivalence of symbolic automata (Section 3). This algorithm is generic enough to support various improvements that have been proposed in the literature for plain automata [1, 6, 14, 42].
- We show how to combine binary decisions diagrams (BDD) and *disjoint set forests*, the efficient data-structure used by Hopcroft and Karp to define their almost linear algorithm [23, 40] for deterministic automata. This results in a new version of their algorithm, for symbolic automata (Section 3.3).
- We study several constructions for building efficiently a symbolic automaton out of a KAT expression (Section 4): we consider symbolic versions of the extensions of Brzozowski's derivatives [11] and Antimirov' partial derivatives [4] to KAT, as well as a generalisation of Ilie and Yu's inductive construction [25]. The latter construction also requires us to generalise the standard procedure consisting of eliminating epsilon transitions.

**Notation**

We denote sets by capital letters $X, Y, S, T \ldots$ and functions by lower case letters $f, g, \ldots$ Given sets $X$ and $Y$, $X \times Y$ is their Cartesian product, $X \uplus Y$ is their disjoint union and $X^Y$ is the set of functions $f\colon Y \to X$. The collection of subsets of $X$ is denoted by $\mathcal{P}(X)$. For a set of letters $A$, $A^\star$ denotes the set of all finite words over $A$; $\epsilon$ the empty word; and $uv$ the concatenation of words $u, v \in A^\star$. We use 2 for the set $\{0, 1\}$.

## 2. Preliminary material

We first recall some standard definitions about finite automata and binary decision diagrams.

For finite automata, the only slight difference with the setting described in [6] is that we work with Moore machines [31] rather than automata: the accepting status of a state is not necessarily a Boolean, but a value in a fixed yet arbitrary set. Since this generalisation is harmless, we stick to the standard automata terminology.

### 2.1 Finite automata

A deterministic finite automaton (DFA) over the input alphabet $A$ and with outputs in $B$ is a triple $\langle S, t, o\rangle$, where $S$ is a finite set of states, $o\colon S \to B$ is the output function, and $t\colon S \to S^A$ is the (total) transition function which returns, for each state $x$ and for each input letter $a \in A$, the next state $t_a(x)$. For $a \in A$, we write $x \xrightarrow{a} x'$ for $t_a(x) = x'$. For $w \in A^\star$, we denote by $x \xrightarrow{w} x'$ the least relation such that (1) $x \xrightarrow{\epsilon} x$ and (2) $x \xrightarrow{au} x'$ if $x \xrightarrow{a} x''$ and $x'' \xrightarrow{u} x'$ for some $x''$.

The *language* accepted by a state $x \in S$ of a DFA is the function $[\![x]\!]\colon A^\star \to B$ defined as follows:

$$[\![x]\!](\epsilon) = o(x) \quad , \qquad [\![x]\!](aw) = [\![t_a(x)]\!](w) \quad .$$

(When the output set is 2, these functions are indeed characteristic functions of formal languages). Two states $x, y \in S$ are said to be *language equivalent* (written $x \sim y$) when they accept the same language.

### 2.2 Coinduction

Checking whether two states of two distinct automata recognise the same language reduces to checking whether two states of a single automaton recognise the same language: one can always build the disjoint union of the two automata. We thus fix a single DFA, and we define bisimulations. We make explicit the underlying notion of progression which we need in the sequel.

```
1  type (s,β) dfa = {t: s → A → s; o: s → β}
2
3  let equiv (M: (s,β) dfa) (x y: s) =
4    let r = Set.empty () in
5    let todo = Queue.singleton (x,y) in
6    while ¬Queue.is_empty todo do
7      (* invariant: r ↣ r ∪ todo *)
8      let (x,y) = Queue.pop todo in
9      if Set.mem r (x,y) then continue
10     if M.o x ≠ M.o y then return false
11     iter_A (fun a → Queue.push todo (M.t x a, M.t y a))
12     Set.add r (x,y)
13   done
14   return true
```

**Figure 1.** Simple algorithm for checking language equivalence.

**Definition 1** (Progression, Bisimulation). *Given two relations $R, R' \subseteq S \times S$ on the states of an automaton,* $R$ progresses to $R'$, *denoted $R \rightarrowtail R'$, if whenever $x \mathrel{R} y$ then*

1. *$o(x) = o(y)$ and*
2. *for all $a \in A$, $t_a(x) \mathrel{R'} t_a(y)$.*

*A* bisimulation *is a relation $R$ such that $R \rightarrowtail R$.*

Bisimulations provide a sound and complete proof technique for checking language equivalence of DFA:

**Proposition 1** (Coinduction). *Two states of an automaton are language equivalent iff there exists a bisimulation that relates them.*

Accordingly, we obtain the simple algorithm described in Figure 1, for checking language equivalence of two states of the given automaton.

This algorithm works as follows: the variable `r` contains a relation which is a bisimulation candidate and the variable `todo` contains a queue of pairs that remain to be processed. To process a pair $(x, y)$, one first checks whether it already belongs to the bisimulation candidate: in that case, the pair can be skipped since it was already processed. Otherwise, one checks that the outputs of the two states are the same ($o(x) = o(y)$), and one pushes all derivatives of the pair to the `todo` queue: all pairs $(t_a(x), t_a(y))$ for $a \in A$. (This requires the type $A$ of letters to be iterable, and thus finite, an assumption which is no longer required with the symbolic algorithm to be presented in Section 3.) The pair $(x, y)$ is finally added to the bisimulation candidate, and we proceed with the remainder of the queue.

The main invariant of the loop (line 7: `r` $\rightarrowtail$ `r` $\cup$ `todo`) ensures that when `todo` becomes empty, then `r` contains a bisimulation, and the starting states were indeed bisimilar. Another invariant of the loop is that for any pair $(x', y')$ in `todo`, there exists a word $w$ such that $x \xrightarrow{w} x'$ and $y \xrightarrow{w} y'$. Therefore, if we reach a pair of states whose outputs are distinct—line 10, then the word $w$ associated to that pair witnesses the fact that the two initial states are not equivalent.

**Remark 1.** *Note that such an algorithm can be modified to check for language inclusion in a straightforward manner: assuming an arbitrary preorder $\leq$ on the output set $B$, and letting language inclusion mean $x \leq y$ if for all $w \in A^\star$, $[\![x]\!](w) \leq [\![y]\!](w)$, it suffices to replace line 10 in Figure 1 by*

```
if ¬(M.o x ≤ M.o y) then return false.
```

### 2.3 Up-to techniques

The previous algorithm can be enhanced by exploiting *up-to techniques* [36, 39]: an up-to technique is a function $f$ on binary relations such that any relation $R$ satisfying $R \rightarrowtail f(R)$ is contained in a bisimulation. Intuitively, such relations, that are not necessarily bisimulations, are constrained enough to contain only language equivalent pairs.

We have recently shown with Bonchi [6] that the standard algorithm by Hopcroft and Karp [23] actually exploits such an up-to technique: on line 9, rather than checking whether the processed pair is already in the candidate relation `r`, Hopcroft and Karp check whether it belongs to the equivalence closure of `r`. Indeed the function $e$ mapping a relation to its equivalence closure is a valid up-to technique, and this optimisation allows the algorithm to stop earlier. Hopcroft and Karp moreover use an efficient data-structure to perform this check in almost constant time [40]: *disjoint sets forests*. We recall this data-structure in Section 3.3.

Other examples of valid up-to techniques include context-closure, as used in antichain based algorithms [1, 14, 42], or congruence closure [6], which combines both context-closure and equivalence closure. These techniques require working with automata whose states carry a semi-lattice structure, as is typically the case for a DFA obtained from a non-deterministic automaton through the powerset construction.

### 2.4 Binary decision diagrams

Assume an ordered set $(A,<)$ and an arbitrary set $B$. Binary decision diagrams are directed acyclic graphs that can be used to represent functions of type $2^A \rightarrow B$. When $B = 2$ is the two elements set, BDDs thus intuitively represent Boolean formulas with variables in $A$.

Formally, a *(multi-terminal, ordered) binary decision diagram* (BDD) is a pair $(N,c)$ where $N$ is a finite set of nodes and $c$ is a function of type $N \rightarrow B \uplus (A \times N \times N)$ such that if $c(n) = (a,l,r)$ and either $c(l) = (a',\_,\_)$ or $c(r) = (a',\_,\_)$, then $a < a'$.

The condition on $c$ ensures that the underlying graph is acyclic, which makes it possible to associate a function $\lceil n \rceil \colon 2^A \rightarrow B$ to each node $n$ of a BDD:

$$\lceil n \rceil(\alpha) = \begin{cases} b & \text{if } c(n) = b \in B \\ \lceil l \rceil(\alpha) & \text{if } c(n) = (a,l,r) \text{ and } \alpha(a) = 0 \\ \lceil r \rceil(\alpha) & \text{if } c(n) = (a,l,r) \text{ and } \alpha(a) = 1 \end{cases}$$

Let us now recall the standard graphical representation of BDDs:

- A node $n$ such that $c(n) = b \in B$ is represented by a square box labelled by $b$.
- A node $n$ such that $c(n) = (a,l,r) \in A \times N \times N$ is a decision node, which we picture by a circle labelled by $a$, with a dotted arrow towards the *left child* $(l)$ and a plain arrow towards the *right child* $(r)$.

For instance, the following drawing represents a BDD with four nodes; its top-most node denotes the function given on the right-hand side.

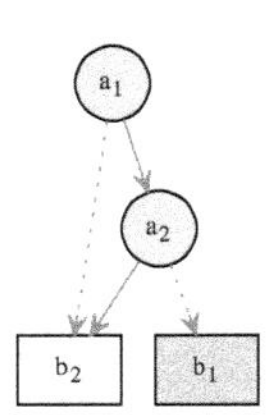


$$\alpha \mapsto \begin{cases} b_1 & \text{if } \alpha(a_1) = 1 \text{ and } \alpha(a_2) = 0 \\ b_2 & \text{otherwise} \end{cases}$$

A BDD is *reduced* if $c$ is injective, and $c(n) = (a,l,r)$ entails $l \neq r$. (The above example BDD is reduced.) Any BDD can be transformed into a reduced one. When $A$ is finite, reduced (ordered)

```
type β node = β descr hash_consed
and β descr = V of β | N of A × β node × β node

val hashcons: β descr → β node
val c: β node → β descr
val memo_rec: ((α'→β'→γ)→α'→β'→γ)→α'→β'→γ
(* with α' = α hash_consed, β' = β hash_consed *)

let constant v = hashcons (V v)
let node a l r = if l==r then l else hashcons (N(a,l,r))

let apply (f: α → β → γ): α node → β node → γ node =
 memo_rec (fun app x y →
 match c(x), c(y) with
  | V v, V w → constant (f v w)
  | N(a,l,r), V _ → node a (app l y) (app r y)
  | V _, N(a,l,r) → node a (app x l) (app x r)
  | N(a,l,r), N(a',l',r') →
    if a=a' then node a (app l l') (app r r')
    if a<a' then node a (app l y) (app r y)
    if a>a' then node a' (app x l') (app x r'))
```

**Figure 2.** An implementation of BDDs.

BDD nodes are in one-to-one correspondence with functions from $2^A$ to $B$ [9, 10]. The main interest in this data-structure is that it is often extremely compact.

In the sequel, we only work with reduced ordered BDDs, which we simply call BDDs. We denote by $\mathrm{BDD}_A[B]$ the set of nodes of a BDD with values in $B$, which is large enough to represent all considered functions. We let $\lfloor f \rfloor$ denote the unique BDD node representing a given function $f\colon 2^A \rightarrow B$. This notation is useful to give abstract specifications to BDD operations: in the sequel, all usages of this notation actually underpin efficient BDD operations.

***Implementation.*** To better explain parts of the proposed algorithms, we give a simple implementation of BDDs in Figure 2.

The type for BDD nodes is given first: we use Filliâtre's hash-consing library [16] to enforce unique representation of each node, whence the two type declarations and the two conversion functions `hashcons` and `c` between those types. The third utility function `memo_rec` is just a convenient operator for defining recursive memoised functions on pairs of hash-consed values.

The function `constant` creates a constant node, making sure it was not already created. The function `node` creates a new decision node, unless that node is useless and can be replaced by one of its two children. The generic function `apply` is central to BDDs [9, 10]: many operations are just instances of this function. Its specification is the following:

$$\texttt{apply}\ f\ x\ y = \lfloor \alpha \mapsto f(\lceil x \rceil(\alpha))(\lceil y \rceil(\alpha)) \rfloor$$

This function is obtained by "zipping" the two BDDs together until a constant is reached. Memoisation is used to exploit sharing and to avoid performing the same computations again and again.

Suppose now that we want to define logical disjunction on Boolean BDD nodes. Its specification is the following:

$$x \vee y = \lfloor \alpha \mapsto \lceil x \rceil(\alpha) \vee \lceil y \rceil(\alpha) \rfloor.$$

We can thus simply use the `apply` function, applied to the Boolean disjunction function:

```
let dsj: bool node → bool node → bool node = apply (||)
```

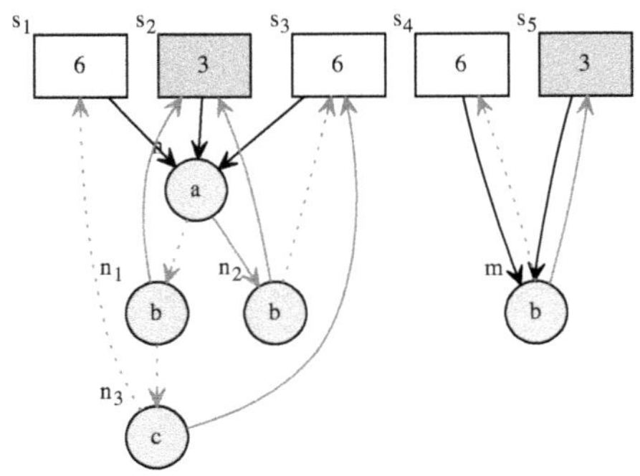


| | $s_1, s_2, s_3$ | | | | | | | | $s_4, s_5$ | | | | | | | |
|---|---|---|---|---|---|---|---|---|---|---|---|---|---|---|---|---|
| $a$ | 0 | 0 | 0 | 0 | 1 | 1 | 1 | 1 | 0 | 0 | 0 | 0 | 1 | 1 | 1 | 1 |
| $b$ | 0 | 0 | 1 | 1 | 0 | 0 | 1 | 1 | 0 | 0 | 1 | 1 | 0 | 0 | 1 | 1 |
| $c$ | 0 | 1 | 0 | 1 | 0 | 1 | 0 | 1 | 0 | 1 | 0 | 1 | 0 | 1 | 0 | 1 |
| $t$ | $s_1$ | $s_3$ | $s_2$ | $s_2$ | $s_3$ | $s_3$ | $s_2$ | $s_2$ | $s_4$ | $s_4$ | $s_5$ | $s_5$ | $s_4$ | $s_4$ | $s_5$ | $s_5$ |

**Figure 3.** A symbolic DFA with five states.

Note that this definition could actually be slightly optimised by inlining apply's code, and noticing that the result is already known whenever one of the two arguments is a constant:

```
let dsj: bool node → bool node → bool node =
 memo_rec (fun dsj x y →
 match c(x), c(y) with
  | V true, _ | _, V false → x
  | _, V true | V false, _ → y
  | N(a,l,r), N(a',l',r') →
    if a=a' then node a (dsj l l') (dsj r r')
    if a<a' then node a (dsj l y ) (dsj r y )
    if a>a' then node a' (dsj x l') (dsj x r'))
```

We ignore such optimisations in the sequel, for the sake of clarity.

## 3. Symbolic automata

A standard technique [10, 13, 20, 41] for working with automata over a large input alphabet consists in using BDDs to represent the transition function: a *symbolic DFA* with output set $B$ and input alphabet $A' = 2^A$ for some set $A$ is a triple $\langle S, t, o\rangle$ where $S$ is the set of states, $t\colon S \to \mathrm{BDD}_A[S]$ maps states into nodes of a BDD over $A$ with values in $S$, and $o\colon S \to B$ is the output function.

Such a symbolic DFA is depicted in Figure 3. It has five states, input alphabet $2^{\{a,b,c\}}$, and natural numbers as output set. We represent the BDD graphically; rather than giving the functions $t$ and $o$ separately, we label the square box corresponding to a state $x$ with its output value $o(x)$ and we link this box to the node $t(x)$ defining the transitions of $x$ using a solid arrow. The explicit transition table is given below the drawing.

The simple algorithm described in Figure 1 is not optimal when working with such symbolic DFAs: at each non-trivial iteration of the main loop, one goes through all letters of $A' = 2^A$ to push all the derivatives of the current pair of states to the queue todo (line 11), resulting in a lot of redundancies.

Suppose for instance that we run the algorithm on the DFA of Figure 3, starting from states $s_1$ and $s_4$. After the first iteration, r contains the pair $(s_1, s_4)$, and the queue todo contains eight pairs:

$(s_1, s_4), (s_3, s_4), (s_2, s_5), (s_2, s_5), (s_3, s_4), (s_3, s_4), (s_2, s_5), (s_2, s_5)$

```
let iter2 (f: α × β → unit): α node → β node → unit =
 memo_rec (fun iter2 x y →
 match c(x), c(y) with
  | V v, V w → f (v,w)
  | V _, N(_,l,r) → iter2 x l; iter2 x r
  | N(_,l,r), V _ → iter2 l y; iter2 r y
  | N(a,l,r), N(a',l',r') →
    if a=a' then iter2 l l'; iter2 r r'
    if a<a' then iter2 l y ; iter2 r y
    if a>a' then iter2 x l'; iter2 x r')
```

**Figure 4.** Iterating over the set of pairs reachable from two nodes.

```
1  type (s,β) sdfa = {t: s → s bdd; o: s → β}
2
3  let symb_equiv (M: (s,β) sdfa) (x y: s) =
4    let r = Set.empty() in
5    let todo = Queue.singleton (x,y) in
6    let push_pairs = iter2 (Queue.push todo) in
7    while ¬Queue.is_empty todo do
8      let (x,y) = Queue.pop todo in
9      if Set.mem (x,y) r then continue
10     if M.o x ≠ M.o y then return false
11     push_pairs (M.t x) (M.t y)
12     Set.add r (x,y)
13   done;
14   return true
```

**Figure 5.** Symbolic algorithm for checking language equivalence.

Assume that elements of this queue are popped from left to right. The first element is removed during the following iteration, since $(s_1, s_4)$ already is in r. Then $(s_3, s_4)$ is processed: it is added to r, and the above eight pairs are appended again to the queue, which now has fourteen elements. The following pair is processed similarly, resulting in a queue with twenty one $(14 - 1 + 8)$ pairs. Since all pairs of this queue are already in r, it is finally emptied through twenty one iterations, and the algorithm returns true.

Note that it would be even worse if the input alphabet was actually declared to be $2^{\{a,b,c,d\}}$: even though the bit $d$ of all letters is irrelevant for the considered DFA, each non-trivial iteration of the algorithm would push even more copies of each pair to the todo queue.

What we propose here is to exploit the symbolic representation, so that a given pair is pushed only once. Intuitively, we want to recognise that starting from the pair of nodes $(n, m)$, the letters 010, 011, 110 and 111 are equivalent[1], since they lead to the same pair, $(s_2, s_5)$. Similarly, the letters 001, 100, and 101 are equivalent: they lead to the pair $(s_3, s_4)$.

This idea is easy to implement using BDDs: like for the apply function (Figure 2), it suffices to zip the two BDDs together, and to push pairs when we reach two leaves. We use for that the procedure iter2 from Figure 3, which successively applies a given function to all pairs reachable from two nodes. Its code is almost identical to apply, except that nothing is constructed (and memoisation is just used to remember those pairs that have already been visited).

We finally modify the simple algorithm from Section 2.1 by using this procedure on line 11; we obtain the code given in Figure 5. We apply iter2 to its first argument once and for all (line 6), so that we maximise memoisation: a pair of nodes that has been vis-

[1] Letters being elements of $2^{\{a,b,c\}}$ here, we represent them with bit-vectors of length three

ited in the past will never be visited again, since all pairs of states reachable from that pair of nodes are already guaranteed to be processed. (As an invariant, we have that all pairs reachable from a pair of nodes memoised in `push_pairs` appear in $\mathtt{r} \cup \mathtt{todo}$.)

Let us illustrate this algorithm by running it on the DFA from Figure 3, starting from states $s_1$ and $s_4$ as previously. During the first iteration, the pair $(s_1, s_4)$ is added to `r`, and `push_pairs` is called on the pair of nodes $(n, m)$. This call virtually results in building the following BDD, where leaves consist of calls to `Queue.push todo`.

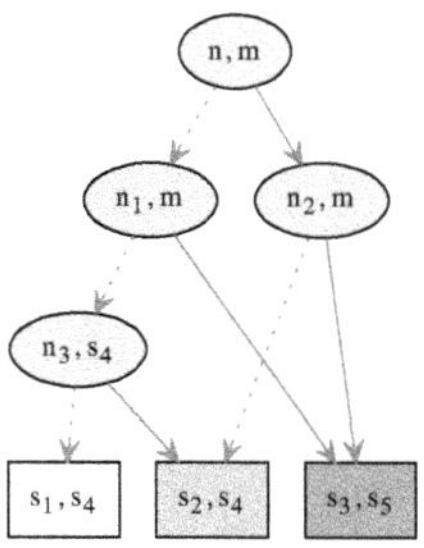


The following three pairs are thus pushed to `todo`.

$$(s_1, s_4), (s_3, s_4), (s_2, s_5)$$

The first pair is removed by a trivial iteration: $(s_1, s_4)$ already belongs to `r`. The two other pairs are processed by adding them to `r`, but without pushing any new pair to `todo`: thanks to memoisation, the two expected calls to `push_pairs n m` are skipped.

All in all, each reachable pair is pushed only once to the `todo` queue. More importantly, the derivatives of a given pair are explored symbolically. In particular, the algorithm would execute exactly in the same way, even if the alphabet was actually declared to be much larger (for instance because the considered states were part of a bigger automaton with more letters). In fact, the main loop is executed at most $n^2$ times, where $n$ is the total number of BDD nodes (both leaves and decision nodes) reachable from the starting states.

Finally note that in the code from Figure 5, the candidate relation `r` is redundant, as the pairs it contains are also stored implicitly in the memoisation table of `iter2` (except for the initial pair). The corresponding lines (4, 9, and 12) can thus be removed.

### 3.1 Displaying symbolic counter-examples.

Bisimulation-based algorithms for language equivalence can be instrumented to produce counter-examples in case of failure, i.e., a word which is accepted by one state and not by the other.

An advantage of the previous algorithm is that those counter-examples can be displayed symbolically; thus enhancing readability. This is particularly important in the context of formal assisted proofs (e.g., when working with KAT in Coq [34]), where a plain guarded string is often too big to be useful to the user, while a 'symbolic' guarded string—where only the bits that are relevant for the counter-example are displayed—can be really helpful to understand which hypotheses have to be used to solve the current goal.

Consider for instance the following automaton.

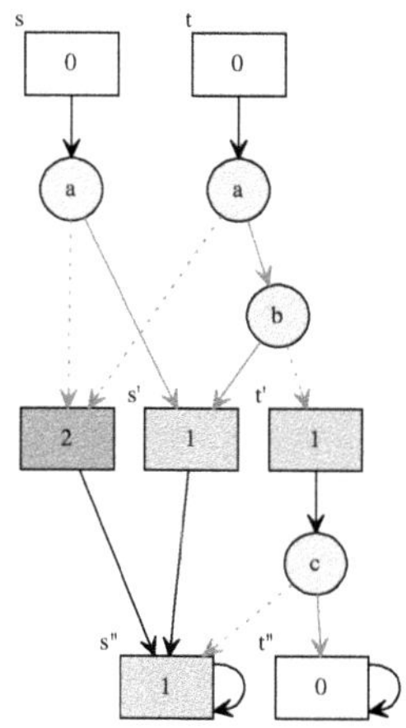


Intuitively, the topmost states $s$ and $t$ are not equivalent because $t$ can take two transitions to reach $t''$, with output 0, while with two transitions, $s$ can only reach $s''$, with output 1.

More formally, the word 100 001 over $2^{\{a,b,c\}}$ is a counter-example: we have

$$\begin{aligned} [\![s]\!](100\,001) &= [\![s']\!](001) = o(s'') = 1 \ , \\ [\![t]\!](100\,001) &= [\![t']\!](001) = o(t'') = 0 \ . \end{aligned}$$

But there are plenty of other counter-examples of length two: it suffices that: $a$ be assigned true and $b$ be assigned false in the first letter, and that $c$ be assigned true in the second letter. The values of the bit $c$ in the first letter, and of the bits $a$ and $b$ in the second letter do not change the above computation. As a consequence, this counter-example is best described as the pseudo-word 10- - -1, or alternatively the word $(a \wedge \neg b)\, c$ whose letters are conjunctions of literals indicating the least requirements to get a counter example.

The algorithm from Figure 5 makes it possible to give this information back to the user:

- modify the queue *todo* to store triples $(w, x, y)$ where $(x, y)$ is a pair of states to process, and $w$ is the associated potential counter-example;
- modify the function `iter2` (Figure 3), so that it uses an additional argument to record the encountered node labels, with negative polarity when going through the recursive call for the left child, and positive polarity for the right child;
- modify line 10 of the main algorithm to return the symbolic word associated with the current pair when the output test fails.

### 3.2 Non-deterministic automata

Standard coinductive algorithms for DFA can be applied to non-deterministic automata (NFA) by using the *powerset construction*. This construction transforms a non-deterministic automaton into a deterministic one; we extend it to symbolic automata in the obvious way.

A *symbolic NFA* is a tuple $\langle S, t, o \rangle$ where $S$ is the set of states, $o\colon S \to B$ is the output function, and $t\colon S \to \mathrm{BDD}_A[\mathcal{P}(S)]$ maps a state and a letter of the alphabet $A' = 2^A$ to a set of possible successor states, using a symbolic representation. The set $B$ of output values must be equipped with a semi-lattice structure $\langle B, \wedge, \bot \rangle$. Assuming such an NFA, one defines a symbolic DFA

$\langle \mathcal{P}(S), t^\sharp, o^\sharp \rangle$ as follows:

$$t^\sharp(\{x_1, \ldots, x_n\}) \triangleq t(x_1) \uplus \ldots \uplus t(x_n) \ ,$$

$$o^\sharp(\{x_1, \ldots, x_n\}) \triangleq o(x_1) \vee \cdots \vee o(x_n) \ .$$

(Where $\uplus$ denotes the pointwise union of two BDDs over sets: $n \uplus m = \lfloor \phi \mapsto \lceil n \rceil(\phi) \cup \lceil m \rceil(\phi) \rfloor$.)

This DFA has exponentially many states. However, when applying bisimulation-based algorithms to such automata, one explores them on the fly, and only those subsets that are reachable from the initial states need to be visited. This number of reachable subsets is usually much smaller than the exponential worst-case bound; in fact it is quite often of the same order as the number of states of the starting DFA (see, e.g., the experiments in Section 5).

### 3.3 Hopcroft and Karp: disjoint sets forests

The previous algorithm can be freely enhanced by using up-to techniques, as described in Section 2.3: it suffices to modify line 9 to skip pairs more or less aggressively, according to the chosen up-to technique. For an up-to technique $f$, line 9 thus becomes

```
if Set.mem (x,y) (f r) then continue .
```

The up-to-equivalence technique used in Hopcroft and Karp's algorithm can however be integrated in a deeper way, by exploiting the fact that we work with BDDs. This leads to a second algorithm, which we describe in this section.

Let us first recall *disjoint sets forests*, the data structure used by Hopcroft and Karp to represent equivalence classes. This standard data-structure makes it possible to check whether two elements belong to the same class and to merge two equivalence classes, both in almost constant amortised time [40].

The idea consists in storing a partial map from elements to elements and whose underlying graph is acyclic. An element for which the map is not defined is the *representative* of its equivalence class, and the representative of an element pointing in the map to some $y$ is the representative of $y$. Two elements are equivalent if and only if they lead to the same representative; to merge two equivalence classes, it suffices to add a link from the representative of one class to the representative of the other class. Two optimisations are required to obtain the announced theoretical complexity:

- when following the path leading from an element to its representative, one should compress it in some way, by modifying the map so that the elements in this path become closer to their representative. There are various ways of compressing paths, in the sequel, we use the method called *halving* [40];
- when merging two classes, one should make the smallest one point to the biggest one, to avoid generating too many long paths. Again, there are several possible heuristics, but we elude this point in the sequel.

As explained above, the simplest thing to do would be to replace the bisimulation candidate $r$ from Figure 5 by a disjoint sets forest over the states of the considered automaton.

The new idea consists in relating the BDD nodes of the symbolic automaton rather than just its states (i.e., just the BDD leaves). By doing so, one avoids visiting pairs of nodes that have already been visited up to equivalence.

Concerning the implementation, we first introduce a BDD unification algorithm (Figure 3.3), i.e., a variant of the function `iter2` which uses disjoint sets forest rather than plain memoisation. This function first creates an empty forest (we use Filliâtre's module `Hmap` of maps over hash-consed values to represent the corresponding partial maps). The function `link` adds a link between two representatives; the recursive terminal function `repr` looks for the representative of a node and implements halving. The inner function

```
1  let unify (f: β × β → unit): β node → β node → unit =
2   (* the disjoint sets forest *)
3   let m = Hmap.empty() in
4   let link x y = Hmap.add m x y in
5   (* representative of a node *)
6   let rec repr x =
7    match Hmap.get m x with
8     | None → x
9     | Some y → match Hmap.get m y with
10       | None → y
11       | Some z → link x z; repr z
12  in
13  let rec unify x y =
14   let x = repr x in
15   let y = repr y in
16   if x ≠ y then
17   match c(x), c(y) with
18    | V v, V w → link x y; f (v,w)
19    | V _, N(_,l,r) → link y x; unify x l; unify x r
20    | N(_,l,r), V _ → link x y; unify l y; unify r y
21    | N(a,l,r), N(a',l',r') →
22      if a=a' then link x y; unify l l'; unify r r'
23      if a<a' then link x y; unify l y ; unify r y
24      if a>a' then link y x; unify x l'; unify x r')
25  in unify
```

**Figure 6.** Unifying two nodes of a BDD, using disjoint set forests.

```
let dsf_equiv (M: (s,β) sdfa) (x y: s) =
 let todo = Queue.singleton (x,y) in
 let push_pairs = unify (Queue.push todo) in
 while ¬Queue.is_empty todo do
  let (x,y) = Queue.pop todo in
  if M.o x ≠ M.o y then return false
  push_pairs (M.t x) (M.t y)
 done;
 return true
```

**Figure 7.** Symbolic algorithm optimised with disjoint set forests.

`unify` is defined similarly as `iter2`, except that it first takes the representative of the two given nodes, and that it adds a link from one to the other before recursing.

Those links can be put in any direction on lines 18 and 22, and we should actually use an appropriate heuristic to take this decision, as explained above. In the four other cases, we put a link either from the node to the leaf, or from the node with the smallest label to the node with the biggest label. By proceeding this way, we somehow optimise the BDD, by leaving as few decision nodes as possible.

It is important to notice that there is actually no choice left in those four cases: we work implicitly with the optimised BDD obtained by mapping all nodes to their representatives, so that we have to maintain the invariant that this optimised BDD is ordered and acyclic. (Notice that this optimised BDD need not be reduced anymore: the children of given a node might be silently equated, and a node might have several representations since its children might be silently equated with the children of another node with the same label)

We finally obtain the algorithm given in Figure 7. It is similar to the previous one (Figure 5), except that we use the new function `unify` to push pairs into the `todo` queue, and that we no longer store the bisimulation candidate `r`: this relation is subsumed by the restriction of the disjoint set forests to BDD leaves.

If we execute this algorithm on the symbolic DFA from Figure 3, between states $s_1$ and $s_4$, we obtain the disjoint set forest depicted below using dashed red arrows. This actually corresponds to the pairs which would be visited by the first symbolic algorithm (Figure 5).

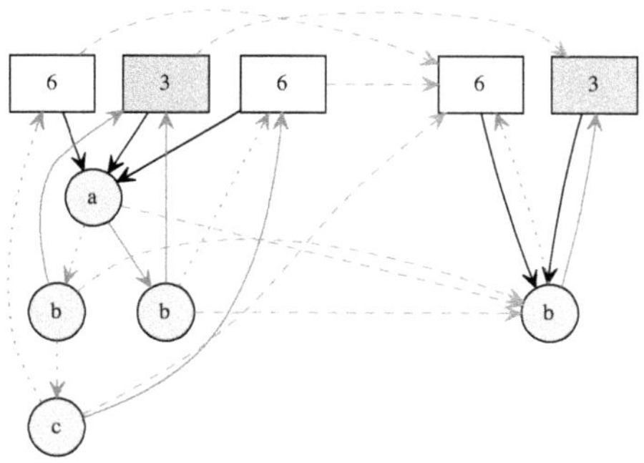


If instead we start from the top-most nodes in the following partly described automaton, we would get the disjoint set forest depicted similarly in red, while the first algorithm would go through all violet lines, one of which is superfluous.

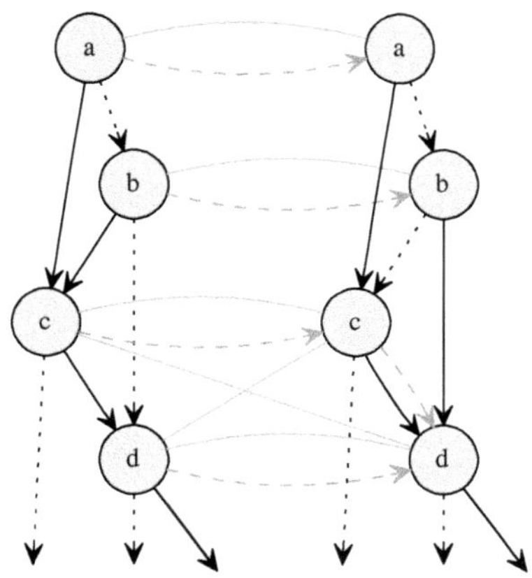


The corresponding optimised BDD consists of the three nodes labelled with $a$, $b$, and $d$ on the right-hand side. This BDD is not reduced, as explained above: the node labelled with $b$ should be removed since it points twice to the node labelled with $d$, and removing this node makes the node labelled with $a$ useless, in turn.

***Complexity.*** Concerning complexity, while the algorithm from Figure 5 is quadratic in the number $n$ of BDD nodes (and leaves) that are reachable from the starting symbolic DFA, the optimised algorithm from Figure 7 performs at most $n$ iterations: two equivalence classes of nodes are merged each time a link is added, and we start with the discrete partition of nodes.

Unfortunately, we cannot immediately deduce that the algorithm is almost linear, as did Tarjan for Hopcroft and Karp's algorithm [40]. The problem is that we cannot always freely choose how to link two representatives (i.e., on lines 19, 20, 23, and 24 in Figure 3.3), so that we cannot guarantee that the amortised complexity of maintaining those equivalence classes is almost constant. We conjecture that such a result holds, however, as the choice we enforce in those cases virtually suppresses binary decision nodes, thus reducing the complexity of subsequent BDD unifications.

***Unification with row types.*** As mentioned in the Introduction, Hopcroft and Karp's algorithm can be seen as an instance of Huet's first-order unification algorithm for recursive terms (i.e., without occur-check). The algorithm presented in Figure 7, and more specifically the BDD unification sub-algorithm (Figure 3.3) is reminiscent of Rémy's extension of this unification algorithm for dealing with *row types*—to obtain an ML-like type inference algorithm in presence of extensible records [33, 37, 38].

More precisely, row types are almost-constant functions from a given set of labels to types, typically represented as association lists with a default value. Unification of such row types is performed pointwise, and is implemented by zipping the two association lists together, as we do here with BDDs (which generalise from almost constant functions to functions with finitely many output values).

It would thus be interesting to understand whether our generalisation of this unification sub-algorithm, from association lists to BDDs, could be useful in the context of unification: either by exploiting the richer structure of functions represented by BDDs, or just for the sake of efficiency, when the set of labels is large (e.g., for type inference on object-oriented programs, where labels correspond to method names).

## 4. Kleene algebra with tests

Now we consider Kleene algebra with tests (KAT), for which we provide several automata constructions that allow us to use the previous symbolic algorithms.

A *Kleene algebra with tests* is a tuple $\langle X, B, \cdot, +, \cdot^\star, \neg, 1, 0\rangle$ such that:

(i) $\langle X, \cdot, +, \cdot^\star, 1, 0\rangle$ is a Kleene algebra [26], i.e., an idempotent semiring with a unary operation, called "Kleene star", satisfying the following axioms:

$$1 + x \cdot x^\star \leq x^\star$$
$$y \cdot x \leq x \Rightarrow y^\star \cdot x \leq x$$
$$x \cdot y \leq x \Rightarrow x \cdot y^\star \leq x$$

(the preorder ($\leq$) being defined by $x \leq y \triangleq x + y = y$);

(ii) $B \subseteq X$;

(iii) $\langle B, \cdot, +, \neg, 1, 0\rangle$ is a Boolean algebra.

The elements of the set $B$ are called "tests"; we denote them by $\phi, \psi$. The elements of $X$, called "Kleene elements", are denoted by $x, y, z$. We sometimes omit the operator "$\cdot$" from expressions, writing $xy$ for $x \cdot y$. The following (in)equations illustrate the kind of laws that hold in all Kleene algebra with tests:

$$\phi + \neg\phi = 1 \qquad \phi \cdot (\neg\phi + \psi) = \phi \cdot \psi = \neg(\neg\phi + \neg\psi)$$

$$x^\star x^\star = x^\star \qquad (x+y)^\star = x^\star(yx^\star)^\star \qquad (x+xxy)^\star \leq (x+xy)^\star$$

$$\phi \cdot (\neg\phi \cdot x)^\star = \phi \qquad \phi \cdot (\phi \cdot x \cdot \neg\phi + \neg\phi \cdot y \cdot \phi)^\star \cdot \phi \leq (x \cdot y)^\star$$

The laws from the first line come from the Boolean algebra structure, while the ones from the second line come from the Kleene algebra structure. The two laws from the last line require both Boolean algebra and Kleene algebra reasoning.

***Binary relations.*** Binary relations form a Kleene algebra with tests; this is the main model we are interested in, in practice. The Kleene elements are the binary relations over a given set $S$, the tests are the predicates over this set, encoded as sub-identity relations, and the star of a relation is its reflexive transitive closure.

This relational model is typically used to interpret imperative programs: such programs are state transformers, i.e., binary relations between states, and the conditions used to define the control-flow of these programs are just predicates on states. Typically, a program "`while` $\phi$ `do p`" is interpreted through the KAT expression $(\phi \cdot p)^\star \cdot \neg\phi$.

***KAT expressions.*** We denote by $\mathcal{R}eg(V)$ the set of *regular expressions* over a set $V$:

$$x, y ::= v \in V \mid x + y \mid x \cdot y \mid x^\star \ .$$

Assuming a set $A$ of elementary tests, we denote by $B(A)$ the set of *Boolean expressions* over $A$:

$$\phi, \psi ::= a \in A \mid 1 \mid 0 \mid \phi \wedge \phi \mid \phi \vee \phi \mid \neg\phi \ .$$

Further assuming a set $\Sigma$ of letters (or atomic Kleene elements), a *KAT expression* is a regular expression over the disjoint union $\Sigma \uplus B(A)$. We let $p, q$ range over elements of $\Sigma$. Note that the constants 0 and 1 from the signature of KAT, and usually found in the syntax of regular expressions, are represented here by injecting the corresponding tests.

***Guarded string languages.*** Guarded string languages are the natural generalisation of string languages for Kleene algebra with tests. We briefly define them.

An *atom* is a valuation from elementary tests to Booleans; it indicates which of these tests are satisfied. We let $\alpha, \beta$ range over atoms, the set of which is denoted by $At$: $At = 2^A$. A Boolean formula $\phi$ is *valid* under an atom $\alpha$, denoted by $\alpha \vDash \phi$, if $\phi$ evaluates to true under the valuation $\alpha$.

A *guarded string* is an alternating sequence of atoms and letters, both starting and ending with an atom:

$$\alpha_1, p_1, \alpha_2, \dots, \alpha_n, p_n, \alpha_{n+1} \ .$$

The concatenation $u * v$ of two guarded strings $u, v$ is a partial operation: it is defined only if the last atom of $u$ is equal to the first atom of $v$; it consists in concatenating the two sequences and removing one copy of the shared atom in the middle.

To any KAT expression, one associates a *guarded string language*, i.e., a set of guarded strings, as follows.

$$\begin{aligned}
G(\phi) &= \{\alpha \in At \mid \alpha \vDash \phi\} && (\phi \in B(A))\\
G(p) &= \{\alpha p \beta \mid \alpha, \beta \in At\} && (p \in \Sigma)\\
G(x + y) &= G(x) \cup G(y)\\
G(xy) &= \{u * v \mid u \in G(x), v \in G(y)\}\\
G(x^\star) &= \{u_1 * \dots * u_n \mid \exists u_1 \dots u_n, \forall i \leq n, u_i \in G(x)\}
\end{aligned}$$

***KAT Completeness.*** Kozen and Smith proved that the equational theory of Kleene algebra with tests is complete over the relational model [30]: any equation that holds universally in this model can be proved from the axioms of KAT. Moreover, two expressions are provably equal if and only if they denote the same language of guarded strings. By a reduction to automata theory this gives algorithms to decide the equational theory of KAT. Now we study several such algorithms, and we show each time how to exploit symbolic representations to make them efficient.

### 4.1 Brzozowski's derivatives

Derivatives were introduced by Brzozowski [11] for (plain) regular expressions; they make it possible to define a deterministic automaton where the states of the automaton are the regular expressions themselves.

Derivatives can be extended to KAT expressions in a very natural way [28]. We recall this extension in Figure 8: one first defines a Boolean function $\epsilon_\alpha$, that indicates whether an expression accepts

$$\begin{aligned}
\epsilon_\alpha(x{+}y) &= \epsilon_\alpha(x){+}\epsilon_\alpha(y)\\
\epsilon_\alpha(x{\cdot}y) &= \epsilon_\alpha(x){\cdot}\epsilon_\alpha(y)\\
\epsilon_\alpha(x^\star) &= 1\\
\epsilon_\alpha(q) &= 0\\
\epsilon_\alpha(\phi) &= \begin{cases} 1 & \text{if } \alpha \vDash \phi\\ 0 & \text{oth.}\end{cases}
\end{aligned}
\qquad
\begin{aligned}
\delta_{\alpha p}(x{+}y) &= \delta_{\alpha p}(x){+}\delta_{\alpha p}(y)\\
\delta_{\alpha p}(x{\cdot}y) &= \begin{cases} \delta_{\alpha p}(x){\cdot}y & \text{if } \epsilon_\alpha(x) = 0\\ \delta_{\alpha p}(x){\cdot}y{+}\delta_{\alpha p}(y) & \text{oth.}\end{cases}\\
\delta_{\alpha p}(x^\star) &= \delta_{\alpha p}(x) \cdot x^\star\\
\delta_{\alpha p}(q) &= \begin{cases} 1 & \text{if } p = q\\ 0 & \text{oth.}\end{cases}\\
\delta_{\alpha p}(\phi) &= 0
\end{aligned}$$

**Figure 8.** Explicit derivatives for KAT expressions

$$\begin{aligned}
\epsilon^{s}(x{+}y) &= \epsilon^{s}(x){\vee}\epsilon^{s}(y)\\
\epsilon^{s}(x{\cdot}y) &= \epsilon^{s}(x){\wedge}\epsilon^{s}(y)\\
\epsilon^{s}(x^\star) &= 1\\
\epsilon^{s}(p) &= 0\\
\epsilon^{s}(\phi) &= \phi
\end{aligned}
\qquad
\begin{aligned}
\delta^{s}(x{+}y) &= \delta^{s}(x) \oplus \delta^{s}(y)\\
\delta^{s}(x{\cdot}y) &= (\delta^{s}(x) \odot y) \oplus (\epsilon^{s}(x) \otimes \delta^{s}(y))\\
\delta^{s}(x^\star) &= \delta^{s}(x) \odot x^\star\\
\delta^{s}(p) &= \lceil p \mapsto 1, _ \mapsto 0 \rceil\\
\delta^{s}(\phi) &= 0
\end{aligned}$$

**Figure 9.** Symbolic derivatives for KAT expressions

the single atom $\alpha$; this function is then used to define the derivation function $\delta_{\alpha p}$, that intuitively returns what remains of the given expression after reading the atom $\alpha$ and the letter $p$. These two functions make it possible to give a coalgebraic characterisation of the characteristic function of $G$. We have:

$$G(x)(\alpha) = \epsilon_\alpha(x) \ , \qquad G(x)(\alpha p u) = G(\delta_{\alpha p}(x))(u) \ .$$

The tuple $\langle \mathcal{R}eg(\Sigma \uplus B(A)), \delta, \epsilon\rangle$ can be seen as a deterministic automaton with input alphabet $At \times \Sigma$, and output set $2^{At}$. Thanks to the above characterisation, a state $x$ in this automaton accepts precisely the guarded string language $G(x)$—modulo the isomorphism $(At \times \Sigma)^\star \to 2^{At} \approx \mathcal{P}((At \times \Sigma)^\star \times At)$.

However, we cannot directly apply the explicit algorithm from Section 2.1, because this automaton is not finite. First, there are infinitely many KAT expressions, so that we have to restrict to those that are accessible from the expressions we want to check for equality. This is however not sufficient: we also have to quotient regular expressions w.r.t. a few simple laws [28]. This quotient is simple to implement by normalising expressions; we thus assume that expressions are normalised in the remainder of this section.

***Symbolic derivatives.*** The input alphabet of the above automaton is exponentially large w.r.t. the number of primitive tests: $At \times \Sigma = 2^A \times \Sigma$. Therefore, the simple algorithm from Section 2.1 is not tractable in practice. Instead, we would like to use its symbolic version (Figure 5).

The output values, in $(2^{At} = 2^A \to 2)$, are also exponentially large, and are best represented symbolically, using Boolean BDDs. In fact, any test appearing in a KAT expression can be pre-compiled into a Boolean BDD: rather than working with regular expressions over $\Sigma \uplus B(A)$ we thus move to regular expressions over $\Sigma \uplus \mathrm{BDD}_A[2]$, which we call *symbolic KAT expressions*. We denote the set of such expressions by SyKAT, and we let $(\!|e|\!)$ denote the symbolic version of a KAT expression $e$.

Note that there is a slight discrepancy here w.r.t. Section 3: the input alphabet is $2^A \times \Sigma$ rather than just $2^{A'}$ for some $A'$. For the sake of simplicity, we just assume that $\Sigma$ is actually of the shape $2^{\Sigma'}$; alternatively, we could work with automata whose transition functions are represented partly symbolically (for $At$), and partly explicitly (for $\Sigma$)—this is what we do in the implementation.

We define the symbolic derivation operations in Figure 9.

The output function, $\epsilon^s$, has type SyKAT $\to$ $\mathrm{BDD}_A[2]$, it maps symbolic KAT expressions to Boolean BDD nodes. The operations used on the right-hand side of this definition are those on Boolean BDDs. The function $\epsilon^s$ is much more efficient than its explicit counterpart ($\epsilon$, in Figure 8): the set of all accepted atoms is computed at once, symbolically.

The function $\delta^s$ has type SyKAT $\to$ $\mathrm{BDD}_{A \uplus \Sigma'}[\mathrm{SyKAT}]$. It maps symbolic KAT expressions to BDDs whose leaves are themselves symbolic KAT expressions. Again, in contrast to its explicit counterpart, $\delta^s$ computes all the transitions of a given expression once and for all. The operations used on the right-hand side of the definition are the following ones:

- $n \oplus m$ is defined by applying pointwise the syntactic sum operation from KAT expressions to the two BDDs $n$ and $m$: $n \oplus m = \lfloor \phi \mapsto \lceil n \rceil(\phi) + \lceil m \rceil(\phi) \rfloor$;
- $n \odot x$ syntactically multiplies all leaves of the BDD $n$ by the expression $x$, from the right: $n \odot x = \lfloor \phi \mapsto \lfloor n \rfloor(\phi) \cdot x \rfloor$;
- $f \otimes n$ "multiplies" the Boolean BDD $f$ with the BDD $n$: $f \otimes n = \lfloor \phi \mapsto \lfloor n \rfloor(\phi)$ if $\lfloor f \rfloor(\phi) = 1, 0$ otherwise$\rfloor$.
- $\lfloor q \mapsto 1, \_ \mapsto 0 \rfloor$ is the BDD mapping $q$ to 1 and everything else to 0 ($q \in \Sigma = 2^{\Sigma'}$ being cast into an element of $2^{A \uplus \Sigma'}$).

By two simple inductions, one proves that for every expression $x \in$ SyKAT, atom $\alpha \in At$, and letter $p \in \Sigma$, we have:

$$\lceil \epsilon^s(\!|x|\!) \rceil(\alpha) = \epsilon_\alpha(x)$$
$$\lceil \delta^s(\!|x|\!) \rceil(\alpha p) = (\!|\delta_{\alpha p}(x)|\!)$$

(Again, we abuse notation by letting the pair $\alpha p$ denote an element of $2^{A \uplus \Sigma'}$.) This ensures that the symbolic deterministic automaton $\langle \mathrm{SyKAT}, \delta^s, \epsilon^s \rangle$ faithfully represents the previous explicit automaton, and that we can use the symbolic algorithms from Section 3.

### 4.2 Partial derivatives

An alternative to Brzozowski's derivatives consists in using Antimirov' *partial derivatives* [4], which generalise to KAT in a straightforward way [34]. The difference with Brzozowski's derivative is that they produce a non-deterministic automaton: states are still expressions, but the derivation function produces a set of expressions. An advantage is that we do not need to normalise expressions on the fly: the set of partial derivatives reachable from an expression is always finite.

We give directly the symbolic definition, which is very similar to the previous one.

$$\delta'^s(x+y) = \delta'^s(x) \uplus \delta'^s(y)$$
$$\delta'^s(x \cdot y) = (\delta'^s(x) \boxdot y) \uplus (\epsilon^s(x) \boxtimes \delta'^s(y))$$
$$\delta'^s(x^\star) = \delta'^s(x) \boxdot x^\star$$
$$\delta'^s(p) = \lfloor p \mapsto \{1\}, \_ \mapsto \emptyset \rfloor$$
$$\delta'^s(\phi) = \emptyset$$

The differences lie in the BDD operations, whose leaves are now sets of expressions:

- $n \uplus m = \lfloor \phi \mapsto \lceil n \rceil(\phi) \cup \lceil m \rceil(\phi) \rfloor$;
- $n \boxdot x = \lfloor \phi \mapsto \{x' \cdot x \mid x' \in \lceil n \rceil(\phi)\} \rfloor$;
- $f \boxtimes n = \lfloor \phi \mapsto \lceil n \rceil(\phi)$ if $\lceil f \rceil(\phi) = 1, \emptyset$ otherwise$\rfloor$.

One can finally relate partial derivatives to Brzozowski's one:

$$\mathrm{KA} \vdash \sum \lceil \delta'^s(x) \rceil(\alpha p) = (\!|\delta_{\alpha p}(x)|\!) \ .$$

(The above $\Sigma$ denotes the iterated sum of the set of partial derivatives—we do not have a syntactic equality because partial derivatives inherently exploit the fact that multiplication distributes over sums.) Using symbolic determinisation as described in Section 3.2, one can thus use the algorithm from Section 3 with Antimirov' partial derivatives.

### 4.3 Ilie & Yu's construction

Other automata constructions from the literature can be generalised to KAT expressions. We can for instance consider Ilie and Yu's construction [25], which produces non-deterministic automata with epsilon transitions with exactly one initial state, and one accepting state.

We consider a slightly simplified version here, where we omit a few optimisations and just proceed by induction on the expression. The four cases are depicted below: $i$ and $f$ are the initial and accepting states, respectively; in the concatenation and star cases, a new state $j$ is introduced.

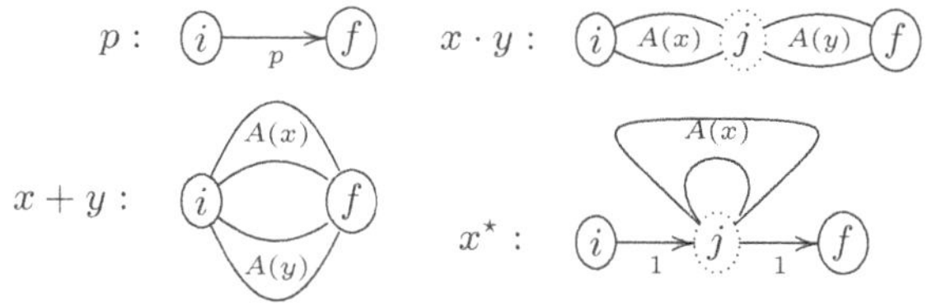


To adapt this construction to KAT expressions, it suffices to generalise epsilon transitions to transitions labelled by tests. In the base case for a test $\phi$, we just add a transition labelled by $\phi$ between $i$ and $f$; the two epsilon transitions needed for the star case just become transitions labelled by the constant test 1.

As expected, when starting from a symbolic KAT expression, those counterparts to epsilon transitions are labelled by Boolean BDD nodes rather than by explicit Boolean expressions.

***Epsilon cycles.*** The most important optimisation we miss with this simplified presentation of Ilie and Yu's construction is that we should merge states that belong to cycles of epsilon transitions. An alternative to this optimisation consists in normalising first the expressions so that for all subexpressions of the shape $e^\star$, $e$ does not contain 1, i.e., $\epsilon^s(e) \neq 1$. Such a normalisation procedure has been proposed for plain regular expressions by Brüggemann-Klein [8]. When working with such normal forms, the automata produced by the above simplified construction (on plain regular expressions) have acyclic epsilon transitions, so that the aforementioned optimisation is unnecessary.

This normalisation procedure generalises easily to (symbolic) KAT expressions. For instance, here are typical normalisations:

$$(\phi + p)^\star \mapsto p^\star \tag{1}$$
$$(p^\star + q)^\star \mapsto (p + q)^\star \tag{2}$$
$$((1 + p)(1 + q))^\star \mapsto (p + q)^\star \tag{3}$$

We say that Symbolic KAT expressions satisfying the above property are in *strict star form*. The normalisation procedure is linear in the size of the expressions; it always produces a smaller expression. As a consequence, when deciding whether a KAT equation holds or not, it is always beneficial to put the expressions in strict star form first, independently from the considered automata construction. (See the experiments in Section 5).

According to the example (1), it might be tempting to strengthen example (3) into $((\phi + p)(\psi + q))^\star \mapsto (p + q)^\star$. Such a step is invalid, unfortunately. (The second expression accepts the guarded string $\alpha p \beta$ for all $\alpha, \beta$, while the starting expression needs $\beta \vDash \psi$.) This example seems to show that one cannot ensure that all starred

| | iterations | | time | | NFA states | DFA states |
|---|---|---|---|---|---|---|
| | symb_equiv | dsf_equiv | symb_equiv | dsf_equiv | | |
| Antimirov ∘ ssf | 6715 | 3980 | 0.53s | 0.47s | 2704 | 4142 |
| Antimirov | 7141 | 4256 | 0.84s | 0.74s | 3039 | 4442 |
| Ilie & Yu ∘ ssf | 6985 | 4209 | 1.77s | 1.73s | 4716 | 4441 |
| Ilie & Yu | 7328 | 4445 | 3.89s | 3.83s | 5730 | 4647 |
| Brzozowski ∘ ssf | 11952 | 6525 | 6.88s | 4.67s | - | 6684 |
| Brzozowski | 19781 | 10080 | 43.00s | 30.00s | - | 10265 |

**Table 1.** Checking random saturated pairs of expressions.

subexpressions are mapped to 0 by $\epsilon^s$. As a consequence we cannot assume that test-labelled transitions generated by Ilie and Yu's construction form an acyclic graph in general.

### 4.4 Test-labelled transitions removal

The above construction produces symbolic NFA with test-labelled transitions, which have to be eliminated in order to apply the algorithms from Section 3. Other constructions from the literature produce automata with epsilon transitions and can be adapted to KAT using test-labelled transitions. A generic procedure for eliminating such transitions is thus desirable.

The usual technique with plain automata consists in computing the reflexive transitive closure of epsilon transitions, to precompose the other transitions with the resulting relation, and declare a state as accepting in the new automaton whenever it can reach an accepting state through this reflexive-transitive closure.

More formally, let us recall Kozen's matricial representation of non-deterministic automaton with epsilon transitions [26], as tuples $\langle n, u, J, N, v\rangle$, where $u$ is a $(1,n)$ 01-matrix denoting the initial states, $J$ is a $(n,n)$ 01-valued matrix denoting the epsilon transitions, $N$ is a $(n,n)$ matrix representing the other transitions (with entries sets of letters in $\Sigma$), and $v$ is a $(n,1)$ 01-matrix encoding the accepting states.

The language accepted by such an automaton can be represented by the following matricial product, using Kleene star on matrices:

$$u \cdot (J+N)^\star \cdot v \ .$$

Thanks to the algebraic law $(a+b)^\star = a^\star \cdot (b \cdot a^\star)^\star$, which is valid in any Kleene algebra, we get

$$\mathrm{KA} \vdash u \cdot (J+N)^\star \cdot v = u \cdot (J^\star N)^\star \cdot (J^\star v) \ .$$

We finally check that $\langle n, u, 0, J^\star N, J^\star v\rangle$ represents a non-deterministic automaton without epsilon transitions. This is how Kozen validates epsilon elimination for plain automata, algebraically [26].

The same can be done here for KAT by noticing that tests (or Boolean BDD nodes) form a Kleene algebra with a degenerate star operation: the constant-to-1 function. One can thus generalise the above reasoning to the case where $J$ is a tests-valued matrix rather than a 01-matrix.

The iteration $J^\star$ of such a matrix can be computed using standard shortest-path algorithms [21], on top of the efficient semiring of Boolean BDD nodes. The resulting automaton has the expected type:

- there is a transition labelled by $\alpha p$ between $i$ and $j$ if there exists a $k$ such that $\alpha \vDash (J^\star)_{i,k}$ and $p \in N_{k,j}$. (The corresponding non-deterministic symbolic transition function can be computed efficiently using appropriate BDD functions.)
- The output value of a state $i$ is the Boolean BDD node obtained by taking the disjunction of all the $(J^\star)_{i,j}$ such that $j$ is an accepting state (i.e., just $(J^\star)_{(i,f)}$ when using Ilie and Yu's construction).

## 5. Experiments

We implemented all presented algorithms in OCaml; the corresponding library is available online, together with an applet allowing to trace them on user-provided examples [35].

Symbolic KAT expressions are hash-consed, which allows us to represent sets of expressions using Patricia trees (e.g., for Antimirov' partial derivates). Expressions are also normalised using smart constructors: sums associated to the left, sorted, and without duplicates; products are associated to the left; consecutive tests are merged; units are cancelled as much as possible. For Antimirov' construction and for Ilie and Yu's construction, the produced symbolic NFA are memoised once and for all, and reindexed so that their states are just natural numbers. This allows us to use bit-vectors to represent sets produced during determinisation. The queue `todo` used for storing the pairs to process is a FIFO queue, so that the automata are explored in a breadth-first manner.

We performed a few experiments to compare the presented algorithms and constructions. We generated random KAT expressions over two sets of seven primitive tests and seven atomic elements, with seventy connectives, and excluding explicit occurrences of the constants 0 and 1. A hundred pairs of random expressions were checked for equality after being saturated by adding the constant $\Sigma^\star$ on both sides. (A difficulty here is that random pairs of expressions are almost always distinguished by a very short guarded string, which is found almost immediately thanks to the breadth-first strategy, independently from the size of the expressions and from the up-to techniques at work. Instead, we would like to evaluate the algorithms based on their running time on more interesting pairs, where the expressions are either equivalent or distinguished only by long guarded strings. By saturating the expressions with the constant $\Sigma^\star$, we artificially make the expressions equivalent. Moreover, looking at an execution of the presented algorithms on such saturated pairs, what happens is that the output test (line 10 on Figure 1) always succeeds, so that the algorithms stop only once the whole automata have been explored and a bisimulation has been found. Moreover, an analysis of the various automata constructions shows that the automata constructed for an expression $p$ are very similar to the automata constructed for the expression $p + \Sigma^\star$: exploring the latter is as hard as exploring the former.)

The results are displayed in Table 1: for each construction and for each of the two symbolic algorithms, we give the total number of iterations (i.e., the number of times we execute line 10 in Figure 5), and the global running time[2]. Each construction is associated to two lines, depending on whether we first put expressions in strict star form or not. We additionally provide the total number of NFA states generated by Antimirov' and Ilie and Yu's constructions, as well as the total number of DFA states generated for the three constructions.

One can notice than Antimirov' partial derivatives provide the fastest algorithms. Ilie and Yu's construction yield approximately

[2] Theses experiments were performed on a MacBook Pro, OS X 10.9.5, 2,4GHz Intel Core i7, 4Go 1333MHz DDR3, OCaml 4.02.1

the same number of iterations as Antimirov' partial derivatives, but require more time: computing the transitive closure for epsilon removal is a costly operation. Brzozowski's construction gives poor results both in terms of time and iterations: the produced automata are larger, and more difficult to compute.

Concerning the equivalence algorithm, one notices that using disjoint set forests significantly reduces the number of iterations. There is almost no difference in the running times with the first two constructions, because most of the time is spent in constructing the automata rather than checking them for equivalence. This is no longer true with Brzozowski's construction, for which the automata are sufficiently big to observe a difference.

## 6. Directions for future work

The equational theory of KAT is PSPACE-complete, but none of the presented algorithms are PSPACE (just because of the use BDDs, but also because the bisimulation candidate, which has to be stored, can be exponentially large). Experiments however suggest that they can be useful in practice: the symbolic DFA produced by the various constructions proposed in this paper tend to be of reasonable size. Quantifying this empirical observation in a formal way seems extremely difficult.

A natural extension of this work would be to apply the proposed algorithms to KAT+B! [19] and NetKAT [2], two extensions of KAT with important applications in verification: while programs with mutable tests in the former case, and network programming in the later case.

KAT+B! has a EXPSPACE-complete equational theory, and its structure makes explicit algorithms completely useless. Designing symbolic algorithms for KAT+B! seems challenging.

NetKAT remains PSPACE-complete, and Foster et al. propose in the present volume a coalgebraic decision procedure relying on a variation of Antimirov' derivatives [17]. To get a practical algorithm, they represent automata transitions using sparse matrices, and they exploit some form of symbolic treatment by using what they call "bases". KAT can be encoded into NetKAT, so that their algorithm could be used for KAT. This encoding is however not streamlined, and it is non-trivial to understand the behaviour of their algorithm on the resulting instances. Conversely, adapting the algorithms presented in the present paper to cope with NetKAT seems feasible, although not straightforward. Concerning the symbolic treatment of automata, our use of BDDs seems more powerful and less ad-hoc than their use of bases, but the precise relationship remains unclear, and we leave its formal analysis for future work.

Moving away from KAT specificities, we leave open the question of the complexity of our symbolic variant of Hopcroft and Karp's algorithm (Figure 7). Tarjan proved that their algorithm is almost linear in amortised time complexity, and he made a list of heuristics for linking and path compression schemes that lead to that complexity [40]; together with Goel, Khanna and Larkin, he recently showed that this complexity is still reached (asymptotically) with randomized linking [18]. A similar study for the symbolic counterpart we propose here remains to be done.

## Acknowledgments

We are grateful to the anonymous referees who provided thorough and detailed reviews, and in particular to the one who noticed the relationship between the present work and Rémy's type inference algorithm for row types.

## References

[1] P. A. Abdulla, Y.-F. Chen, L. Holík, R. Mayr, and T. Vojnar. When simulation meets antichains. In *Proc. TACAS*, volume 6015 of *Lecture Notes in Computer Science*, pages 158–174. Springer Verlag, 2010.

[2] C. J. Anderson, N. Foster, A. Guha, J.-B. Jeannin, D. Kozen, C. Schlesinger, and D. Walker. Netkat: semantic foundations for networks. In *Proc. POPL*, pages 113–126. ACM, 2014.

[3] A. Angus and D. Kozen. Kleene algebra with tests and program schematology. Technical Report TR2001-1844, CS Dpt., Cornell University, July 2001.

[4] V. M. Antimirov. Partial derivatives of regular expressions and finite automaton constructions. *Theoretical Computer Science*, 155(2):291–319, 1996.

[5] S. L. Bloom, Z. Ésik, and G. Stefanescu. Notes on equational theories of relations. *Algebra Universalis*, 33(1):98–126, 1995.

[6] F. Bonchi and D. Pous. Checking NFA equivalence with bisimulations up to congruence. In *Proc. POPL*, pages 457–468. ACM, 2013.

[7] A. Bouajjani, P. Habermehl, and T. Vojnar. Abstract regular model checking. In *Proc. CAV*, volume 3114 of *Lecture Notes in Computer Science*, pages 372–386. Springer Verlag, 2004.

[8] A. Brüggemann-Klein. Regular expressions into finite automata. *Theoretical Computer Science*, 120(2):197–213, 1993.

[9] R. E. Bryant. Graph-based algorithms for boolean function manipulation. *IEEE Trans. Computers*, 35(8):677–691, 1986.

[10] R. E. Bryant. Symbolic Boolean manipulation with ordered binary-decision diagrams. *ACM Computing Surveys*, 24(3):293–318, 1992.

[11] J. A. Brzozowski. Derivatives of regular expressions. *Journal of the ACM*, 11(4):481–494, 1964.

[12] E. Cohen, D. Kozen, and F. Smith. The complexity of Kleene algebra with tests. Technical Report TR96-1598, CS Dpt., Cornell University, 1996.

[13] L. D'Antoni and M. Veanes. Minimization of symbolic automata. In *POPL*, pages 541–554. ACM, 2014.

[14] L. Doyen and J.-F. Raskin. Antichain Algorithms for Finite Automata. In *Proc. TACAS*, volume 6015 of *Lecture Notes in Computer Science*. Springer Verlag, 2010.

[15] Z. Ésik and L. Bernátsky. Equational properties of Kleene algebras of relations with conversion. *Theoretical Computer Science*, 137(2):237–251, 1995.

[16] J.-C. Filliâtre and S. Conchon. Type-safe modular hash-consing. In *ML*, pages 12–19. ACM, 2006.

[17] N. Foster, D. Kozen, M. Milano, A. Silva, and L. Thompson. A coalgebraic decision procedure for NetKAT. In *Proc. POPL*. ACM, 2015.

[18] A. Goel, S. Khanna, D. Larkin, and R. E. Tarjan. Disjoint set union with randomized linking. In *Proc. SODA*, pages 1005–1017. SIAM, 2014.

[19] N. B. B. Grathwohl, D. Kozen, and K. Mamouras. KAT + B! In *Proc. CSL-LICS*. ACM, July 2014.

[20] J. G. Henriksen, J. L. Jensen, M. E. Jørgensen, N. Klarlund, R. Paige, T. Rauhe, and A. Sandholm. Mona: Monadic second-order logic in practice. In *TACAS*, volume 1019 of *Lecture Notes in Computer Science*, pages 89–110. Springer Verlag, 1995.

[21] P. Höfner and B. Möller. Dijkstra, Floyd and Warshall meet Kleene. *Formal Aspects of Computing*, 24(4-6):459–476, 2012.

[22] J. E. Hopcroft. An $n\log n$ algorithm for minimizing states in a finite automaton. Technical report, Stanford University, 1971.

[23] J. E. Hopcroft and R. M. Karp. A linear algorithm for testing equivalence of finite automata. Technical Report 114, Cornell University, December 1971.

[24] G. Huet. *Résolution d'équations dans les langages d'ordre 1,2, ... ,$\omega$*. PhD thesis, Université Paris VII, 1976. Thèse d'État.

[25] L. Ilie and S. Yu. Follow automata. *Information and Computation*, 186(1):140–162, 2003.

[26] D. Kozen. A completeness theorem for Kleene algebras and the algebra of regular events. *Information and Computation*, 110(2):366–390, 1994.

[27] D. Kozen. Kleene algebra with tests. *Transactions on Programming Languages and Systems*, 19(3):427–443, May 1997.

[28] D. Kozen. On the coalgebraic theory of Kleene algebra with tests. Technical report, CIS, Cornell University, March 2008.

[29] D. Kozen and M.-C. Patron. Certification of compiler optimizations using Kleene algebra with tests. In *Proc. CL2000*, volume 1861 of *Lecture Notes in Artificial Intelligence*, pages 568–582. Springer Verlag, 2000.

[30] D. Kozen and F. Smith. Kleene algebra with tests: Completeness and decidability. In *Proc. CSL*, volume 1258 of *Lecture Notes in Computer Science*, pages 244–259. Springer Verlag, September 1996.

[31] E. F. Moore. Gedanken-experiments on sequential machines. *Automata Studies, Annals of Mathematical Studies*, 34:129–153, 1956.

[32] R. Paige and R. E. Tarjan. Three partition refinement algorithms. *SIAM Journal on Computing*, 16(6):973–989, 1987.

[33] F. Pottier and D. Rémy. *Advanced Topics in Types and Programming Languages*, chapter The Essence of ML Type Inference. MIT Press, 2004.

[34] D. Pous. Kleene Algebra with Tests and Coq tools for while programs. In *Proc. ITP*, volume 7998 of *Lecture Notes in Computer Science*, pages 180–196. Springer Verlag, 2013.

[35] D. Pous. Web appendix to this paper, with Ocaml implementation of the proposed algorithms, 2014. `http://perso.ens-lyon.fr/damien.pous/symbolickat`.

[36] D. Pous and D. Sangiorgi. *Advanced Topics in Bisimulation and Coinduction*, chapter about "Enhancements of the coinductive proof method". Cambridge University Press, 2011.

[37] D. Rémy. *Algèbres Touffues. Application au Typage Polymorphe des Objets Enregistrements dans les Langages Fonctionnels*. PhD thesis, Université Paris VII, 1990. Thèse de doctorat.

[38] D. Rémy. Extension of ML type system with a sorted equational theory on types, 1992. Research Report 1766.

[39] D. Sangiorgi. On the bisimulation proof method. *Mathematical Structures in Computer Science*, 8:447–479, 1998.

[40] R. E. Tarjan. Efficiency of a good but not linear set union algorithm. *Journal of the ACM*, 22(2):215–225, 1975.

[41] M. Veanes. Applications of symbolic finite automata. In *CIAA*, volume 7982 of *Lecture Notes in Computer Science*, pages 16–23. Springer Verlag, 2013.

[42] M. D. Wulf, L. Doyen, T. A. Henzinger, and J.-F. Raskin. Antichains: A new algorithm for checking universality of finite automata. In *Proc. CAV*, volume 4144 of *Lecture Notes in Computer Science*, pages 17–30. Springer Verlag, 2006.

# Programming up to Congruence

Vilhelm Sjöberg Stephanie Weirich
University of Pennsylvania, Philadelphia, PA, USA
{vilhelm,sweirich}@cis.upenn.edu

## Abstract

This paper presents the design of ZOMBIE, a dependently-typed programming language that uses an adaptation of a congruence closure algorithm for proof and type inference. This algorithm allows the type checker to automatically use equality assumptions from the context when reasoning about equality. Most dependently-typed languages automatically use equalities that follow from $\beta$-reduction during type checking; however, such reasoning is incompatible with congruence closure. In contrast, ZOMBIE does not use automatic $\beta$-reduction because types may contain potentially diverging terms. Therefore ZOMBIE provides a unique opportunity to explore an alternative definition of equivalence in dependently-typed language design.

Our work includes the specification of the language via a bidirectional type system, which works "up-to-congruence," and an algorithm for elaborating expressions in this language to an explicitly typed core language. We prove that our elaboration algorithm is complete with respect to the source type system, and always produces well typed terms in the core language. This algorithm has been implemented in the ZOMBIE language, which includes general recursion, irrelevant arguments, heterogeneous equality and datatypes.

***Categories and Subject Descriptors*** D.3.1 [*Programming Languages*]: Formal Definitions and Theory

***Keywords*** Dependent types; Congruence closure

## 1. Introduction

The ZOMBIE language [9] aims to provide a smooth path from ordinary functional programming in a language like Haskell to dependently typed programming in a language like Agda. However, one significant difference between Haskell and Agda is that in the latter, programmers must show that every function terminates. Such proofs often require delicate reasoning, especially when they must be done in conjunction with the function definition. In contrast, ZOMBIE includes arbitrary nontermination, relying on the type system to track whether an expression has been typechecked in the normalizing fragment of the language.


*POPL '15*, January 15–17, 2015, Mumbai, India.

ACM 978-1-4503-3300-9/15/01... $15.00.
http://dx.doi.org/10.1145/2676726.2676974

Prior work on ZOMBIE [9, 26] has focused on the metatheory of the core language—type safety for the entire language and consistency for the normalizing fragment—and provides a solid foundation. However, it is not feasible to write programs directly in the core language because the terms get cluttered with type annotations and type conversion proofs. This paper addresses the other half of the design: crafting a programmer-friendly *surface language*, which elaborates into the core.

The reason that elaboration is important in this context is that core ZOMBIE has a weak definition of equivalence. Most dependently-typed languages define terms to be equal when they are (at least) $\beta$-convertible. However, the presence of nontermination makes this definition awkward. To check whether two types are $\beta$-equivalent the type checker has to evaluate expressions inside them, which becomes problematic if expressions may diverge—what if the type checker gets stuck in an infinite loop? Existing languages fix an arbitrary global cut off for how many steps of evaluation the type-checker is willing to do (Cayenne [3]), or only reduce expressions that have passed a conservative termination test (Idris [8]). Core ZOMBIE, somewhat radically, omits automatic $\beta$-conversion completely. Instead, $\beta$-equality is available only through explicit conversion.

Because ZOMBIE does not include automatic $\beta$-conversion, it provides an opportunity to explore an alternative definition of equivalence in a surface language design.

*Congruence closure*, also known as the theory of equality with uninterpreted function symbols, is a basic operation in automatic theorem provers for first-order logic (particularly SMT solvers, such as Z3 [12]). Given some context $\Gamma$ which contains assumptions of the form $a = b$, the congruence closure of $\Gamma$ is the set of equations which are deducible by reflexivity, symmetry, transitivity, and changing subterms.

Although efficient algorithms for congruence closure are well-known [14, 19, 24] this reasoning principle has seen little use in *dependently-typed programming languages*. The problem is not lack of opportunity. Dependently-typed languages feature *propositional equality*, written $a = b$, which is a type that asserts the equality of the two expressions. Programs that use propositional equality build members of this type (using assumptions in the context, and various lemmas) and specify where and how they should be used. Congruence closure can assist with both of these tasks by automating the construction of these proofs and determining the "motive" for their elimination.

However, the adaption of this first-order technique to the higher-order logics of dependently-typed languages is not straightforward. The combination of congruence closure and full $\beta$-reduction makes the equality relation undecidable. As a result, most dependently-typed languages take the conservative approach of only incorporating congruence closure as a meta-operation, such as Coq's `congruence` tactic. While this tactic can assist with the creation of equality proofs, such proofs must still be explicitly eliminated. Proposals to use equations from the context automatically [1, 27, 28] have done so *in addition* to $\beta$-reduction, which makes it hard to characterize exactly which programs will typecheck, and also leaves open the question of how expressive congruence closure is in isolation.

In this work we define the ZOMBIE surface language to be fully "up to congruence", i.e. types which are equated by congruence closure can always be used interchangeably, and then show how the elaborator can implement this type system.

Designing a language around an elaborator—an unavoidably complicated piece of software—raises the risk of making the language hard to understand. Programmers could find it difficult to predict what core term a given surface term will elaborate to, or they may have to think about the details of the elaboration algorithm in order to understand whether a program will successfully elaborate at all.

We avoid these problems using two strategies. First, the syntax of the surface and the core language differ only by *erasable annotations* and the operational semantics ignores these annotations. Therefore the semantics of an expression is apparent just from looking at the source; the elaborator only adds annotations that can not change its behavior. Second, we define a *declarative specification* of the surface language, and prove that the elaborator is complete for the specification. As a result, the programmer does not have to think about the concrete elaboration algorithm.

We make the following contributions:

- We demonstrate how congruence closure is useful when programming, by comparing examples written in Agda, ZOMBIE, and ZOMBIE's explicitly-typed core language (Section 2).
- We define a dependently typed core language where the syntax contains erasable annotations (Section 3).
- We define a typed version of the congruence closure relation that is compatible with our core language, including features (erasure, injectivity, and generalized assumption) suitable for a dependent type system (Section 4).
- We specify the surface language using a bidirectional type system that uses this congruence closure relation as its *definition* of type equality (Section 5).
- We define an elaboration algorithm of the surface language to the core language (Section 6) based on a novel algorithm for typed congruence closure (Section 7). We prove that our elaboration algorithm is complete for the surface language and produces well-typed core language expressions. Our typed congruence closure algorithm both decides whether two terms are in the relation and also produces core language equality proofs.
- We have implemented these algorithms in ZOMBIE, extending the ideas of this paper to a language that includes datatypes and pattern matching, a richer logical fragment, and other features. Congruence closure works well in this setting; in particular, it significantly simplifies the typing rules for case-expressions (Section 8). Our implementation is available.[1]

For space reasons, the full specification of the type systems described in this paper and the details of the proofs are only included in the extended version [25].

[1] `https://code.google.com/p/trellys/`

## 2. Programming up to congruence

Consider this simple proof in Agda, which shows that zero is a right identity for addition.

```
npluszero : (n : Nat) → n + 0 ≡ n
npluszero zero    = refl
npluszero (suc m) = cong suc (npluszero m)
```

The proof follows by induction on natural numbers. In the base case, `refl` is a proof of `0 = 0`. In the next line, `cong` translates a proof of `m + 0 ≡ m` (from the recursive call) to a proof of `suc(m + 0) ≡ suc m`.

This proof relies on the fact that Agda's propositional equality relation (≡) is reflexive and a congruence relation. The former property holds by definition, but the latter must be explicitly shown. In other words, the proof relies on the following lemma:

```
cong : ∀ {A B} {m n : A}
       → (f : A → B) → m ≡ n → f m ≡ f n
cong f refl = refl
```

Now compare this proof to a similar result in ZOMBIE. The same reasoning is present: the proof follows via natural number induction, using the reduction behavior of addition in both cases.

```
npluszero : (n : Nat) → (n + 0 = n)
npluszero n =
  case n [eq] of
   Zero → (join : 0 + 0 = 0)
   Suc m →
     let _ = npluszero m in
       (join : (Suc m) + 0 = Suc (m + 0))
```

Because ZOMBIE does not provide automatic $\beta$-equivalence, reduction must be made explicit above. The term `join` explicitly introduces an equality based on reduction. However, in the successor case, the ZOMBIE type checker is able to infer exactly how the equalities should be put together.

For comparison, the corresponding ZOMBIE core language term includes a number of explicit type coercions:

```
npluszero : (n : Nat) → (n + 0 = n)
npluszero (n : Nat) =
  case n [eq] of
   Zero → join [↝ 0 + 0 = 0]
              ▷ join [~eq + 0 = ~eq]
   Suc m →
     let ih = npluszero m in
      join [↝ (Suc m) + 0 = Suc (m + 0)]
         ▷ join [(Suc m) + 0 = Suc ~ih]
         ▷ join [~eq + 0 = ~eq]
```

Above, an expression of the form $a \triangleright b$ converts the type of the expression $a$, using the equality proof $b$. Equality proofs may be formed in two ways, either via co-reduction (if $a_1$ and $a_2$ both reduce to some common term $b$, then join[$\leadsto a_1 = a_2$ ] is a proof of their equality) or by congruence (if $a$ is a proof of $b_1$=$b_2$, then join[ $\{\sim a/x\}A$ ] is a proof of $\{b_1/x\}A = \{b_2/x\}A$).

Both sorts of equality proofs are constructed in the example. In the base case, The proof `join[↝ 0 + 0 = 0]` follows from reduction, and is converted to be a proof of `(n + 0) = n` by the congruence proof. Here, `eq` is a proof that `0 = n`, an assumption derived from pattern matching. Congruence reasoning constructs a

```
{-# NO_TERMINATION_CHECK #-}
unify : (t1 t2 : Term) → Unify t1 t2
unify leaf leaf = match empty refl
unify leaf (branch t2 t3) = nomatch
unify (branch t1 t2) leaf = nomatch
unify (branch t11 t12) (branch t21 t22)
      with unify t11 t21
...    | nomatch = nomatch
...    | match s p with unify (ap s t12) (ap s t22)
...                | nomatch = nomatch
...                | match s' q
  = match (compose s' s)
       (trans (apCompose (branch t11 t12))
         (trans (cong2 (λ t1 t2 →
                  branch (ap s' t1) t2) p q)
            (sym (apCompose (branch t21 t22)))))
unify t1 (var x) with (x is∈ t1)
...               | no q
  = match (singleton x t1)
       (trans (singleton-∉ t x t q)
         (varSingleton x t))
...               | yes p with t
...                      | var y
  = match empty (cong var (sym (invvar p)))
...                      | _
  = nomatch
unify (var x) t2 with unify t2 (var x)
...               | nomatch   = nomatch
...               | match s p = match s (sym p)
```

```
prog unify : (t1 t2 : Term) → Unify t1 t2
rec unify t1 = \ t2 . case t1, t2 of
    leaf, leaf → match empty _
    leaf, branch _ _ → nomatch
    branch _ _, leaf → nomatch
    branch t11 t12, branch t21 t22 →
      case (unify t11 t21) of
        nomatch → nomatch
        match s p → case (unify (ap s t12) (ap s t22)) of
            nomatch → nomatch
            match s' _ →
              unfold (ap s' (ap s t1)) in
              unfold (ap s' (ap s t2)) in
              let _ = apCompose s' s t1 in
              let _ = apCompose s' s t2 in
                match (compose s' s) _
    _ , var x → case (isin x t1) of
        no q →
           let _ = varSingleton x t1 in
           let _ = singletonNotIn t1 x t1 q in
             match (singleton x t1) _
        yes _ → case t1 of
           var y → let [_] = invvar x y p in
                       match empty _
           _     →
                         nomatch
    var x, _ → case (unify t2 (var x)) of
        nomatch → nomatch
        match s p → match s _
```

**Figure 1.** First-order unification in Agda (left) and in ZOMBIE (right)

proof that that `((0 + 0) = 0) = ((n + 0) = n)`; the parts that differ on each side of the equality are marked by `~eq` in the congruence proof. The successor case uses congruence twice. The equality derived from reduction is first coerced by a congruence derived from the recursive call (`ih : m + 0 = m`), so that it has type `((Suc m) + 0 = Suc m)`. This equality is then coerced by a congruence derived from `eq : (Suc m = n)`, so that the result has type `(n + 0) = n`.

For a larger example, consider unification of first-order terms (Figure 1). For this example, the term language is the simplest possible, consisting only of binary trees constructed by `branch` and `leaf` and possibly containing unification variables, `var`, represented as natural numbers. We also use a type `Substitution` of substitutions, which are built by the functions `singleton` and `compose`, and applied to terms by `ap`.

Proving that `unify` terminates is difficult because the termination metric involves not just the structure of the terms but also the number of unassigned unification variables. (For example, see McBride [18]). To save development effort, a programmer may elect to prove only a partial correctness property: *if* the function terminates then the substitution it returns is a unifier.

In other words, if the `unify` function returns, it either says that the terms do not match, or produces a substitution `s` and a proof that `s` unifies them. We write the data structure in ZOMBIE as follows (the Agda version is similar):

```
data Unify (t1 : Term) (t2 : Term) : Type where
  nomatch
  match of (s : Substitution) (pf : ap s t1 = ap s t2)
```

Comparing the Agda and ZOMBIE implementations, we can see the effect of programming up-to-congruence instead of up-to-$\beta$. When the unifier returns `match`, it needs to supply a proof of equality. The Agda version explicitly constructs the proof using equational reasoning, which involves calling congruence lemmas `sym`, `trans`, `cong` and cong$_2$ from the standard library. The ZOMBIE version leaves such proof arguments as just an underscore, meaning that it can be inferred from the equations in the context. For that purpose, it introduces equalities to the context with `unfold` (for $\beta$-reductions, see Section 8.2) and with calls to relevant lemmas.

Figure 2 demonstrates how congruence closure makes ZOMBIE's version of dependently-typed pattern matching (i.e *smart case*) both simple and powerful. The figure compares (parts of) inductive proofs in ZOMBIE and Agda of an inversion lemma about the `snoc` operation, which appends an element to the end of a list. When both lists are nonempty, the proof argument can be used to derive that `x = y` (using the injectivity of `Cons`), and the recursive call shows that `xs' = ys'`. Congruence closure both puts these together in a proof of `Cons x xs' = Cons y ys'` and supplies the necessary proof for the recursive call.

In Agda, one is tempted to prove the property by pattern matching on the equality between the lists. This approach leads to a "quite fun" puzzle.[2] Here, the equivalence between `x` and `y` cannot be observed until `(snoc xs' z)` and `(snoc xs' z)` are named. The so-called "inspect on steroids" trick provides the equalities `(p : (snoc xs' z = s2)` and `q : (snoc ys' z) = s2)` that are necessary to constructing the fourth argument for the recursive call.

[2] Posed by Eric Mertens on `#agda`.

```
log snoc_inv : (xs ys : List A) → (z : A) → ((snoc xs z) = (snoc ys z)) → xs = ys
ind snoc_inv xs = \ ys z pf.  case xs [xeq], ys of
      Cons x xs' , Cons y ys' →
         let _ = (smartjoin : (snoc xs z) = Cons x (snoc xs' z)) in
         let _ = (smartjoin : (snoc ys z) = Cons y (snoc ys' z)) in
         let _ = snoc_inv xs' [ord xeq] ys' z _ in
            _
      ...

-- Agda pattern matching based solution
snoc-inv : ∀ xs ys z → (snoc xs z ≡ snoc ys z) → xs ≡ ys
snoc-inv (x :: xs')   (y :: ys') z pf with (snoc xs' z) | (snoc ys' z) | inspect (snoc xs') z | inspect (snoc ys') z
snoc-inv (.y :: xs')  (y :: ys') z refl    | .s2  | s2  | [ p ] | [ q ] with (snoc-inv xs' ys' z (trans p (sym q)))
snoc-inv (.y :: .ys') (y :: ys') z refl    | .s2  | s2  | [ p ] | [ q ]  | refl = refl
...

-- Alternative Agda solution based on congruence and injectivity
cons-inj1 : ∀ {x xs y ys} → ((x :: xs) ≡ y :: ys) → x ≡ y
cons-inj1 refl = refl

cons-inj2 : ∀ {x xs y ys} → x :: xs ≡ y :: ys → xs ≡ ys
cons-inj2 refl = refl

snoc-inv' : ∀ xs ys z → (snoc xs z ≡ snoc ys z) → xs ≡ ys
snoc-inv' (x :: xs') (y :: ys') z pf = cong₂ _::_ (cons-inj1 pf) (snoc-inv' xs' ys' z (cons-inj2 pf))
...
```

**Figure 2.** Pattern matching can be tricky in Agda

| | | |
|---|---|---|
| $x, y, f, g, h$ | $\in$ | expression variables |
| expressions $a, b, c, A, B$ | $::=$ | $\mathsf{Type} \mid x$ |
| | $\mid$ | $(x\!:\!A) \to B \mid \mathsf{rec}\, f_A\, x.a \mid a\ b$ |
| | $\mid$ | $\bullet(x\!:\!A) \to B \mid \mathsf{rec}\, f_A\, \bullet_x.a \mid a\ \bullet_b$ |
| | $\mid$ | $a = b \mid \mathsf{join}_\Sigma \mid a_{\triangleright b}$ |
| strategies $\Sigma$ | $::=$ | $\leadsto_{\mathsf{p}}\, i\, j : a = b$ |
| | $\mid$ | $\{\sim v_1/x_1\} \ldots \{\sim v_j/x_j\} c : B$ |
| | $\mid$ | $\mathsf{injdom}\ a \mid \mathsf{injrng}\ a\ b \mid \mathsf{injeq}\ i\ a$ |
| values $v$ | $::=$ | $\mathsf{Type} \mid x$ |
| | $\mid$ | $(x\!:\!A) \to B \mid \mathsf{rec}\, f_A\, x.a$ |
| | $\mid$ | $\bullet(x\!:\!A) \to B \mid \mathsf{rec}\, f_A\, \bullet_x.a$ |
| | $\mid$ | $a = b \mid \mathsf{join}_\Sigma \mid v_{\triangleright b}$ |

**Figure 3.** Syntax

$\boxed{a \leadsto_{\mathsf{cbv}} b}$

$$\frac{}{(\mathsf{rec}\, f\ x.a)\ v \leadsto_{\mathsf{cbv}} \{v/x\}\,\{\mathsf{rec}\, f\ x.a/f\}\ a}\ \textsc{SCAppBeta}$$

$$\frac{}{(\mathsf{rec}\, f\ \bullet.a)\ \bullet \leadsto_{\mathsf{cbv}} \{\mathsf{rec}\, f\ \bullet.a/f\}\ a}\ \textsc{SCIAppBeta}$$

$$\frac{a \leadsto_{\mathsf{cbv}} a'}{a\ b \leadsto_{\mathsf{cbv}} a'\ b}\ \textsc{SCCtx1}$$

$$\frac{a \leadsto_{\mathsf{cbv}} a'}{v\ a \leadsto_{\mathsf{cbv}} v\ a'}\ \textsc{SCCtx2}$$

$$\frac{a \leadsto_{\mathsf{cbv}} a'}{a\ \bullet \leadsto_{\mathsf{cbv}} a'\ \bullet}\ \textsc{SCCtx3}$$

**Figure 4.** Call-by-value operational semantics

Although this development is not long, it is not at all straightforward, requiring advanced knowledge of Agda idioms.

Alternatively, the reasoning used in the ZOMBIE example is also available in Agda, as in the definition of `snoc-inv'`. However, this version requires the use of helper functions to prove that cons is injective and congruent.

## 3. Annotated core language

We now turn to the theory of the system. We begin by describing the target of the elaborator: our annotated core language. This language is a small variant of the dependently-typed call-by-value language defined in prior work [26]. It corresponds to a portion of ZOMBIE's core language, but to keep the proofs tractable we omit ZOMBIE's recursive datatypes and replace its terminating sublanguage [9] with syntactic value restrictions.

The syntax is shown in Figure 3. Terms, types and the sort Type are collapsed into one syntactic category. We use the notation $\{a/x\}\,B$ to denote the capture-avoiding substitution of $a$ for $x$ in $B$. As is standard in dependently-typed languages, our notation for nondependent function types $A \to B$ is syntactic sugar for function types $(x\!:\!A) \to B$, where the variable $x$ is not free in $B$.

Type *annotations*, such as $A$ in rec $f_A\ x.a$, are optional and may be omitted from expressions. Annotations are subscripted in Figure 3. The meta-operator $|a|$ removes these annotations . Expressions that contain no typing annotations are called *erased*.

An expression that includes all annotations is called a *core* or *annotated* expression. The core typing judgement, written $\Gamma \vdash a : A$ and described below, requires that all annotations be present. In this case, the judgement is syntax-directed and trivially decidable. In contrast, type checking for erased terms is undecidable.

The only role of annotations is to ensure decidable type checking. They have no effect on the semantics. In fact, the operational semantics, written $a \rightsquigarrow_{\mathsf{cbv}} b$, is defined only for erased terms and extended to terms with annotations via erasure. This operational semantics is a small-step, call-by-value evaluation relation, shown in Figure 4.

Figure 5 shows the typing rules of the core language typing judgement $\Gamma \vdash a : A$. Additionally, the judgement $\vdash \Gamma$ (elided from the figure) states that each type in $\Gamma$ is well-formed.

Recursive functions are defined using expressions rec $f\ x.a$, with the typing rule TREC. Such expressions are values, and applications step by the rule (rec $f\ x.a)\ v \rightsquigarrow_{\mathsf{cbv}} \{v/x\}\{$rec $f\ x.a/f\}\,a$. If the function makes no recursive calls we also use the syntactic sugar $\lambda x.a$. When a function has a dependent type (TDAPP) then its argument must be a value (this restriction is common for languages with nontermination [16, 30]).

***Irrelevance*** In addition to the normal function type, the core language also include *computationally irrelevant* function types $\bullet(x : A) \rightarrow B$, which are inhabited by irrelevant functions rec $f_A \bullet_x.b$ and eliminated by irrelevant applications $a \bullet_b$. Many expressions in a dependently typed program are only used for type checking, but do not affect the runtime behavior of the program, and these can be marked irrelevant.

Our treatment of irrelevance follows ICC* [5]. Because the treatment of irrelevant functions closely mirrors that of normal functions, we omit the typing rules in this version of the paper. We include this feature in the formalism to show that, besides being generally useful, irrelevance works well with congruence closure. Given that we already handle erasable annotations, we can support full irrelevance for free.

***Equality*** The typing rules at the bottom of Figure 5 deal with propositional equality, a primitive type. The formation rule TEQ states $a = b$ is a well-formed type whenever $a$ and $b$ are two well-typed expressions. There is no requirement that they have the *same* type (that is to say, our equality type is heterogeneous).

Propositional equality is eliminated by the rule TCAST: given a proof, $v$ of an equation $A = B$ we can change the type of an expression from $A$ to $B$. Since our equality is heterogeneous, we need to check that $B$ is in fact a type. We require the proof to be a value in order to rule out divergence. A full-scale language could use a more ambitious termination analysis. (Indeed, our ZOMBIE implementation does so.) However, the congruence proofs generated by our elaborator are syntactic values, so for the purposes of this paper, the simple value restriction is enough. The proof term $v$ in a type cast is an erasable annotation with no operational significance, so the typechecker considers equalities like $a = a_{\triangleright v}$ to be trivially true, and the elaborator is free to insert coercions using congruence closure proofs anywhere.

The rest of the figure shows introduction rules for equality. Equality proofs do not carry any information at runtime, so they all use the same term constructor join, but with different (erasable) annotations, $\Sigma$.

The rule TJOINP introduces equations which are justified by the operational semantics. ZOMBIE source programs must use TJOINP to explicitly indicate expressions that should be reduced. The rule states that join is a proof of $a_1 = a_2$ when the erasures of $a_1$ and $a_2$ reduce to a common expression $b$, using the parallel reduction relation. This common expression, $b$, is not required to be a value. Note that without normalization, we need a cutoff for how long to evaluate, so programmers must specify the number of steps $i$, $j$ of reduction to allow (in ZOMBIE this defaults to 1000 if these numbers are elided).

The rule TJSUBST states that equality is a congruence. The simplest use of the rule is to change a single subexpression, using a proof $v$. The use of the proof is marked with a tilde in the $\Sigma$ annotation; for example, if $\Gamma \vdash v : y = 0$ then we can prove the equality $\mathsf{join}_{\mathsf{Vec\ Nat}\ (\sim v):\mathsf{Vec\ Nat}\ y = \mathsf{Vec\ Nat}\ 0}$. One can also eliminate several different equality proofs in one use of the rule. The syntax of subst includes a type annotation $B$, and the last premise of the TJSUBST rule checks that the ascribed type $B$ matches what one gets after substituting the given equalities into the template $c$. This annotation adds flexibility because the check is only up-to erasure: if needed the programmer can give the left- and right-hand side of $B$ different annotations to make both sides well-typed.

Finally, the rules TJINJEQ, TJINJDOM, and TJIINJRNG state that the equality type and arrow type constructors are injective. (The figure elides similar rules for irrelevant arrow types.) Making type constructors injective is unconventional for a dependent language. It is incompatible with e.g. Homotopy Type Theory, which proves $\mathsf{Nat} \rightarrow \mathsf{Void} = \mathsf{Bool} \rightarrow \mathsf{Void}$. However, in our language we need arrow injectivity to prove type preservation, because type casts are erased and do not block reduction [26]. For example, if a function coerced by type cast steps via $\beta$-reduction, we must use arrow injectivity to derive casts for the argument and result of the application.

We also add injectivity for the equality type constructor (TJINJEQ). This is not required for type safety, but it *is* justified by the metatheory, so it is safe to add. Injectivity is important for the surface language design, see Section 6.

The core language satisfies the usual properties for type systems. For the proofs in Section 6 we rely on the fact that it satisfies weakening, substitution (restricted to values), and regularity. It also satisfies preservation, progress, and decidable type checking. The proofs of these lemmas are in Sjöberg et al. [26].

## 4. Congruence closure

The driving idea behind our surface language is that the programmer should never have to explicitly write a type cast $a_{\triangleright v}$ if the proof $v$ can be inferred by congruence closure. In this section we exactly specify which proofs can be inferred, by defining the typed congruence closure relation $\Gamma \vDash a = b$ shown in Figure 6.

Like the usual congruence closure relation for first-order terms, the rules in Figure 6, specify that this relation is reflexive, symmetric and transitive. It also includes rules for using assumptions in the context and congruence by changing subterms. However, we make a few changes:

First, we add typing premises (in TCCREFL and TCCERASURE) to make sure that the relation only equates well-typed and fully-annotated core language terms. In other words,

$\boxed{\Gamma \vdash a : A}$

$$\frac{\vdash \Gamma}{\Gamma \vdash \mathsf{Type} : \mathsf{Type}}\textsc{TType} \qquad \frac{x : A \in \Gamma \quad \vdash \Gamma}{\Gamma \vdash x : A}\textsc{TVar} \qquad \frac{\Gamma \vdash A : \mathsf{Type} \quad \Gamma, x : A \vdash B : \mathsf{Type}}{\Gamma \vdash (x\!:\!A) \to B : \mathsf{Type}}\textsc{TPi}$$

$$\frac{\Gamma \vdash (x\!:\!A_1) \to A_2 : \mathsf{Type} \quad \Gamma, f : (x\!:\!A_1) \to A_2, x : A_1 \vdash a : A_2}{\Gamma \vdash \mathsf{rec}\ f_{(x A_1) \to A_2}\ x.a : (x\!:\!A_1) \to A_2}\textsc{TRec} \qquad \frac{\Gamma \vdash a : A \to B \quad \Gamma \vdash b : A}{\Gamma \vdash a\ b : B}\textsc{TApp} \qquad \frac{\Gamma \vdash a : (x\!:\!A) \to B \quad \Gamma \vdash v : A}{\Gamma \vdash a\ v : \{v/x\}\,B}\textsc{TDApp}$$

$$\frac{\Gamma \vdash a : A \quad \Gamma \vdash b : B}{\Gamma \vdash a = b : \mathsf{Type}}\textsc{TEq} \qquad \frac{\Gamma \vdash a : A \quad \Gamma \vdash v : A = B \quad \Gamma \vdash B : \mathsf{Type}}{\Gamma \vdash a_{\triangleright v} : B}\textsc{TCast}$$

$$\frac{|a_1| \leadsto_{\mathsf{p}}^{i} b \quad |a_2| \leadsto_{\mathsf{p}}^{j} b \quad \Gamma \vdash a_1 = a_2 : \mathsf{Type}}{\Gamma \vdash \mathsf{join}_{\leadsto_{\mathsf{p}} i\ j : a_1 = a_2} : a_1 = a_2}\textsc{TJoinP}$$

$$\frac{\Gamma \vdash B : \mathsf{Type} \quad \forall k.\ \Gamma \vdash v_k : a_k = b_k \quad |B| = |(\{a_1/x_1\} \ldots \{a_j/x_j\}\, c = \{b_1/x_1\} \ldots \{b_j/x_j\}\, c)|}{\Gamma \vdash \mathsf{join}_{\{\sim v_1/x_1\} \ldots \{\sim v_j/x_j\} c : B} : B}\textsc{TJSubst} \qquad \frac{\Gamma \vdash v : (A_1 = A_2) = (B_1 = B_2)}{\Gamma \vdash \mathsf{join}_{\mathsf{injeq}\ i\ v} : A_i = B_i}\textsc{TJInjEq}$$

$$\frac{\Gamma \vdash v : ((x\!:\!A_1) \to B_1) = ((x\!:\!A_2) \to B_2)}{\Gamma \vdash \mathsf{join}_{\mathsf{injdom}\ v} : A_1 = A_2}\textsc{TJInjDom} \qquad \frac{\Gamma \vdash v_1 : ((x\!:\!A) \to B_1) = ((x\!:\!A) \to B_2) \quad \Gamma \vdash v_2 : A}{\Gamma \vdash \mathsf{join}_{\mathsf{injrng}\ v_1\ v_2} : \{v_2/x\}\,B_1 = \{v_2/x\}\,B_2}\textsc{TJInjRng}$$

**Figure 5.** Typing rules for the annotated core language

$$\frac{\Gamma \vdash a : A}{\Gamma \vDash a = a}\textsc{TCCRefl} \qquad \frac{\Gamma \vDash a = b}{\Gamma \vDash b = a}\textsc{TCCSym} \qquad \frac{\Gamma \vDash a = b \quad \Gamma \vDash b = c}{\Gamma \vDash a = c}\textsc{TCCTrans}$$

$$\frac{|a| = |b| \quad \Gamma \vdash a : A \quad \Gamma \vdash b : B}{\Gamma \vDash a = b}\textsc{TCCErasure} \qquad \frac{x : A \in \Gamma \quad \Gamma \vDash A = (a = b)}{\Gamma \vDash a = b}\textsc{TCCAssumption}$$

$$\frac{\Gamma \vdash A = B : \mathsf{Type} \quad \forall k.\ \Gamma \vDash a_k = b_k \quad |A = B| = |\{a_1/x_1\} \ldots \{a_j/x_j\}\, c = \{b_1/x_1\} \ldots \{b_j/x_j\}\, c|}{\Gamma \vDash A = B}\textsc{TCCCongruence} \qquad \frac{\Gamma \vDash (a_1 = a_2) = (b_1 = b_2)}{\Gamma \vDash a_k = b_k}\textsc{TCCInjEq}$$

$$\frac{\Gamma \vDash ((x\!:\!A_1) \to B_1) = ((x\!:\!A_2) \to B_2)}{\Gamma \vDash A_1 = A_2}\textsc{TCCInjDom} \qquad \frac{\Gamma \vDash (A_1 \to B_1) = (A_2 \to B_2)}{\Gamma \vDash B_1 = B_2}\textsc{TCCInjRng}$$

**Figure 6.** Typed congruence closure relation

If $\Gamma \vDash a = b$, then $\Gamma \vdash a : A$ and $\Gamma \vdash b : B$.

Next, we adapt the congruence rule so that it corresponds to the TJSUBST rule of the core language. In particular, the rule TCCCONGRUENCE includes an explicit erasure step so that the two sides of the equality can differ in their erasable portions.

Furthermore, we extend the relation in several ways.[3] We automatically use computational irrelevance, in the rule TCCERASURE. This makes sure that the programmer can ignore all annotations when reasoning about programs. Also, we reason up to injectivity of datatype constructors (in rules TCCINJDOM, TCCINJRNG, and TCCINJEQ). As mentioned in Section 3 these rules are valid in the core language, and we will see in Section 6 that there is good reason to make the congruence closure algorithm use them automatically. Note that we restrict rule TCCINJRNG so that it applies only to nondependent function types; we explain this restriction in Section 6.

[3] Systems based around congruence closure often strengthen their automatic theorem prover in some way, e.g. Nieuwenhuis and Oliveras [20] add reasoning about natural number equations, and the Coq `congruence` tactic automatically uses injectivity of data constructors [10].

Finally, the rule TCCASSUMPTION is a bit stronger than the classic rule from first order logic. In the first-order logic setting, this rule is defined as just the closure over equations in the context:

$$\frac{x : a = b \in \Gamma}{\Gamma \vDash a = b}$$

However, in a dependently typed language, we can have equations between equations. In this setting, the classic rule does not respect CC-equivalence of contexts. For example, it would prove the first of the following two problem instances, but not the second.

$$x\!:\!\mathsf{Nat}, y\!:\!\mathsf{Nat}, a\!:\!\mathsf{Type}, h_1\!:\!(x = y) = a, h_2\!:\!x = y \vDash x = y$$

$$x\!:\!\mathsf{Nat}, y\!:\!\mathsf{Nat}, a\!:\!\mathsf{Type}, h_1\!:\!(x = y) = a, h_2\!:\!a \qquad \vDash x = y$$

Therefore we replace the rule with the stronger version shown in the figure.

We were led to these strengthened rules by theoretical considerations when trying to show that our elaboration algorithm was complete with respect to the declarative specification (see Section 6). Once we implemented the current set of rules, we found that they were useful in practice as well as in theory, because they improved the elaboration of some examples in our test suite. The stronger assumption rule is useful in situations where type-level computation produces equality types, for example when using custom induction principles.

## 5. Surface language

Next, we give a precise specification of the surface language, which shows how type inference can use congruence closure to infer casts of the form $a_{\triangleright v}$. Note that this process involves determining both the location of such casts and the proof of equality $v$.

Figure 7 defines a *bidirectional type system* for a partially annotated language. This type system is defined by two (mutually defined) judgements: *type synthesis*, written $\Gamma \vdash a \Rightarrow A$, and *type checking*, written $\Gamma \vdash a \Leftarrow A$. Here $\Gamma$ and $a$ are always inputs, but $A$ is an output of the synthesizing judgement and an input of the checking judgement.

Most rules of this type system are standard for bidirectional systems [22], including the rules for inferring the types of variables (IVAR), the well-formedness of types (IEQ, ITYPE, and IPI), non-dependent application (IAPP), and the mode switching rules CINF and IANNOT. Any term that has enough annotations to synthesize a type $A$ also checks against that type (CINF). Conversely, some terms (e.g. functions) require a known type to check against, and so if the surrounding context does not specify one, the programmer must add a type annotation (IANNOT).

The rules ICAST and CCAST in Figure 7 specify that checking and inference work "up-to-congruence." At any point in the typing derivation, the system can replace the inferred or checked type with something congruent. The notation $\Gamma \vDash^{\exists} A = B$ lifts the congruence closure judgement from Section 4 to the partially annotated surface language. These two rules contain kinding premises to maintain well-formedness of types. The invariant maintained by the type system is that (in a well-formed context $\Gamma$) any synthesized type is guaranteed to be well-kinded, while it is the caller's responsibility to ensure that any time the checking judgement is used the input type is well-kinded.

The rule for checking functions (CREC) is almost identical to the corresponding rule in the core language, with just two changes. First, the programmer can omit the types $A_1$, and $A_2$, because in a bidirectional system they can be deduced from the type the expression is checked against. Second, the new premise injrng slightly restricts the use of this rule. The difficulty is that the congruence closure algorithm does not implement the full TJINJRNG rule of the core language, but injective reasoning is needed by the type checker. Therefore, we rule out function types that do not support injectivity for their ranges in certain (pathological) typing contexts. This premise also appears in the rule for dependent application (IDAPP). We return to this issue in Section 6.

Equations that are provable via congruence closure are available via the checking rule, CREFL. In this case the proof term is just join, written as an underscore in the concrete syntax. Because this is a checking rule, the equation to be proved does not have to be written down directly if it can be inferred from the context.

The rule IJOINP proves equations using the operational semantics. We saw this rule used in the `npluszero` example, written `join : 0 + 0 = 0` in the concrete syntax. Note that the programmer must explicitly write down the terms that should be reduced. The rule IJOINP is a synthesizing rather than checking rule in order to ensure that the typing rules are effectively implementable. Although the type system works "up to congruence" the operational semantics do not. So the expression itself needs to contain enough information to tell the typechecker which member of the equivalence class should be reduced—it cannot get this information from the checking context. (In practice, having to explicitly write this annotation can be annoying. The ZOMBIE implementation includes a feature `smartjoin` which can help—see Section 8.2).

It is also interesting to note the rules that do *not* appear in Figure 7. For example, there is no rule or surface syntax corresponding to TCAST, because this feature can be written as a user-level function. Similarly, the rather involved machinery for rewriting subterms and and erased terms (rule TJSUBST) can be entirely omitted, since it is subsumed by the congruence closure relation. The programmer only needs to introduce the equations into the context and they will be used automatically.

Finally we note that the surface language does not satisfy some of the usual properties of type systems. In particular, it lacks a general weakening lemma because the injrng relation cannot be weakened. Similarly, it does not satisfy a substitution lemma because that property fails for the congruence closure relation. (We might expect that $\Gamma, x : C \vDash a = b$ and $\Gamma \vdash v : C$ would imply $\Gamma \vDash \{v/x\}\, a = \{v/x\}\, b$. But this fails if $C$ is an equation and the proof $v$ makes use of the operational semantics.) And it does not satisfy a strengthening lemma, because even variables that do not occur in a term may be implicitly used as assumptions of congruence proofs.

The situations where weakening and substitution fail are rare (we have never encountered one when writing example programs in ZOMBIE) and there are straightforward workarounds for programmers. Furthermore, these properties do hold for fully annotated expressions, so there are no restrictions on the output of elaboration. However, the typing rules for the declarative system must be formulated to avoid these issues, which requires some extra premises. The rule IVAR requires $\Gamma \vdash A \Leftarrow \mathsf{Type}$ (proving this from $\vdash \Gamma \Leftarrow$ would need weakening); IAPP requires $\Gamma \vdash B \Leftarrow \mathsf{Type}$ (proving this from $\Gamma \vdash A \to B : \mathsf{Type}$ would need strengthening); and CREC requires $\Gamma, f : (x : A_1) \to A_2 \vdash (x : A_1) \to A_2 \Leftarrow \mathsf{Type}$ (proving this from $\Gamma \vdash (x : A_1) \to A_2 \Leftarrow \mathsf{Type}$ would need weakening).

## 6. Elaboration

We implement the declarative system using an elaborating typechecker, which translates a surface language expression (if it is well-formed according to the bidirectional rules) to an expression in the core language.

We formalize the algorithm that the elaborator uses as two inductively defined judgements, written $\Gamma' \Vdash a \Rightarrow a' : A'$ ($\Gamma'$ and $a$ are inputs) and $\Gamma' \Vdash a \Leftarrow A' \rightsquigarrow a'$ ($\Gamma'$, $a$, and $A'$ are inputs). The variables with primes ($\Gamma'$, $a'$ and $A'$) are fully annotated expressions in the core language, while $a$ is the surface language term being elaborated. The elaborator deals with each top-level definition in the program separately, and the context $\Gamma'$ is an input containing the types of the previously elaborated definitions.

The job of the elaborator is to insert enough annotations in the term to create a well-typed core expression. It should not otherwise change the term. Stated more formally,

***Theorem* 1** (Elaboration soundness).

1. If $\Gamma \Vdash a \Rightarrow a' : A$, then $\Gamma \vdash a' : A$ and $|a| = |a'|$.
2. If $\Gamma \vdash A : \mathsf{Type}$ and $\Gamma \Vdash a \Leftarrow A \rightsquigarrow a'$, then $\Gamma \vdash a' : A$ and $|a| = |a'|$.

$$\boxed{\Gamma \vdash a \Rightarrow A}$$

$$\frac{\Gamma \vdash a \Rightarrow A \quad \Gamma \vDash^{\exists} A = B \quad \Gamma \vdash B \Leftarrow \mathsf{Type}}{\Gamma \vdash a \Rightarrow B}\ \textsc{ICast}$$

$$\frac{\Gamma \vdash A \Leftarrow \mathsf{Type} \quad \Gamma \vdash a \Leftarrow A}{\Gamma \vdash a_A \Rightarrow A}\ \textsc{IAnnot}$$

$$\frac{\Gamma \vdash a \Rightarrow A \quad \Gamma \vdash b \Rightarrow B}{\Gamma \vdash a = b \Rightarrow \mathsf{Type}}\ \textsc{IEq}$$

$$\frac{\begin{array}{c}\Gamma \vdash a_1 = a_2 \Leftarrow \mathsf{Type} \\ |a_1| \rightsquigarrow^{i}_{\mathsf{p}} b \quad |a_2| \rightsquigarrow^{j}_{\mathsf{p}} b\end{array}}{\Gamma \vdash \mathsf{join}_{\rightsquigarrow_{\mathsf{p}} i\, j : a_1 = a_2} \Rightarrow a_1 = a_2}\ \textsc{IJoinP}$$

$$\frac{\vdash \Gamma \Leftarrow}{\Gamma \vdash \mathsf{Type} \Rightarrow \mathsf{Type}}\ \textsc{IType}$$

$$\frac{\vdash \Gamma \Leftarrow \quad x : A \in \Gamma \quad \Gamma \vdash A \Leftarrow \mathsf{Type}}{\Gamma \vdash x \Rightarrow A}\ \textsc{IVar}$$

$$\frac{\Gamma \vdash A \Leftarrow \mathsf{Type} \quad \Gamma, x : A \vdash B \Leftarrow \mathsf{Type}}{\Gamma \vdash (x : A) \to B \Rightarrow \mathsf{Type}}\ \textsc{IPi}$$

$$\frac{\begin{array}{l}\Gamma \vdash a \Rightarrow A \to B \quad \Gamma \vdash b \Leftarrow A \\ \Gamma \vdash B \Leftarrow \mathsf{Type}\end{array}}{\Gamma \vdash a\ b \Rightarrow B}\ \textsc{IApp}$$

$$\frac{\begin{array}{l}\Gamma \vdash a \Rightarrow (x : A) \to B \quad \Gamma \vdash v \Leftarrow A \\ \Gamma \vDash^{\exists} \mathsf{injrng}\,(x : A) \to B \text{ for } v \\ \Gamma \vdash \{v_A / x\}\, B \Leftarrow \mathsf{Type}\end{array}}{\Gamma \vdash a\ v \Rightarrow \{v_A / x\}\, B}\ \textsc{IDApp}$$

$$\boxed{\Gamma \vdash a \Leftarrow A}$$

$$\frac{\Gamma \vdash a \Leftarrow A \quad \Gamma \vDash^{\exists} A = B \quad \Gamma \vdash B \Leftarrow \mathsf{Type}}{\Gamma \vdash a \Leftarrow B}\ \textsc{CCast}$$

$$\frac{\Gamma \vdash a \Rightarrow A}{\Gamma \vdash a \Leftarrow A}\ \textsc{CInf}$$

$$\frac{\Gamma \vDash^{\exists} a = b}{\Gamma \vdash \mathsf{join} \Leftarrow a = b}\ \textsc{CRefl}$$

$$\frac{\begin{array}{l}\Gamma, f : (x : A_1) \to A_2, x : A_1 \vdash a \Leftarrow A_2 \\ \Gamma, f : (x : A_1) \to A_2, x : A_1 \vDash^{\exists} \mathsf{injrng}\,(x : A_1) \to A_2 \text{ for } x \\ \Gamma, f : (x : A_1) \to A_2 \vdash (x : A_1) \to A_2 \Leftarrow \mathsf{Type}\end{array}}{\Gamma \vdash \mathsf{rec}\, f\ x.a \Leftarrow (x : A_1) \to A_2}\ \textsc{CRec}$$

$$\boxed{\Gamma \vDash^{\exists} a = b}$$

$$\frac{\Gamma' \vDash a' = b' \quad |a| = |a'| \quad |b| = |b'| \quad |\Gamma| = |\Gamma'|}{\Gamma \vDash^{\exists} a = b}\ \textsc{EEq}$$

$$\boxed{\Gamma \vDash^{\exists} \mathsf{injrng}\, A \text{ for } v}$$

$$\frac{\begin{array}{c}\forall A' B'.\ \Gamma \vDash^{\exists} ((x : A) \to B) = ((x : A') \to B') \\ \text{implies } \Gamma \vDash^{\exists} \{v / x\}\, B = \{v / x\}\, B'\end{array}}{\Gamma \vDash^{\exists} \mathsf{injrng}\,(x : A) \to B \text{ for } v}\ \textsc{EIRPi}$$

**Figure 7.** Bidirectional typing rules for surface language

$$\boxed{\Gamma \vDash \mathsf{injrng}\, A \text{ for } v}$$

$$\frac{\begin{array}{l}\Gamma \vdash v : A \quad \Gamma \vdash (x : A) \to B : \mathsf{Type} \\ \forall A'\, B'.((\Gamma \vDash ((x : A) \to B) = ((x : A') \to B')) \text{ implies } (\Gamma \vDash \{v / x\}\, B = \{v_{\triangleright v_0} / x\}\, B' \text{ where } \Gamma \vdash v_0 : A = A'))\end{array}}{\Gamma \vDash \mathsf{injrng}\,(x : A) \to B \text{ for } v}\ \textsc{IRPi}$$

**Figure 8.** Core language injectivity restriction

Furthermore, the elaborator should accept those terms specified by the declarative system. If the type system of Section 5 accepts a program, then the elaborator succeeds (and produces an equivalent type in inference mode).

***Theorem* 2** (Elaboration completeness).

1. If $\Gamma \vdash a \Rightarrow A$ and $\mapsto \Gamma \rightsquigarrow \Gamma'$ and $\Gamma' \mapsto A \Leftarrow \mathsf{Type} \rightsquigarrow A'$, then $\Gamma' \mapsto a \Rightarrow a' : A''$ and $\Gamma' \vDash A' = A''$

2. If $\Gamma \vdash a \Leftarrow A$ and and $\mapsto \Gamma \rightsquigarrow \Gamma'$ and $\Gamma' \mapsto A \Leftarrow \mathsf{Type} \rightsquigarrow A'$, then $\Gamma' \mapsto a \Leftarrow A' \rightsquigarrow a'$.

Designing the elaboration rules follows the standard pattern of turning a declarative specification into an algorithm: remove all rules that are not syntax directed (in this case ICAST and CCAST), and generalize the premises of the remaining rules to create a syntax-directed system that accepts the same terms. At the same time, the uses of congruence closure relation $\Gamma \vDash a = b$, must be replaced by appropriate calls to the congruence closure algorithm. We specify this algorithm using the following (partial) functions:

- $\Gamma \mapsto A \stackrel{?}{=} B \rightsquigarrow v$, which checks $A$ and $B$ for equality and produces core-language proof $v$.
- $\Gamma \mapsto A =^{?} (x : B_1) \to B_2 \rightsquigarrow v$, which checks whether $A$ is equal to some function type and produces that type and proof $v$.
- $\Gamma \mapsto A =^{?} (B_1 = B_2) \rightsquigarrow v$, which is similar to above, except for equality types.

For example, consider the rule for elaborating function applications:

$$\frac{\begin{array}{l}\Gamma \mapsto a \Rightarrow a' : A_1 \quad \Gamma \mapsto A_1 =^{?} (x : A) \to B \rightsquigarrow v_1 \\ \Gamma \mapsto v \Leftarrow A \rightsquigarrow v' \quad \Gamma \vDash \mathsf{injrng}\,(x : A) \to B \text{ for } v'\end{array}}{\Gamma \mapsto a\ v \Rightarrow a'_{\triangleright v_1}\ v' : \{v' / x\}\, B}\ \textsc{EIDApp}$$

In the corresponding declarative rule (IDAPP) the applied term $a$ must have an arrow type, but this can be arranged by implicitly using ICAST to adjust $a$'s type. Therefore, in the algorithmic system, the corresponding condition is that the type of $a$ should be equal to an arrow type $(x : A) \to B$ modulo the congruence closure. Operationally, the typechecker will infer some type $A_1$ for $a$, then run the congruence closure algorithm to construct the set of all expressions that are equal to $A_1$, and check if the set contains some expression which is an arrow type. The elaborated core term uses the produced proof of $A_1 = (x : A) \to B$ in a cast to change the type of $a$.

At this point there is a potential problem: what if $A_1$ is equal to more than one arrow type? For example, if $A_1 = (x : A) \to B = (x : A') \to B$, then the elaborator has to choose whether to check $b$ against $A$ or $A'$. A priori it is quite possible that only one of them will work; for example the context $\Gamma$ may contain an inconsistent equation like $\mathsf{Nat} \to \mathsf{Nat} = \mathsf{Bool} \to \mathsf{Nat}$. We do not wish to introduce a backtracking search here, because that could make type checking too slow.

This kind of mismatch in the domain type can be handled by extending the congruence closure algorithm. Note that things are fine if $\Gamma \vDash A = A'$, since then it does not matter if $A$ or $A'$ is chosen. So the issue only arises if $\Gamma \vDash (x : A) \to B = (x : A') \to B$ and not $\Gamma \vDash A = A'$. Fortunately, type constructors are injective in the core language (Section 3). Including injectivity as part of the congruence closure judgement (by the rule TCCINJDOM) ensures that it does not matter which arrow type is picked.

We also have to worry about a mismatch in the codomain type, i.e. the case when $\Gamma \vDash A_1 = (x : A) \to B$ and $\Gamma \vDash A_1 = (x : A') \to B'$ for two different types. At first glance it seems as if we could use the same solution. After all, the core language includes a rule for injectivity of the range of function types (rule TJINJRNG). There is an important difference between this rule and TJINJDOM, however, which is the handling of the bound variable $x$ in the codomain $B$: the rule says that this can be closed by substituting any value for it. As a result, we cannot match this rule in the congruence closure relation, because the algorithm would have to guess that value. As far as writing an elaborator goes, maybe this is fine—after all, we only want to apply the axiom to the particular value $v$ from the function application $a\ v$. However, there does not seem to be any natural way to write a declarative specification explaining what values $v$ should be candidates.

Instead, we restrict the declarative language to forbid this problematic case. That is, the programmer is not allowed to write a function application unless all possible return types for the function are equal. Note that in cases when an application is forbidden by this check, the programmer can avoid the problem by proving the required equation manually and ensuring that it is available in the context.

In the fully-annotated core language we express this restriction with the rule IRPI (in Figure 8), and then lift this operation to partially annotated terms by rule EIRPI (Figure 7). Operationally, the typechecker will search for all arrow types equal to $A_1$ and check that the the codomains with $v$ substituted are equal in the congruence closure. This takes advantage of the fact that equivalence classes under congruence closure can be efficiently represented—although the rule as written appears to quantify over potentially infinitely many function types, the algorithm in Section 7 will represent these as a finite union-find structure which can be effectively enumerated. In the core language rule we need to insert a type coercion from $A$ to $A'$ to make the right-hand side well typed. By the rule TCCINJDOM that equality is always provable, so the typechecker will use the proof term $v_0$ that the congruence closure algorithm produced.

On the checking side, the mode-change rule ECINF now needs to prove that the synthesized and checked types are equal.

$$\frac{\Gamma \Vdash a \Rightarrow a' : A \quad \Gamma \Vdash A \stackrel{?}{=} B \rightsquigarrow v_1}{\Gamma \Vdash a \Leftarrow B \rightsquigarrow a'_{\triangleright v_1}}\ \text{ECINF}$$

This rule corresponds to a direct call to the congruence closure algorithm, producing a proof term $v_1$. Note that the inputs are fully elaborated terms—in moving from the declarative to the algorithmic type system, we replaced the undecidable condition $\Gamma \vDash^{\exists} A = B$ with a decidable one.

Finally, the rule ECREFL elaborates checkable equality proofs (written as underscores in the concrete ZOMBIE syntax).

$$\frac{\Gamma \Vdash A =^{?} (a = b) \rightsquigarrow v_1 \quad \Gamma \Vdash a \stackrel{?}{=} b \rightsquigarrow v}{\Gamma \Vdash \mathsf{join} \Leftarrow A \rightsquigarrow v_{\triangleright \mathsf{symm}\ v_1}}\ \text{ECREFL}$$

As in the rule for application, the typechecker does a search through the equivalence class of the ascribed type $A$ to see if it contains any equations. If there is more than one equation it does not matter which one gets picked, because the congruence relation includes injectivity of the equality type constructor (TCCINJEQ). In the elaborated term we need to prove $(a = b) = A$ given $A = (a = b)$. This can be done using TJOINP (for reflexivity) and TJSUBST, and we abbreviate that proof term $\mathsf{symm}\ v_1$.

## 7. Implementing congruence closure

Algorithms for congruence closure in the first-order setting are well studied, and our work builds on them. However, in our type system the relation $\Gamma \vDash a = b$ does more work than "classic" congruence closure: we must also handle erasure, terms with bound variables, (dependently) typed terms, the injectivity rules, the "assumption up to congruence" rule, and we must generate proof terms in the core language.

Our implementation proves an equation $a = b$ in three steps. First, we erase all annotations from the input terms and explicitly mark places where the congruence rule can be applied, using an operation called *labelling*. Then we use an adapted version of the congruence closure algorithm by Nieuwenhuis and Oliveras [20]. Our version of their algorithm has been extended to also handle injectivity and "assumption up to congruence", but it ignores all the checks that the terms involved are well-typed. Finally, we take the untyped proof of equality, and process it into a proof that $a$ and $b$ are also related by the typed relation. The implementation is factored in this way because the congruence rule does not necessarily preserve well-typedness, so the invariants of the algorithm are easier to maintain if we do not have to track well-typedness at the same time.

### 7.1 Labelling terms

In $\Gamma \vDash a = b$, the rule TCCCONGRUENCE is stated in terms of substitution. But existing algorithms expect congruence to be applied only to syntactic function applications: from $a = b$ conclude $f\ a = f\ b$. To bridge this gap, we preprocess equations into (erased) *labelled expressions*. A label $F$ is an erased language expression with some designated holes (written –) in it, and a labelled expression is a label applied to zero or more labelled expressions, i.e. a term in the following grammar.

$$a ::= F\,\overline{a_i}$$

$$\frac{}{\Gamma \vdash^{L} a = a}\textsc{LccRefl} \qquad \frac{\Gamma \vdash^{L} a = b}{\Gamma \vdash^{L} b = a}\textsc{LccSym} \qquad \frac{\Gamma \vdash^{L} a_1 = b \quad \Gamma \vdash^{L} b = a_2}{\Gamma \vdash^{L} a_1 = a_2}\textsc{LccTrans}$$

$$\frac{x : A \in \Gamma \quad \Gamma \vdash^{L} A = ((- = -)\ a\ b)}{\Gamma \vdash^{L} a = b}\textsc{LccAssum} \qquad \frac{\forall k.\ \Gamma \vdash^{L} a_k = b_k}{\Gamma \vdash^{L} F\,\overline{a_i} = F\,\overline{b_i}}\textsc{LccCong} \qquad \frac{\Gamma \vdash^{L} F\ a = F\ b \quad F\ \mathsf{injective}}{\Gamma \vdash^{L} a = b}\textsc{LccInj}$$

**Figure 9.** Untyped congruence closure on labelled terms

Typically a label will represent just a single node of the abstract syntax tree. For example, a wanted equation $f\ x = f\ y$ will be processed into $(-\ -)\ f\ x = (-\ -)\ f\ y$, where the label $(-\ -)$ means this is an application. However, for syntactic forms involving bound variables, it can be necessary to be more coarse-grained. For example, given $a = b$ our implementation can prove $\mathsf{rec}\ f\ x.a{+}x = \mathsf{rec}\ f\ x.b{+}x$, which involves using $\mathsf{rec}\ f\ x.{-}{+}x$ as a label. In general, to process an expression $a$ into a labelled term, the implementation will select the largest subexpressions that do not involve any bound variables.

Applying the labelling step simplifies the congruence closure problems in several ways. We show the simpler problem by defining the relation $\Gamma \vdash^{L} a = b$ defined in Figure 9. Compared to Figure 6 we no longer need a rule for erasure, congruence is only used on syntactic label applications, all the different injectivity rules are handled generically, and we do not ensure that the terms are well-typed. In the appendix we formally define the label operation, and prove that it is complete in the following sense.

***Lemma* 3.** If $\Gamma \vDash a = b$ then $\mathsf{label}\,\Gamma \vdash^{L} \mathsf{label}\ a = \mathsf{label}\ b$.

### 7.2 Untyped congruence closure

Next, we use an algorithm based on Nieuwenhuis and Oliveras [20] to decide the $\Gamma \vdash^{L} a = b$ relation. The algorithm first "flattens" the problem by allocating *constants* $c_i$ (i.e. fresh names) for every subexpression in the input. After this transformation every input equation has either the form $c_1 = c_2$ or $c = F(c_1, c_2)$, that is, it is either an equation between two atomic constants or between a constant and a label $F$ applied to constants. Then follows the main loop of the algorithm, which is centered around three data-structures: a queue of input equations, a union-find structure and a lookup table. In each step of the loop, we take off an equation from the queue and update the state accordingly. When all the equations have been processed the union-find structure represents the congruence closure.

The union-find structure tracks which constants are known to be equal to each other. When the algorithm sees an input equation $c_1 = c_2$ it merges the corresponding union-find classes. This deals with the reflexivity, symmetry and transitivity rules. The lookup table is used to handle the congruence rule. It maps applications $F(c_1, c_2)$ to some canonical representative $c$. If the algorithm sees an input equation $c = F(c_1, c_2)$, then $c$ is recorded as the representative. If the table already had an entry $c'$, then we deduce a new equation $c = c'$ which is added to the queue.

In order to adapt this algorithm to our setting, we make three changes. First, we adapt the lookup tables to include the *richer labels* corresponding to the many syntactic categories of our core language. (Nieuwenhuis and Oliveras only use a single label meaning "application of a unary function.")

Second, we deal with *injectivity rules* in a way similar to the implementation of Coq's `congruence` tactic [10]. Certain labels are considered injective, and in each union-find class we identify the set of terms that start with an injective label. If we see an input equation $c = F(c_1, c_2)$ and $F$ is injective we record this in the class of $c$. Whenever we merge two classes, we check for terms headed by the same $F$; e.g. if we merge a class containing $F(c_1, c_2)$ with a class containing $F(c_1', c_2')$, we deduce new equations $c_1 = c_1'$ and $c_2 = c_2'$ and add those to the queue.

Third, our implementation of the *extended assumption rule* works much like injectivity. With each union-find class we record two new pieces of information: whether any of the constants in the class (which represent types of our language) are known to be inhabited by a variable, and whether any of the constants in the class represents an equality type. Whenever we merge two classes we check for new equations to be added to the queue.

The extended version of the paper contains a precise description of our algorithm, and also gives a formal proof of its correctness:

***Lemma* 4.** The algorithm described above is a decision procedure for the relation $\Gamma \vdash^{L} a = b$.

### 7.3 Typing restrictions and generating core language proofs

Along the pointers in the union-find structure, we also keep track of the evidence that showed that two expressions are equal. The syntax of the evidence terms is given by the following grammar. An evidence term $p$ is either an assumption $x$ (with a proof $p$ that $x$'s type is an equation), reflexivity, symmetry, transitivity, injectivity, or an application of congruence annotated with a label $A$.

$$p, q \quad ::= \quad x_{\triangleright p} \mid \mathsf{refl} \mid p^{-1} \mid p; q \mid \mathsf{inj}_i\ p \mid \mathsf{cong}_A\ p_1 .. p_i$$

Next we need to turn the evidence terms $p$ into proof terms in the core calculus. This is nontrivial, because the Nieuwenhuis-Oliveras algorithm does not track types. Not every equation which is derivable by untyped congruence closure is derivable in the typed theory; for example, if $f : \mathsf{Bool} \to \mathsf{Bool}$, then from the equation $(a : \mathsf{Nat}) = (b : \mathsf{Nat})$ we can not conclude $f\ a = f\ b$, because $f\ a$ is not a well-typed term. Worse still, even if the conclusion is well-typed, not every untyped *proof* is valid in the typed theory, because it may involve ill-typed intermediate terms. For example, let $\mathsf{Id} : (A : \mathsf{Type}) \to A \to A$ be the polymorphic identity function, and suppose we have some terms $a : A$, $b : B$, and know the equations $x : A = B$ and $y : a = b$. Then

$$(\mathsf{cong}_{\mathsf{Id}}\ x\ \mathsf{refl}); (\mathsf{cong}_{\mathsf{Id}}\ \mathsf{refl}\ y)$$

is a valid untyped proof of $\mathsf{Id}\ A\ a = \mathsf{Id}\ B\ b$. But it is not a correct typed proof because it involves the ill-typed term $\mathsf{Id}\ B\ a$:

$$\frac{\dfrac{x : A = B \qquad a = a}{\mathsf{Id}\ A\ a = \mathsf{Id}\ B\ a}\,cong \qquad \dfrac{B = B \qquad y : a = b}{\mathsf{Id}\ B\ a = \mathsf{Id}\ B\ b}\,cong}{\mathsf{Id}\ A\ a = \mathsf{Id}\ B\ b}\,trans$$

Corbineau [10] notes this as an open problem. Of course, the above proof is unnecessarily complicated. The same equation can be proved by a single use of congruence. Furthermore, the simpler

$$
\begin{array}{lcl}
p & \mapsto & p \\
\mathsf{refl}^{-1} & \mapsto & \mathsf{refl} \\
\mathsf{refl}; p & \mapsto & p \\
p; \mathsf{refl} & \mapsto & p \\
(p; q); r & \mapsto & p; (q; r) \\
p; p^{-1} & \mapsto & \mathsf{refl} \\
p^{-1}; p & \mapsto & \mathsf{refl} \\
\\
p^{-1^{-1}} & \mapsto & p \\
(p; q)^{-1} & \mapsto & q^{-1}; p^{-1}
\end{array}
\qquad
\begin{array}{rcl}
(\mathsf{cong}_A\ p_1 .. p_i)^{-1} & \mapsto & \mathsf{cong}_A\ {p_1}^{-1} .. {p_i}^{-1} \\
\\
(\mathsf{inj}_i\ p)^{-1} & \mapsto & \mathsf{inj}_i\ (p^{-1}) \\
\\
(\mathsf{cong}_A\ p_1 \ldots p_i); (\mathsf{cong}_A\ q_1 \ldots q_i) & \mapsto & \mathsf{cong}_A\ (p_1; q_1) .. (p_i; q_i) \\
\\
\mathsf{inj}_k\ (\mathsf{cong}_A\ p_1 \ldots p_i) & \mapsto & p_k \\
\mathsf{inj}_k\ ((\mathsf{cong}_A\ p_1 .. p_i); r) & \mapsto & p_k; (\mathsf{inj}_k\ r) \\
\mathsf{inj}_k\ (r; (\mathsf{cong}_A\ p_1 \ldots p_i)) & \mapsto & (\mathsf{inj}_k\ r); p_k \\
x_{\triangleright(r;\mathsf{cong}_=\ p\ q)} & \mapsto & p^{-1}; (x_{\triangleright r}); q
\end{array}
$$

$$
\frac{p \mapsto p'}{x_{\triangleright p} \mapsto x_{\triangleright p'}}\textsc{Assumption}
\qquad
\frac{p \mapsto p' \quad q \mapsto q'}{p; q \mapsto p'; q'}\textsc{Trans}
\qquad
\frac{\forall k.\ p_k \mapsto p'_k}{\mathsf{cong}_A\ p_1 .. p_i \mapsto \mathsf{cong}_A\ p'_1 .. p'_i}\textsc{Cong}
\qquad
\frac{p \mapsto p'}{\mathsf{inj}_k\ p \mapsto \mathsf{inj}_k\ p'}\textsc{Inj}
$$

**Figure 10.** Simplification rules for evidence terms

proof does not have any issues with typing: every expression occurring in the derivation is either a subexpression of the goal or a subexpression of one of the equations from the context, so we know they are well-typed.

Our key observation is that this trick works in general. The only time a congruence proof will involve expressions which were not already present in the context or goal is when transitivity is applied to two derivations ending in cong. We simplify such situations using the following CONGTRANS rule.

$$(\mathsf{cong}_A\ p_1 .. p_i); (\mathsf{cong}_A\ q_1 .. q_i) \mapsto \mathsf{cong}_A\ (p_1; q_1) .. (p_i; q_i)$$

This rule is valid in general, and it does not make the proof larger. We also need rules for simplifying evidence terms that combine transitivity with injectivity or assumption-up-to-CC, such as $\mathsf{inj}_i\ (\mathsf{cong}_A\ p_1 .. p_k)$ and $x_{\triangleright(r;\mathsf{cong}_=\ p\ q)}$, rules for pushing uses of symmetry ($^{-1}$) past the other evidence constructors, and rules for rewriting subterms. The complete simplification relation $\mapsto$ is shown in Figure 10.

Any evidence term $p$ can be simplified into a normalized evidence term $p^*$. (In the extended version of the paper we define an explicit grammar for fully simplified terms $p^*$, and prove than any term can be simplified into that form). And given $p^*$ it is easy to produce a corresponding proof term in the core language. The idea is that one can reconstruct the middle expression in every use of transitivity $(p; q)$, because at least one of $p$ and $q$ will be specific enough to pin down exactly what equation it is proving. Formally, we define the judgement $\Gamma \vdash^{\mathsf{L}} p : a = b$ by adding evidence terms to the rules in Figure 9, and then prove:

***Lemma* 5.** If we have $\mathsf{label}\,\Gamma \vdash^{\mathsf{L}} p^* : \mathsf{label}\, a = \mathsf{label}\, b$ and $\Gamma \vdash a = b : \mathsf{Type}$, then $\Gamma \vDash a = b$.

Simplifying the evidence terms also solves another issue, which arises because of the TCCERASURE rule. Because the input terms are preprocessed to delete annotations (Section 7.1), an arbitrary evidence term will not uniquely specify the annotations. Again, this issue only arises because of the cong-trans pair. Simplifying the evidence term resolves the issue, because in a simplified term every intermediate expression is pinned down.

Putting together the labelling step, the evidence simplification step and the proof term generation step we can relate typed and untyped congruence closure. In the following theorem, the relation $\Gamma \vdash a = b$ is defined by similar rules as Figure 6 except that we omit the typing premises in TCCREFL, TTCERASURE and TTCCONGRUENCE.

***Theorem* 6.** Suppose $\Gamma \vdash a = b$ and $\Gamma \vdash a = b : \mathsf{Type}$. Then $\Gamma \vDash a = b$. Furthermore $\Gamma \vdash v : a = b$ for some $v$.

The computational content of the proof is how the elaborator generates core language evidence for equalities, so this shows the correctness of the ZOMBIE implementation. But it is also interesting as a theoretical result in its own right, and an important part of the proof of completeness of elaboration (Section 6).

## 8. Extensions

The full ZOMBIE implementation includes more features than the surface language described in Section 5. We omitted them from the formal system in order to simplify the proofs, but they are important to make programming up to congruence work well.

### 8.1 Smart case

Although we do not include datatypes in this paper, they are a part of the ZOMBIE implementation, and an important component of any dependently-typed language. The presence of congruence closure elaboration means that the core language [26] can use a specification of dependently-typed pattern matching called *smart case* [1].

With smart case, the rule for case analysis introduces a new equation into the context when checking each branch of a case expression. For example, the rule for an if expression type checks each branch under the assumption that the condition is true or false.

$$
\frac{\Gamma \vdash a : \mathsf{Bool} \quad \Gamma, x : a = \mathsf{true} \vdash b_1 : A \quad \Gamma, x : a = \mathsf{false} \vdash b_2 : A}{\Gamma \vdash \mathsf{if}\ a\ \mathsf{then}\ b_1\ \mathsf{else}\ b_2 : A}\textsc{TFullCase}
$$

This rule is in contrast to specifications that use *unification* to communicate the information gained by pattern matching. In those systems, if the scrutinee and the patterns are not unifiable (in the fragment of higher-order unification supported by the type system) then the case expression must be rejected. Furthermore, the specification of the typing rule for the unification based systems is more complicated. Smart case, by pushing this information to propositional equality, is both simpler and more expressive.

The downside to smart case has been that because this information is recorded as an assumption in the context, it is more work for the programmer. However, with congruence closure, the type system is immediately able to take advantage of these equalities in each branch. Thus, the ZOMBIE surface language has the convenience of the unification-based rule, while the core language enjoys the simplicity of smart case.

### 8.2 Reduction modulo congruence

In the paper all $\beta$-reductions are introduced by expressions `join : a = b`. But in practice some additional support from the typechecker for common patterns can make programming much more pleasant.

First, one often wants to evaluate some expression $a$ "as far as it goes". Then making the programmer write both sides of the equation $a = b$ is unnecessarily verbose. Instead we provide the syntax `unfold a in body`. The implementation reduces $a$ to normal form, $a \rightsquigarrow_{\mathsf{cbv}} a' \rightsquigarrow_{\mathsf{cbv}} a'' \rightsquigarrow_{\mathsf{cbv}} a'''$ (if $a$ does not terminate the programmer can specify a maximum number of steps), and then introduces the corresponding equations into the context with fresh names. That is, it elaborates as

```
let _ = (join : a = a') in
let _ = (join : a' = a'') in
let _ = (join : a'' = a''') in
  body
```

Second, many proofs requires an interleaving of evaluation and equations from the context, particularly in order to take advantage of equations introduced by smart case. One example is `npluszero` in Section 2. The case-expression needs to return a proof of `n+0 = n`. If we try to directly evaluate `n+0`, we would reach the stuck expression `case n of Zero → 0; Succ m' → Succ (m' + 0)`, so instead we used an explicit type annotation in the `Zero` branch to evaluate `0+0`. However, the context contains the equation `n = Zero`, which suggests that there should be another way to make progress.

To take advantage of such equations, we add some extra intelligence to the way unfold handles CBV-evaluation contexts, that is expressions of the form $f\ a$ or (case $b$ of . . . ). When encountering such an expression it will first recursively unfold the function $f$, the argument $a$, or the scrutinee $b$ (as with ordinary CBV-evaluation), and add the resulting equations to the context. However, it will then examine the congruence equivalence class of these expressions to see if they contain any suitable values—any value $v$ is suitable for $a$, a function value rec $f\ x.a_0$ for $f$, and a value headed by a data constructor for $b$—and then unfold the resulting expression (rec $f\ x.a_0$) $v$. (If there are several suitable values, one is selected arbitrarily). This way unfolding can make progress where ordinary CBV-evaluation gets stuck.

Using the same machinery we also provide a "smarter" version of `join`, which first unfolds both sides of the equation, and then checks that the resulting expressions are CC-equivalent. This lets us omit the type annotations from `npluszero`:

```
npluszero n = case n [eq] of
                Zero → smartjoin
                Suc m → ...
```

The unfold algorithm does not fully respect CC-equivalence, because it only converts *into* values. For example, suppose the context contains the equation $f\ a = v$, Then unfold $g\ (f\ a)$ will evaluate $f\ a$ and add the corresponding equations to the context, but unfold $g\ v$ will not cause $f\ a$ to be evaluated. This gives the programmer more control over what expressions are run.

We have not studied the theory of the unfold algorithm, and indeed it is not a complete decision procedure for our propositional equality. If a subexpression of $a$ does not terminate, unfold will spend all its reduction budget on just that subexpression (but this is OK, because the programmer decides what expression $a$ to unfold). And if the context contains e.g. an equation between two unrelated function values, unfold will arbitrarily choose one of them (but it is hard to think of an example where this would happen). We have found unfold very helpful when writing examples.

## 9. Related work

The annotated core language in this paper is a slight variation on previous work [26], which in turn is a subset of the full language implemented by ZOMBIE [9]. In this version, in order to keep the formalism small we omit some features (uncatchable exceptions and general datatypes) and replace the application rule with a slightly less expressive value-dependent version. However, these omissions are not significant (the original system is still compatible with the "up to congruence" approach and is implemented in ZOMBIE). We also took the opportunity to simplify some typing rules, and to emphasize the role of erasable annotations.

***Propositional Equality*** The idea of using congruence closure is not limited to the particular version of propositional equality used by our core language, which has some nonstandard features (we discussed the motivations for them in [26]). Below, we discuss how those features interact with congruence closure and suggest how the algorithm could be adapted to other settings.

First, our equality is *very heterogeneous*, that is we can form and use equations between terms of different types. This has pros and cons: it can be convenient for the programmer to not worry about types, and the metatheory is simple, but it makes it hard to include type-directed $\eta$-rules. However, congruence closure will work just as well with a conventional homogeneous equality.

Second, we use an *$n$-ary congruence rule*, while most theories only allow eliminating one equation at a time. For congruence closure to work equality must be a congruence, e.g. given $a = a'$ and $b = b'$ we should be able to conclude $f\ a\ b = f\ a'\ b'$. Our $n$-ary rule supports this in the most straightforward way possible. An alternative (used in some versions of ETT [11]) would be to use separate $n$-ary congruence rules for each syntactic form. Systems that only allow rewriting by one equation at a time require some tricks to avoid ill-typed intermediate terms (e.g. [6] Section 8.2.7).

Finally, in our system the elimination of propositional equality is *erased*, so equations like $a_{\triangleright b} = a$ are considered trivially true. This is similar to Extensional Type Theory, but unlike Coq and Agda. Having such equations available is important, because the elaborator inserts casts automatically, without detailed control by the programmer. In Coq that would be problematic, because an inserted cast could prevent two terms from being equal. However, making the conversion erasable is not the only possible approach. For example, in Observational Type Theory [2] the conversions are computationally relevant but the theory includes $a_{\triangleright b} = a$ as an axiom. In that system one can imagine the elaborator would use the axiom to make the elaborated program type-check.

***Stronger equational theories*** The theory of congruence closure is one among a number of related theories. One can strengthen it in various ways by adding more reasoning rules, in order to get a more expressive programming language. However, doing so may endanger type inference, or even the decidability of type checking.

One obvious question is whether we could extend the relation $\Gamma \vDash a = b$ to do both congruence reasoning and $\beta$-reduction at the same time. Unfortunately, this extension causes the relation to become undecidable.

This is clearly the case in our language, which directly includes general recursive function definitions. But even if we allowed only terminating functions, the combination of equality assumption and lambdas can be used to encode general recursion. For example, reasoning in a context containing

```
f : Nat → Nat
h : f = (\x. if (even x) then f (n/2) else f (3*n+1))
```

is equivalent to having available a direct recursive definition

```
f x = if (even x) then f (n/2) else f (3*n+1)
```

Another natural generalization is to allow *rewriting by axiom schemes*, i.e. instead of only using ground equations $a = b$ from the context, also instantiate and use quantified formulas like $\forall xyz.a = b$. In general this generalization (the "word problem") is also not decidable, e.g. it is easy to write down an axiom scheme for the equational theory of SKI-combinators. However, there are semi-decision procedures such as *unfailing completion* [4] which form the basis of many automated theorem provers.

Even when preserving decidability one can still extend congruence closure to know about specific axioms schemes, such as for natural numbers with successor and predecessor [20] or lists [19] or injective data constructors [10].

Clearly one could design a programming language around a more ambitious theory than just congruence closure. Many languages, such as Dafny [17] and Dminor [7] call out to an off-the-shelf theorem prover in order to take advantage of all the theories that the prover implements. One reason we focus on a simple theory is that it makes *unification* easier, which seems to offer promising avenues for future work on type inference. Unification modulo congruence closure (rigid E-unification) is NP-complete [15]. This compares favorably with unification modulo $\beta$ (higher-order unification) which is undecidable. Unification modulo other equational theories (E-unification) must be handled on a theory-by-theory basis, and it is not an operation exposed by most provers.

***Simplifying congruence proofs*** Our CONGTRANS simplification rule is quite natural, and in fact the same rule has been studied before for a different reason. For efficiency, users of congruence closure want to make proofs as small as possible by taking advantage of simplifications like $\mathsf{refl}; p \mapsto p$ or $p^{-1}; p \mapsto \mathsf{refl}$ [13, 29]. However, uses of cong can hide the opportunity for such simplifications. De Moura et al. define the same CONGTRANS rule and give the following example [13]. Given assumptions $h_1 : a = b, h_2 : b = d, h_3 : c = b$, consider the proof term

$$(\mathsf{cong}_f\,(h_1; {h_3}^{-1})); (\mathsf{cong}_f\,(h_3; h_2)) : fa = fd$$

We can get rid of the assumption $h_3$ by doing the rewrite

$$(\mathsf{cong}_f\,(h_1; {h_3}^{-1})); (\mathsf{cong}_f\,(h_3; h_2)) \mapsto \mathsf{cong}_f\,(h_1; {h_3}^{-1}; h_3; h_2).$$

***Dependent programming with congruence closure*** CoqMT [28] aims to make Coq's definitional equality stronger by including additional equational theories, such as Presburger arithmetic, so that for example the types $\mathsf{Vec}\ 0$ and $\mathsf{Vec}\ (n \times 0)$ can be used interchangeably. The prototype implementation only looks at the types themselves, but the metatheory also considers using assumptions from the context. This is complicated because CoqMT still wants to consider types modulo $\beta$-convertibility, and in contexts with inconsistent assumptions like $\mathsf{true} = \mathsf{false}$ one could write nonterminating expressions. Therefore CoqMT imposes restrictions on where an assumption can be used. VeriML makes the definitional equality user-programmable [27], and as an example builds a "stack" combining congruence closure, $\beta$-reduction, and potentially other theorem proving.

Neither CoqMT or VeriML prove that their implementation is complete with respect to a declarative specification. For example, the VeriML application rule requires that the applied function has the type $T \to T'$ and then checks that $T$ is definitionally equal to the type of the argument, but there is no attempt to also handle declarative derivations which require definitional equality to create an arrow type.

The Guru language includes a tactic `hypjoin` [21] similar to our `smartjoin` and `unfold`. However, instead of using equations from the context, the programmer has to write an explicit list of equations, and unlike `unfold` it normalizes the given equations.

## 10. Conclusion

We consider this paper as an application of automatic theorem proving to language design. Of course, in a higher-order logic, we always expect that the programmer will have to supply *some* proofs manually; the question is which ones. Intensional Type Theory recognizes that $\beta\eta$-equivalence in a normalizing language is decidable, so such equality proofs can be handled automatically as part of the definitional equality relation. This paper considers a different decidable equational theory, and proposes a language that is "the dual of ITT": while conventional dependently-typed languages automatically use equalities that follow from $\beta$-reductions but do not automatically use assumptions from the context, our language uses assumptions but does not automatically reduce expressions.

We look forward to exploring the ramifications of this design decision more deeply in the context of a full programming language. Our ZOMBIE implementation provides a good baseline, but we would like to add more automation. In particular, the addition of rigid E-unification seems promising. Furthermore, we would like to explore ways in which $\beta$-reduction and congruence closure can co-exist—perhaps there is some way to achieve the benefits of each approach in the same context.


## Acknowledgments

This material is based upon work supported by the National Science Foundation under Grant Nos. 0910500, 1116620, and 1319880. The ZOMBIE implementation was developed with the assistance of the Trellys team. This paper was written with the help of the Ott tool [23]. The authors would also like to thank the anonymous reviewers for their comments.


## References


[1] T. Altenkirch. The case of the smart case: How to implement conditional convertibility? Presentation at NII Shonan seminar 007, Japan, Sept. 2011.

[2] T. Altenkirch, C. McBride, and W. Swierstra. Observational equality, now! In *PLPV '07: Programming Languages meets Program Verification*, pages 57–68. ACM, 2007.

[3] L. Augustsson. Cayenne – a language with dependent types. In *ICFP '98: International Conference on Functional Programming*, pages 239–250. ACM, 1998.

[4] L. Bachmair, N. Dershowitz, and D. A. Plaisted. Completion Without Failure. In A. H. Kaci and M. Nivat, editors, *Resolution of Equations*

*in Algebraic Structures*, volume 2: Rewriting Techniques, pages 1–30. Academic Press, 1989.

[5] B. Barras and B. Bernardo. The Implicit Calculus of Constructions as a Programming Language with Dependent Types. In *11th international conference on Foundations of Software Science and Computational Structures (FOSSACS 2008)*, volume 4962 of *LNCS*, pages 365–379. Springer, 2008.

[6] Y. Bertot and P. Castéran. *Interactive Theorem Proving and Program Development, Coq'Art:the Calculus of Inductive Constructions*. Springer-Verlag, 2004.

[7] G. M. Bierman, A. D. Gordon, C. Hritcu, and D. E. Langworthy. Semantic subtyping with an SMT solver. In *ICFP '10: International Conference on Functional Programming*, pages 105–116, 2010.

[8] E. C. Brady. Idris—systems programming meets full dependent types. In *PLPV'11: Programming languages meets program verification*, pages 43–54. ACM, 2011. ISBN 978-1-4503-0487-0.

[9] C. Casinghino, V. Sjöberg, and S. Weirich. Combining proofs and programs in a dependently typed langauge. In *POPL '14: 41st ACM SIGPLAN-SIGACT Symposium on Principles of Programming Languages*, 2014.

[10] P. Corbineau. Deciding equality in the constructor theory. In T. Altenkirch and C. McBride, editors, *Types for Proofs and Programs*, volume 4502 of *Lecture Notes in Computer Science*, pages 78–92. Springer Berlin Heidelberg, 2007.

[11] K. Crary. *Type-Theoretic Methodology for Practical Programming Languages*. PhD thesis, Cornell University, 1998.

[12] L. De Moura and N. Bjørner. Z3: An efficient SMT solver. In *Proceedings of the Theory and Practice of Software, 14th International Conference on Tools and Algorithms for the Construction and Analysis of Systems*, TACAS'08/ETAPS'08, pages 337–340, Berlin, Heidelberg, 2008. Springer-Verlag.

[13] L. de Moura, H. Rueß, and N. Shankar. Justifying equality. *Electronic Notes in Theoretical Computer Science (ENTCS)*, 125(3):69–85, July 2005.

[14] P. J. Downey, R. Sethi, and R. E. Tarjan. Variations on the common subexpression problem. *J. ACM*, 27(4):758–771, Oct. 1980.

[15] J. Gallier, W. Snyder, P. Narendran, and D. Plaisted. Rigid E-unification is NP-complete. In *Proceedings of the Third Annual Symposium on Logic in Computer Science (LICS '88)*, pages 218–227, 1988.

[16] L. Jia, J. A. Vaughan, K. Mazurak, J. Zhao, L. Zarko, J. Schorr, and S. Zdancewic. AURA: A programming language for authorization and audit. In *ICFP '08: International Conference on Functional Programming)*, pages 27–38, 2008.

[17] K. R. M. Leino. Dafny: an automatic program verifier for functional correctness. In *Proceedings of the 16th international conference on Logic for programming, artificial intelligence, and reasoning*, LPAR'10, pages 348–370. Springer-Verlag, 2010.

[18] C. McBride. First-order unification by structural recursion, 2001.

[19] G. Nelson and D. C. Oppen. Fast decision procedures based on congruence closure. *J. ACM*, 27(2):356–364, Apr. 1980.

[20] R. Nieuwenhuis and A. Oliveras. Fast congruence closure and extensions. *Inf. Comput.*, 205(4):557–580, Apr. 2007.

[21] A. Petcher and A. Stump. Deciding Joinability Modulo Ground Equations in Operational Type Theory. In S. Lengrand and D. Miller, editors, *Proof Search in Type Theories (PSTT)*, 2009.

[22] B. C. Pierce and D. N. Turner. Local type inference. *ACM Trans. Program. Lang. Syst.*, 22(1):1–44, Jan. 2000.

[23] P. Sewell, F. Nardelli, S. Owens, G. Peskine, T. Ridge, S. Sarkar, and R. Strnisa. Ott: Effective tool support for the working semanticist. *J. Funct. Program.*, 20(1):71–122, 2010.

[24] R. E. Shostak. An algorithm for reasoning about equality. *Commun. ACM*, 21(7):583–585, July 1978.

[25] V. Sjöberg and S. Weirich. Programming up to congruence (extended version). Technical Report MS-CIS-14-10, University of Pennsylvania, Philadelphia, PA, Oct. 2014.

[26] V. Sjöberg, C. Casinghino, K. Y. Ahn, N. Collins, H. D. Eades III, P. Fu, G. Kimmell, T. Sheard, A. Stump, and S. Weirich. Irrelevance, heterogeneous equality, and call-by-value dependent type systems. In J. Chapman and P. B. Levy, editors, *MSFP '12*, volume 76 of *EPTCS*, pages 112–162. Open Publishing Association, 2012.

[27] A. Stampoulis and Z. Shao. Static and user-extensible proof checking. In *Proceedings of the 39th Annual ACM SIGPLAN-SIGACT Symposium on Principles of Programming Languages*, POPL '12, pages 273–284, New York, NY, USA, 2012. ACM.

[28] P.-Y. Strub. Coq modulo theory. In *CSL*, pages 529–543, 2010.

[29] A. Stump and L.-Y. Tan. The algebra of equality proofs. In *16th International Conference on Rewriting Techniques and Applications (RTA'05)*, pages 469–483. Springer, 2005.

[30] N. Swamy, J. Chen, C. Fournet, P.-Y. Strub, K. Bhargavan, and J. Yang. Secure Distributed Programming with Value-dependent Types. In *ICFP '11: International Conference on Functional Programming*, pages 285–296. ACM, 2011.

# A Meta Lambda Calculus with Cross-Level Computation

Kazunori Tobisawa
Graduate School of Mathematical Sciences, The University of Tokyo, Japan
tobisawa@ms.u-tokyo.ac.jp

## Abstract

We propose meta lambda calculus $\lambda^*$ as a basic model of textual substitution via metavariables. The most important feature of the calculus is that every β-redex can be reduced regardless of whether the β-redex contains meta-level variables or not. Such a meta lambda calculus has never been achieved before due to difficulty to manage binding structure consistently with α-renaming in the presence of meta-level variables. We overcome the difficulty by introducing a new mechanism to deal with substitution and binding structure in a systematic way without the notion of free variables and α-renaming.

Calculus $\lambda^*$ enables us to investigate cross-level terms that include a certain type of level mismatch. Cross-level terms have been regarded as meaningless terms and left out of consideration thus far. We find that some cross-level terms behave as quotes and 'eval' command in programming languages. With these terms, we show a procedural language as an application of the calculus, which sheds new light on the notions of stores and recursion via meta-level variables.

***Categories and Subject Descriptors*** F.4.1 [*Mathematical Logic and Formal Languages*]: Mathematical Logic – lambda calculus and related systems

***Keywords*** lambda calculus; metavariables; textual substitution; dynamic binding

## 1. Introduction

### 1.1 Metavariables and Meta Lambda Calculi

When discussing a formal language, we use metavariables. A metavariable is a symbol that stands for some syntactic object in a discussed language. For example, we use the following expression when defining β-reduction of the lambda calculus:

"$(\lambda x.M)N \to_\beta M\{N/x\}$ for variables $x$ and terms $M$, $N$."

In this case, '$x$', '$M$' and '$N$' are metavariables. If we instantiate the metavariables '$x$', '$M$', '$N$' with specific syntactic objects in the lambda calculus, for example, $\mathtt{x}$, $\mathtt{xy}$, $\mathtt{z}$ respectively, then we get '$(\lambda\mathtt{x}.\mathtt{xy})\mathtt{z} \to_\beta (\mathtt{xy})\{\mathtt{z}/\mathtt{x}\}$' as an instance of β-reduction. Note that the expression '$(\mathtt{xy})\{\mathtt{z}/\mathtt{x}\}$' signifies the syntactic object $\mathtt{zy}$ in the lambda calculus, since we can calculate as $(\mathtt{xy})\{\mathtt{z}/\mathtt{x}\} = (\mathtt{x}\{\mathtt{z}/\mathtt{x}\})(\mathtt{y}\{\mathtt{z}/\mathtt{x}\}) = \mathtt{zy}$ after the instantiation of the metavariables.

Recently, several formal systems are proposed as extensions of the lambda calculus to internalize the notion of metavariables [9–11, 17, 18]. In this paper, such formal systems are collectively called **meta lambda calculi**. The most important feature of meta lambda calculi is that they include textual substitution to model instantiation of metavariables. The ordinary substitution in the lambda calculus is performed with α-renaming to avoid incidental variable binding, whereas textual substitution is performed without α-renaming by replacing each occurrence of a variable simply with a term. Thus textual substitution generates new bindings *dynamically*.

We illustrate a sketch of meta lambda calculi. Consider an extension of the syntax of the lambda calculus defined by the following BNF presented in [12]:

$$\text{Terms } M ::= x \mid \lambda x.M \mid M\ M \mid X \mid \delta X.M \mid M \odot M$$

where $x$ ranges over the set of object-level variables and $X$ ranges over the set of meta-level variables. The first three in the above BNF represent the object-level constructs, namely, the constructs in the lambda calculus. The last three represent meta-level constructs as counterparts of the object-level constructs. In the syntax, we have the following reduction sequence corresponding to the example discussed before:

$$(\delta\mathtt{M}.((\delta\mathtt{N}.(\lambda\mathtt{x}.\mathtt{M})\mathtt{N})\odot\mathtt{z}))\odot\mathtt{xy}$$
$$\Rightarrow_\beta (\delta\mathtt{M}.(\lambda\mathtt{x}.\mathtt{M})\mathtt{z})\odot\mathtt{xy} \Rightarrow_\beta (\lambda\mathtt{x}.\mathtt{xy})\mathtt{z} \to_\beta \mathtt{zy},$$

where upper-case letters $\mathtt{M}$ and $\mathtt{N}$ are meta-level variables, and lower-case letters $\mathtt{x}$, $\mathtt{y}$ and $\mathtt{z}$ are object-level variables. In this paper, a meta-level application containing a meta-level abstraction as the left part is called a meta-level β-redex, and an object-level counterpart is called an object-level β-redex. For instance, $(\delta\mathtt{N}.(\lambda\mathtt{x}.\mathtt{M})\mathtt{N})\odot\mathtt{z}$ is a meta-level β-redex, and $(\lambda\mathtt{x}.\mathtt{M})\mathtt{N}$ is an object-level β-redex. Meta-level β-reduction, denoted by $\Rightarrow_\beta$ in Section 1 and Section 2, is performed on a meta-level β-redex in a similar way to the ordinary β-reduction but by textual substitution. In the above example, meta-level variable $\mathtt{M}$ is instantiated with the term $\mathtt{xy}$ by meta-level β-reduction, and the object-level variable $\mathtt{x}$ is dynamically bound by the binder $\lambda\mathtt{x}$.

### 1.2 Problem in Designing a Meta Lambda Calculus

When trying to define a meta lambda calculus formally, we face a subtle problem resulting from coexistence of the ordinary substitution with textual substitution [12]. Consider the following cases to examine object-level β-redexes containing meta-level variables.

**(1)** Consider a term $(\lambda\mathtt{x}.\mathtt{M})\mathtt{z}$. We cannot reduce the term simply by the ordinary substitution as $(\lambda\mathtt{x}.\mathtt{M})\mathtt{z} \to_\beta \mathtt{M}\{\mathtt{z}/\mathtt{x}\} = \mathtt{M}$, since such reduction gives us the following two reduction sequences



*POPL '15*, January 15–17, 2015, Mumbai, India.

ACM 978-1-4503-3300-9/15/01...$15.00.
http://dx.doi.org/10.1145/2676726.2676976

that are not confluent:

$$(\delta\mathtt{M}.(\lambda\mathtt{x}.\mathtt{M})\mathtt{z})\odot\mathtt{xy} \rightarrow_\beta (\delta\mathtt{M}.\mathtt{M})\odot\mathtt{xy} \Rightarrow_\beta \mathtt{xy},$$
$$(\delta\mathtt{M}.(\lambda\mathtt{x}.\mathtt{M})\mathtt{z})\odot\mathtt{xy} \Rightarrow_\beta (\lambda\mathtt{x}.\mathtt{xy})\mathtt{z} \rightarrow_\beta \mathtt{zy}.$$

The term zy in the second line is the intended result of the term $(\delta\mathtt{M}.(\lambda\mathtt{x}.\mathtt{M})\mathtt{z})\odot\mathtt{xy}$ as shown before. It is obviously a mistake to consider that $\mathtt{M}\{\mathtt{z}/\mathtt{x}\} = \mathtt{M}$, since M is a meta-level variable to be instantiated later with a term that may contain the object-level variable x.

**(2)** Consider a term $(\lambda\mathtt{x}.\lambda\mathtt{y}.\mathtt{x})\mathtt{M}$. We cannot reduce the term simply as $(\lambda\mathtt{x}.\lambda\mathtt{y}.\mathtt{x})\mathtt{M} \rightarrow_\beta (\lambda\mathtt{y}.\mathtt{x})\{\mathtt{M}/\mathtt{x}\} = \lambda\mathtt{y}.(\mathtt{x}\{\mathtt{M}/\mathtt{x}\}) = \lambda\mathtt{y}.\mathtt{M}$, since such reduction gives us the following two reduction sequences that are not confluent:

$$(\delta\mathtt{M}.(\lambda\mathtt{x}.\lambda\mathtt{y}.\mathtt{x})\mathtt{M})\odot\mathtt{y} \rightarrow_\beta (\delta\mathtt{M}.\lambda\mathtt{y}.\mathtt{M})\odot\mathtt{y} \Rightarrow_\beta \lambda\mathtt{y}.\mathtt{y},$$
$$(\delta\mathtt{M}.(\lambda\mathtt{x}.\lambda\mathtt{y}.\mathtt{x})\mathtt{M})\odot\mathtt{y} \Rightarrow_\beta (\lambda\mathtt{x}.\lambda\mathtt{y}.\mathtt{x})\mathtt{y} \rightarrow_\alpha (\lambda\mathtt{x}.\lambda\mathtt{z}.\mathtt{x})\mathtt{y} \rightarrow_\beta \lambda\mathtt{z}.\mathtt{y}.$$

The second reduction sequence gives us the intended result. Note that we have the following expression with a side condition in the definition of substitution in the lambda calculus:

$$\text{“}(\lambda y.N)\{M/x\} = \lambda y.(N\{M/x\}) \quad \text{if } y \notin \mathrm{FV}(M, x).\text{”}$$

Hence we cannot actually have $(\lambda\mathtt{y}.\mathtt{x})\{\mathtt{M}/\mathtt{x}\} = \lambda\mathtt{y}.(\mathtt{x}\{\mathtt{M}/\mathtt{x}\})$ without satisfying a side condition such as the one above. However, we do not have such side condition in the first place, since we have no information about the free variables occurring in the term for which M stands, namely, the term with which the meta-level variable M is instantiated later.

The above cases indicate that we cannot define easily object-level substitution for terms containing meta-level variables. The heart of the problem is that a meta-level variable is just a placeholder standing for some object-level term *unknown yet*.

### 1.3 Approaches in Previous Works

Approaches in previous works related to modeling metavariables and the problem discussed above are classified broadly into two categories. Here we explain briefly the essential points of the two categories respectively. Features of individual works are mentioned in Section 5.

#### (1) Meta-Level Variables Assigned with Interfaces

One approach is to assign each meta-level variable $X$ with a finite list of object-level variables to be bound dynamically, which is called the **interface** of meta-level variable $X$ in this paper. With assigning an *appropriate* interface to each meta-level variable, and with *embedding* such additional information into terms explicitly, instantiation of meta-level variables can be emulated by computation in calculi dealing with only static binding, in particular, the ordinary lambda calculus [12].

For example, consider the following meta-level β-reduction:

$$(\delta\mathtt{M}.(\lambda\mathtt{x}.(\lambda\mathtt{y}.\mathtt{Mx})\mathtt{x})(\mathtt{My}))\odot(\mathtt{yx})$$
$$\Rightarrow_\beta (\lambda\mathtt{x}.(\lambda\mathtt{y}.(\mathtt{yx})\mathtt{x})\mathtt{x})((\mathtt{yx})\mathtt{y}).$$

The meta-level β-reduction can be emulated by the following lambda term, which is obtained from the above term by assigning meta-level variable M with the interface (x, y):

$$(\lambda\mathtt{m}.(\lambda\mathtt{x}.(\lambda\mathtt{y}.(\underline{\mathtt{mxy}})\mathtt{x})\mathtt{x})((\underline{\mathtt{mxy}})\mathtt{y}))(\underline{\lambda\mathtt{x}.\lambda\mathtt{y}.\mathtt{yx}})$$
$$\rightarrow_\beta^* (\lambda\mathtt{x}.(\lambda\mathtt{y}.(\mathtt{yx})\mathtt{x})\mathtt{x})((\mathtt{yx})\mathtt{y}).$$

To take a familiar example, the above fact corresponds to the fact that the C program with macros in Figure 1 can be emulated by the C program without macros in Figure 2. A meta-level variable assigned with an interface, for example, the list of x and y, is roughly equivalent to an ordinary function of x and y.

**Figure 1.** WithMacros.c

```
int main() {
  int x = 1;
  int y = x + 1;
  #define M y + x
  x = M + y;
  y = x;
  return M + x;
}
```

**Figure 2.** ViaInterface.c

```
int main() {
  int x = 1;
  int y = x + 1;
  int m(int x, int y)
    { return  y + x; }
  x = m(x, y) + y;
  y = x;
  return m(x, y) + x;
}
```

Calculus $\lambda m$ in [18] and the calculi in [4, 12, 14–16] adopt similar approaches to the one discussed above so as to consider metavariables to be assigned with interfaces. These calculi are inherently designed to deal with only static binding as the ordinary lambda calculus, and hence in these calculi, the notion of textual substitution is modeled by a mechanism like the ordinary substitution as illustrated above. As a result, the problem in question disappears from these calculi. In this paper, these calculi are called **lambda calculi with interfaces** distinctively from meta lambda calculi, since there is a difference between the concept modeled in meta lambda calculi and the concept modeled in lambda calculi with interfaces.

In order to clarify the challenge tackled in meta lambda calculi, we explain the essence of the difference between meta lambda calculi and lambda calculi with interfaces. In meta lambda calculi, meta-level variable M must satisfy the following principle for any object-level variables $x$ and $y$:

$$\lambda x.\mathtt{M} \cong \lambda y.\mathtt{M} \quad \text{if and only if} \quad x = y,$$

where $\cong$ denotes the equivalence induced from rewriting rules. This principle is a consequence of the requirement that the term $\lambda x.\mathtt{M}$ is the counterpart of the expression '$\lambda x.M$' in the metalanguage, and the term $\delta\mathtt{M}.\lambda x.\mathtt{M}$ is the counterpart of the function '$M \mapsto \lambda x.M$' on the set of *all* lambda terms. The principle corresponds to the fact that two functions '$M \mapsto \lambda x.M$' and '$M \mapsto \lambda y.M$' are equal if and only if $x = y$. Note that if the principle did not hold and we had some distinct object-level variables $x$ and $y$ such that $\lambda x.\mathtt{M} \cong \lambda y.\mathtt{M}$, then we would have nonsense equivalence such as $\lambda x.y \cong (\delta\mathtt{M}.\lambda x.\mathtt{M})\odot y \cong (\delta\mathtt{M}.\lambda y.\mathtt{M})\odot y \cong \lambda y.y$.

The goal of meta lambda calculi is to add new syntactic objects called meta-level variables satisfying the above principle into the ordinary lambda calculus. In contrast, lambda calculi with interfaces as well as the ordinary lambda calculus do not contain any term that corresponds to a meta-level variable. Namely, they do not contain a term $N$ satisfying the following property for all variables $x$ and $y$:

$$\lambda x.N \cong \lambda y.N \quad \text{if and only if} \quad x = y.$$

In the example shown before, the term mxy can be used in the ordinary lambda calculus to emulate the behavior of meta-level variable M. However, the term mxy itself cannot be an alternative to meta-level variable M generally. For instance, we have distinct variables a and b satisfying $\lambda\mathtt{a}.\mathtt{mxy} =_\alpha \lambda\mathtt{b}.\mathtt{mxy}$ in the ordinary lambda calculus, whereas $\lambda\mathtt{a}.\mathtt{M} \not\cong \lambda\mathtt{b}.\mathtt{M}$ in meta lambda calculi.

#### (2) Level-Controlled Reduction

The other approach to resolve the problem in Section 1.2 is to restrict reduction rules by side conditions taking levels into account. To cite a case of calculus $\lambda\mathcal{M}$ in [18], object-level β-reduction $(\lambda x.M)N \rightarrow_\beta M\{N/x\}$ is defined with the following side condition:

"$M$ and $N$ contain no meta-level constructs."

The other previous meta lambda calculi [9–11] also adopt similar approaches, although there are various technical differences. A reduction defined with such side conditions is called a **level-controlled reduction** in this paper. Level-controlled reductions bring confluence in meta lambda calculi, since wrong reduction sequences mentioned in Section 1.2 are eliminated by such side conditions. However, level-controlled reductions make some β-redexes stuck. For instance, the following object-level β-redex containing meta-level variables cannot be reduced in the previous meta lambda calculi due to such side conditions shown above:

$$(\lambda \mathtt{y}.\lambda \mathtt{z}.\mathtt{yMN})(\lambda \mathtt{x}.\lambda \mathtt{y}.\mathtt{z}).$$

In other words, we cannot reduce an object-level β-redex until we instantiate meta-level variables in the β-redex with some object-level terms.

### 1.4 Our Purpose

In this paper, we propose meta lambda calculus $\lambda^*$ with a new mechanism to reduce object-level β-redexes containing meta-level variables. Calculus $\lambda^*$ enables us to advance computation in the presence of meta-level variables, and hence opens up new possibilities for reduction strategies that have been restricted by level-controlled reductions in previous meta lambda calculi. For example, we are able to introduce the notion of lazy evaluation in the presence of meta-level variables.

Another purpose of calculus $\lambda^*$ is to examine those terms that include a certain type of level mismatch, such as an object-level abstraction applied to a meta-level abstraction like $(\lambda \mathtt{x}.(\mathtt{x}\odot\mathtt{M}))(\delta\mathtt{M}.\mathtt{M})$. Such terms are called cross-level terms in this paper. Cross-level terms have been regarded as meaningless terms, and left out of consideration by type systems or by level-controlled reductions in previous meta lambda calculi. One of distinct features of calculus $\lambda^*$ is that the calculus makes it possible to compute cross-level terms. In Section 4, we show that some cross-level terms behave as quotes and 'eval' command in programming languages through an example. These terms provide us new insight into the notions of stores and recursion via meta-level variables.

## 2. Overview of Our Approach

### 2.1 An Analysis of Calculation in the Metalanguage

In the metalanguage, we can always:

- rewrite a β-redex '$(\lambda x.M)N$' to the expression '$M\{N/x\}$',
- perform α-renaming with some fresh variable, and
- pass down substitution '$\{N/x\}$' on a term to its subterms.

In this way, we can calculate a β-redex to perform substitution of variables even if the β-redex contains metavariables. For example, we can have the following calculation in the metalanguage:

$$\begin{aligned}
&(\lambda \mathtt{x}.(\lambda \mathtt{y}.M\mathtt{x})\mathtt{x})(M\mathtt{y})\\
&\to_\alpha (\lambda \mathtt{x}.(\lambda v.M\{v/\mathtt{y}\}\mathtt{x})\mathtt{x})(M\mathtt{y}) \quad \text{where } v \text{ is fresh,}\\
&\to_\beta (\lambda v.M\{v/\mathtt{y}\}\{M\mathtt{y}/\mathtt{x}\}(M\mathtt{y}))(M\mathtt{y})\\
&= (\lambda v.M\{v/\mathtt{y}, M\mathtt{y}/\mathtt{x}\}(M\mathtt{y}))(M\mathtt{y})\\
&\to_\beta M\{v/\mathtt{y}, M\mathtt{y}/\mathtt{x}\}\{M\mathtt{y}/v\}(M\{M\mathtt{y}/v\}\mathtt{y})\\
&= M\{M\mathtt{y}/\mathtt{y}, M\{M\mathtt{y}/v\}\mathtt{y}/\mathtt{x}, M\mathtt{y}/v\}(M\{M\mathtt{y}/v\}\mathtt{y})\\
&= M\{M\mathtt{y}/\mathtt{y}, M\mathtt{y}/\mathtt{x}\}(M\mathtt{y}) \quad \text{since } v \text{ is fresh.}
\end{aligned}$$

Note that $\mathtt{x}$ and $\mathtt{y}$ are variables as syntactic objects in the lambda calculus, whereas '$v$' is a metavariable that stands for some variable in the lambda calculus. If we instantiate metavariables '$M$' in the last line with term $\mathtt{yx}$, we get the following result:

$$\begin{aligned}
&(\mathtt{yx})\{(\mathtt{yx})\mathtt{y}/\mathtt{y}, (\mathtt{yx})\mathtt{y}/\mathtt{x}\}((\mathtt{yx})\mathtt{y})\\
&= (\mathtt{yxy})(\mathtt{yxy})(\mathtt{yxy}).
\end{aligned}$$

The key factors that enable us to advance calculation in the presence of metavariables are:

- substitution operators, and
- freshness conditions accompanied with α-renaming.

Note that these two factors interact with each other. In the above example, the freshness condition '$v$ is fresh' first arises in association with α-renaming of the binder $\lambda\mathtt{y}$ to $\lambda v$. In the process of the calculation, the freshness condition deletes substitution operators '$\{M\mathtt{y}/v\}$' following metavariables '$M$'. Furthermore, the last β-reduction that yields substitution operator '$\{M\mathtt{y}/v\}$' actually eliminates the freshness condition '$v$ is fresh' at the end of the calculation. Consequently, we have

$$(\lambda \mathtt{x}.(\lambda \mathtt{y}.M\mathtt{x})\mathtt{x})(M\mathtt{y}) \to_\beta^* M\{M\mathtt{y}/\mathtt{y}, M\mathtt{y}/\mathtt{x}\}(M\mathtt{y})$$

for any term $M$.

We attempt to incorporate the two notions of substitution operators and freshness conditions into a meta lambda calculus to achieve our purpose. It is not difficult to embed substitution operators as syntactic objects. A major obstacle is how to deal with freshness conditions and the interaction with substitution operators in a meta lambda calculus. As explained in the subsequent discussion, we overcome the obstacle by adopting indexed variables and skip operators as alternatives of freshness conditions.

### 2.2 Indexed Variables

Consider the extended syntax of the lambda calculus defined by the following BNF:

$$\text{Terms } M ::= v^d \mid \lambda v.M \mid M\ M$$

where $v$ ranges over a set of names and $d$ ranges over the set of nonnegative integers. In this syntax, a variable consists of a name $v$ and a nonnegative integer $d$ called the index of the variable. In a term, variable $v^d$ skips $d$ binders of $v$ and hence is bound by the $(d+1)$-th binder of $v$. For instance, in term $\lambda\mathtt{x}.\lambda\mathtt{y}.\lambda\mathtt{x}.\mathtt{y}^0\mathtt{x}^1$, the variable $\mathtt{y}^0$ is bound by the binder $\lambda\mathtt{y}$ as in the ordinary lambda calculus, whereas the variable $\mathtt{x}^1$ skips the rightmost binder $\lambda\mathtt{x}$ and is bound by the leftmost binder $\lambda\mathtt{x}$. In a word, we consider an extension of the lambda calculus accompanied with de Bruijn indices [5, 16].

The extended syntax enables us to perform β-reduction without α-renaming, although we can still have the notion of α-renaming. For example, we can reduce a term $(\lambda\mathtt{x}.\lambda\mathtt{y}.\mathtt{y}^0\mathtt{x}^0)(\lambda\mathtt{x}.\mathtt{y}^0)$ in the following two ways:

$$(\lambda\mathtt{x}.\lambda\mathtt{y}.\mathtt{y}^0\mathtt{x}^0)(\lambda\mathtt{x}.\mathtt{y}^0) \to_\beta \lambda\mathtt{y}.\mathtt{y}^0(\lambda\mathtt{x}.\mathtt{y}^1) \to_\alpha \lambda\mathtt{z}.\mathtt{z}^0(\lambda\mathtt{x}.\mathtt{y}^0),$$

$$(\lambda\mathtt{x}.\lambda\mathtt{y}.\mathtt{y}^0\mathtt{x}^0)(\lambda\mathtt{x}.\mathtt{y}^0) \to_\alpha (\lambda\mathtt{x}.\lambda\mathtt{z}.\mathtt{z}^0\mathtt{x}^0)(\lambda\mathtt{x}.\mathtt{y}^0) \to_\beta \lambda\mathtt{z}.\mathtt{z}^0(\lambda\mathtt{x}.\mathtt{y}^0).$$

The reduction sequence in the second line is regarded as the one in the ordinary lambda calculus. Note that if we equate α-equivalent terms as we usually do in the ordinary lambda calculus, then the above two reduction sequences are identical. As a result, the extended syntax provides us a more expressive notation virtually without changing the theory of the lambda calculus.

### 2.3 Skip Operators as Alternatives of Freshness Conditions

In the extended syntax, we no longer need the notion of freshness of variables. For example, we can calculate with metavariables as follows:

$$(\lambda\mathtt{x}.\lambda\mathtt{y}.\mathtt{y}^0\mathtt{x}^0)M \to_\beta (\lambda\mathtt{y}.\mathtt{y}^0\mathtt{x}^0)\{M/\mathtt{x}\} = \lambda\mathtt{y}.\mathtt{y}^0(M * \Uparrow_\mathtt{y}),$$

where $\Uparrow_{\mathtt{y}}$ is a skip operator acting on the term $M$ to increment indices of $\mathtt{y}$ in term $M$ appropriately so as to skip the binder $\lambda\mathtt{y}$. For instance, $(\lambda\mathtt{x}.\mathtt{y}^0) * \Uparrow_{\mathtt{y}}$ denotes $\lambda\mathtt{x}.\mathtt{y}^1$. The above calculation corresponds to the following calculation with a freshness condition in the ordinary lambda calculus:

$$(\lambda\mathtt{x}.\lambda\mathtt{y}.\mathtt{yx})M \rightarrow_{\alpha} (\lambda\mathtt{x}.\lambda v.v\mathtt{x})M \rightarrow_{\beta} \lambda v.vM \quad \text{where } v \text{ is fresh.}$$

Skip operators free us from the need to perform α-renaming and the need to keep freshness conditions outside of terms. Consequently, skip operators can be more easily embedded into a meta lambda calculus than freshness conditions.

### 2.4 A Sketch of Meta Lambda Calculus $\lambda^*$

We construct meta lambda calculus $\lambda^*$ in Section 3 by adopting indexed variables and by embedding both substitution operators and skip operators as syntactic objects in the calculus. Here we show a sketch to give an intuition about the calculus.

The syntax defined by the following BNF is a part of the syntax of calculus $\lambda^*$:

$$\begin{aligned} \text{Terms } M &::= v^d \mid \lambda v.M \mid M\ M \mid X[\sigma] \mid \delta X.M \mid M \odot M \\ \text{Substitutions } \sigma &::= \mathrm{id} \mid {}^{v}\!\!\downarrow\!(M) \cdot \sigma \mid \Uparrow_v \cdot\, \sigma \end{aligned}$$

where $v$ ranges over a set of names, $d$ ranges over the set of non-negative integers, $X$ ranges over the set of meta-level variables, and id signifies the empty sequence. The elements of form ${}^{v}\!\!\downarrow\!(M)$, called **push-elements**, are counterparts of substitution operators '$\{M/v\}$', and the elements of form $\Uparrow_v$, called **pop-elements**, are counterparts of skip operators. In calculus $\lambda^*$, a substitution $\sigma$ is dealt with as a finite sequence of push-elements and pop-elements in order to calculate the two kinds of elements in an integrated way to model the interaction between substitution operators and freshness conditions in the metalanguage. Note that a substitution $\sigma$ can occur only with a meta-level variable $X$ in the form $X[\sigma]$. The $\sigma$ represents a substitution that is suspended to wait for instantiation of the meta-level variable $X$. For instance, term $\mathtt{M}[{}^{\mathtt{x}}\!\!\downarrow\!(\mathtt{z}^0)]$ corresponds to the expression '$M\{\mathtt{z}/\mathtt{x}\}$' that cannot be calculated any more in the metalanguage.

Action of a substitution $\sigma$ on a term $M$, denoted by $M * \sigma$, is designed to reflect the behaviors of substitution operators and skip operators as alternatives of freshness conditions. For instance, the expression $(\mathtt{x}^0\mathtt{M}) * {}^{\mathtt{x}}\!\!\downarrow\!(\mathtt{z}^0)$ denotes the term $\mathtt{z}^0\mathtt{M}[{}^{\mathtt{x}}\!\!\downarrow\!(\mathtt{z}^0)]$, as the expression '$(\mathtt{x}M)\{\mathtt{z}/\mathtt{x}\}$' is reduced to '$\mathtt{z}(M\{\mathtt{z}/\mathtt{x}\})$' in the ordinary lambda calculus. Note that the substitution ${}^{\mathtt{x}}\!\!\downarrow\!(\mathtt{z}^0)$ is suspended on the meta-level variable $\mathtt{M}$, since the substitution cannot act any more until $\mathtt{M}$ is instantiated later. Also, the expression $(\lambda\mathtt{y}.\mathtt{y}^0\mathtt{x}^0) * {}^{\mathtt{x}}\!\!\downarrow\!(\mathtt{M})$ denotes $\lambda\mathtt{y}.\mathtt{y}^0\mathtt{M}[\Uparrow_{\mathtt{y}}]$, which corresponds to the expression '$\lambda\mathtt{y}.\mathtt{y}^0(M * \Uparrow_{\mathtt{y}})$' shown in Section 2.3.

The syntax enables us to advance computation in the presence of meta-level variables in the same way as the metalanguage. For example, the calculation shown in Section 2.1 is represented by the following reduction sequence in calculus $\lambda^*$:

$$\begin{aligned} &(\lambda\mathtt{x}.(\lambda\mathtt{y}.\mathtt{Mx})\mathtt{x})(\mathtt{My}) \\ &\rightarrow_{\beta} ((\lambda\mathtt{y}.\mathtt{Mx})\mathtt{x}) * {}^{\mathtt{x}}\!\!\downarrow\!(\mathtt{My}) \\ &= (\lambda\mathtt{y}.\mathtt{M}[{}^{\mathtt{y}}\!\!\downarrow\!(\mathtt{y}) \cdot {}^{\mathtt{x}}\!\!\downarrow\!(\mathtt{M}[\Uparrow_{\mathtt{y}}]\mathtt{y}^1) \cdot \Uparrow_{\mathtt{y}}](\mathtt{M}[\Uparrow_{\mathtt{y}}]\mathtt{y}^1))(\mathtt{My}) \\ &\rightarrow_{\beta} (\mathtt{M}[{}^{\mathtt{y}}\!\!\downarrow\!(\mathtt{y}) \cdot {}^{\mathtt{x}}\!\!\downarrow\!(\mathtt{M}[\Uparrow_{\mathtt{y}}]\mathtt{y}^1) \cdot \Uparrow_{\mathtt{y}}](\mathtt{M}[\Uparrow_{\mathtt{y}}]\mathtt{y}^1)) * {}^{\mathtt{y}}\!\!\downarrow\!(\mathtt{My}) \\ &= \mathtt{M}[{}^{\mathtt{y}}\!\!\downarrow\!(\mathtt{My}) \cdot {}^{\mathtt{x}}\!\!\downarrow\!(\mathtt{M}[\Uparrow_{\mathtt{y}} \cdot {}^{\mathtt{y}}\!\!\downarrow\!(\mathtt{My})]\mathtt{y}) \cdot \Uparrow_{\mathtt{y}} \cdot {}^{\mathtt{y}}\!\!\downarrow\!(\mathtt{My})](\mathtt{M}[\Uparrow_{\mathtt{y}} \cdot {}^{\mathtt{y}}\!\!\downarrow\!(\mathtt{My})]\mathtt{y}) \\ &\rightarrow_{\varepsilon}^{*} \mathtt{M}[{}^{\mathtt{y}}\!\!\downarrow\!(\mathtt{My}) \cdot {}^{\mathtt{x}}\!\!\downarrow\!(\mathtt{My})](\mathtt{My}), \end{aligned}$$

where indices equal to 0 are omitted. In the last line, ε-reduction eliminates substitutions of form $\Uparrow_v \cdot {}^{v}\!\!\downarrow\!(N)$ to simulate the interaction between substitution operators and freshness conditions. If we instantiate the meta-level variables $\mathtt{M}$ in the last line with term $\mathtt{yx}$, we get the following intended result:

$$\begin{aligned} &(\mathtt{M}[{}^{\mathtt{y}}\!\!\downarrow\!(\mathtt{My}) \cdot {}^{\mathtt{x}}\!\!\downarrow\!(\mathtt{My})](\mathtt{My})) * {}^{\mathtt{M}}\!\!\downarrow\!(\mathtt{yx}) \\ &= ((\mathtt{yx}) * ({}^{\mathtt{y}}\!\!\downarrow\!((\mathtt{yx})\mathtt{y}) \cdot {}^{\mathtt{x}}\!\!\downarrow\!((\mathtt{yx})\mathtt{y})))((\mathtt{yx})\mathtt{y}) \\ &= (\mathtt{yxy})(\mathtt{yxy})(\mathtt{yxy}), \end{aligned}$$

where the meta-level push-element ${}^{\mathtt{M}}\!\!\downarrow\!(\mathtt{yx})$ represents the instantiation of $\mathtt{M}$. Note that the suspended substitution for object-level variables $\mathtt{y}$ and $\mathtt{x}$ following the meta-level variable $\mathtt{M}$ in the first line is resumed to obtain the result after the instantiation of $\mathtt{M}$.

In the discussion thus far, we illustrate a sketch of an extension of the lambda calculus added meta-level constructs. In the same way, we can easily add meta-meta-level constructs, meta-meta-meta-level constructs and so on. As a result, we obtain meta lambda calculus $\lambda^*$ that includes infinitely hierarchical levels as meta lambda calculi in [9, 10, 18].

### 2.5 Blocks to Variable Binding

Lastly, we make a remark about a connection between object-level variable binding and meta-level application. In calculus $\lambda^*$, we have the following equality:

$$(M_1 \odot M_2) * {}^{v}\!\!\downarrow\!(N) = (M_1 * {}^{v}\!\!\downarrow\!(N)) \odot M_2.$$

This equality states that object-level variables $v^d$ occurring in the right part $M_2$ of meta-level application $M_1 \odot M_2$ are prevented from being bound by outer binders of $v$ [13]. As an example, we take a term $(\lambda\mathtt{y}.((\delta\mathtt{M}.(\lambda\mathtt{x}.(\lambda\mathtt{y}.\mathtt{Mx})\mathtt{x})(\mathtt{My}))\odot(\mathtt{yx})))(\mathtt{x1})$ that roughly corresponds to a part of the C program with macros in Figure 1. We should consider that the variable $\mathtt{y}$ in the right part '$\mathtt{yx}$' of the meta-level application is not bound by the leftmost binder $\lambda\mathtt{y}$. Otherwise, we could perform substitution for the $\mathtt{y}$ as follows:

$$\begin{aligned} &(\lambda\mathtt{y}.((\delta\mathtt{M}.(\lambda\mathtt{x}.(\lambda\mathtt{y}.\mathtt{Mx})\mathtt{x})(\mathtt{My}))\odot(\mathtt{yx})))(\underline{\mathtt{x1}}) \\ &\rightarrow_{\beta} ((\delta\mathtt{M}.(\lambda\mathtt{x}.(\lambda\mathtt{y}.\mathtt{Mx})\mathtt{x})(\mathtt{My}))\odot(\mathtt{yx})) * {}^{\mathtt{y}}\!\!\downarrow\!(\underline{\mathtt{x1}}) \\ &= ((\delta\mathtt{M}.(\lambda\mathtt{x}.(\lambda\mathtt{y}.\mathtt{Mx})\mathtt{x})(\mathtt{My})) * {}^{\mathtt{y}}\!\!\downarrow\!(\underline{\mathtt{x1}}))\odot((\mathtt{yx}) * {}^{\mathtt{y}}\!\!\downarrow\!(\underline{\mathtt{x1}})) \\ &= ((\delta\mathtt{M}.(\lambda\mathtt{x}.(\lambda\mathtt{y}.\mathtt{Mx})\mathtt{x})(\mathtt{My})) * {}^{\mathtt{y}}\!\!\downarrow\!(\underline{\mathtt{x1}}))\odot((\underline{\mathtt{x1}})\mathtt{x}). \end{aligned}$$

Such a reduction prevents a calculus from satisfying confluence, since we also have the following reduction sequence that generates new bindings dynamically:

$$\begin{aligned} &(\lambda\mathtt{y}.((\delta\mathtt{M}.(\lambda\mathtt{x}.(\lambda\mathtt{y}.\mathtt{Mx})\mathtt{x})(\mathtt{My}))\odot(\underline{\mathtt{yx}})))(\mathtt{x1}) \\ &\Rightarrow_{\beta} (\lambda\mathtt{y}.(((\lambda\mathtt{x}.(\lambda\mathtt{y}.\mathtt{Mx})\mathtt{x})(\mathtt{My})) * {}^{\mathtt{M}}\!\!\downarrow\!(\underline{\mathtt{yx}})))(\mathtt{x1}) \\ &= (\lambda\mathtt{y}.(\lambda\mathtt{x}.(\lambda\mathtt{y}.(\underline{\mathtt{yx}})\mathtt{x})\mathtt{x})((\underline{\mathtt{yx}})\mathtt{y}))(\mathtt{x1}). \end{aligned}$$

Note that in the term *after* the meta-level β-reduction, the variables $\mathtt{y}$ in the two copies '$\mathtt{yx}$' are *newly bound* by one of the two binders $\lambda\mathtt{y}$ respectively. This fact indicates that in the term *before* the meta-level β-reduction, we should consider that the variable $\mathtt{y}$ in the right part '$\mathtt{yx}$' of the meta-level application copied by instantiation is *not bound yet* by any binder. Stated differently, in the C program with macros in Figure 1, the variable `y` in the fifth line signifies the *value* of `y` determined by assignment in the third line, whereas the variable `y` on the right of `#define` command in the fourth line signifies the *text* 'y' itself, which does not refer any value yet.

## 3. Meta Lambda Calculus $\lambda^*$

We formally define meta lambda calculus $\lambda^*$ and show that the calculus satisfies confluence.

### 3.1 Terms and Substitutions

We consider the set $\mathcal{L}$ of **levels** as the set of positive integers. The object-level is 1, the meta-level is 2, the meta-meta-level is 3, and so on. We assume that we are given the set $\mathcal{N}$ of **names** and function Lv of $\mathcal{N}$ into $\mathcal{L}$ that assigns a level to each name.

**Definition 3.1.** We define inductively the set $Ter$ of **terms** and the auxiliary set $Sub_\ell$ for each level $\ell$ as follows:

$$\begin{aligned}
v^d[\sigma] &\in Ter \quad \text{if } v \in \mathcal{N},\ d \in \mathbb{N},\ \sigma \in Sub_{\mathrm{Lv}(v)},\\
\lambda v.M &\in Ter \quad \text{if } v \in \mathcal{N},\ M \in Ter,\\
M \mathbin{@_\ell} N &\in Ter \quad \text{if } \ell \in \mathcal{L},\ M, N \in Ter,\\
\mathrm{id} &\in Sub_\ell,\\
{}^v{\downarrow}(M)\cdot\sigma &\in Sub_\ell \quad \text{if } v \in \mathcal{N}_{<\ell},\ M \in Ter,\ \sigma \in Sub_\ell,\\
\uparrow_v \cdot\, \sigma &\in Sub_\ell \quad \text{if } v \in \mathcal{N}_{<\ell},\ \sigma \in Sub_\ell,
\end{aligned}$$

where $\mathcal{N}_{<\ell} = \{v \in \mathcal{N} \mid \mathrm{Lv}(v) < \ell\}$, $\mathbb{N}$ is the set of nonnegative integers, and id signifies the empty sequence. We define the set $Sub$ of **substitutions** as the union $\bigcup_{\ell\in\mathcal{L}} Sub_\ell$. Note that a substitution is a finite sequence of push-elements ${}^v{\downarrow}(M)$ and pop-elements $\uparrow_v$ for names $v$ and terms $M$. Push-elements and pop-elements are collectively called push-pop-elements.

**Notation.** As defined above, dots ' $\cdot$ ' represent punctuation marks for substitutions. We use the same dot to represent concatenation of substitutions. For instance, if substitution $\sigma$ equals ${}^v{\downarrow}(M)\cdot\uparrow_v$ for name $v$ and term $M$, then $\sigma\cdot\sigma$ denotes ${}^v{\downarrow}(M)\cdot\uparrow_v\cdot{}^v{\downarrow}(M)\cdot\uparrow_v$. In particular, $\mathrm{id}\cdot\sigma = \sigma\cdot\mathrm{id} = \sigma$ holds. We also use exponential notation, namely, $\sigma^0 = \mathrm{id}$ and $\sigma^{n+1} = \sigma\cdot\sigma^n$ for substitutions $\sigma$ and nonnegative integers $n$. We omit superscripts '0' following names and brackets '[id]' around the empty sequence, when no confusion may occur.

**Example 3.2.** The following are terms, where $\mathtt{x}, \mathtt{y}, \mathtt{z}$ are names of level 1, and $\mathtt{M}, \mathtt{N}$ are names of level 2:

$$(\lambda \mathtt{x}.\mathtt{y}^0[\mathrm{id}]) \mathbin{@_1} \mathtt{z}^0[\mathrm{id}],$$
$$\mathtt{M}^0[{}^{\mathtt{x}}{\downarrow}(\mathtt{N}^1[\mathrm{id}])\cdot\uparrow_{\mathtt{x}}\cdot{}^{\mathtt{y}}{\downarrow}(\lambda\mathtt{x}.\mathtt{M}^2[\uparrow_{\mathtt{y}}\cdot\uparrow_{\mathtt{z}}])].$$

We usually represent the term in the first line simply as $(\lambda\mathtt{x}.\mathtt{y}) \mathbin{@_1} \mathtt{z}$.

### 3.2 Action of Substitutions on Terms

**Definition 3.3.** Let $v$ be a name and $d$ a nonnegative integer. The **$\langle v, d\rangle$-component** $\sigma\langle v, d\rangle$ of a substitution $\sigma$ is the term defined inductively as follows:

$$\mathrm{id}\langle v, d\rangle := v^d[\mathrm{id}],$$
$$({}^w{\downarrow}(M)\cdot\sigma)\langle v, d\rangle := \begin{cases} M & \text{if } v = w \text{ and } d = 0,\\ \sigma\langle v, d-\delta_{vw}\rangle & \text{otherwise,}\end{cases}$$
$$(\uparrow_w\cdot\,\sigma)\langle v, d\rangle := \sigma\langle v, d+\delta_{vw}\rangle,$$

where $\delta_{vw}$ is the integer defined by

$$\delta_{vw} := \begin{cases} 1 & \text{if } v = w,\\ 0 & \text{otherwise.}\end{cases}$$

We give an intuitive explanation about $\langle v, d\rangle$-components of a substitution $\sigma$. Consider an $\mathcal{N}$-indexed family of infinite stacks of terms. Such a family of stacks is called an environment here. Push-elements ${}^v{\downarrow}(M)$ and pop-elements $\uparrow_v$ represent operations on the stack indexed by name $v$. Hence substitution $\sigma$ as a composition of push-pop-elements represents an operation on environments. In what follows, the stack indexed by name $v$ in an environment is simply called the $v$-stack. The environment whose $v$-stack consists of the infinite sequence $v^0, v^1, v^2, \ldots$ for each name $v$, is called the identity environment. The $\langle v, d\rangle$-component $\sigma\langle v, d\rangle$ signifies the element at depth $d$ in the $v$-stack in the environment obtained by operating $\sigma$ on the identity environment.

For instance, consider a substitution $\sigma = {}^v{\downarrow}(M)\cdot\uparrow_v\cdot\uparrow_v$. Substitution $\sigma$ means the operation "pop from the $v$-stack, and then pop from the $v$-stack, and then push the term $M$ into the $v$-stack." By operating $\sigma$ on the identity environment, we obtain an environment whose $v$-stack consists of the infinite sequence $M, v^2, v^3, \ldots$, and thus we have $\sigma\langle v, 0\rangle = M$, $\sigma\langle v, 1\rangle = v^2$, $\sigma\langle v, 2\rangle = v^3$, and so on.

**Definition 3.4.** Let $S$ be a subset of the set $\mathcal{N}$ of names. The **$S$-restriction** $\sigma\restriction S$ of a substitution $\sigma$ is the substitution defined inductively as follows:

$$\mathrm{id}\restriction S := \mathrm{id},$$
$$({}^v{\downarrow}(M)\cdot\sigma)\restriction S := \begin{cases} {}^v{\downarrow}(M)\cdot(\sigma\restriction S) & \text{if } v \in S,\\ \sigma\restriction S & \text{otherwise,}\end{cases}$$
$$(\uparrow_v\cdot\,\sigma)\restriction S := \begin{cases} \uparrow_v\cdot(\sigma\restriction S) & \text{if } v \in S,\\ \sigma\restriction S & \text{otherwise.}\end{cases}$$

For levels $\ell$ and substitutions $\sigma$, we define $\sigma_{<\ell}$ and $\sigma_{\geq\ell}$ by

$$\sigma_{<\ell} := \sigma\restriction\{v \in \mathcal{N} \mid \mathrm{Lv}(v) < \ell\},$$
$$\sigma_{\geq\ell} := \sigma\restriction\{v \in \mathcal{N} \mid \mathrm{Lv}(v) \geq \ell\}.$$

We abbreviate $\sigma_{<\mathrm{Lv}(v)}$ and $\sigma_{\geq\mathrm{Lv}(v)}$ to $\sigma_{<v}$ and $\sigma_{\geq v}$ respectively for names $v$.

**Definition 3.5.** We define inductively the term $M*\sigma$ resulting from **action** of a substitution $\sigma$ on a term $M$, and the substitution $\tau\circ\sigma$ resulting from **composition** of substitutions $\sigma$ and $\tau$, as follows:

$$v^d[\tau]*\sigma := \begin{cases} v^d[\sigma] & \text{if } \sigma_{\geq v} = \tau = \mathrm{id},\\ \sigma\langle v, d\rangle * (\tau\circ\sigma)_{<v} & \text{otherwise,}\end{cases}$$
$$(\lambda v.M)*\sigma := \lambda v.(M * \Uparrow_v(\sigma)),$$
$$(M \mathbin{@_\ell} N)*\sigma := (M*\sigma) \mathbin{@_\ell} (N*\sigma_{\geq\ell}),$$
$$\mathrm{id}\circ\sigma := \sigma,$$
$$({}^v{\downarrow}(M)\cdot\tau)\circ\sigma := {}^v{\downarrow}(M*\sigma_{\geq v})\cdot(\tau\circ\sigma),$$
$$(\uparrow_v\cdot\,\tau)\circ\sigma := \uparrow_v\cdot(\tau\circ\sigma),$$

where $\Uparrow_v(\sigma)$ denotes ${}^v{\downarrow}(v^0[\mathrm{id}])\cdot(\sigma\circ\uparrow_v)$.

The first branch in the first line for action on a variable of name $v$ states that substitution $\sigma$ does nothing and stays as the suspended substitution on the variable, if the $\sigma$ does not contain any push-pop-elements of level $\ell \geq \mathrm{Lv}(v)$. The second branch states that substitution $\sigma$ replaces the variable $v^d[\tau]$ with the corresponding term $\sigma\langle v, d\rangle$, and the suspended substitution $\tau$ composed with $\sigma$ further acts on the term. The restriction represented by '$<$' indicates that all push-pop-elements of level $\ell \geq \mathrm{Lv}(v)$ in $\sigma$ are consumed by substitution for the variable $v^d[\tau]$. The expression $\Uparrow_v(\sigma)$ in the second line represents a substitution obtained by adjusting $\sigma$ to skip the binder '$\lambda v$' appropriately. The restriction represented by '$\geq$' in the third line and the fifth line is due to blocks to variable binding discussed in Section 2.5. Note that $v^d[\tau]*\sigma = \sigma\langle v, d\rangle * (\tau\circ\sigma)_{<v}$ always holds by definition.

We show that $M*\sigma$ and $\sigma\circ\tau$ are well-defined for all terms $M$ and all substitutions $\sigma$ and $\tau$ by induction on height of terms and level of substitutions defined below.

**Definition 3.6.** The height $\mathrm{Ht}(M)$ of a term $M$ and the height $\mathrm{Ht}(\sigma)$ of a substitution $\sigma$ are the nonnegative integers defined inductively as follows:

$$\begin{aligned}
\mathrm{Ht}(v^d[\sigma]) &:= \mathrm{Ht}(\sigma),\\
\mathrm{Ht}(\lambda v.M) &:= \mathrm{Ht}(M)+1,\\
\mathrm{Ht}(M \mathbin{@_\ell} N) &:= \max\{\mathrm{Ht}(M), \mathrm{Ht}(N)\}+1,\\
\mathrm{Ht}(\mathrm{id}) &:= 0,\\
\mathrm{Ht}({}^v{\downarrow}(M)\cdot\sigma) &:= \max\{\mathrm{Ht}(M)+1, \mathrm{Ht}(\sigma)\},\\
\mathrm{Ht}(\uparrow_v\cdot\,\sigma) &:= \mathrm{Ht}(\sigma).
\end{aligned}$$

**Definition 3.7.** The level $\mathrm{Lv}(\sigma)$ of a substitution $\sigma$ is the nonnegative integer defined inductively as follows:

$$\mathrm{Lv}(\mathrm{id}) := 0,$$
$$\mathrm{Lv}({}^{v}{\downarrow}(M)\cdot\sigma) := \begin{cases} \mathrm{Lv}(\sigma) & \text{if } M = v^d[\mathrm{id}] \text{ for some } d \in \mathbb{N}, \\ \max\{\mathrm{Lv}(v), \mathrm{Lv}(\sigma)\} & \text{otherwise,} \end{cases}$$
$$\mathrm{Lv}({\uparrow_v}\cdot\sigma) := \mathrm{Lv}(\sigma).$$

**Proposition 3.8.** *Let $M$ be a term and $\sigma$ be a substitution. Then $M * \sigma$ is well-defined.*

*Proof.* We give a detailed proof for this proposition to clarify the mechanism of the calculus. Many other propositions in this section are proved in a similar way.

The above proposition is proved by induction on lexicographic ordering of pairs $\langle \mathrm{Lv}(\sigma), \mathrm{Ht}(M)\rangle$.

(1) Consider the case of $M = v^d[\tau]$.

First, we show that $\tau \circ \sigma$ is well-defined by induction on length of $\tau$. The case of $\tau = \mathrm{id}$ and the case of $\tau = {\uparrow_w}\cdot\tau_1$ are trivial. Consider the case of $\tau = {}^{w}{\downarrow}(N)\cdot\tau_1$. Then $\tau\circ\sigma = {}^{w}{\downarrow}(N * \sigma_{\geq w})\cdot(\tau_1\circ\sigma)$. Note that $N*\sigma_{\geq w}$ is well-defined by induction hypothesis since $\mathrm{Lv}(\sigma_{\geq w}) \leq \mathrm{Lv}(\sigma)$ and $\mathrm{Ht}(N) < \mathrm{Ht}(M)$. Thus $\tau\circ\sigma$ is well-defined.

Next, we show that $\sigma\langle v, d\rangle * (\tau\circ\sigma)_{<v}$ is well-defined. If $\mathrm{Lv}(\sigma) \geq \mathrm{Lv}(v)$, then by induction hypothesis $\sigma\langle v,d\rangle * (\tau\circ\sigma)_{<v}$ is well-defined since $\mathrm{Lv}((\tau\circ\sigma)_{<v}) < \mathrm{Lv}(\sigma)$. If $\mathrm{Lv}(\sigma) < \mathrm{Lv}(v)$, then $\sigma\langle v,d\rangle = v^e$ for some $e\in\mathbb{N}$, and hence $\sigma\langle v,d\rangle*(\tau\circ\sigma)_{<v} = v^e[(\tau\circ\sigma)_{<v}]$ by definition.

(2) Consider the case of $M = \lambda v.M_1$.

We show that $\sigma\circ{\uparrow_v}$ is well-defined and $\mathrm{Lv}(\sigma\circ{\uparrow_v}) = \mathrm{Lv}(\sigma)$ by induction on length of $\sigma$. The case of $\sigma = \mathrm{id}$ and the case of $\sigma = {\uparrow_w}\cdot\sigma_1$ are trivial. Consider the case of $\sigma = {}^{w}{\downarrow}(N)\cdot\sigma_1$. Then $\sigma\circ{\uparrow_v} = {}^{w}{\downarrow}(N*({\uparrow_v})_{\geq w})\cdot(\sigma_1\circ{\uparrow_v})$. We prove below that $N*({\uparrow_v})_{\geq w}$ is well-defined.

If $\mathrm{Lv}(\sigma) > 0$, then $N*({\uparrow_v})_{\geq w}$ is well-defined by induction hypothesis since $\mathrm{Lv}(({\uparrow_v})_{\geq w}) = 0$. If $\mathrm{Lv}(\sigma) = 0$, then $N = w^e$ for some $e\in\mathbb{N}$, and thus $N*({\uparrow_v})_{\geq w} = w^{e+\delta_{vw}}$.

Note that $N = w^e$ for some $e\in\mathbb{N}$ if and only if $N*({\uparrow_v})_{\geq w} = w^c$ for some $c\in\mathbb{N}$. Thus we have $\mathrm{Lv}(\sigma\circ{\uparrow_v}) = \mathrm{Lv}(\sigma)$.

Consequently, $M*\sigma = \lambda v.(M_1 * {\Uparrow_v}(\sigma))$ is well-defined by induction hypothesis since ${\Uparrow_v}(\sigma) = {}^{v}{\downarrow}(v)\cdot(\sigma\circ{\uparrow_v})$ is well-defined and we have $\mathrm{Lv}({\Uparrow_v}(\sigma)) = \mathrm{Lv}(\sigma)$ and $\mathrm{Ht}(M_1) < \mathrm{Ht}(M)$.

(3) The case of $M = M_1 \mathbin{@_\ell} M_2$ is trivial. □

**Corollary 3.9.** *Let $\sigma$ and $\tau$ be substitutions. Then $\sigma\circ\tau$ is well-defined.*

### 3.3 Reductions on Terms

**Definition 3.10.** Let $\rightarrowtail$ be a binary relation on the set *Ter* of terms. We say that $\rightarrowtail$ is a reduction relation if $\rightarrowtail$ satisfies the following conditions:

$$v^d[\sigma\cdot{}^{w}{\downarrow}(M)\cdot\tau] \rightarrowtail v^d[\sigma\cdot{}^{w}{\downarrow}(M')\cdot\tau] \quad \text{if } M\rightarrowtail M',$$
$$\lambda v.M \rightarrowtail \lambda v.M' \quad \text{if } M\rightarrowtail M',$$
$$M \mathbin{@_\ell} N \rightarrowtail M' \mathbin{@_\ell} N \quad \text{if } M\rightarrowtail M',$$
$$N \mathbin{@_\ell} M \rightarrowtail N \mathbin{@_\ell} M' \quad \text{if } M\rightarrowtail M'.$$

We define $\beta$**-reduction** $\to_\beta$ as the least reduction relation satisfying the following expression:

$$(\lambda v.M)\mathbin{@_\ell} N \to_\beta M * {}^{v}{\downarrow}(N) \quad \text{if } \mathrm{Lv}(v) = \ell.$$

We also define $\alpha$**-renaming** $\to_\alpha$ and $\eta$**-reduction** $\to_\eta$ as the least reduction relations satisfying the following expressions:

$$\lambda v.M \to_\alpha \lambda w.(M * ({}^{v}{\downarrow}(w)\cdot{\uparrow_w})) \quad \text{if } \mathrm{Lv}(v) = \mathrm{Lv}(w),$$

and

$$\lambda v.((M * {\uparrow_v})\mathbin{@_\ell} v) \to_\eta M \quad \text{if } \mathrm{Lv}(v) = \ell,$$

respectively.

**Notation.** Let $\rightarrowtail$ and $\rightarrowtail'$ be binary relations on a set. The composition of binary relations $\rightarrowtail$ and $\rightarrowtail'$ is denoted by $\rightarrowtail\cdot\rightarrowtail'$. The transitive closure of $\rightarrowtail$ is denoted by $\rightarrowtail^*$.

**Remark 3.11.** A term is said to be **annotation-free** if all indices in the term equal 0 and all substitutions in the term equal id. Consider the set $\Lambda_1$ of annotation-free terms consisting only of constructs of level 1. Then the set $\Lambda_1$ is just the set of terms in the ordinary lambda calculus under the assumption that we have infinitely many names of level 1 in the set $\mathcal{N}$ of names. Furthermore, $\beta$-reduction, $\alpha$-renaming and $\eta$-reduction on the set $\Lambda_1$ coincide with the counterparts in the ordinary lambda calculus. As a result, the formalization of calculus $\lambda^*$ provides us another definition of the ordinary lambda calculus in which $\beta$-reduction is defined without the notion of free variables and $\alpha$-renaming.

### 3.4 Equivalence on Terms

The $\beta$-reduction defined in Definition 3.10 is not strictly confluent. Consider a term $M = (\lambda\mathtt{x}.((\lambda\mathtt{y}.\mathtt{N})\mathbin{@_1}\mathtt{z}))\mathbin{@_1}\mathtt{y}$ with names $\mathtt{x}$, $\mathtt{y}$, $\mathtt{z}$ of level 1 and name $\mathtt{N}$ of level 2. We can obtain two distinct $\beta$-normal forms from $M$ as follows:

$$M \to_\beta^* \mathtt{N}[{}^{\mathtt{y}}{\downarrow}(\mathtt{z})\cdot{}^{\mathtt{x}}{\downarrow}(\mathtt{y})], \text{ and}$$
$$M \to_\beta^* \mathtt{N}[{}^{\mathtt{y}}{\downarrow}(\mathtt{z})\cdot{}^{\mathtt{x}}{\downarrow}(\mathtt{y})\cdot{\uparrow_{\mathtt{y}}}\cdot{}^{\mathtt{y}}{\downarrow}(\mathtt{z})].$$

The two substitutions $\sigma = {}^{\mathtt{y}}{\downarrow}(\mathtt{z})\cdot{}^{\mathtt{x}}{\downarrow}(\mathtt{y})$ and $\tau = {}^{\mathtt{y}}{\downarrow}(\mathtt{z})\cdot{}^{\mathtt{x}}{\downarrow}(\mathtt{y})\cdot{\uparrow_{\mathtt{y}}}\cdot{}^{\mathtt{y}}{\downarrow}(\mathtt{z})$ in the above are obviously distinct sequences of push-pop-elements. However, $\sigma$ and $\tau$ have the same $\langle v, d\rangle$-component for all names $v$ and nonnegative integers $d$. We introduce an equivalence relation to equate such two substitutions. The equivalence relation leads the $\beta$-reduction to be confluent.

**Definition 3.12.** We define equivalence relations $\simeq_{\mathrm{t}}$ on the set *Ter* of terms and $\simeq_{\mathrm{s}}$ on the set *Sub* of substitutions inductively as follows:

$$\mathrm{id} \simeq_{\mathrm{s}} \mathrm{id},$$
$$\sigma \simeq_{\mathrm{s}} \tau \quad \text{if } \sigma\langle v,d\rangle \simeq_{\mathrm{t}} \tau\langle v,d\rangle \text{ for any } v\in\mathcal{N}, d\in\mathbb{N},$$
$$v^d[\sigma] \simeq_{\mathrm{t}} v^d[\tau] \quad \text{if } \sigma\simeq_{\mathrm{s}}\tau,$$
$$\lambda v.M \simeq_{\mathrm{t}} \lambda v.N \quad \text{if } M\simeq_{\mathrm{t}} N,$$
$$M_1\mathbin{@_\ell} M_2 \simeq_{\mathrm{t}} N_1\mathbin{@_\ell} N_2 \quad \text{if } M_1\simeq_{\mathrm{t}} N_1 \text{ and } M_2\simeq_{\mathrm{t}} N_2.$$

The symbols $\simeq_{\mathrm{t}}$ and $\simeq_{\mathrm{s}}$ are written simply as $\simeq$ by omitting the subscripts, when no confusion may occur.

We give another possible formalization of the equivalence on terms to illustrate the connection between equivalent terms more concretely by providing canonical form of substitutions.

**Definition 3.13.** We define $\varepsilon$**-reduction** on terms as the least reduction relation satisfying the following three expressions:

$$v^d[\sigma\cdot{\uparrow_w}\cdot{}^{w}{\downarrow}(M)\cdot\tau] \to_\varepsilon v^d[\sigma\cdot\tau],$$
$$v^d[\sigma\cdot{}^{w}{\downarrow}(w^e)\cdot{\uparrow_w}^{e+1}] \to_\varepsilon v^d[\sigma\cdot{\uparrow_w}^{e}],$$

and

$$v^d[\sigma\cdot\rho_1\cdot\rho_2\cdot\tau] \to_\varepsilon v^d[\sigma\cdot\rho_2\cdot\rho_1\cdot\tau]$$

for any $\rho_1 \in \{{}^{w}{\downarrow}(M), {\uparrow_w}\}$ and $\rho_2 \in \{{}^{u}{\downarrow}(N), {\uparrow_u}\}$ with $w \neq u$.

**Definition 3.14.** For each term $M$, we define $\#M$ as the number of push-pop-elements in $M$, namely, the number of up-arrows and down-arrows occurring in $M$. A term $M$ is said to be **canonical** if $\#M \leq \#M'$ holds for any term $M'$ satisfying $M \to_\varepsilon^* M'$. A substitution $\sigma$ is also said to be canonical if $v^d[\sigma]$ is a canonical term for some name $v$ and nonnegative integer $d$.

**Remark 3.15.** A substitution $\sigma$ is canonical, if and only if for each name $v$ we have

$$\sigma\lceil\{v\} = {}^v\!\downarrow(M_0^v)\cdot{}^v\!\downarrow(M_1^v)\cdot\dots\cdot{}^v\!\downarrow(M_{p_v-1}^v)\cdot\uparrow_v{}^{q_v}$$

for some nonnegative integers $p_v$, $q_v$ and canonical terms $M_0^v$, $M_1^v$, ..., $M_{p_v-1}^v$, such that $M_{p_v-1}^v \neq v^{q_v-1}$ if $p_v > 0$ and $q_v > 0$. Suppose that the above equality hold. Then we have

$$\sigma\langle v,d\rangle = \begin{cases} M_d^v & \text{if } 0 \le d < p_v, \\ v^{d-p_v+q_v} & \text{otherwise,} \end{cases}$$

for each nonnegative integer $d$.

**Proposition 3.16.** *Let $M$ and $N$ be terms. Then $M \simeq N$ holds if and only if $M \to_\varepsilon^* \cdot \leftarrow_\varepsilon^* N$ holds.*

*Proof.* It is straightforward that $M \to_\varepsilon N$ implies $M \simeq N$. We show that $M \simeq N$ implies $M \to_\varepsilon^* \cdot \leftarrow_\varepsilon^* N$.

We have canonical terms $M_c$ and $N_c$ such that $M \to_\varepsilon^* M_c$ and $N \to_\varepsilon^* N_c$. Note that $M \simeq N$ implies $M_c \simeq N_c$. We can prove that if $M_c \simeq N_c$ then $M_c \to_\varepsilon^* N_c$ by straightforward induction on $\mathrm{Ht}(M_c) + \mathrm{Ht}(N_c)$. □

**Theorem 3.17.** *The following properties hold:*

$$\begin{aligned} M * \sigma &\simeq M' * \sigma' && \text{if } M \simeq M' \text{ and } \sigma \simeq \sigma', \\ \sigma \circ \tau &\simeq \sigma' \circ \tau' && \text{if } \sigma \simeq \sigma' \text{ and } \tau \simeq \tau', \\ \mathrm{id} \circ \sigma &\simeq \sigma \simeq \sigma \circ \mathrm{id}, \\ (\rho \circ \sigma) \circ \tau &\simeq \rho \circ (\sigma \circ \tau), \\ M * \mathrm{id} &\simeq M, \\ (M * \sigma) * \tau &\simeq M * (\sigma \circ \tau), \end{aligned}$$

*for terms $M$, $M'$ and substitutions $\rho$, $\sigma$, $\sigma'$, $\tau$.*

In short, action of substitutions on terms and composition of substitutions preserve equivalence, and the set *Sub* of substitutions amounts to a monoid acting on the set *Ter* of terms up to equivalence. We prove the above properties in what follows.

**Proposition 3.18.** *Let $M$ be a term. Then $M * \mathrm{id} \simeq M$ holds.*

*Proof.* We prove the stronger proposition that $M * \sigma \simeq M$ holds for any term $M$ and any substitution $\sigma$ satisfying the following condition: for any name $v$ there exists a nonnegative integer $p$ such that

$$\sigma\lceil\{v\} = {}^v\!\downarrow(v^0)\cdot{}^v\!\downarrow(v^1)\cdot\dots\cdot{}^v\!\downarrow(v^{p-1})\cdot\uparrow_v{}^p.$$

The stronger proposition is proved by straightforward induction on $\mathrm{Ht}(M)$. □

**Lemma 3.19.** *Let $\sigma$ and $\tau$ be substitutions, $v$ a name, $d$ a nonnegative integer. Then $(\tau \circ \sigma)\langle v,d\rangle \simeq \tau\langle v,d\rangle * \sigma_{\ge v}$ holds.*

*Proof.* By straightforward induction on length of $\tau$. □

**Proposition 3.20.** *Let $M$ and $M'$ be terms, $\sigma$ and $\sigma'$ substitutions. If $M \simeq M'$ and $\sigma \simeq \sigma'$, then $M * \sigma \simeq M' * \sigma'$ holds.*

*Proof.* The proposition is proved by induction on the lexicographic ordering of pairs $\langle \max\{\mathrm{Lv}(\sigma), \mathrm{Lv}(\sigma')\}, \mathrm{Ht}(M) + \mathrm{Ht}(M')\rangle$ as in the proof of Proposition 3.8. □

**Corollary 3.21.** *Let $\sigma$, $\sigma'$, $\tau$ and $\tau'$ be substitutions such that $\sigma \simeq \sigma'$ and $\tau \simeq \tau'$. Then $\tau \circ \sigma \simeq \tau' \circ \sigma'$ holds.*

**Proposition 3.22.** *Let $M$ be a term, $\sigma$ and $\tau$ substitutions. Then $(M * \sigma) * \tau \simeq M * (\sigma \circ \tau)$ holds.*

*Proof.* The proposition is proved by induction on lexicographic ordering of pairs $\langle \mathrm{Lv}(\sigma) + \mathrm{Lv}(\tau), \mathrm{Ht}(M)\rangle$.

(1) Consider the case of $M = v^d[\rho]$.

We can prove that $(\rho\circ\sigma)\circ\tau \simeq \rho\circ(\sigma\circ\tau)$ by induction hypothesis and by the fact that $(\sigma \circ \tau)_{\ge \ell} = \sigma_{\ge \ell} \circ \tau_{\ge \ell}$ for each level $\ell$. We show below that $(v^d[\rho] * \sigma) * \tau \simeq v^d[\rho] * (\sigma \circ \tau)$.

Suppose that $\mathrm{Lv}(\sigma) \ge \mathrm{Lv}(v)$. Then $(v^d[\rho]*\sigma)*\tau = (\sigma\langle v,d\rangle * (\rho\circ\sigma)_{<v})*\tau \simeq \sigma\langle v,d\rangle * ((\rho\circ\sigma)_{<v}\circ\tau) \simeq \sigma\langle v,d\rangle * (\tau_{\ge v}\circ((\rho\circ\sigma)\circ\tau)_{<v}) \simeq (\sigma\langle v,d\rangle * \tau_{\ge v}) * ((\rho\circ\sigma)\circ\tau)_{<v} \simeq (\sigma\circ\tau)\langle v,d\rangle * (\rho\circ(\sigma\circ\tau))_{<v} = v^d[\rho] * (\sigma\circ\tau)$ by induction hypothesis and by the fact that $(\rho\circ\sigma)_{<v}\circ\tau \simeq \tau_{\ge v}\circ((\rho\circ\sigma)\circ\tau)_{<v}$.

Suppose that $\mathrm{Lv}(\sigma) < \mathrm{Lv}(v)$. Then $\sigma\langle v,d\rangle = v^e$ holds for some $e \in \mathbb{N}$. We have $(v^d[\rho] * \sigma) * \tau = v^e[(\rho\circ\sigma)_{<v}] * \tau = \tau\langle v,e\rangle * ((\rho\circ\sigma)_{<v}\circ\tau)_{<v} = \tau\langle v,e\rangle * ((\rho\circ\sigma)\circ\tau)_{<v} \simeq (\sigma\circ\tau)\langle v,d\rangle * (\rho\circ(\sigma\circ\tau))_{<v} = v^d[\rho] * (\sigma\circ\tau)$.

(2) Consider the case of $M = \lambda v.M_1$.

We show that $(\sigma\circ\uparrow_v)\circ\Uparrow_v(\tau) \simeq (\sigma\circ\tau)\circ\uparrow_v$.

Suppose that $\mathrm{Lv}(\sigma) > 0$. Then $((\sigma\circ\uparrow_v)\circ\Uparrow_v(\tau))\langle w,d\rangle \simeq (\sigma\langle w,d\rangle * (\uparrow_v)_{\ge w}) * \Uparrow_v(\tau)_{\ge w} \simeq \sigma\langle w,d\rangle * (\uparrow_v\circ\Uparrow_v(\tau))_{\ge w} \simeq \sigma\langle w,d\rangle * (\tau\circ\uparrow_v)_{\ge w} \simeq (\sigma\langle w,d\rangle * \tau_{\ge w}) * (\uparrow_v)_{\ge w} \simeq ((\sigma\circ\tau)\circ\uparrow_v)\langle w,d\rangle$ by induction hypothesis.

Suppose that $\mathrm{Lv}(\sigma) = 0$. Then $\sigma\langle w,d\rangle = w^e$ holds for some $e \in \mathbb{N}$. We have $((\sigma\circ\uparrow_v)\circ\Uparrow_v(\tau))\langle w,d\rangle \simeq (\sigma\langle w,d\rangle * (\uparrow_v)_{\ge w}) * \Uparrow_v(\tau)_{\ge w} = (w^e * (\uparrow_v)_{\ge w}) * \Uparrow_v(\tau)_{\ge w} = w^{e+\delta_{vw}} * \Uparrow_v(\tau)_{\ge w} \simeq (\tau\circ\uparrow_v)\langle w,e\rangle \simeq \tau\langle w,e\rangle * (\uparrow_v)_{\ge w} \simeq (w^e * \tau_{\ge w}) * (\uparrow_v)_{\ge w} = (\sigma\langle w,d\rangle * \tau_{\ge w}) * (\uparrow_v)_{\ge w} \simeq ((\sigma\circ\tau)\circ\uparrow_v)\langle w,d\rangle$.

Therefore we have $(M*\sigma)*\tau = \lambda v.((M_1 * \Uparrow_v(\sigma)) * \Uparrow_v(\tau)) \simeq \lambda v.(M_1 * (\Uparrow_v(\sigma)\circ\Uparrow_v(\tau))) = \lambda v.(M_1 * ({}^v\!\downarrow(v * \Uparrow_v(\tau)_{\ge v}) \cdot ((\sigma\circ\uparrow_v)\circ\Uparrow_v(\tau)))) \simeq \lambda v.(M_1 * ({}^v\!\downarrow(v)\cdot((\sigma\circ\tau)\circ\uparrow_v))) = \lambda v.(M_1 * \Uparrow_v(\sigma\circ\tau)) = M * (\sigma\circ\tau)$ by induction hypothesis.

(3) The case of $M = M_1 \mathbin{@_\ell} M_2$ is trivial. □

**Corollary 3.23.** *Let $\rho$, $\sigma$ and $\tau$ be substitutions. Then we have $(\rho\circ\sigma)\circ\tau \simeq \rho\circ(\sigma\circ\tau)$.*

### 3.5 Confluence of Reductions

We prove that β-reduction is confluent up to equivalence by the technique of parallel reduction [19]. In other words, we prove confluence of βε-reduction.

**Definition 3.24.** We define auxiliary binary relations $\Rrightarrow_{\mathrm{t}}$ on the set *Ter* of terms and $\Rrightarrow_{\mathrm{s}}$ on the set *Sub* of substitutions inductively as follows:

$$\begin{aligned} (\lambda v.M) \mathbin{@_{\mathrm{Lv}(v)}} N &\Rrightarrow_{\mathrm{t}} M' * {}^v\!\downarrow(N') && \text{if } M \Rrightarrow_{\mathrm{t}} M',\ N \Rrightarrow_{\mathrm{t}} N', \\ v^d[\sigma] &\Rrightarrow_{\mathrm{t}} v^d[\sigma'] && \text{if } \sigma \Rrightarrow_{\mathrm{s}} \sigma', \\ \lambda v.M &\Rrightarrow_{\mathrm{t}} \lambda v.M' && \text{if } M \Rrightarrow_{\mathrm{t}} M', \\ M_1 \mathbin{@_\ell} M_2 &\Rrightarrow_{\mathrm{t}} M_1' \mathbin{@_\ell} M_2' && \text{if } M_1 \Rrightarrow_{\mathrm{t}} M_1',\ M_2 \Rrightarrow_{\mathrm{t}} M_2', \\ \mathrm{id} &\Rrightarrow_{\mathrm{s}} \mathrm{id}, \\ {}^v\!\downarrow(M)\cdot\sigma &\Rrightarrow_{\mathrm{s}} {}^v\!\downarrow(M')\cdot\sigma' && \text{if } M \Rrightarrow_{\mathrm{t}} M',\ \sigma \Rrightarrow_{\mathrm{s}} \sigma', \\ \uparrow_v\cdot\sigma &\Rrightarrow_{\mathrm{s}} \uparrow_v\cdot\sigma' && \text{if } \sigma \Rrightarrow_{\mathrm{s}} \sigma'. \end{aligned}$$

Note that we have $\to_\beta^* = \Rrightarrow_{\mathrm{t}}^*$. The symbols $\Rrightarrow_{\mathrm{t}}$ and $\Rrightarrow_{\mathrm{s}}$ are written simply as $\Rrightarrow$ by omitting the subscripts, when no confusion may occur.

**Lemma 3.25.** *Let $M$ and $M'$ be terms, $\sigma$ and $\sigma'$ substitutions. If $M \Rrightarrow \cdot \simeq M'$ and $\sigma \Rrightarrow \cdot \simeq \sigma'$, then $M * \sigma \Rrightarrow \cdot \simeq M' * \sigma'$ holds.*

*Proof.* By straightforward induction on the lexicographic ordering of pairs $\langle \mathrm{Lv}(\sigma), \mathrm{Ht}(M)\rangle$. □

**Lemma 3.26.** *Let $M$ and $N$ be terms. If $M \simeq \cdot \Rrightarrow N$ holds, then we have $M \Rrightarrow \cdot \simeq N$.*

*Proof.* We can prove the following proposition by straightforward induction on $\mathrm{Ht}(L)$: if $M \simeq L \Rrightarrow N$ for some term $L$, then there exists a term $L'$ such that $M \Rrightarrow L' \simeq N$. □

**Definition 3.27.** For each term $M$ and each substitution $\sigma$, we define term $M^\wedge$ and substitution $\sigma^\wedge$ inductively as follows:

$$
\begin{aligned}
(v^d[\sigma])^\wedge &:= v^d[\sigma^\wedge],\\
(\lambda v.M)^\wedge &:= \lambda v.(M^\wedge),\\
(M \mathbin{@_\ell} N)^\wedge &:= \begin{cases} L^\wedge * {}^v\!\!\downarrow\!(N^\wedge) & \text{if } M = \lambda v.L, \mathrm{Lv}(v) = \ell,\\ M^\wedge \mathbin{@_\ell} N^\wedge & \text{otherwise,}\end{cases}\\
\mathrm{id}^\wedge &:= \mathrm{id},\\
({}^v\!\!\downarrow\!(M)\cdot\sigma)^\wedge &:= {}^v\!\!\downarrow\!(M^\wedge)\cdot\sigma^\wedge,\\
(\Uparrow_v\cdot\sigma)^\wedge &:= \Uparrow_v\cdot\sigma^\wedge.
\end{aligned}
$$

**Lemma 3.28.** *Let $M$ and $N$ be terms such that $M \Rrightarrow N$. Then $N \Rrightarrow \cdot \simeq M^\wedge$ holds.*

*Proof.* By straightforward induction on $\mathrm{Ht}(M)$. □

**Theorem 3.29.** *Let $M$ and $N$ be terms. If $M \leftarrow^*_\beta \cdot \simeq \cdot \rightarrow^*_\beta N$, then $M \rightarrow^*_\beta \cdot \simeq \cdot \leftarrow^*_\beta N$ holds.*

*Proof.* By Lemma 3.26 and Lemma 3.28, we can easily prove that $M \Lleftarrow \cdot \simeq \cdot \Rrightarrow N$ implies $M \Rrightarrow \cdot \simeq \cdot \Lleftarrow N$ for any terms $M$ and $N$. By this proposition and Lemma 3.26, the above theorem is proved. □

**Corollary 3.30.** *Let $M$ and $N$ be terms, and $\rightarrow_{\beta\varepsilon}$ be the union of reduction relations $\rightarrow_\beta$ and $\rightarrow_\varepsilon$. If $M \leftarrow^*_{\beta\varepsilon} \cdot \rightarrow^*_{\beta\varepsilon} N$, then we have $M \rightarrow^*_{\beta\varepsilon} \cdot \leftarrow^*_{\beta\varepsilon} N$.*

## 4. An Application

Calculus $\lambda^*$ provides us a way to manipulate binding structure flexibly with dynamic binding via meta-level variables. We illustrate the feature through an application of the calculus to a procedural language.

### 4.1 Procedural Language PROC

We introduce a simple procedural language PROC as an extension of imperative language IMP in [20]. PROC permits us to store and retrieve not only numbers but also procedures. We implement PROC in $\lambda^*$ by exploiting the feature to manipulate binding structure dynamically. The implementation of PROC demonstrates that some notions related to names in procedural languages, such as stores, recursion, and localization of names, can be realized by dynamic binding via meta-level variables.

**Definition 4.1.** We define the syntax of PROC by the following BNF:

$$
\begin{aligned}
\text{N-expressions } E &::= x \mid n \mid \texttt{plus}\ E\ E \mid \texttt{minus}\ E\ E\\
\text{P-expressions } F &::= z \mid \texttt{proc}\ P\\
\text{Commands } C &::= x\,\texttt{=}\,E \mid z\,\texttt{=}\,F \mid \texttt{exec}\ F \mid \texttt{if}\ E\ P\ P \mid\\
&\qquad \texttt{while}\ E\ P \mid \texttt{local}\ P\ \texttt{export}\ {}^{x_1x_2\cdots x_h}_{z_1z_2\cdots z_k}\\
\text{Procedures } P &::= \mathrm{id} \mid C\,;P
\end{aligned}
$$

where $n$, $h$, $k$ range over the set $\mathbb{N}$ of nonnegative integers, $x$, $x_1$, $x_2, \ldots, x_h$ range over a set $\mathcal{N}_\mathrm{N}$ of names for numbers, $z$, $z_1$, $z_2, \ldots, z_k$ range over a set $\mathcal{N}_\mathrm{P}$ of names for procedures, and id signifies the empty sequence. The sets $\mathcal{N}_\mathrm{N}$ and $\mathcal{N}_\mathrm{P}$ are disjoint. We define $\mathbb{P}$ as the set of all procedures. Note that a procedure $P$ is a finite sequence of commands. We represent concatenation of procedures $P_1$ and $P_2$ as $P_1\,;P_2$.

**Definition 4.2.** A pair $\langle\varphi_\mathrm{N},\varphi_\mathrm{P}\rangle$ of a function $\varphi_\mathrm{N}$ of $\mathcal{N}_\mathrm{N}$ into $\mathbb{N}$ and a function $\varphi_\mathrm{P}$ of $\mathcal{N}_\mathrm{P}$ into $\mathbb{P}$, is called a **state** of stores. We define $\mathbb{S}$ as the set of all states of stores, and call an element of the set $\mathbb{S}$ simply a state. Let $\varphi = \langle\varphi_\mathrm{N},\varphi_\mathrm{P}\rangle$ be a state. Then the value $E^\varphi$ of n-expression $E$ in state $\varphi$ is the nonnegative integer defined inductively as follows:

$$
\begin{aligned}
x^\varphi &:= \varphi_\mathrm{N}(x),\\
n^\varphi &:= n,\\
(\texttt{plus}\ E_1\ E_2)^\varphi &:= E_1{}^\varphi + E_2{}^\varphi,\\
(\texttt{minus}\ E_1\ E_2)^\varphi &:= \max\{E_1{}^\varphi - E_2{}^\varphi, 0\}.
\end{aligned}
$$

Similarly, the value $F^\varphi$ of p-expression $F$ in state $\varphi$ is the procedure defined as follows:

$$
\begin{aligned}
z^\varphi &:= \varphi_\mathrm{P}(z),\\
(\texttt{proc}\ P)^\varphi &:= P.
\end{aligned}
$$

**Definition 4.3.** Let $\varphi = \langle\varphi_\mathrm{N},\varphi_\mathrm{P}\rangle$ be a state. For nonnegative integers $n$ and names $x$ in $\mathcal{N}_\mathrm{N}$, state $\varphi\{n/x\}$ is defined as follows:

$$
\varphi\{n/x\} := \langle\varphi'_\mathrm{N},\varphi_\mathrm{P}\rangle \quad \text{where } \varphi'_\mathrm{N}(x') = \begin{cases} n & \text{if } x' = x,\\ \varphi_\mathrm{N}(x') & \text{otherwise,}\end{cases}
$$

for names $x'$ in $\mathcal{N}_\mathrm{N}$. Similarly, state $\varphi\{P/z\}$ is defined for procedures $P$ and names $z$ in $\mathcal{N}_\mathrm{P}$ as follows:

$$
\varphi\{P/z\} := \langle\varphi_\mathrm{N},\varphi'_\mathrm{P}\rangle \quad \text{where } \varphi'_\mathrm{P}(z') = \begin{cases} P & \text{if } z' = z,\\ \varphi_\mathrm{P}(z') & \text{otherwise,}\end{cases}
$$

for names $z'$ in $\mathcal{N}_\mathrm{P}$.

**Definition 4.4.** For procedures $P$, $P'$, and states $\varphi$, $\varphi'$, we define transition relation $\langle P \mid \varphi\rangle \rightarrow \langle P' \mid \varphi'\rangle$ as follows:

$$
\begin{aligned}
\langle x\,\texttt{=}\,E\,;P \mid \varphi\rangle &\rightarrow \langle P \mid \varphi\{E^\varphi/x\}\rangle,\\
\langle z\,\texttt{=}\,F\,;P \mid \varphi\rangle &\rightarrow \langle P \mid \varphi\{F^\varphi/z\}\rangle,\\
\langle \texttt{exec}\ F\,;P \mid \varphi\rangle &\rightarrow \langle F^\varphi\,;P \mid \varphi\rangle,\\
\langle \texttt{if}\ E\ P_1\ P_2\,;P \mid \varphi\rangle &\rightarrow \langle P_1\,;P \mid \varphi\rangle \quad \text{if } E^\varphi > 0,\\
\langle \texttt{if}\ E\ P_1\ P_2\,;P \mid \varphi\rangle &\rightarrow \langle P_2\,;P \mid \varphi\rangle \quad \text{if } E^\varphi = 0,\\
\langle \texttt{while}\ E\ P_1\,;P \mid \varphi\rangle &\rightarrow \langle \texttt{if}\ E\ \{P_1\,;\texttt{while}\ E\ P_1\}\ \mathrm{id}\,;P \mid \varphi\rangle,
\end{aligned}
$$

and, if $\langle P_1 \mid \varphi\rangle \rightarrow^* \langle \mathrm{id} \mid \varphi'\rangle$ for some state $\varphi'$ then

$$
\langle \texttt{local}\ P_1\ \texttt{export}\ {}^{x_1\cdots x_h}_{z_1\cdots z_k}\,;P \mid \varphi\rangle \rightarrow \langle P \mid \psi\rangle
$$

with $\psi = \varphi\{x_1{}^{\varphi'}/x_1\}\cdots\{x_h{}^{\varphi'}/x_h\}\{z_1{}^{\varphi'}/z_1\}\cdots\{z_k{}^{\varphi'}/z_k\}$.

### 4.2 Implementation of PROC in $\lambda^*$

In the subsequent discussion, we assume that the set $\mathcal{N}_\mathrm{N}$ of names for numbers and the set $\mathcal{N}_\mathrm{P}$ of names for procedures are disjoint finite sets $\{\bar{x}_1, \bar{x}_2, \ldots, \bar{x}_a\}$ and $\{\bar{z}_1, \bar{z}_2, \ldots, \bar{z}_b\}$ respectively for some nonnegative integers $a$ and $b$. Note that we can adopt such assumption when computing a procedure in PROC, since every procedure contains only finitely many names. Furthermore, we assume that the set of names of level 1 in calculus $\lambda^*$ contains all names in PROC.

**Notation.** In this section, applications of each level are left-associative, and the body of an abstraction extends as far right as possible, in a customary way. Upper-case letters are names of level 2, and lower-case letters are names of level 1. We omit marks '$@_1$' for applications of level 1. For instance, $(\lambda\mathtt{M.Mxy}) \mathbin{@_2} \mathtt{M} \mathbin{@_2} \mathtt{N}$ signifies $((\lambda\mathtt{M}.((\mathtt{M} \mathbin{@_1} \mathtt{x}) \mathbin{@_1} \mathtt{y})) \mathbin{@_2} \mathtt{M}) \mathbin{@_2} \mathtt{N}$.

**Definition 4.5.** To n-expressions $E$, p-expressions $F$, commands $C$ and procedures $P$ in PROC, we assign terms $[\![E]\!]$, $[\![F]\!]$, $(\!|C|\!)$ and

$[\![P]\!]$ in calculus $\lambda^*$ respectively, as follows:

$$
\begin{aligned}
&[\![x]\!] := x, \quad [\![0]\!] := \mathit{zero}, \quad [\![n+1]\!] := \mathit{scc}[\![n]\!],\\
&[\![\mathtt{plus}\ E_1\ E_2]\!] := \mathit{plus}[\![E_1]\!][\![E_2]\!],\\
&[\![\mathtt{minus}\ E_1\ E_2]\!] := \mathit{minus}[\![E_1]\!][\![E_2]\!],\\
&[\![z]\!] := z, \quad [\![\mathtt{proc}\ P]\!] := \mathit{block} \mathbin{@_2} [\![P]\!],\\
&(\!|x = E|\!) := \mathit{set}_x \mathbin{@_2} [\![E]\!], \quad (\!|z = F|\!) := \mathit{set}_z \mathbin{@_2} [\![F]\!],\\
&(\!|\mathtt{exec}\ F|\!) := \mathit{unblock} \mathbin{@_2} [\![F]\!],\\
&(\!|\mathtt{if}\ E\ P_1\ P_2|\!) := \mathit{if} \mathbin{@_2} [\![E]\!] \mathbin{@_2} [\![P_1]\!] \mathbin{@_2} [\![P_2]\!],\\
&(\!|\mathtt{while}\ E\ P|\!) := \mathit{while} \mathbin{@_2} [\![E]\!] \mathbin{@_2} [\![P]\!],\\
&(\!|\mathtt{local}\ P\ \mathtt{export}\,{}^{x_1 \ldots x_h}_{z_1 \ldots z_k}|\!) := \mathit{local}^{x_1 \ldots x_h}_{z_1 \ldots z_k} \mathbin{@_2} [\![P]\!],\\
&[\![\mathrm{id}]\!] := \mathit{id}, \quad [\![C\,;P]\!] := \mathit{comp} \mathbin{@_2} (\!|C|\!) \mathbin{@_2} [\![P]\!],
\end{aligned}
$$

where

$$
\begin{aligned}
&\mathit{zero} := \lambda \mathtt{s}.\lambda \mathtt{z}.\mathtt{z}, \quad \mathit{fst} := \lambda \mathtt{a}.\lambda \mathtt{b}.\mathtt{a}, \quad \mathit{snd} := \lambda \mathtt{a}.\lambda \mathtt{b}.\mathtt{b},\\
&\mathit{scc} := \lambda \mathtt{n}.\lambda \mathtt{s}.\lambda \mathtt{z}.\mathtt{s}(\mathtt{nsz}),\\
&\mathit{prd} := \lambda \mathtt{n}.\mathtt{n}(\lambda \mathtt{p}.\lambda \mathtt{c}.\mathtt{c}(\mathtt{p}\ \mathit{snd})(\mathit{scc}(\mathtt{p}\ \mathit{snd})))(\lambda \mathtt{c}.\mathtt{c}(\mathit{zero})\mathit{zero})\mathit{fst},\\
&\mathit{plus} := \lambda \mathtt{m}.\lambda \mathtt{n}.\mathtt{n}(\mathit{scc})\mathtt{m}, \quad \mathit{minus} := \lambda \mathtt{m}.\lambda \mathtt{n}.\mathtt{n}(\mathit{prd})\mathtt{m},\\
&\mathit{block} := \lambda \mathtt{Y}.\lambda \mathtt{x}.(\mathtt{x} \mathbin{@_2} \mathtt{Y}), \quad \mathit{unblock} := \lambda \mathtt{Z}.\mathtt{Z}(\lambda \mathtt{Y}.\mathtt{Y}),\\
&\mathit{set}_v := \lambda \mathtt{E}.\lambda \mathtt{K}.(\lambda v.\mathtt{K})\mathtt{E},\\
&\mathit{if} := \lambda \mathtt{E}.\lambda \mathtt{P}.\lambda \mathtt{Q}.\lambda \mathtt{K}.\mathtt{E}(\lambda \mathtt{z}.\mathit{fst})\mathit{snd}(\mathtt{P} \mathbin{@_2} \mathtt{K})(\mathtt{Q} \mathbin{@_2} \mathtt{K}),\\
&\mathit{while} := \mathit{fix} \mathbin{@_2} (\lambda \mathtt{W}.\lambda \mathtt{E}.\lambda \mathtt{P}.(\mathit{if} \mathbin{@_2} \mathtt{E} \mathbin{@_2} \mathit{loop} \mathbin{@_2} \mathrm{id})),\\
&\mathit{fix} := \lambda \mathtt{F}.((\lambda \mathtt{X}.(\mathtt{F} \mathbin{@_2} (\mathtt{X} \mathbin{@_2} \mathtt{X}))) \mathbin{@_2} (\lambda \mathtt{X}.(\mathtt{F} \mathbin{@_2} (\mathtt{X} \mathbin{@_2} \mathtt{X})))),\\
&\mathit{loop} := \mathit{comp} \mathbin{@_2} \mathtt{P} \mathbin{@_2} (\mathtt{W} \mathbin{@_2} \mathtt{E} \mathbin{@_2} \mathtt{P}),\\
&\mathit{local}^{x_1 \ldots x_h}_{z_1 \ldots z_k} := \lambda \mathtt{P}.\lambda \mathtt{K}.(\mathit{export}^{x_1 \ldots x_h}_{z_1 \ldots z_k})(\lambda \mathtt{K}.\lambda x_1. \ldots .\lambda z_k.\mathtt{K})\mathtt{P},\\
&\mathit{export}^{x_1 \ldots x_h}_{z_1 \ldots z_k} := \lambda \mathtt{e}.\lambda \mathtt{r}.(\mathtt{e} \mathbin{@_2} \mathtt{K})(\mathtt{r} \mathbin{@_2} x_1) \cdots (\mathtt{r} \mathbin{@_2} z_k),\\
&\mathit{id} := \lambda \mathtt{K}.\mathtt{K}, \quad \mathit{comp} := \lambda \mathtt{P}.\lambda \mathtt{Q}.\lambda \mathtt{K}.(\mathtt{P} \mathbin{@_2} (\mathtt{Q} \mathbin{@_2} \mathtt{K})).
\end{aligned}
$$

**Definition 4.6.** For each state $\varphi$ in PROC, we define $[\![\varphi]\!]$ as the substitution $\sigma_{\mathrm{N}} \cdot \sigma_{\mathrm{P}}$ in calculus $\lambda^*$, where $\sigma_{\mathrm{N}}$ and $\sigma_{\mathrm{P}}$ are the substitutions defined as follows:

$$
\begin{aligned}
\sigma_{\mathrm{N}} &:= {}^{\bar{x}_1}{\downarrow}([\![\bar{x}_1^{\varphi}]\!]) \cdot \cdots \cdot {}^{\bar{x}_a}{\downarrow}([\![\bar{x}_a^{\varphi}]\!]),\\
\sigma_{\mathrm{P}} &:= {}^{\bar{z}_1}{\downarrow}(\mathit{block} \mathbin{@_2} [\![\bar{z}_1^{\varphi}]\!]) \cdot \cdots \cdot {}^{\bar{z}_b}{\downarrow}(\mathit{block} \mathbin{@_2} [\![\bar{z}_b^{\varphi}]\!]).
\end{aligned}
$$

We also define a relation $\sigma \approx_0 \tau$ for substitutions $\sigma$ and $\tau$ as follows:

$$\sigma \approx_0 \tau \quad \text{if and only if} \quad \sigma\langle v, 0\rangle = \tau\langle v, 0\rangle \text{ for each name } v.$$

**Notation.** In what follows, the relation $\to_\beta^* \cdot \simeq$ is denoted by $\rightsquigarrow_\beta$, and the relation $\to_\beta^* \cdot \simeq \cdot \leftarrow_\beta^*$ is denoted by $\cong_\beta$.

With the above setting, a transition sequence in PROC is simulated by the corresponding reduction sequence in calculus $\lambda^*$, as stated in the following propositions.

**Proposition 4.7.** *Let $P$ be a procedure, $\varphi$ and $\varphi'$ states, and $\sigma$ a substitution. If $\langle P \mid \varphi\rangle \to^* \langle \mathrm{id} \mid \varphi'\rangle$ and $\sigma \approx_0 [\![\varphi]\!]$ hold, then there exists a substitution $\sigma'$ such that $[\![P]\!] * \sigma \rightsquigarrow_\beta [\![\mathrm{id}]\!] * \sigma'$ and $\sigma' \approx_0 [\![\varphi']\!]$.*

*Proof.* By straightforward induction on size of transition sequence $\langle P \mid \varphi\rangle \to^* \langle \mathrm{id} \mid \varphi'\rangle$. □

**Corollary 4.8.** *Let $P$ and $P'$ be procedures, $\varphi$ and $\varphi'$ states, and $\sigma$ a substitution. If $\langle P \mid \varphi\rangle \to \langle P' \mid \varphi'\rangle$ and $\sigma \approx_0 [\![\varphi]\!]$ hold, then there exists a substitution $\sigma'$ such that $[\![P]\!] * \sigma \cong_\beta [\![P']\!] * \sigma'$ and $\sigma' \approx_0 [\![\varphi']\!]$.*

**Remark 4.9.** Stated differently, we have the following as an alternative to Proposition 4.7. Let $P$ be a procedure, $\varphi$ and $\varphi'$ states, and $\sigma$ a substitution. If $\langle P \mid \varphi\rangle \to^* \langle \mathrm{id} \mid \varphi'\rangle$ and $\sigma \approx_0 [\![\varphi]\!]$ hold, then we have

$$\mathit{comp} \mathbin{@_2} (\lambda \mathtt{K}.\mathtt{K}[\sigma]) \mathbin{@_2} [\![P]\!] \rightsquigarrow_\beta \lambda \mathtt{K}.\mathtt{K}[\sigma']$$

for some substitution $\sigma'$ such that $\sigma' \approx_0 [\![\varphi']\!]$.

**Example 4.10.** Let $P$ be the following procedure in PROC that corresponds to the Ruby program in Figure 3:

```
sum = proc { n = ar;
  ct = plus ct 1;
  if n {
    local {ar = minus n 1; exec sum} export rv, ct;
    rv = n + rv
  } { rv = 0 }
}; ct = 0; local {ar = 3; exec sum} export rv, ct
```

Then $[\![P]\!]$ is reduced to the following term in normal form:

$$[\![P]\!] \rightsquigarrow_\beta \lambda \mathtt{K}.\mathtt{K}[{}^{\mathtt{ct}}{\downarrow}(\hat{4}) \cdot {}^{\mathtt{ct}}{\downarrow}(\hat{0}) \cdot {}^{\mathtt{rv}}{\downarrow}(\hat{6}) \cdot {}^{\mathtt{sum}}{\downarrow}(M)]$$

where $\hat{0}$, $\hat{4}$ and $\hat{6}$ are the Church numerals of 0, 4 and 6 respectively, and $M$ is the term that corresponds to the procedure assigned to name `sum`.

**Figure 3.** Sum.rb

```
def sum(n)
  $ct = $ct + 1
  if n > 0
    n + sum(n - 1)
  else 0 end
end
$ct = 0
sum(3)
```

**Figure 4.** DynamicLiar.rb

```
p = "not(eval(p))"
print eval(p)
```

**Figure 5.** StaticLiar.rb

```
p = not(p)
print p
```

### 4.3 Recursion via Names and Textual Substitution

In PROC, we can write recursive procedures in the usual manner. This feature stems from the fact that we can store and retrieve procedures textually via names, and the feature is implemented with terms *block* and *unblock* in calculus $\lambda^*$. Actually, the terms *block* and *unblock* behave as quotes and 'eval' command in programming languages. For example, consider the following term $L$ that corresponds to the Ruby program in Figure 4:

$$L = (\lambda \mathtt{p}.(\mathit{unblock} \mathbin{@_2} \mathtt{p}))(\mathit{block} \mathbin{@_2} (\mathtt{n}(\mathit{unblock} \mathbin{@_2} \mathtt{p}))).$$

Then we have the following infinite reduction sequence that corresponds to the infinite loop caused by the program in Figure 4:

$$L \rightsquigarrow_\beta M \rightsquigarrow_\beta \mathtt{n}M \rightsquigarrow_\beta \mathtt{n}(\mathtt{n}M) \rightsquigarrow_\beta \mathtt{n}(\mathtt{n}(\mathtt{n}M)) \rightsquigarrow_\beta \cdots$$

where $M$ is the term defined as follows:

$$
\begin{aligned}
M &= (\lambda \mathtt{Z}.\mathtt{Z}[{}^{\mathtt{p}}{\downarrow}(N)](\lambda \mathtt{Y}.\mathtt{Y}[{}^{\mathtt{p}}{\downarrow}(N)])) \mathbin{@_2} \mathtt{p},\\
N &= \mathit{block} \mathbin{@_2} (\mathtt{n}(\mathit{unblock} \mathbin{@_2} \mathtt{p})).
\end{aligned}
$$

Note that the terms *block* and *unblock* play fundamental roles to generate the infinite reduction sequence. In fact, if we remove the applications of the terms *block* and *unblock* in term $L$, then we get the term $(\lambda \mathtt{p}.\mathtt{p})(\mathtt{np})$, which corresponds to the Ruby program in Figure 5 that causes no infinite loops. From viewpoint of variable binding, quotes are considered as blocks to variable binding discussed in Section 2.5, and 'eval' command destroys blocks to variable binding. The terms *block* and *unblock* behave in the same way.

### 4.4 A Comment from Viewpoint of Type Systems

To make a brief comment about properties of calculus $\lambda^*$, we introduce a rough type system similar to the simple type system for the lambda calculus.

**Definition 4.11.** We assume that we are given a set of atomic types. The set *Typ* of types is defined inductively as follows:

$$T \in \mathit{Typ} \quad \text{if } T \text{ is an atomic type,}$$
$$T_1 \to_\ell T_2 \in \mathit{Typ} \quad \text{if } \ell \text{ is a level and } T_1, T_2 \in \mathit{Typ}.$$

**Definition 4.12.** A function of $\mathcal{N}$ into *Typ* is called a **type assignment**. For type assignments $\xi$, terms $M$, substitutions $\sigma$, and types $T$, we define typing relations $\xi \vdash M : T$ and $\xi \vdash \sigma$ inductively as follows:

$\xi \vdash v^d[\sigma] : \xi(v) \quad$ if $\xi \vdash \sigma$,

$\xi \vdash \lambda v.M : \xi(v) \to_\ell T \quad$ if $\ell = \mathrm{Lv}(v)$ and $\xi \vdash M : T$,

$\xi \vdash M_1 @_\ell M_2 : T' \quad$ if $\xi \vdash M_1 : T \to_\ell T'$ and $\xi \vdash M_2 : T$,

$\xi \vdash \mathrm{id}$,

$\xi \vdash {}^v\!\!\downarrow\!(M) \cdot \sigma \quad$ if $\xi \vdash M : \xi(v)$ and $\xi \vdash \sigma$,

$\xi \vdash \Uparrow_v \cdot \sigma \quad$ if $\xi \vdash \sigma$.

With the rough type system defined above, we can have subject reduction property stated by the following proposition.

**Proposition 4.13.** *Let $\xi$ be a type assignment, $T$ a type, $M$ and $M'$ terms. If $\xi \vdash M : T$ and $M \to_\beta M'$, then $\xi \vdash M' : T$ holds.*

However, the rough type system does not provide us strong normalization property, in contrast to the type system for calculus $\lambda\mathcal{M}$ [18]. For example, consider a type assignment $\xi_x$ satisfying the following conditions:

$\xi_x(\mathtt{n}) = B \to_1 B, \quad \xi_x(\mathtt{p}) = \mathit{Block}(B), \quad \xi_x(\mathtt{x}) = B \to_2 B,$
$\xi_x(\mathtt{Y}) = B, \quad \xi_x(\mathtt{Z}) = \mathit{Block}(B),$

where $B$ is a type, and $\mathit{Block}(B)$ signifies $(B \to_2 B) \to_1 B$. Then the following expressions hold:

$$\xi_x \vdash \mathit{block} : B \to_2 \mathit{Block}(B),$$
$$\xi_x \vdash \mathit{unblock} : \mathit{Block}(B) \to_2 B,$$
$$\xi_x \vdash L : B,$$

where $L$ is the term defined in Section 4.3. The term $L$ has type $B$, and thus we may expect that the term $L$ signifies a value of type $B$. However, the term $L$ actually has no normal form and hence signifies nothing, as in the case of the liar paradox.

In order to eliminate such unwanted situations and achieve strong normalization property, we need a more elaborate type system. In fact, the rough type system permits term $L' = \lambda\mathtt{n}.L$ to have type $(B \to_1 B) \to_1 B$ in the type assignment $\xi_x$, whereas $L'$ is a fixed-point operator of level 1 in a sense that we have $L'M \cong_\beta M(L'M)$ for any term $M$. A key difference from calculus $\lambda\mathcal{M}$ providing strong normalization property is caused by the existence of cross-level terms that bring on level-increasing reduction, such as object-level $\beta$-reduction generating new meta-level $\beta$-redexes. A term is said to be **cross-level** if the term can be typed only in cross-level type assignments. A type assignment $\xi$ is said to be cross-level if there exists a name $v$ such that the type $\xi(v)$ of $v$ in the type assignment $\xi$ contains an arrow '$\to_\ell$' of level $\ell$ greater than $\mathrm{Lv}(v)$. For instance, the above $\xi_x$ is a cross-level type assignment, and the terms *block* and $\mathit{export}^{x_1 \ldots x_h}_{z_1 \ldots z_k}$ are cross-level terms as well as the term $L$ mentioned above. Cross-level type assignments and cross-level terms are seemingly meaningless. Hence, cross-level terms have been left out of consideration by type systems or by level-controlled reductions in previous meta lambda calculi. However, we consider that cross-level terms may be worth investigating, since cross-level terms seem to have connections with notions related to names and bindings in programming languages, such as stores, quotes, recursion, and localization of names, as demonstrated in this section. We leave further research about this topic as a future work.

# 5. Related Works

## 5.1 Meta Lambda Calculi

We discuss connections with previous meta lambda calculi that include inherently textual substitution via meta-level variables.

Calculus $\lambda\mathcal{M}$ proposed by Sato, Sakurai, Kameyama and Igarashi [18] is a meta lambda calculus with infinitely hierarchical levels. $\lambda\mathcal{M}$ adopts level-controlled reductions and a type system to achieve preferable properties in coexistence with textual substitution. The type system eliminates cross-level terms mentioned in Section 4.4. $\lambda\mathcal{M}$ is actually a subsystem of $\lambda^*$ consisting only of annotation-free terms. The level-controlled reduction in $\lambda\mathcal{M}$ is viewed as a restriction of $\beta$-reduction in $\lambda^*$ on a set of annotation-free terms.

Calculus LamCC in Gabbay and Lengrand [10] also includes infinitely hierarchical levels. LamCC adopts level-controlled reductions and explicit substitutions. Unlike other meta lambda calculi, LamCC does not have the notion of level of application. In other words, the level of each application occurring in a term is determined dynamically in the process of computation. One of the features of $\lambda^*$ different from LamCC is that substitutions in $\lambda^*$ have canonical representation. By this feature, terms signifying the same substitution, for example, $(\lambda\mathtt{x}.\lambda\mathtt{y}.\mathtt{M})\mathtt{Nz}$ and $(\lambda\mathtt{y}.\lambda\mathtt{x}.\mathtt{M})\mathtt{zN}$ are reduced to the same term $\mathtt{M}[{}^{\mathtt{x}}\!\!\downarrow\!(\mathtt{N}) \cdot {}^{\mathtt{y}}\!\!\downarrow\!(\mathtt{z})]$ by $\beta$-reduction and $\varepsilon$-reduction in $\lambda^*$. In LamCC, the above two terms are reduced to distinct two terms in normal form.

Gabbay's NEW calculus of contexts [9] and two-level lambda calculus [11] adopt level-controlled reductions and freshness contexts. A freshness context is regarded as an assumption about freshness conditions for meta-level variables. Reductions are controlled by freshness contexts. In a word, a term is reduced under some assumption about freshness conditions for meta-level variables.

The NEW calculus and LamCC mentioned above include NEW binders 'И' separately from ordinary lambda binders 'λ'. A NEW binder indicates that an object-level variable is fresh for meta-level variables. For instance, $\text{И}\mathtt{x}.\lambda\mathtt{x}.\mathtt{Mx} \to_\alpha \text{И}\mathtt{y}.\lambda\mathtt{y}.\mathtt{My}$ holds, since the object-level variables '$\mathtt{x}$' and '$\mathtt{y}$' in the above terms are considered to be fresh for meta-level variable $\mathtt{M}$. In calculus $\lambda^*$, such information is represented by pop-elements. The above two terms and the $\alpha$-renaming are represented in $\lambda^*$ as $\lambda\mathtt{x}.\mathtt{M}[\Uparrow_\mathtt{x}]\mathtt{x} \to_\alpha\to_\varepsilon \lambda\mathtt{y}.\mathtt{M}[\Uparrow_\mathtt{y}]\mathtt{y}$.

Bekki's meta-lambda calculus [2] is a study of categorical semantics for metavariables. The type system in the calculus eliminates cross-level terms mentioned in Section 4.4. The formalization shown in Bekki and Asai [3] and in Masuko and Bekki [13] adopts assumption about free variables for meta-level variables in order to perform $\alpha$-renaming in the presence of meta-level variables. The notion of blocks to variable binding discussed in Section 2.5 is pointed out in [13].

## 5.2 Other Works

Attempts to model textual substitution via metavariables in a calculus are originated from Hashimoto and Ohori's typed context calculus [12], which is designed to internalize the notion of lambda contexts. Their calculus adopts level-controlled reductions and a mechanism, called renamers, to manage binding structure consistently with the notion of holes to represent lambda contexts. Holes are regarded as meta-level variables, and lambda contexts are regarded as meta-level abstractions from viewpoint of meta lambda calculi. The technique of renamers is considered a kind of approaches by interfaces assigned to meta-level variables mentioned in Section 1.3. Sato, Sakurai and Kameyama's simply typed context calculus [16], calculus $\lambda m$ in Sato et al. [18], Nanevski, Pientka and Pfenning's calculi [14, 15] with modal types, and Boespflug and Pientka [4] with multi-level modal types are also designed by approaches of interfaces assigned to metavariables. These calculi are called lambda calculi with interfaces distinctively from meta lambda calculi in this paper. The goal of these calculi to provide type systems for meta-level variables seems to lead the design to use information about interfaces assigned to meta-level variables not only in type systems but also in rewriting systems. This feature of the design makes the difference between these calculi and meta lambda calculi as illustrated in Section 1.3. The technique of indexed variables is adopted in [16].

The syntax of calculus $\lambda^{\mathrm{m}}$ in Davies [7] is similar to the syntax of $\lambda^*$ in a sense that variables and applications are assigned with numbers. The numbers in calculus $\lambda^*$ signify levels of variables, which determine *strength* of substitution so that substitution of level $\ell$ is performed by regarding variables of level less than $\ell$ as mere texts. In contrast, the numbers in calculus $\lambda^{\mathrm{m}}$ signify stages of computation, which determine *time* of substitution. In $\lambda^{\mathrm{m}}$, all variables occurring in a term are bound statically as usual, unlike meta lambda calculi.

Methods to deal with substitutions as syntactic objects date back to Abadi, Cardelli, Curien and Lévy's explicit substitutions [1]. Dowek, Hardin and Kirchner [8] applies the method to the nameless lambda calculus with meta-level variables. The formalization of substitutions with push-elements and pop-elements in $\lambda^*$ is almost the same as their formalization, although substitutions in $\lambda^*$ are sorted by names and defined to occur only as suspended substitutions on meta-level variables. The slight difference from their formalization stems from the purpose to make calculus $\lambda^*$ become a supersystem of $\lambda\mathcal{M}$ [18] as well as the ordinary lambda calculus. In other words, this paper does not concern itself about modeling concrete way and cost of performing substitution, which is the original purpose of explicit substitutions in Abadi et al.

Calculus $\lambda$N proposed by Dami [6] is an extension of the lambda calculus to model dynamic binding. The syntax of $\lambda$N includes additional constructs called labels separately from ordinary variables. A main difference between $\lambda$N and $\lambda^*$ is their style of dynamic binding. Calculus $\lambda^*$ deals with dynamic binding by lambda binders via meta-level variables, whereas $\lambda$N deals with dynamic binding by labels, not by lambda binders.

## 6. Conclusion

We have proposed meta lambda calculus $\lambda^*$, in which any $\beta$-redex of any level can be reduced to perform substitution for variables. This feature makes it possible to advance computation even in the presence of meta-level variables, and hence provides us new possibilities for reduction strategies that have been restricted by level-controlled reductions in previous meta lambda calculi.

Also, we have shown a procedural language as an application of calculus $\lambda^*$. Through the implementation of the procedural language, we have observed the connections between dynamic binding via meta-level variables and the notions of stores and recursion in procedural languages. We hope that calculus $\lambda^*$ contributes toward understanding metavariables and the association with notions related to names and bindings in programming languages.


## Acknowledgments

The author wishes to thank his supervisor, Ryu Hasegawa, sincerely for the fruitful discussions. The author also thanks Brigitte Pientka and anonymous reviewers for helpful comments.


## References


[1] M. Abadi, L. Cardelli, P.-L. Curien and J.-J. Lévy. 1991. Explicit substitutions. *Journal of Functional Programming* 1, 4, 375–416.

[2] Daisuke Bekki. 2009. Monads and meta-lambda calculus. In *New Frontiers in Artificial Intelligence (JSAI 2008)*, LNAI 5447, 193–208.

[3] Daisuke Bekki and Kenichi Asai. 2010. Representing covert movements by delimited continuations. In *New Frontiers in Artificial Intelligence (JSAI-isAI 2009)*, LNAI 6284, 161–180.

[4] Mathieu Boespflug and Brigitte Pientka. 2011. Multi-level contextual type theory. In *Proceedings of the 6th International Workshop on Logical Frameworks and Meta-languages: Theory and Practice (LFMTP 2011)*, EPTCS 71, 29–43.

[5] N. G. de Bruijn. 1972. Lambda calculus notation with nameless dummies, a tool for automatic formula manipulation, with application to the Church-Rosser theorem. *Indagationes Mathematicae* 75, 5, 381–392.

[6] Laurent Dami. 1998. A lambda-calculus for dynamic binding. *Theoretical Computer Science* 192, 2, 201–231.

[7] Rowan Davies. 1996. A temporal-logic approach to binding-time analysis. In *Proceedings of the 11th Annual IEEE Symposium on Logic in Computer Science (LICS '96)*, 184–195.

[8] Gilles Dowek, Thérèse Hardin and Claude Kirchner. 2000. Higher order unification via explicit substitutions. *Information and Computation* 157, 183–235.

[9] Murdoch J. Gabbay. 2005. A NEW calculus of contexts. In *Proceedings of the 7th ACM SIGPLAN International Conference on Principles and Practice of Declarative Programming (PPDP '05)*, 94–105.

[10] Murdoch J. Gabbay and Stéphane Lengrand. 2009. The lambda-context calculus (extended version). *Information and Computation* 207, 12, 1369–1400.

[11] Murdoch J. Gabbay and Dominic P. Mulligan. 2009. Two-level lambda-calculus. *Electronic Notes in Theoretical Computer Science* 246, 107–129.

[12] Masatomo Hashimoto and Atsushi Ohori. 2001. A typed context calculus. *Theoretical Computer Science* 266, 249–272.

[13] Moe Masuko and Daisuke Bekki. 2011. Categorical semantics of meta-lambda calculus (in Japanese). In *Informal Proceedings of the 13th JSSST Workshop on Programming and Programming Languages*, 60–74.

[14] Aleksandar Nanevski, Brigitte Pientka and Frank Pfenning. 2003. A modal foundation for meta-variables. In *Proceedings of the 2003 ACM SIGPLAN Workshop on Mechanized Reasoning about Languages with Variable Binding (MERLIN '03)*, 1–6.

[15] Aleksandar Nanevski, Frank Pfenning and Brigitte Pientka. 2008. Contextual modal type theory. *ACM Transactions on Computational Logic* 9, 3, Article 23, 49 pages.

[16] Masahiko Sato, Takafumi Sakurai and Yukiyoshi Kameyama. 2002. A simply typed context calculus with first-class environments. *Journal of Functional and Logic Programming* 2002, 1–41.

[17] Masahiko Sato, Takafumi Sakurai, Yukiyoshi Kameyama and Atsushi Igarashi. 2003. Calculi of meta-variables. In *Computer Science Logic (CSL 2003)*, LNCS 2803, 484–497.

[18] Masahiko Sato, Takafumi Sakurai, Yukiyoshi Kameyama and Atsushi Igarashi. 2008. Calculi of meta-variables. *Frontiers of Computer Science in China* 2, 1, 12–21.

[19] Masako Takahashi. 1995. Parallel reductions in $\lambda$-calculus. *Information and Computation* 118, 1, 120–127.

[20] Glynn Winskel. 1993. *The Formal Semantics of Programming Languages*. The MIT Press.

# Algebraic Effects, Linearity, and Quantum Programming Languages

Sam Staton

Radboud University Nijmegen

## Abstract

We develop a new framework of algebraic theories with linear parameters, and use it to analyze the equational reasoning principles of quantum computing and quantum programming languages. We use the framework as follows:

- we present a new elementary algebraic theory of quantum computation, built from unitary gates and measurement;
- we provide a completeness theorem for the elementary algebraic theory by relating it with a model from operator algebra;
- we extract an equational theory for a quantum programming language from the algebraic theory;
- we compare quantum computation with other local notions of computation by investigating variations on the algebraic theory.

## 1. Introduction

Quantum programming languages test many of the challenges of modern programming language theory: linear use of resources, separation, locality. A good way to understand a programming language is to understand equality of programs. In this paper we develop a general algebraic framework for computational effects involving linear resources. We use it to give a complete axiomatization of equality of quantum programs.

***What is quantum computing?*** From a programming language perspective, quantum computing involves qubits and entanglement:

- *There is a type* $\mathsf{qubit}$ *of qubits.* Viewed as an abstract type, we can imagine a qubit as having an internal state that is a position on the surface of a sphere (called the Bloch sphere), but the accessor functions do not actually permit us to read its position on the surface. The three accessor functions are, informally, as follows. (*Notation:* we underline them.)
  - $\underline{\mathsf{new}}$: allocate a new qubit, with initial position at the top of the $Z$ axis (called $|0\rangle$).
  - $\underline{\mathsf{apply}}_{\mathtt{U}}$: apply a rotation to the qubit on the sphere around a given axis by a given angle, as specified by a unitary matrix $\mathtt{U}$. For example, we can kind-of negate a qubit by rotating it by $180°$ around the $X$ axis, taking the top of the sphere to the bottom; this unitary rotation is notated $\mathtt{X}$, and so the function that applies the rotation is notated $\underline{\mathsf{apply}}_{\mathtt{X}}$.
  - $\underline{\mathsf{measure}}$: make a random boolean choice, with the probability of returning either 0 or 1 depending on the $Z$ co-ordinate of the qubit (this is called the standard basis). For example, if the qubit was on the $X$ axis, the result of measuring will be 0 or 1 with equal probability, like tossing a fair coin; if it was at the very top of the sphere, the result of measuring will be 0 with certainty; if it was at the very bottom of the sphere, the result of measuring will be 1 with certainty. Measuring a qubit destroys it: all that remains is the result of the measurement.
- *For types $A$ and $B$, there is a type $A \otimes B$ of entangled pairs.* For instance the type $\mathsf{qubit} \otimes \mathsf{qubit}$ is a type of pairs of possibly entangled qubits. Entanglement is achieved by controlled unitary rotations. For example, the controlled-$\mathtt{X}$ unitary, $\mathtt{cX}$, affects two qubits, and if $t$ is an expression of type $\mathsf{qubit} \otimes \mathsf{qubit}$ then also $\underline{\mathsf{apply}}_{\mathtt{cX}}(t)$ is an expression of type $\mathsf{qubit} \otimes \mathsf{qubit}$. The computation $\underline{\mathsf{apply}}_{\mathtt{cX}}(a, b)$ is like 'if $a$ is 1 then return $(a, \neg b)$ else return $(a, b)$', so that the second value returned depends on the first value input. The entanglement occurs because this controlled rotation happens without actually measuring $a$, and indeed it is reversible. Yet if $a$ is subsequently measured then the controlled rotation appears to have behaved in this way.

The main contribution of this paper is the fact that the relationship between unitary rotations and measurement can be completely described by three simple axioms (Theorem 9), and allocation by two simple axioms (Theorem 11). This simple axiomatization (combined with the unitary groups and commutativity laws) completely characterizes earlier models that are built from operator algebra and functional analysis.

In the remainder of this introduction, we give an informal overview of these results. To express the equations, we need to first discuss the syntax.

***Quantum programming languages and quantum programs.*** A quantum programming language captures the ideas of quantum computation in a linear type theory. For example, we can write a program of type $\mathsf{qubit} \to \mathsf{qubit}$:

$$\mathsf{fn}\ a : \mathsf{qubit} \Rightarrow \mathsf{if}\ \underline{\mathsf{measure}}\, a = 0\ \mathsf{then}\ \underline{\mathsf{new}}()\ \mathsf{else}\ \underline{\mathsf{apply}}_{\mathtt{X}}(\underline{\mathsf{new}}()) \tag{1}$$

which measures a qubit and returns a new qubit initialized either to $|0\rangle$ or $|1\rangle$, depending on the outcome. In other words, the input qubit is collapsed on to the $Z$ axis.

For another example of a program, we recall the Hadamard rotation, $\mathtt{Had}$, which maps the $Z$ axis onto the $X$ axis by rotating $180°$ around the axis that lies between the $X$ and $Z$ axes. We can use this to define a coin toss operation: first initialize a qubit to the



*POPL '15*, January 15–17 2015, Mumbai, India.
Copyright is held by the owner/author(s). Publication rights licensed to ACM.
ACM 978-1-4503-3300-9/15/01... $15.00.
http://dx.doi.org/10.1145/2676726.2676999

top of the sphere, and then rotate by Hadamard, and then measure: the program

$$\underline{\mathsf{measure}}(\underline{\mathsf{apply}}_{\mathsf{Had}}(\underline{\mathsf{new}}())) \;:\; \mathsf{bit}$$

returns 0 or 1 with equal probability. We can use this to randomly rotate a qubit around the $Z$ axis: writing Z for the rotation of 180° around the $Z$ axis,

$$\mathsf{fn}\ a : \mathsf{qubit} \Rightarrow \mathsf{if}\ \underline{\mathsf{measure}}(\underline{\mathsf{apply}}_{\mathsf{Had}}(\underline{\mathsf{new}}())) = 0$$
$$\mathsf{then}\ a\ \mathsf{else}\ \underline{\mathsf{apply}}_{\mathsf{Z}}(a)\ :\ \mathsf{qubit} \to \mathsf{qubit} \quad (2)$$

It turns out that this program (2) is actually equal to the first program (1): projecting onto the $Z$ axis is the same as randomly flipping around the $Z$ axis. This fact, perhaps counter-intuitive at first, is a consequence of our simple intuitive axiomatization of quantum computation.

***Notions of computation and algebraic theories.*** In programming language theory it is often useful to analyze different features of a programming language separately. In the quantum programs above there are standard features such as sequencing, if-then-else, functions, as well as the aspects specific to quantum computing.

One way of distinguishing the specific 'notions of computation' from the other standard features of programming languages is by using algebraic effects [36]. A key contribution of this paper (§2) is a new algebraic framework for analyzing the effects of a linear-use resource.

A useful step towards the algebraic analysis is to step away from booleans, if-then-else and sums by writing $\mathsf{measure}(a, t, u)$ for the program (if $\underline{\mathsf{measure}}(a) = 0$ then $t$ else $u$). By working with expressions such as $\mathsf{measure}(a, t, u)$, which are in a kind-of continuation-passing normal form, we can forget about structural aspects and typing issues. Indeed to analyze the algebraic theory of quantum computation, we need only distinguish between two kinds of thing: qubits and computations.

Notice our typographic convention: we underline programming-language-style commands ($\underline{\mathsf{measure}}(a)$) but not the corresponding algebraic operations ($\mathsf{measure}(a, t, u)$). We make this correspondence precise in Section 5.

***Algebraic structure of quantum computation.*** We are now in a position to postulate the algebraic structure of quantum computation. It supports four constructions:

- if $t$ is a computation involving a qubit $a$ then there is a computation $\mathsf{new}(a.t)$ that allocates that qubit, initialized to $|0\rangle$, and continues as $t$;
- if $t$ is a computation involving qubits $b_1 \dots b_n$ and U is a unitary matrix over $n$ qubits then there is a quantum computation $\mathsf{apply}_{\mathsf{U}}(a_1 \dots a_n,\ b_1 \dots b_n.t)$ that first performs the unitary U to the qubits $a_1 \dots a_n$ and then binds the resulting qubits $b_1 \dots b_n$ in the continuation $t$;
- if $t$ and $u$ are computations and $a$ is a qubit then there is a computation $\mathsf{measure}(a, t, u)$ that measures $a$ and continues as either $t$ or $u$ depending on the result of the measurement. This construction is linear in the quantum parameters: $t$ and $u$ cannot contain $a$.
- if $x$ is a variable standing for a continuation that expects $n$ qubits (notation, $x : n$) and $a_1 \dots a_n$ are qubits, then $x(a_1 \dots a_n)$ is a computation over $n$ qubits.

We can construct our two programs, (1) and (2), as algebraic expressions as follows:

$$\mathsf{measure}(a, \mathsf{new}(b.x(b)), \mathsf{new}(b.\mathsf{apply}_{\mathsf{X}}(b, b'.x(b'))))$$
$$\mathsf{new}(b.\mathsf{apply}_{\mathsf{Had}}(b, b'.\mathsf{measure}(b', x(a), \mathsf{apply}_{\mathsf{Z}}(a, a'.x(a')))))$$

Here $x$ is a variable standing for the continuation of the computation (as yet unspecified) which is parameterized by the result qubit.

***Diagrammatic notation.*** Informal diagrams are often helpful. Our notion of quantum computation is very similar to the notion described by quantum circuits, for instance in the book by Nielsen and Chuang [31]. The two programs above ((1), (2)) could be written as the following circuits:

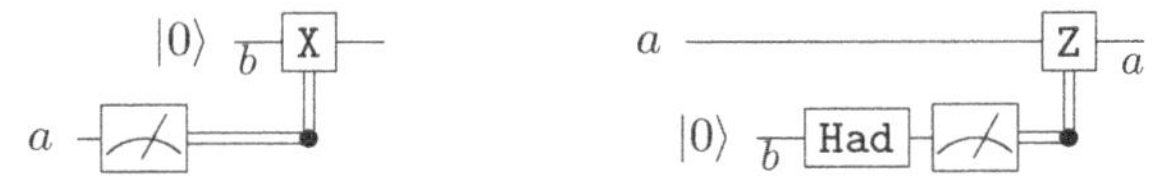


The circuits should be read from left to right. The single wires carry qubits, the double wires carry classical bits. The boxes are the unitary rotations, and the meter device is measurement, which takes a quantum wire to a classical one. The vertical lines indicate control: the outcome of the measurement determines whether the gate is applied.

*Aside:* Just as we wanted to isolate notions of quantum computation from other aspects of programming languages, so we ought to isolate the quantum parts of quantum circuits (qubits, unitaries, measurement) from the classical wires. This leads us to a 3-d notation like

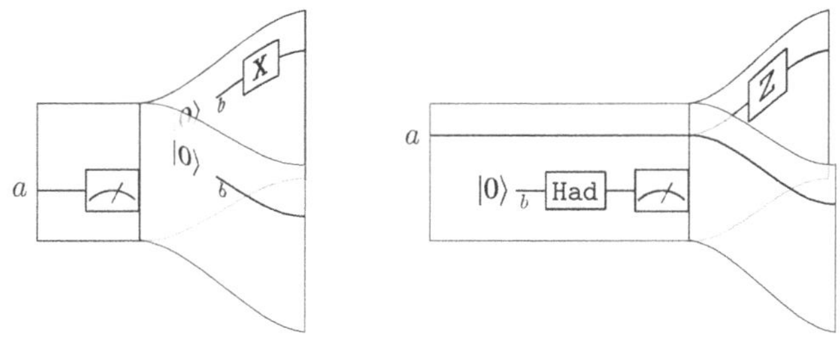


in which measurement causes a branch in the circuit instead of a classical wire. These kinds of diagram are very similar to Melliès' notation for storage of classical bits [28], but they are also common in the many-worlds interpretation of quantum mechanics. In this paper we will only use diagrams in an informal way, and so we will write 2-d circuit diagrams for simplicity. We return to the relationship with classical bits in Section 6.2.

***Axioms of quantum computation.*** We are now in a position to summarize the algebraic laws of quantum computation. A full account is in Section 3. In brief, the laws of measurement are:

- after measurement, quantum negation is like classical negation:

$$\mathsf{apply}_{\mathsf{X}}(a, a'.\mathsf{measure}(a', x, y)) = \mathsf{measure}(a, y, x)$$

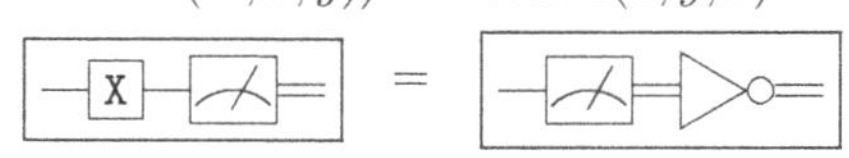


- after measurement, quantum control is like classical control:

$$\mathsf{apply}_{\mathsf{cU}}(a, b, a'b'.\mathsf{measure}(a', x(b'), y(b')))$$
$$= \mathsf{measure}(a, x(b), \mathsf{apply}_{\mathsf{U}}(b, b'.y(b')))$$

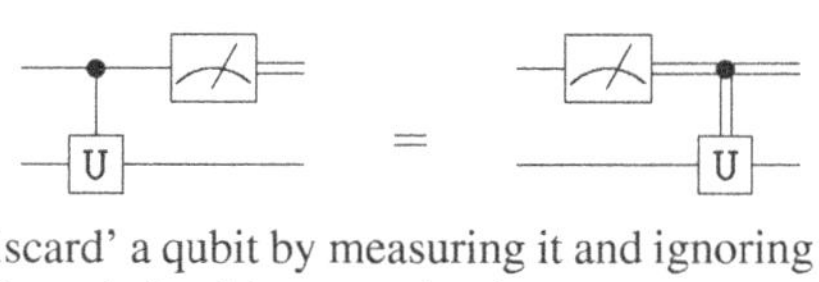


- we can 'discard' a qubit by measuring it and ignoring the result; gates on discarded qubits are redundant:

$$\mathsf{apply}_{\mathsf{U}}(a, a'.\mathsf{measure}(a', x, x)) = \mathsf{measure}(a, x, x)$$

We combine these three axioms with the equations of the unitary groups and the following two sensible axioms for qubit allocation:

- new qubits are initialized to $|0\rangle$, according to measurement

$$\mathsf{new}(a.\mathsf{measure}(a,x,y)) = x$$

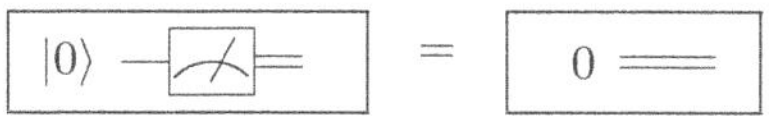


- new qubits are initialized to $|0\rangle$, according to controlled gates:

$$\mathsf{new}(a.\mathsf{apply}_{\mathsf{cU}}(a,b,a'b'.x(a',b'))) = \mathsf{apply}_{\mathsf{U}}(b,b'.\mathsf{new}(a.x(a,b')))$$

***Completeness theorem.*** Other authors have proposed equational theories for quantum computation and quantum programming languages. We discuss this in Section 3.5. What makes this paper special is that it is a *complete* equational theory of quantum computation.

Of course, it is very useful to have some handy equations — they can be used to optimize programs and partially evaluate them. But by giving a fully complete equational theory we can understand quantum computation from the axioms of the theory without having to turn to denotational models built from operator algebra. This is the subject of Section 4.

We have the following result.

**Theorem 11.** *The following data are equivalent:*

- *An algebraic expression, modulo the equality derivable from our axioms;*
- *A completely positive unit-preserving map between finite dimensional C*-algebras.*

(It is already well-known that a completely positive map can be understood in terms of allocating qubits, applying a unitary, and then measuring, and Selinger [42] phrased this in terms of programming languages; the novelty here is our complete axiomatization of equality.)

Thus our simple equational theory provides a justification for the model of quantum computation based on operator algebra. Although linear algebra plays a major role in many models of quantum computation, the non-convex addition in linear algebra often has no direct physical justification. Viewed in this way, our work suggests an alternative technique for reconstructing quantum theory from reasonable postulates, which is a subject of much recent work (e.g. [12, 20]). In our equational theory, vector spaces do *not* have an explicit role. The point is that rather than jumping from physical intuitions directly to linear algebra, one can first set up a precise equational model of the physical intuitions, and then use that to justify the models that use linear algebra.

## 2. Algebraic theories with linear parameters

In this section we introduce a formalism for describing computational effects over linearly-used resources. Our leading example is quantum computations over qubits. To motivate this, we consider some simple examples. If $x$ and $y$ are quantum computations and $a$ is a qubit, then $\mathsf{measure}(a,x,y)$ is a quantum computation that first measures $a$, and, depending on the result, continues as $x$ or as $y$. We can allocate new qubits, writing $\mathsf{new}(a.\mathsf{measure}(a,x,y))$ for the computation that first allocates $a$, then measures it, continuing as either $x$ or $y$. We can also apply unitaries to qubits, writing $\mathsf{apply}_{\mathsf{cX}}(a,b,a'b'.\mathsf{measure}(a',\mathsf{measure}(b',v,x),\mathsf{measure}(b',y,z)))$ for the computation that first applies a controlled-not gate to qubits $a$ and $b$, yielding qubits $a'$ and $b'$, and then measures $a'$ and then $b'$.

We make some informal remarks about this syntax, before introducing a formal system.

1. There are two kinds of variable: in the examples above, $a, b$ stand for qubits whereas $v, x, y, z$ stand for computations.
2. In the example with new, the $a$ is binding, and we could just as well write $\mathsf{new}(b.\mathsf{measure}(b,x,y))$.
3. Computations can involve qubit parameters $a, b$, and the variables $x, y$ stand for computations, so we will also allow variables with qubit parameters. When we write $x(a,b)$, the computation variable $x$ is being passed parameters $a$ and $b$. For instance we can write a computation expression $\mathsf{new}(a.z(a))$ which allocates a new qubit $a$ and passes it as a parameter to the continuation $z$; we can substitute $\mathsf{measure}(a,x,y)$ for $z(a)$, resulting in the term $\mathsf{new}(a.\mathsf{measure}(a,x,y))$. The notation means that we do not consider implicit variable capture.
4. Care must be taken when using qubits. Measuring a qubit destroys it, and so we adopt the convention that, in an expression $\mathsf{measure}(a,t,u)$, the qubit parameter $a$ should not appear free in $t$ or $u$. This kind of linearity also plays a crucial role in the syntax for unitaries: in $\mathsf{apply}_{\mathsf{cX}}(a,b,\dots)$ it is crucial that $a$ and $b$ are different qubits and not aliases for the same qubit. For simplicity we adopt the convention that apply consumes its qubit parameters, creating new ones that are passed to the continuation.

### 2.1 General syntactic framework

Our general syntactic framework is an algebraic framework which is not at all specific to quantum computation. Indeed, it is a new substructural version of the 'parameterized algebraic theories' already used to analyze various kinds of computation including local store, $\pi$-calculus-style communication [47] and logic programming [45], following some other similar syntactic frameworks [11, 18, 30, 35, 40]. There are two kinds of variable:

1. Computation variables (ranged over by $x, y$ etc.). Computations can depend on parameters, and we write $x : p$ if $x$ has $p$ parameters. The number $p$ is sometimes called a valence.
2. Parameter variables (ranged over by $a, b$). In the quantum situation, these stand for qubits.

As in classical algebra, a theory comprises a signature (Def. 1) and axioms (Def. 2).

**Definition 1.** *An* arity, $(p \mid m_1 \dots m_k)$, *is a natural number* ($p \geq 0$) *followed by a list of natural numbers* ($m_1 \dots m_k$).

*A* signature with linear parameters *comprises a set of operations, and for each operation* O *an arity* $(p \mid m_1 \dots m_k)$. *Informally, this specifies that* O *takes* $p$ *parameter arguments and* $k$ *computation arguments, and the* $i$*th computation argument has* $m_i$ *parameters bound in it. We write* $\mathrm{O} : (p \mid m_1 \dots m_k)$.

We define a three-place judgement $\Gamma \mid \Delta \vdash t$ of well-formed terms in context in a given signature. Here, $\Gamma$ is a list of computation variables with their valences, and $\Delta$ is a list of parameter variables. The judgement is the least one closed under the following rules.

$$\frac{-}{\Gamma, x : p, \Gamma' \mid a_1 \dots a_p \vdash x(a_1 \dots a_p)}$$

$$\frac{\Gamma \mid a_1 \dots a_p \vdash t}{\Gamma \mid a_{\sigma(1)} \dots a_{\sigma(p)} \vdash t} \quad (\sigma \text{ is a permutation of } p)$$

$$\frac{\Gamma \mid \Delta, b_1 \dots b_{m_1} \vdash t_1 \quad \dots \quad \Gamma \mid \Delta, b_1 \dots b_{m_k} \vdash t_k \qquad \mathrm{O} : (p \mid m_1 \dots m_k)}{\Gamma \mid \Delta, a_1 \dots a_p \vdash \mathrm{O}(a_1, \dots, a_p,\ b_1 \dots b_{m_1}.t_1,\ \dots,\ b_1 \dots b_{m_k}.t_k)}$$

In the term formation rule for operations, the $b$'s are binding, and we work up to renaming those bound variables, just as in predicate logic ($\forall x.P(x) = \forall y.P(y)$) or $\lambda$-calculus.

We make some remarks about the rules.

- An operation O consumes its parameters, the $a$'s, and they cannot appear free in the continuations, the $t$'s (unless of course one happens to use the same symbol for the $a$'s and the $b$'s).
- Weakening and contraction are admissible in the $\Gamma$ context but not in the $\Delta$ context.
- The syntax admits the following simultaneous substitution law:

$$\frac{x_1 : m_1 \ldots x_k : m_k \mid \Delta \vdash t \qquad \Gamma \mid \Xi, a_1 \ldots a_{m_1} \vdash u_1 \quad \ldots \quad \Gamma \mid \Xi, a_1 \ldots a_{m_k} \vdash u_k}{\Gamma \mid \Delta, \Xi \vdash t[{}^{\Xi, a_1 \ldots a_{m_1} \vdash u_1}/_{x_1} \ldots {}^{\Xi, a_1 \ldots a_{m_k} \vdash u_k}/_{x_k}]}$$

**Definition 2.** *Fix an algebraic signature with linear parameters. An* axiom *is a pair of terms in the same context; it is written* $\Gamma \mid \Delta \vdash t = u$.

*A presentation of an* algebraic theory with linear parameters *comprises an algebraic signature with linear parameters and a set of axioms over the signature.*

In an algebraic theory we form an equivalence relation on terms in each context $(\Gamma|\Delta)$ by closing substitution instances of the axioms under reflexivity, symmetry, transitivity and congruence.

We now proceed to develop the basic model theory of algebraic theories with linear parameters. The reader could now jump to read about the algebraic theory of quantum computation (§3).

### 2.2 Models of algebraic theories with linear parameters

Classical algebraic theories are typically first understood as set-theoretic structures, but it is often profitable to look at models whose carrier is not merely a set and whose structure maps are not merely functions, that is, to look at models in different categories. In Section 4, we will prove our full completeness result by looking at models whose carriers are **C***-algebras.

To account for the parameters, we are urged to look at categories where for each object $X$ and for each natural number $n$ there is a given object $n \bullet X$. We can then think of a morphism $X \to n \bullet Y$ informally as a morphism $X \to Y$ with $n$ parameters. We will interpret operations $\mathrm{O} : (p \mid m_1 \ldots m_k)$ as morphisms $(m_1 \bullet X) \times \cdots \times (m_k \bullet X) \to (p \bullet X)$.

Let us make this more formal. Let $\mathbf{Bij}$ be the category whose objects are natural numbers and whose morphisms are bijections between the natural numbers (considered as sets). We will consider it as a symmetric monoidal category, where the monoidal operation is addition of numbers. Recall (e.g. [23]) that an *action* of $\mathbf{Bij}$ comprises a category $\mathcal{V}$ together with a functor $\bullet : \mathbf{Bij} \times \mathcal{V} \to \mathcal{V}$ and natural isomorphisms, $0 \bullet X \cong X$ and $(m+n) \bullet X \cong m \bullet (n \bullet X)$, satisfying coherence conditions.

Let $\mathcal{V}$ be an action of $\mathbf{Bij}$ such that the category $\mathcal{V}$ has products and each functor $m \bullet - : \mathcal{V} \to \mathcal{V}$ preserves products.

**Definition 3.** *A* structure *for a signature in $\mathcal{V}$ is an object $X$ together with, for each operation $\mathrm{O} : (p \mid m_1 \ldots m_k)$ a morphism $(m_1 \bullet X) \times \cdots \times (m_k \bullet X) \to p \bullet X$.*

Given a structure for a signature, one can interpret each term in context $x_1 : m_1 \ldots x_k : m_k \mid a_1 \ldots a_p \vdash t$ as a morphism in the category, $[\![t]\!] : (m_1 \bullet X) \times \cdots \times (m_k \bullet X) \to p \bullet X$. This interpretation is defined by induction on the structure of terms in a standard way. Informally, the interpretation assigns a value in $X$ for each valuation of its variables. Note that exchange of parameters amounts to the functoriality of the action, and the admissibility of substitution amounts to the composition of the morphisms that interpret the terms.

**Definition 4.** *A* model *of an algebraic theory with linear parameters is a structure for its signature such that for each axiom $x_1 : m_1 \ldots x_k : m_k \mid a_1 \ldots a_p \vdash t = u$ the interpretation morphisms $[\![t]\!], [\![u]\!] : (m_1 \bullet X) \times \cdots \times (m_k \bullet X) \to p \bullet X$ are equal.*

**Proposition 5** (Soundness)**.** *If an equality is derivable in a theory then it is is true in all models.*

This is proved by induction on the derivations of equality.

**Proposition 6.** *Consider terms $x_1{:}m_1 \ldots x_k{:}m_k \mid a_1 ... a_p \vdash t, u$ of an algebraic theory that are equal in all models. Their equality is derivable from the axioms of the theory.*

*Proof.* Fix an algebraic theory with linear parameters. Consider the category of functors $[\mathbf{Bij} \to \mathbf{Set}]$ and natural transformations between them. This has finite products: $(F \times G)(p) = F(p) \times G(p)$. There is an action of $\mathbf{Bij}$ on $[\mathbf{Bij} \to \mathbf{Set}]$ given by $(n \bullet F)(p) = F(p+n)$. For each computation context $\Gamma = (x_1 : m_1 \ldots x_k : m_k)$ we define a functor $T_\Gamma : \mathbf{Bij} \to \mathbf{Set}$ with $T_\Gamma(q)$ the set of terms in context $(\Gamma|b_1 \ldots b_q)$ modulo the derivable equations. This can be given the structure of a model, in the functor category $[\mathbf{Bij} \to \mathbf{Set}]$: notice that $(p \bullet T_\Gamma)(\Delta)$ is the set of terms in context $(\Gamma \mid \Delta, a_1 \ldots a_p)$, and we define the structure maps using the term formation for the operations. In this model, for any term $\Gamma \mid a_1 \ldots a_p \vdash t$ we have in particular a function $[\![t]\!]_0 : T_\Gamma(m_1) \times \cdots \times T_\Gamma(m_k) \to T_\Gamma(p)$, and by definition, $t = [\![t]\!]_0(x_1(b_1 \ldots b_{m_1}), \ldots, x_k(b_1 \ldots b_{m_k}))$ in $T_\Gamma(p)$. So if two terms $\Gamma \mid a_1 \ldots a_p \vdash t, u$ are such that $[\![t]\!] = [\![u]\!]$ in this model, then $t = u$ must be derivable. □

Functors $(\mathbf{Bij} \to \mathbf{Set})$ are called 'species of structure', and have been used to analyze aspects of quantum computation including variations on the Fock space construction (e.g. [7]).

In this paper we are particularly interested in models that are fully complete in the following sense.

**Definition 7.** *A model $X$ in a category is* fully complete *if for all contexts $(x_1 : m_1 \ldots x_k : m_k|a_1 \ldots a_p)$,*

- *for every morphism $f : (m_1 \bullet X) \times \ldots (m_k \bullet X) \to (p \bullet X)$ there is a term $x_1 : m_1 \ldots x_k : m_k \mid a_1 \ldots a_p \vdash t$ such that $[\![t]\!] = f$;*
- *for all terms $x_1 : m_1 \ldots x_k : m_k \mid a_1 \ldots a_p \vdash t, u$, if $[\![t]\!] = [\![u]\!]$ then $t = u$ is derivable.*

# 3. An algebraic theory of quantum computation

### 3.1 Rudiments of unitaries.

The basic idea of quantum computation is that the $2^n \times 2^n$ unitary matrices describe purely quantum circuits over $n$ qubits. We recall some key parts of the theory of unitaries.

Recall that a square matrix U of complex numbers is *unitary* if its conjugate transpose U* is its inverse (U.U* = I = U*.U). Unitaries of the same dimension form a group under matrix multiplication: multiplication of two unitaries is again unitary. If U and V are $2^p \times 2^p$ unitaries, then we can use quantum circuit diagrams to illustrate their multiplication by horizontal juxtaposition.

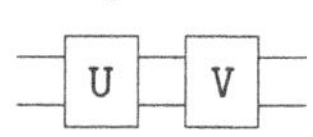


For the simplest example, a 1-dimensional unitary is just a complex number with modulus 1. This is sometimes called a global phase shift. Global phase shifts can ultimately be neglected in quantum computation, indeed that is a consequence of our Axiom (C), but they still play a role in the unitary groups.

Every rotation by some angle about an axis of the sphere can be understood as a $2 \times 2$ unitary. In fact, every $2 \times 2$ unitary arises by combining a global phase shift with such a rotation. We are particularly interested in the rotation by $\pi$ about the $X$ axis, $\mathtt{X} = \left(\begin{smallmatrix} 0 & 1 \\ 1 & 0 \end{smallmatrix}\right)$, rotation by $\theta$ about the $Z$ axis, $\mathtt{Z}^\theta = \left(\begin{smallmatrix} 1 & 0 \\ 0 & e^{i\theta} \end{smallmatrix}\right)$, and the Hadamard rotation, $\mathtt{Had} = \frac{1}{\sqrt{2}}\left(\begin{smallmatrix} 1 & 1 \\ 1 & -1 \end{smallmatrix}\right)$.

To explain the different ways of combining unitaries, we note that the collection of all finite unitaries of different dimensions forms a groupoid, that is, a category where all morphisms are isomorphisms. The objects are natural numbers, and a morphism $\mathtt{U} : n \to n$ is an $n \times n$ unitary. Recall that a monoidal structure on a category is a way of combining objects and morphisms. There are two symmetric monoidal structures on this groupoid of unitaries, coming from the multiplication and addition of dimensions.

One monoidal structure is multiplication: if U and V are unitaries, $m \times m$ and $n \times n$ respectively, the Kronecker product $\mathtt{U} \otimes \mathtt{V}$ is a unitary $(m \times n) \times (m \times n)$ matrix: $(\mathtt{U} \otimes \mathtt{V})_{i+mk,j+ml} = \mathtt{U}_{i,j}\mathtt{U}_{k+1,l+1}$. When $m = 2^p$ and $n = 2^q$ are powers of two, so $m \times n = 2^{p+q}$, we can illustrate this structure on quantum circuit diagrams as vertical juxtaposition.

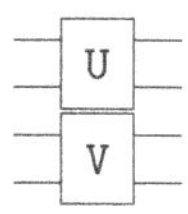


The other monoidal structure is addition of dimensions: if U and V are unitaries, $m \times m$ and $n \times n$ respectively, the block diagonal $(m+n) \times (m+n)$ matrix $\left(\begin{smallmatrix} \mathtt{U} & 0 \\ 0 & \mathtt{V} \end{smallmatrix}\right)$ is also unitary. In general we write $D(\mathtt{U}_1, \ldots, \mathtt{U}_k)$ for a block diagonal.

The block diagonal unitaries are controlled unitaries. The smallest example is $\mathtt{Z}^\theta$, which can be thought of as a controlled global phase shift. More generally if U and V are $2^p \times 2^p$ unitaries, then $D(\mathtt{U}, \mathtt{V})$ is a $2^{p+1} \times 2^{p+1}$ unitary, illustrated as follows:

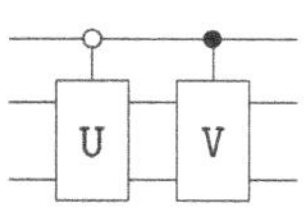

(3)

In particular the block diagonal $\mathtt{cX} \stackrel{\text{def}}{=} D(\mathtt{I}_2, \mathtt{X})$ is sometimes called 'controlled not'.

We have already seen the symmetry structure for $+$ at dimension 1: it is the X gate. The symmetry for the multiplication monoidal structure is $\mathtt{swap} \stackrel{\text{def}}{=} D(1, \mathtt{X}, 1)$.

In fact, every $2^p \times 2^p$ unitary can be built from the two monoidal structures and the single qubit unitaries (e.g. [31, §4.5.2]).

***Remark:*** Our aim in this paper is to study the interaction between the unitaries and qubit allocation and measurement. There is a body of work on axiomatizing unitaries (e.g. [43]), which is complementary to our aims. Moreover the groupoid of unitaries has topological structure. We are ignoring this continuity in this paper, but it is important from a foundational point of view (e.g. [20, Axiom P4']), and it is central to the study of approximation of quantum gates (e.g. [31, Ch. 4.5]) and the notions of estimation inherent to quantum algorithms (e.g. [31, Ch. 5]).

### 3.2 The signature of quantum computation

The signature for quantum computation comprises the following operations.

$$\mathsf{new} : (0 \mid 1) \qquad \mathsf{measure} : (1 \mid 0, 0)$$
$$\mathsf{apply}_\mathtt{U} : (n \mid n) \quad \text{for every } 2^n \times 2^n \text{ unitary } \mathtt{U}$$

Explicitly, these operations induce the following term formation rules:

$$\frac{\Gamma \mid \Delta, a \vdash t}{\Gamma \mid \Delta \vdash \mathsf{new}(a.t)} \qquad \frac{\Gamma \mid \Delta \vdash t \quad \Gamma \mid \Delta \vdash u}{\Gamma \mid \Delta, a \vdash \mathsf{measure}(a, t, u)}$$

$$\frac{\Gamma \mid \Delta, b_1 \ldots b_n \vdash t}{\Gamma \mid \Delta, a_1, \ldots a_n \vdash \mathsf{apply}_\mathtt{U}(\vec{a}, \vec{b}.t)}$$

together with the variables and exchange law (§2.1). (There are no closed terms in this theory, in common with continuation passing style.)

***Examples***

1. We can make a new qubit initialized to $|1\rangle$ and continue as $x$.

   $$x : 1 \mid - \vdash \mathsf{new}(a.\mathsf{apply}_\mathtt{X}(a, b.x(b)))$$

   This is justified by the term formation rules:

   $$\cfrac{\cfrac{\overline{x : 1 \mid b \vdash x(b)}}{x : 1 \mid a \vdash \mathsf{apply}_\mathtt{X}(a, b.x(b))}}{x : 1 \mid - \vdash \mathsf{new}(a.\mathsf{apply}_\mathtt{X}(a, b.x(b)))}$$

   Here, the $a$ and $b$ are binding: this expression is equal to $\mathsf{new}(c.\mathsf{apply}_\mathtt{X}(c, d.x(d)))$ and also equal to the expression $\mathsf{new}(a.\mathsf{apply}_\mathtt{X}(a, a.x(a)))$. The notation $x(b)$ indicates that the continuation $x$ takes a parameter $b$.

   A convenient shorthand:

   $$\mathsf{new}_0(a.t) \stackrel{\text{def}}{=} \mathsf{new}(a.t), \quad \mathsf{new}_1(a.t) \stackrel{\text{def}}{=} \mathsf{new}(a.\mathsf{apply}_\mathtt{X}(a, a.t)).$$

2. We can use quantum operations to make a random choice between continuations $x$ and $y$.

   $$x : 0, y : 0 \mid - \vdash \mathsf{new}(a.\mathsf{apply}_\mathtt{Had}(a, b.\mathsf{measure}(b, x, y)))$$

3. A Bell state comprises two entangled qubits. We can create a Bell state and pass it to $x$:

   $$x : 2 \mid - \vdash \mathsf{new}(a.\mathsf{new}(b.\mathsf{apply}_\mathtt{Had}(a, a.$$
   $$\mathsf{apply}_{D(\mathtt{I}_2, \mathtt{X})}(a, b, ab.x(a, b)))))$$

   This would be written as the following circuit diagram:

   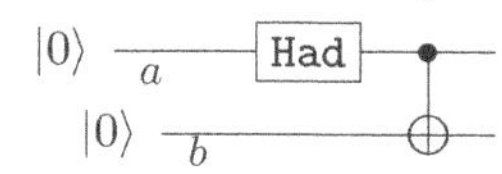
   

4. The linearity constraints mean that we cannot implicitly discard nor duplicate qubits. However we can explicitly discard a qubit $a$, by measuring it and ignoring the result.

   $$x : 0 \mid a \vdash \mathsf{measure}(a, x, x)$$

5. In our formalism, measurement consumes the qubit parameter. Another convention is that measurement retains the qubit but it is now collapsed into one of the basis states. This can be simulated by immediately creating a new qubit with the result of the measurement:

   $$x : 1 \mid a \vdash \mathsf{measure}(a, \mathsf{new}_0(a.x(a)), \mathsf{new}_1(a.x(a)))$$

6. In fact, we will later show that (5) is the same as randomly rotating the phase of $a$ by $\pi$, using the rotation $\mathtt{Z} = \left(\begin{smallmatrix} 1 & 0 \\ 0 & -1 \end{smallmatrix}\right)$.

$$x : 1 \mid a \vdash \mathsf{new}_0(b.\mathsf{apply}_\mathtt{Had}(b, b.\mathsf{measure}(b, x(a),$$
$$\mathsf{apply}_\mathtt{Z}(a, a.x(a)))))$$

### 3.3 Axioms of quantum computation

The terms built from new, apply, measure and variables are subject to the following laws. The axioms are of four main kinds. There are two classes of interesting axioms, relating unitaries and measurement (A–C), and relating qubit allocation with unitaries and measurement (D–E). The remaining axioms are more administrative, relating the properties of unitaries with composition in the syntax (F–I), and commutativity of the theory (J–L).

***Interaction between unitary gates and measurement.*** Our first set of axioms describe the interaction between the unitaries and the standard basis measurement operations. Axiom (A) states that the quantum not gate (X) simply negates a measurement.

$$\mathsf{apply}_{\mathtt{X}}(a, a.\mathsf{measure}(a, x, y)) = \mathsf{measure}(a, y, x) \qquad \text{(A)}$$

Informally,

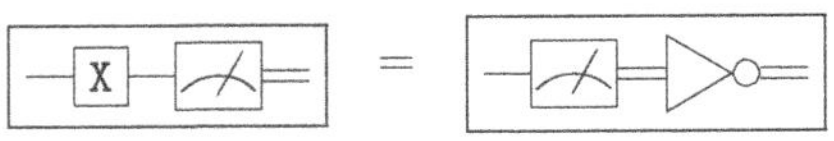


Axiom scheme (B) states that after measurement, quantum control appears the same as classical control. Recall that $D(\mathtt{U}, \mathtt{V})$ is the block diagonal matrix, $\left(\begin{smallmatrix}\mathtt{U} & 0\\ 0 & \mathtt{V}\end{smallmatrix}\right)$.

$$\mathsf{measure}(a, \mathsf{apply}_{\mathtt{U}}(\vec{b}, \vec{b}.x(\vec{b})), \mathsf{apply}_{\mathtt{V}}(\vec{b}, \vec{b}.y(\vec{b}))$$
$$= \mathsf{apply}_{D(\mathtt{U},\mathtt{V})}(a, \vec{b},\ (a, \vec{b}).\mathsf{measure}(a, x(\vec{b}), y(\vec{b}))) \qquad \text{(B)}$$

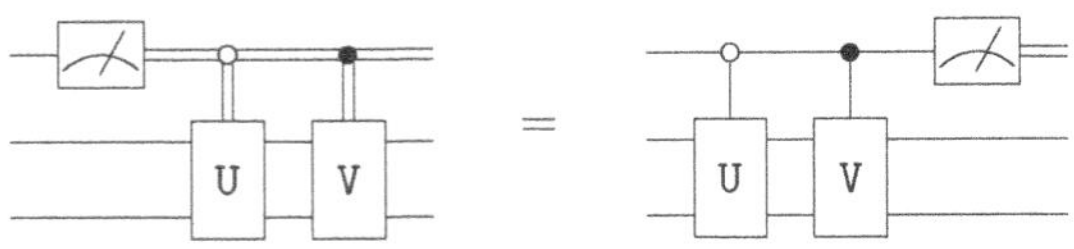


*(B)*

For Axiom (C) we need some shorthand. For a list of $p$ distinct parameter variables $a_1 \ldots a_p$ and a term $t$, define a term $\mathsf{discard}_p(a_1 \ldots a_p, t)$, informally 'measure $a_1 \ldots a_p$ and continue as $t$ regardless'; formally:

$$\mathsf{discard}_0(-, t) = t;$$
$$\mathsf{discard}_{n+1}(a, \vec{b}, t) = \mathsf{measure}(a, \mathsf{discard}_n(\vec{b}, t), \mathsf{discard}_n(\vec{b}, t)).$$

We can now phrase Axiom scheme (C), which asserts that if all the qubits involved in a unitary are to be discarded, the unitary is redundant.

$$\mathsf{apply}_{\mathtt{U}}(\vec{a},\ \vec{a}.\mathsf{discard}_n(\vec{a}, x)) = \mathsf{discard}_n(\vec{a}, x)$$
$$\text{where U is a } 2^n \times 2^n \text{ unitary, } n \geq 0 \qquad \text{(C)}$$

In particular, Axiom (C) for $n = 0$ says when global phase can be ignored.

***Axioms for qubit allocation:*** Our second class of axioms describe the interaction between new and measurement and controlled unitaries. They simply impose the idea that new qubits are initialized to $|0\rangle$. Firstly measuring a new qubit always yields 0:

$$\mathsf{new}(a.\mathsf{measure}(a, x, y)) = x \qquad \text{(D)}$$

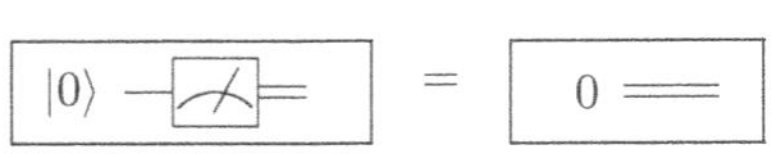


(This axiom is similar to Selinger's axiom for quantum flow charts [42, §6.6].) Secondly a unitary controlled by a new qubit will always be controlled by 0.

$$\mathsf{new}(a.\mathsf{apply}_{D(\mathtt{U},\mathtt{V})}(a, \vec{b},\ a, \vec{b}.x(a, \vec{b})))$$
$$= \mathsf{apply}_{\mathtt{U}}(\vec{b}, \vec{b}.\mathsf{new}(a.x(a, \vec{b}))) \qquad \text{(E)}$$

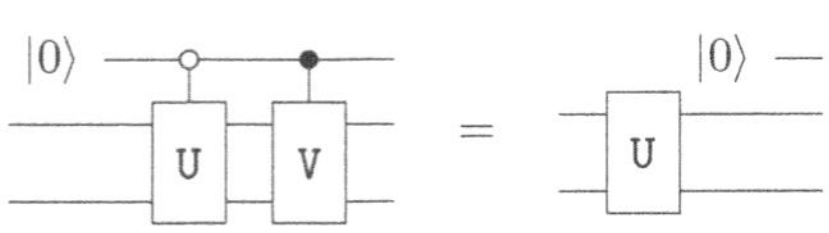


This concludes the interesting axioms. The remaining axioms are more administrative.

***Respecting the symmetric monoidal groupoid of unitaries.*** Our third class of axioms imposes the relationships between the structure of the unitaries and the compositional structure of terms built from $\mathsf{apply}_{\mathtt{U}}$. We can understand axioms (A) and (B) as relating the $+$ monoidal structure of the groupoid of unitaries with the branching structure after measurement. The remaining axiom schemes (F)-(I) relate the other structure of the groupoid (composition and the $\times$ monoidal structure) with the syntax of the algebraic theory.

$$\mathsf{apply}_{\mathtt{swap}}(a, b, (a, b).x(a, b)) = x(b, a) \qquad \text{(F)}$$
$$\mathsf{apply}_{\mathtt{I}}(\vec{a}, \vec{a}.x(\vec{a})) = x(\vec{a}) \qquad \text{(G)}$$
$$\mathsf{apply}_{\mathtt{UV}}(\vec{a}, \vec{a}.x(\vec{a})) = \mathsf{apply}_{\mathtt{U}}(\vec{a}, \vec{a}.\mathsf{apply}_{\mathtt{V}}(\vec{a}, \vec{a}.x(\vec{a}))) \qquad \text{(H)}$$
$$\mathsf{apply}_{\mathtt{U}\otimes\mathtt{V}}(\vec{a}, \vec{b}, (\vec{a}, \vec{b}).x(\vec{a}, \vec{b})) = \mathsf{apply}_{\mathtt{U}}(\vec{a}, \vec{a}.\mathsf{apply}_{\mathtt{V}}(\vec{b}, \vec{b}.x(\vec{a}, \vec{b}))) \qquad \text{(I)}$$

Here are informal illustrations of these equations.

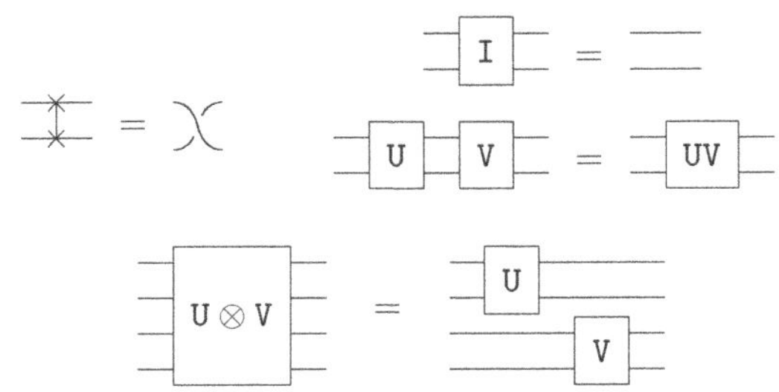


***Commutativity.*** Our final class of axioms ensure that our equational theory is commutative in the sense of [26]. In this parameterized setting, this means that all operations commute as far as is allowed by the variable binding. For instance, the following commutativity equation scheme is already derivable from (I):

$$\mathsf{apply}_{\mathtt{U}}(\vec{b}, \vec{b}.\mathsf{apply}_{\mathtt{V}}(\vec{c}, \vec{c}.x(\vec{b}, \vec{c})) = \mathsf{apply}_{\mathtt{V}}(\vec{c}, \vec{c}.\mathsf{apply}_{\mathtt{U}}(\vec{b}, \vec{b}.x(\vec{b}, \vec{c}))$$

This is in spite of the fact that multiplication of unitaries is not commutative, e.g. $\mathtt{X.Had} \neq \mathtt{Had.X}$. For instance, while

$$\mathsf{apply}_{\mathtt{X}}(a, a.\mathsf{apply}_{\mathtt{Had}}(b, b.x(a, b)))$$
$$= \mathsf{apply}_{\mathtt{Had}}(b, b.\mathsf{apply}_{\mathtt{X}}(a, a.x(a, b)))$$

this does not imply that $\mathsf{apply}_{\mathtt{X}}(a, b.\mathsf{apply}_{\mathtt{Had}}(b, c.x(c)))$ is equal to $\mathsf{apply}_{\mathtt{Had}}(a, b.\mathsf{apply}_{\mathtt{X}}(b, c.x(c)))$: it is not a substitution instance, because one must respect the variable binding. (This is an example of a general technique for converting a non-commutative algebraic structure to a commutative one by passing linear-use parameters; see also [30].)

Several other commutativity equations also follow from our other axioms, but we need to explicitly include the following commutativity axioms:

$$\mathsf{measure}(a, \mathsf{measure}(b, u, v), \mathsf{measure}(b, x, y))$$
$$= \mathsf{measure}(b, \mathsf{measure}(a, u, x), \mathsf{measure}(a, v, y)) \qquad \text{(J)}$$

$$\mathsf{new}(a.\mathsf{new}(b.x(a, b))) = \mathsf{new}(b.\mathsf{new}(a.x(a, b))) \qquad \text{(K)}$$

$$\mathsf{new}(a.\mathsf{measure}(b, x(a), y(a)))$$
$$= \mathsf{measure}(b, \mathsf{new}(a.x(a)), \mathsf{new}(a.y(a))) \qquad \text{(L)}$$

Commutativity laws are essentially built in to the quantum circuits notation. For instance Axiom (L) could be informally written

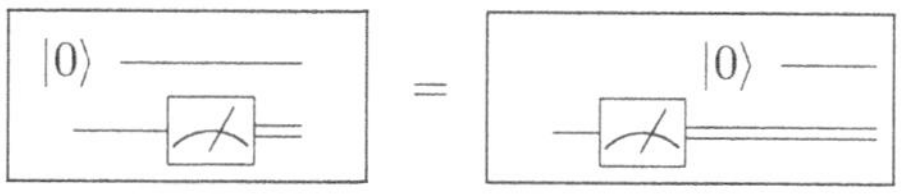


This concludes our axiomatization of quantum computation.

### 3.4 Examples of derivations

***Rotation about $Z$ doesn't affect standard basis measurement.*** Let $\mathtt{Z}^\theta = \left(\begin{smallmatrix}1 & 0\\ 0 & e^{i\theta}\end{smallmatrix}\right) = D(1, e^{i\theta})$. Then

$$
\begin{aligned}
&\mathsf{apply}_{\mathtt{Z}^\theta}(a, a.\mathsf{measure}(a, x, y))\\
&\quad= \mathsf{apply}_{D(1,e^{i\theta})}(a, a.\mathsf{measure}(a, x, y))\\
&\quad= \mathsf{measure}(a, \mathsf{apply}_1(x), \mathsf{apply}_{e^{i\theta}}(y)) && \textit{by (B)}\\
&\quad= \mathsf{measure}(a, x, y) && \textit{by (C)}.
\end{aligned}
$$

Similarly rotation of a new qubit about $Z$ doesn't affect it:

$$
\begin{aligned}
&\mathsf{new}(a.\mathsf{apply}_{\mathtt{Z}^\theta}(a, a.x(a)))\\
&\quad= \mathsf{new}(a.\mathsf{apply}_1(x(a))) && \textit{by (E)}\\
&\quad= \mathsf{new}(a.x(a)) && \textit{by (C)}. && (4)
\end{aligned}
$$

***Notation.*** To save space we introduce shorthand:

$$\nu a.\, t \stackrel{\text{def}}{=} \mathsf{new}(a.t) \qquad t\ ?_a\ u \stackrel{\text{def}}{=} \mathsf{measure}(a, t, u)$$

$$\mathtt{U}_{\vec{a}}(t) \stackrel{\text{def}}{=} \mathsf{apply}_{\mathtt{U}}(\vec{a}, \vec{a}.t) \quad \mathsf{disc}_{\vec{a}}(t) \stackrel{\text{def}}{=} \mathsf{d}_{\vec{a}}(t) \stackrel{\text{def}}{=} \mathsf{discard}(\vec{a}, t)$$

(Note that we use the same variable names for the input and output of the unitary gates.) For example, equation (4) would be written $\nu a.\, \mathtt{Z}^\theta_a(x(a)) = \nu a.\, x(a)$, and the key axioms would be written

$$
\begin{aligned}
\mathtt{X}_a(x\ ?_a\ y) &= y\ ?_a\ x && \textit{(A)}\\
(\mathtt{U}_{\vec{b}}(x)(\vec{b}))\ ?_a\ (\mathtt{V}_{\vec{b}}(y)(\vec{b})) &= D(\mathtt{U},\mathtt{V})_{a,\vec{b}}(x(\vec{b})\ ?_a\ y(\vec{b})) && \textit{(B)}\\
\mathtt{U}_{\vec{a}}(\mathsf{discard}(\vec{a}, x)) &= \mathsf{discard}(\vec{a}, x) && \textit{(C)}\\
\nu a.\, (x\ ?_a\ y) &= x && \textit{(D)}\\
\nu a.\, D(\mathtt{U},\mathtt{V})_{a,\vec{b}}(x(a,\vec{b})) &= \mathtt{U}_{\vec{b}}(\nu a.\, x(a,\vec{b})) && \textit{(E)}
\end{aligned}
$$

***Random choice is symmetric.*** Recall that $\nu a.\, \mathtt{Had}_a(x\ ?_a\ y)$ provides a random choice between $x$ and $y$. We deduce that it is unbiased:

$$
\begin{aligned}
\nu a.\, \mathtt{Had}_a(x\ ?_a\ y) &= \nu a.\, \mathtt{Z}_a(\mathtt{Had}_a(x\ ?_a\ y)) && \textit{using } (4)\\
&= \nu a.\, \mathtt{Had}_a(\mathtt{X}_a(x\ ?_a\ y)) && \textit{since } \mathtt{Z.Had} = \mathtt{Had.X}\\
&= \nu a.\, \mathtt{Had}_a(y\ ?_a\ x). && \textit{using (A)} && (5)
\end{aligned}
$$

NB. Random choice is also idempotent and medial, so it is a mean value algebra (e.g. [2]).

***Random phase flip = measurement.*** Consider the following equation:

$$\nu a.\, \mathtt{Had}_a(x(b)\ ?_a\ \mathtt{Z}_b(x(b))) = (\nu a.\, x(a))\ ?_b\ (\nu a.\, \mathtt{X}_a(x(a)))$$

In full:

$$
\begin{aligned}
&\mathsf{new}_0(a.\mathsf{apply}_{\mathtt{Had}}(a, a.\mathsf{measure}(a, x(b), \mathsf{apply}_{\mathtt{Z}}(b, b.x(b)))))\\
&\quad= \mathsf{measure}(b, \mathsf{new}_0(a.x(a)), \mathsf{new}_1(a.x(a)))
\end{aligned}
$$

It says that randomly flipping the phase of a qubit is the same as measuring it. Nielsen and Chuang discuss the equation to demonstrate the freedom in the operator-sum representation [31, eqns 8.66–8.70]. We can prove it directly in our equational theory.

First we show that measuring a qubit is the same as making an entangled copy using controlled not, $\mathtt{cX} = D(\mathtt{I}_2, \mathtt{X})$, and then discarding the original:

$$
\begin{aligned}
&(\nu a.\, x(a))\ ?_b\ (\nu a.\, \mathtt{X}_a(x(a)))\\
&= \nu a.\, (x(a)\ ?_b\ \mathtt{X}_a(x(a))) && \textit{using (L)}\\
&= \nu a.\, \mathtt{cX}_{b,a}(x(a)\ ?_b\ x(a)) && \textit{using (B)}\\
&= \nu a.\, \mathtt{cX}_{b,a}(\mathsf{disc}_b(x(a)))\\
&= \nu a.\, \mathtt{cX}_{a,b}(\mathtt{cX}_{b,a}(\mathsf{disc}_a(x(b)))) && (\dagger)\\
&= \nu a.\, \mathtt{cX}_{b,a}(\mathsf{disc}_a(x(b))) && \textit{using (E)}
\end{aligned}
$$

†: since $\mathtt{cX.swap.cX} = \mathtt{swap.cX.swap}$ as matrices.

We conclude by showing that the last line is the same as randomly flipping the phase.

$$
\begin{aligned}
&\nu a.\, \mathtt{cX}_{b,a}(\mathsf{disc}_a(x(b)))\\
&= \nu a.\, \mathtt{Had}_a(\mathtt{cZ}_{a,b}(\mathtt{Had}_a(\mathsf{disc}_a(x(b))))) && (\ddagger)\\
&= \nu a.\, \mathtt{Had}_a(\mathtt{cZ}_{a,b}(\mathsf{disc}_a(x(b)))) && \textit{using (C)}\\
&= \nu a.\, \mathtt{Had}_a(x(b)\ ?_a\ \mathtt{Z}_b(x(b))) && \textit{using (B)}.
\end{aligned}
$$

‡: since $\mathtt{swap.cX.swap} = (\mathtt{Had} \otimes I).\mathtt{cZ}.(\mathtt{Had} \otimes I)$, and where $\mathtt{cZ} = D(I_2, \mathtt{Z})$.

***Reasoning without qutrits.*** The following example illustrates a key point in the proof of our completeness theorem (Thm. 11). When reasoning in terms of C*-algebras, one has access to various structures that are not definable in our syntax as it stands, such as base 3 quantum digits, 'qutrits'. We could extend our syntax to have parameter variables of different sorts, for different bases. In fact, we do not need these structures to deduce the relevant equations between computations over qubits. Let

$$\mathtt{U} = D(1, \mathtt{Had}, 1) = \begin{pmatrix} 1 & 0 & 0 & 0\\ 0 & 1/\sqrt{2} & 1/\sqrt{2} & 0\\ 0 & 1/\sqrt{2} & -1/\sqrt{2} & 0\\ 0 & 0 & 0 & 1\end{pmatrix} =$$ 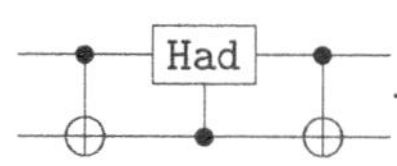 .


Consider the following equation:

$$
\begin{aligned}
&\nu b.\, \mathtt{U}_{a,b}(x(a)\ ?_b\ (y\ ?_a\ u))\\
&\quad= \nu b.\, \mathtt{U}_{a,b}(x(a)\ ?_b\ (y\ ?_a\ v))
\end{aligned} \qquad (6)
$$

By considering this equation for all $x$, $y$, $u$, $v$, we have an equational way of expressing the idea that, after the unitary, the pair $(a, b)$ of qubits will never be in the state $|1, 1\rangle$. In effect we have a qutrit, although qutrits are not expressible in this formalism. We derive equation 6 by introducing an intermediate qubit $c$, as follows. Let $\mathtt{T} = D(\mathtt{I}_6, \mathtt{X})$, the $8 \times 8$ Toffoli gate, and note that if $\mathtt{V}$ is a block 3-1 matrix then $\mathtt{T}.(\mathtt{V} \otimes \mathtt{I}_2) = (\mathtt{V} \otimes \mathtt{I}_2).\mathtt{T}$.

$$
\begin{aligned}
&\nu b.\, \mathtt{U}_{a,b}(x(a)\ ?_b\ (y\ ?_a\ u))\\
&= \nu b.\, \mathtt{U}_{ab}((\nu c.\, \mathsf{d}_c(x(a)))\ ?_b\ ((\nu c.\, \mathsf{d}_c(y))\ ?_a\ (\nu c.\, u?_c v))) && \textit{by (D)}\\
&= \nu c.\, \nu b.\, \mathtt{U}_{a,b}(\mathsf{d}_c(x(a))\ ?_b\ (\mathsf{d}_c(y)\ ?_a\ (u\ ?_c\ v))) && \textit{(commutativity)}\\
&= \nu c.\, \nu b.\, (\mathtt{U} \otimes \mathtt{I})_{abc}(\mathsf{d}_c(x(a))\ ?_b\ (\mathsf{d}_c(y)\ ?_a\ (u\ ?_c\ v))) && \textit{(G),(I)}\\
&= \nu c.\, \nu b.\, \mathtt{T}.(\mathtt{U} \otimes \mathtt{I})_{abc}(\mathsf{d}_c(x(a))\ ?_b\ (\mathsf{d}_c(y)\ ?_a\ (u?_c v))) && \textit{(E)}\\
&= \nu c.\, \nu b.\, (\mathtt{U} \otimes \mathtt{I}).\mathtt{T}_{abc}(\mathsf{d}_c(x(a))\ ?_b\ (\mathsf{d}_c(y)\ ?_a\ (u?_c v)))\\
&= \nu c.\, \nu b.\, (\mathtt{U} \otimes \mathtt{I})_{abc}(\mathsf{d}_c(x(a))\ ?_b\ (\mathsf{d}_c(y)\ ?_a\ \mathtt{X}_c(u?_c v))) && \textit{(B)}\\
&= \nu c.\, \nu b.\, (\mathtt{U} \otimes \mathtt{I})_{a,b,c}(\mathsf{d}_c(x(a))\ ?_b\ (\mathsf{d}_c(y)\ ?_a\ (v\ ?_c\ u))) && \textit{(A)}\\
&= \nu c.\, \nu b.\, \mathtt{U}_{a,b}(\mathsf{d}_c(x(a))\ ?_b\ (\mathsf{d}_c(y)\ ?_a\ (v\ ?_c\ u))) && \textit{(G),(I)}\\
&= \nu b.\, \mathtt{U}_{a,b}(x(a)\ ?_b\ (y\ ?_a\ v)) && \textit{(D)}.
\end{aligned}
$$

### 3.5 Other axiomatizations of quantum computation

Equational reasoning about programs is widely regarded as important, and several authors have already proposed useful equations for reasoning about quantum programs (e.g. [42, §4.9], [55, §6], and [53]), and other aspects of quantum computation [51, 54].

There are two particular equational formalisms that we would like to mention especially: the measurement calculus [15] and the ZX calculus [14] (which comes out of the categorical quantum mechanics programme, see also [1, 52]). Unlike our theory, neither of these axiomatizations of equality are complete for quantum computation. But they are both in a different spirit: they have strong results regarding term rewriting. It seems unlikely that there is a straightforward rewriting system to fully decide equality of quantum computations, firstly because of problems with rewriting expressions over the unitary groups, and secondly because our derivation of (6) was not at all automatic: it required some ingenuity.

## 4. Full completeness

In the previous section we provided a new algebraic description of quantum computation by giving axioms that express the relationship between the unitary gates, measurement and allocation. We now show that this algebraic theory completely characterizes quantum computation.

We show this by reference to a well-established model of quantum mechanics, over 60 years old, based on operator algebra and C*-algebras. We show that terms in our theory correspond bijectively with completely positive maps. Thus, via our axiomatization, one can fully understand quantum computation without first knowing all about operator algebra. Conversely, linear algebra gives an array of techniques for reasoning about the quantum computation that we have axiomatized: one can decide equality of computations by comparing matrix representations of the linear maps.

### 4.1 Rudiments of C*-algebras

The idea of matrix mechanics is that the observables of a quantum system should be elements of a C*-algebra. Recall that a C*-algebra is a vector space over the field of complex numbers that also has multiplication, a unit and an involution, satisfying associativity laws for multiplication, involution laws (e.g. $x^{**} = x$, $(xy)^* = y^*x^*$, $(\alpha x)^* = \bar{\alpha}(x^*)$) and such that the spectral radius provides a norm making it a Banach space. A *-homomorphism between C*-algebras is a linear map that preserves the multiplication, involution and unit. We write **Cstar** for the category of C*-algebras and *-homomorphisms.

A key source of examples of C*-algebras are the algebras $M_k$ of $k \times k$ complex matrices, with matrix addition and multiplication, and where involution is conjugate transpose. In particular the set $M_1 = \mathbb{C}$ of complex numbers has a C*-algebra structure, and the $2 \times 2$ matrices, $M_2$, form the C*-algebra containing the observables of qubits.

The 'direct sum' $X \oplus Y$ of C*-algebras is given by the cartesian product of the underlying sets. It has the universal property of the categorical product. The C*-algebra $\mathbb{C} \oplus \mathbb{C}$ represents classical bits.

If $X$ is a C*-algebra then the $k \times k$ matrices valued in $X$ form a C*-algebra, $M_k(X)$. For instance $M_k(\mathbb{C}) = M_k$, and $M_k(M_l) \cong M_{k \times l}$. Informally, we can think of the C*-algebra $M_k(X)$ as representing $k$ entangled copies of $X$.

Any linear map $f : X \to Y$ extends in the obvious way to a linear map $M_k(f) : M_k(X) \to M_k(Y)$, and $M_k(f)$ is a *-homomorphism if $f$ is. We can thus use this matrix construction to understand **Cstar** as a category suitable for modelling algebraic theories with linear parameters. Consider the action of **Bij** on **Cstar** given by $m \bullet X = M_{2^m}(X)$. The direct sum distributes over the action: $M_k(X \oplus Y) \cong M_k(X) \oplus M_k(Y)$.

In Section 2.2 we defined a notion of model for an algebraic theory with linear parameters. We now investigate models of the theory of quantum computation (§3) whose carrier is the complex numbers, considered as a C*-algebra. Note that $m \bullet \mathbb{C} = M_{2^m}$, the C*-algebra of $2^m \times 2^m$ complex matrices, representing $m$ entangled qubits. Thus a term $a_1 \dots a_p \mid x_1 : m_1 \dots x_k : m_k \vdash t$ is interpreted as a linear map $[\![t]\!] : M_{m_1} \times \cdots \times M_{m_k} \to M_p$. This can be read, informally, as in predicate transformer semantics: 'if $[\![t]\!](o_1 \dots o_k)$ is observed of $a_1 \dots a_p$ then $o_1 \dots o_k$ will be observed of $x_1 \dots x_k$'. Our interpretation of quantum programs as maps between C*-algebras follows other recent work in this direction (e.g. [13, 22, 41]).

### 4.2 Full completeness for measurement

We begin with the subtheory built from measurement and unitaries. We will add qubit allocation in Section 4.3. The operations measure and and $\mathsf{apply}_\mathtt{U}$ are interpreted using the following *-homomorphisms, $\mathsf{measure} : M_1 \oplus M_1 \to M_2$ and $\mathsf{apply}_\mathtt{U} : M_p \to M_p$ (for each $p \times p$ unitary matrix $\mathtt{U}$).

$$\mathsf{measure}(\alpha, \beta) = \begin{pmatrix} \alpha & 0 \\ 0 & \beta \end{pmatrix} \qquad \qquad \mathsf{apply}_\mathtt{U}(A) = \mathtt{U}^* A \mathtt{U}.$$

**Proposition 8.** *In the category of C*-algebras and *-homomorphisms, the complex numbers $\mathbb{C}$ form a model of the subtheory of quantum computation involving* measure *and* $\mathsf{apply}_U$ *(but not* new*), and all the relevant axioms ((A)–(C), (F)–(J)).*

This is shown by direct calculation.

**Theorem 9.** *The complex numbers form a fully complete model:*

1. *For any *-homomorphism $f : M_{2^{m_1}} \oplus \cdots \oplus M_{2^{m_k}} \to M_{2^p}$ there is a term in the algebraic theory not involving* new*, $x_1 : m_1 \dots x_k : m_k \mid a_1 \dots a_p \vdash t$, such that $f = [\![t]\!]$.*
2. *If $\Gamma \mid \Delta \vdash t, u$ and $t$ and $u$ do not contain* new*, and $[\![t]\!] = [\![u]\!]$ then $\Gamma \mid \Delta \vdash t = u$ is derivable.*

We give a rough outline of our proof here, some more detail is in the Appendix. The theorem is proved by noting that a term not involving new can always be rearranged to a term $\mathsf{apply}_\mathtt{U}(\vec{a}, \vec{a}.t)$ where $t$ is built from measure and variables. We can understand a term built only from measure as a Bratteli diagram, which is a combinatorial way of understanding the *-homomorphisms.

### 4.3 Full completeness for all quantum computations

***Completely positive unital maps.*** To interpret allocation, we move beyond *-homomorphisms. Recall that an element $x$ of a C*-algebra is called *positive* if $\exists y. x = y^* y$. A linear map $f : X \to Y$ is *completely positive* if for all $k$ the map $M_k(f) : M_k(X) \to M_k(Y)$ preserves positive elements. (If either $X$ or $Y$ has commutative multiplication then it is sufficient to check the case $k = 1$.) We will focus on the completely positive maps that preserve units. These form a category $\mathbf{Cstar}_{\mathrm{CPU}}$ and the products and **Bij**-action extend from **Cstar** (*-homomorphisms) to $\mathbf{Cstar}_{\mathrm{CPU}}$.

***Interpretation.*** The operation new is interpreted using the following map, $\mathsf{new} : M_2 \to M_1$.

$$\mathsf{new}\begin{pmatrix} \alpha_{11} & \alpha_{12} \\ \alpha_{21} & \alpha_{22} \end{pmatrix} = \alpha_{11}.$$

This is not a *-homomorphism, but it is completely positive and unital.

**Proposition 10.** *In the category of C*-algebras and completely positive unital maps, the complex numbers $\mathbb{C}$ form a model of the theory of quantum computation.*

**Theorem 11.** *The complex numbers form a fully complete model:*

1. *For any linear map $f : M_{2^{m_1}} \oplus \cdots \oplus M_{2^{m_k}} \to M_{2^p}$ that is completely positive and unital, there is a term in the algebraic theory, $x_1 : m_1 \dots x_k : m_k \mid a_1 \dots a_p \vdash t$, such that $f = [\![t]\!]$.*
2. *If $\Gamma \mid \Delta \vdash t, u$ and $[\![t]\!] = [\![u]\!]$ then $\Gamma \mid \Delta \vdash t = u$ is derivable.*

(NB. Part (1) of the theorem is essentially Thm. 6.14 of [42].)

A proof is in the Appendix. In brief, we use Stinespring's theorem (e.g. [34]) to factor a completely positive unital map into a *-homomorphism followed by a restriction. This corresponds to the way that every term can be written with all the new's at the front, then the apply's, and finally the measure's. To obtain full completeness we use the minimal dilation that Stinespring's theorem yields. However, there is a complication: in this model we can only work with C*-algebras of the form $\bigoplus_{i=1}^{k} M_{2^{m_i}}$, and the minimal dilation need not be of this form. For instance, consider example (6): its minimal dilation is a *-homomorphism $M_2 \oplus M_1 \oplus M_1 \to M_3$. We resolve this by generalizing our derivation of (6) from the axioms.

## 5. A quantum programming language

The syntax of our equational theory describes quantum computation but it is not immediately amenable to practical programming because it focuses on continuing computations rather than intermediate results.

There is a standard way of moving between an equational theory like ours and a syntax more oriented towards programming. This applies to many different notions of computation [37]. In the setting of quantum computation, we can illustrate it by suggesting that a programmer might find it helpful to have a typed function $\underline{\mathsf{measure}} : \mathsf{qubit} \to \mathsf{bit}$ which returns the result of a standard basis measurement. Our measurement operation can then be derived: $\mathsf{measure}(a, x, y) = \mathsf{if}\ \underline{\mathsf{measure}}(a) = 0\ \mathsf{then}\ x\ \mathsf{else}\ y$. Conversely, if we have a language with a $\mathsf{bit}$ type that is a model of our equational theory, we can derive $\underline{\mathsf{measure}}(a) = \mathsf{measure}(a, 0, 1)$.

This relationship between 'algebraic operations' (like measure) and 'generic effects' (underlined, like $\underline{\mathsf{measure}}$) is a crucial one in the theory of computational effects [37]. It allows us to pass from our algebraic syntax to a language rather like Selinger's QPL [42]. A categorical way to understand this relationship is in terms of the duality between Lawvere theories, which are an abstract description of algebraic theories, and Freyd categories, which are an abstract description of first order programming languages [49].

***Program equations.*** To be more precise, we briefly demonstrate the programming language that corresponds automatically to our algebraic theory. The types are built from the grammar:

$$A, B \ ::= \ \mathsf{qubit} \mid I \mid A \otimes B \mid 0 \mid A + B.$$

We write bool for $I + I$. A context in this language is just an assignment of types to variables. The typed terms are built from the standard rules for a linear type theory (e.g. [8]), e.g.

$$\frac{-}{x : A \vdash x : A} \qquad \frac{\Gamma \vdash t : A \otimes B \quad \Delta, x : A, y : B \vdash u : C}{\Gamma, \Delta \vdash \mathsf{let}\ (x, y) = t\ \mathsf{in}\ u : C}$$

To this standard linear type theory we add the following generic effects:

$$\frac{-}{\vdash \underline{\mathsf{new}}() : \mathsf{qubit}} \qquad \frac{\Gamma \vdash t : \mathsf{qubit}^{\otimes n}}{\Gamma \vdash \underline{\mathsf{apply}}_{\mathsf{U}}(t) : \mathsf{qubit}^{\otimes n}}$$

$$\frac{\Gamma \vdash t : \mathsf{qubit}}{\Gamma \vdash \underline{\mathsf{measure}}(t) : \mathsf{bool}}$$

The resulting language is essentially Selinger's QPL [42] (see also [3, 19, 33, 53, 55]).

Our axioms (§3.3) between algebraic expressions have counterparts as program equations, e.g. our five key axioms can be written:

$$\underline{\mathsf{measure}}(\underline{\mathsf{apply}}_{\mathsf{X}}(a)) = \neg(\underline{\mathsf{measure}}(a)) \qquad (A)$$

$$\mathsf{let}\ (a', x') = \underline{\mathsf{apply}}_{D(\mathsf{U},\mathsf{V})}(a, x)\ \mathsf{in}\ (\underline{\mathsf{measure}}(a'), x') \qquad (B)$$

$$= \mathsf{if}\ \underline{\mathsf{measure}}(a){=}0\ \mathsf{then}\ (0, \underline{\mathsf{apply}}_{\mathsf{U}}(x))\ \mathsf{else}\ (1, \underline{\mathsf{apply}}_{\mathsf{V}}(x))$$

$$\underline{\mathsf{discard}}(\underline{\mathsf{apply}}_{\mathsf{U}}(x)) = \underline{\mathsf{discard}}(x) \qquad (C)$$

$$\underline{\mathsf{measure}}(\underline{\mathsf{new}}()) = 0 \qquad (D)$$

$$\underline{\mathsf{apply}}_{D(\mathsf{U},\mathsf{V})}(\underline{\mathsf{new}}(), x) = (\underline{\mathsf{new}}(), \underline{\mathsf{apply}}_{\mathsf{U}}(x)) \qquad (E)$$

The commutativity equations amount to the commutativity of let (e.g. [50]). We combine our axioms with the standard equational theory of a linearly typed language (e.g. [8]). In this way we build a language in which every context-type pair is a model of the theory in Section 3. For instance, if $\Gamma, a : \mathsf{qubit} \vdash t : A$ then let

$$\mathsf{new}_{\Gamma,A}(a.t) \ \stackrel{\text{def}}{=}\ t[\underline{\mathsf{new}}()/a];$$

if $\Gamma \vdash t : A$ and $\Gamma \vdash u : A$ then let

$$\mathsf{measure}_{\Gamma,A}(a, t, u) \ \stackrel{\text{def}}{=}\ \mathsf{if}\ \underline{\mathsf{measure}}(a){=}0\ \mathsf{then}\ t\ \mathsf{else}\ u.$$

***Higher order computation and monads.*** By understanding quantum computation as an algebraic effect, we are able to begin applying other techniques developed for algebraic effects in general, such as compiler optimizations and static analyses [24] and normalization by evaluation [4]. Another general method is building models of higher order computation with effects [38] by using monads.

Indeed, the equational theory of quantum computation is not a theory in the sense of classical universal algebra, but rather a theory enriched in the functor category $[\mathbf{Bij}, \mathbf{Set}]$, which is why we used actions of $\mathbf{Bij}$ to discuss models.

To be precise: it is a general fact that to give an algebraic theory with linear parameters in the style of Section 2 is to give a sifted-colimit-preserving strong monad on the symmetric monoidal closed functor category $[\mathbf{Bij} \to \mathbf{Set}]$. This follows from our syntactic completeness result (Prop. 6; see also [45, Cor. 1], [47, §VII]). For each computation context $\Gamma = (x_1 : m_1 \ldots x_k : m_k)$, we define a functor $F_\Gamma : \mathbf{Bij} \to \mathbf{Set}$ by $F_\Gamma = \mathbf{Bij}(m_1, -) + \cdots + \mathbf{Bij}(m_k, -)$. Every functor $\mathbf{Bij} \to \mathbf{Set}$ is a sifted colimit of functors of this form, so to define a sifted-colimit-preserving monad $T$ on the functor category $(\mathbf{Bij} \to \mathbf{Set})$ it suffices to specify its action on functors of the form $F_\Gamma$. Let

$$T(F_\Gamma)p \ = \ \{\Gamma \mid a_1 \ldots a_p \vdash t\}/_= \\ \cong \ \mathbf{Cstar}_{\mathrm{CPU}}(M_{2^{m_1}} \oplus \cdots \oplus M_{2^{m_k}}, M_{2^p}).$$

In the proof of Proposition 6, $T(F_\Gamma)$ was called $T_\Gamma$. (See also e.g. [25] and [5, 9, 29].)

Since our algebraic theory (§3) is commutative, the Kleisli category of the monad $T$ is monoidal [26] (see also [50]). This makes a connection with other work on monoidal categories for quantum computation. The monad-based model seems to be closely related to the one proposed by [27]; it would be interesting to compare it with the model of [33]. One can also study the full subcategory of the Kleisli category that is spanned by objects of the form $F_\Gamma$. This is essentially the syntactic category of our programming language, and its dual can be thought of as the Lawvere theory for our algebraic theory [49]. It is sometimes called a Freyd category, which also makes a connection with [53], since Freyd categories are a categorical formulation of arrows.

## 6. Variations on the algebraic theory

A distinct advantage of specifying notions of computation by algebraic theories is that it is very easy to combine different theories and to investigate the consequences of further operations and equations.

### 6.1 Characterizing different linear maps

***Non-returning computations, sub-unital maps and recursion.*** We can model computations whose results are partially undefined (e.g. they 'fail') by adding to our theory a constant symbol undef : $(0 \mid -)$. This should commute with the other operations:

$$- \mid a \vdash \mathsf{discard}(a, \mathsf{undef}) = \mathsf{undef}.$$

We interpret undef as the zero map undef : $M_0 \to M_1$ between C*-algebras: undef$() = 0$. The correspondence with C*-algebras extends to 'undef' when we relax the preservation of units to the requirement that $(1 - f(1))$ is positive: these maps are called *subunital*.

**Proposition 12.** *In the category of C*-algebras and completely positive subunital maps, the complex numbers form a fully complete model of the algebraic theory of quantum computation extended with* undef.

(In brief, this is because to give a subunital map $f : X \to Y$ is to give a unital map $f : X \oplus \mathbb{C} \to Y$.) Selinger has noted that the sub-unital maps between finite-dimensional C*-algebras form a pointed dcpo, and proposed to use this to interpret recursion in a quantum programming language [42]; this ought to be related to standard algebraic ways of analyzing iteration [10].

***Non-determinism and non-unital maps.*** Some authors drop the requirement of preserving the unit altogether (e.g. [21]). I am not aware of any attempt to justify this with physical intuitions, but we can consider the idea in this algebraic framework. We do this by adding to the algebraic theory a commutative monoid, that is, a binary operation $\oplus : (0 \mid 0, 0)$ satisfying the monoid laws:

$$(x \oplus y) \oplus z = x \oplus (y \oplus z) \quad x \oplus y = y \oplus x \quad \mathsf{undef} \oplus x = x$$

Let us add axioms imposing that $\oplus$ commutes with the other operations (measure, apply and new). The operation $\oplus$ is reminiscent of non-deterministic computation, although we do *not* impose idempotence, $x \oplus x = x$; in fact, there is no non-degenerate commutative algebraic theory that combines idempotent nondeterminism with probabilistic choice.

We can interpret $\oplus$ as a linear map between C*-algebras: let $\oplus : M_1 \oplus M_1 \to M_1$ be given by $\oplus(\alpha, \beta) = \alpha + \beta$. This is completely positive, but it does not preserve units.

**Proposition 13.** *In the category of C*-algebras and all completely positive maps, the complex numbers form a fully complete model of the algebraic theory of quantum computation extended with* undef *and* $\oplus$.

To show this, we define one-sided measurement operation, $\mathsf{m}_0 : (1 \mid 0)$ by $\mathsf{m}_0(a, x) = \mathsf{measure}(a, x, \mathsf{undef})$, so that

$$\mathsf{measure}(a, x, y) = \mathsf{m}_0(a, x) \oplus \mathsf{apply}_{\mathtt{X}}(a, a.\mathsf{m}_0(a, y)).$$

Now all terms can be rearranged into an sum of operators, as in Choi's theorem.

### 6.2 Relationship with classical data and QRAM.

***Changing of unitaries.*** The algebraic presentation of quantum computation does not assume very much about the unitaries, only they that they form a groupoid with two monoidal structures. To focus on classical computation, we can cut down to the $\{0, 1\}$ valued unitary matrices. In this classical setting the following extra axiom is reasonable.

$$x(a) = \mathsf{measure}(a, \mathsf{new}_0(a.x(a)), \mathsf{new}_1(a.x(a))) \qquad \text{(M)}$$

Axiom (M) is consistent with classical computation:

**Proposition 14.** *The two-element set, 2, is a fully complete model in the category* $\mathbf{Set}^{\mathrm{op}}$. *In other words, the following data are equivalent:*

- *A term $x_1{:}m_1 \ldots x_k{:}m_k \mid a_1 \ldots a_p \vdash t$ where all the unitaries are valued in $\{0, 1\}$, modulo all the axioms including (M).*
- *A function $2^p \to (2^{m_1} + \cdots + 2^{m_k})$ between sets.*

Note that Axiom (M) is is inconsistent with quantum computation, since we can use it to derive $x = y$ (for all $x$ and $y$):

$$\begin{aligned}
x &= \nu a.\,(x \mathbin{?_a} y) && \textit{(D)}\\
&= \nu a.\,\mathtt{Had}_a(\mathtt{Had}_a(x \mathbin{?_a} y)) && \textit{(G),(H)}\\
&= \nu a.\,\mathtt{Had}_a((\nu a.\,\mathtt{Had}_a(x?_a y)) \mathbin{?_a} (\nu a.\,\mathtt{X}_a(\mathtt{Had}_a(x?_a y)))) && \textit{(M)}\\
&= \nu a.\,\mathtt{Had}_a((\nu a.\,\mathtt{Had}_a(y?_a x)) \mathbin{?_a} (\nu a.\,\mathtt{X}_a(\mathtt{Had}_a(y?_a x)))) && \textit{(5)}\\
&= \nu a.\,(y \mathbin{?_a} x) && \textit{(M),(H),(G)}\\
&= y && \textit{(D)}
\end{aligned}$$

Notice that the algebraic framework allows us to make this very strong statement: we are not only saying that (M) fails in the particular model of C*-algebras, but moreover that it fails in *every* consistent model of quantum computation.

***Reference cells versus their contents.*** A rather different approach to quantum data is to step away from the actual qubits, and instead consider pointers to memory cells that store qubits (in 'QRAM'). This approach is taken in the QIO monad [6].

We can analyze this in the context of our algebraic theory by understanding the parameter variables $(a, b)$ not as qubits but as distinct references to memory cells. Thus new does not create a new qubit, but rather allocates a new memory cell containing a qubit initialized with $|0\rangle$. With this interpretation, discard is not discarding a bit, but rather discarding the name of the pointer: the memory itself might remain active.

In this context it is appropriate to omit Axiom (C). We now explain this by analogy with the classical situation.

***Algebraic theories with a discard operation.*** The theory of quantum computation has, as a subtheory, the simple theory of discarding. The signature is discard : $(1 \mid 0)$, and there is one equation: $\mathsf{discard}(a, \mathsf{discard}(b, x)) = \mathsf{discard}(b, \mathsf{discard}(a, x))$. In Prop. 6 we saw that the functor category $[\mathbf{Bij}, \mathbf{Set}]$ is a canonical category for models of algebraic theories with linear parameters. In fact, as is quite well known (e.g. [17, 28, 39]), the category of algebras for the theory of discard alone is equivalent to the functor category $[\mathbf{Inj}, \mathbf{Set}]$, where $\mathbf{Inj}$ is the category of natural numbers and injections between them. This means that every algebraic theory with linear parameters and with a discard operation induces a monad on the category $[\mathbf{Inj}, \mathbf{Set}]$. This category has long been used to model dynamic allocation [44] and separation [32].

The category $\mathbf{Inj}$ has a monoidal structure, given by addition of natural numbers, and this extends to a monoidal structure on the category $[\mathbf{Inj}, \mathbf{Set}]$. If we have an algebraic theory with linear parameters and a the discard operation commutes with all other operations, then this induces a strong monad on $[\mathbf{Inj}, \mathbf{Set}]$ for this monoidal structure. There is a well-studied strong monad on $[\mathbf{Inj}, \mathbf{Set}]$ that describes local store of classical data: it is attributed to O'Hearn and Tennant, but first appeared in [36]. We analyze that monad by considering an algebraic theory of classical local store, which is a variation on the theory of quantum computation (§3) found by restricting to $\{0, 1\}$-valued matrices; omitting Axiom (C); and including Axiom (M).

**Proposition 15.** *The (enriched) category of algebras for the theory of classical local store is equivalent to the category of LS-algebras from [36], over* $[\mathbf{Inj}, \mathbf{Set}]$.

(This is proved in much the same way as [28, 36, 39], only within the formal framework of algebraic theories with linear parameters.) An important property of the monad for local store of classical data is that it is enriched in $[\mathbf{Inj}, \mathbf{Set}]$ in two ways: firstly with the monoidal structure, which gives a notion of separation; and secondly with the cartesian product, which enables standard programming with ordinary cartesian products.

If we add Axiom (C) then we retain the enrichment in the monoidal structure (see also [48, §4.2.2]) but the cartesian enrichment is broken. Indeed, no further axioms can be added without breaking the cartesian enrichment [46].

Following Proposition 15, we can also consider an algebraic theory of quantum local store, by omitting Axiom (C) (except for $n = 0$); omitting Axiom (M), but using all the unitaries. This again supports the two different kinds of enrichment in $[\mathbf{Inj}, \mathbf{Set}]$. We propose our algebraic theory of quantum local store as a semantic theory of the notion of computation describing the QRAM model.

| ***Summary.*** | *Axioms omitted* | *Unitaries valued in* |
|---|---|---|
| Quantum computation | (M) | Complex numbers |
| Classical computation | None | $\{0, 1\}$ |
| Classical local store | (C) | $\{0, 1\}$ |
| QRAM | (C),(M) | Complex numbers |

It would be interesting to add other operations to the signature, such as communication primitives, e.g. following [47].

***Overall summary.*** We have presented a framework for algebraic theories with linear parameters (§2) and used it to axiomatize quantum computing (§3). We showed that our axiomatization completely describes quantum computing, by referring to an old model built from operator algebra (§4). We showed how to extend the notion of quantum computing to a programming language (§5), and considered several variations on the theory (§6), demonstrating the flexibility of the algebraic framework.

***Acknowledgements:*** This research was supported by ERC Project QCLS. It wouldn't have been possible without the QCLS group in Nijmegen: Robin Adams, Kenta Cho, Robert Furber, Bart Jacobs, Mathys Rennela, Sander Uijlen, Bas Westerbaan, and Bram Westerbaan.

I presented this work at the Workshop on Quantum Physics and Logic (QPL, Kyoto 2014) and it was included in the informal proceedings of that workshop. I am grateful to the anonymous reviewers and the organizers of QPL 2014, and to the reviewers of POPL 2014, for their valuable comments. It has been helpful to discuss this work with many other people too, including Samson Abramsky, Rasmus Møgelberg, Gordon Plotkin, Jamie Vicary, and Mingsheng Ying.

## References

[1] S. Abramsky and B. Coecke. A categorical semantics of quantum protocols. In *Proc. LICS 2004*, 2004.

[2] J. Aczél. On mean values. *Bull. Am. Math. Soc.*, 54:392–400, 1948.

[3] R. Adams. QPEL: Quantum program and effect language. In *Proc. QPL 2014*, 2014. To appear.

[4] D. Ahman and S. Staton. Normalization by evaluation and algebraic effects. In *Proc. MFPS XXIX*, pages 51–69, 2013.

[5] T. Altenkirch, J. Chapman, and T. Uustalu. Monads need not be endofunctors. In *FOSSACS 2010*.

[6] T. Altenkirch and A. Green. The Quantum IO Monad. In *Semantic Techniques in Quantum Computation*. CUP, 2009.

[7] J. Baez and J. Dolan. From finite sets to Feynman diagrams. In *Mathematics Unlimited — 2001 and Beyond*. Springer, 2001.

[8] N. Benton and P. Wadler. Linear logic, monads and the lambda calculus. In *LICS 1996*.

[9] C. Berger, P.-A. Melliès, and M. Weber. Monads with arities and their associated theories. *J. Pure Appl. Algebra*, 216, 2012.

[10] S. L. Bloom and Z. Esik. *Iteration Theories: The Equational Logic of Iterative Processes*. Springer, 1993.

[11] I. Cervesato and F. Pfenning. A Linear Logical Framework. *Inform. Comput.*, 179(1):19–75, 2002.

[12] G. Chiribella, G. M. D'Ariano, and P. Perinotti. Informational derivation of quantum theory. *Phys. Rev. A*, 84, 2011.

[13] K. Cho. Semantics for a quantum programming language by operator algebras. In *Proc. QPL 2014*, 2014. To appear.

[14] B. Coecke and R. Duncan. Interacting quantum observables. In *Proc. ICALP 2008*, pages 298–310, 2008.

[15] V. Danos, E. Kashefi, and P. Panangaden. The measurement calculus. *J. ACM*, 54(2), 2007.

[16] P. A. Fillmore. *A User's Guide to Operator Algebras*. Wiley-Interscience, 1996.

[17] M. Fiore. Notes on combinatorial functors. Draft, 2001.

[18] M. P. Fiore and C.-K. Hur. Second-order equational logic. In *CSL'10*.

[19] A. S. Green, P. L. Lumsdaine, N. J. Ross, P. Selinger, and B. Valiron. Quipper: a scalable quantum programming language. In *PLDI 2013*.

[20] L. Hardy. Reformulating and reconstructing quantum theory. arXiv:1104.2066, 2011.

[21] C. Heunen, A. Kissinger, and P. Selinger. Completely positive projections and biproducts. arXiv:1308.4557.

[22] B. Jacobs. On block structures in quantum computation. In *Proc. MFPS XXIX*, 2013.

[23] G. Janelidze and G. Kelly. A note on actions of a monoidal category. *Theory Appl. Categ.*, 9(4), 2001.

[24] O. Kammar and G. D. Plotkin. Algebraic foundations for effect-dependent optimisations. In *POPL 2012*, pages 349–360, 2012.

[25] G. M. Kelly and A. J. Power. Adjunctions whose counits are coequalisers. *J. Pure Appl. Algebra*, 89:163–179, 1993.

[26] F. E. J. Linton. Autonomous equational categories. *J. Math. Mech.*, 15:637–642, 1966.

[27] O. Malherbe, P. J. Scott, and P. Selinger. Presheaf models of quantum computation: an outline. In *Computation, Logic, Games, and Quantum Foundations*. Springer, 2013.

[28] P.-A. Melliès. Local stores in string diagrams. In *RTA-TLCA 2014*.

[29] P.-A. Melliès. Segal condition meets computational effects. In *Proc. LICS 2010*, pages 150–159, 2010.

[30] R. E. Møgelberg and S. Staton. Linear usage of state. *Logical Methods Comput. Sci.*, 10(1), 2014.

[31] M. A. Nielsen and I. L. Chuang. *Quantum Computation and Quantum Information*. CUP, 2011.

[32] P. W. O'Hearn. On bunched typing. *J. Funct. Program.*, 2003.

[33] M. Pagani, P. Selinger, and B. Valiron. Applying quantitative semantics to higher-order quantum computing. In *Proc. POPL 2014*.

[34] V. Paulsen. *Completely Bounded Maps and Operator Algebras*. CUP, 2003.

[35] G. Plotkin. Some varieties of equational logic. In *Algebra, meaning and computation*. Springer, 2006.

[36] G. D. Plotkin and J. Power. Notions of computation determine monads. In *Proc. FOSSACS'02*, 2002.

[37] G. D. Plotkin and J. Power. Algebraic operations and generic effects. *Applied Categorical Structures*, 11(1):69–94, 2003.

[38] J. Power. Generic models for computational effects. *Theor. Comput. Sci.*, 364(2):254–269, 2006.

[39] J. Power. Indexed Lawvere theories for local state. In *Models, logics and higher-dimensional categories: a tribute to the work of Mihály Makkai*, pages 213–230. American Mathematical Society, 2011.

[40] J. Power and M. Tanaka. Binding signatures for generic contexts. In *Proc. TLCA 2005*, volume 308–323, 2005.

[41] M. Rennela. Towards a quantum domain theory: Order-enrichment and fixpoints in W*-algebras. In *Proc. MFPS XXX*, 2014.

[42] P. Selinger. Towards a quantum programming language. *Mathematical Structures in Computer Science*, 14(4):527–586, 2004.

[43] P. Selinger. Generators and relations for n-qubit Clifford operators. arXiv:1310.6813, 2013.

[44] I. Stark. Categorical models for local names. *LISP and Symb. Comp.*, 9(1):77–107, 1996.

[45] S. Staton. An algebraic presentation of predicate logic. In *FOSSACS 2013*.

[46] S. Staton. Completeness for algebraic theories of local state. In *FOSSACS 2010*.

[47] S. Staton. Instances of computational effects. In *LICS 2013*.

[48] S. Staton. Two cotensors in one. In *Proc. MFPS XXV*, 2009.

[49] S. Staton. Freyd categories are enriched lawvere theories. In *Proc. Workshop on Algebra, Coalgebra and Topology*, volume 303 of *ENTCS*, pages 197–206, 2013.

[50] S. Staton and P. B. Levy. Universal properties for impure programming languages. In *POPL 2013*, 2013.

[51] A. van Tonder. A lambda calculus for quantum computation. *SIAM J. Comput.*, 33(5):1109–1135, 2004.

[52] J. Vicary. Higher semantics of quantum protocols. In *LICS 2012*.

[53] J. K. Vizzotto, G. R. Librelotto, and A. Sabry. Reasoning about general quantum programs over mixed states. In *SBMF 2009*, 2009.

[54] M. Ying and Y. Feng. An algebraic language for distributed quantum computing. *IEEE Trans. Computers*, 58(6):728–743, 2009.

[55] M. Ying, N. Yu, and Y. Feng. Alternation in quantum programming: from superposition of data to superposition of programs. arXiv:1402.5172, 2014.

## A. Proof of full completeness

We use this appendix to give more details of our proof of the completeness theorems from Section 4. As a first step we consider the case without new.

**Theorem 9.**

1. *For any *-homomorphism* $f : M_{2^{m_1}} \oplus \cdots \oplus M_{2^{m_k}} \to M_{2^p}$ *there is a term in the algebraic theory not involving* new, $x_1 : m_1 \dots x_k : m_k \mid a_1 \dots a_p \vdash t$, *such that* $f = [\![t]\!]$.
2. *If* $\Gamma \mid \Delta \vdash t, u$ *and* $t$ *and* $u$ *do not contain* new, *and* $[\![t]\!] = [\![u]\!]$ *then* $\Gamma \mid \Delta \vdash t = u$ *is derivable.*

*Proof notes.* Recall that if $m_1 \dots m_k, p$ are non-zero natural numbers then the set of Bratteli diagrams, $\mathbf{Brat}(m_1 \dots m_k, p)$, comprises $k$-tuples of natural numbers $s_1 \dots s_k$ ('partial multiplicities') such that $\sum_{i=1}^k s_i m_i = p$. There is a function

$$\mu : \mathbf{Brat}(m_1 \dots m_k, p) \to \mathbf{Cstar}(M_{m_1} \oplus \cdots \oplus M_{m_k}, M_p)$$

where $\mu(s_1 \dots s_k)(A_1, \dots, A_k)$ is the block diagonal matrix formed by $s_1$ copies of $A_1$ followed by $s_2$ copies of $A_2$ and so on.

The following result is standard (e.g. [16, 1.1.3]).

**Proposition 16.** *The function* $\mu$ *has a retraction: there is a function* $\rho : \mathbf{Cstar}(M_{m_1} \oplus \cdots \oplus M_{m_k}, M_p) \to \mathbf{Brat}(m_1 \dots m_k, p)$ *such that* $\rho\mu = \mathrm{id}$. *Moreover* $\rho(f) = \rho(g)$ *if and only if there is a* $p \times p$ *unitary* $U$ *such that* $f(\vec{A}) = U^*(g(\vec{A}))U$. □

Consider a context $(x_1 : m_1 \dots x_k : m_k \mid a_1 \dots a_p)$. Suppose that the second order variables are arranged in order of increasing valence. The following are in bijective correspondence:

1. Terms built only from measure and variables, such that the variables (of both kinds) appear in the same order as in the context. (These terms are not considered modulo any equations.)
2. Sequences of partial multiplicities in $\mathbf{Brat}(2^{m_1} \dots 2^{m_k}, 2^p)$.

To show this, we interpret a term $t$ as a Bratteli diagram $(\!|t|\!)$ so that $\mu(\!|t|\!) = [\![t]\!]$. If the term is a variable $x_i(a_1 \dots a_q)$, then $m_i = q = p$, and we let $(\!|x_i(a_1 \dots a_q)|\!) \in \mathbf{Brat}(2^{m_1} \dots 2^{m_k}, 2^p)$ be given by $s_i = 1$, and $s_j = 0$ for $j \neq i$. If the term is a measurement, $\mathsf{measure}(a_{p+1}, t, u)$, then by induction $t$ and $u$ correspond to Bratteli diagrams $(\!|t|\!), (\!|u|\!) \in \mathbf{Brat}(2^{m_1} \dots 2^{m_k}, 2^p)$, and so $\sum_{i=1}^k (\!|t|\!)_i 2^{m_i} + \sum_{i=1}^k (\!|u|\!)_i 2^{m_i} = 2^{p+1}$. Let $(\!|\mathsf{measure}(a_{p+1}, u, v)|\!)$ in $\mathbf{Brat}(2^{m_1} \dots 2^{m_k}, 2^{p+1})$ be the coordinatewise sum of $(\!|t|\!)$ and $(\!|u|\!)$, i.e. $(\!|\mathsf{measure}(a_{p+1}, u, v)|\!)_i = (\!|t|\!)_i + (\!|u|\!)_i$.

The inverse to this interpretation maps Bratteli diagrams $\vec{s}$ in $\mathbf{Brat}(2^{m_1} \dots 2^{m_k}, 2^p)$ to terms $\mathrm{Measure}(\vec{s})$ of this special form, so that $\mathrm{Measure}((\!|t|\!)) = t$ and $(\!|\mathrm{Measure}(\vec{s})|\!) = \vec{s}$. This inverse is defined by induction on $p$. The special order on the computation variables is needed here.

We can thus define a section of the semantic map

$$[\![-]\!] : \{t \mid (x_1 : m_1 \dots x_k : m_k \mid a_1 \dots a_p \vdash t)\} \to \mathbf{Cstar}(M_{2^{m}_1} \oplus M_{2^{m_k}}, M_{2^p})$$

as follows. Every *-homomorphism $f : M_{2^{m_1}} \oplus \cdots \oplus M_{2^{m_k}} \to M_{2^p}$ factors as $f(x) = \mathtt{U}^* \cdot (\mu\, \vec{s})(x) \cdot \mathtt{U}$, for a $2^p \times 2^p$ unitary $\mathtt{U}$, so that $f = [\![\mathsf{apply}_{\mathtt{U}}(\vec{a}, \vec{a}.\mathrm{Measure}(\vec{s}))]\!]$. Thus the first part of the Theorem 9 is proved.

We show the second part of Theorem 9 in two stages.

1. We show that the section of the semantic map doesn't depend on the choice of U;
2. We show that the section is a surjection, i.e. that every term is equal to one of the form $\mathsf{apply}_{\mathtt{U}}(\vec{a}, \vec{a}.\mathrm{Measure}(\vec{s}))$.

First, we show that for any Bratteli diagram $\vec{s} \in \mathbf{Brat}(2^{m_1} ... 2^{m_k}, 2^p)$ and any $2^p \times 2^p$ unitaries U, V, if

$$\mathtt{U}^* \cdot (\mu\, \vec{s})(-) \cdot \mathtt{U} = \mathtt{V}^* \cdot (\mu\, \vec{s})(-) \cdot \mathtt{V} \tag{7}$$

as linear maps, then we can derive the equality

$$\mathsf{apply}_{\mathtt{U}}(\vec{a}, \vec{a}.\mathrm{Measure}(\vec{s})) = \mathsf{apply}_{\mathtt{V}}(\vec{a}, \vec{a}.\mathrm{Measure}(\vec{s})) \tag{8}$$

between terms. This fact can be understood along the same lines as the freedom in the operator-sum representation of completely positive maps (e.g. [31, Ch. 8]). If $(\mu\, \vec{s})(-) = \mathtt{U}^* \cdot (\mu\, \vec{s})(-) \cdot \mathtt{U}$ then U must be built from a tensor products of unitaries that are conditional on qubits that are being measured and that act on qubits that are being discarded. All this is taken care of by laws (A)–(C), (F)–(J). Thus the section of the semantic map does not depend on the choice of U.

It remains for us to show that the section is a surjection, i.e. that every term is equivalent to one of the form $\mathsf{apply}_{\mathtt{U}}(\vec{a}, \vec{a}.\mathrm{Measure}(\vec{s}))$. In brief, we use the equations to rearrange a term as follows: first we push all measure operations inside apply operations using law (B); next we arrange all the second order variables to appear in the designated order by using controlled nots (possibly controlled-controlled-nots etc), via laws (A), (B) and (J); we arrange all the parameter variables to appear in the designated order, by using controlled swaps, via laws (B), (F); a sequence of apply operations can be combined into one apply operation, using tensors and composition, via laws (G)–(I). This concludes our proof of Theorem 9. □

The remainder of Appendix A, including a proof outline for Theorem 11, is available on my home page, `http://www.cs.ru.nl/personal/sstaton`.

# Proof Spaces for Unbounded Parallelism

Azadeh Farzan Zachary Kincaid
University of Toronto

Andreas Podelski
University of Freiburg

## Abstract

In this paper, we present a new approach to automatically verify multi-threaded programs which are executed by an unbounded number of threads running in parallel.

The starting point for our work is the problem of how we can leverage existing automated verification technology for sequential programs (abstract interpretation, Craig interpolation, constraint solving, etc.) for multi-threaded programs. Suppose that we are given a correctness proof for a trace of a program (or for some other program fragment). We observe that the proof can always be decomposed into a finite set of Hoare triples, and we ask *what can be proved from the finite set of Hoare triples using only simple combinatorial inference rules* (without access to a theorem prover and without the possibility to infer genuinely new Hoare triples)?

We introduce a proof system where one proves the correctness of a multi-threaded program by showing that for each trace of the program, *there exists* a correctness proof in the space of proofs that are derivable from a finite set of axioms using simple combinatorial inference rules. This proof system is complete with respect to the classical proof method of establishing an inductive invariant (which uses thread quantification and control predicates). Moreover, it is possible to algorithmically check whether a given set of axioms is sufficient to prove the correctness of a multi-threaded program, using ideas from well-structured transition systems.

## 1. Introduction

In this paper, we present a new approach to verifying multi-threaded programs which are executed by an unbounded number of concurrent threads. Many important systems and application programs belong to this category, e.g. filesystems, device drivers, web servers, and image processing applications.

We will start by demonstrating our approach on a simple example. Consider a program in which an unknown number of threads concurrently execute the code below. The goal is to verify that, if $g \geq 1$ holds initially, then it will always hold (regardless of how many threads are executing).

```
global int g
local  int x
1: x := g;
2: g := g+x;
```

Consider the set of the Hoare triples (A) - (D) given below.



*POPL'15*, January 15 - 17 2015, Mumbai, India.
Copyright is held by the owner/author(s). Publication rights licensed to ACM.
ACM 978-1-4503-3300-9/15/01... $15.00.
http://dx.doi.org/10.1145/2676726.2677012

| | | | |
|---|---|---|---|
| (A) | $\{g \geq 1\}$ | $\langle x := g : 1\rangle$ | $\{x(1) \geq 1\}$ |
| (B) | $\{g \geq 1 \land x(1) \geq 1\}$ | $\langle g := g + x : 1\rangle$ | $\{g \geq 1\}$ |
| (C) | $\{g \geq 1\}$ | $\langle x := g : 1\rangle$ | $\{g \geq 1\}$ |
| (D) | $\{x(1) \geq 1\}$ | $\langle x := g : 2\rangle$ | $\{x(1) \geq 1\}$ |

Here we use $x(1)$ to refer to Thread 1's copy of the local variable x, and $\langle x := g : 1\rangle$ to indicate the instruction `x := g` executed by Thread 1.

We will discuss how such Hoare triples can be generated automatically shortly. But for now, suppose that we have been given the above set of Hoare triples, and consider a deductive system in which these triples are taken as axioms, and the only rules of inference are *sequencing*, *symmetry*, and *conjunction*. These rules are easily illustrated with concrete examples:

- *Sequencing* composes two Hoare triples sequentially. For example, sequencing (A) and (D) yields

  (A $\circ$ D) $\{g \geq 1\}$ $\langle x := g : 1\rangle\langle x := g : 2\rangle$ $\{x(1) \geq 1\}$

- *Symmetry* permutes thread identifiers. For example, renaming (A) and (C) (mapping $1 \mapsto 2$) yields

  (A') $\{g \geq 1\}$ $\langle x := g : 2\rangle$ $\{x(2) \geq 1\}$
  (C') $\{g \geq 1\}$ $\langle x := g : 2\rangle$ $\{g \geq 1\}$

  and, renaming (D) (mapping $1 \mapsto 2$ and $2 \mapsto 1$) yields

  (D') $\{x(2) \geq 1\}$ $\langle x := g : 1\rangle$ $\{x(2) \geq 1\}$

- *Conjunction* composes two Hoare triples by conjoining pre- and postconditions. For example, conjoining (A') and (C') yields

  (A' $\land$ C') $\{g \geq 1\}$ $\langle x := g : 2\rangle$ $\{g \geq 1 \land x(2) \geq 1\}$

  and conjoining (A) and (D') yields (A $\land$ D')

  $\{g \geq 1 \land x(2) \geq 1\}$ $\langle x := g : 1\rangle$ $\{x(1) \geq 1 \land x(2) \geq 1\}$

Naturally, the deductive system may apply inference rules to deduced Hoare triples as well: for example, by sequencing (A' $\land$ C') and (A $\land$ D'), we get the Hoare triple

$$\{g \geq 1\}\ \langle x := g : 2\rangle\langle x := g : 1\rangle\ \{x(1) \geq 1 \land x(2) \geq 1\}$$

A *proof space* is a set of valid Hoare triples which is closed under sequencing, symmetry, and conjunction (that is, it is a *theory* of this deductive system). Any finite set of valid Hoare triples generates an infinite proof space by considering those triples to be axioms and taking their closure under deduction; we call such a finite set of Hoare triples a *basis* for the generated proof space.

One key insight in this paper is that, although it may be challenging to formalize a correctness argument for a multi-threaded program, any given *trace* (sequence of program instructions) of the program is just a simple (straight-line) sequential program which can be easily proved correct. In fact, just these three simple inference rules (sequencing, symmetry, and conjunction) are sufficient to prove the correctness of *any* trace of the example program. That is, for any trace $\tau$ of the program, $\{g \geq 1\}\ \ \tau\ \ \{g \geq 1\}$ belongs to the proof space generated by (A) – (D), regardless of *which* or *how many* threads execute in $\tau$. Crucially (and *due* to the simplicity of the inference rules), this fact can be checked completely automatically, by leveraging techniques developed in the context of well-structured transition systems [2, 17, 18].

Now let us turn to the problem of how Hoare triples like (A) – (D) can be generated automatically. An important feature of proof spaces is that they are generated from a very simple set of Hoare triples, of the sort one could expect to generate using standard technology for sequential verification. To appreciate the simplicity of these triples, consider the following inductive invariant for the program, the classical notion of correctness proof for multi-threaded programs:

$$g \geq 1 \wedge (\forall i.\mathsf{loc}(i) = 2 \Rightarrow \mathtt{x}(i) \geq 1)$$

(which indicates that g is at least 1, and all threads $i$ at line 2 of the program have $\mathtt{x}(i)$ at least 1). This is a simple invariant for this program, but it is one which we cannot rely on a sequential verifier to find because it makes use of features which are not encountered on sequential programs: thread quantification ($\forall i$), and control predicates ($\mathsf{loc}(i) = 2$). In contrast, the triples (A) – (D) are of the form one might expect to generate using a sequential verifier. Thus, proof spaces are a solution to the problem of *how to use automated proof technology for sequential programs to prove the correctness of programs with unboundedly many threads.*

One possible algorithm (discussed further in Section 7) for automating proof spaces is to build a basis for a proof space iteratively in a manner analogous to a counter-example guided abstraction refinement (CEGAR) loop. While this algorithm is not the focus of this paper, it is important to recognize the context of and motivation behind proof spaces. The algorithm operates as follows: first choose a trace for which there is no correctness theorem in the proof space. For example, suppose that we start with the trace

$$\langle \mathtt{x} := \mathtt{g} : 1\rangle\langle \mathtt{x} := \mathtt{g} : 2\rangle\langle \mathtt{g} := \mathtt{g} + \mathtt{x} : 1\rangle$$

$$\{g \geq 1\}\ \langle \mathtt{x} := \mathtt{g} : 1\rangle\ \{\mathtt{x}(1) \geq 1\}\ \langle \mathtt{x} := \mathtt{g} : 2\rangle\ \{\mathtt{x}(1) \geq 1\}\ \langle \mathtt{g} := \mathtt{g} + \mathtt{x} : 1\rangle\ \{g \geq 1\}$$

This trace can be viewed as a sequential program, and we can use standard technology (e.g., abstract interpretation, constraint solving, Craig interpolation) to construct a proof for it (for example, the one on the right). By extracting the atomic Hoare triples along this sequence, we can arrive at the triples (A), (B), and (D), which we add to our basis. We may then extract a new trace which cannot be proved using just (A), (B), and (D), and restart the loop. The loop terminates when (and if) (1) it finds a feasible counter-example or (2) all traces of the program have correctness theorems in the proof space.

The key contribution of this paper is the notion of *proof spaces*, a proof system which can be used to exploit sequential verification technology for proving the correctness of multi-threaded programs with unboundedly many threads. The merits of proof spaces are as follows:

- Rather than enriching the language of assertions (introducing thread quantification and control predicates) and employing more powerful symbolic reasoning, proof spaces use simple assertions which can be combined using combinatorial reasoning (i.e., without a theorem prover).
- We show that the combinatorial reasoning involved in checking whether all traces of a program have a correctness theorem in a proof space can be automated, and give an algorithm which leverages ideas from well-structured transition systems [18]. We show that this proof space checking problem is undecidable in general, but our algorithm is a decision procedure for an interesting subclass of proof spaces.
- Despite the apparent weakness of our three inference rules and the restricted language of assertions, we show that proof spaces are complete relative to a variant of Ashcroft's classical proof system for multi-threaded programs (which employs universal thread quantification and control predicates).

## 2. Motivating example

Consider a simplified implementation of a thread pool, where there are arbitrarily many threads each executing the code that appears in Figure 1. The global variable `tasks` holds an array of tasks of size `len`, the global variable `next` stores the index of the next available task, and the global variable `m` is a lock which protects access to `next`. We denote the threads of the program by $T_1, T_2, \ldots$. Each thread $T_i$ has two local variables `c(i)` and `end(i)` which represent the current and last task in the block of tasks acquired by $T_i$. Each thread operates by simply acquiring a block of 10 consecutive tasks (lines 1-8) and then performing the tasks in its acquired block in sequence (lines 9-13). The `else` branch (line 6) ensures that once the end of the array is reached, all remaining threads that attempt to acquire a block of tasks acquire an empty block (`c = end`).

The details of the tasks are omitted for simplicity, and we maintain only enough information to assert a desired property: that no two threads are ever assigned the same task. This property is encoded by using the `tasks` array to represent the status of each task (0 = started, 1 = finished); a thread can fail the assertion if, between finishing some task and executing the assertion, some other thread starts that same task.

```
global int : len; // total number of tasks
global int array(len) : tasks; // array of tasks
global int : next; // position of next available task block
global lock : m; // lock protecting next

thread T:
   local int : c;    // position of current task
   local int : end; // position of last task in acquired block
   // acquire block of tasks
1  lock(m);
2     c := next;
3     next := next + 10;
4     if (next <= len):
5        end := next;
6     else:
7        end := len;
8  unlock(m);
   // perform block of tasks
9  while (c < end):
10    tasks[c] := 0; // mark task c as started
      ...            // work on the task c
11    tasks[c] := 1; // mark task c as finished
12    assert(tasks[c] == 1); // no other thread has started task c
13    c := c + 1;
```

**Figure 1.** Thread pooling example, adapted from [36].

The sketch below illustrates a snapshot of the `tasks` array (and other instantiated local and global variables) in the thread pool program, where threads 1 to 35 have all finished acquiring their block of tasks (but have not yet started to complete them), and thread 36 has not started the process yet.

| Group | | | | |
|---|---|---|---|---|
| Locking | $\{true\}$<br>$\langle \texttt{lock(m)} : 1\rangle$<br>$\{m = 1\}$ | $\{m = 1\}$<br>$\langle \texttt{lock(m)} : 1\rangle$<br>$\{false\}$ | | |
| Initialization | $\{true\}$<br>$\langle \texttt{c := next} : 1\rangle$<br>$\{\texttt{c}(1) \le \texttt{next}\}$ | $\{\texttt{c}(1) \le \texttt{next}\}$<br>$\langle \texttt{next := next + 10} : 1\rangle$<br>$\{\texttt{c}(1) < \texttt{next}\}$ | $\{true\}$<br>$\langle \texttt{end := next} : 1\rangle$<br>$\{\texttt{end}(1) \le \texttt{next}\}$ | |
| Initialization | $\{\texttt{end}(1) \le \texttt{next}\}$<br>$\langle \texttt{c := next} : 2\rangle$<br>$\{\texttt{end}(1) \le \texttt{c}(2)\}$ | $\{true\}$<br>$\langle \texttt{assume(next > len)} : 1\rangle$<br>$\{\texttt{len} \le \texttt{next}\}$ | $\{\texttt{len} \le \texttt{next}\}$<br>$\langle \texttt{end := len} : 1\rangle$<br>$\{\texttt{end}(1) \le \texttt{next}\}$ | |
| Loop | $\{true\}$<br>$\langle \texttt{assume(c < end)} : 1\rangle$<br>$\{\texttt{c}(1) < \texttt{end}(1)\}$ | $\{true\}$<br>$\langle \texttt{tasks[c] := 1} : 1\rangle$<br>$\{\texttt{tasks}[\texttt{c}(1)] = 1\}$ | $\{\texttt{tasks}[\texttt{c}(1)] = 1\}$<br>$\langle \texttt{assume(tasks[c] != 1)} : 1\rangle$<br>$\{false\}$ | $\{\texttt{end}(1) \le \texttt{c}(2)\}$<br>$\langle \texttt{c := c + 1} : 2\rangle$<br>$\{\texttt{end}(1) \le \texttt{c}(2)\}$ |
| Loop | $\{\texttt{tasks}[\texttt{c}(1)] = 1 \wedge \texttt{c}(1) < \texttt{end}(1) \le \texttt{c}(2)\}$<br>$\langle \texttt{tasks[c] := 0} : 2\rangle$<br>$\{\texttt{tasks}[\texttt{c}(1)] = 1\}$ | $\{\texttt{tasks}[\texttt{c}(1)] = 1 \wedge \texttt{c}(2) < \texttt{end}(2) \le \texttt{c}(1)\}$<br>$\langle \texttt{tasks[c] := 0} : 2\rangle$<br>$\{\texttt{tasks}[\texttt{c}(1)] = 1\}$ | | |

**Figure 2.** The basis of a proof space for the thread pooling example. The variable `c(1)` denotes the copy of the local variable `c` in Thread 1 and the command $\langle \texttt{c := next} : 1\rangle$ denotes the instance of the command `c := next` in Thread 1, etc. Trivial Hoare triples of the type $\{\varphi\}\ \langle\sigma : \texttt{i}\rangle\ \{\varphi\}$ where the set of variables that $\langle\sigma : \texttt{i}\rangle$ modifies is disjoint from the set of variables in $\varphi$, have been omitted for brevity.

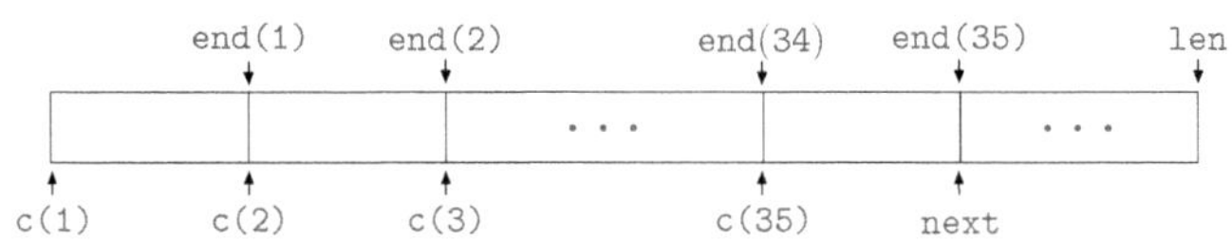


In order to show that two threads, say Threads 1 and 2, cannot be assigned the same task, we may argue that the intervals assigned to them `[c(1), end(1))` and `[c(2), end(2))` are disjoint by proving that `end(1)` is less than or equal to `c(2)`.

***Proof space for thread pooling*** Figure 2 illustrates a finite set of Hoare triples (a basis) that generates a proof space for the thread pooling program. In the figure, the Hoare triples are categorized into three groups (*Locking*, *Initialization*, and *Loop*). We omit Hoare triples that represent trivial invariance axioms of the form $\{\varphi\}\ \langle\sigma : \texttt{i}\rangle\ \{\varphi\}$ where the command $\langle\sigma : \texttt{i}\rangle$ does not write to a variable that appears in $\varphi$; for example,

$$\{\texttt{c}(2) \le \texttt{next}\}\ \langle \texttt{c := next} : 1\rangle\ \{\texttt{c}(2) \le \texttt{next}\}\,.$$

Note that the set of triples in Figure 2 use *mixed assertions* (in the terminology in [12]), which relate the values of local variables to global variables (e.g., $\texttt{c}(1) \le \texttt{next}$), as well as *inter-thread assertions*, which relate the local variables of different threads (e.g., $\texttt{end}(1) \le \texttt{c}(2)$). As discussed in [25], both mixed assertions and inter-thread assertions raise an issue when one attempts to use predicate abstraction techniques. Inter-thread assertions cannot be used in classical compositional proof systems (e.g. thread-modular proofs). In these proof systems, inter-thread relationships can only be accommodated through auxiliary variables [29, 35].

To represent the program in a simple formal model, we encode each conditional branch as a nondeterministic branch between `assume` commands (one for the condition and one for its negation), and we encode `assert(e)` through a command `assume(!e)` (for the negation of the expression `e`) which leads to a new *error location*. We thus encode the correctness of the program (the validity of the assert statement) through the non-reachability of the error location by any thread. An *error trace* is an interleaved sequence of commands of any number of threads which leads *some* thread to the error location (e.g., in Figure 3, the sequence in (a) followed by the sequence in (b)). Thus, we can express the correctness of the program by the validity of the Hoare triple $\{true\}\ \tau\ \{false\}$ for every error trace $\tau$. Given this Hoare triple as the specification of correctness of a trace, we have that *a trace is correct if and only if it is infeasible*.

Let us now demonstrate how the proof space is used to argue for the correctness of the program. We must show that for every error trace $\tau$ *there exists* a derivation of $\{true\}\ \ \tau\ \ \{false\}$ which can be constructed from the triples in Figure 2 using only the combinatorial inference rules of symmetry, conjunction, and sequencing.

Let us first consider the pair of Hoare triples in the *Locking* group. We treat the `lock(m)` command as the atomic sequence $\{$`assume(m = 0); m := 1`$\}$, and `unlock(m)` command as the assignment `m := 0`. Intuitively, the locking Hoare triples encapsulate the reasoning required to prove that the lock `m` provides mutually exclusive access to the variable `next`. Any trace that violates the locking semantics can be proved infeasible using the Hoare triples in the Locking group along with the sequencing and symmetry rules. To see why, consider that any such trace can be decomposed as

$$\tau_1 \cdot \langle \texttt{lock(m)} : \texttt{i}\rangle \cdot \tau_2 \cdot \langle \texttt{lock(m)} : \texttt{j}\rangle \cdot \tau_3$$

such that the following Hoare triples are valid:

$$\begin{array}{ccc} \{true\} & \tau_1 & \{true\} \\ \{true\} & \langle \texttt{lock(m)} : \texttt{i}\rangle & \{m = 1\} \\ \{m = 1\} & \tau_2 & \{m = 1\} \\ \{m = 1\} & \langle \texttt{lock(m)} : \texttt{j}\rangle & \{false\} \\ \{false\} & \tau_3 & \{false\} \end{array}$$

This decomposition exploits the fact that any trace which violates the semantics of locking has a shortest prefix which contains a violation: that is, we may assume that $\tau_2$ contains no `unlock(m)` commands because, if it did, there would be a shorter prefix in which two threads simultaneously hold the lock m. Having justified their semantic validity, we may now consider how to derive these triples using symmetry and sequencing from the Locking axioms in Figure 2. The two triples above concerning the `lock(m)` command are inferred from the triples in the Locking group by renaming thread 1 (i.e. using the symmetry rule) to i and j, respectively. The rest of the triples come from the simple invariance Hoare triples (not depicted in Figure 2, but mentioned in the caption), that allow us to infer $\{m = 1\}$ $\langle \sigma : \mathtt{i} \rangle$ $\{m = 1\}$ for any command $\sigma$ except `unlock(m)`, and $\{\mathit{true}\}$ $\langle \sigma : \mathtt{i} \rangle$ $\{\mathit{true}\}$ and $\{\mathit{false}\}$ $\langle \sigma : \mathtt{i} \rangle$ $\{\mathit{false}\}$ for every command $\sigma$.

We now turn our attention to the error traces which *do* respect locking semantics, and show that they are infeasible. The six Hoare triples in the *Initialization* section of Figure 2 are sufficient to prove that after two threads (say 2 and 9) acquire their block of tasks, those blocks do not overlap (i.e., we have either $\mathtt{end}(9) \leq \mathtt{c}(2)$ or $\mathtt{end}(2) \leq \mathtt{c}(9)$, depending on the order in which the threads acquire their tasks). An example of such a trace (which can be proved using just sequencing and symmetry operations) appears in Figure 3(a). We encourage the reader to show (using conjunction) that if we extend the trace in Figure 3(a) by the initialization sequence of a third thread (say, Thread 5) to obtain a trace $\tau$, then

$$\{\mathit{true}\} \quad \tau \quad \{\mathtt{end}(2) \leq \mathtt{c}(9) \wedge \mathtt{end}(2) \leq \mathtt{c}(5) \wedge \mathtt{end}(9) \leq \mathtt{c}(5)\}$$

belongs to the proof space as well. Following similar proof combination steps, one can see that the argument can be adapted to traces with any number of threads.

Finally, the triples in the *Loop* section can be used to show two things. First, the "non-overlapping" property established in the initialization section is preserved by the loop: for example, if $\mathtt{end}(2) \leq \mathtt{c}(9)$ holds at the beginning of the loop, then if thread 2 or thread 9 (or any other thread) executes the loop, $\mathtt{end}(2) \leq \mathtt{c}(9)$ continues to hold. Second, (assuming the non-overlapping condition holds), if some task has been completed then it remains completed: for example, if `tasks[c(2)] = 1`, then when thread 9 starts task `c(9)` (i.e. assigns 0 to `tasks[c(9)]`), it cannot overwrite the value of the array cell `tasks[c(2)]` (this is ensured by the precondition $\mathtt{c}(2) < \mathtt{end}(2) \leq \mathtt{c}(9)$, which implies $\mathtt{c}(2) \neq \mathtt{c}(9)$). Figure 3(b) gives an example proof which can be derived using the *Loop* section. The sequential composition of traces in Figure 3(a) and Figure 3(b) forms an error trace (i.e. one that leads to the error location), and sequencing their proofs yields a proof that the error trace is infeasible.

We hope that it is now intuitively clear (or at least plausible) that, given any particular error trace $\tau$, it is possible to derive $\{\mathit{true}\}$ $\tau$ $\{\mathit{false}\}$ using the symmetry, sequencing, and conjunction rules starting from the axioms given in Figure 2. The question is: how can one be assured that all (infinitely many) error traces can be proved infeasible in this way? In Section 6 we will show how to formalize such an argument, and moreover, give a procedure for checking that it holds.

## 3. Preliminaries

In this section, we will define our program model and introduce some technical definitions.

We fix a set of global variables GV and a set of local variables LV. Intuitively, these are the variables that can appear in the program text. We will often make use of the set $\mathsf{LV} \times \mathbb{N}$ of *indexed* local variables, and denote a pair $\langle x, \mathtt{i} \rangle \in \mathsf{LV} \times \mathbb{N}$ by $x(\mathtt{i})$. Intuitively, such an indexed local variable $x(\mathtt{i})$ refers to thread i's copy of the local variable $x$.

For simplicity, we will assume that program variables take integer values, and the program is expressible in the theory of linear integer arithmetic. This assumption is made only to simplify the presentation by making it more concrete; our approach and results

```
{true}
lock(m)                      :2
{true}
c := next                    :2
{true}
next := next + 10            :2
{true}
assume(next <= len)          :2
{true}
end := next                  :2
{end(2) ≤ next}
unlock(m)                    :2
{end(2) ≤ next}
lock(m)                      :9
{end(2) ≤ next}
c := next                    :9
{end(2) ≤ c(9)}
next := next + 10            :9
{end(2) ≤ c(9)}
assume(next <= len)          :9
{end(2) ≤ next}
end := next                  :9
{end(2) ≤ c(9)}
unlock(m)                    :9
{end(2) ≤ c(9)}
```

(a) Initialization example

```
{end(2) ≤ c(9)}
assume(c < end)              :2
{c(2) < end(2) ∧ end(2) ≤ c(9)}
tasks[c] := 0                :2
{c(2) < end(2) ∧ end(2) ≤ c(9)}
tasks[c] := 1                :2
{tasks[c(2)] = 1 ∧ c(2) < end(2)
 ∧ end(2) ≤ c(9)}
assume(c < end)              :9
{tasks[c(2)] = 1 ∧ c(2) < end(2)
 ∧ end(2) ≤ c(9)}
tasks[c] := 0                :9
{tasks[c(2)] = 1}
assume(tasks[c] != 1)        :2
{false}
```

(b) Loop example

**Figure 3.** Example traces

do not depend on linear arithmetic in any essential way.

Given a set of variable symbols $V$, we use $\mathsf{Term}(V)$ to denote the set of linear terms with variables drawn from $V$. Similarly, $\mathsf{Formula}(V)$ denotes the set of linear arithmetic formulas with variables drawn from $V$. We here use $V$ as a parameter which we will instantiate according to the context. For example, $\mathsf{Term}(\mathsf{GV} \cup \mathsf{LV})$ denotes the set of terms which may appear in the text of a program (which refers to the thread template), and $\mathsf{Formula}(\mathsf{GV} \cup (\mathsf{LV} \times \mathbb{N}))$ denotes the set of formulas which may appear in a pre- or postcondition (which refers to concrete threads).

We use the notation $[x \mapsto t]$ to denote a substitution which replaces the variable $x$ with the term $t$ and generalize the notation to parallel substitutions in the standard way. The application of a substitution $\rho$ to a formula $\varphi$ (or a term $t$) is denoted $\varphi[\rho]$ (or $t[\rho]$). Two classes of substitutions of particular interest for our technical development are *instantiations* and *permutations*.

- Given an index $\mathtt{i} \in \mathbb{N}$, we use $\iota_{\mathtt{i}}$ to denote the instantiation substitution which replaces each local variable $x \in \mathsf{LV}$ with an indexed local variable $x(\mathtt{i})$. For example, if we take i to be 3 and c is a local variable and next is a global, we have

$$(\mathtt{c} \leq \mathtt{next})[\iota_3] = \mathtt{c}(3) \leq \mathtt{next}$$

- Each permutation $\pi : \mathbb{N} \to \mathbb{N}$ defines a substitution which replaces each indexed local variable $x(\mathtt{i})$ with $x(\pi(\mathtt{i}))$. We abuse notation by identifying each permutation with the substitution it defines. For example if $\pi$ is a permutation which maps $3 \leftrightarrow 1$, then

$$(\mathtt{c}(3) \leq \mathtt{next})[\pi] = \mathtt{c}(1) \leq \mathtt{next}$$

We identify a program $P$ with a control flow graph for a single *thread template* which is executed by an unbounded number of threads. (The extension to more than one thread template is straightforward.) A control flow graph is a directed, labeled graph $P = \langle \mathsf{Loc}, \Sigma, \ell_{\mathsf{init}}, \ell_{\mathsf{err}}, \mathsf{src}, \mathsf{tgt} \rangle$, where $\mathsf{Loc}$ is a set of program locations, $\Sigma$ is a set of program commands, $\ell_{\mathsf{init}}$ is a designated initial location, $\ell_{\mathsf{err}}$ is a designated error location, and $\mathsf{src}, \mathsf{tgt} : \Sigma \to \mathsf{Loc}$ are functions mapping each program command to its source and target location. Note that our definition of a control flow graph (using src and tgt) implies that we distinguish between different occurrences of a program instruction.

A program command $\sigma \in \Sigma$ is of one of two forms:

- an *assignment* of the form $x := t$ where $x \in \mathsf{GV} \cup \mathsf{LV}$ and $t \in \mathsf{Term}(\mathsf{GV} \cup \mathsf{LV})$, or
- an *assumption* of the form $\mathtt{assume}(\varphi)$ where $\varphi \in \mathsf{Formula}(\mathsf{GV} \cup \mathsf{LV})$.

We will denote a pair consisting of a program command $\sigma \in \Sigma$ and an index $\mathtt{i} \in \mathbb{N}$ as the *indexed* command $\langle\sigma : \mathtt{i}\rangle$. Intuitively, such an indexed command $\langle\sigma : \mathtt{i}\rangle$ refers to thread $\mathtt{i}$'s instance of the program command $\sigma$, or: the index $\mathtt{i}$ indicates the identifier of the thread which executes $\sigma$.

A *trace*

$$\tau = \langle\sigma_1 : \mathtt{i}_1\rangle\langle\sigma_2 : \mathtt{i}_2\rangle \cdots \langle\sigma_n : \mathtt{i}_n\rangle$$

is a sequence of indexed commands.

A *Hoare triple* is a triple

$$\{\varphi\} \ \ \tau \ \ \{\psi\}$$

where $\tau$ is a trace and $\varphi$ and $\psi$ are formulas with global variables and indexed local variables, i.e., $\varphi, \psi \in \mathsf{Formula}(\mathsf{GV} \cup (\mathsf{LV} \times \mathbb{N}))$.

The validity of Hoare triples for traces is defined as one would expect. Intuitively, if the command reads or writes the local variable $x$, then the indexed command $\langle\sigma : \mathtt{i}\rangle$ (i.e., the command $\sigma$ executed by thread $\mathtt{i}$) reads or writes thread $\mathtt{i}$'s copy of the local variable $x$. To express this formally, we use the instantiation substitution $\iota_{\mathtt{i}}$ introduced above. In particular, if $x$ is a local variable, $x[\iota_{\mathtt{i}}]$ is the indexed local variable $x(\mathtt{i})$ (and if $x$ is a global variable, $x[\iota_{\mathtt{i}}]$ is simply $x$).

For a trace of length 1 (i.e., for an indexed command), we have:

- $\{\varphi\} \ \ \langle(x := t) : \mathtt{i}\rangle \ \ \{\psi\}$ is valid if
$$\varphi \models \psi[x[\iota_{\mathtt{i}}] \mapsto t[\iota_{\mathtt{i}}]]$$
- $\{\varphi\} \ \ \langle(\mathtt{assume}(\theta)) : \mathtt{i}\rangle \ \ \{\psi\}$ is valid if
$$\varphi \wedge \theta[\iota_{\mathtt{i}}] \models \psi$$

where $\models$ denotes entailment modulo the theory of integer linear arithmetic. For a trace of the form $\tau.\langle\sigma : \mathtt{i}\rangle$, the triple $\{\varphi\} \ \ \tau.\langle\sigma : \mathtt{i}\rangle \ \ \{\psi\}$ is valid if there exists some formula $\psi'$ such that $\{\varphi\} \ \ \tau \ \ \{\psi'\}$ and $\{\psi'\} \ \ \langle\sigma : \mathtt{i}\rangle \ \ \{\psi\}$ are valid.

We call a trace $\tau$ *infeasible* if the Hoare triple $\{true\} \ \ \tau \ \ \{false\}$ is valid. Intuitively, $\tau$ is infeasible if it does not correspond to any execution.

Given a program $P$ (identified by the control flow graph of a single thread template, i.e., a graph with edges labeled by commands $\sigma \in \Sigma$ and with the initial location $\ell_{\mathsf{init}}$ and the error location $\ell_{\mathsf{err}}$), a trace $\tau$ is an *error trace* of $P$ if

- for each index $\mathtt{i} \in \mathbb{N}$, the projection of $\tau$ onto the commands of thread $\mathtt{i}$ corresponds to a path through $P$ starting at $\ell_{\mathsf{init}}$ (i.e., each thread $\mathtt{i}$ starts at the initial location), and
- there is (at least) one index $\mathtt{j} \in \mathbb{N}$ such that the projection of $\tau$ onto the commands of thread $\mathtt{j}$ corresponds to a path through $P$ ending at $\ell_{\mathsf{err}}$ (i.e., some thread $\mathtt{j}$ ends at the error location).

We say that a program $P$ is *correct* if every error trace of $P$ is infeasible (i.e., there is no execution of $P$ wherein some thread reaches the error location $\ell_{\mathsf{err}}$).

The notion of correctness be used to encode many correctness properties including thread-state reachability (and thus the safety of `assert` commands) and mutual exclusion. The encoding is possibly done by introducing monitors (ghost instructions on ghost variables), much in the same way that safety properties can be reduced to non-reachability in sequential programs.

## 4. Proof spaces

We will now introduce *proof spaces*, the central technical idea of this paper. We begin by formalizing the inference rules of SEQUENCING, SYMMETRY, and CONJUNCTION.

The *sequencing rule* is a modification of the familiar one from Hoare logic. We omit the rule of consequence from Hoare logic, and instead incorporate consequence in our sequencing rule: that is, we allow triples $\{\varphi_0\} \ \ \tau_0 \ \ \{\varphi_1\}$ and $\{\varphi_1'\} \ \ \tau_1 \ \ \{\varphi_2\}$ to be composed when $\varphi_1$ and $\varphi_1'$ do not exactly match, but $\varphi_1$ entails $\varphi_1'$. However, a design goal of proof spaces is that the inference rules should be purely combinatorial (and thus, should not require access to a theorem prover to discharge the entailment). Towards this end, we define a *combinatorial entailment* relation $\Vdash$ on formulas: identifying a conjunction with the set of its conjuncts, we have $\varphi \Vdash \psi$ if $\varphi$ is a superset of $\psi$. Formally,

$$\varphi_1 \wedge ... \wedge \varphi_n \Vdash \psi_1 \wedge ... \wedge \psi_m \ \text{ if } \{\varphi_1, ..., \varphi_n\} \supseteq \{\psi_1, ..., \psi_m\}$$

The sequencing rule is formalized as follows:

$$\textsc{Sequencing}\quad \frac{\{\varphi_0\} \ \ \tau_0 \ \ \{\varphi_1\} \qquad \varphi_1 \Vdash \varphi_1' \qquad \{\varphi_1'\} \ \ \tau_1 \ \ \{\varphi_2\}}{\{\varphi_0\} \ \ \tau_0 \, ; \tau_1 \ \ \{\varphi_2\}}$$

The symmetry rule exploits the fact that thread identifiers are interchangeable in our program model, and therefore uniformly permuting thread identifiers in a valid Hoare triple yields another valid Hoare triple:

$$\textsc{Symmetry}\quad \frac{\{\varphi\} \ \ \langle\sigma_1 : \mathtt{i}_1\rangle \cdots \langle\sigma_n : \mathtt{i}_n\rangle \ \ \{\psi\}}{\{\varphi[\pi]\} \ \ \langle\sigma_1 : \pi(\mathtt{i}_1)\rangle \cdots \langle\sigma_n : \pi(\mathtt{i}_n)\rangle \ \ \{\psi[\pi]\}} \quad \begin{array}{c}\pi : \mathbb{N} \to \mathbb{N} \\ \text{is a permutation}\end{array}$$

Lastly, the rule of conjunction allows one to combine two theorems about the same trace by conjoining preconditions and postconditions:

$$\textsc{Conjunction}\quad \frac{\{\varphi_1\} \ \ \tau \ \ \{\psi_1\} \qquad \{\varphi_2\} \ \ \tau \ \ \{\psi_2\}}{\{\varphi_1 \wedge \varphi_2\} \ \ \tau \ \ \{\psi_1 \wedge \psi_2\}}$$

Next, we formalize our notion of a proof space:

**Definition 4.1** (Proof space) A *proof space* $\mathscr{H}$ is a set of valid Hoare triples which is closed under SEQUENCING, SYMMETRY, and CONJUNCTION. ⌟

Our definition restricts proof spaces to contain only valid Hoare triples for the sake of convenience. Clearly, the SEQUENCING, SYMMETRY, and CONJUNCTION rules preserve validity.

The strategy behind using proof spaces as correctness proofs can be summarized in the following proof rule: *If we can find a proof space $\mathscr{H}$ such that for every error trace $\tau$ of the program $P$, we have that the Hoare triple $\{true\} \ \ \tau \ \ \{false\}$ belongs to $\mathscr{H}$, then $P$ is correct.*

Our main interest in proof spaces is using the above proof rule as a foundation for algorithmic verification of concurrent programs. Towards this end, we augment the definition of proof spaces with additional conditions that make them easier to manipulate algorithmically. We call the proof spaces satisfying these conditions *finitely generated proof spaces*. First, we define *basic Hoare triples*, which are the "generators" of such proof spaces.

**Definition 4.2** (Basic Hoare triple) A *basic Hoare triple* is a valid Hoare triple of the form

$$\{\varphi\} \ \ \langle\sigma : \mathtt{i}\rangle \ \ \{\psi\}$$

where

1. the postcondition $\psi$ cannot be constructed by conjoining two other formulas, and

2. for each $j \in \mathbb{N}$, if an indexed local variable of the form $x(j)$ appears in the precondition $\varphi$, then either j is equal to the index i of the command, or $x(j)$ or some other indexed local variable $y(j)$ with the same index j must appear in the postcondition $\psi$ ("the precondition mentions only relevant threads"). ⌟

The asymmetry between the precondition and the postcondition in Condition 1 is justified by the rule of consequence. Given a (non-basic) Hoare triple

$$\{\varphi_0 \wedge \varphi_1\}\ \langle \sigma : \mathtt{i} \rangle\ \{\psi_1 \wedge \psi_2\},$$

we may "split the postcondition" to arrive at two valid triples

$$\{\varphi_0 \wedge \varphi_1\}\ \langle \sigma : \mathtt{i} \rangle\ \{\psi_1\}$$
$$\{\varphi_0 \wedge \varphi_1\}\ \langle \sigma : \mathtt{i} \rangle\ \{\psi_2\}$$

from which the original triple may be derived via CONJUNCTION. As a result, the postcondition restriction on basic Hoare triples does not lose significant generality. Since preconditions cannot be split in this way, Definition 4.2 is asymmetric.

**Definition 4.3** (Finitely generated) We say that a proof space $\mathscr{H}$ is *finitely generated* if there exists a finite set of basic Hoare triples $H$ such that $\mathscr{H}$ is the smallest proof space which contains $H$. In this situation, we call $H$ a *basis* for $\mathscr{H}$. ⌟

Proof spaces give a new proof system for verifying safety properties for multi-threaded programs. The remainder of this paper studies some of the questions which arise from introducing such a proof system. In the next section, we consider the question of the expressive power of proof spaces (that is, what can be proved using proof spaces). In Sections 6 and 7, we discuss how proof spaces may be used in the context of algorithmic verification.

## 5. Completeness

The method of using global inductive invariants to prove correctness of concurrent programs dates back to the seminal work of Ashcroft [4]. Ashcroft's method originally applied to programs with finitely many threads, but can be adapted to the infinite case by admitting into the language of assertions universal quantifiers over threads. In this section, we prove the completeness of proof spaces relative to Ashcroft's method. This establishes that the combinatorial operations of proof spaces are adequate for representing Ashcroft proofs, even though Ashcroft assertions make use of features not available to proof space assertions (namely, universal quantifiers over threads and control assertions).

We start by formalizing Ashcroft proofs. We can treat each local variable as an uninterpreted function symbol of type $\mathbb{N} \to \mathbb{Z}$ (i.e, the interpretation of $x \in \mathsf{LV}$ is a function which maps each thread identifier $\mathtt{i} \in \mathbb{N}$ to the value of thread i's copy of $x$).

We let $\mathsf{TV}$ be a set of *thread variables* which are variables whose values range over the set of thread identifiers $\mathbb{N}$. We typically use $i, j, i_1, \ldots$ to refer to thread variables (note that we use $\mathtt{i}, \mathtt{j}, \mathtt{i}_1, \ldots$ to refer to thread identifiers, i.e., elements of $\mathbb{N}$). We use $\mathsf{LV}[\mathsf{TV}]$ to denote the set of terms $x(i)$ where $x \in \mathsf{LV}$ and $i \in \mathsf{TV}$. A *data assertion* is a linear arithmetic formula $\psi$ built up from global variables and terms of the form $x(i)$ where $x \in \mathsf{LV}$ and $i \in \mathsf{TV}$, i.e., $\psi \in \mathsf{Formula}(\mathsf{GV} \cup \mathsf{LV}[\mathsf{TV}])$.

A *global assertion* is defined to be a sentence of the form

$$\Phi_{\mathsf{inv}} = \forall i_1, \ldots, i_n . \varphi_{\mathsf{inv}}(i_1, \ldots, i_n)$$

where $\varphi_{\mathsf{inv}}$ is a formula built up from Boolean combinations of

- *data assertions*,
- control assertions $\mathsf{loc}(i) = \ell$ (with $i \in \mathsf{TV}$ and $\ell \in \mathsf{Loc}$), and
- thread equalities $i = j$ and disequalities $i \neq j$ (with $i, j \in \mathsf{TV}$).

For any program command $\sigma \in \Sigma$, we use $[\![\sigma]\!]$ to denote the transition formula which represents *some* thread executing $\sigma$. This is a formula over an extended vocabulary which includes a primed copy of each of the global and local variable symbols (interpreted as the post-state values of those variables). This formula is of the form

$$\exists i. \psi^1(i) \wedge (\forall j. \psi^2(i, j))$$

where (intuitively) $\psi^1$ describes the state change for the thread which executes $\sigma$ (thread $i$), and $\psi^2$ describes the state change for all other threads (thread $j$). For example, if $\sigma$ is an assignment $x := x + g$ where $x$ is local, $g$ is global, and $\ell = \mathsf{src}(\sigma)$ and $\ell' = \mathsf{tgt}(\sigma)$, then:

$$[\![\sigma]\!] \equiv \exists i. \Big(\mathsf{loc}(i) = \ell \wedge \mathsf{loc}'(i) = \ell' \wedge x'(i) = x(i) + g \wedge g' = g$$
$$\wedge \forall j \neq i. \big(\mathsf{loc}(j) = \mathsf{loc}'(j) \wedge x(j) = x'(j)\big)\Big).$$

We may now formally define Ashcroft invariants:

**Definition 5.1** (Ashcroft invariant) Given a program $P$, an *Ashcroft invariant* is a global assertion $\Phi_{\mathsf{inv}}$ such that

1. $\forall i. \mathsf{loc}(i) = \ell_{\mathsf{init}}$ entails $\Phi_{\mathsf{inv}}$.
2. For any command $\sigma \in \Sigma$, we have that $\Phi_{\mathsf{inv}} \wedge [\![\sigma]\!]$ entails $\Phi'_{\mathsf{inv}}$ (where $\Phi'_{\mathsf{inv}}$ denotes the formula obtained by replacing the symbols in $\Phi_{\mathsf{inv}}$ with their primed copies)
3. $\Phi_{\mathsf{inv}}$ entails $\forall i. \mathsf{loc}(i) \neq \ell_{\mathsf{err}}$. ⌟

Clearly, the existence of an Ashcroft invariant for a program implies its correctness (that is, that the error location of the program is unreachable). The following theorem is the main result of this section, which establishes the completeness of proof spaces relative to Ashcroft invariants.

**Theorem 5.2** (Relative completeness) Let $P$ be a program. If there is an Ashcroft invariant which proves the correctness of $P$, then there is a finitely generated proof space which proves the correctness of $P$. ⌟

*Proof.* To simplify notation, we will prove the result only for the case that the Ashcroft proof has two quantified thread variables. The generalization to an arbitrary number of quantified thread variables is straightforward.

Let $P$ be a program, and let $\Phi_{\mathsf{inv}}$ be an Ashcroft proof. Without loss of generality, we may assume that $\Phi_{\mathsf{inv}}$ is written as

$$\Phi_{\mathsf{inv}} \equiv (\forall i \bigvee_{\ell \in \mathsf{Loc}} \mathsf{loc}(i) = \ell \wedge \varphi_\ell(i))$$
$$\wedge (\forall i \neq j. \bigvee_{\ell, \ell' \in \mathsf{Loc} \times \mathsf{Loc}} \mathsf{loc}(i) = \ell \wedge \mathsf{loc}(j) = \ell' \wedge \varphi_{\ell, \ell'}(i, j)))$$

where each $\varphi_\ell(i)$ and $\varphi_{\ell,\ell'}(i,j)$ is a integer arithmetic formula (i.e., does not contain loc). Furthermore, we can assume that $\Phi_{\mathsf{inv}}$ is *symmetric* in the sense that $\varphi_{\ell,\ell'}(i,j)$ is syntactically equal to $\varphi_{\ell',\ell}(j,i)$ and that $\varphi_{\ell,\ell'}(i,j)$ entails $\varphi_\ell(i)$ (for any $i, j, \ell, \ell'$). We can prove that any $\Phi_{\mathsf{inv}}$ can be written in this form by induction on $\Phi_{\mathsf{inv}}$ We also assume that $\varphi_{\ell_{\mathsf{err}}}(i) = \mathit{false}$ and $\varphi_{\ell_{\mathsf{init}}}(i) = \varphi_{\ell_{\mathsf{init}}, \ell_{\mathsf{init}}}(i, j) = \mathit{true}$; the fact that this loses no generality is a consequence of conditions 1 and 3 of Definition 5.1. Finally, we assume that each formula $\varphi_\ell(i)$ and $\varphi_{\ell,\ell'}(i,j)$ is not (syntactically) a conjunction (cf. Condition 1 of Definition 4.2): this assumption is validated by observing any formula $\varphi$ is equivalent to $\varphi \vee \mathit{false}$, which is not a (syntactic) conjunction.

We construct a set of basic Hoare triples $H$ by collecting the set of all Hoare triples of the following four types:

$$\{\varphi_{\ell_1}(1)\}\ \langle \sigma : 1 \rangle\ \{\varphi_{\ell_1'}(1)\}$$

$$\{\varphi_{\ell_1, \ell_2}(1, 2)\}\ \langle \sigma : 1 \rangle\ \{\varphi_{\ell_2}(2)\}$$

$$\{\varphi_{\ell_1,\ell_2}(1,2)\}\ \langle\sigma : \mathtt{1}\rangle\ \{\varphi_{\ell_1',\ell_2}(1,2)\}$$

$$\{\varphi_{\ell_1,\ell_2}(1,2) \wedge \varphi_{\ell_1,\ell_3}(1,3) \wedge \varphi_{\ell_2,\ell_3}(2,3)\}\ \langle\sigma : \mathtt{1}\rangle\ \{\varphi_{\ell_2,\ell_3}(2,3)\}$$

where $\mathsf{src}(\sigma) = \ell_1$ and $\mathsf{tgt}(\sigma) = \ell_1'$.

We now must show that (1) each Hoare triple in $H$ is basic (i.e., satisfies Definition 4.2) and (2) for every trace $\tau$ of $P$, $\{true\}\ \ \tau\ \ \{false\}$ belongs to the proof space generated by $H$. Condition (2) is delayed to Section 6, where we prove a stronger result (Proposition 6.14). Here, we will just prove condition (1).

One can easily observe that conditions 1 and 2 of Definition 4.2 hold. It remains to show that each Hoare triple in $H$ is valid. We will prove only the validity of the Hoare triple

$$\{\varphi_{\ell_1,\ell_2}(1,2)\}\ \langle\sigma : \mathtt{1}\rangle\ \{\varphi_{\ell_1',\ell_2}(1,2)\}$$

where $\mathsf{src}(\sigma) = \ell_1$ and $\mathsf{tgt}(\sigma) = \ell_1'$. The other cases are similar.

Let us write $[\![\sigma]\!]$ as $\exists i.\psi^1(i) \wedge (\forall k.\psi^2(i,k))$. For a proof by contradiction, let us suppose that the above Hoare triple is invalid. This means:

$$\varphi_{\ell_1,\ell_2}(1,2) \wedge \psi^1(1) \wedge (\forall k.\psi^2(1,k)) \not\models \varphi_{\ell_1',\ell_2}(1,2)'$$

It follows that there exists a structure $\mathfrak{A}$ such that

$$\mathfrak{A} \models \varphi_{\ell_1,\ell_2}(1,2) \wedge \psi^1(1) \wedge (\forall k.\psi^2(1,k))$$

and $\mathfrak{A} \not\models \varphi_{\ell_1',\ell_2}(1,2)'$. Without loss of generality, we may assume that $\mathsf{loc}(2)^{\mathfrak{A}} = \mathsf{loc}'(2)^{\mathfrak{A}} = \ell_2$. Our strategy will be to construct from $\mathfrak{A}$ a structure $\mathfrak{B}$ such that

$$\mathfrak{B} \models \Phi_{\mathsf{inv}} \wedge \psi^1(1) \wedge (\forall k.\psi^2(1,k))$$

but $\mathfrak{B} \not\models \Phi_{\mathsf{inv}}'$, which contradicts condition 2 of Definition 5.1.

We obtain $\mathfrak{B}$ simply by restricting the interpretation of the $\mathsf{Thread}$ sort to the set $\{1,2\}$ (intuitively: we consider a configuration of the program in which 1 and 2 are the only threads). Then we have

$$\mathfrak{B} \models \varphi_{\ell_1,\ell_2}(1,2) \wedge \psi^1(1) \wedge (\forall k.\psi^2(1,k))$$

by downward absoluteness of universal sentences and $\mathfrak{B} \not\models \varphi_{\ell_1',\ell_2}(1,2)'$ by upward absoluteness of quantifier-free sentences.

From $\mathfrak{B} \models \psi^1(1)$, we have $\mathfrak{B} \models \mathsf{loc}(1) = \ell_1$. By assumption, we have $\mathfrak{B} \models \mathsf{loc}(2) = \ell_2$. It follows that

$$\mathfrak{B} \models \varphi_{\ell_1,\ell_2}(1,2) \wedge \mathsf{loc}(1) = \ell_1 \wedge \mathsf{loc}(2) = \ell_2$$

and thus, from the symmetry condition imposed on $\Phi_{\mathsf{inv}}$, that $\mathfrak{B} \models \Phi_{\mathsf{inv}}$. It is then easy to see that

$$\mathfrak{B} \models \Phi_{\mathsf{inv}} \wedge \psi^1(1) \wedge (\forall k.\psi^2(1,k))$$

holds. Finally, we note that since $\mathfrak{B} \models \mathsf{loc}'(1) = \ell_1' \wedge \mathsf{loc}'(2) = \ell_2$ and $\mathfrak{B} \not\models \varphi_{\ell_1',\ell_2}(1,2)$, $\mathfrak{B}$ is incompatible with every disjunct of

$$\bigvee_{\ell,\ell' \in \mathsf{Loc}\times\mathsf{Loc}} \mathsf{loc}'(1) = \ell \wedge \mathsf{loc}'(2) = \ell' \wedge \varphi_{\ell,\ell'}'(1,2)$$

and thus $\mathfrak{B} \not\models \Phi_{\mathsf{inv}}'$.

□

As we mentioned previously, Ashcroft invariants are able to make use of features which are not available to proof spaces, namely control assertions (i.e., assertions of the form $\mathsf{loc}(i) = \ell$) and universal quantification over thread variables. These "exotic" features are typical for program logics for concurrent programs with unbounded parallelism. As a general rule, classical verification techniques for sequential programs do not synthesize assertions which make use of these features. The price we pay for the relative ease of generating proof spaces is the relative difficulty of checking them. We address this topic in the next section.

## 6. Proof checking

We now turn to the main algorithmic problem suggested by the proof rule for proof spaces presented in Section 4: *given a program $P$ and a finite basis $H$ of a proof space $\mathscr{H}$, how do we check whether for every error trace $\tau$ we have that $\{true\}\ \ \tau\ \ \{false\}$ belongs to $\mathscr{H}$?* Our solution to this problem begins by introducing a new class of automata, *predicate automata*, which can be used to represent both the set of error traces of a program and the set of traces $\tau$ which have the infeasibility theorem $\{true\}\ \ \tau\ \ \{false\}$ in a finitely generated proof space. We show that the problem of checking whether for every error trace $\tau$ we have that $\{true\}\ \ \tau\ \ \{false\}$ belongs to $\mathscr{H}$ can be reduced to the emptiness problem for predicate automata. We show that the general emptiness checking problem is undecidable, and we give a semi-algorithm and show that it is a decision procedure for an interesting sub-class of predicate automata which correspond to thread-modular proofs.

### 6.1 Predicate automata

Predicate automata are a class of infinite-state automata which recognize languages over an infinite alphabet of the form $\Sigma \times \mathbb{N}$.[1] For readers familiar with alternating finite automata (AFA) [8, 9], a helpful analogy might be that predicate automata are to first-order logic what AFA are to propositional logic. A predicate automaton (PA) is equipped with a relational *vocabulary* $\langle Q, ar\rangle$ (in the usual sense of first-order logic) consisting of a finite set of predicate symbols $Q$ and a function $ar : Q \to \mathbb{N}$ which maps each predicate symbol to its arity. A state of a PA is a proposition $q(\mathtt{i}_1, ..., \mathtt{i}_{ar(q)})$, where $q \in Q$ and $\mathtt{i}_1, ..., \mathtt{i}_{ar(q)} \in \mathbb{N}$. The transition function maps such states to formulas in the vocabulary of the PA (where disjunction corresponds to nondeterministic (existential) choice, and conjunction corresponds to universal choice). It is important to note that the symbols $q \in Q$ are "uninterpreted": they have no special semantics, and any subset of $\mathbb{N}^{ar(q)}$ is a valid interpretation of $q$.

Given a vocabulary $\langle Q, ar\rangle$ (and given the set $\mathsf{TV}$ of thread variables, i.e., variables whose values range over the set of thread identifiers $\mathbb{N}$), we define the set of *positive formulas* $\mathcal{F}(Q, ar)$ over $\langle Q, ar\rangle$ to be the set of negation-free formulas where each atom is either (1) a proposition of the form $q(i_1, ..., i_n)$ (where $i_1, ..., i_n \in \mathsf{TV}$), or (2) an equation $i = j$ (where $i, j \in \mathsf{TV}$), or (3) a disequation $i \neq j$ (where $i, j \in \mathsf{TV}$). Predicate automata are defined as follows:

**Definition 6.1** (Predicate automata) A *predicate automaton* (PA) is a 6-tuple $A = \langle Q, ar, \Sigma, \delta, \varphi_{\mathsf{start}}, F\rangle$ where

- $\langle Q, ar\rangle$ is a relational vocabulary
- $\Sigma$ is a finite alphabet
- $\varphi_{\mathsf{start}} \in \mathcal{F}(Q, ar)$ is an initial formula with no free variables.
- $F \subseteq Q$ is a set of accepting predicate symbols
- $\delta : Q \times \Sigma \to \mathcal{F}(Q, ar)$ is a transition function which satisfies the property that for any $q \in Q$ and $\sigma \in \Sigma$, the free variables of $\delta(q,\sigma)$ are members of the set $\{i_0, ..., i_{ar(q)}\}$. ⌟

To understand the restriction on the variables in the formula $\delta(q,\sigma)$, it may be intuitively helpful to think of $q$ as $q(i_1, ..., i_{ar(q)})$ and of $\sigma$ as $\langle\sigma : i_0\rangle$.

We will elucidate this definition by first describing the dynamics of a PA. PA dynamics will be defined by a nondeterministic[2] transition system where edges are labeled by elements of the indexed

[1] Such languages are commonly called *data languages* [32].

[2] Readers familiar with AFA should note that we are effectively describing the "nondeterminization" of PA.

alphabet $\Sigma \times \mathbb{N}$, and where the nodes of the transition system are *configurations* which we will introduce next:

**Definition 6.2** (Configuration) Let $A = \langle Q, ar, \Sigma, \delta, \varphi_{\mathsf{start}}, F\rangle$ be a PA. A *configuration* $\mathcal{C}$ of $A$ is finite set of ground propositions of the form $q(\mathtt{i}_1, ..., \mathtt{i}_{ar(q)})$, where $q \in Q$ and $\mathtt{i}_1, ..., \mathtt{i}_{ar(q)} \in \mathbb{N}$. ⌟

It is convenient to identify a configuration $\mathcal{C}$ with the formula $\bigwedge_{q(\mathtt{i}_1,...,\mathtt{i}_{ar(q)})\in\mathcal{C}} q(\mathtt{i}_1, ..., \mathtt{i}_{ar(q)})$. We define the *initial* configurations of $A$ to be the cubes of the disjunctive normal form (DNF) of $\varphi_{\mathsf{start}}$ (for example, if $\varphi_{\mathsf{start}}$ is $p \wedge (q \vee r)$, then the initial configurations are $p \wedge q$ and $p \wedge r$). A configuration is *accepting* if for all $q(\mathtt{i}_1, ..., \mathtt{i}_{ar(q)}) \in \mathcal{C}$, we have $q \in F$; otherwise, it is *rejecting*.

A PA $A = \langle Q, ar, \Sigma, \delta, \varphi_{\mathsf{start}}, F\rangle$ induces a transition relation on configurations as follows:

$$\mathcal{C} \xrightarrow{\sigma:\mathtt{k}} \mathcal{C}'$$

if $\mathcal{C}'$ is a cube in the DNF of the formula

$$\bigwedge_{q(\mathtt{i}_1,...,\mathtt{i}_{ar(q)})\in\mathcal{C}} \delta(q,\sigma)[i_0 \mapsto \mathtt{k}, i_1 \mapsto \mathtt{i}_1, ..., i_{ar(q)} \mapsto \mathtt{i}_{ar(q)}]$$

The fact that the free variables of $\delta(q, \sigma)$ must belong to the set $\{i_0, ..., i_{ar(q)}\}$ guarantees that the formula above has no free variables, and therefore its DNF corresponds to a set of configurations. Note also that the formula above may contain equalities and disequalities, but since they are ground (have no free variables), they are equivalent to either *true* or *false*, and thus can be eliminated.

We can think of $\delta(q, \sigma)$ as a rewrite rule whose application instantiates the (implicit) formal parameters $i_1, ..., i_{ar(q)}$ of $q$ to the actual parameters $\mathtt{i}_1, ..., \mathtt{i}_n$ and instantiates $i_0$ to $\mathtt{k}$ (the index of the letter being read). In light of this interpretation, we will often write $\delta$ in a form that makes the (implicit) formal parameters explicit: for example, instead of

$$\begin{aligned}\delta(q,\sigma) =& (i_0 \neq i_1 \wedge (q(i_0, i_1) \vee q(i_1, i_2))) \\ &\vee (i_0 = i_1 \wedge q(i_1, i_2) \wedge q(i_2, i_1))\end{aligned}$$

we will typically write

$$\begin{aligned}\delta(q(i,j), \langle\sigma : k\rangle) =& (k \neq i \wedge (q(k, i) \vee q(i, j))) \\ &\vee (k = i \wedge q(i, j) \wedge q(j, i)) \,.\end{aligned}$$

A trace $\tau = \langle\sigma_1 : \mathtt{i}_1\rangle \cdots \langle\sigma_n : \mathtt{i}_n\rangle$ is accepted by $A$ if there is a sequence of configurations $\mathcal{C}_n, ..., \mathcal{C}_0$ such that:

1. $\mathcal{C}_n$ is initial
2. for each $r \in \{1, ..., n\}$, $\mathcal{C}_r \xrightarrow{\sigma_r:\mathtt{i}_r} \mathcal{C}_{r-1}$
3. $\mathcal{C}_0$ is accepting

It is important to note that the definition of acceptance implies that a PA reads its input from right to left rather than left to right. We will discuss the reason behind this when we explain the correspondence between proof spaces and predicate automata (Proposition 6.4).

Our first example of a predicate automaton will be the one constructed to accept the language of error traces of a program:

**Proposition 6.3** Given a program $P$, there is a predicate automaton $A_P$ such that $\mathcal{L}(A_P)$ is the set of error traces of $P$. ⌟

*Proof.* Let $P$ be a program given by the thread template

$$P = \langle \mathsf{Loc}, \Sigma, \ell_{\mathsf{init}}, \ell_{\mathsf{err}}, \mathsf{src}, \mathsf{tgt}\rangle \,.$$

We define a PA $A_P = \langle Q, ar, \Sigma, \delta, \varphi_{\mathsf{start}}, F\rangle$, which closely mirrors the (reversed) control structure of $P$.

- $Q = \{\mathsf{loc}, \mathsf{err}\} \cup \mathsf{Loc}$, where $\mathsf{err}$ and $\mathsf{loc}$ are distinguished predicate symbols, to be explained in the following.
- $ar(\mathsf{loc}) = ar(\mathsf{err}) = 0$ and for all $\ell \in \mathsf{Loc}$, $ar(\ell) = 1$
- Let $\sigma \in \Sigma$ with, say, $\ell_1 = \mathsf{src}(\sigma)$ and $\ell_2 = \mathsf{tgt}(\sigma)$.

  The transition rule for a location $\ell \in \mathsf{Loc}$ is given by

  $$\delta(\ell(i), \langle\sigma : j\rangle) = \begin{cases}(i = j \wedge \ell_1(i)) \vee (i \neq j \wedge \ell(i)) & \text{if } \ell = \ell_2 \\ i \neq j \wedge \ell(i) & \text{if } \ell \neq \ell_2\end{cases}$$

  The transition rule for $\mathsf{loc}$ is given by

  $$\delta(\mathsf{loc}, \langle\sigma : i\rangle) = \mathsf{loc} \wedge \ell_1(i)$$

  The transition rule for $\mathsf{err}$ is given by

  $$\delta(\mathsf{err}, \langle\sigma : i\rangle) = \begin{cases}\ell_1(i) & \text{if } \ell_2 = \ell_{\mathsf{err}} \\ \mathsf{err} & \text{if } \ell_2 \neq \ell_{\mathsf{err}}\end{cases}$$

- $\varphi_{\mathsf{start}} = \mathsf{loc} \wedge \mathsf{err}$
- $F = \{\ell_{\mathsf{init}}, \mathsf{loc}\}$

Intuitively, the distinguished predicate symbol $\mathsf{err}$ represents "some thread is at the error location." The $\mathsf{loc}$ predicate is responsible for "initializing" the program counter of threads (in the backwards direction). That is, $\mathsf{loc}$ ensures that in every reachable configuration $\mathcal{C}$ of $A_P$, every $\sigma \in \Sigma$ and every $\mathtt{i} \in \mathbb{N}$, we have that if $\mathcal{C} \xrightarrow{\sigma:\mathtt{i}} \mathcal{C}'$, then $\ell_1(\mathtt{i}) \in \mathcal{C}'$, where $\ell_1 = \mathsf{src}(\sigma)$. For example, let $\sigma \in \Sigma$ with $\ell_1 = \mathsf{src}(\sigma)$ and $\ell_2 = \mathsf{tgt}(\sigma)$. By reading $\langle\sigma : 3\rangle$, the initial configuration $\mathsf{loc} \wedge \mathsf{err}$ may transition to $\ell_1(3) \wedge \mathsf{loc} \wedge \mathsf{err}$ if $\ell_2$ is not $\ell_{\mathsf{err}}$ or to $\ell_1(3) \wedge \mathsf{loc}$ if $\ell_2$ is $\ell_{\mathsf{err}}$.

We omit a formal proof that $\mathcal{L}(A_P)$ is indeed the set of error traces of $P$. □

As the following proposition states, predicate automata are also sufficiently powerful to represent the set of traces which are proved correct by a given finitely-generated proof space.

**Proposition 6.4** Let $\mathscr{H}$ be a proof space which is generated by a finite set of basic Hoare triples $H$. There exists a PA $A_H$ (which can be computed effectively from $H$) such that $\mathcal{L}(A_H)$ is exactly the set of traces $\tau$ such that $\{\mathit{true}\}\ \tau\ \{\mathit{false}\} \in \mathscr{H}$. ⌟

*Proof.* Let $H$ be a set of basic Hoare triples. The predicate automaton $A_H = \langle Q, ar, \Sigma, \delta, \varphi_{\mathsf{start}}, F\rangle$ closely mirrors the structure of $H$: intuitively, the predicates of $A_H$ correspond to the assertions used in $H$, and each Hoare triple corresponds to a transition in $\delta$.

The key step in defining $A_H$ is to show how each Hoare triple in $H$ corresponds to a transition rule (noting that if there are several Hoare triples with the same postcondition, we may combine their transition rules disjunctively). For a concrete example, consider the Hoare triple:

$$\{\mathtt{t(3)} \geq 0 \wedge \mathtt{t(9)} > \mathtt{t(3)}\}\ \langle \mathtt{t\ :=\ 2*t} : 9\rangle\ \{\mathtt{t(9)} > \mathtt{t(3)}\}$$

This triple corresponds to the transition

$$\begin{aligned}\delta([\mathtt{t(1)} > \mathtt{t(2)}](i,j), \sigma : k) =& i \neq j \wedge i = k \wedge j \neq k \\ &\wedge [\mathtt{t(1)} \geq 0](j) \wedge [\mathtt{t(1)} > \mathtt{t(2)}](k, j)\end{aligned}$$

The predicates which appear in this formula are *canonical names* for the formulas in the Hoare triples (e.g., $[\mathtt{t(1)} \geq 0]$ is the canonical name for $\mathtt{t(3)} \geq 0$).

After constructing the transition relation as in the example, we construct $A_H$ by taking the set of predicates to be the canonical names for formulas which appear in $H$, $[\mathit{false}]$ to be the initial formula, and $\{[\mathit{true}]\}$ to be the set of final formulas. □

The construction of a PA from a set of basic Hoare triples for Proposition 6.4 reveals that the reason we defined predicate automata to read a trace backwards (i.e., the sequence of indexed commands from right to left) is the asymmetry between pre- and postconditions in basic Hoare triples. Definition 4.2 requires that the postcondition of a basic Hoare triple cannot be constructed by conjoining two other formulas, while the precondition is arbitrary (i.e., we may think of the postcondition as a single proposition, while the precondition is a set of propositions). Since the transition function of a PA is defined on single propositions, the action of a transition must transform a postcondition to its precondition, which necessitates reading the traces backwards.

Propositions 6.3 and 6.4 together imply that the problem of checking whether a proof space proves the correctness of every trace of a program can be reduced to the language inclusion problem for predicate automata. The following proposition reduces the problem further to the emptiness problem for predicate automata (noting that $\mathcal{L}(A_P) \subseteq \mathcal{L}(A_H)$ is equivalent to $\mathcal{L}(A_P) \cap \overline{\mathcal{L}(A_H)} = \emptyset$):

**Proposition 6.5** Predicate automata languages are closed under intersection and complement. ⌟

*Proof.* The constructions for intersection and complementation of predicate automata follow the classical ones for alternating finite automata.

Let $A$ and $A'$ be PAs. We form their intersection $A \cap A'$ by taking the vocabulary to be the disjoint union of the vocabularies of $A$ and $A'$, and define the transition relation and accepting predicates accordingly. The initial formula is obtained by conjoining the initial formulas of $A$ and $A'$.

Given a PA $A = \langle Q, ar, \Sigma, \delta, \varphi_{\mathsf{start}}, F\rangle$, we form its complement $\overline{A} = \langle \overline{Q}, \overline{ar}, \Sigma, \overline{\delta}, \overline{\varphi_{\mathsf{start}}}, \overline{F}\rangle$ as follows.

We define the vocabulary $(\overline{Q}, \overline{ar})$ to be a "negated copy" of $(Q, ar)$: $\overline{Q} = \{\overline{q} : q \in Q\}$ and $\overline{ar}(\overline{q}) = ar(q)$. The set of accepting predicate symbols is the (negated) set of rejecting predicate symbols from $A$: $\overline{F} = \{\overline{q} \in \overline{Q} : q \in Q \setminus F\}$. For any formula $\varphi$ in $\mathcal{F}(Q, ar)$, we use $\overline{\varphi}$ to denote the "De Morganization" of $\varphi$, defined recursively by:

- $\overline{q(\vec{i})} = \overline{q}(\vec{i})$
- $\overline{i = j} = i \neq j$ and $\overline{i \neq j} = i = j$
- $\overline{\varphi \wedge \psi} = \overline{\varphi} \vee \overline{\psi}$ and $\overline{\varphi \vee \psi} = \overline{\varphi} \wedge \overline{\psi}$

We define the transition function and initial formula of $\overline{A}$ by De Morganization: $\overline{\delta}(\overline{q}, \sigma) = \overline{\delta(q, \sigma)}$ and the initial formula is $\overline{\varphi_{\mathsf{start}}}$. □

## 6.2 Checking emptiness for predicate automata

In this section, we give a semi-algorithm for checking PA emptiness which is sound (when the procedure terminates, it gives the correct answer) and complete for counter-examples (if the PA accepts a word, the procedure terminates). Our procedure for checking PA language emptiness is a variant of the tree-saturation algorithm for well-structured transition systems (cf. [18]). The algorithm is essentially a state-space exploration of a predicate automaton (starting from an initial configuration, searching for a reachable accepting configuration), but with one crucial improvement: we equip the state space with a *covering* pre-order, and prune the search space by removing all of those configurations which are not minimal with respect to this order. The key insight behind the development of well-structured transition systems is that, if the order satisfies certain conditions (namely, it is a well-quasi order[3]) this pruning strategy is sufficient to ensure termination of the search (i.e., although the search space may be infinite, the pruned search space is finite).

[3] A well-quasi order (wqo) is a preorder $\preceq$ such that for any infinite sequence $\{x_i\}_{i \in \mathbb{N}}$ there exists $i < j$ such that $x_i \preceq x_j$.

We begin by defining the covering relation on PA configurations:

**Definition 6.6** (Covering) Given a PA $A = \langle Q, ar, \Sigma, \delta, \varphi_{\mathsf{start}}, F\rangle$, we define the *covering pre-order* $\preceq$ on the configurations of $A$ as follows: if $\mathcal{C}$ and $\mathcal{C}'$ are configurations of $A$, then $\mathcal{C} \preceq \mathcal{C}'$ ("$\mathcal{C}$ *covers* $\mathcal{C}'$") if there is a permutation $\pi : \mathbb{N} \to \mathbb{N}$ such that for all $q \in Q$ and all $q(\mathtt{i}_1, .., \mathtt{i}_{ar(q)}) \in \mathcal{C}$, we have $q(\pi(\mathtt{i}_1), ..., \pi(\mathtt{i}_{ar(q)})) \in \mathcal{C}'$. ⌟

The idea behind the pruning strategy is that if two configurations $\mathcal{C}$ and $\mathcal{C}'$ are both in the search space and $\mathcal{C} \preceq \mathcal{C}'$, then we may remove $\mathcal{C}'$. The correctness of this strategy relies on the fact that if $\mathcal{C} \preceq \mathcal{C}'$ and an accepting configuration is reachable from $\mathcal{C}'$, then an accepting configuration is reachable from $\mathcal{C}$ (and thus, if an accepting configuration is reachable, then an accepting configuration is reachable without going through $\mathcal{C}'$). This fact follows from a downwards compatibility lemma:

**Lemma 6.7** (Downwards compatibility) Let $A$ be a PA and let $\mathcal{C}$ and $\mathcal{C}'$ be configurations of $A$ such that $\mathcal{C} \preceq \mathcal{C}'$. Then we have the following:

1. If $\mathcal{C}'$ is accepting, then $\mathcal{C}$ is accepting.
2. For any $\langle \sigma : \mathtt{j}\rangle \in \Sigma \times \mathbb{N}$, if we have

$$\mathcal{C}' \xrightarrow{\sigma:\mathtt{j}} \overline{\mathcal{C}}'$$

then there exists a configuration $\overline{\mathcal{C}}$ and an index $\mathtt{k} \in \mathbb{N}$ such that

$$\mathcal{C} \xrightarrow{\sigma:\mathtt{k}} \overline{\mathcal{C}}$$

and $\overline{\mathcal{C}} \preceq \overline{\mathcal{C}}'$. ⌟

We now develop our algorithm in more detail. In the remainder of this section, let us fix a predicate automaton $A = \langle Q, ar, \Sigma, \delta, \varphi_{\mathsf{start}}, F\rangle$.

State-space exploration of PA is complicated by the fact that the alphabet $\Sigma \times \mathbb{N}$ is infinite and therefore PAs are infinitely branching (although for a fixed letter, each configuration has only finitely many successors). The key to solving this problem is that all but finitely many $\mathtt{i} \in \mathbb{N}$ are indistinguishable from the perspective of a given configuration $\mathcal{C}$. With this in mind, let us define the *support* $\mathsf{supp}(\mathcal{C})$ of a configuration $\mathcal{C}$ to be the set of all indices which appear in $\mathcal{C}$; formally,

$$\mathsf{supp}(\mathcal{C}) = \{\mathtt{i}_r : q(\mathtt{i}_1, ..., \mathtt{i}_{ar(q)}) \in \mathcal{C}, 1 \leq r \leq ar(q)\}$$

Intuitively, if $\mathtt{i}, \mathtt{j} \notin \mathsf{supp}(\mathcal{C})$, then $\mathtt{i}$ and $\mathtt{j}$ are effectively indistinguishable starting from $\mathcal{C}$. This intuition is formalized in the following lemma:

**Lemma 6.8** Let $\mathcal{C}$ be a configuration, $\mathtt{k}_1, \mathtt{k}_2 \in \mathbb{N} \setminus \mathsf{supp}(\mathcal{C})$, and $\sigma \in \Sigma$. For all configurations $\mathcal{C}_1$ such that $\mathcal{C} \xrightarrow{\sigma:\mathtt{k}_1} \mathcal{C}_1$, there exists a configuration $\mathcal{C}_2$ such that $\mathcal{C} \xrightarrow{\sigma:\mathtt{k}_2} \mathcal{C}_2$ and $\mathcal{C}_1 \preceq \mathcal{C}_2$ and $\mathcal{C}_2 \preceq \mathcal{C}_1$. ⌟

As a result of this lemma, from a given configuration $\mathcal{C}$, it is sufficient to explore $\langle \sigma : \mathtt{i}\rangle$ such that $\mathtt{i} \in \mathsf{supp}(\mathcal{C})$, plus one additional $\mathtt{j} \notin \mathsf{supp}(\mathcal{C})$. In our algorithm we simply choose the additional $\mathtt{j}$ to be 1 more than the maximum index in $\mathsf{supp}(\mathcal{C})$.

Finally, we state our procedure for PA emptiness in Algorithm 1. This algorithm operates by expanding a reachability forest $(N, E)$ where the nodes $(N)$ are configurations and the edges $(E)$ are labeled by indexed letters. The frontier of the reachability tree is kept in a worklist *worklist*, and the set of *closed* nodes (configurations which have already been expanded) is kept in $Closed$.

**Theorem 6.9** Algorithm 1 is sound and is complete for non-emptiness: given a predicate automaton $A$, if Algorithm 1 returns Empty, then $\mathcal{L}(A)$ is $\emptyset$, and if $\mathcal{L}(A)$ is nonempty, then Algorithm 1 returns a word in $\mathcal{L}(A)$. ⌟

```
Input: predicate automaton A = ⟨Q, Σ, δ, φ_start, F⟩
Output: Empty, if L(A) is empty; a word w ∈ L(A), if not
Closed ← ∅;
N ← ∅;
E ← ∅;
worklist ← dnf(φ_start) ;
while worklist ≠ [] do
    C ← head(worklist);
    worklist ← tail(worklist);
    if ¬∃C' ∈ Closed s.t. C' ⪯ C then
        /* Expand C                                        */
        foreach i ∈ supp(C) ∪ {1 + max supp(C)} do
            foreach σ ∈ Σ do
                foreach C' s.t. C --σ:i--> C' and C' ∉ N do
                    N ← N ∪ {C'};
                    E ← E ∪ {C --σ:i--> C'};
                    if C' is accepting then
                        return word w labeling the path in
                        the graph (N, E) from C' to a root;
                    else
                        worklist ← worklist ++[C'];
                    end
                end
            end
        end
    end
    Closed ← Closed ∪ {C};
end
return Empty
```

**Algorithm 1:** Emptiness check for predicate automata

### 6.3 Decidability results

Although Algorithm 1 is sound and complete for non-emptiness, it is *not* complete for emptiness: Algorithm 1 may fail to terminate in the case that the language of the input PA is empty. In fact, this must be the case for any algorithm, because PA emptiness is undecidable in the general case:

**Proposition 6.10** General PA emptiness is undecidable. ⌟

*Proof.* The idea behind the proof is to reduce the halting problem for two-counter Minsky machines to the problem of deciding emptiness of a predicate automaton. The reduction uses two binary predicates, $ln_1$ and $ln_2$ to encode the value of the two counters: for example, a configuration

$$ln_1(4,3) \wedge ln_1(3,5) \wedge ln_1(5,1) \wedge ln_2(2,8)$$

encodes that the value of counter 1 is 3, while the value of counter 2 is 1 (i.e., the value of counter $i$ corresponds to the length of the chain $ln_i$). The challenging part of this construction is to encode zero-tests, but we omit this technical discussion from the paper. □

***Monadic predicate automata.*** Since PA emptiness is undecidable in general, it is interesting to consider subclasses where it is decidable. We say that a predicate automaton $A = \langle Q, ar, \Sigma, \delta, \varphi_{\mathsf{start}}, F\rangle$ is *monadic* if for all $q \in Q$, $ar(q) \leq 1$. We have the following:

**Proposition 6.11** Algorithm 1 terminates for monadic predicate automata (i.e., emptiness is decidable for the class of monadic predicate automata, and Algorithm 1 is a decision procedure). ⌟

*Proof.* A sufficient (but not necessary) condition for Algorithm 1 to terminate is if $\preceq$ is a well-quasi order (wqo) - this is a standard result from well-structured transition systems. The fact that $\preceq$ is a well-quasi order on configurations of monadic predicate automata follows easily from Dickson's lemma.

The fact that Algorithm 1 is a decision procedure for the emptiness problem for monadic predicate automata follows from Theorem 6.9 and the fact that it terminates. □

The PA for a program (Proposition 6.3) always corresponds to a monadic PA; a finitely generated proof space $\mathscr{H}$ *fails* to be monadic (i.e., correspond to a monadic PA) exactly when one of the basic Hoare triples which generates it $\{\varphi\}$ $\langle\sigma : \mathtt{i}\rangle$ $\{\psi\}$ has a postcondition which relates the local variables of two or more threads together (for example, an assertion of the form $x(1) \leq y(2)$).

Monadic PA have a conceptual correspondence to thread-modular proofs [19], which also disallow assertions which relate the local variables of different threads. Indeed, if there exists a thread-modular proof for a program, then there exists a monadic proof space (i.e., a proof space which corresponds to a monadic PA). This correspondence is not exact, however: monadic proof spaces are strictly more powerful than thread-modular proofs. In particular, one can show that any correct Boolean (or finite-domain) program has a proof space which corresponds to a monadic proof space. To see why, consider that the transition function of a Boolean program corresponds to a finite set of Hoare triples.[4]

***Discussion: decidability beyond monadic predicate automata.*** Note that the converse of Proposition 6.11 is not true, i.e., non-monadic proofs do not necessarily cause Algorithm 1 to diverge. For example, the proof of the thread pooling program from Section 2 is not monadic (for example, the assertion $\mathtt{end(1)} \leq \mathtt{c(2)}$ is dyadic). And yet, Algorithm 1 terminates for this example. We will informally discuss some other classes for which Algorithm 1 terminates.

We can generalize the monadic condition in a number of different ways while maintaining termination. One such generalization is *effectively monadic* PA, where there is a finite set of indices $D \subseteq \mathbb{N}$ such that in any reachable minimal (with respect to $\preceq$) configuration $\mathcal{C}$, for all $q(\mathtt{i}_1, ..., \mathtt{i}_n)$ we have at most one of $\mathtt{i}_1, ..., \mathtt{i}_n$ *not* in $D$. Intuitively, effectively monadic PAs can be used to reason about programs where one or more processes play a distinguished role (e.g., a client/server program, where there is a single distinguished server but arbitrarily many clients). Another alternative is *boundedly non-monadic* PA, where there exists some bound $K$ such that in any reachable minimal (with respect to $\preceq$) configuration $\mathcal{C}$, the cardinality of the set $\{q(\mathtt{i}_1, ..., \mathtt{i}_n) \in \mathcal{C} : ar(q) > 1\}$ is less than $K$. The thread pooling example from Section 2 is boundedly non-monadic with a bound of 3. Intuitively, boundedly non-monadic PAs can be used to reason about programs which do not require "unbounded chains" of inter-thread relationships.

There is a great deal of research on proving that classes of systems are well-quasi ordered which can be adapted to the setting of predicate automata. For example, we may admit a single binary predicate which forms a total order relation (by Higman's lemma), or a tree (by Kruskal's tree theorem). Meyer showed in [30] that depth-bounded processes are well-quasi ordered, which implies that for depth-bounded processes of known depth, the covering problem can be decided using a standard backward algorithm for WSTSs. Intuitively, the covering problem asks whether a system can reach a configuration that contains some process that is

[4] This assumes that every command of the program is deterministic, but this is without loss of generality because for Boolean programs, it is always possible to replace nondeterministic commands (e.g., `b := *`) with a nondeterministic branch between deterministic commands (e.g., `b := 0` and `b := 1`).

in a local error state. The question whether the covering problem is decidable for the entire class of depth-bounded processes was later addressed in [39], where an adequate domain of limits was developed for well-structured transition systems that are induced by depth-bounded processes, and consequently the existence of a forward algorithm for deciding the covering problem was demonstrated.

### 6.4 Completeness of PA

In this section, we strengthen the relative completeness result from Section 5. Theorem 5.2 establishes that any Ashcroft proof for a program $P$ corresponds to a finitely generate proof space $\mathscr{H}$ which covers the traces of $P$. But given our earlier undecidability result (Proposition 6.10), there is cause for concern that, although we can construct a basis $H$ for $\mathscr{H}$, there may be no way to validate that it covers the traces of a program. In this section, we introduce emptiness certificates for PA, and complete the picture by showing that we can construct an emptiness certificate for $A_P \cap \overline{A_H}$.

**Definition 6.12** Let $A = \langle Q, ar, \Sigma, \delta, \varphi_{\text{start}}, F\rangle$ be a PA. An *emptiness certificate* for $A$ is a formula $\varphi \in \mathcal{F}(Q, ar)$ (which may additionally have arbitrary quantification of thread variables) such that:

- $\varphi_{\text{start}} \models \varphi$
- for all $\mathcal{C}, \mathcal{C}', \sigma, \mathtt{i}$ such that $\mathcal{C} \models \varphi$ and $\mathcal{C} \xrightarrow{\sigma:\mathtt{i}} \mathcal{C}'$, we have $\mathcal{C}' \models \varphi$.
- Every model of $\varphi$ is rejecting. ⌟

An emptiness certificate can be seen as a kind of inductive invariant which shows that the language of a given predicate automaton is empty.

The following proposition establishes that emptiness certificates can be viewed as proofs that the language of a given predicate automaton is empty.

**Proposition 6.13** Let $A$ be a PA such that there exists an emptiness certificate for $A$. Then $\mathcal{L}(A) = \emptyset$. ⌟

Finally, we can state a strengthening of the completeness result from Section 5: not only do Ashcroft proofs correspond to finitely generated proof spaces, but they correspond to *checkable* proof spaces:

**Proposition 6.14** (PA Completeness) Let $P$ be a program. If there is an Ashcroft proof of correctness for $P$, then there is a proof space $\mathscr{H}$ which covers the traces of $P$, and there is an emptiness certificate for the predicate automaton $A_P \cap \overline{A_H}$. ⌟

*Proof.* We continue from the point started in the proof of Theorem 5.2: we let $P$ be a program, $\Phi_{\text{inv}}$ be an Ashcroft invariant of the form

$$\begin{aligned}\Phi_{\text{inv}} \equiv & (\forall i. \bigvee_{\ell \in \mathsf{Loc}} \mathsf{loc}(i) = \ell \land \varphi_\ell(i)) \\ & \land (\forall i \neq j. \bigvee_{\ell,\ell' \in \mathsf{Loc}\times\mathsf{Loc}} \mathsf{loc}(i) = \ell \land \mathsf{loc}(j) = \ell' \land \varphi_{\ell,\ell'}(i,j)))\end{aligned}$$

and let $H$ be as in Theorem 5.2.

We must construct an emptiness certificate for the automaton $A_P \cap \overline{A_H}$. Recall that the vocabulary of $A_P \cap \overline{A_H}$ consists of the vocabulary of $A_P$ along with the "negated" vocabulary of $A_H$. That is, the set of predicate symbols is

$$\mathsf{Loc} \cup \{\mathsf{loc}, \mathsf{err}\} \cup \{\overline{\varphi_\ell} : \ell \in \mathsf{Loc}\} \cup \{\overline{\varphi}_{\ell,\ell'} : \ell, \ell' \in \mathsf{Loc}\} \cup \{\overline{[false]}\}$$

For any $\ell \in \mathsf{Loc}$ we use $\overline{\ell(i)}$ as shorthand for

$$\bigvee \{\ell'(i) : \ell' \in \mathsf{Loc} \land \ell \neq \ell'\} .$$

The following formula, which we call $\overline{\Phi}_{\text{inv}}$, is such an emptiness certificate:

$$\begin{aligned}\mathsf{loc} \land \Big( & (\exists i. \bigwedge_{\ell \in \mathsf{Loc}} \overline{\ell(i)} \lor \overline{\varphi_\ell}(i)) \\ & \lor (\exists i, j. i \neq j \land \bigwedge_{\ell,\ell' \in \mathsf{Loc}\times\mathsf{Loc}} \overline{\ell(i)} \lor \overline{\ell'(j)} \lor \overline{\varphi_{\ell,\ell'}}(i,j))) \\ & \lor (\mathsf{err} \land \overline{[false]})\Big)\end{aligned}$$

The conditions of Definition 6.12 can easily be checked. The intuition behind this emptiness certificate comes from the observation that the negation of a forwards inductive invariant is a backwards inductive invariant. □

## 7. Verification algorithm

In this section, we outline a verification algorithm based on the automatic construction of proof spaces, and then discuss how the algorithm can be customized using various heuristics known and some perhaps yet to be discovered. Keep in mind that our aim in this section is not the presentation and/or evaluation of such heuristics, but rather to place proof spaces in their algorithmic context and to discuss some of the interesting research problems which are posed by this specific algorithmic context.

The high-level verification procedure based on proof spaces is given in Algorithm 2. It is essentially a variation of a standard counter-example guided abstraction refinement (CEGAR) loop. $\mathsf{proof\text{-}space}(\tau)$ is a procedure that computes a finite set of basic Hoare triples such that $\{true\}\ \ \tau\ \ \{false\}$ belongs to the proof space generated by $\mathsf{proof\text{-}space}(\tau)$.

One straightforward implementation of $\mathsf{proof\text{-}space}$ is to use sequence interpolation [22]. Given a trace $\tau = \langle \sigma_1 : \mathtt{i}_1\rangle \cdots \langle \sigma_n : \mathtt{i}_n\rangle$, we may use sequence interpolation to compute a sequence of intermediate assertions $\varphi_1, ..., \varphi_{n+1}$ such that $\varphi_1 = true$, $\varphi_{n+1} = false$, and for every $j \leq n$, the Hoare triple $\{\varphi_j\}\ \ \langle \sigma_j : \mathtt{i}_j\rangle\ \ \{\varphi_{j+1}\}$ is valid. We may then take the $\mathsf{proof\text{-}space}(\tau)$ to be the set of all such Hoare triple $\{\varphi_j\}\ \ \langle\sigma_j : \mathtt{i}_j\rangle\ \ \{\varphi_{j+1}\}$.[5]

Algorithm 2 takes as input a program $P$ and, if it terminates, returns either a counter-example $\tau$ showing that the error location of $P$ is reachable or a basis $H$ of a proof space which proves the correctness of $P$. The algorithm operates by repeatedly sampling error traces $\tau$ of $P$ for which $\{true\}\ \ \tau\ \ \{false\}$ is not in the proof space generated by $H$. If $\tau$ is feasible then the program is incorrect and the counter-example $\tau$ is returned. Otherwise, we add the Hoare triples from $\mathsf{proof\text{-}space}(\tau)$ to $H$. If we are *unable* to sample a trace $\tau$ for which $\{true\}\ \ \tau\ \ \{false\}$ is not in the proof space generated by $H$, then $H$ is a basis for a proof space which proves the correctness of $P$, and we return $H$. The high-level properties of this algorithm are summarized in the following theorem.

**Theorem 7.1** Algorithm 2 is sound and is complete for counter-examples: given a program $P$, if Algorithm 2 returns Safe, then $\ell_{\text{err}}$ is unreachable; if $\ell_{\text{err}}$ is reachable, then Algorithm 2 returns a feasible trace which reaches $\ell_{\text{err}}$. ⌟

***Discussion*** There is a great deal of flexibility in the design choices of the proof-space procedure. Let us discuss some of the design considerations and directions for future research concerning the construction of a proof space from a trace. An abstract proof-space procedure can be viewed to include these two steps:

[5] Technically speaking, these triples may not satisfy condition 1 of Definition 4.2, so we must define $\mathsf{proof\text{-}space}(\tau)$ to be the set of all $\{\varphi_j \lor false\}\ \ \langle\sigma_j : \mathtt{i}_j\rangle\ \ \{\varphi_{j+1} \lor false\}$.

Construct program automaton $A_P$;
$H \leftarrow \emptyset$; /* Basis for a proof space */
**while** $(A_P \cap \overline{A_H}) \neq \emptyset$ **do** /* Algorithm 1 */
  Select $\tau$ from $A_P \cap \overline{A_H}$; /* Algorithm 1 */
  **if** $\tau$ *is feasible* **then**
    **return** *Counter-example* $\tau$
  **else**
    $H \leftarrow H \cup$ proof-space($\tau$)
  **end**
**end**
**return** *Proof* $H$

**Algorithm 2:** Verify($P$)

1. Construct a program $P'$ such that $P'$ over-approximates the input trace $\tau$ (in the sense that $\tau$ is an error trace of $P'$ and $\{true\}$ $P'$ $\{false\}$), and construct a proof of correctness for $P'$.
2. Decompose the proof from step 1 to get a finite set of basic Hoare triples.

Step 1 can be replaced by a variety of different algorithms. The straightforward algorithm we suggested above (i.e. sequence interpolants) is one option. One can also view Step 1 to be implemented as a refinement loop, in the sense that an approximation is constructed and if a proof of correctness cannot be constructed for it, it is refined until a proof can be found. There are an array of known techniques that lie in the middle of the spectrum from the sequence interpolants for the trace (where we take $P' = \tau$), to a fully generalized refinement construction of the generalization of the trace (where $P'$ is the most general provably correct program containing $\tau$). For example, path programs [6] can be used to restore some of the looping structure from $P$ in order to take advantage of (sequential) loop invariant generation techniques. Bounded programs [38] are another category of suitable candidates for $P'$, where a loop-free concurrent underapproximation of $P$ is constructed through "de-interleaving" $\tau$; a correctness proof for the bounded program can then be constructed using techniques for fixed-thread concurrent program verification.

Step 2, decomposition of the proof, is more subtle than it might seem. In particular, the requirement that preconditions of basic Hoare triples may contain only relevant threads (condition 2 of Definition 4.2) may be difficult to enforce. An interesting feature of the sequence interpolation procedure outlined above is that the relevance requirement follows immediately from the properties of interpolants. But in general, it may be necessary to develop non-trivial algorithms for decomposing a proof into basic Hoare triples.

An interesting alternative to step 2 is to consider the problem of constructing basic Hoare triples directly rather than to extract them from an existing proof. For example, one possibility is to design an interpolation procedure which yields monadic proof spaces, perhaps borrowing techniques from tree interpolation [10].

## 8. Related work

There is a huge body of work on analysis and verification of concurrent programs. In this section, we limit ourselves to the substantial body of work on verification of programs with unbounded parallelism. Below, we provide some context for our work in this paper, and compare with the most related work.

***Unbounded parallelism and unbounded memory*** The proof checking procedure presented in Section 6 can be viewed as a kind of *pre*$^*$ analysis using the proof space, which may be reminiscent of predicate abstraction. There are two particular approaches to predicate abstraction for programs with unbounded parallelism and unbounded memory which are related to ours: *indexed predicate abstraction* [28] and *dual reference programs* [25]. Indexed predicate abstraction allow predicates to have free (thread) variables (e.g., $x(i) \geq 0$), with the ultimate goal of computing an Ashcroft invariant (i.e., a universally quantified invariant) of a fixed quantifier depth. Admitting free thread variables allows indexed predicates to be combined "under the quantifier" and thus compute complex quantified invariants from simple components. In view of the symmetry closure condition of proof spaces, indexed predicates serve a similar function to our ground Hoare triples, and our use of combinatorial generalization shares the goal of [28] to compute complex invariants from simple components. [28] uses a theorem prover to reason about universal quantifiers and program data simultaneously, and determines an Ashcroft invariant for a program by computing the least fixpoint in a finite abstract domain determined by a set of indexed predicates. Our technique does not require a theorem prover which supports universal quantifiers (or heuristics for quantifier instantiation), and the predicate automata inclusion check algorithm (based on the tree-saturation algorithm for well-structured transition systems) replaces the abstract fixpoint computation. The separation between reasoning about data and thread quantification provides a fresh perspective on what exactly makes reasoning about unbounded parallelism difficult, and enables us to state and prove results such as the decidability of the monadic case (i.e. Proposition 6.11), which has no obvious analogue in the setting of [28].

Dual reference programs allow two types of predicates: *single-thread predicates* (*mixed assertions* in the terminology in [12]), which refer to globals and the locals of one thread, and *inter-thread predicates*, which refer to globals and the locals of two threads, where one thread is universally quantified (e.g., $\forall j.x(i) < x(j)$). Although dual reference programs are not necessarily well-structured transition systems, [25] shows that it is always possible to convert a dual reference program obtained from an asynchronous program via predicate abstraction to a WSTS. In contrast with [25], our technique is complete relative to Ashcroft invariants. Moreover, we are able to use standard techniques from sequential verification to compute refinement predicates, whereas it is less clear how to automatically generate their inter-thread predicates that are of the form $\varphi(l, l_P)$, where $l$ is the local variable of a distinct active thread, and $l_p$ stand for a local variable of *all* passive threads (and therefore the predicates are universally quantified).

*Model checking modulo theories* (MCMT) is a general method for proving safety of array-based systems [20], which generalize finite-state parameterized systems. The MCMT algorithm is essentially a *pre*$^*$ computation which utilizes techniques from well-structured transition systems to guarantee termination for a subclass of array-based systems (which can be expressed in well-quasi ordered theories); this is similar in spirit to the proof checking algorithm presented in Section 6 and the covering relation defined in [20] is strikingly similar to Definition 6.6. In [3], MCMT is combined with interpolation-based abstraction, which in some practical cases terminates when the MCMT algorithm does not. Perhaps the most notable difference between our approach and MCMT is that we separate the verification problem into two sub-problems: constructing a proof space, and checking the adequacy of the proof space.

There is some work on automated invariant generation for programs where the number of threads and memory are unbounded [13, 23, 36]. These methods generally differ from ours in that they compute inductive invariants and are not property driven. In [36], starting with a set of candidate invariants (assertions), the approach builds a reflective abstraction, from which invariants of the concrete system are obtained in a fixpoint process. The number of quantifiers used in the invariants is a parameter of the abstract domain that needs to be fixed a priori. In [13], data flow graphs are used to compute invariants of concurrent programs with unboundedly many threads. Their abstraction is not expressive enough to capture relations between local variables and global variables, or local variables of other threads. In [23], a language of recursively defined formulas about arrays of variables, suitable for specifying safety properties of parameterized systems, is used. Their main contribution is a proof method for implications between such formulas, which accommodates the implementation of an abstract interpreter. Their effort was in the direction of proving entailment between complex formulas; our effort is to avoid them altogether.

The problem of proving data structure invariants for programs with unboundedly many threads is attacked in [5] and [37]. [5] aims to exploit thread-modularity in their proofs, which restricts the ways in which thread-local variables may be correlated (for the practical gain of a faster analysis). Additional correlations can be captured using the technique of [37], in which a universally quantified *environment assertion* is used to keep track of relationships between a distinguished thread and all other threads.

***Unbounded Parallelism and Bounded Memory*** In [1], a border case between unbounded and bounded data is investigated where shared variables range over unbounded domain of naturals but the local states of processes are finite (i.e. local variables of threads range over finite domains). There has been a great deal of work in the area of automated verification and analysis of concurrent programs where the number of threads is unbounded but the threads are finite-state [7, 24, 27, 31, 33]. We skip a detailed discussion of the wealth of techniques in this area, as they are not as closely related to our technique in the sense that they are limited to finite-state threads.

***Automata on infinite alphabets*** One of the main contributions of this paper is a method for determining whether the language of error traces of some program $P$ are included inside the set language of correct traces proved by some proof space $\mathscr{H}$. Classical automata-theoretic techniques cannot directly be applied because the alphabet of program commands is infinite. However, the automata community has developed generalizations of automata to infinite alphabets; the most relevant to our work is *(alternating) register automata (ARA)*, which are closely related to predicate automata.

Register automata were first introduced in [26]. Universality for register automata was shown to be undecidable in [32], which implies ARA emptiness is undecidable in the general case. However, the emptiness problem for ARA with 1 register (cf. monadic predicate automata) was proved to be decidable in [11] by reduction to reachability for lossy counter machines; and a direct proof based on well-structured transition systems was later presented in [16].

***Language-theoretic program verification*** The method presented in this paper is inspired by the language-theoretic approach to program correctness proposed in [21]. Notably, this approach has also been used in the context of concurrent programs with a fixed number of threads [14] and concurrent programs with unboundedly many threads [15]. One fundamental difference between our approach and previous language-theoretic techniques is that in [14, 15, 21], a *finite* set of program statements and therefore a *finite* alphabet was used. In [15], counting proofs were presented as a method for automatically synthesizing auxiliary variables in complex counting arguments for parameterized protocols. Counting proofs, i.e. proofs that use auxiliary counters are not expressible as proof spaces without the use of these auxiliary variables. On the other hand, proof spaces are capable of proving properties of programs which involve reasoning about infinite-domain local variables which is beyond the counting proofs framework. It will be interesting to investigate whether the strengths of the counting proofs and proof spaces can be combined into a single framework.

## 9. Conclusion

We conclude with a discussion of our work in a wider context and with an outlook to future work.

***Abstract interpretation*** From the perspective of abstract interpretation, proof spaces introduce a new class of abstract transformers for multi-threaded programs. We will here only sketch the details of a formalization of proof spaces in the abstract interpretation framework. The main part of the PA emptiness algorithm (Algorithm 1) applied to the predicate automaton $A_P \cap \overline{A_H}$ (for the program $P$ and the basis $H$ of a proof space) iterates an abstraction of the pre-image of the transition function. The corresponding abstract domain is the free lattice generated by the set consisting of the negations of the assertions that are used in the basis $H$ and the set of control assertions. The fact that the lattice is free (i.e., ignores the logical meaning of assertions) justifies our calling the abstract fixpoint computation *combinatorial*. The definition of the abstract transformer can be inferred from the definition of the transition function of the predicate automaton.

In contrast to work on software model checking for unbounded parallelism, we have not phrased abstraction as a source-to-source transformation, i.e., a mapping of a program into another one. Instead, we have taken the more general approach of abstract interpretation, which is to define an abstraction through a mapping of a semantics-defining function over a partially-ordered domain into another one.

***Symbolic vs. combinatorial reasoning*** In program verification, there is a tradition of dividing the problem of proving that a program satisfies a property of interest into two sub-tasks: (1) finding a simplified model of the program which simulates it, and (2) verifying that the property holds in the model. The first is a *symbolic* problem which requires reasoning about the program's (often infinite-domain) data theory (e.g., integers), and the second is *combinatorial* problem over a (possibly very large) finite state space. A classical example of this is the SLAM tool, which computes a recursive Boolean program which abstracts a given program using a finite set of predicates (generated via symbolic reasoning) and then verifies the Boolean program using CFL reachability [34] (a combinatorial algorithm).

Proof spaces achieve a similar separation between symbolic and combinatorial reasoning: symbolic reasoning is required to construct the basis of a proof space, and then checking whether every error trace can be proved infeasible using the sequencing, symmetry, and conjunction rules is a combinatorial problem. From this point of view, our algorithm for predicate automaton emptiness serves a role which is analogous to CFL reachability in SLAM. It is interesting to note that (unlike CFL reachability), the emptiness problem for general predicate automata is undecidable. There is a body of work on other combinatorial verification problems to serve as targets for multi-threaded programs [1, 25], but none are complete (in the sense of Section 5). Thus, our work reflects a fundamental tension between completeness and decidability in the setting of unbounded parallelism which does not exist for sequential programs or even multi-threaded programs with a fixed number of threads.

***Unbounded vs. Infinite*** The number of threads which participate in an error trace of a multi-threaded program is *unbounded* rather than *infinite*. This enables proof spaces to use conjunction and symmetry in place of universal thread quantification, and thus avoid the problem of directly synthesizing quantifiers. One may view using universal quantification to reason about unbounded threads (as in Ashcroft's proof system) as a deficiency, because an entailment is only provable in first order logic if it holds for *all* models, including models which have an infinite universe of threads.

For termination and liveness properties, one needs to reason about infinite traces. This creates the need to distinguish between programs with unboundedly many threads (e.g., computations which are parallelized over a number of processes which is determined at run time) and programs with infinitely many threads (e.g., programs with dynamic thread creation which spawn infinitely many threads over an infinite execution). In the setting of unbounded parallelism, then even if a trace is infinite, it can involve only finitely many threads. Thus, it may in principle be possible to extend proof spaces to termination and liveness properties. This is a topic of future work.

## References


[1] Parosh A. Abdulla, Yu-Feng Chen, Giorgio Delzanno, Frédéric Haziza, Chih-Duo Hong, and Ahmed Rezine. Constrained monotonic abstraction: a CEGAR for parameterized verification. In *CONCUR*, pages 86–101, 2010.

[2] Parosh A. Abdulla, Karlis Čerāns, Bengt Jonsson, and Yih-Kuen Tsay. General decidability theorems for infinite-state systems. In *LICS*, pages 313–321, 1996.

[3] Francesco Alberti, Roberto Bruttomesso, Silvio Ghilardi, Silvio Ranise, and Natasha Sharygina. Lazy abstraction with interpolants for arrays. In *LPAR*, pages 46–61, 2012.

[4] Edward A. Ashcroft. Proving assertions about parallel programs. *J. Comput. Syst. Sci.*, 10(1):110–135, February 1975.

[5] Josh Berdine, Tal Lev-Ami, Roman Manevich, G. Ramalingam, and Shmuel Sagiv. Thread quantification for concurrent shape analysis. In *CAV*, pages 399–413, 2008.

[6] Dirk Beyer, Thomas A. Henzinger, Rupak Majumdar, and Andrey Rybalchenko. Path invariants. In *PLDI*, pages 300–309, 2007.

[7] Ahmed Bouajjani, Bengt Jonsson, Marcus Nilsson, and Tayssir Touili. Regular model checking. In *CAV*, pages 403–418, 2000.

[8] Janusz A. Brzozowski and Ernst L. Leiss. On equations for regular languages, finite automata, and sequential networks. *Theoretical Computer Science*, 10(1):19–35, 1980.

[9] Ashok K. Chandra, Dexter C. Kozen, and Larry J. Stockmeyer. Alternation. *J. ACM*, 28(1):114–133, January 1981.

[10] Jürgen Christ and Jochen Hoenicke. Extending proof tree preserving interpolation to sequences and trees. In *Workshop on SMT Solving*, 2013.

[11] Stéphane Demri and Ranko Lazić. LTL with the freeze quantifier and register automata. *ACM Trans. Comput. Logic*, 10(3):16:1–16:30, April 2009.

[12] Alastair F. Donaldson, Alexander Kaiser, Daniel Kroening, Michael Tautschnig, and Thomas Wahl. Counterexample-guided abstraction refinement for symmetric concurrent programs. *Formal Methods in System Design*, 41(1):25–44, 2012.

[13] Azadeh Farzan and Zachary Kincaid. Verification of parameterized concurrent programs by modular reasoning about data and control. In *POPL*, pages 297–308, 2012.

[14] Azadeh Farzan, Zachary Kincaid, and Andreas Podelski. Inductive data flow graphs. In *POPL*, pages 129–142, 2013.

[15] Azadeh Farzan, Zachary Kincaid, and Andreas Podelski. Proofs that count. In *POPL*, pages 151–164, 2014.

[16] Diego Figueira. Alternating register automata on finite words and trees. *Logical Methods in Computer Science*, 8(1), 2012.

[17] Alain Finkel. A generalization of the procedure of Karp and Miller to well structured transition systems. In *ICALP*, pages 499–508, 1987.

[18] Alain Finkel and Philippe Schnoebelen. Well-structured transition systems everywhere! *Theoretical Computer Science*, 256(1):63–92, 2001.

[19] Cormac Flanagan, Stephen N. Freund, and Shaz Qadeer. Thread-modular verification for shared-memory programs. In *ESOP*, pages 262–277, 2002.

[20] Silvio. Ghilardi, Enrica Nicolini, Silvio Ranise, and Daniele Zucchelli. Towards SMT model checking of array-based systems. In *IJCAR*, pages 67–82, 2008.

[21] Matthias Heizmann, Jochen Hoenicke, and Andreas Podelski. Refinement of trace abstraction. In *SAS*, pages 69–85, 2009.

[22] Thomas A. Henzinger, Ranjit Jhala, Rupak Majumdar, and Kenneth L. McMillan. Abstractions from proofs. In *POPL*, pages 232–244, 2004.

[23] Joxan Jaffar and Andrew E. Santosa. Recursive abstractions for parameterized systems. In *FM*, pages 72–88, 2009.

[24] Alexander Kaiser, Daniel Kroening, and Thomas Wahl. Dynamic cutoff detection in parameterized concurrent programs. In *CAV*, pages 645–659, 2010.

[25] Alexander Kaiser, Daniel Kroening, and Thomas Wahl. Lost in abstraction: Monotonicity in multi-threaded programs. In *CONCUR*, pages 141–155, 2014.

[26] Michael Kaminski and Nissim Francez. Finite-memory automata. *Theor. Comput. Sci.*, 134(2):329–363, November 1994.

[27] Salvatore La Torre, Parthasarathy Madhusudan, and Gennaro Parlato. Model-checking parameterized concurrent programs using linear interfaces. In *CAV*, pages 629–644, 2010.

[28] Shuvendu K. Lahiri and Randal E. Bryant. Predicate abstraction with indexed predicates. *ACM Trans. Comput. Logic*, 9(1), December 2007.

[29] Alexander Malkis. *Cartesian abstraction and verification of multi-threaded programs*. PhD thesis, University of Freiburg, 2010.

[30] Roland Meyer. On boundedness in depth in the pi-calculus. In *IFIP TCS*, pages 477–489, 2008.

[31] Kedar S. Namjoshi. Symmetry and completeness in the analysis of parameterized systems. In *VMCAI*, pages 299–313, 2007.

[32] Frank Neven, Thomas Schwentick, and Victor Vianu. Finite state machines for strings over infinite alphabets. *ACM Trans. Comput. Logic*, 5(3):403–435, July 2004.

[33] Amir Pnueli, Sitvanit Ruah, and Lenore D. Zuck. Automatic deductive verification with invisible invariants. In *TACAS*, pages 82–97, 2001.

[34] Thomas W. Reps, Susan Horwitz, and Shmuel Sagiv. Precise interprocedural dataflow analysis via graph reachability. In *POPL*, pages 49–61, 1995.

[35] Willem-Paul de Roever. *Concurrency verification: introduction to compositional and noncompositional methods*. Cambridge University press, Cambridge, 2001.

[36] Alejandro Sanchez, Sriram Sankaranarayanan, César Sánchez, and Bor-Yuh Evan Chang. Invariant generation for parametrized systems using self-reflection. In *SAS*, pages 146–163. Springer, 2012.

[37] Michal Segalov, Tal Lev-Ami, Roman Manevich, Ramalingam Ganesan, and Mooly Sagiv. Abstract transformers for thread correlation analysis. In *APLAS*, pages 30–46, 2009.

[38] Nishant Sinha and Chao Wang. On interference abstractions. In *POPL*, pages 423–434, 2011.

[39] Thomas Wies, Damien Zufferey, and Thomas A. Henzinger. Forward analysis of depth-bounded processes. In *FOSSACS*, pages 94–108, 2010.

# Equations, contractions, and unique solutions

Davide Sangiorgi
Università di Bologna & INRIA
www.cs.unibo.it/~sangio/

## Abstract

One of the most studied behavioural equivalences is bisimilarity. Its success is much due to the associated bisimulation proof method, which can be further enhanced by means of 'up-to bisimulation' techniques such as 'up-to context'.

A different proof method is discussed, based on unique solution of special forms of inequations called contractions, and inspired by Milner's theorem on unique solution of equations. The method is as powerful as the bisimulation proof method and its 'up-to context' enhancements. The definition of contraction can be transferred onto other behavioural equivalences, possibly contextual and non-coinductive. This enables a coinductive reasoning style on such equivalences, either by applying the method based on unique solution of contractions, or by injecting appropriate contraction preorders into the bisimulation game.

The techniques are illustrated on CCS-like languages; an example dealing with higher-order languages is also shown.

***Categories and Subject Descriptors*** F.3.1 [*Logics and Meaning of Programs*]: Specifying and Verifying and Reasoning about Programs—logics of programs; F.3.2 [*Logics and Meaning of Programs*]: Semantics of Programming Languages—operational semantics.

***General Terms*** Theory

***Keywords*** Bisimulation; Coinduction; Equations; Unique solution; Contraction

## 1. Introduction

Bisimilarity is employed to define behavioural equivalences and reason about them. Originated in concurrency theory, bisimilarity is now widely used also in other areas, as well as outside Computer Science.

In this paper, behavioural equivalences, hence also bisimilarity, are meant to be *weak* because they abstract from internal moves of terms, as opposed to the *strong* ones, which make no distinctions between the internal moves and the external ones (i.e., the interactions with the environment). Weak equivalences are, practically, the most relevant ones: e.g., two equal programs may produce the same result with different numbers of evaluation steps.


*POPL '15*, January 15–17, 2015, Mumbai, India.
Copyright © 2015 ACM 978-1-4503-3300-9/15/01...$15.00.
http://dx.doi.org/10.1145/2676726.2676965

In proofs of bisimilarity results, the bisimulation proof method has become predominant, particularly with the enhancements of the method provided by the so called 'up-to techniques' [26]. Among these, one of the most powerful ones is 'up-to expansion and context', whereby the derivatives of two terms can be rewritten using expansion and bisimilarity and then a common context can be erased. Forms of 'bisimulations up-to context' have been shown to be effective in various fields, including process calculi [24, 26, 34], $\lambda$-calculi [14, 16, 17, 35], and automata [7, 30].

The landmark document for bisimilarity is Milner's CCS book [19]. In the book, Milner carefully explains that the bisimulation proof method is not supposed to be the only method for reasoning about bisimilarity. Indeed, various interesting examples in the book are handled using other techniques, notably *unique solution of equations*, whereby two tuples of processes are componentwise bisimilar if they are solutions of the same system of equations. This method is important in verification techniques and tools based on algebraic reasoning [2, 28, 29].

Milner's theorem that guarantees unique solutions [19] has however limitations: the equations must be 'guarded and sequential', that is, the variables of the equations may only be used underneath a visible prefix and preceded, in the syntax tree, only by the sum and prefix operators. This limits the expressiveness of the technique (since occurrences of other operators above the variables, such as parallel composition and restriction, in general cannot be removed), and its transport onto other languages (e.g., languages for distributed systems or higher-order languages, which usually do not include the sum operator).

In this paper we propose a refinement of Milner's technique in which equations are replaced by special inequations called *contractions*. Intuitively, for a behavioural equivalence $\asymp$, its contraction $\succeq_{\asymp}$ is a preorder in which $P \succeq_{\asymp} Q$ holds if $P \asymp Q$ and, in addition, $Q$ has the *possibility* of being as efficient as $P$. That is, $Q$ is capable of simulating $P$ by performing less internal work. It is sufficient that $Q$ has one 'efficient' path; $Q$ could also have other paths, that are slower than any path in $P$. Uniqueness of the solution of a system of contractions is defined as with systems of equations: any two solutions must be equivalent with respect to $\asymp$. The difference with equations is in the meaning of solution: in the case of contractions the solution is evaluated with respect to the preorder $\succeq_{\asymp}$, rather than the equivalence $\asymp$.

If a system of equations has a unique solution, then the corresponding system of contractions, obtained by replacing the equation symbol with the contraction symbol, has a unique solution too. The converse however is false: it may be that only the system of contractions has a unique solution. More important, the condition that guarantees a unique solution in Milner's theorem about equations can be relaxed: 'sequentiality' is not required, and 'guardedness' can be replaced by 'weak guardedness', that is, the variables of the contractions can be underneath *any* prefix, including a prefix representing internal work. (This is the same constraint in Milner's 'unique solution of equations' theorem for *strong* bisimilarity; the constraint is unsound for equations on weak bisimilarity.)

We show that Milner's theorem is not complete for *pure* equations (equations in which recursion is only expressible through the variables of the equations, without using the recursion construct of the process language): there are bisimilar processes that cannot be solutions to the same system of guarded and sequential pure equations. In contrast, completeness holds for weakly-guarded pure contractions. The contraction technique is also *computationally* complete: any bisimulation $\mathcal{R}$ can be transformed into an equivalent system of weakly-guarded contractions that has the same size of $\mathcal{R}$ (where the size of a relation is the number of its pairs, and the size of a system of contractions is the number of its contractions). An analogous result also holds with respect to bisimulation enhancements such as 'bisimulation up-to expansion and context'. The contraction technique is in fact computationally equivalent to the 'bisimulation up-to contraction and context' technique — a refinement of 'bisimulation up-to expansion and context'.

The contraction technique can be generalised to languages whose syntax is the term algebra derived from some signature, and whose semantics is given as an LTS. In this generalisation the weak-guardedness condition for contractions becomes a requirement of *autonomy*, essentially saying that the processes that replace the variables of a contraction do not contribute to the initial action of the resulting expression. The technique can also be transported onto other equivalences, including contextually-defined equivalences such as barbed congruence, and non-coinductive equivalences such as contextual equivalence (i.e., may testing) and trace equivalence [9, 10, 22]. For each equivalence, one defines its contraction preorder by controlling the amount of internal work performed.

Finally, we show that a contraction preorder can be injected into the bisimulation game. That is, given an equivalence $\asymp$ and its contraction preorder $\succeq_{\asymp}$, we can define the technique of 'bisimulation up-to $\succeq_{\asymp}$ and context' whereby, in the bisimulation game, the derivatives of the two processes can be manipulated with $\succeq_{\asymp}$ and $\asymp$ (similarly to the manipulations that are possible in the standard 'bisimulation up-to expansion and context' using the expansion relation and bisimilarity) and a common context can then be erased. The resulting 'bisimulation up-to $\succeq_{\asymp}$ and context' is sound for $\asymp$. This technique allows us to derive results for $\asymp$ using the (enhanced) bisimulation proof method.

The contraction technique cannot however be transported onto all (weak) behavioural equivalences. For instance, it does not work in the setting of infinitary trace equivalence (whereby two processes are equal if they have the same finite and infinite traces), and must testing [9]. A discussion on this point is deferred to the concluding section.

We conclude the paper with an example of application of contractions to a higher-order language, which exploits the autonomy condition.

***Structure of the paper*** All background material is reported in Section 2. Contractions and their properties are introduced in Section 3, for bisimilarity and the CCS language. The extension to languages defined from a generic signature is presented in Section 4. The transport of contractions onto other behavioural equivalences is discussed in Sections 5 (barbed congruence), 6 (contextual equivalence), 7 (trace equivalence), and 8 (non-applicability to certain equivalences). The injection of contractions into the bisimulation game is described in Section 9. The example with higher-order languages is reported in Section 10.

# 2. Background

## 2.1 CCS

We assume an infinite set of *names* $a, b, \ldots$ and a set of *constant identifiers* (or simply *constants*) for writing recursive processes. The special symbol $\tau$ does not occur in the names and in the constants. The class of the CCS processes is built from the operators of parallel composition, guarded sum, restriction, and constants, and the guard of a sum can be an input, an output, or a silent prefix:

$$P \;:=\; P_1 \mid P_2 \;\Big|\; \Sigma_{i\in I}\mu_i.\, P_i \;\Big|\; \boldsymbol{\nu} a\, P \;\Big|\; K$$

$$\mu \;:=\; a \;\Big|\; \overline{a} \;\Big|\; \tau$$

where $I$ is a countable indexing set. Sums are guarded so to ensure that behavioural equivalences and preorders are substitutive. We write $\mathbf{0}$ when $I$ is empty, and $P + Q$ for binary sums, with the understanding that, to fit the above grammar, $P$ and $Q$ should be sums of prefixed terms. Each constant $K$ has a definition $K \stackrel{\triangle}{=} P$. We sometimes omit trailing $\mathbf{0}$, e.g., writing $a \mid b$ for $a.\mathbf{0} \mid b.\mathbf{0}$. We write $\mu^n.\, P$ for $P$ preceded by $n$ $\mu$-prefixes. In a few examples we write $!\mu.\, P$ as abbreviation for the constant $K_{\mu.P} \stackrel{\triangle}{=} \mu.\,(P \mid K_{\mu.P})$. The operational semantics is given by means of an LTS, and is reported in Figure 1 (the symmetric version of the two rules for parallel composition has been omitted). The *immediate derivatives* of a process $P$ are the elements of the set $\{P' \mid P \xrightarrow{\mu} P' \text{ for some } \mu\}$. We use $\ell$ to range over visible actions (i.e., inputs or outputs, excluding $\tau$).

Some standard notations for transitions: $\Longrightarrow$ is the reflexive and transitive closure of $\xrightarrow{\tau}$, and $\stackrel{\mu}{\Longrightarrow}$ is $\Longrightarrow\xrightarrow{\mu}\Longrightarrow$ (the composition of the three relations). Moreover, $P \xrightarrow{\widehat{\mu}} P'$ holds if $P \xrightarrow{\mu} P'$ or ($\mu = \tau$ and $P = P'$); similarly $P \stackrel{\widehat{\mu}}{\Longrightarrow} P'$ holds if $P \stackrel{\mu}{\Longrightarrow} P'$ or ($\mu = \tau$ and $P = P'$). We write $P(\xrightarrow{\mu})^n P'$ if $P$ can become $P'$ after performing $n$ $\mu$-transitions. Finally, $P \xrightarrow{\mu}$ holds if there is $P'$ with $P \xrightarrow{\mu} P'$, and similarly for other forms of transitions.

***Further notations*** Letters $\mathcal{R}, \mathcal{S}$ range over relations. We use infix notation for relations, e.g., $P \;\mathcal{R}\; Q$ means that $(P, Q) \in \mathcal{R}$. We use a tilde to denote a tuple, with countably many elements; thus the tuple may also be infinite. All notations are extended to tuples componentwise; e.g., $\widetilde{P} \;\mathcal{R}\; \widetilde{Q}$ means that $P_i \;\mathcal{R}\; Q_i$, for each component $i$ of the tuples $\widetilde{P}$ and $\widetilde{Q}$. And $C[\widetilde{P}]$ is the process obtained by replacing each hole $[\cdot]_i$ of the context $C$ with $P_i$. We write $\mathcal{R}^c$ for the closure of a relation under contexts. Thus $P \;\mathcal{R}^c\; Q$ means that there are a context $C$ and tuples $\widetilde{P}, \widetilde{Q}$ with $P = C[\widetilde{P}], Q = C[\widetilde{Q}]$ and $\widetilde{P} \;\mathcal{R}\; \widetilde{Q}$. We use symbol $\stackrel{\text{def}}{=}$ for abbreviations. For instance, $P \stackrel{\text{def}}{=} G$, where $G$ is some expression, means that $P$ stands for the expression $G$ (in contrast, symbol $\stackrel{\triangle}{=}$ is used for the definition of constants, whereas $=$ is used for syntactic equality and for equations). If $\leq$ is a preorder, then $\geq$ is its inverse (and conversely).

## 2.2 Bisimilarity and expansion

We focus on *weak* behavioural equivalences, which abstract from the number of internal steps performed.

DEFINITION 2.1 (bisimilarity). *A process relation* $\mathcal{R}$ *is a* bisimulation *if, whenever* $P \;\mathcal{R}\; Q$*, we have:*

1. $P \xrightarrow{\mu} P'$ *implies that there is* $Q'$ *such that* $Q \stackrel{\widehat{\mu}}{\Longrightarrow} Q'$ *and* $P' \;\mathcal{R}\; Q'$*;*
2. *the converse of (1) on the actions from* $Q$.

$$\Sigma_{i\in I}\mu_i.\,P_i \xrightarrow{\mu_i} P_i \qquad \frac{P \xrightarrow{\mu} P'}{P \mid Q \xrightarrow{\mu} P' \mid Q} \qquad \frac{P \xrightarrow{a} P' \quad Q \xrightarrow{\overline{a}} Q'}{P \mid Q \xrightarrow{\tau} P' \mid Q'} \qquad \frac{P \xrightarrow{\mu} P'}{\nu a\, P \xrightarrow{\mu} \nu a\, P'}\ \mu \neq a, \overline{a} \qquad \frac{P \xrightarrow{\mu} P'}{K \xrightarrow{\mu} P'}\ \text{if } K \triangleq P$$

**Figure 1.** The LTS for CCS

*$P$ and $Q$ are* bisimilar, *written $P \approx Q$, if $P$ $\mathcal{R}$ $Q$ for some bisimulation $\mathcal{R}$.* □

We sometimes call bisimilarity *weak* bisimilarity, to distinguish it from *strong bisimilarity*, $\sim$, obtained by replacing in the above definition the weak answer $Q \stackrel{\widehat{\mu}}{\Longrightarrow} Q'$ with the strong $Q \xrightarrow{\mu} Q'$.

The bisimulation proof method can be enhanced by means of *up-to techniques*. One of the most useful auxiliary relations in up-to techniques is the *expansion* relation $\succeq_{\mathrm{e}}$ [32]. This is an asymmetric version of $\approx$ where $P \succeq_{\mathrm{e}} Q$ means that $P \approx Q$, but also that $Q$ achieves the same as $P$ with no more work, i.e. with no more $\tau$ actions. Intuitively, if $P \succeq_{\mathrm{e}} Q$, we can think of $Q$ as being at least as fast as $P$ or, more generally, we can think that $P$ uses at least as many resources as $Q$.

DEFINITION 2.2 (expansion). *A process relation $\mathcal{R}$ is an* expansion *if, whenever $P$ $\mathcal{R}$ $Q$,*

1. *$P \xrightarrow{\mu} P'$ implies that there is $Q'$ with $Q \xrightarrow{\widehat{\mu}} Q'$ and $P'$ $\mathcal{R}$ $Q'$;*
2. *$Q \xrightarrow{\mu} Q'$ implies that there is $P'$ with $P \stackrel{\mu}{\Longrightarrow} P'$ and $P'$ $\mathcal{R}$ $Q'$.*

$P$ expands $Q$*, written $P \succeq_{\mathrm{e}} Q$, if $P$ $\mathcal{R}$ $Q$, for some expansion $\mathcal{R}$.*

Relation $\succeq_{\mathrm{e}}$ is studied – using a different terminology – by Arun-Kumar and Hennessy [1]: they show that $\succeq_{\mathrm{e}}$ is a mathematically tractable preorder and has a complete proof system for finite terms based on a modification of the standard $\tau$ laws for CCS. In CCS, strong and weak bisimilarity are congruence relations, and expansion is a precongruence. It holds that $\sim\,\subseteq\,\succeq_{\mathrm{e}}$ and $\succeq_{\mathrm{e}}\,\subseteq\,\approx$; moreover each inclusion is strict. The inclusions are obvious. For the strictness, we have that $P \not\sim \tau.\,P$, $P \preceq_{\mathrm{e}} \tau.\,P$, and $\tau.\,P \not\preceq_{\mathrm{e}} P$, $\tau.\,P \approx P$.

A powerful up-to technique is 'bisimulation up-to $\succeq_{\mathrm{e}}$ and context'. It combines 'up-to expansion' (the possibility of rewriting the derivatives of two related processes using $\succeq_{\mathrm{e}}$ and $\approx$), with 'up-to context' (the possibility of removing a common context from the derivatives). We recall that $\mathcal{R}^{\mathrm{c}}$ is the context closure of $\mathcal{R}$.

DEFINITION 2.3 (bisimulation up-to $\succeq_{\mathrm{e}}$ and context). *A process relation $\mathcal{R}$ is a* bisimulation up-to $\succeq_{\mathrm{e}}$ and context *if, whenever $P$ $\mathcal{R}$ $Q$, we have:*

1. *$P \xrightarrow{\mu} P'$ implies that there is $Q'$ with $Q \stackrel{\widehat{\mu}}{\Longrightarrow} Q'$ and $P' \succeq_{\mathrm{e}} \mathcal{R}^{\mathrm{c}} \approx Q'$;*
2. *the converse of (1) on the actions from $Q$.*

The occurrence of $\succeq_{\mathrm{e}}$ on the left of $\mathcal{R}^{\mathrm{c}}$ cannot be replaced by $\approx$, as this would break the soundness of the technique [26]. The technique is sound [33]:

LEMMA 2.4 (soundness of bisimulation up-to $\succeq_{\mathrm{e}}$ and context). *If $\mathcal{R}$ is a bisimulation up-to $\succeq_{\mathrm{e}}$ and context, then $R \subseteq \approx$.*

### 2.3 An example

In examples in the paper, we sometimes use a version of CCS with value passing; this could be translated into pure CCS [19], but having explicit value passing improves readability. In a value-passing calculus, $a(x).\,P$ is an input at $a$ in which $x$ is the placeholder for the value received, whereas $\overline{a}\langle n\rangle.\,P$ is an output at $a$ of the value $n$; and $A\langle n\rangle$ is a parametrised constant. The following example illustrates 'bisimulation up-to $\succeq_{\mathrm{e}}$ and context', and will then be used for comparison with other techniques.

We wish to implement a server that, when interrogated by clients at a channel $c$, starts a certain interaction protocol with the client, after consulting an auxiliary server $A$ at $a$. Here the auxiliary server $A$ is deterministic: at every cycle it outputs an integer value, which changes with the cycle (this change is represented by the successor function, for simplicity).

We consider two implementations of the server. The difference between them is that the first server, $L$, is lazy, and consults $A$ only *after* a request from a client has been received. In contrast, the other server, $E$, consults $A$ beforehand so to be then ready in answering a client:

$$\begin{array}{rcl} L & \triangleq & c(z).\,a(x).\,(L \mid R\langle c,x,z\rangle) \\ E & \triangleq & a(x).\,c(z).\,(E \mid R\langle c,x,z\rangle) \\ A\langle n\rangle & \triangleq & \overline{a}\langle n\rangle.\,A\langle n+1\rangle \end{array}$$

Here $R\langle c,x,z\rangle$ represents the interaction protocol that is started with a client, and can be any process. It may use the values $x$ and $z$ (obtained from the client and the auxiliary server $A$); the interactions produced may actually depend on the values $x$ and $z$. Process $R\langle c,x,z\rangle$ may also use channel $c$, and therefore trigger further interactions with the main server; in contrast, $R\langle c,x,z\rangle$ may not use $a$ (i.e., it may not interrogate the auxiliary server).

We use the 'bisimulation up-to expansion and context' technique to prove that the composition of the two servers with $A$ yields bisimilar lazy and eager systems:

$$\begin{array}{rcl} \mathit{LS}\langle n\rangle & \stackrel{\mathrm{def}}{=} & \nu a\,(A\langle n\rangle \mid L) \\ \mathit{ES}\langle n\rangle & \stackrel{\mathrm{def}}{=} & \nu a\,(A\langle n\rangle \mid E) \end{array}$$

Relation $\mathcal{R} \stackrel{\mathrm{def}}{=} \cup_n\{(\mathit{LS}\langle n\rangle, \mathit{ES}\langle n\rangle)\}$ is a bisimulation up-to expansion and context. Consider a pair $(\mathit{LS}\langle n\rangle, \mathit{ES}\langle n\rangle)$. The two processes have one initial transition; the most interesting case is the challenge transition from $\mathit{ES}\langle n\rangle$, and we only consider this one. We have

$$\mathit{ES}\langle n\rangle \xrightarrow{\tau} \nu a\,(A\langle n+1\rangle \mid c(z).\,(E \mid R\langle c,n,z\rangle)) \stackrel{\mathrm{def}}{=} E'$$

Process $\mathit{LS}\langle n\rangle$ may not produce internal steps, hence its only possible answer is

$$\mathit{LS}\langle n\rangle \Longrightarrow \mathit{LS}\langle n\rangle$$

We can now perform some algebraic manipulations of $E'$: first, we employ CCS expansion law to pull out the prefix at $c$, then a structural law to resize the scope of the restriction at $a$ in which we exploit the property that $R\langle c,n,z\rangle$ may not use $a$. (All these laws are valid for strong bisimilarity, hence also for expansion.) We thus obtain:

$$\begin{array}{rcl} E' & \succeq_{\mathrm{e}} & c(z).\,(\nu a\,(A\langle n+1\rangle \mid E) \mid R\langle c,n,z\rangle) \\ & = & c(z).\,(\mathit{ES}\langle n+1\rangle \mid R\langle c,n,z\rangle) \stackrel{\mathrm{def}}{=} E'' \end{array}$$

We can act similarly on $\mathit{LS}\langle n\rangle$, and in addition also employing the law

$$\nu a\,(a(y).\,P \mid \overline{a}\langle v\rangle.\,Q) \approx \nu a\,(P\{^{v}\!/\!_{y}\} \mid Q) \qquad (1)$$

This gives us:

$$\begin{array}{rcl} LS\langle n\rangle & \approx & c(z).(\boldsymbol{\nu} a\,(A\langle n+1\rangle \mid L) \mid R\langle c,n,z\rangle) \\ & = & c(z).(LS\langle n+1\rangle \mid R\langle c,n,z\rangle) \stackrel{\text{def}}{=} L' \end{array}$$

We have thus obtained two processes, $E''$ and $L'$, in the context closure of $\mathcal{R}$, and we are done.

In the proof, the 'up-to' techniques allow us to work with a relation that has exactly one pair for each integer. Specifically, 'up-to context' avoids us considering processes in parallel with the lazy and eager systems, whereas 'up-to expansion' allows us to reason only on the 'normal forms' $LS\langle n\rangle$ and $ES\langle n\rangle$ for these systems.

### 2.4 Systems of equations

Uniqueness of solutions of equations [19] intuitively says that if a context $C$ obeys certain conditions, then all processes $P$ that satisfy the equation $P \approx C[P]$ are bisimilar with each other.

We need variables to write equations. We use capital letters $X, Y, Z$ for these variables and call them *equation variables*. The body of an equation is a CCS expression possibly containing equation variables. Thus such expressions, ranged over by $E$, live in a CCS grammar extended with equation variables.

DEFINITION 2.5. *Assume that, for each $i$ of a countable indexing set $I$, we have variables $X_i$, and expressions $E_i$ possibly containing such variables. Then*

$$\{X_i = E_i\}_{i\in I}$$

*is a* system of equations. *(There is one equation for each variable $X_i$.)*

We write $E[\widetilde{P}]$ for the expression resulting from $E$ by replacing each variable $X_i$ with the process $P_i$, assuming $\widetilde{P}$ and $\widetilde{X}$ have the same length. (This is syntactic replacement, akin to the substitution of the holes of a context with processes.) The components of $\widetilde{P}$ need not be different from each other, as it must be for the variables $\widetilde{X}$. If the system has infinitely many equations, the tuples $\widetilde{P}$ and $\widetilde{X}$ are infinite too.

DEFINITION 2.6. *Suppose $\{X_i = E_i\}_{i\in I}$ is a system of equations:*

- *$\widetilde{P}$ is a* solution of the system of equations for $\approx$ *if for each $i$ it holds that $P_i \approx E_i[\widetilde{P}]$.*
- *the system has* a unique solution for $\approx$ *if whenever $\widetilde{P}$ and $\widetilde{Q}$ are both solutions for $\approx$, then $\widetilde{P} \approx \widetilde{Q}$.*

Examples of systems with a unique solution for $\approx$ are:

1. $X = a.X$
2. $X_1 = a.X_2$, $X_2 = b.X_1$

The unique solution of the system (1), modulo $\approx$, is the constant $K \stackrel{\triangle}{=} a.K$: for any other solution $P$ we have $P \approx K$. The unique solution of (2), modulo $\approx$, are the constants $K_1, K_2$ with $K_1 \stackrel{\triangle}{=} a.K_2$ and $K_2 \stackrel{\triangle}{=} b.K_1$; again, for any other pair of solutions $P_1, P_2$ we have $K_1 \approx P_1$ and $K_2 \approx P_2$. Examples of systems that do not have unique solution are:

1. $X = X$
2. $X = \tau.X$
3. $X = a \mid X$

All processes are solutions of (1) and (2); examples of solutions for (3) are $K$ and $K \mid b$, for $K \stackrel{\triangle}{=} a.K$.

DEFINITION 2.7. *A system of equations $\{X_i = E_i\}_{i\in I}$ is*

- guarded *if, in each $E_i$, each occurrence of an equation variable is underneath a visible prefix;*
- sequential *if, in each $E_i$, each occurrence of an equation variable only appears underneath prefixes and sums.*

In other words, if the system is sequential, then for every expression $E_i$, any subexpression of $E_i$ in which $X_j$ appears, apart from $X_j$ itself, is a sum (of prefixed terms). For instance,

- $X = \tau.X + \mu.\mathbf{0}$ is sequential but not guarded, because the guarding prefix for the variable is not visible.
- $X = \ell.X \mid P$ is guarded but not sequential.
- $X = \ell.X + \tau.\boldsymbol{\nu} a\,(a.\overline{b} \mid a.\mathbf{0})$, as well as $X = \tau.(a.X + \tau.b.X + \tau)$ are both guarded and sequential.

THEOREM 2.8 (unique solution of equations, [19]). *A system of guarded and sequential equations has a unique solution for $\approx$.*

The proof exploits an invariance property on immediate transitions for guarded and sequential expressions, and then extracts a bisimulation (up-to bisimilarity) out of the solutions of the system.

To see the need of the sequentiality condition, consider the equation (from [19])

$$X = \boldsymbol{\nu} a\,(a.X \mid \overline{a})$$

where $X$ is guarded but not sequential. Any processes that does not use $a$ is a solution.

## 3. Contractions

In Theorem 2.8 the constraints on guardedness and, especially, on sequentiality limit its applicability. Further, the same definitions and examples discussed for bisimilarity (and hence also the same limitations) apply to other behavioural equivalences; e.g., contextual equivalence and trace-based equivalences.

One may wonder if the conditions of Theorem 2.8 can be relaxed by simply requiring that each equation be *sequentially guarded*, that is, of the form $X = \Sigma_j \ell_j.E_j$ (where $\ell_j$ is a visible action). Unfortunately, uniqueness still fails; a counterexample is

$$X = a.\boldsymbol{\nu} a\,(\overline{a} \mid X)\ .$$

Any process $P$ with $P \approx a.P'$, and $P'$ unable to use $a$, is a solution. Examples are $a.\mathbf{0}$ and $a.b.\mathbf{0}$.

An equation $X = a.E$ need not have a unique solution even if we confine ourselves to processes that may only perform $a$ transitions. An example is the equation

$$X = a.\boldsymbol{\nu} b\,(\boldsymbol{\nu} a\,(\overline{a}.!\overline{a}.\overline{b} \mid X) \mid !b.a)\ .$$

Here the body of the equation produces an $a$, cancels the first $a$ from $X$ and then reproduces all other $a$'s. Any process $P$ with $P \approx a.P'$ for some $P'$, is a solution; for instance, $a.\mathbf{0}$ or $a.a.\mathbf{0}$ or even $!a.\mathbf{0}$.

### 3.1 Contraction preorders

The constraints on the unique-solution Theorem 2.8 can be weakened if we move from equations to certain inequations that we call *contractions*.

Intuitively, for a behavioural equivalence $\asymp$, its contraction $\succeq_{\asymp}$ is a preorder in which $P \succeq_{\asymp} Q$ holds if $P \asymp Q$ and, in addition, $Q$ has the *possibility* of being at least as efficient as $P$. That is, if $P$ can do some work (i.e., some interactions with its environment), then $Q$ should be able to do the same work at least as quickly as $P$ (i.e., performing no more $\tau$-steps then those performed by $P$). Process $Q$, however, may be nondeterministic and may have other ways of doing the same work, and these could be slow (i.e., involving more $\tau$-steps than those performed by $P$). We first explain the idea on the concrete case of bisimilarity.

DEFINITION 3.1 (bisimulation contraction). *A process relation $\mathcal{R}$ is a* bisimulation contraction *if, whenever $P \mathcal{R} Q$,*

1. *$P \xrightarrow{\mu} P'$ implies there is $Q'$ such that $Q \xrightarrow{\widehat{\mu}} Q'$ and $P' \mathcal{R} Q'$;*
2. *$Q \xrightarrow{\mu} Q'$ implies there is $P'$ such that $P \stackrel{\widehat{\mu}}{\Longrightarrow} P'$ and $P' \approx Q'$.*

Bisimilarity contraction, *written $\succeq_{\mathrm{bis}}$, is the union of all bisimulation contractions.*

In the first clause $Q$ is required to match $P$'s challenge transition with at most one transition. This makes sure that $Q$ is capable of mimicking $P$'s work at least as efficiently as $P$. In contrast, the second clause of Definition 3.1, on the challenges from $Q$, entirely ignores efficiency: it is the same clause of weak bisimulation — the final derivatives are even required to be related by $\approx$, rather than by $\mathcal{R}$.

Bisimilarity contraction is coarser than the expansion relation $\succeq_{\mathrm{e}}$ of Definition 2.2. Clause (1) is the same in the two definitions. But in clause (2) expansion uses $P \stackrel{\mu}{\Longrightarrow} P'$, rather than $P \stackrel{\widehat{\mu}}{\Longrightarrow} P'$; moreover with contraction the final derivatives are simply required to be bisimilar. An expansion $P \succeq_{\mathrm{e}} Q$ tells us that $Q$ is always more efficient than $P$, whereas the contraction $P \succeq_{\mathrm{bis}} Q$ just says that $Q$ has the possibility of being more efficient than $P$.

EXAMPLE 3.2. We have $a \not\succeq_{\mathrm{bis}} \tau.a$. However, $a + \tau.a \succeq_{\mathrm{bis}} a$, as well as its converse, $a \succeq_{\mathrm{bis}} a + \tau.a$. Indeed, if $P \approx Q$ then $P \succeq_{\mathrm{bis}} P + Q$. The last two relations do not hold with $\succeq_{\mathrm{e}}$, which explains the strictness of the inclusion $\succeq_{\mathrm{e}} \subseteq \succeq_{\mathrm{bis}}$. □

As bisimilarity contraction follows expansion in one direction and bisimilarity in the other, clearly separating the two, the precongruence and congruence for such relations can be combined into a precongruence proof for the contraction.

THEOREM 3.3. *$\succeq_{\mathrm{bis}}$ is a precongruence in CCS.*

### 3.2 Systems of contractions

A *system of contractions* is defined as a system of equations, except that the contraction symbol $\succeq$ is used in the place of the equality symbol $=$. Thus a system of contractions is a set $\{X_i \succeq E_i\}_{i \in I}$ where $I$ is an indexing set and expressions $E_i$ may contain the contraction variables $\{X_i\}_{i \in I}$.

DEFINITION 3.4. *Given a behavioural equivalence $\asymp$ and its contraction $\succeq_{\asymp}$, and a system of contractions $\{X_i \succeq E_i\}_{i \in I}$, we say that:*

- *$\widetilde{P}$ is a* solution for $\succeq_{\asymp}$ of the system of contractions *if $\widetilde{P} \succeq_{\asymp} \widetilde{E}[\widetilde{P}]$;*
- *the system has* a unique solution for $\asymp$ *if whenever $\widetilde{P}$ and $\widetilde{Q}$ are both solutions for $\succeq_{\asymp}$ then $\widetilde{P} \asymp \widetilde{Q}$.*

When we reason about bisimilarity, the contraction symbol $\succeq$ is interpreted as the bisimilarity contraction $\succeq_{\mathrm{bis}}$, and the equivalence $\asymp$ as the bisimilarity $\approx$. Thus $\widetilde{P}$ solution for $\succeq_{\mathrm{bis}}$ of the system of contractions $\{X_i \succeq E_i\}_{i \in I}$ means that $\widetilde{P} \succeq_{\mathrm{bis}} \widetilde{E}[\widetilde{P}]$; and the system having a unique solution for $\approx$ means that whenever $\widetilde{P}$ and $\widetilde{Q}$ are both solutions for $\succeq_{\mathrm{bis}}$ then $\widetilde{P} \approx \widetilde{Q}$.

LEMMA 3.5. *If a system of equations $\{X_i = E_i\}_{i \in I}$ has a unique solution for $\approx$, then also the corresponding system of contractions $\{X_i \succeq E_i\}_{i \in I}$ has a unique solution for $\approx$.*

The lemma holds because any system of equations has at least one solution for strong bisimilarity, obtained by interpreting the equations as recursive process definitions. A solution for strong bisimilarity is also a solution in the system of contractions. Moreover, any solution of the system of contractions is a solution of the system of equations. (The converse, in contrast, is false: as we shall see, systems of contractions more easily have a unique solution.)

### 3.3 Conditions for unique solution of contractions

DEFINITION 3.6. *A system of contractions $\{X_i \succeq E_i\}_{i \in I}$ is* weakly guarded *if, in each $E_i$, each occurrence of a contraction variable is underneath a prefix.*

In proofs about weakly-guarded contractions we will often unfold the contractions, exploiting the substitutivity of the contraction preorder, with the objective of placing processes that are solutions of the contractions underneath a certain number of prefixes. Suppose $\widetilde{P}$ are solutions of a system of contractions $\{X_i \succeq E_i\}_{i \in I}$, and consider a context $C[\widetilde{P}]$. Then the process obtained from $C[\widetilde{P}]$ by unfolding the contractions once is $C[\,\widetilde{E}[\widetilde{P}]\,]$; the process obtained by unfolding the contractions twice is $C[\,\widetilde{E}[\widetilde{E}[\widetilde{P}]]\,]$; and similarly for the $n$-unfolding.

LEMMA 3.7. *Suppose $\widetilde{P}$ and $\widetilde{Q}$ are solutions for $\approx$ of a system of weakly-guarded contractions. For any context $C$, if $C[\widetilde{P}] \stackrel{\mu}{\Longrightarrow} R$, then there is a context $C'$ such that $R \succeq_{\mathrm{bis}} C'[\widetilde{P}]$ and $C[Q] \stackrel{\widehat{\mu}}{\Longrightarrow}\approx C'[\widetilde{Q}]$.*

**Proof** [Sketch] Let $n$ be the length of the transition $C[\widetilde{P}] \stackrel{\mu}{\Longrightarrow} R$ (the number of 'strong steps' of which it is composed), and let $C''[\widetilde{P}]$ and $C''[\widetilde{Q}]$ be the processes obtained from $C[\widetilde{P}]$ and $C[\widetilde{Q}]$ by unfolding the definitions of the contractions $n$ times. Thus in $C''$ each hole is underneath at least $n$ prefixes, and cannot contribute to an action in the first $n$ transitions.

We have $C[\widetilde{P}] \succeq_{\mathrm{bis}} C''[\widetilde{P}]$, and $C[\widetilde{Q}] \succeq_{\mathrm{bis}} C''[\widetilde{Q}]$, by the precongruence properties of $\succeq_{\mathrm{bis}}$. Moreover, since each hole of the context $C''$ is underneath at least $n$ prefixes, applying the definition of $\succeq_{\mathrm{bis}}$ on the transition $C[\widetilde{P}] \stackrel{\mu}{\Longrightarrow} R$, we infer the existence of $C'$ such that $C''[\widetilde{P}] \stackrel{\widehat{\mu}}{\Longrightarrow} C'[\widetilde{P}] \preceq_{\mathrm{bis}} R$ and $C''[\widetilde{Q}] \stackrel{\widehat{\mu}}{\Longrightarrow} C'[\widetilde{Q}]$. Finally, again applying the definition of $\succeq_{\mathrm{bis}}$ on $C[\widetilde{Q}] \succeq_{\mathrm{bis}} C''[\widetilde{Q}]$, we derive $C[\widetilde{Q}] \stackrel{\widehat{\mu}}{\Longrightarrow}\approx C'[\widetilde{Q}]$. □

THEOREM 3.8 (unique solution of contractions for $\approx$). *A system of weakly-guarded contractions has a unique solution for $\approx$.*

**Proof** [Sketch] One shows that if $\widetilde{P}$ and $\widetilde{Q}$ are solutions for $\approx$ of a system of weakly-guarded contractions, then the relation

$$\mathcal{R} \stackrel{\text{def}}{=} \{(R,S) \mid R \approx C[\widetilde{P}], S \approx C[\widetilde{Q}] \text{ for some context } C\}.$$

is a bisimulation, exploiting Lemma 3.7. □

In comparison to Theorem 2.8 for equations, in Theorem 3.8 for contractions the 'guardedness' condition is weakened, allowing variables that are underneath $\tau$ prefixes; most important, the sequentiality condition is removed, allowing variables underneath any process constructs.

EXAMPLE 3.9. The following contractions have a unique solution for $\approx$:

1. $X \succeq \tau.X$
2. $X \succeq a.\boldsymbol{\nu}a\,(\overline{a} \mid X))$
3. $X \succeq a.\boldsymbol{\nu}b\,(\boldsymbol{\nu}a\,(\overline{a}.!a.\overline{b} \mid X) \mid !b.a)$

We have seen in Section 2.4 and at the beginning of Section 3 that the corresponding equations do not have a unique solution. The solutions of the contraction (1) are all inactive processes, where a process is *inactive* if it cannot perform visible actions (i.e., if $P$ is the process, then there is no $P'$ and visible action $\ell$ such that $P \Longrightarrow P' \xrightarrow{\ell}$). The contraction has a unique solution because all inactive processes are bisimilar. It is easy to see that an inactive process is solution. Conversely, suppose $P$ is not inactive, and let $n$ be the least $n \geq 0$ such that $P(\xrightarrow{\tau})^n \xrightarrow{\ell}$ for some $\ell$; then $P$ is not a solution of $P \succeq \tau.P$ because $\tau.P$ needs at least $n+1$ $\tau$-steps before exhibiting any visible action, and therefore can never be more efficient than $P$. Example of solutions for (2) and (3) are $a.P$ and $\tau.a.P$, where $P$ is inactive. Any solution of (2) and (3) is bisimilar with $a.\mathbf{0}$. □

REMARK 3.10. Results such as Lemma 3.7 and Theorem 3.8 also hold if the game played in clause (1) of Definition 3.1 of bisimulation contraction is that of strong simulation (i.e., "$P \xrightarrow{\mu} P'$ implies there is $Q'$ such that $Q \xrightarrow{\mu} Q'$ and $P' \mathcal{R} Q'$"). However, the resulting relation would not be coarse enough to capture expansion – a major goal for this paper is understanding existing 'bisimilarity up-to' techniques, where expansion is important. □

### 3.4 Completeness

An interesting class of contractions are those in which the body $E$ of each contraction $X \succeq E$ does not contain constants. In these systems, all forms of infinity in the behaviour of processes are captured by recursive calls through the contraction variables. We call such systems *pure*. Similarly we call pure a system of equations without constants. In this section we discuss the expressiveness of pure systems of contractions and equations. (With constants the question is vacuous, as the behaviour of any process $P$ is captured by the guarded and sequential equation $X = P$.) We show that the technique of weakly-guarded contractions given by Theorem 3.8 is complete, whereas that of guarded and sequential equations given by Theorem 2.8 is not.

If $\mathcal{R}$ is a relation then we can also view $\mathcal{R}$ as an ordered sequence of pairs (e.g., assuming some lexicographical ordering). Then $\mathcal{R}_i$ indicates the tuple obtained by projecting the pairs in $\mathcal{R}$ on the $i$-th component ($i = 1, 2$).

THEOREM 3.11 (completeness). *Suppose $\mathcal{R}$ is a bisimulation. Then there is a system of weakly-guarded pure contractions of which $\mathcal{R}_1$ and $\mathcal{R}_2$ are solutions for $\succeq_{\text{bis}}$.*

**Proof** [Sketch] Suppose $\mathcal{R}$ is a bisimulation. We define a system of contractions of which $\mathcal{R}_1$ and $\mathcal{R}_2$ are solutions. The variables of the contractions are of the form $X_{P,Q}$ for $P \mathcal{R} Q$, and there is one contraction for each pair in $\mathcal{R}$.

We show how the contraction for a pair $P \mathcal{R} Q$ is built. Consider an enumeration of all the transitions from $P$:

$$P \xrightarrow{\mu_r} P_r$$

where $r$ ranges over some countable set $I_P$. Following the bisimulation game, for each $r$ there is $Q_r$ s.t. $Q \stackrel{\widehat{\mu_r}}{\Longrightarrow} Q_r$ and $P_r \mathcal{R} Q_r$. Proceeding similarly on the challenge transitions from $Q$, i.e. $Q \xrightarrow{\mu_s} Q_s$ for $s \in I_Q$, we find processes $P_s$ with $P \stackrel{\widehat{\mu_s}}{\Longrightarrow} P_s$ and $P_s \mathcal{R} Q_s$. Then the contraction for the pair $P, Q$ is:

$$X_{P,Q} \succeq \Sigma_r \mu_r.\, X_{P_r,Q_r} + \Sigma_s \mu_s.\, X_{P_s,Q_s}$$

□

The contractions in the proof of the theorem are sequential and weakly guarded, but not necessarily guarded. The assertion of Theorem 3.11 can actually be refined: the technique based on weakly-guarded contractions is also *computationally complete* with respect to the bisimulation proof method, in the sense that the size of the structures needed and the subsequent amount of checks are comparable. The *size* of a relation is the number of its pairs. The size of a system of contractions is the number of contractions. The proof of Theorem 3.11 shows that the system of contractions derived from a bisimulation $\mathcal{R}$ has the same size as $\mathcal{R}$; moreover, the work needed to prove that $\mathcal{R}_1$ and $\mathcal{R}_2$ are solutions of the system of contractions is precisely the work needed to check the challenge/response diagrams of the bisimulation game for $\mathcal{R}$.

In contrast, the method for equations resulting from Theorem 2.8 is not complete. For instance, there is no system of guarded and sequential pure equations in which one of the solutions is the process $K$ so defined:

$$K \stackrel{\triangle}{=} \tau.(a \mid K) + \tau.\mathbf{0}\ .$$

To see this, it is useful to express the behaviour of $K$ via the following constants:

$$\begin{aligned} H_0 &\stackrel{\triangle}{=} \tau.H_1 + \tau \\ H_i &\stackrel{\triangle}{=} \tau.H_{i+1} + a.H_{i-1} + \tau.a^i \quad (i > 0) \end{aligned}$$

We have $a^i \mid K \approx H_i$, for each $i$, as witnessed by the relation

$$\mathcal{R} \stackrel{\text{def}}{=} \cup_{i \geq 0}\{(a^i \mid K, H_i)\}\ ,$$

which is a bisimulation up-to strong bisimilarity. Now, for each $n \neq m$, we have $H_n \not\approx H_m$ (because, assuming $n < m$, $H_m$ cannot match the transition $H_n \xrightarrow{\tau} a^n$); moreover, for each $n$ there is a transition $H_n \xrightarrow{\tau} H_{n+1}$. As a consequence, the infinite sequence of transitions

$$H_0 \xrightarrow{\tau} H_1 \xrightarrow{\tau} \cdots H_n \xrightarrow{\tau} H_{n+1} \xrightarrow{\tau} \cdots \tag{2}$$

go through states that are pairwise non-bisimilar. An equation of which $K$ is solution should be able to express the same behaviour. This is impossible, however, if the equation is sequential and guarded, because the equation variables must be underneath a visible prefix, and can only be reached by performing a visible action. Hence an infinite nesting of internal transitions as in (2) cannot be derived.

### 3.5 Relationship with up-to context

The completeness of the contraction technique given by Theorem 3.11, including the computational completeness discussed after the theorem, remains also with respect to powerful enhancements of the bisimulation proof method such as 'up-to context' techniques.

We show that the contraction technique is in fact computationally equivalent to the 'up-to $\succeq_{\text{bis}}$ and context' technique, a refinement of the 'up-to expansion and context' of Definition 2.3 (the former captures a larger set of relations because bisimilarity contraction is coarser than expansion).

DEFINITION 3.12 (bisimulation up-to $\succeq_{\text{bis}}$ and context). *A process relation $\mathcal{R}$ is a* bisimulation up-to $\succeq_{\text{bis}}$ and context *if, whenever $P \mathcal{R} Q$, we have:*

1. *$P \xrightarrow{\mu} P'$ implies there is $Q'$ such that $Q \stackrel{\widehat{\mu}}{\Longrightarrow} Q'$ and $P' \succeq_{\text{bis}} \mathcal{R}^c \approx Q'$*
2. *the converse of (1) on the actions from $Q$.*

THEOREM 3.13. *Suppose $\mathcal{R}$ is a bisimulation up-to $\succeq_{\text{bis}}$ and context. Then there is a system of weakly-guarded contractions, of the same size as $\mathcal{R}$, of which $\mathcal{R}_1$ and $\mathcal{R}_2$ are solutions for $\succeq_{\text{bis}}$.*

*Conversely, suppose $\widetilde{P}$ and $\widetilde{Q}$ are solutions for $\succeq_{\rm bis}$ to the same system of weakly-guarded contractions. Then the relation $\{(P_i, Q_i)\}_i$ is a bisimulation up-to $\succeq_{\rm bis}$ and context.*

The theorem is proved along the lines of Theorem 3.11.

REMARK 3.14. The definition of contraction was derived by attempts at obtaining theorems such as 3.11 and 3.13. The constructions in the theorems do not work with expansion in place of bisimilarity contraction. □

From Theorems 3.13 and 3.8 we derive:

COROLLARY 3.15. (soundness of 'bisimulation up-to $\succeq_{\rm bis}$ and context'). *If $\mathcal{R}$ is a bisimulation up-to $\succeq_{\rm bis}$ and context, then $R \subseteq \approx$.*

Having shown that the techniques of weakly-guarded contractions and 'bisimulation up-to $\succeq_{\rm bis}$ and context' are equivalent, we can derive the soundness of one from the soundness of the other (in Corollary 3.15 we took the contraction technique as primitive). The complexity of the soundness proofs of the two techniques is similar. The main difference is that the expressions in the body of the contractions are weakly guarded, whereas the contexts of the 'up-to context' bisimulation techniques are not. As a consequence, in the proofs for the 'up-to context' techniques one has to reason about all possible interactions between a context and the processes plugged into it, proceeding by transition induction and a case analysis on the last rule used to derive a transition. With contractions this is avoided, exploiting the weak-guardedness condition and the unfolding of the contractions.

### 3.6 Example: the lazy and eager servers

We show a proof of the bisimilarity between the lazy and the eager systems of Section 2.3 using the technique of unique solution of contractions. This serves both as an an illustration of the application of the technique, and as a comparison with the technique based on the bisimulation proof method employed in the proof of Section 2.3.

The proof consists in showing that $\{LS\langle n\rangle\}_n$ and $\{ES\langle n\rangle\}_n$ are solutions of the following system of contractions:

$$\{X_n \succeq c(z).\,(X_{n+1} \mid R\langle c, n, z\rangle)\}_n \qquad (3)$$

We establish that $\{ES\langle n\rangle\}_n$ is a solution using the algebraic laws in the proof in Section 2.3 (noticing that in (1) $\approx$ can be replaced by $\succeq_{\rm bis}$):

$$\begin{array}{rcl} ES\langle n\rangle & \succeq_{\rm bis} & \boldsymbol{\nu} a\,(A\langle n+1\rangle \mid c(z).\,(E \mid R\langle c, n, z\rangle)) \\ & \sim & c(z).\,(\boldsymbol{\nu} a\,(A\langle n+1\rangle \mid E) \mid R\langle c, n, z\rangle) \\ & = & c(z).\,(ES\langle n+1\rangle \mid R\langle c, n, z\rangle)\ . \end{array}$$

We proceed similarly for $LS\langle n\rangle$.

The contraction (3) is not sequential, hence contractions and Theorem 3.8 cannot be replaced by equations and Theorem 2.8.

## 4. Language generalisation

We have shown the property of unique solution of weakly-guarded contractions in CCS. We generalise here the theorem to an arbitrary process language, using a more abstract condition. The generalisation serves both to better understand the validity of the theorem, and for applicability to languages that, unlike CCS, do not have an explicit prefixing construct.

For this generalisation we consider the case — standard in process algebra — in which the syntax of the processes is the term algebra generated by some signature, and the semantics is given as an LTS. We call *process language* any such language. We use $\mathcal{L}$ to denote a generic process language, and $\mathcal{L}(\mathcal{X})$ for its extension with the contraction variables in $\mathcal{X}$. We say that $\mathcal{L}$ is *$\approx$-safe* if, in $\mathcal{L}$, $\approx$ is a congruence relation, and its corresponding contraction $\succeq_{\rm bis}$ is a precongruence.

In Theorem 3.8, the 'weakly guarded' hypothesis makes sure that the body of a contraction alone determines the first interaction. The body is thus autonomous: the interaction occurs without contributions from the terms that replace the contraction variables. Whenever the bodies of the contractions are autonomous in this sense, the unique-solution property holds.

DEFINITION 4.1 (autonomous contractions). *An expression $E$ of $\mathcal{L}(\mathcal{X})$ is* autonomous *if for all processes $\widetilde{P}$ of $\mathcal{L}$ we have:*

- *if $E[\widetilde{P}] \xrightarrow{\mu} R$, then there is a context $C$ such that $R = C[\widetilde{P}]$, and for all $\widetilde{Q}$, also $E[\widetilde{Q}] \xrightarrow{\mu} C[\widetilde{Q}]$.*

*A system of contractions $\{X_i \succeq E_i\}_{i\in I}$ is* autonomous *if each expression $E_i$ is autonomous.*

THEOREM 4.2. *In any $\approx$-safe process language $\mathcal{L}$, a system of autonomous contractions has a unique solution for $\approx$.*

The proof of the theorem is similar to that of Theorem 3.8. Checking the autonomy property is often straightforward. For instance, in the case of the *GSOS* format [5], autonomy holds if, in the body $E$ of a contraction, all variables are underneath an axiom operator, that is, an operator that, as CCS prefix, is defined by means of SOS rules in which the set of hypothesis is empty.

In some cases, autonomy may be better than the weakly-guarded hypothesis even if the calculus has a prefix operator: we shall see an example in Section 10, with the Higher-Order $\pi$-calculus, where autonomy allows us to capture occurrences of the contraction variables *within* output prefixes.

## 5. Barbed congruence

We (briefly) consider the application of the idea of contraction to barbed congruence [20], for various reasons. First, barbed congruence is a contextually-defined form of behavioural equivalence, and it paves the way to the treatment of other forms of contextual equivalence. Second, we want to show that – sometimes – the contraction techniques make it possible to work directly with barbed congruence, even though it is contextually defined (e.g., the example with higher-order processes in Section 10). Third, the definition of barbed congruence applies to any language with a reduction semantics (i.e., a *reduction* relation and a *barb*, or *observation*, predicate), as opposed to the LTS semantics of the languages in earlier sections.

Thus the definitions and results in this section hold for any algebraic calculus (the term algebra over a signature) equipped with a reduction semantics, that is, a reduction relation $\longrightarrow$ and a barb predicate $\downarrow$. We use $\mathcal{RL}$ for referring to a generic such language, and $\mathcal{RL}(\mathcal{X})$ for its extension with the contraction variables in $\mathcal{X}$. (For CCS, $\longrightarrow$ is $\xrightarrow{\tau}$ and $P\downarrow$ holds if $P \xrightarrow{\ell}$, for some visible action $\ell$.) As usual, $\Longrightarrow$ is the reflexive and transitive closure of $\longrightarrow$; and $P \Downarrow$ holds if there is $P'$ with $P \Longrightarrow P'$ and $P'\downarrow$.

DEFINITION 5.1 (barbed bisimulation and congruence). *A relation $\mathcal{R}$ on the processes of $\mathcal{RL}$ is a* barbed bisimulation *if whenever $P \mathrel{\mathcal{R}} Q$:*

1. *$P \longrightarrow P'$ implies there is $Q'$ such that $Q \Longrightarrow Q'$ and $P' \mathrel{\mathcal{R}} Q'$;*
2. *$P\downarrow$ implies $Q \Downarrow$;*
3. *the converse of (1) and (2), on challenges from $Q$.*

Barbed bisimilarity, *written $\approx_{\rm bar}$, is the union of all barbed bisimulations. Two processes $P$ and $Q$ are* barbed congruent, *written*

$P \approx^{c}_{\text{bar}} Q$*, if for each context* $C$*, it holds that* $C[P] \approx_{\text{bar}} C[Q]$. □

REMARK 5.2. The definitions of barbed congruence in the literature often make use of a *set* of barb predicates; we use only *one* barb here for mere simplicity of presentation. A variant of barbed congruence is *reduction-closed barbed congruence* [11], in which the closure under contexts is placed within the definition of bisimilarity. The difference between the two variants has no consequences on the results in the paper. □

In the 'contraction version' of barbed bisimilarity we write $Q \stackrel{\wedge}{\longrightarrow} Q'$ if $Q \longrightarrow Q'$ or $Q = Q'$.

DEFINITION 5.3. (barbed contraction, barbed congruence contraction). *A relation* $\mathcal{R}$ *on the processes of* $\mathcal{RL}$ *is a* barbed contraction *if, whenever* $P \;\mathcal{R}\; Q$:

1. $P \longrightarrow P'$ *implies there is* $Q'$ *such that* $Q \stackrel{\wedge}{\longrightarrow} Q'$ *and* $P' \;\mathcal{R}\; Q'$;
2. $Q \longrightarrow Q'$ *implies there is* $P'$ *such that* $P \Longrightarrow P'$ *and* $P' \approx_{\text{bar}} Q'$;
3. $P \downarrow$ *implies* $Q \downarrow$;
4. $Q \downarrow$ *implies* $P \Downarrow$.

Barbed contraction, *written* $\succeq_{\text{bar}}$*, is the union of all barbed contractions.* Barbed congruence contraction, *written* $\succeq^{c}_{\text{bar}}$*, relates two processes* $P$ *and* $Q$ *if, for each context* $C$*, it holds that* $C[P] \succeq_{\text{bar}} C[Q]$.

We transport the concept of autonomy to reduction-based semantics.

DEFINITION 5.4 (reduction-autonomous contractions). *An expression* $E$ *of* $\mathcal{RL}(\mathcal{X})$ *is* reduction-autonomous *if for all processes* $\widetilde{P}$ *and context* $C$ *of* $\mathcal{RL}$:

- *if* $C[E[\widetilde{P}]] \longrightarrow R$*, then there is a context* $C'$ *such that* $R = C'[\widetilde{P}]$ *and, for all* $\widetilde{Q}$*, also* $C[E[\widetilde{Q}]] \longrightarrow C'[\widetilde{Q}]$;
- *if* $C[E[\widetilde{P}]] \downarrow$ *then, for all* $\widetilde{Q}$*, also* $C[E[\widetilde{Q}]] \downarrow$.

*A system of contractions* $\{X_i \succeq E_i\}_{i \in I}$ *is* reduction-autonomous *is each expression* $E_i$ *is reduction-autonomous.*

Barbed congruence and its contraction are, by definition, fully substitutive. Hence the safety requirement of Theorem 4.2 is not needed. In the property of unique solution for barbed congruence, the symbols $\asymp$ and $\succeq_{\asymp}$ of Definition 3.4 become $\approx^{c}_{\text{bar}}$ and $\succeq^{c}_{\text{bar}}$, respectively.

THEOREM 5.5. *In* $\mathcal{RL}$*, any system of reduction-autonomous contractions has a unique solution for* $\approx^{c}_{\text{bar}}$.

# 6. Uniqueness of solution of contractions for non-coinductive equivalences

We consider now non-coinductive equivalences. We focus on contextual equivalence [22] (i.e., *may testing* [9]), because it is widely studied. As the barbed congruence of Section 5, so contextual equivalence is contextually defined. Thus the setting considered is the same: an algebraic process language equipped with a reduction semantics. We reuse notations and terminologies from Section 5. Intuitively, two terms are contextually equivalent when they are equally observable, in any context.

DEFINITION 6.1 (contextual equivalence). $P \approx_{\text{ctx}} Q$ *holds when* $C[P] \Downarrow$ *iff* $C[Q] \Downarrow$*, for all* $C$.

The definition of the contextual equivalence contraction uses the predicate $P \Downarrow^{n}$, indicating that a barb is reached in at most $n$ steps, i.e., $P(\stackrel{\tau}{\longrightarrow})^{m} P' \downarrow$, for some $P'$, with $0 \leq m \leq n$.

DEFINITION 6.2 (contextual equivalence contraction). $P \succeq_{\text{ctx}} Q$ *if for all* $C$:

1. $C[P] \Downarrow^{n}$ *implies* $C[Q] \Downarrow^{n}$*, for any* $n$;
2. $C[Q] \Downarrow$ *implies* $C[P] \Downarrow$.

Thus, referring to contextual equivalence, the symbols $\asymp$ and $\succeq_{\asymp}$ of Definition 3.4 become $\approx_{\text{ctx}}$ and $\succeq_{\text{ctx}}$.

THEOREM 6.3. *A system of reduction-autonomous contractions has a unique solution for* $\approx_{\text{ctx}}$.

**Proof** [Sketch] Suppose $\widetilde{P}$ and $\widetilde{Q}$ are solutions for $\succeq_{\text{ctx}}$, and consider a context $C$. One shows that $C[\widetilde{P}] \Downarrow$ implies $C[\widetilde{Q}] \Downarrow$. Suppose $C[\widetilde{P}] \Downarrow^{n}$. One proceeds by induction on $n$, exploiting the properties of the unfolding of contractions. □

COROLLARY 6.4. *In CCS, a system of weakly-guarded contractions has a unique solution for* $\approx_{\text{ctx}}$.

### 6.1 Example: the lazy and eager servers, revisited

Contextual equivalence does not have the congruence problems of bisimilarity for summation that motivated, in the presentation of CCS in Section 2, the use of guarded sums. We can therefore admit the full summation construct $\Sigma_i P_i$ in the grammar for the CCS processes. Such a flexibility will be useful in this example.

We revisit the lazy and eager servers in the example of Section 2.3. We modify the auxiliary server $A$, which was consulted by the main server before starting an interaction protocol with a client. In Section 2.3, the server was deterministic; now it is non-deterministic. Thus all definitions remain the same except that $A$ always returns an arbitrary integer:

$$A \stackrel{\triangle}{=} \Sigma_{n \in N}\; \overline{a}\langle n\rangle.\, A$$

The system with the lazy main server is now $\mathit{LS} \stackrel{\text{def}}{=} \boldsymbol{\nu} a\,(A \mid L)$, and the system with the eager main server is $\mathit{ES} \stackrel{\text{def}}{=} \boldsymbol{\nu} a\,(A \mid E)$, where $L$ and $E$ are as in Section 2.3. The timing difference between $\mathit{LS}$ and $\mathit{ES}$ in consulting $A$ is observable under bisimilarity. The reason is that an interaction

$$\mathit{ES} \longrightarrow \boldsymbol{\nu} a\,(A \mid c(z).\,(E \mid R\langle c, n, z\rangle))\,,$$

in which $n$ is received from $A$, is a commitment to using $n$ in the interaction with the next client. In contrast, $\mathit{LS}$ is unable to make such a commitment — its only initial transition is a visible one.

The difference is however not observable under contextual equivalence. We prove $\mathit{LS} \approx_{\text{ctx}} \mathit{ES}$ using the technique of unique solution of weakly-guarded contractions. The proof is similar to that with the deterministic auxiliary server and the bisimilarity contraction in Section 3.6, with a further simplification: a single contraction is sufficient, namely

$$X \succeq c(z).\, \Sigma_n (X \mid R\langle c, n, z\rangle) \tag{4}$$

To show that both $\mathit{LS}$ and $\mathit{ES}$ are solutions for $\succeq_{\text{ctx}}$ of this contraction, we employ the same laws and algebraic reasoning of Section 3.6 (which are sound because bisimilarity implies contextual equivalence). An additional laws is required in the proof of $\mathit{ES}$:

$$\Sigma_i \alpha.\, R_i \succeq_{\text{ctx}} \alpha.\, \Sigma_i R_i \quad (\alpha \text{ is any prefix}) \tag{5}$$

(the law is actually valid for *strong* contextual equivalence, where two equal processes are required to reach an observable in the same number of steps). This is one of the most distinguishing laws of contextual equivalence. Using the laws we have:

$$\begin{array}{rcl} ES = \boldsymbol{\nu} a\,(A \mid E) & \succeq_{\rm ctx} & \Sigma_n c(z).\, \boldsymbol{\nu} a\,(A \mid E \mid R\langle c,n,z\rangle) \\ & \succeq_{\rm ctx} & c(z).\, \Sigma_n(\boldsymbol{\nu} a\,(A \mid E) \mid R\langle c,n,z\rangle) \\ & = & c(z).\, \Sigma_n(ES \mid R\langle c,n,z\rangle) \end{array}$$

which shows that $ES$ is a solution of the contraction (4). The proof that also $LS$ is a solution is simpler.

The above proof is similar to the proofs with the servers in Sections 2.3 and 3.6. All these proofs, explicitly or implicitly, employ 'up-to context' reasoning; above the common context is $c(z).\, \Sigma_n([\cdot] \mid R\langle c,n,z\rangle)$.

A proof that follows the definition of contextual equivalence would be hard due to the quantification on all contexts. In CCS, contextual equivalence coincides with trace equivalence. The equality in the example cannot be proved purely algebraically, using standard axiom systems for trace equivalence, because the systems compared are not finite or finite state (axiomatisations are complete only on these systems). One could show that $ES$ and $LS$ have the same traces proceeding by induction on the length of the traces. The proof is tedious, for instance because $R$ could be any process.

REMARK 6.5. The proof of the equality between $ES$ and $LS$ reveals the essence of the technique based on unique solution of contractions. One employs some simple algebraic laws to prove that two tuples of terms are solutions of a certain system of contractions, from which the equality between the two tuples is derived from the unique-solution theorem. The algebraic laws may have been obtained in various ways (e.g., an axiomatisation of the equality for the finite terms). In our example we have used laws for bisimilarity, because it implies contextual equivalence, plus law (5). Law (5) is a well-known law in axiomatisations of trace equivalence; the law can also be easily proved directly in terms of contextual equivalence, reasoning by induction on the length on the number of $\tau$-steps needed to reach an observable. □

## 7. Trace equivalence

In this section we briefly consider trace equivalence. In CCS and most process algebras, trace equivalence is a direct characterisation of contextual equivalence, in the same way as bisimilarity is for barbed congruence. Aside from this, we look at trace equivalence because it is a behavioural equivalence non-contextual and inductive. We use $s$ to range over *traces*, i.e., non-empty sequences of visible actions.

We assume to be in a generic process language $\mathcal{L}$ with an LTS semantics, as in Section 4. We write $P \stackrel{\mu}{\Longrightarrow}_n P'$ if $P \stackrel{\mu}{\Longrightarrow} P'$ is derived using $n$ strong transitions (i.e., we have $P(\stackrel{\tau}{\longrightarrow})^m \stackrel{\mu}{\longrightarrow} (\stackrel{\tau}{\longrightarrow})^{m'} P'$ and $n = m + m' + 1$. If $s = \ell_1, \ldots, \ell_n$, then we write $P \stackrel{s}{\Longrightarrow}$ if $P \stackrel{\ell_1}{\Longrightarrow} P_1 \stackrel{\ell_2}{\Longrightarrow} P_2 \ldots P_{n-1} \stackrel{\ell_n}{\Longrightarrow} P_n$, for some processes $P_1, \ldots, P_n$. Similarly we write $P \stackrel{s}{\Longrightarrow}_m$ if there are $P_1, \ldots, P_n$ with $P \stackrel{\ell_1}{\Longrightarrow}_{m_1} P_1 \stackrel{\ell_2}{\Longrightarrow}_{m_2} P_2 \ldots P_{n-1} \stackrel{\ell_n}{\Longrightarrow}_{m_n} P_n$, and $m = \Sigma_i m_i$.

DEFINITION 7.1. *Two processes $P, Q$ of $\mathcal{L}$ are* trace equivalent, *written $P \approx_{\rm tr} Q$, if for each trace $s$ we have $P \stackrel{s}{\Longrightarrow}$ iff $Q \stackrel{s}{\Longrightarrow}$.*

*Two processes $P, Q$ are in the* trace equivalence contraction, *written $P \succeq_{\rm tr} Q$, if, for each trace $s$:*

1. *if $P \stackrel{s}{\Longrightarrow}_n$ then $Q \stackrel{s}{\Longrightarrow}_m$ for some $m \leq n$;*
2. *if $Q \stackrel{s}{\Longrightarrow}$ then $P \stackrel{s}{\Longrightarrow}$.*

A process language is $\approx_{\rm tr}$*-safe* if $\approx_{\rm tr}$ is a congruence and $\succeq_{\rm tr}$ a precongruence.

THEOREM 7.2. *In any $\approx_{\rm tr}$-safe process language $\mathcal{L}$, a system of autonomous contractions has a unique solution for $\approx_{\rm tr}$.*

Refined forms of trace equivalence exist. For instance, *ready trace equivalence* [3, 10] combines traces with barbs. The idea of contraction and Theorem 7.2 can be adapted to ready traces by combining the treatment of traces in Definition 7.1 with the treatment of barbs in Definitions 5.3 and 6.2.

## 8. Non-applicability of the technique

The contraction technique may be applied to any equivalence whose observables are *finitary*, in the sense that if an observable holds then it can be reached in a finite number of transitions. Bisimilarity is in this class: the observables are the weak transitions $\stackrel{\mu}{\Longrightarrow}$; each use of $\stackrel{\mu}{\Longrightarrow}$ is finitary because obtained by composing a finite number of strong transitions ($\stackrel{\tau}{\longrightarrow}$ and $\stackrel{\mu}{\longrightarrow}$). Different uses of $\stackrel{\mu}{\Longrightarrow}$ may have different lengths, but each length is finite. The same argument holds for $\Downarrow$, the observable of contextual equivalence. In all these cases, the contraction preorder precisely arises by playing with such finite measures.

There are behavioural equivalences, however, in which the observables are not finitary. For instance, an observable may be inherently coinductive, as for observables such as infinite traces and non-termination. We illustrate the possible failure of the contraction techniques in these cases using *infinitary trace equivalence*, whereby two processes are equated if they have the same traces, including the infinite ones. It is unclear how the contraction of infinitary trace equivalence should be defined. In any case, however, 'unique solution' would fail, even for guarded and sequential contractions. As an example, consider the processes $P \stackrel{\rm def}{=} \Sigma_n a^n$ and $Q \stackrel{\rm def}{=} P + a.\, !a.\, \mathbf{0}$. These processes are not infinitary trace equivalent. However, in an 'infinitary trace' semantics they both are solutions to the (guarded and sequential) contraction

$$X \succeq a + a.\, X$$

The definition of the the contraction for infinitary trace equivalence is irrelevant here, because the processes have no $\tau$-transitions. Similar problems arise for *must equivalence*, where non-termination is observable — the same counterexample of infinitary trace equivalence applies.

## 9. Injecting contractions into the bisimulation game

An advantage of bisimilarity, with respect to other behavioural equivalences, is the locality of the required checks: related states only have to match each other's immediate transitions. We can inject some locality also in other equivalences by introducing the corresponding contraction into a 'bisimulation up-to' game. We illustrate this possibility with contextual equivalence, which is inductive and contextual and therefore faraway from bisimilarity and its local checks. Since we play the bisimulation game, we assume a process language $\mathcal{L}$ with an LTS semantics, on top of which contextual equivalence (and reduction semantics) is defined as in CCS.

DEFINITION 9.1 (bisimulation up-to $\succeq_{\rm ctx}$). *A relation $\mathcal{R}$ on the process language $\mathcal{L}$ is a* bisimulation up-to $\succeq_{\rm ctx}$ *if, whenever $P \mathcal{R} Q$, we have:*

1. *$P \stackrel{\mu}{\longrightarrow} P'$ implies $Q \stackrel{\widehat{\mu}}{\Longrightarrow} Q'$ and $P' \succeq_{\rm ctx} \mathcal{R} \approx_{\rm ctx} Q'$*
2. *the converse of (1) on the actions from $Q$.*

As in the case of ordinary bisimulation, so bisimulation up-to $\succeq_{\rm ctx}$ may be enhanced by combination with further up-to techniques. For instance, in the *bisimulation up-to $\succeq_{\rm ctx}$ and context* the requirement $P' \succeq_{\rm ctx} \mathcal{R} \approx_{\rm ctx} Q'$ on the derivatives of Definition 2.3 becomes

$$P' \succeq_{\rm ctx} \mathcal{R}^{\rm c} \approx_{\rm ctx} Q'$$

It is sufficient to analyse the most powerful technique ('up-to $\succeq_{\rm ctx}$ and context'), and the results will also hold for the weaker 'up-to $\succeq_{\rm ctx}$'. We derive soundness from that of the corresponding contraction technique.

LEMMA 9.2. *In $\mathcal{L}$, suppose $\mathcal{R}$ is a bisimulation up-to $\succeq_{\rm ctx}$ and context. Then there is a system of reduction-autonomous contractions, of the same size as $\mathcal{R}$, of which $\mathcal{R}_1$ and $\mathcal{R}_2$ are solutions for $\succeq_{\rm ctx}$.*

COROLLARY 9.3. (soundness of bisimulation up-to $\succeq_{\rm ctx}$ and context). *Suppose a relation $\mathcal{R}$ on the process language $\mathcal{L}$ is a bisimulation up-to $\succeq_{\rm ctx}$ and context. Then $\mathcal{R} \subseteq \approx_{\rm ctx}$.*

We have seen that, in the case of bisimilarity, the techniques of 'unique solution of contractions for $\approx$' and of 'bisimulation up-to contraction and context' are equivalent. For contextual equivalence, however, the former technique is more powerful. The reason is that, in the 'bisimulations up-to $\succeq_{\rm ctx}$ and context' game, laws and equalities for $\approx_{\rm ctx}$ are applied only *after* the derivatives of the processes in the pairs have been chosen. For instance, the lazy and eager servers of Section 6.1, *LS* and *ES*, cannot be a pair of a bisimulation up-to $\succeq_{\rm ctx}$ and context, for the same reason why they are not bisimilar: the challenge transition

$$ES \xrightarrow{\tau} \boldsymbol{\nu} a\,(A \mid c(z).\,(E \mid R\langle c,n,z\rangle))$$

cannot be matched by *LS*.

In some cases, however, the obstacle can be bypassed. We show this for the processes *LS* and *ES* of the server example. We relate *LS* to a contraction $ES'$ of *ES*, obtained by abstracting the initial private communication with the auxiliary server $A$:

$$ES \succeq_{\rm ctx} \Sigma_n \boldsymbol{\nu} a\,(A \mid c(z).\,(E \mid R\langle c,n,z\rangle)) \stackrel{\rm def}{=} ES' \qquad (6)$$

Now, the singleton relation $\{(LS, ES')\}$ is a bisimulation up-to $\succeq_{\rm ctx}$ and context. The processes in the pair initially may only perform an input at $c$; if $v$ is the value received in the input, then the transitions are

$$\begin{array}{rccl} & ES' & \xrightarrow{c(v)} & \Sigma_n \boldsymbol{\nu} a\,(A \mid E \mid R\langle c,n,v\rangle) \stackrel{\rm def}{=} ES'_1 \\ \text{and} & LS & = & \boldsymbol{\nu} a\,(A \mid c(z).\,a(x).\,(L \mid R\langle c,x,z\rangle)) \\ & & \xrightarrow{c(v)} & \boldsymbol{\nu} a\,(A \mid a(x).\,(L \mid R\langle c,x,v\rangle)) \stackrel{\rm def}{=} LS_1 \end{array}$$

Now we have, using algebraic reasoning similar to that in previous examples with the servers and (6):

$$\begin{array}{rccl} & ES'_1 & \sim & \Sigma_n(\boldsymbol{\nu} a\,(A \mid E) \mid R\langle c,n,v\rangle) \\ & & \succeq_{\rm ctx} & \Sigma_n(ES' \mid R\langle c,n,v\rangle) \\ \text{and} & LS_1 & \succeq_{\rm ctx} & \Sigma_n(\boldsymbol{\nu} a\,(A \mid L) \mid R\langle c,x,v\rangle) \\ & & = & \Sigma_n(LS \mid R\langle c,x,v\rangle) \end{array}$$

This is sufficient, up-to $\succeq_{\rm ctx}$ and context. Finally, having proved $ES \approx_{\rm ctx} ES'$ and $ES' \approx_{\rm ctx} LS$, we derive $ES \approx_{\rm ctx} LS$ by transitivity.

Other behavioural equivalences and their contractions can be injected into the 'bisimulation up to' game, along the lines of what done here for contextual equivalence.

## 10. Higher-order languages

The contraction technique may also be used in higher-order languages such as the $\lambda$-calculus and the Higher-Order $\pi$-calculus [34]. We refrain from attempting to produce a general theory of contractions for higher-order languages, comparable in power to the bisimulation proof method for these languages. We leave this for future work. Here we simply show that the transport to a higher-order setting of the most basic contraction techniques — those involving a reduction semantics and contextually-defined equivalences — can still be useful. We illustrate this on the Higher-Order $\pi$-calculus.

We consider the Higher-Order $\pi$-calculus in its simplest form, where only processes can be communicated. Below is the syntax; see Figure 2 for the reduction semantics.

$$P \quad ::= \quad \overline{a}\langle P\rangle.\,Q \;\Big|\; a(x).\,P \;\Big|\; x \;\Big|\; \boldsymbol{\nu} a\, P \;\Big|\; P \mid Q \;\Big|\; \mathbf{0}$$

We use $a, b, c, \ldots$ to range over names, and $x, y, z, \ldots$ to range over variables; we call them *language variables* (to distinguish them from the contraction or equation variables such as $X, Y$). An input $a(x).\,P$ binds the free occurrences of variable $x$ in $P$; similarly a restriction $\boldsymbol{\nu} a\; P$ binds the free occurrences of name $a$ in $P$. A term is *open* or *closed* depending on whether it may, or may not, have free language variables (in any case, it may have free names).

***Systems of contractions in the Higher-Order $\pi$-calculus*** In the definition of barbed congruence and its contraction, the only technicality of higher-order languages that has to be taken into account is the distinction between open and closed terms. This is dealt with in the expected manner. All running terms are supposed to be closed. Thus the definitions of equivalences and preorders in earlier sections (e.g., barbed congruence and its contraction) are meant to be on closed terms. The definitions are generalised to open expressions by requiring instantiation of the language variables with all closing substitutions, i.e., substitutions that make the terms closed (using, in contextual definitions, closing contexts rather than closing substitutions would yield the same relations).

***An example*** The example is about two ways of modeling the replication operator. We consider the equality (barbed congruence) between the terms $\overline{c}\langle A\rangle$ and $\overline{c}\langle B\rangle$, where

$$A \stackrel{\rm def}{=} b(y).\,\boldsymbol{\nu} a\,(M \mid \overline{a}\langle M\rangle) \qquad \text{for } M \stackrel{\rm def}{=} a(x).\,(y \mid x \mid \overline{a}\langle x\rangle)$$

and

$$B \stackrel{\rm def}{=} b(y).\,\boldsymbol{\nu} a\,(N \mid \overline{a}\langle y \mid N\rangle) \qquad \text{for } N \stackrel{\rm def}{=} a(x).\,(x \mid \overline{a}\langle x\rangle).$$

Terms $\overline{c}\langle A\rangle$ and $\overline{c}\langle B\rangle$ send on $c$ processes ($A$ and $B$) that can receive a process at $b$ and then replicate this process. Indeed, if $P$ is the process so received, assuming $a$ does not occur free in $P$, in one case we obtain the term

$$A_P \stackrel{\rm def}{=} \boldsymbol{\nu} a\,(M\{{}^{P}\!/\!{}_{y}\} \mid \overline{a}\langle M\{{}^{P}\!/\!{}_{y}\}\rangle)$$

and in the other case

$$B_P \stackrel{\rm def}{=} \boldsymbol{\nu} a\,(N \mid \overline{a}\langle P \mid N\rangle)\,,$$

and then we have:

$$A_P \longrightarrow P \mid A_P \longrightarrow P \mid P \mid A_P \longrightarrow \cdots$$

$$B_P \longrightarrow P \mid B_P \longrightarrow P \mid P \mid B_P \longrightarrow \cdots$$

The internal structure of $A_P$ and $B_P$ is however different.

A system of contractions that proves $\overline{c}\langle A\rangle \approx^{\rm c}_{\rm bar} \overline{c}\langle B\rangle$ is the following:

$$\begin{array}{rcl} X & \succeq & \overline{c}\langle Y\rangle.\,\mathbf{0} \\ Y & \succeq & b(y).\,Z \\ Z & \succeq & \tau.\,(y \mid Z) \end{array}$$

These contractions are reduction-autonomous, and therefore have a unique solution for barbed congruence. Note that, in the first contraction, a contraction variable occurs within the initial output prefix. Thus the contraction is *not* weakly guarded. Still, the contraction is reduction-autonomous because a process that replaces the

Structural congruence the least congruence $\equiv$ such that:

- $P \mid Q \equiv Q \mid P, P \mid (Q \mid R) \equiv (P \mid Q) \mid R, P \mid \mathbf{0} \equiv P; \boldsymbol{\nu} a\, \mathbf{0} \equiv \mathbf{0}, \boldsymbol{\nu} a\, \boldsymbol{\nu} b\, P \equiv \boldsymbol{\nu} b\, \boldsymbol{\nu} a\, P; (\boldsymbol{\nu} a\, P) \mid Q \equiv \boldsymbol{\nu} a\, (P \mid Q)$, if $a$ not free in $Q$

The reduction relation $P \longrightarrow Q$ is the least relation such that:

$$a(x).\, R \mid \overline{a}\langle P\rangle .\, Q \longrightarrow R\{^{P}\!/\!_{x}\} \mid Q \qquad \frac{P \longrightarrow P'}{P \mid Q \longrightarrow P' \mid Q} \qquad \frac{P \longrightarrow P'}{\boldsymbol{\nu} a\, P \longrightarrow \boldsymbol{\nu} a\, P'} \qquad \frac{P \equiv P' \longrightarrow P'' \equiv P'''}{P \longrightarrow P''''}$$

**Figure 2.** The reduction semantics for HO$\pi$

variable (and that therefore represents the value emitted in the output) does not contribute to the first action. Note also that the third contraction is open — it has $y$ as a free variable. Two solutions for $\succeq^{\rm c}_{\rm bar}$ (the barbed congruence contraction) to the above system of three contractions are, respectively:

1. $\overline{c}\langle A\rangle$, $A$, and $\boldsymbol{\nu} a\, (M \mid \overline{a}\langle M\rangle)$;
2. $\overline{c}\langle B\rangle$, $B$, and $\boldsymbol{\nu} a\, (N \mid \overline{a}\langle y \mid N\rangle)$.

The third process of each solution has $y$ free, as its corresponding contraction. To prove that these are solutions, we need a few simple algebraic laws.

Using the bisimulation proof method, the proof of the equality between $\overline{c}\langle A\rangle$ and $\overline{c}\langle B\rangle$ is more cumbersome; with the bisimulation techniques currently available, a proof requires an infinite relation. Even in the case of environmental bisimulation, where a form of 'up-to context' is available, the relation used in [35] for the same example is infinite because, intuitively, the values emitted, $A$ and $B$, have to be stored in an environment, and can then be played back at any time, possibly several times. What makes the difference is that contractions here allow us to extract a common context that incorporates the prefix for the initial action. In contrast, in 'up-to context' techniques for bisimulation, contexts are only removed from the derivatives, after firing an initial prefix.

## 11. Further related work

Milner's theorem about unique solution of equations stems from an axiomatisation of bisimulation on finite-state processes [21]. Indeed, in axiomatisations of behavioural equivalences [2, 19], the corresponding rule plays a key role and is called *fixed-point rule*, or *recursive specification principle*; see also [27], for trace equivalence. The possible shapes of the solutions of systems of equations, in connection with conditions on the guardedness of the equations, is studied by Baeten and Luttik [4].

Unique solution of equations has been considered in various settings, including languages, algebraic power series and pushdown automata (see the surveys [15, 23]), as well as in coalgebras (e.g., [18]). These models, however, do not have the analogous of 'internal step', around which all the theory of contractions is built. In functional languages, unique solution of equations is sometimes called 'unique fixed-point induction principle'. See for instance [31], in which the conditions resembles Milner's conditions of Theorem 2.8, and [13], which studies equations on streams advocating a condition based on the notion of 'contractive function' (the word 'contraction' here is unrelated to its use in our paper).

A tutorial on bisimulation enhancements is [26]. 'Up-to context' techniques have been formalised in a coalgebraic setting, and adapted to languages whose LTS semantics adheres to the GSOS format [5]; see for instance [6], which uses lambda-bialgebras, a generalisation of GSOS to the categorical framework.

The techniques in Section 9, transporting the bisimulation proof method and some of its enhancements onto non-coinductive equivalences, remind us of techniques for reducing non-coinductive equivalences to bisimilarity. For instance, trace equivalence on nondeterministic processes can be reduced to bisimilarity on deterministic processes, following the powerset construction for automata [12]; a similar reduction can be made for testing equivalence [8]. These results rely on transformations of transitions systems, which modify the nondeterminism and the set of states, in such a way that a given equivalence on the original systems corresponds to bisimilarity on the altered systems. In contrast, in the techniques of Section 9 the transformation of processes is performed dynamically, alongside the bisimulation game: two processes are manipulated only when necessary, i.e., when their immediate transitions would break the bisimulation game.

Some beautiful results have been obtained in CSP [28, 29] in which systems of equations have unique solutions provided their least fixed point (intuitively obtained by infinite unfolding of the equations) does not contain divergent states. In CSP the semantics has usually a denotational flavour and, most important, the reference behavioural equivalence, failure equivalence, is divergent sensitive. As mentioned in Section 8, currently we do not know how to handle divergence in the theory of contractions, as divergence is not a finitary observable. We note however that (at least in the equivalences considered in the paper) unique solution of contractions holds in cases where the infinite unfolding of the contractions would introduce divergence: e.g., the contractions of Example 3.9, as well as the contractions employed in the examples about the lazy and eager servers (where divergence may appear if, in the interaction protocol with a client, the main server is called back).

## 12. Conclusions and future work

In this paper we have presented operational techniques, based on the idea of contraction, for proving weak behavioural equivalences, that is, equivalences that abstract from internal moves. We have focused on concurrent languages but the techniques are not meant to be specific to concurrency. We have illustrated the techniques with bisimulation, the most natural ground of application, discussing also completeness. We have then shown that the technique of unique solution of contractions can be transported onto other equivalences, with finitary observables (e.g., contextual equivalence, barbed congruence, trace equivalence). We have also seen that the contraction preorders can be injected into the bisimulation game. In the case of bisimulation, this leads to a (minor) improvement of an existing technique, namely 'bisimulation up-to expansion and context'. The case of non-coinductive or contextual equivalences such as contextual equivalence is more interesting: we can use the bisimulation proof method (enhanced with up-to context) for reasoning on these equivalences, combined with algebraic laws for manipulating states whose immediate transitions would break the bisimulation game. Such techniques allow us, implicitly, to transfer 'up-to context' forms of reasoning, originally proposed for labeled bisimilarities and their proof method, onto equivalences that are contextual or non-coinductive.

As for the technique based on equations, so the technique based on contractions is meant to be used in combination with algebraic reasoning, on terms whose behaviour is not finite or finite-state: the recursion on the contraction variables captures the infinite behaviour of terms, and the proof that certain processes are solutions is carried out with pure algebraic reasoning.

In comparison with equations, a drawback of unique solution of contractions for an equivalence $\asymp$ is that the solutions are not $\asymp$-interchangeable: it may be that $P$ is solution and $Q$ is not, even though $P \asymp Q$.

The proof of completeness of the 'unique solution of contractions' method with respect to the bisimulation proof method uses the sum operator to express the possible initial actions of a process. We would like to see how completeness can be recovered in languages in which the sum operator is missing. One may consider the introduction of an operator akin to sum, to be used only for writing contractions. Also, we did not tackle completeness in equivalences other than bisimilarity.

We have related the contraction technique to bisimulation enhancements such as 'up-to expansion and context'. While powerful, these are not the only possible enhancements. It would be interesting to see whether other enhancements can be captured using contractions or similar notions.

We would like to understand on which behavioural equivalences the technique of unique solution of contractions works. We mentioned in Section 8 that it seems to work if the observables of the equivalence are finitary. More experimentation is needed to clarify this point, and formalise appropriate conditions.

In the example with a higher-order language, we have applied the most basic contraction techniques — those for contextually-defined equivalences. The use of other contraction techniques requires further investigation. Such study may shed light on the applicability of up-to context techniques to higher-order languages [14, 16, 17, 24, 35].

Our original motivation for studying contractions was to better understand 'up-to context' enhancements of the bisimulation proof method and their soundness. More broadly, the goal of the line of work reported is to improve our understanding of bisimilarity and the proof techniques for it, including the possibility of exporting the techniques onto other equivalences.

## Acknowledgments

I have benefited from discussions with Luca Aceto, Jos Baeten, Filippo Bonchi, Matthew Hennessy, Bill Roscoe, David Sands, and from the comments of the anonymous referees. This work has been partially supported by the ANR project 12IS02001 'PACE', and the MIUR-PRIN project 'CINA'.

## References

[1] S. Arun-Kumar and M. Hennessy. An efficiency preorder for processes. *Acta Informatica*, 29:737–760, 1992.

[2] J.C.M. Baeten, T. Basten, and M.A. Reniers. *Process Algebra: Equational Theories of Communicating Processes*. Cambridge University Press, 2010.

[3] Jos C. M. Baeten, Jan A. Bergstra, and Jan Willem Klop. Ready-trace semantics for concrete process algebra with the priority operator. *Comput. J.*, 30(6):498–506, 1987.

[4] Jos C. M. Baeten and Bas Luttik. Unguardedness mostly means many solutions. *Theor. Comput. Sci.*, 412(28):3090–3100, 2011.

[5] B. Bloom, S. Istrail, and A.R. Meyer. Bisimulation can't be traced. *Journal of the ACM*, 42(1):232–268, 1995.

[6] F. Bonchi, D. Petrisan, D. Pous, and J. Rot. Coinduction up to in a fibrational setting. Proc. CSL-LICS'14, ACM, 2014.

[7] Filippo Bonchi and Damien Pous. Checking nfa equivalence with bisimulations up to congruence. In *Proc. POPL'13*, pages 457–468. ACM, 2013.

[8] Rance Cleaveland and Matthew Hennessy. Testing equivalence as a bisimulation equivalence. *Formal Asp. Comput.*, 5(1):1–20, 1993.

[9] R. De Nicola and R. Hennessy. Testing equivalences for processes. *Theoretical Computer Science*, 34:83–133, 1984.

[10] R.J. van Glabbeek. The linear time—branching time spectrum II. In *Proc. CONCUR '93*, volume 715. Springer, 1993.

[11] K. Honda and N. Yoshida. On reduction-based process semantics. *Theoretical Computer Science*, 152(2):437–486, 1995.

[12] John E. Hopcroft, Rajeev Motwani, and Jeffrey D. Ullman. *Introduction to Automata Theory, Languages, and Computation*. Addison-Wesley, Boston, MA, USA, 2006.

[13] G. Hutton and M. Jaskelioff. Representing Contractive Functions on Streams. Submitted, 2011.

[14] V. Koutavas and M. Wand. Small bisimulations for reasoning about higher-order imperative programs. In *Proc. POPL'06*, pages 141–152. ACM, 2006.

[15] Michal Kunc. Simple language equations. *Bulletin of the EATCS*, 85:81–102, 2005.

[16] S.B. Lassen. Relational reasoning about contexts. In *Higher-order operational techniques in semantics*, pages 91–135. Cambridge University Press, 1998.

[17] S.B. Lassen. Bisimulation in untyped lambda calculus: Böhm trees and bisimulation up to context. *Electr. Notes Theor. Comput. Sci.*, 20:346–374, 1999.

[18] S. Milius, L. S. Moss, and D. Schwencke. Abstract GSOS rules and a modular treatment of recursive definitions. *Logical Methods in Computer Science*, 9(3), 2013.

[19] R. Milner. *Communication and Concurrency*. Prentice Hall, 1989.

[20] R. Milner and D. Sangiorgi. Barbed bisimulation. In *Proc. 19th ICALP*, volume 623 of *LNCS*, Springer Verlag, 1992.

[21] Robin Milner. A complete axiomatisation for observational congruence of finite-state behaviors. *Inf. Comput.*, 81(2):227–247, 1989.

[22] James H. Morris. *Lambda-Calculus Models of Programming Languages*. Phd thesis MAC-TR-57, M.I.T., project MAC, Dec. 1968.

[23] Ion Petre and Arto Salomaa. Algebraic systems and pushdown automata. In *Handbook of Weighted Automata*, EATCS Series, pages 257–289. Springer, 2009.

[24] Adrien Piérard and Eijiro Sumii. Sound bisimulations for higher-order distributed process calculus. In *Proc. FOSSACS*, volume 6604 of *LNCS*, pages 123–137. Springer, 2011.

[25] Andrew Pitts. Howe's method. In *Advanced Topics in Bisimulation and Coinduction*. Cambridge University Press, 2012.

[26] Damien Pous and Davide Sangiorgi. Enhancements of the bisimulation proof method. In *Advanced Topics in Bisimulation and Coinduction*. Cambridge University Press, 2012.

[27] Alexander Moshe Rabinovich. A complete axiomatisation for trace congruence of finite state behaviors. In *Proc. 9th MFPS*, volume 802 of *LNCS*, pages 530–543. Springer, 1993.

[28] A. W. Roscoe. *The theory and practice of concurrency*. Prentice Hall, 1998.

[29] A. W. Roscoe. *Understanding Concurrent Systems*. Springer, 2010.

[30] Jurriaan Rot, Marcello M. Bonsangue, and Jan J. M. M. Rutten. Coinductive proof techniques for language equivalence. In *Proc. LATA*, volume 7810 of *LNCS*, pages 480–492. Springer, 2013.

[31] David Sands. Computing with Contexts: A simple approach. ENTCS, volume 10, Elsevier, 1998.

[32] Sangiorgi, D. and Milner, R. The problem of "Weak Bisimulation up to". In *Proc. CONCUR '92*, volume 630 of *LNCS*, Springer, 1992.

[33] D. Sangiorgi. Locality and True-concurrency in Calculi for Mobile Processes. In *Proc. TACS '94*, volume 789 of *LNCS*, Springer, 1994.

[34] D. Sangiorgi and D. Walker. *The π-calculus: a Theory of Mobile Processes*. Cambridge University Press, 2001.

[35] Davide Sangiorgi, Naoki Kobayashi, and Eijiro Sumii. Environmental bisimulations for higher-order languages. *ACM Trans. Program. Lang. Syst.*, 33(1):5, 2011.

# Succinct Representation of Concurrent Trace Sets *

Ashutosh Gupta
IST Austria
agupta@ist.ac.at

Thomas A. Henzinger
IST Austria
tah@ist.ac.at

Arjun Radhakrishna
IST Austria, University of Pennsylvania
arjunrad@seas.upenn.edu

Roopsha Samanta
IST Austria
rsamanta@ist.ac.at

Thorsten Tarrach
IST Austria
ttarrach@ist.ac.at

## Abstract

We present a method and a tool for generating succinct representations of sets of concurrent traces. We focus on trace sets that contain all correct or all incorrect permutations of events from a given trace. We represent trace sets as *HB-formulas* that are Boolean combinations of *happens-before* constraints between events. To generate a representation of incorrect interleavings, our method iteratively explores interleavings that violate the specification and gathers generalizations of the discovered interleavings into an HB-formula; its complement yields a representation of correct interleavings.

We claim that our trace set representations can drive diverse verification, fault localization, repair, and synthesis techniques for concurrent programs. We demonstrate this by using our tool in three case studies involving synchronization synthesis, bug summarization, and abstraction refinement based verification. In each case study, our initial experimental results have been promising.

In the first case study, we present an algorithm for inferring missing synchronization from an HB-formula representing correct interleavings of a given trace. The algorithm applies rules to rewrite specific patterns in the HB-formula into locks, barriers, and wait-notify constructs. In the second case study, we use an HB-formula representing incorrect interleavings for bug summarization. While the HB-formula itself is a concise counterexample summary, we present additional inference rules to help identify specific concurrency bugs such as data races, define-use order violations, and two-stage access bugs. In the final case study, we present a novel predicate learning procedure that uses HB-formulas representing abstract counterexamples to accelerate counterexample-guided abstraction refinement (CEGAR). In each iteration of the CEGAR loop, the procedure refines the abstraction to eliminate multiple spurious abstract counterexamples drawn from the HB-formula.

***Categories and Subject Descriptors*** D [2]: 4—Formal methods

***Keywords*** Trace Generalization; Concurrent Programs; Synchronization Synthesis; Bug Summarization; CEGAR


ACM 978-1-4503-3300-9/15/01...$15.00.
http://dx.doi.org/10.1145/2676726.2677008

## 1. Introduction

Sets of concurrent traces containing permutations of events from a given concurrent trace are useful for predictive analysis (e.g., [24, 34, 35, 41]) and synchronization synthesis (e.g., [8, 9]) of shared-memory concurrent programs. Most approaches using such trace sets are restricted to specific aspects of reasoning about concurrent programs such as data race detection [24, 34], detection of safety violations [35, 41] and fixing assertion failures [8, 9]. Moreover, the representations of trace sets and exploration strategies used in some of these approaches [8, 9, 35]) *underapproximate* the target trace sets. In this paper, we present a succinct, *complete* representation of such concurrent trace sets, which can drive diverse verification, fault localization, repair, and synthesis techniques for concurrent programs. The representation is complete in the sense that it encodes every trace in the trace set of interest.

**Concurrent trace sets.** First, we fix some terminology. An *execution* $\pi$ of a concurrent program $\mathcal{P}$ is an alternating sequence of variable valuations and events corresponding to a feasible interleaving of instructions from the threads of $\mathcal{P}$. An execution is *good* if it satisfies a given specification, and *bad* otherwise. A *trace* is a sequence of events corresponding to an interleaving of instructions from the threads of $\mathcal{P}$. The trace of an execution $\pi$ is the sequence of events within $\pi$. The language $\mathcal{L}(\tau)$ of a trace $\tau$ is the set of all executions with trace $\tau$. A trace $\tau$ is feasible if $\mathcal{L}(\tau)$ is non-empty, and infeasible otherwise. A feasible trace $\tau$ is good if all executions in $\mathcal{L}(\tau)$ are good, and bad otherwise.

We group traces into *neighbourhoods*. The neighbourhood $\mathcal{N}_\tau$ of a trace $\tau$ contains all permutations of $\tau$ that preserve $\tau$'s intra-thread event order. The *good neighbourhood* $\mathcal{N}_\tau^g$ of a trace $\tau$ is the set containing all the good traces in $\mathcal{N}_\tau$. The *bad neighbourhood* $\mathcal{N}_\tau^b$ of a trace $\tau$ is a set containing all the bad traces in $\mathcal{N}_\tau$. The languages $\mathcal{L}(\mathcal{N}_\tau)$, $\mathcal{L}(\mathcal{N}_\tau^g)$ and $\mathcal{L}(\mathcal{N}_\tau^b)$ are the unions of the languages of all traces in $\mathcal{N}_\tau$, $\mathcal{N}_\tau^g$ and $\mathcal{N}_\tau^b$, respectively.

**Representation of concurrent trace sets.** There are multiple ways to represent trace sets. Some representations may be more expressive or useful for reasoning about concurrent programs than others. A candidate representation that has been used for certain trace sets is a partial order over events [8, 9, 41]. The neighbourhood of a trace, as defined above, can also be represented as a partial order. However, the good neighbourhood or the bad neighbourhood of a trace is, in general, not a partial order. For instance, for the

*This research was supported in part by the European Research Council (ERC) under grant agreement 267989 (QUAREM), by the Austrian Science Fund (FWF) NFN project S11402-N23 (RiSE), and the NSF Expeditions award CCF 1138996.

**Figure 1** Online banking: This trace is drawn from a program consisting of three threads, one for withdrawing money, one for depositing money, and one for checking consistency of the bank account after completion of a withdrawal and a deposit.[a]

```
globalvars: int x, withdrawal, deposit, balance,
            deposited, withdrawn;
init: x = balance; deposited = 0; withdrawn = 0;
            withdrawal > 0; deposit > 0;

thread_withdraw:
localvars: int temp;
TW[1]: temp := balance;
TW[2]: balance := temp - withdrawal;
TW[3]: withdrawn := 1;

thread_deposit:
localvars: int temp;
TD[1]: temp := balance;
TD[2]: balance := temp + deposit;
TD[3]: deposited := 1;

thread_checkresult:
TC[1]: assume (deposited = 1 and withdrawn = 1);
TC[2]: assert (balance = x + deposit - withdrawal);
```

Exact representation of $\mathcal{N}_\tau^b$:
$hb(\mathtt{T_W}[1], \mathtt{T_D}[2]) \wedge hb(\mathtt{T_D}[1], \mathtt{T_W}[2]) \wedge hb(\mathtt{T_W}[3], \mathtt{T_C}[1]) \wedge hb(\mathtt{T_D}[3], \mathtt{T_C}[1])$
Exact representation of $\mathcal{N}_\tau^g$:
$(hb(\mathtt{T_D}[2], \mathtt{T_W}[1]) \vee hb(\mathtt{T_W}[2], \mathtt{T_D}[1])) \wedge hb(\mathtt{T_W}[3], \mathtt{T_C}[1]) \wedge hb(\mathtt{T_D}[3], \mathtt{T_C}[1])$
Representation of sound overapproximation of $\mathcal{N}_\tau^b$:
$hb(\mathtt{T_W}[1], \mathtt{T_D}[2]) \wedge hb(\mathtt{T_D}[1], \mathtt{T_W}[2])$
Representation of sound overapproximation of $\mathcal{N}_\tau^g$:
$hb(\mathtt{T_D}[2], \mathtt{T_W}[1]) \vee hb(\mathtt{T_W}[2], \mathtt{T_D}[1])$

[a] In all the examples in this paper, we represent traces using typed global variable declarations/initializations, followed by each thread's typed local variable declarations and instructions. Note that this representation depicts a trace and not a program.

trace $\tau$ in Fig. 1, $\mathcal{N}_\tau^g$ is not a partial order, but is a disjunction (i.e., union) of partial orders. In our work, we represent trace sets as *HB-formulas*. An HB-formula is a Boolean combination of *happens-before* causality constraints between events. HB-formulas can represent arbitrary finite sets of finite traces, and in particular, good and bad neighbourhoods (see Fig. 1). As we will see later, HB-formulas are not only expressive, but also versatile enough to be usable for diverse objectives.

Given a trace $\tau$ and a correctness specification, we present a method to generate an HB-formula $\varphi_B$ representing the bad neighbourhood of $\tau$. To generate $\varphi_B$, we first encode all the bad executions in $\mathcal{L}(\mathcal{N}_\tau)$ in a quantifier-free first-order formula $\Phi$ such that an execution $\pi$ is a model of $\Phi$ iff $\pi$ is a bad execution in $\mathcal{L}(\mathcal{N}_\tau^b)$. We then *incrementally* construct $\varphi_B$. Initially, $\varphi_B$ is set to `false`. In each step: (1) we invoke an SMT solver to obtain a model for $\Phi$ that does not belong to the language of the subset of $\mathcal{N}_\tau^b$ represented by the current $\varphi_B$, (2) *generalize* the trace of the model into an HB-formula $\varphi$, and (3) update $\varphi_B$ by adding $\varphi$ as a disjunct. We iterate until there is no new model of $\Phi$. The trace generalization used in each iteration has the following properties: (a) the model obtained in the iteration satisfies $\varphi$, and (b) any trace in $\mathcal{N}_\tau$ that satisfies $\varphi$ is bad. The final HB-formula obtained is an *exact* representation of $\mathcal{N}_\tau^b$.

While an exact representation is a worthy goal, the corresponding $\varphi_B$ may not be succinct. To gain succinctness and utility, we trade in exactness. In particular, we permit the inclusion of infeasible traces to obtain a succinct HB-formula representing a *sound overapproximation* of $\mathcal{N}_\tau^b$. The overapproximation of $\mathcal{N}_\tau^b$ is sound in the sense that it is guaranteed to not include any good traces. To generate such a succinct HB-formula, we enhance the above procedure. We use data-flow analysis and minimal unsatisfiability core (unsat core) computation for generalizing the trace of the model into an HB-formula $\varphi$ in step (2) of each iteration. This new trace generalization step has the following properties: (a) the model obtained in the iteration satisfies $\varphi$, and (b) any trace in $\mathcal{N}_\tau$ satisfying $\varphi$ is either bad or infeasible.

Complementing $\varphi_B$, the succinct representation of a sound overapproximation of $\mathcal{N}_\tau^b$ yields $\varphi_G$, a succinct representation of a sound overapproximation of $\mathcal{N}_\tau^g$. Note that complementing the exact representation of $\mathcal{N}_\tau^b$ does not yield an exact representation of $\mathcal{N}_\tau^g$. In fact, our existing methodology cannot produce an exact representation of $\mathcal{N}_\tau^g$. Fig. 1 shows the exact representation of $\mathcal{N}_\tau^b$ and the representations for sound overapproximations of $\mathcal{N}_\tau^g$ and $\mathcal{N}_\tau^b$ obtained by our method for the example trace shown.

We implemented the above procedure as a tool TARA and used it to generate (succinct) representations of trace sets of programs drawn from the software verification competition (SV-Comp) [3] and the regression suites of ESBMC [31] and CONREPAIR [9].

We demonstrate the applicability of our representations of good and bad neighbourhoods of a trace to three case studies involving synchronization synthesis, bug summarization and verification based on counterexample-guided abstraction refinement (CEGAR).

**Case Study: Synchronization synthesis.** Shared-memory concurrent programs are excellent targets for automated *program completion*, in particular, for synthesis of missing synchronization [8, 9, 13, 30, 39]. We present a novel algorithm that uses $\varphi_G$ to synthesize synchronization for eliminating the bad neighbourhood of $\tau$. The algorithm proceeds by applying rewrite rules to derive synchronization primitives such as mutex locks, barriers, shared exclusive locks and wait-notify statements from easily-identifiable patterns in $\varphi_G$. For example, a missing mutex lock in the example in Fig. 1 that ensures the instructions at $\mathtt{T_W}[1]$ and $\mathtt{T_W}[2]$ in **thread_withdraw** do not interfere with the instructions $\mathtt{T_D}[1]$ and $\mathtt{T_D}[2]$ in **thread_deposit** is identified by the pattern $hb(\mathtt{T_D}[2], \mathtt{T_W}[1]) \vee hb(\mathtt{T_W}[2], \mathtt{T_D}[1])$ in $\varphi_G$. We emphasize that most other synchronization synthesis techniques generate atomic sections rather than locks, wait-notify statements etc. Atomic sections are not directly implementable. Moreover, our synchronization primitives can potentially permit more correct concurrent behaviours than atomic sections. We have implemented this algorithm as an extension of our tool TARA and used it to successfully synthesize synchronization for our benchmarks.

**Case Study: Bug summarization.** Error detection tools based on model checking and static analyses typically provide counterexample traces to help with program debugging. However, these traces can be long and encumbered with unnecessary data, providing little insight about the actual bug. In our second case study, we use $\varphi_B$, the representation for a sound overapproximation of a trace's bad neighbourhood, for counterexample and bug summarization. The HB-formula $\varphi_B$ encodes relevant *ordering* information about all counterexamples in the neighbourhood of $\tau$ and can be viewed as a stand-alone counterexample summary. While this can already be useful feedback for a human debugger, we present a set of rules to infer specific bugs such as data races, atomicity violations, two-stage access bugs and define-use order violations. These rules work by identifying particular patterns in $\varphi_B$ and combining them with some lightweight data-flow information. We have extended TARA for bug summarization and evaluated it on our benchmarks.

**Case Study: Accelerating CEGAR.** We also recognize an application of our representation of bad neighbourhoods of abstract counterexamples in accelerating CEGAR for concurrent programs. CEGAR often takes many iterations to find the right predicates for proving correctness of a program. The choice of refinement procedure usually determines the number of iterations necessary. Many heuristics have been proposed to find relevant predicates quickly, e.g., [4]. This problem is compounded in concurrent program verification, where the existence of a large number of interleavings can delay the discovery of *interesting* spurious counterexamples that lead to relevant predicates. We present a new predicate learning procedure that uses the HB-formula $\varphi_B$ representing the bad neighbourhood of a spurious counterexample of an abstract concurrent program. In each iteration of the CEGAR loop, our procedure refines the abstraction to eliminate multiple spurious abstract counterexamples drawn from $\varphi_B$, using a method similar to *beautiful interpolants* [1]. We have integrated our TARA-based refinement procedure within SATABS [12] and have been able to reduce the number of iterations needed to verify various example programs.

**Highlights.** We introduce a novel representation for concurrent trace sets based on HB-formulas (Sec. 2). HB-formulas have several useful properties. They can express arbitrary finite trace sets. They enable efficient computation and concise expression of unions over trace sets. This is exploited by our tool TARA to compute succinct representations of sound overapproximations of good and bad neighbourhoods of a trace. HB-formulas are an intuitively appealing representation for trace sets. They can reveal specific patterns of causality relations between events that can drive diverse verification, fault localization, repair, and synthesis techniques for concurrent programs. We demonstrate the use of our tool in three applications — synchronization synthesis (Sec. 3), bug summarization (Sec. 4), and CEGAR acceleration (Sec. 5).

## 2. Trace Neighbourhoods and Representations

In this section, we formalize concurrent executions, traces and trace neighbourhoods. We also present algorithms and experimental results for computing good and bad neighbourhoods. The case studies in Sections 3, 4, and 5 are based on the techniques presented here.

### 2.1 Concurrent Programs and Traces

We consider shared-memory concurrent programs composed of a fixed number of sequential threads. In further discussion, we fix a concurrent program $\mathcal{P} = \langle V, \{T_1, \ldots, T_k\}, SV, \langle LV_1, \ldots, LV_k\rangle\rangle$ where $\{T_1, \ldots, T_k\}$ are a set of threads, $SV$ is a set of shared variables, each $LV_i$ is the set of local variables of thread $T_i$, and $V = SV \cup \bigcup_i LV_i$ is the set of all variables. Let $V_i = SV \cup LV_i$ denote the set of variables that can be read from and written by thread $T_i$. As the main objects of study in this paper are traces, we keep the exposition simple by not specifying syntactic and control flow details of threads at this stage. In this paper, we assume that variables range over integers and program instructions perform standard linear arithmetic operations. However, our techniques apply to a much wider variety of variable domains and operations.

**Concurrent executions.** A *concurrent execution* $\pi = \Gamma_0 e_1 \Gamma_1 \ldots \Gamma_{n-1} e_n \Gamma_n$ is an alternating sequence of valuations $\Gamma_i$ of variables $V$ and events $e_i$ corresponding to some interleaving of instructions from the threads in $\mathcal{P}$—for each $i$, execution of $e_i$ from valuation $\Gamma_{i-1}$ leads to valuation $\Gamma_i$. Each event $e$ is a labelled statement of the form $\mathtt{T}[\ell]$ : $stmt$, where T is a thread identifier, $\ell$ is a location identifier*, and $stmt$ is an atomic instruction. We write $pid(e)$ for the thread identifier T. Without loss of generality, we assume that the location identifiers of events from each thread are sequential natural numbers, i.e., the first event from a thread gets location identifier 1, the next gets 2, and so on. Further, we abuse notation by often writing $\mathtt{T}[\ell]$ instead of the event with label $\mathtt{T}[\ell]$. We represent the sequence of events from thread $T$ with location identifiers between $\ell$ and $\ell'$ (inclusive) by $\mathtt{T}[\ell : \ell']$. We also use the symbol $L$ to denote location identifier ranges such as $\ell : \ell'$.

We use two different formalisms to express atomic instructions.

- *Guarded actions.* Here, an instruction from thread $T_i$ is either a guarded action $\mathtt{assume}(G) \rightarrow \mathtt{assign}$ or an assertion $\mathtt{assert}(G)$, where $G$ is a Boolean expression over $V_i$ and $\mathtt{assign}$ is a parallel assignment $\mathtt{v_1}, \ldots, \mathtt{v_m} := expr_1, \ldots, expr_m$ of expressions over $V_i$ to variables in $V_i$.
- *Transition predicates.* Here, an instruction from thread $T_i$ is a predicate over variables from $V_i \cup V_i'$ where $V_i'$ contains primed versions of variables in $V_i$. Intuitively, variables from $V_i$ and $V_i'$ represent the values of program variables before and after the execution of the instruction, respectively. For example, the assignment $\mathtt{x} := \mathtt{x} + \mathtt{y}$ is represented as $x' = x + y$. The advantage of this formalism is that it can express non-deterministic statements which we need to model abstract programs in Sec. 5. Assertions are represented as before, i.e., as $\mathtt{assert}(G)$, where $G$ is a Boolean expression over $V_i$.

An execution $\pi = \Gamma_0 e_1 \Gamma_1 \ldots e_n \Gamma_n$ is *good* if for each assertion $e_i = \mathtt{T}[\ell] : \mathtt{assert}(G)$, the Boolean expression $G$ evaluates to $\mathtt{true}$ under valuation $\Gamma_{i-1}$; the execution is *bad* otherwise.

**Concurrent traces.** A *concurrent trace* $\tau = e_1 \ldots e_n$ is a sequence of events that corresponds to some interleaving of instructions from threads in $\mathcal{P}$. The *language* $\mathcal{L}(\tau)$ of a trace $\tau = e_1 \ldots e_n$ is the set of all executions $\Gamma_0 e_1' \Gamma_1 \ldots e_n' \Gamma_{n+1}$ where $e_i = e_i'$ for $i \in [1, n]$. For a set of traces $\mathcal{N}$, we abuse notation and write $\mathcal{L}(\mathcal{N})$ instead of $\bigcup_{\sigma \in \mathcal{N}} \mathcal{L}(\sigma)$. We denote by $events(\tau)$ the set $\{e_1, \ldots, e_n\}$ of events in $\tau$. For any two events $e_i, e_j \in events(\tau)$, we say $e_i <_\tau e_j$ if $e_i$ occurs before $e_j$ in $\tau$.

A trace $\tau$ is *feasible* if its language has at least one execution (i.e., $\mathcal{L}(\tau) \neq \emptyset$), and is *infeasible* otherwise. A feasible trace $\tau$ is *good* if all executions in $\mathcal{L}(\tau)$ are good, and is *bad* otherwise.

### 2.2 Representing Trace Neighbourhoods

We reason about traces that differ only in the scheduling choices using trace neighbourhoods. The *neighbourhood* $\mathcal{N}_\tau$ of a trace $\tau$ is a set of traces $\mathcal{N}_\tau = \{\sigma \mid events(\sigma) = events(\tau) \wedge \forall e_i, e_j \in events(\tau) : pid(e_i) = pid(e_j) \wedge e_i <_\tau e_j \Rightarrow e_i <_\sigma e_j\}$. Intuitively, $\mathcal{N}_\tau$ contains all traces having the same events as $\tau$ and having the same order of events within each thread. A trace in $\mathcal{N}_\tau$ may be infeasible, good, or bad. We denote the subsets of good and bad traces in $\mathcal{N}_\tau$ by $\mathcal{N}_\tau^g$ and $\mathcal{N}_\tau^b$, respectively. We call $\mathcal{N}_\tau^b$ and $\mathcal{N}_\tau^g$ the *bad* and *good* neighbourhoods of $\tau$.

Note that $\mathcal{N}_\tau$ corresponds to a partial order $(events(\tau), \sqsubseteq)$, with $e_i \sqsubseteq e_j$ iff $e_i <_\tau e_j$ and $pid(e_i) = pid(e_j)$. However, $\mathcal{N}_\tau^g$ and $\mathcal{N}_\tau^b$ do not, in general, correspond to a partial order (cf. the exact representation of $\mathcal{N}_\tau^g$ in Fig. 1).

**Representing subsets of trace neighbourhoods.** We represent subsets of trace neighbourhoods using *happens-before formulas*, or, *HB-formulas*. An HB-formula $\varphi$ for a trace $\tau$ is either a: (a) *basic constraint* of the form $hb(e_i, e_j)$ where $e_i, e_j \in events(\tau)$; or (b) a Boolean combination of HB-formulas, i.e., one of $\varphi_1 \wedge \varphi_2$, $\varphi_1 \vee \varphi_2$, or $\neg\varphi_1$ where $\varphi_1$ and $\varphi_2$ are HB-formulas.

The semantics $[\![\varphi]\!]$ of an HB-formula $\varphi$ for a trace $\tau$ is subset of $\mathcal{N}_\tau$, defined as follows: (a) for a basic constraint $hb(e_i, e_j)$, we have that $[\![hb(e_i, e_j)]\!] = \{\sigma \in \mathcal{N}_\tau \mid e_i <_\sigma e_j\}$; and (b) for Boolean combinations, we have that $[\![\varphi_1 \wedge \varphi_2]\!] = [\![\varphi_1]\!] \cap [\![\varphi_2]\!]$, $[\![\varphi_1 \vee \varphi_2]\!] = [\![\varphi_1]\!] \cap [\![\varphi_2]\!]$, and $[\![\neg\varphi_1]\!] = \mathcal{N}_\tau \setminus [\![\varphi_1]\!]$, respectively.

**Remark 2.1.** *Our HB-formulas only represent constraints on scheduling. One could define more expressive constraints which include constraints not just on scheduling, but also on variable valuations in individual executions. However, our hypothesis is that happens-before constraints on scheduling are sufficient to express many interesting properties of traces and executions. This is also*

*We assume that all location identifiers from one thread are unique. Thus, multiple occurrences of the same instruction (for example, in the body of a loop) are relabelled with unique identifiers.

*supported by empirical data that shows that most concurrency bugs are due to bad ordering of instructions in a trace rather than the interaction between schedules and variable valuations [29].*

### 2.3 Computing Good and Bad Neighbourhoods

In this section, we present an algorithm for computing an exact representation for the bad neighbourhood of a trace. However, as this representation may be unwieldy and complex, we further provide an algorithm to produce sound overapproximations of $\mathcal{N}_\tau^b$ and $\mathcal{N}_\tau^g$, i.e., to find succinct HB-formulas $\varphi_G$ and $\varphi_B$ such that $\mathcal{N}_\tau^g \subseteq [\![\varphi_G]\!]$, $\mathcal{N}_\tau^b \subseteq [\![\varphi_B]\!]$, and $[\![\varphi_G]\!] \cap \mathcal{N}_\tau^b = [\![\varphi_B]\!] \cap \mathcal{N}_\tau^g = \emptyset$.

**Encoding bad executions.** Given a trace $\tau$, our algorithm is based on constructing a quantifier free first-order formula that represents all bad executions in $\mathcal{L}(\mathcal{N}_\tau)$. We use the concurrent trace program encoding [41] which is based on a concurrent single static assignment (CSSA) form of traces. We recall the encoding below to make the presentation self-contained. We present the encoding for the case where instructions are expressed as guarded actions; the case where instructions are expressed as transition predicates is similar. Given a trace $\tau$, we first rewrite it into the CSSA form.

- For each variable $v$, we introduce a unique name $v_{w,e}$ for each event $e$ that may change the value of $v$ (here, $w$ stands for "write"). Further, for each variable $v$, we introduce a unique name $v_\iota$ to represent the value of $v$ at the start of an execution.
- For each event $e$ that reads a variable $v$, we replace $v$ as follows:
  - If $v$ is a local variable, we replace $v$ by $v_{w,e'}$ where $e'$ is the most recent event from the thread that writes to $v$; and
  - If $v$ is a shared variable, we replace $v$ by $v_{r,e}$ (where $r$ stands for "read") and we store an additional constraint, where $v_{r,e} = \pi(v_\iota, v_{w,e_1}, v_{w,e_2},, \ldots, v_{w,e_\ell})$ where $e_i$ ranges over all events from other threads that write to $v$ and the most recent event from the same thread that writes to $v$.

  The $\pi$-functions above are analogous to the $\phi$-functions used to express joins in sequential single static assignment encodings, i.e., $v_{r,e} = \pi(v_\iota, v_{w,e_1}, \ldots, v_{w,e_\ell})$ expresses that $e$ reads either the initial value of $v$, or the value written by one of $e_1, \ldots, e_\ell$.
- Further, for each event $e$, we define the condition that $e$ is feasibly reached. If $e$ is the first event in a thread, we set $cond(e) = \texttt{true}$. Otherwise, $cond(e)$ depends on the previous event from the same thread in $\tau$ (say $e'$). If $e'$ is an assertion, we let $cond(e) = cond(e')$. Otherwise, $e'$ is a guarded action $\texttt{assume}(G) \to \texttt{assign}$, and we let $cond(e) = cond(e') \wedge G$.

**Example 2.2.** *In the running example from Fig. 1, the statement* $\texttt{T}_\texttt{W}[1] : \texttt{temp:=balance};$ *would be encoded as* $temp_{w,\texttt{T}_\texttt{W}[1]} = balance_{r,\texttt{T}_\texttt{W}[1]} \wedge balance_{r,\texttt{T}_\texttt{W}[1]} = \pi(balance_\iota, balance_{w,\texttt{T}_\texttt{D}[2]})$.

Given a trace $\tau$ rewritten in the CSSA form, the following constraints encode executions in the neighbourhood $\mathcal{N}_\tau$ of $\tau$:

- *Thread orders.* In any execution in the neighbourhood of $\tau$, the order of events in each thread is the same as in the trace $\tau$. We define $\Phi_{PO} = \bigwedge\{hb(e_i, e_j) \mid pid(e_i) = pid(e_j) \wedge e_i <_\tau e_j\}$.
- *Variable assignments.* This part of the encoding is a direct translation of the assignments in each event into constraints. We have $\Phi_{VD} = \bigwedge_e \bigwedge_{i=1}^m v_{w,e}^i = expr^i$, where $e$ ranges over events of the form $\texttt{T}[\ell]$ : $stmt$ with $stmt$ being $\texttt{assume(G)} \to \texttt{v}^1_\texttt{w,e}, \ldots, \texttt{v}^\texttt{m}_\texttt{w,e} := expr^1, \ldots, expr^m$.
- *$\pi$-constraints.* Each $\pi$-constraint chooses a value for a read of a shared variable from possible writes. Formally, each condition $v_{r,e} = \pi(v_\iota, v_{w,e_1}, \ldots, v_{w,e_\ell})$ is rewritten as $[v_{r,e} = v_\iota \wedge \bigwedge_i hb(e, e_i)] \vee \bigvee_{i=1}^\ell [v_{r,e} = v_{w,e_i} \wedge cond(e_i) \wedge hb(e_i, e) \wedge \bigwedge_{j \neq i}(hb(e_j, e_i) \vee hb(e, e_j))]$. Intuitively, the above formula states that: (a) the value of $v$ read by $e$ is either the initial value of $v$ or written by one of $e_1, \ldots, e_\ell$; (b) if the value is the initial value, all $e_i$ happen after $e$; and (c) if the value is written by $e_i$, then $e_i$ is feasibly reached and all conflicting writes either happen before $e_i$ or after $e$. We denote by $\Phi_{PI}$ the conjunction of all such $\pi$-constraints. For example, for the $\pi$-function from Example 2.2, the corresponding constraint is $(balance_{r,\texttt{T}_\texttt{W}[1]} = balance_\iota \wedge hb(\texttt{T}_\texttt{W}[1], \texttt{T}_\texttt{D}[2])) \vee (balance_{r,\texttt{T}_\texttt{W}[1]} = balance_{w,\texttt{T}_\texttt{D}[2]} \wedge hb(\texttt{T}_\texttt{D}[2], \texttt{T}_\texttt{W}[1]))$.
- *Correctness condition.* For correctness, if an assertion event $e = \texttt{T}[\ell] : \texttt{assert}(G_e)$ is feasibly reached, then $G_e$ must hold. Hence, the correctness condition is $\Phi_{COR} = \bigwedge_e (cond(e) \Rightarrow G_e)$ where $e$ ranges over assertion events.

The final encoding for bad executions is given by $\Phi_{CTP}(\tau) = \Phi_{PO} \wedge \Phi_{VD} \wedge \Phi_{PI} \wedge \neg\Phi_{COR}$. We also encode the complementary correctness condition as $\Phi_{\overline{CTP}}(\tau) = \Phi_{PO} \wedge \Phi_{VD} \wedge \Phi_{PI} \wedge \Phi_{COR}$.

For convenience, we use an auxilliary formula $\Phi_{FEA}$ to represent the condition that each assumption must hold. We have $\Phi_{FEA} = \bigwedge_e cond(e)$ where $e$ ranges over all events.

An execution $\pi$ *corresponds* to a model $\mathcal{V}$ of $\Phi_{CTP}$ if: (a) the value of each $v_\iota$ in $\mathcal{V}$ is the initial value of $v$ in $\pi$; (b) the value of each $v_{r,e}$ in $\mathcal{V}$ is the value of $v$ read by $e$ in $\pi$; (c) the value of each $v_{w,e}$ in $\mathcal{V}$ is the value of $v$ written by $e$ in $\pi$; and (d) the value of $hb(e_i, e_j)$ in $\mathcal{V}$ is true if and only if $e_i$ occurs before $e_j$ in $\pi$.

**Theorem 2.3** ([41]). *Given a trace $\tau$, (a) for every model $\mathcal{V}$ of $\Phi_{CTP}(\tau)$ there is a bad execution $\pi \in \mathcal{L}(\mathcal{N}_\tau^b)$ such that $\pi$ corresponds to $\mathcal{V}$; and (b) for every $\pi \in \mathcal{L}(\mathcal{N}_\tau^b)$ there is a model $\mathcal{V}$ of $\Phi_{CTP}(\tau)$ such that $\pi$ corresponds to $\mathcal{V}$.*

**Bad neighbourhood computation.** Armed with $\Phi_{CTP}$ — an SMT encoding of bad executions in the neighbourhood of a trace $\tau$ — we now present an algorithm to compute a representation of $\mathcal{N}_\tau^b$. Algo. 1 proceeds by repeatedly computing satisfying assignments to $\Phi_{CTP}$ using an SMT solver (lines 2 and 3), and accumulating the HB-formulas in the models (lines 4 and 5). We conjoin $\Phi_{CTP}$ with additional constraints to ensure that the same satisfying assignments are not returned each time.

**Algorithm 1** Computing the bad neighbourhood of a trace

**Require:** Trace $\tau$
**Ensure:** HB-formula $\varphi_B$ such that $\mathcal{N}_\tau^b = [\![\varphi_B]\!]$.
1: $\Phi \leftarrow \Phi_{CTP}(\tau)$; $\varphi_B \leftarrow \texttt{false}$
2: **while** $\Phi \wedge \neg\varphi_B$ is satisfiable **do**
3: $\quad\mathcal{V} \leftarrow$ satisfying assignment for $\Phi \wedge \neg\varphi_B$
4: $\quad\varphi'_B \leftarrow \bigwedge\{hb(e, e') \mid \mathcal{V} \models hb(e, e')\}$
5: $\quad\varphi_B \leftarrow \varphi_B \vee \varphi'_B$
6: **return** $\varphi_B$

**Overapproximating bad neighbourhoods.** While Algo. 1 computes an exact representation of $\mathcal{N}_\tau^b$, it is inefficient in practice. Hence, we forgo the goal of an exact representation. Instead, we compute a *sound overapproximation* of $\mathcal{N}_\tau^b$, which may include infeasible traces, but not good traces. Given trace $\tau$, Algo. 2 computes sound overapproximations of $\mathcal{N}_\tau^b$ and $\mathcal{N}_\tau^g$. Algo. 2 performs several optimizations with respect to Algo. 1 to accumulate weaker constraints from each model of $\Phi_{CTP}$, i.e., Algo. 2 attempts to accumulate larger subsets of $\mathcal{N}_\tau$ into $\varphi_B$ in each iteration.

- **Data-flow analysis.** From the model $\mathcal{V}$ of $\Phi_{CTP}(\tau)$, the data-flow analysis retains those happens-before constraints ($\varphi'_B$) that are necessary to preserve the data-flow into the failing assertion in the corresponding execution. We use the function $DF_\mathcal{V}(e)$ (line 5) to compute constraints that ensure $e$ can be feasibly reached and can read the same variable values as in $\mathcal{V}$. Given the execution corresponding to $\mathcal{V}$, let $reads(e)$, $readsG(e)$, and $srcEvent(v, e)$ represent the variables read by $e$, the variables read by $e$ in the guard (if $e$ is not a guarded assignment, $readsG(e) = \emptyset$), and the event that writes the value of $v$ read by $e$. We have $DF_\mathcal{V}(e) = DF^1_\mathcal{V}(e) \cup DF^2_\mathcal{V}(e)$ where:

- we let $DF^1_{\mathcal{V}}(e) = \bigcup_{v \in reads(e)} \left[\{(v, srcEvent(v, e), e)\} \cup DF_{\mathcal{V}}(srcEvent(v, e))\right]$; and
- $DF^2_{\mathcal{V}}(e) = \bigcup_{e' \in E, v \in readsG(e')} \left[\{(v, srcEvent(v, e'), e')\} \cup DF_{\mathcal{V}}(srcEvent(v, e'))\right]$ where event $e'$ ranges over $E = \{e' \mid pid(e) = pid(e') \wedge \mathcal{V} \models hb(e', e)\}$.

Intuitively, $DF^1_{\mathcal{V}}$ ensures that $e$ can read the same values as in $\mathcal{V}$ and $DF^2_{\mathcal{V}}$ ensures that $e$ is feasibly reached. We then get additional constraints $ADF$ necessary to ensure conflicting writes do not affect the data-flow into the assertion (line 6).

- **Unsatisfiable core computation.** Next, we perform two rounds of generalization on $\varphi_{B'}$ through unsatisfiable core computation. In the first round, we construct a formula $\varphi_{B'} \wedge Choices(\mathcal{V}) \wedge \Phi_{\overline{CTP}}(\tau)$ where $Choices(\mathcal{V})$ fixes the initial variable values to the ones from $\mathcal{V}$ (line 9). A satisfying assignment to this formula models executions where no failing assertion is feasibly reached. Therefore, if the formula is unsatisfiable, the happens-before constraints from the unsatisfiable core (line 11) ensure that all executions satisfying $Choices(\mathcal{V})$ are bad. Note that if all instructions are deterministic, the above formula is always unsatisfiable. In the second round (line 13), we follow a similar procedure, but with the formula $\varphi_{B'} \wedge \Phi_{FEA} \wedge \Phi_{\overline{CTP}}$. Here, a model is a good execution and hence, the constraints from the unsatisfiable core (line 13) ensure that any feasible execution is necessarily bad.

  Roughly, the first round allows us to generalize the HB-formula in the case of data-dependent bugs. The second round lets us generalize further in the case of data-independent bugs.

The sound overapproximation, $\varphi_G$, of $\mathcal{N}^g_\tau$ is obtained by complementing $\varphi_B$ (line 15). Note that $\varphi_B$ returned is in disjunctive normal form (DNF), while $\varphi_G$ is in conjunctive normal form (CNF).

---

**Algorithm 2** Computing sound overapproximations of the bad and good neighbourhoods of a trace

**Require:** Trace $\tau$

**Ensure:** HB-formulas $(\varphi_B, \varphi_G)$ such that $\mathcal{N}^g_\tau \subseteq [\![\varphi_G]\!]$, $\mathcal{N}^b_\tau \subseteq [\![\varphi_B]\!]$, and $[\![\varphi_G]\!] \cap [\![\varphi_B]\!] = \emptyset$.

1: $\Phi \leftarrow \Phi_{CTP}(\tau)$; $\varphi_B \leftarrow$ `false`
2: **while** $\Phi \wedge \neg\varphi_B$ is satisfiable **do**
3: $\quad\mathcal{V} \leftarrow$ satisfying assignment for $\Phi \wedge \neg\varphi_B$
4: $\quad$ {Data-flow analysis}
5: $\quad DF \leftarrow DF_{\mathcal{V}}(e^*)$ where $e^*$ is the failing assertion in $\mathcal{V}$
6: $\quad ADF \leftarrow \bigcup_{(v,e_i,e_j) \in DF} \bigcup_{\{e_k \mid e_k \text{ writes } v\}} (\{(v, e_k, e_i) \mid \mathcal{V} \models hb(e_k, e_i)\} \cup \{(v, e_j, e_k) \mid \mathcal{V} \models hb(e_j, e_k)\})$
7: $\quad \varphi_{B'} \leftarrow \bigwedge_{(v,e_i,e_j) \in DF \cup ADF} hb(e_i, e_j)$
8: $\quad$ {Unsat-core computation}
9: $\quad Choices(\mathcal{V}) \leftarrow \bigwedge_{v \in V} v_\iota = \mathcal{V}[v_\iota]$
10: $\quad$ **if** $\varphi_{B'} \wedge Choices(\mathcal{V}) \wedge \Phi_{\overline{CTP}}(\tau))$ is unsatisfiable **then**
11: $\quad\quad \varphi_{B'} \leftarrow MinUNSATCore(Soft \leftarrow \varphi_{B'}, Hard \leftarrow Choices(\mathcal{V}) \wedge \Phi_{\overline{CTP}}(\tau))$
12: $\quad$ **if** $\varphi_{B'} \wedge \Phi_{FEA}(\tau) \wedge \Phi_{\overline{CTP}}(\tau))$ is unsatisfiable **then**
13: $\quad\quad \varphi_{B'} \leftarrow MinUNSATCore(Soft \leftarrow \varphi_{B'}, Hard \leftarrow \Phi_{FEA}(\tau) \wedge \Phi_{\overline{CTP}}(\tau))$
14: $\quad \varphi_B \leftarrow \varphi_B \vee \varphi_{B'}$
15: $\varphi_G \leftarrow \neg\varphi_B$; **return** $(\varphi_B, \varphi_G)$

---

**Theorem 2.4.** *For a trace $\tau$, if Algo. 2 returns $(\varphi_B, \varphi_G)$, then $\mathcal{N}^b_\tau \subseteq [\![\varphi_B]\!]$, $\mathcal{N}^g_\tau \subseteq [\![\varphi_G]\!]$, and $[\![\varphi_G]\!] \cap \mathcal{N}^b_\tau = [\![\varphi_B]\!] \cap \mathcal{N}^g_\tau = \emptyset$.*

### 2.4 Implementation and Evaluation

We have implemented Algorithms 1 and 2 in a tool TARA (accessible at `https://github.com/thorstent/TARA`). TARA consists of 4000 lines of C++ code and uses Z3 [15] to discharge SMT queries. We use a new input format, CTRC, for specifying traces. The CTRC format consists of global and thread-local variables along with types and any initial valuations, and the instructions (in SMT-LIB format) in each thread. This makes TARA independent and easy to use with any front-end that can translate instructions to the SMT-LIB syntax. We use a modified version of CONREPAIR [9] to generate CTRC files for bad traces. CONREPAIR, in turn, uses CBMC [11] to find bad traces in programs and CPACHECKER [5] to translate C statements into the SMT-LIB format.

TARA has a number of different output options. Algo. 1 generates an HB-formula in DNF, which is often large. Algo. 2 generates a succinct HB-formula in DNF, the sizes of whose disjuncts are locally minimized. In our experience, the unsat core provided by Z3 is often far from minimal. Hence, we first use Z3 to compute an unsat core and then use a custom minimization technique—we use Z3 incrementally with triggers to activate and deactivate expressions for unsat core minimization. TARA can also generate an HB-formula in CNF representing bad neighbourhoods. However, this is computationally more expensive.

**Experiments.** Our benchmarks are from a diverse set of sources, namely, the concurrency track of the 2014 software verification competition SV-COMP [3] (suite sv) and the regression-test suites of CONREPAIR [9] (suite cr) and ESBMC [31] (suite es). We also use a set of small handmade examples with common bug patterns (suite hm). The cr suite contains simplifed versions of real buggy code from the linux kernel. To test the limits of TARA, we use the `loop-x` examples that have two threads each executing a loop of $x$ iterations. For correct behaviour, each iteration should execute atomically with respect to iterations of the other thread. However, the locks required to ensure this are missing.

We ran our experiments on a laptop with a 4-core Core i5 CPU and 8GB of RAM running Linux. Our results are presented in Table 1. The time reported only includes the time taken by TARA, and not the time needed to find a bad trace in the benchmark program. The #Threads/#Instrs column in Table 1 indicates the complexity of the benchmarks in terms of the number of threads and instructions. The performance of SMT queries involving $\Phi_{CTP}$ is mostly influenced by the number and size of $\pi$-functions. The #$\pi$-functions/#Disjuncts column indicates the number of $\pi$-functions and average number of arguments per $\pi$-function.

The performance of TARA using Algo. 1 and Algo. 2 are in columns marked Algo.1 and Algo.2, respectively. For each algorithm, we report the number of iterations, the total time taken and the size of the generated $\varphi_B$ (as the number of disjuncts and the average number of terms in each disjunct). Algo. 1 times out after 10 minutes in many cases—in such cases, we report the number of loop iterations completed before the timeout. With Algo. 2, TARA terminates within 5 seconds for each benchmark. This time is negligible compared to the time taken to find the initial counterexample trace. For example, CBMC took 2 minutes to find the trace `usb-serial-1`, while our analysis completed exploration of its bad neighbourhood in 2 seconds. We tested the limits of our tool in the `loop-x` examples. With 32 iterations per thread, we exceeded the timeout and hit the limit of our current implementation.

## 3. Case Study: Synchronization Synthesis

In our first case study, we use the representation of a sound overapproximation of the good neighbourhood of a trace $\tau$ (returned as $\varphi_G$ by Algo. 2) to synthesize synchronization that eliminates the bad neighbourhood of $\tau$. Missing synchronization primitives such as locks, barriers, and wait-notify statements present themselves as easily identifiable HB-formula *patterns* in $\varphi_G$. Our procedure derives the required synchronization using rules that rewrite such patterns into the corresponding primitives.

**Table 1** Experiments: $\varphi_B$ generation

| Name | Suite | #Threads/#Instrs | #$\pi$-functions/#Disjuncts | Iterations Algo.1 | Iterations Algo.2 | Total time Algo.1 | Total time Algo.2 | Size of $\varphi_B$ Algo.1 | Size of $\varphi_B$ Algo.2 |
|---|---|---|---|---|---|---|---|---|---|
| reorder_2 | sv | 2/3 | 2/2.0 | 1 | 1 | 18ms | 28ms | 1/2.0 | 1/2.0 |
| define_use | cr | 2/4 | 2/2.0 | 1 | 1 | 15ms | 22ms | 1/2.0 | 1/1.0 |
| em28xx | cr | 2/8 | 4/2.0 | 1 | 1 | 16ms | 25ms | 1/2.0 | 1/1.0 |
| locks | es | 3/8 | 10/1.6 | 12 | 2 | 27ms | 37ms | 12/5.5 | 2/4.0 |
| 2stage | hm | 2/8 | 5/1.4 | 8 | 1 | 26ms | 32ms | 8/3.8 | 1/2.0 |
| drbd_receiver | cr | 2/9 | 5/1.6 | 40 | 1 | 42ms | 28ms | 40/3.9 | 1/1.0 |
| md | cr | 3/11 | 4/1.8 | 40 | 1 | 76ms | 33ms | 40/6.1 | 1/1.0 |
| lazy01 | sv | 3/12 | 6/3.7 | 2 | 2 | 31ms | 57ms | 2/3.0 | 2/2.0 |
| locks_hb | hm | 4/13 | 10/2.2 | >29.0k | 7 | TO | 119ms | TO | 6/3.0 |
| lc_rc | cr | 4/14 | 8/2.0 | 4.6k | 1 | 21.4s | 37ms | 4.6k/16.7 | 1/1.0 |
| barrier_locks | hm | 3/18 | 17/2.6 | 10.6k | 6 | 1.4min | 521ms | 10.6k/10.0 | 4/1.5 |
| stateful01 | sv | 3/19 | 10/3.4 | 2.3k | 2 | 10.5s | 84ms | 2.3k/9.4 | 2/1.0 |
| read_write_lock | sv | 4/22 | 16/3.4 | 9.2k | 4 | 1.6min | 319ms | 9.2k/16.1 | 4/3.0 |
| loop | hm | 2/38 | 14/2.7 | 2 | 1 | 38ms | 72ms | 2/3.0 | 1/2.0 |
| fib_bench | sv | 3/39 | 24/3.6 | >20.5k | 2 | TO | 2.3s | TO | 2/10.0 |
| i2c_hid | cr | 2/42 | 26/4.5 | >23.4k | 3 | TO | 615ms | TO | 3/1.3 |
| rtl8169-1 | cr | 7/71 | 22/2.7 | >20.4k | 1 | TO | 111ms | TO | 1/2.0 |
| rtl8169-2 | cr | 7/116 | 41/2.3 | >7.3k | 1 | TO | 463ms | TO | 1/1.0 |
| rtl8169-5 | cr | 7/134 | 48/3.1 | >5.5k | 1 | TO | 1.5s | TO | 1/1.0 |
| rtl8169-4 | cr | 7/142 | 48/3.0 | >8.4k | 9 | TO | 3.8s | TO | 2/1.0 |
| rtl8169-6 | cr | 7/144 | 52/2.9 | >8.1k | 1 | TO | 887ms | TO | 1/1.0 |
| usb_serial-1 | cr | 7/151 | 87/3.7 | >5.5k | 1 | TO | 1.9s | TO | 1/1.0 |
| usb_serial-2 | cr | 7/163 | 93/3.6 | >4.4k | 3 | TO | 4.4s | TO | 1/1.0 |
| rtl8169-3 | cr | 8/174 | 61/3.6 | >4.2k | 2 | TO | 2.7s | TO | 1/1.0 |
| usb_serial-3 | cr | 7/178 | 100/3.7 | >4.3k | 1 | TO | 2.1s | TO | 1/1.0 |
| loop-2 | N/A | 2/16 | 8/3.0 | >4.0k | 4 | 11.6s | 135ms | 4.0k/8.9 | 4/2.0 |
| loop-4 | N/A | 2/32 | 16/5.0 | >24.6k | 8 | TO | 309ms | TO | 8/2.0 |
| loop-8 | N/A | 2/64 | 32/9.0 | >15.3k | 16 | TO | 3s | TO | 16/2.0 |
| loop-16 | N/A | 2/128 | 64/17.0 | >4.4k | 32 | TO | 1.1min | TO | 32/2.0 |
| loop-32 | N/A | 2/256 | 128/33.0 | >674 | 64 | TO | 35.5min | TO | 64/2.0 |

**Synchronization primitives.** We first describe various synchronization primitives that we derive. Recall from Sec. 2 that we use the notation $\mathtt{T}[\ell]$ to refer to events labelled with $\mathtt{T}[\ell]$, and the notations $\mathtt{T}[\ell : \ell']$ and $\mathtt{T}[\mathtt{L}]$ to refer to corresponding event sequences.

1. *Wait-Notify.* A wait-notify $\mathtt{WaitNotify}(\mathtt{T}_2[\ell_2], \mathtt{T}_1[\ell_1])$ denotes a `wait` to make $\mathtt{T}_2[\ell_2]$ wait for $\mathtt{T}_1[\ell_1]$ to complete, and a `notify` to make $\mathtt{T}_1[\ell_1]$ signal $\mathtt{T}_2[\ell_2]$ upon completion.
2. *Locks.* A lock $\mathtt{Lk}(\mathtt{T}_1[\mathtt{L}_1], \ldots, \mathtt{T}_n[\mathtt{L}_n])$ denotes a common lock protecting each event sequence $\mathtt{T}_i[\mathtt{L}_i]$, $i \in [1, n]$, to ensure that these event sequences cannot execute concurrently.
3. *Barriers.* A barrier $\mathtt{Barrier}(\mathtt{T}_1[\ell_1], \ldots, \mathtt{T}_n[\ell_n])$ at location $\ell_i$ of thread $\mathtt{T}_i$, $i \in [1, n]$, prevents each thread $\mathtt{T}_i$ from proceeding beyond $\ell_i$ until every other thread $\mathtt{T}_j$ reaches $\ell_j$. In other words, $\mathtt{T}_i$ cannot execute the event at $\ell_i$ until every other $\mathtt{T}_j$ executes the event at $\ell_j - 1$.
4. *Shared-exclusive locks.* A shared-exclusive lock (or, a readers-writers lock) $\mathtt{ShExLock}(\mathtt{Sh} : \mathtt{T}_{s1}[\mathtt{L}_{s1}], \ldots, \mathtt{T}_{sn}[\mathtt{L}_{sn}], \mathtt{Ex} : \mathtt{T}_{x1}[\mathtt{L}_{x1}], \ldots, \mathtt{T}_{xm}[\mathtt{L}_{xm}])$ permits concurrent execution of all event sequences $\mathtt{T}_{si}[\mathtt{L}_{si}]$, $i \in [1, n]$, while preventing concurrent execution of (a) any two $\mathtt{T}_{xi}[\mathtt{L}_{xi}]$ and $\mathtt{T}_{xj}[\mathtt{L}_{xj}]$ with $i \neq j$, and (b) any $\mathtt{T}_{xi}[\mathtt{L}_{xi}]$ and $\mathtt{T}_{sj}[\mathtt{L}_{sj}]$.

**Rewriting $\varphi_G$ to derive synchronization.** During the rewrite process below, we use disjunctive formulae (denoted by $\psi$) where each disjunct is either an atomic *hb*-constraint of the form $hb(\mathtt{T}_i[\ell_i], \mathtt{T}_j[\ell_j])$, or a synchronization primitive. For a trace $\tau$, we repeatedly apply the rewrite rules from Fig. 2 on $\varphi_G$ (in CNF, as returned from Algo. 2) until no more rules are applicable. The ADD.WAITNOTIFY, ADD.LOCK and ADD.BARRIER rules *introduce* the wait-notify, locks, and barrier primitives. The MERGE.LOCKS rule *merges* locks across pairs of threads, while the MERGE.LOCKS.DEADLOCKS rule merges locks that can potentially lead to deadlocks. The MULTITHREAD.LOCK and MULTITHREAD.BARRIER rules inductively derive locks and barriers spanning multiple threads. The ADD.SHAREDEXCLUSIVELOCK rule derives a shared exclusive lock from already inferred locks. Since $\varphi_G$, as generated by Algo. 2, is already optimized, we do not merge `WaitNotify` primitives.

We explain two of the above rules here. The premise of the ADD.LOCK rule asks for two event sequences $\mathtt{T}_1[\ell_1 : \ell_1']$ and $\mathtt{T}_2[\ell_2 : \ell_2']$ such that one of them has to finish execution before the other starts, i.e., $hb(\mathtt{T}_1[\ell_1'], \mathtt{T}_2[\ell_2]) \vee hb(\mathtt{T}_2[\ell_2'], \mathtt{T}_1[\ell_1])$. Equivalently, the two event sequences do not execute concurrently. This is enforced by the lock $\mathtt{Lk}(\mathtt{T}_1[\ell_1 : \ell_1'], \mathtt{T}_2[\ell_2 : \ell_2'])$. The premise of the MERGE.LOCKS.DEADLOCKS rule looks for two already derived locks, acquired by two threads in different orders (which may lead to a deadlock), and merges these locks into one.

Note that the rewriting process always terminates. However, depending on the order of rules applied, we may obtain different formulae. Upon termination, we get a CNF formula over synchronization primitives. We pick a set $\mathcal{S}$ of synchronization primitives, consisting of one primitive from each conjunct. Let $\mathcal{P}^{\mathcal{S}}$ be the program obtained by inserting each synchronization primitive in $\mathcal{S}$ into the corresponding position in the original concurrent program $\mathcal{P}$.

**Theorem 3.1** (Soundness of rewrite rules)**.** *Given a trace $\tau$, let $\mathcal{P}^{\mathcal{S}}$ be obtained as described above. Let $\pi \in \mathcal{L}(\mathcal{N}_\tau)$ be a deadlock-free execution of $\mathcal{P}^{\mathcal{S}}$. Then $\pi \notin \mathcal{L}(\mathcal{N}_\tau^b)$, i.e., $\pi$ is not bad.*

While $\mathcal{P}^{\mathcal{S}}$ is not guaranteed deadlock-free, we perform simple consistency checks when choosing $\mathcal{S}$ to prevent obvious deadlocks. For example, we ensure that `WaitNotify` primitives in $\mathcal{S}$ do not introduce *ordering cycles* over $events(\tau)$.

Note that our rewrite rules are by no means complete. It may be possible to derive the above synchronization primitives using different rules that represent other scenarios. Further, our rewrite

**Figure 2** Rewrite rules for synchronization synthesis

$$\frac{hb(\mathtt{T_1}[\ell_1'],\mathtt{T_2}[\ell_2]) \vee hb(\mathtt{T_2}[\ell_2'],\mathtt{T_1}[\ell_1]) \vee \psi \quad \ell_1 \leq \ell_1' \quad \ell_2 \leq \ell_2'}{\mathtt{Lk}(\mathtt{T_1}[\ell_1 : \ell_1'],\mathtt{T_2}[\ell_2 : \ell_2']) \vee \psi}\ \textsc{Add.Lock} \qquad \frac{hb(\mathtt{T_1}[\ell_1],\mathtt{T_2}[\ell_2]) \vee \psi}{\mathtt{WaitNotify}(\mathtt{T_2}[\ell_2],\mathtt{T_1}[\ell_1]) \vee \psi}\ \textsc{Add.WaitNotify}$$

$$\frac{(hb(\mathtt{T_1}[\ell_1 - 1],\mathtt{T_2}[\ell_2]) \vee \psi) \wedge (hb(\mathtt{T_2}[\ell_2 - 1],\mathtt{T_1}[\ell_1]) \vee \psi)}{\mathtt{Barrier}(\mathtt{T_1}[\ell_1],\mathtt{T_2}[\ell_2]) \vee \psi}\ \textsc{Add.Barrier}$$

$$\frac{(\mathtt{Lk}(\mathtt{T_1}[\mathtt{L_1}],..,\mathtt{T_n}[\mathtt{L_n}]) \vee \psi) \wedge \bigwedge_{i=1}^{n} \mathtt{Lk}(\mathtt{T_i}[\mathtt{L_i}],\mathtt{T_{n+1}}[\mathtt{L_{n+1}}]) \vee \psi}{\mathtt{Lk}(\mathtt{T_1}[\mathtt{L_1}],..,\mathtt{T_n}[\mathtt{L_{n+1}}]) \vee \psi}\ \textsc{Multithread.Lock}$$

$$\frac{(\mathtt{Lk}(\mathtt{T_1}[\mathtt{L_1}],\mathtt{T_2}[\mathtt{L_2}]) \vee \psi) \wedge (\mathtt{Lk}(\mathtt{T_1}[\mathtt{L_1}'],\mathtt{T_2}[\mathtt{L_2}']) \vee \psi) \quad \mathtt{T_1}[\mathtt{L_1}'] \subseteq \mathtt{T_1}[\mathtt{L_1}] \quad \mathtt{T_2}[\mathtt{L_2}'] \subseteq \mathtt{T_2}[\mathtt{L_2}]}{\mathtt{Lk}(\mathtt{T_1}[\mathtt{L_1}],\mathtt{T_2}[\mathtt{L_2}]) \vee \psi}\ \textsc{Merge.Locks}$$

$$\frac{(\mathtt{Lk}(\mathtt{T_1}[\ell_1^{\mathtt{a}},\ell_1^{\mathtt{a}'}],\mathtt{T_2}[\ell_2^{\mathtt{a}},\ell_2^{\mathtt{a}'}]) \vee \psi) \wedge (\mathtt{Lk}(\mathtt{T_1}[\ell_1^{\mathtt{b}},\ell_1^{\mathtt{b}'}],\mathtt{T_2}[\ell_2^{\mathtt{b}},\ell_2^{\mathtt{b}'}]) \vee \psi) \quad \ell_1^{\mathtt{a}} \leq \ell_1^{\mathtt{b}} \leq \ell_1^{\mathtt{a}'} \quad \ell_2^{\mathtt{b}} \leq \ell_2^{\mathtt{a}} \leq \ell_2^{\mathtt{b}'}}{\mathtt{Lk}(\mathtt{T_1}[\ell_1^{\mathtt{a}}, \max(\ell_1^{\mathtt{a}'},\ell_1^{\mathtt{b}'})]],\mathtt{T_2}[\ell_2^{\mathtt{b}}, \max(\ell_2^{\mathtt{b}'},\ell_2^{\mathtt{a}'})]) \vee \psi}\ \textsc{Merge.Locks.Deadlocks}$$

$$\frac{(\mathtt{Barrier}(\mathtt{T_1}[\ell_1],\ldots,\mathtt{T_n}[\ell_n]) \vee \psi) \wedge \bigwedge_{i=1}^{n} (\mathtt{Barrier}(\mathtt{T_i}[\ell_i],\mathtt{T_{n+1}}[\ell_{n+1}]) \vee \psi)}{\mathtt{Barrier}(\mathtt{T_1}[\ell_1],\ldots,\mathtt{T_{n+1}}[\ell_{n+1}]) \vee \psi}\ \textsc{Multithread.Barrier}$$

$$\frac{\bigwedge_{i=1}^{n} \bigwedge_{j=1}^{m} (\mathtt{Lk}(\mathtt{T_{s_i}}[\mathtt{L_{s_i}}],\mathtt{T_{x_j}}[\mathtt{L_{x_j}}]) \vee \psi) \quad \bigwedge_{i=1}^{m} \bigwedge_{j=1}^{m} (\mathtt{Lk}(\mathtt{T_{x_i}}[\mathtt{L_{x_i}}],\mathtt{T_{x_j}}[\mathtt{L_{x_j}}]) \vee \psi)}{\mathtt{ShExLock}(\mathtt{Sh} : \mathtt{T_{s_1}}[\mathtt{L_{s_1}}],\ldots,\mathtt{T_{s_n}}[\mathtt{L_{s_n}}], \mathtt{Ex} : \mathtt{T_{x_1}}[\mathtt{L_{x_2}}],\ldots,\mathtt{T_{x_m}}[\mathtt{L_{x_m}}]) \vee \psi}\ \textsc{Add.SharedExclusiveLock}$$

system can also be extended to other synchronization primitives. We now present examples illustrating the application of our rules.

**Example 3.2.** *For the example trace shown in Fig. 1, $\varphi_G$ is given by $hb(\mathtt{T_D}[2],\mathtt{T_W}[1]) \vee hb(\mathtt{T_W}[2],\mathtt{T_D}[1])$. Applying the* ADD.LOCK *rewrite rule yields* $\mathtt{Lk}(\mathtt{T_W}[1:2],\mathtt{T_D}[1:2])$.

**Example 3.3.** *For the example trace shown in Fig. 3(a), $\varphi_G$ is given by $(hb(\mathtt{T_F}[4],\mathtt{T_S}[3]) \vee hb(\mathtt{T_S}[4],\mathtt{T_F}[3])) \wedge hb(\mathtt{T_S}[4],\mathtt{T_F}[5]) \wedge hb(\mathtt{T_F}[4],\mathtt{T_S}[5])$. Applying the* ADD.LOCK *rewrite rule yields:* $\mathtt{Lk}(\mathtt{T_F}[3:4],\mathtt{T_S}[3:4]) \wedge hb(\mathtt{T_S}[4],\mathtt{T_F}[5]) \wedge hb(\mathtt{T_F}[4],\mathtt{T_S}[5])$. *Applying the* ADD.BARRIER *rule yields:* $\mathtt{Lk}(\mathtt{T_F}[3:4],\mathtt{T_S}[3:4]) \wedge \mathtt{Barrier}(\mathtt{T_F}[5],\mathtt{T_S}[5])$.

**Example 3.4.** *For the example trace shown in Fig. 3(b), $\varphi_G$ is as shown. The disjuncts $\psi_1$ and $\psi_2$ are not relevant for this example except for the fact that $\psi_1$ is common to the $3^{rd}$ and $4^{th}$ conjuncts, $\psi_2$ is common to the $5^{th}$ and $6^{th}$ conjuncts and $\psi_1 \neq \psi_2$.*

- *Applying* ADD.LOCK *yields:* $hb(\mathtt{T_I}[2],\mathtt{T_F}[2]) \wedge hb(\mathtt{T_I}[2],\mathtt{T_S}[2]) \wedge (\mathtt{Lk}(\mathtt{T_F}[4],\mathtt{T_S}[3:4]) \vee \psi_1) \wedge (\mathtt{Lk}(\mathtt{T_F}[3:4],\mathtt{T_S}[4]) \vee \psi_1) \wedge (\mathtt{Lk}(\mathtt{T_F}[4],\mathtt{T_S}[3:4]) \vee \psi_2) \wedge (\mathtt{Lk}(\mathtt{T_F}[3:4],\mathtt{T_S}[4]) \vee \psi_2)$.
- *Applying* MERGE.LOCKS *next yields:* $hb(\mathtt{T_I}[2],\mathtt{T_F}[2]) \wedge hb(\mathtt{T_I}[2],\mathtt{T_S}[2]) \wedge (\mathtt{Lk}(\mathtt{T_F}[3:4],\mathtt{T_S}[3:4]) \vee \psi_1) \wedge (\mathtt{Lk}(\mathtt{T_F}[3:4],\mathtt{T_S}[3:4]) \vee \psi_2)$.
- *Finally, applying the* ADD.WAITNOTIFY *rule yields:* $\mathtt{WaitNotify}(\mathtt{T_F}[2],\mathtt{T_I}[2]) \wedge \mathtt{WaitNotify}(\mathtt{T_S}[2],\mathtt{T_I}[2]) \wedge (\mathtt{Lk}(\mathtt{T_F}[3:4],\mathtt{T_S}[3:4]) \vee \psi_1) \wedge (\mathtt{Lk}(\mathtt{T_F}[3:4],\mathtt{T_S}[3:4]) \vee \psi_2)$.

*Note that the* MERGE.LOCKS *rule does not apply to the last two conjuncts as $\psi_1 \neq \psi_2$. One possible solution for $\mathcal{S}$ is* $\{\mathtt{WaitNotify}(\mathtt{T_F}[2],\mathtt{T_I}[2]), \mathtt{WaitNotify}(\mathtt{T_S}[2],\mathtt{T_I}[2]), \mathtt{Lk}(\mathtt{T_F}[3:4],\mathtt{T_S}[3:4])\}$.

### 3.1 Experiments

We implemented the above procedure as an extension to TARA. Given a trace $\tau$, TARA supports synchronization synthesis as an optional step after generating succinct representations of $\mathcal{N}_\tau^g$ and $\mathcal{N}_\tau^b$. The implementation first attempts to apply the rules ADD.BARRIER, ADD.LOCK and ADD.WAITNOTIFY (in that order). Then, the merging rules are applied, first merging locks across thread pairs, and then merging barriers and locks spanning multiple threads. We report the results of synchronization synthesis experiments in Table 2. In each case, we report the numbers of locks (#L), barriers (#B) and wait-notify (#WN) primitives synthesized. The synthesized synchronization matched our (human) intuition about the repairs needed. Since TARA generates fairly small $\varphi_G$ formulae, the synthesis takes less than 50 microseconds in every case.

**Table 2** Experiments: synchronization synthesis

| Name | #L | #B | #WN | Name | #L | #B | #WN |
|---|---|---|---|---|---|---|---|
| reorder_2 | 1 | 0 | 0 | loop | 1 | 0 | 0 |
| define_use | 0 | 0 | 1 | fib_bench | 1 | 0 | 0 |
| em28xx | 0 | 0 | 1 | i2c_hid | 1 | 0 | 2 |
| locks | 1 | 0 | 0 | rtl8169-1 | 0 | 0 | 1 |
| 2stage | 0 | 0 | 1 | rtl8169-2 | 0 | 0 | 1 |
| drbd_receiver | 0 | 0 | 1 | rtl8169-5 | 0 | 0 | 1 |
| md | 0 | 0 | 1 | rtl8169-4 | 0 | 0 | 2 |
| lazy01 | 0 | 0 | 2 | rtl8169-6 | 0 | 0 | 1 |
| locks_hb | 1 | 0 | 2 | usb_serial-1 | 0 | 0 | 1 |
| lc_rc | 0 | 0 | 1 | usb_serial-2 | 0 | 0 | 1 |
| barrier_locks | 1 | 1 | 0 | rtl8169-3 | 0 | 0 | 1 |
| stateful01 | 0 | 0 | 2 | usb_serial-3 | 0 | 0 | 1 |
| read_write_lock | 4 | 0 | 0 | | | | |

## 4. Case Study: Bug Summarization

In our second case study, we use the representation for a sound overapproximation of the bad neighbourhood of a trace $\tau$ (returned as $\varphi_B$ by Algo. 2) for counterexample summarization and bug summarization. The HB-formula $\varphi_B$ encapsulates relevant ordering information about all counterexamples in the neighbourhood of $\tau$ and can be viewed as a stand-alone counterexample summary. For instance, in Fig. 3(c), one may view $\varphi_B = hb(\mathtt{T_N}[2],\mathtt{T_P}[2])$ as a counterexample summary that indicates a possible order violation. While such a bug report can already be useful to a human debugger, a cursory examination of the data-flow through the events in $\varphi_B$ can enable formulation of a more precise bug summary. To this end, we present a set of rules to help infer specific bugs such as data races, define-use order violations and two-stage access bugs.

### 4.1 Inferring Bug Summaries from $\varphi_B$

We assume $\varphi_B$ is in DNF. Our inference rules are presented in Fig. 4. For a thread $T$, a location $\ell$, and a global program vari-

**Figure 3** Example programs

```
globals:float value1, value2, value3, value4, sum;
        int flag1, flag2;
init: value1 = 1, value2 = 2, value3 = 4,
      value4 = 8, sum = 0, flag1 = 0, flag2 = 0;

thread_firsthalf:
locals: float temp, localsum;
init: localsum = 0;
TF[1]: localsum := localsum + value1;
TF[2]: localsum := localsum + value2;
TF[3]: temp := sum;
TF[4]: sum := temp + localsum;
TF[5]: value1 := value1/sum;
TF[6]: value2 := value2/sum;
TF[7]: flag1 := 1;

thread_secondhalf:
locals: temp, localsum;
init: localsum = 0;
TS[1]: localsum := localsum + value3;
TS[2]: localsum := localsum + value4;
TS[3]: temp := sum;
TS[4]: sum := temp + localsum;
TS[5]: value3 := value3/sum;
TS[6]: value4 := value4/sum;
TS[7]: flag2 := 1;

thread_checkresult:
TC[1]: assume (flag1 = 1 and flag2 = 1);
TC[2]: assert (value1 + value2 + value3 + value4 = 1);
```

$\varphi_G$: $(hb(\mathrm{T_F}[4], \mathrm{T_S}[3]) \vee hb(\mathrm{T_S}[4], \mathrm{T_F}[3])) \wedge hb(\mathrm{T_S}[4], \mathrm{T_F}[5]) \wedge hb(\mathrm{T_F}[4], \mathrm{T_S}[5])$

**(a)** Normalization. The goal of the program this trace is drawn from is to normalize a set of values such that their sum computes to 1. The program consists of three threads. The first and second thread process one half each of the set of values. Once the first and second thread run to completion, the third thread checks if the sum of the normalized values is 1.

```
globals: pointer hw_start;
         int registered;
init: registered = 0;

pci_thread:
TP[1]: registered := 1;
TP[2]: hw_start := &drv_hw_start;

network_thread:
TN[1]: assume (registered ≠ 0);
TN[2]: assert (*hw_start = drv_hw_start); /* pointer
                                          dereference */

void drv_hw_start() {
/* does something */
}
```

$\varphi_B$: $hb(\mathrm{T_N}[2], \mathrm{T_P}[2])$

**(c)** Network device initializer. This trace is drawn from a simplified snippet of the Linux RealTek 8169 network driver. The `pci` thread signals that a network device is registered using the variable `registered` and sets `hw_start` to point to the `drv_hw_start` method. The `network` thread calls `drv_open` once the network device is registered. The `drv_open` method dereferences the `hw_start` pointer.

```
globals: int intrmask, initdone, workqueueitems,
         interrupts;
init: intrmask = 0, initdone = 0, workqueueitems = 0,
      interrupts = 0;

thread_interruptmaskset:
TI[1]: intrmask := 1;
TI[2]: initdone := 1;

thread_first_irqhandler:
locals: int temp;
TF[1]: assume (intrmask = 1);
TF[2]: assert (initdone = 1);
TF[3]: temp := workqueueitems;
TF[4]: workqueueitems := temp + 1;
TF[5]: interrupts := interrupts + 1;

thread_second_irqhandler:
locals: int temp;
TS[1]: assume (intrmask = 1);
TS[2]: assert (initdone = 1);
TS[3]: temp := workqueueitems;
TS[4]: workqueueitem := temp + 1;
TS[5]: interrupts := interrupts + 1;

thread_checkworkqueue:
TC[1]: assert (workqueueitems ≥ interrupts);
```

$\varphi_G$: $hb(\mathrm{T_I}[2], \mathrm{T_F}[2]) \wedge hb(\mathrm{T_I}[2], \mathrm{T_S}[2]) \wedge (hb(\mathrm{T_S}[4], \mathrm{T_F}[4]) \vee hb(\mathrm{T_F}[4], \mathrm{T_S}[3]) \vee \psi_1) \wedge (hb(\mathrm{T_F}[4], \mathrm{T_S}[4]) \vee hb(\mathrm{T_S}[4], \mathrm{T_F}[3]) \vee \psi_1) \wedge (hb(\mathrm{T_S}[4], \mathrm{T_F}[4]) \vee hb(\mathrm{T_F}[4], \mathrm{T_S}[3]) \vee \psi_2) \wedge (hb(\mathrm{T_F}[4], \mathrm{T_S}[4]) \vee hb(\mathrm{T_S}[4], \mathrm{T_F}[3]) \vee \psi_2)$

**(b)** Interrupt handler (simplified snippet of the Linux RealTek 8169 network driver). Once the `intrmask` variable is set by the `interruptmaskset` thread, the hardware starts producing interrupts. The handling of these interrupts, by the two `irqhandler` threads, is correct only if the driver initialization is complete (captured by the `initdone` variable). The `irqhandlers` add items to a workqueue; the addition of items is modeled using a counter `workqueueitems`. The variable `interrupts` counts the total number of interrupts handled by the `irqhandler` threads and the thread `checkworkqueue` uses `interrupts` to check for inconsistencies in the workqueue.

```
globals: int[] pagetable, memory;
init: pagetable[1] = 5, memory[5] = 10;

thread_pagetableaccess:
locals: int loc, data, page;
TP[1]: page := 1;
TP[2]: loc := pagetable[page];
TP[3]: data := memory[loc];
TP[4]: assert (data = 10);

thread_datamove:
locals: int page, newloc, loc;
TD[1]: page, newloc := 1, 20;
TD[2]: loc := pagetable[page];
TD[3]: pagetable[page] := newloc;
TD[4]: memory[newloc] := memory[loc];
```

$\varphi_B$: $hb(\mathrm{T_D}[3], \mathrm{T_P}[2]) \wedge hb(\mathrm{T_P}[3], \mathrm{T_D}[4])$

**(d)** Page-table. The `pagetableaccess` thread reads a memory location `loc` from `pagetable` and reads `data` from that memory location. The `datamove` thread reads the current memory location `loc` from `pagetable`, updates `pagetable` with a new memory location `newloc` and copies the data from the old memory location to the new memory location.

**Figure 4** Inference rules for bug summarization[a]

$$\frac{hb(\mathtt{T}_1[\ell_1'], \mathtt{T}_2[\ell_2]) \wedge hb(\mathtt{T}_2[\ell_2], \mathtt{T}_1[\ell_1'']) \wedge \psi \quad read(\mathtt{T}_1[\ell_1'], v) \quad write(\mathtt{T}_1[\ell_1''], v) \quad access(\mathtt{T}_2[\ell_2], v)}{\mathtt{DataRace}(\{\mathtt{T}_1[\ell_1'], \mathtt{T}_1[\ell_1'']\}, \mathtt{T}_2[\ell_2])}\ \textsc{DataRace.1}$$

$$\frac{hb(\mathtt{T}_1[\ell_1'], \mathtt{T}_2[\ell_2'']) \wedge hb(\mathtt{T}_2[\ell_2'], \mathtt{T}_1[\ell_1'']) \wedge \psi \quad read(\mathtt{T}_1[\ell_1'], v) \quad write(\mathtt{T}_1[\ell_1''], v) \quad read(\mathtt{T}_2[\ell_2'], v) \quad write(\mathtt{T}_2[\ell_2''], v)}{\mathtt{DataRace}(\{\mathtt{T}_1[\ell_1'], \mathtt{T}_1[\ell_1'']\}, \{\mathtt{T}_2[\ell_2'], \mathtt{T}_2[\ell_2'']\})}\ \textsc{DataRace.2}$$

$$\frac{hb(\mathtt{T}_1[\ell_1], \mathtt{T}_2[\ell_2]) \wedge hb(\mathtt{T}_2[\ell_2], \mathtt{T}_1[\ell_1']) \wedge \psi \quad access(\mathtt{T}_1[\ell_1], v) \quad access(\mathtt{T}_2[\ell_2], v) \quad access(\mathtt{T}_1[\ell_1'], v)}{\mathtt{AtomicityViolation}(\mathtt{T}_1[\ell_1 : \ell_1'], \mathtt{T}_2[\ell_2])}\ \textsc{AtomicityViolation.1}$$

$$\frac{hb(\mathtt{T}_1[\ell_1], \mathtt{T}_2[\ell_2']) \wedge hb(\mathtt{T}_2[\ell_2], \mathtt{T}_1[\ell_1']) \wedge \psi \quad access(\mathtt{T}_1[\ell_1], v) \quad access(\mathtt{T}_2[\ell_2], v) \quad access(\mathtt{T}_1[\ell_1'], v) \quad access(\mathtt{T}_2[\ell_2'], v)}{\mathtt{AtomicityViolation}(\mathtt{T}_1[\ell_1 : \ell_1'], \mathtt{T}_2[\ell_2 : \ell_2'])}\ \textsc{AtomicityViolation.2}$$

$$\frac{hb(\mathtt{T}_1[\ell_1], \mathtt{T}_2[\ell_2]) \wedge hb(\mathtt{T}_2[\ell_2'], \mathtt{T}_1[\ell_1']) \wedge \psi \quad write(\mathtt{T}_1[\ell_1], v) \quad write(\mathtt{T}_1[\ell_1'], w) \quad read(\mathtt{T}_2[\ell_2], v) \quad read(\mathtt{T}_2[\ell_2'], w)}{\mathtt{TwoStageAccessBug}(\mathtt{T}_1[\ell_1 : \ell_1'], \mathtt{T}_2[\ell_2 : \ell_2'])}\ \textsc{TwoStageAccessBug.1}$$

$$\frac{hb(\mathtt{T}_1[\ell_1], \mathtt{T}_2[\ell_2]) \wedge hb(\mathtt{T}_2[\ell_2'], \mathtt{T}_1[\ell_1']) \wedge \psi \quad read(\mathtt{T}_1[\ell_1], v) \quad read(\mathtt{T}_1[\ell_1'], w) \quad write(\mathtt{T}_2[\ell_2], v) \quad write(\mathtt{T}_2[\ell_2'], w)}{\mathtt{TwoStageAccessBug}(\mathtt{T}_1[\ell_1 : \ell_1'], \mathtt{T}_2[\ell_2 : \ell_2'])}\ \textsc{TwoStageAccessBug.2}$$

$$\frac{\begin{array}{c} hb(\mathtt{T}_1[\ell_1], \mathtt{T}_2[\ell_2]) \wedge \psi \qquad read(\mathtt{T}_1[\ell_1], v) \qquad write(\mathtt{T}_2[\ell_2], v) \\ \exists \sigma \in \mathcal{N}_\tau : \sigma \models hb(\mathtt{T}_1[\ell_1], \mathtt{T}_2[\ell_2]) \wedge \psi \wedge \bigwedge_{\mathtt{T}[\ell]} write(\mathtt{T}[\ell], v) \wedge \mathtt{T}[\ell] \neq \mathtt{T}_1[\ell_1] \Rightarrow hb(\mathtt{T}_1[\ell_1], \mathtt{T}[\ell]) \end{array}}{\mathtt{DefineUse}(\mathtt{T}_1[\ell_1], \mathtt{T}_2[\ell_2])}\ \textsc{DefineUse}$$

[a]In this figure, $\ell_1 < \ell_1' < \ell_1''$ and $\ell_2 < \ell_2' < \ell_2''$.

able $v$, (a) $read(\mathtt{T}[\ell], v)$ denotes that event $\mathtt{T}[\ell]$ reads from $v$, (b) $write(\mathtt{T}[\ell], v)$ denotes that event $\mathtt{T}[\ell]$ writes to $v$, and (c) $access(\mathtt{T}[\ell], v)$ denotes that event $\mathtt{T}[\ell]$ reads from or writes to $v$. In the discussion below, we combine these with ordering constraints in a natural manner. For example, $read(\mathtt{T}_1[\ell_1], v) \rightarrow write(\mathtt{T}_2[\ell_2], v)$ says that event $\mathtt{T}_1[\ell_1]$ happens before $\mathtt{T}_2[\ell_2]$ and that $read(\mathtt{T}_1[\ell_1], v)$ and $write(\mathtt{T}_2[\ell_2], v)$ hold.

**Data races.** Recall that in our framework, every instruction is assumed to execute atomically. This includes statements of the form $\mathtt{v} := \mathtt{v} + \mathtt{1}$, which may execute non-atomically at a low-level. Hence, to infer data races corresponding to *concurrent* accesses of a shared variable $v$, we need to model statements at a lower level, i.e., by separating events into several low-level atomic events. In most cases, these low-level atomic events either read or write variables, but not both. For instance, a decomposition of an event $e_1$ with instruction $\mathtt{v} := \mathtt{v} + \mathtt{1}$ is given by $e_1'; e_1''$, where event $e_1'$ has instruction $\mathtt{r} := \mathtt{v} + \mathtt{1}$, event $e_1''$ has instruction $\mathtt{v} := \mathtt{r}$, and $r$ is a local variable modelling a register. In this case, a data race between event $e_1$ and some other event $e_2$ accessing $v$ in another thread manifests itself in a trace $\sigma$ as the ordering pattern $e_1' <_\sigma e_2 <_\sigma e_1''$. Hence, the DataRace.1 rule infers a possible data race between events labelled $\mathtt{T}_1[\mathtt{l}_1']$,$\mathtt{T}_1[\mathtt{l}_1'']$, and $\mathtt{T}_2[\mathtt{l}_2]$ if the pattern $read(\mathtt{T}_1[\mathtt{l}_1'], v) \rightarrow access(\mathtt{T}_2[\mathtt{l}_2], v) \rightarrow write(\mathtt{T}_1[\mathtt{l}_1''], v)$ is found in $\varphi_B$.

Further, if $e_2$ is also decomposed into $e_2'; e_2''$, where $e_2'$ reads from $v$ and $e_2''$ writes to $v$, a data race can manifest in a trace $\sigma$ as $e_1 <_\sigma e_2' \wedge e_1' <_\sigma e_2$. The DataRace.2 rule infers a possible data race between $\mathtt{T}_1[\ell_1'], \mathtt{T}_1[\ell_1'']$ and $\mathtt{T}_2[\ell_2'], \mathtt{T}_2[\ell_2'']$, if the patterns $read(\mathtt{T}_1[\ell_1'], v) \rightarrow write(\mathtt{T}_2[\ell_2''], v)$ and $read(\mathtt{T}_2[\ell_2'], v) \rightarrow write(\mathtt{T}_1[\ell_1''], v)$ is found in the same disjunct of $\varphi_B$.

**Atomicity violations.** The AtomicityViolation rules generalize the DataRace rules. If the data-flow and ordering pattern $access(\mathtt{T}_1[\ell_1], v) \rightarrow access(\mathtt{T}_2[\ell_2], v) \rightarrow access(\mathtt{T}_1[\ell_1'], v)$ manifests in $\varphi_B$, the first rule infers a possible atomicity violation of the event sequence $\mathtt{T}_1[\ell_1 : \ell_1']$ via event $\mathtt{T}_2[\ell_2]$. If the patterns $access(\mathtt{T}_1[\ell_1], v) \rightarrow access(\mathtt{T}_2[\ell_2'], v)$ and $access(\mathtt{T}_2[\ell_2], v) \rightarrow access(\mathtt{T}_1[\ell_1'], v)$ manifest in the same disjunct of $\varphi_B$, the second rule infers a possible atomicity violation of the event sequence $\mathtt{T}_1[\ell_1 : \ell_1']$ and event sequence $\mathtt{T}_2[\ell_2 : \ell_2']$.

**Two stage access.** The TwoStageAccessBug rules capture two classic scenarios of two-stage access bugs, indicating violations of some *consistency* requirement of accesses to $v$ and $w$. In particular, the values of $v$ and $w$ read by a thread could be inconsistent if either of the following patterns manifest in $\varphi_B$: (a) $write(\mathtt{T}_1[\ell_1], v) \rightarrow read(\mathtt{T}_2[\ell_2], v) \rightarrow read(\mathtt{T}_2[\ell_2'], w) \rightarrow write(\mathtt{T}_1[\ell_1'], w)$; or (b) $read(\mathtt{T}_1[\ell_1], v) \rightarrow write(\mathtt{T}_2[\ell_2], v) \rightarrow write(\mathtt{T}_2[\ell_2'], w) \rightarrow read(\mathtt{T}_1[\ell_1'], w)$.

**Define-use ordering.** The DefineUse rule infers a specific type of order violation indicating the use of a variable before it is defined. Given $\varphi_B$ in DNF, if the ordering $read(\mathtt{T}_1[\ell_1], v) \rightarrow write(\mathtt{T}_2[\ell_2], v)$ manifests in a disjunct $\delta$, the rule infers a define-use order violation if there exists a trace $\sigma \in \mathcal{N}_\tau$ such that $\sigma$ satisfies $\delta$ and $\mathtt{T}_1[\ell_1]$ precedes all events that write to $v$ in $\sigma$.

Starting from $\varphi_B$ given in DNF, we repeatedly apply the inference rules from Fig. 4 until no more rules are applicable. We report all inferred bugs as possible violations. Note that our goal here is only to assist the user in program debugging. Our inference rules are not complete. We do not claim that our inferred bugs will manifest in the program's executions, or that they will match a human debugger's intuition. We now present examples illustrating the application of some of our bug inference rules.

**Example 4.1.** *For the example trace shown in Fig. 1, $\varphi_B$ is given by $hb(\mathtt{T}_\mathtt{W}[1], \mathtt{T}_\mathtt{D}[2]) \wedge hb(\mathtt{T}_\mathtt{D}[1], \mathtt{T}_\mathtt{W}[2])$. Since $read(\mathtt{T}_\mathtt{W}[1], balance)$, $write(\mathtt{T}_\mathtt{W}[2], balance)$, $read(\mathtt{T}_\mathtt{D}[1], balance)$ and $write(\mathtt{T}_\mathtt{D}[2], balance)$ hold, we can apply the* DataRace.2 *rule to infer a* $\mathtt{DataRace}(\mathtt{W}[1:2], \mathtt{Y}[1:2])$. *Note that this bug inference matches the synchronization* $\mathtt{Lk}(\mathtt{T}_\mathtt{W}[1:2], \mathtt{T}_\mathtt{D}[1:2])$ *synthesized in Example 3.2.*

**Example 4.2.** *Consider the example trace shown in Fig. 3(c). In our encoding, the pointer hw_start is modelled as an integer variable hw that is initially 0 (since hw_start is uninitialized). The pointer dereference in $\mathtt{T}_\mathtt{N}[2]$ is modelled as* $\mathtt{assert}(\mathtt{hw} > 0)$. *For this example, $\varphi_B$ is given by $hb(\mathtt{T}_\mathtt{N}[2], \mathtt{T}_\mathtt{P}[2])$. Since $read(\mathtt{T}_\mathtt{N}[2], hw)$ and $write(\mathtt{T}_\mathtt{P}[2], hw)$ hold, and trace $\mathtt{T}_\mathtt{P}[1], \mathtt{T}_\mathtt{N}[1], \mathtt{T}_\mathtt{N}[2], \mathtt{T}_\mathtt{P}[2]$ satisfies the last premise of the* DefineUse *rule, we can apply the rule to infer a define-use order violation between $\mathtt{T}_\mathtt{N}[2]$ and $\mathtt{T}_\mathtt{P}[2]$.*

**Example 4.3.** *For the example trace shown in Fig. 3(d), $\varphi_B$ is given by $hb(\mathtt{T_D}[3], \mathtt{T_P}[2]) \wedge hb(\mathtt{T_P}[3], \mathtt{T_D}[4])$. Since $write(\mathtt{T_D}[3], pagetable)$, $write(\mathtt{T_D}[4], memory)$, $read(\mathtt{T_P}[2], pagetable)$ and $read(\mathtt{T_P}[3], memory)$ hold, we can apply the* TWOSTAGEACCESSBUG.1 *rule to infer* $\mathtt{TwoStageAccessBug}(\mathtt{T_D}[3:4], \mathtt{T_P}[2:3])$.

### 4.2 Experiments

Given a trace $\tau$, TARA supports bug summarization as an optional step after generating $\varphi_B$. Starting from $\varphi_B$ in DNF, the implementation attempts to apply the DATARACE, ATOMICITYVIOLATION, TWOSTAGEACCESSBUG and DEFINEUSE inference rules (in that order). Identical bug reports are merged to avoid duplicates.

The experimental results of using our TARA-based bug summarization on our test-suite are presented in Table 3. We report the numbers of data races (#DR), atomicity violations (#AV), two-stage access bugs (#2S) and define-use bugs (#DU) inferred. The Human column in the table presents a classification of the bugs present in the benchmarks, as reported by an expert user (OV stands for order violation). The last column indicates if TARA's bug summary matched the human classification. For the majority of benchmarks, TARA summarized the bug correctly (Yes). In some cases, TARA did not infer a bug summary (–). For the usb_serial-1 benchmark, TARA's bug summary contradicted the human classification. For each example, the implementation takes at most 12 milliseconds.

**Table 3** Experiments: bug summarization

| Name | #2S | #DR | #AV | #DU | Human | Bug summary right? |
|---|---|---|---|---|---|---|
| reorder_2 | 0 | 0 | 0 | 1 | DU | Yes |
| define_use | 0 | 0 | 0 | 1 | DU | Yes |
| em28xx | 0 | 0 | 0 | 1 | DU | Yes |
| locks | 0 | 2 | 0 | 0 | DR | Yes |
| 2stage | 1 | 0 | 0 | 0 | 2S | Yes |
| drbd_receiver | 0 | 0 | 0 | 0 | OV | – |
| md | 0 | 0 | 0 | 1 | DU | Yes |
| lazy01 | 0 | 0 | 0 | 0 | OV | – |
| locks_hb | 0 | 2 | 0 | 2 | DR, DU | Yes |
| lc_rc | 0 | 0 | 0 | 0 | OV | – |
| barrier_locks | 0 | 2 | 0 | 0 | DR, OV | Yes |
| stateful01 | 0 | 0 | 0 | 0 | OV | – |
| read_write_lock | 0 | 0 | 4 | 0 | AV | Yes |
| hm-loop | 0 | 1 | 0 | 0 | DR | Yes |
| fib_bench | 0 | 0 | 2 | 0 | AV | Yes |
| i2c_hid | 0 | 0 | 1 | 0 | AV, OV | Yes |
| rtl8169-1 | 0 | 0 | 0 | 1 | DU | Yes |
| rtl8169-2 | 0 | 0 | 0 | 1 | DU | Yes |
| rtl8169-5 | 0 | 0 | 0 | 0 | OV | – |
| rtl8169-4 | 0 | 0 | 0 | 0 | OV | – |
| rtl8169-6 | 0 | 0 | 0 | 0 | OV | – |
| usb_serial-1 | 0 | 0 | 0 | 1 | OV | No |
| usb_serial-2 | 0 | 0 | 0 | 0 | OV | – |
| rtl8169-3 | 0 | 0 | 0 | 0 | OV | – |
| usb_serial-3 | 0 | 0 | 0 | 0 | OV | – |

## 5. Case Study: Accelerating CEGAR

In the final case study, we present a procedure for learning predicates for refinement in a CEGAR loop [14], with the help of TARA. An abstraction-refinement loop proceeds by building an abstract model of an input program and applying a model-checker on the abstract model. If the abstract model satisfies the correctness specification, then the input program is correct. Otherwise, the model-checker finds an abstract counterexample, i.e., an execution in the abstract model. The abstraction counterexample is spurious if there is no concrete execution that corresponds to the abstract counterexample. Given a spurious counterexample, the refinement procedure refines the abstract model. This is done by finding predicates that inform the abstraction procedure to construct the next abstract model by adding the relevant details to the current abstract model such that the spurious counterexample is absent from next abstract model. The process starts over with the newly refined abstraction. After a number of iterations, the abstract model may have no more counterexamples, which proves the correctness of the input program. For simpler presentation, we assume that the input program is correct and all the abstract counterexamples are spurious.

An abstraction-refinement loop often takes many iterations to find the right set of predicates to prove correctness of the input program. This usually depends on the design of the refinement procedure. Many heuristics have been proposed to find the relevant predicates in fewer iterations (see, for example, [4]). We aim to use TARA to accelerate the search for the right predicates, i.e., reduce the number of iterations of a CEGAR loop.

Our refinement procedure takes a concurrent abstract counterexample as input and returns refinement predicates. First, we analyse the counterexample using TARA and obtain an HB-formula $\varphi_B$ that encodes a set of incorrect interleavings. We sample a number of interleavings from $\varphi_B$ and attempt to compute refinement predicates that simultaneously remove all the sampled spurious inter-leavings using a method similar to *beautiful interpolants* [1].

### 5.1 Abstraction and Refinement

An *abstract model* of a concurrent program $\mathcal{P} = \langle V, \{T_1, \ldots, T_k\}, SV, \langle LV_1, \ldots, LV_k \rangle\rangle$ is another concurrent program $\hat{\mathcal{P}} = \langle V, \{\hat{T}_1, \ldots, \hat{T}_k\}, SV, \langle LV_1, \ldots, LV_k \rangle\rangle$ such that, for each $i \in [1, k]$ and event $e$ in $T_i$, there is an event $\hat{e}$ in $\hat{T}_i$ such that if $\Gamma_0 e \Gamma_1$ is feasible then $\Gamma_0 \hat{e} \Gamma_1$ is feasible.

In predicate abstraction, the abstract event $\hat{e}$ corresponding to an event $e$ is defined using a set of predicates as follows. Let us suppose predicates $\rho_1, \ldots, \rho_m$ are used for abstraction. Let $i \in [1, m]$. Let $\beta_i$ be the weakest precondition of $e$ over $\rho_i$, and $\gamma_i$ be the weakest precondition of $e$ over $\neg\rho_i$. Let $\hat{\beta}_i$ and $\hat{\gamma}_i$ be the weakest formulas that are Boolean combinations of $\rho_1, \ldots, \rho_m$, and imply $\beta_i$ and $\gamma_i$, respectively. $\Gamma_0 \hat{e} \Gamma_1$ is feasible iff $\forall i \in [1, m] : (\Gamma_0 \models \hat{\beta}_i \to \Gamma_1 \models \rho_i) \wedge (\Gamma_0 \models \hat{\gamma}_i \to \Gamma_1 \models \neg\rho_i)$.

Let $\Gamma_0 \hat{e}_1 \Gamma_1 \ldots \hat{e}_n \Gamma_n$ be a spurious counterexample, i.e., a trace in the abstract model that violates the specification. A refinement procedure computes additional predicates $\alpha_0, \alpha_1, \ldots, \alpha_{n-1}, \alpha_n$ over program variables that satisfy the following constraint.

$$\alpha_0 = true \wedge \alpha_n = false \wedge \bigwedge_{i=1}^{n} \alpha_{i-1} \wedge e_i \to \alpha'_i$$

Note that the primed formula $\alpha'_i$ is the formula $\alpha_i$ where each variable $v$ is replaced by its primed version $v'$. Recall that $v'$ represents the value of $v$ the execution of an instruction. An abstract model computed using predicates $\alpha_1, \ldots, \alpha_{n-1}$ is guaranteed to not exhibit the spurious counterexample [23].

### 5.2 Sampling an HB-formula

We pass trace $\hat{e}_1 \ldots \hat{e}_n$ to TARA and obtain an HB-formula $\varphi_B$ in DNF to represent bad abstract traces. $\varphi_B$ is a formula over events $\hat{e}_1 \ldots \hat{e}_n$. With slight abuse of notation, we assume that $\varphi_B$ is a formula over events $e_1 \ldots e_n$, which can be obtained by replacing abstract events by their corresponding concrete events in $\varphi_B$. We sample a few concrete infeasible traces that satisfy $\varphi_B$ and try to compute the simultaneous refinement predicates, i.e., predicates that eliminate all the sampled traces from the abstract program. Intuitively, learning predicates simultaneously using multiple spurious counterexamples may allow us to find more *general* predicates. Both sampling and simultaneous refinement are heuristics choices.

Here, we present one possible choice for the sampling. However, one can imagine a wide array of heuristics for these choices. In our sampling heuristic, we search for two disjuncts in $\varphi_B$ of the form

$$\varphi_1 \wedge e_a < e_b \quad \text{and} \quad \varphi_2 \wedge e_b < e_a$$

such that negation of any HB-formula in $\varphi_1$ is not in $\varphi_2$. We generate traces $\tau_1$ and $\tau_2$ such that (a) they satisfy $\varphi_1 \wedge \varphi_2 \wedge e_a < e_b$ and $\varphi_1 \wedge \varphi_2 \wedge e_b < e_a$ respectively; and (b) they are of the following form with $e^1_{k_1} = e_a$ and $e^2_{k_2} = e_b$.

$$\tau_1 = \underbrace{e^0_1 \ldots e^0_{k_0}}_{prefix} \underbrace{e^1_1 \ldots e^1_{k_1} \, e^2_1 \ldots e^2_{k_2}}_{\bowtie} \underbrace{e^3_1 \ldots e^3_{k_3}}_{suffix}$$

$$\tau_2 = \overbrace{e^0_1 \ldots e^0_{k_0}} \, \overbrace{e^2_1 \ldots e^2_{k_2}} \, \overbrace{e^1_1 \ldots e^1_{k_1}} \, \overbrace{e^3_1 \ldots e^3_{k_3}}$$

If $\varphi_1 \wedge \varphi_2 \wedge e_a < e_b$ and $\varphi_1 \wedge \varphi_2 \wedge e_b < e_a$ are satisfiable, such traces always exist. Both the traces have a common prefix and suffix, and two middle segments $e^1_1 \ldots e^1_{k_1}$ and $e^2_1 \ldots e^2_{k_2}$ are swapped. From the traces, we obtain refinement predicates $\alpha_1 \ldots \alpha_{k_0}$, $\beta_1 \ldots \beta_{k_1+k_2}$, $\gamma_1 \ldots \gamma_{k_1+k_2}$, and $\delta_1 \ldots \delta_{k_3}$ by solving the following constraints.

$$\alpha_0 = true \wedge \bigwedge_{i=1}^{k_0} (\alpha_{i-1} \wedge e^0_i \rightarrow \alpha'_i) \wedge \alpha_{k_0} = \beta_0 = \gamma_0 \qquad \text{(prefix)}$$

$$\bigwedge_{i=1}^{k_1} (\beta_{i-1} \wedge e^1_i \rightarrow \beta'_i) \wedge \bigwedge_{i=k_1+1}^{k_1+k_2} (\beta_{i-1} \wedge e^2_{i-k_1} \rightarrow \beta'_i) \qquad \text{(mid trace 1)}$$

$$\bigwedge_{i=1}^{k_2} (\gamma_{i-1} \wedge e^2_i \rightarrow \gamma'_i) \wedge \bigwedge_{i=k_2+1}^{k_2+k_1} (\gamma_{i-1} \wedge e^1_{i-k_2} \rightarrow \gamma'_i) \qquad \text{(mid trace 2)}$$

$$\delta_0 = \beta_{k_1+k_2} = \gamma_{k_1+k_2} \wedge \bigwedge_{i=1}^{k_3} (\delta_{i-1} \wedge e^3_i \rightarrow \delta'_i) \wedge \delta_{k_3} = false \qquad \text{(suffix)}$$

In the above equations, the first and last constraints correspond to the prefix and suffix respectively. The second and third constraints correspond to the middle segments of the two traces.

### 5.3 Constraint Solving for Simultaneous Refinement

We discuss how to solve the above constraints for refinement. The above constraints are a set of non-recursive Horn clauses. Many techniques exist to solve such constraints (e.g. [7, 22]). Since we are aiming for simultaneous refinement, we prefer the solutions for the unknown predicates to be simple atomic formulas. If an unknown predicate appears as consequent of multiple implications (for example, $\alpha_{k_0+1}$), then the solver may naturally give a solution that is a disjunction of two atomic formulas. We use the method that is presented in Sec. 4 of [1] for the theory of linear arithmetic that forces a solver to return solutions for the above constraints with single atomic formulas if such a solution exists.

**Table 4** Experiments: CEGAR acceleration

| Example | SATABS | | SATABS[TARA] | |
|---|---|---|---|---|
| | Iterations | Time(s) | Iterations | Time(s) |
| example1 | 55 | 35.4 | 45 | 33.5 |
| example2 | 65 | 45.7 | 60 | 47.9 |
| example3 | 45 | 23.0 | 41 | 23.9 |

### 5.4 Experimental Results

We have implemented the above refinement procedure in SATABS [16] and refer to the modified version as SATABS[TARA]. In Table 4 we present the result of running SATABS and SATABS[TARA] on three hand crafted examples. Each of these examples contain two threads and 15-20 lines of code. Our method reduces the number of iterations in all the examples. However, the total time of verification increases for two examples due to the fact that our refinement procedure is not well optimized.

## 6. Related Work

**Representations of trace sets.** The $\Phi_{CTP}$ encoding used in Sec. 2 was introduced in [41], and subsequently generalized in [27, 37]. We may find more applications and variations of our tool TARA from exploring other suitable happens-before constraint based encodings of "interesting" interleavings from the body of predictive analysis literature (cf. [35, 38]). Concurrent counterexample traces have been generalized into partial order (Mazurkiewicz) traces in [8, 9]. As demonstrated in this paper, partial orders may not be adequate to represent arbitrary trace sets. The work in [20] introduces a new data structure, an inductive data-flow graph (iDFG), to generalize proofs of programs. While iDFGs is also a representation of (concurrent) trace sets, it is not clear how one may apply iDFGs for program debugging or synthesis. In other work, interference scenarios have been proposed in [19] to represent concurrent executions that are behaviourally equivalent under the same input values. For sequential programs, the authors in [2] represent all counterexamples of recursive programs using pushdown automata.

**Synchronization synthesis.** In the formal methods and programming languages community, synchronization synthesis of concurrent programs has been an active area of research for a long time [8, 9, 13, 30, 39, 40]. In the past, the approaches in [13, 40] were based on inferring synchronization by constructing and exploring the entire product graph or tableaux corresponding to a concurrent program. Recent approaches infer synchronization incrementally from traces [39] or generalizations of bad traces [8, 9]. However, the techniques from [8, 9, 39] infer atomic sections rather than locks—atomic sections are not directly implementable and need to be translated into locks either manually, or using other automated techniques (see, for example, [10]). Jin et al. introduce CFIX [26], a tool that fixes bugs in concurrent C programs by matching bug patterns and proposing fixes. However, in their case, the bug patterns are simple (corresponding to only conjunctions of happens-before constraints) and hence, cannot infer synchronization such as barriers. On the other hand, the CFIX tool is very robust and practical, and has generated fixes and corresponding patches for real open-source libraries.

**Bug summarization.** While there have been various techniques for fault localization, error explanation, counterexample minimization and bug summarization for sequential programs, we restrict our attention to relevant works for concurrent programs. In [28], the authors focus on shortening counterexamples in message-passing programs to a set of "crucial events" that are both necessary and sufficient to reach the bug. In [25], the authors introduce a heuristic to simplify concurrent error traces by reducing the number of context-switches. There are several papers that survey and classify common concurrency bug patterns [18, 29]. We can extend our bug inference rules using the bug patterns from the papers. Finally, there is a large body of work on automatic detection of specific bugs such as data races and atomicity violations [17, 32, 34, 43].

**Accelerating CEGAR.** There are several works to enhance the CEGAR loop by finding better predicates, e.g. [4, 36]. In the setting of hardware model-checking (for circuits), Glusman et al. [21] extend the CEGAR loop by adding several predicates if a spurious counterexample is found; they generate all counterexamples of the same length and gather information about valuations crucial to the incorrectness of the counterexamples. In a similar setting, Wang et al. [42] improve the CEGAR by introducing a technique to eliminate all spurious counterexamples for an invariant. Sakunkonchak et al. [33] apply CEGAR optimizations to software model checking and speed up the search for predicates that make the counterexample spurious. However, they do not use interpolants and instead search the counterexample for conflicting predicates. Bjesse et al. [6] use predicates obtained from CEGAR to guide bounded-model checking (BMC) and extend its reach.

## 7. Concluding Remarks

We propose a representation for concurrent trace sets based on HB-formulas. We present a method and a tool TARA for generating succinct representations of sound overapproximations of good and bad neighbourhoods of a trace. We use TARA to successfully drive three applications in concurrent program reasoning — synchronization synthesis, bug summarization and CEGAR. We believe that our representation and algorithms can significantly boost the applicability and utility of trace-based techniques for concurrency.

While the initial experiments using TARA have been promising, there are several avenues for future work. We plan to extend TARA to infer synchronization from traces over different set of events. In the bug summarization domain, we plan to add a larger class of bug inference rules. For accelerating CEGAR based verification, we plan to implement a more efficient refinement procedure and explore other sampling rules for picking abstract counterexamples.

**Acknowledgements.** The authors would like to thank Jyotirmoy Deshmukh, Roderick Bloem, and Bettina Könighofer for enabling fruitful discussions. The authors would also like to thank the anonymous reviewers for their considerable, constructive feedback.

## References

[1] A. Albarghouthi and K. McMillan. Beautiful interpolants. In *CAV*, pages 313–329, 2013.

[2] S. Basu, D. Saha, Y. Lin, and S. Smolka. Generation of all counter-examples for push-down systems. In *FORTE*, pages 79–94. 2003.

[3] D. Beyer. Status report on software verification. In *TACAS*, pages 373–388. 2014. `http://sv-comp.sosy-lab.org/`.

[4] D. Beyer, T. Henzinger, R. Majumdar, and A. Rybalchenko. Path invariants. In *PLDI*, pages 300–309, 2007.

[5] D. Beyer and E. Keremoglu. CPACHECKER: A tool for configurable software verification. In *CAV*, pages 184–190, 2011. `http://cpachecker.sosy-lab.org/`.

[6] P. Bjesse and J. Kukula. Using counter example guided abstraction refinement to find complex bugs. In *DATE*, pages 156–161, 2004.

[7] N. Bjørner, K. McMillan, and A. Rybalchenko. On solving universally quantified horn clauses. In *SAS*, pages 105–125, 2013.

[8] P. Černý, T. Henzinger, A. Radhakrishna, L. Ryzhyk, and T. Tarrach. Efficient synthesis for concurrency by semantics-preserving transformations. In *CAV*, pages 951–967, 2013.

[9] P. Černý, T. Henzinger, A. Radhakrishna, L. Ryzhyk, and T. Tarrach. Regression-free synthesis for concurrency. In *CAV*, pages 568–584. 2014. `https://github.com/thorstent/ConRepair`.

[10] S. Cherem, T. Chilimbi, and S. Gulwani. Inferring locks for atomic sections. In *PLDI*, pages 304–315, 2008.

[11] E. Clarke, D. Kroening, and F. Lerda. A tool for checking ANSI-C programs. In *TACAS*, pages 168–176, 2004. `http://www.cprover.org/cbmc/`.

[12] E. Clarke, D. Kroening, N. Sharygina, and K. Yorav. SATABS: SAT-based predicate abstraction for ANSI-C. In *TACAS*, pages 570–574, 2005.

[13] E. M. Clarke and E. A. Emerson. *Design and synthesis of synchronization skeletons using branching time temporal logic*. Springer, 1982.

[14] E. M. Clarke, O. Grumberg, S. Jha, Y. Lu, and H. Veith. Counterexample-guided abstraction refinement. In *CAV*, pages 154–169, 2000.

[15] L. De Moura and N. Bjørner. Z3: An efficient smt solver. In *CACAS*, pages 337–340. 2008. `http://z3.codeplex.com/`.

[16] A. Donaldson, A. Kaiser, D. Kroening, and T. Wahl. Symmetry-aware predicate abstraction for shared-variable concurrent programs. In *CAV*, pages 356–371, 2011.

[17] D. Engler and K. Ashcraft. Racerx: effective, static detection of race conditions and deadlocks. In *SOSP*, pages 237–252, 2003.

[18] E. Farchi, Y. Nir, and S. Ur. Concurrent bug patterns and how to test them. In *PDPS*, page 7 pp., 2003.

[19] A. Farzan, A. Holzer, N. Razavi, and H. Veith. Con2colic testing. In *FSE*, pages 37–47, 2013.

[20] A. Farzan, Z. Kincaid, and A. Podelski. Inductive data flow graphs. In *POPL*, pages 129–142. 2013.

[21] M. Glusman, G. Kamhi, S. Mador-Haim, R. Fraer, and M. Vardi. Multiple-counterexample guided iterative abstraction refinement: An industrial evaluation. In *TACAS*, pages 176–191. 2003.

[22] A. Gupta, C. Popeea, and A. Rybalchenko. Solving recursion-free horn clauses over li+uif. In *APLAS*, pages 188–203, 2011.

[23] T. A. Henzinger, R. Jhala, R. Majumdar, and K. L. McMillan. Abstractions from proofs. In *POPL*, pages 232–244, 2004.

[24] J. Huang, P. Meredith, and G. Roşu. Maximal sound predictive race detection with control flow abstraction. In *PLDI*, pages 337–348, 2014.

[25] N. Jalbert and K. Sen. A trace simplification technique for effective debugging of concurrent programs. In *FSE*, pages 57–66, 2010.

[26] G. Jin, W. Zhang, D. Deng, B. Liblit, and S. Lu. Automated Concurrency-Bug Fixing. In *OSDI*, pages 221–236. 2012.

[27] V. Kahlon and C. Wang. Universal causality graphs: a precise happens-before model for detecting bugs in concurrent programs. In *CAV*, pages 434–449, 2010.

[28] S. Kashyap and V. Garg. Producing short counterexamples using "crucial events". In *CAV*, pages 491–503. 2008.

[29] S. Lu, S. Park, E. Seo, and Y. Zhou. Learning from mistakes: a comprehensive study on real world concurrency bug characteristics. In *ASPLOS*, pages 329–339, 2008.

[30] Z. Manna and P. Wolper. Synthesis of communicating processes from temporal logic specifications. In *TOPLAS*, pages 68–93, 1984.

[31] J. Morse, M. Ramalho, L. Cordeiro, D. Nicole, and B. Fischer. ESBMC 1.22. In *TACAS*, pages 405–407. 2014. `http://www.esbmc.org/`.

[32] M. Said, C. Wang, Z. Yang, and K. Sakallah. Generating data race witnesses by an smt-based analysis. In *NASA Formal Methods*, pages 313–327. 2011.

[33] T. Sakunkonchak, S. Komatsu, and M. Fujita. Using counterexample analysis to minimize the number of predicates for predicate abstraction. In *ATVA*, pages 553–563. 2007.

[34] S. Savage, M. Burrows, G. Nelson, P. Sobalvarro, and T. Anderson. Eraser: A dynamic data race detector for multithreaded programs. *ACM Trans. on Computer Systems (TOCS)*, pages 391–411, 1997.

[35] K. Sen, G. Roşu, and G. Agha. Detecting errors in multithreaded programs by generalized predictive analysis of executions. In *FMOODS*, pages 211–226, 2005.

[36] R. Sharma, A. V. Nori, and A. Aiken. Interpolants as classifiers. In *CAV*, pages 71–87, 2012.

[37] N. Sinha and C. Wang. On Interference Abstractions. In *POPL*, pages 423–434, 2011.

[38] Y. Smaragdakis, J. Evans, C. Sadowski, J. Yi, and C. Flanagan. Sound predictive race detection in polynomial time. *ACM SIGPLAN Notices*, pages 387–400, 2012.

[39] M. Vechev, E. Yahav, and G. Yorsh. Abstraction-guided synthesis of synchronization. In *POPL*, pages 327–338, 2010.

[40] M. T. Vechev, E. Yahav, and G. Yorsh. Inferring synchronization under limited observability. In *TACAS*, pages 139–154, 2009.

[41] C. Wang, S. Kundu, M. Ganai, and A. Gupta. Symbolic predictive analysis for concurrent programs. In *FM*, pages 256–272. 2009.

[42] C. Wang, B. Li, H. Jin, G. Hachtel, and F. Somenzi. Improving ariadne's bundle by following multiple threads in abstraction refinement. *IEEE TCAD*, pages 2297–2316, 2006.

[43] C. Wang, R. Limaye, M. Ganai, and A. Gupta. Trace-based symbolic analysis for atomicity violations. In *TACAS*, pages 328–342. 2010.

# K-Java: A Complete Semantics of Java

Denis Bogdănaş
Alexandru Ioan Cuza University, Iaşi, Romania
denis.bogdanas@info.uaic.ro

Grigore Roşu
University of Illinois at Urbana-Champaign
grosu@illinois.edu

## Abstract

This paper presents K-Java, a complete executable formal semantics of Java 1.4. K-Java was extensively tested with a test suite developed alongside the project, following the Test Driven Development methodology. In order to maintain clarity while handling the great size of Java, the semantics was split into two separate definitions – a static semantics and a dynamic semantics. The output of the static semantics is a preprocessed Java program, which is passed as input to the dynamic semantics for execution. The preprocessed program is a valid Java program, which uses a subset of the features of Java. The semantics is applied to model-check multi-threaded programs. Both the test suite and the static semantics are generic and ready to be used in other Java-related projects.

***Categories and Subject Descriptors*** D.3.1 [*Programming Languages*]: Formal Definitions and Theory—Semantics

***Keywords*** Java, mechanized semantics, K framework

## 1. Introduction

Java is the second most popular programming language (`http://langpop.com/`), after C and followed by PHP. Both C and PHP have recently been given formal semantics [20, 22]. Like the authors of the C and PHP semantics, and many others, we firmly believe that programming languages *must* have formal semantics. Moreover, the semantics should be public and easily accessible, so inconsistencies are more easily spotted and fixed, and formal analysis tools should be based on such semantics, to eliminate the semantic gaps and thus errors in such tools. Without a formal semantics it is impossible to state or prove anything about the language with certainty, including that a program meets its specification, that a type system is sound, or that a compiler or interpreter is correct. While all analysis tools or implementations for the language invariably incorporate some variant of the language semantics, or a projection of it, these are hard to access and thus to asses.

To the best of our knowledge, the most notable attempts to give Java a formal semantics are ASM-Java [35], which uses abstract state machines, and JavaFAN [21], which uses term rewriting. However, as discussed in Section 2, these semantics are far from being complete or even well tested. Each comes with a few sample Java programs illustrating only the defined features, and each can execute only about half of the other's programs.

We present K-Java, a semantics for Java which systematically defines every single feature listed in the official definition of Java 1.4, which is the Java Language Specification, 2nd edition (JLS) [25], a 456-page 18-chapter document. Moreover, our semantics is thoroughly tested. In fact, we spent about half the time dedicated to this project to write tests, which are small Java programs exercising special cases of features or combinations of them. Specifically, we followed a Test Driven Development methodology to first develop the tests for the feature to be defined and interactions of it with previous features, and then defined the actual semantics of that feature. This way we produced a comprehensive set of 840 tests, which serves as a conformance test suite not only for our semantics, but also for testing various other Java tools. Considering that no such conformance test suite exists for Java, our tests can also be regarded as a contribution made by this paper.

As a semantic framework and development tool for our Java semantics we chose $\mathbb{K}$ [33] (`http://kframework.org`). There are several appealing aspects of $\mathbb{K}$ that made it suitable for such a large project. $\mathbb{K}$ provides a convenient notation for modular semantics of languages, as well as automatically-generated execution and formal analysis tools for the defined languages, such as a parser and interpreter, state-space explorer for reachability, model-checker, symbolic execution engine, deductive program verifier, and, recently, a translator of semantics to Coq. In particular, recent advances in matching and reachability logic [17, 32] have been incorporated in $\mathbb{K}$, making it unnecessary to define multiple semantics for the same language, e.g. an operational semantics for execution and an axiomatic semantics for program verification. The C [20] and PHP [22] semantics mentioned above have both been defined in $\mathbb{K}$, and demonstrated their usefulness using the generic $\mathbb{K}$ tools; the MatchC prover [5, 31], for example, automatically turns the C semantics into a Hoare-style deductive verifier of C programs.

To emphasize that our Java semantics is useful beyond just providing a reference model for the language, we show how the builtin model-checker of $\mathbb{K}$ can be used to model-check multi-threaded Java programs. While this illustrates only one possible application of the semantics, other applications can be similarly derived from the language-independent tools provided by $\mathbb{K}$.

Besides such immediate applications, we believe that our executable semantics of Java is also a convenient platform for experimenting with Java extensions. For example, [9] proposes to extend Java with traits and records, [23] with mixins, and [27] with immutable objects. The proposal to extend Java with generic types [14] made it to the language in Java 5. The widely debated lambda expression feature, with at least three evolving proposals [29], was finally incorporated in Java 8. Such extensions are easy to add to our semantics, and thanks to $\mathbb{K}$ one would immediately benefit not only from a reference model for them but also from all the formal analysis tools automatically offered by $\mathbb{K}$.

This paper makes the following two specific contributions:


*POPL '15*, January 15–17, 2015, Mumbai, India.

ACM 978-1-4503-3300-9/15/01... $15.00.
http://dx.doi.org/10.1145/2676726.2676982

- K-Java, the first complete semantics of Java 1.4, including multi-threading. More generally, K-Java is the first complete semantics for an imperative statically typed object-oriented concurrent language. Section 3 illustrates some challenges of formalising Java, Section 4 describes our definitional methodology and shows selected rules, and Section 5 shows an application to model-checking multithreaded programs.
- Comprehensive test suite covering all Java constructs (Section 6), also used to compare Java semantics in Section 2.

## 2. Related Work

Here we discuss two other major formal executable semantics of Java and compare them with K-Java. We also recall other large language semantics that influenced the design of K-Java.

### 2.1 Other Executable Semantics of Java

**ASM-Java** [35] is the first attempt to define a complete semantics of Java 1.0, and the most complete prior to K-Java, showing that is it feasible to define formal semantics to real-life programming languages. It was defined using Abstract State Machiness (ASMs) and covers almost all major features of Java, except packages. ASM-Java is also executable; with the kind help of its authors we were able make it work. ASM-Java comes with 58 tests that touch all their implemented features, which we used as one of our external test suites for K-Java. ASM-Java contains not only the semantics of Java, but also defines the compiler and the bytecode format, and gives a manual proof for the correctness of their compiler.

While K-Java uses a different formalism, it follows the ASM-Java methodology to separate the static and the dynamic semantics. Except for that, ASM-Java and K-Java are quite different. ASM-Java uses many auxiliary constructs in their preprocessed programs produced by the static semantics, while K-Java uses (a subset of) plain Java. ASM-Java is monolithic, while in K-Java the static and the dynamic semantics are two separate definitions that can be used independently. For example, other projects can use our static semantics to reduce the set of Java programs they need to handle.

**JavaFAN** [21] is another large-scale executable semantics of Java, defined using term rewriting in Maude [16]. Our testing revealed that JavaFAN is overall less complete than ASM-Java, although JavaFAN passed a few tests that ASM-Java failed to pass. However, unlike ASM-Java, thanks to the high-performance Maude model-checker [18], JavaFAN was successfully used to perform state-space exploration and model-checking of Java programs. For example, JavaFAN was able to detect the deadlock in the Dining Philosophers problem and prove the fixed program correct.

**Comparison.** Since both ASM-Java and JavaFAN are executable, we evaluated their completeness by running our comprehensive test suite (Section 6) with each. The results of our findings are presented in Figure 1. The list of Java features is divided into 10 large groups, separated by horizontal bars. The first 8 groups contain features introduced with Java 1.0: literals, expressions, statements, arrays, classes and instance members, interfaces, static members and static initialization, packages and identifier resolution. Group 9 includes features introduced with Java 1.2, and the last group includes the single new feature of Java 1.4 - `assert`.

| Feature | AJ | JF | KJ |
|---|---|---|---|
| Basic integer, boolean, String literals | ● | ● | ● |
| Other literals | ○ | ○ | ● |
| Overflow, distinction between integer types | ● | ○ | ● |
| Prefix `++i --i`, also `+= -= ... , \|\| &&` | ○ | ● | ● |
| Bit-related operators: `\| & ^ >> << >>>` | ○ | ○ | ● |
| Other integer operators | ● | ● | ● |
| String + <other types> | ◐ | ◐ | ● |
| Reference operators | ● | ◐ | ● |
| Basic statements | ● | ● | ● |
| Switch | ○ | ○ | ● |
| Try-catch-finally | ● | ○ | ● |
| Break | ● | ◐ | ● |
| Continue | ● | ○ | ● |
| Array basics | ● | ● | ● |
| Array-related exceptions | ● | ○ | ● |
| Array length | ● | ○ | ● |
| Array polymorphism | ● | ○ | ● |
| Array initializers | ○ | ○ | ● |
| Array default values | ● | ○ | ● |
| Basic OOP - classes, inheritance, polymorphism | ● | ● | ● |
| Method overloading – distinct number of arguments | ● | ● | ● |
| Method overloading without argument conversion | ● | ○ | ● |
| Method overloading with argument conversion | ○ | ○ | ● |
| Method access modes | ○ | ○ | ● |
| Instance field initializers | ● | ◐ | ● |
| Chained constructor calls via `this()` and `super()` | ● | ○ | ● |
| Keyword `super` | ● | ○ | ● |
| Interfaces | ● | ○ | ● |
| Interface fields | ● | ○ | ● |
| Static methods and fields | ● | ● | ● |
| Accessing unqualified static fields | ◐ | ○ | ● |
| Static initialization | ◐ | ◐ | ● |
| Static initialization trigger | ● | ○ | ● |
| Packages | ○ | ○ | ● |
| Shadowing | ◐ | ● | ● |
| Hiding | ● | ○ | ● |
| Instance initialization blocks | ○ | ● | ● |
| Static inner classes | ○ | ○ | ● |
| Instance inner classes | ○ | ○ | ● |
| Local & anonymous classes | ○ | ○ | ● |
| Assert statement | ○ | ○ | ● |

Support level: ● = Full ◐ = Partial ○ = None

AJ represents ASM-Java [35], JF is JavaFAN [21] and KJ is our work.

**Figure 1.** Completeness comparison of various semantics of Java

Besides packages, ASM-Java does not define all literal forms, an important set of operators, the switch statement, array initializers, and complex cases of method overloading and method access modes. The remaining features of Java 1.0 are defined, except for some corner cases. JavaFAN, despite being more recent than ASM-Java, covers a smaller subset of Java. Yet, it surpasses ASM-Java in a few areas. JavaFAN supports a wider set of operators, but still not all of them, and it has better support for local variable shadowing. Yet many other features are not supported: switch and continue, advanced array features, many class-related features and interfaces. Also, JavaFAN makes no distinction between various integer types and integer overflow is not defined. From Java 1.2 and 1.4, it only supports the simplest feature, instance initializers.

**Methodology.** The level of granularity differs widely both among groups and among individual rows in Figure 1. We intentionally compressed large portions of Java into one row when all semantics defined them (e.g., Basic OOP). Yet, when we identified interesting features not supported by some of the semantics, we extracted them into individual rows. We were careful to interpret the test results objectively. In particular, we designed each test to touch as few Java features as possible other than the tested one, to minimize the number of reasons for failure (Section 6). In the rare cases when we were unable to identify why a particular test failed, we gave the semantics the benefit of the doubt (except for K-Java).

### 2.2 Other Large-Scale Executable Semantics

Several large-scale semantics have been defined recently. Due to space constraints, we only mention those which had a direct influence on K-Java. The first large-scale semantics developed in $\mathbb{K}$ was that of C [20]. It covered all the C features, was tested using the GCC torture test suite [24], and was used to explore C undefinedness. A large fragment of PHP [22], also defined in $\mathbb{K}$, was tested for conformance using the PHP standard test suite and applied to prove simple properties using model-checking. Two different semantics of large fragments of Python were defined using $\mathbb{K}$ [26] and resp. PLT Redex [30]. Both were tested against publicly available test suites. The ASM-Java techniques were also successfully reused to define C# [13], benefiting from the fact that Java and C# are similar. JSCert [10] is an almost complete semantics for JavaScript in Coq, using a methodology that ensured a close visual resemblance to the standard, and tested against the JavaScript standard test suite.

## 3. Background and Challenges

Here we give background on Java and $\mathbb{K}$, and discuss some of the major challenges faced when giving semantics to Java.

### 3.1 The Java Language Specification

Java is a statically, strongly typed, object-oriented, multi-threaded language. It is completely defined, i.e., unlike other languages [10, 20], it has no undefined or implementation-dependent features. Except for threads, Java is completely deterministic. The official definition of Java 1.4 is the JLS [25]. JLS has 456 pages and 18 chapters; the part that defines the language has 377 pages. Java is distributed as part of the Java Development Kit (JDK), together with a several thousand class library. The class library, however, is *not* part of the JLS. Nevertheless, we defined semantics to all classes that are central to the language and mentioned in the JLS, such as `Object`, `String`, `Thread` and a dozen exception types.

**Challenges.** The K-Java project faced formidable challenges. The first challenge is the sheer size of Java. At the imperative level the language has 36 operators (JLS §15) and 18 statements (§16). Java values may be subject to a large number of conversions (§5). There are complex rules for resolving an identifier (§6). More precisely, an identifier in Java could mean one of the following: package, class, field, local variable or method. Method name could be decided based on the immediate syntactic context alone. However, disambiguating between the remaining categories is non-trivial and involves many special cases. One of the most complex features of Java is method overloading, that we illustrate in the next subsection. Classes have complex initialization rules that include static initialization (§8.3.2, 12.4) and instance initialization (§8.3.2, 12.5). The matter is further complicated by the ability to call on the first line of a constructor either a constructor of the same class through `this()` or a constructor of the base class through `super()`. Interfaces interact with a wide number of features as they may have methods, static fields, specific rules for initialization and method overwriting.

Java has a number of modularity features, such as packages, imports, and four categories of nested classes: static inner, non-static inner, local and anonymous. Since nested classes may access names from their enclosing classes, they bring a large number of special cases for name resolving. Packages are important to define access modes, and access modes have challenging interactions with the other Java features, as will be illustrated in Section 3.2.

The separation of the whole semantics into static and dynamic definition is a consequence of Java being statically typed. Dynamically typed languages like PHP or JavaScript need just a dynamic semantics. JLS clearly defines what computations should happen before the execution (compile-time) and what should happen during the execution (runtime). In Section 3.2 we present an example that illustrates the difficulties produced by static typing. While it might seem natural to have the two semantics for Java, we did not follow this approach from the beginning. How static typing influenced the design decisions of K-Java is discussed in Section 4.1.

Another challenge was the careful testing and implementation of all corner cases for each new feature. The difficulty arises when the new feature interacts with already defined features. For example, packages were among the last features added. We had to make sure packages were properly resolved in all contexts — in variable declarations, extends/implements clauses, cast expressions, etc. When we later added inner classes, we had to make sure inner classes work equally well in all the contexts above. For each context we had to test that inner classes might be referred both by simple names and by fully qualified names, that might contain package names. Our testing methodology is presented in Section 6.

Despite these challenges, we made no compromises and completely defined every single feature of Java 1.4.

**JLS content unrelated to K-Java.** Java was designed to be compiled into a bytecode format that is executed on a hardware-independent Java Virtual Machine (JVM). Consequently, some details of JLS deal specifically with the bytecode representation and are irrelevant here. Such parts are §12.1-12.3, 12.6-12.8 (details of JVM execution) and §13 (bytecode binary compatibility). JLS also defines all the compile-time errors that might be produced by incorrect programs. We do not cover them, as the focus of K-Java is to model the behavior of valid Java programs only.

Also, we do not cover Dynamic Class Loading (DCL), §12.2. Instead, in K-Java all classes are loaded at the beginning of the execution. JLS mentions the possibility to load classes at runtime, from other formats than bytecode, but sends the reader to the JVM specification for details. No other details are given. For this reason, it is fair to consider DCL a JVM rather than a Java feature, and to regard the default class loader (the one loading classes from ".class" files from the startup classpath) purely as a performance optimization, with no implication to the semantics.

**Limitations.** We do not define the Java Memory Model (JMM) that governs the allowed multi-threaded execution behaviors (§17). Instead, we define a sequentially consistent memory model with a global store and no caches, consistent with the JLS only if all fields are `volatile`. Defining JMM would be a significant effort on its own, relatively orthogonal to the present work. Also, JMM 1.4 was replaced by JMM 5, so is no longer actual. It has been demonstrated that $\mathbb{K}$ allows for modular replacement of the memory model [19, §4.2.6]; we plan to do the same for Java in future work.

### 3.2 A Flavor of Java: Static Typing and Access Modes

Every Java expression has a statically assigned type. Static types have various functions during execution:

- Subexpression types influence the type of the parent expression. For example, `1 + 2` is not the same as `1 + (long)2`.
- Integers' type gives their precise representation within the allowed range. When the range for a certain type is exceeded, overflow occurs: `1000` is different from `(byte)1000`.
- When an object has a member (field or static method) that hides an inherited member one can pick the right member by manipulating the type of the qualifier. Given `b` of type `B`, then `b.v` and `((A)b).v` could refer to different fields.
- Method overloading allows methods with the same name and number of arguments, but with different argument types. Then `f(0)` and `f((long)0)` may invoke different methods.

For most expressions, the static type might be computed at the same time as the actual value of the expression. One might think that static types could be computed during execution at the same time as the value of an expression is computed. We actually did this in an older version of the semantics, and it worked great for a while. However, we had to rethink this approach when the time came to define the ternary conditional operator `_?_:_`. An expression

```
class A {
  private String f(int a) {return "int";}
  String f(long a) {return "long";}

  String test() {
    return f((byte)0); }              //int
}
class B {
  String test() {
    return new A().f((byte)0); }  //long
}
```

**Figure 2.** Method overloading with access modes

```
package a;
public class A {
  void f() { ... }
  void g() { ... }
}

package a;
public class B extends A {
  protected void f() { ... }
  void g() { ... }
}

package b;
import a.*;
public class C extends B {
  protected void f() { ... }
  protected void g() { ... }
}

A c = new C(); c.f();   //C.f()
               c.g();   //B.g()
```

**Figure 3.** Package access mode and method overriding

`a ? b : c` evaluates to `b` when `a` is true, and to `c` otherwise. When `b` and `c` have different static types, the conditional expression will have the *join type* of the two[1]. Thus, the static type of the operator depends on the type of the two arguments, yet only one of these arguments is evaluated at runtime. It would be incorrect to compute the value of both `b` and `c` just for the sake of having their static type (due to possible side effects). Therefore the computation of static types had to be separated from the actual execution.

One of the most complex features of Java is method overloading. First, the arguments of a method call may have types that are different from the parameter types. When the method is overloaded, the version with the *most specific* types that are compatible with the argument types is invoked. Moreover, the choice of available versions of the method is influenced by access modes.

In Figure 2, both versions of `f()` are compatible with the call `f((byte)0)`, yet the set of accessible versions is different for the two call sites. The call from `A.test()` has access to both versions, and it chooses the more specific one. However, the call from `B.test()` cannot access the private `f()`; it calls the one with default access mode. The situation is even more complex when overloading is combined with inheritance and subtype polymorphism.

One might be tempted to think that access modes are only required for static semantics and could be discarded before execution.

[1] JLS §15.25 puts some restrictions on the types of arguments of _?_:_, that makes join in most cases to be the widest type of arguments 2 and 3.

In Java this is not the case. In Figure 3 the two methods `f()` and `g()` are very similar, yet the declaring class of the actually invoked methods is different. Since `A.f()` is declared with package access mode, and class `C` is in a different package, the method `C.f()` does not directly override `A.f()`. However, it does override `A.f()` *indirectly*, through the declaration `B.f()`. The method `A.f()` is accessible to `B` since both `A` and `B` are in the same package. As `B.f()` is declared with protected access mode, the method is accessible to any subclass of `B`, including to `C`. Thus, a link is established that allows `C.f()` to override `A.f()`. The very similar method `g()` is declared with the default (package) access mode in `B`, that prevents the connection between `B.g()` and `C.g()`. Hence, in order to determine the right method to be invoked, it is not sufficient to pick the last one visible to the dynamic (runtime) type of the qualifier. A correct semantics has to analyse the entire chain of classes between the static type of the qualifier and the dynamic type.

The examples above illustrate how static typing allows for a rich set of features, but it also brings significant complexity. Moreover, it is not enough to consider each language feature in isolation. It is required to define and *test* each combination that might lead to non-trivial interactions. Section 6 addresses testing. Some rules related to method invocation are presented in Section 4.3.

### 3.3 $\mathbb{K}$ (`http://kframework.org`)

$\mathbb{K}$ [33] is a framework for engineering language semantics. Given a syntax and a semantics of a language, $\mathbb{K}$ generates a parser, an interpreter, as well as formal analysis tools such as model checkers and deductive theorem provers, at no additional cost. It also supports various backends, such as Maude and, experimentally, Coq, that is, it can translate language semantics defined in $\mathbb{K}$ into Maude or Coq definitions. The interpreter allows the semanticists to continuously test their semantics, significantly increasing their effectiveness. Furthermore, the formal analysis tools facilitate formal reasoning for the given language semantics, which helps both in terms of applicability of the semantics and in terms of engineering the semantics itself; for example, the state-space exploration capability helps the language designer to cover all the non-deterministic behaviors of certain language constructs or combinations of them.

Here we describe $\mathbb{K}$ only very briefly. More details are given on an as-needed basis in the rest of the paper. In $\mathbb{K}$, a language syntax is given using conventional BNF annotated with semantic attributes. A language semantics is given as a set of reduction rules over configurations. A configuration is an algebraic structure of the program state, organized as nested labeled cells holding semantic information, including the program itself. Figure 4 shows a subset of the Java configuration. The order of cells is irrelevant in a configuration. Leaf cells contain pieces of the program state like a computation stack or continuation (e.g., k), environments (e.g., env), stacks (e.g., stack), etc. As this is all best understood through an example, let us consider a typical rule for reading a variable:

$$\left\langle \frac{X}{V} \cdots \right\rangle_{\mathsf{k}} \ \langle \cdots X \mapsto L \cdots \rangle_{\mathsf{env}} \ \langle \cdots L \mapsto V \cdots \rangle_{\mathsf{store}}$$

We see here three cells, k, env and store. The k cell represents a list (or stack) of computations waiting to be performed. The left-most (i.e., top) element of the stack is the next item to be computed. The env cell is simply a map of variables to their locations. And the cell store is a map from locations to values. The rule above says that if the next thing to be evaluated (which here we call a redex) is the variable lookup expression $X$, then one should match $X$ in the environment to find its location $L$ in memory, and match $L$ in the store to find its value $V$. With this information, one should transform the redex into that value, $V$; the horizontal line represents a reduction. A cell with no horizontal line means that it is read

$$\left\langle \left\langle \left\langle \langle K \rangle_{\mathsf{k}}\ \langle List \rangle_{\mathsf{stack}}\ \langle \langle Map \rangle_{\mathsf{env}}\ \langle ClassType \rangle_{\mathsf{crntClass}}\ \langle Int \rangle_{\mathsf{location}} \rangle_{\mathsf{methodContext}} \atop \langle \langle Int \rangle_{\mathsf{tid}}\ \langle Map \rangle_{\mathsf{holds}}\ \langle Bool \rangle_{\mathsf{interrupted}} \rangle_{\mathsf{threadData}} \right\rangle_{\mathsf{thread*}} \right\rangle_{\mathsf{threads}} \atop \left\langle \left\langle \langle ClassType \rangle_{\mathsf{classType}}\ \langle Map \rangle_{\mathsf{methods}} \atop \langle \langle \langle K \rangle_{\mathsf{methodSignature}}\ \langle List \rangle_{\mathsf{methodParams}}\ \langle K \rangle_{\mathsf{methodBody}} \rangle_{\mathsf{methodDec*}} \rangle_{\mathsf{methodDecs}} \right\rangle_{\mathsf{class*}} \right\rangle_{\mathsf{classes}} \atop \langle Map \rangle_{\mathsf{store}}\ \langle List \rangle_{\mathsf{in}}\ \langle List \rangle_{\mathsf{out}}\ \langle Set \rangle_{\mathsf{busy}}\ \langle Map \rangle_{\mathsf{waitingThreads}} \right\rangle_{\mathsf{T}}$$

**Figure 4.** Subset of the Java Configuration

but does not change during the reduction. The "..." are structural frames, that is, they match portions of cells that are irrelevant.

This unconventional notation is actually quite useful. The above rule would be written out as a traditional rewrite rule like this:

$$\langle X \curvearrowright \kappa \rangle_{\mathsf{k}}\ \langle \rho_1, X \mapsto L, \rho_2 \rangle_{\mathsf{env}}\ \langle \rho_3, L \mapsto V, \rho_4 \rangle_{\mathsf{store}}$$
$$\Rightarrow \langle L \curvearrowright \kappa \rangle_{\mathsf{k}}\ \langle \rho_1, X \mapsto L, \rho_2 \rangle_{\mathsf{env}}\ \langle \rho_3, L \mapsto V, \rho_4 \rangle_{\mathsf{store}}$$

Items in the k cell are separated with "$\curvearrowright$", which can now be seen. The $\kappa$ and $\rho_1$, $\rho_2$, $\rho_3$, $\rho_4$ take the place of the "..." above. The most important thing to notice is that nearly the entire rule is duplicated on the right-hand side (RHS). Duplication in a definition requires that changes be made in concert, in multiple places. If this duplication is not kept in sync, it leads to subtle semantic errors. In a complex language like Java, the configuration is much more complex, and would require including additional cells like methodContext, thread and threads (Figure 4). $\mathbb{K}$ automatically infers these intervening cells, keeping the rules local and modular.

In fact, one of the most appealing aspects of $\mathbb{K}$ is its modularity. It is very rarely the case that one needs to touch existing rules in order to add a new feature to the language. There are two $\mathbb{K}$ features specifically targeting modularity. First, the configuration can be structured as nested cells. Second, the language designer needs only to mention the cells that are needed in each rule, and only the needed portions of those cells. For example, the above rule only refers to the k, env and store cells, while the entire configuration contains many other cells as shown in Figure 4. This modularity contributes not only to compact and thus human readable semantics, but also to the overall effectiveness of the semantics development process. For example, even if a new cell is added to the configuration later on in order to support a new feature, the above rule does not change.

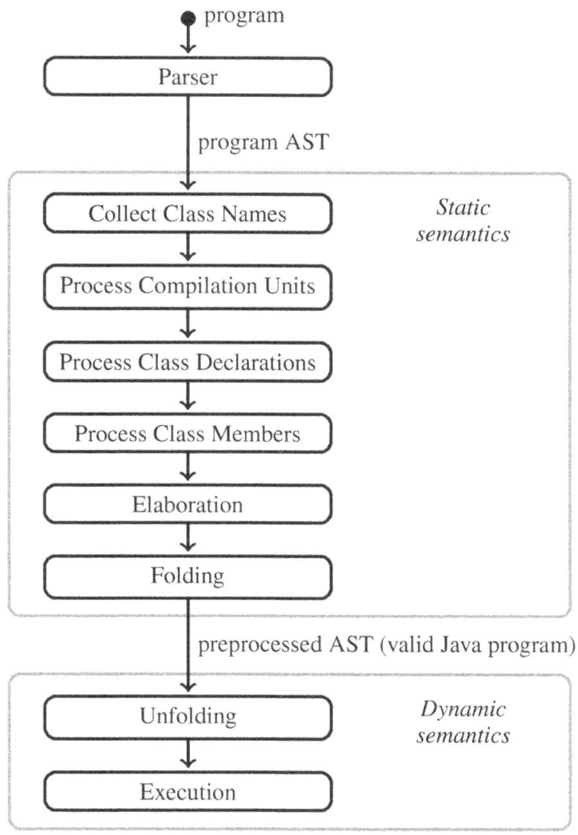


**Figure 5.** The structure of K-Java

## 4. K-Java: The Semantics of Java in $\mathbb{K}$

K-Java is divided into two separate definitions: static semantics and dynamic semantics (Figure 5). For parsing we use JavaFront [15], a Java grammar defined in SDF [28], which we turned into a parser compatible with $\mathbb{K}$ by using the SDF-to-K adapter [11].

The static semantics takes as input the AST representation of a Java program and produces a preprocessed program as the output. It performs computations that could be done statically, and are referred in JLS as compile-time operations. Such computations include converting each simple class name into a fully qualified class name or computing the static type of each expression. The preprocessed AST is passed to the dynamic semantics for execution.

***Statistics*** We define the semantics for all 186 syntactic productions of Java. Here are some statistics for our semantics:

| | Static | Dynamic | Common | Lib | Total |
|---|---|---|---|---|---|
| SLOC | 3112 | 2035 | 539 | 497 | 6183 |
| CLOC | 857 | 1189 | 383 | 98 | 2527 |
| Size (KB) | 168 | 139 | 52 | 22 | 381 |
| N cells | 31 | 36 | 28 | – | 95 |
| N rule | 497 | 347 | 183 | 47 | 1074 |
| N aux | 111 | 83 | 79 | 9 | 282 |

The rows represent source lines of code (SLOC), comment lines of code (CLOC), total files size, number of cells, number of rules, number of auxiliary functions. The columns represent the static semantics, the dynamic semantics except class library, modules common for both static and dynamic semantics, class library (including multi-threading) and the total size.

Next we present an overview of the static semantics and continue with selected rules from the dynamic semantics.

### 4.1 Static Semantics

The static semantics consists of several phases, depicted in Figure 5. Each phase digs deeper into the syntactic structure of Java and either performs a set of transformations over the program or computes some new configuration cells.

***Collect class names phase.*** In this phase the initial program is traversed and all class names are collected into a map. The names map serves two purposes at later phases: to resolve simple class names into fully qualified class names and to determine the set of classes available inside a package. Each class is traversed recursively, so that the inner classes are also registered. Yet the traversing does not proceed inside code blocks, thus classes defined at the block level (local and anonymous) are not discovered at this stage.

***Process compilation units phase.*** In this phase the traversal starts again from the initial program AST and performs two tasks. The first is to move class content from the initial AST to the class cells inside the configuration, from where it will be easier to access during subsequent phases. From this point on the program is no longer a monolithic AST but a collection of class cells. The granularity of the initial class content is very rough. At this stage just the class declaration, including `extends/implements` clauses, is analysed, and not the class members. The class content is analysed recursively like in the the previous phase, to process all the inner classes. The second task of this phase is to process imports and produce the map of class names accessible for each top-level class.

***Process class declarations phase.*** In this phase the simple class names inside `extends/implements` clauses of each class are converted into fully qualified class names. This allows us to compute the map of accessible class names for inner classes. JLS has complex rules for the names accessible inside inner classes that do not allow computing those names at an earlier stage.

***Process class members phase.*** At this stage the body of each class is processed and each member is stored in an appropriate cell. For methods, the parameter and return types are now resolved.

***Elaboration phase.*** This phase involves analysing the code blocks and is the most complex of all phases. The transformations here involve resolving class names inside blocks, resolving expression types and method overloading. Also at this stage block-level classes (local and anonymous) are first detected. Upon their detection, block-level classes must be passed through all the previous phases, to be normalized to the same format as the other classes.

***Transformations.*** Figure 6 depicts most of the transformations performed by static K-Java. Left column contains sample input fragments together with the minimal relevant context. The right column represents the transformed fragment. These transformations illustrate the means by which it was possible to represent the preprocessed program as valid Java, without any extra annotations.

The simple class names are transformed into fully qualified class names (row 1). This allows us to eliminate imports clauses in preprocessed programs. Each expression is additionally wrapped into a cast expression that encodes its static type (row 2). During execution this cast is treated like a regular cast. The example in the figure also illustrates binary numeric promotion: the result type of the addition between an `int` and a `long` is a long.

In addition, for method calls each argument is wrapped into one more cast, namely to the expected parameter type (row 3). This allows us to effectively encode method overloading.

Row 4 illustrates the preprocessing of fields accessed by simple names. Each such field access is converted into a qualified access. If the field is non-static, it will be qualified by `this` (first case in row 4), and `this` should be additionally cast to the current class type, according to rule 2. If the field is static, it will be qualified with the class that defined the field (second case). The same transformation is performed for methods called without a qualifier.

This last transformation allows us to disambiguate among the four roles of a name, namely package, class, field or local variable:

| Syntax | Syntactic Context | Resulting Role |
|---|---|---|
| `Id` | package | package |
| `Id` | package or class | package |
| `Id` | class | class |
| `((Type) Qual.Id)` | expression | field |
| `((Type) Id)` | expression | local var |

An identifier inside a syntactic context where only a package is allowed will be considered a package. If either a package or a class is allowed, then the identifier will also be considered a package

<table>
<tr><th>Initial code</th><th>Preprocessed code</th></tr>
<tr><td>Object</td><td>java.lang.Object</td></tr>
<tr><td>1 + 2L</td><td>(long)((int)1+(long)2)</td></tr>
<tr><td>void f(long a);<br>f(1);</td><td><br>f((long)(int)1);</td></tr>
<tr><td>class A{ int v;<br>  static int s;}<br>v<br>s</td><td><br><br>(int)((A) this).v<br>(int)A.s</td></tr>
<tr><td>class A{ A(){} }</td><td>class A {<br>  A(){ super(); }<br>}</td></tr>
<tr><td>class A {<br> static int a=1;<br> static{a++;}<br>}</td><td>class A {<br> static int a;<br> static{a=1;a++;}<br>}</td></tr>
<tr><td>class A {<br> int a=1;<br> {a++;}<br> A(){<br>  super();<br> }<br>}</td><td>class A {<br> int a;<br> void $init(){<br>  a=1;a++;<br> }<br> A(){<br>  super();<br>  $init();<br> }<br>}</td></tr>
<tr><td>class O {<br> void m() {<br>  final<br>   int a=1,b=2;<br>  class L {<br>   int f(){<br>    return a+b;<br>   }<br>  };<br>  new L().f();<br> }<br>}</td><td>class O {<br> void m() {<br>  final int a=1,b=2;<br>  LEnv $env<br>    =new LEnv();<br>  $env.a=a;<br>  $env.b=b;<br>  new L($env).f();<br> } //m()<br><br> class LEnv{<br>  int a,b;<br> }<br> class L{<br>  LEnv $env;<br>  L(LEnv $env){<br>   this.$env=$env;<br>  }<br>  int f(){<br>   return<br>     $env.a+$env.b;<br>  }<br> } //L<br>} //O</td></tr>
<tr><td>final int a;<br>new A() {<br> int f() {<br>  return a;<br> }<br>}.f();</td><td>final int a;<br>class LocalA<br>  extends A{...};<br>new LocalA().f();</td></tr>
</table>

**Figure 6.** Transformations performed by the static semantics

(here we consider classes that are used as qualifiers to refer to an inner class also as packages). A field or a local variable will always be part of a cast expression, thus will always be inside an expression context. If the respective identifier is qualified, then it is a field. Otherwise it is a local variable.

Continuing with row 5, if a constructor does not call another constructor on the first line, then it should call the base class constructor, `super()`, except if the current class is `Object`. For legibility, we omit the already discussed transformations (e.g., wrapping into cast expressions) in the remaining examples.

Initializers of static fields as well as static initializing blocks are collected into one big static initializing block (row 6), which is invoked during execution when the class is for the first time accessed by the program. For instance initializers the same procedure cannot be followed (row 7). Instead, all the instance initialization code is collected into the method `$init()`, that is called by the constructors right after the base constructor `super()` was called.

Arguably the most complex transformation is that of local classes. It is encoded into a separate module with 26 rules, one of the largest of K-Java. Local classes are converted into instance inner classes within the same enclosing class. The unusual difficulty of this transformation arises from the ability of local classes to access final local variables visible at the point when the class was declared. The most common case is presented in row 8. For each such local class `L`, an additional inner class `LEnv` is defined that stores the enclosing local environment of `L`. `LEnv` contains a field for each variable in the environment. Accesses to the local environment of `L` are encoded as accesses to fields of `LEnv`.

Finally, anonymous classes are first converted into local classes, which are in turn converted into inner classes (the last row).

***Motivation for elaboration phase.*** Initially, K-Java was developed without an elaboration phase. For example expression types were computed along their value each time they were executed. Similarly, other computations that are now done in the elaboration phase were performed on the fly during execution. This approach worked up to a point, and produced a monolithic semantics which was more compact than the present one. However, when we reached the point to define the semantics of the conditional expression `_?_:_` and of the local classes, it eventually became clear that we had to compute the static types upfront. As described in Section 3.2, it is impossible to compute the type of a conditional expression by evaluating its operands dynamically. Also, local classes had to be discovered and preprocessed prior to execution, in order to cover all the corner cases. For this we needed a pre-execution phase capable to dig into code blocks.

***Folding phase.*** The last and simplest phase of preprocessing, Folding, combines the information stored in class cells back into one big AST, acting as an interface to the dynamic semantics. Since all the transformations performed by the static semantics maintain the validity of the program, the resulting preprocessed AST represents a valid Java program as well. This phase is technically unnecessary for the dynamic semantics alone, because Unfolding phase in dynamic K-Java (Figure 5) is the exact mirror of Folding, distributing the AST back into the same cells that were used to produce it. Folding and Unfolding phases were required to complete the division between the static and the dynamic parts of K-Java.

***The preprocessed AST.*** The output of the static semantics is the preprocessed AST. This AST has a valuable property: it corresponds to a valid Java program, equivalent to the initial one. More precisely, for every Java program $P_1$ there is a program $P_2$ such that the preprocessed AST of $P_1$ is equal to the AST of $P_2$. We do not prove this property, we only state it, supported by the observation that every transformation performed by the static semantics preserves program equivalence.

Maintaining this equivalence imposed some challenges. First, we were forced to use only transformations that preserve program validity. All the transformations presented in Figure 6 are also performed by the Java compiler (javac), with the difference that javac produces bytecode. In contrast, not all transformations performed by javac were accessible to static K-Java. For example, javac flattens inner classes into top-level classes. We could not do the same because we would lose method access modes, and access modes have to be preserved (Section 3.2). Also, we could not use any auxiliary constructs in the preprocessed AST. Despite the challenges, we believe producing a preprocessed AST with stated properties was worthwhile, since it enables our static semantics to be usable in conjunction with tools outside the $\mathbb{K}$ ecosystem.

### 4.2 Exceptions

We choose to illustrate the first rules from K-Java through the dynamic semantics of `throw` and `try/catch` (Figure 7). These rules are relatively self-contained and require just the cell k. By default, rules without a cell context (as are all the rules in Figure 7) automatically apply to the current computation task (the first task in k, which holds the current computation). Virtually all the rules in a language definition in $\mathbb{K}$ match the first task of k either explicitly or (like here) implicitly.

The first rule rewrites a `try/catch` into the body of `try`, $S$, followed by catch clauses wrapped into the auxiliary construct `catchBlocks`. The binary associative construct "$\curvearrowright$" (spelled "followed by") is builtin to $\mathbb{K}$ and stands for computation task sequentialization. The constructor's role is to separate individual tasks in the current computation. Now rules for other statements will apply over the content of $S$ until it is either entirely consumed or a `throw` statement becomes the first task.

In the first case, if $S$ was consumed, it means the execution of `try` block completed normally. Then the term `catchBlocks` reaches the top of computation and is discarded by the second rule. In the second rule, "_" is an anonymous variable, which can match anything. Here it can match one or more `catch` clauses. The term `catchBlocks` is rewritten into " $\cdot$ ", the unit (or empty) computation. In words, this rule says that if `catchBlocks` reaches the top of computation then discard it. Now the entire `try/catch` is consumed and the execution continues with the next statement.

In case $S$ throws an exception, a `throw` statement will eventually reach the top of the computation. Figure 7 continues with the syntax definition of `throw`, as it has a semantic role. Before `throw` could be evaluated, the expression inside `throw` has to be evaluated to a value. $\mathbb{K}$ has a compact notation to achieve this — the $[strict]$ annotation, meaning: bring the non-terminals of the annotated syntax to the top of computation, and plug them back when they are evaluated to a final value. Specifically for the statement `throw`, this annotation is compiled into one heating and one cooling rule, as shown in the inner box figure. The heating rule brings the expression to the top of computation for evaluation. The notation "$\square$" (spelled "hole") is a placeholder marking the context from which the expression was heated. The rule should only apply if the expression is not a final result yet (here a typed value); this restriction is encoded in the side condition. The cooling rule brings the produced typed value back to its original context. The typed value is $V :: ThrowT$ — an auxiliary notation of K-Java. The left side of "::" is the value, while the right side is the static type. $\mathbb{K}$ also has more general forms of $[strict]$, allowing to control which arguments should be heated and the evaluation order.

Now the actual rules for `throw` are ready to apply. Rule 3 (THROW-MATCH) matches when the type of the exception carried by `throw` is compatible with the type accepted by the first `catch` clause, so the exception is caught. The compatibility of the exception type and the `catch` clause's type is verified by the expression $\texttt{subtype}(\mathit{ThrowT}, \mathit{CatchT})$ in the side condition. In this case, both the **throw** statement and the **catchBlocks** construct are rewritten into a sequence of three statements: a declaration of the **catch** parameter $X$ of type $\mathit{CatchT}$ as a local variable ($\mathit{CatchT} X$;), an initialization of $X$ with the exception value typed with the type expected by $X$ ($X = V :: \mathit{CatchT}$;), and the body of **catch** — $\mathit{CatchS}$. All three statements are wrapped inside a block `{ }`, to confine the variable `X` to its expected scope.

Rule 4 matches when the two types are not compatible. In this case the first **catch** clause is dissolved, bringing the next one (if any) to the top of the list. Rule 5 matches when **throw** cannot interact with the next statement (the side condition). Statements interacting with **throw** are the non-empty **catchBlocks** and **finally**. Thus, if the next computation item after **throw**, *KI:KItem*, is anything except the two, including the empty **catchBlocks** produced eventually by the fourth rule, that statement will be dissolved. The statement **throw** will remain the top of computation until it reaches a matching **catch** or remains the only rule inside the k cell. The notation *KI:KItem* means that variable *KI* should match only one item in the computation sequence separated by $\curvearrowright$. If we wrote just *KI*, then the entire remaining computation would be matched. If **throw** remains the only task in the computation, another rule will match that will ensure exception propagation outside the current method.

Loop statements with **break**/**continue** are defined similarly.

One may wonder why not desugar a **try** with multiple **catch** clauses into multiple **try** with one **catch** each. We actually did so initially, but it turned out to be incorrect. Indeed, the code

```
try { throw new A(); }
catch(A a) { throw new B(); }
catch(B b) { ... }
```

*cannot* be desugared into

```
try {
  try { throw new A(); }
  catch(A a) { throw new B(); }
}
catch(B b) { ... }
```

because in the second case the exception `B` would get caught by `catch(B b)`, and this is incorrect according to JLS. This (counter) example is now included in our test suite.

### 4.3 Method Invocation

The central rule of method invocation is the first rule in Figure 8. This is actually the last rule to be applied, after a long chain of computations that involves computing the qualifier, the arguments, loading the required information from various cells of configuration and deciding the actual method to be invoked, based on the access mode, as was mentioned in Section 3.2. When the actual invocation of the method is ready to be performed, the top of computation cell contains a term of the form $\mathit{Qual}.\texttt{methodRef}(\mathit{Sig}, \mathit{DecC})(\mathit{Args})$. This term is a Java qualified method invocation expression augmented with K-Java auxiliary syntax. Here $\mathit{Qual}$ is the qualifier—the object or class upon which the method is invoked. The term $\texttt{methodRef}(\mathit{Sig}, \mathit{DecC})$ is a reference to a method with signature $\mathit{Sig}$ declared in the class $\mathit{DecC}$. The variable $\mathit{RestK}$ denotes the remaining computation/-continuation in cell k. This rule performs the following operations:

- The rest of computation ($\mathit{RestK}$) and the current content of methodContext are saved to a new entry (or frame) on top of the cell stack. This data will be used to restore the current computation context by the rules for **return**.
- The new method context is initialized with:
  - An empty local variable environment (env).
  - The declaring class of the invoked method (crntClass).
  - The current object location, computed by auxiliary function $\texttt{getOid}(\mathit{Qual})$ as:
    - The location of the qualifier, if qualifier is an object.
    - No location, if qualifier is a class (for static methods).
- Current computation is rewritten into a sequence of four terms:
  - Static initialization of the new declaring class.
  - Initialization of the parameters.
  - The method body.
  - A return statement with no arguments. This will be reached only if the execution of the method body terminates without reaching another **return** or **throw** statement.

The auxiliary function **staticInit()** triggers static initialization of the qualifying class, in case this class was not initialized yet. Repeated calls of this function have no effect.

RULE TRY

$$\frac{\texttt{try}\ S\ \mathit{CatchList}}{S \curvearrowright \texttt{catchBlocks}\ (\mathit{CatchList})}$$

RULE CATCHBLOCKS-DISSOLVE

$$\frac{\texttt{catchBlocks}\ (\_)}{\cdot}$$

SYNTAX $\mathit{Stmt} ::= \texttt{throw}\ \mathit{Exp}\ ;\ [\underbrace{\mathit{strict}}_{\text{compiled into:}}]$

RULE THROW-HEAT

$$\frac{\cdot}{E} \curvearrowright \texttt{throw}\ \frac{E}{\square}\ ;$$

REQUIRES $\neg_{Bool}\ \texttt{isTypedValue}\ (E)$

RULE THROW-COOL

$$\frac{V :: \mathit{ThrowT}}{\cdot} \curvearrowright \texttt{throw}\ \frac{\square}{V :: \mathit{ThrowT}}\ ;$$

RULE THROW-MATCH

$$\frac{\texttt{throw}\ V :: \mathit{ThrowT}\ ; \curvearrowright \texttt{catchBlocks}\ (\texttt{catch}\ (\mathit{CatchT}\ \ X)\{\mathit{CatchS}\}\ \_)}{\{\mathit{CatchT}\ \ X\ ;\curvearrowright X = V :: \mathit{CatchT}\ ;\curvearrowright \mathit{CatchS}\}}$$

REQUIRES $\texttt{subtype}\ (\mathit{ThrowT}, \mathit{CatchT})$

RULE THROW-NOT-MATCH

$$\texttt{throw}\ V :: \mathit{ThrowT}\ ; \curvearrowright \texttt{catchBlocks}\left(\frac{\texttt{catch}\ (\mathit{CatchT}\ \ X)\{\mathit{CatchS}\}}{\cdot}\ \_\right)$$

REQUIRES $\neg_{Bool}\ \texttt{subtype}\ (\mathit{ThrowT}, \mathit{CatchT})$

RULE THROW-PROPAGATION

$$\texttt{throw}\ \_ :: \_\ ; \curvearrowright \frac{\mathit{KI} : \mathit{KItem}}{\cdot}$$

REQUIRES $\neg_{Bool}\ \texttt{interactsWithThrow}\ (\mathit{KI})$

**Figure 7.** Rules for `try/catch` and `throw`

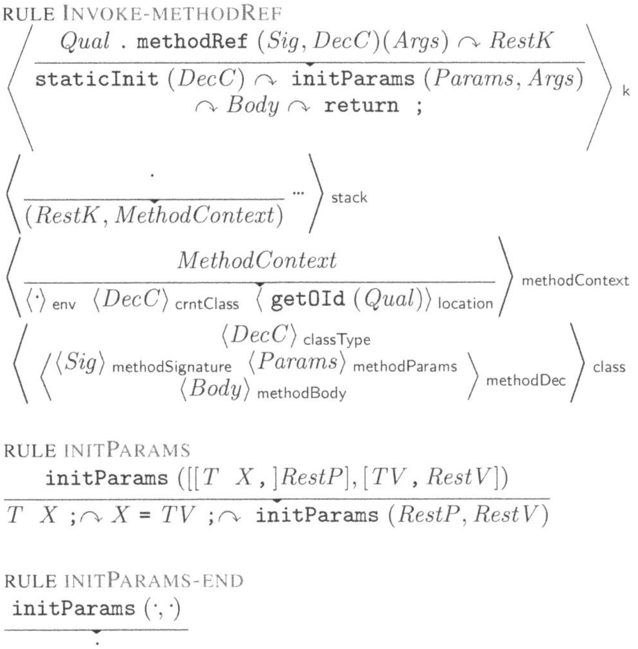


**Figure 8.** Final rules for method invocation

The function `initParams()` is defined by rules 2 and 3 in Figure 8. It takes as arguments two lists—the list of parameter declarations and the list of argument values. The first rule processes the first parameter declaration in the list. The parameter with name $X$ of type $T$ is rewritten into a local variable declaration $T\ X$; followed by an assignment expression that initializes $X$ with the argument value. The third term in the RHS of the rewrite is `initParams` with the processed parameter and argument removed. Here we use `[ ]` as $\mathbb{K}$ brackets, to disambiguate terms grouping.

When all parameters are processed, both arguments of `initParams` become empty lists. In this case the third rule from the figure applies, dissolving the `initParams` term.

The complete semantics of method invocation, as well as the semantics of `new`, are discussed in the companion report [12].

### 4.4 Multithreading and Synchronization

K-Java has basic support for threads. First is the class Thread with methods `start()`, `join()` and `interrupt()`. We also support thread synchronization through the `synchronized` statement (JLS §14.19) and the `synchronized` modifier for methods (JLS §8.4.3.6). For more advanced usage we support threading-related methods from class `Object`: `wait()`, `notify()`, `notifyAll()`.

Below we discuss the key rules for methods `wait()` and `notify()`. Both methods have to be called from a `synchronized` block that holds the monitor (lock) of the target object. When `wait()` is called, the thread releases the lock on target object and blocks until another thread calls `notify()` on the same object. When `notify()` is called, the waiting thread does not wake up immediately, but only after the notifying thread exited the `synchronized` block. When waking up, the thread re-acquires the lock on the target object. When there are multiple threads waiting on the same monitor object, `notify()` will non-deterministically wake up one of them. Finally, if either `wait()` or `notify()` is called in a state where the current thread does not hold the appropriate monitor, an exception is thrown.

The rules are presented in Figure 9 (see Figure 4 for the configuration cells). The first rule [object-wait] corresponds to the invocation of `wait()`. Here the term `objectRef`($Oid$, _) :: _ represents a

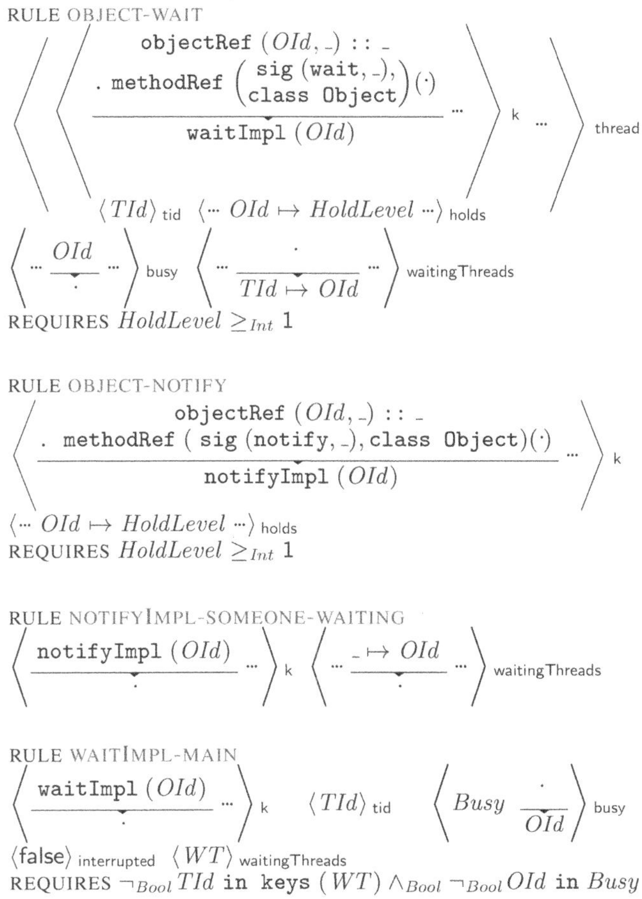


**Figure 9.** Rules for `Object.wait()` and `Object.notify()`

typed object reference—the qualifier of the method call. The only part that is of interest to us from this term is $Oid$—the object identifier in the store, that is also used as synchronization key. The next term, `methodRef(sig(wait,`_`),class Object)`, represents a method reference to the method with signature `sig(wait,` _) (name `wait` and irrelevant arguments), declared in the class `Object`. The expression above the horizontal line (LHS of the rewrite) is a method call expression, for the given object reference, the given method reference and no arguments. This rule replaces the method call expression in cell k with `waitImpl()`—an auxiliary function used later, to exit from the waiting state. The id of the current thread (`TId`) has to be registered in the set in waitingThreads. The cell holds attached to each thread stores the number of times the current thread acquired the lock on each object. Here we use it to make sure that the current thread acquired the lock at least once (see the side condition). Another cell matched here is busy. This one, in contrast with holds is a global cell, unique for the whole configuration. It stores the set of objects that are currently used as synchronization monitors—arguments of blocks `synchronized`. When an object enters the waiting state, it has to release its ownership to the monitor; this is done by deleting `OL` from the set.

The second rule [object-notify] is the starting rule for `notify()`. The side condition ensures that the current thread holds the monitor on the target object. The actual logic of `notify()` is delegated to `notifyImpl()`. The construct `notifyImpl()` requires two rules for two cases—the case when there is at least one thread waiting on the target object, and the case when there is none.

Rule [notifyImpl-someone-waiting] is the rule for the first case. If there is a thread waiting on the current object, then the object identifier `OId` will be present among the map values of waitingThreads. By deleting the whole entry associated to that value we enable the waiting thread to proceed. If there is no thread waiting for this object then term `notifyImpl()` is simply consumed.

At this stage, after a call to `notify()`, the rule for `waitImpl()` could match inside another thread (rule [waitImpl-main]). The rule checks in its side conditions that the current thread identifier, `TId`, is not among the waiting threads anymore. It also checks that the target object, represented by `OId`, is not busy. This is required because the thread exiting from waiting state has to reacquire the monitor on the target object. Finally, the rule has to make sure that the thread was not interrupted while it was waiting. Otherwise another rule will match and will throw the appropriate exception.

We only presented the key rules above, corresponding to the most common execution scenario. The corner cases, such as illegal calls that should result in various exceptions, are not included but are nevertheless fully supported and tested.

## 5. Applications

Here we show how K-Java together with builtin $\mathbb{K}$ tools can be used to explore multi-threaded program behaviors. The first application is state space exploration and the second is LTL model-checking.

### 5.1 State Space Exploration

The next simplest way to use K-Java besides execution is state space exploration. When a program is run with the $\mathbb{K}$ runner and option `--search`, the tool outputs all of the possible executions for the program, exposing any possible non-deterministic behavior. This capability was successfully used in the semantics of C [20] to expose the non-determinism of expression evaluation. While single-threaded Java is deterministic, threads bring non-determinism. By running a multi-threaded Java program in search mode, we can produce all its interleaving behaviors.

Additionally, the option `--pattern` allows us to filter the search results according to a pattern. This feature may be effectively used, for example, to detect deadlocks. In K-Java, the cell $\langle\rangle_{\text{thread}}$ is dissolved when the corresponding thread finishes its execution. Consequently, we can detect successful execution paths by using the pattern $\langle\cdot\rangle_{\text{threads}}$. The pattern will match when there are no threads remaining. Conversely, the pattern $\langle\_\rangle_{\text{thread}}$ would match the final states where at least one thread did not finish its execution, e.g. a deadlock. We successfully used this approach to detect the deadlock in the Dining Philosophers problem.

### 5.2 LTL Model-Checking

While state space search might be used to test some programs, $\mathbb{K}$ offers a more powerful capability for exploring non-deterministic behavior. Specifically, $\mathbb{K}$ provides linear temporal logic (LTL) model-checking capabilities through its Maude [16] backend. In this section we show how K-Java can be seamlessly used to verify LTL properties of multi-threaded applications.

Consider the program in Figure 10 (a modified version of [8]). The program contains a blocking queue – a classical producer-consumer example with one producer and one consumer thread. The inner class BlockingQueue contains two methods - `put()` and `get()`. The methods are synchronized, designed to be called from a multi-threaded environment. When `put()` is called on a full queue, the calling thread has to wait until some other thread dequeues an element. Similarly, the consumer thread calling `get()` has to wait when the queue is empty. The producer (the main thread) calls `put()` four times, while the consumer (anonymous thread inside `main()`) calls `get()` the same four times. Aside from demonstrating multi-threading capabilities, this small program illustrates many other features of Java: expressions with side effects,

```
public class QueueTest {
  static class BlockingQueue {
    int capacity = 2;
    int[] array = new int[capacity];
    int head=0, tail=0;
    synchronized void put(int element)
        throws InterruptedException {
      if (tail-head == capacity) {
        wait();                              // 1
      }
      array[tail++ % capacity] = element;
      System.out.print(0);
      notify();                              // 2
    }
    synchronized int get()
        throws InterruptedException {
      if (tail-head == 0) {
        wait();                              // 3
      }
      int element
          = array[head++ % capacity];
      System.out.print(1);
      notify();                              // 4
      return element;
    }
  }

  public static void main(String[] args)
      throws Exception {
    final BlockingQueue queue
        = new BlockingQueue();
    new Thread() {
      public void run() {
        for(int i=0; i<4; i++) {
          try {
            queue.get();
          }
          catch(InterruptedException e) {}
    } } }.start();
    for(int i=0; i<4; i++) {
      queue.put(i);
    }
  }
}
```

**Figure 10.** A two-threaded blocking queue

exception handling, arrays, static and instance methods, inner and anonymous classes. Running state space exploration for the example above correctly produces all eight expected interleavings of the output text (0 represents a call to `put()`, 1 – a call to `get()`):

```
00101011 00101101 00110011 00110101
01001011 01001101 01010011 01010101
```

The implementation of `BlockingQueue` contains a deliberate, subtle problem. The `wait()` call is within an `if` inside both `get()` and `put()`, thus is executed at most once. This is actually a correct behavior if we have just one producer and one consumer,[2] but leads to problems when the number of threads is at least three. Above, the only way a thread waiting on line labelled "3" could be awakened is from a call to `notify()` from method `put()`, line labeled "2". Since at the end of the method `put()` we have at least one element in the queue, method `get()` can safely extract an element.

In a scenario with one producer and two consumers the thread waiting on "3" could be awakened by a call to `notify()` from ei-

[2] We do not consider spurious wakeups here.

ther "2" or "4". If the thread executing `get()` was awakened by "2" (another `get()`), that other `get()` could have actually extracted the last element from the queue, thus rendering the queue empty. Unaware of the queue state, the freshly-awakened thread will execute the body of `get()` and will extract a non-existing element from the queue. To eliminate this possibility, we need to replace the `if` statements with `while` above both at "1" and "3". A programmer might make such a subtle mistake, when first designing the queue for a two-threaded usage, and then extending the context to more threads. It is difficult to expose this bug through traditional testing. We executed the incorrect three-threaded program a dozen times with the JVM; it never picked the buggy path.

Next, we would like to expose the problem above with LTL. In this implementation of queue `tail` is incremented each time an element is added to the queue, and `head` is incremented each time an element is extracted. They are never decremented. Since it is not possible to extract more elements than are added, a basic invariant of the queue is `head <= tail`. This is the exact invariant that is violated by the example above in the three-threaded scenario.

The LTL model checking capability of the $\mathbb{K}$ framework allows us to find the bug by model checking the following LTL formula:

```
□(this instanceof BlockingQueue
   ⟹ this.head <= this.tail)
```

The property was correctly proven true for the example in Figure 10, but was proven false for the three-threaded version of the same program. When we corrected the queue implementation, the model checker proved the formula correct. The version of the program in Figure 10 took 15 seconds to model check, produced 72 transition states and roughly two million rewrites.

Similar formal program analysis capabilities were demonstrated within the semantics of C [20] and PHP [22].

# 6. Testing

Testing K-Java took almost half of the overall development time. Here we describe our testing efforts, which resulted in what could be the first publicly available conformance test suite for Java.

## 6.1 The Quest for a Test Suite

Virtually all recent executable language semantics projects [10, 20, 22, 30] used an external test suite for validation. Naturally, we tried to do the same. The official test suite for Java, targeting both the language and the class library, is Java Compatibility Kit (JCK) [2] from Oracle. JCK is *not* publicly available. Instead Oracle offers free access for non-profit organisations willing to implement the whole JDK, i.e., *both* the language *and* the class library. After a laborious application, Oracle rejected our request.

We also explored unofficial test suites. Jtreg, part of OpenJDK [7], is a regression test suite for the class library, but not for the language. Another test suite is Mauve [6], containing tests for classes and for the compiler, but not for the runtime. Tests targeting the compiler test its capability to distinguish between correct and incorrect Java programs, and to output the appropriate error message. Unfortunately, all these tests were unsuitable for our purpose.

There were actually two external test suites that we were able to use. One was the set of examples from ACM-Java [35] that we presented in Section 2. Another one was the list of examples from the book Java Precisely [34]. We used 44 out of 58 tests from ASM-Java and 63 out of 114 examples from Java Precisely. The programs that we did not use either illustrated compiler errors, or were not complete Java programs, or used classes that we do not support.

These two sets of examples, while useful, were far from enough. Their purpose was to illustrate Java, not to exercise every single corner case of the language. With no luxury of an available comprehensive test suite, we had no choice but to develop our own.

## 6.2 Test Development Methodology

When writing our tests we followed the Test Driven Development (TDD). The main principle of TDD is to write tests before implementing the actual feature under test. It was advantageous to use TDD for K-Java for two reasons. First, K-Java has a complete and final specification—JLS. Consequently, our tests are not expected to change as a result of changes in the specification. Second, tests for K-Java are self-contained Java programs, they do not depend on any part of the system under test (K-Java) to be written.

For every test, we compared the output produced by K-Java with the output produced by JDK. When developing a new feature, we followed the following steps. First we tried to cover all corner cases of the feature under test in isolation. For example, the first nonterminal of the `for` statement might be a list of variable initializers. In such case we will include in our tests statements with zero, one or more initializers. Second, we would define the new feature in the simplest way possible to pass all the tests. Sometimes, after inspecting the implementation, we would identify some corner cases that were not captured by the tests. We would add additional tests for such cases. Thus our methodology was a combination of white-box and black-box testing. In addition to the steps above, we wrote tests for each *combination* of language features whenever we thought that the two features may possibly unexpectedly interact.

We followed the development of Java starting from low-level features such as literals, expressions, statements, towards the higher level features. The order of development is approximately reflected by the order in which tests were written, which can be found in K-Java public repository [1]. We aimed at testing every detail specified in JLS; e.g., to test the precise order of execution of subexpressions inside an expression, we intentionally used subexpressions with side-effects and verified the correct order of evaluation by observing the correct order in which the side effects occurred.

Some features depended on other features to be properly tested. For example, in order to test the precise static type of various expressions we used method overloading. For example, if an expression `e` has to return type `A`, but a plausible erroneous semantics could also produce `B`, we tested the correct choice by calling `f(e)`, where `f` was an overloaded method that could accept an argument of type `A` or `B`. In all such cases we were careful to postpone the exhaustive testing of the freshly developed feature, and to write the tests later once all prerequisites are available.

Eventually, we produced a test suite consisting of 840 tests.

***Multithreading.*** To test multi-threading we used state space exploration. We designed a test suite comprised of 28 programs explicitly aiming at covering all the behaviours of all the supported multi-threaded language constructs. For each program, we first produce all the possible solutions using $\mathbb{K}$. Then we compare the number of solutions with the expected, manually determined one.

***Later changes, testing ASM-Java and JavaFAN.*** When we first tried to execute ASM-Java and JavaFAN over our test suite, the majority of the tests unexpectedly failed. It was because some very basic feature, used in most of the tests, was not supported. For example ASM-Java did not support addition between a string and a boolean. JavaFAN did not support escape characters, and we were not able to use `"\n"` in our tests for this reason. To overcome this problem, we inspected our tests and eliminated the most common causes of failure, when they were not the actual feature under test. This way we were able to produce the results reported in Section 2.

# 7. Conclusion and Discussion

We have discussed K-Java, which to our knowledge is the first complete formal semantics of Java. The semantics has been split into a static and a dynamic semantics, and the static semantics was framed so that its output is also a valid Java program. This way, it can seamlessly be used as a frontend in other Java semantics or analysis tools. As a side contribution we have also developed a comprehensive conformance test suite for Java, to our knowledge the first public test suite of its kind, comprising more than 800 small Java programs that attempt to exercise all the corner cases of all the language constructs, as well as non-trivial interactions of them.

The skeptical reader may argue that there is no such thing as a 'complete' semantics of a large language like Java, because it is always possible to miss a feature or, worse, an interaction of features. While this is true in principle, we mention that completeness of the semantics was our major objective from the inception of this project, and that we have very carefully considered all possible interactions of features that were explicitly discussed in the JSL or that we could think of. Since there is no other attempt to completely formalize Java that we are aware of in order to formally compare with K-Java, due to all the above we believe that it is fair to claim that K-Java is the first complete formal semantics of Java.

K-Java can serve as a platform to experiment with Java extensions. Not only can one define such extensions rigorously, but one also gets a reference implementation for experimentation.

We plan to extend K-Java with semantics for the the latest versions of Java, starting with Java 5. Most of Java 5 features can be compiled into JVM 1.4 bytecode by using javac option `-target jsr14`: generics, varargs, for-each loop and autoboxing [3]. These features can be similarly defined in the static K-Java. Support in the dynamic K-Java would be required for enumerations and annotations. The best-known feature of Java 8 is lambda expressions. Lambdas could be desugared into anonymous classes implementing a functional interface. JDK uses a different strategy, yet the designers of Java suggest desugaring as an option [4].

We also plan to define dynamic class loading. It has already been defined in K-Python [26], so we see no impediments in adapting it for K-Java. This would allow support for a much wider set of classes from JDK, consequently, for more real life programs.

Finally, using $\mathbb{K}$'s support for Reachability Logic [17], it should be possible to deductively verify Java applications. Deductive verification requires more user involvement that model checking and would be a separate work on its own.

## Acknowledgments

Partly supported by NSF grants CCF-1218605 and CCF-1318191.

## References

[1] K-Java repository. URL `https://github.com/kframework/java-semantics/tree/popl-artifact-evaluation`.

[2] Gaining access to the JCK. URL `http://openjdk.java.net/groups/conformance/JckAccess/`.

[3] Using Java 5 features in earlier JDKs. URL `http://www.ibm.com/developerworks/java/library/j-jtp02277/index.html`.

[4] Translation of lambda expressions. URL `http://cr.openjdk.java.net/~briangoetz/lambda/lambda-translation.html`.

[5] MatchC project. URL `http://fsl.cs.illinois.edu/index.php/Special:MatchCOnline`.

[6] Mauve. URL `https://sourceware.org/mauve/`.

[7] Openjdk project. URL `http://openjdk.java.net/`.

[8] A simple scenario using wait() and notify() in Java. URL `http://stackoverflow.com/questions/2536692/a-simple-scenario-using-wait-and-notify-in-java`.

[9] L. Bettini, F. Damiani, I. Schaefer, and F. Strocco. Traitrecordj: A programming language with traits and records. *Sci. Comput. Program.*, 78(5):521–541, May 2013.

[10] M. Bodin, A. Chargueraud, D. Filaretti, P. Gardner, S. Maffeis, D. Naudziuniene, A. Schmitt, and G. Smith. A trusted mechanised JavaScript specification. In *POPL'14*, pages 87–100. ACM, 2014.

[11] D. Bogdănaş. Label-based programming language semantics in K framework with SDF. In *SYNASC '12*, pages 160–167. IEEE, 2012.

[12] D. Bogdănaş. K-Java: runtime semantics for method invocation and object instantiation. Technical report, University of Illinois, 2014. URL `http://hdl.handle.net/2142/55512`.

[13] E. Börger, N. G. Fruja, V. Gervasi, and R. F. Stärk. A high-level modular definition of the semantics of C#. *Theor. Comput. Sci.*, 336 (2-3):235–284, May 2005.

[14] G. Bracha, M. Odersky, D. Stoutamire, and P. Wadler. Making the future safe for the past: Adding genericity to the java programming language. In *OOPSLA '98*, pages 183–200. ACM, 1998.

[15] M. Bravenboer, R. Vermaas, R. de Groot, and E. Dolstra. Java Front. URL `http://strategoxt.org/Stratego/JavaFront`.

[16] M. Clavel, F. Durn, S. Eker, P. Lincoln, N. Mart-oliet, J. Meseguer, and C. Talcott. Maude manual (version 2.6), 2011. URL `http://maude.cs.uiuc.edu/maude2-manual/`.

[17] A. Ştefănescu, c. Ciobâcă, R. Mereuţă, B. M. Moore, T. F. Şerbănuţă, and G. Roşu. All-path reachability logic. In *RTA-TLCA'14*, LNCS. Springer, 2014.

[18] S. Eker, J. Meseguer, and A. Sridharanarayanan. The Maude LTL model checker and its implementation. In *SPIN'03*, pages 230–234. Springer-Verlag, 2003.

[19] C. Ellison. *A Formal Semantics of C with Applications*. PhD thesis, University of Illinois, July 2012.

[20] C. Ellison and G. Roşu. An executable formal semantics of C with applications. In *POPL '12*, pages 533–544. ACM, 2012.

[21] A. Farzan, F. Chen, J. Meseguer, and G. Roşu. Formal analysis of Java programs in JavaFAN. In *CAV'04*, volume 3114 of *LNCS*, pages 501 – 505, 2004.

[22] D. Filaretti and S. Maffeis. An executable formal semantics of PHP. In *ECOOP'14*, pages 567–592, 2014.

[23] M. Flatt, S. Krishnamurthi, and M. Felleisen. A programmer's reduction semantics for classes and mixins. In *Formal Syntax and Semantics of Java*, pages 241–269. Springer-Verlag, 1999.

[24] FSF. C language testsuites: "C-torture" version 4.4.2, 2010. URL `http://gcc.gnu.org/onlinedocs/gccint/C-Tests.html`.

[25] J. Gosling, B. Joy, G. Steele, and G. Bracha. *Java Language Specification, Second Edition*. Addison-Wesley, 2nd edition, 2000.

[26] D. Guth. A formal semantics of Python 3.3. Master's thesis, University of Illinois at Urbana-Champaign, July 2013.

[27] C. Haack, E. Poll, J. Schfer, and A. Schubert. Immutable objects for a java-like language. In *ESOP'07*, volume 4421 of *LNCS*, pages 347–362. Springer Berlin Heidelberg, 2007.

[28] J. Heering, P. R. H. Hendriks, P. Klint, and J. Rekers. The syntax definition formalism SDF—reference manual—. *SIGPLAN Not.*, 24 (11):43–75, Nov. 1989.

[29] K. Kreft and A. Langer. Understanding the closures debate, 2008. URL `http://www.javaworld.com/article/2077869/scripting-jvm-languages/understanding-the-closures-debate.html`.

[30] J. G. Politz, A. Martinez, M. Milano, S. Warren, D. Patterson, J. Li, A. Chitipothu, and S. Krishnamurthi. Python: The full monty. In *OOPSLA '13*, pages 217–232. ACM, 2013.

[31] G. Roşu and A. Ştefănescu. Checking reachability using matching logic. In *OOPSLA'12*, pages 555–574. ACM, 2012.

[32] G. Roşu, A. Ştefănescu, c. Ciobâcă, and B. M. Moore. One-path reachability logic. In *LICS'13*, pages 358–367. IEEE, June 2013.

[33] G. Roşu and T. F. Şerbănuţă. An overview of the K semantic framework. *JLAP*, 79(6):397–434, 2010.

[34] P. Sestoft. *Java Precisely*. MIT Press, 2002.

[35] R. F. Stärk, E. Börger, and J. Schmid. *Java and the Java Virtual Machine: Definition, Verification, Validation*. Springer-Verlag, 2001.

# Towards the Essence of Hygiene

Michael D. Adams
University of Utah
University of Illinois at Urbana/Champaign
http://michaeldadams.org/

## Abstract

Hygiene is an essential aspect of Scheme's macro system that prevents unintended variable capture. However, previous work on hygiene has focused on algorithmic implementation rather than precise, mathematical definition of what constitutes hygiene. This is in stark contrast with lexical scope, alpha-equivalence and capture-avoiding substitution, which also deal with preventing unintended variable capture but have widely applicable and well-understood mathematical definitions.

This paper presents such a precise, mathematical definition of hygiene. It reviews various kinds of hygiene violation and presents examples of how they occur. From these examples, we develop a practical algorithm for hygienic macro expansion. We then present algorithm-independent, mathematical criteria for whether a macro expansion algorithm is hygienic. This characterization corresponds closely to existing hygiene algorithms and sheds light on aspects of hygiene that are usually overlooked in informal definitions.

***Categories and Subject Descriptors*** D.3.1 [*Programming Languages*]: Formal Definitions and Theory—Semantics

***General Terms*** Algorithms; Languages

***Keywords*** Hygiene; Macros; Nominal logic

## 1. Introduction

Hygiene is an essential aspect of the Scheme macro system that prevents unintended variable capture. For example, suppose we have a short-circuiting `or` macro that expands as follows.

```
(let ([x #t])
  (or (begin (write "!") #f) x)) ⇝
(let ([x #t])
  (let ([tmp (begin (write "!") #f)])
    (if tmp tmp x)))
```

This expansion introduces a `let` binding for `(begin (write "!") #f)` in order to avoid duplicating its side effect. However, this `let` binding can cause trouble. Suppose the original expression used `tmp` instead of `x`. In a naive macro system, the result would be the following expansion.

```
(let ([tmp #t])
  (or (begin (write "!") #f) tmp)) ⇝
(let ([tmp #t])
  (let ([tmp (begin (write "!") #f)])
    (if tmp tmp tmp)))
```

In the result of this expansion, `tmp` is captured and no longer bound to what it was at the call to `or`. Changing the binding name from `x` to `tmp` has changed the result from `#f` to `#t`.

Hygiene prevents these problems. In a hygienic macro expansion system, macros are automatically as well-behaved with regard to variable names as the core forms of the language, and users can rely on the expected alpha equivalences. Essentially, hygiene is the moral equivalent of lexical scoping at the macro level.

Hygiene has a long history in the literature (Kohlbecker et al. 1986; Kohlbecker and Wand 1987; Bawden and Rees 1988; Clinger and Rees 1991; Clinger 1991; Dybvig et al. 1993; Herman and Wand 2008; Herman 2010). However, these works leave hygiene defined informally and focus on the algorithmic aspects or apply to only a restricted set of macros that follow certain typing disciplines and do not handle the general case. Furthermore, while they all purport to implement similar concepts of hygiene, they use divergent implementation approaches that are difficult to formally compare without a precise, formal definition of hygiene.

This paper proposes such a definition of hygiene. This definition is formally precise and connects hygiene to concepts from nominal logic (Gabbay and Pitts 2002). In particular, it shows that hygiene is a combination of alpha equivalence and nominal logic's notion of equivariance. This definition is applicable to a wide variety of macro systems, and deriving a practical algorithm that satisfies it leads to connections with existing hygiene algorithms such as the `syntax-case` expansion algorithm used in Scheme (Dybvig et al. 1993). Finally, we use this definition to highlight important aspects of hygiene that are omitted from traditional, informal descriptions of hygiene.

The organization of this paper is as follows. In Section 2, we give an overview of the basic ideas behind our characterization of hygiene. In Section 3, we review the fundamentals of macro expansion in Scheme. In Section 4, we examine various sorts of hygiene violations and how they occur. We show why traditional notions of alpha equivalence and other naive methods for ensuring hygiene are not sufficient. We show that identifiers in a general hygienic system must be diatomic rather than monatomic, and we present a simple algorithmic method for ensuring hygiene. In Section 5, we develop a formal, mathematical characterization of hygiene in terms of nominal logic. In the process, we demonstrate a new sort of hygiene violation that, while implicitly handled by traditional hygiene algorithms, is not widely discussed. In Section 6, we show how this characterization corresponds to the `syntax-case` algorithm. Finally, in Section 7 we discuss related work, and in Section 8 we conclude.



*POPL '15*, January 15–17, 2015, Mumbai, India.
Copyright © 2015 ACM 978-1-4503-3300-9/15/01...$15.00.
http://dx.doi.org/10.1145/2676726.2677013

## 2. Overview of the Main Ideas

While we give a more complete treatment of the mathematical concepts of hygiene in Section 5, the main ideas are as follows.

We show that a syntactic representation that treats identifiers as simple atomic values with no auxiliary information does not contain enough information to express the structures needed to implement a hygienic macro system as powerful as Scheme's. We can, however, express those structures by splitting identifiers into a pair of atoms. Identifiers are thus diatomic instead of monatomic, and we write them as $<r\ b>$ where $r$ is the *reference part* of the identifier and is inhabited by a *reference atom* while $b$ is the *binder part* and is inhabited by a *binder atom*.

Next, we formally define hygiene in terms of two criteria. The first, the Reference Hygiene Criterion, requires that each macro expansion step respect alpha equivalence with respect to reference atoms in the fully expanded, outer parts of the syntax that have known binding structures.

Unfortunately, we cannot use alpha equivalence in the partially expanded, inner parts of the syntax as their binding structures are unknown. To handle this, the second criterion, the Binder Hygiene Criterion, is expressed in terms of an equivariance condition with respect to binder atoms that must hold on all macro transformation functions.

In essence, the Reference Hygiene Criterion requires that the expansion process respect alpha equivalence in the parts of the syntax with known binding structures. In parts of the syntax where the binding structure is unknown, this will not work, so the Binder Hygiene Criterion requires that macro transformers respect any possible binding structure that that part of the syntax may have.

Together, these two criteria formally define hygiene, and we specify these using nominal logic in Section 5. These criteria are consistent with traditional, informal definitions of hygiene (Bawden and Rees 1988; Clinger and Rees 1991). The Reference Hygiene Criterion ensures that references introduced by a macro are not captured by bindings other than those introduced by the macro. The Binder Hygiene Criterion ensures that binders introduced by a macro are always freshly generated and thus cannot capture reference other than those introduced by the macro.

Finally, though introduced-reference and introduced-binder hygiene are usually described as the two main aspects of hygiene, the equivariance used to define the Binder Hygiene Criterion requires a third aspect. Namely, macro transformers must not observe the values of binders in their inputs other than to compare them with other binders in their inputs. This third form of hygiene is actually enforced by traditional hygiene algorithms even though informal descriptions of those algorithms do not discuss it.

## 3. Basics of Scheme Macros

Before considering hygiene, we briefly review the basics of Scheme macros and how they operate. As shown in Figure 1, macro expansion occurs between the reader, which parses a string into an s-expression, and the interpreter or compiler, which evaluates or compiles the fully expanded term.

At the start of this process, an s-expression is taken from the reader and injected into the domain of syntax objects. For our purposes, a syntax object is an s-expression with identifiers instead of symbols. In a naive expander these identifiers are plain symbols, but in a hygienic expander they carry extra scoping and binding information. In some presentations, syntax objects additionally contain other information such as source locations or data structures that assist the algorithmic performance of macro expansion. We omit these as they are not relevant to the essential theory of hygiene. In the remainder of this paper, we deal only with syntax objects and do not use s-expressions.

$$\text{String} \xrightarrow{\text{Read}} \text{S-expression} \xrightarrow{\text{Inject}} \text{Syntax}_0$$
$$\rightsquigarrow \text{Syntax}_1 \rightsquigarrow \ldots \rightsquigarrow \text{Syntax}_n \xrightarrow{\text{Compile}} \text{Executable}$$

**Figure 1.** Scheme's compilation pipeline

Next comes the core expansion process. We model this as a sequence of small-step rewrites using $\rightsquigarrow$. Each step corresponds to one particular macro invocation or expansion of a core form. The expansion process always proceeds with the outermost expression that can be expanded. We thus divide the program into two parts. We call the inner part that is waiting to be further expanded *u-syntax* as its binding structure is *unknown*, and we call the outer part that is already fully expanded *k-syntax* as its binding structure is *known*.

There is no more expansion to be done in k-syntax, and we know the form of each component of k-syntax. Thus we can represent it using the abstract-syntax representations used internally by the compiler. Conversely, the structure of the u-syntax waiting to expand is not yet manifest. In order to distinguish u-syntax from k-syntax, we adopt the notation of underlining the former. Thus, for example, we may say that the u-syntax `(lambda (x) (+ 1 x))` expands after a number of steps to the k-syntax `(lambda (x) (+ 1 x))`. Note that u-syntax may be modified by macro expansion though k-syntax cannot. Thus, while we might expect the expression `(f x y)` to be a function call, it may instead be a macro call if `f` is bound to a macro definition. Likewise, even though `(lambda (x) y)` is usually a lambda expression, it may be a macro or function call due to a local definition of `lambda`. This is resolved only once this u-syntax is fully expanded into k-syntax. We define both u-syntax and k-syntax in Figure 2 where we use vector notation for repeated elements. For simplicity of presentation, we gloss over which repetitions are zero-or-more versus one-or-more, and we include `let`-style forms as core forms instead of encoding them in terms of `lambda`. Using these forms, the `or` macro can be written as in Figure 3. The full expansion sequence for `(let ([x #t]) (or #f x))` is then as shown in Figure 4.

To define a macro, we use `let-syntax` and `letrec-syntax`. These are similar to `let` and `letrec` except that the left-hand sides of their bindings are the names of macros and the right-hand sides are macro transformers. For example, we use the following to define the `or` macro where *f* is the macro transformer for `or`.

```
(letrec-syntax ([or f]) ...)
```

Macros are generally invoked using a function-call-like syntax.[1] Within the body of this `letrec-syntax`, the `or` macro can thus be invoked using `(or #f x)`.

A *macro transformer* is a function that defines how a macro expands. It takes as argument the syntax object representing the macro invocation and returns the syntax object to which the macro call should expand. For example, the macro invocation `(or #f x)` causes `(or #f x)` to be passed as input to the transformer for `or`. The transformer then returns a syntax object such as `(let ([tmp #f]) (if tmp tmp (or x)))`.

Syntax objects are similar to s-expressions, but they have separate methods for construction and deconstruction. Unlike s-expressions, which use functions like `cons`, `pair?`, `car` and `cdr` to create and examine objects, syntax objects use the pattern matching form `syntax-case` and the quotation form `syntax`.

The first argument of `syntax-case` is the scrutinee and is matched against the patterns in each clause. The second argument

[1] Scheme's `make-variable-transformer` and `identifier-syntax` allow macros to be called in other places. As these are orthogonal to hygiene, we omit them from this paper for the sake of simplicity.

**Identifiers** $i ::=$ `x` | `y` | `z` | $\cdots$

**Constants** $c ::=$ `#f` | `#t` | `1` | `2` | $\cdots$

**Pattern Literals** $lit ::= i$

**U-Syntax** $stx ::= \underline{i} \mid \underline{c} \mid \underline{()} \mid \underline{(stx\ .\ stx)}$

**K-Syntax**

| | |
|---|---|
| $ast ::= c$ | Constants |
| $\mid i$ | Variables |
| \| `(lambda (`$\overrightarrow{i}$`)` $\overrightarrow{ast}$`)` | Functions |
| \| `(`$ast\ \overrightarrow{ast}$`)` | Function App. |
| \| `(if` $ast\ ast\ ast$`)` | Conditionals |
| \| `(let (`$\overrightarrow{[i\ ast]}$`)` $\overrightarrow{ast}$`)` | Local Variables |
| \| `(letrec (`$\overrightarrow{[i\ ast]}$`)` $\overrightarrow{ast}$`)` | |
| \| `(let-syntax (`$\overrightarrow{[i\ ast]}$`)` $\overrightarrow{ast}$`)` | Local Macros |
| \| `(letrec-syntax (`$\overrightarrow{[i\ ast]}$`)` $\overrightarrow{ast}$`)` | |
| \| `(syntax` $stx$`)` | Syntax Constr. |
| \| `(syntax-case` $ast$ `(`$\overrightarrow{lit}$`)` $\overrightarrow{[pat\ ast]}$`)` | Syntax Deconstr. |
| $\mid stx$ | Unexpanded Code |
| $\mid \cdots$ | |

**Patterns**

| | |
|---|---|
| $pat ::=$ _ | Wild Card |
| \| `()` | Nil Constant |
| $\mid i$ | Pattern Variables |
| \| `(`$pat\ .\ pat$`)` | Pairs |
| $\mid \cdots$ | |

**Figure 2.** Syntactic forms

is a list of identifiers that are to be treated as literal constants in the patterns of the `syntax-case`. In this paper, pattern literals are not used, and we use only a subset of the pattern language. However, the techniques we describe trivially generalize to pattern literals and the full pattern language. The subset that we use allows a pattern to be either a wild card that matches anything, the nil constant, a pattern variable or a pair of patterns. As with s-expressions, nested pairs can be represented using list notation.

The `syntax` form is a quotation form for syntax objects. As a notational short-hand, `(syntax` $e$`)` can be written as `#'`$e$ for any $e$ just as `(quote` $e$`)` can be written as `'`$e$. In addition, any pattern variables that are bound by `syntax-case` are automatically substituted for the corresponding identifiers in an enclosed `syntax`. Any identifiers that are not bound by a pattern are simply constants. For example, the following evaluates to the syntax object `(a 1 z)`.

```
(syntax-case #'(1 a) () [(x y) #'(y x z)])
```

Finally, for simplicity of presentation we do not discuss library forms, module forms, `define` or `define-syntax`. In addition, we only briefly discuss, in Section 6, how to handle the `quote` form and the hygiene "bending" operators `datum->syntax` and `syntax->datum`.

```
(letrec-syntax ([or
  (lambda (stx)
    (syntax-case stx ()
      [(_)        #'#f]
      [(_ x)      #'x]
      [(_ x . xs) #'(let ([tmp x])
                      (if tmp tmp (or . xs)))]))])
  ...)
```

**Figure 3.** Definition of the `or` macro

```
(let ([x #t]) (or #f x)) ⇝
(let ([x #t]) (or #f x)) ⇝
(let ([x #t]) (or #f x)) ⇝
(let ([x #t])
  (let ([tmp #f]) (if tmp tmp (or x)))) ⇝
(let ([x #t])
  (let ([tmp #f]) (if tmp tmp (or x)))) ⇝
(let ([x #t])
  (let ([tmp #f]) (if tmp tmp (or x)))) ⇝
(let ([x #t])
  (let ([tmp #f]) (if tmp tmp (or x)))) ⇝
(let ([x #t])
  (let ([tmp #f]) (if tmp tmp (or x)))) ⇝
(let ([x #t])
  (let ([tmp #f]) (if tmp tmp (or x)))) ⇝
(let ([x #t])
  (let ([tmp #f]) (if tmp tmp x))) ⇝
(let ([x #t])
  (let ([tmp #f]) (if tmp tmp x)))
```

**Figure 4.** Example naive expansion of the `or` macro

## 4. Hygiene

Before considering how to mathematically define hygiene in Section 5, we examine the different sorts of hygiene, how they are violated and how to handle them algorithmically. To do this we start with a naive algorithm that uses monatomic identifiers and work our way up to a fully hygienic algorithm. The resulting algorithmic techniques are relatively simple, but they provide useful intuitions about how a hygienic expansion system ought to behave. Later in Section 5, we use these intuitions to develop mathematically precise properties that characterize hygiene.

### 4.1 Types of Hygiene Violations

Hygiene is fundamentally about avoiding unintended variable capture, and there are two primary ways that can happen. The first is by a macro introducing binders, and the second is by a macro introducing references. For example, as seen in the following quote, according to Clinger and Rees (1991) a hygienic macro system is one in which:

> *1. It is impossible to write a high-level macro that inserts a binding that can capture references other than those inserted by the macro.*
>
> *2. It is impossible to write a high-level macro that inserts a reference that can be captured by bindings other than those inserted by the macro.*

Interestingly, once we mathematically characterize hygiene, we will discover that there is a third kind of hygiene violation. Specifically, we must ensure that identifiers that act as binders in the input of a macro transformer are not observed by the macro transformer other than to compare them to other binders from the same input. Though this third kind is not often discussed, it is implicitly averted by traditional hygiene algorithms, and we explore this in Section 5.6.

### 4.1.1 Introduced-Binder Hygiene

As an example of introduced-binder hygiene, consider the following code.

```
(let ([tmp #t]) (or #f tmp))
```

This should evaluate to `#t` since the first argument to `or` is `#f` and the second argument, `tmp`, is bound to `#t`. However, a naive, non-hygienic expander eventually expands this to the following.

```
(let ([tmp #t])
  (let ([tmp #f]) (if tmp tmp tmp)))
```

The `or` macro introduces an inner binding of `tmp` to `#f` that shadows the binding of `tmp` to `#t` and results in this code evaluating to `#f` instead of the expected `#t`.

### 4.1.2 Introduced-Reference Hygiene

Hygiene violations due to introduced binders are certainly the most easily recognized sort of violation. However, violations due to introduced references can also occur. Consider, for example, the following variation of the code we had before.

```
(let ([if #t]) (or #f if))
```

All we have done is rename `tmp` to `if`, so this code should still evaluate to `#t`. However, a naive, non-hygienic expander eventually expands this to the following.

```
(let ([if #t])
  (let ([tmp #f]) (if tmp tmp if)))
```

Note that `if` is bound to `#t`, so `(if tmp tmp if)` is not the core form for `if` as it was before, but rather a function application of the variable `if` to the variable references `tmp`, `tmp` and `if`. This is thus attempting to call `#t` as a function. Aside from being a runtime error, it is unlikely to be what the programmer intended.

This time the binding of `tmp` to `#f` introduced by the `or` macro is not the cause of the problem. Rather, it is the fact that the macro introduces a reference to `if` that it expects to be bound to the core form for `if`. Since the macro is called in a context in which `if` is not bound to the core form, we get an incorrect result.

This problem occurs any time a macro introduces a reference that it expects to be bound in a particular way. Though this particular violation occurred due to the rebinding of a core form, this may happen even in a system with multiple namespaces. For example, a macro that introduces references to non-core forms such as `read` or `eval` has the same problem if it is called in a context where those identifiers are rebound.

## 4.2 Enforcing Hygiene with Binder Renaming

As a first attempt at moving from a naive, non-hygienic macro expander to a hygienic macro expander, let us consider the introduced reference problem more carefully. As before, we start with the following code.

```
(let ([if #t]) (or #f if))
```

As shown before, in a naive expander, this code eventually expands to the following.

```
(let ([if #t])
  (let ([tmp #f]) (if tmp tmp if)))
```

To avoid this problem, we can rename bound variables to freshly generated identifiers as soon as they are exposed. Thus for example, after expanding the outer `let` and before expanding the `or` macro, we can generate a fresh identifier such as `if1` and replace all occurrences of `if` with `if1`. This results in the following code.

```
(let ([if1 #t]) (or #f if1))
```

When this fully expands, we get the following, which has avoided capturing the `if` used by the `or` macro.

```
(let ([if1 #t])
  (let ([tmp #f]) (if tmp tmp if1)))
```

Note that we do not rename bindings until they are fully expanded into k-syntax and thus have a known binding structure that cannot be modified by other macro calls.

## 4.3 Binder Renaming is Insufficient

Since binder renaming is sufficient to ensure introduced-reference hygiene, a natural question is whether it is sufficient to ensure introduced-binder hygiene. Unfortunately, it is not. To see this, consider the following example where we have placed the definition of the `or` macro inside the binding of `tmp`.

```
(let ([tmp #t])
  (letrec-syntax ([or
      ... #'(let ([tmp ...]) ...) ...])
    (or #f tmp)))
```

For the sake of brevity, we elide most of the `or` macro except for the `tmp` binding introduced by it.

After the outer `let` form expands and before the body of the `let` expands, we generate a fresh identifier for it to bind, and we rename all `tmp` references. This results in the following.

```
(let ([tmp1 #t])
  (letrec-syntax ([or
      ... #'(let ([tmp1 ...]) ...) ...])
    (or #f tmp1)))
```

Note that when `tmp` is renamed to `tmp1`, the `tmp` identifier introduced by the `or` macro is also renamed. If we continue expansion, we get the following.

```
(let ([tmp1 #t])
  (letrec-syntax ([or
      ... #'(let ([tmp1 ...]) ...) ...])
    (or #f tmp1)))
```

If we then expand the call to the `or` macro, we get the following.

```
(let ([tmp1 #t])
  (letrec-syntax ([or
      ... #'(let ([tmp1 ...]) ...) ...])
    (let ([tmp1 #f])
      (if tmp1 tmp1 (or tmp1)))))
```

At this point, we can see that even though we have been careful to rename any bindings discovered during the expansion process, introduced-binder hygiene has been violated. The `or` macro has introduced a binding for `tmp1` that shadows the outer binding to `tmp1` and incorrectly captures the reference to `tmp1` in `(or tmp1)`. The renaming of `tmp1` when the inner `let` is expanded will not help us as it will rename all occurrences of `tmp1` and not just those introduced by the `or` macro.

While we will come back to the use of binder renaming for ensuring hygiene, this example demonstrates that it does not ensure introduced-binder hygiene. To find a complete solution for hygiene we must seek something more.

## 4.4 Enforcing Hygiene with Gensym

For the moment, we set aside binder renaming and introduced-reference hygiene to consider hygiene violations due to introduced binders. This happens for example in Section 4.1.1, where the binding for `tmp` that is introduced by the `or` macro shadows the locally defined `tmp`.

The problem is that the introduced `tmp` happens to coincide with the `tmp` being used locally. We can avoid this by using a freshly generated identifier instead of `tmp`. Indeed, this is a widely used technique in systems with non-hygienic macro expanders. For example, if we have a `gensym-identifier` operator that generates fresh identifiers, we could define the `or` macro as follows.

```
(letrec-syntax ([or (lambda (stx)
  (syntax-case stx ()
    [(_)   #'#f]
    [(_ x) #'x]
    [(_ x . xs)
     (syntax-case (gensym-identifier #'tmp) ()
       [g #'(let ([g x])
              (if g g (or . xs)))])]))])
  ...)
```

Here we use `syntax-case` to introduce `g` as a pattern variable that gets replaced with the result of `gensym-identifier`. This ensures that the binder we introduce is unique and thus never conflicts with one from the input to the macro.

If we consider the example from Section 4.1.1 with this definition of `or`, the expansion proceeds thusly. The code immediately before expanding the `or` macro is as follows.

```
(let ([tmp #t]) (or #f tmp))
```

When `or` expands, `gensym-identifier` creates a fresh identifier, say `tmp1`, that is globally unique. The identifier `tmp1` does not conflict with `tmp`, and thus we avoid the hygiene violation due to an introduced binder. The fully expanded expression is then the following.

```
(let ([tmp #t])
  (let ([tmp1 #f]) (if tmp1 tmp1 tmp)))
```

Unfortunately, while using `gensym-identifier` allows us to avoid hygiene violations caused by introduced binders, it provides no help with introduced references. Consider again the following example from Section 4.1.2.

```
(let ([if #t]) (or #f if))
```

If we use `gensym-identifier` but not binder renaming, we get the following when we fully expand the `or` macro.

```
(let ([if #t])
  (let ([tmp1 #f]) (if tmp1 tmp1 if)))
```

The binder introduced by the macro uses the freshly generated identifier `tmp1`, but that is not the identifier causing the problem. It is the binding of `if` that is the problem. That binding is outside the reach of the `or` macro, and thus there is nothing the macro can do to avoid the captured variable. This example demonstrates that, on its own, using freshly generated identifiers for introduced binders is not a complete solution to hygiene either.

## 4.5 Binder Renaming with Gensym is Also Insufficient

Neither the solution in Section 4.2 nor the solution in Section 4.4 is sufficient on its own to ensure hygiene, but they handle complementary aspects. On the one hand, the solution in Section 4.2 handles introduced-reference hygiene. On the other hand, the solution in Section 4.4 handles introduced-binder hygiene. Thus we might consider combining the two. First, we rename identifiers bound by core forms that are discovered during macro expansion. Then, we require that any binders introduced by macro transformers be freshly generated.

Surprisingly, this does not work either. To see why, consider the question of whether `x` should be freshly generated by the `m` macro in the following code.

```
(let ([x 3])
  (let-syntax ([let-inc ...])
    (let-syntax ([m (lambda (stx)
      (syntax-case stx ()
        [(_ y) #'(let-inc x (* x y))]))])
      (m x))))
```

Suppose `let-inc` is defined as follows.

```
(let-syntax ([let-inc (lambda (stx)
  (syntax-case stx ()
    [(_ u v) #'(let ([u 2]) v)]))])
  ...)
```

Whatever is passed to `let-inc` as `u` becomes bound. Thus, the `x` introduced by `m` needs to be freshly generated because it is introducing a new binder. If we do not freshly generate `x`, then the expansion sequence would be the following, which results in the unintended capture of the `x` originally passed to `m` by the binding of `x` introduced by `m`.

```
(m x) ⇝ (let-inc x (* x x)) ⇝
(let ([x 2]) (* x x))
```

On the other hand, freshly generating the `x` introduced by `m` avoids this problem and results in the following expansion sequence where no unintended capture occurs.

```
(m x) ⇝ (let-inc x1 (* x1 x)) ⇝
(let ([x1 2]) (* x1 x))
```

While freshly generating `x` avoids unintended capture in this case, consider if `let-inc` were defined as the following.

```
(let-syntax ([let-inc (lambda (stx)
  (syntax-case stx ()
    [(_ u v) #'(+ 1 u)]))])
  ...)
```

With this definition, `let-inc` ignores its second argument and is not a binding form. If we freshly generate `x` like before, then we get the following expansion sequence.

```
(m x) ⇝ (let-inc x1 (* x1 x)) ⇝ (+ 1 x1)
```

This results in an error since `x1` is now a variable reference and there is no `x1` in scope. If, on the other hand, we do not freshly generate `x`, then we get the following expansion sequence, which behaves correctly.

```
(m x) ⇝ (let-inc x (* x x)) ⇝ (+ 1 x)
```

We might still hold out hope that a sufficiently careful programmer with sufficient information about the binding structure of `let-inc` could write macros like `m` that freshly generate identifiers exactly in those places where they should. However, that hope is dashed once we consider a definition of `let-inc` like the following.

```
(let-syntax ([let-inc (lambda (stx)
  (syntax-case stx ()
    [(_ u v) #'(let ([u (+ 1 u)]) v)]))])
  ...)
```

Here let-inc expands to both the increment and let binding from our previous definitions of let-inc. If m does not freshly generate x, then the expansion sequence is as follows.

```
(m x) ⇝ (let-inc x (* x x)) ⇝
(let ([x (+ 1 x)]) (* x x))
```

This is wrong as the binding of x in the resulting let improperly captures the x from the original call to m.

On the other hand, if m does freshly generate x, then the expansion sequence is as follows.

```
(m x) ⇝ (let-inc x1 (* x1 x)) ⇝
(let ([x1 (+ 1 x1)]) (* x1 x))
```

This is also wrong as there is a reference to the unbound variable x1 in the right-hand side of the let binding.

With this definition of let-inc, we are stuck. The m macro *must* freshly generate the x that it introduces because of the let binding, but the m macro also *must not* freshly generate the x that it introduces because of the reference in the right-hand side of the let binding.

### 4.6 Enforcing Hygiene with Diatomic Identifiers

The problem in Section 4.5 is because some uses of x should use the freshly generated version while others should not. As long as identifiers are atomic symbols, we cannot have both. In order to resolve this, we split identifiers into a reference part and a binder part so they are diatomic instead of monatomic. We thus write identifiers as <*r* *b*> where *r* is the reference part and *b* is the binder part. The reference part is inhabited by a *reference atom* and is used if the identifier eventually ends up in a reference position while the binder part is inhabited by a *binder atom* and is used to determine what identifiers are captured when the identifier ends up in a binding position. These two sorts of atoms are from mutually disjoint domains, and a binder atom is never used in a position that expects a reference atom or vice versa. As a simplifying notation, we write x for <x.r x.b> when the diatomic nature of an identifier is not significant.

With these diatomic identifiers, m can expand with both non-freshly generated and freshly generated atoms in the reference and binder parts of the identifier, respectively. So for example, we could have the following expansion sequence.

```
(m <x.r x.b>) ⇝
(let-inc <x.r x1.b> (* <x.r x1.b> <x.r x.b>)) ⇝
(let ([<x.r x1.b> (+ 1 <x.r x1.b>)])
  (* <x.r x1.b> <x.r x.b>))
```

The binder part of the introduced identifier <x.r x1.b> is freshly generated but the reference part is not. In the right-hand side of the let binding, we use the reference part of the identifier, x.r, which was not freshly generated. On the other hand, in the left-hand side of the let binding, we use the binder part of the identifier, x1.b. Thus, the let does not capture the identifier in the body of the let that has x.b as a binder part.

To account for this change, we define expansion to operate with diatomic identifiers using the small-step relation in Figure 5. This relation is closed under congruence for k-syntax but not u-syntax. Thus expansion always operates at an outermost u-syntax. Also, though it may appear that the third clause (i.e., macro application) overlaps the other clauses, it does not. Binding forms always use fresh reference atoms, so *r* in the third clause never overlaps with reference-atom constants such as lambda.r in the other clauses.

Under this definition, variable references merely expand to their reference parts. For example, we have the following expansion.

```
<x.r x.b> ⇝ x.r
```

In effect, the reference part of an identifier represents what the identifier would refer to if there were no more binding forms discovered during expansion.

Binding forms are a bit more complicated. When expanding a binding form, we use the binder part of the identifier to determine what identifiers it captures. Once that is determined, those identifiers must be modified to refer to the newly expanded binding form. Since variable references expand to a reference atom, the binding forms in k-syntax also use reference atoms for their binding positions. Since the target of a variable reference is determined by the reference part of an identifier, we replace the reference parts of the captured identifiers with freshly generated reference atoms that we then also use in the k-syntax for the binding form. This replacement is implemented using the subst helper function defined in Figure 6. Its first clause replaces the reference part of identifiers that have a particular binder part, and the other clauses are merely a standard traversal over u-syntax.

Considering lambda again, we have the following expansion sequence.

```
(lambda (<x.r x.b>) (<y.r x.b> <x.r z.b>)) ⇝
(lambda (w.r) (<w.r x.b> <x.r z.b>)) ⇝ ... ⇝
(lambda (w.r) (w.r x.r))
```

As with binder renaming, we use w.r, a freshly generated reference atom for the binding form. The y.r in <y.r x.b> is changed to w.r since the binder part of that identifier, x.b, matches the binder part of the identifier, <x.r x.b>, that is in the binding position for the lambda form. In other words, that identifier should be captured by the lambda. On the other hand, the identifier <x.r z.b> is left alone as its binder part does not match x.b.

### 4.7 Diatomic Identifiers are Sufficient

Returning to the final version of the let-inc macro from Section 4.5, we can now see how all of this fits together. First, we start with the following expression.

```
(m <x.r x.b>)
```

When m expands, it freshly generates the binder portion of any identifiers that it introduces, and we thus get the following.

```
(let-inc <x.r x1.b> (* <x.r x1.b> <x.r x.b>))
```

When let-inc expands, the <x.r x1.b> identifier is placed in both the left-hand and right-hand sides of the let binding, which results in the following.

```
(let ([<x.r x1.b> (+ 1 <x.r x1.b>)])
  (* <x.r x1.b> <x.r x.b>))
```

At this point, we expand the let form. This generates a fresh reference atom x2.r, and we use subst to replace the reference part of any identifiers in the body that have the same binder part as the bound identifier. This binder part is x1.b and was freshly generated by the m macro, so the only identifier captured is the first argument to *, and we get the following.

```
(let ([x2.r (+ 1 <x.r x1.b>)])
  (* <x2.r x1.b> <x.r x.b>))
```

We then expand the right-hand side of the let binding. Since the identifier in it is a variable reference, it expands to its reference part to produce the following.

```
(let ([x2.r (+ 1 x.r)])
  (* <x2.r x1.b> <x.r x.b>))
```

$$
\begin{aligned}
\underline{c} &\leadsto c \\
\underline{<r\ b>} &\leadsto r \\
\underline{(<r\ b>\ \overrightarrow{args})} &\leadsto f\ \underline{(<r\ b>\ \overrightarrow{args})} \text{ where } f \text{ is the currently in-scope transformer bound to } r \\
&\qquad \text{and all identifiers introduced by } f \text{ have freshly generated binder parts} \\
\underline{(\texttt{<lambda.r}\ b_0\texttt{>}\ (\overrightarrow{<r\ b>})\ \overrightarrow{body})} &\leadsto (\texttt{lambda}\ (\overrightarrow{r'})\ \overrightarrow{\left(\mathsf{subst}\ \overrightarrow{b}\ \overrightarrow{r'}\ \underline{body}\right)}) \\
\underline{(\texttt{<if.r}\ b_0\texttt{>}\ test\ true\ false)} &\leadsto (\texttt{if}\ \underline{test}\ \underline{true}\ \underline{false}) \\
\underline{(\texttt{<let.r}\ b_0\texttt{>}\ \overrightarrow{[<r\ b>\ rhs]})\ \overrightarrow{body})} &\leadsto (\texttt{let}\ (\overrightarrow{[r'\ \underline{rhs}]})\ \overrightarrow{\left(\mathsf{subst}\ \overrightarrow{b}\ \overrightarrow{r'}\ \underline{body}\right)}) \\
\underline{(\texttt{<letrec.r}\ b_0\texttt{>}\ \overrightarrow{[<r\ b>\ rhs]})\ \overrightarrow{body})} &\leadsto (\texttt{letrec}\ (\overrightarrow{[r'\ \left(\mathsf{subst}\ \overrightarrow{b}\ \overrightarrow{r'}\ \underline{rhs}\right)]})\ \overrightarrow{\left(\mathsf{subst}\ \overrightarrow{b}\ \overrightarrow{r'}\ \underline{body}\right)}) \\
\underline{(\texttt{<let-syntax.r}\ b_0\texttt{>}\ \overrightarrow{[<r\ b>\ rhs]})\ \overrightarrow{body})} &\leadsto (\texttt{let-syntax}\ (\overrightarrow{[r'\ \underline{rhs}]})\ \overrightarrow{\left(\mathsf{subst}\ \overrightarrow{b}\ \overrightarrow{r'}\ \underline{body}\right)}) \\
\underline{(\texttt{<letrec-syntax.r}\ b_0\texttt{>}\ \overrightarrow{[<r\ b>\ rhs]})\ \overrightarrow{body})} &\leadsto (\texttt{letrec-syntax}\ (\overrightarrow{[r'\ \left(\mathsf{subst}\ \overrightarrow{b}\ \overrightarrow{r'}\ \underline{rhs}\right)]})\ \overrightarrow{\left(\mathsf{subst}\ \overrightarrow{b}\ \overrightarrow{r'}\ \underline{body}\right)}) \\
\underline{(\texttt{<syntax.r}\ b_0\texttt{>}\ stx)} &\leadsto (\texttt{syntax}\ \underline{stx}) \\
\underline{(\texttt{<syntax-case.r}\ b_0\texttt{>}\ stx\ lits\ \overrightarrow{[pat\ rhs]})} &\leadsto (\texttt{syntax-case}\ stx\ lits\ \overrightarrow{[pat'\ \left(\mathsf{subst}\ \overrightarrow{b}\ \overrightarrow{r'}\ \underline{rhs}\right)]}) \\
&\qquad \text{where } \overrightarrow{b} \text{ is the binder parts of the non-literal identifiers in the} \\
&\qquad \text{corresponding } \overrightarrow{pat}\text{, and } pat' \text{ is } pat \text{ with each identifier } <r\ b> \\
&\qquad \text{replaced by a corresponding element of } \overrightarrow{r'} \\
\underline{(fun\ \overrightarrow{args})} &\leadsto (\underline{fun}\ \underline{\overrightarrow{args}}) \text{ if none of the above cases apply}
\end{aligned}
$$

**Figure 5.** Macro expansion with diatomic identifiers. In this figure, we let $\overrightarrow{r'}$ be fresh reference atoms and $\mathsf{subst}\ \overrightarrow{b}\ \overrightarrow{r'}\ e$ be the application of subst to $e$ for each pair of corresponding elements from $\overrightarrow{b}$ and $\overrightarrow{r'}$. Closed under congruence for k-syntax.

$$
\begin{aligned}
\mathsf{subst}\ b\, r\ \underline{<r'\ b'>} &= \underline{<r\ b'>} && \text{if } b = b' \\
\mathsf{subst}\ b\, r\ \underline{<r'\ b'>} &= \underline{<r'\ b'>} && \text{if } b \neq b' \\
\mathsf{subst}\ b\, r\ \underline{c} &= \underline{c} && \text{if } c \text{ is a constant} \\
\mathsf{subst}\ b\, r\ \underline{()} &= \underline{()} \\
\mathsf{subst}\ b\, r\ \underline{(stx_1\ .\ stx_2)} &= \underline{(\mathsf{subst}\ b\, r\ stx_1\ .\ \mathsf{subst}\ b\, r\ stx_2)}
\end{aligned}
$$

**Figure 6.** Definition of subst

All the remaining identifiers are references, so the last bit of expansion results in the following.

```
(let ([x2.r (+ 1 x.r)])
  (* x2.r x.r))
```

Note that identifiers for `x` that are introduced by `m` can all capture each other because they have the same freshly generated binder parts, but those introduced identifiers cannot capture anything else as their binder parts are distinct from the binder parts of any other identifiers.

### 4.8 Summary

At this point, we have an algorithm that completely handles hygiene. We summarize the major points as follows.

First, identifiers are diatomic and contain both a reference part and a binder part. The reference part represents what the identifier refers to if it ends up in a reference position. The binder part represents which identifiers can capture each other.

Second, when expanding a binding form, we use the binder part of an identifier to determine what identifiers are captured by it. A freshly generated reference atom is created for the binding form, and the reference parts of the captured identifiers are then replaced with this reference atom so that those identifiers now refer to that binding form.

Finally, we require that the binder parts of any identifiers introduced by a macro call be freshly generated. This ensures that the only identifiers they can capture are ones that were introduced in that macro call.

If we go back to the examples of hygiene violation in the `or` macro with this algorithm, we get the expansion sequence in Figure 7, which shows the enforcement of both introduced-reference hygiene (with the `if` binding) and introduced-binder hygiene (with the `tmp` binding).

## 5. The Mathematics of Hygiene

The algorithm in Section 4 provides useful intuitions about hygiene but does not define what hygiene actually is. We now turn to this question and consider the mathematical properties that characterize hygiene. We do this in terms of permutations, support and equivariance from nominal logic (Gabbay and Pitts 2002), so we review these before turning to the main question of characterizing hygiene. In the process, we expose observed-binder hygiene as a third way hygiene can be violated that is not often discussed but is implicitly averted by traditional hygiene algorithms.

### 5.1 Nominal Logic

#### 5.1.1 Permutations

In nominal logic, permutations are invertible, total mappings over atoms. We write $(\alpha \leftrightarrow \beta)$ for the permutation that maps the atoms

```
(let ([<tmp.r tmp.b> #t])
  (let ([<if.r if.b> 2]) (or #f <tmp.r tmp.b>))) ⇝
(let ([p.r #t])
  (let ([<if.r if.b> 2]) (or #f <p.r tmp.b>))) ⇝
(let ([p.r #t])
  (let ([<if.r if.b> 2]) (or #f <p.r tmp.b>))) ⇝
(let ([p.r #t])
  (let ([q.r 2]) (or #f <p.r tmp.b>))) ⇝
(let ([p.r #t])
  (let ([q.r 2]) (or #f <p.r tmp.b>))) ⇝
(let ([p.r #t])
  (let ([q.r 2])
    (let ([<tmp.r s.b> #f])
      (<if.r if.b> <tmp.r s.b>
        <tmp.r s.b> (or <p.r tmp.b>))))) ⇝
(let ([p.r #t])
  (let ([q.r 2])
    (let ([t.r #f])
      (<if.r if.b> <t.r s.b>
        <t.r s.b> (or <p.r tmp.b>))))) ⇝
(let ([p.r #t])
  (let ([q.r 2])
    (let ([t.r #f])
      (<if.r if.b> <t.r s.b>
        <t.r s.b> (or <p.r tmp.b>))))) ⇝
(let ([p.r #t])
  (let ([q.r 2])
    (let ([t.r #f])
      (if <t.r s.b>
        <t.r s.b> (or <p.r tmp.b>))))) ⇝
(let ([p.r #t])
  (let ([q.r 2])
    (let ([t.r #f])
      (if t.r <t.r s.b> (or <p.r tmp.b>))))) ⇝
(let ([p.r #t])
  (let ([q.r 2])
    (let ([t.r #f])
      (if t.r t.r (or <p.r tmp.b>))))) ⇝
(let ([p.r #t])
  (let ([q.r 2])
    (let ([t.r #f]) (if t.r t.r <p.r tmp.b>)))) ⇝
(let ([p.r #t])
  (let ([q.r 2])
    (let ([t.r #f]) (if t.r t.r p.r))))
```

**Figure 7.** Example hygienic expansion of the `or` macro

**Identifiers and Constants**

$\pi \bullet \texttt{<}r\ \ b\texttt{>} = \texttt{<}\pi \bullet r\ \ \pi \bullet b\texttt{>}$

$\pi \bullet c = c$

**U-Syntax**

$\pi \bullet \underline{i} = \underline{\pi \bullet i}$

$\pi \bullet \underline{c} = \underline{\pi \bullet c}$

$\pi \bullet \underline{()} = \underline{()}$

$\pi \bullet \underline{(stx_1\ \ .\ \ stx_2)} = \underline{(\pi \bullet stx_1\ \ .\ \ \pi \bullet stx_2)}$

**K-Syntax**

$\pi \bullet \texttt{(lambda (}\overrightarrow{i}\texttt{)}\ \overrightarrow{body}\texttt{)} = \texttt{(lambda (}\overrightarrow{\pi \bullet i}\texttt{)}\ \overrightarrow{\pi \bullet body}\texttt{)}$

$\pi \bullet \texttt{(}fun\ \overrightarrow{args}\texttt{)} = \texttt{(}\pi \bullet fun\ \overrightarrow{\pi \bullet args}\texttt{)}$

$\pi \bullet \texttt{(if}\ test\ true\ false\texttt{)}$
$= \texttt{(if}\ \pi \bullet test\ \ \pi \bullet true\ \ \pi \bullet false\texttt{)}$

$\pi \bullet \texttt{(let (}\overrightarrow{\texttt{[}i\ rhs\texttt{]}}\texttt{)}\ \overrightarrow{body}\texttt{)}$
$= \texttt{(let (}\overrightarrow{\texttt{[}\pi \bullet i\ \ \pi \bullet rhs\texttt{]}}\texttt{)}\ \overrightarrow{\pi \bullet body}\texttt{)}$

$\pi \bullet \texttt{(letrec (}\overrightarrow{\texttt{[}i\ rhs\texttt{]}}\texttt{)}\ \overrightarrow{body}\texttt{)}$
$= \texttt{(letrec (}\overrightarrow{\texttt{[}\pi \bullet i\ \ \pi \bullet rhs\texttt{]}}\texttt{)}\ \overrightarrow{\pi \bullet body}\texttt{)}$

$\pi \bullet \texttt{(let-syntax (}\overrightarrow{\texttt{[}i\ rhs\texttt{]}}\texttt{)}\ \overrightarrow{body}\texttt{)}$
$= \texttt{(let-syntax (}\overrightarrow{\texttt{[}\pi \bullet i\ \ \pi \bullet rhs\texttt{]}}\texttt{)}\ \overrightarrow{\pi \bullet body}\texttt{)}$

$\pi \bullet \texttt{(letrec-syntax (}\overrightarrow{\texttt{[}i\ rhs\texttt{]}}\texttt{)}\ \overrightarrow{body}\texttt{)}$
$= \texttt{(letrec-syntax (}\overrightarrow{\texttt{[}\pi \bullet i\ \ \pi \bullet rhs\texttt{]}}\texttt{)}\ \overrightarrow{\pi \bullet body}\texttt{)}$

$\pi \bullet \texttt{(syntax}\ stx\texttt{)} = \texttt{(syntax}\ \pi \bullet stx\texttt{)}$

$\pi \bullet \texttt{(syntax-case}\ ast\ lits\ \overrightarrow{\texttt{[}pat\ rhs\texttt{]}}\texttt{)}$
$= \texttt{(syntax-case}\ \pi \bullet ast\ \ \pi \bullet lits\ \overrightarrow{\texttt{[}\pi \bullet pat\ \ \pi \bullet rhs\texttt{]}}\texttt{)}$

**Patterns**

$\pi \bullet \_ = \_$

$\pi \bullet () = ()$

$\pi \bullet (pat_1\ \ .\ \ pat_2) = (\pi \bullet pat_1\ \ .\ \ \pi \bullet pat_2)$

**Figure 8.** Lifted permutation application

$\alpha$ and $\beta$ to each other while leaving all other atoms unchanged and $(\vec{\alpha} \leftrightarrow \vec{\beta})$ for the permutation that maps corresponding elements of $\vec{\alpha}$ and $\vec{\beta}$ to each other while leaving all other atoms unchanged. We write the application of a permutation $\pi$ to an atom $\alpha$ as $\pi \bullet \alpha$. Finally, since every permutation is invertible, we write $\pi^{-1}$ for the inverse of $\pi$. We lift these permutations from applying over individual atoms to applying over both k-syntax and u-syntax by a straightforward homomorphism as shown in Figure 8. Note that we apply the permutation even to bound variables. If we do not, the permutation could result in unintended captures. For example, consider the permutation $(\alpha \leftrightarrow \beta)$ applied to the term `(lambda` $(\alpha)$ $\beta$`)`. If we do not permute the variable binding, $\alpha$, then we cannot permute the body, $\beta$, without causing unintended variable capture.

Finally, nominal logic lifts permutations to apply to functions. If we let $\circ$ compose permutations with functions, then the application of a permutation $\pi$ to a function $f$ is defined by the equation $\pi \bullet f = \pi \circ f \circ \pi^{-1}$. To see the intuition behind this, consider if we have the intentional representation of $f$. Applying $\pi$ to $f$ should apply $\pi$ to all the atoms in the implementation of $f$. Thus, if $f$ always returns some constant $c$, then $\pi \bullet f$ should return $\pi \bullet c$. We achieve this effect by applying $\pi$ to the output of $f$. However, we have to be careful about inputs to $f$ that end up in the output. For example, if $f$ is the identity function, then $f$ contains no atoms and applying $\pi$ to $f$ should not change it. Applying $\pi$ to the output of $f$ would incorrectly rename elements of the input that end up in the output. We counteract this by applying $\pi^{-1}$ to the input. Any inputs that end up in the output will have the $\pi$ canceled out by the $\pi^{-1}$ and thus be unchanged.

### 5.1.2 Support

From this notion of permutation, nominal logic defines the concept of the support of an object. Intuitively, the support of an object is the set of atoms that "occur free" in it. It is usually defined over a quotiented domain that equates alpha equivalent terms, but for the sake of clarity we make uses of alpha equivalence explicit. If $\simeq$ is

$$\texttt{(lambda (}\vec{i}\texttt{)}\ \overrightarrow{body}\texttt{)} \simeq \texttt{(lambda (}\vec{i'}\texttt{)}\ \overrightarrow{body'}\texttt{)} \quad \text{if } \forall^{\infty}\vec{i''}.\ \overrightarrow{body \overset{\vec{i},\vec{i'},\vec{i''}}{\simeq} body'}$$

$$\texttt{(let (}\overrightarrow{\texttt{[}i\ rhs\texttt{]}}\texttt{)}\ \overrightarrow{body}\texttt{)} \simeq \texttt{(let (}\overrightarrow{\texttt{[}i'\ rhs'\texttt{]}}\texttt{)}\ \overrightarrow{body'}\texttt{)} \quad \text{if } \overrightarrow{rhs \simeq rhs'} \text{ and } \forall^{\infty}\vec{i''}.\ \overrightarrow{body \overset{\vec{i},\vec{i'},\vec{i''}}{\simeq} body'}$$

$$\texttt{(letrec (}\overrightarrow{\texttt{[}i\ rhs\texttt{]}}\texttt{)}\ \overrightarrow{body}\texttt{)} \simeq \texttt{(letrec (}\overrightarrow{\texttt{[}i'\ rhs'\texttt{]}}\texttt{)}\ \overrightarrow{body'}\texttt{)} \quad \text{if } \forall^{\infty}\vec{i''}.\ \overrightarrow{rhs \overset{\vec{i},\vec{i'},\vec{i''}}{\simeq} rhs'} \text{ and } \overrightarrow{body \overset{\vec{i},\vec{i'},\vec{i''}}{\simeq} body'}$$

$$\texttt{(let-syntax (}\overrightarrow{\texttt{[}i\ rhs\texttt{]}}\texttt{)}\ \overrightarrow{body}\texttt{)} \simeq \texttt{(let-syntax (}\overrightarrow{\texttt{[}i'\ rhs'\texttt{]}}\texttt{)}\ \overrightarrow{body'}\texttt{)} \quad \text{if } \overrightarrow{rhs \simeq rhs'} \text{ and } \forall^{\infty}\vec{i''}.\ \overrightarrow{body \overset{\vec{i},\vec{i'},\vec{i''}}{\simeq} body'}$$

$$\texttt{(letrec-syntax (}\overrightarrow{\texttt{[}i\ rhs\texttt{]}}\texttt{)}\ \overrightarrow{body}\texttt{)} \simeq \texttt{(letrec-syntax (}\overrightarrow{\texttt{[}i'\ rhs'\texttt{]}}\texttt{)}\ \overrightarrow{body'}\texttt{)} \quad \text{if } \forall^{\infty}\vec{i''}.\ \overrightarrow{rhs \overset{\vec{i},\vec{i'},\vec{i''}}{\simeq} rhs'} \text{ and } \overrightarrow{body \overset{\vec{i},\vec{i'},\vec{i''}}{\simeq} body'}$$

$$\texttt{(syntax-case } s\ \texttt{(}\vec{l}\texttt{)}\ \overrightarrow{\texttt{[}pat\ rhs\texttt{]}}\texttt{)} \simeq \texttt{(syntax-case } s'\ \texttt{(}\vec{l'}\texttt{)}\ \overrightarrow{\texttt{[}pat'\ rhs'\texttt{]}}\texttt{)} \quad \text{if } s \simeq s' \text{ and } \vec{l} \simeq \vec{l'} \text{ and}$$

$$\overrightarrow{\forall^{\infty}\vec{i''}.\ pat \overset{\vec{i},\vec{i'},\vec{i''}}{\simeq} pat' \text{ and } rhs \overset{\vec{i},\vec{i'},\vec{i''}}{\simeq} rhs'}$$

where $i$ and $i'$ are the non-literal identifiers in the corresponding $pat$ and $pat'$, respectively

**Figure 9.** Alpha equivalence for k-syntax. We write $t_1 \overset{\vec{i},\vec{i'},\vec{i''}}{\simeq} t_2$ as an abbreviation for $\left(\vec{i} \leftrightarrow \vec{i''}\right) \bullet t_1 \simeq \left(\vec{i'} \leftrightarrow \vec{i''}\right) \bullet t_2$ and use $\forall^{\infty}$ for "for all but finitely many". Closed under reflexivity, symmetry, transitivity and congruence.

the alpha equivalence relation, the support of a term $t$ is the smallest finite set, $\mathsf{supp}\, t$, such that the following holds.

$$\forall \alpha, \beta \notin \mathsf{supp}\, t.\ (\alpha \leftrightarrow \beta) \bullet t \simeq t$$

As an example of this, consider the term `(lambda` $(\alpha)$ $(\alpha\ \beta)$`)`. Swapping the atom $\alpha$ with any atom other than $\beta$ results in an alpha-equivalent term. Thus $\alpha$ is *not* in the support of that term. On the other hand, any atom that we swap with $\beta$ results in a non-alpha-equivalent term. Thus $\beta$ *is* in the support of that term.

### 5.1.3 Equivariance

Finally, nominal logic defines equivariance as holding for a function iff its support is empty. Thus, $f$ is equivariant iff any of the following equivalent equations hold, where alpha equivalence over functions is interpreted extensionally (i.e., they take alpha equivalent terms to alpha equivalent terms).

$$\begin{aligned} & \mathsf{supp}\, f = \emptyset \\ \Leftrightarrow\ & \forall \pi . \pi \bullet f \simeq f \\ \Leftrightarrow\ & \forall \pi . \pi \circ f \circ \pi^{-1} \simeq f \\ \Leftrightarrow\ & \forall \pi . \pi \circ f \simeq f \circ \pi \end{aligned}$$

## 5.2 Alpha Equivalence

As already mentioned, hygiene is essentially lexical scoping at the macro level. Thus it would be natural to characterize hygiene by requiring alpha-equivalent terms to expand to alpha-equivalent terms. However, since macro transformers can be any Turing computable function, we cannot in general know the binding structure of u-syntax and thus cannot define a non-trivial alpha-equivalence relation over them. For example, we may have a macro that uses a complicated function of its input to determine whether or not to expand to a `let`. As another example, even a simple `let` may not actually be a binding form if it is nested in some other macro call as the outer macro may rearrange the u-syntax so the `let` becomes some other form.

Fortunately, while we cannot know the binding structure of u-syntax, we know the binding structure of the parts of the code already expanded into k-syntax. For example, after one step of expansion, the example in Section 4.2 becomes the following.

```
(let ([if.r #t]) (or #f <if.r if.b>))
```

Now that the `let` form has expanded into k-syntax, it cannot expand further, and its binding structure is fixed. We do not know the binding structure of its body, though, because the body is u-syntax that may be further expanded.

Nevertheless, we can use a weakened notion of alpha equivalence that accounts for the binding structure manifest in k-syntax but assumes no non-trivial equivalences in u-syntax. This weakened notion of alpha equivalence is a conservative approximation of whatever the actual binding structure may be and is sufficient to formally define when hygiene violations occur due to introduced references. In Figure 9 we formally define this alpha equivalence. It is entirely standard and behaves as usual for alpha equivalence except that it has no equivalences for u-syntax other than reflexivity. For example, the above expression is alpha equivalent to the following.

```
(let ([x.r #t]) (or #f <x.r if.b>))
```

If these two expressions do not expand to alpha-equivalent expressions, then introduced-reference hygiene is violated. We formally define this as follows.

> **Criterion 1** (Reference Hygiene). *A macro expansion step is hygienic with regard to references iff for any partially expanded expressions $e_1$, $e_2$ and $e_1'$ where $e_1 \simeq e_2$ and $e_1 \rightsquigarrow e_1'$, there exists an $e_2'$ such that $e_1' \simeq e_2'$ and $e_2 \rightsquigarrow e_2'$. A macro system is hygienic with regard to references iff all its expansion steps are hygienic with regard to references.*

Since this criterion is independent of the details of the expansion algorithm, we are free to choose from any of the well-known methods for manipulating terms while respecting alpha equivalence. In Section 4.2, we ensured this property by always freshly generating bound reference atoms, but we can also use the binding forms provided by nominal logic.

**Expansion**

$$\underline{\texttt{(<fresh.r }b_0\texttt{> (}\vec{b}\texttt{) }body\texttt{)}} \rightsquigarrow \texttt{(fresh (}\vec{b}\texttt{) }\underline{body}\texttt{)}$$

**Permutation**

$$\pi \bullet \texttt{(fresh (}\vec{b}\texttt{) }body\texttt{)} = \texttt{(fresh (}\overrightarrow{\pi \bullet b}\texttt{) }\pi \bullet body\texttt{)}$$

**Alpha Equivalence**

$$\texttt{(fresh (}\vec{b}\texttt{) }body\texttt{)} \simeq \texttt{(fresh (}\vec{b'}\texttt{) }body'\texttt{)} \qquad \text{if } \forall^{\infty}\vec{b''}.\, body \overset{\vec{b},\vec{b'},\vec{b''}}{\simeq} body'$$

$$\texttt{(fresh () }body\texttt{)} \simeq body$$

$$\texttt{(fresh (}\vec{b}\texttt{) }body\texttt{)} \simeq \texttt{(fresh (}\vec{b} \cup \vec{b_0}\texttt{) }body\texttt{)} \qquad \text{if } b_0 \cap \mathsf{supp}\, body = \emptyset$$

**Figure 10.** Definitions of expansion, permutation and alpha equivalence for `fresh`

Note that, just like binder renaming, the Reference Hygiene Criterion ensures reference hygiene but not binder hygiene. This is due to the fact that we do not know the binding structure of u-syntax and thus have no non-trivial equivalences for it. Tackling that problem is the subject of the remainder of this section.

### 5.3 Fresh Identifiers

As a first step toward handling binder hygiene, recall that the algorithm in Section 4.4 requires that macros freshly generate the binder atoms in any identifiers they introduce. In order to mathematically model this, we introduce a scoping construct for binder atoms. We write this as `(fresh (`$\vec{b}$`)` *body*`)` where the binder atoms in $\vec{b}$ are introduced into the scope of *body*. Duplicates are not allowed in $\vec{b}$ and order is irrelevant, so we treat $\vec{b}$ as a set.

In Figure 10 we define expansion, permutation and alpha equivalence for this form. In addition to the usual alpha equivalences, we may omit atoms bound by `fresh` that are not in the support of its body, and if `fresh` does not bind any atoms, we can replace it with just its body. We include these equivalences because the sole purpose of `fresh` is to bring the elements of $\vec{b}$ into the scope of its body. If they are not used, then we do not need `fresh` to bring them into scope. Just as with other binding constructs, operations such as substitution must rename the binders in `fresh` to avoid unintended capture.

Now instead of using `gensym-identifier`, we make macros return a `fresh` wrapped around a syntax object. For example, the `or` macro expands as follows.

```
(or #f <tmp.r tmp.b>) ⇝
(fresh (tmp1.b)
  (let ([<tmp.r tmp1.b> #f])
    (if <tmp.r tmp1.b>
      <tmp.r tmp1.b> <tmp.r tmp.b>)))
```

This is identical to when we used `gensym-identifier` except that `tmp1.b` now comes from a locally declared scope instead of being a global gensym.

### 5.4 Equivariance

A macro transformer should use `fresh` for any introduced binder atoms, but in order to formally require this, we need to define what counts as an introduced binder atom. For example, if a transformer returns `<x.r y.b>` when passed `<x.r x.b>` as input, clearly `y.b` was introduced by the macro and should be included in the atoms scoped by `fresh`. However, what if a macro returns `<x.r x.b>` when passed `<x.r x.b>` as input? The macro transformer might be the identity function. In that case, `x.b` is not introduced by the macro as it comes from the input. On the other hand, the macro transformer could be the constant function that always returns `<x.r x.b>`. In that case, `x.b` *is* introduced by the macro. We just happen to have chosen an input that coincides with the output.

In order to handle this, note that the binder atoms introduced by a transformer are in its support. Thus we can force macro transformers to use `fresh` for introduced binder atoms by requiring that their supports contain no binder atoms. In other words, we require that macro transformers be equivariant with respect to binder atoms. This allows us to distinguish between transformers that return `<x.r x.b>` when passed `<x.r x.b>` because they are an identity function and those that do so because they are a constant function. In the former case, applying the permutation (`x.b` $\leftrightarrow$ `y.b`) to the function before applying it to `<x.r x.b>` results in the following.

$$\begin{aligned}
&((\texttt{x.b} \leftrightarrow \texttt{y.b}) \bullet f)\, \underline{\texttt{<x.r x.b>}} \\
&= ((\texttt{x.b} \leftrightarrow \texttt{y.b}) \circ f \circ (\texttt{y.b} \leftrightarrow \texttt{x.b}))\, \underline{\texttt{<x.r x.b>}} \\
&= (\texttt{x.b} \leftrightarrow \texttt{y.b}) \bullet (f\ ((\texttt{y.b} \leftrightarrow \texttt{x.b}) \bullet \underline{\texttt{<x.r x.b>}})) \\
&= (\texttt{x.b} \leftrightarrow \texttt{y.b}) \bullet \left(f\, \underline{\texttt{<x.r y.b>}}\right) \\
&= (\texttt{x.b} \leftrightarrow \texttt{y.b}) \bullet \underline{\texttt{<x.r y.b>}}) \\
&= \underline{\texttt{<x.r x.b>}}
\end{aligned}$$

On the other hand, doing the same on a constant function results in the following.

$$\begin{aligned}
&((\texttt{x.b} \leftrightarrow \texttt{y.b}) \bullet f)\, \underline{\texttt{<x.r x.b>}} \\
&= ((\texttt{x.b} \leftrightarrow \texttt{y.b}) \circ f \circ (\texttt{y.b} \leftrightarrow \texttt{x.b}))\, \underline{\texttt{<x.r x.b>}} \\
&= (\texttt{x.b} \leftrightarrow \texttt{y.b}) \bullet (f\ ((\texttt{y.b} \leftrightarrow \texttt{x.b}) \bullet \underline{\texttt{<x.r x.b>}})) \\
&= (\texttt{x.b} \leftrightarrow \texttt{y.b}) \bullet \left(f\, \underline{\texttt{<x.r y.b>}}\right) \\
&= (\texttt{x.b} \leftrightarrow \texttt{y.b}) \bullet \underline{\texttt{<x.r x.b>}} \\
&= \underline{\texttt{<x.r y.b>}}
\end{aligned}$$

In the former case, the transformer function is equivariant with respect to binder atoms, and applying the permutation does not change the output. In the latter case, however, the transformer is not equivariant, and the permutation changes the output.

If a transformer needs to introduce a binder atom, as is the case with `tmp` in the `or` macro, then in order to remain equivariant, it must use `fresh`. For example, instead of returning the constant `<x.r x.b>`, we can have $f$ return `(fresh (x.b) <x.r x.b>)`. In that case, modulo alpha equivalence, applying the permutation to $f$ does not change it. This is seen in the following.

$$\begin{aligned}
&((\texttt{x.b} \leftrightarrow \texttt{y.b}) \bullet f)\, \underline{\texttt{<x.r x.b>}} \\
&= ((\texttt{x.b} \leftrightarrow \texttt{y.b}) \circ f \circ (\texttt{y.b} \leftrightarrow \texttt{x.b}))\, \underline{\texttt{<x.r x.b>}} \\
&= (\texttt{x.b} \leftrightarrow \texttt{y.b}) \bullet (f\ ((\texttt{y.b} \leftrightarrow \texttt{x.b}) \bullet \underline{\texttt{<x.r x.b>}})) \\
&= (\texttt{x.b} \leftrightarrow \texttt{y.b}) \bullet \left(f\, \underline{\texttt{<x.r y.b>}}\right) \\
&= (\texttt{x.b} \leftrightarrow \texttt{y.b}) \bullet \texttt{(fresh (x.b) }\underline{\texttt{<x.r x.b>}}\texttt{)} \\
&= \texttt{(fresh (y.b) }\underline{\texttt{<x.r y.b>}}\texttt{)} \\
&\simeq \texttt{(fresh (x.b) }\underline{\texttt{<x.r x.b>}}\texttt{)}
\end{aligned}$$

This then gives rise to the following criterion defining hygiene with respect to binders.

**Criterion 2** (Binder Hygiene)**.** *A macro transformer is hygienic with respect to binders iff it is equivariant with respect to binder atoms. A macro system is hygienic with respect to binders if all its transformers are hygienic with respect to binders.*

### 5.5 Automating Hygiene

While the Binder Hygiene Criterion provides a formal description of hygiene with respect to binders, it still places the burden of ensuring hygiene on the macro author. While a mechanical proof checker or a type system like in Herman and Wand (2008) or Herman (2010) could verify that a particular transformer is equivariant, we can also have the macro system automatically enforce binder hygiene. A simple way to do this is to use `fresh` to capture any binder atoms in the support of a transformer. Thus we have the following definition where $\mathsf{supp_b}\, f$ is the support of $f$ with respect to binder atoms.

**Definition 3** (Automated Hygiene). Given a transformer $f$, let the hygienic version of that transformer be the following.

$$\mathsf{hyg}\, f = (\texttt{fresh}\ (\mathsf{supp_b}\, f)\ f)$$

Effectively this assumes $f$ is supposed to be equivariant and uses `fresh` to clean up any binder atoms that the macro author left in the support of $f$.

In order to apply the result of hyg to an argument, we lift `fresh` to be a function where application of `fresh` is as follows.

**Definition 4** (Fresh Application). If $s \cap \mathsf{supp_b}\, x = \emptyset$, then

$$(\texttt{fresh}\ (s)\ f)\, x = (\texttt{fresh}\ (s)\ (f\, x))$$

When $s$ and the support of $x$ are not disjoint, we use alpha-equivalence to rename $s$ to not conflict with $x$ before applying this definition.

This definition trivially ensures the equivariance of hyg as shown in the following theorem.

**Theorem 5** (Equivariance of Automated Hygiene). *For any $f$ with a finite support with respect to binder atoms,* hyg $f$ *is equivariant with respect to binder atoms.*

*Proof.* Trivial. The hyg operator produces a `fresh` that captures the binder atoms in the support of $f$, and thus the support of hyg $f$ is empty. □

If the macro system applies hyg to all macro transformers, then all macros are automatically hygienic. For example, consider again the macro that returns the constant <u>`<x.r x.b>`</u>. The support of this with respect to binder atoms is the singleton containing `x.b`. If we apply hyg to this, we get `(fresh (x.b)` $f$`)`. Applying this to <u>`<x.r x.b>`</u> then results in the following.

$$\begin{aligned}
&(\texttt{fresh (x.b)}\ f)\ \underline{\texttt{<x.r x.b>}} \simeq\\
&(\texttt{fresh (x1.b)}\ (\texttt{x.b} \leftrightarrow \texttt{x1.b}) \bullet f)\ \underline{\texttt{<x.r x.b>}} =\\
&(\texttt{fresh (x1.b)}\ (((\texttt{x.b} \leftrightarrow \texttt{x1.b}) \bullet f)\ \underline{\texttt{<x.r x.b>}})) =\\
&(\texttt{fresh (x1.b)}\ (\texttt{x.b} \leftrightarrow \texttt{x1.b}) \bullet \underline{\texttt{<x.r x.b>}}) =\\
&(\texttt{fresh (x1.b)}\ \underline{\texttt{<x.r x1.b>}})
\end{aligned}$$

Of course, computing the support of a function is undecidable in general. To get a practical implementation, we can instead use the following definition.

**Definition 6** (Automated Hygiene, Alternative). Given a transformer $f$ and a syntax object $x$, where $\pi$ is some minimal permutation mapping each element of $\mathsf{supp_b}\, x$ to an atom not in the support of $f$ or $x$, let the application of the hygienic version of that transformer be as follows.

$$\begin{aligned}
&(\mathsf{hyg}\, f)\ x =\\
&\quad (\texttt{fresh}\ (\mathsf{supp_b}\,((\pi \bullet f)\ x) - \mathsf{supp_b}\, x)\ ((\pi \bullet f)\ x))
\end{aligned}$$

Since we can easily compute the support of a syntax object, this definition is practical to implement but behaves the same as Definition 3 as shown in the following theorem.

**Theorem 7** (Equivalance of Automated Hygiene Definitions). *Definition 3 and Definition 6 are equivalent definitions of* hyg *up to alpha equivalence.*

*Proof.* Let $s_1 = \mathsf{supp_b}\, f - \mathsf{supp_b}\, x$, $s_2 = \mathsf{supp_b}\, f \cap \mathsf{supp_b}\, x$ and $s_3 = \mathsf{supp_b}\, x - \mathsf{supp_b}\, f$. Also let $\pi$ be defined as in Definition 6. Finally, let $v = \mathsf{supp_b}\,((\pi \bullet f)\ x)$. Note that $\pi \bullet s_1$, $\pi \bullet s_2$, $s_2$ and $s_3$ are all disjoint and $v \subseteq \mathsf{supp_b}\,(\pi \bullet f) \cup \mathsf{supp_b}\, x = \pi \bullet s_1 \cup \pi \bullet s_2 \cup s_2 \cup s_3$. We then have the following equalities.

$$\begin{aligned}
&(\texttt{fresh}\ (\mathsf{supp_b}\, f)\ f)\, x\\
=\ &(\texttt{fresh}\ (s_1 \cup s_2)\ f)\, x\\
\simeq\ &(\texttt{fresh}\ (\pi \bullet (s_1 \cup s_2))\ \pi \bullet f)\, x\\
=\ &(\texttt{fresh}\ (\pi \bullet (s_1 \cup s_2))\ ((\pi \bullet f)\ x))\\
=\ &(\texttt{fresh}\ ((\pi \bullet s_1) \cup (\pi \bullet s_2))\ ((\pi \bullet f)\ x))\\
\simeq\ &(\texttt{fresh}\ (v \cap (\pi \bullet s_1 \cup \pi \bullet s_2))\ ((\pi \bullet f)\ x))\\
=\ &(\texttt{fresh}\ (v - (s_2 \cup s_3))\ ((\pi \bullet f)\ x))\\
=\ &(\texttt{fresh}\ (\mathsf{supp_b}\,((\pi \bullet f)\ x) - \mathsf{supp_b}\, x)\ ((\pi \bullet f)\ x))
\end{aligned}$$ □

Note that different choices of $\pi$ in Definition 6 may result in different results, but as a corollary of Theorem 7 those results are all alpha equivalent to each other.

### 5.6 Observed-Binder Hygiene

Alert readers may notice that the Binder Hygiene Criterion affects not just binder atoms introduced by transformers but also binder atoms *observed* by macro transformers. For example, consider the following macro transformer where `bound-identifier=?` extracts the binder atoms from two identifiers and tests if they are equal.

```
(let-syntax ([obs (lambda (stx)
  (if (bound-identifier=? stx #'<x.r x.b>)
    #'1 #'2))])
  ...)
```

In a naive expansion system, if the input to this transformer is <u>`<x.r x.b>`</u>, then the output is <u>1</u>. However, if we apply the permutation (`x.b` $\leftrightarrow$ `y.b`) to the transformer, then the result is the following.

$$\begin{aligned}
&((\texttt{x.b} \leftrightarrow \texttt{y.b}) \bullet \mathsf{obs})\ \underline{\texttt{<x.r x.b>}}\\
=\ &((\texttt{x.b} \leftrightarrow \texttt{y.b}) \circ \mathsf{obs} \circ (\texttt{y.b} \leftrightarrow \texttt{x.b}))\ \underline{\texttt{<x.r x.b>}}\\
=\ &(\texttt{x.b} \leftrightarrow \texttt{y.b}) \bullet (\mathsf{obs}\ ((\texttt{y.b} \leftrightarrow \texttt{x.b}) \bullet \underline{\texttt{<x.r x.b>}}))\\
=\ &(\texttt{x.b} \leftrightarrow \texttt{y.b}) \bullet \left(\mathsf{obs}\ \underline{\texttt{<x.r y.b>}}\right)\\
=\ &(\texttt{x.b} \leftrightarrow \texttt{y.b}) \bullet \underline{2}\\
=\ &\underline{2}
\end{aligned}$$

This function does not *introduce* any atoms. Nevertheless, it does *observe* a binder atom in the input. Thus, permuting it changes its output, and it is not equivariant. This is not just an artifact of how we have mathematically defined hygiene but is a distinction present in many hygiene algorithms. Indeed, if `obs` were to take the identifier constant that it is comparing against the input and introduce it into its output, then respecting *introduced*-binder hygiene requires that it not bind over any identifiers from the input. Thus, those identifiers should not be equal when they are observed by `bound-identifier=?`. To achieve this, we must keep the atoms in the input distinct from any atoms internal to the transformer and thus enforce *observed*-binder hygiene. This is not as well known as introduced-binder and reference hygiene but is just as important.

### 5.7 Summary

At this point, we now have a mathematical definition of hygiene and can summarize the main points as follows.

First, we assume identifiers are diatomic as in Section 4.6.

Second, in order to enforce reference hygiene, we require that the Reference Hygiene Criterion holds. In other words, we require that expansion steps respect alpha equivalences over already exposed binding forms in the k-syntax portion of the code.

Third, introduced binder atoms are noted by their presence in the support of a transformer.

Fourth, we require that the Binder Hygiene Criterion hold in order to force transformers to be equivariant with respect to binder atoms and thus enforce binder hygiene. When macros introduce a binder atom, they must thus use `fresh` so they remain equivariant.

Finally, we can automatically make transformers be equivariant by using the hyg operator as defined in Definition 3 or Definition 6.

## 6. Hygiene and `syntax-case`

The definition of hygiene in Section 5 has a close correspondence to the `syntax-case` algorithm described by Dybvig et al. (1993). While a detailed explanation of `syntax-case` is beyond the scope of this paper, we highlight a few of the parallels. In the `syntax-case` algorithm, *wraps* are used to annotate syntax objects with binding information. There are two different algorithms described by Dybvig et al. (1993) for applying these wraps. In one, wraps may be suspended in the middle of applying to a syntax object and are lazily applied to descendant syntax objects. In the other, wraps are eagerly applied and always descend syntax objects until they reach individual identifiers. These two models are semantically equivalent. The former is asymptotically more efficient, but the latter is simpler and more directly corresponds to our definition of hygiene.

In the eager version of the `syntax-case` algorithm, wraps are a sequence of *marks* and *substitutions* surrounding a base symbol for an identifier. Marks are atomic, and substitutions map a set of marks and a particular symbol to a *label*, which is also atomic.

New marks are added to the wrap of an identifier during the macro expansion process. A fresh mark, along with its inverse, called an *anti-mark*, is created each time a macro is called. The anti-mark is placed on the identifiers in the input of the macro transformer while the mark is placed on the output of the macro transformer. When a mark is placed on an identifier that has the corresponding anti-mark, they cancel each other out. Identifiers with different marks are considered to be not `bound-identifer=?`. The behavior of marks in this regard mirrors the behavior of the permutation $\pi$ in Definition 6. The difference is that a mark is essentially an abstract permutation that we treat opaquely without knowing how it maps atoms.

When a binding form expands, a new label is chosen for the binding, and a substitution is created that maps the marks and symbol of the identifier in the binding position to the new label. This substitution is added to the wraps of any identifiers in the body. When an identifier expands in a reference position, the substitutions are consulted to determine to what label it is bound. This models the behavior of how binding forms are expanded in Section 4.6. The freshly generated reference atom corresponds to the new label. The subst operator corresponds to the creation of a substitution.

Finally, note that the operators `bound-identifier=?` and `free-identifier=?` in `syntax-case` are equivalent to comparing the reference and binder parts, respectively, of the diatomic identifiers described in Section 4.6.

In all these regards, the `syntax-case` algorithm corresponds to an almost direct implementation of the mathematical principles in Section 5. The major difference is that `syntax-case` treats permutations as opaque symbolic objects (i.e., marks) and the operations on identifiers are stored in reified forms (i.e., the marks and substitutions in a wrap). This allows operators such as `quote`, `syntax->datum` and `datum->syntax` that "bend" hygiene and either strip wraps from identifiers or transplant the wrap of an identifier to a new symbol. The mathematics in Section 5 can also support these operations if we generalize it to treat permutations as opaque objects and keep subst reified.

## 7. Related Work

Kohlbecker et al. (1986) defined a hygienic macro expansion algorithm by marking identifiers with time stamps indicating the macro expansion step in which they were introduced. However, their definition of hygiene encompasses only introduced-binder hygiene and not introduced-reference hygiene.

Bawden and Rees (1988) then proposed using syntactic closures to handle hygiene. They define hygiene to include both introduced-binder and introduced-reference hygiene. With syntactic closures, macros take syntactic environments as arguments and return expressions that have been closed over particular environments. These environments are then used when interpreting identifiers in those expressions. Clinger (1991) takes a different approach and passes functions for explicitly renaming and comparing identifiers to each macro transformer. In both these systems, macro authors must be careful to correctly use the tools provided for ensuring hygiene as they may otherwise end up with non-hygienic macros.

Clinger and Rees (1991) combined the pattern matching language of Kohlbecker and Wand (1987) with the ideas from Bawden and Rees (1988) to create a system that lets users write high-level macros that are automatically hygienic. Finally, the `syntax-case` algorithm (Dybvig et al. 1993; Dybvig 2007) extended this by allowing macro transformers to be arbitrary functions and providing mechanisms for "bending" the rules of hygiene. The system specified by the $R^6RS$ Scheme standard (Sperber et al. 2007, 2009) is based on this along with extensions for interlibrary macros.

These systems all focus on the algorithmic implementation of hygiene and define hygiene only informally or by way of a particular algorithm. However, the Reference Hygiene Criterion and the Binder Hygiene Criterion are broadly applicable, and we can consider how they apply to these systems. Kohlbecker et al. (1986) satisfies the Binder Hygiene Criterion but not the Reference Hygiene Criterion, which reflects the fact that they are concerned only with binder hygiene. Bawden and Rees (1988) and Clinger (1991) provide the tools for macro authors to satisfy both the Reference Hygiene Criterion and the Binder Hygiene Criterion but do not enforce them. Nevertheless, whether a macro author has used the tools correctly can be determined by whether these criteria are respected by the transformer. Clinger and Rees (1991) and Dybvig et al. (1993) automatically satisfy the Reference Hygiene Criterion and the Binder Hygiene Criterion except when hygiene "bending" operators are used.

A number of systems (Ganz et al. 2001; Culpepper and Felleisen 2003, 2004; Herman and Wand 2008; Herman 2010) use shape types or some other typing discipline to enforce hygiene. These systems generally annotate macros with types that specify their binding structures and enforce the Reference Hygiene Criterion and the Binder Hygiene Criterion as a consequence of typeability. Several of them directly connect their notions of hygiene to nominal logic, albeit in a typed setting. However, these type systems reject many otherwise well-formed, hygienic macros and do not consider hygiene in a general setting without a type system or when not all binding structures are known in advance.

The definition of hygiene that we propose is not only useful for determining whether a particular macro system is hygienic, but also provides a useful perspective on extensions to hygiene that have been proposed. For example, van Tonder (2005) gives examples of macros that use local functions to manipulate the syntax. Since the usual hygiene algorithms do not distinguish between identifiers introduced by different functions within the same macro expansion step, these helper functions may unintentionally capture identifiers introduced by each other. This is easily solved by exposing the `hyg` operator to macro authors so they can annotate these functions as needing to introduce distinct identifiers. Similar techniques can be used with the local transformations in Culpepper and Felleisen (2010) and Culpepper (2012). Another example is anaphoric macros (Barzilay et al. 2011). The classic case of this is a `loop` macro that binds `break` to a continuation that breaks out of the loop. This binding is introduced by the macro but should be visible to the loop body written by the macro user. We conjecture that this can be handled by allowing macros to specify that they have a non-empty support. For example, `loop` would specify that `break` is in its support.

## 8. Conclusion

Hygiene is an essential aspect of the Scheme macro system. There have been multiple implementations of it over the years, but no general, formal definition of what it is. Existing definitions are either informal, tied to a particular expansion algorithm or consider only a restricted subset of macros that follow a certain typing discipline. In this paper we examine several examples of hygiene and how it is violated in naive expanders. From these examples, we then develop a simple expansion algorithm that preserves hygiene. Based on the intuitions developed with that algorithm, we then construct a mathematically precise, formal definition of hygiene. This definition connects hygiene to nominal logic and shows that hygiene is a combination of alpha equivalence and equivariance. It is algorithm independent and can be used to test whether a proposed algorithm is hygienic. This definition closely corresponds to several existing algorithms, and in particular, the `syntax-case` algorithm closely parallels how one would naturally write an algorithm to satisfy this definition.

## Acknowledgments

Thanks go to Mitchell Wand, William Byrd, R. Kent Dybvig, J. Ian Johnson, Michael Ballantyne, Celeste Hollenbeck and the anonymous reviewers for their comments, suggestions and help in improving this paper.

This material is based upon work supported in part by NSF Grant CCF 13-18191. Any opinions, findings, conclusions or recommendations expressed in this material are those of the authors and do not necessarily reflect the views of the NSF.

This article reports on work supported by the Defense Advanced Research Projects Agency under agreement no. FA8750-10-2-0233. The views expressed are those of the authors and do not reflect the official policy or position of the Department of Defense or the U.S. Government.

## References

Eli Barzilay, Ryan Culpepper, and Matthew Flatt. Keeping it clean with syntax parameters. In *Proceedings of the Twelfth Workshop on Scheme and Functional Programming*, October 2011.

Alan Bawden and Jonathan Rees. Syntactic closures. In *Proceedings of the 1988 ACM Conference on LISP and Functional Programming*, LFP '88, pages 86–95, New York, NY, USA, 1988. ACM. ISBN 0-89791-273-X. doi: 10.1145/62678.62687.

William Clinger. Hygienic macros through explicit renaming. *ACM SIGPLAN Lisp Pointers*, IV(4):25–28, October 1991. ISSN 1045-3563. doi: 10.1145/1317265.1317269.

William Clinger and Jonathan Rees. Macros that work. In *Proceedings of the 18th ACM SIGPLAN-SIGACT Symposium on Principles of Programming Languages*, POPL '91, pages 155–162, New York, NY, USA, 1991. ACM. ISBN 0-89791-419-8. doi: 10.1145/99583.99607.

Ryan Culpepper. Fortifying macros. *Journal of Functional Programming*, 22(Special Issue 4–5):439–476, September 2012. ISSN 1469-7653. doi: 10.1017/S0956796812000275.

Ryan Culpepper and Matthias Felleisen. Well-shaped macros. In *Proceedings of the Fourth Workshop on Scheme and Functional Programming*, pages 59–68, November 2003.

Ryan Culpepper and Matthias Felleisen. Taming macros. In Gabor Karsai and Eelco Visser, editors, *Generative Programming and Component Engineering*, volume 3286 of *Lecture Notes in Computer Science*, pages 225–243. Springer Berlin Heidelberg, 2004. ISBN 978-3-540-23580-4. doi: 10.1007/978-3-540-30175-2_12.

Ryan Culpepper and Matthias Felleisen. Fortifying macros. In *Proceedings of the 15th ACM SIGPLAN International Conference on Functional Programming*, ICFP '10, pages 235–246, New York, NY, USA, 2010. ACM. ISBN 978-1-60558-794-3. doi: 10.1145/1863543.1863577.

R. Kent Dybvig. Syntactic abstraction: The `syntax-case` expander. In Andy Oram and Greg Wilson, editors, *Beautiful Code: Leading Programmers Explain How They Think*, Theory in Practice, chapter 25. O'Reilly Media, July 2007. ISBN 978-0-596-51004-6.

R. Kent Dybvig, Robert Hieb, and Carl Bruggeman. Syntactic abstraction in Scheme. *LISP and Symbolic Computation*, 5(4):295–326, December 1993. ISSN 0892-4635 (Print) 1573-0557 (Online). doi: 10.1007/BF01806308.

Murdoch J. Gabbay and Andrew M. Pitts. A new approach to abstract syntax with variable binding. *Formal Aspects of Computing*, 13(3–5): 341–363, July 2002. ISSN 0934-5043 (Print) 1433-299X (Online). doi: 10.1007/s001650200016.

Steven E. Ganz, Amr Sabry, and Walid Taha. Macros as multi-stage computations: type-safe, generative, binding macros in MacroML. In *Proceedings of the Sixth ACM SIGPLAN International Conference on Functional Programming*, ICFP '01, pages 74–85, New York, NY, USA, 2001. ACM. ISBN 1-58113-415-0. doi: 10.1145/507635.507646.

David Herman. *A Theory of Typed Hygienic Macros*. PhD thesis, Northeastern University, Boston, MA, USA, May 2010.

David Herman and Mitchell Wand. A theory of hygienic macros. In Sophia Drossopoulou, editor, *Programming Languages and Systems*, volume 4960 of *Lecture Notes in Computer Science*, pages 48–62. Springer Berlin Heidelberg, 2008. ISBN 978-3-540-78738-9. doi: 10.1007/978-3-540-78739-6_4.

Eugene Kohlbecker, Daniel P. Friedman, Matthias Felleisen, and Bruce Duba. Hygienic macro expansion. In *Proceedings of the 1986 ACM Conference on LISP and Functional Programming*, LFP '86, pages 151–161, New York, NY, USA, 1986. ACM. ISBN 0-89791-200-4. doi: 10.1145/319838.319859.

Eugene E. Kohlbecker and Mitchell Wand. Macro-by-example: Deriving syntactic transformations from their specifications. In *Proceedings of the 14th ACM SIGACT-SIGPLAN Symposium on Principles of Programming Languages*, POPL '87, pages 77–84, New York, NY, USA, 1987. ACM. ISBN 0-89791-215-2. doi: 10.1145/41625.41632.

Michael Sperber, R. Kent Dybvig, Matthew Flatt, and Anton van Straaten (eds.). Revised$^6$ report on the algorithmic language Scheme, September 2007. URL `http://www.r6rs.org/`.

Michael Sperber, R. Kent Dybvig, Matthew Flatt, Anton van Straaten, Robby Findler, and Jacob Matthews. Revised$^6$ report on the algorithmic language Scheme. *Journal of Functional Programming*, 19 (Supplement S1):1–301, August 2009. ISSN 1469-7653. doi: 10.1017/S0956796809990074.

André van Tonder. *SRFI-72: Hygienic macros*, September 2005. URL `http://srfi.schemers.org/srfi-72/srfi-72.html`.

# Self-Representation in Girard's System U

Matt Brown
UCLA
msb@cs.ucla.edu

Jens Palsberg
UCLA
palsberg@ucla.edu

## Abstract

In 1991, Pfenning and Lee studied whether System F could support a typed self-interpreter. They concluded that typed self-representation for System F "seems to be impossible", but were able to represent System F in $F_\omega$. Further, they found that the representation of $F_\omega$ requires kind polymorphism, which is outside $F_\omega$. In 2009, Rendel, Ostermann and Hofer conjectured that the representation of kind-polymorphic terms would require another, higher form of polymorphism. Is this a case of infinite regress? We show that it is not and present a typed self-representation for Girard's System U, the first for a $\lambda$-calculus with decidable type checking. System U extends System $F_\omega$ with kind polymorphic terms and types. We show that kind polymorphic types (i.e. types that depend on kinds) are sufficient to "tie the knot" – they enable representations of kind polymorphic terms without introducing another form of polymorphism. Our self-representation supports operations that iterate over a term, each of which can be applied to a representation of itself. We present three typed self-applicable operations: a self-interpreter that recovers a term from its representation, a predicate that tests the intensional structure of a term, and a typed continuation-passing-style (CPS) transformation – the first typed self-applicable CPS transformation. Our techniques could have applications from verifiably type-preserving metaprograms, to growable typed languages, to more efficient self-interpreters.

***Categories and Subject Descriptors*** D.3.4 [*Processors*]: Interpreters; D.2.4 [*Program Verification*]: Correctness proofs, formal methods

***General Terms*** Languages; Theory

***Keywords*** Lambda Calculus; Self Representation; Types

## 1. Introduction

Typed self-representation is the problem of representing a statically typed language in itself. It can be seen as the intersection of two lines of research: self-representation, which generally studies representations of untyped or dynamically typed languages in themselves, and typed representation, which studies techniques for defining typed representations of statically typed languages that ensure only well-typed programs can be represented.


*POPL '15*, January 15–17, 2015, Mumbai, India.

http://dx.doi.org/10.1145/2676726.2676988

In general, the techniques required for building a representation depend upon both the meta-language (in which the representation is defined) and the object language (which is represented). Representations of expressive object language features tend to require even more expressive meta-language features. In the case of a self-interpreter, the meta-language and the object language are the same. The key challenge of typed self-representation is to identify a single typed language that is expressive enough to represent each of its own features, without additional expressive power.

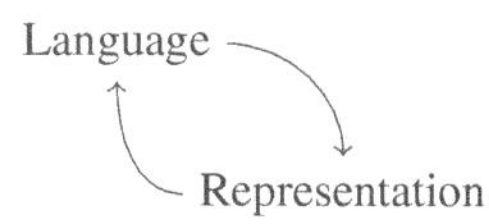


In our case, we are interested in typed $\lambda$-calculi with decidable type checking. It has been an open question since 1991 [26] whether a typed $\lambda$-calculus with decidable type checking can support a meaningful notion of typed self-representation.

**Self Representation.** Self-representation and self-interpretation have many important applications. A self-interpreter can be used to grow a language from a small core implemented in some other meta-language. One can use similar techniques to implement self-optimizers and compilers, as well as debuggers, read-eval-print-loops, and macro systems. A similar idea is the reflective tower, which uses an infinite tower of self-interpreters to add reflective capabilities to a language.

There are many examples of self-interpreters in the literature, including ones for $\lambda$-calculus [4, 7, 8, 18, 22, 23, 28, 31], Haskell [25], JavaScript [13], Lisp [21], Python [36], Ruby [37], Scheme [2], Standard ML [29], and many others [19, 32, 38]. In each of these the representations are untyped, in the sense that (1) it is possible to build representations of ill-typed terms, and (2) all representations are either untyped or else have the same type.

**Typed Representation.** We can contrast this with typed representations, which have two essential properties: (1) only well-typed terms can be represented, and (2) the type of a term is reflected in the type of its representation, in the sense that the former can be determined by the latter. This provides important correctness guarantees for metaprograms. An immediate consequence of (1) is that a metaprogram cannot produce ill-typed terms. We can also ensure that the types of its input and output terms are related in a particular way. For example, we can ensure that a self-interpreter preserves the type of its input, or that a continuation-passing-style transformation modifies the type of the input program in the expected way.

There are many examples in the literature of typed representations. In most cases the techniques rely on the fact that the meta-language has a more powerful type system than the object language.

**Typed Self-Representation.** The goal of typed self-representation is to combine the benefits of self-representation and typed representation. It promises the best of both worlds: on the one hand, it brings the expressive power of self-representation to the world of statically typed languages. On the other hand, it brings the correctness guarantees of types to self-applicable metaprograms. A robust typed self-representation would support typed variants of the kinds of applications enabled by self-representation. It would also narrow the expressiveness gap between dynamically typed languages and statically typed languages, allowing more classical programs from dynamically typed languages to be statically type checked.

What does it mean for a language to support typed self-representation? We have adopted two primary requirements: that our language be a typed $\lambda$-calculus with decidable type-checking, and that a representation support operations that iterate over the structure of the term. Further, we want to allow operations that produce results of different types, possibly related to the type of the input representation.

We target a typed self-recognizer [17], which is a self-interpreter that recovers a term from its representation. The idea of a self-recognizer was first studied by Kleene [18] in 1936 for an untyped $\lambda$-calculus. There are several examples of typed recognizers and self-recognizers [26, 27] that are implemented by iteration. Iteration is desirable because it can be supported by languages that don't include recursion. An operation that iterates or folds over the term is defined by cases – one case for each syntactic form.

In the case of a pure $\lambda$-calculus (that contains only abstractions, applications, and variables), we have identified a core challenge that is related to typed self-representation. The Polymorphic Application (polyapp) problem is to define a polymorphic application function for each form of application in the language. For example, System F terms can be applied to terms and to types. The polyapp problem for System F is to define a polymorphic application function that can apply terms to terms, and a polymorphic application function that can apply terms to types. In Section 3.2 we present a general technique for implementing polyapp functions by decomposing types. In subsequent sections we leverage this technique to represent terms and types.

**History.** Typed self-representation of $\lambda$-calculi has been studied since at least 1991, when Pfenning and Lee [26] considered whether System F could support a typed self-recognizer. Pfenning and Lee concluded that the problem "seems to be impossible", but were able to implement a typed recognizer for System F representations in $F_\omega$. Furthermore, they were able to implement $F_\omega$ in $F^+_\omega$, which extends $F_\omega$ with kind polymorphic terms. They did not study representation of $F^+_\omega$.

In 2009 Rendel, Ostermann and Hofer [27] studied the representation of kind polymorphism, and conjectured that it would require "another, higher form of polymorphism". Their solution was to combine the categories of types and kinds, so that kind polymorphism is represented in the same way as type polymorphism. They demonstrated the first typed self-representation and first typed self-recognizer for a $\lambda$-calculus, though their calculus does not support decidable type checking.

In 2011 Jay and Palsberg [17] implemented a typed self-interpreter for a combinator calculus with System F types. They implemented a self-recognizer and the first typed self-enactor, a self-interpreter that implements multi-step reduction on typed representations. Like [27], type checking is undecidable in their calculus. Their representation technique was designed for combinators, and does not appear to be easily translated to a $\lambda$-calculus.

**Tying the Knot.** A challenge of representing a typed $\lambda$-calculus is to find techniques for representing each form of abstraction and application in the language without adding any new ones. Pfenning and Lee represented System F type abstraction and application using the higher order types of $F_\omega$. In particular, they used higher order types to represent System F type abstractions and applications.

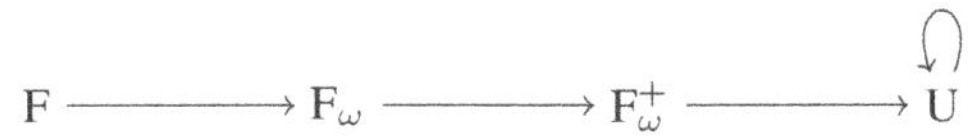


**Figure 1.** Four typed $\lambda$-calculi: $\rightarrow$ denotes "represented in."

We can demonstrate their technique using a polymorphic type application function.

A type application function for System F type applications should map a polymorphic term and a type to the application of the term to the type. For example, given a term of type $\forall\alpha.\ \alpha \rightarrow \alpha$ and a type $\tau$, the type application function should return a term of type $\tau \rightarrow \tau$. We can define the type application function for this case as $\lambda x : (\forall\alpha.\ \alpha \rightarrow \alpha).\ \Lambda\beta.\ x\ \beta$.

A polymorphic type application function for System F should be able to apply any polymorphic term. In other words, it should be polymorphic in the type of the term, and the type of the term must itself be polymorphic. What is needed is a way to abstract over exactly the polymorphic types of System F, excluding monomorphic types like $\alpha \rightarrow \beta$. This is beyond the capabilities of System F type abstraction.

Pfenning and Lee solved this problem by encoding quantified types as second-order types in System $F_\omega$. For example, the type $\forall\alpha.\ \alpha \rightarrow \alpha$ can be encoded as the second-order type $\lambda\alpha : *.\ \alpha \rightarrow \alpha$. The types of $F_\omega$ are classified by a family of kinds. First-order types like $\tau_1 \rightarrow \tau_2$ have kind $*$, and second-order types like $\lambda\alpha : *.\ \alpha \rightarrow \alpha$ have kind $* \rightarrow *$. Type abstractions in $F_\omega$ range over a particular kind that is specified by an annotation. We can abstract over encodings of System F quantified types using a type abstraction annotated with kind $* \rightarrow *$. This enables a polymorphic type application function for System F quantified types to be implemented as:

$$\Lambda\sigma : * \rightarrow *.\ \lambda \mathrm{x} : (\forall\alpha : *.\ \sigma\ \alpha).\ \Lambda\beta : *.\ \mathrm{x}\ \beta$$

In $F_\omega$, the type of this term is $\forall\sigma : * \rightarrow *.\ (\forall\alpha : *.\ \sigma\ \alpha) \rightarrow (\forall\beta : *.\ \sigma\ \beta)$. The type $\forall\alpha : *.\ \sigma\ \alpha$ represents an arbitrary quantified type. Substituting $\sigma$ with an encoded quantified type recovers the quantified type. For example, substituting $\sigma$ with $\lambda\alpha : *.\ \alpha \rightarrow \alpha$ yields $\forall\alpha : *.\ (\lambda\alpha : *.\ \alpha \rightarrow \alpha)\ \alpha$, which is equivalent to $\forall\alpha : *.\ \alpha \rightarrow \alpha$. Note that $\forall\alpha : *.\ \alpha \rightarrow \alpha$ is the $F_\omega$ version of $\forall\alpha.\ \alpha \rightarrow \alpha$. Since every System F quantified type can be encoded as an $F_\omega$ type of kind $* \rightarrow *$, this type application function can apply any polymorphic System F term. It can only apply polymorphic terms, because no substitution for $\sigma$ can make $(\forall\alpha : *.\ \sigma\ \alpha)$ into a monomorphic type.

Pfenning and Lee used this technique to represent System F in $F_\omega$. They were unable to represent System $F_\omega$ in itself, but did achieve a representation of $F_\omega$ in $F^+_\omega$, which extends $F_\omega$ with kind abstraction and application in terms. It is easy to imagine that this is a case of infinite regress; that representing kind-abstractions will require another extension, which will also need to be represented if we hope to achieve self-representation.

The System F type application function discussed above already hints at the question of infinite regress. It can apply any polymorphic term typeable in System F, but is not itself typeable in System F. On the other hand, it is typeable in System $F_\omega$, but can only apply some of the polymorphic terms in $F_\omega$. In particular, it cannot apply itself. This begs the following question, which we name the Polymorphic Application problem: is it possible to define a set of polymorphic application functions in a particular language, one for each form of application in the terms of that language (e.g., for applications of terms to terms, terms to types, terms to kinds, etc.)? We conjecture that a language that supports typed self-representation can also support polymorphic application.

In Section 3.2 we formalize the Polymorphic Application problem and present a solution for Girard's System U. In later sections we use our solution to define our typed self-representation for System U. Our result is summarized in Figure 1. Pfenning and Lee were able to represent System F in $F_\omega$, and $F_\omega$ in $F_\omega^+$. We show that $F_\omega^+$ can be represented in System U, and that System U can represent itself.

**System U.** System U was first introduced by Jean-Yves Girard in his PhD thesis [16], in which he also introduced System F. Girard used System U to formalize a version of the Burali-Forti paradox. Girard's paradox showed that System U is not strongly normalizing, and that every type is inhabited. Thus, as a logic, System U is inconsistent.

System U is a Pure Type System that lies outside the $\lambda$-cube [5], and that does not include dependent types. It is an extension of $F_\omega^+$, and every legal $F_\omega^+$ term is a legal System U term. The terms of System U consist of variables and abstractions and applications of each of terms, types, and kinds. The types of System U consist of variables and abstractions and applications of each of types and kinds. Intuitively, the types of System U are the terms of System F. In Section 3.2 we show that System U can support a polymorphic application function for each form of application. A key property that makes tying the knot possible is that System U does not have higher-order kinds. As a result, there is no "type system" for kinds: all kinds are classified by a single sort $\square$. This is analogous to the types of System F: System F does not have higher-order types, and all types are classified by a single sort $*$. Since System U has only one classifier of kinds, a representation of System U does not need to abstract over classifiers of kinds.

**Representation and Operations.** We represent both terms and the types of terms. We call our term representation procedure "quotation". In section 5, we define a meta-level process of quotation, which formalizes what it means for one term to represent another. In the diagram above, our quotation function quote maps a typed term to its representation. Unlike the other operations in the figure, quote is defined outside the language itself.

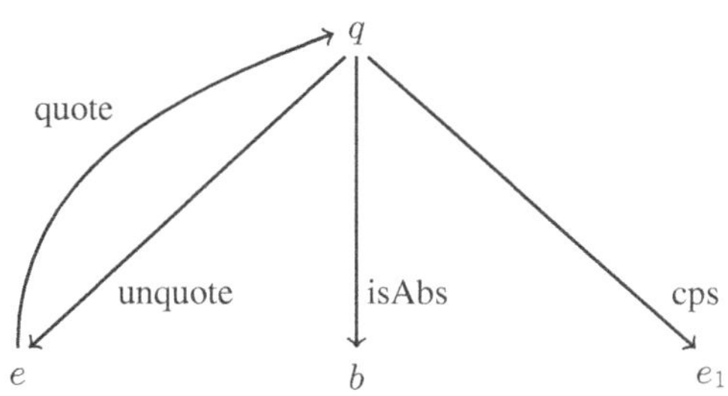


We support operations that iterate or fold over the representation. In section 6 we present three example operations defined as folds: a self-recognizer unquote that recovers a term from its representation, a predicate isAbs that tests the intensional structure of a representation, and a typed continuation-passing style (CPS) transformation. CPS transformation is often used in compilers of functional programming languages.

**Our Results.** We identify System U as the first known typed $\lambda$-calculus with decidable type checking that supports typed self-representation. We represent both terms and the types of terms, which enables operations that transform the type of their input. Type representations are essential to our implementation of the first typed self-applicable CPS transformation. The result type of the CPS transformation is a function of the intensional structure of the input type.

Our type representations are types of a particular kind U. Type representations are used to type check term representations. For example, suppose that e is a term of type $\tau$, that q is the representation of e, and that $\sigma$ is the representation of $\tau$. Then the type of q is Exp $\sigma$. Our self-recognizer unquote recovers a term from its representation, so that unquote $\sigma$ q $\equiv_\beta$ e. The type of unquote is $\Pi\alpha : U.\ \text{Exp}\ \alpha \rightarrow \text{UId}\ \alpha$. In Pure Type Systems, $\Pi$ is analogous to the $\forall$ quantifier of System F and $F_\omega$. The type UId is an operation on type representations that recovers a type from its representation. For example UId $\sigma \equiv_\beta \tau$.

**Rest of the Paper.** Section 2 gives an overview of Pure Type Systems, Section 3 describes System U, Section 4 defines our representation of types, Section 5 defines our representation of terms, Section 6 presents our example operations, Section 7 discusses our implementation and experimental results, Section 8 contains a comparison with related work, Section 9 discusses future work, and Section 10 concludes. Proofs of theorems stated throughout the paper are provided in the appendix of the full paper, which is available from our website [1].

## 2. Pure type systems

We use Barendregt's [5] formalization of System U as a Pure Type System (PTS). This section gives an overview of some important aspects of PTSs for the unfamiliar reader, but does not include a detailed tutorial. Pure Type Systems have a uniform syntax, which helps to clarify both the presentation of our self-representation techniques, and a comparison between System U and other PTS instances like System F and $F_\omega$. The comparison serves to explain what parts of System U are important for achieving a self-representation.

A Pure Type System is defined by a set of expressions $\mathcal{T}$ and a specification. The expressions are defined by the grammar:

$$\mathcal{T} = V \mid C \mid \lambda V : \mathcal{T}.\, \mathcal{T} \mid \mathcal{T}\, \mathcal{T} \mid \Pi V : \mathcal{T}.\, \mathcal{T}$$

Here $V$ ranges over a countable set of variables and $C$ ranges over a set of constants. We use $x$, $y$ to range over variables, $c$ to range over constants, and $a$, $b$, $A$, and $B$ to range over expressions. Functionals are introduced by the $\lambda$ form and eliminated by application. The form $\Pi V : \mathcal{T}.\, \mathcal{T}$ introduces a product, which is used to classify functionals.

The notation A $\rightarrow_\beta$ B denotes that A reduces to B in one step of $\beta$-reduction. Similarly, A $\rightarrow_\eta$ B denotes that A reduces to B in one step of $\eta$-reduction, and A $\rightarrow_{\beta\eta}$ B denotes that either A $\rightarrow_\beta$ B or A $\rightarrow_\eta$ B. The relation $\twoheadrightarrow_\beta$ denotes the reflexive transitive closure of $\rightarrow_\beta$, and $\equiv_\beta$ denotes the least congruence relation generated by $\rightarrow_\beta$. The relations $\twoheadrightarrow_\eta$, $\equiv_\eta$, $\twoheadrightarrow_{\beta\eta}$, and $\equiv_{\beta\eta}$ are defined similarly.

A specification of a PTS consists of a triple $(\mathcal{S}, \mathcal{A}, \mathcal{R})$. The first component $\mathcal{S}$ is a subset of $C$ called sorts. We will use $s$ to range over sorts. In the systems we consider, all constants are sorts. The second component $\mathcal{A}$ is a set of axioms of the form $c : s$, where $c$ is a constant and $s$ a sort. The third component $\mathcal{R}$ is a set of rules of the form $(s_1, s_2, s_3)$, for some sorts $s_1$, $s_2$, and $s_3$. We use the shorthand $(s_1, s_2)$ to denote $(s_1, s_2, s_2)$. The specification and a set of derivation rules determine the derivable typing judgments $\Gamma \vdash$ A : B.

In a judgment of the form $\Gamma \vdash$ A : B, we call A the *subject* and B the *classifier* of A. If $\Gamma \vdash$ A : B can be derived using the rules in Figure 2 with the specification of a particular PTS, then A is *legal* in that system. Some authors call the set of legal expressions the *terms*, though we will use *term* to refer to a subset of the legal expressions defined below.

We call a product derived with the rule $(s_1, s_2, s_3)$ as its side-condition an "$(s_1, s_2, s_3)$ product". The rule ensures that a $(s_1, s_2, s_3)$ product will be classified by $s_3$. A product $\Pi$x : A. B is called a dependent product if x occurs free in $B$. It is standard to abbreviate products $\Pi$x : A. B as A $\rightarrow$ B when x does not occur free in B. It is sometimes possible to determine that an arbitrary $(s_1, s_2, s_3)$ product can be written in this abbreviated form. For

$$\text{axioms}\ \frac{}{\vdash \mathrm{c:s}}\ (\mathrm{c:s}) \in \mathrm{A}$$

$$\text{start}\ \frac{\Gamma \vdash A : s}{\Gamma, x : A \vdash x : A}$$

$$\text{weakening}\ \frac{\Gamma \vdash a : A \qquad \Gamma \vdash B : s}{\Gamma, x : B \vdash a : A}$$

$$\text{product}\ \frac{\Gamma \vdash A : s_1 \qquad \Gamma, x : A \vdash B : s_2}{\Gamma \vdash (\Pi x : A.B) : s_3}\ (s_1, s_2, s_3) \in R$$

$$\text{abstraction}\ \frac{\Gamma, x : A \vdash b : B \qquad \Gamma \vdash (\Pi x : A.B) : s}{\Gamma \vdash (\lambda x : A.b) : (\Pi x : A.B)}$$

$$\text{application}\ \frac{\Gamma \vdash F : (\Pi x : A.B) \qquad \Gamma \vdash a : A}{\Gamma \vdash F\ a : B[x := a]}$$

$$\text{conversion}\ \frac{\Gamma \vdash A : B \qquad \Gamma \vdash B' : s \qquad B \equiv_\beta B'}{\Gamma \vdash A : B'}$$

**Figure 2.** The rules for a PTS $\lambda(\mathcal{S},\mathcal{A},\mathcal{R})$

example, in System F, a $(*,*)$ product has the form $\Pi$x : A. B, where x ranges over terms and A and B are types. Since System F does not include dependent types, x cannot occur free in B, so $\Pi$x : A. B can be written A $\rightarrow$ B.

To demonstrate the uniformity of PTS syntax, consider the System F term $\Lambda\alpha$. $\lambda$x : $\alpha$. x which has the System F type $\forall\alpha.\alpha \rightarrow \alpha$. The symbol $\Lambda$ denotes a type abstraction. The type variable $\alpha$ is not classified, since System F does not classify types. The symbol $\lambda$ denotes a term abstraction, and the term variable x is classified. The universal quantifier $\forall$ forms the types of $\Lambda$ abstractions, and $\rightarrow$ forms the types of $\lambda$ abstractions. In PTS syntax, the term is written $\lambda\alpha : *.\ \lambda$x : $\alpha$. x, and the type is written $\Pi\alpha : *.\ \Pi$x : $\alpha$. $\alpha$. Here the same symbol $\lambda$ is used for the both abstractions, and the type of each $\lambda$ abstraction is a product. Since x does not occur free in $\alpha$, we can also write the type as $\Pi\alpha : *.\ \alpha \rightarrow \alpha$.

**Theorem 2.1** (Subject Reduction for $\rightarrow_{\beta\eta}$ [15]). *If* $\Gamma \vdash$ A : B *and* A $\twoheadrightarrow_{\beta\eta}$ A$'$*, then* $\Gamma \vdash$ A$'$ : B

**Theorem 2.2** (Church-Rosser for $\rightarrow_\beta$ [15]). *If* $\Gamma \vdash$ A : B *and* A $\twoheadrightarrow_\beta$ $A_1$ *and* A $\twoheadrightarrow_\beta$ $A_2$*, then there exists* A$'$ *such that* $A_1 \twoheadrightarrow_\beta$ A$'$ *and* $A_2 \twoheadrightarrow_\beta$ A$'$.

While the focus of this paper is primarily on System U, we also discuss Systems F, $F_\omega$ and $F_\omega^+$. The PTS specification of each system is listed in Figure 3. The sorts of each is a subset of $\{*, \Box, \Delta\}$. We divide the legal expressions of each PTS based on these sorts: the sort $*$ corresponds to the *terms*, the sort $\Box$ corresponds to the *types*, and the sort $\Delta$ corresponds to the *kinds*. More precisely, suppose a legal expression $A$ is derived by $\Gamma \vdash A : B$. If $\Gamma \vdash B : *$, then $A$ is a term. If $\Gamma \vdash B : \Box$, then $A$ is a type. If $\Gamma \vdash B : \Delta$, then $A$ is a kind.

The axioms $\mathcal{A}$ of a PTS instance defines how the different sorts are related to each other. The axioms of each PTS instance listed in Figure 3 are a subset of $\{* : \Box, \Box : \Delta\}$. The axiom $(* : \Box)$ means that $\Box$ is the classifier of $*$ and that types classify terms. The axiom $(\Box : \Delta)$ means that $\Delta$ is the classifier of $\Box$ and that the kinds classify types. We call the classifier of a term its type, and the classifier of a type its kind.

The rules $\mathcal{R}$ determine which products are legal in a PTS instance. The rules $\mathcal{R}$ of each PTS instance listed in Figure 3 are a

| | | |
|---|---|---|
| System F | $\mathcal{S}$ | $*, \Box$ |
| | $\mathcal{A}$ | $* : \Box$ |
| | $\mathcal{R}$ | $(*,*), (\Box,*)$ |
| System $F_\omega$ | $\mathcal{S}$ | $*, \Box, \Delta$ |
| | $\mathcal{A}$ | $* : \Box, \Box : \Delta$ |
| | $\mathcal{R}$ | $(*,*), (\Box,*), (\Box,\Box)$ |
| System $F_\omega^+$ | $\mathcal{S}$ | $*, \Box, \Delta$ |
| | $\mathcal{A}$ | $* : \Box, \Box : \Delta$ |
| | $\mathcal{R}$ | $(*,*), (\Box,*), (\Box,\Box), (\Delta,*)$ |
| System U | $\mathcal{S}$ | $*, \Box, \Delta$ |
| | $\mathcal{A}$ | $* : \Box, \Box : \Delta$ |
| | $\mathcal{R}$ | $(*,*), (\Box,*), (\Box,\Box), (\Delta,*), (\Delta,\Box)$ |

**Figure 3.** PTS specifications of key calculi

subset of $\{(*,*), (\Box,*), (\Box,\Box), (\Delta,*), (\Delta,\Box)\}$. The rule $(*,*)$ derives terms that abstract over other terms, the types of which are $(*,*)$ products. The rule $(\Box,*)$ derives terms that abstract over types, the types of which are $(\Box,*)$ products. The rule $(\Box,\Box)$ derives types that abstract over other types, the kinds of which are $(\Box,\Box)$ products. The rule $(\Delta,*)$ derives terms that abstract over kinds, the types of which are $(\Delta,*)$ products. The rule $(\Delta,\Box)$ derives types that abstract over kinds, the kinds of which are $(\Delta,\Box)$ products.

In each PTS of Figure 3, legal products are either types or kinds. A product type is a legal product that is a type. It is necessarily a $(s,*)$ product. A product kind is a legal product that is a kind. It is necessarily a $(s,\Box)$ product.

We adopt a naming convention to help distinguish between terms, types, and kinds. Names starting with lower-case letters such as $e$ refer to terms. Names starting with upper-case letters and the greek letters $\alpha, \beta, \tau$, and $\sigma$ refer to types. Greek letters $\kappa$ and $\chi$ refer to kinds.

Systems F and $F_\omega$ are part of the $\lambda$-cube [5], while $F_\omega^+$ and U are not because of the rules $(\Delta,*)$ and $(\Delta,\Box)$. All except System U are strongly normalizing. Girard's thesis [16] proved that System U is not strongly normalizing. In particular, there exists a legal term in System U with the type $\Pi\alpha : *.\alpha$ that does not have a normal form. However, the types and kinds of System U are strongly normalizing.

Type checking is decidable for each of System F, $F_\omega$, $F_\omega^+$, and U [6]. This relies on that each system is *injective* [14], a technical property of Pure Type Systems. An injective PTS also has the property that types are unique [5].

None of the PTS instances shown in Figure 3 have dependent types (e.g., types that abstract over terms), which require the rule $(*,\Box)$. A consequence of this is that any $(*,*)$ product $\Pi$x : $\tau_1$. $\tau_2$ can be written $\tau_1 \rightarrow \tau_2$. Types cannot depend on terms, so $x$ cannot occur free in $\tau_2$.

## 3. System U

In this section we define a decomposition of System U product types and use it to solve the Polymorphic Application problem for System U. The ideas in this section recur throughout the paper: in the definition of type representations in Section 4; in the decomposition of type representations in Section 4; and in the definition of term representations in Section 5.

### 3.1 Decomposing Product Types

In a pure type system, products are always classified by a sort. The sort of types is $*$, so product types are products classified by $*$.

The product types of System U are formed by $(*, *)$, $(\square, *)$, and $(\Delta, *)$. In general, if a product $\Pi x : A.\, \tau$ is formed by $(s, *)$, then $\tau$ is classified by $*$ (i.e. $\tau$ is a type) and A is classified by $s$. System U products formed by $(*, *)$ and by $(\Delta, *)$ are special cases. A $(*, *)$ product of the form $\Pi x : \tau_1.\tau_2$ is special because the bound variable $x$ cannot occur free in $\tau_2$ (i.e. types cannot depend on terms). Products formed by $(\Delta, *)$ are special because the only subject classified by $\Delta$ is $\square$.

**Theorem 3.1.** *In System U, if $\Gamma \vdash A : \Delta$, then $A = \square$.*

*Proof.* By induction on the height of the derivation. Assume $\Gamma \vdash A : \Delta$. We proceed by considering the last rule in the derivation. If the last rule is axioms, then $(A : \Delta) \in \mathcal{A}$. The only possibility is $(\square, \Delta)$, so $A = \square$ as required. If the last rule is start, then $(\Delta : s) \in \mathcal{A}$. Contradiction. If the last rule is weakening, then $\Gamma = \Gamma_1, x : C$ and $\Gamma_1 \vdash A : \Delta$. By induction, $A = \square$ as required. If the last rule is product, then there exist sorts $s_1, s_2$ such that $(s_1, s_2, \Delta) \in \mathcal{R}$. Contradiction. If the last rule is abstraction, then $\Delta = \Pi x : A.B$. Contradiction. If the last rule is application, then $B[x := a] = \Delta$. There are two cases: either $B = \Delta$, or $a = \Delta$. If $B = \Delta$, then $(\Pi x : A.\Delta)$ must be legal. This in turn requires a sort $s$ and an axiom $\Delta : s$. Contradiction. If $a = \Delta$, then there must exist a term $A$ such that $\Gamma \vdash \Delta : A$. Contradiction. If derived by conversion, then there must exist a sort $s$ such that $\Gamma \vdash \Delta : s$, which in turn requires an axiom $\Delta : s$. Contradiction. $\square$

In words, Theorem 3.1 states that System U does not include a "type system" for kinds. The situation is similar for the types of System F, as it does not include a kind system (which is a "type system" for types). In the PTS formulation of System F, the only subject classified by $\square$ is $*$. As we will see, Theorem 3.1 is a key property of System U that enables self-representation.

**Theorem 3.2.** *If $\Gamma \vdash \tau : *$, and $\tau$ is a normal form, then $\tau$ is of one of the following forms:*

| | |
|---|---|
| $\alpha\ A_1\ \ldots\ A_n$ | where $\alpha$ is a type variable. |
| $\tau_1 \to \tau_2$ | where $\Gamma \vdash \tau_1 : *$ |
| $\Pi\alpha : \kappa.\ \tau_1$ | where $\Gamma \vdash \kappa : \square$ |
| $\Pi\chi : \square.\ \tau_1$ | |

Since we are only interested in decomposing product types (and not applications of the form $\alpha\ \tau_1\ \ldots\ \tau_n$), we only consider the last three cases. We begin by defining a constructor for each case of product, corresponding to the rule $(s, *)$ that forms the product.

**Definition 3.1** (Constructors for product types)**.** *We define the following constructors for product types:*

$$\begin{aligned} \pi_* &= \lambda\alpha : *.\ \lambda\beta : *.\ \alpha \to \beta \\ \pi_\square &= \lambda\chi : \square.\ \lambda\alpha : \chi \to *.\Pi\beta : \chi.\ \alpha\ \beta \\ \pi_\Delta &= \lambda\alpha : \square \to *.\Pi\chi : \square.\ \alpha\ \chi \end{aligned}$$

It is straightforward to check that the product type constructors have the types given by the following judgments:

$$\begin{aligned} \langle\rangle &\vdash \pi_* : * \to * \to * \\ \langle\rangle &\vdash \pi_\square : \Pi\chi : \square.\ (\chi \to *) \to * \\ \langle\rangle &\vdash \pi_\Delta : (\square \to *) \to * \end{aligned}$$

Every product type formed by $(s, *)$ can be equivalently expressed as an application of the constructor $\pi_s$. This is akin to a higher order abstract syntax encoding of product types [30].

**Theorem 3.3** (Decomposition of product types)**.** *For any legal $(*, *)$ product $\tau_1 \to \tau_2$, any legal $(\square, *)$ product $\Pi\alpha : \kappa.\ \tau$, and any legal $(\Delta, *)$ product $\Pi\chi : \square.\ \tau$, we have:*

$$\begin{aligned} \tau_1 \to \tau_2 &\equiv_\beta \pi_*\ \tau_1\ \tau_2 \\ \Pi\alpha : \kappa.\ \tau &\equiv_\beta \pi_\square\ \kappa\ (\lambda\alpha : \kappa.\ \tau) \\ \Pi\chi : \square.\ \tau &\equiv_\beta \pi_\Delta\ (\lambda\chi : \square.\ \tau) \end{aligned}$$

Below we define the components of a product to be the arguments of the constructor that yield an equivalent type.

**Definition 3.2** (Components of products)**.**

- *The components of a $(*, *)$ product type $\tau_1 \to \tau_2$ are $\tau_1$ and $\tau_2$.*
- *The components of a $(\square, *)$ product type $\Pi\alpha : \kappa.\ \tau$ are $\kappa$ and $\lambda\alpha : \kappa.\ \tau$.*
- *The component of a $(\Delta, *)$ product type $\Pi\chi : \square.\ \tau$ is $\lambda\chi : \square.\ \tau$.*

The following theorem states that the components of a product are always legal in the same environment as the product itself.

**Theorem 3.4** (Types of product components)**.**

1. *If $\Gamma \vdash (\Pi x : \tau_1.\ \tau_2) : *$ and $\Gamma \vdash \tau_1 : *$, then $\Gamma \vdash \tau_2 : *$.*
2. *If $\Gamma \vdash (\Pi\alpha : \kappa.\ \tau) : *$ and $\Gamma \vdash \kappa : \square$, then $\Gamma \vdash (\lambda\alpha : \kappa.\ \tau) : \kappa \to *$.*
3. *If $\Gamma \vdash (\Pi\chi : \square.\ \tau) : *$, then $\Gamma \vdash (\lambda\chi : \square.\ \tau) : \square \to *$.*

As stated earlier, the key properties of System U that enable our self-representation technique are that product types can be decomposed, and that terms and types can abstract over the components. The components of a $(*, *)$ product are two types, and can be abstracted in terms and types by the rules $(\square, *)$ and $(\square, \square)$, respectively. The components of a $(\square, *)$ product are a kind and a type, and can be abstracted in terms by the rules $(\Delta, *)$ and $(\square, *)$, and in types by $(\Delta, \square)$ and $(\square, \square)$. The single component of a $(\Delta, *)$ component is a type, and can be abstracted over in terms and types by $(\square, *)$ and $(\square, \square)$. These properties will play key roles in our solution of the Polymorphic Application problem (Section 3.2), and in the representation of types (Section 4) and terms (Section 5).

### 3.2 Polymorphic Application

We can now formalize the requirements of a polymorphic application functions and state the Polymorphic Application problem for a class of Pure Type Systems.

**Definition 3.3** (Standard PTS)**.** *A PTS $\lambda(\mathcal{S}, \mathcal{A}, \mathcal{R})$ is* standard *if:*

- *The designated sort $* \in \mathcal{S}$ classifies the types of terms.*
- *For each sort $s \in S$, $(s : *) \notin \mathcal{A}$.*
- *If $(s_1, s_2, *) \in \mathcal{R}$, then $s_2 = *$.*

The first condition of a Standard PTS establishes $*$ as the sort corresponding to terms. The second condition states that terms do not classify anything. The third condition states that if a term is an abstraction, then its body is also a term. The systems listed in Figure 3 and those in the $\lambda$-cube are all standard.

**Definition 3.4** (Polymorphic Application Function)**.** *Let $\lambda(\mathcal{S}, \mathcal{A}, \mathcal{R})$ be a Standard PTS, let $(s, *) \in \mathcal{R}$, and let p be a legal closed term. We say that p is a polymorphic application function for the $(s, *)$ products of $\lambda(\mathcal{S}, \mathcal{A}, \mathcal{R})$ if it satisfies the following two conditions:*

- *p is of the form*

  $$\lambda x_1 : A_1.\ \ldots\ \lambda x_n : A_n.\ \lambda x : (\Pi b_1 : B.\tau).\ \lambda b_2 : B.\ x\ b_2$$

  *for some $x_1, \ldots x_n, A_1, \ldots A_n, b_1, b_2, B, \tau$ such that*

  $$x_1 : A_1, \ldots, x_n : A_n \vdash B : s.$$

- *For every closed $(s, *)$ product $\sigma$ of $\lambda(\mathcal{S}, \mathcal{A}, \mathcal{R})$, there exist legal expressions $a_1, \ldots, a_n$ such that*

  $$\langle\rangle \vdash p\ a_1\ \ldots\ a_n : \sigma \to \sigma$$

The first condition defines the form of a polymorphic application function for $(s, *)$ products. The $n$ outermost abstractions are what make it polymorphic: they abstract over the component(s) of such products. The term under the $n$ outermost abstractions,

$\lambda x : (\Pi b_1 : B.\, \tau).\, \lambda b_2 : B.\, x\, b_2$, should be an application function for an arbitrary $(s, *)$ product. The second condition states that we can obtain an application function for particular closed $(s, *)$ product by $n$ applications.

**Definition 3.5** (Polymorphic Application Problem). *For a Standard PTS $\lambda(\mathcal{S}, \mathcal{A}, \mathcal{R})$, we say that $\lambda(\mathcal{S}, \mathcal{A}, \mathcal{R})$ supports polymorphic application if there exists a legal polymorphic application function* $\text{polyapp}_s$ *for every rule $(s, *) \in \mathcal{R}$.*

For example, a solution of the Polymorphic Application problem for System F requires two polyapp functions that are legal System F terms: a $\text{polyapp}_*$ function to apply terms to terms, and a $\text{polyapp}_\Box$ function to apply terms to types. We conjecture that no legal $\text{polyapp}_\Box$ function exists for System F, and therefore that the Polymorphic Application problem for System F is impossible.

We now show how to solve the Polymorphic Application problem for System U. The solution consists of three application functions: $\text{polyapp}_*$, $\text{polyapp}_\Box$, and $\text{polyapp}_\Delta$. Later we will use the techniques from this section to define our representations of types and terms.

**Term applications.** Our first polymorphic application function $\text{polyapp}_*$ applies terms to terms. Terms that can be applied to other terms have $(*, *)$ product types of the form $\tau_1 \to \tau_2$, where $\langle\rangle \vdash \tau_1 : *$. An application function for terms of type $\tau_1 \to \tau_2$ will have the type $(\tau_1 \to \tau_2) \to \tau_1 \to \tau_2$, and can be implemented as:

$$\lambda \mathrm{f} : \tau_1 \to \tau_2.\, \lambda \mathrm{a} : \tau_1.\, \mathrm{f}\, \mathrm{a}$$

By Theorem 3.4, we have that $\langle\rangle \vdash \tau_2 : *$. Therefore, we can make this polymorphic by abstracting out $\tau_1$ and $\tau_2$. The resulting function, $\text{polyapp}_*$, implements application of $(*, *)$ functions:

$$\text{polyapp}_* = \lambda \tau_1 : *.\, \lambda \tau_2 : *.\, \lambda \mathrm{f} : \tau_1 \to \tau_2.\, \lambda \mathrm{a} : \tau_1.\, \mathrm{f}\, \mathrm{a}$$

The abstractions of $\tau_1$ and $\tau_2$ are type abstractions formed by $(\Box, *)$. The type of $\text{polyapp}_*$ is:

$$\Pi \tau_1 : *.\, \Pi \tau_2 : *.\, (\tau_1 \to \tau_2) \to \tau_1 \to \tau_2$$

**Lemma 3.1.** $\text{polyapp}_*$ *is a polymorphic application function for $(*, *)$ products in System U.*

*Proof.* We have already seen that $\text{polyapp}_*$ is legal. It is easily checked that it has the required form, and that $\tau_1 : *, \tau_2 : * \vdash \tau_1 : *$. Let $\sigma_1 \to \sigma_2$ be closed a $(*, *)$ product in System U. By Theorem 3.4, the components $\sigma_1$ and $\sigma_2$ are both closed types of kind $*$. Therefore $\text{polyapp}_*\, \sigma_1\, \sigma_2 : (\sigma_1 \to \sigma_2) \to \sigma_1 \to \sigma_2$ as required. □

**Type applications.** Our second polymorphic application function $\text{polyapp}_\Box$ applies terms to types. Terms that can be applied to types have $(\Box, *)$ product types of the form $\Pi\alpha : \kappa.\, \tau$, where $\alpha$ ranges over types of kind $\kappa$ and $\tau$ is a type. Based on the type rules in Figure 2, an application function for terms of a particular $(\Box, *)$ product type $\Pi\alpha : \kappa.\, \tau$ should have the type:

$$(\Pi\alpha : \kappa.\tau) \to \Pi\beta : \kappa.\, (\tau[\alpha := \beta]) \qquad (\dagger)$$

Here $\tau[\alpha := \beta]$ denotes the type obtained by substituting $\beta$ for $\alpha$ in $\tau$. The syntax $\tau[\alpha := \beta]$ is not part of our language of types, but can be expressed as $(\lambda\alpha : \kappa.\, \tau)\, \beta$. Letting $\tau'$ denote $\lambda\alpha : \kappa.\, \tau$, we can write $(\dagger)$ as:

$$(\Pi\alpha : \kappa.\, \tau'\, \alpha) \to \Pi\beta : \kappa.\, \tau'\, \beta$$

We can implement a polymorphic application function $\text{polyapp}_\Box$ for $(\Box, *)$ products by abstracting over $\kappa$ and $\tau'$, which are the components of $\Pi\alpha : \kappa.\, \tau$. Theorem 3.4 states that $\kappa$ has sort $\Box$ and $\tau'$ has kind $\Box \to *$.

$$\text{polyapp}_\Box = \lambda\kappa : \Box.\lambda\tau' : \kappa \to *.\lambda \mathrm{f} : (\Pi\alpha : \kappa.\, \tau'\alpha).\lambda\beta : \kappa.\, \mathrm{f}\, \beta$$

The first two abstractions of $\text{polyapp}_\Box$ bind the components of an arbitrary $(\Box, *)$ product type. The third abstraction binds a term of the corresponding product type. The final abstraction binds the type argument. The type of $\text{polyapp}_\Box$ is:

$$\Pi\kappa : \Box.\, \Pi\tau' : \kappa \to *.\, (\Pi\alpha : \kappa.\, \tau'\, \alpha) \to \Pi\beta : \kappa.\, \tau'\, \beta$$

**Lemma 3.2.** $\text{polyapp}_\Box$ *is a polymorphic application function for $(\Box, *)$ products in System U.*

*Proof.* We have already seen that $\text{polyapp}_\Box$ is legal and has the required form. It is easily checked that $\kappa : \Box, \tau' : \kappa \to * \vdash \kappa : \Box$. Let $(\Pi\alpha : \kappa_1.\sigma)$ be a closed, legal $(\Box, *)$ product in System U. Then $\kappa_1$ is closed and classified by $\Box$. By Theorem 3.4, we have that $(\lambda\alpha : \kappa_1.\, \sigma)$ is closed and has kind $\kappa_1 \to *$. It is easily checked that we can derive $\langle\rangle \vdash \text{polyapp}_\Box\, \kappa_1\, (\lambda\alpha : \kappa_1.\, \sigma) : (\Pi\alpha : \kappa_1.\, \sigma) \to (\Pi\alpha : \kappa_1.\, \sigma)$, as required. □

**Kind applications.** Our last polymorphic application function $\text{polyapp}_\Delta$ applies terms to kinds. Terms that can be applied to types have $(\Delta, *)$ product types of the form $\Pi\chi : \Box.\, \tau$, where $\chi$ ranges over kinds and $\tau$ is a type. An application function for terms of a particular $(\Delta, *)$ product type $\Pi\chi : \Box.\, \tau$ should have the type:

$$(\Pi\chi_1 : \Box.\tau) \to \Pi\chi_2 : \Box.\tau[\chi_1 := \chi_2] \qquad (\ddagger)$$

This type is similar to $(\dagger)$, with one important difference: whereas the type variables $\alpha$ and $\beta$ are classified by an arbitrary kind $\kappa$, the kind variables $\chi_1$ and $\chi_2$ can only be classified by $\Box$ (by Theorem 3.1). We express the substitution as $(\lambda\chi_1 : \Box.\, \tau)\, \chi_2$. Letting $\tau'$ denote $\lambda\chi_1 : \Box.\, \tau$, we can write $(\ddagger)$ as:

$$(\Pi\chi_1 : \Box.\, \tau'\, \chi_1) \to \Pi\chi_2 : \Box.\, \tau'\, \chi_2$$

Theorem 3.4 states that $\tau'$ has kind $\Box \to *$. Therefore, we can implement a polymorphic application function for $(\Delta, *)$ as:

$$\text{polyapp}_\Delta = \lambda\tau' : \Box \to *.\, \lambda \mathrm{x} : (\Pi\chi_1 : \Box.\, \tau'\, \chi_1).\, \lambda\chi_2 : \Box.\, \mathrm{x}\, \chi_2$$

The first abstraction of $\text{polyapp}_\Delta$ is a type abstraction that binds the sole component of an arbitrary $(\Delta, *)$ product type. The second abstraction binds a term of the corresponding product type. The final abstraction binds the kind argument. The type of $\text{polyapp}_\Delta$ is:

$$\text{polyapp}_\Delta : \Pi\tau' : \Box \to *.\, (\Pi\chi_1 : \Box.\, \tau'\, \chi_1) \to \Pi\chi_2 : \Box.\, \tau'\, \chi_2$$

**Lemma 3.3.** $\text{polyapp}_\Delta$ *is a polymorphic application function for $(\Delta, *)$ products in System U.*

*Proof.* We have already seen that $\text{polyapp}_\Delta$ is legal and has the required form. It is an axiom of System U that $\Box$ is classified by $\Delta$. Let $(\Pi\chi : A.\sigma)$ be a closed, legal $(\Delta, *)$ product in System U. Then $A$ is closed and classified by $\Delta$. By Theorem 3.1, $A = \Box$. By Theorem 3.4, we have that $(\lambda\chi : \Box.\, \sigma)$ is closed and has kind $\Box \to *$. It is easily checked that we can derive $\langle\rangle \vdash \text{polyapp}_\Delta\, (\lambda\chi : \Box.\, \sigma) : (\Pi\chi : \Box.\, \sigma) \to (\Pi\chi : \Box.\, \sigma)$, as required. □

It is notable that the definition of $\text{polyapp}_\Delta$ uses every rule of System U. The abstractions over x, $\tau'$, and $\chi_2$ are formed by $(*, *)$, $(\Box, *)$, and $(\Delta, *)$, respectively. The type constructor $\pi_\Delta$ is type-level function formed by $(\Box, \Box)$, and the kind $\Box \to *$ of $\tau'$ is formed by $(\Delta, \Box)$.

**Theorem 3.5.** *System U solves the Polymorphic Application Problem.*

*Proof.* Lemmas 3.1, 3.2, and 3.3 show that there exist legal polymorphic application functions in System U for each of its $(s, *)$ rules: $(*, *)$, $(\Box, *)$, and $(\Delta, *)$. □

Our polyapp functions we rely on two properties of System U: that we can decompose product types (Theorem 3.3), and that $\Box$ is the only subject classified by $\Delta$ (Theorem 3.1). System U appears to be a local minimum (excluding the trivial PTS with $\mathcal{R} = \emptyset$): each of the rules $(*, *)$, $(\Box, *)$, $(\Box, \Box)$, $(\Delta, *)$, $(\Delta, \Box)$ is important for our solution.

| | $(*,*)$ | $(\Box,*)$ | $(\Delta,*)$ |
|---|---|---|---|
| System F | ✓ | × | |
| System $F_\omega$ | ✓ | × | |
| System $F_\omega^+$ | ✓ | ✓ | × |
| System U | ✓ | ✓ | ✓ |

**Table 1.** Polymorphic application functions in our PTSs.

### 3.3 Polymorphic application in other systems

That $\Box$ is the only subject classified by $\Delta$ is a key to solving the Polymorphic Application problem for System U: it avoids the need to abstract over $\Box$, which is impossible in System U. However, there is more to the story – in System F, $*$ is the only subject classified by $\Box$, and yet it appears that Polymorphic Application is impossible in System F. The question of whether a PTS supports Polymorphic Application seems to require whole-system consideration. We do not know of a simple test that can answer this question for an arbitrary PTS, and leave the formulation of such a test for future work.

We conjecture that Polymorphic Application is not possible for System F, $F_\omega$, or $F_\omega^+$. Table 1 summarizes the polymorphic application functions that can be implemented in each system using the techniques of Section 3.2. Cells marked with ✓ indicate that a $\text{polyapp}_s$ function for $(s,*)$ products can be defined in the system. Cells marked with × indicate that the definition of $\text{polyapp}_s$ in that system seems to be impossible. Empty cells indicate that $(s,*)$ products are outside the system.

The first column shows that polymorphic application functions for $(*,*)$ products can be implemented in all four languages. This is because a $(*,*)$ product can be decomposed into two types of kind $*$, and each language includes terms that abstract over types of kind $*$ via the $(\Box,*)$ rule.

System F does not support a $\text{polyapp}_\Box$ function for applying terms to types. In System F, decomposing $(\Box,*)$ products (i.e. quantified types) requires higher-order types, which in turn require the rule $(\Box,\Box)$.

System $F_\omega$ can implement a polymorphic application function for System F $(\Box,*)$ products, but not for its own $(\Box,*)$ products. Since all System F types have kind $*$, all $(\Box,*)$ products in System F have the form $\Pi\alpha : *.\ \tau$. These can be decomposed into a single component $\lambda\alpha : *.\ \tau$, which has kind $* \to *$ in $F_\omega$. Since $F_\omega$ includes higher kinds, a $\text{polyapp}_\Box$ function for $F_\omega$ should abstract over the kind, as we did in the $\text{polyapp}_\Box$ for System U. Since $F_\omega$ does not include the rule $(\Delta,*)$ needed for kind abstraction in terms, it cannot implement $\text{polyapp}_\Box$.

System $F_\omega^+$ can implement $\text{polyapp}_\Box$ because it includes the rule $(\Delta,*)$. However, it can't implement $\text{polyapp}_\Delta$ because $(\Delta,*)$ product types can't be decomposed in $F_\omega^+$. Decomposing $(\Delta,*)$ products requires kind-polymorphic types, which in turn require the rule $(\Delta,\Box)$.

The techniques used to implement these polymorphic application functions can also be used to build typed representations. Thus, we can interpret the results of Table 1 to mean: System F can be represented in $F_\omega$, $F_\omega$ can be represented in $F_\omega^+$, $F_\omega^+$ can be represented in U, and U can be represented in itself. In sections 4 and 5 we will use the techniques from this section to build representations of types and terms.

## 4. Representing Types

In this section, we define a process for representing types of kind $*$. Type representations are themselves types. We are primarily interested in term representations, and the purpose of type representations is to enable more typed operations on term representations – in particular, operations like CPS transformation that transform the type of a program in a non-trivial way.

Since the purpose of type representations is to support typed operations on term representations, we only represent types of kind $*$, which are the types of terms. We do not represent higher-order types like $\lambda\alpha : *.\ \alpha$, which has the kind $* \to *$. We only represent types in normal form – products, variables, and applications of variables to one or more types. While the terms of System U are not strongly normalizing, the types are. This ensures that any type of kind $*$ can be normalized and represented. While we only represent closed terms, it is important that we can represent open types. This is because we will represent not only the type of the top-level term being represented, but also the type of each of its subterms. Type representations should support type functions that depend on the intensional structure of their inputs. These play an important role in the implementation of our typed CPS transformation in Section 6.3. We summarize the requirements for our representation of types below.

**Definition 4.1.** *The requirements for our type representation procedure are:*

- *Only legal types can be represented.*
- *Every legal normal-form type of kind $*$ can be represented.*
- *Type representations support operations that fold over the structure of the type.*

**Constructors for Type Representations.** We represent types using higher order abstract syntax (HOAS), inspired by [27] and [30]. Type representations are types of kind U, which is defined inductively from four constructors. Theorem 3.2 states that a type of kind $*$ is either an application of a type variable to zero or more arguments, or a product derived from one of the rules $(*,*)$, $(\Box,*)$, or $(\Delta,*)$. Our type representation includes a constructor for each case.

**Definition 4.2** (Constructors of Type Representations)**.** *The kind* U *is defined inductively by the constructors:*

$$\begin{array}{ll} \langle\rangle \vdash \text{Var} & : * \to \text{U} \\ \langle\rangle \vdash \text{Prod}_* & : \text{U} \to \text{U} \to \text{U} \\ \langle\rangle \vdash \text{Prod}_\Box & : (\Pi\chi : \Box.\ (\chi \to \text{U}) \to \text{U}) \\ \langle\rangle \vdash \text{Prod}_\Delta & : (\Box \to \text{U}) \to \text{U} \end{array}$$

The constructor Var builds representations of type variables applied to zero or more types. The constructors of $\text{Prod}_*$, $\text{Prod}_\Box$ and $\text{Prod}_\Delta$ build representations of $(*,*)$, $(\Box,*)$ and $(\Delta,*)$ products, respectively. Their types are similar to those of the constructors $\pi_*$, $\pi_\Box$, and $\pi_\Delta$ defined in Section 3.1, except that they construct types of kind U instead of types kind $*$. The body of this paper will keep the definitions of U and its constructors abstract. The appendix of the full paper gives concrete definitions of U and its constructors as System U terms.

**Building Type Representations.** The procedure $\triangleright$ for building type representations is defined in Figure 4. It takes as input the derivation of a normal form type of kind $*$ and outputs a representation of the type. The representation of a product type depends on whether it is a $(*,*)$ product, a $(\Box,*)$ product, or a $(\Delta,*)$ product.

An application of a variable to zero or more types is represented by applying the constructor Var to it. A product formed by $(*,*)$ has the form $\tau_1 \to \tau_2$, where $\tau_1$ and $\tau_2$ are each of kind $*$. It is represented by applying the constructor $\text{Prod}_*$ to the representations of $\tau_1$ and $\tau_2$. A product formed by $(\Box,*)$ has the form $\Pi\alpha : \kappa.\ \tau$, where $\tau$ has kind $*$ and $\alpha$ may occur free in $\tau$. We build the representation of $\tau$ in the environment $\Gamma, \alpha : \kappa$, and abstract over $\alpha$ in the representation $\sigma$. The result has kind $\kappa \to \text{U}$ in the environment $\Gamma$. We then apply the constructor $\text{Prod}_\Box$ to the kind $\kappa$ and the resulting abstraction. A product formed by $(\Delta,*)$ has the form

$$\frac{}{\Gamma \vdash \alpha\, A_1\, \ldots A_n : * \rhd \text{Var}\,(\alpha\, A_1\, \ldots\, A_n)}$$

$$\frac{\Gamma \vdash \tau_1 : * \rhd \sigma_1 \qquad \Gamma \vdash \tau_2 : * \rhd \sigma_2}{\Gamma \vdash \tau_1 \to \tau_2 : * \rhd \text{Prod}_*\, \sigma_1\, \sigma_2}$$

$$\frac{\Gamma \vdash \kappa : \Box \qquad \Gamma, \alpha : \kappa \vdash \tau : * \rhd \sigma}{\Gamma \vdash (\Pi\alpha : \kappa.\tau) : * \rhd \text{Prod}_\Box\, \kappa\, (\lambda\alpha : \kappa.\sigma)}$$

$$\frac{\Gamma, \chi : \Box \vdash \tau : * \rhd \sigma}{\Gamma \vdash (\Pi\chi : \Box.\tau) : * \rhd \text{Prod}_\Delta\, (\lambda\chi : \Box.\sigma)}$$

**Figure 4.** Type Representation Procedure

$\Pi\chi : \Box.\, \tau$, where $\tau$ has kind $*$ and $\chi$ may occur free in $\tau$. We build the representation of $\tau$ in the environment $\Gamma, \chi : \Box$, and abstract over $\chi$ in the representation $\sigma$. The result has kind $\Box \to \text{U}$ in the environment $\Gamma$. We then apply the constructor $\text{Prod}_\Delta$ to the resulting abstraction.

**Theorem 4.1** (Kinds of type representations)**.** *If* $\Gamma \vdash \tau : *$ *and* $\Gamma \vdash \tau : * \rhd \sigma$, *then* $\Gamma \vdash \sigma : \text{U}$.

**Example 4.1.** The type of the polymorphic identity function, $\Pi\alpha : *.\alpha \to \alpha$, is represented as $\text{Prod}_\Box\, *\, (\lambda\alpha : *.\, \text{Prod}_*\, (\text{Var}\,\alpha)\, (\text{Var}\,\alpha))$.

When context $\Gamma$ of the derivation $\Gamma \vdash \tau : *$ is clear, we write $\overline{\tau}$ to denote the type $\sigma$ such that $\Gamma \vdash \tau : * \rhd \sigma$.

**Folds over type representations.** Our type representation enables operations that fold over the structure of the type. A fold is defined by supplying case functions for each case of the structure of types of kind $*$: variables (or type applications with a variable in function position), $(*, *)$ products, $(\Box, *)$ products, and $(\Delta, *)$ products.

Case functions for type variables have kind $* \to *$. Variables are the base case for our inductive type representation. The fold function maps an input variable to some type of kind $*$. Since we only represent types of kind $*$, the input type variable must have kind $*$. Case functions for $(*, *)$ products of the form $\tau_1 \to \tau_2$ have kind $* \to * \to *$. Its two arguments of kind $*$ correspond the results of folding over $\tau_1$ and $\tau_2$. Case functions for $(\Box, *)$ products of the form $\Pi\alpha : \kappa.\, \tau$ have kind $\Pi\chi : \Box.\, (\chi \to *) \to *$. An argument type of kind $(\chi \to *)$ will be the result of folding over a type in which a type variable of kind $\chi$ can occur free. Case functions for $(\Delta, *)$ products of the form $\Pi\chi : \Box.\, \tau$ have kind $(\Box \to *) \to *$. An argument type of kind $(\Box \to *)$ will be the result of folding over a type in which a kind variable can occur free.

**Definition 4.3.** *Suppose* var, $\text{prod}_*$, $\text{prod}_\Box$, *and* $\text{prod}_\Delta$ *satisfy:*

$$\begin{array}{ll} \langle\rangle \vdash \text{var} & : * \to * \\ \langle\rangle \vdash \text{prod}_* & : * \to * \to * \\ \langle\rangle \vdash \text{prod}_\Box & : \Pi\chi : \Box.\, (\chi \to *) \to * \\ \langle\rangle \vdash \text{prod}_\Delta & : (\Box \to *) \to * \end{array}$$

*Then* $\text{Fold}[\text{var}, \text{prod}_*, \text{prod}_\Box, \text{prod}_\Delta]$ *denotes the type* F *such that* $\langle\rangle \vdash \text{F} : \text{U} \to *$, *and:*

$$\begin{array}{ll} \text{F}\,\overline{\tau} \equiv_\beta \text{var}\,\tau & \text{if } \tau \text{ is of the form } \alpha\, A_1\, \ldots\, A_n \\ \text{F}\,\overline{\tau} \equiv_\beta \text{prod}_*\, (\text{F}\,\overline{\tau_1})\, (\text{F}\,\overline{\tau_2}) & \text{if } \tau = \tau_1 \to \tau_2,\ \Gamma \vdash \tau_1 : * \\ \text{F}\,\overline{\tau} \equiv_\beta \text{prod}_\Box\, \kappa\, (\lambda\alpha : \kappa.\, \text{F}\,\overline{\tau_1}) & \text{if } \tau = \Pi\alpha : \kappa.\tau_1,\ \Gamma \vdash \kappa : \Box \\ \text{F}\,\overline{\tau} \equiv_\beta \text{prod}_\Delta\, (\lambda\chi : \Box.\, \text{F}\,\overline{\tau_1}) & \text{if } \tau = \Pi\chi : \Box.\, \tau_1 \end{array}$$

Our first example of an operation on type representations is listed in Figure 5. UId recovers a type from its representation. The case function for variables is the identity. The case function for each product type is the corresponding constructor.

$$\text{UId} = \text{Fold}[(\lambda\alpha : *.\, \alpha), \pi_*, \pi_\Box, \pi_\Delta]$$

**Figure 5.** A function that recovers a type from its representation

**Theorem 4.2.** If $\Gamma \vdash \tau : *$, then $\text{UId}\,\overline{\tau} \equiv_\beta \tau$.

We define the components of type representations similarly to the components of types:

**Definition 4.4** (Components of product representations)**.**

- *The components of the representation of a* $(*, *)$ *product type* $\overline{\tau_1 \to \tau_2}$ *are* $\overline{\tau_1}$ *and* $\overline{\tau_2}$.
- *The components of the representation of a* $(\Box, *)$ *product type* $\overline{\Pi\alpha : \kappa.\, \tau}$ *are* $\kappa$ *and* $\lambda\alpha : \kappa.\, \overline{\tau}$.
- *The component of a* $(\Delta, *)$ *product type* $\Pi\chi : \Box.\, \tau$ *is* $\lambda\chi : \Box.\, \overline{\tau}$.

## 5. Representing Terms

In this section we define a process quote($\cdot$) that builds representations of terms. We begin by establishing the requirements for our representation. First and foremost,we should be able to represent every legal term in the language, and representations should themselves be legal terms. All representations should be strongly normalizing, even if they represent a non-normalizing term. In order to be considered useful, we require our representations to support operations that fold over the structure of the term. We summarize our requirements typed representation of terms below.

**Definition 5.1** (Requirements for term representation)**.**

- *Only legal terms can be represented.*
- *Every closed legal term can be represented.*
- *All representations are strongly normalizing.*
- *Representations support folds.*

Given these requirements, what is required to type check representations? Since a representation has different semantics than the term it represents, we expect its type to also be different. On the other hand, we expect the types of a term and its representation to be related. This allows typed operations with result types that depend on the type of the input term.

### 5.1 Representation using PHOAS

We represent terms using typed Parametric Higher Order Abstract Syntax (PHOAS) [12, 35]. The use of PHOAS allows our representation to support multiple operations with different result types. Recall that our type representation, which uses a simpler non-parametric HOAS, only supports operations that produce results of kind $*$. In each case we choose the simplest representation for our needs.

Our representations have types of the form $\text{Exp}\,\overline{\tau}$, where $\overline{\tau}$ is a type representation. The type Exp is defined in Figure 6. It is parametric in a type R of kind $\text{U} \to *$, which is supplied by each operation and determines the result type of the operation. Instantiating a representation of type $\text{Exp}\,\overline{\tau}$ with a result type R yields the type $\text{PExp R}\,\overline{\tau}$, which can be read "$\text{Exp}\,\overline{\tau}$ specialized to parameter R".

The specialized representation type PExp is inductively defined by the constructors listed in Figure 6. There is a constructor for each form of the terms of System U. System U terms are either variables, $\lambda$ abstractions, or applications. The abstractions and applications can be formed by the rules $(*, *)$, $(\Box, *)$, or $(\Delta, *)$.

Our quotation procedure quote($\cdot$) is defined in Figure 7. It relies on a pre-quotation procedure ▶ defined in Figure 8. Given a term

$$\begin{aligned}
\text{mkVar} &: \Pi R : U \to *.\ \Pi\alpha : U.\ R\ \alpha \to \text{PExp}\ R\ \alpha \\
\text{mkAbs}_* &: \Pi R : U \to *.\ \Pi\alpha : U.\ \Pi\beta : U. \\
&\quad (R\ \alpha \to \text{PExp}\ R\ \beta) \to \text{PExp}\ R\ (\text{Prod}_*\ \alpha\ \beta) \\
\text{mkApp}_* &: \Pi R : U \to *.\ \Pi\alpha : U.\ \Pi\beta : U. \\
&\quad \text{PExp}\ R\ (\text{Prod}_*\ \alpha\ \beta) \to \text{PExp}\ R\ \alpha \to \text{PExp}\ R\ \beta \\
\text{mkAbs}_\square &: \Pi R : U \to *.\ \Pi\kappa : \square.\ \Pi\alpha : (\kappa \to U). \\
&\quad (\Pi\beta : \kappa.\ \text{PExp}\ R\ (\alpha\ \beta)) \to \text{PExp}\ R\ (\text{Prod}_\square\ \kappa\ \alpha) \\
\text{mkApp}_\square &: \Pi R : U \to *.\ \Pi\kappa : \square.\ \Pi\alpha : (\kappa \to U). \\
&\quad \text{PExp}\ R\ (\text{Prod}_\square\ \kappa\ \alpha) \to \Pi\beta : \kappa.\ \text{PExp}\ R\ (\alpha\ \beta) \\
\text{mkAbs}_\Delta &: \Pi R : U \to *.\ \Pi\alpha : \square \to U. \\
&\quad (\Pi\chi : \square.\ \text{PExp}\ R\ (\alpha\ \chi)) \to \text{PExp}\ R\ (\text{Prod}_\Delta\ \alpha) \\
\text{mkApp}_\Delta &: \Pi R : U \to *.\ \Pi\alpha : \square \to U. \\
&\quad \text{PExp}\ R\ (\text{Prod}_\Delta\ \alpha) \to \Pi\chi : \square.\ \text{PExp}\ R\ (\alpha\ \chi) \\
\\
\text{Exp} &= \lambda\alpha : U.\ \Pi R : U \to *.\ \text{PExp}\ R\ \alpha
\end{aligned}$$

**Figure 6.** Representation Constructors

$$\frac{\langle\rangle \vdash e : \tau \blacktriangleright q}{\text{quote}(e) = \lambda\, R : U \to *.\ q}$$

**Figure 7.** Quotation

$$\frac{\Gamma \vdash \tau : *}{\Gamma \vdash x : \tau \blacktriangleright \text{mkVar}\ R\ \overline{\tau}\ x}$$

$$\frac{\Gamma \vdash \tau_1 : * \qquad \Gamma, x : \tau_1 \vdash e : \tau_2 \blacktriangleright q}{\Gamma \vdash (\lambda x : \tau_1.e) : \tau_1 \to \tau_2 \blacktriangleright \text{mkAbs}_*\ R\ \overline{\tau_1}\ \overline{\tau_2}\ (\lambda x : R\ \overline{\tau_1}.q)}$$

$$\frac{\Gamma \vdash \tau_2 : * \qquad \Gamma \vdash e_1 : \tau_2 \to \tau \blacktriangleright q_1 \qquad \Gamma \vdash e_2 : \tau_2 \blacktriangleright q_2}{\Gamma \vdash e_1\ e_2 : \tau \blacktriangleright \text{mkApp}_*\ R\ \overline{\tau_2}\ \overline{\tau}\ q_1\ q_2}$$

$$\frac{\Gamma \vdash \kappa : \square \qquad \Gamma, \alpha : \kappa \vdash e : \tau \blacktriangleright q}{\Gamma \vdash (\lambda\alpha : \kappa.e) : (\Pi\alpha : \kappa.\tau) \blacktriangleright \text{mkAbs}_\square\ R\ \kappa\ (\lambda\alpha : \kappa.\overline{\tau})\ (\lambda\alpha : \kappa.q)}$$

$$\frac{\Gamma \vdash \kappa : \square \qquad \Gamma \vdash e : (\Pi\alpha : \kappa.\tau) \blacktriangleright q \qquad (\overline{\tau}[\alpha := \tau_1]) \rightsquigarrow (\overline{\tau[\alpha := \tau_1]}) = c}{\Gamma \vdash e\ \tau_1 : (\tau[\alpha := \tau_1]) \blacktriangleright c\ (\text{mkApp}_\square\ R\ \kappa\ (\lambda\alpha : \kappa.\overline{\tau})\ q\ \tau_1)}$$

$$\frac{\Gamma, \chi : \square \vdash e : \tau \blacktriangleright q}{\Gamma \vdash (\lambda\chi : \square.e) : (\Pi\chi : \square.\tau) \blacktriangleright \text{mkAbs}_\Delta\ R\ (\lambda\chi : \square.\overline{\tau})\ (\lambda\chi : \square.q)}$$

$$\frac{\Gamma \vdash e : (\Pi\chi : \square.\tau) \blacktriangleright q}{\Gamma \vdash e\ \kappa : (\tau[x := \kappa]) \blacktriangleright \text{mkApp}_\Delta\ R\ (\lambda\chi : \square.\overline{\tau})\ q\ \kappa}$$

**Figure 8.** Pre-quotation

of type $\tau$, the pre-quoter produces a term of type PExp R $\overline{\tau}$. Then quote($\cdot$) simply abstracts over R in the result.

The pre-quoter embeds type representations within term representations. This is a key to supporting operations like CPS that transform the type of their input. As is common in HOAS representations, we use abstractions to bind the free variables of a representation. For example, if $\alpha : \kappa \vdash$ e $\blacktriangleright$ q, then $\alpha$ may occur free in q. We close q by abstracting over $\alpha$. If q has type PExp R $\overline{\tau}$, then $\lambda\alpha : \kappa.q$ has type $\Pi\alpha : \kappa$. PExp R $\overline{\tau}$. This reflects that the representation has a free variable, and enables substituting for $\alpha$ by application.

The first rule of pre-quotation handles variables. Representations of variables are constructed using mkVar. Variables are represented metacircularly [28], that is, using other variables. In particular, a variable of type $\tau$ is represented using a variable of type R $\overline{\tau}$.

Abstractions formed by $(*, *)$ bind term variables in terms, and have types of the form $\tau_1 \to \tau_2$. Their representations are constructed using mkAbs$_*$. The types $\overline{\tau_1}$ and $\overline{\tau_2}$ are the components of $\overline{\tau_1 \to \tau_2}$. The premise $\Gamma$, x : $\tau_1 \vdash$ e : $\tau_2 \blacktriangleright$ q builds a representation of the body in the extended environment $\Gamma$, x : $\tau_1$. The abstraction $\lambda$x : R $\tau_1$. q binds the free variable $x$ in the representation of e.

Applications formed by $(*, *)$ apply terms to terms. An application $e_1$ $e_2$, where $e_1$ has the type $\tau_2 \to \tau$, is represented by applying the constructor mkApp$_*$ to the components of $\overline{\tau_2 \to \tau}$, and the representations of $e_1$ and $e_2$.

Abstractions formed by $(\square, *)$ bind type variables in terms, and have types of the form $\Pi\alpha : \kappa.\ \tau$. Their representations are constructed using mkAbs$_\square$. The kind $\kappa$ and type $\lambda\alpha : \kappa.\ \overline{\tau}$ are the components of $\overline{\Pi\alpha : \kappa.\ \tau}$. The premise $\Gamma, \alpha : \kappa \vdash$ e : $\tau \blacktriangleright$ q builds a representation of the body in the extended environment $\Gamma, \alpha : \kappa$. The abstraction $\lambda\alpha : \kappa$. q binds the free variable $\alpha$ in the representation of e.

Applications formed by $(\square, *)$ apply terms to types. Only the term is represented; the type argument is not represented, even if it is of kind $*$. The constructor mkApp$_\square$ is applied to the components of the $\overline{\Pi\alpha : \kappa.\ \tau}$, the representation q of the term e, and the type argument $\tau_1$. The result is a term of type PExp R $\overline{\tau}[\alpha := \tau_1]$. A coercion $c$ of type PExp R $(\overline{\tau}[\alpha := \tau_1]) \to$ PExp R $(\overline{\tau[\alpha := \tau_1]})$ is generated by the binary operation $\rightsquigarrow$. Coercions are discussed further below, and full detail is given in the appendix to the full paper.

Abstractions formed by $(\Delta, *)$ bind kind variables in terms, and have types of the form $\Pi\chi : \square.\ \tau$. Their representations are constructed using mkAbs$_\Delta$. The type $\lambda\chi : \square.\ \overline{\tau}$ is the component of $\overline{\Pi\chi : \square.\ \tau}$. The premise $\Gamma, \chi : \square \vdash$ e : $\tau \blacktriangleright$ q builds a representation of the body in the extended environment $\Gamma, \chi : \square$. The abstraction $\lambda\chi : \square$. q binds the free variable $\chi$ in the representation of e.

Applications of products formed by $(\Delta, *)$ apply terms to kinds. Again, only the term is represented. The constructor mkApp$_\Delta$ is applied to the component of $\overline{\Pi\chi : \square.\ \tau}$, the representation of the term, and the kind argument.

**Example 5.1.** *Let id* = $\lambda\alpha : *.\lambda x : \alpha.x$.

$$\begin{aligned}
\text{quote(id)} = &\lambda R : U \to *. \\
&\text{mkAbs}_\square\ R\ *\ (\lambda\alpha : *.\ \overline{\alpha \to \alpha}) \\
&\quad (\lambda\alpha : *.\ \text{mkAbs}_*\ R\ \overline{\alpha}\ \overline{\alpha} \\
&\qquad (\lambda x : R\ \overline{\alpha}.\ \text{mkVar}\ R\ \overline{\alpha}\ x))
\end{aligned}$$

In bottom-up order, the mkVar term corresponds to the output of the pre-quoter $\blacktriangleright$ on the derivation $\alpha : *, x : \alpha \vdash x : \alpha$, the mkAbs$_*$ term to the output on $\alpha : * \vdash (\lambda x : \alpha.\ x) : \alpha \to \alpha$, and the mkAbs$_\square$ term to the output on $\langle\rangle \vdash$ id : $(\Pi\alpha : *.\alpha \to \alpha)$. At the top-level, quote(id) abstracts over R in the pre-quotation of id.

For convenience, we define a notation $\overline{e}$ as we did for type representations, though its definition is slightly different. When e is a term, $\overline{e}$ denotes its pre-quotation, which allows us to use $\overline{e}$ even when e is not closed.

$$\frac{\Gamma \vdash e : \tau \blacktriangleright q \qquad \langle\rangle \vdash F : U \to *}{\overline{e} = q[R := F]}$$

We allow the environment $\Gamma$ and the result type function F to be implied by the context.

Since variables are represented by variables with different types, we define a representation environment $\overline{\Gamma}$ in which pre-quotations are legal. We define $\overline{\Gamma}$ inductively by the following rules. We allow the result type function F to be implied by context.

**Definition 5.2** (Representation Environment)**.**

$$\begin{array}{lll} \overline{\langle\rangle} = \langle\rangle & & \\ \overline{\Gamma, x : \tau} = \overline{\Gamma}, x : F\,\overline{\tau} & \text{if } \Gamma \vdash \tau : * \\ \overline{\Gamma, \alpha : \kappa} = \overline{\Gamma}, \alpha : \kappa & \text{if } \Gamma \vdash \kappa : \Box \\ \overline{\Gamma, \chi : \Box} = \overline{\Gamma}, \chi : \Box & \end{array}$$

We now formalize the types of pre-quotations and quotations:

**Theorem 5.1.** *If* $\Gamma \vdash e : \tau$ *and* $\langle\rangle \vdash F : U \to *$, *then* $\overline{\Gamma} \vdash \overline{e} : \text{PExp F } \overline{\tau}$.

**Theorem 5.2** (Types of quotations)**.** *If* $\langle\rangle \vdash e : \tau : *$, *and* quote(e) = q, *then* $\langle\rangle \vdash q : \text{Exp } \overline{\tau}$.

**Theorem 5.3.** *If* quote(e) = q, *then* q *is strongly normalizing.*

Authors traditionally define a representation in $\lambda$-calculus to be a normal form [22, 23, 27]. We follow Pfenning and Lee [26] and define constructors for our representation, which allow us to abstract away the details of our encoding. Representations built from our constructors are not normal forms, but reduce to normal forms in a few predictable steps. We provide an example in the appendix to the full paper [1]. It is also possible to define a quoter that produces closed normal forms.

### 5.2 Tying the knot

Theorem 5.2 states that our quotation procedure is complete: every legal System U term can be represented. We achieve self-representation using the techniques developed for our solution to the Polymorphic Application problem in Section 3.2. The type of each polyapp$_s$ function is related to the types of the corresponding representation constructors mkAbs$_s$ and mkApp$_s$.

Each polymorphic application function polyapp$_s$ abstracts over the components of $(s, *)$ product types. We can use UId to define a version of polyapp$_s$ that abstracts over the components of $(s, *)$ type representations. For example, polyapp$_\Delta$ could be defined as:

$$\lambda\alpha : \Box \to U.\ \lambda x : \text{UId}\ (\text{Prod}_\Delta\ \alpha).\ \lambda\chi : \Box.\ x\ \chi$$

The application of $x$ to $\chi$ is legal because UId (Prod$_\Delta$ $\alpha$) is equivalent to $\Pi\chi_1 : \Box.\ \text{UId}\ (\alpha\ \chi_1)$. This version of polyapp$_\Delta$ can have either of the following equivalent types:

- $\Pi\alpha : \Box \to U.\ (\Pi\chi : \Box.\ \text{UId}\ (\alpha\ \chi)) \to \text{UId}\ (\text{Prod}_\Delta\ \alpha)$
- $\Pi\alpha : \Box \to U.\ \text{UId}\ (\text{Prod}_\Delta\ \alpha) \to \Pi\chi : \Box.\ \text{UId}\ (\alpha\ \chi)$

If we replace UId with PExp R in the first type and abstract over R, we get the type of mkAbs$_\Delta$. The same operation on the second type yields the type of mkApp$_\Delta$.

We summarize the results of Section 3.2, Section 4, and Section 5 as follows: Every form of product type in System U can be decomposed, and we can implement a polymorphic application function by abstracting over the components. Further, every form of product type in System U can be represented. Type representations can also be decomposed and the components can be also used to define a polymorphic application function. Finally, we can combine our polymorphic application functions with standard representation techniques to achieve self-representation.

$$\begin{aligned}
\text{Abs}_* &= \lambda R : U \to *.\ \Pi\alpha : U.\ \Pi\beta : U. \\
&\quad (R\ \alpha \to R\ \beta) \to R\ (\text{Prod}_*\ \alpha\ \beta) \\
\text{App}_* &= \lambda R : U \to *.\ \Pi\alpha : U.\ \Pi\beta : U. \\
&\quad R\ (\text{Prod}_*\ \alpha\ \beta) \to R\ \alpha \to R\ \beta \\[1em]
\text{Abs}_\Box &= \lambda R : U \to *.\ \Pi\kappa : \Box.\ \Pi\alpha : (\kappa \to U). \\
&\quad (\Pi\beta : \kappa.\ R\ (\alpha\ \beta)) \to R\ (\text{Prod}_\Box\ \kappa\ \alpha) \\
\text{App}_\Box &= \lambda R : U \to *.\ \Pi\kappa : \Box.\ \Pi\alpha : (\kappa \to U). \\
&\quad R\ (\text{Prod}_\Box\ \kappa\ \alpha) \to \Pi\beta : \kappa.\ R\ (\alpha\ \beta) \\[1em]
\text{Abs}_\Delta &= \lambda R : U \to *.\ \Pi\alpha : \Box \to U. \\
&\quad (\Pi\chi : \Box.\ R\ (\alpha\ \chi)) \to R\ (\text{Prod}_\Delta\ \alpha) \\
\text{App}_\Delta &= \lambda R : U \to *.\ \Pi\alpha : \Box \to U. \\
&\quad R\ (\text{Prod}_\Delta\ \alpha) \to \Pi\chi : \Box.\ R\ (\alpha\ \chi)
\end{aligned}$$

**Figure 9.** Types of Case Functions

### 5.3 Folds over term representations

Our representation of terms is designed to support operations that fold over the structure of the term. A fold is defined by six case functions, one each for abstractions and applications formed by $(*, *)$, $(\Box, *)$, and $(\Delta, *)$. The result of a fold is defined by induction on the structure of the term. For each term, the corresponding case function is applied to the the results of folding over its subterms. This is made formal below.

The types of the case functions of a fold are defined in 9. The types App$_*$, App$_\Box$, and App$_\Delta$ and are similar to the types of our Polymorphic Application functions polyapp$_*$, polyapp$_\Box$ and polyapp$_\Delta$ from Section 3.2. Each App$_s$ types and the type of each polyapp$_s$ function relies on the idea of decomposition. The difference is that the App$_s$ types deal with components of type representations, while the types of the polyapp$_s$ functions deal with components of product types.

The specification of an operation on term representations consists of a result type R, a witness of type Witness R, and six case functions. The witness ensures that for all types $\tau$ and $\tau_1$ such that $\Gamma, \alpha : \kappa \vdash \tau : *$ and $\Gamma \vdash \tau_1 : \kappa$, the quoter can synthesize a coercion of type: $\text{PExp R}\ (\overline{\tau}[\alpha := \tau_1]) \to \text{PExp R}\ (\overline{\tau[\alpha := \tau_1]})$. These coercions are necessary in order to represent type applications. The semantics of a coercion thus depends on the witness, which gives us the flexibility needed to support multiple operations on a single generic representation. We will say more about the coercions for each of our operations in the following section. Witnesses and coercions are described in greater detail in the appendix to the full paper.

**Definition 5.3.** Suppose F, w, abs$_*$, app$_*$, abs$_\Box$, app$_\Box$, abs$_\Delta$, and app$_\Delta$ satisfy:

$$\begin{array}{llll}
\langle\rangle \vdash F & : U \to * & & \\
\langle\rangle \vdash w & : \text{Witness F} & & \\
\langle\rangle \vdash \text{abs}_* & : \text{Abs}_*\ F & \langle\rangle \vdash \text{app}_* & : \text{App}_*\ F \\
\langle\rangle \vdash \text{abs}_\Box & : \text{Abs}_\Box\ F & \langle\rangle \vdash \text{app}_\Box & : \text{App}_\Box\ F \\
\langle\rangle \vdash \text{abs}_\Delta & : \text{Abs}_\Delta\ F & \langle\rangle \vdash \text{app}_\Delta & : \text{App}_\Delta\ F
\end{array}$$

Then fold[F, w, abs$_*$, app$_*$, abs$_\Box$, app$_\Box$, abs$_\Delta$, app$_\Delta$] denotes a term f such that $\langle\rangle \vdash f : \Pi\alpha : U.\text{PExp F}\ \alpha \to F\ \alpha$, and for any context $\Gamma$, term e, and type $\tau$ such that $\Gamma \vdash e : \tau$, we have that:

$$
\begin{array}{ll}
\mathsf{w} & : \mathsf{Witness\ UId} \\
\mathsf{id}_* & = \lambda\alpha : \mathsf{U}.\ \lambda\beta : \mathsf{U}.\ \lambda\mathsf{x} : \mathsf{UId}\ \alpha \to \mathsf{UId}\ \beta.\ \mathsf{x} \\
\mathsf{id}_\Box & = \lambda\kappa : \Box.\ \lambda\alpha : \kappa \to \mathsf{U}.\ \lambda\mathsf{x} : (\Pi\beta : \kappa.\ \mathsf{UId}\ (\alpha\ \beta)).\ \mathsf{x} \\
\mathsf{id}_\Delta & = \lambda\alpha : \Box \to \mathsf{U}.\ \lambda\mathsf{x} : (\Pi\chi : \Box.\ \mathsf{UId}\ (\alpha\ \chi)).\ \mathsf{x} \\
\mathsf{unquote} & = \mathsf{fold}[\mathsf{UId}, \mathsf{w}, \mathsf{id}_*, \mathsf{id}_*, \mathsf{id}_\Box, \mathsf{id}_\Box, \mathsf{id}_\Delta, \mathsf{id}_\Delta]
\end{array}
$$

**Figure 10.** Definition of unquote

If e is a variable, then $\mathsf{f}\ \overline{\tau}\ \overline{\mathsf{e}} \equiv_\beta \mathsf{e}$.
If $\tau = \tau_1 \to \tau_2$, $\Gamma \vdash \tau_1 : *$, and $\mathsf{e} = \lambda\mathsf{x} : \tau_1.\ \mathsf{e}_1$, then
$\mathsf{f}\ \overline{\tau}\ \overline{\mathsf{e}} \equiv_\beta \mathsf{abs}_*\ \overline{\tau_1}\ \overline{\tau_2}\ (\lambda\mathsf{x} : \mathsf{F}\ \overline{\tau_1}.\ \mathsf{f}\ \overline{\tau_2}\ \overline{\mathsf{e}_1})$.
If $\mathsf{e} = \mathsf{e}_1\ \mathsf{e}_2$, $\Gamma \vdash \mathsf{e}_2 : \tau_1 : *$, then
$\mathsf{f}\ \overline{\tau}\ \overline{\mathsf{e}} \equiv_\beta \mathsf{app}_*\ \overline{\tau_1}\ \overline{\tau}\ (\mathsf{f}\ \overline{\tau_1 \to \tau}\ \overline{\mathsf{e}_1})\ (\mathsf{f}\ \overline{\tau_1}\ \overline{\mathsf{e}_2})$.
If $\tau = \Pi\alpha : \kappa.\ \tau_1$, $\Gamma \vdash \kappa : \Box$, and $\mathsf{e} = \lambda\alpha : \kappa.\ \mathsf{e}_1$, then
$\mathsf{f}\ \overline{\tau}\ \overline{\mathsf{e}} \equiv_\beta \mathsf{abs}_\Box\ \kappa\ (\lambda\alpha : \kappa.\ \overline{\tau_1})\ (\lambda\alpha : \kappa.\ \mathsf{f}\ \overline{\tau_1}\ \overline{\mathsf{e}_1})$.
If $\mathsf{e} = \mathsf{e}_1\ \tau_2$, $\Gamma \vdash \kappa : \Box$, and $\Gamma \vdash \mathsf{e}_1 : \Pi\alpha : \kappa.\ \tau_1$, then
$\mathsf{f}\ \overline{\tau}\ \overline{\mathsf{e}} \equiv_\beta c\ (\mathsf{app}_\Box\ \kappa\ (\lambda\alpha : \kappa.\ \overline{\tau_1})\ (\mathsf{f}\ \overline{\Pi\alpha : \kappa.\ \tau_1}\ \overline{\mathsf{e}_1})\ \tau_2)$
for some coercion c.
If $\tau = \Pi\chi : \Box.\ \tau_1$, and $\mathsf{e} = \lambda\chi : \Box.\ \mathsf{e}_1$, then
$\mathsf{f}\ \overline{\tau}\ \overline{\mathsf{e}} \equiv_\beta \mathsf{abs}_\Delta\ (\lambda\chi : \Box.\overline{\tau_1})\ (\lambda\chi : \Box.\ \mathsf{f}\ \overline{\tau_1}\ \overline{\mathsf{e}_1})$.
If $\mathsf{e} = \mathsf{e}_1\ \kappa$, $\Gamma \vdash \kappa : \Box$, and $\Gamma \vdash \mathsf{e}_1 : \Pi\chi : \Box.\ \tau_1$, then
$\mathsf{f}\ \overline{\tau}\ \overline{\mathsf{e}} \equiv_\beta \mathsf{app}_\Delta\ (\lambda\chi : \Box.\ \overline{\tau_1})\ (\mathsf{f}\ \overline{\Pi\chi : \Box.\tau_1}\ \overline{\mathsf{e}_1})\ \kappa$.

Definition 5.3 states that the operation specified by fold[F, w, $\mathsf{abs}_*$, $\mathsf{app}_*$, $\mathsf{abs}_\Box$, $\mathsf{app}_\Box$, $\mathsf{abs}_\Delta$, $\mathsf{app}_\Delta$] has the semantics expected of a fold. The seven cases are mutually exclusive and exhaustive: a term in System U is either a variable, an abstraction, or an application. Abstractions and applications can be formed by one of three rules: $(*, *)$, $(\Box, *)$, $(\Delta, *)$.

## 6. Operations

In this section we show how to program three benchmark operations on our representation. The first, called unquote, is a typed self-recognizer – a self-interpreter that recovers an term from its representation. The second, called isAbs, is a simple example of an intensional predicate. It tests whether its input represents an abstraction or an application. The third, and most complex, is a typed self-applicable continuation-passing-style (CPS) transformation.

### 6.1 Unquote

Our self-recognizer unquote is defined in Figure 10. It produces results with types determined by UId. Each case function in the definition of unquote is an identity function. If a term e has type $\tau$, then unquoting a representation of e produces a term of type UId $\overline{\tau}$. Theorem 4.2 states that UId $\overline{\tau}$ is equivalent to $\tau$.

**Theorem 6.1** (Type of unquote).

$$\langle\rangle \vdash \mathsf{unquote} : (\Pi\alpha : \mathsf{U}.\ \mathsf{Exp}\ \alpha \to \mathsf{UId}\ \alpha)$$

Unquote folds identity functions over the term. The result is equivalent to the original term.

**Theorem 6.2** (Correctness of unquote).
*If* $\langle\rangle \vdash \mathsf{e} : \tau$ *and* quote(e) = q, *then* unquote $\overline{\tau}$ q $\equiv_\beta$ e.

The coercions produced by the witness for unquote are always identity functions. Consider the type UId $(\overline{\tau}[\alpha := \tau_1]) \to$ UId $\overline{\tau[\alpha := \tau_1]}$, which is the type of an arbitrary coercion for unquote. This type is equivalent to $\tau[\alpha := \tau_1] \to \tau[\alpha := \tau_1]$.

### 6.2 isAbs

Our second benchmark operation isAbs is shown in Figure 11. isAbs tests if its input is a representation of an abstraction. This demonstrates that we can define operations on a representation that cannot be defined directly on the represented term. The result type UBool of isAbs is the constant Bool function. Each case function in the definition of isAbs is a constant function. It discards the result of folding over its subterm(s), since we are only interested in the outermost constructor of the representation. The case functions for abstractions are constant true functions and the case functions for applications are constant false functions.

$$
\begin{array}{ll}
\mathsf{Bool} = & \Pi\alpha : *.\ \alpha \to \alpha \to \alpha \\
\mathsf{true} = & \lambda\alpha : *.\ \lambda t : \alpha.\ \lambda f : \alpha.\ t \\
\mathsf{false} = & \lambda\alpha : *.\ \lambda t : \alpha.\ \lambda f : \alpha.\ f
\end{array}
$$

$$\mathsf{UBool} = \lambda\alpha : \mathsf{U}.\ \mathsf{Bool}$$

$$
\begin{array}{ll}
\mathsf{w} & : \mathsf{Witness\ UBool} \\
\mathsf{abs}_* & = \lambda\mathsf{T}_1 : *.\ \lambda\mathsf{T}_2 : *.\ \lambda\mathsf{f} : \mathsf{Bool} \to \mathsf{Bool.true} \\
\mathsf{app}_* & = \lambda\mathsf{T}_1 : *.\ \lambda\mathsf{T}_2 : *.\ \lambda\mathsf{f} : \mathsf{Bool}.\ \lambda\mathsf{e}_1 : \mathsf{Bool.\ false} \\
\mathsf{abs}_\Box & = \lambda\chi : \Box.\ \lambda\mathsf{F} : \chi \to *.\ \lambda\mathsf{e}_1 : \chi \to \mathsf{Bool.\ true} \\
\mathsf{app}_\Box & = \lambda\chi : \Box.\ \lambda\mathsf{F} : \chi \to *.\ \lambda\mathsf{e}_1 : \mathsf{Bool}.\ \lambda\mathsf{x} : \chi.\ \mathsf{false} \\
\mathsf{abs}_\Delta & = \lambda\mathsf{T}_1 : \Box \to *.\ \lambda\mathsf{e}_1 : \Box \to \mathsf{Bool.\ true} \\
\mathsf{app}_\Delta & = \lambda\mathsf{T}_1 : \Box \to *.\ \lambda\mathsf{e}_1 : \mathsf{Bool}.\ \lambda\chi : \Box.\mathsf{false} \\
\mathsf{isAbs} & = \mathsf{fold}[\mathsf{UBool}, \mathsf{w}, \mathsf{abs}_*, \mathsf{app}_*, \mathsf{abs}_\Box, \mathsf{app}_\Box, \mathsf{abs}_\Delta, \mathsf{app}_\Delta]
\end{array}
$$

**Figure 11.** Specification of isAbs

**Theorem 6.3** (Type of isAbs).

$$\langle\rangle \vdash \mathsf{isAbs} : (\Pi\alpha : \mathsf{U}.\ \mathsf{Exp}\ \alpha \to \mathsf{Bool})$$

The application of isAbs to the representation of a term of type $\tau$ produces a term of type UBool $\overline{\tau}$, which is equivalent to Bool. Like those for UId, coercions for UBool types are identity functions. Consider the type UBool $(\overline{\tau}[\alpha := \tau_1]) \to$ UBool $\overline{\tau[\alpha := \tau_1]}$, which is the type of an arbitrary coercion for isAbs. Since UBool is a constant function, this type is equivalent to Bool $\to$ Bool.

**Theorem 6.4** (Correctness of isAbs).
*If* $\langle\rangle \vdash \mathsf{e} : \tau : *$ *and* quote(e) = q *then:*

- *If* $\mathsf{e} = \lambda x : \mathsf{A}.\mathsf{e}_1$, *then* isAbs $\overline{\tau}$ q $\equiv_\beta$ true.
- *If* $\mathsf{e} = \mathsf{e}_1\ \mathsf{A}$, *then* isAbs $\overline{\tau}$ q $\equiv_\beta$ false.

### 6.3 Continuation-Passing Style

In this section, we implement a type call-by-name continuation-passing style (CPS) transformation on our representation. CPS transformation is commonly used in compilers for functional languages. It makes the evaluation order (call-by-name in our case) explicit, and eliminates the need for a control-stack. There are examples of typed CPS transformations in the literature, though ours is the first that is self-applicable. We extend the typed CPS transformation of [27], which operates on typed representations of simply typed $\lambda$ calculus. To transform abstractions and applications of types and kinds, we extend the technique used by Morrisett et al [24] to transform System F type abstractions and applications.

The result of applying the CPS transformation to the representation of a term of type $\tau$ is a term of type CPS $\overline{\tau}$. The type CPS is shown in Figure 12. CPS is defined via a fold $\mathsf{CPS}_1$ and a helper function Ct. The CPS-transformation itself is defined in Figure 13.

**Theorem 6.5** (Type of cps).

$$\langle\rangle \vdash cps : (\Pi\alpha : U.\ Exp\ \alpha \to CPS\ \alpha)$$

Coercions for CPS types are not identity functions, unlike those for UId and UBool types. As a simple example, note that for type variables $\alpha$ and $\beta$, CPS $(\overline{\alpha}[\alpha := \beta \to \beta])$ is not equivalent to CPS $(\overline{\alpha[\alpha := \beta \to \beta]})$. The former simplifies to CPS (Var $(\beta \to$

$$\begin{aligned}
\text{Ct} &= \lambda \text{T} : *. \, \Pi \, \text{V} : *. \, (\text{T} \to \text{V}) \to \text{V} \\
\\
\text{var} &= \lambda \alpha : *. \, \alpha \\
\text{prod}_* &= \lambda \alpha : *. \, \lambda \beta : *. \, \text{Ct} \, \alpha \to \text{Ct} \, \beta \\
\text{prod}_\square &= \lambda \chi : \square. \, \lambda \alpha : \chi \to *. \, \Pi \beta : \chi. \, \text{Ct} \, (\alpha \, \beta) \\
\text{prod}_\Delta &= \lambda \text{T}_1 : \square \to *. \, \Pi \chi : \square. \, \text{Ct} \, (\text{T}_1 \, \chi) \\
\text{CPS}_1 &= \text{Fold}[\text{var}, \text{prod}_*, \text{prod}_\square, \text{prod}_\Delta] \\
\\
\text{CPS} &= \lambda \text{T} : \text{U}. \, \text{Ct} \, (\text{CPS}_1 \, \text{T})
\end{aligned}$$

**Figure 12.** The result type of CPS transformation

$$\begin{aligned}
\text{w} &: \text{Witness CPS} \\
\text{abs}_* &= \lambda \alpha : \text{U}. \, \lambda \beta : \text{U}. \, \lambda \text{f} : \text{CPS} \, \alpha \to \text{CPS} \, \beta. \\
&\quad \lambda \text{V} : *. \, \lambda \text{k} : (\text{CPS} \, \alpha \to \text{CPS} \, \beta) \to \text{V}. \, \text{k} \, \text{f} \\
\\
\text{app}_* &= \lambda \alpha : \text{U}. \, \lambda \beta : \text{U}. \, \lambda \text{f} : \text{CPS} \, (\text{Prod}_* \, \alpha \, \beta). \, \lambda \text{x} : \text{CPS} \, \alpha. \\
&\quad \lambda \text{V} : *. \, \lambda \text{k} : (\text{CPS}_1 \, \beta) \to \text{V}. \\
&\quad \text{f} \, \text{V} \, (\lambda \text{g} : \text{CPS} \, \alpha \to \text{CPS} \, \beta. \, \text{g} \, \text{x} \, \text{V} \, \text{k}) \\
\\
\text{abs}_\square &= \lambda \chi : \square. \, \lambda \alpha : \chi \to \text{U}. \, \lambda \text{e} : (\Pi \beta : \chi. \, \text{CPS} \, (\alpha \, \beta)). \\
&\quad \lambda \text{V} : *. \, \lambda \text{k} : (\text{CPS}_1 \, (\text{Prod}_\square \, \chi \, \alpha)) \to \text{V}. \, \text{k} \, \text{e} \\
\\
\text{app}_\square &= \lambda \chi : \square. \, \lambda \alpha : (\chi \to \text{U}). \, \lambda \text{e} : \text{CPS} \, (\text{Prod}_\square \, \chi \, \alpha). \, \lambda \beta : \chi. \\
&\quad \lambda \text{V} : *. \, \lambda \text{k} : (\text{CPS}_1 \, (\alpha \, \beta)) \to \text{V}. \\
&\quad \text{e} \, \text{V} \, (\lambda \text{e}_1 : (\Pi \beta_1 : \chi. \, \text{CPS} \, (\alpha \, \beta_1)).\text{e}_1 \, \beta \, \text{V} \, \text{k}) \\
\\
\text{abs}_\Delta &= \lambda \alpha : \square \to \text{U}. \, \lambda \text{e} : \Pi \chi : \square. \, \text{CPS} \, (\alpha \, \chi). \\
&\quad \lambda \text{V} : *. \, \lambda \text{k} : \text{CPS}_1 \, (\text{Prod}_\Delta \, \alpha) \to \text{V}. \, \text{k} \, \text{e} \\
\\
\text{app}_\Delta &= \lambda \alpha : \square \to \text{U}. \, \lambda \text{e} : \text{CPS} \, (\text{Prod}_\Delta \, \alpha). \, \lambda \chi : \square. \\
&\quad \text{e} \, \text{V} \, (\lambda \text{e}_1 : (\Pi \chi_1 : \square. \, \text{CPS} \, (\alpha \, \chi_1)).\text{e}_1 \, \chi \, \text{V} \, \text{k}) \\
\\
\text{cps} &= \text{fold}[\text{CPS}, \text{w}, \text{abs}_*, \text{app}_*, \text{abs}_\square, \text{app}_\square, \text{abs}_\Delta, \text{app}_\Delta]
\end{aligned}$$

**Figure 13.** Specification of cps

$\beta$)), and the latter to CPS (Prod$_*$ (Var $\beta$) (Var $\beta$)). Coercions for CPS types add and remove continuations as necessary.

We don't attempt to formally verify the correctness of cps, though we validate it by testing it on the polyapp functions from Section 3.2.

## 7. Experiments

We conduct experiments using an implementation of System U, which is available from our website [1]. We implement a parser in Ohm, a domain specific language for writing parsers and the successor to OMeta [34]. The parser generates abstract syntax for our Haskell implementation of System U, which includes type and term quoters, a validity checker, an evaluator, and an incomplete $\beta,\eta$-equivalence checker. We have used the implementation to mechanically check that all System U terms, types and kinds presented in the paper are legal, and to verify the equivalence theorems. We have verified that self-applications of unquote, isAbs, and cps are legal and have normal forms. Furthermore, self-application of unquote is equivalent to unquote itself, and self-application of isAbs evaluates to the Church boolean true:

$$\frac{\text{quote(unquote)} = \text{q}}{\text{unquote} \; \overline{(\Pi \alpha : \text{U}. \, \text{Exp} \, \alpha \to \text{UId} \, \alpha)} \; \text{q} \equiv_{\beta,\eta} \text{unquote}}$$

| | | |
|---|---|---|
| $\text{F}_\omega^*$ | $\mathcal{S}$ | $*, \square$ |
| | $\mathcal{A}$ | $* : \square, \square : \square$ |
| | $\mathcal{R}$ | $(*, *), (\square, *), (\square, \square)$ |

**Figure 14.** PTS specification of $\text{F}_\omega^*$

$$\frac{\text{quote(isAbs)} = \text{q}}{\text{isAbs} \; \overline{(\Pi \alpha : \text{U}. \, \text{Exp} \, \alpha \to \text{UBool} \, \alpha)} \; \text{q} \equiv_{\beta,\eta} \text{true}}$$

We have validated cps by applying it to each of our polyapp functions from Section 3.2.

## 8. Related Work

The problem of typed self-representation has been studied since 1991, when Pfenning and Lee considered whether System F ($\lambda 2$) could represent itself [26]. They found that "metacircularity seems to be impossible" for System F. However, they developed several typed representations of one language in another – System F in System $\text{F}_\omega$ , and $\text{F}_\omega$ in $\text{F}_\omega^+$. Their representation technique inspired our own. They use higher order abstract syntax similar to ours, with two important differences. They don't represent types, and their quoter does not change the types of variables. Each of these is important for our typed cps transformation.

The key idea of decomposition of product types is already present in Pfenning and Lee [26]. The idea recurs throughout the literature on typed HOAS representations. In the setting of pure type systems, the pattern becomes more clear. We identify decomposition of product types and abstraction of the resulting components as key requirements for typed representation of a pure type system.

Rendel, Ostermann, and Hofer [27] defined the first typed self-representation and self-recognizer (which they called eval). They study a language $\text{F}_\omega^*$ defined in Figure 14. Like $\text{F}_\omega$, System $\text{F}_\omega^*$ contains the rule $(\square, \square)$ which allows formation of higher-order types. Unlike $\text{F}_\omega$, which classifies types using a family of kinds induced by the sort $\Delta$ and axiom $\square : \Delta$, System $\text{F}_\omega^*$ adds an axiom $\square : \square$, which forms types that classify other types. Types that classify other types play the role of "kind" in System $\text{F}_\omega^*$. This is sufficient to tie the knot: abstractions formed by $(\square, *)$ can abstract over both types and "kinds" in terms. Similarly, $(\square, \square)$ can abstract over both types and "kinds" in types.

Our type representation is partly inspired by that of [27], which represents the types of simply typed $\lambda$-calculus in $\text{F}_\omega^*$. They use type representations in a representation of simply-typed $\lambda$-calculus in $\text{F}_\omega^*$, which supports a typed CPS transformation. Our self-representation of System U and CPS transformation are also inspired by their representation and CPS transformation of simply-typed $\lambda$-calculus.

Like System U, System $\text{F}_\omega^*$ is not normalizing. Unlike System U, type checking of $\text{F}_\omega^*$ is undecidable due to the $(\square, \square)$ rule. We conjecture that System U can be embedded into $\text{F}_\omega^*$, but that System $\text{F}_\omega^*$ cannot be embedded into System U.

Our representation of types is also inspired by Saha et al. [30]. They study intensional type analysis for $\lambda_i^\omega$ which, like System U, includes type and kind polymorphism. They encode base types of kind $\Omega$ (analogous to $*$ in System U) using HOAS. The kinds of their HOAS type constructors parallel the kinds of the constructors of our type representations.

| $\lambda_i^\omega$ | Kind | System U | Kind |
|---|---|---|---|
| $\to$ | $\Omega \to \Omega \to \Omega$ | $\text{Prod}_*$ | $\text{U} \to \text{U} \to \text{U}$ |
| $\forall$ | $\forall \chi.(\chi \to \Omega) \to \Omega$ | $\text{Prod}_\square$ | $\Pi \chi : \square.(\chi \to \text{U}) \to \text{U}$ |
| $\forall^+$ | $(\forall \chi.\Omega) \to \Omega$ | $\text{Prod}_\Delta$ | $(\square \to \text{U}) \to \text{U}$ |

Despite notational differences, there is a direct correspondence between the kinds of the constructors for $\lambda_i^\omega$ types and our type representations. The binders $\forall$ and $\Pi$ play the same role in each calculus. Furthermore, in System U $\Box \rightarrow$ U is shorthand for $\Pi\chi : \Box.$U (since $\chi$ does not occur free in U). A subtle difference is that there is no classifier for the kinds of $\lambda_i^\omega$ (they use a well-formedness condition), while in our PTS formulation of System U all kinds are classified by $\Box$. Saha et al. include a type operator Typerec for intensional type analysis of base types based on folds. They support fold operations that produce higher-kinded results. The Typerec operator is primitive, which avoids the need for type representations. They did not study self-representation of System $\lambda_i^\omega$, and it is an open question whether it would be possible. We conjecture that System U can be embedded into $\lambda_i^\omega$, but $\lambda_i^\omega$ cannot be embedded into System U.

Typed representation has been extensively studied, and is still an active area of research. Chen and Xi [10, 11] studied typed representation and typed meta-programming. Carette, Kiselyov and Shan [9] use typed representation to build tagless interpretations. McBride [20] achieved a metacircular representation of dependently typed languages in Agda. Axelsson [3] developed a technique for building generic, composable typed representations as a solution to the expression problem [33]. Each of these is important related work, and we have learned from and been inspired by them, even though they did not study self-representation.

## 9. Future Work

*Size.* Our representations do not support operations that measure the size of a term. This is a limitation of our higher order abstract syntax representation. Abstractions in the representation, particularly type abstractions, can block access to the size of subterms. Assuming the size operation should produce results of some closed type Nat, we would need a way to convert a term of type $\Pi\alpha : \kappa.$ Nat to Nat. The quantification $\alpha$ is redundant, since $\alpha$ does not occur free in Nat. In order to recover the Nat, we would have to apply the term of type $\Pi\alpha : \kappa.$Nat to a type of kind $\kappa$. This is not always possible, since not all System U kinds are inhabited. In [27] this was addressed by adding a type constant $\bot : \Pi\alpha : \Box.\alpha$, which could be used to apply these abstractions.

*Beyond kind* $*$. Our representation of types is limited to types of kind $*$. Full representation of types is desirable, as it may eliminate the need for coercions and the witnesses that enable coercions. Full representation may also enable more operations. It is an open question whether full type representation is possible in System U.

*Without type representation.* At the other end of the type representation spectrum, we can consider representation of terms that don't require representation of types. We represent types in order to support our typed CPS transformation. In particular, type representations allow us to give cps the polymorphic type $\Pi\alpha :$ U.Exp $\alpha \rightarrow$ CPS $\alpha$. The input and output types Exp $\alpha$ and CPS $\alpha$ are both defined in terms of the quantified variable $\alpha$. Our other operations, unquote and isAbs, do not require any representation of types. It is possible to define a simpler representation type $\text{Exp}_1$ of kind $* \rightarrow *$, and a quotation procedure that represents terms of type $\tau$ with terms of types $\text{Exp}_1\ \tau$. The representation type and quoter would be similar to those from Rendel, Ostermann, Hofer [27]. In particular, we would no longer require coercions.

*Strong normalization.* Of the two $\lambda$-calculi System $F_\omega^*$ and System U known to support typed self-representations, neither is strongly normalizing. It is an open question whether a language with decidable type checking and strong normalization can support typed self-representation.

*Representing open terms.* Our quoter changes the types of variables, which is important for our cps transformation, but also limits our representations to closed terms. Pfenning and Lee did not change the type of variables, which enabled them to represent free variables (i.e. those bound outside the representation) in the same way as bound variables. It is possible to extend our representation type with a new constructor for representing free variables, with the type:

$$\Pi \text{R} : \text{U} \rightarrow *.\Pi\alpha : *.\alpha \rightarrow \text{PExp R (Var } \alpha)$$

To represent a free variable of type $\tau$, the quoter would first apply this constructor, producing a term of type PExp R (Var $\tau$). Then it would synthesize a coercion to change the type to PExp R $\overline{\tau}$. Note that Var $\tau \equiv \overline{\alpha}[\alpha := \tau]$ and that $\overline{\tau} \equiv \overline{\alpha[\alpha := \tau]}$.

*Dependent Types.* We can extend System U with dependent types by adding to $\mathcal{R}$ the rule $(*, \Box)$ that forms types that abstract over terms. The resulting system still supports polymorphic application, which indicates that it might also support self-representation. Compared to the polyapp functions for System U, the only change required is to $\text{polyapp}_*$, since $(*, *)$ products can now be dependent. For example, in a product type $\Pi x : \tau_1.\ \tau_2$ formed by $(*, *)$, the bound variable $x$ can now occur free in $\tau_2$. The $\text{polyapp}_*$ function for the extended system could be defined as:

$$\lambda\tau_1 : *.\ \lambda\tau_2 : \tau_1 \rightarrow *.\ (\Pi x : \tau_1.\tau_2\ x) \rightarrow \Pi y : \tau_1.\ \tau_2\ y$$

Note that the kind $\tau_1 \rightarrow *$ is formed by $(*, \Box)$. We still have the property that $\Box$ is the only element of $\Delta$, which is key to tying the knot. However, the addition of dependent types would raise two challenges for type representation. The first is due to the introduction of non-normalizing types (e.g. because types can contain non-normalizing terms). Our type representation in this paper only applies to types in normal form. Second, the type representation must consider how to represent types that depend on terms.

## 10. Conclusion

The question of whether a meaningful notion of typed self-representation is possible for a language with decidable type checking has been open since 1991 [26]. We answer in the affirmative by presenting the first typed self-representation for a $\lambda$-calculus with decidable type checking. Our calculus is System U, which was introduced in Girard's PhD thesis [16]. We embed representations of types into representations of terms, which enable operations like CPS transformation that change the type of a term. Our representation supports operations that iterate over the term, and we provide three example self-applicable operations: a typed self-recognizer that recovers a term from its representation, a predicate that tests the intensional structure of a term, and a typed CPS transformation. Ours is the first typed self-applicable CPS transformation. We have validated our results by conducting experiments using an implementation of System U in Haskell.

*Acknowledgments.* We thank John Bender, Mahdi Eslamimehr, Barry Jay, Todd Millstein, Cody Roux, Aaron Stump, and the POPL reviewers for helpful comments, discussions, and suggestions. This material is based upon work supported by the National Science Foundation under Grant Number 1219240.

## References

[1] The webpage accompanying this paper is available at http://compilers.cs.ucla.edu/popl15/. The full paper with the appendix is available there, as are the source code for our implementation of System U and our operations.

[2] Harold Abelson, Gerald Jay Sussman, and Julie Sussman. *Structure and Interpretation of Computer Programs.* MIT Press, 1985.

[3] Emil Axelsson. A generic abstract syntax model for embedded languages. *SIGPLAN Not.*, 47(9):323–334, September 2012.

[4] Henk Barendregt. Self-interpretations in lambda calculus. *J. Funct. Program*, 1(2):229–233, 1991.

[5] HP Barendregt. *Handbook of Logic in Computer Science (vol. 2): Background: Computational Structures: Abramski, S. (ed)*, chapter Lambda Calculi with Types. Oxford University Press, Inc., New York, NY, 1993.

[6] Gilles Barthe. Type-checking injective pure type systems. *J. Funct. Program.*, 9(6):675–698, November 1999.

[7] Michel Bel. A recursion theoretic self interpreter for the lambda-calculus. http://www.belxs.com/michel/#selfint.

[8] Alessandro Berarducci and Corrado Böhm. A self-interpreter of lambda calculus having a normal form. In *CSL*, pages 85–99, 1992.

[9] Jacques Carette, Oleg Kiselyov, and Chung-chieh Shan. Finally tagless, partially evaluated: Tagless staged interpreters for simpler typed languages. *Journal of Functional Programming*, 19(5):509–543, 2009.

[10] Chiyan Chen and Hongwei Xi. Meta-Programming through Typeful Code Representation. In *Proceedings of the Eighth ACM SIGPLAN International Conference on Functional Programming*, pages 275–286, Uppsala, Sweden, August 2003.

[11] Chiyan Chen and Hongwei Xi. Meta-Programming through Typeful Code Representation. *Journal of Functional Programming*, 15(6):797–835, 2005.

[12] Adam Chlipala. Parametric higher-order abstract syntax for mechanized semantics. In *Proceedings of the 13th ACM SIGPLAN International Conference on Functional Programming*, ICFP '08, pages 143–156, New York, NY, USA, 2008. ACM.

[13] Brendan Eich. Narcissus. `http://mxr.mozilla.org/mozilla/source/js/narcissus/jsexec.js`, 2010.

[14] Herman Geuvers and Mark-Jan Nederhof. Modular proof of strong normalization for the calculus of constructions. *J. Funct. Program.*, 1(2):155–189, 1991.

[15] Jan Herman Geuvers. *Logics and type systems*. 1993.

[16] Jean-Yves Girard. *Interprétation fonctionelle et élimination des coupures de l'arithmétique d'ordre supérieur*. PhD thesis, Université Paris VII, 1972.

[17] Barry Jay and Jens Palsberg. Typed self-interpretation by pattern matching. In *Proceedings of ICFP'11, ACM SIGPLAN International Conference on Functional Programming*, pages 247–258, Tokyo, September 2011.

[18] Stephen C. Kleene. $\lambda$-definability and recursiveness. *Duke Math. J.*, pages 340–353, 1936.

[19] Oleg Mazonka and Daniel B. Cristofani. A very short self-interpreter. http://arxiv.org/html/cs/0311032v1, November 2003.

[20] Conor McBride. Outrageous but meaningful coincidences: Dependent type-safe syntax and evaluation. In *Proceedings of the 6th ACM SIGPLAN Workshop on Generic Programming*, WGP '10, pages 1–12, New York, NY, USA, 2010. ACM.

[21] John McCarthy. Recursive functions of symbolic expressions and their computation by machine, part i. *Commun. ACM*, 3(4):184–195, April 1960.

[22] Torben Æ. Mogensen. Efficient self-interpretations in lambda calculus. *Journal of Functional Programming*, 2(3):345–363, 1992. See also DIKU Report D–128, Sep 2, 1994.

[23] Torben Æ. Mogensen. Linear-time self-interpretation of the pure lambda calculus. *Higher-Order and Symbolic Computation*, 13(3):217–237, 2000.

[24] Greg Morrisett, David Walker, Karl Crary, and Neal Glew. From System F to typed assembly language. *ACM Trans. Program. Lang. Syst.*, 21(3):527–568, May 1999.

[25] Matthew Naylor. Evaluating Haskell in Haskell. *The Monad.Reader*, 10:25–33, 2008.

[26] Frank Pfenning and Peter Lee. Metacircularity in the polymorphic $\lambda$-calculus. *Theoretical Computer Science*, 89(1):137–159, 1991.

[27] Tillmann Rendel, Klaus Ostermann, and Christian Hofer. Typed self-representation. In *Proceedings of PLDI'09, ACM SIGPLAN Conference on Programming Language Design and Implementation*, pages 293–303, June 2009.

[28] John C. Reynolds. Definitional interpreters for higher-order programming languages. In *Proceedings of 25th ACM National Conference*, pages 717–740. ACM Press, 1972. The paper later appeared in Higher-Order and Symbolic Computation, 11, 363–397 (1998).

[29] Andreas Rossberg. HaMLet. http://www.mpi-sws.org/ rossberg/hamlet, 2010.

[30] Bratin Saha, Valery Trifonov, and Zhong Shao. Intensional analysis of quantified types. *ACM Trans. Program. Lang. Syst.*, 25(2):159–209, 2003.

[31] Fangmin Song, Yongsen Xu, and Yuechen Qian. The self-reduction in lambda calculus. *Theoretical Computer Science*, 235(1):171–181, March 2000.

[32] John Tromp. Binary lambda calculus and combinatory logic. In *Kolmogorov Complexity and Applications*, 2006. A Revised Version is available at http://homepages.cwi.nl/ tromp/cl/LC.pdf.

[33] Philip Wadler. The expression problem. http://www.daimi.au.dk/ madst/tool/papers/expression.txt.

[34] Alessandro Warth and Ian Piumarta. Ometa: An object-oriented language for pattern matching. In *Proceedings of the 2007 Symposium on Dynamic Languages*, DLS '07, pages 11–19, New York, NY, USA, 2007. ACM.

[35] Geoffrey Washburn and Stephanie Weirich. Boxes go bananas: Encoding higher-order abstract syntax with parametric polymorphism. In *Proceedings of the Eighth ACM SIGPLAN International Conference on Functional Programming*, ICFP '03, pages 249–262, New York, NY, USA, 2003. ACM.

[36] Wikipedia. PyPy. http://en.wikipedia.org/wiki/PyPy, 2010.

[37] Wikipedia. Rubinius. http://en.wikipedia.org/wiki/Rubinius, 2010.

[38] Tetsuo Yokoyama and Robert Glück. A reversible programming language and its invertible self-interpreter. In *Proceedings of PEPM'07, ACM Symposium on Partial Evaluation and Semantics-Based Program Manipulation*, 2007.

# Coding by Everyone, Every Day

Peter Lee
Microsoft Research
petelee@microsoft.com

**Abstract**

In recent years, advances in machine learning and related fields have led to significant advances in a range of user-interface technologies, including audio processing, speech recognition, and natural language processing. These advances in turn have enabled speech-based digital assistants and speech-to-speech translation systems to become practical to deploy on a large scale. In essence, machines are becoming capable of hearing what we are saying. But will they understand what we want them to do when we talk to them? What are the prospects for getting useful work done – in essence, by synthesizing programs – through the act of having a conversation with a computer?

In this lecture, I will speculate on the central role that programming-language design and program synthesis may have in this possible – and I will argue, likely – future of computing, one in which every user writes programs, every day, by conversing with a computing system.

**ACM Classification:** D.1.2 [Automatic Programming]; I.2.2 [Automatic Programming]---Program synthesis

**Author Keywords:** natural user interaction; digital assistants

**Biography**

Dr. Peter Lee is Corporate Vice President, Microsoft Research. He manages Microsoft's worldwide research operations, comprising twelve laboratories and over 1,000 researchers, engineers, and support personnel dedicated to advancing the state of the art in computing and creating new technologies for Microsoft's products and services. Prior to joining Microsoft, Lee held key positions in both government and academia, most recently at the Defense Advanced Research Projects Agency (DARPA), where he founded and directed a major technology office that supported research in computing and related areas in the social and physical sciences. Prior to DARPA, Lee served as head of Carnegie Mellon University's nationally top-ranked computer science department. He also served as the university's vice provost for research.

Lee has shown executive-level leadership in world-class research organizations spanning academia, government, and industry. He is a Fellow of the Association for Computing Machinery and serves the research community at the national level, including policy contributions to the President's Council of Advisors on Science and Technology and membership on both the National Research Council's Computer Science and Telecommunications Board and the Advisory Council of the Computer and Information Science and Engineering Directorate of the National Science Foundation. He was the former chair of the Computing Research Association and has testified before both the US House Science and Technology Committee and the US Senate Commerce Committee.

Lee holds a Ph.D. in computer and communication sciences from the University of Michigan at Ann Arbor and bachelor's degrees in mathematics and computer sciences, also from the University of Michigan at Ann Arbor.


*POPL'15*, January 15–17, 2015, Mumbai, India.
ACM 978-1-4503-3300-9/15/01.
http://dx.doi.org/10.1145/2676726.2682622

# Databases and Programming: Two Subjects Divided by a Common Language?

Peter Buneman
University of Edinburgh

## Abstract

The 1990s saw a hugely productive interaction between database and programming language research. Ideas about type systems from programming languages played a central role in generalizing and adapting relational database systems to new data models. At the same time databases provided some of the best concrete examples of the application of concurrency theory and of the benefits of high-level optimization in functional programming languages. One of the driving ambitions behind this research was the idea that database access should be properly embedded in programming languages: one should not have to be bilingual in order to use a database from a programming language; and that goal has to some extent been realized.

In the past fifteen years, new data models, both for data storage and for data exchange have appeared with depressing regularity and with each such model, the inevitable query language. Does programming language research have anything to contribute to these new languages? Should we take the time to to worry about embedding these models in conventional languages? Over the same period, some interesting new connections between databases and programming languages have emerged, notably in the areas of scientific databases, annotation and provenance. Will this provide new opportunities for cross-fertilization?

**ACM Classification:**
D.3 Programming Languages; H.2 Database management

## Biography

Peter Buneman is Professor of Database Systems at the University of Edinburgh. His work in computer science has focused mainly on databases and programming languages, specifically: active databases, database semantics, approximate information, query languages, types for databases, data integration, bioinformatics and semistructured data. He has recently worked on issues associated with scientific and curated databases such as data provenance, archiving and annotation. He has served on numerous programme committees, editorial boards and working groups, and has been programme chair for ACM SIGMOD, ACM PODS and ICDT.

He is a fellow of the Royal Societies of London and Edinburgh, a fellow of the ACM and the recipient of a Royal Society Wolfson Merit Award.

Before joining the University of Edinburgh, Buneman was a Professor at the Department of Computer and Information Science at the University of Pennsylvania. He received his undergraduate degree from Cambridge University, his graduate degree from the University of Warwick, and he did postdoctoral work at the University of Edinburgh. He has held visiting positions at the University of Glasgow, Imperial College, Kyoto University and INRIA. In addition to computer science he has made contributions to graph theory; to the mathematics of phylogeny. Recently he has helped to build systems for the delivery of affordable rural Internet.

*POPL'15*, January 15–17, 2015, Mumbai, India.
ACM 978-1-4503-3300-9/15/01.
http://dx.doi.org/10.1145/2676726.2682620

# Probabilistic Termination

## Soundness, Completeness, and Compositionality

Luis María Ferrer Fioriti    Holger Hermanns
Saarland University

## Abstract

We propose a framework to prove almost sure termination for probabilistic programs with real valued variables. It is based on ranking supermartingales, a notion analogous to ranking functions on non-probabilistic programs. The framework is proven sound and complete for a meaningful class of programs involving randomization and bounded nondeterminism. We complement this foundational insight by a practical proof methodology, based on sound conditions that enable compositional reasoning and are amenable to a direct implementation using modern theorem provers. This is integrated in a small dependent type system, to overcome the problem that lexicographic ranking functions fail when combined with randomization. Among others, this compositional methodology enables the verification of probabilistic programs *outside* the complete class that admits ranking supermartingales.

***Categories and Subject Descriptors*** D.2.4 [*Software Engineering*]: Software/Program Verification; F.3.1 [*Logic and Meanings of Programs*]: Specifying and Verifying and Reasoning about Programs

***General Terms*** Probabilistic Programs; Termination.

***Keywords*** Probabilistic Programs; Program Verification; Termination; Supermartingales.

## 1. Introduction

Termination is one of the simplest and yet most important liveness properties. If the program involves randomization, or is operating in a randomized environment, the natural analogon of termination is *almost sure termination*, saying that the probability of eventually terminating is one, so divergence has zero probability.

Proving termination of non-probabilistic programs is equivalent to constructing a *ranking function* [14]. That is a mapping $v : S \to D$ such that $v(s) \succ v(s')$ for all transitions $s \to s'$ in the program, where $(D, \succ)$ is well-founded (a partial order without infinite descending chains). In case of programs over countable state spaces and bounded branching, one can restrict to $(\mathbb{N}, >)$ as well-founded relation. Having a numeric domain allows one to synthesize ranking functions via the solution of convex optimization problems [5, 9, 33, 34]. In addition, the value $v(s)$ provides an upper bound on the maximum number of steps before termination if assuming the program to start at state $s$.

For probabilistic programs, ranking functions provide a sound method to prove termination, but are far from being complete. To illustrate this, consider the following probabilistic program:

```
while n > 0 do
    c := uniform(0, 1)
    if c < 0.5 then
        n := n − 1
    fi
od
```

Clearly, the program terminates with probability one, since ignoring the decrementing command forever has probability zero. Yet, there cannot exist a ranking function proving termination, because each time the conditional branch is skipped the program state remains unchanged, but well-founded relations are anti-reflexive. However, with probability $\frac{1}{2}$ the next value of $n$ will be decremented to $n - 1$, and with the same probability it will be $n$. This means that the expected value of variable $n$ after each iteration is decreased by $0.5$.

Bournez and Garnier [3] were the first to connect probabilistic program termination to *Lyapunov ranking functions* [15] (or Foster-Lyapunov functions). These constitute the analogon of ranking functions for probabilistic programs, by considering expected values instead of values: They allow the value of some states to increase when executing some transitions, as long as the expected value (i.e. its average) decreases. Formally a mapping $v : S \to \mathbb{R}^+$ is a Lyapunov ranking functions if there exists a constant $\varepsilon > 0$, such that:

$$v(s) \geq \sum_{s' \in S} \mathbb{P}(s, \alpha, s') v(s') + \varepsilon \qquad (1)$$

whenever $\alpha$ is a program instruction enabled at state $s$, and $\mathbb{P}(s, \alpha, s')$ is the probability of going from $s$ to $s'$ using the command $a$. Notably, $(\mathbb{R}^+, \succ)$ is a well-founded relation on the positive reals, where $a \succ b \equiv a > b + \varepsilon$. Lyapunov ranking functions provide a sound method to prove almost sure (a.s.) termination, and in analogy to ranking functions, $v(s)/\varepsilon$ is an upper bound on the expected number of steps before termination [15]. Thus, in fact, Lyapunov ranking functions guarantee a stronger property, namely, that the expected time to termination is finite. This is sometimes referred to as *positive almost sure termination* [3]. For probabilistic programs with countable state spaces, Lyapunov ranking functions not only are a sound method to prove positive almost sure termination *but* a complete one – but only as long as non-determinism is absent. We overcome this foundational restriction with this paper and embed the resulting theory into a practical, compositional proof method. When dealing with nondeterminism and probabilism, families of schedulers play an important role. As we will see, one of the


*POPL '15*, January 15–17, 2015, Mumbai, India.

ACM 978-1-4503-3300-9/15/01.
http://dx.doi.org/10.1145/2676726.2677001

distinct technical aspects of our approach is that the *semantic space* of a probabilistic program is set up in such a way that all possible schedulers share a common probability space. This enables correct reasoning about measurability of the quantities involved. In our setting the base quantities are ranking supermartingales, which in turn are a generalization of Lyapunov ranking functions. The main contributions of the paper are:

- We present a new semantics for non-deterministic programs where schedulers share a common probability space. (Section 4)
- We demonstrate that the Lyapunov ranking functions proposed by Bournez and Garnier [3] are *not* complete for positive almost sure termination in the non-deterministic case, and the same holds for ranking supermartingales. (Section 2)
- We extend the ranking supermartingale approach of Chakarov and Sankaranarayanan [7] to the bounded non-deterministic case, arriving at a sound and complete characterization of terminating programs. (Section 5)
- We provide a compositional and sound proof method for almost sure termination. The framework only relies on the synthesis of probabilistic linear loop invariants [7, 19]. (Sections 6, and 7)
- We provide a method to identify program variables that must have finite expectation. (Theorem 7.6)

## 2. Motivating Counter-Examples

Lyapunov ranking functions provide the apparatus to bound the expected number of steps a probabilistic program will take. As such, they are sound and complete for positive almost sure termination provided the probabilistic program is deterministic. In the presence of (bounded) non-determinism the notion appears to have a natural extension, obtained by requiring that the expected number of steps needed is finite for all possible resolutions of the non-determinism. However, as we illustrate below, and in contrast to results that were undisputed for a decade [3, Theorem 3], the completeness results for (positive) almost sure termination do not extend to the case of non-deterministic programs. Moreover, we show below that Lyapunov ranking functions are still incomplete even if besides all expectations also the supremum of all expectations is known to be finite.

***A simple quiz show.*** Consider the program illustrated in Figure 1. It represents a quiz show, where after the quiz and prior to termination (state \$) the gained money is spent one unit at a time. A participant can initially (state ?) either answer a yes/no question or decide to stop the game immediately. If the participant decides to finish, he obtains a prize $f(n)$, where $n$ is the number of questions answered thus far. If the participant answers correctly he can continue playing. In case of failing a question, he loses the game immediately and receives a consolation prize $g(n)$. For the participant in question, the quiz is so difficult that he realizes that the best strategy is to answer at random (state ¢). Analyzing this game, we first observe that the participant will receive (with probability one) a finite amount of money, because the event of answering questions correctly forever has probability zero. We now analyze the expected amount of money that the participant will receive. This depends on the number $n$ of questions the participant is willing to answer before stopping, and of course on the choice of $f$ and $g$:

$$E_n = \frac{f(n)}{2^n} + \sum_{1 \le k \le n} \frac{g(k-1)}{2^k} \qquad E_\infty = \sum_{1 \le k} \frac{g(k-1)}{2^k}$$

The quantity $E_\infty$ corresponds to the expected gain if the participant never stops answering questions. Thus, he always gets the consolation prize.

***$\forall_n E_n < \infty$ does not work.*** In a scenario where $f(n) = 3^n$, and $g(n) = n$, we see that clearly $E_n < E_{n+1} < \infty$ and $E_n \to \infty$ as $n \to \infty$. So it seems that the best strategy is to never give up. However, $E_\infty = 1$. This is because the limit of the expectation is *not* the expectation of the limit. In other words, there is *no* optimal strategy. Despite being able to find a Lyapunov ranking function for each particular resolution of the non-determinism (as all $E_n$ are finite), we are unable to build a single, universal Lyapunov ranking function. It would require assigning $\infty$ to some of the states.

***$\sup_n E_n < \infty$ neither.*** Consider now the case where $f(n) = 2^n$ and $g(n) = n$. Now we have $E_n \to 2$ as $n \to \infty$, so now the prize earned is bounded, and our participant will not get rich for sure. In this case the aspect of interest is the expected money that the participant will receive under the assumption that he already answered $m$ questions correctly:

$$E_{n,m} = \frac{2^n}{2^{n-m}} + \sum_{m+1 \le k \le n} \frac{k-1}{2^{k-m}} \quad \text{with } m \le n$$

Here, the maximum expectation after answering $m$ questions turns out to be $2^m + m + 1$, obtained by $n \to \infty$. Yet, the maximum expectation after answering the $m+1$-th question (right or wrong) is $\frac{1}{2}\left(2^{m+1} + (m+1) + 1\right) + \frac{1}{2}m$, and that value is again $2^m + m + 1$. Therefore, the expectation remains invariant, i.e. a function assigning to each state the maximum expected termination time does not "rank" in expectation. And this function cannot be twisted to a ranking one without assigning $\infty$ to at least one of the states.

***Cheating works!*** Now suppose that we, but not the participant, are able to record all results of the random choices and their effects prior to the show. Suppose also, that the results of the random choices are independent of the strategy of the participant about when to stop answering. We might for instance know that the fourth random choice will make the participant miss the fourth question, thus we are sure that he will get the consolation prize if he decides to answer at least four questions. We can then also infer that he will win the prize if he is prudent enough to withdraw before the fourth question. In other words, we know the maximum amount of money the participant is capable of winning *regardless* of his strategy. As this quantity is random we can analyze its expected value $E^*$. If $f(k+1) > f(k) > g(k)$, then:

$$E^* = \sum_{1 \le k} \frac{f(k)}{2^k}$$

In the above two examples, $E^*$ is infinite because $f(k) \ge 2^k$. In Section 5 we show that a Lyapunov ranking function can only be constructed if and only if $E^*$ is finite. The proper definition of $E^*$ which implicitly ranges over all possible strategies, relies on a novel semantics for non-deterministic and probabilistic programs, introduced in Section 4.

## 3. Preliminaries

In this section we present some basic concepts of probability and measure theory, as needed for this paper. More detailed descriptions can be found in reference books such as Ash [1] and Williams [35].

***Measure Theory.*** An arbitrary set $\Omega$ that contains all possible outcomes of an experiment is called a *sample space*. A *$\sigma$-algebra* $\mathcal{F}$ is a collection of subsets of $\Omega$ that is closed under complement and countable union, and $\Omega \in \mathcal{F}$. The elements of $\mathcal{F}$ are called *events*. We say that $A$ is *$\mathcal{F}$-measurable* if $A \in \mathcal{F}$. In case $\Omega = \mathbb{R}$, the *Borel $\sigma$-algebra* denoted by $\mathcal{B}(\mathbb{R})$ is the $\sigma$-algebra generated by the class of open sets. A function $f : \Omega \to \Omega'$ is *measurable* with respect to $\mathcal{F}$ and $\mathcal{F}'$ if $f^{-1}(B) \in \mathcal{F}$ for all $B \in \mathcal{F}'$. A *probability measure* $\mu$ is a function of signature $\mathcal{F} \to [0, 1]$ such that $\mu(\Omega) = 1$, and it

```
n, i, c := 0, 0, 0
while c < 0.5 do
    if * then
        c := uniform(0, 1)
        if c < 0.5 then n := n + 1 else i := g(n) fi
    else
        c, i := 1, f(n)
    fi
od

while 0 < i do i := i − 1 od
```

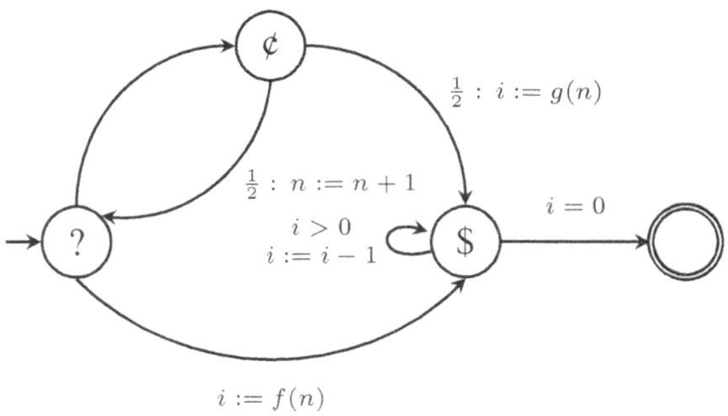


**Figure 1.** Quiz show example.

is countably additive: the probability of a countable disjoint union of events is given by the sum of the individual probabilities. An event $A$ occurs *almost surely* (a.s.) if $\mu(A) = 1$. Similarly $A$ is a *null event* if $\mu(A) = 0$. Two events $A$ and $B$ are *independent* when $\mu(A \cap B) = \mu(A)\mu(B)$. Two $\sigma$ algebras $\mathcal{F}$ and $\mathcal{G}$ are independent if all events $A \in \mathcal{F}$ and $B \in \mathcal{G}$ are independent. Given an element $x \in \Omega$, $\delta_x$ is the *Dirac distribution* of $x$ and satisfies $\delta_x(\{x\}) = 1$. The *conditional measure* of $\mu$ under a non-null event $B$ is $\mu|_B(A) = \frac{\mu(A \cap B)}{\mu(B)}$ A *probability space* is a triple $(\Omega, \mathcal{F}, \mu)$, where $\mathcal{F}$ is a $\sigma$-algebra of $\Omega$, and $\mu$ is a probability measure for $\mathcal{F}$.

***Random Variables.*** A function $X : \Omega \to \mathbb{R}$ is a *random variable* (r.v.) on $(\Omega, \mathcal{F}, \mu)$, if it is $(\mathcal{F}, \mathcal{B}(\mathbb{R}))$-measurable. A r.v. $X$ is *discrete* provided the range of $X$ is countable. A particular discrete r.v. is the *indicator function* of a measurable set $A$. It takes values in $\{0, 1\}$, and satisfies $(\mathbf{1}_A(\omega) = 1) \equiv (\omega \in A)$. The *expected value* of a random variable $X$ is the quantity:

$$\mathbb{E}(X) \triangleq \int_\Omega X d\mu$$

where $\int$ is the Lebesgue integral, see Ash [1] for a detailed explanation. In case of a discrete r.v., the expected value can be expressed as a weighted average. In particular, $\mathbb{E}(\mathbf{1}_A) = \mu(A)$. If $\mathbb{E}(|X|)$ is a finite value, we say $X$ is *integrable*. It ensures that $\mathbb{E}(X\mathbf{1}_A)$ is finite for any measurable event $A$.

***Filtrations.*** A finite or infinite sequence $\{\mathcal{F}_n\}$ of $\sigma$-algebras is a *filtration* if $\mathcal{F}_k \subseteq \mathcal{F}_{k+1} \subseteq \mathcal{F}$ for all $k \in \mathbb{N}$. For example consider the experiment of tossing two coins, i.e. the sample space $\Omega$ is $\{HH, TT, HT, TH\}$. A possible filtration is $\mathcal{F}_0 = \{\emptyset, \Omega\}$, $\mathcal{F}_1 = \{\emptyset, \{HH, HT\}, \{TT, TH\}, \Omega\}$, and $\mathcal{F}_2 = \mathcal{P}(\Omega)$. A sequence of random variables $\{X_n\}$ is *adapted* to a filtration $\{\mathcal{F}_n\}$ if $X_n$ is $\mathcal{F}_n$-measurable for all $n$, and it is *predictable* if $X_n$ is $\mathcal{F}_{n-1}$-measurable for all $n$.

***Stopping Times.*** A discrete random variable $T$ that takes values in $\mathbb{N} \cup \{\infty\}$ is a *stopping time* with respect to a filtration $\{\mathcal{F}_n\}$ if the event $\{T \leq n\}$ is $\mathcal{F}_n$-measurable. Since each element $\mathcal{F}_n$ of a filtration is a $\sigma$-algebra, then the events $\{T > n\}$ and $\{T = n\}$ are also $\mathcal{F}_n$-measurable. From the previous example a stopping time is the r.v. $T_H$ that satisfy $T_H(H\_) = 1, T_H(TH) = 2$, and is infinity otherwise. We have $T_H^{-1}(0) = \emptyset \in \mathcal{F}_0$, $T_H^{-1}(1) = \{HH, HT\} \in \mathcal{F}_1$, and $T_H^{-1}(2) = \{TH\} \in \mathcal{F}_2$. Stopping times posses several properties that we will exploit in this paper. For example if $T_1$ and $T_2$ are stopping times so are $T_1 \wedge T_2$ (minimum), $T_1 \vee T_2$ (maximum), and $T_1 + T_2$. Also, any random variable that takes a constant value in $\mathbb{N}$ is trivially a stopping time. The expected value of a stopping time can be expressed in a very convenient form:

$$\mathbb{E}(T) = \sum_{1 \leq k} \mathbb{P}(T \geq k) \tag{2}$$

We can also define the $\sigma$-algebra $\mathcal{F}_T$ of events that occur up to time $T$ as follows:

$$A \in \mathcal{F}_T \equiv \forall n : A \cap \{T \leq n\} \in \mathcal{F}_n. \tag{3}$$

Notice that $T$ is measurable in $\mathcal{F}_T$. If $S$ and $T$ are stopping times with $S \leq T$, then $\mathcal{F}_S \subseteq \mathcal{F}_T$. Thus, sequences of increasing stopping times define a filtration.

***Conditional Expectation.*** Given an integrable r.v. $X$ on a probability space $(\Omega, \mathcal{F}, \mu)$, and $\mathcal{G}$ a sub-$\sigma$-algebra of $\mathcal{F}$, the *conditional expectation* $\mathbb{E}(X \mid \mathcal{G})$ is a r.v. measurable in $\mathcal{G}$ that satisfies:

$$\int_A X \, d\mu = \int_A \mathbb{E}(X \mid \mathcal{G}) \, d\mu \quad \text{for all } A \in \mathcal{G}$$

Intuitively $\mathbb{E}(X \mid \mathcal{G})$ is the expected outcome of a random experiment (represented by $X$), if some partial information of the result is available (represented by $\mathcal{G}$). Consider again the experiment of tossing two coins. The expected number of observed heads is one. However, if the result of one of the coins is already known, then the expected value changes. It would be 1.5 in case the revealed coin landed heads, and 0.5 otherwise. Some important properties about conditional expectations are the following:

$$\mathbb{E}(X \mid \{\emptyset, \Omega\}) = \mathbb{E}(X) \tag{4}$$

$$\mathbb{E}(X + Y \mid \mathcal{G}) = \mathbb{E}(X \mid \mathcal{G}) + \mathbb{E}(Y \mid \mathcal{G}) \tag{5}$$

$$\mathbb{E}(\mathbb{E}(X \mid \mathcal{H}) \mid \mathcal{G}) = \mathbb{E}(X \mid \mathcal{G}) \quad \text{if } \mathcal{G} \subset \mathcal{H} \tag{6}$$

$$\mathbb{E}(XY \mid \mathcal{G}) = X\mathbb{E}(Y \mid \mathcal{G}) \quad \text{if } X \text{ is } \mathcal{G}\text{-measurable} \tag{7}$$

Their intuitive meaning is as follows: (4) if no information is available it is the same as taking the expected value; (6) the conditional expectation depends on the maximum amount of available information; (7) the expectation depends only on unknown information.

***Uniform Integrability.*** The concept of uniform integrability is an extension of integrability of a r.v. to a family of random variables, similar to the notion of uniform convergence in real analysis. A collection $\{X_n\}$ is *uniformly integrable* (UI), if the following holds:

$$\lim_{K \to \infty} \sup_n \mathbb{E}(|X_n| \mathbf{1}_{[|X_n| > K]}) = 0 \tag{8}$$

Informally, the expected values of a UI family are bounded and the probability mass is globally concentrated within this boundary, i.e. for any constant $\varepsilon > 0$, we can find a constant $\delta > 0$ such that $\mathbb{E}(|X_n|\mathbf{1}_A) \leq \varepsilon$ for all $n$, and all events $A$ such that $\mu(A) \leq \delta$. Uniform integrability is a central concept in probability theory. It is a necessary and sufficient condition to guarantee that a sequence of r.v. converging in probabilities also converges in expectation, and it ensures that $\mathbb{E}(|X_n|)$ is finite, thus integrability. It will also play an important role in our findings.

## 4. Probabilistic Programs

In this section we present the syntax of our idealized probabilistic programs, and we provide a semantics in terms of random vectors over a probability space.

### 4.1 Syntax

Our programs will be composed by the following grammar:

$\langle statement\rangle$ ::= $\langle ident\rangle$ ':=' $\langle expr\rangle$
| $\langle ident\rangle$ ':=' $\langle distribution\rangle$
| **'if'** $\langle ndbexpr\rangle$ **'then'** $\langle statement\rangle$ **'else'** $\langle statement\rangle$ **'fi'**
| **'while'** $\langle bexpr\rangle$ **'do'** $\langle statement\rangle$ **'od'**
| $\langle statement\rangle$ ';' $\langle statement\rangle$

$\langle expr\rangle$ ::= $\langle constant\rangle$ | $\langle ident\rangle$ | $\langle expr\rangle$ '+' $\langle expr\rangle$
| $\langle expr\rangle$ '*' $\langle expr\rangle$ | $\langle expr\rangle$ '-' $\langle expr\rangle$

$\langle bexpr\rangle$ ::= $\langle expr\rangle$ '<' $\langle expr\rangle$ | $\langle expr\rangle$ '>' $\langle expr\rangle$
| $\langle bexpr\rangle$ **'and'** $\langle bexpr\rangle$ | $\langle bexpr\rangle$ **'or'** $\langle bexpr\rangle$

$\langle ndbexpr\rangle$ **::= '*'** | $\langle bexpr\rangle$

Here, $\langle distribution\rangle$ stands for any probability distribution that is integrable, and has a known expected value, like uniform, exponential, normal, etc. The program **if** $*$ **then** $P_1$ **else** $P_2$ **fi** represents a non-deterministic choice between the statement $P_1$, and $P_2$. If $P'$ is a statement contained inside a program $P$, we say $P$ is the parent of $P'$ and we denote it by $P' \lhd P$. $P' \unlhd P$ is the reflexive version of $\lhd$. It is worth mentioning that probabilistic choices $P_1 \oplus_p P_2$ in the style of McIver and Morgan [30] can be encoded in our framework as $c := uniform(0,1)$; **if** $c < p$ **then** $P_1$ **else** $P_2$ **fi** .

Given an arithmetic or boolean expression $e$, the set of variables that occur syntactically in $e$ is denoted by $vars(e)$. The set of variables that are modified by a program $P$, i.e. all the program variables that appear on the left of assignment instructions, is denoted by $lvars(P)$.

### 4.2 Semantics

There are several ways to define semantics of probabilistic programs. Kozen [27] provides a denotational semantics in terms of continuous linear transformations of probability distributions. Given an initial distribution of the program variables, the semantics is a sub-probability distribution indicating the distribution of the program variables at termination time. The sub-distribution is a probability distribution provided the program a.s. terminates. Non-determinism is not considered in this semantics, but can be introduced using probabilistic power-domains [24]. On another route, probabilistic non-deterministic programs can be represented operationally as Markov Decision Processes [20]. The usual approach then is to define the sample space as the set of possible path executions, after non-determinism is resolved by means of a scheduler. The latter is basically a mapping from finite paths (determining the program state) to enabled commands. Each scheduler induces a dedicated probability measure on measurable paths. Therefore, the same program under two different schedulers yields two different probability spaces.

The approach we follow is closer to the latter but is equipped with a more refined semantics. The core innovation is that all schedulers are defined over the *same* probability space, still they induce distinct random processes. This will allow us to break conceptual limitations of the earlier approaches. An event may then have distinct interpretations, according to the scheduler considered. Other events have a global meaning. These "global" events in turn will enable us to identify the set of programs where Lyapunov ranking functions provide a complete proof methodology.

Another feature of our semantics is that it does not have a built-in distinction between probabilistic and non-probabilistic commands. At each step a value is sampled from a distribution, but the executed command is free to use or to entirely ignore the sampled outcome.

**Definition 4.1** (Guarded Command)**.** Given a finite set of real valued variables $Vars = \{X_1, \dots, X_N\}$ a *guarded command* is a tuple $(l^i, G, \mathbf{f}, l^f)$ that consists of an initial location $l^i$, a final location $l^f$, a guard $G$ that is a $\mathcal{B}(\mathbb{R})^N$-measurable set, an update vector $\mathbf{f} = (f_1, \dots, f_N)$ of $(\mathcal{B}(\mathbb{R})^{N+1}, \mathcal{B}(\mathbb{R}))$-measurable functions.

A command is *enabled* if the program counter is $l^i$, and the variables satisfy $G$. After firing an enabled command, the program counter is set to $l^f$. The values of the program variables are modified according to the update vector. The value of $X_k$ is determined by $f_k : \mathbb{R}^{N+1} \to \mathbb{R}$. The new valuation depends on the old values and a single sampled value at each step. The underlying probability space is assumed to ensure that the sampled value adheres to the right probability distribution.

**Definition 4.2** (Probabilistic Program)**.** A *probabilistic program* is a tuple $(L, Vars, Cmds, l_0, l_\perp)$, where $L$ is the program counter, $Vars = \{X_k\}_{k=1}^N$ is a finite set of real valued program variables, $Cmds = \{cmd_k\}_{k=1}^M$ is a finite set of guarded commands, $l_0$ is the initial program location, and $l_\perp$ is the location reached upon program termination. We require that for each location and variable valuation at least one command is enabled, except for the final location.

It is possible to have multiple commands enabled simultaneously, namely when several commands have the same initial location and their guards overlap. The resulting non-determinism in such programs is resolved by means of a *scheduler*. A realistic scheduler can at each step base its decision on the information currently available, including information accumulated about the past. In particular, a scheduler cannot decide to perform an action based on information about events that will occur in the future. Also, it must satisfy certain measurability conditions, so as to obtain a fully stochastic process when removing non-determinism. Before we dive into the formal definition of schedulers we first need to formalize the notion of "available information". This formalization will be provided by a filtration of the probability space of our program, and will be the same for *all* schedulers. This in turn will allow us to observe the behavior of all scheduler simultaneously.

**Definition 4.3** (Semantic Space of Programs)**.** Let $P$ be a probabilistic program with $N$ variables. A *semantic space of* $P$ is a tuple $(\Omega, \mathcal{F}, \mu, \{\mathcal{F}_n\}_{n=0}^\infty, \mathbf{X}_0, \{C_n\}_{n=1}^\infty)$, such that:

- $(\Omega, \mathcal{F}, \mu)$ is a probability space.
- $\{\mathcal{F}_n\}_{n=0}^\infty$ is a filtration of $\mathcal{F}$.
- $\mathbf{X}_0$ is a random vector of size $N$ that is measurable in $\mathcal{F}_0$.
- $\{C_n\}_{n=1}^\infty$ is a sequence of identically distributed random variables, with $C_n$ integrable, $\mathcal{F}_n$-measurable, and independent of $\mathcal{F}_{n-1}$.

$\mathbf{X}_0$ is the *initial valuation* of the program variables. $C_n$ plays the role of a (possibly continuous-valued, finite-dimensional) coin, and represents a value sampled at step $n$.

This definition does not define a unique semantic space for a program, but instead specifies the minimum requirements to obtain a meaningful semantics. This generality is essential for the decomposition presented in Section 6. However, the most basic filtration with the desired properties is $\{\sigma(C_1, \dots, C_n)\}_{n=1}^\infty$ where

$$
\begin{aligned}
[\![X_k := E]\!] &= \{(l_0, true, (\pi_1, \ldots, \pi_{k-1}, E, \pi_{k+1}, \ldots, \pi_N), l_\perp)\}\\
[\![X_k := \langle distribution\rangle]\!] &= \{(l_0, true, (\pi_1, \ldots, \pi_{k-1}, \pi_{N+1}, \pi_{k+1}, \ldots, \pi_N), l_\perp)\}\\
[\![P_1; P_2]\!] &= [\![P_1]\!] \cup [\![P_2]\!]\\
[\![\textbf{if } G \textbf{ then } P_t \textbf{ else } P_f \textbf{ od}]\!] &= \{(l_0, G, (\pi_1, \ldots, \pi_N), l_0^{P_t}), (l_0, \overline{G}, (\pi_1, \ldots, \pi_N), l_0^{P_f})\} \cup [\![P_t]\!] \cup [\![P_f]\!]\\
&\cup \{(l_\perp^{P_t}, true, (\pi_1, \ldots, \pi_N), l_\perp), (l_\perp^{P_f}, true, (\pi_1, \ldots, \pi_N), l_\perp)\}\\
[\![\textbf{if } * \textbf{ then } P_t \textbf{ else } P_f \textbf{ od}]\!] &= \{(l_0, true, (\pi_1, \ldots, \pi_N), l_0^{P_t}), (l_0, true, (\pi_1, \ldots, \pi_N), l_0^{P_f})\} \cup [\![P_t]\!] \cup [\![P_f]\!]\\
&\cup \{(l_\perp^{P_t}, true, (\pi_1, \ldots, \pi_N), l_\perp), (l_\perp^{P_f}, true, (\pi_1, \ldots, \pi_N), l_\perp)\}\\
[\![\textbf{while } G \textbf{ do } P_W \textbf{ od}]\!] &= \{(l_0, G, (\pi_1, \ldots, \pi_N), l_0^{P_W}), (l_0, \overline{G}, (\pi_1, \ldots, \pi_N), l_\perp)\}\\
&\cup [\![P_W]\!] \cup \{(l_\perp^{P_W}, true, (\pi_1, \ldots, \pi_N), l_0)\}
\end{aligned}
$$

**Table 1.** Semantics of probabilistic programs (all the program locations are assumed to be unique)

$\sigma(C_1, \ldots, C_n)$ is the smallest $\sigma$-algebra that makes $C_1, \ldots, C_n$ measurable.

Definition 4.3 implicitly assumes all sampling instructions of $P$, modeled by $C_n$, to have the same distribution. We impose this restriction for the sake of clarity of the exposition. It can be relinquished by fixing the uniform unit distribution for coins and reconstructing all other integrable distributions from there by inversion. But this forces us to explicitly deal with Polish spaces, which obfuscates our arguments with technicalities. All the proofs contained in this paper can be adapted to that general setting.

The filtration $\{\mathcal{F}_n\}$ faithfully characterizes the information available after executing the first $n$ commands: the result of the initial distribution of the program variables (measurable in $\mathcal{F}_0 \subseteq \mathcal{F}_n$), and the sampled values of $C_1, \ldots, C_n$ (all measurable in $\mathcal{F}_n$). The independence requirement does not only guarantee $C_n$ being independent of $C_m$, it also ensures that $\mathcal{F}_n$ does not leak any information about the future. That is $C_n$ is sampled *precisely* at time $n$. To see this, take $C_m$ with $m > n$. Independence implies $\mu(C_m \in [a,b) \cap A) = \mu(C_m \in [a,b))\mu(A)$ for all events $A \in \mathcal{F}_n$ and all real intervals $[a,b)$. If the random variable $C_m$ were $\mathcal{F}_n$-measurable we would be able to take $C_m \in [a,b)$ as $A$ with $0 < \mu(C_m \in [a,b)) < 1$, rendering a contradiction in the above equality.

**Definition 4.4** (Scheduler). Given a semantic space $(\Omega, \mathcal{F}, \mu, \{\mathcal{F}_n\}, \mathbf{X}_0, \{C_n\})$, a *scheduler* $\phi$ is a collection $\{\phi_n\}_{n=1}^{\infty}$ of functions with signatures $\Omega \to \{1, \ldots, M\}$ such that $\phi_n$ is $\mathcal{F}_{n-1}$-measurable.

The measurability condition imposed on schedulers is crucial. The function $\phi_n$ selects the command to be executed at step $n$. The decision depends only on the initial state and the past observed samples, $\mathcal{F}_{n-1}$-measurable events. The value of the current and future samples, measurable in $\mathcal{F} \setminus \mathcal{F}_{n-1}$, have no influence on how the scheduler resolves the non-determinism present. Notice that the probability measure $\mu$ in the semantic space does *not* depend on the scheduler, thus different schedulers can be defined under the same probability space. This is the key feature of our semantics.

Schedulers that do incorporate randomization in their decisions can be modeled in our framework by augmenting the filtration in our semantic space. For example we can use $\{\sigma(U_0, C_1, U_1, \ldots C_n, U_n)\}$ with $U_k$ uniform in the interval $(0,1)$. The scheduler $\phi_n$ can use the result of $U_{n-1}$ as it is $\mathcal{F}_{n-1}$ measurable.

**Definition 4.5** (Operational Semantics). Let $P = (L, Vars, Cmds, l_0, l_\perp)$ be a probabilistic program with $(\Omega, \mathcal{F}, \mu, \{\mathcal{F}_n\}, \mathbf{X}_0, \{C_n\})$ being its semantic space. The semantics of $P$ under a scheduler $\phi = \{\phi_n\}$, is given by the following sequence of random vectors on the probabilistic space $(\Omega, \mathcal{F}, \mu)$ that is adapted to $\{\mathcal{F}_n\}$:

$$
\begin{aligned}
(L, \mathbf{X})_0^\phi(\omega) &\triangleq (l_0, \mathbf{X}_0(\omega))\\
(L, \mathbf{X})_{n+1}^\phi(\omega) &\triangleq (l_{k_{n+1}}^f, \mathbf{f}_{k_{n+1}}(\mathbf{X}_n^\phi(\omega), C_{n+1}(\omega)))
\end{aligned}
$$

where $k_{n+1} = \phi_{n+1}(\omega)$, the command selected by the scheduler to be executed at time $n+1$.

A scheduler is *valid* if every selected command is enabled in the respective state i.e., the following holds.

$$\phi_{n+1}(\omega) = k \quad \Rightarrow \quad L_n^\phi = l_k^i \wedge \mathbf{X}_n^\phi \in G_k \tag{9}$$

A valid scheduler $\phi$ is *memoryless* if it picks the next command to execute based solely on the current value of the program variables:

$$(L, \mathbf{X})_n^\phi(\omega) = (L, \mathbf{X})_m^\phi(\omega) \Rightarrow \phi_{n+1}(\omega) = \phi_{m+1}(\omega) \tag{10}$$

In the rest of the paper we only consider valid non-randomized memoryless schedulers. This restriction does not affect any of our results since this class is provably enough to prove almost sure termination [13]. However, it simplifies our proofs as $\phi$ can be viewed as a function $\phi : L \times \mathbb{R}^N \to \{1, \ldots M\}$.

The connection between our program syntax and guarded commands, i.e. the intuitive semantics of probabilistic programs is given in Table 1, where $\pi_k$ is the projection of a tuple of size $N+1$ on the $k$-th component and $^-$ denotes set complementation. (Note that the structure displayed on the right of figure 1 is a compressed version of what is obtained when applying this semantics to the program on its left.)

## 5. Almost Sure Termination

In this section we revise the notion of almost sure termination and its variants. For this, we introduce the notion of ranking supermartingales, which are a generalization of Lyapunov ranking functions. We prove that the synthesis of ranking supermartingales is a sound and complete proof method for positive almost sure termination for a restricted, yet useful, class of programs.

A program terminates if the time (i.e. number of steps) until the location $l_\perp$ is reached is finite. For this to hold, one has to prove that the program eventually reaches that location. We introduce two random variable $T^\phi$ and $T^*$ that measure these times. The former indicates the time step when the program under scheduler $\phi$ reaches the final location $l_\perp$. The latter is the earliest time step for which it is guaranteed that *any* valid scheduler has already terminated. We stress that $T^*$ can be defined in our setting just because all schedulers share a common probability space. The formal definition of these r.v. is as follows:

$$T^\phi(\omega) \triangleq \min\{n : L_n^\phi(\omega) = l_\perp\} \quad (11)$$

$$T^* \triangleq \sup_\phi T^\phi \quad (12)$$

It is not difficult to prove that $T^\phi$ is indeed a stopping time. More elaborated is the argument for $T^*$. The definition of $T^*$ involves a supremum over an uncountable set of stopping times, and an uncountable number of operations over measurable sets does not necessarily yield a measurable object.

**Lemma 5.1.** *$T^\phi$ and $T^*$ are stopping times.*

*Proof.* $T^\phi$ is a first arrival time, and is as such the typical example of stopping times [1, 35]. To see that $T^*$ is also a stopping time it is enough to see that $\{T^* > n\} \in \mathcal{F}_n$. Take any sequence of length $c_1, \ldots, c_n$, such as $c_k \in \{1, \ldots, M\}$, and consider the scheduler $\phi^{c_1,\ldots,c_n} \triangleq \{\phi^{c_1,\ldots,c_n}{}_k\}_{k=1}^\infty$ where:

$$\phi^{c_1,\ldots,c_n}{}_k(\omega) \triangleq \begin{cases} c_k & k \leq n \text{ and } c_k \text{ enabled,} \\ i & \text{otherwise, with } i \text{ the minimum} \\ & \text{enabled command after } k \text{ steps.} \end{cases}$$

The definition for the case $c_k$ not being enabled is to ensure that $\phi^{c_1,\ldots,c_n}{}_k$ is measurable. The command $c_i$ is always well defined as each non terminal state has at least one enabled command. Any path that terminates in more than $n$ steps, will be included in $\{T^{\phi^{c_1,\ldots,c_n}} > n\}$ for a proper sequence $c_1, \ldots, c_n$. The number of such sequences is exactly $M^n$, a finite quantity, and thus $\{T^* > n\} \equiv \bigcup\{T^{\phi^{c_1,\ldots,c_n}} > n\}$. □

*Remark* 5.2. The change in the program counter from step $n-1$ to step $n$ depends only on the selected command, and not on the result of the probabilistic experiment performed at step $n$. Therefore, we can infer whether or not the program terminates at step $n$ by inspecting the resolution of the scheduler at step $n$. That depends only on $\mathcal{F}_{n-1}$-measurable events. However, $\{T^\phi \leq n\}$ is still $\mathcal{F}_n$-measurable since $\mathcal{F}_{n-1} \subseteq \mathcal{F}_n$.

We are now in the position to define some important notions of termination in the presence of probability:

**Definition 5.3** (Almost Sure Termination [3]). Given a program and its semantics $\{(L, \mathbf{X})_n^\phi\}$ for any valid schedulers $\phi$ the program is said to be *almost surely terminating* if for all $\phi$, $\mathbb{P}(T^\phi < \infty) = 1$. If in addition $\mathbb{E}(T^\phi) < \infty$ for all valid schedulers, then it is said to be *positive almost surely terminating*.

Lyapunov ranking functions have been introduced to reason about programs involving discrete probability measures and countable state spaces. A Lyapunov ranking function $v$ can be interpreted as a random variable $V_n^\phi$ as follows:

$$V_n^\phi(\omega) = v((L, \mathbf{X})_n^\phi(\omega)). \quad (13)$$

From this perspective, condition (1) implies $\{V_n^\phi\}$ is a discrete supermartingale [35]. Thus, the natural generalization of Lyapunov ranking functions on continuous distributions are supermartingales:

**Definition 5.4** (Ranking Supermartingale). A sequence of r.v. $\{Y_n\}$ adapted to $\{\mathcal{F}_n\}$ is a *supermartingale* if $\mathbb{E}(|Y_n|) < \infty$, and $\mathbb{E}(Y_{n+1} \,|\, \mathcal{F}_n) \leq Y_n$. In addition, it is a *ranking supermartingale* if $Y_n \geq 0$, and $\mathbb{E}(Y_{n+1} \,|\, \mathcal{F}_n) \leq Y_n - \varepsilon \mathbf{1}_{\{Y_n > 0\}}$ for some constant $\varepsilon > 0$.

This definition is a slight variation of ranking martingales from Chakarov and Sankaranarayanan [7], the difference being that we give an explicit lower bound. Thus, if $\mathbb{E}(Y_n^\phi) = 0$, then $Y_n^\phi = 0$ a.s. and therefore termination can be ensured. Another difference is a technicality, namely we do not require that the expectation always decreases. By $\mathbf{1}_{\{Y_n > 0\}}$ we require that only as long as the program is still running.

The connection of ranking supermartingales and positive almost sure termination is given by the following lemma. The result is similar to [3, 7] but we provide an alternative proof.

**Lemma 5.5.** *Let $\{Y_n\}$ be a ranking supermartingale with $\varepsilon$ as required in the definition above, and $T(\omega) = \min_n \{n : Y_n(\omega) = 0\}$. Then, $\mathbb{P}(T < \infty) = 1$, and $\mathbb{E}(T) \leq \frac{\mathbb{E}(Y_0)}{\varepsilon}$.*

*Proof.* First, we prove by induction that $\mathbb{E}(Y_n) \leq \mathbb{E}(Y_0) - \varepsilon \sum_{0 \leq k < n} \mathbb{P}(Y_k > 0))$. The base case $n = 0$ is immediate since the sum ranges over an empty set. For the inductive case:

$$\begin{aligned}
& \mathbb{E}(Y_{n+1} \,|\, \mathcal{F}_n) \leq Y_n - \varepsilon \mathbf{1}_{\{Y_n > 0\}} \\
\Rightarrow \quad & \wr\; X \leq Y \Rightarrow \mathbb{E}(X) \leq \mathbb{E}(Y) \;\wr \\
& \mathbb{E}(\mathbb{E}(Y_{n+1} \,|\, \mathcal{F}_n)) \leq \mathbb{E}(Y_n - \varepsilon \mathbf{1}_{\{Y_n > 0\}}) \\
\equiv \quad & \wr\; \text{(4), (6), and linearity} \;\wr \\
& \mathbb{E}(Y_{n+1}) \leq \mathbb{E}(Y_n) - \varepsilon \mathbb{E}(\mathbf{1}_{\{Y_n > 0\}}) \\
\equiv \quad & \wr\; \text{Inductive hypothesis, } \mathbb{E}(\mathbf{1}_A) = \mathbb{P}(A) \;\wr \\
& \mathbb{E}(Y_{n+1}) \leq \mathbb{E}(Y_0) - \varepsilon \textstyle\sum_{0 \leq k < n} \mathbb{P}(Y_k > 0) - \varepsilon \mathbb{P}(Y_n > 0) \\
\equiv \quad & \wr\; \text{Arithmetic} \;\wr \\
& \mathbb{E}(Y_{n+1}) \leq \mathbb{E}(Y_0) - \varepsilon \textstyle\sum_{0 \leq k < n+1} \mathbb{P}(Y_k > 0)
\end{aligned}$$

Since $Y_n \geq 0$, and $\varepsilon$ then $\sum_{0 \leq k < n} \mathbb{P}(Y_k > 0) \leq \frac{\mathbb{E}(Y_0)}{\varepsilon}$ for all $n$. Therefore the series $\sum_{0 \leq k} \mathbb{P}(Y_k > 0)$ converges. This implies that $\mathbb{P}(Y_n > 0) \to 0$ as $n \to \infty$, and hence in particular $\mathbb{P}(T < \infty) = 1$. It remains to prove that the expectation of $T$ is bounded by $\mathbb{E}(Y_0)/\varepsilon$.

$$\begin{aligned}
& \mathbb{E}(T) \\
= \quad & \wr\; (2) \;\wr \\
& \textstyle\sum_{1 \leq k} \mathbb{P}(T \geq k) \\
= \quad & \wr\; \text{definition of } T \;\wr \\
& \textstyle\sum_{1 \leq k} \mathbb{P}(Y_k > 0) \\
\leq \quad & \wr\; \text{previous derivation, } \mathbb{P}(Y_0 \geq 0) \geq 0 \;\wr \\
& \frac{\mathbb{E}(Y_0)}{\varepsilon}
\end{aligned}$$

□

**Theorem 5.6** (Soundness). *Let $P$ be a probabilistic program with semantics $\{(L, \mathbf{X})_n^\phi\}$, and a ranking supermartingale $\{Y_n\}$ such that $Y_n = 0$ implies $T^\phi \leq n$ for all valid schedulers $\phi$. Then, $P$ almost sure terminates, and $T^*$ is integrable.*

*Proof.* This is a direct consequence of Lemma 5.5. □

The counterexample in Section 2 motivates the following incompleteness result.

**Theorem 5.7** (Incompleteness). *There exists a program $P$ with $T^\phi$ integrable for all valid schedulers $\phi$, and $\sup_\phi \mathbb{E}(T^\phi)$ finite such that there is no ranking supermartingale that guarantees $P$ terminates.*

However, we can characterize the programs on which supermartingales can be used to prove termination:

**Theorem 5.8** (Completeness). *If $T^*$ is integrable, then there exists a ranking supermartingale.*

*Proof.* We propose the random process $\{Y_n\}$ as a ranking supermartingale, where

$$Y_n \triangleq \mathbb{E}(T^* \mid \mathcal{F}_n) - T^* \wedge n \tag{14}$$

Notably, the conditional expectation is well defined since $0 \leq \mathbb{E}(T^*) < \infty$. To see that $\{Y_n\}$ is adapted to $\{\mathcal{F}_n\}$, we note that the first term is $\mathcal{F}_n$-measurable, by the definition of conditional expectation. The second term is $\mathcal{F}_n$-measurable since $T^*$ is a stopping time and thus $\{T^* > n\} \in \mathcal{F}_n$. In fact for $n > 0$ the previous event is in $\mathcal{F}_{n-1}$. Lets prove that $\{Y_n\}$ is a ranking supermartingale:

$$\begin{aligned}
& \mathbb{E}(Y_{n+1} \mid \mathcal{F}_n) \\
= & \quad \wr \text{ Definition of } Y_{n+1} \ \wr \\
& \mathbb{E}(\mathbb{E}(T^* \mid \mathcal{F}_{n+1}) - T^* \wedge (n+1) \mid \mathcal{F}_n) \\
= & \quad \wr \text{ Linearity } \wr \\
& \mathbb{E}(\mathbb{E}(T^* \mid \mathcal{F}_{n+1}) \mid \mathcal{F}_n) - \mathbb{E}(T^* \wedge (n+1) \mid \mathcal{F}_n) \\
= & \quad \wr \text{ (6), (7), and } T^* \wedge (n+1) \text{ is } \mathcal{F}_n\text{-measurable } \wr \\
& \mathbb{E}(T^* \mid \mathcal{F}_n) - T^* \wedge (n+1) \\
= & \quad \wr\ a \wedge (b+1) = a \wedge b + \mathbf{1}_{[a>b]} \ \wr \\
& \mathbb{E}(T^* \mid \mathcal{F}_n) - T^* \wedge n - \mathbf{1}_{\{T^*>n\}} \\
= & \quad \wr \text{ (14) twice, and } a > b \equiv a > (a \wedge b) \ \wr \\
& Y_n - \mathbf{1}_{\{Y_n>0\}}
\end{aligned}$$

□

Theorem 5.8 is concise, elegant and seems constructive, but one needs to know about the terminating behavior beforehand to apply it, and still one might face that the synthesis of distributions is in general non-computable [18]. In the remainder of this paper we attack this problem by building a practical framework to synthesize ranking supermartingales compositionally.

## 6. Program Manipulation

We now turn to the question how to analyze properties of complex probabilistic programs. The general idea is to decompose them into ones that are smaller and easier to reason about. For example if our programs is a sequential composition of several subprograms, we would like to infer properties for each subprogram and then transfer the results to the original program. Kozen [27] showed that sequential programs correspond to function composition, conditional branching to conditional probabilities, and iterations to fixed points or to infinite summations. The results presented in this section echo the Kozen decomposition in the context of filter-based semantics. For a program $P$ we have a semantic space ($\Omega$, $\mathcal{F}$, $\mu$, $\{\mathcal{F}_n\}$, $\mathbf{X}_0$, $\{C_n\}$) for the program semantics, and we would like to distill an adequate semantics for a subprogram $P'$ of $P$. That is, we need to build a semantic space ($\Omega$, $\mathcal{F}$, $\mu$, $\{\mathcal{F}'_n\}$, $\mathbf{X}'_0$, $\{C'_n\}$) for $P'$ in such a way that we can relate the semantics $\mathbf{X}$ of $P$ with the semantics $\mathbf{X}'$ of $P'$, in the probability space $(\Omega, \mathcal{F}, \mu)$.

It does not come as a surprise that the $\{\mathcal{F}'_n\}$ should correspond to the events that occur once $l'_0$ is reached in $P$, i.e. $\mathcal{F}'_n = \mathcal{F}_{T+n}$, where $T$ is a stopping time such that $L^\phi_T = l'_0$. Similarly, the candidates for $C'_n$ are also $C_{T+n}$, yet we must prove that they satisfy the conditions of Definition 4.3. This is only the case if $l'_0$ is a.s. reached.

**Lemma 6.1.** *Let $T$ be an a.s. finite stopping time with respect to the filtration $\{\mathcal{F}_n\}$, and $\{C_n\}$ be as in Definition 4.3. Then, for all $n \geq 1$ $C_{T+n}$ has the same distribution as $\{C_n\}$. Moreover, $C_{T+n}$ is $\mathcal{F}_{T+n}$-measurable and independent of $\mathcal{F}_{T+n-1}$.*

*Proof.* The result follows from the fact that the event $\{T = \infty\}$ can be ignored. We first prove that $C_{T+n}$ has the same distribution as $\{C_n\}$.

$$\begin{aligned}
& \mathbb{P}(C_{T+n} \in A) \\
= & \quad \wr\ T \text{ a.s. finite } \wr \\
& \textstyle\sum_{0\leq k} \mathbb{P}(C_{T+n} \in A \wedge T = k) \\
= & \quad \wr \text{ substitution } \wr \\
& \textstyle\sum_{0\leq k} \mathbb{P}(C_{k+n} \in A \wedge T = k) \\
= & \quad \wr\ C_{k+n} \text{ independent of } \mathcal{F}_{k+n-1} \supseteq \mathcal{F}_k \ \wr \\
& \textstyle\sum_{0\leq k} \mathbb{P}(C_{k+n} \in A)\mathbb{P}(T = k) \\
= & \quad \wr\ \{C_n\} \text{ identically distributed } \wr \\
& c_A \textstyle\sum_{0\leq k} \mathbb{P}(T = k) \\
= & \quad \wr\ T \text{ a.s. finite } \wr \\
& c_A
\end{aligned}$$

The proof of $C_{T+n}$ being independent of $\mathcal{F}_{T+n-1}$ is similar and thus omitted. We now prove that $C_{T+n}$ is $\mathcal{F}_{T+n}$-measurable.

$$\begin{aligned}
& \{C_{T+n} \in A\} \cap \{T + n = m\} \in \mathcal{F}_m \\
\equiv & \quad \wr\ A \cap B \equiv (A \cap B) \cap B \ \wr \\
& \{C_m \in A\} \cup \{T = m - n\} \in \mathcal{F}_m \\
\equiv & \quad \wr\ C_m \text{ is } \mathcal{F}_m\text{-measurable, and } \mathcal{F}_{m-n} \subseteq \mathcal{F}_m \ \wr \\
& \mathit{true}
\end{aligned}$$

□

### 6.1 Sequential programs

Consider a sequential program $P$ of the form $P_1; \ldots; P_M$. We can define the random variable $T^{k,\phi}$ as the time when the subprogram $P_k$ is reached, and $\Delta T^{k,\phi}$ as the amount of time spent on it.

$$T^{k,\phi} \triangleq \min_n \{n : L^\phi_n = l^i_k\} \tag{15}$$

$$\Delta T^{k,\phi} \triangleq T^{k+1,\phi} - T^{k,\phi} \tag{16}$$

Being a first hitting time indicator, $T^{k,\phi}$ *is* a stopping time. The other random variable, $\Delta T^{k,\phi}$, is however not necessarily a stopping time, as it measures a relative amount of time. However, we can transform it into a stopping time by adjusting the time frame.

**Lemma 6.2.** *$\Delta T^{k,\phi}$ is a stopping time with respect to the filtration $\{\mathcal{F}_{T^{k,\phi}+n}\}$.*

*Proof.* We need to prove $\{\Delta T^{W,\phi} \leq n\}$ is $\mathcal{F}_{T^{k,\phi}+n}$-measurable:

$$\begin{aligned}
& \{\Delta T^{k+1,\phi} \leq n\} \in \mathcal{F}_{T^{k,\phi}+n} \\
\equiv & \quad \wr \text{ definition of } \mathcal{F}_T \ \wr \\
& \forall m \quad \{\Delta T^{k+1,\phi} \leq n\} \cap \{T^{k,\phi} + n \leq m\} \in \mathcal{F}_m \\
\equiv & \quad \wr \text{ (16) } \wr \\
& \forall m \quad \{T^{k+1,\phi} \leq m\} \in \mathcal{F}_m \\
\equiv & \quad \wr\ T^{k+1,\phi} \text{ is a stopping time } \wr \\
& \mathit{true}
\end{aligned}$$

□

Another interesting property is that if an event $\omega$ is not terminating in $P_k$, i.e. $T^{k,\phi} < \infty$ and $T^{k+1,\phi} = \infty$, then $\Delta T^{k,\phi} = \infty$ and $\Delta T^{l,\phi} = 0$ for all $l > k$. Also $T^{k,\phi}$ can be reconstructed as $\sum_{l<k} \Delta T^{l,\phi}$.

**Lemma 6.3.** *Let $P_1; \ldots ; P_M$ be a probabilistic program with semantic space $(\Omega,\ \mathcal{F},\ \mu, \{\mathcal{F}_n\},\ \mathbf{X}_0,\ \{C_n\})$, a memoryless scheduler $\phi$ and its associated semantics $\{(L, \mathbf{X})^\phi_n\}$, such that $T^{k,\phi}$ a.s. finite. Then, $(\Omega,\ \mathcal{F},\ \mu', \{\mathcal{F}'_n\},\ \mathbf{X}'_0,\ \{C'_n\})$ is a valid semantic space for program $P_k$, where:*

$$\mu' \triangleq \mu \qquad \mathbf{X}_0 \triangleq \mathbf{X}_{T^{k,\phi}}$$
$$\mathcal{F}'_n \triangleq \mathcal{F}_{T^{k,\phi}+n} \qquad C'_n \triangleq C_{T^{k,\phi}+n}$$

*Moreover, both semantics are related as follows:*

$$(L', \mathbf{X}')^\phi_n = (L, \mathbf{X})^\phi_{T^{k,\phi}+n}$$
$$T'^\phi = \Delta T^{k,\phi}$$

The identities in the previous Lemma are well defined because all random variables belong to the *same* probability space $(\Omega, \mathcal{F}, \mu)$.

### 6.2 Conditional Branching and Non-Determinism

For branching structures like $\mathbf{if}\, G\, \mathbf{then}\, P_t\, \mathbf{else}\, P_f\, \mathbf{od}$ we define the following stopping times:

$$T^{t,\phi} \triangleq \min_n\{n\ :\ L^\phi = l^t_\perp\} \tag{17}$$
$$T^{f,\phi} \triangleq \min_n\{n\ :\ L^\phi = l^f_\perp\} \tag{18}$$

Since both branches cannot be taken simultaneously, the statement $T^{t,\phi} = \infty \vee T^{f,\phi} = \infty$ holds with *certainty*. In turn, we can reconstruct the time of termination of the original program as follows:

$$T^\phi = (T^{t,\phi} \wedge T^{f,\phi}) + 1$$

The second summand corresponds to the execution of the join transition from Table 1. One may be tempted to analyze $P_t$ and $P_f$ in $(\Omega,\ \mathcal{F},\ \mu,\ \{\mathcal{F}_{n+1}\},\ \mathbf{X}_1,\ \{C_{n+1}\})$. In fact, if both $P_t$ and $P_f$ terminate then the full program does, but the converse does not hold. For example a non-terminating $P_t$ does not prohibit termination for initial valuations that do not satisfy the condition. Thus, we should "eliminate" such events from the semantics of $P_t$ and $P_f$. To do so, we define the semantics of both branches in different probability spaces, but we maintain the same measurable space $(\Omega, \mathcal{F})$. Moreover, null events in one probability space are a.s. valid in the other one.

**Lemma 6.4.** *Let $\mathbf{if}\, G\, \mathbf{then}\, P_t\, \mathbf{else}\, P_f\, \mathbf{od}$ be a probabilistic program with a semantic space $(\Omega,\ \mathcal{F},\ \mu, \{\mathcal{F}_n\},\ \mathbf{X}_0,\ \{C_n\})$ and $\phi$ a memoryless scheduler defining a semantics $\{(L, \mathbf{X})^\phi_n\}$. Then, $(\Omega,\ \mathcal{F},\ \mu^t, \{\mathcal{F}^t_n\},\ \mathbf{X}^t_0,\ \{C^t_n\})$ is a valid semantic space for $P_t$, with*

$$\mu^t \triangleq \mu|_{G_0} \qquad \mathbf{X}^t_0 \triangleq \mathbf{X}_0$$
$$\mathcal{F}^t_n \triangleq \mathcal{F}_{n+1} \qquad C^t_n \triangleq C_{n+1}$$

*and similarly for $(\Omega,\ \mathcal{F},\ \mu^f, \{\mathcal{F}^f_n\},\ \mathbf{X}^f_0,\ \{C^f_n\})$ and $P_f$. where $\mu^f \triangleq \mu|_{\overline{G}_0}$. The semantics are related as follows:*

$$(L^t, \mathbf{X}^t)^\phi_n = (L, \mathbf{X})^\phi_{n+1} \qquad \textit{in } (\Omega, \mathcal{F}, \mu^t)$$
$$(L^f, \mathbf{X}^f)^\phi_n = (L, \mathbf{X})^\phi_{n+1} \qquad \textit{in } (\Omega, \mathcal{F}, \mu^f)$$
$$(L, \mathbf{X})^\phi_{n+1} = \mathbf{1}_{G_0}(L^t, \mathbf{X}^t)^\phi_n + \mathbf{1}_{\overline{G}_0}(L^f, \mathbf{X}^f)^\phi_n \qquad \textit{in } (\Omega, \mathcal{F}, \mu)$$

Notice that $\mathbf{X}_n$, $\mathbf{X}^t_n$, and $\mathbf{X}^f_n$, are all random vectors in the probability spaces $(\Omega, \mathcal{F}, \mu)$, $(\Omega, \mathcal{F}, \mu^t)$, and $(\Omega, \mathcal{F}, \mu^f)$, since they are $(\mathcal{F}, \mathcal{B}(\mathbb{R}))$-measurable. The different probability measures just induce different stochastic behaviors, as characterized in the above lemma. Notice that since $\phi$ is memoryless we can use the same analysis for the non-deterministic case, because the non-deterministic condition '$*$' can be replaced by a measurable set.

### 6.3 While Loops

The last program construction that we have to decompose is the while loop $W \triangleq \mathbf{while}\, G\, \mathbf{do}\, P_W\, \mathbf{od}$. There are some important random variables that characterize $W$.

$$T^{W,\phi}_k \triangleq \min_n\{n\ :\ L^\phi_n = l_G \wedge \#_n\, l_G = k\} \wedge T^\phi \tag{19}$$
$$\Delta T^{W,\phi}_k \triangleq T^{W,\phi}_{k+1} - T^{W,\phi}_k \tag{20}$$
$$S^{W,\phi} \triangleq \#_\infty\, l_G \tag{21}$$

where $\#_n\, l(\omega) = \sum_{0 \le k \le n} \mathbf{1}_{[L^\phi_k = l]}(\omega)$ is the number of times location $l$ was reached in the first $n$ steps. The random variable $T^{W,\phi}_k$ indicates the time when $W$ starts the $k$-th iteration. In case $W$ performs the loop body less than $k$ times, we could consider $T^{W,\phi}_k$ to be infinite, but instead we consider the $k$-th iteration to take place immediately at the time $W$ terminates. This technicality ensures that $T^{W,\phi}_k \le T^{W,\phi}_{k+1} \le T^\phi$, i.e. we have a partial order on the stopping times, with $T^\phi$ as a supremum. Similar to our handling of the sequential operator, $\Delta T^{W,\phi}_k$ indicates the time spent at the $k$-th iteration, with $\Delta T^{W,\phi}_k = 0$ in case the loop finishes or diverges prior to the $k$th iterations. The last random variable introduced above, $S^{W,\phi}$, counts the numbers of times the guard of the loop is evaluated before termination. Some important identities can be derived:

$$T^{W,\phi}_k = \sum_{l<k} \Delta T^{W,\phi}_l \tag{22}$$
$$T^\phi = \sum_{l \le S^{W,\phi}} \Delta T^{W,\phi}_l \tag{23}$$

Similar random variables are to be defined in case of nested while loops. For the present work we only need the analogon of $S^{W,\phi}$. Considering the case where $W \lhd W_m \lhd \ldots \lhd W_1$, and $k_j$ indicates the current iteration of loop $W_j$, we define

$$S^{W,\phi}_{k_1,\ldots,k_m} \triangleq \sum_{0 \le n} \mathbf{1}_{[L^\phi_n = l_G \wedge \forall_{j \le m}\, \#_n\, l_{G_k} = k_j]} \tag{24}$$

Notice that $S^{W,\phi}_{k_1,\ldots,k_m} = 0$ whenever one of the parent loops $W_j$ terminated before $k_j$ iterations.

**Lemma 6.5.** *Let $W$ be a program of the form $\mathbf{while}\, G\, \mathbf{do}\, P_W\, \mathbf{od}$ equipped with a semantic space $(\Omega,\ \mathcal{F},\ \mu, \{\mathcal{F}_n\},\ \mathbf{X}_0,\ \{C_n\})$, and a memoryless scheduler $\phi$ that defines a semantics $\{(L, \mathbf{X})^\phi_n\}$. Then $(\Omega,\ \mathcal{F},\ \mu^k, \{\mathcal{F}^k_n\},\ \mathbf{X}^k_0,\ \{C^k_n\})$ is a valid semantic space for $P_W$ where*

$$\mu^k \triangleq \mu|_{G^\phi_k} \qquad \mathbf{X}^k_0 \triangleq \mathbf{X}^\phi_{T^{W,\phi}_k}$$
$$\mathcal{F}^k_n \triangleq \mathcal{F}_{T^{W,\phi}_k+n+1} \qquad C^k_n \triangleq C_{T^{W,\phi}_k+n+1}$$

*Then the following equalities a.s. hold, provided $G^\phi_k$ is not empty, and $T^{W,\phi}_k$ is a.s. finite.*

$$(L^k, \mathbf{X}^k)^\phi_n = (L, \mathbf{X})^\phi_{T^{W,\phi}_k+n} \qquad \textit{in } (\Omega, \mathcal{F}, \mu^k)$$
$$\mathbf{X}^\phi_{T^{W,\phi}_{k+1}} = \mathbf{1}_{G^\phi_k}\mathbf{X}^k_{T^k} + \mathbf{1}_{\overline{G}^\phi_k}\mathbf{X}^k_0 \qquad \textit{in } (\Omega, \mathcal{F}, \mu)$$
$$(L, \mathbf{X})^\phi_{T^{W,\phi}_k+n+1} = \mathbf{1}_{G^\phi_k}(L^k, \mathbf{X}^k)^\phi_n + \mathbf{1}_{\overline{G}^\phi_k}(L^k, \mathbf{X}^k)^\phi_{T^{W,\phi}_k} \qquad \textit{in } (\Omega, \mathcal{F}, \mu)$$

A (maybe) surprising result is that $S^{W,\phi}$ *is a stopping time for* a specific filtration.

**Lemma 6.6.** *The random variable $S^{W,\phi}$ is a stopping time with respect to the filtration $\{\mathcal{F}_{T^{W,\phi}_n}\}$.*

*Proof.* We need to prove $\{S^{W,\phi} \leq n\}$ is $\mathcal{F}_{T_n^{W,\phi}}$-measurable:

$$
\begin{array}{ll}
& \{S^{W,\phi} \leq n\} \in \mathcal{F}_{T_n^{W,\phi}} \\
\equiv & \quad \wr \text{ definition of } \mathcal{F}_T \ \wr \\
& \forall m \quad \{S^{W,\phi} \leq n\} \cap \{T_n^{W,\phi} \leq m\} \in \mathcal{F}_m \\
\equiv & \quad \wr \ S^{W,\phi} \leq n \equiv T_n^{W,\phi} = T^{W,\phi} \ \wr \\
& \forall m \quad \{T^{W,\phi} \leq m\} \in \mathcal{F}_m \\
\equiv & \quad \wr \ T^{W,\phi} \text{ is an stopping time } \wr \\
& true
\end{array}
$$

□

The above lemma turns out to be very important to prove termination. It suggests that we only have to look at the random process $\{(L, \mathbf{X})^{\phi}_{T_n^{W,\phi}}\}$ in order to prove termination of $W$.

## 7. Compositional Reasoning about Termination

In this section we present a compositional framework for almost sure termination that fully exploits the program structure. In general we are facing a loop $W = \textbf{while}\, G\, \textbf{do}\, P_1 \ldots P_N\, \textbf{od}$, where each $P_k$ can be another loop. We aim to prove $W$ is a.s. terminating by showing that each nested loop of $W$ is a.s. terminating, together with an a.s. termination proof for a sliced, unnested version of $W$. We take great care to make the resulting framework apt for implementation.

### 7.1 A probabilistic lexicographic argument

If $W$ does not involve any randomization, them we can apply a very simple compositional variant rule [14, 26] using Floyd-Hoare logic:

$$
\text{V-RULE}\ \frac{\begin{array}{c}\forall k : P_k \text{ terminates and } \{\, R = z \,\}\, P_k \,\{\, R \leq z \,\} \\ \exists k \,\{\, R = z \,\}\, P_k \,\{\, R < z \,\} \qquad < \text{is well-founded}\end{array}}{\textbf{while}\, G\, \textbf{do}\, P_1 \ldots P_N\, \textbf{od} \quad \text{terminates}}
$$

This proof rule induces a lexicographic ranking function on well-structured programs. To apply this rule we need to prove the termination of each inner loop separately, and ensure that the variant argument $R$ does not increase in any $P_k$. Additionally, we need to find at least one $P_k$ where $R$ indeed decreases. The inference rule V-RULE is sound but not complete as $R$ can be increased in an inner loop as long as that gets compensated later. Despite its simplicity, it is a powerful inference rule, since it can be applied recursively until a simple while loop without nesting remains. Thus, one only needs a procedure to synthesize ranking functions for simple loops, combined with effective decision procedures to verify the non-increasing and strictly decreasing conditions.

Condition $\{\, R = z \,\}\, P_k \,\{\, R \leq z \,\}$ is basically another way of expressing $R' \leq R$ where $R'$ is the value of the expression $R$ after executing $P_k$. Such a predicate, involving primed and unprimed expressions, can be regarded as a *transition invariant* [32]. Also, predicates $R' \leq R$ and $R' < R$ correspond to conditions *Unaffecting* and *Ranking* in the work of Bradley, Manna and Sipma [5].

We aim for an extension of the V-RULE to the probabilistic case, implying the need to synthesize ranking supermartingales instead of ranking functions. We thus need to construct the probabilistic counterpart of transition invariants, or more precisely of conditions *Unaffecting* and *Ranking*. Since we are dealing with decreasing expectations, the natural way forward considers *probabilistic transition invariants* as relations between unprimed expressions and the conditional expectation of primed ones. This means requiring $\mathbb{E}(R' \mid R) \leq R$ for *Unaffecting*. An effective way of ensuring this is given by the following inductive definition:

$$
\begin{aligned}
Dec_{\leq}(E, X := e) &\triangleq \mathbb{E}(E[X/e] \mid Vars) \leq E \\
Dec_{\leq}(E, P_1; P_2) &\triangleq Dec_{\leq}(E, P_1) \wedge Dec_{\leq}(E, P_2) \\
Dec_{\leq}(E, \textbf{if} \ldots) &\triangleq Dec_{\leq}(E, P_t) \wedge Dec_{\leq}(E, P_f) \\
Dec_{\leq}(E, \textbf{while} \ldots) &\triangleq Dec_{\leq}(E, P_W)
\end{aligned}
$$

Notice that the base case corresponds to the weakest precondition of that simple assignment. In case that $E$ is *propositionally linear*, i.e. an expression of the form $\mathbf{1}_{G_1} E_1 + \ldots + \mathbf{1}_{G_n} E_n$ where $G_k$ is a conjunctive linear predicate, and $E_k$ is a linear expression, the Motzkin transposition theorem can be applied to check $Dec_{\leq}(E, P)$ as pointed out by Katoen et al. [25]. If $Dec_{\leq}(E, P)$ is satisfied, it ensures that $\{E_n^{\phi}\}$ is a supermartingale irrespective of the scheduler $\phi$, provided all $E_k$ are integrable.

The probabilistic counterpart of the *Ranking* condition is similar:

$$
\begin{aligned}
Dec_{<}(E, X := e) &\triangleq \mathbb{E}(E[X/e] \mid Vars) \leq E - \varepsilon \\
Dec_{<}(E, P_1; P_2) &\triangleq (Dec_{<}(E, P_1) \wedge Dec_{\leq}(E, P_2)) \vee \\
&\phantom{\triangleq} \ (Dec_{\leq}(E, P_1) \wedge Dec_{<}(E, P_2)) \\
Dec_{<}(E, \textbf{if} \ldots) &\triangleq Dec_{<}(E, P_t) \wedge Dec_{<}(E, P_f) \\
Dec_{<}(E, \textbf{while} \ldots) &\triangleq false
\end{aligned}
$$

where $\varepsilon > 0$, is existentially quantified. $Dec_{<}(E, P)$ guarantees that the expectation of $E$ strictly decreases by the execution of $P$. Notably, $E$ is not necessarily decreased after the execution of a loop, because the loop body might be executed zero times. The conditions $Dec_{\leq}$ and $Dec_{<}$ constitute an over approximation and can be weakened so as to provide a more precise but costly analysis.

**Definition 7.1** (Compositional Ranking Supermartingale)**.** Given a loop $\textbf{while}\, G\, \textbf{do}\, P_W\, \textbf{od}$, a *compositional ranking supermartingale* $R$ is a propositionally linear expression over the program variables such that $Dec_{\leq}(R, P_W)$ and $Dec_{<}(R, P_W)$.

### 7.2 A counter-example

Although it does appear plausible that with this probabilistic interpretation the V-RULE is sound in the context of probabilistic programs, this is *not* the case in general. Consider the following non-terminating program $P$ with a nested loop $P'$:

$X := 1;$
**while** $X > 0$ **do**
  $C := 0$
  **while** $C < 0.5$ **do**
    $C := uniform(0, 1);$
    **if** $C < 0.5$ **then** $X := 2(X - 1)$ **else** $X := 2$ **fi**
  **od**
  $X := X - 1$
**od**

The inner loop $P'$ finishes once the sampled value is greater than $0.5$, in that case the variable $X$ is set to 2. The next instruction decrements the value of $X$ to 1, and thus the guard of the outer loop remains satisfied. Suppose that we overlook that the program never terminates, and we instead want to find a compositional ranking supermartingale for $P$ so as to prove a.s. termination. The obvious choice would be $X$: It is decremented in every outer iteration, and the program finishes as soon as $X$ is 0 in the guard of $P$. We only need to prove that, the value of $X$ decreases in expectation after $P'$ terminates, i.e. we aim to show

$$
\mathbb{E}(X_T \mid \mathcal{F}_0) \leq X_0 \tag{25}
$$

where $X_0$, and $X_T$ are the values of $X$ before and after executing $P'$. We want to prove the above by showing that the value of $X$ does not increase in expectation after a single iteration:

$$\mathbb{E}(X_{n+1} \mid \mathcal{F}_n) \leq X_n \quad \text{for all } n \tag{26}$$

The latter is true because $\mathbb{E}(X_{n+1} \mid \mathcal{F}_n) = \frac{1}{2}\mathbb{E}(2(X_n - 1) \mid \mathcal{F}_n) + \frac{1}{2}\mathbb{E}(2 \mid \mathcal{F}_n) = X_n$. Effectively $X$ is a compositional ranking supermartingale according to Definition 7.1. But, $\mathbb{E}(X_T \mid \mathcal{F}_0) = 2 > 1 = X_0$ since $X_T = 2$, i.e. condition (26) does not imply (25), while it should be implied if the probabilistic version of the V-RULE were sound. The root of this problem is that $Dec_{\leq}$ cannot be used to prove (25). In the following section we show under which circumstances $Dec_{\leq}$ can indeed be used safely.

### 7.3 Preserving probabilistic transition invariants

In this subsection we present sufficient conditions to guarantee that supermartingale properties are kept after almost sure termination. We also give stronger conditions that are relatively straightforward to automate. As a basis we use that the supermartingale properties are ensured at a stopping time whenever the underlying supermartingale is uniformly integrable:

**Theorem 7.2** (Optional Sampling [1]). *Let $\{X_n\}$ be a supermartingale and $\{T_n\}$ a sequence of increasing stopping times, then $\{X_{T_n}\}$ is a supermartingale in $\{\mathcal{F}_{T_n}\}$ if either one of the following conditions holds:*

- *$T_n \leq c_n$ for all $n$ where $c_n$ are constants.*
- *$\{X_n\}$ is uniformly integrable.*

The first condition allows us to infer the supermartingale property on bounded terminating programs, for example without loops. For the general case however, we are left with the second condition, which in turn forces us to prove condition (8). Unfortunately, the latter is not readily mechanizable in contemporary theorem provers, and thus is an impediment for our efforts to arrive at a directly implementable framework. We therefore embark on making it more manageable.

**Lemma 7.3** (UI of Dominated Sequences [35]). *Let $\{X_n\}$ be a random process, and $Y$ be an integrable r.v. such that $|X_n| \leq Y$ for all $n$. Then the random process $\{X_n\}$ is uniformly integrable.*

**Lemma 7.4.** *Let $\{X_n\}$ a random process adapted to $\{\mathcal{F}_n\}$ such that $X_n$ integrable and $\mathbb{E}(|X_{n+1} - X_n| \mid \mathcal{F}_n) \leq c$ for some fixed constant $c$, and let $T$ an integrable stopping time. Then $\{X_{n \wedge T}\}$ is uniformly integrable.*

*Proof.* Let $D_n \triangleq |X_n - X_{n-1}|\mathbf{1}_{\{T \geq n\}}$, for all $0 < n$, then $|X_{n \wedge T}| \leq |X_0| + \sum_{1 \leq k} D_k$ for all $n$. Using Lemma 7.3, we only need to prove that the expectation of the summation is finite.

$$\begin{array}{ll} & \mathbb{E}(D_{n+1} \mid \mathcal{F}_n) \\ = & \quad \wr \text{ definition of } D_n \; \wr \\ & \mathbb{E}(|X_{n+1} - X_n|\mathbf{1}_{\{T \geq n+1\}} \mid \mathcal{F}_n) \\ = & \quad \wr \; \{T > n\} \text{ is } \mathcal{F}_n\text{-measurable, and (7)} \; \wr \\ & \mathbb{E}(|X_{n+1} - X_n| \mid \mathcal{F}_n)\mathbf{1}_{\{T \geq n+1\}} \\ \leq & \quad \wr \text{ hypothesis } \wr \\ & c\mathbf{1}_{\{T \geq n+1\}} \end{array}$$

Applying (4) we obtain $\mathbb{E}(D_n) \leq c\mathbb{P}(T \geq n)$, then:

$$\begin{array}{ll} & \mathbb{E}(\sum_{1 \leq k} D_k) \\ = & \quad \wr \text{ linearity } \wr \\ & \sum_{1 \leq k} \mathbb{E}(D_k) \\ \leq & \quad \wr \text{ previous derivation } \wr \\ & c\sum_{1 \leq k} \mathbb{P}(T \geq k) \\ = & \quad \wr \text{ characterization of } \mathbb{E}(T) \; \wr \\ & c\mathbb{E}(T) \\ < & \quad \wr \; T \text{ integrable } \wr \\ & \infty \end{array}$$

□

As we use supermartingales to guarantee a.s. termination, requiring $T$ integrable is not a impediment in our framework. The main implementation benefit of this lemma is that the condition $\mathbb{E}(|X_{n+1} - X_n| \mid \mathcal{F}_n) \leq c$ can be directly inferred from a program statement using normal static analysis or the following function that take into account the expected behavior:

$$BM(x := e) \triangleq \begin{cases} Vars & \text{if } \mathbb{E}(|e - X| \mid Vars) \leq c \\ Vars \setminus \{x\} & \text{otherwise} \end{cases}$$

$$BM(P_1; P_2) \triangleq BM(P_1) \cap BM(P_2)$$
$$BM(\,\mathbf{if}\; G\; \mathbf{then}\; P_t\; \mathbf{else}\; P_f\; \mathbf{od}\,) \triangleq BM(P_t) \cap BM(P_f)$$
$$BM(\mathbf{while}\; G\; \mathbf{do}\; P_W\; \mathbf{od}\,) \triangleq Vars \setminus lvars(S)$$

As uniform integrable families preserve martingale properties in general, one can use Lemma 7.4 also as a means to prove that a program is *not* positive a.s. terminating: This boils down to finding a positive *submartingale* that is 0 only when the program terminates.

**Corollary 7.5.** *Let $\{Y_n\}$ a positive submartingale with respect to the filtration $\{\mathcal{F}_n\}$, i.e. $\mathbb{E}(Y_{n+1} \mid \mathcal{F}_n) \geq Y_n$ and $Y_n \geq 0$ for all $n$, such that $\mathbb{E}(|Y_{n+1} - Y_n| \mid \mathcal{F}_n) \leq c$. Then, the stopping time $T = \min_n\{n : Y_n = 0\}$ is not integrable unless $Y_0 = 0$.*

### 7.4 Probabilistic V-RULE + typechecking ⇒ a.s. termination

The theory developed thus far revolves around probabilistic assertions on the program variables, and we discussed the basis of obtaining these assertions in a symbolic manner. However, the results are correct only if we guarantee that the program variables appearing in the assertions are integrable. This task is in itself not trivial. A program could induce an arbitrary distribution on the program variables, including some with for example infinite expectation. We know that all variables are of type $\mathbb{R}$, but we need means to infer which ones are integrable. We will attack this remaining problem now, by means of static typechecking with dependent types. To guarantee that the relevant expressions are integrable we again rely on uniform integrability as this implies bounded expectation.

We shall label each program instruction with two sets of program variables yielding the form $\{\, Y_1, \ldots, Y_n \,\}\, P \,\{\, Z_1, \ldots, Z_m \,\}$. Informally, it means that if variables $Y_1, \ldots, Y_n$ are integrable before executing $P$, then $Z_1, \ldots, Z_m$, will be integrable after $P$ terminates. A program will be *well-labeled* if the labeling is obtained using the inference rules in Table 2. The rule for loops is based on the requirements of Lemma 7.4. The linear combination of integrable random variables is also integrable. A r.v. of the form $X * Y$ is not necessarily integrable even if both $X$ and $Y$ are. As an example, consider $X$ that is $(\sqrt{2})^n$ with probability $\frac{1}{2^n}$, then $\mathbb{E}(X) = \frac{\sqrt{2}}{\sqrt{2}-1}$, but $\mathbb{E}(X^2) = \infty$. This restriction can be relaxed if a previous static analysis of the program shows that at least one the two variables is bounded. The rest of the rules are straightforward.

$$\text{BASE}\ \frac{}{\{\,\emptyset\,\}\,P\,\{\,\emptyset\,\}} \qquad \text{SEQ}\ \frac{\{\,A_1\,\}\,P_1\,\{\,B_1\,\} \quad \{\,A_2\,\}\,P_2\,\{\,B_2\,\} \quad A_2 \subseteq B_1}{\{\,A_1\,\}\,P_1; P_2\,\{\,B_2\,\}}$$

$$\text{MOD}\ \frac{\{\,A_1\,\}\,P\,\{\,B_1\,\} \quad A_1 \subseteq A_2 \quad B_1 \supseteq B_2}{\{\,A_2\,\}\,P\,\{\,B_2\,\}}$$

$$\text{ASSIG-L}\ \frac{e \text{ linear} \quad vars(e) \subseteq A}{\{\,A\,\}\,x := e\,\{\,A \cup \{x\}\,\}} \qquad \text{ASSIG-NL}\ \frac{e \text{ non-linear} \quad vars(e) \subseteq A}{\{\,A\,\}\,x := e\,\{\,A \setminus \{x\}\,\}}$$

$$\text{WHILE}\ \frac{\{\,A\,\}\,P\,\{\,B\,\} \quad A \subseteq B}{\{\,A\,\}\,\textbf{while}\,G\,\textbf{do}\,P\,\textbf{od}\,\{\,A \cap BM(P)\,\}} \qquad \text{IF}\ \frac{\{\,A_1\,\}\,P_1\,\{\,B_1\,\} \quad \{\,A_2\,\}\,P_2\,\{\,B_2\,\}}{\{\,A_1 \cup A_2\,\}\,\textbf{if}\,G\,\textbf{then}\,P_1\,\textbf{else}\,P_2\,\textbf{fi}\,\{\,B_1 \cap B_2\,\}}$$

**Table 2.** Inference Rules

**Theorem 7.6.** *Given a well-labeled program* $\{\,A\,\}\,P\,\{\,B\,\}$ *with semantic space* $(\Omega,\ \mathcal{F},\ \mu, \{\mathcal{F}_n\},\ \mathbf{X}_0,\ \{C_n\})$*, and a valid scheduler* $\phi$ *such that:*

*(i)* $\mathbb{P}(T^\phi < \infty) = 1$,

*(ii)* $Y_0^\phi$ *integrable for all variables* $Y \in A$*, and*

*(iii)* $S^{W,\phi}_{k1,\ldots,k_m}$ *integrable for all while-loops* $W \trianglelefteq P$.

*Then,* $Z^\phi_{T^\phi}$ *is integrable for all* $Z \in B$*, and for all propositionally linear expressions* $E$ *such that* $vars(E) \subseteq A_S \cap B_S$ *for all* $\{\,A_S\,\}\,S\,\{\,B_S\,\}$ *with* $S \trianglelefteq P$*:*

*(a)* $Dec_{\leq}(E, P) \Rightarrow \mathbb{E}(E^\phi_{T^\phi} \mid \mathcal{F}_0) \leq E^\phi_0$

*(b)* $Dec_{<}(E, P) \Rightarrow \mathbb{E}(E^\phi_{T^\phi} \mid \mathcal{F}_0) \leq E^\phi_0 - \varepsilon$*, for some fixed* $\varepsilon > 0$

*(c)* $E \subseteq BM(P) \Rightarrow \mathbb{E}(|E^\phi_{T^\phi} - E^\phi_0| \mid \mathcal{F}_0) \leq c$*, for some fixed* $c > 0$.

*Proof.* Structural induction on $P$ for *any* semantic space. For the base case $\{\,A\,\}\,X := e\,\{\,B\,\}$ we only need to analyze the case when $X \in B$. The only rule from Table 2 that can be applied is ASSIGN-L. Thus, $e$ is linear; $vars(e) \subseteq A$; $Y^\phi_0$ integrable for all $Y \in vars(e)$; $X^\phi_{T^\phi} = e^\phi_0$ is integrable. Properties (a)-(c) follow immediately from the definition of $Dec_{\leq}$, $Dec_{<}$, and $BM$.

For the sequential composition $\{\,A\,\}\,P_1\,\{\,B\,\}\,P_2\,\{\,C\,\}$ and using (i), we have $\Delta T^{1,\phi}$, and $\Delta T^{2,\phi}$ a.s. finite. Applying the induction hypothesis (IH) on $\{\,A\,\}\,P_1\,\{\,B\,\}$ using the same semantic space, we obtain $Y^\phi_{\Delta T^{1,\phi}}$ integrable for all $Y \in B$, and (a)-(c) for all propositionally linear expressions. We can apply IH on $\{\,B\,\}\,P_2\,\{\,C\,\}$ and the semantic space $(\Omega,\ \mathcal{F},\ \mu,\ \{\mathcal{F}_{\Delta T^{1,\phi}+n}\},\ \mathbf{X}_0,\ \{C_{\Delta T^{1,\phi}+n}\})$. Using Lemma 6.2 we obtain $Z^\phi_{T^\phi} = Z^\phi_{\Delta T^{1,\phi}+\Delta T^{2,\phi}}$ is integrable for all $Z \in C$. Properties (a)-(c) are again straightforward from the function definitions. The conditional branching case proceeds similar, but uses Lemma 6.4.

Let's prove the looping case $\{\,A\,\}\,\textbf{while}\,G\,\textbf{do}\,P_W\,\textbf{od}\,\{\,B\,\}$. From (i) we can deduce $\Delta T^{W,\phi}_k$ a.s. finite. We also have that $\{\,A\,\}\,P_W\,\{\,A\,\}$ is well-labeled, thus we can apply IH with respect to the semantic space $(\Omega,\ \mathcal{F},\ \mu^k, \{\mathcal{F}^k_n\},\ \mathbf{X}^k_0,\ \{C^k_n\})$ as defined in Lemma 6.5. By induction on $k$, we obtain $Y$ integrable at time $T^{W,\phi}_k$ for all $Y \in A$, and conditions (a)-(c) are satisfied at time $T^{W,\phi}_k$. If the program variable $Z \in B$ then $Z \in BM(P_W)$. In turn, we can apply Lemma 7.4 as $S^{W,\phi}$ is integrable, and obtain $Z$ uniform integrable when sampled at times $\{T^{W,\phi}_k\}$. Thus, $Z$ is integrable when the program terminates. Condition (a) follows from Lemma 7.4 and Theorem 7.2. Conditions (b) and (c) are trivial since $Dec_{<}(E, W) = false$, and $BM(W) \cap lvars(W) = \emptyset$. □

The previous theorem ensures uniform integrability of program variables at specific points in the execution. However, it requires to prove that loops are expected to be executed a finite number of times. This is weaker than requiring positive a.s. termination, but is clearly stronger than a.s. termination in case of nested loops. The next theorem shows that the probabilistic lexicographic argument is sound if a well-labeling is provided. Yet, such a labeling must ensure that compositional ranking supermartingales employed are integrable.

**Theorem 7.7** (Compositional Termination)**.** *Given a well-labeled program* $\{\,A\,\}\,P\,\{\,B\,\}$ *and a semantic space* $(\Omega,\ \mathcal{F},\ \mu, \{\mathcal{F}_n\},\ \mathbf{X}_0,\ \{C_n\})$*, such that* $Y_0$ *is integrable for all* $Y \in A$ *and for each while-loop* $\{\,A_L\,\}\,W\,\{\,B_L\,\}$ *in* $P$ *we have a compositional ranking supermartingale* $R$ *satisfying*

*(i)* $vars(R) \in A_L$.

*(ii)* $P' \triangleleft W$ *and* $\{\,A'\,\}\,P'\,\{\,B'\,\}$ *imply* $vars(R) \in A' \cap B'$

*Then,* $\mathbb{P}(T^\phi < \infty) = 1$*, and* $\mathbb{E}(S^{W,\phi}) < \infty$ *for all loops, and all schedulers* $\phi$.

*Proof.* By induction on the structure of $P$ for *any* semantic space. The base case is trivially terminating. For the sequence and conditional branching we have to apply similar arguments as in Theorem 7.6, thus we omit them.

We turn to proving that $\textbf{while}\,G\,\textbf{do}\,P_W\,\textbf{od}$ is a.s. terminating. We can assume that $\{\,A\,\}\,P_W\,\{\,A\,\}$ is well-labeled, i.e. that the MOD rule was not applied to $P$ and therefore $A = A_W \subseteq B_W$. Nesting an induction on $k$ we can prove using IH that $P_W$ a.s. terminates with the semantic space $(\Omega,\ \mathcal{F},\ \mu^k, \{\mathcal{F}^k_n\},\ \mathbf{X}^k_0,\ \{C^k_n\})$. Using Lemma 6.5 and Theorem 7.6 we can then infer that $\Delta T^{W,\phi}_k$ is a.s. finite, and that:

$$\mathbb{E}(R_{T^{W,\phi}_{k+1}} \mid \mathcal{F}_{T^{W,\phi}_k}) \leq R_{T^{W,\phi}_k} - \varepsilon \mathbf{1}_{G_0 \cap \ldots G_{T^{W,\phi}_k}}$$

in the original semantic space of $P$ because $Dec_{<}(R, P_W)$ and $vars(R) \in A$. Thus $\{R_{T^{W,\phi}_n} \mathbf{1}_{R_{T^{W,\phi}_n} > 0}\}$ is a ranking supermartingale with respect to the filtration $\{\mathcal{F}_{T^{W,\phi}_n}\}$, and from Lemma 5.5 $S^{W,\phi}$ is integrable. We are only left with the need to prove that $T^\phi$ is a.s. finite. Here, the identity (22) comes in handy to ensure that, since all the involved r.v. are a.s. finite. □

Theorem 7.7 only ensures a.s. termination, i.e. the random variable $T^*$ is not necessarily integrable. The terminating argument built into the proof is not a global supermartingale that decreases in expectation at each step, instead it is a ranking supermartingale that decreases after a.s. finite random steps.

As a concrete example, the following labelled program will be used to demonstrate that our proof system is indeed capable of proving a.s. termination of programs where $\mathbb{E}(T^*)$ is not finite. In other words it exemplifies that we can prove a.s. termination compositionally in settings where global supermartingales arguments must fail.

$\{X\}$
$C, U := 0, 1;$
$\{C, U, X\}$
**while** $C < 0.5$ **do**
    $\{C, U, X\}$
    $X := U$
    **while** $X > 0$ **do**
        $\{C, U, X\}$
        $X := X - uniform(0, 1);$
        $\{C, U, X\}$
    **od**
    $\{C, U, X\}$
    $C, U := uniform(0, 1), 2U;$
    $\{C, U, X\}$
**od**
$\{C\}$

It is easy to see that the program is well-labeled according to the rules in Table 2. Furthermore, $\mathbf{1}_{[C<0.5]}$ is an obvious ranking supermartingale for the outer loop, and so is $X$ for the inner loop. Thus we can apply Theorem 7.7 to decide that the program a.s. terminates. Furthermore, we can infer that $S^W$ (the number of times the outer loop is executed), and $\Delta T_k^W$ (the number of steps in the $k$-th iteration) are all integrable. In particular, $\mathbb{E}(S^W) = 2$ since $S^W$ is a simple geometric distribution, and $\mathbb{E}(\Delta T_k^W) \leq 4^k$ as the value of $X$ is decreased by 0.5 on average, starting off from $2^k$ at the beginning of the $k$-th iteration. Also $\Delta T_k^W > 2^k$, as $X$ is decreased by at most 1. This plausibilises why the program a.s. terminates. However $\mathbb{E}(\sum_{k\leq S^W} T_k^W) \geq \sum_{0<k} \mathbb{P}(S = k)2^k = \infty$, i.e. the program does not terminate in finite mean time.

### 7.5 An extensible framework

Independent of the above type system, one would intuitively expect that if a program almost surely terminates for all possible initial states (i.e. initializing via Dirac distributions), then the program terminates under any arbitrary distribution, including those violating the initial precondition in our labeling.

**Theorem 7.8.** *A program $P$ with variables $\{X_n\}$ terminates for all initial valuations such that $\{X_{n,0} = \infty\} = \emptyset$ if and only if it terminates for all initial valuations such that $\mathbb{E}(X_{n,0}) < \infty$.*

*Proof.* Notice that one implication is trivially true. Suppose $P$ terminates for all initial valuations that make the variables integrable. Let us fix an arbitrary probability space $(\Omega, \mathcal{F}, \mu)$, and an initial valuation $\mathbf{X}_0$, such that all $X_{n,0}(\omega)$ are finite. Consider the semantics of this program under a memoryless scheduler $\phi$, and define $A \triangleq \{T^\phi < \infty\}$. We want to prove $\mu(A) = 1$. Let's consider the semantics of the same program under the same probability space, but with a different initial valuation. Namely, $X_{n,0}^m \triangleq X_{n,0}\mathbf{1}_{[|X_{n,0}|\leq m]}$. Thus, we can consider the following measurable sets $A_m \triangleq \{T^{\phi,m} < \infty\}$, and $I_m \triangleq \{\exists_n |X_{n,0}| > m\}$. Notice that $X_{n,0}^m$ is integrable, and therefore $\mu(A_m) = 1$. We also have $A_m \setminus I_m \subseteq A$, $A_m \uparrow A$ and $I_m \downarrow \emptyset$. Thus, $\mu(A_m \setminus I_m) \uparrow 1$, and in turn $\mu(A) = 1$ as needed. □

This theorem is weaker than expected, namely we guarantee termination for those initial distributions that make integrable the program variables. But inside our framework we get this for free owed to the MOD rule. On the other hand, Theorem 7.8 allows us to incorporate a powerful inference rule into our framework

$$\text{ABS}\frac{P \text{ a.s. terminating} \quad A \subseteq Vars \setminus lvars(P)}{\{A\}P\{A\}}$$

thereby relaxing the requirements on compositional ranking supermartingales so that they only need to ensure integrability of unmodified variables. This rule makes it possible to feed into our framework background knowledge about program fragments, especially obtainable by standard non-probabilistic termination arguments.

## 8. Related work

Termination of concurrent probabilistic programs was first studied by Hart, Sharir and Pnueli [22]. They focused on finite state programs under fairness assumptions. In that setting termination is a pure topological property, actual probabilities do not play a role. Later, they gave a sound and complete characterization for almost sure termination in case of countable state spaces [21]. Esparza, Gaiser and Kiefer [12], proposed a sound and complete method for proving termination of finite state programs. Their approach is based on [22] and proceeds by finding a $\omega$-regular expression on the possible outcomes of the random experiments that guarantees termination regardless of the actual state. Monniaux [31] used abstract interpretation techniques to approximate the probability distribution of un-nested loops. He proved termination in cases where the probability of executing a loop more than $n$ times decreases exponentially with $n$. Brázdil et al. [6] proved a.s. termination in the context of probabilistic push-down automata using Azuma's Lemma. McIver and Morgan [30] propose a sound variant rule for probabilistic programs. Their notion is less general than ranking supermartingales as they require variants to be upper bounded. Bournez and Garnier [3] studied positive a.s. termination in the context of term rewriting systems, Gnaedig [17] developed a proof system for positive a.s. termination for rewrite systems under innermost strategies using induction. It is not clear how the author dealt with the integrability problems discussed throughout this paper. Chakarov and Sankaranarayanan [7] applied aspects of martingale theory in the context of verification of deterministic probabilistic programs, presenting sound conditions to prove termination using global ranking supermartingales.

Termination analysis for non-probabilistic programs has grown immensely in the last decade. There are several approaches to prove termination of functional programs and rewriting systems including the size change principle [29], and dependency pairs [16]. In case of imperative programs modern approaches rely on synthesizing several small ranking functions and combining them. Lexicographic approaches [4, 5, 10] try to find an order in the ranking functions in such that the largest modification always decreases. Ramsey methods [2, 8, 11, 28, 32] exploit the fact that a relation is well-founded if its transitive closure is contained in a disjunction of well-founded relation. For a summary on both methods we refer to [10] that proposes a hybrid approach.

## 9. Discussion

Based on a novel filtration-based treatment of probabilistic program semantics, this paper has successfully addressed several intriguing open questions in probabilistic program termination research. On the foundational side, we have extended the theory of ranking supermartingales to provably work with bounded nondeterministic programs. This is complemented with a sound and complete proof method for almost sure termination, together with a safe method to identify the set of program variables having finite expectation. The framework is strictly decoupled from the distributions appearing in a program, as long as they are integrable and their expectations are known. Care has been taken to make the entire approach readily implementable. Our framework is thus capable of proving automatically a.s. termination on programs that state of the art methods like [3, 7, 12] are unable to verify. Moreover, it goes strictly beyond positive a.s. termination that is the largest setting where Lyapunov ranking functions are complete.

Among others, our contributions can be used to improve the weakest expectation calculus of McIver and Morgan [30] in two dimensions. First, we can drastically weaken their requirement to provide a proof of termination so as to ensure total correctness. The second aspect to improve upon is related to the fact that soundness of their method is in practice restricted to weakly finite programs (i.e. where the number of reachable states from any initial states is finite). This is rooted in a requirement that all variables are bounded, which in turn directly ensures that all relevant expressions are integrable. Our Theorem 7.6 in conjunction with Theorem 7.7 can be used to drop boundedness restrictions, and thereby extend the scope of analyzable programs considerably.

Probabilistic programming [18] is a relatively new area of research that merges concepts form programming languages, machine learning, static analysis, and probabilistic model checking. Probabilistic models are described as probabilistic programs, and inference methods are used to compute exact or approximate values of probabilities and expectations. Our work can be used in these contexts to perform static analysis of probabilistic programs prior to using Monte Carlo methods, as simulation results on non-terminating programs or programs where first moments do not exist are misleading and usually meaningless. Furthermore, termination analysis is also an important ingredient to guarantee the correctness of probabilistic program slicing [23].

## Acknowledgments

This work is supported by the EU 7th Framework Programme under grant agreements 295261 (MEALS) and 318490 (SENSATION), the DFG Transregional Collaborative Research Centre SFB/TR 14 AVACS, and by the CAS/SAFEA International Partnership Program for Creative Research Teams. We would would like to thank Pedro R. D'Argenio and Jan Krčál for their comments in a preliminary version of this paper, Hassan Hatefi for many insightful discussions, and the many anonymous reviewers for their invaluable comments.

## References

[1] R. B. Ash and C. Doléans-Dade. *Probability and Measure Theory*. Harcourt, 2000.

[2] J. Berdine, A. Chawdhary, B. Cook, D. Distefano, and P. W. O'Hearn. Variance analyses from invariance analyses. In *POPL*, pages 211–224. ACM, 2007.

[3] O. Bournez and F. Garnier. Proving positive almost-sure termination. In *RTA*, *LNCS* 3467:323–337. Springer, 2005.

[4] A. R. Bradley, Z. Manna, and H. B. Sipma. The polyranking principle. In *ICALP*, *LNCS* 3580:1349–1361. Springer, 2005.

[5] A. R. Bradley, Z. Manna, and H. B. Sipma. Linear ranking with reachability. In *CAV*, *LNCS* 3576:491–504. Springer, 2005.

[6] T. Brázdil, J. Esparza, S. Kiefer, and A. Kucera. Analyzing probabilistic pushdown automata. *Formal Methods in System Design*, 43 (2):124–163, 2013.

[7] A. Chakarov and S. Sankaranarayanan. Probabilistic program analysis with martingales. In *CAV*, *LNCS* 8044:511–526. Springer, 2013.

[8] M. Codish and S. Genaim. Proving termination one loop at a time. In *WLPE*, *CW371 Report*, pages 48–59. K. U. Leuven, 2003.

[9] M. Colón and H. Sipma. Synthesis of linear ranking functions. In *TACAS*, *LNCS* 2031:67–81. Springer, 2001.

[10] B. Cook, A. See, and F. Zuleger. Ramsey vs. lexicographic termination proving. In *TACAS*, *LNCS* 7795:47–61. Springer, 2013.

[11] N. Dershowitz, N. Lindenstrauss, Y. Sagiv, and A. Serebrenik. A general framework for automatic termination analysis of logic programs. *Appl. Algebra Eng. Commun. Comput.*, 12(1/2):117–156, 2001.

[12] J. Esparza, A. Gaiser, and S. Kiefer. Proving termination of probabilistic programs using patterns. In *CAV*, *LNCS* 7358:123–138. Springer, 2012.

[13] J. Filar and K. Vrieze. *Competitive Markov Decision Processes*. Springer-Verlag New York, Inc., New York, NY, USA, 1996.

[14] R. W. Floyd. Assigning meanings to programs. *Mathematical aspects of computer science*, 19:19–32, 1967.

[15] F. G. Foster. On the stochastic matrices associated with certain queuing processes. *The Annals of Mathematical Statistics*, 24(3):355–360, 09 1953.

[16] J. Giesl, R. Thiemann, and P. Schneider-Kamp. The dependency pair framework: Combining techniques for automated termination proofs. In *LPAR*, *LNCS* 3452:301–331. Springer, 2004.

[17] I. Gnaedig. Induction for positive almost sure termination. In *PPDP*, pages 167–178. ACM, 2007.

[18] A. D. Gordon, T. A. Henzinger, A. V. Nori, and S. K. Rajamani. Probabilistic programming. In *FOSE*, pages 167–181. ACM, 2014.

[19] F. Gretz, J.-P. Katoen, and A. McIver. Prinsys - on a quest for probabilistic loop invariants. In *QEST*, *LNCS* 8054:193–208. Springer, 2013.

[20] F. Gretz, J.-P. Katoen, and A. McIver. Operational versus weakest pre-expectation semantics for the probabilistic guarded command language. *Perform. Eval.*, 73:110–132, 2014.

[21] S. Hart and M. Sharir. Concurrent probabilistic programs, or: How to schedule if you must. *SIAM J. Comput.*, 14(4):991–1012, 1985.

[22] S. Hart, M. Sharir, and A. Pnueli. Termination of probabilistic concurrent program. *ACM Trans. Program. Lang. Syst.*, 5(3):356–380, 1983.

[23] C.-K. Hur, A. V. Nori, S. K. Rajamani, and S. Samuel. Slicing probabilistic programs. In *PLDI*, pages 133–144. ACM, 2014.

[24] C. Jones. *Probabilistic non-determinism*. PhD thesis, University of Edinburgh, 1989.

[25] J.-P. Katoen, A. McIver, L. Meinicke, and C. C. Morgan. Linear-invariant generation for probabilistic programs: - automated support for proof-based methods. In *SAS*, *LNCS* 6337:390–406. Springer, 2010.

[26] S. Katz and Z. Manna. A closer look at termination. *Acta Inf.*, 5: 333–352, 1975.

[27] D. Kozen. Semantics of probabilistic programs. *J. Comput. Syst. Sci.*, 22(3):328–350, 1981.

[28] D. Kroening, N. Sharygina, A. Tsitovich, and C. M. Wintersteiger. Termination analysis with compositional transition invariants. In *CAV*, *LNCS* 6174:89–103. Springer, 2010.

[29] C. S. Lee, N. D. Jones, and A. M. Ben-Amram. The size-change principle for program termination. In *POPL*, pages 81–92. ACM, 2001.

[30] A. McIver and C. Morgan. *Abstraction, Refinement And Proof For Probabilistic Systems*. Springer, 2004.

[31] D. Monniaux. An abstract analysis of the probabilistic termination of programs. In *SAS*, *LNCS* 2126:111–126. Springer, 2001.

[32] A. Podelski and A. Rybalchenko. Transition invariants. In *LICS*, pages 32–41. IEEE Computer Society, 2004.

[33] A. Podelski and A. Rybalchenko. A complete method for the synthesis of linear ranking functions. In *VMCAI*, *LNCS* 2937:239–251. Springer, 2004.

[34] K. Sohn and A. V. Gelder. Termination detection in logic programs using argument sizes. In *PODS*, pages 216–226. ACM Press, 1991.

[35] D. Williams. *Probability with Martingales*. Cambridge University Press, 1991.

# Leveraging Weighted Automata in Compositional Reasoning about Concurrent Probabilistic Systems

Fei He[1,2,3] Xiaowei Gao[1,2,3] Bow-Yaw Wang[4] Lijun Zhang[5]

[1] Tsinghua National Laboratory for Information Science and Technology (TNList)
[2] School of Software, Tsinghua University
[3] Key Laboratory for Information System Security, Ministry of Education, China
[4] Academia Sinica, Taiwan
[5] State Key Laboratory of Computer Science, Institute of Software, Chinese Academy of Sciences
hefei@tsinghua.edu.cn, syczgxw@163.com, bywang@iis.sinica.edu.tw, zhanglj@ios.ac.cn

## Abstract

We propose the first sound and complete learning-based compositional verification technique for probabilistic safety properties on concurrent systems where each component is an Markov decision process. Different from previous works, weighted assumptions are introduced to attain completeness of our framework. Since weighted assumptions can be implicitly represented by multi-terminal binary decision diagrams (MTBDD's), we give an $L^*$-based learning algorithm for MTBDD's to infer weighted assumptions. Experimental results suggest promising outlooks for our compositional technique.

***Categories and Subject Descriptors*** D.2.4 [*Software/Program Verification*]: Model Checking

***General Terms*** Theory, Verification

***Keywords*** Compositional verification; probabilistic model checking; algorithmic learning

## 1. Introduction

Probabilistic programs are widely deployed in various systems. For problems requiring substantial computation resources, their solutions can be too costly for practice purposes. For many such problems, probabilistic algorithms may attain better expected worst-case running time than the worst-case running time of any classical algorithm [36]. Probabilistic methods hence become a viable technique to solve hard problems in practice. Indeed, the IEEE 802.11 standard has employed probabilistic methods to avoid the transmission collision in wireless networks [2].

Similar to classical systems, probabilistic systems are not always free of errors. In order to ensure their correctness, verification techniques have been developed to analyze probabilistic systems. Just like classical systems, a probabilistic system may consist of several concurrent components. The number of system states also increases exponentially in the number of concurrent components. Addressing the state explosion problem is crucial to probabilistic verification techniques.

For classical systems, compositional verification aims to mitigate the state explosion problem by divide and conquer. Suppose a classical system $M_0 \| M_1$ composed of two concurrent components $M_0, M_1$, and $P$ an intended property about the system. Consider the assume-guarantee reasoning proof rule for classical systems [13]:

$$\frac{M_0 \preceq A \qquad A \| M_1 \models P}{M_0 \| M_1 \models P} \tag{1}$$

The notation $M_0 \preceq A$ means that $A$ simulates all behaviors of $M_0$. Informally, the rule says that to show the composed system satisfying $P$, it suffices to find a classical assumption $A$ such that $A$ simulates $M_0$, and $A$ composed with $M_1$ satisfies $P$ as well.

A useful assumption needs to be small (at least smaller than $M_0$) and able to establish the intended property. Finding useful assumptions in assume-guarantee reasoning appears to require ingenuity. Although heuristics have been proposed to construct such assumptions automatically, they are not always applicable. Oftentimes, verifiers have to provide assumptions manually. Such laborious tasks are very time consuming and can be extremely difficult to carry out on large systems.

Interestingly, the problem of finding useful classical assumptions can be solved by active machine learning [13]. In active machine learning [3], a learning algorithm infers a representation of an unknown target by making queries to a teacher. The learning-based framework thus devises a mechanical teacher to answer such queries. Together with a learning algorithm, the framework is able to find assumptions automatically. For classical systems, the $L^*$ learning algorithm for regular languages [3] suffices to infer classical finite automata as classical assumptions [13]. Other techniques have also been developed to find useful assumptions for compositional verification of classical systems [11, 20, 22, 25].

From the classical learning-based framework, one gathers that two ingredients are essential to finding probabilistic assumptions. First, a sound and invertible assume-guarantee reasoning proof rule for probabilistic systems is needed. A sound proof rule allows us to analyze compositionally by finding probabilistic assumptions. An invertible proof rule additionally guarantees the existence of such probabilistic assumptions when probabilistic systems satisfy intended properties. Second, a learning algorithm for probabilistic assumptions is also needed. With a carefully designed mechanical teacher, probabilistic assumptions can then be inferred by the learning-based framework for probabilistic systems.


*POPL '15*, January 15–17, 2015, Mumbai, India.

ACM 978-1-4503-3300-9/15/01... $15.00.
http://dx.doi.org/10.1145/2676726.2676998

Finding a sound and invertible assume-guarantee reasoning proof rule does not appear to be a problem. Indeed, the classical proof rule (1) can be extended to probabilistic systems via probabilistic simulation [39]. Learning probabilistic assumptions however is more difficult. To the best of our knowledge, an active learning algorithm for probabilistic systems is yet to be found. In fact, it is undecidable to infer labeled probabilistic transition systems under a version of Angluin's learning model [30]. Learning algorithms for general probabilistic systems may not exist after all.

Given the absence of learning algorithms for probabilistic systems, some authors propose restricted proof rules with only classical assumptions [16, 32]. Since classical assumptions can be represented by classical finite automata, the $L^*$ algorithm is employed to infer such assumptions in restricted probabilistic assume-guarantee reasoning proof rules. Yet classical assumptions are incapable of expressing general probabilistic behaviors. Such restricted proof rules are not invertible. Subsequently, existing probabilistic assume-guarantee reasoning frameworks are sound but incomplete.

We propose a sound and complete assume-guarantee reasoning framework for verifying probabilistic safety properties on Markov decision processes (MDP's). Let $M_0$ and $M_1$ be MDP's, and $P_{\leq p}[\psi]$ a probabilistic safety property. Our most ingenious idea is to consider *weighted* assumptions in our new assume-guarantee reasoning proof rule:

$$\frac{M_0 \preceq_e A \qquad A \| M_1 \models P_{\leq p}[\psi]}{M_0 \| M_1 \models P_{\leq p}[\psi]} \tag{2}$$

where $A$ is a weighted automaton. Intuitively, $M_0 \preceq_e A$ means that every transition of $A$ has a weight not less than the probability of the corresponding transition in $M_0$. Compared to the proof rules in [16, 32], ours relaxes but does not restrict the expressive power of assumptions. More precisely, we consider 0/1-weighted automata whose weights are between 0 and 1 inclusively as weighted assumptions. Since transition functions of 0/1-weighted automata can be probability distributions, the class of 0/1-weighted automata subsumes MDP's. Our assume-guarantee reasoning proof rule is trivially invertible.

In order to find weighted assumptions in our learning-based framework, we also need a learning algorithm for such assumptions. Although active learning algorithms for probabilistic systems are still unknown, weighted assumptions on the other hand are learnable due to the relaxation on transition functions. Our second innovation is to adopt a well-known representation that enables a simple $L^*$-based learning algorithm for weighted assumptions. Observe that weighted automata can be implicitly represented by multi-terminal binary decision diagrams (MTBDD's) [6, 15, 18]. We hence develop an $L^*$-based learning algorithm for MTBDD's and deploy it to infer implicitly represented weighted assumptions. With the two ingredients, a mechanical teacher is designed to guide our learning algorithm to find weighted assumptions for probabilistic safety properties. We successfully develop a sound and complete learning-based assume-guarantee reasoning framework by circumventing the unsolved problem of learning probabilistic systems.

In addition to completeness and learnability, adopting weighted assumptions can also be very efficient. Note that assumptions are not unique oftentimes. If a probabilistic assumption establishes a probabilistic property, a slightly different weighted (but not necessarily probabilistic) assumption most likely will establish the property as well. Since there are more useful weighted assumptions, our new framework can be more effective in finding one of them. Additionally, inferring weighted assumptions implicitly allows us to better integrate the learning-based framework with symbolic probabilistic model checking. Indeed, experimental results from realistic test cases such as IEEE 802.11 and 1394 standards are promising.

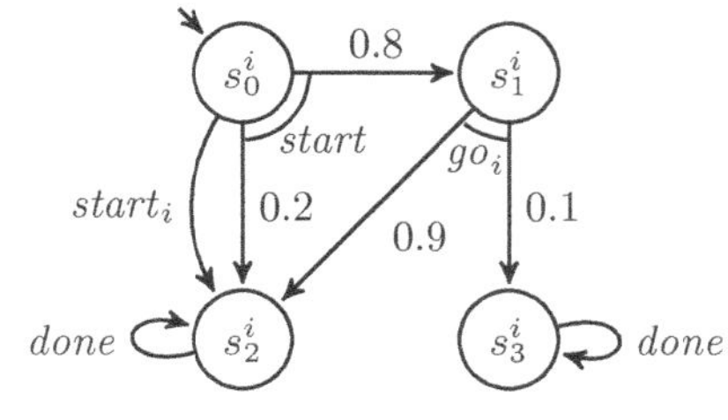


Figure 1: $\mathsf{node}_i$

Compositional verification can alleviate the state explosion problem even for probabilistic programs.

Our technical contributions are summarized as follows.

- We propose the first sound and invertible assume-guarantee reasoning proof rule with weighted assumptions for probabilistic safety properties on MDP's.
- We give an MTBDD learning algorithm under Angluin's active learning model. It uses a polynomial number of queries in the sizes of target MTBDD's and variable sets.
- With our new proof rule and learning algorithm, we give the first sound and complete learning-based assume-guarantee reasoning framework for probabilistic safety properties on MDP's.
- We compare our new technique with the monolithic probabilistic model checker PRISM [38]. Experimental results suggest promising outlooks for our compositional technique.

This paper is organized as follows. In Section 2, we illustrate our learning-based compositional verification technique by a small example. In Section 3, backgrounds of probabilistic systems and probabilistic model checking are provided. Section 4 presents our sound and invertible assume-guarantee reasoning proof rule. The MTBDD learning algorithm is described in Section 5. Our learning-based assume-guarantee reasoning framework is given in Section 6. Section 7 reports the experimental results on parameterized test cases. Finally, Section 9 concludes this paper.

## 2. A Motivating Example

Consider the probabilistic system $\mathsf{node}_1 \| \mathsf{node}_2$ composed of two MDP's $\mathsf{node}_i$ ($i = 1, 2$) in Figure 1. The process $\mathsf{node}_i$ has four states: the initial state ($s_0^i$), the ready state ($s_1^i$), the succeeded state ($s_2^i$), and the failed state ($s_3^i$). Initially, both $\mathsf{node}_1$ and $\mathsf{node}_2$ begin at their respective initial states $s_0^1$ and $s_0^2$. The system may start up all nodes (by the $start$ action), or choose one node to start (by either the $start_1$ or $start_2$ action). The two processes $\mathsf{node}_1$ and $\mathsf{node}_2$ synchronize on shared actions. When the system starts up all nodes by the $start$ action, $\mathsf{node}_1$ transits to its ready state $s_1^1$ with probability 0.8, or to its succeeded state $s_2^1$ with the probability 0.2. Simultaneously, $\mathsf{node}_2$ transits to its ready and succeeded states $s_1^2$ and $s_2^2$ with probabilities 0.8 and 0.2 respectively. Note that the sum of probabilities on each action is 1. Each action hence gives a probabilistic distribution over states. For non-shared actions, only the acting process moves; other processes stay. Hence $\mathsf{node}_1$ transits to its succeeded state $s_2^1$ while $\mathsf{node}_2$ remains in its initial state $s_0^2$ when the system chooses to start up $\mathsf{node}_1$ with the action $start_1$. Similarly, when the process $\mathsf{node}_i$ is at its ready state $s_1^i$, it transits to its succeeded state $s_2^i$ with probability 0.9, or to its failed state $s_3^i$ with probability 0.1 on the action $go_i$. Observe that the probability of a transition is not shown when it is 1. Hence $\mathsf{node}_i$ transits from $s_0^i$ to $s_2^i$ with probability 1 on the action $start_i$.

In the system $\mathsf{node}_1 \| \mathsf{node}_2$, the system state $s_3^1 s_3^2$ is the failed state. The system is designed so that the probability of reaching the failed state is no more than 0.01. Formally, the intended property is

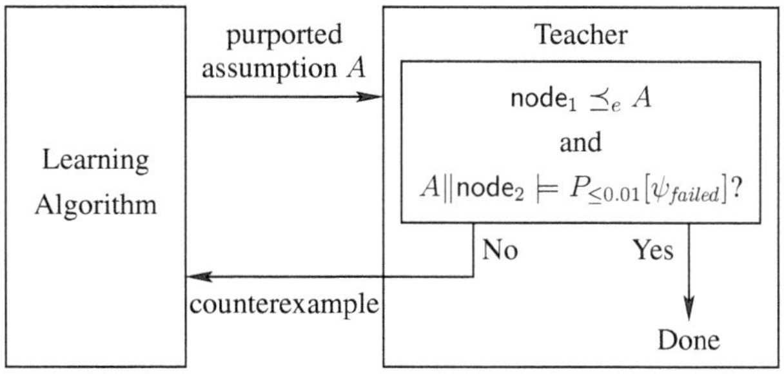


Figure 2: Overview

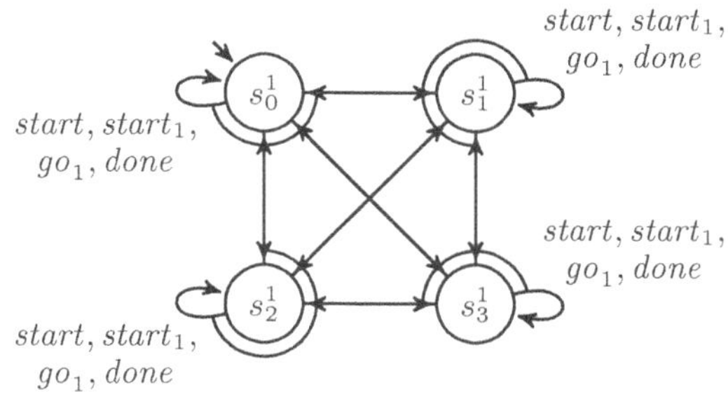


Figure 3: Weighted Assumption $A$

specified by the probabilistic computation tree logic formula

$$P_{\leq 0.01}[\psi_{failed}]$$

where $\psi_{failed}$ stands for $F\ \langle s_3^1 s_3^2 \rangle$ and $F$ is the "in the future" temporal operator. We would like to check whether the system satisfies the probabilistic property by compositional verification.

### 2.1 Compositional Reasoning

With the proof rule (2), to show $\mathsf{node}_1 \| \mathsf{node}_2 \models P_{\leq 0.01}[\psi_{failed}]$, it suffices to find a weighted assumption $A$ that

- $\mathsf{node}_1 \preceq_e A$, equivalently, $A$ performs every transition of $\mathsf{node}_1$ with no less probability; and
- $A \| \mathsf{node}_2 \models P_{\leq 0.01}[\psi_{failed}]$, equivalently, the system $A \| \mathsf{node}_2$ satisfies the probabilistic property.

Clearly, one could choose $A$ to be $\mathsf{node}_1$ if the system satisfies the intended probabilistic property. But then the premise $A \| \mathsf{node}_2 \models P_{\leq 0.01}[\psi_{failed}]$ is precisely the conclusion $\mathsf{node}_1 \| \mathsf{node}_2 \models P_{\leq 0.01}[\psi_{failed}]$. Verifiers would not benefit from compositional verification by choosing $\mathsf{node}_1$ as a weighted assumption.

### 2.2 Overview

We follow the learning-based framework to infer a weighted assumption satisfying the two conditions in the last subsection [11, 13, 25, 32]. In the framework, a learning algorithm is deployed to infer weighted assumptions with the help of a mechanical teacher. The learning algorithm presents purported assumptions to the teacher. The teacher checks if a purported weighted assumption fulfills the premises in the assume-guarantee reasoning proof rule (2). If not, the mechanical teacher will help the learning algorithm refine purported assumptions by counterexamples.

Figure 2 gives an overview of the learning-based framework. On a purported weighted assumption $A$, the teacher checks $\mathsf{node}_1 \preceq_e A$ and invokes a model checker to verify $A \| \mathsf{node}_2 \models P_{\leq 0.01}[\psi_{failed}]$. If both premises are fulfilled, we are done. Otherwise, the teacher provides a counterexample to the learning algorithm. The learning algorithm then modifies the purported weighted assumption $A$ accordingly. We illustrate the framework with concrete examples.

### 2.3 A Purported Assumption

Consider a purported weighted assumption $A$ in Figure 3. On the actions $start$, $start_1$, $go_1$, and $done$, the assumption $A$ can transit from a state to any state. Similar to MDP's, the weight of a transition is not shown when it is 1. For instance, $A$ transits from the state $s_1^1$ to the state $s_j^1$ on the action $go_1$ with weight 1 for every $0 \leq j \leq 3$. In comparison, the process $\mathsf{node}_1$ moves from the state $s_1^1$ to the states $s_0^1, s_1^1, s_2^1, s_3^1$ on the action $go_1$ with probabilities $0, 0, 0.9, 0.1$ respectively (Figure 1). Observe that $A$ is not an MDP since the sum of weights from the state $s_1^1$ on the action $go_1$ is 4.

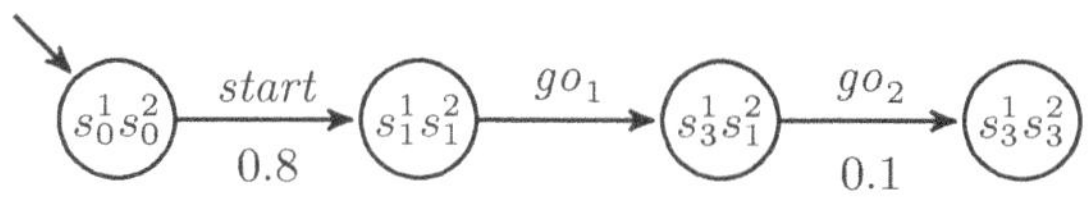


Figure 4: Witness to $A \| \mathsf{node}_2 \not\models P_{\leq 0.01}[\psi_{failed}]$

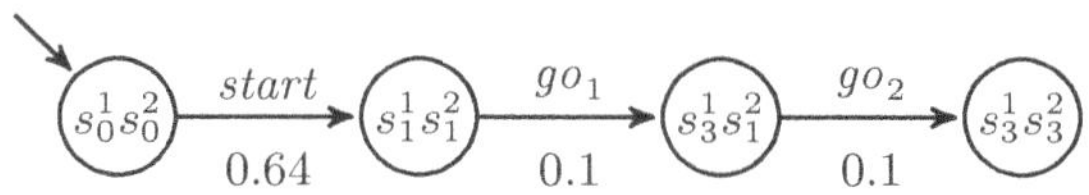


Figure 5: Corresponding Path in $\mathsf{node}_1 \| \mathsf{node}_2$

On receiving the weighted assumption $A$, the mechanical teacher decides whether the assumption $A$ fulfills both premises in our probabilistic compositional verification proof rule. It first checks if the assumption $A$ performs every transition of $\mathsf{node}_1$ with a weight not less than the probability in $\mathsf{node}_1$. This is clearly the case. Consider, for instance, the transitions from $s_1^1$ to $s_0^1, s_1^1, s_2^1, s_3^1$ on the action $go_1$. The weights associated with these transitions of $A$ are all equal to 1. They are not less than the probabilities $0, 0, 0.9, 0.1$ associated with the corresponding transitions of $\mathsf{node}_1$ respectively. The premise $\mathsf{node}_1 \preceq_e A$ is fulfilled. The mechanical teacher then checks the other premise by model checking.

### 2.4 Model Checking

Technically, a probabilistic model checker does not take weighted assumptions as inputs. Since $A$ is a weighted assumption, $A \| \mathsf{node}_2$ need not be an MDP. A probabilistic model checker can not verify whether $A \| \mathsf{node}_2 \models P_{\leq 0.01}[\psi_{failed}]$ directly. We need to lift the probabilistic model checking algorithm to weighted assumptions.

After model checking, we find that the property $P_{\leq 0.01}[\psi_{failed}]$ does not hold on $A \| \mathsf{node}_2$. A witness to $A \| \mathsf{node}_2 \not\models P_{\leq 0.01}[\psi_{failed}]$ is shown in Figure 4. The witness has only one path from the initial state $s_0^1 s_0^2$ to the failed state $s_3^1 s_3^2$. Its weight is $0.8 \times 1 \times 0.1 = 0.08 > 0.01$. $P_{\leq 0.01}[\psi_{failed}]$ is not satisfied on $A \| \mathsf{node}_2$.

### 2.5 Witness Checking

Since $A \| \mathsf{node}_2 \not\models P_{\leq 0.01}[\psi_{failed}]$, the mechanical teacher concludes that the weighted assumption $A$ does not establish the intended probabilistic property. On the other hand, the mechanical teacher cannot conclude that the system $\mathsf{node}_1 \| \mathsf{node}_2$ does not satisfy the property either. Since $A$ has larger weights than $\mathsf{node}_1$, a weighted witness to $A \| \mathsf{node}_2 \not\models P_{\leq 0.01}[\psi_{failed}]$ is not necessarily a witness to $\mathsf{node}_1 \| \mathsf{node}_2 \not\models P_{\leq 0.01}[\psi_{failed}]$. Before revising the weighted assumption $A$, the mechanical teacher checks if the witness to $A \| \mathsf{node}_2 \not\models P_{\leq 0.01}[\psi_{failed}]$ is spurious or not.

Recall that the weighted assumption $A$ contains all transitions in $\mathsf{node}_1$. The witness to $A \| \mathsf{node}_2 \not\models P_{\leq 0.01}[\psi_{failed}]$ therefore corresponds to a path in $\mathsf{node}_1 \| \mathsf{node}_2$ (Figure 5). Also recall that the weight associated with a transition in the weighted assumption

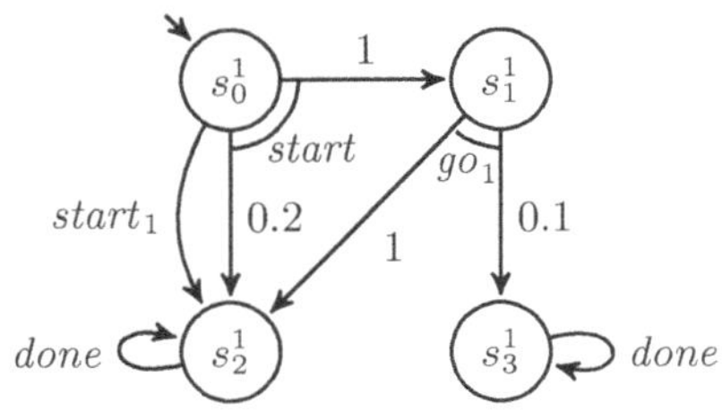


Figure 6: Weighted Assumption $A'$

$A$ is not less than the probability of the corresponding transition in $\mathsf{node}_1$. The probability of the corresponding path in $\mathsf{node}_1 \| \mathsf{node}_2$ can be much smaller than the weight of the witness to $A \| \mathsf{node}_2 \not\models P_{\leq 0.01}[\psi_{failed}]$. Indeed, the corresponding path in $\mathsf{node}_1 \| \mathsf{node}_2$ has probability $0.64 \times 0.1 \times 0.1 = 0.0064 \leq 0.01$. It does satisfy the intended probabilistic property. The witness to $A \| \mathsf{node}_2 \not\models P_{\leq 0.01}[\psi_{failed}]$ is hence spurious. The mechanical teacher then should help the learning algorithm revising the weighted assumption by sending a counterexample.

### 2.6 Selecting Counterexamples

In order to remove the spurious witness in Figure 4 from the weighted assumption $A$, the mechanical teacher selects a transition in the weighted assumption $A$ which contributes most to the spurious witness. In Figure 4, the transitions $s_0^1 \xrightarrow{start} s_1^1$ and $s_1^1 \xrightarrow{go_1} s_3^1$ in the weighted assumption $A$ contribute to the spurious witness. The mechanical teacher can send either of the transitions as a counterexample to the learning algorithm. Here, let us say the mechanical teacher sends the transition $s_1^1 \xrightarrow{go_1} s_3^1$ as the counterexample. The learning algorithm will then update the weight of the selected transition in revised weighted assumptions.

### 2.7 Learning Assumption

After receiving a counterexample, the learning algorithm will purport another weighted assumption. Suppose the learning algorithm purports the weighted assumption $A'$ (Figure 6). For any transition, its weight in $A'$ is no less than the probability of the corresponding transition in $\mathsf{node}_1$. For example, the weighted assumption $A'$ transits from the state $s_1^1$ to the states $s_0^1, s_1^1, s_2^1, s_3^1$ with weights $0, 0, 1, 0.1$ respectively on the action $\mathsf{go}_1$. The corresponding transitions in $\mathsf{node}_1$ have probabilities $0, 0, 0.9, 0.1$ respectively. We have $\mathsf{node}_1 \preceq_e A'$. $A' \| \mathsf{node}_2 \models P_{\leq 0.01}[\psi_{failed}]$ moreover holds by model checking. According to our compositional verification proof rule, the mechanical teacher concludes that the system $\mathsf{node}_1 \| \mathsf{node}_2$ satisfies the intended probabilistic property.

Note again that $A'$ is a not a probabilistic assumption. Although $A'$ and $\mathsf{node}_1$ have the same number of states in the explicit representation, their implicit MTBDD representations are different. $A'$ has 26 nodes and 4 terminals; $\mathsf{node}_1$ has 27 nodes with 6 terminals in the implicit representation. Compositional verification replaces the component $\mathsf{node}_1$ with a slightly smaller weighted assumption $A'$. In fact, $\mathsf{node}_1$ is the only probabilistic assumption that can establish the probabilistic property. If only probabilistic assumptions were considered, assume-guarantee reasoning would not be effective in this example. Adopting weighted assumptions gives our framework more useful assumptions in compositional verification.

## 3. Preliminaries

### 3.1 Weighted Automata and Markov Decision Processes

Given a finite set $S$, a *weighted function* on $S$ is a mapping $\delta : S \to \mathbb{Q}$. A weighted function on $S$ is denoted as a vector of length $|S|$. A *probability distribution* on $S$ is a function $\delta^D : S \to [0, 1] \cap \mathbb{Q}$ that $\sum_{s \in S} \delta^D(s) = 1$. A *point distribution* $\varepsilon_s$ on $s \in S$ is a probability distribution where $\varepsilon_s(t) = 1$ if $t = s$ and $\varepsilon_s(t) = 0$ otherwise. Denote the set of weighted functions and probability distributions on $S$ by $\Delta(S)$ and $\Delta^D(S)$ respectively. Clearly, $\Delta^D(S) \subseteq \Delta(S)$.

**Definition 1** *A* weighted automaton *(WA) is a 4-tuple* $M = (S, \bar{s}, Act, T)$ *where* $S$ *is a finite set of* states, $\bar{s} \in S$ *is an* initial state, *$Act$ is a finite alphabet of* actions, *and* $T : S \times Act \to \Delta(S)$ *is a* weighted transition function.

A *finite path* $\pi$ in $M$ is a non-empty finite sequence $s_0 \xrightarrow{\alpha_0} s_1 \xrightarrow{\alpha_1} \dots \xrightarrow{\alpha_{n-1}} s_n$ where $s_0 = \bar{s}$, $\alpha_i \in Act$, and $s_i \xrightarrow{\alpha_i} s_{i+1}$ is a *transition* with $T(s_i, \alpha_i)(s_{i+1}) \neq 0$ for all $0 \leq i < n$. We denote by $\pi[i] = s_i$ the $(i+1)$th state, and $|\pi| = n$ its *length*. The *weight* $Wt(\pi)$ of a finite path $\pi$ is $T(s_0, \alpha_0)(s_1) \times T(s_1, \alpha_1)(s_2) \times \cdots \times T(s_{n-1}, \alpha_{n-1})(s_n)$. Denote $Path_M$ the set of all finite paths in $M$. Let $\Pi \subseteq Path_M$ be a set of finite paths. $\Pi$ is *prefix containment free* if for every $\pi, \pi' \in \Pi$, $\pi$ is not a proper prefix of $\pi'$. When $\Pi$ is prefix containment free, the *weight* $Wt(\Pi)$ of $\Pi$ is $\sum_{\pi \in \Pi} Wt(\pi)$.

**Definition 2** *A* $0/1$-weighted automaton $(0/1\text{-WA})$ $M = (S, \bar{s}, Act, T)$ *is a WA where* $0 \leq T(s, \alpha)(t) \leq 1$ *for every* $s, t \in S$ *and* $\alpha \in Act$.

A WA is nondeterministic. There may be multiple transitions between two states on different actions. Adversaries are used to resolve nondeterministic choices in WA's [5]. Let $S^+$ denote a nonempty sequence of states in $S$, and $Act(s)$ the set $\{\alpha \in Act : T(s, \alpha)(t) > 0 \text{ for some } t\}$. An (deterministic) *adversary* is a function $\sigma : S^+ \to Act$ such that $\sigma(s_0 s_1 \dots s_n) \in Act(s_n)$. More general notion of adversaries involving randomizations exists, but deterministic ones are sufficient for our problem. A WA $M$ under an adversary $\sigma$ is therefore deterministic. Let $Adv_M$ denote the set of adversaries of $M$. We write $M^\sigma$ for the WA whose transitions are determinized by the adversary $\sigma \in Adv_M$.

**Definition 3** *A* Markov decision process *(MDP)* $M = (S, \bar{s}, Act, T)$ *is a* $0/1$*-WA where* $T(s, \alpha) \in \Delta^D(S)$ *or* $T(s, \alpha)$ *is the constant zero weighted function for every* $s \in S$ *and* $\alpha \in Act$.

Since the weighted functions returned by weighted transition functions of MDP's are probability distributions, the weight associated with each transition in MDP's is referred to as probability.

Let $S_i$ be a finite set and $\delta_i \in \Delta(S_i)$ for $i = 0, 1$. Define $(\delta_0 \otimes \delta_1)(s_0, s_1) = \delta_0(s_0) \times \delta_1(s_1)$. Observe that $\delta_0 \otimes \delta_1 \in \Delta(S_0 \times S_1)$; and if $0 \leq \delta_0(s_0) \leq 1$ and $0 \leq \delta_1(s_1) \leq 1$, then $0 \leq (\delta_0 \otimes \delta_1)(s_0, s_1) \leq 1$.

**Definition 4** *Let* $M_i = (S_i, \bar{s}_i, Act_i, T_i)$ *be WA for* $i = 0, 1$. *The* parallel composition *of* $M_0$ *and* $M_1$ *(written* $M_0 \| M_1$*) is a WA* $M_0 \| M_1 = (S_0 \times S_1, (\bar{s}_0, \bar{s}_1), Act_0 \cup Act_1, T)$ *where*

$$T((s_0, s_1), \alpha) = \begin{cases} T_0(s_0, \alpha) \otimes \varepsilon_{s_1} & \text{if } \alpha \notin Act_1 \\ \varepsilon_{s_0} \otimes T_1(s_1, \alpha) & \text{if } \alpha \notin Act_0 \\ T_0(s_0, \alpha) \otimes T_1(s_1, \alpha) & \text{if } \alpha \in Act_0 \cap Act_1 \end{cases}$$

Observe that parallel composition of two $0/1$-WAs yields a $0/1$-WA, and parallel composition of two MDP's yields an MDP.

**Example 1** *The process* $\mathsf{node}_1$ *in Figure 1 is an MDP with* $S_{\mathsf{node}_1} = \{s_0^1, s_1^1, s_2^1, s_3^1\}$, $\bar{s}_{\mathsf{node}_1} = s_0^1$, $Act_{\mathsf{node}_1} = \{start, start_1, go_1, done\}$, *and* $T_{\mathsf{node}_1}(s, \alpha) = \langle 0, 0.8, 0.2, 0 \rangle$ *if* $s = s_0^1, \alpha = start$ *(others are defined similarly). On the other hand, A in Figure 3 is a* $0/1$*-WA since its weighted transition function does not return probability distributions.*

### 3.2 Probabilistic Model Checking for MDP's

Fix a finite set $AP$ of *atomic propositions*. We focus on *probabilistic safety properties* specified by *Probabilistic Computation Tree Logic (PCTL)* [8, 24] in the form of $P_{\leq p}[\psi]$ with $p \in [0, 1]$ and

$$\phi ::= true \mid a \mid \phi \wedge \phi \mid \neg \phi$$
$$\psi ::= \phi U \phi$$

where $a$ is an atomic proposition, $\phi$ a *state formula*, $\psi$ a *path formula*, and $U$ the "until" temporal operator. For example, "the probability of an error occurrence is at most 0.01" is specified as $P_{\leq 0.01}[true\, U \phi_{err}]$ where $\phi_{err}$ is a state formula indicating the occurrence of an error.

PCTL and the safety fragment in general allow nested probabilistic operators [27]. In this paper, we consider a fragment, known as *conditional reachability probability*, and leave the extension to general PCTL safety property as our future work.

Given $M = (S, \bar{s}, Act, T)$ and $P_{\leq p}[\psi]$ with $\psi = \phi_1 U \phi_2$. We define $p^{\sigma}_{M,s}(\psi) = Wt(\Pi)$ where $\Pi = \{\pi \in Path_{M^\sigma} \mid \forall i = 0..|\pi| - 1.\ (\pi[i] \models \phi_1 \wedge \neg\phi_2) \wedge (\pi[|\pi|] \models \phi_2)\}$. Observe that $\Pi$ is prefix containment free, and $prob(\Pi)$ is the probability of reaching $\phi_2$ states along $\phi_1$ states under the adversary $\sigma$.

Let $p^{max}_{M,s}(\psi) = \max_{\sigma \in Adv_M} p^{\sigma}_{M,s}(\psi)$ denote the maximal probability that $\psi$ is satisfied at $s$ over all adversaries. We say that $s$ *satisfies* $P_{\leq p}[\psi]$ (written $M, s \models P_{\leq p}[\psi]$) if $p^{max}_{M,s}(\psi) \leq p$; $M$ *satisfies* $P_{\leq p}[\psi]$ (written $M \models P_{\leq p}[\psi]$) if $M, \bar{s} \models P_{\leq p}[\psi]$. We write $p^{\sigma}_{M,s}(\psi)$ and $p^{max}_{M,s}(\psi)$ as $p^{\sigma}_{s}(\psi)$ and $p^{max}_{s}(\psi)$ respectively if $M$ is clear.

Let $\psi = \phi_1 U \phi_2$. The probability $p^{max}_{s}(\psi)$ can be approximated by an iterative algorithm [5]. The computation starts from the states satisfying $\phi_2$ and iterates backward to compute the maximum probability of reaching these states from the states satisfying $\phi_1$. More precisely, define

$$p^{max}_{s,i}(\psi) = \begin{cases} 1 & \text{if } s \models \phi_2 \\ 0 & \text{if } s \not\models \phi_2 \wedge s \not\models \phi_1 \\ 0 & \text{if } s \not\models \phi_2 \wedge s \models \phi_1 \wedge i = 0 \\ \max_{\alpha} \left\{ \sum_{t \in S} T(s, \alpha)(t) \times p^{max}_{t,i-1}(\psi) \right\} & \text{otherwise} \end{cases}$$

Then $p^{max}_{s}(\psi) = \lim_{i \to \infty} p^{max}_{s,i}(\psi)$. The computation iterates until $p^{max}_{s,i}(\psi)$ converges.

A *weighted witness* [23, 41, 42] to $M \not\models P_{\leq p}[\psi]$ is a pair $(\sigma, c)$ where $\sigma \in Adv_M$ is an adversary with $p^{\sigma}_{\bar{s}}(\psi) > p$, and $c$ is a set of finite paths in $M^\sigma$ such that (1) for all $\pi \in c$, $\pi \models \psi$; (2) for all proper prefix $\pi'$ of $\pi$, $\pi' \not\models \psi$; and (3) $Wt(c) > p$. Observe that the set $c$ is prefix containment free. Hence $Wt(c)$ is well-defined. We obtain the *$(\sigma, c)$-fragment* of $M$ (written $M^{\sigma,c}$) by removing all transitions not appearing in any path of $c$ from $M^\sigma$.

**Example 2** *Consider the weighted witness $(\sigma, c)$ shown in Figure 4 where $\sigma(\langle s^1_0 s^2_0 \rangle) = start$, $\sigma(\langle s^1_0 s^2_0 \rangle \langle s^1_1 s^2_1 \rangle) = go_1$, $\sigma(\langle s^1_0 s^2_0 \rangle \langle s^1_1 s^2_1 \rangle \langle s^1_3 s^2_1 1 \rangle) = go_2$, and $c = \{\langle s^1_0 s^2_0 \rangle \xrightarrow{start} \langle s^1_1 s^2_1 \rangle \xrightarrow{go_1} \langle s^1_3 s^2_1 \rangle \xrightarrow{go_2} \langle s^1_3 s^2_3 \rangle\}$. The weight of $c$ is $0.8 \times 1 \times 0.1 = 0.08$.*

### 3.3 Model Checking for 0/1-WA's

Consider our assume-guarantee proof rule (2), where $A$ is a 0/1-weighted assumption, the parallel composition $A \| M_1$ usually yields a 0/1-WA, but not an MDP. The probabilistic model checking algorithm in preceding section needs be adapted to 0/1-WA's.

Given a state $s$ of a 0/1-WA $M$ and a probabilistic safety property $P_{\leq p}[\psi]$, we say $s$ *satisfies* $P_{\leq p}[\psi]$ (written $M, s \models P_{\leq p}[\psi]$) if the weight $w^{max}_{s}(\psi) \leq p$ where $w^{max}_{s}(\psi)$ is defined similarly as for MDP's. Here $w^{max}_{s}(\psi)$ is referred to as *weights* rather than *probability*. Note we again omit the subscript $M$ when it is clear. We say that $M$ *satisfies* $P_{\leq p}[\psi]$ (written $M \models P_{\leq p}[\psi]$) if $M, \bar{s} \models P_{\leq p}[\psi]$. An iterative algorithm similar to the one for MDP's is used to compute $w^{max}_{s}(\psi)$ for 0/1-WAs. A notable difference is that the iterative computation may not converge in a 0/1-WA. To avoid divergent computation, define

$$\underline{w}^{max}_{s,i}(\psi) = \min \left\{ 1, \max_{\alpha} \left\{ \sum_{t \in S} T(s, \alpha)(t) \times \underline{w}^{max}_{t,i-1}(\psi) \right\} \right\}$$

if $s \not\models \phi_2 \wedge s \models \phi_1 \wedge i > 0$. Effectively, $\underline{w}^{max}_{s,i}(\psi)$ truncates the value of $w^{max}_{s,i}(\psi)$ when the latter exceeds 1. Let $\underline{w}^{max}_{s}(\psi) = \lim_{i \to \infty} \underline{w}^{max}_{s,i}(\psi)$. We have $\underline{w}^{max}_{s}(\psi) \leq 1$, and $\underline{w}^{max}_{s}(\psi) = w^{max}_{s}(\psi)$ when $w^{max}_{s} \leq 1$.

Note that the properties we are interested in are of the form $P_{\leq p}[\psi]$ with $p \in [0, 1]$. When $p = 1$, such properties are trivially satisfied. For $0 \leq p < 1$, we have $p < w^{max}_{s}(\psi)$ if $p < \underline{w}^{max}_{s}(\psi)$.[1]

## 4. An Assume-Guarantee Reasoning Proof Rule

Assume-guarantee reasoning proof rules for probabilistic systems are proposed in [16, 32]. Those proof rules replace a probabilistic component in a composition with a classical assumption. Since classical assumptions can not characterize all probabilistic behaviors of the replaced component, such rules are not invertible. We propose an assume-guarantee reasoning proof rule that replaces a probabilistic component with a weighted automaton. We begin with the weighted extension of the classical simulation relation.

**Definition 5** *Let $M = (S, \bar{s}, Act, T)$ and $M' = (S', \bar{s}', Act', T')$ be WA's, we say $M$ is* embedded *in $M'$ (written $M \preceq_e M'$) if $S = S'$, $\bar{s} = \bar{s}'$, $Act = Act'$, and $T(s, \alpha)(t) \leq T'(s, \alpha)(t)$ for every $s, t \in S$ and $\alpha \in Act$.*

**Lemma 1** *Let $M$, $M'$, $N$ be 0/1-WA's, and $P_{\leq p}[\psi]$ a probabilistic safety property.*

1. *$M \preceq_e M'$ implies $M \| N \preceq_e M' \| N$;*
2. *$M \preceq_e M'$ and $M' \models P_{\leq p}[\psi]$ imply $M \models P_{\leq p}[\psi]$.*

**Proof:** *Let $M = (S, \bar{s}, Act, T)$, $M' = (S', \bar{s}', Act', T')$, and $N = (S_N, \bar{s}_N, Act_N, T_N)$ be WA's. By $M \preceq_e M'$, we have $S = S'$, $\bar{s} = \bar{s}'$, and $Act = Act'$. Hence $M \| N$ and $M' \| N$ have the same state space, initial state, and alphabet. Since $T(s, \alpha)(t) \leq T'(s, \alpha)(t)$ and $T_N(p, \alpha)(q) \geq 0$, $T(s, \alpha)(t) \times T_N(p, \alpha)(q) \leq T(s, \alpha)(t) \times T_N(p, \alpha)(q)$ for every $s, t \in S$, $p, q \in S_N$, and $\alpha \in Act \cap Act_N$. Hence $T_{M\|N}((s, p), \beta)(t, q) \leq T_{M'\|N}((s, p), \beta)(t, q)$ for every $\beta \in Act \cup Act_N$ by Definition 4.*

*Since $T(s, \alpha)(t) \leq T'(s, \alpha)(t)$, $w^{max}_{M,\bar{s}}(\psi) \leq w^{max}_{M',\bar{s}}(\psi)$. $w^{max}_{M',\bar{s}}(\psi) \leq p$ for $M' \models P_{\leq p}[\psi]$. Thus $w^{max}_{M,\bar{s}}(\psi) \leq w^{max}_{M',\bar{s}}(\psi) \leq p$. $M \models P_{\leq p}[\psi]$ as well.* □

Lemma 1 shows that the operator $\preceq_e$ is compositional and preserves probabilistic safety properties. Hence

**Theorem 1** *Let $M_i = (S_i, \bar{s}_i, Act_i, T_i)$ be MDP's for $i = 0, 1$ and $P_{\leq p}[\psi]$ a probabilistic safety property, Then the following proof rule is both sound and invertible:*

$$\frac{M_0 \preceq_e A \qquad A \| M_1 \models P_{\leq p}[\psi]}{M_0 \| M_1 \models P_{\leq p}[\psi]}$$

*where $A = (S_A, \bar{s}_A, Act_A, T_A)$ is a 0/1-WA.*

**Proof:** *Soundness of the proof rule follows from Lemma 1. By $M_0 \preceq_e A$, $M_0 \| M_1 \preceq_e A \| M_1$ (Lemma 1(1)). Since $A \| M_1 \models P_{\leq p}[\psi]$, we have $M_0 \| M_1 \models P_{\leq p}[\psi]$ (Lemma 1(2)). The proof rule is also invertible. When the conclusion holds, $M_0$ itself is a weighted assumption. The two premises are trivially fulfilled.* □

[1] Note here we need $p < 1$ to conclude $p < w^{max}_{s}(\psi)$.

# 5. Learning $0/1$-Weighted Automata

We adopt the learning-based framework [13, 16] to generate an assumption $A$ in the assume-guarantee reasoning proof rule (Theorem 1). To apply our new proof rule, a weighted assumption is needed. One could employ learning algorithms that infer explicit quantitative models like multiplicity automata [7]. Those learning algorithms require complex and accurate matrix operations. They hence induce substantial computation and implementation overheads. To avoid such overheads, we adopt a different representation to enable a simple and efficient learning technique. More precisely, we use MTBDD's to represent weighted assumptions implicitly. To infer implicitly represented weighted assumptions, we then develop an MTBDD learning algorithm under Angluin's learning model.

## 5.1 Multi-Terminal Binary Decision Diagrams

Let $\mathbb{B}$ denote the *Boolean domain* $\{0,1\}$. Fix a finite ordered set of Boolean variables $\mathbf{x} = \langle x_1, x_2, \ldots, x_n \rangle$. A *valuation* $\nu = \langle v_1, v_2, \ldots, v_n \rangle$ of $\mathbf{x}$ assigns the Boolean value $v_i$ to the Boolean variable $x_i$. Let $\mu$ and $\nu$ be valuations of $\mathbf{x}$ and $\mathbf{y}$ respectively with $\mathbf{x} \cap \mathbf{y} = \emptyset$. The *concatenation* of $\mu$ and $\nu$ is the valuation $\mu\nu$ of $\mathbf{x} \cup \mathbf{y}$ such that $\mu\nu(z) = \mu(z)$ if $z \in \mathbf{x}$ and $\mu\nu(z) = \nu(z)$ if $z \in \mathbf{y}$. For $\mathbf{y} \subseteq \mathbf{x}$, the *restriction* $\nu\!\uparrow_{\mathbf{y}}$ of $\nu$ on $\mathbf{y}$ is a valuation of $\mathbf{y}$ that $\nu\!\uparrow_{\mathbf{y}}(y) = \nu(y)$ for $y \in \mathbf{y}$. Let $f(\mathbf{x}) : \mathbb{B}^n \to \mathbb{Q}$ be a function over $\mathbf{x}$. We write $f(\nu)$ for the *function value* of $f$ under the valuation $\nu$. Let $f_1(\mathbf{x})$ and $f_2(\mathbf{x})$ be functions over $\mathbf{x}$, $f_1(\mathbf{x}) \leq f_2(\mathbf{x})$ denotes $f_1(\nu) \leq f_2(\nu)$ for every valuation $\nu$ of $\mathbf{x}$.

A *multi-terminal binary decision diagram* (MTBDD) [18] over $\mathbf{x}$ is a rooted, directed, acyclic graph representing a function $f(\mathbf{x}) : \mathbb{B}^n \to \mathbb{Q}$. An MTBDD has two types of nodes. A *non-terminal* node is labeled with a variable $x_i$; it has two outgoing edges with labels 0 and 1. A *terminal* node is labeled with a rational number. The representation supports binary operations. For instance, the MTBDD of the sum of two functions is computed by traversing the MTBDD's of the two functions.

Given a valuation $\nu$ of $\mathbf{x}$, $f(\nu)$ can be obtained by traversing the MTBDD of $f(\mathbf{x})$. Starting from the root, one follows edges by values of the Boolean variables labeling the nodes. When a terminal node is reached, its label is the value $f(\nu)$. Since a function $f(\mathbf{x})$ and its MTBDD are equivalent, $f(\mathbf{x})$ also denotes the MTBDD of the function $f(\mathbf{x})$ by abusing the notation.

It is straightforward to represent a WA by MTBDD's [26]. Let $M = (S, \bar{s}, Act, T)$ be a WA. Without loss of generality, we assume $|S| = 2^n$ and $|Act| = m$. We use $\mathbf{x} = \langle x_1, x_1, \ldots, x_n \rangle$, $\mathbf{x}' = \langle x_1', x_2', \ldots, x_n' \rangle$ to encode states and next states in $S$, and $\mathbf{z} = \langle z_1, z_2, \ldots, z_m \rangle$ to encode actions in $Act$. Let $\nu, \nu'$ be valuations of $\mathbf{x}, \mathbf{x}'$ and $\alpha$ a valuation of $\mathbf{z}$. The action valuation $\alpha$ of $\mathbf{x}$ is *valid* if it maps at most one variable to 1 (at most one action can be taken). A valuation $\nu$ of $\mathbf{x}$ or $\mathbf{x}'$ encodes a state $\lceil \nu \rceil \in S$. A valid action valuation $\alpha$ encodes an action $\lceil \alpha \rceil \in Act$. Define

$$l_M(\nu) = \begin{cases} 1 & \text{if } \lceil \nu \rceil = \bar{s} \\ 0 & \text{otherwise} \end{cases}$$

$$f_M(\alpha\nu\nu') = \begin{cases} T(\lceil \nu \rceil, \lceil \alpha \rceil)(\lceil \nu' \rceil) & \text{if } \alpha \text{ is valid} \\ 0 & \text{otherwise} \end{cases}$$

Then the MTBDD encoding of $M$ is $(\mathbf{x}, l_M(\mathbf{x}), \mathbf{z}, f_M(\mathbf{z}, \mathbf{x}, \mathbf{x}'))$. We will represent a WA by its MTBDD encoding from now on.

**Example 3** *Consider the process* node$_1$ *in Figure 1 where the states are* $s_i^1$ *for* $i = 0, \ldots, 3$, *and the alphabet of actions is* $Act = \{start, start_1, go_1, done\}$. *We use* $\mathbf{x} = \langle s^1.0, s^1.1 \rangle$ *to encode the set of states, and* $\mathbf{z} = \langle start, start_1, go_1, done \rangle$ *to encode the alphabet of actions. The MTBDD of* $f_{\mathsf{node}_1}(\mathbf{z}, \mathbf{x}, \mathbf{x}')$ *is shown in Figure 7. In the figure, the terminal node labled by the number* 0 *and its incoming edges are not shown. Solid edges are labeled by* 1 *and dotted edges are labeled by* 0. *Hence, for instance, the process* node$_1$ *transits from* $s_1^1 = \lceil \langle 0, 1 \rangle \rceil$ *to* $s_2^1 = \lceil \langle 1, 0 \rangle \rceil$ *on the action* $go_1$ *with probability* 0.9 *by the shaded path. Note that valuations of* $\mathbf{z}$ *need be valid. Thus only the valuations* $\langle 1,0,0,0 \rangle$, $\langle 0,1,0,0 \rangle$, $\langle 0,0,1,0 \rangle$, *and* $\langle 0,0,0,1 \rangle$ *of* $\mathbf{z}$ *yield non-zero values of* $f_{\mathsf{node}_1}$.

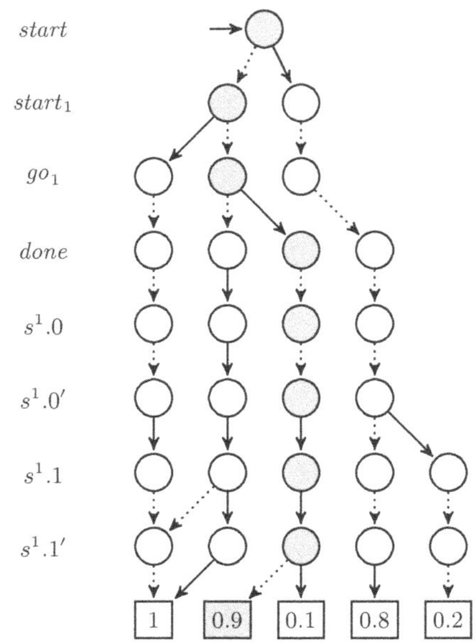


Figure 7: MTBDD of $f_{\mathsf{node}_1}$

Using MTBDD's, Theorem 1 is rephrased as follows.

**Corollary 1** *Let* $M_i = (\mathbf{x}_i, l_{M_i}(\mathbf{x}_i), \mathbf{z}, f_{M_i}(\mathbf{z}, \mathbf{x}_i, \mathbf{x}_i'))$ *be MDP's for* $i = 0, 1$ *and* $P_{\leq p}[\psi]$ *a probabilistic safety property. Then*

$$\frac{M_0 \preceq_e A \qquad A \| M_1 \models P_{\leq p}[\psi]}{M_0 \| M_1 \models P_{\leq p}[\psi]}$$

*where* $A = (\mathbf{x}_0, l_{M_0}(\mathbf{x}_0), \mathbf{z}, f_A(\mathbf{z}, \mathbf{x}_0, \mathbf{x}_0'))$ *is a* $0/1$*-WA.*

## 5.2 The $L^*$ Learning Algorithm for Regular Languages

We adapt the $L^*$ algorithm to infer an MTBDD representing a weighted assumption [3]. $L^*$ is a learning algorithm for regular languages. Assume a target regular language only known to a teacher. The $L^*$ algorithm infers a minimal deterministic finite automaton recognizing the target regular language by posing the following queries to the teacher:

- A membership query asks if a string belongs to the target language; and
- An equivalence query asks if a conjectured finite automaton recognizes the target language. If not, the teacher has to provide the learning algorithm a string as a counterexample.

The $L^*$ algorithm uses membership queries to construct the transition function of a deterministic finite automaton. When it constructs a deterministic finite automaton consistent with previous membership queries, $L^*$ poses an equivalence query to check if the automaton does recognize the target regular language. If so, the algorithm has learned the target language correctly. Otherwise, the counterexample is used to improve the conjectured finite automaton.

It can be shown [3] that the $L^*$ algorithm always infers the minimal deterministic finite automaton recognizing any target regular language within a polynomial number of queries.

### 5.3 An MTBDD Learning Algorithm

Since any 0/1-WA can be represented by MTBDD's, we develop an MTBDD learning algorithm to infer weighted assumptions. Let $f(\mathbf{x})$ be an unknown target MTBDD. We assume a *teacher* to answer the following types of queries:

- On a *membership query* $MQ(\nu)$ with a valuation $\nu$ of $\mathbf{x}$, the teacher answers $f(\nu)$;
- On an *equivalence query* $EQ(g)$ with a *conjecture* MTBDD $g(\mathbf{x})$, the teacher answers *YES* if $f = g$. Otherwise, she returns a valuation $\nu$ of $\mathbf{x}$ with $f(\nu) \neq g(\nu)$ as a *counterexample*.

Observe that a valuation of $\mathbf{x}$ can be represented by a binary string of length $|\mathbf{x}|$. To illustrate how our MTBDD learning algorithm works, consider an unknown MTBDD $f(\mathbf{x})$ with exactly 2 values 0 and $r$. Since there are finitely many binary strings of length $|\mathbf{x}|$, the language $R$ of binary strings representing valuations of $\mathbf{x}$ that evaluate $f$ to $r$ is regular. The $L^*$ learning algorithm for regular languages hence can be used to infer a finite automaton recognizing the language $R$ [3]. The learning algorithm applies the Myhill-Nerode theorem for regular languages. It constructs the transition function of the minimal deterministic finite automaton for any unknown regular language by posing membership and equivalence queries about the unknown target. Since the minimal deterministic finite automaton for $R$ is structurally similar to the MTBDD $f$ with two terminal nodes [28], the $L^*$ algorithm can be modified to infer MTBDD's with two terminal nodes [19].

Generally, an unknown MTBDD $f(\mathbf{x})$ has $k$ values $r_1, r_2, \ldots, r_k$. It evaluates to a value $r_i$ on a valuation of $\mathbf{x}$. Moreover, the language $R_i$ of binary strings representing valuations of $\mathbf{x}$ that evaluate $f$ to $r_i$ is regular for every $1 \leq i \leq k$. Consider generalized deterministic finite automata with $k$ acceptance types. On any binary string, the computation of a generalized deterministic finite automaton ends in a state of an acceptance type. Formally, define a *$k$-language* $\mathcal{L}$ over an alphabet $\Sigma$ to be a partition $\{L_1, L_2, \ldots, L_k\}$ of $\Sigma^*$. That is, $\cup_i L_i = \Sigma^*$ and $L_i \cap L_j = \emptyset$ when $i \neq j$. A *$k$-deterministic finite automaton ($k$-DFA)* $D = (Q, \Sigma, \delta, q_0, \mathcal{F})$ consists of a finite *state set* $Q$, an *alphabet* $\Sigma$, a *transition function* $\delta : Q \times \Sigma \to Q$, an *initial state* $q_0 \in Q$, and *acceptance types* $\mathcal{F} = \{F_1, F_2, \ldots, F_k\}$ where $F_i$'s form a partition of $Q$. Define $\delta^*(q, \epsilon) = q$ and $\delta^*(q, aw) = \delta^*(\delta(q, a), w)$ where $a \in \Sigma$ and $w \in \Sigma^*$. For a string $w \in \Sigma^*$, we say *$D$ accepts $w$ with type $i$* if $\delta^*(q_0, w) \in F_i$. Let $L_i(D) = \{w : D \text{ accepts } w \text{ with type } i\}$. A $k$-DFA hence *accepts* a $k$-language $\mathcal{L}(D) = \{L_i(D) : 1 \leq i \leq k\}$. It is almost straightforward to show a generalized Myhill-Nerode theorem for $k$-DFA.

**Theorem 2** *The following statements are equivalent:*

1. *A $k$-language $\mathcal{L} = \{L_1, L_2, \ldots, L_k\}$ is accepted by a $k$-DFA;*
2. *Define the relation $R$ over $\Sigma^*$ such that $xRy$ if and only if for every $z \in \Sigma^*$, $xz, yz \in L_i$ for some $i$. $R$ is of finite index.*

In order to learn general MTBDD's, we modify the $L^*$ algorithm to generate $k$-DFA. Consider binary strings of length $|\mathbf{x}|$ representing valuations of $\mathbf{x}$. Since an MTBDD evaluates a valuation to a value, the values of an MTBDD partition $\Sigma^{|\mathbf{x}|}$. With $\Sigma^* \setminus \Sigma^{|\mathbf{x}|}$, an MTBDD in fact gives a partition of $\Sigma^*$. In other words, an MTBDD defines a $k$-language. By Theorem 2, the modified $L^*$ algorithm infers a minimal $k$-DFA that accepts the $k$-language defined by an unknown MTBDD. It remains to derive an MTBDD learning algorithm from the modified $L^*$ algorithm for $k$-DFA.

Two minor problems need to be addressed in the design of our MTBDD learning algorithm. First, the modified $L^*$ algorithm makes membership queries on binary strings of arbitrary lengths. The teacher for learning MTBDD's only answers membership queries on valuations over fixed variables. Second, the modified $L^*$ algorithm presents a $k$-DFA as a conjecture in an equivalence query. The MTBDD teacher however accepts MTBDD's as conjectures. To solve these problems, we apply the techniques in [19].

When the modified $L^*$ algorithm asks a membership query on a binary string, our MTBDD learning algorithm checks if the string has length $|\mathbf{x}|$. If not, the MTBDD learning algorithm returns 0 to denote the weight 0. Otherwise, the MTBDD learning algorithm forwards the corresponding valuation of $\mathbf{x}$ to the teacher and returns the teacher's answer to the modified $L^*$ algorithm. When the modified $L^*$ algorithm gives a $k$-DFA in an equivalence query, the MTBDD learning algorithm transforms the automaton into an MTBDD. It basically turns the initial state into a root, each state at distance less than $n$ into a non-terminal node labeled with variable $x_i$, and each state at distance $n$ into a terminal node.

**Theorem 3** *Let $f(\mathbf{x})$ be a target MTBDD. The MTBDD learning algorithm outputs $f$ in polynomial time, using $O(|f|^2 + |f| \log |\mathbf{x}|)$ membership queries and at most $|f|$ equivalence queries.*

**Proof:** *The modified $L^*$ algorithm outputs the minimal $k$-DFA $F$, using $O(|F|^2 + |F| \log m)$ membership queries and at most $|F|$ equivalence queries where $m$ is the length of the longest counterexample. Every membership or equivalence query of the modified $L^*$ algorithm induces at most one query in the MTBDD learning algorithm. When the modified $L^*$ algorithm makes an equivalence query with a $k$-DFA, the MTBDD learning algorithm transforms it into an MTBDD of the same size in polynomial time. Whenever a counterexample is obtained from the MTBDD teacher, the MTBDD learning algorithm forwards the corresponding binary string of length $|\mathbf{x}|$ to the modified $L^*$ algorithm. Hence the learning algorithm infers the MTBDD $f$ with $O(|f|^2 + |f| \log |\mathbf{x}|)$ membership and $|f|$ equivalence queries.* □

## 6. The Learning-based Verification Framework

With our new assume-guarantee reasoning proof rule (Section 4) and learning algorithm for MTBDD's (Section 5), we can now describe our sound and complete learning framework.

Let $M_i = (\mathbf{x}_i, l_{M_i}(\mathbf{x}_i), \mathbf{z}, f_{M_i}(\mathbf{z}, \mathbf{x}_i, \mathbf{x}_i'))$ be MDP's ($i = 0, 1$), and $P_{\leq p}[\psi]$ a probabilistic safety property. To verify if $M_0 || M_1 \models P_{\leq p}[\psi]$ holds, we aim to generate a 0/1-WA $A = (\mathbf{x}_0, l_{M_0}(\mathbf{x}_0), \mathbf{z}, f_A(\mathbf{z}, \mathbf{x}_0, \mathbf{x}_0'))$ to fulfill the premises $M_0 \preceq_e A$ and $A || M_1 \models P_{\leq p}[\psi]$. To find such a weighted assumption $A$, we use the MTBDD learning algorithm to infer an MTBDD $f_A(\mathbf{z}, \mathbf{x}_0, \mathbf{x}_0')$ as the weighted transition function. Recall that the MTBDD learning algorithm relies on a teacher to answer queries about the target MTBDD. We therefore will design a mechanical teacher to answer queries from the learning algorithm (Figure 8).

Let $\alpha$ be a valuation encoding an action, $\nu$ and $\nu'$ valuations encoding states. The mechanical teacher consists of the membership query resolution algorithm $ResolveMQ(\alpha\nu\nu')$ and the equivalence query resolution algorithm $ResolveEQ(f_A)$. The membership query resolution algorithm answers a membership query $MQ(\alpha\nu\nu')$ by the weight associated with the transition from $\lceil \nu \rceil$ to $\lceil \nu' \rceil$ on action $\lceil \alpha \rceil$ in a weighted assumption fulfilling the premises of the assume-guarantee reasoning proof rule. Similarly, the equivalence query resolution algorithm answers an equivalence query $EQ(f_A)$ by checking whether the MTBDD $f_A$ represents the weighted transition function of a weighted assumption. The equivalence query resolution algorithm should return a counterexample when $f_A$ does not represent a suitable weighted transition function. Recall that $M_0$ itself is trivially a weighted assumption. Our teacher simply uses the weighted transition function $f_{M_0}$ of $M_0$ as the target. In the worst case, our framework will find the weighted assumption $M_0$ and hence attain completeness. In practice, it often finds useful weighted assumptions before $M_0$ is inferred.

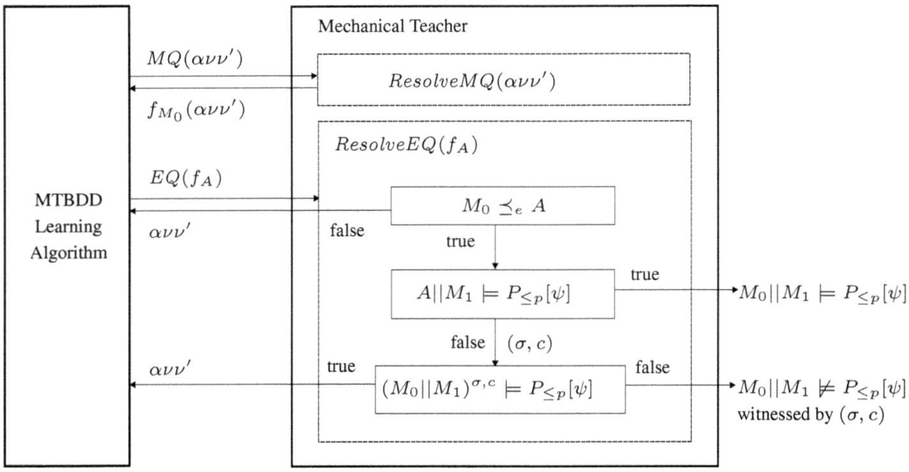


Figure 8: Learning Framework for Compositional Verification

### 6.1 Resolving Membership Queries

Our membership query resolution algorithm targets the weighted transition function of $M_0$. Clearly, $M_0$ embeds itself and hence can be used as a weighted assumption. On the membership query $MQ(\alpha\nu\nu')$, the mechanical teacher simply returns $f_{M_0}(\alpha\nu\nu')$.

**Input** : $MQ(\alpha\nu\nu')$
**Output**: a rational number
answer $MQ(\alpha\nu\nu')$ with $f_{M_0}(\alpha\nu\nu')$;

**Algorithm 1:** $ResolveMQ(\alpha\nu\nu')$

### 6.2 Resolving Equivalence Queries

On an equivalence query $EQ(f_A)$, the mechanical teacher is given an MTBDD $f_A(\mathbf{z}, \mathbf{x}_0, \mathbf{x}_0')$. Consider the WA $A = (\mathbf{x}_0, l_{M_0}(\mathbf{x}_0), \mathbf{z}, f_A(\mathbf{z}, \mathbf{x}_0, \mathbf{x}_0'))$. We need to verify if both premises of the assume-guarantee reasoning proof rule in Corollary 1 hold. The equivalence query resolution algorithm first checks if $M_0 \preceq_e A$. If not, there are valuations $\alpha, \nu$, and $\nu'$ with $f_{M_0}(\alpha\nu\nu') > f_A(\alpha\nu\nu')$. The equivalence query resolution algorithm returns $\alpha\nu\nu'$ as a counterexample to $EQ(f_A)$.

If $M_0 \preceq_e A$, the equivalence query resolution algorithm continues to check whether $A \| M_1 \models P_{\leq p}[\psi]$ holds by model checking. If $A \| M_1 \models P_{\leq p}[\psi]$ holds, the MTBDD learning algorithm has inferred a weighted assumption that establishes $M_0 \| M_1 \models P_{\leq p}[\psi]$ by the assume-guarantee reasoning proof rule in Corollary 1. Otherwise, the equivalence query resolution algorithm obtains a weighted witness $(\sigma, c)$ to $A \| M_1 \not\models P_{\leq p}[\psi]$ from model checking. It then checks if the weighted witness is spurious. Recall that $M_0 \| M_1$ and $A \| M_1$ have the same state set and action alphabet due to $M_0 \| M_1 \preceq_e A \| M_1$. The $(\sigma, c)$-fragment $(M_0 \| M_1)^{\sigma,c}$ is well-defined. If $(M_0 \| M_1)^{\sigma,c} \models P_{\leq p}[\psi]$, the weighted witness $(\sigma, c)$ is spurious. The algorithm then analyzes the spurious weighted witness $(\sigma, c)$ and returns a valuation as the counterexample. Otherwise, the algorithm concludes $(M_0 \| M_1)^{\sigma,c} \not\models P_{\leq p}[\psi]$ with the weighted witness $(\sigma, c)$ (Algorithm 2).

**Example 4** *Consider the weighted witness in Figure 4. The $(\sigma, c)$-fragment* $(\mathsf{node}_1 \| \mathsf{node}_2)^{\sigma,c}$ *is shown in Figure 5. There is but one path in* $(\mathsf{node}_1 \| \mathsf{node}_2)^{\sigma,c}$. *This path ends in $\langle s_3^1 s_3^2 \rangle$ and hence satisfies $\psi_{failed}$. Its weight however is* $0.64 \times 0.1 \times 0.1 = 0.0064 \leq 0.01$. *Thus* $(\mathsf{node}_1 \| \mathsf{node}_2)^{\sigma,c} \models P_{\leq 0.01}[\psi_{failed}]$. *The weighted witness in Figure 4 is spurious.*

**Input** : $EQ(f_A)$
**Output**: $YES$, a counterexample to $EQ(f_A)$
$A \leftarrow (\mathbf{x}_0, l_{M_0}(\mathbf{x}_0), \mathbf{z}, f_A(\mathbf{z}, \mathbf{x}_0, \mathbf{x}_0'))$;
**if** $\exists \alpha\nu\nu'. f_A(\alpha\nu\nu') < f_{M_0}(\alpha\nu\nu')$ **then**
  answer $EQ(f_A)$ with the counterexample $\alpha\nu\nu'$;
  receive a new equivalence query $EQ(f_{A'})$;
  **call** $ResolveEQ(f_{A'})$;
**if** $A||M_1 \models P_{\leq p}[\psi]$ **then**
  answer $EQ(f_A)$ with $YES$;
  **return** "$M_0||M_1 \models P_{\leq p}[\psi]$";
**else**
  let $(\sigma, c)$ be a weighted witness to $A||M_1 \not\models P_{\leq p}[\psi]$;
  **if** $(M_0||M_1)^{\sigma,c} \models P_{\leq p}[\psi]$ **then**
    select a transition $\lceil \mu \rceil \xrightarrow{\lceil \alpha \rceil} \lceil \mu' \rceil$ with the maximal contribution from $(A||M_1)^{\sigma,c}$;
    answer $EQ(f_A)$ with $\alpha{\uparrow_{\mathbf{x}_0}}\mu'{\uparrow_{\mathbf{x}_0'}}$;
    receive a new equivalence query $EQ(f_{A'})$;
    **call** $ResolveEQ(f_{A'})$;
  **else**
    **return** "$M_0||M_1 \not\models P_{\leq p}[\psi]$" with $(\sigma, c)$;
  **end**
**end**

**Algorithm 2:** $ResolveEQ(f_A)$

**Selecting Counterexamples**. Given a spurious weighted witness $(\sigma, c)$, the mechanical teacher selects a transition from $c$ as a counterexample to the MTBDD learning algorithm. The counterexample is intended to remove the spurious weighted witness $(\sigma, c)$ from weighted assumptions.

Let $(\sigma, c)$ be a spurious weighted witness with $(A \| M_1)^{\sigma,c} \not\models P_{\leq p}[\psi]$ and $(M_0 \| M_1)^{\sigma,c} \models P_{\leq p}[\psi]$. Recall that $(M_0 \| M_1)^{\sigma,c}$ and $(A \| M_1)^{\sigma,c}$ have the same state set, initial state, and alphabet. The only differences between $(M_0 \| M_1)^{\sigma,c}$ and $(A \| M_1)^{\sigma,c}$ are the weights associated with transitions. In order to remove the spurious weighted witness $(\sigma, c)$, we would like to select transitions which differentiate $(M_0 \| M_1)^{\sigma,c}$ from $(A \| M_1)^{\sigma,c}$ most significantly.

More precisely, for any transition $t$ in $c$, let $\Pi_A(t)$ and $\Pi_0(t)$ be the sets of paths in respectively $(A \| M_1)^{\sigma,c}$ and $(M_0 \| M_1)^{\sigma,c}$ which contain transition $t$. Define $\omega(t) = Wt(\Pi_A(t)) - Wt(\Pi_0(t))$ to be the *contribution* of transition $t$ in the spurious weighted witness $(\sigma, c)$. The mechanical teacher simply selects a transition $t$

with the maximal contribution. The weight of the selected transition in $A$ will be revised to the probability of the corresponding transition in $M_0$. Its contribution will be 0 in following revisions. Note that contributions of transitions are computed using MTBDD's for efficiency. Details are omitted due to space limit.

Observe moreover that selecting one transition may not eliminate the spurious weighted witness. Since a spurious weighted witness contains several transitions, the weight of the witness may not be reduced sufficiently after revising a few transitions. Subsequently, the same spurious weighted witness may be recomputed by model checking the premises with a revised weighted assumption. In order to reduce the number of model checking invocations, we reuse the same spurious weighted witness to compute counterexamples [25]. More precisely, our implementation checks if the current spurious weighted witness is eliminated from revised weighted assumptions. If not, the mechanical teacher selects another transition from the spurious weighted witness to further refine the revised weighted assumptions. Since a spurious weighted witness is used to revise several weighted assumptions, the number of model checking invocations is reduced.

### 6.3 Correctness

The correctness of our assume-guarantee reasoning framework for probabilistic systems follows from Theorem 1. We establish the soundness, completeness, and termination of the new learning-based framework in the remainder of this section.

**Theorem 4 (Soundness)** *Let $M_i = (\mathbf{x}_i, l_{M_i}(\mathbf{x}_i), \mathbf{z}, f_{M_i}(\mathbf{z}, \mathbf{x}_i, \mathbf{x}'_i))$ be MDP's for $i = 0, 1$, $P_{\leq p}[\psi]$ a probabilistic safety property, and $f_A(\mathbf{z}, \mathbf{x}_0, \mathbf{x}'_0)$ an MTBDD.*

- *If $ResolveEQ(f_A)$ returns "$M_0 \| M_1 \models P_{\leq p}[\psi]$," then $M_0 \| M_1 \models P_{\leq p}[\psi]$ holds.*
- *If $ResolveEQ(f_A)$ returns "$M_0 \| M_1 \not\models P_{\leq p}[\psi]$" with $(\sigma, c)$, then $(\sigma, c)$ is a weighted witness to $M_0 \| M_1 \not\models P_{\leq p}[\psi]$.*

**Proof:** *When our learning-based framework reports "$M_0 \| M_1 \models P_{\leq p}[\psi]$" in Algorithm 2, a weighted assumption $A = (\mathbf{x}_0, l_{M_0}(\mathbf{x}_0), \mathbf{z}, f_A(\mathbf{z}, \mathbf{x}_0, \mathbf{x}'_0))$ such that $M_0 \preceq_e A$ and $A \| M_1 \models P_{\leq p}[\psi]$ has been inferred. By the soundness of the assume-guarantee reasoning proof rule (Theorem 1), $M_0 \| M_1 \models P_{\leq p}[\psi]$. On the other hand, suppose our learning-based framework reports "$M_0 \| M_1 \not\models P_{\leq p}[\psi]$." The weighted witness $(\sigma, c)$ to $A \| M_1 \not\models P_{\leq p}[\psi]$ has been verified to be a witness to $M_0 \| M_1 \not\models P_{\leq p}[\psi]$.* □

**Theorem 5 (Completeness)** *Let $M_i = (\mathbf{x}_i, l_{M_i}(\mathbf{x}_i), \mathbf{z}, f_{M_i}(\mathbf{z}, \mathbf{x}_i, \mathbf{x}'_i))$ be MDP's for $i = 0, 1$, and $P_{\leq p}[\psi]$ a probabilistic safety property.*

- *If $M_0 \| M_1 \models P_{\leq p}[\psi]$, then $ResolveEQ(f_A)$ returns "$M_0 \| M_1 \models P_{\leq p}[\psi]$" for some MTBDD $f_A(\mathbf{z}, \mathbf{x}_0, \mathbf{x}'_0)$.*
- *If $M_0 \| M_1 \not\models P_{\leq p}[\psi]$, then $ResolveEQ(f_A)$ returns "$M_0 \| M_1 \not\models P_{\leq p}[\psi]$" with a weighted witness $(\sigma, c)$.*

**Proof:** *In our framework, the MTBDD learning algorithm targets the weighted transition function of $M_0$. It will infer $f_{M_0}(\mathbf{z}, \mathbf{x}_0, \mathbf{x}'_0)$ eventually (Theorem 3). If $M_0 \| M_1 \models P_{\leq p}[\psi]$, the learning algorithm always infers a weighted assumption $A$ (in the worst case, $A$ is $M_0$) such that $M_0 \preceq_e A$ and $A \| M_1 \models P_{\leq p}[\psi]$. Hence $ResolveEQ(f_A)$ returns "$M_0 \| M_1 \models P_{\leq p}[\psi]$." Otherwise, the learning algorithm always infers a weighted assumption $A$ (in the worst case, $A$ is $M_0$) such that $M_0 \| M_1 \not\models P_{\leq p}[\psi]$ is witnessed by $(\sigma, c)$. $ResolveEQ(f_A)$ returns "$M_0 \| M_1 \not\models P_{\leq p}[\psi]$."* □

**Theorem 6 (Termination)** *Let $M_i = (\mathbf{x}_i, l_{M_i}(\mathbf{x}_i), \mathbf{z}, f_{M_i}(\mathbf{z}, \mathbf{x}_i, \mathbf{x}'_i))$ be MDP's for $i = 0, 1$, and $P_{\leq p}[\psi]$ a probabilistic safety property. Our learning-based framework reports "$M_0 \| M_1 \models P_{\leq p}[\psi]$" or "$M_0 \| M_1 \not\models P_{\leq p}[\psi]$" within a polynomial number of queries in $|f_{M_0}(\mathbf{z}, \mathbf{x}_0, \mathbf{x}'_0)|$ and $|\mathbf{z} \cup \mathbf{x}_0 \cup \mathbf{x}'_0|$.*

**Proof:** *In our learning-based framework, the MTBDD learning algorithm targets the weighted transition function of $M_0$. It will infer the target MTBDD $f_{M_0}(\mathbf{z}, \mathbf{x}_0, \mathbf{x}'_0)$ using $O(n^2 + n \log m)$ membership queries and at most $n$ equivalence queries where $n = |f_{M_0}(\mathbf{z}, \mathbf{x}_0, \mathbf{x}'_0)|$ and $m = |\mathbf{z} \cup \mathbf{x}_0 \cup \mathbf{x}'_0|$ (Theorem 3). At this point, the weighted assumption $A$ is $M_0$. The mechanical teacher reports either "$M_0 \| M_1 \models P_{\leq p}[\psi]$" or "$M_0 \| M_1 \not\models P_{\leq p}[\psi]$."* □

## 7. Experiments

We have implemented a prototype of our compositional verification technique on top of PRISM 4.0.1 [38]. It accepts an MDP specified in the PRISM modeling language and a probabilistic safety property. The MTBDD learning algorithm is implemented by modifying the $L^*$ algorithm in libalf 0.3 library [9] with CUDD 2.5.0 package.[2] The membership query resolution algorithm (Algorithm 1) and the embedded checking algorithm (Algorithm 2) are implemented using CUDD. Probabilistic model checking in the equivalence query resolution algorithm (Algorithm 2) is performed by PRISM (using the MTBDD engine). We generate counterexamples by the techniques in [23]. All experiments were run on a virtual machine with 2.6GHz CPU and 4GB RAM.

Our compositional approach is evaluated on several parameterized examples. All examples are derived from the PRISM website.[3] For each model, we check a probabilistic safety property. All models and properties are briefly described below:

- *Consensus* models a randomized coin algorithm [4] which allows $N$ processes in a distributed network to reach a consensus by accessing a global shared counter parameterized by $K$. The specification describes "the probability that eventually all processes make a decision but some two processes do not agree on the same value is at most $p$".
- *WLAN* models the wireless local area networks specified in the IEEE 802.11 standard [2]. Stations of a wireless network cannot listen to their own transmission. Each station has a backoff counter (with the maximal value of $B$) to minimize the likelihood of transmission collision. The time bounded version of this model is considered. The specification describes "the probability that either station's backoff counter hits the number $K$ within some time is at most $p$".
- *FireWire* models the tree identify protocol of the IEEE 1394 high performance serial bus [1]. Among nodes connected in a network, a root node needs to be elected to act as the manager of the bus in the network. The time bound for message transmission is parameterized by $deadline$. The implementation version of this model is considered. The specification describes "the probability that a root node is elected eventually before some time deadline passes is at most $p$".
- *Philo* models a randomized solution to the dining philosophers problem [33]. $N$ philosophers sit around a circular table. Neighboring philosophers share a resource. A philosopher can eat if he obtains the resources from both sides. The specification describes "the probability that neighboring philosophers do not obtain their shared resource simultaneously is at most 0.00001."

Our tool selects one process of the model as $M_0$ and the composition of other processes as $M_1$. Selecting the composition of multiple processes as $M_0$ can be done by solving the two-way decomposition problem [14, 43]. Here we employ a simple heuristic:

[2] `http://vlsi.colorado.edu/~fabio/CUDD/`

[3] `http://www.prismmodelchecker.org`

choose the process with the minimal *interface alphabet*. The interface alphabet of a process is the set of shared actions. For example, the *WLAN* model consists of four processes: *medium, station1, station2* and *timer*, with interface alphabets $\{send1, send2, finish1, finish2\}$, $\{time, finish1, send1\}$, $\{time, finish2, send2\}$ and $\{time\}$, respectively. We choose *timer* as $M_0$ by our heuristic.

The first experiment compares the performance of our compositional approach (*compositional*) with the monolithic probabilistic model checking in PRISM (*monolithic*). Experimental results are listed in Table 1. For each model and a corresponding probabilistic safety property $P_{\leq p}[\psi]$, we compute the property of $P_{max=?}[\psi]$ by PRISM and report it in the $P_{max}$ column. Note that the property $P_{\leq p}[\psi]$ holds on the model if and only if $p \geq P_{max}$. The satisfiability of the property $P_{\leq p}[\psi]$ on the model is reported in the *Result* column. For each test case, we show the model size (*size*) and run time (*time*). The model size counts the number of MTBDD nodes for the weighted transition function of the composed model.[4] The run time includes the time spent on all stages, including model construction, model checking, witness analysis, and assumption learning. For monolithic approach, both PRISM with the MTBDD engine (PRISM-M) and PRISM with the hybrid engine (PRISM-H) are tested. Their run times are listed in $T_M$ and $T_H$ columns respectively. For compositional approach, the number of PRISM calls (*#Call*) is also reported. The last column (*reduction*) shows the reduction of model size and time of our compositional approach to PRISM-M. All time is in seconds, and the symbol "–" indicates either time-out (4 hours) or memory-out (4GB).

The results are very encouraging. In 20 of 23 cases, the compositional verifier outperforms PRISM-M significantly. Moreover, a reduction of 90% in time is achieved in 9 cases; and a reduction of 80% in model sizes is attained in 8 cases. Our compositional approach benefits the verification by avoiding the construction of the whole model. In the *size reduction* column of Table 1, our compositional approach succeeds in learning an assumption $A$ such that the size of $A \| M_1$ is much smaller than that of $M_0 \| M_1$ in most cases. Only for the two smallest unsatisfied cases in the *Consensus* example, our compositional approach performs worse. One possible reason is that the sizes of the models are so small that compositional verification is redundant. Also, observe that PRISM-H performs much better then PRISM-M in the *Consensus* example. MTBDD-based techniques (monolithic or not) may not be the best choice for this example.

Hybrid (PRISM-H) and MTBDD-based (PRISM-M and ours) techniques can also be compared in Table 1. The results heavily depend on the examples. Similar phenomenons were also reported in [31]. For all cases in the *Consensus* example, PRISM-H performs much better than both MTBDD-based techniques. For all cases in the *Philos* example, the performances of PRISM-H and PRISM-M are similar. However, in the more realistic *WLAN* and *FireWire* examples, PRISM-H runs out of memory quickly when the model size becomes large.

The second experiment evaluates the impact of the probability bound $p$ on the effectiveness of compositional verification. This experiment is performed on examples with different probability bounds. The results on the *WLAN* example with $(B, K) = (4, 2)$ are plotted in Figure 9(a). When $p$ is above or nearly above $P_{max}$ ($\approx 0.1836$), the performance of our approach goes down quickly. The reason is that the property becomes satisfied when $p \geq P_{max}$. More equivalence queries are then required to infer a proper assumption to prove both premises of the reasoning rule. On the other hand, if the probability bound $p$ is less than $P_{max}$, a coarse weighted assumption suffices to verify the property. Similar phenomenons can be observed on the *Consensus* example with $(N, K) = (4, 2)$ (Figure 9(b)). The result from the *FireWire* example with *deadline* = 400 (Figure 9(c)) is quite different. Observe that the actual probability $P_{max}$ of the *FireWire* examples is 1. Its properties are trivially unsatisfied for any $p$. Thus there is no rising edge in Figure 9(c) as in other figures. In the *Philos* example, the probability $P_{max}$ is 0 and hence the properties are always satisfied for any $p$. Similar to *FireWire*, we do not observe any rising edge and hence skip the figure of the *Philos* example. Compositional verification however always outperforms the monolithic algorithm regardless of satisfiability of properties in both examples.

[4] By composed model, we mean $M_0 \| M_1$ for monolithic checker and $A \| M_1$ for our checker.

## 8. Related Works

The most relevant works to ours are [16, 17, 32]. In their proof rules, assumptions are classical deterministic finite automata. The $L^*$ algorithm has been applied to infer classical assumptions in [16]. As discussed above, classical assumptions cannot express general probabilistic behaviors. Such techniques are sound but incomplete. We adopt weighted automata as assumptions to have a sound and invertible proof rule. Our technique is both sound and complete. A sound and invertible assume-guarantee reasoning proof rule for probabilistic I/O systems is given in [17]. The framework however only works for fully probabilistic discrete time Markov chains and may not terminate. Our technique in contrast applies to Markov decision processes and always terminates.

Undecidability of inferring labeled probabilistic transition systems under Angluin's active learning model is shown in [30]. A (necessarily) restricted learning algorithm for such probabilistic systems is also proposed in the same paper. In addition to learning different concepts, the restricted algorithm does not utilize membership queries whereas ours does. An alternative direction for generating probabilistic assumptions is to use abstraction refinement (AGAR) techniques [21]. In [29], probabilistic assumptions are conservative abstractions of system components. They are iteratively refined by counterexamples [12]. However, AGAR relies on partitioning the explicit state space to construct assumptions [21, 29]. We are not aware of any symbolic implementation of AGAR techniques for classical or probabilistic systems.

Various learning algorithms have been proposed for probabilistic systems [10, 34, 35, 40]. These learning algorithms adopt passive learning model. They are not applicable to the learning-based assume-guarantee reasoning framework in [13].

Learning algorithms for binary decision diagrams were proposed in [19, 37]. In [19], an $L^*$-based algorithm was developed. The work in [37] used a classification tree-based learning algorithm for regular languages. Both algorithms inferred deterministic finite automata and transformed them into decision diagrams.

## 9. Conclusion

We proposed a sound and complete learning-based assume-guarantee reasoning technique for probabilistic safety properties on MDP's. Instead of probabilistic assumptions, we infer weighted assumptions for compositional verification. Using an MTBDD learning algorithm, our technique generates implicit representations of weighted assumptions. Experimental results show that the assume-guarantee reasoning technique outperforms the monolithic probabilistic model checking in most of the test cases.

Our technique can be applied to sequential probabilistic systems. Let $M$ be an MDP and $P_{\leq p}[\psi]$ a probabilistic safety property. One generates a 0/1-WA $A$ such that $M \preceq_e A$ and $A \models P_{\leq p}[\psi]$ by our learning-based technique. It is however not recommended when $M$ is composed of concurrent MDP's. Since the construction of the composition can be very expensive, the computation should

Table 1: Experimental Results: Monolithic vs. Compositional

| Example | Param | $P_{max}$ | Result | Monolithic | | | Compositional | | | Reduction(%) | |
|---|---|---|---|---|---|---|---|---|---|---|---|
| | | | | $T_H$ | $T_M$ | Size | #Call | $T$ | Size | Time | Size |
| Consensus ($p$=0.01) | (2, 6) | 0.04 | false | 0.16 | 3.86 | 393 | 6 | 6.08 | 423 | -57.5 | -7.6 |
| | (2, 10) | 0.02 | false | 0.50 | 17.36 | 417 | 6 | 24.87 | 460 | -43.3 | -10.3 |
| | (4, 2) | 0.29 | false | 2.86 | 40.22 | 2288 | 6 | 35.79 | 2211 | 11.0 | 3.4 |
| | (4, 6) | 0.10 | false | 42.15 | 1109.71 | 2340 | 6 | 703.53 | 2269 | 36.6 | 3.0 |
| | (4, 10) | 0.06 | false | 169.21 | 4747.15 | 2384 | 6 | 3051.72 | 2327 | 35.7 | 2.4 |
| | (6, 2) | 0.36 | false | 411.57 | 1611.16 | 7075 | 6 | 1068.06 | 6753 | 33.7 | 4.6 |
| | (6, 4) | 0.19 | false | 2841.36 | 10270.29 | 7055 | 6 | 5751.38 | 6728 | 44.0 | 4.6 |
| WLAN ($p$=0.1) | (2, 2) | 0.18 | false | 430.21 | 381.38 | 304314 | 4 | 5.91 | 33237 | 98.5 | 89.1 |
| | (3, 2) | 0.18 | false | – | 675.15 | 626744 | 4 | 5.94 | 40945 | 99.1 | 93.5 |
| | (3, 3) | 0.02 | true | – | 687.04 | 626744 | 11 | 977.89 | 664801 | -42.3 | -6.1 |
| | (4, 2) | 0.18 | false | – | 2620.32 | 1321221 | 4 | 7.64 | 52129 | 99.7 | 96.1 |
| | (4, 3) | 0.02 | true | – | 2530.00 | 1321221 | 11 | 1776.14 | 1421456 | 29.8 | -7.6 |
| | (4, 4) | 0.00 | true | – | 2683.98 | 1321221 | 11 | 2061.69 | 1421456 | 23.2 | -7.6 |
| FireWire ($p$=0.1) | 200 | 1.00 | false | 182.58 | 86.04 | 836852 | 4 | 37.06 | 129750 | 56.9 | 84.5 |
| | 400 | 1.00 | false | 1897.39 | 507.58 | 1220933 | 4 | 38.92 | 129761 | 92.3 | 89.4 |
| | 600 | 1.00 | false | – | 954.33 | 1243547 | 4 | 39.17 | 129778 | 95.9 | 89.6 |
| | 800 | 1.00 | false | – | 1380.22 | 1243552 | 4 | 39.21 | 129772 | 97.2 | 89.6 |
| | 1000 | 1.00 | false | – | 1803.40 | 1243551 | 4 | 39.52 | 129780 | 97.8 | 89.6 |
| Philos ($p$=0.01) | 20 | 0.00 | true | 29.80 | 29.74 | 58565 | 1 | 13.43 | 19328 | 54.9 | 67.0 |
| | 25 | 0.00 | true | 55.98 | 56.36 | 91325 | 1 | 31.48 | 29908 | 44.1 | 67.3 |
| | 30 | 0.00 | true | 109.01 | 108.84 | 131260 | 1 | 54.71 | 42763 | 49.7 | 67.4 |
| | 35 | 0.00 | true | 1006.60 | 1022.58 | 178370 | 1 | 96.45 | 57893 | 90.6 | 67.5 |
| | 40 | 0.00 | true | 2370.48 | 2348.22 | 232655 | 1 | 168.14 | 75298 | 92.8 | 67.6 |

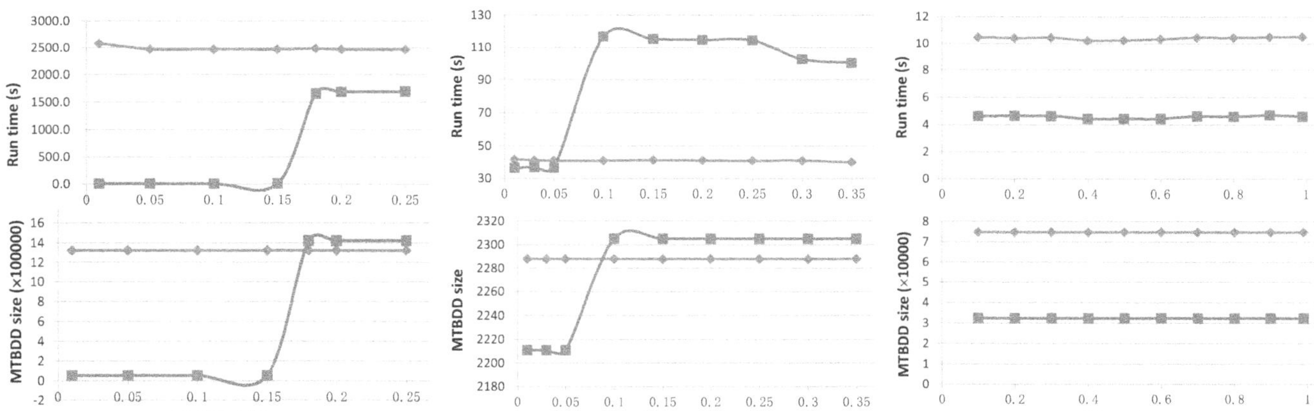


(a) WLAN (b) Consensus (c) FireWire

Figure 9: Impacts of $p$ on the Performance of MTBDD-Based Approaches (red for compositional, blue for monolithic).

be deferred after concurrent components are simplified. Assume-guarantee reasoning presented in this paper is certainly preferred.

Currently, our PRISM-based implementation receives a finite set of paths as weighted witnesses to $M \not\models P_{\leq p}[\psi]$. Generally, weighted witnesses to $M \not\models P_{\lhd p}[\psi]$ where $\lhd \in \{<, \leq\}$ are represented as graphs with strongly connected components [41, 42]. We plan to generalize transition contributions to select counterexamples from spurious weighted witnesses with strongly connected components. We moreover would like to extend our learning framework to verifying richer properties such as general probabilistic safety or liveness properties.

## Acknowledgments

Fei He (corresponding author) and Xiaowei Gao are supported by the Chinese National 973 Plan (2010CB328003); the NSF of China (61272001, 60903030, 91218302); the Chinese National Key Technology R&D Program (SQ2012BAJY4052), the Importation and Development of High-Caliber Talents Project of Beijing Municipal Institutions (YETP0167), and the Tsinghua University Initiative Scientific Research Program; Bow-Yaw Wang (corresponding author) is supported by the Ministry of Science and Technology of Taiwan (103-2221-E-001 -020 -MY3); Lijun Zhang (corresponding author) is supported by the Natural Science Foundation of China (NSFC) under grant No. 61472473, 61428208, 61361136002, the CAS/SAFEA International Partnership Program for Creative Research Teams.

## References

[1] IEEE standard for a high-performance serial bus. *IEEE Std 1394-2008*, pages 1–954, Oct 2008.

[2] IEEE standard for information technology–telecommunications and information exchange between systems local and metropolitan area networks–specific requirements part 11: Wireless LAN medium access control (MAC) and physical layer (PHY) specifications. *IEEE Std 802.11-2012 (Revision of IEEE Std 802.11-2007)*, pages 1–2793, March 2012.

[3] D. Angluin. Learning regular sets from queries and counterexamples. *Information and Computation*, 75(2):87–106, 1987.

[4] J. Aspnes and M. Herlihy. Fast randomized consensus using shared memory. *Journal of Algorithms*, 11(3):441–460, 1990.

[5] C. Baier and J.-P. Katoen. *Principles of model checking*. MIT Press, 2008.

[6] C. Baier, E. M. Clarke, V. Hartonas-Garmhausen, M. Kwiatkowska, and M. Ryan. Symbolic model checking for probabilistic processes. In *ICALP*, volume 1256 of *LNCS*, pages 430–440. Springer, 1997.

[7] A. Beimel, F. Bergadano, N. H. Bshouty, E. Kushilevitz, and S. Varricchio. Learning functions represented as multiplicity automata. *Journal of ACM*, 47(3):506–530, May 2000. .

[8] A. Bianco and L. de Alfaro. Model checking of probabalistic and nondeterministic systems. In *FSTTCS*, volume 1026 of *LNCS*, pages 499–513. Springer, 1995.

[9] B. Bollig, J.-P. Katoen, C. Kern, M. Leucker, D. Neider, and D. R. Piegdon. libalf: The automata learning framework. In *CAV*, volume 6174 of *LNCS*, pages 360–364. Springer, 2010.

[10] Y. Chen, H. Mao, M. Jaeger, T. Nielsen, K. Guldstrand Larsen, and B. Nielsen. Learning Markov models for stationary system behaviors. In *NASA Formal Methods*, volume 7226 of *LNCS*, pages 216–230. Springer, 2012.

[11] Y.-F. Chen, E. M. Clarke, A. Farzan, M.-H. Tsai, Y.-K. Tsay, and B.-Y. Wang. Automated assume-guarantee reasoning through implicit learning. In *CAV*, volume 6174 of *LNCS*, pages 511–526. Springer, 2010.

[12] E. Clarke, O. Grumberg, S. Jha, Y. Lu, and H. Veith. Counterexample-guided abstraction refinement. In *CAV*, volume 1855 of *LNCS*, pages 154–169. Springer, 2000.

[13] J. M. Cobleigh, D. Giannakopoulou, and C. S. Păsăreanu. Learning assumptions for compositional verification. In *TACAS*, volume 2619 of *LNCS*, pages 331–346. Springer, 2003.

[14] J. M. Cobleigh, G. S. Avrunin, and L. A. Clarke. Breaking up is hard to do: An evaluation of automated assume-guarantee reasoning. *ACM Transactions on Software Engineering and Methodology (TOSEM)*, 17 (2):7, 2008.

[15] L. De Alfaro, M. Kwiatkowska, G. Norman, D. Parker, and R. Segala. Symbolic model checking of probabilistic processes using MTBDDs and the Kronecker representation. In *TACAS*, volume 1758 of *LNCS*, pages 395–410. Springer, 2000.

[16] L. Feng, M. Kwiatkowska, and D. Parker. Compositional verification of probabilistic systems using learning. In *QEST*, pages 133–142. IEEE, 2010.

[17] L. Feng, T. Han, M. Kwiatkowska, and D. Parker. Learning-based compositional verification for synchronous probabilistic systems. In *ATVA*, volume 6996 of *LNCS*, pages 511–521. Springer-Verlag, 2011.

[18] M. Fujita, P. C. McGeer, and J.-Y. Yang. Multi-terminal binary decision diagrams: An efficient data structure for matrix representation. *Formal Methods in System Design*, 10(2/3):149–169, 1997.

[19] R. Gavaldà and D. Guijarro. Learning ordered binary decision diagrams. In *ALT*, volume 997 of *LNCS*, pages 228–238. Springer, 1995.

[20] M. Gheorghiu, D. Giannakopoulou, and C. S. Păsăreanu. Refining interface alphabets for compositional verification. In *TACAS*, volume 4424 of *LNCS*, pages 292–307. Springer, 2007.

[21] M. Gheorghiu Bobaru, C. S. Păsăreanu, and D. Giannakopoulou. Automated assume-guarantee reasoning by abstraction refinement. In *CAV*, volume 5123 of *LNCS*, pages 135–148. Springer, 2008.

[22] A. Gupta, K. L. McMillan, and Z. Fu. Automated assumption generation for compositional verification. In *CAV*, volume 4590 of *LNCS*, pages 420–432. Springer, 2007.

[23] T. Han, J.-P. Katoen, and D. Berteun. Counterexample generation in probabilistic model checking. *IEEE Transactions on Software Engineering*, 35(2):241–257, 2009.

[24] H. Hansson and B. Jonsson. A logic for reasoning about time and reliability. *Formal aspects of computing*, 6(5):512–535, 1994.

[25] F. He, B.-Y. Wang, L. Yin, and L. Zhu. Symbolic assume-guarantee reasoning through BDD learning. In *ICSE*, pages 1071–1082. ACM, 2014.

[26] A. Hinton, M. Kwiatkowska, G. Norman, and D. Parker. PRISM: A tool for automatic verification of probabilistic systems. In *TACAS*, volume 3920 of *LNCS*, pages 441–444. Springer, 2006.

[27] J.-P. Katoen, L. Song, and L. Zhang. Probably safe or live. In *Proceedings of the Joint Meeting of the Twenty-Third EACSL Annual Conference on Computer Science Logic (CSL) and the Twenty-Ninth Annual ACM/IEEE Symposium on Logic in Computer Science (LICS)*, pages 55:1–55:10. ACM, 2014.

[28] S. Kimura and E. M. Clarke. A parallel algorithm for constructing binary decision diagrams. In *ICCD*, pages 220–223. IEEE, 1990.

[29] A. Komuravelli, C. S. Păsăreanu, and E. M. Clarke. Assume-guarantee abstraction refinement for probabilistic systems. In *CAV*, volume 7358 of *LNCS*, pages 310–326. Springer, 2012.

[30] A. Komuravelli, C. S. Păsăreanu, and E. M. Clarke. Learning probabilistic systems from tree samples. In *LICS*, pages 441–450. IEEE, 2012.

[31] M. Kwiatkowska, G. Norman, and D. Parker. Probabilistic symbolic model checking with PRISM: A hybrid approach. *International Journal on Software Tools for Technology Transfer*, 6(2):128–142, 2004.

[32] M. Kwiatkowska, G. Norman, D. Parker, and H. Qu. Assume-guarantee verification for probabilistic systems. In *TACAS*, volume 6015 of *LNCS*, pages 23–37. Springer, 2010.

[33] D. Lehmann and M. O. Rabin. On the advantage of free choice: A symmetric and fully distributed solution to the dining philosophers problem (extended abstract). In *POPL*, pages 133–138. ACM, 1981.

[34] H. Mao, Y. Chen, M. Jaeger, T. D. Nielsen, K. G. Larsen, and B. Nielsen. Learning probabilistic automata for model checking. In *QEST*, pages 111–120. IEEE, 2011.

[35] H. Mao, Y. Chen, M. Jaeger, T. D. Nielsen, K. G. Larsen, and B. Nielsen. Learning Markov decision processes for model checking. *arXiv preprint arXiv:1212.3873*, 2012.

[36] R. Motwani and P. Raghavan. *Randomized Algorithms*. Cambridge University Press, 1995.

[37] A. Nakamura. An efficient query learning algorithm for ordered binary decision diagrams. *Information and Computation*, 201(2):178–198, 2005.

[38] D. A. Parker. *Implementation of symbolic model checking for probabilistic systems*. PhD thesis, University of Birmingham, 2002.

[39] R. Segala and N. Lynch. Probabilistic simulations for probabilistic processes. In *CONCUR*, volume 836 of *LNCS*, pages 481–496. Springer, 1994.

[40] W.-G. Tzeng. Learning probabilistic automata and Markov chains via queries. *Machine Learning*, 8(2):151–166, 1992.

[41] R. Wimmer, N. Jansen, E. Ábrahám, B. Becker, and J.-P. Katoen. Minimal critical subsystems for discrete-time Markov models. In *TACAS*, volume 7214 of *LNCS*, pages 299–314. Springer, 2012.

[42] R. Wimmer, N. Jansen, A. Vorpahl, E. Ábrahám, J.-P. Katoen, and B. Becker. High-level counterexamples for probabilistic automata. In *QEST*, pages 39–54. IEEE, 2013.

[43] H. Zhu, F. He, W. N. Hung, X. Song, and M. Gu. Data mining based decomposition for assume-guarantee reasoning. In *FMCAD*, pages 116–119. IEEE, 2009.

# Full Abstraction for Signal Flow Graphs

Filippo Bonchi
ENS Lyon, U. Lyon, CNRS, INRIA
filippo.bonchi@ens-lyon.fr

Paweł Sobociński
U. Southampton, UK
ps@ecs.soton.ac.uk

Fabio Zanasi
ENS Lyon, U. Lyon, CNRS, INRIA
fabio.zanasi@ens-lyon.fr

## Abstract

Network theory uses the string diagrammatic language of monoidal categories to study graphical structures formally, eschewing specialised translations into intermediate formalisms. Recently, there has been a concerted research focus on developing a network theoretic approach to signal flow graphs, which are classical structures in control theory, signal processing and a cornerstone in the study of feedback. In this approach, signal flow graphs are given a relational denotational semantics in terms of formal power series.

Thus far, the operational behaviour of such signal flow graphs has only been discussed at an intuitive level. In this paper we equip them with a structural operational semantics. As is typically the case, the purely operational picture is too concrete – two graphs that are denotationally equal may exhibit different operational behaviour. We classify the ways in which this can occur and show that any graph can be *realised* – rewritten, using the graphical theory, into an *executable* form where the operational behavior and the denotation coincides.

***Categories and Subject Descriptors*** D.3.1 [*Formal Definitions and Theory*]: Semantics; F.3.2 [*Semantics of Programming Languages*]: Algebraic approaches to semantics

***Keywords*** Signal Flow Graphs, String Diagrams, PROPs, Structural Operational Semantics, Full Abstraction

## 1. Introduction

Signal flow graphs (SFGs) are foundational structures in control theory and signal processing studied since at least the 1950s [23]. They can be constructed from small set of basic components (displayed below) and feedbacks.

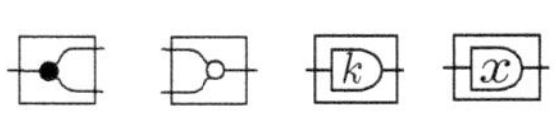

(1)

Signals, which take values over a field k, flow from left to right. The leftmost component *duplicates* the signal, the second *sums* the two signals arriving on the left and the third *multiplies* the signal by a scalar $k \in \mathsf{k}$. The rightmost one is a *delay*: when a sequence of signals $k_0, k_1, k_2, \ldots$ arrives on the left, it outputs the sequence $0, k_0, k_1 \ldots$ It can be thought as a synchronous one place buffer initialised with 0.



*POPL '15*, January 15–17, 2015, Mumbai, India.

http://dx.doi.org/10.1145/2676726.2676993

A simple mathematical meaning can be given to those SFGs where feedbacks pass through (at least) one delay component. It is well known (see e.g. [21]) that SFGs with this restriction denote rational functions. In traditional approaches, however, SFGs are not treated as interesting mathematical structures per se: formal analyses typically mean translations into systems of linear equations—although, more recently, they have also attracted the use of coalgebraic tools [4, 26]. Another series of recent works [3, 5, 7, 14, 31] embraces SFGs as graphical structures known as *string diagrams* and studies them as mathematical objects of interest in their own right—this approach is known as *network theory* [2]. The majority of the attention so far has been focused on what we call the *denotational semantics*: differently from the classical approach, string diagrams, in general, give rise to *linear relations* rather than functions. The string diagrams that are considered are not restricted by any side conditions on feedbacks, being all those diagrams generated from the basic components (1), together with their duals:

(2)

Intuitively, in 2 the signal flows from right to left. This means that diagrams constructed using both components in (1) and (2) have no univocal flow direction and require a relational model.

Network theory brings fundamentally new ingredients to the field of signal flow graphs. First, the relational semantics is a *compositional* account of their behavior that enjoys a sound and complete axiomatisation independently discovered in [5, 7] and [3]. Second, the axiomatisation has uncovered a rich underlying mathematical playground – featuring two Hopf algebras and two Frobenius algebras – which also reveals connections with quantum phenomena [3, 6, 31]. Third, it has resulted in a subtle re-evaluation of *causality* as a central ingredient of SFGs. In 1953 Mason [23] wrote: "flow graphs differ from electrical network graphs in that their branches are directed. In accounting for branch directions it is necessary to take an entirely different line of approach from that adopted in electrical network topology." Instead, our results suggest that *direction of signal flow is not a primitive notion*: this argument has been made informally already in [3, 5] but is rigorously shown at the end of this paper (Section 6). Similar ideas are prominent in the *behavioural approach* in control theory [30].

In this paper, we introduce *operational semantics* to the network theoretic accounts of signal flow graphs: we show that string diagrams can be thought of as terms of a process calculus and executed as state machines. For this reason we shall call our string diagrams *circuit diagrams* or simply *circuits*. Reconciling the operational perspective with the established denotational model turns out to be quite subtle. Indeed, the denotational semantics is in a sense too abstract: finite computations that reach *deadlocks* are ignored. Such deadlocks can arise for instance when components of (1) are composed with the those of (2) and, intuitively, the signal flows from the left and right toward the middle. For an example, consider the circuit below on the left.

 (3)

In a first step, the signals arriving from left and right are stored in the two buffers. Then, the stored values are compared in the middle of the circuit: if they do not agree then the computation gets stuck. The circuit on the right features another problem, which we call *initialisation*. Intuitively, the flow goes from the middle toward left and right. All its computations are forced to start by emitting on the left and on the right the value 0 which is initially stored in the two buffers. The two circuits are denotationally equivalent, but their operational behaviour can be obviously distinguished: the leftmost does not have initialisation and the rightmost cannot deadlock.

Deadlock and initialisation are dual problems at the heart of the mismatch of operational and denotational semantics. We show that circuits in *cospan form*, namely circuits built from components in (1) followed by those in (2) (like the leftmost circuit in (3)), are free from initialisation. Instead, circuits in *span form*, i.e., those built from components in (2) followed by (1) (like the rightmost in (3)) are free from deadlock. This is interesting because the equational theory developed in [3, 5] asserts that any circuit is equivalent to both one in cospan and one in span form. This duality of deadlock and initialisation helps us in proving a *full abstraction* result: for those circuits that are free from both deadlock and initialisation, the operational and the denotational semantics agree.

Our second main theorem is a *realisability* result: for any denoted behaviour there exists some circuit that properly, without deadlocks or initialisation, *realises* it. The key for the proof is the fact that any circuit in [3, 5] is equivalent (according to the denotational semantics) to a signal flow graph up to some "rewiring". This result allow us to impose a syntactic restriction to our circuits to guarantee deadlock and initialisation freedom. By virtue of the full abstraction results we can thus safely use the axiomatization of [3, 5] to reason about the operational behaviour of these circuits.

Summarising, the main results of this paper are:

- a structural operational semantics for the network-theoretic account of SFGs;
- a full abstraction theorem relating the operational and the denotational semantics previously introduced in [3, 5];
- a realisability theorem: every behaviour can be implemented by a circuit without deadlock and initialisation;
- a formal explanation of the fact that direction of flow is a derivative notion.

***Related work.*** String diagrams originally came to the fore in the study of monoidal categories because they clear away swathes of cumbersome coherence bureaucracy, thereby dramatically simplifying algebraic arguments: in particular, they are useful for characterising *free* monoidal categories [16, 18, 27].

In this paper we work with particular symmetric monoidal categories, called PROPs [19, 22] (PROduct-and-Permutation categories). PROPs are a useful setting for the study of string diagrams and especially monoidal theories—Lack's theory of composing PROPs [19] was used to derive the axiomatisation in [5, 7]. PROPs have also recently been used by computer scientists: Lafont's study of boolean circuits [20], Bruni, Montanari, Plotkin, and Terreni [8] have used them to give an alternative presentation of Milner's bigraphs while Fiore and Campos [13] presented a theory of directed acyclic graphs. Our operational semantics is related to Katis, Sabadini and Walters' [17] Span(Graph) algebra of transition systems and the algebra of connectors of Bruni, Lanese and Montanari [9]. String diagrams are increasingly used by computer scientists: for instance we mention Pavlovic's monoidal computer [24, 25] where they are employed to study classical notions of computability and computational complexity.

The interplay of Hopf algebras and Frobenius algebras, at the core of the axiomatisation of the denotational semantics, appeared first in the work of Coecke, Duncan and Kissinger [11, 12] on the ZX-calculus, used in the study of quantum circuits. Similar algebraic interactions emerged in the study of Petri nets [28] and in string-diagrammatic theories of asynchronous circuits [15].

***Structure.*** In §2 we introduce the operational semantics. In §3 we recall the denotational semantics from [3, 5] and we prove full abstraction in §4. In §5 we prove the realisability theorem and in §6 we consider a directed syntax in order to capture classical SFGs.

***Notational conventions.*** $\mathbb{C}[a, b]$ is the set of arrows from $a$ to $b$ in a small category $\mathbb{C}$. Composition of $f : a \to b$, $g : b \to c$ is written $f ; g : a \to c$. When $\mathbb{C}$ is monoidal, $\oplus$ is the monoidal product.

## 2. The Signal Flow Calculus: Syntax and Operational Semantics

Here we give the syntax and the structural operational semantics of a simple process calculus, to which we shall refer to as the *Signal Flow Calculus*. Fix an arbitrary field $\mathsf{k}$. The syntax, given below, does not feature binding nor primitives for recursion, while $k$ ranges over $\mathsf{k}$.

$c ::=$ 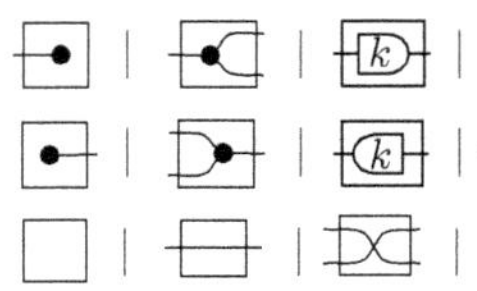 $\mid c \oplus c \mid c ; c$ (4) (5) (6)

A *sort* is a pair $(n, m)$, with $n, m \in \mathbb{N}$. We shall consider only terms that are sortable, according to the rules of Fig. 1. A simple inductive argument confirms uniqueness of sorting: if $c : (n, m)$ and $c : (n', m')$ then $n = n'$ and $m = m'$. We will refer to sortable terms as *circuits* since, intuitively, a term $c : (n, m)$ represents a circuit with $n$ ports on the left and $m$ ports on the right. The wires carry elements of a field $\mathsf{k}$.

The operational semantics is a transition system with states augmented circuits where each *delay* component (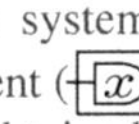 and ) is assigned some value $k \in \mathsf{k}$. Thus *states* are obtained by replacing the delays in the syntax specification with *registers* 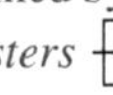 $^k$ and 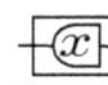 $^k$ for each $k \in \mathsf{k}$. As for circuits, we only consider sortable states, which are defined by adding

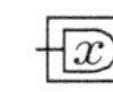 $^k : (1, 1)$ and 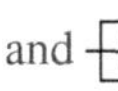 $^k : (1, 1)$.

to the rules in Fig. 1.

Structural inference rules for operational semantics are given in Fig. 2 where we use strings of length $n$ to represents vectors in $\mathsf{k}^n$. So, the empty string stands for $()$, the only vector of $\mathsf{k}^0$, and $v = k_1 \dots k_n$ for the column vector $\begin{pmatrix} k_1 \\ \vdots \\ k_n \end{pmatrix}$ in $\mathsf{k}^n$.

If state $s : (n, m)$ is the source of a transition $\xrightarrow[w]{v} t$ then $t$ is also a state with sort $(n, m)$ and $v$ and $w$ are strings representing vectors of $\mathsf{k}^n$ and $\mathsf{k}^m$, respectively. Intuitively, $s \xrightarrow[w]{v} t$ means that $s$ can become $t$ whenever the signals on the $n$ ports on the left agree with $v$ and the signals on the $m$ ports on the right agree with $w$. Each circuit $c$ then yields a transition system with a chosen *initial state* $s_0$ of $c$, obtained by replacing the delays 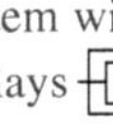 and 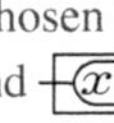 in $c$ with registers 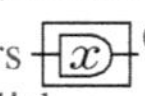 $^0$ and 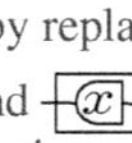 $^0$ containing 0.

To establish a preliminary intuition, we can consider circuits built up of the components in (4) as taking signals from the left

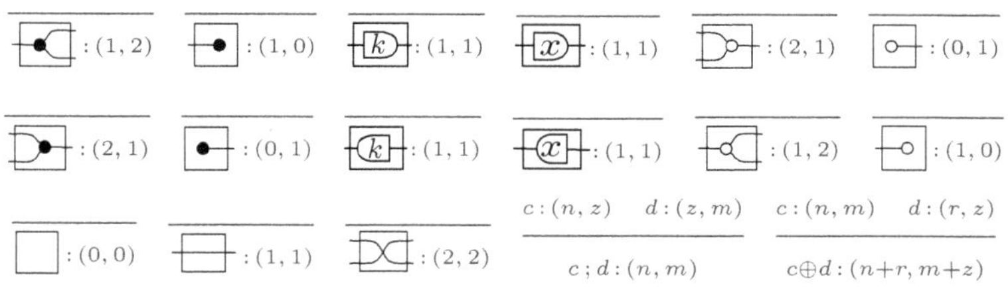

**Figure 1.** Sort inference rules.

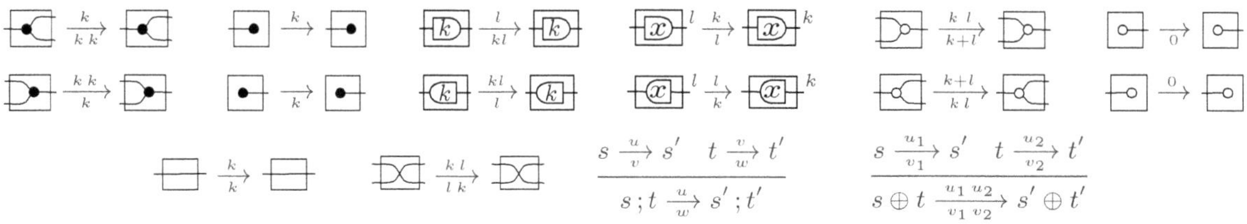

**Figure 2.** Structural rules for operational semantics, with $k, l$ ranging over k and $u, v, w$ vectors of elements of k of the appropriate size.

boundary to the right: thus is a *copier*, duplicating the signal arriving on the left; accepts any signal on the left and discards it, producing nothing on the right; is an *adder* that takes two signals on the left and emits their sum on the right, and constantly emits the signal 0 on the right; is an *amplifier*, multiplying the signal on the left by the scalar $k \in$ k. Finally, is a *delay*, a synchronous one place buffer initialised with 0.

The terms of row (5) are those of row (4) "reflected about the $y$-axis". Their behaviour is symmetric—indeed, here it is helpful to think of signals flowing from right to left.

In row (6), is a *twist*, swapping two signals, is the empty circuit and is the *identity* wire: the signals on the left and on the right ports are equal. Terms can be combined by two binary operators: sequential ; and parallel $\oplus$ composition.

In the syntax specification we purposefully used a graphical rendering of the components. Indeed, we will seldom write terms in the traditional way and instead represent them as 2-dimensional diagrams. We adopt the following common convention:

$c\,;c'$ is drawn 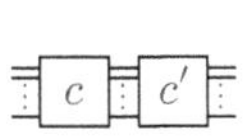 $c \oplus c'$ is drawn 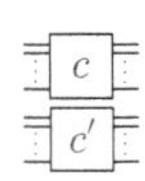 .

A *computation* of a circuit $c$, is a (possibly infinite) path $s_0 \xrightarrow[w_0]{v_0} s_1 \xrightarrow[w_1]{v_1} \ldots$ in the transition system of $c$, starting from its initial state $s_0$. When $c$ has sort $(n, m)$, each $v_i$ and $w_i$ consist of strings over k, say $k_{i1} \ldots k_{in}$ and $l_{i1} \ldots l_{im}$, respectively. The *trace* of a computation $s_0 \xrightarrow[w_0]{v_0} s_1 \xrightarrow[w_1]{v_1} \ldots$ is then a pair of vectors $\begin{pmatrix} \alpha_1 \\ \vdots \\ \alpha_n \end{pmatrix}, \begin{pmatrix} \beta_1 \\ \vdots \\ \beta_m \end{pmatrix}$ where $\alpha_j = k_{0j}k_{1j}\ldots$ and $\beta_j = l_{0j}l_{1j}\ldots$. Occasionally we will use the notation $(\overrightarrow{\alpha}, \overrightarrow{\beta})$ for such a pair and, to make the notation lighter, we will write $\alpha_j = k_0k_1\ldots$ and $\beta_j = l_0l_1\ldots$. Moreover, with $\alpha_j(i)$ and $\beta_j(i)$ we will denote the $i$-th elements of $\alpha_j$ and $\beta_j$.

Note that in a computation of length $z$, all $\alpha_j, \beta_j$ have length $z$, while for an infinite computation all $\alpha_j, \beta_j$ are infinite. In the former case, we say that a trace is finite, in the latter that it is infinite. We use $ft(c)$ to denote the set of all finite traces of $c$ and $it(c)$ for the set of all infinite ones.

**Example 1.** Consider the two circuits below.

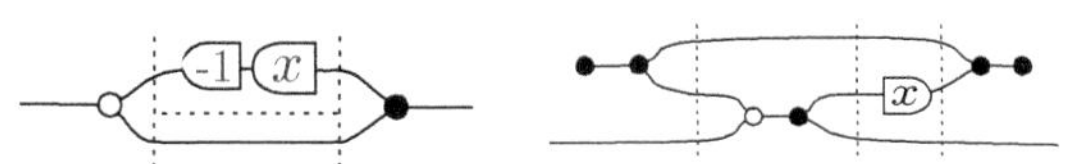


The first is a graphical representation of the term

$c_1 =$ 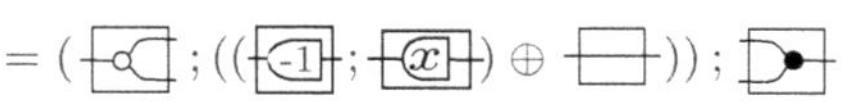

the second of the term

$c_2 =$ 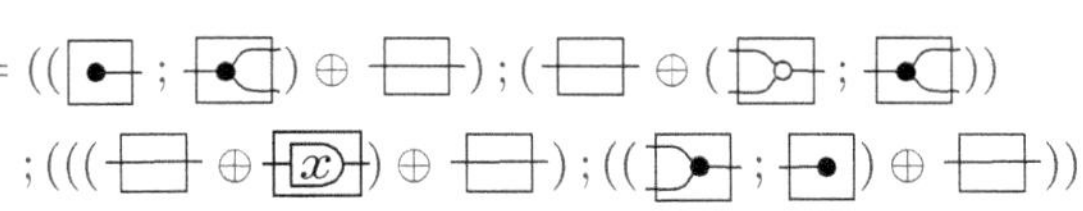

Note that, according to our intuition, in the leftmost circuit the signal flows from right to left, while the rightmost, the signal flows from left to right – indeed, the terms ; and ; serve as "bent identity wires" which allow us to form a feedback loop. Let $c_1[k]$ and $c_2[k]$ represent the states of $c_1$ and $c_2$, with $k$ denoting the value at the register. The rules of Fig. 2 yield the computation

$$c_i[0] \xrightarrow[1]{1} c_i[1] \xrightarrow[1]{0} c_i[1] \xrightarrow[1]{0} c_i[1] \cdots$$

for $i \in 0, 1$, which yields the trace $(1000\ldots), (1111\ldots)$. In fact, as we shall show via a sound and complete axiomatisation, despite of the signal intuitively flowing in different directions, the two circuits have the same observable behaviour.

A slightly more involved example is given below.

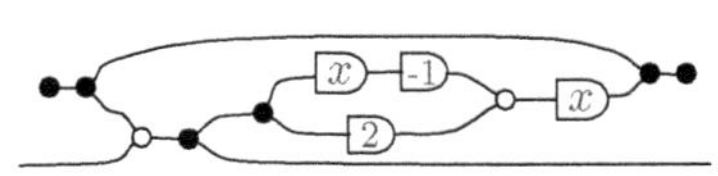


We leave the reader to write down a term that is represented by the diagram above: call it $c_3$ and let $c_3[k_1, k_2]$ represent the state where the two registers, reading from from left to right, have values $k_1$ and $k_2$. Then, the operational semantics allows us to derive the following computation

$$c_3[0,0] \xrightarrow[1]{1} c_3[1,2] \xrightarrow[2]{0} c_3[2,3] \xrightarrow[3]{0} c_3[3,4] \xrightarrow[4]{0} \cdots$$

that yields the trace $(1000\ldots, 1234\ldots)$.

***Circuits Diagrams.*** In the first two diagrams of Example 1 we used dotted lines to ease the passage from each diagram to the corresponding syntactic term. Indeed, it is clear that syntax carries more information than the diagrammatic notation (e.g. associativity). From the point of view of operational behaviour, however, this extra information is irrelevant and is conveniently discarded by the graphical notation: we will never again blemish our diagrams with dotted lines.

**Remark 1.** Checking that this "forgetting" is sound amounts to verifying that for any circuits $c_1, c_2, c_3, c_4$, the following circuits (when sortable) yield isomorphic transition systems:

- $(c_1 \,;\, c_2) \,;\, c_3$ and $c_1 \,;\, (c_2 \,;\, c_3)$,
- ; $c_1$, $c_1$ and $c_1$ ; ,
- $(c_1 \oplus c_2) \oplus c_3$ and $c_1 \oplus (c_2 \oplus c_3)$,
- $\oplus\, c_1$, $c_1$ and $c_1 \oplus$ ,
- $(c_1 \,;\, c_3) \oplus (c_2 \,;\, c_4)$ and $(c_1 \oplus c_2) \,;\, (c_3 \oplus c_4)$.

Of course, the reader will notice a close connection with the axioms of monoidal categories — we make explicit use of this fact below. In fact we will use *symmetric* monoidal categories (SMCs) of a specific kind, namely PROPs [19, 22]: a PROP (product and permutation category) is a strict SMC with objects the natural numbers, where $\oplus$ on objects is by addition. Morphisms between PROPs are strict symmetric monoidal functors that act as identity on objects: PROPs and their morphisms form the category $\mathbf{PROP}$.

**Definition 1.** The PROP Circ of *circuit diagrams* is defined as:

- arrows $n \to m$ are circuit terms of sort $(n, m)$ quotiented by the axioms of symmetric monoidal categories (see *e.g.* [27]). Composition ; and monoidal product $\oplus$ of circuits are given by the syntax operations in (6).
- The identities are $id_0 :=$ and $id_{n+1} := id_n \oplus$ . The symmetries $\sigma_{n,m}\colon n+m \to m+n$ are defined in the obvious way starting from $\sigma_{1,1} :=$ . For instance, $\sigma_{2,3}$ is (up-to the axioms of SMCs) the circuit below.

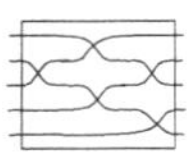

Observe that all the axioms of SMCs are sound (à la Remark 1) with respect to the operational semantics given in Figure 2: for two state terms $c$ and $d$ representing the same state diagram, the corresponding transition systems are isomorphic. This means that there is not any problem in reasoning up to the axioms of SMCs. For this reason, in the rest of the paper we shall refer to circuits diagrams and state diagrams just as *circuits* and *states*, purposefully blurring the line between diagrams and traditional syntax.

We identify two sub-PROPs of Circ: $\overrightarrow{\mathsf{Circ}}$ has as arrows only those circuits in Circ that are built from the components of (4) and (6) and $\overleftarrow{\mathsf{Circ}}$ only those circuits built from the components of (5) and (6). The notation emphasises that for circuits in $\overrightarrow{\mathsf{Circ}}$, signal flow is from left to right, and in $\overleftarrow{\mathsf{Circ}}$ from right to left. Formally, observe that $\overleftarrow{\mathsf{Circ}}$ is the opposite category of $\overrightarrow{\mathsf{Circ}}$: any circuit of $\overleftarrow{\mathsf{Circ}}$ can be seen as one of $\overrightarrow{\mathsf{Circ}}$ reflected about the $y$-axis. We also remark that Circ is the coproduct in $\mathbf{PROP}$ of $\overrightarrow{\mathsf{Circ}}$ and $\overleftarrow{\mathsf{Circ}}$.

Beyond $\overrightarrow{\mathsf{Circ}}$ and $\overleftarrow{\mathsf{Circ}}$, we can identify another class of circuits of Circ which adhere to the classical notion of *signal flow graph* (see *e.g.* [23]). In these circuits, the signal flows from left to right, like in $\overrightarrow{\mathsf{Circ}}$, but with the possibility of having *feedback loops*, provided that these pass through at least one delay. Formally, this amounts to defining, for each $n$ and $m$, an assignment $\mathsf{Tr}(\cdot)\colon \mathsf{Circ}[n+1, m+1] \to \mathsf{Circ}[n,m]$ mapping a circuit $c\colon n+1 \to m+1$ into the $n$-to-$m$ circuit below:

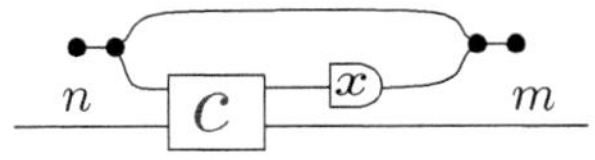


In the picture above and in the sequel, we use the shorthand notation for a circuit of the form $id_z$. The intuition is that $\mathsf{Tr}(\cdot)$ equips the circuit $c$ with a feedback loop carrying the signal from its topmost right to its topmost left port.

Signal flow graphs form a PROP SF, which is the sub-PROP of Circ inductively defined as follows:

- if $c \in \overrightarrow{\mathsf{Circ}}[n,m]$, then $c \in \mathsf{SF}[n,m]$
- if $c \in \mathsf{SF}[n+1, m+1]$, then $\mathsf{Tr}(c) \in \mathsf{SF}[n,m]$
- if $c_1 \in \mathsf{SF}[n,z]$ and $c_2 \in \mathsf{SF}[z,m]$, then $c_1 ; c_2 \in \mathsf{SF}[n,m]$
- if $c_1 \in \mathsf{SF}[n,m]$ and $c_2 \in \mathsf{SF}[r,z]$, then $c_1 \oplus c_2 \in \mathsf{SF}[n+r, m+z]$.

For instance, the second and third circuit of Example 1 are in SF, whereas the first one is in $\overleftarrow{\mathsf{Circ}}$.

**Remark 2.** The rules of Figure 2 describe the step-by-step evolution of state machines without relying on a fixed flow orientation. This operational semantics is not meant to be executable for all circuits: the rule for sequential composition implicitly quantifies existentially on the middle value $v$, resulting in potentially unbounded non-determinism. However, for circuits where flow directionality can be assigned, like the class SF above, existential quantification becomes deterministic subject to a choice of inputs to the circuit at each step of evaluation. We will see in Section 6 that any circuit can be transformed into this form, where the valid transformations are those allowed by the equational theory, presented below.

## 3. Denotational Semantics

Here we define the denotational domain of interpretation for circuits; all the results in this section are proven in or immediately follow from [5, 7]. We begin by recalling some background.

A formal Laurent series (fls) is a function $\sigma\colon \mathbb{Z} \to \mathsf{k}$ for which there exists $i \in \mathbb{Z}$ such that $\sigma(j) = 0$ for all $j < i$. The *degree* of $\sigma$ is the smallest $d \in \mathbb{Z}$ such that $\sigma(d) \neq 0$. We write $\sigma$ as $\ldots, \sigma(-1), \underline{\sigma(0)}, \sigma(1), \ldots$ with position 0 underlined, or as formal sum $\sum_{i=d}^{\infty} \sigma(i)x^i$. With the latter notation, we define the sum and product of $\sigma = \sum_{i=d}^{\infty} \sigma(i)x^i$ and $\tau = \sum_{i=e}^{\infty} \tau(i)x^i$ as

$$\sigma + \tau \;=\; \sum_{i=min(d,e)}^{\infty} \big(\sigma(i) + \tau(i)\big)x^i \tag{7}$$

$$\sigma \cdot \tau \;=\; \sum_{i=d+e}^{\infty} \Big(\sum_{k+j=i} \sigma(j)\cdot\tau(k)\Big)x^i \tag{8}$$

The units for $+$ and $\cdot$ are $\ldots 0, \underline{0}, 0 \ldots$ and $\ldots 0, \underline{1}, 0 \ldots$. Fls form a field $\mathsf{k}((x))$, where the inverse $\sigma^{-1}$ of fls $\sigma$ with degree $d$ is:

$$\sigma^{-1}(i) = \begin{cases} 0 & \text{if } i < -d \\ \sigma(d)^{-1} & \text{if } i = -d \\ \frac{\sum_{i=1}^{n}\left(\sigma(d+i)\cdot\sigma^{-1}(-d+n-i)\right)}{-\sigma(d)} & \text{if } i = -d+n \text{ for } n>0 \end{cases} \tag{9}$$

A *formal power series* (fps) is a fls with degree $d \geq 0$. By (7) and 8 fps are closed under $+$ and $\cdot$, but not under inverse: it is immediate from (9) that $\sigma^{-1}$ is a fps iff $\sigma$ has degree $d = 0$. Therefore fps form a ring which we denote by $\mathsf{k}[[x]]$.

Other algebras of interest are the ring $\mathsf{k}[x]$ of *polynomials* and its field of *fractions* $\mathsf{k}(x)$. A polynomial $k_0 + k_1x + \cdots + k_nx^n$ can also be regarded as the fps $\sum_{i=0}^{\infty} k_ix^i$ with $k_i = 0$ for all $i > n$. Instead, in order to express fractions we need the full generality of fls: there is a unique field morphism mapping $k \in \mathsf{k}(x)$ into the fls $\ldots 0, \underline{k}, 0 \ldots$ and the indeterminate $x$ into $\ldots 0, \underline{0}, 1, 0 \ldots$. This morphism will map, in particular, the fraction $\frac{1}{x}$ into the fls $\ldots 0, 1, \underline{0}, 0, 0 \ldots$.

In Section 4.1, we will use polynomials to encode finite sequences, and fps for streams. In this perspective, fls can be thought of as sequences with an infinite future, but a "finite past". Note that, differently from polynomials, fractions can express infinite sequences. For instance, $\frac{1}{(1-x)^2}$ denotes (along the field morphism introduced above) the fls $\ldots, 0, 0, \underline{1}, 2, 3, \ldots$

**Definition 2.** Let $\mathsf{Rel}_{\mathsf{k}((x))}$ be the following PROP:

- arrows $n \to m$ are subsets of $\mathsf{k}((x))^n \times \mathsf{k}((x))^m$.
- composition is relational: given $G = \{(u, v) \mid u \in \mathsf{k}((x))^n, v \in \mathsf{k}((x))^z\}$ and $H = \{(v, w) \mid v \in \mathsf{k}((x))^z, w \in \mathsf{k}((x))^m\}$, their composition is $\{(u, w) \mid \exists v.(u, v) \in G \wedge (v, w) \in H\}$.
- $G \oplus H = \{\left(\begin{pmatrix} u \\ u' \end{pmatrix}, \begin{pmatrix} v \\ v' \end{pmatrix}\right) \mid (u, v) \in G, (u', v') \in H\}$.
- The symmetries $n \to n$ are induced by bijections of finite sets: $\rho : n \to n$ is associated with the subset $\{(v, w) \mid v, w \in \mathsf{k}((x))^n,\ v_i = w_{\rho i}\}$.

$\mathsf{Rel}_{\mathsf{k}((x))}$ serves as the domain for the denotational semantics.

**Definition 3.** The PROP morphism $[\![\cdot]\!] : \mathsf{Circ} \to \mathsf{Rel}_{\mathsf{k}((x))}$ is inductively defined on circuits as follows. For the components in (4)

$$\longmapsto \{(\sigma, \begin{pmatrix} \sigma \\ \sigma \end{pmatrix}) \mid \sigma \in \mathsf{k}((x))\}$$

$$\longmapsto \{(\sigma, (\,)) \mid \sigma \in \mathsf{k}((x))\}$$

$$\longmapsto \{(\begin{pmatrix} \sigma \\ \tau \end{pmatrix}, \sigma + \tau) \mid \sigma, \tau \in \mathsf{k}((x))\}$$

$$\longmapsto \{((\,), 0)\}$$

$$\longmapsto \{(\sigma, \sigma \cdot k) \mid \sigma \in \mathsf{k}((x))\}$$

$$\longmapsto \{(\sigma, \sigma \cdot x) \mid \sigma \in \mathsf{k}((x))\}$$

where $0$, $k$ and $x$ denote fls. The semantics of components in (5) is symmetric, e.g. is mapped to $\{((\,), \sigma) \mid \sigma \in \mathsf{k}((x))\}$. For (6)

$$\longmapsto \{((\,), (\,))\}$$

$$\longmapsto \{(\sigma, \sigma) \mid \sigma \in \mathsf{k}((x))\}$$

$$\longmapsto \{(\begin{pmatrix} \sigma \\ \tau \end{pmatrix}, \begin{pmatrix} \tau \\ \sigma \end{pmatrix}) \mid \sigma, \tau \in \mathsf{k}((x))\}$$

$$c_1 \oplus c_2 \longmapsto [\![c_1]\!] \oplus [\![c_2]\!] \qquad c_1 \,;\, c_2 \longmapsto [\![c_1]\!] \,;\, [\![c_2]\!]$$

**Remark 3.** It is easy to verify that for any circuit $c \in \mathsf{Circ}[n, m]$, $[\![c]\!]$ forms a subspace of $\mathsf{k}((x))^n \times \mathsf{k}((x))^m$, considered as a vector space over $\mathsf{k}((x))$. See [5] for more details.

**Example 2.** Consider the circuit . We have that

$$\begin{aligned} [\![\ \ ]\!] &= [\![\ \ ]\!] \,;\, [\![\ \ ]\!] \\ &= \{(\sigma, \sigma \cdot x) \mid \sigma \in \mathsf{k}((x))\} \,;\, \{(\sigma \cdot x, \sigma) \mid \sigma \in \mathsf{k}((x))\} \\ &= \{(\sigma, \sigma) \mid \sigma \in \mathsf{k}((x))\} \end{aligned}$$

which is equal to $[\![\ \ ]\!]$. Note that any fls $\ldots \sigma(-1), \underline{\sigma(0)}, \sigma(1) \ldots$ on the left of is related to $\ldots \underline{\sigma(-1)}, \sigma(0), \sigma(1) \ldots$ on its right and this is in turn related to $\ldots \sigma(-1), \underline{\sigma(0)}, \sigma(1) \ldots$ on the right of . The circuit is thus the inverse of : while delays $\sigma$, accelerates it.

Similarly, consider a circuit . Its semantics is the composite of $[\![\ \ ]\!]$ (pairing $\sigma$ with $\sigma \cdot k$) and $[\![\ \ ]\!]$ (pairing $k \cdot \sigma$ with $\sigma$): if $k \neq 0$, we can see it as first multiplying and then dividing $\sigma$ by $k$. Thus for $k \neq 0$ and have the same denotation.

### 3.1 Equational Theory

The equivalence induced by the denotational semantics is axiomatized in Figures 3, 4 and 5. There, $p$, $p_1$, $p_2$ range over $\mathsf{k}[x]$ and $q$ over $\mathsf{k}[x] \setminus \{0\}$. Given a polynomial $p = k_0 + k_1x + k_2x^2 + \cdots + k_nx^n$, and are notation for the circuit on the left and on the right respectively:

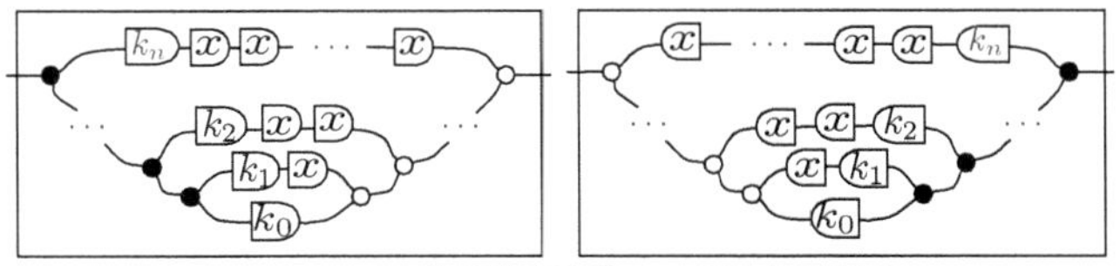

Observe that components , and , become specific cases of , respectively. Instead the notation indicates both the circuits and : indeed, they are provably equal from the other axioms (for instance, using (I5) and (A5)).

Let $\stackrel{\mathbb{IH}}{=}$ be the smallest congruence on circuits generated by these axioms and $\mathbb{IH}$ the PROP obtained by quotienting $\mathsf{Circ}$ by $\stackrel{\mathbb{IH}}{=}$.

**Theorem 1.** Let $c$, $d$ be circuits in $\mathsf{Circ}$. Then $[\![c]\!] = [\![d]\!]$ iff $c \stackrel{\mathbb{IH}}{=} d$.

The equational theory of $\mathbb{IH}$ equips circuits with a very rich algebraic structure, that can be presented in a modular way:

- Figure 3 describe the interaction of components in (4). (A1)-(A3) and (A6)-(A8) impose a commutative monoid and a cocommutative comonoid structure on the components , and , respectively. Together they form a bialgebra, by laws (A9)-(A12). Instead, (A4), (A5), (A17), (A18) describe the behavior of derived components of shape , saying in particular that they are compatible with the bialgebra structure. Finally, note that the bialgebra is in fact an Hopf algebra, with antipode the circuit .

  It is convenient to fix this "module" of $\mathbb{IH}$ as a sub-PROP, which we call $\mathbb{HA}$ because of the Hopf algebra structure. It can be equivalently defined as the PROP having as arrows the circuits of $\overrightarrow{\mathsf{Circ}}$ quotiented by the equations in Figure 3.
- The algebraic structure described above is dualised for components in (5), in the sense that the axioms (An)* in Figure 4 are exactly those (An) of Figure 3 reflected about the y-axis. This means that , satisfy the equations of commutative comonoids, , the ones of commutative monoids, and together they form an Hopf Algebra with antipode . The corresponding sub-PROP is $\mathbb{HA}^{op}$, that is, the opposite category of $\mathbb{HA}$: for a circuit $c \in \mathbb{HA}[n, m]$, we draw the corresponding one in $\mathbb{HA}^{op}[m, n]$ as $c$ reflected about the y-axis. Equivalently, $\mathbb{HA}^{op}$ can be defined as the PROP having as arrows the circuits of $\overleftarrow{\mathsf{Circ}}$ quotiented by the equations in Figure 4.

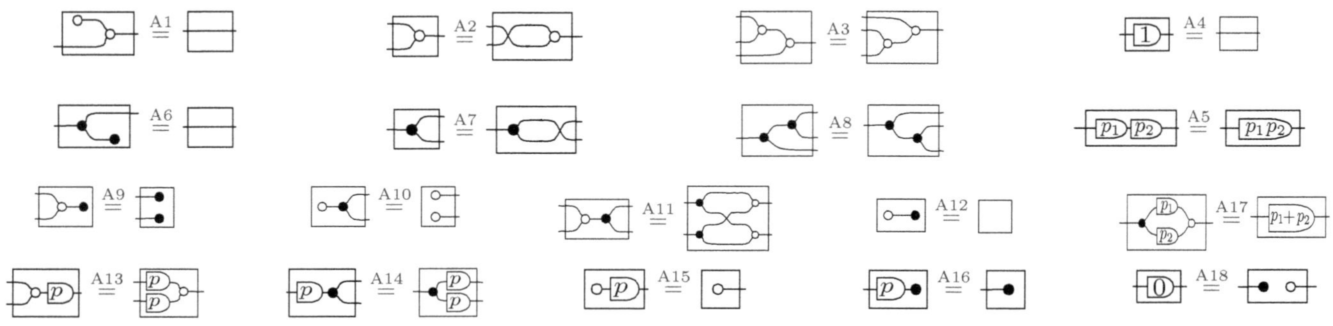


**Figure 3.** Interaction of components in (4)

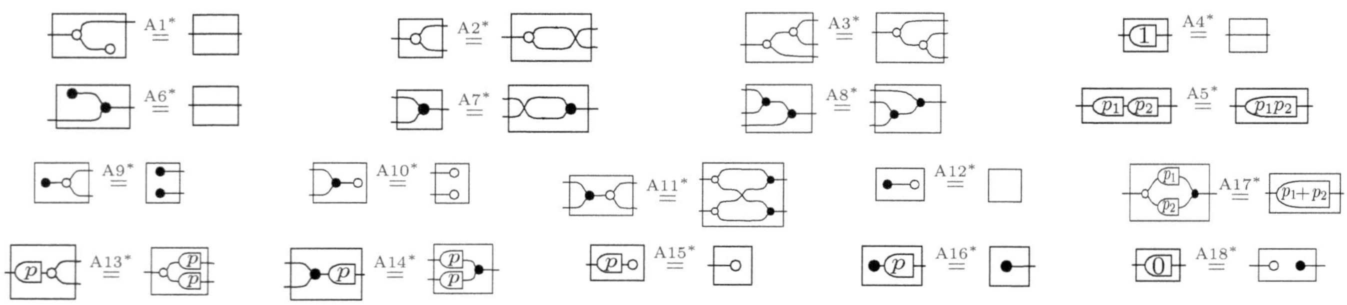


**Figure 4.** Interaction of components in (5)

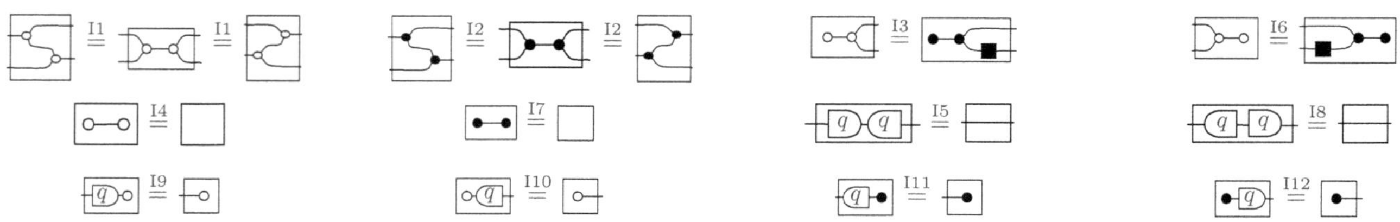


**Figure 5.** Interaction of components in (4) with the ones in (5)

- Finally, equations in Figure 5 describe the interaction of components in (4) with components in (5). This motivates the name $\mathbb{IH}$ for the theory of $\mathbb{I}$nteracting $\mathbb{H}$opf algebras. The axioms of interaction describe a separable Frobenius algebra [10] for both the white and the black family of components.

The subtheories $\mathbb{HA}$ and $\mathbb{HA}^{op}$ actually have an interesting life of their own: they characterise circuits with simple functional behaviors, in the following sense. Let $\mathsf{Mat}\,\mathsf{k}[x]$ be the PROP where arrows $n$ to $m$ are $m \times n$-matrices over $\mathsf{k}[x]$, composition ; is matrix multiplication, $A \oplus B$ is the matrix $\begin{pmatrix} A & 0 \\ 0 & B \end{pmatrix}$ and the symmetries are the rearrangements of the rows of the identity matrix. Then $\mathbb{HA}$ is a presentation of $\mathsf{Mat}\,\mathsf{k}[x]$, that is, they are isomorphic as PROPs [5, 7]. Dually, $\mathbb{HA}^{op}$ is isomorphic to $\mathsf{Mat}\,\mathsf{k}[x]^{op}$.

The circuits of $\mathbb{HA}$ and $\mathbb{HA}^{op}$ are not the only ones exhibiting a functional behavior. As shown in [5], by quotienting the PROP of signal flow graphs $\mathsf{SF}$ by the axioms of $\mathbb{IH}$, one obtains a PROP, hereafter referred to as $\mathbb{SF}$, that presents the PROP $\mathsf{Mat}\,\mathsf{k}\langle x\rangle$ of matrices over the *rationals*, i.e, fractions of polynomials $\frac{k_0+k_1x+k_2x^2\cdots+k_nx^n}{l_0+l_1x+l_2x^2\cdots+l_nx^n}$ where $l_0 \neq 0$. The definition of $\mathsf{Mat}\,\mathsf{k}\langle x\rangle$ is formally the same as the one of $\mathsf{Mat}\,\mathsf{k}[x]$, with the ring $\mathsf{k}\langle x\rangle$ of rationals replacing $\mathsf{k}[x]$.

The equational theory of $\mathbb{IH}$ allows us to factorise circuits of $\mathsf{Circ}$ in terms of those of $\overrightarrow{\mathsf{Circ}}$ and $\overleftarrow{\mathsf{Circ}}$. We say that $c \in \mathsf{Circ}[n,m]$ is in *cospan form* if it is of shape $c_1 \,;c_2$, with $c_1 \in \overrightarrow{\mathsf{Circ}}[n,z]$ and $c_2 \in \overleftarrow{\mathsf{Circ}}[z,m]$ for some $z$. Dually, $d \in \mathsf{Circ}[n,m]$ is in *span form* if it is of shape $d_1 \,; d_2$, with $d_1 \in \overleftarrow{\mathsf{Circ}}[n,r]$ and $d_2 \in \overrightarrow{\mathsf{Circ}}[r,m]$ for some $r$.

**Proposition 1.** For all circuits $c$ of $\mathsf{Circ}$, there exist circuits $c'$ in span form and $c''$ in cospan form such that $c \stackrel{\mathbb{IH}}{=} c' \stackrel{\mathbb{IH}}{=} c''$.

## 4. Full abstraction

In this section we tackle the question of relating the operational and the denotational semantics of the Signal Flow Calculus, introduced in Section 2 and 3 respectively.

To this aim, an elementary observation is that the denotational semantics seems to be too coarse, since it abstracts away from the finite behaviours that might arise during the executions of the circuits. For example, consider 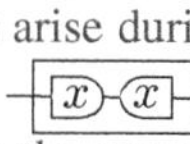 and 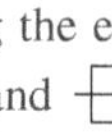: as we have shown in Example 2, they have the same denotational semantics, namely the set of all pairs $(\sigma, \sigma)$ of fls. However, some computations of the former circuit can reach a *deadlock*. For instance, we can make a transition from the initial state with labels $k \neq l$, but there are no further possible transitions from the resulting state:

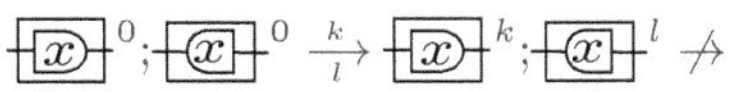

Such failures are not taken into account by the denotational semantics: intuitively, this only considers the successful computations, which are the ones yielding infinite traces. If we restrict to these situations, then 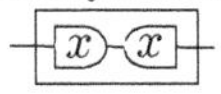 behaves exactly as the identity circuit 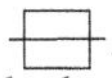. Here are more examples of circuits that may reach a deadlocked state.

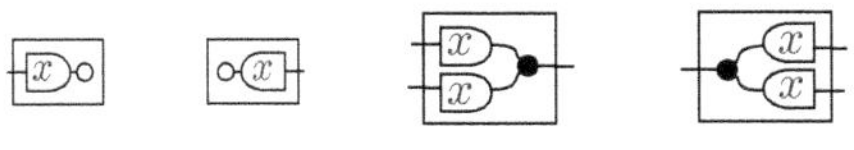

(10)

Our diagnosis is that problematic circuits are those in which internal components (in particular, the delays) have a conflicting design. Note that all the above examples are in *cospan form*, that is, they are of shape $c = c_1 \,;\, c_2$ with $c_1$ a circuit of $\overrightarrow{\mathsf{Circ}}$ and $c_2$ one of $\overleftarrow{\mathsf{Circ}}$. Intuitively, the signal in $c$ is flowing from the left/right boundaries towards the middle, that is, the boundary shared by circuits $c_1$ and $c_2$.

According to our analysis, we can avoid deadlocks by considering instead circuits $d$ in *span form*, i.e. $d = d_1 \,;\, d_2$ for $d_1$ in $\overleftarrow{\mathsf{Circ}}$ and $d_2$ in $\overrightarrow{\mathsf{Circ}}$. Circuits of this shape cannot deadlock since, intuitively, the signal is flowing from the middle boundary towards the left (transmitted by $d_1$) and the right (transmitted by $d_2$).

In order to formalize our observations, first we say that a circuit is *deadlock free* when none of its computations can reach a deadlock - namely, a state from which no transition is derivable. Then we have the following result.

**Theorem 2.** Circuits of Circ in span form are deadlock free.

Together with Proposition 1, this theorem asserts that, for each circuit of Circ, there exists an equivalent one in $\mathbb{IH}$ that is deadlock free. This could give us some hope of reconciling the operational and the denotational semantics but, unfortunately, also for some circuits in span form they do not agree: for instance, 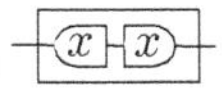 and 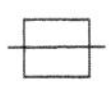 have the same denotational semantics, but all the computation of the former are forced to start with $\xrightarrow[0]{0}$. Indeed

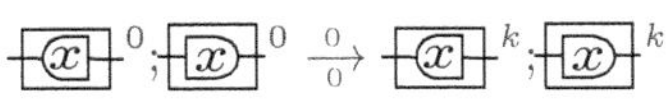 for any $k$.

Note that after the first transition 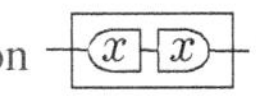 behaves exactly as 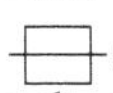: in some sense, the former circuit exhibits a proper behaviour only after an initialisation step. To make this formal, we say that a circuit $c$ is *initialisation free* if, whenever $s_0 \xrightarrow[0\ldots0]{0\ldots0} s_1$, then $s_1 = s_0$, where $s_0$ is the initial state of $c$. Other basic circuits that suffer from initialisation are displayed below.

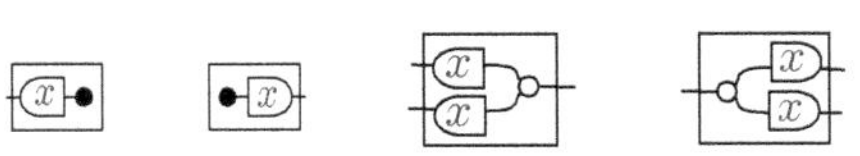

(11)

All problematic circuits above are in span form, meaning that they can be decomposed into $c_1 \,;\, c_2$, with $c_1$ in $\overleftarrow{\mathsf{Circ}}$ and $c_2$ in $\overrightarrow{\mathsf{Circ}}$. The intuition is that any delay in $c_1$ and $c_2$ sends the signal from the common middle boundary towards the outer boundaries, thus requiring a step in which the default value 0 of each delay is emitted before behaving properly. According to this analysis, such a situation is avoided when we can see all the delays as pointing towards the middle of the circuit. This leads to the following statement.

**Theorem 3.** Circuits of Circ in cospan form are initialisation free.

Theorems 2 and 3 suggest a duality between deadlock and initialisation, expressible in terms of span and cospan decompositions of circuits of Circ. In fact, this is reflected also by the displayed problematic circuits: the ones in (10) are dual to the ones in (11) in a precise sense, namely by changing the black/white colouring and the direction of delays[1]. Moreover, according to our analysis circuits with deadlocks have *more* behaviours (traces) than those prescribed by the denotational semantics, while circuits with initialisation have *fewer* behaviours. We would then expect circuits which are both deadlock and initialisation free to yield exactly the right amount of behavior: this will be the content of the next section, leading to the full abstraction result (Corollary 2).

### 4.1 Reconciling Observation and Denotation

Given a circuit $c$ of Circ, we define its *observable behavior* $\langle c \rangle$ as the pair $(ft(c), it(c))$ of its finite and infinite traces. Like the denotational semantics $[\![\cdot]\!]$, also the observable behaviour $\langle \cdot \rangle$ can be expressed in a compositional way, as a PROP morphism from Circ to a certain target PROP that we are going to define below. In order to do that, we first observe that finite and infinite traces can be equivalently described in terms of polynomials and of fps respectively. Indeed, in a trace $(\overrightarrow{\alpha}, \overrightarrow{\beta})$ of length $z$, each sequence $\alpha_j = k_0 k_1 \ldots k_z$ and $\beta_j = l_0 l_1 \ldots l_z$ can be encoded as polynomials $k_0 x + k_1 x + \cdots + k_z x^z$ and $l_0 x + l_1 x + \cdots + l_z x^z$ respectively. Similarly, in an infinite trace $(\overrightarrow{\alpha}, \overrightarrow{\beta})$, each stream $\alpha_j = k_0 k_1 \ldots$ and $\beta_j = l_0 l_1 \ldots$ defines fps $\Sigma_{i=0}^{\infty} k_i x^i$ and $\Sigma_{i=0}^{\infty} j_i x^i$ respectively. We can then see $ft(c)$ as a relation between vectors of polynomials and $it(c)$ as a relation between vectors of fps.

On the base of this observation, we take $\mathsf{Rel}_{\mathsf{k}[x]} \times \mathsf{Rel}_{\mathsf{k}[[x]]}$ as target of $\langle \cdot \rangle$. Here $\mathsf{Rel}_{\mathsf{k}[x]}$ and $\mathsf{Rel}_{\mathsf{k}[[x]]}$ are PROPs defined as $\mathsf{Rel}_{\mathsf{k}((x))}$ (Definition 2), but with $\mathsf{k}[x]$ and $\mathsf{k}[[x]]$ respectively in place of $\mathsf{k}((x))$. Arrows of $\mathsf{Rel}_{\mathsf{k}[x]} \times \mathsf{Rel}_{\mathsf{k}[[x]]}$ from $n$ to $m$ are pairs $(f, g)$ with $f \in \mathsf{Rel}_{\mathsf{k}[x]}[n, m]$ and $g \in \mathsf{Rel}_{\mathsf{k}[[x]]}[n, m]$. The following statement guarantees that $\langle \cdot \rangle$ is compositional:

**Proposition 2.** $\langle \cdot \rangle \colon \mathsf{Circ} \to \mathsf{Rel}_{\mathsf{k}[x]} \times \mathsf{Rel}_{\mathsf{k}[[x]]}$ is a morphism of PROPs.

We have now all the ingredients to build a bridge between the domain of observations $\mathsf{Rel}_{\mathsf{k}[x]} \times \mathsf{Rel}_{\mathsf{k}[[x]]}$ and the denotational domain $\mathsf{Rel}_{\mathsf{k}((x))}$.

For this purpose, we first illustrate how to relate infinite traces (i.e., pairs of vectors of fps) and vectors of fls. We say that a trace $\left(\overrightarrow{\alpha}, \overrightarrow{\beta}\right) \in \mathsf{k}[[x]]^n \times \mathsf{k}[[x]]^m$ *generates* $\left(\overrightarrow{\sigma}, \overrightarrow{\tau}\right) \in \mathsf{k}((x))^n \times \mathsf{k}((x))^m$ if there exist an *instant* $z \in \mathbb{Z}$ such that

(i) $\alpha_j(i) = \sigma_j(i + z)$ and $\beta_h(i) = \tau_h(i + z)$ for all $i \in \mathbb{N}$ and $k$, $j$ with $1 \leq j \leq n$, $1 \leq h \leq m$;

(ii) $z$ is smaller or equal than any degree of $\sigma_1 \ldots \sigma_n, \tau_1 \ldots \tau_m$.

To see the intuition behind this notion, recall from Section 3 that, whereas fps give a way of encoding streams, fls encode streams "with a (finite) past". If we see it as a translation from $(\overrightarrow{\alpha}, \overrightarrow{\beta})$ to $(\overrightarrow{\sigma}, \overrightarrow{\tau})$, our correspondence takes the fps in $(\overrightarrow{\alpha}, \overrightarrow{\beta})$ and fix for them all a common "present" moment. For example, the trace $(k_0 k_1 k_2 \ldots, l_0 l_1 l_2 \ldots) \in \mathsf{k}[[x]] \times \mathsf{k}[[x]]$ generates infinitely many pairs of fls, among which we have:

$$(\ldots 0\underline{0}k_1 k_2 k_3 \ldots, \ldots 0\underline{0}l_1 l_2 l_3 \ldots)$$
$$(\ldots 00\underline{k_1} k_2 k_3 \ldots, \ldots 00\underline{l_1} l_2 l_3 \ldots)$$
$$(\ldots 00\underline{k_1 k_2} k_3 \ldots, \ldots 00\underline{l_1 l_2} l_3 \ldots)$$

[1] See [7, §7.2] for a more detailed account of this transformation in a denotational context.

with choice of present moment $(0, 0)$, $(k_1, l_1)$ and $(k_2, l_2)$ respectively. The instant $z \in \mathbb{Z}$ will be 1 for the first, 0 for the second and $-1$ for the third pair above.

Conversely, we can start from all the fls in $(\overrightarrow{\sigma}, \overrightarrow{\tau})$ and forget about their present moment to obtain streams. The requirement that the instant $z$ is chosen not bigger than any degree implies that only 0s are removed in the process, that is, there is no information loss. For instance, $(\dots 00k_1\underline{k_2}k_3 \dots, \dots 00\underline{l_1}l_2l_3 \dots) \in \mathsf{k}((x)) \times \mathsf{k}((x))$ is generated by infinitely many traces, including:

$$(k_1k_2k_3 \dots, 0l_1l_2l_3 \dots)$$
$$(0k_1k_2k_3 \dots, 00l_1l_2l_3 \dots)$$
$$(00k_1k_2k_3 \dots, 000l_1l_2l_3 \dots).$$

The instant $z$ is chosen to be $-1$ for the first, $-2$ for the second and $-3$ for the third pair above.

To complete the picture, we relate finite and infinite traces. A trace $(\overrightarrow{\alpha}, \overrightarrow{\beta}) \in \mathsf{k}[x]^n \times \mathsf{k}[x]^m$ of length $z$ is a *prefix* of an infinite trace $(\overrightarrow{\gamma}, \overrightarrow{\delta}) \in \mathsf{k}[[x]]^n \times \mathsf{k}[[x]]^m$ iff $\alpha_j(i) = \gamma_j(i)$ and $\beta_h(i) = \delta_h(i)$ for all $0 \le i \le z$, $1 \le j \le n$ and $1 \le h \le m$.

We are now ready to define our correspondence between arrows of $\mathsf{Rel}_{\mathsf{k}[x]} \times \mathsf{Rel}_{\mathsf{k}[[x]]}$ and arrows of $\mathsf{Rel}_{\mathsf{k}((x))}$.

**Definition 4.** Let $(f, g)$ be an arrow of $\mathsf{Rel}_{\mathsf{k}[x]} \times \mathsf{Rel}_{\mathsf{k}[[x]]}$. We define $\mathcal{F}(f, g)$ as the following arrow in $\mathsf{Rel}_{\mathsf{k}((x))}[n, m]$:

$$\left\{\left(\overrightarrow{\sigma}, \overrightarrow{\tau}\right) \;\middle|\; \begin{array}{l}\text{there exist a trace } \left(\overrightarrow{\alpha}, \overrightarrow{\beta}\right) \in g \\ \text{generating } \left(\overrightarrow{\sigma}, \overrightarrow{\tau}\right)\end{array}\right\}$$

In the converse direction, given an arrow $S \in \mathsf{Rel}_{\mathsf{k}((x))}[n, m]$, we define $\mathcal{U}(S)$ as the pair $(f, g) \in \mathsf{Rel}_{\mathsf{k}[x]} \times \mathsf{Rel}_{\mathsf{k}[[x]]}[n, m]$ where $g \in \mathsf{Rel}_{\mathsf{k}[[x]]}[n, m]$ is given as

$$\left\{\left(\overrightarrow{\alpha}, \overrightarrow{\beta}\right) \;\middle|\; \begin{array}{l}\text{there exist a pair } \left(\overrightarrow{\sigma}, \overrightarrow{\tau}\right) \in S \\ \text{generated by } \left(\overrightarrow{\alpha}, \overrightarrow{\beta}\right)\end{array}\right\}$$

and $f \in \mathsf{Rel}_{\mathsf{k}[x]}[n, m]$ is the set of all prefixes of the traces in $g$.

Intuitively, the action of $\mathcal{F}$ on $(f, g)$ is to forget the first component and generate all the vectors of fls generated by vectors of fps in $g$. Instead we can describe $\mathcal{U}$ as abstracting away the choice of the present for all fls and represent them as fps. This gives the second element in the target pair $(f, g)$: the first is irrelevant, since it only consists of the prefixes of traces in $g$ (in particular, we do not generate any deadlock trace). To see how $\mathcal{F}$ and $\mathcal{U}$ work more precisely, we shall consider the following example.

**Example 3.** Recall that, for $c =$ 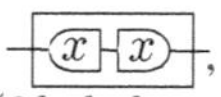, the set $it(c)$ consists of all infinite traces of the form $(0k_0k_1k_2 \dots, 0k_0k_1k_2 \dots)$, that is, $c$ behaves as the identity after one initialisation step. Since this circuit is deadlock free, the set $ft(c)$ instead contains all and only those finite traces which are prefixes of some infinite trace in $it(c)$.

One can check that $\mathcal{F}\langle c \rangle$ is the identity relation $\{(\sigma, \sigma) \mid \sigma \in \mathsf{k}((x))\}$ (which is actually equal to $[\![c]\!]$). For instance, the pair of fls

$$(\dots 00\underline{k_0}k_1k_2k_3 \dots, \dots 00\underline{k_0}k_1k_2k_3 \dots) \qquad (12)$$

is generated by $(0k_0k_1k_2 \dots, 0k_0k_1k_2 \dots)$. If we then apply $\mathcal{U}$ to $\mathcal{F}\langle c \rangle$, we obtain a pair $(f, g) \in \mathsf{Rel}_{\mathsf{k}[x]} \times \mathsf{Rel}_{\mathsf{k}[[x]]}[1, 1]$ where $f$ coincides with the original $ft(c)$, while $g$ is strictly larger than $it(c)$. Indeed $(k_0k_1k_2 \dots, k_0k_1k_2 \dots) \notin it(c)$ but it belongs to $g$ since it generates the pair (12).

We now focus on circuit $d =$ 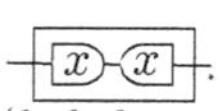. The set $it(d)$ consists of all infinite traces of the form $(k_0k_1k_2 \dots, k_0k_1k_2 \dots)$ and the set $ft(d)$ consists of either prefixes of $it(d)$ or traces leading to deadlocks having the form $(k_0k_1 \dots k_ul, k_0k_1 \dots k_ul')$ with $l \neq l'$. It is easy to check that these traces are lost when applying $\mathcal{UF}$ to $\langle d \rangle$, while no infinite trace is added or removed.

The example above suggests that the composite mapping $\mathcal{FU}$ *enlarges* the set of observable behaviors for circuits with initialisation (e.g. 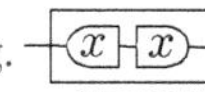) and, dually, *restricts* it for circuits with deadlocks (e.g. 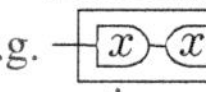). The next statement illustrates the extent of these observations.

**Theorem 4.** Let $c$ be a circuit of Circ. Then the following holds:

(a) $\mathcal{F}\langle c \rangle = [\![c]\!]$.
(b) If $c$ is deadlock free, then $\langle c \rangle \subseteq \mathcal{FU}[\![c]\!]$. [2]
(c) If $c$ is initialisation free, then $\langle c \rangle \supseteq \mathcal{FU}[\![c]\!]$.

Statement (a) above is instrumental in showing full abstraction (Corollary 2), but is also of independent interest. Indeed it allows to immediately derive that

**Corollary 1.** For any two circuits $c, d \in$ Circ, $[\![c]\!] = [\![d]\!]$ if and only if $\mathcal{F}\langle c \rangle = \mathcal{F}\langle d \rangle$.

In some sense, Corollary 1 tells us under which conditions an external observer cannot distinguish circuits that have the same denotation. This is the case whenever $\mathcal{F}\langle c \rangle = \mathcal{F}\langle d \rangle$, that is, the observation of $c$ and $d$ can be only made "up-to $\mathcal{F}$". Intuitively, this amounts to imposing the following two conditions, stemming from the definition of $\mathcal{F}$. First, we prevent the observation of finite behavior — because $\mathcal{F}$ disregards $ft(c)$ and $ft(d)$. This means that we cannot detect deadlock and, for instance, 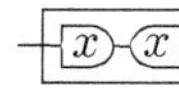 and 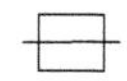 become indistinguishable. Second, we prevent an external agent from choosing *when* to begin the observation. For instance, take $c =$ 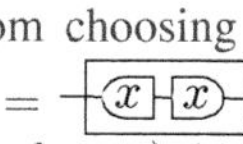. By observing the pair $(\dots 00k_0\underline{k_1}k_2 \dots, \dots 00k_0\underline{k_1}k_2 \dots)$ in $\mathcal{F}\langle c \rangle$, on principle we are not able to judge whether it has been generated by a trace $(k_0k_1k_2 \dots, k_0k_1k_2 \dots)$ or $(0k_0k_1k_2 \dots, 0k_0k_1k_2 \dots)$ in $\langle c \rangle$: the definition of $\mathcal{F}$ allows for both (and infinitely many other) options. Since our view is restricted to $\mathcal{F}\langle c \rangle$, we cannot tell if the observation of the actual stream starts with 0 or $k_0$. Therefore, from that viewpoint 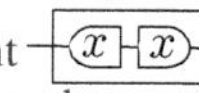 and 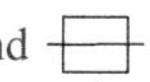 are indistinguishable.

In general, when observations can be made without the restrictions of $\mathcal{F}$, one *can* distinguish amongst circuits that are denotationally equivalent, as explained in Example 3. Statements (b) and (c) in Theorem 4 allow us to derive that observations and denotations do coincide for the class of well-behaved circuits that do not suffer from deadlocks and initialisation steps.

**Corollary 2** (Full Abstraction)**.** For any two circuits $c$ and $d$ of Circ that are deadlock and initialisation free,

$$[\![c]\!] = [\![d]\!] \text{ if and only if } \langle c \rangle = \langle d \rangle.$$

## 5. Realisability

In the previous section, we have seen two different canonical forms for circuits of Circ: the span form, preventing deadlocks, and the cospan form, avoiding initialisation steps. We now tackle the question of transforming, within the equational theory of $\mathbb{IH}$, any circuit $c$ of Circ into one $d$ featuring both properties. This is appealing because, by Corollary 2, $d$ properly *realises* the denoted behaviour $[\![c]\!]$. To this aim, we first observe that our desiderata are fulfilled for the class SF, introduced in Section 2:

**Proposition 3.** Every $c$ in SF is deadlock and initialisation free.

[2] The inclusion is meant to be component-wise, i.e. $it(c) \subseteq g$ and $ft(c) \subseteq f$ where $(ft(c), it(c)) = \langle c \rangle$ and $(f, g) = \mathcal{FU}[\![c]\!]$.

The intuition behind Proposition 3 is that the rules for inductively constructing circuits of SF do not allow for the conflicting design originating the phenomena of initialisation and deadlock. In particular, adding feedbacks to a circuit of SF preserves initialisation and deadlock freedom.

In order to achieve our goal, we will introduce a canonical form for circuits in Circ which is based on SF. Roughly speaking, such form consists of signal flow graphs where "the wires have been jumbled up". We make this intuition precise in the sequel.

First, for each $n, m \in \mathbb{N}$, we take circuits $\eta_n : n \to 1+1+n$ and $\epsilon_m : 1+1+m \to m$ as illustrated below.

$\eta_n :=$ 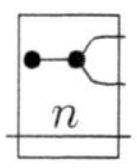 $\epsilon_m :=$ 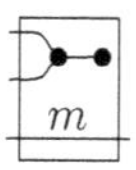

Then, we define the families of operators $\mathsf{L}_{n,m} : \mathsf{Circ}[n+1, m] \to \mathsf{Circ}[n, 1+m]$ and $\mathsf{R}_{n,m} : \mathsf{Circ}[n, 1+m] \to \mathsf{Circ}[1+n, m]$ as follows: for any circuit $c \in \mathsf{Circ}[n+1, m]$,

$$\mathsf{L}_{n,m}(c) = \eta_n \,; (id_1 \oplus c)$$

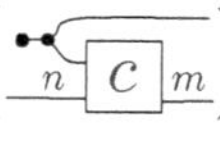

and, for any circuit $d \in \mathsf{Circ}[n, m+1]$

$$\mathsf{R}_{n,m}(d) = (id_1 \oplus d)\,; \epsilon_m.$$

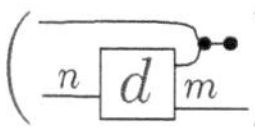

**Remark 4.** When defined on $\mathbb{IH}$, $\mathsf{L}_{n,m}$ and $\mathsf{R}_{n,m}$ enjoy some interesting properties. Let $1 + - : \mathbb{IH} \to \mathbb{IH}$ be the functor acting on objects as $k \mapsto 1 + k$ and on arrows as $f \mapsto id_1 \oplus f$. This functor is self-adjoint: the unit and the counit are the $\eta_n$ and $\epsilon_m$ defined as above. The fact that $\mathbb{IH}$ is a SMC implies naturality of $\eta$ and $\epsilon$. They satisfy the triangle inequalities because of the following "snake" lemma, provable in $\mathbb{IH}$ using (I2), (A5) and (A5)*:

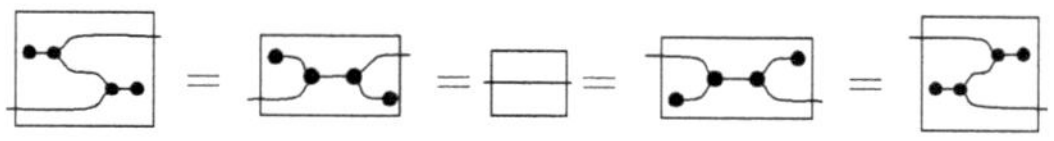 (13)

The canonical isomorphisms between hom-sets, induced by the adjunction, are $\mathsf{L}_{n,m} : \mathbb{IH}[n+1, m] \to \mathbb{IH}[n, 1+m]$ and $\mathsf{R}_{n,m} : \mathbb{IH}[n, 1+m] \to \mathbb{IH}[1+n, m]$ defined as above. We can understand $\mathsf{L}_{n,m}$ intuitively as "rewiring" the connection to the first port on the left to the right of the circuit. The fact that $\mathsf{L}_{n,m}$ and $\mathsf{R}_{n,m}$ are isomorphisms means that no information is lost – all such circuits can be "rewired" back to their original form.

**Definition 5.** Any $c_2 \in \mathsf{Circ}[n_2, m_2]$ is a *rewiring* of $c_1 \in \mathsf{Circ}[n_1, m_1]$ when $c_2$ can be obtained from $c_1$ by a combination of the following operations:

- application of $\mathsf{L}_{n,m}$, for some $n$ and $m$,
- application of $\mathsf{R}_{n,m}$, for some $n$ and $m$,
- post-composition with a permutation,
- pre-composition with a permutation.

Permutations are needed to rewire any port on the boundaries. For instance, they allow to rewire the second port on the right as the third on the left in the circuit $c: 2 \to 2$ below:

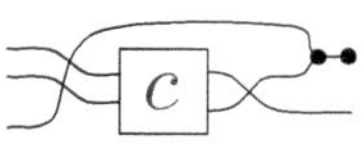

For our purposes, it is of importance to observe that

**Lemma 1.** Rewiring preserves deadlock and initialisation freedom.

The remainder of this section will be devoted to showing that we can put circuits of Circ into the desired shape.

**Theorem 5.** Every circuit in Circ is equal in $\mathbb{IH}$ to the rewiring of some circuit in SF.

By Theorem 5, Proposition 3 and Lemma 1 we achieve the realisability result claimed at the beginning of this section.

**Corollary 3** (Realisability). Every circuit $c$ of Circ is equal in $\mathbb{IH}$ to some circuit $d$ of Circ that is deadlock and initialisation free.

### 5.1 Proof of Theorem 5

In order to prove Theorem 5, we first need some preliminaries on matrices and their circuit representations. Indeed, there is a natural way of representing matrices over the field $\mathsf{k}(x)$ of fractions of polynomials as circuits of Circ. To illustrate it, consider the following example:

$$\begin{pmatrix} p_1/q_1 & p_4/q_4 & p_7/q_7 \\ p_2/q_2 & p_5/q_5 & p_8/q_8 \\ p_3/q_3 & p_6/q_6 & p_9/q_9 \end{pmatrix}$$

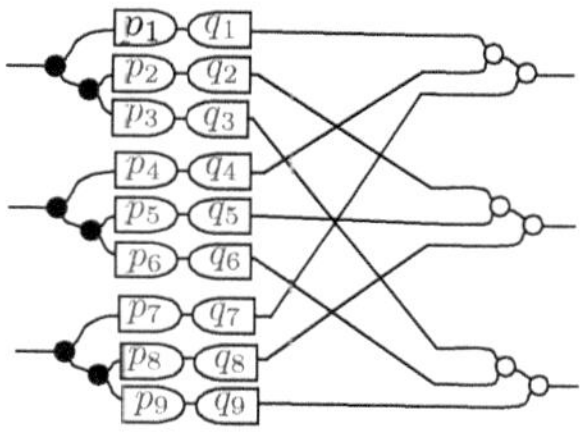

The circuit $c$ on the right encodes the matrix $M$ on the left in the following way: for each boundary of $c$, we assume a top-bottom enumerations of the ports, starting from 1. Then the entry $M_{j,i}$ (column $j$, row $i$) has value $\frac{p}{q} \in \mathsf{k}(x)$ if and only if, reading the circuit from the left to the right, one finds a path connecting the $j^{th}$ port on the left to the $i^{th}$ port on the right passing through a circuit 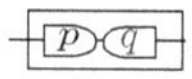. Intuitively, the ports on the left represent columns, the ones on the right rows, and the links between them carry the values in the matrix. One can verify the correspondence between $c$ and $M$ formally: $[\![c]\!]$ is the relation $\{(\vec{\sigma}, M \cdot \vec{\sigma}) \mid \vec{\sigma} \in \mathsf{k}((x))^3\}$.

It will be convenient to work with matrices (and the corresponding circuits) of a particular shape. We say that a matrix over $\mathsf{k}(x)$ is in *rational form* if all its entries are in fact rationals (in $\mathsf{k}\langle x \rangle$) and:

1. for each non-zero row, there is a pivot entry with value 1.
2. in the column of a pivot, the pivot is the only non-zero entry.

An example is displayed below where $r_1, r_2, r_3 \in \mathsf{k}\langle x \rangle$.

$$\begin{pmatrix} r_1 & 0 & 1 & 0 \\ r_2 & 1 & 0 & 0 \\ r_3 & 0 & 0 & 1 \\ 0 & 0 & 0 & 0 \end{pmatrix}$$

The following lemma is the final ingredient for the proof of Theorem 5—its proof is an easy exercise in linear algebra.

**Lemma 2.** Every $\mathsf{k}(x)$ matrix is row equivalent to one in rational form.

*Proof of Theorem 5.* Let us fix a circuit $c \in \mathsf{Circ}[n, m]$. In the following, we will sketch a recipe, using the equational theory of $\mathbb{IH}$, with which $c$ is transformed into the rewiring of a circuit in SF. To improve readability, we shall draw any circuit as if both $n$ and $m$ were 2. It should be fairly clear how our argument generalizes.

(i) First we transform $c$ into the circuit $c_1$ on the right: the two are equal in $\mathbb{IH}$ by virtue of (13).

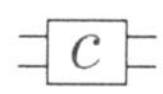 $\overset{\mathbb{IH}}{\Rightarrow}$ 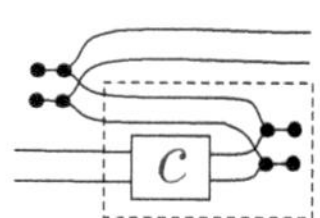

Let us call $c_2$ the circuit from $n + m$ to 0 delimited by a dotted square in the picture above. Since $c_0$ is obtained by rewiring on

$c_2$, it should be clear that, if $c_2$ can be rearranged as the rewiring of a circuit in SF, then this property also holds for $c_0$. Therefore, in the sequel we shift our focus to $c_2$.

(ii) Proposition 1 allows us to rewrite $c_2$ in cospan form, as the composition along a middle boundary $z$ of circuits $c_3$ and $c_4$ below, while preserving equality in $\mathbb{IH}$. By definition of cospan form, $c_3$ is an arrow of $\overrightarrow{\mathsf{Circ}}$, while $c_4$ is an arrow of $\overleftarrow{\mathsf{Circ}}$. For the sake of readability, we will draw $z$ as if it were 2.

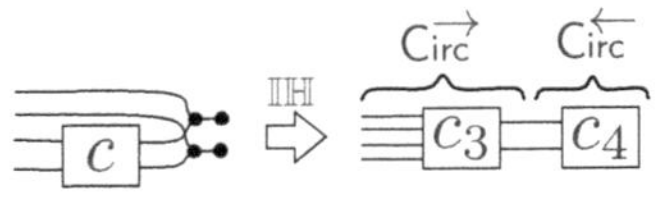


(iii) Since we are reasoning in $\mathbb{IH}$, in particular all the equations of $\mathbb{HA}^{op}$ hold. Now, 0 is both the initial and the terminal object in $\mathsf{Mat}\,\mathsf{k}[x]$; because $\mathbb{HA}^{op} \cong \mathsf{Mat}\,\mathsf{k}[x]^{op}$, this means that there is exactly one circuit of $\overleftarrow{\mathsf{Circ}}$, up to equivalence in $\mathbb{HA}^{op}$, from $z$ to 0. It follows that $c_4$ and the $z$-tensor of (a circuit that we call $c_5$) are equal in $\mathbb{HA}^{op}$ — and thus in $\mathbb{IH}$. We can thus write $c_3 ; c_4$ as $c_3 ; c_5$:

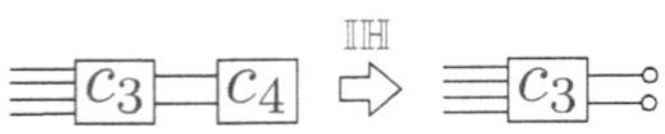


(iv) Since $c_3$ is in $\overrightarrow{\mathsf{Circ}}$ we can use the results about $\mathbb{HA}$ to reason about it. In particular, $c_3$ can be mapped into an $z \times (m+n)$ matrix of polynomials $M$, because $\mathbb{HA} \cong \mathsf{Mat}\,\mathsf{k}[x]$. As we remarked at the beginning of this section, there is a canonical way of representing $M$ as a circuit $c_6$ of Circ:

$$\begin{pmatrix} p_{11} & p_{21} & p_{31} & p_{41} \\ p_{12} & p_{22} & p_{32} & p_{42} \end{pmatrix}$$

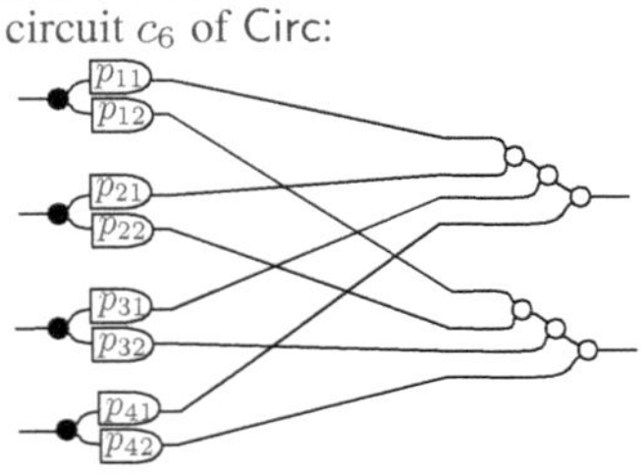


Since $c_3$ corresponds to $M$ along the isomorphism $\mathbb{HA} \cong \mathsf{Mat}\,\mathsf{k}[x]$, it follows that $[\![c_3]\!]$ is $\{(\sigma, M \cdot \sigma \mid \sigma \in \mathsf{k}((x))^n\}$. Therefore $[\![c_3]\!] = [\![c_6]\!]$ meaning by Theorem 1 that $c_3 \stackrel{\mathbb{IH}}{=} c_6$. It follows that we can rewrite our circuit $c_3 ; c_5$ as $c_6 ; c_5$:

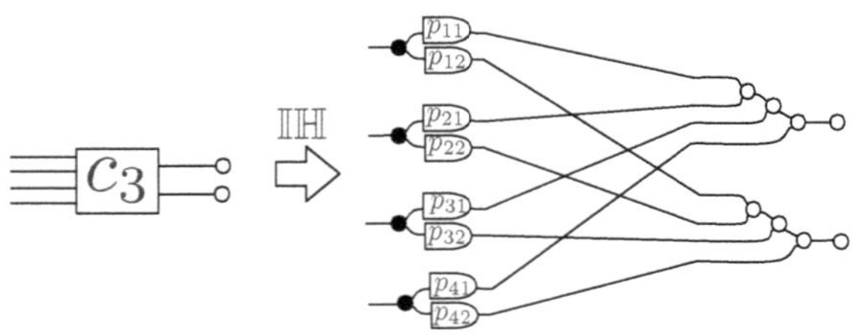


(v) Using Lemma 2, we can then transform $M$ into a matrix $M^*$ in rational form (for instance, the one on the left below). Since $M^*$ is a matrix over $\mathsf{k}(x)$, we have a canonical circuit $c_7$ of $\mathbb{IH}$ (on the right) representing it.

$$\begin{pmatrix} 1 & p_1/q_1 & 0 & p_3/q_3 \\ 0 & p_2/q_2 & 1 & p_4/q_4 \end{pmatrix}$$

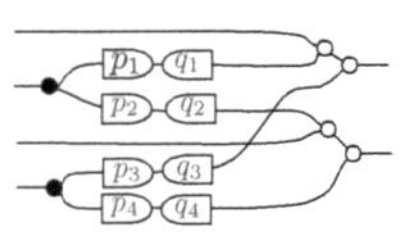


By definition of rational form, each non-zero row $R$ in $M^*$ is associated with a pivot column $C$ with the only non-zero value 1 at the intersection of $R$ and $C$. In order to graphically represent such property in $c_7$, we supposed the following choice of pivots: the first and the third column for the first and second row respectively. Observe that an entry with value 0 corresponds to the circuit, which in $\mathbb{IH}$ is equal to : therefore we could avoid drawing the corresponding link in the circuit $c_7$.

We now claim that $c_6 ; c_5 \stackrel{\mathbb{IH}}{=} c_7 ; c_5$. By Theorem 1, to check this it suffices to show that $[\![c_6 ; c_5]\!] = [\![c_7 ; c_5]\!]$, that is:

$$\{(\sigma, M \cdot \sigma \mid M \cdot \sigma = \overrightarrow{0}\} = \{(\sigma, M^* \cdot \sigma) \mid M^* \cdot \sigma = \overrightarrow{0}\}.$$

This is true because the two relations above describe the kernel of $M$ and $M^*$ respectively, and $M^*$ is row-equivalent to $M$. It follows that we can rewrite $c_6 ; c_5$ as $c_7 ; c_5$, while preserving equality in $\mathbb{IH}$:

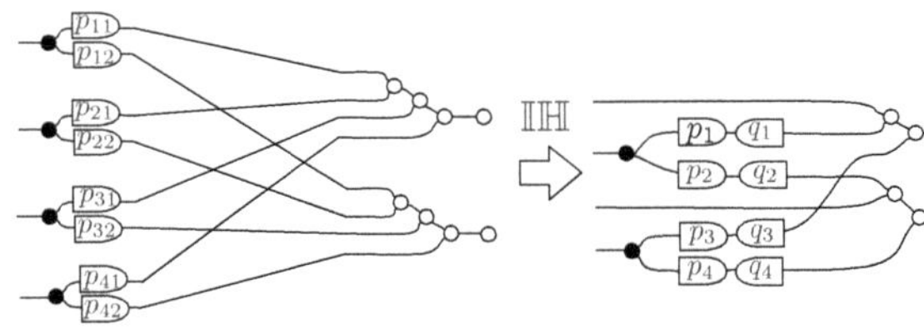


(vi) We now focus on circuit $c_7 ; c_5$. Our next step is to use associativity and commutativity of to make one of the two legs of each component be always attached to the pivot-wire of the corresponding row. Also, we use the axioms of SMCs and naturality of the symmetry to push the pivot-wires towards the top of the circuit, as follows:

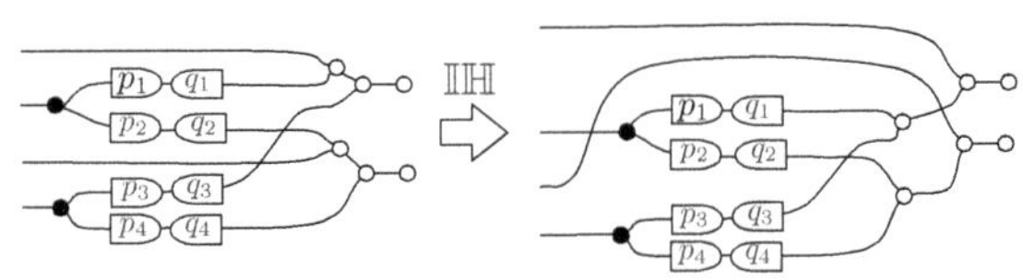


(vii) We can now remove the components of shape by turning them into rewiring structure. This can be done by simply applying axiom (I6) of $\mathbb{IH}$:

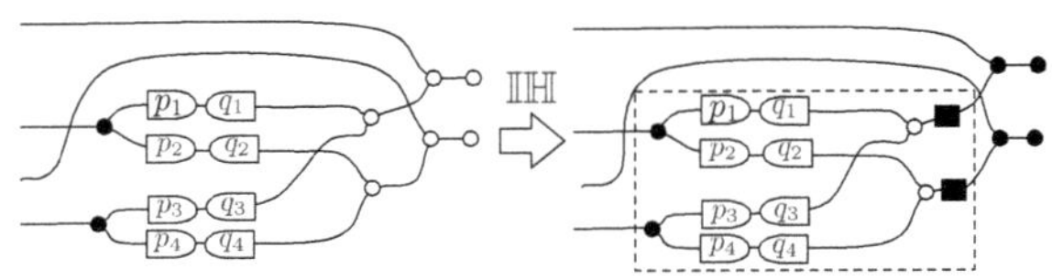


(viii) Let us call $c_8$ the rightmost circuit above: it is a rewiring of the circuit inscribed into the dotted square, which we call $c_9$. Since $c_7$ was constructed starting by a matrix in rational form, for all the components in $c_8$, $\frac{p}{q}$ is a rational. Thus, using the fact that $\mathbb{SF} \cong \mathsf{Mat}\,\mathsf{k}\langle x \rangle$, we can rewrite in $\mathbb{IH}$ each such component as a circuit $\tilde{c}$ in SF:

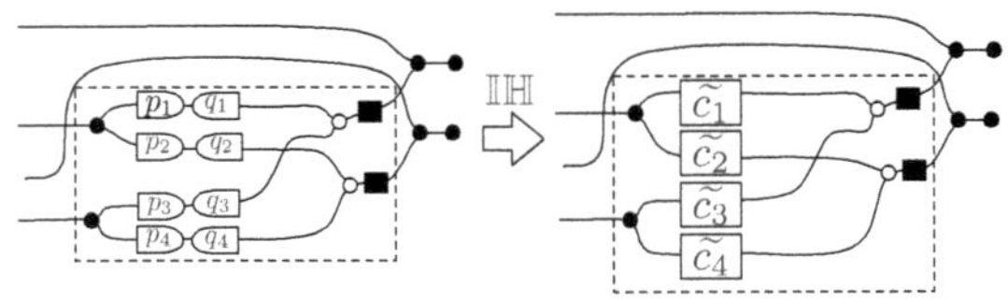


Now, observe that $c_9$ can be seen as the composition (via $\oplus$ and ; ) of circuits that are all in SF.

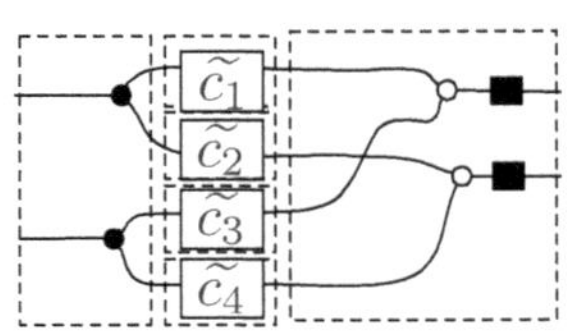

It follows that $c_9$ is also in SF and thus $c_8$ is the rewiring of a circuit in SF. Since $c_8$ was obtained by $c_2$ by only using rewriting steps allowed by the equational theory of $\mathbb{IH}$, the statement of the theorem follows. □

## 6. Directing the Flow

In the classical presentation of signal flow graphs (see e.g. [23]), wires are directed, signifying the direction of signal flow. Throughout the previous sections, we have been referring to flow direction only on an intuitive level. We now introduce directionality explicitly, claiming that it can be really treated as a *derivative* notion of our theory of circuits. We then present some applications and examples supporting our statement.

In order to model classical signal flow graphs we first need to introduce an alternative syntax, which we call the *directed* signal flow calculus. We will need components that resemble those of $\overrightarrow{\mathsf{Circ}}$, but which are explicitly oriented from left to right.

$e ::=$ 

We also require some "pure" wiring: since signal flow is explicit, we include two versions of the identity wire and four of the twist:

$w ::=$ 

These basic components above are given a sorting $(u, v)$ where $u, v \in \{◄, ►\}^*$; for instance:

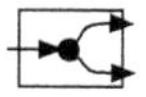 : (►, ►►) and 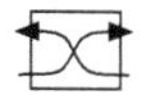 : (◄►, ►◄).

Classical signal flow graphs are obtained by composing components $e$ and $w$ using the operations ; and $\oplus$, for which we reuse the sorting rules of Fig. 1, together with guarded feedback operations $\mathsf{Tr}^{►}(\cdot)$ that take a circuit of sort $(►^{1+m}, ►^{1+n})$ and yield a circuit of sort $(►^m, ►^n)$. The associated sorting rule is thus:

$$\frac{c : (►^{1+n}, ►^{1+m})}{\mathsf{Tr}^{►}(c) : (►^n, ►^m)}$$

This is represented graphically as follows:

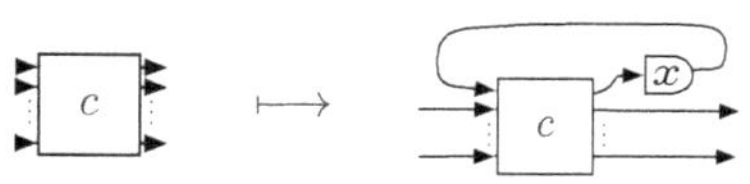

The syntax for directed signal flow graphs is thus:

$$sf ::= e \mid w \mid sf \,;sf \mid sf \oplus sf \mid \mathsf{Tr}^{►}(sf)$$

Finally, we include top-level operations reminiscent of the rewiring in §5: $L^{►}$, $L^{◄}$, $R^{►}$ and $R^{◄}$, with sorting rules:

$$\frac{c : (►u, v)}{L^{►}(c) : (u, ◄v)} \qquad \frac{c : (◄u, v)}{L^{◄}(c) : (u, ►v)} \qquad \frac{c : (u, ►v)}{R^{►}(c) : (◄u, v)} \qquad \frac{c : (u, ◄v)}{R^{◄}(c) : (►u, v)}$$

In the graphical rendering below we leave out the arrowheads on wires where direction is arbitrary:

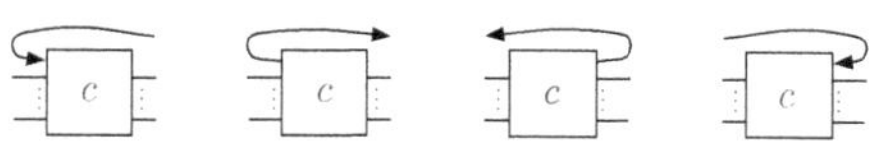

Circuits of the directed signal flow calculus are thus specified by following grammar:

$$d ::= sf \mid L^{►}d \mid L^{◄}d \mid R^{►}d \mid R^{◄}d \mid d;w \mid w;d$$

Note that the composition at the top level is restricted to disallow the introduction of unguarded feedback.

Rather than defining the operational semantics directly, we can obtain the expected behaviour by first translating directed terms to the signal flow calculus. Intuitively, the inductively defined translation $\mathcal{E}$ "erases directions" from the wires:

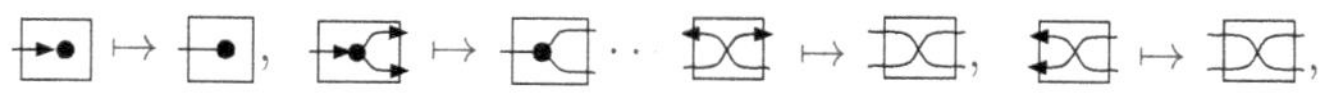

$$sf_1\,;sd_2 \mapsto \mathcal{E}(sf_1)\,;\mathcal{E}(sf_2), \quad sf_1 \oplus sf_2 \mapsto \mathcal{E}(sd_1) \oplus \mathcal{E}(sf_2),$$
$$\mathsf{Tr}^{►}(sf) \mapsto \mathsf{Tr}(\mathcal{E}(sf)), \quad \mathsf{L}^{\star}(d) \mapsto \mathsf{L}(\mathcal{E}(d)) \quad \mathsf{R}^{\star}(d) \mapsto \mathsf{R}(\mathcal{E}(d)).$$

where $\star \in \{◄, ►\}$ and Tr, L and R are defined as in §2 and §5.

A key observation is that directed sort discipline prevents us from writing problematic circuits where signal flow is incompatible, like in the examples in §4. In fact, using Proposition 3 and Lemma 1 we get:

**Proposition 4.** For any circuit $d$ of the directed signal flow calculus, $\mathcal{E}(d)$ is deadlock and initialisation free.

Moreover, this syntactic restriction does not affect the expressiveness since, thanks to Theorem 5, rewirings of signal flow graphs denote all the possible behaviours. Thus, informally speaking, all circuits in Circ can be directed (modulo the theory of $\mathbb{IH}$).

**Proposition 5.** For any circuit $c$ of Circ, there exists a directed circuit $d$ such that $\mathcal{E}(d) \stackrel{\mathbb{IH}}{=} c$

Propositions 4 and 5 have two interesting consequences. First, Proposition 4 and the full-abstraction result mean that we can use the equational theory of $\mathbb{IH}$ to safely reason about classical signal flow graphs and extensions—indeed, all the circuits in the directed signal flow calculus. Roughly speaking, the procedure is: forget the directions and then use $\stackrel{\mathbb{IH}}{=}$. This confirms the intuition that, like for electrical circuits, also for signal flow graphs directionality is *not* a primitive notion as originally advocated in [23].

Second, Proposition 4, Proposition 5 and full-abstraction tell us that the denotational semantics of any circuit of the signal flow calculus can be properly realised by some directed circuit. We can therefore use the "more liberal" signal flow calculus to specify circuits and the "more restrictive" directed calculus to implement them. One can then check that an implementation $d$ adheres to a specification $c$ by mean of the graphical reasoning supported by $\mathbb{IH}$. Indeed $\mathcal{E}(d) \stackrel{\mathbb{IH}}{=} c$, means that $d$ implements, without deadlocks or initialisation, the behaviour denoted by $c$. Note that while an implementation is a directed circuit—typically featuring feedbacks—we are being deliberately vague about what kind of circuit in Circ constitutes a specification: in examples that we consider these are typically generating functions that can be obtained in a standard way (see e.g. [29]) from recurrence formulas. We illustrate these ideas with the aid of the simple example below.

**Example 4.** Consider the circuits displayed below. The leftmost serves as specification ($\frac{1}{1-x}$) and the rightmost, a directed circuit, as its implementation.

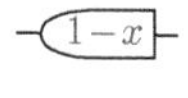

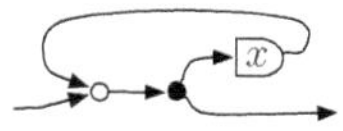

To prove that the implementation realises the specification, we first throw away all the directions from the wires and then we proceed with a graphical derivation in $\mathbb{IH}$:

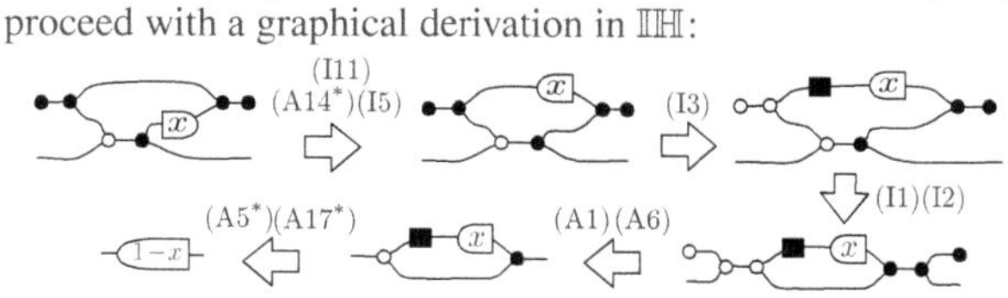

(14)

We annotated the key axioms of $\mathbb{IH}$ justifying each derivation step. Note that the first and the second to last circuit, that we have just proved equivalent, are $c_2$ and $c_1$ from Example 1 (modulo the notation $\boxed{\blacksquare}$ adopted for $\boxed{-1}$ since Section 3).

A similar procedure can be used to check the observational equivalence of directed signal flow graphs. For instance, take:

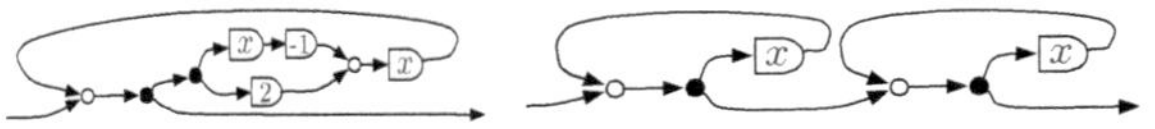
(15)

First, we forget the direction of the flow and we obtain the circuits $c_3$ and $c_4$ depicted below, on the left and on the right.

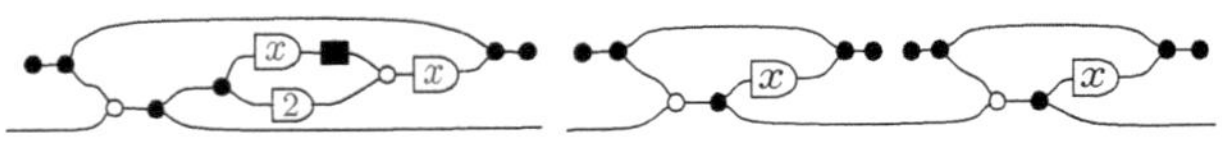

Then, by virtue of Proposition 4 and full abstraction, we can safely use $\stackrel{\mathbb{IH}}{=}$ to check $\langle c_3 \rangle = \langle c_4 \rangle$. Observe that $c_3$ is like in Example 1 and $c_4$ is just the sequential composition $c_2 \,; c_2$. We can thus reuse (14) to see that

$$c_4 = c_2 \,; c_2 \stackrel{\mathbb{IH}}{=} \boxed{1-x} \,;\, \boxed{1-x} \stackrel{\mathbb{IH}}{=} \boxed{(1-x)^2}$$

To conclude, we only have to check that $c_3$ is equal in $\mathbb{IH}$ to the rightmost circuit above. This is shown as follows, along the same lines of derivation (14):

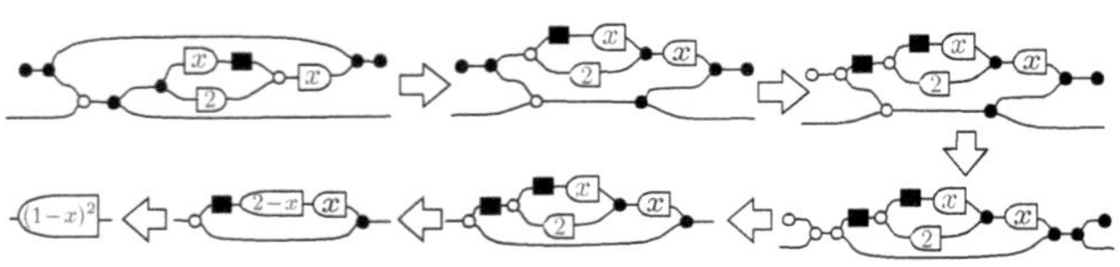

The circuits in (15) can also be thought of as two different implementations of $\boxed{(1-x)^2}$. Indeed, $\frac{1}{(1-x)^2}$ is the generating function of the sequence $1, 2, 3, 4, \ldots$.

## 7. Conclusions

The network theoretic approach combines algebra and topology–the circuits of the theory that we presented have an algebraic nature, as demonstrated by the axiomatisations, as well as a topological nature, when viewed as string diagrams. Our contribution adds an operational understanding to the previously discovered denotational insights. Throughout the paper we have tried to illustrate the fruitful interplay between algebra, topology, the operational and denotational approaches.

Although our attention in this work was restricted to signal flow graphs, the same methodology could be beneficial in other areas where diagrammatic notation is employed: in addition to the examples we mentioned in the introduction there are Kahn process networks, Bayesian networks and automata, amongst many others. Typically, such diagrammatic formalisms are translated to more traditional mathematics, but seldom reasoned about directly. The broad picture of the work in this paper is a deep connection between a denotational view and a fully-fledged operational approach that is intimately related to the hallmark of network theory: the interplay between algebra and topology. Our vision is close to that advocated by Abramsky for concurrency theory [1]: we believe that this approach will eventually lead to less a specialised, fragmented and sometimes overly syntax-focussed landscape.

***Acknowledgements*** We thank the anonymous referees for the fruitful discussion. The first and the third author acknowledge support from the ANR project 12IS02001 PACE.

## References


[1] S. Abramsky. What are the fundamental structures of concurrency? we still don't know! *CoRR*, abs/1401.4973, 2014.

[2] J. C. Baez. Network theory. `http://math.ucr.edu/home/baez/networks/`, 2014.

[3] J. C. Baez and J. Erbele. Categories in control. *CoRR*, abs/1405.6881, 2014. `http://arxiv.org/abs/1405.6881`.

[4] H. Basold, M. Bonsangue, H. H. Hansen, and J. Rutten. (co)algebraic characterizations of signal flow graphs. In *To appear in LNCS*, 2014.

[5] F. Bonchi, P. Sobociński, and F. Zanasi. A categorical semantics of signal flow graphs. In *CONCUR*, 2014.

[6] F. Bonchi, P. Sobociński, and F. Zanasi. Interacting bialgebras are Frobenius. In *FoSSaCS '14*. Springer, 2014.

[7] F. Bonchi, P. Sobociński, and F. Zanasi. Interacting Hopf algebras. *CoRR*, abs/1403.7048, 2014. `http://arxiv.org/abs/1403.7048`.

[8] R. Bruni, U. Montanari, G. Plotkin, and D. Terreni. On hierarchical graphs: reconciling bigraphs, gs-monoidal theories and gs-graphs.

[9] R. Bruni, I. Lanese, and U. Montanari. A basic algebra of stateless connectors. *Theor Comput Sci*, 366:98–120, 2006.

[10] A. Carboni and R. F. C. Walters. Cartesian bicategories I. *J Pure Appl Algebra*, 49:11–32, 1987.

[11] B. Coecke and R. Duncan. Interacting quantum observables. In *ICALP'08*, pages 298–310, 2008.

[12] B. Coecke, R. Duncan, A. Kissinger, and Q. Wang. Strong complementarity and non-locality in categorical quantum mechanics. In *LiCS'12*, pages 245–254, 2012.

[13] M. P. Fiore and M. D. Campos. The algebra of directed acyclic graphs. In *Abramsky Festschrift*, volume 7860 of *LNCS*, 2013.

[14] B. Fong. A compositional approach to control theory. PhD Transfer Report, 2013.

[15] D. R. Ghica. Diagrammatic reasoning for delay-insensitive asynchronous circuits. In *Abramsky Festschrift*, pages 52–68, 2013.

[16] A. Joyal and R. Street. The geometry of tensor calculus, I. *Adv. Math.*, 88:55–112, 1991.

[17] P. Katis, N. Sabadini, and R. F. C. Walters. Span(Graph): an algebra of transition systems. In *AMAST '97*, pages 322–336. Springer, 1997.

[18] G. M. Kelly and M. L. Laplaza. Coherence for compact closed categories. *J. Pure Appl. Algebra*, 19:193–213, 1980.

[19] S. Lack. Composing PROPs. *Theor App Categories*, 13(9):147–163, 2004.

[20] Y. Lafont. Towards an algebraic theory of boolean circuits. *J Pure Appl Alg*, 184:257–310, 2003.

[21] B. Lahti. *Signal Processing and Linear Systems*. Oxford University Press, 1998.

[22] S. Mac Lane. Categorical algebra. *B Am Math Soc*, 71:40–106, 1965.

[23] S. J. Mason. *Feedback Theory: I. Some Properties of Signal Flow Graphs*. MIT Research Laboratory of Electronics, 1953.

[24] D. Pavlovic. Monoidal computer i: Basic computability by string diagrams. *Inf. Comput.*, 226:94–116, 2013.

[25] D. Pavlovic. Monoidal computer ii: Normal complexity by string diagrams. *CoRR*, abs/1402.5687, 2014.

[26] J. J. M. M. Rutten. A tutorial on coinductive stream calculus and signal flow graphs. *Theor. Comput. Sci.*, 343(3):443–481, 2005.

[27] P. Selinger. A survey of graphical languages for monoidal categories. arXiv:0908.3347v1 [math.CT], 2009.

[28] P. Sobociński. Nets, relations and linking diagrams. In *CALCO '13*, 2013.

[29] H. Wilf. *Generatingfunctionology*. A. K. Peters, 3rd edition, 2006.

[30] J. C. Willems. The behavioural approach to open and interconnected systems. *IEEE Contr. Syst. Mag.*, 27:46–99, 2007.

[31] W. J. Zeng and J. Vicary. Abstract structure of unitary oracles for quantum algorithms. *CoRR*, abs/1406.1278, 2014.

# Conjugate Hylomorphisms

## *Or:* The Mother of All Structured Recursion Schemes

Ralf Hinze Nicolas Wu Jeremy Gibbons

Department of Computer Science, University of Oxford, Wolfson Building, Parks Road, Oxford, OX1 3QD, England

{ralf.hinze,nicolas.wu,jeremy.gibbons}@cs.ox.ac.uk

## Abstract

The past decades have witnessed an extensive study of structured recursion schemes. A general scheme is the *hylomorphism*, which captures the essence of divide-and-conquer: a problem is broken into sub-problems by a coalgebra; sub-problems are solved recursively; the sub-solutions are combined by an algebra to form a solution. In this paper we develop a simple toolbox for assembling *recursive coalgebras*, which by definition ensure that their hylo equations have unique solutions, whatever the algebra. Our main tool is the *conjugate rule*, a generic rule parametrized by an adjunction and a conjugate pair of natural transformations. We show that many basic adjunctions induce useful recursion schemes. In fact, almost every structured recursion scheme seems to arise as an instance of the conjugate rule. Further, we adapt our toolbox to the more expressive setting of *parametrically recursive coalgebras*, where the original input is also passed to the algebra. The formal development is complemented by a series of worked-out examples in Haskell.

***Categories and Subject Descriptors*** D.1.1 [*Programming Techniques*]: Applicative (Functional) Programming; D.3.2 [*Programming Languages*]: Language Classifications—applicative (functional) languages; F.3.2 [*Logics and Meanings of Programs*]: Semantics of Programming Languages—algebraic approaches to semantics

***General Terms*** Languages, Theory, Verification

***Keywords*** recursion schemes, hylomorphisms, adjunctions

## 1. Introduction

Over forty years ago, Hoare [14] observed that "there are certain close analogies between the methods used for structuring data and the methods for structuring a program which processes that data". These days, the relationship between data structure and program structure is often expressed via structured recursion schemes, which are widely used in functional languages such Haskell.

Although such schemes are less powerful than general recursion, their importance echoes the philosophy [23] that functional programmers who are not interested in recursion patterns are like imperative programmers who use `GOTO` instead of `WHILE-DO`. For instance, even in Haskell, accidentally writing a non-terminating dynamic programming algorithm is all too easy using explicit recursion, when this can be prevented by using an appropriate recursion scheme.

Canonical examples are provided by *folds* (catamorphisms), which consume data structures, and *unfolds* (anamorphisms), which produce them, solutions $h$ and $k$ of the following recursion equations:

$$h \cdot in = a \cdot \mathsf{F}\, h \qquad out \cdot k = \mathsf{F}\, k \cdot c \ ,$$

which are shaped by a *base functor* $\mathsf{F}$. Categorically, these recursion schemes arise from constructions in which *in* and *out* are *initial algebras* and *final coalgebras* respectively. Initiality and finality each correspond to both existence and uniqueness of solutions to the equations above, traditionally written $h = (\!|a|\!)$ and $k = [\!(c)\!]$.

Folds and unfolds have been thoroughly studied and are now well understood and widely used, but they are rather restrictive patterns of computation. Thus, there have been many generalizations, extensions, and combinations in an attempt to improve expressivity. Ultimately, most of these are variations on a single theme, the *hylomorphism* [23], which arises as a solution to the equation:

$$h = a \cdot \mathsf{F}\, h \cdot c \ .$$

This generalization comes with a catch: there is no guarantee that a solution exists for a hylo equation with a given coalgebra $c$ and algebra $a$, let alone that such a solution is uniquely determined. A candidate solution is $(\!|a|\!) \cdot [\!(c)\!]$, but this only works if the carriers of initial algebras and final coalgebras coincide.

A number of workarounds to the catch have been proposed over the years. One could work in an algebraically compact category such as **Cpo** [23]; then the carriers of initial algebras and final coalgebras do coincide, but one has to relax uniqueness of solutions to ordering them (for example, picking the least solution). Similarly, one could work in a self-dual category such as **Rel** [4]; again, the carriers coincide, this time because final coalgebras are exactly the converses of initial algebras, but again one has to resort to least solutions and deal with inequalities rather than equalities.

Alternatively, rather than restricting the setting in such ways, we can instead constrain the programs under consideration. In particular, we can restrict ourselves to so-called recursive coalgebras [6]—those that by definition yield unique solutions to the hylo equation, whatever the algebra. Dually, we can work with corecursive algebras—those that yield unique solutions whatever the coalgebra. This is a trade-off: only certain coalgebras (or dually, algebras) are admissible, but in return there need be no restriction on the setting, and no resort to inequalities rather than equalities.

The cost side of the trade-off is mitigated by providing a toolbox of techniques for assembling the admissible components, rather than requiring their admissibility to be proved from first principles. For example, because an initial algebra *in* is an isomorphism, it has an inverse $in^{\circ}$, and this inverse turns out to be a recursive coalgebra. Hylomorphisms with $c = in^{\circ}$ are just folds, so by itself this is not



*POPL '15*, January 15–17, 2015, Mumbai, India.

ACM 978-1-4503-3300-9/15/01…$15.00.
http://dx.doi.org/10.1145/2676726.2676989

very interesting; it becomes more interesting when we develop a powerful theory of constructions on recursive coalgebras, as we set out to do. Our theory is based on adjunctions, and, of course, it all dualizes nicely to corecursive algebras.

Perhaps surprisingly, the entire theory is based on only two tools, which we call the *rolling rule* and the *conjugate rule*. The former applies when the base functor shaping the recursion is composed from two other functors, and allows the two functors to be swapped. The latter allows us to shunt functors between the producer and consumer parts of the hylo. The conjugate rule is parametrized by an adjunction and a conjugate pair of natural transformations. In a sense the ensuing recursion scheme, *conjugate hylomorphisms*, can be considered the *mother of all recursion schemes*, as almost every recursion scheme can be framed as an instance: folds and unfolds [10, 21, 23], folds with parameters [26], mutu- and zygomorphisms [8, 20], histo- and futumorphisms [29], generalized folds [5], recursion schemes from comonads [31], and adjoint folds [11].

This is not the first time this topic has been visited, and indeed most of the results in Section 3 appear in Capretta et al. [6], albeit using different machinery—comonads and distributive laws—and with substantially longer proofs. We demonstrate that each of their comonadic schemes also arises by instantiating the conjugate rule to an adjunction that generates the comonad. Indeed, in many ways the present work extends the unification of structured recursion schemes presented in [13], which showed that recursion schemes from comonads [31] are subsumed by adjoint folds [11]. Rather pleasingly, the generalization from initial algebras to recursive coalgebras streamlines many of the proofs. A distinct advantage of adjunctions over comonads is that the former compose nicely: we can build advanced recursion schemes out of simple ones by composing the underlying adjunctions (Section 3.5).

Folds are equivalent to paramorphisms [22], the Squiggol rendering of primitive recursion, where the input is also passed to the algebra. However, when we generalize initial algebras to recursive coalgebras this equivalence no longer holds. Practical considerations suggest that providing the inputs is useful, and this motivates us to extend the theory to include so-called parametrically recursive coalgebras [27]. (There is also a dual variation [24] corresponding to apomorphisms [32], which allow the coalgebra to stop the recursion early.) Here is where we feel the benefit of a unified approach: we show that the rolling and the conjugate rule can be generalized to this more expressive setting, generalizing all of their instances in one go. (There is only one exception; see Section 5.6.)

In summary, this paper makes the following novel contributions:

- we unify and substantially simplify prior work on structured recursion schemes;
- we identify two central adjunction-like techniques for proving the uniqueness of a wide range of recursion equations;
- we generalize these techniques to the more expressive setting of parametrically recursive coalgebras.

The rest of the paper is structured as follows. Section 2 provides some background category theory, with an overview of important adjunctions. In Section 3 we discuss hylomorphisms, and introduce the two cornerstones of our theory: the rolling rule and the conjugate rule. We provide all of the proofs, as they serve as templates for the development in Section 5. We support our claim that almost all known structured recursion schemes can be expressed as instances of the conjugate rule. We illustrate the schemes through a number of Haskell examples as we go. More elaborate examples based on dynamic programming are given in Section 4. We then extend the theory in Section 5 to cover parametrically recursive coalgebras; in particular, we adapt the rolling and the conjugate rule to the new setting. We follow this with further examples in Section 6. Finally, Section 7 discusses related work, and Section 8 concludes.

## 2. Background

This paper assumes a basic knowledge of category theory: the reader should be familiar with the notions of functors and natural transformations. In this section we fix the notation and establish the concepts that will be used in the remainder of the paper. For the most part this material is standard, and can safely be glossed over on an initial reading, except perhaps the material on conjugates.

### 2.1 Algebras and Coalgebras

Algebras and coalgebras form the basis for the categorical description of structured recursion schemes.

Given an endofunctor $\mathsf{F} : \mathscr{C} \to \mathscr{C}$, a so-called *base functor*, an $\mathsf{F}$-algebra is a pair $(a, A)$, where $a : \mathsf{F}\,A \to A$ is an arrow and $A : \mathscr{C}$ is an object, which are known respectively as the *action* and *carrier* of the algebra. (We deviate a little from the standard notation $(A, a)$, in order to have a syntax that distinguishes algebras from coalgebras.) Since the action determines its carrier, it is often used by itself to refer to the $\mathsf{F}$-algebra. An $\mathsf{F}$-homomorphism between algebras $(a, A)$ and $(b, B)$ is an arrow $h : A \to B : \mathscr{C}$ such that $h \cdot a = b \cdot \mathsf{F}\,h$.

$$\begin{array}{ccc} \mathsf{F}\,A & \xrightarrow{\mathsf{F}\,h} & \mathsf{F}\,B \\ {\scriptstyle a}\downarrow & & \downarrow{\scriptstyle b} \\ A & \xrightarrow[h]{} & B \end{array}$$

$\mathsf{F}$-homomorphisms compose, and there is an identity, so $\mathsf{F}$-algebras and $\mathsf{F}$-homomorphisms form a category, which we call $\mathsf{F}\text{-}\mathbf{Alg}(\mathscr{C})$. The initial object of this category, if it exists, is given by $(in, \mu\mathsf{F})$ and called the *initial* $\mathsf{F}$*-algebra*. Initiality implies that to each $\mathsf{F}$-algebra, $(a, A)$, there corresponds a unique $\mathsf{F}$-homomorphism, $(\!|a|\!) : (in, \mu\mathsf{F}) \to (a, A)$, called a *fold*. The algebra *in* is, in fact, an isomorphism, so $\mu\mathsf{F}$ is a fixed-point of $\mathsf{F}$ (in a certain sense, the least fixed-point); this fact is known as Lambek's Lemma [18].

Dually, given an endofunctor $\mathsf{G} : \mathscr{C} \to \mathscr{C}$, a $\mathsf{G}$-coalgebra is a pair $(C, c)$, where $C : \mathscr{C}$ is the carrier and $c : C \to \mathsf{G}\,C$ is the action of the coalgebra. A $\mathsf{G}$-homomorphism between coalgebras $(C, c)$ and $(D, d)$ is an arrow $h : C \to D : \mathscr{C}$ that satisfies $\mathsf{G}\,h \cdot c = d \cdot h$. Just as before, a category $\mathsf{G}\text{-}\mathbf{Coalg}(\mathscr{C})$ can be formed from $\mathsf{G}$-coalgebras and $\mathsf{G}$-homomorphisms. The final object of this category, if it exists, is given by $(\nu\mathsf{G}, out)$ and called the *final* $\mathsf{G}$*-coalgebra*. The unique homomorphism to the $\mathsf{G}$-algebra $(C, c)$, called an *unfold*, is written $[\![c]\!] : C \to \nu\mathsf{G}$.

Throughout, we use Haskell as a lingua franca for exemplifying categorical constructions. However, we are careful to distinguish between inductive and coinductive types, which Haskell conflates.

**Example 2.1.** The semantics of the inductive datatype *Tree* defined

$$\mathbf{data}\ \mathit{Tree} = \mathit{Empty} \mid \mathit{Node}\ \mathit{Tree}\ \mathbb{Z}\ \mathit{Tree}$$

is given by the initial algebra $(in, \mu\mathsf{Tree})$, where the *base functor*

$$\mathbf{data}\ \mathsf{Tree}\ \mathit{tree} = \mathsf{Empty} \mid \mathsf{Node}\ \mathit{tree}\ \mathbb{Z}\ \mathit{tree}$$

abstracts away from the recursive occurrences of *Tree*. The Haskell rendering of the isomorphism *in*, the action of the initial algebra, amounts to a simple renaming of constructors. □

The category $\mathsf{F}\text{-}\mathbf{Alg}(\mathscr{C})$ has more structure than $\mathscr{C}$. The forgetful or underlying functor $\mathsf{U}^{\mathsf{F}} : \mathsf{F}\text{-}\mathbf{Alg}(\mathscr{C}) \to \mathscr{C}$ forgets about the additional structure: $\mathsf{U}^{\mathsf{F}}\,(a, A) = A$ and $\mathsf{U}^{\mathsf{F}}\,h = h$. An analogous functor can be defined for coalgebras: $\mathsf{U}_{\mathsf{G}} : \mathsf{G}\text{-}\mathbf{Coalg}(\mathscr{C}) \to \mathscr{C}$.

***Liftings and coliftings*** A functor $\overline{\mathsf{H}} : \mathsf{F}\text{-}\mathbf{Alg}(\mathscr{C}) \to \mathsf{G}\text{-}\mathbf{Alg}(\mathscr{D})$ is called a *lifting* of $\mathsf{H} : \mathscr{C} \to \mathscr{D}$ iff $\mathsf{H} \circ \mathsf{U}^{\mathsf{F}} = \mathsf{U}^{\mathsf{G}} \circ \overline{\mathsf{H}}$. For liftings, the action on the carrier and on homomorphisms is fixed; the action on the algebra can be specified using a natural transformation

$\lambda : \mathsf{H} \circ \mathsf{F} \dot{\leftarrow} \mathsf{G} \circ \mathsf{H}$. Then the lifting $\mathsf{H}^{\lambda}$ is characterised by:

$$\mathsf{H}^{\lambda}\ (a,A) = (\mathsf{H}\ a \cdot \lambda\ A, \mathsf{H}\ A) \qquad \mathsf{H}^{\lambda}\ h = \mathsf{H}\ h\ . \tag{2.1}$$

Since we use the action of an algebra to refer to the algebra itself, we often abbreviate $\mathsf{H}\ a \cdot \lambda\ A$ by $\mathsf{H}^{\lambda}\ a$.

Dually, $\underline{\mathsf{H}} : \mathsf{F}\text{-}\mathbf{Coalg}(\mathscr{C}) \to \mathsf{G}\text{-}\mathbf{Coalg}(\mathscr{D})$ is a colifting of $\mathsf{H} : \mathscr{C} \to \mathscr{D}$ iff $\mathsf{U}_{\mathsf{G}} \circ \underline{\mathsf{H}} = \mathsf{H} \circ \mathsf{U}_{\mathsf{F}}$. Given $\lambda : \mathsf{H} \circ \mathsf{F} \dot{\to} \mathsf{G} \circ \mathsf{H}$ we can define a colifting as follows:

$$\mathsf{H}_{\lambda}\ (C,c) = (\mathsf{H}\ C, \lambda\ C \cdot \mathsf{H}\ c) \qquad \mathsf{H}_{\lambda}\ h = \mathsf{H}\ h\ . \tag{2.2}$$

### 2.2 Adjunctions

Adjunctions were introduced by Kan [17] and are so pervasive in the study of category theory that Mac Lane [19, p.vii] noted "Adjoint functors arise everywhere." Our work supports this view: adjunctions provide a unified framework for program transformation.

Given categories $\mathscr{C}, \mathscr{D}$, we say that functors $\mathsf{L} : \mathscr{C} \leftarrow \mathscr{D}$ and $\mathsf{R} : \mathscr{C} \to \mathscr{D}$ form an adjunction, written $\mathsf{L} \dashv \mathsf{R} : \mathscr{C} \rightharpoonup \mathscr{D}$ or

$$\mathscr{C} \underset{\mathsf{R}}{\overset{\mathsf{L}}{\underset{\longrightarrow}{\overset{\longleftarrow}{\bot}}}} \mathscr{D}\quad ,$$

iff there is a bijection between the sets of arrows

$$\lfloor - \rfloor : \mathscr{C}(\mathsf{L}\ A, B) \cong \mathscr{D}(A, \mathsf{R}\ B) : \lceil - \rceil$$

that is natural both in $A$ and $B$. We say that $\mathsf{L}$ is a *left adjoint* for $\mathsf{R}$, and $\mathsf{R}$ a *right adjoint* for $\mathsf{L}$; the isomorphism $\lfloor - \rfloor$ is called the *left adjunct*, and its inverse $\lceil - \rceil$ the *right adjunct*.

That the adjuncts $\lfloor - \rfloor$ and $\lceil - \rceil$ are mutually inverse can be captured using an equivalence:

$$f = \lceil g \rceil \iff \lfloor f \rfloor = g\ , \tag{2.3}$$

for all $f : \mathsf{L}\ A \to B : \mathscr{C}$ and $g : A \to \mathsf{R}\ B : \mathscr{D}$. The naturality properties of the adjuncts are alternatively expressed as fusion laws.

$$\mathsf{R}\ k \cdot \lfloor f \rfloor \cdot h = \lfloor k \cdot f \cdot \mathsf{L}\ h \rfloor \tag{2.4a}$$

$$k \cdot \lceil g \rceil \cdot \mathsf{L}\ h = \lceil \mathsf{R}\ k \cdot g \cdot h \rceil \tag{2.4b}$$

An alternative definition of adjunctions is based on the natural transformations $\epsilon = \lceil id \rceil$ and $\eta = \lfloor id \rfloor$, which are called the *counit* $\epsilon : \mathsf{L} \circ \mathsf{R} \dot{\to} \mathsf{Id}$ and the *unit* $\eta : \mathsf{Id} \dot{\to} \mathsf{R} \circ \mathsf{L}$ of the adjunction. All in all, an adjunction consists of six entities: two functors, two adjuncts, and two units. Each can be defined in terms of the others:

$$\begin{array}{lll} \lceil g \rceil = \epsilon\ B \cdot \mathsf{L}\ g & \epsilon = \lceil id \rceil & \mathsf{L}\ h = \lceil \eta\ B \cdot h \rceil \\ \lfloor f \rfloor = \mathsf{R} f \cdot \eta\ A & \eta = \lfloor id \rfloor & \mathsf{R}\ k = \lfloor k \cdot \epsilon\ A \rfloor\ . \end{array} \tag{2.5}$$

**Example 2.2.** Coproducts and products arise as left and right adjoints $(+) \dashv \Delta \dashv (\times)$ of the diagonal functor $\Delta : \mathscr{C} \to \mathscr{C} \times \mathscr{C}$ defined by $\Delta A = (A, A)$ and $\Delta f = (f, f)$.

$$\mathscr{C} \underset{\Delta}{\overset{(+)}{\underset{\longrightarrow}{\overset{\longleftarrow}{\bot}}}} \mathscr{C} \times \mathscr{C} \qquad \mathscr{C} \times \mathscr{C} \underset{(\times)}{\overset{\Delta}{\underset{\longrightarrow}{\overset{\longleftarrow}{\bot}}}} \mathscr{C}$$

The bijections express that pairs of arrows with the same target (respectively, source) are in 1-1 correspondence with arrows from a coproduct (respectively, to a product). In the case of products, the left adjunct $\lfloor (f_1, f_2) \rfloor = f_1 \vartriangle f_2$ is known as the 'split' combinator, and the counit $\epsilon = (outl, outr)$ arises from the projections.

$$(f_1, f_2) = (outl, outr) \cdot \Delta\ g \iff f_1 \vartriangle f_2 = g \tag{2.6a}$$

Note that the equation on the left lives in a product category. For products, the fusion law (2.4a) specializes to

$$(k_1 \times k_2) \cdot (f_1 \vartriangle f_2) \cdot h = (k_1 \cdot f_1 \cdot h) \vartriangle (k_2 \cdot f_2 \cdot h)\ . \tag{2.6b}$$

Both laws will be frequently used in calculations. □

**Example 2.3.** Perhaps the best-known example of an adjunction is currying: a function of two arguments can be treated as a function of the first argument whose values are functions of the second.

$$\mathscr{C} \underset{(-)^P}{\overset{-\times P}{\underset{\longrightarrow}{\overset{\longleftarrow}{\bot}}}} \mathscr{C}$$

The right adjoint of pairing with $P$ is the exponential from $P$. The function $\Lambda$ (pronounce: "curry") corresponds to the left adjunct:

$$\Lambda : \mathscr{C}(A \times P, B) \cong \mathscr{C}(A, B^P)\ .$$

In **Set**, the object $B^P$ is the set of total functions from $P$ to $B$. □

Left adjoints preserve initial objects, $\mathsf{L}\ 0 \cong 0$. Dually, right adjoints preserve final objects, $\mathsf{R}\ 1 \cong 1$. In general, <u>l</u>eft <u>a</u>djoints <u>p</u>reserve <u>c</u>olimits (LAPC) and <u>r</u>ight <u>a</u>djoints <u>p</u>reserve <u>l</u>imits (RAPL).

**Example 2.4.** Possibly infinite trees with branching structure determined by $\mathsf{G}$ and labels drawn from $A$ constitute the *cofree* $\mathsf{G}$*-coalgebra* $\mathsf{Cofree}_{\mathsf{G}}\ A$, which arises as the right adjoint of the underlying functor $\mathsf{U}_{\mathsf{G}}$.

$$\mathscr{C} \underset{\mathsf{Cofree}_{\mathsf{G}}}{\overset{\mathsf{U}_{\mathsf{G}}}{\underset{\longrightarrow}{\overset{\longleftarrow}{\bot}}}} \mathsf{G}\text{-}\mathbf{Coalg}(\mathscr{C})$$

The action of $\mathsf{Cofree}_{\mathsf{G}}\ A = (\mathsf{G}_{\infty}\ A, \mathsf{tail}\ A)$ maps a tree to a $\mathsf{G}$-structure of subtrees. The counit $\epsilon = \mathsf{head}$ extracts the label of the root of a tree, and $\eta\ (A,a) = [\![a]\!]$ constructs a tree. The bijection instantiating (2.3) expresses that the tree for a given start state and a given state-transition function expressed as a coalgebra is uniquely determined by a mapping from states to observations:

$$f = \mathsf{head}\ B \cdot \mathsf{U}_{\mathsf{G}}\ g \iff \mathsf{Cofree}_{\mathsf{G}} f \cdot [\![a]\!] = g\ , \tag{2.7}$$

for all $f : \mathsf{U}_{\mathsf{G}}\ (A,a) \to B$ and $g : (A,a) \to \mathsf{Cofree}_{\mathsf{G}}\ B$.

Since $\mathsf{Cofree}_{\mathsf{G}}$ is a right adjoint, final coalgebras arise as a special case (RAPL): $(\nu\mathsf{G}, out) \cong \mathsf{Cofree}_{\mathsf{G}}\ 1$.

Conversely, cofree coalgebras can be implemented in terms of final coalgebras: $(\mathsf{T}\ B, \mathsf{tail}\ B)$ with $\mathsf{head}\ B : \mathsf{T}\ B \to B$ is a cofree $\mathsf{G}$-coalgebra if and only if $(\mathsf{T}\ B, \mathsf{head}\ B \vartriangle \mathsf{tail}\ B)$ is a final $\mathsf{G}_B$-coalgebra where $\mathsf{G}_B\ X = B \times \mathsf{G}\ X$. It suffices to show that $h : A \to \mathsf{T}\ B$ with $\mathsf{head}\ B \cdot h = hd$ is a $\mathsf{G}$-coalgebra homomorphism if and only if it is a $\mathsf{G}_B$-coalgebra homomorphism. The proof is standard, but instructive:

$$\begin{array}{ll} & \mathsf{head}\ B \cdot h = hd \ \wedge\ \mathsf{tail}\ B \cdot h = \mathsf{G}\ h \cdot tl \\ \iff & \{ \vartriangle \text{ is an isomorphism (2.6a)} \} \\ & \mathsf{head}\ B \cdot h \vartriangle \mathsf{tail}\ B \cdot h = hd \vartriangle \mathsf{G}\ h \cdot tl \\ \iff & \{ \text{product fusion (2.6b)} \} \\ & (\mathsf{head}\ B \vartriangle \mathsf{tail}\ B) \cdot h = hd \vartriangle \mathsf{G}\ h \cdot tl \\ \iff & \{ \text{definition of } \mathsf{G}_B \text{ and product fusion (2.6b)} \} \\ & (\mathsf{head}\ B \vartriangle \mathsf{tail}\ B) \cdot h = \mathsf{G}_B\ h \cdot (hd \vartriangle tl) \end{array}$$

Note that every $\mathsf{G}_B$-coalgebra is of the form $hd \vartriangle tl$, since $c = outl \cdot c \vartriangle outr \cdot c$. Consequently,

$$\mathsf{G}_{\infty}\ B \cong \nu X\ .\ B \times \mathsf{G}\ X\ . \tag{2.8}$$

This implies that $\mathsf{head}\ B \vartriangle \mathsf{tail}\ B$ is an isomorphism; we use $\mathsf{cons}\ B$ to denote its inverse. As an aside, (2.8) motivates the nomenclature: $\mathsf{G}_{\infty}\ B$ can be seen as the type of generalized streams—'generalized' because the 'tail' is a $\mathsf{G}$-structure of 'streams' rather than just a single one; we obtain standard streams for $\mathsf{G} = \mathsf{Id}$. □

***Conjugates*** At the heart of several of our core proofs are conjugate natural transformations [19]. Just as natural transformations relate functors, conjugates relate adjoint pairs of functors. Given the adjunctions $\mathsf{L} \dashv \mathsf{R} : \mathscr{C} \rightharpoonup \mathscr{D}$ and $\mathsf{L}' \dashv \mathsf{R}' : \mathscr{C}' \rightharpoonup \mathscr{D}'$, and functors $\mathsf{H} : \mathscr{C} \to \mathscr{C}'$ and $\mathsf{K} : \mathscr{D} \to \mathscr{D}'$, the natural transformations $\sigma : \mathsf{L}' \circ \mathsf{K} \dot{\to} \mathsf{H} \circ \mathsf{L}$ and $\tau : \mathsf{K} \circ \mathsf{R} \dot{\to} \mathsf{R}' \circ \mathsf{H}$ are *conjugates*, written $\sigma \dashv \tau$, if one of the equivalent equations

$$\lfloor \mathsf{H} f \cdot \sigma A \rfloor' = \tau B \cdot \mathsf{K} \lfloor f \rfloor \ , \tag{2.9a}$$

$$\mathsf{H} \lceil g \rceil \cdot \sigma A = \lceil \tau B \cdot \mathsf{K} g \rceil' \ , \tag{2.9b}$$

holds, for all $f : \mathsf{L}\, A \to B : \mathscr{C}$ and $g : A \to \mathsf{R}\, B : \mathscr{D}$. An important property is that each component uniquely determines the other.

## 3. Recursive Coalgebras

Hylomorphisms, or hylos for short, are solutions to a recursion scheme that captures the essence of *divide-and-conquer* algorithms. Such algorithms have three phases: first, a problem is broken into sub-problems by a coalgebra; second, sub-problems are recursively and independently turned into sub-solutions; and finally, sub-solutions are combined by an algebra to form a solution. The recursive call structure of the hylo is determined by the common base functor of the coalgebra and the algebra. Depending on the shape, hylomorphisms capture while-programs, binary-subdivision-schemes etc. In fact, practically any program can be cast into the hylo form [15]. However, there is no a priori guarantee that a solution exists for a hylo equation with a given coalgebra and algebra, let alone that such a solution is uniquely determined.

### 3.1 Basic Definitions

***Hylomorphisms*** Let $\mathsf{F} : \mathscr{C} \to \mathscr{C}$ be an endofunctor, let $(a, A)$ be an $\mathsf{F}$-algebra, and let $(C, c)$ be an $\mathsf{F}$-coalgebra. An arrow $h : A \leftarrow C$ is a *hylomorphism* (or algebra-from-coalgebra homomorphism), $h : (a, A) \leftarrowtail (C, c)$, if it satisfies

$$h = a \cdot \mathsf{F}\, h \cdot c \ . \tag{3.1}$$

The *control functor* $\mathsf{F}$ governs the recursive call structure. We use $(a, A) \leftarrowtail (C, c)$ or $(C, c) \rightarrowtail (a, A)$ to denote the set of all hylomorphisms that satisfy (3.1).

**Example 3.1.** The functor $(A + -)$ can be used to model tail recursion: a loop either terminates producing an $A$ value, or it goes through another iteration. Tail-recursive programs are captured by

$$h = (id \triangledown id) \cdot (A + h) \cdot c \iff h = (id \triangledown h) \cdot c \ ,$$

where $id \triangledown id : A + A \to A$ is the so-called *codiagonal*. □

Unlike algebra or coalgebra homomorphisms, hylomorphisms do *not* compose, so they do *not* form a category. However, they do compose with algebra and coalgebra homomorphisms.

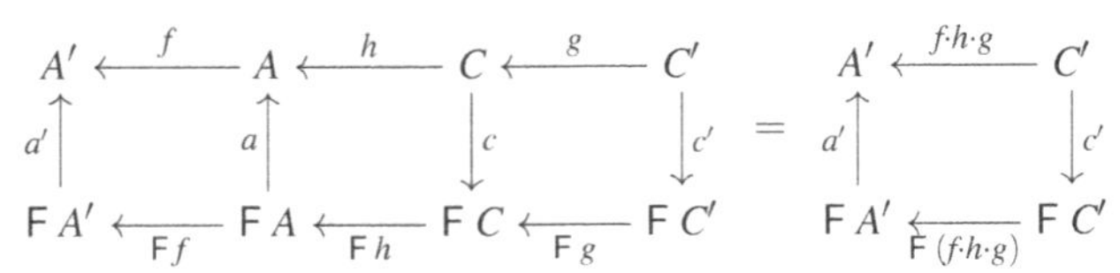


Thus, the assignment $((C, c), (a, A)) \mapsto ((C, c) \rightarrowtail (a, A))$ can be turned into a functor of type $(\mathsf{F}\text{-}\mathbf{Coalg}(\mathscr{C}))^{\mathsf{op}} \times \mathsf{F}\text{-}\mathbf{Alg}(\mathscr{C}) \to \mathbf{Set}$.

We are particularly interested in situations where (3.1) has a unique solution. In general, the algebra and coalgebra work hand-in-hand to achieve uniqueness. However, at the extreme, uniqueness can be shown by focusing on either the coalgebra or the algebra.

***Recursive Coalgebras*** A coalgebra $(C, c)$ is *recursive* (or algebra-initial) if for every algebra $(a, A)$ there is a *unique* hylo $(a, A) \leftarrowtail (C, c)$. We denote such hylos by $(\!| a \leftarrow c |\!)$ to emphasize the source of uniqueness. This notation is reminiscent of that of folds, since a recursive coalgebra provides a kind of initiality: post-composing a hylo with any algebra homomorphism $h : (a, A) \to (b, B)$ yields again a unique hylo, $h \cdot (\!| a \leftarrow c |\!) = (\!| b \leftarrow c |\!)$. The full subcategory of $\mathsf{F}\text{-}\mathbf{Coalg}(\mathscr{C})$ of recursive coalgebras is denoted $\mathsf{F}\text{-}\mathbf{Rec}(\mathscr{C})$.

**Example 3.2.** Lambek's Lemma states that the action of the initial algebra $(in, \mu\mathsf{F})$ has an inverse, which implies

$$h \cdot in = a \cdot \mathsf{F}\, h \iff h = a \cdot \mathsf{F}\, h \cdot in^{\circ} \ .$$

Consequently, $(\mu\mathsf{F}, in^{\circ})$ is recursive and $(\!| a |\!) = (\!| a \leftarrow in^{\circ} |\!)$. □

***Corecursive Algebras*** Dually, an algebra $(a, A)$ is *corecursive* (or coalgebra-final) if for every coalgebra $(C, c)$ there is a *unique* hylo $(a, A) \leftarrowtail (C, c)$. We denote such hylos by $[\![ a \leftarrow c ]\!]$ to emphasize the source of this uniqueness. The full subcategory of $\mathsf{F}\text{-}\mathbf{Alg}(\mathscr{C})$ of corecursive algebras is denoted $\mathsf{F}\text{-}\mathbf{Corec}(\mathscr{C})$.

For example, the algebras $(out^{\circ}, \nu\mathsf{G})$ and $(\mathsf{cons}\, B, \mathsf{G}_{\infty}\, B)$ are corecursive (recall that $\mathsf{cons}\, B = (\mathsf{head}\, B \vartriangle \mathsf{tail}\, B)^{\circ}$).

With these definitions in place, we proceed by describing two fundamental techniques for establishing uniqueness: Eppendahl's Basic Lemma [7], which we call the *rolling rule*, and a symmetric version of Proposition 12 of [6], which we call the *conjugate rule*. Indeed, we will be careful to emphasize symmetry, even though our main focus is on recursive coalgebras.

### 3.2 Rolling Rule

We now consider algebras and coalgebras where *two* functors compose to create the base functor. The rolling rule allows us to swap the underlying functors, and establishes a means of deriving new recursive coalgebras and corecursive algebras from old ones. We start with the situation described in the following diagram.

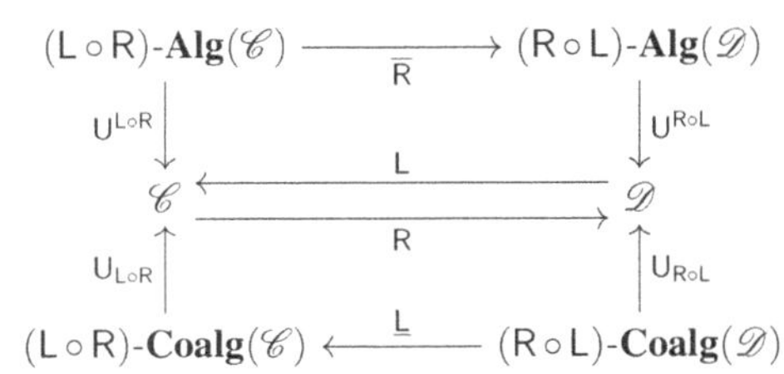

(3.2a)

Since the base functors are compositions, the functor $\mathsf{L}$ (not necessarily adjoint) has a trivial colifting to categories of coalgebras. Recall that we need a natural transformation of type $\mathsf{L} \circ (\mathsf{R} \circ \mathsf{L}) \dot{\to} (\mathsf{L} \circ \mathsf{R}) \circ \mathsf{L}$; the identity will do nicely: $\underline{\mathsf{L}} = \mathsf{L}_{id}$, and, likewise $\overline{\mathsf{R}} = \mathsf{R}^{id}$.

The *rolling rule* establishes an adjunction-like correspondence between two types of hylomorphisms.

**Theorem 3.1** (Rolling Rule)**.** *Assuming the data in* (3.2a)*, there is a bijection between the sets of hylos*

$$\underline{\mathsf{L}}\, (C, c) \rightarrowtail (a, A) \ \cong \ (C, c) \rightarrowtail \overline{\mathsf{R}}\, (a, A) \ , \tag{3.2b}$$

*natural in* $(C, c) : (\mathsf{R} \circ \mathsf{L})\text{-}\mathbf{Coalg}(\mathscr{D})$ *and* $(a, A) : (\mathsf{L} \circ \mathsf{R})\text{-}\mathbf{Alg}(\mathscr{C})$.

*Proof.* The correspondence is witnessed by the functions $\lfloor - \rfloor$ and $\lceil - \rceil$, defined $\lfloor x \rfloor = \mathsf{R}\, x \cdot c$ and $\lceil y \rceil = a \cdot \mathsf{L}\, y$. These trivially form a bijection between fixed-points of $\lceil \lfloor - \rfloor \rceil$ and fixed-points of $\lfloor \lceil - \rceil \rfloor$:

$$x = \lceil \lfloor x \rfloor \rceil \iff y = \lfloor \lceil y \rceil \rfloor \ ,$$

where $y = \lfloor x \rfloor$ and $x = \lceil y \rceil$. Unrolling the definitions we obtain

$$x = a \cdot \mathsf{L}\, (\mathsf{R}\, x) \cdot \mathsf{L}\, c \iff y = \mathsf{R}\, a \cdot \mathsf{R}\, (\mathsf{L}\, y) \cdot c \ ,$$

which shows that $x : \underline{\mathsf{L}}\, (C, c) \rightarrowtail (a, A)$ and $y : (C, c) \rightarrowtail \overline{\mathsf{R}}\, (a, A)$. The proof of naturality is straightforward. □

The 1-1 correspondence (3.2b) allows us to conclude that $\underline{\mathsf{L}}\, (C, c)$ is recursive if $(C, c)$ is. Thus, the colifting $\underline{\mathsf{L}}$ preserves recursiveness, and, dually, the lifting $\overline{\mathsf{R}}$ preserves corecursiveness.

$$\underline{\mathsf{L}} : (\mathsf{L} \circ \mathsf{R})\text{-}\mathbf{Rec}(\mathscr{C}) \leftarrow (\mathsf{R} \circ \mathsf{L})\text{-}\mathbf{Rec}(\mathscr{D}) \tag{3.3a}$$

$$\overline{\mathsf{R}} : (\mathsf{L} \circ \mathsf{R})\text{-}\mathbf{Corec}(\mathscr{C}) \to (\mathsf{R} \circ \mathsf{L})\text{-}\mathbf{Corec}(\mathscr{D}) \tag{3.3b}$$

### 3.3 Final Recursive Coalgebras

An important special case of the rolling rule is where we substitute $\mathsf{L}, \mathsf{R} := \mathsf{F}, \mathsf{Id}$. We use this to prove the following

**Theorem 3.2.** *The recursive coalgebra* $(C, c)$ *is final if and only if* $c$ *is an isomorphism.*

The unique $\mathsf{F}$-coalgebra homomorphism from the recursive coalgebra $(C, c)$ to the final recursive coalgebra is written $[\![c]\!]_*$, which emphasizes that this unfolds into a *recursive* coalgebra.

*Proof.* "$\Longrightarrow$": The inverse of $c$ is the unique coalgebra homomorphism $c^\circ = [\![\mathsf{F}\, c]\!]_*$—using the rolling rule we know that $\mathsf{F}\, c$ is recursive if $c$ is recursive (3.3a).

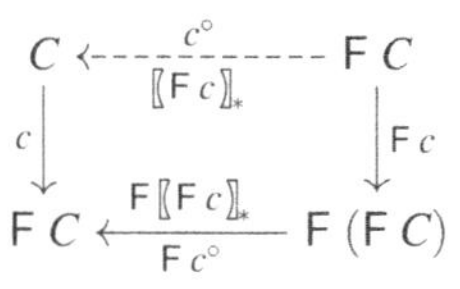

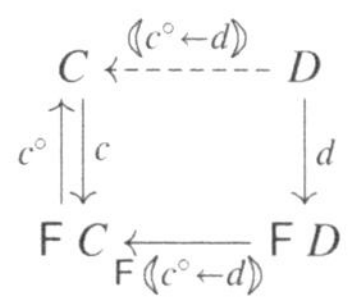

Now, $c^\circ \cdot c = id$ because $(C, c)$ is final. Conversely, $c \cdot c^\circ = \mathsf{F}\, c^\circ \cdot \mathsf{F}\, c = id$, see diagram on the left above.

"$\Longleftarrow$": if $c$ is an iso, then $(\!|c^\circ \leftarrow d|\!)$ is the unique coalgebra homomorphism to $(C, c)$ from the recursive coalgebra $(D, d)$, see diagram on the right above. Hence, $(C, c)$ is final. □

**Corollary 3.3.** *The final recursive* $\mathsf{F}$*-coalgebra is* $(\mu\mathsf{F}, in^\circ)$.

Corollary (3.3) is an important result as it allows us to freely mix folds $(\!|a|\!)$ as consumers with recursive unfolds $[\![c]\!]_*$ as producers.

### 3.4 Conjugate Rule

The rolling rule can only be applied when a pair of functors form the base functor of the (co)algebra. We can lift this restriction to simple endo-functors $\mathsf{F} : \mathscr{C} \to \mathscr{C}$ and $\mathsf{G} : \mathscr{D} \to \mathscr{D}$ when there is an adjunction between $\mathscr{C}$ and $\mathscr{D}$. Given $\mathsf{L} \dashv \mathsf{R} : \mathscr{C} \rightharpoonup \mathscr{D}$, and conjugates

$$\sigma : \mathsf{L} \circ \mathsf{G} \dot{\to} \mathsf{F} \circ \mathsf{L} \dashv \tau : \mathsf{G} \circ \mathsf{R} \dot{\to} \mathsf{R} \circ \mathsf{F} \ ,$$

we have the following situation.

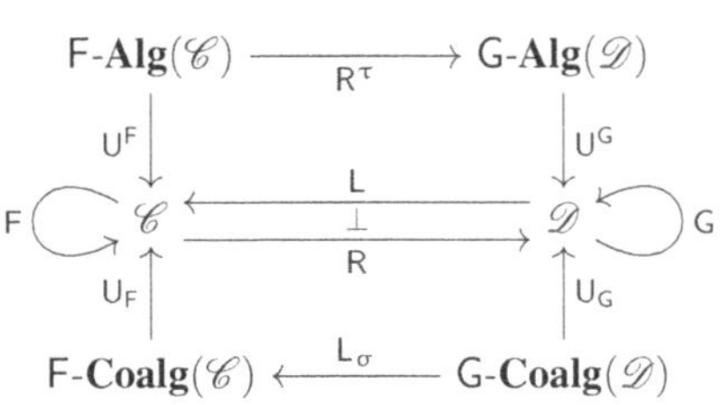

(3.4a)

Using the conjugates we colift $\mathsf{L}$ to categories of coalgebras (2.2) and lift $\mathsf{R}$ to categories of algebras (2.1).

The *conjugate rule* uses an adjunction to establish a correspondence between hylomorphisms and, unlike the rolling rule, does not require (co)algebras that involve the composition of functors.

**Theorem 3.4** (Conjugate Rule)**.** *Assuming the data in* (3.4a)*, there is a bijection between the sets of conjugate hylomorphisms*

$$\mathsf{L}_\sigma\,(C, c) \rightarrowtail (a, A) \ \cong\ (C, c) \rightarrowtail \mathsf{R}^\tau\,(a, A) \ , \qquad (3.4b)$$

*that is natural in* $(C, c) : \mathsf{G}\text{-}\mathbf{Coalg}(\mathscr{D})$ *and* $(a, A) : \mathsf{F}\text{-}\mathbf{Alg}(\mathscr{C})$.

Using the conjugates is a natural choice: just as adjoint functors determine one another (up to $\cong$), so too do conjugates. It is this property that allows us to move between algebras and coalgebras.

*Proof.* We have to show

$$x = a \cdot \mathsf{F}\, x \cdot \mathsf{L}_\sigma\, c \iff \lfloor x \rfloor = \mathsf{R}^\tau\, a \cdot \mathsf{G}\, \lfloor x \rfloor \cdot c \ , \qquad (3.4c)$$

where $\lfloor - \rfloor$ is the left adjunct of $\mathsf{L} \dashv \mathsf{R}$.

$$\begin{aligned}
& x = a \cdot \mathsf{F}\, x \cdot \mathsf{L}_\sigma\, c \ :\ A \leftarrow \mathsf{L}\, C \\
\iff & \ \{ \text{ definition of colifting (2.2) } \} \\
& x = a \cdot \mathsf{F}\, x \cdot \sigma\, C \cdot \mathsf{L}\, c \\
\iff & \ \{ \ \lfloor - \rfloor \text{ and } \lceil - \rceil \text{ are isomorphisms (2.3) } \} \\
& \lfloor x \rfloor = \lfloor a \cdot \mathsf{F}\, x \cdot \sigma\, C \cdot \mathsf{L}\, c \rfloor \\
\iff & \ \{ \ \lfloor - \rfloor \text{ is natural (2.4a) } \} \\
& \lfloor x \rfloor = \mathsf{R}\, a \cdot \lfloor \mathsf{F}\, x \cdot \sigma\, C \rfloor \cdot c \\
\iff & \ \{ \ \sigma \dashv \tau \text{ conjugates (2.9a) } \} \\
& \lfloor x \rfloor = \mathsf{R}\, a \cdot \tau\, A \cdot \mathsf{G}\, \lfloor x \rfloor \cdot c \\
\iff & \ \{ \text{ definition of lifting (2.1) } \} \\
& \lfloor x \rfloor = \mathsf{R}^\tau\, a \cdot \mathsf{G}\, \lfloor x \rfloor \cdot c \ :\ \mathsf{R}\, A \leftarrow C \ .
\end{aligned}$$

Naturality of (3.4b) is inherited from the underling adjunction. □

The 1-1 correspondence (3.4b) between what we call *conjugate hylomorphisms* implies that $\mathsf{L}_\sigma\,(C, c)$ is recursive if $(C, c)$ is. Thus, $\mathsf{L}_\sigma$ preserves recursiveness; dually, $\mathsf{R}^\tau$ preserves corecursiveness.

$$\mathsf{L}_\sigma : \mathsf{F}\text{-}\mathbf{Rec}(\mathscr{C}) \leftarrow \mathsf{G}\text{-}\mathbf{Rec}(\mathscr{D}) \qquad (3.5a)$$

$$\mathsf{R}^\tau : \mathsf{F}\text{-}\mathbf{Corec}(\mathscr{C}) \to \mathsf{G}\text{-}\mathbf{Corec}(\mathscr{D}) \qquad (3.5b)$$

Moreover, using our notation for hylos, (3.4c) gives:

$$\lfloor (\!| a \leftarrow \mathsf{L}_\sigma\, c |\!) \rfloor = (\!| \mathsf{R}^\tau\, a \leftarrow c |\!) \ , \qquad (3.6a)$$

$$\lceil [\![ \mathsf{R}^\tau\, a \leftarrow c ]\!] \rceil = [\![ a \leftarrow \mathsf{L}_\sigma\, c ]\!] \ . \qquad (3.6b)$$

#### 3.4.1 Data and Control Functors

The conjugate rule involves six entities—four functors and two natural transformations—which can be a little daunting. When the adjunction $\mathsf{L} \dashv \mathsf{R}$ is fixed, what remains is the choice of functors $\mathsf{F}$ and $\mathsf{G}$, and the conjugate $\sigma \dashv \tau$. Often one of the functors can be identified as a *data functor* as it is either part of the input or output type of a hylo. Then there is a canonical choice for the other functor, the *control functor* that governs the recursive call structure.

Focusing on the input, the framework of the conjugate rule can be instantiated with the data functor $\mathsf{G} := \mathsf{D}$, and the control functor $\mathsf{F} := \mathsf{C} = \mathsf{L} \circ \mathsf{D} \circ \mathsf{R}$ with the following conjugate pair:

$$\sigma = \mathsf{L} \circ \mathsf{D} \circ \eta : \mathsf{L} \circ \mathsf{D} \dot{\to} \mathsf{C} \circ \mathsf{L} \ \dashv\ \tau = \eta \circ \mathsf{D} \circ \mathsf{R} : \mathsf{D} \circ \mathsf{R} \dot{\to} \mathsf{R} \circ \mathsf{C} \ .$$

The control functor $\mathsf{C}$ is obtained by going round in a circle, see Diagram (3.4a). It is canonical in the following sense: any hylo equation $x = a \cdot \mathsf{C}'\, x \cdot \mathsf{L}_{\sigma'}\, c$ with $\sigma' : \mathsf{L} \circ \mathsf{D} \dot{\to} \mathsf{C}' \circ \mathsf{L}$ is equivalent to one that uses the canonical control functor [13].

For this particular instance the conjugate rule can be simplified: using (2.5) it is straightforward to show that $\mathsf{R}^\tau\, a = \lfloor a \rfloor$ and $\mathsf{C}\, x \cdot \mathsf{L}_\sigma\, c = \mathsf{L}\,(\mathsf{D}\, \lfloor x \rfloor \cdot c)$. Thus, (3.4c) becomes:

$$x = a \cdot \mathsf{L}\,(\mathsf{D}\, \lfloor x \rfloor \cdot c) \iff \lfloor x \rfloor = \lfloor a \rfloor \cdot \mathsf{D}\, \lfloor x \rfloor \cdot c \ . \qquad (3.7)$$

Dually, we can focus on the output. Then the roles of $\mathsf{F}$ and $\mathsf{G}$ are interchanged: we instantiate the conjugate rule to $\mathsf{F}, \mathsf{G} := \mathsf{D}, \mathsf{C}$ with the canonical control functor $\mathsf{C} = \mathsf{R} \circ \mathsf{D} \circ \mathsf{L}$, and conjugates:

$$\sigma = \epsilon \circ \mathsf{D} \circ \mathsf{L} : \mathsf{L} \circ \mathsf{C} \dot{\to} \mathsf{D} \circ \mathsf{L} \ \dashv\ \tau = \mathsf{R} \circ \mathsf{D} \circ \epsilon : \mathsf{C} \circ \mathsf{R} \dot{\to} \mathsf{R} \circ \mathsf{D} \ .$$

To illustrate the versatility of the conjugate rule we instantiate the rule to the adjunctions discussed in Section 2.2. Since we focus on recursive coalgebras, we consider instances of the equation

$$x = a \cdot \mathsf{F}\, x \cdot \mathsf{L}_\sigma\, c$$

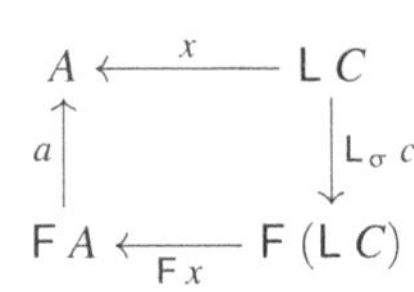

, (3.8)

and of this equation, which builds on the canonical control functor:

$$x = a \cdot \mathsf{L}\,(\mathsf{D}\,\lfloor x \rfloor \cdot c) \qquad \begin{array}{ccc} A & \xleftarrow{\;x\;} & \mathsf{L}\,C \\ {\scriptstyle a}\uparrow & & \downarrow{\scriptstyle \mathsf{L}\,c} \\ \mathsf{L}\,(\mathsf{D}\,(\mathsf{R}\,A)) & \xleftarrow[\mathsf{L}\,(\mathsf{D}\,\lfloor x \rfloor)]{} & \mathsf{L}\,(\mathsf{D}\,C) \end{array} \quad . \tag{3.9}$$

We already know that both equations have unique solutions if $c$ is recursive. We shall see that each of the adjunctions induces a useful recursion scheme. In fact, almost every structured recursion scheme seems to arise this way (an obvious exception being schemes that make use of the rolling rule, but that do not involve adjoint functors). The reader is invited to dualize.

### 3.4.2 Instance: Hylo-shift Law: $\mathsf{Id} \dashv \mathsf{Id}$

As a warm-up, consider the adjunction $\mathsf{Id} \dashv \mathsf{Id}$. For this trivial case, a conjugate pair is given by a natural transformation $\alpha : \mathsf{G} \dot{\to} \mathsf{F}$.

$$\alpha : \mathsf{Id} \circ \mathsf{G} \dot{\to} \mathsf{F} \circ \mathsf{Id} \quad \dashv \quad \alpha : \mathsf{G} \circ \mathsf{Id} \dot{\to} \mathsf{Id} \circ \mathsf{F}$$

Then (3.6a) specializes to the so-called *hylo-shift law* [23]:

$$(\!| a \leftarrow \alpha\, C \cdot c |\!) = (\!| a \cdot \alpha\, A \leftarrow c |\!) \ , \tag{3.10}$$

which allows us to shift a natural transformation between the algebra and coalgebra part of a hylomorphism.

### 3.4.3 Instance: Mutual Recursion: $\Delta \dashv (\times) : \mathscr{C} \times \mathscr{C} \rightharpoonup \mathscr{C}$

Mutual recursion describes the situation where a number of functions rely on one another in calculating their results.

**Example 3.3** (Minimax). An example of mutual recursion is the minimax algorithm. Consider a two-player game where starting at the root of a finite tree, the players take it in turn to choose whether the left or right branch of the tree is taken. The final score is the sum of all the nodes that have been visited before the final leaf. The task of one player is to maximize this score, while the other player tries to minimize it. The two mutually recursive functions are:

$$\begin{array}{l} \mathit{maximize}, \mathit{minimize} :: \mathit{Tree} \to \mathbb{Z} \\ \mathit{maximize}\ (\mathit{Empty}) \qquad = 0 \\ \mathit{maximize}\ (\mathit{Node}\ l\ v\ r) = v + (\mathit{minimize}\ l\ `\mathit{max}`\ \mathit{minimize}\ r) \\ \mathit{minimize}\ \ (\mathit{Empty}) \qquad = 0 \\ \mathit{minimize}\ \ (\mathit{Node}\ l\ v\ r) = v + (\mathit{maximize}\ l\ `\mathit{min}`\ \mathit{maximize}\ r) \ . \end{array}$$

These functions rely symmetrically on each other's results before proceeding to the next step. □

**Example 3.4** (Perfect trees). Another example of mutual recursion is where the dependence is asymmetric. Consider the function *perfect*, which checks to see whether a tree is perfectly balanced.

$$\begin{array}{l} \mathit{perfect} :: \mathit{Tree} \to \mathbb{B} \\ \mathit{perfect}\ (\mathit{Empty}) \qquad = \mathit{True} \\ \mathit{perfect}\ (\mathit{Node}\ l\ v\ r) = \mathit{perfect}\ l \wedge \mathit{perfect}\ r \wedge \mathit{height}\ l == \mathit{height}\ r \\ \mathit{height} :: \mathit{Tree} \to \mathbb{Z} \\ \mathit{height}\ (\mathit{Empty}) \qquad = 0 \\ \mathit{height}\ (\mathit{Node}\ l\ v\ r) = 1 + (\mathit{height}\ l)\ `\mathit{max}`\ (\mathit{height}\ r) \end{array}$$

The calculation of *perfect* depends on *height*, but the result of *height* is independent of *perfect*. □

In both examples, the mutually recursive functions have the same source type and both use the coalgebra $in^{\circ}$, which suggests instantiating the conjugate rule to the adjunction $\Delta \dashv (\times)$.

***Mutu-hylo*** When we pick the canonical control functor, we obtain mutually recursive hylos, or *mutu-hylos* for short. Given $x = (x_1, x_2)$ and $a = (a_1, a_2)$, Equation (3.9) specializes to

$$x = a \cdot \Delta\,(\mathsf{D}\,\lfloor x \rfloor \cdot c) \iff \left\{ \begin{array}{l} x_1 = a_1 \cdot \mathsf{D}\,(x_1 \vartriangle x_2) \cdot c \ : \ A_1 \leftarrow C \\ x_2 = a_2 \cdot \mathsf{D}\,(x_1 \vartriangle x_2) \cdot c \ : \ A_2 \leftarrow C \ . \end{array} \right.$$

The algebras $a_1 : \mathsf{D}\,(A_1 \times A_2) \to A_1$ and $a_2 : \mathsf{D}\,(A_1 \times A_2) \to A_2$ can avail themselves of the results of both recursive calls. The coalgebra has to be the same, and it must be recursive.

A special case of the mutu-hylo is the *zygo-hylo*, where only one of the algebras is dependent on both results: $a_2 := a_2' \cdot \mathsf{D}\,\mathit{outr}$.

***Banana-split*** Here is an amusing variation on the theme. The diagonal functor $\Delta$ satisfies a simple property: $\Delta \circ \mathsf{D} = (\mathsf{D} \times \mathsf{D}) \circ \Delta$. Let us instantiate the conjugate rule to $\mathsf{F}, \mathsf{G} := \mathsf{D} \times \mathsf{D}, \mathsf{D}$ with

$$\mathit{id} : \Delta \circ \mathsf{D} = (\mathsf{D} \times \mathsf{D}) \circ \Delta \quad \dashv \quad \tau : \mathsf{D} \circ (\times) \dot{\to} (\times) \circ (\mathsf{D} \times \mathsf{D}) \ .$$

Note that $\tau = \mathsf{D}\,\mathit{outl} \vartriangle \mathsf{D}\,\mathit{outr}$. Then Equation (3.8) specializes to

$$x = a \cdot (\mathsf{D} \times \mathsf{D})\, x \cdot \Delta_{\mathit{id}}\, c \iff \left\{ \begin{array}{l} x_1 = a_1 \cdot \mathsf{D}\, x_1 \cdot c \ : \ A_1 \leftarrow C \\ x_2 = a_2 \cdot \mathsf{D}\, x_2 \cdot c \ : \ A_2 \leftarrow C \ . \end{array} \right.$$

We obtain a system of two independent functions, which appears unexciting. However, we can invoke (3.6a), which gives us

$$(\!| a_1 \leftarrow c |\!) \vartriangle (\!| a_2 \leftarrow c |\!) = (\!| a_1 \cdot \mathsf{D}\,\mathit{outl} \vartriangle a_2 \cdot \mathsf{D}\,\mathit{outr} \leftarrow c |\!) \ ,$$

as $(\times)^{\tau}\,(a_1, a_2) = a_1 \cdot \mathsf{D}\,\mathit{outl} \vartriangle a_2 \cdot \mathsf{D}\,\mathit{outr}$. We obtain a generalization of the-called *banana-split law* [4], an important program optimization that replaces a double recursion by a single one. (The law is called 'banana-split', because the fold brackets look like bananas and $\vartriangle$ is pronounced 'split'.)

### 3.4.4 Instance: Accumulators: $- \times P \dashv (-)^P : \mathscr{C} \rightharpoonup \mathscr{C}$

A useful form of recursion is where an additional parameter, an accumulator, is passed in for use by the algebra.

**Example 3.5** (Append). Our first example of recursion with a parameter is in the definition of *cat*, which takes two lists and appends them together by structural induction on the first list.

$$\begin{array}{l} \mathit{cat} :: ([a], [a]) \to [a] \\ \mathit{cat}\ ([\,], \quad \mathit{ys}) = \mathit{ys} \\ \mathit{cat}\ (x : \mathit{xs}, \mathit{ys}) = x : \mathit{cat}\ (\mathit{xs}, \mathit{ys}) \end{array}$$

The second parameter is not changed during the recursion, and is simply passed through until the base case is reached. □

**Example 3.6** (Tree flattening). A slightly more elaborate example is an efficient version of turning a tree of values into a list. The naive version flattens both subtrees independently and appends the results. Since appending is of linear complexity in its first argument, the following variant is more desirable.

$$\begin{array}{l} \mathit{flattenCat} :: (\mathit{Tree}, [\mathbb{Z}]) \to [\mathbb{Z}] \\ \mathit{flattenCat}\ (\mathit{Empty}, \quad \mathit{xs}) = \mathit{xs} \\ \mathit{flattenCat}\ (\mathit{Node}\ l\ x\ r, \mathit{xs}) = \mathit{flattenCat}\ (l, x : \mathit{flattenCat}\ (r, \mathit{xs})) \end{array}$$

The function spawns off two new invocations of itself, but only in the second does the parameter $\mathit{xs}$ remain unchanged. □

The handling of parameters is a case for the curry adjunction.

***Varying parameters*** Using the canonical control functor, Equation (3.9) specializes to the *accu-hylo*

$$x = a \cdot ((\mathsf{D}\,(\Lambda\, x) \cdot c) \times P) \ : \ A \leftarrow C \times P \ .$$

This models the situation where the parameter varies during the recursion; $a : \mathsf{D}\,(A^P) \times P \to A$ receives a $\mathsf{D}$-structure of curried variants of $x$, and can supply each of them with a different argument.

***Constant parameters*** The case where the parameter is passed unchanged can be modelled using the so-called *strength* of a functor:

$$\sigma : (\times P) \circ \mathsf{D} \dot{\to} \mathsf{D} \circ (\times P) \quad \dashv \quad \tau : \mathsf{D} \circ (-)^P \dot{\to} (-)^P \circ \mathsf{D} \ .$$

The strength $\sigma\, A : \mathsf{D}\, A \times P \to \mathsf{D}\,(A \times P)$ broadcasts a value across a structure. (Every endofunctor on **Set** has a canonical strength.) For this data, Equation (3.8) specializes to

$$x = a \cdot \mathsf{D}\, x \cdot \sigma\, C \cdot (c \times P) \quad : \quad A \leftarrow C \times P \ .$$

The strength copies the parameter to each of the recursive calls.

### 3.4.5 Instance: Course-of-Values Recursion: $\mathsf{U_G} \dashv \mathsf{Cofree_G}$

The one remaining adjunction introduced in Section 2.2 that we have not yet discussed is $\mathsf{U_G} \dashv \mathsf{Cofree_G}$. It turns out that this instance gives us *course-of-values recursion*. We postpone a discussion of interesting programming examples until Section 4, where we look at various dynamic programming algorithms.

This instance is more challenging as it involves coalgebras over coalgebras! Consider the categories involved.

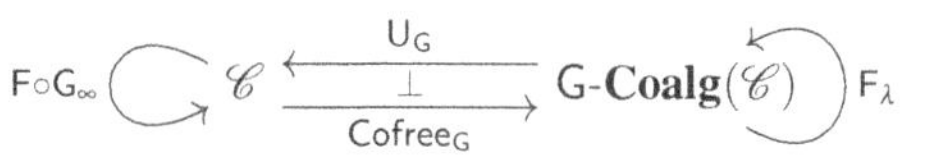


The data functor is now a functor over $\mathsf{G}$-**Coalg**($\mathscr{C}$), for example, the colifting $\mathsf{F}_\lambda$ where $\lambda : \mathsf{F} \circ \mathsf{G} \dot{\to} \mathsf{G} \circ \mathsf{F}$; the corresponding canonical control functor is $\mathsf{U_G} \circ \mathsf{F}_\lambda \circ \mathsf{Cofree_G} = \mathsf{F} \circ \mathsf{U_G} \circ \mathsf{Cofree_G} = \mathsf{F} \circ \mathsf{G}_\infty$. For this data, Equation (3.9) specializes to

$$\begin{aligned} & x = a \cdot \mathsf{U_G}\,(\mathsf{F}_\lambda\, \lfloor x \rfloor \cdot c) \quad : \quad A \leftarrow \mathsf{U_G}\,(C,d) \\ \iff & \quad \{\ \mathsf{U_G} \circ \mathsf{F}_\lambda = \mathsf{F} \circ \mathsf{U_G}\ \} \\ & x = a \cdot \mathsf{F}\,(\mathsf{U_G}\, \lfloor x \rfloor) \cdot \mathsf{U_G}\, c \quad : \quad A \leftarrow \mathsf{U_G}\,(C,d) \\ \iff & \quad \{\ \lfloor x \rfloor = \mathsf{Cofree_G}\, x \cdot [\![ d ]\!]\, (2.7) \text{ and definition of } \mathsf{U_G}\ \} \\ & x = a \cdot \mathsf{F}\,(\mathsf{G}_\infty\, x \cdot [\![ d ]\!]) \cdot c \quad : \quad A \leftarrow C \ , \end{aligned}$$

where $a : \mathsf{F}\,(\mathsf{G}_\infty\, A) \to A$ and $c : (C,d) \to \mathsf{F}_\lambda\,(C,d)$. The coalgebra $c$ lives in $\mathsf{F}_\lambda$-**Coalg**($\mathsf{G}$-**Coalg**($\mathscr{C}$)); it is an $\mathsf{F}$-coalgebra that is simultaneously a $\mathsf{G}$-coalgebra homomorphism. If we wish to apply this instance of the conjugate rule, we have to ensure that $((C,d),c)$ is a recursive $\mathsf{F}_\lambda$-coalgebra. The following lemma shows that $\mathsf{F}_\lambda$-recursiveness is actually a weaker notion than $\mathsf{F}$-recursiveness.

**Lemma 3.5.** *Let $\mathscr{D}$ be a full subcategory of $\mathsf{G}$-**Coalg**($\mathscr{C}$), let $\mathsf{F}_\lambda : \mathscr{D} \to \mathscr{D}$, and let $((C,d),c) : \mathsf{F}_\lambda$-**Coalg**($\mathscr{D}$). Then*

$$(C,c) : \mathsf{F}\text{-}\mathbf{Rec}(\mathscr{C}) \quad \Longrightarrow \quad ((C,d),c) : \mathsf{F}_\lambda\text{-}\mathbf{Rec}(\mathscr{D}) \ .$$

*Proof.* We have to show that the equation in $h$

$$h = a \cdot \mathsf{F}\, h \cdot c \quad : \quad (A,b) \leftarrow (C,d) \tag{3.11}$$

has a unique solution for each $\mathsf{F}_\lambda$-algebra $(a,(A,b))$. (An $\mathsf{F}_\lambda$-algebra is also known as a $\lambda$-bialgebra; $\mathsf{F}_\lambda$-coalgebras have been called $\lambda$-dicoalgebras [6].) If $(C,c)$ is a recursive $\mathsf{F}$-coalgebra, we know that (3.11) has a unique solution in $\mathscr{C}$. Since $\mathscr{D}$ is a full subcategory of $\mathsf{G}$-**Coalg**($\mathscr{C}$), it suffices to show that $h$ is a $\mathsf{G}$-coalgebra homomorphism of type $(A,b) \leftarrow (C,d)$.

$$\begin{aligned} & b \cdot h \\ = & \quad \{\ h \text{ solves } (3.11)\ \} \\ & b \cdot a \cdot \mathsf{F}\, h \cdot c \\ = & \quad \{\ a : \mathsf{F}_\lambda\,(A,b) \to (A,b)\ \} \\ & \mathsf{G}\, a \cdot \lambda\, A \cdot \mathsf{F}\, b \cdot \mathsf{F}\, h \cdot c \end{aligned} \qquad \begin{aligned} & \mathsf{G}\, h \cdot d \\ = & \quad \{\ h \text{ solves } (3.11)\ \} \\ & \mathsf{G}\, a \cdot \mathsf{G}\,(\mathsf{F}\, h) \cdot \mathsf{G}\, c \cdot d \\ = & \quad \{\ c : (C,d) \to \mathsf{F}_\lambda\,(C,d)\ \} \\ & \mathsf{G}\, a \cdot \mathsf{G}\,(\mathsf{F}\, h) \cdot \lambda\, C \cdot \mathsf{F}\, d \cdot c \\ = & \quad \{\ \lambda \text{ is natural}\ \} \\ & \mathsf{G}\, a \cdot \lambda\, A \cdot \mathsf{F}\,(\mathsf{G}\, h) \cdot \mathsf{F}\, d \cdot c \ . \end{aligned}$$

Since $x = \mathsf{G}\, a \cdot \lambda\, A \cdot \mathsf{F}\, x \cdot c$ has a unique solution as $c$ is recursive, we can conclude that $b \cdot h = \mathsf{G}\, h \cdot d$. □

Combining the conjugate rule and Lemma 3.5 we obtain

**Corollary 3.6.** *Let $((C,d),c)$ be a $\mathsf{F}_\lambda$-coalgebra, then*

$$(C,c) : \mathsf{F}\text{-}\mathbf{Rec}(\mathscr{C}) \quad \Longrightarrow \quad (C, \mathsf{F}\,[\![ d ]\!] \cdot c) : (\mathsf{F} \circ \mathsf{G}_\infty)\text{-}\mathbf{Rec}(\mathscr{C}) \ .$$

An important special case arises if we identify $\mathsf{F}$ and $\mathsf{G}$, setting $\mathsf{F} := \mathsf{G}$ and $\lambda = id : \mathsf{F} \circ \mathsf{F} \dot{\to} \mathsf{F} \circ \mathsf{F}$. Since a $\mathsf{G}$-coalgebra $c : C \to \mathsf{G}\, C$ is also a $\mathsf{G}$-coalgebra homomorphism $c : (C,c) \to \mathsf{G}_{id}\,(C,c)$, the nested coalgebra $((C,c),c)$ is a $\mathsf{G}_{id}$-coalgebra. For this special case we can further simplify Equation (3.9) to

$$x = a \cdot \mathsf{G}\,(\mathsf{G}_\infty\, x \cdot [\![ c ]\!]) \cdot c \quad : \quad A \leftarrow C \ . \tag{3.12}$$

Operationally, $\mathsf{G}\,[\![ c ]\!] \cdot c = \mathsf{tail}\, C \cdot [\![ c ]\!]$ builds a table of all reachable arguments of $x$, excluding the current one. The hylomorphism $x$ is then recursively applied to all of these, making the results available to the algebra $a : \mathsf{G}\,(\mathsf{G}_\infty\, A) \to A$. In other words, $a$ can access the entire computational history, implementing *course-of-values recursion*. Incidentally, it may seem somewhat odd that a potentially infinite structure is used for tabulation, even though we know that $c$ is recursive; we come back to this point in Section 5.4.

***Efficiency*** Equation (3.12) specifies the notion of course-of-values recursion. However, it does not serve as a blue-print for an implementation, as it realizes the naive recursive definition, which typically leads to an exponential running time. A first step towards an efficient implementation is to define $x$ in terms of its conjugate: $x = \mathsf{head}\, A \cdot \lfloor x \rfloor$ (2.7) where $\lfloor x \rfloor = \lfloor a \rfloor \cdot \mathsf{G}\, \lfloor x \rfloor \cdot c$ (3.7). The conjugate $\lfloor x \rfloor : (C,c) \to (\mathsf{G}_\infty\, A, \mathsf{tail}\, A)$ builds an entire memo-table bottom-up using $\lfloor a \rfloor = \mathsf{G}_\infty\, a \cdot [\![ \mathsf{G}\,(\mathsf{tail}\, A) ]\!]$. This is a vast improvement, but we can do better still, avoiding the costly $\mathsf{G}_\infty\, a$. Using the fact that $\lfloor x \rfloor$ is a $\mathsf{G}$-coalgebra homomorphism, we reason

$$\begin{aligned} & \lfloor x \rfloor = \lfloor a \rfloor \cdot \mathsf{G}\, \lfloor x \rfloor \cdot c \ \wedge\ \mathsf{tail}\, A \cdot \lfloor x \rfloor = \mathsf{G}\, \lfloor x \rfloor \cdot c \\ \Longrightarrow & \quad \{\ \text{Leibniz's law and } \mathsf{head}\, A \cdot \lfloor a \rfloor = a\ (2.7)\ \} \\ & \mathsf{head}\, A \cdot \lfloor x \rfloor = a \cdot \mathsf{G}\, \lfloor x \rfloor \cdot c \ \wedge\ \mathsf{tail}\, A \cdot \lfloor x \rfloor = \mathsf{G}\, \lfloor x \rfloor \cdot c \\ \iff & \quad \{\ \vartriangle \text{ is an isomorphism } (2.6\text{a})\ \} \\ & \mathsf{head}\, A \cdot \lfloor x \rfloor \vartriangle \mathsf{tail}\, A \cdot \lfloor x \rfloor = a \cdot \mathsf{G}\, \lfloor x \rfloor \cdot c \vartriangle \mathsf{G}\, \lfloor x \rfloor \cdot c \\ \iff & \quad \{\ \text{product fusion } (2.6\text{b})\ \} \\ & (\mathsf{head}\, A \vartriangle \mathsf{tail}\, A) \cdot \lfloor x \rfloor = (a \vartriangle id) \cdot \mathsf{G}\, \lfloor x \rfloor \cdot c \\ \iff & \quad \{\ \mathsf{head}\, A \vartriangle \mathsf{tail}\, A \text{ is an isomorphism}\ \} \\ & \lfloor x \rfloor = \mathsf{cons}\, A \cdot (a \vartriangle id) \cdot \mathsf{G}\, \lfloor x \rfloor \cdot c \ . \end{aligned}$$

Thus, $\lfloor x \rfloor = (\!| \mathsf{cons}\, A \cdot (a \vartriangle id) \leftarrow c |\!)$ and consequently

$$x = \mathsf{head}\, A \cdot (\!| \mathsf{cons}\, A \cdot (a \vartriangle id) \leftarrow c |\!) \ . \tag{3.13}$$

This implementation builds an entire memo-table, invoking $a$ exactly once per node. Note that this does not depend on laziness.

### 3.5 Combining Adjunctions

Up to now we have considered various recursion schemes in isolation. Of course, in practice more complex algorithms are composed by combining different schemes. Consider as an example two mutually recursive functions, of which one has a parameter.

$$\begin{aligned} x_1 &= a_1 \cdot \mathsf{D}\,(x_1 \vartriangle \Lambda\, x_2) \cdot c \\ x_2 &= a_2 \cdot (\mathsf{D}\,(x_1 \vartriangle \Lambda\, x_2) \times P) \cdot (c \times P) \end{aligned}$$

One of the attractive features of adjunctions is that we can easily combine simple adjunctions to form more complex ones. The recursion scheme above, for instance, is given by

$$(\mathsf{Id} \times (- \times P)) \circ \Delta \ \dashv\ (\times) \circ (\mathsf{Id} \times (-)^P) \quad : \quad \mathscr{C} \times \mathscr{C} \rightharpoonup \mathscr{C} \ ,$$

which combines pairing, $\mathsf{L}_1 \times \mathsf{L}_2 \dashv \mathsf{R}_1 \times \mathsf{R}_2$, and composition of adjunctions, $\mathsf{L}_2 \circ \mathsf{L}_1 \dashv \mathsf{R}_1 \circ \mathsf{R}_2$. (Do not be confused by the four occurrences of $\times$: the formula involves products both in **Cat**, eg $\mathsf{Id} \times (-)^P$, and in $\mathscr{C}$, eg $- \times P$.) Indeed, all of the machinery introduced for *adjoint folds* [11] is immediately applicable here.

## 4. Application: Dynamic Programming I

We now discuss two examples of course-of-values recursion, introduced in Section 3.4.5, via dynamic programming algorithms.

***The knapsack problem*** A classic use of dynamic programming is to solve the *unbounded knapsack problem*. The goal is to maximize the total value of elements that are placed into a knapsack with a fixed weight capacity $c$. The elements are represented as a list of pairs $(w, v)$ where $w$ is the weight and $v$ is the value; elements are unbounded in multiplicity. The problem can be solved with the following recursion, where $wvs$ is implicitly provided:

$$\begin{aligned}
&knapsack :: \mathbb{N} \to \mathbb{R} \\
&knapsack\ c = maximum_0\ [\,v + knapsack\ (c - w) \\
&\qquad\qquad\qquad\qquad\quad \mid (w, v) \leftarrow wvs, 0 < w \wedge w \leqslant c\,]\ .
\end{aligned}$$

The value of a knapsack is determined by finding the item in $wvs$ that maximizes the total value while also decreasing the capacity of the knapsack. The function $maximum_0$ returns 0 when given an empty list, and otherwise returns the maximum value in the list.

Dynamic programming optimizes equations like *knapsack* by replacing the recursive calls with look-ups into a memo-table. Since the guard $0 < w \wedge w \leqslant c$ ensures that the recursive calls are always on smaller arguments, this fits perfectly into the framework of Equation (3.12). The base functor is $\mathsf{G} := \mathsf{Nat}$ defined

$$\mathbf{data}\ \mathsf{Nat}\ nat = Zero \mid Succ\ nat\ ,$$

and $c$ is simply the final recursive coalgebra $in^\circ : \mathbb{N} \to \mathsf{Nat}\ \mathbb{N}$. The memo-table $\mathsf{Nat}_\infty$ can be seen as the type of *non-empty colists*. The coalgebra $\mathsf{Nat}\,[\![ in^\circ ]\!] \cdot in^\circ$ of (3.12) generates the colist of all predecessors in decreasing order; for example, for 3 we obtain the colist $Succ\ (Cons\ 2\ (Succ\ (Cons\ 1\ (Succ\ (Cons\ 0\ Zero)))))$. To retrieve values from the memo-table we use

$$\begin{aligned}
&lookup_\infty :: (\mathbb{N}, \mathsf{Nat}_\infty\ v) \to Maybe\ v \\
&lookup_\infty\ (0, \quad Cons\ a\ _) \qquad\qquad = Just\ a \\
&lookup_\infty\ (n+1, Cons\ a\ (Zero)) \qquad = Nothing \\
&lookup_\infty\ (n+1, Cons\ a\ (Succ\ as)) = lookup_\infty\ (n, as)\ .
\end{aligned}$$

Table look-up amounts to an accu-hylo where the memo-table is the accumulator and the recursive coalgebra is $in^\circ : \mathbb{N} \to \mathsf{Nat}\ \mathbb{N}$.

From the specification of *knapsack* we extract an algebra (named the same to emphasise their relationship, but in a different font) $\mathsf{knapsack}$ by making a case distinction on the structure of the naturals, and replacing boundary guards with pattern matching.

$$\begin{aligned}
&\mathsf{knapsack} :: \mathsf{Nat}\ (\mathsf{Nat}_\infty\ \mathbb{R}) \to \mathbb{R} \\
&\mathsf{knapsack}\ (Zero) \qquad = 0 \\
&\mathsf{knapsack}\ (Succ\ table) = maximum_0 \\
&\quad [\,v + u \mid (w, v) \leftarrow wvs, Just\ u \leftarrow [lookup_\infty\ (w-1, table)]\,]
\end{aligned}$$

The effect of $lookup_\infty\ (i, table)$ is to return the result that was computed $i+1$ 'steps before' the current point of call. Thus, the key difference to the specification is that recursive calls with *absolute* indexing, $knapsack\ i$, are replaced by *relative* table look-ups, $lookup_\infty\ (c-1-i, table)$ where $c$ is the current input. The call $knapsack\ (c-w)$ is turned into $lookup_\infty\ (c-1-(c-w), table) = lookup_\infty\ (w-1, table)$, which works out nicely as the original input $c$ is actually not available to the algebra!

Now, if we capture Equation (3.13) as a higher-order function

$$\begin{aligned}
&dyna :: (Functor\,f) \Rightarrow (f\ (f_\infty\ a) \to a) \to (c \to f\ c) \to (c \to a) \\
&dyna\ a\ c = \mathsf{head} \cdot h\ \mathbf{where}\ h = \mathsf{cons} \cdot (a \vartriangle id) \cdot fmap\ h \cdot c\ ,
\end{aligned}$$

then the efficient implementation of knapsack is a breeze.

$$knapsack = dyna\ \mathsf{knapsack}\ in^\circ$$

From now on we just present the algebra and omit this final step.

***Catalan numbers*** The Catalan numbers determine how many distinct well-formed arrangements can be made with a given number of pairs of matching parentheses. They are given by a simple recursive equation, summing the results of splitting the parentheses at all possible points, and computing a convolution of the results of independent solutions:

$$\begin{aligned}
&catalan :: \mathbb{N} \to \mathbb{N} \\
&catalan\ 0 \qquad\quad = 1 \\
&catalan\ (n+1) = sum\ [catalan\ i * catalan\ (n-i) \mid i \leftarrow [0\,..\,n]]\ .
\end{aligned}$$

This is an instructive example, since it illustrates a deficiency of the recursion scheme: the upper bound for $i$ depends on the input parameter, but the input is not available to the algebra. We present a work-around here, and approach the problem in a more principled way in Section 5. The basic idea is to store the arguments in the memo-table: we use $(\mathsf{Nat}_{\mathbb{N}})_\infty$, where $\mathsf{F}_C$ is defined in Haskell by

$$\mathbf{type}\,f_c\ x = (c, f\ x)\ .$$

Instead of the coalgebra $in^\circ$ we use $id \vartriangle in^\circ : \mathbb{N} \to \mathsf{Nat}_{\mathbb{N}}\ \mathbb{N}$. We show in Section 5 that $id \vartriangle in^\circ$ is indeed a recursive coalgebra. The algebra $\mathsf{catalan}$ can then be written as follows:

$$\begin{aligned}
&\mathsf{catalan} :: \mathsf{Nat}_{\mathbb{N}}\ ((\mathsf{Nat}_{\mathbb{N}})_\infty\ \mathbb{N}) \to \mathbb{N} \\
&\mathsf{catalan}\ (n, Zero) \qquad\ = 1 \\
&\mathsf{catalan}\ (n, Succ\ table) = sum\ (zipWith\ (*)\ xs\ (reverse\ xs)) \\
&\quad \mathbf{where}\ xs = take_\infty\ (n, table)\ .
\end{aligned}$$

The key here is that the algebra knows about the current depth of its application, which is held in $n$. Thus, the appropriate number of values can be extracted from the memo-table, and convolved to form a solution. The function $take_\infty :: (\mathbb{N}, (\mathsf{Nat}_c)_\infty\ v) \to [v]$, which accomplishes the first step, has a straightforward implementation.

We have shown that the examples can be implemented using course-of-values recursion, but there are some remaining issues. In particular, the lack of an absolute reference point in the recursion has made the expression of the algorithms somewhat inelegant. In *knapsack*, we were fortunate that the indexing was essentially relative to begin with, but this is not always the case. The root of the problem lies in the fact that the original argument of the hylo is not available to the algebra. The next section introduces a cure, which will also allow us to replace infinite by finite memo-tables.

## 5. Para-recursive Coalgebras

As we have seen, hylos are restrictive, since the algebra can in general not access the argument of the hylo. It can reconstruct the argument only in the special case that the coalgebra has a left inverse. And indeed, for initial algebras, folds and so-called paramorphisms are interdefinable [22]. For practical considerations, we ensure that inputs can always be reconstructed and focus on coalgebras of the form $id \vartriangle c$, as these have the trivial left inverse *outl*.

### 5.1 Basic Definitions

***Para-hylomorphisms ("have your cake and eat it too")*** Recall that $\mathsf{F}_C\ X = C \times \mathsf{F}\ X$. Let $(a, A)$ be an $\mathsf{F}_C$-algebra, and let $(C, c)$ be an $\mathsf{F}$-coalgebra. An arrow $h : A \leftarrow C$ is a *para-hylomorphism*, or para-hylo for short, if it satisfies

$$h = a \cdot (id \vartriangle \mathsf{F}\ h \cdot c) \quad (\iff \quad h = a \cdot \mathsf{F}_C\ h \cdot (id \vartriangle c))\ . \qquad (5.1)$$

The argument is passed both to the coalgebra $c$ and the algebra $a$. (This is closely related to Haskell's @-patterns.) But note the asymmetry: $c$ is a standard $\mathsf{F}$-coalgebra, whereas $a$ is an $\mathsf{F}_C$-algebra.

***Para-recursive coalgebras*** The $\mathsf{F}$-coalgebra $(C, c)$ is parametrically recursive [27], or *para-recursive* for short, if Equation (5.1) has a unique solution for each $\mathsf{F}_C$-algebra $(a, A)$. In other words, $(C, c)$ is a para-recursive $\mathsf{F}$-coalgebra if and only if $(C, id \vartriangle c)$ is a recursive $\mathsf{F}_C$-coalgebra. The full subcategory of $\mathsf{F}$-$\mathbf{Coalg}(\mathscr{C})$ of para-recursive coalgebras is denoted $\mathsf{F}$-$\mathbf{PRec}(\mathscr{C})$.

A coalgebra that is para-recursive is also recursive—this is a simple application of the hylo-shift law (3.10) with $outr : \mathsf{F}_C \dot\to \mathsf{F}$. The converse holds if $c$ has a left inverse. Then the para-hylo is equivalent to a zygo-hylo. Consequently, the recursive coalgebra $(\mu\mathsf{F}, in^{\circ})$ is also para-recursive.

***Apo-hylomorphisms ("stop'n'go")*** Dualizing the notion of para-hylos, we replace the product in the source type of the algebra by a coproduct in the target type of the coalgebra. This allows the coalgebra to stop the recursion early (cf Example 3.1). Dual to $\mathsf{F}_C$ we define $\mathsf{F}^A\ X = A + \mathsf{F}\ X$. Let $(a,A)$ be an $\mathsf{F}$-algebra, and let $(C,c)$ be an $\mathsf{F}^A$-coalgebra. An arrow $h : A \leftarrow C$ is an *apo-hylomorphism*, or apo-hylo for short, if it satisfies

$$h = (id \triangledown a \cdot \mathsf{F}\ h) \cdot c \quad (\Longleftrightarrow \quad h = (id \triangledown a) \cdot \mathsf{F}^A\ h \cdot c) \qquad (5.2)$$

***Apo-corecursive algebras*** The $\mathsf{F}$-algebra $(a,A)$ is *apo-corecursive* (aka completely iterative), if Equation (5.2) has a unique solution for each $\mathsf{F}^A$-coalgebra $(C,c)$.

Next we adapt the rolling and conjugate rules to the new setting. Recall that both rules capture perfectly symmetric situations, showing that certain coliftings preserve recursiveness and, dually, certain liftings preserve corecursiveness. Now the symmetry is broken, in that we need two separate proofs. For reasons of space, we concentrate on para-recursive coalgebras.

### 5.2 Para-Rolling Rule

Our goal is to show that $x = a \cdot (id \vartriangle \mathsf{L}\ (\mathsf{R}\ x) \cdot \mathsf{L}\ c) : A \leftarrow \mathsf{L}\ C$, where $a : \mathsf{L}\ C \times \mathsf{L}\ (\mathsf{R}\ A) \to A$ and $c : C \to \mathsf{R}\ (\mathsf{L}\ C)$, has a unique solution if $c$ is para-recursive. We take the same approach as in Section 3.2 and write the right-hand side of the equation as a composition of two transformations: $x = \lceil \lfloor x \rfloor \rceil$ where

$$\lfloor x \rfloor = \mathsf{R}\ x \cdot c \qquad\qquad \lceil y \rceil = a \cdot (id \vartriangle \mathsf{L}\ y) \ . \qquad (5.3)$$

Clearly, solutions of $x = \lceil \lfloor x \rfloor \rceil$ are in 1-1 correspondence to solutions of $y = \lfloor \lceil y \rceil \rfloor$. However, it is not immediate that the latter equation is actually a para-hylo equation. Let's calculate.

$$\begin{array}{ll} & y = \lfloor \lceil y \rceil \rfloor \\ \Longleftrightarrow & \{ \text{ definition of } \lfloor - \rfloor \text{ and } \lceil - \rceil \text{ (5.3) } \} \\ & y = \mathsf{R}\ (a \cdot (id \vartriangle \mathsf{L}\ y)) \cdot c \\ \Longleftrightarrow & \{ \textit{ assumption: } \mathsf{R} \text{ is zippable, see (5.4) below } \} \\ & y = \mathsf{R}\ a \cdot \mathsf{zip} \cdot (\mathsf{R}\ id \vartriangle \mathsf{R}\ (\mathsf{L}\ y)) \cdot c \\ \Longleftrightarrow & \{ \text{ product fusion (2.6b) } \} \\ & y = \mathsf{R}\ a \cdot \mathsf{zip} \cdot (c \times id) \cdot (id \vartriangle \mathsf{R}\ (\mathsf{L}\ y) \cdot c) \end{array}$$

The last equation is indeed a para-hylo equation. However, we have to assume that $\mathsf{R}$-structures are *zippable*: that there exists a natural transformation $\mathsf{zip} : \mathsf{R}\ A \times \mathsf{R}\ B \dot{\to} \mathsf{R}\ (A \times B)$ such that $\mathsf{zip} \cdot (id \vartriangle id) = \mathsf{R}\ (id \vartriangle id)$. Because of naturality this implies

$$\mathsf{zip} \cdot (\mathsf{R} f \vartriangle \mathsf{R}\ g) = \mathsf{R}\ (f \vartriangle g) \ . \qquad (5.4)$$

Many but not all functors are zippable; for instance, $\mathsf{Id}$, $P+$, and $P\times$ are zippable but $+$ is not. We have established

**Theorem 5.1.** *Assume the data in* (3.2a). *If* $\mathsf{R}$ *is zippable, then*

$$\underline{\mathsf{L}} : (\mathsf{L} \circ \mathsf{R})\text{-}\mathbf{PRec}(\mathscr{C}) \leftarrow (\mathsf{R} \circ \mathsf{L})\text{-}\mathbf{PRec}(\mathscr{D}) \ . \qquad (5.5)$$

### 5.3 Final and Cofree Para-recursive Coalgebras

**Theorem 5.2.** *The para-recursive coalgebra* $(C,c)$ *is final if and only if* $c$ *is an isomorphism.*

*Proof.* The proof is exactly the same as for recursive coalgebras (Theorem 3.2), except that the para-rolling rule is used to show that $\mathsf{F}\ c$ is para-recursive if $c$ is ($\mathsf{Id}$ is trivially zippable). □

**Corollary 5.3.** *The final para-recursive* $\mathsf{F}$*-coalgebra is* $(\mu\mathsf{F}, in^{\circ})$.

Just as final coalgebras can be generalized to cofree coalgebras, final para-recursive coalgebras can be generalized to *cofree para-recursive coalgebras*, which we write $\mathsf{Cofree}_*\ B = (\mathsf{G}_*\ B, \mathsf{tail}_*\ B)$. The functor $\mathsf{Cofree}_*$ arises as the right adjoint of the forgetful functor $\mathsf{U}_* : \mathsf{G}\text{-}\mathbf{PRec}(\mathscr{C}) \to \mathscr{C}$.

$$\mathscr{C} \underset{\mathsf{Cofree}_*}{\overset{\mathsf{U}_*}{\underset{\longrightarrow}{\overset{\longleftarrow}{\bot}}}} \mathsf{G}\text{-}\mathbf{PRec}(\mathscr{C})$$

We have characterized $\mathsf{G}_\infty$ as the type of possibly infinite trees whose branching structure is determined by $\mathsf{G}$. Roughly speaking, $\mathsf{G}_*$ is the finite counterpart of $\mathsf{G}_\infty$. So the counit $\epsilon = \mathsf{head}_*$ extracts the root label of a tree, and $\eta\ (A,a) = [\![a]\!]_*$ constructs a finite tree.

$$\mathsf{G}_*\ B \cong \mu X\, .\, B \times \mathsf{G}\ X \qquad\qquad \mathsf{G}_\infty\ B \cong \nu X\, .\, B \times \mathsf{G}\ X$$

The proof of the isomorphism on the left is almost the same as the one for the isomorphism on the right (Example 2.4). We prove that $(\mathsf{T}\ B, \mathsf{tail}_*\ B)$ with $\mathsf{head}_*\ B : \mathsf{T}\ B \to B$ is a cofree para-recursive $\mathsf{G}$-coalgebra if and only if $(\mathsf{T}\ B, \mathsf{head}_*\ B \vartriangle \mathsf{tail}_*\ B)$ is a final para-recursive $\mathsf{G}_B$-coalgebra. It suffices to show that $h : A \to \mathsf{T}\ B$ with $\mathsf{head}_*\ B \cdot h = hd$ is a $\mathsf{G}$-coalgebra homomorphism if and only if it is a $\mathsf{G}_B$-coalgebra homomorphism.

$$\begin{array}{ll} & \mathsf{head}_* \cdot h = hd \ \wedge\ \mathsf{tail}_* \cdot h = \mathsf{G}\ h \cdot tl \\ \Longleftrightarrow & \{ \text{ see Example 2.4 } \} \\ & (\mathsf{head}_* \vartriangle \mathsf{tail}_*) \cdot h = \mathsf{G}_A\ h \cdot (hd \vartriangle tl) \end{array}$$

As the arrows now range over a sub-category, there is one additional proof obligation: we have to show that $tl$ is a para-recursive $\mathsf{G}$-coalgebra if and only if $hd \vartriangle tl$ is a para-recursive $\mathsf{G}_B$-coalgebra.

**Lemma 5.4.** *Let* $f : C \to D$ *and let* $(C,c)$ *be an* $\mathsf{F}$*-coalgebra. Then*

$$(C,c) : \mathsf{F}\text{-}\mathbf{PRec}(\mathscr{C}) \quad \Longleftrightarrow \quad (C, f \vartriangle c) : \mathsf{F}_D\text{-}\mathbf{PRec}(\mathscr{C}) \ . \qquad (5.6)$$

*Proof.* "$\Longrightarrow$": First of all, note that $\mathsf{F}_C = (C \times -) \circ \mathsf{F}$ and

$$(\mathsf{F}_D)_C = (C \times -) \circ (D \times -) \circ \mathsf{F} \cong ((C \times D) \times -) \circ \mathsf{F} = \mathsf{F}_{C \times D} \ .$$

The isomorphism is witnessed by $\alpha : (X \times Y) \times Z \cong X \times (Y \times Z)$, which is natural in $Z$, that is, $\alpha : \mathsf{F}_{C \times D} \dot{\to} (\mathsf{F}_D)_C$. The proof then amounts to a simple application of the hylo-shift law (3.10) with $\alpha \cdot ((id \vartriangle f) \times id) : (\mathsf{F}_D)_C \dot{\leftarrow} \mathsf{F}_{C \times D} \dot{\leftarrow} \mathsf{F}_C$.

"$\Longleftarrow$": Again, we apply the hylo-shift law (3.10), this time with $C \times outr : \mathsf{F}_C \dot{\leftarrow} (\mathsf{F}_D)_C$. □

The characterization of $\mathsf{G}_*$ implies that $\mathsf{head}_*\ B \vartriangle \mathsf{tail}_*\ B$ is an isomorphism; we use $\mathsf{cons}_*\ B$ to denote its inverse.

### 5.4 Course-of-Values Recursion Revisited: $\mathsf{U}_* \dashv \mathsf{Cofree}_*$

When we discussed course-of-values recursion in Section 3.4.5 we noted the oddity that a potentially infinite structure is used for tabulation, even though only recursive coalgebras are involved. The oddity turned into a nuisance for the examples in Section 4, as many desirable functions such as *reverse* are not total functions on coinductive types. Using $\mathsf{G}_*$ we can remedy the problem. As usual, let us first consider the categories involved.

$$\mathsf{F} \circ \mathsf{G}_* \circlearrowright \mathscr{C} \underset{\mathsf{Cofree}_*}{\overset{\mathsf{U}_*}{\underset{\longrightarrow}{\overset{\longleftarrow}{\bot}}}} \mathsf{G}\text{-}\mathbf{PRec}(\mathscr{C}) \circlearrowleft \mathsf{F}_\lambda$$

The data functor is now a functor over $\mathsf{G}\text{-}\mathbf{PRec}(\mathscr{C})$. Coliftings $\mathsf{F}_\lambda$ do not automatically preserve para-recursiveness, so this entails a *proof obligation* for the user of the scheme (see also below). The rest is, however, routine. Equation (3.9) specializes to

$$x = a \cdot \mathsf{F}\ (\mathsf{G}_*\ x \cdot [\![d]\!]_*) \cdot c \ : \ A \leftarrow C \ ,$$

where $a : \mathsf{F}\ (\mathsf{G}_* A) \to A$ and $c : (C,d) \to \mathsf{F}_\lambda\ (C,d)$. As an instance of the conjugate rule, Lemma 3.5 is applicable, and we record

**Theorem 5.5.** *Let $((C,d),c)$ be an $\mathsf{F}_\lambda$-coalgebra, then*

$$(C,c) : \mathsf{F}\text{-}\mathbf{Rec}(\mathscr{C}) \implies (C, \mathsf{F}\,[\![d]\!]_* \cdot c) : (\mathsf{F} \circ \mathsf{G}_*)\text{-}\mathbf{Rec}(\mathscr{C}) \ .$$

The special case where we identify F and G also works out nicely. The para-rolling rule instantiated to $\mathsf{L}, \mathsf{R} := \mathsf{G}, \mathsf{Id}$ implies that $\mathsf{G}_{id}$ preserves para-recursiveness. Consequently,

$$x = a \cdot \mathsf{G}\ (\mathsf{G}_*\, x \cdot [\![c]\!]_*) \cdot c \ \ : \ \ A \leftarrow C \qquad (5.7)$$

has a unique solution if $c : C \to \mathsf{G}\ C$ is *para*-recursive. The coalgebra $c$ has to be para-recursive, because it is used as an argument of $[\![-]\!]_*$. The algebra $a : \mathsf{G}\ (\mathsf{G}_* A) \to A$ now receives a G-structure of *finite* memo-tables that record the entire computational history.

### 5.5 Para-Conjugate Rule

Right adjoints preserve limits, in particular, binary products. Recall that the functor R preserves products if $\mathsf{R}\ (B_1 \times B_2)$ with $\mathsf{R}\ outl$ and $\mathsf{R}\ outr$ is a product of $\mathsf{R}\ B_1$ and $\mathsf{R}\ B_2$. This implies that there is a natural isomorphism $\iota : \mathsf{R}\ B_1 \times \mathsf{R}\ B_2 \cong \mathsf{R}\ (B_1 \times B_2)$ such that

$$\iota \cdot (\lfloor f_1 \rfloor \vartriangle \lfloor f_2 \rfloor) = \lfloor f_1 \vartriangle f_2 \rfloor \ , \qquad (5.8)$$

for all $f_i : A \to \mathsf{R}\ B_i$. Because of RAPL the conjugate rule can be adapted without further ado.

**Theorem 5.6.** *Assume the data in* (3.4a). *Then*

$$\mathsf{L}_\sigma : \mathsf{F}\text{-}\mathbf{PRec}(\mathscr{C}) \leftarrow \mathsf{G}\text{-}\mathbf{PRec}(\mathscr{D}) \ . \qquad (5.9)$$

*Proof.* Adopting the calculation for Theorem 3.4 we reason

$$\begin{array}{ll}
& x = a \cdot (id \vartriangle \mathsf{F}\, x \cdot \mathsf{L}_\sigma\, c) \ \ : \ \ A \leftarrow \mathsf{L}\ C \\
\iff & \{ \text{ definition of colifting (2.2) } \} \\
& x = a \cdot (id \vartriangle \mathsf{F}\, x \cdot \sigma\, C \cdot \mathsf{L}\, c) \\
\iff & \{ \lfloor - \rfloor \text{ and } \lceil - \rceil \text{ are isomorphisms (2.3) } \} \\
& \lfloor x \rfloor = \lfloor a \cdot (id \vartriangle \mathsf{F}\, x \cdot \sigma\, C \cdot \mathsf{L}\, c) \rfloor \\
\iff & \{ \lfloor - \rfloor \text{ is natural (2.4a) } \} \\
& \lfloor x \rfloor = \mathsf{R}\, a \cdot \lfloor id \vartriangle \mathsf{F}\, x \cdot \sigma\, C \cdot \mathsf{L}\, c \rfloor \\
\iff & \{ \text{ R preserves products (5.8) } \} \\
& \lfloor x \rfloor = \mathsf{R}\, a \cdot \iota \cdot (\lfloor id \rfloor \vartriangle \lfloor \mathsf{F}\, x \cdot \sigma\, C \cdot \mathsf{L}\, c \rfloor) \\
\iff & \{ \lfloor - \rfloor \text{ is natural (2.4a) } \} \\
& \lfloor x \rfloor = \mathsf{R}\, a \cdot \iota \cdot (\lfloor id \rfloor \vartriangle \lfloor \mathsf{F}\, x \cdot \sigma\, C \rfloor \cdot c) \\
\iff & \{ \sigma \dashv \tau \text{ conjugates (2.9b) } \} \\
& \lfloor x \rfloor = \mathsf{R}\, a \cdot \iota \cdot (\lfloor id \rfloor \vartriangle \tau\, A \cdot \mathsf{G}\, \lfloor x \rfloor \cdot c) \\
\iff & \{ \text{ product fusion (2.6b) } \} \\
& \lfloor x \rfloor = \mathsf{R}\, a \cdot \iota \cdot (\lfloor id \rfloor \times \tau\, A) \cdot (id \vartriangle \mathsf{G}\, \lfloor x \rfloor \cdot c) \ \ : \ \ \mathsf{R}\, A \leftarrow C \ .
\end{array}$$

The proof works by pushing $\lfloor - \rfloor$ inwards to work on the hylo $x$. □

The conjugate rule allows for a unified treatment of most if not all recursion schemes. Now we feel the benefit of this unified approach: using the para-conjugate rule, generalizing the different schemes to para-hylos is a piece of cake. Table 1 summarizes our findings. There is only one exception: course-of-values recursion. This particular instance of the conjugate rule relates hylos in the ambient category to hylos in the category of coalgebras. However, for para-hylos we need products, but these do not necessarily exist in categories of coalgebras. Fortunately, there is an easy way out. We postpone the treatment of course-of-values recursion until Section 5.6 and first turn our attention to the easy cases.

In their most general form, the recursion schemes build on the canonical control functor. For the induced conjugate pair $\mathsf{L} \circ \mathsf{D} \circ \eta \dashv \eta \circ \mathsf{D} \circ \mathsf{R}$, the para-hylo equation becomes

$$x = a \cdot (id \vartriangle \mathsf{L}\ (\mathsf{D}\ \lfloor x \rfloor \cdot c)) \ \ : \ \ A \leftarrow \mathsf{L}\ C \ ,$$

where $a : \mathsf{C}_C\, A \to A$ and $c : C \to \mathsf{D}\ C$. Unravelling the definitions, $\mathsf{C} = \mathsf{L} \circ \mathsf{D} \circ \mathsf{R}$ and $\mathsf{F}_C\, X = C \times \mathsf{F}\ X$, the algebra $a$ is assigned the impressive type $\mathsf{L}\ C \times \mathsf{L}\ (\mathsf{D}\ (\mathsf{R}\ A)) \to A$. The entries in Table 1 specialize the equation above to various adjunctions. There is a slight twist for accumulators: we use $outl \vartriangle \ldots$ instead of $id \vartriangle \ldots$, otherwise $a$ would receive $P$ twice. (This is a cosmetic change.)

### 5.6 Course-of-Values Recursion Re-Revisited

It remains to show that

$$x = a \cdot (id \vartriangle \mathsf{G}\ (\mathsf{G}_\infty\, x \cdot [\![c]\!]) \cdot c) \ \ : \ \ A \leftarrow C \qquad (5.10)$$

has a unique solution if $c$ is para-recursive. The proof is inspired by the treatment of Catalan numbers in Section 4: we integrate the arguments of $x$ into the memo-table using $(\mathsf{G}_C)_\infty$.

To convert between different types of memo-tables we make use of a natural transformation that changes the base functor. Let $\alpha : \mathsf{F} \mathbin{\dot\to} \mathsf{G}$, then $\alpha_\infty : \mathsf{F}_\infty \mathbin{\dot\to} \mathsf{G}_\infty$ is given by

$$\alpha_\infty = \mathsf{cons} \cdot (id \times \alpha \circ \alpha_\infty) \cdot (\mathsf{head} \vartriangle \mathsf{tail}) \ .$$

Since cons is corecursive, $\alpha_\infty$ is uniquely defined. (If all the necessary cofree coalgebras exist, $(-)_\infty : \mathscr{C}^\mathscr{C} \to \mathscr{C}^\mathscr{C}$ can be turned into a *higher-order* functor, whose action on arrows is given by $\alpha_\infty$.) The transformation enjoys the attractive *functor fusion* property:

$$\alpha_\infty\, C \cdot [\![c]\!] = [\![\alpha\, C \cdot c]\!] \ . \qquad (5.11)$$

The proof is left as the obligatory exercise for the reader. Using functor fusion we can rewrite Equation (5.10) into the standard form for course-of-values recursion (3.12).

$$\begin{array}{ll}
& x = a \cdot \mathsf{G}_C\ (\mathsf{G}_\infty\, x \cdot [\![c]\!]) \cdot (id \vartriangle c) \\
\iff & \{ \text{ functor fusion (5.11) and } outr \cdot (f \vartriangle g) = g \ \} \\
& x = a \cdot \mathsf{G}_C\ (\mathsf{G}_\infty\, x \cdot outr_\infty \cdot [\![id \vartriangle c]\!]) \cdot (id \vartriangle c) \\
\iff & \{ \ outr_\infty : (\mathsf{G}_C)_\infty \mathbin{\dot\to} \mathsf{G}_\infty \text{ is natural } \} \\
& x = a \cdot \mathsf{G}_C\ (outr_\infty \cdot (\mathsf{G}_C)_\infty\, x \cdot [\![id \vartriangle c]\!]) \cdot (id \vartriangle c) \\
\iff & \{ \ \mathsf{G}_C \text{ is a functor } \} \\
& x = a \cdot \mathsf{G}_C\ outr_\infty \cdot \mathsf{G}_C\ ((\mathsf{G}_C)_\infty\, x \cdot [\![id \vartriangle c]\!]) \cdot (id \vartriangle c)
\end{array}$$

The results of Section 3.4.5 imply that the latter equation has a unique solution if $id \vartriangle c$ is recursive, that is, if $c$ is para-recursive.

As an aside, the algebra $a \cdot \mathsf{G}_C\ outr_\infty$ discards a lot of useful information. Noting that $(\mathsf{G}_C)_\infty\, A \cong \mathsf{G}_\infty\ (C \times A)$, the algebra has type $C \times \mathsf{G}\ (\mathsf{G}_\infty\ (C \times A)) \to A$: it receives the original argument and a memo-table that pairs each prior argument with its result, which has potentially useful applications.

Using an entirely analogous argument, we can also show that the variant that uses a finite memo-table

$$x = a \cdot (id \vartriangle \mathsf{G}\ (\mathsf{G}_*\, x \cdot [\![c]\!]_*) \cdot c) \ \ : \ \ A \leftarrow C$$

has a unique solution if $c$ is para-recursive. Only the reason why the equations are uniquely defined changes: we essentially replace the statement "... is unique as the algebra $a$ is corecursive" by "... is unique as the coalgebra $c$ is para-recursive". Consider the base transformer $\alpha_* : \mathsf{F}_* \mathbin{\dot\to} \mathsf{G}_*$ given by

$$\alpha_* = \mathsf{cons}_* \cdot (id \times \alpha \circ \alpha_*) \cdot (\mathsf{head}_* \vartriangle \mathsf{tail}_*) \ .$$

This equation uniquely defines $\alpha_*$, as $\mathsf{tail}_*$ is para-recursive. Using the analogue of functor fusion, $\alpha_*\, C \cdot [\![c]\!]_* = [\![\alpha\, C \cdot c]\!]_*$, we have

$$\begin{array}{ll}
& x = a \cdot \mathsf{G}_C\ (\mathsf{G}_*\, x \cdot [\![c]\!]_*) \cdot (id \vartriangle c) \\
\iff & \{ \text{ see above } \} \\
& x = a \cdot \mathsf{G}_C\ outr_* \cdot \mathsf{G}_C\ ((\mathsf{G}_C)_*\, x \cdot [\![id \vartriangle c]\!]_*) \cdot (id \vartriangle c) \ .
\end{array}$$

Note that $id \vartriangle c$ is used as an argument to $[\![-]\!]_*$. By Lemma (5.4) we know that $id \vartriangle c$ is para-recursive if $c$ is.

| *recursion scheme* | *adjunction* | *conjugates* | *para-hylo equation* | *algebra* |
|---|---|---|---|---|
| (hylo-shift law) | $\mathsf{Id} \dashv \mathsf{Id}$ | $\alpha \dashv \alpha$ | $x = a \cdot (id \vartriangle \mathsf{D}\, x \cdot \alpha\, C \cdot c) \; : \; A \leftarrow C$ | $a : C \times \mathsf{D}\, A \to A$ |
| mutual recursion | $\Delta \dashv (\times)$ | ccf | $x_1 = a_1 \cdot (id \vartriangle \mathsf{D}\,(x_1 \vartriangle x_2) \cdot c) \; : \; A_1 \leftarrow C$<br>$x_2 = a_2 \cdot (id \vartriangle \mathsf{D}\,(x_1 \vartriangle x_2) \cdot c) \; : \; A_2 \leftarrow C$ | $a_1 : C \times \mathsf{D}\,(A_1 \times A_2) \to A_1$<br>$a_2 : C \times \mathsf{D}\,(A_1 \times A_2) \to A_2$ |
| accumulator | $- \times P \dashv (-)^P$ | ccf | $x = a \cdot (outl \vartriangle ((\mathsf{D}\,(\Lambda x) \cdot c) \times P)) \; : \; A \leftarrow C \times P$ | $a : C \times \mathsf{D}\,(A^P) \times P \to A$ |
| course-of-values (§5.6) | $\mathsf{U}_{\mathsf{D}} \dashv \mathsf{Cofree}_{\mathsf{D}}$ | ccf | $x = a \cdot (id \vartriangle \mathsf{D}\,(\mathsf{D}_\infty\, x \cdot [\![ c ]\!]) \cdot c) \; : \; A \leftarrow C$ | $a : C \times \mathsf{D}\,(\mathsf{D}_\infty\, A) \to A$ |
| finite memo-table (§5.6) | $\mathsf{U}_* \dashv \mathsf{Cofree}_*$ | ccf | $x = a \cdot (id \vartriangle \mathsf{D}\,(\mathsf{D}_*\, x \cdot [\![ c ]\!]_*) \cdot c) \; : \; A \leftarrow C$ | $a : C \times \mathsf{D}\,(\mathsf{D}_*\, A) \to A$ |

**Table 1.** Different types of para-hylos building on the canonical control functor (ccf); the coalgebra is $c : C \to \mathsf{D}\, C$ in each case.

## 6. Application: Dynamic Programming II

***Catalan numbers revisited*** We have laboured hard to make the implementation of dynamic programming algorithms simpler, and now we can reap the rewards. For the Catalan numbers we replace $Nat_\infty$, the type of non-empty colists, by $Nat_*$, the type of non-empty *lists*. Since $Nat_*$ is an inductive type, we can actually convert memo-tables into standard non-empty lists.

$$\begin{array}{l}
nelist :: \mathsf{Nat}_*\; v \to [v] \\
nelist\; (Cons_*\; a\; (Zero)) \quad = [a] \\
nelist\; (Cons_*\; a\; (Succ\; as)) = a : nelist\; as
\end{array}$$

This allows us to frame *catalan* as an instance of (5.7), where the coalgebra is simply $in^\circ : \mathbb{N} \to \mathsf{Nat}\, \mathbb{N}$, and the algebra implements a convolution. Using the hylo-shift law with $\mathsf{Nat} \circ nelist$, the algebra can actually work directly on lists.

$$\begin{array}{l}
\mathsf{catalan} :: \mathsf{Nat}\; [\mathbb{N}] \to \mathbb{N} \\
\mathsf{catalan}\; (Zero) \quad = 1 \\
\mathsf{catalan}\; (Succ\; xs) = sum\; (zipWith\; (*)\; xs\; (reverse\; xs))
\end{array}$$

***Chain matrix multiplication*** In *chain matrix multiplication* we must find the minimum number of scalar operations required to multiply a chain of matrices $A_0 \ldots A_n$, where each matrix $A_k$ has dimensions given by $a_k \times a_{k+1}$. Multiplying a $p \times q$ matrix by a $q \times r$ matrix yields a $p \times r$ matrix, costing (we assume) $pqr$ scalar operations. Matrix multiplication is associative, of course, but different parenthesisations can lead to different costs.

The recurrence that solves this problem works by considering all the different splits, and minimizing the combined cost:

$$\begin{array}{l}
chain :: (\mathbb{N}, \mathbb{N}) \to \mathbb{N} \\
chain\; (i,j) \mid i == j = 0 \\
\qquad\qquad\;\; \mid i < j = minimum\; [a_i * a_{k+1} * a_{j+1} + \\
\qquad\qquad\qquad\qquad chain\; (i,k) + chain\; (k+1,j) \mid k \leftarrow [i\,..\,j-1]] \;.
\end{array}$$

The final answer for this is held in $chain\; (0, n-1)$, where $n$ is the number of matrices that are being multiplied.

This is quite unlike previous examples, since the input type is not immediately inductive. To work around this, we can show that it is isomorphic to an inductive type. Some bounds checking reveals that the domain of *chain* is actually a subset of $(\mathbb{N}, \mathbb{N})$, since the function is only defined when $0 \leqslant i \leqslant j$. Thus, the algebra needs access to only a triangle of previous values that can be represented as a set of pairs $\mathbb{T} = \{(i,j) \mid 0 \leqslant i \leqslant j\}$. It is easy to show that there is an isomorphism $tri : \mathbb{N} \cong \mathbb{T} : tri^\circ$ between the set of triangle pairs and the natural numbers, and this gives us that $(tin, \mathbb{T})$ is initial, where $tin = tri \cdot in \cdot Nat\; tri^\circ$. Thus, the coalgebra $tin^\circ$ is corecursive, and with appropriate choice of *tri*, can be given by:

$$\begin{array}{l}
tin^\circ :: \mathbb{T} \to \mathsf{Nat}\; \mathbb{T} \\
tin^\circ\; (0,0) \qquad\qquad\;\; = Zero \\
tin^\circ\; (i,j) \mid i == j \qquad = Succ\; (0, j-1) \\
\qquad\qquad\; \mid otherwise = Succ\; (i+1, j) \;.
\end{array}$$

Here we record an efficient version of $tri^\circ$ that is based on the formula for triangle numbers, $T(n) = \sum_{i=1}^{n} i = n(n+1)/2$:

$$\begin{array}{l}
tri^\circ :: \mathbb{T} \to \mathbb{N} \\
tri^\circ\; (i,j) = j * (j+1)\; `div`\; 2 + j - i \;.
\end{array}$$

The definition of the algebra $\mathsf{chain}$ requires particular attention to the relative indices: the base case is straightforward, but when $i < j$ we must calculate the offset carefully.

$$\begin{array}{l}
\mathsf{chain} :: (\mathbb{T}, \mathsf{Nat}\; (\mathsf{Nat}_*\; \mathbb{N})) \to \mathbb{N} \\
\mathsf{chain}\; ((i,j), Zero) = 0 \\
\mathsf{chain}\; ((i,j), Succ\; table) \\
\quad \mid i == j = 0 \\
\quad \mid i < j = minimum\; [a_i * a_{k+1} * a_{j+1} + u + v \mid k \leftarrow [i\,..\,j-1], \\
\qquad Just\; u \leftarrow [extract\; (i,k)], Just\; v \leftarrow [extract\; (k+1,j)]] \\
\quad \textbf{where}\; extract\; (r,s) = lookup_*\; (tri^\circ\; (i,j) - tri^\circ\; (r,s) - 1, table)
\end{array}$$

This definition closely mirrors the specification given by *chain*, except that rather than being recalculated, results are now extracted from the lookup table using $lookup_* :: (\mathbb{N}, \mathsf{Nat}_*\; a) \to Maybe\; a$, which, like its coinductive counterpart, is an accu-hylo. Although we are certain to have a unique solution, not all proof obligations are discharged yet: naturally, the correctness relies on whether the appropriate elements are indexed in the intermediate table.

The two examples have shown that the arguments provided to the algebra by para-recursive coalgebras are particularly convenient for dynamic programming algorithms with tricky indices.

## 7. Related Work

***Recursive coalgebras*** The study of recursive coalgebras goes back to the work of Osius [25] on categorical set theory, where he showed that every well-founded coalgebra of the powerset functor is recursive. Taylor [27] generalized this result to set functors that preserve inverse images. Adámek et al. [1] further demonstrated that for finitary set functors preserving inverse images, recursive coalgebras are equivalent both to parametrically recursive coalgebras and to the existence of homomorphisms into the initial algebra. Completely iterative algebras are dual to parametrically recursive coalgebras, and were investigated by Milius [24], where we can glean the dual of some of the technical material in Section 5. Backhouse and Doornbos [2] worked on reductivity of recursive *relational* coalgebras, including applications to hylo equations.

***Rolling rule*** The origins of the rolling rule can be traced back at least to the work of Freyd [9] on algebraically complete categories, which was later extended by Backhouse et al. [3] to form the categorical fixed-point calculus. However, they only considered algebras and algebra-homomorphisms. Eppendahl [7] analyzed Freyd's proof of the Iterated Square Lemma and noticed that an adjunction-like correspondence formed a core part of the proof. (He calls the correspondence a *pro-adjunction*, as hylomorphisms form a profunctor.) He further generalized (a weak form of) the Square Lemma to recursive coalgebras.

***Conjugate rule*** An early instance of the conjugate rule can be found in the work of Bird and Paterson [5]. In order to show that generalized folds are uniquely defined, they discuss conditions to ensure that the equation $x \cdot \mathsf{L}\, in = \Psi\, x$ (or equivalently, $x = \Psi\, x \cdot \mathsf{L}\, in^{\circ}$) uniquely defines $x$. Two solutions are provided to this problem, the second of which requires $\mathsf{L}$ to have a right adjoint.

Technically our work is closest to the seminal paper by Capretta et al. [6] on using recursive coalgebras as a tool for structured recursion, which is essentially a generalization of results in [28, 29, 31]. Ironically, they introduce the conjugate rule, but do not use it to full effect, relying on comonads and distributive laws instead. We apply the conjugate rule more liberally, leading to substantially shorter proofs. We can do so because we use adjunctions rather than comonads as our building blocks: adjunctions are a more flexible concept as they can be easily composed.

Capretta et al. instantiate their theory to two main examples: the product comonad, which gives rise to zygo-hylos, and the cofree comonad, which gives rise to course-of-values recursion. We saw in Section 3.4.3 that zygo-hylos are a special case of mutual recursion from the adjunction $\Delta \dashv (\times)$. Section 3.4.5 demonstrated that course-of-values recursion arises out of the adjunction $\mathsf{U_G} \dashv \mathsf{Cofree_G}$, based on $\mathsf{F}_\lambda$-recursiveness, which is more general. They also discuss the so-called co-solution theorem, which corresponds to our development of para-recursive course-of-values recursion in Section 5.6. Similarly, the work of Uustalu and Vene [30] discusses the comonad $\mathsf{G}_*$, which we covered in detail in Section 5.4. As an aside, zygo-hylos precisely fall out of the adjunction $\mathsf{U_Z} \dashv \mathsf{P_Z} : \mathscr{C} \rightharpoonup \mathscr{C} \downarrow Z$, between $\mathscr{C}$ and the slice category $\mathscr{C} \downarrow Z$, where the pairing functor $\mathsf{P_Z}$ is right adjoint to the forgetful functor $\mathsf{U_Z}$. In fact, whatever the comonad $\mathsf{N}$, we can apply the machinery of the Eilenberg–Moore construction and use the adjunction $\mathsf{U_N} \dashv \mathsf{Cofree_N} : \mathscr{C} \rightharpoonup \mathscr{C}_\mathsf{N}$ to integrate the ensuing comonadic recursion scheme into our framework. Such an approach mimics the techniques of Hinze et al. [13], which further shows that our theory based on adjunctions subsumes the use of comonads, but not the other way round.

For brevity, we have not shown all interesting adjunctions. For example, *natural* hylomorphisms between parametric datatypes arise from the adjunction $(- \circ \mathsf{P}) \dashv \mathsf{Ran_P}$ between pre-composition and the right Kan extension, covering generalized folds [5].

***Recursion schemes*** In this paper we have paid particular attention to course-of-values recursion, which was first captured as *histomorphisms* [29]. This scheme was identified as an instance of comonadic recursion in [31]. The adaption of histomorphisms for use in dynamic programming was worked out in detail by [16], although in an algebraically compact setting. This was later modified to the setting of recursive coalgebras in [12]. Both of these works focus on the efficiency of these schemes.

## 8. Conclusion

We believe that this work is a significant step towards a unifying theory of datatype-generic programming. It is quite amazing that all of the well-studied structured recursion schemes can be framed as instances of a single construction, conjugate hylomorphisms, aptly justifying the title "mother of all structured recursion schemes".

## Acknowledgments

We are especially grateful to the reviewers for their detailed comments and suggestions. This work has been funded by EPSRC grant number EP/J010995/1.

## References

[1] J. Adámek, D. Lücke, and S. Milius, "Recursive coalgebras of finitary functors," *RAIRO-Theoretical Informatics and Applications*, vol. 41, no. 04, pp. 447–462, 2007.

[2] R. Backhouse and H. Doornbos, "Datatype-generic termination proofs," *Theory of Comput. Sys.*, vol. 43, no. 3-4, pp. 362–393, 2008.

[3] R. Backhouse, M. Bijsterveld, R. van Geldrop, and J. van der Woude, "Categorical fixed point calculus," in *Category Theory and Computer Science*, ser. LNCS, vol. 953. Springer, Aug. 1995, pp. 159–179.

[4] R. Bird and O. de Moor, *Algebra of Programming*. Prentice Hall Europe, 1997.

[5] R. Bird and R. Paterson, "Generalised folds for nested datatypes," *Form. Asp. Comput.*, vol. 11, no. 2, pp. 200–222, 1999.

[6] V. Capretta, T. Uustalu, and V. Vene, "Recursive coalgebras from comonads," *Inform. Comput.*, vol. 204, no. 4, pp. 437–468, 2006.

[7] A. Eppendahl, "Coalgebra-to-algebra morphisms," *Electronic Notes in Theoretical Computer Science*, vol. 29, no. 0, pp. 42–49, 1999.

[8] M. M. Fokkinga, "Tupling and mutumorphisms," *The Squiggolist*, vol. 1, no. 4, pp. 81–82, Jun. 1990.

[9] P. Freyd, "Algebraically complete categories," in *Category Theory*, ser. Lect. Notes Math. Springer, 1991, vol. 1488, pp. 95–104.

[10] T. Hagino, "Category theoretic approach to data types," Ph.D. dissertation, University of Edinburgh, 1987.

[11] R. Hinze, "Adjoint folds and unfolds—an extended study," *Sci. Comput. Program.*, vol. 78, no. 11, pp. 2108–2159, 2013.

[12] R. Hinze and N. Wu, "Histo- and dynamorphisms revisited," in *Workshop on Generic Program.* ACM, 2013, pp. 1–12.

[13] R. Hinze, N. Wu, and J. Gibbons, "Unifying structured recursion schemes," in *ICFP*. ACM, 2013, pp. 209–220.

[14] C. A. R. Hoare, "Notes on data structuring," in *Structured Programming*, ser. APIC studies in data processing. Academic Press, 1972, pp. 83–174.

[15] Z. Hu, H. Iwasaki, and M. Takeichi, "Deriving structural hylomorphisms from recursive definitions," in *ICFP*. ACM, 1996, pp. 73–82.

[16] J. Kabanov and V. Vene, "Recursion schemes for dynamic programming," in *Math. of Prog. Construction*, ser. LNCS. Springer, 2006, pp. 235–252.

[17] D. M. Kan, "Adjoint functors," *Trans. Am. Math. Soc.*, vol. 87, no. 2, pp. 294–329, 1958.

[18] J. Lambek, "A fixpoint theorem for complete categories," *Math. Z.*, vol. 103, pp. 151–161, 1968.

[19] S. Mac Lane, *Categories for the Working Mathematician*, 2nd ed., ser. Graduate Texts in Mathematics. Springer, 1998.

[20] G. Malcolm, "Algebraic data types and program transformation," Ph.D. dissertation, University of Groningen, 1990.

[21] ——, "Data structures and program transformation," *Sci. Comput. Program.*, vol. 14, no. 2–3, pp. 255–280, 1990.

[22] L. Meertens, "Paramorphisms," *Form. Asp. Comput.*, vol. 4, pp. 413–424, 1992.

[23] E. Meijer, M. Fokkinga, and R. Paterson, "Functional programming with bananas, lenses, envelopes and barbed wire," in *Functional Programming Languages and Computer Architecture*, ser. LNCS, vol. 523. Springer, 1991, pp. 124–144.

[24] S. Milius, "Completely iterative algebras and completely iterative monads," *Inform. Comput.*, vol. 196, no. 1, pp. 1–41, 2005.

[25] G. Osius, "Categorical set theory: A characterization of the category of sets," *J. Pure Appl. Algebra*, vol. 4, no. 1, pp. 79–119, 1974.

[26] A. Pardo, "Generic accumulations," in *IFIP TC2 Working Conference on Generic Program.*, vol. 243. Kluwer Academic Publishers, Jul. 2002, pp. 49–78.

[27] P. Taylor, *Practical Foundations of Mathematics*, ser. Cambridge Studies in Adv. Math. Cambridge University Press, 1999, no. 59.

[28] T. Uustalu and V. Vene, "Coding recursion à la Mendler," in *Workshop on Generic Program.*, Jul. 2000, pp. 69–85.

[29] ——, "Primitive (co)recursion and course-of-value (co)iteration, categorically," *Informatica, Lith. Acad. Sci.*, vol. 10, no. 1, pp. 5–26, 1999.

[30] ——, "The recursion scheme from the cofree recursive comonad," *Electronic Notes in Theoretical Computer Science*, vol. 229, no. 5, pp. 135–157, 2011, Math. Structured Functional Program. 2008.

[31] T. Uustalu, V. Vene, and A. Pardo, "Recursion schemes from comonads," *Nordic J. Comput.*, vol. 8, pp. 366–390, Sep. 2001.

[32] V. Vene and T. Uustalu, "Functional programming with apomorphisms (corecursion)," *Proceedings of the Estonian Academy of Sciences: Physics, Mathematics*, vol. 47, no. 3, pp. 147–161, 1998.

# Quantitative Interprocedural Analysis *

Krishnendu Chatterjee
Andreas Pavlogiannis
IST Austria (Institute of Science and Technology Austria) Klosterneuburg, Austria
{krish.chat, pavlogiannis}@ist.ac.at

Yaron Velner
Tel Aviv University, Israel
yaronvel@post.tau.ac.il

## Abstract

We consider the quantitative analysis problem for interprocedural control-flow graphs (*ICFG*s). The input consists of an *ICFG*, a positive weight function that assigns every transition a positive integer-valued number, and a labelling of the transitions (events) as good, bad, and neutral events. The weight function assigns to each transition a numerical value that represents a measure of how good or bad an event is. The quantitative analysis problem asks whether there is a run of the *ICFG* where the ratio of the sum of the numerical weights of good events versus the sum of weights of bad events in the long-run is at least a given threshold (or equivalently, to compute the maximal ratio among all valid paths in the *ICFG*). The quantitative analysis problem for *ICFG*s can be solved in polynomial time, and we present an efficient and practical algorithm for the problem. We show that several problems relevant for static program analysis, such as estimating the worst-case execution time of a program or the average energy consumption of a mobile application, can be modeled in our framework. We have implemented our algorithm as a tool in the Java Soot framework. We demonstrate the effectiveness of our approach with two case studies. First, we show that our framework provides a sound approach (no false positives) for the analysis of inefficiently-used containers. Second, we show that our approach can also be used for static profiling of programs which reasons about methods that are frequently invoked. Our experimental results show that our tool scales to relatively large benchmarks, and discovers relevant and useful information that can be used to optimize performance of the programs.

***Categories and Subject Descriptors*** D.3.4 [*Programming Languages*]: Processors—Optimization; F.3.2 [*Logics and Meanings of Programs*]: Semantics of Programming Langugages—Program Analysis

***General Terms*** Algorithms, Languages, Performance

***Keywords*** Interprocedural analysis, Quantitative objectives, Mean-payoff and ratio objectives, Memory bloat, Static profiling.

* This work has been supported by the Austrian Science Foundation (FWF) under the NFN RiSE (S11405-07), FWF Grant P23499-N23, ERC Start grant (279307: Graph Games), ERC grant 321174-VSSC, Israel Science Foundation grant 652/11, and Microsoft faculty fellows award.


*POPL '15*, January 15–17, 2015, Mumbai, India.

ACM 978-1-4503-3300-9/15/01... $15.00.
http://dx.doi.org/10.1145/2676726.2676968

## 1. Introduction

**Static and interprocedural analysis.** Static analysis techniques provide ways to obtain information about programs without actually running them on specific inputs. Static analysis explores the program behavior for *all* possible inputs and *all* possible executions. For non-trivial programs, it is impossible explore all the possibilities, and hence static analysis uses approximations (abstract interpretations) to account for all the possibilities [16]. Static analysis algorithms generally operate on the interprocedural control-flow graphs (for brevity *ICFG*s). An *ICFG* consists of a collection of control-flow graphs (CFGs), one for each procedure of the program. The CFG of each procedure has a *unique entry* node and a *unique exit* node, and other nodes represent statements of the program and conditions (in other words, basic blocks of the program). In addition, there are *call* and *return* nodes for each procedure which represent invoking of procedures and return from procedures. Call-transitions connect call nodes to entry nodes; and return-transitions connect exit nodes to return nodes. Algorithmic analysis of *ICFG*s provides the mathematical framework for static analysis of programs. Interprocedural analysis with objectives such as reachability, set-based information, etc have been deeply studied in the literature [10, 24, 29, 31–33].

**Quantitative objectives.** A *qualitative* (or Boolean) objective assigns to every run of a program a Boolean value (accept or reject). A *quantitative* objective assigns to every run of a program a real value that represents a quality measure of the run. The analysis of programs with quantitative objectives is gaining huge prominence due to embedded systems with requirements on resource consumption, promptness of responses, performance analysis etc. Quantitative objectives have been proposed in several applications such as for worst-case execution time (see [41] for survey), power consumption [37], prediction of cache behavior for timing analysis [20], performance measures [5, 13, 21], to name a few. Another important feature of quantitative objectives is that they are very well-suited for *anytime algorithms* [8] (where anytime algorithms generate imprecise answers quickly, and proceed to construct progressively better approximate solutions with refinements) (for a more elaborate discussion see [12]).

**Mean-payoff and ratio objectives.** One of the most well-studied and mathematically elegant quantitative objectives is the *mean-payoff* objective, where a rational-valued weight is associated with every transition and the goal is to ensure that the long-run average of the weights along a run is at least a given threshold [3, 19, 46]. For example, consider a weight function that assigns to every transition the resource (such as power) consumption, then the mean-payoff objective measures the average resource consumption along a run. Along with *ICFG*s with mean-payoff objectives, we also consider *ratio* objectives. For ratio objectives, the transitions (events) of the *ICFG*s are labelled as good, bad, or neutral events, and a positive weight function assigns a positive integer-valued weight to every transition, and the weight function represents how good or bad an event is. The quantitative analysis problem asks if there is a run of the program such that the ratio of the sum of the weights of the good events versus the weights of the bad events in the long-run is at least a given threshold. For example, consider a weight function that assigns weight 1 to each transition, and a labeling of events as follows: whenever a request is made is a bad event, whenever a request is pending is a good event, and whenever no request is pending is a neutral event. The ratio objective assigns the long-run average time between requests and the corresponding grant per request for a run, and measures timeliness of responses to requests. Finite-state systems (or intraprocedural finite-state programs) with mean-payoff objectives have been studied in the literature in [19, 21, 26, 46] for performance modeling, and more recently applied in synthesis of reactive systems with quality guarantee [5] and robustness [6], reliability requirements and resource bounds of reactive systems [9, 13, 17].

**Interprocedural quantitative analysis.** Quantitative objectives such as mean-payoff and ratio objectives provide the appropriate framework to express several important system properties such as resource consumption and timeliness. While finite-state systems with mean-payoff objectives have been studied in the literature, the static analysis of $ICFG$s with mean-payoff and ratio objectives has largely been ignored. An interprocedural analysis is *precise* if it provides the meet-over-all-*valid*-paths solution (a path is valid if it respects the fact that when a procedure finishes it returns to the site of the most recent call). In the quantitative setting, the problem corresponds to finding the maximal value over all valid paths and to produce a witness (symbolic) path for that value. In this work, we consider precise interprocedural quantitative analysis for $ICFG$s with mean-payoff and ratio objectives.

**Our contributions.** In this work we present a flexible and general modelling framework for quantitative analysis and show how it can be used to reason about quantitative properties of programs and about potential optimizations in the program. We present an efficient polynomial-time algorithm for precise interprocedural quantitative analysis, which is implemented as a tool. We demonstrate the efficiency of the algorithm with two case studies, and show that our approach scales to programs with thousands of methods.

1. *(Theoretical modeling).* We show that $ICFG$s with mean-payoff and ratio objectives provide a robust framework that naturally captures a wide variety of static program analysis optimization and reasoning problems.
   (a) *(Detecting container usage).* An exceedingly important problem for performance analysis is detection of runtime bloat that significantly degrades the performance and scalability of programs [27, 45]. A common source of bloat is inefficient use of containers [45]. We show that the problem of detecting usage of containers can be modeled as $ICFG$s with ratio objectives. A good use of a container corresponds to a good event and no use of the container is a bad event, and a misuse is represented as a low ratio of good vs bad events. Hence the container usage problem is naturally modeled as ratio analysis of $ICFG$s. While the problem of detecting container usage was already considered in [45], our different approach has the following benefits (see Section 5.2 for a comparison). First, our approach can handle recursion ([45] does not handle recursion). Second, our approach is sound, and does not yield false positives. Third, the approach of [45] ignored DELETE operations and we are able to take into consideration both ADD and DELETE operations (thus provide a more refined analysis). Moreover, our algorithmic approach for analysis of $ICFG$s is polynomial, whereas the algorithmic approach of [45] in the worst case can be exponential.
   (b) *(Static profiling of programs).* We use our framework to model a conceptually new way for static profiling of programs for performance analysis. A line in the code (or a code segment) is referred as *hot* if there exists a run of the program where the line of code is frequently executed. For example, a function is referred as *hot* if there exists a run of the program where the function is frequently invoked, i.e., the frequency of calls to the function among all function calls is at least a given threshold. Again this problem is naturally modeled as ratio problem for $ICFG$s, and our approach statically detects methods that are more frequently invoked. Optimization of frequently executed code would naturally lead to performance improvements and reasoning about hot spots in the code can assist the complier to apply optimization such as function inlining and loop unrolling (see Subsection 3.2 for more details).
   (c) *(Other applications).* We show the generality of our framework by demonstrating that it provides an appropriate framework for theoretical modeling of diverse applications such as interprocedural worst-case execution time analysis, evaluating speedup in parallel computation, and interprocedural average energy consumption analysis.
2. *(Algorithmic analysis).* The quantitative analysis of $ICFG$s with mean-payoff objectives can be achieved in polynomial time by a reduction to pushdown systems with mean-payoff objectives (which can be solved in polynomial time [14]). However, the resulting algorithm in the worst case has time complexity that is a polynomial of degree thirteen and space complexity that is a polynomial of degree six (which is prohibitive in practice). We exploit the special theoretical properties of $ICFG$s in order to improve the theoretical upper bound and get an algorithm that in the worst case runs in cubic time and with quadratic space complexity. In addition, we exploit the properties of *real-world* programs and introduce optimizations that give a practical algorithm that is much faster than the theoretical upper bound when the relevant parameters (the total number of entry, exit, call, and returns nodes) are small, which is typical in most applications. Finally we present a linear reduction of the quantitative analysis problem with ratio objectives to mean-payoff objectives.
3. *(Tool and experimental results).* We have implemented our algorithm and developed a tool in the Java Soot framework [38]. We show through two case studies that our approach scales to relatively large programs from well-known benchmarks. The details of the case studies are as follows:
   (a) *(Detecting container usage).* Our experimental results show that our tool scales to relatively large benchmarks (DaCapo 2009 [4]), and discover relevant and useful information that can be used to optimize performance of the programs. Our tool could analyze all containers in several benchmarks (like muffin) whereas [45] could analyze them partially (in muffin only half of the containers were analyzed in [45] — before the predefined time bound was exceeded). Our sound approach allows us to avoid false reports (that were reported by [45]) and our simple mathematical modelling even allows us to report misuses that were not reported by [45].
   (b) *(Static profiling of programs).* We run an analysis to detect hot methods for various thresholds. Our experimental results on the benchmarks report only a small fraction of the functions as hot for high threshold values, and thus give useful information about potential functions to be optimized for performance gain. In addition we perform a dynamic profiling and mark the top 5% of the most frequently invoked functions as hot. Our experiments show a significant correlation between the results of the static and dynamic analysis. In addition, we show that the sensitivity and specificity of the static classification can be controlled by considering different thresholds, where lower thresholds increase the sensitivity and higher thresholds increase the specificity. We in-

vestigate the trade-off curve (ROC curve) and demonstrate the prediction power of our approach.

Thus we show that several conceptually different problems related to program optimizations are naturally modeled in our framework, and demonstrate that we present a flexible and generic framework for quantitative analysis of programs. Moreover, our case studies show that our tool scales to benchmarks with real-world programs.

## 2. Definitions

In this section we present formal definitions of interprocedural control-flow graphs, and the quantitative analysis problems. We will use an example program, described in Figure 1 and Figure 2, to demonstrate each definition.

**Interprocedural control-flow graphs (*ICFG*s).** A program $P$ with $m$ methods is modeled by an interprocedural control-flow graph $(ICFG)$ $\mathcal{A}$ which consists of a tuple $\langle A_1, \ldots, A_m \rangle$ of $m$ modules, where each module $A_i = \langle N_i, En_i, Ex_i, Calls_i, Retns_i, \delta_i \rangle$ represents a method (or the control-flow graph of a method) in the program. A module $A_i$ contains the following components:

- A finite set of nodes $N_i$.
- An entry node $En_i$, which represents the first node of the method.
- An *exit* node $Ex_i$, which represents termination of the method.
- A finite set $Calls_i$ that denotes the set of *calls* of the method, and a finite set $Retns_i$ that denotes the set of *returns*.
- A transition relation $\delta_i$ defined as follows: A transition in $A_i$ is either (i) between two nodes in the same module (internal transitions) or between a return node and a node in the same module (i.e., $u, v$ such that $u \in N_i \cup Retns_i$ and $v \in N_i \cup Calls_i$); or (ii) between a call node of a module $A_i$ and the entry node of a module $A_j$ (which models the invocation of method $j$ from method $i$); or (iii) between the exit node of module $A_i$ and a return node of a module $A_j$ (which models the case that method $i$ terminated and the run of the program continues in method $j$ which invoked method $i$).

We denote by $N = \bigcup_{1 \le i \le m} N_i$ and similarly, $En = \bigcup_{1 \le i \le m} \{En_i\}$; $Ex = \bigcup_{1 \le i \le m} \{Ex_i\}$; $Calls = \bigcup_{1 \le i \le m} Calls_i$; $Retns = \bigcup_{1 \le i \le m} Retns_i$; and $\delta = \bigcup_{1 \le i \le m} \delta_i$. In the sequel we use $N$ (resp. $N_i$) to denote all nodes in $\mathcal{A}$ (resp. $A_i$), and refer to the nodes of $N \setminus (Calls \cup Retns \cup En \cup Ex)$ as *internal nodes*.

**Quantitative *ICFG*s.** A *quantitative ICFG* (*QICFG* for brevity) consists of an *ICFG* $\mathcal{A}$ and a weight function $w$ that assigns a rational-valued weight $w(e) \in \mathbb{Q}$ to every transition $e$, where $\mathbb{Q}$ is the set of all rationals.

**Example 1.** *Consider an example program shown in Figure 1 and Figure 2. In this example, (i)* Modules: *$A_1$ = main, $A_2$ = foo; (ii)* Nodes: *$N_2$ = {f:Entry, if(x>1), f:call foo, f:foo ret, x++, f:Exit}; (iii)* Entry and exit: *$En_2$ = f:Entry and $Ex_2$ = f:Exit; (iv)* Calls and returns: *$Calls_2$ = {f:call foo} and $Retns_2$ = {f:foo ret}; and (v)* Transition: *for example, (x++,f:Exit) $\in \delta_2$, (f:Exit,f:foo ret) $\in \delta_2$ and (f:Exit,m:foo ret) $\in \delta_2$.*

**Configurations and paths.** A *configuration* consists of a sequence $c = (r_1, \ldots, r_j, u)$, where each $r_i$ is a return node (i.e., $r_i \in Retns$) and $u \in N$ is a node in one of the modules. Intuitively, when the module that $u$ belongs to terminates, the program will continue in $r_j$. A sequence of configurations is *valid* if it does not violate the transition relation, and a *path* $\pi$ is a valid sequence of configurations. We note that a path can be equivalently represented by the first configuration and a sequence of transitions. For a path $\pi = \langle c_1, c_2, \ldots, c_\ell \rangle$ we denote by (i) $n_i$: the node of configuration $c_i$ (i.e., $c_i = (r_1, \ldots, r_j, n_i)$), and (ii) $\alpha_i$: the stack string of $c_i$ (i.e., $\alpha_i = r_1, \ldots, r_j$). For a path $\pi$ let $\pi[1, i]$ denote the prefix of length $i$ of $\pi$. A run of the program is modeled by a path in $\mathcal{A}$.

```
void main(){
    while( x ){
        if( y > 0 )
            foo( x );
        else
            z = 7;
    }
    z++;
    return;
}
```

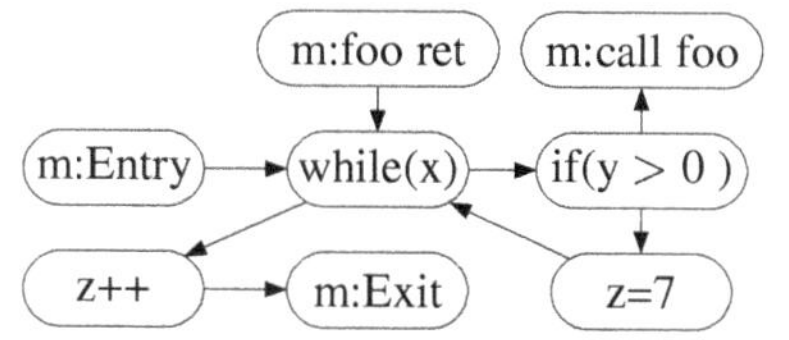


**Figure 1.** main

```
int foo( int x ){
    if( x > 1 )
        foo(x − 1);
    x++;
    return x;
}
```

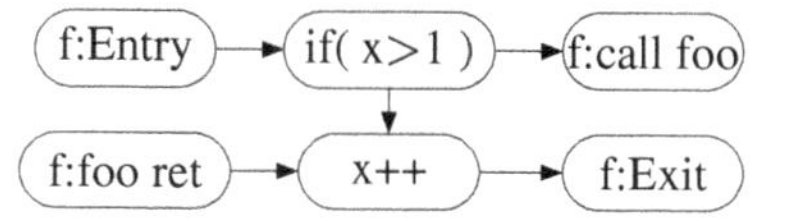


**Figure 2.** foo

**Example 2.** *Consider the program and the corresponding ICFG shown in Figure 1 and Figure 2. An example of a run in the program modeled as a path in the ICFG is as follows: $\langle$($\epsilon$, m:Entry), ($\epsilon$, while(x)), ($\epsilon$, if (y > 0)), ($\epsilon$, m:call foo), (m:foo ret, f:Entry), (m:foo ret, if (x > 1)), (m:foo ret, f:call foo), (m:foo ret, f:foo ret, f:Entry), $\ldots\rangle$, where $\epsilon$ denotes the empty stack.*

**Ratio analysis problem.** In this work we consider the *ratio analysis* problem, where every transition of a *ICFG* has a label from the set $\{good, bad, neutral\}$. Intuitively, desirable events are labelled as $good$, undesirable events are labelled as $bad$, and other events are labelled as $neutral$. The ratio analysis problem, given a *ICFG*, a labeling of the events, and a threshold $\lambda > 0$, asks to determine whether there is a run where the ratio of sum of weights of *good* events vs the sum of weights of the *bad* events that is greater than the threshold $\lambda$. Formally, we consider a positive integer-weight function $w$, that assigns a positive integer-valued weight to every transition, and for good and bad events the weight denotes how good or how bad the respective event is. For a finite path $\pi$ we denote by $good(w(\pi))$ (resp., $bad(w(\pi))$) the sum of weights of the good (resp., bad) events in $\pi$. In particular, for the weight function $w$ that assigns weight 1 to every transition, we have that $good(w(\pi))$ (resp. $bad(w(\pi))$) represents the number of good (resp. bad) events. We denote $Rat(w(\pi)) = \frac{good(w(\pi))}{\max\{1, bad(w(\pi))\}}$ the ratio of the sum of weights of good and bad events in $\pi$ (note that in denominator we have $\max\{1, bad(w(\pi))\}$ to remove the pathological case of division by zero). For an infinite path $\pi$ we denote

$$LimRat(w(\pi)) = \begin{cases} \liminf_{i \to \infty} Rat(w(\pi[1,i])) & \text{if } \pi \text{ has infinitely many good or bad events;} \\ 0 & \text{otherwise;} \end{cases}$$

informally this represents the ratio as the number of relevant (good/bad) events goes to infinity. Our analysis focuses on paths with unbounded number of relevant events, and infinitely many events provide an elegant abstraction for unboundedness. Hence, we investigate the following problem:

> Given a *ICFG* with labeling of good, bad, and neutral events, a positive integer weight function $w$, and a threshold $\lambda \in \mathbb{Q}$ such that $\lambda > 0$, determine whether there exists an infinite path $\pi$ such that $LimRat(w(\pi)) > \lambda$.

**Remark 1.** *Our approach can be extended to reason about finite runs by a adding an auxiliary transition, labeled as a neutral event, from the final state of the program to its initial state (also see Section 3.3).*

**Mean-payoff analysis problem.** In the mean-payoff analysis problem we consider a $QICFG$ with a rational-valued weight function $w$. For a finite path $\pi$ in a $QICFG$ we denote by $w(\pi)$ the total weight of the path (i.e., the sum of the weights of the transitions in $\pi$), and by $Avg(w(\pi)) = \frac{w(\pi)}{|\pi|}$ the average of the weights, where $|\pi|$ denotes the length of $\pi$. For an infinite path $\pi$, we denote $LimAvg(w(\pi)) = \liminf_{i \to \infty} Avg(w(\pi[1,i]))$. The mean-payoff analysis problem asks whether there exists an infinite path $\pi$ such that $LimAvg(w(\pi)) > 0$. In Section 4 we show how the ratio analysis problem of $ICFG$s reduces to the mean-payoff analysis problem of $QICFG$s.

**Assigning context-dependent and path-dependent weights.** In our model the numerical weights are assigned to every transition of a $ICFG$. First, note that since we consider weight functions as an input and allow all weight functions, the weights could be assigned in a dependent way. Second, in general, we can have an $ICFG$, and a finite-state deterministic automaton (such as a deterministic mean-payoff automaton [13]) that assigns weights. The deterministic automaton can assign weights depending on different contexts (or call strings) of invocations, or even independent of the context but dependent on the past few transitions (i.e., path-dependent), i.e., the automaton has the stack alphabet and transition of the $ICFG$ as input alphabet and assigns weights depending on the current state of the automaton and an input letter. We call such a weight function *regular weight function*. Given a regular weight function specified by an automaton $A$ and an $ICFG$ we can obtain a $ICFG$ (that represents the path-dependent weights) by taking their synchronous product, and hence we will focus on $ICFG$s for algorithmic analysis. The regular weight function can also be an *abstraction* of the real weight function, e.g., the regular weight function is an *over-approximation* if the weights that it assigns to the good (resp. bad) events are higher (resp. lower) than the real weights. If the original weight function is bounded, then an over-approximation with a regular weight function can be obtained (which can be refined to be more precise by allowing more states in the automaton of the regular weight function). Note that the new $ICFG$ which is obtained from an $ICFG$ and automaton $A$ has a blowup in the number of states of $A$, and thus there is a tradeoff between the precision of $A$ and the size of the new $ICFG$ constructed.

## 3. Applications: Theoretical Modeling

In this section we show that many diverse problems for static analysis can be reduced to ratio analysis of $ICFG$s. We will present experimental results (in Section 5) for the problems described in Section 3.1 and Section 3.2.

### 3.1 Container analysis

The inefficient use of containers is the cause of many performance issues in Java. An excellent exposition of the problem with several practical motivations is presented in [45]. The importance of accurate identification of misuse of containers that minimizes (and ideally eliminates) the number of false warnings was emphasized in [45] and much effort was spent to avoid false warnings for real-world programs. We show that the ratio analysis for $ICFG$s provides a mathematically sound approach for the identification of inefficient use of containers.

**Two misuses.** We aim to capture two common misuses of containers following the definitions in [45]. The first inefficient use is an *underutilized container* that always holds very few number of elements. The cause of inefficiency is two-fold: (i) a container is typically created with a default number of slots, and much more memory is allocated than needed; and (ii) the functionality that is associated with the container is typically not specialized to the case that it has only very few elements. The second inefficiency is caused by *overpopulated containers* that are looked up rarely, though potentially they can have many elements. This causes a memory waste and performance penalty for every lookup. Thus we consider the following two cases of misuse:

1. A container is *underutilized* if there exists a constant bound on the number of elements that it holds for all runs of the program.
2. For a threshold $\lambda$, a container is *overpopulated* if for all runs of the program the ratio of GET vs ADD operations is less than $\lambda$.

We note that our approach is demand-driven (where users can specify to check the misuse of a specific container).

**Modeling.** The modeling of programs as $ICFG$s is standard. We describe how the weight function and the ratio analysis problem can model the problem of detecting misuses. We abstract the different container operations into GET, ADD, and DELETE operations. For this purpose we require the user to annotate the relevant class methods by GET, ADD, or DELETE; and by a weight function that corresponds to the number of GET, ADD, or DELETE operations that the method does (typically this number is 1). For example, in the class **HashSet**, the **add** method is annotated by ADD, the **contains** method is annotated by GET and the **remove** operation is annotated by DELETE. The **clear** operation which removes all elements from the set is annotated by DELETE but with a large weight (if **clear** appears in a loop, it dominates the add operations of the loop). We note that the annotation can be automated with the approach that is described in [45].

1. When detecting underutilized containers we define ADD operations as good events and DELETE operations as bad events, and check for threshold 1. Note that the relevant threshold is 1: if the (long-run) ratio of ADD vs DELETE is not greater than 1, then the total number of elements in the container is bounded by a constant.
2. When detecting overpopulated containers we define GET operations as good events and ADD operations as bad events, and check for the given threshold $\lambda$.

In addition, since we wish to analyze heap objects, the allocation of the container is a bad event with a large weight (i.e., similar effect as of **clear**); see Example 3. The container is misused iff the answer to the ratio analysis problem is NO (note that in the problem description for container analysis we have quantification over all paths and for ratio analysis of $ICFG$s the quantification is existential). The detection is demand-driven and done for an allocated container **c**.

*Details of modeling.* Intuitively, a transition in the call graph is good if it invokes a functionality that is annotated by a good operation (i.e., ADD operation for the underutilized analysis and GET operation for the overpopulated analysis) and the object that invokes the operation points to container **c**, and it is bad if the invoked operation is annotated as bad. Formally, for a given allocated container **c**: If at a certain line a variable **t** that *may point to* **c** invokes a good functionality, then we denote the transition as good. If **t** *must point to* **c** and invokes a bad functionality, then we denote it as a bad events. All other transitions are neutral. Note that our modeling is conservative. The misuse is detected for the container **c** if all runs of the program have a ratio of good vs bad events that is below the threshold (in other words, the container is not misused if there exists a path where the ratio of good vs bad events is above the threshold, and this exactly corresponds to the ratio analysis of $ICFG$s).

**Example 3.** *We illustrate some important aspects of the container analysis problem with an example. Consider the program shown in Figure 3. We consider the containers that are allocated in line 9 and in line 20 and analyze them for underutilization. There exist runs that go through line 14 and properly use the container that is allocated in line 9, since qux method can add unbounded number of elements to the hash table (due to its recursive call). However, the container in line 20 is underutilized, since in every run the number of elements is bounded by 2. However, note that if the* DELETE *operation is not handled, then the container is reported as properly used. We note that since we assign large weights to*

```
1  void qux( Hashtable h, int x ){
2     h.put( x, x/2 );
3     if( x > 0 ){
4        qux( h, x/2 );
5     }
6  }
7
8  Hashtable bar( int x ){
9     return new Hashtable(x*x);
10 }
```

```
12 void foo( int x ){
13    if( x % 2){
14       Hashtable h1 = bar(x);
15       qux(h1, x);
16    }
17    else
18    {
19       for( int y = 0 ; y < x ; y++ ){
20          Hashtable h2 = new Hashtable(y);
21          h2.put(y,x);
22          for( int z = 0 ; z < y ; z++ )
23          {
24             h2.put(z,y);
25             ...
26             h2.remove(z);
27          }
28       }
29    }
30 }
```

**Figure 3.** An example for underutilized container analysis.

*the allocation of the container, this prevents the analysis from reporting that h2 properly uses the container that is allocated in line 20. In summary, the example illustrates the following important features: (1) the proper usage of the container should be tested also outside of its allocation site*[1] *(as opposed to the approach of [45]); (2) sometimes the proper usage of a container is due to recursion; and (3) handling* DELETE *operations appropriately increases the precision of analysis. While these important features are illustrated with the toy example, such behaviors were also manifested in the programs of the benchmarks (see Subsection 5.2 for details).*

*Soundness.* Our ratio analysis approach for $ICFG$s is both sound and complete (with respect to the weighted abstracted $ICFG$). Since we use a conservative approach for assigning bad and good events, the $ICFG$ we obtain for the misuse analysis of containers is sound and we get the following result.

**Theorem 1.** (SOUNDNESS). *The underutilized and overpopulated container analysis through the ratio analysis problem on ICFGs is sound (do not report false positives, i.e., any reported misused container is truly misused).*

**Remark 2.** *We remark about the significance of the soundness of our approach.*

- *The soundness criteria is a very important and desirable feature for container analysis (for details see [43, 45]), because a reported misused container needs to be analyzed manually and incurs a substantial effort for optimization. Hence as argued in [43, 45], spurious warnings (false positive) of misuse must be minimized. In our approach, a misuse is reported iff in every run a misuse is detected, and with a sound (over approximation) annotation of the weights our approach is sound.*
- *The soundness of our approach is with respect to a sound (over approximation) annotation of the* ADD , DELETE *and* GET *operations. In addition, for a given ICFG, our ratio analysis is* precise *(i.e.. both sound and complete), hence, our container analysis is sound.*

### 3.2 Static profiling

Finding the most frequently executed lines in the code can help the programmer to identify the critical parts of the program and focus on the optimization of these parts. It can also assist the compiler (e.g., a C compiler) to decide whether it should apply certain optimizations such as *function inlining* (replacing a function call by the body of the called function) and *loop unrolling* (re-write the loop as a repeated sequence of similar independent statements). These optimizations can reduce the running time of the program, but on the other hand, they increase the size of the (binary) code. Hence, knowing whether the function or loop is *hot* (frequently invoked) is important when considering the time vs. code size tradeoff. In this subsection we present the model for profiling the frequency of function calls (which allows finding hot functions), and we note that our profiling technique is generic and can be scaled to detect other hot spots in the code (e.g., hot loops).

**Problem description.** Given a program with several functions, a function $f$ is called $\lambda$-hot, if there exists a run (of unbounded length) of the program where the frequency of calls to $f$ (among all function calls in the run) is at least $\lambda$. Formally, for a run, given a prefix of length $i$, let $\#f(i)$ denote the number of calls to $f$ and $\#c(i)$ denote the number of function calls in the prefix of length $i$. The function is $\lambda$-hot if there exists a run such that $\liminf_{i\to\infty} \frac{\#f(i)}{\#c(i)} > \lambda$.

**Modeling.** The modeling of programs as $ICFG$s is straightforward. We describe the labeling of events and weight function in $ICFG$s to determine if a function $f$ is $\lambda$-hot. First we label call-transitions to $f$ as good events and assign weight 1; then we label all other call-transitions as bad events and assign them weight 1. To ensure that the number of calls to $f$ also appear in the denominator (in the total number of calls) we label transitions from the entry node of $f$ as bad events with weight 1. The function $f$ is $\lambda$-hot iff the answer to the ratio analysis problem with threshold $\lambda$ is YES.

### 3.3 Estimating worst-case execution time

The approach of [12] for estimating worst-case execution time (WCET) is also naturally captured by ratio analysis. While the intraprocedural problem was considered in [12], our approach allows the more general interprocedural analysis. In this approach, we consider (as in [12]) that each program statement is assigned a cost that corresponds to its running time (e.g., number of CPU cycles).

**Modeling.** The modelling of WCET analysis of the program is as follows: We add to the $ICFG$ of the program a transition from every terminal node to the initial node, and every such transition is a bad event with weight 1. All the other transitions are good events and their weight is their cost (running time). The WCET of the program is at most $N$ cycles if and only if the answer to the ratio analysis problem with threshold $N$ is NO.

### 3.4 Evaluating the speedup in a parallel computation

The speed of a parallel computing is limited by the time needed for the sequential fraction of the program. For example, if a program runs for 10 minutes on a single processor core, and a certain part of the program that takes 2 minutes to execute cannot be parallelized, then the minimum execution time cannot be less than two minutes (regardless of how many processors are devoted to a parallelized execution of this program). Hence, the speedup is at most 5. Amdahl's law [1] states that the theoretical speedup that can be obtained by executing a given algorithm on a system capable of executing $n$ threads of execution is at most $\frac{1}{B+\frac{1}{n}(1-B)}$, where $B$ is the fraction of the algorithm that is strictly serial. Our ratio analysis technique can be used to (conservatively) estimate the value of $B$ and thus to evaluate the outcome of Amdahl's law.

**Modeling.** As in Section 3.3, we consider that the cost of every program statement is given, and we add to the $ICFG$ of the program a transition from every terminal node to the initial node, this time as a neutral event with weight 0. All the transitions of the code that cannot be parallelized are defined as good events, and the other transitions are defined as bad events. We denote by $P$ the fraction of the code that can be parallelized and by $S$ the fraction of the code that is strictly serial. The value of $\frac{S}{P}$ is at most $\lambda$ if and only if the answer to the ratio analysis problem with threshold $\lambda$ is NO. Hence $B$ is bounded by $\frac{1}{1+\frac{1}{\lambda}}$ for which the answer to the ratio analysis problem with threshold $\lambda$ is NO.

[1] E.g., an HashTable is allocated in bar function but the proper usage is done outside the allocation site, namely, after the termination of bar.

### 3.5 Average energy consumption

In the case of many consumer electronics devices, especially mobile phones, battery capacity is severely restricted due to constraints on size and weight of the device. This implies that managing energy well is paramount in such devices. Since most mobile applications are non-terminating (e.g., a web browser), the most important metric for measuring energy consumption is the average memory consumption per time unit [11], e.g., watts per second.

**Modeling.** We consider that the running time and energy consumption of each statement in the application code is given (or is approximated). In our modeling we split each transition in the $ICFG$ into two consecutive transitions, the first is a good event and the next is a bad event. The good event is assigned with a weight that corresponds to the energy consumption of the program statement and the bad event is assigned with a weight that corresponds to the running time of the statement. The average energy consumption of the application is at most $\lambda$ if and only if the answer to the ratio analysis problem is NO.

## 4. Algorithm for Quantitative Analysis of $QICFG$s

In this section we present three results. The mean-payoff analysis problem for $QICFG$s can be solved in polynomial time, this can be derived from [14]. First, we present an algorithm that significantly improves the current theoretical bound for the problem for $QICFG$s. Second, we present an efficient algorithm that in most practical cases is much faster as compared to the theoretical upper bound. Finally, we present a linear reduction of the ratio analysis problem to the mean-payoff analysis problem for $QICFG$s.

### 4.1 Improved algorithm for mean-payoff analysis

In this section we first discuss the basic polynomial-time algorithm for mean-payoff analysis of $QICFG$s that can be obtained from the results on pushdown systems shown in [14]. Due to space constraints the technical proofs are relegated to the supplementary material.

**Results of [14] and reduction.** The results of [14] show that pushdown systems with mean-payoff objectives can be solved in polynomial time. Given a pushdown system with state space $Q$ and stack alphabet $\Gamma$, the polynomial-time algorithm of [14] can be described as follows. The algorithm is iterative, and in each iteration it constructs a finite graph of size $O(|Q| \cdot |\Gamma|^2)$ and runs a Bellman-Ford style algorithm on the finite graph from each vertex. The Bellman-Ford algorithm on the finite graph from all vertices in each iteration requires $O(|Q|^3 \cdot |\Gamma|^6)$ time and $O(|Q|^2 \cdot |\Gamma|^4)$ space. The number of iterations required is $O(|Q|^2 \cdot |\Gamma|^2)$. Thus the time and space requirement of the algorithm are $O(|Q|^5 \cdot |\Gamma|^8)$ and $O(|Q|^2 \cdot |\Gamma|^4)$, respectively. A $QICFG$ can be interpreted as a pushdown system where $N$ corresponds to $Q$ and $Retns$ corresponds to $\Gamma$.

**Theorem 2.** (BASIC ALGORITHM [14]). *The mean-payoff analysis problem for QICFGs can be solved in* $O(|N|^5 \cdot |Retns|^8)$ *time and* $O(|N|^2 \cdot |Retns|^4)$ *space, respectively.*

**Improved algorithm.** We will present an improved polynomial-time algorithm for the mean-payoff analysis of $QICFG$s. The improvement relies on the following properties of $QICFG$s:

1. The transitions of a module are independent of the stack of a configuration, while in pushdown systems the transitions can depend on the top symbol of the stack. This enables to reduce the size of the finite graphs to be considered in every iteration.
2. Every call node has only one corresponding return node. Therefore, if a module $A_1$ invokes a module $A_2$, then the behavior of $A_1$ after the termination of $A_2$ is independent of $A_2$. This enables us to reduce the number of iterations to $O(|Calls|)$.

To present the improved algorithm and its correctness formally, we need a refined analysis and extensions of the results of [14]. We first describe a key aspect and present an overview of the solution.

**Remark 3.** *(Infinite-height lattice). Our algorithm will be an iterative algorithm till some fixpoint is reached. However, for interprocedural analysis with finite-height lattices, fixpoints are guaranteed to exist. Unfortunately in our case for mean-payoff objectives, it is an infinite-height lattice. Thus a fixpoint is not guaranteed. For this reason the analysis for mean-payoff objectives is more involved, and this is even in the case of finite graphs. For example, for reachability objectives in finite graphs linear-time algorithms exist, whereas for finite graphs with mean-payoff objectives the best-known algorithms (for over three decades) are quadratic [23].*

**Solution overview.** In finite graphs the solution for the mean-payoff analysis is to check whether the graph has a cycle $C$ such that the sum of weights of $C$ is positive. If such a cycle exists, then a *lasso* path that leads to the cycle and then follows the cyclic path forever has positive mean-payoff value. For $QICFG$s we show that it is enough to find either a loop in the program such that the sum of weights of the loop is positive or a sequence of calls and returns with positive total weight such that the last invoked module is the same as the first invoked module. For this purpose we compute a *summary function* that finds the maximum weight (according to the sum of weights) path between every two statements of a method (i.e., between every two nodes of a module). The computation is an extension of the Bellman-Ford algorithm to $QICFG$s. We show that it is enough to compute a summary function for $QICFG$s with a *stack height* that is bounded by some constant, and then all that is left is to mark pairs of nodes such that the weight of a maximal weight path between them is unbounded. In finite graphs the maximum weight between two vertices is unbounded only if the graph has a cycle with positive sum of weights (i.e., a path with positive total weight that can be pumped). For $QICFG$s it is also possible to *pump* special types of acyclic paths. We first characterize these pumpable paths (up to Lemma 2). We then show how to compute a bounded summary function (Lemma 3 and the paragraph that follows it and Example 5). Finally we show how to use the summary function to solve the mean-payoff analysis problem. We start with the basic notions related to stack heights and pumpable paths, and their properties which are crucial for the algorithm.

*Stack heights.* The *configuration stack height* of $c = (r_1, \ldots, r_j, u)$, denoted as $\mathsf{SH}(c)$, is $j$. For a finite path $\pi = \langle(\alpha_1, n_1), \ldots, (\alpha_\ell, n_\ell)\rangle$, the stack height of the path (denoted by $\mathsf{SH}(\pi)$) is the maximal stack height of all the configurations in the path. Formally $\mathsf{SH}(\pi) = \max\{|\alpha_1|, \ldots, |\alpha_\ell|\}$. The *additional stack height* of $\pi$ is the additional height of the stack in the segment of the path, i.e., the additional stack height $\mathsf{ASH}(\pi)$ is $\mathsf{SH}(\pi) - \max(|\alpha_1|, |\alpha_\ell|)$.

*Pumpable pair of paths.* Let $\pi = \langle c_1 t_1 t_2 \ldots\rangle$ be a finite or infinite path (where each $t_i$ is a transition in the $QICFG$). A *pumpable pair of paths* for $\pi$ is a pair of non-empty sequences of transitions: $(p_1, p_2) = (t_{i_1} t_{i_1+1} \ldots t_{i_1+\ell_1}, t_{i_2} t_{i_2+1} \ldots t_{i_2+\ell_2})$, for $\ell_1, \ell_2 \geq 0$, $i_1 \geq 0$ and $i_2 > i_1 + \ell_1$ such that for every $j \geq 0$ the path $\pi^j_{(p_1,p_2)}$ obtained by pumping the pair $p_1$ and $p_2$ of paths $j$ times each is a valid path, i.e., for every $j \geq 0$ we have

$$\pi^j_{(p_1,p_2)} = \langle c_1 t_1 \ldots t_{i_1-1} (p_1)^j t_{i_1+\ell_1+1} \ldots t_{i_2-1} (p_2)^j t_{i_2+\ell_2+1} \ldots\rangle$$

is a valid path. We illustrate the above definitions with the next example.

**Example 4.** *Consider the program from Figure 1 and Figure 2 and the corresponding ICFG. A possible path in the program is*

*m:Entry* $\rightarrow$ *while(x)* $\rightarrow$ *if(y>0)* $\rightarrow$ *m:call foo* $\rightarrow$ *f:Entry* $\rightarrow$ *if(x>1)* $\rightarrow$ *f:call foo* $\rightarrow$ *f:Entry* $\rightarrow$ *if(x>1)* $\rightarrow$

x++ $\rightarrow$ f:Exit $\rightarrow$ f:foo ret $\rightarrow$ x++ $\rightarrow$ f:Exit $\rightarrow$ m:foo ret $\rightarrow$ while(x)

*and we denote this path with $\pi$. Then $\mathsf{ASH}(\pi) = 2$, and the pair of paths f:Entry $\rightarrow$ if(x>1) $\rightarrow$ f:call foo and f:foo ret $\rightarrow$ x++ $\rightarrow$ f:Exit is a pumpable pair of paths.*

In the next lemmas we first show that every path with large additional stack has a pumpable pair of paths, and then establish the connection of additional stack height and the existence of pumpable pair of paths with positive weights in Lemma 2. The key intuition for the proof of the next lemma is that a path with $\mathsf{ASH}(\pi) > |Calls| + 1$ must contain a recursive call that can be pumped.

**Lemma 1.** *Let $\pi$ be a finite path with $\mathsf{ASH}(\pi) = d > |Calls| + 1$. Then $\pi$ has a pumpable pair of paths.*

**Lemma 2.** *Let $c_1, c_2$ be two configurations and $j \in \mathbb{Z}$. Let $d \in \mathbb{N}$ be the minimal additional stack height of all paths between $c_1$ and $c_2$ with total weight at least $j$. If $d > |Calls| + 1$, then there exists a path $\pi^*$ from $c_1$ to $c_2$ with additional stack height $d$ that has a pumpable pair $(p_1, p_2)$ with $w(p_1) + w(p_2) > 0$.*

*Proof.* Let us consider the set of paths $\Pi$ between $c_1$ and $c_2$ with total weight at least $j$, and let $\Pi_{\min}$ be the subset of $\Pi$ that has minimal additional stack height. The proof is by induction on the length of paths in $\Pi_{\min}$. Consider a path $\pi$ from $\Pi_{\min}$ that has the shortest length among all paths in $\Pi_{\min}$. Since $\mathsf{ASH}(\pi) = d > |Calls| + 1$, then by Lemma 1 it contains a pumpable pair. Let us consider the path $\pi_1$ obtained from $\pi$ by pumping the pumpable pair zero times (i.e., the pumpable pair is removed). Since we remove a part of the path we have that $\mathsf{ASH}(\pi_1) \leq \mathsf{ASH}(\pi)$. If $w(\pi_1) \geq w(\pi)$, then we obtain a path $\pi_1$ with weight at least $j$, with either smaller additional stack height than $\pi$, or of shorter length, contradicting that $\pi$ is the shortest length minimal additional stack height path with weight at least $j$. Hence we must have $w(\pi_1) < w(\pi)$, and hence the pumpable pair has positive weight. Now for an arbitrary path $\pi$ in $\Pi_{\min}$ we obtain that it has a pumpable pair. Either the pumpable pair has positive weight and we are done, else removing the pumpable pair we obtain a shorter length path of the same stack height, and the result follows by inductive hypothesis on the length of paths. □

Our algorithm for the mean-payoff analysis problem is based on detecting the existence of certain *non-decreasing* paths with positive weight. The maximal weights of such non-decreasing paths between node pairs are captured with the notion of a *summary function* and *bounded summary functions* (with bounded additional stack height). We now define them, and establish the lemma related to the number of bounded summary functions to be computed.

*Local minimum and non-decreasing paths.* A configuration $c_i$ in a path $\pi = \langle c_1, \ldots, c_\ell \rangle$ is a *local minimum* if the stack height of $c_i$ is minimal in $\pi$, i.e., $|\alpha_i| = \min(|\alpha_1|, \ldots, |\alpha_\ell|)$. A path from configuration $(\alpha, n_1)$ to $(\alpha\beta, n_2)$ is a *non-decreasing $\alpha$-path* if $(\alpha, n_1)$ is a local minimum. Note that if a sequence of transitions is a non-decreasing $\alpha$-path for some $\alpha \in Retns^*$, then the same sequence of transitions is a non-decreasing $\gamma$-path for every $\gamma \in Retns^*$. Hence, we say that $\pi$ is a non-decreasing path if there exists $\alpha \in Retns^*$ such that $\pi$ is a non-decreasing $\alpha$-path.

*Summary function.* Given the *QICFG* $\mathcal{A}$ and $\alpha \in Retns^*$, we define a summary function $s_\alpha : \bigcup_{1 \leq \ell \leq m}(N_\ell \times N_\ell) \rightarrow \{-\infty\} \cup \mathbb{Z} \cup \{\omega\}$ as:

1. $s_\alpha(n_1, n_2) = z \in \mathbb{Z}$ iff the weight of the maximum weight non-decreasing path from configuration $(\alpha, n_1)$ to configuration $(\alpha, n_2)$ is $z$.
2. $s_\alpha(n_1, n_2) = \omega$ iff for all $j \in \mathbb{N}$ there exists a non-decreasing path from $(\alpha, n_1)$ to $(\alpha, n_2)$ with weight at least $j$.
3. $s_\alpha(n_1, n_2) = -\infty$ iff there is no non-decreasing path from $(\alpha, n_1)$ to $(\alpha, n_2)$.

We note that for every $\alpha, \beta \in Retns^*$ it holds that $s_\alpha \equiv s_\beta$. Hence, we consider only $s \equiv s_\epsilon$ (where $\epsilon$ is the empty string and corresponds to empty stack). The computation of the summary function is done by considering stack height bounded summary functions defined below.

*Stack height bounded summary function.* For every $d \in \mathbb{N}$, the *stack height bounded summary function* $s_d : \bigcup_{1 \leq \ell \leq m}(N_\ell \times N_\ell) \rightarrow \{-\infty\} \cup \mathbb{Z} \cup \{\omega\}$ is defined as follows: (i) $s_d(n_1, n_2) = z \in \mathbb{Z}$ iff the weight of the maximum weight non-decreasing path from $(\epsilon, n_1)$ to $(\epsilon, n_2)$ with additional stack height at most $d$ is $z$; (ii) $s_d(n_1, n_2) = \omega$ iff for all $j \in \mathbb{N}$ there exists a non-decreasing path from $(\epsilon, n_1)$ to $(\epsilon, n_2)$ with weight at least $j$ and additional stack height at most $d$; and (iii) $s_d(n_1, n_2) = -\infty$ iff there is no non-decreasing path with additional stack height at most $d$ from $(\epsilon, n_1)$ to $(\epsilon, n_2)$.

*Facts of summary functions.* We have the following facts: (i) for every $d \in \mathbb{N}$, we have $s_{d+1} \geq s_d$ (monotonicity); and (ii) $s_{d+1}$ is computable from $s_d$ and the *QICFG*. By the above facts we get that if $s_d \equiv s_{d+1}$, i.e., if a fix point is reached, then $s \equiv s_d$. For interprocedural analysis with finite-height lattices, fix points are guaranteed to exist. Unfortunately in our case, the image of $s_i$ is infinite and moreover, it is an infinite-height lattice. Thus a fix point is not guaranteed. The next lemma shows that we can compute all the non-$\omega$ values of $s$ with the bounded summary function.

**Lemma 3.** *Let $d = |Calls| + 1$. For all $n_1, n_2 \in N$, if $s(n_1, n_2) \in \mathbb{Z} \cup \{-\infty\}$, then $s(n_1, n_2) = s_d(n_1, n_2)$.*

By Lemma 3 we get that if $s_{d+1}(n_1, n_2) > s_d(n_1, n_2)$ (for $d = |Calls| + 1$), then $s(n_1, n_2) = \omega$. Hence, the summary function $s$ is obtained by the fix point of the following computation: (i) Compute $s_{i+1}$ from $s_i$ up to $s_d$ for $d = |Calls| + 1$; (ii) for $i \geq |Calls| + 1$, if $s_{i+1}(n_1, n_2) > s_i(n_1, n_2)$, then set $s_{i+1}(n_1, n_2) = \omega$; (iii) a fix point is reached after at most $O(|Calls|)$ iterations (say $j$ iterations), and then we set $s \equiv s_j$. This establishes that we require only $O(|Calls|)$ iterations as compared to $O(|N|^2 \cdot |Retns|^2)$ iterations. The number of returns and calls are the same and thus we significantly improve the number of iterations required from the quartic worst-case bound to linear bound. We now describe the computation of every iteration to obtain $s_{i+1}$ from $s_i$.

*Computation of $s_{i+1}$ from $s_i$.* We first compute a partial function, namely, $s'_{i+1} : En \times Ex \rightarrow \{-\infty, \omega\} \cup \mathbb{Z}$ that satisfies $s'_{i+1}(n_1, n_2) = s_{i+1}(n_1, n_2)$ for every $n_1 \in En$ and $n_2 \in Ex$. We initialize $s'_0(n_1, n_2) = s_0(n_1, n_2)$. For every module $A_\ell$ we construct a finite graph $G^i_\ell$ by taking all the nodes and transitions of $A_\ell$ and by adding a transition between every call node and its corresponding return node. For every transition between a pair of nodes $n_1, n_2 \in N_\ell \setminus (Calls_\ell \cup Retns_\ell)$ we assign the weight according to the original weight in $\mathcal{A}$. For every transition between a call node that invokes module $A_p$ and a corresponding return node we assign the weight $s'_i(En_p, Ex_p)$. To compute $s'_{i+1}$ for module $A_\ell$ we run one Bellman-Ford iteration over $G^i_\ell$ for source node $En_\ell$ and target node $Ex_\ell$. We observe the next two key properties of $s'_i$:

- For every iteration $i$, a module $A_\ell$, and pair of nodes $n_1, n_2 \in N_\ell$ we have that the weight of the maximum weight path between $n_1$ and $n_2$ in $G^i_\ell$ is exactly $s_{i+1}(n_1, n_2)$ (the proof is by a simple induction over $i$).
- If $s'_{i+1} \equiv s'_i$, then $s_{i+1} \equiv s_i$ (follows from the first key property).

Hence, to compute $s$ we compute $s'_{i+1}$ from $s'_i$ until we get $s'_{i+1} \equiv s'_i$, and then we compute all pairs maximum weight paths (e.g., by the Floyd-Warshall algorithm) over every $G^i_\ell$ and get $s_{i+1}$ (and $s_{i+1} \equiv s$). The Floyd-Warshall algorithm has a cubic time complexity and quadratic space complexity [15]. Therefore, the time complexity for computing every iteration of $s_i$ is $O(\sum |N_\ell|^2)$ and the complexity of the last step is $O(\sum |N_\ell|^3)$. The space complexity of the last step is $O(\max\{|N_1|, \ldots, |N_m|\}^2)$, but to store $s_i$ we require $O(\sum |N_\ell|^2)$ space.

*Summary graph.* Given *QICFG* $\mathcal{A}$ with a summary function $s$, we construct the *summary graph* $\mathsf{Gr}(\mathcal{A}) = (V, E)$ of $\mathcal{A}$ with a weight function $w : E \to \mathbb{Z} \cup \{\omega\}$ as follows: (i) $V = N \setminus (Ex \cup Retns)$; and (ii) $E = E_{internal} \cup E_{calls}$ where $E_{internal} = \{(n_1, n_2) \mid n_1, n_2 \in N_\ell$ for some $\ell$, and $s(n_1, n_2) > -\infty\}$ contains the transitions in the same module and $E_{calls} = \{(n_1, n_2) \mid n_1 \in Calls$ and $n_2 \in En$ and $n_1$ is a call to a module with entry node $n_2\}$ contains the call transitions. The weights of $E_{internal}$ are according to the summary function $s$ and the weights of $E_{calls}$ are according to the weights of these transitions in $\mathcal{A}$ (i.e., according to $w$). A simple cycle in $\mathsf{Gr}(A)$ is a *positive simple cycle* iff one of the following conditions hold: (i) the cycle contains an $\omega$ edge; or (ii) the sum of the weights of the cycles according to the weights of the summary graph is positive. Lemma 4 shows the equivalence of the mean-payoff analysis problem and positive cycles in the summary graph.

**Lemma 4.** *A QICFG $\mathcal{A}$ has a path $\pi$ with $LimAvg(w(\pi)) > 0$ iff the summary graph $\mathsf{Gr}(\mathcal{A})$ has a (reachable) positive cycle.*

*Proof.* If $\mathsf{Gr}(\mathcal{A})$ does not contain a positive cycle, then it follows that the weight of every non-decreasing path in $\mathcal{A}$ is bounded by the weight of the maximum weight path in $\mathsf{Gr}(\mathcal{A})$. Hence, for every infinite path $\pi$ we get that every prefix of $\pi$ is a non-decreasing path from the initial configuration with bounded weight (sum of weights bounded from above), and therefore $LimAvg(w(\pi)) \leq 0$. Conversely, if $\mathsf{Gr}(\mathcal{A})$ has a positive cycle, then it follows that there is a path $\pi_0\pi_1$ in $\mathsf{Gr}(\mathcal{A})$ such that $\pi_0$ and $\pi_1$ are non-decreasing paths, $\pi_1$ begins and ends in the same node (possibly at higher stack height) and $w(\pi_1) > 0$. Hence, the path $\pi_0\pi_1^\omega$ is a valid path and satisfies $LimAvg(w(\pi_0\pi_1^\omega)) = \frac{w(\pi_1)}{|\pi_1|} > 0$, where $\pi_1^\omega = \pi_1 \cdot \pi_1 \cdot \pi_1 \ldots$ is the infinite concatenation of the finite path $\pi_1$. The desired result follows. □

*Algorithm and analysis.* Algorithm 1 solves the mean-payoff analysis problem for *QICFG*s. The computation of the summary function requires $O(|Calls|)$ computations of the partial summary function $s'_i$, which requires $m$ runs of Bellman-Ford algorithm, each run over a graph of size $|N_\ell|$ (hence, each run takes $O(|N_\ell|^2)$ time). In addition the computation requires $m$ runs of all pairs maximum weight path (Floyd-Warshall) algorithm. Each run is over a graph of size $O(|N_\ell|)$ (hence, each run takes $O(|N_\ell|^3)$ time and $O(|N_\ell|^2)$ space). Finally we detect positive cycles by running Bellman-Ford algorithm once over the summary graph, which takes $O(|N|^2)$ time and $O(|N|)$ space. Thus we obtain the following result.

**Theorem 3.** (IMPROVED ALGORITHM). *Algorithm 1 solves the mean-payoff analysis problem for QICFGs in $O\left((|Calls| \cdot (\sum |N_\ell|^2)) + (\sum |N_\ell|^3) + |N|^2\right)$ time and $O(\sum |N_\ell|^2)$ space.*

**Remark 4.** *Note that in the worst case the running time of Algorithm 1 is cubic and the space requirement is quadratic.*

The next example is an illustration of a run of Algorithm 1.

**Example 5.** *Consider the QICFG that consists of modules f and g (Figures 4 and 5) and the entry of f is the initial entry of the program. We now describe the run of Algorithm 1 over the QICFG. For simplicity, we denote the graph of f by F and the graph of g by G (and not by $G_1$ and $G_2$). Note that the number of call nodes is 3.*

*We first compute the summary function $s'$ and the first step is to compute $s'_0$. We have $s'_0$(f:entry,f:exit) $= -35$, and $s'_0$(g:entry,g:exit) $= -25$.*

*In order to compute $s'_1$(f:entry,f:exit) we construct a graph $F^0$ from F by adding a transition from the node f:call g to the node f:ret g with weight $s'_0$(g:entry,g:exit) and find the maximum weight*

**Algorithm 1** Mean-payoff *QICFG* Analysis

**for** $\ell \leftarrow 1$ to $m$ **do**
  $s'_0(En_\ell, Ex_\ell) \leftarrow$ BELLMAN-FORD$(A_\ell)$ {Compute $s'_0$ by running Bellman-Ford algorithm on $A_\ell$}
**end for**
$i \leftarrow 1$
**loop**
  **for** $\ell \leftarrow 1$ to $m$ **do**
    Construct $G_\ell^{i-1}$ according to $s'_{i-1}$
    $s'_i(En_\ell, Ex_\ell) \leftarrow$ BELLMAN-FORD$(G_\ell^{i-1})$ {Compute $s'_i$ by running Bellman-Ford algorithm over $G_\ell^{i-1}$}
  **end for**
  **if** $s'_i \equiv s'_{i-1}$ **then**
    **break**
  **end if**
  **if** $i > |Calls| + 1$ **then**
    **for** $\ell \leftarrow 1$ to $m$ **do**
      **if** $s'_i(En_\ell, Ex_\ell) > s'_{i-1}(En_\ell, Ex_\ell)$ **then**
        $s'_i(En_\ell, Ex_\ell) = \omega$
      **end if**
    **end for**
  **end if**
  $i \leftarrow i + 1$
**end loop**
$s \leftarrow$FLOYD-WARSHALL$(s'_i)$
Construct $\mathsf{Gr}(\mathcal{A})$ from $s$
BELLMAN-FORD$(\mathsf{Gr}(\mathcal{A}))$ {Run Bellman-Ford over $\mathsf{Gr}(\mathcal{A})$}
**if** $\mathsf{Gr}(\mathcal{A})$ has a positive cycle **then**
  **return** YES
**else**
  **return** NO
**end if**

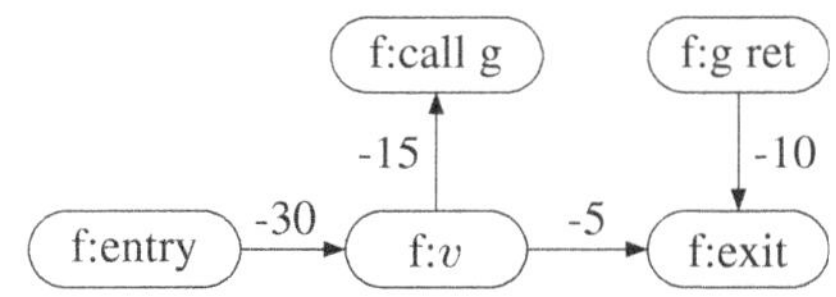


**Figure 4.** Module f

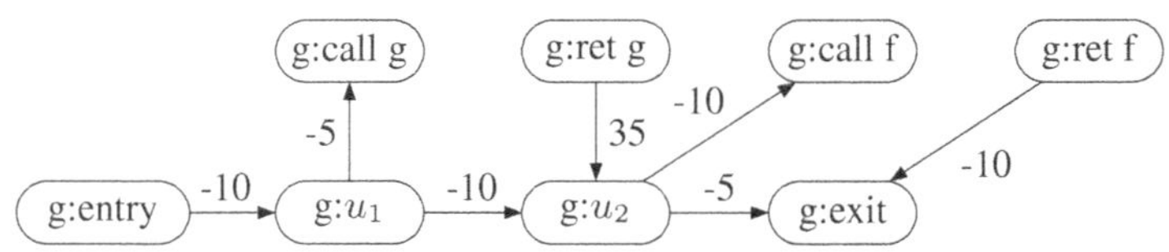


**Figure 5.** Module g

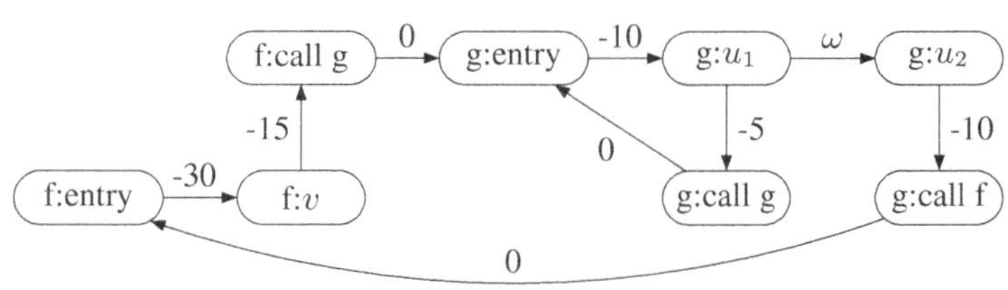


**Figure 6.** Summary graph of f and g

*path from f:entry to f:exit in $F^0$. We get $s'_1$(f:entry,f:exit) $= -35$. In order to compute $s'_1$(g:entry,g:exit) we construct a graph $G^0$ from G by adding a transition from g:call g to g:ret g with weight $s'_0$(g:entry,g:exit) and a transition from g:call f to g:ret f with weight $s'_0$(f:entry,f:exit) and find the maximum weight path from g:entry to g:exit in $G^0$. We get $s'_1$(g:entry,g:exit) $= -10$.*

*Since $s'_1 \neq s'_0$, we continue to compute $s'_2$. We construct $F^1$ and $G^1$ in the same manner as we constructed $F^0$ and $G^0$ (but take the values of $s'_1$ instead of $s'_0$) and get $s'_2$(f:entry,f:exit) $= -35$, $s'_2$(g:entry,g:exit) $= 5$. For $i = 3$ we get $s'_3$(f:entry,f:exit) $= -35$, $s'_3$(g:entry,g:exit) $= 20$. For $i = 4$, $s'_4$(f:entry,f:exit) $= -35$, $s'_4$(g:entry,g:exit) $= 35$.*

*For $i = 5$ we get $s'_5$(f:entry,f:exit) $= -20$ and $s'_5$(g:entry,g:exit) $= 50$. Since $i > |Calls| + 1$ and $s'_5$(f:entry,f:exit) $>$ $s'_4$(f:entry,f:exit) and $s'_5$(g:entry,g:exit) $>$ $s'_4$(g:entry,g:exit) we assign assign $s'_5$(f:entry,f:exit) $= \omega$ and $s'_5$(g:entry,g:exit) $= \omega$. In the sixth iteration we get a fix point (that is, $s'_6 \equiv s'_5$) and exit the loop block.*

*From $F^5$ and $G^5$ we compute the summary function s. For example s(g:entry,g:$u_1$) $= \omega$ and s(f:entry,f:v) $= -30$. Finally, we construct the summary graph (see Figure 6) and check whether a positive cycle exists. The cycle f:entry→f:v→f:call g→g:entry→g:$u_1$→g:$u_2$→g:call f→f:entry contains an $\omega$-edge and thus, it is a positive cycle. Hence algorithm returns YES.*

### 4.2 Efficient algorithm for mean-payoff analysis

In this section we further improve the algorithm for the mean-payoff analysis problem for *QICFG*s, and the improvement depends on the fact that typically the number of entry, exit, call, and returns nodes is much smaller than the size of the *QICFG*s. Formally, in most typical cases we have $|Ex \cup Retns \cup Calls \cup En| << |N|$. Let $X_\ell = \{Ex_\ell, En_\ell\} \cup Retns_\ell \cup Calls_\ell$ and $X = \bigcup_\ell X_\ell$. We present an improvement that enables us to construct the summary function over graphs of size $O(|X_\ell|)$ (instead of graphs of size $O(|N_\ell|)$ of Section 4.1), and with at most $O(|Calls|)$ iterations. Hence, the algorithm in most typical cases will be much faster and require much smaller space.

**Compact representation.** The key idea for the improvement is to represent the modules in *compact form*. The compact form of a module $A_\ell$, denoted by $\mathsf{Comp}(A_\ell)$, consists of the entry, exit, call, and returns node of $A_\ell$. There is transition between every node in $\mathsf{Comp}(A_\ell)$, and the weight of each transition is the maximum weight path between the nodes with additional stack height 0 (and if there is no such path, then the weight is $-\infty$). Formally, $\mathsf{Comp}(A_\ell) = (V, E)$; where $V = X_\ell$; $E = V \times V$, and $w(v_1, v_2) = s_0(v_1, v_2)$ (where $s_0$ is the bounded height summary function of height 0). If in $\mathsf{Comp}(A_\ell)$ there is a cycle with positive weight that is reachable from the entry node, then we say that $A_\ell$ is a *positive mean-payoff witness*. The computation of the compact form for a module $A_\ell$ requires $O(|X_\ell| \cdot |N_\ell|^2)$ time and $O(|N_\ell|)$ space (running Bellman-Ford on each $A_\ell$), and thus the compact form for all modules can be computed in $O(\sum |X_\ell| \cdot |N_\ell|^2)$ time and $O(\max |N_\ell|)$ space (note that the space can be reused).

*Witness in summary graph of compact forms.* After constructing the compact forms, we compute a summary function for $\mathsf{Comp}(A_1), \ldots, \mathsf{Comp}(A_m)$, and a corresponding summary graph. We say that there is a path with positive mean-payoff iff there exists a positive cycle in the summary graph or there exists a path to the entry node of a positive mean-payoff witness. The correctness of the algorithm relies on the next lemma.

**Lemma 5.** *Let $\mathcal{A} = \langle A_1, \ldots, A_m \rangle$ be a QICFG, let $\mathsf{Gr}(\mathcal{A})$ be its summary graph and let $\mathsf{Comp}(\mathsf{Gr}(\mathcal{A}))$ be the summary graph that is formed by $\mathsf{Comp}(A_1), \ldots, \mathsf{Comp}(A_m)$. The following assertions are equivalent:*

1. *$\mathsf{Gr}(\mathcal{A})$ has a (reachable) positive cycle.*
2. *$\mathsf{Comp}(\mathsf{Gr}(\mathcal{A}))$ has a (reachable) positive cycle or a positive mean-payoff witness.*

The above lemma establishes the correctness of the computation on compact form graphs, and gives us the following result. The following result is obtained from Theorem 3 by replacing $|N_\ell|$ with $|X_\ell|$ and $|N|$ by $|X|$, and the additional $\sum |X_\ell| \cdot |N_\ell|^2$ time and $\max |N_\ell|$ space are required for the compact form computation.

**Theorem 4.** (Efficient algorithm). *The mean-payoff analysis problem for QICFGs can be solved in $O\left((|Calls| \cdot (\sum |X_\ell|^2)) + (\sum |X_\ell|^3) + |X|^2 + \sum |X_\ell| \cdot |N_\ell|^2\right)$ time and $O(\sum |X_\ell|^2 + \max |N_\ell|)$ space, where $X_\ell = \{Ex_\ell, En_\ell\} \cup Retns_\ell \cup Calls_\ell$ and $X = \bigcup_\ell X_\ell$.*

### 4.3 Reduction: Ratio analysis to mean-payoff analysis

We now establish a linear reduction of the ratio analysis problem to the mean-payoff analysis problem. Given a *ICFG* $\mathcal{A}$ with labeling of good, bad, and neutral events, a positive integer weight function $w$, and rational threshold $\lambda > 0$, the reduction of the ratio analysis problem to the mean-payoff analysis problem is as follows. We consider a *QICFG* $\mathcal{A}'$ with weight function $w_\lambda$ for the mean-payoff objective defined as follows: for a transition $e$ we have

$$w_\lambda(e) = \begin{cases} w(e) & \text{if } e \text{ is labelled with } \mathit{good} \\ -\lambda \cdot w(e) & \text{if } e \text{ is labelled with } \mathit{bad} \\ 0 & \text{otherwise (if } e \text{ is labelled with } \mathit{neutral}) \end{cases}$$

The next lemma establishes the correctness of the reduction.

**Lemma 6.** *Given a ICFG $\mathcal{A}$ with labeling of good, bad, and neutral events, a positive integer weight function $w$, and rational threshold $\lambda > 0$, let $\mathcal{A}'$ be the QICFG with weight function $w_\lambda$.*

*There exists a path $\pi$ in $\mathcal{A}$ with $LimRat(w(\pi)) > \lambda$ iff there exists a path $\pi$ in $\mathcal{A}'$ with $LimAvg(w_\lambda(\pi)) > 0$.*

**Remark 5.** *Note that in our reduction from ratio analysis to mean-payoff analysis we do not change the QICFG, but only change the weight function. Thus our algorithms from Theorem 3 and Theorem 4 can also solve the ratio analysis problem for QICFGs. Moreover, our proof of lemma 6 shows that for all paths $\pi$, if we have $LimAvg(w_\lambda(\pi)) > 0$, then we also have $LimRat(w(\pi)) > \lambda$, i.e., any witness for the mean-payoff analysis is also a witness for the ratio analysis.*

## 5. Experimental Results: Two Case Studies

In this section we present our experimental results on two case studies described in Section 3.1 and Section 3.2. We run our case studies on several benchmarks in Java, including DaCapo 2009 benchmarks [4], and we use [7, 25] to assist Soot for the construction of the control-flow graphs. First we present some optimizations that proved useful for speed-up in the benchmarks.

### 5.1 Optimization for case studies

We present four optimizations for the case studies: the first two are general, and the last two are specific to our case studies.

**Faster computation of stack height bounded summary function.** We note that if module $A_\ell$ invokes only modules $A_{j_1}, \ldots, A_{j_k}$, and $s'_i(En_{j_h}, Ex_{j_h}) = s'_{i-1}(En_{j_h}, Ex_{j_h})$ for all $h \in \{1, \ldots, k\}$, then $s'_i(En_\ell, Ex_\ell) = s'_{i-1}(En_\ell, Ex_\ell)$. Hence, when computing $s'_i$, we maintain a set $\mathcal{L}^i = \{\ell \mid s'_i(En_\ell, Ex_\ell) > s'_{i-1}(En_\ell, Ex_\ell)\}$, and in the next iteration we run Bellman-Ford algorithm only for the modules that invoke modules from $\mathcal{L}^i$.

**Reducing the number of iterations for fix point.** We now present an optimization that allows us to reduce the number of bounded height summary functions from $O(|Calls|)$ to a practically constant number. We note that the $O(|Calls|)$ theoretical bound is tight. However, only pathological cases can reach even a fraction of this bound. We note that in typical programs the average nesting of function calls is practically constant (say 10). So if we do not get a fix point after 10 iterations (i.e., $s'_{11} > s'_{10}$), then it is probably because there is a recursive call with positive weight. If this is the case, then if we build the summary graph according to $s_{11}$, we will get a positive cycle in the summary graph, that is, we will get a witness for a path with a positive mean-payoff, and we can stop the computation (since by definition $s \geq s_{11}$, we get that this witness is valid). Hence, our optimized algorithm is to compute the bounded height summary function $s'_i$ and if $s'_i > s'_{i-1}$ and $i = 10, 20, 30, \ldots$, then we construct the summary graph and look for a witness path. If a path is found, then we are done. Otherwise we continue and compute $s'_{i+1}$.

**Removing redundant modules.** Consider an $ICFG$ $\mathcal{A} = \langle A_1, \ldots, A_m \rangle$ in which every node is reachable from the program entry (the entry node of the main method). We say that module $A_i$ is *non-redundant* if (i) the module has non-zero weight transitions (good or bad events); or (ii) it invokes a non-redundant module, and is called *redundant* otherwise. Let $A_i$ be a redundant module. For every path $\pi$ that contains a transition to $En_i$ (an invocation of $A_i$), the segment of $\pi$ between that transition and the first transition to $Ex_i$ contains only neutral transitions. Because all nodes of $\mathcal{A}$ are reachable, we can safely replace each call node that invokes $A_i$ by an internal node that leads to the corresponding return node, and label it as a neutral event. Our optimization then consists of removing redundant modules, as follows:

1. First, we perform a single-source interprocedural reachability from the program entry, which requires linear time ([31]), and discard all non-reachable nodes in all modules.
2. Then, we perform a backwards reachability computation on the call graph of $\mathcal{A}$, starting from the set of all modules that contain non-zero weight transitions. All detected redundant modules are discarded, and calls to them are replaced according to the above description.

Hence, when computing the bounded height summary function, the size of the graph is smaller and the Bellman-Ford algorithm takes less time. Additionally, the number of calls $|Calls|$ decreases, which reduces the number of iterations required in the main loop of Algorithm 1. In the first case study, typically more than half of the methods are eliminated in this process.

**Incremental computation of summary functions.** We present the final optimization which is relevant for our second case study. Let $\mathcal{A}^1$ be a $QICFG$ and let $\mathcal{A}^2$ be a $QICFG$ that is obtained from $\mathcal{A}^1$ only by increasing some of the transitions weights. Let $s^1$ be the summary function of $\mathcal{A}^1$. Then we can compute the summary function of $\mathcal{A}^2$ by setting $s'^2_0 \equiv s^1$ and by computing $s'^2_i$ from $s'^2_{i+1}$ in the usual way. The correctness is almost trivial. Since the weights of $\mathcal{A}^2$ are at least as the weights of $\mathcal{A}^1$, we get that if we conceptually add a transition $(n_1, n_2)$ with weight $s^1(n_1, n_2)$ for every two nodes (in the same module) in $\mathcal{A}^2$, then the weights of the paths with the maximal weight in $\mathcal{A}^2$ remain the same. By assigning $s'^2_0 = s^1$ we only add such conceptual transitions. Hence, the correctness follows. We now describe how this optimization speed up the analysis of the second case study. In the static profiling for function frequencies, we need to build a summary graph for every function $f$, and then run the mean-payoff analysis for every such graph. Given this optimization, we can first compute (only once) a summary graph for the case that all method invocations are bad events. We denote this $QICFG$ by $\mathcal{A}^*$ and the corresponding summary function by $s^*$. Note that in $\mathcal{A}^*$ all weights are negative, and the mean-payoff analysis answer is trivially NO. But still the summary function computation, which computes the quantitative information about the maximum weight context-free paths, provides useful information and saves recomputation. To determine the frequency of $f$ we assign weights to $\mathcal{A}$ and get $\mathcal{A}^f$, and the difference between $\mathcal{A}^f$ and $\mathcal{A}^*$ is only in the weight that is assigned to the invocation of $f$. We then compute the summary function $s^f$ for $\mathcal{A}^f$ by first assigning $s'^f_0 = s^*$. In practical cases, programs can have thousands of methods, but only small portion of them will have a path to $f$. So along with the previous optimizations we get that only few Bellman-Ford runs are required to compute $s^f$. Overall, the computation of $s^*$ is expensive, and may take several minutes for a large program, but it is done only once, and then the computation of each $s^f$ is much faster.

### 5.2 Container analysis

*Technical details about experimental results.* We discuss a few relevant details about our experiments and results.

- We use the points-to analysis tool of [36]. This tool provides interprocedural on demand analysis for a may-alias relationship of two variables. We say that a variable may point to an allocated container if it may-alias the container, and a variable must point to an allocated container if it may-alias only one allocated container.
- For the underutilized containers the threshold is 1, and for the analysis of overpopulated containers we set a threshold of 0.1 for our experimental results. That is, if the ratio between the number of added elements to the number of lookup operations is more than 10, then the container is overpopulated.

**Experimental results.** Our experimental results on the benchmarks are reported in Table 1. In the table, **# M** and **# CO** represent the number of methods and containers that are reachable from the main entry of the program, respectively; **# OP** and **# UC** represent the number of overpopulated and underutilized containers discovered by our tool, respectively; and **TA(s)** and **TQ(s)** represent the time required for alias analysis and the time required for the quantitative analysis of $QICFG$s (in seconds), respectively; and the entries of the respective columns represent the time for overpopulated/underutilized container analysis. We now highlight some interesting aspects of our experimental results. First, our approach for container analysis discovers containers that are overpopulated or underutilized, while maintaining soundness. Second, the cases that we identify reveal useful information for optimization, for example, in the first (batik-rasterizer) and the second (batik-svgpp) benchmarks we identify containers that always have a small bounded number of elements.

| Benchmark | # M | # CO | # OP | # UC | TA(s) | TQ(s) |
|---|---|---|---|---|---|---|
| batik-rasterizer | 21433 | 9 | 1 | 2 | 124/125 | 144/143 |
| batik-svgpp | 7859 | 3 | 0 | 3 | 20/20 | 14/13 |
| mrt | 9798 | 10 | 1 | 0 | 70/13 | 41/59 |
| java_cup | 8173 | 10 | 0 | 0 | 19/19 | 25/22 |
| xalan | 8729 | 6 | 3 | 2 | 5/5 | 41/43 |
| polyglot | 8068 | 8 | 2 | 2 | 0/0 | 17/17 |
| antlr | 8607 | 15 | 5 | 2 | 11/12 | 25/24 |
| jflex | 21852 | 43 | 3 | 6 | 2473/2614 | 178/210 |
| avrora | 13331 | 75 | 9 | 9 | 145/141 | 111/113 |
| muffin | 22503 | 50 | 3 | 5 | 2500/157 | 352/173 |
| bloat06 | 10675 | 211 | 32 | 14 | 399/250 | 2241/2165 |
| eclipse06 | 9335 | 74 | 8 | 4 | 37/22 | 222/164 |
| jython06 | 12210 | 66 | 9 | 5 | 154/68 | 13593/8376 |

**Table 1.** Experimental results for container usage analysis

**Comparison with the work of [45].** While the notion of underutilized and overpopulated containers is the same in our work and in [45], the concrete mathematical definition is different.

- *(Conceptual difference in modeling).* The formal definitions in [45] rely on properties of a specifically constructed *inequality graph* that in practice gives a good approximation on whether a container is properly used (for details, see Definition 8 in [45]). Our formal definition is conceptually simpler and relies on a very general and flexible mathematical framework, but on the

| Benchmark | # M | # I | T |
|---|---|---|---|
| antlr | 768 | 326 | 1.2 |
| bloat | 2576 | 676 | 30.8 |
| eclipse | 1056 | 215 | 2.3 |
| fop | 429 | 47 | 0.4 |
| luindex | 567 | 239 | 0.7 |
| lusearch | 842 | 237 | 2.5 |
| pmd | 2547 | 589 | 11.5 |

**Table 2.** Experimental results for frequency of functions.

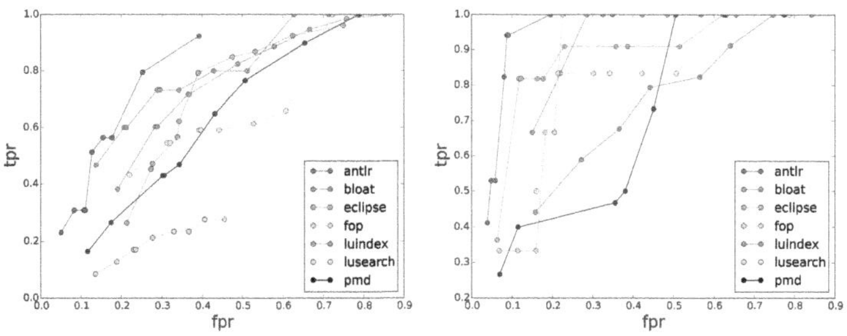


**Figure 7.** The ROC curves. The left plot shows the results when all methods are analyzed. The right plot shows the results when only the active methods are analyzed.

other hand it crucially relies on the accuracy of the constructed *QICFG*. For example, our technique may not report a container as underutilized even if the witness path for proper utilization is very complex, e.g., has 20 nested function calls, and therefore it is unlikely to be realizable on practice.

- *(Advantages and disadvantages).* Our approach has several advantages: (1) First, our approach can handle recursion, whereas [45] does not handle recursion. (2) Second, we present a sound and complete approach for ratio analysis of *QICFG*s, and with a conservative modeling we have a sound analysis approach for detecting containers misuse. (3) Third, our algorithm is polynomial time (once the points-to relation is computed), whereas the algorithmic approach of [45] in the worst case is exponential. (4) Finally, our approach also allows us to handle DELETE operations: in [45] loops with only ADD operations (in ADD vs DELETE) were identified as proper usage, whereas we identify loops where the difference of the ADD and DELETE operations is positive as proper usage (this subsumes the loops of [45] and for example, also loops with two ADD operations and one DELETE operation). Example 3 illustrates the advantages of our approach. One drawback of our approach is that it is conservative: while for underutilized containers analysis (ADD vs DELETE) our approach captures all cases of [45] (as explained above), our approach for overpopulated containers analysis is more conservative (to obtain soundness).
- *(Comparison of experimental outcomes).* With our approach we were able to fully analyze all the containers in all benchmarks, whereas in [45] the analysis for few benchmarks (e.g., muffin) was not done for all containers since a timeout was reached. Below we present example snippets of code from the benchmarks where our analysis gives different results from the analysis of [45]. The example in Figure 8 shows that handling DELETE operations leads to more refined analysis: in the example, if DELETE operations are not handled, then the misuse is not detected. The example in Figure 9 shows that the proper utilization of containers might depend on the recursive calls. Finally, the example in Figure 10 illustrates that the proper use of containers can be outside its allocation site.

```
public void cleared() {
    ...
    if (list != null){
        ...
    }
    else{
        Object o = elementsById.remove(id);
        if (o != this) // oops not us!
            elementsById.put(id, o);
    }
}
```

```
public void run() {
    while(true) {
        ...
        if (...) {
            ...
            rc.cleared();
        }
        ...
    }
    ...
}
```

**Figure 8.** An example from benchmark batik. The method **run** invokes **cleared** in a loop, and in every invocation, one element of elementsById is removed and one element is added. Thus in this loop the total number of elements in elementsById is bounded.

```
void addCNAME(CNAMERecord cname) {
    if (backtrace == null)
        backtrace = new Vector();
    backtrace.insertElementAt(cname, 0);
}

public SetResponse findRecords(Name name, short type) {
    ...
    if (type != Type.CNAME && type != Type.ANY && rrset.getType() == Type.CNAME)
    {
        zr = findRecords(cname.getTarget(), type);
        zr.addCNAME(cname);
        ...
    }
    ...
    return zr;
}
```

**Figure 9.** An example from benchmark muffin. The method **findRecords** has a recursive call, and method **addCNAME** adds an element to vector backtrace. A path with recursion depth $n$ adds $n$ elements to backtrace. Hence, backtrace may have unbounded number of elements and it is not underutilized.

```
Hashtable cgi(Request request)
{
    Hashtable attrs = new Hashtable(13);
    ...
    if (query != null)
    {
        StringTokenizer st = new StringTokenizer(decode(query), "&");
        while (st.hasMoreTokens())
        {
            ...
            attrs.put(key, value);
        }
    }
    ...
    return attrs;
}

public Reply recvReply(Request request)
{
    ...
    else if (request.getPath().equals("/admin/set"))
    {
        Hashtable attrs = cgi(request);
        ..
        for (int i = 0; i < enabled.size(); i++)
        {
            ...
            prefs.put(key, (String) attrs.get(key));
        }
        ...
    }
    ...
    return reply;
}
```

**Figure 10.** An example from benchmark muffin. The method **cgi** allocates the container attrs and potentially adds it many elements. The method **recvReply** performs a **get** operation over attrs in a loop. Since we analyze not only the operations that are nested in the allocation site, we detect that attrs is not overpopulated (the analysis of [45] reports it as overpopulated).

### 5.3 Static profiling: frequency of function calls

**Experimental results.** We examined ten thresholds, namely $1/30, 2/30, 3/30, ..., 10/30$, and for each threshold $\lambda$ we say that a method is *statically hot* if it is $\lambda$-hot (according to the definition in Subsection 3.2). We compared the results to dynamic profiling from the DaCapo benchmarks [4]. In the dynamic profiling we define the top 5% of the most frequently invoked functions as *dynamically hot*. For example, if a program has 1000 functions, and in the benchmark 500 functions were invoked at least once, then the 25 most frequently invoked functions are dynamically hot. We note that theoretically speaking, the definitions of dynamic and static hotness are incomparable (basically for any $\lambda$), but our experimental results show a good correlation between the two notions. To illustrate the correlation we treat our static analysis as a *classifier* of hot methods, and the *specificity* and *sensitivity* of the classifier are controlled by the threshold $\lambda$. The sensitivity of a classifier is measured by the *true positive rate* (tpr), which is

$$\frac{\text{\#dynamically hot methods that are reported as statically hot}}{\text{\#dynamically hot methods}}$$

The specificity is determined by the *false positive rate* (fpr):

$$\frac{\text{\#non-dynamically hot methods that are reported as statically hot}}{\text{\#methods}}$$

For high values of $\lambda$, the classifier is expected to capture only dynamically hot methods (but it will miss most of the dynamically hot methods), and thus it will have very high fpr but very low tpr. For very low values of $\lambda$ the classifier will report most of the methods as hot, so most of the hot methods will be reported as hot, and we will have very high tpr but very low fpr. A fundamental metric for classifier evaluation is a *receiver operating characteristic (ROC) graph*. A ROC graph is a plot with the false positive rate on the X axis and the true positive rate on the Y axis. The point (0,1) is the perfect classifier, and the area beneath an ROC curve can be used as a measure of accuracy of the classifier.

In our experimental evaluation we only considered application functions (and not library functions), and the results are presented in Table 2. In the table, **# M** represents the number of application methods (that are reachable from the main entry of the program), **# I** represents the number of application methods that were actually invoked in the benchmark, **T** represents the average running time for the static analysis of a single method (i.e., to check whether a single method is $\lambda$-hot for a fixed $\lambda$) (in seconds). For each $\lambda$ we present the tpr and fpr values of the classifications. We present an evaluation for two cases. In the first case we statically analyze all the methods and calculate the tpr and fpr accordingly. In the second case we consider only the *active methods*, namely, the methods that were invoked at least once in the program, and we remove all the other methods from the program control flow graph. This simulates a typical case where the programmer has prior knowledge on methods that are definitely not hot and can instruct the static analysis to ignore them. The ROC curves are presented in Figure 7, where the most left points on the graph are for $\lambda = 10/30$ and the fpr and tpr increases as $\lambda$ decreases (until it finally reaches $1/30$). In general, for most of the programs the static analysis gives useful and quite accurate information. Specifically, the threshold $\lambda = 7/30$ captures more than half of the hot methods for most benchmarks (i.e., except fop and antlr) and with a fpr less than 0.3 which means that if a method was statically reported as not hot, then with probability 0.7 it is really not hot. We note that the analysis over fop gives quite poor results because only 10% of the methods were active. However, when we analyzed only the active methods we get better results for fop, see the right hand graph in Figure 7. When we only consider the active methods, the threshold $\lambda = 9/30$ captures most of the dynamically hot methods while maintaining a fpr less than 0.1 (for most programs).

*Remarks.* We run the experiments on a single thread Intel Pentium 3.80GHz. For Table 1 results, the alias analysis did not complete for some benchmarks (e.g. fop, pmd). In Table 2 we only show benchmarks for which we managed to obtain dynamic profiles. For a few benchmarks (e.g. jython) the quantitative analysis took too long for the entire benchmark. In such cases, our tool could be used to focus on specific functions.

## 6. Related Work

**Interprocedural analysis.** Algorithms that operate on the interprocedural control-flow graphs provide the framework for static analysis of programs, and have numerous applications. Precise interprocedural analysis is crucial for dataflow analysis and has been studied in several works [29, 31]. The study of interprocedural analysis has also been extended to weighted pushdown systems, where the weight domain is a bounded idempotent semiring [10, 33]. Analysis of such weighted pushdown systems has been used in many applications of program analysis [24, 32, 33]. Our work is different because the objectives (mean-payoff and ratio analysis) we consider are very different from reachability and bounded domains. The mean-payoff objective is a function that assigns a real-valued number to every path. In contrast to bounded domain functions, the range of a mean-payoff function is potentially uncountable. We develop novel techniques to extend the summary graph approach for finite-height lattices to solve mean-payoff analysis of $QICFG$s (which requires computing fix points for infinite-height lattices).

**Mean-payoff analysis.** Mean-payoff objectives are quantitative metrics for performance modeling in many applications and very well-studied in the context of finite-state graphs and games. Finite-state graphs and games with mean-payoff objectives have been studied in [19, 21, 23, 46] for performance modeling, and robust synthesis of reactive systems [5, 6]. Quantitative abstraction-refinement frameworks for finite-state systems with mean-payoff objectives have also been studied in [12]. While the mean-payoff objectives have been considered in depth for finite-state systems, they have not been considered in depth for interprocedural analysis. Pushdown systems with mean-payoff objectives were considered in [14]. We significantly improve the complexity of the polynomial-time algorithm for interprocedural mean-payoff analysis that can be obtained by a reduction to the results of [14].

**Detecting inefficiently-used containers.** Bloat detection and detecting inefficiently used containers have been identified in many previous works as a major reason for program inefficiency. Dynamic approaches for the problem were studied in many works such as [18, 27, 28, 30, 34, 35, 44]. A static approach to analyze the problem was first considered in [45], which is the most closely related work to our case study. The work of [45] provides an excellent exposition of the problem with several practical motivations. It also describes the clear advantages of the static analysis tools, and identifies that soundness in detecting inefficiently used containers (with no or low false positive rates) is a very important feature. Our approach for the problem is significantly different from the approach of [45]. A big part of the contribution of [45] is an automated annotation for the functionality of the containers operation. The main algorithmic approach of [45] is to use CFL-reachability (context-free reachability) to identify nesting loop depths and then use this information for detecting misuse of containers. Our algorithmic approach is very different: we use a quantitative analysis approach, i.e., ratio analysis of $QICFG$s to model the problem.

**Static profiling of programs.** Static and dynamic profiling of programs is in the heart of program optimization. Static profiling are typically used in branch predictions where the goal is to assign probabilities to branches, and typically require some prior knowledge on the probability of inputs. Static profiling of programs for branch predictions has been considered in [2, 22, 39, 42]. Dynamic profiling has also been used in many applications related to performance optimizations, see [40] for a collection of dynamic profiling tools. Two main drawbacks of dynamic profiling are that they require inputs, and they cannot be used for compiler optimizations. We use static profiling to determine if a function is invoked frequently along some run of the program, and do not require any prior knowledge on inputs. The techniques used in [2, 39, 42] involves solving linear equations with sparse matrix solvers, whereas our solution method is different (by quantitative analysis of $QICFG$s).

## 7. Conclusion

In this work we considered the quantitative (ratio and mean-payoff) analysis for interprocedural programs. We demonstrated how interprocedural quantitative analysis can aid to automatically reason about properties of programs and potential program optimizations. We significantly improved the theoretical known upper-bound for the polynomial-time solution, and presented several practical optimizations that proved to be useful in real programs. We have implemented the algorithm in Java, and showed that it scales to DaCapo benchmarks of real-world programs. This shows that interprocedural quantitative analysis is feasible and useful. Some possible directions of future works are as follows: (1) extend our framework with multiple quantitative objectives and study their applications; and (2) extend [12] to have an abstraction-refinement framework for quantitative interprocedural analysis.

**Acknowledgments.** We thank Mooly Sagiv for pointing us to reference [45], Nimrod Zibil for discussions on C optimizations, and anonymous reviewers for their helpful comments.

## References

[1] G. M. Amdahl. Validity of the single processor approach to achieving large scale computing capabilities. In *Proceedings of the April 18-20, 1967, spring joint computer conference*, pages 483–485. ACM, 1967.

[2] T. Ball and J. R. Larus. Branch prediction for free. In *PLDI*, pages 300–313, 1993.

[3] H. Bjorklund, S. Sandberg, and S. Vorobyov. A combinatorial strongly subexponential strategy improvement algorithm for mean payoff games. In *MFCS'04*, pages 673–685, 2004.

[4] S. M. Blackburn, R. Garner, C. Hoffmann, A. M. Khang, K. S. McKinley, R. Bentzur, A. Diwan, D. Feinberg, D. Frampton, S. Z. Guyer, M. Hirzel, A. Hosking, M. Jump, H. Lee, J. E. B. Moss, A. Phansalkar, D. Stefanović, T. VanDrunen, D. von Dincklage, and B. Wiedermann. The dacapo benchmarks: java benchmarking development and analysis. *SIGPLAN Not.*, 41(10):169–190, 2006.

[5] R. Bloem, K. Chatterjee, T. A. Henzinger, and B. Jobstmann. Better quality in synthesis through quantitative objectives. In *CAV*, pages 140–156, 2009.

[6] R. Bloem, K. Greimel, T. A. Henzinger, and B. Jobstmann. Synthesizing robust systems. In *FMCAD*, pages 85–92, 2009.

[7] E. Bodden, A. Sewe, J. Sinschek, M. Mezini, and H. Oueslati. Taming reflection: Aiding static analysis in the presence of reflection and custom class loaders. In *ICSE '11*, pages 241–250. ACM, 2011.

[8] M. S. Boddy. Anytime problem solving using dynamic programming. In *AAAI*, pages 738–743, 1991.

[9] U. Boker, K. Chatterjee, T. A. Henzinger, and O. Kupferman. Temporal specifications with accumulative values. In *LICS*, 2011.

[10] A. Bouajjani, J. Esparza, and T. Touili. A generic approach to the static analysis of concurrent programs with procedures. In *POPL*, 2003.

[11] A. Carroll and G. Heiser. An analysis of power consumption in a smartphone. In *USENIX*, 2010.

[12] P. Cerný, T. A. Henzinger, and A. Radhakrishna. Quantitative abstraction refinement. In *POPL*, pages 115–128, 2013.

[13] K. Chatterjee, L. Doyen, and T. A. Henzinger. Quantitative languages. *ACM Trans. Comput. Log.*, 11(4), 2010.

[14] K. Chatterjee and Y. Velner. Mean-payoff pushdown games. In *LICS*, pages 195–204, 2012.

[15] T. H. Cormen, C. E. Leiserson, R. L. Rivest, and C. Stein. *Introduction to Algorithms*. The MIT Press, 3rd edition, 2009.

[16] P. Cousot and R. Cousot. Abstract interpretation: A unified lattice model for static analysis of programs by construction or approximation of fixpoints. In *POPL*, pages 238–252, 1977.

[17] M. Droste and I. Meinecke. Describing average- and longtime-behavior by weighted MSO logics. In *MFCS*, pages 537–548, 2010.

[18] B. Dufour, B. G. Ryder, and G. Sevitsky. A scalable technique for characterizing the usage of temporaries in framework-intensive java applications. In *SIGSOFT FSE*, pages 59–70, 2008.

[19] A. Ehrenfeucht and J. Mycielski. Positional strategies for mean payoff games. *Int. Journal of Game Theory*, 8(2):109–113, 1979.

[20] C. Ferdinand, F. Martin, R. Wilhelm, and M. Alt. Cache behavior prediction by abstract interpretation. *Sci. Comput. Program.*, 99.

[21] J. Filar and K. Vrieze. *Competitive Markov Decision Processes*. Springer-Verlag, 1997.

[22] J. L. Hennessy and D. A. Patterson. *Computer Architecture, Fourth Edition: A Quantitative Approach*. Morgan Kaufmann, 2006.

[23] R. Karp. A characterization of the minimum cycle mean in a digraph. *Discrete Mathematics*, 23:309–311, 1978.

[24] A. Lal, T. W. Reps, and G. Balakrishnan. Extended weighted pushdown systems. In *CAV*, pages 434–448, 2005.

[25] O. Lhoták and L. J. Hendren. Scaling java points-to analysis using spark. In *CC*, pages 153–169, 2003.

[26] T. A. Liggett and S. A. Lippman. Stochastic games with perfect information and time average payoff. *Siam Review*, 11:604–607, 1969.

[27] N. Mitchell and G. Sevitsky. The causes of bloat, the limits of health. In *OOPSLA*, pages 245–260, 2007.

[28] N. Mitchell, G. Sevitsky, and H. Srinivasan. Modeling runtime behavior in framework-based applications. In *ECOOP*, 2006.

[29] M. Müller-Olm and H. Seidl. Precise interprocedural analysis through linear algebra. In *POPL*, pages 330–341, 2004.

[30] G. Novark, E. D. Berger, and B. G. Zorn. Efficiently and precisely locating memory leaks and bloat. In *PLDI*, pages 397–407, 2009.

[31] T. W. Reps, S. Horwitz, and S. Sagiv. Precise interprocedural dataflow analysis via graph reachability. In *POPL*, pages 49–61, 1995.

[32] T. W. Reps, A. Lal, and N. Kidd. Program analysis using weighted pushdown systems. In *FSTTCS*, pages 23–51, 2007.

[33] T. W. Reps, S. Schwoon, S. Jha, and D. Melski. Weighted pushdown systems and their application to interprocedural dataflow analysis. *Sci. Comput. Program.*, 58(1-2):206–263, 2005.

[34] O. Shacham, M. T. Vechev, and E. Yahav. Chameleon: adaptive selection of collections. In *PLDI*, pages 408–418, 2009.

[35] A. Shankar, M. Arnold, and R. Bodík. Jolt: lightweight dynamic analysis and removal of object churn. In *OOPSLA*, 2008.

[36] M. Sridharan and R. Bodík. Refinement-based context-sensitive points-to analysis for java. In *PLDI*, pages 387–400, 2006.

[37] V. Tiwari, S. Malik, and A. Wolfe. Power analysis of embedded software: a first step towards software power minimization. *IEEE Trans. VLSI Syst.*, 2(4):437–445, 1994.

[38] R. Vallée-Rai, P. Co, E. Gagnon, L. Hendren, P. Lam, and V. Sundaresan. Soot - a java bytecode optimization framework. In *CASCON'99*.

[39] T. A. Wagner, V. Maverick, S. L. Graham, and M. A. Harrison. Accurate static estimators for program optimization. In *PLDI*, 1994.

[40] Wikipedia. List of performance analysis tools.

[41] R. Wilhelm, J. Engblom, A. Ermedahl, N. Holsti, S. Thesing, D. B. Whalley, G. Bernat, C. Ferdinand, R. Heckmann, T. Mitra, F. Mueller, I. Puaut, P. P. Puschner, J. Staschulat, and P. Stenström. The worst-case execution-time problem - overview of methods and survey of tools. *ACM Trans. Embedded Comput. Syst.*, 7(3), 2008.

[42] Y. Wu and J. R. Larus. Static branch frequency and program profile analysis. In *MICRO 27*, pages 1–11. ACM, 1994.

[43] Y. Xie, M. Naik, B. Hackett, and A. Aiken. Soundness and its role in bug detection systems. In *Proc. of the Workshop on the Evaluation of Software Defect Detection Tools*, 2005.

[44] G. H. Xu, N. Mitchell, M. Arnold, A. Rountev, E. Schonberg, and G. Sevitsky. Finding low-utility data structures. In *PLDI*, 2010.

[45] G. H. Xu and A. Rountev. Detecting inefficiently-used containers to avoid bloat. In *PLDI*, pages 160–173, 2010.

[46] U. Zwick and M. Paterson. The complexity of mean payoff games on graphs. *Theoretical Computer Science*, 158:343–359, 1996.

# Specification Inference Using Context-Free Language Reachability


Osbert Bastani
Stanford University
obastani@cs.stanford.edu

Saswat Anand
Stanford University
saswat@cs.stanford.edu

Alex Aiken
Stanford University
aiken@cs.stanford.edu



## Abstract

We present a framework for computing context-free language reachability properties when parts of the program are missing. Our framework infers candidate specifications for missing program pieces that are needed for verifying a property of interest, and presents these specifications to a human auditor for validation. We have implemented this framework for a taint analysis of Android apps that relies on specifications for Android library methods. In an extensive experimental study on 179 apps, our tool performs verification with only a small number of queries to a human auditor.



***Categories and Subject Descriptors*** F.3.2 [*Semantics of Programming Languages*]: Program analysis; F.3.1 [*Specifying and Verifying and Reasoning about Programs*]: Mechanical verification

***Keywords*** program analysis; verification; specification inference


## 1. Introduction

Interprocedural analyses are the building blocks for many applications of program analysis, including program slicing [23], bug finding [1, 6, 18], and taint analysis [32]. One limitation of most interprocedural analyses is that they assume the entire program's source code can be analyzed. In practice, many programs call methods in libraries that may be written in lower-level languages, use dynamic features such as Java reflection, or do not have source code available for analysis. In fact, in our experience, for large systems it is unusual if any of these situations does *not* occur many times. Handling missing or hard-to-analyze code in a fully automatic way generally results in using either very pessimistic and imprecise assumptions or very optimistic and unsound assumptions.

One pragmatic approach to address these problems is to manually write specifications encoding the relevant behavior of the library (or hard-to-analyze) methods so that the library source code does not need to be analyzed. For this approach to work, it is critical that (i) the manual effort of writing the specifications is small, and (ii) the analysis produces sound results even if some specifications are missing. Prior work has addressed these issues to some extent: [3, 4, 7, 15, 16, 21, 22, 25, 33] have applied data mining techniques to infer specifications, which helps address (i), and [34] has developed techniques for inferring minimal sets of specifications needed for program verification, which addresses both (i) and (ii).

In this paper we consider the problem of inferring missing specifications in the context of solving a general context-free language (CFL) reachability problem. Many important interprocedural analyses can be formulated as CFL reachability problems, and our framework makes these algorithms more practical and easier to apply to large programs where parts of the code are either missing or too difficult to analyze statically.

We instantiate our framework for taint analysis of Android apps, and perform an extensive experimental study on 179 apps. Many of these apps have hundreds of thousands of bytecode instructions and thousands of calls to Android library methods. Instead of analyzing the Android library methods, we infer two kinds of specifications that help capture their taint behavior:

- missing taint flows between parameters and return values of library methods, and
- missing alias relations introduced by library methods.

Our work has three main contributions. First, we develop a general framework for describing potentially missing specifications for CFL reachability analyses (Section 4). In particular, the framework can be instantiated to compute the two kinds of specifications above, among others. Second, we present a specification inference algorithm based on this framework (Section 5) that produces sound results, infers accurate specifications, scales to large applications, and allows a human auditor to refine the results. Third, we evaluate an implementation (Section 6) of our specification inference framework with the aforementioned experimental study in which our tool infers a large collection of library specifications and verifies whether or not apps have taint flows (Section 7).

## 2. Motivating Example

We begin with an example that motivates the need for specification inference to verify reachability properties of partial programs. The technical development begins in Section 3.

The popularity of the Android framework (which is installed on over 1 billion phones) has led to a proliferation of Android malware. These malicious apps exhibit behaviors including theft of contact information, sending SMS text messages to premium phone numbers, and unauthorized location tracking. Many of the malicious behaviors exhibited by current Android malware can be described as the flow of sensitive data to untrusted recipients, such as location data flowing to an untrusted web server, or an untrusted phone number flowing to an SMS send request. In principle, standard static taint analysis can identify such malware.

For example, suppose we want to look for malware that leaks location data via SMS messages. Consider the Java-like code in




*POPL '15*, January 15–17, 2015, Mumbai, India.



http://dx.doi.org/10.1145/2676726.2676977

Figure 1. In principle, a static analysis can track the data returned by `getLatitude`, and determine that it is passed to `sendSMS`. Unfortunately, the Android library (written in Java, with calls to native code) is a classic example of how system libraries cause difficulties for static analyses. Android library methods frequently use reflection and native methods, making it very difficult to construct a precise call graph or to perform a sound and precise context sensitive points-to analysis. Examples of such problems in practice include:

- `System.arraycopy` is a native method.
- `Bundle.putLong` indirectly calls the native Android library method `Parcel.nativeWriteLong` (bundles are used to pass data to and receive data from the Android system).
- `GeoPoint.getLatitudeE6` is part of a closed-source Google library, so the source code is unavailable.

While implementations of the Android library methods may be missing, the net taint flows through these methods are generally simple. For example, we can summarize the net taint flows through `List.add`, `List.get`, and `Double.toString` as follows: (i) $\mathtt{arg}_{\mathtt{add}}$ may be *aliased* with $\mathtt{ret}_{\mathtt{get}}$ (i.e., they may point to the same object), and (ii) if taint flows to $\mathtt{this}_{\mathtt{toString}}$, then taint also flows to $\mathtt{ret}_{\mathtt{toString}}$. Here, $\mathtt{ret}_{\mathtt{fn}}$ is the return value of `fn`, $\mathtt{this}_{\mathtt{fn}}$ is the receiver of `fn`, and $\mathtt{argName}_{\mathtt{fn}}$ is the parameter passed to `fn` named `argName`. The library specifications in Figure 2 capture these properties. Note that the code in Figure 2 is only a specification for the `List` and `Double` classes (i.e., it soundly captures the information flows and aliasing introduced by their methods), and is not a valid implementation of the classes. There are two kinds of specifications:

1. An *alias specification* summarizes the potential aliases caused by a library method. These are written as short methods that do nothing except introduce the desired aliasing. For example, the specification for `List.add` means that calling `List.add` may cause $\mathtt{arg}_{\mathtt{add}}$ and $\mathtt{this}_{\mathtt{add}}$`.val` to be aliased. Also, the specification for `List.get` says that calling `List.get` may cause $\mathtt{this}_{\mathtt{get}}$`.val` and $\mathtt{ret}_{\mathtt{get}}$ to be aliased. Note that if $\mathtt{this}_{\mathtt{arg}}$ and $\mathtt{this}_{\mathtt{get}}$ are aliased, then these specifications cause $\mathtt{arg}_{\mathtt{add}}$ and $\mathtt{ret}_{\mathtt{get}}$ to be aliased.
2. A *taint specification* describes how taint flows through a library method. These specifications are expressed as `@Flow` annotations, where the taint on the first argument (either a parameter `arg`, a return value `ret`, the receiver `this`, or a special label such as `LOC` representing a taint source) is transfered to the second argument (similar to the first argument, except in this case a special label would represent a sink, e.g. `SMS`). For example, the specification of `Double.toString` means that if $\mathtt{this}_{\mathtt{toString}}$ is tainted, then $\mathtt{ret}_{\mathtt{toString}}$ is also tainted.

The specifications in Figure 2 enable the analysis to find the flow from the source label `LOC` to the sink label `SMS` in Figure 1. First, the return value $\mathtt{ret}_{\mathtt{getLatitude}}$ is tainted with the source label `LOC`. Second, this taint is passed to `lat`, which is stored in `list.val`. Third, the value is retrieved from `list` and stored in `latAlias`, before being converted into a string and passed as the `text` argument of the Android library method `sendSMS(String text)`. Finally, our specification says that the `text` argument of the method `sendSMS` is sent to the sink labeled `SMS`, so the code exhibits a flow from `LOC` to `SMS`.

Naïvely, we may expect that flow specifications are sufficient to capture all information flows. For example, we may consider using taint specifications that handle field accesses, and replace the alias specification for `List.add` with the flow specification `@Flow(arg, this.val)`. However, this specification is unsound—it fails to capture the flow from `LOC` to `SMS` in Figure 3:

```
Double lat = getLatitude();
List list = new List();
list.add(lat);
Double latAlias = list.get(0);
String latStr = latAlias.toString();
sendSMS(latStr);
```

**Figure 1.** A flow through the List and Double classes.

```
class List:
  Object val;
  void add(Object arg) { val = arg; }
  Object get(Integer index) { return val; }
class Double:
  @Flow(this, return)
  String toString() {}
class LocationManager:
  @Flow(LOC, return)
  static String getLatitude() {}
class SMS:
  @Flow(text, SMS)
  static void sendSMS(String text) {}
```

**Figure 2.** Specifications for Android library classes.

```
class Box: String f;
List list = new List();
Box box = new Box();
list.add(box);
Box boxAlias = list.get(0);
boxAlias.f = getLatitude();
sendSMS(box.f);
```

**Figure 3.** An information flow not captured by taint specifications.

`boxAlias.f` is tainted by `LOC`, so `list.val.f` is tainted (since `boxAlias` and `list.val` are aliased), but the proposed specification for `List.add` does not transfer this taint to `box.f` (even though taint flows to `box.f`). In general, we need alias specifications to precisely and soundly capture flows due to aliasing.

Manually writing library specifications is expensive: the Android library contains over 5000 classes, many exhibiting complex taint flow behavior. Typically, a human auditor must search the application for calls to potentially important library methods, and then manually write specifications for these methods. Even moderately large apps contain thousands of library method calls, but most of them are irrelevant to finding taint flows. Our experience is likely representative: over a one year period spent analyzing potential Android malware, we have written specifications for just 179 library classes, and we continue to find important new specifications.

Missing specifications can cause false negatives in the static analysis. For example, suppose we remove the library specification for `List.add` from Figure 2. Then the static analysis cannot find the flow from `LOC` to `SMS` (since the taint path between them is broken), causing a false negative. Unlike false positives, where the auditor has a list of flows to inspect in detail, false negatives are difficult to track down—ensuring that a tool has not produced a false negative such as the missing flow from `LOC` to `SMS` may require examining every library method call made by the application.

Intuitively, the visible application code contains useful information about the correct specifications for the library methods. For example, if we remove the specification for `List.add`, then there is still a flow from the `LOC` to $\mathtt{arg}_{\mathtt{add}}$, and a flow from $\mathtt{this}_{\mathtt{get}}$`.val` to SMS. However, $\texttt{arg}_{\texttt{add}}$ and $\texttt{this}_{\texttt{add}}\texttt{.val}$ are no longer aliased, so the flow is broken. Only one additional assumption (i.e., that $\texttt{arg}_{\texttt{add}}$ is aliased with $\texttt{this}_{\texttt{add}}\texttt{.val}$) is needed to complete the flow.

This example motivates an approach to specification inference that searches for specifications that complete broken flows. Our approach proceeds in two steps. First, our tool finds *potential flows* by making worst-case assumptions about the missing specifications. Second, for each potential flow, our tool keeps track of which assumptions are sufficient to prove that the potential flow is a true flow, which we call *sufficient assumptions* for the potential flow. Finally, the tool proposes that these sufficient assumptions are true. These assumptions correspond to specifications that are the *inferred specifications* produced by the tool.

Continuing our example, our tool would find a potential flow from `LOC` to `SMS` by making worst-case assumptions about the specification for `List.add`, which includes introducing aliasing between $\texttt{arg}_{\texttt{add}}$ and $\texttt{this}_{\texttt{add}}\texttt{.val}$. This specification for `List.add` is a sufficient assumption for the potential flow from `LOC` to `SMS`, so it is inferred by our tool. Upon seeing this inferred specification, the human auditor can confirm that it is correct and thereby determine that the potential flow is a true flow.

In practice, there may be multiple sufficient assumptions for each potential flow. Our tool keeps track of a *minimal* set of sufficient assumptions—i.e., it looks for flows that are broken in the fewest places possible. The guiding principle is that *potential flows that require fewer assumptions are more likely to be real flows than potential flows that require more assumptions*. By extension, potential flows that produce the fewest inferred specifications are most likely to be correct and should be checked first by an auditor.

We use (interprocedural) taint analysis to motivate and validate our general framework. Taint analysis is a prototypical example of a program analysis that can be expressed as a CFL reachability problem and has many practical applications. Furthermore, it is built on top of points-to analysis, which is a key part of many interprocedural program analyses. One of our goals is to infer aliasing relationships potentially introduced by library methods that are missing specifications.

## 3. CFL Reachability for Explicit Taint Flows

In this section we present a static analysis for finding explicit taint flows and illustrate it using the example in Section 2. Our analysis performs CFL reachability on the portion of the code that is available, and uses specifications for the portion of the code that is unavailable. The specifications are usually manually generated, for example by a human auditor. Our understanding is that many practical systems have this design, and we do not claim that it is novel. However, as far as we know this approach is not well-documented in the literature, so we describe it in some detail. In Section 4, we generalize this analysis to one where some specifications (in addition to the code) are also unavailable (for example, because the auditor has only produced partial specifications), and the task is to infer the possible missing specifications.

Let $C = (U, \Sigma, P, T)$ be a context-free grammar (CFG), where $U$ is the set of non-terminals, $\Sigma$ is the set of terminals, $P$ is the set of productions, and $T$ is the start symbol. We assume $C$ is normalized so that every production has at most two symbols on the right-hand side [19]. We write $A \stackrel{*}{\Rightarrow} \alpha$, where $A$ is a non-terminal and $\alpha$ is a string of terminals and non-terminals, if $\alpha$ can be derived from $A$.

Let $G$ be a directed graph such that the edges $v \xrightarrow{\sigma} v'$ in $G$ are labeled with terminal symbols $\sigma \in \Sigma$. A *path* $v \stackrel{\alpha}{\dashrightarrow} v' \in G$ is a sequence of edges $v \xrightarrow{\sigma_1} w_1 \xrightarrow{\sigma_2} \dots \xrightarrow{\sigma_k} v'$ such that $\alpha = \sigma_1 \dots \sigma_k$. The transitive closure of $G$ under $C$ is the graph $G^C$ such that $v \xrightarrow{A} v' \in G^C$ if and only if there exists $v \stackrel{\alpha}{\dashrightarrow} v' \in G$ such that $A \stackrel{*}{\Rightarrow} \alpha$. If $v \xrightarrow{T} v'$, we say $v'$ is $C$-*reachable* from $v$.

DEFINITION 3.1. Given a CFG $C$, a graph $G = (V, E)$, and subsets of vertices $V_{\text{source}}, V_{\text{sink}} \subseteq V$, the *CFL reachability problem* is to determine whether there exist $v \in V_{\text{source}}$ and $v' \in V_{\text{sink}}$ such that $v'$ is $C$-reachable from $v$.

Typically, formulating a program analysis as a CFL reachability problem involves converting the input program into a graph $G = (V, E)$ and a CFG $C$, and then solving the CFL reachability problem for $C$ and $G$ for some given sets of sources and sinks $V_{\text{source}}, V_{\text{sink}} \subseteq V$. This problem can be solved by finding the closure of $G$ under $C$ using a dynamic programming algorithm [19].

### 3.1 Explicit Taint Flows

We now describe a standard flow- and path-insensitive explicit taint analysis. *Explicit* taint analysis only tracks taint through data flows—i.e., it follows tainted data as it is copied in the course of program execution. We defer discussion of *implicit* flows, where the information transferred depends on control flow decisions, to Section 3.2. As a part of the explicit taint analysis, we perform points-to analysis to find taint flows due to aliasing. For Java, points-to analysis can be expressed as a CFL reachability problem [26]. We extend the points-to analysis to a taint analysis by including source and sink edges that pass taint into and out of the system.

A set of *taint specifications* $\mathcal{S}$ consists of three relations: the *source specifications* $\text{Src}(v, \ell)$, the *sink specifications* $\text{Sink}(v, \ell)$, and the *flow specifications* $\text{Flow}(v, v')$. Here, $v, v' \in G$ are formal method parameters or return values, and $\ell \in \mathcal{L} = \mathcal{L}_{\text{source}} \cup \mathcal{L}_{\text{sink}}$ is a *label* representing a taint source ($\ell \in \mathcal{L}_{\text{source}}$) or a sink ($\ell \in \mathcal{L}_{\text{sink}}$). The relations have the following semantics:

- $\text{Src}(v, \ell)$ says $v$ is tainted with source $\ell \in \mathcal{L}_{\text{source}}$,
- $\text{Sink}(v, \ell)$ says $v$ is passed to sink $\ell \in \mathcal{L}_{\text{sink}}$, and
- $\text{Flow}(v, v')$ says that any taint on $v$ flows to $v'$.

Given a program $P$, the *taint graph* for $P$ is $G = (V, E)$, where $V = \mathcal{O} \cup \mathcal{U} \cup \mathcal{L}$. Here, $\mathcal{O}$ is the set of abstract objects in the program (each of which uniquely corresponds to an object allocation site), $\mathcal{U}$ denotes the program's set of reference variables, and $\mathcal{L}$ is the set of labels introduced above. Figure 4 gives rules for generating an initial set of edges for the graph. Rules 1-4 handle primitive forms of statements. Rule 1 says that the contents of the abstract object $o$ flow to the reference $v$ on the left-hand side of the assignment (more formally, $v$ may *point to* $o$). Rule 2 similarly encodes the flow when a reference variable $v$ is assigned to another reference variable $u$. Rules 3 and 4 record the flows induced by field writes (or *puts*) and field reads (or *gets*) respectively; note that there is a distinct put/get operation for each field $f$.

Rules 5-7 formalize the description of the taint specifications $\mathcal{S}$ given above. Rule 5 (symbol SrcRef) says that a source taints a reference variable, Rule 6 (symbol RefSink) says that the contents of a reference variable flow to a particular sink, and Rule 7 (symbol RefRef) says that the contents of one reference variable flow to another reference variable. Rules 8 and 9 are technical devices. Intuitively, Rule 8 ensures at least one abstract object flows to the target reference variable of any flow specification, which eliminates the need to include alias specifications for every method allocating a non-primitive return value (Rule 8 is discussed further in Section 3.2). Finally, Rule 9 allows us to express paths with "backwards" edges by introducing a label $\overline{\sigma}$ to represent the reversal of an edge labeled $\sigma$.

We handle interprocedural taint flow as follows: arguments passed by the caller are assigned to formal parameters, which are assigned to the corresponding references in the callee. Values returned by the callee are assigned to a formal return value, which is assigned to the corresponding reference in the caller. Vertices representing formal parameters and formal return values are added to $G$ by the analysis, for example $\texttt{lat} \xrightarrow{\text{Assign}} \texttt{this}_{\texttt{add}}^{\texttt{formal}} \xrightarrow{\text{Assign}} \texttt{this}_{\texttt{add}}$ and $\texttt{ret}_{\texttt{toString}} \xrightarrow{\text{Assign}} \texttt{ret}_{\texttt{toString}}^{\texttt{formal}} \xrightarrow{\text{Assign}} \texttt{latString}$. This indirection ensures that method boundaries are clear.

Figure 6 shows the taint graph generated from the code in Figure 1 and the specifications in Figure 2 using the rules in Figure 4. For clarity, we have not included formal parameters and formal return values in the graph, but have assigned caller arguments directly to the corresponding callee references and callee return values directly to corresponding caller reference. The graph describes the explicit flows in the program. For example, the edges

$$\texttt{arg}_{\texttt{add}} \xrightarrow{\text{Put[val]}} \texttt{this}_{\texttt{add}} \xleftarrow{\text{Assign}} \texttt{list} \xrightarrow{\text{Assign}} \texttt{this}_{\texttt{get}} \xrightarrow{\text{Get[val]}} \texttt{ret}_{\texttt{get}}$$

capture the fact that any value stored in the list through the `List.add` method can potentially be the result of the `List.get` method. More precisely, the middle two edges show that the reference `list`, the receiver of `List.add`, and the receiver of `List.get` all potentially point to the same abstract object.

The next step is to identify the paths through the graph that correspond to explicit taint flows, which we specify using the CFG $C_{\text{taint}}$ defined as follows (with $\mathcal{F}$ denoting the set of fields in $P$):

$$\Sigma_{\text{taint}} = \{\text{New}, \text{Assign}, \text{SrcRef}, \text{RefSink}, \text{RefRef}\} \cup \{\text{Put}[f], \text{Get}[f] \mid f \in \mathcal{F}\}$$

$$U_{\text{taint}} = \{\text{FlowsTo}, \text{SrcObj}, \text{SrcSink}\} \cup \{\text{FlowsTo}[f] \mid f \in \mathcal{F}\}$$

We also include symbols $\overline{\sigma}$ and $\overline{A}$ in $\Sigma_{\text{taint}}$ and $U_{\text{taint}}$, respectively. The start symbol of $C_{\text{taint}}$ is $T_{\text{taint}} = \text{SrcSink}$. The source vertices we consider are the taint source labels (i.e. $V_{\text{source}} = \mathcal{L}_{\text{source}}$), and the sink vertices we consider are the sink labels (i.e. $V_{\text{sink}} = \mathcal{L}_{\text{sink}}$).

The productions are shown in Figure 5. Rules 10-13 build the points-to relation $o \xrightarrow{\text{FlowsTo}} v$, which means that the reference variable $v \in \mathcal{U}$ may point to the abstract object $o \in \mathcal{O}$. For example, because Figure 6 contains the path

$$\texttt{o}_{\texttt{lat}} \xrightarrow{\text{FlowsTo}} \texttt{arg}_{\texttt{add}} \xrightarrow{\text{Put[val]}} \texttt{this}_{\texttt{add}} \xrightarrow{\overline{\text{FlowsTo}}} \texttt{o}_{\texttt{list}},$$

Rule 12 adds edge $\texttt{o}_{\texttt{lat}} \xrightarrow{\text{FlowsTo[val]}} \texttt{o}_{\texttt{list}}$. Here, $\texttt{o}_{\texttt{lat}}$ and $\texttt{o}_{\texttt{list}}$ are the abstract objects allocated to `lat` and `list`, respectively. Then we have path

$$\texttt{o}_{\texttt{lat}} \xrightarrow{\text{FlowsTo[val]}} \texttt{o}_{\texttt{list}} \xrightarrow{\text{FlowsTo}} \texttt{this}_{\texttt{get}} \xrightarrow{\text{Get[val]}} \texttt{ret}_{\texttt{get}}.$$

Therefore Rule 13 adds $\texttt{o}_{\texttt{lat}} \xrightarrow{\text{FlowsTo}} \texttt{ret}_{\texttt{get}}$, which causes Rule 11 to add $\texttt{o}_{\texttt{lat}} \xrightarrow{\text{FlowsTo}} \texttt{latAlias}$. This means that $\texttt{ret}_{\texttt{getLatitude}}$ and `latAlias` may point to the same abstract object $\texttt{o}_{\texttt{lat}}$, i.e. $\texttt{ret}_{\texttt{getLatitude}}$ and `latAlias` are aliased.

The backwards edge $\texttt{this}_{\texttt{add}} \xrightarrow{\overline{\text{FlowsTo}}} \texttt{o}_{\texttt{list}}$ in the example path above is added by Rule 17, which introduces a reversed edge $v' \xrightarrow{\overline{A}} v$ for every non-terminal edge $v \xrightarrow{A} v'$. In this way, Rule 17 plays the same role for non-terminal edges that Rule 9 plays for terminal edges. Note that the (forward, non-reversed) edge $\texttt{o}_{\texttt{list}} \xrightarrow{\text{FlowsTo}} \texttt{this}_{\texttt{add}}$ arises from the path of terminal edges

$$\texttt{o}_{\texttt{list}} \xrightarrow{\text{New}} \texttt{list} \xrightarrow{\text{Assign}} \texttt{this}_{\texttt{add}}$$

and the application of Rule 10 followed by Rule 11.

### 3.2 Implicit (Library) Taint Flows

Because $\texttt{ret}_{\texttt{getLatitude}}$ and `latAlias` can point to the same object, if one of them is tainted, then the other should be tainted as well.

1. $\texttt{v=new X()} \Rightarrow o \xrightarrow{\text{New}} v$
2. $\texttt{u=v} \Rightarrow v \xrightarrow{\text{Assign}} u$
3. $\texttt{u.f=v} \Rightarrow v \xrightarrow{\text{Put}[f]} u$
4. $\texttt{u=v.f} \Rightarrow v \xrightarrow{\text{Get}[f]} u$
5. $\text{Src}(v, \ell) \in \mathcal{S} \Rightarrow \ell \xrightarrow{\text{SrcRef}} v$
6. $\text{Sink}(v, \ell) \in \mathcal{S} \Rightarrow v \xrightarrow{\text{RefSink}} \ell$
7. $\text{Flow}(v, v') \in \mathcal{S} \Rightarrow v \xrightarrow{\text{RefRef}} v'$
8. $\exists v\ (\text{Flow}(v, v') \in \mathcal{S}) \Rightarrow o_{v'} \xrightarrow{\text{New}} v'$
9. $v \xrightarrow{\sigma} v' \Rightarrow v' \xrightarrow{\overline{\sigma}} v$ (where $\overline{\overline{\sigma}} = \sigma$)

**Figure 4.** Program fact extraction rules for taint analysis. In Rule 8, $o_{v'}$ is a fresh vertex.

10. $\text{FlowsTo} \rightarrow \text{New}$
11. $\text{FlowsTo} \rightarrow \text{FlowsTo Assign}$
12. $\text{FlowsTo}[f] \rightarrow \text{FlowsTo Put}[f]\ \overline{\text{FlowsTo}}$
13. $\text{FlowsTo} \rightarrow \text{FlowsTo}[f]\ \text{FlowsTo Get}[f]$
14. $\text{SrcObj} \rightarrow \text{SrcRef}\ \overline{\text{FlowsTo}}$
15. $\text{SrcObj} \rightarrow \text{SrcObj FlowsTo RefRef}\ \overline{\text{FlowsTo}}$
16. $\text{SrcSink} \rightarrow \text{SrcObj FlowsTo RefSink}$
17. $A \rightarrow A_1 \ldots A_k \Rightarrow \overline{A} \rightarrow \overline{A_k} \ldots \overline{A_1}$ (where $\overline{\overline{A}} = A$)

**Figure 5.** Productions for $C_{\text{taint}}$.

Instead of keeping track of taint on the reference variables, it is simpler to keep track of taint on the objects. In Figure 6, Rule 14 adds the edge $\texttt{LOC} \xrightarrow{\text{SrcObj}} \texttt{o}_{\texttt{lat}}$, which says that $\texttt{o}_{\texttt{lat}}$ is tainted. For this taint to flow to the sink, the analysis must be able to pass the taint to $\texttt{o}_{\texttt{ret}_{\texttt{toString}}}$ (the object allocated to $\texttt{ret}_{\texttt{toString}}$).

But here we encounter a problem: there is no explicit flow through `Double.toString`, because no data is copied from the input to the output of the method. Instead, there is an *implicit* flow through a sequence of look-ups converting digits in the double value to characters in the string. That is, information still flows from the input to the output of the method, but through control flow decisions rather than through explicit data flow.

Implicit flows are much more difficult to analyze precisely than explicit flows, because it is much harder to avoid tainting far too much of the program when analyzing implicit flows. Another way to handle implicit flows is to use explicit taint analysis but include appropriate specifications for methods that have implicit flows. We consider the set of specifications that pass taint from one argument to another argument or to the return value. In our specification $\mathcal{S}$, this behavior is described by the relation $\text{Flow}(v, v')$, where $v \in V$ is a library method parameter and $v' \in V$ is a library method parameter or return value. Such specifications require Rule 8 from Figure 4, which adds *phantom objects* to the graph.

Recall that we attach taint to objects, not references. Thus, no taint can flow to parts of the code that have no objects associated with them. If a library method does not have an alias specification, then the method will have no object associated with its return value. Rather than manually add alias specifications for every method with a non-primitive return object, Rule 8 in Figure 4 automatically adds a (fresh) abstract object that the return value points to. For example, Rule 8 adds $\texttt{o}_{\texttt{ret}_{\texttt{toString}}} \xrightarrow{\text{New}} \texttt{ret}_{\texttt{toString}}$, causing Rule 10 to add

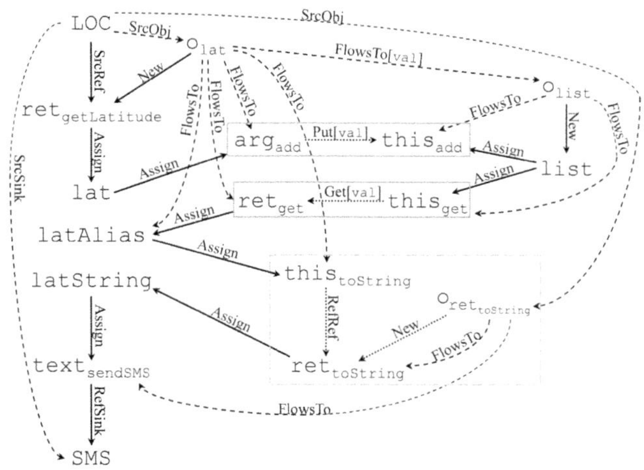


**Figure 6.** The taint graph $G$ corresponding to the code in Figure 1 and the library specifications in Figure 2. Solid edges are facts extracted from the code in Figure 1 (backwards edges added by Rule 9 are not shown). Dotted edges are facts extracted from the library specifications in Figure 2. Edges corresponding to alias specifications are boxed in a solid red line, and edges corresponding to flow specifications are boxed in a dashed blue line. Dashed edges are edges added by productions in Figure 5 (not all such edges are shown).

$o_{\texttt{ret}_{\texttt{toString}}} \xrightarrow{\text{FlowsTo}} \texttt{ret}_{\texttt{toString}}$. Now we can capture the flow in Figure 1. In Figure 6, we have the path

$$\texttt{LOC} \xrightarrow{\text{SrcObj}} o_{\texttt{lat}} \xrightarrow{\text{FlowsTo}} \texttt{this}_{\texttt{toString}}$$
$$\xrightarrow{\text{RefRef}} \texttt{ret}_{\texttt{toString}} \xrightarrow{\overline{\text{FlowsTo}}} o_{\texttt{ret}_{\texttt{toString}}}.$$

Rule 15 adds the edge $\texttt{LOC} \xrightarrow{\text{SrcObj}} o_{\texttt{ret}_{\texttt{toString}}}$. Now we have

$$\texttt{LOC} \xrightarrow{\text{SrcObj}} o_{\texttt{ret}_{\texttt{toString}}} \xrightarrow{\text{FlowsTo}} \texttt{text}_{\texttt{sendSMS}} \xrightarrow{\text{RefSink}} \texttt{SMS},$$

so Rule 16 adds the edge $\texttt{LOC} \xrightarrow{\text{SrcSink}} \texttt{SMS}$.

## 4. Problem Statement

In this section, we formulate the problem of performing a sound and precise CFL reachability analysis when some specifications are missing, along with the problem of inferring the missing specifications. Our formulation extends the framework defined in Section 3.

### 4.1 Missing Specifications CFL Reachability

Suppose we want to perform a CFL reachability analysis on a program $P$. Assume $G^* = (V^*, E^*)$ is the graph constructed from $P$ with complete specifications. If specifications are missing, then the constructed graph $\widehat{G} = (\widehat{V}, \widehat{E})$ may be missing vertices and edges, i.e. $\widehat{V} \subseteq V^*$ and $\widehat{E} \subseteq E^*$. The goal is to perform a sound and precise worst-case analysis given some information about the missing vertices and edges. We encode the possible missing data as a family of graphs $\mathcal{G}$, where we only know that $G^* \in \mathcal{G}$.

DEFINITION 4.1. Suppose we are given $\widehat{G} = (\widehat{V}, \widehat{E})$, a set of sources $V_{\text{source}} \subseteq \widehat{V}$, a set of sinks $V_{\text{sink}} \subseteq \widehat{V}$, along with some family $\mathcal{G}$ of graphs such that for each $G \in \mathcal{G}$, $\widehat{G}$ is a subgraph of $G$, i.e. $\widehat{G} \subseteq G$. We call $G$ a *completion* of $\widehat{G}$. Let $\mathcal{A} : V_{\text{source}} \times V_{\text{sink}} \to$ Bool be the result of a static analysis, where $\mathcal{A}(v, v') = \mathit{true}$ indicates that taint flows from $v$ to $v'$.

```
class List:
  void add(Object arg) {
     arg.f = arg;
     this.val = arg; }
```

**Figure 7.** An alternative (and incorrect) specification for `List.add`.

- $\mathcal{A}$ is *sound* if for every $v \in V_{\text{source}}$ and $v' \in V_{\text{sink}}$, $\mathcal{A}(v, v') =$ false if and only if there does not exist any $G \in \mathcal{G}$ such that $v \xrightarrow{T} v' \in G^C$.
- $\mathcal{A}$ is *precise* if for every $v \in V_{\text{source}}$ and $v' \in V_{\text{sink}}$, $\mathcal{A}(v, v') =$ true if and only if there exists $G \in \mathcal{G}$ such that $v \xrightarrow{T} v' \in G^C$.

The idea behind this definition is that an analysis is sound if it does not miss any taint flow present in at least one of the possible completions of $\widehat{G}$, and the algorithm is precise if it does not report any flows that do not occur in any completion of $\widehat{G}$. An analysis $\mathcal{A}$ solves the *missing specifications CFL reachability problem* for a family $\mathcal{G}$ if it is both sound and precise.

While Definition 4.1 captures the notion of performing a worst-case analysis that is sound and precise, we are also interested in keeping track of the assumptions that the worst-case analysis makes about missing specifications. In practice, many assumptions may produce the same results. Therefore we are interested in producing a minimal set of assumptions. Suppose we have a partial order $(\mathcal{G}, \leq)$, where $G_1 \leq G_2$ should mean that the graph $G_1$ makes at most as many assumptions as $G_2$. The definition of $\leq$ depends on the family $\mathcal{G}$. In addition to producing sound and precise results $\mathcal{A}$, we would like to produce a minimal $G \in \mathcal{G}$ (with respect to $\leq$) such that performing the CFL reachability analysis on $G$ yields $\mathcal{A}$.

DEFINITION 4.2. Suppose we are given the inputs as in Definition 4.1, along with a partial order $(\mathcal{G}, \leq)$. We use the notation $e \overset{?}{\in} G$; this expression evaluates to true if $e \in G$ and false otherwise. The *CFL reachability specification inference problem* is to produce sound and precise results $\mathcal{A}$, along with *sufficient assumptions*, encoded as a graph $G \in \mathcal{G}$ satisfying $\mathcal{A}(v, v') = (v \xrightarrow{T} v' \overset{?}{\in} G^C)$ for every $v \in V_{\text{source}}$ and $v' \in V_{\text{sink}}$. Furthermore, we require that $G$ is *minimal*, i.e. there does not exist sufficient assumptions $G' \in \mathcal{G}$ such that $G' < G$.

In the remainder of this section, we describe how we apply this framework to inferring alias and flow specifications.

### 4.2 $\mathcal{G}$ Using Regular Languages

To design an algorithm for solving a missing specifications CFL reachability problem, we must first specify the family $\mathcal{G}$ of graphs to which $G^*$ may belong. Our goal is to define a family $\mathcal{G}$ that is simultaneously general, retains precision in practice, and admits efficient algorithms. We confine our presentation to inferring specifications for missing methods. This restriction is without loss of generality and is done to simplify notation and discussion throughout the rest of the paper.

One restriction we do make is that inferred specifications do not access static fields. Our algorithms in fact work without this restriction, but the results are almost always not useful. It is easy to see why: if there are at least two missing methods that can access static fields, it is possible for one to store a tainted value in a static field and the other to read it, whether or not these methods have anything else to do with each other. Furthermore, specifications involving static fields are rare: none of the specifications we have manually written have involved static fields.

Consider the taint graph $G$ in Figure 6. Suppose the specification for the method `List.add` in Figure 2 is missing, so the edge

$\texttt{arg}_{\texttt{add}} \xrightarrow{\text{Put[val]}} \texttt{this}_{\texttt{add}}$ in Figure 6 is missing, giving us the graph $\widehat{G}$. Without access to static fields, the only way to complete a flow through $\widehat{G}$ is if there is a path connecting $\texttt{arg}_{\texttt{add}}$ to $\texttt{this}_{\texttt{add}}$. In general, for a method $m$, the only possible taint flows through $m$ are from a parameter of $m$ to $m$'s return value, or from one parameter to another parameter. We use $V_m \subseteq \widehat{V}$ to denote the vertices of $\widehat{G}$ corresponding to the formal parameters and return value of $m$.

To be sound, we must assume that the specification of `List.add` could execute any sequence of operations. In other words, $G$ consists of $\widehat{G}$ with some additional subgraph $G_{\texttt{arg}_{\texttt{add}},\texttt{this}_{\texttt{add}}}$ connecting $\texttt{arg}_{\texttt{add}}$ to $\texttt{this}_{\texttt{add}}$. Note that for any subgraph $G_{\texttt{arg}_{\texttt{add}},\texttt{this}_{\texttt{add}}}$ corresponding to a possible specification of `List.add`'s behavior, the only information relevant to the CFL reachability problem is the possible sequences of terminals $\alpha \in \Sigma^*$ that can occur along paths $\texttt{arg}_{\texttt{add}} \overset{\alpha}{\dashrightarrow} \texttt{this}_{\texttt{add}}$. Generalizing from this example, for a missing method $m$ it suffices to consider the family of graphs $\mathcal{G}$ consisting of all graphs containing $\widehat{G}$ as a subgraph with additional paths $w \overset{\alpha}{\dashrightarrow} w'$, where $w, w' \in V_m$.

For example, one completion of $\widehat{G}$ is the taint graph $G$ in Figure 6, which is just $\widehat{G}$ with the edge $\texttt{arg}_{\texttt{add}} \xrightarrow{\text{Put[val]}} \texttt{this}_{\texttt{add}}$ added back in. But there are other ways to complete $\widehat{G}$, even for this simple example. Consider the graph $G'$ obtained when the specification for `List.add` is given in Figure 7. Then $G'$ is $\widehat{G}$ with the additional path

$$\texttt{arg}_{\texttt{add}} \xrightarrow{\text{Put[f]}} \texttt{arg}_{\texttt{add}} \xrightarrow{\text{Put[val]}} \texttt{this}_{\texttt{add}}$$

In general, there may be infinitely many possible paths $\texttt{arg}_{\texttt{add}} \overset{\alpha}{\dashrightarrow} \texttt{this}_{\texttt{add.this}}$ because the sequence of operations $\alpha$ can be arbitrarily long. Thus, we need some compact way to represent an infinite language of strings; the regular languages are a natural choice. This discussion motivates our definition of the family $\mathcal{G}_W^R$:

DEFINITION 4.3. Let $W \subseteq \widehat{V} \times \widehat{V}$ and let $R$ be a regular language over $\Sigma$. The family of graphs $\mathcal{G}_W^R$ contains the graph $G$ if

- $\widehat{G} \subseteq G$
- If $(w, w') \in W$, then the nondeterministic finite automaton (NFA) $N$ with the transition matrix given by the subgraph $G_{w,w'}$ satisfies $L(N) \subseteq L(R)$.

Here, $G_{w,w'}$ is the subgraph connecting $w$ to $w'$ (not including $w$ or $w'$). This definition exploits the insight that we can think of the subgraph $G_{w,w'}$ as the transition graph of an NFA $N$ with start state $w$ and final state $w'$. Any path $w \overset{\alpha}{\dashrightarrow} w' \in G_{w,w'}$ satisfies $\alpha \in L(N)$. Conversely, for any $\alpha \in L(N)$, there exists a path $w \overset{\alpha}{\dashrightarrow} w' \in G_{w,w'}$.

In general, choosing $R = \Sigma^*$ will produce sound results, since this choice imposes no constraints on the allowed paths connecting $w$ and $w'$. In practice, a more restrictive language may be chosen either to incorporate known constraints on potential specifications, or to trade some soundness for improved scalability.

### 4.3 Inferring Specifications for $\mathcal{G}_W^R$

We now formulate the corresponding missing specifications problem. Our goal is to infer specifications of the following form: there exists a path (or set of paths) connecting $w$ and $w'$. As discussed above, both alias and flow specifications can be described in this manner. We need to define a partial order $\leq$ on $\mathcal{G}_W^R$ that captures the notion of making minimal assumptions about missing specifications. Because we are searching for source-sink paths, it is natural to define $\leq$ in terms of source-sink paths through $G$. To simplify notation, we assume there is a single source and a single sink, i.e. $V_{\text{source}} = \{v_{\text{source}}\}$ and $V_{\text{sink}} = \{v_{\text{sink}}\}$. Let $\mathcal{P}(G) = \{v_{\text{source}} \overset{\alpha}{\dashrightarrow} v_{\text{sink}} \in G \mid T \overset{*}{\Rightarrow} \alpha\}$ denote the set of all possible source-sink paths in $G$. We define the *weight* of a source-sink path $p \in \mathcal{P}(G)$ to be

$$\text{weight}(p) = \sum_{(w,w') \in W} (\#\text{ times } p \text{ passes through } G_{w,w'}).$$

In other words, the weight of a path $p$ equals the number of assumptions $G_{w,w'} \neq \emptyset$ used along $p$. Note that if an assumption is used multiple times (i.e., $p$ passes through $G_{w,w'}$ multiple times), then each use is counted separately. Define the weight of $G \in \mathcal{G}_W^R$ to be the minimum weight of any source-sink path in $G$: $\text{weight}(G) = \arg\min_{p \in \mathcal{P}(G)} \text{weight}(p)$. Now define $G_1 \leq G_2$ if $\text{weight}(G_1) \leq \text{weight}(G_2)$. In other words, we want to find $G \in \mathcal{G}_W^R$ with the source-sink path of lowest weight. In Section 5, we show how to reduce this problem to the shortest-path CFL reachability problem.

We are interested in inferring both flow and alias specifications. Let $V_m = V_m^{\text{arg}} \cup \{r_m\}$, where $V_m^{\text{arg}}$ is the set of formal parameters of a method $m$, and $r_m$ is the formal return value of $m$. First, we infer missing flow specifications (i.e., specifications $\text{Flow}(v, v')$, which describe implicit taint flows through library methods):

$$W_{\text{flow}} = \{(w, w') : w \in V_m^{\text{arg}} \text{ and } w' \in V_m\}$$
$$R_{\text{flow}} = \text{RefRef}$$

For example, we could use the family $\mathcal{G}_{W_{\text{flow}}}^{R_{\text{flow}}}$ to infer the specification for `Double.toString` if it were missing.

Second, we infer missing alias specifications (which describe alias relations potentially introduced by calls to methods such as `List.add` and `List.get`):

$$\begin{aligned} W_{\text{alias}} &= \{(w, w') : w, w' \in V_m\} \\ R_{\text{alias}} &= (\text{Assign} + \overline{\text{Assign}}) \\ &\quad (\text{New} + \text{Assign} + \text{Put}[f]_{f \in \mathcal{F}} + \text{Get}[f]_{f \in \mathcal{F}} \\ &\quad + \overline{\text{New}} + \overline{\text{Assign}} + \overline{\text{Put}[f]}_{f \in \mathcal{F}} + \overline{\text{Get}[f]}_{f \in \mathcal{F}})^* \\ &\quad (\text{Assign} + \overline{\text{Assign}}) \end{aligned}$$

The possible sequences of operations are bracketed by $(\text{Assign} + \overline{\text{Assign}})$ because allocation and field access operations cannot be performed on formal parameters and formal return values (since they are added to $\widehat{G}$ by the static analysis and do not correspond to references in the program, as described in Section 3).

## 5. Algorithms for Specification Inference

In this section we present an algorithm that solves the missing specifications problem stated in Definition 4.1 for $\mathcal{G}_W^R$. Next, we discuss an optimization that enables our algorithm to scale to large programs. Finally, we describe how to extend the algorithm to solve the specification inference problem stated in Definition 4.2 by using a shortest-path extension of the CFL reachability algorithm. This allows us to construct an algorithm that interacts with a human auditor to produce results that are sound and precise with respect to $G^*$. An overview of our system is given in Figure 8.

### 5.1 Algorithms for $\mathcal{G}_W^R$

Consider $(w, w') \in W$. Recall that every potential path $w \overset{\alpha}{\dashrightarrow} w'$ satisfies $\alpha \in L(R)$. To be sound and precise with respect to $\mathcal{G}_W^R$, it suffices to construct a subgraph connecting $w$ and $w'$ such that there is a path $w \overset{\alpha}{\dashrightarrow} w'$ through this subgraph if and only if $\alpha \in L(R)$.

The subgraphs that satisfy this property are the transition graphs for nondeterministic finite automata (NFAs) that accept $L(R)$. For every $(w, w') \in W$, Algorithm 1 constructs the transition graph $\mathcal{N}(s \xrightarrow{R} f)$ for one such NFA, and then adds this transition graph to $\widehat{G}$ to connect $w$ to $w'$, resulting in graph $G'$. Finally, we compute

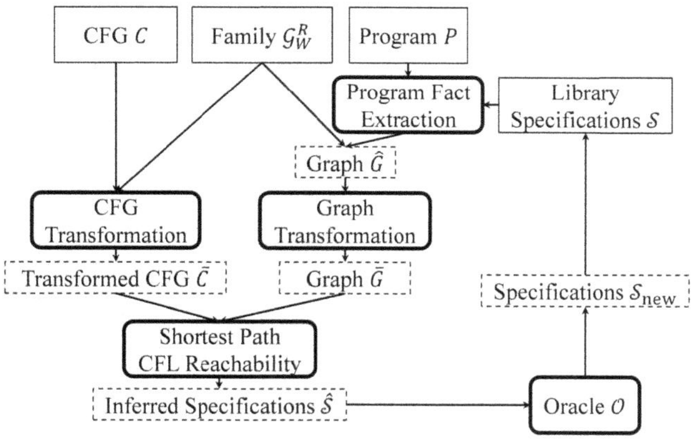


**Figure 8.** An overview of our specification inference system. The system infers specifications $\widehat{\mathcal{S}}$ and proposes them to the oracle $\mathcal{O}$ (i.e., the human auditor), who examines the proposals and generates a new set of specifications $\mathcal{S}_{\text{new}}$. Then $\mathcal{S} \leftarrow \mathcal{S} \cup \mathcal{S}_{\text{new}}$, and the process repeats. Program fact extraction is described in Section 3. While not depicted here, $C$ may depend on $P$. The graph transformation and CFG transformation are computed by Algorithm 2. The shortest-path CFL reachability algorithm is described in Section 5.3 and Appendix A. The specification refinement loop is performed by Algorithm 3.

1. $\mathcal{N}(v \xrightarrow{\sigma} v') = \{v \xrightarrow{\sigma} v'\}$ for all $\sigma \in \Sigma$
2. $\mathcal{N}(v \xrightarrow{R_1 R_2} v') = \mathcal{N}(v \xrightarrow{R_1} t) \cup \mathcal{N}(t \xrightarrow{R_2} v')$
3. $\mathcal{N}(v \xrightarrow{R_1 + R_2} v') = \mathcal{N}(v \xrightarrow{R_1} v') \cup \mathcal{N}(v \xrightarrow{R_2} v')$
4. $\mathcal{N}(v \xrightarrow{R_1^*} v') = \{v \xrightarrow{\epsilon} t\} \cup \mathcal{N}(t \xrightarrow{R_1} t) \cup \{t \xrightarrow{\epsilon} v'\}$

**Figure 9.** Given $v \xrightarrow{R} v'$, $\mathcal{N}$ constructs the transition graph for a NFA that accepts $R$ with start state $v$ and final state $v'$. In Rules 2 and 4, $t$ is a fresh vertex.

the transitive closure $(G')^C$ of $G'$ with respect to the context-free language $C$. The following correctness result follows from the correspondence between $L(R)$ and $\mathcal{N}(s \xrightarrow{R} f)$ described above.

THEOREM 5.1. Algorithm 1 is sound and precise for $\mathcal{G}_W^R$.

### 5.2 Optimizations

Consider the subgraph $G_i = \mathcal{N}(s_i \xrightarrow{R} f_i)$ constructed by Algorithm 1 for a pair $(w_i, w_i') \in W$ (where $i$ is an index over pairs $(w_i, w_i')$). One issue scaling Algorithm 1 is that the CFL reachability algorithm may add a large number of edges that are only among the vertices within $G_i$. Any such *internal edge* $n_i \xrightarrow{A} m_i$, where $n_i$ and $m_i$ are vertices in $G_i$, is added whenever there is a path $n_i \overset{\alpha}{\dashrightarrow} m_i \in G_i$ such that $A \overset{*}{\Rightarrow} \alpha$. The problem is that the subgraphs $G_i$ are all isomorphic—thus, the same edges are recomputed many times by the standard CFL reachability algorithm. This observation suggests that we can benefit from precomputing the internal edges.

One convenient way to implement this optimization is to preprocess the grammar $C$ instead of adding graphs to $\widehat{G}$. That is, we embed an (optimized) version of $G_i$ in $C$. Since the graphs $G_i$ are all isomorphic to one another, this embedding only needs to be performed once. Intuitively, such an transformation is possible because $G_i$ encodes a regular language and $C$ is context-free.

The essential idea is that for every $(w_i, w_i') \in W$, we replace $G_i$ by a single vertex. Because we are only interested in summarizing the transitive closure of $G_i$ with respect to $C$, we only need one vertex to represent the net effect of $G_i$, though this vertex may have many incident edges. More specifically, we modify $\widehat{G}$ in the following ways to define a new graph $\overline{G}$:

- We add a new vertex $v_i$ to $\widehat{G}$; here the single vertex $v_i$ will represent $G_i$.
- We add two new, distinct terminal symbols $b$ and $e$ to $\Sigma$, standing for "beginning $G_i$ at $w_i$" and "exiting $G_i$ at $w_i'$", respectively. These terminals are needed to mark in the modified grammar where we enter and exit $G_i$.
- We add the edges $w_i \xrightarrow{b} v_i \xrightarrow{e} w_i'$ to $\widehat{G}$.

**Algorithm 1** A sound and precise algorithm for $\mathcal{G}_W^R$. Here, $\mathcal{N}(s \xrightarrow{R} f)$ is defined in Figure 9.

**function** EXPANSION($C, \widehat{G}, W, R, v, v'$)
  **return** $v \xrightarrow{T} v' \overset{?}{\in} (\text{EXPANSIONHELPER}(\widehat{G}, W, R))^C$
**end function**
**function** EXPANSIONHELPER($\widehat{G}, W, R$)
  $G' \leftarrow \widehat{G}$
  **for all** $(w, w') \in W$ **do**
    // $s$ and $f$ are fresh vertices
    $G' \leftarrow G' \cup \{w \xrightarrow{\epsilon} s, f \xrightarrow{\epsilon} w'\} \cup \mathcal{N}(s \xrightarrow{R} f)$
  **end for**
  **return** $G'$
**end function**

We now turn to incorporating the transitions of each $G_i$ into $C$, defining a new grammar $\overline{C}$. Let $n_i$, $m_i$, and $r_i$ denote vertices in $G_i$ (corresponding to NFA states $n$, $m$, and $r$, respectively). Let $v \in \widehat{V}$ (recall that $\widehat{V}$ is the set of vertices of $\widehat{G}$—i.e., all the vertices not in any $G_i$). Finally, $G'$ is the graph constructed by Algorithm 1. We want $C$ and $\overline{C}$ to correspond in the following way:

1. If there is an edge $v \xrightarrow{A} n_i \in (G')^C$, then there should be an edge $v \xrightarrow{A_n} v_i \in \overline{G}^{\overline{C}}$. Intuitively, the non-terminal $A_n$ records that $A$ was matched ending at the vertex in $G_i$ corresponding to state $n$.
2. If there is an edge $n_i \xrightarrow{A} v \in (G')^C$, then there should be an edge $v_i \xrightarrow{A^n} v \in \overline{G}^{\overline{C}}$. Intuitively, the non-terminal $A^n$ records that $A$ was matched starting at the vertex in $G_i$ corresponding to state $n$.
3. If there is an edge $n_i \xrightarrow{A} m_j \in (G')^C$ (that is *not* an internal edge), then there should be an edge $v_i \xrightarrow{A_m^n} v_j \in \overline{G}^{\overline{C}}$. Intuitively, the non-terminal $A_m^n$ records that $A$ was matched starting at the vertex in $G_i$ corresponding to state $n$, and ending at the vertex in $G_j$ corresponding to state $m$.

Finally, we need to define the productions for each of the additional non-terminals so that conditions 1-3 above are satisfied. We generate these additional productions of $\overline{C}$ from the productions in $C$ and the $C$-closure of $G_i$ using the rules in Figure 10. In the figure, we refer to vertices $s_i$ and $f_i$ in $G_i$ introduced by Algorithm 1, which correspond to the start state $s$ and end state $e$ of the NFA, respectively.

We briefly explain Rules 1a-f (the rules for non-terminals of the form $A_n$) for producing productions of $\overline{C}$ in Figure 10; Rules 2a-f and 3a-h are similar.

(a) Suppose we have edge $v \xrightarrow{A} w_i \in (G')^C$. Because we have edge $w_i \xrightarrow{\epsilon} s_i \in G'$, we produce $v \xrightarrow{A} s_i \in (G')^C$. In $\overline{G}^{\overline{C}}$, we

1. Productions for $A_n$:

(a) $\dfrac{}{A_s \to Ab \in \overline{C}}$

(b) $\dfrac{s_i \xrightarrow{A} n_i \in G_i^C}{A_n \to b \in \overline{C}}$

(c) $\dfrac{n_i \xrightarrow{\epsilon} m_i \in G_i^C}{A_m \to A_n \in \overline{C}}$

(d) $\dfrac{A \to B \in C}{A_n \to B_n \in \overline{C}}$

(e) $\dfrac{A \to BD \in C}{A_n \to BD_n \in \overline{C}}$

(f) $\dfrac{A \to BD \in C \quad n_i \xrightarrow{D} m_i \in G_i^C}{A_m \to B_n \in \overline{C}}$

2. Productions for $A^n$:

(a) $\dfrac{}{A^f \to eA \in \overline{C}}$

(b) $\dfrac{n_i \xrightarrow{A} f_i \in G_i^C}{A^n \to e \in \overline{C}}$

(c) $\dfrac{m_i \xrightarrow{\epsilon} n_i \in G_i^C}{A^m \to A^n \in \overline{C}}$

(d) $\dfrac{A \to B \in C}{A^n \to B^n \in \overline{C}}$

(e) $\dfrac{A \to BD \in C}{A^n \to B^n D \in \overline{C}}$

(f) $\dfrac{A \to BD \in C \quad m_i \xrightarrow{B} n_i \in G_i^C}{A^m \to D^n}$

3. Productions for $A_m^n$:

(a) $\dfrac{}{A_s^n \to A^n b \in \overline{C}}$

(b) $\dfrac{}{A_n^f \to eA_n \in \overline{C}}$

(c) $\dfrac{n_i \xrightarrow{\epsilon} m_i \in G_i^C}{A_m^r \to A_n^r \in \overline{C}}$

(d) $\dfrac{m_i \xrightarrow{\epsilon} n_i \in G_i^C}{A_r^m \to A_r^n \in \overline{C}}$

(e) $\dfrac{A \to B \in C}{A_n^m \to B_n^m \in \overline{C}}$

(f) $\dfrac{A \to BD \in C}{A_n^m \to B^m D_n \in \overline{C}}$

(g) $\dfrac{A \to BD \in C \quad n_i \xrightarrow{D} m_i \in G_i^C}{A_m^r \to B_n^r \in \overline{C}}$

(h) $\dfrac{A \to BD \in C \quad m_i \xrightarrow{B} n_i \in G_i^C}{A_r^m \to D_r^n \in \overline{C}}$

4. Stitching productions:

(a) $\dfrac{}{A \to A_f e \in \overline{C}}$

(b) $\dfrac{}{A \to bA^s \in \overline{C}}$

(c) $\dfrac{A \to BD \in C}{A \to B_n D^n \in \overline{C}}$

(d) $\dfrac{A \to BD \in C}{A_n \to B_m D_n^m \in \overline{C}}$

(e) $\dfrac{A \to BD \in C}{A^n \to B_m^n D^m \in \overline{C}}$

(f) $\dfrac{A \to BD \in C}{A_m^n \to B_r^n D_m^r \in \overline{C}}$

**Figure 10.** Productions for $\overline{C}$.

**Algorithm 2** Optimized algorithm for $\mathcal{G}_W^R$. Here, $\mathcal{T}(G_i, C)$ applies the rules in Figure 10 to $C$ for the given graph $G_i$. Also, $s$ and $f$ are fresh vertices.

**function** PREPROCESS($C, \widehat{G}, W, R, v, v'$)
  $G_i \leftarrow \mathcal{N}(s \xrightarrow{R} f)$; $\overline{C} \leftarrow \mathcal{T}(G_i, C)$
  **return** $v \xrightarrow{T} v' \overset{?}{\in} (\text{PREPROCESSHELPER}(\widehat{G}, W))^{\overline{C}}$
**end function**
**function** PREPROCESSHELPER($\widehat{G}, W$)
  $\overline{G} \leftarrow \widehat{G}$
  **for all** $(w, w') \in W$ **do**
    // $v$ is a fresh vertex
    $\overline{G} \leftarrow \overline{G} \cup \{w \xrightarrow{b} v, v \xrightarrow{e} w'\}$
  **end for**
  **return** $\overline{G}$
**end function**

1. $\text{FlowsTo}_n \to \text{FlowsTo}_s$ (Rule 1f)
2. $\text{FlowsTo}_n \to \text{FlowsTo}[f]_n$ (Rule 1f)
3. $\text{FlowsTo}_n \to \text{FlowsTo}[f]\ \text{FlowsTo}_n$ (Rules 1e & 1f)
4. $\text{FlowsTo}[f]_n \to \text{FlowsTo}_n$ (Rule 1f)
5. $\text{FlowsTo}[f]_n \to \text{FlowsTo}\ \text{Put}[f]\ \overline{\text{FlowsTo}_n}$ (Rule 1e)

**Figure 11.** Examples of production rules added by Figure 10, along with the rules that generate them.

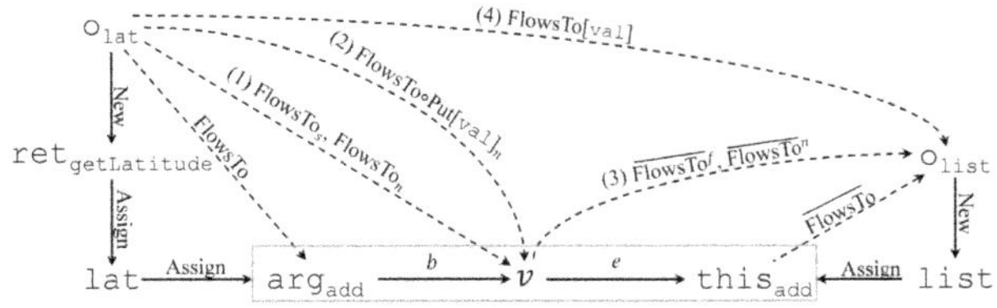


**Figure 12.** Algorithm 2 adds the dashed edges to Figure 6 if the specification for `List.add` is missing. We only show edges relevant to the production of the edge labeled (4).

have edges $v \xrightarrow{A} w_i \xrightarrow{b} v_i$, and we need to produce $v \xrightarrow{A_s} v_i$. This is achieved by the production $A_s \to Ab \in \overline{C}$.

(b) Suppose we have internal edge $s_i \xrightarrow{A} n_i \in G_i^C$. Because we have edge $w_i \xrightarrow{\epsilon} s_i \in G'$, we produce $w_i \xrightarrow{A} n_i \in (G')^C$. In $\overline{G}^{\overline{C}}$, we have edge $w_i \xrightarrow{b} v_i$ and we need to produce $w_i \xrightarrow{A_n} v_i$. This is achieved by the production $A_n \to b \in \overline{C}$.

(c) Suppose we have internal edge $n_i \xrightarrow{\epsilon} m_i \in G_i^C$ and edge $v \xrightarrow{A} n_i \in (G')^C$. Then we produce $v \xrightarrow{A} m_i \in (G')^C$. In $\overline{G}^{\overline{C}}$, we have edge $v \xrightarrow{A_n} v_i$, and we need to produce $v \xrightarrow{A_m} v_i$. This is achieved by the production $A_m \to A_n \in \overline{C}$.

(d) Suppose we have edge $v \xrightarrow{B} n_i \in (G')^C$ and production $A \to B \in C$. Then we produce $v \xrightarrow{A} n_i \in (G')^C$. In $\overline{G}^{\overline{C}}$, we have edge $v \xrightarrow{B_n} v_i$, and we need to produce $v \xrightarrow{A_n} v_i$. This is achieved by the production $A_n \to B_n \in \overline{C}$.

(e) Suppose we have edges $v \xrightarrow{B} v' \xrightarrow{D} n_i \in (G')^C$ and production $A \to BD \in C$. Then we produce $v \xrightarrow{A} n_i \in (G')^C$. In $\overline{G}^{\overline{C}}$, we have edges $v \xrightarrow{B} v' \xrightarrow{D_n} v_i$, and we need to produce $v \xrightarrow{A_n} v_i$. This is achieved by the production $A_n \to BD_n \in \overline{C}$.

(f) Suppose we have edge $v \xrightarrow{B} n_i \in (G')^C$, internal edge $n_i \xrightarrow{D} m_i \in G_i^C$, and production $A \to BD \in C$. Then we produce $v \xrightarrow{A} m_i \in (G')^C$. In $\overline{G}^{\overline{C}}$, we have edge $v \xrightarrow{B_n} v_i$, and we need to produce $v \xrightarrow{A_m} v_i$. This is achieved by the production $A_m \to B_n \in \overline{C}$.

Note that cases (e) and (f) correspond to two possibilities for binary productions, (e) handling the case where one edge is fully outside of $G_i$ and (f) handling the case where one edge is fully inside $G_i$. In the case where only the middle vertex is in $G_i$ and both endpoints are outside, then we need the "stitching production" (c) in Figure 10. We describe stitching productions (a), (b), and (c):

(a) Suppose we have edge $v \xrightarrow{A} f_i \in (G')^C$. Because we have edge $f_i \xrightarrow{\epsilon} w_i' \in G'$, we produce $v \xrightarrow{A} w_i' \in (G')^C$. In $\overline{G}^{\overline{C}}$, we have edges $v \xrightarrow{A_f} v_i \xrightarrow{e} w_i'$, and we need to produce $v \xrightarrow{A} w_i'$. This is achieved by the production $A \to A_f e \in \overline{C}$.

(b) Suppose we have edge $s_i \xrightarrow{A} v \in (G')^C$. Because we have edge $w_i \xrightarrow{\epsilon} s_i \in G'$, we produce $w_i \xrightarrow{A} v \in (G')^C$. In $\overline{G}^{\overline{C}}$, we have edges $w_i \xrightarrow{b} v_i \xrightarrow{A^s} v$, and we need to produce $w_i \xrightarrow{A} v$. This is achieved by the production $A \to bA^s \in \overline{C}$.

(c) Suppose we have edges $v \xrightarrow{B} n_i \xrightarrow{D} v' \in (G')^C$ and production $A \to BD \in C$. Then we produce $v \xrightarrow{A} v' \in (G')^C$. In $\overline{G}^{\overline{C}}$, we have edges $v \xrightarrow{B_n} v_i \xrightarrow{D^n} v'$, and we need to produce $v \xrightarrow{A} v'$. This is achieved by the production $A \to B_n D^n$.

The stitching productions (d), (e), and (f) are similar to (c).

Finally, we show that the rules given in Figure 10 are complete. As above, we focus on Rules 1a-f first. Note that we need to add an edge $v \xrightarrow{A_n} v_i$ whenever there exists a path $v \overset{\alpha}{\dashrightarrow} w_i$ and there exists $\beta \in \Sigma^*$ such that $A \overset{*}{\Rightarrow} \alpha\beta$ and $s_i \overset{\beta}{\dashrightarrow} n_i \in G_i$. In other words, $\alpha$ is the portion of the path in $\widehat{G}$ and $\beta$ is the portion of the path in $G_i$, and the path ends at vertex $n_i \in G_i$. Consider the production that is the first step in the derivation of $A \overset{*}{\Rightarrow} \alpha\beta$:

- Case $A \to \epsilon$: then $\alpha = \epsilon$, so $v = w_i$, and we need to add edge $w_i \xrightarrow{A_n} v_i$. The fact that $\alpha = \epsilon$ also implies that $A \overset{*}{\Rightarrow} \beta$, so $s_i \xrightarrow{A} n_i \in G_i^C$. Hence this case is handled by Rule 1b.
- Case $A \to BD$: either $\alpha$ is a prefix of $BD$ and $\beta$ is a suffix of $D$ (handled by Rule 1e), or $\alpha$ is a prefix of $B$ and $\beta$ is a suffix of $BD$ (handled by Rule 1f).
- Case $A \to B$: then $\alpha$ is a prefix of $B$ and $\beta$ is a suffix of $B$, so this case is handled by Rule 1d.

Rule 1a is added to satisfy the semantics of the symbol $b \in \Sigma$. Finally, we have to consider $\epsilon$ transitions that occur in $G_i^C$—i.e., $n_i \xrightarrow{\epsilon} m_i \in G_i^C$ (these transitions are used in conjunction with the implicit productions $A \to \epsilon A$ and $A \to A\epsilon$). These transitions are handled by Rule 1c. Rules 2a-f and 3a-h follow similarly.

Next, we show that Rules 4a-f are complete. Note that we need to add an edge $v \xrightarrow{A} v'$ whenever there exist paths $v \overset{\alpha}{\dashrightarrow} w_i$ and $w_i' \overset{\gamma}{\dashrightarrow} v'$, and there exists $\beta \in L(R)$ such that $A \overset{*}{\Rightarrow} \alpha\beta\gamma$. Here, $\alpha$ and $\gamma$ are the portions of the path in $\widehat{G}$, and $\beta$ is the portion of the path in $G_i$. As before, we can consider production that is the first step in the derivation of $A \overset{*}{\Rightarrow} \alpha\beta\gamma$. This time, we only need to handle the case where the production is split at vertex $v_i$—i.e., $A \to BD$, where $B \overset{*}{\Rightarrow} \alpha\beta_1$ and $D \overset{*}{\Rightarrow} \beta_2\gamma$ (and $\beta = \beta_1\beta_2$); this is handled by Rule 4c. Rules 4d-f follow similarly when considering productions for $A_n$, $A^n$, and $A_n^m$. Finally, the semantics of the symbols $b$ and $e$ are handled by Rules 4b and 4a, respectively. While we only described the case where the path passes through a single pair $(w_i, w_i')$, the general case follows because the first step in the derivation can be split only at a single vertex $v_i$.

We denote the subroutine constructing $\overline{C}$ by $\mathcal{T}$, i.e. $\overline{C} = \mathcal{T}(G_i, C)$. Note that any $G_i$ can be used, since $G_i$ (and hence $G_i^C$) is the same for every $(w_i, w_i') \in W$. Algorithm 2 calls $\mathcal{T}$ to obtain a new grammar $\overline{C}$. It then computes the transitive closure $\overline{G}^{\overline{C}}$. We have the following correctness result:

THEOREM 5.2. Algorithm 2 is sound and precise for $\mathcal{G}_W^R$.

We briefly discuss the complexity of Algorithm 2. The rules in Figure 10 are not recursive, so the number of productions in $\overline{C}$ is a constant multiple of the number of productions in $C$. Similarly, the graph $\overline{G}$ constructed by Algorithm 2 is a constant mulitple of the size of $\widehat{G}$. The complexity of Algorithm 2 is dominated by the complexity of computing the transitive closure $\overline{G}^{\overline{C}}$. This is $O(|G|^3|C|^3)$ (where $|G|$ is the number of vertices in $G$, and $|C|$ is the number of terminals and non-terminals in $C$) [19].

As an example, consider $\mathcal{G}_{W_{\text{alias}}}^{R_{\text{alias}}}$ defined in Section 4. Let

$$\Sigma_{\text{pt}} = \{\text{New}, \text{Assign}\} \cup \{\text{Get}[f'], \text{Put}[f'] \mid f' \in \mathcal{F}\}.$$

As before, we include symbols $\overline{\sigma}$ in $\Sigma_{\text{pt}}$. Recall that $R_{\text{alias}} = (\text{Assign} + \overline{\text{Assign}})\Sigma_{\text{pt}}^*(\text{Assign} + \overline{\text{Assign}})$. Then $\mathcal{N}(s \xrightarrow{R_{\text{alias}}} f)$ produces the transition graph for the NFA $N = (\{s, n, f\}, \delta, s, f)$, where $n \in \delta(s, \text{Assign})$, $n \in \delta(s, \overline{\text{Assign}})$, $n \in \delta(\sigma, n)$ for all $\sigma \in \Sigma_{\text{pt}}$, $f \in \delta(\text{Assign}, n)$, and $f \in \delta(\overline{\text{Assign}}, n)$. Productions for $\text{FlowsTo}_n$ and $\text{FlowsTo}[f']_n$ ($f' \in \mathcal{F}$) are shown in Figure 11.

Consider the code in Figure 1, and suppose the specification for `List.add` is missing, so $W_{\text{alias}} = V_{\texttt{List.add}}$. In Figure 12, we show the following edges that are added by Algorithm 2:

1. This edge represents two edges: $\text{FlowsTo}_s$ is added by $\text{FlowsTo}_s \to \text{FlowsTo}\ b$ (Rule 1a), and $\text{FlowsTo}_n$ is added by $\text{FlowsTo}_s \to \text{FlowsTo}_n$ (Rule 1f, because $\text{FlowsTo} \to \text{FlowsTo Assign}$).
2. This edge is added by $\text{FlowsTo} \circ \text{Put}[f]_n \to \text{FlowsTo}_n$ (Rule 1f, because $\text{FlowsTo} \circ \text{Put}[f] \to \text{FlowsTo Put}[f]$).
3. This edge represents two edges: $\overline{\text{FlowsTo}}^f$ is added by $\overline{\text{FlowsTo}}^f \to e\ \overline{\text{FlowsTo}}$ (Rule 2a), and $\overline{\text{FlowsTo}}^n$ is added by $\overline{\text{FlowsTo}}^n \to \overline{\text{FlowsTo}}^f$ (Rule 2f, because $\overline{\text{FlowsTo}} \to \overline{\text{Assign}}\ \overline{\text{FlowsTo}}$).
4. This edge is added by $\text{FlowsTo}[f] \to \text{FlowsTo}{\circ}\text{Put}[f]_n\ \overline{\text{FlowsTo}}^n$ (Rule 4c, because $\text{FlowsTo}[f] \to \text{FlowsTo} \circ \text{Put}[f]\ \overline{\text{FlowsTo}}$).

We have used the production $\text{FlowsTo}{\circ}\text{Put}[\texttt{val}] \to \text{FlowsTo Put}[\texttt{val}]$ that comes from normalizing the CFG. Once Algorithm 2 adds the edge $\texttt{o}_{\texttt{lat}} \xrightarrow{\text{FlowsTo}[\texttt{val}]} \texttt{o}_{\texttt{list}}$, it will add the edge $\texttt{LOC} \xrightarrow{\text{SrcSink}} \texttt{SMS}$ as a consequence of the productions in $C_{\text{taint}}$.

### 5.3 Interactive Refinement

We extend Algorithm 2 to find *sufficient assumptions* for the edge $e' = v_{\text{source}} \xrightarrow{T} v_{\text{sink}}$ (recall that sufficient assumptions are encoded as graphs $G \in \mathcal{G}_W^R$ such that $\mathcal{A}(v_{\text{source}}, v_{\text{sink}}) = e' \overset{?}{\in} G^C$). If Algorithm 2 does not produce any source-sink edge $e'$, then we simply return $\widehat{G}$. Otherwise, we record the inputs for each edge produced by Algorithm 2 when computing the closure $\overline{G}^{\overline{C}}$. Recursively searching through the inputs of $e'$, we reconstruct a path $p = v_{\text{source}} \overset{\alpha}{\dashrightarrow} v_{\text{sink}}$ such that $T \overset{*}{\Rightarrow} \alpha$. We record the index of every pair of edges $w_i \xrightarrow{b} v_i \xrightarrow{e} w_i'$ that occurs along $p$, which we denote by $\mathcal{I}$. Then we add the corresponding graphs $G_i = \mathcal{N}(s_i \xrightarrow{R} f_i)$ to $\widehat{G}$, i.e. $G = \widehat{G} \cup \{G_i \mid i \in \mathcal{I}\}$. The resulting graph $G$ has the desired property $e' \in G^C$.

There may exist multiple paths $p = v_{\text{source}} \overset{\alpha}{\dashrightarrow} v_{\text{sink}}$ such that $T \overset{*}{\Rightarrow} \alpha$, each of which may yield different sufficient assumptions $G$. We further extend Algorithm 2 to find minimal sufficient assumptions $G$ for $e'$. Recall that this corresponds to minimizing $\text{weight}(G)$, i.e. finding $G \in \mathcal{G}_W^R$ with source-sink path $p$ of minimum $\text{weight}(p)$. To do so, we define a weight function on $\Sigma$ by setting $\text{weight}(b) = \text{weight}(e) = \frac{1}{2}$, and $\text{weight}(\sigma) = 0$ for all other $\sigma \in \Sigma$. This extends to $\Sigma^*$ by setting $\text{weight}(\sigma_1 ... \sigma_k) = \sum_{i=1}^k \text{weight}(\sigma_i)$. Note that for source-sink path $p = v_{\text{source}} \overset{\alpha}{\dashrightarrow} v_{\text{sink}} \in \mathcal{P}(\overline{G})$, $\text{weight}(p) = \text{weight}(\alpha)$. Consider the following:

DEFINITION 5.3. Let $\overline{G}$ be the graph defined above. The *shortest-path CFL reachability problem* is to return the shortest path $p^* = \arg\min_{p \in \mathcal{P}(\overline{G})} \text{weight}(\alpha)$, or return $\emptyset$ if $\mathcal{P}(\overline{G}) = \emptyset$.

Knuth describes a generalization of Djikstra's algorithm to find the shortest string in a context-free grammar [14]. This algorithm generalizes to solving the shortest-path CFL reachability problem: we replace the worklist of edges in [19] with a heap of edges, where the priority of an edge is the weight of its shortest path (see Algorithm 4 in Appendix A for details). By using Algorithm 4 to compute the closure $\overline{G}^{\overline{C}}$, we find the source-sink path $p^* \in \mathcal{P}(\overline{G})$

**Algorithm 3** Iterative refinement of results. Here, $s$ and $f$ are fresh vertices.

**function** ORACLEREFINE($C, \widehat{G}, W, R, v, v', \mathcal{O}$)
  $G_i \leftarrow \mathcal{N}(s \xrightarrow{R} f); \overline{C} \leftarrow \mathcal{T}(G_i, C)$
  **repeat**
    $\overline{G} \leftarrow$PREPROCESSHELPER($\widehat{G}, W$)
    $p^* \leftarrow$SHORTESTPATH($\overline{C}, \overline{G}, v \xrightarrow{T} v'$)
    **for all** $w \xrightarrow{b} v \xrightarrow{e} w' \in p^*$ **do**
      $\widehat{G} \leftarrow \widehat{G} \cup \mathcal{O}(w, w')$
      $W \leftarrow W - \{(w, w')\}$
    **end for**
  **until** $v \xrightarrow{T} v' \notin \overline{G}^{\overline{C}}$ or weight$(p^*) = 0$
  **return** $v \xrightarrow{T} v' \overset{?}{\in} \overline{G}^{\overline{C}}$
**end function**

that passes through the fewest possible edges $w \xrightarrow{b} v \xrightarrow{e} w'$. Then the sufficient assumptions $G$ constructed from $p^*$ has minimum weight.

Finally, we describe an algorithm for interactively refining the static analysis results with the help of an auditor. Recall that the graph $\widehat{G}$ is missing some vertices and edges from $G^*$. Suppose we can query an oracle to obtain information about $G^*$:

DEFINITION 5.4. We say $\mathcal{O}$ is an *oracle* for $G$ if for every $(w, w') \in W$, $\mathcal{O}(w, w') = G^*_{w,w'}$.

We use a human auditor as an oracle $\mathcal{O}$. On input $(w, w')$, the auditor examines the library documentation and return the true specification $G^*_{w,w'}$. The problem is to produce static analysis results that are sound and precise with respect to $G^*$, while making as few queries $\mathcal{O}(w, w')$ as possible.

Algorithm 3 solves this problem. It obtains the shortest path $p^* \in \mathcal{P}(\overline{G})$ for the edge $e' = v_{\text{source}} \xrightarrow{T} v_{\text{sink}}$ by calling $p^* \leftarrow$ SHORTESTPATH($\overline{C}, \overline{G}, e'$). Then the algorithm replaces every edge $w \xrightarrow{b} v \xrightarrow{e} w'$ in $p^*$ with $\mathcal{O}(w, w')$. Algorithm 3 repeats this process until either weight$(p^*) = 0$, or until $\mathcal{P}(G') = \emptyset$. In the former case, the path $p^*$ does not contain any symbols $b$ or $e$, i.e. $p^*$ does not pass through any potentially missing specifications. This proves that $p^* \in \widehat{G}$, i.e. $e' \in \widehat{G}^C \subseteq (G^*)^C$. In the latter case, because Algorithm 2 is sound, it only returns $p^* = \emptyset$ if there does not exist *any* $G \in \mathcal{G}_W^R$ such that $e' \in G$. Since we have assumed that $G^* \in \mathcal{G}_W^R$, this proves that $e' \notin (G^*)^C$. Therefore:

THEOREM 5.5. Algorithm 3 computes $v_{\text{source}} \xrightarrow{T} v_{\text{sink}} \overset{?}{\in} (G^*)^C$.

## 6. Implementation

We have implemented the system described in Figure 8 for Java, and specifically for the Android framework. A number of extensions are required beyond the essentials we have described, but these extensions do not introduce any new ideas. For example, we include rules for primitive variables that are essentially rules for reference variables without fields. Our current implementation does not consider specifications involving static fields; as discussed in Section 4, in our experience such specifications lead to many false positives as there are few constraints on the possible flows between static variables, and in practice there are few flows among them.

Prior to this work, we had manually written many specifications over a period of more than one year. These *baseline specifications* $S$ cover 176 Android library classes, including a number of taint sources (location, device ID, SIM data, contacts, and calendar data) and a number of sinks (network sockets, SMS messages, and user settings modifications). This baseline also includes specifications for important container objects including ArrayList, LinkedList, and HashMap. Since our focus in on the long tail of missing specifications, we bootstrap our implementation of the specification inference framework with these baseline specifications.

In our implementation, program fact extraction is performed using the Chord platform [20] modified to work with the Jimple intermediate representation provided by Soot [30]. In order to improve precision of our analysis, we extend the points-to rules (Rules 10-13 in Figure 5) so that they are context sensitive—more precisely, we use a 1-CFA points-to analysis. Additionally, because Java is type safe, we use type filters in the points-to analysis (i.e., a reference of type $T$ can only point to an object of type $T'$ if $T'$ is a subtype of $T$). Our solver detects and discards points-to edges that are not consistent with the type constraints of the program. Our shortest-path CFL solver is based on the CFL solver in [19], modified with the algorithm from [14] to compute shortest paths; details are given in Appendix A.

Within our specification inference framework we implement both flow ($R_{\text{flow}}, W_{\text{flow}}$) and alias ($R_{\text{alias}}, W_{\text{alias}}$) specifications. For each inferred specification, we manually reference the Android library documentation to determine if the specification is correct, and rerun the analysis with the updated specifications. We repeat this process until no new specifications are inferred.

When inferring alias specifications, the large size of the sound points-to analysis makes it difficult to scale the inference algorithm. We implemented a demand-driven optimization. First, we perform the entire analysis using BDDBDDB [31] as the solver. However, BDDBDDB cannot compute shortest paths. Instead, we use the results from BDDBDDB to prune irrelevant edges (i.e., edges that do not contribute to a source-sink path) from $\overline{G}$. Finally, we recompute the analysis using our shortest-path CFL solver.

Ideally we would infer alias and flow specifications simultaneously. However, worst-case flow specifications introduce a large number of incorrect taint flows, causing the demand-driven optimization to fail to eliminate enough edges for the specification inference algorithm to scale for some benchmarks. As a result, we perform the two analyses separately in our experiments. Nevertheless, inferring alias specifications alone is already sufficient to be sound with respect to finding explicit taint flows.

| Spec. Type | Flow | Alias |
|---|---|---|
| **# Android apps** | 179 | 156 |
| **Total Correct Specifications Proposed** | 486 | 35 |
| **Total Specifications Proposed** | 1122 | 63 |
| **Overall Accuracy** | 0.433 | 0.556 |
| **Average # Specifications Proposed** | 23.8 | 0.813 |
| **Accuracy of Random Sample** | 0.140 | N/A |

**Figure 13.** Statistics on inferred Android library specifications.

## 7. Experimental Results

We ran our tool on a corpus of 179 Android apps. Our results are for the optimized version of our specification inference algorithm, i.e. Algorithm 2, since preliminary experiments with Algorithm 1 did not scale even to apps of moderate size. The running time for one iteration of Algorithm 3 is plotted in Figure 16(c). The flow specification inference algorithm ran on all 179 apps, running in fewer than 10 seconds per iteration on average for most apps, which is fast enough to allow a human auditor to interactively run the analysis. The alias specification inference algorithm successfully ran on 156 apps. The worst-case assumptions cause a substantial increase in the points-to relation size (see Figure 16(d)), which proved to be too large on the remaining 23 apps. Still, inferring alias specifications runs in under 100 seconds for most apps with up to 100,000 lines of Jimple code.

| App Name | Jimple LOC | # Spec. | # Critical Spec. | Total # Spec. | Rounds | Accuracy | Flows | Run Time (s) | Spec. Type |
|---|---|---|---|---|---|---|---|---|---|
| 411524 | 497178 | 43 | 20 | 6478 | 5 | 0.5116 | 42 | 178.6 | Flow |
| APG-M | 471943 | 20 | 9 | 5553 | 5 | 0.5 | 16 | 22.30 | Flow |
| browser | 421026 | 139 | 24 | 10361 | 16 | 0.2662 | 48 | 607.3 | Flow |
| 0C2B78 | 395053 | 244 | 11 | 4726 | 78 | 0.1066 | 222 | 10.38 | Flow |
| highrail | 265875 | 142 | 15 | 4242 | 18 | 0.1690 | 64 | 12.20 | Flow |
| iwz | 263014 | 38 | 17 | 4937 | 5 | 0.5789 | 38 | 14.24 | Flow |
| ce667f | 193518 | 48 | 26 | 4388 | 5 | 0.6042 | 44 | 10.38 | Flow |
| ConnectBot | 136800 | 4 | 4 | 3454 | 2 | 1.0 | 2 | 2.357 | Flow |
| yaaic | 109286 | 0 | 0 | 5440 | 1 | N/A | 0 | 3.769 | Flow |
| tomdroid | 44478 | 14 | 5 | 3029 | 6 | 0.3571 | 2 | 1.607 | Flow |
| highrail | 265875 | 2 | 2 | 5167 | 2 | 1.0 | 1 | 9623 | Alias |
| andmj | 239227 | 0 | 0 | 5229 | 1 | N/A | 0 | 1555 | Alias |
| ce667f | 193518 | 0 | 0 | 5509 | 1 | N/A | 0 | 3234 | Alias |
| ConnectBot | 136800 | 0 | 0 | 3293 | 1 | N/A | 0 | 3193 | Alias |
| 05ed92 | 134235 | 1 | 1 | 12632 | 2 | 1.0 | 3 | 2254 | Alias |
| SMSBot | 134230 | 15 | 3 | 4693 | 7 | 0.467 | 2 | 284.3 | Alias |
| yaaic | 109286 | 0 | 0 | 4161 | 1 | N/A | 0 | 816.1 | Alias |
| ca70f4 | 81974 | 3 | 0 | 3307 | 3 | 0.0 | 0 | 45.57 | Alias |
| tomdroid | 44478 | 0 | 0 | 3697 | 1 | N/A | 0 | 68.154 | Alias |
| a1d58b | 41682 | 2 | 1 | 2285 | 3 | 0.5 | 1 | 7.847 | Alias |

**Figure 14.** Specification inference results on large Android apps. *Critical specifications* are both correct and lie along a true source-sink path. "Total # specifications" is the number of worst-case specifications, "Rounds" is the number of iterations in Algorithm 3, "Accuracy" is the proportion of proposed specifications that are correct, and "Flows" is the number of new flows discovered (accuracy is N/A if no specifications are inferred).

| Class | Method Signature | Specification | Spec. Type |
|---|---|---|---|
| com.google.android.maps.GeoPoint | int getLatitudeE6() | (`this`, `return`) | Flow |
| java.lang.Double | double parseDouble(java.lang.String) | (`arg1`, `return`) | Flow |
| org.json.JSONObject | org.json.JSONObject getJSONObject(java.lang.String) | (`this`, `return`) | Alias |
| android.telephony.gsm.SmsMessage | java.lang.String getMessageBody() | (`this`, `return`) | Alias |
| android.content.ContentValues | void put(java.lang.String, java.lang.String) | (`arg2`, `this`) | Alias |

**Figure 15.** Sample of inferred specifications. "Specification" is the pair $(w, w') \in W$ returned by Algorithm 3.

Results for selected apps, including the largest four that ran successfully for each analysis, are shown in Figure 14. We show the number of specifications proposed by our tool (# Spec.), along with the number of worst-case specifications (Total # Spec.). Our tool may propose specifications that are correct (i.e., represent valid paths throughs library methods), but do not contribute to a correct source-sink path in the program. Therefore, we also show the number of specifications that are both correct *and* contribute to a true source-sink flow (# Critical Spec.), which is a lower bound for the number of specifications proposed. We call such specifications *critical specifications*, because they are the specifications that an auditor must examine in order to find all source-sink flows. The number of inferred specifications is plotted as black circles in Figure 16(a) and (b), along with the number of inferred specifications that are correct (plotted as red triangles), and the number of critical specifications (plotted as blue diamonds). For readability, (a) is a log-log plot, and the $x$-axis of (b) is log-scale. The accuracy of the aggregated specifications are shown in Figure 13. Note that the accuracy is directly correlated with the manual labor required by the oracle: higher accuracy means that the oracle will have to examine fewer incorrect specifications.

### 7.1 Specification Inference Accuracy

Our first experiment demonstrates the accuracy of the specifications inferred. For each app, we ran our inference algorithm with the baseline specifications $\mathcal{S}$. The inferred alias specifications are very accurate, in part because of type filters. We show some examples of inferred specifications in Figure 15.

We compare our results to randomly chosen specifications. We randomly chose 50 possible flow specifications in the following way: randomly choose a method, randomly choose a pair of formal parameters $v$ and $v'$ (or a formal parameter $v$ and the formal return value $v'$), and propose the flow specification $v \xrightarrow{\text{RefRef}} v'$. The accuracy of a specification randomly chosen in this way is only 0.140, whereas the overall accuracy of the specifications inferred by our tool is 0.433.

The number of specifications proposed, which grows roughly linearly with app size, is very manageable. It is usually a small multiple of the number of critical specifications. For alias specification inference, each app produced fewer than 20 proposals, each of which could be checked in under a minute. Significantly more flow specifications are inferred, but these are even faster to check. All but five of the apps required fewer than 100 proposals. In total, the tool helped discover hundreds of new specifications and flows, a task that we estimate would have taken weeks without the tool.

### 7.2 Specification Aggregation

Our second experiment demonstrates how our tool can be used to quickly build a useful collection of library specifications. Consider analyzing the apps in some arbitrary order and aggregating specifications along the way; that is, the $i$th app is analyzed using all of the correct specifications discovered in analyzing the first $i-1$ apps. Intuitively, the most frequently used methods should have their specifications discovered relatively early in the process and we should subsequently benefit from already having those specifications and not needing to infer them again.

Figure 16(e) shows the proportion of new specifications proposed by Algorithm 3 with aggregation to the number of specifications proposed when Algorithm 3 starts from the baseline. The red, triangle series shows, for each app, the percentage of new specifica-

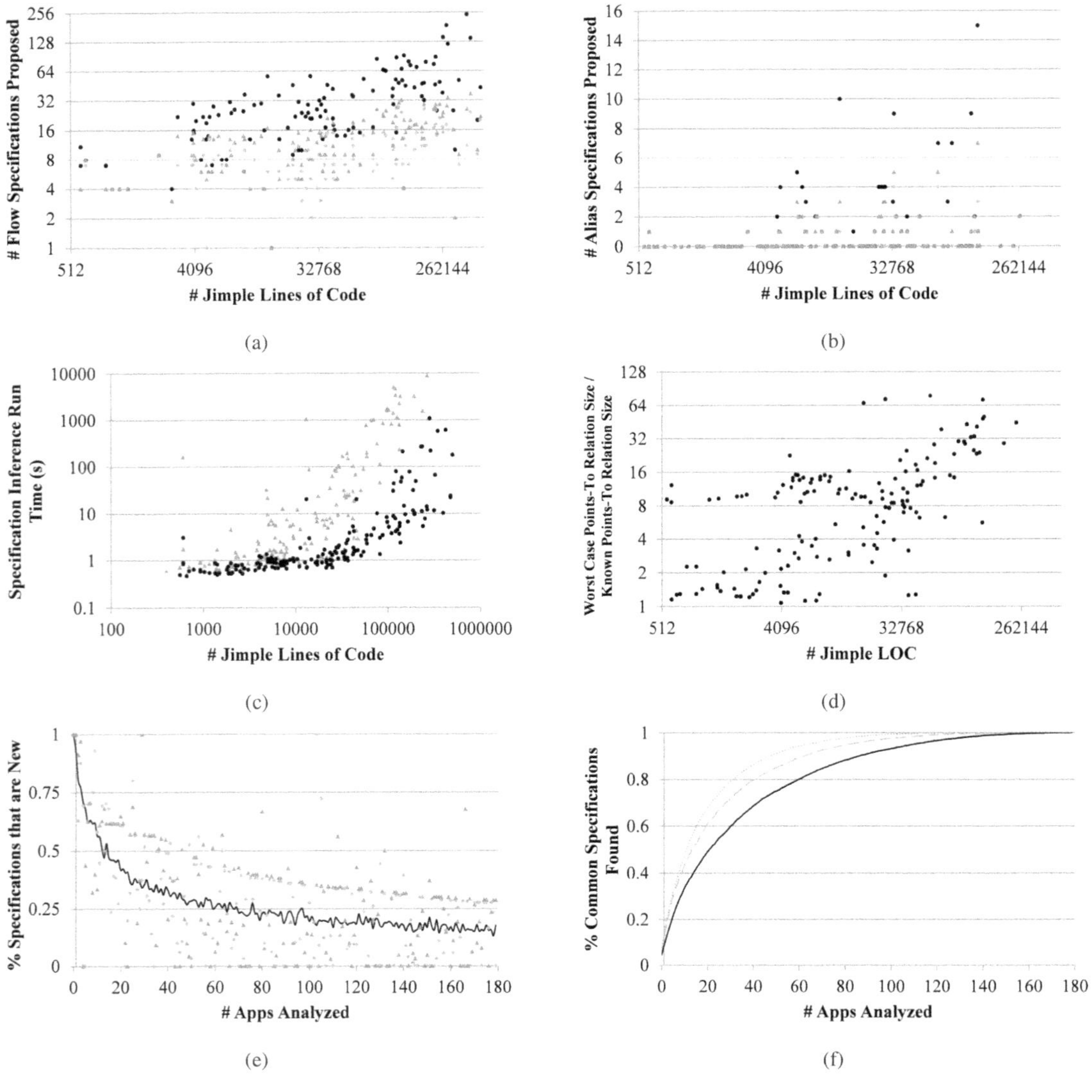


**Figure 16.** For (a) flow and (b) alias: # specifications proposed (black, circle), # correct (red, triangle), and # critical (blue, diamond). (c) Run time of the flow (black, circle) and alias (red, triangle) specification inference algorithms. (d) Ratio of worst-case points-to relation size to known points-to relation size. (e) Ratio of # specifications with aggregation to # specifications from baseline, averaged over 100 random orders (black line), and for two different random orders (red triangle, blue diamond). (f) Proportion of common specifications proposed, for $c = 2$ (black, solid), 3 (blue, dashed), and 4 (red, dotted), averaged over 100 random orders.

tions that the auditor must examine. After the 100th app, more than 2/3 of the needed specifications are already known, and for many apps no new specifications are needed. The blue, diamond series shows the same effect from processing the apps in a different random order. The black line shows the average number of new specifications over 100 such runs (varying the order of the apps each time); as can be seen, the auditor's workload for a new app with aggregation approaches about 20% of that without aggregation. The red and blue series give a sense of the considerable variance, but the overall trend is clear: regardless of chosen order, the proportion of new specifications quickly becomes small and the auditor only does a fraction of the work compared to starting from the baseline. The required work would drop further after processing more apps.

Figure 16(f) shows the proportion of *common* specifications that are identified after analyzing each number of apps. We say a specification is common if it is proposed by the tool for at least $c \in \{2, 3, 4\}$ apps. In this graph, the black, solid curve corresponds to $c = 2$; the blue, dashed curve corresponds to $c = 3$; and the red, dotted curve corresponds to $c = 4$. Each line shows the average proportion over 100 random permutations. The tool quickly picks up a large fraction of the common specifications, reaching more than 82% after just a quarter of the apps have been analyzed in the case $c = 3$.

### 7.3 Verification

We ran Algorithm 3 to termination, i.e., until no new specifications for missing parts of the program could add any more taint flows, which means that the remaining taint flows all occur in the original graph $\widehat{G}$. In the case of alias inference, this also proves that no additional explicit taint flows can occur. Figure 16(b) shows the number of specifications that had to be checked by an auditor to completely verify the absence of explicit taint flows in an app. This number is very reasonable (at most 15), showing that the tool makes verification of large apps practical. In the case of flow specification inference, taint flows due to missing alias specifications can still occur, and verification requires that the auditor supply all relevant alias specifications. In practice, this analysis still discovers many library methods that need alias specifications, since taint often flows forwards through these methods. Thus our tool finds many taint flows even if alias specifications are missing.

There are currently two primary limitations to our tool. One we have already discussed: inferring both alias and flow specifications simultaneously is too expensive for our tool on some apps. The second is that while we can infer missing flow and alias specifications, we still require a complete list of the possible sources and sinks in the program to be able to find flows at all. While manually annotating sources and sinks is a much easier problem (by orders of magnitude) than finding flows, it would still be useful to consider how to provide automatic assistance in discovering sources and sinks in large apps.

As can be seen from the total number of potential specifications shown in Figure 14, without our tool an auditor would have to examine a huge number of potential specifications. Even if many of these can be easily eliminated, our experience has been that without the aid of our tool, performing verification on moderately sized apps can take hours or even days, and performing verification on large apps is almost impossible.

## 8. Related Work

**Sound analysis with missing specifications.** There has been previous work that shares our goal of inferring specifications for verification based on abductive inference [19]. There are several differences in the two approaches. First, we handle the general class of CFL reachability problems, whereas [34] addresses standard graph reachability problems. Second, abductive inference is a very general tool and solving abductive inference problems is NP-hard. Our algorithm, which is tailored to specification inference, runs in polynomial time. As a result, our system appears to scale considerably better, and we are able to conduct a much larger experiment on many more apps than [34]. There has also been prior work on sound call graph generation [2]. Their work constructs a placeholder library that exhibits every possible behavior that can affect the call graph. Our technique, in addition to being more general, actually proposes library specifications and allows an auditor to interactively refine analysis results.

**Specification inference.** There has been work using data mining to infer specifications [3, 4, 7, 15, 16, 21, 22, 25, 33]. Several of these techniques use dynamic traces to propose specifications [4, 33], while others apply domain knowledge and statically infer specifications from the source code [7, 15, 16, 22, 25]. Our tool differs in that it applies to CFL reachability problems. Furthermore, our tool produces sound results, which enables interactive verification.

**CFL reachability for program analyses.** A large number of program analyses have been expressed as CFL reachability problems, for example points-to analysis [26, 28], many set constraint problems [11, 13, 19], various interprocedural analyses [23, 24], and type qualifier inference [10]. Our work makes these techniques more applicable for whole-program analysis by providing a practical and sound approach to dealing with missing or hard-to-analyze portions of the program. Our work makes use of ideas for combining context-free reachability with additional regular language properties such as [12].

**Applications of program analysis to security.** Work on taint analysis for Android includes SCanDroid [9], which statically tracks taint flows between applications, TaintDroid [8], which is a dynamic system that performs real time monitoring, and FlowDroid [5], which uses static analysis to find information leaks. Static analysis has also been applied to finding vulnerabilities in web applications [17, 27, 29, 32].

**Algorithm 4** Algorithm for computing shortest-path CFL reachability.

**function** SHORTESTPATH($G, C, e$)
  $G^C \leftarrow$GRAPH(); $I \leftarrow$MAP(); $H \leftarrow$HEAP()
  **for all** $v \xrightarrow{\sigma} v' \in G$ **do**
    $H$.UPDATE($v \xrightarrow{\sigma} v'$, weight($\sigma$))
    $I[v \xrightarrow{\sigma} v'] \leftarrow \emptyset$
  **end for**
  **while** $\neg H$.EMPTY() **do**
    $[v \xrightarrow{A} v', P_{\text{cur}}] \leftarrow H$.DELETEMIN()
    $G^C \leftarrow G^C \cup \{v \xrightarrow{A} v'\}$
    **for all** $D \to AB \in C$ **do**
      **for all** $v' \xrightarrow{B} v'' \in G^C$ **do**
        $P_{\text{new}} \leftarrow P_{\text{cur}} + H$.PRIORITY($v' \xrightarrow{B} v''$)
        **if** $P_{\text{new}} < H$.PRIORITY($v \xrightarrow{D} v''$) **then**
          $H$.UPDATE($v \xrightarrow{D} v''$, $P_{\text{new}}$)
          $I[v \xrightarrow{D} v''] \leftarrow [v \xrightarrow{A} v', v' \xrightarrow{B} v'']$
        **end if**
      **end for**
    **end for**
    **for all** $D \to BA \in C$ **do**
      **for all** $v'' \xrightarrow{B} v \in G^C$ **do**
        $P_{\text{new}} \leftarrow H$.PRIORITY($v'' \xrightarrow{B} v$)$+P_{\text{cur}}$
        **if** $P_{\text{new}} < H$.PRIORITY($v'' \xrightarrow{D} v'$) **then**
          $H$.UPDATE($v'' \xrightarrow{D} v'$, $P_{\text{new}}$)
          $I[v'' \xrightarrow{D} v'] \leftarrow [v'' \xrightarrow{B} v, v \xrightarrow{A} v']$
        **end if**
      **end for**
    **end for**
    **for all** $B \to A \in C$ **do**
      **if** $P_{\text{cur}} < H$.PRIORITY($v \xrightarrow{B} v'$) **then**
        $H$.UPDATE($v \xrightarrow{B} v'$, $P_{\text{cur}}$)
        $I[v \xrightarrow{B} v'] \leftarrow [v \xrightarrow{A} v']$
      **end if**
    **end for**
  **end while**
  **if** $e \in I$ **then**
    **return** GETPATH($I, e$)
  **end if**
  **return** $\emptyset$
**end function**
**function** GETPATH($I, e$)
  **if** $I[e] = \emptyset$ **then**
    **return** $[e]$
  **end if**
  $[e_1, ..., e_k] \leftarrow I[e]$
  **return** GETPATH($e_1$)+...+GETPATH($e_k$)
**end function**

## 9. Conclusions

We have developed a general framework that applies to any program analysis formulated as a CFL reachability problem. Our framework allows us to perform a sound analysis by inferring missing specifications, and furthermore allows an auditor to interactively refine the results. We have demonstrated the quality of the specifications inferred by our tool on a corpus of 179 real-world Android apps. Our results show that our tool can both help build large collections of specifications very efficiently, and make it practical for an auditor to perform verification.

## A. Shortest-Path CFL Reachability

The shortest-path algorithm in Algorithm 4 generalizes Knuth's algorithm for finding shortest strings in CFLs to computing shortest-path CFL reachability. Essentially, Knuth's algorithm [14] builds on an algorithm for determining emptiness of a context-free grammar: it adds a heap that keeps track of the shortest sequence of terminals that can be derived from each non-terminal symbol. Similarly, Algorithm 4 generalizes the algorithm for computing CFL reachability described in [19]. In the pseudocode, arrays are denoted as $[x_1, ..., x_k]$, and addition of arrays is defined to be $[x_1, ..., x_k] + [y_1, ..., y_h] = [x_1, ..., x_k, y_1, ..., y_h]$.

We introduce a heap $H$ that keeps track of the shortest path for each edge $v \xrightarrow{A} v'$. The current priority of the edge $v \xrightarrow{A} v'$ is the length of the current shortest path. If a shorter path is found, then the heap is updated with the new path and the new priority. At every iteration of the algorithm, the lowest priority edge $v \xrightarrow{A} v'$ (with priority $P_{\text{cur}}$) is removed from the heap, added to $G^C$, and then processed. Note that once this happens, there can be no way of producing $v \xrightarrow{A} v'$ with lower priority: every subsequent edge removed from $H$ must have priority at least $P_{\text{cur}}$, so any edge produced while processing such an edge must also have priority at least $P_{\text{cur}}$. Since every possible way of producing $v \xrightarrow{A} v'$ is considered, the shortest path is correctly identified.

The heap $H$ supports the following operations: UPDATE($e$) updates the priority of edge $e$ (and adds $e$ to $H$ if $e \notin H$), EMPTY() returns true if the heap contains no edges, PRIORITY($e$) returns the current priority of edge $e$, and DELETEMIN() removes the lowest priority element in the heap and returns it (along with its current priority). We assume that PRIORITY returns $\infty$ for edges not yet added to $H$, and 0 for edges already removed from $H$. The complexity of Algorithm 4 is $O(|G|^3|C|^3(\log|G| + \log|C|))$ because of the additional cost of updating the heap (as before, $|G|$ is the number of vertices in $G$, and $|C|$ is the number of terminals and non-terminals in $C$).

The shortest path itself is stored in a map $I$, which keeps track of the edges $[e_1, ..., e_k]$ (where $k \in \{0, 1, 2\}$) used to produce $v \xrightarrow{A} v'$. The shortest path itself is reconstructed by recursively querying the shortest path for each edge in $I[v \xrightarrow{A} v']$.

Algorithm 4 does not handle edges labeled with the empty string $\epsilon$, or productions $A \to \epsilon$. In order to handle the former, our solver introduces a fresh terminal symbol $\widehat{\epsilon}$, replaces every edge $v \xrightarrow{\epsilon} v'$ with $v \xrightarrow{\widehat{\epsilon}} v'$, and adds productions $A \to \widehat{\epsilon}A$ and $A \to A\widehat{\epsilon}$ for every non-terminal $A$ in the input grammar. The latter is handled by adding self loops $v \xrightarrow{A} v$ for every $v \in V$ and every $A \in U$ such that $A \to \epsilon \in C$ (see [19]).

## Acknowledgments

This material is based on research sponsored by the Air Force Research Laboratory, under agreement number FA8750-12-2-0020. The U.S. Government is authorized to reproduce and distribute reprints for Governmental purposes notwithstanding any copyright notation thereon.

## References

[1] A. Aiken, S. Bugrara, I. Dillig, T. Dillig, B. Hackett, P. Hawkins. An overview of the Saturn project. In *PASTE*, 43-48, 2007.

[2] K. Ali, O. Lhoták. Averroes: whole-program analysis without the whole program. In *ECOOP*, 2013.

[3] R. Alur, P. Černý, P. Madhusudan, W. Nam. Synthesis of interface specifications for Java classes. In *POPL*, 2005.

[4] G. Ammons, R. Bodík, J. Larus. Mining specifications. In *POPL*, 2002.

[5] S. Arzt, S. Rasthofer, C. Fritz, E. Bodden, A. Bartel, J. Klein, Y. L. Traon, D. Octeau, P. McDaniel. FlowDroid: precise context, flow, field, object-sensitive and lifecycle-aware taint analysis for Android apps. In *PLDI*, 2014.

[6] T. Ball, S. Rajamani. The SLAM project: debugging system software via static analysis. In *POPL*, 2002.

[7] N. Beckman, A. Nori. Probabilistic, modular and scalable inference of typestate specifications. In *PLDI*, 2011.

[8] W. Enck, P. Gilbert, B. Chun, L. Cox, J. Jung, P. McDaniel, A. Sheth. TaintDroid: an information-flow tracking system for realtime privacy monitoring on smartphones. In *OSDI*, 2010.

[9] A. P. Fuchs, A. Chaudhuri, J. S. Foster. SCanDroid: automated security certification of Android applications. In *IEEE Symposium on Security and Privacy*, 2010.

[10] D. Greenfieldboyce, J. S. Foster. Type qualifier inference in Java. In *OOPSLA*, 2007.

[11] J. Kodumal, A. Aiken. Banshee: a scalable constraint-based analysis toolkit. In *SAS*, 2005.

[12] J. Kodumal, A. Aiken. Regularly annotated set constraints. In *PLDI*, 2007.

[13] J. Kodumal, A. Aiken. The set constraint/CFL reachability connection in practice. In *PLDI*, 2004.

[14] D. Knuth. A generalization of Dijkstra's algorithm. In *Information Processing Letters*, 6(1):1-5, 1977.

[15] T. Kremenek, P. Twohey, G. Back, A. Ng, D. Engler. From uncertainty to belief: inferring the specification within. In *OSDI*, 2006.

[16] B. Livshits, A. V. Nori, S. K. Rajamani, A. Banerjee. Merlin: specification inference for explicit information flow problems. In *PLDI*, 2009.

[17] B. Livshits, M. S. Lam. Finding security vulnerabilities in Java applications with static analysis. In *USENIX Security Symposium*, 2005.

[18] B. Livshits, M. S. Lam. Tracking pointers with path and context sensitivity for bug detection in C programs. In *FSE*, 2003.

[19] D. Melski, T. Reps. Interconvertibility of a class of set constraints and context-free language reachability. In *Theoretical Computer Science*, 248(1):29-98, 2000.

[20] M. Naik, A. Aiken, J. Whaley. Effective static race detection for Java. In *PLDI*, 2006.

[21] J. W. Nimmer, M. D. Ernst. Automatic generation of program specifications. In *ISSTA*, 2002.

[22] M. K. Ramanathan, A. Grama, S. Jagannathan. Static specification inference using predicate mining. In *PLDI*, 2007.

[23] T. Reps. Program analysis via graph reachability. In *ILPS*, 1997.

[24] T. Reps, S. Horwitz, M. Sagiv. Precise interprocedural data flow analysis via graph reachability. In *POPL*, 1995.

[25] S. Shoham, E. Yahav, S. Fink, M. Pistoia. Static specification mining using automata-based abstractions. In *ISSTA*, 2007.

[26] M. Sridharan, D. Gopan, L. Shan, R. Bodik. Demand-driven points-to analysis for Java. In *OOPSLA*, 2005.

[27] M. Sridharan, S. Artzi, M. Pistoia, S. Guarnieri, O. Tripp, R. Berg. F4F: taint analysis of framework-based web applications. In *OOPSLA*, 2011.

[28] M. Sridharan, R. Bodik. Refinement-based context-sensitive points-to analysis for Java. In *PLDI*, 2006.

[29] O. Tripp, M. Pistoia, S. J. Fink, M. Sridharan, O. Weisman. TAJ: effective taint analysis of web applications. In *PLDI*, 2009.

[30] R. Vallée-Rai, P. Co, E. Gagnon, L. Hendren, P. Lam, V. Sundaresan. Soot: a Java bytecode optimization framework. In *CASCON*, 1999.

[31] J. Whaley, M. S. Lam. Cloning-based context-sensitive pointer alias analysis using binary decision diagrams. In *OOPSLA*, 2004.

[32] Y. Xie, A. Aiken. Static detection of security vulnerabilities in scripting languages. In *USENIX Security Symposium*, 2006.

[33] J. Yang, D. Evans, D. Bhardwaj, T. Bhat, M. Das. Perracotta: mining temporal API rules from imperfect traces. In *ICSE*, 2006.

[34] H. Zhu, T. Dillig, I. Dillig. Automated inference of library specifications for source-sink property verification. In *APLAS*, 2013.

# On Characterizing the Data Access Complexity of Programs

Venmugil Elango
The Ohio State University
elango.4@osu.edu

Fabrice Rastello
Inria
Fabrice.Rastello@inria.fr

Louis-Noël Pouchet
The Ohio State University
pouchet@cse.ohio-state.edu

J. Ramanujam
Louisiana State University
ram@cct.lsu.edu

P. Sadayappan
The Ohio State University
saday@cse.ohio-state.edu

## Abstract

Technology trends will cause data movement to account for the majority of energy expenditure and execution time on emerging computers. Therefore, computational complexity will no longer be a sufficient metric for comparing algorithms, and a fundamental characterization of data access complexity will be increasingly important. The problem of developing lower bounds for data access complexity has been modeled using the formalism of Hong & Kung's red/blue pebble game for computational directed acyclic graphs (CDAGs). However, previously developed approaches to lower bounds analysis for the red/blue pebble game are very limited in effectiveness when applied to CDAGs of real programs, with computations comprised of multiple sub-computations with differing DAG structure. We address this problem by developing an approach for effectively composing lower bounds based on graph decomposition. We also develop a static analysis algorithm to derive the asymptotic data-access lower bounds of programs, as a function of the problem size and cache size.

***Categories and Subject Descriptors*** F.2 [*Analysis of Algorithms and Problem Complexity*]: General; D.2.8 [*Software*]: Metrics—Complexity measures

***General Terms*** Algorithms, Theory

***Keywords*** Data access complexity; I/O lower bounds; Red-blue pebble game; Static analysis

## 1. Introduction

Advances in technology over the last few decades have yielded significantly different rates of improvement in the computational performance of processors relative to the speed of memory access. Because of the significant mismatch between computational latency and throughput when compared to main memory latency and bandwidth, the use of hierarchical memory systems and the exploitation of significant data reuse in the faster (i.e., higher) levels of the memory hierarchy is critical for high performance. With future systems, the cost of data movement through the memory hierarchy is expected to become even more dominant relative to the cost of performing arithmetic operations [6, 17, 32], both in terms of time and energy. It is therefore of critical importance to limit the volume of data movement to/from memory by enhancing data reuse in registers and higher levels of the cache. Thus the characterization of the inherent data access complexity of computations is extremely important.

```
for(i=1;i<N-1;i++)
  for(j=1;j<N-1;j++)
    A[i,j]=A[i-1,j]+A[i,j-1];
```

(a) Untiled code

```
for(it=1;it<N-1;it+=T)
  for(jt=1;jt<N-1;jt+=T)
    for(i=it;i<min(it+T,N-1);i++)
      for(j=jt;j<min(jt+T,N-1);j++)
        A[i,j]=A[i-1,j]+A[i,j-1];
```

(b) Equivalent tiled code

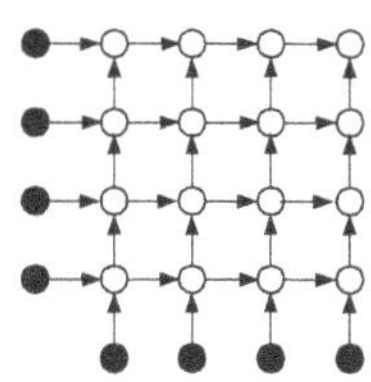

(c) CDAG

Figure 1: Single-sweep two-point Gauss-Seidel code

Let us consider the code shown in Fig. 1(a). Its computational complexity can be simply stated as $(N-2)^2$ arithmetic operations. Fig. 1(b) shows a functionally equivalent form of the same computation, after a tiling transformation. The tiled form too has exactly the same computational complexity of $(N-2)^2$ arithmetic operations. Next, let us consider the data access cost for execution of these two code forms on a processor with a single level of cache. If the problem size $N$ is larger than cache capacity, the number of cache misses would be higher for the untiled version (Fig. 1(a)) than the tiled version (Fig. 1(b)). But if the cache size were sufficiently large, the tiled version would not offer any benefits in reducing cache misses.

Thus, unlike the computational complexity of an algorithm, which stays unchanged for different valid orders of execution of its operations and also independent of machine parameters like cache


*POPL '15*, January 15–17, 2015, Mumbai, India.

ACM 978-1-4503-3300-9/15/01... $15.00.
http://dx.doi.org/10.1145/2676726.2677010

size, the data access cost depends both on the cache capacity and the order of execution of the operations of the algorithm.

A fundamental question therefore is: *Given a computation and the amount of storage at different levels of the cache/memory hierarchy, what is the minimum possible number of data transfers at the different levels, among all valid schedules that perform the operations?*

In order to model the range of valid scheduling orders for the operations of an algorithm, it is common to use the abstraction of the computational directed acyclic graph (CDAG), with a vertex for each instance of each computational operation, and edges from producer instances to consumer instances. Fig. 1(c) shows the CDAG for the codes in Fig. 1(a) and Fig. 1(b), for $N$=6; although the relative order of operations is different between the tiled and untiled versions, the set of computation instances and the producer-consumer relationships for the flow of data are exactly the same (special "input" vertices in the CDAG represent values of elements of $A$ that are read before they are written in the nested loop).

While in general it is intractable to precisely answer the above fundamental question on the absolute minimum number of data transfers between main memory and caches/registers among all valid execution schedules of a CDAG, it is feasible to develop *lower bounds* on the optimal number of data transfers.

An approach to developing a lower bound on the minimal data movement for a computation in a two-level memory hierarchy was addressed in the seminal work of Hong & Kung by using the model of the red/blue pebble game on a computational directed acyclic graph (CDAG) [20]. While the approach has been used to develop I/O lower bounds for a small number of homogeneous computational kernels, as elaborated later, it poses challenges for effective analysis of full applications that are comprised of a number of parts with differing CDAG structure.

In this paper, we address the problem of analysis of affine loop programs to develop lower bounds on their data movement complexity. The work presented in this paper makes the following contributions:

- **Enabling composition in analysis of data access lower bounds**: It adapts the Hong & Kung pebble game model on CDAGs and the associated model of *S-partitioning* under a restriction that disallows recomputation, thereby enabling effective composition of I/O lower bounds for composite CDAGs from lower bounds for component CDAGs.
- **Static analysis of programs for lower bounds characterization**: It develops an approach for asymptotic parametric analysis of data-access lower bounds for arbitrary affine loop programs, as a function of cache size and problem size. This is done by analyzing linearly independent families of non-intersecting dependence chains.

## 2. Background

### 2.1 Computational Model

We are interested in modeling the inherent data access complexity of a computation, defined as the minimum number of data elements to be moved between local memory (with limited capacity but fast access by the processor) and main memory (much slower access but unlimited capacity) among all valid execution orders for the operations making up the computation. While the key developments in this paper can be naturally extended to address multi-level memory hierarchies and parallel execution, using an approach like the MMHG (Multiprocessor Memory Hierarchy Game) model of Savage & Zubair [29], we restrict the treatment in this paper to the case of only two levels of memory hierarchy and sequential execution.

The model of computation we use is a computational directed acyclic graph (CDAG), where computational operations are represented as graph vertices and the flow of values between operations is captured by graph edges. Fig. 2 shows an example of a CDAG corresponding to a simple loop program. Two important characteristics of this abstract form of representing a computation are that (1) there is no specification of a particular order of execution of the operations: although the program executes the operations in a specific sequential order, the CDAG abstracts the schedule of operations by only specifying partial ordering constraints as edges in the graph; (2) there is no association of memory locations with the source operands or result of any operation. (labels in Fig. 2 are only shown for aiding explanation; they are not part of the formal description of a CDAG).

```
for (i = 1; i < 4; ++i)
  S += A[i-1] + A[i];
```

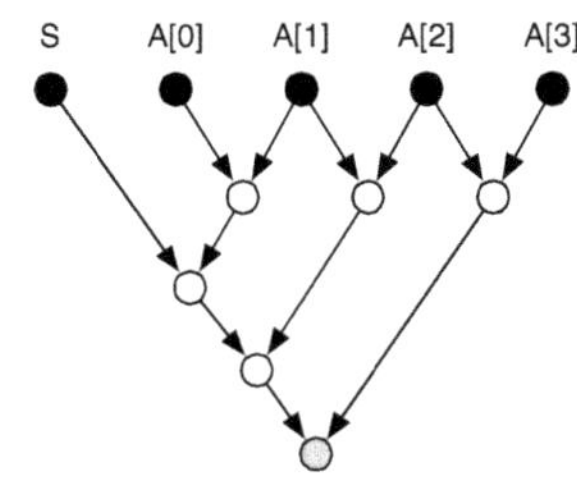


Figure 2: Example of a CDAG. Input vertices are represented in black, output vertices in grey.

We use the notation of Bilardi & Peserico [7] to formally describe the CDAG model used by Hong & Kung:

DEFINITION 1 (CDAG-HK). *A computational directed acyclic graph (CDAG) is a 4-tuple $C = (I, V, E, O)$ of finite sets such that: (1) $I \subset V$ is the input set and all its vertices have no incoming edges; (2) $E \subseteq V \times V$ is the set of edges; (3) $G = (V, E)$ is a directed acyclic graph; (4) $V \setminus I$ is called the operation set and all its vertices have one or more incoming edges; (5) $O \subseteq V$ is called the output set.*

### 2.2 The Red-Blue Pebble Game

Hong & Kung used this computational model in their seminal work [20]. The inherent I/O complexity of a CDAG is the minimal number of I/O operations needed while optimally playing the *Red-Blue pebble game*. This game uses two kinds of pebbles: a fixed number of red pebbles that represent the small fast local memory (could represent cache, registers, etc.), and an arbitrarily large number of blue pebbles that represent the large slow main memory.

DEFINITION 2 (Red-Blue pebble game [20]). *Let $C = (I, V, E, O)$ be a CDAG such that any vertex with no incoming (resp. outgoing) edge is an element of $I$ (resp. $O$). Given $S$ red pebbles and an arbitrary number of blue pebbles, with an initial blue pebble on each input vertex, a complete calculation is any sequence of steps using the following rules that results in a final configuration with blue pebbles on all output vertices:*

**R1 (Input)** *A red pebble may be placed on any vertex that has a blue pebble (load from slow to fast memory),*

**R2 (Output)** *A blue pebble may be placed on any vertex that has a red pebble (store from fast to slow memory),*

**R3 (Compute)** *If all immediate predecessors of a vertex $v \in V \setminus I$ have red pebbles, a red pebble may be placed on (or moved to)* [1] *$v$ (execution or "firing" of operation),*

[1] The original red-blue pebble game in [20] does not allow moving/sliding a red pebble from a predecessor vertex to a successor; we chose to allow it since it reflects real instruction set architectures. Others [27] have also considered a similar modification. But all our proofs hold for both the variants.

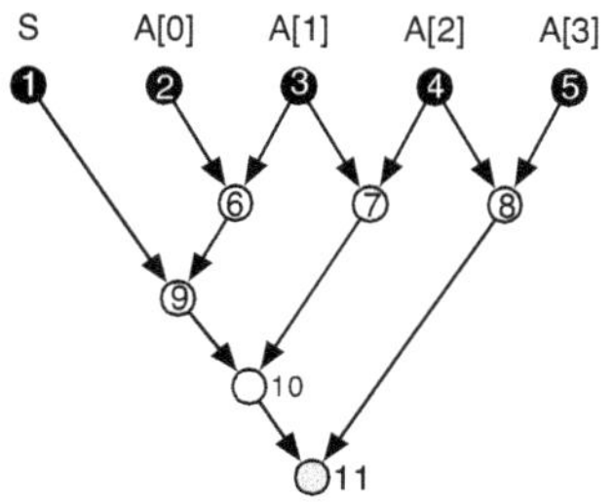


Figure 3: Example of schedule for a *complete calculation* on CDAG in Fig. 2. The vertex numbers represent the order of execution.

**R4 (Delete)** *A red pebble may be removed from any vertex (reuse storage).*

The number of I/O operations for any complete calculation is the total number of moves using rules R1 or R2, i.e., the total number of data movements between the fast and slow memories. The inherent I/O complexity of a CDAG is the smallest number of such I/O operations that can be achieved, among all complete calculations for that CDAG. An *optimal* calculation is a complete calculation achieving the minimum number of I/O operations.

Fig. 3 shows an example schedule for the CDAG in Fig. 2. Given $S$ red pebbles and unlimited blue pebbles, goal of the game is to begin with blue pebbles on all input vertices, and finish with blue pebbles on all output vertices by following the rules in Definition 2 without using more than $S$ red pebbles. Considering the case with three red pebbles ($S = 3$), one possible complete calculation for the CDAG in Fig. 3 is: $\{R1_2, R1_3, R3_6, R4_2, R1_1, R3_9, R4_1, R4_6, R1_4, R3_7, R4_3, R3_{10}, R4_9, R4_7, R1_5, R3_8, R4_4, R4_5, R3_{11}, R2_{11}\}$. The I/O cost of this complete calculation is 6 (which corresponds to the number of moves using rules $R1$ and $R2$). A different complete calculation for the same CDAG with I/O cost of 12 is given by: $\{R1_2, R1_3, R3_6, R4_2, R1_4, R2_6, R3_7, R4_3, R1_5, R2_7, R3_8, R2_8, R1_1, R1_6, R3_9, R4_1, R4_6, R1_7, R3_{10}, R4_7, R4_9, R1_8, R3_{11}, R2_{11}\}$. The I/O complexity of the CDAG is the minimum I/O cost of all such complete calculations.

### 2.3 Lower Bounds on I/O Complexity via $S$-Partitioning

While the red-blue pebble game provides an operational definition for the I/O complexity problem, it is generally not feasible to determine an optimal calculation on a CDAG. Hong & Kung developed a novel approach for deriving I/O lower bounds for CDAGs by relating the red-blue pebble game to a graph partitioning problem defined as follows.

DEFINITION 3 (Hong & Kung $S$-partitioning of a CDAG [20]). *Let $C = (I, V, E, O)$ be a CDAG. An $S$-partitioning of $C$ is a collection of $h$ subsets of $V$ such that:*

**P1** $\forall i \neq j,\ V_i \cap V_j = \emptyset$, *and* $\bigcup_{i=1}^{h} V_i = V$
**P2** *there is no cyclic dependence between subsets*
**P3** $\forall i,\ \exists D \in \mathit{Dom}(V_i)$ *such that* $|D| \leq S$
**P4** $\forall i,\ |\mathit{Min}(V_i)| \leq S$

*where a dominator set of $V_i$, $D \in \mathit{Dom}(V_i)$ is a set of vertices such that any path from $I$ to a vertex in $V_i$ contains some vertex in $D$; the minimum set of $V_i$, $\mathit{Min}(V_i)$ is the set of vertices in $V_i$ that have all its successors outside of $V_i$; and for a set $A$, $|A|$ is the cardinality of the set $A$.*

Hong & Kung showed a construction for a $2S$-partition of a CDAG, corresponding to any complete calculation on that CDAG using $S$ red pebbles, with a tight relationship between the number of vertex sets $h$ in the $2S$-partition and the number of I/O moves $q$ in the complete calculation, as shown in Theorem 1. The tight association between any complete calculation and a corresponding $2S$-partition provides the key Lemma 1 that serves as the basis for Hong & Kung's approach for deriving lower bounds on the I/O complexity of CDAGs typically by reasoning on the maximal number of vertices that could belong to any vertex-set in a valid $2S$-partition.

THEOREM 1 (Pebble game, I/O and $2S$-partition [20]). *Any complete calculation of the red-blue pebble game on a CDAG using at most $S$ red pebbles is associated with a $2S$-partition of the CDAG such that $S\,h \geq q \geq S\,(h-1)$, where $q$ is the number of I/O moves in the complete calculation and $h$ is the number of subsets in the $2S$-partition.*

LEMMA 1 (Lower bound on I/O [20]). *Let $H$ be the minimal number of vertex sets for any valid $2S$-partition of a given CDAG (such that any vertex with no incoming – resp. outgoing – edge is an element of $I$ – resp. $O$). Then the minimal number $Q$ of I/O operations for any complete calculation on the CDAG is bounded by: $Q \geq S \times (H-1)$*

This key lemma has been useful in proving I/O lower bounds for several CDAGs [20] by reasoning about the maximal number of vertices that could belong to any vertex-set in a valid $2S$-partition.

## 3. Challenges in Composing I/O Lower Bounds from Partitioned CDAGs

Application codes are typically constructed from a number of sub-computations using the fundamental composition mechanisms of sequencing, iteration and recursion. As explained in Sec. 1, in contrast to analysis of computational complexity of such composite application codes, I/O complexity analysis poses challenges. With computational complexity, the operation counts of sub-computations can simply be added. However, using the red/blue pebble game model of Hong & Kung, as elaborated below, it is problematic to analyze the I/O complexity of sub-computations and simply combine them by addition. In the next section, we develop an approach to overcome the problem.

### 3.1 The Decomposition Problem

The Hong & Kung red/blue pebble game model places blue pebbles on all CDAG vertices without predecessors, since such vertices are considered to hold inputs to the computation, and therefore assumed to start off in slow memory. Similarly, all vertices without successors are considered to be outputs of the computation, and must have blue pebbles at the end of a complete calculation. If the vertices of a CDAG corresponding to a composite application are disjointly partitioned into sub-DAGs, the analysis of each sub-DAG will require the initial placement of blue pebbles on all vertices without predecessors in the sub-DAG, and final placement of blue pebbles on all vertices without successors in the sub-DAG. So an optimal calculation for each sub-DAG will require at least one load (R1) operation for each input and a store (R2) operation for each output. But in a complete calculation on the full composite CDAG, clearly it may be possible to pass values in a red pebble between vertices in different sub-DAGs, so that the I/O complexity could be less than the sum of the I/O costs for optimal calculations on each sub-DAG. This is illustrated by the following example.

Fig. 4(b) shows the CDAG for the computation in Fig. 4(a). Fig. 4(c) shows the CDAG partitioned into two sub-DAGs, where the first sub-DAG contains vertices of $S1$ and $S2$ (and the input vertices corresponding to `a[i]` and `b[i]`), and the second sub-DAG contains vertices of $S3$ and $S4$. Considering the full CDAG, with just two red pebbles, it can be computed at an I/O cost of 12, incurring I/O just for the initial loads of inputs `a[i]` and `b[i]`, and the final stores for outputs `f[i]`. In contrast, with the partitioned sub-DAGs, the first sub-DAG will incur additional output stores

```
for(i = 0; i < 4; i++)
  c[i] = a[i] + b[i]; // S1
for(i = 0; i < 4; i++)
  d[i] = c[i] * c[i]; // S2
for(i = 0; i < 4; i++)
  e[i] = c[i] + d[i]; // S3
for(i = 0; i < 4; i++)
  f[i] = d[i] * e[i]; // S4
```

(a) Original code

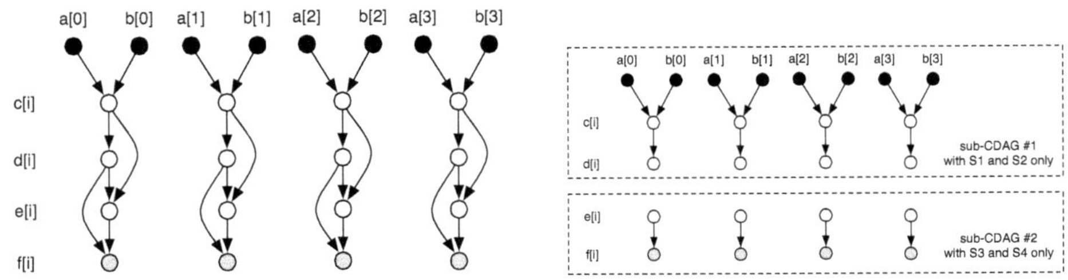


(b) Full CDAG (c) CDAG partitioning

Figure 4: Example illustrating limitation of Hong & Kung model regarding composition of lower bounds from sub-components of CDAG

for the successor-free vertices $S2[i]$, and the second sub-DAG will incur input loads for predecessor-free vertices $S3[i]$. Thus the sum of optimal red/blue pebble game I/O costs for the two sub-DAGs amounts to 20 moves, i.e., it exceeds the optimal I/O cost for the full CDAG.

The above example illustrates a fundamental problem with the Hong & Kung red/blue pebble game model: a simple combining of I/O lower bounds for sub-DAGs of a CDAG cannot be used to generate an I/O lower bound for the composite CDAG. But the ability to perform complexity analysis by combining analyses of component sub-computations is important for the analysis of real applications. Such decomposition of data-access complexity analysis can be enabled by making a change to the Hong & Kung pebble game model, as discussed next.

### 3.2 Flexible Input/Output Vertex Labeling to Enable Composition of Lower Bounds

With the Hong & Kung model, all vertices without predecessors must be input vertices, and all vertices without successors must be output vertices. By relaxing this constraint, we show that composition of lower bounds from sub-CDAGs is valid. With such a modification, vertices without predecessors will not be required to be input vertices, and such predecessor-free non-input vertices do not have an initial blue pebble placed on them. However, such vertices are allowed to fire using rule R3 at any time, since they do not have any predecessor nodes without red pebbles. Vertices without successors are similarly not required to be output vertices, and those not designated as outputs do not need a blue pebble on them at the end of the game. However, all compute vertices (i.e., vertices in $V \setminus I$) in CDAG are required to have fired for any complete calculation.

Using the modified model of the red/blue pebble game with flexible input/output vertex labeling, it is feasible to compose I/O lower bounds by adding lower bounds for disjointly partitioned sub-CDAGs of a CDAG. The following theorem formalizes it.

THEOREM 2 (Decomposition). *Let $C = (I,V,E,O)$ be a CDAG. Let $\{V_1,V_2,\ldots,V_p\}$ be an arbitrary (not necessarily acyclic) disjoint partitioning of $V$ ($\bigcap_{i=1}^{p} V_i = \emptyset$ and $\bigcup_{i=1}^{p} V_i = V$) and $C_1,C_2,\ldots,C_p$ be the induced partitioning of $C$ ($I_i = I \cap V_i$, $E_i = E \cap V_i \times V_i$, $O_i = O \cap V_i$). If $Q$ is the I/O complexity for $C$ and $Q_i$ is the I/O complexity for $C_i$, then $\sum_{i=1}^{p} Q_i \leq Q$. In particular, if $L_i$ is the I/O lower bound for $C_i$, then $\sum_{i=1}^{p} L_i$ is an I/O lower bound for $C$.*

*Proof.* Consider an optimal calculation $\mathcal{P}$ for $C$, with cost $Q$. We define the cost of $\mathcal{P}$ restricted to $V_i$, denoted as $Q_{|V_i}$, as the number of $R1$ or $R2$ transitions in $\mathcal{P}$ that involve a vertex of $V_i$. Clearly $Q = \sum_{i=1}^{p} Q_{|V_i}$. We will show that we can build from $\mathcal{P}$, a valid complete calculation $\mathcal{P}_{|V_i}$ for $C_i$, of cost $Q_{|V_i}$. This will prove that $Q_i \leq Q_{|V_i}$, and thus $\sum_{i=1}^{p} Q_i \leq \sum_{i=1}^{p} Q_{|V_i} = Q$. $\mathcal{P}_{|V_i}$ is built from $\mathcal{P}$ as follows: (1) for any transition in $\mathcal{P}$ that involves a vertex $v \in V_i$, apply this transition in $\mathcal{P}_{|V_i}$; (2) delete all other transitions in $\mathcal{P}$. Conditions for transitions $R1$, $R2$, and $R4$ are trivially satisfied. Whenever a transition $R3$ on a vertex $v$ is performed in $\mathcal{P}$, all the predecessors of $v$ must have a red pebble on them. Since all transitions of $\mathcal{P}$ on the vertices of $V_i$ are maintained in $\mathcal{P}_{|V_i}$, when $v$ is executed in $\mathcal{P}_{|V_i}$, all its predecessor vertices must have red pebbles, enabling transition $R3$. □

With this modified model of the red/blue pebble game that permits predecessor-free vertices to be non-input vertices, complex CDAGs can be decomposed and lower bounds for the composite CDAG can be obtained by composition of the bounds from the sub-CDAGs. However, sub-CDAGs that have no "true" input and output vertices in them will have trivial I/O lower bounds of zero – the entire set of vertices in the sub-CDAG can fit in a single vertex set for a valid 2S-partition, for any value of S, since conditions **P1-P4** are trivially satisfied.

In the next section, we present a solution to the problem. The main idea is to impose restrictions on the red/blue pebble game to disallow re-pebbling or multiple firings of any vertex using rule R3. We show that by imposing such a restriction, we can develop an input/output tagging strategy for sub-CDAGs that enables stronger lower bounds to be generated by CDAG decomposition.

## 4. S-Partitioning when Re-Pebbling is Prohibited

With the pebble game model of Hong & Kung, the compute rule R3 could be applied multiple times in a complete calculation. This is useful in modeling algorithms that perform re-computation of multiply used values rather than incur the overhead of storing and loading it. However, the majority of practically used algorithms do not perform any redundant recomputation. Hence several efforts [1, 3, 7, 10, 12, 21, 24–28, 30, 31] have modeled I/O complexity under a more restrictive model that disallows recomputation, primarily because it eases or enables analysis with some lower bounding techniques. In this section, we consider the issue of composing bounds via CDAG decomposition under a model that disallows recomputation, i.e., prohibits re-pebbling. We develop a modified definition of S-partition that is adapted to enable I/O lower bounds to be developed for the restricted red/blue pebble game. This provides two significant benefits:

1. It enables non-trivial I/O lower bound contributions to be accumulated from sub-CDAGs of a CDAG, even when the sub-CDAGs do not have any true inputs. This is achieved via input/output tagging/untagging strategies we develop in this section.
2. It enables static analysis of programs to develop parametric expressions for asymptotic lower bounds as a function of cache and problem size parameters. This is described in the following sections.

A pebble game model that does not allow recomputation can be formalized by changing rule R3 of the red/blue pebble game to R3-NR (NR denotes No-Recomputation or No-Repebbling) and the definition of a complete calculation as follows:

DEFINITION 4 (Recompute-restricted Red-Blue pebble game). *Let $C = (I,V,E,O)$ be a CDAG. Given S red pebbles and arbitrary number of blue pebbles, with an initial blue pebble on each input vertex, a complete calculation is any sequence of steps using the following rules that causes each vertex in $V \setminus I$ to be fired once using Rule R3-NR, and results in a final configuration with blue pebbles on all output vertices:*

**R1 (Input)** *A red pebble may be placed on any vertex that has a blue pebble (load from slow to fast memory),*

**R2 (Output)** *A blue pebble may be placed on any vertex that has a red pebble (store from fast to slow memory),*

**R3-NR (Compute)** *If all immediate predecessors of a vertex $v \in V \setminus I$ have red pebbles on them, and a red pebble has not previously been placed on v, a red pebble may be placed on v.*

**R4 (Delete)** *A red pebble may be removed from any vertex (reuse storage).*

We next present an adaptation of Hong and Kung's S-partition that will enable us to develop larger lower bounds for the restricted pebble game model that prohibits repebbling.

DEFINITION 5 ($S^{NR}$-partitioning of CDAG). *Given a CDAG C, an $S^{NR}$-partitioning of C is a collection of h subsets of $V \setminus I$ such that:*

**P1** $\forall i \neq j,\ V_i \cap V_j = \emptyset$, *and* $\bigcup_{i=1}^{h} V_i = V \setminus I$

**P2** *there is no cyclic dependence between subsets*

**P3** $\forall i,\ |\mathsf{In}(V_i)| \leq S$

**P4** $\forall i,\ |\mathsf{Out}(V_i)| \leq S$

*where the input set of $V_i$, $\mathsf{In}(V_i)$ is the set of vertices of $V \setminus V_i$ that have at least one successor in $V_i$; the output set of $V_i$, $\mathsf{Out}(V_i)$ is the set of vertices of $V_i$ that are also part of the output set O or that have at least one successor outside of $V_i$.*

THEOREM 3 (Restricted pebble game, I/O and $2S^{NR}$-partition). *Any complete calculation of the red-blue pebble game, without repebbling, on a CDAG using at most S red pebbles is associated with a $2S^{NR}$-partition of the CDAG such that $S \times h \geq q \geq S \times (h-1)$, where q is the number of I/O moves in the game and h is the number of subsets in the $2S^{NR}$-partition.*

*Proof.* Consider a complete calculation $\mathcal{P}$ that corresponds to some scheduling (i.e., execution) of the vertices of the graph $G = (V,E)$ that follows the rules R1–R4 of the restricted pebble game. We view this calculation as a string that has recorded all the transitions (applications of pebble game rules). Suppose that $\mathcal{P}$ contains exactly $q$ transitions of type $R1$ or $R2$. Let $(\mathcal{P}_1, \mathcal{P}_2, \ldots, \mathcal{P}_h)$ correspond to a partitioning of the transitions of $\mathcal{P}$ into $h = \lceil q/S \rceil$ consecutive sub-sequences such that each $\mathcal{P}_i \in (\mathcal{P}_1, \ldots, \mathcal{P}_{h-1})$ contains exactly $S$ transitions of type $R1$ or $R2$.

The CDAG contains no node isolated from the output nodes, and any vertex of $V \setminus I$ is computed exactly once in $\mathcal{P}$. Let $V_i$ be the set of vertices computed (transition R3-NR) in the sub-calculation $\mathcal{P}_i$. Property $P1$ is trivially fulfilled.

As transition R3-NR on a vertex $v$ is possible only if its predecessor vertices have red pebbles on them, those predecessors are necessarily executed in some $\mathcal{P}_j$, $j \leq i$ and are thus part of a $V_j$, $j \leq i$. This proves property $P2$.

To prove $P3$, for a given $V_i$ we consider two sets: $V_R$ is the set of vertices that had a red pebble on them just before the execution of $P_i$; $V_{BR}$ is the set of vertices on which a red pebble is placed according to rule $R1$ (input) during $\mathcal{P}_i$. We have, $\mathsf{In}(V_i) \subseteq V_R \cup V_{BR}$. Thus $|\mathsf{In}(V_i)| \leq |V_R| + |V_{BR}|$. As there only $S$ red pebbles, $|V_R| \leq S$. Also by construction of $\mathcal{P}_i$, $|V_{RB}| \leq S$. This proves that $|\mathsf{In}(V_i)| \leq 2S$ (property $P3$).

Property $P4$ is proved in a similar way: $V'_R$ is the set of vertices that have a red pebble on them just after the execution of $\mathcal{P}_i$; $V'_{RB}$ is the set of vertices of $V_i$ on which a blue pebble is placed during $\mathcal{P}_i$ according to rule $R2$. We have that $\mathsf{Out}(V_i) \subseteq V'_R \cup V'_{RB}$. Thus $|\mathsf{Out}(V_i)| \leq |V'_R| + |V'_{RB}|$. As there are only $S$ red pebbles, $|V'_R| \leq S$. Also by construction of $\mathcal{P}_i$, $|V'_{RB}| \leq S$. This proves that $|\mathsf{Out}(V_i)| \leq 2S$ (property $P4$). □

LEMMA 2 (I/O lower bound for restricted pebble game). *Let $H^{NR}$ be the minimal number of vertex sets for any valid $2S^{NR}$-partition of a given CDAG. Then the minimal number Q of I/O operations for any complete calculation on the CDAG, without any repebbling, is bounded by: $Q \geq S \times (H^{NR} - 1)$*

The above theorem and lemma establish the relationship between complete calculations of the restricted pebble game and 2S-NR partitions. The critical difference between the standard S-partition of Hong & Kung and the S-NR partition is the validity condition pertaining to incoming edges into a vertex set in the partition: for the former the size of dominator sets is constrained to be no more than S, while for the latter the number of external vertices with edges into the vertex set is constrained by S. When a CDAG is decomposed into sub-CDAGs, very often some of the sub-CDAGs get isolated from the CDAG's input and output vertices. This will lead to trivial (i.e., zero) lower bounds for such component sub-CDAGs. For the restricted pebble game, below we develop an approach to obtain tighter lower bounds for component sub-CDAGs that have become isolated from inputs and outputs of the full CDAG. The key idea is to allow any vertex without predecessors (resp. successors) to simulate an input (resp. output) vertex by specially tagging it so, and then adjusting the obtained lower bound to account for a one-time access cost for loading (resp. storing) such a tagged input (resp. output). The vertices of a CDAG remain unchanged, but the labeling (tag) of some vertices as inputs/outputs in the CDAG is changed.

THEOREM 4 (Input/Output (Un)Tagging – Restricted pebble game). *Let C and C′ be two CDAGs of the same DAG $G = (V,E)$: $C = (I,V,E,O)$, $C' = (I \cup dI, V, E, O \cup dO)$, where, $dI \subseteq V$ and $dO \subseteq V$. If Q is the I/O complexity for C and Q′ is the I/O complexity for C′ then, Q can be bounded by Q′ as follows (tagging):*

$$Q' - |dI| - |dO| \leq Q \tag{1}$$

*Reciprocally, Q′ can be bounded by Q as follows (untagging):*

$$Q \leq Q' \tag{2}$$

*Proof.* Consider an optimal calculation $\mathcal{P}$ for $C$, of cost $Q$. We will build a valid complete calculation $\mathcal{P}'$ for $C'$, of cost no more than $Q + |dI| + |dO|$. This will prove that $Q' \leq Q + |dI| + |dO|$. We build $\mathcal{P}'$ from $\mathcal{P}$ as follows: (1) for any input vertex $v \in dI$, the (only) transition $R3$ involving $v$ in $\mathcal{P}$ is replaced in $\mathcal{P}'$ by a transition $R1$; (2) for any output vertex $v \in dO$, the (only) transition $R3$ involving $v$ in $\mathcal{P}$ is complemented by an $R2$ transition; (3) any other transition in $\mathcal{P}$ is reported as is in $\mathcal{P}'$.

Consider now an optimal calculation $\mathcal{P}'$ for $C'$, of cost $Q'$. We will build a valid complete calculation $\mathcal{P}$ for $C$, of cost no more than $Q'$. This will prove that $Q \leq Q'$. We build $\mathcal{P}$ from $\mathcal{P}'$ as follows: (1) for any input vertex $v \in dI$, the first transition $R1$ involving $v$ in $\mathcal{P}'$ is replaced in $\mathcal{P}$ by a transition $R3$ followed by a transition $R2$; (2) any other transition in $\mathcal{P}'$ is reported as is in $\mathcal{P}$. □

We note that such a construction is only possible for the restricted pebble game where repebbling is disallowed. It enables tighter lower bounds to be developed via CDAG decomposition. In the next section, we use S-NR partitioning and the untagging theorem in developing a static analysis approach to characterizing data-access lower bounds of loop programs.

## 5. Parametric Lower Bounds via Static Analysis of Programs

In this section, we develop a static analysis approach to derive asymptotic parametric I/O lower bounds as a function of cache size and problem size, for *affine computations*. Affine computations can be modeled using (union of) convex sets of integer points, and (union of) relations between these sets. The motivation is twofold. First, there exists an important class of affine computations whose control and data flow can be modeled exactly at compile-time using only affine forms of the loop iterators surrounding the computation statements, and program parameters (constants whose values are unknown at compile-time). Many dense linear algebra computations, image processing algorithms, finite difference methods, etc., belong to this class of programs [18]. Second, there exist readily available tools to perform complex geometric operations on such sets and relations. We use the Integer Set Library (ISL) [36] for our analysis.

In Subsection 5.1, we provide a description of the program representation for affine programs. In Subsection 5.2, we detail the geometric reasoning that is the basis for the developed I/O lower bounds approach. Subsection 5.3 describes the I/O lower bound computation using examples.

### 5.1 Background and Program Representation

In the following, we use ISL terminology [36] and syntax to describe sets and relations. We now recall some key concepts to represent program features.

***Iteration domain*** A computation vertex in a CDAG represents a dynamic instance of some operation in the input program. For example, given a statement $S1$ : `A[i] += B[i+1]` surrounded by one loop `for(i = 0; i < n; ++i)`, the operation += will be executed $n$ times, and each such dynamic instance of the statement corresponds to a vertex in the CDAG. For affine programs, this set of dynamic instances can be compactly represented as a (union of) $\mathcal{Z}$-polyhedra, i.e., a set of integer points bounded by affine inequalities intersected with an affine integer lattice [19]. Using ISL notation, the iteration domain of statement $S1$, $D_{S1}$, is denoted: `[n]->{S1[i]:0<=i<n}`. The left-hand side of `->`, `[n]` in the example, is the list of all parameters needed to define the set. `S1[i]` models a set with one dimension (`[i]`) named $i$, and the set space is named `S1`. Presburger formulae are used on the right-hand side of : to model the points belonging to the set. In ISL, these sets are disjunctions of conjunctions of Presburger formulae, thereby modeling unions of convex and strided integer sets. The *dimension* of a set $S$ is denoted as $\dim(S)$. $\dim(S1) = 1$ in the example above. The *cardinality* of set $S$ is denoted as $|S|$. $|S1| = n$ for the example. Standard operations on sets, such as union, intersection, projection along certain dimensions, are available. In addition, key operations for analysis, such as building counting polynomials for the set (i.e., polynomials of the program parameters that model how many integer points are contained in a set; $n$ in our example) [4], and parametric (integer) linear programming [16] are possible on such sets. These operations are available in ISL.

We remark that although our analysis relies on integer sets and their associated operations, it is not limited to programs that can be exactly captured using such sets (e.g., purely affine programs). Since we are interested in computing lower bounds on I/O, an under-approximation of the statement domain and/or the set of dependences is acceptable, since an I/O lower bound for the approximated system is a valid lower bound for the actual system. For instance, if the iteration domain $D_S$ of a statement $S$ is not described exactly using Presburger formulae, we can under-approximate this set by taking the largest convex polyhedron $\underline{D_S} \subseteq D_S$. Such a polyhedron can be obtained, for instance, by first computing the convex hull $\overline{D_S} \supseteq D_S$ and then shifting its faces until they are strictly included in $D_S$. We also remark that such sets can be extracted from an arbitrary CDAG (again using approximations) by means of trace analysis, and especially trace compression techniques for vertices modeling the same computation [22].

***Relations*** In the graph $G = (V,E)$ of a CDAG $C = (I,V,E,O)$, vertices are connected by producer-consumer edges capturing the data flow between operations. Similar to iteration domains, affine forms are used to model the *relations* between the points in two sets. Such relations capture which data is accessed by a dynamic instance of a statement, as in classical data-flow analysis. In the example above, elements of array `B` are read in statement $S1$, and the relation $R1$ describing this access is: `[n]->{S1[i] -> B[i+1] : 0<=i<n}`. This relation models a single edge between each element of set $S1$ and an element of set $B$, described by the relationship $i \rightarrow i+1$. Several operations on relations, such as $\mathsf{domain}(R)$, which computes the domain (e.g., input set) of the relation ($\mathsf{domain}(R1) =$ `[n] -> {[i] : 0<=i<n}`), $\mathsf{image}(R)$ computing the image (e.g., range, or output set) of $R$ ($\mathsf{image}(R1) =$ `[n] -> {[i] : 1<=i<n+1}`), the composition of two relations $R1 \circ R2$, their union $\cup$, intersection $\cap$, difference $\setminus$ and the transitive closure $R^+$ of a relation, are available. All these operations are supported by ISL.

Relations can also be used to directly capture the connections between computation vertices. For instance, given two statements $S1$ and $S2$ with a producer-consumer relationship, the edges connecting each dynamic instance of $S1$ and $S2$ in a CDAG can be expressed using relations. For example, `[n]->{S1[i,j] -> S2[i,j-1,k] : ...}` models a relation between a 2D statement and a 3D statement. Each point in $S1$ is connected to several points in $S2$ along the $k$-dimension.

We note that in a similar manner to iteration domains for vertices, relations can also be extracted from non-affine programs via convex under-approximation or from the CDAG via trace analysis. Again, care must be taken to always properly under-approximate the relations capturing data dependences: it is safe to ignore a dependence (it can only lead to under-approximation of the data flow and therefore the I/O requirement), and therefore we only consider must-dependences in our analysis framework.

### 5.2 Geometric Reasoning for I/O Lower Bounds by 2S-partitioning

Given a CDAG, Lemma 2 establishes a relation between a lower bound on its data movement complexity for execution with $S$ fast storage elements and the minimal possible number of vertex sets among all valid $2S^{NR}$-partitions of the CDAG. The minimum possible number of vertex sets in a $2S^{NR}$-partition is inversely related to the largest possible size of any vertex set for a valid $2S^{NR}$-partition. A geometric reasoning based on the Loomis-Whitney inequality [23] and its generalization [5, 34] has been used to establish I/O lower bounds for a number of linear algebra algorithms [1, 2, 11, 21]. A novel approach to determining I/O lower bounds for affine computations in perfectly nested loops has been recently developed [11] using similar geometric reasoning. The approach developed in this paper is inspired by that work and also uses a similar geometric reasoning, but improves on the prior work in two significant ways:

1. *Generality*: It can be applied to a broader class of computations, handling multiple statements and imperfectly nested loops.
2. *Tighter Bounds*: For computations with loop-carried dependences that are not oriented perfectly along one of the iteration space dimensions, it provides tighter I/O lower bounds, as illustrated by the Jacobi example in the next section.

Before presenting the details of the static analysis for lower bounds characterization of affine computations, we use a simple example to illustrate the geometric approach based on the Loomis-Whitney inequality and its generalizations that have been used to develop I/O lower bounds for matrix-multiplication and other linear algebra computations. Consider the code exemplifying an N-body force calculation in Fig. 5(a). We have a 2D iteration space with $\Theta(N^2)$ points. The net force on each of $N$ particles from the other particles is computed using the function `f()`, which uses the mass and position of a pair of particles to compute the force between them. The total number of input data elements for the computation is $\Theta(N)$. If $S < N$, it will be necessary to bring in at least some of the input data elements more than once from slow to fast memory. A geometric reasoning for a lower bound on the amount of I/O to/from fast memory proceeds as follows. Consider an arbitrary vertex set from any valid $2S^{NR}$-partition. Let the set of points $\mathsf{P}$ in the iteration space, illustrated by a cloud in Fig. 5(b), denote the vertex set. The projections of each of the points onto the two iteration space axes are shown. Let $|\mathsf{P}_i|$ and $|\mathsf{P}_j|$ respectively denote the number of distinct points on the $i$ and $j$ axes. $|\mathsf{P}_i|$ represents the number of distinct elements of input arrays `pos` and `mass` that are accessed in the computation, for references `pos(i)` and `mass(i)`. Similarly, $|\mathsf{P}_j|$ corresponds to the number of distinct elements accessed via the references `pos(j)` and `mass(j)`. For any vertex set from a valid $2S^{NR}$-partition, the size of the input set cannot exceed $2S$. Hence $2 \times |\mathsf{P}_i| \leq 2S$ and $2 \times |\mathsf{P}_j| \leq 2S$. For this 2D example, the Loomis-Whitney inequality asserts that the number of points in $\mathsf{P}$ cannot exceed $|\mathsf{P}_i| \times |\mathsf{P}_j|$. Combining the two inequalities, we can conclude that $S^2$ is an upper bound on the size of the vertex set. Thus, the minimum number of vertex sets in a valid 2S-partition, $H = \Omega(N^2/S^2)$. By Lemma 2, a lower bound on I/O is $(H-1) \times S$, i.e., $\Omega(N^2/S)$.

```
for(i=0;i<N;i++)
 for(j=0;j<N;j++)
  if (i <> j) force(i)
  += f(mass(i),mass(j),pos(i),pos(j));
```

(a) Code for N-body force calculation

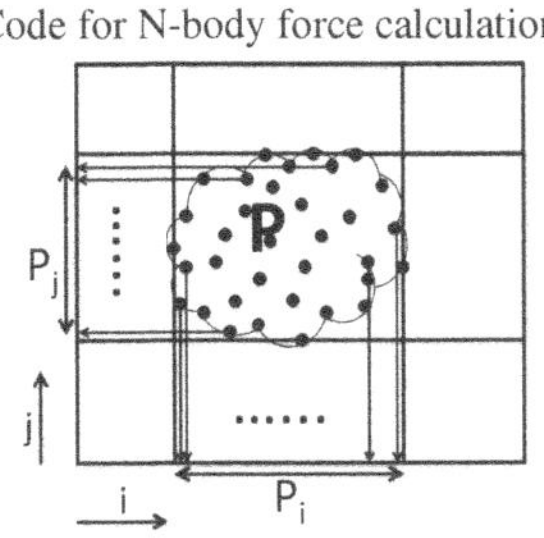


(b) Geometric Projection

Figure 5: Illustration of Geometric Reasoning for I/O Lower Bounds

More generally, for a $d$-dimensional iteration space, given some bounds on the number of elements on some projections of $\mathsf{P}$, a bound on $|\mathsf{P}|$ can be derived using a powerful approach developed by Christ et al. [11]. Christ et al. [11, Theorem 3.2] extended the discrete case of the Brascamp-Lieb inequality [5, Theorem 2.4] to obtain these bounds. Since our goal here is to develop asymptotic parametric bounds, the extension of the continuous Brascamp-Lieb inequality, stated below (in the restricted case of orthogonal projections and using the Lebesgue measure for volumes), is sufficient for our analysis. We use the notation $H \leq \mathbb{R}^d$ to denote that $H$ is a linear subspace of $\mathbb{R}^d$.

THEOREM 5. *Let $\phi_j : \mathbb{R}^d \rightarrow \mathbb{R}^{d_j}$ be an orthogonal projection for $j \in \{1,2,\ldots,m\}$ such that $\phi_j(x_1,\ldots,x_d) = (y_1,\ldots,y_{d_j})$ where $\{y_1,\ldots,y_{d_j}\} \subseteq \{x_1,\ldots,x_d\}$.*
*Then, for $(s_1,\ldots,s_m) \in [0,1]^m$:*

$$\forall H \leq \mathbb{R}^d,\ \dim(H) \leq \sum_{j=1}^{m} s_j \dim(\phi_j(H)) \quad (3)$$

$$\Longleftrightarrow \qquad \forall E \subseteq \mathbb{R}^d,\ |E| \leq \prod_{j=1}^{m} |\phi_j(E)|^{s_j} \quad (4)$$

Since the linear transformations $\phi_j$ are orthogonal projections, the following Theorem enables us to limit the number of inequalities of Eq. (3) required for Theorem 5 to hold. Only one inequality per subspace $H_i$, defined as the linear span of the canonical vector $e_i$, is required ($\langle e_i \rangle$ represents the subspace spanned by the vector with a non-zero only in the $i^{th}$ coordinate):

THEOREM 6. *Let $\phi_j : \mathbb{R}^d \rightarrow \mathbb{R}^{d_j}$ be an orthogonal projection for $j \in \{1,2,\ldots,m\}$ such that $\phi_j(x_1,\ldots,x_d) = (y_1,\ldots,y_{d_j})$ where $\{y_1,\ldots,y_{d_j}\} \subseteq \{x_1,\ldots,x_d\}$.*
*Then, for $(s_1,\ldots,s_m) \in [0,1]^m$ :*

$$\forall H \leq \mathbb{R}^d,\ \dim(H) \leq \sum_{j=1}^{m} s_j \dim(\phi_j(H)) \quad (5)$$

$$\Longleftrightarrow \qquad \forall H_i = \langle e_i \rangle,\ 1 = \dim(H_i) \leq \sum_{j=1}^{m} s_i \delta_{i,j} \quad (6)$$

*where,* $\delta_{i,j} = \dim(\phi_j(H_i))$

The proof of Theorem 6 directly corresponds to the proof of [11, Theorem 6.6] and is omitted (see also [5, Prop. 7.1]). It shows that if $s = (s_1,\ldots,s_m) \in [0,1]^m$ are such that $\forall H_i,\ 1 \leq \sum_{j=1}^{m} s_i \delta_{i,j}$, then the volume of any measurable set $E \subseteq \mathbb{R}^d$ can be bounded by $U_s = \prod_{j=1}^{m} |\phi_j(E)|^{s_j}$. In order to obtain as tight an asymptotic bound as possible, we seek $s$ such that $U_s$ is as small as possible. Since we have $|\phi_j(H)| \leq S$, this corresponds to finding $s_j$ such that $\prod_{j=1}^{m} S^{s_j}$ is minimized, or equivalently, $S^{\sum_{j=1}^{m} s_j}$ is minimized. In other words, $\sum_{j=1}^{m} s_j$ has to be minimized. For this purpose, if $\forall i,\ \exists j$, s.t., $\delta_{i,j} = 1$, we solve:

$$\text{Minimize} \sum_{j=1}^{m} s_j, \text{ s.t., } \forall i,\ 1 \leq \sum_{j=1}^{m} s_j \delta_{i,j} \quad (7)$$

We can instead solve the following dual problem, whose solution gives an indication of the shape of the optimal "cube."

$$\text{Maximize} \sum_{i=1}^{d} x_i, \text{ s.t., } \forall j,\ \sum_{i=1}^{d} x_i \delta_{i,j} \leq 1 \quad (8)$$

We use an illustrative example:

```
for(i=0;i<N;i++)
 for(j=0;j<N;j++)
  for(k=0;k<N;k++)
   C[i][j] = C[i][j] + A[i][k]*B[k]
```

Consider the following three projections (we explain how the projection directions are obtained later in this section)

$$\phi_1 : (i,j,k) \rightarrow (i,j);\ \phi_2 : (i,j,k) \rightarrow (i,k);\ \phi_3 : (i,j,k) \rightarrow (k)$$

Let $H_1$, $H_2$ and $H_3$ denote the three subspaces spanned by the canonical bases of $\mathbb{R}^3$. Consider, for example, the linear map $\phi_1$. We have $\delta_{1,1} = \dim(\phi_1(h_1)) = 1$ for any $h_1 \in H_1$, $\delta_{2,1} = \dim(\phi_1(h_2)) = 1$ for any $h_2 \in H_2$, and $\delta_{3,1} = \dim(\phi_1(h_3)) = 0$ for any $h_3 \in H_3$. Thus, we obtain the constraint $x_1.1 + x_2.1 + x_3.0 \leq 1$, or $x_1 + x_2 \leq 1$. Similarly, we obtain the remaining two constraints for the projections $\phi_2$ and $\phi_3$.

This results in the following linear programming problem:

$$\text{Maximize } x_1 + x_2 + x_3 \quad (9)$$

s.t. $x_1 + x_2 \le 1;\ x_1 + x_3 \le 1;\ x_3 \le 1$

Solving Eq. (9) provides the solution $(x_1, x_2, x_3) = (0, 1, 1)$, i.e., $x_1 + x_2 + x_3 = 2$. The solution corresponds to considering a cube of asymptotic dimensions $1 \times S \times S$ and volume $O(S^{\sum_{j=1}^{3} x_j}) = O(S^2)$ as the largest vertex-set. This provides an I/O lower bound of $\Omega(N^3/S)$, when the problem size $N$ is sufficiently large.

### 5.3 Automated I/O Lower Bound Computation

We present a static analysis algorithm for automated derivation of expressions for parametric asymptotic I/O lower bounds for programs. We use two illustrative examples to explain the various steps in the algorithm before providing detailed pseudo-code for the algorithm.

***Illustrative example 1:*** Consider the following example of Jacobi 1D stencil computation.

```
Parameters: N, T
Inputs: I[N]
Outputs: A[N]
    for (i=0; i<N; i++)
S1:  A[i] = I[i];

    for (t=1; t<T; t++)
    {
      for (i=1; i<N-1; i++)
S2:     B[i] = A[i-1] + A[i] + A[i+1];

      for (i=1; i<N-1; i++)
S3:     A[i] = B[i];
    }
```

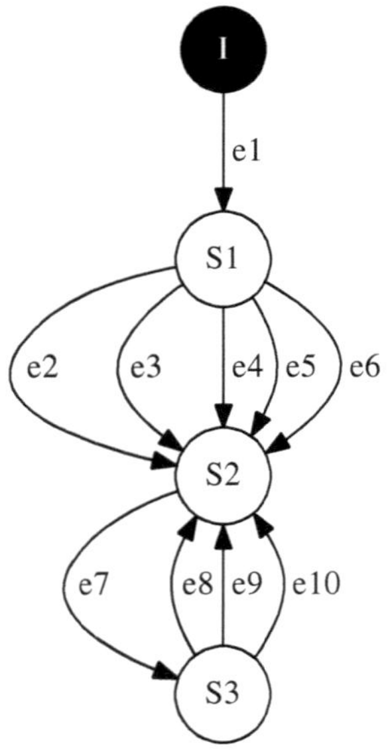


Figure 6: Data-flow graph for Jacobi 1D

Fig. 6 shows the static data-flow graph $G_F = (V_F, E_F)$ for Jacobi 1D. $G_F$ contains a vertex for each statement in the code. The input array `I` is also explicitly represented in $G_F$ by node $I$ (shaded in black in Fig. 6). Each vertex has an associated domain as shown below:

- $D_I$ = `[N]->{I[i]:0<=i<N}`
- $D_{S1}$ = `[N]->{S1[i]:0<=i<N}`
- $D_{S2}$ = `[T,N]->{S2[t,i]:1<=t<T and 1<=i<N-1}`
- $D_{S3}$ = `[T,N]->{S3[t,i]:1<=t<T and 1<=i<N-1}`

The edges represent the true (read-after-write) data dependences between the statements. Each edge has an associated affine dependence relation as shown below:

- Edge $e1$: This edge corresponds to the dependence due to copying the inputs `I` to array `A` at statement $S1$ and has the following relation.
  `[N]->{I[i]->S1[i]:0<=i<N}`
- Edges $e2$, $e3$ and $e4$: The use of array elements `A[i-1]`, `A[i]` and `A[i+1]` at statement $S2$ are captured by edges $e2$, $e3$ and $e4$, respectively.
  `[T,N]->{S1[i]->S2[1,i+1]:1<=i<N-2}`
  `[T,N]->{S1[i]->S2[1,i]:1<=i<N-1}`
  `[T,N]->{S1[i]->S2[1,i-1]:2<=i<N-1}`
- Edges $e5$ and $e6$: Multiple uses of the boundary elements `I[0]` and `I[N-1]` by `A[t][1]` and `A[t][N-2]`, respectively, for `1<=t<T` are represented by the following relations.
  `[T,N]->{S1[0]->S2[t,1]:1<=t<T}`
  `[T,N]->{S1[N-1]->S2[t,N-2]:1<=t<T}`
- Edge $e7$: The use of array `B` in statement `S3` corresponds to edge $e7$ with the following relation.
  `[T,N]->{S2[t,i]->S3[t,i]:1<=t<T and 1<=i<N-1}`
- Edges $e8$, $e9$ and $e10$: The uses of array `A` in statement $S2$ from $S3$ are represented by these edges with the following relations.
  `[T,N]->{S3[t,i]->S2[t+1,i+1]:1<=t<T-1 and 1<=i<N-2}`
  `[T,N]->{S3[t,i]->S2[t+1,i]:1<=t<T-1 and 1<=i<N-1}`
  `[T,N]->{S3[t,i]->S2[t+1,i-1]:1<=t<T-1 and 2<=i<N-1}`

Given a path $p = (e_1, \dots, e_l)$ with associated edge relations $(R_1, \dots, R_l)$, the relation associated with $p$ can be computed by composing the relations of its edges, i.e., $\mathsf{relation}(p) = R_l \circ \cdots \circ R_1$. For instance, the relation for the path $(e7, e8)$ in the example, obtained through the composition $R_{e8} \circ R_{e7}$, is given by $R_p$ = `[T,N] -> {S2[t,i] -> S2[t+1,i+1]}`. Further, the domain and image of a composition are restricted to the points for which the composition can apply, i.e., $\mathsf{domain}(R_j \circ R_i) = R_i^{-1}(\mathsf{image}(R_i) \cap \mathsf{domain}(R_j))$ and $\mathsf{image}(R_j \circ R_i) = R_j(\mathsf{image}(R_i) \cap \mathsf{domain}(R_j))$. Hence, $\mathsf{domain}(R_p)$ = `[T,N] -> {S2[t,i] : 1<=t<T-1 and 1<=i<N-2}` and $\mathsf{image}(R_p)$ = `[T,N] -> {S2[t,i] : 2<=t<T and 2<=i<N-1}`.

Two kinds of paths, namely, *injective circuit* and *broadcast path*, defined below, are of specific importance to the analysis.

DEFINITION 6 (Injective edge and circuit). *An* injective edge *$a$ is an edge of a data-flow graph whose associated relation $R_a$ is both affine and injective, i.e., $R_a = \mathbf{A}.\vec{x} + \vec{b}$, where $\mathbf{A}$ is an invertible matrix. An* injective circuit *is a circuit $E$ of a data-flow graph such that every edge $e \in E$ is an injective edge.*

DEFINITION 7 (Broadcast edge and path). *A* broadcast edge *$b$ is an edge of a data-flow graph whose associated relation $R_b$ is affine and* $\dim(\mathsf{domain}(R_b)) < \dim(\mathsf{image}(R_b))$. *A* broadcast path *is a path $(e_1, \dots, e_n)$ of a data-flow graph such that $e_1$ is a broadcast edge and $\forall_{i=2}^{n} e_i$ are injective edges.*

Injective circuits and broadcast paths in a data-flow graph essentially indicate multiple uses of same data, and therefore are good candidates for lower bound analysis. Hence only paths of these two kinds are considered in the analysis. The current example of Jacobi 1D computation illustrates the use of injective circuits to derive I/O lower bounds, while the use of broadcast paths for lower bound analysis is explained in another example that follows.

**Injective circuits:** In the Jacobi example, we have three circuits to vertex $S2$ through $S3$. The relation for each circuit is computed by composing the relations of its edges as explained earlier. The relations, and the dependence vectors they represent, are listed below.

- Circuit $c_1 = (e7, e8)$:
  $R_{c_1}$ = `[T,N] -> {S2[t,i]->S2[t+1,i+1] : 1<=t<T-1 and`

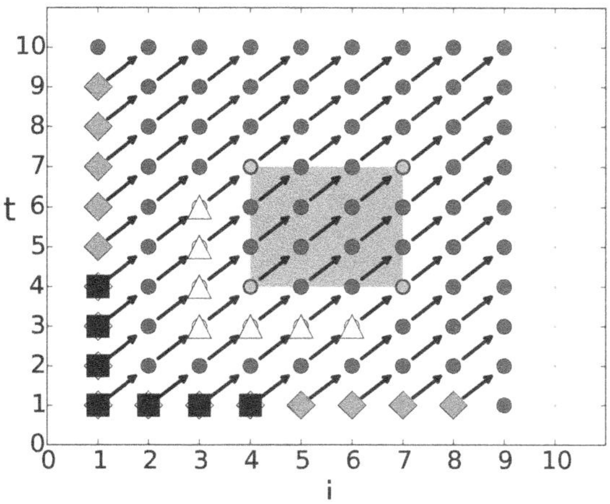


Figure 7: Original iteration domain space for Jacobi 1D. Blue circles: Integer points of domain $D_{S2}$; Black arrows: Relation $R_{c1}$ of circuit $(e7, e8)$; Red diamonds: Frontier $F_1$; Gray box: subset $E$ and corresponding vertex-set $\upsilon_1$; Yellow triangles: $\mathsf{In}(\upsilon_1)$; Black squares: Projection of the points inside gray box along the direction of black arrows onto the frontier.

```
1<=i<N-2}
```
$\vec{b_1} = (1,1)^T$

- Circuit $c_2 = (e7, e9)$:
  $R_{c_2}$ = `[T,N] -> {S2[t,i]->S2[t+1,i] : 1<=t<T-1 and 1<=i<N-1}`
  $\vec{b_2} = (1,0)^T$
- Circuit $c_3 = (e7, e10)$:
  $R_{c_3}$ = `[T,N] -> {S2[t,i]->S2[t+1,i-1] : 1<=t<T-1 and 2<=i<N-1}`
  $\vec{b_3} = (1,-1)^T$

Fig. 7 pictorially shows the domain $D_{S2}$ and the relation $R_{c_1}$ as a $\mathcal{Z}$-polyhedron for $T = N = 11$.

DEFINITION 8 (Frontier). *The frontier, $F$, of a relation $R$, with domain $D$, is the set of points with no incoming edges in the corresponding $\mathcal{Z}$-polyhedron.*

$F$ can be calculated using the set operation $F = D \setminus R(D)$. The frontiers $F_1$, $F_2$ and $F_3$ for the three relations, $R_{c_1}$, $R_{c_2}$ and $R_{c_3}$ respectively, are listed below.

- $F_1$ = `[T,N]->{S2[1,i]:2<=i<N-2; S2[t,1]:1<=t<T-1}`
- $F_2$ = `[T,N]->{S2[1,i]:1<=i<N-1}`
- $F_3$ = `[T,N]->{S2[1,i]:2<=i<N-1; S2[t,N-2]:2<=t<T-1}`

In Fig. 7, points of frontier $F_1$ are shown as red diamond shaped points. Due to the correspondence between a $\mathcal{Z}$-polyhedron and a (sub-)CDAG (refer to Sec. 5.1), each point in a frontier represents a source vertex (i.e., vertex with no incoming edges) of the (sub-)CDAG. It could be seen that there are $|F_i|, 1 \leq i \leq 3$, disjoint paths $P_i, 1 \leq i \leq 3$ (as a consequence of the injective property of the relations) in the sub-CDAG $C_1 = (I_1, V_1, E_1, O_1)$ (corresponding to the instances of statements $S2$ and $S3$), each with a distinct source vertex that corresponds to a point in $F_i$. These source vertices are tagged as inputs for the lower bounds analysis and their count, $|F_i|$, is later subtracted from the final I/O lower bound using Theorem 4.

Let $\upsilon_1 \subseteq V_1$ be a vertex-set of a valid $2S$-partition of $C_1$. There are a set of points $E$ in the $\mathcal{Z}$-polyhedron (e.g., the set of points inside the gray colored box in Fig. 7) corresponding to $\upsilon_1$. The set of points outside $E$ with an edge to a point in $E$ corresponds to $\mathsf{In}(\upsilon_1)$ (e.g., points marked with yellow triangles in Fig. 7). Since there is no cyclic dependence between the vertex-sets of the $2S$-partition and the paths are disjoint, by starting from the vertices of $\mathsf{In}(\upsilon_1)$ and tracing backwards along the paths in any $P_i$, $1 \leq i \leq 3$, we should reach $|\mathsf{In}(\upsilon_1)| \leq 2S$ distinct source vertices. This process corresponds to projecting the set $E$ along each of the directions $\vec{b_i}$, $1 \leq i \leq 3$ onto the frontier $F_i$, $1 \leq i \leq 3$. Hence we have $|E_{\downarrow \vec{b_i}}| \leq 2S$ (here, $E_{\downarrow \vec{b_i}}$ denotes projecting $E$ along the direction $\vec{b_i}$). The points of the frontier obtained by projection are shown as black squares (over red diamonds) in Fig. 7. We ensure that $E \subseteq D^R_{S2} = \mathsf{domain}(R_{c_1}) \cap \mathsf{image}(R_{c_1}) \cap \mathsf{domain}(R_{c_2}) \cap \mathsf{image}(R_{c_2}) \cap \mathsf{domain}(R_{c_3}) \cap \mathsf{image}(R_{c_3})$. This allows us to apply the geometric reasoning discussed in Sec. 5.2 to restrict the size of the set $E$ as shown below. Since $\dim(D_{S2}) = 2$, it is sufficient to consider any two linearly independent directions.

Theorem 6 applies only for projections along the orthogonal directions. In case projection vectors are non-orthogonal, a simple change of basis operation is used to transform the space to a new space where the projection directions are the canonical bases. In the example, if we consider vectors $\vec{b_1}/|\vec{b_1}|$ and $\vec{b_3}/|\vec{b_3}|$ as the projection directions in the original space, then the linear map $\left( \vec{b_1}/|\vec{b_1}| \quad \vec{b_3}/|\vec{b_3}| \right)^{-1}$ will transform the $\mathcal{Z}$-polyhedron to a new space where the projection directions are the canonical bases. In the example, after such transformation, the projection vectors are $(1,0)^T$ and $(0,1)^T$, and hence we have the following two projections: $\phi_1 : (i,j) \rightarrow (i)$; $\phi_2 : (i,j) \rightarrow (j)$. From Eq. 6, we obtain the following inequalities for the dual problem (refer (8)): $x_1 \leq 1$; $x_2 \leq 1$.

In addition, we also need to include constraints for the degenerate cases where the problem size considered may be small relative to the cache size, $S$. Hence, we have the following additional constraints for the example: $|\phi_1(E)|^{x_1} \leq (N+T)$; $|\phi_2(E)|^{x_2} \leq (N+T)$, or (after taking log with base $S$), $x_1 \log_S(|\phi_1(E)|) \leq \log_S(N+T)$; $x_2 \log_S(|\phi_1(E)|)) \leq \log_S(N+T)$. Since $|\phi_j(E)| \leq S$, we have $\log_S(|\phi_j(E)|) \leq 1$. Hence, we obtain the constraints $x_1 \leq \log_S(N+T)$ and $x_2 \leq \log_S(N+T)$. Thus, we solve the following following parametric linear programming problem.

$$\text{Maximize } \Theta = x_1 + x_2 \tag{10}$$

$$\begin{array}{llll} \text{s.t.} & x_1 & \leq & 1 \\ & x_2 & \leq & 1 \\ & x_1 & \leq & \log_S(N+T) \\ & x_2 & \leq & \log_S(N+T) \end{array}$$

Solving Eq. (10) using PIP [16] provides the following solution: If $\log_S(N+T) \geq 1$ then, $x_1 = x_2 = 1$, else, $x_1 = x_2 = \log_S(N+T)$.

This specifies that when $N+T = \Omega(S)$, $|\upsilon_1| = O(S^2)$, and hence $Q = \Omega\left(\frac{NT}{S} - (N+T)\right)$ (here, $(N+T)$ is subtracted from the lower bound to account for I/O tagging), otherwise, $|\upsilon_1| = O\left((N+T)^2\right)$ and $Q = \Omega\left(\frac{NTS}{(N+T)^2} - (N+T)\right)$.

In the example, since the vectors $\vec{b_1}/|\vec{b_1}|$ and $\vec{b_3}/|\vec{b_3}|$ are already orthonormal, the change of basis transformation that we performed earlier is unimodular. But, in general this need not be the case. Since we focus only on asymptotic parametric bounds, any constant multiplicative factors that arise due to the non-unimodular transformation are ignored.

***Illustrative example 2:*** The following example is composed of a scaled matrix-multiplication and a Gauss-Seidel computation within an outer iteration loop.

```
Parameters: W, N, T
Inputs: A[N][N], C[N][N], Temp[N][N]
Outputs: A[N][N], C[N][N]
   // Iterative loop with scaled Matmult
```

```
    // followed by Stencil
    for(it=0;it<W;it++)
    {
      // Scaled Matmult split out into a sequence of
      // mat-vec and vector scaling ops for each row
      for(i=0;i<N;i++)
      {
        for(j=0;j<N;j++)
          for(k=0;k<N;k++)
S1:         Temp[i][j] += A[i][k]*A[k][j];

        for(j=0;j<N;j++)
S2:       Temp[i][j] = 2*Temp[i][j];

        for(j=0;j<N;j++)
S3:       C[i][j] += Temp[i][j];
      }

      // Seidel stencil
      for(t=0;t<T;t++)
        for (i=1; i<N-1; i++)
          for (j=1; j<N-1; j++)
S4:         A[i][j] = 0.5 * (A[i-1][j] + A[i][j-1] \
              + A[i][j] + A[i+1][j] + A[i][j+1]);
    }
```

The decomposition theorem (Theorem 2) allows us to split this code into individual components, analyze each sub-program separately and obtain the I/O lower bounds for the whole program through simple summation of the individual bounds. Hence, given the CDAG $C$ of the above example, the analysis proceeds with the following steps:

- The CDAG $C$ and thus the underlying program is decomposed as follows: (1) Each iteration of the outer loop, with trip-count `W`, is split into $W$ sub-programs. (2) Each of this sub-program is further decomposed by separating the matmult (consisting of statements $S1$, $S2$ and $S3$) and Seidel operations (consisting of statement $S4$) into individual sub-programs.
- The vertices corresponding to the input arrays of the matmult and Seidel computations are tagged as inputs in their corresponding sub-CDAGs.
- The matmult (with sub-CDAG $C_m = (I_m, V_m, E_m, O_m)$) and the Seidel computation (with sub-CDAG $C_s = (I_s, V_s, E_s, O_s)$) are separately analyzed for their I/O lower bounds.
- If $L_m$ and $L_s$ are the I/O lower bounds obtained in the previous step for matmult and Seidel computation, respectively, Theorem 2 and Theorem 4 provides us an I/O lower bound of $\Omega(W \times ((L_m - |I_m|) + (L_s - |I_s|)))$ for the whole program.

The analysis of the Seidel computation is similar to the analysis of the Jacobi 1D computation detailed in the previous example. Hence, we skip the analysis and provide the following result: If $N = \Omega(\sqrt{S})$ and $T = \Omega(\sqrt{S})$ then, $Q_s = \Omega\left(\frac{N^2T}{\sqrt{S}} - N^2 - NT\right)$, else $Q_s \geq 0$. where, $Q_s$ is the I/O complexity for the Seidel computation.

Now, we consider the analysis of the scaled matmult. The dataflow graph, $G_F$ consists of six vertices: vertices $A$, $C$ and $Temp$ correspond to the input arrays `A`, `C` and `Temp`, respectively; vertices $S1$, $S2$ and $S3$ correspond to the statements $S1$, $S2$ and $S3$, respectively. The domain corresponding to each vertex (in the order $A$, $C$, $Temp$, $S1$, $S2$ and $S3$) is listed below:

- $D_A =$ `[N]->{A[i,j]:0<=i<N and 0<=j<N}`
- $D_C =$ `[N]->{C[i,j]:0<=i<N and 0<=j<N}`
- $D_{Temp} =$ `[N]->{Temp[i,j]:0<=i<N and 0<=j<N}`
- $D_{S1} =$ `[N]->{S1[i,j,k]:0<=i<N and 0<=j<N and 0<=k<N}`
- $D_{S2} =$ `[N]->{S2[i,j]:0<=i<N and 0<=j<N}`
- $D_{S3} =$ `[N]->{S3[i,j]:0<=i<N and 0<=j<N}`

The relations corresponding to various edges are listed below.

- relation$(e1 = (A, S1)) = R_{e1} =$ `[N] -> {A[i, j] -> S1[i,j',j] : 0<=i<N and 0<=j<N and 0<=j'<N}`
- relation$(e2 = (A, S1)) = R_{e2} =$ `[N] -> {A[i,j] -> S1[i',j,i] : 0<=i'<N and 0<=i<N and 0<=j<N}`
- relation$(e3 = (C, S3)) = R_{e3} =$ `[N] -> {C[i,j] -> S3[i,j] : 0<=i<N and 0<=j<N}`
- relation$(e4 = (Temp, S1)) = R_{e4} =$ `[N] -> {Temp[i,j] -> S1[i,j,0] : 0<=i<N and 0<=j<N}`
- relation$(e5 = (S1, S1)) = R_{e5} =$ `[N] -> {S1[i,j,k] -> S1[i,j,k+1] : 0<=i<N and 0<=j<N and 0<=k<N-1}`
- relation$(e6 = (S1, S2)) = R_{e6} =$ `[N] -> {S1[i,j,N-1] -> S2[i,j] : 0<=i<N and 0<=j<N}`
- relation$(e7 = (S2, S3)) = R_{e7} =$ `[N] -> {S2[i,j] -> S3[i,j] : 0<=i<N and 0<=j<N}`

**Broadcast paths:** The paths $p_1 = (e1)$ and $p_2 = (e2)$ are of type broadcast. As $p_1$ and $p_2$ are composed of a single edge, their relations, $R_{p_1}$ and $R_{p_2}$ respectively, are the same as their edge. Thus, $R_{p_1} = R_{e1}$ and $R_{p_2} = R_{e2}$. We are specifically interested in the broadcast paths whose inverse-relations (e.g., $R_{p_1}^{-1}$) can be expressed as affine maps. In our example, the two inverse-relations $R_{p_1}^{-1}$ and $R_{p_2}^{-1}$ can be expressed as affine maps as shown below:

$$R_{p_1}^{-1} \equiv \begin{pmatrix} 1 & 0 & 0 \\ 0 & 0 & 1 \end{pmatrix} \cdot \begin{pmatrix} i \\ j' \\ j \end{pmatrix} + \begin{pmatrix} 0 \\ 0 \\ 0 \end{pmatrix}$$

$$R_{p_2}^{-1} \equiv \begin{pmatrix} 0 & 0 & 1 \\ 0 & 1 & 0 \end{pmatrix} \cdot \begin{pmatrix} i' \\ j \\ i \end{pmatrix} + \begin{pmatrix} 0 \\ 0 \\ 0 \end{pmatrix}$$

Further, we have an injective circuit $p_3 = (e5)$ with $R_{p_3} = R_{e5}$, whose direction vector $\vec{b_3} = (0,0,1)^T$.

We next calculate the frontiers $F_1$, $F_2$ and $F_3$ of the relations $R_{p_1}$, $R_{p_2}$ and $R_{p_3}$, respectively, by taking the set-difference of their domain and image (e.g., $F_1 = D_{p_1} \setminus R_{p_1}(D_{p_1})$), where, $D_{p_1} = \mathsf{domain}(p_1)$). The three frontiers are shown using the ISL notation below:

- $F_1 =$ `[N] -> {A[i,j] : 0<=i<N and 0<=j<N}`
- $F_2 =$ `[N] -> {A[i,j] : 0<=i<N and 0<=j<N}`
- $F_3 =$ `[N] -> {S1[i,j,0] : 0<=i<N and 0<=j<N}`

In the case an injective circuit (with associated relation, say, $R_a$), we chose the direction of projection to be the vector representing $R_a$. Here, in case of a broadcast path (with associated relation, say, $R_b = \mathbf{A}.\vec{x} + \vec{b}$), we choose the kernel of the matrix $\mathbf{A}$, $\ker(\mathbf{A})$, to be the projection direction. The intuition behind choosing this direction is that the kernel represents the plane of reuse, and hence, the set of points obtained by projecting a set $E$ along the kernel directions represents the $\mathsf{In}(E)$. In general, the kernel can be of dimension higher than one (but has to be at least one due to the definition of a broadcast path). The kernels ($\vec{k_1}$ and $\vec{k_2}$) of the inverse-relations of the paths $p_1$ and $p_2$ are: $\vec{k_1} = (0,1,0)^T$ and $\vec{k_2} = (1,0,0)^T$, respectively.

By choosing $\vec{k_1}, \vec{k_2}$ and $\vec{b_3}$ as the projection directions, we obtain $\phi_1 : (i,j,k) \rightarrow (i,k)$; $\phi_2 : (i,j,k) \rightarrow (j,k)$; $\phi_3 : (i,j,k) \rightarrow (i,j)$. This provides us the following inequalities: $x_1 + x_3 \leq 1$; $x_2 + x_3 \leq 1$; $x_1 + x_2 \leq 1$. Further, to handle the degenerated cases, we have the additional constraints that specify that the size of the projections onto the subspaces $\{\vec{i}\}$, $\{\vec{j}\}$ and $\{\vec{k}\}$ should not exceed $N$ and the size of the projections onto the subspaces $\{\vec{i},\vec{j}\}$, $\{\vec{j},\vec{k}\}$ and $\{\vec{i},\vec{k}\}$ should not exceed $N^2$. Hence, we obtain the following parametric linear programming problem.

$$\text{Maximize } \Theta = x_1 + x_2 + x_3 \tag{11}$$

$$
\begin{aligned}
\text{s.t.}\quad x_1+x_2 &\leq 1\\
x_2+x_3 &\leq 1\\
x_1+x_3 &\leq 1\\
x_1 &\leq \log_S(N)\\
x_2 &\leq \log_S(N)\\
x_3 &\leq \log_S(N)\\
x_1+x_2 &\leq 2\log_S(N)\\
x_2+x_3 &\leq 2\log_S(N)\\
x_1+x_3 &\leq 2\log_S(N)
\end{aligned}
$$

Solving Eq. (11) using PIP [16] provides the following solution: If $2\log_S(N) \geq 1$ then, $x_1 = x_2 = x_3 = 1/2$, else, $x_1 = x_2 = x_3 = \log_S(N)$. Hence, when $N = \Omega(\sqrt{S})$, $Q_m = \Omega\left(\frac{N^3}{\sqrt{S}} - N^2\right)$, otherwise, $Q_m \geq 0$.

Finally, by applying Theorem 2, we obtain the I/O lower bound for the full program, $Q \geq Q_m + Q_s = \Omega\left(W \times \left(\frac{N^3}{\sqrt{S}} + \frac{N^2T}{\sqrt{S}} - N^2 - NT\right)\right)$ when $N$ and $T$ are sufficiently large.

***Putting it all together:*** Algorithm 1 provides a pseudo-code for our algorithm. Because the number of possible paths in a graph is highly combinatorial, several choices are made to limit the overall practical complexity of the algorithm. First, only edges of interest, i.e., those that correspond to relations whose image is representative of the iteration domain, are kept. Second, paths are considered in the order of decreasing expected profitability. One criterion detailed here corresponds to favoring injective circuits over broadcast paths with one-dimensional kernel (to reduce the potential span), and then broadcast paths with decreasing kernel dimension (the higher the kernel, the more the reuse, the lower the constraint).

For a given vertex $v$, once the directions associated with the set of paths chosen so far span the complete space of the domain of $v$, no more paths are considered. The role of the function try() (on lines 20, 26 and 32 in Algorithm 1) amounts to finding a set of paths that are linearly independent, compatible (i.e., a base can be associated to them), and representative. The funtion try() is shown in Algorithm 3. The function best($v$) (shown in Algorithm 2) selects a set of paths for a vertex $v$ and computes the associated complexity. The function solve() (shown in Algorithm 4) writes the linear program and returns the I/O lower bound (with cases) for a domain $D$ and a set of compatible subspaces.

Various operations used in the pseudo-code are detailed below.

- Given a relation $R$, domain($R$) and image($R$) return the domain and image of $R$, respectively.
- For an edge $e$, the operation relation($e$) provides its associated relation. If $R_e$ = relation($e$) has acceptable number of disjunctions, then the edge can be split into multiple edges with count equal to the number of disjunctions, otherwise, a convex under-approximation can be done.
- For a given path $p = (e_1, e_2, \ldots, e_l)$ with associated relations $(R_{e_1}, R_{e_2}, \ldots, R_{e_l})$ we can compute the associated relation for $p$ by composing the relations of its edges, i.e., relation($p$) computes $R_{e_l} \circ \cdots \circ R_{e_2} \circ R_{e_1}$. Note that the domain of the composition of two relations is restricted to the points for which the composition can apply, i.e. $\text{domain}(R_i \circ R_j) = R_j^{-1}(\text{image}(R_j) \cap \text{domain}(R_i))$ and $\text{image}(R_i \circ R_j) = R_i(\text{image}(R_j) \cap \text{domain}(R_i))$.
- For a given domain $D$, dim($D$) returns its dimension. If the cardinality of $D$ (i.e., number of points in $D$) is represented in terms of the program parameters, its dimension can be obtained by setting the values of the parameters to a fixed big value (say $\mathcal{B}$), and computing $\log_B(|D|)$, and rounding the result to the nearest integer. For example, if $|D| = C(n,m) = nm + n + 3$, setting $\mathcal{B} = 10^3$, we get $\dim(D) = \text{round}(\log_{\mathcal{B}}(C(\mathcal{B},\mathcal{B}))) = 2$.
- If a relation $R$ is injective and can be expressed as an affine map of the form $\mathbf{A}.\vec{x} + \vec{b}$, then the operation ray($R$) computes $\vec{b}$, otherwise, returns $\perp$.
- For a relation $R$, if its inverse can be expressed as an affine relation $\mathbf{A}.\vec{x} + \vec{b}$, rkernel($R$) computes the kernel of the matrix $A$ (and returns $\perp$ otherwise).
- For a set of vectors $b = \{\vec{b_1}, \ldots, \vec{b_l}\}$, subspace($b$) provides the linear subspace spanned by those vectors.
- For a set of linear subspaces $K = \{k_1, \ldots, k_l\}$, base($K$) gives a set of linearly independent vectors $b = \{\vec{b_1}, \ldots, \vec{b_d}\}$ such that for any $k_i$, there exists $b_i \subseteq b$ s.t. $k_i$ = subspace($b_i$). If such a set could not be computed, it returns $\perp$.
- For a path $p$, vertices($p$) returns its set of vertices.
- Given an expression $X$, the operation simplify($X$) simplifies the expression by eliminating the lower order terms. For example, simplify($NT + N^2 - N + T$) returns $NT + N^2$.

```
1  G_F = (V_F, E_F);
2  F_I := ∅; F_B := ∅; F_BB := ∅;
3  foreach e = (u, v) ∈ E_F do
4      R := relation(e);
5      if dim(image(R)) < dim(v) then next;
6      if R is invertible then F_I := F ∪ {e};
7      if dim(domain(R)) = dim(image(R)) − 1 then
8          F_B := F_B ∪ {e}
9      end
10     if dim(domain(R)) < dim(image(R)) − 1 then
11         F_BB := F_BB ∪ {e}
12     end
13 end
14 foreach v ∈ V_F do
15     d := dim(v);
16     foreach circuit p from v to v in F_I do
17         R := relation(p);
18         if (b := ray(R)) = ⊥ then next p;
19         if dim(image(R)) < d then next p;
20         if try(v, subspace(b), p) then next v;
21     end
22     foreach cycle-free path p to v in F_B F_I^* do
23         R := relation(p);
24         if (k := rkernel(R)) = ⊥ then next p;
25         if dim(image(R)) < d then next p;
26         if try(v, k, p) then next v;
27     end
28     foreach cycle-free path p to v in F_BB F_I^* do
29         R := relation(p);
30         if (k := rkernel(R)) = ⊥ then next p;
31         if dim(image(R) < d) then next p;
32         if try(v, k, p) then next v;
33     end
34     best(v);
35 end
36 simplify(Σ_{v∈V_F} v.complexity);
```

**Algorithm 1:** For each vertex $v$ in a data-flow graph $G_F$, finds a set of paths and computes the corresponding complexity.

```
Function best(vertex v)
let (k, K, D, T) ∈ v.clique with maximum lexicographic value of
    (dim(D), dimension(k), −Σ_{k_i∈K} dimension(k_i), solve(D, K), −|T|);
Q := solve(D, K);
v.complexity := Q;
```

**Algorithm 2:** For a vertex $v$, selects a set of paths and computes the associated complexity.

```
Function try(vertex v, subspace k′, path p)
{v.clique is a set of quadruples (k, K, D, T) where:
    - k is a subspace,
    - K is a set of subspaces,
    - D is a domain,
    - T is a set of vertices}
{v.complexity is an asymptotic complexity (with cases)}
if k′ ∈ v.subspaces then return false;
v.subspaces := v.subspaces ∪ {k′};
foreach (k, K, D, T) ∈ v.clique ∪ (⊥, ⊥, ⊥, ⊥) do
    if dimension(k + k′) > dimension(k) and
    base(K ∪ {k′}) ≠ ⊥ then
        D′ = image(relation(p)) ∩ D;
        if D = ⊥ or dim(D′) = dim(D) then
            T′ := T ∪ vertices(p);
            K′ := K ∪ {k′};
            v.clique := v.clique ⋃ (k + k′, K′, D′, T′);
            if dimension(k + k′) ≥ dim(domain(v)) then
                Q := solve(D′, K′);
                v.complexity := Q;
                return true;
            end
        end
    end
end
return false;
```

**Algorithm 3:** For a vertex $v$, try to add path $p$ to some other paths. Return true if a good bound is found.

```
Function solve(domain D, set of subspaces K)
b := base(K);
LP := objective(maximize Θ = Σ_{b_i∈b} α_i);
foreach k ∈ K do LP := LP.constraint(Σ_{b_i∉k} α_i ≤ 1);
foreach b′ ⊂ b do
    D_{b′} := projection(subspace(b′), D);
    LP := LP.constraint(Σ_{b_i∈b′} α_i ≤ log_S(|D_{b′}|));
end
F := Σ_{k∈K} |projection(¬k, D)|;
Θ := solution(LP);
U := S^Θ;
Q := Ω(|D|S / U) − Ω(F);
return Q;
```

**Algorithm 4:** For a domain $D$ and a set of compatible subspaces, writes the linear program, and returns the I/O lower bound (with cases).

## 6. Related Work

Hong & Kung provided the first formalization of the I/O complexity problem for a two-level memory hierarchy using the red/blue pebble game on a CDAG and the equivalence to 2S-partitions of the CDAG. We perform an adaptation of Hong & Kung 2S-partitioning to constrain the size of the input set of each vertex set rather than a dominator set, which is suitable for bounding the minimum I/O for a CDAG with the restricted red/blue pebble game where repebbling is disallowed. This adaptation enables effective composition of lower bounds of sub-CDAGs to form I/O lower bounds for composite CDAGs. A similar adaptation has previously been used by modifying the red/blue pebble game through addition of a third kind of pebble [14, 15]. The composition of lower bounds for sequences of linear algebra operations has previously been addressed by the work of Ballard et al. [1] by use of "imposed" reads and writes in between segments of operations, adding the lower bounds on data access for each of the segments, and subtracting the number of imposed reads and writes. Our use of tagged inputs and outputs in conjunction with application of the decomposition theorem bears similarities to the use of imposed reads and writes by Ballard et al., but is applicable to the more general model of CDAGs that model data dependences among operations.

Bilardi et al. [8] proposed an approach to obtain lower bounds on the access complexity of a DAG in terms of space lower bounds that apply to disjoint components of the DAG, when recomputation is not allowed. The approach was later extended to the case when recomputation is allowed, by means of the notion of free-input space complexity [9].

Irony et al. [21] used a geometric reasoning with the Loomis-Whitney inequality [23] to present an alternate proof to Hong and Kung's [20] for I/O lower bounds on standard matrix multiplication. More recently, Demmel's group at UC Berkeley has developed lower bounds as well as optimal algorithms for several linear algebra computations including QR and LU decomposition and the all-pairs shortest paths problem [1, 3, 13, 33].

Extending the scope of the Hong & Kung model to more complex memory hierarchies has also been the subject of research. Savage provided an extension together with results for some classes of computations that were considered by Hong & Kung, providing optimal lower bounds for I/O with memory hierarchies [27]. Valiant proposed a hierarchical computational model [35] that offers the possibility to reason in an arbitrarily complex parametrized memory hierarchy model. While we use a single-level memory model in this paper, the work can be extended in a straight forward manner to model multi-level memory hierarchies.

Unlike Hong & Kung's original model, several models have been proposed that do not allow recomputation of values (also referred to as "no repebbling") [1, 3, 7, 10, 12, 21, 24–28, 30, 31]. Savage [27] developed results for FFT using no repebbling. Bilardi and Peserico [7] explore the possibility of coding a given algorithm so that it is efficiently portable across machines with different hierarchical memory systems, without the use of recomputation. Ballard et al. [1, 3] assume no recomputation in deriving lower bounds for linear algebra computations. Ranjan et al. [25] develop better bounds than Hong & Kung for FFT using a specialized technique adapted for FFT-style computations on memory hierarchies. Ranjan et al. [26] derive lower bounds for pebbling r-pyramids under the assumption that there is no recomputation. As discussed earlier, we also use a model that disallows recomputation of values. But our focus in this regard is different from previous efforts – we formalize an adaptation of the the 2S-partitioning model of Hong & Kung that facilitates effective composition of lower bounds from sub-CDAGs of a composite CDAG.

```
for(i=0;i<N;i++)
 for(j=0;j<N;j++)
  for(k=0;k<N;k++)
   C[i][j]+=A[i][k]+B[k][j];
```

(a) Matrix Multiplication Code

```
for(i=0;i<N;i++)
 for(j=0;j<N;j++)
  for(k=0;k<N;k++)
  {
   C[i][j]  +=  1;
   A[i][k]  +=  1;
   B[k][j]  +=  1;
  }
```

(b) Code with same array accesses as Mat-Mult

Figure 8: Example illustrating difference between CDAG model and computational model used by Christ et al. [11]

The previously described efforts on I/O lower bounds have involved manual analysis of algorithms to derive the bounds. In contrast, in this paper we develop an approach to automate the analysis of I/O lower bounds for programs. The only other such effort to our knowledge is the recent work of Christ et al. [11]. Indeed, the approach we have develop in this paper was inspired by their work, but differs in a number of significant ways:

1. The models of computation are different. Our work is based on the CDAG and pebbling formalism of Hong & Kung, while the lower bound results of Christ et al. [11] are based on a different abstraction of an indivisible loop body of affine statements within a perfectly nested loop. For example, under that model, the lower bounds for codes in Fig. 8(a) (standard matrix multiplication) and Fig. 8(b) would be exactly the same – $O(N^3/\sqrt{S})$ – since the analysis is based only on the array accesses in the computation. In contrast, with the red/blue pebble-game model, the CDAGs for the two codes are very different, with the matrix-multiplication code in Fig. 8(a) representing a connected CDAG, while the code in Fig. 8(b) represents has a CDAG with three disconnected parts corresponding to the three statements, and computation has a much lower I/O complexity of $O(N^2)$.
2. The work of Christ et al. [11] does not model data dependencies between statement instances, and can therefore produce weak lower bounds. In contrast, the approach developed in this paper is based on using precise data dependence information as the basis for geometric reasoning in the iteration space to derive the I/O lower bounds. For example, with the 2D-Jacobi example discussed earlier, the lower bound obtained by the approach of Christ et al. would be $O(N^2)$ instead of the tight bound of $O(N^2T/\sqrt{S})$ that is obtained with the algorithm developed in this paper.
3. This work addresses a more general model of programs. While the work of Christ et al. [11] only models perfectly nested loop computations, the algorithms presented in this paper handle sequences of imperfectly nested loop computations.

## 7. Discussion

We conclude by raising some issues and open questions, some of which are being addressed in ongoing work.

**Tightness of lower bounds**: A very important question is whether a lower bound is tight – clearly, zero is a valid but weak and useless I/O lower bound for any CDAG. The primary means of assessing tightness of lower bounds is by comparison with upper bounds from algorithm implementations that have been optimized for data locality. For example, tiling (or blocking) is a commonly used approach to enhance data locality of nested loop computations. An open question is whether any automatic tool can be designed to systematically explore the space of valid schedules to generate good parametric upper bounds based on models and/or heuristics that minimize data movement cost.

**Lower bounds when recomputation is allowed**: The vast majority of existing application codes do not perform any redundant recomputation of any operations. But with data movement costs becoming increasingly dominant over operation execution costs, both in terms of energy and performance, there is significant interest in devising implementations of algorithms where redundant recomputation of values may be used to trade off additional inexpensive operations for a reduction in expensive data movements to/from off-chip memory. It is therefore of interest to develop automated techniques for I/O lower bounds under the original model of Hong & Kung that permits re-computation of CDAG vertices. Having lower bounds under both models can offer a mechanism to identify which algorithms have a potential for a trade-off between extra computations for reduced data movement and which do not.

If the CDAG representing a computation has matching and tight I/O lower bounds under both the general model and the restricted model, the algorithm does not have potential for such a trade-off. On the other hand, if a lower bound under the restricted model (that prohibits re-pebbling) is higher than a tight lower bound under the general model, the computation has potential for trading off extra computations for a reduction in volume of data movement. This raises an interesting question: *Is it possible to develop necessary and/or sufficient conditions on properties of the computation, for example on the nature of the data dependencies, which will guarantee matching (or differing) lower bounds under the models allowing/prohibiting re-computation?*

**Relating I/O lower bounds to machine parameters**: I/O lower bounds can be used to determine whether an algorithm will be inherently limited to performance far below a processor's peak because of data movement bottlenecks. The collective bandwidth between main memory and the last level cache in multicore processors in words/second on current systems is over an order of magnitude lower than the aggregate computational performance of the processor cores in floating-point operations per second; this ratio is a critical machine balance parameter. By comparing this machine balance parameter to the ratio of the I/O lower bound (calculated for $S$ set to the capacity of the last level on-chip cache) to the total number of arithmetic operations in the computation, we can determine if the algorithm will be inherently limited by data movement overheads. However, such an analysis will also require tight assessment of the constants for the leading terms in the asymptotic expressions of the order complexity for I/O lower bounds. This is not addressed by the approach presented in this paper.

**Modeling associative operators**: Reductions using associative operators like addition occur frequently in computations. With the CDAG model, some fixed order of execution is enforced for such computations, resulting in an over-constrained linear chain of dependencies between the vertices corresponding to instances of an associative operator. Some previously developed geometric approaches to modeling I/O lower bounds [1, 11, 21] have developed I/O lower bounds for a family of algorithms that differ in the order of execution of associative operations. It would be of interest to extend the automated lower bounding approach of this paper to also model lower bounds among a family of CDAGs corresponding to associative reordering of the operations.

**Finding good decompositions**: The second illustrative example in Sec. 5 demonstrated the benefit of judiciously decomposing CDAGs to obtain good lower bounds by combining bounds for sub-CDAGs via the decomposition theorem. However, if the decomposition is performed poorly, the result will be a very weak lower bound. In the same example, if the computation within the second level `i` loop had also been used to further decompose the CDAG, we would have a sequence of matrix-vector multiplications with order complexity $O(N^2)$ from which the tagged I/O nodes of the same order of complexity must be subtrated out, resulting in a weak lower bound of zero. Conversely, if the computation within the outer `it` loop were not decomposed into sub-CDAGs, it would again have resulted in weak lower bounds. The question of automatically finding effective decompositions of CDAGs to enable tight lower bounds is an open problem.

## 8. Conclusion

Characterizing the I/O complexity of a program is a cornerstone problem, that is particularly important with current and emerging power-constrained architectures where data movement costs are the dominant energy bottleneck. Previous approaches to modeling the I/O complexity of computations have several limitations that this paper has addressed. First, by suitably modifying the pebble game model used for characterizing I/O complexity, analysis of large composite computational DAGs is enabled by decomposition into smaller sub-DAGs, a key requirement to allow the analysis of complex programs. Second, a static analysis approach has been developed to compute I/O lower bounds, by generating asymptotic parametric data-access lower bounds for programs as a function of cache size and problem size.

## Acknowledgment

We thank the anonymous referees for the feedback and many suggestions that helped us significantly in improving the presentation of the work. We thank Gianfranco Bilardi, Jim Demmel, and Nick Knight for discussions on many aspects of lower bounds modeling and their suggestions for improving the paper. This work was supported in part by the U.S. National Science Foundation through awards 0811457, 0926127, 0926687 and 1059417, by the U.S. Department of Energy through award DE-SC0012489, and by Louisiana State University.


## References


[1] G. Ballard, J. Demmel, O. Holtz, and O. Schwartz. Minimizing communication in numerical linear algebra. *SIAM J. Matrix Analysis Applications*, 32(3):866–901, 2011.

[2] G. Ballard, J. Demmel, O. Holtz, B. Lipshitz, and O. Schwartz. Brief announcement: Strong scaling of matrix multiplication algorithms and memory-independent communication lower bounds. In *Proc. SPAA '12*, pages 77–79, 2012.

[3] G. Ballard, J. Demmel, O. Holtz, and O. Schwartz. Graph expansion and communication costs of fast matrix multiplication. *J. ACM*, 59(6): 32, 2012.

[4] A. Barvinok. Computing the Ehrhart polynomial of a convex lattice polytope. *Discrete and Computational Geometry*, 12:35–48, 1994.

[5] J. Bennett, A. Carbery, M. Christ, and T. Tao. Finite bounds for Holder-Brascamp-Lieb multilinear inequalities. *Mathematical Research Letters*, 55(4):647–666, 2010.

[6] K. Bergman, S. Borkar, et al. Exascale computing study: Technology challenges in achieving exascale systems. *DARPA IPTO, Tech. Rep*, 2008.

[7] G. Bilardi and E. Peserico. A characterization of temporal locality and its portability across memory hierarchies. *Automata, Languages and Programming*, pages 128–139, 2001.

[8] G. Bilardi and F. P. Preparata. Processor - Time Tradeoffs under Bounded-Speed Message Propagation: Part II, Lower Bounds. *Theory Comput. Syst.*, 32(5):531–559, 1999.

[9] G. Bilardi, A. Pietracaprina, and P. D'Alberto. On the space and access complexity of computation DAGs. In *Graph-Theoretic Concepts in Computer Science*, volume 1928 of *LNCS*, pages 81–92. 2000.

[10] G. Bilardi, M. Scquizzato, and F. Silvestri. A lower bound technique for communication on bsp with application to the fft. In *Euro-Par*, pages 676–687, 2012.

[11] M. Christ, J. Demmel, N. Knight, T. Scanlon, and K. Yelick. Communication Lower Bounds and Optimal Algorithms for Programs That Reference Arrays Part 1. EECS Technical Report EECS–2013-61, UC Berkeley, May 2013.

[12] S. A. Cook. An observation on time-storage trade off. *J. Comput. Syst. Sci.*, 9(3):308–316, 1974.

[13] J. Demmel, L. Grigori, M. Hoemmen, and J. Langou. Communication-optimal parallel and sequential QR and LU factorizations. *SIAM J. Scientific Computing*, 34(1), 2012.

[14] V. Elango, F. Rastello, L.-N. Pouchet, J. Ramanujam, and P. Sadayappan. Data access complexity: The red/blue pebble game revisited. Technical report, OSU/INRIA/LSU/UCLA, Sept. 2013. OSU-CISRC-7/13-TR16.

[15] V. Elango, F. Rastello, L. Pouchet, J. Ramanujam, and P. Sadayappan. On characterizing the data movement complexity of computational dags for parallel execution. In *26th ACM Symposium on Parallelism in Algorithms and Architectures, SPAA '14*, pages 296–306, 2014.

[16] P. Feautrier. Parametric integer programming. *RAIRO Recherche Opérationnelle*, 22(3):243–268, 1988.

[17] S. H. Fuller and L. I. Millett. *The Future of Computing Performance: Game Over or Next Level?* The National Academies Press, 2011.

[18] S. Girbal, N. Vasilache, C. Bastoul, A. Cohen, D. Parello, M. Sigler, and O. Temam. Semi-automatic composition of loop transformations for deep parallelism and memory hierarchies. *Intl. J. of Parallel Programming*, 34(3), 2006.

[19] G. Gupta and S. Rajopadhye. The Z-polyhedral model. In *ACM SIGPLAN Symposium on Principles and Practice of Parallel Programming (PPoPP'07)*, pages 237–248. ACM, 2007.

[20] J.-W. Hong and H. T. Kung. I/O complexity: The red-blue pebble game. In *Proc. of the 13th annual ACM sympo. on Theory of computing (STOC'81)*, pages 326–333. ACM, 1981.

[21] D. Irony, S. Toledo, and A. Tiskin. Communication lower bounds for distributed-memory matrix multiplication. *J. Parallel Distrib. Comput.*, 64(9):1017–1026, 2004.

[22] A. Ketterlin and P. Clauss. Profiling data-dependence to assist parallelization: Framework, scope, and optimization. In *MICRO*, pages 437–448, 2012.

[23] L. Loomis and H. Whitney. An inequality related to the isoperimetric inequality. *Bull. Am. Math. Soc.*, 55:961–962, 1949.

[24] D. Ranjan and M. Zubair. Vertex isoperimetric parameter of a computation graph. *Int. J. Found. Comput. Sci.*, 23(4):941–964, 2012.

[25] D. Ranjan, J. Savage, and M. Zubair. Strong I/O lower bounds for binomial and FFT computation graphs. In *Computing and Combinatorics*, volume 6842 of *LNCS*, pages 134–145. Springer, 2011.

[26] D. Ranjan, J. E. Savage, and M. Zubair. Upper and lower I/O bounds for pebbling r-pyramids. *J. Discrete Algorithms*, 14:2–12, 2012.

[27] J. Savage. Extending the Hong-Kung model to memory hierarchies. In *Computing and Combinatorics*, volume 959 of *LNCS*, pages 270–281. 1995.

[28] J. E. Savage. *Models of Computation*. Addison-Wesley, 1998.

[29] J. E. Savage and M. Zubair. A unified model for multicore architectures. In *Proceedings of the 1st International Forum on Next-generation Multicore/Manycore Technologies*, page 9. ACM, 2008.

[30] J. E. Savage and M. Zubair. Cache-optimal algorithms for option pricing. *ACM Trans. Math. Softw.*, 37(1), 2010.

[31] M. Scquizzato and F. Silvestri. Communication lower bounds for distributed-memory computations. *CoRR*, abs/1307.1805, 2013.

[32] J. Shalf, S. Dosanjh, and J. Morrison. Exascale computing technology challenges. *High Performance Computing for Computational Science–VECPAR 2010*, pages 1–25, 2011.

[33] E. Solomonik, A. Buluç, and J. Demmel. Minimizing communication in all-pairs shortest paths. In *IPDPS*, 2013.

[34] S. I. Valdimarsson. The Brascamp-Lieb polyhedron. *Can. J. Math.*, 62(4):870–888, 2010.

[35] L. G. Valiant. A bridging model for multi-core computing. *J. Comput. Syst. Sci.*, 77:154–166, Jan. 2011.

[36] S. Verdoolaege. isl: An integer set library for the polyhedral model. In *Mathematical Software–ICMS 2010*, pages 299–302. Springer, 2010.

# Sound Modular Verification of C Code Executing in an Unverified Context

Pieter Agten Bart Jacobs Frank Piessens

iMinds-DistriNet, KU Leuven

{firstname}.{lastname}@cs.kuleuven.be

## Abstract

Over the past decade, great progress has been made in the static modular verification of C code by means of separation logic-based program logics. However, the runtime guarantees offered by such verification are relatively limited when the verified modules are part of a whole program that also contains unverified modules. In particular, a memory safety error in an unverified module can corrupt the runtime state, leading to assertion failures or invalid memory accesses in the verified modules. This paper develops runtime checks to be inserted at the boundary between the verified and the unverified part of a program, to guarantee that no assertion failures or invalid memory accesses can occur at runtime in any verified module. One of the key challenges is enforcing the separation logic frame rule, which we achieve by checking the integrity of the footprint of the verified part of the program on each control flow transition from the unverified to the verified part. This in turn requires the presence of some support for module-private memory at runtime. We formalize our approach and prove soundness. We implement the necessary runtime checks by means of a program transformation that translates C code with separation logic annotations into plain C, and that relies on a protected module architecture for providing module-private memory and restricted module entry points. Benchmarks show the performance impact of this transformation depends on the choice of boundary between the verified and unverified parts of the program, but is below 4% for real-world applications.

***Categories and Subject Descriptors*** D.2.4 [*Software Engineering*]: Software/Program Verification

***Keywords*** separation logic; verification; runtime checking

## 1. Introduction

The construction of reliable software in unsafe languages like C or C++ is known to be challenging. Yet, because of the excellent performance of these languages, and because they can give the programmer access to low-level details of the machine on which the program is executing, they are often the languages of choice for infrastructural software such as hypervisors, operating systems and servers, and for embedded software.



*POPL '15*, January 15–17 2015, Mumbai, India.



http://dx.doi.org/10.1145/2676726.2676972

One way of significantly increasing assurance in the reliability of software is the use of program verification. Over the past decade, program verification technology for C-like programming languages has reached a level of maturity that makes it possible to verify real-world software, albeit with considerable effort. Two high-profile examples are the verification of Microsoft's hypervisor Hyper-V using the VCC verifier [11], and the verification of seL4 [24], a microkernel of the L4 family. But there are many other examples of projects that formally verify the safety and/or functional correctness of (parts of) C programs.

For large systems, it is essential that the verification technique used is *modular*. Each module (for instance each function) is verified to comply with its specification, relying only on the *specification* of the other modules that the verified module is interacting with. Several sound modular verification tools for C have been proposed [10, 22]. However, the soundness properties of these verifiers have an important limitation. To the best of our knowledge, all soundness results for modular C verifiers have the form: under the condition that *all* modules of a program have been verified, any execution of that program will comply with the specification. In other words, as soon as there is one unverified module, all bets are off. The implementations of modules that are not verified are part of the *trusted computing base*; it is *assumed* that they comply with the specifications for these modules that were used to verify the verified part of the program. Such assumptions are particularly troublesome for memory-unsafe languages such as C, as a single memory-safety error (such as a buffer overflow) in one unverified module can in principle mess up the runtime state of *all* modules. This has several undesirable consequences:

- While testing a partially verified program, failures may still occur in the verified part of the program, and the root cause for such failures may be hard to track down. This includes both memory safety failures (e.g. dereferencing invalid memory addresses) as well as failures of assertions that were statically verified to hold.
- Security properties verified to hold in a module are not guaranteed to hold when that module is used as part of a larger, unverified program. Hence, the benefits of partial verification for security purposes are limited. In particular, in a security setting, one must consider that memory safety errors may be *exploited* by means of code injection attacks [14]. Maintaining the integrity of a verified module in such a setting is very challenging.

What is needed is a technique for ensuring that failures cannot occur in the verified part of the program. Any runtime error should either (1) lead to a failure in the unverified part, or (2) be detected on entry to the verified part. This will entail that the state of the verified module is always valid, and that no properties that were verified to hold for this module state will ever be violated.

The approach we suggest is based on performing *runtime checks* at the *boundary* between the verified and unverified part of the program. While sound approaches for such dynamic contract checking exist for safe languages [15, 16], to the best of our knowledge there is no system that achieves such sound contract checking for unsafe languages such as C. Furthermore, existing approaches instrument *each* memory access in the unverified part [29] or verified part [34], entailing a large performance cost, while we will perform our checks only when crossing the verified-unverified boundary.

The main contribution of this paper is the development of a program transformation that, given a C program partitioned into an unverified module and a module verified by means of separation logic, transforms the verified module into a *hardened* module that includes sound and complete runtime checks at the boundaries of the module. A key problem that needs to be solved is how to make sure that memory errors (or alternatively, malicious code) in the unverified part cannot corrupt the state of the verified module, while still only performing explicit checks at the boundary. We solve this problem in two steps. First, the boundary checks perform integrity checks on the heap footprint of the verified module: on re-entry to the verified module, we check that the heap memory "owned" by the verified part has not been changed by the unverified part of the program. This ensures that bad writes to the heap performed by the unverified part are detected. Second, we need a mechanism for protecting the integrity of local variables and control flow metadata of the verified module. For this, we rely on the recent work on *protected module architectures* (PMAs), which are low-level security architectures providing support for module-private data regions and restricted module code entry points. Early prototypes [26, 35] are hypervisor-based [37], while the most recent research prototypes [30] implement this protection in hardware, thereby reducing the trusted computing base to just the processor itself. Intel recently announced hardware support for PMA's under the name Intel Software Guard Extensions (SGX) [20], hence this type of protection mechanisms will be broadly available in the near future.

The combination of the module boundary checks and the PMA protection of local variables and control flow gives us a very strong modular soundness guarantee: *no verified assertion in the verified module will ever fail at runtime, even if the module runs as part of a vulnerable application that is subject to code injection attacks.* The main contributions of this paper are:

- The development of runtime checks for separation logic contracts at the boundary between a verified and an unverified part of a C program.
- A formal correctness proof of these runtime checks.
- The observation that existing fully abstract secure compilation techniques [2, 31] to a PMA ensure the soundness of these runtime checks even in the presence of code injection attacks exploiting memory safety errors in the unverified part.
- The development of a robust prototype, based on the VeriFast [22] verifier.
- The quantification of the performance cost of the technique by means of micro and macro benchmarks.

The remainder of this paper is structured as follows. First, we elaborate on the problem we solve and on our proposed solution in Sections 2 and 3. Section 4 gives an informal explanation of our program transformations, and Section 5 illustrates them using an example program. Section 6 formalizes the transformations. In Section 7 we discuss our prototype implementation and the results of our benchmarks. Finally, we discuss related work in Section 8 and conclude in Section 9.

## 2. Problem Statement

We assume as given a separation logic-based program logic for C [33], and a sound modular static verifier that checks compliance of C functions with contracts expressed in the program logic. For concreteness, we work in this paper with the VeriFast verifier [22], but our results are not specific to VeriFast. We use VeriFast syntax in our examples: separating conjunction is written as `&*&`, and `?x` introduces an existentially quantified logic variable.

For programs in which each function is statically verified and where the `main` function has an empty precondition, verification ensures that no routine ever performs an illegal memory operation and each routine upholds its contract. However, verifying the entire code base of a program is often infeasible, for instance because it is too costly in terms of programmer effort. Trying to prove full program correctness properties for partially verified programs would clearly be overambitious, since there are no guarantees about the behavior of the unverified parts. However, as this section will point out, even statements concerned only with the verified parts of the program cannot be proven in general for partially verified programs written in memory unsafe languages.

We consider single-threaded C programs consisting of two parts: an unverified *context* and a statically verified module. Each function of the verified module and each function prototype used by it specifies a separation logic contract, consisting of a precondition (**req**uires) and a postcondition (**ens**ures). Static verification ensures that the verified functions are memory safe and comply with their specifications, but only under the assumption that the precondition holds on function entry and that any function called from those functions complies to its own specification.

```
// Prototypes
int med(struct lst *l);


// Unverified functions
int main()
{
  struct lst *l =
    read_list();
  print(med(l));
}

void srt(struct lst *l)
{
  < unverified sort
    implementation >
}
```

```
// Prototypes
void srt(struct lst *l);
 req list(l, ?v0);
 ens list(l, ?v1) &*&
     val_eq(v0, v1) &*&
     sorted(v1);

// Verified functions
int med(struct lst *l)
 req list(l, ?v0) &*&
     0 < length(v0);
 ens list(l, v0) &*&
     res == median(v0);
{
  int s = len(l);
  struct lst *l0 = copy(l);
  srt(l0);
  <proof statements>
  return nth(l0, s/2);
}
```

Consider the example program shown above. On the left is the context, consisting of a `main` function, a `srt` function and a prototype for a function `med`. On the right is the verified module, which contains the function `med` and a prototype for `srt`. The `med` function takes as input a non-empty list and claims that, after execution, the list still contains the original values and the return value will be the median of the input list. This function relies on functions `len`, `nth` and `srt` to perform its task. The verifier relies on the contracts of those functions, in addition to the proof statements in `med` itself, to prove that the function will uphold its contract. The implementation of `len` and `nth` is not shown in the example, but they are assumed to be part of the verified module, hence the verifier can verify those functions as well. On the other hand, for the `srt` function the verified module only contains a prototype. Hence the verifier can only *assume* that its implementation will uphold the specified contract.

Linking the two parts of the example program together and executing them may still lead to violations of the verified module specifications, if one of the functions has a *bug*. We say that a function has a bug if it does not comply with its contract. That is, there exists an execution of the function that satisfies its precondition, but exhibits an invalid memory access, violates the postcondition, or performs another function call and violates the precondition of the called function. We assume that the static verifier is *sound*, i.e., it rejects any function with a bug. Hence there are only bugs in the unverified context, not in the verified module.

For instance, if `read_list` (called from `main`) has a bug and returns an invalid (e.g., unallocated) memory address, the `len` function or some other verified function could perform an illegal memory operation. Likewise, if `srt` has a bug and violates the contract specified in its function prototype, then the verified function `med` might not uphold its contract either. Furthermore, because C is a memory unsafe language, `srt` can write to arbitrary memory locations, thereby modifying data belonging to the `med` function. For instance, `srt` could write to the original list `l`, instead of the copy `l0` that it was given. Hence, any properties verified to hold by the verifier about $l$ while verifying `med` might be violated at runtime after a call to the unverified function `srt`. Note that `srt` can also *read* memory that it is not allowed to by its contract. This is also a bug, but it will not violate any property of the verified module assumed by the verifier, hence our runtime checks will allow this.

How bad the effects of bugs in the unverified part of the program can be, depends on how the program is executed. A *safe* execution performs complete runtime checking and will detect bugs as soon as they appear. Nguyen et al. [29] propose a way to perform such executions. Every memory access is checked and contracts are checked on each function entry and exit. Hence, safe executions are expensive. It is sound to remove the runtime checks from the verified module, as the soundness of verification implies that these checks will never fail in the safe execution. But as long as there is a significant unverified part, the performance cost will be high.

Because of this performance cost, executions of C programs are usually *not* safe. Hence, executions can enter an *error state* and continue executing. We say an execution is in an error state if it has performed memory accesses resulting in undefined behavior according to C semantics or if the execution has violated some of the separation logic specifications. An execution can only *enter* an error state in a function with a bug. That function is the *root cause* of the error state. An execution *fails* at the point where it detects the error state and terminates. Safe executions fail immediately at the root cause of a bug, but other executions may continue after entering an error state. Typically what happens then is implementation-dependent: the program behavior depends on details of the compiler and the machine on which the compiled code is executed. Most C compilers will generate code that may detect some error states such as the dereference of a memory address that the operating system has not even allocated to the program. But in general, failure of the execution may happen long after going into an error state. As a consequence, executions may enter an error state in the unverified context, but then fail in the verified module. The verified module may also be operating while in an error state, yet *not* fail, and possibly further mess up the runtime state and worsen the error state of the execution. This is exactly why partial verification is less useful than it could be, as discussed in the introduction.

Our approach is to develop efficient runtime checks to be inserted at the boundary between verified and unverified code, that make sure that no failures can occur in the verified module. Executions can enter an error state while executing in the unverified context and the execution may then continue in an error state, but we have the guarantee that *any error state that might impact the verified module will be detected before control flow enters the verified module.* As a consequence, we have that the execution never fails while control is inside the verified module.

# 3. Overview of our solution

To guarantee that error states never impact verified modules, we need to model the execution of programs with memory safety errors. We describe two such models below.

## 3.1 Control-flow safe execution

The *control-flow safe* execution models programs as commands that operate on a heap. This is a standard model of unsafe imperative programs in the separation logic literature [33]. Memory safety errors may impact any part of the heap, but they cannot modify local variables or the control flow. In other words, code-injection attacks or stack smashing are not modeled.

For the control-flow safe execution, it is sufficient to perform runtime checks at the boundary between the verified module and the unverified context. Roughly speaking, the checks that need to be performed at the boundary are the following. Each function of the verified module should (1) check that its precondition holds on entry from an unverified function, (2) check that the callee's postcondition holds after an *outcall* (i.e., a call from the verified module to an unverified function), and (3) ensure that unverified functions did not modify any heap locations that could affect the verified function's correct execution. In our approach, the first two checks are based on a translation of separation logic pre- and postconditions into equivalent C code that will check the validity of those conditions at runtime. For the third check, our approach keeps track of the *footprint* of the verified module, i.e., the memory locations that the module can read or write, and it uses an integrity check to ensure that unverified functions do not modify the contents of those locations (except for the locations explicitly allowed by the precondition of the called unverified function). Right before performing a call from a verified function to a function of the unverified context, a cryptographic checksum is calculated over the contents of the verified module's footprint, which is recalculated and compared against the original on re-entry of the verified module.

We develop a program transformation on the verified module that injects the necessary runtime checks in Section 4, and we prove them correct for the control-flow safe execution of programs in Section 6.

## 3.2 Unsafe execution

Of course, for most realistic C compilers, the control-flow safe execution model is too abstract. Control flow information and local variables (i.e., the runtime stack) are stored in the same memory space as the heap, and hence memory safety errors can also modify control flow or contents of local variables. This is particularly relevant if we consider the possibility that our program might be under attack, and an adversary provides input that triggers a memory safety error in the unverified part of the program by performing one of the many possible low level attacks against C programs [14].

Hence, we also consider *unsafe* executions, where programs are compiled in the standard way to a Von Neumann style processor architecture. Under such unsafe executions, the boundary checks discussed above are insufficient, as memory safety errors might corrupt the integrity checksum that the boundary checks compute. Also corruption of the control flow or of local variables in the verified functions may lead to failures in the verified module.

To restore the property that no failures occur in the verified module, we build on a recently proposed fully abstract secure compilation technique towards protected module architectures [2, 31]. This compilation technique protects modules from a potentially malicious context and ensures that any possible effect that the malicious context can have on the hardened module can be understood at source code level. By composing this secure compilation technique with the program transformation for the control-flow safe execution, we get the desired property that no failures can occur in the verified module, even in the presence of stack-smashing, code injection attacks or other exploitations of memory safety errors in the unverified context.

# 4. Program transformations

This section describes how a verified module can be transformed into a *hardened* module containing runtime boundary checks, and how our prototype implements these checks. At an architectural level, the hardened module can be divided into a *functional* part and a *boundary checking* part. The former is essentially a copy of the verified module given as input, where the separation logic contracts and proof statements have been removed and the functions have been given a fresh name and marked `static` in order to remove them from the module's public interface. The latter part contains new functions and data structure definitions to actually perform the runtime boundary checks. The hardened module is constructed such that each transition between the context and the functional part passes through the appropriate function of the boundary checking part. The transformation is based solely on the source code of the verified module and the annotated function *prototypes* of the unverified part. Hence, the transformation does not require access to the source code of the unverified part. The resulting hardened module can be linked with the unverified part as-is: no recompilation of the unverified part is necessary.

The sections below explain concretely how different kinds of separation logic constructs can be translated into C code for checking them. We assume the control-flow safe execution model, since it is the execution model provided to us by the fully abstract compilation scheme, as described in Section 3.2.

## 4.1 Pure assertions

*Pure* assertions, as opposed to *spatial* assertions, only reference local variables and hence do not make claims about the heap. Such assertions can be translated straightforwardly into a C expression, as shown by the example below.

```
// Original module
int fac(int x)
 req x >= 0;
 ens res > 0;
{
  if (x == 0) return 1;
  int p = prod(x,
    fac(x-1));
  return p;
}

int prod(int x, int y);
 req true;
 ens res == x * y;
```

```
// Hardened module
// (Functional part)
static int _fac(int x) {
  if (x == 0) return 1;
  int p = _prod(x,
    _fac(x-1));
  return p;
}

// (Boundary checking part)
static
int _prod(int x, int y) {
  int r = prod(x, y);
  if (! (r == x * y)) trap();
  return r;
}

int fac(int x) {
  if (! (x >= 0)) trap();
  return _fac(x);
}
```

All assertions in this example, i.e., the contracts of `fac` and `prod`, are pure. In the hardened module, `fac` has been replaced by an *entry stub* that first checks the precondition, before calling `_fac`, which is a slightly modified version of the original `fac`. The only functional difference is that the modified version calls the `_prod` *outcall stub* instead of the original function `prod` in the context. The outcall stub first calls `prod` in the context and then checks whether the postcondition holds. If any check fails, the `trap` function is called, which ends execution. The functions `_prod` and `_fac` have been marked `static` to indicate they are not in the public interface of the hardened module.

## 4.2 Spatial assertions

Spatial assertions describe (parts of) the heap: they indicate that a certain memory region should contain certain values. The assertions need not necessarily specify exactly what those values are, they can instead existentially quantify over them, by binding a logic variable (see, for instance, the logic variable bindings `?a` and `?b` in the precondition of the original module in the example below). The difficulty with spatial assertions is that a function in the context can overwrite these values, even though that function might not be allowed to do so by its contract, thereby possibly violating properties of the verified module verified to hold by the verifier. In separation logic terms, this corresponds to a violation of the *frame rule*. As described in Section 3, we use a cryptographic checksum over the memory footprint of the hardened module to solve this problem.

```
// Original module
struct pair {int a, b;};

void f(struct pair* p)
 req p->a |-> ?a &*&
     p->b |-> ?b
 ens p->a |-> _ &*&
     p->b |-> _;
{
 <...>
 ct(p);
 <...>
}

void ct(struct pair* p);
 req p->a |-> ?n;
 ens p->a |-> ?m &*&
     m == n + 1;
```

```
// Hardened module
struct pair {int a, b;};

static
void _f(struct pair* p) {
 <...>
 _ct(p);
 <...>
}

static
void _ct(struct pair* p) {
 char h0[32], h1[32];
 int n = intp(&(p->a),C);
 fp_hash(h0);
 ct(p);
 fp_hash(h1);
 if (!eq(h0, h1)) trap();
 int m = intp(&(p->a),P);
 if (m != n+1) trap();
}

void f(struct pair* p) {
 a = intp(&(p->a),P);
 b = intp(&(p->b),P);
 _f(p);
 intp(&(p->a),C);
 intp(&(p->b),C);
}
```

The code above shows our approach. In the hardened module on the right, the verified function `f` has been replaced by an entry stub that first calls `intp` for both integer *points-to* assertions in the precondition of the original `f`, then calls `_f` and finally calls `intp` again for both integer *points-to* assertions in the postcondition.

The `intp` function is a *data type checking function* provided by our runtime checking system. It takes as arguments a pointer `p` to an integer and an enumeration value, and performs two important functions. The function first checks whether `p` points to a valid integer, which it does by simply reading `*p`. Secondly, the function adds or removes the memory region occupied by the integer (i.e., the memory region of `sizeof(int)` bytes starting at address `p`) to or from a global data structure describing the hardened module's footprint. When the enumeration value is `P` (for *produce*), the memory region is added to the footprint and when it is `C` (for *consume*) the region is removed. When adding a region to the footprint, `intp` checks that the region does not overlap with the existing footprint. This corresponds to the semantics of the separating conjunction, which requires that the footprint of each of its conjuncts occupies a *disjoint* part of the heap. We do not support non-separating conjunction but argue in Section 6.3 that this does not pose expressibility problems. If all checks pass, the `intp` function returns the integer value at the given address, or ends execution by calling `trap` otherwise. Functions similar to `intp` are provided for other primitive data types (`char`, `unsigned int`, ...) and pointers, because the memory sizes of those data types can differ.

In the function `_f` of the hardened module, the call to the `ct` function of the context has been replaced by a call to the `_ct` outcall stub. This stub first removes (consumes) the footprint of `ct`'s precondition from the hardened module's footprint, before calculating a hash over the memory regions described by the remaining footprint. This hash is stored in the local variable `h0`, where it is protected from the context by the secure compilation scheme. Next, the stub calls `ct`, handing over control to the context. When the context function returns, the outcall stub verifies that the memory described by the footprint has not been tampered with, by recalculating the hash and comparing it to the original value stored in `h0`. Finally, the stub checks whether the postcondition of `ct` holds by producing its footprint and checking whether the values in the corresponding memory region adhere to the contract. Note that we do not prevent the context from *reading* memory it is not supposed to by its contract, because this can never violate properties of the verified module assumed by the verifier.

For our prototype, we implemented the footprint data structure as a radix trie. This data structure supports $O(k)$ addition, removal and overlap testing, and $O(n)$ traversal, with $k$ the number of bits in a memory address (e.g. 64 for a 64-bit CPU) and $n$ the number of memory regions in the trie. The footprint description must be protected from being overwritten by memory safety errors in the unverified context and hence we store it in the module-private memory section provided by the PMA.

### 4.3 Predicates

Separation logic predicates are named, parameterized assertions, used to provide data encapsulation and to describe recursive data structures. For instance, the following predicate describes a linked list of integers of a certain size.

```
struct list { int value; struct list* next; };

pred list_pred(struct list* l; int size) =
  l == 0 ? size == 0 : l->value |-> _ &*& l->next |-> ?n
      &*& list_pred(n, ?size0) &*& size == size0 + 1;
```

Predicates can have an arbitrary number of parameters and separation logic allows us to existentially quantify over each of them. For instance, a valid precondition could be `list_pred(?l, 5)`, meaning that there must be a linked list of size 5 somewhere on the heap. Translating this quantification into a runtime check would however be problematic, since in general the entire heap would need to be examined in order to bind a value to `l` at runtime. Hence, we require predicates to be *precise*: predicates must separate their parameters into input and output parameters and only output parameters can be quantified over when using a predicate. In a predicate definition, each output parameter of the predicate must be assigned a value in all execution paths of the predicate's body. We discuss the implications of this requirement in Section 6.3. In VeriFast syntax, parameters before the semicolon in the parameter list of a predicate definition are input parameters and the other parameters are output parameters. Hence, for `list_pred` defined above, `l` is an input parameter and `size` is an output parameter.

```
static void
list_pred(struct list* l, int* size, enum op_type op) {
  if (l == 0) { *size = 0; }
  else {
    intp(&(l->value), op);
    struct list* n = ptrp(&(l->next), op);
    int size0;
    list_pred(n, &size0, op);
    *size = size0 + 1;
  }
}
```

The code above shows the transformation of the `list_pred` predicate. It is a *predicate checking function* with one more parameter than the original predicate. This extra parameter is an enumeration value indicating whether the predicate will be used for consumption or production and its value is simply passed on to the data type checking functions (e.g. `intp`) described in Section 4.2. Input parameters have the same type in the runtime checking function as in the original predicate and output parameters are *pointers* to the type of the parameter in the original predicate. The predicate's body is transformed straightforwardly into equivalent C code. When an output parameter is assigned a value in the predicate body, the corresponding pointer parameter in the runtime checking function is assigned a value as well. As exemplified by the recursive call to `list_pred`, a predicate call assertion is transformed into a call to the corresponding predicate checking function. If an assertion uses a constant value or previously bound variable for an output argument instead of binding a new variable (e.g. `list_pred(l, s)` with `s` already bound, instead of `list_pred(l, ?s)`), then this is pre-transformed to first binding a fresh variable to the output parameter and then constraining it with an equality (e.g. `list_pred(l, ?s0) &*& s0 == s`). This allows the core transformation to assume that output arguments are always existentially quantified.

### 4.4 Inductive data types

While spatial assertions and predicates are in some cases sufficient to prove memory safety, they are insufficient to prove full functional correctness for most programs. For instance, the `list_pred` predicate defined in the previous section specifies the size and memory footprint of a linked list, but does not say anything about its *contents*. VeriFast supports a rich specification language with inductive data types and fixpoint functions (i.e., primitive recursive functions) over them. The example below shows how such constructs can be used for specifying functional correctness properties.

```
induct ints = ints_nil() | ints_cons(int, ints);

pred list_pred(struct list* l; ints values) =
  l == 0 ?
    values == ints_nil()
  :
    l->value |-> ?v &*& l->next |-> ?n &*&
    list_pred(n, ?vs_tail) &*&
    values == ints_cons(v, vs_tail);

fixpoint int head(ints lst) {
  switch (lst) {
    case ints_nil(): return 0;
    case ints_cons(v, tail): return v;
  }
}

int get_first(struct list* l)
  req list_pred(l, ?values);
  ens list_pred(l, values) &*& res == head(lst);
{
  <implementation omitted>
}
```

The behavior of `get_first` is completely specified by its contract. Our transformation translates such inductive data type specifications into *tagged structures*, a known technique for implementing variant types in C. The code below shows the data structure definitions corresponding to `ints` and its two constructors.

```
struct ints { int tag; };
                                   struct ints_cons {
struct ints_nil {                    int tag;
  int tag;                           int _1;
  // No members                      struct ints* _2;
};                                 };
```

To prevent the context from tampering with instances of these data structures when the context is in control, the data must either be stored in the private memory section provided by the PMA, or be included in the module's footprint such that it's incorporated in the cryptographic checksum described in Section 4.2. We chose to store the data in the private memory section, which is faster than the checksum-based approach, but does require more private memory.

Besides these structure declarations, the transformation also generates an equality comparison function for each inductive data type. Finally, fixpoint function definitions are translated straightforwardly into equivalent C functions.

### 4.5 Function pointers

VeriFast allows programs using function pointers to be verified, by letting users associate contracts with *classes* of functions. The code below shows how a verified module can use a function pointer to call a function in the unverified part.

```
typedef
int int_func(int x);
  req true;
  ens result > 0;
```

```
void f(int_func* g, int x)
  req is_int_func(g);
  ens true;
{
  int y = g(x);
  <...>
}
```

The typedef on the left defines `int_func` as the class of functions that take an integer argument and return a strictly positive integer result. On the right, the function `f` takes a pointer `g` to such a function, applies it to a local variable `x` and stores the result in `y`. The contract for `g` is specified by the `is_int_func(g)` assertion in the precondition of `f`, which refers to the typedef on the left.

Our transformation handles function pointer calls almost the same way it handles regular calls. That is, an outcall stub is generated for each defined function pointer typedef, and the hardened module calls this outcall stub instead of calling corresponding function pointers directly. Function pointer outcall stubs take as an argument a pointer to the concrete function to call. For instance, for the example code above, the function pointer outcall stub would be:

```
static int _int_func(int_func* f, int x) {
  <calculate footprint hash>
  int result = f(x);
  <verify footprint hash, check postcondition>
  return result;
}
```

Indirect function calls from the context to the hardened module are also supported naturally. Since all functions of the functional part of the hardened module have been made `static`, the only publicly accessible functions of the module are those in the boundary checking part. The fully abstract compilation scheme uses the PMA's restriction on module entry points to ensure that only those public functions can be called from the context at runtime. Hence, the necessary runtime checks are performed whenever the unverified part calls the hardened module through a function pointer.

## 5. Example program

This section uses an example program to illustrate how the transformations described above affect the hardened module's footprint description. Figure 1 depicts the example program and the footprint at various execution points. Note that the program is an abstract example created to illustrate the footprint evolution under various control flow transitions, and is not intended to model any useful computation. The program consists of the verified functions `vf1`, `vf2` and `vf3`, and, in addition to the standard C library, two unverified functions `main` and `uvf`. The unverified function `uvf` is annotated with a separation logic contract, so it can be called from

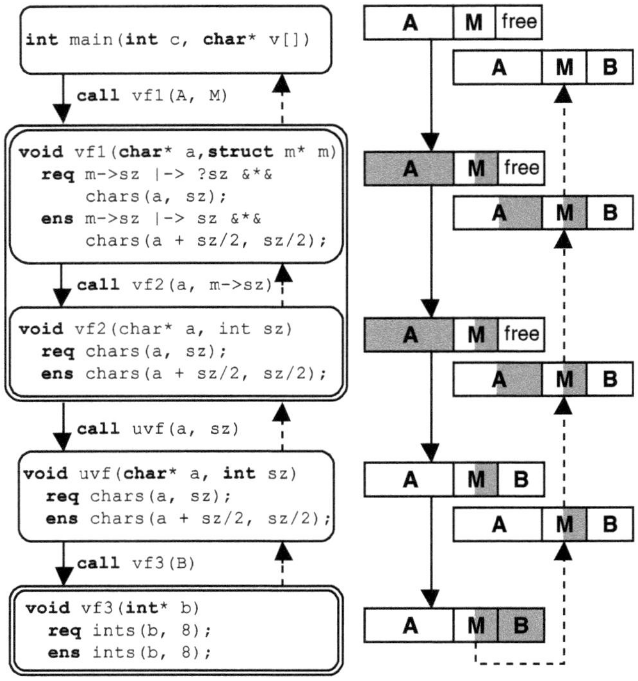


**Figure 1.** When executing the example program on the left, the footprint evolves as shown on the right. The single-bordered boxes on the left are unverified functions while the double-bordered boxes are verified functions. The boxes on the right represent the heap, with the grayed-out parts representing the hardened module's footprint. Solid lines are function calls and dashed lines are returns.

the verified functions. The function signatures and contracts shown in Figure 1 refer to a `struct m` and predicate `chars`, defined as:

```
struct m {
  int x; int sz;
};
```

```
pred chars(char *a, int sz) =
  sz <= 0 ? true :
  char(a) &*& chars(a+1, sz-1);
```

A `chars(a, sz)` instance represents a character array of size `sz`, starting at heap address `a`. The `char` predicate used by `chars` is a VeriFast primitive which asserts that its argument points to a valid character in memory. Its translation is a call to the `charp` data type checking function (similar to `intp` described in Section 4.2).

We now discuss how each of the function calls shown in Figure 1 affects the hardened module's footprint description. Assume `main` allocates an array `A` of `N` bytes and an instance `M` of `struct m`, using the standard (unverified) `malloc` function, and assigns the value `N` to `M`'s `sz` field. At this point, the heap contains `A` and `M` and the footprint description is empty. Next, `main` calls the verified function `vf1(A, M)`, and hence this function's entry stub will check whether its precondition holds. The precondition check consists of reading the `sz` field of `M` and verifying that `A` is in fact a character array of size `N`. As part of this check, the memory occupied by `M`'s `sz` field and the entire array `A` will be added to the footprint description. The memory occupied by `M`'s `x` field is not mentioned in `vf1`'s precondition and hence is not added to the footprint description.

Next, `vf1` calls `vf2(a, m->sz)` directly, without passing through a boundary checking function, because both caller and callee are in the hardened module. No runtime checks are performed and hence the footprint description remains the same.

The `vf2` function now makes an outcall `uvf(a, sz)`, which passes through the corresponding outcall stub. The stub first removes the array `A` from the footprint description, because it is referenced in `uvf`'s precondition, and then hashes the memory in the remaining footprint description (consisting of only the `sz` field of `M`), before calling `uvf`.

We assume `uvf` allocates an array `B` of eight integers, again using the standard `malloc` function, and then calls `vf3(B)`. This function's entry stub will verify that `B` is a valid array of eight integers and will add `B` to the footprint description. The `vf3` function now executes its (unspecified) body and then returns, thereby removing `B` from the footprint description, as specified by its postcondition.

Now `uvf` is back in control and returns to its outcall stub in the hardened module. The stub will first check that the memory in the footprint (still consisting of only `M`'s `sz` field) has not been modified, by recalculating the hash and comparing it to the original. Execution is aborted if any change is detected. If the new hash matches the original, the stub checks whether `uvf`'s postcondition holds and adds the second half of `A` back to the footprint description, as specified by `uvf`'s postcondition. The stub then returns control to `vf2`. Note that it is impossible that `vf2` now tries to access the first half of `A`, since this would have been detected by the static verifier when verifying `vf2`.

The `vf2` function now returns to `vf1`, without any change in the footprint description, because both functions are part of the hardened module. Finally, `vf1` returns to `main`, removing the second half of `A` and `M`'s `sz` field from the footprint description, as specified by `vf1`'s postcondition. Control is now back at the `main` function and the footprint description is empty.

# 6. Formalization

This section formalizes the transformations described in Section 4 and shows that they are *safe* and *precise*. Safety means that the hardened module does not fail, even when it is interacting with a context that does not uphold its contracts. Precision means that the hardened module behaves exactly like the original verified module when interacting with a context that *does* uphold its contracts. Focusing on the essentials of the transformation, we do not formalize inductive data types nor function pointers. Due to space constraints, we only give a high-level overview of the formalization here and leave the full text and proofs for our extended technical report [3].

## 6.1 Programming language

We first define a simple imperative programming language that models C. The syntax of this language is defined in Figure 2 and its operational semantics are described in Figure 3. We write $[\![e]\!]_s$ to indicate the value of an expression $e$ evaluated under a store $s$, assuming standard non-negative integer expression evaluation. In addition to standard imperative language constructs such as heap lookup, mutation, allocation and deallocation, the language provides two assertion commands. The first is **assert**$(b)$, which asserts that the boolean expression $b$ holds and the other is **alloced**$(l)$, which asserts that the memory address $l$ is allocated. Both commands evaluate to **skip** if the assertion succeeds and to **trap** otherwise. Trapping (as opposed to failing) is a clean way of indicating an abnormality: our runtime checks trap whenever they discover a bug in the context. Once a program traps, it remains in the trapped state forever (i.e., it diverges).

Program states $\Sigma \vdash \langle \overline{s}, h\rangle \mid c$ consist of a map $\Sigma$ from routine names to routine definitions, a stack $\overline{s}$, a heap $h$ and the program under execution $c$. The stack is a list of stores $s$, each of which is a partial function from $\mathit{Vars}$ to $\mathbb{N}^+$. The heap is a partial function from memory locations in $\mathbb{N}^+$ to values in $\mathbb{N}^+$. Execution starts from an empty store and heap.

We assume our programs are well-formed. That is, they never try to use a variable that was not defined earlier in the code, and they do not refer to undefined routines.

**Definition 1** (Failure). *We say a program $c$* fails *when it is stuck. For well-formed programs this corresponds to reading, writing or deallocating an unallocated memory location.*

Since we prove safety for *any* hardened module, absence of failure according to this definition also implies absence of assertion failures.

## 6.2 Separation logic

We define separation logic triples of the form $\Gamma \vdash \{P\}\ c\ \{Q\}$ and $\Delta \vDash \{P\}\ c\ \{Q\}$. Triples of the first form mean that the *static verifier* asserts that, given the function $\Gamma$ mapping routine names to contracts, if $P$ holds then $c$ will not fail and $Q$ will hold after executing $c$. The $\Gamma$ corresponds to the *prototypes* of the functions of the context (including their contracts). Triples of the latter form mean that if $P$ holds in some state (stack and heap), then *executing $c$ under the context $\Delta$* won't fail and $Q$ will hold in the resulting state. The $\Delta$ corresponds to a concrete context, in the form of a map from routine names to routine definitions.

Because the verifier is sound, $\Gamma \vdash \{P\}\ c\ \{Q\}$ implies $\Delta \vDash \{P\}\ c\ \{Q\}$, under the critical condition that *the routines of $\Delta$ uphold the contracts defined in $\Gamma$*. The essence of our formalization is to show that our program transformation will allow us to discard this critical condition. We are only concerned with partial correctness, so $c$ is allowed to diverge, which is what happens when our runtime checks trap (see Figure 3). The assertions $P$ and $Q$ are defined as:

$$P, Q ::= b \mid b\ ?\ P : Q \mid e \mapsto ?x \mid p(e, ?x) \mid y := e \mid P * Q \mid P \wedge Q \mid P \vee Q \mid \neg P \mid \top$$

where booleans $b$ and expressions $e$ are defined as in Figure 2, $p$ refers to a user-defined predicate **pred** $p(x, y) = a$ and $?x$ introduces a logic variable $x$. The first parameter of a user-defined predicate is an input parameter and the second is an output parameter. The assignment assertion $y := e$ is used to bind a value to predicate output parameters. The formal semantics of this assertion language are defined in Figure 4, where a judgment $s, h \vDash P \rightsquigarrow s'$ means that $P$ holds under store $s$ and heap $h$ and binds new logic variables (using $e \mapsto ?x$ and $p(e, ?x)$) to end up with the updated store $s'$.

## 6.3 Contract assertion language

Although assertions in our meta-theory range over the full language defined above, routine and predicate contracts come from a more restricted language of *precise* assertions.

$$a ::= b \mid b\ ?\ a : a \mid e \mapsto ?x \mid p(e, ?x) \mid y := e \mid a * a$$

In particular, routine and predicate assertions do not include standard conjunction, disjunction, negation nor top. Furthermore, we require user-defined predicates to constrain their output parameter to a single value (using the $y := e$ construct) exactly once on each possible execution path of their body. These requirements make existential quantification *constructive*: assertions indicate how each variable can be assigned a value, thereby avoiding an exhaustive search which would entail an enormous runtime performance cost.

While excluding disjunction, negation and non-separating conjunction between spatial predicates might seem to limit the expressiveness of the contract assertion language, this language subset corresponds exactly to the assertion languages supported by VeriFast [22], Smallfoot [6] and other separation logic-based program verifiers [8, 13]. Extensive experience with these tools has shown that this subset is sufficiently expressive for practical purposes [32].

In the rest of the text, we will consistently use symbols $P$ and $Q$ for meta-level assertions and symbol $a$ for contract assertions.

### 6.4 Transformations

In this section, we formalize the transformations described in Section 4. We start by defining a function $\mathsf{prod}(a)$ from assertions to commands that models the *production* of $a$ (see Section 4.2). The code generated by this function assumes there is a program variable `fp` containing a set of memory locations that represents the hardened module's current footprint. The generated code will (1) trap if $a$ does not hold or if its footprint would overlap with the footprint in `fp`, (2) create a program variable $x$ for each logic variable $?x$ in $a$ and (3) add the assertion's footprint to `fp`. The function is defined as follows.

$$\begin{aligned}\mathsf{prod}(y := e) &= (y := e)\\ \mathsf{prod}(b) &= \textbf{assert}(b)\\ \mathsf{prod}(b\ ?\ a_1 : a_2) &= \textbf{if } b \textbf{ then } \mathsf{prod}(a_1) \textbf{ else } \mathsf{prod}(a_2)\\ \mathsf{prod}(e \mapsto ?x) &= \begin{cases} x := e;\ x := \mathtt{in}(x, \mathtt{fp});\\ \textbf{assert}(x = 0);\ x := e;\ \textbf{alloced}(x);\\ \mathtt{fp} := \mathtt{add}(x, \mathtt{fp});\ x := [x]\end{cases}\end{aligned}$$

where `fp` is the program variable that stores the footprint, $\mathtt{in}(x, y)$ returns 1 if $x$ is in the list represented by $y$ and 0 otherwise, and $\mathtt{add}(x, y)$ adds $x$ to the list represented by $y$.

$$\mathsf{prod}(p(e, ?x)) = (x := e;\ \{\mathtt{fp}, x\} := prod_p(\mathtt{fp}, x))$$

where $prod_p$ implements the production part of the *predicate checking routine* for $p$, defined as **routine** $prod_p(\mathtt{fp}, x) = \mathsf{prod}(a)$; $\mathtt{res} := \{\mathtt{fp}, y\}$ with $a$ the body of **pred** $p(x, y)$. The $\{\mathtt{fp}, x\}$ is syntactic sugar for a tuple consisting of `fp` and $x$.

$$\mathsf{prod}(a_1 * a_2) = \mathsf{prod}(a_1); \mathsf{prod}(a_2)$$

Next we define the additional transformation functions required to safely perform *outcalls* from a hardened module to routines of the context that might not uphold their contract. We first define $\mathsf{cons}(a)$, a function that models the *consumption* of an assertion. As explained in Section 4.2, this function needs to be called right before making an outcall, to consume (remove) the footprint of the context function's precondition from the current footprint `fp`. The structure of $\mathsf{cons}(a)$ is identical to that of $\mathsf{prod}(a)$, but it has to *remove* $a$'s footprint instead of adding it. Furthermore, there is no need for $\mathsf{cons}(a)$ to check that $a$ actually holds, because the static verifier already ensured this when checking the verified module. Hence, we do not need to use the **assert** and **alloced** commands in the definition of $\mathsf{cons}()$. The function is defined as follows.

$$\begin{aligned}\mathsf{cons}(y := e) &= (y := e)\\ \mathsf{cons}(b) &= \textbf{skip}\\ \mathsf{cons}(b\ ?\ a_1 : a_2) &= \textbf{if } b \textbf{ then } \mathsf{cons}(a_1) \textbf{ else } \mathsf{cons}(a_2)\\ \mathsf{cons}(e \mapsto ?x) &= x := e;\ \mathtt{fp} := \mathtt{rem}(x, \mathtt{fp});\ x := [x]\end{aligned}$$

where $\mathtt{rem}(x, y)$ removes $x$ from the list represented by $y$.

$$\mathsf{cons}(p(e, ?x)) = (x := e;\ \{\mathtt{fp}, x\} := cons_p(\mathtt{fp}, x))$$

where $cons_p$ implements the consumption part of the *predicate checking routine* for $p$, defined as **routine** $cons_p(\mathtt{fp}, x) = \mathsf{cons}(a)$; $\mathtt{res} := \{\mathtt{fp}, y\}$ with $a$ the body of predicate **pred** $p(x, y)$

$$\mathsf{cons}(a_1 * a_2) = \mathsf{cons}(a_1); \mathsf{cons}(a_2)$$

Now we just need a function $\mathsf{harness}_\Gamma(r)$ that can generate outcall stubs for routines $r(\overline{x})$ of the context. This function takes a mapping $\Gamma$ from routines to contracts, corresponding to the prototypes of functions defined in the context. For $\Gamma(r) = (a_{pre}, a_{post})$, $\mathsf{harness}_\Gamma(r)$ is defined as:

$$\begin{aligned}&\textbf{routine } stub_r(fp, \overline{x}) =\\ &\quad \mathsf{cons}(a_{pre});\ s := \mathtt{snap}(fp);\\ &\quad res := r(\overline{x});\\ &\quad s' := \mathtt{snap}(fp);\ \textbf{assert}(s = s');\\ &\quad \mathsf{prod}(a_{post});\ res := \{fp,\ res\}\end{aligned}$$

where we assume all introduced variables are fresh and $\mathtt{snap}(x)$ returns a snapshot of the contents of the footprint $x$ (corresponding to calculating the hash of the footprint, as described in Section 4.2).

Finally, we can define the full transformation function $[c]_{\Gamma,a}$, using a helper function $[c]'_\Gamma$, as follows:

$$[x := r(\overline{x})]'_\Gamma = \{fp,\ x\} := stub_r(fp, \overline{x})$$

where $r$ is a routine of the context and $stub_r$ is the name of the outcall stub routine generated by $\mathsf{harness}_\Gamma(r)$

$$\begin{aligned}[c_1;\ c_2]'_\Gamma &= [c_1]'_\Gamma;\ [c_2]'_\Gamma\\ [\textbf{if } b \textbf{ then } c_1 \textbf{ else } c_2]'_\Gamma &= \textbf{if } b \textbf{ then } [c_1]'_\Gamma \textbf{ else } [c_2]'_\Gamma\\ [x := \textbf{alloc}]_\Gamma &= x := \textbf{alloc};\ \mathtt{fp} := \mathtt{add}(x, \mathtt{fp})\\ [\textbf{dealloc}(x)]_\Gamma &= \textbf{dealloc}(x);\ \mathtt{fp} := \mathtt{rem}(x, \mathtt{fp})\\ [c]'_\Gamma &= c \qquad \text{(for all other kinds of } c\text{)}\end{aligned}$$

The full transformation function $[c]_{\Gamma,a}$ then is

$$[c]_{\Gamma,a} = (\mathtt{fp} := \emptyset;\ \mathsf{prod}(a);\ [c]'_\Gamma)$$

### 6.5 Safety and precision

We now come to the two crucial properties our transformation must have: safety and precision.We only state the theorems here, but leave the full proofs for our extended technical report [3]. We first need a new definition before we can state these main theorems.

**Definition 2** (No-fail). *The function* $\mathsf{nofail}(\Delta)$ *returns a non-failing variant of the program* $\Delta$.

How nofail works is of no importance to our formalization, but one can see that the **alloced** command could be used to check each memory location before accessing it, thereby preventing failure.

The safety theorem states that if the context does not fail, but does not necessarily uphold its contracts either, then the hardened module will never fail.

**Theorem 1** (Safety). *For any command c, environment* $\Gamma$, *assertions* $a_{pre}$ *and* $a_{post}$ *such that* $\Gamma \vdash \{a_{pre}\}\ c\ \{a_{post}\}$, *and an arbitrary context* $\Delta$, *we have* $\mathsf{nofail}(\Delta) \vDash \{\top\}\ [c]_{\Gamma,a_{pre}}\ \{\top\}$.

Finally, our precision theorem states that our transformations do not change the expected behavior of the hardened module when the context upholds its contracts.

**Theorem 2** (Precision). *For any command c and assertions* $a_{pre}$ *and* $a_{post}$ *such that* $\Gamma \vdash \{a_{pre}\}\ c\ \{a_{post}\}$, *we have that* $\forall\Delta.\ \Delta \vDash \Gamma \Rightarrow \Delta \vDash \{a_{pre}\}\ [c]_{\Gamma,a_{pre}}\ \{a_{post}\}$.

The $\Delta \vDash \Gamma$ condition means that the context $\Delta$ upholds the contracts specified by $\Gamma$. Under standard separation logic, this means (amongst other conditions) that context functions cannot read outside the footprint specified by their precondition. However, our precision theorem can actually be slightly stronger than this, because the theorem holds even if the context is allowed to read outside its designated footprint, as argued in Section 4.2.

## 7. Prototype performance

We have implemented the transformations described in Section 4 as a source-to-source translator written in OCaml. This translator

$$e ::= n \mid x \mid e + e \mid e - e$$

$$c ::= x := e \mid x := [x] \mid [x] := x \mid x := r(\overline{x}) \mid \textbf{if } b \textbf{ then } c \textbf{ else } c \mid x := \textbf{alloc} \mid \textbf{dealloc}(x) \mid \textbf{assert}(b) \mid \textbf{alloced}(x) \mid \textbf{skip} \mid c; c$$

$$b ::= true \mid false \mid e = e \mid e < e \mid \neg b$$

$$l, n \in \mathbb{N}^+ \quad x, y, z \in Vars$$

$$Routine ::= \textbf{routine } r(\overline{x}) \ = c$$

$$Program := \mathcal{P}(Routine)$$

**Figure 2.** Syntax definition of our imperative language

$$E ::= \ \langle\,\rangle \mid E; c \qquad \text{Evaluation contexts}$$

$$\frac{}{\Sigma \vdash \langle \overline{s}, h \rangle \mid \textbf{trap} \to \Sigma \vdash \langle \overline{s}, h \rangle \mid \textbf{trap}}\ \text{trapLoop}$$

$$\frac{\overline{s} = s :: \overline{s_t} \qquad [\![e]\!]_s = n \qquad \overline{s'} = s[x \to n] :: \overline{s_t}}{\Sigma \vdash \langle \overline{s}, h \rangle \mid E[x := e] \to \Sigma \vdash \langle \overline{s'}, h \rangle \mid E[\textbf{skip}]}\ \text{varAssign}$$

$$\frac{}{\Sigma \vdash \langle \overline{s}, h \rangle \mid E[\textbf{skip}; c] \to \Sigma \vdash \langle \overline{s}, h \rangle \mid E[c]}\ \text{skip}$$

$$\frac{\overline{s} = s :: \overline{s_t} \qquad [\![e]\!]_s = true}{\Sigma \vdash \langle \overline{s}, h \rangle \mid E[\textbf{if } e \textbf{ then } c \textbf{ else } c'] \to \Sigma \vdash \langle \overline{s}, h \rangle \mid E[c]}\ \text{ifTrue}$$

$$\frac{\overline{s} = s :: \overline{s_t} \qquad [\![e]\!]_s = false}{\Sigma \vdash \langle \overline{s}, h \rangle \mid E[\textbf{if } e \textbf{ then } c \textbf{ else } c'] \to \Sigma \vdash \langle \overline{s}, h \rangle \mid E[c']}\ \text{ifFalse}$$

$$\frac{\overline{s} = s :: \overline{s_t} \qquad s(x') = l \qquad l \to n \in h \qquad \overline{s'} = s[x \to n] :: \overline{s_t}}{\Sigma \vdash \langle \overline{s}, h \rangle \mid E[x := [x']] \to \Sigma \vdash \langle \overline{s'}, h \rangle \mid E[\textbf{skip}]}\ \text{heapRead}$$

$$\frac{\overline{s} = s :: \overline{s_t} \qquad s(x) = l \qquad l \to n' \in h \qquad h' = h[l \to s(x')]}{\Sigma \vdash \langle \overline{s}, h \rangle \mid E[[x] := x'] \to \Sigma \vdash \langle \overline{s}, h' \rangle \mid E[\textbf{skip}]}\ \text{heapWrite}$$

$$\frac{\overline{s} = s :: \overline{s_t} \qquad s(\overline{y}) = \overline{n} \qquad \overline{s'} = \{\overline{x} \to \overline{n}\} :: \overline{s} \qquad \Sigma(r) = (\textbf{routine } r(\overline{x}) \ = c)}{\Sigma \vdash \langle \overline{s}, h \rangle \mid E[z := r(\overline{y})] \to \Sigma \vdash \langle \overline{s'}, h \rangle \mid E[c;\ z := \textbf{ret}]}\ \text{call}$$

$$\frac{\overline{s} = s :: s' :: \overline{s_t} \qquad \overline{s'} = s'[x \to s(\text{‘res’})] :: \overline{s_t}}{\Sigma \vdash \langle \overline{s}, h \rangle \mid E[x := \textbf{ret}] \to \Sigma \vdash \langle \overline{s'}, h \rangle \mid E[\textbf{skip}]}\ \text{return}$$

$$\frac{\overline{s} = s :: \overline{s_t} \qquad l \notin \{l' | l' \to n \in h\} \qquad \overline{s'} = s[x \to l] :: \overline{s} \qquad h' = h[l \to n']}{\Sigma \vdash \langle \overline{s}, h \rangle \mid E[x := \textbf{alloc}] \to \Sigma \vdash \langle \overline{s'}, h' \rangle \mid E[\textbf{skip}]}\ \text{alloc}$$

$$\frac{\overline{s} = s :: \overline{s_t} \qquad s(x) = l \qquad l \to n \in h \qquad h' = h \setminus \{l \to n\}}{\Sigma \vdash \langle \overline{s}, h \rangle \mid E[\textbf{dealloc}(x)] \to \Sigma \vdash \langle \overline{s}, h' \rangle \mid E[\textbf{skip}]}\ \text{dealloc}$$

$$\frac{\overline{s} = s :: \overline{s_t} \qquad [\![x]\!]_s = l \qquad l \mapsto n \in h}{\Sigma \vdash \langle \overline{s}, h \rangle \mid E[\textbf{alloced}(x)] \to \Sigma \vdash \langle \overline{s}, h \rangle \mid E[\textbf{skip}]}\ \text{allocedTrue}$$

$$\frac{\overline{s} = s :: \overline{s_t} \qquad [\![x]\!]_s = l \qquad l \mapsto n \notin h}{\Sigma \vdash \langle \overline{s}, h \rangle \mid E[\textbf{alloced}(x)] \to \Sigma \vdash \langle \overline{s}, h \rangle \mid \textbf{trap}}\ \text{allocedFalse}$$

$$\frac{\overline{s} = s :: \overline{s_t} \qquad [\![b]\!]_s = true}{\Sigma \vdash \langle \overline{s}, h \rangle \mid E[\textbf{assert } b] \to \Sigma \vdash \langle \overline{s}, h \rangle \mid E[\textbf{skip}]}\ \text{assertTrue}$$

$$\frac{\overline{s} = s :: \overline{s_t} \qquad [\![b]\!]_s = false}{\Sigma \vdash \langle \overline{s}, h \rangle \mid E[\textbf{assert } b] \to \Sigma \vdash \langle \overline{s}, h \rangle \mid \textbf{trap}}\ \text{assertFalse}$$

**Figure 3.** Small-step operational semantics of our imperative language

$$\frac{[\![b]\!]_s = true \qquad h = \emptyset}{s, h \vDash b \rightsquigarrow s}\ \text{pure}$$

$$\frac{[\![e]\!]_s = l \qquad h = \{l \to n\}}{s, h \vDash e \mapsto ?x \rightsquigarrow s[x \to n]}\ \text{pointsTo}$$

$$\frac{[\![b]\!]_s = true \qquad s, h \vDash P \rightsquigarrow s'}{s, h \vDash b\ ?\ P : Q \rightsquigarrow s'}\ \text{condTrue}$$

$$\frac{[\![b]\!]_s = false \qquad s, h \vDash Q \rightsquigarrow s'}{s, h \vDash b\ ?\ P : Q \rightsquigarrow s'}\ \text{condFalse}$$

$$\frac{\textbf{pred } p(x, y) = P \qquad [\![e]\!]_s = n \qquad \{x \to n\}, h \vDash P \rightsquigarrow s' \qquad m = s'(y)}{s, h \vDash p(e, ?z) \rightsquigarrow s[z \to m]}\ \text{predicate}$$

$$\frac{s, h_1 \vDash P \rightsquigarrow s' \qquad s', h_2 \vDash Q \rightsquigarrow s'' \qquad h_1 \perp h_2 \qquad h = h_1 \cup h_2}{s, h \vDash P * Q \rightsquigarrow s''}\ \text{sepConj}$$

Where $h_1 \perp h_2 \Leftrightarrow dom(h_1) \cap dom(h_2) = \emptyset$

$$\frac{s, h \vDash P \rightsquigarrow s'}{s, h \vDash P \vee Q \rightsquigarrow s'}\ \text{disjL} \qquad \frac{s, h \vDash Q \rightsquigarrow s'}{s, h \vDash P \vee Q \rightsquigarrow s'}\ \text{disjR}$$

$$\frac{s, h_1 \vDash P \rightsquigarrow s' \qquad s', h_2 \vDash Q \rightsquigarrow s'' \qquad h = h_1 = h_2}{s, h \vDash P \wedge Q \rightsquigarrow s''}\ \text{conj}$$

$$\frac{\textbf{pred } p(x, y) = P \qquad [\![e]\!]_s = n \qquad \{x \to n\}, h \vDash P \rightsquigarrow s' \qquad s(z) = s'(y)}{s, h \vDash p(e, z) \rightsquigarrow s}\ \text{concrPredicate}$$

$$\frac{[\![e]\!]_s = l \qquad h = \{l \to n\} \qquad s(x) = n}{s, h \vDash e \mapsto x \rightsquigarrow s}\ \text{concrPointsTo}$$

$$\frac{[\![e]\!]_s = n \qquad h = \emptyset}{s, h \vDash y := e \rightsquigarrow s[y \to n]}\ \text{assign} \qquad \frac{}{s, h \vDash \top \rightsquigarrow s}\ \text{top}$$

$$\frac{\neg \exists s' : s, h \vDash P \rightsquigarrow s'}{s, h \vDash \neg P \rightsquigarrow s}\ \text{negation} \qquad \frac{s, h \vDash P \rightsquigarrow s'}{s, h \vDash P}\ \text{assertion}$$

**Figure 4.** Semantics of our assertion language

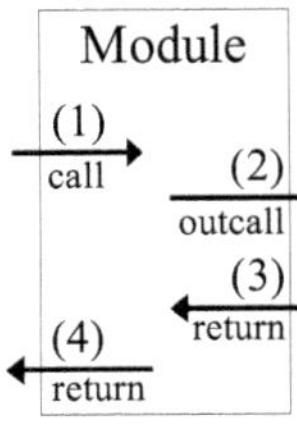


| | Check assertion validity | Add/remove assertion footprint | Hash module footprint |
|---|---|---|---|
| (1) | X (pre) | X | |
| (2) | | X | X |
| (3) | X (post) | X | X |
| (4) | | X | |

**Figure 5.** Actions performed for all types of boundary transitions.

takes as input a verified C module with VeriFast annotations (including annotated function prototypes for any function of the context called from the verified module), and outputs a hardened version of the module. The translator reuses significant parts of the existing VeriFast codebase, such as its lexer, parser and typechecker. Although VeriFast's license prevents us from releasing the source code at this time, a binary version of the translator is available online[1]. The translator has been approved by the POPL Artifact Evaluation Committee.

In the sections below, we describe the results of measuring the performance impact of the inserted runtime checks versus the verified module without any runtime checks. We ran micro and macro benchmarks on a standard desktop system, without a protected module architecture, in order to quantify the overhead of *just* the runtime checks, and we discuss the additional overhead introduced by a PMA in Section 7.3. All benchmarks were compiled with GCC 4.8.2, using optimization level 3, and were executed on a system with a 3.10 GHz Intel Core i5-2400 CPU with 8 GiB of RAM, running Ubuntu 14.04. The hash function used to calculate the hash over the footprint when performing an outcall is BLAKE2b [19].

### 7.1 Micro benchmarks

Since our transformations introduce checks at the *boundary* between the verified and unverified part, there will be a performance overhead when crossing the verified-unverified boundary. During a boundary check, up to three actions are performed: (1) checking whether the assertion (pre- or postcondition) holds, (2) adding or removing the assertion's footprint from the footprint description maintained by the module, and (3) hashing the memory in the module's footprint description. Figure 5 shows which actions are performed for each kind of boundary transition. We measured the contribution of each of these factors using two micro benchmarks based on simple data structures, similar to those used in [29].

The first micro benchmark is a verified module that takes as input a linked list of integers and sorts it using insertion sort. The second micro benchmark is another verified module that does an in-order traversal of a binary search tree to produce a sorted linked list. Both modules have been verified for memory safety (i.e., not for full functional correctness). The entry point signatures of these two modules are as follows.

```
struct list_node* insertion_sort(struct list_node* l);
  req list_pred(l);
  ens list_pred(result);

struct list_node* bst_to_list(struct bst_node* bst);
  req bst_pred(bst, ?v);
  ens bst_pred(bst, v) &*& list_pred(result);
```

Figure 6 shows the distribution of execution time over the different actions performed by the runtime checks for these benchmarks, for input lengths of $10^1$, $10^2$, $10^3$ and $10^4$ elements. The number

[1] https://distrinet.cs.kuleuven.be/software/sound-verification

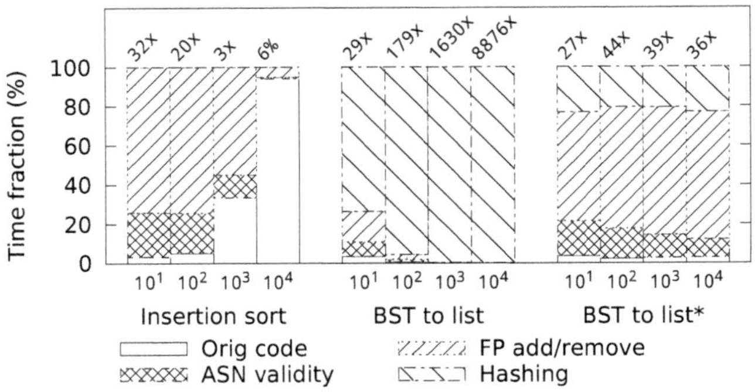


**Figure 6.** The execution time distribution over the different runtime checking actions for our micro benchmarks, for different input lengths. The numbers above the bars indicate the total execution time overhead in comparison to the unhardened code.

above each bar indicates the total overhead in comparison to the unhardened code.

The left bar chart shows that, for small input sizes, the insertion sort module spends significant time modifying the footprint description and checking assertion validity. As the input size increases however, the relative overhead due to these actions drops to the point where it becomes insignificant. This is because modifying the footprint and checking assertion validity are $\mathcal{O}(n)$ operations that are only performed when entering or exiting the module, and insertion sort is a $\mathcal{O}(n^2)$ algorithm. Hence, the time spent doing useful calculations inside the module increases faster than the time spent performing runtime checks. No time is spent on hashing, because the benchmark does not make any outcalls.

The middle bar chart shows that the BST module spends almost all of its time hashing its footprint, resulting in a huge performance overhead that increases with increasing input size. This is because the benchmark performs an outcall to `malloc` for each node of the input BST that it visits: the memory for the output list is allocated piece-by-piece while traversing the input. Because hashing the module footprint is an $\mathcal{O}(n)$ operation and it is performed $n$ times, we have an $\mathcal{O}(n^2)$ hashing overhead. Since the BST to list algorithm itself is only $\mathcal{O}(n)$, the hashing overhead quickly dominates the execution time. It is however possible to reduce the hashing overhead to $\mathcal{O}(n)$ by using a slightly modified algorithm that first calculates the size of input BST and then allocates memory for the entire output list with a single `malloc` call. This will cause the module footprint to be hashed only once, instead of $n$ times. The performance overhead of this algorithm is shown in the right bar chart of Figure 6. While the relative overhead is still significant, it now remains constant with increasing input size. This shows that the choice of boundary between verified and unverified code, and the number of times this boundary is crossed, can have a large impact on performance.

### 7.2 Macro benchmarks

While the micro benchmarks from Section 7.1 show how the execution time overhead is distributed over the different actions performed during a runtime check, they do not show the major advantage of our approach: the fact that there is no performance impact on code running completely in the verified or in the unverified part but not transitioning between the two. To show this effect and to assess the real-world feasibility of our approach, we have constructed three realistic macro benchmarks in which we verify and harden a small, security-critical part of an application, but leave the bulk of the application unverified. We measured both the execution time and memory overhead for these macro benchmarks.

### 7.2.1 Apache httpd modules

The first two macro benchmarks are modified Apache httpd authentication modules, which are used by the web server for verifying user credentials (for instance as part of HTTP Basic Authentication). The first Apache benchmark is based on the `mod_authn_anon` module, and uses a single pair of valid username/password credentials hardcoded in memory. The other benchmark is based on `mod_authn_file`, which reads the list of valid credentials from a file on disk. Both modules provide a single entry point function that takes client credentials (sent to the web server by the browser) as input and returns an integer indicating whether or not they are valid. The signatures of these functions are shown below.

```
int check_password_mem(char *u, char *p);
  req string(u, ?user) &*& string(p, ?pass);
  ens string(u, user) &*& string(p, pass) &*&
      result == 1 ?
        user == "username" &*& pass == "secret"
      :
        result == 0 ? true : result == 2;

int check_password_file(char *u, char *p);
  req string(u, ?user) &*& string(p, ?pass);
  ens string(u, user) &*& string(p, pass);
```

The modules' code consists mainly of a number of outcalls to various I/O and string processing functions of the standard library. In particular, the memory-based module performs 2 such outcalls per HTTP request, while the file-based module performs 34. As can be seen from the signatures above, the memory-based module has been verified for full functional correctness, while the file-based module has only been verified for memory safety, but this makes no difference at runtime. The path of the valid credentials file has been hardcoded in the source of the file-based module.

We set up the pre-forked version of Apache httpd 2.4.7 to serve the default WordPress 3.9.1 sample website with a MySQL 5.5.37 database backend. We used the Apache HTTP server benchmarking tool `ab` to measure the time required to perform 5,000 HTTP requests using 10 concurrent client threads. The client and server were executed on the same host to eliminate any network bottlenecks, and we made sure the web server did not use any form of credential caching. The memory overhead was measured by comparing the peak resident set size of the modules.

The first two rows of Table 1 show the results for the Apache benchmarks. The execution time overhead is low, averaging at 0.68% and 3.74% over three benchmarking runs for the memory-based and file-based module respectively. The memory overhead is also low, averaging at 0.08% and 6.60%. The difference in overhead between the two modules is due to the different number of outcalls they perform and because the file-based module needs a relatively large buffer for reading lines from the password file. This buffer is part of the module's footprint and hence needs to be described by the footprint description and hashed when making outcalls.

### 7.2.2 NetKit FTP daemon

The NetKit FTP daemon is an FTP daemon shipped with many current Linux distributions. It contains a `checkuser` function that is used to determine whether the names of users trying to log in appear in the `/etc/ftpusers` file of blocked users. We have verified this function and have moved it into a separate module, which we then hardened with our prototype translator. The signature of this function is shown below.

```
int checkuser(char *fname, char *name);
  req string(fname, ?fn) &*& string(name, ?n);
  ens string(fname, fn) &*& string(name, n);
```

The implementation of this function is quite similar to the `mod_authn_file` Apache module, performing 30 outcalls to various I/O and string processing functions per FTP session. The benchmark consists of performing 500 FTP sessions using 10 concurrent client threads, where each session consists of a user logging in, downloading a 1 KiB file and then disconnecting again.

The third row of Table 1 shows the results obtained by taking the average of three benchmarking runs. Both the execution time and memory overhead are again low, confirming our claim that real-world applications consisting mainly of unverified code plus a small hardened module, incur only a small performance overhead.

## 7.3 PMA overhead

As explained in Section 3, our runtime checks assume a control-flow safe execution model, which we propose to achieve using a fully abstract compilation [2, 31] of the hardened source code to a PMA. Since the micro and macro benchmarks described above were performed on a standard desktop system without a PMA, their results do not yet represent the overhead of our full end-to-end approach. While recent developments [20] indicate low-overhead hardware-based PMA platforms will be available for commodity desktop systems in the near future, the currently available PMAs for desktop systems are still in an experimental state, which prohibits us from running our benchmarks on top of them.

In order to still quantify the overhead of a fully abstract compiler and a PMA, we developed a benchmark to be run on Sancus [30], which is a fully-functional PMA for low-end networked microcontrollers. The Sancus prototype consists of a fully abstract compiler towards a small PMA-enabled 16-bit microcontroller (based on the TI MSP430) featuring 48 KiB of ROM and 10 KiB of RAM. The benchmark consists of a hardened module that provides a function for calculating the median of a linked list of integers, similar to the code example given in Section 2. The function's precondition asserts that the list is a valid non-empty linked list and its body performs three outcalls: one to copy the list, one to sort the copy and one to free the copy before returning. The hash function used for this benchmark was SHA-256. The results indicate the overhead of Sancus (both the compiler and the platform) is below 1%.

## 7.4 Reducing hashing overhead

The micro benchmarks show that considerable time can be spent hashing the module's footprint. One way of reducing this overhead is to do away with hashing and instead copy the entire module footprint contents to a secure location in memory (e.g., the PMA's private memory region) when making an outcall and to check the footprint against this copy on return. Experiments show that this gives a performance benefit of between 0% and 20% in comparison with hashing, but it obviously requires much more memory.

Another potential performance issue is that, as the verified codebase of an application grows, the size of the hardened module's footprint grows as well, which means more data must be hashed on each boundary transition. However, as the verified codebase grows, the part of the data that is used *exclusively* by the verified part of the application is likely to grow as well. Hence, this data can be placed in private memory, where it can be accessed only by the hardened module and hence need not be hashed on boundary transitions.

An interesting way to solve both issues is by taking advantage of hardware page protection support to reduce the amount of data needing to be hashed on boundary transitions. If an entire memory page is part of the module's footprint, it can be marked read-only in hardware before making an outcall and be reverted to read-write access on return. However, memory pages are typically at least 4 KiB in size, making this approach too coarse-grained to be used directly. A hybrid approach where pages that are completely in the footprint description are set read-only and the rest of the footprint is hashed or copied, is viable, but we consider it out of scope for this paper.

| | Execution time (s) | | | Peak resident set size (KiB) | | |
|---|---|---|---|---|---|---|
| | **unhardened** | **hardened** | **overhead** | **unhardened** | **hardened** | **overhead** |
| **mod_authn_anon** | 33.164 | 33.388 | 0.224 (0.68)% | 33,356 | 33,384 | 28 (0.08%) |
| **mod_authn_file** | 33.554 | 34.809 | 1.255 (3.74)% | 33,324 | 35,524 | 2,200 (6.60%) |
| **ftpd** | 23.193 | 23.242 | 0.049 (0.21)% | 952 | 976 | 24 (2.52%) |

**Table 1.** The macro benchmarks show a low real-world performance overhead in terms of execution time and memory consumption.

### 7.5 Summary

Our micro benchmarks show that the performance overhead of the runtime checks can be significant if there is little computation in- or outside the verified module, compared to the computation required for the boundary checks. Most of this overhead is due to hashing the module's footprint and adding/removing memory regions to/from the footprint description. Nevertheless, the macro benchmarks show that this overhead becomes negligible once more computation is performed in the unverified context. Hence, when developing modules to be verified and hardened, it is critical that the boundary between verified and unverified code is chosen wisely. That is, developers should try to minimize the number of verified/unverified boundary crosses in order to minimize the performance overhead. Although we could not run our full set of benchmarks on a PMA-enabled system, a separate benchmark performed on Sancus indicates the platform overhead is negligible. These results demonstrate the practical feasibility of our approach.

## 8. Related work

Separation logic-based formal verification ensures memory safety, which can be considered one of its main advantages for memory unsafe languages such as C. There are however many other notable solutions for making C memory safe, such as Safe-C [4], CCured [28] and Cyclone [23]. These systems rely on a combination of type system extensions, static analyses and runtime checks to ensure memory safety, but make no attempt at providing correctness guarantees beyond that. Furthermore, these solutions protect against input-providing attackers, while we protect against more powerful in-code attackers (i.e., attackers that have already gained the ability to execute code in the unverified part).

The idea that software modules should specify contracts in the form of pre- and post-conditions was popularized by Meyer [27] in the programming language Eiffel. Such contracts can then be checked statically or dynamically, and there is a huge amount of literature both on static and on dynamic checking of contracts. Some notable examples include the Java Modeling Language (JML) based tools [7], and .NET Contracts [5].

We rely on fully abstract secure compilation for providing a control-flow safe execution platform and ensuring the soundness of our runtime checks in the presence of code injection attacks. Full abstraction was pioneered by Abadi [1], and has recently been used as a basis for secure compilation to machine code [2, 31] and JavaScript [17]. A related approach is that of TS* [36], a gradually-typed subset of JavaScript that ensures type-safety even when interacting with an untrusted JavaScript context. Although the techniques used in TS* are different from our approach, this work shares our goal of providing a robust foundation for security-sensitive code, while still allowing interaction with an untrusted environment. In the remainder of this section, we limit our attention to the most relevant and closely related works.

Our approach combines modular static verification with runtime checking, to achieve a non-trivial soundness property in the context of an unsafe programming language. The approach is based on separation logic [33] so that there is a clear notion of memory ownership and we can compute the footprint (i.e., the owned region of memory) of a module and take a snapshot of that region's contents. For our implementation and experiments we have used the VeriFast [21, 22] separation logic-based assertion language and static program verification tool for C and Java. Other separation logic-based program verifiers include Smallfoot [6], JStar [13], HIP [9], and Space Invader/Infer [8]. Another notable modular static verification tool for C programs is VCC [10]. However, instead of separation logic, it uses a verification logic that is heavily based on ghost variables, so it is not clear how one would generate runtime checks for module specifications written in VCC's annotation language.

Runtime checking of separation logic assertions is known to be challenging because of the frame rule. A related approach is that of Nguyen et al. [29]. Although some of the techniques used in their approach are similar to ours (e.g., tracking footprints and splitting predicate parameters into input and output parameters), their objective is different from ours. Their runtime checker aims to stay as close to the standard separation logic semantics as possible, while our approach only aims to ensure that no failures can occur in verified code. We can hence allow unverified code to read arbitrary memory, which is not allowed under standard separation logic. Nguyen et al. use a heap coloring technique and runtime checks at every method invocation and field access in unverified code to check framing. This introduces a large performance overhead (on the order of $10,000\times$ if all necessary checks are done) that increases as the size of the unverified code grows. As shown in Section 7, the relative performance impact of our approach decreases with a larger unverified codebase. Also, since the implementation of Nguyen et al. needs to instrument unverified code, the entire codebase must be recompiled, whereas we only need access to the verified module. Finally, the implementation of Nguyen et al. is for Java, so they do not address the complications related to the lack of memory safety of C.

Another related approach is that of Yarra [34], in which runtime checks are used to protect C programs from non-control data attacks. Developers must annotate *critical data structures* with special type declarations, from which point on they should only access those data structures using those special types. In its *whole program protection mode*, runtime checks are inserted throughout the entire codebase to detect illegal accesses to the critical data structures, causing a large performance overhead. In its *library protection mode* however, only the memory accesses of a small core of the application (loosely corresponding to the verified module of our approach) are instrumented. Critical memory writes in the core are modified to maintain a shadow copy of critical objects on separate memory pages, which are made read-only using hardware page protections before calling untrusted code. Critical memory reads in the core are instrumented to check consistency of both copies, thereby detecting unauthorized writes to critical objects from untrusted code. The library protection mode is similar to how we enforce the separation logic frame rule, in the sense that critical regions of memory are integrity protected when calling untrusted code. Our solution provides stronger guarantees than Yarra, since we ensure validity of arbitrary separation logic assertions, instead of only data structure integrity. Also, Yarra does not prevent untrusted code from disabling the shadow page protections, making it vulnerable to code-injection attacks in the unprotected part. Finally, although the performance cost of Yarra's library protection mode is low, it grows with both the number of boundary crossings *and* the number of reads and writes to critical data in the core part of the application.

Kosmatov et al. [25] described the runtime checking of E-ACSL annotations for C programs, in the context of the Frama-C platform. E-ACSL is an executable subset of ACSL, a behavioral specification language for C programs. Both function contracts and in-body annotations can be specified and can be translated into runtime checks by the E-ACSL2C translator. In order to perform such runtime checks, each memory allocation, deallocation and variable assignment is instrumented to record information about the modified region of memory into a dedicated *data store*. This store hence contains a copy of the program's data and some meta data about it. The runtime pre, post and in-body annotation checks query the store in order to determine the annotations' validity. Although the approach mentions the use of static analyses to statically discard some of the runtime checks, there is no notion of a verified and an unverified part. Hence, the entire program must be instrumented for the checks to be sound and complete. This results in a high overall performance cost, ranging from 13× to 800×.

The problem of checking contracts at the boundary between statically checked modules and unchecked modules has also been studied extensively in higher-order programming languages. Findler and Felleisen pioneered this line of work and proposed higher-order contracts [15], which have been implemented in the Racket programming language [16]. The main challenge addressed is that of function values passed over the boundary. Compliance of such function values with their specified contract is generally undecidable. But it can be handled by wrapping the function with a wrapper that will check the contract of the function value at the point where the function is called. This is similar to how we handle function pointers: the corresponding contract is checked when the function is called. One concern that has received extensive attention is the proper assignment of *blame* once a contract violation is detected [12, 18]. While this line of research shares our goal of safely composing a statically checked module with an unchecked module, the issues of higher order contracts and blame assignment are largely orthogonal to the problems we address in this paper.

## 9. Conclusion

Separation logic-based verification of C code is a powerful technique for guaranteeing the absence of code failures. However, verifying large programs is difficult and requires significant expertise and developer effort. Modular verification tools support partial verification, where only the most critical modules are verified, and where over time more and more modules get verified. Unfortunately, this kind of partial verification gives only limited guarantees at runtime. Bugs in the unverified part of the program can also impact the state of the *verified* part, and hence might trigger failures in verified modules.

We have proposed a way to transform and compile partially verified programs such that the runtime guarantees are significantly better, without imposing severe performance penalties. After our code transformations, no failures can ever occur in the verified module; if a bug is triggered in the unverified part of the program, this is detected before it can impact the state or control flow of the verified module. This is useful for testing, as it detects bugs faster, and for security as it can guarantee verified properties of modules even in the presence of code injection attacks against the unverified part of the program.


## Acknowledgments

We thank Greta Yorsh and our anonymous reviewers for their valuable comments and suggestions that have improved the quality of this paper. This work has been supported in part by the Intel Lab's University Research Office, and by the Research Fund KU Leuven. Pieter Agten holds a PhD fellowship of the Research Foundation - Flanders (FWO).


## References


[1] M. Abadi. Protection in programming-language translations. In *Proceedings of the 25th International Colloquium on Automata, Languages and Programming*, ICALP '98, pages 868–883, London, UK, UK, 1998. Springer-Verlag. ISBN 3-540-64781-3.

[2] P. Agten, R. Strackx, B. Jacobs, and F. Piessens. Secure compilation to modern processors. In *Proceedings of the 2012 IEEE 25th Computer Security Foundations Symposium*, CSF '12, pages 171–185, Washington, DC, USA, 2012. IEEE Computer Society. ISBN 978-0-7695-4718-3. . URL `http://dx.doi.org/10.1109/CSF.2012.12`.

[3] P. Agten, B. Bart Jacobs, and F. Piessens. Sound modular verification of C code executing in an unverified context: extended version. Technical Report CW 676, KU Leuven, 2014. URL `http://www.cs.kuleuven.be/publicaties/rapporten/cw/CW676.abs.html`.

[4] T. M. Austin, S. E. Breach, and G. S. Sohi. Efficient detection of all pointer and array access errors. In *Proceedings of the ACM SIGPLAN 1994 Conference on Programming Language Design and Implementation*, PLDI '94, pages 290–301, New York, NY, USA, 1994. ACM. ISBN 0-89791-662-X. . URL `http://doi.acm.org/10.1145/178243.178446`.

[5] M. Barnett and W. Schulte. Runtime verification of .net contracts. *J. Syst. Softw.*, 65(3):199–208, Mar. 2003. ISSN 0164-1212. . URL `http://dx.doi.org/10.1016/S0164-1212(02)00041-9`.

[6] J. Berdine, C. Calcagno, and P. W. O'Hearn. Smallfoot: Modular automatic assertion checking with separation logic. In *Proceedings of the 4th International Conference on Formal Methods for Components and Objects*, FMCO'05, pages 115–137, Berlin, Heidelberg, 2006. Springer-Verlag. ISBN 3-540-36749-7, 978-3-540-36749-9. . URL `http://dx.doi.org/10.1007/11804192_6`.

[7] L. Burdy, Y. Cheon, D. R. Cok, M. D. Ernst, J. R. Kiniry, G. T. Leavens, K. R. M. Leino, and E. Poll. An overview of jml tools and applications. *Int. J. Softw. Tools Technol. Transf.*, 7(3):212–232, June 2005. ISSN 1433-2779. . URL `http://dx.doi.org/10.1007/s10009-004-0167-4`.

[8] C. Calcagno, D. Distefano, and V. Vafeiadis. Bi-abductive resource invariant synthesis. In *Proceedings of the 7th Asian Symposium on Programming Languages and Systems*, APLAS '09, pages 259–274, Berlin, Heidelberg, 2009. Springer-Verlag. ISBN 978-3-642-10671-2. . URL `http://dx.doi.org/10.1007/978-3-642-10672-9_19`.

[9] W.-N. Chin, C. David, H. H. Nguyen, and S. Qin. Automated verification of shape, size and bag properties via user-defined predicates in separation logic. *Sci. Comput. Program.*, 77(9):1006–1036, Aug. 2012. ISSN 0167-6423. . URL `http://dx.doi.org/10.1016/j.scico.2010.07.004`.

[10] E. Cohen, M. Dahlweid, M. Hillebrand, D. Leinenbach, M. Moskal, T. Santen, W. Schulte, and S. Tobies. Vcc: A practical system for verifying concurrent c. In *Proceedings of the 22nd International Conference on Theorem Proving in Higher Order Logics*, TPHOLs '09, pages 23–42, Berlin, Heidelberg, 2009. Springer-Verlag. ISBN 978-3-642-03358-2. . URL `http://dx.doi.org/10.1007/978-3-642-03359-9_2`.

[11] M. Dahlweid, M. Moskal, T. Santen, S. Tobies, and W. Schulte. Vcc: Contract-based modular verification of concurrent c. In *31st International Conference on Software Engineering, ICSE 2009*, pages 429–430, May 2009. .

[12] C. Dimoulas, R. B. Findler, C. Flanagan, and M. Felleisen. Correct blame for contracts: No more scapegoating. In *Proceedings of the 38th Annual ACM SIGPLAN-SIGACT Symposium on Principles of*

*Programming Languages*, POPL '11, pages 215–226, New York, NY, USA, 2011. ACM. ISBN 978-1-4503-0490-0. . URL `http://doi.acm.org/10.1145/1926385.1926410`.

[13] D. Distefano and M. J. Parkinson J. jstar: Towards practical verification for java. In *Proceedings of the 23rd ACM SIGPLAN Conference on Object-oriented Programming Systems Languages and Applications*, OOPSLA '08, pages 213–226, New York, NY, USA, 2008. ACM. ISBN 978-1-60558-215-3. . URL `http://doi.acm.org/10.1145/1449764.1449782`.

[14] U. Erlingsson. Low-level software security: Attacks and defenses. In A. Aldini and R. Gorrieri, editors, *Foundations of Security Analysis and Design IV*, pages 92–134. Springer-Verlag, Berlin, Heidelberg, 2007. ISBN 3-540-74809-1, 978-3-540-74809-0. URL `http://dl.acm.org/citation.cfm?id=1793914.1793919`.

[15] R. B. Findler and M. Felleisen. Contract soundness for object-oriented languages. In *Proceedings of the 16th ACM SIGPLAN Conference on Object-oriented Programming, Systems, Languages, and Applications*, OOPSLA '01, pages 1–15, New York, NY, USA, 2001. ACM. ISBN 1-58113-335-9. . URL `http://doi.acm.org/10.1145/504282.504283`.

[16] M. Flatt and PLT. Reference: Racket. Technical Report PLT-TR-2010-1, PLT Inc., 2010. `http://racket-lang.org/tr1/`.

[17] C. Fournet, N. Swamy, J. Chen, P.-E. Dagand, P.-Y. Strub, and B. Livshits. Fully abstract compilation to javascript. In *Proceedings of the 40th Annual ACM SIGPLAN-SIGACT Symposium on Principles of Programming Languages*, POPL '13, pages 371–384, New York, NY, USA, 2013. ACM. ISBN 978-1-4503-1832-7. . URL `http://doi.acm.org/10.1145/2429069.2429114`.

[18] M. Greenberg, B. C. Pierce, and S. Weirich. Contracts made manifest. In *Proceedings of the 37th Annual ACM SIGPLAN-SIGACT Symposium on Principles of Programming Languages*, POPL '10, pages 353–364, New York, NY, USA, 2010. ACM. ISBN 978-1-60558-479-9. . URL `http://doi.acm.org/10.1145/1706299.1706341`.

[19] J. Guo, P. Karpman, I. Nikolic, L. Wang, and S. Wu. Analysis of blake2. Cryptology ePrint Archive, Report 2013/467, 2013. `http://eprint.iacr.org/`.

[20] Intel Corporation. Intel software guard extensions, 2013. URL `http://software.intel.com/en-us/intel-isa-extensions#pid-19539-1495`.

[21] B. Jacobs and F. Piessens. Expressive modular fine-grained concurrency specification. In *Proceedings of the 38th Annual ACM SIGPLAN-SIGACT Symposium on Principles of Programming Languages*, POPL '11, pages 271–282, New York, NY, USA, 2011. ACM. ISBN 978-1-4503-0490-0. . URL `http://doi.acm.org/10.1145/1926385.1926417`.

[22] B. Jacobs, J. Smans, and F. Piessens. A quick tour of the verifast program verifier. In *Proceedings of the 8th Asian Conference on Programming Languages and Systems*, APLAS'10, 2010.

[23] T. Jim, J. G. Morrisett, D. Grossman, M. W. Hicks, J. Cheney, and Y. Wang. Cyclone: A safe dialect of c. In *Proceedings of the General Track of the Annual Conference on USENIX Annual Technical Conference*, ATEC '02, pages 275–288, Berkeley, CA, USA, 2002. USENIX Association. ISBN 1-880446-00-6. URL `http://dl.acm.org/citation.cfm?id=647057.713871`.

[24] G. Klein, K. Elphinstone, G. Heiser, J. Andronick, D. Cock, P. Derrin, D. Elkaduwe, K. Engelhardt, R. Kolanski, M. Norrish, T. Sewell, H. Tuch, and S. Winwood. sel4: Formal verification of an os kernel. In *Proceedings of the ACM SIGOPS 22nd Symposium on Operating Systems Principles*, SOSP '09, pages 207–220, New York, NY, USA, 2009. ACM. ISBN 978-1-60558-752-3. . URL `http://doi.acm.org/10.1145/1629575.1629596`.

[25] N. Kosmatov, G. Petiot, and J. Signoles. An optimized memory monitoring for runtime assertion checking of C programs. In *Runtime Verification - 4th International Conference, RV 2013, Rennes, France, September 24-27, 2013. Proceedings*, pages 167–182, 2013. . URL `http://dx.doi.org/10.1007/978-3-642-40787-1_10`.

[26] J. M. McCune, B. J. Parno, A. Perrig, M. K. Reiter, and H. Isozaki. Flicker: An execution infrastructure for tcb minimization. In *Proceedings of the 3rd ACM SIGOPS/EuroSys European Conference on Computer Systems 2008*, Eurosys '08, pages 315–328, New York, NY, USA, 2008. ACM. ISBN 978-1-60558-013-5. . URL `http://doi.acm.org/10.1145/1352592.1352625`.

[27] B. Meyer. Applying "design by contract". *Computer*, 25(10):40–51, Oct. 1992. ISSN 0018-9162. . URL `http://dx.doi.org/10.1109/2.161279`.

[28] G. C. Necula, S. McPeak, and W. Weimer. Ccured: Type-safe retrofitting of legacy code. In *Proceedings of the 29th ACM SIGPLAN-SIGACT Symposium on Principles of Programming Languages*, POPL '02, pages 128–139, New York, NY, USA, 2002. ACM. ISBN 1-58113-450-9. . URL `http://doi.acm.org/10.1145/503272.503286`.

[29] H. H. Nguyen, V. Kuncak, and W.-N. Chin. Runtime checking for separation logic. In *Proceedings of the 9th International Conference on Verification, Model Checking, and Abstract Interpretation*, VMCAI'08, pages 203–217, Berlin, Heidelberg, 2008. Springer-Verlag. ISBN 3-540-78162-5, 978-3-540-78162-2. URL `http://dl.acm.org/citation.cfm?id=1787526.1787545`.

[30] J. Noorman, P. Agten, W. Daniels, R. Strackx, A. Van Herrewege, C. Huygens, B. Preneel, I. Verbauwhede, and F. Piessens. Sancus: Low-cost trustworthy extensible networked devices with a zero-software trusted computing base. In *Proceedings of the 22nd USENIX Conference on Security*, SEC'13, pages 479–494, Berkeley, CA, USA, 2013. USENIX Association. ISBN 978-1-931971-03-4. URL `http://dl.acm.org/citation.cfm?id=2534766.2534808`.

[31] M. Patrignani, P. Agten, R. Strackx, B. Jacobs, D. Clarke, and F. Piessens. Secure compilation to protected module architectures. *ACM Transactions on Programming Languages and Systems (TOPLAS)*, accepted for publication in ACM TOPLAS.

[32] P. Philippaerts, J. T. Mühlberg, W. Penninckx, J. Smans, B. Jacobs, and F. Piessens. Software verification with VeriFast: Industrial case studies. *Science of Computer Programming*, 82(1):77–97, Mar. 2014. URL `https://lirias.kuleuven.be/handle/123456789/388689`.

[33] J. C. Reynolds. Separation logic: A logic for shared mutable data structures. In *Proceedings of the 17th Annual IEEE Symposium on Logic in Computer Science*, LICS '02, pages 55–74, Washington, DC, USA, 2002. IEEE Computer Society. ISBN 0-7695-1483-9. URL `http://dl.acm.org/citation.cfm?id=645683.664578`.

[34] C. Schlesinger, K. Pattabiraman, N. Swamy, D. Walker, and B. Zorn. Modular protections against non-control data attacks. In *Proceedings of the 2011 IEEE 24th Computer Security Foundations Symposium*, CSF '11, pages 131–145, Washington, DC, USA, 2011. IEEE Computer Society. ISBN 978-0-7695-4365-9. . URL `http://dx.doi.org/10.1109/CSF.2011.16`.

[35] R. Strackx and F. Piessens. Fides: Selectively hardening software application components against kernel-level or process-level malware. In *Proceedings of the 2012 ACM Conference on Computer and Communications Security*, CCS '12, pages 2–13, New York, NY, USA, 2012. ACM. ISBN 978-1-4503-1651-4. . URL `http://doi.acm.org/10.1145/2382196.2382200`.

[36] N. Swamy, C. Fournet, A. Rastogi, K. Bhargavan, J. Chen, P.-Y. Strub, and G. Bierman. Gradual typing embedded securely in javascript. In *Proceedings of the 41st ACM SIGPLAN-SIGACT Symposium on Principles of Programming Languages*, POPL '14, pages 425–437, New York, NY, USA, 2014. ACM. ISBN 978-1-4503-2544-8. .

[37] A. Vasudevan, S. Chaki, L. Jia, J. McCune, J. Newsome, and A. Datta. Design, implementation and verification of an extensible and modular hypervisor framework. In *Proceedings of the 2013 IEEE Symposium on Security and Privacy*, SP '13, pages 430–444, Washington, DC, USA, 2013. IEEE Computer Society. ISBN 978-0-7695-4977-4. . URL `http://dx.doi.org/10.1109/SP.2013.36`.

# Deep Specifications and Certified Abstraction Layers

Ronghui Gu  Jérémie Koenig  Tahina Ramananandro  Zhong Shao
Xiongnan (Newman) Wu  Shu-Chun Weng  Haozhong Zhang[†]  Yu Guo[†]

Yale University  [†]University of Science and Technology of China

## Abstract

Modern computer systems consist of a multitude of abstraction layers (e.g., OS kernels, hypervisors, device drivers, network protocols), each of which defines an interface that hides the implementation details of a particular set of functionality. Client programs built on top of each layer can be understood solely based on the interface, independent of the layer implementation. Despite their obvious importance, abstraction layers have mostly been treated as a system concept; they have almost never been formally specified or verified. This makes it difficult to establish strong correctness properties, and to scale program verification across multiple layers.

In this paper, we present a novel language-based account of abstraction layers and show that they correspond to a strong form of abstraction over a particularly rich class of specifications which we call *deep specifications*. Just as *data abstraction* in typed functional languages leads to the important *representation independence* property, abstraction over deep specification is characterized by an important *implementation independence* property: any two implementations of the same deep specification must have *contextually equivalent* behaviors. We present a new layer calculus showing how to formally specify, program, verify, and compose abstraction layers. We show how to instantiate the layer calculus in realistic programming languages such as C and assembly, and how to adapt the CompCert verified compiler to compile certified C layers such that they can be linked with assembly layers. Using these new languages and tools, we have successfully developed multiple certified OS kernels in the Coq proof assistant, the most realistic of which consists of 37 abstraction layers, took less than one person year to develop, and can boot a version of Linux as a guest.

***Categories and Subject Descriptors*** D.2.4 [*Software Engineering*]: Software/Program Verification—Correctness proofs, formal methods; D.3.3 [*Programming Languages*]: Languages Constructs and Features; D.3.4 [*Programming Languages*]: Processors—Compilers; D.4.5 [*Operating Systems*]: Reliability—Verification; D.4.7 [*Operating Systems*]: Organization and Design—Hierarchical design; F.3.1 [*Logics and Meanings of Programs*]: Specifying and Verifying and Reasoning about Programs

***Keywords*** Abstraction Layer; Modularity; Deep Specification; Program Verification; Certified OS Kernels; Certified Compilers.


*POPL '15*, January 15–17, 2015, Mumbai, India.

ACM 978-1-4503-3330-9/15/01...$15.00.
http://dx.doi.org/10.1145/2676726.2676975

## 1. Introduction

Modern hardware and software systems are constructed using a series of abstraction layers (e.g., circuits, microarchitecture, ISA architecture, device drivers, OS kernels, hypervisors, network protocols, web servers, and application APIs), each defining an interface that hides the implementation details of a particular set of functionality. Client programs built on top of each layer can be understood solely based on the interface, independent of the layer implementation. Two layer implementations of the same interface should behave in the same way in the context of any client code.

The power of abstraction layers lies in their use of a very rich class of specifications, which we will call *deep specifications* in this paper. A deep specification, in theory, is supposed to capture the precise functionality of the underlying implementation as well as the assumptions which the implementation might have about its client contexts. In practice, abstraction layers are almost never formally specified or verified; their interfaces are often only documented in natural languages, and thus cannot be rigorously checked or enforced. Nevertheless, even such informal instances of abstraction over deep specifications have already brought us huge benefits. Baldwin and Clark [1] attributed such use of abstraction, modularity, and layering as the key factor that drove the computer industry toward today's explosive levels of innovation and growth because *complex products can be built from smaller subsystems that can be designed independently yet function together as a whole*.

Abstraction and modularity have also been heavily studied in the programming language community [31, 30]. The focus there is on abstraction over "shallow" specifications. A module interface in existing languages cannot describe the full functionality of its underlying implementation, instead, it only describes type specifications, augmented sometimes with simple invariants. Abstraction over shallow specifications is highly desirable [24], but client programs cannot be understood from the interface alone—this makes modular verification of correctness properties impossible: verification of client programs must look beyond the interface and examine its underlying implementation, thus breaking the modularity.

Given the obvious importance, formalizing and verifying abstraction layers are highly desirable, but they pose many challenges:

- *Lack of a language-based model.* It is unclear how to model abstraction layers in a language-based setting and how they differ from regular software modules or components. Each layer seems to be defining a new "abstract machine;" it may take an existing set of mechanisms (e.g., states and functions) at the layer below and expose a different view of the same mechanisms. For example, a virtual memory management layer—built on top of a physical memory layer— would expose to clients a different view of the memory, now accessed through virtual addresses.
- *Lack of good language support.* Programming an abstraction layer formally, by its very nature, would require two languages: one for writing the layer implementation (which, given the low-

level nature of many layers, often means a language like C or assembly); another for writing the formal layer specification (which, given the need to precisely specify full functionality, often means a rich formal logic). It is unclear how to fit these two different languages into a single setting. Indeed, many existing formal specification languages [34, 18, 16] are capable of building accurate *models* with rich specifications, but they are not concerned with connecting to the actual running code.

- *Lack of compiler and linking support.* Abstraction layers are often deployed in binary or assembly. Even if we can verify a layer implementation written in C, it is unclear how to compile it into assembly and link it with other assembly layers. The CompCert verified compiler [19] can only prove the correctness of compilation for whole programs, not individual modules or layers. Linking C with assembly adds a new challenge since they may have different memory layouts and calling conventions.

In this paper, we present a formal study of abstraction layers that tackles all these challenges. We define a *certified abstraction layer* as a triple $(L_1, M, L_2)$ plus a mechanized proof object showing that the layer implementation $M$, built on top of the interface $L_1$ (the *underlay*), indeed faithfully *implements* the desirable interface $L_2$ above (the *overlay*). Here, the *implements* relation is often defined as some *simulation* relation [22]. A certified layer can be viewed as a "parameterized module" (from interfaces $L_1$ to $L_2$), *a la* an SML functor [23]; but it enforces a stronger contextual correctness property: a correct layer is like a "certified compiler," capable of converting any *safe* client program running on top of $L_2$ into one that has the same behavior but runs on top of $L_1$ (e.g., by "compiling" abstract primitives in $L_2$ into their implementation in $M$).

A regular software module $M$ (built on top of $L_1$) with interface $L_2$ may not enjoy such a property because its client may invoke another module $M'$ which shares some states with $M$ but imposes different state invariants from those assumed by $L_2$. An abstraction layer does not allow such a client, instead, such $M'$ must be either built on top of $L_2$ (thus respecting the invariants in $L_2$), or below $L_2$ (in which case, $L_2$ itself must be changed).

Our paper makes the following new contributions:

- We present the first language-based account of certified abstraction layers and show how they correspond to a *rigorous* form of abstraction over deep specifications used widely in the system community. A certified layer interface describes not only the precise functionality of any underlying implementation but also clear assumptions about its client contexts. Abstraction over deep specifications leads to the powerful *implementation independence* property (see Sec. 2): any two implementations of the same layer interface have contextually equivalent behaviors.
- We present a new layer calculus showing how to formally specify, program, verify, and compose certified abstraction layers (see Sec. 3). Such a layer language plays a similar role as the module language in SML [23], but its interface checking is not just typechecking or signature matching; instead, it requires formal verification of the *implements* relation in a proof assistant.
- We have instantiated the layer calculus on top of two core languages (see Sec. 4 and 5): **ClightX**, a variant of the CompCert Clight language [5]; and **LAsm**, an x86 assembly language. Both ClightX and LAsm can be used to program certified abstraction layers. We use the Coq logic [35] to develop all the layer interfaces. Each ClightX or LAsm layer is parameterized over its underlay interface, implemented using CompCert's external call mechanisms. We developed new tools and tactic libraries to help automate the verification of the *implements* relation.
- We have also modified CompCert to build a new verified compiler, **CompCertX**, that can compile ClightX abstraction layers into LAsm layers (see Sec. 6). CompCertX is novel because it can prove a stronger correctness theorem for compiling individual functions in each layer—such a theorem requires reasoning about *memory injection* [21] between the memory states of the source and target languages. To support linking between ClightX and LAsm layers, we show how to design the *implements* relation so that it is stable over memory injection.
- Using these new languages and tools, we have successfully constructed several feature-rich certified OS kernels in Coq (see Sec. 7). A certified kernel $(L_{x86}, K, L_{ker})$ is a verified LAsm implementation $K$, built on top of $L_{x86}$, and it *implements* the set of system calls as specified in $L_{ker}$. The correctness of the kernel guarantees that if a user program $P$ runs *safely* on top of $L_{ker}$, running the version of $P$ linked with the kernel $K$ on $L_{x86}$ will produce the same behavior. All our certified kernels are built by composing a collection of smaller layers. The most realistic kernel consists of 37 layers, took less than one person year to develop, and can boot a version of Linux as a guest.

The *POPL Artifact Evaluation Committee* reviewed the full artifact of our entire effort, including ClightX and LAsm, the CompCertX compiler, and the implementation of all certified kernels with Coq proofs. The reviewers unanimously stated that our implementation *exceeded their expectations.* Additional details about our work can be found in the companion technical report [13].

## 2. Why abstraction layers?

In this section, we describe the main ideas behind deep specifications and show why they work more naturally with abstraction layers than with regular software modules.

### 2.1 Shallow vs. deep specifications

We introduce shallow and deep specifications to describe different classes of requirements on software and hardware components. Type information and program contracts are examples of "shallow" specifications. Type-based module interfaces (e.g., ML signatures) are introduced to support compositional static type checking and separate compilation: a module $M$ can be typechecked based on its import interface $L_1$ (without looking at $L_1$'s implementation), and shown to have types specified in its export interface $L_2$.

To support compositional verification of strong functional correctness properties on a large system, we would hope that all of its components are given "deep" specifications. A module $M$ will be verified based on its import interface $L_1$ (without looking at $L_1$'s implementation), and shown to *implement* its export interface $L_2$.

To achieve true modularity, we would like to reason about the behaviors of $M$ **solely** based on its import interface $L_1$; and we would also like its export interface $L_2$ to describe the full functionality of $M$ while omitting the implementation details.

More formally, a deep specification captures everything we want to know about any of its implementations—it must satisfy the following important "implementation independence" property:

> **Implementation independence:** *Any two implementations (e.g., $M_1$ and $M_2$) of the same deep specification (e.g., $L$) should have* contextually equivalent *behaviors.*

Different languages may define such contextual equivalence relation differently, but regardless, we want that, given any *whole-program* client $P$ built on top of $L$, running $P \oplus M_1$ (i.e., $P$ linked with $M_1$) should lead to the same observable result as running $P \oplus M_2$.

Without implementation independence, running $P \oplus M_1$ and $P \oplus M_2$ may yield different observable results, so we can prove a specific whole-program property that holds on $P \oplus M_1$ but not on $P \oplus M_2$—such whole-program property cannot be proved based on the program $P$ and the specification $L$ alone.

```
typedef enum {
  TD_READY, TD_RUN,
  TD_SLEEP, TD_DEAD
} td_state;

struct tcb {
  td_state tds;
  struct tcb *prev, *next;
};

struct tdq {
  struct tcb *head, *tail;
};
// ν_tcbp and ν_tdqp
struct tcb tcbp[64];
struct tdq tdqp[64];
// κ_dequeue
struct tcb *
dequeue(struct tdq *q){
  struct tcb *head,*next;
  struct tcb *pid=null;
  if(q == null)
    return pid;
  else {
    head = q -> head;
    if (head == null)
     return pid;
    else {
     pid = head;
     next = head -> next;
     if(next == null) {
      q -> head = null;
      q -> tail = null;
     } else {
      next -> prev = null;
      q -> head = next;
     }
    }
  }
  return pid;
} ...
```

```
Inductive td_state :=
| TD_READY | TD_RUN
| TD_SLEEP | TD_DEAD.


Inductive tcb :=
| TCBUndef
| TCBV (tds: td_state)
       (prev next: Z)

Inductive tdq :=
| TDQUndef
| TDQV (head tail: Z)

Record abs:={tcbp:ZMap.t tcb;
             tdqp:ZMap.t tdq}

Function σ̂_dequeue a i :=
match (a.tdqp i) with
|TDQUndef => None
|TDQV h t =>
 if zeq h 0 then
  Some (a, 0)
 else
 match a.tcbp h with
 |TCBUndef => None
 |TCBV _ _ n =>
  if zeq n 0 then
  let q':=(TDQV 0 0) in
   Some (set_tdq a i q', h)
  else
  match a.tcbp n with
  |TCBUndef => None
  |TCBV s' _ n' =>
   let q':=(TDQV n t) in
   let a':=set_tdq a i q' in
   let b:=(TCBV s' 0 n') in
    Some (set_tcb a' n b, h)
  end
 end
end ...
```

**Figure 1.** Concrete (in C) vs. abstract (in Coq) thread queues

```
Definition tcb := td_state.

Definition tdq := List Z.

Record abs':={tcbp:ZMap.t tcb;
              tdqp:ZMap.t tdq}
```

```
Function σ̂'_dequeue a i :=
match (a.tdqp i) with
| h :: q' =>
  Some(set_tdq a i q', h)
| nil => None
end ......
```

**Figure 2.** A more abstract queue (in Coq)

Hoare-style partial correctness specifications are rarely deep specifications since they fail to satisfy implementation independence. Given two implementations of a partial correctness specification for a factorial function, one can return the correct factorial number and another can just go into infinite loop. A program built on top of such specification may not be reasoned about based on the specification alone, instead, we have to peek into the actual implementation in order to prove certain properties (e.g., termination).

In the rest of this paper, following CompCert [20], we will focus on languages whose semantics are *deterministic* relative to external events (formally, these languages are defined as both *receptive* and *determinate* [33] and they support external nondeterminism such as I/O and concurrency by making events explicit in the execution traces). Likewise, we only consider interfaces whose primitives have deterministic specifications. If $L$ is a deterministic interface, and both $M_1$ and $M_2$ implement $L$, then $P \oplus M_1$ and $P \oplus M_2$ should have identical behaviors since they both follow the semantics of running $P$ over $L$, which is deterministic. Deterministic specifications are thus also deep specifications.

Deep specifications can, of course, also be nondeterministic. They may contain resource bounds [6], numerical uncertainties [7], etc. Such nondeterminism should be unobservable in the semantics of a *whole* program, allowing implementation independence to still hold. We leave the investigation of nondeterministic deep specifications as future work.

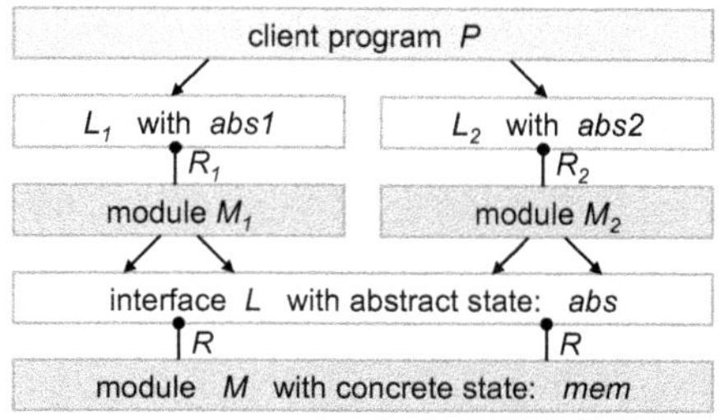


**Figure 3.** Client code with conflicting abstract states?

## 2.2 Layers vs. modules

When a module (or a software component) implements an interface with a shallow specification, we often hide its private memory state completely from its client code. In doing so, we can guarantee that the client cannot possibly break any invariants imposed on the private state in the module implementation.

If a module implements an interface with a deep specification, we would still hide the private memory state from its client, but we also need to introduce an *abstract state* to specify the full functionality of each primitive in the interface.

For example, Fig. 1 shows the implementation of a concrete thread queue module (in C) and its interface with a deep specification (in Coq). The local state of the C implementation consists of 64 thread queues (tdqp) and 64 thread control blocks (tcbp). Each thread control block consists of the thread state, and a pair of pointers (prev and next) indicating which linked-list queue it belongs to. The dequeue function takes a pointer to a queue; it returns the head block if the queue is not empty, or null if the queue is empty.

In the Coq specification (Fig. 1 right; we omitted some invariants to make it more readable), we introduce an abstract state of type abs where we represent each C array as a Coq finite map (ZMap.t), and each pointer as an integer index (Z) to the tdq or tcb array. The dequeue primitive $\hat{\sigma}_{\text{dequeue}}$ is a mathematical function of type abs $\rightarrow$ Z $\rightarrow$ option (abs $\times$ Z); when the function returns None, it means that the abstract primitive faults. This dequeue specification is intentionally made very similar to the C function, so we can easily show that the C module indeed *implements* the specification.

We define that a module implements a specification if there is a *forward simulation* [22] from the module implementation to its specification. In the context of determinate and receptive languages [33, 20], if the specification is also deterministic, it is sufficient to find a forward simulation from the specification to its implementation (this is often easier to prove in practice).

In the rest of this paper, following CompCert, we often call the forward simulation from the implementation to its specification as *upward (forward) simulation* and the one from the specification to its implementation as *downward (forward) simulation*.

Fig. 2 shows a more abstract specification of the same queue implementation where the new abstract state abs' omits the prev and next links in tcb and treats each queue simply as a Coq list. The dequeue specification $\hat{\sigma}'_{\text{dequeue}}$ is now even simpler, which makes it easier to reason about its client, but it is now harder to prove that the C module implements this more abstract specification. This explains why we often introduce less abstract specifications (e.g., the one in Fig. 1) as intermediate steps, so a complex abstraction can be decomposed into several more tractable abstraction steps.

Deep specification brings out an interesting **new challenge** shown in Fig. 3: *what if a program $P$ attempts to call primitives defined in two different interfaces $L_1$ and $L_2$, which may export two* *conflicting views (i.e., abstract states* abs1 *and* abs2*) of the same abstract state* abs *(thus also the same concrete memory state* mem*)?*

Here we assume that modules $M, M_1, M_2$ implement interfaces $L, L_1, L_2$ via some simulation relations $R, R_1, R_2$ (lines marked with a dot on one end) respectively. Clearly, calling primitives in $L_2$ may violate the invariants imposed in $L_1$, and vice versa, so $L_1$ and $L_2$ are breaking each other's abstraction when we run $P$. In fact, even without $M_2$ and $L_2$, if we allow $P$ to directly call primitives in $L$, similar violation of $L_1$ invariants can also occur.

This means that we must prohibit client programs such as $P$ above, and each deep specification must state the clear assumptions about its valid client contexts. Each interface should come with a single abstract state (abs) used by its primitives; and its client can only access the same abs throughout its execution.

This is what *abstraction layers* are designed for and why they are more compositional (with respect to deep specification) than regular modules! Layers are introduced to limit interaction among different modules: only modules with identical state views (i.e., $R_1, R_2$ and abs1, abs2 must be identical) can be composed horizontally.

A layer interface seems to be defining a new "abstract machine" because it only supports client programs with a particular view of the memory state. The correctness of a certified layer implementation allows us to transfer formal reasoning (of client programs) on one abstract machine (the overlay) to another (the underlay).

Programming with certified abstraction layers enables a disciplined way of composing a large number of components in a complex system. Without using layers, we may have to consider arbitrary module interaction or dependencies: an invariant held in one function can be easily broken when it calls a function defined in another module. A layered approach aims to sort and isolate all components based on a carefully designed set of abstraction levels so we can reason about one small abstraction step at a time and eliminate most unwanted interaction and dependencies.

## 3. A calculus of abstraction layers

***Motivation*** A user of an abstraction layer $(L_1, M, L_2)$ wants to know that its implementation $M$ (on top of the underlay interface $L_1$) can be used to run any program $P$ written against the overlay interface $L_2$. If we consider $L_1, L_2$ as abstract machines and $M$ as a program transformation (which transforms a program $P$ into $M(P)$), then for some notion of refinement $\sqsubseteq$, this property can be stated as $\forall P \,.\, M(P)@L_1 \sqsubseteq P@L_2$, meaning that the behavior of $M(P)$ executing on top of the underlay specification $L_1$ refines that of the program $P$ executing on top of the overlay specification $L_2$.

This view of abstraction layers captures a wide variety of situations. Furthermore, two layers $(L_1, M, L_2)$ and $(L_2, N, L_3)$ can be composed as $(L_1, M \circ N, L_3)$, and the correctness of the layer implementation $M \circ N$ follows from that of $M$ and $N$.

However, the layer interfaces are often not arbitrary abstract machines, but simply instances of a base language, specialized to provide layer-specific primitives and abstract state. The implementation is not an arbitrary transformation, but instead consists of some library code to be linked with the client program. In order to prove this transformation correct, we will verify the implementation of each primitive separately, and then use these proofs in conjunction with a general template for the instrumented language.

Abstract machines and program transformations are too general to capture this redundant structure. The layer calculus presented in this section provides fine-grained notions of layer interfaces and implementations. It allows us to describe what varies from one layer to the next and to assemble such layers in a generic way.

### 3.1 Prerequisites

To keep the formalism general and simple, we initially take the syntax and behavior of the programs under consideration to be abstract parameters. Specifically, in the remainder of this section we will assume that the following are given:

- a set of identifiers $i \in \mathbb{I}$ which will be used to name variables, functions, and primitives (e.g., dequeue and tcbp in Fig. 1);
- sets of function definitions $\kappa \in \mathrm{K}$, and variable definitions $\nu \in \mathrm{T}$, as specified by the language (e.g., $\kappa_{\mathsf{dequeue}}$ and $\nu_{\mathsf{tcbp}}$ in Fig. 1);
- a set of behaviors $\sigma \in \Sigma$ for the individual primitives of layers, and the individual functions of programs (e.g., the step relation $\sigma_{\mathsf{dequeue}}$ derived from the Coq function $\hat{\sigma}_{\mathsf{dequeue}}$ in Fig. 1).

More examples can be found in Sec. 4.

We also need to define how the behaviors refine one another. This is particularly important because our layer interfaces bundle primitive specifications, and because a relation between layer interfaces is defined pointwise over these primitives. Ultimately, we wish to use these fine-grained layers and refinements to build complete abstract machines and whole-machine simulations. This can only be done if the refinements of individual primitives are consistent; for example, if they are given in terms of the same simulation relation.

Hence, we index behavior refinement by the elements of a partial monoid $(\mathbb{R}, \circ, \mathbf{id})$. We will refer to the elements $R \in \mathbb{R}$ of this monoid as *simulation relations*. However, note that at this stage, the elements of $\mathbb{R}$ are entirely abstract, and we require only that the composition operator $\circ$ and identity element $\mathbf{id}$ satisfy the monoid laws $R \circ (S \circ T) = (R \circ S) \circ T$ and $R \circ \mathbf{id} = \mathbf{id} \circ R = R$.

Finally, we need to interpret these abstract simulation relations as refinement relations between behaviors. That is, for each $R \in \mathbb{R}$, we require a relation $\leqslant_R$ on $\Sigma$. For instance, if the behaviors $\sigma_1, \sigma_2 \in \Sigma$ are taken to be step relations over some sets of states, $\sigma_1 \leqslant_R \sigma_2$ may be interpreted as the following simulation diagram:

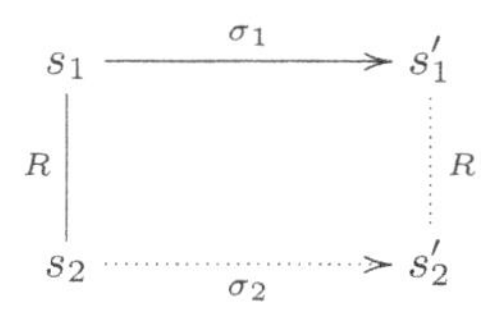


That is, whenever two states $s_1, s_2$ are related by $R$ in some sense, and $\sigma_1$ takes $s_1$ to $s_1'$ in one step, then there exists $s_2'$ such that $\sigma_2$ takes $s_2$ to $s_2'$ in zero or more steps, and $s_2'$ and $s_1'$ are also related by $R$. The relations $\leqslant_{-}$ should respect the monoid structure of $\mathbb{R}$, so that for any $\sigma \in \Sigma$ we have $\sigma \leqslant_{\mathbf{id}} \sigma$, and so that whenever $R, S \in \mathbb{R}$ and $\sigma_1, \sigma_2, \sigma_3 \in \Sigma$ such that $\sigma_1 \leqslant_R \sigma_2$ and $\sigma_2 \leqslant_S \sigma_3$, it should be the case that $\sigma_1 \leqslant_{S \circ R} \sigma_3$.

### 3.2 Layer interfaces and modules

The syntax of the calculus is defined as follows:

$$L ::= \varnothing \mid i \mapsto \sigma \mid i \mapsto \nu \mid L_1 \oplus L_2$$
$$M ::= \varnothing \mid i \mapsto \kappa \mid i \mapsto \nu \mid M_1 \oplus M_2$$

The layer interfaces $L$ and modules $M$ are essentially finite maps; constructions of the form $i \mapsto \_$ are elementary single-binding objects, and $\oplus$ computes the union of two layers or modules. This is illustrated by the proof-of-concept interpretation given in the companion technical report [13]. For example, the thread queue module, shown in Fig. 1, can be defined as $M_{\mathsf{thread\_queue}} := \mathsf{tcbp} \mapsto \nu_{\mathsf{tcbp}} \oplus \mathsf{tdqp} \mapsto \nu_{\mathsf{tdqp}} \oplus \mathsf{dequeue} \mapsto \kappa_{\mathsf{dequeue}}$, while the overlay interface can be defined as $L_{\mathsf{thread\_queue}} := \mathsf{dequeue} \mapsto \sigma_{\mathsf{dequeue}}$.

The rules are presented in Fig. 4. The inclusion preorder defined on modules corresponds to the intuition that when $M \subseteq N$, any definition present in $M$ must be present in $N$ as well. The composition operator $\oplus$ behaves like a join operator. However, while $M \oplus N$ is an upper bound of $M$ and $N$, we do not require it to be the *least* upper bound. The order on layer interfaces extends the

$\boxed{M_1 \subseteq M_2}$

$$M \subseteq M \qquad \text{MLE-REFL}$$
$$\varnothing \subseteq M \qquad \text{MLE-EMPTY}$$
$$M \oplus \varnothing \subseteq M \qquad \text{MLE-ID-RIGHT}$$
$$(M_1 \oplus M_2) \oplus M_3 \subseteq M_1 \oplus (M_2 \oplus M_3) \qquad \text{MLE-ASSOC}$$
$$M_2 \oplus M_1 \subseteq M_1 \oplus M_2 \qquad \text{MLE-COMM}$$
$$M_1 \subseteq M_1 \oplus M_2 \qquad \text{MLE-UB-LEFT}$$
$$M_1 \subseteq M_2 \wedge M_2 \subseteq M_3 \Rightarrow M_1 \subseteq M_3 \qquad \text{MLE-TRANS}$$
$$M_1 \subseteq M_1' \wedge M_2 \subseteq M_2' \Rightarrow M_1 \oplus M_2 \subseteq M_1' \oplus M_2' \qquad \text{MLE-MON}$$

$\boxed{L_1 \leqslant_R L_2}$

$$L \leqslant_{\mathsf{id}} L \qquad \text{LLE-REFL}$$
$$\varnothing \leqslant_R L \qquad \text{LLE-EMPTY}$$
$$L \oplus \varnothing \leqslant_{\mathsf{id}} L \qquad \text{LLE-ID-RIGHT}$$
$$(L_1 \oplus L_2) \oplus L_3 \leqslant_{\mathsf{id}} L_1 \oplus (L_2 \oplus L_3) \qquad \text{LLE-ASSOC}$$
$$L_2 \oplus L_1 \leqslant_{\mathsf{id}} L_1 \oplus L_2 \qquad \text{LLE-COMM}$$
$$L_1 \leqslant_{\mathsf{id}} L_1 \oplus L_2 \qquad \text{LLE-UB-LEFT}$$
$$L \oplus L \leqslant_{\mathsf{id}} L \qquad \text{LLE-IDEMPOTENT}$$
$$L_1 \leqslant_R L_2 \wedge L_2 \leqslant_S L_3 \Rightarrow L_1 \leqslant_{S \circ R} L_3 \qquad \text{LLE-TRANS}$$
$$L_1 \leqslant_R L_1' \wedge L_2 \leqslant_R L_2' \Rightarrow L_1 \oplus L_2 \leqslant_R L_1' \oplus L_2' \qquad \text{LLE-MON}$$
$$\sigma_1 \leqslant_R \sigma_2 \Rightarrow i \mapsto \sigma_1 \leqslant_R i \mapsto \sigma_2 \qquad \text{LLE-INTRO-PRIM}$$

$\boxed{L_1 \vdash_R M : L_2}$

$$\frac{}{L \vdash_{\mathsf{id}} \varnothing : L}\ \text{EMPTY}$$

$$\frac{}{L \vdash_{\mathsf{id}} i \mapsto \nu : i \mapsto \nu}\ \text{VAR}$$

$$\frac{L_1 \vdash_R M : L_2 \qquad L_2 \vdash_S N : L_3}{L_1 \vdash_{R \circ S} M \oplus N : L_3}\ \text{VCOMP}$$

$$\frac{L \vdash_R M : L_1 \qquad L \vdash_R N : L_2}{L \vdash_R M \oplus N : L_1 \oplus L_2}\ \text{HCOMP}$$

$$\frac{L_1 \leqslant_R L_1' \qquad L_1 \vdash_S M : L_2 \qquad L_2' \leqslant_T L_2}{L_1' \vdash_{R \circ S \circ T} M : L_2'}\ \text{CONSEQ}$$

**Figure 4.** The fine-grained layer calculus

underlying simulation preorder $\leqslant_R$ on behaviors. Compared to $\subseteq$, it should satisfy the additional property LLE-IDEMPOTENT.

The judgment $L_1 \vdash_R M : L_2$ is akin to a typing judgment for modules. It asserts that, using the simulation relation $R$, the module $M$—running on top of $L_1$—faithfully implements $L_2$. Because modules consist of code ultimately intended to be linked with a client program, the empty module $\varnothing$ acts as a unit, and can implement any layer interface $L$ (EMPTY). Moreover, appending first $N$, then $M$ to a client program is akin to appending $M \oplus N$ in one step (VCOMP). These rules correspond to the identity and composition properties already present in the framework of abstract machines and program transformations. However, the fine-grained calculus also provides a way to split refinements (HCOMP): when two different layer interfaces are implemented *in a compatible way* by two different modules on top of a common underlay interface, then the union of the two modules implements the union of the two interfaces.

This allows us to break down the problem of verifying a layer implementation in smaller pieces, but ultimately, we need to handle individual functions and primitives. The consequence rule (CONSEQ) can be used to tie our notion of behavior refinement into the calculus. However, to make the introduction of certified code possible, we need a semantics of the underlying language.

### 3.3 Language semantics

Assume that layers and modules are interpreted in the respective sets $\mathbb{L}$ and $\mathbb{M}$. The semantics of a module can be understood as the effect of its code has on the underlay interface, as specified by a function

$$[\![-]\!] : \mathbb{M} \to (\mathbb{L} \to \mathbb{L})$$
$$i \mapsto \nu \leqslant_{\mathsf{id}} [\![i \mapsto \nu]\!] L \qquad \text{SEM-VAR}$$
$$[\![M]\!](L \oplus [\![N]\!] L) \leqslant_{\mathsf{id}} [\![M \oplus N]\!] L \qquad \text{SEM-COMP}$$
$$M_1 \subseteq M_2 \wedge L_1 \leqslant_R L_2 \Rightarrow [\![M_1]\!] L_1 \leqslant_R [\![M_2]\!] L_2 \qquad \text{SEM-MON}$$

**Figure 5.** Semantics of modules

$[\![-]\!] : \mathbb{M} \to \mathbb{L} \to \mathbb{L}$. Given such a function, we can interpret the typing judgment as:

$$L_1 \vdash_R M : L_2 \quad \Leftrightarrow \quad L_2 \leqslant_R L_1 \oplus [\![M]\!] L_1 .$$

Then the properties in Fig. 5 are sufficient to ensure the soundness of the typing rules with respect to this interpretation.

Here, surprisingly, we require that the specification refine the implementation! This is because our proof technique involves turning such a *downward* simulation into the converse *upward* simulation, as detailed in Sec. 5 (Theorem 1) and Sec. 4.3. Also, we included $L_1$ on the right-hand side of $\leqslant_R$ to support pass-through of primitives in the underlay $L_1$ into the overlay $L_2$.

The property SEM-COMP can be understood intuitively as follows. In $[\![M]\!](L \oplus [\![N]\!] L)$, the code of $M$ is able to use the functions defined in $N$ in addition to the primitives of the underlay interface $L$, but conversely the code of $N$ cannot access the functions of $M$. However, in $[\![M \oplus N]\!] L$, the functions of $M$ and $N$ can call each other freely, and therefore the result should be more defined. The property SEM-MON states that making the module and underlay larger should also result in a more defined semantics.

Once a language semantics is given, we introduce a language-specific rule to prove the correctness of individual functions:

$$\frac{\mathsf{VC}(L, \kappa, \sigma)}{L \vdash_{\mathsf{id}} i \mapsto \kappa : i \mapsto \sigma}\ \text{FUN}$$

where the language-specific predicate $\mathsf{VC}(L, \kappa, \sigma)$ asserts that the function body $\kappa$ faithfully implements the primitive behavior $\sigma$ on top of $L$. This rule can be combined with the rules of the calculus to build up complete certified layer implementations.

Similarly, given a concrete language semantics, we will want to tie the calculus back into the framework of abstract machines and program transformations. For a layer interface $L$, we will define a corresponding abstract machine meant to execute programs written in a version of the language augmented with the primitives specified in $L$. The program transformation associated with a module $M$ will simply concatenate the code of $M$ to the client program. Then, for a particular notion of refinement $\sqsubseteq$, we will want to prove that the typing judgments entail the contextual refinement property:

$$\frac{L_1 \vdash_R M : L_2}{\forall P \,.\, (P \oplus M) @ L_1 \sqsubseteq P @ L_2}$$

Informally, if $M$ faithfully implements $L_2$ on top of $L_1$, then invocations in $P$ of a primitive $i$ with behavior $\sigma$ in $L_2$, can be satisfied by calling the corresponding function $\kappa$ in $M$.

Indeed in Sec. 4 and Sec. 5, the primitive specifications in $[\![M]\!] L$, based on step relations, are defined to reflect the possible executions of the function definitions in $M$. Therefore, $L_2 \leqslant_R L_1 \oplus [\![M]\!] L_1$ implies that, for any primitive implementation in $M$, the corresponding deep specification in $L_2$ refines the execution of that function definition. Hence the execution of program $P$ with underlay $L_2$ refines that of $P \oplus M$ with underlay $L_1$ (the properties enumerated in Fig. 5 hold for a similar reason). Properties of the language (i.e., being determinate and receptive) can then be used to reverse this refinement into the desired $(P \oplus M) @ L_1 \sqsubseteq P @ L_2$.

## 4. Layered programming in ClightX

In this section, we provide an instantiation of our framework for a C-like language. This instantiation serves two purposes: it illustrates a common use case for our framework, showing its usability and practicality; and it shows that our framework can add modularization and proof infrastructure to existing language subsets at minimal cost.

***Our starting point: CompCert Clight*** Clight [5] is a subset of C and is formalized in Coq as part of the CompCert project. Its formal semantics relies on a memory model [21] that is not only realistic enough to specify C pointer operations, but also designed to simplify reasoning about non-aliasing of different variables. From the programmer's point of view, Clight avoids most pitfalls and peculiarities of C such as nondeterminism in expressions with side effects. On the other hand, Clight allows for pointer arithmetic and is a true subset of C. Such simplicity and practicality turn Clight into a solid choice for certified programming. However, Clight provides little support for abstraction, and proving properties about a Clight program requires intricate reasoning about data structures. This issue is addressed by our layer infrastructure.

### 4.1 Abstract state, primitives, and layer interfaces

We enable abstraction in Clight and other CompCert languages by instrumenting the memory states used by their semantics with an *abstract state* component. This abstract state can be manipulated using *primitives*, which are made available through CompCert's external function mechanism. We call the resulting language ClightX.

***Abstract state and external functions*** The abstract state is not just a ghost state for reasoning: it does influence the outcome of executions! However, we seek to minimize its impact on the existing proof infrastructure for program and compiler verification. We do not modify the semantics of the basic operations of Clight, or the type of values it uses. Instead, the abstract state is accessed exclusively through Clight's external function mechanism.

***Primitives and layer interfaces*** CompCert offers a notion of *external functions*, which are useful in modeling interaction with the environment, such as input/output. Indeed, CompCert models compiler correctness through traces of events which can be generated only by external functions. CompCert axiomatizes the behaviors of external functions without specifying them, and only assumes they do not behave in a manner that violates compiler correctness. We use the external function mechanism to extend Clight with our primitive operations, and supply their specifications to make the semantics of external functions more precise.

**Definition 1** (Primitive specification)**.** *Let mem denote the type of memory state, and let* val *denote the type of concrete values. A primitive specification $\sigma$ over the abstract state type $A$ is a predicate on $(\mathsf{val}^* \times \mathsf{mem} \times A) \times (\mathsf{val} \times \mathsf{mem} \times A)$: when $\sigma(args, m, a, res, m', a')$ holds, we say that the primitive takes arguments $args$, memory state $m$ and abstract state $a$, and returns a result $res$, a memory state $m'$ and an abstract state $a'$.*

The type of abstract state and the set of available primitives will constitute our notion of layer interface.

**Definition 2** (Layer interface)**.** *A layer interface $L$ is a tuple $L = (A, P)$ where $A$ is the type of abstract state, and $P$ is the set of primitives as a finite map from identifiers to primitive specifications over the abstract state $A$.*

### 4.2 The ClightX parametric language

***Syntax*** The syntax of ClightX (parameterized over a layer interface $L$) is identical to that of Clight. It features global variables (including function pointers), stack-allocated local variables, and temporary variables $t$. Expressions have no side effects; in particular, they cannot contain any function call. They include full-fledged pointer arithmetics (comparison, offset, C-style "arrays").

$$\begin{array}{rcll} e & ::= & n \mid x \mid t & \text{Constant, variable, temporary} \\ & \mid & \&e \mid *e \mid e_1 \ op\ e_2 \mid \ldots & \end{array}$$

Statements include assignment to a memory location or a temporary, function call and return, and structured control (loops, etc.).

$$\begin{array}{rcll} S & ::= & e_1 = e_2 & \text{Assignment to a memory location} \\ & \mid & t := e & \text{Assignment to a temporary variable} \\ & \mid & t \leftarrow e(e_1, \ldots) & \text{Function call} \\ & \mid & \mathtt{return}(e) & \text{Function return} \\ & \mid & S_1; S_2 \mid \mathtt{if}(e)\ S_1\ \mathtt{else}\ S_2 \mid \mathtt{while}(e)\ S & \end{array}$$

Function calls may refer to internal functions defined as part of a module, or to primitives defined in the underlay $L$. However these two cases are not distinguished syntactically. In fact, the layer calculus allows for replacing primitive specifications with actual code implementation, with no changes to the caller's code.

**Definition 3** (Functions, modules)**.** *A ClightX function is a tuple $\kappa = (targs, lvars, S)$, where targs is the list of temporaries to receive the arguments, lvars is the list of local stack-allocated variables with their sizes, and $S$ is a statement, the function body. A module $M$ is a finite map from identifiers to ClightX functions.*

***Semantics*** Compared with Clight, the semantics of ClightX($L$) adds a notion of abstract state, and permits calls to the primitives of $L$. We will write $L(i)(args, m, a, res, m', a')$ to denote the semantics of the primitive associated with identifier $i$ in $L$.

We present the semantics of ClightX under the form of a big-step semantics. We fix an injective mapping $\Gamma$ from global variables to memory block identifiers. We write $[\![e]\!](l, \tau, m)$ for the evaluation of expression $e$ under local variables $l$, temporaries $\tau$ and memory state $m$. We write $\Gamma, L, M, l \vdash S : (\tau, m, a) \downarrow (res; \tau', m', a')$ for the semantics of statements: from the local environment $l$, the temporary environment $\tau$, the memory state $m$, and the abstract state $a$, execution of $S$ terminates and yields result $res$ (or $\cdot$ if no result), temporary environment $\tau'$, memory state $m'$, and abstract state $a'$. For instance, the rule for `return` statements is:

$$\frac{[\![e]\!](l, \tau, m) = res}{\Gamma, L, M, l \vdash \mathtt{return}(e) : (\tau, m, a) \downarrow (res; \tau, m, a)}$$

We write $\Gamma, L, M \vdash f : (args; m, a) \Downarrow (res; m', a')$ to say that a function $f$ defined either as an internal function in the module $M$, or as a primitive in the layer interface $L$, called with list of arguments $args$, from memory state $m$ and abstract state $a$, returns result $res$, memory $m'$ and abstract state $a'$.

For internal function calls, we first initialize the temporary environment with the arguments, and allocate the local variables of the callee ($\mathsf{next}(m)$ denotes the next available block identifier in memory $m$, not yet allocated). Then, we execute the body. Finally, we deallocate the stack-allocated variables of the callee.

$$\frac{\begin{array}{c} M(f) = ((t_1, \ldots, t_n), ((x_1, sz_1), \ldots, (x_k, sz_k)), S) \\ m_1 = \mathsf{alloc}(sz_k) \circ \cdots \circ \mathsf{alloc}(sz_1)(m) \\ l = \varnothing[x_1 \leftarrow \mathsf{next}(m)] \ldots [x_k \leftarrow \mathsf{next}(m) + k - 1] \\ \tau = \varnothing[t_1 \leftarrow v_1] \ldots [t_n \leftarrow v_n] \\ \Gamma, L, M, l \vdash S : (\tau, m_1, a) \downarrow (res; \tau', m_2, a') \\ m' = \mathsf{free}(\mathsf{next}(m), sz_1) \circ \cdots \circ \mathsf{free}(\mathsf{next}(m) + k - 1, sz_k)(m_2) \end{array}}{\Gamma, L, M \vdash f : (v_1, \ldots, v_n; m, a) \Downarrow (res; m', a')}$$

For primitive calls, we simply query the layer interface $L$:

$$\frac{L(f)(args, m, a, res, m', a')}{\Gamma, L, M \vdash f : (args; m, a) \Downarrow (res; m', a')}$$

Using the function judgment, we can state the rule for function call statements as:

$$\frac{\begin{array}{cc} & \forall i, [\![e_i]\!](l, \tau, m) = v_i \qquad [\![e]\!](l, \tau, m) = (b, 0) \\ \Gamma(f) = b & \Gamma, L, M \vdash f : (v_1, \ldots, v_n; m, a) \Downarrow (res; m', a') \\ & \tau' = \tau[t \leftarrow res] \end{array}}{\Gamma, L, M, l \vdash t \leftarrow e(e_1, \ldots, e_n) : (\tau, m, a) \downarrow (\cdot; \tau', m', a')}$$

$$\frac{\dfrac{\forall i \,.\, L_1 \vdash_{\mathbf{id}} i \mapsto \kappa_i : i \mapsto \sigma_i'}{L_1 \vdash_{\mathbf{id}} M : L_1'} \qquad \dfrac{\dfrac{\forall i \,.\, \sigma_i \leqslant_R \sigma_i'}{\forall i \,.\, i \mapsto \sigma_i \leqslant_R i \mapsto \sigma_i'}}{L_2 \leqslant_R L_1'}}{L_1 \vdash_R M : L_2}$$

where $L_1$ is the underlay, the module $M = \bigoplus_i i \mapsto \kappa_i$, the intermediate layer $L_1' = \bigoplus_i i \mapsto \sigma_i'$, and the overlay $L_2 = \bigoplus_i i \mapsto \sigma_i$.

**Figure 6.** Building a certified ClightX layer

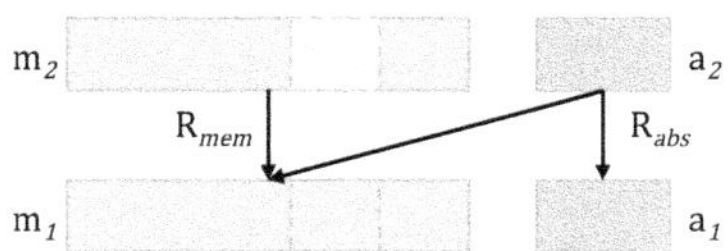


**Figure 7.** Layer simulation relation

The full semantics of ClightX is given in the companion TR [13].

**Definition 4** (Semantics of a module). *Let $M$ be a ClightX module, and $L$ be a layer interface. Let $\Gamma$ be a mapping from global variables to memory blocks. The semantics of a module $M$ in ClightX($L$), written $[\![M]\!]L$, is the layer interface defined as follows:*

- *the type of abstract state is the same as in $L$;*
- *the semantics of primitives are defined by the following rule:*

$$\frac{f \in \mathrm{dom}(M) \qquad \Gamma, L, M \vdash f : (args; m, a) \Downarrow (res; m', a')}{([\![M]\!]L)(f)(args, m, a, res, m', a')}$$

### 4.3 Layered programming and verification

To construct a certified abstraction layer $(L_1, M, L_2)$, we need to find a simulation $R$ such that $L_1 \vdash_R M : L_2$ holds. Fig. 6 gives an overview of this process. We write $M = \bigoplus_i i \mapsto \kappa_i$, where $i$ ranges over the function identifiers defined in module $M$, and $\kappa_i$ is the corresponding implementation. Global variables in $M$ should not be accessible from the layers above: their permissions are removed in the overlay interface $L_2$. The interface $L_2$ also includes a specification $\sigma_i$ for each function $i$ defined in $M$.

We decouple the task of code verification from that of data structure abstraction. We introduce an intermediate layer interface, $L_1' = \bigoplus_i i \mapsto \sigma_i'$, with its specifications $\sigma_i'$ expressed in terms of the underlay states. We first prove that $L_1 \vdash_{\mathbf{id}} M : L_1'$ holds. For each function $i$ in $M$, we show that its implementation $\kappa_i$ is a downward simulation of its "underlay" specification $\sigma_i'$, that is, $L_1 \vdash_{\mathbf{id}} i \mapsto \kappa_i : i \mapsto \sigma_i'$. We apply the HCOMP rule to compose all the per-function simulation statements. Note the simulation relations here are all **id**, meaning there is no abstraction of data structures in these steps. We then prove $L_2 \leqslant_R L_1'$, which means that each specification $\sigma_i$ in $L_2$ is an abstraction of the intermediate specification $\sigma_i'$ via a simulation relation $R$. From $i \mapsto \sigma_i \leqslant_R i \mapsto \sigma_i'$, we apply the monotonicity rule LLE-MON to get $L_2 \leqslant_R L_1'$. Finally, we apply the CONSEQ rule to deduce $L_1 \vdash_R M : L_2$.

***Verifying ClightX functions*** $L_1$ and $L_1'$ share the same views of both concrete and abstract states, so no simulation relation is involved during this step of verification (the FUN rule in Sec. 3.3). Using Coq's tactical language, we have developed a proof automation engine that can handle most of the functional correctness proofs of ClightX programs. It contains two main parts: a ClightX statement/expression interpreter that generates the verification conditions by utilizing rules of ClightX big-step semantics, and an automated theorem prover that discharges the generated verification conditions on the fly. The automated theorem prover is a first order prover, extended with different theory solvers, such as the theory of integer arithmetic and the theory of CompCert style partial maps. The entire automation engine is developed in Coq's Ltac language.

```
typedef enum {
  PG_RESERVED, PG_KERNEL,
  PG_NORMAL
} pg_type;

struct page_info {
  pg_type t;
  uint u;
};
struct page_info AT[1<<20];
```

```
Notation RESV := 0.
Notation KERN := (RESV + 1).
Notation NORM := (KERN + 1).

Inductive page_info :=
| ATV (t: Z) (u: Z)
| ATUndef.

Record abs'' :=
  {AT: ZMap.t page_info}.
```

**Figure 8.** Concrete (C) vs. abstract (Coq) memory allocation table

```
// κat_get
uint at_get (uint i){
  uint allocated;
  allocated = AT[i].u;
  if (allocated != 0)
      allocated = 1;
  return allocated;
}

// κat_set
void at_set (uint i, uint b){
   AT[i].u = b;
}
```

```
Function σ̂at_get a i :=
match (a.AT i) with
| ATV _ 0 => Some 0
| ATV _ _ => Some 1
| _ => None
end.

Function σ̂at_set a i b :=
match (a.AT i) with
| ATV t _ =>
Some (set_AT a i (ATV t b))
| _ => None
end.
```

**Figure 9.** Concrete vs. abstract getter-setter functions for AT

```
Inductive σ'at_set :=
| ∀ m m' a ofs v n,
  m.store AT ofs v = m'
  -> ofs = n * 8 + 4
  -> 0 <= n < 1048576
  -> σ'at_set (n::v::nil)
        m a Vundef m' a.
```

```
Inductive σat_set :=
| ∀ m a a' n v,
    σ̂at_set a n v = Some a'
  -> 0 <= n < 1048576
  -> σat_set (n::v::nil)
        m a Vundef m a'.
```

**Figure 10.** High level and low level specification for at_set

***Data abstraction*** Since primitives in $L_1'$ and $L_2$ are atomic, we prove the single-step downward simulation between $L_1'$ and $L_2$ only at the specification level. The simulation proof for the abstraction can be made language independent. The simulation relation $R$ captures the relation between the underlay state (concrete memory and abstract state) and the overlay state, and can be decomposed as $R_{\mathrm{mem}}$ and $R_{\mathrm{abs}}$ (see Fig. 7). The relation $R_{\mathrm{mem}}$ ensures that the concrete memory states $m_1$ and $m_2$ contain the same values, while making sure the memory permissions for the part to be abstracted are erased in the overlay memory $m_2$. The component $R_{\mathrm{abs}}$ relates the overlay abstract state $a_2$ with the full underlay state $(m_1, a_1)$.

Through this decomposition, we achieve the following two objectives: the client program can directly manipulate the abstract state without worrying about its underlying concrete implementation (which is hidden via $R_{\mathrm{mem}}$), and the abstract state in the overlay is actually implementable by the concrete memory and abstract state in the underlay (via $R_{\mathrm{abs}}$).

***Common patterns*** We have developed two common design patterns to further ease the task of verification. The *getter-setter* pattern establishes memory abstraction by introducing new abstract states and erasing the corresponding memory permissions for the overlay. The overlay only adds the get and set primitives which are implemented using simple memory load/store operations at the underlay. The *abs-fun* pattern implements key functionalities, but does not introduce new abstract state. Its implementation (on underlay) does not touch concrete memory state. Instead, it only accesses the states

```
// κ_palloc
uint palloc(uint nps){
  uint i = 0, u;
  uint freei = nps;
  while(freei == nps
       && i < nps) {
    u = at_get(i);
    if (u == 0)
      freei = i;
    i ++;
  }
  if (freei != nps)
    at_set(freei, 1);
  return freei;
}
```

```
Definition first_free a n:
  {v| 0<= fst v < n
   /\ a.AT (fst v) = ATV (snd v) 0
   /\ ∀x, 0 <= x < fst v
       -> ~ a.AT x = ATV _ 0}
+ {∀x, 0 <= x < n
       -> ~ a.AT x = ATV _ 0}.

Function σ̂_palloc a nps :=
match first_free a nps with
 | inleft (exist (i, t) _) =>
   (set_AT a i (ATV t 1), i)
 | _ => (a, nps)
end.
```

**Figure 11.** Concrete (in C) vs. abstract (in Coq) palloc function

```
Inductive σ'_palloc : spec :=
| ∀ m a a' nps n,
   σ̂_palloc a nps = (a', n)
   -> 0 <= nps < 1048576
   -> σ'_palloc (nps::nil) m a n m a'.

Definition σ_palloc := σ'_palloc.
```

**Figure 12.** High level and low level specification for palloc function

that have already been abstracted, and it only does so using the primitives provided by the underlay interface.

Figs. 8-12 show how we use the two patterns to implement and verify a simplified physical memory allocator palloc, which allocates and returns the first free entry in the physical memory allocation table. Fig. 8-10 shows how we follow the *getter-setter* pattern to abstract the allocation table into a new abstract state. As shown in Fig. 8, we first turn the concrete C memory allocation table implementation into an abstract Coq data type. Then we implement the getter and setter functions for the memory allocation table, both in C and Coq (see Fig. 9). The Coq functions $\hat{\sigma}_{\text{at\_get}}$ and $\hat{\sigma}_{\text{at\_set}}$ are just intermediate specifications that are used later in the overlay specifications. The actual underlay and overlay specifications of the setter function at_set are shown in Fig. 10.

We then prove $L_1 \vdash_{\textbf{id}} \mathsf{at\_set} \mapsto \kappa_{\text{at\_set}} : \mathsf{at\_set} \mapsto \sigma'_{\text{at\_set}}$, and also $\mathsf{at\_set} \mapsto \sigma_{\text{at\_set}} \leqslant_R \mathsf{at\_set} \mapsto \sigma'_{\text{at\_set}}$.

The code verification (first part) is easy for this pattern because the memory load and store operations in the underlay match the source code closely. The proof can be discharged by our automation tactic. The main task of this pattern is to prove refinement (second part): we design a simulation relation $R$ relating the memory storing the global variable at underlay with its corresponding abstract data at overlay. The component $R_{\text{mem}}$ ensures that there is no permission for allocation table AT in overlay memory state $m_2$, while the component $R_{\text{abs}}$ is defined as follows:

- $\forall i \in [0, 2^{20})$, $R_{\text{abs}}$ enforces the *writable* permission on AT[i] at underlay memory state $m_1$, and requires ($a_2$.AT i) at overlay to be (ATV AT[i].t AT[i].u).
- Except for AT, $R_{\text{abs}}$ requires all other abstract data in underlay and overlay to be the same.

The refinement proof for $L_2 \leqslant_R L'_1$ involves the efforts to prove that this relation $R$ between underlay memory and overlay abstract state is preserved by all the atomic primitives in both $L'_1$ and $L_2$.

After we abstract the memory and get/set operations, we implement palloc on top of $L_2$, following the *abs-fun* pattern. The previous overlay now becomes the new underlay ("$L_1$"). Fig. 11 shows both the implementation of palloc in ClightX and the abstract function in Coq. As before, we separately show that $L_1 \vdash_{\textbf{id}} \mathsf{palloc} \mapsto \kappa_{\text{palloc}} : \mathsf{palloc} \mapsto \sigma'_{\text{palloc}}$, and $\mathsf{palloc} \mapsto \sigma_{\text{palloc}} \leqslant_R \mathsf{palloc} \mapsto \sigma'_{\text{palloc}}$ holds. For the *abs-fun* pattern, the refinement proof is easy. Since we do not introduce any new abstract states in this pattern, the implementation only manipulates the abstract states through the primitive calls of the underlay. Thus, as shown in Fig. 12, the corresponding underlay and overlay specifications are exactly the same, so the relation $R$ here is the identity (**id**) and the proof of refinement is trivial. The main task for the *abs-fun* pattern is to verify the code, which is done using our automation tactic.

The above examples show that for the *getter-setter* pattern, the primary task is to prove data abstraction, while for the *abs-fun* pattern, the main task is to do simple program verification. These two tasks are well understood and manageable, so the decoupling (via these two patterns) makes the layer construction much easier.

## 5. Layered programming in LAsm

In this section, we describe LAsm, the *Layered Assembly language*, and the extended machine model which LAsm is based on.

The reason we are interested in assembly code and behavior is threefold. First of all, even though we provide ClightX to write most code, we are still interested in the actual assembly code running on the actual machine. In Section 6, we will provide a verified compiler to transport all proofs of code written in ClightX to assembly.

Secondly, there are parts of software that have to be manually written in assembly for various reasons. For example, the standard implementation of kernel context switch modifies the stack pointer register ESP, which does not satisfy the C calling convention and has to be verified in assembly. A linker will be defined in Section 6 to link them with compiled C code.

Last but not least, we are interested not only in the behavior of our code, but also in the behavior of the *context* that will call functions defined in our code. To be as general as possible, we allow the context to include all valid assembly code sequences. To this end, it is necessary to transport per-function refinement proofs to a whole-machine *contextual refinement* proof.

***The LAsm assembly language*** We start from the 32-bit x86 assembly subset specified in CompCert. CompCert x86 assembly is modeled as a state machine with a register set and a memory state. The register set consists of eight 32-bit general-purpose registers and eight XMM registers designated as scalar double-precision floating-point operands. The memory state is same as the one in Clight. In particular, each function executes with its stack frame modeled in its own memory block, so that the stack is not a contiguous piece of memory. Another anomaly regarding function calls in CompCert x86 assembly is that the return address is stored in pseudo-register RA instead of being pushed onto the stack, so that the callee must allocate its own stack frame and store the return address.

Similarly to ClightX, we extend the machine state with an abstract state, which will be modified by primitives. This yields LAsm, whose syntax is the same as that of CompCert x86 assembly, except that the semantics will be parameterized over the type of abstract states and the specifications of primitives. Most notably, primitive calls are syntactically indistinguishable from normal function calls, yet depend on the specifications semantically.

Moreover, in our Coq formalization, the semantics of LAsm is also equipped with memory accessors for address translation in order to handle both kernel memory linear mapping and user space virtual memory. However, for the sake of presentation, we are going to describe a simplified version of LAsm where memory accesses only use the kernel memory.

We define the semantics of LAsm in small-step form. The machine state is $(\rho, m, a)$ where $\rho$ contains the values of registers, $m$ is the concrete memory state and $a$ is the abstract state. Let $M$ be an LAsm module, which is a finite map from identifiers to arrays of LAsm instructions, we write $\Gamma, L, M \vdash (\rho, m, a) \rightarrow (\rho', m', a')$

a transition step in the LAsm machine. The full syntax and formal semantics of LAsm is described in the companion technical report.

***Assembly layer interfaces*** The semantics of LAsm is parameterized over a layer interface. Different from C-style primitives (see Def. 1), which are defined using argument list and return value, primitives implemented in LAsm often utilize their full control over the register set and are not restricted to a particular calling convention (e.g. context switch). Therefore, it is necessary to extend the structure of layer interfaces to allow assembly-style primitives modifying the register set.

**Definition 5** (Assembly-style primitive). *An assembly-style primitive specification $p$ over the abstract state type $A$ is a predicate on $((\mathsf{preg} \to \mathsf{val}) \times \mathsf{mem} \times A) \times ((\mathsf{preg} \to \mathsf{val}) \times \mathsf{mem} \times A)$. $p(\rho, m, a, \rho', m', a')$ says that the primitive $p$ takes register set $\rho$, memory state $m$ and abstract state $a$ as arguments, and returns register set $\rho'$, memory state $m'$ and abstract state $a'$ as result.*

By "*style*," we mean the calling convention, not the language in which they are actually implemented. C-style primitives may very well be implemented as hand-written assembly code at underlay.

We can then define assembly layer interfaces by replacing the primitive specification with our assembly-style one in Def. 2. But, to make reasoning simpler, when defining assembly layer interfaces, we distinguish C-style from assembly-style primitives. First, C-style primitives can be refined by other C-style primitives. Second and most importantly, it becomes possible to instantiate the semantics of ClightX with an *assembly* layer interface by just considering C-style primitives and ignoring assembly-style primitives (which might not follow the C calling convention). In this way, ClightX code is only allowed to call C-style primitives, whereas LAsm can actually call both kinds of primitives.

**Definition 6** (Assembly layer interface). *An assembly layer interface $L$ is a tuple $L = (A, P_{\mathrm{ClightX}}, P_{\mathrm{LAsm}})$ where:*

- *$(A, P_{\mathrm{ClightX}})$ is a C layer interface (see Def. 2)*
- *$P_{\mathrm{LAsm}}$ is a finite map from identifiers to assembly-style primitive specifications over the abstract state $A$. The domains of $P_{\mathrm{ClightX}}$ and $P_{\mathrm{LAsm}}$ shall be disjoint.*

***Whole-machine semantics and contextual refinement*** Based on the relational transition system which we just defined for LAsm, we can define the whole-machine semantics including not only the code that we wrote by hand or that we compile, but also the *context* code that shall call our functions. To this end, it suffices to equip the semantics with a notion of initial and final state, in a way similar to the CompCert x86 whole-program assembly semantics.

In CompCert, the initial state consists of an empty register set with only EIP (instruction pointer register) pointing to the `main` function of the module, and the memory state is constructed by allocating a memory block for each global variable of the program. We follow the same approach for LAsm, except that we also need an initial abstract state, provided by the layer interface, so we need to extend its definition:

**Definition 7** (Whole-machine layer interface). *A whole-machine layer interface $L$ is a tuple $L = (A, P_{\mathrm{ClightX}}, P_{\mathrm{LAsm}}, a_0)$ where:*

- *$(A, P_{\mathrm{ClightX}}, P_{\mathrm{LAsm}})$ is an assembly layer interface*
- *$a_0 : A$ is the initial abstract state.*

**Definition 8** (Whole-machine initial state). *The whole-machine LAsm initial state for layer interface $L$ and module $M$ is the LAsm state $(\rho_0, m_0, a_0)$ defined as follows:*

- $\rho_0(r) = \begin{cases} (\Gamma(\mathtt{main}), 0) & \textit{if } r = \mathsf{EIP} \\ 0 & \textit{if } r = \mathsf{RA} \\ \bot & \textit{otherwise} \end{cases}$
- *$m_0$ is constructed from the global variables of $\Gamma$, $L$, $M$*
- *$a_0$ is the whole-machine initial state specified in $L$*

**Definition 9** (Whole-machine final state). *A whole-machine LAsm state $(\rho, m, a)$ is final with return code $n$ if, and only if, $\rho(\mathsf{EAX}) = n$ and $\rho(\mathsf{EIP}) = 0$, where EAX is the accumulator register.*

Notice that $\rho(\mathsf{EIP})$ contains the *integer* 0, which is also the initial return address and is not a valid pointer. This ensures that executions do not go beyond a final state, following the CompCert x86 whole-program semantics: `main` has returned to its "caller", which does not exist. Thus, the final state is uniquely determined (there can be no other possible behavior once such a state is reached), so the whole-machine semantics is deterministic once the primitives are.

**Definition 10** (Whole-machine behavior). *Let $\Gamma$ be a mapping of global variables to memory blocks. Then, we say that*

- $LAsm(\Gamma, L, M)$ diverges *if there is an infinite execution sequence from the whole-machine initial state for $L$*
- $LAsm(\Gamma, L, M)$ terminates with return code $n$ *if there is a finite execution sequence from the whole-machine initial state for $L$ to a whole-machine final state with return code $n$*
- $LAsm(\Gamma, L, M)$ goes wrong *if there is a finite execution sequence from the whole-machine initial state for $L$ to a non-final state that can take no step.*

Then, we are interested in *refinement* between whole machines:

**Definition 11** (Whole-machine refinement). *Let $L_{high}, L_{low}$ be two whole-machine assembly layer interfaces, and $M_{high}, M_{low}$ be two LAsm modules. Then, we say that $M_{low}@L_{low}$ refines $M_{high}@L_{high}$, and write $M_{low}@L_{low} \sqsubseteq M_{high}@L_{high}$ if, and only if, for any $\Gamma$ such that $\mathrm{dom}(L_{high}) \cup \mathrm{dom}(M_{high}) \cup \mathrm{dom}(L_{low}) \cup \mathrm{dom}(M_{low}) \subseteq \mathrm{dom}(\Gamma)$ and $LAsm(\Gamma, L_{high}, M_{high})$ does not go wrong, then (1) $LAsm(\Gamma, L_{low}, M_{low})$ does not go wrong; (2) if $LAsm(\Gamma, L_{low}, M_{low})$ terminates with return code $n$, then so does $LAsm(\Gamma, L_{high}, M_{high})$; (3) if $LAsm(\Gamma, L_{low}, M_{low})$ diverges, so does $LAsm(\Gamma, L_{high}, M_{high})$.*

In our Coq implementation, we actually formalized the semantics of LAsm with a richer notion of observable behaviors involving CompCert-style events such as I/O. Thus, we define the whole-machine behaviors and refinement using event traces *a la* CompCert [20, 3.5 sqq.]: if the higher machine does not go wrong, then every valid behavior of the lower machine is a valid behavior of the higher.

Finally, we can define *contextual refinement* between layer interfaces through a module $M$:

**Definition 12** (Contextual refinement). *We say a module $M$ implements an overlay $L_{high}$ on top of an underlay $L_{low}$, and write $L_{low} \models M : L_{high}$ if, and only if, for any module* (context) *$M'$ disjoint from $M, L_{low}, L_{high}$, we have $(M \oplus M')@L_{low} \sqsubseteq M'@L_{high}$.*

***Per-module semantics*** As for ClightX, we can also specify the semantics of an LAsm module as a layer interface. However, a major difference between ClightX and LAsm is that it is not possible to uniquely characterize the "per-function final state" at which function execution should stop. Indeed, as in LAsm there is no control stack, when considering the per-function semantics of a function $f$, it is not possible to distinguish $f$ exiting and returning control to its caller, from a callee $g$ returning to $f$.

Thus, even though both the step relation of the LAsm semantics and the primitive specifications (of a layer interface) are deterministic, the semantics of a function could still be non-deterministic.

**Definition 13.** *Let $L = (A, \_, \_)$ be an assembly layer interface, and $M$ be an LAsm module. The module semantics $[\![M]\!]L$ is then the assembly layer interface $[\![M]\!]L = (A, \varnothing, P)$, where the assembly-style primitive specification $P$ is defined for each $f \in \mathrm{dom}(M)$*

*using the small-step semantics of LAsm as follows:*

$$P(f)(\rho, m, a, \rho', m', a') \Leftrightarrow \Gamma(f) = b \wedge \rho(\mathsf{EIP}) = (b, 0) \wedge \Gamma, L, M \vdash (\rho, m, a) \rightarrow^{+} (\rho', m', a')$$

***Soundness of per-module refinement*** In this paper, we aim at showing that the layer calculus given in Section 3 is a powerful device to prove contextual refinement: instead of proving the whole-machine contextual refinement directly, we only need to prove the *downward simulation* relations about individual modules, notated as $L_{\text{low}} \vdash_R M : L_{\text{high}}$, and apply the soundness theorem to get the contextual refinement properties at the whole-machine level.

**Lemma 1** (Downward simulation diagram). *Let $(L_{low}, M, L_{high})$ be a certified layer, such that $L_{low} \vdash_R M : L_{high}$. Then, for any module $M'$, we have the following downward simulation diagram:*

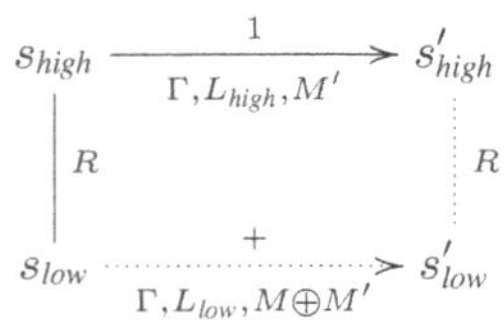


**Theorem 1** (Soundness). *Let $(L_{low}, M, L_{high})$ be a certified layer. If the primitive specifications of $L_{low}$ are deterministic and if $L_{low} \vdash_R M : L_{high}$, then $L_{low} \models M : L_{high}$.*

*Proof.* Since the whole machine $LAsm(\Gamma, L_{\text{low}}, M)$ is deterministic, we can flip the downward simulation given by Lemma 1 to an upward one, hence the whole-machine refinement. □

Since the per-function semantics is non-deterministic due to its final state not being uniquely defined, we can only flip the downward simulation to contextual refinement at the whole-machine level.

## 6. Certified compilation and linking

We would like to write most parts of our kernel in ClightX rather than in LAsm for easier verification. This means that, for each layer interface $L$, we have to compile our ClightX($L$) source code to the corresponding LAsm($L$) assembly language in such a way that all proofs at the ClightX level are preserved at the LAsm level.

This section describes how we have modified the CompCert compiler to compile certified C layers into certified assembly layers. It also talks about how we link compiled certified C layers with other certified assembly layers.

### 6.1 The CompCertX verified compiler

To transport the proofs at ClightX down to LAsm, we adapt the CompCert verified compiler to parameterize all its intermediate languages over the layer interface $L$ similarly to how we defined ClightX($L$), including the assembly language. This gives rise to CompCertX($L$) (for "CompCert eXtended", where external functions are instantiated with layer interface $L$).

CompCertX goes from ClightX to the similarly parameterized AsmX and then to LAsm. We retain all features and optimizations of CompCert, including function inlining, dead code elimination, common subexpression elimination, and tail call recognition.

***Compiler correctness for CompCertX*** Because CompCert only proves semantics preservation for whole programs, the major challenge is to adapt the semantics preservation statements of all compilation passes (from Clight to assembly) to per-function semantics.

The operational semantics of all CompCert languages are given through small-step transition relations equipped with sets of whole-program initial and final states, so we have to redesign those states to per-function setting. For the initial state, whereas CompCert constructs an initial memory and calls `main` with no arguments, we take the function pointer to call, the initial memory, and the list of arguments as parameters. For the final state, we take not only the return value, but also the memory state when we exit the function.

Consequently, the compiler correctness proofs have to change. Currently, CompCert uses a downward simulation diagram [20, 2.1] for each pass from Clight, then, thanks to the fact that the CompCert assembly language is deterministic (up to input values given by the environment), CompCert composes all of them together before turning them to a single upward simulation which actually entails that the compiled code refines the source code.

In this work, we follow a similar approach: for each individual pass, we prove per-function semantics preservation in a downward simulation flavor. We do not, however, turn it into an upward simulation, because the whole layer refinement proof is based on downward simulation, which is in turn turned into an upward simulation at whole-machine contextual refinement thanks to the determinism (up to the environment) of LAsm($L$).

***Memory state during compilation*** The main difference between CompCert and CompCertX lies in the memory given at the beginning of a function call.

In the whole-program setting, the initial state is the same across all languages, because it is uniquely determined by the global variables (which are preserved by compilation). On the other hand, in the middle of the execution when entering an arbitrary function, the memory in Clight is different from its assembly counterpart because CompCert introduces *memory transformations* such as memory injections or extensions [21, 5.4] to manage the callees' stack frames. This is actually advantageous for compilation of handling arguments and the return address.

For CompCertX, within the module being compiled, the same memory state mismatch also exists. At module entry, however, we cannot assume much about the memory state because it is given as a parameter to the semantics of each function in the module. In fact, this memory state is determined by the caller, so it may very well come from non-ClightX code (e.g., arbitrary assembly user code), thus we have to take the same memory as initial state across all the languages of CompCertX. It follows then that the arguments of the function already have to be present in the memory, following the calling convention imposed by the assembly language, even though ClightX does not read the arguments from memory.

Another difference between CompCert and CompCertX is the treatment of final memory states. In CompCert, only the return value of a program is observable at the end; the final memory state is not. By contrast, in CompCertX, the final memory state is passed back to the caller hence observable. Thus, it is necessary to account for memory transformations when relating the final states in the simulation diagrams.

***Compilation refinement relation*** Finally, the per-function compiler correctness statement of CompCertX can be roughly summarized as this commutative diagram and formally defined below.

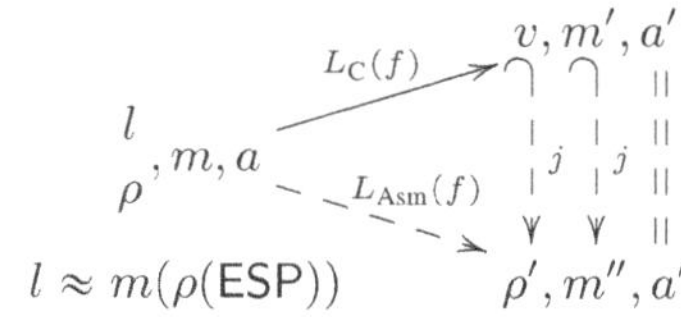


**Definition 14.** *Let $L_C$ be a C layer interface, and $L_{Asm}$ be an assembly layer interface. We say that $L_C$ is simulated by $L_{Asm}$ by compilation, written $L_C \leqslant^{comp} L_{Asm}$, if and only if, for any $\Gamma$, and for any execution $L_C(f)(l, m, a, v, m', a')$ of a primitive $f$ of $L_C$ for some list $l$ of arguments and some return value $v$, from memory state $m$ and abstract state $a$ to $m'$ and $a'$, and for any register map $\rho$ such that the following requirements hold:*

1. *the memory $m$ contains the arguments $l$ in the stack pointed to by $\rho(\mathsf{ESP})$*
2. $\mathsf{EIP}$ *points to the function $f$ being called: $\rho(\mathsf{EIP}) = (\Gamma(f), 0)$*

*Then, there is a primitive execution $L_{Asm}(f)(\rho, m, a, \rho', m'', a')$ and a memory injection $j$ from $m'$ to $m''$ preserving the addresses of $m$ such that the following holds:*

- *the values of callee-save registers in $\rho$ are preserved in $\rho'$;*
- *$\rho'(\mathsf{EIP})$ points to return address $\rho(\mathsf{RA})$;*
- *the return value contained in $\rho'(\mathsf{EAX})$ (for integers/pointers) or $\rho'(\mathsf{FP0})$ (for floating-points) is related to $v$ by $j$;*

**Theorem 2.** *Let $L$ be an assembly layer interface with all C-style primitives preserving memory transformations. Then, for any $M$:*

$$[\![M]\!]L \leqslant^{comp} [\![\mathrm{CompCertX}(M)]\!]L$$

More details can be found in the companion technical report.

### 6.2 Linking compiled code with assembly code

Contrary to traditional separate compilation, we target compiling ClightX functions that may be called by LAsm assembly code. Since the caller may be arbitrary LAsm code, not necessarily well-behaved code written in or compiled from ClightX, we have to assume that the memory we are given follows LAsm layout. When reasoning about memory states that involve compiled code, we then have to accommodate memory injections introduced by the compiler.

During a whole-machine refinement proof, the two memory states of the overlay and the underlay are related with a simulation relation $R$. However, consider when the higher (LAsm) code calls an overlay primitive, that, in the underlay, is compiled from ClightX. Because during the per-primitive simulation proofs we ignored the effects of the compiler, the memory injection introduced by the compiler may become a source of discrepancy. That is why we encapsulate, in $R$, a memory injection between the higher memory state and the lower memory state. This injection is identity until the lower state calls a compiled ClightX function. Then, at every such call, the layer simulation relation $R$ can "absorb" compilation refinement on its right-hand side:

**Lemma 2.** *If $L'$ and $L_C$ are C overlays and $L_{Asm}$ is an assembly underlay, with $L' \leqslant_R L_C$ and $L_C \leqslant^{comp} L_{Asm}$, then $L' \leqslant_R L_{Asm}$.*

*Proof.* If $R$ encapsulates a memory injection $j_0$, and compilation introduces a memory injection $j$, then, the simulation relation $R$ will still hold with the composed memory injection $j \circ j_0$. □

***Summary of the refinement proof with compilation and linking*** Finally, the outline of proving layer refinement $L_1 \vdash M : L_2$, where $M = \mathrm{CompCertX}(M_C) \oplus M_{\mathrm{Asm}}$ is the union of a compiled ClightX module and an LAsm module, is summarized in the following steps, also shown in Fig. 13:

1. Split the overlay $L_2$ into two layer interfaces $L_{2,\mathrm{C}}$ and $L_{2,\mathrm{Asm}}$ where $L_{2,\mathrm{C}}$ is a C layer interface containing primitive specifications to be implemented by ClightX code (necessarily C-style) and $L_{2,\mathrm{Asm}}$ is an assembly layer interface containing all other primitives (implemented in LAsm), so that $L_2 = L_{2,\mathrm{C}} \oplus L_{2,\mathrm{Asm}}$.
2. For each such part of the overlay, design an intermediate layer interface $L'_{1,\mathrm{C}}$ and $L'_{1,\mathrm{Asm}}$ with the same abstract state type as $L_1$ (see Section 4.3), and prove $L_{2,\mathrm{C}} \leqslant_R L'_{1,\mathrm{C}}$ and $L_{2,\mathrm{Asm}} \leqslant_R L'_{1,\mathrm{Asm}}$ independently of the implementation.
3. For both intermediate layer interfaces, prove that they are implemented by modules $M_{\mathrm{C}}$ and $M_{\mathrm{Asm}}$ on top of $L_1$ respectively, i.e. $L'_{1,\mathrm{C}} \leqslant_{\mathbf{id}} [\![M_{\mathrm{C}}]\!]L_1$ and $L'_{1,\mathrm{Asm}} \leqslant_{\mathbf{id}} [\![M_{\mathrm{Asm}}]\!]L_1$.
4. Then, compile $M_{\mathrm{C}}$: $[\![M_{\mathrm{C}}]\!]L_1 \leqslant^{\mathrm{comp}} [\![\mathrm{CompCertX}(M_{\mathrm{C}})]\!]L_1$.

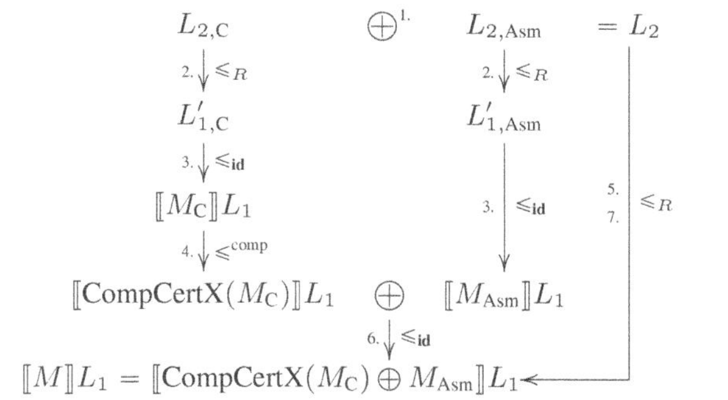

**Figure 13.** Proof steps of layer refinement $L_1 \vdash_R M : L_2$

5. Using LLE-TRANS and LLE-MON to combine 2. and 3., we have: $L_{2,\mathrm{C}} \oplus L_{2,\mathrm{Asm}} \leqslant_R L'_{1,\mathrm{C}} \oplus L'_{1,\mathrm{Asm}} \leqslant_{\mathbf{id}} [\![M_{\mathrm{C}}]\!]L_1 \oplus [\![M_{\mathrm{Asm}}]\!]L_1$
   On the C side (left of $\oplus$), Lemma 2 shows that $\leqslant_R$ absorbs $\leqslant^{\mathrm{comp}}$. By 4.: $L_{2,\mathrm{C}} \oplus L_{2,\mathrm{Asm}} \leqslant_R [\![\mathrm{CompCertX}(M_{\mathrm{C}})]\!]L_1 \oplus [\![M_{\mathrm{Asm}}]\!]L_1$
6. From the soundness of HCOMP (proof in TR [13]), and because $M = \mathrm{CompCertX}(M_{\mathrm{C}}) \oplus M_{\mathrm{Asm}}$, we have:
   $$[\![\mathrm{CompCertX}(M_{\mathrm{C}})]\!]L_1 \oplus [\![M_{\mathrm{Asm}}]\!]L_1 \leqslant_{\mathbf{id}} [\![M]\!]L_1$$
7. Finally, by combining 5. and 6., we have $L_{2,\mathrm{C}} \oplus L_{2,\mathrm{Asm}} \leqslant_R [\![M]\!]L_1$. Since $L_2 = L_{2,\mathrm{C}} \oplus L_{2,\mathrm{Asm}}$, by using LLE-UB-LEFT and LLE-COMM, we have: $L_2 \leqslant_R [\![M]\!]L_1 \leqslant_{\mathbf{id}} [\![M]\!]L_1 \oplus L_1 \leqslant_{\mathbf{id}} L_1 \oplus [\![M]\!]L_1$, thus we get $L_1 \vdash_R M : L_2$.

## 7. Case study: certified OS kernels

To demonstrate the power of our new languages and tools, we have applied our new layered approach to specify and verify four variants of mCertiKOS kernels in the Coq proof assistant. This section describes these kernels and the benefits of the approach.

The mCertiKOS base kernel is a simplified uniprocessor version of the CertiKOS kernel [12] designed for the 32 bit x86 architecture. It provides a multi-process environment for user-space applications using separate virtual address space, where the communications between different applications are established by message passing. The mCertiKOS-hyp kernel, built on top of the base kernel, is a realistic hypervisor kernel that can boot recent versions of unmodified Linux operating systems (Debian 6.0.6 and Ubuntu 12.04.2). The mCertiKOS-rz kernel extends the hypervisor supporting "ring 0" processes, hosting "certifiably safe" services and application programs inside the kernel address space. Finally, we strip the last kernel down to the mCertiKOS-emb kernel, removing virtualization, virtual memory, and user-space interrupt handling. This results in a minimal operating system suitable for embedded environments.

The layer structures of these kernels are shown in the top half of Fig. 14; each block in the top half represents a collection of sub-layers shown in the bottom half (as we zoom in on mCertiKOS-hyp).

***mCertiKOS*** The layered approach is the key to our success in fully certifying a kernel. In Sec. 4.3, we have shown how to define getters and setters for abstract data types like those in Fig. 8, allowing higher layers to manipulate abstract states. Furthermore, layering is also crucial to certification of thread queues as discussed in Sec. 2. Instead of directly proving that a C linked-list implements a functional list, we insert an intermediate layer as shown in Fig. 1 to divide the difficult task into two steps.

These may look like mere proof techniques for enabling abstract states or reducing proof effort, but they echo the following mantra which makes our certification more efficient and scalable:

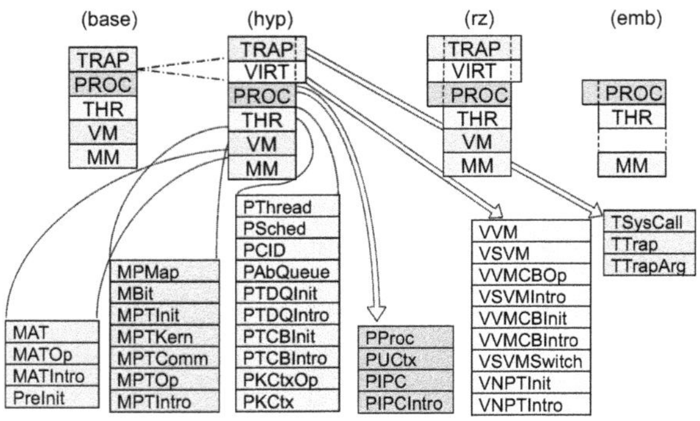


**Figure 14.** Various mCertiKOS layer structures. Layer short-hands: TRAP: interrupt handling; VIRT: virtualization; PROC: process management; THR: thread management; VM: virtual memory; MM: physical memory management.

> *Abstract in minimal steps, specify* full *behavior, and hide* all *underlying details.*

This is also how we prove the overall contextual correctness guarantees for all system calls and interrupt handlers. Fig. 15 shows the call graph of the page fault handler, including all functions called both directly and indirectly. Circles indicate functions, solid arrows mean primitive invocations, and faint dashed lines are primitives that are translated by all the layers they pass through.

Defined in TSysCall layer interface, the page fault handler makes use of proc_exit and proc_start, both defined in PProcd layer interface. Since the invocations of them are separated by other primitive calls, one may expect that the invariants need to be re-established or the effects of the in-between calls re-interpreted. Fortunately, as our mantra suggests, when the in-between layers translate the two primitives to TTrap layer interface, the behaviors of them are *fully* specified in terms of TTrap's abstract states, and the invariants of PProc layer interface are considered the underlying details and have *all* been hidden. This is especially important for calls like proc_exit to ikern_set which span over 20 layers with the abstract states so different that direct translation is not feasible.

Finally, kernel initialization is another difficult task that has been missing from other kernel verification projects. The traditional kernel initialization process is not compatible with *"specify full behavior and hide all underlying details."* For example, start_kernel in Linux kernel makes a sequence of calls to module initializations. mCertiKOS's initialization (see its call graph in Fig. 16) is a *chain* of calls to layer initializations; this pattern complies with the guideline that initializing one layer should hide the detail about initializing the lower layers. Without layering, the specifications of *all* functions will be populated with initialization flags for each module they depend on. This makes encapsulation harder and could also lead to a quadratic blowup in size and proving effort.

***mCertiKOS-hyp*** The mCertiKOS-hyp kernel provides core primitives to build full-fledged user-level hypervisors by supporting one of the two popular hardware virtualization technologies – AMD SVM. The primitives include the operations for manipulating the virtual machine status, handling VMEXITs, starting or stopping a virtual machine, *etc.* The details of virtualization, e.g., the virtual machine control block and the nested page table, are hidden from the guest applications. The hypervisor functionalities are implemented in nine layers and then inserted in between process management and interrupt handling layers. The layered approach allows us to do so while (1) only modeling virtualization-specific structures when needed; (2) retaining primitives in the layer interface PProc by systematic lifting; and (3) adding new primitives (including a new initialization function) guaranteed not to interfere with existing primitives.

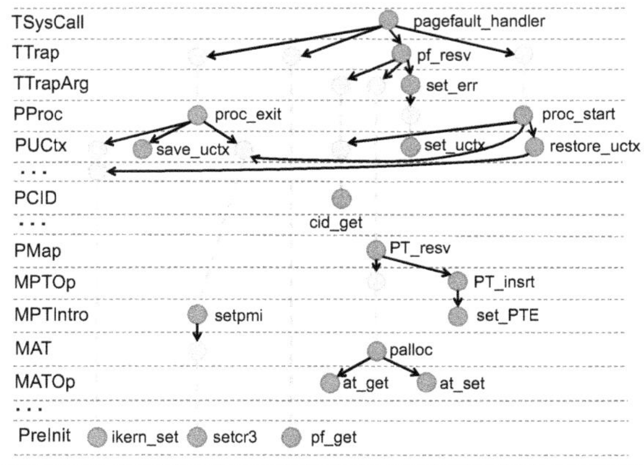


**Figure 15.** Call graph of the page fault handler

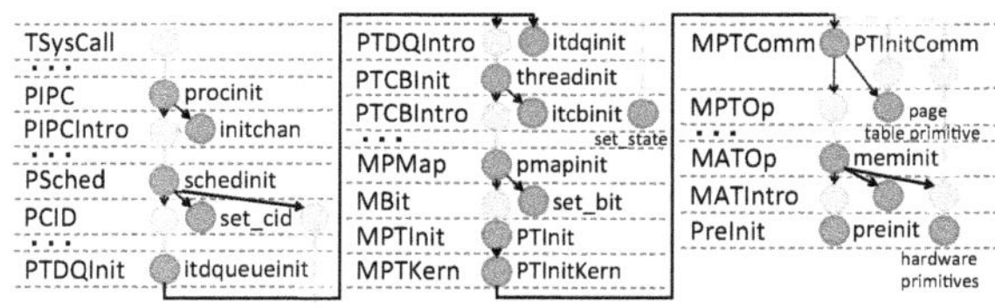


**Figure 16.** Call graph of mCertiKOS initializer

***mCertiKOS-rz*** The mCertiKOS-rz kernel explores a different dimension—instead of adding intermediate layers, we augmented a few existing layers (in mCertiKOS-hyp) with support of ring 0 processes. The main modification is at PProc, where an additional kind of threads is defined. However, all the layers between PProc and TSysCall also need to be extended to expose the functionality as system calls. Thankfully, since all the new primitives are already described in deep specifications, lifting them to system calls only requires equality reasoning in Coq.

***mCertiKOS-emb*** The mCertiKOS-emb kernel cuts features down to a bare minimum: it does not switch to user mode, hence does not require memory protection and does not provide system call interfaces. This requires *removing* features instead of adding them. Since the layered structure minimizes entanglements by eliminating unnecessary dependencies and code coupling, the removal process was relatively easy and straightforward. Moreover, removing the top 12 layers requires no additional specifications for those now top-level primitives—deep specifications are suitable for both internal reasonings and external descriptions. Thread and process management layers now sit directly on top of physical memory management; virtual memory is never enabled. The layers remain largely the same barring the removal of primitives mentioning page tables.

***Evaluation and limitations*** The planning and development of mCertiKOS took 9.5 person months plus 2 person months on linking and code extraction. With the infrastructure in place, mCertiKOS-hyp only took 1.5 person months to finish, and mCertiKOS-rz and mCertiKOS-emb take half a person month each. The kernels are written, layer by layer, in LAsm and ClightX abstract syntaxes along with driver functions specifying how to compose (link) them. All of those are in Coq for the proofs to refer to. We utilize Coq's code extraction to get an OCaml program which contains CompCertX, the abstract syntax trees of the kernels, and the driver functions, which invoke CompCertX on pieces of ClightX code and generate the full assembly file. The output of the OCaml program is then fed to an assembler to produce the kernel executable.

With the device drivers (running as user processes) and a cooperative scheduler, most of the benchmarks in lmbench are under 2x slowdown running in mCertiKOS-hyp, well within expected overhead. Ring 0 processes, not used in the above experiment, can easily lower the number as we measured one to two orders of magnitude reduction in the number of cycles needed to serve system calls.

Because the proof was originally developed directly in terms of abstract machines and program transformations, the current code base does not yet reflect the calculus presented in Sec. 3 in its entirety. Notably, vertical composition is done at the level of the whole-machine contextual refinements obtained by applying the soundness theorem to each individual abstraction layer.

Outside our verified kernels (mCertiKOS-hyp consists of about 3000 lines of C and assembly), there are 300 lines of C and 170 lines of x86 assembly code that are not verified yet: the preinit procedure, the ELF loader used by user process creation, and functions such as memcpy which currently cannot be verified because of a limitation arising from the CompCert memory model. Device drivers are not verified because LAsm lacks device models for expressing the correctness statement. Finally, the CompCert assembler for converting LAsm into machine code remains unverified.

## 8. Related work

***Hoare-style program verification*** Hoare logic [14] and its modern variants [32, 2, 26] were introduced to prove strong (partial or total) correctness properties of programs annotated with pre- and postconditions. A total-correctness Hoare triple $[P]C[Q]$ often means a refinement between the implementation $C$ and the specification $[P, Q]$: given any state $S$, if the precondition $P(S)$ holds, then the command $C$ can run safely and terminate with a state that satisfies $Q$. Though not often done, it is also possible to introduce auxiliary/ghost states to serve as "abstract states" and prove that a program implements a specification via a simulation.

Our layer language can be viewed as a novel way of imposing a module system over Hoare-style program verification. We insist on using interfaces with deep specifications and we address the "conflicting abstract states" problem mentioned in Sec. 2. Traditional program verification does not always use deep specification (for pre- and post-conditions) so the module interfaces (e.g., $[P, Q]$) may allow some safe but unwanted behaviors. Such gap is fine if the goal is to just prove safety (as in static type-checking), but if we want to prove the strong contextual correctness property across module boundaries, it is important that each interface accurately describes the functionality and scope of the underlying implementation.

In addition to the obvious benefits on compositionality, our layered approach also enables a new powerful way of combining programming- and specification languages in a single setting. Each layer interface enables a new programming language at a specific abstraction level, which is then used to implement layers at even higher levels. As we move up the layer hierarchy, our programming language gets closer and closer to the specification language—it can call primitives at higher abstraction levels but it still supports general-purpose programming (e.g., in ClightX).

Interestingly, we did not need to introduce any program logic to verify our OS kernel code. Instead, we verify it directly using the ClightX (or LAsm) language semantics (which is already conveniently parameterized over a layer interface). In fact, unlike Hoare logic which shows that a program (e.g., $C$) refines a specification (e.g., $[P, Q]$), we instead show there is a downward simulation from the specification to the program. As in CompCert, we found this easier to prove and we can do this because both our specification and language semantics are deterministic relative to external events.

***Stepwise program refinement*** Dijkstra [9] proposed to "realize" a complex program by decomposing it into a hierarchy of linearly ordered "abstract machines." Based on this idea, the PSOS team at SRI [27] developed the Hierarchical Development Methodology (HDM) and applied HDM to design and specify an OS using 20 hierarchically organized modules. HDM was difficult to be rigorously applied in practice, probably because of the lack of powerful specification and proof tools. In this paper, we advance the HDM paradigm by using a new formal layer language to connect multiple layers and by implementing all certified layers and proofs in a modern proof assistant. We also pursued decomposition more aggressively since it made our verification task much easier.

Morgan's refinement calculus [25] is a formalized approach to Dijkstra's stepwise refinement. Using this calculus, a high-level specification can be refined through a series of correctness-preserving transformations and eventually turned into an efficient executable. Our work imposes a new layer language to enhance compositional reasoning. We use ClightX (or LAsm) and the Coq logic as our "refinement" language, and use a certified layer (with deep specification) to represent each such correctness-preserving transformation. All our ClightX and LAsm instances have executable semantics and can be compiled and linked using our new CompCertX compiler.

***Separate compilation for CompCert*** Compositional compiler correctness is an extremely challenging problem [3, 15], especially when it involves an open compiler with multiple languages [29]. In the context of CompCert, a recent proposal [4] aims to tackle the full Clight language but it has not been fully implemented in the CompCert compiler. While our CompCertX compiler proves a stronger correctness theorem for each ClightX layer, the ClightX language is subtly different from the original full-featured Clight language. Within each ClightX layer, all locally allocated memory blocks (e.g., stack frames) cannot be updated by functions defined in another layer. This means that ClightX does not support the same general "stack-allocated data structures" as in Clight. This is fine for our OS kernels since they do not allocate any data structures on stack, but it means that CompCertX can not be regarded as a full featured separate compiler for CompCert.

***OS kernel verification*** The seL4 team [17] were the first to build a proof of functional correctness for a realistic microkernel. The seL4 work is impressive in that all the proofs were done inside a modern mechanized proof assistant. They have shown that the behaviors of 7500 lines of their C code always follow an abstract specification of their kernel. To make verification easier, they introduced an intermediate executable specification to hide C specifics. Both their abstract and executable specifications are "monolithic" as they are not divided into layers to support abstraction among different kernel modules. These kernel interdependencies led to more complex invariants which may explain why their effort took 11 person years.

The initial seL4 effort was done completely at the C level so it does not support many assembly level features such as address translation. This also made verification of assembly code and kernel initialization difficult (1200 lines of C and 500 lines of assembly are still unverified). It is also unclear how to use their verified kernel to reason about user-level programs since they would be running in a different address space. Our certified kernels, on the other hand, directly model assembly-level machines that support all kernel/user and host/guest programs. Memory access to a user-level address space must go through a page table, and memory access in a guest virtual machine must go through a nested page table. We thus had no problem verifying our kernel initialization or assembly code.

***Modular verification of low-level code*** Vaynberg and Shao [36] also used a layered approach to verify a small virtual memory manager. Their layers are not linearly ordered; instead, their seven abstract machines form a DAG with potential upcalls (i.e., calls from a lower layer to upper ones). As a result, their initialization function (an upcall) was much harder to verify. Their refinement proofs between layers are insensitive to termination, from which they can only prove partial correctness but not the strong contextual correctness property which we prove in our current work.

Feng *et al.* [11] developed OCAP, an open framework for linking components verified in different domain-specific program logics. They verified a thread library with hardware interrupts and preemption [10] using a variant of concurrent separation logic [28]. They decomposed the thread implementation into a sequential layer (with interrupts disabled) and a concurrent layer (with interrupts enabled). Chlipala [8] developed Bedrock, an automated Coq library to support verified low-level programming. All these systems aimed to prove *partial correctness* only, so they are quite different from the layered simulation proofs given in this paper.

## 9. Conclusions

Abstraction layers are key techniques used in building large-scale computer software and hardware. In this paper, we have presented a novel language-based account of abstraction layers and shown that they are particularly suitable for supporting abstraction over deep specifications, which is essential for compositional verification of strong correctness properties. We have designed a new layer language and imposed it on two different core languages (ClightX and LAsm). We have also built a verified compiler from ClightX to LAsm. By aggressively decomposing each complex abstraction into smaller abstraction steps, we have successfully developed several certified OS kernels that prove deeper properties (contextual correctness), contain smaller trusted computing bases (all code verified at the assembly level), require significantly less effort (3000 lines of C and assembly code proved in less than 1 person year), and demonstrate strong support for extensibility (layers are heavily reused in different certified kernels). We expect that both deep specifications and certified abstraction layers will become critical technologies and important building blocks for developing large-scale certified system infrastructures in the future.

***Acknowledgments*** We thank Quentin Carbonneaux, David Costanzo, Rance DeLong, Xinyu Feng, Bryan Ford, Liang Gu, Jan Hoffmann, Hongjin Liang, Joshua Lockerman, Peter Neumann, David Pichardie, members of the CertiKOS team at Yale, and anonymous referees for helpful comments and suggestions that improved this paper and the implemented tools. This research is based on work supported in part by DARPA grants FA8750-10-2-0254 and FA8750-12-2-0293, NSF grants 1065451 and 0915888, and ONR Grant N00014-12-1-0478. It is also supported in part by China Scholarship Council and National Natural Science Foundation of China (NSFC grants 61229201 and 61202052). Any opinions, findings, and conclusions contained in this document are those of the authors and do not reflect the views of these agencies.

## References

[1] C. Y. Baldwin and K. B. Clark. *Design Rules: Volume 1, The Power of Modularity*. MIT Press, March 2000.

[2] M. Barnett, B.-Y. E. Chang, R. DeLine, B. Jacobs, and K. R. M. Leino. Boogie: A modular reusable verifier for object-oriented programs. In *Proc. 4th Symp on Formal Methods for Components and Objects*, 2005.

[3] N. Benton and C.-K. Hur. Biorthogonality, step-indexing and compiler correctness. In *ICFP'09*, pages 97–108, 2009.

[4] L. Beringer, G. Stewart, R. Dockins, and A. W. Appel. Verified compilation for shared-memory C. In *ESOP'14*, pages 107–127, 2014.

[5] S. Blazy and X. Leroy. Mechanized semantics for the Clight subset of the C language. *J. Automated Reasoning*, 43(3):263–288, 2009.

[6] Q. Carbonneaux, J. Hoffmann, T. Ramananandro, and Z. Shao. End-to-end verification of stack-space bounds for C programs. In *PLDI'14*.

[7] S. Chaudhuri, S. Gulwani, and R. Lublinerman. Continuity analysis of programs. In *POPL'10*, pages 57–69, 2010.

[8] A. Chlipala. Mostly-automated verification of low-level programs in computational separation logic. In *PLDI'11*, pages 234–245, 2011.

[9] E. W. Dijkstra. Notes on structured programming. In *Structured programming*, pages 1–82. Academic Press, 1972.

[10] X. Feng, Z. Shao, Y. Dong, and Y. Guo. Certifying low-level programs with hardware interrupts and preemptive threads. In *PLDI'08*, pages 170–182, June 2008.

[11] X. Feng, Z. Shao, Y. Guo, and Y. Dong. Combining domain-specific and foundational logics to verify complete software systems. In *VSTTE'08*, pages 54–69, 2008.

[12] L. Gu, A. Vaynberg, B. Ford, Z. Shao, and D. Costanzo. CertiKOS: a certified kernel for secure cloud computing. In *APSys '11*, 2011.

[13] R. Gu, J. Koenig, T. Ramananandro, Z. Shao, X. Wu, S.-C. Weng, H. Zhang, and Y. Guo. Deep specifications and certified abstraction layers. Yale Univ. Technical Report YALEU/DCS/TR-1500; `http://flint.cs.yale.edu/publications/dscal.html`, Oct. 2014.

[14] C. A. R. Hoare. An axiomatic basis for computer programming. *Communications of the ACM*, 12(10):576–580, Oct. 1969.

[15] C.-K. Hur, D. Dreyer, G. Neis, and V. Vafeiadis. The marriage of bisimulations and Kripke logical relations. In *POPL'12*, pages 59–72.

[16] D. Jackson. *Software abstractions: logic, languages, and analysis*. The MIT Press, 2012.

[17] G. Klein, K. Elphinstone, G. Heiser, J. Andronick, D. Cock, P. Derrin, D. Elkaduwe, K. Engelhardt, et al. seL4: Formal verification of an OS kernel. In *SOSP'09*, pages 207–220, October 2009.

[18] L. Lamport. The temporal logic of actions. *ACM Transactions on Programming Languages and Systems*, 16(3), May 1994.

[19] X. Leroy. The CompCert verified compiler. `http://compcert.inria.fr/`, 2005–2014.

[20] X. Leroy. A formally verified compiler back-end. *Journal of Automated Reasoning*, 43(4):363–446, 2009.

[21] X. Leroy and S. Blazy. Formal verification of a C-like memory model and its uses for verifying program transformation. *J. Automated Reasoning*, 41(1):1–31, 2008.

[22] N. A. Lynch and F. W. Vaandrager. Forward and backward simulations: I. Untimed systems. *Inf. Comput.*, 121(2):214–233, 1995.

[23] R. Milner, M. Tofte, R. Harper, and D. MacQueen. *The Definition of Standard ML (Revised)*. MIT Press, Cambridge, Massachusetts, 1997.

[24] J. C. Mitchell. Representation independence and data abstraction. In *POPL'86*, pages 263–276, January 1986.

[25] C. C. Morgan. *Programming from specifications, 2nd Edition*. Prentice-Hall, 1994.

[26] A. Nanevski, G. Morrisett, and L. Birkedal. Polymorphism and separation in Hoare type theory. In *ICFP'06*, pages 62–73, Sept. 2006.

[27] P. G. Neumann, R. S. Boyer, R. J. Feiertag, K. N. Levitt, and L. Robinson. A provably secure operating system: its system, its applications, and proofs. Technical Report CSL-116, SRI, May 1980.

[28] P. W. O'Hearn. Resources, concurrency and local reasoning. In *CONCUR'04*, pages 49–67, 2004.

[29] J. T. Perconti and A. Ahmed. Verifying an open compiler using multi-language semantics. In *ESOP'14*, pages 128–148, 2014.

[30] B. C. Pierce. *Types and Programming Languages*. The MIT Press, 2002.

[31] J. C. Reynolds. *Theories of Programming Languages*. Cambridge University Press, 1998.

[32] J. C. Reynolds. Separation logic: A logic for shared mutable data structures. In *LICS'02*, pages 55–74, 2002.

[33] J. Sevcík, V. Vafeiadis, F. Z. Nardelli, S. Jagannathan, and P. Sewell. CompCertTSO: A verified compiler for relaxed-memory concurrency. *J. ACM*, 60(3), 2013.

[34] M. Spivey. *The Z Notation: A reference manual*. Prentice Hall, 1992.

[35] The Coq development team. The Coq proof assistant. `http://coq.inria.fr`, 1999 – 2014.

[36] A. Vaynberg and Z. Shao. Compositional verification of a baby virtual memory manager. In *CPP'12*, pages 143–159, Dec 2012.

# From Network Interface to Multithreaded Web Applications

## A Case Study in Modular Program Verification

Adam Chlipala
MIT CSAIL
adamc@csail.mit.edu

## Abstract

Many verifications of realistic software systems are *monolithic*, in the sense that they define single *global invariants* over complete system state. More *modular* proof techniques promise to support reuse of component proofs and even reduce the effort required to verify one concrete system, just as modularity simplifies standard software development. This paper reports on one case study applying modular proof techniques in the Coq proof assistant. To our knowledge, it is the first modular verification certifying a system that combines infrastructure with an application of interest to end users. We assume a nonblocking API for managing TCP networking streams, and on top of that we work our way up to certifying multithreaded, database-backed Web applications. Key verified components include a cooperative threading library and an implementation of a domain-specific language for XML processing. We have deployed our case-study system on mobile robots, where it interfaces with off-the-shelf components for sensing, actuation, and control.

***Categories and Subject Descriptors*** F.3.1 [*Logics and Meanings of Programs*]: Specifying and Verifying and Reasoning about Programs - Mechanical verification; D.2.4 [*Software Engineering*]: Software/Program Verification - Correctness proofs

***Keywords*** modular program verification; proof assistants; thread libraries; Internet servers; domain-specific languages

## 1. Introduction

Program verification for realistic systems is very labor-intensive. The proof engineer faces all of the usual challenges of the software engineer and then some. Typically a machine-checked proof of program correctness requires more human effort than implementing the software system in the first place. *Modularity* is an essential part of the programmer's arsenal in mastering complexity, and we might ask for the same in verification. We want a program's proof to mirror its natural decomposition into encapsulated components. Each component should be proved to respect a formal interface, and thereafter we reason about the component only through its interface. Not only does this style allow us to reuse component proofs in verifications of different full systems, but it also frequently lowers the effort to verify just one system, for the same reason the author of a program with a special-purpose data structure may choose to encapsulate that data structure in its own class or module, even with no expectation for future reuse in other programs.

The most recent impressive system verifications are not modular. The L4.verified [22] and Verve [37] projects have both verified operating-system kernels with different semi-automated proof tools. Their proofs are structured around *global invariants* relating all state of all system components, both in the kernel and in relevant parts of applications. When one part of a kernel changes, the global invariant must often be modified, and the proofs of all other components must be reconsidered. Ideally, proof automation is able to use already-written annotations and proof scripts to reconstruct the new proofs, but in practice the proof engineer is often required to revisit old proof details of system modules beside the one he has changed. Such coupling between proof pieces is undesirable, and we instinctively feel that it should be avoidable for certain kinds of changes, like applying an optimization that does not affect a component's API-level behavior.

A variety of impressive results have also been published for *modular* verification systems. Modular program logics have been demonstrated for a variety of tricky features of low-level code including dynamic thread creation [9], function pointers [29], stack-based control operators [12], self-modifying code [3], garbage collection [28], and interrupts [10]. However, these past projects never applied modular verification *at scale*, certifying a full system of interest to end users. In theory, the frameworks were set up to allow black-box linking of proofs about systems infrastructure and applications, to produce full-system proofs, but the devil is in the details. This paper is about those details.

We present **the first realistic case study in modular mechanized program verification, establishing properties of a deployed application**. What exactly we mean by "realistic" we will spell out below. One key element is separate proof of an application and reusable systems infrastructure. In our case, the application is a *database-backed dynamic Web application* and the infrastructure is a *cooperative multithreading library*. One subtle source of difficulty is supporting infrastructure that itself needs to play nicely with other modules of infrastructure, some of which may not even have been written or specified yet. Contrast that complication with the L4.verified [22] and Verve [37] proofs, which show correctness of OS kernels assumed to have exclusive control over all privileged elements of machine state; or the proof of the CompCert C compiler [23], which assumes that no other compiler will be used to produce code in the final program. Other elements of realism have produced further challenges, which we needed to solve on the way to deploying an application with real users who are not formal-methods experts.


*POPL '15*, January 15–17, 2015, Mumbai, India.

ACM 978-1-4503-3300-9/15/01... $15.00.
http://dx.doi.org/10.1145/2676726.2677003

What properties would we expect to see of modular verifications, in a hypothetical future world where such activities are standard, at least for code of particular importance?

- **Not all verified components will have theorems at the same level of detail.** The reason is the classic formal-methods complaint that "a word processor does not have an obvious specification worth proving." Also, different parts of a system may be of varying importance, where the proof engineer wants to invest more effort in more important components via more precise theorems.
- **Not all software in the final system will be verified.** It is necessary to have some kind of "foreign function interface" to connect to conventional components.
- **There will be further modular structure within infrastructure components, and this structure must be designed to facilitate effective reasoning in client code.** For instance, in the components of a thread library, we need to think carefully about which interfaces to assign to the data structures used to implement the scheduler, where we feel pressure to make the interfaces as *weak* as possible to minimize proof effort. However, we are building these modules so that they may eventually be linked with client code, where we feel pressure to make the infrastructure interfaces as *strong* as possible to give the client flexibility.
- **Some components will be implemented in domain-specific languages (DSLs)**, but we do not want to have to trust anything about those languages or their implementations. Our case study uses a DSL for declarative XML processing and access to a relational database.
- **Most proof details should be automated.** It is unacceptable to require detailed manual proof for each line of program code.
- Most importantly, **we must actually link our proofs of infrastructure components with proofs of applications, to form full-program theorems.** A proof of infrastructure is only as good as the sorts of proof composition it enables.

To the best of our knowledge, no past work in modular verification has produced a runnable case study demonstrating any of the above principles, whereas ours involves all of them.

Our verification was done in the Coq proof assistant using the Bedrock library [4, 5], whose basic functionality we review in more detail shortly. Bedrock is a platform for producing verified assembly code by programming, proving, and compiling entirely within Coq.

Our application is a replacement for the so-called Master Server of the popular open-source Robot Operating System (ROS) [32]. ROS is a platform for component-based implementation of robotics software. Systems are structured as networks of nodes (processes) that communicate only via message-passing (mostly with TCP). Messages are largely exchanged via a publish-subscribe architecture. Among other services, the Master Server processes node requests to publish or subscribe to particular named topics. It must maintain an in-memory database mapping node names to IP addresses and ports, mapping topics to their publishers and subscribers, and so on. The Master Server speaks the XML-RPC protocol and runs as a Web server. Our version of it has been deployed on several semi-autonomous vehicles and used to coordinate the interaction of nodes for sensors, actuators, and control algorithms.

The system infrastructure we have verified is a cooperative threading library. As unverified primitives, we assume system-call functions for opening TCP sockets and sending and receiving byte streams over them. Furthermore, we require system calls for efficient polling, to determine which sockets have new data to process. All the assumed primitives beside polling are nonblocking. On top of them, we implement a threading library that supports the standard abstraction of threads blocking during calls to IO functions, without forcing programmers to refactor their code into continuation-passing style.

We prove a deep functional correctness theorem for the thread library, where bugs can lead to particularly vexing misbehavior where one thread overwrites the private state of another. To demonstrate the possibility to mix proofs at different granularities in one verification, we verify the application at the level of data-structure shape invariants, mostly pertaining to the in-memory relational database. We link the module proofs together into a whole-program proof.

The *unifying specification style* applied to the final program is: various points in the assembly code (e.g., entry labels of crucial functions) are labeled with invariants in higher-order logic, formalizing properties of machine state that should always hold upon reaching those points. We prove that, starting from an initial program location whose invariant is satisfied, execution will proceed safely forever, never reaching a program point whose invariant is false, regardless of what nondeterministic results system calls return. These invariants can be at many different levels of specificity. Invariants within our thread library encode detailed requirements for functional correctness, while invariants in our application code focus more on shape invariants of data structures like the in-memory relational database. All invariants, throughout the program, must formalize enough of essential isolation properties to guarantee lack of corruption of other modules' data structures.

Section 2 gives a more detailed outline of what we have proved, and Section 3 reviews the relevant aspects of the Bedrock framework. The next few sections present our **main contributions**:

- Section 4 explains how to extend Bedrock with a treatment of system calls, to model *interaction with conventional, unverified libraries*.
- Section 5 introduces three *verification design patterns* that we found essential to meet our standard of proof modularity and automation. We present a new style of definition for recursive predicates that are higher-order and stateful, a new formal interface style for components of thread libraries or others working with first-class code pointers, and a new take on classic separation-logic [33] rules that is compatible with verifying the building blocks of domain-specific languages.
- The next two sections present *particular modular verification architectures that we found work well for our components*. Section 6 presents the architecture of our *cooperative threading library* and Section 7 the architecture of our *verified compiler for a DSL for XML processing and relational database operations*.
- Finally, one contribution that we want to highlight most is that our proofs apply to real code that has been deployed outside a formal-methods context. Section 8 gives some *empirical analysis of our proofs and executable code*, which we do not believe has been done before for modularly verified systems.

The complete source code of this project, for both rechecking proofs and generating executable Linux programs, is available on the project Web site:

`http://plv.csail.mit.edu/bedrock/`

## 2. System Architecture Summary

Before proceeding to technical details, we take a moment to sketch the full layered architecture that we have verified. Different levels of this architecture have separately encapsulated proofs, and we combine all the proofs, treated as black boxes, into one final theorem about a particular linked assembly program.

To summarize our results: the unifying verification formalism is based on *invariant checking*. Programs contain assertions written in higher-order logic. That is, they may express much more intricate properties than in executable code-based assertions. Each module contains code with assertions, plus assumptions on other modules, plus proofs that the assumptions imply that *no assertions are violated while we are running code from this module*. Our final program is a large assembly source file (about 500,000 lines) where each basic block begins with an assertion, but we produce this code by (verified) compilation from higher-level languages with their own notions of where assertions (again, in higher-order logic, not just executable code) are allowed. The *final theorem* is that the assembly code runs without assertion violations.

The Bedrock platform is fundamentally single-threaded at its lowest level. We verify assembly programs with respect to a single-core operational semantics. We do not take advantage of parallelism as a performance optimization, but rather we use concurrency as a convenient program-structuring idiom, with multiple threads running and participating in different IO interactions. The thread model is *cooperative*, where threads yield control of the processor explicitly by calling particular library functions.

We prove *functional (partial) correctness* of our thread library, by giving it very expressive assertions, sufficient to enable easy verification of similar functional correctness of simple applications, e.g., proving that a factorial program really computes factorial despite context switches to other threads in the middle of its computation. Application assertions that we prove are about data-structure shape invariants. For instance, we have an in-memory relational database involving nontrivial use of arrays (with index arithmetic unchecked at runtime) and linked lists. In future work we would hope to establish stronger properties, but we also consider it worthwhile to demonstrate that modular verification is not "all or nothing." Rather, different parts of a system may be verified at different granularities, while still allowing fully rigorous linking into useful whole-program results.

Our proof is structured into several software layers. We expand on each layer in later sections, but here is a quick summary.

1. **Device Abstraction API**. We begin from a nonverified layer providing a set of system calls for basic, nonblocking access to a network card and TCP/IP stack. Without impacting our proofs, this layer could just as well be a simple interprocess communication mechanism, as the details of message-passing are orthogonal to the properties we verify.

2. **Data Structures & Algorithms** (systems-level). Our first verified layer considers core data structures, such as the free list of a `malloc()` implementation and the FIFO queue at the heart of a round-robin thread scheduler. Challenges here have to do with reasoning about heap-allocated data structures, pointer aliasing, and their connection to higher-level interfaces like "finite multiset" to be exported to higher layers.

3. **Thread Context Management**. Next, we provide an abstraction of *queues of suspended threads*. Verification challenges center on the relationship between memory and first-class code pointers (i.e., saved instruction pointers of threads). Each thread must be considered to own some private memory but also to access some shared memory, containing data structures that other threads access as well. Functions at this level must break basic abstractions of C-like code, implementing a coroutine style by storing function return pointers in heap data structures, rather than just returning to them as usual. The interface for this level should *hide* such details, so that higher layers may pretend that a normal function-call discipline is being followed.

4. **Blocking IO Abstraction**. The next challenge is to provide a simple interface that enables easy overlapping of IO and computation. While the lowest layer of our system exposes nonblocking IO functions, we combine them with thread queues to implement *blocking IO* plus *dynamic thread creation and destruction*. The interface of this level should make blocking IO calls appear very similar to the nonblocking calls, hiding the fact that threads may suspend themselves into queues while waiting for IO events to be enabled.

5. **Data Structures & Algorithms** (application-level). We implement a simple in-memory relational database, with standard data structures for representing table state.

6. **Domain-Specific Language** (application-level). Our application must both access the database and do parsing and generation of XML, since it provides an XML-RPC Web service. We implemented a domain-specific language (DSL) called the Bedrock Web Service Language (BWS), which more or less allows us to execute intuitive pseudocode for such operations. Our language has a verified compiler, so programmers do not need to do *any manual proof* to generate a theorem corresponding to a compiled application, showing that it maintains the invariants of the database, does not interfere with other threads, etc.

7. **Application Logic**. Finally, we implement the ROS Master service as a BWS program in about 400 lines of code, calling BWS library tactics to automate its proof.

Layers 2 through 4 would be considered as a "user-level thread library" in UNIX parlance. They implement functionality similar to what has been treated in operating-systems-verification projects like L4.verified [22]. Those projects have generally given *operational* specifications to kernels, via nondeterministic programs expressing how the kernel should respond to hardware and user-level events. In the modular verification style we adopt here, we instead specify all layers of the system in terms of *invariants* that are respected and with *preconditions* and *postconditions* of functions. The two approaches can be related to each other formally, and the invariant style tends to make for easier verification of application-level properties.

Of course, one can always ask for more specific theorems about programs, and it is hard to come up with a formal characterization of "full functional correctness for a full system." For instance, most theorems assume correctness of hardware at some level, and our proof goes even further in considering a TCP/IP stack to be outside the scope of what we verify. However, we do not assume any other services traditionally provided by an operating system: we need no virtual memory, no process preemption interrupts, and so on. The program style is set up to be compatible with "bare-metal" execution in future work. We start modestly with our application-level specifications, as this case study is targeted at learning pragmatic lessons about modular program proofs from first principles.

## 3. Review of Bedrock

Our verification is done using Bedrock, a Coq library that provides formal definitions, proof procedures, and syntax macros, which together enable implementing, specifying, verifying, and compiling low-level programs within Coq. At the core of Bedrock is the Bedrock IL, a kind of cross-platform assembly language. In the end, every program we verify is compiled to the Bedrock IL, and our correctness theorems are stated in terms of this language and its semantics. Every assembly basic block begins with an invariant, and we prove that each invariant holds each time it is visited. We compile Bedrock IL to 32-bit or 64-bit x86 assembly code for

| | | | |
|---|---|---|---|
| 2nd-order vars. | $\alpha$ | | |
| Coq propositions | $P$ | $\in$ | Prop |
| Machine words | $w$ | $\in$ | $\mathbb{W}$ |
| Machine states | $\gamma$ | $\in$ | $\mathbb{S}$ |
| Coq terms | $v$ | | |
| PropX | $\phi$ | $::=$ | $\lceil P \rceil \mid \{\vert\, \lambda\gamma.\ \phi \,\vert\}w \mid \phi \wedge \phi \mid \phi \vee \phi$ |
| | | | $\mid \phi \Rightarrow \phi \mid \forall x.\ \phi \mid \exists x.\ \phi$ |
| | | | $\mid \alpha(v) \mid \forall \alpha.\ \phi \mid \exists \alpha.\ \phi$ |

**Figure 1.** Syntax of the XCAP assertion logic

execution in Linux. That final translation is currently unverified, but it works in a particularly simple way, essentially macro-expanding each Bedrock IL opcode into a sequence of opcodes in the target language.

Though the core features deal with an assembly language, Bedrock provides infrastructure for combined verification and compilation of an extensible C-like language, the Bedrock Structured Programming System (BSPS) [5], and our explanation in this paper begins at that abstraction layer. We will write code that looks broadly like C. It is important to note that these programs appear within Coq source files that also contain theorem statements and proofs; Bedrock takes advantage of Coq's extensible parser to embed syntax of other languages. We make further use of the same facility to embed our new Bedrock Web Service Language, whose verified compiler is also built on top of BSPS to avoid redundant proofs about low-level code generation. We refer readers to past Bedrock publications [5] for details of the lower abstraction levels that we elide for the rest of this paper.

Bedrock implements the XCAP [29] program logic and inherits the sorts of final program correctness theorems that XCAP supports. XCAP is designed for modular verification of programs that manipulate code pointers as data. In such a setting, it is not obvious what is an appropriate notion of *specification* for functions. One might try defining a domain of specifications like $\mathbb{P} \triangleq (\mathbb{W} \rightharpoonup \mathbb{P}) \rightarrow \mathbb{S} \rightarrow \mathsf{Prop}$. That is, a specification is a predicate over both machine states $\mathbb{S}$ and mappings from program counters $\mathbb{W}$ to the specifications of the associated code blocks. Some sort of ability for specifications to refer to specifications or code of other blocks is essential for verifying higher-order programs. Unfortunately, the naïve recursive equation has no solution, as a simple cardinality argument shows.

Several more involved notions of specification have been studied. Many are based on *step indexing* [2], where otherwise troubling recursive definitions are made well-founded by adding extra parameters counting steps of program execution that remain. XCAP, and thus our work in this paper, is based on an alternative approach. A specification language is defined with a *deep embedding*, or an explicit definition of syntax trees in Coq. XCAP uses the PropX language shown in Figure 1.

PropX is a second-order assertion language that includes most of the usual connectives. Unusual features include $\lceil P \rceil$, for *lifting* a normal Coq proposition into PropX; and $\{\vert\, \lambda\gamma.\ \phi \,\vert\}w$, a kind of *Hoare double*, for asserting that the precondition of the code block pointed to by $w$ is the function $\lambda\gamma.\ \phi$, from Bedrock IL machine states to PropX formulas. Introducing this connective solves the problem with specifications that reference other specifications. Just as a classic static type system allows, e.g., a map function to constrain its argument using a syntactic function type, XCAP allows, e.g., an assembly-level map function to constrain its argument using a syntactic Hoare double nested within map's precondition. The soundness of either reasoning pattern is justified by considering that, at each point in program execution, we are running some code fragment that has been proved to meet a syntactic specification, which accurately describes the current state.

```
// Standard TCP socket operations
fd_t listen(int port);
fd_t accept(fd_t sock);
int read(fd_t sock, void *buf, int n_bytes);
int write(fd_t sock, void *buf, int n_bytes);
void close(fd_t sock);

// epoll-style IO event notification
res_t declare(fd_t sock, bool isWrite);
res_t wait(bool isBlocking);
```

**Figure 2.** List of system calls

Usually one wants a more semantic notion $\{\lambda\gamma.\ \phi\}w$ of a Hoare double, saying not that the given specification is literally attached to code block $w$, but rather that the given specification *implies* $w$'s specification semantically. Both this notation and the *Hoare triple* of separation logic [33] are defined by macro expansion to uses of $\{\vert \cdot \vert\}\cdot$ and other connectives.

Also crucial to the expressiveness of PropX is the inclusion of *second-order quantification* over predicate variables $\alpha$. For instance, in our thread library verification, we use this feature to quantify over invariants describing the private state of individual threads. The semantics of PropX formulas is given by a set of natural-deduction rules, where the second-order quantifiers receive the peculiar treatment of being given *introduction rules but no elimination rules*. As a result, elimination-style reasoning may only be done at the meta level, in Coq's normal logic, reasoning about the syntactic definition of PropX deduction. Here is where we run into the friction that seems always to accompany sound specification regimes for higher-order, stateful programs, as the soundness proof for the PropX deduction system cannot be adapted naturally to cover elimination rules for these quantifiers.

In the rest of this paper, we often adopt convenient shorthands like omitting lifting brackets $\lceil \cdot \rceil$ in PropX formulas, pretending that we are instead working in a more conventional higher-order logic.

Earlier we sketched the basic idea of a *verified module*: a unit of *code* annotated with *invariant assertions*, plus *assumptions* about which invariants (e.g., as precondition-postcondition pairs) are associated with code labels in other modules, plus *proof* that our own code never encounters assertion violations, if our assumptions are accurate. XCAP instantiates this style to the case of assembly code. Modules encapsulate sets of basic blocks, and a *linking theorem* justifies combining the basic blocks of two modules, when their assumptions are consistent. Linking module A with B may remove A's assumptions about B, and vice versa. Eventually, we link enough modules to empty out the assumptions, and we have a *closed program*. The final theorem about a verified closed program is that it never encounters violations of its invariant assertions. We also get a standard *memory safety* property, where code never accesses unmapped memory addresses or jumps to nonexistent program labels.

Once again, however, in this paper we take the assembly-level details for granted, hiding below the abstractions that BSPS provides. We think in terms of verified modules, invariants, linking, etc., for modules of C-like code.

## 4. System Calls

The last section reviewed existing tools that we rely on, and we now turn to new contributions. The next few sections discuss elements of modular verification that only show up when scaling to more

$$\frac{\begin{array}{c}[r.\mathsf{Sp}, r.\mathsf{Sp}+16) \in \mathsf{ValidMem} \\ m[r.\mathsf{Sp}+8] = buf \quad m[r.\mathsf{Sp}+12] = len \\ [buf, buf+len) \in \mathsf{ValidMem} \quad r'.\mathsf{Sp} = r.\mathsf{Sp} \\ (\forall a.\ a \notin [buf, buf+len) \to m'[a] = m[a])\end{array}}{(m, \texttt{read}, r) \longrightarrow (m', r.\mathsf{Rp}, r')}$$

**Figure 3.** Operational-semantics rule for `read()` system call

realistic systems. We begin here with the question, **how do we support integration with unverified support code**?

We extended the Bedrock IL with new *system calls*, trusted primitives outside the scope of our verification, upon which we depend to provide an efficient interface to the outside world. Since we focus on Internet servers, our system calls all relate to TCP network connections and IO. These system calls expose only nonblocking operations, with no controls on sharing resources (e.g., the network card) across different software components. Instead, we implement such controls in Bedrock and verify our implementations.

Figure 2 shows C prototypes for our trusted system calls. The first group of functions provides a simplified version of the standard BSD sockets API. We write `fd_t` for the type of file descriptors, standing here for open socket connections. Again we emphasize that all of these socket operations are *nonblocking*. For example, any call to `read()` will return immediately with an error code if no bytes are available to read.

On top of this interface, we built a verified implementation of the standard cooperative multithreading abstraction with blocking IO. To enable efficient polling of the kind needed to implement blocking IO, we use two additional system calls in the style of Linux's `epoll`[1]. A function `declare()` is called to register intent to read or write a particular socket, producing a value called a *reservation*. Later, when the program makes a `wait()` system call, the result is a reservation whose associated IO operation is now ready to execute. A call to `wait()` itself may either be blocking, if the program has no other useful work to do without further IO opportunities; or nonblocking, if there is further CPU-bound work to do while waiting for IO. Conceptually, in the former case, the system blocks until one of the reserved IO events becomes enabled, at which point that reservation ID is returned.

We have extended the Bedrock IL semantics to include these system calls as primitive operations, explained via one new operational-semantics rule per system call. Figure 3 gives an example rule for `read()`. The semantics is small-step, operating on states of the form $(m, pc, r)$, where $m$ is memory, $pc$ the program counter, and $r$ values of registers. Two registers in particular matter here, to formalize the calling convention that `read()` expects: the stack pointer $\mathsf{Sp}$ and the return pointer $\mathsf{Rp}$, which stores a code address to return to after the call.

The first few premises in Figure 3 formalize the precondition of `read()`. In order, we have that the stack pointer indicates a valid memory segment lasting at least 16 bytes (containing the values of passed parameters), two particular stack slots contain the values of parameters $buf$ and $len$, and the memory region signified by those parameters is valid. The remaining premises constrain the result state of this step. We say that the stack pointer $\mathsf{Sp}$ is guaranteed to be restored, and that only memory addresses within the passed buffer may be modified.

Note that the rule is quite nondeterministic. We give a conservative characterization of the unverified code that we link against. In particular, rather than formalizing the effect of the function, we just describe which parts of state it may change.

[1] `http://en.wikipedia.org/wiki/Epoll`

Though it is convenient to state our final theorems in terms of this relatively simple operational semantics, reasoning about this style of specification directly is unwieldy, so we restate it in the higher-level separation-logic [33] notation that Bedrock provides (and we prove that each restatement implies the original). For a concrete example, consider this Hoare triple that we prove for the `read()` function.

$$\{\mathsf{buf} \overset{?}{\mapsto} \mathsf{len}\}\mathsf{read}(\mathsf{sock}, \mathsf{buf}, \mathsf{len})\{\mathsf{buf} \overset{?}{\mapsto} \mathsf{len}\}$$

The notation $a \overset{?}{\mapsto} n$ asserts that memory address $a$ is the beginning of an accessible memory region of $n$ bytes.

The `read()` specification is not fully precise. For instance, the file descriptor `sock` is not mentioned at all. We do not model the detailed semantics of network access, instead conservatively modeling reading from the network as *nondeterministic*. Our concern is more with verifying the correct management of resources internal to a single server, so specifications focus on memory layout and transfers of control.

We implemented the system calls mostly in C, with some assembly code to mediate between the Bedrock calling convention and the native conventions of target platforms.

## 5. Three Verification Design Patterns

The last section discussed the operational semantics that we use to state our final theorem. Recall that programs at any level of Bedrock are annotated with *invariant assertions*, and we prove that assertions always hold whenever we reach them. We now describe three design patterns we developed in the course of choosing good invariants and good ways of proving that they always hold.

### 5.1 Defining Higher-Order Recursive Predicates

A challenging question arising in many verification tasks is **how should we define recursive, stateful, higher-order predicates**? That is, we need self-referential logical predicates that constrain both mutable state and first-class code pointers. Small changes in the formalism may bring large consequences for the ease of **proof automation**. Past work on verifying a thread library in XCAP [30] faced this challenge by extending XCAP with a new recursive $\mu$ connective. That specification style turns out to make automation especially challenging, for reasons that we explain shortly.

The natural use of recursive predicates in our setting is for queues of suspended threads. The associated data representation predicate must be *higher-order* because it deals with code pointers (for suspended threads) and *recursive* because the preconditions of those pointers must mention the same predicate we are defining. The last condition follows because we expect threads to be able to call into the thread library, whose methods will naturally be specified in terms of the same thread queue predicate.

In this section, we discuss sound encodings of such predicates, using a simpler motivating example, that of a function memo table structure that stores both a function and an optional cached return value for it. We would like to expose our memo table as an *abstract data type* with an *abstraction relation* that hides implementation details. The code module implementing memo tables should expose methods for allocating new tables, setting the function stored in a table, and querying the return value of a current function. For simplicity, we consider only stored functions with no arguments and no private state, satisfying deterministic specifications.

Since we model simple pure functions, a number $n$ serves as a "specification" for such a function, giving the result that it must always return, so it makes sense to define the invariant of memo tables as a predicate $\mathsf{MemoTable}(p, n)$, over the pointer $p$ to the table and the function specification $n$. Here is a first cut at the

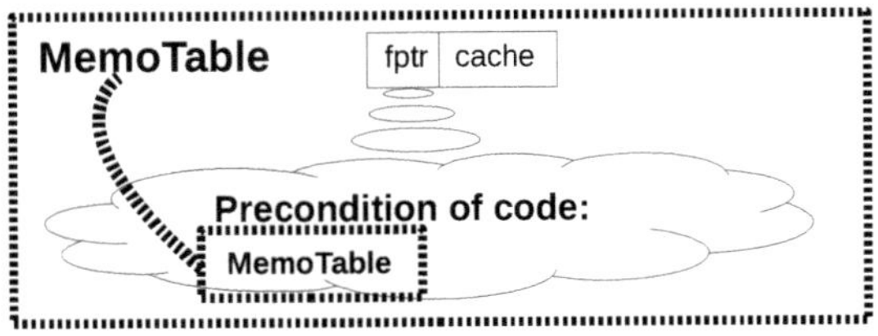


**Figure 4.** Sketch of a recursive higher-order specification for a simple memo table

predicate definition in separation-logic style [33], which makes intuitive sense but has a formal weakness that we come to shortly.

$$\mathsf{MemoTable}(p,n) \triangleq \exists f,c.\ (p \mapsto f,c) \wedge (c \neq 0 \Rightarrow c = n) \\ \wedge\ \{\mathsf{MemoTable}(p,n)\}f\{\mathsf{MemoTable}(p,n) \wedge \mathsf{result} = n\}$$

We write that a memo table is a record in memory, indicated by the multiword points-to operator $\mapsto$. In particular, $p$ points to a record containing some values $f$, a function pointer; and $c$, a cache of the current function's result, or 0 to indicate that the cache is invalid. The next clause of the definition enforces cache validity, where any nonzero $c$ value must match the expected function return value. The final clause ascribes a specification to $f$ via a Hoare triple: it must be legal to call in any state where the memo table itself remains present with the same parameters, and (if it terminates) it must return the expected result $n$ while preserving a functionally indistinguishable memo table in memory.

Figure 4 visualizes this predicate definition. We introduce a convention followed throughout this paper of indicating encapsulation boundaries with dashed borders. In this example, the only component is the memo table module. We indicate the *recursive* reference within the predicate definition with a dashed line connecting the overall predicate name to a smaller copy of the predicate's box elsewhere. Here the smaller copy appears within a thought bubble indicating a specification ascribed to a code pointer.

This programming pattern is associated with the idea of Landin's knot, where a program without explicit recursion may nonetheless become recursive by stashing first-class function values in a mutable store. Application to abstract data types in separation logic has been studied before, not just for the XCAP thread library project [30] that we build on, but also in a variety of other recent work, e.g. with impredicative concurrent abstract predicates [35]. Our solution here also uses impredicative quantification (which is built into XCAP's PropX language) in an essential way.

A predicate like this one can be used in ascribing an abstract specification to a method, such as the following ones for overwriting the function stored in a memo table and querying the current function result, respectively. (The latter case ought to be implemented by consulting and updating the cache as appropriate, so that the stored function only needs to be called once.)

$$\{\mathsf{MemoTable}(p,n) \\ \wedge\ \{\mathsf{MemoTable}(p,n')\}f\{\mathsf{MemoTable}(p,n') \wedge \mathsf{result} = n'\}\} \\ \mathtt{SetFunc}(p,f) \\ \{\mathsf{MemoTable}(p,n')\}$$

$$\{\mathsf{MemoTable}(p,n)\} \\ \mathtt{QueryFunc}(p) \\ \{\mathsf{MemoTable}(p,n) \wedge \mathsf{result} = n\}$$

Unfortunately, it is not obvious that the recursion in our definition of MemoTable is well-founded. Certainly treated like a recursive function in a programming language, this definition does not "terminate," since one call invokes itself with the same arguments. We might try to phrase it as an *inductive* definition as in Coq and other proof assistants, expressed as the least relation satisfying a set of inference rules. Here we are still out of luck, as proof assistants must generally impose a *positivity restriction*, where an inference rule for a predicate $P$ may not contain a premise like $P(x) \Rightarrow \ldots$, with an implication from the same predicate being defined. It is hard to see how to encode Hoare-triple preconditions such that the formulas inside them do not show up in just that kind of *negative* position.

This sort of puzzle is not a consequence of our choice of XCAP's assertion logic; related challenges appear in all work on semantics for higher-order programs with state. One popular solution uses *step-indexed relations* [2] to break circularities in recursive definitions. We instead use the syntactic features of XCAP to make our definition legal.

Past work on verifying a thread library in XCAP [30] extended the XCAP assertion logic with a new $\mu$ connective for anonymous recursive predicates. Of course, to retain soundness, this connective cannot be given the obvious natural-deduction rules establishing $(\mu\alpha.\ P) \leftrightarrow P[(\mu\alpha.\ P)/\alpha]$, since then we would summon the usual logical unsoundnesses of systems supporting definitions like $P \triangleq \neg P$. So, this past work dealt with the inconvenience of a restricted set of proof rules for $\mu$. In particular, $\mu$ gets an introduction rule but no elimination rule, forcing elimination-style reasoning to take place only in the meta logic, Coq, in terms of explicit syntactic statements about formula provability.

In our work, we apply a new approach to recursive predicate definitions in XCAP that imposes fewer restrictions on reasoning patterns, which is especially helpful for the simpler proof automation that it enables. Rather than applying the analogue of *anonymous* recursive types from programming, we instead apply an analogue of *named* recursive types. We derive a connective $\mathtt{name} \equiv P$ for looking up the predicate associated with a textual name `name`, and we allow program modules to include such definitions of named predicates, which the connective will consult.

$$\mathsf{MemoTable}(p,n) \triangleq \exists f,c.\ (p \mapsto f,c) \wedge (c \neq 0 \Rightarrow c = n) \\ \wedge\ (\exists P.\ \mathtt{MemoTable} \equiv P \\ \wedge\ \{P(p,n)\}f\{P(p,n) \wedge \mathsf{result} = n\})$$

Note that this definition is not explicitly recursive. The predicate name MemoTable does not appear in its own definition. Instead, we see the monospaced `MemoTable`, referring to a label within an XCAP code module. Our actual implementation gives each module its own separate label namespace, so there is no danger of predicate-name clash across modules. We note that this approach to recursive definition can be seen as an analogue to the well-known "recursion through the store" at the level of specifications.

An interesting implementation detail is how we can derive the new connective from the original XCAP connectives. First, a recursive definition of predicate `name` as $P$ in a module is encoded as a code block labeled `name` whose specification is $\lambda\_.\ \forall x.\ P(x)$, embedding $P$ into an XCAP assertion in an arbitrary way. Next, we define $\mathtt{name} \equiv P$ as $\{\!|\ \lambda\_.\ \forall x.\ P(x)\ |\!\}\mathtt{name}$, using the syntactic Hoare double to look up the specification associated with the right code block and assert it equal to a template built from $P$. One subtle point here is that we want to allow any module to include predicates over any Coq types. The $\forall$ quantifiers in the templates above are implicitly annotated with the predicate type, and at some point in a related proof we need to reason from the equality of two such formulas to the equality of their embedded predicates. That reasoning step turns out to require the opaquely named Axiom K [34], which is the only Coq axiom used anywhere in our development.

An important benefit of this new encoding compared to past work on a $\mu$ connective for XCAP shows up in the definition of MemoTable above: the higher-order quantification over $P$ appears

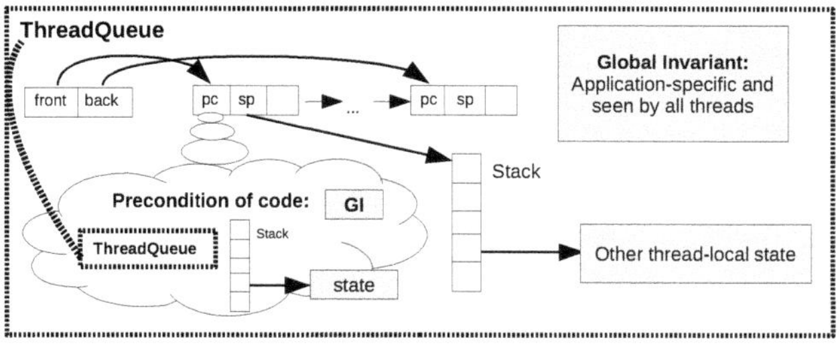


**Figure 5.** Zooming in on ThreadQueue invariant

only in one conjunct of the definition of MemoTable, so only when reasoning about that conjunct do we need to deal with the "incompleteness" of XCAP's natural-deduction rules for higher-order quantification. Only lines of code in the memo table implementation that actually call the function $f$ will need to venture into that conjunct, so straightforward proof automation can help us verify the rest of the code automatically, applying the usual manipulations to the connectives. This pattern persists into our verification of thread queues, where manual human proving effort is only necessary for lines of code that resume suspended threads.

### 5.2 Specifying Layers of Threading Abstractions

In verifying a thread library and its client code, we benefit from several dimensions of modularity. Most obviously, it should be possible to verify client code without knowing library implementation details. However, we also want to take advantage of proof modularity *within* the library, raising the question, **which specification idioms apply effectively to modules within a thread library, where each layer of the library manages suspended threads in some form**? Past work with XCAP on cooperative [30] and preemptive [11] thread libraries dodges this question by not attempting to verify any actual application code against the libraries, let alone focus on minimizing human effort to verify a new client program. Creating a pleasant client experience requires widening the library specifications, and in turn that widening reveals the benefits of decomposing the somewhat intricate proofs across modules with encapsulated state.

Take as an example our lowest-level component that encapsulates suspended threads: ThreadQueue, providing a FIFO queue of thread entries. Our definition is very close to that from a prior XCAP cooperative threading library [30], but the key difference is in modeling *parts of memory shared across threads*. That past work forced threads to operate only on their own private memory partitions, modulo the ability to allocate and free memory blocks. Realistic applications need to share some state. For instance, in our final application, the in-memory database is shared across worker threads.

Consider the schematic presentation of (most of) ThreadQueue's data-structure invariant in Figure 5. We maintain a queue as a linked list of saved instruction pointer/stack pointer pairs. Each saved stack pointer points to some memory region that is private to the associated thread, and there is also a shared memory region described by the global invariant. The trickiness appears in deciding which requirements to assert for the saved code pointers. We face the challenges in recursive predicate definition from the prior subsection, plus additional complexities associated with state, both thread-local and shared.

Figure 6 gives the formal definition that we settled on, which we will explain in pieces.

Though many single-threaded data structures have obvious notions of correctness, a concurrent structure like the ThreadQueue raises questions of how we specify the rules for sharing of state across threads. Many options are possible, and we adopted one simple choice here. Our specifications would be quite inflexible if we took literally the idea of a global invariant, or a fixed property that must always hold of shared memory. Invariants may evolve over time. For instance, in the overall thread scheduler, we want the invariant to change as the set of *open files* expands, since the invariant ought to enforce that certain pointers only go to valid open files.

We formalize a more general shared-state regime using the idea of *monotonically evolving state*. A client programmer of ThreadQueue is allowed to choose a set of *worlds* $\mathcal{W}$, such as "sets of open file pointers." Furthermore, an *evolution relation* $\sqsubseteq$ must be provided, to characterize how the world is allowed to change over time. This relation must be reflexive and transitive, but no further restrictions are enforced. Monotonic evolution of state is not sufficient for stating all of the invariants one might care about, like that there are no dangling references to *closed* file records, but it provides a useful starting point for investigating logical interfaces to expose to applications. (In higher layers of our stack, we dodge the need to rule out dangling file references by recycling freed file records in a free list and keeping dummy data in any free records.)

The global invariant may now be given as a predicate over $\mathcal{W}$ and the root pointer of the ThreadQueue. Concretely, the ThreadQueue module in Coq is a *functor* in the sense of ML module systems [24]. Its parameters are $\mathcal{W}$, $\sqsubseteq$, and the global invariant predicate ginv, plus some logical axioms that must be proved about them (e.g., transitivity).

This use of worlds and an evolution relation is inspired by the various semantic techniques based on Kripke structures, such as Kripke logical relations for compiler verification [19]. Binary state-evolution relations for concurrent program verification have a long history, including in rely-guarantee proof methods [20], which have been used both for Hoare-logic-style proofs and in concert with refinement types [14]; and in the two-state object invariants of VCC [7].

As an example of one of the proved specifications for ThreadQueue's methods, here is the specification for `yield()`.

$$\forall w \in \mathcal{W}.\ \{\mathsf{tq}(w,q) \star \mathsf{ginv}(w,q) \star \mathsf{malloc}\}$$
$$\mathtt{yield}(q)$$
$$\{\exists w' \in \mathcal{W}.\ w \sqsubseteq w' \wedge \mathsf{tq}(w',q) \star \mathsf{ginv}(w',q) \star \mathsf{malloc}\}$$

The specification is in the style of separation logic [33], which uses the $\star$ operator to indicate by $P \star Q$ that memory can be split into two disjoint regions, one satisfying $P$ and the other satisfying $Q$. We write tq for the invariant sketched in Figure 5, ginv for the global invariant predicate, and malloc for the free-list data-structure invariant of our `malloc` library. Universal quantification over $w$ captures the abstract global state at the point where `yield()` is called, while in the postcondition, existential quantification over $w'$ introduces the new, possibly *evolved*, world that characterizes state when the yielding thread is finally resumed.

Note that this specification hides an important complexity: `yield()` does not behave as a normal function, but rather grabs the function return pointer and *stores it in a heap data structure*. Nonetheless, the specification looks like one for a normal function, and we successfully encapsulate the details of code-pointer manipulation within the correctness proof for ThreadQueue.

Verification of methods like `yield()` depends on giving a proper definition of tq, drawing on the recursive definition approach from Section 5.1. First, we define what is a valid *suspension* of a paused thread in Figure 6, via a predicate $\mathsf{susp}(w,q,p,s)$ over world (at time of suspension) $w$, thread queue pointer $q$, saved program counter $p$, and saved stack pointer $s$. The definition starts by using Section 5.1's trick to obtain in local predicate variable $P$ a reference to tq. Next, we quantify existentially (and impredica-

$$\begin{array}{l}\mathsf{susp}(w,q,p,s) \triangleq \lambda m.\ \exists P.\ \texttt{ThreadQueue} \equiv P \\ \quad \wedge\ \exists \mathcal{I}.\ \mathcal{I}(m) \wedge \{\lambda\gamma. \\ \quad\quad \gamma.\mathsf{Sp} = s \wedge \exists w'.\ w \sqsubseteq w' \\ \quad\quad \wedge\ [\mathcal{I} \star P(w',q) \star \mathsf{ginv}(w',q) \star \mathsf{malloc}]\gamma \\ \quad \}p \end{array}$$

$$\begin{array}{l}\mathsf{tq}(w,q) \triangleq \exists \overline{t}, q', s'.\ (q \mapsto q', s') \star \mathsf{backupStack}(s') \\ \quad \star\ \mathsf{queue}(\overline{t}, q') \star \bigotimes_{(p,s)\in\overline{t}} \mathsf{susp}(w,q,p,s)\end{array}$$

**Figure 6.** The thread queue predicate and an auxiliary definition

tively) over another predicate variable $\mathcal{I}$, capturing the suspended thread's local memory invariant. We assert that this invariant does indeed describe $m$, the partial memory that is the implicit parameter to a separation-logic predicate like susp.

The final part of the definition is a semantic Hoare double ascribing a precondition to the saved program counter. Where $\gamma$ is the Bedrock IL state at the point where the thread is resumed, we require first that the stack pointer of $\gamma$ has been restored to the saved value $s$. Next, we require that the world $w$ has evolved legally to some $w'$. A separation-logic assertion applied to $\gamma$ breaks memory into four pieces, satisfying the local invariant $\mathcal{I}$, the thread queue invariant tq (referenced via its local name $P$), the global invariant in the new world, and the `malloc` library invariant.

Figure 6 also gives the final definition of the tq predicate, for parameters current world $w$ and queue pointer $q$. We quantify over a *bag* (or multiset) $\overline{t}$ of suspended threads, represented as pairs of saved program counters and stack pointers, as well as over two values $q'$ and $s'$ that $q$ points to. The pointer $q'$ is to a more primitive queue structure, while $s'$ points to the backup stack used while deallocating the current thread in `exit()`. Multisets form the interface with queues via the queue predicate. The most interesting part of the specification is its last conjunct, which uses $\bigotimes$ as a notation for iterated separating conjunction over some index bag. Here we generate one susp conjunct per suspended thread in $\overline{t}$.

All the quantifiers appearing directly in tq's definition are first-order, since their domains do not involve specifications. As a result, this definition stays within the fragment of XCAP assertions that support simple proof automation, using connectives that have both introduction and elimination rules. In contrast, susp uses second-order quantification, so less clean proofs are required to reason about indirect jumps to suspended threads. Fortunately, only four such jumps appear in the ThreadQueue implementation, and we are able to apply predictable proof automation for the other 60-some lines of executable code. Past work on verifying a similar library with XCAP [30] used a new $\mu$ recursive predicate connective that also lacks an elimination rule, and perhaps partly as a result, their proofs were highly manual, using about 10 times more lines of proof to establish a weaker interface for a library with fewer features.

### 5.2.1 Layering More Instances of the Same Pattern

Not only does the world-based specification style facilitate flexible use of shared state in applications, it also composes nicely in layers within a thread library. To demonstrate, we discuss verifying two further components on top of ThreadQueue: ThreadQueues, which exposes multiple queues corresponding to multiple possible IO events; and Scheduler, which exposes standard blocking IO operations on TCP sockets. To our knowledge, ours is the first work to consider a certified implementation of blocking IO in a modular verification framework.

First consider ThreadQueues, which abstracts over a dynamically growing set of thread queues. It provides our first chance to take advantage of the generality of ThreadQueue's handling of global invariants. Specifically, ThreadQueues asks the programmer to choose $\mathcal{W}$ and $\sqsubseteq$ like before, though now ginv is a predicate over $\mathcal{W}$ and *bags* of queues, where the latter component was just a single queue for ThreadQueue. For any such choices by the programmer for the parameters of ThreadQueues, we must come up with appropriate parameters to use internally for ThreadQueue. Concretely, both of these modules are ML-style functors, and ThreadQueues instantiates the ThreadQueue functor with derived parameters based on its own parameters.

The main idea is to define a ThreadQueue-level world to contain not just a ThreadQueues-level world, but also *the set of all queues that have been allocated so far*. To formalize this notion for given $\mathcal{W}$, $\sqsubseteq$, and ginv, here is how we derive the ThreadQueue parameters, where $\mathcal{P}(Q)$ stands for the set of sets of queue pointers:

$$\begin{array}{rcl}\mathcal{W}' & \triangleq & \mathcal{P}(Q) \times \mathcal{W} \\ (\overline{q}_1, s_1) \sqsubseteq' (\overline{q}_2, s_2) & \triangleq & \overline{q}_1 \subseteq \overline{q}_2 \wedge s_1 \sqsubseteq s_2 \\ \mathsf{ginv}'((\overline{q}, s), q) & \triangleq & \mathsf{ginv}(\overline{q}, s) \star \bigotimes_{q' \in \overline{q} - \{q\}} \mathsf{tq}((\overline{q}, s), q')\end{array}$$

We focus on explaining the ginv′ definition, which formalizes what a particular thread queue expects to see in the remainder of memory. The definition above says "a thread queue sees the global invariant plus all of the *other* thread queues." The "other" part is encoded via the $-$ operator in the index bag of $\bigotimes$. This sort of explicit capture of all library state may seem verbose compared to state-hiding approaches like anti-frame rules [31] and dynamic locks with invariants [15] for separation logic. An advantage of our approach here is that it may be developed as a "specification design pattern" on top of XCAP's simple Hoare logic, with no requirement to build supporting features into the trusted base, while state-hiding approaches seem to require such support.

Thankfully for the application programmer, these details are encapsulated inside the ThreadQueues correctness proof. In the end, we export method specifications that refer to an abstract predicate tqs, whose arguments are a world value and a set of available queues. Here is the revised specification for `yield()` at the ThreadQueues level, for enqueuing a thread into *inq* while dequeuing a thread to resume from *outq*.

$$\begin{array}{c}\forall w \in \mathcal{W}, \overline{q} \in \mathcal{P}(Q).\ \{inq \in \overline{q} \wedge outq \in \overline{q} \\ \wedge\ \mathsf{tqs}(w, \overline{q}) \star \mathsf{ginv}(w, \overline{q}) \star \mathsf{malloc}\} \\ \texttt{yield}(inq, outq) \\ \{\exists w' \in \mathcal{W}, \overline{q}' \in \mathcal{P}(Q).\ w \sqsubseteq w' \wedge \overline{q} \subseteq \overline{q}' \\ \wedge\ \mathsf{tqs}(w', \overline{q}') \star \mathsf{ginv}(w', \overline{q}') \star \mathsf{malloc}\}\end{array}$$

We come finally to Scheduler, which encapsulates ThreadQueues along with other state to provide both thread management and blocking TCP IO. Scheduler is parameterized over a choice of a simple global invariant whose only argument is $\overline{f}$, a set of available file record pointers. We thus instantiate ThreadQueues with $\mathcal{W}$ as the set of sets of file pointers, $\sqsubseteq$ as the subset relation, and ginv as the invariant that we sketch later in Figure 8. Our choice of this particular interface prevents the final clients of Scheduler from choosing global invariants that depend on custom world concepts. The proof architecture would support a stronger interface preserving such freedom, but we decided to compromise flexibility in favor of more straightforward proof automation.

Now we arrive at a specification for the final repackaging of `yield()`, where $F$ is the set of file record pointers:

$$\begin{array}{c}\forall \overline{f} \in \mathcal{P}(F).\ \{\mathsf{sched}(\overline{f}) \star \mathsf{ginv}(\overline{f}) \star \mathsf{malloc}\} \\ \texttt{yield}() \\ \{\exists \overline{f}' \in \mathcal{P}(F).\ \overline{f} \subseteq \overline{f}' \wedge \mathsf{sched}(\overline{f}') \star \mathsf{ginv}(\overline{f}') \star \mathsf{malloc}\}\end{array}$$

The final interface hides all details of code-pointer manipulation, using just an abstract predicate to capture the state of the scheduler library. The four layers ThreadQueue, ThreadQueues, Scheduler, and application are truly modular, where proofs in each layer treat only the next lower layer, only through Hoare triples for methods specified with abstract predicates. We may tweak each layer without needing to reexamine proofs for others, so long as we maintain its formal interface. For instance, the specifications of the lower-level components are general enough to allow us to hone the data structures of the scheduler without modifying any other module or its proofs.

The reader may have noticed an apparent weakness in our functor-based approach to specifying global invariants: when multiple applications are sharing a Scheduler instance, they must somehow coordinate to choose a mutually satisfactory global invariant. However, it is fairly straightforward to build a little plumbing that still allows each application to be proved modularly, when global state of each application can be kept in a distinct region that other applications may not touch. Each application (with proof) is implemented as a functor over the part of the global invariant contributed by *other* applications, and the overall global invariant is denoted as the conjunction of the part known locally and the part passed as functor parameter. A single global invariant may be seen through a different lens of this kind for each application. Variants of this approach may also support different modes of state-sharing between applications. The point is that the Scheduler specification allows these modularity disciplines to be constructed on top, with Scheduler's implementation and proof remaining a black box.

One last note may be worthwhile, about the malloc predicate used throughout our example specifications. Why does this predicate not take some kind of state-tracking argument, too, which we are forced to propagate through the spec of Scheduler? For instance, one might expect to see malloc parameterized over a description of which memory blocks have been allocated so far, so that we can require that any block being freed really did come from a past allocation. Our `malloc` library dodges this complication by allowing any block of memory (disjoint from the current malloc state) to be donated via "deallocation," even if it previously had nothing to do with `malloc`.

### 5.3 Patterns for DSL Implementation

Many verification tasks are practical to carry out over code in low-level languages like C, but, in scaling to larger systems, we may realize large productivity improvements by coding in and reasoning about higher-level languages. Ideally we raise the abstraction level while keeping our final theorems at the level of assembly code. The relevant question is, **what is the right way to incorporate a verified DSL implementation within a modular proof**?

In particular, we focus on how the DSL implementation and proof may themselves be factored into modules. We developed our DSL, the Bedrock Web Services Language (BWS), modularly at the level of *language constructs*. BWS supports the mostly orthogonal features of relational database access and XML processing. Each of these factors is further decomposed into constructs, like database querying vs. modification, and XML pattern-matching vs. generation. Each construct is implemented with a separately encapsulated proof. We hope these building blocks are suitable to assemble in different ways to build different DSLs, but we also found that modularity paid off, even just for the construction of this one DSL.

The Bedrock Structured Programming System [5] already provides a notion of *certified low-level macro*, where we package a code generator with a Hoare-logic proof rule and a proof that the two are compatible. Thus, it was natural for us to implement our DSL building blocks as BSPS macros.

$$\begin{array}{rcl}
\mathsf{SE}(\texttt{""}, \mathit{offset}) & \triangleq & \texttt{output} \leftarrow 1 \\
\mathsf{SE}(c :: s, \mathit{offset}) & \triangleq & \mathsf{If}\ (\texttt{pos} + \lceil \mathit{offset} \rceil < \texttt{len} \\
& & \quad \&\&\ \texttt{str}[\texttt{pos} + \lceil \mathit{offset} \rceil] = \lceil c \rceil)\ \{ \\
& & \lceil \mathsf{SE}(s, \mathit{offset} + 1) \rceil \\
& & \}\ \mathsf{else}\ \{\ \texttt{output} \leftarrow 0\ \}
\end{array}$$

**Figure 7.** Definition of a code generator for string equality

The Bedrock module formalism does not currently support statically allocated data, such as for string literals extracted from source code. No doubt a more practical evolution of the framework would add such a feature, but we can take advantage of the omission to motivate an example macro, for checking whether a byte array matches a string literal. In other words, we effectively represent static character arrays by inlining appropriate unrolled loops into assembly code.

BSPS includes basic combinators for, e.g., sequencing, conditionals, and loops. Merely composing these combinators and their proof rules leads to a *derived* proof rule that may expose too much code detail. We often want to *wrap* a macro, applying an equivalent of the *rule of consequence* to assign a more abstract proof rule. The BSPS design includes a basic wrapping combinator, which exposes a view of programs at the level of Bedrock IL control-flow graphs, with no concept of local variables. We found that interface to be too cumbersome for the more abstract macros that interest us in this project, so we built a higher-level wrapping combinator that allows the preconditions and postconditions of chunks to mention the set $\mathcal{V}$ of declared local variables.

To illustrate, consider our example of a macro to check whether some substring of a string equals a constant. Let us fix four program variable names: `str`, for a pointer to the string we should check; `len`, a variable holding its length; `pos`, indicating the first index of the substring to check; and `output`, a variable where we write either 0 or 1, to indicate the Boolean result of the test. In Figure 7, a simple recursive definition of a function SE suffices to generate the code, on top of more primitive BSPS macros.

We implement definitions like this one in Coq's functional programming language Gallina. The $\lceil \ldots \rceil$ syntax indicates antiquoting some computed code pieces within BSPS syntax. We define the overall macro via $\mathsf{StringEq}(s) \triangleq \mathsf{SE}(s, 0)$.

BSPS automatically builds a sound Hoare-style proof rule for any concrete application of StringEq. However, the rule reveals the exact low-level code structure, when we would prefer a more abstract presentation, encapsulating details like checking array bounds. Here is the rule we derive with our expanded wrapping combinator; we will step through explaining it in stages. We make the four variable names (e.g., `str`) into explicit parameters of the macro (e.g., str), so that client code may choose appropriate concrete names for its context.

$$\begin{array}{l}
\forall I, P.\ \{P \star \mathsf{array8}(I, \mathsf{str}) \land |I| = \mathsf{len} \land \mathsf{pos} \leq \mathsf{len} \\
\quad \land \{\mathsf{str}, \mathsf{len}, \mathsf{pos}, \mathsf{output}\} \subseteq \mathcal{V} \\
\quad \land \mathsf{NoDup}([\mathsf{str}, \mathsf{len}, \mathsf{pos}, \mathsf{output}]) \land |s| < 2^{32} \\
\quad \land \mathsf{FV}(P) \cap \{\mathsf{output}, \mathsf{pos}\} = \emptyset\} \\
\quad \texttt{StringEq}(\mathsf{str}, \mathsf{len}, \mathsf{pos}, \mathsf{output}, s) \\
\{P \star \mathsf{array8}(I, \mathsf{str}) \land |I| = \mathsf{len} \land \mathsf{pos} \leq \mathsf{len}\}
\end{array}$$

Most of the precondition and postcondition are heap-independent facts combined with $\land$. The only heap-dependent parts of the predicates are $P$, some frame predicate; and $\mathsf{array8}(I, \mathsf{str})$, indicating that the requested variable str points to a byte array whose contents are $I$. These parts repeat verbatim before and after, indicating that the macro may only produce code that has no heap effects (or fails to terminate).

Most of the heap-independent parts of the precondition are variable-related side conditions, of the sort familiar to users of separation logic. We require that the variable parameters are all members of the set $\mathcal{V}$ of declared local variables, and we also require that no variable name is duplicated as the value of multiple parameters.

The last precondition conjunct imposes a condition on the free variables of the frame predicate $P$, which is inspired by conditions in the classic separation-logic frame rule. That rule assumes $\{P\}c\{Q\}$ and concludes $\{P \star F\}c\{Q \star F\}$ for an arbitrary $F$ that *does not mention variables that command c could modify*. The classic rule is able to inspect $c$ syntactically to determine which variables it may write, but in the macro setting we want to hide code details through encapsulation. Thus, we expose a formal interface for `StringEq` that in effect promises not to change any variable outside the set $\{\mathsf{output}, \mathsf{pos}\}$, by only allowing useful postconditions with $P$ that does not depend on those variables.

This technique generalizes to macros that take blocks of code as arguments. For instance, consider some macro $\mathsf{Iterate}(\texttt{buf}, \texttt{len}, k)$ implementing a `foreach` loop over all cells of a buffer (indicated by base-pointer variable `buf` and length variable `len`), running some body code $k$ for each. Where $\mathbb{V}$ is some set of program variables that the macro needs to use in generated bookkeeping code, we might assign this proof rule:

$$\frac{\begin{array}{c}\forall I.\ \{P \star \mathsf{array8}(I, \mathsf{buf}) \wedge |I| = \mathsf{len}\} \\ k\ \{P \star \mathsf{array8}(I, \mathsf{buf}) \wedge |I| = \mathsf{len}\}\end{array}}{\begin{array}{c}\forall I.\ \{P \star \mathsf{array8}(I, \mathsf{buf}) \wedge |I| = \mathsf{len} \\ \wedge\ \{\mathsf{buf}, \mathsf{len}\} \cup \mathbb{V} \subseteq \mathcal{V} \wedge \mathsf{FV}(P) \cap \mathbb{V} = \emptyset\} \\ \mathsf{Iterate}(\mathsf{buf}, \mathsf{len}, k)\ \{P \star \mathsf{array8}(I, \mathsf{buf})\}\end{array}}$$

Let us read the conclusion first. We assert a particular Hoare triple for the macro, for arbitrary choices of buffer contents $I$ (which should remain unchanged by execution). As before, two pieces of state appear identically in precondition and postcondition: a frame predicate $P$ and the buffer itself via the $\mathsf{array8}$ predicate. We require that variable $\mathsf{len}$ hold an accurate array length, that all variables we need are included in the available variables $\mathcal{V}$, and that the frame predicate $P$ does not depend on any of the bookkeeping variables $\mathbb{V}$ that may be modified.

The premise formalizes expectations for the body code block $k$. We require that a Hoare triple is valid for $k$, again for any buffer contents $I$. Specifically, $k$ must preserve a familiar-looking statement about $P$, $\mathsf{buf}$, and $\mathsf{len}$. Technically, $k$ might change the values of these variables, but at least the new versions must still satisfy the invariant that $\mathsf{buf}$ points to an array whose length is $\mathsf{len}$. Note that $P$ may be chosen to include any state known only to $k$ and not to the $\mathsf{Iterate}$ macro.

We want to emphasize one key element of rules like this one: the body $k$ may be instantiated with *arbitrary assembly code that can be proved semantically to satisfy the Hoare triple*. That is, in coding and verifying our DSL building blocks, we need not commit to the DSL design in advance. Subsets of our building blocks ought to be usable to construct different verified DSL implementations, though so far we have only assembled them into the DSL of Section 7.

## 6. A Thread-Library Component Stack

This section overviews our **concrete architecture for a modularly verified (cooperative) thread library that exposes a rich interface to client code**. Sections 5.1 and 5.2 presented the two key novel design patterns that enabled this architecture, and we show the details in Figure 8.

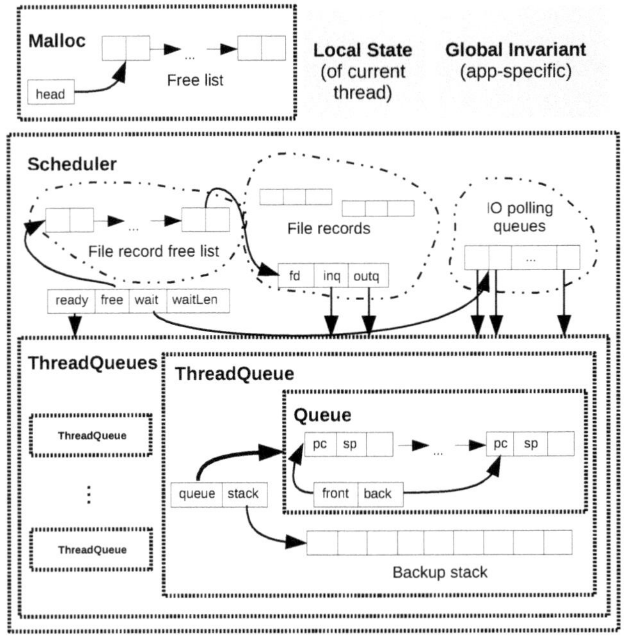


**Figure 8.** Thread-library architecture

We follow visual conventions introduced in Figure 4. Mixed dotted and dashed borders group elements of state within a single encapsulation boundary, to aid understanding. Arrows indicate pointers, which terminate at precise memory elements, when they do not span encapsulation boundaries; or terminate at the edges of dashed boxes, when pointing to abstract objects provided by other modules. Basically, this picture shows how to take a snapshot of memory in a running system and divide it into pieces encapsulated within separately verified modules.

The bulk of the diagram portrays state of the **Scheduler**, which provides functions for thread creation and destruction, TCP connection management, and blocking IO. These functions are built on top of the nonblocking IO system calls from Figure 2. The Scheduler is implemented via a number of data structures, including three more encapsulated components (sketched in Section 5.2), but an abstract interface is exported for use by client code.

The Scheduler manages both *threads* and *open files*. A Scheduler instance is rooted in a four-element struct, containing *ready*, a pointer to a queue of suspended threads ready to be resumed; *free*, a pointer to a pool of available structs to use in representing open files; *wait*, a pointer to a table to be consulted in interpreting the results of polling via the `wait()` system call; and *waitLen*, the length of the *wait* array.

The Scheduler maintains a pool of file records, which are recycled after previous open files are closed. Each file record includes an underlying file descriptor and pointers to two queues of suspended threads, one for threads waiting to read from the file and the other for threads waiting to write. In any blocking IO call associated with one of these file records, a pointer to the appropriate one of the two queues is saved in the *wait* array, at an offset equal to the *reservation* assigned to this request by the `declare()` system call. Thus, when a `wait()` system call returns, its return value may be treated as an index into *wait*, determining which thread is woken up to handle the new IO event. Since the trusted specs of `declare()` and `wait()` are simple and nondeterministic, we do dynamic checking of reservations returned by `wait()`, to make sure they are in-bounds for the *wait* array. We also check that the

```
bfunctionNoRet "handler"("buf", "listener", "accepted", "n", "Sn")
  [handlerS]
  "listener" ← Call "scheduler"!"listen"(port)
  [∀ fs, PREmain[_, R] ⌈ R ∈ fs ⌉ ⋆ sched fs ⋆ mallocHeap 0];;
  "buf" ← Call "buffers"!"bmalloc"(inbuf_size)
  [∀ fs, PREmain[V, R] R ↦? bsize ⋆ ⌈ R ≠ 0 ⌉ ⋆ ⌈ freeable R inbuf_size ⌉
     ⋆ ⌈ V "listener" ∈ fs⌉ ⋆ sched fs ⋆ mallocHeap 0];;
  "accepted" ← Call "scheduler"!"accept"("listener")
  [∀ fs, PREmain[V, R] ⌈ R ∈ fs ⌉ ⋆ V "buf" ↦? bsize ⋆ ⌈ V "buf" ≠ 0 ⌉ ⋆ ⌈
     freeable (V "buf") inbuf_size ⌉ ⋆ ⌈ V "listener" ∈ fs⌉ ⋆ sched fs
     ⋆ mallocHeap 0];;
  "n" ← Call "scheduler"!"read"("accepted", "buf", bsize)
  [∀ fs, PREmain[V] ⌈ V "accepted" ∈ fs ⌉ ⋆ V "buf" ↦? bsize ⋆ ⌈ V "buf"
     ≠ 0 ⌉ ⋆ ⌈ freeable (V "buf") inbuf_size ⌉ ⋆ ⌈ V "listener" ∈ fs⌉ ⋆
     sched fs ⋆ mallocHeap 0];;
  "Sn" ← "n" + 1;;
  Call "scheduler"!"close"("accepted")
  [∀ fs, PREmain[V] V "buf" ↦? bsize ⋆ ⌈ V "buf" ≠ 0 ⌉ ⋆ ⌈ freeable (V "
     buf") inbuf_size ⌉ ⋆ ⌈ V "listener" ∈ fs⌉ ⋆ sched fs ⋆ mallocHeap
     0 ⋆ ⌈ V "Sn" = V "n" ^+ $1 ⌉ ];;
  Call "scheduler"!"close"("listener")
  [∀ fs, PREmain[V] V "buf" ↦? bsize ⋆ ⌈ V "buf" ≠ 0 ⌉ ⋆ ⌈ freeable (V "
     buf") inbuf_size ⌉ ⋆ sched fs ⋆ mallocHeap 0 ⋆ ⌈ V "Sn" = V "n" ^+ $
     1 ⌉ ];;
  Call "buffers"!"bfree"("buf", inbuf_size)
  [∀ fs, PREmain[V] sched fs ⋆ mallocHeap 0 ⋆ ⌈ V "Sn" = V "n" ^+ $1 ⌉ ];;
  Call "sys"!"printInt"("Sn")
  [∀ fs, PREmain[V] sched fs ⋆ mallocHeap 0 ⋆ ⌈ V "Sn" = V "n" ^+ $1 ⌉ ];;
  Exit 100
end

Ltac t := try solve [ sep unf hints; auto ];
  unf; unfold localsInvariantMain; post; evaluate hints; descend;
    try match_locals; sep unf hints; auto.

Theorem ok : moduleOk m.
Proof.
  vcgen; abstract t.
Qed.
```

**Figure 9.** An example client program of the thread library

corresponding array cell has been initialized with a non-null queue pointer. Failure of either check signals a top-level runtime program error.

The concept of *threads* in Scheduler is lighter-weight than in most thread libraries. There is no persistent data structure in the library standing for a thread. Instead, we think of each queue as storing continuations allocated opportunistically as "threads" decide to block. The notations in our specification style so far have been hiding details of call-stack representation. Effectively, we require each thread to have a valid stack at the point where it calls any library function, but it is legal for thread code to grow and shrink its stack through manual reallocation between blocking operations. When such an operation is triggered, the associated stack is folded into the idea of local state for the continuation that we save.

Figure 9 shows an example of a client program verified against the thread library. We refer the reader to the BSPS paper [5] for more detail on the C-like programming language used here. At a high level, the code alternates between executable statements and *invariants* enclosed in square brackets. The former are mostly assignments and function calls. We prove that every invariant holds every time it is reached.

This program accepts a TCP connection on a port, reads some bytes from that connection, and then stashes in a local variable a value one greater than the number of bytes read. After a few more calls into the thread library, that saved value is printed. Invariants ensure that the proper value is printed in the end, modulo the non-

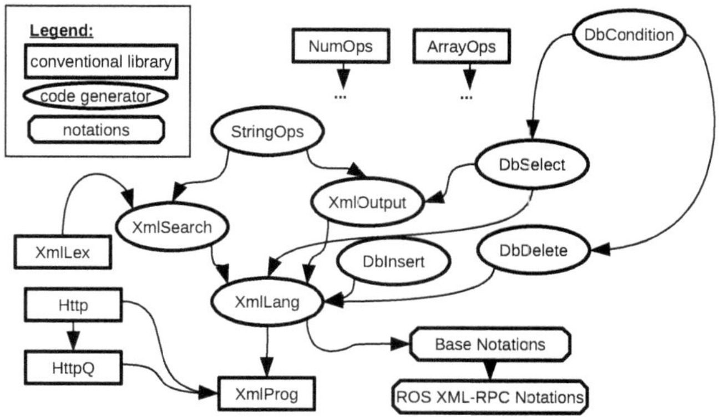


**Figure 10.** Architecture of verified DSL implementation

determinism of our specs for the underlying IO operations. For instance, the later invariants include clauses `V "Sn" = V "n" ^+ $1`, asserting that the value of local variable `Sn` equals the value of variable `n` plus one, in the domain of 32-bit machine words. Other interesting conjuncts appearing throughout the function include `sched fs`, representing the state of the scheduler with open-file set `fs`; and `V "accepted" ∈ fs`, indicating that local variable `accepted` holds a file pointer belonging to that set.

Figure 9 shows an excerpt from a real Coq source file, ending in the full code to *prove* that invariants are never violated. The proof is almost entirely automated, appealing to the separation-logic proof procedures that Bedrock provides [25]. This level of automation persists in verifications of more featureful client code, and it represents a qualitative improvement to the ease of building on verified systems libraries, compared to past work.

## 7. A Library of Verified Compiler Features

We summarize our **architecture for modular verification of a DSL implementation for database access and XML processing**. Section 5.3 introduced the basic design patterns we use for splitting a language implementation into a set of *certified macros*, whose definitions and proofs are independent of the full language that they will be used to implement. Recall that we decided to verify our thread library at the level of functional correctness, and verify client applications mostly at the level of data-structure shape invariants. Figure 10 shows how we decomposed the verification effort at that level for the implementation of our DSL, the Bedrock Web Service Language (BWS). Arrows indicate dependencies between modules.

The two core sets of features are relational database access and XML processing. We decompose the former into macros for filtering (DbCondition), querying (DbSelect), adding (DbInsert), and removing (DbDelete) database rows; and the latter into macros for XML pattern-matching (XmlSearch) and generation (XmlOutput). All of the above are combined into a macro XmlLang, whose parameter is a syntactic BWS program in an AST type. We are able to write the equivalent of a type-checker as a functional program over these ASTs. The final theorem for our main BWS macro establishes that any type-correct program is compiled to assembly code that maintains the invariants of the database and does not interfere with the state of other components.

Figure 11 shows an example BWS function definition from our ROS Master Server. Any such function is callable remotely over HTTP, following the XML-RPC protocol. This particular function installs a key-value pair in the configuration store that the Master maintains. One complication is that ROS nodes are allowed to *subscribe* to updates on particular keys, and we must initiate further

```
RosCommand "setParam"(!string $"caller_id",
                      !string $"key", !any $$"value")
Do
 Delete "params" Where ("key" = $"key");;
 Insert "params" ($"key", $"value");;

 From "paramSubscribers" Where ("key" = $"key") Do
  Callback "paramSubscribers"#"subscriber_api"
  Command "paramUpdate"(!string "/master", !string $"key", $"value");;

 Response Success
  Message "Parameter set."
  Body ignore
 end
end

Theorem Wf : wf ts pr buf_size outbuf_size.
Proof.
  wf.
Qed.
```

**Figure 11.** Example BWS function with proof

HTTP callbacks to all interested parties. In order, the body commands of this function delete any old mapping for the key, insert the new mapping, loop over callbacks to all nodes subscribed to updates, and return a response document to the calling node. The code here uses special ROS-specific Coq notations to hide the details of XML parsing and generation, but we use BWS macros for those functions under the hood.

We show the complete program-specific correctness proof at the end of the figure. This proof actually applies to the full set of 20 methods in the Master. It works by calling a BWS library tactic `wf` for discharging program well-formedness obligations automatically. We only need that sort of shallow fact to instantiate the generic correctness proof of the BWS implementation, yielding an assembly-level result that can be composed with the main theorem about our thread library. The generated `main()` function spawns a set of worker threads servicing HTTP requests.

## 8. Empirical Results

The premise of this paper is that some lessons about modular verification can only be learned by building and deploying systems at realistic scales. Our ROS Master Server application has both an assembly-level Coq proof and real users without formal-methods expertise. In this section, we summarize the human cost of carrying out our case study, the run-time performance of our application, and its usability.

### 8.1 Developing the Proofs

Overall, we spent about *2 person-months* implementing and verifying the thread library, and then another *2 person-months* doing the same for the BWS implementation. The ROS Master Server itself is trivial to code and verify with that infrastructure in place. The thread library includes about 600 lines of implementation code and about 3000 additional lines to state and prove theorems, making for a ratio of verification code to implementation of about 5:1. The BWS implementation includes about 1000 lines for actual executable code generation plus about 20,000 lines for verification, for a ratio of about 20:1. We ascribe the higher overhead in the latter case to the greater "meta-ness" of a compiler, where the code has a higher density of interesting operations. These ratios in general compare reasonably to related projects, like L4.verified [22] with a ratio of 20:1 in a project over 2.2 person-years (with non-modular proofs); and past work in modular verification of thread libraries [11, 30] achieving ratios on the order of 100:1, spending person-months just on developing libraries without interfacing them formally with realistic verified applications.

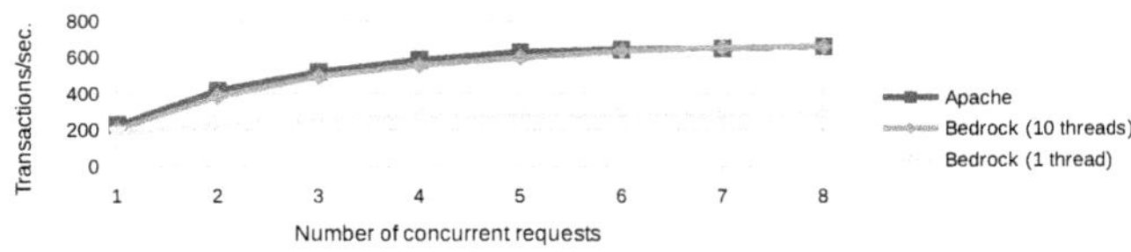


**Figure 12.** Throughput of our Web server (static content)

Our general workflow is to verify each component fully before testing it. We have been pleasantly surprised that not a single bug has been found in the systems components through testing; verification caught every mistake we have found so far. Testing has revealed about 10 bugs in the application-level components, for which we prove only the sorts of invariant annotations from Figure 9. In each case, we corrected the implementation and found that our automation adjusted the proofs without any need to edit proof code manually.

The current biggest practical obstacle to our verification methodology is the performance of the proof automation (taking several hours to check our whole stack), which we hope to ameliorate in the future by running proof search in parallel on compute clusters.

### 8.2 Running the Code

We have not attempted to build a competitive high-performance Web server, but we wanted to make sure that we had not simplified our program code too much during verification, in a way that led to performance too poor to support any real use. Therefore, we ran a basic load test experiment between two servers in the same cloud data center. Our benchmark input is the full set of static files from a recent snapshot of a conference Web site. There are about 60 different files, with one outlier at size about 3 MB and the rest each smaller than 1 MB, with several HTML files of only a few kB each. Our experiment compares our verified server against the Apache server from Ubuntu 13 with default configuration. We load-test each server by launching on one of the two machines a set of concurrent processes to send repeated requests to a server running on the other machine.

Figure 12 shows the results of our experiment, comparing the throughput of Apache and our verified server running either 1 worker thread or 10. As expected, the single-threaded server fails to scale throughput well with increased request concurrency. In contrast, our 10-thread verified server keeps up with Apache. Here the network link and the underlying Linux implementation are the real limiting factors. Our coarse experimental results show just that we (and Apache) attain sufficient performance to saturate that substrate. If anything, the results are skewed in favor of Apache, which runs multiple hardware threads, while the Bedrock model is inherently single-core. We can serve real Web sites at rates that will not aggravate users, where to our knowledge previous mechanized verifications of applications had not yielded any such practical results.

The real test of our case-study program is the reactions of its real users. The robotics experts who helped us with our test deployment pay little attention to verification details and are much more interested in how our Master server performs in practice. In the demo set-up, ROS nodes split across the two computers (robot and control terminal) include those associated with a joystick, wheel controls, and sensors including GPS and radar. Where the traditional Python Master server leads to a 2-second start-up process for the robot to enable driving it with the joystick, our BWS server requires 8 seconds, which our users deem tolerable in a high-assurance context.

Bedrock-based programs should have an inherent performance advantage over interpreted Python, thanks to specialized generation of assembly code doing manual memory management. However, our very elementary database implementation, which does not use any kind of index structures, should bring an offsetting asymptotic performance disadvantage, compared to the standard dictionaries used to store corresponding data in the Python server. We also, to make proofs more straightforward, simplified some aspects of our code in ways that hurt performance, like always allocating certain buffers at a fixed size and zeroing them out in full per request, even when network inputs do not take up the full space; and making copies of buffers before sending them, to deal with a library specification weakness that we explain in the next paragraph. We believe that the performance differential stems from these coding patterns.

In the process of building and deploying the application, we noticed a few weaknesses in the thread-library formal interface. For instance, the blocking `write()` function is assigned a specification like:

$$\{\mathsf{sched} \star \mathsf{ginv} \star \mathsf{buf} \overset{?}{\mapsto} \mathsf{len}\}\mathtt{write}(\mathsf{sock}, \mathsf{buf}, \mathsf{len})\{\ldots\}$$

We realized late that this specification precludes sending from string buffers that logically belong within the global invariant, such as strings for column values within the database. To compensate, we copy column values into temporary buffers before sending them, incurring additional overhead.

Our server does defend successfully against a security attack that works on the Python server. A carefully crafted XML input[2] leads the Python server to loop allocating an effectively unbounded amount of memory. In contrast, our final theorem establishes a modest static bound on how much memory our server can allocate, by defining the set ValidMem (demonstrated in Figure 3) to be small enough.

## 9. Related Work

Several recent projects have verified systems infrastructure mechanically. L4.verified [22] is the best-known project in this space, based on an Isabelle/HOL proof that a C-language microkernel refines a specification of system calls and so forth, given by a functional program. There has been preliminary work [21] on using the L4.verified proof to establish theorems about applications running on the kernel, but we are not aware of results with applications on the scale of those reported here with our Web service. The Verve project [37] establishes type safety but not functional correctness of .NET programs running on a platform that includes a verified garbage collector. The Verisoft project [1] has also produced kernel correctness proofs, using a decomposition of the proof effort via layering several abstract machines, from hardware to user-level. Theorems have been proved for kernel composed with embedded applications [8] following a simple communication model without dynamic thread creation or freeform calls to IO operations.

Past work has designed verification frameworks to support modular reasoning. For instance, the CAP project has demonstrated several verification frameworks for systems-level programs, including the XCAP logic [29] that we use here.

One project used XCAP to verify a user-level thread library [30] that inspired our new work. Our library follows theirs roughly to the level of ThreadQueue, where their work ends. They also assign their version of this module a weaker specification that does not support sharing of memory across threads in application-specific ways, and they did not report on experience verifying applications against the library.

A follow-on project applied a compositional program logic for hardware interrupts to certify kernel-level code for process scheduling (without dynamic process creation) plus user-level code implementing synchronization primitives [11]. Here the focus was on exporting a convenient interface for user-level systems library work, rather than for applications of interest to end users, and no such applications were verified. Even in the proofs of user-level code that rely on abstract interfaces exported by kernel-level modules, the verification overhead is about 10 times greater than in our new work, though it is hard to make a direct comparison, since our library is based on cooperative scheduling rather than interrupt-based preemption.

Gotsman and Yang presented a framework for on-paper modular correctness proofs of preemptive process schedulers [16]. They designed a domain-specific separation logic to enable proofs of this kind for a variety of schedulers that are more realistic than those tackled in other verification work, including ours. No application-level proof approach is suggested for linking of whole-system theorems, and none of their proofs are mechanized so far, so it is hard to predict what human cost they would impose on authors of schedulers or applications.

Ours is not the first project to implement a verified compiler for a higher-level language on top of BSPS. The Cito project [36] has verified semantics preservation for a C-like language with built-in support for data abstraction. That compiler theorem is stronger than ours for BWS, which only establishes preservation of data-structure shape invariants, but it also applies to a programming language at a lower abstraction level, requiring more proof work by programmers to establish basic properties of source code.

The Frenetic project has verified an implementation [17] of a domain-specific language for software-defined networking. They compile to the OpenFlow language rather than general-purpose assembly, establishing in Coq rich semantic correctness properties of network controllers, without the sort of feature-modular DSL decomposition we introduce in this paper.

Other projects have verified elements of database-backed Web applications. The Ynot project [6] produced proofs for a Web-based application [27] and a relational database engine [26]. That work established more semantic properties than in this paper, for a more realistic database system, but in the setting of interpretation in a high-level functional language, rather than compilation to optimized assembly; and they require new manual proof about each program using the database library.

Several programming languages have been developed to help programmers reason about XML manipulation, including Xtatic [13] and XDuce [18]. These languages use features like *regular expression types* to bring static typing features like pattern-match exhaustiveness checking from the world of ML and Haskell to XML processing. This sort of static type system would be a complementary addition to BWS.

## 10. Conclusion

We have described the first modular mechanized verification of a deployed software system, combining proofs about systems infrastructure (primarily a thread library) and an application (an XML-based Web service backed by a relational database). Our summary of the project focuses on lessons that are difficult to learn when not applying modular verification *at scale*, where formal interfaces must be flexible at the same time as machine-checked proofs are kept automated, short, and maintainable. We sketch one decomposition that we found effective, into about 20 separately encapsulated pieces, which we hope can provide a model for future verifications in this style.

## Acknowledgments

We thank our collaborators at SRI and UIUC, for their help getting our verified server running on real robots; and the anony-

[2] `http://en.wikipedia.org/wiki/Billion_laughs`

mous reviewers, for their helpful comments on an earlier version of this paper. This work has been supported in part by NSF grant CCF-1253229 and by DARPA under agreement number FA8750-12-2-0293. The U.S. Government is authorized to reproduce and distribute reprints for Governmental purposes notwithstanding any copyright notation thereon. The views and conclusions contained herein are those of the authors and should not be interpreted as necessarily representing the official policies or endorsements, either expressed or implied, of DARPA or the U.S. Government.

## References

[1] E. Alkassar, W. J. Paul, A. Starostin, and A. Tsyban. Pervasive verification of an OS microkernel: inline assembly, memory consumption, concurrent devices. In *Proc. VSTTE*, pages 71–85. Springer-Verlag, 2010.

[2] A. W. Appel and D. McAllester. An indexed model of recursive types for foundational proof-carrying code. *TOPLAS*, 23(5):657–683, Sept. 2001.

[3] H. Cai, Z. Shao, and A. Vaynberg. Certified self-modifying code. In *Proc. PLDI*, pages 66–77. ACM, 2007.

[4] A. Chlipala. Mostly-automated verification of low-level programs in computational separation logic. In *Proc. PLDI*, pages 234–245. ACM, 2011.

[5] A. Chlipala. The Bedrock structured programming system: Combining generative metaprogramming and Hoare logic in an extensible program verifier. In *Proc. ICFP*, pages 391–402. ACM, 2013.

[6] A. Chlipala, G. Malecha, G. Morrisett, A. Shinnar, and R. Wisnesky. Effective interactive proofs for higher-order imperative programs. In *Proc. ICFP*, pages 79–90. ACM, 2009.

[7] E. Cohen, M. Dahlweid, M. Hillebrand, D. Leinenbach, M. Moskal, T. Santen, W. Schulte, and S. Tobies. VCC: A practical system for verifying concurrent C. In *Proc. TPHOLs*, pages 23–42. Springer-Verlag, 2009.

[8] M. Daum, N. W. Schirmer, and M. Schmidt. From operating-system correctness to pervasively verified applications. In *Proc. IFM*, pages 105–120. Springer-Verlag, 2010.

[9] X. Feng and Z. Shao. Modular verification of concurrent assembly code with dynamic thread creation and termination. In *Proc. ICFP*, pages 254–267. ACM, 2005.

[10] X. Feng, Z. Shao, Y. Dong, and Y. Guo. Certifying low-level programs with hardware interrupts and preemptive threads. In *Proc. PLDI*, pages 170–182. ACM, 2008.

[11] X. Feng, Z. Shao, Y. Guo, and Y. Dong. Combining domain-specific and foundational logics to verify complete software systems. In *Proc. VSTTE*, pages 54–69. Springer-Verlag, 2008.

[12] X. Feng, Z. Shao, A. Vaynberg, S. Xiang, and Z. Ni. Modular verification of assembly code with stack-based control abstractions. In *Proc. PLDI*, pages 401–414. ACM, 2006.

[13] V. Gapeyev, M. Y. Levin, B. C. Pierce, and A. Schmitt. The Xtatic experience. In *Proc. PLAN-X*, 2005. University of Pennsylvania Technical Report MS-CIS-04-24, Oct 2004.

[14] C. S. Gordon, M. D. Ernst, and D. Grossman. Rely-guarantee references for refinement types over aliased mutable data. In *Proc. PLDI*. ACM, 2013.

[15] A. Gotsman, J. Berdine, B. Cook, N. Rinetzky, and M. Sagiv. Local reasoning for storable locks and threads. In *Proc. APLAS*, pages 19–37. Springer-Verlag, 2007.

[16] A. Gotsman and H. Yang. Modular verification of preemptive OS kernels. In *Proc. ICFP*, pages 404–417. ACM, 2011.

[17] A. Guha, M. Reitblatt, and N. Foster. Machine-verified network controllers. In *Proc. PLDI*, pages 483–494. ACM, 2013.

[18] H. Hosoya and B. C. Pierce. XDuce: A statically typed XML processing language. *ACM Transactions on Internet Technology*, 3(2):117–148, May 2003.

[19] C.-K. Hur and D. Dreyer. A Kripke logical relation between ML and assembly. In *Proc. POPL*, pages 133–146. ACM, 2011.

[20] C. B. Jones. Tentative steps toward a development method for interfering programs. *ACM Trans. Program. Lang. Syst.*, 5(4):596–619, Oct. 1983.

[21] G. Klein. From a verified kernel towards verified systems. In *Proc APLAS*, pages 21–33. Springer-Verlag, 2010.

[22] G. Klein, K. Elphinstone, G. Heiser, J. Andronick, D. Cock, P. Derrin, D. Elkaduwe, K. Engelhardt, R. Kolanski, M. Norrish, T. Sewell, H. Tuch, and S. Winwood. seL4: Formal verification of an OS kernel. In *Proc. SOSP*, pages 207–220. ACM, 2009.

[23] X. Leroy. Formal certification of a compiler back-end or: programming a compiler with a proof assistant. In *Proc. POPL*, pages 42–54. ACM, 2006.

[24] D. MacQueen. Modules for Standard ML. In *Proc. LFP*, pages 198–207. ACM, 1984.

[25] G. Malecha, A. Chlipala, and T. Braibant. Compositional computational reflection. In *Proc. ITP*, pages 374–389. Springer-Verlag, 2014.

[26] G. Malecha, G. Morrisett, A. Shinnar, and R. Wisnesky. Toward a verified relational database management system. In *Proc. POPL*, pages 237–248. ACM, 2010.

[27] G. Malecha, G. Morrisett, and R. Wisnesky. Trace-based verification of imperative programs with I/O. *J. Symb. Comput.*, 46(2):95–118, Feb. 2011.

[28] A. McCreight, Z. Shao, C. Lin, and L. Li. A general framework for certifying garbage collectors and their mutators. In *Proc. PLDI*, pages 468–479. ACM, 2007.

[29] Z. Ni and Z. Shao. Certified assembly programming with embedded code pointers. In *Proc. POPL*, pages 320–333. ACM, 2006.

[30] Z. Ni, D. Yu, and Z. Shao. Using XCAP to certify realistic systems code: Machine context management. In *Proc. TPHOLs*, pages 189–206. Springer-Verlag, 2007.

[31] F. Pottier. Hiding local state in direct style: A higher-order anti-frame rule. In *Proc. LICS*, pages 331–340. IEEE Computer Society, 2008.

[32] M. Quigley, B. Gerkey, K. Conley, J. Faust, T. Foote, J. Leibs, E. Berger, R. Wheeler, and A. Ng. ROS: an open-source robot operating system. *ICRA Workshop on Open Source Software*, 2009.

[33] J. C. Reynolds. Separation logic: A logic for shared mutable data structures. In *Proc. LICS*, pages 55–74. IEEE Computer Society, 2002.

[34] T. Streicher. *Investigations into intensional type theory*. Habilitation thesis, 1993.

[35] K. Svendsen and L. Birkedal. Impredicative concurrent abstract predicates. In *Proc. ESOP*, pages 149–168. Springer-Verlag, 2014.

[36] P. Wang, S. Cuellar, and A. Chlipala. Compiler verification meets cross-language linking via data abstraction. In *Proc. OOPSLA*, pages 675–690. ACM, 2014.

[37] J. Yang and C. Hawblitzel. Safe to the last instruction: automated verification of a type-safe operating system. In *Proc. PLDI*, pages 99–110. ACM, 2010.

# A Calculus for Relaxed Memory

Karl Crary  Michael J. Sullivan
Carnegie Mellon University
crary@cs.cmu.edu  mjsulliv@cs.cmu.edu

## Abstract

We propose a new approach to programming multi-core, relaxed-memory architectures in imperative, portable programming languages. Our memory model is based on explicit, programmer-specified requirements for order of execution and the visibility of writes. The compiler then realizes those requirements in the most efficient manner it can. This is in contrast to existing memory models, which—if they allow programmer control over synchronization at all—are based on inferring the execution and visibility consequences of synchronization operations or annotations in the code.

We formalize our memory model in a core calculus called RMC. Outside of the programmer's specified requirements, RMC is designed to be strictly more relaxed than existing architectures. It employs an aggressively nondeterministic semantics for expressions, in which actions can be executed in nearly any order, and a store semantics that generalizes Sarkar, *et al.*'s and Alglave, *et al.*'s models of the Power architecture. We establish several results for RMC, including sequential consistency for two programming disciplines, and an appropriate notion of type safety. All our results are formalized in Coq.

***Categories and Subject Descriptors*** D.3.3 [*Language Constructs and Features*]: Concurrent programming structures

***Keywords*** Relaxed memory concurrency

## 1. Introduction

Modern multi-core computer architectures employ relaxed memory models, interfaces to memory that are considerably weaker than the conventional model of sequential consistency [17]. In a sequentially consistent setting, an execution is consistent with some interleaving of the individual memory operations. Thus, the programmer may assume that (a) all threads have a common view of memory that agrees on the order in which memory operations are performed, and (b) that commonly-agreed order respects program-order in regard to operations issued by the same thread.

Relaxed memory architectures provide no such common view of memory. Although most do enforce a globally agreed order on writes to individual locations, the order does not extend to multiple locations. Indeed, on some architectures (notably Power [15] and ARM [13]) it is more useful to start from a view of memory as simply a pool of available writes [5, 22] (and then impose structure), than it is to start from memory as a mapping of locations to values and then try to weaken it.

Moreover, modern architectures also execute instructions out of order. While most do out-of-order execution in a fashion that is undetectable to single-threaded programs, on some important relaxed-memory architectures (*e.g.,* Power and ARM again) it is possible for multi-threaded programs to expose out-of-order execution.

As illustrated by Adve and Gharachorloo [1] and others [2, 22], these are two distinct phenomena. Relaxed memory behaviors cannot always be reduced to just one or the other. This point is often not clearly understood by programmers, or even by authors of documentation, which sometimes give rules governing when reads and writes might be reordered, without specifying the "order" in question.

Relaxed memory architectures can be challenging to program. Single-threaded code, and also concurrent code free of data races (in which accesses to shared variables are protected by mutexes), usually require no special effort, but implementing lock-free data structures, or implementing the mutexes themselves can be very delicate indeed.

In the past the problem was made particularly challenging by the lack of clear specifications of the memory models. Recent work has addressed this difficulty for some important architectures [3–5, 22, 23], but for portable, imperative programming languages the memory models are either insufficiently expressive or quite complex:

In Java [18] and C/C++ [7, 8, 11] the memory model is divided into two parts: a simple mechanism for data-race-free programming, and a less simple one for lock-free data structures and for low-level implementation of synchronization utilities. Like much of the work on architecture models, our primary concern in this paper is the second aspect; our approach to data-race-free programs—discussed in Section 9—is conventional.

Java's `volatile` variables and C/C++'s `atomic` variables need not be used within a mutex, and thus are suitable for lock-free data structures and synchronization implementation. Java's volatiles are guaranteed to be sequentially consistent; this provides a convenient programming model, but it also imposes a cost which can be undesirable in particularly performance-critical code. C/C++'s atomics are more flexible. The programmer annotates each operation on an atomic with a "memory order" that indirectly dictates the semantics of the operation, which may be as strong as sequentially consistent or may be weaker.

Some of the rules governing C/C++ memory orders are quite complicated. Consider the example below (for illustrative purposes only, the details will not be important in the sequel) which has the standard "message passing" idiom at its core:


*POPL '15,* January 15–17, 2015, Mumbai, India.

http://dx.doi.org/10.1145/2676726.2676984

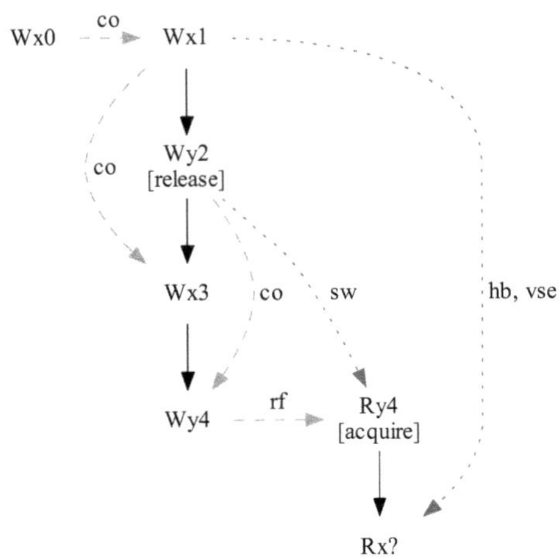


The unlabelled edges are the program order. The dashed red edges are witness relations[1] derived directly from the trace: Ry4 reads from ($\xrightarrow{\text{rf}}$) Wy4. The coherence order ($\xrightarrow{\text{co}}$, the global ordering among writes to the same location) on x is Wx0, Wx1, Wx3, and on y is Wy2, Wy4. From these edges[2] the rules of C/C++ define a plethora of derived edges (shown in dotted blue):

Since Wy2 is marked with "release" order, it is considered a *release action* and forms the head of a *release sequence* (not shown, to avoid cluttering the diagram) that also includes Wy4. Since Ry4 is marked with "acquire" order and reads from Wy2's release sequence, Wy2 *synchronizes-with* Ry4. (Wy4 does not synchronize with Ry4 because Wy4 has relaxed order and thus is not a release action.) Consequently, Wx1 *happens-before* Rx?. Thus Wx1 is a *visible side effect* to Rx? (because there is no other write to x that intervenes by happens-before), and its *visible sequence of side effects* (not shown) consists of itself and Wx3. An atomic read must come from its visible sequence of side effects, so Rx? must read from either Wx1 or Wx3, not Wx0.

On the other hand, if Wy4 had "release" order, then Wy4 (not Wy2) would synchronize-with Ry4, which would mean that Wx3 happens-before Rx?, so Wx3 (not Wx1) would be a visible side effect to Rx?. The visible sequence of side effects would contain only Wx3, so Rx? could read only from Wx3.

This is just a simple example; the required reasoning can be much more complex. Indeed, the key C/C++ notion of *happens-before* is intentionally not transitive (!), to enable certain optimizations on architectures like Power and ARM when using the "consume" memory order.

### 1.1 The RMC Memory Model

We propose a different model for low-level programming on relaxed memory architectures. Rather than have the programmer specify annotations that indirectly determine the relations governing which writes can satisfy which reads, we allow the programmer to specify the key relations *directly*. It is then the compiler's job to generate code to realize them.

[1] in the terminology of Batty, *et al.* [7]

[2] C/C++ refers to program order as "sequenced before" and to the coherence order as "modification order". We use our terms to maintain consistent terminology throughout the paper.

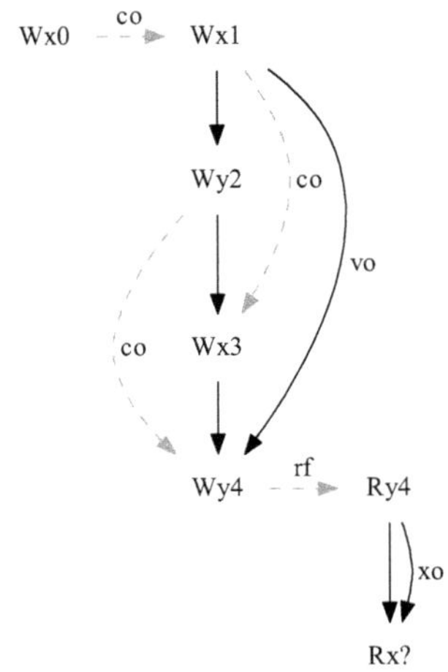


As before, the solid black edges are given by the program, and the dashed red edges are witness relations derived from the trace. The unlabelled edges are again program order. In addition, the program specifies *visibility-order* ($\xrightarrow{\text{vo}}$) and *execution-order* ($\xrightarrow{\text{xo}}$) edges. In this example, to bring about the same outcome as the C/C++ example, the programmer indicates that Wx1 is visibility-ordered before Wy4, and that Ry4 is execution-ordered before Rx?. The visibility specification means that any thread that can see Wy4 must also see Wx1, and the execution specification means that Rx? must occur after Ry4. Thus, Rx? can see Wy4 (since Rx? takes place after its thread reads from Wy4), so it must also see Wx1, and consequently it cannot read from the overwritten Wx0. A programmer who wanted to exclude Wx1 as well would indicate that Wx3 is visibility-ordered before Wy4.

In this paper we present RMC (for Relaxed Memory Calculus), a core calculus for imperative computing with relaxed memory that realizes this memory model. RMC is intended to admit all the strange (to a sequentially consistent eye) executions permitted by relaxed memory architectures. Thus, an RMC program can be implemented on such architectures with no synchronization overhead beyond what is explicitly specified by the programmer.

Importantly, we do *not* attempt to capture the *precise* behavior of any architecture. On the contrary, RMC is specifically intended to be *strictly more relaxed* (in other words, even more perverse) than any existing architecture. This is for two reasons: First, because we find it more elegant to do so. Second, because we hope that by doing so, we can future-proof RMC against further innovations by computer architects.

Thus, RMC makes only five assumptions regarding the architecture: (1) Single-threaded computations (meaning single-threaded programs, and also the critical sections of properly synchronized programs) respect sequential consistency. (2) There exists a strict partial order (called coherence order) on all writes to the same location, and it is respected by reads. (3) The message passing idiom (illustrated above, and discussed in more detail in Section 7) works. (4) There exists a push mechanism (this corresponds to Power's `sync`, ARM's `dmb`, and x86's `mfence`). (5) There exists a mechanism for atomic read-write operations (also known as atomic test-and-set).

Some older architectures might not satisfy 3, 4, or 5, but the importance of those assumptions is now well-understood and we expect that future architectures will. An architecture might also provide some atomic read-modify-write operations; RMC accounts for such, but does not require them. Alglave, *et al.* [5], another architecture-independent formalism, proposes axioms similar in spirit to these assumptions. We compare them to ours in Section 10.

We take as our reference points the (broadly similar) Power and ARM architectures, and the x86 architecture, because they enjoy rigorous, usable specifications [5, 22, 23]. We focus on the former because in all cases relevant to this paper, the complexities of Power and ARM subsume those of x86.

Like Sarkar, *et al.*'s model for Power [22], and Sewell, *et al.*'s model for x86 [23], our calculus is based on an operational semantics, not an axiomatic semantics. Nevertheless, one aspect of our system does give it some axiomatic flavor. Our rules for carrying out storage actions require that the coherence order remain acyclic (assumption 2, above), but to afford maximum flexibility, we do not impose any particular protocol to ensure this. Thus, when reasoning about code, this requirement functions much like an axiom. Alglave, *et al.*'s intermediate machine [5] has a somewhat similar flavor.

The paper makes several contributions:

- We show how to program relaxed-memory architectures using programmer-specified visibility- and execution-order edges.
- We give an elegant calculus capturing out-of-order and speculative execution.
- We give an aggressively relaxed model of memory. It accounts for the write-forwarding behavior of Power and ARM, and a "leapfrogging write" behavior on ARM, in addition to other possible phenomena not yet observed or even implemented.
- We prove three main theorems: (1) A type safety result (including a novel adaptation of progress to nondeterministic execution). (2) A sequential-consistency theorem showing that sequential consistency can be obtained by interleaving instructions with memory barriers. This theorem generalizes a theorem of Batty, *et al.* [9] for the more permissive semantics of RMC, and also streamlines the proof. (3) A second sequential-consistency theorem showing that data-race-free programs enjoy sequential consistency. This theorem adapts a standard result to RMC.

All the results of the paper are formalized in Coq. The formalization may be found at:

`www.cs.cmu.edu/~crary/papers/2014/rmc.tgz`

A version of this paper with a full appendix [12] containing all the inference rules may be found at:

`www.cs.cmu.edu/~crary/papers/2014/rmc.pdf`

## 2. Tagging

RMC's main tool for coping with relaxed memory is user-specified edges indicating visibility order (anyone who sees the latter action can see the former) and execution order (the former action must be executed before the latter). It is easy enough to indicate required orderings between operations by drawing edges on an execution trace, but, of course, execution traces are not programs. How are specified orders rendered in source code?

We do this by using tags to identify operations, and including a declaration form to express required edges between tags. This is illustrated in the following piece of code, which implements the middle thread of the example from Section 1.1 in an extension of C using the RMC memory model:

```
VEDGE(before, after);
L(before, x = 1);
y = 2;
x = 3;
L(after, y = 4);
```

Here, the write `x = 1` (*i.e.*, Wx1) is tagged **before**, and the write `y = 4` (*i.e.*, Wy4) is tagged **after**. The declaration "`VEDGE(before, after)`" indicates that a visibility edge exists between operations tagged **before** and **after**. If we wanted to make Wx3 also visibility ordered before Wy4, we could declare additional tags and edges, or just add the **before** tag to `x = 3`.

Visibility order implies execution order, because it makes little sense to say that $i$ should be visible to anyone who can see $i'$, if $i'$ can be seen before $i$ even takes place. We can get execution order alone using the `XEDGE` keyword.

Tagging creates edges only between operations in program order. Thus, we cannot require an operation to execute before an earlier operation.

This is particularly important when tags appear within loops:

```
VEDGE(before, after);
for (i = 0; i < 2; i++) {
  L(after, x = i);
  L(before, y = i + 10);
}
```

Here, the visibility edge reaches from each y-assignment to the x-assignment in the next iteration of the loop:

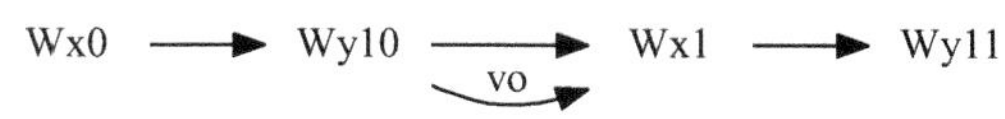


We do not generate nonsensical edges upstream from Wy10 to Wx0, or from Wy11 to Wx1.

Also observe that tags generate edges between all operations with appropriate tags, not only the nearest ones. For example, reversing the tags in the previous code to obtain:

```
VEDGE(before, after);
for (i = 0; i < 2; i++) {
  L(before, x = i);
  L(after, y = i + 10);
}
```

generates:

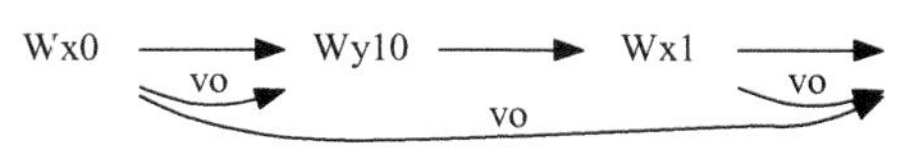


Note the long edge from Wx0 to Wy11. This long edge is desired, as we will see in an example in Section 5.

It is also sometimes useful to impose visibility and execution order more broadly than can be done with individual edges. For example, the code to enter a mutex needs to be execution-ordered before everything in the following critical section, and the code to exit a mutex needs to be visibility-ordered after everything in the preceding critical section. Drawing individual edges between the operations of the mutex and the critical section would be tedious, and would break the mutex abstraction. Instead, RMC allows the programmer to draw edges between an operation and *all* its program-order predecessors or successors using the special quasi-tags `pre` and `post`.

## 3. Visibility

The model recognizes five kinds of actions: reads, writes, read-writes, pushes (see below), and no-ops. Although the primary interest of the visibility order is writes, it can also be useful to impose visibility among other actions. One reason is that visibility order is transitive, so edges can create new paths even when inconsequential in isolation. For instance, if $i_1 \stackrel{\text{vo}}{\rightarrow} i_2 \stackrel{\text{vo}}{\rightarrow} i_3$, the transitive edge $i_1 \stackrel{\text{vo}}{\rightarrow}^{+} i_3$ might be important even if $i_1 \stackrel{\text{vo}}{\rightarrow} i_2$ were unimportant in its own right. (This is the only use for no-ops.)

More substantially, consider the following trace. (In this and subsequent traces, all locations are initialized to zero. These writes are omitted from the diagrams to reduce clutter.) The Wx1 $\xrightarrow{rf}$ Rx1 edge induces visibility order between Wx1 and Rx1. Thus, Wx1 is visibility-ordered before Wy2 by transitivity. Consequently, Rx? can see Wx1, so it cannot read from Wx0.

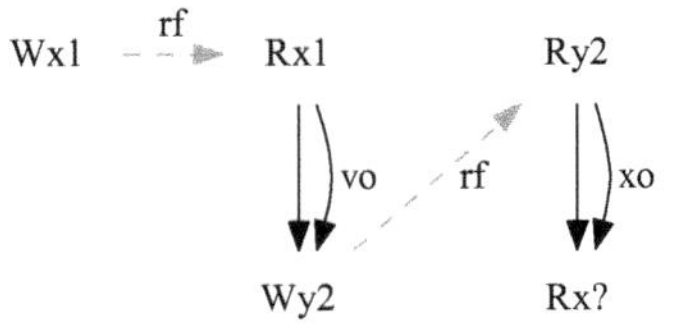


Pushes perform a global synchronization, like `sync` on Power, `dmb` on ARM, or `mfence` on x86. Once a push is executed, it is visible to all threads. Consider the following trace, adapted from Boehm and Adve's [11] read-to-write causality example.

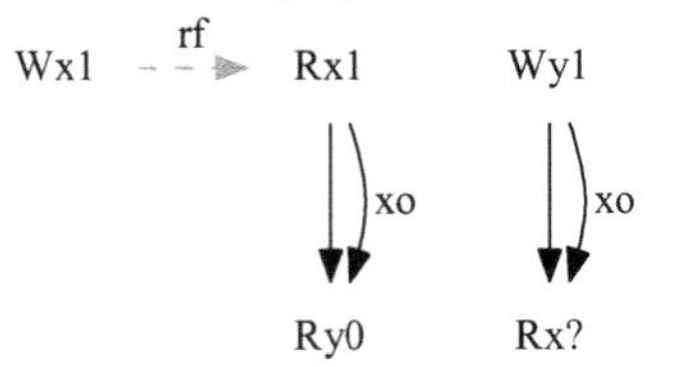


Rx? can read 0, because nothing forces Wx1 to be visible to Rx?. Changing the xo edges to vo has no effect, because visibility-order edges to reads have no more effect than execution order (except possibly to create other paths by transitivity, which would not happen here). However, introducing pushes does change matters:

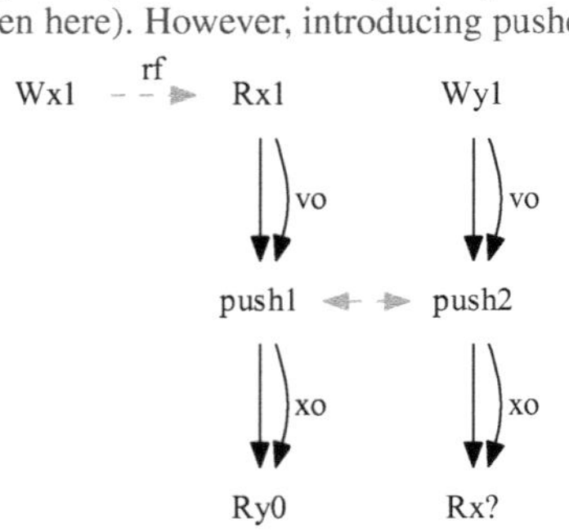


Now Rx? must read 1. Pushes are totally ordered (a consequence of being globally visible), so either push1 is visible to push2 or vice versa. If the former, then Wx1 is visible to Rx?. If the latter, then the trace is impossible because Wy1 is visible to Ry0. This reasoning is generalized in the Sequential Consistency theorem (Section 9).

For another example of reasoning using pushes, consider:

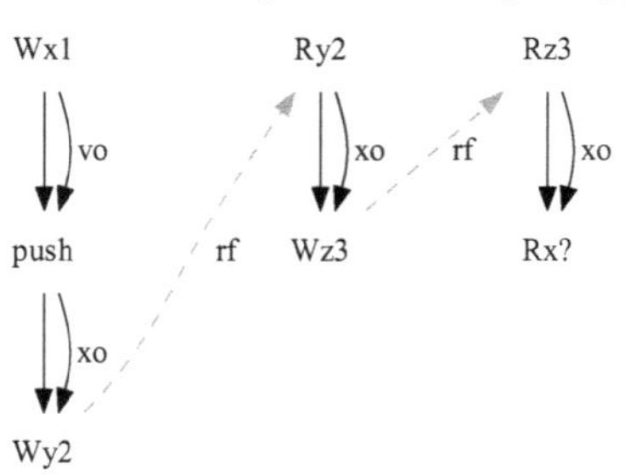


Observe that Wx1 is visibility-ordered before the push, but has no specified relationship to Wz3, so we do not know immediately that Wx1 is visible to Rx?. However, Wy2 takes place after the push, and Ry2, Wz3, Rz3 and Rx? happen later still. Therefore, since pushes are globally visible, Rx? must see the push, and consequently must see Wx1.

## 4. Out-of-order and speculative execution

An RMC expression consists of a monadic sequence of actions. In a conventional monadic language, an action's lifecycle goes through two phases: first, resolve the action's arguments (purely), then execute the action (generating effects). In RMC we add an intermediate phase. Once an action's arguments are resolved, we *initiate* the action, which replaces the action by an action identifier. Later, an initiated action can be executed, at which time the identifier is replaced by the action's result.

Once an action is initiated, execution may proceed out of order. The semantics may nondeterministically choose to execute the action immediately, or it may delay it and process a later action first.

For example, consider an expression that reads from $a$ then writes to $b$. One possible execution executes the write before the read:

$$
\begin{array}{lll}
 & x \leftarrow \mathsf{R}[a] \text{ in } \_ \leftarrow \mathsf{W}[b, 12] \text{ in ret } x & \\
\mapsto & x \leftarrow i_1 \text{ in } \_ \leftarrow \mathsf{W}[b, 12] \text{ in ret } x & \\
\mapsto & x \leftarrow i_1 \text{ in } \_ \leftarrow i_2 \text{ in ret } x & \\
\mapsto & x \leftarrow i_1 \text{ in } \_ \leftarrow \text{ret ()} \text{ in ret } x & \text{(with write effect)} \\
\mapsto & x \leftarrow i_1 \text{ in ret } x & \\
\mapsto & x \leftarrow \text{ret } 10 \text{ in ret } x & \text{(with read effect)} \\
\mapsto & \text{ret } 10 &
\end{array}
$$

The purpose of the initiation phase is to require the execution to commit to the arguments of earlier actions before executing later ones. This is important because program-order earlier actions often affect the semantics of later ones, even when the later actions are actually executed first.

Out-of-order execution makes it possible for execution to proceed out of program order, but not out of dependency order. For example, suppose the write to $b$ depends on the value read from $a$:

$$
\begin{array}{ll}
 & x \leftarrow \mathsf{R}[a] \text{ in } \_ \leftarrow \mathsf{W}[b, x] \text{ in ret } x \\
\mapsto & x \leftarrow i_1 \text{ in } \_ \leftarrow \mathsf{W}[b, x] \text{ in ret } x \\
\mapsto & ??
\end{array}
$$

The write to $b$ cannot initiate because its arguments are not known. However, RMC permits execution to *speculate* on the value of unknown quantities. For, example we may speculate that $x$ will eventually become 10, producing the execution:

$$
\begin{array}{lll}
 & x \leftarrow i_1 \text{ in } \_ \leftarrow \mathsf{W}[y, x] \text{ in ret } x & \\
\mapsto & 10 \leftarrow i_1 \text{ in } \_ \leftarrow \mathsf{W}[y, 10] \text{ in ret } 10 & \text{(NB!)} \\
\mapsto & 10 \leftarrow i_1 \text{ in } \_ \leftarrow i_2 \text{ in ret } 10 & \\
\mapsto & \ldots & \\
\mapsto & 10 \leftarrow i_1 \text{ in ret } 10 & \\
\mapsto & 10 \leftarrow \text{ret } 10 \text{ in ret } 10 & \text{(with read effect)} \\
\mapsto & \text{ret } 10 &
\end{array}
$$

Here, the syntax $v \leftarrow e \text{ in } e'$ is a distinct syntactic form[3] from the usual monadic bind ($x \leftarrow e \text{ in } e'$). Unlike the usual form, it binds no variables, and instead indicates the value that the bound expression is required to return. Speculation allows us to step from $x \leftarrow e \text{ in } e'$ to $v \leftarrow e \text{ in } [v/x]e'$. Eventually, once the expression has been executed, we can discharge the speculation, stepping from $v \leftarrow \text{ret } v \text{ in } e$ to $e$.

The combination of out-of-order and speculative execution allows us to execute the program in nearly any order, subject only to the constraints imposed by the programmer and those inherent in the actions themselves.

[3] In fact, it is actually a derived form, built from a more primitive speculation form in Section 6.

RMC uses nondeterminism in a variety of ways, but speculation is the most aggressive. Unlike our other uses (*e.g.*, interleaving of threads, out-of-order execution, the choice of which read satisfies a write), speculation can take execution down a blind alley. In the above example, we speculated $i_1$ would return 10. But suppose it did not? Then we find ourselves in a state like $10 \leftarrow \mathsf{ret}\ 11\ \mathsf{in}\ \mathsf{ret}\ 10$ from which we can make no further progress.

We do not refer to states like this as "stuck", since stuck usually connotes an unsafe state. Instead we call such states "moot", since they arise in executions that cannot actually happen. When reasoning about RMC programs, one may ignore any executions that become moot.

Although the use of speculation above might seem fanciful at the architectural level, it could very easily arise in an optimizing compiler, which might be able to determine statically that $\mathsf{R}[a]$ would (or at least could) return 10.

A more common use of speculation by the hardware is to execute past a branch when the discriminating value is not yet known. For example:[4]

$$
\begin{array}{ll}
 & x \leftarrow \mathsf{R}[a]\ \mathsf{in}\ \mathsf{force}(\mathsf{if}\ x = 0\ \mathsf{then}\ \mathsf{susp}\, e\ \mathsf{else}\ \mathsf{susp}\, e') \\
\mapsto & x \leftarrow i_1\ \mathsf{in}\ \mathsf{force}(\mathsf{if}\ x = 0\ \mathsf{then}\ \mathsf{susp}\, e\ \mathsf{else}\ \mathsf{susp}\, e') \\
\mapsto & 10 \leftarrow i_1\ \mathsf{in}\ \mathsf{force}(\mathsf{if}\ 10 = 0\ \mathsf{then}\ \mathsf{susp}\, e\ \mathsf{else}\ \mathsf{susp}\, e') \\
\mapsto & 10 \leftarrow i_1\ \mathsf{in}\ \mathsf{force}(\mathsf{susp}\, e') \\
\mapsto & 10 \leftarrow i_1\ \mathsf{in}\ e' \\
\mapsto & \cdots
\end{array}
$$

## 5. An example

As a realistic example of code using the RMC memory model, consider the code in Figure 1. This code—adapted from the Linux kernel [14]—implements a ring-buffer, a common data structure that implements an imperative queue with a fixed maximum size. The ring-buffer maintains front and back pointers into an array, and the current contents of the queue are those that lie between the back and front pointers (wrapping around if necessary). Elements are inserted by advancing the back pointer, and removed by advancing the front pointer.

The ring-buffer permits at most one writer at a time, and at most one reader at a time, but allows concurrent, unsynchronized access by a writer and a reader.

Note that the buffer is considered empty, not full, when the front and back coincide. Thus, the buffer is full—and enqueueing fails—when exactly one empty cell remains. This seemingly minor implementation detail complicates the analysis of the code in an interesting way.

We wish the ring-buffer to possess two important properties: (1) the elements dequeued are the same elements that we enqueued (that is, threads do not read from an array cell without the pertinent write having propagated to that thread), and (2) no enqueue overwrites an element that is still current.

The key lines of code are those tagged `echeck`, `write`, and `eupdate` (in `enqueue`), and `dcheck`, `read`, and `dupdate` (in `dequeue`). (It is not necessary to use disjoint tag variables in different functions; we do so only to simplify the exposition.)

For property (1), consider an enqueue-dequeue pair. We have $\mathtt{write} \overset{\mathsf{vo}}{\rightarrow} \mathtt{eupdate} \overset{\mathsf{rf}}{\rightarrow} \mathtt{dcheck} \overset{\mathsf{xo}}{\rightarrow} \mathtt{read}$. It follows that `write` is visible to `read`.

Property (2) is a bit more complicated. Since a full ring-buffer has an empty cell, it requires two consecutive enqueues to risk overwriting a cell. The canonical trace we wish to prevent appears in Figure 2. In it, $\mathtt{read}_1$ reads from $\mathtt{write}_2$, a "later" write that finds

[4] Here, susp suspends an expression (forming a thunk), and force forces a suspension.

```
bool enqueue(buffer *buf, char ch)
{
    XEDGE(echeck, write);
    VEDGE(write, eupdate);

    unsigned back = buf->back;
    L(echeck, unsigned front = buf->front);

    int enqueued = false;
    if (ring_increment(back) != front) {
        L(write, buf->arr[back] = ch);
        L(eupdate,
          buf->back = ring_increment(back));
        enqueued = true;
    }
    return enqueued;
}

int dequeue(buffer *buf)
{
    XEDGE(dcheck, read);
    XEDGE(read, dupdate);

    unsigned front = buf->front;
    L(dcheck, unsigned back = buf->back);

    int ch = -1;
    if (front != back) {
        L(read, ch = buf->arr[front]);
        L(dupdate,
          buf->front = ring_increment(front));
    }
    return ch;
}
```

**Figure 1.** A ring-buffer

room in the buffer only because of a dequeue operation subsequent to $\mathtt{read}_1$. Hence, a current entry is overwritten.

This problematic trace is impossible, since $\mathtt{read}_1 \overset{\mathsf{xo}}{\rightarrow} \mathtt{dupdate}_1 \overset{\mathsf{rf}}{\rightarrow} \mathtt{echeck}_1 \overset{\mathsf{xo}}{\rightarrow} \mathtt{write}_2 \overset{\mathsf{rf}}{\rightarrow} \mathtt{read}_1$. (Alternatively, $\mathtt{read}_1 \overset{\mathsf{xo}}{\rightarrow} \mathtt{dupdate}_2 \overset{\mathsf{rf}}{\rightarrow} \mathtt{echeck}_2 \overset{\mathsf{xo}}{\rightarrow} \mathtt{write}_2 \overset{\mathsf{rf}}{\rightarrow} \mathtt{read}_1$.) In RMC, if $i \overset{\mathsf{rf}}{\rightarrow} i'$ then $i$ must be executed earlier than $i'$ (you cannot read from a write that hasn't yet executed), so it follows that $\mathtt{read}_1$ must execute strictly before itself, which is a contradiction.

Note that this argument relies on $\mathtt{echeck}_1 \overset{\mathsf{xo}}{\rightarrow} \mathtt{write}_2$ (or $\mathtt{read}_1 \overset{\mathsf{xo}}{\rightarrow} \mathtt{dupdate}_2$). Merely having, say, $\mathtt{echeck}_1 \overset{\mathsf{xo}}{\rightarrow} \mathtt{write}_1$ would be insufficient, since nothing in the code as written gives us $\mathtt{write}_1 \overset{\mathsf{xo}}{\rightarrow} \mathtt{write}_2$.

***Contrasted with C/C++*** To implement the ring-buffer in C/C++, one can mark the `eupdate` and `dupdate` operations as "release", and the `echeck` and `dcheck` operations as "acquire".

For property (1), in an enqueue-dequeue pair we get `eupdate` synchronizes-with `dcheck`, since `eupdate` reads from `dcheck`. This implies that `write` happens-before `read`.[5]

For property (2), consider the trace in Figure 3. In this trace, $\mathtt{dupdate}_1$ synchronizes-with $\mathtt{echeck}_1$ (alternatively, $\mathtt{dupdate}_2$ synchronizes-with $\mathtt{echeck}_2$), so $\mathtt{read}_1$ happens-before $\mathtt{write}_2$. Thus $\mathtt{read}_1$ cannot read from $\mathtt{write}_2$.

[5] The latter inference is a bit subtle, since happens-before is not transitive. It includes program order on the left, but includes it on the right only after synchronizes-with.

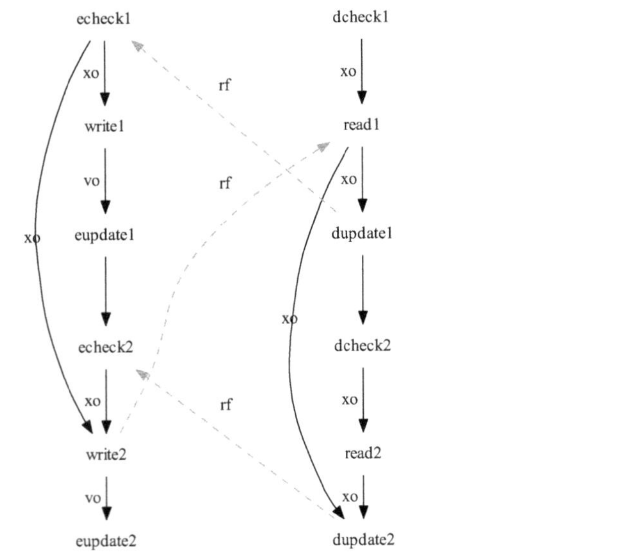


**Figure 2.** Impossible ring-buffer trace

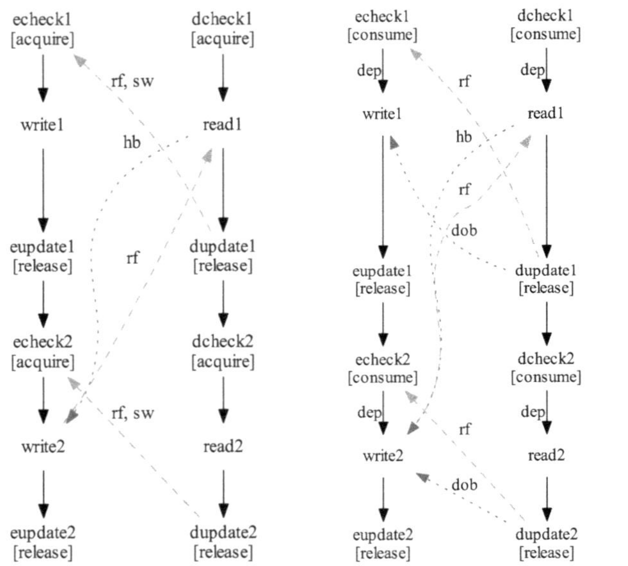


**Figure 3.** Impossible ring-buffer traces in C/C++

These correctness arguments for RMC and C/C++ are broadly similar. In part, this is because the C/C++ ring-buffer code is fairly simple, without any nontrivial release sequences or visible sequences of side-effects [7]. And, in part, this is because the C/C++ implementation uses release/acquire synchronization instead of release/consume (which may be cheaper on certain architectures, such as Power and ARM).

To obtain potentially better performance in C/C++, one may instead mark `echeck` and `dcheck` as "consume" and introduce spurious data dependencies from `echeck` to `write`, and `dcheck` to `read`. This makes the correctness argument more delicate. For property (1), in an enqueue-dequeue pair we get (using the former data dependency) that `eupdate` is dependency-ordered-before `read`, which (using the delicate definition of happens-before) once again ensures that `write` happens-before `read`.

| | | | |
|---|---|---|---|
| types | $\tau$ | $::=$ | $\mathsf{unit} \mid \mathsf{nat} \mid \tau\ \mathsf{ref} \mid \tau\ \mathsf{susp} \mid \tau \to \tau$ |
| numbers | $n$ | $::=$ | $0 \mid 1 \mid \cdots$ |
| tags | $T$ | $::=$ | $\cdots$ |
| locations | $\ell$ | $::=$ | $\cdots$ |
| identifiers | $i$ | $::=$ | $\cdots$ |
| threads | $p$ | $::=$ | $\cdots$ |
| terms | $m$ | $::=$ | $x \mid () \mid \ell \mid n \mid \mathsf{ifz}\ m\ \mathsf{then}\ m\ \mathsf{else}\ m$ |
| | | $\mid$ | $\mathsf{susp}\ e \mid \mathsf{fun}\ x(x{:}\tau){:}\tau.m \mid m\ m$ |
| values | $v$ | $::=$ | $x \mid () \mid \ell \mid n \mid \mathsf{susp}\ e \mid \mathsf{fun}\ x(x{:}\tau){:}\tau.m$ |
| attributes | $b$ | $::=$ | $\mathsf{vis} \mid \mathsf{exe}$ |
| labels | $\varphi$ | $::=$ | $t \mid T \mid \overset{b}{\lhd} \mid \overset{b}{\rhd}$ |
| expr's | $e$ | $::=$ | $\mathsf{ret}\ m \mid x{:}\tau \leftarrow e\ \mathsf{in}\ e \mid v = v\ \mathsf{in}\ e$ |
| | | $\mid$ | $\mathsf{R}[m] \mid \mathsf{W}[m, m] \mid \mathsf{RW}[m, m]$ |
| | | $\mid$ | $\mathsf{RMW}[m, x{:}\tau.m] \mid \mathsf{Push} \mid \mathsf{Nop} \mid i$ |
| | | $\mid$ | $\mathsf{force}\ m \mid \mathsf{new}\ t \overset{b}{\Rightarrow} t.e \mid \varphi \# e$ |
| execution states | $\xi$ | $::=$ | $\epsilon \mid \xi \parallel p : e$ |
| tag sig | $\Upsilon$ | $::=$ | $\epsilon \mid \Upsilon, T$ |
| loc'n sig | $\Phi$ | $::=$ | $\epsilon \mid \Phi, \ell{:}\tau$ |
| ident sig | $\Psi$ | $::=$ | $\epsilon \mid \Psi, i{:}\tau@p$ |
| contexts | $\Gamma$ | $::=$ | $\epsilon \mid \Gamma, t{:}\mathsf{tag} \mid \Gamma, x{:}\tau$ |

**Figure 4.** Syntax

The argument for property (2) is a bit more subtle, because happens-before is not transitive. In the argument for RMC, and for C/C++ with "acquire", we can construct the illegal path using either $\mathtt{dupdate}_1 \xrightarrow{\mathsf{rf}} \mathtt{echeck}_1$ or $\mathtt{dupdate}_2 \xrightarrow{\mathsf{rf}} \mathtt{echeck}_2$. In contrast, with "consume" we can only use the latter. We can observe that $\mathtt{dupdate}_1$ is dependency-ordered-before $\mathtt{write}_1$, and that $\mathtt{dupdate}_2$ is dependency-ordered-before $\mathtt{write}_2$. However, since happens-before respects program on the left but not (in general) on the right, only the latter suffices to show $\mathtt{read}_1$ happens-before $\mathtt{write}_2$.

In RMC, the programmer need not concern him or herself with acquire vs. consume. He or she simply specifies what is needed—such as execution order between `echeck` and `write`—and the compiler synthesizes the most efficient code it can to implement the specification.

Conversely, RMC also allows the programmer to make finer distinctions. In C/C++, both `eupdate` and `dupdate` must be marked "release". This entails the same overhead for each, tantamount to a visibility order specification in RMC. But, as we have seen, visibility order is necessary only in `enqueue`; `dequeue` requires merely the less-expensive execution order.

## 6. RMC

The syntax of RMC given in Figure 4. Tags ($T$) and identifiers ($i$) range over actual dynamically generated tags and identifiers; they do not appear in user programs. We do not discuss the allocation primitives in this paper so memory locations ($\ell$) can appear in RMC programs here, but not in real RMC-based programs. There are two sorts of variables: $x$ ranges over values and $t$ ranges over tags.

We make a standard syntactic distinction between pure terms ($m$) and effectful expressions ($e$). The terms are standard, and most of the expression forms we have discussed already. The speculation form $v = v'$ in $e$ indicates that the values $v$ and $v'$ are speculated to be identical while evaluating $e$. The monadic speculation form from Section 4 is actually a derived form:

$$v \leftarrow e\ \mathsf{in}\ e' \overset{\mathrm{def}}{=} x \leftarrow e\ \mathsf{in}\ (x = v\ \mathsf{in}\ e')$$

$$\frac{\Upsilon;\Phi;\Gamma\vdash m:\tau}{\Upsilon;\Phi;\epsilon;\Gamma\vdash \mathsf{ret}\, m:\tau} \qquad \frac{}{\Upsilon;\Phi;(i{:}\tau@p);\Gamma\vdash i:\tau}$$

$$\frac{\Upsilon;\Phi;\Psi;\Gamma\vdash e_1:\tau_1 \quad \Upsilon;\Phi;\Psi';(\Gamma,x{:}\tau_1)\vdash e_2:\tau_2 \quad e_1\ \mathsf{init}}{\Upsilon;\Phi;(\Psi,\Psi');\Gamma\vdash x{:}\tau_1\leftarrow e_1\ \mathsf{in}\ e_2:\tau_2}$$

$$\frac{\Upsilon;\Phi;\Psi;\Gamma\vdash e_1:\tau_1 \quad \Upsilon;\Phi;\epsilon;(\Gamma,x{:}\tau_1)\vdash e_2:\tau_2}{\Upsilon;\Phi;\Psi;\Gamma\vdash x{:}\tau_1\leftarrow e_1\ \mathsf{in}\ e_2:\tau_2}$$

**Figure 5.** Static Semantics (abridged)

| | | | |
|---|---|---|---|
| actions | $\alpha$ | $::=$ | $\mathsf{R}[\ell] \mid \mathsf{W}[\ell,v] \mid \mathsf{RW}[\ell,v]$ |
| | | $\mid$ | $\mathsf{Push} \mid \mathsf{Nop}$ |
| transactions | $\delta$ | $::=$ | $\emptyset \mid \vec{\varphi}\,\#\,i=\alpha \mid i\downarrow v \mid T \overset{b}{\Rightarrow} T$ |
| events | $\theta$ | $::=$ | $\mathsf{init}(i,p) \mid \mathsf{is}(i,\alpha) \mid \mathsf{label}(\varphi,i)$ |
| | | $\mid$ | $\mathsf{edge}(b,T,T) \mid \mathsf{exec}(i) \mid \mathsf{rf}(i,i)$ |
| | | $\mid$ | $\mathsf{co}(i,i)$ |
| histories | $H$ | $::=$ | $\epsilon \mid H,\theta$ |

**Figure 6.** Dynamic Semantics, syntax

The tag allocation form new $t\overset{b}{\Rightarrow}t'.e$ generates two new tags bound to variables $t$ and $t'$ in the scope $e$. Those tags express either a visibility or execution edge, as indicated by the attribute $b$.[6] The labelling form $\varphi\ \#\ e$ attaches a *label* to an expression, which is either a tag or a quasi-tag $\overset{b}{\lhd}$ and $\overset{b}{\rhd}$ (representing `pre` and `post`).

Finally, an execution state is an association list, pairing thread identifiers ($p$) with the current expression on that thread.

***Static Semantics*** The static semantics of RMC expressions is largely standard. Expressions are typechecked relative to three ambient signatures and a context. The ambient signatures specify the valid tags, locations, and identifiers, giving the types for location and identifiers, and the threads for identifiers. Terms are not passed an identifier signature because identifiers cannot appear within well-formed terms. Execution states are not passed a context, because well-formed execution states must be closed.

The only interesting aspect is in the treatment of the identifier signature, which we use to ensure that each unexecuted identifier appears exactly once, and that the store's view of program order agrees with the code. Thus, on a given thread, the identifier signature is used like a linear, ordered context [19], as shown in Figure 5. There are two rules for bind: Since actions must be initiated in order, identifiers may appear in the second expression of a bind only when the first is fully initiated (*i.e.,* all of its actions have been converted to identifiers). At the top level (not shown, for space reasons), the identifier signature lists unexecuted identifiers in the same order they appear in the store, and the typing rules for execution states filter out the identifiers for other threads.

***Dynamic Semantics*** Threads and the store communicate by synchronously agreeing on a *transaction*. The empty transaction ($\emptyset$)—which most thread transitions use—indicates there is no store effect. The initiation transaction $\varphi_1,\ldots,\varphi_n\ \#\ i=\alpha$ indicates that the action $\alpha$ is being initiated with labels $\varphi_1,\ldots,\varphi_n$, and is assigned identifier $i$. The execution transaction $i\downarrow v$ indicates that $i$ has been executed and yielded result $v$. The edge transaction $T \overset{b}{\Rightarrow} T'$ indicates that $T$ and $T'$ are fresh tags, expressing a $b$ edge.

The key rules of the dynamic semantics of expressions and execution states appear in Figure 7. The dynamic semantics depends on typing because we want the speculation rule to speculate only well-typed values. Consequently the dynamic semantics for expressions and execution states depends on a tag and location signature, and (for expressions) on a context. The evaluation step judgement for expressions indicates the transaction on which that step depends, and the judgement for execution states indicates both the transaction and the thread on which the step took place.

[6] Thus, in RMC, each tag has exactly one partner. From this primitive, the compiler builds up a more flexible mechanism that allows tags to be used in multiple edges, as in the example of Section 5.

In the interest of brevity, we elide the ambient signatures and context in most of the rules, where they are just ignored or passed to premises. We also leave out the rules that just evaluate subterms (except when they are interesting), and we leave out the dynamic semantics of terms, which is standard.

The rules for out-of-order execution (third row) are straightforward. Speculation (fourth row) allows execution to step from $[v/x]e$ to $v=v'$ in $[v'/x]e$, provided $v$ and $v'$ have the same type. Note that variables are considered values, so an important instance is $e\mapsto(x=v\ \mathsf{in}\ [v/x]e)$.

The heart of the system is the bottom row. Once the subterms of an action are evaluated (and thus it matches the grammar of actions given in Figure 6), the action initiates, synchronizing on a transaction $\epsilon\ \#\ i=\alpha$, and is replaced by $i$. As the transaction bubbles up, it collects any labels that the action lay within. Once all the actions within a label have been initiated, the label can be eliminated. Later, the action executes and is replaced by a return of its value.

***Read-modify-writes*** The semantics deals with read-modify-write expressions by speculating them into read-write expressions. Conceptually, the expression $\mathsf{RMW}[m_1,x{:}\tau.m_2]$ reads location $m_1$ (a $\tau$ location), substitutes the read value for $x$ in $m_2$, and writes $m_2$, all in one atomic operation. To implement this, the dynamic semantics first evaluates the location (this is necessary for type safety[7]) to obtain $\mathsf{RMW}[\ell,x{:}\tau.m_2]$. Then the semantics speculates that the read will return some value $v$, which it substitutes for $x$ to obtain a read-write expression. That read-write expression is then wrapped with speculation scaffolding to ensure that the read-write does in fact return $v$:

$$\frac{\Upsilon;\Phi;\Gamma\vdash v:\tau}{\begin{array}{l}\Upsilon;\Phi;\Gamma\vdash \mathsf{RMW}[\ell,x{:}\tau.m_2]\overset{\emptyset}{\mapsto}\\ \qquad (x{:}\tau\leftarrow \mathsf{RW}[\ell,[v/x]m_2]\ \mathsf{in}\ x=v\ \mathsf{in}\ \mathsf{ret}\,v)\end{array}}$$

Thus, while read-writes are actions seen by the store, read-modify-writes are handled exclusively by the thread semantics. Note that while RMC admits read-modify-write expressions in great generality, we do not assume that languages using the RMC memory model provide such full generality; on the contrary, we expect that they will provide a small set of such operations (*e.g.* fetch-and-add or compare-and-swap) supported by the architecture.

***The Store*** RMC's store is modelled in spirit after the storage subsystem of Sarkar, *et al.*'s [22] model for Power, with adaptations made for RMC's generality. As in Sarkar, *et al.*, the store is represented, not by a mapping of locations to values, but by a *history* of all the events that have taken place. The syntax of events appears in Figure 6.

Three events pertain to the initiation of actions: $\mathsf{init}(i,p)$ records that $i$ was initiated on thread $p$, $\mathsf{is}(i,\alpha)$ records that $i$ rep-

[7] If the location diverges, then there might be no actual location to which values of type $\tau$ have been written. Consquently, the type $\tau$ might be empty, so no speculation transition would be possible.

$$\boxed{\Upsilon; \Phi \vdash \xi \xmapsto{\delta @ p} \xi'}$$

$$\frac{\Upsilon; \Phi; \epsilon \vdash e \overset{\delta}{\mapsto} e'}{\Upsilon; \Phi \vdash (\xi \parallel p : e) \xmapsto{\delta @ p} (\xi \parallel p : e')} \qquad \frac{\xi \xmapsto{\delta @ p'} \xi'}{(\xi \parallel p : e) \xmapsto{\delta @ p'} (\xi' \parallel p : e)}$$

$$\boxed{\Upsilon; \Phi; \Gamma \vdash e \overset{\delta}{\mapsto} e' \qquad e\ \mathsf{init} \qquad \varphi \# \delta}$$

$$\frac{}{\mathsf{ret}\, m\ \mathsf{init}} \qquad \frac{}{i\ \mathsf{init}} \qquad \frac{e_1\ \mathsf{init} \quad e_2\ \mathsf{init}}{x{:}\tau \leftarrow e_1\ \mathsf{in}\ e_2\ \mathsf{init}} \qquad \frac{e\ \mathsf{init}}{v_1 = v_2\ \mathsf{in}\ e\ \mathsf{init}} \qquad \frac{}{\mathsf{force}(\mathsf{susp}\, e) \overset{\emptyset}{\mapsto} e} \qquad \frac{}{\mathsf{new}\, t \overset{b}{\Rightarrow} t'.e \xmapsto{T \overset{b}{\Rightarrow} T'} [T, T'/t, t']e}$$

$$\frac{e_1 \overset{\delta}{\mapsto} e_1'}{(x{:}\tau \leftarrow e_1\ \mathsf{in}\ e_2) \overset{\delta}{\mapsto} (x{:}\tau \leftarrow e_1'\ \mathsf{in}\ e_2)} \qquad \frac{e_1\ \mathsf{init} \quad \Upsilon; \Phi; (\Gamma, x{:}\tau) \vdash e_2 \overset{\delta}{\mapsto} e_2' \quad x \notin \mathsf{FV}(\delta)}{\Upsilon; \Phi; \Gamma \vdash (x{:}\tau \leftarrow e_1\ \mathsf{in}\ e_2) \overset{\delta}{\mapsto} (x{:}\tau \leftarrow e_1\ \mathsf{in}\ e_2')} \qquad \frac{}{(x{:}\tau \leftarrow \mathsf{ret}\, v\ \mathsf{in}\ e) \overset{\emptyset}{\mapsto} [v/x]e}$$

$$\frac{\Upsilon; \Phi; \Gamma \vdash v : \tau \quad \Upsilon; \Phi; \Gamma \vdash v' : \tau}{\Upsilon; \Phi; \Gamma \vdash [v/x]e \overset{\emptyset}{\mapsto} (v = v'\ \mathsf{in}\ [v'/x]e)} \qquad \frac{e \overset{\delta}{\mapsto} e'}{v = v'\ \mathsf{in}\ e \overset{\delta}{\mapsto} v = v'\ \mathsf{in}\ e'} \qquad \frac{}{(v = v\ \mathsf{in}\ e) \overset{\emptyset}{\mapsto} e}$$

$$\frac{}{\alpha \xmapsto{\epsilon \# i = \alpha} i} \qquad \frac{e \overset{\delta}{\mapsto} e'}{\varphi \# e \xmapsto{\varphi \# \delta} \varphi \# e'} \qquad \frac{e\ \mathsf{init}}{\varphi \# e \overset{\emptyset}{\mapsto} e} \qquad \frac{}{i \xmapsto{i \downarrow v} \mathsf{ret}\, v} \qquad \varphi \# \delta = \begin{cases} (\varphi, \vec{\varphi}) \# i = \alpha & \text{if } \delta = (\vec{\varphi} \# i = \alpha) \\ \delta & \text{otherwise} \end{cases}$$

**Figure 7.** Dynamic Semantics, threads (abridged)

resents action $\alpha$, and $\mathsf{label}(\varphi, i)$ records that label $\varphi$ is attached to $i$. These three events always occur together, but it is technically convenient to treat them as distinct events.

The event $\mathsf{edge}(b, T, T')$ records the allocation of two tags and an edge between them.

Two events pertain to executed actions: $\mathsf{exec}(i)$ records that $i$ is executed, and $\mathsf{rf}(i, i')$ records both that $i'$ is executed and $i'$ read from $i$.

The final form, $\mathsf{co}(i, i')$, adds a coherence-order edge from $i$ to $i'$. This is not used in the operational semantics, but it is useful in some proofs to have a way to add extraneous coherence edges.

Store transitions take the form $H \xmapsto{\delta @ p} H'$, in which the $\delta$ is a transaction that is shared synchronously with a transition in thread $p$.

In the store transition rules, we write $H(\theta)$ to mean the event $\theta$ appears in $H$, where $\theta$ may contain wildcards $(*)$ indicating parts of the event that don't matter. As usual, we write $\rightarrow^+$ and $\rightarrow^*$ for the transitive, and the reflexive, transitive closures of a relation $\rightarrow$. We write the composition of two relations as $\overset{x}{\rightarrow}\overset{y}{\rightarrow}$. We say that $\rightarrow$ is *acyclic* if $\neg \exists x.\, x \rightarrow^+ x$.

We can give three store transitions immediately. An empty transaction generates no new events. An edge transaction simply records the new edge, provided both tags are distinct and fresh. (We define $\mathsf{tagdecl}_H(T)$ to mean $H(\mathsf{edge}(*, T, *)) \vee H(\mathsf{edge}(*, *, T))$.) An initiation transaction records the thread, the action, and any labels that apply, provided the identifier is fresh.

$$\frac{}{H \xmapsto{\emptyset @ p} H}\ (\textsc{None}) \qquad \frac{T \neq T' \quad \neg\mathsf{tagdecl}_H(T) \quad \neg\mathsf{tagdecl}_H(T')}{H \xmapsto{T \overset{b}{\Rightarrow} T' @ p} H, \mathsf{edge}(b, T, T')}\ (\textsc{Edge})$$

$$\frac{\neg H(\mathsf{init}(i, *))}{H \xmapsto{\vec{\varphi} \# i = \alpha @ p} H, \mathsf{init}(i, p), \mathsf{is}(i, \alpha), [\mathsf{label}(\varphi, i) \mid \varphi \in \vec{\varphi}]}\ (\textsc{Init})$$

The remaining rules require several auxiliary definitions:

- Identifiers are in *program order* if they are initiated in order and on the same thread:

$$i \overset{\mathsf{po}}{\rightarrow}_H i' \overset{\text{def}}{=}$$
$$\exists H_1, H_2, H_3, p.\ H = H_1, \mathsf{init}(i, p), H_2, \mathsf{init}(i', p), H_3$$

  The operational semantics ensures that this notion of program order agrees with the actual program, since (recall) no expression can be executed out-of-order until any preceding actions are initiated.

- An identifer is marked as executed by either an exec or an rf event: $\mathsf{exec}_H(i) \overset{\text{def}}{=} H(\mathsf{exec}(i)) \vee H(\mathsf{rf}(*, i))$.
- *Trace order* is the order in which identifiers were actually executed: $i \overset{\mathsf{to}}{\rightarrow}_H i' \overset{\text{def}}{=} \exists H_1, H_2.\ H = H_1, H_2 \wedge \mathsf{exec}_{H_1}(i) \wedge \neg\mathsf{exec}_{H_1}(i')$. Note that this definition makes executed identifiers trace-order-earlier than non-yet-executed identifiers.
- *Specified order,* which realizes the tagging discipline, is defined by the rules:

$$\frac{i \overset{\mathsf{po}}{\rightarrow}_H i' \quad H(\mathsf{label}(T, i)) \quad H(\mathsf{label}(T', i')) \quad H(\mathsf{edge}(b, T, T'))}{i \overset{b}{\Rightarrow}_H i'}$$

$$\frac{i \overset{\mathsf{po}}{\rightarrow}_H i' \quad H(\mathsf{label}(\overset{b}{\lhd}, i'))}{i \overset{b}{\Rightarrow}_H i'} \qquad \frac{i \overset{\mathsf{po}}{\rightarrow}_H i' \quad H(\mathsf{label}(\overset{b}{\rhd}, i))}{i \overset{b}{\Rightarrow}_H i'}$$

- The key notion of *execution order* is defined in terms of specified order: $i \overset{\mathsf{xo}}{\rightarrow}_H i' \overset{\text{def}}{=} \exists b.\, i \overset{b}{\Rightarrow}_H i'$.
- An identifier is *executable* if it has not been executed, and all its execution-order predecessors have been: $\mathsf{executable}_H(i) \overset{\text{def}}{=} \neg\mathsf{exec}_H(i) \wedge \forall i'.\, i' \overset{\mathsf{xo}}{\rightarrow}_H i \supset \mathsf{exec}_H(i')$.
- A read action is either a read or a read-write: $\mathsf{reads}_H(i, \ell) = H(\mathsf{is}(i, \mathsf{R}[\ell])) \vee H(\mathsf{is}(i, \mathsf{RW}[\ell, *]))$.
- Similarly, a write action is either a write or a read-write: $\mathsf{writes}_H(i, \ell, v) = H(\mathsf{is}(i, \mathsf{W}[\ell, v])) \vee H(\mathsf{is}(i, \mathsf{RW}[\ell, v]))$.

- *Reads-from:* $i \xrightarrow{\mathsf{rf}}_H i' \stackrel{\text{def}}{=} H(\mathsf{rf}(i,i'))$.
- Identifiers $i$ and $i'$ are *push-ordered* if $i$ is a push and is trace-order-earlier than $i'$: $i \xrightarrow{\pi\mathsf{o}}_H i' \stackrel{\text{def}}{=} H(\mathsf{is}(i,\mathsf{Push})) \wedge i \xrightarrow{\mathsf{to}}_H i'$. Since pushes are globally visible as soon as they execute, this means that $i$ should be visible to $i'$.
- The key notion of *visibility order* is defined as the union of specified visibility order, reads-from, and push order: $i \xrightarrow{\mathsf{vo}}_H i' \stackrel{\text{def}}{=} i \xRightarrow{\mathsf{vis}}_H i' \vee i \xrightarrow{\mathsf{rf}}_H i' \vee i \xrightarrow{\pi\mathsf{o}}_H i'$.

Finally, there is the central notion of coherence order (written $i \xrightarrow{\mathsf{co}}_H i'$), a strict partial order on actions that write to the same location. The coherence order is inferred *ex post* from the events that transpire in the store, in a manner that we discuss in detail in Section 7. For now, the important property is coherence order must always be acyclic.

Note that our *ex post* view of coherence order is in contrast to the *ex ante* view taken by Sarkar, *et al.* [22]. In our *ex post* view, coherence order is inferred from events that have already occurred; in the *ex ante* view, coherence edges must *already* exist (introduced nondeterministically and asynchronously) in order for events to occur.

With these definitions in hand, we give the remaining rules:

$$\frac{\begin{array}{l} H(\mathsf{init}(i,p)) \quad H(\mathsf{is}(i,\alpha)) \quad \alpha = \mathsf{R}[\ell] \vee \alpha = \mathsf{RW}[\ell,v'] \\ \mathsf{executable}_H(i) \quad \mathsf{acyclic}(\xrightarrow{\mathsf{co}}_{H;\mathsf{rf}(i_w,i)}) \\ \mathsf{writes}_H(i_w,\ell,v) \quad \mathsf{exec}_H(i_w) \end{array}}{H \overset{i\downarrow v@p}{\longmapsto} H, \mathsf{rf}(i_w,i)} \ (\textsc{Read})$$

$$\frac{\begin{array}{c} H(\mathsf{init}(i,p)) \quad H(\mathsf{is}(i,\alpha)) \\ \alpha = \mathsf{W}[\ell,v] \vee \alpha = \mathsf{Push} \vee \alpha = \mathsf{Nop} \\ \mathsf{executable}_H(i) \quad \mathsf{acyclic}(\xrightarrow{\mathsf{co}}_{H;\mathsf{exec}(i)}) \end{array}}{H \overset{i\downarrow ()@p}{\longmapsto} H, \mathsf{exec}(i)} \ (\textsc{Nonread})$$

Observe that read actions (reads and read-writes) are treated the same, and non-read actions (writes, pushes, and no-ops) are treated the same. However, their presence in the history can have very different effects on other actions.

Also observe that Read has no explicit premise ensuring that the read returns the "right value," beyond ensuring that $i_w$ writes to the same location $i$ reads from. The validity of the read is enforced implicitly by the premise $\mathsf{acyclic}(\xrightarrow{\mathsf{co}}_{H,\mathsf{rf}(i_w,i)})$. If $i_w$ is an improper write for $i$ to read from—for example, if $i_w$ is coherence-older than some other write visible to $i$—then adding $\mathsf{rf}(i_w,i)$ to the history will create a cycle in coherence order.

***The top level*** The top-level dynamic semantics appears in Figure 8. RMC's top-level state consists of the three ambient signatures, a history, and an execution state.

$$\begin{array}{llcl} \text{signature} & \Sigma & ::= & (\Upsilon,\Phi,\Psi) \\ \text{state} & s & ::= & (\Sigma,H,\xi) \end{array}$$

An auxiliary judgement over ambient signatures updates them according to the transaction. The state can make a transition when all three components agree on a transaction.

## 7. Coherence order

The ultimate question to be resolved is which writes are permitted to satisfy a given read. In a sequentially consistent setting, the only write permitted to satisfy a given read is the unique, most-recent write to the read's location. In relaxed memory setting, the "most-recent write" is no longer unique. Nevertheless, we assume that there exists an order on writes that is respected by all reads. Following Sarkar, *et al.* [22], we call this the *coherence order*.

$$\boxed{\Sigma \overset{\delta@p}{\longmapsto} \Sigma'}$$

$$\frac{}{\Sigma \overset{\emptyset@p}{\longmapsto} \Sigma} \qquad \frac{\forall \varphi \in \vec{\varphi}.\ \Upsilon;\epsilon \vdash \varphi : \mathsf{label} \quad \Upsilon,\Phi,\Psi,\epsilon \vdash \alpha : \tau}{(\Upsilon,\Phi,\Psi) \overset{\vec{\varphi}\#i=\alpha@p}{\longmapsto} (\Upsilon,\Phi,(\Psi, i{:}\tau@p))}$$

$$\frac{\Psi = \Psi_1, i{:}\tau@p, \Psi_2 \quad \vdash v : \tau}{(\Upsilon,\Phi,\Psi) \overset{i\downarrow v@p}{\longmapsto} (\Upsilon,\Phi,(\Psi_1,\Psi_2))} \qquad \frac{\begin{array}{c}\Upsilon' = \Upsilon, T, T' \\ T \neq T' \quad T,T' \notin \Upsilon\end{array}}{(\Upsilon,\Phi,\Psi) \overset{T \overset{b}{\Rightarrow} T'@p}{\longmapsto} (\Upsilon',\Phi,\Psi)}$$

$$\boxed{s \mapsto s'}$$

$$\frac{\begin{array}{c}\Sigma = (\Upsilon,\Phi,\Psi) \\ \Sigma \overset{\delta@p}{\longmapsto} \Sigma' \quad H \overset{\delta@p}{\longmapsto} H' \quad \Upsilon;\Phi \vdash \xi \overset{\delta@p}{\longmapsto} \xi'\end{array}}{(\Sigma,H,\xi) \mapsto (\Sigma',H',\xi')}$$

**Figure 8.** Dynamic Semantics, top-level

As in Sarkar, *et al.*, the coherence order is a strict partial order that relates only writes to the same location. In an effort to future-proof our calculus, we place only the minimum constraints on coherence order necessary to accomplish three goals: First, single-threaded computations should exhibit the expected behavior. Second, the message passing idiom—expressed via RMC's visibility and execution order—should work. Third, read-write operations should be atomic in an appropriate sense. These three aims result in three rules defining coherence order, which we explore below.

The first coherence rule states that a read always reads from the most recent of all writes (to its location) that it has seen:

$$\frac{i \xrightarrow{\mathsf{wrp}}_H i_r \quad i' \xrightarrow{\mathsf{rf}}_H i_r \quad i \neq i'}{i \xrightarrow{\mathsf{co}}_H i'} \ (\textsc{Co-Read})$$

Here we write $i \xrightarrow{\mathsf{wrp}} i_r$ (pronounced "$i$ is *write-read-prior* to $i_r$") to say that the read $i_r$ has already seen the write $i$. (Other writes may also have been seen; the prior writes are the ones we know for certain have been seen.) Since $i_r$ reads from $i'$ instead of $i$, we infer that $i'$ is coherence-later than $i$.

We know that $i_r$ has seen $i_w$ in one of two ways. First, $i_w$ is program-order-earlier than $i_r$ (thus ensuring that single-threaded computations work properly). Second, $i_w$ is visibility-order-previous to some action that is execution-order-previous to $i_r$ (thus ensuring that the message-passing idiom works properly).

$$\frac{i \xrightarrow{\mathsf{po}}_H i' \quad \mathsf{writes}_H(i,\ell,v) \quad \mathsf{reads}_H(i',\ell)}{i \xrightarrow{\mathsf{wrp}}_H i'} \ (\textsc{Wrp-po})$$

$$\frac{i \xrightarrow{\mathsf{vo}}{}^{+}_{H} \xrightarrow{\mathsf{xo}}{}^{*}_{H} i' \quad \mathsf{writes}_H(i,\ell,v) \quad \mathsf{reads}_H(i',\ell)}{i \xrightarrow{\mathsf{wrp}}_H i'} \ (\textsc{Wrp-vis})$$

The second coherence rule says that a write is always more recent than all other writes (to its location) it has seen:

$$\frac{i \xrightarrow{\mathsf{wwp}}_H i'}{i \xrightarrow{\mathsf{co}}_H i'} \ (\textsc{Co-write})$$

Here we write $i \xrightarrow{\mathsf{wwp}} i'$ (*write-write-prior*) to say that the write $i'$ has already seen the write $i$. This has two rules similar to write-read priority:

$$\frac{i \xrightarrow{\mathsf{po}}_H i' \quad \mathsf{writes}_H(i,\ell,v) \quad \mathsf{writes}_H(i',\ell,v')}{i \xrightarrow{\mathsf{wwp}}_H i'} \ (\textsc{Wwp-po})$$

$$\frac{i \xrightarrow{\mathsf{vo}}{}^{+}_{H} \xrightarrow{\mathsf{xo}}{}^{*}_{H} i' \quad \mathsf{writes}_H(i,\ell,v) \quad \mathsf{writes}_H(i',\ell,v')}{i \xrightarrow{\mathsf{wwp}}_H i'} \ (\textsc{Wwp-vis})$$

Another write-write-priority rule says that $i'$ has seen $i$, if $i'$ has seen some read $i_r$ that has seen $i$:

$$\frac{i \overset{\mathsf{wrp}}{\rightarrow}_H i_r \quad i_r \overset{\mathsf{rwp}}{\rightarrow}_H i'}{i \overset{\mathsf{wwp}}{\rightarrow}_H i'} \quad (\text{WWP-READ})$$

Read-write-priority ($\overset{\mathsf{rwp}}{\rightarrow}$), used here, has only a program-order rule. Although a visibility rule would also be sound, it is easy to show that it would not add any new coherence edges, so we omit it for simplicity.

$$\frac{i \overset{\mathsf{po}}{\rightarrow}_H i' \quad \mathsf{reads}_H(i, \ell) \quad \mathsf{writes}_H(i', \ell, v)}{i \overset{\mathsf{rwp}}{\rightarrow}_H i'} \quad (\text{RWP-PO})$$

The third coherence rule says that when an atomic read-write action $i$ reads from a write $i_w$, no other write $i'$ can come between them in coherence order:

$$\frac{i_w \overset{\mathsf{rf}}{\rightarrow}_H i \quad H(\mathsf{is}(i, \mathsf{RW}[*,*])) \quad i_w \overset{\mathsf{co}}{\rightarrow}_H i' \quad i \neq i'}{i \overset{\mathsf{co}}{\rightarrow}_H i'} \quad (\text{CO-RW})$$

The fourth and final coherence rule says that extra coherence edges can be given in the history. This is a technical device for Corollary 8; the operational semantics never introduces any such events.

$$\frac{H(\mathsf{co}(i, i'))}{i \overset{\mathsf{co}}{\rightarrow}_H i'} \quad (\text{CO-FIAT})$$

### 7.1 Discussion

The definition of coherence order works in tandem with the requirement for coherence order to be acyclic to prevent illegal resolution of reads. For example, suppose $i_w \overset{\mathsf{co}}{\rightarrow} i'_w$ and $i_r$ has seen $i'_w$. Then $i_r$ cannot read from $i_w$. If it did, we would infer that $i'_w \overset{\mathsf{co}}{\rightarrow} i_w$, which would introduce a cycle in coherence order.

***Write-write conflicts*** An alert reader may have observed that RMC enforces execution order *only* for programmer-specified execution-order edges. Execution order does not respect program order even for conflicting memory accesses. This is an unusual design, and it merits a little discussion.

Suppose $i_w$ and $i'_w$ are writes to the same location, and suppose $i_w \overset{\mathsf{po}}{\rightarrow} i'_w$. It does not follow from any principle identified above that $i_w$ must execute before $i'_w$. All that is required is that $i_w$ be coherence-earlier than $i'_w$, so that any read that sees both must choose the latter.

In fact, existing architectures do this. Both Power and ARM employ *write forwarding* [22], wherein a write that is not yet eligible to be sent to the storage system can nevertheless satisfy subsequent reads on the same processor. In RMC's view, such a write was executed as soon as it became eligible to be read from,[8] which might well be sooner than some program-order-previous write.

***Read-write conflicts*** Suppose $i_r$ reads from the same location $i_w$ writes to, and suppose $i_r \overset{\mathsf{po}}{\rightarrow} i_w$. Again, it does not follow that $i_w$ must execute after $i_r$. All that is required is that $i_r$ ultimately read from a write coherence-earlier than $i_w$.

In fact, existing architectures do this also! Some ARM processors will sometimes aggressively carry out a write even when preceding reads are not yet complete, and rely on the storage system to ensure that those preceding reads are satisfied by earlier writes. The left-hand trace in Figure 9 can be observed (rarely) on the APQ8060 processor [5, figure 32]. For this trace to occur, the processor must execute Rx0 before the push, and hence it must execute Wy2 before Ry1. We call this phenomenon a "leapfrogging write."

[8] Hence, RMC's "executed" is not the same thing as Sarkar, *et al.*'s "committed" [22].

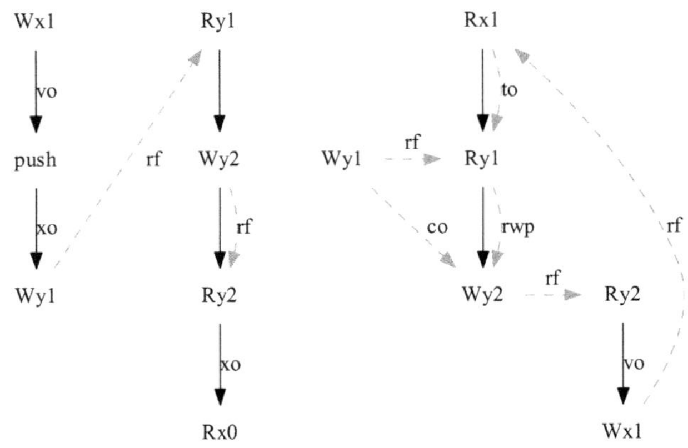


**Figure 9.** Leapfrogging writes (left observed, right allowed by Sarkar, *et al.* revised model)

The leapfrogging write phenomenon also illustrates why priority-via-visibility (*e.g.,* WRP-VIS) must be defined using execution order, and not merely trace order, as might otherwise seem attractive. If trace order ($\overset{\mathsf{to}}{\rightarrow}$) were used, RMC would not admit the right-hand trace in Figure 9 because then $\text{Wy2} \overset{\mathsf{vo}}{\rightarrow}{}^{+} \text{Rx1} \overset{\mathsf{to}}{\rightarrow} \text{Ry1}$ would give us $\text{Wy2} \overset{\mathsf{wrp}}{\rightarrow} \text{Ry1}$, so $\text{Wy2} \overset{\mathsf{co}}{\rightarrow} \text{Wy1}$ (by CO-READ), which would contradict $\text{Wy1} \overset{\mathsf{co}}{\rightarrow} \text{Wy2}$ (which we have by CO-WRITE). This trace, although not yet observed on any processor, is admitted by the revision [21] of the Sarkar, *et al.* model [22], to account for leapfrogging writes. Thus, our definition of the message-passing idiom that we seek to respect is based only on *deliberate* ordering using execution order, and not accidental ordering observed by trace order.

***Write-read conflicts*** Suppose $i_w$ writes to the same location $i_r$ reads from, and suppose $i_w \overset{\mathsf{po}}{\rightarrow} i_r$. Again, it does not follow that $i_r$ must execute after $i_w$. Instead, it is conceivably possible that the architecture could aggressively complete the read and then ensure that $i_w$ is coherence-earlier that the write that satisfied $i_r$.

This behavior has not been observed on any architecture, and we certainly do not advocate it. But in light of the existence of leapfrogged writes, this sort of "leapfrogged read" does not seem inconceivable.

Note, however, that this behavior can only occur in the presence of a data race. If $i_w$ is coherence-later than all other writes to the relevant location, as would be the case in properly synchronized code, then $i_r$ cannot read from any other write. In that case, $i_r$ must read from $i_w$, and thus it cannot execute until $i_w$ does.

***Semantic deadlock*** One consequence of the very loose semantics of RMC's stores is that execution can find its way into a dead end in which no more progress is possible. We call this phenomenon *semantic deadlock.* To be clear, this is a distinct phenomenon from ordinary deadlock, in which a buggy program is unable to make progress, often due to a faulty locking protocol. In *semantic* deadlock a correct program is nevertheless unable to make progress due to inconsistent choices made by the nondeterministic semantics.

Semantic deadlock arises when any progress would create a cycle in coherence order. This can happen because of reads or pushes. An example of the former is shown in the left-hand trace in Figure 10. In this trace, Rx? cannot read from Wx1, because if $\text{Wx1} \overset{\mathsf{rf}}{\rightarrow} \text{Rx?}$ then $\text{Wy2} \overset{\mathsf{vo}}{\rightarrow}{}^{+} \text{Rx?}$, so $\text{Wy2} \overset{\mathsf{wwp}}{\rightarrow} \text{Wy1}$, which would create a cycle in coherence order. However, no other write to x is available, so Rx? cannot execute.

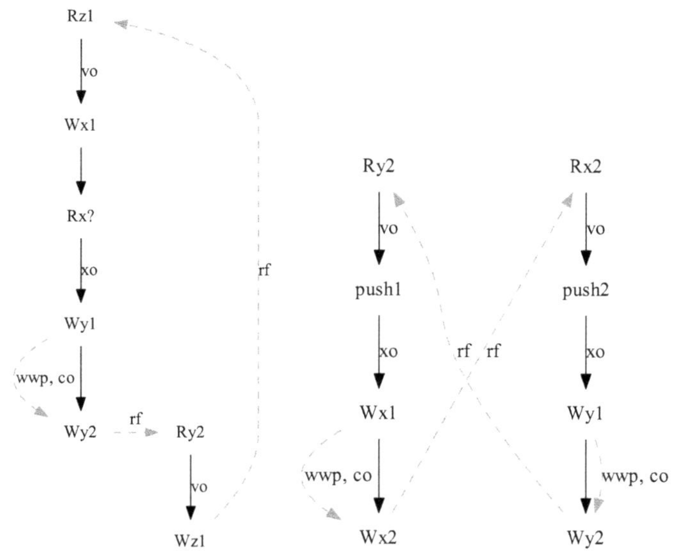


**Figure 10.** Semantic deadlock

An example of the latter is shown in the right-hand trace of Figure 10. In this trace, neither push nor Wx1 nor Wy1 can execute. Suppose push1 executes before Wy1. Then push1 $\stackrel{\pi o}{\rightarrow}$ Wy1, so Wy2 $\stackrel{vo}{\rightarrow}^{+}$ Wy1, and so Wy2 $\stackrel{wwp}{\rightarrow}$ Wy1, which creates a cycle in coherence order. Thus Wy1 must execute before push1. Similarly, Wx1 must execute before push2. But push1 $\stackrel{xo}{\rightarrow}$ Wx1 and push2 $\stackrel{xo}{\rightarrow}$ Wy1 so no progress can be made.

Obviously, semantic deadlock cannot occur in a real execution. Therefore we restrict our attention to *consistent histories*, which are histories that can be extended so that every action is executed, without initiating any new actions. (Resolving the former example by adding a new write for Rx? to read from would be cheating. The storage system must function on its own; it cannot rely on a thread to break its deadlock.) This leads to a subtlety in type safety (Theorem 3), similar to our treatment of moot states resulting from inaccurate speculation.

## 8. Implementation

Implementing the RMC memory model on x86 architectures is easy. The total-store-ordering semantics [23] provides that all instructions are executed in program order (or, more precisely, cannot be observed to be executed out of program order), each write is visible either globally or only to its own thread, and writes become globally visible in program order. Consequently, visibility- and execution-order edges compile away to nothing, and pushes can be implemented by `mfence`s.

Power [22] and ARM [5] are more interesting. Pushes are again implemented by a fence (`sync` on Power, `dmb` on ARM). Necessary visibility edges—many can be eliminated statically—are realized by a lightweight fence lying between the two actions. On Power, the lightweight fence is `lwsync`; ARM does not have one, so a full fence (`dmb`) is required.

Power and ARM do not provide an analogous execution-order fence, but execution order can be enforced using a number of standard devices, including data or address dependencies (possibly spurious), control dependencies to an `isync` (Power) or `isb` (ARM) instruction, and control dependencies to writes.

Note that we do not give a direct mapping of RMC constructs onto the instruction set architecture, such as the mappings for

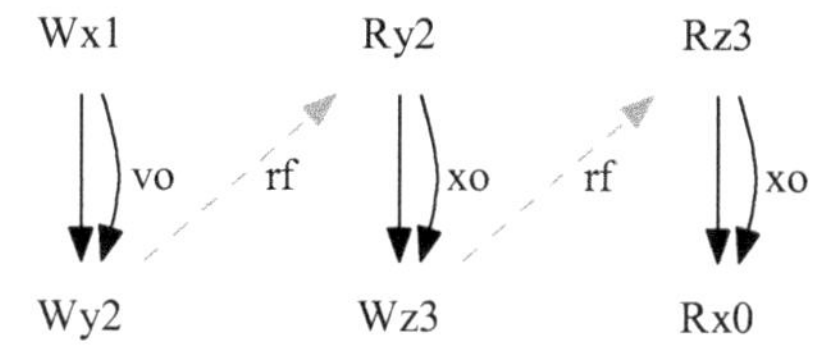


**Figure 11.** ISA2 litmus test

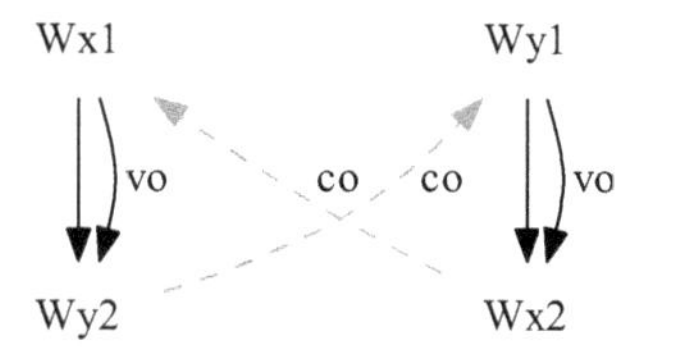


**Figure 12.** 2+2W litmus test

C/C++ considered in Batty, *et al.* [9]. In C/C++, the synchronization code is determined by the memory-order of an action, so such a mapping is meaningful. In contrast, in RMC the synchronization code is determined by *the edges connecting* two actions, and the resulting code might appear anywhere between the two. Thus, a direct mapping is not meaningful.

For example, a C/C++ store-release is implemented on Power by `lwsync; st`. Peephole optimization might improve this, but not much. In RMC, a visibility edge $i \stackrel{vo}{\rightarrow} i'$ can be realized by a `sync` or `lwsync` appearing anywhere between $i$ and $i'$. Indeed, multiple visibility edges might well be realized by the same instruction.

***The cost of minimality*** As always, one can sometimes obtain better performance with hand-crafted assembly language than with compiled code.

Consider the classic ISA2 litmus test [5, 22] in Figure 11. This trace is possible in RMC. The edge `Ry2` $\stackrel{xo}{\rightarrow}$ `Wz3` breaks up the chain of visibility order between `Wx1` and `Rz3`, so we cannot show that `Wx1` is prior to `Rx0`.

However, when compiled into Power, using an `lwsync` for $\stackrel{vo}{\rightarrow}$, and a dependency for $\stackrel{xo}{\rightarrow}$, this trace is forbidden. Power guarantees *B-cumulativity* [5, 15, 22], which says that accepting a memory barrier from another thread has the same effect as generating it on your own thread. For `Ry2` to happen on Power, the second thread must accept the `lwsync` barrier and the `Wx1` before it, thus placing a barrier between `Wx1` and `Wz3`. In our terminology we would say B-cumulativity results in `Wx1` $\stackrel{vo}{\rightarrow}$ `Wz3`, and causes `Wx1` to be prior to `Rx0`.

To prevent this, the programmer would need to insert a push between `Wx1` and `Wy2`, or upgrade the `Ry2` $\rightarrow$ `Wz3` edge to visibility order. Either way, some additional overhead might be incurred.

As another example, consider the 2+2W litmus test [5, 22] in Figure 12. Nothing in RMC prevents this trace from taking place. However, when compiled into Power, using an `lwsync` for $\stackrel{vo}{\rightarrow}$, this trace is forbidden. Power guarantees [5, 22] the acyclicity of a relation that in RMC we would write $\stackrel{co}{\rightarrow} \cup \stackrel{vo}{\rightarrow}$, which is plainly violated by the trace. RMC makes no such guarantee.

To prevent this, the programmer would need to insert pushes between both pairs of writes. Again, some additional overhead might be incurred.

Both traces are also possible when translated into C/C++, so C/C++ shares these potential overheads. In RMC we could avoid them by basing our design on stronger assumptions, but we prefer to make the weakest possible assumptions. Thus, some possible additional overhead in cases such as these can be seen as the cost of our minimal assumptions.

## 9. Theorems

***Type safety*** The first property we establish for RMC is type safety. RMC's typing judgement for top-level states is $\vdash (\Sigma, H, \xi)\,\mathsf{ok}$ with the one rule:

$$\frac{\vdash H : \Sigma \quad \Sigma \vdash \xi\ \mathsf{ok}}{\vdash (\Sigma, H, \xi)\ \mathsf{ok}}$$

The auxiliary judgement $\vdash H : \Sigma$ states that $H$ is *trace coherent* (which basically means it could be generated by RMC's dynamic semantics), and $H$'s contents match $\Sigma$. The details appear in the appendix [12].

Now we can state the preservation theorem:

THEOREM 1 (Preservation). *If $s \mapsto s'$ and $\vdash s\ \mathsf{ok}$ then $\vdash s'\ \mathsf{ok}$.*

The progress theorem is trickier. The standard formulation of progress—well-formed states either are final or take a step—is inappropriate for RMC because of nondeterminism. The goal of type safety is to show that bad states are not reachable from well-formed programs, and the standard formulation identifies bad states with "stuck" states. This is very convenient, provided we can design our operational semantics so that good states have at least one transition and bad ones have no transitions. In a deterministic setting, this is usually feasible.

But for RMC it is both too weak and too strong. Suppose our state has two threads, running $e$ and $e'$, and suppose further that $e$ is in a bad state. Even if $e$ is stuck, the state as a whole may not be, because we might still be able to take a step on $e'$. In other words, "stuckness" fails to capture "badness" when we can nondeterministically choose which thread to execute.

Indeed, for RMC the problem is even more pronounced, because no expression can ever be stuck. It is always possible to take a step using the speculation rule.

Conversely, "unstuckness" is also too strong a condition (or would be, if the speculation rule did not make it trivial). We call a state *moot* if it contains an unresolvable speculation ($v = v'$ in $e$, where $v$ and $v'$ are closed but not equal), or if it is semantically deadlocked. A moot state might well be stuck (except for gratuitous speculation), if it had no work left to do other than undischargeable speculations or deadlocked actions, but it is not a bad state. It is simply a state that resulted from nondeterministically exploring a blind alley.

Instead, we characterize the good states directly with a judgement $s\ \mathsf{right}$. The details can be found in the appendix [12]. Then, instead of "unstuckness", we prove:

THEOREM 2 (Rightness). *If $\vdash s\ \mathsf{ok}$ then $s\ \mathsf{right}$.*

This is similar to Wright and Felleisen's original technique [24], except they characterized the faulty states instead of the good ones, and for them faultiness was a technical device, not the notion of primary interest.

By itself this is a little unsatisfying because we might have made a mistake in the definition of rightness. To ameliorate this, we anchor rightness back to the operational semantics:

THEOREM 3 (Progress). *If $s\ \mathsf{right}$, then either (1) for every thread $p : e$ in $s$, $e$ is final, or (2) there exists $s'$ such that $s \mapsto s'$ without using the speculation rule, or (3) $s$ is moot.*

***Sequential consistency*** We also prove two results that establish sequential consistency for different programming disciplines. Our first shows that the programmer can achieve sequential consistency by interleaving actions with pushes.

The proof follows the general lines of Batty, *et al.*'s [8] sequential consistency proof, but it is generalized to account for the looseness of RMC (*e.g.*, leapfrogging writes) and our main lemma is simpler. We begin with three definitions: *Specified sequential consistency* indicates that the two actions are separated by a push.[9] A *from-read* edge between $i$ and $i'$ means that $i$ reads from a write that is coherence-earlier than $i'$. *Sequentially consistent order* [2] is the union of $\xrightarrow{\mathsf{ssc}}$, $\xrightarrow{\mathsf{co}}$, $\xrightarrow{\mathsf{rf}}$, and $\xrightarrow{\mathsf{fr}}$:

$$\begin{aligned} i \xrightarrow{\mathsf{ssc}}_H i' &\stackrel{\text{def}}{=} \exists i_p.\, H(\mathsf{is}(i_p, \mathsf{Push})) \wedge i \xrightarrow{\mathsf{vo}}{}^{+}_H i_p \xrightarrow{\mathsf{xo}}{}^{+}_H i' \\ i \xrightarrow{\mathsf{fr}}_H i' &\stackrel{\text{def}}{=} \exists i_w.\, i_w \xrightarrow{\mathsf{rf}}_H i \wedge i_w \xrightarrow{\mathsf{co}}{}^{+}_H i' \\ i \xrightarrow{\mathsf{sc}}_H i' &\stackrel{\text{def}}{=} i \xrightarrow{\mathsf{ssc}}_H i' \vee i \xrightarrow{\mathsf{co}}_H i' \vee i \xrightarrow{\mathsf{rf}}_H i' \vee i \xrightarrow{\mathsf{fr}}_H i' \end{aligned}$$

We also define *communication order* [2] as sequentially consistent order without $\xrightarrow{\mathsf{ssc}}$:

$$i \xrightarrow{\mathsf{com}}_H i' \stackrel{\text{def}}{=} i \xrightarrow{\mathsf{co}}_H i' \vee i \xrightarrow{\mathsf{rf}}_H i' \vee i \xrightarrow{\mathsf{fr}}_H i'$$

An important property of communication order is that it relates only accesses to the same location, and it agrees with coherence order on writes.

LEMMA 4 (Main Lemma). *Suppose $H$ is trace coherent, complete (that is, every identifier in $H$ is executed), and coherence acyclic (that is, $\mathsf{acyclic}(\xrightarrow{\mathsf{co}}_H)$). If $i_1 \xrightarrow{\mathsf{xo}}{}^{+}_H i_2 \xrightarrow{\mathsf{com}}{}^{*}_H i_3 \xrightarrow{\mathsf{vo}}{}^{+}_H i_4$, where $i_1$ and $i_4$ are pushes, then $i_1 \xrightarrow{\mathsf{to}}_H i_4$.*

**Proof**

We may assume, without loss of generality, that $i_3$ is a write: If $i_3$ is a push or no-op, then $i_2 = i_3$ (because $\xrightarrow{\mathsf{com}}$ relates only reads and writes) and the result follows immediately. If $i_3$ is a read, then it reads from some write $i_3'$, and we can rearrange to obtain $i_1 \xrightarrow{\mathsf{xo}}{}^{+}_H i_2 \xrightarrow{\mathsf{com}}{}^{*}_H i_3' \xrightarrow{\mathsf{vo}}{}^{+}_H i_4$ (since $i_3' \xrightarrow{\mathsf{vo}}_H i_3$).

Since $H$ is complete, $i_1$ and $i_4$ are executed, so either $i_1 \xrightarrow{\mathsf{to}}_H i_4$ or $i_4 = i_1$ or $i_4 \xrightarrow{\mathsf{to}}_H i_1$. In the first case we are done. In both of the remaining cases we have $i_4 \xrightarrow{\mathsf{vo}}{}^{*}_H i_1$, either trivially or using push order. Therefore $i_3 \xrightarrow{\mathsf{vo}}{}^{+}_H i_1$. From this we draw a contradiction.

Suppose $i_2$ is a write. Then $i_2 \xrightarrow{\mathsf{co}}{}^{*}_H i_3$ (since $i_2 \xrightarrow{\mathsf{com}}{}^{*}_H i_3$). However, we also have $i_3 \xrightarrow{\mathsf{wwp}}_H i_2$ so $i_3 \xrightarrow{\mathsf{co}}_H i_2$, which is a contradiction.

On the other hand, suppose $i_2$ is a read. Let $i_w \xrightarrow{\mathsf{rf}}_H i_2$. Then $i_w \xrightarrow{\mathsf{com}}{}^{+}_H i_3$, so $i_w \xrightarrow{\mathsf{co}}{}^{+}_H i_3$. However, $i_3 \xrightarrow{\mathsf{wrp}}_H i_2$ so $i_3 \xrightarrow{\mathsf{co}}_H i_w$, which is a contradiction. □

COROLLARY 5. *Suppose $H$ is trace coherent, complete, and coherence acyclic. If $i_1 \xrightarrow{\mathsf{xo}}{}^{+}_H i_2 \xrightarrow{\mathsf{sc}}{}^{*}_H i_3 \xrightarrow{\mathsf{vo}}{}^{+}_H i_4$, where $i_1$ and $i_4$ are pushes, then $i_1 \xrightarrow{\mathsf{to}}_H i_4$.*

**Proof**

By induction on the number of $\xrightarrow{\mathsf{ssc}}$ steps in $i_2 \xrightarrow{\mathsf{sc}}{}^{*}_H i_3$.

THEOREM 6. *Suppose $H$ is trace coherent, complete, and coherence acyclic. Then $\xrightarrow{\mathsf{sc}}_H$ is acyclic.*

[9] In practice the execution-order edge from $i_p$ to $i'$ is ordinarily provided by labelling the push with $\overset{\mathsf{exe}}{\rhd}$.

**Proof**

Suppose $i \overset{\mathsf{sc}}{\to}{}^{+}_{H} i$. We show there must be at least one $\overset{\mathsf{ssc}}{\to}$ edge in the cycle. Suppose the contrary. Then $i \overset{\mathsf{com}}{\to}{}^{+}_{H} i$. If $i$ is a write, then $i \overset{\mathsf{co}}{\to}{}^{+}_{H} i$, which is a contradiction. If $i$ is a read, then $i \overset{\mathsf{com}}{\to}{}^{*}_{H} i_w \overset{\mathsf{rf}}{\to}_{H} i$, so $i_w \overset{\mathsf{co}}{\to}{}^{+}_{H} i_w$, which is a contradiction.

Thus suppose that $i_1 \overset{\mathsf{ssc}}{\to}_{H} i_2 \overset{\mathsf{sc}}{\to}{}^{*}_{H} i_1$. Expanding $\overset{\mathsf{ssc}}{\to}$ we obtain $i_1 \overset{\mathsf{vo}}{\to}{}^{+}_{H} i_p \overset{\mathsf{xo}}{\to}{}^{+}_{H} i_2 \overset{\mathsf{sc}}{\to}{}^{*}_{H} i_1$ for a push $i_p$. By Corollary 5, $i_p \overset{\mathsf{to}}{\to}_{H} i_p$, which is a contradiction. □

DEFINITION 7. A history $H$ is *consistent* if there exists $H'$ containing no is events, such that $H, H'$ is trace coherent, complete, and coherence acyclic.

COROLLARY 8 (Sequential consistency). *Suppose $H$ is consistent. Suppose further that $S$ is a set of identifiers such that for all $i, i' \in S$, $i \overset{\mathsf{po}}{\to}_{H} i'$ implies $i \overset{\mathsf{ssc}}{\to}_{H} i'$. Then there exists a sequentially consistent ordering for $S$ (in the sense of Lamport [17]).*

**Proof Sketch**

Let $H'$ extend $H$ so that $H'$ is complete and $\overset{\mathsf{co}}{\to}_{H'}$ totally orders writes to the same location. By Theorem 6, $\overset{\mathsf{sc}}{\to}_{H'}$ is acyclic, so there exists a total order containing it. By Alglave [2, §4.2.1.3], such an order is a sequentially consistent order for the actions in $S$.

Observe that the sequentially consistent order includes *all* of $H$'s writes, not only those belonging to $S$. Thus, writes not belonging to $S$ are adopted into the sequentially consistent order. This means that the members of $S$ have a consistent view of the order in which *all* writes took place, not just the writes belonging to $S$. However, for non-members that order might not agree with program order. (The order contains non-$S$ reads too, but for purposes of reasoning about $S$ we can ignore them. Only the writes might satisfy a read in $S$.)

Our second is a standard result establishing sequential consistency for data-race-free programs. We define *synchronized-before* as follows:

$$i \overset{\mathsf{sb}}{\to}_{H} i' \overset{\text{def}}{=} \exists i_s.\, i \overset{\mathsf{vo}}{\to}{}^{+}_{H} i_s \overset{\mathsf{po}}{\to}{}^{*}_{H} i' \wedge H(\mathsf{label}(\overset{\mathsf{exe}}{\rhd}, i_s))$$

In essence $i \overset{\mathsf{sb}}{\to} i'$ says that $i$ is visible to some synchronization operation $i_s$ that is execution-order before $i'$. That $i_s$ must be labelled $\overset{\mathsf{exe}}{\rhd}$ so that $i$ will also be synchronized before any program-order successors of $i'$. Note that this definition is insensitive to the mechanism of synchronization: it might use an atomic read-write, the Bakery algorithm, or any other.

We say that a program is data-race-free if any two conflicting actions on different threads are ordered by synchronized-before. Boehm and Adve [11] refer to this sort of data race as a "type 2 data race." We may then show that data-race-free programs are sequentially consistent:

THEOREM 9. *Suppose $H$ is trace coherent, coherence acyclic, and data-race-free. Let $\overset{\mathsf{scdrf}}{\to}_{H}$ be the union of $\overset{\mathsf{po}}{\to}_{H}$, $\overset{\mathsf{co}}{\to}_{H}$, $\overset{\mathsf{rf}}{\to}_{H}$, and $\overset{\mathsf{fr}}{\to}_{H}$. Then $\overset{\mathsf{scdrf}}{\to}_{H}$ is acyclic.*

**Proof Sketch**

Let $\overset{\mathsf{sq}}{\to}_{H}$ be the union of $\overset{\mathsf{po}}{\to}_{H}$ and $\overset{\mathsf{sb}}{\to}_{H}$. We show that $\overset{\mathsf{sq}}{\to}_{H}$ is acyclic and contains $\overset{\mathsf{scdrf}}{\to}_{H}$.

COROLLARY 10 (Sequential consistency). *Suppose $H$ is consistent and data-race-free. Then there exists a sequentially consistent ordering for all identifiers in $H$.*

These two sequential consistency results can also be combined into a single theorem for programs that contain some data-race-free code and also use specified sequential consistency. Details appear in the Coq formalization.

## 10. Conclusion

***The "thin-air" problem*** As given above, RMC makes no effort to rule out "thin-air reads", in which a write of a speculated value justifies itself, thereby allowing a value to appear which has no cause to exist (out of thin air, so to speak). This could be done by adapting the parallel trace mechanism in Jagadeesan, *et al.* [16], as follows:

First we break the execute transaction $(i \downarrow v)$ into two forms: write execution $(i \Downarrow v)$ for writes, and benign execution (still $i \downarrow v$) for everything else. The important difference is that write execution is not passed up by speculation expressions:

$$\frac{e \overset{\delta}{\mapsto} e' \quad \delta \text{ not of the form } i \Downarrow v}{v = v' \text{ in } e \overset{\delta}{\mapsto} v = v' \text{ in } e'}$$

By itself, this prevents speculated values from being written to the store, since speculated values appear only in actions that arise within speculation expressions. We do not want to go so far as to rule out speculated writes entirely. Instead, we allow a benign execution in the thread (which might be speculated) to rendezvous with a write execution, provided there exists an alternative trace in which that write could have taken place without speculation:

$$\frac{\begin{array}{c} \Sigma = (\Upsilon, \Phi, \Psi) \qquad \Sigma_{alt} = (\Upsilon_{alt}, \Phi_{alt}, \Psi_{alt}) \\ \Sigma \overset{i \Downarrow v @ p}{\longmapsto} \Sigma' \qquad H \overset{i \Downarrow v @ p}{\longmapsto} H' \qquad \Upsilon; \Phi \vdash \xi \overset{i \downarrow v @ p}{\longmapsto} \xi' \\ (\Sigma, H, \xi) \mapsto^{*} (\Sigma_{alt}, H_{alt}, \xi_{alt}) \\ H_{alt} \overset{i \Downarrow v @ p}{\longmapsto} H'_{alt} \qquad \Upsilon_{alt}; \Phi_{alt} \vdash \xi_{alt} \overset{i \Downarrow v @ p}{\longmapsto} \xi'_{alt} \end{array}}{(\Sigma, H, \xi) \mapsto (\Sigma', H', \xi')}$$

However, this is not a complete solution to the problem. It prevents thin-air reads, but at the cost of preventing some desirable compiler optimizations. As Batty and Sewell [6] illustrate, it is very difficult to distinguish between thin-air traces and some desirable traces.

We are not troubled by the fact that real architectures do not exhibit thin-air traces, as RMC is designed to be looser than real architectures anyway. Thin-air traces do not implicate type safety; our speculation construct produces only well-typed values. Batty, *et al.* [10] observe that thin-air traces can create difficulties for modular reasoning, but they also observe that the problem can be resolved by type-checking.

However, one negative consequence of thin-air reads that is still relevant to RMC is a failure of abstraction. They allow a program to produce a member of an abstract type by means other than calling the module that defines it, which makes Reynolds-style abstraction [20] fail. We see this as the central problem for thin-air traces.

Yet the problem also suggests a possible path forward. As yet there is no rigorous theory of Reynolds-style abstraction that even comes close to supporting RMC anyway. Such a theory would offer some structure more compelling than mere intuition for identifying problematic thin-air traces, and hopefully for ruling them out. This is an important avenue for future work.

***Related work*** RMC's store is inspired by the storage subsystem of Sarkar, *et al.* [22]. However, the RMC store is more general, as it is not intended to capture the behavior of a specific architecture, and the RMC's thread semantics is entirely different from Sarkar, *et al.*'s thread subsystem.

Another similar formalism is the axiomatic framework of Alglave, *et al.* [5] (hereafter "Cats"), which builds on Alglave [2]. Like RMC, Cats is a generic system, not specific to any architecture. RMC is an operational framework and Cats is axiomatic, but this difference is less than it might seem since (as noted in Section 1.1), RMC's acyclic-coherence requirement gives it an axiomatic flavor. Moreover, Cats also defines a operational system in a similar fashion (transitions may take place provided they violate no axiom), and show it equivalent to the axiomatic system.

The greatest differences between RMC and Cats stem from their differing aims: First, Cats is not intended to serve as a programming language. Second, while RMC aims to be *weaker* than all real architectures, Cats aims to model them. Thus, Cats includes a variety of parameterized machinery that can be instantiated to obtain the behavior of a specific architecture, machinery that RMC omits.

Cats includes four axioms that relate to RMC's five assumptions. Their "sc per location" axiom corresponds to our first two assumptions (sequential consistency for single-threaded computations, and an acyclic coherence order), except that unlike RMC, Cats chooses to forbid read-read hazards. (Nevertheless Cats could easily be altered to permit them, and RMC could forbid them with an additional coherence rule.) Their "observation" axiom includes our third assumption (message-passing works), but also includes B-cumulativity (recall Section 8) which RMC does not. Their "propagation" axiom includes our fourth assumption (pushes exist), and defines a propagation order similar to our visibility order. However, the propagation axiom goes further, requiring (in RMC terminology) that $\xrightarrow{co} \cup \xrightarrow{vo}$ be acyclic (recall Section 8), which we do not. We omit Cats's "no thin air" axiom, while Cats omits our fifth assumption (atomic read-writes exist), although Cats includes much of the machinery necessary to support them.

RMC's speculation mechanism is inspired by the one suggested in Jagadeesan, *et al.* [16]. Like RMC, they allow a speculated value to be invented out of whole cloth, provided that speculation is subsequently discharged. However, the details are quite different. In their system, the speculated value is written immediately into the store. This makes speculation an effectful operation, while in RMC it is pure.

Moreover, the means of discharge is quite different. In RMC, speculation is tied to a value, and is discharged when it becomes equal to the speculated value. In Jagadeesan *et al.* speculation is tied to a location in the store. Discharge occurs when the speculated value is written to that location, but that condition would be trivial if employed naively, since such a write already happened at the moment of speculation. Instead, they maintain a parallel trace without the speculated write, and the speculation is discharged when the write occurs in the parallel trace.

Putting speculation in the thread semantics, as we do, rather than the store semantics, makes for a cleaner formalism, since it separates orthogonal concerns, and since it does not require a parallel-trace mechanism. On the other hand, their approach automatically rules out thin-air reads, which ours does not. As discussed above, doing so in our setting requires the addition of a parallel-trace mechanism reminiscent of theirs.

***Formalization*** All the results of this paper are formalized in Coq. The formalization consists of 29 thousand lines of code (including comments and whitespace), and takes 93 seconds to check on a 3.4 GHz Intel Core i7.

## References


[1] S. Adve and K. Gharachorloo. Shared memory consistency models: A tutorial. *IEEE Computer*, 1995.

[2] J. Alglave. *A Shared Memory Poetics*. PhD thesis, Université Paris VII, Nov. 2010.

[3] J. Alglave. A formal hierarchy of weak memory models. *Formal Methods in System Design*, 41:178–210, 2012.

[4] J. Alglave, L. Maranget, S. Sarkar, and P. Sewell. Fences in weak memory models. In *Twenty-Second International Conference on Computer Aided Verification*, 2010.

[5] J. Alglave, L. Maranget, and M. Tautschnig. Herding cats: Modelling, simulation, testing, and data-mining for weak memory. *ACM Transactions on Programming Languages and Systems*, 2014. To appear.

[6] M. Batty and P. Sewell. The thin-air problem. Working note, available at `http://www.cl.cam.ac.uk/~pes20/cpp/notes42.html`, Feb. 2014.

[7] M. Batty, S. Owens, S. Sarkar, P. Sewell, and T. Weber. Mathematizing C++ concurrency: The post-Rapperswil model. Technical Report N3132, ISO IEC JTC1/SC22/WG21, Aug. 2010. Available electronically at `www.open-std.org/jtc1/sc22/wg21/docs/papers/2010/n3132.pdf`.

[8] M. Batty, S. Owens, S. Sarkar, P. Sewell, and T. Weber. Mathematizing C++ concurrency. In *Thirty-Eighth ACM Symposium on Principles of Programming Languages*, Austin, Texas, Jan. 2011.

[9] M. Batty, K. Memarian, S. Owens, S. Sarkar, and P. Sewell. Clarifying and compiling C/C++ concurrency: from C++11 to POWER. In *Thirty-Ninth ACM Symposium on Principles of Programming Languages*, Philadelphia, Pennsylvania, Jan. 2012.

[10] M. Batty, M. Dodds, and A. Gotsman. Library abstraction for C/C++ concurrency. In *Fortieth ACM Symposium on Principles of Programming Languages*, Rome, Italy, Jan. 2013.

[11] H.-J. Boehm and S. V. Adve. Foundations of the C++ concurrency memory model. In *2008 SIGPLAN Conference on Programming Language Design and Implementation*, Tucson, Arizona, June 2008.

[12] K. Crary and M. J. Sullivan. A calculus for relaxed memory. Technical Report CMU-CS-14-139, Carnegie Mellon University, School of Computer Science, 2014.

[13] R. Grisenthwaite. ARM barrier litmus tests and cookbook. `http://infocenter.arm.com/help/topic/com.arm.doc.genc007826/Barrier_Litmus_Tests_and_Cookbook_A08.pdf`, 2009.

[14] D. Howells and P. E. McKenney. Circular buffers. `https://www.kernel.org/doc/Documentation/circular-buffers.txt`.

[15] IBM. Power ISA$^{TM}$ version 2.06 revision B, 2010.

[16] R. Jagadeesan, C. Pitcher, and J. Riely. Generative operational semantics for relaxed memory models. In *Nineteenth European Symposium on Programming*, 2010.

[17] L. Lamport. How to make a multiprocessor computer that correctly executes multiprocess programs. *IEEE Transactions on Computers*, C-28(9), Sept. 1979.

[18] J. Manson, W. Pugh, and S. V. Adve. The Java memory model. In *Thirty-Second ACM Symposium on Principles of Programming Languages*, Long Beach, California, Jan. 2005.

[19] J. Polakow. *Ordered Linear Logic and Applications*. PhD thesis, Carnegie Mellon University, School of Computer Science, Pittsburgh, Pennsylvania, Aug. 2001.

[20] J. C. Reynolds. Types, abstraction and parametric polymorphism. In *Information Processing '83*, pages 513–523. North-Holland, 1983. Proceedings of the IFIP 9th World Computer Congress.

[21] S. Sarkar, P. Sewell, J. Alglave, and L. Maranget. ppcmem executable model (ARM version). Unpublished code, 2011.

[22] S. Sarkar, P. Sewell, J. Alglave, L. Maranget, and D. Williams. Understanding POWER multiprocessors. In *2011 SIGPLAN Conference on Programming Language Design and Implementation*, San Jose, California, June 2011.

[23] P. Sewell, S. Sarkar, S. Owens, F. Z. Nardelli, and M. O. Myreen. x86-TSO: A rigorous and usable programmer's model for x86 multiprocessors. *Communications of the ACM*, 53(7), July 2010.

[24] A. K. Wright and M. Felleisen. A syntactic approach to type soundness. *Information and Computation*, 115:38–94, 1994.

# Iris: Monoids and Invariants as an Orthogonal Basis for Concurrent Reasoning

Ralf Jung
MPI-SWS & Saarland University
jung@mpi-sws.org

David Swasey
MPI-SWS
swasey@mpi-sws.org

Filip Sieczkowski
Aarhus University
filips@cs.au.dk

Kasper Svendsen
Aarhus University
ksvendsen@cs.au.dk

Aaron Turon
Mozilla Research
aturon@mozilla.com

Lars Birkedal
Aarhus University
birkedal@cs.au.dk

Derek Dreyer
MPI-SWS
dreyer@mpi-sws.org

## Abstract

We present Iris, a concurrent separation logic with a simple premise: *monoids and invariants are all you need.* Partial commutative monoids enable us to express—and invariants enable us to enforce—user-defined *protocols* on shared state, which are at the conceptual core of most recent program logics for concurrency. Furthermore, through a novel extension of the concept of a *view shift*, Iris supports the encoding of *logically atomic specifications, i.e.,* Hoare-style specs that permit the client of an operation to treat the operation essentially as if it were atomic, even if it is not.

***Categories and Subject Descriptors*** D.3.1 [*Programming Languages*]: Formal Definitions and Theory; D.3.3 [*Programming Languages*]: Language Constructs and Features; F.3.1 [*Logics and Meanings of Programs*]: Specifying and Verifying and Reasoning about Programs

***Keywords*** Separation logic, fine-grained concurrency, atomicity, partial commutative monoids, invariants, higher-order logic, compositional verification.

## 1. Introduction

Concurrency is fundamentally about shared state. This is true not only for shared-memory concurrency, where the state takes the form of a "heap" that threads may write to and read from, but also for message-passing concurrency, where the state takes the form of a "network" that threads may send to and receive from (or a sequence of "events" on which threads may synchronize). Thus, to scalably verify concurrent programs of any stripe, we need compositional methods for reasoning about shared state.

This goal has sparked a long line of work, especially in recent years, during which a synthesis of *rely-guarantee reasoning* [21] and *separation logic* [31, 28] has led to a series of increasingly advanced program logics for concurrency: RGSep [37], SAGL [13], LRG [12], CAP [10], HLRG [15], CaReSL [34], iCAP [33], FCSL [27], TaDA [8], and others. In this paper, we present a logic called **Iris** that explains some of the complexities of these prior separation logics in terms of a simpler unifying foundation, while also supporting some new and powerful reasoning principles for concurrency.

Before we get to Iris, however, let us begin with a brief overview of some key problems that arise in reasoning compositionally about shared state, and how prior approaches have dealt with them.

### 1.1 Invariants and their limitations

The canonical model of concurrency is *sequential consistency* [23]: threads take turns interacting with the shared state (reading/writing, sending/receiving), with each turn lasting for one step of computation.[1] Although the semantics of sequentially consistent (SC) concurrency is simple to define, that does not mean it is easy to reason about. In particular, the key question is how to do *thread-local* reasoning—that is, verifying one thread at a time—even though other threads may *interfere* with (*i.e.,* mutate) the shared state in between each step of computation in the thread we are verifying.

***The invariant rule.*** The simplest (and oldest) way in which concurrent program logics account for such interference is via *invariants* [5]. An invariant is a property that holds of some piece of shared state at all times: each thread accessing the state may assume the invariant holds *before* each step of its computation, but it must also ensure that it continues to hold *after* each step.

Formally, in concurrent separation logics, the invariant rule looks *something like* the following (omitting some important details that we explain later in §4):

$$\frac{\{R * P\}\ e\ \{R * Q\} \qquad e \text{ physically atomic}}{\boxed{R} \vdash \{P\}\ e\ \{Q\}}$$

Here, the assertion $\boxed{R}$ states the knowledge that there exists an invariant $R$ governing some piece of shared state. Given this knowledge, the rule tells us that $e$ may gain (exclusive) control of the shared state satisfying $R$, so long as it ensures that $R$ continues to hold of it when it is finished executing. Note the crucial side condition that $e$ be *physically atomic*, meaning that it takes exactly one step of computation. If $e$ were not physically atomic, then another thread might access the shared state governed by $\boxed{R}$ during $e$'s execution, in which case it would not be safe for the rule to grant $e$ exclusive control of the shared state throughout its execution.

[1] There is much recent work on weaker models of concurrency, which are in many ways more realistic, but in this paper we focus on SC concurrency.



*POPL '15*, January 15–17, 2015, Mumbai, India.

ACM 978-1-4503-3300-9/15/01...$15.00.
http://dx.doi.org/10.1145/2676726.2676980

The invariant rule is simple and elegant. Unfortunately, it also suffers from two major limitations, which a significant amount of follow-on work has attempted to overcome.

***Limitation #1: The need for protocols.*** The first limitation pertains to the seemingly static nature of invariants. For the kinds of interference found in more sophisticated concurrent programs, one may require something a bit more "dynamic" than fixed invariants. It is often necessary, for instance, to have a way of expressing:

- *Irreversibility:* once a certain change to some shared state has occurred, it is irreversible—we cannot go back.
- *Rights:* certain changes to the shared state may only be made by privileged threads that have the "rights" to make those changes.

At first glance, at least, neither of these seems to be expressible in the limited language of invariants. As a consequence, many more recent logics provide some mechanism—such as rely-guarantee assertions [21, 37, 12], regions [10, 33, 8], STSs [34], and concurroids [27]—to account for irreversibility and rights. All of these mechanisms are effectively different ways of describing *protocols* on shared state, which assert how the shared state is permitted to evolve over time.

Although the protocol mechanisms of modern logics are clearly useful, each logic bakes in its own somewhat different mechanism (and corresponding proof rules) as primitive, leading us to wonder: Is this really necessary? *Might there be a simpler logical mechanism for legislating interference, from which more advanced mechanisms could be easily derived?*

***Limitation #2: The need for logical atomicity.*** The second limitation pertains to the side condition of the invariant rule requiring the operation $e$ to be physically atomic (take exactly one step of computation). Obviously, this side condition makes it much more desirable (as a client) to program with physically atomic operations than with non-atomic ones. But there are many operations that *appear* to be atomic even though they take more than one step of computation, and for such operations the invariant rule is not applicable.

Specifically, it is often desirable to construct concurrent programs so that the interference on shared state is only observable within the limited scope of some mutable ADT (abstract data type). For instance, consider concurrent stacks. A sophisticated implementation [16] may rely on fine-grained synchronization between threads in order to maximize parallelism, and thus proving it correct demands the use of invariants (or protocols) to account for the rampant interference. But this internal interference need not infect the verification of client code. In particular, the canonical notion of correctness for concurrent stacks is that it should appear to clients as if all stack operations take effect atomically (*i.e.,* in some sequential order), which is typically formalized via *linearizability* [17] or *contextual refinement* [14, 34]. In this case, we say that the operations provided by the stack ADT are *observably atomic.*

Ideally, we would like to be able to treat observably atomic operations *as if they were* physically atomic. That way, clients of the stack ADT could establish invariants on the contents of the stack and then use the invariant rule when reasoning about push and pop operations. This *can* be done to some extent with contextual refinement (see the layered verification in [34]), but it requires going *outside the logic* in order to connect up the verification of an ADT with that of its clients. Moreover, the refinement approach is only applicable in higher-level languages where the type system is strong enough to support hiding the internals of an ADT from its clients.

A more flexible approach, we argue, would be to *internalize* the notion of observable atomicity as a logical specification, so that both the proof obligation for establishing atomicity and the proof principle it provides to clients take the form of a single Hoare-style specification written *within the logic itself.* We refer to such a

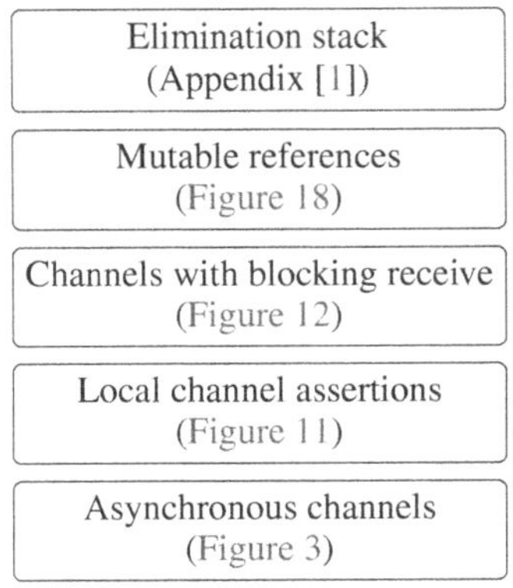


**Figure 1.** Case study: A stack of abstractions.

specification as being *logically atomic*. Intuitively, the key benefit of working with a logically atomic spec is to enable a version of the invariant rule *without the side condition that $e$ be physically atomic.* This allows clients to treat operations providing such specs as if they were actually atomic, without requiring any extra-logical reasoning.

Very recent work by da Rocha Pinto *et al.* on their logic TaDA [8] supports precisely such a notion of logically atomic specs, together with a number of useful but nonstandard proof rules, but all of these are baked into the logic as primitive. Furthermore, TaDA is currently not able to reason about a significant class of sophisticated concurrent data structures that employ inter-thread cooperation (aka "helping") [35, 33].

This begs the question: *Might there be a way to define logical atomicity in terms of simpler logical primitives, and to derive the associated reasoning principles within the logic?*

### 1.2 Iris: An orthogonal basis for concurrent reasoning

In this paper, we propose Iris, a concurrent separation logic based on a very simple premise: *monoids and invariants are all you need.*

Invariants we have already discussed at length. As for monoids: Partial commutative monoids (PCMs) are widely known to provide a generic model of *resources*—both physical resources (like the heap) and logical resources (like ghost state)—suitable for use in a separation logic. A number of modern logics involve PCMs either in the model of the logic [33, 34] or as a feature in the logic itself [22, 24, 9]. What does not seem to be widely known, however, is that monoids and invariants form a kind of orthogonal basis for concurrent reasoning. In particular:

- Monoids enable us to *express* protocols on shared state.
- Invariants enable us to *enforce* protocols on shared state.

These two mechanisms, put together, are unexpectedly powerful. In particular, using monoids and invariants, we show how to:

- Encode a variety of the advanced *protocol* mechanisms from modern logics (§2 and §3).
- Derive *proof rules* that are taken as primitive proof rules in other modern logics (§4 and §5).
- Encode TaDA-style *logically atomic specs*, and derive their most important associated proof rules (§7).
- Go beyond TaDA and verify logically atomic specs for fine-grained concurrent ADTs that employ *helping* (§8).

A key technical novelty of Iris that facilitates the above contributions is an extension of the concept of *view shift* that has been proposed in recent work [10, 9, 33]. We explain this mechanism in §4. Furthermore, the soundness of Iris's primitive proof rules, which we discuss briefly in §6, has been fully mechanized in Coq [1].

***Syntax***

(Fix disjoint, infinite sets *Chan* and *Var* of channel names and variables.)

$$c, d \in Chan$$
$$x, y, f \in Var$$
$$v, w ::= x \mid c \mid \textbf{rec}\ f(x).\ e \mid () \mid (v, v) \mid \textbf{inj}_i\ v$$
$$e ::= v \mid e\ e \mid (e, e) \mid e.i \mid \textbf{inj}_i\ e \mid \textbf{case}\ e\ \textbf{of inj}_1\ x \Rightarrow e \mid \textbf{inj}_2\ x \Rightarrow e \mid \textbf{newch} \mid \textbf{send}(e, e) \mid \textbf{tryrecv}\ e \mid \textbf{fork}\ e$$
$$K ::= [] \mid \textbf{send}(K, e) \mid \textbf{send}(v, K) \mid \textbf{tryrecv}\ K \mid \cdots$$

***Derived forms***

$$\mathsf{None} \triangleq \textbf{inj}_1\ () \qquad \mathsf{Some}(e) \triangleq \textbf{inj}_2\ e$$

***Machine states***

$$M \in Bag \text{ (finite bags of values)}$$
$$C \in Chan \xrightarrow{\text{fin}} Bag$$
$$T \in \mathbb{N} \xrightarrow{\text{fin}} Exp$$

***Pure reduction (omitted)*** $\boxed{e \xrightarrow{\text{pure}} e'}$

***Per-thread reduction*** $\boxed{C; e \to C'; e'}$

$$C; e \to C; e' \quad \text{when } e \xrightarrow{\text{pure}} e'$$
$$C; \textbf{newch} \to C[c \mapsto \emptyset]; c$$
$$C[c \mapsto M]; \textbf{send}(c, v) \to C[c \mapsto M \uplus \{v\}]; ()$$
$$C[c \mapsto \emptyset]; \textbf{tryrecv}\ c \to C[c \mapsto \emptyset]; \mathsf{None}$$
$$C[c \mapsto M \uplus \{v\}]; \textbf{tryrecv}\ c \to C[c \mapsto M]; \mathsf{Some}(v)$$

***Machine reduction*** $\boxed{C; T \to C'; T'}$

$$\frac{C; e \to C'; e'}{C; T[i \mapsto K[e]] \to C'; T[i \mapsto K[e']]}$$
$$C; T[i \mapsto K[\textbf{fork}\ e]] \to C; T[i \mapsto K[()], j \mapsto e]$$

**Figure 2.** A language with asynchronous channels. (We denote the disjoint union $f \uplus [x \mapsto y]$ by $f[x \mapsto y]$.)

To demonstrate the effectiveness of abstraction and modular reasoning in Iris, we have applied it to a significant case study that builds a stack of abstractions, with each layer exporting only an abstract atomic specification to the layers above (Figure 1). The bottom two layers are physically atomic, while the top three are logically atomic.

At the bottom of the stack we start with a large-footprint physically atomic specification of channels in a λ-calculus with asynchronous message passing (§2). On top of that we first develop small-footprint specs (§5.2), followed by channels with a logically atomic blocking receive operation (§7.2). We then show that we can use channels (via a standard encoding [26]) to implement a logically atomic spec for mutable references, which we finally use in the verification of a fine-grained elimination stack ADT (§8). Put together, this constitutes a modular verification of elimination stacks running on a message-passing machine, performed completely within the Iris logic. Full details of the case study, as well as all other omitted technical details, appear in our technical appendix [1].

## 2. Iris – Part I: Monoids

Iris is a higher-order separation logic parameterized by the language of program expressions that one wishes to reason about.

For the purpose of this paper, we instantiate the programming language to the one shown in Figure 2, which provides primitive operations $\textbf{send}(e, e)$ and $\textbf{tryrecv}\ e$ for asynchronous (non-blocking) message passing via channels. We have chosen this language, rather than the usual heap-manipulating command language one finds in most separation-logic papers, in order to emphasize (1) that nothing about Iris is fundamentally tied to shared-memory concurrency, and (2) that heap-like abstractions can in fact be built up within the logic (§8).

The logic includes the usual connectives and rules of higher-order separation assertion logic as generated by the grammar below.

$$\Sigma ::= 1 \mid \mathsf{Exp} \mid \mathsf{Val} \mid \mathsf{Prop} \mid \Sigma \times \Sigma \mid \Sigma \to \Sigma \mid \cdots$$
$$t, P, \varphi ::= () \mid (t, t) \mid \pi_1\ t \mid \pi_2\ t \mid \lambda x : \Sigma.\ t \mid \varphi\ t \mid t =_\Sigma t \mid \mathsf{False} \mid \mathsf{True} \mid P \wedge P \mid P \vee P \mid P \Rightarrow P \mid \exists x : \Sigma.\ P \mid \forall x : \Sigma.\ P \mid P * P \mid P \mathrel{-\!\!*} P \mid \cdots$$

Here, Σ denotes the type of a term (written $t$, $P$, or $\varphi$ among others) in the logic. Terms include language expressions and values, propositions, and products and function spaces over these. The typing rules are standard and omitted (see the appendix [1]). The judgment $\Gamma \mid \mathcal{P} \vdash Q$ says that for all instantiations of the variables in Γ, the propositions $\mathcal{P}$ entail $Q$. The contexts are often left implicit. In the following sections, we will gradually introduce and motivate key features of the logic along with their associated terms and types.

$$\{\lfloor C \rfloor\}\ \textbf{newch}\ \{c.\ \lfloor C[c \mapsto \emptyset] \rfloor\}$$
$$\{\lfloor C[c \mapsto M] \rfloor\}\ \textbf{send}(c, m)\ \{v.\ v = () \wedge \lfloor C[c \mapsto M \uplus \{m\}] \rfloor\}$$
$$\{\lfloor C[c \mapsto M \uplus \{m\}] \rfloor\}\ \textbf{tryrecv}\ c\ \{v.\ v = \mathsf{Some}(m) \wedge \lfloor C[c \mapsto M] \rfloor\}$$
$$\{\lfloor C[c \mapsto \emptyset] \rfloor\}\ \textbf{tryrecv}\ c\ \{v.\ v = \mathsf{None} \wedge \lfloor C[c \mapsto \emptyset] \rfloor\}$$

**Figure 3.** Rules derived from the semantics of asynchronous channels (see Figure 2).

***Physical state.*** To specify and reason about the behavior of programs, the logic features Hoare triples, written $\{P\}\ e\ \{v.\ Q\}$. Here $v$ serves as a binder for the return value in postcondition $Q$.

The logic is parametric in the syntax and semantics of the underlying programming language. As such, the logic only features basic structural rules and lacks Hoare axioms for primitive expressions. However, the logic provides a canonical way of adding such axioms, by internalizing the reduction semantics of the underlying language as axioms about the entire physical machine state.

To express this, Iris features a *physical state assertion*, written $\lfloor \varsigma \rfloor$, and a type State of physical states of the underlying language. For every term $\varsigma$ of type State, $\lfloor \varsigma \rfloor$ asserts exclusive ownership of the physical state, along with the knowledge that the physical state is exactly $\varsigma$. Using this assertion we can directly translate the reduction relation defined in Figure 2 into the axioms given in Figure 3. The physical state assertion only supports reasoning about the entire physical state; however, as we will see in §5.2, through the combination of monoids and invariants, it is possible to define more local reasoning principles.

Figure 4 summarizes the syntax and proof rules for physical states and selected structural Hoare rules. For now, ignore the $\Rrightarrow$ in Csq and the □ in VSimp. Combined, these rules simply yield the standard rule of consequence with implication. In the next section, we will explain how Iris generalizes that rule.

***Ghost state.*** In addition to physical state assertions, Iris also supports assertions about *ghost state* (aka auxiliary state). Ghost state was originally proposed as a way to abstractly characterize some

***Syntax***

$$P ::= \cdots \mid P \Rrightarrow P \mid \{P\}\, e\, \{\varphi\} \mid \lfloor\varsigma\rfloor \mid \Box P \qquad \Sigma ::= \cdots \mid \mathsf{State}$$

***Physical state axioms***

$$\lfloor\varsigma\rfloor * \lfloor\varsigma'\rfloor \Rightarrow \mathsf{False}$$

***Structural Hoare rules***

$$\textsc{Frame}\ \frac{\{P\}\, e\, \{v.\, Q\}}{\{P * R\}\, e\, \{v.\, Q * R\}} \qquad \textsc{Ret}\ \{\mathsf{True}\}\, w\, \{v.\, v = w\}$$

$$\textsc{Bind}\ \frac{\{P\}\, e\, \{v.\, Q\} \qquad \forall v.\, \{Q\}\, K[v]\, \{w.\, R\}}{\{P\}\, K[e]\, \{w.\, R\}} \qquad \textsc{VSImp}\ \frac{\Box(P \Rightarrow Q)}{P \Rrightarrow Q}$$

$$\textsc{Csq}\ \frac{P \Rrightarrow P' \qquad \{P'\}\, e\, \{v.\, Q'\} \qquad \forall v.\, Q' \Rrightarrow Q}{\{P\}\, e\, \{v.\, Q\}}$$

**Figure 4.** Physical state and selected structural rules.

knowledge about the history of a computation that is essential to verifying it [29]. More generally, ghost state is useful for modularly describing a thread's *knowledge* about some shared state, as well as the *rights* it has to modify it [7, 22].

In many logics, ghost state takes the form of a ghost heap. However, as the name implies, ghost state is a purely logical construct, introduced solely for the purpose of verification, and thus there is no need to tie it to a particular language or machine model. Consequently, in Iris, following several recent logics [22, 9, 24], we model ghost state as a *partial commutative monoid (PCM)*, which is taken as a parameter of the logic. We call the elements of this PCM *ghost resources*, and we use the term "resources" to refer both to physical states and ghost resources. (Assertions in Iris represent predicates over both kinds of resources.)

We represent the partial commutative monoid as a (total) commutative monoid with a zero element. The term $a \cdot b$ is thus always well formed. Formally, we require a set $|M|$ with two distinguished elements $\bot$ (zero, undefined) and $\epsilon$ (unit) and an operation $\cdot$ (compose) such that the following properties hold:

$$a \cdot b = b \cdot a \qquad \epsilon \cdot a = a \qquad (a \cdot b) \cdot c = a \cdot (b \cdot c)$$
$$\bot \cdot a = \bot \qquad \bot \neq \epsilon$$

We call $|M|$ the carrier of the monoid $M = (|M|, \bot, \epsilon, \cdot)$ and use $|M|^+$ to refer to the carrier without the zero element: $|M| \setminus \{\bot\}$.

To reason about these monoid elements, the logic features a type $\mathsf{Monoid}$ of monoid elements and internalizes the composition operation as a function on $\mathsf{Monoid}$. For each term $a$ of type $\mathsf{Monoid}$, the logic features a corresponding ghost assertion $\boxed{a}$, which asserts $a \neq \bot$, along with ownership of an $a$ fragment of the *global* ghost state. The global ghost state is the composition of all locally owned fragments. Ghost resources can thus be split and combined arbitrarily according to the chosen $\cdot$ operation: $\boxed{t \cdot u} \Leftrightarrow \boxed{t} * \boxed{u}$.

Since the ghost state is unrelated to the underlying physical state, we can update the current global ghost state arbitrarily at any time. We express updates of ghost state using *view shifts*. A view shift from $P$ to $Q$, written $P \Rrightarrow Q$, asserts that it is possible to update the state from $P$ to $Q$ without changing the underlying physical state. The rule of consequence Csq in Figure 4 thus allows view shifts (and not just implications) to be applied in pre- and postconditions.

If we own a fragment $a$ of the global ghost state, we must ensure that any updates of the ghost state are consistent with any fragments potentially owned by the environment (*e.g.,* other threads). The FpUpd rule in Figure 5 expresses that we can update a ghost fragment $a$ to an element $b \in B$ if this update is frame-preserving ($a \rightsquigarrow B$);

***Syntax***

$$a, P ::= \cdots \mid \boxed{a} \mid a \cdot a \qquad \Sigma ::= \cdots \mid \mathsf{Monoid}$$

***Ghost resource axioms***

$$\boxed{a} * \boxed{b} \Leftrightarrow \boxed{a \cdot b} \qquad \mathsf{True} \Rrightarrow \boxed{\epsilon} \qquad \boxed{\bot} \Rightarrow \mathsf{False}$$

***Ghost resource updates***

$$\textsc{FpUpd}\ \frac{a \rightsquigarrow B}{\boxed{a} \Rrightarrow \exists b \in B.\, \boxed{b}} \qquad \text{where } a \rightsquigarrow B \text{ is shorthand for } \Box\forall a_f.\, a \# a_f \Rightarrow \exists b \in B.\, b \# a_f$$

**Figure 5.** Syntax and proof rules for ghost resources.

that is, if it preserves an arbitrary composable frame $a_f$:

$$a \rightsquigarrow B \triangleq \Box\forall a_f.\, a \# a_f \Rightarrow \exists b \in B.\, b \# a_f$$
$$a \rightsquigarrow b \triangleq a \rightsquigarrow \{b\}$$

where $a \# a_f$ is notation for $a \cdot a_f \neq \bot$.

Note that the premise of rule FpUpd is merely a "fact": it does not express ownership of any state. To express such facts, the logic features an *always* modality, written $\Box P$, for asserting that $P$ holds and does not assert any ownership. Such assertions are called *pure* and can be freely duplicated (*i.e.,* we have $\Box P \Rightarrow \Box P * \Box P$ and $\Box P \Rightarrow P$). View shifts and Hoare triples are other examples of pure assertions: the knowledge that a view shift or Hoare triple holds can thus be freely duplicated.

## 3. Monoid constructions

The monoid representing ghost resources—together with the frame-preserving update rules that it supports—can be seen as a way of *expressing a protocol* on logical state: given ownership of a particular monoid element, what does the owner know about the global ghost state and how are they permitted to update it? In this section, we present a number of useful monoid constructions (and their attendant frame-preserving update rules), representing different types of protocols. These protocols are not (yet) related to anything else; they just exist on their own. We will see in §5 how to *enforce* a protocol governing some other shared state.

The main novelty in this section is an encoding of *State Transition Systems* as a monoid. State Transistion Systems (STSs) provide a general and intuitive way of describing possible interference, expressed as a directed graph. The nodes of the graph represent possible ghost states, while edges describe how the ghost state may evolve. In §3.7, we show how to internalize this way of describing interference in Iris, through a general STS-as-monoid construction.

Recall that we represent PCMs as commutative monoids with zero. When defining monoid carriers, we leave this zero element $\bot$ implicit. Furthermore, we will not explicitly define the cases of the composition function that involve $\epsilon$ or $\bot$.

### 3.1 The exclusive monoid

The exclusive monoid over a set $X$ supports two notions of ownership: exclusive ownership of an element $x \in X$ vs. no ownership. The owner of an element $x \in X$ thus has exact knowledge about the state. Formally, $\mathrm{Ex}(X)$ is the monoid with carrier $X \uplus \{\epsilon\}$ and composition only defined when one of the operands is $\epsilon$.

This gives rise to the following frame-preserving update, which captures the ownership intuition given above.

$$x \rightsquigarrow a$$

Any non-trivial element of the monoid can be updated to any element. In terms of separation-logic reasoning, the already described physical assertions $\lfloor\varsigma\rfloor$ behave like ghost assertions about an exclusive monoid over physical states $\varsigma$ (see the axiom in Figure 4), except that of course one cannot use view shifts to update them.

### 3.2 The fractional monoid

It is often desirable to share knowledge about some piece of ghost state (*e.g.,* between different threads). A simple way to do that would be to reuse the carrier from $\text{Ex}(X)$, but let $a \cdot a = a$. This captures the right idea of knowledge, but gives up any notion of ownership: since all elements are duplicable, no frame-preserving update is possible. Instead, we would like a way to keep track of how much the knowledge about ghost state has spread, so that, after gathering it all up again, we can do a frame-preserving update.

This is achieved by the monoid $\text{FRAC}(X)$ which has carrier $((0, 1] \cap \mathbb{Q}) \times X \uplus \{\epsilon\}$ and composition

$$(q, x) \cdot (q', x') \triangleq (q + q', x) \qquad \text{if } q + q' \leq 1 \text{ and } x = x'$$

With this monoid, we can do any frame-preserving update *after collecting all the pieces*:

$$(1, x) \rightsquigarrow a$$

### 3.3 The product monoid

Using a product construction, we can combine any family of monoids $(M_i)_{i \in I}$ into a single monoid, while maintaining their individual reasoning principles (*i.e.,* frame-preserving updates). We define the carrier of the product monoid $\prod_{i \in I} M_i$ to be the product of the monoid carriers $\prod_{i \in I} |M_i|^+$. Composition is defined pointwise, if all of the constituent compositions are well defined (otherwise it is $\perp$).

We would like to operate on the $i$th component of this product monoid just as we would act on the individual monoid $M_i$, and indeed the following frame-preserving update rule holds.

$$a \rightsquigarrow_{M_i} B \vdash f[i \mapsto a] \rightsquigarrow \{f[i \mapsto b] \mid b \in B\}$$

### 3.4 Finite partial functions

A very common monoid in separation logics is the *heap*, modeled as a finite partial function from locations to values. We can obtain this monoid from the product monoid, by adding just one new piece.

Given a countably infinite domain $X$ and a monoid (codomain) $M$, define $\text{FPFUN}(X, M)$ to be the product monoid $\prod_{x \in X} M$, with the additional restriction of the carrier to elements $f$ where the set $\text{dom}(f) \triangleq \{x \mid f(x) \neq \epsilon_M\}$ is finite. This is well defined, since the set of these $f$ contains the unit (which is the function mapping everything to $\epsilon_M$) and is closed under composition. You can think of these $f$ as finite partial functions to $|M|^+ \setminus \{\epsilon\}$, where the elements outside their domains are mapped to $\epsilon$.

Since the domain of $f \in \text{FPFUN}(X, M)$ is finite, an additional frame-preserving update becomes possible: a new element can be allocated.

FPFUNALLOC

$$a \in |M|^+ \vdash f \rightsquigarrow \{f[x \mapsto a] \mid x \notin \text{dom}(f)\}$$

Note that $x$ is bound by the set comprehension: in applying this update, one cannot choose which $x$ one gets.

Consider the monoid $\text{HEAP} \triangleq \text{FPFUN}(Loc, \text{Ex}(Val))$, where *Loc* is a set of locations. The carrier of this monoid consists of finite partial functions from locations to values, and composition of $h$ and $h'$ is defined if all pointwise compositions are defined. From the composition on $\text{Ex}(Val)$, it follows that this is the case iff $\text{dom}(h)$ and $\text{dom}(h')$ are disjoint. This is exactly the standard composition of heaps in separation logic!

Now consider $\text{FHEAP}(Loc) \triangleq \text{FPFUN}(Loc, \text{FRAC}(Val))$. This models a fractional heap, another commonly used monoid in separation logics. It can be used as ghost heap. We define the syntactic sugar $x \overset{q}{\hookrightarrow} w$ to mean $\boxed{[x \mapsto (q, v)]}$ if $q \in (0, 1]$, and $\mathsf{False}$ otherwise. Then we can show:

$$\forall v.\ \mathsf{True} \Rrightarrow \exists x.\ x \overset{1}{\hookrightarrow} v \tag{1}$$

$$\forall x, q_1, q_2, v, w.\ x \overset{q_1}{\hookrightarrow} v * x \overset{q_2}{\hookrightarrow} w \Leftrightarrow x \overset{q_1+q_2}{\hookrightarrow} v * v = w \tag{2}$$

$$\forall x, q, v.\ x \overset{q}{\hookrightarrow} v \Rightarrow x \overset{q}{\hookrightarrow} v \wedge q \in (0, 1] \tag{3}$$

$$\forall x, v, w.\ x \overset{1}{\hookrightarrow} v \Rrightarrow x \overset{1}{\hookrightarrow} w \tag{4}$$

We can use (1) to allocate a new ghost heap cell. Knowledge about the value and ownership of the location can be split and combined using (2). This is useful, in particular, when combining two pieces of a cell that were handed out earlier: one can learn that they point to the same value. Rule (3) says that fractional assertions have well-formed fractions. Having full ownership, the value in the ghost heap can be updated using (4).

### 3.5 Named monoid instances and multiple monoids

In the previous section, we had to fix the global monoid to provide a particular derived construction. We may, however, want to use two different constructions in the same proof without requiring them to share their monoid. It is also useful to be able to obtain a fresh *instance* of a monoid at any time. As it turns out, all the tools we need to mitigate this are already at hand. Given a family of monoids $(M_i)_{i \in I}$, we use a combination of the product and finite partial function monoids to define a global monoid $M$ as follows:

$$M \triangleq \prod_{i \in I} \text{FPFUN}(\mathbb{N}, M_i)$$

The product construction allows us to use a different monoid for independent parts of the proof, while the finite partial function construction provides named instances of these monoids. For the remainder of the article, we assume Iris has been instantiated with the monoid $M$ given above, constructed from a family of monoids $(M_i)_{i \in I}$, taken as a parameter.

We write $\boxed{a : M_i}^{\gamma}$ (or just $\boxed{a}^{\gamma}$ if $M_i$ is clear from the context) for $\boxed{[i \mapsto [\gamma \mapsto a]]}$ when $a \in |M_i|^+$, and for $\mathsf{False}$ when $a = \perp_{M_i}$. The ghost resource $\boxed{a : M_i}^{\gamma}$ thus asserts ownership of a part $a$ of the instance named $\gamma$ of monoid $M_i$ in the current state. From the rules for ghost resources (Figure 5) and the frame-preserving updates in §3.3 and §3.4, we can derive the following rules for allocating, updating, and combining named monoid ghost resources.

NEWGHOST

$$\frac{a \in |M_i|^+}{\mathsf{True} \Rrightarrow \exists \gamma.\ \boxed{a : M_i}^{\gamma}}$$

GHOSTUPD

$$\frac{a \rightsquigarrow_{M_i} B}{\boxed{a : M_i}^{\gamma} \Rrightarrow \exists b \in B.\ \boxed{b : M_i}^{\gamma}}$$

GHOSTEQ

$$\boxed{a : M_i}^{\gamma} * \boxed{b : M_i}^{\gamma} \Leftrightarrow \boxed{a \cdot b : M_i}^{\gamma}$$

### 3.6 The authoritative monoid

A common pattern in concurrent reasoning is to put "someone" in charge of owning the global, *authoritative* state of some ghost resource, while "everyone else" owns fragments of that resource together with the knowledge that their fragments are all contained within the authoritative state.

We can capture this pattern with the monoid $\text{AUTH}(M)$ where

$$|\text{AUTH}(M)|^+ \triangleq \left\{ (x, a) \;\middle|\; \begin{array}{l} x \in |\text{Ex}(|M|^+)|^+ \wedge a \in |M|^+ \wedge \\ (x = \epsilon_{\text{Ex}(|M|^+)} \vee a \leq_M x) \end{array} \right\}$$

So the monoid consists of pairs, where the right component behaves just like $M$ and the left component asserts exclusive ownership of a (non-zero) element of $M$. We impose the additional restriction that if an authoritative element is present, it must be an extension of the current fragment ($a \leq_M x$, which is shorthand for $\exists b.\ a \cdot_M b = x$). Composition is defined pointwise, and undefined if it is not in the carrier—*i.e.*, if the combined fragment exceeds the combined authoritative element, or if two authoritative elements are present. Note that $(\epsilon_{\text{Ex}(|M|+)}, \epsilon_M)$ is the unit and asserts no ownership or knowledge whatsoever, but $(\epsilon_M, \epsilon_M)$ asserts that the authoritative element is $\epsilon_M$.

We write $\bullet x$ to assert full ownership $(x, \epsilon_M)$ and $\circ a$ to assert fragmental ownership $(\epsilon_{\text{Ex}(|M|+)}, a)$. For consistency, we write $\bullet x, \circ a$ for $(x, a)$.

The frame-preserving update for this monoid says that, if we own the authoritative element and some fragment, then we can exchange that fragment for anything that's compatible with "the rest":

AUTHUPD
$M$ cancellative $\wedge\, b \# a_f \;\vdash\; (\bullet a \cdot a_f, \circ a) \rightsquigarrow (\bullet b \cdot a_f, \circ b)$

The rule requires that $M$ be *cancellative*, which means

$$\forall a_f, a, b.\ a_f \cdot a = a_f \cdot b \neq \bot \Rightarrow a = b$$

The monoids $\text{Ex}(X)$ and $\text{Frac}(X)$ are cancellative for any $X$, and monoid products preserve cancellativity.

Building on an example from §3.4, consider $\text{Auth}(\text{Heap})$. This monoid allows us to assert authoritative ownership of some complete heap $\bullet h$ as well as fragmental ownership of, *e.g.*, individual memory locations as $\circ \ell \mapsto v$. Since HEAP is cancellative, we obtain the following frame-preserving updates.

AHEAPUPD
$(\bullet h \cdot \ell \mapsto v, \circ \ell \mapsto v) \rightsquigarrow (\bullet h \cdot \ell \mapsto w, \circ \ell \mapsto w)$

AHEAPADD
$\ell \notin \text{dom}(h) \;\vdash\; (\bullet h) \rightsquigarrow (\bullet h \cdot \ell \mapsto v, \circ \ell \mapsto v)$

Owning $(\bullet h, \circ \ell \mapsto v)$, we can deduce that $h = h' \cdot \ell \mapsto v$ for some $h'$ by the definition of the carrier. Moreover, we can add a new location $\ell$ to $\text{Auth}(\text{Heap})$ *at any point we wish*, provided we can show that $\ell$ is not allocated in the current authoritative heap. This contrasts sharply with the frame-preserving update FPFUNALLOC for HEAP, where we can never be sure which location we get—we just know it will be fresh.

### 3.7 STSs with tokens

In their logic CaReSL [34], Turon *et al.* show how to usefully characterize the possible interference in a concurrent computation using *State Transition Systems (STSs)* with *tokens* [35]. As suggested in §1.1, these mechanisms serve to express *irreversibility* of state change and the *rights* to make state changes. Concretely, an STS comes equipped with a set of states and transitions between them, as well as a set of tokens and a mapping from states to tokens. The transition relation enforces irreversibility by restricting which states are accessible from which other states. The tokens assigned to a particular state are "owned" by the STS, and can be picked up by any thread when transitioning to other states. Tokens must be *conserved*: when taking transitions, the (disjoint) union of the tokens owned locally and the tokens owned by the STS's current state cannot change. The tokens owned locally by a given thread thus serve to limit the rights of other threads to make certain transitions.

As an example, consider the possible states of a remote procedure call (RPC) between a client and a server. Initially, a call has been sent, and it is the server's turn to send back a reply. Only after that has happened can the client receive the reply and terminate.

The corresponding STS is given in Figure 6. The second state, Rx, contains the token SRV. This means that the token is owned by the STS if we are at this state. To satisfy conservation of tokens, a transition from Tx to Rx can only be performed by giving up SRV. Owning SRV thus limits the possible interference from the environment: nobody but the owner of SRV can make this transition. Thus, saying we are *at least* in state Tx and we own token SRV amounts to saying we are *exactly* in state Tx.

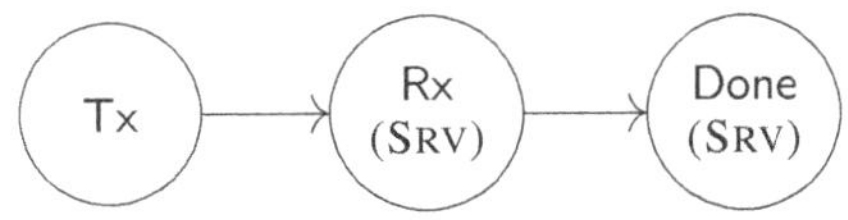


**Figure 6.** STS for a remote procedure call.

$$(s, T) \rightarrow (s', T') \triangleq s \rightarrow s' \wedge \mathcal{T}(s) \uplus T = \mathcal{T}(s') \uplus T'$$
$$\mathsf{frm}(s, T) \triangleq (s, \mathsf{TokSet} \setminus (\mathcal{T}(s) \uplus T))$$
$$\uparrow(S, T) \triangleq \{s' \in \mathcal{S} \mid \exists s \in S.\ \mathsf{frm}(s, T) \rightarrow^* \mathsf{frm}(s', T)\}$$

$$|\text{STS}_{\mathcal{S}}| \triangleq \left\{ (s, S, T) \;\middle|\; \begin{array}{l} (s, S, T) \in \text{Ex}(\mathcal{S}) \times \mathcal{P}(\mathcal{S}) \times \mathcal{P}(\mathcal{T}) \wedge \\ (s = \epsilon \vee s \in S) \wedge \uparrow(S, T) = S \wedge \\ S \neq \emptyset \wedge \forall s \in S.\ \mathcal{T}(s) \cap T = \emptyset \end{array} \right\}$$

$$(s, S, T) \cdot (s', S', T') \triangleq (s \cdot s', S \cap S', T \uplus T')$$

(where composition is undefined if the result is not in $|\text{STS}_{\mathcal{S}}|$)

**Figure 7.** Monoid encoding of STSs.

The monoid $\text{STS}_{\mathcal{S}}$ for an STS $(\mathcal{S}, \rightarrow)$ with token set $\mathsf{TokSet}$ and token assignment $\mathcal{T} : \mathcal{S} \rightarrow \mathsf{TokSet}$ is defined in Figure 7. It has three parts. First is the STS's current authoritative state $s$. Ownership and knowledge of this state can only ever be held by one party—hence we use an exclusive monoid to represent it. Even if we do not own the authoritative $s$, we can use the second part of the monoid, $S$, to describe what we know about the set of *possible* states $s$ could be, *e.g.*, that it is *accessible* from a certain state $s_0$. Composition on these sets is simply intersection, and knowledge about possible states is freely duplicable (as $S = S \cap S$). Finally, there is a set of locally owned tokens $T$: since we own them locally, we know that no other party owns them (composition is defined by $\uplus$), and that the protocol does not own them either ($\forall s \in S.\ \mathcal{T}(s) \cap T = \emptyset$).

Regarding the second part of the monoid, not all possible sets of states $S$ are sensible. Every such set we define to exist will be *stable* knowledge, meaning it cannot be invalidated by actions of the environment. We thus restrict the set of possible states to be closed under transitions by the environment, as formalized by the upward-closure $\uparrow$ in Figure 7: $\uparrow(S, T) = S$. The figure also shows how to lift the relation $\rightarrow$ between states to a relation between state-token pairs: $(s, T) \rightarrow (s', T')$ says that, owning the tokens in $T$, one can move from $s$ to $s'$ and end up with the tokens in $T'$. In our RPC STS, for example, we have $(\mathsf{Tx}, \{\text{SRV}\}) \rightarrow (\mathsf{Rx}, \emptyset)$. On the other hand, $(\mathsf{Tx}, \emptyset)$ has no successor.

This definition gives rise to the following frame-preserving update. Owning the authoritative state and some tokens, we can make any transition that is justified by the tokens we own:

STSUPD
$$\frac{(s, T) \rightarrow^* (s', T')}{(s, S, T) \rightsquigarrow (s', \uparrow(\{s'\}, T'), T')}$$

Note how we use $\uparrow$ to stabilize knowledge—having transitioned to $s'$, we know that we are *at least* in $s'$.

While encoding STSs as monoids is interesting, we can only unleash its true power—recovering CaReSL's workhorse, the "island update" rule—once we have a way of enforcing STSs as protocols over the evolution of some shared state. For that, we need invariants.

## 4. Iris – Part II: Invariants

So far, Iris only supports reasoning about state that is owned by one thread or another. There is no mechanism yet for sharing state between threads. To support such sharing, we extend the logic now with *invariants*. Given a proposition $P$, the assertion $\boxed{P}^{\iota}$ asserts the existence of a shared invariant named $\iota$, which governs resources satisfying $P$. Since invariant assertions just assert the existence of a shared invariant, they are pure and thus freely duplicable: $\boxed{P}^{\iota} \Leftrightarrow \Box\boxed{P}^{\iota}$.

To access the shared resource they govern, invariants can be *opened* for the duration of a physically atomic expression. Opening an invariant grants temporary ownership of the shared resource. Once the invariant is reestablished (possibly after resources have been transferred in or out), it can be *closed* again. The following INV rule (which will turn out to be derivable from other rules) grants $e$ ownership of shared resource $R$ for the duration of its execution.

INV

$$\frac{\{\triangleright R * P\}\; e\; \{v.\, \triangleright R * Q\}_{\mathcal{E}} \qquad e \text{ phys. atomic}}{\boxed{R}^{\iota} \vdash \{P\}\; e\; \{v.\, Q\}_{\mathcal{E} \uplus \{\iota\}}}$$

For now, ignore the *later* modality $\triangleright$, we will come back to it later. The rule (read backwards) says that, if you know that an invariant $R$ with name $\iota$ exists, you can add its resources to the precondition. The verification of $e$ can then freely use those resources as it wishes, but it must give back control of some resources satisfying $R$ when it is done.

***Masks.*** To ensure that each invariant is opened at most once, we annotate Hoare triples with an invariant mask. For the Hoare triple $\{P\}\; e\; \{v.\, Q\}_{\mathcal{E}}$ we can assume the invariants in $\mathcal{E}$ hold prior to the execution and must reestablish them after each single physical step. We say that the invariants in $\mathcal{E}$ are *enabled*, which means that they hold on some portion of the shared (physical and logical) state. Here $\mathcal{E}$ is a term of type $\mathsf{InvMask}$—the type of invariant masks, which are simply sets of invariant names.

***Mask-changing view shifts.*** It is helpful to think about the INV rule as combining three separate steps of reasoning. First, note that, in the conclusion, $\iota$ is enabled, which means that it can be opened (disabled), and the resource satisfying $\triangleright R$ can be transferred from shared control to the local control of $e$. Second, this resource, together with $P$, is used to reason about $e$, which reestablishes $\triangleright R$ and some additional $Q$ under the assumption that $\iota$ is disabled. Third, the invariant is closed (reenabled), which returns the resource satisfying $\triangleright R$ to shared control and restores the original invariant mask. For reasons that will become clear in §7, we find it useful to be able to reason about the opening and closing steps of this rule independently of the reasoning about $e$ that goes on in between. Consequently, instead of taking INV as primitive, Iris employs a *novel notion of view shifts that can open or close invariants*.

This is achieved by annotating view shifts with two sets of invariants: those that are enabled *before* and *after* the update. The view shift $P \;{}^{\mathcal{E}_1}\!\!\Rrightarrow^{\mathcal{E}_2} Q$ expresses that it is possible to update the local state from $P$ to $Q$ without updating the physical state, where *only* the invariants in $\mathcal{E}_1$ and $\mathcal{E}_2$ are required to hold before and after the update, respectively. We write $P \Rrightarrow_{\mathcal{E}} Q$ as syntactic sugar for $P \;{}^{\mathcal{E}}\!\!\Rrightarrow^{\mathcal{E}} Q$. The INVOPEN and INVCLOSE rules in Figure 8 express invariant opening and closing as mask-changing view shifts.

The rule of atomic consequence (ACSQ in Figure 9) allows us to open invariants $\mathcal{E}'$ for the duration of an expression $e$, provided we close them again afterwards. This rule can be composed with INVOPEN and INVCLOSE to obtain INV as a derived rule.

Note that ACSQ can only be sound for *physically atomic* expressions: After doing one step in $e$, another thread may be next to compute, and it may rely on invariants in $\mathcal{E}'$. We will see in §7 how to give specifications for functions that are *not physically atomic*, while still allowing opening invariants. Our more general notion of mask-changing view shifts will prove to be very helpful there.

***View shift rules.*** View shifts permit a frame rule VSFRAME similar to the usual frame rule for Hoare triples. However, this rule serves not only to frame resources around a view shift. It can also be used to frame invariants: if some invariant $\iota$ not covered by either mask of the view shift is known to be enabled, it remains so when the view shift is applied. Hence, view shifts may only affect invariants that they explicitly name in one of their masks. The same kind of framing is possible for Hoare triples; we refer the reader to the appendix [1] for the full set of rules.

***Syntax***

$$P, \iota, \mathcal{E} ::= \cdots \mid \boxed{P}^{\iota} \mid \triangleright P \qquad \Sigma ::= \cdots \mid \mathsf{Name} \mid \mathsf{InvMask}$$

***Proof rules***

NEWINV

$$\mathsf{infinite}(\mathcal{E}) \vdash \triangleright P \Rrightarrow_{\mathcal{E}} \exists \iota \in \mathcal{E}.\, \boxed{P}^{\iota}$$

INVOPEN

$$\boxed{P}^{\iota} \vdash \mathsf{True} \;{}^{\{\iota\}}\!\!\Rrightarrow^{\emptyset} \triangleright P$$

INVCLOSE

$$\boxed{P}^{\iota} \vdash \triangleright P \;{}^{\emptyset}\!\!\Rrightarrow^{\{\iota\}} \mathsf{True}$$

**Figure 8.** Syntax and proof rules for invariants.

VSTRANS

$$\frac{\mathcal{E}_2 \subseteq \mathcal{E}_1 \cup \mathcal{E}_3 \qquad P \;{}^{\mathcal{E}_1}\!\!\Rrightarrow^{\mathcal{E}_2} Q \qquad Q \;{}^{\mathcal{E}_2}\!\!\Rrightarrow^{\mathcal{E}_3} R}{P \;{}^{\mathcal{E}_1}\!\!\Rrightarrow^{\mathcal{E}_3} R}$$

VSFRAME

$$\frac{P \;{}^{\mathcal{E}_1}\!\!\Rrightarrow^{\mathcal{E}_2} Q}{P * R \;{}^{\mathcal{E}_1 \uplus \mathcal{E}'}\!\!\Rrightarrow^{\mathcal{E}_2 \uplus \mathcal{E}'} Q * R}$$

VSTIMELESS

$$\frac{\mathsf{timeless}(P)}{\triangleright P \Rrightarrow P}$$

ACSQ

$$\frac{P \;{}^{\mathcal{E} \uplus \mathcal{E}'}\!\!\Rrightarrow^{\mathcal{E}} P' \qquad \{P'\}\; e\; \{v.\, Q'\}_{\mathcal{E}} \qquad \forall v.\, Q' \;{}^{\mathcal{E}}\!\!\Rrightarrow^{\mathcal{E} \uplus \mathcal{E}'} Q \qquad e \text{ phys. atomic}}{\{P\}\; e\; \{v.\, Q\}_{\mathcal{E} \uplus \mathcal{E}'}}$$

**Figure 9.** Most important view shift rules (cf. our appendix [1]).

The view shift transitivity rule VSTRANS allows two view shifts to be combined, provided they agree on the invariants that are enabled between the two view shifts and that those invariants are not forgotten in the conclusion ($\mathcal{E}_2 \subseteq \mathcal{E}_1 \cup \mathcal{E}_3$). This side condition is necessary to ensure soundness of the VSFRAME rule.

New invariants are created by transferring local resources satisfying the invariant to the shared state. As this involves a relabeling of resources (from "local" to "shared") but not any actual change to physical state, it can be expressed as a view shift. The NEWINV rule in Figure 8 allocates an invariant with a name $\iota$, chosen from a set of possible names $\mathcal{E}$. We require $\mathcal{E}$ to be infinite to make sure that there is some invariant name in there that is not taken already. And since we can pick the infinite set, we can reason that the different invariants we create have different names (by creating them with applications of NEWINV with disjoint $\mathcal{E}$'s). Disjointness of invariant names is important if we wish to apply INV in nested fashion, since we will have to prove that each invariant is opened at most once.

***Later modality.*** Since any Iris assertion can serve as an invariant, one can define invariants that refer to other invariants or even themselves. This *impredicativity* introduces a potential circularity. Following iCAP [33] and CaReSL [34], we use step-indexing to break this circularity, and internalize the notion of steps using a *later* modality. The assertion $\triangleright P$ expresses that $P$ holds one step later. To ensure that invariants are well defined, the shared resource backing up $\boxed{P}^{\iota}$ need only satisfy $\triangleright P$. Thus, opening an invariant (INVOPEN) grants ownership of the shared resource one step later. Conversely, to close an invariant (INVCLOSE), it suffices to reestablish the shared resource one step later. If a resource $P$ holds now, it also holds later: $P \Rrightarrow \triangleright P$.

With *timeless* propositions, things are simpler. Timeless propositions are not affected by $\triangleright$, as expressed in rule VSTIMELESS. Examples of such propositions include physical state assertions and ghost assertions. Timelessness matters primarily when reasoning about propositions appearing in invariants: if an invariant is timeless, we can immediately view shift from $\boxed{P}^{\iota}$ to $P$ by opening the invariant to obtain $\triangleright P$, then applying VSTIMELESS. The formal definition of timelessness can be found in the appendix [1].

## 5. Invariant constructions

In combination with invariants, the monoid constructions presented in §3 let us encode powerful patterns for local reasoning about protocols on shared resources, including several that were developed in previous work [34, 33, 8]. To achieve this, an abstract *protocol* (as defined by a monoid) is tied to an *interpretation* of what the protocol is intended to guarantee about some shared resources, and the desired connection between the two is enforced with an invariant. It is then possible to derive Hoare triples for expressions that update the shared resources in accordance with the protocol.

### 5.1 STSs with interpretation

The whole point of the encoding of STSs from §3.7 was to be able to define protocols capable of governing some shared resource (*e.g.,* the pointer structure implementing some concurrent mutable ADT, although in general the shared resource need not be physical). To support this functionality, we begin by extending the STSs from §3.7 with an interpretation $\varphi(s)$ for each state $s$, which will say what property should hold of the underlying shared resource when the current (*i.e.,* authoritative) state of the STS is $s$.

Let the STS $(\mathcal{S}, \rightarrow)$, interpretation function $\varphi : \mathcal{S} \rightarrow \mathsf{Prop}$, and instance name $\gamma$ be given. We then define the following invariant:

$$\mathsf{STSInv}(\mathcal{S}, \varphi, \gamma) \triangleq \exists s.\ \boxed{(s, \mathcal{S}, \emptyset) : \mathrm{STS}_{\mathcal{S}}}^{\gamma} * \varphi(s)$$

By creating this invariant, we enforce that the current authoritative state $s$ of the STS instance $\gamma$ is a shared resource, as is whatever shared resource backs up its interpretation $\varphi(s)$, which is the state that multiple threads want to access concurrently.

Returning to the RPC example from §3.7, let us assume knowledge of an STS invariant governing an instance $\gamma$ of the RPC STS in Figure 6. Suppose we own resources $P$ and the STS resource $\boxed{(\mathsf{Rx}, \emptyset)}^{\gamma}$ and want to transition the STS to state Done and establish $Q$. Our ghost resource represents knowledge that the STS is at least in state Rx (and ownership of no tokens). When we open the invariant, we learn the authoritative state, $s \in \{\mathsf{Rx}, \mathsf{Done}\}$, and take ownership of $\triangleright\varphi(s)$. (The knowledge we started with ensures $s \neq \mathsf{Tx}$.) Since we want to transition to Done, our primary proof obligation is to show that, no matter what $s$ is, we can update the resources on hand, $P * \triangleright\varphi(s)$, to $\triangleright\varphi(\mathsf{Done}) * Q$. Having proven that, we can then close the invariant and walk away with $\boxed{(\mathsf{Done}, \emptyset)}^{\gamma} * Q$. (The ghost represents our updated knowledge about the STS.)

This general reasoning pattern is reflected in the derived rule STS in Figure 10. If we ignore the tokens (for simplicity), the rule says: if we know the STS instance $\gamma$ is at least in state $s_0$ and want to update the STS, then it suffices to show that for any future state $s$ of $s_0$ we can, adding $\triangleright\varphi(s)$ to our precondition, establish $\triangleright\varphi(s')$ in our postcondition (for some future state $s'$ of $s$).

The rule matches exactly CaReSL's island update rule [34]. As with INV from the previous section, it is derived using ACSQ, and the proof follows the same decomposition: open invariant, reason with additional resources, close invariant. The only difference is an additional frame-preserving update using STSUPD right before closing the invariant.

### 5.2 Authoritative monoids with interpretation

In this section, we implement the second layer of our stack (Figure 1) using reasoning principles similar to those Krishnaswami *et al.* developed for "superficially substructural types" [22]. We derive these principles by marrying an interpretation to the monoid $\mathrm{AUTH}(M)$, much as we did for the monoid $\mathrm{STS}_{\mathcal{S}}$ in §5.1.

Consider the Hoare triples we obtained in Figure 3 to reason about language primitives. They all carry in their precondition a physical assertion, $\lfloor \varsigma \rfloor$, about the global machine state, which can only ever be held by a single party. These are called *large-footprint specifications*, as opposed to the *small-footprint specifications* given in Figure 11, which only mention the channel they operate on [31]. We aim to derive these small-footprint specs. We will achieve this by putting ownership of the entire physical state into an invariant, so that it is shared by everybody. The invariant ties this physical state to a ghost resource so that fragments of the ghost resource (which can be split up among different threads) effectively control fragments of the physical state.

We can model the state of a network using the monoid $\mathrm{NET} \triangleq \mathrm{FPFUN}(\mathsf{Chan}, \mathrm{EX}(\mathsf{Bag}))$. This gives us an adequate level of sharing: we can make assertions about individual channels, without mentioning all the others. Next, we define the interpretation $\varphi : |\mathrm{NET}|^{+} \rightarrow \mathsf{Prop}$ that we wish to hold for the *authoritative* state of this monoid, *i.e.,* the composition of all fragments:

$$\varphi(C) \triangleq \lfloor C \rfloor$$

(Here, we implicitly coerce between the finite partial functions in $|\mathrm{NET}|^{+}$, and the ones comprising the possible physical states).

To tie the two together, we use an instance $\gamma$ of $\mathrm{AUTH}(\mathrm{NET})$ and the following invariant.

$$\mathsf{ChanInv} \triangleq \exists C.\ \boxed{\bullet C : \mathrm{AUTH}(\mathrm{NET})}^{\gamma} * \varphi_{\bot}(C)$$

We extend $\varphi$ to $\varphi_{\bot} : |\mathrm{NET}| \rightarrow \mathsf{Prop}$ by setting $\varphi_{\bot}(\bot) = \mathsf{False}$.

Now assume that we own $\boxed{\circ\, c \mapsto M}^{\gamma}$ (which we will write $c \prec M$), and consider what we obtain upon opening the invariant ChanInv. While we cannot know which $C$ witnesses the existential, we know from the definition of $\mathrm{AUTH}(\mathrm{NET})$ that $c \mapsto M \leq C$, and thus $C(c) = M$. With our temporary ownership of the shared physical state $\lfloor C \rfloor$, we can justify operating on our channel $c$. All of this follows just from owning $c \prec M$, which is a purely logical assertion that has nothing to do *per se* with the physical state—it is the invariant which lets *us* decide how we want to tie the two together. After the operation on $c$, we make us of the fact that we own both the authoritative state and the fragment governing $c$, so we know nobody else can hold any knowledge about this channel. Hence we can do a frame-preserving update synchronizing the ghost state with the new physical state, and closing the invariant.

In general, we may want to give an interpretation $\varphi : |M|^{+} \rightarrow \mathsf{Prop}$ to every (non-zero) element of some cancellative monoid $M$. We can do so with the invariant

$$\mathsf{AuthInv}(M, \varphi, \gamma) \triangleq \exists c.\ \boxed{\bullet c : \mathrm{AUTH}(M)}^{\gamma} * \varphi_{\bot}(c)$$

The reasoning pattern enabled by this construction is codified by rule AUTH in Figure 10.

The rule says that if we know an invariant tying the authoritative part of $\gamma$ to $\varphi$, and if we own the fragment $a$ in $\gamma$, then we can gain access to the interpretation $\varphi_{\bot}(a \cdot a_f)$ of the current authoritative state (where $a_f$ is everything owned by the environment). If, using the resources of the interpretation together with the $P$ that we carried in, we can establish $\varphi_{\bot}(b \cdot a_f)$ (which implies $b \;\#\; a_f$) together with $Q$, then we are allowed to carry out whatever was left in $Q$, and update our ghost fragment to $b$. Like STS, this rule combines opening and closing an invariant with a frame-preserving update (except here the update uses AUTHUPD rather than STSUPD).

The triples given in Figure 11 are derived using AUTH. The mask $\mathcal{E}_{\mathsf{chan}}$ will contain the name of the invariant governing ChanInv. Note that we make crucial use of the VSTIMELESS rule here: After opening the invariant, we actually obtain $\triangleright\lfloor C \rfloor$. But physical state assertions are timeless, so we can immediately view shift that to

STS
$$\frac{\forall s \in \uparrow(\{s_0\}, T).\ \{\triangleright\varphi(s) * P\}\ e\ \{v.\ \exists s', T'.\ (s, T) \rightarrow^* (s', T') * \triangleright\varphi(s') * Q\}_{\mathcal{E}} \qquad e \text{ phys. atomic}}{\boxed{\mathsf{STSInv}(\mathcal{S}, \varphi, \gamma)}^{\iota} \vdash \left\{\boxed{(s_0, T)}^{\gamma} * P\right\}\ e\ \left\{v.\ \exists s', T'.\ \boxed{(s', T')}^{\gamma} * Q\right\}_{\mathcal{E} \uplus \{\iota\}}}$$

INV
$$\frac{\{\triangleright R * P\}\ e\ \{v.\ \triangleright R * Q\}_{\mathcal{E}} \qquad e \text{ phys. atomic}}{\boxed{R}^{\iota} \vdash \{P\}\ e\ \{v.\ Q\}_{\mathcal{E} \uplus \{\iota\}}}$$

AUTH
$$\frac{e \text{ phys. atomic} \qquad M \text{ cancellative} \qquad \forall a_f.\ \{\triangleright\varphi_{\perp}(a \cdot a_f) * P\}\ e\ \{v.\ \exists b.\ \triangleright\varphi_{\perp}(b \cdot a_f) * Q\}_{\mathcal{E}}}{\boxed{\mathsf{AuthInv}(M, \varphi, \gamma)}^{\iota} \vdash \left\{\boxed{a}^{\gamma} * P\right\}\ e\ \left\{v.\ \exists b.\ \boxed{b}^{\gamma} * Q\right\}_{\mathcal{E} \uplus \{\iota\}}}$$

**Figure 10.** Derived rules to reason about shared state.

$$\{\mathsf{True}\}\ \textbf{newch}\ \{c.\ c \prec \emptyset\}$$

$$\{c \prec M\}\ \textbf{send}(c, m)\ \{v.\ v = () \wedge c \prec M \uplus \{m\}\}_{\mathcal{E}_{\mathsf{chan}}}$$

$$\{c \prec M\}\ \textbf{tryrecv}\ c$$
$$\left\{\begin{array}{l} v.\ (M = \emptyset \wedge v = \mathsf{None} \wedge c \prec \emptyset) \vee \\ \quad (\exists m.\ m \in M \wedge v = \mathsf{Some}(m) \wedge c \prec M \setminus \{m\}) \end{array}\right\}_{\mathcal{E}_{\mathsf{chan}}}$$

**Figure 11.** Derived rules for language primitives (see Figure 3 for the basic rules).

$$\{\mathsf{True}\}\ \textbf{newch}\ \{c.\ c \prec \emptyset\}$$

$$\langle M.\ c \prec M\rangle\ \textbf{send}(c, m)\ \langle v.\ c \prec M \uplus \{m\} \wedge v = ()\rangle^{\mathcal{E}_{\mathsf{chan}}}$$

$$\langle M.\ c \prec M\rangle\ \mathsf{recv}\ c\ \langle m.\ c \prec M \setminus \{m\} \wedge m \in M\rangle^{\mathcal{E}_{\mathsf{chan}}}$$

where

$$\begin{array}{l} \mathsf{recv} \triangleq \textbf{rec}\ \mathit{recv}(c). \\ \quad \textbf{let}\ v = \textbf{tryrecv}\ c\ \textbf{in} \\ \quad \textbf{case}\ v\ \textbf{of}\ \mathsf{None} \Rightarrow \mathit{recv}\ c \mid \mathsf{Some}(m) \Rightarrow m \end{array}$$

**Figure 12.** Logically atomic spec for channels with blocking recv.

$\lfloor C \rfloor$ and not bother with the $\triangleright$. Furthermore, we obtain a single unified description of **tryrecv** by case distinction on $M$.

This pattern turns out to be very expressive. It is applicable whenever it is necessary to collect some state in a central place, and useful to spread ownership and knowledge about parts of this state. For example, in a heap-manipulating language, this pattern easily scales to provide fractional permissions. Also note that AUTH corresponds closely to Krishnaswami *et al.*'s "sharing rule" [22]. This is yet another example of Iris's ability to derive powerful reasoning principles that are built fixed into prior logics.

## 6. Semantics

The semantics of Iris is defined in the accompanying technical appendix and formalized in the accompanying Coq development [1]. In this section we give a very brief overview of the model.

To model invariants, assertions in Iris are modeled relative to a *world* that describes the invariants allocated so far. Since invariants are themselves expressed as assertions, this introduces a circularity in the modeling of assertions and worlds. This is the standard type-world circularity that also arises in models of type systems with dynamic allocation and higher-order store [3]. We use standard metric-based techniques to solve the circularity [4, 6] and, in particular, Sieczkowski *et al.*'s library [32] for solving such circularities in Coq. Crucially, the construction of the semantic domain of assertions—which allows us to model invariants—is parametric in the ghost state monoid. Invariants and monoids are thus also orthogonal semantically.

Iris's adequacy theorem expresses that if $\{\lfloor \varsigma \rfloor\}\ e\ \{v.\ \varphi(v)\}$ is derivable and $e$ executes to a value $v$ when started in physical state $\varsigma$, then $v$ satisfies $\varphi$. Here, $\varphi(v)$ is a pure predicate, *i.e.*, it describes a property of $v$ and cannot mention resources or invariants. Formally:

**Theorem 1** (Adequacy).
*If* $\vdash \{\lfloor \varsigma \rfloor\}\ e\ \{v.\ \varphi(v)\}$ *and* $\varsigma; [i \mapsto e] \rightarrow^* \varsigma'; [i \mapsto v] \uplus T'$, *then* $\varphi(v)$.

The $T'$ in the final state permits $e$ to fork off other threads.

Soundness of the underlying higher-order separation logic, the rules in Figures 4, 5, 8, and 9, and the adequacy theorem have all been proven in Coq [1].

## 7. Logical atomicity

How can triples like the ones in Figure 11 be used? Of course, one could just use them as normal Hoare triples, and establish $c \prec M$ before calling them. This, however, would effectively sequentialize access to the channel: every caller would have to prove that they exclusively own the channel in order to access it.

Moreover, we often *want* several threads to be able to "race" for access to the resource. For example, consider the case where there is an invariant $\iota_{\mathsf{even}}$ governing the channel, making sure it only ever contains even numbers:

$$\boxed{\exists M.\ c \prec M \wedge \forall m \in M.\ m \in \mathbb{N} \wedge m \text{ is even}}^{\iota_{\mathsf{even}}}$$

Since **send** is a *physically atomic* operation, we can use INV to gain access to the channel. We can open the invariant *around* the call to **send**, atomically observing the current state of the channel. If we are sending an even number, we can reestablish the invariant after **send** is done, and close it again. This is sound because no other thread can interfere with the physically atomic call to **send**. In this case, we say that we have a *physically atomic triple* for **send**.

Now consider the blocking implementation of recv defined in Figure 12. We would like to do the same kind of reasoning, *e.g.*, to verify that recv $c$ always returns an even number. But recv is not physically atomic, so INV does not apply. However, intuitively, recv *behaves as if it were atomic*: there is a single point in time (often called the *linearization point*) where the receiving action is (logically) committed, namely the instant when **tryrecv** succeeds. We ought to be able to exploit this, and call recv based on the channel assertion that is governed by $\iota_{\mathsf{even}}$—but if we only have a normal Hoare triple for recv, there is no way to do this. Our goal is thus to find a notion of a *logically atomic triple* that admits the reasoning principles given in Figure 10, but is applicable to functions like recv.

Now, note that all of our reasoning principles in Figure 10 were derived using ACSQ, which lets us compose physically atomic triples with view shifts *that open and close invariants*, whereas the corresponding rule for general expressions, CSQ, works only for view shifts with the same set of invariants enabled on both sides. It is thus justified to say that ACSQ *logically captures the essence of what it means to be atomic*. Hence, logically atomic triples should support the same kind of reasoning, and we will use this insight in determining how to define them.

### 7.1 Logically atomic triples

In order to motivate the definition of logical atomic specifications, it is helpful to consider the needs of both a client *using* such a specification, and a module *proving* it.

***Client perspective.*** What would it mean for recv to support a reasoning principle like ACSQ? Well, for example, we would like to have the following instantiation of ACSQ:

$$\frac{\begin{array}{c}\{c \prec M\}\ \mathsf{recv}\ c\ \{m.\ c \prec M \setminus \{m\} \land m \in M\}_{\mathcal{E}_{\mathsf{chan}}} \\ P\ {}^{\mathcal{E}_{\mathsf{chan}} \uplus \mathcal{E}'}\!\!\Rrightarrow^{\mathcal{E}_{\mathsf{chan}}}\ c \prec M \\ \forall m.\ c \prec M \setminus \{m\} \land m \in M\ {}^{\mathcal{E}_{\mathsf{chan}}}\!\!\Rrightarrow^{\mathcal{E}_{\mathsf{chan}} \uplus \mathcal{E}'}\ Q(m)\end{array}}{\{P\}\ \mathsf{recv}\ c\ \{m.\ Q(m)\}_{\mathcal{E}_{\mathsf{chan}} \uplus \mathcal{E}'}} \tag{5}$$

As a client of the module implementing recv , we would expect that module to prove the first premise. We would then give proofs for the two view shifts, and obtain the conclusion.

Now, recv is not physically atomic, so (5) is not sound. However, we can transform (5) into the "elimination form" of its first premise, *i.e.,* into the statement that ACSQ can be applied to recv:

$$\begin{array}{l}\forall P, Q, \mathcal{E}', M.\ (P\ {}^{\mathcal{E}_{\mathsf{chan}} \uplus \mathcal{E}'}\!\!\Rrightarrow^{\mathcal{E}_{\mathsf{chan}}}\ c \prec M) \land \\ (\forall m.\ c \prec M \setminus \{m\} \land m \in M\ {}^{\mathcal{E}_{\mathsf{chan}}}\!\!\Rrightarrow^{\mathcal{E}_{\mathsf{chan}} \uplus \mathcal{E}'}\ Q(m)) \\ \Rightarrow \{P\}\ \mathsf{recv}\ c\ \{v.\ Q(v)\}_{\mathcal{E}_{\mathsf{chan}} \uplus \mathcal{E}'}\end{array} \tag{6}$$

If *this* is the interface provided by the module, then we as client can do exactly the reasoning that (5) would allow us to do! The key observation is that such a statement can be made about any operation, be it physically atomic or not.

There are still some problems, though. Suppose we want to call recv on the channel $c$ governed by the invariant $\iota_{\mathsf{even}}$. To do this, we have to choose some $M$ and then prove that we can view shift from $P$ to $c \prec M$. However, we only learn the current $M$ *after* opening the invariant (*inside* the proof of the the view shift), so we have no way to fix it *a priori*! Furthermore, we cannot prove the second view shift: at that point, we have forgotten that all messages in $M$ are even numbers, so we cannot reestablish the invariant.

To solve this, we introduce a special treatment for $M$ such that it only has to be fixed after opening the invariant. We will also bake in an application of FRAME, similar to how ACSQ was baked into (6). This leads us to the following:

$$\begin{array}{l}\forall P, Q, R, \mathcal{E}'.\ (P\ {}^{\mathcal{E}_{\mathsf{chan}} \uplus \mathcal{E}'}\!\!\Rrightarrow^{\mathcal{E}_{\mathsf{chan}}}\ \exists M.\ c \prec M * R(M)) \land \\ \left(\begin{array}{l}\forall M, m.\ c \prec M \setminus \{m\} \land m \in M * R(M) \\ \qquad {}^{\mathcal{E}_{\mathsf{chan}}}\!\!\Rrightarrow^{\mathcal{E}_{\mathsf{chan}} \uplus \mathcal{E}'}\ Q(M, m)\end{array}\right) \\ \Rightarrow \{P\}\ \mathsf{recv}\ c\ \{m.\ \exists M.\ Q(M, m)\}_{\mathcal{E}_{\mathsf{chan}} \uplus \mathcal{E}'}\end{array} \tag{7}$$

This is strong enough to be useful in our example. We choose:

$$P \triangleq \mathsf{True} \qquad Q(\_, m) \triangleq m \in \mathbb{N} \land m \text{ is even} \qquad \mathcal{E}' \triangleq \{\iota_{\mathsf{even}}\}$$

$$R(M) \triangleq \forall m \in M.\ m \in \mathbb{N} \land m \text{ is even}$$

The view shifts are then easy to show. Applying (7), this yields the desired triple, stating that recv $c$ always returns an even number:

$$\{\mathsf{True}\}\ \mathsf{recv}\ c\ \{m.\ m \in \mathbb{N} \land m \text{ is even}\}_{\mathcal{E}_{\mathsf{chan}} \uplus \{\iota_{\mathsf{even}}\}}$$

Note how our ability to prove the postcondition (that $m$ is even) relies crucially on the fact that the frame $R$ can depend on $M$.

***Module perspective.*** Let us now switch roles, and consider the case of a module that wants to *provide* a specification like (7). This means we get to *assume* some arbitrary $P$, $Q$, $R$, $\mathcal{E}'$ and the associated view shifts, and we have to prove an (ordinary) Hoare triple. Unlike in the normal case of proving a triple, we do not have access to the resource $c \prec M$ that we operate on. Instead, we own some $P$, about which we only know that we can view shift to the desired resource. How can that be enough?

$$\begin{array}{l}\langle x.\ \alpha \rangle\ e\ \langle v.\ \beta \rangle^{\mathcal{E}_M}_{\mathcal{E}} \triangleq \mathcal{E}_M \# \mathcal{E} \land \\ \square \left(\begin{array}{l}\forall P, Q, R, \mathcal{E}_R. \\ \quad \langle x.\ P \Lleftarrow\!\!\Rrightarrow \alpha \mid R(x), \mathcal{E}_R \mid v.\ \beta \Rrightarrow Q(x, v) \rangle^{\mathcal{E}_M}_{\mathcal{E}} \\ \quad \Rightarrow \{P\}\ e\ \{v.\ \exists x.\ Q(x, v)\}_{\top}\end{array}\right) \\ \langle x.\ P \Lleftarrow\!\!\Rrightarrow \alpha \mid R, \mathcal{E}_R \mid v.\ \beta \Rrightarrow Q \rangle^{\mathcal{E}_M}_{\mathcal{E}} \triangleq \\ \quad \mathsf{timeless}(P) \land \mathcal{E}_R \# \mathcal{E} \cup \mathcal{E}_M \land \\ \quad (P\ {}^{-\mathcal{E}_M}\!\!\Lleftarrow\!\!\Rrightarrow^{-\mathcal{E}_M - \mathcal{E}_R}\ \exists x.\ \alpha * R) \land \\ \quad (\forall x, v.\ \beta * R\ {}^{-\mathcal{E}_M - \mathcal{E}_R}\!\!\Rrightarrow^{-\mathcal{E}_M}\ Q)\end{array}$$

**Figure 13.** Definition of logically atomic triples and atomic shifts.

The key is this: at the "linearization point" (as explained above, the single step of execution where the operation "commits"), we will make use of the view shifts we have been given, together with rule ACSQ, to grant us temporary access to $c \prec M$ for that one step. Formally, at the linearization point, we will use the view shift from $P$ to $c \prec M$, which may open some islands $\mathcal{E}'$—hence, we call it the *opening view shift*. After operating on the resource, the only way to complete the proof is to use a corresponding *closing view shift*, of which we have only one, to view shift the updated resource back to $Q$. Since this marks the point in time where the atomic action commits, we also call this the *committing view shift*. Note that since we do not know anything about $R$, we have no choice but to use the same $M$ with $Q$ that we originally got from the opening view shift.

Sometimes, however, one has to deal with an operation that *could* be the linearization point, but it is not known up front (*i.e.,* until reasoning about the postcondition) whether that will be the case. For this reason, it is necessary to be able to *abort* an atomic update. For example, recv internally uses **tryrecv**, which has two possible outcomes: either a message was received, in which case we can commit and are done, or the channel was empty, in which case we loop again. Thus, in the proof, we would be stuck if the only closing view shift we had at our disposal was the committing one. Hence we extend (7) to assume an additional *aborting view shift* (as another closing view shift), which lets us go back to $P$ if the commit did not happen. We arrive at the following, general pattern:

$$\begin{array}{l}\forall P, Q, R, \mathcal{E}'.\ (P\ {}^{\mathcal{E} \uplus \mathcal{E}'}\!\!\Lleftarrow\!\!\Rrightarrow^{\mathcal{E}}\ \exists x.\ \alpha(x) * R(x)) \land \\ (\forall x, v.\ \beta(x, v) * R(x)\ {}^{\mathcal{E}}\!\!\Rrightarrow^{\mathcal{E} \uplus \mathcal{E}'}\ Q(x, v)) \\ \Rightarrow \{P\}\ e\ \{v.\ \exists x.\ Q(x, v)\}_{\mathcal{E} \uplus \mathcal{E}'}\end{array} \tag{8}$$

Leaving aside the generalization of the predicates, the only difference from (7) is that the first view shift is now bidirectional.

***Formal definition.*** We define logically atomic triples in Figure 13. Note that $x$ is free in $\alpha$, $R$, $\beta$ and $Q$, while $v$ is free in $\beta$ and $Q$, and also note that $\mathcal{E}_1 \# \mathcal{E}_2$ denotes disjointness of invariant masks. The definition differs from (8) only in a few technical details.

First of all, we collect the antecedent of the implication (8) into its own syntactic sugar, which we call an *atomic shift*. An atomic triple is, roughly, an implication from an atomic shift to a normal Hoare triple that ties the pre- and postconditions of the triple and the shift together. We give this Hoare triple a fixed mask, $\top$. Since $e$ will generally not be physically atomic, ACSQ cannot be applied, so a smaller mask would be of no use to a client.

The definition mentions three masks: $\mathcal{E}$, $\mathcal{E}_M$, and $\mathcal{E}_R$. What are they? Well, it turns out that rather than talking about the invariants that the client *may* rely on being enabled (that would be $\mathcal{E} \uplus \mathcal{E}'$ in (8)), it is often more convenient to talk about those invariants the client *may not* rely on. (In Figure 13, we write $-\mathcal{E}$ to denote $\top \setminus \mathcal{E}$.)

LAAtomic
$$\frac{e \text{ phys. atomic} \qquad \forall x.\ \{\alpha\}\ e\ \{v.\ \beta\}_{\mathcal{E}_M}}{\langle x.\ \alpha\rangle\ e\ \langle v.\ \beta\rangle^{\mathcal{E}_M}}$$

LAHoare
$$\frac{\langle x.\ \alpha\rangle\ e\ \langle v.\ \beta\rangle^{\mathcal{E}_M}_{\mathcal{E}} \qquad \forall x.\ \mathsf{timeless}(\alpha)}{\forall x.\ \{\alpha\}\ e\ \{v.\ \beta\}_{\top}}$$

LAFrame
$$\frac{\langle x.\ \alpha\rangle\ e\ \langle v.\ \beta\rangle^{\mathcal{E}_M}_{\mathcal{E}} \qquad \mathcal{E}' \# \mathcal{E}_M}{\langle x.\ \alpha * P\rangle\ e\ \langle v.\ \beta * P\rangle^{\mathcal{E}_M}_{\mathcal{E}\uplus\mathcal{E}'}}$$

LAExist
$$\frac{\langle x, y.\ \alpha\rangle\ e\ \langle v.\ \beta\rangle^{\mathcal{E}_M}_{\mathcal{E}}}{\langle x.\ \exists y.\ \alpha\rangle\ e\ \langle v.\ \beta\rangle^{\mathcal{E}_M}_{\mathcal{E}}}$$

LACsq
$$\frac{\forall x.\ \alpha\ {}^{\mathcal{E}\uplus\mathcal{E}'}{\Lleftarrow\!\!\!\Rrightarrow}^{\mathcal{E}}\ \alpha' \qquad \langle x.\ \alpha'\rangle\ e\ \langle v.\ \beta'\rangle^{\mathcal{E}_M}_{\mathcal{E}} \qquad \forall x, v.\ \beta'\ {}^{\mathcal{E}}{\Rrightarrow}^{\mathcal{E}\uplus\mathcal{E}'}\ \beta \qquad \mathcal{E}' \# \mathcal{E}_M}{\langle x.\ \alpha\rangle\ e\ \langle v.\ \beta\rangle^{\mathcal{E}_M}_{\mathcal{E}\uplus\mathcal{E}'}}$$

LAInv
$$\frac{\langle x.\ \triangleright R * \alpha\rangle\ e\ \langle v.\ \triangleright R * \beta\rangle^{\mathcal{E}_M}_{\mathcal{E}} \qquad \iota \notin \mathcal{E}_M}{\boxed{R}^{\iota} \vdash \langle x.\ \alpha\rangle\ e\ \langle v.\ \beta\rangle^{\mathcal{E}_M}_{\mathcal{E}\uplus\{\iota\}}}$$

LASts
$$\frac{\langle x, s.\ s \in \uparrow(\{s_0\}, T) * \triangleright\varphi(s) * \alpha\rangle\ e\ \langle v.\ \exists s', T'.\ (s, T) \rightarrow^* (s', T') * \triangleright\varphi(s') * \beta\rangle^{\mathcal{E}_M}_{\mathcal{E}} \qquad \iota \notin \mathcal{E}_M}{\boxed{\mathsf{STSInv}(\mathcal{S}, \varphi, \gamma)}^{\iota} \vdash \left\langle x.\ \boxed{(s_0, T) : \mathrm{STS}_{\mathcal{S}}}^{\gamma} * \alpha\right\rangle\ e\ \left\langle v.\ \exists s', T'.\ \boxed{(s', T') : \mathrm{STS}_{\mathcal{S}}}^{\gamma} * \beta\right\rangle^{\mathcal{E}_M}_{\mathcal{E}\uplus\{\iota\}}}$$

**Figure 14.** Selected proof rules for logically atomic triples.

$$\text{Context: } \left\langle \begin{array}{l} M.\ P \Lleftarrow\!\!\!\Rrightarrow c \prec M \mid R, \mathcal{E}_R \mid \\ m.\ c \prec M \setminus \{m\} \wedge m \in M \Rrightarrow Q(M, m) \end{array} \right\rangle^{\mathcal{E}_{\mathsf{chan}}}_{\emptyset}$$

$$\{P\}_{\top}$$

(LAHoare)

$$\langle P\rangle_{-\mathcal{E}_{\mathsf{chan}}}$$

(Open $\mathcal{E}_R$)

$$\langle c \prec M * R(M)\rangle_{-\mathcal{E}_{\mathsf{chan}}, \mathcal{E}_R}$$

$$\textbf{let } v = \ \textbf{tryrecv}\ c\ \textbf{in}$$

$$\left\langle \begin{array}{l} (c \prec \emptyset \wedge v = \mathsf{None} \wedge M = \emptyset \vee \\ \exists m.\ c \prec M \setminus \{m\} \wedge m \in M \wedge \\ v = \mathsf{Some}(m)) * R(M) \end{array} \right\rangle_{-\mathcal{E}_{\mathsf{chan}}, \mathcal{E}_R}$$

$$\left\langle \begin{array}{l} P * v = \mathsf{None} \vee \\ \exists M, m.\ Q(M, m) * v = \mathsf{Some}(m) \end{array} \right\rangle_{-\mathcal{E}_{\mathsf{chan}}}$$

$$\{P * v = \mathsf{None} \vee \exists M, m.\ Q(M, m) * v = \mathsf{Some}(m)\}_{\top}$$

$$\textbf{case}\ v\ \textbf{of}\ \mathsf{None} \Rightarrow\ \{P\}_{\top}\ \mathit{recv}\ c\ \{m.\ \exists M.\ Q(M, m)\}_{\top}$$

$$\mid \mathsf{Some}(m) \Rightarrow\ \{\exists M, v.\ Q(M, m)\}_{\top}\ m\ \{m.\ \exists M.\ Q(M, m)\}_{\top}$$

**Figure 15.** Proof outline for recv.

The first two masks describe invariants that the module knows and cares about. We call $\mathcal{E}_M$ the *module mask*: these are the invariants the module wants to be able to open up before calling client view shifts, so it is essential that the client *not* depend on these invariants at all. We call $\mathcal{E}$ the *shared mask*: these are the invariants that both the module and the client may depend on, and that therefore the client may not disable in its atomic shift. Both of these masks show up in logically atomic triples themselves.

The third mask, $\mathcal{E}_R$, we call the *client mask*. This is a set of invariants that the client depends on *and* disables in its atomic shift. The module does not know or care about these invariants, and thus the client can choose $\mathcal{E}_R$ arbitrarily, so long as it is disjoint from the first two masks.

The atomic shift imposes a (somewhat odd) restriction that $P$ must be timeless, the reason for which is as follows. It is necessary, when opening an invariant, to surround it with the $\triangleright$ modality (see InvOpen). But with logically atomic triples, it is often the case that invariants are opened in a nested fashion, *i.e.,* the caller opens an invariant "around" the triple (using LAInv, Figure 14), and the module itself opens another invariant at the linearization point. Ultimately, however, this all happens in an application of ACsq around a single, physical step of the underlying language. So there is just one physical step available to strip off a single $\triangleright$. This issue is solved by making $P$ timeless, which means we can use VSTimeless to deal with the $\triangleright$. In practice, this is not a serious restriction: The assertions we use are typically either timeless (like ghost resources) or pure (like invariant assertions). It is thus possible to move the pure assertions into the context (which means we can make them available anywhere), and to put the (timeless) resources into $P$.

Finally, note that atomic shifts and atomic triples (like view shifts and Hoare triples) are pure facts and can therefore be duplicated.

***Derived rules.*** These definitions support the derived rules given in Figure 14. Most important is the rule of consequence (LACsq), which (like the original ACsq) may be applied to view shifts that change masks. But with LACsq, we can open invariants around expressions like recv that are not physically atomic! In other words, for any expression satisfying a logically atomic specification, we can apply well-established reasoning patterns (*e.g.,* LAInv, LASts) that, in most logics, work only for physically atomic expressions.

LAAtomic shows that any physically atomic triple is also logically atomic. The rule LAExist permits us to bind a variable in the atomic shift. Unlike in the standard existential rule for Hoare triples (cf. our appendix [1]), it would be unsound here to move $y$ all the way out of the triple to a universal quantifier. Finally, LAHoare can be used to convert logically atomic triples to normal ones. This is where the timeless restriction rears its (only slightly ugly) head.

## 7.2 Proof of blocking receive

As an example of working with logically atomic specifications, we are going to derive the already mentioned specification for recv:

$$\forall c.\ \langle M.\ c \prec M\rangle\ \mathsf{recv}\ c\ \langle m.\ c \prec M \setminus \{m\} \wedge m \in M\rangle^{\mathcal{E}_{\mathsf{chan}}} \quad (9)$$

First, we unfold the syntactic sugar for atomic triples. We thus get to assume some $P$, $Q$, $R$, $\mathcal{E}_R$ such that the atomic shift shown at the top of Figure 15 holds.

The most important step of the proof (outlined in Figure 15) is to establish the following triple:

$$\langle P\rangle \quad \textbf{tryrecv}\ c \\ \left\langle \begin{array}{l} v.\ P * v = \mathsf{None} \vee \\ \quad \exists M, m.\ Q(M, m) * v = \mathsf{Some}(m) \end{array} \right\rangle^{\mathcal{E}_{\mathsf{chan}}}_{-\mathcal{E}_{\mathsf{chan}}} \quad (10)$$

Intuitively, **tryrecv** either returns some message and completes the update (yielding $Q$), or it returns None and maintains $P$.

Once we have shown this, we can use LAHoare to obtain a normal Hoare triple, and complete the proof with standard reasoning.

To show (10), we will have to use the atomic shift. It is clear what to do in the precondition: we are going to open the invariants $\mathcal{E}_R$ with the opening view shift, obtaining $c \prec M$. For the postcondition, we are going to use the committing view shift in case **tryrecv** succeeded, and the aborting view shift otherwise. Hence we have to show:

$$\langle \exists M.\, c \prec M * R(M) \rangle \quad \textsf{tryrecv}\ c \quad \left\langle \begin{array}{l} v.\ c \prec \emptyset * R(\emptyset) * v = \mathsf{None} \lor \\ \quad \exists M, m.\ c \prec M \setminus \{m\} \land m \in M * \\ \qquad R(M) * v = \mathsf{Some}(m) \end{array} \right\rangle^{\mathcal{E}_{\mathsf{chan}}}_{-\mathcal{E}_{\mathsf{chan}}, \mathcal{E}_R} \tag{11}$$

Now we can apply LAExist to bind the $M$, followed by LACsq (but without changing masks) to make use of this bound variable in the postcondition.

$$\langle M.\, c \prec M * R(M) \rangle \quad \textsf{tryrecv}\ c \quad \left\langle \begin{array}{l} v.\ \big(c \prec \emptyset \land v = \mathsf{None} \land M = \emptyset \lor \\ \quad \exists m.\ c \prec M \setminus \{m\} \land m \in M \land \\ \qquad v = \mathsf{Some}(m)\big) * R(M) \end{array} \right\rangle^{\mathcal{E}_{\mathsf{chan}}}_{-\mathcal{E}_{\mathsf{chan}}, \mathcal{E}_R} \tag{12}$$

Note that after framing $R(M)$ with LAFrame, this is exactly a logically atomic version of the spec for **tryrecv** given in Figure 11. We are thus just a single application of LAAtomic away from completing the proof. This also shows that our construction only requires a logically atomic spec for **tryrecv**—it does not depend on **tryrecv** being physically atomic.

Together with the triples for **send** and **newch** in Figure 11 and an application of LAAtomic, this completes the proof of the channel specification from Figure 12. With this example, we have illustrated (1) how to prove a logically atomic specification for recv, and (2) how the logically atomic specification of **tryrecv** supports reasoning principles normally reserved for physically atomic expressions.

## 8. Putting logical atomicity to work

Now that we have proven a logically atomic spec for recv, we are in a position to state and prove a logically atomic spec for mutable references, using the well-known encoding [26] in Figure 16.

The idea behind this encoding is to represent a reference as a channel, on which a background "server" process listens for requests. Allocating a reference (ref $e$) involves allocating a fresh channel $r$ (which represents the reference) and forking off a server process (srv $r$ $e$). This server process will listen for messages from client processes that send it Get, Set, and Cas requests on $r$ in order to perform reads and writes on the reference. Each such request includes a freshly generated reply channel $d$, along which the server sends the result of the requested operation.

By analogy with ML-style modules, we wish to show that this encoding is a "functor":[2] If $e_{\mathsf{newch}}$, $e_{\mathsf{send}}$, and $e_{\mathsf{recv}}$ satisfy a logically atomic spec for channels, then ref, !, :=, and cas satisfy such a spec for references.

In Figures 17 and 18, we define predicates $\varphi_{\mathsf{chan}}$ and $\varphi_{\mathsf{ref}}$ to represent the "signatures" of channels and references, in which the specific masks, expressions, and abstract predicates (that a particular implementation would define) are held abstract. The concrete predicate $\prec$ in Figure 12 satisfies these properties: we can implement $\varphi_{\mathsf{chan}}$. Note that we require the abstract predicates to be timeless so they can be used with LAHoare.

In our appendix [1], we verify references as channels by proving

$$\begin{array}{l} \forall \mathcal{E}_{\mathsf{chan}}, \mathcal{E}_{\mathsf{ref}}, e_{\mathsf{newch}}, e_{\mathsf{send}}, e_{\mathsf{recv}}. \\ \quad \varphi_{\mathsf{chan}}(\mathcal{E}_{\mathsf{chan}}, e_{\mathsf{newch}}, e_{\mathsf{send}}, e_{\mathsf{recv}}) \land \\ \quad \mathcal{E}_{\mathsf{chan}} \subseteq \mathcal{E}_{\mathsf{ref}} \land \mathsf{infinite}(\mathcal{E}_{\mathsf{ref}} \setminus \mathcal{E}_{\mathsf{chan}}) \\ \quad \Rrightarrow_{\mathcal{E}_{\mathsf{ref}}} \varphi_{\mathsf{ref}}(\mathcal{E}_{\mathsf{ref}}, \mathsf{ref}, !, :=, \mathsf{cas}) \end{array} \tag{13}$$

[2] To our knowledge, the correctness of this encoding has not been specified and proven in this modular style before. Prior work [38] has shown that an entire language with references can be faithfully translated into $\pi$-calculus.

Let expressions $e_{\mathsf{newch}}$, $e_{\mathsf{send}}$, and $e_{\mathsf{recv}}$ be given. Define

$$\begin{aligned} \mathsf{ref}\ e &\triangleq \textbf{let}\ r = e_{\mathsf{newch}}\ \textbf{in fork}\ \mathsf{srv}\ r\ e; r \\ !e &\triangleq \mathsf{rpc}\ e\ \mathsf{Get} \\ e := e' &\triangleq \mathsf{rpc}\ e\ \mathsf{Set}(e') \\ \mathsf{cas}(e, e_1, e_2) &\triangleq \mathsf{rpc}\ e\ \mathsf{Cas}(e_1, e_2) \end{aligned}$$

where

$$\begin{array}{l} \mathsf{rpc} \triangleq \lambda r.\ \lambda m. \\ \qquad \textbf{let}\ d = e_{\mathsf{newch}}\ \textbf{in} \\ \qquad e_{\mathsf{send}}(r, (d, m)); e_{\mathsf{recv}}\ d \\ \mathsf{srv} \triangleq \lambda r.\ \textbf{rec}\ loop(v). \\ \qquad \textbf{let}\ (d, m) = e_{\mathsf{recv}}\ r\ \textbf{in} \\ \qquad \textbf{let}\ reply = \lambda m'.\ \lambda v'.\ (e_{\mathsf{send}}(d, m'); loop\ v')\ \textbf{in} \\ \qquad \textbf{case}\ m\ \textbf{of} \\ \qquad\quad \mathsf{Get} \Rightarrow reply\ v\ v \\ \qquad\quad \mid \mathsf{Set}(w) \Rightarrow reply\ ()\ w \\ \qquad\quad \mid \mathsf{Cas}(v_1, v_2) \Rightarrow \textbf{let}\ b = (v = v_1)\ \textbf{in} \\ \qquad\qquad\qquad \textbf{let}\ v' = \textbf{if}\ b\ \textbf{then}\ v_2\ \textbf{else}\ v\ \textbf{in} \\ \qquad\qquad\qquad reply\ b\ v' \end{array}$$

**Figure 16.** Implementing references as channels.

Since the reference operations use the channel interface, we require that all invariants needed by the channel operations are available in $\mathcal{E}_{\mathsf{ref}}$. Furthermore, the reference module allocates an invariant in order to enforce a protocol on the ghost state underlying the abstract points-to predicate. Thus there need to be infinitely many invariant names it can use for its own purposes ($\mathcal{E}_{\mathsf{ref}} \setminus \mathcal{E}_{\mathsf{chan}}$) to satisfy NewInv. This is also the reason that (13) is a view shift rather than an implication. Note that we can completely abstract away from how the channel operations treat their invariant names, just as users of $\varphi_{\mathsf{ref}}$ do not have to care about the fact that some of the invariants in $\mathcal{E}_{\mathsf{ref}}$ actually belong to the channel module. This shows that, with some small effort, proper abstraction is possible in Iris despite our use of global invariant masks at view shifts and Hoare triples.

In our proof of (13), the server thread for a reference is the one that actually commits all operations on it by performing logical updates on behalf of client requests. Hence, a client thread must transfer its atomic shift and precondition $P$ to the server, which it does using the invariant of the reference module. (This transfer is made possible by the fact that invariants in Iris are impredicative, as explained at the end of §4.) The server can then apply the client's opening and committing view shift, sending $Q$ back to the client. This is a particularly simple example of *helping* [35, 33], a common phenomenon in fine-grained concurrent algorithms.

To make the proof work out, we had to change the code in Figure 16 slightly: at some places, we introduced **skip** to be able to strip off a $\triangleright$. Since InvOpen adds a $\triangleright$ to the invariant, this means we have to take a physical step if (1) the invariant is opened around the last operation a function is performing and (2) the function's postcondition does not specify a $\triangleright$. The need to insert such **skip**s is a known irritation in the world of step-indexed logics, but it is perfectly sound: adding **skip**s does not affect the observable behavior of a program for the kind of observations we are considering.

As logically atomic triples are compatible with advanced techniques for reasoning with shared state (*e.g.*, LASTs), it is perfectly straightforward to verify clients of the references-as-channels module against the abstract spec $\varphi_{\mathsf{ref}}$. To drive this point home, our appendix [1] includes a verification of elimination stacks [16, 35],

$$\varphi_{\mathsf{chan}}(\mathcal{E}_{\mathsf{chan}}, e_{\mathsf{newch}}, e_{\mathsf{send}}, e_{\mathsf{recv}}) \triangleq \Box\exists(\cdot \prec \cdot) \in \mathsf{Val} \times \mathsf{Bag} \to \mathsf{Prop}.$$
$$\forall c, M.\ \mathsf{timeless}(c \prec M) \land$$
$$\forall c, M, M'.\ c \prec M * c \prec M' \Rightarrow \mathsf{False} \land$$
$$\{\mathsf{True}\}\ e_{\mathsf{newch}}\ \{c.\ c \prec \emptyset\} \land$$
$$\forall c, m.\ \langle M.\ c \prec M\rangle\ e_{\mathsf{send}}(c, m)\ \langle x.\ c \prec M \uplus \{m\} \land x = ()\rangle^{\mathcal{E}_{\mathsf{chan}}}$$
$$\land\ \forall c.\ \langle M.\ c \prec M\rangle\ e_{\mathsf{recv}}\ c\ \langle m.\ c \prec M \setminus \{m\} \land m \in M\rangle^{\mathcal{E}_{\mathsf{chan}}}$$

**Figure 17.** Specification for channels with blocking receive.

$$\varphi_{\mathsf{ref}}(\mathcal{E}_{\mathsf{ref}}, e_{\mathsf{ref}}, e_{\mathsf{get}}, e_{\mathsf{set}}, e_{\mathsf{cas}}) \triangleq \Box\exists(\cdot \mapsto \cdot) \in \mathsf{Val} \times \mathsf{Val} \to \mathsf{Prop}.$$
$$\forall r, v.\ \mathsf{timeless}(r \mapsto v) \land$$
$$\forall r, v, w.\ r \mapsto v * r \mapsto w \Rightarrow \mathsf{False} \land$$
$$\forall v.\ \{\mathsf{True}\}\ e_{\mathsf{ref}}\ v\ \{r.\ r \mapsto v\} \land$$
$$\forall r.\ \langle v.\ r \mapsto v\rangle\ e_{\mathsf{get}}\ r\ \langle x.\ r \mapsto v \land x = v\rangle^{\mathcal{E}_{\mathsf{ref}}} \land$$
$$\forall r, v.\ \langle r \mapsto \_\rangle\ e_{\mathsf{set}}\ r\ v\ \langle x.\ r \mapsto v \land x = ()\rangle^{\mathcal{E}_{\mathsf{ref}}} \land$$
$$\forall r, v_1, v_2.\ \langle v.\ r \mapsto v\rangle\quad e_{\mathsf{cas}}(r, v_1, v_2)\quad \left\langle \begin{matrix} b.\ b = \mathsf{true} \land v = v_1 \land r \mapsto v_2 \lor \\ b = \mathsf{false} \land v \neq v_1 \land r \mapsto v \end{matrix} \right\rangle^{\mathcal{E}_{\mathsf{ref}}}$$

**Figure 18.** Specification for references.

a challenging example from the literature that employs helping in a more complex way than the references-as-channels module does. This verification is parameterized by an arbitrary implementation of references that is assumed to satisfy the logically atomic spec $\varphi_{\mathsf{ref}}$. The code and proof closely follow those in the technical appendix of iCAP [33], the chief difference being that the iCAP proof depends on the reference operations being physically atomic, whereas ours does not. With this, we complete our stack of abstractions (Figure 1).

## 9. Related work

In the introduction, we motivated Iris in relation to the state of the art in modular concurrency verification. Here, we give a few more detailed comparisons with the most closely related work.

***Monoids.*** The centrality of partial commutative monoids dates back to the earliest models of separation logic, but only recently did a number of different models and logics begin to employ PCMs as a way of characterizing more fine-grained notions of interference [22, 9, 24]. The Views framework [9], in particular, enables the user to tie logical resources (represented as a PCM of the user's choice) to physical resources, according to a particular user-defined interpretation of logical resources as assertions about physical ones. In this way, Views, like Iris, supports protocol-based reasoning.

However, Views is limited in that it effectively requires the user to bake in a fixed invariant tying logical to *physical* resources, with no logical support for layering further invariants on top of those logical resources. Iris, in contrast, provides built-in logical support for user-defined invariants over *logical* (ghost) resources; these are crucial, *e.g.,* for enabling the verification of elimination stacks to impose its own invariants over the *logical* points-to assertions exported by the references-as-channels module one layer below. Furthermore, although we have not emphasized it in this paper, Iris invariants can be defined using higher-order, guarded recursive predicates akin to [33] (unlike in Views, which only supported first-order logics).

View shifts were introduced by the Views framework as a specialization of the notion of "repartitioning" from CAP [10]. A repartitioning describes an update of ghost state in terms of an update of the underlying physical state. A view shift in [9] is thus simply a repartitioning that preserves the underlying physical state. CAP uses a two-level approach for reasoning about atomic expressions: one has to prove how the expression updates the physical state and separately prove a repartitioning that relates this back to the abstract level. In Iris, rule ACsq offers more fine-grained control. Instead of going all the way to the concrete physical state, it is possible to open just as many levels of abstraction as are needed to justify the execution of the atomic expression.

Although we believe our monoid encoding of STSs with tokens is novel, most of the monoid constructions we used have been described previously. In particular, Dockins *et al.* [11] treat monoids in an algebraic manner, as separation algebras (SA). They provide various generic building blocks like discrete SAs (equivalent to our exclusive monoid), products and sums, as well as a generalization of fractional monoids they call *shares*. To facilitate the treatment of sums, their monoids can have multiple units. We believe that our restriction to a single unit (and a single zero) can be lifted easily. Unlike SAs, our monoids do not generally have to be cancellative.

***Invariants.*** The idea of relating logical resources with physical resources through invariants is also present in Pilkiewicz and Pottier's work on monotonic state [30], Jensen and Birkedal's work on "fictional separation logic" [20], and Krishnaswami *et al.*'s work on "superficially substructural types" [22]. They are all restricted to a sequential setting. Pilkiewicz and Pottier's type-and-capability system uses "fates"—ghost variables whose values grow monotonically—to reason locally about lower bounds on ghost state. Using invariants, they lift these reasoning principles to monotonic physical state. Invariants and fates are orthogonal, independent principles. Iris supports similar reasoning principles for monotonic state, through an encoding of fates as STSs. Fictional separation logic (FSL) combines monoids with indirect Hoare triples specifying an interpretation map, which serves as invariant. Their approach is based on a syntactic translation into a standard separation logic and it is not clear how this approach extends to a concurrent setting. Superficially substructural types (SST) combines the approach of a type system with the more flexible forms of sharing supported by arbitrary monoids in FSL. As we have shown in §5.2 (rule Auth), we can support reasoning in the style of SST's "sharing rule".

In the concurrent setting, previous work—*e.g.,* on CaReSL [34], iCAP [33], and TaDA [8]—has typically fixed a particular and very useful monoid construction. Iris can be used to encode the patterns of reasoning found in these logics, but with a simpler set of primitive mechanisms and proof rules (whose soundness we have verified in Coq [1]). In addition, on a technical level, Iris is more general and expressive than these earlier logics. Like iCAP but unlike CaReSL and TaDA, Iris supports full higher-order logic and impredicative invariants, which are useful for giving modular specifications of libraries. Going beyond iCAP, Iris supports mask-changing view shifts; these are essential to our ability to encode TaDA-style logically atomic specs, as shown in §7. The notions of logical atomicity developed in TaDA and Iris are closely related, as is evident by the extra binder both had to introduce (the "funny" universal quantifier in TaDA, and the binder in the precondition of Iris's logically atomic triples), as well the similarity of the proof rules. At this point, Iris lacks the "private" pre- and postcondition of TaDA, but they would be easy to add to the syntactic sugar.

Like Iris, Cohen *et al.* [7] strive to provide a minimal basis for concurrent reasoning, but theirs is based on a ghost heap and two-state invariants, whereas ours is based on arbitrary ghost PCMs and one-state invariants. The two approaches are optimizing for different goals. Our logic is substructural and supports more expressive—*e.g.,* higher-order and logically atomic—specifications. Theirs is not, making it better suited to use with automated verification tools like

SMT solvers. However, more work remains to be done to sort out the precise formal relationship between the two orthogonal bases.

***Atomicity.*** Concerning the proving of logically atomic specs, TaDA is currently not able to reason about fine-grained data structures that employ inter-thread cooperation (aka "helping"). In Iris, this is possible thanks to the impredicative invariants (see the example in §8), similar to the approach taken in iCAP, which in turn was inspired by previous work of Jacobs and Piessens [19] on VeriFast. To support impredicativity and thus also helping, our model of Iris is based on a solution to a recursive domain equation. That is avoided in VeriFast, which instead attempts to use a kind of Gödel encoding of predicates. However, according to Jacobs [18], the soundness and the generality of this encoding approach of VeriFast are unclear.

Liang and Feng [25] propose another approach to observable atomicity, based on linearizability. Like CaReSL, they appeal to an extra-logical theorem when verifying clients against modules with observably atomic behavior. However, following ideas from Turon *et al.* [35], their logic also supports *speculative* execution of linearization points, which they use to establish soundness of the reasoning patterns developed by Vafeiadis in his thesis [36].

Further work remains to be done in order to extend Iris with support for such speculative reasoning [2]. (The same goes for iCAP and TaDA as well.) Speculation is important in verifying fine-grained concurrent ADTs in which the ordering of a sequence of linearization points may not be known "in real time" but only after the corresponding operations have completed. Intuitively, speculation is challenging in Iris because, when we verify that a module satisfies a logically atomic spec, we perform updates to the state of the module using view shifts provided by the client, so the client *can* (in theory) observe the linearization points in real time. To address this problem, a natural starting point would be to try to follow the model of speculation in Turon *et al.* [35] and generalize Iris assertions from predicates over resources to predicates over *sets* of resources, but it is not yet clear how this would fit into our general approach to logical atomicity.

## Acknowledgments

This research is supported in part by a Microsoft Research PhD Scholarship, and in part by the ModuRes Sapere Aude Advanced Grant from The Danish Council for Independent Research for the Natural Sciences (FNU). We thank Lisa Kohl for fruitful discussions during her internship at MPI-SWS, and we also thank the anonymous reviewers for extremely helpful and detailed feedback.

## References

[1] Appendix and Coq development. `http://plv.mpi-sws.org/iris`.

[2] M. Abadi and L. Lamport. The existence of refinement mappings. *Theor. Comput. Sci.*, 82(2):253–284, 1991.

[3] A. Ahmed, D. Dreyer, and A. Rossberg. State-dependent representation independence. In *POPL*, 2009.

[4] P. America and J. Rutten. Solving reflexive domain equations in a category of complete metric spaces. *J. Comput. Syst. Sci.*, 39(3):343–375, 1989.

[5] E. A. Ashcroft. Proving assertions about parallel programs. *Journal of Computer and System Sciences*, 10(1):110–135, 1975.

[6] L. Birkedal, B. Reus, J. Schwinghammer, K. Støvring, J. Thamsborg, and H. Yang. Step-indexed Kripke models over recursive worlds. In *POPL*, 2011.

[7] E. Cohen, *et al.* Invariants, modularity, and rights. In *PSI*, 2009.

[8] P. da Rocha Pinto, T. Dinsdale-Young, and P. Gardner. TaDA: A logic for time and data abstraction. In *ECOOP*, 2014.

[9] T. Dinsdale-Young, L. Birkedal, P. Gardner, M. J. Parkinson, and H. Yang. Views: Compositional reasoning for concurrent programs. In *POPL*, 2013.

[10] T. Dinsdale-Young, M. Dodds, P. Gardner, M. Parkinson, and V. Vafeiadis. Concurrent abstract predicates. In *ECOOP*, 2010.

[11] R. Dockins, A. Hobor, and A. W. Appel. A fresh look at separation algebras and share accounting. In *APLAS*, 2009.

[12] X. Feng. Local rely-guarantee reasoning. In *POPL*, 2009.

[13] X. Feng, R. Ferreira, and Z. Shao. On the relationship between concurrent separation logic and assume-guarantee reasoning. In *ESOP*, 2007.

[14] I. Filipović, P. O'Hearn, N. Torp-Smith, and H. Yang. Blaming the client: On data refinement in the presence of pointers. In *FACS*, 2009.

[15] M. Fu, Y. Li, X. Feng, Z. Shao, and Y. Zhang. Reasoning about optimistic concurrency using a program logic for history. In *CONCUR*, 2010.

[16] D. Hendler, N. Shavit, and L. Yerushalmi. A scalable lock-free stack algorithm. In *SPAA*, 2004.

[17] M. P. Herlihy and J. M. Wing. Linearizability: a correctness condition for concurrent objects. *TOPLAS*, 12(3):463–492, 1990.

[18] B. Jacobs. Personal communication, 2014.

[19] B. Jacobs and F. Piessens. Expressive modular fine-grained concurrency specification. In *POPL*, 2011.

[20] J. B. Jensen and L. Birkedal. Fictional separation logic. In *ESOP*, 2012.

[21] C. B. Jones. Tentative steps toward a development method for interfering programs. *TOPLAS*, 5(4):596–619, 1983.

[22] N. R. Krishnaswami, A. Turon, D. Dreyer, and D. Garg. Superficially substructural types. In *ICFP*, 2012.

[23] L. Lamport. How to make a multiprocessor computer that correctly executes multiprocess programs. *IEEE Trans. Comput.*, 28(9):690–691, 1979.

[24] R. Ley-Wild and A. Nanevski. Subjective auxiliary state for coarse-grained concurrency. In *POPL*, 2013.

[25] H. Liang and X. Feng. Modular verification of linearizability with non-fixed linearization points. In *PLDI*, 2013.

[26] R. Milner. *Communicating and Mobile Systems: the $\pi$-Calculus*. Cambridge University Press, 1999.

[27] A. Nanevski, R. Ley-Wild, I. Sergey, and G. A. Delbianco. Communicating state transition systems for fine-grained concurrent resources. In *ESOP*, 2014.

[28] P. O'Hearn. Resources, concurrency, and local reasoning. *TCS*, 375(1):271–307, 2007.

[29] S. Owicki and D. Gries. Verifying properties of parallel programs: An axiomatic approach. *CACM*, 19(5):279–285, 1976.

[30] A. Pilkiewicz and F. Pottier. The essence of monotonic state. In *TLDI*, 2011.

[31] J. C. Reynolds. Separation logic: A logic for shared mutable data structures. In *LICS*, 2002.

[32] F. Sieczkowski, A. Bizjak, Y. Zakowski, and L. Birkedal. Modular reasoning about concurrent higher-order imperative programs: a Coq tutorial. `http://users-cs.au.dk/birke/modures/tutorial/index.html`, 2014.

[33] K. Svendsen and L. Birkedal. Impredicative concurrent abstract predicates. In *ESOP*, 2014.

[34] A. Turon, D. Dreyer, and L. Birkedal. Unifying refinement and Hoare-style reasoning in a logic for higher-order concurrency. In *ICFP*, 2013.

[35] A. Turon, J. Thamsborg, A. Ahmed, L. Birkedal, and D. Dreyer. Logical relations for fine-grained concurrency. In *POPL*, 2013.

[36] V. Vafeiadis. *Modular fine-grained concurrency verification*. PhD thesis, University of Cambridge, 2007.

[37] V. Vafeiadis and M. Parkinson. A marriage of rely/guarantee and separation logic. In *CONCUR*, 2007.

[38] D. Walker. Objects in the pi-calculus. *Inf. Comput.*, 116(2):253–271, 1995.

# Tractable Refinement Checking for Concurrent Objects

Ahmed Bouajjani
LIAFA, Université Paris Diderot
abou@liafa.univ-paris-diderot.fr

Michael Emmi
IMDEA Software Institute
michael.emmi@imdea.org

Constantin Enea Jad Hamza
LIAFA, Université Paris Diderot
{cenea,jhamza}@liafa.univ-paris-diderot.fr

## Abstract

Efficient implementations of concurrent objects such as semaphores, locks, and atomic collections are essential to modern computing. Yet programming such objects is error prone: in minimizing the synchronization overhead between concurrent object invocations, one risks the conformance to reference implementations — or in formal terms, one risks violating *observational refinement*. Testing this refinement even within a single execution is intractable, limiting existing approaches to executions with very few object invocations.

We develop a polynomial-time (per execution) approximation to refinement checking. The approximation is parameterized by an accuracy $k \in \mathbb{N}$ representing the degree to which refinement violations are visible. In principle, more violations are detectable as $k$ increases, and in the limit, all are detectable. Our insight for this approximation arises from foundational properties on the partial orders characterizing the happens-before relations between object invocations: they are *interval orders*, with a well defined measure of complexity, i.e., their *length*. Approximating the happens-before relation with a possibly-weaker interval order of bounded length can be efficiently implemented by maintaining a bounded number of integer counters. In practice, we find that refinement violations can be detected with very small values of $k$, and that our approach scales far beyond existing refinement-checking approaches.

***Categories and Subject Descriptors*** F.3.1 [*Specifying and Verifying and Reasoning about Programs*]: Mechanical verification

***General Terms*** Reliability, Verification

***Keywords*** Concurrency; Refinement; Linearizability

## 1. Introduction

Efficient implementations of concurrent objects such as semaphores, locks, and atomic collections including stacks and queues are vital to modern computer systems. Programming them is however error prone. To minimize synchronization overhead between concurrent object-method invocations, implementors avoid blocking operations like lock acquisition, allowing methods to execute concurrently. However, concurrency risks unintended inter-operation interference, and risks conformance to reference implementations. Conformance is formally captured by *observational refinement*: given two libraries $L_1$ and $L_2$ implementing the methods of some concurrent object, we say $L_1$ *refines* $L_2$ if and only if every computation of every program using $L_1$ would also be possible were $L_2$ used instead.

Verifying observational refinement is intrinsically hard, and generally undecidable [4]. Here we develop a tractable algorithmic approach to detecting refinement violations, in two parts.

The first part, outlined in Section 1.1, establishes a foundational characterization of refinement in terms of sets of so-called *histories*. Histories abstract executions into the happens-before (partial) order between object-method invocations. We show that refinement between libraries is equivalent to a history-set inclusion problem. Consequently, violations correspond to excluded histories.

Since refinement-violation detection for even a single execution is NP-hard [8], the second part, outlined in Section 1.2, develops a novel approximation for refinement checking. We demonstrate that our approach is feasible, leading to scalable refinement-violation-detection algorithms. The insight behind our approximation exploits fundamental properties of the histories arising from shared-memory concurrent executions: they are a special class of partial orders called interval orders. Such orders admit convenient representations leading to efficient automation, and reveal a useful parameter for refining our approximation. In practice we find that even coarse approximations uncover refinement violations, and can be implemented much more efficiently than existing approaches.

### 1.1 Characterizing Observational Refinement

Naturally, automating observational refinement verification is challenging. The most immediate obstacle arises from the quantification over the infinitely-many possible library-client programs: a library $L_1$ refines another library $L_2$ if every observation of every client program using $L_1$ is also admitted using $L_2$. Our first contribution is to provide a *precise* characterization of refinement as a set-inclusion problem, defined independently from libraries' execution contexts, between the partial orders of operations admitted by each library. More precisely, we associate to each execution $e$ a partial order $H(e)$ on its object-method invocations, called a *history*. An operation $o_1$ is considered to happen before an operation $o_2$ in $H(e)$ if $o_1$ completes before $o_2$ is invoked in $e$. We prove that a library $L_1$ refines another $L_2$ if and only if the set $H(L_1)$ of $L_1$'s histories (i.e., associated with $L_1$'s executions) is included in $H(L_2)$.

This characterization is a fundamental result that offers a fresh view for reasoning about refinement. Thus far, the principal approach for checking observational refinement in the literature is based on *linearizability* [11], requiring that operations of every execution of $L_1$ can be permuted into a serial execution of $L_2$ while preserving the return-call order between operations. While linearizability implies observational refinement [6], we demonstrate that the converse does not generally hold. To shed light on the subtle relationship between these concepts, we investigate the link between history inclusion and linearizability. We prove that when $L_2$ is atomic, which is often the case for reference implementations, history inclusion between $L_1$ and $L_2$, and therefore observational refinement, is equivalent to linearizability.



*POPL '15*, January 15–17, 2015, Mumbai, India.

ACM 978-1-4503-3300-9/15/01... $15.00.
http://dx.doi.org/10.1145/2676726.2677002

### 1.2 Approximating Observational Refinement

Besides offering a fresh perspective on observational refinement, our characterization leads to an efficient approximation-based approach for detecting refinement violations, exploiting fundamental properties of library executions and their histories. We consider a *weakening preorder* $\preceq$ on histories as a means for approximation: a history $h_1$ is *weaker* than another history $h_2$, written $h_1 \preceq h_2$, essentially if $h_1$ is obtained from $h_2$ by relaxing order constraints. We show that if a library $L$ admits a history $h$, then $L$ also admits every weaker history $h' \preceq h$. Our approximation principle considers weakenings $A(h) \preceq h$ of histories $h \in H(L_1)$, such that checking $A(h) \in H(L_2)$ is *tractable*. If $A(h) \notin H(L_2)$ then $h \notin H(L_2)$, and thus a violation is found.

The challenge is to design a parameterized approximation $A_k$, for $k \in \mathbb{N}$, such that $A_k(h) \in H(L_2)$ is decidable in *polynomial time* in the size of $h$. The approximation should also be *complete*, in the sense that for any history $h$, there exists $k \in \mathbb{N}$ such that $h \preceq A_k(h)$, ensuring that any violation can be captured with a large enough parameter value. Finally, the approximation should be easy to implement, and catch violations with small parameter values.

Our approximation scheme exploits a fundamental property of shared-memory library executions: their histories are *interval orders*, a special case of partial orders which admit *canonical representations* in which each operation $o$ is mapped to a positive-integer-bounded interval $I(o)$. An operation $o_1$ happens before another operation $o_2$ if and only if the interval $I(o_1)$ ends before $I(o_2)$ begins [9]. Interval orders are equipped with a natural notion of *length*, which corresponds to the smallest integer constant for which an interval mapping exists. Our approximation $A_k$ maps each history $h$ to a weaker history $A_k(h)$ of interval length at most $k$.

Bounded-interval-length orders admit a convenient representation of histories using counting: each interval is represented by a counter whose value reflects the number of operations spanning that interval. Such a representation conveniently opens the door to symbolic manipulation of history sets using arithmetic constraints, which we describe using a simple *operation counting logic (OCL)*. We demonstrate that this logic has a polynomial-time model-checking problem, and is suitable for reasoning about commonly-used concurrent object libraries including atomic collections like stacks and queues. We also demonstrate that OCL formulæ can be systematically constructed for a broad class of concurrent objects.

Moreover, counting-based representations can be efficiently monitored in polynomial-time and space using simple counter increments and decrements at the precise moments when operations begin and end. By maintaining a $k$-interval-length approximation $A_k(H(e))$ of an execution $e$, we effectively reduce our approximate refinement-checking problem to a *safety verification* problem by periodically checking whether $A_k(H(e)) \models \Psi$, where $\Psi$ is an OCL formula characterizing the $k$-interval-length histories of $H(L_2)$.

Empirically, we demonstrate that our approach is effective in both dynamic-checking and static-checking contexts. Used in the dynamic setting, we maintain relatively-low runtime overhead which does not increase in the length of executions. Our approach scales far beyond the existing approaches based on linearizability, in which enumerating linearizations explodes exponentially in the length of executions. Furthermore, our approximation $A_k$ is well-suited for catching refinement violations with small parameter values: violations are most often detected with $k \leq 2$, and almost always with $k \leq 4$. In fact, we even prove that many violations to atomic collection objects including stacks and queues can always be caught with $k \leq 3$. In the static-checking context, our counting-based representation allows us to leverage off-the-shelf SAT/SMT-based symbolic program exploration tools including CSeq [7] (with backend CBMC [13]) and SMACK [24] (with backend Corral [15]) to discover refinement violations.

```
struct node *Top;                    int pop():
                                       struct node *n,*t;
void push(int v):                      do {
  struct node *n,*t;                     *t = Top;
  n = malloc(sizeof( *n));               if (t==NULL) return EMPTY;
  n->data = v;                           n = t->next;
  do {                                 } while (! CAS (&Top, t, n))
    struct node *t = Top;              int result = t->data;
    n->next = t;                       free(t);
  } while (! CAS (&Top, t, n));        return result;


struct node {           void Thread1():      void Thread2():
  int data;               push(1);             int y = pop();
  struct node *next;      int x = pop();       push(2);
}                                              push(3);
                                               int z = pop();
```

**Figure 1.** An implementation of Treiber's stack. The pop operation returns the value EMPTY when the stack is empty.

### 1.3 Summary of Contributions

This work makes the following contributions:

- A characterization of observational refinement as a history-set-inclusion problem (§4), and a proof of equivalence with linearizability for atomic reference implementations (§5).
- An under-approximation for detecting observational refinement violations based on a weakening preorder on histories, exploiting the fact that library histories are interval orders (§6).
- An efficient implementation of our approximation using counters. Specifically, we reduce refinement checking to safety-property checking (§6.2) using symbolic arithmetic representations of bounded-interval-length history sets (§6.1), demonstrate cut-off bounds for atomic-collection objects (§7), and develop an automatic construction of counting representations (§8).
- Experimental validation of our approximation-based approach in both dynamic-checking and static-checking settings (§9).

## 2. Motivating Example

Figure 1 lists a non-blocking Treiber's stack [26] implementation providing `push` and `pop` methods. This implementation stores pushed elements into a singly-linked list rooted at `Top`, and avoids blocking lock acquisitions in favor of non-blocking compare-and-swap (`CAS`) operations in order to maximize parallelism, allowing methods to interleave their internal actions. In one atomic step, the `CAS` operation assigns `Top = n` only if `Top == t`.

Unfortunately this implementation suffers from a subtle concurrency bug, now commonly known as an "ABA" bug [17]. The bug manifests in the two-thread program of Figure 1, via the execution depicted in Figure 2(a). Essentially, Thread 1 wrongfully assumes the absence of interference from other threads on the successful `CAS` operation. Thread 1 is preempted right before executing its `CAS` in the `pop` method; at that moment, its `t` variable points to the first element in the list at address `0xFF` added by `push(1)`, and `n == NULL`. While Thread 2 updates the list with two additional elements, added by `push(2)` and `push(3)`, the `t` variable of Thread 1 still points to the list's first element at address `0xFF`, which was freed by Thread 2's call to `pop`, and reallocated in the call to `push(3)`. When Thread 1 resumes, its `CAS` succeeds, effectively removing two elements from the list instead of one. The final `pop` of Thread 2 thus erroneously returns `EMPTY`. Intuitively, this is a problem because the `EMPTY` value should not have been returned since more elements have been pushed than popped prior to Thread 2's final `pop` operation.

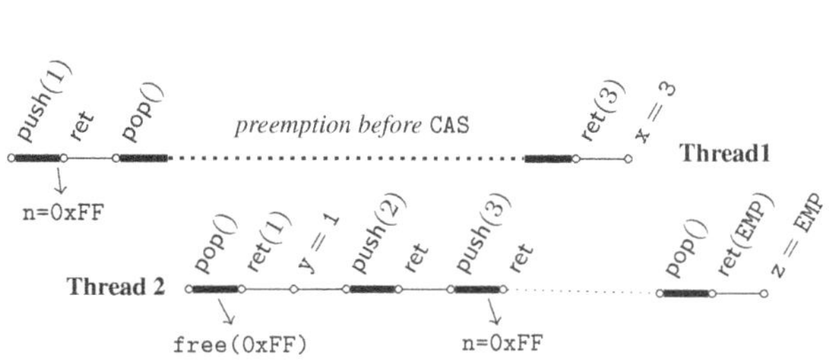


(a) An execution $e$ of the program; it depicts calls, returns, and assignments, and time progresses from left to right.

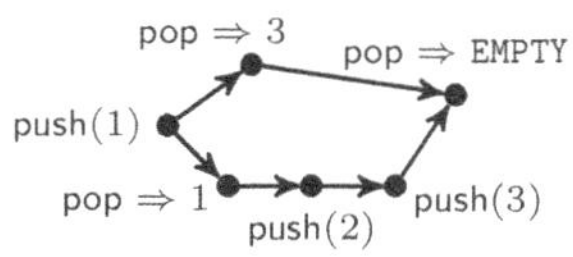


(b) The history $H(e)$ of execution $e$.

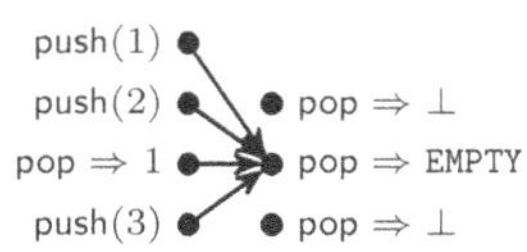


(c) A history weaker than $H(e)$.

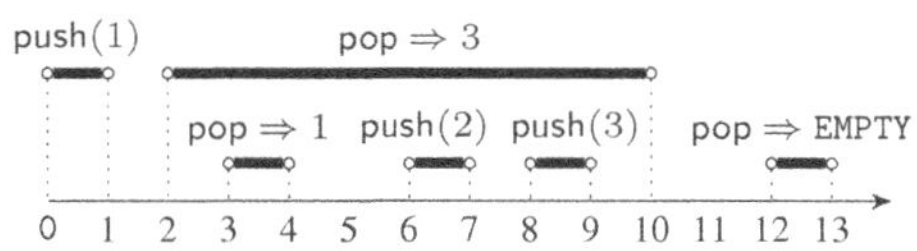


(d) The history $H(e)$ as an interval order.

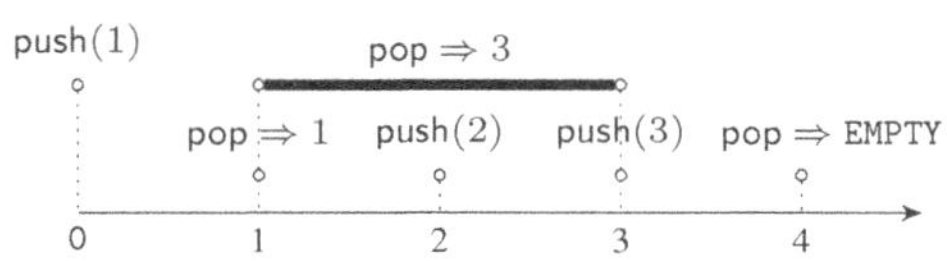


(e) The canonical representation of $H(e)$.

**Figure 2.** An execution and its history.

This bug exposes the fact that our CAS-based implementation does not conform to programmers' expectations of a stack object whose operations execute atomically, e.g., by holding a lock for the duration of each operation. In particular, the assignment `z = EMPTY` should never have occurred.

This idea of conformance is rigorously captured by the formal notion of *observational refinement*. Essentially, an implementation $L_1$ of a concurrent object *refines* another implementation $L_2$ if every observable behavior of a program using $L_1$ is also observable using $L_2$. This property clearly does not hold between the CAS-based implementation of Figure 1 and a correct atomic lock-based implementation, since `y = 1; x = 3; z = EMPTY` is observable using the CAS-based implementation, yet not using the atomic one.

## 3. Observational Refinement

We formalize the criterion of *observational refinement* using a simple yet universal model of computation, namely labeled transition systems (LTS). This model captures shared-memory programs with an arbitrary number of threads, abstracting away the details of any particular programming system irrelevant to our development.

A *labeled transition system* $A = (Q, \Sigma, q_0, \delta)$ over the possibly-infinite alphabet $\Sigma$ is a possibly-infinite set $Q$ of states with initial state $q_0 \in Q$, and a transition relation $\delta \subseteq Q \times \Sigma \times Q$. The $i$th symbol of a sequence $e \in \Sigma^*$ is denoted $e_i$. An *execution* of $A$ is a sequence $e \in \Sigma^*$ such that for some $q_1, q_2, \ldots, q_{|e|} \in Q$, we have $\delta(q_i, e_i, q_{i+1})$ for each $i$ such that $0 \le i < |e|$. The projection $e|\Gamma$ is the maximum subsequence of $e$ over alphabet $\Gamma$. $E(A)$ denotes the set of $A$'s executions, and $E(A)|\Gamma$ their projections over $\Gamma$ (note that $E(A)$ is prefix closed). The *synchronous product* $A_1 \times A_2$ of two LTSs is defined as usual, respecting $E(A_1 \times A_2)|(\Sigma_1 \cap \Sigma_2) = E(A_1)|\Sigma_2 \cap E(A_2)|\Sigma_1$.

### 3.1 Libraries

Programs interact with libraries by calling named library *methods*, which receive *parameter values* and yield *return values* upon completion. We fix arbitrary sets $\mathbb{M}$ and $\mathbb{V}$ of method names and parameter/return values.

**Example 3.1.** *The method and value sets for the stack implementation in Figure 1 are* $\mathbb{M} = \{\mathsf{push}, \mathsf{pop}\}$ *and* $\mathbb{V} = \mathbb{N} \cup \{\mathtt{EMPTY}\}$.

We fix an arbitrary set $\mathbb{O}$ of operation identifiers, and for given sets $\mathbb{M}$ and $\mathbb{V}$ of methods and values, we fix the sets

$$C = \{m(v)_o : m \in \mathbb{M}, v \in \mathbb{V}, o \in \mathbb{O}\}, \text{ and}$$
$$R = \{\mathsf{ret}(v)_o : v \in \mathbb{V}, o \in \mathbb{O}\}$$

of *call actions* and *return actions*; each call action $m(v)_o$ combines a method $m \in \mathbb{M}$ and value $v \in \mathbb{V}$ with an *operation identifier* $o \in \mathbb{O}$. Operation identifiers are used to pair call and return actions. We denote the operation identifier of a call/return action $a$ by $\mathsf{op}(a)$. Call and return actions $c \in C$ and $r \in R$ are *matching*, written $c \mapsto r$, when $\mathsf{op}(c) = \mathsf{op}(r)$. A word $e \in \Sigma^*$ over alphabet $\Sigma$, such that $(C \cup R) \subseteq \Sigma$, is *well formed* when:

- Each return is preceded by a matching call: $e_j \in R$ implies $e_i \mapsto e_j$ for some $i < j$.
- Each operation identifier is used in at most one call/return: $\mathsf{op}(e_i) = \mathsf{op}(e_j)$ and $i < j$ implies $e_i \mapsto e_j$.

We say that the well-formed word $e \in \Sigma^*$ is *sequential* when

- Operations do not overlap: $e_i, e_k \in C$ and $i < k$ implies $e_i \mapsto e_j$ for some $i < j < k$.

Well-formed words represent executions. We assume every set of well-formed words is closed under isomorphic renaming of operation identifiers. For notational convenience, we often associate $\mathbb{O}$ with $\mathbb{N}$, e.g., writing $m(u)_1$ and $\mathsf{ret}(v)_2$ in place of $m(u)_{o_1}$ and $\mathsf{ret}(v)_{o_2}$. An operation $o$ of an execution $e$ is *completed* when both call and return actions $m(u)_o$ and $\mathsf{ret}(v)_o$ of $o$ occur in $e$, and is otherwise *pending*.

**Example 3.2.** *The well-formed words*

$\mathsf{push}(0)_1\ \mathsf{pop}_2\ \mathsf{pop}_3\ \mathsf{ret}_1\ \mathsf{ret}(0)_3\ \mathsf{ret}(0)_2$, *and* $\mathsf{push}(0)_1\ \mathsf{pop}_2\ \mathsf{pop}_3\ \mathsf{ret}_1\ \mathsf{ret}(0)_2$

*represent executions in which one call to the* $\mathsf{push}(0)$ *method overlaps with two calls to* $\mathsf{pop}$. *In the first execution both calls to* $\mathsf{pop}$ *have matching return actions* $\mathsf{ret}(0)$, *i.e., the operations* 2 *and* 3 *are completed, while operation* 3 *is pending in the second, it has no matching return.*

Libraries dictate the execution of methods between their call and return points. Accordingly, a library cannot prevent a method from being called, though it can decide not to return. Furthermore, any library action performed in the interval between call and return points can also be performed should the call have been made earlier, and/or the return made later. Our technical results rely on these properties. A library thus allows any sequence of invocations to its methods made by *some* program.

**Definition 3.1.** *A* library $L$ *is an LTS over alphabet* $C \cup R$ *such that each execution* $e \in E(L)$ *is well formed, and*

- *Call actions* $c \in C$ *cannot be disabled:* $e \cdot e' \in E(L)$ *implies* $e \cdot c \cdot e' \in E(L)$ *if* $e \cdot c \cdot e'$ *is well formed.*
- *Call actions* $c \in C$ *cannot disable other actions:* $e \cdot a \cdot c \cdot e' \in E(L)$ *implies* $e \cdot c \cdot a \cdot e' \in E(L)$.
- *Return actions* $r \in R$ *cannot enable other actions:* $e \cdot r \cdot a \cdot e' \in E(L)$ *implies* $e \cdot a \cdot r \cdot e' \in E(L)$.

We write $e_1 \rightsquigarrow e_2$ when $e_2$ can be derived from $e_1$ by applying zero or more of the above rules. The *closure* of a set $E$ of executions under $\rightsquigarrow$ is denoted $\overline{E}$.

Note that even a library that implements *atomic methods*, e.g., by guarding method bodies with a global-lock acquisition, admits executions in which method calls and returns overlap. A library which accesses the client's thread identifiers can be modeled by taking thread identifiers as method parameters.

**Example 3.3.** *Any library which admits the execution*

$$\mathsf{push}(0)_1\ \mathsf{ret}_1\ \mathsf{pop}_2\ \mathsf{ret}(0)_2$$

*with sequential calls to* push *and* pop *must also admit*

$$\mathsf{push}(0)_1\ \mathsf{pop}_2\ \mathsf{ret}_1\ \mathsf{ret}(0)_2 \text{ and } \mathsf{push}(0)_1\ \mathsf{pop}_2\ \mathsf{pop}_3\ \mathsf{ret}_1\ \mathsf{ret}(0)_2,$$

*among others, yet need not admit an execution*

$$\mathsf{push}(0)_1\ \mathsf{pop}_2\ \mathsf{pop}_3\ \mathsf{ret}_1\ \mathsf{ret}(0)_3\ \mathsf{ret}(0)_2$$

*with two completed* pop *operations returning* 0.

A library $L$ is called *atomic* if it is defined by the closure of some set $E$ of sequential executions, i.e., $E(L) = \overline{E}$. When such a set $E$ exists, it is unique, and we call it *the kernel of* $L$, denoted by ker $L$. Note that ker $L$ contains only completed operations since $e_1 \cdot e_2 \rightsquigarrow e_1 \cdot c \cdot e_2$, for any unmatched call $c$. Atomic libraries are often considered as specifications for concurrent objects.

**Example 3.4.** *The* atomic stack *is the library whose kernel is the set of sequential executions for which the return value of each* pop *operation is either*

- *the argument value* $v$ *to the last unmatched* push *operation, or*
- EMPTY *if there are no unmatched* push *operations.*

*In practice, the atomic stack can be implemented by guarding the methods of a "sequential" stack object by global-lock acquisition.*

### 3.2 Refinement between Libraries

Refinement between libraries is defined with respect to the observable actions of programs which invoke library methods. Complementary to libraries, programs control their execution outside of method call and return points. Accordingly, any program action performed in the interval between call and return points can also be performed should the call have been made later, and/or the return made earlier. A program thus allows any sequence of matching returns generated by *some* implementation of the methods it invokes.

**Definition 3.2.** *A program* $P$ *over actions* $\Sigma$ *is an LTS over alphabet* $(\Sigma \uplus C \uplus R)$ *where each execution* $e \in E(P)$ *is well formed, and*

- *Call actions* $c \in C$ *cannot enable other actions:* $e \cdot c \cdot a \cdot e' \in E(P)$ *implies* $c \mapsto a$ *or* $e \cdot a \cdot c \cdot e' \in E(P)$.
- *Return actions* $r \in R$ *cannot disable other actions:* $e \cdot a \cdot r \cdot e' \in E(P)$ *implies* $a \mapsto r$ *or* $e \cdot r \cdot a \cdot e \in E(P)$.
- *Return actions* $r \in R$ *cannot be disabled:* $e \cdot e' \in E(P)$ *implies* $e \cdot r \cdot e' \in E(L)$ *if* $e \cdot r \cdot e'$ *is well formed.*

**Example 3.5.** *Any program which admits the execution*

$$\mathsf{push}(0)_1\ \mathsf{pop}_2\ \mathsf{ret}(0)_2\ \mathsf{pop}_3\ \mathsf{ret}_1,$$

*with two sequential* pop *calls concurrent with* push, *must also admit*

$$\mathsf{push}(0)_1\ \mathsf{ret}_1\ \mathsf{pop}_2\ \mathsf{ret}(0)_2\ \mathsf{pop}_3 \quad \text{and}$$
$$\mathsf{push}(0)_1\ \mathsf{ret}_1\ \mathsf{pop}_2\ \mathsf{ret}(0)_2\ \mathsf{pop}_3\ \mathsf{ret}(\mathsf{EMPTY})_3,$$

*among others, in which all three calls are sequential and the second* pop *may return (with any value), yet need not admit an execution*

$$\mathsf{push}(0)_1\ \mathsf{ret}_1\ \mathsf{pop}_3\ \mathsf{pop}_2\ \mathsf{ret}(0)_2,$$

*in which the two calls to* pop *are concurrent. The set of executions admitted by a program allows any possible implementation of the methods. While programs cannot force methods to execute concurrently, they can force methods to execute sequentially, e.g., by waiting for one to return before calling the next.*

Refinement between libraries $L_1$ and $L_2$ means that any program execution possible with $L_1$ is also possible with $L_2$.

**Definition 3.3.** *The library* $L_1$ refines $L_2$, *written* $L_1 \leq L_2$, *iff*

$$E(P \times L_1)|\Sigma \subseteq E(P \times L_2)|\Sigma$$

*for all programs* $P$ *over actions* $\Sigma$.

Note that $\leq$ is a preorder over libraries. As library and program alphabets only intersect on call and return actions $C \cup R$, our formalization supposes that programs and libraries communicate only through method calls and returns, and not, e.g., through shared random-access memory.

**Example 3.6.** *The incorrect Treiber's stack implementation of Figure 1 does not refine an atomic lock-based reference implementation, since the execution of Figure 2 is admitted by its composition with the two-thread program of Figure 1.*

## 4. History Inclusion

Though we seek to develop automated techniques to check observational refinement between libraries, the definition of Section 3 does not suggest any practical means; it only suggests enumerating every possible execution of every possible program. In this section we introduce an equivalent notion based on concise abstractions of program executions called *histories*. Besides being independent of programs, this equivalent notion helps expose the structure of the refinement problem, and suggests practical means of automation which we develop in Section 6.

### 4.1 Histories

For given sets $\mathbb{M}$ and $\mathbb{V}$ of methods and values, we fix a set $\mathbb{L} = \mathbb{M} \times \mathbb{V} \times (\mathbb{V} \cup \{\bot\})$ of *operation labels*, and denote the label $\langle m, u, v \rangle$ by $m(u) \Rightarrow v$. A *history* $h = \langle O, <, f \rangle$ is a partial order $<$ on a set $O \subseteq \mathbb{O}$ of operation identifiers labeled by $f : O \to \mathbb{L}$ for which $f(o) = m(u) \Rightarrow \bot$ implies $o$ is maximal in $<$. The *history* $H(e)$ of a well-formed execution $e \in \Sigma^*$ labels each operation with a method-call summary, and orders non-overlapping operations:

- $O = \{\mathsf{op}(e_i) : 0 \leq i < |e| \text{ and } e_i \in C\}$,
- $\mathsf{op}(e_i) < \mathsf{op}(e_j)$ iff $i < j$, $e_i \in R$, and $e_j \in C$.
- $f(o) = \begin{cases} m(u) \Rightarrow v & \text{if } m(u)_o \in e \text{ and } \mathsf{ret}(v)_o \in e \\ m(u) \Rightarrow \bot & \text{if } m(u)_o \in e \text{ and } \mathsf{ret}(\_)_o \notin e \end{cases}$

An operation of $h$ labeled by $\ell \in \mathbb{L}$ is called an $\ell$ *operation*. The histories admitted by $L$ are $H(L) = \{H(e) : e \in E(L)\}$.

**Example 4.1.** *Figure 2(b) depicts the history of the execution in Figure 2(a). Arrows depict the order relation modulo transitivity. Operations* $o_1$ *and* $o_2$ *are ordered in* $h$ *if* $o_1$*'s return precedes* $o_2$*'s call. For example,* push(1) *precedes* pop $\Rightarrow$ 3. *However,* pop $\Rightarrow$ 1 *is incomparable to* pop $\Rightarrow$ 3 *because* pop $\Rightarrow$ 1*'s return comes after* pop $\Rightarrow$ 3*'s call, and* pop $\Rightarrow$ 3*'s return comes after* pop $\Rightarrow$ 1*'s call. The order among operations' call actions is irrelevant, as is the order among their return actions.*

While the general concept of histories allows arbitrary partial orders of operations, any history $H(e)$ arising from an LTS execution $e$ falls into a restricted class called *interval orders*. Intuitively, this is because our execution model assumes that operations share a common notion of global time: the actions in an execution are linearly ordered.

**Definition 4.1.** *An* interval order *is a partial order* $\langle O, < \rangle$ *such that* $o_1 < o_3$ *and* $o_2 < o_4$ *implies* $o_1 < o_4$ *or* $o_2 < o_3$.

**Lemma 4.1.** *The history $H(e) = \langle O, f, <\rangle$ of a well-formed execution e forms an interval order $\langle O, <\rangle$.*

*Proof.* Suppose $o_1 < o_3$ and $o_2 < o_4$ in $H(e)$, and fix $i_1, i_2, i_3, i_4$ such that $e_{i_1}$ and $e_{i_2}$ are the return actions of $o_1$ and $o_2$, and $e_{i_3}$ and $e_{i_4}$ are the call actions of $o_3$ and $o_4$; note that $i_1 < i_3$ and $i_2 < i_4$. Since $<$ linearly orders $\{i_1, i_2, i_3, i_4\}$, either $i_1 < i_4$, in which case $o_1 < o_4$, or $i_4 < i_1$, in which case $i_2 < i_4 < i_1 < i_3$, so $o_2 < o_3$. □

**Example 4.2.** *Figure 2(d) pictures the history in Figure 2(b) as an interval order. Each operation is represented by an integer-bounded interval on the real number line such that $o_1 < o_2$ iff the interval associated to $o_1$ finishes before the interval associated to $o_2$.*

In this work we consider only histories of well-formed executions, i.e., those forming interval orders, without explicit qualification.

This notion of histories gives rise to a natural order relating histories by their operation ordering. Basically, a history $h_1$ is *weaker* than another history $h_2$ if $h_2$ contains all completed operations of $h_1$, and preserves the order between $h_1$'s operations. The pending operations of $h_1$ can be either omitted or completed in $h_2$.

**Definition 4.2.** *Let $h_1 = \langle O_1, <_1, f_1\rangle$ and $h_2 = \langle O_2, <_2, f_2\rangle$. We say $h_1$ is* weaker than *$h_2$, written $h_1 \preceq h_2$, when there exists an injection $g : O_2 \to O_1$ such that*

- *$o \in \text{range}(g)$ when $f_1(o) = m(u) \Rightarrow v$ and $v \neq \bot$,*
- *$g(o_1) <_1 g(o_2)$ implies $o_1 <_2 o_2$ for each $o_1, o_2 \in O_2$,*
- *$f_1(g(o)) \ll f_2(o)$ for each $o \in O_2$.*

*where $(m_1(u_1) \Rightarrow v_1) \ll (m_2(u_2) \Rightarrow v_2)$ iff $m_1 = m_2$, $u_1 = u_2$, and $v_1 \in \{v_2, \bot\}$. We say $h_1$ and $h_2$ are* equivalent *when $h_1 \preceq h_2$ and $h_2 \preceq h_1$.*

**Example 4.3.** *Figure 2(c) pictures a history $h'$ weaker than the history h in Figure 2(b). Note that $h'$ contains two pending* pop$\Rightarrow\bot$ *operations, one of them is completed in h (it corresponds to the* pop $\Rightarrow 3$ *operation) and one of them is omitted in h.*

Throughout this work we do not distinguish between equivalent histories, and we assume every set $H$ of histories is closed under inclusion of equivalent histories, i.e., if $h_1$ and $h_2$ are equivalent and $h_1 \in H$, then $h_2 \in H$ as well.

### 4.2 History Inclusion is Equivalent to Refinement

Our notion of histories has two important properties which makes refinement between libraries equivalent to inclusion between their history sets. The first property is that libraries are closed under the weakening relation $\preceq$. Essentially when $L$ admits the history $H(e)$ of an execution $e$, then it also admits the history $H(e')$ of any $e'$ which is $\rightsquigarrow$-derivable from $e$. Our definitions of $\rightsquigarrow$ and $\preceq$ coincide to imply $H(e') \preceq H(e)$.

**Lemma 4.2.** *If $h_1 \in H(L)$ and $h_2 \preceq h_1$ then $h_2 \in H(L)$.*

A history $h$ is essentially an abstraction of the set $\{e : H(e) = h\}$ of executions which preserve an order between returns preceding calls. The closure properties of Definition 3.1 ensure that a library $L$ admits all executions $e$ with $H(e) \in H(L)$.

**Lemma 4.3.** $E(L) = \{e \in (C \cup R)^* : H(e) \in H(L)\}$.

Lemmas 4.2 and 4.3 ultimately imply the equivalence between refinement and history inclusion. Essentially, any given history $h$ of a library $L_1$ can be captured by a program $P_h$ whose observations witness the ordering among $h$'s operations. However, its observations cannot forbid additional orderings between $h$'s operations (this is due to the closure properties in Definition 3.2). The refinement $L_1 \leq L_2$ implies that $L_2$ also admits those observations, through one or more possibly-stronger histories $h'$. It then follows from Lemma 4.2 that $L_2$ also admits $h \preceq h'$. For the reverse direction, it follows from Lemma 4.3 that history inclusion implies inclusion of executions, and ultimately observations.

**Theorem 1.** $L_1 \leq L_2$ *iff* $H(L_1) \subseteq H(L_2)$.

*Proof.* ($\Rightarrow$) Let $h = \langle O, <, f\rangle \in H(L_1)$; we show $h \in H(L_2)$ by constructing a program $P_h$ over actions $\Sigma$ which only admits executions with histories stronger than $h$:

$$\forall e \in E(P_h).\ |(e|\Sigma)| = n \implies h \preceq H(e),$$

where $n = |\{o \in O : f(o) = m(u) \Rightarrow v \neq \bot\}|$ is the number of completed operations in $h$. Given such a program $P_h$, taking any execution $e_1 \in E(P_h \times L_1)$ with $|(e_1|\Sigma)| = n$, we must also have an execution $e_2 \in E(P_h \times L_2)$ such that $(e_2|\Sigma) = (e_1|\Sigma)$ by definition of $L_1 \leq L_2$. Since $|(e_2|\Sigma)| = n$ and $e_2 \in E(P_h)$, we also know that $h \preceq H(e_2)$, and since $(e_2|C \cup R) \in E(L_2)$, we have $H(e_2) \in H(L_2)$, along with any history weaker than $H(e_2)$ by Lemma 4.2, namely $h$.

We construct $P_h = \langle Q, \Sigma, q_0, \delta\rangle$ over alphabet $\Sigma = C \cup R \cup \{a\}$ whose states $Q : O \to \mathbb{B}^2$ track operations called/completed status. The initial state is $q_0 = \{o \mapsto \langle\bot, \bot\rangle : o \in O\}$. Transitions are given by,

$$
\begin{array}{l}
\text{for each } q \in Q, o \in O, m \in \mathbb{M}, v \in \mathbb{V} \\
\quad \text{if } f(o) = m(v) \Rightarrow \_ \text{ and } q(o') \text{ for all } o' < o \text{ then} \\
\qquad q[o \mapsto \bot, \bot] \xrightarrow{m(v)_o} q[o \mapsto \top, \bot] \\
\quad \text{if } f(o) = m(\_) \Rightarrow v \text{ then} \\
\qquad q[o \mapsto \top, \bot] \xrightarrow{\mathsf{ret}(v)_o} \cdot \xrightarrow{a} q[o \mapsto \top, \top] \\
\quad \text{if } f(o) = m(\_) \Rightarrow \bot \text{ then} \\
\qquad q[o \mapsto \top, \bot] \xrightarrow{\mathsf{ret}(v)_o} q[o \mapsto \top, \top]
\end{array}
$$

It is routine to verify that $P_h$ is a program according to Definition 3.2. Moreover, in any execution $e \in E(P_h)$, the call $m(u)_o$ of any operation $o$ must come after the return $\mathsf{ret}(v)_{o'}$ of each $o' < o$. Furthermore, all completed operations of $h$ are completed in $e$ if and only if $(e|\Sigma) = a^n$. Note that $e$ may contain more completed operations than $h$ (because of the last transition rule) but less pending operations (because the transition rule corresponding to the call of a pending operation may not have been applied in $e$). It follows that $|(e|\Sigma)| = n \implies h \preceq H(e)$.

($\Leftarrow$) Let $P$ be a program over actions $\Sigma$, and $e \in E(P \times L_1)$; we show that $e \in E(P \times L_2)$. Since $(e|C \cup R) \in E(L_1)$, we know $H(e) \in H(L_1)$ by definition of $H(L_1)$, and then $H(e) \in H(L_2)$ by hypothesis. By Lemma 4.3 we deduce $(e|C \cup R) \in E(L_2)$, and thus by definition of LTS composition, $e \in E(P \times L_2)$. □

## 5. Comparison with Linearizability

The linearizability criterion [11] provides an alternative characterization of library conformance which implies observational refinement [6]. In this section we demonstrate that linearizability is generally stricter than observational refinement, yet the two criteria coincide when the reference implementation is atomic.

Linearizability [11] is defined by an execution order: $e_1 \sqsubseteq e_2$ iff there exists a well-formed execution $e_1'$ obtained from $e_1$ by appending return actions, and deleting call actions, such that:

> $e_2$ is a permutation of $e_1'$ that preserves the order between return and call actions, i.e., a given return action occurs before a given call action in $e_1'$ iff the same holds in $e_2$.

For example, the second and the third executions in Example 3.3 are $\sqsubseteq$-smaller than the first (with sequential calls to push and pop).

An execution $e_1$ is *linearizable* w.r.t. a library $L_2$[1] iff there exists a sequential execution $e_2 \in E(L_2)$, with only completed operations, such that $e_1 \sqsubseteq e_2$. A library $L_1$ is *linearizable* w.r.t. $L_2$, written $L_1 \sqsubseteq L_2$, iff each execution $e_1 \in E(L_1)$ is linearizable w.r.t. $L_2$.

Since linearizability compares executions of $L_1$, which may contain pending operations, with executions of $L_2$, in which every operation is completed, observational refinement need not imply linearizability when $L_2$ contains non-terminating methods, i.e., where the calls to these methods are pending in all executions.

**Example 5.1.** *Let L be the library whose kernel contains the single execution $e = m(u)_1\ m'(u)_2\ \mathsf{ret}(v)_1$, in which the call to $m'$ is pending. Although L refines itself, since refinement is reflexive, L is not linearizable w.r.t. itself, since e could only be linearizable w.r.t. L if $E(L)$ were to contain one of the following executions:*

$$m(u)_1\ \mathsf{ret}(v)_1 \quad m(u)_1\ m'(u)_2\ \mathsf{ret}(v)_1\ \mathsf{ret}(\_)_2$$

$$m(u)_1\ \mathsf{ret}(v)_1\ m'(u)_2\ \mathsf{ret}(\_)_2 \quad m'(u)_2\ \mathsf{ret}(\_)_2 m(u)_1\ \mathsf{ret}(v)_1.$$

*Yet $E(L) = \overline{\{e\}}$ clearly contains none of them.*

A typical correctness criterion for concurrent objects is linearizability with respect to atomic versions of themselves. Despite the negative general result of Example 5.1, when restricted to atomic libraries, linearizability and history inclusion, and thus observational refinement, coincide. This relationship essentially follows from the relationship between the order relations $\sqsubseteq$ and $\preceq$.

**Lemma 5.1.** $e_1 \sqsubseteq e_2$ *iff* $H(e_1) \preceq H(e_2)$.

*Proof.* By definition $e_1 \sqsubseteq e_2$ means that there exists $e_1'$ such that $e_2$ is a permutation of $e_1'$ preserving the order between return and call actions, thus $e_2 \leadsto e_1'$, and thus $H(e_1') \preceq H(e_2)$. Furthermore, since $e_1'$ is obtained from $e_1$ by appending returns and deleting calls, $H(e_1) \preceq H(e_1')$. By transitivity, $H(e_1) \preceq H(e_2)$. The other direction is equally straightforward. □

**Theorem 2.** $L_1 \sqsubseteq L_2$ *iff* $H(L_1) \subseteq H(L_2)$, *if* $L_2$ *is atomic.*

*Proof.* ($\Rightarrow$) Let $h \in H(L_1)$. By hypothesis, any execution $e_1$ with $H(e_1) = h$ is linearizable w.r.t. $L_2$, i.e., there exists an execution $e_2 \in L_2$ with only completed operations such that $e_1 \sqsubseteq e_2$. By Lemma 5.1, this implies $H(e_1) \preceq H(e_2)$. By the closure property in Lemma 4.2, if $H(e_2) \in H(L_2)$ then $h = H(e_1) \in H(L_2)$.

($\Leftarrow$) Let $e_1$ be an execution of $L_1$. By hypothesis, $H(e_1) \in H(L_2)$, which by Lemma 4.3, implies $e_1 \in E(L_2)$. Since $L_2$ is an atomic library, there exists a sequential execution $e_2 \in \ker E(L_2)$ with only completed operations such that $e_1 \sqsubseteq e_2$. Thus, $e_1$ is linearizable w.r.t. $L_2$. □

## 6. Approximating History Inclusion

By the equivalences of Section 5, checking whether a given history $H(e)$ is included in a set $H(L)$ of library histories is equivalent to checking whether $H(e)$ is linearizable with respect to $L$, for a atomic library $L$. It follows that deciding $H(e) \in H(L)$ is NP-hard for an arbitrary library $L$, since it is NP-hard for the atomic register object [8]. Generally speaking, the only known algorithms to decide $H(e) \in H(L)$ must check whether each possible linearization of the partially-ordered history $H(e)$ is equivalent to some sequential execution of operations according to $L$, backtracking to try alternate linearizations on each failed attempt. Recent work implies that the more general problem of checking whether *all histories* $H(L_1)$ of a given library $L_1$ are included in the set of histories $H(L_2)$ of a fixed library $L_2$ is undecidable, since it is equivalent to checking whether $L_1$ is linearizable w.r.t. $L_2$ when $L_2$ is atomic [4].

[1] The original definition of Herlihy and Wing [11] assumes that $L_2$ is a set of sequential executions. Here we consider a slight extension adapted to concurrent executions, faithful to the original intention, where $\ker L_2$ may be a set of sequential executions.

These complexity obstacles suggest investigating approximations to the history inclusion problems — i.e., both $h \in H(L)$ and its more general variation $H(L_1) \subseteq H(L_2)$ — in order to devise tractable algorithms.

In this work, we focus on parameterized *under approximations* for detecting violations to observational refinement, achieving increasing accuracy with decreasing efficiency. For this, we design a notion of parameterized history-weakening approximation functions $A_k$ which map any history $h$ to a weaker history $A_k(h) \preceq h$, and which have the following properties:

**Strength-increasing:** $A_0(h) \preceq A_1(h) \preceq \ldots \preceq A_k(h) \preceq h$.

**Completeness:** there exists $k \in \mathbb{N}$ such that $h \preceq A_k(h)$.

**Tractable inclusion:** $A_k(h) \in H(L)$ is decidable in polynomial time when $k$ is fixed.

This weakening-based approximation is convenient since whenever $A_k(h)$ is not included in $H(L)$, then neither is $h$, since $H(L)$ is closed under weakening; if $h$ were to belong to $H(L)$, then any weakening, and in particular $A_k(h)$, would also belong to $H(L)$. While completeness means that increasing $k$ increases the ability to detect observational refinement violations, this must incur a decrease in efficiency since the inclusion problem $A_k(h) \in H(L)$ is NP-hard when $k$ is not fixed. By design, the approximation function $A_k$ allows us to solve the approximate history inclusion problem $A_k(h) \in H(L)$ in polynomial time for fixed $k$. For the more general problem of refinement between libraries $L_1$ and $L_2$, our approximation asks whether $A_k(h) \in H(L_1) \setminus H(L_2)$, and becomes decidable for fixed $k$, so long as the set $\{A_k(h) : h \in H(L_1)\}$ is computable. Completeness of $A_k$ ensures overall completeness, i.e., that for any $h \in H(L_1) \setminus H(L_2)$ there is some $k \in \mathbb{N}$ such that $A_k(h) \in H(L_1) \setminus H(L_2)$.

Our key challenge is to develop approximation functions $A_k$ for which history inclusion can be computed in polynomial time for fixed $k$, and for which observational refinement violations surface with small $k$. We demonstrate the latter in Section 7–9.

In this section we develop a schema of approximation functions for which the approximate history inclusion problem is polynomial-time computable. Our development exploits structural aspects of the history inclusion problem; in particular, we exploit the fact that histories are *interval orders*, with a natural measure of complexity, i.e., the interval order *length* [9]. Leveraging this notion of length, we abstract each history $h$ to a weaker history $A_k(h)$ whose length is bounded by $k$, and represent the set $H(L)$ of histories, restricted to interval length $k$, by a formula against which $A_k(h)$ can be evaluated in polynomial time (§6.1). Finally, we exhibit a program monitoring scheme which can be used to decide our approximate observational refinement problem $\exists h.\ A_k(h) \in H(L_1) \setminus H(L_2)$, or as a general-purpose runtime-execution monitor (§6.2).

### 6.1 Bounded-Interval-Length History Inclusion

The *past* of an element $o \in O$ of a poset $\langle O, < \rangle$ is the set

$$\mathrm{past}(o) = \{o' \in O : o' < o\}$$

of elements ordered before $o$.

**Example 6.1.** *In the history h from Figure 2(b), the* $\mathsf{pop} \Rightarrow 3$ *and* $\mathsf{pop} \Rightarrow 1$ *operations have the same past, namely the operation* $\mathsf{push}(1)$, *while the past of the* $\mathsf{push}(3)$ *operation consists of the* $\mathsf{push}(1)$, $\mathsf{pop} \Rightarrow 1$, *and* $\mathsf{push}(2)$ *operations.*

This notion of operations' pasts induces a linear notion of time into execution histories due to the following fact.

**Lemma 6.1** (Rabinovitch [23]). *The set* $\{\text{past}(o) : o \in O\}$ *of pasts of an interval order* $\langle O, < \rangle$ *is linearly ordered by set inclusion.*

Furthermore, this linear notion of time has an associated notion of *length*, which corresponds to the length of the linear order on operation's pasts.

**Definition 6.1** (Greenough [9]). *The* length *of an interval order* $\langle O, < \rangle$ *is one less than the number of its distinct pasts.*

We denote the length of the interval order $\langle O, < \rangle$ underlying a history $h = \langle O, f, < \rangle$ as $\text{len}\, h$.

Our history-weakening approximation functions $A_k$ map histories to weaker histories whose corresponding interval orders have length at most $k$. While there are various ways to define such a function $A_k$, any such function enables the polynomial-time inclusion check $A_k(h) \in H(L)$ which we demonstrate in the following; Section 6.2 describes a polynomial-time computable instantiation of $A_k$ which we have found useful in practice.

Interval orders have canonical representations which associate to operations integer-bounded intervals on the real number line; their canonical representations minimize the interval bounds to the interval-order length.

**Lemma 6.2** (Greenough [9]). *An interval order* $\langle O, < \rangle$ *of length* $n \in \mathbb{N}$ *has a canonical representation* $I : O \to [n]^2$ *mapping each* $o \in O$ *to the interval* $I(o) = [i, j] \subseteq [0, n]$, *with*

$$i = |\{\text{past}(o') : o' < o\}| \text{ and } j = |\{\text{past}(o') : \neg o < o'\}| - 1$$

*such that* $o_1 < o_2$ *iff* $\sup I(o_1) < \inf I(o_2)$.

The canonical representation thus associates the interval $[i, j]$ to an operation $o$ which succeeds the $i$th past, and precedes the $(j+1)$st past. Note that the interval of an operation can be determined in polynomial time by counting the distinct pasts among operations.

**Example 6.2.** *Figure 2(e) pictures the canonical representation of the history in Figure 2(b). Note that* $\text{len}\, H(e) = 4$.

We define the *counting representation* $\Pi(h)$ of a history $h = \langle O, f, < \rangle$, whose underlying interval order $\langle O, < \rangle$ has the canonical representation $I : O \to [n]^2$, as the multiset

$$\Pi(h) = \{\{\langle f(o), I(o) \rangle : o \in O\}\}$$

of label-and-interval pairs; defining $\Pi(L) = \{\Pi(h) : h \in H(L)\}$ yields a criterion equivalent to history inclusion based on counting representations (which follows from Lemmas 4.1 and 6.2).

**Lemma 6.3.** $H(e) \in H(L)$ *iff* $\Pi(H(e)) \in \Pi(L)$.

**Example 6.3.** *The counting representation of the history* $h$ *in Figure 2(b) is the multiset*

$$\{\{\langle \mathsf{push}(1), [0,0] \rangle, \langle \mathsf{pop} \Rightarrow 1, [1,1] \rangle, \langle \mathsf{pop} \Rightarrow 3, [1,3] \rangle, \langle \mathsf{push}(2), [2,2] \rangle, \langle \mathsf{push}(3), [3,3] \rangle, \langle \mathsf{pop} \Rightarrow \mathtt{Empty}, [4,4] \rangle\}\}.$$

This counting representation leads to an effective logical characterization of history sets using arithmetic operations, inequalities, and a counting function $\#$. Formally, *operation counting logic* is the first-order logic whose syntax is listed in Figure 3. The $\#$ function is interpreted over a history $h = \langle O, f, < \rangle$ as

$$[\![\#(\ell, i, j)]\!]_h = |\{o \in O : f(o) = \ell \text{ and } I(o) = [i, j]\}|$$

where $I$ is the canonical representation of $\langle O, < \rangle$.

We allow predicates $P$ of arbitrary arity over operation labels, so long as they are evaluated in polynomial time. Furthermore, operation-label variables are quantified only over the operation labels which occur in the history over which a formula is evaluated. The satisfaction relation $\models$ for quantified formulæ is defined by:

$$h \models \exists x.\, F \quad \text{iff} \quad \exists o \in O.\, h \models F[x \leftarrow f(o)].$$

$i, j \in \mathbb{N}$ integer constants
$\ell \in \mathbb{L}$ operation-label constants
$x : \mathbb{L}$ operation-label variables
$X ::= \ell \mid x$
$T ::= i \mid \#(X, i, j) \mid T + T$
$F ::= T \leq T \mid P(X, \dots, X) \mid \neg F \mid F \wedge F \mid \exists x.\, F$

**Figure 3.** The syntax of Operation Counting Logic.

where $h = \langle O, f, < \rangle$. The *quantifier count* of an operation counting formula $\Psi$ is the number of quantified variables in $\Psi$. An operation counting formula $\Psi$ *represents a library* $L$ *up to* $k$ when $h \in H(L)$ iff $h \models \Psi$ for every history $h$ of length at most $k$.

**Lemma 6.4.** *Checking if a history* $h$ *satisfies an operation counting formula* $\Psi$ *of fixed quantifier count is decidable in polynomial time.*

*Proof.* This follows from the facts that: (1) the canonical representation of $h$ is polynomial-time computable (see Lemma 6.2), (2) functions and predicates are polynomial-time computable, and (3) quantifiers are only instantiated over labels occurring in $h$. The latter implies that quantifiers can be replaced by a disjunction over the labels occurring in $h = \langle O, f, < \rangle$:

$$h \models \exists x.\, F \quad \text{iff} \quad h \models \bigvee_{o \in O} F[x \leftarrow f(o)]. \qquad \square$$

## 6.2 Monitoring Bounded-Interval-Length Histories

Though there are numerous ways to define a function $A_k$ which approximates histories to weaker $k$-interval-length histories, the natural solution we consider here is an $A_k$ which maintains the last $k$ interval bounds precisely, abstracting all previous interval bounds with equality. Formally, given a history $h = \langle O, <, f \rangle$ such that $\text{len}\, h = n$, and $k \in \mathbb{N}$, we define $A_k(h) = \langle O, <', f \rangle$ by

$$o_1 <' o_2 \text{ iff } o_1 < o_2 \text{ and } n - k < \inf I(o_2)$$

where $I$ is the interval map of $h$. Intuitively, $A_k$ remembers only the ordering between "recent" operations which have started after interval $n - k$. It follows by definition that $A_k(h) \preceq h$, since ordering constraints are only removed from $<$. Note that $A_k(h) = h$ if $\text{len}\, h \leq k$.

**Lemma 6.5.** *Let* $I$ *and* $I_k$ *be the interval maps of* $h$ *and* $A_k(h)$. *For each* $o \in O$ *with* $I(o) = [i, j]$:

$$I_k(o) = [\max(i - n + k, 0), \max(j - n + k, 0)].$$

We reduce the online maintenance of $k$-interval-length histories to the maintenance of integer counters. As the first step in establishing the link between history and counter maintenance, we define the $\oplus$ operator: For a given history $h = \langle O, f, < \rangle$ let

$$h \oplus m(u)_o = \langle O \cup \{o\}, f[o \mapsto m(u) \Rightarrow \bot], <' \rangle$$
$$h \oplus \mathsf{ret}(v)_o = \langle O, f[o \mapsto m(u) \Rightarrow v], < \rangle \text{ s.t. } f(o) = m(u) \Rightarrow \bot$$

where $<'$ is the transitive closure of $< \cup \{\langle o', o \rangle : f(o') = \_(\_) \Rightarrow v \neq \bot\}$ relating all completed operations to $o$. As the following lemma shows, the $\oplus$ operator allows us to manipulate our $k$-approximations $A_k(H(e))$ directly, without having to maintain the precise history $H(e)$ of an execution $e$. Note that besides maintaining $A_k(H(e))$, this formulation requires us to compute $A_{k-1}(H(e))$ periodically as well.

**Lemma 6.6.** *Let* $e' = e \cdot m(u)_o$.

- $A_k(H(e')) = A_k(H(e)) \oplus m(u)_o$ *if* $\text{len}\, H(e') = \text{len}\, H(e)$.

**Data**: Interval length $k \in \mathbb{N}$
**Data**: Stream $e \in (C \cup R)^\omega$ of call/return actions
**Result**: counting representation $\Pi(A_k(H(e)))$
**initially** $n = 0$, $s = \emptyset$, $\pi = \emptyset$
**switch** *input action* **do**
  **if** *call action* $m(u)_o$ **then**
    **if** *previous action was return* **then**
      **incr** $n$
      **if** $n > k$ **then** $\pi \leftarrow \overleftarrow{\pi}$
    **end**
    $s(o) \leftarrow n$
    **incr** $\pi(m(u) \Rightarrow \bot, [\min(n,k), k])$
  **end**
  **case** *return action* $\mathsf{ret}(v)_o$
    $i = s(o) - \max(n-k, 0)$
    **decr** $\pi(m(u) \Rightarrow \bot, [i,k])$
    **incr** $\pi(m(u) \Rightarrow v, [i, \min(n,k)])$
  **end**
**endsw**
**yield** $\pi$

**Algorithm 1:** An online operation algorithm for computing the approximation $\Pi(A_k(H(e)))$ of a given history $H(e)$.

- $A_k(H(e')) = A_{k-1}(H(e)) \oplus m(u)_o$ *if* $\operatorname{len} H(e') > \operatorname{len} H(e)$.

*Additionally,*

- $A_k(H(e \cdot \mathsf{ret}(v)_o)) = A_k(H(e)) \oplus \mathsf{ret}(v)_o$.

The second step in establishing the link between history and counter maintenance is given by the following lemma, which implies that history extension, i.e., execution step, corresponds to either a single counter increment, or a single decrement and a single increment.

**Lemma 6.7.** *Let* $\operatorname{len} h' = k$. *If* $h' = h \oplus m(u)_o$ *then*

- $\Pi(h') = \Pi(h) \cup \{\langle m(u) \Rightarrow \bot, [k,k] \rangle\}$.

*If* $h' = h \oplus \mathsf{ret}(v)_O$ *then*

- $\Pi(h') = \Pi(h) \cup \{\langle m(u) \Rightarrow v, [i,k] \rangle\} \setminus \{\langle m(u) \Rightarrow \bot, [i,k] \rangle\}$,

*where* $I$ *is the interval map of* $h'$ *and* $I(o) = [i,k]$.

As noted before Lemma 6.6, besides incrementing/decrementing counters as operations begin and complete, we must occasionally compute $A_{k-1}(H(e))$ as well, thus merging the least-recent interval bounds, in order to maintain a bounded-length history approximation. We achieve this with an interval shifting operation $\overleftarrow{\pi}$ applied to a counting representation $\pi$. Formally, for all $\ell \in \mathbb{L}$, and $0 \le i \le j \le k$, if $\ell$ is completed then

$$\begin{aligned} \overleftarrow{\pi}(\ell, [i,j]) = {} & \eta(\pi(\ell, [i+1, j+1]), i < k \wedge j < k) \\ & + \eta(\pi(\ell, [i, j+1]), i = 0 \wedge j < k) \\ & + \eta(\pi(\ell, [i,j]), i = 0 \wedge j = 0), \end{aligned}$$

and if $\ell$ is pending then

$$\overleftarrow{\pi}(\ell, [i,j]) = \eta(\pi(\ell, [i+1, k]), i < k) + \eta(\pi(\ell, [i,k]), i = 0),$$

where the conditional function $\eta : \mathbb{N} \times \mathbb{B} \to \mathbb{N}$ is defined by

$$\eta(n, \varphi) = \begin{cases} n & \text{if } \varphi \text{ is valid} \\ 0 & \text{otherwise.} \end{cases}$$

The following lemma establishes the intended effect of $\overleftarrow{\pi}$.

**Lemma 6.8.** *If* $\operatorname{len} h = k$ *and* $\pi = \Pi(h)$, *then* $\overleftarrow{\pi} = \Pi(A_{k-1}(h))$.

Algorithm 1 computes the counting representation of a given history incrementally, according to the increment/decrement and shift operations of Lemmas 6.7 and 6.8. The variable $n$ maintains the interval length of the execution history $H(e)$, while the variable $s$ maintains the infimum $s(o)$ of the interval of each operation $o$ in $H(e)$; $s(o)$ can be discarded once $o$ completes. The corresponding infimum in $A_k(H(e))$ when $o$ is invoked is given by $\min(n,k)$, as the interval bounds used in $A_k(H(e))$ may not exceed $k$. When $o$ completes, it is possible that some number of shift operations have translated its interval in $A_k(H(e))$. As the number of performed shift operations is equal to $\min(n-k, 0)$, $o$'s infimum in $A_k(H(e))$ when completing is given by $s(o) - \min(n-k, 0)$. It follows by Lemmas 6.7 and 6.8 that Algorithm 1 computes $A_k(H(e))$.

**Theorem 3.** *Algorithm 1 computes the history approximation* $\Pi(A_k(H(e)))$ *of an execution* $e$ *in* $O(|\mathbb{L}| \cdot k^2 + \operatorname{width}(e))$ *space*[2] *and* $O(|e|)$ *time, where* $\operatorname{width}(e)$ *is the maximum number of concurrent operations in* $e$.

In the worst case $\operatorname{width}(e) = |e|$. In practice however one expects the number of threads, and thus concurrent operations, to be bounded, nullifying the effect of $|e|$ on asymptotic space complexity.

**Corollary 1.** *The approximate inclusion problem* $A_k(h) \in H(L)$ *is decidable in polynomial time, for fixed* $k$, *given an operation counting formula* $\Psi$ *for* $L$ *up to* $k$, *of fixed quantifier count.*

As an online monitor program $P_k$ for history approximation, Algorithm 1 effectively reduces the approximate refinement checking problem between $L_1$ and $L_2$ to a safety verification problem on the composition $P_k \times L_1$: as $P_k$ tracks the counting representation $\pi = \Pi(A_k(H(e)))$ of the current execution $e$'s approximation, we must only verify whether $\pi$ satisfies the operation-counting formula $\Psi$ for $L_2$ up to $k$.

**Corollary 2.** *Given* $\Psi$ *an operation counting formula for* $L_2$ *up to* $k$, *the approximate inclusion* $\exists h.\ A_k(h) \in H(L_1) \setminus H(L_2)$ *is equivalent to the safety verification problem*

$$(P_k \times L_1) \models \Box\Psi$$

*where* $\Psi$ *is interpreted over* $P_k$*'s counting representation.*

## 7. Atomic Collections

Atomic collection objects including stacks and queues are among the most heavily investigated concurrent objects [19]. We demonstrate that our approximation is effective in uncovering refinement violations for these objects, in the sense that most violations can be uncovered with coarse approximations, i.e., $k \le 3$, depending on the data structure. We achieve this by exhibiting families of operation counting formulæ characterizing these structures with "cutoff" (or "small-model") properties: informally, if $n \in \mathbb{N}$ is a cutoff for $\Psi$, then for any history $h$ violating $\Psi$, there exists a weaker history $h' \preceq h$ violating $\Psi$ with $\operatorname{len} h' \le n$. While this $h'$ may not correspond directly to $A_k(h)$, for $k \le n$, we can deduce there exists some $h'$ whose $k$-approximation $A_k(h')$ violates $\Psi$.

Our results build off of previous characterizations of concurrent data structures [1, 10] into a small set of constituent properties. For ease of presentation, in the following we consider only completed histories, i.e., in which no operation is pending. This restriction comes without loss of generality for library implementations which ensure that each operation can complete when uninterrupted by others [10]. In any case, our formulæ can be extended to handle pending operations as well.

[2] The space complexity of Algorithm 1 is constant in the number of operations when the size of integers is fixed, as in the case of modern computer architectures; otherwise, the space complexity is logarithmic in the number of operations, i.e., in execution length.

$$\mathsf{total}(x,i,j) = \sum_{i \le i' \le j' \le j} \#(x,i',j')$$

$$\mathsf{before}_k(x,y) = \bigvee_{0 \le i < k} \left( \begin{array}{l} \mathsf{total}(x,0,i) > 0 \wedge \\ \mathsf{total}(y,0,i) = 0 \wedge \mathsf{total}(x,i{+}1,k) = 0 \end{array} \right)$$

$$\mathsf{match}(x,y) = \mathsf{Push}(x) \wedge \mathsf{Pop}(y) \wedge \mathsf{SameVal}(x,y)$$

$$\Psi_{\mathrm{rv}} = \exists x,y.\ \mathsf{match}(x,y) \wedge \mathsf{before}_k(y,x)$$

$$\Psi_{\mathrm{ev}} = \exists x,y,z.\ \mathsf{match}(x,z) \wedge \mathsf{EmptyVal}(y) \wedge \mathsf{before}_k(x,y) \wedge \mathsf{before}_k(y,z)$$

$$\Psi_{\mathrm{fv}} = \exists x_1,x_2,y_1,y_2.\ \mathsf{match}(x_1,y_1) \wedge \mathsf{match}(x_2,y_2) \wedge \mathsf{before}_k(x_1,x_2) \wedge \mathsf{before}_k(y_2,y_1)$$

$$\Psi_{\mathrm{lv}} = \exists x_1,x_2,y_1,y_2.\ \mathsf{match}(x_1,y_1) \wedge \mathsf{match}(x_2,y_2) \wedge \mathsf{before}_k(x_1,x_2) \wedge \mathsf{before}_k(y_1,y_2) \wedge \mathsf{before}_k(x_2,y_1)$$

**Figure 4.** Four families of operation-counting formulæ characterizing atomic data structure violations, parameterized by the interval length $k \in \mathbb{N}$. The predicates $\mathsf{Push}(x)$, $\mathsf{Pop}(x)$, $\mathsf{EmptyVal}(x)$ hold when $x$ is the label of a push, pop, or empty-pop operation, respectively, and $\mathsf{SameVal}(x,y)$ holds when $x$ and $y$ are labels with the same value, either in the argument or return position. All formulæ are of size polynomial in $k$, and have fixed quantifier counts.

### 7.1 Small-Model Formulæ for Stacks and Queues

A *formula family* $\Psi$ is an indexed set $\{\Psi_i : i \in \mathbb{N}\}$. We say a history $h$ *satisfies* $\Psi$, written $h \models \Psi$, when $h \models \Psi_i$ for $i = \operatorname{len} h$. We say that a family $\Psi$ has a *cutoff* $n \in \mathbb{N}$ when for each history $h \models \Psi$ there exists some $h' \preceq h$ such that $A_n(h') \models \Psi$. Figure 4 defines four families of operation-counting formulæ:

- $\Psi_{\mathrm{rv}}$ characterizes *remove violations* in which a pop operation returns a value for which there is no corresponding push.
- $\Psi_{\mathrm{ev}}$ characterizes *empty violations* in which some pop operation returns EMPTY, yet whose span is covered by the presence of some pushed element which has not (yet) been popped.
- $\Psi_{\mathrm{fv}}$ characterizes *FIFO violations* in which some pair of pops occur in the *opposite* order of their corresponding pushes.
- $\Psi_{\mathrm{lv}}$ characterizes *LIFO violations* in which some pair of pops occur in the *same* order as their corresponding pushes, and the second push occurs before the first pop.

As in previous work [1, 10], our arguments for the (partial) completeness of these properties rely on *data independence* [28], i.e., that library executions are closed under consistent renaming $\mathbb{V} \to \mathbb{V}$ of method call/return values, and assume that each value is pushed at most once. In practice, collection-based data structures are data independent, and the second condition can always be met by tagging each value with a unique identifier. However, in order to achieve bounded counting representations, we may only distinguish between these values up to equivalence relations with finite quotients. Formally, we say a history $\langle O, f, < \rangle$ uses *unique values* when $f(o_1) = m_1(u) \Rightarrow v_1$ and $f(o_2) = m_2(u) \Rightarrow v_2$ implies $o_1 = o_2$.

**Theorem 4.** *The families $\Psi_{\mathrm{rv}}$, $\Psi_{\mathrm{ev}}$, $\Psi_{\mathrm{fv}}$, and $\Psi_{\mathrm{lv}}$, of operation-counting formulæ have cutoffs* 0, 2, 2, *and* 3, *respectively.*

*Proof.* Here we prove the theorem for $\Psi_{\mathrm{rv}}$ and $\Psi_{\mathrm{fv}}$; the others follow similarly. Since $\Psi_{\mathrm{rv}}$ does not discriminate between intervals, $h = \langle O, <, f \rangle \models \Psi_{\mathrm{rv}}$ iff $A_0(h) = \langle O, \emptyset, f \rangle \models \Psi_{\mathrm{rv}}$.

Next, let $h = \langle O, <, f \rangle \models \Psi_{\mathrm{fv}}$ and let $\ell_1$, $\ell_2$, $\ell_1'$, and $\ell_2'$ be the instances of the variables $x_1$, $x_2$, $y_1$, and $y_2$, respectively. Let $\Psi_{\mathrm{fv},k}$ denote the formula parametrized by $k$ in the family $\Psi_{\mathrm{fv}}$. By definition $h \models \Psi_{\mathrm{fv},k}$, where $k = \operatorname{len} h$. We consider only the case when $\mathsf{total}(y_1) > 0$ holds (the other case is similar). Besides the constraints on operation labels, the formula $\Psi_{\mathrm{fv},k}$ states that all $\ell_1$ operations end before an $\ell_1'$ operation starts and all $\ell_2$ operations end before an $\ell_2'$ operation starts. Let $I : O \to [n]^2$ be the canonical representation of $h$. Also, let $j_1$ (resp., $j_2$) be the maximum upper bound of an interval associated to an $\ell_1$ (resp., $\ell_3$) operation, i.e.,

$$j_1 = \max \{ j : \exists o \in O.\ I(o) = [i,j] \wedge f(o) = \ell_1 \},$$
$$j_2 = \max \{ j : \exists o \in O.\ I(o) = [i,j] \wedge f(o) = \ell_2 \}.$$

We define a weaker history $h' \preceq h$, that contains exactly the same set of operations as $h$ but it preserves only the ordering constraints $o_1 < o_2$ s.t. $I(o_1) \subseteq [0, j_1]$ and $I(o_2) \subseteq [j_1, \infty]$, or $I(o_1) \subseteq [0, j_2]$ and $I(o_2) \subseteq [j_2, \infty]$. The length of $h'$ is at most 2 and $h' \models \Psi_{\mathrm{fv},2}$. Since $A_2(h') = h'$, $\Psi_{\mathrm{rv}}$ has cutoff 2. □

**Corollary 3.** *The families of operation-counting formulæ,*

$$\Psi_{\mathrm{stack}} = \Psi_{\mathrm{rv}} \vee \Psi_{\mathrm{ev}} \vee \Psi_{\mathrm{lv}}, \textit{ and}$$
$$\Psi_{\mathrm{queue}} = \Psi_{\mathrm{rv}} \vee \Psi_{\mathrm{ev}} \vee \Psi_{\mathrm{fv}}$$

*have cutoffs* 3 *and* 2, *respectively.*

While $\Psi_{\mathrm{rv}}$ and $\Psi_{\mathrm{fv}}$ are complete, in the sense that they characterize every possible remove and FIFO violation, the $\Psi_{\mathrm{lv}}$ and $\Psi_{\mathrm{ev}}$ families are incomplete: Example 7.1 demonstrates this for $\Psi_{\mathrm{ev}}$ by exhibiting a parameterized history $h(n)$ for $n \ge 1$ such that $h(n) \notin H(L_{\mathrm{queue}})$,[3] yet $h(n) \models \neg\Psi_{\mathrm{ev}}$ for all $n > 1$. While it is theoretically possible to define a family $\Psi'_{\mathrm{ev},k}$ which catches all empty violations in histories with interval length at most $k$ — a fact that we demonstrate in Section 7.2 — we do not currently know whether it is possible to construct a formula which catches all empty violations in histories with arbitrarily-large interval length.

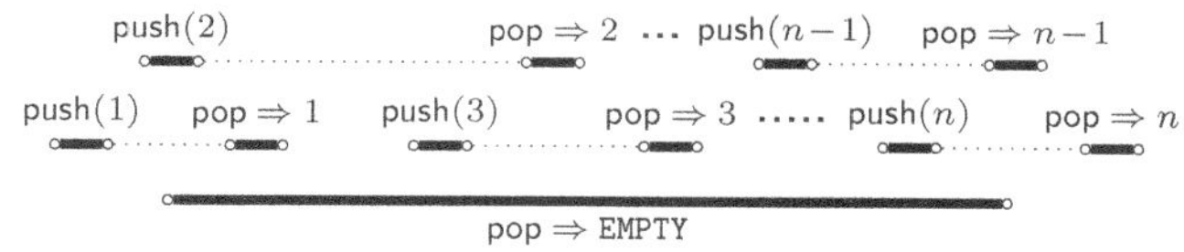


**Figure 5.** A family of empty violations, parameterized by $n \in \mathbb{N}$.

**Example 7.1.** *In the history of Figure 5, n pairs of* push *and* pop *operations ensure that throughout the span of the* pop(EMPTY), *some element is always present; i.e., at every time between the call and return of* pop(EMPTY), *there exists some element $v \in \mathbb{V}$ such that* push($v$) *has completed, yet* pop $\Rightarrow v$ *has not yet begun. It follows that any such history would not be included in the histories $H(L_{\mathrm{queue}})$ of an atomic queue library. The empty-violation family $\Psi_{\mathrm{ev}}$ however only captures such violations for $n = 1$, i.e., with a single* push-pop *pair spanning* pop(EMPTY).

Despite the theoretical possibility for empty violations which only surface for large $n$, our practical experience suggests small $n$ tends to suffice. The bug $B_5$ of our static analysis experiment in Section 9.3 surfaced as an empty violation, and was detected with approximation $A_1$, implying $n \le 1$, i.e., where some unmatched push operation precedes pop(EMPTY). Similarly, although the history of Figure 2(b) satisfies the empty-violation formula $\Psi_{\mathrm{ev}}$, so does the weaker length-1 history of Figure 2(c). Furthermore, we have found that the same bugs which manifest as empty violations often manifest as order violations as well. The ABA bug of Figure 2(a) is such a case: had the first thread executed another push(4) before push(1), then the final pop of Thread 2 would have returned 4, yielding the order violation push(4); push(2); pop $\Rightarrow$ 4.

[3] $L_{\mathrm{queue}}$ denotes an atomic FIFO queue library with push and pop methods.

### 7.2 Completeness for Bounded Interval Length

While Section 7.1 demonstrates complete families $\Psi_{\text{queue}}$ and $\Psi_{\text{stack}}$ of operation counting formulæ for the $L_{\text{queue}}$ and $L_{\text{stack}}$ objects for histories of interval length up to 2 and 3, respectively, this section exhibits complete formulæ for histories of any bounded interval length $k \in \mathbb{N}$.

For the rest of this section, we fix an interval length $k \in \mathbb{N}$ and demonstrate that a bounded enumeration of histories suffices to characterize every possible violation.

Given a history $h = \langle O, <, f \rangle$, an *element* $\langle o_1, o_2 \rangle \in O^2$ is a pair of operations such that $f(o_1) = \mathsf{push}(v)$ and $f(o_2) = \mathsf{pop}{\Rightarrow}v$ for some $v \in \mathbb{V}$. We say that two distinct elements $\langle o_1, o_2 \rangle$ and $\langle o_3, o_4 \rangle$ are *redundant with* $h$ when their operations have the same pasts and futures,[4]

$$\begin{aligned} \text{past}(o_1) &= \text{past}(o_3) & \text{future}(o_1) &= \text{future}(o_3) \\ \text{past}(o_2) &= \text{past}(o_4) & \text{future}(o_2) &= \text{future}(o_4) \end{aligned}$$

(and thus will share the same canonical intervals). We say the element $\langle o_1, o_2 \rangle$ is *redundant with* $h$ when there exists an element of $h$ with which it is redundant. We say that $h' = \langle O \cup O', <', f' \rangle$ *extends* $h = \langle O, <, f \rangle$ *with* $O'$ when $o_1 < o_2$ iff $o_1 <' o_2$ for all $o_1, o_2 \in O$, and $f(o) = f'(o)$ for all $o \in O$.

**Lemma 7.1.** *Let $x \in \{\text{stack}, \text{queue}\}$. If $h'$ extends $h$ with $\{o_1, o_2\}$ and $\langle o_1, o_2 \rangle$ is redundant with $h$, then $h \in H(L_x)$ iff $h' \in H(L_x)$.*

To enumerate the non-redundant $k$-length histories, let $\mathbb{I}_k = \{[i,j] : i, j \in \mathbb{N},\ 0 \le i \le j \le k\}$ be the set of integral intervals up to $k \in \mathbb{N}$, and fix an arbitrary total order $\ll$ over $\mathbb{I}_k^2$. We define the function $H^1$ mapping any subset $\{\langle I_{1,1}, I_{1,2} \rangle, \ldots, \langle I_{n,1}, I_{n,2} \rangle\} \subseteq \mathbb{I}_k^2$ to the history $\langle O, <, f \rangle$ where

$$\begin{aligned} O &= \{\langle i, 1 \rangle, \langle i, 2 \rangle : 1 \le i \le n\} \\ \langle i_1, j_1 \rangle < \langle i_2, j_2 \rangle &\text{ iff } I_{i_1, j_1} < I_{i_2, j_2} \\ f(\langle i, j \rangle) &= \begin{cases} \mathsf{push}(i) & \text{if } j = 1 \\ \mathsf{pop} \Rightarrow i & \text{if } j = 2 \end{cases} \end{aligned}$$

such that $\langle I_{1,1}, I_{1,2} \rangle \ll \langle I_{2,1}, I_{2,2} \rangle \ll \ldots \ll \langle I_{n,1}, I_{n,2} \rangle$. Then we define the finite set $H_k^1 = \{H^1(X) : X \subseteq \mathbb{I}_k^2\}$. Notice that the histories of $H_k^1$ do not contain redundant elements. Finally, we define the finite subset $H_{x,k}^1 = H_k^1 \setminus H(L_x)$ of histories which are not admitted by $L_x$, for $x \in \{\text{stack}, \text{queue}\}$, and enumerate them to write the formula characterizing length $k$ violations to $L_x$:

$$\Psi_{x,k} = \bigvee \{\Psi_h : h \in H_{x,k}^1\}$$

where $\Psi_h$ characterizes the history $h = \langle O, <, f \rangle$ with operations $\{o_1, \ldots, o_n\}$ and elements $\xi$, and its extensions:

$$\Psi_h = \exists x_1, \ldots, x_n. \bigwedge_{o_i < o_j} \mathsf{before}_k(x_i, x_j) \wedge \bigwedge_{\langle o_i, o_j \rangle \in \xi} \mathsf{match}(x_i, x_j)$$

Note that $\Psi_{x,k}$ is polynomial in size, and has fixed quantifier count, for fixed $k \in \mathbb{N}$.

**Theorem 5.** *Let $x \in \{stack, queue\}$. If $\text{len}\, h \le k$ and $h$ uses unique values, then $h \in H(L_x)$ iff $h \models \neg \Psi_{x,k}$.*

## 8. Atomic Libraries with Context-Free Kernels

While the previous section provides operation-counting formulae for particular classes of atomic objects, here we provide a systematic technique to derive operation-counting formulae for any atomic library that can be written as a context-free language, including objects such as (reader-writer) locks and semaphores, or context-free approximations of arbitrary libraries. For this construction we require finite sets $\mathbb{M}$ and $\mathbb{V}$ of methods and values. Given an atomic library $L$ such that $\ker E(L)$ is context free, and an interval bound $k \in \mathbb{N}$, we generate a formula $\Psi_{L,k}$ representing $L$ up to $k$.

Our construction relies on Parikh's Theorem [22]. We recall that the *Parikh image* of $w \in \Sigma^*$ is the multiset $\Pi(w) : \Sigma \to \mathbb{N}$ mapping each symbol $a \in \Sigma$ to its number of occurrences in $w$, and the *Parikh image* of a language $E \subseteq \Sigma^*$ is the set $\Pi(E) = \{\Pi(w) : w \in L\}$ of its words' images. If $\ker E(L)$ is context free, then the language $E_k = \{e \in E(L) : \text{len}\, H(e) \le k\}$ of $L$'s executions with bounded-length histories has the same Parikh image as a context-free language, and by Parikh's Theorem, $\Pi(E_k)$ can be represented as a Presburger formula, from which we derive $\Psi_{L,k}$.

**Theorem 6.** *Let $L$ be an atomic library over finite sets $\mathbb{M}$ and $\mathbb{V}$ of methods and values such that $\ker E(L)$ is a context-free language, and let $k \in \mathbb{N}$. Then there exists an effectively-computable operation-counting formula $\Psi_{L,k}$ representing $L$ up to $k$.*

This construction is useful in practice, allowing us to derive the formulæ used in our static-checking experiments of Section 9.3.

## 9. Experimental Evaluation

To demonstrate the practical value of our approach to refinement checking, we argue that our $k$-approximation:

- uncovers violations with small values of $k$,
- can be efficiently implemented for use in systematic concurrency testing and long-term runtime monitoring, and
- can be efficiently implemented for use in static analysis.

To argue these points, we have studied actual concurrent data structure implementations in C/C++, including the Scal[5] High-Performance Multicore-Scalable Computing suite. Some of these implementations, such as the Michael-Scott Queue [18], are meant to preserve observational refinement[6], while others, such as Kirsch et al.'s $k$-FIFO [12], are meant to preserve weaker properties. Unless otherwise noted, we use these implementations without modification, except to annotate methods with a fixed set of possible preemption points, e.g., preceding shared-memory accesses. While space prohibits including the entirety of our study, the sample and analysis which we do include is representative.

For our first two experiments (§9.1, §9.2) we have developed a tool for systematically enumerating a large number of alternate executions involving a limited number of object method invocations. We run each operation on a separate thread, and execute all thread schedules up to a given number $n \in \mathbb{N}$ of thread preemptions, at specified preemption points, similarly to Microsoft's Chess tool [20]. With $n = 0$ preemptions, there is only one schedule to execute, though the number of schedules grows exponentially as $n$ increases. For instance, with our annotation of preemptions in Scal's Michael-Scott Queue, we execute $f(n)$ schedules of a program with 8 method invocations at a rate of roughly one million schedules per minute, where $f$ is given by

$$f(1) = 33, f(2) = 612, f(3) = 8343, f(4) = 95434, f(5) = 930141$$

While similar in spirit to the second, our third experiment (§9.3) executes all round-robin thread schedules up to a given number $n \in \mathbb{N}$ of rounds *symbolically*: we use CSeq [7] to sequentialize a simple program which invokes a limited number of library methods, and then CBMC [13] (version 4.5) to perform bounded model checking up to a given loop-unroll bound. All measurements were made on similar MacBook Pro 2.XGHz Intel Core i5/i7 machines.

[4] Similarly to the definition of past from Section 6.1, we define the *future* of an operation $o$ in an history $\langle O, <, f \rangle$ by $\text{future}(o) = \{o' \in O : o < o'\}$.

[5] `http://scal.cs.uni-salzburg.at`

[6] More precisely, they have been designed to be linearizable.

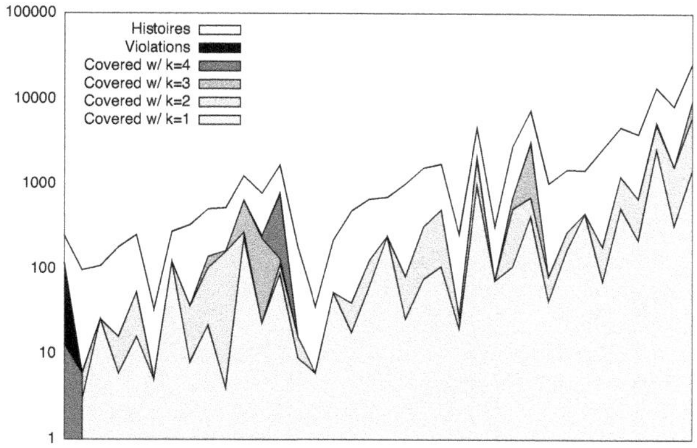


**Figure 6.** Comparison of violations covered with $k \leq 4$. Each data point counts histories on a logarithmic scale over all executions up to 5 preemptions on Scal's nonblocking bounded-reordering queue with $i \leq 4$ enqueue operations and $j \leq 4$ dequeue operations. The x-axis is ordered by increasing number of executions (1023–2359292) over $i+j$; we show only points with over 1000 executions. The largest data points measure the total number of unique histories encountered over a given set of executions. Second are the number of those histories violating refinement. Following are the numbers of those violations covered by $A_k$, for varying values of $k$. In this experiment $A_0$ exposed no violations.

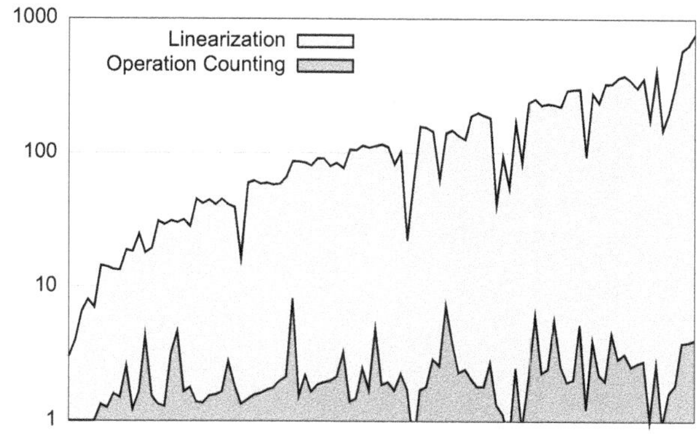


**Figure 7.** Comparison of runtime overhead between linearization-based monitoring and operation counting (for $A_2$) for up to 20 operations. Each data point measures runtime on a **logarithmic scale**, normalized to unmonitored execution time, over all executions up to 3 preemptions on Scal's nonblocking Michael-Scott queue with $i \leq 10$ enqueue operations and $j \leq 10$ dequeue operations. The x-axis is ordered by increasing $i+j$, and each data point is sampled from up to 126600 executions. Times do not include pre-calculation of sequential histories for linearization-based monitoring. While our $A_k$ monitor scales well, usually maintaining under 3x overhead, the linearization monitor scales **exponentially**, running with nearly **1000x overhead** with 20 operations.

### 9.1 Coverage of Refinement Violations

To show that our approximation $A_k$ uncovers observational refinement violations with small values of $k$, we measure the number of history violations detected by a traditional linearizability checker[7] versus those caught by $A_k$. The linearizability checker serves as an exact measure due to the equivalence of Section 5. While the approximation $A_k(H(e))$ of a violation $H(e)$ may not itself be a violation, one hopes to encounter some execution $e'$ for which the violation $A_k(H(e'))$ *covers* $H(e)$, i.e., for which $A_k(H(e')) \preceq H(e)$.

Figure 6 demonstrates that $A_k$ covers most or all violations with small values of $k$. While $A_4$ suffices to cover all violations at nearly all data points — besides the first point, where the sample size of 1023 executions is small relative to the 8 operations — all values $k > 0$ capture a nontrivial and increasing number of violations. Note that our cutoff results of Section 7 are not undermined by the fact that $A_3$ and $A_4$ have missed violations; violations were missed due to not having encountered a diverse enough sample of executions. In fact, as the execution-sample size increases (the x-axis is ordered by number of executions over operations) the value of $k$ required to capture a violation appears to decrease, all violations being captured by $A_3$ after a certain point.

### 9.2 Operation Counting for Testing & Runtime Monitoring

Figure 7 compares the runtime overhead of our $A_2$ approximation versus a traditional linearizability checker[8] sampling executions with up to 20 operations on Scal's nonblocking Michael-Scott queue. Since computing the set ker $H(L_{\text{queue}})$ of sequential queue histories over $n$ operations becomes prohibitively expensive as $n$ increases, surpassing a timeout of 5m for $n = 7$, we bypass the computation of ker $H(L_{\text{queue}})$ entirely, simply enumerating the linearizations of a given execution history without checking inclusion. Despite our best-effort implementation, one observes the cost incurred by linearization: as the number of operations increases, the number of linearizations increases exponentially, and performance plummets. With only 20 operations, instrumentation overhead is nearly 1000x. Our counting-based implementation of $A_2$ avoids this dramatic overhead: though not seriously optimized, we observe a 2.01x geometric-mean runtime overhead. This scalability suggests that our approximation can be used not only for systematic concurrency testing with few method invocations, but also for runtime monitoring, where the number of operations grows without limit.

[7] We implement a linearization-enumerating monitor, as in Line-Up [5].

[8] See footnote 7.

### 9.3 Operation Counting for Static Analysis

Our approximation $A_k$ also leads to an effective static means of refinement checking, due to the simplicity of operation-counting. By using only simple increment and decrement operations on integer counters, and program assertions[9] on those counters, we are able to leverage static verification tools capable of integer reasoning. We have found that the major obstacle in applying static tools is concurrency: even though the required counter reasoning is simple, reasoning precisely about thread interleavings is challenging, with or without our operation-counting instrumentation.

Despite the difficultly of precise static reasoning about thread interleavings, we have successfully applied our approach using two different static-verification backends: one based on SMACK [24] and Corral [15], and the other based on CSeq [7] and CBMC [13]. Both toolchains are based on sequentialization [14] and SAT/SMT-based bounded model checking. Our results in Table 1 report on the latter. Among 5 data structure implementations, we manually injected 9 realistic concurrency bugs. All bugs were uncovered as refinement violations with approximation $A_0$ or $A_1$, in round-robin executions of up to 4 rounds, of a program with at most 4 push and 4 pop operations, and with loops unrolled up to 2 times. Although the time complexity of concurrent exploration is high independently of our operation-counting instrumentation, particularly as the number of rounds increases, one clearly observes that our approximation is effective in detecting violations statically.

[9] We constructed program assertions automatically via Theorem 6.

| Library | Bug | $P$ | $k$ | $m$ | $n$ | Time |
|---|---|---|---|---|---|---|
| Michael-Scott Queue | $B_1$ (head) | $2 \times 2$ | 1 | 2 | 2 | 24.76s |
| Michael-Scott Queue | $B_1$ (tail) | $3 \times 1$ | 1 | 2 | 3 | 45.44s |
| Treiber Stack | $B_2$ | $3 \times 4$ | 1 | 1 | 2 | 52.59s |
| Treiber Stack | $B_3$ (push) | $2 \times 2$ | 1 | 1 | 2 | 24.46s |
| Treiber Stack | $B_3$ (pop) | $2 \times 2$ | 1 | 1 | 2 | 15.16s |
| Elimination Stack | $B_4$ | $4 \times 1$ | 0 | 1 | 4 | 317.79s |
| Elimination Stack | $B_5$ | $3 \times 1$ | 1 | 1 | 4 | 222.04s |
| Elimination Stack | $B_2$ | $3 \times 4$ | 0 | 1 | 2 | 434.84s |
| Lock-coupling Set | $B_6$ | $1 \times 2$ | 0 | 2 | 2 | 11.27s |
| LFDS Queue | $B_7$ | $2 \times 2$ | 1 | 1 | 2 | 77.00s |

**Table 1.** Runtimes for the static detection of injected refinement violations with CSeq & CBMC. For a given program $P_{i \times j}$ with $i$ and $j$ invocations to the push and pop methods, we explore the $n$-round round-robin schedules of $P_{i \times j}$ with $m$ loop iterations unrolled, with a monitor for our $A_k$ approximation. Bugs are ($B_1$) non-atomic lock operation, ($B_2$) ABA bug [17], ($B_3$) non-atomic CAS operation, ($B_4$) misplaced brace, ($B_5$) forgotten assignment, ($B_6$) misplaced lock, ($B_7$) predetermined capacity exceeded.

## 10. Related Work

Previous work on automated verification for concurrent objects focuses on the *linearizability* criterion [11]. While folklore has long held that linearizability implies observational refinement, Filipovic et al. [6] recently proved this fact; they also proved that the two criteria coincide when considering only library executions in which all operations have completed. Our results in Section 5 expound further: we show that the two criteria coincide for atomic object specifications, and that in general, observational refinement can hold for non-linearizable objects.

The theoretical limits of linearizability are well studied. Gibbons and Korach [8] show NP-completeness for checking a single execution. Alur et al. [2] show EXPSPACE membership for checking finite-state implementations against atomic specifications, but only when the number of program threads is bounded. Bouajjani et al. [4] show the same problem is undecidable with unbounded threads, and introduce a decidable variant for a restricted class of executions.

Several semi-automated approaches for proving linearizability, and thus observational refinement, have relied on annotating method bodies with *linearization points* [3, 16, 21, 27, 29], to reduce the otherwise-exponential space of possible history linearizations to one single linearization. These methods often rely on programmer annotation, and do not admit conclusive evidence of a violation in the case of a failed proof.

Automated approaches for detecting linearizability violations such as Line-Up [5] enumerate the exponentially-many possible history linearizations. This exponential cost effectively limits such approaches to executions with few operations, as noted in Section 9.2. Colt [25]'s approach mitigates this cost with programmer-annotated linearization points, as in the previously-mentioned approaches, and ultimately suffers from the same problem: a failed proof only indicates incorrect annotation.

## References


[1] P. A. Abdulla, F. Haziza, L. Holík, B. Jonsson, and A. Rezine. An integrated specification and verification technique for highly concurrent data structures. In *TACAS*, pages 324–338, 2013.

[2] R. Alur, K. L. McMillan, and D. Peled. Model-checking of correctness conditions for concurrent objects. *Inf. Comput.*, 160(1-2):167–188, 2000.

[3] D. Amit, N. Rinetzky, T. W. Reps, M. Sagiv, and E. Yahav. Comparison under abstraction for verifying linearizability. In *CAV '07*, volume 4590 of *LNCS*, pages 477–490, 2007.

[4] A. Bouajjani, M. Emmi, C. Enea, and J. Hamza. Verifying concurrent programs against sequential specifications. In *ESOP '13*, volume 7792 of *LNCS*, pages 290–309. Springer, 2013.

[5] S. Burckhardt, C. Dern, M. Musuvathi, and R. Tan. Line-Up: a complete and automatic linearizability checker. In *PLDI '10*, pages 330–340. ACM.

[6] I. Filipovic, P. W. O'Hearn, N. Rinetzky, and H. Yang. Abstraction for concurrent objects. *Theor. Comput. Sci.*, 411(51-52):4379–4398, 2010.

[7] B. Fischer, O. Inverso, and G. Parlato. CSeq: a concurrency pre-processor for sequential C verification tools. In *ASE '13*, pages 710–713. IEEE, 2013.

[8] P. B. Gibbons and E. Korach. Testing shared memories. *SIAM J. Comput.*, 26(4):1208–1244, 1997.

[9] T. L. Greenough. *Representation and Enumeration of Interval Orders and Semiorders*. PhD thesis, Dartmouth College, 1976.

[10] T. A. Henzinger, A. Sezgin, and V. Vafeiadis. Aspect-oriented linearizability proofs. In *CONCUR*, pages 242–256, 2013.

[11] M. Herlihy and J. M. Wing. Linearizability: A correctness condition for concurrent objects. *ACM Trans. Program. Lang. Syst.*, 12(3):463–492, 1990.

[12] C. M. Kirsch, M. Lippautz, and H. Payer. Fast and scalable, lock-free k-FIFO queues. In *PaCT 13*, volume 7979 of *LNCS*, pages 208–223, 2013.

[13] D. Kroening and M. Tautschnig. CBMC - C bounded model checker - (competition contribution). In *TACAS '14*, volume 8413 of *LNCS*, pages 389–391, 2014.

[14] A. Lal and T. W. Reps. Reducing concurrent analysis under a context bound to sequential analysis. *Formal Methods in System Design*, 35(1): 73–97, 2009.

[15] A. Lal, S. Qadeer, and S. K. Lahiri. A solver for reachability modulo theories. In *CAV '12*, volume 7358 of *LNCS*, pages 427–443.

[16] Y. Liu, W. Chen, Y. A. Liu, and J. Sun. Model checking linearizability via refinement. In *FM '09*, volume 5850 of *LNCS*, pages 321–337.

[17] M. M. Michael. ABA prevention using single-word instructions. Technical Report RC 23089, IBM T. J. Watson Res. Ctr., 2004.

[18] M. M. Michael and M. L. Scott. Simple, fast, and practical non-blocking and blocking concurrent queue algorithms. In *PODC '96*, pages 267–275. ACM, 1996.

[19] M. Moir and N. Shavit. Concurrent data structures. In D. Metha and S. Sahni, editors, *Handbook of Data Structures and Applications*, pages 47:14–30. Chapman and Hall/CRC Press, San Jose, CA, 2007.

[20] M. Musuvathi, S. Qadeer, T. Ball, G. Basler, P. A. Nainar, and I. Neamtiu. Finding and reproducing heisenbugs in concurrent programs. In *OSDI '08*, pages 267–280. USENIX Association, 2008.

[21] P. W. O'Hearn, N. Rinetzky, M. T. Vechev, E. Yahav, and G. Yorsh. Verifying linearizability with hindsight. In *PODC '10*, pages 85–94. ACM.

[22] R. Parikh. On context-free languages. *J. ACM*, 13(4):570–581, 1966.

[23] I. Rabinovitch. The dimension of semiorders. *Journal of Combinatorial Theory, Series A*, 25(1):50 – 61, 1978. ISSN 0097-3165.

[24] Z. Rakamaric and M. Emmi. SMACK: Decoupling source language details from verifier implementations. In *CAV '14*, volume 8559 of *LNCS*, pages 106–113. Springer, 2014.

[25] O. Shacham, N. G. Bronson, A. Aiken, M. Sagiv, M. T. Vechev, and E. Yahav. Testing atomicity of composed concurrent operations. In *OOPSLA '11*, pages 51–64. ACM, 2011.

[26] R. Treiber. Systems programming: Coping with parallelism. Technical Report RJ5118, IBM Almaden Res. Ctr., 1986.

[27] V. Vafeiadis. Automatically proving linearizability. In *CAV '10*, volume 6174 of *LNCS*, pages 450–464.

[28] P. Wolper. Expressing interesting properties of programs in propositional temporal logic. In *POPL '86*, pages 184–193. ACM Press, 1986.

[29] S. J. Zhang. Scalable automatic linearizability checking. In *ICSE '11*, pages 1185–1187. ACM.

# Decentralizing SDN Policies

Oded Padon
Tel Aviv University
odedp@mail.tau.ac.il

Neil Immerman
University of Massachusetts, Amherst
immerman@cs.umass.edu

Aleksandr Karbyshev
Tel Aviv University
karbyshev@post.tau.ac.il

Ori Lahav
Tel Aviv University
orilahav@post.tau.ac.il

Mooly Sagiv
Tel Aviv University
msagiv@post.tau.ac.il

Sharon Shoham
The Academic College of Tel Aviv Yaffo
sharon.shoham@gmail.com

## Abstract

Software-defined networking (SDN) is a new paradigm for operating and managing computer networks. SDN enables logically-centralized control over network devices through a "controller" — software that operates independently of the network hardware. Network operators can run both in-house and third-party SDN programs on top of the controller, e.g., to specify routing and access control policies.

In practice, having the controller handle events limits the network scalability. Therefore, the feasibility of SDN depends on the ability to efficiently decentralize network event-handling by installing forwarding rules on the switches. However, installing a rule too early or too late may lead to incorrect behavior, e.g., (1) packets may be forwarded to the wrong destination or incorrectly dropped; (2) packets handled by the switch may hide vital information from the controller, leading to incorrect forwarding behavior. The second issue is subtle and sometimes missed even by experienced programmers.

The contributions of this paper are two fold. First, we formalize the correctness and optimality requirements for decentralizing network policies. Second, we identify a useful class of network policies which permits automatic synthesis of a controller which performs optimal forwarding rule installation.

***Categories and Subject Descriptors*** D.3.2 [Programming Languages]: Language Classifications—Specialized application languages; I.2.2 [Artificial Intelligence]: Automatic Programming—Program synthesis

***Keywords*** Software-defined networking; Network programming languages; Synthesis; Logic programming; Distributed systems

## 1. Introduction

Software-defined networking (SDN) is a paradigm for operating and managing computer networks [1]. SDN enables logically-centralized control over network devices through a "controller" — software that operates independently of the network hardware. In practice, having the controller handle all network events limits network scalability. Therefore, the feasibility of SDN depends on the ability to efficiently and correctly decentralize handing of network events by installing forwarding rules on the switches. This problem can be difficult and error prone even for experienced programmers.

In particular, there is a subtle local-versus-global issue that is a frequent cause of errors in SDN implementations. Namely, when a packet arrives at a switch, the switch's forwarding rules determine whether the packet is handled locally or sent to the controller. But when should a packet be sent to the controller?

We say that an event $e$ is *relevant* if there is *some sequence of future events* that can only be handled correctly if the controller knows about $e$. If $e$ is relevant then the switch *must* inform the controller about it. On the other hand, if $e$ is irrelevant, then from the viewpoint of network traffic and efficiency, it is best for the switch to handle $e$ locally and *not* inform the controller about it. Thus, a switch needs to test whether or not an incoming event is relevant. However, relevance is in general a second-order property — does there exist a sequence of future events — that may be difficult or impossible for the switch to test.

In this paper, we solve this problem. We show how to automatically go from the specification of a network policy to its decentralized implementation as forwarding rules to be initially installed on the switches and updated in response to events occurring on the switches.

We make the following contributions:

1. We define the correctness and optimality of a decentralized implementation of a network policy. Our definitions are given in English and more formally in second-order logic.
2. We specify a first-order language, $\mathcal{L}_1$, for expressing network policies. $\mathcal{L}_1$ is reasonably expressive. Furthermore, we show how to automatically synthesize an optimal decentralized implementation of any network policy expressible in $\mathcal{L}_1$.
3. We identify a property that we call *$k$-bounded causality* and show that any network policy $F$ expressed in $\mathcal{L}_1$ satisfies $k$-bounded causality with the parameter $k$ easily determined from $F$. Intuitively, if a network policy has $k$-bounded causality, then instead of considering all possible sequences of future events, we only need to consider sequences of length at most $k$.
4. Using the *$k$-bounded causality* of $F$, we show that the above second-order definitions of correctness and optimality for a decentralized implementation of $F$ can be written simply in a fragment of first-order logic with equality.


*POPL '15*, January 15–17, 2015, Mumbai, India.
Copyright © 2015 ACM 978-1-4503-3300-9/15/01... $15.00.
http://dx.doi.org/10.1145/2676726.2676990

5. Using quantifier elimination on the resulting formulas, we show how to automatically derive quantifier-free implementation rules for $F$. The latter can be automatically translated to forwarding rules which when installed on the switches, result in a correct and optimal decentralized implementation of the input network policy $F$.

**What this paper does not do:** There are many fascinating issues about the **distributed** control of a network, i.e., how to send forwarding rules over the network to keep all the switches in a correct state as cheaply as possible. We will consider some of these questions in future work.

In this paper, we consider the problem of computing the local forwarding rules, not how we send them over the network to the switches. A related interesting question which we also do not consider in this paper is how to compute the incremental changes of the forwarding rules. That is, which rules should we add and remove in reaction to each new relevant event.

This paper is organized as follows: Section 2 provides an informal overview of the problem addressed by this paper. The terminology used in this paper is described in Section 3. The problem addressed by this paper is defined formally in Section 4. Section 5 provides necessary and sufficient conditions for decentralization and optimality. Our first order policy language is defined in Section 6. The algorithm for synthesizing forwarding rules is described in Section 7. Related work is described in Section 8.

## 2. Overview

This section provides an informal overview of the decentralization problem and how we solve it. The reader need not be familiar with Software-Defined Networks (SDNs).

### 2.1 Forwarding policies

We assume that we have a finite set of switches, each of which has a fixed set of ports, `Ports`, connected to hosts and other switches. The events of interest are "packet-receive" events, each of which represents a packet arriving at some switch $s$ on some input port. The possible resulting action is for $s$ to forward the packet along some set of ports $P \subseteq \texttt{Ports}$. A policy is a specification of what action to take given an event and the history of all previous events. The policy dictates the behavior of every switch as a function of the global history of events.

As a running example, consider the well-studied policy of a *learning switch* with host migration. The learning switch learns locations of hosts in the network by analyzing the packets incoming on its ports. Initially, it is supposed to flood any arriving packet (i.e., send it to all ports except where it came from), while learning the location of its sender. Future packets, whose destination's location is already learned, should be forwarded directly to the learned port(s) instead of flooding it to all ports. This eliminates unnecessary traffic. It is possible for hosts to change their location, i.e., to *migrate*. The learning switch that supports host migration should forward the packet to the port where the packet's destination was last seen. More precisely, for a packet with destination $d$ arriving at switch $s$ on port $p$, if the history does not include any previous packet that arrived at $s$ with source $d$, then $s$ should flood the packet, i.e., send it over all ports except $p$. On the other hand, if there was such a packet and the most recent of these arrived on port $p'$, then $s$ should send the packet only on port $p'$.

### 2.2 Distributed forwarding

SDNs implement forwarding policies using switches that have limited expressive power, along with a centralized controller. Events can either be handled locally by the switch receiving the event, or communicated to the controller.

**Algorithm 1** Controller ⟨Policy⟩

> *State* := *initial_state*
> **while** new packet-receive event $e$ **do**
>     action := *compute_action*(Policy, *State*, $e$)
>     *update_state*(*State*, $e$)
>     rules := ***infer_rules*** (Policy, *State*)
>     *configure_switches*(rules)
>     *send_to_switches*(action)
> **end while**

The switches follow forwarding rules that determine the port(s) to which the arriving packets are forwarded according to the attributes of the packet. These rules also determine when the switch must forward the packet to the controller.[1] Each set of rules defines a "stateless" behaviour in the sense that it does *not* refer to the previous history of events. The rules are installed and removed from the switches only by the controller.

In contrast to the switches, the centralized controller is *stateful*: its behavior, which includes instructing the switches how to forward packets that were sent to it, as well as installing forwarding rules on the switches for future packets, may depend on the entire log of events that it has seen so far. For that, the controller may maintain the history of events it has received as part of its state. Algorithm 1 depicts a simple scheme of a stateful controller, parametrized by the policy.

Note that the policy of the learning switch described above cannot be implemented by a switch alone as the handling of the current packet requires access to the history of previous events.

In this work, we focus on the rule inference component of the controller. For scalability and performance, as many events as possible should be handled locally by the switches. However, as shown next it is subtle to correctly install forwarding rules. In fact even current high-level network programming languages including [6, 14, 18] essentially require that the programmer specifies conditions that determine when forwarding rules can be installed (see Section 8).

### 2.3 Correctness of forwarding rule installation

This paper formulates the notion of correctness of forwarding rule installation. Our formulation is inspired by the OPENFLOW standard [2], but it can be adapted to other distributed systems.

Roughly speaking, we say that a forwarding rule installation policy is *correct* with respect to a policy if all packets are forwarded to the right ports as defined by the policy. Since the policy defines the actions to be performed based on the full sequence of events, while rule installation depends only on the packets that arrive to the controller, correctness is in fact divided to the following two conditions: (1) every packet is forwarded to the right ports (either by the installed rules or by the controller), and (2) packets are sent to the controller whenever necessary.

To formalize (2) we define a notion of relevance. We call an event *relevant* if it may affect the future behavior of the system. Thus the second condition for correctness requires that all relevant events must be forwarded to the controller.

***Learning switch forwarding rules*** Table 1 contains several rule installation policies for the learning switch example. Each of them specifies a set of switch forwarding rules for any history $H$. In the rules, $e$ denotes the current event (arriving packet). Notice that $H$ does not appear in the rules themselves, as the switches cannot access the history.

[1] For simplicity, we assume that the switches send a packet to the controller iff the installed forwarding rules do not determine any local action for the packet. Our techniques can also deal with rules that explicitly send some events to the controller.

| | Rule Installation Policy |
|---|---|
| **trivial** | none |
| **LS$_1$** | for any $e_1 \in H$ :<br>`forward`$(e_1.in) \quad \leftarrow \quad e.sw = e_1.sw,\ e.dst = e_1.src$ |
| **LS$_2$** | for any $e_1, e_2 \in H$ :<br>`forward`$(e_2.in) \quad \leftarrow \quad e.sw = e_1.sw = e_2.sw,\ e.src = e_1.src,\ e.dst = e_2.src$ |
| **LS$_3$** | for any $e_1 \in H$ such that $\forall e' \in H. (e'.sw = e_1.sw \wedge e' > e_1 \implies e'.src \neq e_1.src)$ and<br>$e_2 \in H$ such that $\forall e' \in H. (e'.sw = e_2.sw \wedge e' > e_2 \implies e'.src \neq e_2.src)$ :<br>`forward`$(e_2.in) \quad \leftarrow \quad e.sw = e_1.sw = e_2.sw,\ e.src = e_1.src,\ e.dst = e_2.src,\ e.in = e_1.in$ |

**Table 1.** Sample rule installation policies for the learning switch in terms of current events and histories, $e, H$ respectively. $e_1 > e_2$ means that $e_1$ occurred later than $e_2$ in $H$.

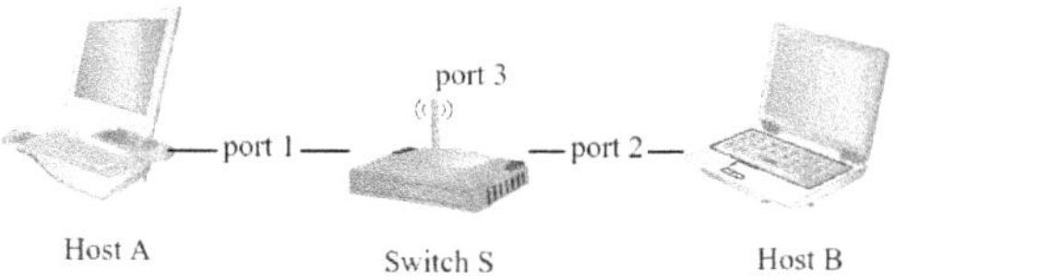


**Figure 1.** A sample topology for a learning switch $s$ with three ports 1, 2, and 3.

The trivial rule installation policy does not install any rules and thus is correct, but it is far from optimal, as all events are handled by the centralized controller. The **LS$_1$** policy installs a rule to forward an event $e$ to port $p$ if the history includes an event that arrived to the same switch as $e$ on the port $p$ and its source is the destination of $e$. While this policy seems natural, it is *incorrect* since it installs rules "too early". Figure 1 shows a sample topology (with a single switch $s$ and two hosts $A$ and $B$) and Table 2 presents a scenario where following **LS$_1$** results in incorrect behaviour. The first event is a packet from $A$ to $B$ that occurred in the switch $s$ and arrived on port 1. Since the switch initially has no rules, this packet is sent to the controller which floods it, and also installs a forwarding rule (according to **LS$_1$**) to forward all packets arriving in switch $s$ whose destination is $A$ to port 1. This appears to be a correct forwarding. As a result of this rule, the next event of a packet from $B$ to $A$ is (correctly) forwarded to port 1 by the switch, but it is not sent to the centralized controller. Hence, the controller does not learn that $B$ is connected to port 2. Consequently, the third event (another packet from $A$ to $B$) is flooded, while it should have been forwarded only to output port 2.

The **LS$_2$** installation policy avoids the bug of premature rule installations, as it installs rules matching packets for which both the source and the destination locations have already been learned. **LS$_2$** is implemented in most SDN systems. It installs a rule to forward $e$ to port $p$ if the history includes: (1) an event that arrived on switch $s$ in input port $p$ and its source is the destination of $e$; and (2) another event that arrived on $s$ with the same source as $e$. This is a more modest installation policy which installs rules "per-flow". However, it cannot cope with host migration. Table 3 demonstrates an incorrect behaviour that happens when host $A$ relocates from port 1 to port 3. Indeed, after the second event, when both the locations of hosts $A$ and $B$ were learned, the switch will locally handle packets between $A$ and $B$. The third event, a packet from $A$ to $B$ that arrived on port 3 after $A$ migrated, is handled locally and is not sent to the controller. Accordingly, the controller is not aware of $A$'s migration. This, again, results in an incorrect behaviour, as the fourth event from $B$ to $A$ is forwarded to port 1, while $A$ informed its new location in port 3.

**LS$_3$** is a correct rule installation policy with correct handling of host migration. It installs a rule to forward $e$ to port $p$: if (1) the last event in the history at switch $s$ whose source is the destination of $e$ arrived in input port $p$; (2) the last event in the history at switch $s$ whose source is the source of $e$ arrived in the same input port as $e$. Thus, it only installs rules for handling packets that come from the last known location of some host. Table 4 demonstrates how **LS$_3$** properly handles the scenario presented in Table 3. After the second event, the rules installed match only events coming on the *known* locations of $A$ and $B$. Consequently, the third event (after $A$ migrates), is handled by the controller, and thus the controller learns that $A$ migrated. As a result, the controller replaces the previously installed forwarding rules with two new rules, and the forth event is handled correctly by the switch.

The example of the learning switch with migration shows that deriving a correct rule installation policy for a given forwarding policy is challenging even for simple and well-studied examples.

### 2.4 Optimality of forwarding rule installation

With correctness being the first criterion, our goal is to also ensure that the forwarding rules installed on the switches allow the switches to handle as many events as possible locally. Such a forwarding rule installation policy is called *optimal*. The trivial installation is suboptimal, whereas **LS$_3$** is optimal.

We show that having the installed rules handle *all* irrelevant events is both necessary and sufficient condition for optimality.

### 2.5 Our approach

Our approach for inferring optimal rule installation consists of a "static" part, which takes place at compile time, and a "dynamic" part which operates at runtime. The static part derives from the given policy a description of the optimal rule installation policy which determines for each history the rules that should be installed (for the learning switch example, this corresponds to obtaining **LS$_3$**, see Table 1). The runtime component is executed by the controller whenever an event is forwarded to it, and it is responsible for computing the updated rules to be installed on the switches by applying the rule installation policy on the current history of events. We consider the history of events received by the controller as its state.

#### 2.5.1 Inferring rule installation policies

In general inferring correct forwarding rule installation is undecidable (see Section 6.4). In this paper we define a restricted variant of first-order logic, called $\mathcal{L}_1$, which is powerful enough to capture many useful forwarding policies, and is amenable to automatic synthesis of optimal rule installation policies. We then describe an algorithm for synthesizing an optimal rule installation policy for any given forwarding policy expressed in our logic. For example, for the learning switch, it infers **LS$_3$**.

Applying our procedure to the Firewall example from [8] actually improves its implementation by proactively installing more rules, as demonstrated in Section 7.4.

| event | action | rule-updates |
|---|---|---|
| $\langle s, 1, A \rightarrow B\rangle$ | flood | **install:** forward(1) $\leftarrow$ $e.sw = s,\ e.dst = A$ |
| $\langle s, 2, A \rightarrow B\rangle$ | forward(1) | |
| $\langle s, 1, A \rightarrow B\rangle$ | flood | |

**Table 2.** A scenario which reveals a bug in the forwarding rule installation policy $\mathbf{LS}_1$. Controller actions are underlined.

| event | action | rule-updates |
|---|---|---|
| $\langle s, 1, A \rightarrow B\rangle$ | flood | |
| $\langle s, 2, B \rightarrow A\rangle$ | forward(1) | **install:** forward(2) $\leftarrow$ $e.sw = s,\ e.src = A,\ e.dst = B$; forward(1) $\leftarrow$ $e.sw = s,\ e.src = B,\ e.dst = A$ |
| | | A migrates from 1 to 3 |
| $\langle s, 3, A \rightarrow B\rangle$ | forward(2) | |
| $\langle s, 2, B \rightarrow A\rangle$ | forward(1) | |

**Table 3.** A scenario which reveals a bug in the the forwarding rule installation policy $\mathbf{LS}_2$. Controller actions are underlined.

| event | action | rule-updates |
|---|---|---|
| $\langle s, 1, A \rightarrow B\rangle$ | flood | |
| $\langle s, 2, B \rightarrow A\rangle$ | forward(1) | **install:** forward(2) $\leftarrow$ $e.sw = s,\ e.src = A,\ e.dst = B,\ e.in = 1$; forward(1) $\leftarrow$ $e.sw = s,\ e.src = B,\ e.dst = A,\ e.in = 2$ |
| | | A migrates from 1 to 3 |
| $\langle s, 3, A \rightarrow B\rangle$ | forward(2) | **remove the previous two rules** **install:** forward(2) $\leftarrow$ $e.sw = s,\ e.src = A,\ e.dst = B,\ e.in = 3$; forward(3) $\leftarrow$ $e.sw = s,\ e.src = B,\ e.dst = A,\ e.in = 2$ |
| $\langle s, 2, B \rightarrow A\rangle$ | forward(3) | |

**Table 4.** A scenario demonstrating the correct forwarding rule installation policy $\mathbf{LS}_3$. Controller actions are underlined.

***Formulation of correctness and optimality in first-order logic*** The correctness and optimality conditions of installation policies refer to irrelevant events, where irrelevance of events is examined with respect to unbounded future sequences of events, which naturally requires second-order quantifiers. Nevertheless, we identify a "bounded causality" property of policies and show that for policies admitting this property the condition for an event being irrelevant can be equivalently specified in first-order logic. The bounded causality property states that there is a (computable) bound $k$, such that if an event affects the behaviour for some sequence of future events, then it will also affect the behaviour for some sequence of $k$ future events. This allows us to construct first-order definitions of an optimal (correct) installation policy.

***Specification of policies*** We specify policies by formulas in $\mathcal{L}_1$, which are interpreted with respect to a history and a "current" event. $\mathcal{L}_1$ allows any Boolean combination of components, where components are existentially quantified formulas, in which all (existential) quantifiers are *guarded*: they either refer to the existence of an event in the history (denoted by $\exists \bar{y} \in \mathbb{H}$, where $\mathbb{H}$ is a special symbol and $\bar{y}$ is an event variable), or they refer to the last event in the history that has some property $\psi$ (denoted by $\exists \bar{y} = Last_{\psi}$, where $\bar{y}$ is an event variable and $\psi$ is a formula).

For example, the policy for the learning switch that supports migrations of hosts is specified in $\mathcal{L}_1$ by the collection of formulas $\varphi^p$, one for each port $p$, that define when to forward to $p$:

$$\varphi^p_{\mathsf{ls}} = \exists \bar{y} = Last_{(\bar{x}.sw \approx \bar{y}.sw) \wedge (\bar{x}.dst \approx \bar{y}.src)}.\ (\bar{y}.in \approx p)$$

In addition, the formula that defines when to perform `flood` is given by:

$$\varphi^{\mathtt{flood}}_{\mathsf{ls}} = \bigwedge_{p \in \mathtt{Ports}} \neg \varphi^p$$

If instead of $\varphi^p$ above one takes

$$\varphi^p_{\mathsf{ls}} = \exists \bar{y} \in \mathbb{H}.\ (\bar{x}.sw \approx \bar{y}.sw) \wedge (\bar{x}.dst \approx \bar{y}.src) \wedge (\bar{y}.in \approx p),$$

this results in a policy that forwards each packet to all ports in which the destination of the packet was seen before.

Our design of $\mathcal{L}_1$ was guided by common SDN applications, as well as by the ability to obtain the bounded causality property: $\mathcal{L}_1$-policies have this property. $\mathcal{L}_1$ allows us to express restricted temporal properties, using the "last" quantifiers (or similar variants, see Section 6.2, Remark 4). A possible extension is to also explicitly refer to order on events. We did not augment this into $\mathcal{L}_1$ since it complicates the presentation of our approach.

On the other hand, $\mathcal{L}_1$ formulas cannot express policies that involve counting events in the history or require arithmetic operations such as advanced load balancing (we can, however, handle simple load balancing based on fixed IP distributions). Another source of limitation is the restriction to Boolean combinations of alternation-free quantified formulas. If we allow alternation of quantifiers, the bounded causality property breaks (see Section 7.1).

***Static computation of rule installation policy*** For a policy expressed in $\mathcal{L}_1$ which enjoys the bounded causality property, we are able to specify the optimal rule installation policy in first-order logic (extended with guarded quantifiers). For example, for a learning switch with migration, for each port $p$, we obtain the following formula:

$$\varphi^p = \varphi^p_{\mathsf{ls}} \wedge \exists \bar{y} = Last_{(\bar{x}.sw \approx \bar{y}.sw) \wedge (\bar{x}.src \approx \bar{y}.src)}.\ (\bar{y}.in \approx \bar{x}.in)$$

Note that when the rule installation policy refers to the history of events via guarded quantifiers, it refers to the filtered history that only consists of events that were sent to the controller, as opposed to the forwarding policy that refers to the full history.

### 2.5.2 Runtime rule installation

After generating the first-order formulas that express the optimal installation policy, it remains to show that given a concrete history of events that arrived to the controller, the controller can dynamically compute the rules that need to be installed on the switches based on the installation policy (where the installed rules do not refer to the history of events).

For this purpose, we first remove the guarded quantifiers (that still exist in the definition of the installation policy) by using the actual history at hand. Next we remove the unguarded quantifiers using a quantifier elimination process. The result is a set of quantifier-free formulas describing the forwarding rules to be installed.

## 3. Terminology

SDN is a particular form of a distributed event-driven system, composed of a collection of *decentralized components* and a single *centralized controller*. The decentralized components are configurable switches, and the centralized controller is the OPENFLOW network controller. Events are packet-receive events occurring in the switches.

Next, we precisely formulate the notions involved in defining the decentralization problem.

***Events.*** $\mathcal{Q}$ is a finite set of event attributes. Each attribute $q \in \mathcal{Q}$ is associated with a (possibly, infinite) set of values $\mathcal{E}_q$. Events are records with one field for each event attribute. We will denote by $\mathcal{E}$ the set of all events.

In the context of SDN, events are packet-receive events (packets that arrive at a switch and may or may not be forwarded to the centralized controller). The event attributes $\mathcal{Q}$ include $sw$, $in$, $src$, $dst$, where $sw$ is the switch receiving the packet; $in$ is the port through which the packet is received ($\mathcal{E}_{in} = \texttt{Ports}$ is a finite set of ports); $src$ is the source field in the packet header; and $dst$ is the destination field in the packet header. If needed, other fields may be included in $\mathcal{Q}$ (e.g. time stamp, logical port, VLAN information etc.).

***Histories.*** A *history* is a finite sequence of events from $\mathcal{E}$. In particular, an event $e$ is considered a history of length one. $H_1 \cdot H_2$ denotes the concatenation of sequences $H_1$ and $H_2$. We write $H_1 \preceq H_2$ to mean that $H_1$ is a subsequence of $H_2$. $\mathcal{H}$ is the set of all histories. The *size* $|H|$ of a history is the number of elements it contains, $|e_1 \cdot \ldots \cdot e_n| = n$.

***Actions.*** $\mathcal{A}$ is a finite nonempty set of *actions*. In SDN-related examples in this paper, the set of actions is $\mathcal{A} = \texttt{Ports} \cup \{\texttt{drop}, \texttt{flood}\}$, where an action $p \in \texttt{Ports}$ represents forwarding a given packet to port $p$, the action `flood` represents "flooding" the packet, i.e. forwarding it to all ports except for the port in which it was received, and the action `drop` means dropping the packet without forwarding it.

***Policies.*** A *policy* is a function from $\mathcal{H}$ to $\mathcal{E} \to P^+(\mathcal{A})$, the set of non-empty subsets of $\mathcal{A}$. A policy defines the behaviour of the system, where its input is the sequence of events (history) that occurred so far. Given a history $H$ and a "current" event $e_1$, $F(H)(e_1)$ determines the (nonempty) set of actions that should be performed in reaction to $e_1$. When the next event $e_2$ occurs, the considered history also includes $e_1$, meaning that the reaction to $e_2$ will be each action in $F(H \cdot e_1)(e_2)$.

Here are some examples of policies for SDN:

**Hub (flooding switch)** Flood all arriving packets (i.e., on all switches forward each packet to all ports except for its input port).

**Firewall** Forward to port 2 all packets arriving on port 1; forward to port 1 a packet arriving on port 2 from source $s$ if the history includes an incoming event on port 1 whose destination is $s$. In this scenario, we assume that ports 1 and 2 are the only ports of any switch in the network, where trusted hosts are all connected through port 1, and untrusted hosts are connected through port 2.

**Learning switch (w/o migration)** For a packet arriving in switch $s$ with destination $d$, forward it to port $p$ if the history includes a packet that arrived in $s$ on the input port $p$ and its source was $d$ (the port $p$ must be unique since there is no migration of hosts). If no such packet exsits in the history, flood the arriving packet.

**Learning switch with migration** For a packet arriving in switch $s$ with destination $d$, forward it to port $p$ if the history includes a packet that arrived in $s$ from source $d$ and the most recent such packet has input port $p$. If no such packet exists in the history, flood the arriving packet.

**Authorization Server** There is a designated host $h_a$ serving as an *authorization server*, which sends special *authorization* and *deauthorization* packets to the controller. Communication is allowed only between *authorized* hosts. A host becomes authorized when the controller receives an authorization packet authorizing the host, and may become deauthorized if the controller receives a deauthorization packet for that host.

It is also possible to compose several of the aforementioned policies by applying different policies in each switch.

Note that any computable policy, $F$, may be implemented via a *centralized controller* that keeps track of the entire history: whenever an event $e$ occurs corresponding to switch $s$ receiving packet $p$, $s$ informs the controller about $e$. The controller then instructs $s$ to perform the actions $F(H)(e)$ and adds $e$ to its log, $H' := H \cdot e$.

However, sending all events to a centralized controller creates a bottleneck and makes the system not scalable. A scalable system requires that many events will be handled locally by stateless decentralized components, implementing the policy in a decentralized and scalable way.

***Event Handlers.*** To formalize the concept of locally handling events by the decentralized components, we introduce *event handlers*. An event handler is a *partial* function from $\mathcal{E}$ to $P^+(\mathcal{A})$, which returns a set of actions to perform for the events for which it is defined. At any point in time, the behaviour of the decentralized components is defined by an event handler $R$. The domain of $R$ is the set of events that are locally processed by the decentralized components without informing the controller. Whenever an event $e$ occurs in some decentralized component, if $R(e)$ is defined then each action in $R(e)$ is performed locally. If $R(e)$ is not defined, then the decentralized component informs the controller and awaits further instructions. Below $\mathcal{R}$ denotes the set of all event handlers.

In the context of SDN, event handlers correspond to sets of forwarding rules, e.g., "drop all packets arriving into port 1, and flood all packets arriving into port 2 with source field `192.168.1.123`". The empty event handler corresponds to the empty set of forwarding rules. Note that the controller also implements a (total) event handler at each point in time.

*Remark* 1. We view the set of switches as one abstract unit that implements a single, joint, event handler. In practice, the joint event handler is divided between the individual switches by taking into account the $sw$ attribute of the events.

***Event handler generators.*** An *event handler generator* is a function from $\mathcal{H}$ to $\mathcal{R}$ (it assigns event handlers to histories).

In the context of SDN, event handler generators correspond to forwarding rule installation policies. Whenever the controller processes a packet-receive event (sent to it by some switch), it also computes a new event handler and installs it on the switches. Note that if there are different types of switches, then a given switch only needs the forwarding rules pertaining to its type. In practice, only relevant changes to the set of forwarding rules must be sent to each switch.

Let $I$ be an event handler generator. The $I$*-history*, $\mathcal{C}_I(H)$, for a history $H$ is defined inductively: $\mathcal{C}_I(\epsilon) = \epsilon$, and

$$\mathcal{C}_I(H \cdot e) = \begin{cases} \mathcal{C}_I(H) \cdot e & \text{if } I(\mathcal{C}_I(H))(e) \text{ is not defined} \\ \mathcal{C}_I(H) & \text{otherwise} \end{cases}$$

For a sequence of events $H = e_1 \cdots e_n$, $\mathcal{C}_I(H)$ is the subsequence consisting of those events that are forwarded to the controller, i.e., not handled locally. Thus, $\mathcal{C}_I(H)$ is the log that is saved in the controller. Since $\mathcal{C}_I$ strips out exactly those events that are handled locally and thus not forwarded to the controller, we have,

**Lemma 1.** *For any event handler generator $I$, $\mathcal{C}_I$ is idempotent, i.e., for every history $H$, $\mathcal{C}_I(\mathcal{C}_I(H)) = \mathcal{C}_I(H)$.*

*Proof.* By induction on $H$. □

**Definition 1.** Given an event handler generator $I$, we say that a history $H$ is $I$*-reachable* if $H = \mathcal{C}_I(H')$ for some history $H'$.

Namely, $H$ is $I$-reachable if there is a sequence of events for which $H$ is the corresponding log. By Lemma 1 we have that $H$ is $I$-reachable iff $H = \mathcal{C}_I(H)$.

***Combined policies.*** Let $F$ be a policy and $I$ an event handler generator. To see how well $F$ and $I$ play together, we define the *combined policy* of $F$ with respect to $I$, $F_I : \mathcal{H} \to \mathcal{E} \to P^+(\mathcal{A})$ as follows:

$$F_I(H)(e) = \begin{cases} I(\mathcal{C}_I(H))(e) & \text{if } I(\mathcal{C}_I(H))(e) \text{ is defined} \\ F(\mathcal{C}_I(H))(e) & \text{otherwise.} \end{cases}$$

Thus $F_I$ is the policy that decentralizes according to $I$ and defers to $F$ when $I$ is not defined.

## 4. The Decentralization Problem

In this section we precisely define the decentralization problem.

**Definition 2** (Decentralization). An event handler generator $I$ *decentralizes* a policy $F$ if $F_I = F$.

**Definition 3** (Optimality). An event handler generator $I$ that decentralizes a policy $F$ is *optimal* if for every history $H$ and every event handler generator $I'$ that decentralizes $F$, $\mathcal{C}_I(H) \preceq \mathcal{C}_{I'}(H)$.

Let $I$ be a decentralizer of $F$. $I$ is optimal if it sends to the controller exactly those events that every decentralizer of $F$ sends to the controller, i.e., it only sends those events that it must send.

In the decentralization problem we are given a policy $F$ and the goal is to produce an optimal event handler generator $I$ that decentralizes $F$. In addition to the challenge of decentralization, another challenge stems from the fact that the event handlers generated by $I$ should be implemented in some restricted language that is amenable for installation on the decentralized components. More formally, suppose we have some restricted programming language $T$ such that programs of this language can run on the decentralized components. This language is used to implement event handlers, i.e. partial functions from $\mathcal{E}$ to $2^{\mathcal{A}}$.

*Remark* 2. In this paper we assume that the rules supported by the decentralized components are Boolean conditions on event attributes. Each rule defines a Boolean condition (involving event attributes and perhaps some constants) and an action that should be performed if the condition is satisfied by the current packet-receive event. In the context of SDN, the decentralized components are the switches, which support forwarding rules according to the OPENFLOW standard [2]. The translation of Boolean conditions of this kind to OPENFLOW rules was addressed in [13] in the context of the NetCore network programming language.

An event handler generator $I$ is called $T$*-suitable* if there is an algorithm that given a history $H$, produces a $T$-description of $I(H)$.

**Definition 4.** The *Decentralization Problem* of a policy $F$ relative to $T$ is given by:

**Input.** A specification of a computable policy $F$.
**Output.** A $T$-suitable event handler generator $I$ that decentralizes $F$ and is optimal.

Note that without the optimality requirement, this problem has a trivial solution: let $I_\emptyset$ be the event handler generator that always returns the empty event handler. For this generator, we obviously have $F_{I_\emptyset} = F$.

In general, the problem of decentralization is undecidable (for example, if $F$ is defined in some Turing-complete formalism, or using full first-order logic, as shown in Section 6.4). In the sequel, we will identify a useful family of policies for which the decentralization problem can be solved automatically.

## 5. Characterization of Decentralization and Optimality

In this section, we provide necessary and sufficient conditions for decentralization and optimality. The results presented in this section were verified by means of the proof assistant COQ [17][2].

### 5.1 Decentralization

We show that an event handler generator $I$ decentralizes $F$ if and only if $I$ agrees with $F$ and does not hide any events relevant to the behaviour of the system.

**Definition 5** (Compatibility). An event handler generator $I$ is *compatible* with a policy $F$ if for every event $e$ and $I$-reachable history $H$, $I(H)(e) = F(H)(e)$ whenever $I(H)(e)$ is defined.

Intuitively, $I$ is compatible with $F$ if the event handlers generated by $I$ always perform exactly the actions defined by the policy $F$.

**Definition 6** (Transparency). An event handler generator $I$ is *transparent* with respect to a policy $F$ if $F(\mathcal{C}_I(H)) = F(H)$ holds for every history $H$.

Recall that $\mathcal{C}_I(H)$ is the subsequence of $H$ that is sent to the controller when using $I$. Thus, events in $\mathcal{C}_I(H)$ are those events that the centralized controller "sees", and the only ones that can affect its behaviour. In general, this filtering of events can compromise the correctness of the whole system. An event handler generator $I$ is transparent with respect to a policy $F$ exactly if this filter does not break the policy $F$.

The following theorem gives a useful characterization of when an event handler generator decentralizes a policy (Def. 2).

**Theorem 1.** *An event handler generator $I$ decentralizes a policy $F$ iff it is both compatible and transparent with respect to $F$.*

We now obtain an equivalent definition for transparency, using the notion of an *irrelevant event*:

**Definition 7.** An event $e$ is *irrelevant* with respect to a policy $F$ and a history $H$ if $F(H \cdot e \cdot H') = F(H \cdot H')$ for every history $H'$.

[2] The COQ scripts are available at `https://github.com/karbyshev/decentralize`

**Theorem 2.** *I is transparent with respect to F iff for every I-reachable history H, I(H) is only defined for events that are irrelevant with respect to F and H.*

From the inductive proof of the previous theorem, we get the following as a corollary.

**Corollary 1.** *I is transparent with respect to F iff for all histories H and H′,* $F(H \cdot H') = F(\mathcal{C}_I(H) \cdot H')$.

### 5.2 Optimality

We call an event handler generator *proactive* for a policy $F$ if it is defined on all possible events:

**Definition 8** (Proactiveness). An event handler generator $I$ is *proactive* with respect to a policy $F$ if for every $I$-reachable history $H$, $I(H)$ is defined for all events that are irrelevant with respect to $F$ and $H$.

**Theorem 3.** *An event handler generator I that decentralizes a policy F is optimal iff it is proactive with respect to F.*

### 5.3 Optimal decentralizing event handler generator

Combining Theorems 1 and 3, we obtain that an event handler generator $I$ optimally decentralizes $F$ iff it is compatible, transparent, and proactive with respect to $F$. For any policy $F$, we define the event handler generator $I_F^{\text{opt}}$ that decentralizes $F$ and is optimal with respect to $F$ as follows:

**Definition 9.** Given a policy $F$, the event handler generator $I_F^{\text{opt}}$ is defined by:

$$I_F^{\text{opt}}(H)(e) = \begin{cases} F(H)(e) & e \text{ is irrelevant w.r.t. } H, F \\ \text{undefined} & \text{otherwise} \end{cases}$$

Obviously, $I_F^{\text{opt}}$ is compatible with $F$ and proactive with respect to $F$. Its transparency follows directly from Theorem 2. Therefore, $I_F^{\text{opt}}$ optimally decentralizes $F$. However, note that even when $F$ is computable, $I_F^{\text{opt}}$ may not be computable, since irrelevance is defined in terms of all possible histories $H'$. In the following section we show that for a useful family of policies, the above definition can be used to automatically produce an optimal event handler generator.

## 6. First-Order Specifications of Policies

In this section we introduce a formalism for describing policies via a fragment of first-order logic. This fragment is expressive enough for a variety of useful and interesting policies in the context of SDN. In the next section we provide a solution to the decentralization problem for policies specified in this fragment, i.e., an algorithm that synthesizes an optimal suitable event handler generator for a given policy.

### 6.1 The language $\mathcal{L}$

***Syntax.*** We use an extension of many-sorted first-order language, that we call $\mathcal{L}$, as the basis for our specification languages:

- $\mathcal{L}$'s sorts are the attributes in $\mathcal{Q}$.
- Equality, denoted by $\approx$, is the only predicate symbol.
- $\mathcal{L}$ includes a constant symbol for any element $d \in \bigcup_{q \in \mathcal{Q}} \mathcal{E}_q$ (we will use the elements themselves as constant symbols).
- $\mathcal{L}$ employs ordinary connectives and quantifiers as in first-order logic.
- To succinctly represent events, $\mathcal{L}$ allows "event variables", "event constants" and "selector functions" as syntactic sugar. For example, assuming that $\mathcal{Q} = \{sw, in, src, dst\}$ and $1 \in \mathcal{E}_{src}$, the expression $\forall \bar{y}. (1 \approx \bar{y}.src) \wedge (2 \not\approx \bar{y}.dst)$ is a shorthand for the $\mathcal{L}$-formula $\forall v_1 : sw, v_2 : in, v_3 : src, v_4 : dst. (1 \approx v_3) \wedge (2 \not\approx v_4)$ (to have shorter formulas, one can equivalently take $\forall v_1 : src, v_2 : dst. (1 \approx v_1) \wedge (2 \not\approx v_2)$ in this case).
- $\mathcal{L}$ has a designated free event variable, $\bar{x}$, which we will use to refer to the current event.
- $\mathcal{L}$ has two additional kinds of quantifiers:
  - History-guarded existential quantifiers of the form $\exists \bar{y} \in \mathbb{H}$, where $\mathbb{H}$ is a special symbol and $\bar{y}$ is an event variable.
  - *Last*-quantifiers of the form $\exists \bar{y} = Last_\psi$ where $\bar{y}$ is an event variable and $\psi$ is a quantifier-free formula whose only free variables are $\bar{y}$ and possibly the designated variable $\bar{x}$.

***Semantics.*** Define the many-sorted logical structure $\mathcal{M} = \mathcal{M}(\mathcal{Q}, \mathcal{E}_q : q \in \mathcal{Q})$ as follows:

- $\mathcal{M}$ has a domain $\mathcal{E}_q$ for each sort $q \in \mathcal{Q}$.
- $\approx$ is interpreted as equality.
- Each constant symbol $d$ is interpreted as the element $d \in \mathcal{E}_q$.

The model $\mathcal{M}$ and a given event $e$ naturally induce a satisfaction relation for quantifier-free $\mathcal{L}$-formulas $\varphi$ with $\bar{x}$ as their only free variable. Since $\mathcal{M}$ is usually fixed, we write $e \models \varphi$ to mean that $\mathcal{M}$ is a model (in the usual sense) of $\varphi\{e/\bar{x}\}$.

The semantics of $\mathcal{L}$ extends usual first-order semantics. It is defined with respect to the model $\mathcal{M}$, and a given history $H$ and event $e$. Since $\mathcal{M}$ is usually fixed, we write $H, e \models \varphi$ to mean $\mathcal{M}, H, e \models \varphi$, defined inductively as follows:

- If $\varphi$ is a quantifier-free formula with $\bar{x}$ as its only free variable, then $H, e \models \varphi$ iff $e \models \varphi$.
- The propositional connectives are interpreted as usual.
- $H, e \models \forall v : q. \theta$ if $H, e \models \theta\{d/v\}$ for every $d \in \mathcal{E}_q$.
- $H, e \models \exists v : q. \theta$ if $H, e \models \theta\{d/v\}$ for some $d \in \mathcal{E}_q$.
- $H, e \models \exists \bar{y} \in \mathbb{H}. \theta$ if there is some $e'$ in $H$ for which $H, e \models \theta\{e'/\bar{y}\}$.
- $H, e \models \exists \bar{y} = Last_\psi. \theta$ if $H, e \models \theta\{e'/\bar{y}\}$ where $e'$ is the last event in $H$ for which $e \models \psi\{e'/\bar{y}\}$. If no such event $e'$ exists then $H, e \not\models \exists \bar{y} = Last_\psi. \theta$.

***$\mathcal{L}$-specification of event handler generators.*** Recall that the set of event handlers, $\mathcal{R}$, is the set of partial functions from $\mathcal{E}$ to $P^+(\mathcal{A})$ and an event handler generator is a function from $\mathcal{H}$ to $\mathcal{R}$. Let $I : \mathcal{H} \to \mathcal{R}$ be an event handler generator. Let $\Phi = \{\varphi^a \mid a \in \mathcal{A}\}$ be a set of $\mathcal{L}$-formulas, where each $\varphi^a$ includes the variable $\bar{x}$ as its only free variable. We say that $\Phi$ *defines* $I$, if for every history $H$ and event $e$:

- $I(H)(e) = \{a \in \mathcal{A} \mid H, e \models \varphi^a\} \neq \emptyset$ whenever $I(H)(e)$ is defined.
- $\{a \in \mathcal{A} \mid H, e \models \varphi^a\} = \emptyset$ whenever $I(H)(e)$ is not defined.

### 6.2 Specifications of policies

Policies are functions from $\mathcal{H}$ to $\mathcal{E} \to P^+(\mathcal{A})$. As with event handler generators, we specify a policy via a set of formulas $\Phi = \{\varphi^a \mid a \in \mathcal{A}\}$. Since policies define total event handlers, it must be the case that for all histories $H$ and events $e$, $\{a \in \mathcal{A} \mid H, e \models \varphi^a\} \neq \emptyset$.

We will define policies in a restriction $\mathcal{L}_1$ of $\mathcal{L}$ which we now define. First define a *component* to be a prenex formula of $\mathcal{L}$ that has only history-guarded and last-quantifiers:

$$\exists \bar{y}_1 = Last_{\psi_1} \ldots \exists \bar{y}_m = Last_{\psi_m} \exists \bar{z}_1 \in \mathbb{H} \ldots \exists \bar{z}_r \in \mathbb{H}. \theta$$

where $\theta$ is quantifier-free. The language $\mathcal{L}_1$ consists of all Boolean combinations of components.

*Notation* 1. For an $\mathcal{L}_1$-formula $\varphi$, we denote by $k_{Last}(\varphi)$ the number of occurrences of last-quantifiers in $\varphi$, and by $k_{\exists}(\varphi)$ the number of occurrences of guarded existential quantifiers in $\varphi$. We also define $k_\varphi = k_{Last}(\varphi) + k_{\exists}(\varphi)$.

An $\mathcal{L}_1$*-policy* is a policy defined by a set of $\mathcal{L}_1$-formulas. The following property of $\mathcal{L}_1$-formulas will be crucial for our main results. Among other things, it will allow us to automatically check that a set $\Phi = \{\varphi^a \mid a \in \mathcal{A}\} \subseteq \mathcal{L}_1$ indeed defines a policy, $F_\Phi$, i.e., that for all histories $H$, $F_\Phi(H)$ is total. We first introduce the following definition.

**Definition 10.** Let $\varphi$ be an $\mathcal{L}_1$-formula, $e$ an event, and $H = e_1 \cdot \ldots \cdot e_n$ a history. The *kernel* of $H$ w.r.t. $\varphi$ and $e$, denoted $kernel_{\varphi,e}(H)$, is defined to be a minimal set of indices $\subseteq \{1, \ldots, n\}$ such that for every component $\alpha$ of $\varphi$ of the form

$$\exists \bar{y}_1 = Last_{\psi_1} \ldots \exists \bar{y}_m = Last_{\psi_m} \exists \bar{z}_1 \in \mathbb{H} \ldots \exists \bar{z}_r \in \mathbb{H}.\, \theta :$$

- for every $1 \leq j \leq m$, $kernel_{\varphi,e}(H)$ contains the maximal index $i_j^{Last}$ such that $e \models \psi_j\{e_{i_j^{Last}}/\bar{y}_j\}$, if such an index exists ($e_{i_j^{Last}}$ is the *last* event in $H$ that satisfies the above), and
- if $H, e \models \alpha$ then $kernel_{\varphi,e}(H)$ includes some indices $i_1^{\exists}, \ldots, i_r^{\exists}$ s.t. $e \models \theta\{e_{i_1^{Last}}/\bar{y}_1\} \ldots \{e_{i_m^{Last}}/\bar{y}_m\}\{e_{i_1^{\exists}}/\bar{z}_1\} \ldots \{e_{i_r^{\exists}}/\bar{z}_r\}$.

Note that the size of $kernel_{\varphi,e}(H)$ is at most $k_\varphi$. Intuitively, $kernel_{\varphi,e}(H)$ includes the indices of all events from $H$ that determine whether $H, e \models \varphi$. Therefore:

**Theorem 4.** *Let $\varphi$ be an $\mathcal{L}_1$-formula. Then for every history $H = e_1 \cdot \ldots \cdot e_n$ and event e, and for every subsequence $H_1 = e_{j_1} \cdot \ldots \cdot e_{j_\ell}$ of $H$ such that $kernel_{\varphi,e}(H) \subseteq \{j_1, \ldots, j_\ell\}$, we have $H_1, e \models \varphi$ iff $H, e \models \varphi$.*

*Proof.* Let $H = e_1 \cdot \ldots \cdot e_n$ be some history and $e$ some event. Let $H_1 = e_{j_1} \cdot \ldots \cdot e_{j_\ell}$ be a subsequence of $H$ such that $kernel_{\varphi,e}(H) \subseteq \{j_1, \ldots, j_\ell\}$. We claim that for every component $\alpha$ of $\varphi$ we have: $H, e \models \alpha$ iff $H_1, e \models \alpha$. Indeed, consider some component $\alpha = \exists \bar{y}_1 = Last_{\psi_1} \ldots \exists \bar{y}_m = Last_{\psi_m}. \exists \bar{z}_1 \in \mathbb{H} \ldots \exists \bar{z}_r \in \mathbb{H}.\, \theta$ of $\varphi$. A crucial observation is that for $1 \leq j \leq m$, any event $e'$ that is the last event in $H$ that satisfies $e \models \psi_j\{e'/\bar{y}\}$ is also the last event in $H_1$ that satisfies this property. Furthermore, there is no event $e'$ in $H$ that satisfies $e \models \psi_j\{e'/\bar{y}\}$ iff there is no such event in $H_1$. Suppose that $H, e \models \alpha$. Then $H_1, e \models \alpha$ by definition of $kernel_{\varphi,e}(H)$ (and due to the fact that any last event in $H$ satisfying $\psi$ remains a last event in $H_1$). For the converse, suppose that $H_1, e \models \alpha$. Then since all last elements of $H_1$ are maintained in $H$, and since $H_1 \preceq H$ which ensures that the events satisfying the history guarded quantifiers are also maintained, we get that $H, e \models \alpha$. □

*Remark* 3. In Theorem 4 we use the set $kernel_{\varphi,e}(H)$ of indices to define a subsequence $H_0$ of $e_1 \cdot \ldots \cdot e_n$ and we require inclusion of $kernel_{\varphi,e}(H)$ in the set of indices defining the subsequence $H_1 = e_{j_1} \cdot \ldots \cdot e_{j_\ell}$ rather than requiring that $H_0 \preceq H_1$. The reason for that is that $e_1 \cdot \ldots \cdot e_n$ may contain duplicates of the same event. For an event that appears more than once we must make sure to keep in $H_1$ the correct *occurrence* (index) of the event to preserve the last elements. Therefore, it is not enough to require that $H_0 \preceq H_1 \preceq H$. For example, suppose that $\varphi = \exists \bar{y} = Last_\psi.\theta$ and let $H = e_1 e_2 e_1$, where $e_1$ and $e_2$ both satisfy $\psi$ but only $e_1$ satisfies $\theta$. Then in this case $H, e \models \varphi$ and $kernel_{\varphi,e}(H) = \{3\}$, consisting of the index of the last element satisfying $\psi$. If we just consider the corresponding subsequence $H_0 = e_1$, then for $H_1 = e_1 e_2$ we cannot guarantee $H_1, e \models \varphi$ iff $H, e \models \varphi$, even though $H_0 \preceq H_1$. This is because we kept in $H_1$ the first occurrence of $e_1$ where in fact we needed the second occurrence, thus changing the last element. When considering the sets of indices we see that indeed $\{3\} \not\subseteq \{1, 2\}$.

Using Theorem 4 and the property that $|kernel_{\varphi,e}(H)| \leq k_\varphi$, we can check if $\Phi = \{\varphi^a \mid a \in \mathcal{A}\} \subseteq \mathcal{L}_1$ defines a policy. We need to check that for all histories and events, at least one of the $\mathcal{L}_1$-formulas in $\{\varphi^a \mid a \in \mathcal{A}\}$ holds. This amounts to checking that the $\mathcal{L}_1$-formula $\bigvee_{a \in \mathcal{A}} \varphi^a$ is valid. Theorem 4 ensures that for the validity (or satisfiability) of an $\mathcal{L}_1$-formula $\varphi$ it suffices to consider only histories that include up to $k_\varphi$ events. Furthermore, if we want to check that some set $S$ of actions should never take place together (e.g. $\{\texttt{flood}, \texttt{drop}\}$), we can verify that the policy admits these restrictions by checking that the formula $\bigwedge_{a \in S} \varphi^a$ is unsatisfiable.

*Remark* 4. The last quantifiers allow us to select some (occurrences of) events from a history and refer to their properties. One can extend $\mathcal{L}_1$ to include additional selectors, such as "last $k$", "first $k$" etc., as long as they select a fixed number of (occurrences of) events from the history, and in addition have the property that applying the selection on a subsequence of the history that includes all the selected indices will result in the same selection. These properties ensure that Theorem 4 still holds, when Definition 10 (kernel) is adapted accordingly.

### 6.2.1 $\mathcal{L}_1$-specifications of SDN policies.

Now, we give $\mathcal{L}_1$ specifications for the example policies from Section 3. Recall that in the context of SDN, $\mathcal{Q} = \{sw, in, src, dst\}$, and the set of actions is $\mathcal{A} = \texttt{Ports} \cup \{\texttt{flood}, \texttt{drop}\}$, where $\texttt{Ports} = \mathcal{E}_{in}$ is a finite set of ports present in each switch. In the following, we use $p$ to denote a port in $\texttt{Ports}$, and the formulas for the actions that are not specified are assumed to be $\bot$.

***Hub (flooding switch).*** The policy for the hub is specified by:

$$\varphi_{\text{hub}}^{\texttt{flood}} = \top$$

***Firewall*** The policy for the firewall is specified by:

$$\varphi_{\text{fw}}^1 = (\bar{x}.in \approx 2) \wedge \exists \bar{y} \in \mathbb{H}.(\bar{y}.in \approx 1) \wedge (\bar{y}.dst \approx \bar{x}.src)$$
$$\varphi_{\text{fw}}^2 = (\bar{x}.in \approx 1)$$
$$\varphi_{\text{fw}}^{\texttt{drop}} = \neg\varphi_{\text{fw}}^1 \wedge \neg\varphi_{\text{fw}}^2$$

***Learning switch*** The policy for the learning switch is specified by:

$$\varphi_{\text{ls}}^p = \exists \bar{y} \in \mathbb{H}.\, (\bar{x}.sw \approx \bar{y}.sw) \wedge (\bar{x}.dst \approx \bar{y}.src) \wedge (\bar{y}.in \approx p)$$
$$\varphi_{\text{ls}}^{\texttt{flood}} = \bigwedge_{p \in \texttt{Ports}} \neg\varphi_{\text{ls}}^p$$

***Learning switch with migrations*** The policy for the learning switch that supports migrations of hosts is specified by:

$$\varphi_{\text{lsm}}^p = \exists \bar{y} = Last_{(\bar{x}.sw \approx \bar{y}.sw) \wedge (\bar{x}.dst \approx \bar{y}.src)}.\, (\bar{y}.in \approx p)$$
$$\varphi_{\text{lsm}}^{\texttt{flood}} = \bigwedge_{p \in \texttt{Ports}} \neg\varphi_{\text{lsm}}^p$$

***Authorization server*** To model the scenario, we introduce an attribute *type* in $\mathcal{Q}$, along with two constants $A$ and $D$ meaning that the sent message is an authorization or deauthorization massage, respectively. We assume that the authorization server connects directly to the switch, so we can model the authorization (deauthorization) of host $h$ by a packet whose source is $h_a$, its destination is $h$, and its type is $A$ ($D$).

The policy for the switch connected to an authorization server is specified by:

$$\varphi_{\text{auth}}^{\texttt{flood}} = \bar{x}.src \not\approx h_a \wedge \bar{x}.dst \not\approx h_a \implies$$
$$(\exists \bar{y} = Last_{\psi(\bar{x}.src)}.\, \bar{y}.type = A) \wedge$$
$$(\exists \bar{y} = Last_{\psi(\bar{x}.dst)}.\, \bar{y}.type = A)$$
$$\varphi_{\text{auth}}^{\texttt{drop}} = \neg\varphi_{\text{auth}}^{\texttt{flood}}$$

where $\psi(h) = \bar{y}.src = h_a \wedge \bar{y}.dst = h$.

### 6.3 Specification of event handlers

We finally complete the description of the specification language by choosing the programming language $T$ for the decentralized components to be the quantifier-free fragment of $\mathcal{L}$. The rationale is that this is convenient for us and even very primitive components, such as switches in the context of SDN, can run this $T$. More precisely, $T$ is the fragment $\mathcal{L}_0$ of $\mathcal{L}$ consisting of quantifier-free $\mathcal{L}$-formulas whose only free variable is $\bar{x}$. A collection $\{\varphi^a_R \mid a \in \mathcal{A}\}$ of such formulas *defines* an event handler $R$ if the following hold for every event $e$:

- $R(e) = \{a \in \mathcal{A} \mid e \models \varphi^a_R\} \neq \emptyset$ whenever $R(e)$ is defined.
- $\{a \in \mathcal{A} \mid e \models \varphi^a_R\} = \emptyset$ whenever $R(e)$ is not defined.

For example, the event handler $R$ which drops all packets arriving in port 1, and is undefined for all other events, is specified in $\mathcal{L}_0$ as $\varphi^{\texttt{drop}}_R = (\bar{x}.in \approx 1)$, and $\varphi^a_R = \bot$ for all other actions $a$.

### 6.4 Undecidability of decentralization of $\mathcal{L}$-policies

If we allow to define policies using formulas in the unrestricted language $\mathcal{L}$ instead of $\mathcal{L}_1$, the decentralization problem becomes undecidable. To prove this, we show that the finite satisfiability problem for first-order logic with a single binary predicate can be reduced to the problem of (optimally) decentralizing a policy expressed using $\mathcal{L}$-formulas. Let $\psi$ be a formula in (unsorted) first-order logic with one binary predicate $B$. We transform $\psi$ into an $\mathcal{L}$-formula by simulating every pair of elements satisfying $B$ by an event in the history. Technically, let $\psi'$ be the formula obtained from $\psi$ by replacing any occurrence of the binary predicate $B(u, w)$ by the formula $(\exists \bar{y} \in \mathbb{H}.(\bar{y}.src \approx u) \wedge (\bar{y}.dst \approx w))$. In addition, all the original variables (and quantifiers) in $\psi$ which are unsorted, become sorted with sort "host". Finally, all free variables in $\psi$ are existentially quantified in $\psi'$. $\psi'$ is an $\mathcal{L}$-formula (note that it has no free variable), and it can be used to define the following policy $F$: $\varphi^{\texttt{flood}} = \psi', \varphi^{\texttt{drop}} = \neg\psi'$.

We now claim that $\psi$ has no finite model iff $I^{\text{opt}}_F(\epsilon) = R_{\texttt{drop}}$ such that $R_{\texttt{drop}}(e) = \texttt{drop}$ for every event $e$, where $I^{\text{opt}}_F$ is the optimal event handler generator for $F$.

The construction of $\psi'$ ensures that $\psi$ has no finite model iff there is no finite history that satisfies $\psi'$. In addition, if there is no finite history that satisfies $\psi'$, then the policy simply instructs to always drop all events. This means that $I^{\text{opt}}_F(\epsilon) = R_{\texttt{drop}}$. For the converse, assume that $I^{\text{opt}}_F(\epsilon) = R_{\texttt{drop}}$. Then by induction, for every history $H$, $C_{I^{\text{opt}}_F}(H) = \epsilon$ and hence $F_{I^{\text{opt}}_F}(H) = I^{\text{opt}}_F(C_{I^{\text{opt}}_F}(H)) = I^{\text{opt}}_F(\epsilon) = R_{\texttt{drop}}$, meaning all events are always dropped, and by the assumption that $I^{\text{opt}}_F$ is correct with respect to $F$, we get that $F(H) = R_{\texttt{drop}}$ for any $H$, hence no (finite) history satisfies $\psi'$.

## 7. Our Solution

In this section, we introduce a method for synthesizing programs that implement optimal event handler generators for given $\mathcal{L}_1$-policies. We start by showing that for any given set of $\mathcal{L}_1$-formulas that defines the policy $F$, one can automatically derive a set of $\mathcal{L}$-formulas that defines the optimal decentralizing event handler generator $I^{\text{opt}}_F$ (see Definition 9).

Then, we will show that any event handler generator $I$ that is defined by a set of $\mathcal{L}$-formulas is $\mathcal{L}_0$-suitable. That is, we present an algorithm (see Section 7.3) that given $I$ and a history $H$, produces an $\mathcal{L}_0$-description of $I(H)$.

Using these ingredients we obtain an implementation of a controller in the context of SDN, as described in Algorithm 2. The controller is parametrized by the policy $F$, and by $I^{\text{opt}}_F$, which is expressed in $\mathcal{L}$ and precomputed from $F$ by the method described in Section 7.2. The controller accumulates the sequence $H$ of events it receives as its state. For a new event, it computes the action to be performed by evaluating the $\mathcal{L}_1$-formulas defining the policy on the current history. It then infers rules by applying the algorithm from Section 7.3 to compute $I^{\text{opt}}_F(H)$.

**Algorithm 2** Runtime System $\langle F, I^{\text{opt}}_F\rangle$

```
H := ε
while new packet-receive event e do
    action := F(H, e)        # compute an action
    H := H · e               # update state
    rules := I_F^opt(H)      # compute rules (Section 7.3)
    configure_switches(rules)
    send_to_switches(action)
end while
```

### 7.1 Bounded causality

For a general policy $F$, $I^{\text{opt}}_F$ may not be computable. This is due to the fact that the relevance of an event may depend on the behavior of the policy for infinitely many possible future sequences of events (see Definition 7). However, we now show that for $\mathcal{L}_1$-definable policies, we can bound the size of future sequences of events that must be considered.

**Definition 11.** For an integer $k$, an event $e$ is *$k$-relevant* with respect to policy $F$ and history $H$ if there exists a history $H'$ of size at most $k$ that distinguishes whether $e$ occurred, i.e., $F(H \cdot e \cdot H') \neq F(H \cdot H')$.

**Definition 12** ($k$-bounded causality)**.** For an integer $k$, we say that a policy $F$ has *$k$-bounded causality* if for any event $e$ and history $H$, if $e$ is relevant with respect to $F$ and $H$ then it is also $k$-relevant.

In other words, a policy $F$ has $k$-bounded causality if whenever an event $e$ is relevant, it can cause a change after at most $k$ additional events.

**Theorem 5.** *Let $\Phi = \{\varphi^a \mid a \in \mathcal{A}\} \subseteq \mathcal{L}_1$ define a policy $F_\Phi$. Then $F_\Phi$ has $k_\Phi$-bounded causality, for*

$$k_\Phi := \max\{k_{Last}(\varphi^a) + 2 \cdot k_\exists(\varphi^a) \mid a \in \mathcal{A}\}. \quad (1)$$

*Proof.* We show that $F$ has $k_\Phi$-bounded causality. Given $H, H'$ and $e$ such that $F(H \cdot e \cdot H') \neq F(H \cdot H')$, it follows that there exists an event $e'$ and an action $a \in \mathcal{A}$ such that $a \in F(H \cdot e \cdot H')(e')$ but $a \notin F(H \cdot H')(e')$ or vice versa. W.l.o.g. assume the former. This means that $H \cdot e \cdot H', e' \models \varphi^a$ but $H \cdot H', e' \not\models \varphi^a$. We construct a history $H_0 \preceq H'$ of size at most $k_\Phi$ such that the same holds when $H'$ is replaced by $H_0$.

In order to construct $H_0$, we construct the set of indices of the events in $H'$ that participate in $H_0$. Let

$$J'_1 = \mathit{kernel}_{\varphi^a, e'}(H \cdot e \cdot H') \cap \{|H \cdot e| + 1, \ldots, |H \cdot e \cdot H'|\}$$

be all the indices in $\mathit{kernel}_{\varphi^a, e'}(H \cdot e \cdot H')$ which refer to events taken from $H'$. To consider the actual indices in $H'$ we subtract $|H \cdot e|$ from all of the indices. The result, $J^{H'}_1 = \{i - |H \cdot e| \mid i \in J'_1\}$, is a set of indices from $H'$. Similarly, let

$$J'_2 = \mathit{kernel}_{\varphi^a, e'}(H \cdot H') \cap \{|H| + 1, \ldots, |H \cdot H'|\}$$

be all the indices in $\mathit{kernel}_{\varphi^a, e'}(H \cdot H')$ of events taken from $H'$, and let $J^{H'}_2 = \{i - |H| \mid i \in J'_2\}$ be the corresponding set of indices in $H'$.

We define a set of indices $J_0 = J^{H'}_1 \cup J^{H'}_2$ of events in $H'$ and define a subsequence $H_0$ of $H'$ accordingly. Namely, suppose that $H' = e_1 \cdot \ldots \cdot e_{|H'|}$. Then $H_0 = e_{i_1} \cdot \ldots \cdot e_{i_k}$ where $1 \le e_{i_1} < \ldots < e_{i_k} \le |H'|$ and $J_0 = \{e_{i_1}, \ldots, e_{i_k}\}$.

Recall that the kernel size of a history w.r.t. $\varphi^a$ is at most $k_{\varphi^a} = k_{Last}(\varphi^a) + k_{\exists}(\varphi^a)$. Since both $J_1^{H'}$ and $J_2^{H'}$ include all the indices of the "last" events from $H'$ (see Definition 10), which are the same, then the size of $J_0$ and therefore also the size of $H_0$ is bounded by $k_{Last}(\varphi^a) + 2 \cdot k_{\exists}(\varphi^a) \leq k_\Phi$. Further, since $H \cdot e \cdot H_0 \preceq H \cdot e \cdot H'$ such that the set of indices of $H \cdot e \cdot H_0$ in $H \cdot e \cdot H'$ is $(\{1, \ldots, |H \cdot e|\} \cup J_1') \supseteq \mathit{kernel}_{\varphi^a, e'}(H \cdot e \cdot H')$, then by Theorem 4, $H \cdot e \cdot H', e' \models \varphi^a$ iff $H \cdot e \cdot H_0, e' \models \varphi^a$. Similarly, since $H \cdot H_0 \preceq H \cdot H'$ such that the set of indices of $H \cdot H_0$ in $H \cdot H'$ is $(\{1, \ldots, |H|\} \cup J_2') \supseteq \mathit{kernel}_{\varphi^a, e'}(H \cdot H')$, then by Theorem 4, $H \cdot H', e' \models \varphi^a$ iff $H \cdot H_0, e' \models \varphi^a$. We conclude that $H \cdot e \cdot H_0, e' \models \varphi^a$ but $H \cdot H_0, e' \not\models \varphi^a$ as required. □

*Remark* 5. By inspecting Definition 10 and the proof of Theorem 4 and Theorem 5, it follows that in several cases we can obtain a slightly better bound (lower $k_\Phi$), that will simplify our examples below. In particular:

- If the given set of formulas $\Phi = \{\varphi^a \mid a \in \mathcal{A}\}$ defining $F$ contains *only* history guarded quantifiers, then we can take

$$k_\Phi := \max\{k_\exists(\varphi^a) - 1 \mid a \in \mathcal{A}\}. \quad (2)$$

  To see this, note that without last quantifiers, it cannot be the case that $H \cdot H', e' \models \alpha$ but $H \cdot e \cdot H', e' \not\models \alpha$ for some component $\alpha$. Furthermore, if we have $H \cdot H', e' \models \theta\{e_1/\bar{z}_1\} \ldots \{e_r/\bar{z}_r\}$ for some $e_1, \ldots, e_r$, then $H \cdot e \cdot H', e' \models \theta\{e_1/\bar{z}_1\} \ldots \{e_r/\bar{z}_r\}$ for the same events (none of these properties is guaranteed in the presence of last quantifiers). This allows us to choose $k_\exists(\varphi^a)$ elements (indices) to comprise $H_0$, instead of $2 \cdot k_\exists(\varphi^a)$: for components that are satisfied in both $H \cdot H'$ and $H \cdot e \cdot H'$ it suffices to choose the elements based on $H \cdot H'$ (rather than both). Finally, we need one event less since there is at least one component $\alpha$ for which $H \cdot e \cdot H', e' \models \alpha$ but $H \cdot H', e' \not\models \alpha$. For this component we can choose $k_\exists(\alpha) - 1$ events, knowing that the additional event must be $e$ itself.
- If the formulas $\varphi^a$ contain only last quantifiers then we can take

$$k_\Phi := \max\{k_{Last}(\varphi^a) - 1 \mid a \in \mathcal{A}\}. \quad (3)$$

  By the proof of Theorem 5 it suffices to consider $k_{Last}(\varphi^a)$ "last" events from $H'$ in the construction of $H_0$. In fact, since there is at least one component $\alpha$ for which $H \cdot e \cdot H', e' \models \alpha$ but $H \cdot H', e' \not\models \alpha$ or vice versa, while the last events in $H'$ are clearly the same, then the difference must stem from a last event in $H$ or $H \cdot e$. Either way, this event is not in $H'$ making the size of $H_0$ at most $k_{Last}(\varphi^a) - 1$.

***Unbounded causality in the presence of quantifier alternation*** If we allow alternation of quantifiers in the specification of policies, then the $k$-bounded causality property does not necessarily hold. As an example, consider a policy $F$ which defines two possible actions, $a$ and $b$, where $\varphi^a = \forall \bar{z}_1 \in \mathbb{H}. \exists \bar{z}_2 \in \mathbb{H}. \bar{z}_1.\mathit{src} = \bar{z}_2.\mathit{dst} \wedge \bar{z}_1.\mathit{dst} = \bar{z}_2.\mathit{src}$ and $\varphi^b = \neg\varphi^a$. Namely, if in the current history $H$ every event has a matching event with opposite source and destination, then action $a$ is performed on the current event $e$ (for any $e$). Otherwise $b$ is performed. Assume to the contrary that $F$ has the $k$-bounded causality property for some $k$. Consider a history $H$ of length $k+1$ which consists of events such that all sources are different, all destinations are different, and all sources are different from all destinations. Further, consider an event $e$ whose source and destination also differ from all sources and destinations in $H$. Clearly, $e$ is relevant. However, $e$ is not $k$-relevant. Indeed, for any future sequence of events $H''$ with $\leq k$ events, at least one of the events in $H$ remains unmatched, whether $H''$ follows $H$ or $H \cdot e$. Thus, $F(H \cdot H'')(e') = F(H \cdot e \cdot H'')(e') = b$ for any $e'$.

### 7.2 Construction of an optimal event handler generator

In this section we show that for any policy $F$ defined by a set of $\mathcal{L}_1$ formulas, we can define the optimally decentralizing event handler generator $I_F^{\mathrm{opt}}$ using a set of $\mathcal{L}$-formulas. First, we introduce the following notation.

*Notation* 2. Let $\varphi$ be an $\mathcal{L}$-formula with one free event variable $\bar{x}$. Let $\bar{y}_1, \ldots, \bar{y}_n$ be event variables. We denote by $\varphi[\bar{y}_1, \ldots, \bar{y}_n]$ the formula obtained from $\varphi$ as follows:

- Each subformula of $\varphi$ of the form $\exists \bar{y} \in \mathbb{H}. \psi$ is replaced by

$$(\exists \bar{y} \in \mathbb{H}. \psi) \vee \bigvee_{1 \leq i \leq n} \psi\{\bar{y}_i/\bar{y}\}.$$

- Each subformula of $\varphi$ of the form $\exists \bar{y} = \mathit{Last}_\psi. \theta$ is replaced by

$$(\exists \bar{y} = \mathit{Last}_\psi. \theta \wedge N_\psi^0[\bar{y}_1, \ldots, \bar{y}_n]) \vee \bigvee_{1 \leq i \leq n} \left(\theta\{\bar{y}_i/\bar{y}\} \wedge \psi\{\bar{y}_i/\bar{y}\} \wedge N_\psi^i[\bar{y}_1, \ldots, \bar{y}_n]\right)$$

  where $N_\psi^i[\bar{y}_1, \ldots, \bar{y}_n] = \bigwedge_{i < j \leq n} \neg\psi\{\bar{y}_j/\bar{y}\}$

Intuitively, the notation $\varphi[\bar{y}_1, \ldots, \bar{y}_n]$ is used to encode the formula $\varphi$ when the history is extended by a suffix of events described by $\bar{y}_1, \ldots, \bar{y}_n$. This affects both the history-guarded quantifiers and the last quantifiers. Formally, this is stated by the following lemma.

**Lemma 2.** *For any $\mathcal{L}$-formula $\varphi$ with one free variable $\bar{x}$, history $H$, events $e_1, \ldots, e_n, e$, and distinct event variables $\bar{y}_1, \ldots, \bar{y}_n$, we have $H \cdot e_1 \cdot \ldots \cdot e_n, e \models \varphi$ iff $H, e \models \varphi[\bar{y}_1, \ldots, \bar{y}_n]\{e_1/\bar{y}_1\} \ldots \{e_n/\bar{y}_n\}$.*

Using this notation, the synthesis of $\{\varphi^a_{I_F^{\mathrm{opt}}} \mid a \in \mathcal{A}\}$ from $\{\varphi^a \mid a \in \mathcal{A}\}$ is done using the following definition:

**Definition 13.** Given $\{\varphi^a \mid a \in \mathcal{A}\}$, for any action $a \in \mathcal{A}$ the formula $\varphi^a_{I_F^{\mathrm{opt}}}$ is defined by: $\varphi^a_{I_F^{\mathrm{opt}}} := \varphi^a \wedge \bigwedge_{0 \leq m \leq k_\Phi, a' \in \mathcal{A}} \psi_m^{a'}$ where:

- $k_\Phi$ is the bound defined in Theorem 5, such that $F$ has the $k_\Phi$-bounded causality property.
- $\psi_m^{a'}$ denotes the formula:

$$\forall \bar{y}_1, \ldots, \bar{y}_m, \bar{y}.$$
$$\varphi^{a'}\{\bar{y}/\bar{x}\}[\bar{x}, \bar{y}_1, \ldots, \bar{y}_m] \iff \varphi^{a'}\{\bar{y}/\bar{x}\}[\bar{y}_1, \ldots, \bar{y}_m]$$

We present several clarifications:

- The formulas $\varphi^a$, $\psi_m^{a'}$, and therefore also $\varphi^a_{I_F^{\mathrm{opt}}}$, all have $\bar{x}$ as their only free event variable, which represents the "current" event.
- Each $\varphi_I^a$ is an $\mathcal{L}$-formula, but not an $\mathcal{L}_1$-formula since it includes unguarded quantifiers.
- The conjunction of the formulas $\psi_m^{a'}$ over all actions $a' \in \mathcal{A}$ encodes the property that the (current) event $e$, represented by $\bar{x}$, is irrelevant when considering exactly $m$ events into the future (where to obtain $k_\Phi$-irrelevance we consider the conjunction over all $0 \leq m \leq k_\Phi$). Technically, $\bar{y}_1, \ldots, \bar{y}_m$ represent the $m$ future events $e_1, \ldots, e_m$, and $\bar{y}$ represents an event to which $F$ is applied in the future with or without considering $e$. On the left hand side of the comparison we therefore apply $\varphi^{a'}$ on $\bar{y}$ and use $[\bar{x}, \bar{y}_1, \ldots, \bar{y}_m]$ to extend the history by the events $e, e_1, \ldots, e_m$. Similarly, on the right hand side we use $[\bar{y}_1, \ldots, \bar{y}_m]$ to extend the history by only $e_1, \ldots, e_m$ (excluding $e$).

The above explanations can be straightforwardly summarized in the following theorem that establishes the correctness of our construction. In particular, note that since $F$ is defined by $\mathcal{L}_1$-formulas, it has $k_\Phi$-bounded causality, and so $k_\Phi$-irrelevance is equivalent to full irrelevance.

**Theorem 6.** *Let $F$ be a policy defined by a set $\Phi = \{\varphi^a \mid a \in \mathcal{A}\}$ of $\mathcal{L}_1$-formulas. Then the set of $\mathcal{L}$ formulas $\Phi^{opt} = \{\varphi^a_{I_F^{opt}} \mid a \in \mathcal{A}\}$ as in Definition 13 defines the event handler generator $I_F^{opt}$.*

*Proof.* Follows from Theorem 2, Theorem 5 and Lemma 2. □

This completes the construction of an $\mathcal{L}$-definition of an optimal event handler generator $I$ that decentralizes $F$.

*Remark* 6. In Definition 13, in the construction of $\varphi^a_{I_F^{\text{opt}}}$, it is sufficient to include only $m = 0$ and $m = k_\Phi$ in the conjunction $\bigwedge_{\substack{0 \le m \le k_\Phi \\ a' \in \mathcal{A}}} \psi^{a'}_m$, omitting the intermediate values. The reason is that $\mathcal{L}_1$-formulas cannot detect stuttering in non-empty histories. Namely, for any $\varphi \in \mathcal{L}_1$, we have

$$H \cdot e_1 \cdot H', e \models \varphi \iff H \cdot e_1 \cdot e_1 \cdot H', e \models \varphi.$$

As a result, if $\psi^{a'}_m$, which considers $m$ events into the future, does not hold for some $0 < m < k_\Phi$, it also does not hold for $m = k_\Phi$ by repeating one of the $m$ future "refuting" elements.

### 7.3 $\mathcal{L}_0$-suitability of $\mathcal{L}$-definitions

Here we show that the event handler generator $I$ defined before as a set of $\mathcal{L}$-formulas is $\mathcal{L}_0$-suitable. Assume we are given such a set $\{\varphi^a_I \mid a \in \mathcal{A}\}$. We describe a general algorithm that will take as input a concrete history $H$, and produce a set $\{\varphi^a_{I(H)} \mid a \in \mathcal{A}\}$ of $\mathcal{L}_0$-formulas that defines the event handler $I(H)$.

Let $H$ be a particular history. For $\{\varphi^a_{I(H)} \mid a \in \mathcal{A}\}$ to define $I(H)$ the following has to hold:

**Correctness** For any event $e$ and action $a$:

$$H, e \models \varphi^a_I \quad \text{iff} \quad e \models \varphi^a_{I(H)}$$

The computation is done in two steps, as described next.

***Step 1.*** First, we eliminate the history guarded quantifiers and the last quantifiers according to their semantics. Suppose $H = e_1 \cdot \ldots \cdot e_n$. Then:

- Every subformula in each $\varphi^a_I$ that begins with a history guarded quantifier $\exists \bar{y} \in \mathbb{H}.\theta$ is replaced by a disjunction: $\bigvee_{1 \le i \le n} \theta\{e_i/\bar{y}\}$
- Every subformula in each $\varphi^a_I$ that begins with a last quantifier $\exists \bar{y} = Last_\psi.\theta$ is replaced with the following disjunction:

$$\bigvee_{1 \le i \le n} \Big(\theta\{e_i/\bar{y}\} \wedge \psi\{e_i/\bar{y}\} \wedge N^i_\psi[e_1, \ldots, e_n]\Big)$$

where $N^i_\psi[e_1, \ldots, e_n] = \bigwedge_{i<j\le n} \neg\psi\{e_j/\bar{y}\}$

Note that this transformation is similar to the one defined in Notation 2, where we assume that the full history is $e_1 \cdot \ldots \cdot e_n$. The next proposition justifies correctness.

**Proposition 1.** *Let $\varphi$ be an $\mathcal{L}$-formula with one free event variable $\bar{x}$, and suppose that $\varphi'$ was obtained from $\varphi$ as described above. Then $H, e \models \varphi$ iff $e \models \varphi'$.*

***Step 2.*** In this stage we have a set of formulas in which equality is the only predicate symbol. To make them $\mathcal{L}_0$-formulas, it remains to eliminate the quantifiers. For this simple case, it can be done by "equality enumeration" as explained next.

**Definition 14.** For a quantifier-free $\mathcal{L}$-formula $\varphi$ in which equality is the only predicate symbol and a variable $v$, $\varphi^{\not\approx v}$ is the $\mathcal{L}$-formula, inductively denied by:

$$\varphi^{\not\approx v} = \begin{cases} \top & \varphi = (v \approx v) \\ \bot & \varphi = (v \approx t) \text{ or } \varphi = (t \approx v) \text{ where } t \ne v \\ \varphi & \varphi = (t_1 \approx t_2) \text{ where } t_1 \ne v \text{ and } t_2 \ne v \\ \varphi_1^{\not\approx v} \circ \varphi_2^{\not\approx v} & \varphi = \varphi_1 \circ \varphi_2 \text{ where } \circ \in \{\wedge, \vee, \rightarrow, \leftrightarrow\} \\ \neg\varphi_1^{\not\approx v} & \varphi = \neg\varphi_1 \end{cases}$$

Intuitively, this operator resolves any equality involving $v$ in $\varphi$ under the assumption that the value of $v$ is different from the values of all other variables and constants that appear in $\varphi$. Note that the variable $v$ does not occur anymore in $\varphi^{\not\approx v}$, and the following is valid in first-order logic: $\left(\bigwedge_{t \in \mathcal{V}_\varphi} v \not\approx t\right) \implies (\varphi \iff \varphi^{\not\approx v})$ where $\mathcal{V}_\varphi$ is the set of free variables and constant symbols that occur in $\varphi$, except for the variable $v$ itself.

Equipped with this operator, we can now explain what we mean by equality enumeration.

The elimination of quantifiers from the formulas that we obtained after step 1 directly follows from the following two equivalences, that hold for any quantifier-free formula $\varphi$ that has only equality as a predicate symbol:

1. If $\mathcal{E}_q$ is infinite then $\forall v : q.\varphi \equiv \left(\bigwedge_{t \in \mathcal{V}_\varphi} \varphi\{t/v\}\right) \wedge \varphi^{\not\approx v}$, where $\mathcal{V}_\varphi$ is the set of free variables and constants in $\varphi$ except for $v$.
2. If $\mathcal{E}_q$ is finite then $\forall v : q.\varphi \equiv \left(\bigwedge_{t \in \mathcal{E}_q} \varphi\{t/v\}\right)$.

The second equivalence is obvious (recall that we assume a constant symbol for any element in the domain), and the first can be explained as follows:

$$\begin{aligned} \forall v : q.\varphi &\equiv (\bigwedge_{t \in \mathcal{V}_\varphi} \varphi\{t/v\}) \wedge \forall v : q.((\bigwedge_{t \in \mathcal{V}_\varphi} v \not\approx t) \rightarrow \varphi) \\ &\equiv (\bigwedge_{t \in \mathcal{V}_\varphi} \varphi\{t/v\}) \wedge \forall v : q.((\bigwedge_{t \in \mathcal{V}_\varphi} v \not\approx t) \rightarrow \varphi^{\not\approx v}) \\ &\equiv (\bigwedge_{t \in \mathcal{V}_\varphi} \varphi\{t/v\}) \wedge ((\exists v : q. \bigwedge_{t \in \mathcal{V}_\varphi} v \not\approx t) \rightarrow \varphi^{\not\approx v}) \\ &\equiv (\bigwedge_{t \in \mathcal{V}_\varphi} \varphi\{t/v\}) \wedge \varphi^{\not\approx v} \end{aligned}$$

where the last equivalence is due to the fact that $\mathcal{E}_q$ is infinite.

By repeatedly applying these equivalences from the inner-most to the outer-most quantifier, one obtains an equivalent quantifier-free formula. Hence, the second step amounts to performing this simple quantifier elimination on all formulas in the set, producing $\{\varphi^a_{I(H)} \mid a \in \mathcal{A}\}$ as a result.

To summarize, if we are given $\Phi$, an $\mathcal{L}_1$ specification of a policy $F$, we showed in Theorem 6 that we can automatically construct $\Phi^{\text{opt}}$, an $\mathcal{L}$ specification of an optimal event handler generator $I_F^{\text{opt}}$. Now we have given an algorithm to go from $\Phi^{\text{opt}}$ and a history $H$ to the quantifier-free specification of forwarding rules that implement $I_F^{\text{opt}}(H)$. In conclusion, we have shown the following:

**Theorem 7.** *Given an $\mathcal{L}_1$-specification of a policy $F$, we can automatically produce a program which takes a history $H$ and produces the quantifier-free specification of forwarding rules that implement an optimal implementation of $F$.*

*Remark* 7. The running time of our solution to the decentralization problem is determined by the complexity of the static part and the complexity of the dynamic part. For a policy formula $\psi$ expressed in $\mathcal{L}_1$ with causality bound $k$, the static translation produces an

$\mathcal{L}$-formula for $I_{\psi}^{\text{opt}}$ of the length $\mathcal{O}(|\psi| \cdot k^2)$ with $k+1$ nested universal quantifiers, where $|\psi|$ is the length of formula $\psi$. Denote the resulting formula by $\psi'$. In the dynamic part, for the current history $H$ of length $h = |H|$, Step 1 eliminates guarded quantifiers from $\psi'$ and produces a formula $\psi''$ of size $\mathcal{O}(|\psi'| \cdot h^{2k})$ with the same nesting depth of universal quantifiers as $\psi'$. Step 2 eliminates (unguarded) universal quantifiers from $\psi''$ and returns a formula of size $\mathcal{O}(|\psi''| \cdot m^{k+1})$ where $m$ is a maximum of $k$, $h$, the number of constants occurring in $\psi$ and of all $|\mathcal{E}_q|$, for finite $\mathcal{E}_q$. In total, the running time of the algorithm of Theorem 7 is in $\mathcal{O}(|\psi| \cdot k^2 \cdot h^{2k} \cdot m^{k+1})$. In all the examples in this paper, the algorithm is linear in $|\psi|$, as $k$ can be taken to be 0 according to Remark 5.

It is important to note that (1) the complexity is measured with respect to $|H|$ where $H$ is the log kept by the controller, and not the full history. This is especially important as the optimal event handler generator minimizes the size of this log; and (2) the running time analysis refers to the processing of events handled by the controller, whose number is minimized, and not of events handled by the switches.

### 7.4 Examples

We demonstrate our technique on two examples: the firewall and the learning switch that supports migrations.

***Firewall*** Recall the policy for the firewall, given by:

$$\begin{aligned}
\varphi^1 &= (\bar{x}.in \approx 2) \land \exists \bar{z} \in \mathbb{H}.(\bar{z}.in \approx 1) \land (\bar{z}.dst \approx \bar{x}.src) \\
\varphi^2 &= (\bar{x}.in \approx 1) \\
\varphi^{\texttt{drop}} &= \neg\varphi^1 \land \neg\varphi^2
\end{aligned}$$

In the above we renamed $\bar{y}$ to $\bar{z}$ in order to avoid confusion. For the simplicity of the presentation, we focus here on just one switch. To obtain the $\mathcal{L}$-description of the optimal decentralizing event handler generator, we use Definition 13. For each $a \in \{1, 2, \texttt{drop}\}$, we get $\varphi_I^a = \varphi^a \land \tau$ where

$$\begin{aligned}
&\tau = \forall \bar{y}, \bar{y}_1, \ldots, \bar{y}_{k_\Phi}. \\
&\bigwedge_{a' \in \mathcal{A}} \varphi^{a'}\{\bar{y}/\bar{x}\}[\bar{x}, \bar{y}_1, \ldots, \bar{y}_{k_\Phi}] \iff \varphi^{a'}\{\bar{y}/\bar{x}\}[\bar{y}_1, \ldots, \bar{y}_{k_\Phi}]
\end{aligned}$$

Since the policy formulas have only one history-guarded quantifier, we can take $k_\Phi = 0$, as explained in Remark 5. Then we can compute an equivalent formula for $\tau$ as follows.

$$\begin{aligned}
\tau \equiv \forall \bar{y}. &\bigwedge_{a' \in \mathcal{A}} \varphi^{a'}\{\bar{y}/\bar{x}\}[\bar{x}] \iff \varphi^{a'}\{\bar{y}/\bar{x}\} \\
\overset{(1)}{\equiv} \forall \bar{y}. &(\varphi^1\{\bar{y}/\bar{x}\}[\bar{x}] \iff \varphi^1\{\bar{y}/\bar{x}\}) \land \\
&(\varphi^2\{\bar{y}/\bar{x}\}[\bar{x}] \iff \varphi^2\{\bar{y}/\bar{x}\}) \land \\
&(\varphi^{\texttt{drop}}\{\bar{y}/\bar{x}\}[\bar{x}] \iff \varphi^{\texttt{drop}}\{\bar{y}/\bar{x}\}) \\
\overset{(2)}{\equiv} \forall \bar{y}. &(\varphi^1\{\bar{y}/\bar{x}\}[\bar{x}] \iff \varphi^1\{\bar{y}/\bar{x}\}) \\
\overset{(3)}{\equiv} \forall \bar{y}. &(\bar{y}.in \approx 2) \land (\bar{x}.in \approx 1) \land (\bar{x}.dst \approx \bar{y}.src) \implies \\
&\exists \bar{z} \in \mathbb{H}.\, (\bar{z}.in \approx 1) \land (\bar{z}.dst \approx \bar{y}.src)
\end{aligned}$$

In step (2), we omit the conjunct for $\varphi^{\texttt{drop}}$, since $\varphi^{\texttt{drop}}$ is a Boolean combination of $\varphi^1$ and $\varphi^2$. Furthermore, the conjunct for $\varphi^2$ can be omitted as tautological. Step (3) is by applying standard equivalences of propositional logic. By applying rules of FOL with equality, it is also easy to see that the last formula can be further simplified to:

$$\tau \equiv (\bar{x}.in \approx 1) \implies \exists \bar{z} \in \mathbb{H}.(\bar{z}.in \approx 1) \land (\bar{z}.dst \approx \bar{x}.dst)$$

In particular, for the empty history one obtains:

$$\varphi_I^{\texttt{drop}} \equiv \neg\varphi^1 \land \neg\varphi^2 \land (\bar{x}.in \not\approx 1) \equiv \bar{x}.in \not\approx 1$$

which is equivalent to $(\bar{x}.in \approx 2)$. This means that the synthesized rule installation policy will initially install a rule to drop all packets arriving on port 2. This actually improves the SDN program implementing a stateful firewall policy from [8] by proactively installing more rules.

***Learning switch with migrations*** Recall the policy for the learning switch that supports migrations of hosts, given by:

$$\begin{aligned}
\varphi^p &= \exists \bar{z} = Last_{(\bar{x}.sw \approx \bar{z}.sw) \land (\bar{x}.dst \approx \bar{z}.src)}.\, (\bar{z}.in \approx p) \\
\varphi^{\texttt{flood}} &= \bigwedge_{p \in \texttt{Ports}} \neg\varphi^p
\end{aligned}$$

Again, we renamed $\bar{y}$ to $\bar{z}$ in order to avoid confusion.

For each $a \in \texttt{Ports} \cup \{\texttt{flood}\}$, we have $\varphi_I^a = \varphi^a \land \tau$ where

$$\begin{aligned}
\tau \equiv \forall \bar{y}. &\bigwedge_{a' \in \mathcal{A}} \varphi^{a'}\{\bar{y}/\bar{x}\}[\bar{x}] \iff \varphi^{a'}\{\bar{y}/\bar{x}\} \\
\overset{(1)}{\equiv} \forall \bar{y}. &\bigwedge_{p \in \texttt{Ports}} (\varphi^p\{\bar{y}/\bar{x}\}[\bar{x}] \iff \varphi^p\{\bar{y}/\bar{x}\}) \land \\
&(\varphi^{\texttt{flood}}\{\bar{y}/\bar{x}\}[\bar{x}] \iff \varphi^{\texttt{flood}}\{\bar{y}/\bar{x}\}) \\
\overset{(2)}{\equiv} \forall \bar{y}. &\bigwedge_{p \in \texttt{Ports}} (\varphi^p\{\bar{y}/\bar{x}\}[\bar{x}] \iff \varphi^p\{\bar{y}/\bar{x}\}) \\
\overset{(3)}{\equiv} \forall \bar{y}. &\bigwedge_{p \in \texttt{Ports}} [((\exists \bar{z} = Last_{\bar{y}.sw \approx \bar{z}.sw \land \bar{y}.dst \approx \bar{z}.src}.\, \bar{z}.in \approx p) \land \\
&\quad \neg(\bar{y}.sw \approx \bar{x}.sw \land \bar{y}.dst \approx \bar{x}.src)) \lor \\
&\quad (\bar{x}.in \approx p \land \bar{y}.sw \approx \bar{x}.sw \land \bar{y}.dst \approx \bar{x}.src) \iff \\
&\quad \exists \bar{z} = Last_{\bar{y}.sw \approx \bar{z}.sw \land \bar{y}.dst \approx \bar{z}.src}.\, \bar{z}.in \approx p] \\
\overset{(4)}{\equiv} &\bigwedge_{p \in \texttt{Ports}} \forall \bar{y}.\, [\bar{y}.sw \approx \bar{x}.sw \land \bar{y}.dst \approx \bar{x}.src \implies \\
&((\exists \bar{z} = Last_{\bar{y}.sw \approx \bar{z}.sw \land \bar{y}.dst \approx \bar{z}.src}.\, \bar{z}.in \approx p) \iff \bar{x}.in \approx p)] \\
\overset{(5)}{\equiv} &\bigwedge_{p \in \texttt{Ports}} [(\exists \bar{z} = Last_{\bar{x}.sw \approx \bar{z}.sw \land \bar{x}.src \approx \bar{z}.src}.\, \bar{z}.in \approx p) \iff \\
&\quad \bar{x}.in \approx p] \\
\overset{(6)}{\equiv} &\exists \bar{z} = Last_{\bar{x}.sw \approx \bar{z}.sw \land \bar{x}.src \approx \bar{z}.src}.\, \bar{z}.in \approx \bar{x}.in
\end{aligned}$$

In the initial description of $\tau$ we used the property that the policy formulas have only last quantifiers. Therefore, we can take $k_\Phi = 0$, as explained in Remark 5. We can omit the conjunct for $\varphi^{\texttt{flood}}$ in step (2), since $\varphi^{\texttt{flood}}$ is a Boolean combination of $\varphi^p$, $p \in \texttt{Ports}$. In step (4), we used the propositional equivalence

$$((A \land \neg B) \lor (C \land B) \iff A) \equiv (B \implies (A \iff C))$$

and the first-order equivalence $\forall x. \bigwedge A_i \equiv \bigwedge(\forall x.\, A_i)$. In steps (5) and (6), we used rules of FOL with equality.

We demonstrate the computation done at the runtime for the topology from Figure 1 and scenario from Table 4. As the current history we consider

$$H = \langle s, 1, A \to B\rangle \cdot \langle s, 2, B \to A\rangle$$

Consider the current event $e = \langle s, 3, A \to B\rangle$, which means that the host $A$ has migrated to port 3. After eliminating the last-quantifier with respect to the current history and omitting the conjuncts for equalities of switch components, we get for $\tau$:

$$1 \approx \bar{x}.in \land \bar{x}.src \approx A \land \bar{x}.src \not\approx B \lor 2 \approx \bar{x}.in \land \bar{x}.src \approx B$$

We see that for the current event, the above formula is equivalent to $\bot$, which means that the current event $e$ must be forwarded to the controller.

Consider as a current history

$$H = \langle s, 1, A \to B\rangle \cdot \langle s, 2, B \to A\rangle \cdot \langle s, 3, A \to B\rangle$$

after the migration of host $A$ to port 3. Consider the current packet $e = \langle s, 2, B \to A\rangle$. After applying Step 1, we get for $\tau$

$$\begin{aligned} &1 \approx \bar{x}.in \wedge \bar{x}.src \approx A \wedge \bar{x}.src \not\approx B \wedge \bar{x}.src \not\approx A \vee \\ &2 \approx \bar{x}.in \wedge \bar{x}.src \approx B \wedge \bar{x}.src \not\approx A \vee \\ &3 \approx \bar{x}.in \wedge \bar{x}.src \approx A \\ \equiv\ &2 \approx \bar{x}.in \wedge \bar{x}.src \approx B \vee 3 \approx \bar{x}.in \wedge \bar{x}.src \approx A \end{aligned}$$

Since $e$ satisfies the formula $\varphi_I^3 = \varphi^3 \wedge \tau$, the current event is forwarded to port 3, as intended.

## 8. Related Work

***Verification and Synthesis of Correct SDN Programs*** Verifying the correctness of SDN programs has recently received a lot of attention [3–5, 9, 12, 16]. These works aim to verify a given controller program which implements a forwarding rule installation policy. In contrast, this paper identifies a specific correctness criterion. We also automatically infer correct and optimal forwarding rule installation policies for forwarding policies expressed in a useful fragment of first-order logic.

***Atomicity of Rule Installation*** This paper assumes that events are executed atomically, ignoring out-of-order rule installations. Consistently updating a software-defined network is an important challenge in SDN (see [15]). One can enforce the atomicity of the inferred forwarding rules using barriers. In the future, it may be possible also infer the minimal barriers for a given forwarding policy using techniques similar to [11].

***Language Abstractions for SDNs.*** [6, 10, 14, 18] introduce abstractions for programming controllers in order to simplify the task of programming controllers and to enable more efficient implementations. Our work can be combined with these abstractions in order to further simplify the task or SDN programming and to reduce the number of errors for limited policies expressible in our language.

[18] transforms algorithmic policies into forwarding rules which drastically simplifies SDN programming. However, unlike our work, they do not analyze the dependencies between the forwarding policies and the packet histories. Therefore that cannot guarantee correctness for forwarding policies which depend on the histories.

[6] provides a high level level language called *Pyretic* for programming SDN controllers. Pyretic provides a mechanism to define functions which update the forwarding rules in an abstract way. These functions are called when new packets arrive to the controller, according to filters defined by the programmer. Note that the programmer has to write the update code, and also to explicitly define the filter stating which packets should trigger an update. The programmer is also responsible for assuring that the filter definition is consistent with the update code which requires non-trivial temporal reasoning. In contrast we provide a higher level of abstraction for expressing the forwarding policy and automatically infer correct and optimal installation of forwarding rules.

Figure 2 shows the learning switch (w/o host migration) expressed in Pyretic. In lines 2–7 the programmer defines the update and in line 8 the programmer defines the filter. Maintaining consistency between the filter and the update code is error prone and subtle. For instance, the consistency between lines 2–7 and line 8 depends on the assumption that there is no host migration, and this assumption is not explicit anywhere in the code. Therefore, it may be worthwhile to integrate our inference mechanism into Pyretic by limiting the expressive power of the update code.

```
1: def learn(self):
2:     def update(pkt):
3:         self.P =
4:         if_(match(dstmac=pkt['srcmac'],
5:                   switch=pkt['switch']),
6:             fwd(pkt['inport']),
7:             self.P)
8:     q = packets(1,['srcmac','switch'])
9:     q.when(update)
```

**Figure 2.** A learning switch in Pyretic.

```
1: ON packet_in(p):
2:   DO forward(new) WHERE
3:     learned(p.locSw, new.locPt, p.dlDst);
4:
5: ON packet_in(p):
6:   INSERT (p.locSw, p.locPt, p.dlSrc)
7:     INTO learned WHERE
8:     NOT learned(p.locSw, p.locPt, p.dlSrc);
```

**Figure 3.** A learning switch in FlowLog.

FlowLog [14] is an innovative tierless programming language for SDNs. It allows the programmer to express the forwarding policy in an SQL like language.

Figure 3 shows the learning switch expressed in FlowLog. Lines 1–3 express the forwarding behavior using the relation `learned`. Lines 5–8 express updating of the `learned` relation in response to new packets. Line 8 (the `WHERE`-clause), defines for which packets the update should take place. At first glance, it looks as if the programmer can declare the forwarding policy w/o worrying about rule installation. However, the installation of rules is determined by the `WHERE`-clause, which has to be specified by the programmer. Requiring that the programmer manually specifies the `WHERE`-clause may lead to subtle performance and correctness issues. For example, the programmer can naively interpret these rules according to SQL semantics and replace the condition in the `WHERE`-clause by `true`. In SQL semantics, both variants are equivalent since adding an element to a relation does nothing if the element is already in the relation. However, in FlowLog, changing the `WHERE`-clause to `true` results in sending all packets to the controller since they will all satisfy the `WHERE`-clause, leading to a performance issue. Similarly, if the `WHERE`-clause is inconsistent with the update that takes place (e.g., over-restrictive), then relevant packets will not be sent to the controller, and the correctness of the system may be compromised.

Indeed, FlowLog and Pyretic both split the task of updating the controller state into two interleaved mechanisms, and it is up to the programmer to make sure they are used consistently. In contrast, we propose a way to automatically infer one from the other and guarantee correctness and optimality.

NetCore [13] is a novel framework for programming SDN controllers. It includes a mechanism to transform Boolean combinations of conditions on events into OPENFLOW rules, which can be used to translate the installation rules inferred by this paper into OPENFLOW. Because NetCore is Turing complete, it requires that the programmers specify the conditions under which rules need to be installed in the form of an auxiliary hand-written function. As argued in this paper, this approach is error prone and requires non-trivial temporal reasoning on all possible sequences of events which may occur. Our approach in this paper limits the expressive power of the policy language to avoid the need to supply unchecked conditions.

***Datalog as a Specification Language*** Datalog is another good candidate for expressing network forwarding policies [7]. This means expressing the forwarding policy as a Datalog query over the history. For policies expressed in Datalog with recursion (with or without allowing stratified negation), $k$-bounded causality does not necessarily hold. This is also the case for policies expressed in Datalog without recursion and with negation. As for Datalog without recursion and without negation, policies expressed in it can also be expressed using $\mathcal{L}_1$-formulas, and therefore have the $k$-bounded causality for some $k$. However, not every policy expressible using $\mathcal{L}_1$ formulas can be expressed in Datalog without recursion and without negation, including simple policies such as the learning switch (since the forwarding behavior is non-monotonic in the history).

## 9. Conclusion

In this work we have investigated the decentralization problem of SDN. We characterized correctness and optimality of forwarding rule installation policies. While the problem of finding an optimal correct installation policy is undecidable in general, we show how to construct such installation policies for forwarding policies expressed in a natural restricted variant of first order logic. As a future work, it is worthwhile to study the applicability of our approach in a broader setting of distributed systems and distributed databases.

***Extensions*** Our approach can be straightforwardly extended in several ways.

Our specification language of policies, $\mathcal{L}_1$, includes two kinds of guarded quantifiers: one which examines existence of some event in the history, and one which refers to the last event in the history that has some property. As discussed in Remark 4, our results also apply if we extend $\mathcal{L}_1$ by additional guarded quantifiers, such as "last $k$" or "first $k$".

We consider a finite set of actions $\mathcal{A}$, which allows us to describe functions from $\mathcal{E}$ to $\mathcal{A}$ using a finite set of formulas, one for each action. In order to handle packet rewriting (performed for example in NAT boxes and supported by OpenFlow) one needs to consider an infinite set of actions since in this context, an action may be "forward to port 2 and change the source field to `1.2.3.4`". This means that the (infinite) set of addresses will be added to the set of actions. Our approach can be adapted to handle this as well by adding another sort, representing an action, to be used in $\mathcal{L}_1$ formulas, such that actions will be specified internally in $\mathcal{L}_1$. A policy will then be defined by a single formula with an additional free variable describing the action to be performed. The conjunction over all actions that is used when defining the formulas of the optimal event handler generator (Definition 13) will simply be replaced by a universal quantifier which will later be eliminated.

Our approach can also handle multiple types of events, by adding an attribute that describes the event type, and any other type specific attributes needed.

It is also possible to develop synthesis methods which are applied incrementally each time a history is changed and to produce only the new rules to be installed or removed.

## Acknowledgments

Padon, Immerman, Karbyshev, Lahav and Sagiv were funded by the European Research Council under the European Union's Seventh Framework Program (FP7/2007–2013) / ERC grant agreement no. [321174-VSSC], and by a grant from the Israel Science Foundation (652/11). Immerman was partially supported by NSF grant CCF 1115448. Shoham was partially supported by BSF grant no. 2012259. We thank Nate Foster, Daniel Jackson, Tova Milo, Aurojit Panda, Michael Schapira and the anonymous referees for insightful comments which improved this paper.

## References

[1] The Open Networking Foundation. `http://opennetworking.org`.

[2] *OpenFlow Switch Specification*, Oct. 2013. Version 1.4.0.

[3] ANDERSON, C. J., FOSTER, N., GUHA, A., JEANNIN, J.-B., KOZEN, D., SCHLESINGER, C., AND WALKER, D. NetKAT: Semantic foundations for networks. In *POPL* (2014), S. Jagannathan and P. Sewell, Eds., ACM, pp. 113–126.

[4] BALL, T., BJØRNER, N., GEMBER, A., ITZHAKY, S., KARBYSHEV, A., SAGIV, M., SCHAPIRA, M., AND VALADARSKY, A. Vericon: Towards verifying controller programs in software-defined networks. In *PLDI* (June 2014), SIGPLAN, ACM.

[5] CANINI, M., VENZANO, D., PERES, P., KOSTIC, D., AND REXFORD, J. A NICE Way to Test OpenFlow Applications. In *NSDI* (2012).

[6] FOSTER, N., GUHA, A., REITBLATT, M., STORY, A., FREEDMAN, M. J., KATTA, N. P., MONSANTO, C., REICH, J., REXFORD, J., SCHLESINGER, C., WALKER, D., AND HARRISON, R. Languages for software-defined networks. *IEEE Communications Magazine 51*, 2 (2013), 128–134.

[7] HUANG, S. S., GREEN, T. J., AND LOO, B. T. Datalog and emerging applications: an interactive tutorial. In *Proceedings of the 2011 ACM SIGMOD International Conference on Management of Data* (2011), ACM, pp. 1213–1216.

[8] KATTA, N. P., REXFORD, J., AND WALKER, D. Logic programming for software-defined networks. In *ACM SIGPLAN Workshop on Cross-model Language Design and Implementation* (Sept. 2012).

[9] KAZEMIAN, P., VARGHESE, G., AND MCKEOWN, N. Header Space Analysis: Static Checking For Networks. In *NSDI* (2012).

[10] KOPONEN, T., AMIDON, K., BALLAND, P., CASADO, M., CHANDA, A., FULTON, B., GANICHEV, I., GROSS, J., GUDE, N., INGRAM, P., JACKSON, E., LAMBETH, A., LENGLET, R., LI, S.-H., PADMANABHAN, A., PETTIT, J., PFAFF, B., RAMANATHAN, R., SHENKER, S., SHIEH, A., STRIBLING, J., THAKKAR, P., WENDLANDT, D., YIP, A., AND ZHANG, R. Network virtualization in multi-tenant datacenters. In *NSDI* (2014).

[11] KUPERSTEIN, M., VECHEV, M. T., AND YAHAV, E. Automatic inference of memory fences. *SIGACT News 43*, 2 (2012), 108–123.

[12] KUZNIAR, M., PERESINI, P., CANINI, M., VENZANO, D., AND KOSTIC, D. A SOFT Way for OpenFlow Switch Interoperability Testing. In *CoNEXT* (2012), pp. 265–276.

[13] MONSANTO, C., FOSTER, N., HARRISON, R., AND WALKER, D. A compiler and run-time system for network programming languages. *SIGPLAN Not. 47*, 1 (Jan. 2012), 217–230.

[14] NELSON, T., FERGUSON, A. D., SCHEER, M. J. G., AND KRISHNAMURTHI, S. Tierless programming and reasoning for software-defined networks. In *NSDI* (2014), USENIX Association, pp. 519–531.

[15] REITBLATT, M., FOSTER, N., REXFORD, J., SCHLESINGER, C., AND WALKER, D. Abstractions for network update. In *ACM SIGCOMM* (2012), pp. 323–334.

[16] SKOWYRA, R., LAPETS, A., BESTAVROS, A., AND KFOURY, A. A verification platform for sdn-enabled applications. In *HiCoNS* (2013).

[17] THE COQ DEVELOPMENT TEAM. *The Coq proof assistant reference manual*. TypiCal Project (formerly LogiCal), 2012. Version 8.4.

[18] VOELLMY, A., WANG, J., YANG, Y. R., FORD, B., AND HUDAK, P. Maple: simplifying SDN programming using algorithmic policies. In *ACM SIGCOMM* (2013), pp. 87–98.

# Program Boosting: Program Synthesis via Crowd-Sourcing

Robert A Cochran
University of North Carolina
rac@cs.unc.edu

Loris D'Antoni
University of Pennsylvania
lorisdan@seas.upenn.edu

Benjamin Livshits
Microsoft Research
livshits@microsoft.com

David Molnar
Microsoft Research
dmolnar@microsoft.com

Margus Veanes
Microsoft Research
margus@microsoft.com

## Abstract

In this paper, we investigate an approach to program synthesis that is based on crowd-sourcing. With the help of crowd-sourcing, we aim to capture the "wisdom of the crowds" to find good if not perfect solutions to inherently tricky programming tasks, which elude even expert developers and lack an easy-to-formalize specification.

We propose an approach we call *program boosting*, which involves crowd-sourcing imperfect solutions to a difficult programming problem from developers and then *blending* these programs together in a way that improves their correctness.

We implement this approach in a system called CROWDBOOST and show in our experiments that interesting and highly non-trivial tasks such as writing regular expressions for URLs or email addresses can be effectively crowd-sourced. We demonstrate that carefully blending the crowd-sourced results together consistently produces a *boost*, yielding results that are better than any of the starting programs. Our experiments on 465 program pairs show consistent boosts in accuracy and demonstrate that program boosting can be performed at a relatively modest monetary cost.

***Categories and Subject Descriptors*** F.4.3 [*Theory of Computation*]: Formal languages; H.5.3 [*Information Systems*]: Collaborative Computing; D.1.2 [*Programming Techniques*]: Automatic Programming

***Keywords*** Program Synthesis; Crowd-sourcing; Symbolic Automata; Regular Expressions

## 1. Introduction

Everyday programming involves solving numerous small but necessary tasks. Some of these tasks are fairly routine; others are surprisingly challenging. Examples of challenging self-contained tasks include coming up with a regular expression to recognize email addresses or sanitizing an input string to avoid SQL injection attacks. Both of these tasks are easy to describe to most developers succinctly, yet both are surprisingly difficult to "get right," i.e., to implement while properly addressing all the tricky corner cases. Furthermore, there is plenty of room for ambiguity in both tasks: for example, even seasoned developers can disagree as to whether `john+doe@acm.org` or `john..doe.@acm.com` are valid email addresses or whether removing all characters outside of the [`a` − `zA` − `Z`] set is a valid sanitization strategy for preventing SQL injection attacks. These tasks are *under-specified*; there may not be absolute consensus on what solution is correct; moreover, different people may get different parts of the solution wrong.

What if we could pose these tricky programming tasks as a crowd-sourcing challenge? Ideally, we would be able to describe the task in question in English, admittedly, a very loose form of specification, with all its inherent ambiguities and under-specified corner cases. We would subsequently use the "wisdom of the crowds" to arrive at a solution, without having a precise specification *a priori*, but perhaps armed with some positive and negative examples, giving us a partial specification. This paper explores this deceptively simple idea and expands on previous investigations into the use of crowd-sourcing to help with technically challenging programming problems. Our implementation, CROWDBOOST, shares some of the high-level goals with systems such as TurkIt [27], Deco [33], and Collabode [13].

### 1.1 In Search of Perfect URL Validation

In December 2010, Mathias Bynens, a freelance web developer from Belgium, set up a page to collect possible regular expressions for matching URLs. URL matching turns out to be a surprisingly challenging problem. While RFCs may define formal grammars for URLs, it is non-trivial to construct a regular expression that can be used in practice from these specifications. To help with testing the regular expressions, Mathias posted a collection of both positive and negatives examples, that is, strings that should be accepted as proper URLs or rejected. While some example URLs are as simple as `http://foo.com/blah_blah`, others are considerably more complex and require the knowledge of allowed protocols (`ftps://foo.bar/` should be rejected) or the range of numbers in IP addresses (which is why `http://123.123.123` should be rejected).

Mathias posted this challenge to his followers on Twitter. Soon, a total of 12 responses were collected, as summarized in Figure 1. Note that the majority of responses were incorrect at least in part: while all regular expressions correctly captured simple URLs such as `http://www.cnn.com`, they often would disagree on some of the more subtle inputs. Only one participant with a Twitter handle


*POPL '15*, January 15–17, 2015, Mumbai, India.

http://dx.doi.org/10.1145/2676726.2676973

of @diegoperini managed to get all the answers right[1]. Twitter user @stephenhay came close, getting all positive inputs right, but missing some of the negative inputs. Notably, this experiment performed by Mathias was a specific form of *program crowd-sourcing*.

### 1.2 Key Observations

While a detailed analysis of this experiment is available at `http://mathiasbynens.be/demo/url-regex`, a few things are clear:

- The problem posed by Mathias is *surprisingly* complex; moreover, it is a problem where it is easy to get started and get to a certain level or accuracy, but getting to perfect precision on the example set is very difficult;
- potential answers provided by developers range in length (38–1,347) and accuracy (.56–1), a great deal, as measured on a set of examples. Note that the most accurate answer provided by @diegoperini is in this case *not* the longest;
- developers get *different* portions of the answer wrong; while a particular developer may forget the `ftp://` URL scheme but remember to include optional port numbers that follow the host name, another developer may do exactly the opposite;
- cleverly combining (or *blending*) partially incorrect answers may yield a correct one.

Inspired by these observations, *program boosting* is a technique that combines crowd-sourced programs using the technique of genetic programming to yield a solution of higher quality. A way of combining individual classifiers to improve the accuracy is referred to as *classifier boosting* in machine learning [37], hence of our choice of the term program boosting. This technique is especially helpful for problems that elude a precise specification.

### 1.3 Other Domains for Program Boosting

The experimental results in this paper focus heavily on the regular expression domain; regular expressions represent a limited but very important class of programming tasks, which maintain decidability of many important properties, unlike programs written in general-purpose languages like C or Java. However, we feel that a wide range of problems are captured by the mental model outlined above. Just like with other general techniques, we cannot really foresee all domains in which boosting may be valuable, but we give several examples below.

**Security sanitizers:** Security sanitizers are short, self-contained string-manipulation routines that are crucial in preventing cross-site scripting attacks in web applications, yet programming these sanitizers is widely-recognized to be a difficult task [17]. Sanitizers written in domain specific languages have properties that allow for automated manipulation and reasoning about program behavior, but human intervention is still required when a specification is not precise. Reasoning about sanitizers amounts to reasoning about transducers; we feel that algorithms similar to those presented in this paper can be developed for transducers as well. Program boosting can incorporate powerful new techniques for program analysis with the on-demand efforts of both expert and non-expert human insight.

**Merging code patches:** We envision the application of program boosting in other domains as well. For example, while it would be difficult to mix the code from several Java program directly, we can imagine how the space of possible combinations of *code patches* written by different developers could be explored to find an optimal result as judged by the crowd.

[1] The full regex from @diegoperini can be obtained from the address `https://gist.github.com/dperini/729294`.

| Regex source | Regex length | True positive | True negative | Overall accuracy |
|---|---|---|---|---|
| @krijnhoetmer | 115 | .78 | .41 | .59 |
| @gruber | 71 | .97 | .36 | .65 |
| @gruber v2 | 218 | 1.00 | .33 | .65 |
| @cowboy | 1,241 | 1.00 | .15 | .56 |
| @mattfarina | 287 | .72 | .44 | .57 |
| @stephenhay | 38 | 1.00 | .64 | .81 |
| @scottgonzales | 1,347 | 1.00 | .15 | .56 |
| @rodneyrehm | 109 | .83 | .36 | .59 |
| @imme_emosol | 54 | .97 | .74 | .85 |
| @diegoperini* | **502** | **1.00** | **1.00** | **1.00** |

**Figure 1:** Representative regular expressions for URLs obtained from http://mathiasbynens.be/demo/url-regex. For every possible solution we show its length, true and false positive rates, and the overall accuracy. The last row is the winner.

**Combining static analysis checkers:** The precision of static analysis *checkers* or bug finding tools can be improved via cleverly blending them together. One scheme could be to have multiple checkers for NULL dereferences vote on a particular potential violation. Another would be to blend machine learning and program analysis by training a decision tree which determines which checker to apply in response to a range of local static features.

**Web site layout:** In web site design, A/B testing is often used to measure design changes and their observable influence on behavior [20]. Building on the idea that the customer is always right, program boosting could be used to construct a layout engine that renders results which are most pleasing to the user.

The key thread linking these application areas together is that a problem exists where the overall specification and how it should be implemented are difficult to pin down, but it is easy to indicate whether a given solution is correctly operating on a single input. Defining effective blending operations for each of these domains remains a separate research challenge, which we only address for regular expressions.

### 1.4 Contributions

Our paper makes these contributions:

- We propose a technique we dub *program boosting*. Program boosting is a semi-automatic program generation or synthesis technique that uses a set of initial crowd-sourced programs and combines (or blends) them to provide a better result, according to a fitness function.
- We show how to implement program boosting for regular expressions. We propose a genetic programming technique [2, 21, 35] with custom-designed *crossover* and *mutation* operations. We propose a new genetic programming paradigm in which the fitness function is evolved along with the candidate programs.
- We implement our program boosting technique in a tool, CrowdBoost, to generate complex regular expressions. We represent regular expressions using *Symbolic Finite Automata* (SFAs), which enable succinct representation, while supporting large alphabets. We adapt classic algorithms, such as *string-to-language* edit distance, to the symbolic setting. To the best of our knowledge, ours is also the first work that uses genetic programming on automata over complex alphabets such as UTF-16.
- We evaluate program boosting techniques on four case studies. In our experiments on a set of 465 pairs of regular expression programs, we observe an average boost in accuracy of 16.25%, which is a significant improvement on already high-quality

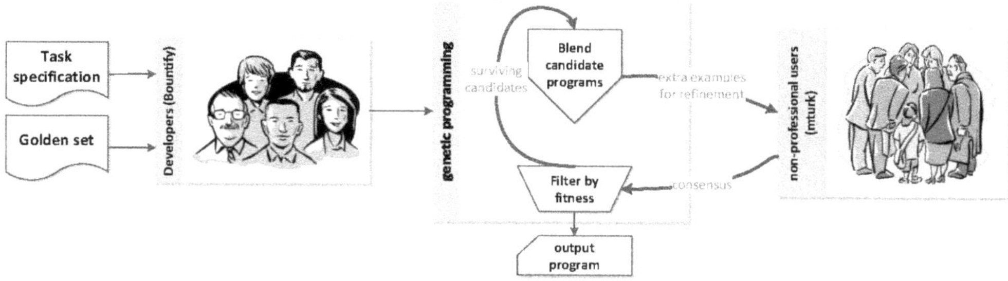


**Figure 2:** System architecture.

initial solutions. Importantly, the boosting effect is *consistent* across the tasks and sources of initial regular expressions, which enhances our belief in the generality of our approach.

### 1.5 Paper Organization

The rest of the paper is organized as follows. Section 2 gives an outline of our approach of using two crowds in tandem to generate programs. Section 3 gives the details of our approach to boosting regular expression-based programs based on symbolic finite automata or SFAs. Section 4 provides an experimental evaluation in the context of four case studies. Section 5 contains a discussion of some of the outstanding challenges we see for future research. Finally, Sections 6 and 7 describe related work and conclude.

## 2. Program Boosting

This section provides an overview of program boosting. Much of the motivation for our approach comes from experimenting with different tasks that can be captured via regular expressions. For example, the following imperfect initial regular expressions for matching US phone numbers `^[0-9]{3}-[0-9]*-[0-9]{4}$` and `^[0-9]{3}-[0-9]{3}-[0-9]*$` can be combined to yield `^[0-9]{3}-[0-9]{3}-[0-9]{4}$`. While still probably not the final solution, the resulting regex avoids the obvious pitfalls in the initial two, namely, initial regexes allow digit sequences of arbitrary length.

### 2.1 Background on Crowd-Sourcing

In the last several years we have seen a rise in the use of crowd-sourcing for both general tasks that do not require special skills (recognize if there is a cat in the picture, reformat text data, correct grammar in a sentence) and skilled tasks such as providing book illustrations or graphic design assignments on request or perhaps writing short descriptions of products.

A good example of a crowd-sourcing site for unskilled work is Amazon's Mechanical Turk (frequently abbreviated as *mturk*); oDesk is another widely-used platform, this one primarily used for skilled tasks. Both Mechanical Turk and oDesk can be used for sourcing programming tasks, although neither is specialized for that. Note that one can consider StackOverflow and other similar programming assistance sites as an informal type of crowd-sourcing. Indeed, these sites are so good at providing *ingredients* for solving difficult programming problems that some developers routinely keep StackOverflow open in their browsers as they code.

Bountify (`http://bountify.co`) allows people to post programming tasks, some involving writing new code from scratch (*Write a JavaScript function to generate multiple shades of a given color*), and others involving fixing bugs in existing code (*Why does my HTML table not look the way I expect and how should I tweak my CSS to make it look right?*). These programming tasks generally are not overly time-consuming; a typical task pays about $5. Responses are posted publicly, leading to other developers learning from partial answers. Finally, the poster decides which developer(s) to award the bounty to.

Note that *interactive* crowd-sourcing is not the only source of code for a particular programming task. Indeed, one can easily use a code search engine to find the insight one is looking for in open-source projects. Searching for terms such as `url_regex` using a dedicated code engine will yield some possible regular expressions for URL filtering; so will exploring a programming advice site such as StackOverflow.

### 2.2 Overview of Program Boosting

Figure 2 shows the architecture of our system. We start with a textual task specification and an initial training set of (positive and negative) examples (also called "golden set"). To crowd-source a solution to the specified task, we take advantage of two crowds, the *skilled crowd* consisting of developers and the *untrained crowd* consisting of regular computer users. The former contains developers for hire via services such as Bountify, typically skilled in one or more languages such as Java and C++, the latter consists of regular computer users found on Mechanical Turk.

**Two-crowd approach:** For simplicity, in this paper we focus on *binary classification tasks*, that is programs that (1) consume a single input; (2) produce a boolean (*yes*/*no*) output; and (3) for any input, a non-specialist computer user can decide if the answer for it should be a *yes* or a *no*. Examples of such tasks include programs that decide if the input is a properly formatted phone number or programs that decide if the input image contains a giraffe.

The last requirement is necessary for *refinement*, i.e., deciding the proper outcome for tricky corner cases with the help of an untrained crowd. Our observation is that while the untrained crowd is not going to help us to source programs, they will be able to *recognize* correct or incorrect program behaviors. By way of analogy, while a layperson may not be able to write a computer vision program that recognizes the presence of a giraffe in an image, humans are remarkably good at recognizing whether a given picture has a giraffe in it. This two-crowd approach helps us to both *collect* or *source* candidate programs and to systematically expand the space of considered inputs by asking the untrained crowd for disambiguation.

While other fitness criteria are possible, in this paper we focus on improving the *accuracy* of blended programs on a training set of positive and negative examples.

### 2.3 Program Boosting via Genetic Programming

To generalize the approach advocated in our example above, a natural technique to consider is *genetic programming* [2, 21, 35], a specialized form of genetic algorithms. Genetic programming is a search technique in the space of programs, whose goal is to improve program fitness over a series of generations. A successful genetic programming formulation relies on implementing two operations that may be familiar to the reader: *crossover* and *mutation*.

```
1: Input: Programs σ, examples φ, crossover function β, mutation function μ,
   example generator δ, fitness function η, budget θ
2: Output: Boosted program
3: function Boost(⟨σ, φ⟩, β, μ, δ, η, θ)
4:   while (η̂ < 1.0 ∧ θ > 0) do                         ▷ Until perfect or no money
5:     ϕ = ∅                                           ▷ New examples for this generation
6:     for all ⟨σ_i, σ_j⟩ ∈ FindCrossoverCandidates(σ) do
7:       for all σ' ∈ β(⟨σ_i, σ_j⟩) do                  ▷ Crossover σ_i and σ_j
8:         ϕ = ϕ ∪ δ(σ', φ)                            ▷ Generate new examples
9:         σ = σ ∪ {σ'}                                ▷ Add this candidate to σ
10:      end for
11:    end for
12:    for all ⟨σ_i⟩ ∈ FindMutationCandidates(σ) do
13:      for all σ' = μ(σ_i) do                        ▷ Mutate σ_i
14:        ϕ = ϕ ∪ δ(σ', φ)                            ▷ Generate new examples
15:        σ = σ ∪ {σ'}                                ▷ Add this candidate to σ
16:      end for
17:    end for
                                   ▷ Get consensus on these new examples via mturk
18:    ⟨φ_ϕ, θ⟩ = GetConsensus(ϕ, θ)                    ▷ and update budget
19:    φ = φ ∪ φ_ϕ                                     ▷ Add the newly acquired examples
20:    σ = Filter(σ)                                   ▷ Update candidates
21:    ⟨σ̂, η̂⟩ = GetBestFitness(σ, η)
22:  end while
23:  return σ̂                                         ▷ Return program with best fitness
24: end function
```

**Figure 3:** Program boosting implemented as an iterative genetic programming algorithm.

Given a set of initial crowd-sourced programs, the program boosting algorithm proceeds in generations. In the context of our phone number example, these initial programs may be the two initial regular expressions. At every generation, it performs a combination of crossover and mutation operations. (In our example, this may tweak individual parts of the regular expression to handle phone number separators like `-` and `.`) As a form of refinement, new examples are added to the training set. As an example, in our regular expression implementation the goal of refinement is to attain 100% *state coverage* by considering non-obvious cases such as `212.555-1212` or `1-)212) 555-1212` as either valid or invalid phone numbers to be added to the evolving training set. Finally, the candidates with the highest fitness are chosen to continue to the next generation.

Crowd-sourcing initial programs and continuous refinement of the training set are key differeniators of program boosting and more standard genetic programming [2, 21, 35].

### 2.4 Program Boosting Algorithm

Figure 3 shows our program boosting algorithm as pseudo-code. Let $\Sigma$ be the set of all programs and $\Phi$ be the set of all inputs. In every generation, we update the set of currently considered programs $\sigma \subset \Sigma$ and the set of current examples $\phi \subset \Phi$.

Note that the algorithm is iterative in nature: the process of boosting proceeds in *generations*, similar to the way genetic programming is typically implemented. The overall goal is to find a program with the best fitness in $\Sigma$. At each generation, new examples in $\Phi$ are produced and sent to the crowd to obtain consensus. The algorithm is parametrized as follows:

- $\sigma \subset \Sigma$ is the initial set of programs;
- $\phi \subset \Phi$ is the initial set of positive and negative examples;
- $\beta : \Sigma \times \Sigma \to 2^{\Sigma}$ is the crossover function that takes two programs and produces a set of possible crossovers;
- $\mu : \Sigma \to 2^{\Sigma}$ is the mutation function that given a program produces a set of possible mutated programs;
- $\delta : \Sigma \times 2^{\Phi} \to 2^{\Phi}$ given a program and a set of examples generates a new set of training examples;
- $\eta : \Sigma \to \mathbb{N}$ is the fitness function;
- $\theta \in \mathbb{N}$ is the budget for Mechanical Turk crowd-sourcing.

Later we show how to implement operations that correspond to functions $\beta$, $\mu$, $\delta$, and $\eta$ for regular expressions using SFAs. Note that in practice in the interest of completing faster we usually limit the number of iterations to a set limit such as 10.

Our implementation, CROWDBOOST, benefits greatly from parallelism. In particular, we make the two loops on lines 6 and 12 of the algorithm parallel. While we need to be careful in our implementation to avoid shared state, this relatively simple change ultimately leads to near-full utilization on a machine with 8 or 16 cores.

Unfortunately, our call-outs to the crowd on line 16 to get the consensus are in-line. This does lead to an end-to-end slowdown in practice, as crowd workers tend to have a latency associated with finding and starting new tasks, even if their throughput is quite high. In the future, we envision a slightly more streamlined architecture where allowing speculative exploration of the space of programs may allow us to invoke crowd calls asynchronously.

## 3. Boosting Regular Expressions

In this section we instantiate the different parts of the program boosting algorithm for the regular expression domain. We first describe Symbolic Finite Automata and show how they are used to represent regular expressions in our implementation, CROWDBOOST. Next, we present algorithms for crossover, mutation, and example generation, used by the algorithm in Figure 3.

### 3.1 Symbolic Finite Automata

While regular expressions are succinct and relatively easy to understand, they are not easy to manipulate algebraically. In particular, there is algorithm for complementing or intersecting them directly. We therefore opt for finite automata. Classic deterministic finite automata (DFAs) enjoy many closure properties and friendly complexities, however each DFA transition can only carry one character, causing the number of transitions in the DFA to be proportional to the size of the alphabet. When the alphabet is large (UTF-16 has $2^{16}$ elements) this representation becomes impractical.

Symbolic Finite Automata (SFAs) [41] extend classic automata with symbolic alphabets. In an SFA, each edge is labeled with a predicate rather than a single input character and this allows the automaton to represent multiple concrete transitions succinctly. For example, in the SFA of Figure 7 the transition from state 10 to state 11 is labeled with the predicate `[^#--\/?\s]`. Because of the size of the UTF-16 set, this transition in classic automata would be represented by thousands of concrete transitions.

Before defining SFAs we first need to introduce several preliminary concepts. Since the guards of SFA transitions are predicates, operations such as automata intersection need to "manipulate" such predicates. Let's consider the problem of intersecting two DFAs. In classic automata intersection, if the two DFAs respectively have transitions $(p, a, p')$ and $(q, a, q')$ the intersected DFA (also called the product) will have a transition $(\langle p, q\rangle, a, \langle p', q'\rangle)$. Now if we want to intersect two SFAs this simple synchronization would not work. If two SFAs respectively have transitions $(p, \varphi, p')$ and $(q, \psi, q')$ (where $\varphi$ and $\psi$ are predicates), the intersected SFA will need to synchronize the two transitions only on the values that are both in $\varphi$ and $\psi$, therefore the new transition will be $(\langle p, q\rangle, \varphi \wedge \psi, \langle p', q'\rangle)$ where the guard is the conjunction of the two predicates $\varphi$ and $\psi$. Moreover if the predicate $\varphi \wedge \psi$ defines an empty set of characters, this transition should be removed. This example shows how the set of predicates used in the SFA should at least be closed under $\wedge$ (conjunction), and the underlying theory should be decidable (we can check for satisfiability). It can be shown that in general in order to achieve the classic closure properties of regular language the set of predicates must also be closed under negation.

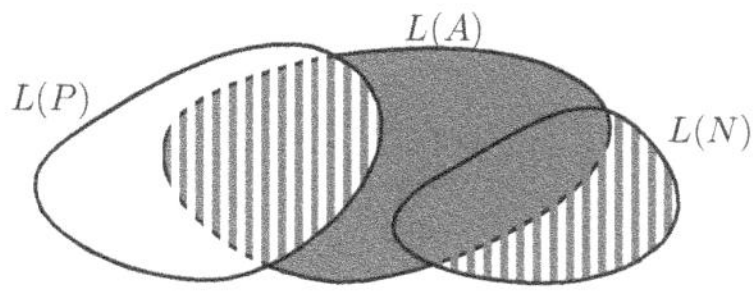


**Figure 4:** Fitness computation for an SFA $A$. The dashed regions represent the strings on which $A$ is correct.

**Definition 1.** A Boolean algebra $B$ has components $(\mathcal{D}_B, P_B, f, \bot, \top, \wedge, \neg)$. $\mathcal{D}_B$ is a set of domain elements, and $P_B$ is a set of predicates closed under Boolean connectives $\wedge, \neg$, and $\bot, \top \in P_B$. The denotation function $f : P_B \mapsto 2^{\mathcal{D}_B}$ is such that $f(\top) = \mathcal{D}_B$, $f(\bot) = \emptyset$, $f(\varphi \wedge \psi) = f(\varphi) \cap f(\psi)$, and $f(\neg\varphi) = \mathcal{D}_B \setminus f(\varphi)$. For $\varphi \in P_B$, we write $IsSat(\varphi)$ when $f(\varphi) \neq \emptyset$, and say that $\varphi$ is *satisfiable*. We say that $B$ is decidable if $IsSat$ is decidable.

We can now define Symbolic Finite Automata.

**Definition 2.** A Symbolic Finite Automaton, SFA, $A$ is a tuple $(B, Q, q_0, F, \delta)$ where $B$ is a decidable Boolean algebra, called the *alphabet*, $Q$ is a finite set of *states*, $q_0 \in Q$ is the *initial state*, $F \subseteq Q$ is the set of *final states*, and $\delta \subseteq Q \times P_B \times Q$ is a finite set of *moves* or *transitions*.

In the following definitions we refer to a generic SFA $A$. We say that $A$ is deterministic if for every state $q \in Q$ there do not exist two distinct transitions $(q, \varphi, q_1)$, and $(q, \psi, q_2)$ in $\delta$, such that $IsSat(\varphi \wedge \psi)$. We say that $A$ is complete if for every state $q \in Q$ and every symbol $a \in \mathcal{D}_B$ there exists a transition $(q_1, \varphi, q_2)$ such that $a \in f(\varphi)$. In this paper we only consider deterministic and complete SFAs, and for this class of SFAs we can then define the reflexive-transitive closure of $\delta$ as, $\delta^*(q, \varepsilon) = q$, and for all $a \in \mathcal{D}$ and $s \in \mathcal{D}^*$, $\delta^*(q, as) = \delta(q', s)$, if $\exists(q, \varphi, q') \in \delta$ such that $a \in f(\varphi)$. The language accepted by $A$ is $L(A) = \{s \mid \delta^*(q_0, s) \in F\}$.

**BDD algebra:** We describe the Boolean algebra of binary decision diagrams (BDDs), which is used in this paper to model sets of UTF-16 characters that are used in regular expressions. A BDD algebra $2^{bv_k}$ is the powerset algebra whose domain is the finite set $bv_k$, for some $k > 0$, consisting of all non-negative integers less than $2^k$, or equivalently, all $k$-bit bit-vectors. A predicate is represented by a BDD [40] of depth $k$. The variable order of the BDD is the reverse bit order of the binary representation of a number, in particular, the most significant bit has the lowest ordinal. The Boolean operations correspond directly to the BDD operations, $\bot$ is the BDD representing the empty set. The denotation $f(\varphi)$ of a BDD $\varphi$ is the set of all integers $n$ such that a binary representation of $n$ corresponds to a solution of $\varphi$. For example, in the case of URLs over the alphabet UTF-16, we use the BDD algebra $2^{bv_{16}}$ to naturally represent sets of UTF-16 characters (bit-vectors). We consider the SFA and BDD implementations from the symbolic automata toolkit [41].

### 3.2 Fitness Computation

Recall that as part of the genetic programming approach employed in program boosting we need to be able to assess the fitness of a particular program. For regular expressions this amounts to calculating the *accuracy* on a training set. The process of fitness calculation can by itself be quite time-consuming. This is because running a large set of examples and counting how many of them are accepted correctly by each produced SFA is a process that scales quite poorly when we consider thousands of SFAs and hundreds of examples. Instead, we construct SFAs $P$ and $N$, which represent the languages of all positive and all negative examples, respectively. For any SFA $A$, we then compute the cardinality of the intersection sets $L(A) \cap L(P)$ and $L(N) \setminus L(A)$ (see dashed regions in Figure 4), both of which can be computed fast using SFA operations. The accuracy can be then computed as $(|L(A \cap P)| + |L(N \setminus A)|)/|L(P \cup N)|$ and will range from 0 to 1. A challenge inherent with our refinement technique is that our evolved example set can greatly deviate from the initial golden set. While imperfect, we still want to treat the golden set as a more reliable source of truth; to this end, we use weighting to give the golden set a higher weight in the overall fitness calculation. In our experimental evaluation, we get reliably good results if we set golden:evolved weights to 9:1.

```
Input: SFAs A1 = (Q1, q0^1, F1, δ1), A2 = (Q2, q0^2, F2, δ2)
Output: All crossovers of A1 and A2
function CROSSOVERS(A1, A2)
 C1 := COMPONENTS(A1)
 C2 := COMPONENTS(A2)
 for all c1 ∈ C1 do
  C1' := {c1' | c1 ≺_A1 c1'}
  for all t→ = (p1, φ, p2) ∈ EXIT_MOVES(c1, A1) do
   for all c2 ∈ C2 do
    for all i2 ∈ ENTRY_STATES(c2, A2) do
     C2' := {c2' | c2 ⪯_A2 c2'}
     for all c2' ∈ C2' do
      for all t← = (q1, φ, q2) ∈ EXIT_MOVES(c2', A2) do
       for all c1' ∈ C1' do
        for all i1 ∈ ENTRY_STATES(c1', A1) do
         t'→ := (p1, φ, i2), t'← := (q1, φ, i1)
         δ_new := δ1 ∪ δ2 \ {t→, t←} ∪ {t'→, t'←}
         yield return (Q1 ∪ Q2, q0^1, F1 ∪ F2, δ_new)
end function
function EXIT_MOVES(c, A)
 return {(p, φ, q) ∈ δ_A | p ∈ c ∧ q ∉ c}
end function
function ENTRY_STATES(c, A)
 return {q ∈ Q_A | (∃(p, φ, q) ∈ δ_A.p ∉ c ∧ q ∈ c) ∨ (q = q0^A)}
end function
```

**Figure 5:** Crossover algorithm.

### 3.3 Crossover

A crossover operation interleaves two SFAs into a single SFA that "combines" their behaviors. An example of this operation is illustrated in Figure 6. Given two SFAs $A$ and $B$, the crossover algorithm creates a new SFA by redirecting two transitions, one from $A$ to $B$, and one from $B$ to $A$. The goal of such an operation is that of using a component of $B$ inside $A$. The crossover algorithm is shown in Figure 5. In all of the following algorithms we assume the SFAs to be minimal [8].

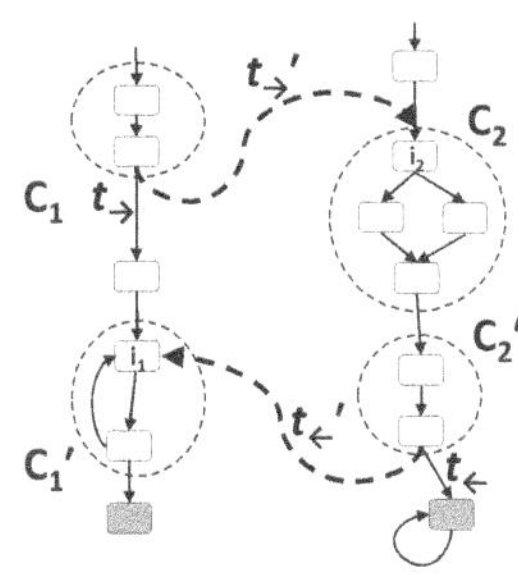


**Figure 6:** Crossover.

An SFA can have many transitions and trying all the possible crossovers can be impractical. Concretely, if $A$ has $n_1$ states and $m_1$ transitions, and $B$ has $n_2$ states and $m_2$ transitions, there will be $O(n_1 n_2 m_1 m_2)$ possible crossovers, and checking fitness for this many SFAs would not scale.

We devise several heuristics that try to mitigate such blowup by limiting the number of possible crossovers. The first technique we use is to guarantee that: 1) if we leave $A$ by redirecting a transition $(q, \varphi, q_1)$ to $B$, and come back to $A$ from $B$ with a transition that reaches a state $q_2$ in $A$, then $q_2$ is reachable from $q_1$, but different from it (we write $q_1 \prec q_2$), and 2) if we reach $B$ in a state $p_1$, and leave it by redirecting a transition $(p_2, \varphi, p)$, then $p_2$

is reachable from $p_1$ (we write $p_1 \preceq p_2$). Following these rules, we only generate crossover automata for which there always exists an accepted string that traverses both the redirected transitions.

The next heuristics limit the number of "interesting" edges and states to be used in the algorithm by grouping multiple states into single component and only considering those edges that travel from one component to another one. In the algorithm in Figure 5, the reachability relation $\prec$ is naturally extended to components (set of states). The function COMPONENTS returns the set of state components computed using one or more of the heuristics described below.

**Strongly-connected components:** Our first strategy collapses states that belong to a single strongly connected component (SCCs). SCCs are easy to compute and often capture interesting blocks of the SFA.

**Collapsing stretches:** In several cases SCCs do not collapse enough states. Consider the SFA in Figure 7. In this example, the only SCC with more than one state is the set $\{11–12\}$. Moreover, most of the phone number regexes are represented by acyclic SFAs causing the SCCs to be completely ineffective. To address this limitation we introduce a collapsing strategy for "stretches". A *stretch* is a maximal connected acyclic sub-graph where every node has degree smaller or equal than 2. In the SFA in Figure 7, $\{1, 3, 5\}$, $\{2, 4\}$, and $\{9, 10\}$ are stretches.

**Single-entry, single-exit components:** Even using stretches the collapsing is often ineffective. Consider again the SFA in Figure 7. The set of nodes $\{0, 1, 2, 3, 4, 5, 6, 7, 8\}$ looks like it should be treated as a single component, since it has a single entry point, and a single exit point, however it is not a stretch. This component clearly captures an independent part of the regex which accepts the correct protocols of a URL. Such a component is characterized by the following features:

1. it is a connected direct acyclic sub-graph,
2. it has a single entry and exit point,
3. it does not start or end with a stretch, and
4. it is *maximal*: it is not contained in a bigger component with properties 1–3.

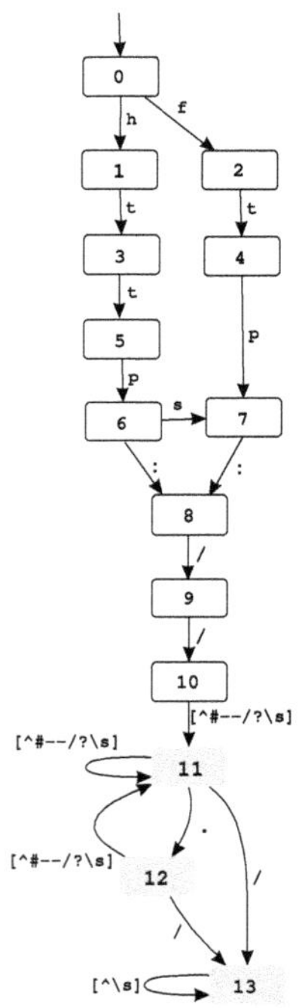


**Figure 7:** Identifying components.

Such components can be computed in linear time by using a variation of depth-first search starting in each node with in-degree smaller or equal than 1. The requirement 4) is achieved by considering the nodes in topological sort (since SCCs are already collapsed the induced graph is acyclic). Since this technique is generally more effective than stretches, we use it before the stretch collapsing.

In the SFA in Figure 7, the final components will then be: $\{0, 1, 2, 3, 4, 5, 6, 7, 8\}$, $\{9, 10\}$, $\{11, 12\}$, and $\{13\}$. Finally, if $A$ has $c_1$ components and $t_1$ transitions between different components, and $B$ has $c_2$ components and $t_2$ transitions between different components, then there will be $O(c_1 c_2 t_1 t_2)$ possible crossovers. In practice this number is much smaller than $O(n_1 n_2 m_1 m_2)$.

**One-way crossovers:** One way crossovers are a variant of those described above in which we redirect one edge from $A$ to $B$ but we do not come back to $A$ on any edge. If $A$ has $t_1$ transitions between different components, and $B$ has $c_2$ components, then there will be $O(c_2 t_1)$ possible one-way crossovers.

```
Input: SFA A = (Q, q, F, δ) and "seed" string w
Output: Set of new training strings
function COVER(A, w)
    C := Q
    while C ≠ ∅ do
        q := REMOVE_FIRST(C)
        A' := SFA_PASSING(A, q)
        s := CLOSEST_STRING(A', w)
        C := C \ STATES_COVERED(s, A)
        yield return s
    end while
end function
// Language of all strings in A passing through state q
function SFA_PASSING(A, q)
    return CONCATENATE((Q, q0, {q}, δ), (Q, q, F, δ))
end function
```

**Figure 8:** Example generation.

### 3.4 Mutation

In its classic definition a mutation operator alters one or more values of the input program and produces a mutated one. SFAs have too many values to be altered (every transition can carry $2^{16}$ elements), and a "blind" approach would produce too many mutations. Instead we consider a guided approach, in which mutations take as input an SFA $A$ and a counterexample $s$, such that $s$ is incorrectly classified by $A$ ($s$ is a positive example but it doesn't belong to $L(A)$, or $s$ is a negative example but it belongs to $L(A)$). Using this extra bit of information we mutate $A$ only in those ways that will cause $s$ to be correctly classified. The intuition behind such operations is to perform a minimal syntactic change in order to correctly classify the counterexample.

**Diminishing mutations:** Given a negative example and an SFA $A$ such that $s \in L(A)$ generate an SFA $A'$, such that $L(A') \subseteq L(A)$ and $s \notin L(A')$. Given a string $s = a_1 \dots a_n$ that is accepted by $A$, the algorithm finds a transition $(q, \varphi, q')$ that is traversed using the input character $a_i$ (for some $i$) when reading $s$ and either removes the whole transition, or simply shrinks the guard to $\varphi \wedge \neg a_i$ disallowing the symbol $a_i$. Given a string of length $k$, this mutation can generate at most $2k$ mutated SFAs. Given the state $q \in F$ such that $\delta^*(q_0, s) = q$, we also output The SFA $A' = (q_0, Q, F \setminus \{q\}, \delta)$, in which the input SFA is mutated by removing a final state.

**Augmenting mutations:** Given a positive example and an SFA $A$ such that $s \notin L(A)$ generate an SFA $A'$, such that $L(A) \subseteq L(A')$ and $s \in L(A')$. Given a string $s = a_1 \dots a_n$ that is not accepted by $A$, the algorithm finds a state $q$ such that, for some $i$, $\delta^*(q_0, a_1 \dots a_i) = q$, and a state $q'$ such that, for some $j > i$, $\delta^*(q', a_j \dots a_n) \in F$. Next, it adds a path from $q$ to $q'$ on the string $a_{mid} = a_{i+1} \dots a_{j-1}$. This is done by adding $|a_{mid}| - 1$ extra states. It is easy to show that the string $s$ is now accepted by the mutated SFA $A'$. Given a string of length $k$ and an SFA $A$ with $n$ states this mutation can generate at most $nk^2$ mutated SFAs. When there exists a state $q$ such that $\delta^*(q_0, s) = q$ we also output the SFA $A' = (q_0, Q, F \cup \{q\}, \delta)$, in which the input SFA is mutated by adding a new final state.

### 3.5 Example Generation

Generating one string is often not enough to "characterize" the language of an SFA. In generating examples, we aim to follow

```
https://f.o/..Q/                  https://f68.ug.dk.it.no.fm
ftp://1.bd:9/:44ZW1               ftp://hz8.bh8.fzpd85.frn7..
http://h:68576/:X                 ftp://i4.ncm2.lkxp.r9..:5811
http://n.ytnsw.yt.ee8             ftp://bi.mt..:349/
```

**(a)** Examples generated randomly

```
Whttp://youtu:e.com               http://y_:outube.com
0.http//youtu:e.com               ht:tpWWW://youtube.com
h_ttp://youtu:e.com               ht:tpWWW0://youtube.com
WWW000http://youtu:e.com          http://youtube.com/
```

**(b)** Examples generated with the edit distance approach starting with the string `http://youtube.com`.

**Figure 9:** Two approaches to examples generation compared.

the following invariant: we attain *full state coverage* for the SFAs we allow to proceed to the next generation. For each SFA $A = (Q, q_0, F, \delta)$, we generate a set of strings $S \subseteq L(A)$, such that for every state $q \in Q$, there exists a string $a_1 \dots a_n \in S$, such that for some $i$, $\delta^*(q_0, a_1 \dots a_i) = q$. The example generation algorithm is described in Figure 8; given an SFA with $k$ state it terminates in at most $k$ iterations. The algorithm simply generates a new string at every iteration, which is forced to cover at least one state which hasn't yet been covered.

Unfortunately, this naïve approach tends to generate strings that look "random", causing untrained crowd workers to be overly conservative by classifying virtually all of the generated strings as negative examples, even when they are not. For example, we have observed a strong negativity bias towards strings that use non-Latin characters. In the case of URLs, we often get strings containing upper Unicode elements such as Chinese characters, which look unfamiliar to US-based workers. Ideally, we would like to generate strings that *look* as close to normal URLs as possible.

**Edit distance:** We solve this problem by using the knowledge encoded in our training set of inputs. We choose to look for strings in $A$ that are close to some example string $e$ in the training set. We can formalize this notion of closeness by using the classic metric of string edit distance. The edit distance between two strings $s$ and $s'$, $ED(s, s')$, is the minimum number of edits (insertion, deletion, and character replacement) that transforms $s$ into $s'$. Given an SFA $A$ and a string $s \notin L(A)$, we want to find a string $s' \in A$ such that $ED(s, s')$ is minimal. In the case of DFAs there exists an algorithm that given a string $s$ and a DFA $A$ computes the metric $min\{ED(s, s') | s' \in L(A)\}$, representing the minimum edit distance between $s$ and all the strings in $L(A)$ [42]. We symbolically extend the algorithm in [42] to compute the minimum string-to-language edit distance for SFAs, and we modify it to actually generate the witness string.[2] The algorithm has complexity $O(|s|n^2)$, where $n$ is the number of states in the SFA.

As an illustration, Figure 9a shows some examples of randomly generated strings, and Figure 9b several strings generated using the edit distance technique. Clearly, the second set looks less "random" and less intimidating to an average Mechanical Turk worker.

## 4. Experimental Evaluation

To evaluate CrowdBoost, our implementation of program boosting, we face a fundamental challenge; there is no easy definition of correctness because the problems we are attempting to solve do not have a clearly defined specification. Recall that our framework is designed to evolve a notion of correctness as the crowd provides more feedback, which is then incorporated into the solution. Therefore, our goal in this section is to describe the experiments on four different regular expression tasks and demonstrate that our technique can both refine an initial specification and construct a solution that performs well (on the both evolved and initial specification). Before we describe our experiments, we first outline our crowd-sourcing setup.

**Bountify:** In addition to sourcing regular expressions from an online library of user-submitted regexes (Regexlib.com) and other sources (blogs, StackOverflow, etc.), we crowd-sourced the creation of initial regular expressions using Bountify, a service that allows users to post a coding task or technical question to the site, along with a monetary reward starting at as little as $1. Typical rewards on Bountify are $5–10. We posted four separate "bounties"

[2] The algorithm in [42] actually has a mistake in the base case of the dynamic program. When computing the value of $V(T, S, c)$ in page 3, the "otherwise" case does not take into account the case in which $T = S$ and $T$ has a self loop on character $c$. We fix the definition in our implementation.

| Task | Specification | Examples + | Examples − |
|---|---|---|---|
| Phone numbers | `https://bountify.co/5b` | 5 | 4 |
| Dates | `https://bountify.co/5v` | 9 | 9 |
| Emails | `https://bountify.co/5c` | 10 | 7 |
| URLs | `https://bountify.co/5f` | 14 | 9 |

**Figure 10:** Specifications provided to Bountify workers. The last two columns capture the number of positive and negative examples (a subset of the golden set) given to workers in the task specifications.

| Time | iurisilvio | vmas | 7aRPnjkn | alixaxel | shobhit |
|---|---|---|---|---|---|
| Wed 7:32 PM | posted solution | | | | |
| Wed 7:32 PM | updated solution | | | | |
| Wed 8:15 PM | | posted solution | | | |
| Wed 8:15 PM | | updated solution | | | |
| Wed 8:17 PM | | updated solution | | | |
| Wed 9:04 PM | | | posted solution | | |
| Wed 9:13 PM | | updated solution | | | |
| Wed 11:00 PM | | | asked question | | |
| Wed 11:01 PM | | | asked question | | |
| Wed 11:36 PM | | | | posted solution | |
| Thu 10:03 AM | | | updated solution | | |
| Thu 10:03 AM | | | | posted solution | |
| Fri 1:02 AM | | | | | posted solution |
| Mon 7:00 PM | left comment | | | | |
| **Mon 7:01 PM** | **updated solution** | | | | |
| Mon 7:08 PM | left comment | | | | |
| Mon 7:10 PM | | | | updated solution | |
| Mon 7:12 PM | | | left comment | | |
| Mon 7:12 PM | | | left comment | | |

**Figure 11:** Illustrating the experience of crowd-sourcing initial regexes for URLs at `https : //bountify.co/5f`.

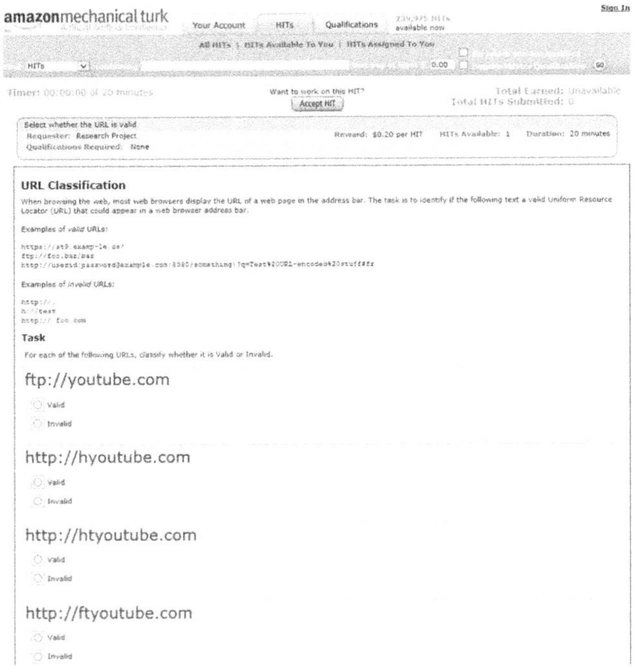


**Figure 12:** Mechanical Turk UI for string classification.

| |
|---|
| I did this HIT a few minutes ago and have a feeling that I did not do it right. If that is the case, could you please let me fix any mistakes so that I do not get rejected? |
| I have a doubt regarding Your valid URL finding HITs . Eg: http://t.jw/s Can I consider the above URL as Invalid. |
| I look forward to doing your HITS. Thanks for posting them! |
| Thank you for providing such type of hits. Keep on posting jobs like this. It will be helpful to me as a financial support for my family. |

**Figure 13:** Examples of real-life Mechanical Turk feedback.

| | Golden set | | Candidate | Candidate regex source: | | |
|---|---|---|---|---|---|---|
| | + | - | regexes | Bountify | Regexlib | Other |
| Phone numbers | 20 | 29 | 8 | 3 | 0 | 5 |
| Dates | 31 | 36 | 6 | 3 | 1 | 2 |
| Emails | 7 | 7 | 10 | 4 | 3 | 3 |
| URLs | 36 | 39 | 9 | 4 | 0 | 5 |

**Figure 14:** The number of examples in the golden set and the number of candidate regexes in each case study.

or requests, each consisting of a high-level specification, and asked for a regular expressions implementations of these specifications.

Over the course of our experiments, freelance developers on Bountify submitted 14 regular expressions that were used in the experiments. Interactions with developers on Bountify sometimes get fairly involved, as illustrated in Figure 11. This figure captures a process of getting the best regular expressions for URLs. Each column of the table corresponds to an individual developer who participated in this bounty. The winner was `iurisilvio`, who was also the first to post a solution—this task was posted on Wednesday evening, with the first solution from `iurisilvio` arriving almost instantaneously. However, in this case, the winning solution did not emerge until the following Monday, after several interactions and clarifications from the poster (us), and refinements of the original solution. Note that this was not done in "real time"; we could have been more aggressive in responding to potential solutions to have this process converge more quickly.

We supplemented the regular expressions created by users on Bountify with regular expressions gathered from Regexlib.com and other online sources total of 33 regular expressions, as detailed in Figure 14.

**Mechanical Turk:** We used Amazon's Mechanical Turk to classify additional examples discovered as part of boosting and generated using the technique described earlier. For each example, we used 5 Mechanical Turk workers provided with a high-level specification of the task. For each string, the Mechanical Turk workers had to classify it as either *Valid* or *Invalid*. As example of a Mechanical Turk user interface is shown in Figure 12.

These strings were grouped in batches containing up to 50 strings and workers were paid a maximum of $0.25 and a minimum of $0.05. These rates were scaled linearly depending on the number of strings within a batch. Classified strings were added to the training set assuming they reached an agreement consensus rate of 60%. Figure 18 shows additional data on Mechanical Turk consensus.

Overall, the workers we encountered on Mechanical Turk have been fairly positive towards our automatically-generated tasks. A few even chose to send us comments such as the ones shown in Figure 13 via email. Clearly, some workers are concerned about doing a good job and also about their reputation. Others asked questions about some of the corner cases.

## 4.1 Experimental Setup

We applied our technique to all unordered pairs of regular expressions (including reflexive pairs $\langle x, x \rangle$) within each of the four specification categories: Phone numbers, Dates, Emails, and URLs. Overall, we considered a total of 465 initial pairs. We evaluated boosting in two separate scenarios: first, using only the genetic algorithm techniques of crossover and mutations and second, using these techniques *and* example generation and refinement with the help of Mechanical Turk workers.

**Initial test set:** In Figure 14 we characterize our initial test set. Columns 2 and 3 show the number of positive and negative examples included in the golden set for each task. Recall that only a subset of these examples was provided to the Bountify workers. Note, that it is difficult to select a comprehensive test set for evaluation, given the complexity of the tasks and the lack of a specification. An ideal test set would contain all the corner cases of the final program, but that program is not known. Consider coming up with a comprehensive set of test cases for phone numbers; numbers direct from a phone book will not provide a lot of the needed complexity. Finding a set of "misshapen" phone numbers that is comprehensive is similarly tough, this is why testing on the evolved set presents a harder challenge for boosting than alternatives. In our experiments, the evolved examples "push the envelope" by considering difficult cases and are generated with help from the crowd, which are difficult to find elsewhere.

**Initial regular expressions:** In Figure 14 we also characterize the size and source of the candidate regular expressions used in our experiments. Columns 4–7 show where our 33 regular expressions come from. Bountify is the most popular source, with 14 coming from there. In Figure 15, we characterize the inputs used in our experiment by length and by the number of states in each resulting SFA. These values convey the varying levels of complexity across the input regular expressions. The regular expression length shown in columns 2–5 of Figure 15 is quite high, with the median frequently being as high as 288 for Dates. To some degree, regular expression length reflects the complexity of these tasks. The state count shown in columns 6–9 of Figure 15 is generally relatively low, due to the natural compression achieved via symbolic representation.

| | Regex character length | | | | SFA state count | | | |
|---|---|---|---|---|---|---|---|---|
| | 25% | 50% | 75% | Max | 25% | 50% | 75% | Max |
| Phone numbers | 44.75 | 54 | 67.75 | 96 | 14.75 | 27 | 28 | 30 |
| Dates | 154 | 288 | 352.25 | 434 | 19 | 39.5 | 72 | 78 |
| Emails | 33.5 | 68.5 | 86.75 | 357 | 7.25 | 8.5 | 10 | 20 |
| URLs | 70 | 115 | 240 | 973 | 12 | 25 | 30 | 80 |

**Figure 15:** Summarized size and complexity of the candidate regexes in our case studies.

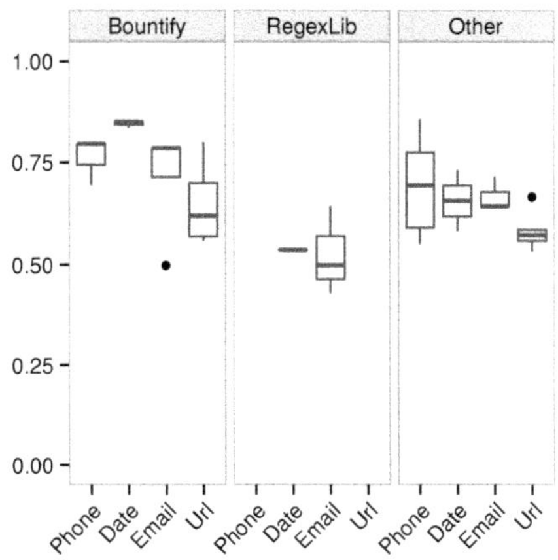


**Figure 16:** Fitness of candidate regular expressions.

| EVALUATED ON... | GOLDEN SET | | | EVOLVED SET | | |
|---|---|---|---|---|---|---|
| | | Boosted | | | Boosted | |
| Task | initial | no crowd | crowd | initial | no crowd | crowd |
| Phone numbers | 0.80 | 0.90 | 0.90 | 0.79 | 0.88 | 0.91 |
| Dates | 0.85 | 0.99 | 0.97 | 0.78 | 0.78 | 0.95 |
| Emails | 0.71 | 0.86 | 0.86 | 0.79 | 0.72 | 0.90 |
| URLs | 0.67 | 0.91 | 0.88 | 0.64 | 0.75 | 0.89 |

**Figure 17:** In each task category, boosting results are shown via fitness values measured on either the golden set or the evolved set for three separate regexes; initial, "no crowd" and "crowd".

Figure 16 shows the distribution of initial accuracy (fitness) values by source. Somewhat surprisingly, the initial values obtained through Bountify are higher than those obtained from RegexLib, a widely-used library of regular expression *specifically designed* to be reused by a variety of developers. Overall, initial fitness values hover between .5 and .75, with none of the regexes being either "too good" or "too bad". Of course, starting with higher-quality initial regular expressions creates less room for growth.

## 4.2 Boosting Results

Our experiments center around pairwise boosting for the four chosen tasks: Phone numbers, Emails, Dates, URLs. We test the quality of the regular expressions obtained through boosting by measuring the *accuracy* on both positive and negative examples. Our measurements are performed both the *golden* set and the *evolved* set. We consider the measurements on the evolved set to be more representative, because the golden set is entirely under our control and could be manipulated by adding and removing examples to influence accuracy measurements. The evolved set, on the other hand, evolves "naturally", through refinement and obtained Mechanical Turk consensus.

Figure 17 captures our high-level results obtained from the boosting process. We display the the mean values for the experiments on each task. We show results as measured both on the golden set of examples and the evolved, expanded set. We see that our process *consistently* results in boosting *across the board*. Significant improvements can be observed by comparing columns 5 and 7. The average boost across all the tasks is 16.25%. It is worth pointing out that having a stable technique that produces consistent boosting for a range of programs is both very difficult and tremendously important to make our approach predictable. Note also that on the larger evolved set the advantage of having a crowd (columns 4 and 7) is more pronounced than on the smaller golden set.

| Task | Generations | | | | Generated strings | | | | Consensus | | | |
|---|---|---|---|---|---|---|---|---|---|---|---|---|
| | 25% | 50% | 75% | Max | 25% | 50% | 75% | Max | 25% | 50% | 75% | Max |
| Phone numbers | 7 | 8 | 10 | 10 | 0 | 6.5 | 20.25 | 83 | 1 | 1 | 1 | 1 |
| Dates | 10 | 10 | 10 | 10 | 29 | 45 | 136 | 207 | 1 | 1 | 1 | 1 |
| Emails | 5 | 5 | 6.5 | 10 | 2 | 7 | 17 | 117 | 1 | 1 | 1 | 1 |
| URLs | 10 | 10 | 10 | 10 | 54 | 72 | 107 | 198 | 0.99 | 1 | 1 | 1 |

**Figure 18:** Characterizing the boosting process. The Generated Strings column, demonstrates that the size of the evolved set varies for each experiment pair, depending on the number of strings created to cover the generated regexes.

## 4.3 Boosting Process

Figure 18 characterizes the boosting process in three dimensions: the number of generations, the number of generated strings, and the measured consensus for classification tasks. For each of these dimensions, we provide 25%, 50%, 75%, and *Max* numbers in lieu of a histogram.

Note that we artificially limit the number of generations to 10. However, about half the pairs for the Emails task finish in 5 generations only. For URLs, there are always 10 generations required — none of the results converge prematurely. The number of generated strings is relatively modest, peaking at 207 for Dates. This suggests that the total crowd-sourcing costs for Mechanical Turk should not be very high. Lastly, the classification consensus is very high overall. This is largely due to the our candidate string generation technique . By making strings look "nice" it prevents a wide spread of opinions.

Figure 19 provides additional statistics for the crossover and mutation process across the tasks in the 25%, 50%, 75%, and Max format used before. Across the board, the number of crossovers produced during boosting is in tens of thousands. Yet only a very small percentage of them *succeed*, i.e survive to the next generation. This is because for the vast majority, the fitness is too small to warrant keeping them around. The number of mutations is smaller, only in single thousands, and their survival rate is somewhat higher. This can be explained by the fact that mutations are relatively local transformations and are not nearly as drastic as crossovers. The overall experience is not uncommon in genetic algorithms.

**Running times:** Figure 20a shows the overall running time for pairwise boosting for each task. The means vary from about 4 minutes per pair and 37 minutes per pair. Predictably, Phone numbers completes quicker than URLs. Note that for Emails, the times are relatively low. This correlates well with the low number of generated strings in Figure 18. Making the boosting process run faster may involve having low-latency Mechanical Turk workers on retainer and is the subject of future work.

**Boosting costs:** Figure 20b shows the costs of performing program boosting across the range of four tasks. The overall costs are quite modest, ranging between 41¢ and $3 per pair. We do see occasional outlets on the high end costing about $12. Some pairs do not require Mechanical Turk call-outs at all, resulting in zero cost.

| Task | Crossovers (thousands) | | | | % Successful crossovers | | | | Mutations (thousands) | | | | % Successful mutations | | | |
|---|---|---|---|---|---|---|---|---|---|---|---|---|---|---|---|---|
| | 25% | 50% | 75% | Max | 25% | 50% | 75 | Max% | 25% | 50% | 75% | Max | 25% | 50% | 75% | Max |
| Phone numbers | 73 | 98 | 113 | 140 | 0.002 | 0.071 | 1.888 | 17.854 | 5 | 6 | 8 | 13 | 3.8 | 5.5 | 11.6 | 34.0 |
| Dates | 14 | 108 | 162 | 171 | 0.21 | 1.51 | 7.22 | 38.92 | 8 | 12 | 17 | 37 | 16 | 31 | 35 | 53 |
| Emails | 3 | 8 | 22 | 165 | 0.45 | 1.62 | 5.11 | 15.04 | 0 | 0 | 2 | 15 | 41 | 54 | 78 | 100 |
| URLs | 116 | 178 | 180 | 180 | 0.88 | 6.62 | 34.29 | 50.15 | 9 | 20 | 52 | 114 | 30 | 35 | 41 | 64 |

**Figure 19:** Successful propagation of candidates.

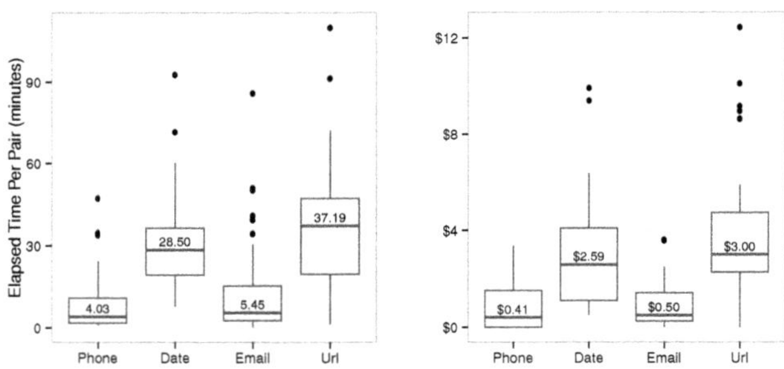


(a) Running times for each task. (b) Costs for Mechanical Turk.
**Figure 20:** Running times and costs.

## 5. Discussion

We see the following main challenges with the program boosting approach. In this paper, we aim to provide solutions to only *some* of these challenges. Addressing all of them in a comprehensive manner will undoubtedly require much subsequent research.

**Low quality of responses:** Just like with other crowd-sourcing tasks, our approach suffers from response quality challenges, both because the crowd participant is honestly mistaken (American Mechanical Turk workers think that Unicode characters are not allowed within URLs) or because they are trying to game the system by providing an answer that is either random or obviously too broad (such as /.*/ for regular expression sourcing tasks).

**Everyone makes the same mistake:** If every developer gets the same corner case incorrect, voting and consensus-based approaches are not going to be very helpful: everyone will incorrectly vote for the same outcome, falsely raising our confidence in the wrong solution. Analysis of *security sanitizers* in [17] illustrates that sometimes that may be the case.

**Over-fitting on the training data:** Just like with any other learning tasks, over-fitting the answer (model) to the data is a potential problem. One way to mitigate this is to force generalization, either explicitly or through limiting the size (length or number of states or another similar metric) of the selected program. For instance, we could favor smaller regular expressions in our selection.

**Program complexity is too high:** While it is possible to blend programs together to achieve good results on training and testing data, it is desirable to produce resulting programs that are too complex to be understood. In some cases, since these programs will be used as black boxes, this is fine; in others, this is not the case.

**Knowing when to stop:** In the context of crowd-sourcing, knowing when to stop soliciting answers is difficult: even if you have absolute agreement among existing workers, it is not clear that asking more questions may not eventually yield disagreement about a non-obvious corner case. The current approach in this paper does not use a more flexible approach to getting the desired level of confidence, although several techniques have been proposed.

**Monetization and payment:** It is not clear how to properly compensate the workers whose (programming) efforts become blended into the end-product. There are thorny intellectual property issues to grapple with. There is the question of whether the workers should be compensated beyond their initial payment, as the software to which they have contributed becomes successful.

**Crowd latency:** The time it takes to gather solutions from the crowd is a major issue in getting program boosting results faster. In the future, it may be possible to have a set of workers on retainer with faster response times. Another option is to design a more asynchronous approach that would speculatively explore the program space.

**Sub-optimality:** Because we are evolving the training set, it is possible that in earlier generations we abandoned programs that in later generations would appear to be more fit. One way to compensate for this kind of sub-optimality is to either revisit the evaluation once the evolved set has been finalized, or to inject some of the previously rejected programs from past generations into the mix at later stages.

## 6. Related Work

**Crowd-sourcing:** Recent work has investigated the incorporation of human computation into programming systems. Several platforms have been proposed to abstract the details of crowd-sourcing services away for the programmer, making the issues of latency, quality control, and cost easier to manage [3, 33, 36]. TurkIt [27] and Collabode [13] take different approaches to the problem of making programming easier; the former enabling usage of non-experts to solve tasks well suited for humans and the latter enabling collaboration between programmers. Another approach to using crowd-sourcing is to break large programming tasks into small independent "microtasks" [25]. Our work furthers progress towards the goal of solving difficult programming problems by leveraging a crowd of mixed skill levels and using formal methods to combine efforts from these multiple workers.

**Genetic algorithms:** In general, genetic algorithms alter structures that represent members of a population to produce a result that is better according to fitness or optimality conditions. Early work [9] evolved finite state machines to predict symbol sequences. Others have extended these techniques to build modular systems that incorporate independent FSMs to solve maze and grid exploration problems [5] or to predict note sequences in musical compositions [18]. In software engineering, genetic algorithms have been applied to fixing software bugs [10] and software optimization [6]. Genetic *programming* is a sub-area of genetic algorithms focused on evolving programs [2, 21, 35]. An evolutionary approach has also been applied to crowd-sourcing creative design, where workers iteratively improved and blended design sketches of a chairs and alarm clocks [31]. Our work introduces a novel use of crowd-sourcing to both crowd-source initial programs and to automatically refine the training set and the fitness function through crowd-sourcing.

**Program analysis and synthesis:** In the theory of abstract interpretation, widening operators are used to compute a valid abstraction for some function [7]. Our use of the mutation and crossover operations to refine or blend SFAs follows the spirit of this approach and may be one path towards applying program boosting to domains where abstract interpretation has seen much success, e.g., static analysis. Recent work has investigated automatic synthesis of program fragments from formal and example based specifications [15, 16, 38, 39]. A specification which defines program behavior can be viewed as a search problem for which constraint solvers or customized strategies can be applied. These approaches use formal methods to aid in the construction of the low-level implementation of a specification. In our technique, the initial specification may be open to interpretation or not fully defined. We take advantage of the crowd to refine our specification and improve the correctness of a collection of implementations.

**Learning regular expressions:** Automatic generation of regular expressions from examples has been explored in the literature for information extraction. In the context of DNA analysis, events can be extracted from DNA sequences by learning simple regular expressions that anchor the relevant strings [11]. Others use transformations on regular expressions themselves, rather than a DFA representation [4, 14, 26]. In contrast, our approach uses the power of symbolic automata to manipulate complex expressions containing large alphabets. We are not aware of traditional learning approaches suitable for learning regular expressions that contain Unicode, due to the large alphabet size.

**Learning DFAs:** Grammatical inference is the study of learning a grammar by observing examples of an unknown language. It has been shown that a learning algorithm can produce a new grammar that can generate all of the examples seen so far in polynomial time [12]. Many variants of this problem have been studied, including different language classes and different learning models. Relevant to this paper is the study of producing a regular language from labeled strings, where the learning algorithm is given a set of positive and negative examples. This problem has been shown to be hard in the worst case [19, 34], but many techniques have been demonstrated to be practical in the average case. The L-star algorithm [1] can infer a minimally accepting DFA but assumes that the target language is known and that hypothesized grammars can be checked for equivalence with the target language. Recent results [30] extend to large alphabets but still require strong assumptions about the oracle. State merging algorithms [23] relax the requirement for a minimal output, and work by building a prefix-tree acceptor for the training examples and then merge states together that map to the same suffixes. A number of extensions to this technique have been proposed [22, 24, 32]. Evolutionary approaches to learning a DFA from positive and negative examples have also been proposed [28, 29].

## 7. Conclusions

This paper presents a novel crowd-sourcing approach to program synthesis called *program boosting*. Our focus is difficult programming tasks, which even the most expert of developers have trouble with. Our insight is that the wisdom of the crowds can be brought to bear on these challenging tasks. In this paper we show how to use two crowds, a crowd of skilled developers and a crowd of untrained computer workers to successfully produce solutions to complex tasks that involve crafting regular expressions.

We have implemented program boosting in a tool called CROWDBOOST and have tested it on four complex tasks, we have crowd-sourced 33 regular expressions from Bountify and several other sources, and performed pairwise boosting on them. We find that our program boosting technique is stable: it produces *consistent* boosts in accuracy when tested on 465 pairs of crowd-sourced programs. Even when starting with initial programs of high quality (fitness), crowd-sourced from qualified developers, we are consistently able to achieve boosts in accuracy, averaging 16.25%.

## References


[1] D. Angluin. Learning regular sets from queries and counterexamples. *Information and Computation*, 75(2), 1987.

[2] W. Banzhaf, P. Nordin, R. E. Keller, and F. D. Francone. *Genetic Programming: An Introduction*. 1997.

[3] D. W. Barowy, C. Curtsinger, E. D. Berger, and A. McGregor. Automan: a platform for integrating human-based and digital computation. In *Proceedings of the Conference on Object-Oriented Programming, Systems, Languages, and Applications*, 2012.

[4] D. F. Barrero, D. Camacho, and M. D.R-Moreno. Automatic web data extraction based on genetic algorithms and regular expressions. In *Data Mining and Multi-agent Integration*. 2009.

[5] K. Chellapilla and D. Czarnecki. A preliminary investigation into evolving modular finite state machines. In *Proceedings of the Congress on Evolutionary Computation*, 1999.

[6] B. Cody-Kenny and S. Barrett. Self-focusing genetic programming for software optimisation. In *Proceedings of the Conference on Genetic and Evolutionary Computation*, 2013.

[7] P. Cousot and R. Cousot. Formal language, grammar and set-constraint-based program analysis by abstract interpretation. In *Proceedings of the Conference on Functional Programming Languages and Computer Architecture*, 1995.

[8] L. D'Antoni and M. Veanes. Minimization of symbolic automata. In *Proceedings of the Symposium on Principles of Programming Languages*, 2014.

[9] L. J. Fogel, A. J. Owens, and M. J. Walsh. *Artificial Intelligence through Simulated Evolution*. 1966.

[10] S. Forrest, T. Nguyen, W. Weimer, and C. L. Goues. A genetic programming approach to automated software repair. In *Proceedings of the Conference on Genetic and Evolutionary Computation*, 2009.

[11] U. Galassi and A. Giordana. Learning regular expressions from noisy sequences. In *Proceedings of the Symposium on Abstraction, Reformulation and Approximation*, 2005.

[12] E. M. Gold. Language identification in the limit. *Information and Control*, 10(5), 1967.

[13] M. Goldman, G. Little, and R. C. Miller. Collabode: Collaborative coding in the browser. In *Proceedings of the Workshop on Cooperative and Human Aspects of Software Engineering*, 2011.

[14] A. González-Pardo and D. Camacho. Analysis of grammatical evolutionary approaches to regular expression induction. In *Proceedings of the Congress on Evolutionary Computation*, 2011.

[15] S. Gulwani. Automating string processing in spreadsheets using input-output examples. In *Proceedings of the Symposium on Principles of Programming Languages*, 2011.

[16] T. Gvero, V. Kuncak, and R. Piskac. Interactive synthesis of code snippets. In *Proceedings of the Converence on Computer Aided Verification*, 2011.

[17] P. Hooimeijer, B. Livshits, D. Molnar, P. Saxena, and M. Veanes. Fast and precise sanitizer analysis with Bek. In *Proceedings of the USENIX Security Symposium*, 2011.

[18] Y. Inagaki. On synchronized evolution of the network of automata. *IEEE Transactions on Evolutionary Computation*, 6(2), 2002.

[19] M. Kearns and L. Valiant. Cryptographic limitations on learning boolean formulae and finite automata. *Journal of the ACM*, 41(1), 1994.

[20] R. Kohavi, R. Longbotham, D. Sommerfield, and R. M. Henne. Controlled experiments on the web: survey and practical guide. *Data Mining and Knowledge Discovery*, 18(1), 2009.

[21] J. R. Koza. *Genetic Programming: On the Programming of Computers by Means of Natural Selection*. 1992.

[22] B. Lambeau, C. Damas, and P. Dupont. State-merging DFA induction algorithms with mandatory merge constraints. In *Proceedings of the International Colloquim on Grammatical Inference*, 2008.

[23] K. J. Lang. Random DFA's can be approximately learned from sparse uniform examples. In *Proceedings of Workshop on Computational Learning Theory*, 1992.

[24] K. J. Lang, B. A. Pearlmutter, and R. Price. Results of the abbadingo one DFA learning competition and a new evidence-driven state merging algorithm. In *Proceedings of the International Colloquim on Grammatical Inference*, 1998.

[25] T. D. LaToza, W. B. Towne, C. M. Adriano, and A. van der Hoek. Microtask programming: Building software with a crowd. In *Proceedings of the Symposium on User Interface Software and Technology*, 2014.

[26] Y. Li, R. Krishnamurthy, S. Raghavan, S. Vaithyanathan, and H. V. Jagadish. Regular expression learning for information extraction. In *Proceedings of the Conference on Empirical Methods in Natural Language Processing*, 2008.

[27] G. Little, L. B. Chilton, M. Goldman, and R. C. Miller. TurKit: tools for iterative tasks on mechanical turk. In *Proceedings of the SIGKDD Workshop on Human Computation*, 2009.

[28] S. M. Lucas and T. J. Reynolds. Learning DFA: evolution versus evidence driven state merging. In *Proceedings of the Congress on Evolutionary Computation*, 2003.

[29] S. M. Lucas and T. J. Reynolds. Learning deterministic finite automata with a smart state labeling evolutionary algorithm. *IEEE Transactions on Pattern Analysis and Machine Intelligence*, 27(7), 2005.

[30] O. Maler and I. E. Mens. Learning regular languages over large alphabets. In *Tools and Algorithms for the Construction and Analysis of Systems*, 2014.

[31] J. V. Nickerson, Y. Sakamoto, and L. Yu. Structures for creativity: The crowdsourcing of design. In *CHI Workshop on Crowd-sourcing and Human Computation*, 2011.

[32] J. Oncina and P. García. Identifying regular languages in polynomial time. In *Advances in Structural and Syntactic Pattern Recognition*, Series in Machine Perception and Artificial Intelligence. 1992.

[33] A. G. Parameswaran, H. Park, H. Garcia-Molina, N. Polyzotis, and J. Widom. Deco: declarative crowdsourcing. In *Proceedings of the Conference on Information and Knowledge Management*, 2012.

[34] L. Pitt and M. K. Warmuth. The minimum consistent DFA problem cannot be approximated within any polynomial. *Journal of the ACM*, 40(1), 1993.

[35] R. Poli, W. B. Langdon, and N. F. McPhee. *A Field Guide to Genetic Programming*. Lulu Enterprises, 2008.

[36] A. J. Quinn, B. B. Bederson, T. Yeh, and J. Lin. Crowdflow: Integrating machine learning with mechanical turk for speed-cost-quality flexibility. Technical Report HCIL-2010-09, University of Maryland, College Park, 2010.

[37] R. E. Schapire. The boosting approach to machine learning: An overview. `https://www.cs.princeton.edu/courses/archive/spring07/cos424/papers/boosting-survey.pdf`, 2002.

[38] A. Solar-Lezama. Program sketching. *STTT*, 15(5-6):475–495, 2013.

[39] S. Srivastava, S. Gulwani, and J. S. Foster. From program verification to program synthesis. In *Proceedings of the Symposium on Principles of Programming Languages*, 2010.

[40] T. E. Uribe and M. E. Stickel. Ordered binary decision diagrams and the davis-putnam procedure. In *Proceedings of the Conference on Constraints in Computational Linguistics*, 1994.

[41] M. Veanes and N. Bjørner. Symbolic automata: The toolkit. In *Proceedings of the Conference on Tools and Algorithms for the Construction and Analysis of Systems*, 2012.

[42] R. A. Wagner. Order-n correction for regular languages. *Communications of the ACM*, 17(5), 1974.


# A. Appendix

To provide intuition on the type of results produced by our technique we present two examples. These are not necessarily the the highest fitness results; some of these are sampled after several generations. The complexity of the evolved results is due to two factors: the regular expressions are obtained using the classical transformation from automata which in general produces large results, and the classifiers have to take into account many corner cases.

```
Task: Email
Fitness: 0.935714285714286
Result:
^(([+-0-9A-Z\_a-z](([+-0-9A-Z_a-z]|\(\)*[+-0-9A-Z_a-z]))*
(@[-0-9A-Za-z]([-0-9A-Za-z])*.[A-Za-z][A-Za-z]|\(\)*@[-0-
9A-Za-z]([-0-9A-Za-z])*@[-0-9A-Za-z]([-0-9A-Za-z])*.[A-Za
-z][A-Za-z])(([A-Za-z]|))*|[+-0-9A-Z\_a-z](([+-0-9A-Z_a-z
]|\(\)*[+-0-9A-Z_a-z]))*(.[^\x0A][-0-9A-Z_a-z]|\(\)*(([\0
-\x09\x0B-*,./:-?[]^`{-\uFFFF][-0-9A-Z_a-z]|@_)|@[-0-9A-Z
a-z]([-0-9A-Za-z])*_))(([-0-9A-Z_a-z]|\[^\x0A][-0-9A-Z_a-
z]))*@[-0-9A-Za-z]([-0-9A-Za-z])*.[A-Za-z][A-Za-z](([A-Za
-z]|))*))$

Task: Phone numbers
Fitness: 0.897959183673469
Result:
^(((((((([02-9]|+1([0-9]|[\x20-.][0-9]))|((|+1((|[\x20-.](
))[0-9])([0-9][0-9][0-9][0-9][0-9][0-9][0-9][0-9][0-9]|[0
-9][0-9][0-9][0-9][0-9][\x20-.][0-9][0-9][0-9][0-9])|(([0
2-9]|+1([0-9]|[\x20-.][0-9]))|((|+1((|[\x20-.]())[0-9])[0
-9][0-9][\x20-.]([0-9][0-9][0-9][0-9][0-9][0-9][0-9]|[0-9
][0-9][0-9][\x20-.][0-9][0-9][0-9][0-9]))|(([02-9]|+1([0-
9]|[\x20-.][0-9]))|((|+1((|[\x20-.]())[0-9])[0-9][0-9])((
[0-9][0-9][0-9][0-9][0-9][0-9][0-9]|[0-9][0-9][0-9][\x20-
.][0-9][0-9][0-9][0-9])|[\x20-.]([0-9][0-9][0-9][0-9][0-9
][0-9][0-9]|[0-9][0-9][0-9][\x20-.][0-9][0-9][0-9][0-9]))
)|1(_)*((([0-9][0-9][0-9]([0-9][0-9][0-9][0-9][0-9][0-9](
[0-9])?|([0-9][0-9][\x20-.]|[0-9][0-9][0-9][\x20-.])[0-9]
[0-9][0-9][0-9])|([0-9]([0-9][0-9][0-9][0-9][0-9][0-9][0-
9][0-9][0-9]|[0-9][0-9][0-9][0-9][0-9][\x20-.][0-9][0-9][
0-9][0-9]))|(([0-9][0-9][\x20-.]|[0-9][0-9][0-9][\x20-.])
|([0-9][0-9][0-9][\x20-.])([0-9][0-9][0-9][0-9][0-9][0-9]
[0-9]|[0-9][0-9][0-9][\x20-.][0-9][0-9][0-9][0-9]))|(([0-
9][0-9])|[0-9][0-9][0-9]))|([0-9][0-9][0-9]))(([0-9][0-9]
[0-9][0-9][0-9][0-9][0-9]|[0-9][0-9][0-9][\x20-.][0-9][0-
9][0-9][0-9])|[\x20-.]([0-9][0-9][0-9][0-9][0-9][0-9][0-9
]|[0-9][0-9][0-9][\x20-.][0-9][0-9][0-9][0-9]))))|1(_)*[\
x20-.](1_)*((((((((([0-9][0-9]([0-9][0-9][0-9][0-9][0-9][0
-9]([0-9])?|([0-9][0-9][\x20-.]|[0-9][0-9][0-9][\x20-.])[
0-9][0-9][0-9][0-9])|(([0-9][\x20-.]|([0-9][0-9][\x20-.])
([0-9][0-9][0-9][0-9][0-9][0-9][0-9]|[0-9][0-9][0-9][\x20
-.][0-9][0-9][0-9][0-9]))|1[0-9][0-9][0-9]([0-9][0-9][0-9
][0-9][0-9][0-9]([0-9])?|([0-9][0-9][\x20-.]|[0-9][0-9][0
-9][\x20-.])[0-9][0-9][0-9][0-9]))|(([02-9]|+1([0-9]|([0-
9]))|1([0-9])([0-9][0-9][0-9][0-9][0-9][0-9][0-9][0-9][0-
9]|[0-9][0-9][0-9][0-9][0-9][\x20-.][0-9][0-9][0-9][0-9])
)|(1([0-9][0-9][\x20-.]|[0-9][0-9][0-9][\x20-.])|(([02-9]
|+1([0-9]|([0-9]))|1([0-9])[0-9][0-9][\x20-.])([0-9][0-9]
[0-9][0-9][0-9][0-9][0-9]|[0-9][0-9][0-9][\x20-.][0-9][0-
9][0-9][0-9]))|(+1[\x20-.]|1[\x20-.])(([0-9]|([0-9])([0-9
][0-9][0-9][0-9][0-9][0-9][0-9][0-9][0-9]|[0-9][0-9][0-9]
[0-9][0-9][\x20-.][0-9][0-9][0-9][0-9])|([0-9]|([0-9])[0-
9][0-9][\x20-.]([0-9][0-9][0-9][0-9][0-9][0-9][0-9]|[0-9]
[0-9][0-9][\x20-.][0-9][0-9][0-9][0-9])))|(([0-9])|([0-9]
[0-9]))(([0-9][0-9][0-9][0-9][0-9][0-9][0-9]|[0-9][0-9][0
-9][\x20-.][0-9][0-9][0-9][0-9])|[\x20-.]([0-9][0-9][0-9]
[0-9][0-9][0-9][0-9]|[0-9][0-9][0-9][\x20-.][0-9][0-9][0-
9][0-9])))|((1([0-9][0-9])|[0-9][0-9][0-9]))|(([02-9]|+1(
[0-9]|([0-9]))|1([0-9])[0-9][0-9]))|(+1[\x20-.]|1[\x20-.]
)([0-9]|([0-9])[0-9][0-9]))(([0-9][0-9][0-9][0-9][0-9][0-
9][0-9]|[0-9][0-9][0-9][\x20-.][0-9][0-9][0-9][0-9])|[\x2
0-.]([0-9][0-9][0-9][0-9][0-9][0-9][0-9]|[0-9][0-9][0-9][
\x20-.][0-9][0-9][0-9][0-9])))))$
```

# Fiat: Deductive Synthesis of Abstract Data Types in a Proof Assistant

Benjamin Delaware    Clément Pit–Claudel    Jason Gross    Adam Chlipala
MIT CSAIL
{bendy, cpitcla, jgross, adamc}@csail.mit.edu

## Abstract

We present Fiat, a library for the Coq proof assistant supporting refinement of declarative specifications into efficient functional programs with a high degree of automation. Each refinement process leaves a proof trail, checkable by the normal Coq kernel, justifying its soundness. We focus on the synthesis of abstract data types that package methods with private data. We demonstrate the utility of our framework by applying it to the synthesis of *query structures* – abstract data types with SQL-like query and insert operations. Fiat includes a library for writing specifications of query structures in SQL-inspired notation, expressing operations over relations (tables) in terms of mathematical sets. This library includes a suite of tactics for automating the refinement of specifications into efficient, correct-by-construction OCaml code. Using these tactics, a programmer can generate such an implementation completely automatically by only specifying the equivalent of SQL indexes, data structures capturing useful views of the abstract data. Throughout we speculate on the new programming modularity possibilities enabled by an automated refinement system with proved-correct rules.

> *"Every block of stone has a statue inside it and it is the task of the sculptor to discover it."*
>
> — Michelangelo

## 1. Introduction

Deductive synthesis allows users to derive correct-by-construction programs interactively via *stepwise refinement of specifications*. The programmer starts with a very underconstrained nondeterministic program, which may be nonobvious how to execute efficiently. Step by step, the developer applies *refinement* rules, which replace program subterms with others that are "at least as deterministic," introducing no *new* behaviors beyond those of the terms they replace. Eventually, the program has been refined to a completely deterministic form, ideally employing efficient data structures and algorithms. At its core, deductive synthesis decomposes a program into a high-level specification of its *functionality* and a sequence of semantics-preserving *optimizations* that produces an efficient, executable implementation. So long as the library of primitive refinement steps is sound, developers using this approach can modify the optimizations to suit their performance requirements, remaining confident that the implementation produced meets the original specification.

This paper introduces an approach for the deductive synthesis of *abstract data types* (ADTs) combining computational refinement [ ] and abstraction relations [ , ]. An important novelty of our approach is that all refinement derivations are carried out inside the Coq proof assistant, thereby achieving a previously unmatched degree of confidence in the correctness of the resulting implementations. Derivations in our prototype system **Fiat** are *optimization scripts* that transform programs in correctness-preserving ways, possibly resolving nondeterminism. These optimization scripts yield machine-checkable refinement theorems certifying the correctness of the resulting implementations.

Systems like Specware [ ] and its predecessors [ , ] at the Kestrel Institute have enabled interactive synthesis by refinement since the 1970s. Only recently has Specware supported any kind of mechanized proof about refinement correctness, by instrumenting refinement primitives to generate Isabelle/HOL proof scripts, although each of these generators expands Specware's trusted code base. Specware also follows a very *manual model of choosing refinement steps*, which is understandable given the challenging problems it has been used to tackle, in domains like artificial intelligence and programming-language runtime systems.

With Fiat, we instead focus (for now, at least) on more modest programming tasks, like those faced by mainstream Web application developers interacting with persistent data stores. The ultimate goal of Fiat is to enable refinement derivations using the sort of push-button automation found in traditional SQL query planners, while adding a high level of assurance about their correctness by carrying them out inside of Coq with full proofs. At the same time, the framework allows seamless integration with manual derivations where they are called for, without weakening the formal guarantee that a derived implementation meets its specification.

By combining the core of Fiat with domain-specific libraries, programmers can write derivations with a high degree of automation. These libraries combine domain-specific refinement theorems and automation tactics to build what amount to first-class, semantics-preserving compilers. Our main case study to date involves a library for synthesizing ADTs with SQL-like operations, operating in the style of *query planners* from the database community. We start with declarative queries over relational tables, transforming them into efficient, correct-by-construction OCaml code. This library implements "domain compilers" at varying levels of automation; users can do completely automated planning for a common class of queries, and with more work they can apply some of our more advanced strategies for choosing data structures or algorithms.

Figure 1 shows an example Fiat derivation for a simple data structure representing a book store. We consider this example in


*POPL '15*, January 15–17, 2015, Mumbai, India.

ACM 978-1-4503-3300-9/15/01...$15.00.
http://dx.doi.org/10.1145/2676726.2677006

```
Definition BookstoreSpec := QueryADTRep BookstoreSchema {
  const Init (_: unit) : rep := empty,

  update AddBook (book: Book) : bool :=
    Insert book into Books,

  update PlaceOrder (order: Order) : bool :=
    Insert order into Orders,

  query GetTitles (author: string) : list string :=
    For (b in Books)
    Where (author = b!Author)
    Return (b!Title),

  query NumOrders (author: string) : nat :=
    Count (For (o in Orders) (b in Books)
           Where (author = b!Author)
           Where (b!ISBN = o!ISBN)
           Return ())
}.

Definition BookStorage : IndexFor Book.
  mkIndex [ BookSchema/Author; BookSchema/ISBN ].
Defined.

Definition OrderStorage : IndexFor Order.
  mkIndex [ OrderSchema/ISBN ].
Defined.

Definition Bookstore_AbsR abs
(conc : BookStorage × OrderStorage) :=
     abs!Books ≃ benumerate (fst conc)
   ∧ abs!Orders ≃ benumerate (snd conc).

Definition Bookstore : Sharpened BookstoreSpec.
  plan Bookstore_AbsR.
  finish sharpening.
Defined.
```

**Figure 1.** Specification for a bookstore ADT

more detail later in the paper, but for now we just want to give a basic sense of how Fiat may be used. The code excerpt begins with a definition of a data type as a set of methods over a relational database schema (whose definition we give later, in Figure 8). Methods are written in SQL-inspired syntax, saying more of what we want computed than how to compute it. These expressions have rigorous meanings in Coq, standing for mathematical sets. For each of our two database tables, we define an *index*, a data structure useful to look up entries by values of certain keys. The two Definitions of IndexFor values accomplish that purpose in the figure. Next, we define an *abstraction relation*, explaining how we propose to implement set-based relations using the concrete indexes we have defined. Finally, we begin an *optimization script* to generate a correct-by-construction implementation (shown later in Figure 11). Most of the work is done by a "domain compiler" called **plan**, which knows how to use indexes to implement queries efficiently. The programmer is free to chain sequences of library invocations and more manual steps, as needed to meet his performance target. Any sequence accepted by Coq is guaranteed to preserve correctness, just as in conventional programming any sequence of calls to an encapsulated data type is guaranteed to preserve its invariants. Instead of just decomposing a program into "data structures + algorithms," implementations synthesized by Fiat are decomposed into "functionality + optimizations," with a similar kind of *enforced modularity* to what we are used to with encapsulated data types.

Considering this idea more carefully, we can spot opportunities for these domain-specific libraries to provide automation that goes beyond the programmer's usual relationship with her compilers. Compilers generally do not play too well with each other, and any optimization not built into a compiler goes unapplied in the final code. By relying on Fiat's core as a common foundation, users can freely *compose* the automation tactics provided by domain-specific libraries. Furthermore, this foundation enables programmers to take an existing domain-specific library and safely extend it with novel optimizations, without affecting the soundness of any program optimized with the extended library.

Section 2 introduces Fiat's basic notions of *computations* and their *refinement* and then lifts these ideas to *abstract data types*, which expose private data through methods with specifications. Section 3 describes how these foundations are utilized to synthesize correct-by-construction ADTs. Section 4 presents *query structures*, a library for synthesizing ADTs with SQL-style operations on relational tables. This library augments the core of Fiat with new notations for specifying *functionality* at a high level and *optimization-script* building blocks for implementing ADTs at varying levels of automation. We have used this machinery to generate correct-by-construction OCaml programs; Section 5 includes more detail. We close with more discussion of related work. The entire Fiat framework, including all the examples discussed in this paper, can be found at `http://plv.csail.mit.edu/fiat/` and can be built and run using the standard distribution of Coq 8.4pl2.

## 2. Refinement

The foundation of deductive synthesis in Fiat is *refinement*: a user starts out with a high-level specification that can be implemented in any number of different ways and iteratively refines the possible implementations until producing an executable (and hopefully efficient) implementation.

Specifications in Fiat are represented as *computations*, or sets of values satisfying some defining property. Figure 2 lists the three combinators Fiat uses to define these sets: **ret** builds a singleton set, set comprehension $\{\_ \mid \_\}$ "picks" an arbitrary element satisfying a characteristic property, and the "bind" combinator, "$\_ \leftarrow \_; \_$", combines two computations. Throughout the text we will use the notation $c \leadsto v \equiv v \in c$ to emphasize that computations denote sets of "computed" values.

$$\textbf{ret}\ a \equiv \{a\} \qquad \{a \mid P\ a\} \equiv \{a \mid P\ a\}$$
$$x \leftarrow c_a; c_b(x) \equiv \{b \mid \exists a \in c_a.\ b \in c_b(a)\}$$

**Figure 2.** Computation combinators

Consider the following (particularly permissive) specification of an insert function for a cache represented as a list of key-value pairs:

$$\text{insert}\ k\ v\ l \equiv \{l' \mid l' \subseteq [(k, v)] \cup l\}$$

This specification only requires that insert does not inject extraneous elements in the list. When a key is not included in the original cache, the specification imposes no ordering on the result and somewhat counterintuitively does not require that the result include the new key-value pair. Such underspecification is not a bug. It allows for a wide range of caching behaviors: existing keys can be replaced or retained when they are reinserted, new keys can be inserted in an order that facilitates lookup, and old values can be dropped from the cache to maintain a constant memory footprint.

Each of these choices represents a more refined version of insert, with refinement defined by the superset relation $\supseteq$ between the set of implementations of insert and that of each choice. Refinement forms a partial order on computations. Intuitively, a computation $c'$ is a refinement of a computation $c$ if $c'$ only "computes" to values that $c$ can "compute" to. Figure 3 shows a subset of the

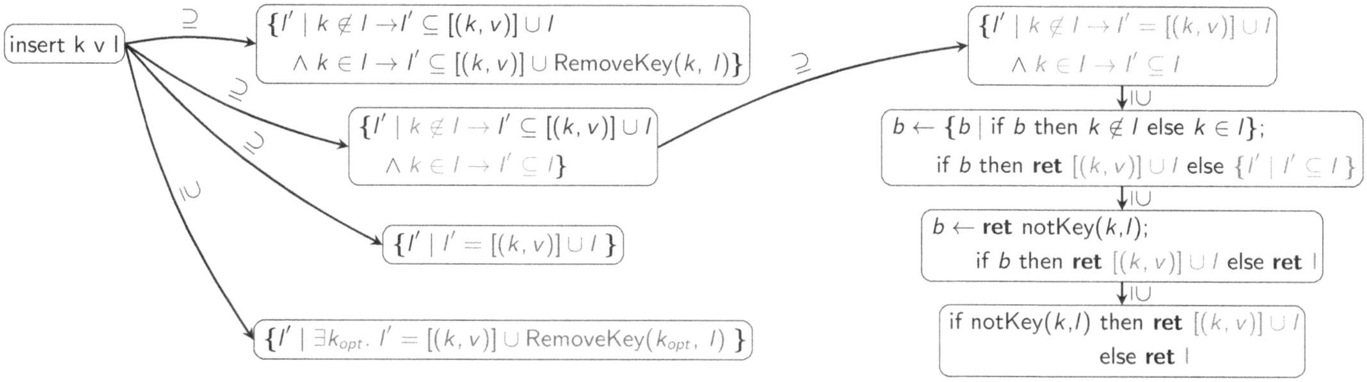


**Figure 3.** A space of possible refinements of insert.

space of computations that we can explore through sequences of refinements from the initial definition of insert. The second column shows a number of refinements of the initial specification, each of which admits a smaller set of implementations. The computation in the second row of this column, for example, only permits implementations that ignore the insertion of duplicate keys.

The third column shows a sequence of refinements progressing towards such an implementation. The first entry further requires implementations to add new keys to the cache. The next computation is an equivalent but more operational version that decomposes the pick into

$$b \leftarrow \{b \mid \text{if } b \text{ then } k \notin l \text{ else } k \in l\};$$
$$\text{if } b \text{ then } \mathbf{ret}\ [(k, v)] \cup l \text{ else } \{l' \mid l' \subseteq l\}$$

where $b$ is bound to the negation of a nondeterministic membership check for key $k$ in list $l$. $b$ is passed to a computation that adds the key-value pair to the list if $k$ is not already used and nondeterministically shrinks $l$ otherwise. The third entry moves closer to an implementation by implementing the membership check using a notKey function and the pick in the else case with **ret** l. A few basic properties of our computation combinators justify implementing each of these subterms of the bind. Refinement may be pushed down through "bind" in two different ways:

$$c_a \supseteq c'_a \longrightarrow (x \leftarrow c_a; c_b(x)) \supseteq (x \leftarrow c'_a; c_b(x))$$
$$(\forall x, c_b(x) \supseteq c'_b(x)) \longrightarrow (x \leftarrow c_a; c_b(x)) \supseteq (x \leftarrow c_a; c'_b(x))$$

The usual monad laws [ ] hold for computations under set equality $=$.

$$(x \leftarrow \mathbf{ret}\ a; c(x)) = c(a)$$
$$(x \leftarrow c; \mathbf{ret}\ x) = c$$
$$(y \leftarrow (x \leftarrow c_a;\ c_b(x));\ c_c(y) = x \leftarrow c_a;\ y \leftarrow c_b(x);\ c_c(y)$$

These laws justify the final refinement in the third column; by transitivity of refinement, it is also a refinement of the initial specification of insert.

### 2.1 Refinement of Abstract Datatypes

Fiat defines abstract data types [ ] (ADTs) as records of state types and computations implementing operations over states. Figure 4 gives a specification of a cache as an abstract data type. In the CacheSig type signature, **rep** stands for an arbitrary abstract implementation type, to be threaded through the methods; this type placeholder has a special status in signatures. The CacheSpec functional specification is a *nondeterministic reference implementation* of a cache. That is, it uses a simple data representation type and its associated method implementations to clearly express how any implementation of this ADT ought to behave. The representation type of CacheSpec does not even obviously lead to computable execution, since it is phrased in terms of mathematical sets. CacheSpec adds to our running example of insert a lookup *method* for retrieving values from the cache, an update method for updating keys already in the cache, and a *constructor* called empty for creating a fresh cache.

```
ADTSig CacheSig :=
  empty : () → rep,
  insert : rep × Key × Value → rep,
  update : rep × Key × (Value → Value) → rep,
  lookup : rep × Key → Maybe Value

ADT CacheSpec implementing CacheSig :=
  rep := Set of (Key × Value)
  constructor empty := Return ∅
  method insert (r : rep, k : Key, v : Value) : rep :=
    {r′ | ∀kv. kv ∈ r′ → kv = (k, v) ∨ kv ∈ r}
  method update (r : rep, k : Key, f : Value → Value) : rep :=
    {r′ | ∀v. (k, v) ∈ r → ∀kv. kv ∈ r′ → kv = (k, f(v))
                                         ∨ kv ∈ RemoveKey(k, r)}
  method lookup (r : rep, k : Key) : Maybe Value :=
    {v_opt | ∀v. v_opt = Some v → (k, v) ∈ r}
```

**Figure 4.** An abstract data type for caches

While mathematical sets provide a clean way to specify the methods of a Cache, they are unsuitable for an ADT implementation, which requires a computational representation type for method implementations to operate on. Fiat uses *abstraction relations* [ , ] to enable refinement of representation types. An abstraction relation $A \approx B$ between two ADTs implementing a common signature ASig is a binary relation on the representation types A.**rep** and B.**rep** that is preserved by the operations specified in ASig. In other words, the operations of the two ADTs take "similar" input states to "similar" output states. Since operations in Fiat are implemented as computations, the methods of B may be computational refinements of A. Thus, an ADT method B.m is a refinement of A.m if

$$\begin{aligned} \mathrm{A.m} \simeq \mathrm{B.m}\ \equiv\ & \\ & \forall\, r_A\, r_B.\ r_A \approx r_B \rightarrow \\ & \quad \forall\, i\, r'_B\, o.\quad \mathrm{B.m}(r_B, i) \rightsquigarrow (r'_B, o) \rightarrow \\ & \qquad \exists r'_A.\ \mathrm{A.m}(r_A, i) \rightsquigarrow (r'_A, o) \wedge r'_A \approx r'_B \end{aligned}$$

The quantified variable $i$ stands for the method's other inputs, beside the "self" value in the data type itself; and $o$ is similarly the parts of the output value beside "self."

The statement of constructor refinement is similar:

$$\mathsf{A.c} \simeq \mathsf{B.c} \;\equiv\; \forall\, i\; r'_B.\ \mathsf{B.m}(i) \leadsto r'_B \rightarrow \exists r'_A.\ \mathsf{A.m}(i) \leadsto r'_A \wedge r'_A \approx r'_B$$

B is a refinement of A if all the operations of B are refinements of the operations of A:

$$\mathsf{A} \simeq \mathsf{B} \;\equiv\; \forall \mathsf{o} \in \mathsf{ASig}.\ \mathsf{A.o} \simeq \mathsf{B.o}$$

To be completely formal, this relation $\simeq$ should be indexed by the abstraction relation $\approx$, so that we write $\mathsf{A} \simeq_{\approx} \mathsf{B}$ to indicate that relation $\approx$ demonstrates the compatibility between the representation types of A and B. Then we can define more general refinement as:

$$\mathsf{A} \simeq \mathsf{B} \;\equiv\; \exists R.\ \mathsf{A} \simeq_R \mathsf{B}$$

Note that by picking equality as the abstraction relation, we can justify the refinement of the code of a particular method using any $\subseteq$ proof. The transitivity of $\simeq$ justifies chaining such steps with others that make representation changes, allowing us to decompose proofs of ADT refinement into applications of basic refinement facts and optimizations of the representation type.

## 3. Synthesis by Fiat

The core of the Fiat framework includes a Coq formalization of refinement that can be used to write machine-checked proofs certifying that an implementation is a valid refinement of an ADT specification. The implementation of a computation $\mathsf{C_S}$ can be expressed in Coq as a computation $\mathsf{C_I}$ paired with a proof that it is a valid refinement of $\mathsf{C_S}$:

$$\mathsf{SharpenedComputation}\ \mathsf{C_S} \;\equiv\; \Sigma\, \mathsf{C_I}.\ \mathsf{C_S} \supseteq \mathsf{C_I}$$

The derivation of an implementation of a computation in Fiat is simply a user-guided search for the two components of this dependent product. By applying transitivity of refinement, a user may take a single step towards an eventual implementation:

$$\forall \mathsf{C_S}\ \mathsf{C'_S}.\ \mathsf{SharpenedComputation}\ \mathsf{C'_S} \rightarrow \mathsf{C_S} \supseteq \mathsf{C'_S} \rightarrow \mathsf{SharpenedComputation}\ \mathsf{C_S}$$

A user satisfied with an implementation of a computation can finish the derivation by reflexivity of refinement:

$$\forall \mathsf{C_I}.\ \mathsf{SharpenedComputation}\ \mathsf{C_I}$$

These two lemmas allow derivations to be decomposed into sequences of applications of basic refinement facts. The refinement proof in Figure 3 gives the recipe for such an *optimization script*. Beginning with an initial goal of SharpenedComputation (insert k v l), the user can progressively apply transitivity with a proof of each refinement step until arriving at

$$\text{if noKey}(k,l) \text{ then } \mathbf{ret}\ [(k,v)] \cup l \text{ else } \mathbf{ret}\ l$$

Moving the **ret**s outside of the if and applying reflexivity to this goal finishes the derivation.

The core of Fiat includes a collection of proofs of basic refinement facts to use in derivations. One example lemma is REFINEPICKDECIDES', which can be used to justify the first refinement step in the third column of Figure 3.

$$\forall P_c\ P_t\ P_e. \{x \mid P_c \rightarrow P_t\ x \wedge \neg P_c \rightarrow P_e\ x\} \supseteq b \leftarrow \{b \mid \text{if } b \text{ then } P_c \text{ else } \neg P_c\}; \text{if } b \text{ then } \{x \mid P_t\ x\} \text{ else } \{x \mid P_e\ x\} \quad (\text{REFINEPICKDECIDES}')$$

Users can freely augment the set of refinements available by writing their own refinement lemmas. These facts are safe to use in any derivation without any expansion of the trusted code base and without breaking the guarantees of refinement. Fiat automates applying these facts using Coq's setoid rewriting tactics, which extend Coq's rewriting machinery with support for partial-order relations other than Leibniz equality[1].

A synthesis goal involving an ADT is expressed as an ADT B paired with a proof that it is a valid refinement of a reference ADT A:

$$\mathsf{Sharpened}\ A \;\equiv\; \Sigma\, \mathsf{B}.\ \mathsf{A} \simeq \mathsf{B}$$

A user can interactively derive a Sharpened ADT implementation in a similar manner as above, by transitively applying basic ADT refinement facts. Once a satisfactorily refined ADT has been derived, users can transform it into a version suitable for extraction to OCaml by refining its method bodies to **ret**s.

In addition to the definitions making up the refinement framework discussed so far, Fiat includes a library of *honing tactics* to help automate the derivation of Sharpened ADTs[2]. As an illustration of these honing tactics, we consider a derivation of an implementation of the cache specified by CacheSpec. Figure 5 shows this derivation, with single-bordered boxes framing honing tactics and double-bordered boxes framing the goals they produce.

***Honing Data Representations*** One of the key design choices when implementing a bounded cache is the policy used to evict entries from a full cache. Many selection algorithms depend on more information than the reference implementation provides. Conceptually, these algorithms associate an index with each key in the cache, which the insertion algorithm uses to select a key for eviction when the cache is full. By augmenting the reference type with an additional set holding the indexes that are assigned to active keys, we are able to refine toward a whole family of cache algorithms. The particular abstraction relation we will use is

$$r_v \approx_i (r'_v, r'_i) \equiv r'_v = r_v \wedge \forall k.\ (k, \_) \in r'_i \leftrightarrow (k, \_) \in r'_v$$

Importantly, it is always possible to build a default (very nondeterministic!) implementation for any abstraction relation:

$$\mathsf{default}^{\approx}_{m}(\mathsf{A.m},\ r_B,\ i) \equiv \{(r'_B, o) \mid \forall r_A.\ r_A \approx r_B \rightarrow \exists r'_A.\ \mathsf{A.m}(r_A,\ i) \leadsto (r'_A, o) \wedge r'_A \approx r'_B\}$$

$$\mathsf{default}^{\approx}_{c}(\mathsf{A.c},\ i) \equiv \{r'_B \mid \exists r'_A.\ \mathsf{A.c}(i) \leadsto r'_A \wedge r'_A \approx r'_B\}$$

Fiat includes a honing tactic "hone representation using $R$" which, when given an abstraction relation $R$, soundly changes the refinement goal from Sharpened A to Sharpened A', where A' is an ADT with the new representation type and with methods and constructors built by the $\mathsf{default}_m$ and $\mathsf{default}_c$ functions, respectively. Applying hone representation to CacheSpec produces the $\mathsf{Cache_2}$ ADT in Figure 5.

***Honing Operations*** After honing the representation of CacheSpec, we can now specify the key replacement policy of a bounded cache as a refinement of the insert method. Fiat includes a honing tactic "hone method $m$" that generates a new subgoal for interactively refining $m$. Figure 5 shows the result of using "hone method insert" to sharpen $\mathsf{Cache_2}$. We can refine the initial specification of insert in this goal to

$$\{l' \mid \exists k_{opt}.\ l' = [(k, v)] \cup \mathsf{RemoveKey}(k_{opt},\ l)\}$$

by rewriting with the refine_ReplaceUsedKeyAdd refinement fact, as in Figure 3. We then use a sequence of rewrites to select the key with the smallest index in $r_i$ once $r_v$ is full.

After selecting the replacement policy, the refined insert method still has dangling nondeterministic choices, with constraints like

[1] The Coq documentation[ ] has a full explanation of the machinery involved.

[2] As the keywords refine, replace, and change are already claimed by standard Coq tactics, Fiat uses the keyword hone in many of the tactics it provides – hence the name of the Sharpened predicate.

$\{r'_n \mid r'_n \approx r'_o\}$, arising from the default$_o$ implementations. Determinizing these picks in every method amounts to selecting the particular replacement key policy. Initializing the index of a key to zero after insert and incrementing the index of a key after each lookup, for example, implements a least frequently used policy. Alternatively, we can use these indexes as logical timestamps by initializing the index of a key to a value greater than every index in the current map and having lookup leave indexes unchanged, implementing a least recently used policy. Once we have rewritten the goal further to select the latter policy, the "finish honing" tactic presents the original Sharpened goal updated with the refined method body. Figure 6 presents the full optimization script for Figure 5.

***Invariants via Abstraction*** The idea of abstraction relations turns out to subsume the idea of *representation invariants* that must always hold on an ADT's state. Consider that an LRU implementation can "cache" the value of the greatest timestamp in its representation and use it in insert to select the next timestamp efficiently. In order to justify this refinement, however, we must maintain the invariant that this cached value holds the latest timestamp. To do so, we can include the invariant in the abstraction relation:

$$r_{vi} \approx_n (r'_{vi}, r'_n) \equiv r'_{vi} = r_{vi} \land r'_n = \max_{(k,i)\in r_{vi}} i$$

Now when honing insert, we can exploit the invariant on $r'_n$ from $\approx_n$ to implement the selection of the timestamp. Since the abstraction relation formalizes the requirements on the saved index, the default implementation of insert automatically keeps the new piece of state up-to-date, albeit in a nondeterministic way that needs further refinement.

***Implementing the Cache*** Once we are satisfied that the cache is sufficiently specified, we can implement it by honing the representation type to a data structure efficiently implementing the remaining nondeterministic operations on sets. For this example, we choose the finite maps implementation in Coq's standard library. We have proven a library of lemmas showing that the operations provided by finite maps correctly implement mathematical set operations used to specify the cache behaviors. The refinement lemmas can be used to implement a number of different high-level specifications. Conversely, since intermediate specifications (such as Cache$_3$) are independent from the implementation data structure, a library of refinement facts about a different data structure can be used to synthesize a different implementation. As an example, we could implement Cache$_3$ with a single map of keys to pairs of values and timestamps, or as two separate maps, one from keys to values and another from timestamps to keys. The former implementation uses less memory, but looking up the key to evict takes $O(n)$ time, whereas the latter can use the second map to do this lookup in $O(1)$ time.

***Taking Stock*** We pause here to put the last two sections in context. Fiat provides a number of simple concepts for organizing the refinement of specifications into efficient code, where abstract data types are a central idea for packaging methods with private data. We apply refinements step-by-step with *optimization scripts*, which apply to Sharpened goals in Coq. These scripts are implemented in Ltac, Coq's Turing-complete tactic language, so it is possible to implement arbitrarily involved heuristics to choose good refinement sequences, packaged as callable tactic functions. The Coq kernel ensures that only semantically valid refinements will be admitted, providing a kind of *enforced modularity* that allows users to write their own refinements to use in optimization scripts. This idea is simple but powerful, supporting decomposition of programming tasks into uses of separate encapsulated components for *functionality* and *optimization*.

The next section shows how to automate the synthesis of ADTs in a domain with a well-known functionality/optimization split.

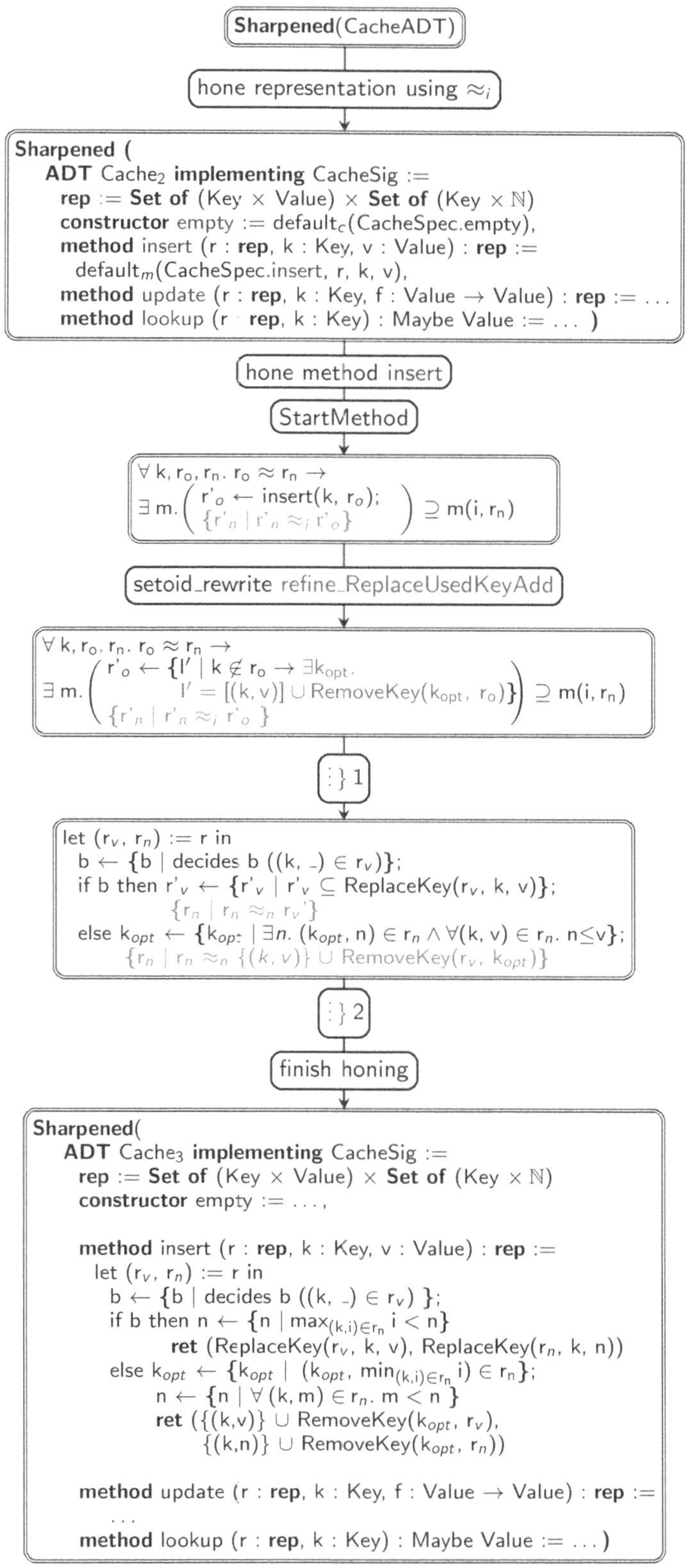


**Figure 5.** Derivation of an LRU implementation of CacheSpec

In particular, we demonstrate the versatility of our approach on specifications inspired by SQL-style relational databases, almost completely automating derivations in this domain with a set of honing tactics that act like database query planners.

## 4. Query Structures

This section presents a library for writing specifications of ADTs using reference implementations called *query structures* and with SQL-like query and insert operations. The library also provides tactic support for automatically refining those specifications into correct and efficient implementations, allowing users to generate custom database-like ADTs. Figure 8 shows the definition of a schema describing a query structure for a simple bookstore ADT, which we used in Figure 1 from the introduction. This code is taken almost verbatim from the QueryStructure library.

### 4.1 Specification of Query Structures

The Fiat query structure library includes a DSL for specifying reference query structures implemented in convenient notation, thanks to Coq's extensible parser. Figure 7 presents the grammar of this embedded DSL; the types $t$, terms $v$, and propositions $P$ are exactly those of Coq itself. The grammar also draws on an infinite set of identifiers I.

Query structures are designed to align with the conceptual abstraction of SQL databases as sets of named *relations* (i.e. tables) containing *tuples*. The query structure library defines tuples as functions from *attributes* (i.e. column names) to values; the type of each value is described by a *heading* mapping attributes to types. Tuple projection is denoted using the ! notation:

$$\langle \text{Author}{::}\text{"T. Pynchon"}, \text{Title}{::}\text{"Bleeding Edge"}\rangle!\text{Title} \\ = \text{"Bleeding Edge"}$$

To align with the standard SQL notion of tables, relations are multisets (mathematical sets that can have repeated elements) of tuples. We implement that concept more concretely by pairing each tuple with a unique numeric index, storing these pairs as sets. Subsection 4.2 discusses how these indexes can be dropped for query structure implementations that only have SQL-like operations. A *relation (S) schema* specifies the heading of the tuples contained in a relation and also a set of constraints describing properties that included tuples must satisfy. Relations themselves are implemented as records, with a field for a mathematical set containing the relation's tuples, and a field for a proof that the schema constraints hold for every pair of tuples in the relation. A query structure is similarly described by a *query structure (Q) schema* that contains a set of schemas and a set of cross-relation constraints describing properties that must hold between tuples of different tables. A query structure is implemented as a record that contains a list of relations and proofs that each pair of relations satisfies its cross-relation constraints. The relations of a query structure are accessed using the ! notation: $qs!i$.

```
hone method insert. {
  StartMethod.
  setoid_rewrite refine_ReplaceUsedKeyAdd.
  setoid_rewrite refine_SubEnsembleInsert.
  autorewrite with monad laws.
  setoid_rewrite refine_pick_KeyToBeReplaced_min.        } 1
  setoid_rewrite refine_If_Then_Else_Bind.
  autorewrite with monad laws.
  setoid_rewrite refine_If_Opt_Then_Else_Bind.
  autorewrite with monad laws.
  setoid_rewrite refine_pick_CacheADTwLogIndex_AbsR.
  setoid_rewrite refine_pick_KVEnsembleInsertRemove
                 with (1 := EquivKeys_H).
  setoid_rewrite refine_pick_KVEnsembleInsert            } 2
                 with (1 := EquivKeys_H).
  autorewrite with monad laws; simpl.
  finish honing. }
```

**Figure 6.** Complete optimization script for Figure 5

$t \in \text{Set}$ (* Types *)
$v \in \text{V}$ (* Terms *)
$P \in \text{Prop}$ (* Propositions *)
$i\ g\ h \in \text{I}$ (* Identifiers *)

$H ::= \langle \overline{i :: t} \rangle$ (*Headings*)
$T ::= \langle \overline{i :: v} \rangle$ (*Tuples*)

$S ::=$ relation $i$ schema $H$ where $P$ (*Relation Schemas*)
(*Query Structure Schemas*)
$Q ::=$ QueryStructure Schema $\overline{S}$ enforcing $P$

(*Functional Dependencies*)
attributes $\overline{i}$ depend on $\overline{g}$ $\equiv$ $\forall t_1\ t_2\ .\ \overline{t_1!g = t_2!g} \rightarrow \overline{t_1!i = t_2!i}$
(*Foreign Keys*)
attribute $i$ for $g$ references $h$ $\equiv$ $\forall t_1 \in g\ .\ \exists t_2 \in h\ .\ t_1!i = t_2!i$

**Figure 7.** Syntax for reference query structure implementations

```
Query Structure Schema
  [ relation Books has schema
      ⟨Author :: string, Title :: string, ISBN :: nat⟩
      where attributes [Title; Author] depend on [ISBN];
    relation Orders has schema
      ⟨ISBN :: nat, Date :: nat⟩ ]
  enforcing [ attribute ISBN for Orders references Books ]
```

**Figure 8.** Query structure schema for a bookstore

***Data-Integrity Constraints*** The constraints contained in relation and query structure schemas are familiar to SQL programmers in the form of data-integrity properties like functional dependencies and foreign-key constraints. In our library, these constraints are simply representation invariants over the state of query structures, enforced by the proof fields of the relation and query structure records. Fiat's query structure library includes notations for these common SQL constraints (listed in Figure 7), but $S$ and $Q$ schema constraints are not limited to them: query structures can include arbitrary predicates over tuples. It is possible to specify that the population of a nation is always equal to the sum of the populations of its cities, for example. Since query structure notations are simply an embedded DSL for writing ADTs, it is possible to write non-SQL-like operations for these ADTs – in addition to conforming with the standard data-integrity properties SQL programmers are familiar with, explicitly including these constraints allows users to be sure that they cannot write operations that go wrong.

### 4.2 Specification of Operations

The query structure library also provides a set of definitions and notations for specifying query and insertion operations mimicking standard SQL queries. Note that ADTs using query structures as reference implementations can support a mix of these operations and operations with arbitrary specifications, and can furthermore use SQL-style notations in the specifications of nonstandard operations. The most basic definition is **empty**, which returns a query structure containing only empty relations. All the operation specifications provided by the library have two implicit arguments: $qs$, the $Q$ schema of the reference implementation; and $q$, the **rep** argument used by each method.

***Querying Query Structures*** Figure 9 presents the notations the query structure library provides for specifying query operations.

$$\textbf{empty} \equiv \{q \mid \forall i \in qs.\ q!i = \emptyset\}$$

$$\textbf{For}\ b \equiv result \leftarrow b;\ \{l \mid \textbf{Permutation}\ l\ result\}$$

$$(x\ \textbf{in}\ i)\ b \equiv table \leftarrow \{l \mid q!i \sim l\};\ \text{fold\_right}\ (\lambda a\, b\, .\ l \leftarrow a;\ l' \leftarrow b;\ \textbf{ret}\ (l +\!\!+ l'))\ (\textbf{ret}\ [])\ (\text{map}\ (\lambda x.b)\ table)$$

$$\textbf{Where}\ P\ b \equiv \{l \mid P \to b \leadsto l \wedge \neg P \to l = []\}$$

$$\textbf{Return}\ a \equiv \textbf{ret}\ [a]$$

$$\textbf{Count}\ b \equiv results \leftarrow b; \textbf{ret}\ \text{length}(results)$$

**Figure 9.** Notations for initializing a query structure and defining query operations

Queries specified by the **For** notation compute any permutation of a list of *result* tuples generated by a body expression. We use permutations in order to avoid fixing a result order in advance. Since queries are specified over relations implemented as mathematical sets, the definitions of these operations are a straightforward lifting of the standard interpretation of queries using comprehensions [ ] and the list monad to handle computations. The **in** notation picks a *result* list that is equivalent ($\sim$) to the mathematical set of relation $i$; this is a placeholder for an enumeration method that is filled in by an implementation. This equivalence relation ignores the indexes of the tuples and only considers their multiplicities, and *result* thus disregards the indexes of the tuples in $i$. The body $b$ is a function that is mapped over each tuple in *result*, producing a list of computations of query results for each element. This list of computations is then flattened into a single list of query results. Finally, **Where** clauses are allowed to use arbitrary predicates. Decision procedures for these predicates are left for an implementation to fill in.

***Query Structure Inserts*** Whereas queries are *observers* for the query structure, insertion operations are *mutators* returning modified query structures, which by definition must satisfy the data-integrity constraints specified by their $Q$ schema. The naïve specification of insertion always inserts a tuple into a query structure:

$$\textbf{Insert}\ t\ \textbf{into}\ i \equiv \{q' \mid \forall u.\ u \in q'!i \leftrightarrow u \in (q!i \cup \{t\})\}$$

This specification is unrealizable in general, however, as there does not exist a proof of consistency for a query structure containing a tuple violating its data-integrity constraints. The specification of **Insert** given in Figure 10 thus only specifies insertion behavior when the tuple satisfies both the $S$ and $Q$ schema constraints. This definition highlights Fiat's ability to specify method behavior at a high level without regard for implementation concerns. The specification delays the decision of how to handle conflicts (i.e. ignore the insertion, drop conflicting tuples, etc.) to subsequent refinements[3]. As we shall see in the following section, this specification can be transformed automatically into a more readily implementable form.

### 4.3 Honing Query Structures

Figure 1 contains the specification of an ADT using a query structure with the bookstore schema from Figure 8 and insert and query operations specified with the notations from the query structure library. As an initial step in implementing this specification, the library provides a fully automated tactic for removing the data-integrity constraints from the representation type of the ADT, building an ADT that uses *unconstrained* query structures, i.e. collections of mathematical sets with no proof components, freeing subsequent refinements from having to consider these proof terms. We pick an abstraction relation enforcing that a query structure is equivalent to an unconstrained query structure if the two contain equivalent sets of tuples:

$$q \approx q' \equiv \forall i \in qs.\ q!i = q'!i \qquad (1)$$

[3] Note that regardless of how conflicts are resolved, the synthesis process ensures that any result must be equivalent to *some* query structure satisfying the data-integrity constraints of the schema.

$$\text{QuerySpec}(i,\ t,\ q') \equiv$$

Schema Constraints:
$$i.P(t,\ t) \to (\forall u \in q!i.\ i.P(u,\ t)) \to (\forall u \in q!i.\ i.P(t,\ u))$$

Query Structure Schema Constraints:
$$\to (\forall g \neq i.\ qs.P_{i,g}(t,\ q!g)) \to (\forall g \neq i, u \in q!g.\ qs.P_{g,i}(u,\ q'!i))$$

$$\to q'.i \subseteq q.i \cup \{t\} \wedge (\forall g \neq i.\ q!g = q'!g)$$

$$\textbf{Insert}\ t\ \textbf{into}\ i \equiv$$
$$id \leftarrow \{id \mid \forall u \in q!i.\ u.id \neq id\};$$
$$q' \leftarrow \{q' \mid \text{QuerySpec}(i,\ (id,\ t),\ q')\};$$
$$b \leftarrow \{b \mid b = true \leftrightarrow (\forall u.\ u \in q'!i \leftrightarrow u \in (q!i \cup \{t\}))\};$$
$$\textbf{Return}\ (q',\ b)$$

**Figure 10.** Notations for insert operations

The implementation of this tactic is straightforward for the **empty** constructor. Queries over unconstrained query structures can also be constructed trivially if they are built from the notations in Figure 10, as those definitions do not reference the proof components of a query structure. For insertions, the tactic applies a lemma showing that if a tuple passes a series of consistency checks, it is possible to build the proof component of a query structure containing that tuple. By running these consistency checks before inserting a tuple into the unconstrained query structure, this lemma shows that there *exists* some query structure, i.e. that the abstraction relation is preserved. For a concrete query structure schema, these checks are materialized as a set of nondeterministic choices of decision procedures for the constraints. If there are no constraints, the tactic simplifies these checks away entirely. Figure 11 shows the result of applying this tactic to the bookstore ADT.

Refining the decision procedures for the remaining constraints into a concrete implementation is easily done by first transitioning to a query-based representation. In the foreign-key case, we refine

```
{b | b decides (∃ book∈ Books. book!ISBN = order!ISBN)}
```

into

```
c ← Count (For (book in Books)
           Where (book!ISBN = order!ISBN)
           Return ()); ret (c ≠ 0).
```

Similarly, functional-dependency checks are refined from

```
{b | b decides (∀ book'∈ Books.
           book!ISBN = book'!ISBN →
           book!Author = book'!Author ∧
           book!Title = book'!Title)}
```

into

```
c ← Count (For (book' in Books)
           Where (book!ISBN = book'!ISBN)
           Where (book!Author ≠ book'!Author ∨
                  book!Title ≠ book'!Title)
           Return ()); ret (c = 0)
```

```
ADTRep (UnConstrQueryStructure BookStoreSchema) {
  const Init (_: ()) : rep :=
    ret (DropQSConstraints (QSEmptySpec BookStoreSchema)),

  meth PlaceOrder (u: rep , order: Order) : bool :=
    id ← {id | ∀ order'∈ u!Orders. order'!id ≠ id};
    b ← {b | b decides (∃ book∈ Books.
                       book!ISBN = order!ISBN)};
    ret if b then (u!Books, u!Orders ∪ {(order, id)}, true)
           else (u!Books, u!Orders, false),

  meth AddBook (u: rep , book: Book) : bool :=
    id ← {id | ∀ book'∈ u!Books. book'!id ≠ id};
    b ← {b | b decides (∀ book'∈ Books.
                       book!ISBN = book'!ISBN →
                       book!Author = book'!Author ∧
                       book!Title = book'!Title)}
    ret if b then (u!Books ∪ {(book, id)}, u!Orders, true)
           else (u!Books, u!Orders, false),

  meth GetTitles (u: rep , author: string) : list string :=
    titles ← For (b in u!Books)
           Where (author = b!Author)
           Return b!Title;
    ret (u, titles),

  meth NumOrders (u: rep , author: string) : nat :=
    num ← Count (For (b in u!Books) (o in u!Orders)
                 Where (author = b!Author)
                 Where (b!ISBN = o!ISBN)
                 Return ());
    ret (u, num) }
```

**Figure 11.** The bookstore ADT after removing data-integrity proofs

This type of refinement allows clients of the library to reuse the existing query machinery to implement these checks and facilitate the automatic derivation of efficient query plans.

Importantly, this tactic only removes constraints from operations built from the notations provided by the library – any "exotic" operations will have to be refined manually to show that they preserve (1). Having removed the constraints automatically for "standard" queries, we now consider how to construct data structures that efficiently implement query and insertion operations.

### 4.4 The Bag Interface

The data structures used to store and retrieve data records are created, accessed, and modified through a unified Bag interface, which guarantees that all underlying implementations behave as multisets. This interface is implemented as a Coq type class parametrized over three types: TContainer, the type of the underlying representation (e.g. lists); TItem, the type of the items stored in the bag (e.g. tuples); and TSearchTerm, the type of the search terms used to look up items matching specific conditions (e.g. a function mapping tuples to Booleans). These types are augmented with a set of operations whose behavior is described by a small number of consistency properties. While maintaining sufficient expressive power to allow for efficient retrieval of information, keeping the interface reduced makes it relatively simple to implement new instances.

The bag interface is split between constants, methods, and axioms. Methods operate on containers and include benumerate, which returns a list of all items stored in a container; binsert, which returns a copy of a container augmented with one extra item; and bfind, which returns all items matching a certain search term. Axioms specify the behavior of these transformations, in relation to two constants: bempty, the empty bag; and bfind_matcher, a matching function used to specify the behavior of bfind: calling bfind on a container must return the same results, modulo permutation, as filtering the container's elements using the bfind_matcher function (including this function allows us to retain maximal generality by allowing different bag instances to provide widely varying types of find functions). Finally, for performance reasons, a bag implementation is required to provide a bcount method (elided here), used to count elements matching a given search term instead of enumerating them.

```
Class Bag (TContainer TItem TSearchTerm : Type) := {
  bempty : TContainer;
  bfind_matcher : TSearchTerm → TItem → bool;

  benumerate : TContainer → list TItem;
  bfind : TContainer → TSearchTerm → list TItem;
  binsert : TContainer → TItem → TContainer;

  binsert_enumerate :
    ∀ inserted container,
      Permutation
        (benumerate (binsert container inserted))
        (inserted :: benumerate container);
  benumerate_empty : benumerate bempty = [];
  bfind_correct :
    ∀ container search_term,
      Permutation (filter (bfind_matcher search_term)
                          (benumerate container))
                  (bfind container search_term)}.
```

### 4.5 Bag Implementations

Fiat provides two instances of the Bag interface, one based on lists and the other based on AVL trees through Coq's finite map interface. The definitions making up the list instance are extremely simple and can thus be reproduced in their entirety below:

```
Instance ListAsBag (TItem TSearchTerm: Type)
        (matcher : TSearchTerm → TItem → bool) :
Bag (list TItem) TItem TSearchTerm :=
    {|bempty := nil;
    bfind_matcher := matcher;

    benumerate container := container;
    bfind container search_term := filter (matcher search_term)
         container;
    binsert container item := item :: container |}.
```

The tree-based implementation, though lengthier, is also readily explained: it organizes elements of a data set by extracting a key from each element and grouping elements that share the same key into smaller bags. The smaller bags are then placed in a map-like data structure, which allows for quick access to all elements sharing the same key. Tree-based bags can thus be used to construct a nested hierarchy of bags, with each level representing a further partition of the full data set (in that case, smaller bags are tree-based bags themselves). In practice, tree bags are implemented as AVL trees mapping projections (keys) to sub-trees whose elements all project to the key under which the sub-tree is filed.

The search terms used to query tree-based bags are pairs, each consisting of an optional key and a search term for sub-bags. The bfind operation behaves differently depending on the presence or absence of a key; if a key is given, then bfind returns the results of calling bfind with the additional search term on the smaller bag whose elements project to the given key. If no key is given, then bfind calls bfind on each smaller bag and then merges all results (a process usually called a skip-scan, in the database world). Finally, benumerate is implemented by calling benumerate on each sub-tree and concatenating the resulting lists, and binsert is implemented by finding (or creating) the right sub-bag to insert into and calling binsert on it. This design is similar to that found in most database management systems, where tuples are indexed on successive columns, with additional support for skip-scans. Figure 12 presents an example of such an indexed bag structure.

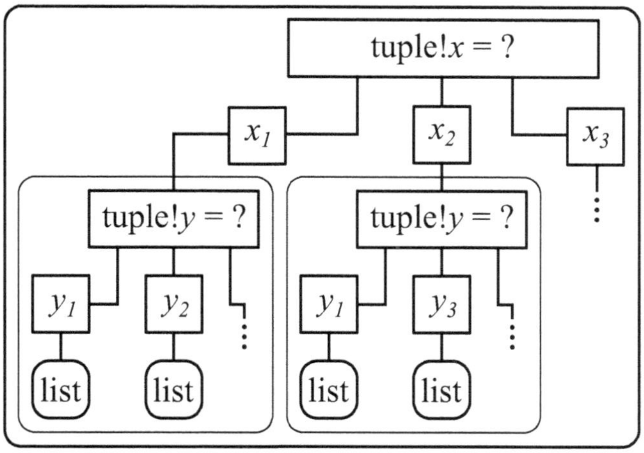


**Figure 12.** Indexed data is organized in a hierarchy of nested bags. In this example, the data set is first partitioned by column $x$, then by column $y$. Since our nested bags implementation supports skip-scanning, this same index can be used to answer queries related to $x$, to $y$, and to both $x$ and $y$.

### 4.6 Automation

As an example of a very general optimization script, we implemented a tactic plan, which works automatically and is able to synthesize efficient implementations of a variety of query structures containing at most two tables, based on index structures backed by our bags library. Figure 13 shows an example of the code output by plan for our running Bookstore example. To produce this code from the reference implementation, the programmer only needs to specify a bag structure for each table, as shown in the part of Figure 1 after the method definitions. The plan tactic applies heuristics to rewrite each method into a more efficient form, given a set of available bag-based indexes. We describe query heuristics in the most detail before briefly covering mutator refinement.

The query heuristics run to refine default (nondeterministic) method bodies induced by choices of abstraction relations. Here a relevant abstraction relation connects each table to a bag-based index. Default query bodies will compute with table contents specified as mathematical sets, and we need to rewrite those operations to use the indexes efficiently. Every actual code transformation is implemented as a Coq setoid rewrite; we just need to determine a useful sequence of rules.

1. The **starting point** of refinement is expressions that work directly with mathematical sets. For example:

   $$\textbf{For } (r \textbf{ in } T) \textbf{ Where } (r.c_1 = 7) \textbf{ Return } (r.c_2)$$

2. A **concretization step** replaces all references to sets with references to *lists* built by enumerating all members of index structures. For instance, the abstraction relation might declare that table $T$ is implemented with index structure $I$, in which case we may rewrite the above to:

   $$\{\ell \mid \textbf{Permutation } \ell \ (\textbf{map } (\lambda r.\ r.c_2) \ (\textbf{filter } (\lambda r.\ r.c_1 == 7) \ (\textbf{benumerate } I)))\}$$

   That is, we convert set operations into standard functional-programming operations over lists, starting from the list of all table elements. Note that we use nondeterministic choice to select any permutation of the list that we compute. We do not want to commit to ordering this early, since we hope to find more efficient versions with different orders.

3. A **rewriting-modulo-permutation** step simplifies the list expression, possibly with rules that change ordering. Here we use standard algebraic laws, like $\textbf{map } f \ (\textbf{map } g \ \ell) = \textbf{map } (f \circ g) \ \ell$. Less standard rules locate opportunities to apply our index structures. Our example query would be refined as follows, assuming the index structure only covers table column $c_1$:

   $$\{\ell \mid \textbf{Permutation } \ell \ (\textbf{map } (\lambda r.\ r.c_2) \ (\textbf{bfind } I \ (7, [])))\}$$

   Our tactic analyzes **filter** functions syntactically to figure out useful ways of applying index structures. In full generality, the heuristics of this phase apply to filter conditions over two tables, and they are able to decompose conjunctive conditions into some use of indexes and some use of less efficient filtering for conditions that do not map neatly to the indexes.

4. A **commitment** step accepts the current list expression as the final answer, commiting to an ordering. Our example is refined in one simple step to:

   $$\textbf{ret } (\textbf{map } (\lambda r.\ r.c_2) \ (\textbf{bfind } I \ (7, [])))$$

```
Sharpened ADTRep (TBookStorage × TOrderStorage) {
  const Init (_: ()) : rep :=
    ret (bempty, bempty)

  meth PlaceOrder (r_n: rep , o: Order) : bool :=
    let (books, orders) := r_n in
    if bcount books (None, Some o!ISBN, []) ≠ 0
    then ret (books, binsert orders o, true)
    else ret (books, orders, false)

  meth AddBook (r_n: rep , b: Book) : bool :=
    let (books, orders) := r_n in
    if bcount books (None, Some b!ISBN, [λ b'.
                     b!Title ≠ b'!Title ||
                     b!Author ≠ b'!Author]) == 0
    then ret (binsert books b, orders, true)
    else ret (books, orders, false)

  meth GetTitles (p: rep , author: string) : list string :=
    let (books, orders) := p in
    ret (books, orders,
         map (λ tuple. tuple!Title)
             (bfind books (Some author, None, [])))

  meth NumOrders (p: rep , author: string) : nat :=
    let (books, orders) := p in
    ret (books, orders,
        fold_left
          (λ count tup.
              count + bcount orders (Some tup!ISBN, []))
          (bfind books (Some author, None, [])) 0)
}
```

**Figure 13.** Synthesized code for Bookstore example

This basic three-step process can be extended quite flexibly. Our implementation handles aggregate functions (e.g., count or max) in the same way. A use of such an operation is **concretized** to a fold over a list, and we apply **rewriting** to incorporate chances to use index structures to compute folds more directly.

One further subtlety applies in the rewriting step for queries over multiple tables. Concretization rewrites a join of two tables into a Cartesian-product operation **Join_Lists**, defined as follows, where

**flat_map** is a variant of **map** that concatenates together the lists produced by its function argument.

$$\textbf{Join\_Lists}\ \ell_1\ \ell_2 \equiv \textbf{flat\_map}\ (\lambda a.\ \textbf{map}\ (\lambda b.\ (a, b))\ \ell_2)\ \ell_1$$

This code pattern is known as a nested loop join, in the database world. Notice that it is inherently asymmetric: we handle one table in an "outer loop" and the other in an "inner loop." Imagine that, because of a **Where** clause, our nested loop has been concretized within a **filter** call, like so:

$$\textbf{filter}\ (\lambda(a, b).\ a.c_1 = 7)\ (\textbf{Join\_Lists}\ \ell_1\ \ell_2)$$

Note that this filter condition is highly selective when it comes to rows of $\ell_1$, but it accepts any row of $\ell_2$. Rewriting will apply the following algebraic law to push the **filter** inside the **Join_Lists**:

$$\begin{aligned} & \textbf{filter}\ f\ (\textbf{Join\_Lists}\ \ell_1\ \ell_2) \\ = \ & \textbf{flat\_map}\ (\lambda a.\ \textbf{map}\ (\lambda b.\ (a, b))\ (\textbf{filter}\ (\lambda b.\ f\ (a, b))\ \ell_2))\ \ell_1 \end{aligned}$$

Here we see that the inner **filter** can be refined into an efficient use of **bfind**, *if* we first swap the order of the **Join_Lists** arguments. The plan tactic attempts heuristically to orchestrate this style of strategic rewriting.

The heuristics for queries are the heart of what plan does, but it also optimizes insert operations. Subsection 4.3 explained how we refine constraint checks into queries, to reuse query-based refinement tools. A plan invocation is responsible for noticing opportunities to apply a suite of formal checks-to-queries rules. We also apply a set of refinements that remove trivially true checks and prune duplicate checks. After the set of checks has been simplified as much as possible, we do a case analysis on all the ways that all the checks could turn out, performing an actual table insert only in cases whose checks imply validity.

### 4.7 Caching Queries

Expressing refinement using the small set of core ideas presented so far allows us to soundly and cleanly integrate optimizations from different domains. As a demonstration, this section will show how we integrate the cache ADTs developed in Subsection 2.1 to cache query results. Importantly, we will apply this refinement after dropping the data-integrity constraints, but *before* implementing the query structure. Moreover, we perform this refinement using the CacheSpec reference implementation, allowing users to choose any caching implementation independently of the query structure. We will be refining a variation of the bookstore ADT that replaces the GetTitles method with one that counts the number of books an author has written:

```
query NumTitles (author: string) : list string :=
  Count (For (b in Books)
           Where (author = b!Author)
           Return ())
```

We begin by honing the representation of the reference query structure to include a cache ADT keyed on author names. The abstraction relation used to hone the representation maintains the invariant that the cache of the new representation only holds valid book counts for each author:

$$\begin{aligned} r_v \approx_c (r'_v, r'_i)\ & \equiv r'_v = r_v \\ & \wedge\ \forall k, v.\ (k, v) \in r'_i \rightarrow \text{NumTitles}(r_v, k) \rightsquigarrow v \end{aligned}$$

We can use the cache consistency predicate to refine NumTitles so that it first nondeterministically picks a key in the cache using lookup, returns that value if it exists, and otherwise runs the query and adds a new key to the cache (this updated cache trivially satisfies the representation invariant). NumOrders and PlaceOrder are unchanged. Since AddBook can increase the number of books for an author in the cache, it needs to update the cache if the author of the new book is in the cache. Applying all these refinements to the bookstore ADT from Figure 11 yields the refined ADT in Figure 14.

```
ADT BookstoreCache implementing BookstoreSig {
  rep := UnConstrQS BookstoreSchema × (CacheSpec 𝕊 ℕ).rep
  const Init (_: unit) : rep := (empty, ∅),

  meth AddBook (r : rep, book: Book) : rep :=
    (r_q, r_c) ← Insert book into Books;
    c ← Count (For (b in Books)
                 Where (author = b!Author)
                 Return ());
    ret (r_q, CacheSpec.update (r_c, book!Author, λ_.c)),

  meth NumTitles (r : rep, author : string) : nat :=
    let (r_q, r_c) := r in
      n ← CacheSpec.lookup(r_c, author);
      if n = Some n' then ret n'
      else c ← Count (For (b in Books)
                        Where (author = b!Author)
                        Return ());
        ret (r_q, CacheSpec.insert (r_c, c) , c),

   query GetTitles (author: string) : list string := ...}
```

**Figure 14.** Version of the bookstore ADT that caches queries

Observe that the following refinement holds:

$$\textbf{For}\ (x\ \textbf{in}\ R \cup \{a\})\ b \ \supseteq \ \begin{array}{l} l \leftarrow b\ a; \\ l' \leftarrow \textbf{For}\ (x\ \textbf{in}\ R)\ b; \\ \text{Return}\ (l \mathbin{+\!\!+} l') \end{array} \tag{2}$$

thus allowing us to refine the query in AddBook:

```
Count( l ← Where (author = a!Author) Return ();
       l' ← For (b in Books)
              Where (author = b!Author) Return ();
       Return (l ++ l'))
```

which can be further refined into:

```
n ← Count (Where (author = a!Author)
             Return ());
n' ← Count (For (b in Books)
              Where (author = b!Author)
              Return ());
Return (n + n')
```

Due to the representation invariant in the abstraction relation, we know that the query bound to $n'$ returns precisely the cache contents, allowing us to refine the update to simply increment the value of author currently in the cache:

```
meth AddBook (r : rep, book: Books) : rep :=
  (r_q, r_c) ← Insert book into Books;
  ret (r_q, CacheSpec.update (r_c, book!Author, increment))
```

This case is actually an example of the broader *finite differencing* [ ] refinement for improving the performance of an expensive operation $f$ whose input can be partitioned into two pieces, old $y$ and new $x$, such that $f(x \oplus y) = f'(x) \oplus' f(y)$. The representation invariant ensures that each value in the cache already stores $f(y)$, allowing us to reduce the computation of $f(x \oplus y)$ to computing $f'(x)$ and updating the value in the cache appropriately. Note that Fiat's refinement process supports finite differencing of *any* ADT operation, through the use of abstraction relations to express cache invariants and refinements to replace repeated computations. In particular, (2) allows us to easily cache **For** queries by partitioning their results into novel results and the portion already in the cache when performing **Insert** updates.

## 5. Evaluation

### 5.1 Extraction of the Bookstore Example

Once they have been fully refined, our data structures can be extracted to produce verified OCaml database management libraries. We performed such an extraction for the bookstore example and benchmarked it. The observed performance is reasonable, and the operations scale in a way that is consistent with the indexing scheme used, as demonstrated by Figure 15. Starting with an empty database, for instance, it takes about 480 ms on an Intel Core i5-3570 CPU @ 3.40GHz to add 10 000 randomly generated books filed under 1 000 distinct authors, and then 6.8 s to place 100 000 orders. Afterward, the system is able to answer about 350 000 GetTitles queries per second and about 160 000 NumOrders queries per second.

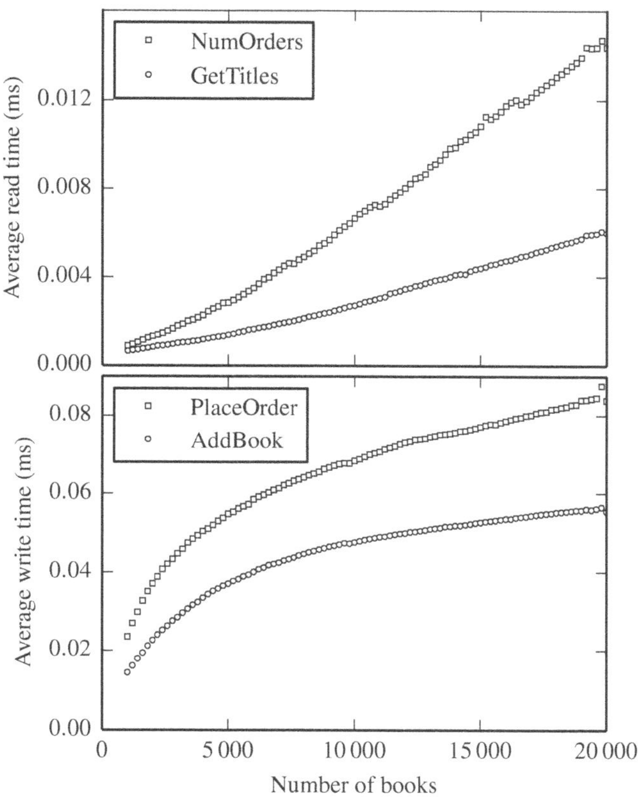


**Figure 15.** Average query execution time, for increasingly large bookstores

### 5.2 Further Examples

To demonstrate the generality of our automated refinement strategies, the code base also includes two more examples: a weather-data database and a stock-market database, both of which are included in the Fiat distribution.

The weather example includes two tables – one to hold information about the weather stations and one to log the measurements – and supports operations such as counting the number of stations in a given geographic area or computing the highest temperature on one day. The stock market example includes one table listing information about stocks and one table keeping track of transactions, and it allows clients to compute the total volume of shares exchanged on one day for a particular stock, plus the largest transaction for a given type of stock.

In both cases skip-scanning allowed for space-efficient indexing (in the weather case, stations could produce a small number of different measurement types: wind speed, temperature, air pressure, or humidity; in the stocks case, different types of stocks were distinguished), and in both cases nontrivial functional dependencies were expressed (for examples, two transactions occurring at the same time and concerning the same stock could differ in the number of shares exchanged but not in price). The plan tactic synthesizes correct, efficient implementation code in both cases.

## 6. Related Work

The concept of deriving implementations that are correct by construction via stepwise refinement of specifications has been around since at least the late sixties [ ].

***Deductive Synthesis*** Specware [ ] and its predecessors KIDS [ ] and DTRE [ ] are deductive synthesis tools for deriving correct-by-construction implementations of high-level specifications. Specware is accompanied by a library of domain theories that describe how to do iterative decomposition of high-level specifications into subproblems until an implementation can be constructed. At each step, Specware checks the validity of the refinement, although only recently have they begun generating Isabelle/HOL proof obligations justifying these transformations. Each of these proof obligation generators makes up part of Specsware's trusted code base; by implementing Fiat completely in Coq we rely on a considerably smaller trusted code base. At the end of refinement, Specware has a series of automated and quite sophisticated transformations that generate C code, though these final steps are currently unverified. In contrast, derivations of ADTs with Fiat are completely verified by Coq, and these derivations may be integrated within larger, more general proof developments. We have also demonstrated more automated refinement for more restrictive domains, as in our query structure examples.

***Synthesis of Abstract Data Types*** There is also a philosophical difference between Fiat and Specware – Kestrel has focused on using Specware to develop families of complex algorithms, including families of garbage collectors [ ], SAT solvers [ ], and network protocols. In contrast, we envision Fiat being used to generate high-assurance code for algorithmically "simple" domains that are amenable to automation. A number of domains have been shown to have this property: Paige et. al [ ] demonstrate how efficient implementations of ADTs supporting set-theoretic operations can be derived by applying fixed-point iteration [ ] to generate initial implementations, using finite differencing [ ] to further optimize the resulting implementation, before finally selecting data structure implementations. The generation of data types supporting query-like operations is another such domain. P2 [ ] was a DSL extension to C that allowed users to specify the layout of container data structures using a library of structures implementing a common interface, akin to Fiat's Bag interface. This interface included an iterator method for querying contents of the container – implementations of these iterators would dynamically optimize queries at runtime. More recently, Hawkins et. al [ ] have shown how to synthesize the implementations of abstract data types specified by abstract relational descriptions supporting query and update operations. They also provide an autotuner for selecting the best data representation implementation in the space of possible decompositions. Our work with Fiat expands on these past projects by adding proofs of correctness in a general-purpose proof assistant, which also opens the door to sound extension of the system by programmers, since Coq will check any new refinement rules.

***Constraint-Based Synthesis*** Constraint-based synthesis formulates the synthesis problem as a search over a space of candidate solutions, with programmers providing a set of constraints to help prune the search space. The Sketch [ ] synthesis system, for example, allows programmers to constrain the search space by encoding their algorithmic insight into skeleton programs with "holes" that a synthesizer automatically completes. Sketching-based approaches have been used to synthesize low-level data-structure manipulating algorithms [ ], concurrent data structures [ ], and programs with numeric parameters that are optimized over some quantitative metric [ ]. These approaches fit into the broad decomposition of "functionality + optimization" proposed here, with the initial sketch representing the former and the synthesizer providing the optimization. Excitingly, Fiat enables opportunities for programmers to inject further insight into the synthesis process by chaining together honing tactics with various degrees of automation. Subsection 4.7 provides an example of such a development, with the user first automatically dropping data-integrity constraints via a honing tactic before manually specifying how to cache certain queries.

***Reasoning with Refinements*** Cohen et al. rely on a similar foundation of refinement to verify an algebra library in Coq using data type refinement [ ] by verifying algorithms parametrized over the data type and its operations. Verification is done using a simple, "proof-oriented" data type. The authors then show how to transport the proof of correctness to a version of the algorithm using a more efficient implementation that is related to the proof-oriented data type by a refinement relation. In contrast, Fiat is a system for (semi-) automatically *deriving* efficient ADTs that are valid refinements. The two approaches could certainly be combined to enable users to build and verify clients of ADTs synthesized by Fiat.

## 7. Future Work and Conclusion

We have reported here on the start of a project to explore the use of proof assistants to enable a new modularity pattern in programming: separating *functionality* from *performance*, where programmers express their functionality and then apply *optimization scripts* to refine it to efficient implementations. Special-case systems like SQL engines have provided this style of decomposition, but only for hardcoded domains of functionality. We explained how the design of Fiat allows programmers to define new functionality domains and new optimization techniques, relying on Coq to check that no optimization technique breaks program semantics. Programmers think of implementing a new database engine as a big investment, but they think of implementing a new container data structure as a reasonable component of a new project. The promise of the Fiat approach is to make the former as routine as the latter, by giving that style of optimization strategy more first-class status within a programming environment, with *enforced modularity* via checking of optimization scripts by a general-purpose proof kernel.

We plan to explore further applications of Fiat, both by identifying other broad functionality domains that admit effective libraries of optimization scripts, and by narrowing the gap with hand-tuned program code by generating low-level imperative code instead of functional code, using the same framework to justify optimizations that can only be expressed at the lower abstraction level.

## Acknowledgments

We thank Eddy Westbrook, Arthur Charguéraud, and the anonymous reviewers for their feedback on earlier versions of this paper. The second author would like to thank École Polytechnique for allowing and supporting the internship during which his contributions were made. This work has been supported in part by NSF grant CCF-1253229 and by DARPA under agreement number FA8750-12-2-0293. The U.S. Government is authorized to reproduce and distribute reprints for Governmental purposes notwithstanding any copyright notation thereon. The views and conclusions contained herein are those of the authors and should not be interpreted as necessarily representing the official policies or endorsements, either expressed or implied, of DARPA or the U.S. Government.

## References

[1] Don Batory, Vivek Singhal, Marty Sirkin, and Jeff Thomas. Scalable software libraries. In *Proceedings of the 1st ACM SIGSOFT Symposium on Foundations of Software Engineering*. ACM, 1993.

[2] Lee Blaine and Allen Goldberg. DTRE – a semi-automatic transformation system. In *Constructing Programs from Specifications*, pages 165–204. Elsevier, 1991.

[3] Peter Buneman, Leonid Libkin, Dan Suciu, Val Tannen, and Limsoon Wong. Comprehension syntax. *SIGMOD Rec.*, 23(1), March 1994.

[4] Swarat Chaudhuri, Martin Clochard, and Armando Solar-Lezama. Bridging boolean and quantitative synthesis using smoothed proof search. In *Proceedings of the 41st ACM SIGPLAN-SIGACT Symposium on Principles of Programming Languages*. ACM, 2014.

[5] Cyril Cohen, Maxime Dénès, and Anders Mörtberg. Refinements for free! In *Certified Programs and Proofs*. Springer International Publishing, 2013.

[6] http://coq.inria.fr/distrib/current/refman/Reference-Manual029.html.

[7] Edsger W. Dijkstra. A constructive approach to the problem of program correctness. Circulated privately, August 1967.

[8] Peter Hawkins, Alex Aiken, Kathleen Fisher, Martin Rinard, and Mooly Sagiv. Data representation synthesis. In *Proceedings of the 32nd ACM SIGPLAN Conference on Programming Language Design and Implementation*. ACM, 2011.

[9] J. He, C.A.R. Hoare, and J.W. Sanders. Data refinement refined. In Bernard Robinet and Reinhard Wilhelm, editors, *ESOP 86*, volume 213 of *Lecture Notes in Computer Science*, pages 187–196. Springer Berlin Heidelberg, 1986.

[10] C.A.R. Hoare. Proof of correctness of data representations. *Acta Informatica*, 1(4):271–281, 1972.

[11] Barbara Liskov and Stephen Zilles. Programming with abstract data types. In *Symposium on Very High Level Languages*, New York, NY, USA, 1974. ACM.

[12] Robert Paige and Fritz Henglein. Mechanical translation of set theoretic problem specifications into efficient RAM code – a case study. *J. Symb. Comput.*, 4(2):207–232, October 1987.

[13] Robert Paige and Shaye Koenig. Finite differencing of computable expressions. *ACM Trans. Program. Lang. Syst.*, 4(3), July 1982.

[14] Dusko Pavlovic, Peter Pepper, and Douglas R. Smith. Formal derivation of concurrent garbage collectors. In *Mathematics of Program Construction*, pages 353–376. Springer Berlin Heidelberg, 2010.

[15] Rishabh Singh and Armando Solar-Lezama. Synthesizing data structure manipulations from storyboards. In *Proceedings of the 19th ACM SIGSOFT Symposium and the 13th European Conference on Foundations of Software Engineering*. ACM, 2011.

[16] Douglas R. Smith. KIDS: A semi-automatic program development system. In *Client Resources on the Internet, IEEE Multimedia Systems '99*, pages 302–307, 1990.

[17] Douglas R. Smith and Stephen J. Westfold. Synthesis of propositional satisfiability solvers, 2008.

[18] Armando Solar-Lezama. *Program Synthesis by Sketching*. PhD thesis, University of California, Berkeley, 2008.

[19] Armando Solar-Lezama, Christopher Grant Jones, and Rastislav Bodik. Sketching concurrent data structures. In *Proceedings of the 2008 ACM SIGPLAN Conference on Programming Language Design and Implementation*. ACM, 2008.

[20] http://www.kestrel.edu/home/prototypes/specware.html.

[21] Philip Wadler. Comprehending monads. In *Mathematical Structures in Computer Science*, pages 61–78, 1992.

# Author Index

www.ingramcontent.com/pod-product-compliance
Ingram Content Group UK Ltd.
Pitfield, Milton Keynes, MK11 3LW, UK
UKHW051419290926
15471UKWH00009B/1692

9 781450 333009